The Grove Dictionary of

American Music

Volume One

The Grove Dictionary of American Music

Second Edition

Volume One

AAMC – Brown, Clifford

Edited by
Charles Hiroshi Garrett

OXFORD
UNIVERSITY PRESS

OXFORD
UNIVERSITY PRESS

Oxford University Press is a department of the University of Oxford. It furthers the University's objective of excellence in research, scholarship, and education by publishing worldwide.

Oxford New York
Auckland Cape Town Dar es Salaam Hong Kong Karachi
Kuala Lumpur Madrid Melbourne Mexico City Nairobi
New Delhi Shanghai Taipei Toronto

With offices in
Argentina Austria Brazil Chile Czech Republic France Greece
Guatemala Hungary Italy Japan Poland Portugal Singapore
South Korea Switzerland Thailand Turkey Ukraine Vietnam

Published in the United States of America by
Oxford University Press
198 Madison Avenue, New York, NY 10016

The first edition was published as *The New Grove Dictionary of American Music*
Edited by H. Wiley Hitchcock and Stanley Sadie (Macmillan, 1986)

The Library of Congress Cataloging-in-Publication Data

The New Grove Dictionary of American Music
The Grove dictionary of American music / edited by Charles Hiroshi Garrett. -Second edition.
volumes ; cm.
Revision of *The New Grove dictionary of American music*, originally published in 1986.
Includes bibliographical references.
ISBN 978-0-19-531428-1 (print set : alk. paper)—978-0-19-999059-7 (v.1 : alk. paper)—978-0-19-999060-3 (v.2 : alk. paper)—978-0-19-999061-0 (v.3 : alk. paper)—978-0-19-999062-7 (v.4 : alk. paper)—978-0-19-999063-4 (v.5 : alk. paper)—978-0-19-999064-1 (v.6 : alk. paper)—978-0-19-999065-8 (v.7 : alk. paper)—978-0-19-999066-5 (v.8 : alk. paper)—ISBN (invalid) 978-0-19-973925-7 (e-book) 1. Music—United States—Encyclopedias. 2. Music—United States—Bio-bibliography. I. Garrett, Charles Hiroshi, 1966– II. Title.
ML101.U6N48 2013
780.973'03—dc23 2012002055

1 3 5 7 9 8 6 4 2

Printed in the United States of America
on acid-free paper

Contents

Preface

The 1986 edition of *The New Grove Dictionary of American Music* (Macmillan), edited by H. Wiley Hitchcock and Stanley Sadie, stands as a landmark in American music studies. The *AmeriGrove*, as it has become commonly known, was the first reference work dedicated to the music of the United States that was comprehensive in approach, academically rigorous, and written by a team of specialists. Its four authoritative volumes, examining the music of the United States in close detail and great depth, heralded the arrival and nourished the field of American music studies.

In response to the enormous growth of scholarship in American music spurred in part by the 1986 edition as well as to the wide-ranging musical activities and transformative developments since its publication, Oxford University Press initiated plans to publish a revised and greatly expanded dictionary of American music. By 2005, organizational and administrative planning was well underway and, by the following year, the advisory and editorial boards had begun to take shape. As the advisory board and editorial team gauged the extent to which the study of American music has blossomed, publication plans grew from an initial six to seven to, finally, eight printed volumes.

As in the first edition of the dictionary, "American" music here refers to musical life and cultures within the region now covered by the 50 states, the District of Columbia, and US territories. The present work likewise features coverage of the music-making practices of native cultures whose occupation of these regions predates European contact. The dictionary's inclusive definition of American music embraces music-making in the United States both by Americans and by selected foreign musicians, with special attention to Canadian and Latin American figures. The dictionary also contains articles on selected American musicians who have made their careers abroad.

This is not a general dictionary of music. It does not include entries on a complete range of musical terminology or of instruments, such as might be found in a comprehensive music dictionary; it does, however, include such terminology and such instruments as have a particular meaning or occupy a particular place in American music. The entry "Synclavier" concerns an instrument that is specifically an American creation; "Opera" deals with American traditions of opera composition, production, and performance. Dictionary entries on émigré musicians such as Arnold Schoenberg as well as groups based overseas, such as the Beatles, focus on their activities and impact within the United States. An American approach will also be seen in the dictionary's focus on scholars whose work has centered on American music; entries on music scholars with other specialties can be found in *Grove Music Online*.

A quarter century of musical activity and burgeoning scholarship has led to new articles in this dictionary on contemporary figures such as singer Mariah Carey and conductor Gustavo Dudamel, as well as on historical ensembles such as the 19th-century touring orchestra, the Germania Musical Society. Some articles in the present work offer updates of articles published either in the 1986 edition or in *Grove Music Online* (initially published in 2001 in print as *The New Grove Dictionary of Music and Musicians*, 2nd ed.), while many articles are newly written. Describing the relationship between coverage of country music in previous Grove dictionaries and the present dictionary demonstrates the way in which content has expanded. The 1986 edition of the dictionary included a substantial article on "country music" as well as nearly 90 additional articles on country music figures and topics. *Grove Music Online* contains a shorter entry on "country music" and a modest number of articles on individual country artists. In response to the sustained impact of and scholarly interest in country music, the present work features a newly commissioned, updated, and extensive article on "country music" as well as nearly 300 articles dedicated to individual country musicians, groups, and subgenres. While all subject areas have received close attention, coverage of certain subject areas has seen extensive growth, including African American music, Asian American music, choral music, cities and regions, concert music, film music, Hawaiian music, Latino music, Native American music, 19th-century music, music and dance, music education, music librarians and libraries, musical theater, opera, popular music, sacred music, and music technology.

The dictionary includes more than 9000 entries on significant people, places, objects, practices, genres, concepts, themes, and traditions. Entries range very widely, from coverage of ABBA and Albuquerque to zydeco and Ellen Zwilich. Given such room to explore its subject, the dictionary features not only general entries on broad topics such as awards, fellowships, patronage, and nonprofit organizations, but also devoted articles to individual patrons and selected granting institutions. The present work also features a newly designed set of entries that address musical life at significant junctures in American history, including the Revolutionary War, the Civil War, the Great Depression, the Cold War, the Civil Rights Movement, and 9/11. Repertories of American music are considered under such headings as "chamber music," "choral music," "percussion music," and "piano music." Many entries treat aspects of American musical life with significant traditions of their own (including "band," "criticism," "electronic dance music," "improvisation," "musical theater," "orchestra," "recorded sound," and "tuning systems"). Various musical institutions—societies, colleges and universities, conservatories—have individual entries; those within cities that are entered in the dictionary are typically discussed within the appropriate city entry.

The preparation of this dictionary involved a large-scale and extended collaboration among individual authors, a board of advisors, and a team of editors, as well as administrative, computing, and publishing staff. The initial steps of our procedure involved dividing the content of the planned dictionary into separate subject areas and inviting advisory board members to suggest updates, alterations, and additions to existing content from the 1986 edition and *Grove Music Online*. Individual responsibilities were assigned to individual subject areas, purposely designed to overlap as a means of achieving more thorough coverage. Incorporating suggestions from the advisory board, a team of senior editors (each responsible for several hundred dictionary entries) and contributing editors (each carrying similar responsibilities involving smaller subject areas), in consultation with the dictionary editor, decided which entries should be reprinted with little or no change, which should be more substantially altered, which should be replaced in whole or in part by new entries, which might be omitted altogether, and which new topics should be considered for inclusion.

The dictionary does not aim at completeness—it is a repository of historically significant information, not a directory. We have tried to provide generous representation of American musical life across the widest possible spectrum.

Despite our best intentions, errors and omissions are inevitable in a work of this size. We encourage readers to send any communications to the editor of *Grove Music Online* (editor@grovemusic.com).

Acknowledgments. First thanks must go to the dictionary contributors, nearly 1500 in number, whose names, together with the titles of the articles they wrote, are listed at the beginning of the first volume. Many of them drew attention to additional material worthy of inclusion, reframed articles, and offered productive suggestions. Claude Conyers merits special commendation for substantially expanding the dictionary's coverage of dance. The editorial team also wishes to recognize the remarkable efforts of Jonas Westover, who contributed more than 400 articles, both new and updated, across the entire dictionary.

I wish to thank all the specialists on the advisory board for sharing expertise, insightful commentary, and thoughtful suggestions concerning the dictionary's design and content. A small group of advisors took on the challenging task of envisioning dictionary entries across particularly large spectrums of musical activity: Frances R. Aparicio (Latino music), Ellen Koskoff (European American music), Portia K. Maultsby (African American music), Josephine Wright (African American music), and Deborah Wong (Asian American music). A number of advisors offered their expertise on more focused subject areas, including Harris M. Berger (ethnomusicology), Philip V. Bohlman (music and religion), David Brackett (popular music, post-1945), Dale Cockrell (sacred music), James Deaville (scholarly approaches and Canadian music), Robert Fink (concert music, post-1950), Kyle Gann (concert music, post-1950), Elise K. Kirk (opera singers), Judith McCulloh (folk music), Martin Miller Marks (film music), David Nicholls (experimentalism), Carol J. Oja (concert music, 1900–50), Katherine K. Preston (19th-century music), Thomas L. Riis (musical theater and opera), Deane L. Root (popular music, pre-1945), David Sanjek (music publishing and recording), Magen Solomon (choral music), Amy Ku'uleialoha Stillman (Hawaiian music), Timothy D. Taylor (technology), Judith Tick (women in music), Sherrie Tucker (jazz), and Paul F. Wells (country music). Advisors who offered expertise on specific groups of musicians included Lynne Aspnes (harpists), José Antonio Bowen (conductors), Mark Katz (violinists), Craig B. Parker (winds and brass performers), Ann Sears (pianists), James A. Strain (percussionists), and Graham Wade (guitarists).

The project flourished thanks to the tireless efforts of the members of the editorial team, all of whom volunteered an enormous amount of time and energy to shape and refine coverage in assigned subject areas, to identify and contact appropriate authors, and to edit and finalize submitted articles. Their work represents a tremendous collective gift of expertise, service, and commitment to American music studies, and I am deeply thankful for the opportunity to work closely with all of them. The following members of the senior editorial board handled large subject areas or shared responsibility for separate subject areas: E. Douglas Bomberger (19th-century music), Carolyn Bryant (musical instruments and instrument makers), Mark Clague (cities, regions, and musical institutions), Kevin Fellezs (Asian American music, Hawaiian music, jazz), Tammy L. Kernodle (blues, gospel, jazz), Daniel Goldmark (film music and music publishing), Jere T. Humphreys (music education), Beth E. Levy (concert music, 1900–50), Alejandro L. Madrid (Latino music), Travis D. Stimeling (country music), and Jacqueline Warwick (popular music, post-1945). The wide scope of the dictionary necessitated the enlistment of additional experts who shaped, commissioned, and edited articles in specialized subject areas: Elizabeth Aldrich (music and dance), Bryan Burton (Native American music), Raoul F. Camus (band music), Esther R. Crookshank (19th-century sacred music), David P. DeVenney (choral music), William A. Everett (musical theater), Emily Daus Ferrigno (electronic music), Thomas V. Fraschillo (winds and brass performers), Brian Harker (jazz), Loren Kajikawa (hip hop), John Koegel (concert music, pre-1825), Paul R. Laird (musical theater), Stephen A. Marini (sacred music), Drew Massey (critics and writers), Michael Meckna (literary figures), N. Lee Orr (organs and organists), Michael V. Pisani (opera), Arian Sheets (musical instruments and instrument makers), Joanna R. Smolko (popular music, pre-1945), Stephanie N. Stallings (concert music, 1900–present), Judy S. Tsou (scholars and librarians), Paul F. Wells (folk music), Ron Wiecki (concert music, 1900–present), and Stephen D. Winick (European American music). Sylvia R. Martin served as associate contributing editor in the area of sacred music.

In a number of specialized areas, expert advice and guidance was needed. The editors wish to thank Cari Geer Alexander, Robert Christgau, Paula Conlon, Richard Crawford, Kyle Devine, J. Richard Haefer, David Hildebrand, Edmond Johnson, Victoria Lindsay Levine, Laurence Libin, Thomas MacCracken, Rick Mattingly, Marie McCarthy, Brian Moon, Renee Lapp Norris, William Osborne, Barbara Owen, Ron Pen, Jody Rosen, Alex Ross, Sally Sommers Smith, Steve Swayne, Thane Tierney, and James Wierzbicki for their generous assistance.

Research assistants, working at the University of Michigan and other institutions, made very significant contributions to the dictionary. We are grateful to Chevauna Adams, Alexander Bonus, Leah Branstetter, TajRoy Calhoun, Joshua Duchan, Sarah Gerk, Mariah Gillespie, Andrew Hoppert, Craig Jennex, Laura Kennedy, Amy Kimura, Ryan Kirk, Michael Mauskapf, Elia Pepps, Christopher Paul Phillpott, Nathan Platte, Judson Cole Ritchie, Rebecca Schwartz-Bishir, Tim Smolko, Garrett Thorson, Leah Weinberg, and Catherine Wojtanowski.

The editorial team also wishes to acknowledge the various helpful forms of institutional support provided by Case Western Reserve University, Elizabethtown College, the Library of Congress, Millikin University, and Texas Christian University.

The primary editorial and administrative work for the dictionary project was carried out at the School of Music, Theatre & Dance at the University of Michigan, an especially generous host institution that provided consistent support for the dictionary. Dean Christopher Kendall served as a tremendous advocate for the project, as did Associate Deans Steven M. Whiting and Mary Simoni. James Borders, chair of the Department of Musicology, and my faculty colleagues were especially supportive and understanding about the editorial demands of this project. University funding for research support, student assistants, and technological support was provided by the School of Music, Theatre & Dance, the Office of the Vice President for Research, the Rackham Graduate School, and the University Research Opportunity Program. University of Michigan professor Jonathan Maybaum, the principal inventor of UM.SiteMaker—a web-based platform that supported the project's extensive development website—provided vital design assistance, contributed specialized programming, and offered timely technical support throughout.

Deepest thanks go to Mark Clague, whose dedication to the project proved absolutely vital. In addition to serving as a senior editor, he offered generous and valuable advice over the entire course of the project. As project editor, he also designed an extensive project website that served as a shared database that facilitated communication between all participants in the project. The dictionary would not have taken its final shape or have been completed on schedule without his many contributions.

I am also extremely thankful to everyone at *Grove Music Online* whose efforts showed such devotion to this project. The dictionary would not exist without Laura Macy, who championed the project from the start and collaborated on the design of its shape, basic features, and editorial structure. Her leadership, vision, and boundless energy enabled the project to become reality. In her role as Laura's assistant, Catriona Hopton handled a variety of administrative details that also helped the project get off the ground. Tim Sachs next took over the reins as publishing editor for the dictionary, and he offered extremely valuable advice, publishing wisdom, creative suggestions, and patient support. As Tim's successor, Anna-Lise Santella skillfully guided the project to its completion with great care and good cheer. I am fortunate as well to have worked closely with Lucie McGee, Jenny Doster, and Jessica Barbour—all of whom provided timely, frequent, and helpful support in their roles assisting Tim and Anna-Lise. Kudos go out to Mary Araneo and her copyediting and production staff for their thorough, detailed, and consistent work on the dictionary. Thanks as well are deserved by Shira Bistricer for her assistance with illustrations.

On a personal note, I wish to thank my family members for being so supportive throughout the course of this project and, most of all, Saleema Waraich for her infinitely generous kindness, love, and patience.

Charles Hiroshi Garrett

September 2013

List of Contributors

The following contributors wrote new articles or heavily revised articles from *The New Grove Dictionary of American Music* or *Grove Music Online:*

Abadía-Rexach, Bárbara Idalissee
Abel, Ernest Lawrence
Acker, Anne Beetem
Adams, Byron
Adams, Daniel
Adams, Kyle
Adams, Sarah
Adams, Stephen J.
Adelt, Ulrich
Ades, David
Ahlquist, Karen
Aitken, Paul A.
Akenson, James E.
Akindes, Fay Yokomizo
Alan, David C.
Albertson, Chris
Albiez, Sean
Albo, Francisco J.
Alburger, Mark
Alcorn, Allison A.
Aldrich, Elizabeth
Alger, Dean
Allen, Aaron S.
Allen, Matthew Harp
Allen, Ray
Allen, Virginia
Alleyne, Mike
Alonso-Minutti, Ana R.
Ambalal, Monica F.
Amchin, Robert A.
Ancelet, Barry Jean
Anderson, David M.
Anderson, Donna K.
Anderson, Gene H.
Anderson, Michael J.
Anderson, Roger C.
Anderson, Tim J.
Andre, Naomi
Andres, Robert
Ansari, Emily Abrams
Antokoletz, Elliott
Aparicio, Frances R.
Apolloni, Alexandra M.
Archdeacon, Dan
Ardito, Linda
Arévalo Mateus, Jorge
Argyropoulos, Erica K.
Arndt, Elizabeth A.
Arnold, Alison E.
Asai, Susan Miyo
Ashworth, Jack
Au, Susan
Auslander, Philip
Avant-Mier, Roberto
Avila, Jacqueline
Avorgbedor, Daniel
Azcona, Estevan César

Baade, Christina
Badger, Reid
Badolato, Nicola
Baker, Hilary
Baker, Valerie Anne
Ball, Steven
Ballard, Lincoln
Balme, Christopher
Bañagale, Ryan Raul
Banks, Margaret Downie
Barber, Barbara G.
Barber, Charles
Bares, William Kirk
Barg, Lisa
Bargreen, Melinda
Barkin, Elaine
Barnhart, Stephen L.
Baron, John H.
Barretta, Scott
Bartlett, Andrew
Barzel, Tamar
Basart, Ann P.
Bash, James
Bass, John
Battier, Marc
Baumgartner, Michael
Baur, Steven
Bazzana, Kevin
Beasley, Steven
Beaster-Jones, Jayson
Beck, Guy L.
Beck, John R.
Beckerman, Michael
Behling, John
Beissinger, Margaret H.
Beisswenger, Drew
Belfy, Jeanne M.
Bell, Brian
Bell, Gelsey
Bellaviti, Sean
Bellemare, Luc
Beltrán, Mary
Bempéchat, Paul-André
Bennett, Dina M.
Benson, Mark
Bergman, Jason S.
Berish, Andrew
Berkman, Franya
Berlin, Edward A.
Bernard, Shane K.
Berresford, Mark
Berry, David Carson
Berry, Michael
Berz, William
Betz, Marianne
Bevan, Clifford

Bickford, Tyler
Bidgood, Lee
Bierley, Paul E.
Birenbaum Quintero, Michael
Bishop, Paula J.
Bithell, David
Bjorn, Lars
Black Junttonen, Mary
Blackburn, Allison
Blake, Daniel
Blaustein, Richard
Blažeković, Zdravko
Blim, Dan
Block, Geoffrey
Blumhofer, Edith
Blumhofer, Jonathan E.
Blunsom, Laurie
Bodiford, J. Ryan
Boettcher, Bonna J.
Bohlman, Andrea F.
Bohlman, Philip V.
Bomberger, E. Douglas
Bomberger, Joseph A.
Boone, Will
Booth, Susan Badger
Borders, James
Borgo, David
Bosse, Joanna
Bothwell, Beau
Botstein, Leon
Bourgeois, John
Boutwell, Brett
Bowen, Michele
Bowers, Nathan D.
Bowles, Edmund A.
Bowman, Durrell
Bowman, Rob
Boyd, Joe Dan
Boyd, Michael
Boyer, Bill Bahng
Boyer, D. Royce
Boyle, Mark A.
Boziwick, George
Brackett, David
Brackett, John
Bradley, Ian
Brady, Erika
Brantley, K. Thomas
Bratus, Alessandro
Breckbill, Anita
Brenner, Helmut
Brett, Thomas
Bridwell-Briner, Kathryn
Brill, Mark
Briscoe, James R.
Britt, Edmund J.
Brockmann, Nicole M.
Brook, Claire
Brookes, Ian
Brooks, Tim
Brophy, Philip
Brown, Gwynne Kuhner
Brown, Jessica L.
Brown, Joseph A.
Brown, Sara Black
Broyles, Michael
Bruce, Ryan D.W.
Brucher, Katherine
Brunelle, Carolyn
Bryan, Karen M.
Bryant, Brooke
Bryant, Carolyn
Bubsey, David R.
Buccio, Daniele
Büchmann-Møller, Frank
Budasz, Rogerio
Buehner, Katie
Buja, Maureen
Bunbury, Richard R.
Burford, Mark
Burgess, Geoffrey
Burkart, Patrick
Burkholder, J. Peter
Burleson, Jill L.
Burlingame, Jon
Burns, Lori
Burton, J. Bryan
Butler, H. Joseph
Butler, J. Michael
Butler, Nicholas Michael

Caldwell, Judi
Cale, Eric M.
Camacho-Azofeifa, Tania
Campana, Deborah
Campbell, Brett
Campbell, Murray
Campbell, Jennifer L.
Campbell, Sharon O'Connell
Camus, Raoul F.
Camus, Renée E.
Candelaria, Lorenzo
Caneva, Thomas E.
Cannon, Alexander M.
Cano, Rubén López
Cantrell, Brent
Cantwell, Robert
Carder, Polly
Care, Ross
Carey, Christian
Carli, Alice
Carlin, Bob
Carlin, Richard
Carner, Gary
Carpenter, Alexander
Carr, Daphne G.
Carroll, Brendan G.
Carroll, Daniel John
Carson, Charles
Carter, Marva Griffin
Carter, Walter
Case, Alex U.
Cassaro, James P.
Castro, Christi-Anne
Catalano, Nick
Cateforis, Theo
Cavicchi, Daniel
Cayward, Margaret
Cederquist, G.J.
Cerchiari, Luca
Ceriani, Davide
Chafin, Theresa
Chambers, Jack
Chapman, Dale E.
Charry, Eric
Chattah, Juan R.
Cheney, Charise
Chevan, David
Chew, Geoffrey
Chute, James
Chybowski, Julia J.
Cifaldi, Susan
Cipolla, Frank J.
Clague, Mark
Clark, Joe C.
Clark, John L., Jr.
Clark, Thomas
Clark, Walter Aaron
Clarke, Donald
Clarke, Garry E.
Clayton, Matthew D., II
Clemente, John
Clendinning, Elizabeth A.
Clifton, Keith E.
Cline, John
Coates, Norma
Cochran, Alfred W.
Cochran, Keith
Cockrell, Dale
Coffman, Don D.
Cohen, Jacob A.
Cohen, Judah M.
Cohen, Noal
Cohen, Norm
Cohen, Ronald D.
Coldwell, Maria V.
Collins, Karen
Colwell, Richard J.
Commanday, Robert
Conklin, Michael
Conlon, Paula J.
Conn, Stephanie
Conrad, Charles
Conrad, Jon Alan
Conway, Cecelia
Conyers, Claude
Cook, James H.
Cook, Susan C.
Cooley, Timothy J.
Cooper, Shelly C.
Copeland, Robert M.
Corey, Charles
Coscarelli, William F.

Cottrell, Stephen
Cowger, Kelsey
Cox, G. Paul
Craft, Elizabeth Titrington
Crain, Timothy M.
Crawford, Richard
Crispin, Judith
Crookshank, Esther R.
Crosby, Jill Flanders
Cumming, Duncan J.
Cunningham, Carl
Cunningham, James E.
Currie, A. Scott
Curtis, Liane
Cusic, Don
Cusick, Suzanne G.

Dalphond, Denise M.M.
Corey, Christi L.
Daniel, Linda J.
Danielson, Virginia
Danner, Peter
Darden, Robert
Darrow, Alice-Ann
Daubney, Kate
Davidson, Mary Wallace
Davis, William B.
Dayal, Geeta
de Graaf, Melissa
de Lerma, Dominique-René
de Valk, Jeroen
Deaville, James
Decker, Todd
DeLapp-Birkett, Jennifer
Dell'Antonio, Andrew
DeLucia, Dennis
Dembski, Stephen
Demorest, Steven M.
Dent, Cedric
Determeyer, Eddy
DeVeaux, Scott
DeVenney, David P.
Devine, Kyle
DeVoto, Mark
Dewar, Andrew Raffo
DeWitt, Mark F.
Diamond, Jody
Díaz Díaz, Edgardo
Díaz, Álvaro Aurelio Vega
Dickson, Jean
Dirksen, Rebecca
Dobney, Jayson Kerr
Doering, James
Döhl, Frédéric
Dohoney, Ryan
Doll, Christopher
Donahue, Matthew A.
Doran, Carol A.
Dorsey, Sarah B.
dos Santos, Silvio J.
Doukhan, Lilianne
Downey, Greg
Dreisbach, Tina Spencer
Drillock, David
Driver, Richard D.
Druesedow, John E.
Dubnov, Shlomo
Duchan, Joshua S.
Dudgeon, Ralph T.
Duerksen, George L.
Dumas, Anthony C.
Dunlay, Kate

Eanes, Edward
Ebright, Ryan
Echard, William
Eden, Bradford Lee
Edwards, J. Michele
Edwards, Kay
Edwards, Leigh H.
Eidsheim, Nina Sun
Eisler, Garrett
Elafros, Athena
Elavsky, C. Michael
Eldredge, Jeffrey T.
Eldredge, Niles
Eli Rodríguez, Victoria
Eliason, Robert E.
Eliassen, Meredith
Elkus, Jonathan
Ellzey, Michael
Elmore, Charles J.
Emoff, Ron
Erickson, Stephen P.
Ertan, Deniz
Erviti, Manuel
Eskew, Harry
Ethen, Michael
Evans, Allan
Evans, DavidEvans, Meredith
Everett, Walter
Everett, William A.
Exner, Ellen
Eyerly, Sarah

Falk, Gary
Fallon, Robert
Fanelli, Michael Paul
Farrar, Lloyd P.
Farrington, Jim
Farrugia, Rebekah
Fast, Susan
Faulkner, Scott
Fawcett-Lothson, Amanda
Feilotter, Melanie
Feintuch, Burt
Feisst, Sabine
Feldman, Evan
Fellezs, Kevin
Fenimore, Ross J.
Ferencz, George J.
Ferencz, Jane Riegel
Fernandez, Raul
Ferre, Stephen
Ferrigno, Emily
Fetterley, Leanne
Feustle, Maristella
Fields, Warren
Fischer, Paul D.
Fiske, Harold
Fitzgerald, Michael
Flaig, Vera H.
Flandreau, Suzanne
Fleiner, Carey
Fleming, BonnieElizabeth
Flory, Andrew
Folkman, Benjamin
Fonarow, Wendy
Fonder, Mark
Font-Navarrete, David
Ford, Phil
Foreman, George C.
Forrest, Rebecca A.
Forry, Mark
Forss, Matthew J.
Fountain, Marcia
Fragman, Dominic A.
Franke, Matthew
Freed, Richard
Freedman, Jean R.
Freeman, Charles S.
Freer, Patrick K.
Frengel, Michael C.
Fresne, Jeannette
Friesen, Michael D.
Froehlich, Hildegard
Froom, David
Fry, Robert Webb, II
Fry, Stephen M.
Fulton, Will

Galván, Gary
Gann, Kyle
Ganson, Paul
Gansz, David
Garber, Michael G.
Garcia, David F.
García, León
Garcia, Luis-Manuel
Garcia, Thomas
Gardner, Kara
Garrett, Charles Hiroshi
Gates, J. Terry
Gattegno, Eliot
Gaztambide-Fernández, Rubén A.
Geduld, Victoria Phillips
Gelfand, Janelle
Gentry, Philip
George-Warren, Holly
Geringer, John M.
Gerk, Sarah
Geston, Mary K.
Getman, Jessica L.

Gibson, Chris
Gibson, Christina Taylor
Gibson, Maya
Gibson, Nathan D.
Giedl, Linda L.
Gilbert, Joel
Gillespie, Robert
Gioia, Ted
Givan, Benjamin
Gloag, Kenneth
Goble, J. Scott
Goertzen, Chris
Goins, Wayne E.
Goldberg, Bethany
Goldin-Perschbacher, Shana
Goldmark, Daniel
Goldschmitt, Kariann
Goldsmith, Melissa Ursula Dawn
Goldsmith, Thomas
Goldstein, Howard
Goldstein, Perry
Gonzalez, G. Mancho
Gonzalez, Melissa
Good, Edwin M.
Goodman, Glenda
Goodman, Linda J.
Gopinath, Sumanth
Gorzelany-Mostak, Dana C.
Gottlieb, Jane
Graham, Sandra Jean
Granade, S. Andrew
Graves, Darlene
Graves, Michael
Grazian, David
Graziano, John
Greco, Nicholas P.
Green, Douglas B.
Green, Edward
Green, Jeffrey
Green, Lucy
Greenberg, Jonathan
Greene, Gary A.
Greene, Jayson
Greene, Kimberly
Greene, Oliver
Greenland, Thomas H.
Greenwald Strom, Laura
Greer, Lowell
Grella, George J., Jr.
Griffiths, Paul
Grimminger, Daniel Jay
Grimshaw, Jeremy N.
Griscom, Richard
Groce, Nancy
Grolman, Ellen K.
Guillén, Lorena
Guion, David M.
Guzski, Carolyn
Gwozdz, Lawrence

Haas, Ain
Habib, Kenneth S.
Haddix, Chuck
Haefer, J. Richard
Hagedorn, Katherine
Hagen, Ross
Hairston O'Connell, Monica
Hajduk, John C.
Hall, Roger L.
Hallman, Diana R.
Hamilton, Andy
Hamilton, Jack
Hammond, Bruce
Hancock, Carl B.
Handel, Greg A.
Hansen, Lindsay
Hanson, Christopher T.F.
Hanson-Dvoracek, Andrew
Haramaki, Gordon
Harbert, Benjamin J.
Harker, Brian
Harnish, David
Harris, Eric Lynn
Hartsock, Ralph
Hash, Phillip M.
Hatch, Martin
Havighurst, Craig
Haws, Barbara
Hayes, Deborah
Hayes, Eileen M.
Hayes, Elaine M.
Hayes, Micah
Heavner, Tabitha W.
Hedden, Debra Gordon
Heffley, Mike
Hegarty, Paul
Heintze, James R.
Heisler, Wayne, Jr.
Helgert, Lars
Heller, Jack
Heller, Michael C.
Hellman, Rick
Henderson, Chip
Henderson, Scott
Henigan, Julie
Hennessey, Patrick
Henriques, Donald A.
Henry, James
Henry, Murphy Hicks
Henry, Warren
Herbert, Trevor
Heriger, Stephanie
Hernández, Ramón
Herrmann, Irene
Hess, Debra L.
Hettrick, William E.
Heyman, Barbara B.
Higgins, Brendan
Higgins, Nicholas
Hildebrand, David
Hill, Matthew
Hill, Megan E.
Hillman, Jessica
Hinkle-Turner, Elizabeth
Hinterbichler, Karl
Hirshberg, Jehoash
Hisama, Ellie M.
Hischak, Thomas S.
Hiser, Kelly
Hitchner, Earle
Hix, Michael
Hlynka, Denis
Ho, Allan B.
Holden, Jonathan
Holley, Whitney B.
Holmes, Jeffrey
Holz, Ronald W.
Hooker, Lynn M.
Hoover, Cynthia Adams
Hoover, Sarah Adams
Hope, Samuel
Hopkins, Christopher
Hoppert, Andrew
Horowitz, Joseph
Horton, E. Ron
Houle, Michelle E.
Housez, Lara E.
Hovland, Michael
Howe, Blake
Howe, Sondra Wieland
Hsu, Wendy F.
Hubbert, Julie
Hubbs, Nadine
Huber, Patrick
Hudson, Kathleen
Hughes, R. Daniel, Jr.
Humphrey, Mary Lou
Humphreys, Jere T.
Hung, Eric
Hunsberger, Donald
Hunter, David
Huston, Spencer A.
Hutchinson, Sydney

Inaba, Mitsutoshi
Isacoff, Stuart
Isoardi, Steven L.

Jabbour, Alan
Jackson, Margaret R.
Jackson, Travis A.
Jamison, Philip A.
Janikian, Leon
Jarnow, Jesse
Jeffrey, Dean
Jenkins, Chadwick
Jennex, Craig
Jensen-Moulton, Stephanie
Jewanski, Jörg
Johnson, Birgitta J.
Johnson, Brett D.
Johnson, Edmond T.
Johnston, Jesse A.
Johnston, Richard
Joiner, Lauren
Jones, Alyson E.

Jones, M. Rusty
Jones, Patrick M.
Jones, Patti
Jones, Roben
Jones, Ryan Patrick
Jovanovic, Rob
Joyce, John
Judd, Robert
Junker, Jay W.
Jurgensmeier, Charles

Kajikawa, Loren
Kaloyanides, Michael G.
Kalra, Ajay
Kamtman, Leslie E.
Kang, You Young
Kaplan, Amelia S.
Karchin, Louis
Kasel, Marco
Kass, Philip J.
Kassabian, Anahid
Kattari, Kimberly A.
Katz, Israel J.
Kawamoto, Akitsugu
Kayali, Francis
Kays, John
Keel, Beverly
Kehrberg, Kevin
Keightley, Keir
Keller, Kate Van Winkle
Kelly, Jennifer W.
Kelly, Steven N.
Kennedy, Gary W.
Kennedy, Laura E.
Kernan, Thomas J.
Kernodle, Tammy L.
Key, Susan
Kienzle, Rich
Kijas, Anna E.
Kimura, Amy Kazuye
Kinnear, Tyler
Kinzer, Charles E.
Kirk, Elise K.
Kirk, Ryan
Kisiedu, Harald
Kite, Rebecca
Klassen, Doreen Helen
Klaus, Sabine K.
Kleszynski, Kenneth
Knapp, Raymond
Knauer, Wolfram
Knight, Ellen
Knouse, Nola Reed
Kobuskie, Jennifer M.
Koegel, John
Koehler, Elisa
Koenig, Theresa
Koeppe, Douglas
Kolt, Robert Paul
Komara, Edward
Kopp, James B.
Koster, John

Kottick, Edward L.
Kovacs, Ingrid M.
Kramer, Katherine
Krasner, Orly Leah
Krawitz, Justin
Kreitner, Kenneth
Kreitner, Mona
Krims, Adam
Kroeger, Karl
Kubicki, Judith M.
Kuntz, Danielle M.
Kuronen, Darcy
Kushner, David Z.
Kuuskoski, Jonathan
Kwon, Donna Lee
Kyger, David J.

LaBrew, Arthur R.
La Chapelle, Peter
Laird, Paul R.
Laird, Tracey E.W.
Lamb, Andrew
Lambert, Philip
Lansky, Paul
Largey, Michael
Lasocki, David
Latimer, Marvin E., Jr.
Laurel, Heather
Laurence, Anya
Lawrence, Tim
Leafstedt, Carl
Lee, Douglas A.
Lee, William R.
Lefferts, Peter M.
Leimseider, John
Lenti, Vincent A.
León, Javier F.
Leonard, Kendra Preston
Leonard, Marion
Leotsakos, George
Lerner, Neil
Leve, James
Levine, Mike
Levine, Victoria Lindsay
Levy, Beth E.
Levy, Mark
Lewis, Alan
Lewis, George E.
Lewis, Hannah
Lewis, Thomas
Libby, Cynthia Green
Libin, Laurence
Lien, Jennifer
Lien, Joelle L.
Lilly, John
Lin, Hsun
Linde, Brad
Linick, Anthony
Linklater, Christina
Lis, Anthony S.
Lister, Rodney
Livingston, Carolyn

Lobaugh, H. Bruce
Lockard, Craig A.
Locke, Ralph P.
Lodge, Mary Jo
Logan, Kathryn
Lomanno, Mark
Lomax, John Nova
Long, Barry
Lopes, Luiz Fernando
Lornell, Kip
Lorre, Sean
Lott, R. Allen
Love, Randolph
Lovell, Jeff
Lovensheimer, Jim
Low, Andrea
Loza, Steven
Lucas, Heidi
Luongo, Paul
Lush, Paige Clark
Luster, Michael
Lyman, Anne

MacAulay, Mark
Macdonald, Claudia
MacInnis, John
MacKinney, Lisa
Madrid, Alejandro L.
Magee, Jeffrey
Mahar, William J.
Mahon, Maureen
Maldonado, Melanie
Maloney, S. Timothy
Manabe, Noriko
Manfredo, Joseph
Manuel, Peter
March, Richard
Mari, Licia
Marini, Stephen A.
Mark, Michael L.
Marshall, Wayne
Martin, Andrew R.
Martin, Margaret
Martin, Sarah L.
Martínez, Katynka Z.
Marvin, Jameson
Masotti, Christian
Massey, Drew
Mather, Olivia Carter
Mathews, Peter
Mathieson, Kenny
Matson, Joseph R.
Matthews, Jennifer
Mattingly, Rick
Maus, Fred Everett
Mauskapf, Michael
Maxile, Horace J., Jr.
May, Eldonna L.
Mazo, Margarita
Mazor, Barry
McBride, Jerry L.
McCabe, Matthew L.

McCain, Martin
McCarthy, David
McCarthy, Marie
mcclung, bruce d.
McCracken, Allison
McCreless, Patrick
McDonald, Chris
McDowell, Amy D.
McFarland, Ann
McGhee, Michael
McGinnis, Beth
McGraw, Ted
McGuire, Julie
McHugh, Dominic
McIlwain, Ben
McKay, Janis L.
McKnight, Mark
McLeod, Ken
McLucas, Anne Dhu
McMillan, Jeffery S.
McMullen, Tracy
McNutt, Ryan R.
McTyre, Ruthann B.
Meacham, Matt
Meckna, Michael
Medwin, Marc
Mehrens, Christopher E.
Meizel, Katherine
Mellard, Jason
Melnick, Jeffrey
Menehan, Kelsey
Menius, Art
Meyer-Frazier, Petra
Mezzadri, Danilo
Miller, Leta E.
Miller, Michael
Miller, Timothy D.
Miner, Gregg
Mirchandani, Sharon
Mitchell, Ian
Mitchell, Jon Ceander
Mitchell, Scott A.
Mitroulia, Eugenia
Miyakawa, Felicia M.
Moehn, Frederick
Mok, April H.
Mondelli, Peter
Montague, Stephen
Mook, Richard
Moon, Brian A.
Moon, Krystyn
Moon, Kyung-Suk
Mooney, Kevin E.
Moore, Laura
Moore, Robin
Moore, Ryan
Moreno, Jairo
Morey, Carl
Morgan, Elizabeth N.
Morgan, Joseph E.
Morgenstern, Dan
Moricz, Klara
Morrison, Matthew D.
Morton, David C.
Moskowitz, David
Moss, Patricia
Motley, Clay
Moulton-Gertig, Suzanne L.
Moyle, Richard M.
Mueller, Gavin
Mugmon, Matthew
Muir, Peter C.
Munger, Philip
Murchison, Gayle
Murdock, Tina
Music, David W.
Musto, Russ

Nachman, Myrna S.
Natvig, Mary
Neal, Brandi A.
Neal, Jocelyn R.
Neal, Mark Anthony
Near, John R.
Neely, Daniel
Neely, Jack
Neff, Severine
Negron, Marisol
Nekola, Anna
Nettl, Bruno
Neuls-Bates, Carol
Newland, Marti
Newman, Nancy
Niblock, Howard
Nicholls, David
Niebur, Louis
Noe, George T.
Noonan, Jeffrey J.
Norris, Renee Lapp
Norton, Kay
Novara, Vincent J.
Nuzzo, Nancy

Obregón, Mireya
O'Brien, Kevin
Ochs, Michael
O'Connell, Christian
O'Connor, Patrick
Ohl, Vicki
Oja, Carol J.
Olmstead, Andrea
O'Loughlin, Niall
O'Meara, Caroline Polk
Ord-Hume, Arthur W.J.G.
Orr, N. Lee
Osborne, William
Ostling, Acton, Jr.
Ota, Diane O.
Oteri, Frank J.
Otfinoski, Steve
Ottenberg, June C.
Ouellette, Dan
Owen, Barbara
Owen, Norton
Oyen, Meredith
Ozment, Elizabeth Whittenburg

Packwood, Gary D.
Page, Janet K.
Palfy, Barbara
Palmer, Larry
Palomares, Carlos
Pappas, Nikos
Parler, Sam
Party, Daniel
Pauley, Jared
Pawlak, Keith
Payette, Jessica
Payne, Alyson
Pearse, Lukas
Pearson, Robert D.
Peck, Ellen Marie
Peck, Robert William
Pecknold, Diane
Pehl, Christa
Pellegrinelli, Lara
Pen, Ron
Pendle, Karin
Pennington, Anna
Pennington, Stephan
Pepping, Amanda
Perea, Jessica Bissett
Perea, John-Carlos
Pérez-Rolón, Jorge A.
Perrone, Dina
Perry, David L.
Perry, Jeff
Perry, Mark E.
Perry, Richard H.
Perten, Elizabeth
Pesce, Dolores
Petersen, Barbara A.
Peterson, Elaine L.
Peterson, Jason
Petteys, M. Leslie
Peyser, Joan
Piekut, Benjamin
Pieslak, Jonathan
Pilgrim, Neva
Pillsbury, Glenn T.
Pinel, Stephen L.
Pinkerton, Emily
Piorkowski, Peter
Piras, Marcello
Pisani, Michael V.
Pita, Laura
Place, Jeff
Platte, Nathan
Pohly, Linda L.
Pollack, Howard
Pollard, Deborah Smith
Polman, Bert F.
Pond, Steven F.

Pool, Jeannie Gayle
Porcaro, Mark D.
Poriss, Hilary
Porter, Cecelia H.
Porter, Lewis
Poutiainen, Ari
Powell, Ardal
Powers, Richard
Pratt, Ray
Preston, Katherine K.
Price, Emmett G., III
Price, Harry E.
Price, William
Prichard, Laura
Priestley, Brian
Proksch, Bryan
Provost, Sarah Caissie
Pruett, David B.
Pruett, Laura Moore
Purcell, Ronald C.
Purciello, Maria
Purin, Peter

Quevedo, Marysol

Radice, Mark, A.
Radomski, James
Raeburn, Bruce Boyd
Raftery, Brian
Ragland, Cathy
Rahaim, Matt
Raizor, Karen
Raley, Lynn
Ramos-Kittrell, Jesús A.
Ramsey, Doug
Ramsey, Guthrie P., Jr.
Randall, Annie J.
Randall, James
Rao, Nancy Yunwha
Rapport, Evan
Raser, Harold E.
Rasmussen, Anne K.
Rausch, Robin
Ravas, Tammy
Reali, Chris
Reed, Roxanne R.
Regelski, Thomas A.
Rehrig, William H.
Reish, Gregory N.
Reitz, Christina L.
Reitzell, James Dobes
Remson, Michael
Renton, Barbara A.
Resta, Craig
Revill, David
Rey, Mario
Reynolds, Christopher A.
Rezak, David M.
Rhodes, Lisa L.
Rice, Albert R.
Rice, Marc
Richards, Patrick
Richardson, John
Richardson, Paul A.
Richardson, Sarah K.
Richmond, John W.
Riehl, Jeffrey S.
Riis, Thomas L.
Riley, Nancy P.
Rivera, Mareia Quintero
Rizzuti, Marida
Robb, Mary
Robinson, Chris
Robinson, Harlow
Rockwell, Joti
Rodger, Gillian M.
Rodman, Ronald W.
Rodnitzky, Jerry
Roholt, Tiger C.
Roman, Zoltan
Romero, Brenda M.
Root, Deane L.
Rosenberg, Ruth E.
Rosenblum, Martin Jack
Rosengard, Robert S.
Rourke, Kelley
Roust, Colin
Royko, David
Rubin, Nick
Ruckert, George
Rumble, John W.
Rumson, Gordon
Ruppa, Paul
Russell, Craig H.
Rye, Howard

Saavedra, Leonora
Sabatini, Arthur J.
Sachs, Joel
Saffle, Michael
Sajnovsky, Cynthia B.
Sakakeeny, Matt
Sala, Aaron J.
Saloman, Ora Frishberg
Samet, Rachel
Samples, Mark C.
Sampsel, Laurie J.
Sanchez, Luis
Sanford, Sally
Sanjek, David
Santella, Anna-Lise P.
Sapoznik, Henry
Saunders, Steven
Saylor, Eric
Scarbrough, Michael
Scheer, Christopher
Schelonka, Greg
Schenbeck, Lawrence
Schiller, David
Schimpf, Peter
Schleifer, Martha Furman
Schlicht, Ursel
Schlitz, J.M.
Schloss, Joseph G.
Schmalenberger, Sarah
Schmidt, Charles P.
Schmidt, John C.
Schmidt, Paul
Schnitker, Laura B.
Schnurr, Stephen J., Jr.
Schrader, Barry
Schroeder, Ilana
Schüler, Nico
Schwartz-Bishir, Rebecca
Scoggin, Lisa
Scott, Andrew
Scott, L. Brett
Scotto, Robert
Seachrist, Denise A.
Sears, Benjamin
Sebesta, Judith A.
Seemann, Charlie
Selfridge-Field, Eleanor
Selvin, Joel
Sercombe, Laurel
Seter, Ronit
Sewell, Stacey
Sewright, Kathleen
Shadle, Douglas W.
Shaffer, Karen A.
Shaftel, Matthew R.
Shardlow, Marilyn Fritz
Sharp, Dan
Shearon, Stephen
Sheets, Arian
Sheinbaum, John J.
Shelley, Anne
Shenton, Andrew
Shepherd, John
Sheppard, W. Anthony
Sherk, Warren M.
Shim, Eunmi
Shirley, Wayne D.
Shirts, Peter
Shockley, Alan
Sholes, Jacquelyn
Shulman, Laurie
Siek, Stephen
Siemers, Brian J.
Siepmann, Jeremy
Silverman, Carol
Simmons, Michael John
Simmons, Walter
Simonett, Helena
Simonot, Colette
Singer, Roberta L.
Skinner, Robert
Slatford, Rodney
Slawek, Stephen
Slominski, Tes
Smigel, Eric
Smiley, Marilynn J.
Smith, Brandon

Smith, Catherine Parsons
Smith, Gareth Dylan
Smith, Hope Munro
Smith, Jewel A.
Smith, Jordan A. Yamaji
Smith, Richard R.
Smolko, Joanna R.
Smolko, Tim
Sneed, Bonnie Borshay
Snelson, John
Snyder, JeanSnyder, Suzanne
Sorce Keller, Marcello
Solis, Gabriel
Solomon, Alan L.
Sommers Smith Wells, Sally K.
Soria, Harry B., Jr.
Southard, Scott Alan
Spackman, Stephen
Sparks, Richard
Spilker, John D.
Spitzer, John
Sposato, Jeffrey S.
Spottswood, Dick
Spring, Howard
Spurgeon, Alan L.
Spurgeon, Debra L.
Stackhouse, Rochelle A.
Stallings, Stephanie
Stanislawski, John
Stanyek, Jason
Steel, David Warren
Stein, Alex Harris
Stein, Eric M.
Steinitz, Richard
Steinke, Greg A
Sterling, Christopher H.
Sternfeld, Jessica
Stewart, Abel
Stewart, Jack
Still, Mary Helen
Stillman, Amy
Stimeling, Travis D.
Stoner-Hawkins, Sylvia
Stover, Chris
Strain, James A.
Straus, Joseph N.
Strickler, Fred
Strong, Willie
Sturman, Janet
Suhadolnik, Sarah E.
Suisman, David
Sullivan, Anita
Sullivan, Jack
Sullivan, Jill
Sumera, Matthew Michael
Summer, Lisa
Summerville, Suzanne
Summit, Jeffrey A.
Sun, Cecilia
Surles, Elizabeth
Suzuki, Yoko
Swayne, Steve
Swenson-Eldridge, Joanne E.
Symonds, Dominic

Taborn, Karen
Talusan, Mary
Tanenbaum, Susie J.
Tarr, Edward H.
Tashiro, Mimi
Tawa, Nicholas
Taylor, Jeffrey
Taylor, Timothy D.
Temperley, Nicholas
Tesser, Neil
Teves, Stephanie Nohelani
Thomas, David W.
Thomas, Jean W.
Thomas, Matthew Alan
Thomas, Susan
Thomas, John
Thompson, Brian C.
Thorson, Garrett
Thuerauf, Jeffrey P.
Tick, Judith
Tierney, Thane
Timbrell, Charles
Tingler, Stephanie
Tipton, Carrie Allen
Titon, Jeff Todd
Tobiason, Anders
Tolbert, Patti M.
Tome, Vanessa
Tommasini, Anthony
Tovey, David G.
Treybig, Joel A.
Trippett, David
Trotter, Herman
Tschmuck, Peter
Tsou, Judy
Tubbs, Jeremy M.
Tucker, Karen B. Westerfield
Turnbull, Gillian
Tychinski, Bruce

Ulaby, Laith
Urrows, David Francis

Vallee, Mickey
Vallier, John B.
van de Leur, Walter
van der Merwe, Ann
Van der Slice, John
Vander Wel, Stephanie
Vandermeer, Philip
Veitch-Olson, Jenni
Vellutini, Claudio
Vickers, Steve
Vigneau, Michelle
Volk Tuohey, Terese
Von Glahn, Denise
Vosen, Elyse Carter

Wade, Graham
Wagner, Lavern John
Wagstaff, John
Wakefield, John C.
Waksman, Steve
Wald, Elijah
Walsh, Thomas J.
Wang, Jui-Ching
Wang, Oliver
Wanser, Jeffery
Warden, Nolan
Ward-Steinman, Patrice Madura
Warfield, Patrick
Warfield, Scott
Warner, Simon
Warwick, Jacqueline
Washburne, Christopher
Waters, Keith
Watkins, Clifford E.
Watson, Jada
Weber, Elisa
Weinberg, Leah G.
Weinert, William
Weinstein, Deena
Weir, Gillian
Weitz, Jay
Welch, Myron
Wells, David Atkinson
Wells Robson, Kate
Wells, Paul F.
Wenderoth, Valeria
West, Aaron J.
West, Paul R.
West, Sandra L.
Westby, James
Westermeyer, Paul
Westover, Jonas
Wetzel, Richard D.
Wheeler, Barbara L.
Wheeler, Scott
Wheelwright, Lynn
White, Miles
Whitesell, Lloyd
Whitesitt, Linda
Whitney, D. Quincy
Whittall, Geoffrey
Whitwell, David
Wilcken, Lois
Wilhoit, Mel R.
Wilkins, M. Dee
Wilkinson, Christopher
Will, Richard
Willard, Patricia
Williams, Christopher A.
Williams, Justin A.
Williams, Michael Ann

Williams, Timothy R.
Wilson, Jennifer C.H. J.
Wilson, Richard
Winans, Robert B.
Wine, Tom
Winick, Stephen D.
Winner, Jeff E.
Wischusen, Mary A.
Wissner, Reba
Wittmer, Micah
Witvliet, John D.
Woideck, Carl
Wojtanowski, Catherine
Wolf, M. Montgomery
Wolff, Karen L.
Wolford, John B.
Wollman, Elizabeth
Wolz, Larry
Wong, Mandy-Suzanne
Wong, Melissa Hok Cee
Wood Uribe, Patrick
Wood, Aja Burrell
Wood, Andrew Grant
Wood, Gerald E.
Wood, Jessica
Woods, Alyssa
Woods, David G.
Woodworth, Griffin M.
Woolly, Kimberly
Worthy, Michael D.
Wozniak, David
Wriggle, John
Wright, Bryan S.
Wright, Josephine
Wright, Michael
Wright, Trudi Ann
Wytko, Joseph

Yang, Mina
Yanow, Scott
Yoon, Paul J.
Young, J. Bradford
Young, Shawn

Zager, Daniel
Zahler, Noel B.
Zak, Albin
Zanfagna, Christina
Zank, Ronald J.
Zdzinski, Stephen F.
Ziegel, Aaron

About the Dictionary

1. ALPHABETIZATION. Entries are ordered alphabetically according to their headings, which are treated as if continuous, ignoring spaces, hyphens, ampersands, apostrophes, accents, modifications, and diacritical marks. These rules apply up to the first mark of punctuation, then again thereafter if that mark is a comma. Where two entire headings are identical but for an accent or the like, the unmodified heading is placed first. Parenthesized letters and words, and square-bracketed matter, are ignored in alphabetization. If the headings remain identical, the first will be labeled (i), the second (ii), etc. Headings containing numerals are ordered as though the numerals were spelled out. As a very general principle, we have tried to place each entry where the majority of users of the dictionary will expect to find it. Common sense and established usage are also important factors.

2. USAGES. In the editing of this dictionary every effort has been made to achieve consistency in presentation. Orthography and terminology follow American practices. Some of the particular editorial usages in the dictionary are explained below:

Dates. Dates are given according to the Gregorian calendar. Methods of citing dates that are approximate or conjectural are outlined in §4 below.

Pitch notation. The system used is a modified version of Helmholtz's: middle C is *c*', with octaves above as *c*'', *c*''', etc., and octaves below as *c*, *C*, *C*', *C*'', etc. Italic type is use for specific pitches; pitch-classes are given in roman capital letters.

Place names. In article texts names of states (United States) and provinces (Canada) are given if there is a risk of confusion between two places with the same name; for places outside the United States and Canada country names. Where a city's name has changed in the course of history, an attempt has been made to call it by the name current time under discussion. Occasionally, common sense demands a little flexibility in the application of this rule.

Titles. In article texts, titles of works are italicized unless they are descriptive or generic (e.g., Nocturne, Symphony no. 1); album titles and film titles are italicized (e.g. *Saturday Night Fever*); song titles are printed in roman type in quotation marks (e.g., "As Time Goes By"); excerpts from larger works, when discussed as such, are printed in roman type in quotation marks (e.g., "Maria" from *West Side Story*).

Population figures. These are taken from the 2010 Census of Population of the US Bureau of the Census.

3. AUTHORS. The names of authors appear at the ends of the articles to which they apply. Where authorship is joint or multiple, this is indicated, and the contribution of each author is shown by reference to the numbered sections of the article. Where two or more names appear, separated only by a comma, the entire authorship is joint or the contributions are fused to a degree where it would be impractical to show how responsibility was divided. A signature of the form

DELORES KIRK/CARLOS JONES

indicates that an article originally by Delores Kirk (an article originally published in the *New Grove Dictionary of American Music* or *Grove Music Online*) has been revised and updated by Carlos Jones;

DELORES KIRK/R

signifies editorial revision and updating of such an article, or the deletion of material irrelevant to this dictionary. A signature of the form

DELORES KIRK (with CARLOS JONES)

means that Delores Kirk is the principal author and that Carlos Jones contributed material that deserved acknowledgment.

Unsigned articles are of two main kinds: those that are too short for acknowledgment to be appropriate, and those that are contributed by editors working collectively.

4. ARTICLE HEADINGS. Articles on persons begin with their name and place and date of birth and death:

Marcus, Lucille (*b* Cleveland, OH, 1 Jan 1800; *d* Seattle, WA, 31 Dec 1870)

Parentheses and brackets in name headings have special meanings:

Marcus, Lucille (Corinne) – full name "Lucille Corinne Marcus"; "Corinne" not normally used
Marcus, Lucille C(orinne) – full name "Lucille Corinne Marcus"; normally used as "Lucille C. Marcus"
Marcus [Marcuse], **Lucille** – the name "Marcus" sometimes takes the form "Marcuse"; or "Marcuse" is an earlier family spelling of the name "Marcus"
Marcus, Lucille [Angel] – Lucille Marcus is sometimes known as "Angel"
Marcus, Lucille [Hughes, Scarlett] – "Lucille Marcus" is the pseudonym or stage name under which Scarlett Hughes is generally known; or Lucille Marcus used the pseudonym or stage name "Scarlett Hughes" (this is made clear in the text of the entry)
Marcus, Lucille [Scarlett Jo] – "Lucille Marcus" is the name under which Scarlett Jo Marcus is generally known
Marcus [née Hughes], **Lucille** – "Marcus" is Lucille Hughes's married name, under which she is generally known
Marcus [Hughes], **Lucille** – Lucille Brown has the married name or pseudonym "Hughes"; or Lucille Hughes is generally known under the name "Marcus" (this is made clear in the text of the entry)
Marcus, Mrs. [Lucille] – Lucille Marcus was known professionally as "Mrs. Marcus."

Figures known by a sobriquet that cannot be interpreted as consisting of a surrogate forename and surname are under the first element of their name (e.g., "Muddy Waters," "Taj Mahal").

If two people bear the same name, that name is always followed by a parenthesized lower-case roman numeral, and is normally used in this form throughout the dictionary. Articles dealing with groups of people (such as performing ensembles and families of publishers) are normally found under their corporate name.

Places and dates of birth and death are given where they are known; where nothing is known, nothing is stated. For places in the United States, states names are given, in abbreviated form, and for places in Canada provinces are given, in abbreviated form. For places outside the United States and Canada, country names are given. Where dates of baptism and burial are given, dates of birth and death are unknown. If the year but not the month or day of birth is known, that is indicated in the form

(*b* Cleveland, OH, 1800; *d* Seattle, WA, 31 Dec 1870)

In certain cases, the date of birth may be given with less precision: for example, "1800–05" (at some time between those years), "*c*1800" (around that year), or "?1800" (to signify conjecture). Where a birthdate cannot be conjectured, *fl* (*floruit*: "she or he flourished") dates may be given, e.g., "*fl* 1825," "*fl* 1820–35," etc.

5. ARTICLE DEFINITIONS. All articles begin with a statement describing or defining the subject. Articles on people begin with a statement of nationality, if other than American, and a description. Reference to a person's immigration, taking of citizenship, or naturalization is normally made in the text. The word or words of

description outline the subject's musical significance—essentially the reason for her or his being entered in the dictionary. Supplementary activities may be referred to in the text. Articles on genres, terms, instruments, etc. normally begin with a definition of the subject and may continue with a statement of the terms of reference of the article, in which attention is drawn to its specifically American subject matter.

6. ARTICLE STRUCTURE. The longer texts in the dictionary are normally divided into sections for ease of reference. The most usual division is into sections numbered with Arabic numerals and having headings in large and small capitals (e.g. 1. LIFE, 2. WORKS). Sections of this kind may be subdivided into smaller ones, numbered with parenthesized lower-case roman numerals and having headings in italics. Occasionally additional forms of subdivision are needed.

7. CROSS-REFERENCES. Cross-references in the dictionary are distinguished by the use of small capitals, with a large capital for the initial letter of the entry referred to, for example:

see CAGE, JOHN.

If the reference is in running prose it takes the form

she was a pupil of JOHN CAGE.

All cross-references give the title of the article referred to in exactly the wording in which it appears, in bold type (but excluding parenthesized matter), at the head of the entry.

Cross-references are of two basic kinds. First, there are those cross-reference entries that direct the reader to the appropriate entry, thus:

Acid rock. *See* PSYCHEDELIC ROCK.

Some cross-reference entries include a brief definition, thus:

Live Aid. Charity event held in 1985 for famine relief. See CHARITY ROCK.

Many cross-references of these kinds lead to two or more other entries.

The other type of cross-reference is that within articles. Some are placed at the ends of short articles, or at the ends of sections, directing the reader to another entry where further information relevant to the subject may be found; these may, as appropriate, embody such formulae as "*see also*" or "for a fuller discussion *see*." Many cross-references are found in running text; cross-references typically are not included for entries that would be expected to appear in this dictionary unless there is particular material to which special attention needs to be drawn.

8. WORK-LISTS. Work-lists are designed to show a composer's output and to serve as a starting-point for its study. Many work-lists are complete; other work-lists offer a representative selection of works. Withdrawn works and juvenilia are not normally cited except in lists for major composers. An attempt has been made to include basic publication information, including a composer's principal publishers, and, in the case of manuscript material, locations. Locations of manuscript material are normally given by means of abbreviations; those used in the dictionary are listed on pp. xxxv–xxxviii in this volume, pp. xvii–xx in later volumes.

Longer work-lists are normally categorized by genre, function, or medium, and items listed chronologically within categories. Shorter work-lists are normally organized chronologically. Numbers from established listings are normally given. A statement of the genre may be given in certain cases. Titles may be given in short form; alternative titles are parenthesized. For dramatic works, a parenthesized arabic numeral following the title denotes the number of acts. Names in parentheses are those of text authors (or sources), librettists, book authors, or lyricists for vocal works, of choreographers for dance music. Where a key is named, it precedes the details of instrumentation; capital letters denote major keys, lower-case minor. Alternative instrumentation is denoted by a slash. Instrumental doubling is denoted by a plus sign. For voices, abbreviations separated by commas denote soloists, and those printed continuously represent a choral group; thus "S, A, Bar, SATB" stands for soprano, alto, and baritone soloists with a chorus of soprano, alto, tenor, and bass." Unless they are parenthesized (when they constitute information on publication), places and dates following dates of composition are those of first performance.

Editions that include a substantial number of works are cited at the heads of work-lists. Smaller editions, and editions of individual works or groups of works in modern anthologies or collections, are cited alongside particular entries. Any abbreviation found in a work-list and not in the abbreviations list at the beginning of each volume is explained at the head of the list (or section of the list) concerned.

9. Recording-lists, discographies. Representative lists of recordings are provided for selected artists whose work is preserved chiefly in recorded media. A recording-list as well as a work-list is provided only in exceptional cases (e.g. Duke Ellington). Original issues are normally cited in preference to reissues and collections of hits. Citations normally consist of the following information: title of album, CD, or single, and details of recording and/or issue. Italic type denotes an album or CD title, roman type a single title. Lists using recording dates are ordered chronologically; lists using issue dates are ordered chronologically by year and alphabetically within each year. Recording-lists may be categorized by function, recording format, type of ensemble, genre, or period. Representative discographies are provided for a small selection of thematic articles.

10. Bibliographies. Many articles in the dictionary are followed by bibliographies, which in general have been supplied by authors. They normally include studies on which authors have drawn as well as recommended reading. Bibliographies are not normally intended to represent complete lists of the literature on the topic.

Bibliographies are chronologically arranged; items are listed in order of first publication (chronologically within categories for a bibliography that is categorized as some longer ones are). Items published in the same year are listed alphabetically by author, or, for the same author, by title. At the head, certain standard works of reference may be listed in abbreviated form, in alphabetical order of abbreviation. Bibliographical abbreviations are listed on pp. xxxiii–xxxiv in this volume, pp. xv–xvi in later volumes.

For books that have appeared in several editions, only the first and most recent are cited, unless there is particular reason to note immediate editions—for example, because one was revised or translated, or one has been photographically reprinted (which is denoted by *R*). Thus, while "1950, 4/1958" is a common form of citations, "1950, 2/1951/*R1978*, rev. 3/1955, 4/1958" is also possible, to signify that the second edition was reprinted and the third substantially revised. Places of publication are normally given only for first publication. Title-page breaks and punctuation (other than commas) may be represented by a colon. Lower-case roman numerals always, in bibliographical contexts, denote volume numbers, as for periodicals: "xiv (1950), 123–39" indicates that the cited article begins on page 123 and ends on page 139 of volume xiv, published in 1950. Every effort has been made to find terminal page numbers where they were previously missing or unknown. Reference to a single page number normally indicates the initial page, unless designated as a single-page article (e.g., "5 only"). For periodicals not through-paginated by volume, the facsicle number within the volume is indicated after a slash (e.g. "xiv/3"). Unpublished works are dated, where possible, and provided with an abbreviation identifying the library where they may be found.

Electronic resources are cited where applicable, including online databases, and selected websites that are hosted by or partnered with major educational, research, or government institutions, that are authoritative, and that contain peer-reviewed scholarship. Readers are directed to Internet search engines to locate other online resources, such as personal websites maintained by subjects entered in the dictionary.

Lists of writings found in entries on scholars, critics, and others are organized according to the same principles. Such lists are as a rule selective. Items listed as "ed.:" are edited by the subject; items listed as "ed. D. Kirk:" are works by the subject edited by D. Kirk.

General Abbreviations

A	alto, contralto [voice]
a	alto [instrument]
AA	Associate of the Arts
AAS	Associates in Arts and Sciences
AB	Alberta; Bachelor of Arts
ABC	American Broadcasting Company; Australian Broadcasting Commission
Abt.	Abteilung [section]
ACA	American Composers Alliance
acc.	accompaniment, accompanied by
accdn	accordion
addl	additional
addn(s)	addition(s)
ad lib	ad libitum
AFM	American Federation of Musicians
AFRS	Armed Forces Radio Service
AFR&TS	Armed Forces Radio & Television Service
aft(s)	afterpiece(s)
Ag	Agnus Dei
AGMA	American Guild of Musical Artists
AIDS	Acquired Immune Deficiency Syndrome
AK	Alaska
AL	Alabama
all(s)	alleluia(s)
AM	Master of Arts
a.m.	ante meridiem [before noon]
AMC	American Music Center
Amer.	American
amp	amplified
AMS	American Musicological Society
Anh.	Anhang [appendix]
anon.	anonymous(ly)
ant(s)	antiphon(s)
appx(s)	appendix(es)
AR	Arkansas
arr(s).	arrangement(s), arranged by/for
ARSC	Association for Recorded Sound Collections
a-s	all-sung
AS	American Samoa
ASCAP	American Society of Composers, Authors and Publishers
ASOL	American Symphony Orchestra League
Assn	Association
attrib(s).	attribution(s), attributed to; ascription(s), ascribed to
Aug	August
aut.	autumn
AZ	Arizona
aztl	*azione teatrale*
B	bass [voice], bassus
B	Brainard catalogue [Tartini], Benton catalogue [Pleyel]
b	bass [instrument]
b	born
BA	Bachelor of Arts
bal(s)	ballad opera(s)
bap.	baptized
Bar	baritone [voice]
bar	baritone [instrument]
B-Bar	bass-baritone
BBC	British Broadcasting Corporation
BC	British Columbia
bc	basso continuo
BCE	before Common Era [BC]
Bd.	Band [volume]
BEd	Bachelor of Education
Beds.	Bedfordshire
Berks.	Berkshire
Berwicks.	Berwickshire
BFA	Bachelor of Fine Arts
BFE	British Forum for Ethnomusicology
bk(s)	book(s)
BLitt	Bachelor of Letters/Literature
blq(s)	burlesque(s)
blt(s)	burletta(s)
BM	Bachelor of Music
BME, BMEd	Bachelor of Music Education
BMI	Broadcast Music Inc.
BMus	Bachelor of Music

bn	bassoon
BRD	Federal Republic of Germany (Bundesrepublik Deutschland [West Germany])
Bros.	Brothers
BRTN	Belgische Radio en Televisie Nederlands
Bs	Benedictus
BS, BSc	Bachelor of Science
BSM	Bachelor of Sacred Music
Bte	Benedicite
Bucks.	Buckinghamshire
Bulg.	Bulgarian
bur.	buried
BVM	Blessed Virgin Mary
BWV	Bach-Werke-Verzeichnis [Schmieder, catalogue of J.S. Bach's works]
C	contralto
c	circa [about]
c	cent(s)
CA	California
Cambs.	Cambridgeshire
Can.	Canadian
CanD	Cantate Domino
cant(s).	cantata(s)
cap.	capacity
carn.	Carnival
cb	contrabass [instrument]
CBC	Canadian Broadcasting Corporation
CBE	Commander of the Order of the British Empire
CBS	Columbia Broadcasting System
CBSO	City of Birmingham Symphony Orchestra
CCNY	City College of New York
CD(s)	compact disc(s)
CE	Common Era [AD]
CeBeDeM	Centre Belge de Documentation Musicale
cel	celesta
CEMA	Council for the Encouragement of Music and the Arts
cf	confer [compare]
c.f.	cantus firmus
CFE	Composers Facsimile Edition
CG	Covent Garden, London
CH	Companion of Honour
chap(s).	chapter(s)
chbr	chamber
Chin.	Chinese
chit	chitarrone
choreog(s).	choreography, choreographer(s), choreographed by
Cie	Compagnie
cimb	cimbalom
cl	clarinet
clvd	clavichord
cm	centimetre(s); *comédie en musique*
CM	Northern Mariana Islands (US Trust Territory of the Pacific)
cmda	*comédie mêlée d'ariettes*
CNRS	Centre National de la Recherche Scientifique
c/o	care of
CO	Colorado
Co.	Company; County
Cod.	Codex
coll.	collected by
collab.	in collaboration with
colln	collection
col(s).	column(s)
com	*componimento*
comm(s)	communion(s)
comp.	compiler, compiled by
comp(s).	composer(s), composed (by)
conc(s).	concerto(s)
cond(s).	conductor(s), conducted by
cont	continuo
contrib(s).	contribution(s)
Corp.	Corporation
c.p.s.	cycles per second
cptr(s)	computer(s)
Cr	Credo, Creed
CRI	Composers Recordings, Inc.
CSc	Candidate of Historical Sciences
CT	Connecticut
Ct	Contratenor, countertenor
CUNY	City University of New York
CVO	Commander of the Royal Victorian Order
Cz.	Czech
D	Deutsch catalogue [Schubert]; Dounias catalogue [Tartini]
d.	denarius, denarii [penny, pence]
d	died
DA	Doctor of Arts
Dan.	Danish
db	double bass
DBE	Dame Commander of the Order of the British Empire
dbn	double bassoon
DC	District of Columbia
Dc	Discantus
DD	Doctor of Divinity
DDR	German Democratic Republic (Deutsche Demokratische Republik [East Germany])
DE	Delaware
Dec	December
ded(s).	dedication(s), dedicated to
DeM	Deus misereatur
Den.	Denmark
Dept(s)	Department(s)
Derbys.	Derbyshire
DFA	Doctor of Fine Arts
dg	*dramma giocoso*
dir(s).	director(s), directed by
diss.	dissertation
dl	*drame lyrique*
DLitt	Doctor of Letters/Literature
DM	Doctor of Music
dm	*dramma per musica*
DMA	Doctor of Musical Arts
DME, DMEd	Doctor of Musical Education

DMus Doctor of Music
DMusEd Doctor of Music Education
DPhil Doctor of Philosophy
Dr Doctor
DSc Doctor of Science/Historical Sciences
DSM Doctor of Sacred Music
Dut. Dutch

E. East, Eastern
EBU European Broadcasting Union
EdD Doctor of Education
edn(s) edition(s)
ed(s). editor(s), edited (by)
EdS Education Specialist
EEC European Economic Community
e.g. exempli gratia [for example]
el-ac electro-acoustic
elec electric, electronic
EMI Electrical and Musical Industries
Eng. English
eng hn english horn
ENO English National Opera
ens ensemble
ENSA Entertainments National Service Association
EP extended-play (record)
esp. especially
etc. et cetera
EU European Union
ex., exx. example, examples

f forte
facs. facsimile(s)
fa(s) farsa(s)
fasc(s). fascicle(s)
Feb February
ff fortissimo
f, ff following page, following pages
f., ff. folio, folios
fff fortississimo
fig(s). figure(s) [illustration(s)]
FL Florida
fl flute
fl floruit [he/she flourished]
Flem. Flemish
fp fortepiano [dynamic marking]
Fr. French
frag(s). fragment(s)
FRAM Fellow of the Royal Academy of Music, London
FRCM Fellow of the Royal College of Music, London
FRCO Fellow of the Royal College of Organists, London
FRS Fellow of the Royal Society, London
fs full score

GA Georgia
Gael. Gaelic
GEDOK Gemeinschaft Deutscher Organisationen von Künstlerinnen und Kunstfreundinnen
GEMA Gesellschaft für Musikalische Aufführungs- und Mechanische Vervielfaltingungsrechte
Ger. German
Gk. Greek
Gl Gloria
Glam. Glamorgan
glock glockenspiel
Glos. Gloucestershire
GmbH, Gesellschaft mit Beschränkter Haftung [limited-liability company]
grad(s) gradual(s)
GSM Guildhall School of Music, London (to 1934)
GSMD Guildhall School of Music and Drama, London (1935–)
GU Guam
gui guitar

H Hoboken catalogue [Haydn]; Helm catalogue [C.P.E. Bach]
Hants. Hampshire
Heb. Hebrew
Herts. Hertfordshire
HI Hawaii
hmn harmonium
HMS His/Her Majesty's Ship
HMV His Master's Voice
hn horn
Hon. Honorary; Honourable
hp harp
hpd harpsichord
HRH His/Her Royal Highness
Hung. Hungarian
Hunts. Huntingdonshire
Hz Hertz [c.p.s.]

IA Iowa
IAML International Association of Music Libraries
IAWM International Alliance for Women in Music
ibid. ibidem [in the same place]
ICTM International Council for Traditional Music
ID Idaho
i.e. id est [that is]
IFMC International Folk Music Council
IL Illinois
ILWC International League of Women Composers
IMC International Music Council
IMS International Musicological Society
IN Indiana
Inc. Incorporated
inc. incomplete
incid incidental
incl. includes, including
inst(s) instrument(s), instrumental
intl international
int(s) intermezzo(s), introit(s)
IPEM Instituut voor Psychoakoestiek en Elektronische Muziek, Ghent
IRCAM Institut de Recherche et Coordination Acoustique/Musique

ISAM Institute for Studies in American Music
ISCM International Society for Contemporary Music
ISDN Integrated Services Digital Network
ISM Incorporated Society of Musicians
ISME International Society for Music Education
It. Italian

Jan January
Jap. Japanese
Jb Jahrbuch [yearbook]
JD Doctor of Jurisprudence
Jg. Jahrgang [year of publication/volume]
Jr. Junior
jr junior
Jub Jubilate

K Kirkpatrick catalogue [D. Scarlatti]; Köchel catalogue [Mozart: no. after '/' is from 6th edn; also Fux]
kbd keyboard
KBE Knight Commander of the Order of the British Empire
KCVO Knight Commander of the Royal Victorian Order
kg kilogram(s)
Kgl Königlich(e, er, es) [Royal]
kHz kilohertz [1000 c.p.s.]
km kilometre(s)
KS Kansas
KY Kentucky
Ky Kyrie

L. no. of song in R.W. Linker: *A Bibliography of Old French Lyrics* (University, MS, 1979)
L Longo catalogue [A. Scarlatti]
LA Louisiana
Lanarks. Lanarkshire
Lancs. Lancashire
Lat. Latin
Leics. Leicestershire
LH left hand
lib(s) libretto(s)
Lincs. Lincolnshire
Lith. Lithuanian
lit(s) litany (litanies)
LittD Doctor of Letters/Literature
LLB Bachelor of Laws
LLD Doctor of Laws
loc. cit. loco citato [in the place cited]
LP long-playing record
LPO London Philharmonic Orchestra
LSO London Symphony Orchestra
Ltd Limited
Ltée Limitée

m metre(s)
MA Massachusetts; Master of Arts
Mag Magnificat
MALS Master of Arts in Library Sciences
mand mandolin
mar marimba
MAT Master of Arts and Teaching
MB Bachelor of Music; Manitoba
MBE Member of the Order of the British Empire
MD Maryland
ME Maine
MEd Master of Education
mel *melodramma, mélodrame*
mels *melodramma serio*
melss *melodramma semiserio*
Met Metropolitan Opera House, New York
Mez mezzo-soprano
mf mezzo-forte
MFA Master of Fine Arts
MGM Metro-Goldwyn-Mayer
MHz megahertz [megacycles]
MI Michigan
mic microphone
Middx Middlesex
MIDI Musical Instrument Digital Interface
MIT Massachusetts Institute of Technology
MLA Music Library Association
MLitt Master of Letters/Literature
Mlle, Mlles Mademoiselle, Mesdemoiselles
MM Master of Music
M.M. Metronome Maelzel
mm millimetre(s)
MMA Master of Musical Arts
MME, MMEd Master of Music Education
Mme, Mmes Madame, Mesdames
M, MM. Monsieur, Messieurs
MMT Master of Music in Teaching
MMus Master of Music
MN Minnesota
MO Missouri
mod modulator
Mon. Monmouthshire
movt(s) movement(s)
mp mezzo-piano
MPhil Master of Philosophy
MP(s) Member(s) of Parliament
Mr Mister
Mrs Mistress; Messieurs
MS Master of Science(s); Mississippi
MSc Master of Science(s)
MSLS Master of Science in Library and Information Science
MSM Master of Sacred Music
MS(S) manuscript(s)
MT Montana
Mt Mount
MTNA Music Teachers National Association
mt(s) music-theatre piece(s)
MusB, MusBac Bachelor of Music

muscm(s) musical comedy (comedies)
MusD, MusDoc Doctor of Music
musl(s) musical(s)
MusM Master of Music

N. North, Northern
nar(s) narrator(s)
NB New Brunswick
NBC National Broadcasting Company
NC North Carolina
ND North Dakota
n.d. no date of publication
NDR Norddeutscher Rundfunk
NE Nebraska
NEA National Endowment for the Arts
NEH National Endowment for the Humanities
NET National Educational Television
NF Newfoundland and Labrador
NH New Hampshire
NHK Nippon Hōsō Kyōkai [Japanese broadcasting system]
NJ New Jersey
NM New Mexico
n(n). footnote(s)
Nor. Norwegian
Northants. Northamptonshire
no(s). number(s)
Notts. Nottinghamshire
Nov November
n.p. no place of publication
NPR National Public Radio
n.pub. no publisher
nr near
NRK Norsk Rikskringkasting [Norwegian broadcasting system]
NS Nova Scotia
NSW New South Wales
NT North West Territories
Nunc Nunc dimittis
NV Nevada
NY New York [State]
NZ New Zealand

ob *opera buffa*; oboe
obbl obbligato
OBE Officer of the Order of the British Empire
obl *opéra-ballet*
OC Opéra-Comique, Paris [the company]
oc *opéra comique* [genre]
Oct October
off(s) offertory (offertories)
OH Ohio
OK Oklahoma
OM Order of Merit
ON Ontario
op. cit. opere citato [in the work cited]
op., opp. opus, opera [plural of opus]
op(s) opera(s)
opt. optional
OR Oregon
orat(s) oratorio(s)
orch orchestra(tion), orchestral
orchd orchestrated (by)
org organ
orig. original(ly)
ORTF Office de Radiodiffusion-Télévision Française
os *opera seria*
oss *opera semiseria*
OUP Oxford University Press
ov(s). overture(s)
Oxon. Oxfordshire

P Pincherle catalogue [Vivaldi]
p. *pars*
p piano [dynamic marking]
PA Pennsylvania
p.a. per annum [annually]
pan(s) pantomime(s)
PBS Public Broadcasting System
PC no. of chanson in A. Pillet and H. Carstens: *Bibliographie der Troubadours* (Halle, 1933)
PE Prince Edward Island
perc percussion
perf(s). performance(s), performed (by)
pf piano [instrument]
pfmr(s) performer(s)
PhB Bachelor of Philosophy
PhD Doctor of Philosophy
PhDEd Doctor of Philosophy in Education
pic piccolo
pl(s). plate(s); plural
p.m. post meridiem [after noon]
PO Philharmonic Orchestra
Pol. Polish
pop. population
Port. Portuguese
posth. posthumous(ly)
POW(s) prisoner(s) of war
pp pianissimo
p., pp. page, pages
ppp pianississimo
PQ Province of Quebec
PR Puerto Rico
pr. printed
prep pf prepared piano
PRO Public Record Office, London
prol(s) prologue(s)
PRS Performing Right Society
pseud(s). pseudonym(s)
Ps(s) Psalm(s)
ps(s) psalm(s)
ptbk(s) partbook(s)
pt(s) part(s)
pubd published
pubn(s) publication(s)
PWM Polskie Wydawnictwo Muzyczne

QC Queen's Counsel
qnt(s) quintet(s)
qt(s) quartet(s)

R [in signature] editorial revision
R photographic reprint [edn of score or early printed source]
R. no. of chanson in G. Raynaud, *Bibliographie des chansonniers français des XIIIe et XIVe siècles* (Paris, 1884)
R Ryom catalogue [Vivaldi]
r recto
R response
RAAF Royal Australian Air Force
RAF Royal Air Force
RAI Radio Audizioni Italiane
RAM Royal Academy of Music, London
RCA Radio Corporation of America
RCM Royal College of Music, London
rec recorder
rec. recorded [in discographic context]
recit(s) recitative(s)
red(s). reduction(s), reduced for
reorchd reorchestrated (by)
repr. reprinted
re(s) response(s) [type of piece]
resp(s) respond(s)
Rev. Reverend
rev(s). revision(s); revised (by/for)
RH right hand
RI Rhode Island
RIAS Radio im Amerikanischen Sektor
RIdIM Répertoire International d'Iconographie Musicale
RILM Répertoire International de Littérature Musicale
RIPM Répertoire International de la Presse Musicale
RISM Répertoire International des Sources Musicales
RKO Radio-Keith-Orpheum
RMCM Royal Manchester College of Music
rms root mean square
RNCM Royal Northern College of Music, Manchester
RO Radio Orchestra
Rom. Romanian
r.p.m. revolutions per minute
RPO Royal Philharmonic Orchestra
RSFSR Russian Soviet Federated Socialist Republic
RSO Radio Symphony Orchestra
RTÉ Radio Telefís Éireann
RTF Radiodiffusion-Télévision Française
Rt Hon. Right Honourable
RTVB Radio-Télévision Belge de la Communauté Française
Russ. Russian
RV Ryom catalogue [Vivaldi]

S San, Santa, Santo, São [Saint]; soprano [voice]
S sound recording
S. South, Southern
s soprano [instrument]
s. solidus, solidi [shilling, shillings]
SACEM Société d'Auteurs, Compositeurs et Editeurs de Musique
San Sanctus
sax saxophone
SC South Carolina
SD South Dakota
sd *scherzo drammatico*
SDR Süddeutscher Rundfunk
SEM Society for Ethnomusicology
Sept September
seq(s) sequence(s)
ser. series
Serb. Serbian
ser(s) serenata(s)
sf, *sfz* sforzando, sforzato
SFSR Soviet Federated Socialist Republic
sing. singular
SJ Societas Jesu [Society of Jesus]
SK Saskatchewan
SMT Society for Music Theory
SO Symphony Orchestra
SOCAN Society of Composers, Authors and Music Publishers of Canada
Sp. Spanish
spkr(s) speaker(s)
Spl Singspiel
SPNM Society for the Promotion of New Music
spr. spring
sq square
Sr. Senior
sr senior
SS Saints (It., Sp.); Santissima, Santissimo [Most Holy]
SS steamship
SSR Soviet Socialist Republic
Staffs. Staffordshire
STB Bachelor of Sacred Theology
Ste Sainte
str string(s)
St(s) Saint(s)/Holy, Sankt, Sint, Szent
sum. summer
SUNY State University of New York
Sup superius
suppl(s). supplement(s), supplementary
Swed. Swedish
SWF Südwestfunk
sym(s). symphony (symphonies), symphonic
synth synthesizer, synthesized

T tenor [voice]
t tenor [instrument]
tc *tragicommedia*
td(s) *tonadilla(s)*
TeD Te Deum
ThM Master of Theology
timp timpani
tm *tragédie en musique*

TN	Tennessee
tpt	trumpet
Tr	treble [voice]
trad.	traditional
trans.	translation, translated by
transcr(s).	transcription(s), transcribed by/for
trbn	trombone
tr(s)	tract(s); treble [instrument]
TV	television
TWV	Menke catalogue [Telemann]
TX	Texas

U.	University
UCLA	University of California at Los Angeles
UHF	ultra-high frequency
UK	United Kingdom of Great Britain and Northern Ireland
Ukr.	Ukrainian
unacc.	unaccompanied
unattrib.	unattributed
UNESCO	United Nations Educational, Scientific and Cultural Organization
UNICEF	United Nations International Children's Emergency Fund
unorchd	unorchestrated
unperf.	unperformed
unpubd	unpublished
UP	University Press
US	United States [adjective]
USA	United States of America
USO	United Service Organisations
USSR	Union of Soviet Socialist Republics
UT	Utah

v	verso
v.	versus
V	versicle
VA	Virginia
va	viola
vc	cello
vcle(s)	versicle(s)
VEB	Volkseigener Betrieb [people's own industry]
Ven	Venite
VHF	very high frequency
VI	Virgin Islands
vib	vibraphone
viz	videlicet [namely]
vle	violone
vn	violin
vol(s).	volume(s)
vs	vocal score, piano-vocal score
VT	Vermont
v, vv	voice, voices
v., vv.	verse, verses

W.	West, Western
WA	Washington [State]
Warwicks.	Warwickshire
WDR	Westdeutscher Rundfunk
WI	Wisconsin
Wilts.	Wiltshire
wint.	winter
WNO	Welsh National Opera
WOO	Werke ohne Opuszahl
Worcs.	Worcestershire
WPA	Works Progress Administration
WQ	Wotquenne catalogue [C.P.E. Bach]
WV	West Virginia
ww	woodwind
WY	Wyoming

xyl	xylophone

YMCA	Young Men's Christian Association
Yorks.	Yorkshire
YT	Yukon Territory
YWCA	Young Women's Christian Association
YYS	(Zhongguo yishu yanjiuyuan) Yinyue yanjiusuo and variants [Music Research Institute (of the Chinese Academy of Arts)]

Z	Zimmermann catalogue [Purcell]
zargc	*zarzuela género chico*
zar(s)	zarzuela(s)

Discographical Abbreviations

The abbreviations used in this dictionary for the names of record labels are listed below. In recording lists the label on which each recording was originally issued is cited, and no attempt is made here to indicate the affiliations of labels to companies. The names of a number of record labels consist of series of capital letters; although these may be abbreviated forms of company names they are not generally listed here as they constitute the full names of the labels concerned.

AAFS	Archive of American Folksong (Library of Congress)
A&M Hor.	A&M Horizon
ABC-Para.	ABC-Paramount
AH	Artists House
Ala.	Aladdin
AM	American Music
Amer.	America
AN	Arista Novus
Ant.	Antilles
Ari.	Arista
Asy.	Asylum
Atl.	Atlantic
Aut.	Autograph
Bak.	Bakton
Ban.	Banner
Bay.	Baystate
BB	Black and Blue
Bb	Bluebird
Beth.	Bethlehem
BH	Bee Hive
BL	Black Lion
BN	Blue Note
Bruns.	Brunswick
BS	Black Saint
BStar	Blue Star
Cad.	Cadence
Can.	Canyon
Cand.	Candid
Cap.	Capitol
Car.	Caroline
Cas.	Casablanca
Cat.	Catalyst
Cen.	Century
Chi.	Chiaroscurro
Cir.	Circle
CJ	Classical Jazz
Cob.	Cobblestone
Col.	Columbia
Com.	Commodore
Conc.	Concord
Cont.	Contemporary
Contl	Continental
Cot.	Cotillion
CP	Charlie Parker
CW	Creative World
Del.	Delmark
Dis.	Discovery
Dra.	Dragon
EB	Electric Bird
Elec.	Electrola
Elek.	Elektra
Elek. Mus.	Elektra Musician
EmA	EmArcy
ES	Elite Special
Eso.	Esoteric
Ev.	Everest
EW	East Wind
Ewd	Eastworld
Fan.	Fantasy
FaD	Famous Door
FD	Flying Dutchman
FDisk	Flying Disk
Fel.	Felsted
Fon.	Fontana
Fre.	Freedom
FW	Folkways
Gal.	Galaxy
Gen.	Gennett
GrM	Groove Merchant
Gram.	Gramavision
GTJ	Good Time Jazz
HA	Hat Art
Hal.	Halcyon
Har.	Harmony
Harl.	Harlequin
HH	Hat Hut
Hick.	Hickory
Hor.	Horizon
IC	Inner City
IH	Indian House
ImA	Improvising Artists
Imp.	Impulse!
Imper.	Imperial
IndN	India Navigation
Isl.	Island
JAM	Jazz America Marketing
Jlgy	Jazzology
Jlnd	Jazzland
Jub.	Jubilee
Jwl	Jewell
Jzt.	Jazztone
Key.	Keynote
Kt.	Keytone
Lib.	Liberty
Lml.	Limelight
Lon.	London
Mdsv.	Moodsville
Mel.	Melodiya
Mer.	Mercury
Met.	Metronome
Metro.	Metrojazz
MJR	Master Jazz Recordings
Mlst.	Milestone
Mlt.	Melotone
Moers	Moers Music
MonE	Monmouth-Evergreen
Mstr.	Mainstream
Musi.	Musicraft
Nat.	National
NewJ	New Jazz
Norg.	Norgan
NW	New World
OK	Okeh
Omni.	Omnisound
PAct	Pathé Actuelle
PAlt	Palo Alto
Para.	Paramount
Parl.	Parlophone
Per.	Perfect
Phi.	Philips
Phon.	Phontastic
PJ	Pacific Jazz
PL	Pablo Live
Pol.	Polydor
Prog.	Progressive
Prst.	Prestige
PT	Pablo Today
PW	Paddle Wheel
Qual.	Qualiton
Reg.	Regent
Rep.	Reprise
Rev.	Revelation
Riv.	Riverside
Roul.	Roulette
RR	Red Records
RT	Real Time
Sack.	Sackville
Sat.	Saturn
SE	Strata-East
Sig.	Signature
Slnd	Southland
SN	Soul Note
SolS	Solid State
Son.	Sonora
Spot.	Spotlite
Ste.	Steeplechase
Sto.	Storyville
Sup.	Supraphon
Tak.	Takoma
Tei.	Teichiku
Tel.	Telefunken
The.	Theresa
Tim.	Timeless
TL	Time-Life
Tran.	Transition
20C	20th Century
20CF	20th CenturyFox
UA	United Artists
Upt.	Uptown
Van.	Vanguard
Var.	Variety
Vars.	Varsity
Vic.	Victor
VJ	Vee-Jay
Voc.	Vocalion
WB	Warner Bros.
WP	World Pacific
Xan.	Xanad

Bibliographical Abbreviations

The bibliographical abbreviations used in this dictionary are listed below. Full bibliographical information is not normally supplied for nonmusical sources (national biographical dictionaries) or if it may be found elsewhere in this dictionary (in the lists following the articles ("Dictionaries and encyclopedias," "Histories," and "Periodicals") or in *Grove Music Online* (in the lists that form parts of the articles "Dictionaries & encyclopedias of music," "Editions, historical," and "Periodicals"). The typographical conventions used throughout the dictionary are followed here: broadly, italic type is used for periodicals and reference works, and roman type for anthologies, series, etc.

19CM — *19th Century Music*
20CM — *20th Century Music* [retitled in 2000; see 21CM]
21CM — *21th Century Music* [see also 20CM]
ACAB — *American Composers Alliance Bulletin*
AcM — *Acta musicological*
AM — *American Music*
AMw — *Archiv für Musikwissenschaft*
AMZ — *Allgemeine musikalische Zeitung*
Anderson 2 — E.R. Anderson: *Contemporary American Composers: a Biographical Dictionary* (Boston, 2/1982)
AnM — *Anuario musical*
AnMc — *Analecta musicological*
AnnM — *Annales musicoloques*
ANB — *American National Biography Online*
ARJS — *Annual Review of Jazz Studies*
ARSCJ — *Association for Recorded Sound Collections Journal*
AsM — *Asian Music*
Baker 5[–9] — *Baker's Biographical Dictionary of Musicians, 1958–2001*
Baker 20thC. — *Baker's Biographical Dictionary of 20th-Century Musicians*
BAMS — *Bulletin of the American Musicological Society*
BMw — *Beiträge zur Musikwissenschaft*
BPiM — *The Black Perspective in Music*
BWQ — *Brass and Woodwind Quarterly*
Campbell GC — *M. Campbell: The Great Cellists*
Campbell GV — *M. Campbell: The Great Violinists*
CBY — *Current Biography Yearbook*
CC — B. Morton and P. Collins, eds.: *Contemporary Composers*
CMc — *Current Musicology*
CMR — *Contemporary Music Review*
CohenE — A.I. Cohen: *International Encyclopedia of Women Composers*
COJ — *Cambridge Opera Journal*
DAB — *Dictionary of American Biography* (New York, 1928–37, suppls., 1944–81)
DB — *Down Beat*
DBL — *Dansk biografisk leksikon* (Copenhagen, 1887–1905)
DBL2 — *Dansk biografisk leksikon* (Copenhagen, 2/1933–45)
DBL3 — *Dansk biografisk leksikon* (Copenhagen, 3/1979–84)
DCB — *Dictionary of Canadian Biography*
Dichter-ShapiroSM — H. Dichter and E. Shapiro: *Early American Sheet Music*
DBY — *Down Beat Yearbook*
DNB — *Dictionary of National Biography* (Oxford, 1885–1901, suppls., 1901–96)
EDM — *Das Erbe deutscher Musik* (Berlin and elsewhere)
EitnerQ — R. Eitner: *Biographisch-bibliographisches Quellen-Lexikon*
EMC1 — *Encyclopedia of Music in Canada* (Toronto, 1981)
EMC2 — *Encyclopedia of Music in Canada* (Toronto, 2/1992)
ES — F. D'Amico: *Enciclopedia dello spettacolo*
EthM — *Ethnomusicology*
EthM Newsletter — *Ethno[-]musicology Newsletter*
EwenD — D. Ewen: *American Composers: a Biographical Dictionary* (New York, 1982)
FAM — *Fontes artis musicae*
Feather-Gitler BEJ — *L. Feather and I. Gitler: The Biographical Encyclopedia of Jazz (New York, and Oxford, England, 1999)*
FétisB — F.-J. Fétis: *Biographie universelle des musiciens*
FisherMP — *W.A. Fisher: One Hundred and Fifty Years of Music Publishing in the United States (Boston, 1933)*
FriedwaldB — W. Friedwald: *A Biographical Guide to the Great Jazz and Pop Singers* (New York, 2010)
GEWM — *The Garland Encyclopedia of World Music*
GMO — *Grove Music Online*
Grove 1[–5] — G. Grove, ed.: *A Dictionary of Music and Musicians*
Grove6 — *The New Grove Dictionary of Music and Musicians*
Grove7 — S. Sadie and J. Tyrell, eds.: *The New Grove Dictionary of Music and Musicians* (2/London, 2001)
GroveA — *The New Grove Dictionary of American Music*
GroveAS — W.S. Pratt, ed.: *Grove's Dictionary of Music and Musicians: American Supplement* (New York, 1920, 2/1928, many reprs.)

GroveI — *The New Grove Dictionary of Musical Instruments*
GroveJ — *The New Grove Dictionary of Jazz*
Grove J2 — *The New Grove Dictionary of Jazz* (2/2002)
GroveO — *The New Grove Dictionary of Opera*
GroveW — *The New Grove Dictionary of Women Composers*
GSJ — *The Galpin Society Journal*
GV — *R. Celletti: Le grandi voci: dizionario critico-biografico dei cantanti*
HDM4 — *Harvard Dictionary, 4th ed.*
HiFi — *High Fidelity*
HiFi/*MusAm* — *High Fidelity/Musical America*
HMYB — *Hinrichsen's Musical Year Book*
IAJRCJ — *International Association of Jazz Record Collectors Journal*
IMSCR — *International Musicological Society Congress Report*
IRASM — *International Review of the Aesthetics and Sociology of Music*
ISAMm — *Institute for Studies in American Music* (New York)
ITO — *In Theory Only*
JAMIS — *Journal of the America Musical Instrument Society*
JAMS — *Journal of the American Musicological Society*
JazzM — *Jazz Monthly*
JbMP — *Jahrbuch der Musikbibliothek Peters*
JEFDSS — *The Journal of the English Folk Dance and Song Society*
JEMF — *J[ohn] E[dwards] M[emorial] F[oundation] Quarterly*
JFSS — *The Journal of the Folk-song Society*
JIFMC — *Journal of the International Folk Music Council*
JJI — *Jazz Journal International*
Jm — *Jazz magazine (Paris)*
JMT — *Journal of Music Theory*
JRBM — *Journal of Renaissance and Baroque Music*
JRME — *Journal of Research in Music Education*
JSAM — *Journal of the Society for American Music*
JT — *Jazz Times*
JVdGSA — *Journal of the Viola da Gamba Society of America*
KdG — *Komponisten der Gegenwart,* ed. H.-W. Heister and W.-W. Sparrer
LAMR — *Latin American Music Review*
LaMusicaD — G.M. Gatti and A. Basso: *La musica: dizionario*
MB — *Musica britannica* (London)
MEJ — *Music Educators Journal*
MF — *Die Musickforschung*
MGG — F. Blume, ed.: *Die Musik in Geschichte und Gegenwart*
MJ — *Music Journal*
ML — *Music and Letters*
MM — *Modern Music*
MMR — *The Monthly Musical Record*
MO — *Musical Opinion*
MQ — *The Musical Quarterly*
MR — *The Music Review*
MSD — *Musicological Studies and Documents* (Rome)
MT — *The Musical Times*
MTNAP — *Music Teachers National Association: Proceedings*
MusAm — *Musical America*
NAW — E.T. James, J.W. James, and P.S. Boyer, eds.: *Notable American Women* (Cambridge, MA, 1971; suppl., 1980)
NOHM — *The New Oxford History of Music*, ed. E. Wellesz, J.A. Westrup, and G. Abraham (London, 1954–)
NRMI — *Nuova rivista musicale italiana*
NZM — *Neue Zeitschrift für Musik* [retitled 1920, see ZfM]
ÖMz — *Österreichische Musikzeitschrift*
ON — *Opera News*
OQ — *Opera Quarterly*
PAMS — *Papers of the American Musicological Society*
PASUC — *Proceedings of the American Society of University Composers*
PMA — *Proceedings of the Musical Association* [retitled 1944, see PRMA]
PNM — *Perspectives of New Music*
PRMA — *Proceedings of the Royal Music Association* [see *PMA*]
RaM — *La rassegna musicale*
RBM — *Revue belge de musicologie*
RdM — *Revue de musicology*
ReM — *La revue musicale*
RiemannL — *Riemann Musik Lexicon,* rev. W. Gurlitt (Mainz, Germany, 12/1959–75)
RISM — *Répertoire international des sources musicales*
RN — *Renaissance News*
RRAM — *Recent Researches in American Music* (Madison, WI)
RS — *Rolling Stone*
Schuller-EJ — G. Schuller: *Early Jazz* (New York, 1968/R)
Schuller-SE — G. Schuller: *The Swing Era* (New York, 1989)
Schwarz GM — *B. Schwarz: Great Masters of the Violin*
SIMG — *Sammelbände der Internationalen Musik-Gesellschaft*
SMA — *Studies in Music*
SMz — *Schweizerische Musikzeitung/Revue musicale suisse*
SouthernB — E. Southern: *Biographical Dictionary of Afro-American and African Musicians*
Thompson — O. Thompson: *The International Cyclopedia of Music and Musicians*
VintonD — J. Vinton, ed.: *Dictionary of Contemporary Music* (New York, 1974)
VMw — *Vierteljahrsschrift für Musikwissenschaft*
Waterhouse-LangwillI — W. Waterhouse: *The New Langwill Index: a Dictionary of Musical Wind-Instrument Makers and Inventors*
YIFMC — *Yearbook of the International Folk Music Council*
ZfM — *Zeitschrift für Musik* [see *NZM*]
ZIMG — *Zeitschrift der Internationalen Musik-Gesellschaft*

Library Abbreviations

AAu Ann Arbor, University of Michigan, Music Library
AB Albany (NY), New York State Library
AKu Akron (OH), University of Akron, Bierce Library
AtaT Talladega (AL) Talladega College
ATS Athens (GA), University of Georgia Libraries
ATet Atlanta (GA), Emory University, Pitts Theology Library
ATu Atlanta (GA), Emory University Library
AU Aurora (NY), Wells College Library
AUS Austin, University of Texas at Austin, The Harry Ransom Humanities Research Center
AUSm Austin, University of Texas at Austin, Fine Arts Library

BAR Baraboo (WI), Circus World Museum Library
BAep Baltimore, Enoch Pratt Free Library
BAhs Baltimore, Maryland Historical Society Library
BApi Baltimore, Arthur Friedheim Library, Johns Hopkins University
BAu Baltimore, Johns Hopkins University Libraries
BAue Baltimore, Milton S. Eisenhower Library, Johns Hopkins University
BAw Baltimore, Walters Art Gallery Library
BER Berea (OH), Riemenschneider Bach Institute Library
BETm Bethlehem (PA), Moravian Archives
BEm Berkeley, University of California at Berkeley, Music Library
BL Bloomington (IN), Indiana University Library
BLl Bloomington (IN), Indiana University, Lilly Library
BLu Bloomington (IN), Indiana University, Cook Music Library
BO Boulder (CO), University of Colorado at Boulder, Music Library
BU Buffalo (NY), Buffalo and Erie County Public Library
Ba Boston, Athenaeum Library
Bc Boston, New England Conservatory of Music, Harriet M. Spaulding Library
Bfa Boston, Museum of Fine Arts
Bgm Boston, Isabella Stewart Gardner Museum, Library
Bh Boston, Harvard Musical Association, Library
Bhs Boston, Massachusetts Historical Society Library
Bp Boston, Public Library, Music Department
Bu Boston, Boston University, Mugar Memorial Library, Department of Special Collections

CA Cambridge (MA), Harvard University, Harvard College Library
CAe Cambridge (MA), Harvard University, Eda Kuhn Loeb Music Library
CAh Cambridge (MA), Harvard University, Houghton Library
CAt Cambridge (MA), Harvard University Library, Theatre Collection
CAward Cambridge (MA), John Milton Ward, private collection [on loan to CA]
CF Cedar Falls (IA), University of Northern Iowa, Library
CHAhs Charleston (SC), The South Carolina Historical Society
CHH Chapel Hill (NC), University of North Carolina at Chapel Hill
CHua Charlottesville (VA), University of Virginia, Alderman Library
CHum Charlottesville (VA), University of Virginia, Music Library
CIhc Cincinnati, Hebrew Union College Library: Jewish Institute of Religion, Klau Library
CIp Cincinnati, Public Library
CIu Cincinnati, University of Cincinnati College - Conservatory of Music, Music Library
CLAc Claremont (CA), Claremont College Libraries
CLU USA, Los Angeles, CA, University of California, Los Angeles

CLp Cleveland, Public Library, Fine Arts Department
CLwr Cleveland, Western Reserve University, Freiberger Library and Music House Library
COhs Columbus (OH), Ohio Historical Society Library
COu Columbus (OH), Ohio State University, Music Library
CP College Park (MD), University of Maryland, McKeldin Library
CR Cedar Rapids (IA), Iowa Masonic Library
Cn Chicago, Newberry Library
Cp Chicago, Chicago Public Library, Music Information Center
CtY USA, New Haven, CT, Yale University
Cu Chicago, University, Joseph Regenstein Library, Music Collection
Cum Chicago, University of Chicago, Music Collection

DAVu Davis (CA), University of California at Davis, Peter J. Shields Library
DAu Dallas, Southern Methodist University, Music Library
DLC USA, Washington, DC, Library of Congress
DMu Durham (NC), Duke University Libraries
DN Denton (TX), University of North Texas, Music Library
DO Dover (NH), Public Library
DSI (JOHP) USA, Washington, DC, Smithsonian Institution: Jazz Oral History Program
Dp Detroit, Public Library, Main Library, Music and Performing Arts Department

E Evanston (IL), Garrett Biblical Institute
EDu Edwardsville (IL), Southern Illinois University
EU Eugene (OR), University of Oregon
Eu Evanston (IL), Northwestern University
FAy Farmington (CT), Yale University, Lewis Walpole Library
FW Fort Worth (TX), Southwestern Baptist Theological Seminary

G Gainesville (FL), University of Florida Library, Music Library
GB Gettysburg (PA), Lutheran Theological Seminary
GR Granville (OH), Denison University Library
GRB Greensboro (NC), University of North Carolina at Greensboro, Walter C. Jackson Library

HA Hanover (NH), Dartmouth College, Baker Library
HG Harrisburg (PA), Pennsylvania State Library
HO Hopkinton (NH), New Hampshire Antiquarian Society
Hbc Hartford (CT), Hartt College of Music Library, The University of Hartford
Hm Hartford (CT), Case Memorial Library, Hartford Seminary Foundation [in ATet]
Hs Hartford (CT), Connecticut State Library
Hw Hartford (CT), Trinity College, Watkinson Library

I Ithaca (NY), Cornell University
ICJic USA, Chicago, IL, Jazz Institute of Chicago
ICU USA, Chicago, IL, University of Chicago
IDt Independence (MO), Harry S. Truman Library
IO Iowa City (IA), University of Iowa, Rita Benton Music Library
InUAtm USA, Bloomington, IN, Indiana University Archives of Traditional Music

K Kent (OH), Kent State University, Music Library
KC Kansas City (MO), University of Missouri: Kansas City, Miller Nichols Library
KCm Kansas City (MO), Kansas City Museum, Library and Archives
KN Knoxville (TN), University of Tennessee, Knoxville, Music Library

LAcs Los Angeles, California State University, John F. Kennedy Memorial Library
LApiatigorsky Los Angeles, Gregor Piatigorsky, private collection [in STEdrachman]
LAs Los Angeles, The Arnold Schoenberg Institute Archives
LAuc Los Angeles, University of California at Los Angeles, William Andrews Clark Memorial Library
LAum Los Angeles, University of California at Los Angeles, Music Library
LAur Los Angeles, University of California at Los Angeles, Special Collections Dept, University Research Library
LAusc Los Angeles, University of Southern California, School of Music Library
LBH Long Beach (CA), California State University
LEX Lexington (KY), University of Kentucky, Margaret I. King Library
LNT USA, New Orleans, LA, Tulane University [transcripts of interviews held at LNT were published on microfilm as New York Times Oral History Program: New Orleans Jazz Oral History Collection (1978–9)]
LOu Louisville, University of Louisville, Dwight Anderson Music Library
LT Latrobe (PA), St Vincent College Library
Lu Lawrence (KS), University of Kansas Libraries

M Milwaukee, Public Library, Art and Music Department
MAhs Madison (WI), Wisconsin Historical Society

MAu Madison (WI), University of Wisconsin
MB Middlebury (VT), Middlebury College, Christian A. Johnson Memorial Music Library
MED Medford (MA), Tufts University Library
MG Montgomery (AL), Alabama State Department of Archives and History Library
MT Morristown (NJ), National Historical Park Museum
Mc Milwaukee, Wisconsin Conservatory of Music Library
MoKmh Kansas City, MO, Kansas City Museum of History
MoUSt USA, St. Louis, MO, University of Missouri

NA Nashville (TN), Fisk University Library
NAu Nashville (TN), Vanderbilt University Library
NBu New Brunswick (NJ), Rutgers - The State University of New Jersey, Music Library, Mabel Smith Douglass Library
NCH (HCJA) USA, Clinton, NY, Hamilton College: Hamilton College Jazz Archive
NEij Newark (NJ), Rutgers - The State University of New Jersey, Rutgers Institute of Jazz Studies Library
NH New Haven (CT), Yale University, Irving S. Gilmore Music Library
NHoh New Haven (CT), Yale University, Oral History Archive
NHub New Haven (CT), Yale University, Beinecke Rare Book and Manuscript Library
NNC USA, New York, NY, Columbia University
NNSc USA, New York, NY, Schomburg Collection, New York Public Library
NNSc (HBC) USA, New York, NY, Schomburg Collection, New York Public Library, Hatch-Billops Collection
NNSc (LAJOHP) USA, New York, NY, Schomburg Collection, New York Public Library, Louis Armstrong Jazz Oral History Project
NO Normal (IL), Illinois State University, Milner Library, Humanities/Fine Arts Division
NORsm New Orleans, Louisiana State Museum Library
NORtu New Orleans, Tulane University, Howard Tilton Memorial Library
NYamc New York, American Music Center Library
NYbroude New York, Broude private collection
NYcc New York, City College Library, Music Library
NYcu New York, Columbia University, Gabe M. Wiener Music & Arts Library
NYcub New York, Columbia University, Rare Book and Manuscript Library of Butler Memorial Library
NYgo New York, University, Gould Memorial Library [in NYu]
NYgr New York, The Grolier Club Library
NYgs New York, G. Schirmer, Inc.
NYhs New York, New York Historical Society Library
NYhsa New York, Hispanic Society of America, Library
NYj New York, The Juilliard School, Lila Acheson Wallace Library
NYkallir New York, Rudolf F. Kallir, private collection
NYlehman New York, Robert O. Lehman, private collection [in NYpm]
NYlibin New York, Laurence Libin, private collection
NYma New York, Mannes College of Music, Clara Damrosch Mannes Memorial Library
NYp New York, Public Library at Lincoln Center, Music Division
NYpl New York, Public Library, Center for the Humanities
NYpm New York, Pierpont Morgan Library
NYpsc New York, New York Public Library, Schomburg Center for Research in Black Culture in Harlem
NYq New York, Queens College of the City University, Paul Klapper Library, Music Library
NYu New York, University Bobst Library
NYw New York, Wildenstein Collection
NYyellin New York, Victor Yellin, private collection
Nf Northampton (MA), Forbes Library
NjR USA, Newark, NJ, Rutgers, the State University of New Jersey
NjR (JOHP) USA, Newark, NJ, Rutgers, the State University of New Jersey: Jazz Oral History Project
Nsc Northampton (MA), Smith College, Werner Josten Library

OAm Oakland (CA), Mills College, Margaret Prall Music Library
OB Oberlin (OH), Oberlin College Conservatory of Music, Conservatory Library
OX Oxford (OH), Miami University, Amos Music Library

PHci Philadelphia, Curtis Institute of Music, Library
PHf Philadelphia, Free Library of Philadelphia, Music Dept
PHff Philadelphia, Free Library of Philadelphia, Edwin A. Fleisher Collection of Orchestral Music
PHgc Philadelphia, Gratz College
PHhs Philadelphia, Historical Society of Pennsylvania Library
PHlc Philadelphia, Library Company of Philadelphia
PHmf Philadelphia, Musical Fund Society [on loan to PHf]
PHphs Philadelphia, The Presbyterian Historical Society Library [in PHlc]
PHps Philadelphia, American Philosophical Society Library
PHu Philadelphia, University of Pennsylvania, Van Pelt-Dietrich Library Center
PO Poughkeepsie (NY), Vassar College, George Sherman Dickinson Music Library

PRObs Providence (RI), Rhode Island Historical Society Library
PROu Providence (RI), Brown University
PRV Provo (UT), Brigham Young University
PRs Princeton (NJ), Theological Seminary, Speer Library
PRu Princeton (NJ), Princeton University, Firestone Memorial Library
PRw Princeton (NJ), Westminster Choir College
Pc Pittsburgh, Carnegie Library, Music and Art Dept
Ps Pittsburgh, Theological Seminary, Clifford E. Barbour Library
Pu Pittsburgh, University of Pittsburgh
Puf Pittsburgh, University of Pittsburgh, Foster Hall Collection, Stephen Foster Memorial

R Rochester (NY), Sibley Music Library, University of Rochester, Eastman School of Music

SA Salem (MA), Peabody and Essex Museums, James Duncan Phillips Library
SBm Santa Barbara (CA), Mission Santa Barbara
SFp San Francisco, Public Library, Fine Arts Department, Music Division
SFs San Francisco, Sutro Library
SFsc San Francisco, San Francisco State University, Frank V. de Bellis Collection
SJb San Jose (CA), Ira F. Brilliant Center for Beethoven Studies, San José State University
SL St Louis, St Louis University, Pius XII Memorial Library
SLC Salt Lake City, University of Utah Library
SLug St Louis, Washington University, Gaylord Music Library
SM San Marino (CA), Huntington Library
SPma Spokane (WA), Moldenhauer Archives
SR San Rafael (CA), American Music Research Center, Dominican College
STEdrachmann Stevenson (MD), Mrs Jephta Drachman, private collection; Mrs P.C. Drachman, private collection
STO Stony Brook (NY), State University of New York at Stony Brook, Frank Melville jr Memorial Library
STu Palo Alto (CA), University, Memorial Library of Music, Department of Special Collections of the Cecil H. Green Library
SY Syracuse (NY), University Music Library
SYkrasner Syracuse (NY), Louis Krasner, private collection [in CAh and SY]
Su Seattle, University of Washington, Music Library

TA Tallahassee (FL), Florida State University, Robert Manning Strozier Library
TNF Nashville (TN) Fisk University
TxU Austin (TX) University of Texas

U Urbana (IL), University of Illinois, Music Library
Uplamenac Urbana (IL), Dragan Plamenac, private collection [in NH]

V Villanova (PA), Villanova University, Falvey Memorial Library

WB Wilkes-Barre (PA), Wilkes College Library
WC Waco (TX), Baylor University, Music Library
WGc Williamsburg (VA), College of William and Mary, Earl Gregg Swenn Library
WI Williamstown (MA), Williams College Library
WOa Worcester (MA), American Antiquarian Society Library
WS Winston-Salem (NC), Moravian Music Foundation, Peter Memorial Library
Wc Washington, DC, Library of Congress, Music Division
Wca Washington, Cathedral Library
Wcf Washington, Library of Congress, American Folklife Center and the Archive of Folk Culture
Wcg Washington, General Collections, Library of Congress
Wcm Washington, Library of Congress, Motion Picture, Broadcasting and Recorded Sound Division
Wcu Washington, Catholic University of America, Music Library
Wdo Washington, Dumbarton Oaks
Wgu Washington, Georgetown University Libraries
Whu Washington, Howard University, College of Fine Arts Library
Ws Washington, Folger Shakespeare Library

Y York (PA), Historical Society of York County, Library and Archives

Volume One

AAMC – Brown, Clifford

A Note on the Use of the Dictionary

This note is intended as a short guide to the basic procedures and organization of the dictionary. A fuller account will be found in "About the Dictionary," pp. xxi–xxiv.

Alphabetization of headings is based on the principle that words are read continuously, ignoring spaces, hyphens, accents, parenthesized and bracketed matter, etc., up to the first punctuation mark, then again thereafter if that mark is a comma. "Mc" and "Mac" are alphabetized as "Mac," "St." as "Saint."

Cross-references are shown in small capitals, with a large capital at the beginning of the first word of the entry referred to. Thus "The UNIVERSITY OF MICHIGAN was founded in Detroit in 1817" means that the entry referred is not "University of Michigan" but "Michigan, University of."

Abbreviations used in the dictionary are listed on pp. xxv–xxxviii, in the order General (beginning on p. xxv), Discographical (p. xxxii), Bibliographical (p. xxxiii), and Library (p. xxxv).

Work-lists are normally arranged chronologically (within section, where divided), in order of year of composition or first publication (in the latter case dates are given in parentheses). Italicized abbreviations (such as *DLC*) stand for libraries holding sources and are explained on p. xxxv.

Recording-lists are arranged chronologically (within section, where divided), typically in order of date of issue. Abbreviations standing for record labels are explained on p. xxxii.

Bibliographies are arranged chronologically (within section, where divided), in order of year of first publication, and alphabetically by author within years. Abbreviations standing for periodicals and reference works are explained on p. xxxiii.

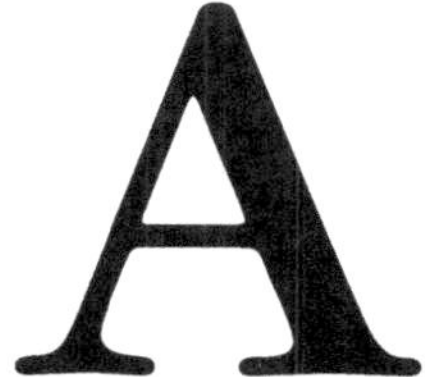

AACM. *See* ASSOCIATION FOR THE ADVANCEMENT OF CREATIVE MUSICIANS (AACM).

A&M. Record company. It was founded in Los Angeles in 1962 by the former US army trumpeter Herb Alpert and the promoter-producer Jerry Moss. For its first few years, A&M depended largely on revenues from Alpert's own recordings. His easy-listening instrumental music recorded with the Tijuana brass had sold over 20 million copies by 1968, when the company's turnover was $50 million. In 1966 A&M also scored success with Sergio Mendes and the Sandpipers' single, "Guantanamera." Moss, however, was keen to broaden the appeal of A&M, and began recording such West Coast artists as Captain Beefheart and Dr John. In 1969 the label opened its first British office and by the early 1970s A&M also signed American recording deals with such artists as Procol Harum, The Move, Joe Cocker, Jimmy Cliff, and Cat Stevens.

By the 1970s A&M were established as the most successful independent record label in the United States. In March 1977 it signed the British punk group the Sex Pistols, but dropped it after six days after complaints from other A&M artists. A&M showed more commitment to the new wave by signing the radio-friendly act The Police. In 1989, Polygram bought A&M for $460 million; Albert and Moss stayed at the helm until 1993. In the late 1990s the A&M roster included international recording stars such as Sting, Sheryl Crow, and Bryan Adams. Seagram bought PolyGram in 1998, and merged with MCA Records to form Universal Music; A&M thus became a subsidiary of the UNIVERSAL MUSIC GROUP and the original company closed its doors. In 2007, the label was relaunched as part of a joint venture, A&M/Octone, which landed popular artists such as K'naan and Maroon 5.

See also ALPERT, HERB

DAVID BUCKLEY/R

ABBA. Swedish pop group. Its members were Benny Andersson (*b* Stockholm, 16 Dec 1946), Agnetha Fältskog (*b* Jönköping, 5 April 1950), Anni-Frid Lyngstad (*b* Ballangen, Norway, 15 Nov 1945), and Björn Ulvaeus (*b* Göteborg, 25 April 1945). Having established separate careers within Swedish pop they started working together in 1970, from 1972 under the name Björn, Benny, Agnetha och Anni-Frid. The acronym ABBA, which uses the first letter of each member's first name, was adopted in 1973. Their victory in the Eurovision Song Contest in 1974, with "Waterloo," launched the most successful international career to emerge from that context. During the period 1974–82 the group attained global popularity with songs such as "Mama Mia" (1975), "Fernando" (1976), "Dancing Queen: (1976), "The Name of the Game" (1977), "Take a chance on me" (1978), and "Super Trouper" (1980), and albums such as *Waterloo* (1974), *ABBA* (1975), *Arrival* (1976), *The Album* (1977), *Voulez-Vous* (1979), and *The Visitors* (1981). In terms of chart performance, ABBA was the world's most successful pop group in the 1970s; by 1983 their cumulative record sales were estimated at 180 million units.

ABBA's music, most of which was written by Andersson and Ulvaeus with some lyrics by their manager Stig Anderson, features carefully designed, eclectic syntheses of 1970s pop and dance music with European and Latin American popular styles, most notably in stylistic pastiches such as the 'Italian' "Andante andante," the 'Greek' "I have a dream" or the 'Andean' "Fernando." Its prominent characteristics are sensuous combinations of diatonic melody and tonal harmony, often involving harmonic motion alternating between two or three chords. A further important factor contributing to ABBA's sound is the meticulously crafted production. The engineer Michael B. Tretow created dense but transparent combinations of multi-tracked vocals with skillfully balanced instrumentation, setting new production standards for mainstream pop. In addition to the music, the group's success was also facilitated by their pioneering use of visual media for promotion, as exemplified by music videos and the concert film *ABBA: the Movie* (1977).

The group disbanded in 1982, after which the members have pursued separate careers with varying degrees of success. Andersson and Ulvaeus wrote the musical *Chess* (with lyricist Tim Rice, 1984), *Kristina från Duvemåla* (1995), based on Vilhelm Moberg's tetralogy of novels about 19th-century Swedish immigrants to the United States, and the extremely successful musical *Mamma Mia* (2000), which was also made into a popular film.

BIBLIOGRAPHY

C. Irwin, A. L. Oldham, and T. Calder: *ABBA: The Name of the Game* (London, 1995)

A. Fältskog: *As I Am: ABBA Before & Beyond* (London, 1997)

C.-M. Palm: *Bright Lights, Dark Shadows: The Real Story of ABBA* (London, 2001)

P. F. Broman: "'When Bll Is Said and Done': Swedish ABBA Reception During the 1970s and the Ideology of Pop," *Journal of Popular Music Studies*, xvii/1 (2005), 45–66

ALF BJÖRNBERG/R

Abbott, Emma (*b* Chicago, IL 9 Dec 1849; *d* Salt Lake City, UT 5 Jan 1891). Soprano and impresario. The product of a musical family, she was performing professionally by the age of nine with her father and older brother in Peoria (where she grew up) and environs. When she was 16 Abbott joined an itinerant concert troupe, and made her Chicago debut in April 1867. After leaving this company Abbott toured solo for several years. In 1869 she met Clara Louise Kellogg, who introduced her to ACHILLE ERRANI, with whom she subsequently studied in New York; her concert debut there was in December 1871. A group of wealthy New Yorkers paid for study abroad and she spent 1872–76 in Europe, studying with Sangiovanni in Milan and Marchesi, Wartel, and Delle Sedie in Paris. During this time she was secretly married to Eugene Wetherell (*d* 1889), who would become her manager. Abbott's operatic debut was at Covent Garden as Marie in *La fille du régiment* (2 May 1876) with Frederick Gye's Royal Italian Opera Company. A disagreement resulted in cancellation of her contract; James Mapleson quickly signed her to his company and took her on provincial tour. She earned critical praise and seemed on the verge of a successful operatic career when she refused to sing Violetta on moral grounds. The subsequent termination of her contract ended her career in Italian opera.

Abbott returned to the United States in December 1876 and made her American operatic debut in New York on 23 February 1877, again as Marie. With no hope of securing another position in Italian opera, she turned instead to opera in English. Her Grand English Opera Company performed widely in the United States from 1879–91, when she died suddenly of pneumonia while performing in Salt Lake City.

Abbott had a pure clear soprano voice of great flexibility and volume, and sang a repertory that included English operas, translations of the standard continental repertory (excepting Wagner), and some operettas. She was phenomenally successful; her company never had a losing season, in part because she and Wetherell were masters at creating and disseminating an image that resonated with Americans. She never cancelled performances, was a proud American from the heartland, appealed to a church-going public through upright behavior, championed the rights of women, and personified a rags-to-riches story. She endeavored to please her audiences by interpolating songs and performing works that were in some fashion abridged; both were common performance practices for the time. Abbott's critical reputation was mixed: some critics labeled her a charlatan, others praised her performances. Some of the negative criticism—and to a certain extent her historical reputation—can be attributed to a cadre of critics (most Wagnerians) who were attempting in the 1880s to make opera into high culture. Abbott provided Americans with opera-as-entertainment and was quite influential despite the critics; as "the people's prima donna," she introduced opera to hundreds of thousands of Americans.

BIBLIOGRAPHY

NAW (H.E. Johnson); *ANB* (K. K. Preston)

G. Greenwood: *Emma Abbott* (n.p., 1878?)

S.E. Martin: *The Life and Professional Career of Emma Abbott* (Minneapolis, 1891)

F.E. Willard and M.A. Livermore: 'Abbott, Emma', *A Woman of the Century* (Chicago, 1893), 2

H.C. Lahee: *Famous Singers of Today and Yesterday* (Boston, 1898)

G. Upton: *Musical Memories* (Chicago, 1908)

O. Thompson: *The American Singer* (New York, 1937/*R*)

KATHERINE K. PRESTON

Abbott, George (*b* Forestville, NY, 25 Jan 1887; *d* Miami Beach, FL, 31 Jan 1995). Stage director and, producer, playwright, and actor. During a 92-year career in the theater Abbott influenced the development of musical comedy and helped launch many important careers. He made his Broadway acting debut in 1913 and continued to act during the 1920s. He also began working as both a playwright and director. After his first hit, *The Fall Guy*, Abbott began to write and stage fast-paced melodramas. In 1932 he co-produced a farce called *20th Century*; it was in this genre that he defined a fast-paced theatrical style that became known as the Abbott Touch. He was the leading director of musical comedies. Abbott also wrote the books for *On your Toes* (1936), *The Boys from Syracuse* (1938), and *Pal Joey* (1940), the scores of which were composed by Richard Rodgers and Lorenz Hart. In 1944 he assisted the original production of *On the Town* by streamlining the plot; it was his authority on timing in musicals that earned him the nickname Play Doctor. Abbott directed productions of many well known musicals including *High Button Shoes*, *Where's Charley?*, *Call me Madam*, *Wonderful Town*, *The Pajama Game*, *Damn Yankees*, *Fiorello!*, and *A Funny Thing Happened On the Way to the Forum*.

BIBLIOGRAPHY

G. Abbott: *Mister Abbott* (New York, 1963)

E. Mordden: *Coming up Roses: the Broadway Musical in the 1950s* (New York, 1998)

SYLVIA STONER-HAWKINS

ABC-Paramount [ABC]. Record company. Founded in 1955 in New York by American Broadcasting-Paramount Theaters, it was coeval with the birth of rock and roll, although a couple of years passed before the label produced hits in that genre, with such songs as Danny and the Juniors' "At the Hop" (1957) and "Rock and roll is here to stay" (1958). It achieved sustained success with less boisterous pop music, particularly the work of Paul Anka ("Diana," "Put your head on my shoulder," and "Puppy Love"). The rest of the company's output comprised children's, spoken word, ethnic, jazz, and rhythm-and-blues records.

From the late 1950s the label attracted many successful African-American artists, including Fats Domino and B.B. King; after signing in 1959 Ray Charles scored his first number one pop single in 1960 with "Georgia on my Mind" and his first number one album in 1962 with *Modern Sounds in Country and Western Music*. In 1966 the label's name was shortened to ABC. Despite subsequently producing some original music—notably that of the Impressions and Steely Dan—the company wound down in the late 1970s. It was sold to and dismantled by MCA in 1979.

CHRISTOPHER DOLL

à Becket, Thomas, Jr. (*b* Philadelphia, PA, 19 July 1843; *d* Philadelphia, PA, 1918). Pianist, singer, educator, and composer. He studied music with his father Thomas à Becket Sr. (*b* 17 March 1808; *d* 6 Jan 1890) and in Philadelphia public schools. The father, a music teacher, actor and composer, wrote "Columbia, the Gem of the Ocean." In 1855 Thomas à Becket Jr. performed at the Walnut Street Theatre in a work written by his father. He developed into one of the finest, most sought after accompanists in the city, joining with leading artists and singing groups. Member and president of the Mendelssohn Club, he sang in a series of 35 light operas produced at the Amateur Drawing Room (1868–72) and accompanied the Orpheus Club (1877–98). An important educator, from 1873 until he died à Becket taught and played the organ at Girard College, a residential school for orphaned boys. À Becket became a member of a group of professional musicians who evaluated music teaching methods in the Philadelphia Public Schools. À Becket family archives at The New York Public Library for the Performing Arts include diaries (1862–80), appointment books, prompt books, and a picture of Thomas à Becket Jr. His compositions include the vocal piece *The Farmer Feeds us All* (Boston, 1874) and *Rural Pictures*, twelve piano pieces published by Hatch in 1900.

BIBLIOGRAPHY

Grove2, Amer. suppl.
L.C. Elson: *The National Music of America* (Boston, 1900)
R.A. Gerson: *Music in Philadelphia* (Philadelphia, 1940)

MARTHA FURMAN SCHLEIFER

Abejo, Rosalina (*b* Tagoloan, Oriental Misamis, 13 July 1922; *d* Fresno, CA, 5 June 1991). Filipina composer and conductor. She studied music at Lourdes College, the piano at St. Scholastica's College and composition at the Philippine Women's University (MM 1957). Later she attended the Labunski School of Composition in Ohio, the Eastman School, and the Catholic University of America, Washington, DC. A nun of the Order of the Virgin Mary, she taught music theory and composition, conducted fund-raising concerts, and travelled widely to take part in international music conferences. In 1977 she moved to the United States, teaching at Kansas University and St. Pius Seminary in Kentucky before moving to Fremont, California; in 1980 she was elected president of the Philippine Foundation of Performing Arts in America. Among the honors she received were the Republic Culture Heritage Award (1967) and the Philippines' Independence Day Award (1973). She produced over 300 compositions and some published music textbooks. Her style is marked by neo-classical and Impressionist features, with quartal harmonies, added-note chords, pentatonic, and modal scales.

WORKS
(selective list)

Orch: Vespers in a Convent Garden, sym. suite, 1956; 13 Variations, 2 pf, orch, 1957; Valle de los caidos, rhapsody, 1964; Sym. "The Trilogy of Man," 1971; Sym. "Guerilla," 1972; Ov. 1081, 1974

Choral: Advent Cant., 1957; The Conversion of King Humabon, cant., 1967; Redemption Orat, 1969; masses, other pieces

Solo vocal: Pamuhat-Buhat [Faith Healing], Bar, wind, native perc, str, 1973; Larawan ng Isang Babae [Woman's Portrait], S, orch, 1965; Buhay [Life], S, orch, 1969; sacred songs

Other inst: 5 str qts, 1949–59; Academic Festival Qt, 1966; Pf Qnt, 1966; Octet, wind, str, 1970; Maranaw Trail, 2 mar, pf, perc, 1971; Octet, brass, perc, 1972; Strings on the Dignity of Man, 1979; The Absent Baritone, 1985

LUCRECIA R. KASILAG

Abeles, Harold F(red) (*b* New York, NY, 10 March 1945). Music educator and scholar. He received degrees from the University of Connecticut (BS 1966, MA 1968) and the University of Maryland, College Park (PhD 1971). He served on the faculties of the University of North Carolina at Greensboro (1972–5), Indiana University (1975–82), and Teachers College, Columbia University (1982–). At Teachers College he served as coordinator of music education, chair of the Arts and Humanities Department, and director of the Division of Instruction. He is coauthor (with C.R. Hoffer and R.H. Klotman) of *Foundations of Music Education* (1984, 2/1994) and coeditor (with L. Custodero) of *Critical Issues in Music Education: Contemporary Theory and Practice* (2010). He wrote chapters for the *Handbook of Music Psychology* (1980, 2/1996) and *The New Handbook of Research on Music Teaching and Learning* (2002), among others. He was founding editor of *The Music Researchers Exchange*, an international music research newsletter (1974–2002). His research has focused on the evaluation of community-based arts organizations and their education programs, assessment of instrumental instruction, sex-stereotyping of musical instruments, evaluation of applied music instructors, evaluation of ensemble directors, technology-based music instruction, and verbal communication in studio instruction.

JERE T. HUMPHREYS

Abenaki [Abnaki]. Native American tribe of the Wabenaki confederacy.

Abercrombie, John (*b* Port Chester, NY, 16 Dec 1944). Jazz guitarist, composer, and bandleader. He grew up in Greenwich, CT, and began playing guitar at the age of 14. He was primarily self-taught until he studied at the Berklee College of Music (1962–6) and with Jack Petersen. Abercrombie joined Johnny Hammond's touring band after the blues organist had spotted him performing with other Berklee students at Paul's Mall in Boston. After studying briefly at the University of North Texas, in 1969 he moved to New York where he performed and recorded in Billy Cobham's jazz-rock band Dreams (1970), joined Chico Hamilton's group, and recorded with Gato Barbieri (1971), Barry Miles (1972), and Gil Evans (1974). Abercrombie attracted wider attention performing with Cobham's fusion band Spectrum from 1974. He also toured with Jack DeJohnette and recorded his debut album, *Timeless* (1974), which marked the start of a prolific relationship with Manfred Eicher and his ECM label. As leader of the trio Gateway he performed and recorded (*Gateway* and *Gateway 2*) with DeJohnette and Dave Holland, departing from earlier fusion works in favor of the more subdued, "chamber" jazz style featured on his debut. Between 1978 and 1980, Abercrombie toured with DeJohnette's band New Directions and with Ralph Towner, and recorded three albums for ECM in a traditional quartet with the pianist Richie Beirach, the bass player George Mraz, and the drummer Peter Donald.

During the early 1980s Abercrombie worked in a number of duos: with Towner and Mraz, he explored originals and standards, with John Scofield he examined bebop, and with Beirach he played guitar synthesizer. He continued to perform on that instrument during the mid-1980s in a trio with the bass player Marc Johnson and Peter Erskine; their recording *Getting There* also featured Michael Brecker. In 1986 he worked with Paul Bley's free-jazz ensemble. Abercrombie spent the early 1990s performing and recording with a new trio that included the drummer Adam Nussbaum and the Hammond organist Dan Wall. He was also a member of Kenny Wheeler's large and small ensembles and worked again with Gateway (*Homecoming*) and Johnson and Erskine. Subsequent collaborations with Andy LaVerne, Joe LaBarbera, Jan Garbarek, and Mark Feldman and his continued relationship with ECM maintained his reputation as one of the foremost modern jazz guitarists.

SELECTED RECORDINGS

As leader: *Timeless* (1974, ECM), *Arcade* (1978, ECM), *Getting There* (1987, ECM), *Speak of the Devil* (1993, ECM), *Open Land* (1999, ECM); of Gateway (with J. DeJohnette and D. Holland): *Gateway* (1975, ECM), *Gateway 2* (1977, ECM), *Homecoming* (1994, ECM)

As sideman: G. Barbieri: *Bolivia/Under Fire* (1973, RCA); D. Liebman: *Lookout Farm* (1973; B. Cobham: *Crosswinds* (1974, Atl.); J. DeJohnette: *New Directions* (1978); K. Wheeler: *The Widow in the Window* (1990, ECM), *Music for Large and Small Ensembles* (1990)

BIBLIOGRAPHY

C. Berg: "John Abercrombie's Six-string Stylistic Summit," *DB*, xliii/4 (1976), 16

B. Milkowski: "John Abercrombie: Seduced by Synths," *DB*, liii/9 (1986), 17

K. Franckling: "John Abercrombie: Low Cholesterol Organ Trio," *JT*, xxiii/6 (1993), 28

C. Stern: "Gateway Trio: an Axis as Bold as Love," *JT*, xxv/10 (1995), 30

BARRY LONG

Abercromby [Abercrombie], **John Joseph** (*fl* 1773–1820). Scottish violinist, viola d'amore player, and teacher. Abercromby was born in Scotland but educated in French Flanders. After hearing Abercromby play at a St. Cecilia Society concert in Charleston in 1773, Josiah Quincy Jr. of Boston wrote, "A Frenchman just arrived, [who] played a first fiddle and solo incomparably, better than any I ever had heard." During the American Revolutionary War, Abercromby remained in Charleston, where he advertised to teach guitar and dance, and performed at concerts during the British occupation of the city. He left Charleston in 1791, and over the next two decades lived in Bucks County, Pennsylvania, Baltimore, Richmond, and Lexington. By 1815 he was in Tennessee, where he opened a music academy in Nashville.

BIBLIOGRAPHY

J. Wooldridge, E. E. Hoss, and W. B. Reese: *History of Nashville, Tennessee* (Nashville, TN, 1890)

J. Carden: *Music in Lexington before 1840* (Lexington, KY, 1980)

N.B. Butler: *Votaries of Apollo: the St Cecilia Society and the Patronage of Concert Music in Charleston, South Carolina, 1766–1820* (Columbia, SC, 2007)

NICHOLAS MICHAEL BUTLER

Abolition. From the mid-1830s through the Civil War, abolitionists systematically deployed songs as spiritual weaponry in the fight to eradicate slavery in the United States. Although anti-slavery sentiment was apparent as early as the 1680s, among the Quakers and Mennonites, and gained momentum as anti-slavery legislation was gradually enacted in the North, music became central to the movement only when anti-slavery societies proliferated in the 1830s. With slavery virtually eliminated in the northern states, William Lloyd Garrison engaged northern white abolitionists and African Americans in agitating for slavery's complete and immediate end, using poetry and music to intensify the evangelical theology and fervor of this moralist crusade. In 1834 he compiled the first anti-slavery songster, *A Selection of Anti-Slavery Hymns*. To be sung at meetings of the American Anti-Slavery Society (founded by Garrison in 1833) and at monthly Concerts of Prayer, the hymns united formal poetry by white authors with a suggested classic hymn tune (such as "Old Hundred" or "Italian Hymn"). The last hymn in the collection was an exception: written in the voice of a slave, it was topical—decrying repatriation to Africa—and was assigned a popular rather than a sacred tune (John Payne Howard's "Sweet Home," 1823). Two other compilations supporting Garrisonian ideology were those of abolitionist Maria Weston Chapman (1836), which assigned hymn meters rather than specific tunes to the poems, and of Presbyterian minister Edwin F. Hatfield (1840). Poets whose work is represented in these three anthologies include John Greenleaf Whittier, Rev. John Pierpont, Lydia H. Sigourney, Elizabeth M. Chandler, Harriet

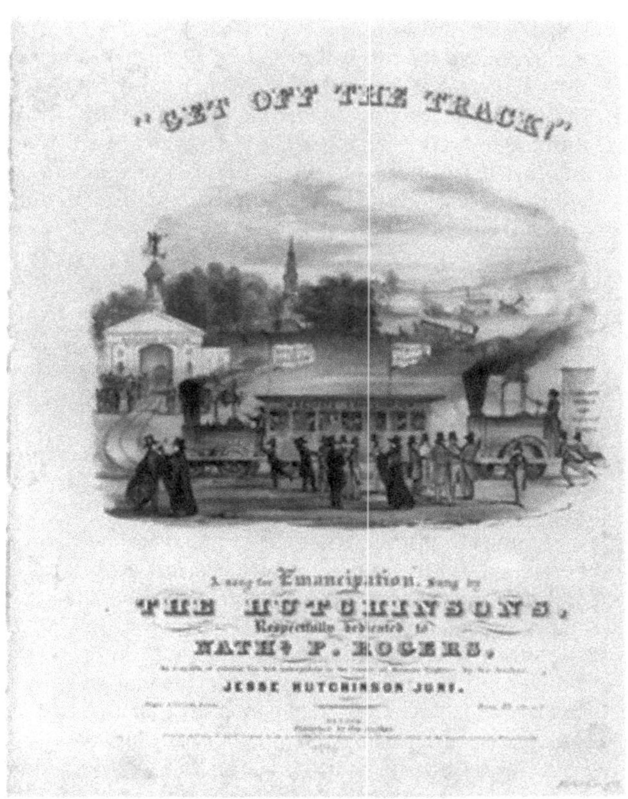

"Get off the Track," abolitionist song by Jesse Hutchinson Jr., 1844. (Library of Congress, Prints and Photographs Division, LOT 10615–59)

Martineau, Garrison, and Chapman, as well as such well-loved hymnists as Watts and the Wesley brothers.

In the 1840s political abolitionism emerged as a competing faction to Christian abolitionism and spawned a wealth of new songs into the 1850s. Whereas Jairus Lincoln's *Anti-Slavery Melodies* (1843) belonged to the Garrisonian mold of morality hymns, activist/singer George Whitefield Clark's compilations traced the course of political abolitionism, from the Liberty Party (*Liberty Minstrel*, 1844, with seven editions through 1848) to the Free Soil Party (*Free Soil Minstrel*, 1848), to the Republican Party (*Harp of Freedom*, 1856). Lyrics became increasingly topical, referring to specific instances of imprisonment, insurrections, and controversies that led up to the war, such as the Fugitive Slave Laws, the Brooks–Sumner incident, and the Kansas–Nebraska Act. Secular tunes predominated: patriotic airs ("The Marseilles Hymn," "America"), Scottish airs ("Scots Wha Hae," "Auld Lang Syne"), popular melodies ("Dan Tucker," "Nelly Bly"), and a large number composed by Clark himself. As with previous books, Clark's songs reflected a white viewpoint, with the rare exceptions of "Stolen we were," with "words by a Colored Man," and "Song of the Coffle Gang," with words by "the Slaves." Clark also supplied musical scores.

These abolitionist songs were performed not only at anti-slavery meetings, rallies, and prayer meetings in northern free states, but in the home and at school (see compilations by Collins and by Gilmore, which drew on Garrisonian-style hymns). Meetings typically included a songleader or chorus on the platform next to the speakers. The chorus might have been an African American juvenile choir (especially at Garrison's meetings), a community group, or a singing troupe like the Hutchinson Family and the African American Luca family. Jesse Hutchinson would take notes during the speeches and compose impromptu songs on the platform, most of which do not survive. There is little evidence that African Americans sang these white compositions, however, unless they were invited guests at white meetings (as were Frederick Douglass, Harriet Tubman, and Sojourner Truth). Black anti-slavery meetings favored Watts and Wesley hymns that expressed messages of freedom and equality.

Abolitionist music composed by and for African Americans was more heterogeneous in concept. William Wells Brown's *Anti-Slavery Harp* (1848) collected previously published as well as new songs, whereas Joshua McCarter Simpson (1820?–76), of Zanesville, Ohio, self-published two books of original songs: *Original Anti-Slavery Songs* (1852) and *The Emancipation Car* (1854). Simpson's choice of tune was often an ironic comment on the text, as illustrated by his setting of "To the White People of America" to the tune of Stephen Foster's "Massa's in the cold, cold ground." Whether Simpson's songs were ever sung is unknown. Much of the anti-slavery music that African Americans created and sang circulated in oral tradition and has been lost, although references to these songs survive in histories and slave narratives. For example Sojourner Truth, who began traveling and preaching abolition in 1843, was noted for improvising religious songs on the lecture platform. Black anti-slavery music in the South necessarily relied on coded meanings, especially since the consequences of singing about freedom became more extreme in the years leading up to the war.

The Civil War inspired a new category of abolitionist song, particularly after 1861, when General Benjamin Butler declared escaped slaves seeking asylum with the Union Army to be "contrabands" of war. Contraband songs quickly appeared and multiplied; some appear in *The Harp of Freedom* (1862), and many were published as sheet music. White abolitionists gave the Negro spiritual "Go down, Moses" the subtitle "The Song of the Contrabands," and enlisted the song's message of liberation in their activism. On New Year's Eve 1862 African Americans in the Contraband Camp in the District of Columbia sang one of its many parodies: "Go down, Abraham, away down in Dixie's land / Tell Jeff. Davis to let my people go." Henry C. Work's immensely popular "Kingdom Coming: the Contraband's Song," introduced by the Christy Minstrels and published as sheet music in 1862, traveled to the South with white and black soldiers, where African Americans transformed it and even claimed the song as their own creation.

Setting abolitionist words to minstrel tunes was both controversial and effective. Authors believed that the tunes would lose their degrading influence when divorced from the minstrel stage and united with righteous lyrics, and the tunes' popularity ensured widespread circulation. Abolitionist songs were disseminated not only in songsters but in white and black newspapers and periodicals, a small body of sheet music, and oral tradition. By 1868 abolitionist song had run its course as songwriters began to focus their efforts on civil rights.

See also Civil war, the.

COLLECTIONS

(selective list)

W.L. Garrison: *A Selection of Anti-Slavery Hymns for the Use of Friends of Emancipation* (Boston, 1834)

M.W. Chapman, ed.: *Songs of the Free and Hymns of Christian Freedom* (Boston, 1836)

E.F. Hatfield, ed.: *Freedom's Lyre: or, Psalms, Hymns, and Sacred Songs for the Slave and His Friends* (New York, 1840)

J.A. Collins, ed.: *The Anti-Slavery Picknick: a Collection of Speeches, Poems, Dialogues and Songs; Intended for Use in Schools and Anti-Slavery Meetings* (Boston, 1842) [contains musical scores]

J. Lincoln: *Anti-Slavery Melodies: for the Friends of Freedom* (Hingham, MA, 1843) [contains musical scores]

H. Wood: *Hartley Wood's Anniversary Book of Music, for the Fourth of July, Temperance, and Anti-Slavery Occasions* (Boston, 1843)

[G.W. Clark, ed.:] *The Liberty Minstrel* (New York, 1844) [contains musical scores]

H.S. Gilmore, ed.: *A Collection of Miscellaneous Songs, from the Liberty Minstrel, Mason's Juvenile Harp &c.; for the Use of the Cincinnati High School* (Cincinnati, 1846)

W.W. Brown, ed.: *The Anti-Slavery Harp: a Collection of Songs for Anti-Slavery Meetings* (Boston, 1848)

G.W. Clark, ed.: *The Free Soil Minstrel* (New York, 1848) [contains musical scores]

Anti-Slavery Songs: a Selection from the Best Anti-Slavery Authors (Salem, OH, 1849)

J. McCarter Simpson: *Original Anti-Slavery Songs* (Zanesville, OH, 1852)

J. McCarter Simpson: *The Emancipation Car* (Zanesville, OH, 1854)

J.H. Camp, ed.: *The Freemen's Glee Book: a Collection of Songs, Odes, Glees and Ballads, with Music, Original and Selected, Harmonized, and Arranged for Each* (New York, 1856)

G.W. Clark, ed.: *The Harp of Freedom* (New York, 1856) [contains musical scores]

BIBLIOGRAPHY

W.W. Brown: *The Negro in the American Rebellion: his Heroism and his Fidelity* (Boston, 1867)

V.L. Eaklor: *Antislavery Songs: a Collection and Analysis* (New York, 1988)

J.M. Spencer: *Protest and Praise: Sacred Music of Black Religion* (Minneapolis, 1990)

J.R. Sherman: *African-American Poetry of the Nineteenth Century: an Anthology* (Urbana, IL, 1992)

E. Southern: *Music of Black Americans* (New York, 3/1997)

K. Masur: "'A Rare Phenomenon of Philological Vegetation': the Word 'Contraband' and the Meanings of Emancipation in the United States," *Journal of American History*, xciii/4 (2007), 1050–84

M.C. Cohen: "Contraband Singing: Poems and Songs in Circulation during the Civil War," *American Literature*, lxxxii (2010), 271–304

SANDRA JEAN GRAHAM

Abrams, Muhal Richard [Abrams, Richard Louis] (*b* Chicago, IL, 19 Sept 1930). Pianist, composer, and administrator. After receiving private piano lessons, he studied at the Chicago Musical College and taught himself the system of composition devised by Joseph Schillinger. He began to work professionally in 1948 and performed regularly at the Cotton Club in Chicago during the 1950s, accompanying visiting musicians such as Dexter Gordon, Sonny Stitt, and Max Roach. After composing and arranging for the Walter "King" Fleming band in the mid-1950s, Abrams joined the hard bop ensemble MJT+3 and made his recording debut on the group's album *Daddy-O Presents MJT+3* (1957, VJ 1013). Beginning in 1961 Abrams led the Experimental Band, a composer-centered rehearsal ensemble whose members included the double bass player Donald Rafael Garrett, Jack DeJohnette, Roscoe Mitchell, and the reed player Joseph Jarman. He subsequently co-founded the Association for the Advancement of Creative Musicians (AACM) in 1965; he was its first president and the founder of the AACM School of Music. Abrams made his first recording as a leader, *Levels and Degrees of Light* (Del. 413), in 1967.

Abrams performed in Europe for the first time in 1973, appearing with his sextet at the Berlin Jazz Days. Since moving to New York in 1976, he has performed as an unaccompanied soloist, and composed for and performed with small ensembles and orchestras. He has recorded in a variety of styles, with the Art Ensemble of Chicago, Anthony Braxton, Leroy Jenkins, Wadada Leo Smith, Henry Threadgill, Amina Claudine Myers, and George E. Lewis. Abrams was the first recipient of the Danish Jazz Center's generous Jazzpar Prize in 1990 and was awarded the NEA Jazzmasters Award in 2010. His explorations of sound textures have influenced improvisational practices in experimental music since the 1960s. Abrams plays the clarinet in addition to his principal instrument.

BIBLIOGRAPHY

E. Jost: *Jazzmusiker: Materialien zur Soziologie der afro-amerikanischen Musik* (Frankfurt am Main, Germany, Berlin, and Vienna, 1981)

G.E. Lewis: *A Power Stronger than Itself: the AACM and American Experimental Music* (Chicago, 2008)

HARALD KISIEDU

Abravanel, Maurice (de) (*b* Thessaloniki, Greece, 6 Jan 1903; *d* Salt Lake City, UT, 22 Sept 1993). Conductor of Greek birth and Spanish-Portuguese descent. He was taken to Switzerland at the age of six and studied medicine at the University of Lausanne before, on Busoni's recommendation, he moved to Berlin in 1922 to study with Kurt Weill. He conducted in provincial German theaters and finally in Berlin until 1933, when he moved to Paris to conduct the Balanchine ballet company and the premiere of Weill's ballet *Die sieben Todsünden*. The following year he toured Australia with the British National Opera Company. On the recommendation of Walter and Furtwängler, he was hired by the Metropolitan Opera, making his debut with *Samson et Dalila* in 1936. In an era of specialization, the mainly negative reviews for his mixed repertory of French opera and Wagner forced him out in 1938. He turned to Broadway, where he renewed his association with Weill, conducting the premieres in New York of *Knickerbocker Holiday* (1938), *Lady in the Dark* (1941), *One Touch of Venus* (1943), *The Firebrand of Florence* (1945), and *Street Scene* (1947). He also spent a season with the Chicago Opera Company (1940–41) and conducted the premiere of Blitzstein's *Regina* in 1949, for which he won a Tony Award.

In 1947 Abravanel was appointed music director of the newly reorganized Utah SO, and by his retirement in 1979 had transformed this unknown community orchestra into a leading US ensemble. He made more than 100 recordings in Utah, including major works by Gould, Rorem, and Schuman, and the first Mahler symphony cycle recorded by a single orchestra. He led the campaign for construction of a 2812-seat symphony hall in Salt Lake City, renamed Abravanel Hall in 1993, but was never to conduct there. He also created touring, educational, and outreach programs which were a model in their time. From 1954 to 1980 he served as music director of the Music Academy of the West in Santa Barbara, from 1981 taught conducting at Tanglewood, and in the same year was awarded the Golden Baton by the American Symphony Orchestra League.

BIBLIOGRAPHY

P. Hart: *Orpheus in the New World: the Symphony Orchestra as an American Cultural Institution* (New York, 1973), 169–91

L.M. Durham: *Abravanel!* (Salt Lake City, 1979)

C.B. Harrison: *Five Thousand Concerts: a Commemorative History of the Utah Symphony* (Salt Lake City, UT, 1986)

A.D. Smith: *The Symphony in America: Maurice Abravanel, and the Utah Symphony Orchestra :the Battle for Classical Music* (M.A. thesis, Bringham Young U., 2002)

CHARLES BARBER, JOSÉ A. BOWEN/R

Abril, Mario (*b* Havana, Cuba, 26 Feb 1942). Cuban-American guitarist, composer, arranger, and educator; immigrated to the United States and naturalized in 1975. He studied piano and composition at the Conservatorio Orbón in Havana, and guitar under Héctor García and Julian Bream. Abril participated in the Bay of Pigs invasion (1961) and was consequently incarcerated for 22 months in Cuba. Returning to the United States, he established a performing and recording career as a classical guitarist, whose arrangements for the instrument have been published worldwide. He holds the PhD degree in music theory from Florida State University.

A series of medical issues with his hands during the 1980s subsequently redirected his focus to composition. Rejecting atonality and traditional developmental procedures in his early works, Abril cultivated a compositional style characterized by tonal and often polytonal harmony and linear writing. Although not a folklorist, he shows an affinity for Cuban musical culture, particularly in the rhythmic component. His compositions include *Migrations* (1996) for narrator and orchestra, *A Mademoiselle Marie* (2000) for soprano and orchestra, and Fantasía for clarinet and piano (2002). The ballet *Amethyst* (1994) was also the subject of an award-winning documentary. Abril is currently professor of guitar and music theory at The University of Tennessee.

MARIO REY

Absaroke. *See* Crow.

Abshire, Nathan (*b* nr Gueydan, LA, 27 June 1913; *d* Basile, LA, 13 May 1981). Cajun accordionist, singer, and songwriter. He came from a musical family; his father, mother, and at least one uncle played instruments. He was among the second generation of Cajun musicians to record, in the 1930s, and helped lead a revival of accordion and traditional Cajun music after World War II. He sometimes performed with Amédé Ardoin. The titles of some of his best known songs, such as "Service Blues" and "French Blues," indicate that blues was a major influence. In 1949 Abshire had a regional (Gulf Coast) hit with "The Pine Grove Blues," after which he named his band, the Pine Grove Boys. Its various lineups included such musicians as Will Kegley (fiddle), Ernest Thibodeaux (guitar), Atlas Frugé (steel guitar), and Robert Bertrand (fiddle and vocals), and its best known recordings were released by Swallow Records. In the 1960s Abshire performed with Dewey Balfa and his brothers at colleges and festivals across the country and in doing so helped bring Cajun music to the national folk music circuit. He was featured in several documentary films, including *Spend it all* (1972) and *The good times are killing me* (1975). He spent his final years in his adopted hometown of Basile, where he also worked as watchman of the town trash dump.

BIBLIOGRAPHY

B. J. Ancelet and E. Morgan, Jr.: *Cajun and Creole Music Makers* (Jackson, MS, 1984 R/1999)

R. Brasseaux and K. Fontenot, eds.: *Accordions, Fiddles, Two Steps and Swing* (Lafayette, LA, 2006)

BARRY JEAN ANCELET

ACA. *See* American composers alliance (aca).

Academia [Academia-Magda], **Eleanor** (*b* Honolulu, HI, 13 August 1958). Recording artist and performer of Filipino descent. A Filipino American artist, she grew up in National City, CA, and excelled at piano, violin, and percussion during her childhood. While an undergraduate at the University of Southern California, she played keyboards in various Los Angeles jazz clubs and attracted the attention of Quincy Jones. Having been introduced to traditional Philippine music by Bayani de Leon, she studied *kulintang* (gong-chime) with Aga Mayo Butocan. The influence of Philippine music may be heard on her first album *Adventure* (Japan Sony/Epic, 1987), which was released in the United States as *Jungle Wave* (CBS, 1987). Her single "Adventure" reached number one on the Billboard Hot Dance/Club Play Charts in 1988. In the same year Academia received a grant from the National Endowment for the Humanities to found the World Kulintang Institute and Research Studies Center; the institute released the album *Kulintang: Ancient Gong/Drum Music from the Southern Philippine* in 1994. Academia worked with master *kulintang* musicians Danongan Kalanduyan and Dr Usopay Cadar. On her indie-rock label, Black Swan Records, she released *Oracle of the Black Swan* (2002) and *When You Live* (2009). She performed as a keyboard player and singer with Ray Parker Jr. Academia's music offers a distinctive blend of rock, funk, pop, classical, R&B, and indigenous Philippine music.

BIBLIOGRAPHY

K. Tuber: "Riding the Jungle Wave," *Orange Coast Magazine* (1988), 179–80

D. Cordova,"Eleanor Academia: Musician," *Distinguished Asian Americans*, ed. H.-C. Kim (Westport, CT, 1999), 4–6

MARY TALUSAN

A cappella, collegiate. *See* COLLEGIATE A CAPPELLA.

Accordion. A family of portable, bellows fueled, free-reed instruments. The right hand typically has access to a series of piano-like keys or circular buttons that activate melodic tones by allowing air to flow over reeds and set them in oscillation. The left hand has access to a separate set of buttons that regulate bass, chord, and in some cases independent tone sonorities. The term "accordion" may apply to instruments that are either diatonically or chromatically scaled. More specifically, a melodeon is a smaller, diatonic button accordion. Another type, known as a concertina, is made in both diatonic and chromatic tunings and is sometimes distinguished by its polygonal sound box. Most accordions have left-hand side air buttons that, when depressed, allow the bellows to be moved rapidly without sounding a reed tone, or provide more bellows when a performer reaches either the bellows' conventional limits of extension (draw out) or compression (push in).

Diatonic button accordions are bisonorically tuned, meaning that a different tone is played on the push in and draw out of the bellows when any particular button is depressed. This tends to result in a more staccato style of playing, since brief pauses or breaks commonly occur with the change in direction of the bellows. This may result in more frequent reliance upon the air button on such instruments. Piano accordions are chromatic and unisonic—in other words the same tone is produced by any key on either the push in or draw out of the bellows. The right-hand side of these accordions features black and white keys that resemble those of a piano. On some larger instruments specific timbral voicings may be created with shift levers. There are various configurations for the left-hand side. The most common is the stradella system, which usually has 120 buttons, comprising rows of bass tones and chords, the latter used to play major, minor, dominant 7th, and diminished chords for each of the 12 keys.

Many accordion-family instruments, including those distributed by North American brands such as Bell, Excelsior, Gabbanelli, Imperial, Monarch, Noble, Silvertone, Titano, and Wurlitzer, are manufactured and exported from Italy. Pietro Deiro, his brother Guido, Pietro Frosini, and Anthony Galla Rini are among the virtuoso accordionists and composers from Italy and other European nations who helped to popularize the instrument in the United States during the early 20th century.

Cajun accordionists in south and southwest Louisiana prefer a diatonic accordion with a single row of ten buttons and four adjustable sets of reeds available for each button's tone. Each reed may be activated or silenced with a knob on the upper right side of the instrument. On early European factory-built instruments, three of these reeds were tuned in octaves, while the fourth was tuned a few cents lower or higher than its neighbor reed, yielding a "wet" tuned tremolo-like sound. Because Cajun performers tend to prefer a "dry" tuned sound based on octave or unison reed relationships, Cajun accordion builders began to replace the "wet" reed with a unison tone on the neighboring reed. Accordionists who play zydeco in south and southwest Louisiana commonly perform on the Cajun-style accordion, on instruments with two or three rows of buttons, or on the piano accordion.

Musicians who perform Irish music prefer a two-row diatonic button accordion on which the rows are tuned a half step apart (B/C, or C/C#, for example), allowing access to a chromatic scale by combining two diatonically tuned rows. Accordionists that perform *norteño* music, which has its roots in northern Mexico and Texas, most often play a three-row diatonic button accordion with 12 left-hand bass and chord buttons. This music has had a strong influence on the Tonoho O'Odham people in southern Arizona, who play a button-accordion-based dance music known as *waila* (or CHICKEN SCRATCH). In communities of people with Polish, Romani, or other Eastern European heritage, the piano accordion is often popular. Among those who perform Arab music—especially Egyptian music for ensembles—performers often retune the piano accordion's reeds to produce microtones.

The bandoneon, a type of concertina used in Argentine tango practice, and the Russian bayan are examples of chromatic button accordions with freebass configurations. Transposition on the bayan is relatively accessible because the symmetrical ordering of its buttons ensures that fingering order remains the same in various keys. The bayan is particularly popular among Russian and Finnish musicians. The converter accordion, a hybrid instrument, allows the performer to switch from stradella to freebass configurations on the left hand by depressing a lever on the left-hand side.

The Chemnitzer concertina (which originated in the Bohemian border region between Germany and the Czech Republic) is related to the bandoneon. Older versions of the instrument typically had 38 buttons with two or three reeds sounding per button ("dry"-tuned in octaves or in unison); more recent versions may have 52 buttons and 4 or 5 sets of reeds sounding for each button. This bisonoric instrument remains popular in the Midwest, especially in southern Minnesota, where the respected Hengel concertina is now made by the accordion builder and player Jerry Minar.

In US folk music, especially that which emanates from the southeastern states, English- and German-style concertinas have been popular. Both of these are smaller than the Chemnitzer and the bandoneon. The English-style instrument is unisonoric, chromatic, and usually hexagonal in shape. Its German counterpart is typically bisonoric and diatonic. Some German-style concertinas are "wet" tuned. Lead Belly as well as other southern African American musicians sometimes performed upon diatonic button accordions.

Luciano Berio, Henry Cowell, David Diamond, Roy Harris, Alan Hovhaness, Robert Rodriguez, and William

Schimmel are among US composers to produce concert works featuring accordion. The composer and accordionist PAULINE OLIVEROS has integrated the instrument into many of her experimental music compositions and has employed it as part of what she terms "deep listening" practices.

The accordion became established as a dance band component with performers such as LAWRENCE WELK, Myron Floren (who played regularly on the Lawrence Welk Show), FRANKIE YANKOVIC (known as "America's Polka King"), and Joey Miskulin. Large accordion dance communities exist in Cleveland, Milwaukee, and Buffalo, as well as other urban centers throughout the country. Virtuosos like Dick Contino demonstrate the accordion's entertainment appeal, and the jazz-influenced style of Art Van Damme, Joe Mooney, Eddie Monteiro, Frank Marocco, and Amy Jo Sawyer have also become popular. Teachers such as Willard Palmer (1917–96) and his partner Bill Hughes, Joan Cochran Sommers, Robert Davine, and Lana Gore have influenced the development of generations of students. Since the 1990s there has been a resurgence of interest in accordion- or bandoneon-led traditional musics such as tango and the polka. Some of today's manufacturers have also introduced digital sequencing accordions that feature a large variety of sounds as well as MIDI capability.

BIBLIOGRAPHY

E.M. Bennett: "William Grant Still and Accordion Music," *BPM*, iii (1975), 193–195

R. Walser: "The Polka Mass: Music of Postmodern Modernity," *EthM*, x (1992), 183–202

J. Snyder: "Leadbelly and His Windjammer: Examining the African American Button Accordion Tradition," *American Music*, xii (1994), 148–66

C. Keil, A. V. Keil, and D. Blau: *Polka Happiness* (Philadelphia, 1996)

G. Smith: "Modern-Style Irish Accordion Playing: History, Biography and Class," *EthM*, xli (1997), 433–63

J. Snyder: "Squeezebox: the Legacy of the Afro-Mississippi Accordionists," *Black Music Research Journal*, xvii (1997), 37–57

D. Blau, C. Keil, A. V. Keil, and S. Feld: *Bright Balkan Morning: Romani Lives and the Power of Music in Greek Macedonia* (Middletown, CT, 2002)

L.J. Rippley: *The Chemnitzer Concertina: a History and an Accolade* (Northfield, MN, 2006)

M.S. Jacobson: "Searching for Rockordion: the Changing Image of the Accordion in America," *American Music*, xxv (2007), 216–47

C. Ragland: *Música Norteña: Mexican Americans Creating a Nation between Nations* (Philadelphia, 2009)

I. Szeman: "Gypsy Music and Deejays: Orientalism, Balkanism, and Romani Musicians," *The Drama Review*, liii/3 (2009), 98–116

RON EMOFF

AC/DC. Australian heavy metal band. Formed in Sydney in 1973 by the brothers Angus Young (*b* Glasgow, Scotland, 31 March 1955; guitar) and Malcolm Young (*b* Glasgow, Scotland, 6 Jan 1953; guitar), its best-known line-up stabilized in 1975 with Mark Evans (*b* Melbourne, Australia, 2 March 1956; bass), Phil Rudd (*b* Melbourne, 19 May 1954; drums), and Bon Scott (Ron Belford Scott; *b* Kirriemuir, Scotland, 9 July 1946 *d* East Dulwich, London, England, 19 Feb 1980; vocals). Cliff Williams (*b* 14 Dec 1949) replaced Evans in 1977, and upon Scott's death, he was replaced by Brian Johnson (*b* 5 Oct 1947). By 1976, they were Australia's leading rock band and decided to move to London in the hope of broader success, which they achieved in the UK and the United States by the end of the decade. They are known for crude, rowdy, and sometimes juvenile lyrics that celebrate excess, transgression, and communal bonding, delivered through very hoarse, sometimes screaming, vocals. Their music is blues-based, displaying few of the Baroque influences that strongly affected most heavy metal bands. It is usually built around riffs that are primarily chordal and rhythmic rather than melodic. Their ensemble work is both forceful and precise, featuring effective use of the two guitars for complementary rhythm parts. Their most popular and critically respected album was *Back in Black* (Atl., 1980), which sold more than 20 million copies in the United States and around 50 million worldwide.

ROBERT WALSER/R

Ace, Johnny [Alexander, John Marshall] (*b* Memphis, TN, 9 June 1929; *d* Houston, TX, 25 Dec 1954). Rhythm-and-blues singer and songwriter. He served in the US Navy in World War II, then played piano with the Memphis-based group the Beale Streeters alongside Bobby Bland, Junior Parker, Roscoe Gordon, and B.B. King; they played electric blues in the style of Sonny Boy Williamson, and in the early 1950s recorded for Ike Turner and Sam Phillips. Ace then signed a contract as a solo artist with Don Robey's Duke recording company; his record "My Song" reached number one on the rhythm-and-blues chart in 1952, as did "The Clock" the following year. Using a smoother style, he made a series of successful recordings in 1953 and 1954, and became a popular live performer. After his death, his song "Pledging my Love" (1955) became his greatest hit; it was later recorded by Elvis Presley, among others. Ace developed a sophisticated type of rhythm and blues, and had more success as a performer of emotional ballads than as a bluesman. His earnest, suppliant style became a model for later romantic singers.

BIBLIOGRAPHY

J.M. Salem: *The Late Great Johnny Ace and the Transition from R&B to Rock 'n' Roll* (Urbana, IL, 2001)

JOHN PICCARELLA/R

Achron, Isidor (*b* Warsaw, Poland, 24 Nov 1892; *d* New York, NY, 12 May 1948). Pianist and composer of Polish birth and Lithuanian descent, brother of JOSEPH ACHRON. Having studied the piano with Anna Esipova, composition with Anatol Liadov, and orchestration with Maximilian Shteynberg at the St. Petersburg Conservatory, he moved to the United States in 1922 and became an American citizen six years later. Until 1933 he was accompanist to Jascha Heifetz, with whom he had first performed in Russia in 1909. Achron then began a successful solo career and gave joint recitals occasionally with his brother Joseph and with his wife, Lea Karina, a Finnish-born mezzo-soprano. His works include two piano concertos (1937, 1942), the first given its premiere by the composer with the New York PO (9 Dec 1937); *Suite grotesque* (1941), first performed by the

St Louis SO (30 Jan 1942); and several pieces for piano and violin.

R. ALLEN LOTT

Achron, Joseph (*b* Lozdzieje, Poland [now Lazdijai, Lithuania], 13 May 1886; *d* Hollywood, CA, 29 April 1943). Violinist and composer of Lithuanian birth. He was the brother of the pianist and composer ISIDOR ACHRON. He began the study of the violin with his father at the age of five, and first performed in public three years later in Warsaw. At the St Petersburg Conservatory, from which he graduated in 1904, he studied the violin with LEON AUER and composition with Lyadov. In 1913 he went to Russia, becoming head of the violin and chamber music departments at the Kharkiv Conservatory, and served in the Russian Army between 1916 and 1918. In the years after World War I he toured extensively as a concert artist in Europe, the Near East and Russia. He was appointed head of the violin masterclass and chamber music department at the Leningrad Artists' Union. In 1925 he immigrated to the United States and settled in New York, where he taught the violin at the Westchester Conservatory. He performed his Violin Concerto no.1 with the Boston SO in 1927. His Golem Suite, also written during this period, was chosen by the ISCM for performance in Venice in 1932; its opening section is recapitulated in exact retrograde to symbolize the downfall of the monster referred to in the title. In 1934 he moved to Hollywood, where he composed music for films and continued his career as a concert violinist. He performed his second violin concerto with the Los Angeles PO in 1936 and his third (commissioned by Heifetz) with the same orchestra in 1939. Atonality and polytonality are among the techniques used in his later works.

WORKS

(selective list)

ORCHESTRAL

Hebrew Melody, op.33, vn, orch, 1911; Hazen, op.34, vc, orch, 1912; 2 Hebrew Pieces, op.35, 1913; Dance Improvisation, op.37, c1913; Shar, op.42, dance, cl, orch, 1917; 2 Pastels, op.44, vn, orch, 1917

The Fiddle's Soul, op.50, 1920; Vn Conc. no.1, op.60, 1925; Konzertanten-Kapelle, op.64, vn, orch, 1928

Golem, suite, chbr orch, 1932; Dance Ov., 1932; Little Dance Fantasy, 1933; Vn Conc. no.2, op.68, 1933; Vn Conc. no.3, op.72, 1937

CHORAL

Epitaph [in memory of Skryabin], op.38, 4vv, orch, 1915; Salome's Dance, op.61, mixed vv, pf, perc, 1925 (1966); Evening Service of the Sabbath, op.67, Bar, 4vv, org, 1932

CHAMBER AND INSTRUMENTAL

1ère suite en style ancien, op.21, vn, pf, c1914 (1923); Chromatic Str Qt, op.26, c1915; Sonata no.1, vn, pf, op.29, c1915; Sym. Variations and Sonata on a Palestinian Theme, op.39, pf, c1916; Suite bizarre, op.41, vn, pf, c1917; Sonata no.2, vn, pf, op.45, c1917

Children's Suite, op.57, cl, str qt, pf, c1925; Elegy, op.62, str qt, 1927; 4 Improvisations, op.65, str qt, 1927; Golem, vc, tpt, hn, pf, 1931; Sinfonietta, op.71, str qt, 1935

MISCELLANEOUS

Spring Night, ballet music for a short film, 1935; incid music for the stage; songs; pf works; pieces for pf, vn; vn transcrs.

MSS in IL-J

Principal publishers: C. Fischer, Boosey & Hawkes (New York), Bloch Publishing Co., Israeli Music Publications

BIBLIOGRAPHY

J.S. Walden: "Music of the 'folks-neshome': 'Hebrew Melody' and Changing Musical Representations of Jewish Culture in the Early Twentieth Century Ashkenazi Diaspora," *Journal of Modern Jewish Studies*, xiii/2 (2009), 151–72

A.M. Friedman, *The sacred choral works of three composers of the St. Petersburg Society for Jewish Folk Music: Theoretical Analysis and Historical Context* (diss., Boston University, 2005)

P. Moddel: *Joseph Achron* (Tel Aviv, 1966) [includes full list of works]

PEGGY GLANVILLE-HICKS/R

Achúcarro, Joaquín (*b* Bilbao, Spain, 1 Nov 1932). Spanish pianist. He began music studies at an early age at the Bilbao Conservatory and later studied with Nikita Magaloff, Walter Gieseking, and Bruno Seidlhofer. After winning awards and international competitions in France, Italy, and Switzerland during his years as a student, Achúcarro scored a triumph at the 1959 Liverpool International Piano Concerto Competition. This led to his debut with the London SO, marking the beginning of an extensive career as concert performer that has taken him to over 60 countries where he has performed with over two hundred orchestras, including the Berlin PO, London PO, Tokyo PO, Sydney SO, and La Scala PO. Achúcarro made his US debut in 1968 with the Chicago SO under Seiji Ozawa. Since then, Achucarro has performed frequently in recitals and concerts with the premiere American orchestras. Since 1989, Achucarro has held the Joel Estes Chair at Southern Methodist University in Dallas. He also teaches master classes at the Accademia Musicale Chigiana of Siena while continuing to maintain a full touring schedule.

Achúcarro's interpretations are characterized by a poetic sound quality along with an impeccable technique that avoids distortions and ostentatious display. Achúcarro maintains a comprehensive repertory from Bach to Impressionistic composers, and has become a celebrated interpreter of Brahms, Rachmaninoff, and Ravel as well as an advocate of Spanish composers including Granados, Falla, and Joaquín Rodrigo. In 1995, by request of Rodrigo, Achúcarro completed a revised edition of *Concierto heroico* (1942), which relieves the work of virtuosic excess through a greater balance between piano and orchestra. Achúcarro premiered the work in Valencia in 1996.

LAURA PITA

Acid jazz. Hybrid genre with origins in London's acid house scene of the late 1980s. Originating with the English DJ and producer Gilles Peterson, the label denotes a craze, a marketing category, and a durable transatlantic jazz subculture with links to hip-hop, rave, and club music. Notable bands include the Brand New Heavies, Jamiroquai, Galliano, and Us3 in the UK and Digable Planets, Groove Collective, and Brooklyn Funk Essentials in the United States. During the music's heyday in the 1990s, groups fused improvised live jazz with soul-jazz beats and elements of hip hop, including lyrics by established rappers like Guru and MC Solaar. The dance-oriented music tapped into the era's fascination with jazz history, DJ culture, and retro kitsch. Jazz publications of the 1990s, including the UK-based *Straight No Chaser* (devoted entirely to acid jazz), debated whether acid jazz was innovative or derivative, genuinely or only superficially jazz. Its advocates touted its accessibility and potential to revive neglected jazz artists and grooves. Collaborations with veteran jazz musicians like Donald Byrd, Roy Ayers, and Ron Carter added credibility to the movement.

The question of whether acid jazz amounts to mass-market pastiche or politically sophisticated jazz is largely a matter of perspective. The populist utopianism of Galliano's dance hit "Prince of Peace" (Talkin' Loud, 1992) may have appealed to club-goers, but aficionados could appreciate the group's subtle dialogue with Pharaoh Sanders' "Hum-Allah" from his album *Jewels of Thought* (1969, Imp.). Us3's "Cantaloop (Flip Fantasia)" (BN, 1993), similarly transformed Herbie Hancock's "Cantaloupe Island" (*Empyrian Isles*, 1964, BN) and was the most famous of the hits to follow in the wake of Blue Note Records' decision to make its back catalog available for sampling. Such successes paved the way for Nu-Jazz offshoots such as the French artist St. Germain and the Norwegian group Jaga Jazzist. These and other European groups declared a greater independence from American jazz oversight by extending the technological and populist innovations of acid jazz at the expense of its historical dialogism.

WILLIAM KIRK BARES

Acid rock. *See* PSYCHEDELIC ROCK.

Ackerman, Paul (*b* New York, NY, 18 Feb 1908; *d* 31 Dec 1977). Journalist. After studying English literature, he worked for *Billboard* from 1934 to 1973, although he left during World War II to serve in the US Coast Guard. Ackerman began his career as a reporter and covered several subjects including vaudeville, radio, and TV before moving to music. He became music editor in 1949. His tenure at *Billboard* accompanied the emergence of rhythm and blues, country music, and rock 'n' roll. Ackerman championed these new styles, recognizing their roots in earlier music traditions and their impact on popular music and culture in general. He published several articles in *High Fidelity* and received numerous awards including an honor from the Recording Industry Association of America for his outstanding service to American music. He also served on the President's commission to select music for the White House Library and in 1995 was inducted into the Rock and Roll Hall of Fame.

JOSEPH E. MORGAN

Ackley, Alfred H(enry) (*b* Spring Hill, PA, 21 Jan 1887; *d* Whittier, CA, 3 July 1960). Gospel composer and editor, brother of BENTLEY DEFOREST ACKLEY. He studied harmony and composition in New York and London, and later became an accomplished cellist. Ackley was ordained by the Presbyterian Church in 1914 and served as a pastor in Pennsylvania and California. He worked with his brother as an editor and composer for Homer A. Rodeheaver's publishing company and wrote approximately 1500 hymns, gospel songs, children's songs, secular songs, and glees, many of which were used in the firm's publications. His most popular composition is the gospel song "He Lives," for which Ackley wrote both the text and tune. (For further information see T. H. Porter: *Homer Alvan Rodeheaver (1880–1955): Evangelistic Musician and Publisher* (diss., New Orleans Baptist Theological Seminary, 1981).

THOMAS HENRY PORTER

Ackley, Bentley DeForest (*b* Spring Hill, PA, 27 Sept 1872; *d* Winona Lake, IN, 3 Sept 1958). Gospel composer and editor, brother of ALFRED H. ACKLEY. He learned to play several instruments, including melodeon, piano, reed organ, alto horn, cornet, piccolo, and clarinet. He studied shorthand and typing and then worked as a stenographer in New York and Philadelphia. Several of his secular songs were published in the 1890s. From 1908 to 1915 Ackley was pianist and private secretary to the evangelist Billy Sunday, and during this period he began to compose gospel songs. In 1910 he and Homer A. Rodeheaver founded the Rodeheaver–Ackley publishing company in Chicago, which became the Rodeheaver Co. the following year. He worked for the firm as a composer and editor until his death; with his brother and Charles H. Gabriel, he provided many of the firm's copyrighted publications. More than 2000 of Ackley's gospel songs were published, including "If your Heart Keeps Right" (1912), "I walk with the king" (1913), and "Sunrise" (1924).

BIBLIOGRAPHY

W.G. McLoughlin Jr.: *Billy Sunday was his Real Name* (Chicago, 1955)

T.H. Porter: *Homer Alvan Rodeheaver (1880–1955): Evangelistic Musician and Publisher* (diss., New Orleans Baptist Theological Seminary, 1981)

HARRY ESKEW

ACMP—The Chamber Music Network [Amateur Chamber Music Players]. Association founded as the Amateur Chamber Music Players in 1947 by Leonard A. Strauss of Indianapolis as an information center for those who play chamber music at home. Its directory, established in 1949, facilitates the meeting of ensemble participants, who rate their performing proficiency by responding to a detailed questionnaire. Singers and piano-duet players were included in 1974. The directory is now available as an online database (<http://www.acmp.net>). One of ACMP's founding members, Helen Rice, was its secretary until 1980. Since 1994 the ACMP Foundation has awarded more than $3.6 million in grants to members of the chamber music community. In 2009 the association had more than 5,000 members from 57 countries. ACMP also publishes the *Chamber Music Network Newsletter*. Its headquarters are in New York.

JOHN SHEPARD/R

Acocella [née Ross], **Joan (B.)** (*b* San Francisco, CA, 13 April 1945). Dance critic. She studied at the University of California, Berkeley (BA 1966), and wrote on the

Ballets Russes for her doctorate in comparative literature at Rutgers University (1984). With an enthusiasm for dance that has anchored her prolific career, Acocella was the senior critic and reviews editor for *Dance Magazine* and became the dance critic for the *New Yorker* in 1998. She has written about dance for many other publications including the *Financial Times*, the *New York Review of Books*, the *New York Times Book Review*, *Art in America*, and the *Times Literary Supplement*. In her books Acocella demonstrates a sustained interest in connecting the public with artistic personae and their voices, as illustrated in her biography of Mark Morris (1993), the essay collection *Twenty-Eight Artists and Two Saints* (2007), and three edited volumes of artists' writings (*Andre Levinson on Dance*, 1991; *The Diary of Vaslav Nijinsky: Unexpurgated Edition*, 1999; *Mission to Siam: the Memoirs of Jessie MacKinnon Hartzell*, 2001). Conveying the vitality of performance through critical prose, Acocella writes of novels' plot twists and authors' struggles with the same energetic and informal style as she does dance performances and their choreographers. Her reviews often serve as germs for larger projects: *Willa Cather and the Politics of Criticism* (2004) was developed from an article published in the *New Yorker* in 1995 that was subsequently awarded the Front Page Award by the Newswomen's Club of New York. Acocella received a Guggenheim Fellowship in 1993 and has been a fellow at the New York Institute for the Humanities.

ANDREA F. BOHLMAN

Acuff, Roy (Claxton) (*b* Maynardville, TN, 15 Sept 1903; *d* Nashville, TN, 23 Nov 1992). Country music singer, fiddler, songwriter, and publisher. He was an active sportsman at high school, but was denied a professional athletic career by a bout of sunstroke. While recovering, he began singing and playing fiddle. In the summer of 1932 he toured eastern Tennessee with a medicine show, and from 1933 to 1935 he performed with his band the Tennessee Crackerjacks (later the Crazy Tennesseans) on Knoxville radio stations KNOX and WROL. Acuff made his first recordings in 1936 for the American Record Corporation, which included a cover of the gospel song "Great Speckle Bird," and two years later began performing regularly on the radio show "Grand Ole Opry" as Roy Acuff and the Smoky Mountain Boys. He subsequently hosted a segment of the show which was broadcast nationwide on the NBC Red Network. Acuff's appearances on "Grand Old Opry" as well as the popularity of such recordings as "Wabash Cannonball" (ARC, 1936) and "Fire Ball Mail" (OK, 1942) and his performances in nine films including *Grand Ole Opry* (1940) established him as the best-known country music performer by the mid-1940s.

In 1942 Acuff, his wife Mildred, and Fred Rose founded Acuff-Rose Publications, the United States's first country-music publishing house. The firm's success helped establish Nashville as the centre of the country-music industry; its catalog includes such songs as "Blue Eyes Crying in the Rain," "Faded Love," and "Oh, Pretty Woman." In 1953 Rose and the Acuffs founded Hickory Records, which recorded Acuff as well as other performers including Don Gibson, and Wilma Lee and Stoney Cooper. In 1966 Acuff became the first living performer to be elected to the Country Music Hall of Fame. He later recorded with the Nitty Gritty Dirt Band (*Will the Circle be Unbroken*, United Artists, 1971, and *Will the Circle be Unbroken: Volume Two*, MCA, 1989). In 1974 Acuff performed for President Richard Nixon during opening ceremonies at the new Opryland Opry House; he lived out his last days in a home on the Opryland grounds.

Influenced by fundamentalist-church singing, Acuff's big, emotive voice and showmanship helped shift the focus of the "Grand Ole Opry" from string bands to singers. His performances also helped introduce the resonator guitar to the show; the instrument was played first in his band by James Clell Summey and from 1939 by Beecher Kirby (aka Bashful Brother Oswald). Acuff's mountain-based repertoire of religious, tragic, and sentimental songs presented an alternative to the newer, western influences then infusing country music.

BIBLIOGRAPHY

E. Schlappi: "Roy Acuff," *Stars of Country Music*, ed. B. C. Malone and J. McCulloh (Urbana, IL, 1975/R), 179–201

E. Schlappi: *Roy Acuff: the Smoky Mountain Boy* (Gretna, LA, 1978, 2/1993)

C.K. Wolfe: "Roy Acuff," *Classic Country: Legends of Country Music* (New York, 2000), 19–26

T. Russell: "Roy Acuff," *Country Music Originals: the Legends and the Lost* (New York, 2007), 195–7

ANTHONY S. LIS

Adam, Claus (*b* Sumatra, Indonesia, 5 Nov 1917; *d* New York, 4 July 1983). Cellist and composer. He spent the first six years of his life in Dutch East Indies (now Indonesia), where his father, Tassilo Adam, worked as an ethnologist; after the family returned to Europe he studied at the Salzburg Mozarteum. In 1929 the family moved to New York, where Adam studied the cello with E. Stoffnegen, D.C. Dounis, and (from 1938 to 1940) Emanuel Feuermann; he also studied conducting with Leon Barzin and composition with Blatt, and was a member of the National Orchestral Association, a training group for young instrumentalists (1935–40). From 1940 to 1943 he was principal cellist of the Minneapolis SO. After serving in the US Air Force during World War II, he studied composition in New York with Stefan Wolpe. In 1948 he formed the New Music Quartet, with which he performed until 1955, when he joined the Juilliard string quartet; he left the group in 1974 to devote his full energies to composition. Adam also had an active teaching career, with positions at the Aspen Music Festival (from 1953), the Juilliard School of Music (from 1955), and the Mannes College (from 1974). His compositions include a Piano Sonata (1948), String Trio (1967), String Quartet (1975), Cello Concerto (1973), and Concerto-variations for orchestra (1976). Like his cello playing, they are characterized by robust expressiveness and infectious rhythmic energy.

JAMES WIERZBICKI

Adamowski, Timothée [Tymoteusz] (*b* Warsaw, Poland, 24 March 1858; *d* Boston, MA, 18 April 1943). Polish violinist. He began violin studies at age seven and later studied under Apolinary Katski and Gustaw Robusky at the Warsaw Conservatory, where he graduated with honors in 1874; he also studied with Massart at the Paris Conservatoire. He made his first American tour in 1879, appearing with Clara Louise Kellogg and Max Strakosch before undertaking his own tour. He settled in Boston thereafter, playing with the Boston SO from 1884 until 1907 (except in 1887–8 when he made a European tour) and teaching at the New England Conservatory. Adamowski appeared 82 times as soloist with the orchestra and conducted the summer popular concerts from 1890–4 and again from 1900–7. He also appeared with orchestras in London, Paris, and Warsaw. In 1888 he formed the Adamowski Quartet with violinist Emmanuel Fiedler, violist Daniel Kuntz, and cellist Giuseppe Campanari; the group was reconstituted the following year with A. Moldauer, Max Zach, and Adamowski's brother Joseph (who immigrated to the United States in 1889), and gave as many as 30 subscription concerts each year. This quartet gave the premiere of a movement of C.M. Loeffler's String Quartet in A minor in 1889; nine years later the ensemble also gave the premiere of G.W. Chadwick's String Quartet No. 5 in D minor, dedicated to the Adamowski brothers. Gustav Strube dedicated his Violin Concerto in F-sharp minor (1905) to him. In 1896 Adamowski formed the Adamowski Trio with his brother Joseph and Joseph's pianist wife Antoinette. He was named second concertmaster of the Boston SO in 1907, but resigned at the end of that season to devote more time to chamber music. He nonetheless continued to teach violin at the New England Conservatory until 1933. Adamowski was known for his fluent technique and musical tone.

BIBLIOGRAPHY

Grove5; *MGG2*

M.A.D. Howe: *The Boston Symphony Orchestra: an Historical Sketch* (Boston, 1914, rev. and enlarged/1931)

B. McPherson and J. Klein: *Measure by Measure: a History of New England Conservatory from 1867* (Boston, 1995)

JEFFREY R. REHBACH/CHARLES S. FREEMAN

Adams, Alton Augustus, Sr. (*b* Charlotte Amalie, St. Thomas, Danish West Indies, 4 Nov 1889; *d* Charlotte Amalie, St. Thomas, US Virgin Islands, 23 Nov 1987). Bandmaster, composer, educator, journalist, and hotelier. Adams became the first African American bandmaster in the US Navy in 1917.

Adams studied piccolo and then flute as a child, growing up within the islands' black artisan class and writing his first compositions for Charlotte Amalie's Municipal Band. In 1911, he founded the Adams Juvenile Band, teaching each instrumentalist himself. After the United States purchased the islands from Denmark in 1917, Adams and his bandsmen were inducted into the US Navy as a cultural bridge between the islands' majority black populace and its new white naval administrators. Adams's *Virgin Islands March* (1919) celebrated his excitement as both an Islander and an American, as it pays homage to his primary musical influence—John Philip Sousa.

Adams became known in US band circles through his idealistic monthly columns in the *Jacob's Band Monthly*. He traveled to the US mainland in 1922 to research music education programs that informed his own plans for the islands' public schools. In 1924, Adams's band toured the East Coast to acclaim; while in New York City, he directed the Goldman Band in Central Park. In 1931 a civilian administration on the islands replaced the navy, and Adams's band was transferred en masse to Guantanamo Bay, Cuba, because its black instrumentalists could not be integrated into the service.

A dozen music manuscripts, including Adams's earlier publications, survived a 1932 fire. Adams's best known compositions are the *Virgin Islands March, The Governor's Own* (1921), and *Spirit of the U.S.N.*, dedicated to President Calvin Coolidge (1924). In 1982, the *Virgin Islands March* became the Virgin Islands' official territorial anthem.

Adams retired from the navy in 1933, returning in 1942 to serve in World War II as director of the navy's first racially integrated band and then of the second all-black Virgin Islands band (1943–5). Adams opened a guesthouse (1947), serving as first president of the Virgin Islands Hotel Association (1952–71). In the 1950s and 60s he worked as the Virgin Islands stringer for several US newspapers and magazines.

BIBLIOGRAPHY

S.A. Floyd Jr.: "Alton Augustus Adams: The First Black Bandmaster in the United States Navy," *BPM*, v (1977), 173–87

M. Clague: "Instruments of Identity: Alton Augustus Adams, Sr., the Navy Band of the Virgin Islands, and the Sounds of Social Change," *Black Music Research Journal*, xviii/1–2 (1998), 21–65

M. Clague: "Adams, Alton Augustus," *International Dictionary of Black Composers*, ed. S. Floyd Jr., i (Chicago, 1999), 9–16

M. Clague, ed.: *The Memoirs of Alton Augustus Adams, Sr., First Black Bandmaster of the United States Navy* (Berkeley, 2008)

MARK CLAGUE

Adams, Bryan (Guy) (*b* Kingston, ON, 5 Nov 1959). Canadian rock singer, songwriter, and guitarist, and photographer. The son of a diplomat, he spent his youth in England, Israel, Portugal, and Austria. After returning with his family to North America, he began performing and recording at the age of 15 with rock bands in British Columbia and Ontario. In 1978 he began what became a long and successful songwriting partnership with Jim Vallance, with whom he created most songs recorded under his name up to 1987, as well as songs recorded by Rod Stewart, Kiss, Bonnie Raitt, Neil Diamond, and the Canadian groups Prism, BTO, and Loverboy.

Adams' albums characteristically alternate between down-tempo piano ballads and straight-ahead rock numbers. His third solo album, *Cuts like a Knife* (1983) launched him to the status of an international celebrity; its singles included the ballad "Straight from the Heart" and the anthem "Cuts like a Knife," which both featured for weeks on magazine charts and music television. The next album, *Reckless* (1984), was even more successful and included the singles "Run to You," "Heaven," and "Summer of '69." Having achieved international fame, Adams directed his career towards composing film soundtracks. He also began to use his celebrity to undertake charity work, beginning in 1984 when he co-wrote "Tears are not enough," the Canadian contribution to Ethiopian famine relief. In 1985 he opened the Philadelphia portion of Bob Geldof's Live Aid and the following year participated in the Amnesty International Conspiracy of Hope tour alongside the Police, Peter Gabriel, and U2. Other beneficiaries include victims of the 2004 Indian Ocean earthquake, Pakistani schoolchildren, and People for the Ethical Treatment of Animals. Adams first worked in the film industry in 1991, co-writing the power ballad "(Everything I do) I do it for you" with Michael Kamen and Robert "Mutt" Lang for the soundtrack of *Robin Hood: Prince of Thieves*; the song won a Grammy Award in 1992. Canada's emblematic rock soloist, Adams has been nominated for 14 additional Grammys and won 18 Juno Awards. He has also been awarded the Order of Canada and the Order of British Columbia for his contributions to popular music and his philanthropic work.

MICHAEL ETHEN

Adams, Charles R. (*b* Charlestown, MA, 9 Feb 1834; *d* West Harwich, MA, 4 July 1900). Tenor. Adams was one of the most prominent American singers in European opera houses throughout the 19th century. He studied singing in Boston and in 1856 was soloist in the Handel and Haydn Society's performance of Haydn's *The Creation*. In 1861 he made concert and opera appearances in the West Indies and Holland. He studied in Vienna with Carlo Barbieri and was engaged for three years by the Berlin Royal Opera, then for eight out of nine years (1867–76) as principal tenor of the Vienna Imperial Opera. He also sang at La Scala and Covent Garden. In 1877 he returned to the United States. During the 1877–8 season at the Academy of Music in New York he sang the title role in the first American production of Wagner's *Rienzi*. An excellent singer and fine actor, he had a commanding stage presence. His voice was described as very powerful and "a very sweet one and one of great range." Adams made his way to Chicago in the 1880s, where he regularly performed oratorios with the Chicago Musical Union. Tannhäuser, Lohengrin, Manrico, and Rienzi were his most celebrated parts. From 1879 Adams lived in Boston as a successful singing teacher; DAME NELLIE MELBA and EMMA EAMES were among his pupils.

BIBLIOGRAPHY

DAB (F.L. Gwinner Cole)

O. Thompson: *The American Singer* (New York, 1937/*R*), 85–9

G.P. Upton: *Musical Memories: My Recollections of Celebrities of the Half Century, 1850–1900* (Chicago, IL, 1908)

H. WILEY HITCHCOCK/JUNE C. OTTENBERG/JONAS WESTOVER

Adams, John (Coolidge) (*b* Worcester, MA, 15 Feb 1947). Composer and conductor. Known for his operatic and orchestral works on contemporary subjects, he is one of the most frequently performed living composers.

1. Life. 2. Works.

1. LIFE. The son of jazz musicians and a fan of rock, Adams studied clarinet with his father and Felix Viscuglia, of the Boston SO. At age ten he began theory and composition lessons, and by age 14 he had his first piece performed by the community orchestra with which he practiced conducting. He also performed with the orchestra alongside his father, often appearing before patients at the New Hampshire State Hospital. As a student at Harvard University (BA 1971, MA 1972) he studied composition with DAVID DEL TREDICI, LEON KIRCHNER, EARL KIM, ROGER SESSIONS, and HAROLD SHAPERO. During this period Adams conducted the Bach Society Orchestra, was a reserve clarinetist for the Boston SO and the Opera Company of Boston, and played Walter Piston's *Clarinet Concerto* at Carnegie Hall.

12-tone composition dominated academia at the time, and Adams compared class to a "mausoleum where we would sit and count tone-rows in Webern." His earliest cataloged works date from these years, among them the *Piano Quintet* and a tape piece, *Heavy Metal* (both from 1970), and *American Standard* (1973), one of the first pieces allowed to be submitted for a Harvard undergraduate thesis.

After moving to San Francisco in 1971, Adams taught at the San Francisco Conservatory of Music (1972–82), working in the electronic music studio, building his own analog synthesizer, and conducting the New Music Ensemble, for which he commissioned and premiered new works by important experimental composers. In this manner, he quickly became involved in the Bay Area's thriving new music scene and began to forge associations with local composers and musicians. In 1973 Adams read John Cage's *Silence* (1961), which he claimed "dropped into [his] psyche like a time bomb."

American Standard was recorded (23 March 1973) at the San Francisco Museum of Modern Art by the San Francisco Conservatory of Music Ensemble; it was released on Brian Eno's Obscure Records label in 1975, with two works by Christopher Hobbs and one by Gavin Bryars, on the album *Ensemble Pieces*. The second movement of *American Standard—Christian Zeal and Activity*—evolved into an ensemble-specific stand-alone composition. At this point Adams began to experiment further with electronic music in such works as *Ktaadn* (1974), *Grounding* (1975), *Onyx* (1976), and *Studebaker Love Music* (1976). Adams explained that working with synthesizers caused a "diatonic conversion," a reversion to the belief that tonality was a force of nature. These experiences are reflected in the writing of the acoustic works *Wavemaker* and *China Gates* (both from 1977), *Phrygian Gates* (1977), and *Shaker Loops* (1978).

In 1978 Adams became new music advisor to the San Francisco SO and wrote *Common Tones in Simple Time* the following year. It was during his time with the San Francisco SO that *Harmonium* for large orchestra and chorus (1980–81) began, as quietly insistent repetitions of the note D on the syllable "no." The work's successful premiere was the first performance of Adams's music by a major mainstream organization, and it established him as a major figure in American music.

With music director Edo de Waart, Adams created the Symphony's New and Unusual Music series, introducing major American and European avant-garde composers to San Francisco audiences. His collaborations with the orchestra served as the model for the Meet the Composer residency program, through which he was appointed the Symphony's composer-in-residence (1982–5). Other works from this period include *Grand Pianola Music* (1982) and *Light over Water* (1983).

In 1983 the director PETER SELLARS approached Adams about writing an opera on the improbable subject of Richard Nixon's momentous six-day visit to China to meet Mao Zedong (21–28 February 1972). After the time of *Harmonielehre* (1984–85), *The Chairman Dances* (1985, an outgrowth of the Nixon opera-in-progress) and *Short Ride in a Fast Machine* (*Fanfare for Great Woods*; 1986), *Nixon in China*, in three acts directed by Sellars, was premiered by the Houston Grand Opera in 1987 and performed over 70 times in the following few years. The opera, the composer's second major work on a text (after *Harmonium*), was televised by PBS and received both Emmy and Grammy awards. The Nonesuch recording of the opera was named "one of the ten most important recordings of the decade" by *Time* magazine.

Reaction was not uniform. Donal Henahan, special to the *New York Times*, called the Houston Grand Opera world premiere "worth a few giggles but hardly a strong candidate for the standard repertory...visually striking but coy and insubstantial." James Wierzbicki for the *St. Louis Post-Dispatch* described Adams's score as the weak point in an otherwise well-staged performance, noting the music as "inappropriately placid...cliché-ridden in the abstract" and "[trafficking] heavily in Adams's worn-out Minimalist clichés." With time, however, the opera has come to be revered. Almost a quarter century after its premiere, *Nixon in China* remains an impressive, memorable, and vivid work, finding a balance between innovation and tradition that has merited numerous presentations around the world.

As a conductor, Adams also maintained an active schedule. In 1988 he was named creative chair of the St Paul Chamber Orchestra, for which he served as conductor and music advisor until 1990. He has served as artistic director and conductor of the Ojai and Cabrillo Music Festivals in California, and he has conducted the New York Philharmonic, the Chicago SO, the Cleveland Orchestra, the Los Angeles Philharmonic, the LSO, the London Sinfonietta, the Halle Orchestra, the Oslo PO, the Royal Concertgebouw Orchestra, the Santa Cecilia Orchestra, and the Deutsches Symphonie-Orchester Berlin. He has often programmed his own works alongside those by composers as diverse as Frank Zappa, Jean Sibelius, Igor Stravinsky, Charles Ives, Aaron Copland, Steve Reich, and Philip Glass.

Between 1989 and 1991 Adams and Alice Goodman created a second opera on a contemporary event, the 1985 hijacking of the Italian cruise liner *Achille Lauro* by a small group of Palestinian terrorists. *The Death of Klinghoffer* received its first performance in Brussels in March 1991, days after the end of the Gulf War. Directed by Sellars with choreography by the Mark Morris Dance Group, the original production was also staged in Lyons, Vienna, Brooklyn, and San Francisco. A film version was made in 2003. The political sensitivity of the subject, however, remained an issue of debate and misunderstanding throughout the run of performances. Although the opera is carefully balanced, with eloquent and profane language given roughly equally to Jews, Muslims, and Christians, the San Francisco performances were picketed, and the work was not fully staged again in the United States until June 2011 at the Opera Theatre of Saint Louis, under the direction of James Robinson. Newspaper critics, the Klinghoffer family, and music scholars have debated the controversies spawned by the opera.

Adams's third stage work, *I was Looking at the Ceiling and Then I Saw the Sky*, an "earthquake/romance" staged by Sellars, with libretto by June Jordan, opened in May 1995 in Berkeley, California. The original production completed a five-month tour to Montreal, New York, Edinburgh, Helsinki, Paris, and Hamburg.

In 1997 Adams celebrated his 50th birthday with a concert in the Concertgebouw (Amsterdam), which featured his own music and works for big band by Gil Evans, Miles Davis, and Duke Ellington. The same year, Emanuel Ax gave the premiere of *Century Rolls* (1996) with the Cleveland Orchestra. In 1999 Adams toured Europe with the Ensemble Modern, conducting his *Naive and Sentimental Music* (1997–8) and Ives's *Symphony No.4*. Also in 1999, Nonesuch released *The John Adams Earbox*, a ten-CD compilation gathering together nearly all of the composer's music over a 20-year period.

Adams's interest in Spanish idioms and the legacy of G.F. Handel led to the creation of *El Niño*, a retelling of the Nativity story using Biblical texts and poetry set in Spanish and English by Hispanic women. Composed for the celebration of the millennium, it was first performed in Paris in December of 2000.

In the wake of the events of 11 September 2001, the New York Philharmonic commissioned Adams to write a memorial to the victims. The resulting work, *On the Transmigration of Souls* (2002), won the Pulitzer Prize in 2003 and three Grammy Awards in 2005. Adams was the first composer to have earned the latter award in three separate years, having previously won for *Nixon in China* (1989) and *El Dorado* (1998).

In 2003 Adams paid homage to his fellow California composers Terry Riley and Lou Harrison, as well as to the writers Jack Kerouac and Gary Snyder, with *The Dharma at Big Sur* (2003), a concerto for six-string electric violin and orchestra, calling for some instruments (harp, piano, samplers) to use just intonation; the concerto was composed for the opening of Disney Hall in Los Angeles.

Adams characterized *My Father Knew Charles Ives* (2003) as "a musical autobiography, an homage and encomium to a composer whose influence on me has been huge." In true Ivesian fashion, all three movements begin quietly and swell to cacophony. The piece, ranging from mysterious harmonies in long tones to full-scale marches, was first performed by Michael Tilson Thomas and the San Francisco Symphony.

After a ten-year hiatus from opera, Adams teamed up once again with Sellars in 2005 for *Doctor Atomic*, which explores the moral dilemma of the creation of the world's first atomic bomb in 1945. Sellars's libretto draws on original source material, including personal memoirs, recorded interviews, technical manuals of nuclear physics, declassified government documents, and the poetry of the *Bhagavad Gita*, John Donne, Charles Baudelaire, and Muriel Rukeyser.

Creative libretto choices figure again in the one-act opera *A Flowering Tree*, composed for the Orquesta Simon Bolivar Youth Orchestra of Caracas, Venezuela, and premiered in Vienna in November of 2006. Adams, collaborating once more with Sellars, created the libretto from a folktale in the Kannada language of southern India as translated by A.K. Ramanujan.

Doctor Atomic Symphony and *Fellow Traveler* both date from 2007, the latter commissioned for the Kronos Quartet by Greg G. Minshall, in honor of Sellars's 50th birthday. Recent projects have included the orchestral works *City Noir* (2009) and *Absolute Jest* (2010), the film score for *I Am Love* (*Io Sono l'Amore*, 2010), and the oratorio *The Gospel According to the Other Mary* (2011).

Adams's numerous honors have included the Royal Philharmonic Society Music Award (1993) for his *Chamber Symphony*, the Grawemeyer Award (1995) for *Violin Concerto,* the title Composer of the Year from *Musical America* (1997), the Pulitzer Prize (2003) for *On the Transmigration of Souls*, the Michael Ludwig Nemmers Prize in Musical Composition (2004), the Harvard Arts Medal (2007), and the Centennial Medal of Harvard University's Graduate School of Arts and Sciences (2004). He has an honorary doctorate from Cambridge University and an honorary membership in Phi Beta Kappa. In 1995 Adams was made a Knight of the Order of Arts and Letters by the French Ministry of Culture, and in 1997 he was elected to the American Academy and Institute of Arts and Letters. He has served as Composer in Residence at Carnegie Hall and Artist in Association with the BBC Symphony Orchestra.

He lives with his wife, the photographer Deborah O'Grady, in Berkeley, California.

2. Works. At a young age, Adams made a conscious decision to break away from both the European postwar aesthetic and the American academic avant-garde of the time. Even as he found his compositional voice, he integrated aspects of popular American culture into his work.

The early unspecified ensemble *American Standard* (named after an appliance brand), for instance, consists of a march, a hymn, and a jazz standard. The work is aleatoric—free of barlines and the necessity of a conductor. Adams has noted that the first movement, "John Philip Sousa," is "stripped down to a plodding pulse, with no melody or harmony" and that it sounds "like the retreat from battle of a badly wounded army (not my original intention, but curiously evocative all the same)." All of the players play an inverted B♭ chord repeated about 60 times with an addition of narration and what the composer calls "corny march rhythms." The second section, "Christian Zeal and Activity" (later reworked as an independent piece), manifests an Ivesian *Unanswered Question*–like collision of a slowed-down *Onward, Christian Soldiers* (Arthur Sullivan, 1871) with tape loops of a fundamentalist preacher reminiscent of Steve Reich's *It's Gonna Rain* (1965). The third-movement, "Sentimentals," has been described by the composer as an "arrangement or reworking" of Duke Ellington's "Sophisticated Lady" (1932), separating melody from harmony.

Phrygian Gates (1977) is minimalist in its hypnotic pulsation, slowly unfolding modulations, and ecstatic levels of energy. Its shifts between modules in Lydian and Phrygian refers to activating electronic gates rather than architectural ones.

If such a work can lead one to conclude that its composer is indeed a minimalist, Adams has proved to be one of the practitioners most anchored in Western classical tradition. Roving tonal centers, fluid tempos, and complex formal schemes have characterized his brand of minimalism/postminimalism. At this time, Adams drew inspiration from modality and the rhythmic energy of repetition.

Shaker Loops (1978), a reworking of *Wavemaker* (1977) for string septet (3 vn, va, 2 vc, b) with conductor, began as a modular composition somewhat in the spirit of Terry Riley's *In C* (1964), in that it has differing numbers of beats in subsequent repeated patterns. It is divided, however, into four distinct movements, each of which grows gradually into the next. Adams worked with a group of string players at the San Francisco Conservatory, at times composing during rehearsal. The composer arranged this piece for string orchestra in 1983, withdrawing the modular concept in favor of a more traditionally notated score.

Adams's gift for setting the intrinsic rhythms of poetry emerged in *Harmonium* (1980–81), which set poems by John Donne and Emily Dickinson in a work of magic, orchestrational inventiveness, and purity, anticipating Reich's large-scale choral-orchestral *The Desert Music* (1983) by several years. In the ensuing decade, Adams's style contained frequent implications of bitonality, contrary musics, and eclecticism.

Indeed, Adams has often remarked on a kind of split personality that emerged during this time, as he alternated regularly between stylistic polarities: irreverent, almost confrontational, self-characterized "Trickster" works and more sober, introspective ones. The Trickster allowed Adams to use the repetitive style and rhythmic drive of minimalism, while simultaneously poking fun at it ("a minimalist bored with minimalism"), joyriding on "those Great Prairies of non-event."

In *Grand Pianola Music* (1982) Adams commented, "Dueling pianos, cooing sirens, Valhalla brass, thwacking bass drums, gospel triads, and a Niagara of cascading flat keys all learned to cohabit as I wrote the piece." It is a humorous work that purposely draws its content from musical clichés. By contrast, *Light over Water: the*

Genesis of Music (1983), commissioned by the Museum of Contemporary Art in Los Angeles, choreographed by Lucinda Childs, with set design by architect Frank Gehry, is a long, unbroken essay in contrasting electro-acoustic sections whose boundaries are subtle, indeed almost imperceptible.

Harmonielehre (1984–5), inspired by a dream of an oil tanker taking flight out of San Francisco Bay and by Arnold Schoenberg's 1911 book of the same name (i.e., *Theory of Harmony*), is a bipolar romp between points of comedy and tragedy. In this piece, the composer fuses repetitive motifs with a lush, highly expressive neoromanticism. Informed by dreams, Jungian analysis, mystical poetry, and transcendentalist writings, such compositions established his reputation as a composer of "accessible" scores. Tonal and emotional, but still elusively complex, these works predated the appearance of related post-minimalist composers of the late 1980s and 90s.

The Chairman Dances (*Foxtrot for Orchestra*; 1985), an outgrowth of the evolving *Nixon in China* (1985–7), sets a colorful, exuberant, witty tone in its amalgamation of East and West, as does *Short Ride in a Fast Machine* (1986), with its trick pony of half-notes (woodblock, soon joined by the four trumpets) and eighths (clarinets and synthesizers).

Behind the mischief of these "trickster" pieces is Adams's characteristic celebration of American vernacular music—the fox-trots, marches, and big band music of his youth. In this regard, Ives, Copland, and Leonard Bernstein are his predecessors. Like them, he manages to dissolve boundaries between "high" and "low" art by drawing freely on the country's vast and fertile sonic traditions.

In his operas Adams has proven that his sensitivity to language has been equal to his talent for individual characterization and drama on a large scale. The 34-piece *Nixon in China* orchestra, brightened by saxophones and synthesizer, emphasizes the wry humor and poignant intellect of Goodman's rhymed couplets. Full of fantasy sequences, photo opportunities, and echoes of big bands, *Nixon* depicts an American icon with playful irony, emphasizing the comic potential of repeated minimalist lyrics, something usually avoided by such colleagues as Glass. Adams manifests the traditional framework of opera in instrumental preludes, choruses, recitatives, and arias and evokes such disparate musics as Chinese pentatonicism, Wagner, Holst, and Stravinsky. The result is, as can be the case in Adams, a work that is at once heroic and banal, comic and tragic.

The composer has noted that, "in almost all cultures other than the European classical one, the real meaning of the music is in between the notes. The slide, the portamento, the 'blue note'—all are essential to the emotional expression, whether it's a great Indian master improvising on a raga or whether it's Jimi Hendrix or Johnny Hodges bending a blue note right down to the floor." Such notions have informed many of Adams's influential pieces post-*Nixon in China*.

The dichotomy of moods continued in 1988 with *Fearful Symmetries* and *The Wound-Dresser*, the second to texts of Walt Whitman (on wounded American Civil War soldiers), and scored for baritone voice, two flutes (piccolos), two oboes, clarinet, bass clarinet, two bassoons, two horns, trumpet (piccolo trumpet), timpani, synthesizer, and strings. The latter work's depiction of graphic violence coexisting with disembodied spiritual transcendence was expanded in *The Death of Klinghoffer* (1989–91), a musical and choreographic passion play that moves between deep meditation and gripping brutality, showing the influence of Bach's Passions in grave, symbolic narratives supported by a full chorus. As in Monteverdi's *L'Orfeo*, the tension between a *prima pratica*, in this case the post-minimalist choruses, and a *seconda* of recitative seems very evident, and a default modus often takes the form of a minimalist accompanimental underpinning, simultaneously overlain with vocal declamation and one or more interior obbligato instrumental lines. Chromatically descending scales mingle with repetitive figures and lyrical vocal lines to create a protracted sense of time.

Adams's later compositions have continued to involve polyphony, chromaticism, and virtuosity, while often retaining the rhythmically charged motoric propulsion of earlier works. Indeed, a "hyperlyrical" and linear quality has informed much of his output.

In 1992 Adams again faced the specter of Schoenberg, a confrontation mostly avoided for two decades (save for *Harmonielehre*), in the *Chamber Symphony*. Commissioned by the Gerbode Foundation for the San

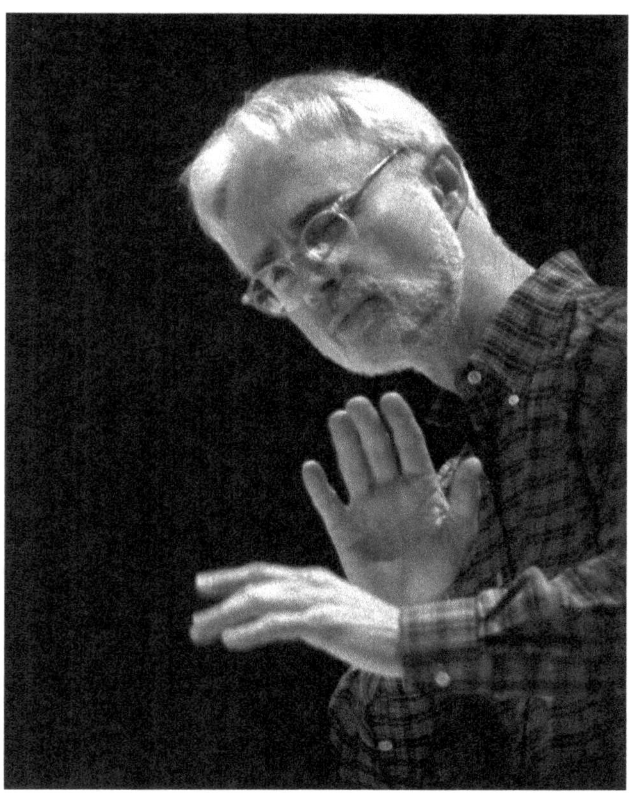

John Adams, c2004. (Laurie Lewis/Lebrecht Music & Arts)

Francisco Contemporary Chamber Players, the work had its genesis when the composer was studying the score to Schoenberg's Op. 9 while overhearing the soundtracks to cartoons that his son was watching. While Adams provides a New Viennese echo in tonality and instrumentation, his additional forces include synthesizer, drum set, trumpet, and trombone. The three movements—"Mongrel Airs," "Aria with Walking Bass," and "Roadrunner"—are aggressive and invigorating (alluding to Warner Brothers composers Carl Stalling, Milt Franklyn, and Treg Brown), as well as chromatic, linear, and virtuosic.

Adams's abiding interest in electronic media, apparent in the addition of synthesizers to his operatic scores and large ensemble pieces, reached a pinnacle in *Hoodoo Zephyr* (1992–3). Throughout the 1990s, the composer's use of modes continued to evolve, especially after discovering Nicolas Slonimsky's *Thesaurus of Scales and Melodic Patterns* (1947) and developing the "earbox," a modal transposition technique of his own creation. Dense counterpoint, simultaneously conflicting meters, and asymmetrical phrases have remained distinctive elements, put to striking use in the darkly new-Viennese *Violin Concerto* (1993). Adams has described the piece, with its sinuous lines, as "a study in 'hypermelody'—the violin sings almost constantly throughout the full 35 minutes of the piece," while the orchestra provides an evocative, post-minimal backdrop. With its rhapsodic and lyrical first movement, tender chaconne, and extroverted toccata, the concerto combines transcendent introspection with virtuoso kineticism. The work, for all its intricate melodic detail, is still underpinned by pattern, with a fantastic orchestration that would whimsically suggest that reincarnated Schoenbergs and Stravinskys had taken up the mantle of minimalism.

The informational concentration of such work, leavened with polyrhythms and highly virtuosic writing, makes considerable demands on instrumentalists. This has led Adams to form close relationships with particular groups (Ensemble Modern, the Schoenberg Ensemble, and the Kronos Quartet; the latter notably in *John's Book of Alleged Dances* [1994], which features triggered prepared-piano tracks) and soloists (Emanuel Ax, Michael Collins, and Gidon Kremer) who are able to meet the challenges.

Such is also the case in *I was Looking at the Ceiling and Then I Saw the Sky* (1995), a daring contemporary crossover told in 25 songs, originally showcased in Berkeley with the Paul Dresher Ensemble Electro-Acoustic Band. While Adams called the piece "essentially a polyphonic love story in the style of a Shakespeare comedy," it is also a social satire on the lives of seven young Americans of varied ethnicities, all living in Los Angeles at the moment of the devastating Northridge earthquake (1994). With its facile evocations of popular music, Adams again shows his chameleon-like ability to evoke style, in a score that captures the clip of Berkeley poet June Jordan's urban and urbane speech patterns, along with Peter Sellars's innovative staging.

Hallelujah Junction (1996), for two pianos, also comes directly from the landscape of Southern California, named after a truck stop on US Highway 395 near the California–Nevada border. Adams noted, "Here we have a case of a great title looking for a piece. So now the piece finally exists: the 'junction' being the interlocking style of two-piano writing which features short, highly rhythmicized motives bouncing back and forth between the two pianos in tightly phased sequences." The work beautifully expands on Reich's phase music of the 1960s.

A balance of modality and chromaticism with humor and earnestness continued to infuse such works as *Slonimsky's Earbox* (1996), *Gnarly Buttons* (1996), and *Century Rolls* (1996)—the latter a very different kind of concerto, which pays tribute to the intricate mechanisms of piano rolls of the 1920s, as well as to Conlon Nancarrow's *Studies for Player Piano*. Considering Adams's penchant for punning titles (e.g., "Dogjam," from *John's Book of Alleged Dances* and "Hail Bop," from *Century Rolls*), it is perhaps not surprising that the title of his *Naive and Sentimental Music* (1997–8) refers not only to Friedrich Schiller's essay, but to the perceived state of contemporary music.

Adams's work in the 2000s has continued to enthrall and surprise. The ambitious nativity-oratorio *El Niño* ("The Child," punning on Christ and the weather phenomenon) is a worthy successor both to *Harmonium* and the operas, a dizzy spin on baroque and Hispanic conceits, interlaced with colorful orchestrations, energetic patternings, and vivid choral writing (Stravinsky's "double-bass" God in *The Flood* superseded by a trio of divine counter-tenors). A poignant *On the Transmigration of Souls* finds a respectful way to combine an overlay of prerecorded voices (harkening back to *Christian Zeal and Activity* as well as to Reich's tape loops) with *Unanswered Question*–influenced music that is somber, heartbreakingly beautiful, and downright dangerous. *Doctor Atomic*, both as opera and symphony, calls forth a cacophony reminiscent of Edgard Varèse, communal muted recitative-like passages, and evocative arioso.

With all this, Adams has maintained that originality is not the urgent concern that it was for the minimalist composers ten years his senior. He has compared his position to that of J.S. Bach, Johannes Brahms, and Gustav Mahler, who "were standing at the end of an era and were embracing all of the evolutions that occurred over the previous 30 to 50 years." The comparison is apt, as Adams has become, like such predecessors, among the most original voices of his time.

WORKS

DRAMATIC

Matter of Heart (film score), 1982, unpubd

Nixon in China (op, 3, A. Goodman), 1985–7; Orchestra of St. Luke's, cond. E. de Waart, Houston, Houston Grand Opera, 22 Oct 1987

The Death of Klinghoffer (op, 2, Goodman), 1989–91; English Opera Chorus, Lyon Opera Orchestra, cond. K. Nagano, Brussels, Theatre Royal de la Monnaie, 19 Mar 1991

I was Looking at the Ceiling and Then I Saw the Sky (music drama, 2, J. Jordan), 1995; Paul Dresher Ensemble, cond. G. Gershon, Berkeley, Zellerbach Playhouse, 11 May 1995

An American Tapestry (film score), 1999

El Niño: a Nativity Oratorio (or, various), 1999–2000; London Voices and Theatre of Voices, Deutsche SO, cond. Nagano, Paris, Théâtre du Chatelet, 15 Dec 2000

Doctor Atomic (op, 2, various), 2004–5; San Francisco Opera, cond. D. Runnicles, San Francisco, War Memorial Opera House, 1 Oct 2005

A Flowering Tree (op, 1, various), 2006; E. Owens, R. Thomas, J. Rivera, Schola Cantorum Caracas, Orquesta Joven Camerata de Venezuela, cond. Adams, Vienna, MuseumsQuartier, 14 Nov 2006

I Am Love (Io Sono l'Amore; film score), 2010

The Gospel According to the Other Mary (orat, P. Sellars), 2011; Los Angeles Master Chorale, Los Angeles PO, cond. G. Dudamel, Los Angeles, Walt Disney Concert Hall, 31 May 2012

ORCHESTRAL

Common Tones in Simple Time, 1979; Harmonium (E. Dickinson, J. Donne), chorus, orch, 1980–81; Shaker Loops, str orch, 1983 [rev. of chbr work]; Harmonielehre, 1984–5; The Chairman Dances, foxtrot, 1985; Tromba lontana, fanfare, 1985; Short Ride in a Fast Machine, fanfare, 1986; Fearful Symmetries, 1988; Eros Piano, pf, orch, 1989; El Dorado, 1991; Vn Conc, 1993; Lollapalooza, 1995; Century Rolls, pf, orch, 1996; Slonimsky's Earbox, 1996; Naive and Sentimental Music, 1997–8; Guide to Strange Places, 2001; My Father Knew Charles Ives, 2003; The Dharma at Big Sur, electric vn, orch, 2003; Doctor Atomic Symphony (2007); City Noir (2009); Absolute Jest (2010).

VOCAL

Ktaadn, chorus, oscillators, filters, 1974, unpubd; Harmonium (E. Dickinson, J. Donne), chorus, orch, 1980–81; Grand Pianola Music, 3 female vv, 2 pf, wind, brass, perc, 1982; The Nixon Tapes (from Nixon in China), solo vv, chorus, orch, 1987; The Wound-Dresser (W. Whitman), Bar, orch, 1988; Choruses from the Death of Klinghoffer (Goodman), 1991; On the Transmigration of Souls (missing persons notices, personal reminiscences, victims' names, comp. Adams), chorus, children's chorus, orch, sound design, 2002

CHAMBER AND SOLO INSTRUMENTAL

Pf Qnt, 1970, unpubd; American Standard, unspecified ens, 1973, unpubd; Christian Zeal and Activity, unspecified ens, 1973; Grounding, 6vv, 3 sax, live elecs, 1975, unpubd; China Gates, pf, 1977; Phrygian Gates, pf, 1977; Shaker Loops, 7 str, 1978; Grand Pianola Music, 3 female vv, 2 pf, wind, brass, perc, 1982; Chbr Sym., 15 insts, 1992; John's Book of Alleged Dances, str qt, sampler, 1994; Road Movies, vn, pf, 1995; Gnarly Buttons, cl, ens, 1996; Hallelujah Junction, 2 pf, 1996; Scratchband, amp ens, 1996; Nancy's Fancy, wind ens, 2001; American Berserk, pf, 2001; Son of Chbr Sym., 2007; Fellow Traveler, str qt, 2007; String Quartet, 2008

ELECTRO-ACOUSTIC

Heavy Metal, 2-channel tape, 1970, unpubd; Grounding, 6vv, 3 sax, live elecs, 1975, unpubd; Onyx, 4-channel tape, 1976, unpubd; Studebaker Love Music, 2-channel tape, 1976, unpubd; Light over Water: the Genesis of Music, 2-channel tape, 1983; Hoodoo Zephyr, 1992–3

ARRANGEMENTS AND ORCHESTRATIONS

6 Songs by Charles Ives, 1v, chbr orch, 1989–93; Wiegenlied, 1989 [orch of Liszt]; The Black Gondola, 1989 [orch of Liszt: La lugubre Gondola]; Berceuse élégiaque, 1991 [orch of Busoni]; Le livre de Baudelaire, Mez, orch, 1993 [orch of 4 poems from Debussy: 5 poèmes (C. Baudelaire)]; La mufa, tango, 1995 [orch of A. Piazzolla]; Revolucionario, tango, 1996 [orch of Piazzolla], withdrawn; Todo Buenos Aires, tango, 1996 [orch of Piazzolla]

OTHER

Recorded interview in NHoh

Principal publishers: Boosey & Hawkes, Associated. Principal recording companies: Nonesuch, Argo, EMI, Philips

WRITINGS

Halleluiah Junction: Composing an American Life (New York, 2008)

BIBLIOGRAPHY

K.R. Schwarz: "Young American Composers: John Adams," *Music and Musicians* (Mar 1985), 10–11

D. Henahan: "Opera: Nixon in China," *New York Times* (24 Oct 1987)

A. Porter: "Nixon in China: John Adams in Conversation with Andrew Porter," *Tempo*, clxvii (1988), 25–30

B. Heisinger: "American Minimalism in the 1980s," *AM*, vii (1989) 430–47

K.R. Schwarz: "Process vs. Intuition in the Recent Works of Steve Reich and John Adams," *AM*, viii (1990), 245–73

R.H. Kornick: *Recent American Opera: a Production Guide* (New York, 1991), esp. 3–5

E. Strickland: *American Composers: Dialogues on Contemporary Music* (Bloomington, IN, 1991)

J.H. Warrack and E. West: *The Oxford Dictionary of Opera* (New York, 1992)

J. Wierzbicki: "John Adams: Nixon in China," *St. Louis Post-Dispatch* (6 Dec 1992)

T.A. Johnson: "Harmonic Vocabulary in the Music of John Adams: a Hierarchical Approach," *JMT*, xxxvii (1993), 117–56

E. Schwartz and D. Godfrey: *Music since 1945: Issues, Materials, and Literature* (New York, 1993)

D. Schwarz: "Listening Subjects: Semiotics, Psychoanalysis, and the Music of John Adams and Steve Reich," *PNM*, xxxi/2 (1993), 24–56

J.T. Rimer: "Recording Reviews," *AM*, xii (1994), 338–41 [review of *Nixon in China*]

R. Jemian and A.M. De Zeeuw: "An Interview with John Adams," *PNM*, xxxiv/2 (1996), 88–104

K.R. Schwarz: *Minimalists* (London, 1996)

M. Daines: "An Interview with John Adams," *OQ*, xiii/1 (1996), 37–54

F.J. Oteri: "John Adams: in the Center of American Music," *NewMusicBox* (1 Jan 2001), <http://www.newmusicbox.org/articles/john-adams-in-the-center-of-american-music/>

C. Pellegrino: "Aspects of Closure in the Music of John Adams," *PNM*, xl/1 (2002), 147–75

D.B. Beverly: *John Adams's Opera* The death of Klinghoffer (diss., U. of Kentucky, 2002)

J.W. Bernard: "Minimalism, Postminimalism, and the Resurgence of Tonality in Recent American Music," *AM*, xxi (2003), 112–33

M. Broyles: *Mavericks and Other Traditions in American Music* (New Haven, CT, 2004)

R. Fink: "Klinghoffer in Brooklyn Heights," *COJ*, xvii (2005), 173–213

T. May: *The John Adams Reader: Essential Writings on an American Composer* (Pompton Plains, NJ, 2006)

A. Tommasini: "Doing Everything but Playing the Music," *New York Times* (30 Apr 2007)

A. Ross: "Countdown: John Adams and Peter Sellars Create an Atomic Opera," *New Yorker* (3 Oct 2005)

R.S. Longobardi: "Re-producing *Klinghoffer*: Opera and Arab Identity before and after 9/11," *JSAM*, iii (2009), 273–310

SARAH CAHILL/MARK ALBURGER

Adams, John Luther (*b* Meridian, MS, 23 Jan 1953). Composer. Growing up in the American South and on the Northeastern seaboard, Adams began his musical career with piano and trumpet lessons, rock drumming, and songwriting in his teens. However, it was the music of Frank Zappa that shifted his focus to contemporary classical music, above all the works of Cage, Feldman, and Varèse. Adams studied composition with Leon Stein and James Tenney at the California Institute of the Arts (BFA 1973). Drawn to environmentalism during his music studies in overdeveloped Southern California, Adams traveled to Alaska in 1975 to campaign for the passage of the Alaska National Interest Lands Conservation Act. He settled there in 1978 to serve as executive director of the Northern Alaska Environmental Center, but soon thereafter established himself as the composer most strongly associated with Alaska, paying tribute in his compositions almost exclusively to his chosen environment. In the 1980s and 1990s Adams was also active as a performer: as timpanist and principal percussionist of the Fairbanks SO and the Arctic Chamber Orchestra (1982–9) and as percussionist in performances of his own music. The author of two books and numerous other writings on music and the environment, Adams has taught at the University of Alaska, at Bennington College, at the Oberlin Conservatory of Music and at Harvard University. Among his many awards are the 2010 Michael Ludwig Nemmers Prize in Music Composition, Rasmuson Foundation Distinguished Artist Award, United States Artists Fellowship, Foundation for Contemporary Arts Fellowship, grants from the Alaska State Council on the Arts, the American Music Center, Meet the Composer, the National Endowment for the Arts, Opera America, and the Rockefeller Foundation, commissions from the American Composers Orchestra, Arctic Chamber Orchestra, Museum of the North, and Paul Allen Foundation, among many other institutions, and residencies with the Anchorage SO, Anchorage Opera, and Alaska Public Radio.

Adams's love of nature, concern for the environment and interest in the resonance of specific places led him to pursue the concept of sonic geography. Early examples of this idea include two works written during Adams's sojourn in rural Georgia: *songbirdsongs* (1974–80), a collection of indeterminate miniature pieces for piccolos and percussion based on free translations of bird songs, and *Night Peace* (1977), a vocal work capturing the nocturnal soundscape of the Okefenokee Swamp through slow-changing and sparse sonic textures. In the 1980s Adams composed his first works inspired by the Arctic north, including *A Northern Suite* (1979–80) and *The Far Country of Sleep* (1988) for orchestra, drawing again on meditative open sonorities and bird song motives. *Earth and the Great Weather* (1989–93), an expansive music theater work for voices, strings, percussion, and recorded sound, constitutes his first mature realization of sonic geography and reveals a greater adherence to abstract and experimental musical means. Inspired by the Arctic National Wildlife Refuge, the work features the language and poetry of the Iñupiat and Athabascan Indian people, natural sounds from the Arctic on tape, justly intoned string and vocal harmonies derived from aeolian wind harp sounds and rhythmically complex percussion movements, reflecting Inuit drumming and Adams's own background as a percussionist. Stylistically and technically, Adams builds on the work of such musical experimentalists as Cage, Cowell, Feldman, and Partch. In the 1990s, aiming at sonic equivalents to the treeless and white northern expanses, he composed a series of meditative orchestral works in one movement, including *Dream in White on White* (1992) and *In the White Silence* (1998), using diatonic non-developmental harmonies, polyrhythm, reiterative techniques, delicate instrumentation, spatially deployed sound, and extended length. *Clouds of Forgetting, Clouds of Unknowing* (1991–5), another spacious orchestral work, however, documents his interest in abstract dimensions of places and features chromaticism and dissonance. In *Strange and Sacred Noise* (1991–7) for percussion quartet, one of several remarkable percussion works, Adams translated ideas from chaos theory and fractal geometry into music to suggest through dissonance and rhythmic complexity primordial noise and the sonic violence of nature. In recent years he has explored electronic media in such works as *Veils and Vesper* (2005), and *The Place Where You Go to Listen* (2004–6), a continuous sound and light environment at the Museum of the North in Fairbanks, which transforms in real-time the Alaskan interior's cycles of daylight and nighttime, phases of the moon, meteorological, seismic and geomagnetic activities, and the aurora borealis into music. Much of Adams's music, perhaps most overtly his settings of John Haines's poetry in *Forest Without Leaves* (1984), exhibits an eco-critical dimension. It reflects his indebtedness to such philosophies as acoustic ecology, deep ecology and bioregionalism, drawing attention to the fragility of Arctic land- and soundscapes threatened by (noise) pollution and global warming. In *Inuksuit* (2009) for nine to 99 percussionists, Adams moved outdoors, creating music in direct response to the soundscape of the performance site, encouraging what he calls "ecological listening."

WORKS

(selective list)

Orch: A Northern Suite, 1979–80, rev. 2004; The Far Country of Sleep, 1988; Clouds of Forgetting, Clouds of Unknowing, chbr orch, 1991–5; Dream in White on White, hp/pf, str qt, str orch, 1992; Sauyatugvik: The Time of Drumming, 1995, arr. 2 pf, timp, 4 perc, 1996; In the White Silence, cel, hp, 2 vib, str qt, str, 1998; Dark Waves, orch, elecs, 2007, arr. 2 pf, elecs, 2007; for Lou Harrison, str qt, pf, str orch, 2007; Inuksuit, 9–99 perc, 2009

Chbr and solo inst: Always Very Soft, 3 perc, 1973, rev. 2007; Green Corn Dance, 6 perc, 1974; songbirdsongs, 2 pic, 3 perc, opt. vn, 1974–80; Strange Birds Passing, fl ens, 1983; Giving Birth to Thunder, Sleeping with his Daughter, Coyote builds North American, nar, E♭ cl + cb cl, vn, db, 4 perc, 1986–90; 5 Yup'ik Dances, pf/hp, 1991–4; Strange and Sacred Noise, perc qt, 1991–7; 5 Athabascan Dances, hp, perc, 1992, arr. gui, hp, perc, 1996; Crow and Weasel (after B. Lopez), pic + b cl, 4 perc, cel, hp, str qnt, 1993–4; Make Prayers to the Raven, fl, vn, vc, hp/pf, perc, 1996–2000; Qilyaun, 4 b drums/(1 b drum, elecs), 1998; The Immeasurable Space of Tones, vn, cb inst, pf, perc, sustaining kbd, 1998–2001; In a Treeless Place, Only Snow, cel, hp/pf, 2 vib, str qt, 1999; The Light That Fills the World, vn, db/cbn, perc, sustaining kbd, 1999, arr. orch, 2000; Time Undisturbed, (pic, fl, a fl)/3 shakuhachis, 3 hp/(cel, pf, hp)/3 kotos, vc, sustaining kbd/sho, 1999; After the Light, a fl, vib, hp, 2001; Among Red Mountains, pf, 2001; Dark Wind, b cl, pf, perc, 2001; The Farthest Place, vn, db, pf, perc, 2001; The Mathematics of Resonant Bodies, perc, elecs, 2002; Red Arc/Blue Veil, pf, perc, elecs, 2002; . . . and bells remembered . . . , perc, 2005; For Jim (Rising), 3 tpt, 3 trbn, 2006; The Light Within, vn, vc, a fl, b cl, pf, perc, elecs, 2007, arr. orch, elecs, 2010; Nunataks, pf, 2007; Three High Places, vn, 2007

Vocal: Night Peace, S, 2 chorus, hp, perc, 1976; up into the silence (e.e. cummings), 1v, pf, 1978, rev. 1984; Forest Without Leaves (J. Haines), chorus, orch, 1984; How the Sun Came to the Forest (Haines), SA, pf/(a fl, eng hn, pf, hp, str), 1984; Earth and the Great Weather, 4 vv, vn, va, vc, db, 4 perc, elecs, natural sounds, 1990–93; Magic song for one who wishes to live and the dead who climb up to the sky, 1v, pf, 1990; Poem of the Forgotten, 1v, pf, 2004; Little Cosmic Dust Poem (Haines), 1v, pf, 2007; Sky with Four Suns and Sky with Four Moons, 4 choirs, 2007–8

Sound Installations: Veils and Vesper, 2005; The Place Where You Go to Listen, 2004–6; The Place We Began, 2008

BIBLIOGRAPHY

M. Morris: "Ecotopian Sounds, or The Music of John Luther Adams and Strong Environmentalism," *Crosscurrents and Counterpoints: Offerings in Honor of Bengt Hambraeus at 70*, ed. P.F. Broman, N.A. Engebretsen, and B. Alphonce (Göteborg, 1998), 129–41

S. Feisst: "Klanggeographie–Klanggeometrie. Der US-amerikanische Komponist John Luther Adams," *MusikTexte*, xci (2001), 4–14
J.L. Adams: *Winter Music: Composing the North* (Middletown, CT, 2004)
A. Ross: "Song of the Earth," *The New Yorker* (12 May 2008)
J.L. Adams: *The Place Where You Go to Listen. In Search of an Ecology of Music* (Middletown, CT, 2009)
B. Herzogenrath, ed.: *The Farthest Place: Music of John Luther Adams* (Lebanon, NH, 2012)

SABINE FEISST

Adams, Lee (Richard) (*b* Mansfield, OH, 14 Aug 1924). Lyricist and writer. Adams began his career as a writer after earning degrees from Ohio State University and Columbia University. He worked initially as a journalist, while also writing lyrics for summer camp productions and night club revues. In 1949, he met CHARLES STROUSE, and over the next decade the two created songs and specialty material for nightclub and television performers. Their first published notices came for several minor productions in the mid-1950s. Adams and Strouse broke through on Broadway in 1960 with *Bye Bye Birdie*, which won the Tony for Best Musical. Other notable shows by this team were *Golden Boy* and *Applause* (1970 Tony Award for Best Musical), which is perhaps their best work together. The pair had no successes together after 1970, save for "Those Were the Days," the theme song for the hit television show *All in the Family*. Adams's later collaboration with Mitch Leigh was not successful. Adams was inducted into the Songwriters Hall of Fame in 1989. His list of over 200 published songs includes such standards as "Put on a happy face," "Lot of Livin' to Do," "Kids," and "Applause."

SCOTT WARFIELD

Adams, [Harrison] **Leslie** (*b* Cleveland, OH, 20 Dec 1932). Composer. He attended Oberlin College (BM 1955), California State University, Long Beach (MA 1967), and Ohio State University (PhD 1973), and studied privately with HERBERT ELWELL, ROBERT STARER, VITTORIO GIANNINI, Leon Dallin, Edward Mattila, Eugene O'Brien, and Marcel Dick. He has taught at Stillman College (1963–4), Florida A&M University (1968–9), and the University of Kansas (1969–78). His honors include composition awards from the National Association of Negro Women (1963) and the Christian Arts Annual National Competition for Choral Music (1979), fellowships from the Rockefeller Foundation Study and Conference Center at Bellagio (1979), Yaddo (1980, 1984), the National Association of Negro Musicians (2004), and the National Opera Association (2006), and commissions from the Center for Black Music Research, the Cleveland Orchestra, and the Ohio Chamber Orchestra. Adams writes in a lyrical style that fuses elements of jazz and black folksong with 20th-century compositional techniques. A few of his works, including *Hymn to Freedom* (1989) and *Christmas Lullaby* (1996), have been recorded.

WORKS
(selective list)

Op: Blake (4, D. Mayers), 1980–86; Slaves (Sidney Goldberg, 2006)
Inst: Pastorale, vn, pf, 1952; 3 Preludes, pf, 1961; Sonata, vc, pf, 1964–5; Ode to Life, orch, 1979, rev. 1982, 1989; Prelude and Fugue, org, 1979; Sym., orch, 1978; Night Song, fl, hp, 1983; Western Adventures, orch, 1985; Offering of Love, org, 1991; Twenty-six Études, pf, 1997–2007
Choral: Hosanna to the Son of David, SATB, 1969; Madrigal, SATB, 1969; Ps cxxi, 4 solo vv, SATB, 1969; The Righteous Man (cant., D. Mayers), SATB, chbr orch/pf, 1985; Christmas Lullaby, children's choir, orch, 1996
Songs: 5 Millay Songs (E. St Vincent Millay), (high/medium v, pf)/(medium v, orch), 1960; 6 Afro-American Songs (L. Hughes, G. Johnson, C. Delany, J. Weldon Johnson, L.M. Collins), (high v, pf)/(medium v/B, orch), 1961; 3 Dunbar Songs (P.L. Dunbar), high v, chbr orch, 1981; The Wider View (Dunbar, G. Johnson, Hughes, R.H. Grenville), high/medium v, pf, 1988; Hymn to Freedom, 3 solo vv, chbr orch, 1989
MSS and correspondence in Leslie Adams Music Archives *CLp*

BIBLIOGRAPHY

Y.C. Williams: "The Making of the Opera *Blake* by Leslie Adams," *New Perspectives on Music*, ed. J. Wright with S.A. Floyd Jr. (Warren, MI, 1992)
W.C. Banfield: *Musical Landscapes in Color: Conversations with Black American Composers* (Lanham, MD, 2003)

JOSEPHINE WRIGHT

Adams, Nathan (*b* Dunstable, NH, 21 Aug 1783; *d* Milford, NH, 16 March 1864). Brass instrument maker. He invented a valve with movable tongues or flaps within the windway. A trumpet in F by Adams with three such valves is displayed on board the *USS Constitution*; it dates from about 1830. A similar instrument, unsigned, with three primitive rotary valves, is in the Essig Collection, Warrensburg, Missouri. Adams is listed as a musical instrument maker in *Longworth's American Almanack, New-York Register, and City Directory* for 1824. For the next four years he was bandmaster on the *USS Constitution*. About 1828 he settled in Lowell, Massachusetts, continuing there as a musical instrument maker until 1835. The latter part of his life was spent as a machinist and repairer of ships' chronometers in Provincetown, Massachusetts. He was the composer of at least one published song, *The Ruins of Troy*, written while on board the *Constitution*.

BIBLIOGRAPHY

WaterhouseLangwillI
Contributions of the Old Residents' Historical Association, Lowell, Massachusetts, v (Lowell, 1894), 179–83
G.A. Ramsdell: *The History of Milford* (Concord, NH, 1901), 229–30
R.E. Eliason: "Early American Valves for Brass Instruments," *GSJ*, xxiii (1970), 86–96

ROBERT E. ELIASON

Adams, Pepper [Park Frederick, III] (*b* Highland Park, MI, 8 Oct 1930; *d* Brooklyn, NY, 10 Sept 1986). Jazz baritone saxophonist and composer. He grew up in Rochester where he took up tenor and baritone saxophones and clarinet, but settled on baritone after moving to Detroit in 1947 as a means of finding work in the city's fiercely competitive music scene. After serving for two years in the US Army Band, Adams returned to Detroit in 1953 and worked there with Tommy Flanagan, Barry Harris, Kenny Burrell, and Elvin Jones, in the house band at the Blue Bird and at Klein's. In 1956 he moved to New York and was a member of Stan Kenton's big band for six months following a recommendation from Oscar Pettiford. From the following year, Adams spent 20 years working in big bands led by Maynard Ferguson, Benny Goodman, Quincy Jones, Lionel Hampton, and Thad Jones and Mel Lewis. During this period he also performed in small ensembles whenever possible and was in demand as a recording artist. Notably, he co-led a quintet with Donald Byrd from 1958 to 1961. By the mid-1970s Adams had worked with many of the best known jazz musicians, including John Coltrane, Wes Montgomery, Thelonious Monk, Dizzy Gillespie, and Charles Mingus. In 1977 he ended a 12-year association with the Jones–Lewis band and began performing internationally as a soloist. During this time he wrote nearly half of his 43 compositions. By the end of his career Adams had recorded 20 albums as a leader and taken part in 600 sessions as a sideman. He was arguably the most accomplished soloist on the baritone saxophone in jazz history and succeeded in elevating it to the level of all other solo instruments. His blinding speed, penetrating timbre, distinctive sound, harmonic ingenuity, precise articulation, confident time-feel, and use of melodic paraphrase—often for comedic effect—make him one of jazz's great postwar stylists, a model to which all subsequent baritone saxophonists have aspired.

BIBLIOGRAPHY

P. Danson: "Pepper Adams," *Coda*, no.191 (1983), 4–9

G. Carner: "Pepper Adams," *Cadence*, xii (1986), no.1, p.13; no.2, p.5; no.3, p.11; no.4, p.5

G. Carner: "Pepper Adams' 'Rue Serpente,'" *JJ*, xxii (1990), 119–38

B. Sidran: *Talking Jazz: an Oral History: 43 Jazz Conversations* (New York, 1995), 209–20

GARY CARNER

Adams, Suzanne (*b* Cambridge, MA, 28 Nov 1872; *d* London, England, 5 Feb 1953). Soprano. She studied with Mathilde Marchesi and Jacques Bouhyin Paris and made her debut at the Paris Opera in 1895 as Juliet; she seems to have studied both Juliet and *Faust*'s Marguerite with Gounod himself, who greatly admired her brilliant yet flexible tone and fine technique. She sang at Covent Garden (1898–1904), where she created Hero in Stanford's *Much Ado about Nothing*, and was also a member of the Metropolitan Opera (1899–1903). Her repertory included Gluck's Eurydice, Donna Elvira, Micaëla (*Carmen*), and Meyerbeer's Marguerite de Valois. She also earned distinction as an oratorio singer in England and the United States. She retired in 1904 and then taught singing in London.

BIBLIOGRAPHY

A. Sterling: "Great Singers Discuss the Voice," *Harper's Bazaar* (27 Jan 1900), 82

J. Freestone: "Suzanne Adams, 1873–1953," *Gramophone*, xxxi (1953–4), 361–6 [with discography]

HERMAN KLEIN/HAROLD ROSENTHAL/R

Adams, Yolanda (Yvette) (*b* Houston, TX, 27 Aug 1961). Gospel music singer. Adams credits her earliest musical influences as James Cleveland, the Edwin Hawkins Singers, Nancy Wilson, and Stevie Wonder. She worked in a variety of jobs, including stints as a fashion model, television news anchor, and schoolteacher, before devoting herself to gospel music. She began her career as a lead singer touring with the Southeast Inspirational Choir, with whom she garnered the attention of composer/producer Thomas Whitfield who oversaw her debut solo album *Just As I Am* (1988) with Sound of Gospel Records. Grounded in traditional church music but open to diverse musical influences, Adams is known for infusing traditional gospel with urban musical influences such as jazz, R&B, and hip hop. Her mainstream album *Mountain High... Valley Low* (Elektra, 1999) is of particular importance in this regard because its diversity of musical styles had the ability to reach both Contemporary Christian and urban music listeners. The album achieved multi-platinum status and went on to earn a Grammy for Best Contemporary Soul Gospel Album (2000), and earned Adams the first American Music Award for Inspirational Artist of the Year.

BIBLIOGRAPHY

B. Carpenter: "Yolanda Adams," *Uncloudy Days: the Gospel Music Encyclopedia* (San Francisco, 2005), 9–11

T. Kernodle: "Work the Works: the Role of African-American Women in the Development of Contemporary Gospel," *Black Music Research Journal*, xxvi/1 (2006), 89–109

MAYA GIBSON

Adderley, Cannonball [Julian Edwin] (*b* Tampa, FL, 15 Sept 1928; *d* Gary, IN, 8 Aug 1975). Jazz alto saxophonist, bandleader, and composer, brother of NAT ADDERLEY. He acquired his nickname (a corruption of "cannibal") in elementary school on account of his large appetite. His father played cornet, and Adderley took up piano and trumpet before settling on alto saxophone. He performed in big bands and directed the Dillard High School band and after three years in the army (1950–53) worked as a teacher. In June 1955 Adderley made an unscheduled debut in New York, sitting in with Oscar Pettiford at Café Bohemia. On the strength of his performance he joined Pettiford's band and recorded with Kenny Clarke for Savoy. Around this time he also recorded for Savoy and EmArcy as a leader, before returning to Florida and forming a band with his brother Nat. From late 1957 he worked with Miles Davis, during which time he performed on a number of Davis's most important recordings, notably *Milestones*, *Porgy & Bess* and *Kind of Blue*. While a member of Davis's group, he recorded his own album (*Somethin' Else*) with Davis as a sideman and another (*Quintet in Chicago*) with the remaining members of the trumpeter's group.

Adderley achieved his greatest success between 1959 and 1975 with a band that included his brother Nat. The group was one of the early proponents of soul jazz and had a number of hits, including Bobby Timmons's "This Here" (aka "Dis Here"), Adderley's "Sack O' Woe," and Joe Zawinul's "Mercy, Mercy, Mercy" The band was generally a quintet, although between 1962 and 1965 it was a sextet with the addition of first Yusef Lateef and then Charles Lloyd. It enjoyed success and performed in Europe, Japan, and South America. Adderley recorded a substantial number of sessions for Orrin Keepnews at Riverside (1958–62) before switching to Capitol.

Adderley's saxophone playing was firmly rooted in blues, gospel, and the jazz styles of Coleman Hawkins,

Benny Carter, and Charlie Parker. He was no great innovator, but instead built his reputation on consolidating and blending existing jazz styles in his own fashion. He combined something of Parker's mercurial flair with Carter's creamy, elegant sonority and displayed a masterly command of bop harmony and a hard, driving swing feel. His music was sometimes dismissed as too formulaic and his style either too traditional or too populist for a time when jazz was undergoing radical change. Nonetheless, he experimented with African drumming in 1968 (*Accent on Africa*) and electronics in the early 1970s. He renewed his association with Keepnews when he moved to Fantasy in 1973 and was working on another record for the label when he died following a stroke in 1975.

SELECTED RECORDINGS

As leader: *Presenting Cannonball Adderley* (1955, Savoy); *Portrait of Cannonball* (1958, Riv.); *Somethin' Else* (1958, BN); *Quintet in San Francisco* (1959, Riv.); *At the Lighthouse* (1960, Riv.); *Know What I Mean?* (1961, Riv.); *Nancy Wilson/Cannonball Adderley* (1962, Cap.); *Nippon Soul* (1963, Cap.); *Mercy, Mercy, Mercy!* (1966, Cap.); *Accent on Africa* (1968, Cap.); *Country Preacher* (1969, Cap.); *Inside Straight* (1973, Fan.)

As sideman with M. Davis: *Milestones* (1958, Col.); *Porgy & Bess* (1958, Col.); *Kind of Blue* (1959, Col.)

BIBLIOGRAPHY

D. Baker: *The Jazz Style of Cannonball Adderley* (Lebanon, IN, 1980)

O. Keepnews: *The View from Within: Jazz Writings, 1948–1987* (New York, 1988)

C. Sheridan: *Dis Here: a Bio-discography of Julian "Cannonball" Adderley* (Westport, CT, 2000)

K. Mathieson: *Cookin': Hard Bop and Soul Jazz 1954–65* (Edinburgh, 2002)

R.P. Jones: "You Know What I Mean? The Pedagogical Canon of Cannonball," *CMc*, nos.79–80 (2005), 169–205

KENNY MATHIESON

Adderley, Nat(haniel, Sr.) (*b* Tampa, FL, 25 Nov 1931; *d* Lakeland, FL, 2 Jan 2000). Jazz cornetist, bandleader, and composer, brother of CANNONBALL ADDERLEY. He took up trumpet as a child at the suggestion of his father, a cornetist, but switched to cornet in 1950. His career was closely linked with that of Cannonball. They formed their first band as children and played together through school, college, and the Army. Adderley then played with Lionel Hampton (1954–5), before joining Cannonball's new band after the saxophonist's Café Bohemia debut (1955). He then worked with J.J. Johnson and Woody Herman (1957–9) while his brother was with Miles Davis, after which he spent 16 years as a member of Cannonball's successful quintet (1959–75). During this period he played the trumpet part for Sammy Davis Jr. in the film *A Man Called Adam* (1966). Following Cannonball's death in 1975, he led his own bands for the rest of his career; in 1980 he also led the Adderley Brotherhood, which featured several former members of Cannonball's quintet. He later played in the Paris Reunion Band (mid-1980s) and the Riverside Reunion Band (1993–4) and continued to perform in his characteristic straight-ahead style until complications from diabetes led to a leg amputation in 1997. His compositions include "Work Song," which became a hard bop standard, and *Shout up a Morning* (1986), a musical based on the folk tale of John Henry.

BIBLIOGRAPHY

O. Keepnews: *The View from Within: Jazz Writings, 1948–1987* (New York, 1988)

K. Mathieson: *Cookin': Hard Bop and Soul Jazz 1954–65* (Edinburgh, 2002)

KENNY MATHIESON

Addison, Adele (*b* New York, NY, 24 July 1925). Soprano. Her vocal and musical abilities won her scholarships to Westminster Choir College, Princeton (BM 1946), and the Berkshire Music Center, where she studied with BORIS GOLDOVSKY. She made her recital debut at Boston in April 1948 and, after further coaching with POVLA FRIJSH in New York, appeared at Town Hall in January 1952. This established her reputation and led to engagements with many American orchestras and the New England and New York City Opera companies. She dubbed the title role in Samuel Goldwyn's film *Porgy and Bess* (1959). On 23 September 1962 she sang in the inaugural concert at Lincoln Center; she toured the USSR in 1963. The silvery timbre of her voice, her agility, and her distinguished musicianship all made her an ideal performer of Baroque music, as her recordings of Bach (*St. Matthew Passion*) and Handel (*Ode for St. Cecilia's Day*) attest. These qualities also made her an admired exponent of contemporary music—she gave the first performances of Foss's *Time Cycle* (1960) and Poulenc's *Gloria* (1961), among many other works. She has taught at the Eastman School, Philadelphia College of the Performing Arts, Aspen Music School, and SUNY, Stony Brook. She has also served on the faculty of the Manhattan School of Music, where she was awarded an honorary doctorate in 2001.

BIBLIOGRAPHY

H. Taubman: "Adele Addison," *New York Times* (28 Jan 1957)

"On the Front Cover," *MusAm*, lxxix/8 (1959), 4

RICHARD BERNAS/KATIE BUEHNER

Addy, Yacub Tetteh (*b* Accra, Ghana, 1931). Master drummer of the Ga ethnic group, West Africa. Born in Accra, Ghana, Yacub is the eldest living member of the revered Addy family of drummers. His father, Jacob Kpani Addy, was a powerful *jinni* whose medicine name was Okonfo Akoto. Yacub has explained that he and his brothers began drumming out of necessity: "One day when they [his father's drummers] were very late, my father lost patience with them, and told his senior sons to start the drumming." While the brothers had never played the drums before, they were familiar with the complex rhythms that accompanied their father's medicine. When the drummers finally arrived, they were shocked by how well the brothers could play. In 1956, before Ghana's independence, Yacub organized the first staged performances of traditional music at the Accra Community Center. By 1968 he started a professional touring group, Oboade, with some of his brothers. This group, based in London from 1972–5, and made three US tours. At first his younger brother, Mustapha Teddey, insisted on leading the group but then left in 1973 to pursue his own career.

In 1975, after Oboade disbanded, Yacub married an American, Amina Addy, and moved to Seattle, Washington.

In 1982, Yacub moved to New York City and created the traditional drum ensemble, Odadaa. While performing during President Clinton's 1993 inauguration, Yacub met Wynton Marsalis, with whom he later worked on the ground-breaking collaboration, the album *Congo Square: Love, Libation, Liberation* (2007). In 2010, he was named an NEA National Heritage Fellow.

VERA H. FLAIG

Adgate, Andrew (*b* Norwich, CT, 22 March 1762; *d* Philadelphia, PA, *c*30 Sept 1793). Singing teacher, concert organizer, conductor, tune book compiler, and wool-card manufacturer. Adgate assisted Andrew Law at a singing-school in Philadelphia in April 1783, and by 1784 had set up an Institution for the Encouragement of Church Music in the city. This was superseded the next year by his "Free School…for diffusing more generally the knowledge of vocal music," which came to be called the Uranian Society, and was finally reorganized in 1787 as the Uranian Academy. Unlike traditional singing-schools, which were private institutions with each scholar paying his or her own way, Adgate's schools were supported by subscription and charged no fees—an early instance of educational democracy. Subscribers received tickets for concerts devoted chiefly to sacred music, given by the singing scholars and their associates under Adgate's direction. These concerts, which took place between 1785 and 1790, were probably the first of their kind in Philadelphia, and perhaps the first anywhere in the United States. A "Grand Concert" on 4 May 1786, which included works by Handel, Billings, James Lyon, and William Tuckey, performed by 230 choristers and an orchestra of 50, was a benefit held for the Pennsylvania Hospital, the Philadelphia Dispensary, and "the Poor." Later Adgate worked in the city as a wool-card manufacturer and merchant; he was a volunteer in the citizens' committee organized during Philadelphia's yellow-fever epidemic of 1793, and died of that disease.

Adgate's first known compilation is an anthology of sacred texts: *Select Psalms and Hymns for the Use of Mr. Adgate's Pupils* (Philadelphia, 1787), although he probably wrote the *Introductory Lessons, Practised by the Uranian Society* (Philadelphia, 1785). He published an instruction manual, the *Rudiments of Music* (Philadelphia, 1788); with Ishmael Spicer, he also compiled the *Philadelphia Harmony* (Philadelphia, 1789), a tune book made up of popular American and European sacred music. Published in one volume, the two items ran through 12 editions in Philadelphia by 1811, but by the fourth edition of 1791 Spicer's name was dropped from the title page. Questions regarding authorship and identity linger as some authorities maintain that Adgate was indeed Absalom Aimwell, the compiler of *The Philadelphia Songster* (Philadelphia, 1789).

BIBLIOGRAPHY

DAB (W.S. Pratt)
O.G. Sonneck: *Early Concert-Life in America (1731–1800)* (Leipzig, 1907/*R*), 103–20
F.J. Metcalf: *American Writers and Compilers of Sacred Music* (New York, 1925/*R*), 29–31
C. Rourke: *The Roots of American Culture* (New York, 1942/*R*), 170–76
R. Crawford: *Andrew Law, American Psalmodist* (Evanston, IL, 1968/*R*)
H.D. Cummings: *Andrew Adgate: Philadelphia Psalmodist and Music Educator* (diss., U. of Rochester, 1975)
A. Perdue Britton, I. Lowens, and R. Crawford: *American Sacred Music Imprints 1698–1810: A Bibliography* (Worcester, MA, 1990)

RICHARD CRAWFORD/NYM COOKE/R

Adkins, Trace (*b* Springhill, LA, 13 Jan 1962). Country music singer. In line with country "hat acts" and neo-traditionalists such as Toby Keith and Tim McGraw, Trace Adkins has forged a working-class image and hard-driving sound by merging honky-tonk with Southern rock, gospel, and blues. His masculine bravado and allegiance to a blue-collar ethos has solidified his position as one of country's top acts.

After time spent working on an oil rig, Adkins moved to Nashville in 1992 to pursue his musical career. There he met producer Scott Hendricks, who signed him to Capitol Records. His 1996 debut album, *Dreamin' Out Loud*, yielded the successful singles "Every Light in the House," "I Left something turned on at home," and "(This Ain't) No Thinkin' Thing," which became his first number-one country hit. Despite problems with alcoholism and a drunk-driving charge, his 2001 album *Chrome* reached the top five on *Billboard*'s Country Albums chart. In 2003, Adkins's *Greatest Hits Collection: Volume 1* and the studio album *Comin' On Strong* reached platinum status and solidified the artist as a commercial force. In the same year, Adkins was also inducted into the Grand Ole Opry. Adkins's presence on the country charts continued with *Songs About Me* (2005), which featured the crossover pop hit, "Honkytonk Badonkadonk." His 2006 album, *Dangerous Man*, again propelled Adkins to the top of the charts with "Ladies Love Country Boys," his first number-one country single since "(This Ain't) No Thinkin' Thing" in 1996. In 2010, Adkins parted ways with Capitol Records, debuted the single "This Ain't No Love Song" on Toby Keith's Show Dog-Universal Records, and, in August, released *Cowboy's Back In Town*.

BIBLIOGRAPHY

T. Roland: "Trace Adkins: The Last Cowboy," *Billboard* (2010), Vol. 122 Issue 29, p. 24–5

JOHN STANISLAWSKI

Adler, Kurt Herbert (*b* Vienna, 2 April 1905; *d* Ross, CA, 9 Feb 1988). Conductor and opera director of Austrian birth. He was educated at the Musikakademie and university in Vienna, and made his debut in 1925 as a conductor for the Max Reinhardt Theatre, then conducted at the Volksoper and opera houses in Germany, Italy, and Czechoslovakia. He assisted Toscanini in Salzburg (1936) and went to the United States in 1938 for an engagement with the Chicago Opera. He worked for the San Francisco Opera from 1943 to 1981, initially as chorus master, then as artistic director in 1953 and general director from 1956. Although he occasionally conducted, most of his time was devoted to administrative duties. During his regime the San Francisco Opera grew increasingly adventurous in repertory and became noted for the engagement of unproven talent and the implementation of modern staging techniques. By 1972 Adler had lengthened the season from five weeks to ten and he also formed subsidiary organizations in San Francisco to stage experimental works, to perform in schools and other unconventional locales, and to train young singers. He retired in 1981 after conducting a performance of *Carmen* with Teresa Berganza and Placido Domingo. His work received citations from the governments of Italy, West Germany, Austria, and Russia.

BIBLIOGRAPHY

K. Lockhart, ed.: *The Adler Years* (San Francisco, 1981)
J. Rockwell: Obituary, *New York Times*, 11 February 1988

MARTIN BERNHEIMER/R

Adler, Larry [Lawrence] (*b* Baltimore, MD, 10 Feb 1914; *d* London, England, 6 Aug 2001). Harmonica player. He was acknowledged as the first harmonica player to achieve recognition and acceptance in classical musical circles and to have elevated the instrument to concert status. At the age of 14 he won a local harmonica contest and soon thereafter started to earn a living performing in movie houses across the United States. Spotted by the British impresario Sir Charles Cochran in 1934, he moved to London, initially to play in Cochran's revue *Streamline*. Adler emerged as a classical musician following his return to the United States in 1939, eventually performing adaptations of works such as Vivaldi's *Violin Concerto in A Minor* with the New York PO and other leading orchestras. His greatest success came through his partnership with dancer Paul Draper. In concert they performed individually and as a duo, frequently improvising on requests from the audience. In 1949 the two were accused of being Communist sympathizers; after they sued their attacker unsuccessfully for libel, Adler settled in London, not returning to the United States until the late 1950s.

Adler's ability was recognized by such composers as Vaughan Williams, Milhaud, Gordon Jacob, Malcolm Arnold, Arthur Benjamin, and Joaquín Rodrigo, all of whom wrote orchestral works with Adler as soloist. He toured extensively and broadcast frequently on radio and television in many countries, and took a keen interest in all aspects of harmonica pedagogy. Adler wrote scores for a number of films, including *Genevieve* (for which he received an Academy nomination), *King and Country*, and *A High Wind in Jamaica*. During the 1980s he appeared mostly in nightclubs, introducing each piece of music with a celebrity-related anecdote from his long career. These stories also appear in his 1984 autobiography, *It Ain't Necessarily So*, which provides a lively if, at times, embellished account of middlebrow performance in the United States during the 20th century.

BIBLIOGRAPHY

"Seeking a Mark," *Time*, lxxxix (30 June 1967), 48
L. Adler: "Larry Adler—my Life on the Blacklist," *New York Times* (15 June 1975)

Larry Adler. (AP Photo)

G. Giddins: "Larry Adler's Ghost Stories," *Village Voice* (20 Aug 1979), 70
L. Adler: *It Ain't Necessarily So* (London, 1984)
R. Bañagale: *Rhapsodies in Blue: New Narratives for an Iconic American "Composition"* (diss., Harvard U., 2011)

IVOR BEYNON/RYAN RAUL BAÑAGALE

Adler, Lou (*b* Chicago, IL, 13 Dec 1933). Record producer, songwriter, artist manager, label owner, and entrepreneur. He was most active in the popular-music industry from the 1950s to the 1970s. He held jobs in publishing and became co-manager of Jan and Dean with Herb Alpert. Under the pseudonym Barbara Campbell, the pair co-wrote "Only Sixteen" for Sam Cooke. Adler also co-wrote "Wonderful World" with Alpert and Cooke. In 1964 he founded Dunhill Records, which was sold to ABC in 1966. He later brought the songwriter P.F. Sloan and the singer Barry McGuire together for "Eve of Destruction." While the manager and producer of the Mamas and Papas, he co-produced the Monterey International pop festival in 1967, insisting that the event be filmed and retaining those rights. The following year he founded Ode Records, which is noted for releasing Carole King's album *Tapestry*. He also produced records and directed a series of "stoner" films for Cheech and Chong. He also served as an executive producer for and bought the US rights to the film *The Rocky Horror Picture Show* (1975).

PAUL D. FISCHER

Adler, Peter Herman (*b* Jablonec, 2 Dec 1899; *d* Ridgefield, CT, 2 Oct 1990). Conductor. After studying composition and conducting with Zemlinsky at the Prague Conservatory, he became music director of the Bremen Staatsoper (1929–32) and the Ukrainian State Philharmonia, Kiev (1932–7), and also appeared as a guest conductor throughout Europe. He left for the United States in 1939 and made his debut with the New York PO in 1940, after which he toured in the United States. From 1949 to 1959 he was music and artistic director of the NBC-TV Opera Company, sharing artistic responsibility with Toscanini. Adler was musical director of the Baltimore SO from 1959 to 1968, and in 1969 became music and artistic director of WNET (National Educational Television). His Metropolitan Opera debut was in 1972. He was director of the American Opera Center at the Juilliard School from 1973 to 1981. Adler was a pioneer director of television opera in the United States and commissioned many works for the medium; among them Menotti's *Amahl and the Night Visitors* and *Maria Golovin* (of which he conducted the premiere at the 1958 Brussels Exposition Universelle), Dello Joio's *The Trial at Rouen,* and Martinů's *The Marriage* (all at NBC), and Pasatieri's *The Trial of Mary Lincoln,* and Henze's *La cubana* (at WNET).

ELLIOTT W. GALKIN

Adler, Richard (*b* New York, NY, 3 Aug 1921; *d* Southhampton, NY, 21 June 2012). Composer and lyricist. Although the son of the distinguished pianist and pedagogue Charles Adler, he received no musical training and instead studied playwriting with Paul Green at the University of North Carolina, graduating in 1943. In 1950, after completing service in the navy (1943–6), he began to compose radio programs and special material with co-composer-lyricist, Jerry Ross (*b* Bronx, NY, 9 March 1926; *d* New York, 11 Nov 1955). By 1953, Adler and Ross had written a number one popular song hit recorded by Tony Bennett, "Rags to Riches" and contributed songs for their debut billing in the Broadway revue *John Murray Anderson's Almanac.* Over the next two years the promising new team were tutored, marketed, and promoted by FRANK LOESSER, who had arranged for their participation in the *Almanac* and then introduced them to the veteran GEORGE ABBOTT, who would mentor, direct, and co-author Adler's two collaborations with Ross, critically acclaimed musicals that each ran to more than one thousand performances on Broadway: *Pajama Game* (1954; revived 1973 and 2006), a musicalization of labor relations in a pajama factory, and *Damn Yankees* (1955; revived 1994 and 2008), the Faust legend in a baseball setting. In addition to establishing a distinctive vernacular musical and lyrical voice, both musicals exhibited the strong personal stamp, originality, and flair, of Abbott (sharing director's billing with Jerome Robbins in *Pajama Game*), and several talented newcomers in *Damn Yankees,* choreographer Bob Fosse and producers Frederick Brisson, Robert E. Griffith, and Harold Prince (the first and perhaps only joint collaboration of Abbott and his protégés Adler and Ross, Robbins, Fosse, and Prince). Several Adler and Ross songs from these shows became popular standards, including "Hey There" (long rumored to be an intentional borrowing from the opening of Mozart's C major piano sonata, K545) and "Hernando's Hideaway" in *Pajama Game,* reaching numbers one and two, respectively, on the Hit Parade, and "Heart" and "Whatever Lola Wants" in *Damn Yankees.* Both shows won the Tony Award for Best Musical and were soon adapted into successful and reasonably faithful films.

Ross succumbed to chronic bronchiectasis in 1955 at the age of 29, and within a few years Adler had mastered the craft of musical composition. His remaining work without a collaborator would nevertheless fall far short of the popular success he enjoyed with Ross. A musical based on Somerset Maugham's *Of Human Bondage* remained unproduced in the late 1950s. *Kwamina* (1961), an ambitious musical depicting the conflict between western and native medical practices in an emerging African nation as well as a then-daring romance between a black man and a white woman, and *Music Is* (1976), a setting of Shakespeare's *Twelfth Night,* had brief Broadway runs (32 and eight performances, respectively). *A Mother's Kisses* (1968) closed before reaching Broadway. Adler also mounted unsuccessful Broadway productions of *Pajama Game* in 1973, directed by Abbott, and Richard Rodgers's and Sheldon Harnick's *Rex* in 1976 (a 1994 revival of *Damn Yankees* was more successful). Working with Robert Allen in 1958 Adler composed the hit song "Everybody Loves a Lover" and in solo efforts he wrote successful jingles for Newport cigarettes and Hertz rental cars ("Let Hertz Put You in the Driver's Seat") that played for more than a decade. He was also the producer and director for various star-studded productions in the Kennedy and Johnson administrations, including Marilyn Monroe's celebrated appearance in Madison Square Garden singing "Happy Birthday" to President Kennedy.

WORKS

MUSICALS

Dates are those of first New York performances. Librettists and lyricists are listed in that order in parentheses

John Murray Anderson's Almanac (Adler music; lyrics by Adler and J. Ross; music and lyrics also by others), 10 Dec 1953;

The Pajama Game (G. Abbott, R. Bissell, after Bissell: *7 1/2 Cents*), collab. J. Ross, orchd D. Walker, 13 May 1954 (incl. "Hey There," "Hernanado's Hideaway"); film, 1957;

Damn Yankees (Abbott, D. Wallop, after Wallop; *The Year the Yankees Lost the Pennant*), collab. Ross, orchd Walker, 5 May 1955 (incl. "Heart," "Whatever Lola Wants"); film 1958;

Kwamina (R.A. Aurthur), orchd S. Ramin and I. Kostal, 23 Oct 1961;

A Mother's Kisses, New Haven, CT, 1968;

Music Is (Abbott, W. Holt, after Shakespeare: *Twelfth Night*), orchd H. Kay, 20 Dec 1976

OTHER WORKS

Television musicals: Little Women, 1957; The Gift of the Magi, 1958; Olympus 7-0000, 1966

Orch: Memory of a Childhood, 1978; Retrospection, 1979; Yellowstone, ov., 1978; Wilderness Suite, 1983; The Lady Remembers (The Statue of Liberty Suite) (1985)

BIBLIOGRAPHY

S. Green: *The World of Musical Comedy* (New York, 1960, 4th ed., rev. and enlarged, 1980)

R. Adler (with Lee Davis): *"You Gotta Have Heart"* (New York, 1990)

S. Suskin: *Show Tunes: the Songs, Shows and Careers of Broadway's Major Composers* (New York, 1992, rev. and expanded, 4/2010)

GEOFFREY BLOCK

Adler, Samuel (Hans) (*b* Mannheim, 4 March 1928). Composer and conductor of German birth. Both of his parents were musical, his father being a cantor and composer of Jewish liturgical music. The family came to the United States in 1939 and Adler attended Boston University (BM 1948) and Harvard University (MA 1950).

He studied composition with AARON COPLAND, PAUL FROMM, PAUL HINDEMITH, Hugo Norden, WALTER PISTON, and RANDALL THOMPSON; musicology with Karl Geiringer, A.T. DAVISON, and PAUL A. PISK; and conducting with SERGEY KOUSSEVITZKY at the Berkshire Music Center. In 1950 he joined the US Army and organized the Seventh Army SO, which he conducted in more than 75 concerts in Germany and Austria; he was awarded the Army Medal of Honor for his musical services. Subsequently he conducted concerts and operas, and lectured extensively throughout Europe and the United States. In 1957 he was appointed professor of composition at North Texas State University, and in 1966 he joined the faculty of the Eastman School of Music, where he served as chair of the composition department from 1974 until his retirement in 1995. He has been a member of the composition faculty at Juilliard School since 1997, and was awarded the 2009–10 William Schuman Scholars Chair. His honors include grants from the Rockefeller (1965) and Ford (1966–71) foundations, a Koussevitzky Foundation commission (1983), a Guggenheim Fellowship (1984–5), an award from the American Academy and Institute of Arts and Letters (1990), a special citation by the American Foundation of Music Clubs (2001), and a number of teaching awards, and several honorary doctorates. In 2003, he received the Aaron Copland Award from ASCAP, for Lifetime Achievement in Music. His works have been performed by major symphony orchestras, choral and chamber ensembles throughout the United States, Europe, South America, and Israel. His book *A Study of Orchestration* (New York, 1982, 2/1989) received the ASCAP-Deems Taylor award in 1983.

Adler is a prolific composer whose music embraces a wide variety of contemporary styles. His works exhibit great rhythmic vitality, with a predilection for asymmetrical rhythms and meters, and a keen sensitivity to counterpoint. His harmonic materials vary from diatonicism and pan-diatonicism (in the works before 1969) to serial techniques (substantial use beginning with *Symphony no.4*, 1967) and occasional improvisatory and aleatory elements (e.g. in the *Concerto for Wind, Brass and Percussion*, 1968, and the *Symphony no.5*, 1975). Clustered effects and a colorful orchestral palette typify works such as the *Concerto for Flute and Orchestra* (1977). Adler's vocal compositions range from large-scale pieces reflecting a strong liturgical background to secular miniatures that are often lighthearted and humorous in nature. A number of his works have been recorded and more than 400 have been published.

SELECTED WORKS

STAGE

The Outcasts of Poker Flat (op, 1, J. Stampfer), 1959, Dallas, April 1961; The Wrestler (op, 1, Stampfer), 1971, Dallas, June 1972; The Lodge of Shadows (musical drama, J. Ramsey), Bar, orch, dancers, 1973, Fort Worth, TX, 1988; The Disappointment (op, A. Barton), 1974 [reconstruction of an early ballad opera]; The Waking (ballet, T. Roethke and others), chorus, orch, 1978

INSTRUMENTAL

Orch: Sym. no.1, 1953; Sym. no.2, 1957; Southwestern Sketches, wind, 1960; Sym. no.3 "Diptypch," 1960, rev. 1980; Requiescat in pace, 1963; Sym. no.4 "Geometrics," 1967; Conc., ww, brass, perc, 1968; Org Conc., 1970; Conc. for Orch, 1971; Sym. no.5 "We are the Echoes" (C. Adler, A.J. Heschel, J.R. Oppenheimer, M. Rukeyser, K. Wolfskehl), Mez, orch, 1975; Concertino no.2, 1976; Fl Conc., 1977; Pf Conc., 1983; Sym. no.6, 1985; Conc., ww qnt, orch, 1991; Concertino no.3, 1993; Time in Tempest Everywhere, 1993; Gui Conc., 1994; Vc Conc., 1995; Pf Conc. no.2, 1996; Max und Moritz, 1997; Horn Conc., 2000; Show an Affirming Flame, 2001; other works, incl. for wind ens, brass

Chbr and solo inst: Sonata, hn, pf, 1948; Str Qt no.3, 1953; Sonata, vn, pf, 1956; Introduction and Capriccio, hp, 1964; Pf Trio no.1, 1964; Sonata no.3, vn, pf, 1965; Sonata, vc, pf, 1966; Cantos I–XVI, various insts, 1968–2004; 4 Dialogues, euphonium, mar, 1974; Str Qt no.6 (W. Whitman), Mez/Bar, str qt, 1975; Aeolus, God of the Winds, cl, vn, vc, pf, 1977; Pf Trio no.2, 1978; Sonata, fl, pf, 1981; Str Qt no.7, 1981; Gottschalkiana, brass qnt, 1982; Sonata, va, pf, 1984; Sonata, gui, 1985; Sonata, ob, pf, 1985; Str Qt no.8, 1990; Brahmsania for 8 Horns, 1997; Pf Qt, 1999; Sonata, fl, pf, 2004; other works

Kbd: Toccata, Recitation and Postlude, org, 1959; Sonata breve, pf, 1963; Pf Sonatina, 1979; Hpd Sonata, 1982; Duo Sonata, 2 pf, 1983; other works

VOCAL

Shir chadash (Sabbath service), B, SAB, org, 1960; The Vision of Isaiah (Bible), B, SATB, orch, 1962; B'Shaaray tefilah (Sabbath service), B, SATB, org/orch, 1963; Shiru Ladonay (Sabbath service), solo/unison vv, org, 1965; Behold your God (cant., Bible), 1966; The Binding (orat, A. Friedlander, after Bible: *Genesis*, Midrash), 1967; From out of Bondage (Bible), S, A, T, B, SATB, brass qnt, perc, org, 1968; A Whole Bunch of Fun (cant., G.V. Catullus, Finjan, Moore, O. Nash, Roethke, Dr Seuss), vv, orch, 1969; We Believe (liturgical), mixed vv, 8 insts, 1974; Of Saints and Sinner (I. Feldman, W. Kaufmann, others), medium v, pf, 1976; A Falling of Saints (Rosenbaum), T, B, chorus, orch, 1977; It is to God I shall Sing (Pss), chorus, org, 1977; Of Musique, Poetrie, Nature and Love (R. Herrick), Mez, fl, pf, 1978; Snow Tracks (Amer. poets), high v, wind, 1981; Choose Life, Mez, T, SATB, orch, 1986; Five Sephardic Choruses, SATB, pf, 1998; Those were the Days, S, pf, 2000; Psalm 24, SATB, brass, org, 2003; other large choral works; numerous smaller sacred and secular choral works; works for solo vv, acc. and unacc.; works for children; arrs.

MSS in *R*

Principal publishers: Theodore Presser Company, Oxford University Press, G. Schirmer, Carl Fischer, E.C. Schirmer, Peters Edition, Ludwig Music, Southern Music Publishers, Transcontinental Music Publishers.

WRITINGS

Anthology for the Teaching of Choral Conducting (New York, 1971, 2/1985)

Sightsinging, Pitch, Interval, Rhythm (New York, 1979, 2/1997)

A Study of Orchestration (New York, 1982, 2/1989, 3/2001)

BIBLIOGRAPHY

EwenD

A.M. Rothmüller: *The Music of the Jews: an Historical Appreciation* (South Brunswick, NJ, rev. 2/1967)

J.D. Lucas: *The Operas of Samuel Adler: an Analytical Study* (diss., Louisiana State U., 1978)

H. Pollack: *Harvard Composers: Walter Piston and his Students, from Elliott Carter to Frederic Rzewski* (Metuchen, NJ, 1992)

M.-Y. Tang: *Pedagogical Works for Piano by Samuel Adler* (diss., Texas Tech Univ., 2003)

M. Shrude: "Teaching Composition in Twenty-First-Century America: A Conversation with Samuel Adler," *American Music*, xxvi/2 (2008), 223–45

MARIE ROLF/R

Adolphe, Bruce (*b* New York, NY, 31 May 1955). Composer. A graduate of the Juilliard School (BM 1976, MM 1976), he taught at the New York University Tisch School of the Arts (1983–93), at Yale University (1984–5), and in the pre-college division of the Juilliard School (1974–93). In 1992 he was appointed education director and music administrator of the Chamber Music Society of Lincoln Center. He was composer-in-residence at the Santa Fe Chamber Music Festival (1989), Music from Angel Fire (1988), the 92nd Street Y School Concert Series (1988–90), and Mannes College New School for Music (2003–4). A prolific composer of chamber music, Adolphe has been the recipient of numerous commissions, including those from the Metropolitan Opera Guild (*The Amazing Adventure of Alvin Allegretto*), the Concert Artists Guild (*Whispers of Mortality*), and the Dorian Wind Quintet (*Night Journey*). His brass quintet, *Triskelion*, was commissioned by the Music Library Association in celebration of its 60th anniversary in 1991.

Adolphe's style is characterized by harmonies built on extended tonal chords that relate in non-key-centered progressions. Like Stravinsky, Messiaen, and Takemitsu, these progressions often derive from alternative modes. Lyrical melodies in his works are treated both contrapuntally and heterophonically, with the texture remaining transparent over distinct harmonic underpinnings. In his later works (e.g., *Whispers of Mortality*, 1994; *In Memories of*, 1994; and *Body Loops*, 1995) a single rhythmic pattern appears in extremely contrasting speeds while the overall tempo remains constant, resulting in a dizzy, spinning effect. Many of his works, like *Urban Scenes* and *The Bitter, Sour, Salt Suite*, reveal a strong jazz sensibility.

Adolphe has composed several works for the stage. His first opera, *The Tell-Tale Heart* (1978), based on the short story by Edgar Allan Poe, interpolates characters other than the sole narrator of the original story. His next two works in the genre, *Mikhoels the Wise* (1982) and *The False Messiah* (1982), investigate aspects of his Jewish heritage. *The Amazing Adventure of Alvin Allegretto* (1994), his only comic opera, focuses on the title character's need to assert his individuality by speaking in the town of Harmony, where everyone sings everything; his rebellion results in child–parent conflict. The work aims to bring together the sometime disparate worlds of traditional opera and popular culture.

Adolphe is a prolific composer of music written especially for families and schools. Works like *Urban Scenes* (1993) and *Three Pieces for Kids and Orchestra* (1988), where children perform along with the orchestra in an interactive exploration of orchestral music making, and classic fairy tales such as *Little Red Riding Hood* (1997) and *Goldilocks and the Three Bears* (1998) demonstrate the composer's agility in composing works that are tonally sophisticated and accessible to audiences of all ages. His *Piano Puzzlers* (2004), a set of 30 popular tunes in the style of famous composers, have been broadcast on US public radio stations.

WRITINGS

GroveO

The Mind's Ear: Exercises for Improving the Musical Imagination for Performers, Listeners, and Composers (St Louis, 1991)

What to Listen for in the World (New York, 1996)

Of Mozart, Parrots, and Cherry Blossoms in the Wind: a Composer Explores Mysteries of the Musical Mind (New York, 1999)

WORKS
(selective list)

STAGE

The Tell-Tale Heart (opera, 1, B. Adolphe, after E.A. Poe), 1978; cond. J. Moriaty, Boston, Opera Theater of the Boston and New England Conservatories, 22 Jan 1982

Mikhoels the Wise (opera, 2, M. Gordon), 1982; cond. A. Kaiser, New York, Theresa L. Kaufmann Concert Hall, 8 May 1982

The False Messiah (opera, 2, Gordon, after G. Scholem: Life of Shabtai Zvi), 1982; Y Chorale, cond. Kaiser, New York, Theresa L. Kaufmann Concert Hall, 9 Apr 1983

The Amazing Adventure of Alvin Allegretto (comic opera, 1, S. Schlesinger, after Adolphe), 1994; cond. S. Crawford, New York, John Jay, 28 Jan 1995

Let Freedom Sing: the Story of Marian Anderson (opera, 1, C. Herron), 2009; cond. M. Rossi, Washington, DC, Atlas Performing Arts Center, 19 Mar 2009

OTHER

Orch: Nex et Maeror (conc.), vn, vc, str, 1976; 3 Pieces for Kids and Orch, 1989; 3 More Pieces for Kids and Orch, 1990; Voices of Moonlight, ob, orch, 1990; After the End, pf, orch, 1993; Body Loops, pf, orch, 1995; Songs of Radical Innocence, 1996; Carry on, Caramoor!, nar, orch, 1999; What Dreams May Come?, chbr orch, 2004; Vn Conc., vn, chbr orch, 2005

Chbr and solo inst: Desperate Measures, hn, 2 tpt, trbn, 1982; Momentum, vn, pf, 1982; Chiaroscuro, double wind qnt, 1984; 3 Lyric Pieces, vc, pf, 1984; Quartet, ob, vn, va, vc, 1984; Troika, cl, vn, vc, 1984; Dream Dance, cl, vn, vc, pf, 1985; Ballade, fl, cl, vn, vc, pf, 1986; Kaleidoscope Sextet, ob, cl, bn, vn, va, vc, 1986; Night Journey, wind qnt, 1986, arr orch; Trio, cl, vn, vc, 1986; Rikudim, fl, hp, 1988; At the Still Point, there the Dance is, cl, str qt, 1989; By a Grace of Sense Surrounded (Str Qt no.1), 1989; Dreamsong, va, pf, 1989; Triskelion, hn, 2 tpt, trbn, b trbn, 1990; Bridgehampton Conc., fl, ob, hpd, 2 vn, va, vc, db, 1991; A White Light Still and Moving, vc, 1991; And All is Always Now, vn, pf, 1992; In Memories of, pf, str qt, 1992; Turning, Returning (Str Qt no.2), 1992; Urban Scenes for Str Qt and Kids!, str qt, children's toys, 1993; Hoodoo Duos: no.1, 2 vn; no.2, vn, vc; no.3, va, db, 1994; Whispers of Mortality (Str Qt no.4), 1994; Couple, vc, pf, 1998; Memories of a Possible Future, pf, str qrt, 1999, rev. 2001; Oh Gesualdo, Divine Tormentor, str qt, 2004; The Tiger's Ear: Listening to Abstract Expressionist Paintings, fl, ob, vn, va, vc, pf, 2006; Self Comes to Mind (A. Damasio), vc, 2 perc, nar, collab. Damasio, 2008

Vocal: She is thy Life (cant., Bible: *Proverbs*), S, A, T, Bar, chorus, 2 tpt, hn, trbn/org, 1982; To his Imaginary Mistress (R. Herrick), T, pf, 1982; Ladino Songs of Love and Suffering (folk poetry), S, hn, gui, 1984; Canticum arcanum (medieval incantations), T, vv, pf, vn, 1986; Marita and her Heart's Desire (L. Gikow), nar, fl + pic, ob, cl, bn, trbn, hp, str, 1994; The Bitter, Sour, Salt Suite (L. Gikow), nar, vn, 1995; A Thousand Years of Love (love poems spanning 1000 years), S, pf, 1998; Out of the Whirlwind (texts written by survivors and victims of the Holocaust), Mez, T, wind ens, 2004; Songs of Life and Love (poems by Iranian, Palestinian, Lebanese, and Israeli women), 2004; Wind across the Sky (traditional poems by Iroquois Indians and other Amerindians), S, pf trio, 2005; Dell'arte e delle cipolle: Omaggio al Bronzino (A. Bronzino, F. Petrarch), SSATB, b viol., hpd, vib, 2010

Young Audiences: Urban Scenes for Str Qt and Kids!, str qt, children's toys, 1993; Little Red Riding Hood (text based on the original story and language by C. Perrault, with additions and alterations by the composer), nar, vn, va, ob, pf, 1997; Goldilocks and the Three Bears (text by the composer), nar, vn, va, vc, ob, pf, 1998; Piano Puzzlers, pf, 2004

JAMES P. CASSARO

Adorno, Theodor (Ludwig) W[iesengrund] (*b* Frankfurt, Germany, 11 Sept 1903; *d* Brig, Switzerland, 6 Aug 1969). German philosopher, social theorist, writer on music, and composer. He came of age during the *Amerikanismus* of the Weimar Republic, becoming a confidant of the Schoenberg circle, was a prominent member of the

Institute for Social Research in Frankfurt from 1931, spent 15 years in exile (1934–49, in Oxford, New York, and Los Angeles), and returned to Germany to accept the chair in philosophy at Frankfurt University. He was one of the foremost music intellectuals of the 20th century. His pervasive influence is traceable across a number of scholarly disciplines, where he is known not only as a principal figure associated with the Frankfurt School and its Marxist orientations, and a leading advocate of critical theory in postwar Germany, but also as a radical commentator on modernism more generally, and a trenchant critic of what he called the culture industry.

Born to a Jewish father and a Catholic mother, Adorno received piano and composition lessons from an early age. From 1918, his weekly readings from Kant's *Critique of Pure Reason* with Siegfried Kracauer led him—he explains—to interpret conceptual contradictions as symptoms of historical antagonisms sedimented within the concepts and organization of philosophical texts. In 1921 he began studying philosophy at Frankfurt University under Hans Cornelius, with secondary fields in musicology, sociology, and psychology; by 1924 he had gained his doctorate with a dissertation on Husserl (*Die Transzendenz des Dinglichen und Noematischen in Husserls Phänomenologie*). It was during these student years that he met Max Horkheimer and Walter Benjamin, who would prove so influential in his later writings. From 1925, Adorno studied composition with Alban Berg, and piano with EDUARD STEUERMANN in Vienna, cementing his Second Viennese School affiliation through further contact with Schoenberg and Webern. Adorno completed his *Habilitationschrift* at the second attempt under Paul Tillich in 1931 with a study of Kirkegaard's aesthetics (his first attempt, drawing together Freudian psychoanalysis and Kantian Idealism, had not been successful in 1927). At this time he began working as a lecturer in philosophy at Frankfurt University. But in 1933, after just two years in the post, he was expelled by the Nazis as a left-leaning Jew; he left Germany the following spring.

While in exile he enrolled for a DPhil at Oxford University, but left for New York in 1938, where Frankfurt's Institute for Social Research had itself resettled under Horkheimer at Columbia University. While his first essays for the Institute from the 1930s had appeared under the aggressive pseudonym Hektor Rottweiler—"On Jazz" (1936) and "The Fetish Character of Music and the Regression of Listening" (1938)—it was in exile that Adorno began writing his major works: *Dialectic of Enlightenment* (with Horkheimer; 1947), *Philosophy of New Music* (1949), *The Authoritarian Personality* (collaboratively authored; New York, 1950), and *Minima Moralia* (Frankfurt, 1951). Against the aftermath of wartime atrocities, he sets out virulent critiques of the culture industry, incorporating the failure of the Enlightenment into a dual perspective where "myth is already enlightenment, and enlightenment reverts to mythology" (*Dialectic of Enlightenment*, xviii). He also evaluated the potential musical "material," that is, the ordering and arrangement of notes as well as a work's formal structure, in ethical terms as a seismographic register of the intricate traumas of each historical age, and, within modernism in particular, as a means of either resisting music's fate as a commodity (at the price of its popular appeal) or of giving in to this fate through reified, regressive structures and meaningless kitsch. A number of recent scholars have criticized Adorno's sustained polemic against jazz and popular music, while others have situated it in the broader context of his critique of commoditized culture.

On returning to Frankfurt's philosophy department in 1949 as full professor, Adorno's work for the institute intensified; he became co-director with Horkheimer, taking over as sole director in 1958. He also began taking part in the summer courses at Darmstadt from 1954, co-teaching courses on performance with the violinist Rudolf Kolisch, as well as lecturing on serialism and music criticism. Writings from this period include monographs on Wagner (1952), Mahler (1960), and Berg (1968); the socio-cultural studies collected in *Prisms* (1955); the diatribe against metaphysics *Against Epistemology* (1956); and his lecture course *Introduction to the Sociology of Music* (1962).

Adorno's leadership profile within postwar West-German academia embroiled him in debates with other prominent intellectuals, student activist groups, and their right-wing critics, including the "positivist dispute" with Karl Popper (1969), Adorno's assault on Heideggerian phenomenology (1964), and even naked sit-ins by students in the lecture halls of the Frankfurt Institute (1969). In his final years, Adorno's two major projects were *Negative Dialectics* (1966) and the incomplete *Aesthetic Theory* (1970), a paradoxical defence both of modernism and its illusions that tackles the problem of discussing art—the "sedimented history of human misery"—in an age when "it is self-evident that nothing concerning art is self-evident anymore."

WRITINGS

with M. Horkheimer: *Dialektik der Aufklärung: philosophische Fragmente* (Amsterdam, 1947/*R*; Eng. trans., 1972, 2002)
Philosophie der neuen Musik (Tübingen, 1949, 3/1967; Eng. trans., 1973/*R*)
Prismen (Berlin and Frankfurt, 1955; Eng. trans., 1967/*R*)
Mahler: Eine musikalische Physiognomik (Frankfurt, 1960/*R*, 2/1963; Eng. trans., 1992)
Negative Dialektik (Frankfurt, 1967; Eng. trans., 1973)
Ästhetische Theorie (Frankfurt, 1970; Eng. trans., 1984, 1997)

BIBLIOGRAPHY

Grove7 (M. Paddison)
R.R. Subotnik: *Developing Variations: Style and Ideology in Western Music* (Minneapolis, 1991)
L. Zuidervaart: *Adorno's Aesthetic Theory: The Redemption of Illusion* (Cambridge, MA, 1991)
M. Paddison: *Adorno's Aesthetics of Music* (Cambridge and New York, 1993)
C. Menke: *The Sovereignty of Art: Aesthetic Negativity in Adorno and Derrida*, trans. N. Solomon (Cambridge, MA, 1998)
M. O'Neill, ed.: *Adorno, Culture and Feminism* (London, 1999)
N. Gibson and A. Rubin, eds.: *Adorno: a Critical Reader* (Oxford and Malden, MA, 2002)
T. DeNora: *After Adorno: Rethinking Music Sociology* (Cambridge, 2003)
S. Müller-Doohm: *Adorno: a Biography*, trans. Rodney Livingstone (Cambridge, 2005)

DAVID TRIPPETT

Adult contemporary. A term used to describe popular music that appeals to listeners between the ages of 25 and 55. Because it is based primarily on marketing demographics rather than being strictly defined by musical elements, it embraces a wide range of genres. In the 1950s the moniker "middle of the road" (or "MOR") was given to radio stations that played music intended for older audiences, including swing- and big band-influenced tunes. These stations arranged their playlists to be separate from youth-oriented rock and roll. When *Billboard* began to echo this format in 1961, their adult-oriented chart was entitled EASY LISTENING. After changing names several times, the chart officially became known as Adult Contemporary in 1979. The distinction between youth-oriented and adult-oriented music has remained important into the 21st century, notably with the television stations MTV (youth-oriented) and VH-1 (adult-oriented).

As musical genres, radio formats, and industry charts have split and morphed, so too have the categories of adult contemporary music. In the 2010s the largest subgenre was hot adult contemporary, which typically featured a mix of hits from previous decades alongside contemporary light rock and softer R&B. Rap music, heavy metal, and dance club music are types of youth-oriented music typically excluded from this admittedly ambiguous format. Mainstream adult contemporary concentrated on somewhat lighter fare. Soft adult contemporary featured more acoustic numbers and ballads by such artists as Mariah Carey and Josh Grobin. While soft adult contemporary has been often geared towards white middle-class audiences, urban adult contemporary has been targeted to reach African American audiences with soft R&B music from such artists as Anita Baker, Whitney Houston, and Luther Vandross.

JONAS WESTOVER

Advertising. Music has been used for the purpose of selling goods for millennia, probably as long as there has been commerce. Street cries, medicine shows, and many other situations offered ways to employ songs that sell before the advent of recording or broadcasting. Medicine show musicians seldom performed songs extolling the virtue of a particular product, but their entertainment made sales pitches less unwelcome, a strategy that persists to this day.

Sheet music published in the 19th century frequently included advertisements, though seldom related to the songs. By the very early 20th century, songs were composed to sell goods, such as "Under the Anheuser Bush" (1903), or mentioned the name of a product, such as, most famously, "In My Merry Oldsmobile" (1905). Lyrics to popular songs would also be replaced with those that mentioned the names of products.

With the rise of radio in the 1920s, music was employed for advertising purposes, though convincing advertising executives, accustomed to advertising in print, that the new medium could be suitable for advertising took some time. There was considerable wariness about placing commercial messages on the radio in the early 1920s for fear of alienating listeners. And there was some public resistance to using the new medium for advertising. The advertising and nascent broadcasting industries thus decided on what was called a "goodwill" model, in which programs were largely produced by advertising agencies for sponsors. Audiences, it was hoped, would be grateful for free entertainment and would not mind an occasional sales message embedded in the program. It was also common in this era to employ the sponsor's name in the program's title, resulting in programs with titles such as *The Eveready Hour*, an early variety program featuring music.

There were frequent debates in the radio and advertising trade press about what kind of music was most suitable to be played on the radio. Since most radio programs before World War II were sponsored by corporations and produced by advertising agencies, this was an important question for advertisers. Most programming was aimed at an audience characterized as middlebrow, a term that came into frequent usage in this era.

In this era, musicians frequently took the name of sponsors, so, for example, the singing duo of Billy Jones and Ernest Hare became known as the Happiness Boys, since their program was sponsored by the Happiness Candy Company. Some confections could be subtler. Virginia Rea and Frank Munn became known as Olive Palmer and Paul Oliver, the featured singers on *The Palmolive Hour*. The practice of naming performers for their sponsors proved to be detrimental to the careers of many musicians, whose sponsors would change, as did the names of the musicians or groups. The Happiness Boys later became the Interwoven Pair, for Interwoven Socks. Audiences struggled to keep up with their favorite musicians as their sponsors shifted.

In the absence of pictures, music on the radio was used almost exclusively to animate a product, to give it, as workers in the industry said, a personality. Thus, for the *Clicquot Club Eskimos* program, the musicians used were mainly a banjo ensemble under the direction of the virtuoso Harry Reser, for it was thought that the sound of banjos vivified the snap and effervescence of Clicquot Club ginger ale.

Sponsored programs frequently employed theme songs that inevitably mentioned the name of the sponsor's product since that was usually in the program's title. These theme songs were part of the genesis of the JINGLE, which emerged during the Great Depression as advertisers became increasingly aggressive, willing to jettison the goodwill model in difficult economic times. There were countless local and regional jingles before the rise of the nationally broadcast jingles of the 1940s, beginning with the massive success of "Pepsi-Cola Hits the Spot," which appeared in 1939. The Pepsi jingle, like many that followed, was based on public domain songs, so that copyright fees could be avoided, though many jingles were specially composed as well. This was the first standalone jingle, not attached to a program, made possible by Pepsi-Cola's president's purchase of the jingle from its composers, and subsequent lease of short amounts of time on a struggling New Jersey radio station. Before this, airtime was leased in units longer than the 60 seconds necessary for the standalone commercial. The jingle is thus responsible for the rise of short commercials of any type.

Music production companies, commonly known as jingle houses, sprang up in the 1950s and after. Jingles and other advertising songs from their inception tracked the popular music styles of the day, usually lagging behind so as to avoid the risk of offending audiences. With the rise of rock-and-roll in the mid-1950s, many Broadway and Tin Pan Alley musicians found it difficult to make a living and turned to jingle writing. Frank Loesser formed his own jingle company and employed Hoagy Carmichael, Vernon Duke, and Harold Rome, among others. Loesser and other Broadway musicians frequently leased their songs for commercial use, sometimes even before the songs appeared before the public. Loesser arranged with the Ford Motor Company to reuse "Standin' on the Corner," from *The Most Happy Fella* (1956), so the line "watchin' all the girls go by" became "watchin' all the Fords go by."

The production of advertising music became increasingly professionalized in this era with the entry of established composers into the ranks of advertising musicians. Large budgets facilitated the production of lavish, Hollywood musical-style numbers such as "See the U.S.A. in Your Chevrolet" from 1952. Composers who specialized in jingles arose, as did jingle singers, who had to cultivate extremely clear diction in order to enunciate lyrics—and, most importantly, the product name.

The rise of television after World War II did not have a noticeable impact on the sound of advertising music, for early television, as many in the advertising industry noted at the time, was conceived simply as radio with pictures. But by the late 1950s some musicians began to speak of employing music for its affective purposes. Affect was almost never discussed with respect to music in the radio era, but as television production matured, composition for television became increasingly like composition for films, with the exception of the continued use of the jingle. Interest in affect in this period was related to new modes of selling that employed various psychological theories to pitch goods, the employment of which was decried in Vance Packard's best-selling *The Hidden Persuaders* of 1957.

The rise of multitrack recording in the 1950s eventually led to a practice of recording a single jingle singer multiple times, resulting in a homogenous sound that was known in the industry as the "Madison Avenue Choir," a sound that was widely employed throughout the 1960s and 1970s and featured a chorus singing in ecstatic and energetic approbation about a product in a kind of secularized gospel style. With this sound, advertising music came into its own as a distinct, recognizable genre, no longer simply mimicking popular styles.

At almost the same moment, however, the advertising industry's growing cultivation of the youth market began to affect advertising music production. While there were attempts to address youth through music before the early 1960s, the most notable campaigns to seek the attention of youth were conducted by Pepsi-Cola and Coca-Cola. Pepsi's first attempts, in the early 1960s, did not employ music that would likely attract the notice of youths (a jazzy version of "Makin' Whoopee" from 1928). The Pepsi Generation series of campaigns, however, were a milestone in the history of advertising, the first time that the youth market had been assiduously sought over multiple campaigns, culminating in the 1980s with Pepsi's hiring of Michael Jackson for several commercials in 1984, and more in 1987. It was Coca-Cola, however, that produced the most memorable and influential of all these commercials, the famous "Hilltop" advertisement from 1971, with music by Bill Backer, Billy Davis, Roger Cook, and Roger Greenaway, better known as "I'd Like to Teach the World to Sing."

This discovery of baby-boom youth was to have profound consequences for the advertising industry, and not just as a new market to exploit. When baby boomers began to achieve positions of authority in the industry in the 1980s, they did not hesitate to denigrate and eschew the jingle—by this period, the workhorse of the industry for decades—and began to use the music of their youth in commercials instead, either re-recording the original music, or licensing the original recording, which frequently prompted fan outrage. The most notorious case was Nike's use of the Beatles' "Revolution" in 1987, the first use of the Beatles' music in a commercial. Even though this music was legally licensed, Nike's advertising agency's use of it prompted a lawsuit by Apple Records, which was settled out of court in 1989; Nike had voluntarily ceased using the song in commercials the previous year.

Focus on the baby boom market didn't wane, but was only the beginning of the advertising industry's long infatuation with the youth market. Many in the advertising industry realized the profit potential of licensing existing music by popular musicians for use in advertising to capture the youth market, despite the outcry over the use of "Revolution." Two publications appeared to help educate those in the advertising industry about using popular music in commercials: *RockBill* (similar to *Playbill*), which was published from 1976 to the mid-1980s, and *Marketing through Music*, a newsletter published by *Rolling Stone* from 1986 to 1989. Regardless of the effectiveness of these publications, the music and advertising industries were coming closer together in this era, and it became increasingly common for corporations to sponsor rock musicians' tours as part of a broader arrangement that could include the use of those musicians' music in commercials.

The world of advertising music was a proving ground for many musicians, who learned how to work in recording studios, for producers would occasionally place young bands in studios for advertising work so that they could become comfortable in the studio. And many aspiring singers or songwriters or instrumentalists or composers learned their craft in advertising, musicians such as Herbie Hancock, Mitch Leigh, and, perhaps most famously, Barry Manilow, who wrote memorable jingles such as "I am stuck on Band-Aid brand" and

"Like a Good Neighbor" for State Farm Insurance in the 1970s, jingles that can still be heard today.

Several major shifts in the 1980s and into the 1990s greatly altered the landscape of the production of advertising music. One was the rise of digital technologies, which had a massive impact on the field, as it did in the realm of the production of popular music more generally. Advertising music composers accustomed to virtually unlimited budgets that allowed them to hire major popular musicians to record advertising music, frequently as part of a large number of musicians, found themselves increasingly constrained by these new technologies. Many musicians who had been in the business for a long time quit, as they were unable or unwilling to learn new technologies and participate in the never-ending race to acquire the best and newest expensive equipment. This provided an opening for younger musicians from the world of rock, who were more proficient in this area. They also tended not to be members of the American Federation of Musicians, which meant that they could be hired for less money. Today, as a result of these new technologies, advertising musicians are frequently expected to produce music in extremely short amounts of time, sometimes less than 24 hours, a far cry from the big-budget era in which a national campaign with music could take a year to mount.

The second significant change in this era was Ronald Reagan's promulgation of neoliberal policies that resulted in a raft of mergers and acquisitions in the advertising industry that put more pressure on firms to be profitable. Music budgets were reduced, and musicians' work was increasingly subject to audience testing and other sorts of measures, which musicians found greatly disheartening, prompting some to leave the business.

Neoliberal policies continued into the 1990s, ushering in another major shift with the passage of the Communications Act of 1996, a law that permitted for the first time the ownership by a single entity of more than one radio station in the same format in the same market. Major corporations quickly streamlined and consolidated radio playlists, resulting in far fewer opportunities for musicians to be heard. With this decline of radio broadcast opportunities, many musicians soon lost their aversion to appearing in television commercials, and the number of such commercials rose to the extent that advertising industry workers began comparing themselves to disc jockeys of the past, the taste arbiters who found new music to promote to the masses. The measure of success for many popular musicians has ceased to be the position achieved on the *Billboard* charts, but the number of appearances in commercials for major brands and usages in popular television programs and films.

A new phase of the complicity of the advertising with the music industries emerged in 2000, when English rock musician Sting recorded a single entitled "Desert Rose," for which a video that featured a Jaguar automobile was produced. His manager forged an agreement with Jaguar to produce a commercial that employed Sting's music. This arrangement, which was part of which became increasingly known in the industry as the "convergence of commerce and content," served as a model of future arrangements in which popular musicians and national and international brands are increasingly intertwined. Today, major brands sponsor musicians' Las Vegas shows, musicians sing songs in commercials that they later include on albums, major brands invite fans to remix the music of an old jingle online, promising to air the best judged remix in a commercial, and much more. A new industry has emerged that seeks to link musicians to advertising and broadcasting opportunities, and major record labels have created offices that similarly help to place music. Far from following trends in popular music, the advertising industry, working in concert with the music industry, is today in a position to create them.

See also TELEVISION MUSIC.

BIBLIOGRAPHY

F. Presbrey: *The History and Development of Advertising* (New York, 1929)

L.M. Scott: "Understanding Jingles and Needledrop: a Rhetorical Approach to Music in Advertising," *Journal of Consumer Research*, xvii (1990), 223–36

S. Smulyan: *Selling Radio: The Commercialization of American Broadcasting 1920–1934* (Washington, DC, 1994)

T. Frank: *The Conquest of Cool: Business Culture, Counterculture, and the Rise of Hip Consumerism* (Chicago, 1997)

B. Klein: *As Heard on TV: Popular Music in Advertising* (Burlington, VT, 2009)

T.D. Taylor: *The Sounds of Capitalism: Advertising, Music, and the Conquest of Culture* (Chicago, 2012)

TIMOTHY D. TAYLOR

AEC. *See* ART ENSEMBLE OF CHICAGO (AEC).

Aeolian. Name associated with a series of piano, organ, and player piano manufacturers.

1. Aeolian Co. 2. American Piano Co. 3. Aeolian Corporation.

1. AEOLIAN CO. Founded by William B(urton) Tremaine (1840–1907), who had begun as a piano maker with Tremaine Brothers in New York. He formed the Mechanical Orguinette Co. (1878) and the Aeolian Organ & Music Co. (1887; from 1895 the Aeolian Co.) to manufacture automatic organs that used perforated music rolls (*see* PLAYER ORGAN). EDWIN SCOTT VOTEY, inventor of the Pianola, the first practical piano player and the most famous name among automatic piano brands, joined the Aeolian Co. in 1897. Henry B. Tremaine (1866–1932), the founder's son, tapped a larger market with an extensive advertising campaign for player pianos in the first three decades of the 20th century. In 1913 Aeolian introduced the Duo-Art reproducing piano, a mechanism (fitted in high-quality pianos) that made it possible to record on paper rolls the slightest nuances of dynamics, tempo and phrasing. Many leading pianists were recorded on Duo-Art machines.

At the turn of the century self-playing organs were becoming a status symbol in the homes of the wealthy, a trend that would continue for the ensuing three decades. Aeolian had begun applying player mechanisms to pipe organs as early as 1895, initially in conjunction with the Ferrand & Votey firm, but eventually established its own factory at Garwood, New Jersey, directed after 1916 by Edwin Votey. The application of the Duo-Art technology in this period enhanced the popularity of Aeolian's residential organs, as well as their ability to reproduce the playing of notable organists such as Yon, Shelley, Eddy, Bonnet, Courboin, and Dupré, who were among the many artists who cut player rolls for Aeolian. While the majority of Aeolian residential player-organs were built for North American clients (including the largest, with four manuals, installed in 1929 at "Longwood," the estate of industrialist Pierre S. DuPont), such instruments were also exported, a significant number going to England; a smaller number went to purchasers in Argentina, Australia, Belgium, France, Germany, and Spain. Although Aeolian had always had a few non-residential clients, during the late 1920s the firm made a conscious effort to branch out into the field of larger church and concert-hall organs, usually without self-players. However, their major stock-in-trade was still residential organs, a market devastated by the stock market crash of 1929; such a large market loss could not be sustained, and following the completion of the large four-manual organ for Duke University Chapel in 1930, Aeolian closed its organ-building operation, selling its assets the following year to the competing firm of the E.M. Skinner firm of Boston, which then became known as the Aeolian-Skinner Organ Co.

In 1903 Tremaine formed the Aeolian, Weber Piano & Pianola Co., of which the Aeolian Co. was a significant part. It took control of a number of important but failing American firms, such as George Steck & Co., Stroud Piano Co., and Weber Piano Co.; some significant reed organ and automatic organ companies, such as Vocalion and Votey Organ Co.; and overseas companies such as Choralian Co. of Germany and Austria, Orchestrelle Co. of Britain, and Pianola Company Proprietary Ltd of Australia. In addition to pianos and the Duo-Art mechanism, the company developed and aggressively promoted such self-playing mechanical instruments as the Aeriole, the Aeolian Orchestrelle Pianola and reed organ, the Metrostyle Pianola, and Aeolian pipe organs. The firm maintained the Aeolian Concert Hall in New York essentially as a showroom for its instruments, although many noted musicians performed there. In 1932 the Aeolian, Weber Piano & Pianola Co. merged with the American Piano Corporation to form the Aeolian American Corporation.

2. American Piano Co. Incorporated in June 1908, it consolidated such earlier American piano companies as Chickering & Sons of Boston and Knabe & Co. of Baltimore with companies owned by the Foster-Armstrong Co. Foster-Armstrong, founded in 1894 in Rochester, New York, by George G. Foster and W.B. Armstrong, had bought the Marshall & Wendell Piano Co. of Albany, New York, in 1899. After the construction of a new factory in East Rochester, New York, in 1906, the company acquired other piano makers and incorporated with a capital of $12 million.

Formed to manufacture pianos ranging from concert grands to mass-produced commercial uprights, the American Piano Co. established a player piano department in 1909. Its Ampico reproducing system, invented in 1913 by Charles Fuller Stoddard, dominated the American automatic piano market along with Aeolian's Duo-Art and the German Welte-Mignon mechanism. The company acquired the Mason & Hamlin Piano Co. in 1922 and sold it to the Aeolian Co. in the early 1930s. Becoming the American Piano Corporation in 1930, it merged with its primary competitor, the Aeolian Co., on 1 September 1932 to form the Aeolian American Corporation in an effort to survive the crises of the Depression and the new technologies of radio and phonograph as rivals to the piano.

3. Aeolian Corporation. The successor to the Aeolian Co. and the American Piano Co. It was called the Aeolian American Corporation from 1932 until 1959. In May of that year Winter & Co. purchased the assets of the corporation, renaming the company the Aeolian Corporation, but retaining the name Aeolian American Corporation for the East Rochester, New York, division until 1971, when it was changed to the Aeolian American Division of the Aeolian Corporation.

The company owned the assets of many earlier American piano manufacturers and made pianos in Toronto, East Rochester, and Memphis under the following trade names: Mason & Risch; Mason & Hamlin; Chickering & Sons; Knabe & Co.; Cable; Winter; Hardman, Peck; Kranich & Bach; J. & C. Fischer; George Steck; Vose & Sons; Henry F. Miller; Ivers & Pond; Melodigrand; Duo-Art; Musette; and Pianola Player Piano.

Peter Perez, former president of Steinway & Sons, bought the Aeolian Corporation in 1983 and operated it until 1985, when the firm declared bankruptcy and closed the East Rochester factory. Its assets were distributed among Sohmer & Co., Wurlitzer Piano Co. and Young Chang. Some brand names have since been retired; others have come under the control of companies in the United States, Korea, and China.

See also Chickering; Knabe; Mason & Hamlin; Hugo Sohmer; Wurlitzer.

BIBLIOGRAPHY

A. Dolge: *Pianos and their Makers* (Covina, CA, 1911/*R*)

G. Kobbé: *The Aeolian Pipe-Organ* (New York, *c*1917)

Q.D. Bowers: *Encyclopedia of Automatic Music Instruments* (Vestal, NY, 1972)

A.W.J.G. Ord-Hume: *Pianola: the History of the Self-Playing Piano* (London, 1984)

H. Jüttemann: "Die mechanischen Harmonien der Firma Aeolian," *Das mechanische Musikinstrument*, no.46 (1988), 15–23

N. Barden: "A History of the Aeolian Company," *American Organist*, xxiv (1990), 254–60

R. Smith: *The Aeolian Pipe Organ and its Music* (Richmond, VA, 1998)

CYNTHIA ADAMS HOOVER/EDWIN M. GOOD, BARBARA OWEN/R

Aeolian Chamber Players. Ensemble. Formed in New York in 1961 by the violinist Lewis Kaplan, the Aeolian Chamber Players were the first American ensemble of mixed instruments to perform together on a permanent basis. The group, which first played at Mount Holyoke

College, Massachusetts, in October 1961 and made its New York debut shortly thereafter (Town Hall, January 1962), originally consisted of Kaplan, flutist Harold Jones, clarinetist Robert Listokin, and pianist Gilbert Kalish. A cello was added in 1966, with the flute rarely used since 1977. The group has been the resident ensemble at Bowdoin College in Brunswick, Maine, since 1964, where the Bowdoin Summer Music Festival, co-founded and directed by Kaplan, takes place. Former members of the ensemble include Jennifer Langbaum and Ronald Thomas (cello), and Charles Neidrich and Thomas Hill (clarinet). The present group includes Kaplan (violin), André Emelianoff (cello), and Peter Basquin (piano). The group, which is recognized for its commitment to both traditional and contemporary repertoire, has toured throughout the United States and Europe. At the Salzburg Festival of 1992, it performed a four-concert series of 20th-century American music. Since its debut, the ensemble has commissioned and performed works by Babbitt, Berio, Bolcom, Chou Wen-chung, Crumb, Davidovsky, Carman Moore, Rochberg, Elliott Schwartz, Ralph Shapey, Subotnick, and Chinary Ung. It has made a number of recordings, the best-known of which is Crumb's *Night of the Four Moons*, nominated for a Grammy award in 1998.

KAREN MONSON/MICHAEL BAUMGARTNER

Aeolian-Skinner Organ Co. Organ-building firm. Founded in 1901 by Ernest M. Skinner, it became one of the leading builders in the country during the first half of the 20th century. It absorbed the organ division of the failing Aeolian firm in 1931 and became known as Aeolian-Skinner from that time onward. With the advent and eventual leadership of G. Donald Harrison, beginning in the 1930s, its tonal emphasis gradually shifted from a suave mastery of orchestral sound to leadership in the realm of a brighter, more classically oriented and eclectic tonal aesthetic that made it an industry leader in the midpoint of the century, and the standard-bearer of what Harrison termed the "American Classic" sound. Both Skinner and Harrison had possessed the technical and musical skill to keep that position of leadership through good times and bad, but upon Harrison's sudden demise in 1956 leadership fell on the shoulders of Joseph S. Whiteford, a lawyer and the majority stockholder, who then became president. Although he attempted to perpetuate Harrison's legacy, he was ill-equipped to do so, and the company began to decline in favor and in quality. During the early 1960s Whiteford withdrew his interest and Donald M. Gillett, the firm's head voicer, became president. In an attempt to attract new talent, Robert L. Sipe, who had been building organs in Dallas, came to the company in 1968, becoming vice president and tonal director in 1970. Under Gillett and Sipe some major organs were still being built, notably those for Lincoln Center in New York (1962) and Kennedy Center in Washington (1969). In 1969 the company moved from its deteriorating Boston buildings to a new location in nearby Randolph, and in an attempt to keep up with some of the newer trends of the period, a few modest mechanical-action organs were built there beginning in 1970. However, the firm's financial position continued to worsen, and by 1972 it was forced to leave its new quarters. Gillett left to become tonal director of the rival M. P. Möller firm and Sipe returned to Texas. Emil David Knutson, chairman of the board, briefly assumed the presidency, but less than a year later Aeolian-Skinner's few remaining assets were sold, and the company ceased to exist.

BIBLIOGRAPHY

N. Barden: "A History of the Aeolian-Skinner Co.: The Post-Harrison Years," *The American Organist,* xxiv/5 (1990)

J. Tyrell: "My Years at Aeolian-Skinner," *Journal of American Organbuilding,* x/4 (1995)

C. Callahan: *Aeolian-Skinner Remembered* (Minneapolis, 1996)

A. Kinzey and S. Lawn: *E. M. Skinner/Aeolian-Skinner Opus List* (Richmond, VA, 1997)

C. R. Whitney: *All the Stops* (New York, 2003)

BARBARA OWEN

Aeolian Vocalists. Vocal trio, nucleus of the group later known as the Hutchinson Family; *see* HUTCHINSON.

Aerosmith. Rock group formed in Boston in 1970. The band's best-known lineup featured Tom Hamilton (*b* Colorado Springs, CO, 31 Dec 1951; bass guitar), Joey Kramer (*b* New York, NY, 21 June 1950; drums), Joe Perry (*b* Boston, MA, 10 Sept 1950; electric guitar), Steven Tyler (Tallarico) (*b* New York, NY, 26 March 1948; vocals), and Brad Whitford (*b* Reading, MA, 23 Feb 1952; electric guitar). Its first material comprised a deft blend of rock and blues. With Tyler's supple voice and convincing rock swagger, the group's technical proficiency produced a refined, confident sound beyond mere flash.

Aerosmith were initially dismissed by critics, who perceived them as imitators of the Rolling Stones. Until 1975 their cocksure boogie riffs and thick studio mixing won them support in Boston and the Midwest, but left them ignored on the West Coast and in the South. Among their early recordings, their power ballad "Dream On" stands out. A breakthrough came with *Rocks* (1976), their most critically celebrated album. In its wake, however, Aerosmith peaked then receded unceremoniously, as drug dependency, delayed album production, and artistic differences precipitated the departures of Perry and Whitford (1979 and 1981 respectively). Reunited in 1985, the group staged an impressive comeback, regaining the commercial success they enjoyed in the mid-1970s. Collaborating with Run-D.M.C., Perry and Tyler helped bring rap music into the mainstream through a crossover version of their song "Walk this Way" which they had originally released in 1975 and was awarded the Soul Train Music Award for Best Rap Single of 1986. Equally successful were mainstream singles "Janie's got a gun" and "Dude (Looks like a Lady)". A trio of power ballads, "Cryin'," "Crazy," and "Amazing" and associated music videos assured the group's success into the 1990s. Aerosmith remained relevant in the grunge era with touring and appearances in Hollywood films and at the festival Woodstock '94. They fully embraced pop sensibilities, beginning with

"Pink" (1996) and culminating with their Super Bowl XXXV performance alongside *NSYNC, Britney Spears, Mary J. Blige, and Nelly. Their starring role in the video game *Guitar Hero: Aerosmith* as well as their tour with KISS appeared to revive their rock credibility.

America's best-selling rock band, Aerosmith have succeeded throughout with riff-oriented rock songs and power ballads in support of Tyler's diverse lyrical topics. With 21 top 40 hits to their credit, four Grammy Awards, and ten MTV Video Music Awards, they were inducted into the Rock and Roll Hall of Fame in 2001.

ROBERT WALSER/MICHAEL ETHEN

Aesop Rock [Bavitz, Ian Matthias] (*b* Northport, Long Island, NY, 5 June 1976). Hip-hop lyricist, vocalist, and producer. Aesop Rock began his career in alternative/underground hip-hop music with two self-financed albums that blended an eclectic approach to sample-based production with poetic, figurative lyrics. His creative output has helped to establish him as a prolific solo artist with a commitment to renovating the rap genre with politically charged songs and experimental production techniques.

Aesop's abstract lyrics have met divided critical responses: some dismiss them as meaningless wordplay, while others argue that more identifiable themes are present across his work. These include contemplations of urban life in New York City, consumerism, wage slavery/labor issues, religion in modern society, and media constructions of reality. Some songs clearly balance abstraction with thoroughly contextualized scenarios; for example, "No Regrets" from the *Labor Days* LP features the story of a young girl evolving from sidewalk chalk drawings through a full life devoted to her passion for art; and "One of Four (Thank You)" from the *Daylight* EP depicts the Aesop's real-life nervous breakdown and expresses gratitude for four friends who aided his psychological recovery. Aesop's vocal style features multiple, intercut audio tracks recorded in contrasting tones and caricatured voices. This approach creates the effect of a dialogue or, perhaps, a monologue of split personalities.

The beats behind Aesop's music have evolved over time. Early self-produced albums such as *Music for Earthworms* featured tracks produced by Dub-L and Blockhead, and also included contributions from DJs such as DJ JS-One, Plain Pat, and Mattimal. Collaborations with Blockhead increased on *Labor Days*, his first album with the Definitive Jux label. Starting with *Bazooka Tooth*, however, Aesop began to produce more of his own music, resulting in what some hear as an unconventional sound departing from mainstream hip hop.

RECORDINGS
(selected)

Music for Earthworms, no label (1997); *Appleseed* (EP), no label (1999); *Float*, Mush Records, MH-202 (2000); *Labor Days*, Definitive Jux, DJX13 (2001); *Daylight* (EP), Definitive Jux, DJX21 (2002); *Bazooka Tooth*, Definitive Jux, DJX068-2 (2003); *Fast Cars, Danger, Fire and Knives* (EP), Definitive Jux, DJX106 (2005); *None Shall Pass*, Definitive Jux, DJX144 (2007)

JORDAN A. YAMAJI SMITH

AFM. *See* AMERICAN FEDERATION OF MUSICIANS (AFM).

African American music. A term applied to distinct configurations of sound organization linked historically and socially to people of African descent living within the United States. While scholarship has identified a shared body of conceptual approaches to sound among the numerous idioms of African American music, musicians have employed them across various functional divides in American culture such as written and oral, sacred and secular, art and popular. Although African American people have been the primary innovators among these idioms, due to mass mediation, the contiguous nature of culture sharing among American ethnic groups, an ever developing and sophisticated global market system, technological advances, and music's ability to absorb the different meanings ascribed to it, people of all backgrounds have shaped, contributed to, and excelled in this fluid yet distinct body of music making. In addition, many historians of African American music have included the activities of blacks that participated as performers and composers in the Eurological concert tradition under this rubric.

1. SLAVERY, CULTURE, AND THE BLACK ATLANTIC. Between the 15th century and mid-19th century close to 12 million Africans were captured and transported to the New World, with the greatest number imported to Brazil and other locations in the Caribbean sugar industry. Reaching its apex between 1700 and 1820 when 6.5 million Africans were taken, the Atlantic slave trade represented one of the largest forced migrations in world history. Only 6% of the total number exported came directly to what is known now as the United States. These captured Africans were distributed along the eastern seaboard from New England to the mid-Atlantic colonies to the Southeast, but the greatest concentration landed in the South.

The nature of slavery in the United States was a singular enterprise, categorically different from various iterations of the "peculiar institution" throughout South America and the Caribbean. These distinct qualities shaped the development of African American cultural forms in dance, literature, visual culture, and especially music. Despite the ingenious and hideous development of laws and social practices designed to keep black slaves subservient they nonetheless asserted their aspirations, senses of beauty and the sublime, their frustrations, pain, and humanity through sound organization.

North America began its philosophically "Western" existence as commercial and religious extensions of European powers. As such early black music making in this context must be understood in its relationship to European-derived musical practices. Although early religious music in the colonies represented a direct transplant from the Old World it was soon indigenized by

"Contraband Children Dancing the Breakdown," Frank Leslie's Illustrated Newspaper, *January 31, 1863. (Courtesy American Antiquarian Society)*

the Pilgrims, whose music became rooted and influential. Musically simplistic and textually derivative, early American religious music would through a series of sonic and ideological developments become wholly "American," though in a persistent relationship—adaptations, rejections, and importations—with European models.

African American musical traditions mirrored these processes with respect to their relationship to the growing musical practices of the larger culture. These traditions constituted a confluence of broad African-derived approaches to sound organization and European-derived song structures and musical systems in a constant state of dynamic and historically specific interactions. What emerged is a composite: an indigenized conceptual framework of music making that has functioned through the years as a key symbol of an African American cultural identity.

The paradox of living as slaves and later as second-class citizens in a society founded on the principles of democracy and freedom produced a social structure in which black cultural production was mapped on a continuum between participation in what the scholar George Lewis has conceptualized as Eurological traditions and those reflecting Afrological aesthetic and structural priorities. Blacks who received training in Colonial-era singing schools are part of a long tradition of participating in Eurological practices that continues into the 21st century. Black music scholarship has generally included such musical activities by African Americans under the rubric "African American music." From New Orleans to the mid-Atlantic to New York the historical record indicates a robust and varied musical culture among a new people created by forced mass migration, social domination, and heroic cultural resilience.

In letters from missionaries, slave advertisements, runaway slave notices, personal travel journals, and memoirs, white observers noted both the musical talents of and the distinct body of music making taking place among the slaves. Their writings, permeated in some instances with the desire to sensationalize what was considered "barbaric" in this practices, described the sounds they heard in rich and colorful detail. An 1867 account of a Pinkster Festival held in the 1770s describes an annual days-long celebration among slaves in Albany, New York. A conglomeration of dance, drum, and song, the musical components of the event provides a telling example of the cultural priorities of a people enjoying themselves during a rare time of repose from their lives as the "nonhuman" tools of their masters:

> The dance had it peculiarities, as well as everything else connected with this august celebration. It consisted chiefly of couples joining in the performance at varying times, and continuing it with their

utmost energy until extreme fatigue or weariness compelled them to retire and give space to a less exhausted set; and in this successive manner was the excitement kept up with unabated vigor, until the shades of night began to fall slowly over the land, and at length deepen into the silent gloom of midnight.

The music made use of on this occasion, was likewise singular in the extreme. The principal instrument selected to furnish this important portion of the ceremony was a symmetrically formed wooded article usually denominated an *eel-pot*, with a cleanly dressed sheep skin drawn tightly over its wide and open extremity....Astride this rude utensil sat Jackey Quackenboss, then in his prime of life and well known energy, beating lustily with his naked hands upon its loudly sounding head, successively repeating the ever wild, though euphonic cry of *Hi-a-bomba, bomba, bomba*, in full harmony with the thumping sounds. These vocal sounds were readily taken up and as oft repeated by the female portion of the spectators not otherwise engaged in the exercises of the scene, accompanied by the beating of time with their ungloved hands, in strict accordance with the eel-pot melody. (James Eights, 1867)

Researchers have historically stressed the "functionality" of black music in comparison to that of the larger society and as a viable link to its "African past." Nonetheless, Anglo-Saxon Protestant religious expression was functional as well in Colonial America and as such became an important structural space for the development of African American music. As early New Englanders debated the value of oral and written modes of pedagogy and dissemination in their churches and singing schools well into the 19th century, African Americans codified their own musical sensibilities within the framework of their gradual acculturation into American Christianity. These qualities included performance practices with a predilection for antiphonal response, timbral heterogeneity, rhythmic variety, improvisation, corporeal activity, and open-ended structures encouraging endless repetition as well as oral dissemination. In 1819, John F. Watson, a black Northern minister, criticized integrated camp meetings in which black musical practices were absorbed into the white church world, and his comments pointed toward a long-term pattern of cultural interdependence:

In the blacks' quarter, the coloured people get together and sing for hours together, short scraps of disjointed affirmations, pledges, or prayers, lengthened out with long repetition choruses. These are all sung in merry chorus-manner of the southern harvest field or husking frolic method, of the slave blacks. (Watson, 1819)

These practices made sonically porous the boundaries separating secular and sacred realms as slave festivals, holidays, and even revolts were accompanied by similar musical components, although the degree of "Africanisms"—those musical qualities with analogous connections to the historical (and in some cases, recent) homeland of the slaves—varied according to regional differences determined by the density of the black population in relation to that of the white ruling classes. Music became an iconic symbol of black difference and a recognized source of communal identity and, thus, inspired the passing of laws in selected states to control the social environment for fear of white safety.

Between 1650 and 1750, the idea that African peoples formed a unified racial unit flourished in Europe as plantation slavery and its cultures shaped race ideology, trade economies, and social practices on both sides of the Atlantic. This construction of African identity was further entrenched in North America as black people founded churches, schools, and fraternal institutions during the decades surrounding 1800, many including the term "African" in their designations. The 1816 founding of the African Methodist Episcopal Church in Philadelphia formally established a black religious tradition in the United States that would continue to develop within the institutional and structural systems of the larger society. The publication of an ex-slave, Reverend Richard Allen's hymnal *A Collection of Spiritual Songs and Hymns* in 1801, affirms that the desire to engage in musical practices of their own making was part of the reason for the establishment of separate denominations. Following the tradition of printed metrical psalters of the New England compilers, Allen's hymnal contains songs by Isaac Watts and others whose forms encourage antiphonal response among participants.

2. Black cultural diversity in the North and the South. Among free blacks in the North, black brass bands that played popular songs of the day could be found in Philadelphia, New York, and Boston as well as in the Midwest and in New Orleans. Some of the music performed by these groups was their own and, thus, a school of composition written for popular consumption emerged employing the styles, tastes, and conventions of their white counterparts. Nonprofessional black itinerant musicians and vendors also roamed public urban spaces peddling their wares with street cries and song fragments analogous to those heard in the fields of Southern plantations. The African Grove Theater in New York City began as a private tea garden in 1816 and opened its doors to the public in 1821. In spite of constant hostility from the neighboring whites, the theater nonetheless remained open until around 1829, mounting productions that typically included overtures, ballad operas, ballets, and intermittent dances and "fashionable" songs or marches.

Frank Johnson, another pioneer Philadelphian, was central in establishing a black instrumental band tradition as a composer, virtuoso musician on the violin and keyed bugle, a bandleader, music instructor, entrepreneur, community organizer, a master music promoter, and the first African American to have his musical works published. He was among the first American musicians to take a band to Europe. Johnson received music instruction from a white teacher who thoroughly grounded him in music theory, composition, and performance. He formed his ensemble between the years 1819 and 1821, playing for many occasions among Philadelphia's white elites. He traveled with equally talented black musicians whose performance practices surely set them apart because of their ability to "distort" the notes on written page into a dynamic style that was drawn from musical traits from black culture. The overwhelming popularity of Johnson's contribution to the various traditions of American band music in his time foreshadowed that of John Philip Sousa, another towering giant in this realm.

During the first 60 years of the 19th century, the United States continued its expansion across the continent, and slavery continued even though an 1808

Congressional Act officially ended the lawful importation of slaves. The demand for slaves in the interior South increased with the dramatically growing plantation economy, solidifying the interdependence of both institutions. Communities of both free and enslaved blacks, the numbers of which rose from three quarters of a million in 1790 to well over 4 million by 1860, continued their resistance to their status in American society. The formation of the Free People of Color, the courageous slave revolts, the establishments of black newspapers, and the growth of independent black churches affirm the presence of a vital black cultural agency.

In the South, the internal slave trade destabilized traditional familial and communal ties but cultural practices such as music making became crucial sites of resistance and community building. With the overwhelming majority of blacks living in the plantation culture of the South in the 19th century, it was natural that their musical practices would become widespread and recognized for their extraordinary qualities. The music of slave religious expression and secular work songs reveal their preferred sonic ideals. In their public working and festival settings sanctioned by the masters, the slaves were encouraged to perform "cultural difference" according to practices from their African cultural heritage and as such expressed their own perspectives toward time, work, and their status as human beings. The new cultural formations that emerged had a tremendous impact on white Southern culture as well, a pattern that would continue in subsequent centuries.

Non-religious music making flourished among slave populations and free blacks in all regions. Documentary evidence shows that the talented fiddlers, and players of the banjo, an instrument of African origin, provided dance music for both black and white populations. Reports of musicians "pattin' juba," a rhythmic technique involving striking the hands on various parts of the body while stamping the feet and singing, detail a propensity for rhythmic complexity. Dancing and drumming often went hand-in-hand in various festivals or weekend occasions for leisure. Work songs, children's game and ring songs, corn husking songs, and songs of protest offer convincing evidence of the rich variety of secular music making taking place in slave populations. Broadly speaking, the creative processes underlying these widespread and varied musical practices operated on a continuum between newly composed materials and that which transformed existing material into something uniquely African American.

During the antebellum period, local customs and laws, black population patterns, and the distinct political histories of various regions determined the shape and geographic diversity of African American musical expression. Where free blacks were in the minority, such as they were in the North, a musician such as Johnson could get training and compete in an integrated, though still unequal, environment. In some regions of the slave-holding South, where blacks were subjected to more harsh and extreme control measures, Christianity strongly shaped the development of a distinctive system of black musical expression. Some areas restricted black music making by suppressing drumming at various historical moments. In New Orleans, part of a larger region with strong French and Spanish cultural roots, a rich heritage of Creole of color, black, and white cultural mixing distinguished the city's musical profile. The Marigny Theater, for example, opened in 1838 for Creoles of color to enjoy light comedies in French together with other kinds of variety shows that included music. New Orleans's black musical life was among the most vibrant in the

Robert Nathanial Dett's opera The Ordering of Moses, *performed by the National Negro Opera Company, Washington, DC, 1950. (National Negro Opera Company Collection, Music Division, Library of Congress)*

nation, boasting special seating for free blacks and slaves at opera houses, freelance instrumentalists, brass bands and orchestras, and the Negro Philharmonic Society, formed during the 1830s to present concerts by local and visiting musicians.

3. The new popular culture. As new musical expressions continued to emerge among black populations during the 19th century, a process through which musical practice embodied the social energies of black historical actors. In the larger world of popular entertainment, blackface minstrelsy emerged as a complex set of performance genres—songs, sketches, dances, novelty acts—whose conventions and functions changed over time and whose influence remained intact for many years. (*See* Minstrelsy.) At the peak of its popularity between 1850 and 1870, it featured white men in blackface executing caricatures of expressive practices observed among slaves, black street vendors, and roving musicians in cities. Minstrelsy's sensational stereotypes and popularity became a paradigm with which black performers would have to contend publicly well into the 20th century. Understood as a uniquely American form of entertainment at a time when the country's cultural elite still looked to European performers, repertoire, and practice as the measure of "good" music, 19th-century periodicals ran articles that disparaged minstrelsy's popularity among the masses. Important to black music history is the fact that contemporary audiences collapsed minstrelsy with musical styles developed by African Americans themselves. Minstrelsy set the tone for "black" performance as a "guilty pleasure," an act of transgression against established social mores for an expanding white middle class with anxiety about upper mobility and distinguishing themselves from those lower on the social ladder.

By the middle of the 19th century, Americans could pursue a number of occupations in the music industry such as performing, composing, teaching, concert management, and publishing. While black amateur musicians abounded, professional opportunities that appeared after Emancipation offered rapid advancement for these musicians whose talents became a growing component of the nation's musical profile. As the century proceeded, musical practice began to settle into categories of valuation: art, mass or popular, and traditional or folk. Issues of repertoire, training, heritage, patterns of consumption, and venue were factors determining the pedigree of a musical practice. As blacks made their socio-political transition from slavery to freedom, their musical culture continually transformed and was transformed by the structures that governed the creation, dissemination, and interpretation of artistic production in America.

For the African American performer after the Civil War participation in theater could involve three related forms: musical theater, minstrel shows, and vaudeville. The black musical theater tradition began when the Hyers Sisters, two women who had already built careers on the concert stage, created together with the white writer Joseph Bradford, the musical comedy *Out of Bondage* in 1876. The first of many such productions, their plots included plantation scenes and topics of racial progress within a format that featured plantation songs, ballads, operatic numbers, and folk dances.

In the realms of performance and composition, the minstrel show became a crucial route to financial security for many black musicians, even those trained in classical music. What was often billed as Ethiopian minstrelsy created the most ample opportunities for African Americans to break into show business with over 100 black minstrel troupes formed between 1865 and 1890. Their entertainment comprised a traveling one hour and 45 minute variety show consisting of three general categories of songs: ballads, comic songs, and specialty numbers. Representative shows featured singers and a small ensemble of instrumentalists and performed the works of such black songwriters as James Bland, Gussie Davis, and Samuel Lucas, as well as Stephen Foster, a white writer. The repertory of the typical black minstrel show also included religious songs and operatic arias.

It was perhaps because of this range of stylistic possibilities on the minstrel stage that black female concert singers such as sissieretta Jones (popularly known as Black Patti) and others of her ilk could transition from the concert stage to the minstrelsy trope circuit when "black prima donnas" fell out of vogue around the turn of the century. Nonetheless, the years after the Civil War saw the rise and popularity of many black women on the concert stage singing European art music. Touring widely in the United States and Europe, Black Patti, soprano Marie Selika Williams, and the Hyers Sisters, among others, maintained active careers with good management and engagements in prestigious concert halls.

Black male instrumentalists achieved significant popularity during this time. Born a slave, the unsighted pianist and composer Thomas Bethune (1849–1908), known as "Blind Tom," received musical training from his masters, learning thousands of works of the classical repertory by ear. Routinely subjected to tests of his powers of extraordinary musical memory, Bethune toured Europe, the United States, and South America for 30 years under the aegis of his owners, who continued to manage his career even after slavery ended. Other black male pianists, organists, and violinists trained as concert artists, breaking new ground first by obtaining formal training in conservatories and next by building reputations in the art world.

4. Spirituals, black culture, and the art idea. A musical development that countered the pervasiveness of black cultural stereotypes in minstrelsy occurred when the Fisk Jubilee Singers, a group of 11 men and women under the directorship of George L. White, began performing art songs designed for the concert stage. (*See* Jubilee singers.) Founded in 1866, six months after the end of the Civil War, Fisk University was established to educate newly freed slaves. White, being charged by the school's administration to provide music instruction to promising students, provided lessons that included

musicianship, classical repertory, and music from the own culture: spirituals. (*See* SPIRITUAL.) With the melodies of the "folk" spirituals as an emotional focal point, these songs were arranged into strict part-singing and performed vocally in bel canto style. A new American genre was born. When White took the group on a tour in 1871 to raise funds for the struggling institution they performed a program similar to that of white singers but that also included spirituals.

Other black colleges would follow suit, using singing groups to raise funds, a tradition that has continued to the present. The Fisk Jubilee Singers and subsequent groups created a new framework for understanding black musical performance. The creation and popularity of the concert spiritual fit into the larger functions of commercialism, religion, and structural integration through education that has long defined African American culture. It also represented another example of the indigenization of culture seen in the initial "invention" of the spiritual in which Eurological poetic and song forms were transformed into a new genre through Afrological performance practice. In this latest turn, however, the Eurological ideas about the fully composed and bounded musical "work," bel canto singing techniques, and concert decorum and praxis was applied to an African American body of song, producing a new form of indigenization that would become an important symbol of history, progress, and the idea of an expansive African American identity.

As awareness of black music continued its surge into the public sphere, it inspired numerous responses across the American culture industry. The anthology *Slave Songs of the United States*, published in 1867, compiled 136 melodies with lyrics collected and edited by Northern abolitionists William Francis Allen, Charles Pickard Ware, and Lucy McKim. Transcribed from songs collected from various geographical locations in the South, the book was the first of its kind, designed to share with readers the mostly religious songs heard by the book's authors. According to the editors, standard notation could not capture all of qualities of performance of these sacred and plantation songs. Represented in print as monophonic melodies, they in fact were performed as improvised heterophony. The compilers desired to capture slave culture's "difference" in written form, an act that for them would at once save a sonic world for posterity and represent the nobility of an enslaved people in the contemporaneous moment.

James Monroe Trotter's *Music and Some Highly Musical People* (New York, 1878) represented another approach to disciplining black musical activity in the United States through literary means. Written by a black amateur musician and impresario, Trotter's book, although focusing exclusively on 19th-century African American musicians, is the first general survey of American music of any kind, making it a landmark in American music historiography. The book contains an appendix with the scores of compositions by black writers, the act of which intended to instill race pride, a sense of cultural nationalism, and "relations of mutual respect and good feeling" between the races.

In the concert world, the pursuit of establishing a language of American musical nationalism came to an apex among composers, patrons, and institutions in the 1890s. This goal was explored along many lines—aesthetic, historical, political, and stylistic. When Bohemian composer Antonín Dvořák visited America as director of the National Conservatory between 1892 and 1895, he created a stir when he pronounced that composers could use African American and Native American melodies to build an indigenous art music culture because of their beauty.

HENRY T. BURLEIGH (1866–1949), one of Dvořák's black students, published *Jubilee Songs of the United States* (1916), arranged for piano and voice, a landmark collection that created the genre of solo black art song. A concert artist, arranger, music editor, and composer, Burleigh wrote more than 300 works, many of which were popular in their time among singers of all backgrounds. While the largescale impact of Dvořák's proclamations may be debated, the fact that Burleigh and many other composers—both black and white—responded creatively to his admonition and wrote music that began an important tradition, confirms its importance.

The last years of the 19th century saw the rise of "public amusements," an explosion of commercialized leisure that indexed America's turn from Victorian sensibilities. Advances in technology, the emergence of cultures of consumerism, and unprecedented black mobility together with increasing educational opportunities created a social milieu in which black musicians became a strong presence in the culture industry. As the specter of minstrelsy still prevailed, many black musicians would have to engage its practices in order to gain opportunities in the newly emerging mass-market enterprise.

5. BLACK MUSIC AND THE MODERN POP CULTURE INDUSTRY. The new technology of recording, pioneered by Thomas Edison in 1877, began as an experiment to reproduce the spoken word and soon became a way to disseminate music. When GEORGE W. JOHNSON, a former slave, recorded "The Whistling Coon" in 1890 for the New Jersey Phonograph company, it made him the first African American recording artist. As a child he was assigned to be the "bodyservant" to his master's young son to whom he was close in age. Johnson sat in on his young master's flute lessons, imitated the notes, and could eventually whistle any tune he heard. He was "discovered" as an adult by the New Jersey Phonograph Company which was looking for something "cheap and loud." Johnson recorded a COON SONG written by the white vaudevillian Sam Devere and filled with lyrics poking fun at physical stereotypes of African Americans.

Close to a decade later black musicians countered these coon song stereotypes when Bert Williams and George Walker recorded songs from the new tradition of the black musical theater for the Victor Talking Machine Company in 1901. The jubilee and quartet singing tradition, made popular by the touring Fisk singers a generation prior, also attracted the attention of the company the following year as they recorded Dinwiddie

Colored Quartet and the Fisk Jubilee Quartet. Nonetheless, distancing themselves from the coon aesthetic of minstrelsy and at the same time riding the crest of its popularity for financial gain proved to be an arduous balancing act for the black musician.

As African Americans became an increasing presence in the popular sphere, traveling troupes began to produce bona fide stars that gained international fame. Bob Cole (1868–1911) and Billy Johnson (c1858–1916) both left Black Patti's Troubadours to produce *A Trip to Coontown*, which debuted in 1898 and toured successfully for two years. That same year, WILL MARION COOK (1869–1944), violinist, composer, choral and orchestral director, and organizer debuted his *Clorindy; or the Origin of the Cakewalk* (co-written by poet Paul Laurence Dunbar) on Broadway, a landmark in the history of black musical theater.

Cook had already established himself as a presence as early as 1890 while directing a touring chamber orchestra and composing for *Scenes from the Opera of Uncle Tom's Cabin* in 1893. Like Burleigh, he was a student of Dvořák and wrote numerous works for voice and chorus, some of which was published in the 1912 anthology *A Collection of Negro Songs*. Cook belonged to a group of institutionally trained nationalistic composers devoted to using materials from black vernacular culture in a wide range of music from the concert stage to theater. Others included James Rosamond Johnson, R. Nathaniel Dett, Charles Cameron White.

6. BLACK MUSICAL WORLDS IN ART AND POP. Musical activities among concert musicians during this period moved in two directions: attempts to break the color line in the established art world and numerous acts of institution building among African Americans for their own constituents. Black singers and instrumentalists continued to make inroads through their artistic endeavors by touring and concertizing in prestigious venues throughout America, the West Indies, and Europe. Emma Azalia Hackley (1867–1922), R. Nathaniel Dett, Carl Diton (1886–1962), Hazel Harrison (1883–1969), and Helen Hagan (1891–1964) were among the pioneers who toured extensively and built careers of which both the black and white press took notice. Although their careers were progressive in many ways, these artists met many obstacles because of the racial climate. As such, together with teaching at historically black colleges, they began to build their own institutions—concert series, music schools and studios, opera companies, chorale societies, symphonies—that perpetuated the performance and study of art music in African American communities.

The combination of commercial markets, individual innovations, and communal sensibilities continued to produce a rich variety of musical forms beyond the concert stage from the 1890s onward. Circulating through written and oral means of dissemination and gathering stylistic coherence gradually over time, ragtime, blues, and early gospel music can all be considered products of eclectic heritages and performance practices. Each would prove to be foundational to many forms of 20th century music making.

7. EXPANDING THE BLACK VERNACULAR: RAGTIME, BLUES, JAZZ, AND GOSPEL. In the 1890s, the term RAGTIME embraced a wide range of music, including syncopated coons songs from minstrelsy, arrangements of these songs for large ensembles, any syncopated music for dancing, and solo piano music. As early as 1876 one finds reference to a stylistic precursor named "jig time" in the musical theater production *Out of Bondage*. Describing an energetic music played on the piano, it was also known as "jig piano," which simulated the rhythms and melodic phrasings of banjo and fiddle dance music. It was the coon song, however, that was more ubiquitous in American society due to minstrelsy's popularity and its association with the cakewalk dance. The publication of William Krell's *Mississippi Rag* (actually a cakewalk) and African American composer Thomas Turpin's *Harlem Rag*, both in 1897, promoted a definition of ragtime as a solo piano composition that codified in score form the elements of the improvised versions. However, the idea of "ragging" an improvisation of a popular song still remained a living tradition along side the new "classic ragtime." SCOTT JOPLIN became particularly well known as a composer of piano ragtime, writing syncopated pieces with multiple strains or themes similar to the march. Sheet music and piano rolls allowed ragtime composers to reach a broad swath of the American public.

The melodic sources of the BLUES grew from the same moans, field hollers, and timbral qualities upon which the spirituals were built. Popular ballads from the Eurological tradition provided the song form models, and they were performed in a variety of non-religious venues and public spaces such as cafes, saloons, streets, theaters, and railroad stations, among other places where money could be earned for performances. The lyrics of the blues, usually performed in first person narrative form, address a large variety of specific everyday experiences often with irony and humor. Guitars, pianos, and small ensembles with a variety of instruments provided the accompaniment for singers in a tightly interactive manner. The genre's codified poetic structure (A-A-B) and the repeating 12-bar harmonic form that became convention has become one of the most important practices of 20th-century American music. Like "ragtime," the term "the blues" once denoted a variety of expressions although it was first developed in the interior South. Women performers like MAMIE SMITH, who became the first black singer to record the blues with "Crazy Blues" (1920), pioneered the new RACE RECORD phenomenon, which targeted African American consumers. It should be noted as well that sheet music by individuals like W.C. Handy (1873–1958) and touring vaudeville stage shows also played a large role in circulating the blues widely.

While the African American church remained the principal venue for early GOSPEL MUSIC in years leading up to the 1930s, it shared with ragtime and blues similar relationships to vernacular cultural sensibilities and to the culture industry. Many rural and urban churches

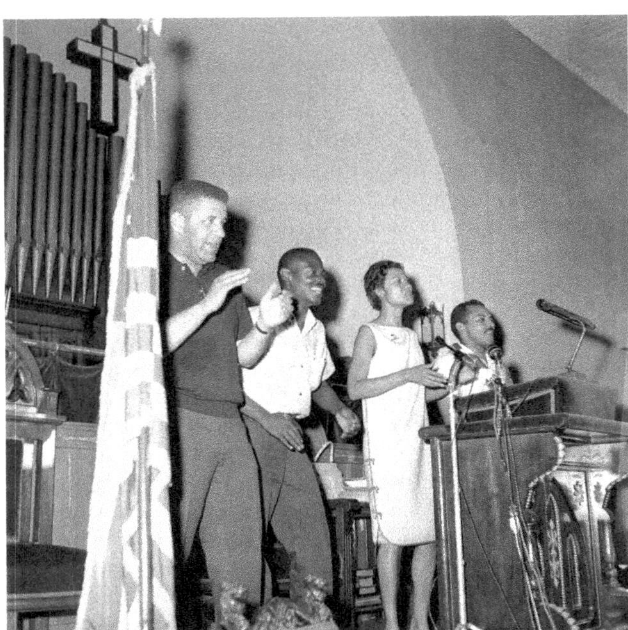

Singing at demonstration at Bethel AME Church, Cambridge, Maryland, led by Stanley Branche (NAACP), Reginald Robinson (Student Non-Violent Coordinating), Gloria Richardson (Cambridge Non-Violent Action Committee), and Phillip H. Savage (NAACP), 1963. (AP Photo/Willliam A. Smith)

maintained the energetic, kinetic, and vocally dramatic conventions established in the spirituals tradition. A shift occurred when composers such as Minister Charles A. Tindley, began to write and publish religious songs made specifically for his own services, innovating the gospel hymn with accompaniment, verse/chorus structure, and improvisation. Recordings began to circulate other forms of early 20th-century religious music as well, including the energizing blues-shouting vocals and "jig time" piano of Holiness singer Arizona Dranes and rural church music for solo vocalist and guitar accompaniment. All three streams would inform the genre of gospel music which emerged in Chicago in the 1930s.

American involvement in World War I, a boom in Northern industry, and the restriction of foreign immigration from Europe created unprecedented opportunities for African Americans living in the South. During the so-called "Great Migration" up to 1 million southern blacks left for the urban north. This mass movement created a cultural milieu in which new musical forms appeared and older styles continued to transform as a result of this move from rural to urban and agrarian to industrial lifestyles. In all aspects of the culture industry—recording, publishing, performance, teaching, and composition—an African American presence made an indelible mark.

One of the most dramatic developments occurred in the continued ascendancy of instrumental improvised music, as the ragtime era led into the jazz age. Jazz, also a genre developed through black musical innovation, grew from many sources, including jig or ragtime piano, the blues, popular song, wind bands, and social dance music. New Orleans, the site of most early jazz activity, supported a strong tradition of wind bands and dance orchestras, many of which emphasized a wide range of styles fully scored arrangements that included "hot" improvisational techniques. Charles "Buddy" Bolden (1877–1931), a popular bandleader, was legendary in his highly idiosyncratic approach on the cornet. From these beginnings, jazz would continue to develop into a dynamic amalgam of tributaries from a continually evolving range of sources, including blues, various popular song forms, marching band instruments together with electric and non-Western ones, other contemporaneous genres from the popular sphere, and art world conceptualizations that when taken together would come to symbolize both African American ingenuity and a broader American sensibility that privileged the notion of cultural crosscurrents.

By the 1920s New York had become the center of the music industry, drawing black musicians to its numerous cabarets, dance halls, nightclubs, and recording opportunities; its lively community of musicians forged new ideas that would attract worldwide attention. Musicians such as bandleaders James Reese Europe (1881–1919), composer and arranger Will Vodery (1885–1951), and William C. Handy, together with many others, had laid the foundation in the preceding decade for the sharp, subsequent demand for black entertainment. Many of the most influential musicians moved between activities in the black theater and the creation of syncopated music for large orchestras that became America's dance soundtrack. Improvising ragtime pianists such as Eubie Blake, Jelly Roll Morton, Willie "the Lion" Smith, Luckey Roberts, and James P. Johnson wrote and performed piano dance music that became foundational to what would be known as the "Jazz Age." Although they have been up until recently largely written out of this history, female musicians such as Hallie Anderson (1885–1927) and Marie Lucas (1880s–1947) were abundantly present on the scene.

Something labeled "jazz" made its debut on recordings in 1917 when the Original Dixieland Jazz Band, a group of white musicians from New Orleans, released "Livery Stable Blues" and "Dixie Jass Band One-Step." Teeming with novelty sounds—including simulated animal noises—these recordings managed to excite enough from the public to usher in an era of recording that encompassed a wide range of idioms grouped under the rubric jazz. The music of black musicians such as King Oliver, Jelly Roll Morton, and Louis Armstrong—all from New Orleans—introduced a culturally commingled sound into the musical landscape, one grounded in blues, robust polyphony, and based on various dance forms. Indeed, the words jazz and "modern" became linked and stretched at this time to describe many idioms. Paul Whiteman, a popular white bandleader who once claimed that jazz "sprang into existence...from nowhere in particular," infused his music with jazz feeling. A notable contribution was George Gershwin's stylishly grand *Rhapsody in Blue*

(1924), a work commissioned by Whiteman that channeled referents from an array of musical tributaries, including jazz.

Between World War I and II, jazz grew from a localized phenomenon and into an internationally known genre. Musicians on both sides of America's racial divide—Duke Ellington, Louis Armstrong, Count Basie, Bix Beiderbecke, Benny Goodman, Mary Lou Williams, and many others—became well-known jazz figures, and in some cases, true icons. Ellington's career, in particular, was symbolic of jazz's ascendance on many levels. His idiosyncratic approach to composition, arranging, and orchestration demonstrated the artistic potential of popular music. The impact of jazz could be measured not only in record sales—it would become by the late 1930s America's popular music choice—but also by its emergent (and international) written criticism, which over time bloomed from discographical surveys for collectors to record reviews, essays, and book-length studies.

With the rise of modernism in the United States, black music, particularly in the hands of black musicians, became a point of debate and speculation. Its value in the public sphere took on a variety of non-mutually exclusive configurations: as an expression of cultural nationalism; as an avenue for commercial gain; as propaganda in the fight for equal rights; and in a variety of other ideas imposed by record companies, critics, "slumming" white audiences, and black intellectuals. Similarly to other expressive arts—film, photography, and literature—during the 1920s and 1930s, black music informed and was influenced by large, sometimes incongruent, cultural movements such as primitivism, the Harlem Renaissance, and Negritude. This, together with the overwhelming popularity of popular dances like the cakewalk, the charleston, the jitterbug, and the lindy hop—all of which became international sensations—worked to saturate the sensibilities of black popular music into all sectors of global society—in mind, body, and spirit.

8. Black classical music in the art world. In the concert world, other ideas about musical modernism beyond the jazz revolution were taking shape. The establishment of first-rate schools of music in America, the growth of urban, in-residence symphony orchestras and opera companies, and a new avant-garde musical language that turned away from diatonicism, all created a larger chasm between art and popular realms. Some black performers with designs on concert careers responded by specializing in art music and by dabbling less in the popular arena as in years past. Some continued to make a living in both realms. From 1921, when Eubie Blake's and Noble Sissle's production *Shuffle Along* premiered, black musical theater produced an aesthetic middle ground as its conventions embodied a mixture of popular song, blues, ballads, choral number, expert arrangements, and symphonic orchestrations. Duke Ellington's *Symphony in Black: a Rhapsody of Negro Life* (1935) extended this musical language of entertainment that was shared by composers across racial lines.

The National Association of Negro Musicians, chartered in 1919, has up to the present, provided a haven of institutional support for black performers, teachers, and composers whose work remained primarily situated in the art world. Singers Roland Hayes, Marian Anderson, Paul Robeson, and Dorothy Maynor built careers that took them to concert stages around the world in recitals, opera companies, and before symphony orchestras. They developed a large following among black audiences and therefore developed repertory that featured art songs based on black thematic materials. The Negro String Quartet, the National Negro Opera Company, the Negro Symphony Orchestra, and professional choruses formed by Hall Johnson and Eva Jessye continued the legacy of institution building among musicians who continued to face varying degrees of discrimination in the concert world. In 1935 Jessye was appointed the choral director for Gershwin's iconic opera *Porgy and Bess*, a work that would become a major platform for black opera singers for decades to come. Dubbed "An American Folk Opera," the opera's embodiment of the spirit of black vernacular music, evocations based on Gershwin's research in South Carolinian black communities, could be interpreted in the legacy of the black cultural nationalism espoused by earlier composers.

The 1930s saw the emergence of full-fledged symphonic works based on thematic material derived from black culture. William Grant Still's *Afro-American Symphony* premiered in 1931 and made history as the first work of its kind by a black composer to be played by a major symphony orchestra, the Rochester PO. Still's prolific output spanned popular music, orchestral work, film and television work, opera, and chamber works, all contributing to his designation as "Dean of Afro-American composers." Florence Bea Price (1888–1953), one of the few female composers at this time to find acclaim, wrote pedagogical pieces, radio commercials, and serious concert works, including the *Piano Concerto in One Movement* and Symphony in E minor (1932). Many of the pieces written by black composers during this time expressed what might be called an "Afro-Romanticism"—works that used black thematic materials couched in the language of 19th-century Romanticism. William Levi Dawson's *Negro Folk Symphony*, which premiered in 1934 with the Philadelphia Orchestra, was such a work. Shirley Graham, the versatile and dynamic musician who later married W.E.B. DuBois, composed and wrote the libretto for *Tom-Tom* (1932), an opera in three acts that made history as the first of its kind by an African American woman.

9. Music in the black church. Within the community theater of the black church, one of the most vibrant and autonomous institutions in African American communities, publications such as *Gospel Pearls*, first appearing in 1921, served to canonize the "on the ground" musical tastes of congregations. The collection is drawn from several origins: standard Protestant hymns, hymns from the lining-out tradition, spirituals, songs by Charles Tindley and other black writers. From the 1930s on, songwriters Lucie Campbell (1885–1963), W. Herbert

Aretha Franklin, 1960s. (D. Hunstein/Lebrecht Music & Arts)

Brewster, Sr. (1897–1987), singer and music publisher Sallie Martin (1896–1988), and pianist, singer, and publisher Roberta Martin (1907–69) all contributed to creating gospel music, a newly formed genre that combined the melodic inflection of the blues, the ragged rhythms of "jig" piano, the fervor and intensity of the ring shout, and the entrepreneurial instincts of popular music. At the center of this creative force was THOMAS A. DORSEY (1899–1993), a preacher's son, who moved to Chicago from Atlanta in 1916 while pursuing an active career in show business. Dorsey maintained performing and songwriting activities in both the church and entertainment worlds but by 1931 he had organized two firsts: a "gospel" choir and a publishing company the following year devoted to original gospel compositions. Dorsey also accompanied a singer who became arguably the first gospel performer to become a star outside the church, MAHALIA JACKSON (1911–72), a performer whose blues-based vocal singing style became the gold standard of the genre for decades.

Since the codification of ragtime piano, pianists developed highly idiosyncratic approaches to solo and ensemble-based improvisation that constituted key elements in the generic codes of various black popular musics. The stride piano of James P. Johnson and Fats Waller, the boogie-woogie style of Meade "Lux" Lewis, and the rollicking "keyboard style" of Roberta Martin's gospel piano would come to define genres and also supply rhetorical gestures for subsequent styles. Likewise, the conventions of both male and female quartet singing styles moved across the porous boundaries of secular and sacred contexts. Not only did quartet singing continually expand its conventions, groups like the Soul Stirrers, Swan Silvertones, Dixie Hummingbirds, Original Gospel Harmonettes of Birmingham, Southern Harps Spiritual Singers, the well-known Five Blind Boys of Alabama, and the Five Blind Boys of Mississippi stood as paradigms for popular singing groups across genres and up to the 1990s.

10. NEW AMALGAMATIONS: BEBOP AND RHYTHM-AND-BLUES. Although commercial markets thrived on strategies of categorization and containment—"race records" for blacks, country or "hillbilly" music for southern whites, and Hit Parade for middle-class whites—musicians and audiences, in truth, borrowed and listened across these social and sonic categories, creating new styles and extending audience bases as a matter of course. The steady migration of southerners to the North exploded once again during the years surrounding World War II and together with a surge toward the abandonment of Jim Crow practices and laws new social patterns emerged, and with them, new musical forms. The infectious swing music of the 1930s, perhaps best personified in the bands of Count Basie, would influence and be supplanted by two new musical styles—bebop and rhythm-and-blues—each articulating various, though not competing, views about leisure, entrepreneurism, art practice, modernism, and identity.

Bebop, also known as modern jazz, emerged in the early to mid-1940s as an instrumental approach to the swing dance aesthetic, an innovation that abstracted some of swing's core conventions. (See BOP.) Drummers disrupted the steady dance beat by dropping offbeat, dramatic accents called "bombs." In order to sidestep paying copyright fees, musicians wrote compositions by writing new, more challenging melodies on the harmonic structures of existing popular songs. The harmonic structures themselves featured a sophisticated approach that exploited the upper partials—9ths, 11ths, and 13ths—and a strong emphasis on the tritone relationships and flatted fifths. The virtuosic improvisations of instrumentalists Charlie Parker, Dizzy Gillespie, Bud Powell, and Max Roach set jazz on a new artistic and demanding course. Vocalists Sarah Vaughan and Betty Carter influenced legions of singers with their command of bebop techniques. Pianist Thelonious Monk's idiosyncratic compositional approach and acerbic solo approach emerged as the quintessential voice of new era in jazz.

If bebop abstracted swing and popular song then early RHYTHM-AND-BLUES—an umbrella label for a constellation of black vernacular styles that appeared somewhat contemporaneously—took swing aesthetics and intensified its dance feeling with a heavier backbeat, a proclivity for 12-bar blues form, repetitious and riff-based melodies, and lyrics whose subject matter comprised all of the earthiness and humor of traditional blues, though, with an urbane twist. Perhaps best exemplified by Ruth Brown and Louis Jordan, the style was sonically related to rock and roll, which emerged in the 1950s as a way to market the new dance music to white teenagers during the beginning years of the Civil Rights Movement and fears of desegregation. Although black performers such as Little Richard, Chuck Berry, and Fats Domino certainly counted among early Rock and roll stars—many believed it to be another strain of rhythm-and-blues—as the style became codified as a genre with its own race-specific social contract, it became understood as primarily "white." The mainstream of rhythm and blues styles featured elements from gospel, blues, and jazz, an imaginative repertoire of lyrics employing vivid imagery from black life together with qualities derived from specific locations such as the "urban blues" sound from Chicago and Los Angeles. Independent record labels were primarily responsible for recording and disseminating early rhythm and blues.

11. Black music in the academy. An important generation of black composers would benefit from opportunities that opened up in education for African Americans as a result of the Civil rights movement. As a result of this shifting tide, many would secure professorships at American universities in addition to securing major prizes and commissions. Their works, ranging from neo-classical styles to uses of more avant-garde materials, were written for chamber groups, opera, solo singer, and symphonies, among other settings. Howard Swanson, Ulysses Kay, George Walker, Hale Smith, and T.J. Anderson were among those who led the way, establishing reputations within the academy and the larger art music world. In the realm of performance, black musicians continued to build active careers, although relatively fewer inroads were gained in the nation's symphony orchestras, still the most prestigious vehicles for concert instrumentalists. African American conductors found greater success abroad, securing positions in Europe after obtaining rigorous training in American institutions. By contrast, the opera and concert stage proved more generous to singers such as Robert McFerrin, Leontyne Price, George Shirley, Grace Bumbry, Shirley Verrett, and Jessye Norman, all of whom made history by singing roles traditionally assigned to white singers. The predominance of black male composers in this period was striking. Julie Perry, despite formidable forerunners such as Florence Price and Shirley Graham, was singular in her prominence as a black female composer of her generation.

12. Post–World War II: black music into the mainstream. From the mid-20th century on, stimulated in part by another south-to-north mass migration during and after World War II, black music with roots in the popular sphere—jazz, gospel, rhythm and blues and all their multifarious sonic iterations—defined, for many, the aesthetic core of what was singular about American music culture. Despite their divergent social functions in the public sphere, they shared qualitative and conceptual characteristics. Independent record labels were key in disseminating the music as their owners sought to maximize profits as major labels initially ignored these styles. Ultimately, major labels would seek out, record, and distribute the music, and by doing so, facilitate their dominant national and international impact. Black popular music came to be seen as an important expressive force for the richness of African American culture, as a metaphor for the processes of creativity in such fields as literature, visual arts, and dance, and as a key symbol for the structural integration of black people into the mainstream of American society.

These genres moved along a trajectory that combined a sturdy grounding in historical traditions as well as a

Jay-Z and Beyoncé, 2006. (Mario Anzuoni/Reuters/Landov)

perpetual avant-gardism, the latter describing how musicians constantly pushed stylistic conventions into new configurations. Gospel music, while continuing its relationship to the aesthetics of the spiritual and the blues and to the combination of religion and entrepreneurialism that characterized the colonial and antebellum eras, developed into an important incubator of talent for other genres. Gospel singing techniques developed in the black church proved especially impacting as by the end of the 20th century they defined how many "pop" singers would approach a song. As the decades progressed, innovators such as Rosetta Tharpe, James Cleveland, Edwin and Walter Hawkins, and Albertina "Twinkie" Clark, among others, built on the earlier contributions of pioneers Lucie Campbell, Willie Mae Ford Smith, and Roberta Martin to establish gospel music as a bastion of cutting-edge creativity, marketing savvy, and stylistic influence. It is important to note the centrality of female musicians in gospel music, which in many ways remains singular in the realm of modern African American music production. Beginning in the 1990s, other cities beyond the recognized centers of Chicago, Detroit, Los Angeles, and Philadelphia became important producers of gospel music, including Houston, Charlotte, and Atlanta.

Ray Charles, Sam Cooke, James Brown, and Aretha Franklin were all important throughout the 1950s and 1960s in infusing the techniques of gospel into the mainstream. Their contributions to the emergent styles dubbed Soul music and Funk defined an era that might be considered the "Afro-Americanization" of global pop culture as their conventions shaped music making internationally in styles ranging from West African High Life to Trinidadian "Gospelypso." Like gospel and rhythm and blues, jazz also continually regenerated itself, sometimes by absorbing the qualities of other styles, including rock and funk. Developments such as free jazz and fusion—both representing the reframing of improvisation in rhythmic and harmonic structures and qualities of interaction that departed significantly from previous conventions in the genre—inspired intense debates about the stability of the art form. The various bands of drummer Art Blakey and trumpeter Miles Davis proved to be incubators for an impressive string of performers who became leading figures in the 1970s, 80s, and 90s.

Beginning in the 1960s academic research on African American music laid the groundwork for the explosion of university-sponsored work appearing throughout the 1990s and into the millennium. Writings by LeRoi Jones (Amiri Baraka), Dena Epstein, Charles Keil, Portia Maultsby, Albert Murray, Samuel A. Floyd Jr., Olly Wilson, Josephine Wright, and especially Eileen Southern, all contributed to a literature that considered the historical, ethnological, and sonic dimensions of black music. Wilson's dual career as an experimental composer and author of key writings on black musical aesthetics was exemplar of the "observing participant" that would define many scholars of African American music of the last 25 years.

If early rhythm-and-blues began its existence in the margins of the music industry, by the 1960s and 1970s its family of idioms had moved to the center of the mainstream. Against the backdrop of the Civil Rights and Black Power Movements, rhythm-and-blues, soul, and funk addressed on the levels of both style and message many of the ideals, aspirations, and urgent sense of socio-political efficacy that marked the moment. At the same time, mass mediation also played a key role in the ubiquity of black popular music in the public sphere as television shows from *American Bandstand*, *Soul Train*, and later the appearance of *BET* broadcast the music into American homes on a large scale. Black films in the early 1970s such as *Shaft* and *Superfly* contained scores by Issac Hayes and Curtis Mayfield respectively, thus providing another platform for the dissemination of the music. The output of record labels such as Curtom and Chess (Chicago), Stax (Memphis) Motown (Detroit), to name but a few, demonstrated the continued significance of regional difference in the styles despite the potential for homogenization in the mass mediation context.

Subsequent to the high years of protests and legal challenges for equal rights by African Americans, urban centers decayed into post-industrial spaces fraught with poor educational systems, drug epidemics, and widespread economic depression. Even as superstars such as Michael Jackson, Prince, Whitney Houston, Janet Jackson, and others had careers that "crossed over" into the pop charts, a growing disaffection and creative surge within urban communities spawned new forms of music directed at their own communities. Hip hop, a popular genre appearing in the late-1970s and coming of age in the 1980s and 90s, represented a dramatic sonic development based on the inventive manipulation of previously recorded music and semi-to-non melodic oral declamation as its emotional focal point. Attention to and understanding of the genre has benefitted from a generation of scholars who grew up as fans and wrote about it within a paradigm of literary and cultural studies, a framework that moved easily among journalistic, ethnographic, and scholarly modes of discourse.

The digital age of musical creativity and dissemination, of which hip hop is perhaps most emblematic, triggered debates about the relativism of musicianship, ownership and copyright, and cultural authenticity. Despite these tensions, musicians have continued to mix genres: hip-hop symphonies, jazz inflected hip hop, and gospel's "holy hip hop" demonstrate the inter-musicality of black musical practices. At the same time, contemporary musicians—whether jazz neoclassicists, revivalist black string bands, or neosoul artists—continue to turn to musical practices of previous decades to both honor the past and to cultivate new audiences.

BIBLIOGRAPHY

J. Watson: *Methodist Error, or Friendly Christian Advice, to Those Methodists who Indulge in Extravagant Religious Emotions and Bodily Exercises* (Trenton, NJ, 1819); excerpts repr. in *Readings in Black American Music*, ed. E. Southern (New York, 1971, rev. 2/1983)

J. Eights: "Pinkster Festivities in Albany" [1867]; repr. in *Readings in Black American Music*, ed. E. Southern (New York, 2/1983), 45–6

W. Allen: "Introduction," *Slave Songs of the United States* (New York, 1867)

J.M. Trotter: *Music and Some Highly Musical People* (New York, 1878/*R*)

H.E. Krehbiel: *Afro-American Folksongs* (New York, 1914/*R*)
J.W. Johnson: *Black Manhattan* (New York, 1930)
M.C. Hare: *Negro Musicians and their Music* (Washington, DC, 1936)
J.W. Work: *Negro Songs and Spirituals* (New York, 1940)
T. Fletcher: *100 Years of the Negro in Show Business* (New York, 1954)
H. Courlander: *Negro Folk Music U.S.A.* (New York, 1963)
L. Jones: *Blues People* (New York, 1963/*R*)
C. Keil: *Urban Blues* (Chicago, 1966)
D.-R. de Lerma, ed.: *Black Music in our Culture* (Kent, OH, 1970)
E. Southern: *The Music of Black Americans: a History* (New York, 1971, rev. 3/1997)
E. Southern, ed.: *Readings in Black American Music* (New York, 1971, rev. 2/1983)
L.F. Emery: *Black Dance in the United States from 1619 to 1970* (Palo Alto, CA, 1972)
D.-R. de Lerma, ed.: *Reflections on Afro-American Music* (Kent, OH, 1973)
H. Roach: *Black American Music: Past and Present*, i (Malabar, FL, 1973, rev. 2/1985)
O. Wilson: "The Significance of the Relationship between Afro-American and West-African Music," *BPM*, ii (1974), 3–22
P. Maultsby: *Afro-American Religious Music, 1619–1861* (diss., U. of Wisconsin, 1975)
P.K. Maultsby: "Selective Bibliography: U.S. Black Music," *EthM*, xix (1975), 421–99
H. Courlander: *A Treasury of Afro-American Folklore* (New York, 1976)
D. Epstein: *Sinful Tunes and Spirituals: Black Folk Music to the Civil War* (Urbana, IL, 1977)
L. Levine: *Black Culture and Black Consciousness* (New York, 1977)
D.N. Baker, L.M. Belt, and H.C. Hudson: *The Black Composer Speaks* (Metuchen, NJ, 1978)
D.A. Handy: *Black Women in American Bands and Orchestras* (Metuchen, NJ, 1981)
S.A. Floyd and M.J. Reisser: *Black Music in the United States: an Annotated Bibliography of Selected Reference and Research Materials* (Millwood, NY, 1983)
M. Green: *Black Women Composers: a Genesis* (Boston, 1983)
A. Woll: *Dictionary of the Black Theatre* (Westport, CT, 1983)
T. Brooks: *America's Black Musical Heritage* (Englewood Cliffs, NJ, 1984)
P. Oliver: *Songsters and Saints: Vocal Traditions on Race Records* (New York, 1984)
J. Gray, ed.: *Blacks in Classical Music: a Bibliographical Guide to Composers, Performers, and Ensembles* (New York, 1988)
T.L. Riis: *Just Before Jazz: Black Musical Theater in New York, 1890–1915* (Washington, DC, 1989)
S.A. Floyd Jr., ed.: *Black Music in the Harlem Renaissance: a Collection of Essays* (New York, 1990)
T. Rose: *Black Noise: Rap Music and Black Culture in Contemporary America* (Hanover, NH, 1993)
S.A. Floyd Jr.: *The Power of Black Music: Interpreting Its History from Africa to the United States* (New York, 1995)
G.E. Lewis: "Improvised Music After 1950: Afrological and Eurological Perspectives," *Black Music Research Journal*, xvi/1 (1996), 215-46
S.A. Floyd Jr., ed.: *International Dictionary of Black Composers* (Chicago, 1999)
M.A. Neal: *What the Music Said: Black Popular Music and Black Public Culture* (New York, 1999)
C. Werner: *A Change is Gonna Come: Music, Race and the Soul of America* (New York, 1999, rev. and expanded 2/2006)
H.C. Boyer: *The Golden Age of Gospel* (Urbana, 2000)
R. Crawford: *America's Musical Life: a History* (New York, 2001)
L. Abbott and D. Seroff: *Out of Sight: the Rise of African American Popular Music, 1889–1895* (Jackson, MS, 2002)
M.A. Neal: *Songs in the Key of Black Life: a Rhythm and Blues Nation* (New York, 2003)
R.M. Radano: *Lying Up a Nation: Race and Black Music* (Chicago, 2003)
G.P. Ramsey Jr.: *Race Music: Black Cultures from Bebop to Hip-Hop* (Berkeley, 2003)
R. Darden: *People Get Ready!: a New History of Black Gospel Music* (New York, 2004)
T. Brooks: *Lost Sounds: Blacks and the Birth of the Recording Industry, 1890–1919* (Urbana and Chicago, IL, 2004)
J. Chang: *Can't Stop, Won't Stop: A History of the Hip-Hop Generation* (New York, 2005)
M.V. Burnim and P.K. Maultsby, eds.: *African American Music: An Introduction* (New York, 2006)
E.M. Hayes and L.F. Williams: *Black Women and Music: More than the Blues* (Urbana, IL, 2007)
L. Abbott and D. Seroff: *Ragged but Right: Black Traveling Shows, "Coon Songs," and the Dark Pathway to Blues and Jazz* (Jackson, MS, 2007)
D.S. Pollard: *When the Church Becomes Your Party: Contemporary Gospel Music* (Detroit, 2008)
K. Lornell, ed.: *From Jubilee to Hip Hop: Readings in African American Music* (Upper Saddle River, NJ, 2010)
W.F. Brundage, ed.: *Beyond Blackface: African Americans and the Creation of American Popular Culture, 1890-1930* (Chapel Hill, NC, 2011)
L. Schenbeck: *Racial Uplift and American Music, 1878–1943* (Jackson, MS, 2012)

GUTHRIE P. RAMSEY JR.

African Methodist Episcopal Church. The oldest and largest black Methodist denomination in the world, with approximately four million members in the United States and abroad. The first independent African American Christian denomination, it was founded by RICHARD ALLEN and other former members of St. George's Methodist Episcopal Church in Philadelphia, Pennsylvania. Allen and Absalom Jones had formed the Free African Society in 1787 to protest the rise in discriminatory treatment faced by growing numbers of blacks in the white church. They and other African American ministers were being denied advancement to pastorate positions, and after white church officials tried to physically remove blacks from the gallery during prayer, Allen and other black members walked out of worship. Efforts toward gaining equal treatment and representation in Methodist congregations were ignored or denied, and in 1794 Allen and Jones organized a separate congregation under the Protestant Episcopal Church. Jones was appointed as its first bishop. Allen, however, wanted to remain in the Methodist tradition, so he and part of the group who had left St. George's founded Bethel African Methodist Episcopal Church during that same year.

Allen, the denomination's first bishop, collected songs that were popular among black Christians as he traveled the countryside starting churches. In 1801 he compiled the first black denominational hymnbook, *A Collection of Spiritual Songs and Hymns Selected from Various Authors*. It included the lyrics of 54 Methodist hymns, several hymns by Allen himself, and some of the earliest printings of American revival camp meeting songs. This pocket hymnal is the earliest known American hymnbook to include "wandering refrains," unrelated choruses freely attached to one or more hymns. It was reprinted in the same year with ten additional hymns and retitled *A Collection of Hymns and Spiritual Songs from Various Authors, by Richard Allen, Minister of the African Methodist Episcopal Church*. These works were the first to include songs of the black oral tradition and reflect the musical tastes of early 19th-century black Protestants.

Bishops of the AME Church, *lithograph by J.-H. Daniels, showing Richard Allen surrounded by portraits of other bishops and scenes of AME activity, c1876. (Library of Congress, Prints and Photographs Division, LC-DIG-pga-03643*

The AME Church's highly organized, jurisdictionally based leadership structure contributed to its growth throughout the 19th century and to its expansion from the Midwest and Northeastern United States into the South after the Civil War. The church's dedication to music for worship is reflected not only in letters and writings circulated on the topic within the denomination but also the high rate of hymn publication. After the 1801 books, the AME Church published eight editions of its denominational hymnal through the AME Book Concern and later the AMEC Sunday School Union. The fourth edition, *The Hymn Book of the African Methodist Episcopal Church* (1876), reflected the theological and social impetus the church took on following Reconstruction. With 1115 songs and 958 pages, it was the largest AME hymnbook, and featured Wesleyan hymnody and hymns by black Methodists and AME bishops. It included 59 camp meeting and revival songs such as those made popular by Ira Sankey (known as "old Zion songs"), despite some leaders' disapproval.

Negro spirituals, however, were not included in this edition or previous editions. This exclusion reflected the controversial stance that AME leadership took against some of the musical and worship practices of rural, ex-slave, and new southern converts. Whereas Richard Allen was known to support emotional and exuberant worship styles, succeeding AME bishops, Daniel Payne in particular, took extreme action toward promoting a more subdued, less emotional, Anglo-American tone, labeling revival songs "corn-field ditties" and surviving African styles of worship like the ring-shout and spirit possession "heathenish." Organized and trained church choirs singing approved hymn tunes were heavily promoted over communally created and maintained congregational songs. Hymnody and Western sacred art music became the core repertoire of many AME church choirs, while non-Methodist blacks began gravitating toward gospel hymns and Thomas Dorsey-style gospel songs in the early decades of the 20th century. Usually financially more well off, AME churches were among the first black congregations to purchase pianos and pipe organs for church services at the turn of the 20th century.

Bodily movements such as hand clapping, swaying, jumping, or dancing were broadly shunned, thus adding to the long-time characterization of AME worship as "high church," as in restrained and cerebral. In the mid-19th century Payne and other leaders were engaged in a social and religious battle for respectability for blacks in American society. Instructions for proper church decorum and an outlined order of worship were featured in each hymnal edition and enforced by presiding bishops and elders during church visits. These actions caused many to leave the AME Church and join other Methodists groups or, as was common in the South, to join black independent Baptist conventions or the more musically exuberant black Pentecostal denominations. In 1898, the AME Church published the first black hymnal with musical notation, *The African Methodist Episcopal Hymn and Tune Book*. Though this hymnal featured more compositions by black Methodists, it did not include any late-19th-century spirituals or any of the newly emerging gospel hymns being composed by Charles Tindley (Methodist Episcopal) and Lucie Campbell (Baptist).

By the 1940s, the AME hymnal was starting to fall out of use and faced competition from other denominational hymnals and supplemental song books such as Tindley's *New Songs of Paradise* (1909) and *Gospel Pearls* (1921) published by the National Baptist Convention, USA. This trend threatened the consistent liturgy of the AME Church, and after a failed attempt at a joint hymnal with the AME Zion Church (New York), the AME Church published *The Richard Allen AME Hymnal* (1946), quickly followed by the *AMEC Hymnal* (1954) from Nashville, Tennessee. Renowned music educators, composers, and arrangers connected with the AME Church such as E.C. Deas, Frederick Hall, and F.A. Clark compiled both editions. Songs by Tindley and Methodist laymen, and for the first time, spirituals, were among the 645 pieces in the 1954 edition.

The most recent edition, the *AMEC Bicentennial Hymnal* (1984), reflects gradually changing attitudes toward music in church services and worship styles. The ninth edition is larger than previous 20th-century editions. Owing to the church's expansion to five continents, the hymnal's foreword reflects such current theological concerns as sexist language, ethnic identity, theological relevance, and contemporary style. It includes 25 spirituals arranged by Harry T. Burleigh, John Wesley Work Jr., and Wendell Whalum. "Lift Every Voice and Sing," written in 1900 by James Weldon Johnson and J. Rosamond Johnson and regarded as "the Negro national anthem," was added for the first time. Gospel songs by Thomas Dorsey, Doris Akers, Kenneth Morris, and Andraé Crouch are present. A decrease in Wesleyan hymnody is also evident in this edition, while the number of social gospel hymns such as "O Beautiful for Spacious Skies" and "God Save America" increased. Compositions by female AME leaders such as Vivienne L. Anderson and Edith Ming are also included. The 2000 reprint is titled *African Methodist Episcopal Church Hymnal*.

In the 21st century AME churches more freely supplement music from their denominational hymnals with other popular sacred music collections such as the black United Methodists' *Songs of Zion* (1980), black gospel music, and in some less conservative or neo-Pentecostal leaning congregations, urban contemporary gospel and songs from the contemporary Christian music sub-genre of praise and worship. Resistance to drums, electric guitars, synthesizers, and brass and wind instruments in non-classical contexts has relaxed since the late 20th century, and some contemporary AME churches also actively support dance ministries.

See also METHODISM.

BIBLIOGRAPHY

C.E. Lincoln and L.H. Mamiya: *The Black Church in the African American Experience* (Durham, NC, 1990)

J.M. Spencer: "The Hymnody of the African Methodist Episcopal Church," *American Music*, viii (1990), 274–93

J.T. Campbell: *Songs of Zion: the African Methodist Episcopal Church in the United States and South Africa* (New York, 1995)

E. Southern: *The Music of Black Americans A History* (New York, 3/1997)

J. Abbington, ed.: *Readings in African American Church Music and Worship* (Chicago, 2001) [incl. E. Southern: "Hymnals of the Black Church"; D. L. White: "Hymnody of the African American Church"]

BIRGITTA J. JOHNSON

African Methodist Episcopal Zion Church [AMEZ]. The second-largest black Methodist denomination, with 1.4 million members in the United States and abroad. The first AMEZ congregation was organized in New York in 1796. Its members were African Americans who left the John Street Methodist Episcopal Church due to rising racial discrimination, especially in worship, from the predominantly white members of the congregation. Similar circumstances had previously led Richard Allen and the black Methodists in Philadelphia to found the AFRICAN METHODIST EPISCOPAL CHURCH in 1794. In 1801 the AMEZ denominational charter was established, and in 1821 James Varick was appointed the first bishop. In order to distinguish themselves from the AME Church, the New York group officially added "Zion" to their name in 1848. The Zion Church became known as the "Freedom Church," with abolitionist members such as Harriet Tubman, Sojourner Truth, and Frederick Douglass, and missionary efforts that emphasized social service and education.

Hymnody was very important in English Methodism and was the main music tradition in Methodist churches of the northern United States in the late 18th century. In 1838 Christopher Rush and others compiled and published the AME Zion Church's first hymnal, *Hymns for the Use of the African Methodist Episcopal Zion Church in America*. Like many hymnals of the period it did not include musical notation. In 1869 an "Improved Edition" was published that included 582 hymns. Compiled by Rush, Samuel M. Giles, and Joseph P. Thompson, each hymn text provided a metrical indication as well as a tune suggestion. The growth of the AME Zion Church, particularly its expansion in the American South after the Civil War, led to the publication of another edition of this hymnal in 1872. With 1129 hymns, it is still the largest collection of songs the denomination has published. Following the general practice of early African American hymnals, editions of AME Zion hymns identified black contributors by name. Early hymnwriters of the AME Zion Church include W.J. Wells, Stephen Gill Spottwood, Bettye Lee Roberts Alleyne, and C.C. Alleyne. Church music at the turn of the 20th century included unaccompanied congregational song, hymns accompanied on the piano, arranged spirituals, and sacred art music. Urban AME Zion churches were among the first independent black churches to purchase organs. With the exception of some congregations in the rural South, AMEZ churches did not actively maintain musical folk performance traditions and worship styles with overt African-derived aesthetics, as did some black Baptist and Pentecostal groups.

In the mid-20th century the AMEZ headquarters relocated to Charlotte, North Carolina, and published an updated hymnal, *AME Zion Hymnal*, in 1957. It consisted of 721 songs, including musical notation and liturgical guidelines. The edition included popular hymns and songs from previous editions, African American spirituals, 20th-century hymns, devotional songs, and gospel hymns. Whereas many middle-class AMEZ churches were reluctant to accept blues-tinged gospel songs in Sunday worship during the 1920s and 1930s, by the 1960s the gospel music by Thomas Dorsey, Sallie Martin, Roberta Martin, Thurston Frazier, and James Cleveland had crossed most denominational borders and become part of the musical repertoire of many AME Zion churches. The current hymnbook, *The AME Zion Bicentennial Hymnal,* published in 1996, includes songs by these and other gospel composers. At the beginning of the 21st century, choirs and instrumentalists have become an important part of music-making in churches. Instrumentation often includes electric keyboard, the Hammond B3 organ, electric guitars, and drums, while some congregations employ small chamber ensembles of string, woodwind, and brass instruments.

BIBLIOGRAPHY

Hymns for the Use of the African Methodist Episcopal Zion Church in America (New York, 1872)

C.E. Lincoln and L.H. Mamiya: *The Black Church in the African American Experience* (Durham, NC, 1990)

D. Miller, ed.: *The AME Zion Bicentennial Hymnal* (Charlotte, 1996)

E. Southern: *The Music of Black Americans: a History* (New York, 3/1997)

J. Abbington: *Readings in African American Church Music and Worship* (Chicago, 2001) [incl. E. Southern: "Hymnals of the Black Church"; D.L. White: "Hymnody of the African American Church"]

BIRGITTA J. JOHNSON

Afrika Bambaataa [Aasim, Kevin Donovan] (*b* New York, NY, 10 April 1960). Hip-hop DJ. DJ Afrika Bambaataa's musical eclecticism and his vision of African American unity helped to shape rap music's early sound, and he is often credited with lending the burgeoning musical style, and the larger culture from which it emerged, the name "hip hop."

Born Kevin Donovan, he grew up amidst an omnipresent gang culture that emerged in the wake of urban planning and deindustrialization that devastated New York's South Bronx neighborhoods. He became a founding member and warlord of one such street gang, the Black Spades. Exposed as a youth to the politics of the black liberation movement, however, he sought ways to transcend gang life. As an expression of racial unity and spiritual rebirth, he changed his name to Afrika Bambaataa Asim, adopting the name of a Zulu chief who led an armed insurrection in pre-Apartheid South Africa. In 1973, he organized local hip-hop luminaries into the Universal Zulu Nation in an effort to promote peace and unity among Bronx gangs. He subsequently founded the community organization Bronx River Organization.

Like Bronx compatriots DJ Grandmaster Flash and DJ Kool Herc, Bambaataa and his crew hosted parties for local youth. As a DJ, he looped the percussive sections (breakbeats) from obscure rock, funk, and electro-pop records as rhythm tracks for rappers, adding unexpected layers to these beats using bits of cartoon melodies and film themes. During the late 1970s, Bambaataa formed two rap crews: the Jazzy 5, including MC Ice, Master D.E.E., AJ Les, and Mr. Freeze, and Soulsonic Force, including Emcee G.L.O.B.E., Mr. Biggs, and Pow Wow. Both groups debuted 12-inch singles under the Paul Winley Record label in 1980, a time when hip hop was moving from school gymnasium dances to recording studios.

Disappointed with Winley's production on "Death Mix," and "Zulu Nation Throwdown," Bamabaataa signed with Tommy Boy Records, collaborating with Tom Silverman, Soul Sonic Force, John Robie, and engineer Arthur Baker to record the pop-rap hit "Planet Rock" (1982). Incorporating the melodies of Kraftwerk and film composer Ennio Morricone—the latter by way of "The Mexican," a track by British rock group Babe Ruth—the record became an international hit and ignited a trend for futuristic electronic dance music. Bambaataa and a group of dancers, graffiti artists, and DJs soon embarked on the first international hip-hop tour. Bambaataa, together with Soulsonic Force, next recorded

Afrika Bambaataa, 2006. (CHIP EAST/Reuters/Landov)

"Looking for the Perfect Beat" and "Renegades of Funk" (1983). He then developed two groups, Time Zone and Shango, with Celluloid Records, releasing the full-length album *Shango Funk Theology* (1984). That same year he appeared in the hip-hop film *Beat Street* and recorded the song "Unity" with James Brown. Since the mid-1990s Bambaataa has collaborated on numerous electronica albums, including *Dark Matter Moving at the Speed of Light* (2004). Although no longer at the forefront of the rap music industry, Bambaataa continues to be an active participant and leader in hip-hop culture worldwide.

BIBLIOGRAPHY

C. Keyes: "At the Crossroads: Rap Music and Its African Nexus," *EthM*, xl/2 (1996), 223–48

J. Fricke and C. Ahearn: *Yes Yes Y'All: the Experience Music Project Oral History of Hip-Hop's First Decade* (Cambridge, MA, 2002)

J. Chang: *Can't Stop Won't Stop: a History of the Hip Hop Generation* (New York, 2005)

DAVID TOOP/MARGARET JACKSON

Afro-American music. *See* African American music.

Afro-Caribbean Music. The field of Afro-Caribbean music comprises a vast and heterogeneous corpus of genres and practices, with most forms of Caribbean music evolving as syncretic products of diverse African- and European-derived elements. Many of these genres have established substantial presences in or influences on music culture in the mainland United States, whether through the activities of diasporic communities or via cross-cultural interactions.

Afro-Caribbean musics may be regarded as spanning a gamut of styles. On one end would lie various neo-African traditional genres that bear close affinities to counterparts or predecessors in Africa and may even embody marginal survivals of entities now obscure in that continent. Particularly prominent in the neo-African category are the many Afro-Caribbean genres—both recreational as well as religious—that feature a West African-derived format of three drums playing ostinato-based rhythms, accompanying call-and-response singing and dancing by groups, couples, or an individual.

The 20th century saw the emergence of a rich and dynamic variety of creole commercial popular music genres whose styles evolved in connection with the new mass media of records and, from the 1920s, radio. Most of these genres were distinctively Afro-Caribbean both in stylistic features as well as the social milieus that generated them and the personnel that performed them. Several came to enjoy considerable popularity in the United States, and especially in New York City, whose mass media infrastructure, immigrant enclaves, and receptive non-Caribbean audiences enabled it to become a dynamic secondary center of Caribbean popular music. At the same time, African American popular musics, from rock to rap, exerted their own sorts of influences on Caribbean popular music scenes, resulting in a dynamic and ongoing process of mutual inspiration and cross-fertilization.

The Spanish-speaking islands of Cuba, Puerto Rico, and the Dominican Republic contain some 60% of the insular Caribbean population and may be said to host the richest diversity of Afro-Caribbean musics. Neo-African music has flourished with particular vigor in Cuba, for several reasons; unlike in the British colonies and the United States, most slaves were imported in the 1800s, with some arriving as late as 1873. Further, from the early colonial period, Spanish manumission practices facilitated the presence of substantial communities of free people of color, many of whom were able to congregate in urban mutual-support societies called *cabildos* where they could cultivate traditional musical practices with only irregular interference. Bantu speakers from the Western Congo region tended to predominate among 17th- and 18th-century slaves, providing a sort of stylistic foundation for much subsequent Afro-Cuban and even creole music culture. Generally ascribed to Congolese derivation are the now-common Conga drums and the traditional Rumba (i)—a recreational dance-music genre featuring three congas and an extended responsorial final section accompanying dancing by a couple or a solo male.

Most of the enslaved Africans brought to Cuba in the 19th century were Yorubas from present-day Nigeria. In *cabildos* and other contexts the Yoruba or *lucumí* were able to cultivate a sort of consolidated and streamlined version of their traditional religion and its associated musics. Especially basic to the music of this religion—called Santería or *regla de ocha*—was a standardized ritual repertoire of Yoruba-language songs (of diverse regional and ritual origins) that came to be accompanied by a trio of *batá* hourglass drums. Despite inconsistent forms of repression, Santería has been able to flourish not only in Cuba but also in Puerto Rico and among Spanish Caribbean communities in urban mainland United States. Both ritual performers as well as interested others have been able to cultivate their interest in Santería music, freely availing themselves, as needed, of websites, commercial recordings, pedagogical literature, and other resources. A few ethnomusicologists lead *batá* ensembles at American universities, and knowledgeable performers of diverse backgrounds abound in New York, Miami, and elsewhere.

The primary Afro-Caribbean traditional dance music genre in Puerto Rico, whose slave population was considerably smaller, has been *bomba*, documented since the early 1800s, and most typically comprising a trio of squat barrel drums accompanying informal responsorial singing and dancing by an individual who interacts with the lead drummer (as in such genres as Cuban *rumba columbia,* Guadeloupean *gwo ka*, and the *tambú* of Curaçao). In the Dominican Republic, the neo-African music presence is also less conspicuous than in Cuba, as the importation of slaves declined much sooner, and a cattle-based mode of production favored racial and cultural creolization rather than persistence of Old World traditions. Nevertheless, Afro-Dominican *palo* drumming, with its responsorial singing and occasional spirit possession, is widespread. Since the latter 20th century, both *bomba* and *palo* have been benefiting from a new valorization of Afro-Caribbean heritage and are occasionally performed in

New York and other American cities both as folkloric stage items and in immigrant festivities.

It was also in Cuba that creole Caribbean vernacular music and dance genres emerged earliest and with greatest vigor. Outstanding in this category was the *contradanza*, which—although primarily derived from European counterparts—had, by the early 1800s, acquired local character in the form of creole and ultimately Afro-Caribbean-derived syncopations, especially the "habanera" or "tango" rhythm. Within a few decades local *contradanza* variants were also flourishing in Puerto Rico and the Dominican Republic, under the names DANZA and merengue, and also in New Orleans, where the interactions of French Caribbean creole musicians with African American counterparts would in the early 1900s century generate both ragtime—related to contradance variants—as well as early jazz.

In early twentieth-century Havana, the son emerged as the first of a series of dynamic commercial Afro-Cuban popular music genres that would in the mid-century decades include the mambo and cha cha chá. Although by that period watered-down forms of Cuban dance music had become popular in the United States, there was nothing diluted about the dynamic big-band mambo of the 1950s that flourished with equal vigor in Havana and New York, where it was avidly danced by Anglo- and Afro-Americans as well as Latinos. The 1950s also saw the emergence of Latin jazz, typically involving small combos foregrounding improvised solos over Afro-Cuban rhythms, in a format meant for listening rather than dance.

The advent of the Cuban Revolution in 1959 vitiated that island's dance music milieu for decades, but in the years around 1970 Puerto Rican and "Nuyorican" musicians rearticulated and modernized the modern *son* under the rubric SALSA (i), a genre whose popularity spread to much of Latin America. Afro-Caribbean features are somewhat less overt in the Dominican *merengue*, although its responsorial *jaleo* sections and often syncopated melodies enable it to be broadly characterized as Afro-Latin. Since the 1980s New York, with its large and dramatically increasing Dominican immigrant community, has itself become a secondary hub for *merengue*.

Afro-Caribbean musics in the French Caribbean can be seen to comprise categories akin to those in the Spanish Caribbean. The predominant syncretic neo-African religion, Haitian Vodun, derives primarily from Dahomeyan and Congolese sources. Its ceremonial music most characteristically features three drums accompanying responsorial singing in mixed Haitian creole and West African-derived "*langaj*." In Martinique and Guadeloupe, *belé* and *gwo ka*, respectively, would come to flourish as neo-African dance-music genres—*belé* most typically as a couple dance, and *gwo ka* as a solo dance in front of a trio of drummers. In the 1950s, Haitian *konpa* (*compas*) emerged as the dominant commercial dance music of the French Caribbean, thriving equally in New York, Miami, and Quebec with the growth of Haitian diasporic communities. The more modernized *zouk* emanating from Martinique and Guadeloupe in the 1980s found greater international presence in France than in North America.

In the former plantation colonies of the British West Indies, persistence of neo-African musics was limited by the early cessation (in 1804) of slave imports and a more culturally repressive and Christianizing milieu. Hence, many traditional dance music genres, such as Trinidadian *bongo* dancing, have largely died out. However, neo-African genres, typically using the familiar three-drum format, do survive in select West Indian locales, such as the eclectic "big drum" socio-religious dances of Carriocou. Still found in some rural Jamaican parishes is the syncretic *kumina* religion, with its distinctive singing and drumming tradition. Another persistent and presently re-Africanizing music tradition is that of the Orisha or Shango religion brought to Trinidad by Yoruba indentured workers in the 1850s.

The absence of settler nationalism in the British colonies tended to retard the emergence of distinctive creole music cultures. Since around 1970, Jamaica nevertheless became an international musical powerhouse, as "roots" reggae, with its idiosyncratic Afrocentricity, burst upon the world music scene, enjoying mass appeal especially among white American youth. REGGAE, however, evolved less from any deep neo-African folk traditions than from local ska, itself a Jamaicanized version of 1950s American rhythm-and-blues disseminated by sound systems playing imported records. From the mid-1970s such sound systems typically included vocalists who voiced lyrics over vinyl records played by a "selector" manipulating turntables, foreshadowing practices that a few years later would become standard in New York hip hop. In the early 1980s this "dancehall" format, in which a "deejay" voiced over a pre-recorded instrumental track, largely replaced roots reggae and subsequently established its own niche in American music culture, peopled by West Indian immigrants and a mix of African and Anglo-American fans.

Throughout the region and its diasporic extensions in the United States, Afro-Caribbean popular music genres have continued to hybridize and proliferate, as in the case of the Spanish-language dancehall variant reggaeton, which burst on the scene in the new millennium. The resiliency of primordial Afro-Caribbeanisms is evident in the way that both reggaeton and Trinidadian soca rearticulate the hoary "habanera" rhythm whose original inspiration may be primarily Congolese. Alongside such atavisms continues the ongoing engagement with contemporary American and especially African American popular musics, inspiring, for example, the Puerto Rican and Cuban rap enlivening the margins of the Latin music scene since the 1990s.

See also LATIN AMERICAN MUSIC; LATINO MUSIC.

BIBLIOGRAPHY

J. Guilbault: *Zouk: World Music in the West Indies* (Chicago, 1993)
R. Glasser: *My Music is My Flag: Puerto Rican Musicians and Their New York Communities, 1917–1940* (Berkeley, 1995)
P. Austerlitz: *Merengue: Dominican Music and Dominican Identity* (Philadelphia, 1997)
G. Averill: *A Day for the Hunter, A Day for the Prey: Music and Power in Haiti* (Chicago, 1997)
J.S. Roberts: *The Latin Tinge: The Impact of Latin American Music on the United States* (New York, 2/1998)
J.S. Roberts: *Latin Jazz: The First of the Fusions: 1880s to Today* (New York, 1999)

S. Barrow and P. Dalton: *The Rough Guide to Reggae* (London, 2001)
M. Salazar: *Mambo Kingdom: Latin Music in New York* (New York, 2002)
N. Sublette: *Cuba and Its Music from the First Drums to the Mambo* (Chicago, 2004)
P. Manuel, with K. Bilby and M. Largey: *Caribbean Currents: Caribbean Music from Rumba to Reggae* (Philadelphia, 2006)
C. Washburne: *Sounding Salsa: Performing Latin Music in New York City* (Philadelphia, 2008)

PETER MANUEL

Afro-Cuban jazz. *See* LATIN JAZZ.

Afshar, Lily (*b* Tehran, Iran, 9 March 1960). Guitarist and educator of Iranian birth. She took up the guitar at the age of ten, later moving to the United States. She received BM and MM degrees in guitar from the Boston Conservatory and the New England Conservatory of Music. In 1986, she was among 12 guitarists selected by Andrés Segovia to perform in his master classes held at the University of Southern California. In 1989, she earned a Doctorate of Music degree in guitar performance from Florida State University, under the direction of Bruce Holzman. She was the first woman worldwide to receive this degree. She studied with Oscar Ghiglia at the Banff School of Fine Arts, Aspen Music Festival, and Siena (Accademia Musicale Chigiana). Among her awards are a Grand Prize in the 1986 Aspen Music Festival Guitar Competition, Top Prize in the 1988 Guitar Foundation of America Competition, a NEA recording award, and selection by the United States Information Agency to Africa as an Artistic Ambassador in 1995. Her scholarship on composer Mario Castelnuovo-Tedesco's *24 Caprichos de Goya*, op.195, includes both her doctoral thesis, as well as a complete recording (1994, Summit Records). She is notable as a strong advocate for new composition for the classical guitar. Her Archer Records CDs *Possession* (2002) and *Hemispheres* (2006) feature eight world premieres. *Hemispheres* showcases a new technical possibility on the instrument: the performance of quarter-tone melodies through the inclusion of added "fretlets." She heads the University of Memphis guitar program.

M. RUSTY JONES

Agee, James Rufus (*b* Knoxville, TN, 27 Nov 1909; *d* New York, NY, 16 May 1955). Novelist, screenwriter, journalist, poet, and film critic. Son of Laura Tyler Agee and Hugh James (Jay) Agee, James Agee graduated from Exeter Academy and Harvard University (1932), before becoming a staff writer for *Fortune* magazine, eventually writing film reviews for both *Time* (1939) and *The Nation* (1942). On assignment from *Fortune*, Agee worked in collaboration with the photographer Walker Evans on the study of Alabama tenant farmers, *Let Us Now Praise Famous Men* (Boston, 1941). His book of poetry, *Permit Me Voyage*, was published by the Yale Series of Younger Poets (New Haven, CT, 1934). In 1951, Agee published the novella, *The Morning Watch* (Boston). He was the principal author of the screenplay for *The African Queen* (1950) and *The Night of the Hunter* (1954). His last major work, the autobiographical novel, *A Death in the Family*, was posthumously published in 1957 (New York), winning the Pulitzer Prize, which was also bestowed on the novel's stage adaptation, *All the Way Home* (New York, 1960).

The composer Samuel Barber had a long association with the writings of Agee, beginning with his settings of poems from *Permit Me Voyage* (1938) and culminating in the musical setting (for soprano and orchestra) of Agee's well-regarded prose-poem, *Knoxville, Summer of 1915* (1947). S. Cumberworth, D. Diamond, W. Meyer, T. Pasatieri, and D. Welcher, among others, have used Agee's poems in various settings.

BIBLIOGRAPHY

D. Madden, ed.: *Remembering James Agee* (Baton Rouge, 1974)
N.L. Huse: *John Hersey and James Agee: a Reference Guide* (Boston, 1978)
L. Bergreen: *James Agee: a Life* (New York, 1984)
M.A. Lofaro, ed.: *A Death in the Family: a Restoration of the Author's Text, The Works of James Agee*, i (Knoxville, 2007)

JOSEPH A. BROWN

Ager, Milton (*b* Chicago, IL, 6 Oct 1893; *d* Los Angeles, CA, 6 May 1979). Composer. He began his career as a song plugger and arranger for the publishing companies of George M. Cohan and Irving Berlin, and had his first success as a songwriter (in collaboration with the composer George W. Meyer) with "Everything's peaches down in Georgia" (G. Clarke, 1918), introduced by Al Jolson. He wrote many songs to lyrics by Jack Yellen (with whom he founded the publishing firm Ager, Yellen & Bornstein in 1922), including "I wonder what's become of Sally" (1924), "Ain't she sweet?" (1927) and "Happy days are here again" (1930); the last became closely associated with the presidential campaigns of Franklin D. Roosevelt. Other well-known songs by Ager are "I'm nobody's baby" (lyrics by B. Davis; 1921), "Auf Wiedersehen, my dear" (A. Hoffman, E.G. Nelson, A. Goodhart; 1932), and, in collaboration with Jean Schwartz, "Trust in me" (N. Wever; 1936). His contributions to stage scores include songs for *What's in a Name?* (1920, with "A Young Man's Fancy"), *Rain or Shine* (1928), and *John Murray Anderson's Almanac* (1929). He also wrote music for the films *Honky Tonk* (1929), *Chasing Rainbows* (1930), and *King of Jazz* (1930).

BIBLIOGRAPHY

J. Burton: *Blue Book of Tin Pan Alley* (Watkins Glen, NY, 1950, 2/1965), 288, 303
Obituary, *New York Times* (8 May 1979)

SAMUEL S. BRYLAWSKI

AGMA. *See* AMERICAN GUILD OF MUSICAL ARTISTS.

Agramonte y Piña, Emilio (*b* Puerto Príncipe, Cuba, ?28 Nov 1844; *d* Havana, ?31 Dec 1918). Pianist, music teacher, arranger, conductor, composer, and lawyer of Cuban birth, naturalized American. Born into a prominent family in Puerto Príncipe, Cuba (present-day Camagüey), Agramonte strongly supported the movement for independence from Spain. He studied music and the law in Cuba, Spain, and France. After vocal studies with Enrico Delle Sedie (1822–1907) and François Delsarte (1811–71) at the Paris Conservatory, he immigrated to the United States, settling in New York in 1869, where he remained until after Cuban independence in 1898. He became a US citizen in 1886.

In the 1870s and 1880s, Agramonte taught music at the Academy of Mount Saint Vincent in the Bronx. In the 1890s he taught with Dudley Buck and William Mason at the Metropolitan College of Music and ran his own School of Opera and Oratorio at his home, teaching singers such as Emilio de Gogorza and Rosalía Chalía, as well as students from the Cuban émigré and European-American communities. José Martí, the "father of Cuban independence" and editor of the New York-based revolutionary newspaper *Patria*, praised Agramonte for his educational work, for his promotion of Wagner's music, and for his 1892 arrangement of Pedro Figuredo y Cisneros's (1819–70) Cuban patriotic hymn "La Bayamesa" (now the Cuban national anthem).

Besides teaching voice, Agramonte sponsored annual recitals at Chickering and Steinway Halls in which he accompanied his most talented pupils and invited guest musicians, and for which he favored a contemporary, international repertory along with a heavy dose of American music, especially the works of Edward MacDowell, Arthur Foote, and George W. Chadwick. He founded the American Composers' Choral Association in 1890, presenting two seasons of American choral concerts before merging with the Manuscript Society of New York. To raise funds for the Cuban revolution, Agramonte and his Latin American compatriots, such as violinists Rafael Díaz Albertini and Carlos Hasselbrink, and singer Emilio de Gogorza, often performed at soirees, periodically performing Spanish and Cuban music. From 1888 to the time of his return to Cuba in 1902, Agramonte directed the Gounod Society of New Haven, Connecticut, one of the best choruses in New England, which grew to include 300 singers. Back in Cuba, he established the Sociedad Coral Chaminade in Havana and taught at the Municipal Music Academy there (now the Conservatorio Amadeo Roldán). He later returned to live in the United States.

BIBLIOGRAPHY

Grove2, Amer. suppl.

F. Calcagno: "Agramonte, Emilio," *Diccionario biográfico cubano* (New York, 1878)

W.S.B. Mathews, ed.: *A Hundred Years in America: an Account of Musical Effort in America* (Chicago, 1889), 202–5

S. Ramírez: "Agramonte, Emilio," *La Habana artística: Apuntes históricos* (Havana, 1891), 365

C. Ripoll, ed.: *Escritos desconocidas de José Martí* (New York, 1971)

A. León: *Del canto y el tiempo* (Havana, 1974), 229–30

J. Koegel: "José Martí's *Patria*, Cuban Émigré Musicians, and the Cuban Independence Movement in New York City in the 1890s," *Music, American Made: Essays in Honor of John Graziano*, ed. J. Koegel (Sterling Heights, MI, 2011), 63–90

JOHN KOEGEL

Aguabella, Francisco (*b* Simpson, Matanzas, Cuba, 10 Oct 1925; *d* Los Angeles, CA, 7 May 2010). Cuban drummer. A master drummer, Francisco Aguabella's expertise in Afro-Cuban sacred drumming traditions included Lucumí *batá*, Iyesá, Arará, and Abakwá, as well as the popular genres of *rumba*, *comparsa*, *salsa*, rock, and Latin jazz. At age 12, Aguabella began playing Lucumí *batá* drums with friend and mentor Esteban "Chacha" Vega. At 18, he joined the local Abakwá society Efi Yumane, befriending fellow drummer Julito Collazo. In 1947 Aguabella moved to Havana to work as a longshoreman and musician. He played sacred *batá* drums for Lucumí ceremonies and performed in the popular "Sun Sun Babae" show at the Sans Souci Club with Trinidad Torregrosa, Raul Díaz, and Merceditas Valdés until the early 1950s. He also played lead *quinto* for the *comparsa* band "Los Dandys de Belen." In 1953 choreographer Katherine Dunham invited Aguabella to join her dance company, with whom he toured Europe, South America, the United States, and Australia for the next four years. In 1957, after the dance company dissolved, Aguabella settled in California. A versatile composer and musician, Aguabella performed, recorded, and toured with Tito Puente, Mongo Santamaría, Dizzy Gillespie, Peggy Lee, Frank Sinatra, Eddie Palmieri, Cachao, Lalo Schifrin, Cal Tjader, MALO, Paul Simon, and many others. He was awarded the NEA National Heritage Fellowship in 1992 and the Durfee Foundation's Master Musicians' Fellowship in 1997.

BIBLIOGRAPHY
(and other resources)

Sworn to the Drum: A Tribute to Francisco Aguabella, film, dir. L. Blank, Flower Films (United States, 1995)

R. Fernandez: *From Afro-Cuban Rhythms to Latin Jazz* (Berkeley, 2006)

KATHERINE HAGEDORN

Aguilar, Gustavo (*b* Brownsville, TX, 2 Nov 1962). Percussionist, improviser, and composer. He received his bachelor's degree from Corpus Christi State University; his master's degrees in percussion performance from the California Institute of the Arts, where he studied with John Bergamo; and a DMA in contemporary music performance from the University of California, San Diego, where he studied with Steven Schick and Anthony Davis. An experimental performer and composer, he also studied with AACM member Wadada Leo Smith, who shaped his interest in the improvisatory and free jazz elements of Chicago's creative music scene. Aguilar's interdisciplinary approach to composition combines improvised and fully notated musical elements with the use of new technologies and informed by an interest in cultural and critical studies. His compositions, such as *Different Paths, Same Destination* (2003), incorporate elements of free jazz, structured improvisation, industrial sound, white noise, guitar as a hand-percussion instrument, and spatial sound relationships—while using instrumentation that relies primarily on various percussion instruments. Aguilar's compositional processes include what he calls "imaginative reaction compositions" whereby he shares with musicians a number of elements—such as poetry, a variety of musical excerpts, and random thoughts and ideas—prior to recording their collective improvisation. The musicians listen to pre-recorded melodic and rhythmic structures Aguilar has composed and create collective, free improvisations, incorporating their interpretation of the shared elements. Dedicated to Julio Estrada, Aguilar's *Xochicalco* (2004) is a fine example of this process.

Aguilar has performed at major festivals throughout the Americas, Europe, and Asia, and has presented lectures and masterclasses at universities and symposia across the United States and abroad. Although he has a long history of collaboration with dancers, filmmakers, poets, painters, dramaturges, and sound installation artists, including Estrada, Annea Lockwood, and Roger Reynolds, he also demonstrates an interest in obscuring the relationships between composer/performer and between media. Aguilar's recent endeavors include work with the Gustavo Aguilar Get Libre Collective, the Aguilar/Howard Duo with saxophonist and electronics pioneer, Earl Howard, and soNu, an electro-acoustic ensemble. His discography includes solo and collaborative releases on Acoustic Levitation Records, Circumvention Music, Edition Modern, Mode Records, Mutable Music, Nine Winds Records, Samsung-Ak, Sang-Joong-Ha Music, and TaRaGa. Aguilar is Assistant Professor of Experimental Performance for the Department of Sound, Performance, and Visual Inquiry at the University of Maine, Farmington, and music director with GroundWorks Dance Theater of Cleveland, Ohio.

WORKS
(selective list)

Heart and Vine, 2002; RoKaMaYoHa, 2002; Ah, Raza! The Making of an American Artist, 2006; Dirac's Theory, 2007; Contrafactum for Scelsi, 2007; Xochicalco (for Julio), 2007; Free Fall and the Acceleration of Gravity (Part I), 2008; Not Knowing The Cart Got In Front (Part II), 2009; Magnolia Wars, 2011; Borrowed Time, 2011; Small Acts, 2011

ELDONNA L. MAY

Aguilera, Christina (María) (*b* New York, NY, 18 Dec 1980). Singer. She is one of the most popular singers of her generation. Her father (originally from Ecuador), a sergeant in the US Army, and her American mother, a Spanish teacher, divorced when Aguilera was seven. As a child, Aguilera placed second on the television show *Star Search*, and performed on the *Mickey Mouse Club* along with Justin Timberlake and Britney Spears. In 1998, she launched her recording career with a track for Disney's animated film *Mulan*. In 1998 she also signed with RCA, and her first album, *Christina Aguilera* (1999) reached number one on the Billboard 200. Her singles from that album, "Genie in a Bottle," "What a Girl Wants," and "Come on Over Baby" reached Number 1 on the Billboard Hot 100. Her first Spanish language album, *Mi reflejo* (2000), stood for 20 weeks at Number 1 on the Billboard Latin charts and earned her a Latin Grammy for Best Female Pop Vocal Album. In 2002 Aguilera released a more adult album with BMG, *Stripped*, which reached Number 2 on the Billboard 200. Her third English language album, *Back to Basics* (2006), also reached Number 1 but her fourth, *Bionic* (2010), received mixed reviews and only limited commercial success. In 2010, Aguilera co-starred with Cher in Steven Antin's film *Burlesque*. Known for the power and range of her voice, as well as her frequent melismatic displays, she has received four Grammys and one Latin Grammy, and made *Rolling Stone*'s list of the 100 Greatest Singers of All Time, the youngest to do so. In 2005, Aguilera married music executive Jordan Bratman, with whom she had a son in 2008. The two later filed for divorce in 2010.

BIBLIOGRAPHY

L. Degnen: *Christina Aguilera* (New York, 2000)
M. Marron: *Christina Aguilera* (New York, 2000)
M. Donovan: *Christina Aguilera: a Biography* (Greenwood, CA, 2010)

ABEL STEWART

Aguinaldo. A sacred and secular traditional song type in Puerto Rico and other areas of the Circum-Caribbean region (Trinidad, Venezuela), as well as in Mexico, Chile, Spain, and the Puerto Rican community in the United States. In Puerto Rico it is particularly associated with Christmas and is related to the non-polyphonic *villancico*. References to the aguinaldo date from the 17th century onwards, and the word has several meanings: a form of traditional *jíbaro* (rural Puerto Rican) music; a devotional song and musical genre performed at Christmas time to a repeated melodic, rhythmic, and harmonic pattern; a song sung in a secular context; a poetic form in hexasyllabic verse arranged in *décimas* (ten-line stanzas); and a gift given at Christmas or Epiphany. Aguinaldos are sung at the *Misa de aguinaldo* (Aguinaldo Mass), celebrated early in the morning each day for the nine days before Christmas. It is played and sung in church services by *comparsas* (ensembles) made up of the traditional *cuatro*, *guiro*, maracas, guitar, *pandareta*, and singers; by the organ; and sometimes by an ensemble of traditional instruments and modern ones such as the electric guitar and drum set. Traveling musicians also go from house to house performing aguinaldos as part of a *parranda* (itinerant group); in return for a song a gift might be given. Some Puerto Rican aguinaldos are named after the locations where the individual variants originated: *aguinaldo orocoveño* (from Orocovis) or *aguinaldo cageño* (from Caguas). Although the pseudonymous writer Guajataca, writing in 1860, regretted that rural traditions such as the aguinaldo were disappearing, the form has endured.

BIBLIOGRAPHY

Guajataca: "Los aguinaldos de Puerto Rico," *Almanaque-aguinaldo de la isla de Puerto Rico para el año de 1861* (n.p. [San Juan, Puerto Rico], 1860), 53–6
J.A. McCoy: *The Bomba and Aguinaldo of Puerto Rico as They Have Evolved from Indigenous, African, and European Cultures* (diss., Florida State U., 1969)
F. López Cruz: *El aguinaldo en Puerto Rico (Su evolución)* (San Juan, Puerto Rico, 1972)
D. Thompson and A.F. Thompson: *Music and Dance in Puerto Rico from the Age of Columbus to Modern Times: an Annotated Bibliography* (Metuchen, NJ, 1991)
P. Manuel, K. Bilby, and M. Largey: *Caribbean Currents: Caribbean Music from Rumba to Reggae* (Philadelphia, rev. 2/2006)

JOHN KOEGEL

Ahlert, Fred(erick) E. (*b* New York, NY, 19 Sept 1892; *d* New York, NY, 20 Oct 1953). Songwriter and arranger. He was raised in Manhattan and, after graduating from the City College of New York and Fordham Law School, took a job with publishers Waterson, Berlin, and Snyder. He began writing songs for vaudeville acts and had his first notable success with the 1920 song "I'd love to fall asleep and wake up in my mammy's arms" (co-written with Sam Lewis and Joe Young). In the 1920s and 1930s, he wrote arrangements for such dance orchestras as Irving Aaronson's Commanders and Fred Waring's Pennsylvanians. He is perhaps best remembered for his Tin Pan Alley collaborations with lyricist Roy Turk, with whom he wrote such songs as "I'll get by (as long as I have you)," "Mean to Me," "Walkin' My Baby Back Home," "Where the Blue of the Night Meets the Gold of the Day" (which became Bing Crosby's theme song), and "Love, You Funny Thing!" For a time in the early 1930s, Ahlert lived in Los Angeles where he wrote scores for films such as *Marianne* (1929) and Buster Keaton's *Free and Easy* (1930). Ahlert served on ASCAP's board of directors from 1933 until his death and also served as the society's president from 1948–50.

BRYAN S. WRIGHT

Ahlstrom, David C. (*b* Lancaster, NY, 22 Feb 1927; *d* San Francisco, CA, 23 Aug 1992). Composer. He studied at the Cincinnati Conservatory of Music, the Eastman School, and the California Institute of Asian Studies. His principal teachers were ALAN HOVHANESS, SIDNEY ROBERTSON COWELL, and BERNARD ROGERS. He taught at Northwestern University (1961–2), Southern Methodist University (1962–7), and Eastern Illinois University (1967–76) before moving to San Francisco as a freelance composer and writer. In 1982 he founded VOICES/SF, Bay Area Youth Opera, an ensemble specializing in new American musical theater. Ahlstrom's one-act chamber opera *Three Sisters who are not Sisters*, to a libretto by Gertrude Stein, was first performed on 1 March 1953 at the Cincinnati Conservatory. Two years later he set another Stein text, *Doctor Faustus Lights the Lights*; it was first performed by VOICES/SF on 29 Oct 1982. Both works recall the Thomson-Stein operas in their mixture of straightforward tonality and sophisticated prosody. His musical comedy *America, I love, You*, to poems by e.e. cummings, was first heard in New Orleans on 6 Jan 1981. Ahlstrom also wrote numerous children's operas and "mini-operas" intended for both children and adults; some of his several symphonies and his chamber works incorporate electronic sound.

HARRY HASKELL

Ahrens, Lynn (*b* New York, NY, 1 Oct 1948). Lyricist. She has collaborated frequently with STEPHEN FLAHERTY.

Aiken, Charles (*b* Goffstown, NH, 13 March 1818; *d* College Hill, OH, 4 Oct 1882). Music educator. He was born into a musical family and graduated from Dartmouth College (BA 1838). He then journeyed west conducting singing schools, eventually settling in Cincinnati in 1842 where he established a singing school at a Presbyterian church. He began his career in public school music in 1848 and was eventually appointed Cincinnati's first superintendent of music. He implemented an innovative primary and secondary school curriculum that culminated in yearly examinations of students and teachers. To assist teachers in his charge, he arranged for the publication of *The Young Singer Part I* and co-compiled *Part II* (Cincinnati, 1860). He expanded those works into *The Young Singer's Manual* (Cincinnati, 1866). That same year he published *The High School Choralist* (Boston), and later *The Choralist's Companion* (Cincinnati, 1872) and the *Cincinnati Music Readers* series (Cincinnati, 1875). Aiken retired in 1879 and was inducted into the Music Educators Hall of Fame in 1986.

BIBLIOGRAPHY

C.F. Goss and S.J. Clarke: *Cincinnati, the Queen City, 1788–1912* (Chicago, 1912), 350–5
C.L. Gary: *A History of Music Education in the Cincinnati Public Schools* (diss., U. of Cincinnati, 1951)
M.L. Mark and C.L. Gary: *A History of American Music Education* (New York, 1992, 3/2007)

VINCENT J. NOVARA

Aiken, Conrad (Potter) (*b* Savannah, GA, 5 Aug 1889; *d* Savannah, GA, 17 Aug 1973). Poet. A prolific writer throughout most of his long career, he produced thirty-three volumes of poetry, five novels, five short story collections, two books of criticism, and a play. When Aiken was eleven years of age, his father killed his mother and then himself, and he spent the rest of his childhood with an aunt in Cambridge, Massachusetts. He became an admirer of Freud, and his works often stress psychological themes. Other influences include T. S. Eliot (a fellow student at Harvard) and Emily Dickinson (whose *Selected Poems* he edited in 1924). In many of his early poems, Aiken experimented with quasi-musical forms. Most notable among these are the six poetic sequences that he called "symphonies": *The Charnel Rose* (1918), *The Jig of Forslin* (1916), *The House of Dust* (1920), *Senlin* (1918), *The Pilgrimage of Festus* (1923), and *Changing Mind* (written in 1925). These works were revised, rearranged in the above order, and presented together in 1949 as *The Divine Pilgrim*. Aiken admitted that he used the word symphony "with considerable license," as he did not attempt to imitate symphonic forms. Instead he achieved a "symphonic" effect through the use of many recurring lyric motives and highly connotative or suggestive language. He described it as poetry that "will not so much present an idea as use its resonance." He also used a great deal of musical imagery, both in these works and in works not specifically related to musical forms.

One of Aiken's lyrics has been especially popular with composers—"Discordants," which was first published in *Turns and Movies and other Tales in Verse* (1916). Its first 12 lines have been extracted for use in several anthologies and variously retitled "Bread and Music," "Music I heard," or "Music I heard with you." Many musical settings of this excerpt have been published, including versions by Bernstein (in *Songfest*), Nordoff, and Hageman. Nordoff, Persichetti, and Crist have set other Aiken excerpts. Although many critics prefer the greater clarity and precision of his later poetry (especially the *Preludes* of the 1930s), composers have clearly concentrated on the more elusive, lyrical expressiveness found in the earlier poems.

BIBLIOGRAPHY

C.S. Lenhart: *Musical Influence on American Poetry* (Athens, GA, 1956)
J. Martin: *Conrad Aiken: a Life of his Art* (Princeton, NJ, 1962)

V. Mizelle: "Conrad Aiken's 'Music Strangely Subtle'," *Georgia Review*, xix (1965), 81–92
R.E. Carlile: "Great Circle: Conrad Aiken's Musico-literary Technique," *Georgia Review*, xxii (1968), 27–36
R.E. Carlile: *Conrad Aiken's Prose: the Musico-literary Perspective* (diss., U. of Georgia, 1971)
H. Hagenbuechle: "Epistemology and Musical Form in Conrad Aiken's Poetry," *Studies in the Literary Imagination*, xiii (1980), 7–25
R.J. Nicolosi: "T.S. Eliot and Music: an Introduction," *MQ*, lxvi (1980), 192–204
M. Hovland: *Musical Settings of American Poetry: a Bibliography* (Westport, CT, 1986)
T.R. Spivey and A. Waterman, eds.: *Conrad Aiken: a Priest of Consciousness* (New York, 1989)

HOWARD NIBLOCK

Aikin, Jesse B(owman) (*b* Chester Co., PA, 5 Mar 1808; *d* Montgomery Co., PA, 1900). Tune book compiler. He introduced a system of seven-shape notation in *The Christian Minstrel* (Philadelphia, 1846), a tune book containing many pieces found in the publications of Lowell Mason. The book underwent one revision and at least 171 reprintings by 1873 and reportedly sold more than 180,000 copies. Aikin's notation found widespread acceptance, particularly in the South, and eventually supplanted all other forms of shape-notation. It continues to be used in denominational hymnals and books of the southern gospel-music tradition. His other publications include *The Juvenile Minstrel* (Philadelphia, 1847), *Harmonia ecclesiae, or Companion to the Christian Minstrel* (Philadelphia, 1853), *The Sabbath-School Minstrel* (Philadelphia, 1859), *The Imperial Harmony* (with Chester G. Allen and Hubert P. Main, New York, 1876), and *The True Principles of the Science of Music* (Philadelphia, 1891, rev. 2/1893; round notation). Aikin was a singing-school teacher; he also sold organs in association with his son-in-law, Isaac R. Hunsberger, in Hatfield, Pennsylvania.

See also SHAPE-NOTE HYMNODY

BIBLIOGRAPHY

G.P. Jackson: *White Spirituals in the Southern Uplands* (Chapel Hill, NC, 1953/*R*)
P.G. Hammond: *A Study of "The Christian Minstrel" (1846) by Jesse B. Aikin* (thesis, Southern Baptist Theological Seminary, 1969)
P. D. Perrin, "Systems of scale notation in nineteenth-century American tune-books," *JRME*, xviii/3 (Fall 1970), 257–64
P.G. Hammond: "Jesse B. Aikin and *The Christian Minstrel*," *American Music*, iii (1985), 442–51

PAUL G. HAMMOND

Ailey, Alvin (*b* Rogers, TX, 5 Jan 1931; *d* New York, NY, 1 Dec 1989). Dancer, choreographer, and dance company director. He began to study dance at Lester Horton's studio in Los Angeles in 1949 and went to the East Coast as a member of Horton's dance company in 1953. After Horton's sudden death and the company's disbandment he joined the cast of the Broadway musical *House of Flowers* (1954), the first of several musicals and plays in which he appeared. In 1958 he assembled a group of dancers to perform his choreography at the 92nd Street YM-YWHA in New York City, and this group eventually grew into the company now called the Alvin Ailey American Dance Theater. His choreographic style combined modern dance, ballet, jazz dance, and elements of social and ethnic dance forms. Many of his works reflect the African American experience in their themes and music; his best-known work, *Revelations* (1960), is danced to spirituals that evoke images of the suffering of slavery, a joyous baptismal ritual, and an exuberant church choir. Although his company initially comprised only African American dancers, it was integrated in 1962, and his artistic vision became more universal in scope, exploring the emotions and dilemmas that all humans share. After retiring as a performer in 1965, he devoted his energies to choreography, both for his own company and others. He created dances for Samuel Barber's *Antony and Cleopatra*, which inaugurated the Metropolitan Opera's new home at Lincoln Center in 1966, and for Leonard Bernstein's *Mass* (1971), marking the opening of the John F. Kennedy Center for the Performing Arts in Washington, DC. *The River* (1970), created for American Ballet Theatre, was one of several works he choreographed to the music of Duke Ellington. Their association was later commemorated by CBS-TV in the telecast *Ailey Celebrates Ellington* (1974). *Cry*, which along with *Revelations* became a signature piece of his company, was a solo created in 1971 for Judith Jamison. Dedicated to his mother and danced to music by Alice Coltrane, Laura Nyro, and Voices of East Harlem, it was a tribute to the indomitable spirit of African American women. During Ailey's lifetime his company was named resident company of Clark Center for the Performing Arts (1960) and Brooklyn Academy of Music (1969), and the first resident modern dance company of City Center (1972). It made numerous tours abroad, often acting as an official goodwill ambassador. The difficult business of running a dance company, along with other pressures, resulted in an emotional breakdown in 1980 that interrupted but did not curtail his creative flow. His desire to make dances that spoke of and to the people has won a wholehearted response from audiences, and his company's popularity continues undiminished today.

WRITINGS

with A.P. Bailey: *Revelations: the Autobiography of Alvin Ailey* (Secaucus, NJ, 1996)

BIBLIOGRAPHY

S. Cook and J. Mazo: *The Alvin Ailey American Dance Theater* (New York, 1978)
J. Dunning: *Alvin Ailey: a Life in Dance* (Reading, MA, 1996)
International Dictionary of Modern Dance (Detroit, 1998)
International Encyclopedia of Dance (New York, 1998)
T. DeFrantz: *Dancing Revelations: Alvin Ailey's Embodiment of African American Culture* (New York, 2004)

SUSAN AU

Ainsworth, Henry (*b* Swanton Morley, Norfolk, England, 1570; *d* Amsterdam, Netherlands, *c*1622–3). English minister and biblical scholar. Ainsworth was expatriated as a "Brownist" in 1593 and settled in Amsterdam in 1597. He was the author of a number of religious tracts and translations, including *The Book of Psalmes: Englished both in Prose and Metre. With Annotations* (1612, 5/1644). This psalter, which includes 39 monophonic psalm tunes, "most taken from our former Englished psalms [and also] the gravest and easiest tunes of the French and Dutch psalms," was brought by the Pilgrim settlers to the Plymouth Colony in 1620, and was used in public worship until 1692, thereby establishing the tradition of PSALMODY in New England. By the late 17th century, however, it was no longer in use there, having been replaced by the Bay Psalm Book (1640) and other psalters.

See also PSALMS, METRICAL.

BIBLIOGRAPHY

Grove7 (H. Wiley Hitchcock/Nicholas Temperley); *DNB* (W.E.A. Axon and E. Axon)

W.E.A. Axon and E. Axon: "Henry Ainsworth, the Puritan Commentator," *Transactions of the Lancashire and Cheshire Antiquarian Society*, vi (1888), 42–57

W.S. Pratt: *The Music of the Pilgrims* (Boston, MA, 1921/*R*)

G. Chandler: *A Study of the 1618 and 1644 Editions of Henry Ainsworth's Psalter* (thesis, Union Theological Seminary, 1951)

J.H. Dorenkamp: "The 'Bay Psalm' Book and the Ainsworth Psalter," *Early American Literature*, viii (1972), 3–16

The Music of Henry Ainsworth's Psalter, ISAMm, xv, 1981 [incl. facs. and transcrs. of all 39 tunes]

M.E. Moody: "'A Man of a Thousand': the Reputation and Character of Henry Ainsworth, 1569/70–1622," *Huntington Library Quarterly*, vliii (1982), 200–214

H. WILEY HITCHCOCK/R

Aitken, Hugh (*b* New York, NY, 7 Sept 1924). Composer. He studied at the Juilliard School (where he later taught) with VINCENT PERSICHETTI, BERNARD WAGENAAR, and ROBERT WARD. In 1970 he was appointed chairman of the music department at William Paterson College in Wayne, New Jersey, where he became professor of music in 1973.

With firm musical principles rooted in Classical models, Aitken uses various effects to produce what he considers to be appropriate moods for his works. His style can be characterized as conservative and neoclassical, with rich polyphonic textures reminiscent of Hindemith, although more lyrical. His style is best demonstrated in works such as the *Aspen Concerto* (1989) and the Violin Concerto (1986), the first of which emphasizes line and development, while the second employs long, angular melodies that are tossed between soloist and orchestra. Later works like *Songs and Caprices* (2001) are not harmonically adventurous, but use popular and international styles as inspiration. The percussion writing in this work is perhaps its most striking feature. Like Stravinsky and Wuorinen, Aitken has looked to earlier music as an inspiration for several of his works. In *Rameau Remembered* (1980), based on airs and dances borrowed primarily from Rameau's *Castor and Pollux*, sections of the original are reworked or juxtaposed in a way that casts them in a new and interesting light. Aitken's contrapuntal skills are in evidence in works such as *In Praise of Ockeghem* (1977), where the dense texture of the string writing is juxtaposed with frequent shifts of tempo relationships like those found in Ockeghem's works.

Aitken has written two operas, *Fables* (1973–4) and *Felipe* (1980). The first is based on ten of Aesop's fables as retold by the 17th-century French poet La Fontaine. Translated and expanded by the composer, these tales explore issues of manners and morals and questions such as selfishness versus altruism and the nature of morality. The 30 roles are shared between four singers, and the episodic nature of the work is held together by a framing device in which the singers portray a band of travelling players. The composer characterizes the mainly tonal music as "eclectic," employing various musical styles resulting in "affectionate parody." Musical quotations, largely from Rameau, appear with ironic effect at certain moments in the plot. Rhythmic intricacy is evident throughout a score that is governed by subtlety of meter changes and nuance.

Felipe, set in 16th-century Seville, focusses on the unforeseen and serious consequences of a lighthearted attempt at seduction. The music is freely tonal, melodic, and rhythmically and metrically sophisticated. The use of Spanish Renaissance tunes, along with some Spanish text and guitar-like accompaniments, gives the opera its regional and cultural flavor.

WORKS
(selective list)

Stage: Fables, a Diversion (chbr op, 2, after La Fontaine), 1973–4, Wayne, NJ, William Paterson College, 23 Oct 1975; Felipe (op, 3, after M. de Cervantes: *El viejo celoso*), 1982, unperf.

Orch: In Praise of Ockeghem, str orch (1977), Rameau Remembered, fl, orch, 1980; Vn Conc., 1984; Aspen Conc., vn, orch, 1989; Sym., 1998; Songs and Caprices, chbr orch, 2001

Band: Suite in Six, 1964; 4 Quiet Pieces, 1967

Chbr and inst: Four Pieces, Four Hands, pf 4 hands, 1965; Suite, cl, 1965; 8 Studies, wind qnt, 1966; Partita, vn, 1968

BIBLIOGRAPHY

M. Redmond: 'Music in New Jersey: Fabulous *Fables*', *The Star-Ledger* (25 Oct 1975)

S. Wadsworth: 'Katonah, N.Y.', *Opera News* 41 (Sept 1976): 69.

R.H. Kornick: *Recent American Opera: a Production Guide* (New York, 1991), 12–14

H. Aitken: *The Piece as a Whole: Studies in Holistic Musical Analysis* (Westport, CT, 1997)

JAMES P. CASSARO

Aitken, John (*b* Dalkeith, Scotland, *c*1746; *d* Philadelphia, PA, 8 Sept 1831). Composer, music engraver, publisher, music dealer, and metalsmith of Scottish birth. Aitken worked as a metalsmith for much of his life, and arrived in Philadelphia by 1785. He began his career as a music publisher in 1787 with three large works: Alexander Reinagle's *A Selection of the Most Favorite Scots Tunes*, William Brown's *Three Rondos for the Piano Forte or Harpsichord*, and his own *A Compilation of the Litanies and Vespers Hymns and Anthems* (1/1787; 2/1791), the only 18th-century Anglo-American published collection of music for the Roman Catholic Church. In 1788 he issued another anthology by Reinagle and may have printed Francis Hopkinson's *Seven Songs*; a few pieces of sheet music and more of Reinagle's song collections followed in 1789. By 1793 he had brought out at least 20 titles, but between then and 1806 he published only the compendious *Scots Musical Museum* (1797) and one of his own songs, *The Goldsmith's Rant* (1802). From 1806 to 1811, however, Aitken was one of Philadelphia's busiest music publishers, bringing out many secular songs and several secular collections as well as more sacred music—a total of perhaps 200 titles—including *Aitken's Collection of Divine Music* (1/1806). His musical activity seems to have ceased after 1811, though he continued in the metalworking and printing trades in Philadelphia until at least 1825.

Aitken has been identified by Wolfe as the first professional publisher of secular music in the United States. His publications of the 1780s mark the earliest sustained commitment to the printing and sale of music of this type, and were also the first-known American publications to have been produced using the intaglio method of engraving metal plates with steel punches rather than by hand.

BIBLIOGRAPHY

WolfeMEP

F.J. Metcalf: *American Writers and Compilers of Sacred Music* (New York, 1925/*R*), 45–6

D.W. Krummel: *Philadelphia Music Engraving and Publishing 1800–1820: a Study in Bibliography and Cultural History* (diss., U. of Michigan, 1958)

R.J. Wolfe: *Secular Music in America, 1801–1825: a Bibliography* (New York, 1964)

A. Britton, I. Lowens, and R. Crawford: *American Sacred Music Imprints 1698–1810: A Bibliography* (Worcester, MA, 1990), 32, 88–91, 478

R.R. Grimes: *How Shall We Sing in a Foreign Land?: Music of Irish Catholic Immigrants in the Antebellum United States* (Notre Dame, IN, 1996), 46, 84, 176

R.R. Grimes: "John Aitken and Catholic Music in Federal Philadelphia," *American Music*, xvi/3 (1998), 289–310

RICHARD CRAWFORD/KIMBERLY GREENE

Aitken, Webster (*b* Los Angeles, CA, 17 June 1908; *d* Santa Fe, NM, 11 May 1981). Pianist. After studying in California under Alexis Kall and Alfred Mirovitch, and at the Curtis Institute under Herbert Simpson, he departed for Berlin to pursue further studies with three pupils of Liszt—Arthur Friedheim, MORIZ ROSENTHAL, and Emil Sauer—as well as with ARTUR SCHNABEL and Marie Prentner (Theodor Leschetizky's principal assistant). He made his professional début in Vienna in 1929 and his New York début at Town Hall on 17 November 1935. In 1938 he played the complete cycle of Schubert's piano sonatas both in London and in New York. During the 1940s Aitken commanded the esteem of Virgil Thomson and of the intellectual public as Schnabel had in the previous generation; his wide-ranging repertory included contemporary works such as Elliott Carter's Piano Sonata, of which Aitken gave the first performance in a radio broadcast in 1947. He also gave the first known complete performance of Charles Ives's *Four Transcriptions from Emerson*. He gave performances of Beethoven's late piano music in New York and at Harvard University in 1950, and through the next decade appeared often in concert, although chiefly in academic settings. From 1961–2 he served as Visiting Artist at the School of Music of the University of Illinois at Urbana-Champaign. In the 1960s he gradually withdrew from public performance but continued to play privately, expanding his repertory to include works by Boulez and Stockhausen. Aitken's recordings of familiar works by Handel, Beethoven, Schubert, and Webern are remarkable for the disturbing intensity of their unconventional interpretations.

RICHARD DYER/JUSTIN KRAWITZ

Akers, Doris (Mae) [Dot] (*b* Brookfield, MO, 21 May 1923; *d* Minneapolis, MN, 26 July 1995). Gospel music composer, pianist, and singer. Akers is credited as the most prolific of the early West Coast African American gospel songwriters, based primarily in Los Angeles. A prodigious talent, Akers wrote "Keep the fire burning in me" at age ten. She arrived in Los Angeles in 1945 and between then and 1948 sang with the Sallie Martin Singers. She joined with Dorothy Simmons in 1948 to form the Simmons-Akers Singers. They were together for approximately ten years and achieved national recognition. Akers received more acclaim in the late 1950s and 1960s as a solo artist and director of the Sky Pilot Choir, a racially mixed group that performed black gospel. She was the first to bridge black and white gospel music; her songs were popularized by leading black and white artists. Akers earned the designation "writer of tomorrow's songs today" for her intricate harmonic and lyrical style and the resonances of popular music. Her songs incorporate typical religious themes including songs about joy, the blood (of Jesus), and the Holy Spirit. "Sweet, Sweet Spirit" (1962) remains one of her most recognized songs, along with "You can't beat God giving" (1957) and "Lord, don't move this mountain" (1958). Her song "Trouble" (1957) was used for a play entitled *Praise House* (1958), and later for a 1980s touring production, *Bessie and Me*. Akers moved to Columbus, Ohio in 1970 and remained active in gospel music, particularly in the white community. She moved to Minneapolis in the early 1990s and served as Minister of Music for Grace Temple Deliverance Center.

BIBLIOGRAPHY

J.C. DjeDje: "Los Angeles Composers of African-American Gospel Music: the First Generations," *American Music*, ii (1993), 412–57

H.C. Boyer: *How Sweet the Sound: the Golden Age of Gospel* (Washington, DC, 1995)

HORACE CLARENCE BOYER/ROXANNE R. REED

Akiyoshi, Toshiko (*b* Dairen, China, 12 Dec 1929). Japanese jazz composer, pianist, and bandleader. She was born to Japanese parents in Manchuria. She began classical piano at seven and was playing professionally in her teens. She studied classical music and turned to jazz only in 1947 after moving to Japan. There she was discovered by Oscar Peterson, who urged her to take up a career in the United States. After studying at Berklee College of Music (1956–9) she became a highly regarded bop pianist, especially in groups with the alto saxophonist Charlie Mariano (to whom she was married from 1959 to 1967). She worked in Japan (1961), joined Charles Mingus in the United States (1962–3), then returned to Japan until 1965. In 1973 she founded a large rehearsal band in Los Angeles with the tenor saxophonist and flautist Lew Tabackin, whom she had married in 1969. Its first album, *Kogun* (1974, RCA), was commercially successful in Japan, and the group attracted increasing popularity and critical acclaim until, by 1980, it was generally regarded as the leading big band in jazz. The band allowed Akiyoshi to write a number of rich, subtle scores in the modern big-band tradition of Gil Evans, Thad Jones, and Mel Lewis, though they were often enriched by elements from Japanese music: *shakuhachi*-style flute solos; *tsuzumi* drums and *biwa*; and *nōh* vocal recitations. This can be heard to advantage on the album *Road Time* (1976, RCA) which was recorded during a concert tour of Japan and includes a second version of *Kogun*. She has continued to play the piano in a delicate, accurate bop style. In 1984 she was the subject of a documentary film, *Toshiko Akiyoshi: Jazz is my Native Language*. The same year she and Tabackin disbanded their group and in 1985 Akiyoshi formed a new big band in New York. The 35th anniversary of her arrival in the United States was celebrated with a big-band concert at Carnegie Hall in 1991. In 1996, she published her autobiography, *Life with Jazz* (Tokyo, 1996). She has continued to record and perform regularly around the world. In 2007, she was named a Jazz Master by the NEA.

SELECTED RECORDINGS

Small group: *Toshiko's Piano* (1953, Norg.); with C. Mariano: *Toshiko–Mariano Quartet* (1960, Can.), Mariano–Toshiko Quartet (1963, Takt); *Dedications* (1976, 1977, Disco Mate); *Toshiko Akiyoshi Plays Billy Strayhorn* (1978, Disco Mate); *Finesse* (1978, Conc.); *Time Stream* (1983, Toshiba East World); *Remembering Bud: Cleopatra's Dream* (1990, Nippon Crown); *Sketches of Japan* (1999, Nippon Crown); *50th Anniversary Concert in Japan* (2006, Tic-Toc); with L. Tabackin: *Vintage: Duke Ellington Songbook* (2008, Tic-Toc); with R. Honshoh: *Classic Encounters* (2010, Studio Songs)

Big band: with L. Tabackin: *Kogun* (1974, RCA); *Long Yellow Road* (1974–5, RCA); *Tales of a Courtesan* (1975, RCA); *Road Time* (1976, RCA); *Insights* (1976, RCA); *Sumi-e* (1979, Insights); *Tanuki's Night Out* (1981); *Live at Carnegie Hall* (1991, Col.); *Four Seasons of Morita Village* (1996, BMG); *Hiroshima—Rising from the Abyss* (2001, Video Arts); *Toshiko Jazz Orchestra in Shanghai* (2011, Pony Canyon)

BIBLIOGRAPHY

C. Sheridan: "The Manchurian Candidate," *Jazz Journal International*, xxxii/1 (1979), 6–7

L. Feather: "Akiyoshi/Tabackin," *The Passion for Jazz* (New York, 1980), 109–11

C. Kuhl: "Akiyoshi & Tabackin: Interview," *Cadence*, viii/7 (1982), 8–10

L. Lyons: "Toshiko Akiyoshi," *The Great Jazz Pianists, Speaking of their Lives and Music* (New York, 1983), 249–56

L. Koplewitz: "Toshiko Akiyoshi: Jazz Composer, Arranger, Pianist, and Conductor," *The Musical Woman*, ii (1984–5), 256–79

W. Minor: *Jazz Journeys to Japan: the Heart within* (Ann Arbor, MI, 2004)

K. Fellezs: "Deracinated Flower: Toshiko Akiyoshi's 'Trace in History'," *Jazz Perspectives*, iv/1 (2010), 35–57

J. BRADFORD ROBINSON/R

Akwid. Musical group formed in 2002 in Los Angeles. The most successful exponents of the Southern California style known as "banda rap" or "urban regional" music, Akwid is a duo of brothers Francisco and Sergio Gómez. Born in Michoacan and raised in Los Angeles, the Gomezes made their debut in the mid 1990s as English-language rappers Juvenile Style, then switched to Spanish and renamed themselves Akwid (a combination of their deejay pseudonyms, A.K. and Wikid) in 2000.

Their first album gained only lackluster sales, but after they signed with a subsidiary of Univision in 2003, their second, *Proyecto Akwid*, sold a third of a million CDs. Its sound mixed traditional Mexican music—especially the West Coast brass band style known as *banda*—with rhythms and studio techniques adapted from gangsta rap. Other groups were attempting similar fusions, but where most had to rely on outside producers, Akwid controlled their own sound and created a particularly organic musical combination, driven by the thump of tuba samples and clever use of familiar *ranchera* singers, whether sampled or as guest stars. Their videos reinforced their musical approach and the rowdy humor of their lyrics, showing the brothers dressed like gang-bangers, with shaven heads and football jerseys, alongside full brass bands in Mexican *charro* suits.

ELIJAH WALD

Alabado/alabanza (Spanish-American: "praise"). Spanish-language Roman Catholic devotional songs of praise and penitence for the sacraments, including the Eucharist, as well as the Passion narrative, the Blessed Virgin Mary, and the saints. It was brought to North America at least as early as 1716 by the Franciscans, and was associated with the missionary Fray Antonio Margil de Jesús (1657–1726). The Franciscans continued the Spanish custom of singing the *alabado*, or *alabanza*, as it is called in Spain, in their Southwestern missions in New Mexico, Texas, and California. The form still survives in some parts of Argentina and Mexico, and most particularly in New Mexico. The melismatic, unaccompanied New Mexican *alabado,* frequently in four-line stanzas of octosyllabic verse, is especially associated with the devotional rites for Holy Week of the Penitential Brotherhood (the *penitentes*). The singing of the *alabado* during Holy Week can be preceded by the sound of the *pito* (end-blown flute with a limited range) and the *matraca* (rattle). The sharp sounds of these instruments reinforce the penitential nature of this type of *alabado*. The devotional *alabanza*, also usually in octosyllabic four-line stanzas, is set syllabically, however, and is sung in Hispano New Mexico throughout the church year. Both the *alabado* and *alabanza* are genres intended for communal singing. Music for the *alabado* survives from the Franciscan missions in California, as sung by Indian musicians, but the form as known there was closer to the *alabanza* than the traditional New Mexican *alabado*.

The largest published collection of devotional *alabados* and *alabanzas* from New Mexico was first compiled by the French priest Jean Baptiste Rallière (1858–1913), the pastor of Tomé, New Mexico. His *Cánticos espirituales* was published by the Jesuit press in 13 editions in New Mexico and Texas between 1884 and 1956 (nine text-only editions and three editions with music). *Cánticos espirituales* grew from 94 devotional songs in the first edition of 1884 to include 305 songs in the last edition of 1956. Later collectors of *alabados* and *alabanzas* include Juan B. Rael, Vicente T. Mendoza, John Donald Robb, Rubén Cobos, and Thomas J. Steele; all published studies of the genre. *Alabado* and *alabanza* music and texts are at the University of New Mexico (John Donald Robb Collection and personal *cancioneros* [songbooks] of individual singers, Center for Southwest Research); American Folklife Center, Library of Congress (Juan B. Rael Collection, online at Hispano Music and Culture of the Northern Rio Grande, <http://memory.loc.gov/ammem/rghtml/rghome.html>); Cobos Collection, Colorado College; and the Museum of New Mexico (Santa Fe).

EDITIONS

J.B. Rallière: *Colección de cánticos espirituales sacados de varios autores* (Las Vegas, NM, 1884/*R*1892)

J.B. Rallière: *Colección de cánticos espirituales recogidos por el Rev. [erendo] P[adre] J[uan] B[autista] Ralliere, cura parroco de Tomé, Nuevo Mexico* (Las Vegas, NM, 1900/*R*1908, 1913, ?1917)

J.B. Rallière: *Cánticos espirituales con música recogidos por la Revista Católica* (Las Vegas, NM, 1916/*R*1927, 1944)

J.B. Rallière: *Cánticos espirituales recogidos por el p[adre] J[uan] B. Ralliere y dispuestos en nuevo orden por un p[adre] d[e] l[a] C[ompañia] d[e] J[esus]* (El Paso, TX, *c*1918–27/*R*1928, 1956)

BIBLIOGRAPHY

J.B. Rael: *The New Mexican Alabado* (Stanford, CA, 1951)

V.T. Mendoza and V.R.R. de Mendoza: *Estudio y clasificación de la música tradicional hispánica de Nuevo México* (Mexico City, 1986)

J.D. Robb: *Hispanic Folk Music of New Mexico and the Southwest: A Self-portrait of a People* (Norman, OK, 1980)

R.B. Stark: "Notes On a Search for Antecedents of New Mexican Alabado Music," *Hispanic Arts and Ethnohistory in the Southwest: New Papers Inspired by the Work of E. Boyd*, ed. M. Weigle (Santa Fe, NM, 1983), 117–27

J. Koegel: "Village Musical Life along the Río Grande: Tomé, New Mexico since 1739," *LAMR*, xviii/2 (1997), 171–248

L. Lindsay Levine and A. Chase: *Music in the Rubén Cobos Collection of Spanish New Mexican Folklore: A Descriptive Catalogue* (Colorado Springs, CO, 1999)

J. Koegel: "Spanish and French Mission Music in Colonial North America," *Journal of the Royal Musical Association*, cxxvi/1 (2001), 1–53

M. Montaño: *Tradiciones nuevomexicanas: Hispano Arts and Culture of New Mexico* (Albuquerque, NM, 2001)

T.J. Steele, ed.: *The Alabados of New Mexico* (Albuquerque, NM, 2005)

C.H. Russell: *From Serra to Sancho: Music and Pageantry in the California Missions* (New York, 2009)

K.D. Mann: *The Power of Song: Music and Dance in the Mission Communities of Northern New Spain, 1590–1810* (Stanford, CA, 2010)

JOHN KOEGEL

Alabama. Country music group. Acknowledged by the Academy of Country Music (ACM) in 1989 as the Artist of the Decade, Alabama is arguably the most celebrated country music group in the history of the genre. Three of the band's members—lead vocalist Randy Owen (*b* Fort Payne, AL, 13 Dec 1949), multi-instrumentalist Jeff Cook (*b* Fort Payne, AL, 27 Aug 1949), and bassist Teddy Gentry (*b* Fort Payne, AL, 22 Jan 1952)—had been performing their unique blend of southern rock and country pop together throughout the American South since 1969. Beginning in 1974, the group began playing regular shows in Myrtle Beach, South Carolina, where drummer Mark Herndon (*b* Springfield, MA, 11 May 1955) became the group's fourth and final member in 1979, one year before Alabama signed with RCA. The group's first major label release *My Home's in Alabama* (RCA, 1980) was an instant success, selling more than two million copies and producing the group's first two number-one *Billboard* country singles, "Tennessee River" and "Why Lady Why." Alabama distinguished themselves from other popular country vocal groups of the period such as the Oak Ridge Boys and the Statler Brothers because the group was self-contained, providing both rich vocal harmonies and virtuosic instrumental accompaniment. The clear, refined studio sound of Alabama's recordings combined with their crossover musical style, which contained influences from country, rock, pop, and bluegrass, resulting in mass appeal among diverse audiences. Alabama would later include 31 additional number-one *Billboard* country singles to their list of credits, including "Mountain Music" (1982), "Dixieland Delight" (1983), "Roll On (Eighteen Wheeler)" (1984), "If you're gonna play in texas (you gotta have a fiddle in the band)" (1984), "Forty-Hour Week (For a Livin')" (1985), "Song of the South" (1989), and "Reckless" (1993). During its career, Alabama received most of the industry awards available to country groups, including most notably the Academy of Country Music's (ACM) Entertainer of the Year award (1981–5), the Country Music Association's Entertainer of the Year award (1982–4), and the American Music Award for Favorite Country Band, Duo or Group (1983–96, 1998). The group officially disbanded in 2003, having received the prestigious Cliffie Stone Pioneer Award by the ACM and sold more than 46 million career albums in the United States. They were inducted into the Country Music Hall of Fame in 2005.

DAVID B. PRUETT

Alabama, University of. State university system with a main campus in Tuscaloosa and satellite campuses in Birmingham and Huntsville. The main campus opened in 1831 and the music department was established in 1918 with the appointment of Robert Lawrence, who taught voice and choir. The first BM degree was awarded in 1938. The music faculty established the Southeastern Composers' League in 1951 and for 20 years hosted the Regional Composers' Forum (1951–70). In 1955 Alabama Educational Television's network telecast of the School of Music's production of Puccini's *La bohème* was the earliest known live opera broadcast for educational television. Currently the School of Music offers the BM, BA, BS, MA, MM, DMA, EdS, EdD, and PhD degrees in such fields as administration, arranging, composition, conducting, education, jazz studies, musicology, performance, theory, therapy, and church music. In 2009 enrollment surpassed 350 students served by a full-time faculty of 37. Since 1984, over 185 eminent scholars and musicians have held residences in the Board of Trustees' Endowed Chair in Music program. The University of Alabama System, consisting of three autonomous public universities, was established in 1969. The Department of Music at the University of Alabama in Birmingham enrolls approximately 190 students and offers the MA in education and BA in education, music, and technology. The Department of Music at the University of Alabama in Huntsville offers the BA in music and enrolls approximately 74 students.

CARL B. HANCOCK

Aladdin. Record company. Brothers Edward and Leo Messner founded the company as Philo Records in 1945 and changed the name to Aladdin the next year. Aladdin's records, which appeared on the Aladdin label and over a half-dozen subsidiaries, were among the most popular "race" (later rhythm-and-blues) records of the time, and represented many facets of African American popular music following World War II. Based in Los Angeles, the company released upbeat boogie by Amos Milburn, such as the 1948 hit "Chicken-Shack Boogie," and group vocal music by artists like the Five Keys. Blues also appeared on Aladdin by artists such as Charles Brown and Lightnin' Hopkins. Jazz saxophonist Lester Young also recorded extensively for Aladdin during the 1950s. Several songs released on Aladdin foreshadowed the development of rock and roll, such as Shirley and Lee's 1956 classic "Let the Good Times Roll." In 1962, the company was sold to Lew Chudd's Imperial Records.

ANDREW FLORY

Alarm Will Sound. Ensemble. Originally a group of students performing in new music concerts at the Eastman School of Music, Alarm Will Sound was formed professionally by artistic director Alan Pierson and managing director Gavin Chuck in 2001. The group made its debut in May of that year at Miller Theater, Columbia University, with *Desert Music* and *Tehillim* by Steve Reich. After giving several programs, each devoted to a single contemporary composer, the group began to both commission new works—including John Adams's *Son of Chamber Symphony*, Wolfgang Rihm's *Will Sound*, and David Lang's *Increase*—and to perform arrangements of other music, notably Varèse's *Poeme Electronique*, by the composer Evan Hause, and the rhythmically complex electronic dance music of Aphex Twin, Mochipet and Autechre, and the Beatles' "Revolution 9," all arranged by ensemble musicians. The group also began adding staging and other theatrical elements to their live performances, developed with director Nigel Maister. These took a range of forms, from stage blocking to the musical theater piece *1969*, which premiered in 2010 and combined pop and classical music from 1969 arranged for the ensemble, actors, and acting roles for several of the musicians in the group. As of 2010, they can be heard on six recordings, including performances of the Reich pieces from their premiere concert, a collection of the Aphex Twin arrangements, *Acoustica*, Michael Gordon's *Van Gogh*, and *a/rhythmia*, the group's exploration of complex rhythmic ideas from the Renaissance to contemporary music.

GEORGE J. GRELLA JR.

Alaska. US state (pop. 721,231; 2010 US Census). Although Alaska's population grew rapidly from World War II through the end of the 20th century, this growth slowed subsequently with population declines in the rural interior. State support for cultural organizations and for arts education in schools and universities has not remained consistent. A high percentage of corporate gifts to arts organizations has come from oil companies, and, in the early 21st century, from the financial services industry.

The city of Anchorage (pop. 291,826; 2010 US Census) is the main hub for musical activity in the vast yet sparsely populated state. Few records exist of the frontier town's musical life before 1928, when the local high school engaged Lorene Harrison, a young college graduate from Kansas, to teach music and home economics; she also sang, produced shows, founded groups, and directed the choir at the First Presbyterian Church of Anchorage. For many years she guided virtually all of the city's musical activities; during World War II, when most civilians were evacuated from Alaska, she stayed on as director of the United Service Organizations, and arranged and conducted concerts at which military personnel and local residents performed.

In 1946 the orchestra members of the Anchorage Little Theatre formed the Anchorage SO; starting as a small group by the 1960s it was a full symphony orchestra performing six subscription concerts a year. In 1947 the Little Theatre produced Handel's *Messiah*, and the chorus members formed the Anchorage Community Chorus under Harrison's direction. One of the first guest artists to appear with the Anchorage SO was the Russian-born pianist Maxim Shapiro, who began organizing Alaskan tours for other performers; these were sponsored by an informal organization known as the Alaska Music Trail. The tours were at first confined to Alaska's larger cities—Ketchikan, Juneau, Anchorage, and Fairbanks—but eventually included as many as 18 communities in Alaska and western Canada; in Anchorage they led to the formation of the Anchorage Concert Association, which continues to present performances by well-known musicians. In 1955 the Anchorage Community Chorus invited ROBERT SHAW to conduct a summer festival; soon after, the Alaska Festival of Music was begun, and Shaw continued as its director for a number of years.

In the late 1940s and 1950s there were no regular presentations of musical theater in Anchorage, though occasional productions of light opera were mounted. In 1955 the Anchorage Civic Opera was formed under the direction of the opera singer Marita Ferall; it generally produced one opera and one Broadway musical per year. In the mid-1960s the Lyric Opera Theatre mounted several productions, but it was not until 1975 that a revitalized Anchorage Civic Opera, under the direction of Elvera Voth, began regularly to present the standard operatic repertory. Voth also conducted the Community Chorus and founded and directed the Anchorage Boys Choir, which formed in the early 1970s. It combined with the Anchorage Girls Choir in 1979, then became the Anchorage Children's Choir in 1986.

As of 2011 music education in voice, strings, winds, and percussion begins at the sixth-grade level, and continues through high school. The Anchorage Youth Symphony (established in 1965) and the Anchorage School District's Junior Youth Symphony (established in 1979) perform three concerts per year in Anchorage. The AYS occasionally tours internationally. The Alaska Children's Choir (established in 1979) and its training groups perform frequently on their own, and collaborate widely with adult choral and orchestral forces.

As of 2011 the University of Alaska Anchorage Department of Music has nine full-time faculty plus adjunct professors. A notable addition to the department's degree programs has been the Master of Arts in Teaching, initiated by Mark Wolbers and now led by Christopher Sweeney. This one-year program involves an internship in an elementary or secondary school, combined with close mentoring from UAA faculty. Since 2004, the opera workshop, initiated by Mari Hahn, has produced one or more operas or musical plays per year.

Anchorage's leading professional ensemble is the Anchorage Symphony Orchestra. Founded in 1948, the orchestra discovered firm footing in the mid-1980s, as the first of three out-of-state conductors was hired as music director. In 1988, the Anchorage Center for the Performing Arts and its three performance spaces opened, which gave the ASO and other groups a first-class venue at which to perform. Under the batons of Stephen Stein, George Hanson, and Randall Craig Fleischer, the ASO brought works such as Gustav Holst's

The Planets, Igor Stravinsky's *Petroushka* and *Le Sacre du Printemps*, and Gustav Mahler's Second and Fifth Symphonies to Anchorage. In 2003, the ASO formed a commissioning club, *Musica Nova*, to commission a new orchestral work every year for the ensemble. Beginning with Philip Munger's Piano Concerto, and including Fairbanks composer John Luther Adams's award-winning *Dark Wave*, the club has now commissioned nine new works.

The Anchorage Concert Chorus, directed by Grant Cochran, has shown innovative approaches to programming, including their 2003 production of Benjamin Britten's *War Requiem* and their production of Leonard Bernstein's *Mass* in 2011.

Fairbanks, Alaska (pop. 97,581; 2010 US Census) is the home of the University of Alaska, with a department of music comparable in size to that of UAA, with 11 full-time faculty plus adjuncts. UAF offers a Masters of Arts in Music program. The university collaborates with the community by directly supporting the Fairbanks Symphony and Arctic Chamber Orchestras, under the direction of Eduard Zilberkant, who also is also chairman of UAF's music department. Alaska's most notable classical composer, JOHN LUTHER ADAMS, resides in Fairbanks. His sound installation, *The Place Where You Go to Listen*, is housed at UA Museum of the North. UAF has taken the lead in statewide support of the arts through its sponsorship of the Annual Festival of Native Arts (founded 1973) as well as its Summer Music Academy (established in 1980), both of which draw performers and students from rural Alaska.

Juneau (pop. 31,275; 2010 US Census) is home of Alaska's most innovative music festival, the CrossSound Festival. Started by Stefan Hakenberg and Jocelyn Clark in 1999, it has commissioned more than 50 composers to create new works for an array of ensembles and soloists. The Juneau Symphony Orchestra, founded in 1962, performs four concerts per season. Under the direction of Kyle Wylie Pickett they have produced Mahler's Second Symphony in 2010, and Alban Berg's Violin Concerto in 2011, among other works.

Other communities, including those in rural Alaska, have their own musical education, presentation, festival, and ensemble structures. The most highly regarded town festival is the Sitka Summer Music Festival (founded 1972), and created by violinist Paul Rosenthal.

Alaska Native musical traditions are quite diverse, and are regarded as a vital component for the upkeep and passing on of these rich, longstanding cultures. The Alaska State Council on the Arts and the Rasmuson Foundation have funded many Alaska Native musicians and ensembles. (See INUIT.)

Statewide, the Alaska Music Educators Association and the Alaska School Activities Association sponsor the All-State Festival (an annual all-state choral, orchestral and band event) and a statewide solo and ensemble contest.

A few Alaska popular musicians have gained national and international fame. Jewel Kilcher, known as JEWEL, grew up in Homer, a small fishing town south of Anchorage. While pursuing high school operatic studies at Interlochen Arts Academy, she began playing guitar and writing her own songs. In 1995, at 19, she recorded her debut album, *Pieces of You*. An Alaskan heavy metal scene has produced popular bands such as 36 Crazyfists. Their move to Portland, Oregon spurred a number of other Alaska bands (including psychedlic rock band Portugal. The Man) to relocate there in the mid-2000s.

The best known Alaska Native popular musical group is the Inuit fusion band Pamyua. Founding members Phillip Blanchett, Stephen Blanchett, and Ossie Kairaiuak are from the Yukon/Kuskokwim River Delta region in southwestern Alaska. Karina Moeller, also a founding member, is from Nuuk, Greenland. The band performs frequently at Native American events in the United States, and at Northern Peoples' events worldwide.

GEORGE R. BELDEN/PHILIP MUNGER

Alaskan Eskimo. *See* INUIT.

Albani [Lajeunesse], **Dame Emma** (Marie Louise Cécile) (*b* Chambly, nr Montreal, PQ, 1 Nov 1847; *d* London, England, 3 Apr 1930). Canadian soprano. Her father was a professor of the harp, piano, and organ. She was educated at the Couvent du Sacré-Coeur in Montreal. She gave concerts in some Quebec towns before her family moved to Albany, New York, in 1864; there she became a soloist at St Joseph's church, and the Albany bishop and others advised Lajeunesse that his daughter should pursue a musical career. In 1868, she went to Paris, where she was taught by Gilbert-Louis Duprez. Later she studied with Francesco Lamperti in Milan. In 1870 she made her debut at Messina as Amina in Bellini's *La sonnambula*, adopting, as suggested by her elocution teacher, the name of Albani, borrowed from an old Italian family. She then sang successfully at Malta and Florence.

On 2 April 1872 she made her London debut at Covent Garden as Amina. The beautiful qualities of her voice and the charm of her appearance were at once appreciated. She sang nearly every season there until 1896, in a great variety of parts, notably as Elsa (1875) and Elisabeth (1876) in the first London performances of *Lohengrin* and *Tannhäuser*. In 1878 she married Ernest Gye, who became lessee of Covent Garden on his father's death. Later she was very successful as Eva (*Die Meistersinger*) and Desdemona (she sang in the first Covent Garden and Metropolitan Opera productions of *Otello*). The last and greatest triumph of her career was on 26 June 1896, when she performed as Isolde in Wagner's *Tristan und Isolde*, playing opposite Jean de Reszke's Tristan and Edouard de Reszke's King Mark.

Albani was a great favorite at the Handel and provincial festivals for many years, and she sang in many new works, notably in those of Charles Gounod, Arthur Sullivan, Alexander Mackenzie, Frederic Cowen, Antonin Dvořák, and Edward Elgar (*The Apostles*). In 1886 she sang in *St Elizabeth* on the occasion of Liszt's farewell visit to England. She also sang in operas and concerts in Paris, Brussels, Germany, the United States, Mexico, and Canada, and on tour in India, Australia, and South Africa. Her voice was a rich soprano of remarkably sympathetic quality. The higher registers were of exceptional beauty, and she had perfected the art of singing *mezza voce*.

On 14 October 1911 she gave a farewell concert at the Royal Albert Hall, afterwards devoting herself to teaching the Lamperti method. In June 1925 she was created DBE.

BIBLIOGRAPHY

E. Albani: *Forty Years of Song* (London, 1911/*R*)

H. Charbonneau: *L'Albani* (Montreal, 1938)

N.A. Ridley: "Emma Albani," *Record Collector*, xii/4–5 (1959), 76–101 [with discography by W.R. Moran]; addenda, xii/8–9 (1959), 197–8; xiv/9–10 (1961); 236 only

C. MacDonald: *Emma Albani: Victorian Diva* (Toronto, 1984)

F. Lindsay: *Répertoire numérique détaillé du fonds Albani* (Chambly, PQ, 1993)

M.-T. Lefebvre and J.-P. Pinson, eds.: *Les cahiers de la Société Québécoise de Recherche en Musique*, iv/1 (June 2000) [incl. several articles on Albani]

ALEXIS CHITTY/GILLES POTVIN

Albanian American music. *See* EUROPEAN AMERICAN MUSIC.

Albert. Family of violin makers and dealers. John Albert (*b* Liel, Baden, Germany, 24 June 1809; *d* Philadelphia, PA, 2 Jan 1900) began as an engineer and inventor. He came to New York from Freiburg, Germany, in 1854 as a refugee of the 1848 revolution, settling in Philadelphia where in 1857 established a shop. His particular interest was in commercial violin manufacture, in which he held several patents; he established the American Star violin factory which, after his retirement in 1887, was run by his son Eugene John Albert (*b* Freiburg, 1851; *d* Philadelphia, 1922). The E.J. Albert firm, under other ownership, continued well into the 1950s.

John's eldest son, Charles Francis Albert (*b* Freiburg, Germany, 25 Dec 1842; *d* Philadelphia, PA, 1 July 1901), established his own shop in Philadelphia in 1865. His interest was in fine instruments and repairs, and as such gained wide respect and admiration. His son and successor, Charles Francis Albert Jr. (*b* Philadelphia, PA, 1869; *d* Philadelphia, PA, 1915), was also a fine maker and restorer, although not at the same level as his father.

Although the Alberts were not the first violin makers to establish themselves in Philadelphia, they were the most exceptional of their period; their violins were modeled on fine Saxon work of the period. Charles Francis Albert, considered the best maker in the family, received highest honors in the Philadelphia Centennial Exposition of 1876. He was noted as an excellent repairer and connoisseur and also introduced numerous advancements in violin accessories; his wound strings and chin rests, for example, were very popular.

PHILIP J. KASS

Albert, Donnie Ray (*b* Baton Rouge, LA, 10 Jan 1950). Baritone. Albert was born, raised, and trained in the South; he received his first degree from Louisiana State University (BM) in 1972 and a few years later completed his Master's degree in Music from Southern Methodist University. He made his debut in the Houston Grand Opera's 1975 production of Joplin's *Treemonisha*. The following year was an extraordinary one for Albert, who returned to Houston to take roles in Puccini's *La Fanciulla del West* and the lead male role in Gershwin's *Porgy and Bess*. The latter production was so successful it was moved to Broadway and, when recorded, won the Grammy for Best Opera Recording of 1978. Albert soon became known for his portrayal of Porgy, reprising the role throughout the world, especially with a major European tour that began in 1988. In 1978, he appeared at the Washington National Opera and New York City Opera, and in the next year at the Lyric Opera of Chicago. After making impressive appearances throughout North America in the early 1980s, he began to receive attention in Europe after performing at the Teatro Comunale in Florence. In the 1990s, Albert began to take on Wagnerian roles, including Wotan and The Flying Dutchman. He won another Grammy for Best Opera Recording in 2009 for Weill's *The Rise and Fall of the City of Mahagonny*. Albert's powerful voice is respected for its commanding quality and varied timbres, and many reviewers have also commented on the strength of his acting abilities.

JONAS WESTOVER

Albert, Stephen (Joel) (*b* New York, NY, 6 Feb 1941; *d* Truro, MA, 27 Dec 1992). Composer. His musical training began as a youngster with piano, french horn, and trumpet lessons. At the age of 15 he began composition studies with ELIE SIEGMEISTER. He later studied with DARIUS MILHAUD, BERNARD ROGERS, Karl-Birger Blomdahl, Joseph Castaldo, and GEORGE ROCHBERG. He completed the BM degree at the Philadelphia Musical Academy in 1962. An appointment at the Juilliard School numbered among his several teaching positions. His many commissions included works for the Chicago SO, National SO, Philadelphia Orchestra, New York PO, Chamber Music Society of Lincoln Center, Library of Congress, and the Fromm and Ford foundations. From 1985 to 1988 he served as composer-in-residence of the Seattle SO. He was awarded the 1985 Pulitzer Prize for his symphony *RiverRun* and received a posthumous Grammy Award for his Cello Concerto.

In the mid-1960s, influenced by the music of Mahler and Brahms, Albert turned from serialism to modified 19th-century compositional techniques. He sought to discover new connections with the music of the past and to capture the gestures of Romanticism within a 20th-century idiom inspired by Bartók, early Stravinsky, and Sibelius. His powerfully dramatic and colorful music characteristically integrates melodic and harmonic structures through the exploitation of selected scale patterns and intervallic relationships. Together these interwoven patterns create a unified, freely flowing musical environment with a strong sense of direction and inevitability. Another favorite technique, the juxtaposition and gradual unification of fragmentary musical ideas, is first evident in early works such as *Cathedral Music* (1971–2) and *Voices Within* (1975).

The works of James Joyce provided the stimulus for four of Albert's mature compositions. Albert's first major work, *To Wake the Dead* (1977–8), is a large-scale song cycle inspired by *Finnegans Wake*. Employing both straightforward and surrealistic styles, the music complements, counterbalances, and occasionally elucidates Joyce's fragmented and dissociated texts. The author's Irish sentiment and bawdy zest for living are captured in fragmented marches, children's songs, music-box tunes, and raucous pub songs. Allusions in *Finnegans Wake* to the legend of Tristan and Isolde prompted Albert to write *TreeStone* (1983–4), a song cycle incorporating themes of humanity's fall from innocence and the cyclic nature of history, as well as archetypes from Jungian psychology. Albert won the Pulitzer Prize with his symphony *RiverRun* (1983–4), an instrumental adaptation of *TreeStone*, which deals abstractly with Joyce's recollections of the Liffey River, from its origin as driving morning rain to its final surge to sea at dusk. *Flower of the Mountain* (1985), inspired by *Ulysses*, is the most lushly romantic of Albert's works. In it, Molly Bloom poignantly recalls her husband's marriage proposal of 16 years earlier; *Sun's Heat* (1989), a companion piece, reveals Leopold Bloom's version of the betrothal. *Distant Hills* (1989) is a pairing of these two monologues. Also intrigued by Greek myths, Albert creates in the two *Bacchae* works (1967 and 1968) and the chamber version of *Into Eclipse* (1981) hard-edged sound worlds that reflect the emotional atmosphere of their terror-filled texts.

During the last five years of his life, Albert composed much instrumental music, including concertos for the violin, cello, and clarinet. The epic Cello Concerto (1990), written for Yo-Yo Ma, reveals Albert at the height of his creative powers. Its sophisticated, abstract instrumental style is imbued with the melodic breadth of his vocal works. Traditional structural forms are used in novel ways that become integral to the motivic development. At the time of his death, Albert had just finished a detailed short score for his Symphony no.2, commissioned by the New York PO for its 150th anniversary.

WORKS

VOCAL

With orch: Supernatural Songs (W.B. Yeats), S, chbr orch, 1964; Winter Songs (R. Frost, W.C. Williams, W.D. Snodgrass), T, orch, 1965; Bacchae Canticles (Euripides, trans. W. Arrowsmith), solo vv, SATB, nar, sax, elec gui, elec db, orch, 1968; Wolf Time (10th-century Icelandic edda), S, amp chbr orch, 1968–9; TreeStone (J. Joyce: *Finnegan's Wake*), S, T, orch/12 insts, 1983–4; Flower of the Mountain (Joyce: *Ulysses*), S, orch/chbr orch, 1985; Sun's Heat (from Joyce: *Ulysses*), T, orch/chbr orch/11 insts, 1989; Distant Hills (Joyce: *Ulysses*), S, T, orch/chbr orch/11 insts, 1989

With chbr ens or solo pf: Wedding Songs (E. Dickinson, R. Frost, R.M. Rilke, W.C. Williams), S, pf, 1964; To Wake the Dead (Joyce: *Finnegans Wake*), S, fl + a fl, cl + b cl, hmn, pf, vn + va, vc, 1977–8; Into Eclipse (after T. Hughes, after Seneca: *Oedipus*), T, 13 insts, 1981, orchd 1986; The Stone Hp (J. Haines), T, timp, hp, 1988, withdrawn; rev. S/T, perc, hp, 2 va, 2 vc, 1989; Rilke Song (Rilke), S, fl, cl, vn, vc, pf, 1991; Ecce puer (Joyce), S, ob, hn, pf, 1992

INSTRUMENTAL

Orch: Illuminations, brass, 2 pf, perc, hp, 1962; Bacchae Prologue, 1967; Leaves from the Golden Notebook, 1970–72; Voices Within, 1975; RiverRun, sym., 1983–4; In Concordiam, vn conc., 1986, rev. 1988; Anthem and Processionals, 1988; Vc Conc., 1990; Wind Canticle, cl conc., 1991; Sym. no.2, 1992, orch completed by S. Currier, 1994

Chbr: 2 Toccatas, pf, 1958–9; Imitations (after Bartók), str qt, 1963; Canons, str qt, 1964; Cathedral Music (Conc. for 4 Qt), (2 amp fl, 2 amp vc), (2 hn, tpt, trbn), (2 perc, amp gui, amp hp), (2 pf, elec org, elec pf), 1971–2; Music from the Stone Hp, 7 pfmrs, 1979–80, withdrawn; Tribute, vn, pf, 1988

Principal publishers: G. Schirmer, Carl Fischer

BIBLIOGRAPHY
and other resources

EwenD

R. Dreier: "Musician of the Month: Stephen Albert," *High Fidelity/Musical America*, xxxv/9 (1985), 4–5, 40

E. Grimes: "Stephen Albert," recorded interview (Newton, MA, 12 Dec 1986), *Major Figures in American Music, Oral History of American Music* (New Haven, CT), 184 a-i

J. McLellan: "Melody as its own Reward," *Washington Post* (30 May 1987)

M.L. Humphrey: "The Music of Stephen Albert," *Stephen Albert* (New York, 1993), 7–16

S. Ledbetter: *Stephen Albert Concerto for Violoncello and Orchestra* (Boston, Feb 1993) [programme notes]

R. Freed: *RiverRun, to Wake the Dead* (Delos 1016, 1998) [disc notes]

C. Kendall: "In Conversation with Stephen Albert," *The Music of Stephen Albert* (Nonesuch, 9 79153-2, 1987) [disc notes]

MARY LOU HUMPHREY

Alberti, Solon (*b* Mt Clemens, MI, 6 Dec 1889; *d* Chicago, IL, 16 Oct 1981). Pianist and accompanist. He was one of 11 children, all musical. His early years were spent in Chicago where he studied cello and piano. He graduated from the Chicago Musical College at 18 and taught there from 1910 to 1914. He conducted the college orchestra, directed its opera workshop, and began his career as an accompanist. At the age of 24 he moved to Kansas City to head the piano, theory, and music history departments at the Conservatory of Music (1914–19); he was also conductor of the Kansas City Opera Association. In 1920 he went to New York, where he lived for the rest of his professional life. His summers were spent conducting opera workshops in various universities and conservatories. He toured extensively with such artists as Melchior, Schumann-Heink, Ruffo, Kullman, Bonelli, Teyte, Meisle, and De Luca. First working as a coach, he became well known as a singing teacher. He was organist and choir director at the Park Avenue Christian Church, 1932–67. In 1978 he retired and moved to Chicago. He composed a number of piano pieces and songs.

PHILIP LIESON MILLER

Alberts, Eunice (*b* Boston, MA, 1927). Contralto. She studied singing at the Longy School of Music, earning a performance certificate, and also at Tanglewood. In 1946 she made her professional debut with Koussevitzky and the Boston Symphony at Tanglewood as a soloist in Beethoven's Ninth Symphony. She continued to appear with them through the early 1950s.

In 1950 Alberts moved to New York, where she continued her work as a concert soloist, garnering the attention of New York City Opera. She made her NYCO debut on 4 October 1951 as the Elderly Woman in the world premiere of Tamkin's *The Dybbuk*. 1955 was an important year for Alberts, which included solo work with the Philadelphia Orchestra in Bach's *St Matthew's Passion*, their world premiere of Hanson's *Sinfonia Sacra*, and Beethoven's *Missa Solemnis* with the New

York Philharmonic under Bernstein. In that year she also became a member of Lyric Opera of Chicago, singing opposite Maria Callas in *I puritani*, *Il Travatore*, and *Madama Butterfly*.

Alberts also performed leading roles with Kansas City Opera, Cincinnati Opera, and Houston Grand Opera. In 1961, she returned to NYCO to play Rebecca Nurse in Robert Ward's *The Crucible* and became a member of Sarah Caldwell's Opera Company of Boston, a group with which she would continue to perform through the late 1980s. In 1963 she sang in the nationally broadcasted Memorial Mass for John F. Kennedy. After Alberts's performance career ended in 1988, she joined the voice faculty of the University of Massachusetts, Lowell.

TRUDI ANN WRIGHT

Albrecht [Albright], **Charles** (*b* Germany, 1759/60; *d* Montgomery, PA, 28 June 1848). Piano maker of German birth. He was active in Philadelphia as a piano maker by the 1790s, probably arriving there on the ship *Hamburgh* in October 1785. (His marriage to Maria Fuchs is listed in the records of St Michael's and Zion's Lutheran Church, Philadelphia, for 17 June 1787; they had no children.) His name appears in tax records, census entries and city directories from 1788 until his death in 1848. First described as a "joiner," he is listed in newspapers and real estate documents as "Musical Instrument Maker" at the address of 95 Vine Street from 1791 to at least 1824, when he retired from piano making but continued to purchase property in Philadelphia and the surrounding counties. Albrecht made some of the earliest surviving American square pianos, over 20 of which are still extant (four are at the Smithsonian Institution, Washington, DC; the date of 1789 on the nameboard of the square piano at the Historical Society of Pennsylvania, Philadelphia, is doubtful). All have handsome cabinet work and a range of from five to five and a half octaves (F' to c''''), with knee levers or hand stops or one pedal. Most are fitted with English single action, several have German *Prellmechanik*, while the later examples (dated 1812 and 1814 inside, under the keyframe) have English double action. While inscriptions inside some instruments indicate the collaboration of Joshua Baker or Albrecht's nephew Charles Deal, no evidence of a relationship between Charles Albrecht, C.F.L. Albrecht, and Albrecht & Co. has been established.

CYNTHIA ADAMS HOOVER

Albrecht, Christian Frederick Ludwig (*b* Hanover, 6 Jan 1788; *d* Philadelphia, PA, March 1843). Piano maker of German birth. He immigrated to the United States, arriving in Philadelphia on 17 October 1822, and from 1823 to 1824 ran a business there at 106 St John Street; from 1830 to 1843 his address was 144 South 3rd Street. On his death his small business was bequeathed to his wife Maria. His pianos exhibit excellent craftsmanship; pianos by him (one upright and one square) at the Smithsonian Institution, Washington, DC, are in empire style and have six octaves. No relationship between Christian Albrecht, Charles Albrecht, and Albrecht & Co. has yet been established.

CYNTHIA ADAMS HOOVER

Albrecht, Henry [Heinrich] **F.** (*b* Grevesmühlen, Mecklenburg, Germany, 13 March 1822; *d* at sea, 7 May 1875). Viola player, clarinettist, writer, and collector of music literature of German birth. An original member of the Germania Musical Society, Albrecht toured the United States with the orchestra 1848–54. His *Skizzen aus dem Leben der Musik-Gesellschaft Germania* is the only known recollection of the ensemble by a member. A shorter, unsigned, but very similar account appeared in the *New York Musical World* (2 September 1854). A lifelong follower of Etienne Cabet's Icarian communism, Albrecht described the Germania as sharing its precepts of equality in rights, duties, and rewards.

Albrecht's passion for music literature had been encouraged by Siegfried Dehn in Berlin, where the future Germanians met. While touring with the orchestra, Albrecht amassed a collection of at least 661 volumes. *Dwight's Journal* acknowledged in 1854 that this was the largest collection in the United States. Albrecht sold his library to Joseph Drexel in 1858 and moved to Philadelphia. He helped Drexel expand his collection and publish a catalog of its holdings in 1869; their combined effort formed the basis of the New York Public Library's Drexel Collection. Albrecht was also active in the Germania Orchestra of Philadelphia with his former Musical Society colleagues Sentz and Plagemann. In 1875 he attempted to retire to Germany, but drowned with his wife and children in the shipwreck of the *Schiller*.

BIBLIOGRAPHY

H. Albrecht: "*Alphabetisch geordnetes Verzeichniss einer Sammlung musikalischer Schriften: Catalogue of H. Albrecht's Collection of Musical Writings*," 1854, NYpl

H. Albrecht: "Les Rappistes," *Colonie Icarienne* (22 Nov 1854)

H. Albrecht: *Skizzen aus dem Leben der Musik-Gesellschaft Germania (Germania Musical Society)* (Philadelphia, 1869)

N. Newman: *Good Music for a Free People: the Germania Musical Society in Nineteenth-Century America* (Rochester, NY, 2010)

NANCY NEWMAN

Albrecht, Otto E(dwin) (*b* Philadelphia, PA, 8 July 1899; *d* Philadelphia, PA, 6 July 1984). Musicologist, music bibliographer, and music librarian. Albrecht was a lifelong resident of Philadelphia and was affiliated with the University of Pennsylvania throughout his career. He studied Romance languages (BA 1921, MA 1925, PhD 1931) and began his teaching career in 1923 as an instructor in French. Soon after his 1935 appointment as assistant professor, he traveled to Berlin on an Oberländer Trust fellowship to study settings of Goethe's poetry. He began teaching music courses in 1938, and in 1962 he transferred from the French Department to the Music Department with an appointment as associate professor.

In 1937, after voicing concerns to the university's president about the state of the library's music collections, he was named Curator of the Music Library, a position he held until his retirement in 1970, at which time the library was named in his honor. As curator, he transformed the small, undistinguished music collection into a significant research library. With the help of benefactor Henry Drinker, he acquired several significant collections, including part of the personal library of Alfred Einstein (1940), the scores and books of the Philadelphia Art Alliance (1940), and the Francis Hopkinson collection of music (1948–50), which comprised hundreds of 18th-century editions and four manuscript volumes of keyboard music copied for his use. Many of Albrecht's summers were spent searching European bookshops for music manuscripts and early editions to add to the shelves of the library. He also assembled a significant personal library of early music editions, which he bequeathed to the university.

Except for his study of medieval music with Jean Beck at Penn in the mid-1920s, Albrecht was a self-taught musicologist. His research interests included music publishing, Philadelphia music history, medieval drama, the music of Johannes Brahms, and 19th-century song, particularly settings of Goethe. He made his most significant contributions in the field of music bibliography, and his work in this area was distinguished by its thoroughness and attention to detail; *A Census of Autograph Music Manuscripts* (Philadelphia, 1953) is particularly notable as a model of its kind. In 1974 Albrecht became chair of the AMS-MLA Joint Committee on RISM and assumed primary responsibility for reporting American holdings of pre-1800 prints and manuscripts. In 1975 he undertook a larger role in RISM by serving as coeditor of series A/I, *Einzeldrucke vor 1800*. He also cataloged the manuscripts in the Mary Flagler Cary Music Collection at the Pierpont Morgan Library, New York.

Albrecht was an active member of several professional organizations. He twice served as vice-president of the Music Library Association (1940–45; 1950–52) and was awarded the MLA Citation (1979). He joined the American Musicology Society in 1935, serving on its board of directors (1939 and 1945), as its treasurer (1954–70), and as business manager of *JAMS* (1958–80). In 1971 he was elected an honorary fellow of the Pierpont Morgan Library. A Festschrift was published in celebration of his seventy-fifth birthday (*Studies in Musicology in Honor of Otto E. Albrecht*, ed. J.W. Hill, Kassel, 1980).

WRITINGS

Grove7 (P. Morgan)

"Microfilm Archives and Musicology," *PAMS 1938*, 62–8

"Adventures and Discoveries of a Manuscript Hunter," *MQ*, xxxi (1945), 492–503

ed., with C.D. Saltonstall and H.C. Smith: *Catalogue of Music for Small Orchestra* (Washington, DC, 1947)

A Census of Autograph Music Manuscripts of European Composers in American Libraries (Philadelphia, 1953)

with H. Cahoon and D. Ewing: *The Mary Flagler Cary Music Collection* (New York, 1970)

"Musical Treasures in the Morgan Library," *Notes*, xxviii (1971–2), 643–51

"Autographs of Viennese Composers in the USA," *Beiträge zur Musikdokumentation: Franz Grasberger zum 60. Geburtstag*, ed. G. Brosche (Tutzing, 1975), 17–25

Checklist of Early Music and Books on Music in the University of Pennsylvania Libraries (Philadelphia, 1977)

"Opera in Philadelphia, 1800–1830," *JAMS*, xxxii (1979), 499–515

PAULA MORGAN/RICHARD GRISCOM

Albrecht & Co. Firm of piano makers. Charles Albright (Albrecht by 1864) is listed in Philadelphia city directories from 1863. He was in partnership with Frederick Riekes (as Albrecht & Riekes, 1864–5), with Riekes and Richard T. Schmidt (as Albrecht, Riekes & Schmidt, 1866–74), and with Riekes and Edmund Wolsieffer (as Albrecht & Co., 1875–86). From 1887 to 1916 the firm was owned by Blasius & Sons, which in turn was owned by Rice-Wuerst & Co., a manufacturer based in Woodbury, New Jersey, from around 1916; Albrecht pianos were listed by Rice-Wuerst until 1920. Although some advertisements for Albrecht & Co. stated that the firm was established in 1789, there is no evidence to support this claim; no relationship between Albrecht & Co., Charles Albrecht, and Christian Albrecht, all piano makers active in Philadelphia, has been established.

CYNTHIA ADAMS HOOVER

Albright, Charles. *See* ALBRECHT, CHARLES.

Albright, Gerald (Anthony) (*b* Hollywood, CA, 30 Aug 1957). Jazz and pop saxophonist. With Grover Washington Jr., and George Benson he was at the forefront of a movement in the 1970s that combined a jazz sensibility with more mass-market styles such as funk, rock, and rhythm and blues. Albright attended Locke High School where Patrice Rushen was a fellow student. At the University of Redlands, he read business management with a minor in music; during this time he refined his saxophone technique and learned to play bass guitar. He subsequently performed and recorded with Rushen, playing the well-known saxophone solo on her hit single "Forget me nots" (Rhino, 1982). Thereafter, his career flourished as he worked with a range of artists including Anita Baker, the Winans Family, Lola Folana, Whitney Houston, Phil Collins, and Quincy Jones. One of Bill Clinton's favorite saxophonists, Albright performed at the president's inauguration as well as at several of his private functions. As a leader, he has made nine albums and sold more than one million records in the United States; his recordings *Pushing the Envelope* and *Sax for Stax* received Grammy nominations for Best Pop Instrumental Album in 2009 and 2010 respectively. Albright has been successful performing both acoustic and electronic music, and he has often integrated sequencing and drum machines into the latter. In addition to his main instrument, he plays bass guitar, flute, and keyboards and produces and arranges for his own projects.

E. RON HORTON

Albright, William (Hugh) (*b* Gary, IN, 20 Oct 1944; *d* Ann Arbor, MI, 17 Sept 1998). Composer, organist, and pianist. He attended the Juilliard Preparatory Department (1959–62), the University of Michigan (1963–70), and the Paris Conservatoire (1968–9), studying composition with ROSS LEE FINNEY, GEORGE ROCHBERG, and OLIVIER MESSIAEN, and the organ with MARILYN MASON. His many commissions and honors included two awards from the Koussevitzky Foundation, the Queen Marie-José Prize (for his *Organbook I*), and an award from the American Academy of Arts and Letters. In 1979 he was selected to represent the United States in UNESCO's International Rostrum of Composers. The American Guild of Organists honored him with the Composer of the Year Award in 1993. He joined the composition department at the University of Michigan in 1970, where, as associate director of the electronic music studio, he pursued research into live and electronic modification of acoustic instruments. Through his own modern rag compositions and his performances and recordings of classical ragtime, stride piano, and boogie-woogie, which include a recording of the complete works of Scott Joplin, Albright was a principal figure in the revival of interest in ragtime and stride masters. He gave many first performances of organ and piano works by American and European composers and commissioned a series of organ works that has substantially enriched the contemporary repertory for that instrument.

Although Albright's early organ works reflect the influence of Messiaen in their colorful registration and chromaticism, his later works, in a variety of mediums, combine a complex rhythmic and atonal style with elements of American popular and non-Western music. Albright's compositional philosophy stresses the value of music as communication and the supremacy of intuition, imagination, and beauty of sound. Much of his music displays exuberant humor and a fresh improvisatory spirit. A section of *Organbook III* (1977–8) briefly evokes "a wandering improvisation by an inebriated Sunday School organist"; *The King of Instruments* (1978) affectionately parodies the composer's own world of the pipe organ, with admonitions to the organist to add "the funniest sounding stop," to perform "in Chicago Blues style," and, with samba rhythms, to "keep repeating ad nauseam." *Flights of Fancy: Ballet for Organ* (1992) contains a "fight song" for the American Guild of Organists as well as a "strip-tease." *Seven Deadly Sins* (1974) subtly satirizes contemporary musical styles and concludes with a *grand galop* finale. Albright's seeming spontaneity and his shifts from Romantic ebullience to nostalgic lyricism are held firmly in balance by rigorous formal concision and control. In the virtuoso *Five Chromatic Dances* for piano (1976), for example, opening pitches outline the tonal centers and harmonic direction for a large-scale structure filled with contrasting textures, colors, and moods.

Albright's music exploits oppositions of all kinds. In addition to Albright's propensity for juxtaposing the traditional and novel, he often blurs the distinction between sacred and secular in his works. His concern for the spiritual resulted in such works as the *Chichester Mass* (1974), commissioned for the 900th anniversary of Chichester Cathedral, the oratorio *A Song to David* (1983), *Sphaera* (1985), commissioned by MIT, and *Chasm* (1989), written for the American Composers Orchestra.

WORKS

DRAMATIC

Alliance, 3 pts, orch, 1967–70; Beulahland Rag, nar, jazz qt, improvisation ens, tape, film, slide projections, 1967–9; Tic, soloist, 2 ens, tape, film, 1967; Seven Deadly Sins (after C. Marlowe and W. Dunbar), opt. nar, 7 players, 1974; Cross of Gold, chorus, insts, actors, 1975; Full Moon in March (incid music, W.B. Yeats), 1978; The Magic City (op, G. Garrett), 1978, inc.

VOCAL

An Alleluia Super-Round, 8 or more vv, 1973; Chichester Mass, chorus, 1974; Mass, D, chorus, congregation, org, perc, 1974; 6 New Hymns, unison vv, kbd, 1974–83; The birth of Jesus/Alleluia, SA, org, 1979; Pax in terra, A, T, chorus, 1981; David's Songs (Pss cxlix, cxvi, cxxxvii), (S, A, T, B)/SATB, 1982; A Song to David (C. Smart), solo vv, 2 choruses, org, 1983; Take up the Song (E. St Vincent Millay), S, SATB, pf, 1986; Antigone's Reply (Sophocles), S, Bar, SATB, pf, 1987; Deum de Deo, SATB, org/pf, 1988; 6 More New Hymns, SATB, pf/org, 1990; Dona nobis pacem, SATB, pf, 1992; Missa brevis, S, org, 1996

INSTRUMENTAL

Orch: Foils, wind, perc, 1963–4; Night Procession, chbr orch, 1972; Gothic Suite, str, org, perc, 1973; Heater, a sax, band, 1977; Bacchanal, org, orch, 1981; Chasm (Sym. Frag.), orch, 1989; Conc., hpd, str, 1991

Chbr and solo: Frescos, ww qt, 1964; 2 Pieces, 9 insts, 1965–6; Caroms, 8 players, 1966; Marginal Worlds, 12 players, 1969–70; Danse macabre, fl, cl, vn, vc, pf, 1971; Take That, 4 perc, 1972; Introduction, Passacaglia and Rondo capriccioso, tack pf, wind, perc; Doo-dah, 3 a sax, 1975; Jericho, tpt, org, 1976; Peace Pipe, 2 bn, 1976; Saints Preserve Us, cl, 1976; Shadows, gui, 1977; Romance, hn, org, 1981; The Enigma Syncopations, fl, db, org, perc, 1982; Brass Tacks, ragtime march, brass qt, 1983; Canon, D, db, hpd, 1984; Sonata, a sax, pf, 1984; Qnt, cl, str qt, 1987; Abiding Passions, ww qnt, 1988; Valley of Fire, sax qt, org, 1989; The Great Amen, fl, pf, 1992; Pit Band, a sax, b cl, pf, 1993; Rustles of Spring, 1994, fl, a sax/cl, vn, vc, pf, 1994; Fantasy Etudes, sax qt, 1995

KEYBOARD

Org: Juba, 1965; Pneuma, 1966; Organbook I, 1967; Organbook II, org, tape, 1971; Stipendium peccati, org, pf, perc, 1973; Dream and Dance, org, perc, 1974; Sweet Sixteenths, 1975; Organbook III, 1977–8; De spiritum, org, 2 pfmrs, 1978; Halo, org, metal insts, 1978; The King of Instruments (E. Haun, W. Albright), nar, org, 1978; That Sinking Feeling, 1982; In memoriam, 1983; 1732: In memoriam Johannes Albrecht, 1984; Chasm, org, opt. echo inst, 1985; Sym. org, 1986; Flights of Fancy (ballet), org, 1992; Cod Piece, org, 1996; Bells in the Air, carillon, 1996; Chorale Prelude "Nun Komm der Heiden Heiland," org, 1997

Other (pf, unless otherwise stated): Pianoàgogo, 1965–6; 3 Original Rags, 1967–8; Grand Sonata in Rag, 1968; 3 Novelty Rags, 1968; The Dream Rags, 1970; 5 Chromatic Dances, 1976; 4 Fancies, hpd, 1978; Sphaera, pf, 2/4-track tape, 1985; 3 New Chestnuts, hpd, 1986; 4 Dance Tributes, 1987–96; The Machine Age, 1988; New Leaves, 1991

Principal publishers: Peters, Elkan-Vogel, Jobert, Marks

BIBLIOGRAPHY

E. Hantz: "An Introduction to the Organ Music of William Albright," *The Diapason*, lxvii/6, (1973), 1, 4–5

D. Burge: "An Interview with William Albright," *Contemporary Keyboard*, iii/3 (1977), 52

J. Perone: *Pluralistic Strategies in Musical Analysis: a Study of Selected Works by William Albright* (diss., SUNY, Buffalo, 1988)

J. Perone: "The Choral Music of William Albright," *American Organist*, xxviii/3 (1993), 60–2

D. Reed: "William Albright: Organ Music of the '80s," *American Organist*, xxvii/4 (1993), 60–3

"Albright Remembered: Remembrances by Bassett, Bolcom, Lerdahl and Gompper," *Newsletter* [Society of Composers, Iowa City, IA], xxviii/9 (1998), 1, 3

DON C. GILLESPIE/MICHAEL McGHEE

Album. The term was first applied to a collection of 78 r.p.m. discs used to record a long work, such as a symphony, that would not fit onto a single disc (*see* SINGLE); these collections were presented in a format resembling a family album, although containing sleeves for discs rather than pages for photographs. The term was later adopted for long-playing records of over 30 minutes of music, and later again also denoted the aesthetic qualities of the music contained within. In the mid-1960s certain musicians created albums that presented a collection of songs organized around one central theme; thus artists such as the Mothers of Invention and the Beatles were described as making "concept" albums. These consisted of a selection of songs either unified by one pivotal idea or built around a narrative sequence, often supported by thematic cover art and appropriate marketing. Album-based music invited admiration for its technical excellence and studio craft. The album as a portfolio or representative selection of work is shown in the popularity of "Best Of" and "Greatest Hits" compilations. Certain top-selling acts such as Pink Floyd and Led Zeppelin, who seldom, or never, released single material, were thought of as "album artists," and the late 1960s saw the rise of progressive rock groups that depended predominantly on album sales for their success.

Album-Oriented Rock (AOR) was used as a marketing term in the 1970s to describe stadium acts such as the Eagles, Toto, Foreigner, and Styx. Such music became the staple of American FM radio in the 1970s. With the rise of the CD (compact disc) in the early 1980s the term album was often used interchangeably with CD. Musicians would record a new "album," which was sold in "record" stores, even if the resulting material was almost exclusively disseminated via the media of the CD. The album remained the most lucrative format produced by the MUSIC INDUSTRY into the 1990s, as record labels targeted consumers over 25, whose spending power ensured a high demand for both new music and old products in the form of reissues. The rise of the digital age and the introduction of Internet-based exchange and distribution eventually led to a precipitous decline in album sales by the start of the 21st century. Aesthetic strategies, business models, and consumer expectations all have redirected much of the music industry toward the production of singles, now typically sold as digitized audio files, as an increasingly significant medium for packaging contemporary music.

DAVID BUCKLEY/CHARLES HIROSHI GARRETT

Albuquerque. City in New Mexico (pop. 541,615; metropolitan area 869,684; 2010 US Census). The Rio Grande Valley has been populated and cultivated since as far back as 2000 BCE. The Pueblo people who lived in the area when Europeans arrived had a sophisticated culture and advanced skills in stone masonry, ceramics, and a wide range of arts and crafts. Although the Spanish settled in New Mexico in 1598, a city charter was not granted to this small outpost until 1706, when provincial governor Don Francisco Cuervo y Valdes named it in honor of Don Francisco Fernández de la Cueva, viceroy of New Spain (1653–60). One of de la Cueva's aristocratic titles was Duke of Alburquerque, referring to the Spanish town of Alburquerque, which led to Albuquerque, New Mexico becoming known as the Duke City. Present-day Albuquerque retains much of its Spanish and Native American cultural heritage, but long ago dropped the additional "r" found in the Spanish name. The spectacular Sandia Mountains run along the eastern side of Albuquerque, and the Rio Grande flows through the city, north to south.

Western art music of various types has been performed in Albuquerque since its establishment in 1706, including sacred liturgical music performed from the colonial period; salon music performed in 19th-century households; Spanish zarzuelas, European operas in English translation, and Gilbert and Sullivan operettas performed by touring companies from the mid-19th century on; and military band performances of waltzes, marches, and opera overtures. The establishment of the music department at the University of New Mexico further encouraged the development of art music. Among its earliest faculty members were Grace Edminster Thompson, first conductor of the Albuquerque Civic SO; JOHN DONALD ROBB, a composer and collector of southwestern folk music; and Kurt Frederick, a Viennese violist/conductor who joined the faculty in 1941. Frederick was instrumental in the establishment of the University Symphony Orchestra, Albuquerque Youth Symphony, and Albuquerque Opera Theatre, as well as the expansion of the UNM Music Department. The university has been an important force in training music educators and performers active throughout the state and the region. Its graduates have become members of major national and international opera companies, symphony orchestras, premier service bands, and university faculties. The department currently offers BM, BA, and MM degrees in performance, music education, jazz studies, composition/theory, and music history. There are 61 full and part time faculty serving a student population of more than 300 undergraduate and 100 graduate majors. The collection of field recordings built by Robb eventually grew to more than 1800 items, including Native American, Hispano, Mexican, and African American music. The Robb Collection is housed by The UNM Fine Arts and Design Library and the University of New Mexico's Center for Southwest Research.

Grace Edminster Thompson founded the Albuquerque Civic Symphony Orchestra in 1932; its name was changed first to the Albuquerque Symphony Orchestra, and then, in 1976, to the New Mexico Symphony Orchestra. Its conductors have included Frederick (under whom it gave the world premiere of Schoenberg's *A Survivor from Warsaw* in 1948), Hans Lange, Maurice Bonney, and Iturbi. In the 1970s the orchestra gradually became fully professional under the direction of Yoshimi Takeda (1970–84). Guillermo Figueroa was named music director in 2000. The NMSO was the largest year-round performing arts organization in the state, employing more than 100 full and part-time musicians and staff. In addition to a subscription series in UNM's Popejoy Hall and the Hispanic Cultural Center, it offered concerts in neighborhood and community centers as well as popular, youth, and small-ensemble concerts.

Due to a number of factors the NMSO declared bankruptcy in the spring of 2011. It was reconstituted by the musicians as the New Mexico Philharmonic. The Albuquerque community also supports a full-time commercial radio station devoted solely to classical music (KHFM).

Numerous chamber music ensembles are active in the city. The June Music Festival, founded in 1940, initially offered a summer series of chamber music concerts and has since changed its name to Chamber Music Albuquerque, presenting a year-round program of concerts by internationally recognized ensembles and soloists. As an adjunct to Chamber Music Albuquerque, the Albuquerque Chamber Soloists offer a series of four concerts that showcases the talents of outstanding New Mexico musicians, many of whom are members of New Mexico's leading orchestras and academic institutions. CHATTER promotes the performance of 20th- and 21st-century music, offering a series of chamber music concerts, educational activities and outreach initiatives in various venues in the city. The Albuquerque Baroque Players, a professional chamber ensemble, formed in the summer of 1997 to perform Baroque music on period instruments. Founded in 1978, Música Antigua de Albuquerque, also a professional chamber ensemble, performs medieval, Renaissance, and Baroque music with voices and period instruments.

Many choral ensembles offer regular concerts, including New Mexico Symphonic Chorus, Albuquerque Civic Chorus, New Mexico Women's Chorus, New Mexico Gay Men's Chorus, Quintessence, The New MexiChords, Enchanted Mesa Show Chorus, Albuquerque Boy Choir, Albuquerque Girl Choir, de Profundis, and Polyphony.

Opera Southwest, incorporated in 1972 as Albuquerque Opera Theatre, is a professional, regional company that produces two to three major operas per year. To date it has produced 117 major operas for nearly 250,000 patrons, and has mounted 23 world premieres by local composers, including original operas created especially for children.

The Albuquerque Youth Symphony was formed in 1955–6 with Frederick as its first conductor. Dale Kempter served as conductor from 1964 until his retirement in 2002. Under his leadership the program grew from a single orchestra to the current six, in addition to a youth band. The top group, the Albuquerque Youth Symphony, now under the direction of Gabriel Gordon, has performed across the United States and toured internationally.

The city supports a broad range of other musical institutions. Dating back to 1960, Musical Theatre Southwest offers several fully staged (with orchestra) Broadway shows each year. Through four different annual concert series, the New Mexico Jazz Workshop presents a wide diversity of music including jazz, blues, salsa and Latin jazz. Offering dozens of concerts and assembly programs each year, it presents local musicians and top visiting artists. The group Los Reyes de Albuquerque, co-founded by Roberto Martínez and Ray Flores in 1962, performs traditional New Mexican music as well as Mexican popular styles, including mariachi and *música ranchera*. Mariachi Spectacular, a five-day celebration of mariachi music held in several indoor and outdoor venues around Albuquerque, features mariachi groups from Mexico, New Mexico, and across the nation. Workshops, competitions, concerts, a mass, and various educational activities are part of this annual event.

Many Albuquerque venues host musical performances. Since 1988, the Outpost Performing Arts Center, an intimate venue seating 175, stages more than 100 events annually—from jazz, folk, blues, and roots music to experimental music to theater and performance art. Since opening in 2000, the National Hispanic Cultural Center, the nation's largest, has staged hundreds of programs in the visual, performing, and literary arts. The KiMo, built in 1927 as a movie theater, is one of the city's best-known landmarks. The historic 700-seat theater, renovated in 1980 and restored in 2000, hosts theatrical and musical events featuring both homegrown and touring productions. It is home to Opera Southwest and various dance companies. Many venues offer classical music concerts, from a number of local churches to the African American Performing Arts Center and Exhibit Hall, from the South Broadway Cultural Center to Robertson and Sons Violin Shop. Fans of popular music can be found at the El Rey Theater, the Journal Pavilion, Route 66 Casino Hotel Legends Theatre, and the Sunshine Theater.

BIBLIOGRAPHY

P. Hart: "Albuquerque Symphony Orchestra," *Orpheus in the New World: the Symphony Orchestra as an American Cultural Institution* (New York, 1973), 239–40

M. Simmons: *Albuquerque: a Narrative History* (Albuquerque, NM, 1982)

K. Hinterbichler: "New Mexico Symphony Orchestra," *Symphony Orchestras of the United States: Selected Profiles*, ed. R.R. Craven, (Westport, CT, 1986), 230–32

M. Simmons: *Hispanic Albuquerque, 1706–1846* (Albuquerque, NM, 2003)

C. Lazell and M. Payne: *Historic Albuquerque: an Illustrated History* (San Antonio, TX, 2007)

KARL HINTERBICHLER

Alburger, Mark (*b* Upper Darby, PA, 2 April 1957). Composer and writer on music. As a young man, Alburger studied the oboe, playing with such groups as the Philadelphia and Delaware Youth Orchestras, where he had the opportunity to work with George Crumb and George Rochberg. His interest in composition had already been ignited before college, and he studied with Karl Kohn at Pomona College (1978) and with James Freeman, Gerald Levinson, and Joan Panetti at Swarthmore College (BA 1979). He spent a short time working with composer Thomas Wubbenhorst in the 1980s, and then obtained his Master's degree at the Dominican University of California in 1991, training with Jules Langert. At Claremont Graduate University (PhD, 1996), Alburger studied with Roland Jackson, Thomas Flaherty, and Christopher Yavelow. His own postminimalist style was further sharpened through his experience working with Terry Riley from 1997 to 1999. Alburger has taught in many locations, including Marin Academy (1986–90), Dominican UC (1992–7), and Diablo Valley College (from 2002). He is also an active performer and arts administrator as well as a music critic; he is Founder and Music Director of the San Francisco Composers Chamber Orchestra, Music Director and Resident Composer of San Francisco Cabaret Opera/Goat Hall Productions, and the Founder and Editor-Publisher of the journals *20th-Century Music* (1994–9) and *21st-Century Music* (2000–), for which he has interviewed an extremely wide range of modern composers. He also contributes to *Commuter Times* and *San Francisco Classical Voice*. Alburger keeps a regular blog (<http://markalburger.blogspot.com/>) in which he refers to his work as "postminimal, postpopular, and postcomedic." He makes terrific use of the internet to disseminate his music, including the many hundreds of videos available on YouTube that capture live performances of his pieces. Alburger's music has been recorded on the labels North/South Consonance, I Kill Me Music, and New Music, which will release his complete catalog; much of his music also can be heard through his blog. His music, at some times steeped in the sounds of the past, at others using modern formal structures, frequently references Biblical subjects. Alburger has received a significant number of accolades, from multiple ASCAP awards and Meet the Composer fellowships to composer's grants from Getty and MetLife, among others.

WORKS
(selective)

Opera: Mice and Men, op.45 (1992); Henry Miller in Brooklyn, op.77 (1999); Job: a Masque, op.79 (1999); Antigone, op.88 (2000); The Little Prince, op.89 (2000); Diocletian: a Pagan Opera, op.90 (2000); The Bald Soprano, op.94 (2001); Animal Opera: an Orwellian Comedy, op.95 (2001); Camino Real, op.110 (2003); The Playboy of the Western World, op.111 (2003); On the Road, op.112 (2004); The Pied Piper of Hamelin: a Child's Opera, op.116 (2004); Waiting for Godot, op.128 (2005); The Ring of Harriet, op.142 (2006); Sex and the Bible: the Opera (Part I), op.169 (2009)

Orch: 9 syms.; 16 concs. (fl, ob, tpt, hn, hp, pf, vn, va, others); overtures, suites

Other: duets, trios, quartets, quintets; works for piano; vocal music

JONAS WESTOVER

Alda [Davies], **Frances (Jeanne)** (*b* Christchurch, New Zealand, 31 May 1883; *d* Venice, Italy, 18 Sept 1952). New Zealand soprano. After the death of her parents, she was brought up by her maternal grandparents in Australia. Her first engagements were in light opera at Melbourne. She then went to Paris and studied with Marchesi, who suggested that she adopt the name Alda; she also arranged Alda's debut as Manon at the Opéra-Comique in 1904. After successful appearances at the Monnaie in Brussels (1905), Covent Garden (1906), and La Scala (1908), where she met Toscanini and Gatti-Cassazza, she was engaged by the Metropolitan (debut, December 1908), where she sang until her retirement in 1930. In 1908 Gatti-Cassazza left La Scala to become director of the Metropolitan; he married Alda in 1910. Her pure, lyrical voice, technically almost faultless, was ideally suited to such roles as Gilda, Violetta, Desdemona, Manon (Massenet), Louise, Mimi, and Cio-Cio-San. She created the leading soprano roles in Damrosch's *Cyrano de Bergerac*, Victor Herbert's *Madeleine*, and Henry Hadley's *Cleopatra's Night*. She is well represented on record.

BIBLIOGRAPHY

F. Alda: *Men, Women and Tenors* (Boston, 1937)

A. Favia-Artsay: "Frances Alda," *Record Collector*, vi (1951), 228 [with discography]

A. Simpson: "'New Zealand's most famous daughter': A profile of Frances Alda (1879–1952)," *Women's Studies*, v/1 (1989), 60–73

ALAN BLYTH/R

Alden, Christopher (*b* New York, NY, 16 Sept 1949). Director, twin brother of DAVID ALDEN. The son of the playwright Jerome Alden and the Broadway dancer Barbara Gaye, he studied at the University of Pennsylvania and began his professional career as an actor, appearing in Joseph Papp's New York Shakespeare Festival Tony Award-winning rock musical *Two Gentlemen of Verona* (1971). After a brief period in the Broadway musical theater, he was an assistant to Jean-Pierre Ponnelle from 1978 to 1982 in Houston, Paris, and Salzburg. Since then he has staged operas in many American cities, and has been director of production at Long Beach Opera (California) and associate director of Opera at the Academy in New York City. These two smaller companies encourage innovation, and Alden has pursued an enlivening approach that has proved controversial but seldom dull; his version of Purcell's *Dido and Aeneas* was presented as a cautionary tale of the flesh for British schoolgirls, while Offenbach's *La vie parisienne* was updated to reflect the drug culture of present-day New York. The results may sometimes be controversial, but they invariably show a questing spirit, a lively theatrical imagination, and genuine love for the work at hand. Alden made his European debut in 1980, directing Mozart's *Don Giovanni* in Basle. His productions for other companies have included the premiere of Stewart Wallace's *Harvey Milk* (1995, Houston), *Turandot* for the ENO, *Faust* for the WNO, and an acclaimed postmodern *Fliegender Holländer* for the Canadian Opera Company, Toronto (all 1996). As an opera director, Alden is known for his use of contemporary imagery and a minimalist visual style. For example, he has likened his own 1984 production of Monteverdi's *L'incoronazione di Poppea* to a new wave rock video and has frequently expressed his desire to connect the inner world of opera theater to the modern sensibility of a younger audience. His use of explicit sexuality, brutal violence, and exaggerated satirical humor has soured his relationship with more conservative patrons.

BIBLIOGRAPHY

D.J. Levin: "Interview with Christopher Alden," *Opera Cues* [Houston Grand Opera Magazine] xxxix/2 (1999), 17

D.J. Levin: "Opera out of Performance: Verdi's 'Macbeth' at San Francisco Opera," *Cambridge Opera Journal*, xvi (2004), 249–67

PETER G. DAVIS/NICOLA BADOLATO

Alden, David (*b* New York, NY, 16 Sept 1949). Opera producer, twin brother of CHRISTOPHER ALDEN. His early productions in America in the late 1970s were well received but gave no hint of the Brechtian, often violent bent that later characterized his stagings in Europe. His staging of *Wozzeck* first at the Metropolitan in 1980 and then at the Scottish Opera later that year was favorably noted by *Opera* magazine, reversing the disdain that had greeted his *Rigoletto* for the same company in 1979. A punk version of *The Rake's Progress* (1982, Amsterdam) led to a notorious *Mazepa* (1984), his first work for the English National Opera, which with its chainsaws and strip lighting entered local operatic folklore as an extreme of director's folly. This established his reputation, however, and his ENO *Simon Boccanegra* (1987) and *Un ballo in maschera* (1989), both designed by David Fielding, were seen to create a new house style that, though controversial and alienating, was both musical and dramatically stimulating. Alden has staged the American premières of Szymanowski's *King Roger* (1988, Long Beach) and Siegfried Matthus's *Judith* (1990, Santa Fe), and the world premières of Bolcom's *Casino Paradise* (1990, Philadelphia) and Josef Tal's *Josef* (1995, Tel Aviv), among other works. With his brother, he co-directed in 1992 semi-staged versions of the three Mozart/Da Ponte operas for the Chicago SO, conducted by Barenboim. Alden has contributed regularly to the Bavarian Opera from the mid-1990s until 2006, working closely with director Peter Jonas.

Alden's preference for abstract settings, often using images of pendulums, chairs and narrow slopes, has worked more effectively with 18th- and 19th-century operas, which were perceived as ripe for reinterpretation, than with modern works, which required clarification rather than obfuscation.

BIBLIOGRAPHY

R. Milnes: "Genoa, Watergate and Trauma: the Theatrical World of Alden and Fielding," *Opera*, xxxix (1988), 1290–301

A. Clements: "David Alden," *Opera*, xlvii (1996), 146–54

PATRICK O'CONNOR/R

Aldrich, Richard (*b* Providence, RI, 31 July 1863; *d* Rome, Italy, 2 June 1937). Critic. Aldrich attended Harvard University, where he studied music under JOHN KNOWLES PAINE, graduating in 1885. That same year he became music critic for the *Providence Journal* after serving his apprenticeship in general journalism. In 1889 he became private secretary to US Senator Nathan F. Dixon, simultaneously serving as music critic to the *Washington Evening Star*. In 1891 he relinquished both posts to join the staff of the *New York Tribune*, where he held various editorial posts, including assistant critic to H.E. Krehbiel, until 1902, when he became music editor of the *New York Times*; he retired in 1923, remaining on the editorial staff in an advisory capacity.

Throughout his career Aldrich was notable for the breadth of his musical knowledge and the soundness of his judgment. To readers, he offered an American perspective on European music, championing the work of the German romantics, especially Wagner. In general Aldrich was sympathetic to modern music, though vehemently opposed to extreme trends. As a member of the National Institute of Arts and Letters, he was distinguished for the excellence of his style and for the wit and urbanity of his writing. He collected an important library of books on music, which he cataloged during the leisure of his later years; it remained intact in the possession of his heirs until 1955, when it was donated by his son to Harvard University.

WRITINGS

A Guide to Parsifal (Boston, 1904)
A Guide to the Ring of the Nibelung (Boston, 1905)
Musical Discourse (London, 1928/*R*)
A Catalogue of Books Relating to Music in the Library of Richard Aldrich (New York, 1931)
Concert Life in New York 1902–1923 (New York, 1941/*R*)

BIBLIOGRAPHY

O. Thompson: "An American School of Criticism," *MQ*, xxiii (1937), 428–39

H.C. COLLES/MALCOLM TURNER/SAMUEL PARLER

Aldrich, Thomas Bailey (*b* Portsmouth, NH, 11 Nov 1836; *d* Boston, MA, 19 March 1907). Poet. He held various editorial positions in New York and Boston from 1855 to 1890 and produced four novels as well as several volumes of poetry, short stories, and essays. With the publication in 1855 of his poem *The Ballad of Babie Bell,* Aldrich achieved almost instant success. He went on to become one of the leading poets and writers of his age. He exerted perhaps his greatest influence on American literature during his years as editor of the *Atlantic Monthly,* succeeding William Dean Howells in that position in 1881. Along with E.C. Stedman, Bayard Taylor, R.H. Stoddard, and other writers of the genteel tradition, Aldrich faded into obscurity in the early 20th century.

In his poetry and prose Aldrich was at his best in shorter forms. His carefully crafted poems are noted for their neatness, precision, and delicacy. Like Oliver Wendell Holmes, he excelled in the type of poetry commonly called "vers de société" or "familiar verse." His light, bright, and easy lyrics were very popular as song and choral texts, especially in the years 1875–1900. The poems most often set were *Nocturne, Cradle Song, Forever and a Day,* and the song "Sweetheart, sigh no more" from the longer narrative poem *Wyndham Towers.* C. Henshaw Dana, Sebastian Schlesinger, and William H. Pommer set the most poems; other composers of Aldrich settings include Arthur Foote and Alfred Pease. Comparatively few settings appeared after 1910.

BIBLIOGRAPHY

C.E. Samuels: *Thomas Bailey Aldrich* (New York, 1965)

R.C. Friedberg: *American Art Song and American Poetry* (Metuchen, NJ, 1981)

M.A. Hovland: *Musical Settings of American Poetry: a Bibliography* (Westport, CT, 1986) [incl. list of settings]

MICHAEL HOVLAND

Aleatory. A term applied to music whose composition and/or performance is, to a greater or lesser extent, undetermined by the composer.

1. Introduction. 2. History. 3. Aleatory composition. 4. Indeterminate notation, graphic notation, and texts. 5. The role of the performer. 6. The aesthetics of chance.

1. Introduction. As defined above, the term "aleatory" applies to all music: it is impossible for a composer to prescribe every aspect in the realization of a composition; even the sound of playback will depend on the equipment used and the acoustic conditions. However, the term is usually restricted to music in which the composer has made a deliberate withdrawal of control, excluding certain established usages which fall within this category: for example, keyboard improvisation, the cadenza, unmeasured pauses, and alternative scorings. Three types of aleatory technique may be distinguished, although a given composition may exhibit more than one of them, separately or in combination: (i) the use of random procedures in the generation of fixed compositions; (ii) the allowance of choice to the performer(s) among formal options stipulated by the composer; and (iii) methods of notation which reduce the composer's control over the sounds in a composition. The liberty offered by these means can extend from a choice between two dynamic markings to almost unguided improvisation.

2. History. Until the mid-20th century Western composers were constantly seeking notational developments that would enable them to determine sounds with greater exactness, an attitude entirely opposed to the aleatory. There were, however, some trivial examples of aleatory music in the 18th century, when schemes were published for generating simple pieces in response to the results of dice throws. One might also consider the art of keyboard improvisation as a precursor of aleatory music, but here the creator and the performer are identical. In most aleatory music, on the other hand, the creator provides a score which gives a degree of freedom to any performer. Similarly, other improvised musics, such as jazz and folk traditions, were not initially the most important influences on aleatory music.

The first composer to make a significant use of aleatory features was Ives, whose scores include exhortations to freedom, alternatives of an unprecedentedly important character, and unrealizable notations that silently invite the performer to find his own solution. From the 1930s Henry Cowell followed Ives's lead in such works as the String Quartet no.3 "Mosaic" (1934), which allows the players to assemble the music from fragments provided. He used other "elastic" (his own word) notations to introduce chance or choice into the performance. His sometime pupil Cage began to use what he called "chance operations" in composition during the early 1950s, notably in the *Music of Changes* for piano (1951). At first Cage's work had most influence on his immediate associates: Morton Feldman wrote a number of "graph" pieces, such as the *Intersection* and *Projection* series, in which notes are replaced by boxes, determining pitch only relatively; and Earle Brown abandoned all conventional notation in, for example, *December 1952*, consisting of 31 black rectangles printed on a single sheet.

European composers were more hesitant in taking up aleatory techniques. Such early examples as Karlheinz Stockhausen's *Klavierstück IX* (1956) and Pierre Boulez's Piano Sonata no.3 (1956–7) allow the player no more than limited freedom in the ordering of composed sections. By this time Cage had gone much further in abandoning the control exercised by the composer, or even the performer(s), reaching an extreme point in *4' 33"* (1952), whose only sounds—those of the environment—are quite unpredictable. About 1960 purely verbal scores were introduced by La Monte Young and others, and the following decade saw the pursuit of aleatory methods to a wide range of ends throughout the world.

After an explosion of interest in the late 1960s, coinciding with a revolutionary period in Western culture generally, aleatory music became a dead or at least dormant issue. Many European composers returned to conventional notation and wrote fully determined works again. And though Cage remained true to non-intention, even he went back to staff notation in *Cheap Imitation* (1969) and many later works. A kind of superficial looseness remained as part of the lingua franca of moderate modernism, and improvisation continued as the mainstay of experimental music. But Cage's later music is unusual in the period for the precision of its invitations to chance.

3. Aleatory composition. Aleatory composition involves the use of random procedures in determining musical aspects that are to be notated; unless other aleatory techniques are also used, the resultant score is no less fixed than a conventional composition. Chance procedures in composition have been most fully and diversely exploited by Cage. In producing the *Music of Changes*, for example, he tossed coins to decide how he should make choices from charts of pitches, durations, intensities and other sound aspects, deriving his chance operations from the "I Ching," the Chinese book of changes. Similar methods were used in assembling *Williams Mix* for tape (1952) and in notating the parts for 12 radio receivers in *Imaginary Landscape no.4* (1951). Other random techniques employed by Cage include placing notes on imperfections in the music paper (*Music for Piano*, 1952–6) and using templates drawn from maps of the constellations (*Atlas eclipticalis*, 1961–2). In contrast with Cage, other composers have often avoided introducing any randomness into their composing or notation, but have permitted the performer some flexibility in realization by means of the provision of alternative orderings. When Cage used formal variability, as in *Winter Music* or the Concert for Piano and Orchestra (1957–8), he left options as open as possible: any amount of the solo part of the Concert may be omitted, as may any or all of the orchestral parts, and the piece may be performed simultaneously with others by the composer.

4. Indeterminate notation, graphic notation, and texts. The types of aleatory music so far described use conventional notation to determine sounds, although, in compositions of mobile form, new signs may be necessary to guide performers in choosing a route. Many composers have

introduced new notations which render the sounds themselves indeterminate, frequently by abandoning traditional signs for graphics or texts. The composer can allow flexibility in the interpretation of conventional symbols by giving alternatives or by specifying sound aspects in only relative terms. Relative notation has often been employed to specify a more or less narrowly defined register rather than a determined pitch, particularly in vocal music. Greater indeterminacy is introduced, still with conventional notation, when performers are asked to improvise on the basis of given pitches or rhythms, to interpret a given pitch sequence with any rhythm, to interpret a given rhythm with any pitches, and so on.

Graphic notation—which may be distinguished from the preceding by the fact that it signifies, if at all, by analogy instead of by symbol—has been employed to supplement conventional notation where the latter proves inadequate. For example, the "shape" of a glissando (i.e. the variation of pitch with time) can be shown by a curved line on a staff; though the aleatory character of such notations is an inevitable concomitant rather than a deliberate addition. Alternatively, graphics may be used as a total replacement for standard symbols, as in Brown's *December 1952*. Some composers raised graphic notation to the level of visual art, but beyond the level of musical intelligibility, since such scores often provide the performer with little or no information as to how the signs are to be interpreted, and the possibilities for sound realization are exceedingly diverse.

Like graphics of this latter sort, verbal texts can be used to give the performer a very large degree of freedom in determining both form and content. The text may be a straightforward instruction for action—often a far from conventionally musical action, as in Young's *Composition 1960 no.5*, whose principal requirement is "Turn a butterfly (or any number of butterflies) loose in the performance area." Other text scores are more inscrutable; Young's *Piano Piece for David Tudor no.3*, for example, consists of the text: "most of them were very old grasshoppers." More usually, texts have been used to give a more or less clearly stated basis for ensemble improvisation.

5. The role of the performer. Aleatory music implies a quite new inventive role for the performer, and its evolution has been closely linked with the technical innovations and accomplishments of individuals and of ensembles.

In some respects, compositions of mobile form introduce the fewest new problems, since the material can be fully composed. When more than one performer is involved and when the composer does not want an anarchic result, either the performers must make all decisions in advance, or else the composer must supply a system of cues and other signals. Where the notation, or lack of it, renders the music still more indeterminate, the performer's responsibility becomes weightier. It is often difficult for the composer to make his intentions clear without hampering the player more than he wishes. The common reaction to this problem in the 1960s was the establishment by composers of performing traditions within their own ensembles, such as the Sonic Arts Union (consisting of the four composers Ashley, Behrman, Lucier and Mumma). Their collective teamwork meant that very little had to be specified in the score. Other composers welcomed the extreme variability with which minimally notated scores may be interpreted, and made no attempt to form a tradition of performance. Their interest was, rather, in exciting the players to awareness of their own and their colleagues' potentialities, a position exemplified by Wolff's work. Some performing ensembles dispensed even with this unassuming stimulus from a composer, and engaged in "free improvisation," though most continued to play composed music as well.

6. The aesthetics of chance. The introduction of chance into a work of art undermines the notion that creation requires, at each moment and on every level, a definite choice on the part of the artist. In general the Western work of art was, until the mid-20th century, supposed to have an ideal identity, and, in the case of performed arts, a performance might be judged by the extent to which it was held to correspond with that identity.

In the works of most European composers, the operation of aleatory technique does not fundamentally disturb that conception. The composition is still the product of an individual mind, though some aspects are left indefinite; the performer has still to realize the composer's intentions. Aleatory music in Europe might, in general, be considered as a matter of choice rather than chance, and the most significant choices have usually remained with the composer, whether he exercised them in notating a score or in directing a performance. Even improvisation groups in Europe customarily retained a traditional regard for achievement, finish and the expression of defined ideas, although few succeeded in establishing a code of practice, such as exists in most jazz, within which their improvisations may be understood.

Cage's use of chance was, from the first, more destructive of the traditional notion of a work of art (just as, previously, his "automatic" procedures had been). Influenced by Zen Buddhism as well as by the musics of the east, his aim was to remove the barrier of his discrimination: any sound was to be admitted, freed to "be itself." It was a persistent search for means of avoiding willed choice that led him to investigate procedures that took music out of the control of both composer and performer. Although his associates, Brown and Feldman, found a parallel for their ideas in the work of visual artists (Alexander Calder's mobiles and Jackson Pollock's action paintings, for example), the central Cagean idea was to remove from music any reference to tradition or any trace of subjectivity, and chance, not choice, was the obvious means. This extreme aleatory position was stated at its most exact in Cage's lecture "Indeterminacy":

> Finally I said that the purpose of this purposeless music would be achieved if people learned to listen; that when they listened they might discover that they preferred the sounds of everyday life to the

ones they would presently hear in the musical program; that that was alright as far as I was concerned.

See also CAGE, JOHN; NOTATION.

BIBLIOGRAPHY

J. Cage: *Silence* (Middletown, CT, 1961)

Source (Sacramento, CA, 1967–) [magazine of short articles on aleatory music, scores and discs]

R. Kostelanetz, ed.: *John Cage* (New York, 1970)

G.M. Potter: *The Role of Chance in Contemporary Music* (diss., Indiana U., 1971)

M. Nyman: *Experimental Music: Cage and Beyond* (London, 1974, 2/1999)

C. Gagne and T. Caras: *Soundpieces: Interviews with American Composers* (Metuchen, NY, 1982)

J. Pritchett: *The Music of John Cage* (Cambridge, 1993)

P. Griffiths: *Modern Music and After* (Oxford, 1995, 2/2011)

K. Gann: *American Music in the Twentieth Century* (New York, 1997)

A. Beal: *New Music, New Allies: American Experimental Music in West Germany from the Zero Hour to Reunification* (Berkeley, CA, 2006)

PAUL GRIFFITHS/R

Aler, John (*b* Baltimore, MD, 4 Oct 1949). Tenor. He was trained by Rilla Mervine and Raymond McGuire at Catholic University, Washington, DC (1969–72), by Oren Brown at the American Opera Center at the Juilliard School (1972–6), and by Marlene Malas. While at the American Opera Center he made his debut as Ernesto (in Donizetti's *Don Pasquale*). In 1977 he won two first prizes at the Concours International de Chant de Paris; his European debut, two years later, was as Belmonte (*Die Entführung aus dem Serail*) at the Théâtre Royal de la Monnaie, Brussels. He first sang at the Santa Fe Opera in 1978 and has subsequently appeared at Covent Garden, Glyndebourne, the Deutsche Oper Berlin, the Vienna Staatsoper, the New York City Opera, the Washington Opera, and with the leading American orchestras. Aler's clear, agile, and appealing tenor is well suited to the operas of Mozart, Rossini, Donizetti, and Bellini. The range of his repertory, however, extends from the French Baroque through the 20th century, including composers as diverse as Rameau, Handel, Berlioz, Britten, and Messiaen. He has made over 60 recordings, three of which—Handel's *Semele* with the English Chamber Orchestra, Bartok's *Cantata Profana* with the Chicago SO, and Berlioz's *Requiem* with the Atlanta Symphony—have been awarded Grammys.

MICHAEL WALSH/PETER MONDELLI

Alexander, Alger(non) Texas (*b* Jewett, TX, 12 Sept 1900; *d* Richards, TX, 18 April 1954). Blues singer. He spent most of his life in east Texas, where he worked as a farmhand in Leon and Grimes counties and as a storeman in Dallas. There he was heard by the record salesman and blues pianist Sam Price, who arranged his first recording session. Alexander became one of the most popular recording blues singers of the 1920s. He was imprisoned for at least two offenses in the course of his career, and his earliest recordings, including "Levee Camp Moan" (1927, OK), are strongly influenced by work song. Unlike most male folk blues singers, he did not accompany himself; on this and the well-known "West Texas Blues" (1928, OK) among others, he was supported by the guitarist Lonnie Johnson, who was able to complement his irregular timing and verse structure. Alexander had a low, moaning singing style and used hummed choruses to good effect, as on "St. Louis Fair Blues" (1928, OK) and "Awful Moaning Blues" (1929, OK), with Dennis "Little Hat" Jones on guitar. His lyrics were often unusual and poetic, but he favored a limited number of tunes and sang almost exclusively in the three-line blues form. A variety of accompanists saved his recordings from the monotony that might have ensued, an example being the sympathetic violin playing of Bo Carter on "Days is lonesome" (1934, OK). After 1934 Alexander made only one more recording, "Bottom's Blues" (1950, Freedom), but his singing is poorly integrated with the accompaniment. Eventually, his health deteriorated and he died of syphilis.

BIBLIOGRAPHY

G. Van Rijn and H. Vergeer: disc notes, *Texas Troublesome Blues: Alger "Texas" Alexander*, Agram 1082 (2009)

PAUL OLIVER/R

Alexander, Charles [Charlie] **M(cCallon)** (*b* Meadow, TN, 24 Oct 1867; *d* Birmingham, UK, 13 Oct 1920). Evangelistic musician and gospel song publisher. He attended Maryville College, Tennessee, later returning as part-time instructor in voice and instrumental music. In 1892 he attended Moody Bible Institute in Chicago to prepare for the gospel ministry. Years earlier he had heard evangelist Dwight L. Moody preach and Ira D. Sankey sing in revival services, and he became determined to develop his musical gifts. While at the school, Alexander was influenced by gospel composer DANIEL BRINK TOWNER, a highly trained musician and teacher who led both choirs and congregations, employing standard conducting patterns and a baton. In 1893, during the World's Columbian Exposition in Chicago, Alexander assisted Moody in services designed to reach visitors at the fair. The following year, he became music director for evangelist Milan B. Williams, holding meetings throughout small towns on the Midwest "Kerosene Circuit," perfecting his approach to leading congregations in singing popular gospel songs. He joined the Moody Institute's president, Reuben A. Torrey, in 1902 on a highly successful mission to Australia. It was there he met pianist Robert Harkness and formed a partnership that popularized a new model for congregational song in revival services. It was based on Alexander's charisma and ability to inspire large crowds in which he employed standard conducting patterns and often rehearsed them like a choir. Harkness provided accompaniment on the piano (rather than the organ) in an improvisatory style, more idiomatic to gospel hymnody. Additional meetings were held in New Zealand, India, and Great Britain. In 1904 Alexander married the English woman, Helen Cadbury, heiress to the famous chocolate empire, and resided in Birmingham on the family estate, which they named Tennessee. He joined Presbyterian evangelist J. Wilbur Chapman in 1906, holding meetings in the United States, Australia, and Asia. Alexander published revival songbooks and owned the international copyrights to highly popular gospel songs such as Charles Gabriel's "His eye is on the sparrow" ("Why should I feel discouraged") and "The Glory Song" ("When all my labors and trials are o'er"). He secured copyrights to many songs in the public domain, and his collections such as *Alexander's Hymns No.3* (1915) remained in circulation for nearly a century. He made a gramophone recording of "The Glory Song" and "Tell Mother I'll be there" (with narration) in 1905. While Alexander was not a hymn writer (composer or poet) and did not possess a particularly appealing solo voice, as did many other evangelistic musicians, he elevated congregational song and gospel music to unprecedented levels of popularity, setting the stage for gospel musicians such as Homer Rodeheaver. Alexander died in Birmingham, England, and was buried in Lodge Hill Cemetery.

See also GOSPEL MUSIC; HYMNODY.

BIBLIOGRAPHY

G. Davis: *Twice Around the World with Alexander: Prince of Gospel Singers* (New York, 1907)

H.C. Alexander and M.J. Kennedy: *Charles M. Alexander: a Romance of Song and Soul-Winning* (New York, 1920)

M.R. Wilhoit: "Alexander, Charles McCallum [sic]," *Encyclopedia of American Gospel Music*, ed. W.K. McNeil (New York, 2005), 7–8

M.R. Wilhoit: "Alexander the Great: Or, Just Plain *Charlie*," *The Hymn: a Journal of Congregational Song*, xlvi/2, (1995), 20–28

HARRY ESKEW/MEL R. WILHOIT

Alexander, Dorothy [Dorothea Moses] (*b* Atlanta, GA, 22 April 1904; *d* Atlanta, GA, 17 Nov 1986). Ballet dancer, choreographer, teacher, and company director. Having suffered osteomylitis in early childhood, she was given ballet lessons to restore her strength. They not only did that but set her on course for her life's work. Dismayed by the lack of training and performing opportunities for ballet dancers in Atlanta, she vowed to create them if she could. After continued study with teachers in Atlanta and New York, she opened her own studio in Atlanta in 1921 and originated a dance enrichment program in Atlanta public schools in 1927. Two years later she founded the Dorothy Alexander Dance Concert Group and began to present public programs with her pupils. This group eventually became the Atlanta Ballet, the nation's oldest regional company. From its inception until the mid-1950s, "Miss Dorothy" created some eighty ballets for the company, including lyrical works for adult audiences as well as story ballets for children. Although she usually worked to the music of popular European composers, she sometimes commissioned works from local composers. Notable are *Valse Classique* (1944; music by C. Michael Ehrhardt), *American Suite* (1951; music by Albert Coleman), and *Fireworks Suite* (1955; music by Hugh Hodgson).

BIBLIOGRAPHY

H.C. Smith: "The Atlanta Ballet: Fifty Golden Years," *Dance Magazine* (Nov 1979), 88–94

D. Hering: "Alexander, Dorothy," *American National Biography Online* (New York, 2000) <http://www.anb.org>

CLAUDE CONYERS

Alexander, James Woodie (*b* Hamilton, MS, 21 Jan 1916; *d* Los Angeles, CA, 8 July 1996). Gospel singer, manager, and promoter. He moved to Los Angeles in the early 1940s to become a member of the Southern Gospel Singers, an all-male quartet. In 1946 he joined the Pilgrim Travelers, another male quartet, of which he soon became the guiding force. During its period of greatest popularity in the 1950s and 1960s the group became known for its close and smooth harmonies. Its members have included Kylo Turner and Keith Barber (leads), Jesse Whitaker (baritone), and Raphael Taylor (bass); jazz singer Lou Rawls also sang with the group in the late 1950s. Among their popular recordings were "Mother Bowed" (1950) and "I was there when the spirit came" (1952). The group performed in concert throughout the United States and won acclaim for their appearances at the Apollo Theater in New York. When the Travelers disbanded following a car accident that left Rawls hospitalized, Alexander shifted his focus to production and management. Alexander was instrumental in securing a recording contract for Dorothy Love Coates and the Original Gospel Harmonettes, recommended the singer Jessy Dixon to Brother Joe May and is credited as one of Little Richard's early mentors and managers. He started working with Sam Cooke, who left gospel music in the late 1950s to pursue a career in pop music, and together they formed SAR records in 1961. Their business briefly would make them two of the most powerful men in the popular music industry. In the years following the death of Cooke in 1963, Alexander continued to manage artists and served as music publishing consultant for Motown songwriters Norman Whitfield and Willie Hutch.

BIBLIOGRAPHY

H. Boyer: *The Golden Age of Gospel Music* (Chicago and Urbana, IL, 2000)

P. Guralnick: *Dream Boogie: The Triumph of Sam Cooke* (New York and Boston, 2005)

D. Thomas: "J.W. Alexander, Legendary Industry Giant Dies," *New York Beacon* (25 July 1996)

HORACE CLARENCE BOYER/TAMMY L. KERNODLE

Alexander, John (*b* Meridian, MS, 21 Oct 1923; *d* Meridian, MS, 8 Dec 1990). Tenor. He trained at the Cincinnati Conservatory and made his debut as Faust with the Cincinnati Opera in 1952. He joined the New York City Opera as Alfredo five years later. In 1961 he made his Metropolitan debut as Ferrando, and performed there regularly until 1987. He also collaborated with other major American opera companies. He was heard at the San Francisco Opera beginning in 1967 (debut as Julien in Gustave Charpentier's *Louise*). In May 1973 he sang the title role in the American premiere of the original French version of *Don Carlos*, staged by the Boston Opera. Two years later he appeared for the first time at the Opera Company of Philadephia as Calaf. Important European engagements included Korngold's *Die tote Stadt* at the Vienna Volksoper (1967), *La bohème* at the Vienna Staatsoper (1968), and Pollione at Covent Garden (1970). The Bellini opera became one of his specialities, and he sung it in a single season opposite the three most celebrated Normas of the time, Sutherland, Sills, and Montserrat Caballé; he recorded the opera with Sutherland and Marilyn Horne (Decca, 1964). Other recordings include Beethoven's Ninth Symphony (1967), Donizetti's *Anna Bolena* (Decca, 1968–9), and, on video, Massenet's *Manon* (VAI, 1967), Donizetti's *Roberto Devereux* with Beverly Sills (VAI, 1967), and Mozart's *Idomeneo* (DG, 1982). Alexander's value to leading American opera companies rested partly with his remarkable versatility and reliability in an enormous repertory, from bel canto to such Germanic roles as Bacchus and Walther von Stolzing. Although his acting sometimes lacked ardor and his singing was not invariably notable for dynamic finesse, he made the most of taste, fervor, stamina, and a voice that commanded an exceptionally brilliant ring at the top.

BIBLIOGRAPHY

J. Hines: *Great Singers on Great Singing* (Garden City, NY, 1982), 25–9

MARTIN BERNHEIMER/CLAUDIO VELLUTINI

Alexander, Josef (*b* Boston, MA, 15 May 1907; *d* Seattle, WA, 23 Dec 1990). Composer. He graduated from the New England Conservatory in 1925 and the following year received a postgraduate diploma. At Harvard University (BA 1938, MA 1939) he was a composition pupil of Walter Piston; his other teachers there included Edward Burlingame Hill, Hugo Leichtentritt (orchestration), and Apel (musicology). Alexander also studied with Nadia Boulanger in Paris and with Aaron Copland at the Berkshire Music Center. He taught at the St. Rosa Convent, Boston College, Harvard, and Brooklyn College, CUNY (1943–77). A spokesman for American composers, he received numerous awards, including both a Naumburg and a Fulbright fellowship.

Although he wrote in nearly every instrumental and non-dramatic vocal medium, Alexander concentrated on works for solo piano, mixed chamber ensembles, and large orchestra. He took a middle ground stylistically between staunch conservatism and unrelenting modernity or complexity, refusing to be influenced by any particular school or current trend of composition. Many of his works are programmatic, but they are never too literally explicit. With the musical portraits in *Epitaphs* (1947) he sought "to capture an essence and cross section of humanity." He often chose colorful and unusual combinations of instruments, as in *Triptych* for cornet, marimba, and guitar, and *Dyad* for four tubas.

WORKS

4 syms.: 1948, 1954, 1961, 1968

Other orch: Pf Conc., 1938; The Ancient Mariner, sym. poem, 1938; Doina, 1940; Dialogues spirituels (Bible), chorus, orch, 1945; Dithyrambe, 1947; Epitaphs, 1947; Campus Suite, sym. band, 1950; Canticle of Night (R. Tagore), low v, orch, 1955; Concertino, tpt, str, 1959; Quiet Music, str, 1965; Duo concertante, trbn, perc, str, 1965; Salute to the Whole World (W. Whitman), nar, orch, 1976; Trinity, brass, perc, 1979; a few shorter works

Chbr and solo inst: 3 Pieces for 8, 1965; Festivities, 4 brass, org, 1968; Triptych, cornet, mar, gui, 1969; Requiem and Coda, Bar/tuba, hn, pf, 1974; 3 Diversions, timp, pf, 1975; Interplay, 4 hn, 1975; Dyad, 4 tubas, 1979; Hexagon, wind qnt, pf, 1980; 5 Fables, ob, bn, pf, 1981; 3 Conversation Pieces, cl, b cl, 1982; Of Masks and Mirrors, s sax/cl, vc, pf, perc, 1983; Synchronizations, fl ens, 1983; Threesome, 2 cl, pf, 1986; 4 qnts, incl. 2 for brass; 2 qts; 2 trios; sonatas for vn, fl, vc, cl, va, trbn, tuba, hn; over 10 other works

Vocal: Songs for Eve (A. MacLeish), S, eng hn, vn, vc, hp, 1957; 4 Preludes on Playthings of the Wind (C. Sandburg), high v, chorus, 7 brass, pf, 1969; Gitanjali: Song Offerings (Tagore), S, hpd, perc ens, 1973; Aspects of Love, 9 songs, S, fl/pic, cl/b cl, vn/va, vc, pf, 1974; Adventures of Alice (L. Carroll), female vv, pf, 1976; Rossettiana (C. Rossetti), S, str qt, 1982; Contrasts (Sandburg), SATB, 1984; over 20 other choruses; other songs

Pf: 2 sonatas, 1936, 1943; 4 Incantations, 1964; 10 Bagatelles, 1967; 12 Pieces in the Attic, 1972; 12 Signs of the Zodiac (Astral Preludes), 1974; Games Children Play, 1976; 9 Etudes, 1979; Of Chinese New Years, 1980; many other works

MSS in GRB

Principal publishers: General/EMI, Lawson-Gould, Peer-Southern

BARBARA A. PETERSEN/MICHAEL MECKNA

Alexander, Roberta (Lee) (*b* Lynchburg, VA, 3 March 1949). Soprano. She studied at the University of Michigan, and continued her training at the Royal Conservatory, The Hague, and the Netherlands Opera Studio, with which she made her debut in *La cambiale di matrimonio* (Rossini). Making her home in Amsterdam, she sang a variety of roles with the Netherlands Opera, one of them in the premiere of Viktor Ullmann's *Der Kaiser von Atlantis* (1975). Her European engagements included performances in Berlin and Zürich (Fiordiligi, Elettra in Mozart's *Idomeneo*, Countess Almaviva). She made her American operatic debut at Houston in 1980 as Pamina; she sang Richard Strauss's Daphne at Santa Fe (1981), and Zerlina at the Metropolitan Opera (1983), where she later sang Bess (Gershwin), Countess Almaviva, Vitellia (*La clemenza di Tito*), Jenůfa, and Mimì. Her British operatic debut was at Covent Garden as Mimì (1984) and she sang the role in English at the English National Opera (1992). She was a highly acclaimed Jenůfa at Glyndebourne in 1989. She made her first appearance in Vienna as Cleopatra (*Giulio Cesare*) at the Theater an der Wien (1985); she later sang at the Staatsoper (debut in 1986). In 2009, aged 60, she sang Maria in Gershwin's *Porgy and Bess* under Nikolaus Harnoncourt (a live recording was issued in 2010). Alexander is an accomplished African American actress with a smoothly produced soprano of wide expressive range. Her operatic recordings include Mozart's Elvira (1990, with Harnoncourt) and Elettra (1991, with Colin Davis), the title role in Goldschmidt's *Beatrice Cenci*, and Stella in his *Der gewaltige Hahnrei* (1994–5). She also has a flourishing concert career and is a notable interpreter of Bach, Mahler, and various American composers. She has recorded Ives and Bernstein songs, and works for soprano and orchestra by Barber and Gershwin.

NOËL GOODWIN/CLAUDIO VELLUTINI

Alexander, Russell (*b* Nevada, MO, 26 Feb 1877; *d* Liberty, NY, 1 Oct 1915). Composer. Little is known of his early life, although he seems to have become involved in the circus. He toured Europe with the Barnum and Bailey Circus Band as a euphonium player in 1897–1902; he also arranged all the music for the tour, producing some of his finest works. He returned to the United States, and in 1903 joined the Exposition Four, which included his brothers Newton and Woodruff, and James Brady. He is considered by many to be one of

America's finest march composers; his best known marches include *Colossus of Columbia*, *From Tropic to Tropic*, and *Olympia Hippodrome*. Many of his compositions are recorded in the Heritage of the March series compiled by Robert Hoe (7, U, AA, ZZ, CCC, and RRR).

WORKS

(selective list; all marches and galops for band)

The Crimson Flush, 1896; The Darlington, 1896; Belford's Carnival, 1897; Burr's Triumphal, 1897; International Vaudeville, 1897; From Tropic to Tropic, 1898; Olympia Hippodrome, 1898; Across the Atlantic, 1899; Rival Rovers, 1899; Memphis, the Majestic, 1900; The Steeplechase, 1900; Colossus of Columbia, 1901; Shoot the Chutes, 1901; Embossing the Emblem, 1902; The Exposition Four, 1903; Storming El Caney Galop, 1903; Paramour of Panama, 1904; Salute to Seattle, 1905; Song of the South, 1905; The Comedy Club, 1907; La Reine, 1907; Baltimore's Boast, 1908; Bastinado Galop, 1908; The Cantonians, 1908; The Southerner, 1908; Hampton Roads, 1909; Pall Mall Famous, 1909; The Conquest, 1913; Patriots of the Potomac, 1913; Round-Up, 1916

Principal publisher: Barnhouse

BIBLIOGRAPHY

R. Hoe Jr.: "Brief Biographies of Famous March Composers," *Journal of Band Research*, xiv/1 (1978), 54 only

W.H. Rehrig: *The Heritage Encyclopedia of Band Music* (Westerville, OH, 1991, suppl. 1996); CD-ROM (Oskaloosa, IA, 2005)

LOREN D. GEIGER

Alford, Harry LaForrest (*b* Hudson, MI, 3 Aug 1875; *d* Chicago, IL, 4 March 1939). Composer and arranger. Alford's musical interests began with learning the trombone and keyboard instruments; this quickly led him to composition, which became the focus of his career. He was encouraged to move to Toledo, Ohio, where he found work as a trombonist in a theater. He enrolled in Dana's Musical Institute in Warren, Ohio, and then traveled widely as an itinerant trombonist. In 1903 Alford settled in Chicago where he began to arrange for dance-bands and theaters. By 1910 he had a large staff of copyists and assistants. The studio he founded eventually became one of the most successful in the country, arranging works by noteworthy composers, including Irving Berlin, W.C. Handy, Sousa, Conway, Pryor, and Merle Evans. Today, however, Alford's marches are his best known works, especially *Purple Carnival* and *Glory of the Gridiron*. A number of his works are recorded in Robert Hoe's *Heritage of the March* series.

DISCOGRAPHY

Paragon Ragtime Orchestra: *Knockout Drops* (1999, PRO 6002) [incl. *Drumology*, *Glances* and *Lucy's Sextette*]

BIBLIOGRAPHY

H.A. VanderCook: "Harry L. Alford," *The Musical Messenger*, xvii/3 (1921)

W.H. Rehrig: *The Heritage Encyclopedia of Band Music* (Westerville, OH, 1991, suppl. 1996); CD-ROM (Oskaloosa, IA, 2005) [includes selective list of works]

JONAS WESTOVER

Alfred Music Publishing. Publishing company. Alfred is a family-owned publisher, started in 1922 and headquartered in Van Nuys, California. They are particularly known for their educational music, but since their acquisition of Warner Publishing in 2005, they now own copyrights estimated to be over one million songs. Created by Alfred Piantadosi, the composer and bandleader, to distribute his own songs, it did not take the publisher long to develop a catalog, which included hits such as "Waiting for the Robert E. Lee" and "Ragtime Cowboy Joe." The New York-based company was sold in 1928 to Sam Manus, and he and his family significantly expanded the group's holdings with a focus in educational materials. Soon after, they developed method books for violin, accordion, guitar, and piano. Alfred's *Basic Piano Library* has been adopted worldwide as a fundamental piano text; other "Library" editions are likewise considered important contributions to music pedagogy. Their work for school ensembles is also substantial, with *Band Expressions* and *Orchestra Expressions* providing several pieces appropriate for beginning groups. In 1975, Alfred was moved to Los Angeles, and soon opened satellite offices in cities across the United States and around the globe, including in Australia, Germany, Singapore, and the United Kingdom. As a distributor, Alfred has connections to several other publishers, such as Belwin, Dover, Faber, Kalmus, and Penguin. Alfred rose from annual sales of $12 million to figures surpassing $60 million after the international expansion of the company and its acquisition of Warner. They now hold printed music for stars as varied as Duke Ellington, Led Zeppelin, and Green Day, and produce over 90,000 active titles.

JONAS WESTOVER

Algonquian. Native American language family; *see* Arapaho, Blackfoot (i), Ojibwe, and Wabenaki.

Ali, Rashied [Patterson, Robert, Jr.] (*b* Philadelphia, PA, 1 July 1935; *d* New York, NY, 13 Aug 2009). Jazz drummer. He learned congas from the age of nine and studied percussion while in the US Army (1952–5). After attending the Granoff School in Philadelphia, he worked in jazz and rhythm-and-blues bands and in 1963 moved to New York, where he was a key figure in the free-jazz movement, performing with Albert Ayler, Don Cherry, Sun Ra, and Archie Shepp. In addition he collaborated with John Coltrane, including the albums *Expression* and *Interstellar Space* (both 1967, Imp.), on which Ali's performance displays the influence of Sunny Murray and Milford Graves. Ali also learned from Elvin Jones, with whom he competed for the drum chair in Coltrane's band. In 1967 Ali worked in Europe with Niels-Henning Orsted Pedersed, studied with Philly Joe Jones, and worked at Ronnie Scott's, London, with Jon Hendricks and Dave Holland. The following year he returned to New York, where he played with Sonny Rollins and Jackie McLean, and for five years from 1974 he ran a club called Studio 77 (also known as Ali's Alley) from his home. Ali played with the Funkyfreeboppers, Jaco Pastorius, Sonny Fortune, and Hot Tuna during the 1980s and worked with Evan Parker and led a free-jazz quartet, By Any Means, in the 1990s. He subsequently toured and recorded with the his own quintet. Ali typically played with relentless energy but no clear pulse. His feel for "multi-directional" rhythms and "circular" time led Coltrane to describe him as "one of the great drummers."

BIBLIOGRAPHY

GroveJ2

V. Wilmer: *As Serious as your Life: the Story of the New Jazz*—John Coltrane and Beyond. (London, 1999 [1977])

A. Budofsky: *The Drummer: 100 Years of Rhythmic Power and Invention* (Cedar Grove, 2006)

GARETH DYLAN SMITH

Alice Cooper. Both a Detroit-based hard rock band and the adopted name of its singer and main creative force Vincent Damon Furnier (*b* Detroit, MI, 4 Feb 1946). Cooper was the son of a minister and the nephew of the storyteller Damon Runyon, after whom he was named. He moved to Arizona, where he attended high school and formed the Nazz. This band eventually took the name Alice Cooper and developed an over-the-top, theatrical shock-rock style that influenced a host of other rock performers.

With snide and clever lyrics, Alice Cooper's style was mainly hard rock, but some tunes were psychedelic and others would be suitable in a Broadway musical. After moving to Michigan, the band scored numerous hits in the early 1970s. Many of the songs were rebellious youth-focused anthems, including "Eighteen" (Warner, 1971) and "School's Out" (Warner, 1972). Others centered on ghoulish menace or mere gothic gruesomeness like "Dead Babies" (Warner, 1971) and "Cold Ethyl" (Atlantic, 1975).

Although the band's songs stand alone as significant developments in rock music they are best understood as embedded in albums themed on one type of shock or another. Their thematic cover art was as lurid as any horror-movie poster. Three of the releases went platinum: *Killer* (Warner, 1971), *School's Out* (Warner, 1972), and *Billion Dollar Babies*, which reached number one in 1973 (Warner).

Emphasizing the theatricality in rock, Alice Cooper's stage shows brought to life, and death, the "little psycho dramas," as Cooper has called them. In macabre make-up and often draped in a live boa constrictor, Cooper brought horror movies to musical life using a guillotine and dolls simulating dead babies as props.

By the mid-1970s the band Alice Cooper was defunct. Since then Cooper, as a solo performer working with various musicians, has released numerous albums. In 2011 Alice Cooper, the band, was inducted into the Rock and Roll Hall of Fame.

DEENA WEINSTEIN

Allanbrook, Douglas Phillips (*b* Melrose, MA, 1 April 1921; *d* Annapolis, MD, 29 Jan 2003). Composer. Early studies with NADIA BOULANGER at the Longy School of Music (1941–2) were halted by service in the US Army in World War II, which he later documented in his memoir *See Naples* (Boston, 1995). Afterwards he studied with WALTER PISTON at Harvard (BA, 1948), Boulanger in Paris (1948–50), and harpsichordist Ruggero Gerlin in Naples (1950–52). In 1952 he became Tutor at St John's College, Annapolis, MD, teaching music, mathematics, and languages, in addition to giving keyboard and chamber music concerts. He married twice; his second wife was musicologist Wye Jamison Allanbrook (1943–2010).

There are 65 works in Allanbrook's musical oeuvre. Important premieres have been the Harpsichord Concerto by Ralph Kirkpatrick (1956, Baltimore), the Third String Quartet by the Kronos Quartet (1977, Annapolis), and the opera *Ethan Frome* by the composer's son John Allanbrook (1998, Harvard University). His collaboration with the Annapolis Brass Quintet resulted in several new works for brass, including *Night and Morning Music* (1977). His style was derived from tonal and atonal idioms, but not serial techniques and electronic instruments. Several works were developed according to formal processes such as the eight rotations of a set of five free variations in *Forty Changes* (1965), while others are rooted in dances like the tarantella of *Naples Music* (1975). His papers are housed at the St. John's College Library, Annapolis.

WORKS
(selected)

Dramatic: Ethan Frome (lyric drama, 3 and epilogue, J.C. Hunt after E. Wharton), 1950–52; Nightmare Abbey (op, 3, D. Allanbrook after T. Love Peacock), 1960–62

Orch: Hpd Conc., 1950; 7 syms.: 1960, 1962, 1967, 1970, 1976, 1977, 1980

Choral: Psalm 130, SATB, org, 1955; Psalm 131, SATB, org, 1955; Seven Last Words (*Bible*), Mez, Bar, chorus, orch, 1970

Songs: In Morte Di Madonna Laura (Petrarch), 1946; 2 Chinese Poems (trans. Waley), 1950; Les Hirandelles (P. de Ronsard), 1950; 3 Love and Death Songs (W. Shakespeare, E. Dickinson), 1982–3

Chamber: 6 str qts: 1955, 1956-57, 1958, 1972, 2001, 2002; Night and Morning Music, brass qnt, 1977; Invitation to the Sideshow, brass qnt, 1982; Commencement Exercises, brass qnt, 1985; 25 Building Blocks, hn, pf, 1985

Kbd: Little Sonatas, hpd, 1949; Forty Changes, pf, 1965; Preludes For All Seasons, pf, 1970; Studies in Black and White, hpd, 1971; Venice Music, pf, 1974; Naples Music, pf, 1975; Night Pieces, pf, 1983–5; New American Preludes, pf, 1990

Principal publishers: Boosey and Hawkes, Atlantis

EDWARD KOMARA

Alleghanians. Mixed troupe of popular vocalists and bell ringers. Organized at New York City in 1846 and billed early as the "Alleghanians, or American Singers," the group, usually a quartet, toured widely from 1847. Members at that time included James M. Boulard (bass), Richard Dunning (tenor), Carrie Hiffert (contralto), and William H. Oakley (alto). From the start, comparisons to the Rainer and Hutchinson family troupes were common. Miriam G. Goodenow, a young soprano, replaced Hiffert, evidently in 1849. This lineup, managed and promoted expansively by Jesse Hutchinson Jr., toured Gold Rush California in 1852. Frank Stoepel, renowned for dazzling performances on a novel "wood and straw instrument," is said to have introduced handbell ringing to the company in 1857. This ensemble, renamed the Alleghanians Vocalists and Swiss Bell Ringers, embarked on a world tour in 1858, presenting American popular music to audiences in many lands.

Guided by agent Daniel G. Waldron, the Alleghanians traveled with evident success from San Francisco to Honolulu, through the South Seas, and back via South

America. The group, at times, included pioneers of their instruments, such as concertina player Alfred B. Sedgwick in the early 1860s and harmonica soloist L. Percy Williams a decade later. In 1871, the Alleghanians split into two companies. One, headed by Boulard, notably included revival singer George S. Weeks (tenor), off and on for several years. It performed extensively in the United Kingdom. The other troupe, managed by Waldron, varied considerably in size. Mary E. Packard, soprano, was the featured vocalist, while Frank L. Benjamin served as music director. This company, which entertained in the United States and Canada, included a "Silver Orchestral Band" of male and female horn players for a year or more. Boulard's group, with Hiffert, was still giving concerts in 1884. An unnamed manager—evidently Waldron—tried to revive his company in 1893 and 1894. The Alleghanians, with a repertoire ranging from glees, simple sentimental songs, and comic ditties to ornate arias, enjoyed lavish praise for sweet, close quartet harmony, and eye-catching, virtuoso bell playing. Brown University holds a collection of important Alleghanians music and memorabilia.

BIBLIOGRAPHY

Alleghanians. Songs and Quartettes, Sung by the Alleghanians (New York, 1850)

Alleghanians: The Alleghanians, Vocalists and Swiss Bell Ringers' Songster: Sketches and Travels (?Portsmouth, NH, 1873)

P.D. Jordan: *Singin' Yankees* (Minneapolis, 1946), 173–89

ALAN LEWIS

Allen [Lee], **Betty** [Elizabeth] **(Louise)** (*b* Campbell, near Youngstown, OH, 17 March 1930; *d* Bronxville, NY, 22 June 2009). Mezzo-soprano. Allen was first exposed to opera listening to a neighbor's radio while growing up in a working-class neighborhood. She entered foster care aged 12 and later studied on scholarships at the historically black Wilberforce University, where the tenor Theodore Heimann steered her towards opera. Allen continued on scholarships at the Hartford School of Music, working with Sarah Peck More, ZINKA MILANOV, and PAUL ULANOWSKY. She was part of the first wave African American opera singers to perform internationally during the post–World War II years. While studying at Berkshire Music Center, Bernstein selected her to sing as mezzo-soprano soloist of his *Jeremiah* Symphony in 1951. Allen made her opera debut the following year in Thomson's *Four Saints in Three Acts*, later participating in the first complete recording. She married Ritten Edward Lee II in 1953 before making her debut with the New York City Opera as Queenie in Kern's *Show Boat*. *New York Times* critic Harold C. Schonberg praised her, writing "When she was onstage everything came to life, and everything around her dimmed." Allen also performed Azucena, Mistress Quickly, Jocasta, Eurycleia in *Il ritorno d'Ulisse in patria*, Teresa in *La sonnambula* and the title role in Joplin's *Treemonisha*. She first appeared at the Colón, Buenos Aires, in 1964 as Jocasta in *Oedipus Rex* and also appeared with Boston, Houston, San Francisco, and Santa Fe opera companies. During the 1970s, she acquired a contralto-like deepening, heard on her recording of Prokofiev's *Alexander Nevsky* under Ormandy. Allen mentored African American singers and introduced poor children to classical music. She taught at the Manhattan School of Music and Curtis Institute of Music in Philadelphia, and was appointed Executive Director for the Harlem School of the Arts in 1979, retiring in 1992 to serve as President Emeritus.

BIBLIOGRAPHY

J. Gruen: "Betty is busy figuring out Betty," *New York Times* (19 Aug 1973)

J. Gray: *Blacks in Classical Music* (Westport, CT, 1988)

Obituary, *New York Times* (25 June 2009)

MEREDITH ELIASSEN

Allen, Carl (Lee) (*b* Milwaukee, WI, 25 April 1961). Jazz drummer. His mother was a gospel singer and his brother Eddie is a jazz trumpeter and arranger. After taking up drums at an early age, Allen studied the instrument in Milwaukee public schools and performed as a teenager with visiting bands led by Sonny Stitt, Red Holloway, and James Moody. From 1979 to 1981 he attended the University of Wisconsin at Green Bay and during the same period was a member of Richard Davis's Wisconsin Connection. After moving to the New York area in 1981, he studied at William Paterson College until 1983. From 1982 to 1991 he played regularly with Freddie Hubbard and had a prolific career as a freelance sideman, working with Terence Blanchard and Donald Harrison, Jackie McLean, Woody Shaw, Art Farmer, and George Coleman, among others. During the 1990s he played with Benny Green, Donald Byrd and Vincent Herring. In 1989, upon the recommendation of Art Blakey, Allen recorded his first albums as a leader, *Dreamboat* and *Piccadilly Square*. He subsequently recorded for Atlantic and Mack Avenue and became a successful producer. An active teacher from 1984, Allen joined the faculty of the Juilliard Institute for Jazz Studies in 2001 and was named its artistic director in 2007. He performs with the Juilliard Jazz Quintet and his own bands, notably the Carl Allen–Rodney Whitaker Project.

BIBLIOGRAPHY

A. Lewis and L. Lewis: "Carl Allen Interview," *Cadence*, xxiv/5 (1998), 5–12, 137–8

M. Dawson: "Carl Allen: Embracing the Journey," *Modern Drummer*, xxxi/11 (2007), 64–78

RUSS MUSTO

Allen, Eugene Womack (*b* Morgan, TX, 13 June 1927). Conductor, composer, arranger, and trumpeter. Allen began trumpet lessons at age seven with his father, a 50-year Texas school band director, and later studied with Jimmy Burke of the Goldman Band and Lloyd Geisler of the National SO. During 45 years of military service, he conducted US Army bands, including the 101st Airborne Division Band. His career culminated with his appointment as Leader and Commander of The United States Army Band (Pershing's Own) in Washington, DC, 1976–90. He led and supervised the band, chorus, orchestra, Army Blues, and Herald Trumpets in more than 5,000 performances annually at the White House, Pentagon, US Capitol, and Arlington National Cemetery, throughout the United States, and in Canada, the US Virgin Islands, Japan, and Australia. He composed *Salute to Veterans*, the official march of the Veterans Administration, and *The Major of St. Lo*, the official march of the 29th Infantry Division. He is a past president of the American Bandmasters Association.

BIBLIOGRAPHY

W.H. Rehrig: *The Heritage Encyclopedia of Band Music* (Westerville, OH, 1991, suppl. 1996); CD-ROM (Oskaloosa, IA, 2005) [includes list of works]

VIRGINIA ALLEN

Allen, Geri (Antoinette) (*b* Pontiac, MI, 12 June 1957). Jazz pianist and composer. She began classical piano study at age seven with Patricia Wilhelm, who also encouraged her interest in jazz. After graduating from Detroit's Cass Technical High School in 1975 (where trumpeter Marcus Belgrave was one of her teachers), she studied with John Malachi at Howard University (BA 1979, jazz studies) and with Nathan Davis at the University of Pittsburgh (MA 1982, ethnomusicology). She also took private piano lessons with Kenny Barron in 1979. She moved to New York in the early 1980s, where she became a member of the M-BASE collective. Allen recorded her first album as a leader, *The Printmakers*, in 1984 (Minor Music). Since then she has performed on more than 100 recordings in a variety of capacities. She worked in trios with Ron Carter and Tony Williams (on albums such as *Twenty One*, 1994, Blue Note) and with Charlie Haden and Paul Motian (*Live at the Village Vanguard*, 1990, DIW). Allen is musical director of the Mary Lou Williams Collective, a group devoted to perpetuating Williams' musical legacy. She also has recorded with Ornette Coleman, Wayne Shorter, James Newton, Betty Carter, and several others. Her albums often feature a mixture of original compositions and standards. As a composer, she has written pieces such as *Sister Leola, An American Portrait* (1993, a Jazz at Lincoln Center commission), *For the Healing of the Nations* (2006, a "sacred jazz suite" dedicated to 9/11 victims), and *Refractions: Flying toward the Sound* (a solo piano work composed for a 2008 Guggenheim Fellowship). Allen has served on the faculties of Howard University (1989–92), the New England Conservatory (1989–91), and the New School (2005–6). In 2004, she joined the University of Michigan, where she is Associate Professor of Jazz and Contemporary Improvisation. Allen's musical style assimilates African music, bebop, free jazz, gospel, and soul. She has cited Cecil Taylor, Herbie Hancock, and McCoy Tyner as her main pianistic influences.

SELECTED RECORDINGS

As unaccompanied soloist: *Home Grown* (1985, Minor Music); *Flying toward the Sound* (2010, Motema)

As leader: *The Printmakers* (1984, Minor Music); *Segments* (1989, DIW); *The Nurturer* (1990, Blue Note); *Eyes… in the Back of your Head* (1995–6, Blue Note); *The Life of a Song* (2004, Telarc); *Timeless Portraits and Dreams* (2006, Telarc); with the Mary Lou Williams Collective: *Zodiac Suite Revisited* (2006, Mary Records)

BIBLIOGRAPHY

G. Santoro: "Geri Allen's Keyboard Koncepts," *Musician*, no. 151 (1991), 66–72

L. Gourse: *Madame Jazz: Contemporary Women Instrumentalists* (New York, 1995)

G. Giddins: *Visions of Jazz: the First Century* (New York, 1998)

L. Blumenfeld: "Geri Allen and the Night Sky: One Pianist's Brilliance Returns to Full View," *Jazziz*, xxi/11 (2004), 36–40

M. Clayton: *M-Base: Envisioning Change for Jazz in the 1980s and Beyond* (diss., Harvard U., 2009)

LARS HELGERT

Allen, Henry "Red" [Red; Allen, Henry (James), Jr.] (*b* Algiers, LA, 7 Jan 1908; *d* New York, NY, 17 April 1967). Jazz trumpeter, singer, and bandleader. His mother introduced him to the violin and he was playing upright alto horn in his father's brass band by the age of eight. His father, a trumpeter, taught him sight-reading, but he took trumpet lessons from Manuel Manetta, among others. After playing in New Orleans cabarets and marching bands as a teenager, in 1927 Allen joined King Oliver's orchestra in St Louis. Oliver had been sideman with Allen Sr.'s band, and Allen traveled with him to New York for an engagement at the Savoy Ballroom where he played alongside Chick Webb. After returning home, he found work with the riverboat orchestras of Fate Marable and Fats Pichon. However, eager to be involved with the musical developments taking place in New York, he subsequently made that city his home. There he joined Luis Russell's orchestra in 1929, then played briefly in Charlie Johnson's band before joining Fletcher Henderson in 1933. Allen's 15 months in Henderson's stellar trumpet section had profound effect on his playing, inspiring solos that tested new boundaries and sometimes were incorporated by Fletcher or Horace Henderson into the band's charts. When the Depression forced the group to disband, Allen began a two-year association with the Mills Blue Rhythm Band.

Allen's ability to adapt his playing to a variety of idiomatic approaches ensured he was in demand at recording sessions in New York and he made his first recordings as a sideman and a leader for Victor in 1927. He continued to record under his own name and with such musicians as Jelly Roll Morton (1929 and 1940), Fats Waller (1929), Clarence Williams (1930), Don Redman (1931), Teddy Wilson (1931), Lionel Hampton, and Coleman Hawkins. He also accompanied blues stars including Victoria Spivey (1929) and Ida Cox (1939). In 1933 he was among the musicians chosen by the visiting English bandleader Spike Hughes to participate in a celebrated series of American sessions in which Benny Carter also took part. From 1954 to 1965 Allen held a residency at the Metropole Café in Times Square. During this period he appeared on two noteworthy network TV specials, "The Sound of Jazz" (1957) and "Chicago and All that Jazz" (1961). He also toured Europe three times: for the first of these, in 1959, he was a member of a New Orleans-style group led by Kid Ory that sought to emulate the success of the Louis Armstrong All Stars; for subsequent visits, in 1963 and 1964, he returned on his own. After the Metropole's jazz programming ended in 1965, Allen held residencies at various venues in the northeast, mainly around New York, Boston and Washington, DC. He died at age 59 from pancreatic cancer.

Allen's trumpet style remained deeply rooted in the New Orleans tradition throughout his career even though he absorbed elements from the musics that emerged during its early stages. Although he stood out from his tradition-bound New Orleans contemporaries, he made no attempt to absorb any of the musical developments of the post-war era. Nevertheless, in the 1960s several trumpeters from a new generation claimed that they heard avant-garde elements in his playing.

SELECTED RECORDINGS

As leader: It should be you/Biff'ly Blues (1929, Vic.); Body and Soul (1935, Voc.); Get the Mop (1946, Vic. 201808); *Ride, Red, Ride in Hi-fi* (1957, RCA); *Feeling Good* (1965, Col.)

As sideman: L. Armstrong: I ain't got nobody (1929, OK); L. Russell: Song of the Swanee (1930, OK); F. Henderson: Wrappin' it up (1934, Decca); T. Wilson: Sentimental and Melancholy (1937, Bruns.); S. Bechet: Egyptian Fantasy (1941, Vic.)

BIBLIOGRAPHY

D. Ellis: "Henry (Red) Allen is the most Avant-Garde Trumpet Player in New York City," *DB*, xxxii/2 (1965), 13

W. Balliett: "The Blues is a Slow Story," *Such Sweet Thunder* (Indianapolis, 1966); repr. in *Improvising* (New York, 1977)

M. Williams: "Henry Red," *Jazz Masters of New Orleans* (New York, 1967)

H. Allen and A.J. McCarthy: "The Early Years," *Jazz Monthly*, no. 180 (1970), 2

J. Evensmo and P. Borthen: *The Trumpet and Vocal of Henry Red Allen, 1927–1942* (Hosle, Norway, 1977)

F. Hoffman: *Henry "Red" Allen/J.C. Higginbotham Discography* (Berlin, 1982)

J. Chilton: *Ride, Red, Ride* (London, 1999)

CHRIS ALBERTSON

Allen, J(oseph) Lathrop (*b* Holland, MA, 24 Sept 1815; *d* c1905). Brass instrument maker. About 1853 he designed a very efficient rotary valve, featuring flattened windways, string linkage, and enclosed stops. This valve was very successful in the United States during the second half of the 19th century. Other makers who adopted the Allen valve included B.F. Richardson, D.C. Hall, and B.F. Quinby, all of whom had at one time worked with Allen; Henry Lehnert, who worked in Boston for a time before moving to Philadelphia; and E. Glier of Cochecton, New York.

Allen began making brass instruments about 1838 in Sturbridge, Massachusetts, a short distance from his birthplace. He moved to Boston in 1842, and is known to have worked in Norwich, Connecticut, from 1846 to 1849; in 1852 he returned to Boston. He is known to have made at least one keyed bugle early in his career, and a number of instruments with double-piston Vienna valves. During the late 1850s in Boston his flat-windway valve won respect among leading musicians and his instruments received favorable comment at mechanics exhibitions. From 1862 until at least 1897 Allen worked in New York, where he continued to make some musical instruments but was also engaged in other types of manufacture.

There are many instruments with Allen valves in American collections of 19th-century brass instruments. Several instruments signed by Allen are found in the John H. Elrod Memorial Collection, Germantown, Maryland, and The Henry Ford, Dearborn, Michigan.

BIBLIOGRAPHY

Waterhouse-LangwillI

R.E. Eliason: "Early American Valves for Brass Instruments," *GSJ*, xxiii (1970), 86–96

R.E. Eliason: *Early American Brass Makers* (Nashville, TN, 1979/Vuarmarens, 1999)

R.E. Eliason: "D.C. Hall and the Quinby Brothers," *JAMIS* xxxiii (2007), 84–161

N. Groce: *Musical Instrument Makers of New York: a Directory of Eighteenth- and Nineteenth-Century Urban Craftsmen* (Stuyvesant, NY, 1991)

ROBERT E. ELIASON

Allen, Marshall (*b* Louisville, KY, 25 May 1924). Alto saxophonist and bandleader. He began clarinet lessons when he was ten and later took up alto saxophone. After joining the US Army at 18 years of age, Allen performed in military bands and, while stationed in Paris, formed a trio with Art Simmons and Don Byas. Allen remained in Europe following his discharge, touring with James Moody and studying clarinet at the Paris Conservatory with Ulysse Delécluse. He returned to the United States in 1951 and led dance bands and worked as a composer in Chicago. After hearing a demo recording of Sun Ra's Arkestra in a record store, Allen sought out the bandleader during a rehearsal and began an apprenticeship. He subsequently rehearsed with the Arkestra for more than a year before joining officially in 1958. His association with the ensemble has lasted more than 50 years.

Allen worked closely with Sun Ra for much of his professional career, composing for the bandleader and performing both in concert and on more than 200 albums; he even shared a house with him. Alongside John Gilmore Allen anchored the reed section, adding flute, clarinet, oboe, and in later years wind synthesizer. He invented the morrow, a woodwind instrument combining a saxophone mouthpiece with an open-holed wooden body, and learned to play and build the kora, a West African multi-string instrument. Allen rarely worked outside the Arkestra, although he made a notable recording with Paul Bley (*Barrage*, ESP, 1964) and performed and recorded with Babatunde Olatunji and his group Drums of Passion (*Drums! Drums! Drums!*, Roulette, 1964). In later collaborations he crossed genres to work with such groups as Sonic Youth, Phish, and Medeski Martin & Wood. Allen assumed leadership of the Arkestra following the deaths of Sun Ra in 1993 and Gilmore in 1995.

SELECTED RECORDINGS

As sideman with Sun Ra: *Jazz in Silhouette* (1959, Sat.); *Visits Planet Earth* (1966, Sat.); *The Magic City* (1966, Sat.); *Cosmic Tones for Mental Therapy* (1967, Sat.); *We Travel the Spaceways* (1967, Sat.)

As sideman with P. Bley: *Barrage* (1964, ESP)

BIBLIOGRAPHY

V. Wilmer: *As Serious as your Life: the Story of the New Jazz* (London, 1977, 3/1987)

J.F. Szwed: *Space is the Place: the Lives and Times of Sun Ra* (New York, 1997)

M. Shanley: "Marshall Allen: the Marshall Plan," *JT*, (12/2002); also available at <http://jazztimes.com/articles/19722-marshall-allen-the-marshall-plan>

BARRY LONG

Allen, Nancy (*b* Mineola, NY, 11 July 1954). Harpist and pedagogue. She studied early with Marion Bannerman, Pearl Chertok, and Mario di Steffano, and in Paris with Lily Laskine in summer 1972. She received degrees from the Juilliard School (BM, MM), working with MARCEL GRANDJANY, Jane Weidensaul, and SUSANN MCDONALD. She won first prize at the Fifth International Harp Competition in Israel (1973). Allen made her New York Carnegie Recital Hall debut in 1975 and became head of the harp department at the Juilliard School in 1985. In 1999, she became principal harpist of the New York Philharmonic. She is also on the faculty of the Aspen Music School. She has performed solo concerts for more than 30 years throughout the world and has been the recipient of the National Endowment Solo Recitalist Grant and sponsorship by the Pro Musicis foundation. Allen appears regularly with the Orpheus Chamber Orchestra and the Chamber Music Society of Lincoln Center, and has appeared as soloist with numerous ensembles including the English Chamber Orchestra, Los Angeles Chamber Orchestra, and Mostly Mozart Festival. She received a Grammy nomination in 1983 for her recording of Ravel's *Introduction and Allegro* on Angel/EMI. Other notable recordings include *Nancy Allen Plays Bach* (EMI, 1985), Ginastera's Harp Concerto (ASV, 1993), *A Celebration for Harp* (Angel/EMI, 1987), Rochberg's *Slow Fires of Autumn* (CRI, 1980), Richard Wilson's *Battle of Longwood Glen* (CRI, 1991), and *Impressions for Flute* (with Ransom Wilson; Angel, 1978).

BIBLIOGRAPHY

W. M. Govea: *Nineteenth- and Twentieth-Century Harpists: a Bio-Critical Sourcebook* (Westport, CT, 1995)

R. Rensch: *Harps and Harpists* (Bloomington, IN, 1989, rev. and expanded, 2/2007)

SUZANNE L. MOULTON-GERTIG

Allen, Paul Hastings (*b* Hyde Park, MA, 28 Nov 1883; *d* Boston, MA, 28 Sept 1952). Composer. After graduating from Harvard University (BA 1903), he moved to Florence, serving in the US diplomatic service in Italy during World War I. He returned to the United States in 1920 and settled in Boston. He was a prolific composer, particularly of operas (e.g., *L'ultimo dei Mohicani*, 1916) and chamber music (much of it for unusual combinations, such as a Quartet for two clarinets, two basset horns, and a bass clarinet). His instrumental works combine careful construction and Romantic gestures, while the operas reflect 19th-century Italian techniques. His *Pilgrim Symphony* (1910) won the Paderewski Prize.

WORKS

Ops: O munasterio, 1911; Il filtro, 1912; Milda, 1913; L'ultimo dei Moicani (after J.F. Cooper), 1916; Cleopatra, 1921; La piccola Figaro, 1931; 6 other ops

8 syms.: "Al mare," g; "Cosmopolitan," C; "Liberty," E; "Lyra," A; "Phoebus," E; "Pilgrim," D; "Somerset," E♭; "Utopia," D

Chbr: Over 100 works for str qt/str qnt/str orch; Suite, chbr orch, 1944; 15 pf sonatas; 8 sonatas, vn, pf; 2 sonatas, vn; Sonata, vc, pf; Pf Trio; Heaven's Gifts, 2 cl, a cl/basset hn, b cl; The Muses, wind ens; Ww Trio; short works for vn, pf; other sonatas and pf pieces

Over 150 songs; choral works; 9 other orch works incl. Serenade (1928), suite

Principal publishers: Whitney Blake; G. Mignani; Riker, Brown & Wellington; L. Sonzogno

H. WILEY HITCHCOCK/MICHAEL MECKNA

Allen, Rex (Elvie) (*b* near Willcox, AZ, 31 Dec 1924; *d* Tucson, AZ, 19 Dec 1999) Singing cowboy, songwriter, actor, and radio and recording artist. Born on a remote ranch, Allen had a powerful voice of tremendous range, was a world-class yodeler, and a prolific songwriter. He had begun a performing career straight out of high school and, after a stint at WTTM in Trenton, NJ, was added to the *National Barn Dance* cast in 1945. A true westerner and a good horseman, he seemed a natural for the singing cowboy film genre, but it was a genre in decline, and his was the last singing series any studio launched. Allen's first film for Republic was the fittingly titled *Arizona Cowboy* (1950), and his last of 19 movies was *Phantom Stallion* (1954).

Allen then turned to television, starring in *Frontier Doctor* (1958). He was able to keep up an active recording and touring career, supplemented by Disney Studios' (and other studios') frequent use of his avuncular and authoritative speaking voice as a narrator of documentaries, television features, and feature films such as *Charlotte's Web* (1973). He recorded for Decca, Mercury, and Buena Vista through the 1950s and 1960s, and landed top-five *Billboard* hits with "Crying in the chapel" (Decca, 1953) and "Don't go near the Indians" (Mercury, 1962). He matured into a gracious elder statesman for western music and was one of the founders of the Western Music Association.

DOUGLAS B. GREEN

Allen, Richard (*b* Philadelphia, PA, 14 Feb 1760; *d* Philadelphia, PA, 26 March 1831). Tunebook compiler, minister, and abolitionist. A former slave, he joined others in forming the Free African Society of Philadelphia in 1787. He began preaching at St. George's Methodist Church and gathered a following within the African American community. He founded his own church, the Bethel AME Church (1801), and joined with other African American congregations to form the first independent black denomination, the African Methodist Episcopal Church; he was appointed its first bishop in 1816. To preserve the tradition of African American worship, he compiled a hymnbook of 54 hymns, *A Collection of Spiritual Songs and Hymns from Various Authors* (1801). An enlarged version was published later that year, and the third and fourth editions were issued in 1808 and 1818. It was the first hymnbook published by an African American for use by African Americans, and many of the hymns later became sources for black spirituals. With Daniel Coker and James Champion,

Allen also compiled the first official hymnbook of the AME Church in 1818.

(*See also* African American music, Gospel music, and Methodism).

BIBLIOGRAPHY

R. Allen: *The Life Experience and Gospel Labors of the Right Reverend Richard Allen* (Philadelphia, 1887/*R*1960)

C. Wesley: *Richard Allen, Apostle of Freedom* (Washington, DC, 1935)

C.V.R. George: *Segregated Sabbaths: Richard Allen and the Rise of the Independent Black Churches, 1760–1840* (New York, 1973)

E. Southern: "Musical Practices in Black Churches in Philadelphia and New York, ca. 1800–1844," *JAMS*, xxx/2 (1977), 296–312

E. Southern: *Readings in Black American Music* (New York, 2/1983), 52–61

E. Southern: "Hymnals of the Black Church," *The Black Perspective in Music*, xvii/1–2 (1989), 153–70

J.R. Braithwaite: "Originality in the 1801 Hymnals of Richard Allen," *New Perspectives on Music: Essays in Honor of Eileen Southern*, ed. J. Wright and S.A. Floyd (Warren, MI, 1992), 71–99

E. Southern: *The Music of Black Americans: A History* (New York, 3/1997)

R.S. Newman: *Freedom's Prophet: Bishop Richard Allen, the AME Church, and the Black Founding Fathers* (New York, 2008)

KIMBERLY GREENE

Allen, Ross (Clearman) (*b* Kirksville, MO, 10 March 1921; *d* Bloomington, IN, 31 Dec 2003). Opera director and teacher. He pursued graduate study at Indiana University, where he staged the choral episodes of Britten's *Billy Budd* for the first American production (1952). While a member of the Indiana University faculty (1953–88), he directed more than 130 works, including the first presentation outside New York of Bernstein's *Candide* (1958), American premieres of Rimsky-Korsakov's *Christmas Eve* (1977) and Martinů's *The Greek Passion* (1981 at the Metropolitan Opera House), and world premieres of John Eaton's *Myshkin* (1973) and (for children) *The Lion and Androcles* (1974). He was a guest director for the Houston Opera, Kansas City Lyric Opera, Cincinnati Summer Opera, Detroit Opera, and New York Pro Musica. He was also involved in modern recreations of liturgical drama and Renaissance entertainments. In 1969 he won a Peabody Award for his television production of Henze's *Elegy for Young Lovers*.

FRANK MERKLING/KAREN M. BRYAN

Allen, Sanford (*b* *c*1930). Violinist. He began his studies at the age of seven and entered the Juilliard School of Music three years later. He completed his formal studies with Vera Fonaroff at the Mannes College of Music. In 1962, he was the first African American musician to become a regular member of the New York PO. He has appeared as a soloist with the Baltimore, Detroit, and Quebec symphony orchestras, and the New York Philharmonic. In 1998, he gave the first performance of Roland Hanna's Sonata for Violin and Piano at the Kennedy Center for the Performing Arts. He was first violinist for the recording of Olly Wilson's *Of Visions & Truth*, as well as the soloist for the recording of Roque Cordero's Violin Concerto, which was released as part of the Columbia label's pioneering Black Composers Series. Allen served on the advisory panel of the New York State Arts Council and was a member of the Executive Board of the Kennedy Center's National Black Music Colloquium and Competition. He has been described as "a violinist who can meet the virtuosity challenges thrillingly. He has extraordinary commitment and finesse and the intensity generated by his impassioned performance is nothing short of overwhelming" (*The Strad*). Sanford married Indian actress and cooking star Madhur Jaffrey.

ANYA LAURENCE

Allen, Steve [Stephen Valentine Patrick William] (*b* New York, NY, 16 Dec 1921; *d* Encino, CA, 30 Oct 2000). Composer, radio and television personality, pianist, singer, and comedian. The son of Belle Montrose and Billy Allen, both of whom worked in vaudeville, he moved from place to place as a child, attending many schools for short periods of time. He played piano from an early age, although his musical training was mainly informal. He began a professional career in Los Angeles as a disc jockey on radio during the 1940s, then turned to television in the 1950s; he established himself as a comedian, and often played the piano during his shows, improvising jazz and singing his own songs. Among the musicians who appeared with him regularly was the vibraphonist Terry Gibbs. Allen's most popular television program was "The Tonight Show," which he began broadcasting locally in New York in 1953, subsequently leading it to nationwide success the following year. Allen performed the title role in the film *The Benny Goodman Story* (1955). In 1956 he began hosting a popular variety hour, "The Steve Allen Show," and in 1957 he briefly produced a jazz television series, "Jazz Scene USA." In the late 1950s he made a number of recordings, combining his musical and comic talents, including an album of boogie-woogie piano music under the name Buck Hammer and an album of modern jazz as Miss Maryanne Jackson. Allen composed a musical, *Sophie* (1963), on the life of Sophie Tucker and music for television and such films as *A Man Called Dagger*. He is said to have written more than 4000 songs; recordings of some of these, notably "Let's go to church next Sunday," "Cotton Candy and a Toy Balloon," and "This could be the start of something big," have been modest hits. Allen also appeared on the stage on Broadway, notably in *The Pink Elephant*, and published several novels, as well as autobiographical works, poems, plays, and dozens of books.

See also Television music.

WRITINGS

Mark it and Strike it (New York, 1960)

Bigger than a Breadbox (New York, 1967)

Make 'em Laugh (Buffalo, 1993)

BIBLIOGRAPHY

Oral history material in *NCH* (HCJA)

"Steve Allen: Man in Motion," *Down Beat*, xxv/23 (1958), 16

"Allen, Steve," *CBY* 1982

R. Severo: Obituary, *New York Times* (1 Nov 2000)

MARK TUCKER

Allen, William Duncan (*b* Portland, OR, 15 Dec 1906; *d* Richmond, CA, 19 Aug 1999). Pianist, organist, accompanist, educator, and critic. After childhood training in piano and organ, Allen received his formal music education at the Oberlin College Conservatory of Music, Ohio (BM, 1928, MM 1936), where he studied piano with George C. Hastings and Frank H. Shaw; in the interim he studied with Gordon Stanley and JAMES FRISKIN at the Juilliard School (1928–9). He taught at Howard University, Washington, DC (1929–35), and at Fisk University in Nashville, Tennessee (1936–43, 1951). Allen held a fellowship from the US Department of Education to study piano with EGON PETRI in Kraków, Poland (1938–9). When his visit was cut short by the German invasion of Poland in September 1939, he used the remainder of his fellowship to study with ISABELLE VENGEROVA at the Mannes College of Music in New York City (1939–40). He toured internationally as accompanist for the baritone Todd Duncan (1943–53). He later accompanied other notable African American singers such as Adele Addison, Betty Allen, Helen Thigpen, Leontyne Price, George Shirley, and William Warfield, and he toured with Robeson (1957–8). Allen settled in San Francisco where he taught privately, worked as music director for local organizations, published music criticism for the *San Francisco Sun-Reporter* and *Oakland Post*, and served as minister of music and organist at the South Berkeley Community Church (1954–79). He left the Bay Area briefly to serve as a visiting professor at Talladega College, Alabama (1980–82). In 1978 Allen was awarded an honorary doctorate of music from the University of California, Berkeley.

BIBLIOGRAPHY

W.E. Terry: "Conversation with William Duncan Allen: the Consummate Collaborator," *BPM*, xv/2 (1987), 182–218

C.C. Crawford, ed.: "Teacher, Pianist, and Accompanist to Concert Artists: William Duncan Allen," Bancroft Library, University of California, Berkeley, 1995 <http://www.oac.cdlib.org/view?docId=hb1779n73k> [interviews]

ROBERT PAUL KOLT

Allen, William Francis (*b* Northborough, MA, 5 Sept 1830; *d* Madison, WI, 9 Dec 1889). Classical scholar, teacher, editor, and writer. Allen is best known musically as an editor of *Slave Songs of the United States* (New York, 1867), also edited by Charles Pickard Ware and Lucy McKim Garrison, who were white collectors of black music.

Allen graduated from Harvard in 1851, subsequently studied in Europe, and returned to the United States in 1856. In 1863 he began an eight-month stint as a teacher on St Helena Island in South Carolina, home to former slaves who remained after plantation owners left in 1861. Here, Allen gained first-hand experience of slave singing that contributed to the detailed explanations of his 36-page prologue to *Slave Songs*. In 1867 Allen was appointed chair of ancient languages at the University of Wisconsin in Madison, where he remained until his death.

Allen's interest in philology is evident in the many pages of the prologue to *Slave Songs* devoted to black speech. The prologue is best known, however, for Allen's musical descriptions. Although Allen did not receive a collegiate musical education, he was a talented amateur musician. Passages from the prologue, particularly Allen's precise descriptions of musical characteristics and his account of the shout, have been quoted frequently by music scholars as rare and accurate descriptions of slave singing.

BIBLIOGRAPHY

D.J. Epstein: *Sinful Tunes and Spirituals: Black Folk Music to the Civil War* (Chicago, 1977)

E. Southern: *The Music of Black Americans: A History* (New York, 3/1997)

RENEE LAPP NORRIS

Allen organ. An electronic organ designed by Jerome Markowitz (1917–91) between 1937 and 1939, and manufactured from 1939 in Allentown, Pennsylvania, and from 1953 in nearby Macungie. The Allen Organ Co. was founded in 1945; besides many models of the organ, it has manufactured electronic harpsichords and an electronic piano (from 1965). After Markowitz's death his son Steve Markowitz succeeded him as president.

The Allen organ was the first fully-electronic organ to become commercially available. A three-manual instrument was produced in 1946, and a four-manual one in 1954. In 1949 a two-speed rotating loudspeaker unit, the Gyrophonic Projector, was introduced. The company was one of the first to develop a fully transistorized organ (1959), and in the digital Computer Organ (1971) it pioneered the replacement of oscillators by a computer that generates sounds by means of digital waveform synthesis (based on recordings of pipe organ spectra). The original organ was designed for use in churches, but later models included concert and home organs. The concert models have frequently taken solo and obbligato roles in orchestras, under conductors such as Barenboim, Bernstein, Dorati, Karajan, Mehta, Ormandy, and Stokowski. Four-manual touring organs were commissioned in the mid-1970s by Carlo Curley (380 loudspeakers) and Virgil Fox (over 500 loudspeakers).

From the mid-1960s to the early 80s Allen's RMI division (Rocky Mount Instruments) manufactured portable electronic pianos and keyboards, including the Electra-Piano (1967), Rock-Si-Chord (1967), and RMI Keyboard Computer KC-I (1974) and KC-II (1977), two of the first polyphonic synthesizers. Other subsidiaries have manufactured digital components, speaker cabinets, and sound systems. Their digital organs, which have retained their broad appeal, constitute the company's primary strength.

BIBLIOGRAPHY

R.L. Eby: *Electronic Organs: a Complete Catalogue, Textbook and Manual* (Wheaton, IL, 1953), 25–47

R.H. Dorf: *Electronic Musical Instruments* (Mineola, NY, 1954, 3/1968), 153–64

W.H. Barnes: *The Contemporary American Organ: its Evolution, Design and Construction* (Glen Rock, NJ, 7/1959), 356–9

J. Markowitz: *Triumphs and Trials of an Organ Builder* (Macungie, PA, 1989)

B. Carson: "A Parade of Exotic Electric Pianos and Fellow Travelers," *Keyboard*, xix/12 (1993), 143, 146–9
B. Carson: "Vintage RMI: the World's First Digital Sample-Playback Synthesizers," *Keyboard*, xxi/3 (1995), 38–46

HUGH DAVIES/R

Aller, Eleanor (*b* New York, NY, 20 May 1917; *d* Los Angeles, CA, 12 Oct 1995). Cellist of Russian parentage. She studied with her father, and at the age of 12 appeared at Carnegie Hall. She subsequently studied with FELIX SALMOND at the Juilliard School of Music, and toured as a soloist. In 1936 she became principal cellist of the Warner Brothers Studio Orchestra, the first woman to hold such an appointment; she held this position until 1972. In 1946 Korngold wrote his Cello Concerto for Aller to play in the film *Deception*, and she also gave the work's first concert performance with the Los Angeles PO. In 1947 Aller and her husband, the violinist FELIX SLATKIN, founded the HOLLYWOOD STRING QUARTET with other principal players from Hollywood studio orchestras. The quartet, which disbanded in 1961, achieved distinction through its many recordings. From 1972 to 1985 Aller was principal cellist for 20th Century Fox. Her playing was accurate and stylish, and she was uncompromising in her musical beliefs.

BIBLIOGRAPHY

M. Campbell: "Allergando con spirito," *The Strad*, xcviii (1987), 831–3
M. Campbell: Obituary, *The Independent* (13 Nov 1995)
M. Campbell: "Hollywood Star," *The Strad*, cvii (1996), 145–7

MARGARET CAMPBELL

Allessi, Joseph, Jr. (*b* Detroit, MI, 9 Sept 1959). Trombonist. Widely regarded as one of the finest trombonists of the later 20th and the 21st centuries, Joseph Alessi began his studies with his father in San Rafael, California prior to enrolling at the Curtis Institute of Music from 1977–80. While still a student, he was appointed acting Second Trombone of the Philadelphia Orchestra, eventually won the position, and remained with the orchestra for four seasons. Prior to his 1985 appointment as Principal with the New York Philharmonic, he performed for one season as Principal with the Montreal Symphony. As a soloist he has performed with the New York Philharmonic on several occasions, including the world première of Christopher Rouse's *Trombone Concerto*, which won the 1993 Pulitzer Prize for Music. Since 1992, with the release of his first compact disc, Alessi has become the preeminent American trombone soloist. He has released more than ten compact disc recordings, commissioned new works, and appeared as soloist throughout the world. A noted master teacher, Alessi has been a member of the faculty at the Juilliard School since 1986. His students hold positions in many major orchestras, and his summer trombone workshop, the Alessi Seminar, attracts performers from around the globe.

BRUCE TYCHINSKI

Alley, Joseph (*b* Kennebunk, ME, 4 March 1804; *d* Newburyport, MA, 8 March 1880). Organ builder and inventor. He is said to have learned about organ building from Joshua Furbush of Wells, who is known to have made a few small reed and pipe organs, and he later built at least one organ for George W. Bourne of Kennebunk before moving in 1826 to Newburyport, Massachusetts, where he began making pianos and chamber organs. He is said to have eventually built 37 church organs, the largest of which was built in 1834 for the Unitarian Church in Newburyport. His unique achievement, however, derives from the two patented "euharmonic" organs built between 1849 and 1851 in conjunction with Henry Ward Poole (1826–90). While having a normal keyboard, these organs had more than one pipe for each black key (e.g., both C♯ and D♭), and the intervals were tuned pure rather than tempered. To bring the properly tuned pipes into operation the player depressed a "selector" pedal for the key in which he desired to play. There was considerable coverage of this instrument in the musical press of the day, and in 1869, again in collaboration with Poole, Alley also constructed a reed organ with an experimental keyboard that allowed purely-tuned playing in several keys. Discouraged by the lack of patronage for these unique instruments, however, Alley later gave up building organs to operate a small pipe-making business with his eldest son, Joseph.

BIBLIOGRAPHY

H.W. Poole: "Essay on Perfect Intonation." *American Journal of Arts and Sciences*, ix (1850)
S.H. Hooker: "Joseph Alley's Enharmonic Organ," *Music Magazine*, xi/4 (1897), 677–687
B. Owen: *The Organ in New England* (Raleigh, NC, 1979), 118–133
B. Owen: "Early Organs and Organ Building in Newburyport," *Essex Institute Historical Collections*, cxxi/3 (1985), 172, 178–182

BARBARA OWEN

Allison, Margaret (*b* McCormick, SC, 25 Sept 1921; *d* Philadelphia, PA, 30 July 2008). Gospel singer, pianist, and composer. She moved to Philadelphia at an early age and sang and played at a local Church of God in Christ. In 1942 she joined a female quartet, the Spiritual Echoes, and served as their pianist for two years, leaving the group in 1944 to organize the Angelic Gospel Singers with her sister Josephine McDowell and two friends, Lucille Shird and Ella Mae Norris. Their first recording, "Touch me, Lord Jesus" (1950), sold 500,000 copies in less than six months. Her most famous composition is "My Sweet Home" (1960). The incidental harmony of their rural singing style and Allison's sliding technique appealed to a large number of supporters who otherwise found the gospel music of the period controlled and calculated. The group traveled and recorded with the Dixie Hummingbirds during the 1950s. Allison toured, recorded, and performed gospel music for over seven decades.

BIBLIOGRAPHY

T. Heilbut: *The Gospel Sound: Good News and Bad Times* (New York, 1971/*R*)
H.C. Boyer: "Gospel Music," *Music Educators Journal*, lxiv/9 (1978), 34

HORACE CLARENCE BOYER/R

Allison, Mose (John, Jr.) (*b* Tippo, MI, 11 Nov 1927). Jazz and blues pianist, singer and songwriter. His style was influenced by the blues music he heard on the juke box at his father's general store. Primarily self taught on piano and trumpet, Allison began playing professionally in Delta roadhouses and attended the University of Mississippi, Oxford. He left school to enlist in the US Army, and during his service he played trumpet and piano and wrote arrangements for an army band. After completing a degree in English at Louisiana State University, he moved to New York in the late 1950s and attracted attention nationally playing piano with such leaders as Chet Baker, Al Cohn, Zoot Sims, Gerry Mulligan, and Stan Getz.

Allison created a hybrid style that integrated country blues with urbane jazz; it can be heard on his first album, *Back Country Suite* (1959, Prst.), which includes what became his signature tune, "Young Man's Blues." In the 1960s Allison's music influenced British rock musicians, and this tune was covered by The Who. During the same period Allison recorded for Atlantic and wrote pithy lyrics about public service and social commentary ("Everybody Cryin' Mercy") and personal crisis ("Hello There, Universe"), some with a playful sense of humor ("Your Mind's on Vacation"). Later songs such as "Ever Since the World Ended" and "Certified Senior Citizen" focused on contemporary culture and aging. Allison has also interpreted blues and jazz standards such as Willie Dixon's "Seventh Son," Muddy Waters' "Rollin' Stone," and Duke Ellington's "I ain't got nothin' but the blues." His elaborate piano instrumentals and improvisations draw upon the music of Charles Ives and Alexander Scriabin and reflect his experimentation with conventional ideas of time.

BIBLIOGRAPHY

P. Jones: *One Man's Blues: the Life and Music of Mose Allison* (London, 1995)

PATTI JONES

Allman Brothers Band, the. Rock group. Its original members were (Howard) Duane Allman (*b* Nashville, TN, 20 Nov 1946; *d* Macon, GA, 29 Oct 1971; guitar), Gregg (Gregory Lenoir) Allman (*b* Nashville, TN, 8 Dec 1947; guitar, keyboard, and vocals), Dickey (Richard) Betts (*b* West Palm Beach, FL, 12 Dec 1943; guitar and vocals), Jaimoe (Jai Johanny) Johanson (John Johan Johanson; *b* Ocean Springs, MS, 8 July 1944; drums and percussion), Berry Oakley (*b* Chicago, IL, 4 April 1948; *d* Macon, GA, 11 Nov 1972; bass guitar), and Butch (Claude Hudson) Trucks (*b* Jacksonville, FL, 11 May 1947; drums). The two Allman brothers grew up in Florida and worked during the 1960s in several short-lived groups, including the Hourglass with whom they recorded two albums for Liberty Records in Los Angeles. In 1968 they moved to Fame Studios in Muscle Shoals, Alabama, where Duane Allman was engaged as a studio guitarist; he participated in sessions with Wilson Pickett, King Curtis, and Aretha Franklin among others. Having signed a recording contract with Atlantic Records, Duane Allman with his brother Gregg formed the Allman Brothers Band, though even after the release of its first album and during its early tours he continued his session work, most significantly with Eric Clapton on Derek and the Dominos' single, "Layla" (1971). The group's second album, *Idlewild South* (1970), and constant touring strengthened its reputation in the United States.

By 1971 the Allman Brothers Band had developed a consistent sound that amalgamated various southern musical styles: Muscle Shoals soul, blues, and country music, and improvisatory hard rock. They kept their rhythms and song structures tight and Gregg Allman used a gruff tenor voice effectively, while Betts and Duane Allman often executed harmonized guitar runs over memorable melodic lines, as in Betts's song "In Memory of Elizabeth Reed" (1970). Capable of fiercely eloquent solos, Duane Allman was also an articulate slide guitarist. The band's style is well captured on the live album *At Fillmore East* (1971), which placed the group in the commercial and artistic forefront of American rock. After Duane Allman's death the group did not replace him, but its album *Eat a Peach* (1972), which included studio and concert material recorded before his death, reached the US top ten. In 1972 Oakley also died and was replaced by Lamar Williams. The group split up in 1976 after recording two more albums, reunited without Williams, and then dissolved again in 1982. In 1989 Gregg Allman and Betts reformed the group, with further personnel changes, to make *Seven Turns* (1990) and other albums. Known for their memorable, improvisatory live performances, and acclaimed for their pivotal role in shaping SOUTHERN ROCK, the band was inducted into the Rock and Roll Hall of Fame in 1995.

BIBLIOGRAPHY

J. Obrect: "Duane Allman," *Guitar Player*, xv/10 (1981), 68–70, 76–84; repr. in *Secrets from the Masters: Conversations with Forty Great Guitar Players*, ed. D. Menn (New York, 1992), 1–6

S. Freeman: *Midnight Riders: The Story of the Allman Brothers Band* (New York, 1995)

CHRIS WALTERS/R

Allusion. A reference in a piece of music to a musical style, type, or convention, or to another piece, in a manner akin to an allusion in speech or literature; also, the act of making such a reference. Allusion to a particular piece is generally distinguished from QUOTATION in that material is not quoted directly, but a reference is made through some other similarity; some writers consider quotation one type of allusion. Typically an allusion is made to evoke associations with the style, repertoire, convention, or piece alluded to and thus to convey meaning, as in Charles Ives's allusion to hymn style to suggest humble submission in *Paracelsus* and Frank Zappa's allusions to popular styles to create irony in *Broadway the Hard Way*; to invoke a work or style as a model for the new work or in homage to another composer, as in George Crumb's allusions to Mahler; or in some other way to suggest a link with the music alluded to that calls for interpretation. Stylistic allusions are often used in operas, program music, and film music to invoke a type of music and the people or activities associated with it, or to suggest a place or time through musical style, as in the African American blues and spiritual styles in William Grant Still's *Afro-American Symphony* and George Gershwin's *Porgy and Bess* or the Mozartean music of the opera-within-an-opera in John Corigliano's *The Ghosts of Versailles*.

See also BORROWING; QUOTATION.

BIBLIOGRAPHY

Grove7 (J. Peter Burkholder)

S.M. Bruns: "'In stilo Mahleriano': Quotation and Allusion in the Music of George Crumb," *American Music Research Center Journal,* iii (1993), 9–39

J.P. Burkholder: *All Made of Tunes: Charles Ives and the Uses of Musical Borrowing* (New Haven, CT, 1995)

C. Smith: "Broadway the Hard Way: Techniques of Allusion in the Music of Frank Zappa," *College Music Symposium,* xxxv (1995), 35–60

A.C. Shreffler: "Phantoms at the Opera: *The Ghosts of Versailles* by John Corigliano and William Hoffman," *CMR,* xx/4 (2001), 117–35

J. PETER BURKHOLDER

Allyson, June [Geisman, Ella] (*b* Bronx, NY, 7 Oct 1917; *d* Ojai, CA, 8 July 2006). Singer and actress. Trained as a dancer and with a career which began on Broadway, she became known as the perennial "girl next door" in MGM motion pictures. Her early career in film was as a dancer in shorts such as *Dime a Dance* (1937), but she gained attention with her first major Broadway role in *Best Foot Forward* (1941) and reprised her role in the 1943 film version. Other musical films in which she appeared include *Thousands Cheer* (1943), *Girl Crazy* (1943), *Two Girls and a Sailor* (1944), *Music for Millions* (1944), *Two Sisters from Boston* (1946), and *Good News* (1947). In 1948, she began to appear in non-musical films, including dramas and comedies. She received a Golden Globe Award in 1952 for *Too Young to Kiss*. She was married to fellow singing actor DICK POWELL from 1945 until his death in 1963.

The distinctive quality of her singing voice was that it closely resembled her speaking voice. Both rested in a relatively low register and exhibited an attractive aspirant quality. Possessing a legitimate stage voice, Allyson was able to be heard easily in theaters without either belting or using electronic enhancement.

WILLIAM A. EVERETT, LEE SNOOK

Almanac Singers. Singing group and political activists. In late 1940 Pete Seeger met Lee Hays, a preacher and labor organizer from Arkansas, and his New York roommate, Millard Lampell, a writer from New Jersey. By February 1941 they had launched the Almanac Singers, a loose collection of musicians devoted to performing original and traditional folksongs, many with a hard political edge. Soon joined by Bess Lomax (sister of Alan), Baldwin ("Butch") and Peter Hawes, Josh White, Woody Guthrie, Agnes ("Sis") Cunningham, and others, they performed before various labor and left-wing groups. Their first album of peace songs, *Songs for John Doe*, appeared in early 1941. This was followed by two albums of traditional songs, *Sod Buster Ballads* and *Deep Sea Chanties*, and the pro-labor *Talking Union*. Their final album, *Dear Mr. President*, which consisted of pro-war songs, was released in 1942. Their left-wing politics led to much negative publicity, and with the start of World War II the group began to fragment. Seeger joined the Army, Guthrie entered the Merchant Marine, and the others went in various directions, but their creative songs and folk style would live on.

BIBLIOGRAPHY

R.A. Reuss and J.C. Reuss: *American Folk Music and Left-Wing Politics, 1927–1957* (Lanham, MD, 2000)

RONALD D. COHEN

Almario, Justo (Pastor Gomez) (*b* Sincelejo, Colombia, 18 Feb 1949). Saxophonist of Colombian birth. His father was a percussionist who performed traditional Colombian music and Almario began his career playing in this style. Influenced by the Cuban music that was popular along the Caribbean coast of Colombia, Almario studied wind instruments and theory in Barranquilla, where he later moved. After a tour of the United States in 1967, he accepted an invitation to move to Miami and in 1969 was offered a scholarship to the Berklee School of Music. Two years later, while he was still studying, Almario was invited to sit in with Mongo Santamaria, who subsequently hired him as musical director for his ensemble; Almario can be heard on a number of Santamaria's recordings, including *Afro-Indio* (1975, Fania). In the following years, Almario worked with Duke Ellington, Machito, Willie Bobo, and Charles Mingus. His group Koinonia, which he formed with Alex Acuña, performed West Coast jazz and promoted Christian spirituality, such as on the album *Celebration* (1984, Sparrow). With Acuña, he later formed Tolú to perform pan-American repertoire, and its albums *Rumbero's Poetry* (1998, Tonga) and *Bongo the VanGogh* (2002, TNG) were well received. Almario also recorded three albums with Cachao (including *Ahora Sí!*, 2004, Univision) that were critically acclaimed. In 1998, in conjunction with Berklee, he instituted a Latin jazz curriculum at Claremont McKenna College. He has also taught at UCLA and worked in film and television.

BIBLIOGRAPHY

L. Tamargo and R. Mangual: "Justo Almario and Alex Acuna: the Return to Planet Tolu," *Latin Beat,* viii/6 (1998), 16–20

R. Bassa Labarrera: "La herencia musical de Justo Almario," *Herencia Latina* (June 2007); also available at <http://www.herencialatina.com/Justo_Almario/Justo_Almario.htm>

MARK LOMANNO

Almeida, John Kameaaloha [Celestino] (*b* Honolulu, HI, 28 Nov 1897; *d* Honolulu, HI, 9 Oct 1985) singer, musician, composer, and bandleader. Almeida lost his eyesight completely by age ten, and left school after the sixth grade. His father returned to Portugal, and his Hawaiian mother and adoptive Hawaiian father nurtured him, immersing him in the music and culture of the rural community. At age 15, Almeida formed his first musical group, the Waianae Star Glee Club, and soon achieved local fame as "John C. Almeida, Hawaii's Blind Musician." Eventually, he replaced his birth middle name of Celestino, with the name of his adoptive father, Kameaaloha, and is remembered today as John Kameaaloha Almeida.

Almeida could not read or write, but shared the poetry of over 200 Hawaiian language compositions, earning him the title of "the Dean of Hawaiian Music." Almeida also popularized numerous other Hawaiian compositions from the 19th century. Among his most famous recordings are "Ku'u Ipo Pua Rose," "'A 'Oia," "Gorgeous Hula," "Holoholo Ka'a," "Noho Paipai," "Kiss Me Love," "Roselani Blossoms," and his radio theme song, "'O Ko'u Aloha Ia 'Oe." Over his 70-year career, Almeida mastered the mandolin, ukulele, guitar, steel guitar, violin, banjo, bass, saxophone, and piano. Almeida was a prolific recordings artist on numerous labels, and a successful radio host on several Hawaii stations. He served as mentor to numerous protégés, including Bill Ali'iloa Lincoln, Joe Keawe, Billy Hew Len, Genoa Keawe, and Almeida's adopted son, Pua Almeida.

BIBLIOGRAPHY

H.B. Soria Jr. and K. Donaghy: *John Kameaaloha Almeida: the Dean of Hawaiian Music* (Honolulu, 2003)

HARRY B. SORIA JR.

Almeida (Nobrega Neto), Laurindo (José) (de Araujo) (*b* Santos, Brazil, 2 Sept 1917; *d* Sherman Oaks, CA, 26 July 1995). Brazilian guitarist, composer, and arranger. He was taught the piano by his mother but secretly taught himself the guitar (borrowing his sister's instrument) from the age of nine. He first worked for radio stations in São Paulo and Rio de Janeiro, and in 1936 made a tour of Europe. For the 1940 Carnival he and Ubirajara Nesdan wrote "Aldeia da roupa branca" (later called "Johnny Peddlar"), which became internationally popular. From 1936 to 1947 Almeida worked with Brazilian artists such as Garoto, Villa-Lobos, Radames Gnatalli, Carmen Miranda and her sister Aurora, and Pixinguinha. After immigrating to the United States in 1947, he appeared in a Danny Kaye film, *A Song is Born*. Soon afterwards he joined Stan Kenton's orchestra, staying with him as a soloist, arranger, and composer until 1952. While with Kenton he introduced the classical guitar tradition to jazz, and his recordings from this time set the standard for jazz guitarists. In the early 1950s he cultivated "samba jazz," a combination of cool jazz with samba elements. He also toured throughout the world and recorded with the Modern Jazz Quartet and his own group, the LA 4.Almeida's guitar works, which include a concerto (1979), were influenced by his classical background, Afro-Brazilian rhythms, traditional Brazilian music, and American jazz. He composed or contributed to a large number of film scores, including *Old Man and the Sea* and *Goodbye, my Lady*. In 1961 his *Discantus* for three guitars tied with Stravinsky's Moments for piano and orchestra in a major composition prize. He also wrote a guitar tutor (1950) and ten Studies for guitar (1988). He made numerous recordings, some featuring his own works, and was created a Comendador da Ordem do Rio Branco by the Brazilian government.

BIBLIOGRAPHY

R. Purcell and B. Hodel: "Laurindo Almeida: celebração dos Setenta," *Soundboard*, xiv/4 (1987–8), 245–7

R. Purcell: "Big Brother: Laurindo Almeida," *Guitar Review*, no.107 (1996), 1–9; no.110 (1997), 18–27

R. Purcell: "Big Brother: Laurindo Almeida (1917–1995)," International Guitar Research Archive, <http://library.csun.edu/igra/bios/almeida.html>

RONALD C. PURCELL

Almeida, Santiago (*b* Skidmore, TX, 25 July 1911; *d* Sunnyside, WA, 8 July 1999). Conjunto musician. Santiago Almeida is best known for playing the *bajo sexto* on some of the earliest and best known recordings of Texas-Mexican conjunto music. Almeida was born into a farmworker family that played music to make ends meet. At 15, he joined the family band, Orquesta Almeida, and played numerous dances in the lower Rio Grande Valley. It was at these dances that he likely encountered accordionist NARCISO MARTÍNEZ. The duo performed together at dances before making their first recording in 1936 for Bluebird Records, a low budget sub-label of RCA records marketed to regional and ethnic audiences. It was a 78-rpm disk of a polka, "La Chicharronera" and a schottische, "El Troconal," which sold well and is now regarded as the first modern conjunto recording. The pairing of these two instruments was significant as it established the musical "core" of the modern Texas-Mexican CONJUNTO ensemble. Over the years, bajo sexto players have imitated Almeida's distinctive cross-picking style, which perfectly balanced Martínez's expressive accordion leads.

CATHY RAGLAND

Alpert, Herb (*b* Los Angeles, CA, 31 March 1935). Trumpeter, composer, bandleader, and record company executive. He studied trumpet as a child and left college to play in the army for a two-year period. After three years of producing records on his own, he launched A&M Records with Jerry Moss in 1962. A&M's first issue was also Alpert's first recording as a trumpeter and bandleader, *The Lonely Bull* (A&M, 1962). The title track included sounds from the bullring in Tijuana, Mexico, so Alpert dubbed his band the Tijuana Brass. His music exploited a distinctive combination of Mexican *mariachi*-style brass with jazz rhythms, which was dubbed Ameriachi. A string of hits including "Mexican Shuffle" (A&M, 1964) and "Tijuana Taxi" (A&M, 1965) followed. In 1966 Alpert had five recordings simultaneously listed on the Billboard Top 20. His cover of "This guy's in love with you" reached no.1 in 1968 (A&M, 1968). The band's instrumental accompaniments influenced the music of Diana Ross and the Supremes and the Beatles. A&M Records became a highly successful company, signing performers such as Joe Cocker, Carole King, and the Flying Burrito Brothers in the 1960s, and the Carpenters, the Police, and Supertramp in the 1970s. Increasingly devoted to A&M's business activities and facing lowering popularity on the charts, Alpert disbanded the Tijuana Brass in 1970.

Alpert began to perform again in 1974, playing in an eclectic style drawing on diverse influences: African (*Herb Alpert and Hugh Masekela*, A&M, 1978), funk and disco (*Rise*, A&M, 1979), big band (*My Abstract Heart*, A&M, 1989), hip hop (*North on South Street*,

A&M, 1991), and jazz (*Midnight Sun*, A&M, 1992). In 1990 he and Moss sold A&M to PolyGram for approximately $500 million. In 1994 the two incorporated Almo Records, with which Alpert recorded *Second Wind* (Almo, 1996), the salsa-inspired *Passion Dance* (Almo, 1997), and *Colors* (Almo, 1999). After a hiatus in which he focused on painting and sculpture, Alpert toured in 2008 with his wife, the jazz vocalist Lani Hall, and recorded *Anything Goes* (Conc., 2009).

Alpert has undertaken extensive philanthropic activities in support of the arts and music education under the auspices of the Herb Alpert Foundation. In 1994 he endowed scholarship awards at the California Institute of the Arts. A $30 million gift in 2007 to UCLA and an additional $15 million gift to the California Institute of the Arts in 2008 led both universities to rename their music schools in his honor. Alpert also underwrites the Carmine Caruso International Jazz Trumpet Solo Competition, named after one of his trumpet teachers.

BIBLIOGRAPHY

B. Rollin: "Small Band, Big Sound: the Tijuana Brass," *Look*, xxx (1966), 104–07

G.H. Lewis: "Ghosts, Ragged but Beautiful: Influences of Mexican Music on American Country-Western and Rock 'n' Roll," *Popular Music and Society*, xv/4 (1991), 85–103

T. Erdmann: "A Passion for Creativity: an Interview with Herb Alpert," *International Trumpet Guild Journal* xxix/2 (2005), 21–30

TERENCE J. O'GRADY/BRYAN PROKSCH

Alsop, Marin (*b* New York, NY, 16 Oct 1956). Conductor. As the daughter of two professional classical musicians—concertmaster and cellist with the NYC Ballet—Alsop was always surrounded by music. She studied piano early and then shifted to violin at age five. From age seven she studied at the Juilliard Pre-College Division. She attended Yale University (1973–6) and earned degrees in violin performance at the Juilliard School (BM 1977, MM 1978). Using money from her freelance work as a violinist, she founded (1984) her own 50-piece orchestra, Concordia, specializing in 20th-century American music, including jazz. LEONARD BERNSTEIN, whose example first inspired her to conduct, later became a significant mentor and influence. In 1988 she studied at Tanglewood with Bernstein, GUSTAV MEIER and SEIJI OZAWA; the following year she returned there and won the Koussevitzky Conducting Prize. Alsop has paid tribute to Bernstein by conducting his works, from her European debut at the Schleswig-Holstein Festival (1993) to an Emmy-Award-nominated production of *Candide* (2005) to the critically acclaimed recording of his *Mass* (2009, Naxos) with the Baltimore Symphony.

In 1989 Alsop accepted music director appointments with the Eugene (Oregon) Symphony Orchestra (1990–96) and the Long Island Philharmonic (1990–96, designate during the 1989–90 season). Since her appointment as music director of the Colorado Symphony Orchestra (1993–2005, conductor laureate from 2006), Alsop's career has moved through added conducting responsibilities, growing artistic recognition, and more prestigious artistic situations: principal guest conductor, City of London Sinfonia (1999–2003) and Royal Scottish National Orchestra (1999–2003); principal conductor, Bournemouth Symphony (2002–8, conductor emeritus from 2008); music director, Baltimore Symphony Orchestra (appointed 2005, interim director 2006–7, MD since September 2007, current contract extended through 2015); chief conductor, Orquestra Sinfônica do Estadual de São Paulo (appointed 2011, begins in 2012); long-term music director, Cabrillo Festival of Contemporary Music, Santa Cruz (since 1992); and Artist-in-Residence, London's Southbank Centre (since 2011). Alsop, who has conducted most of the major American orchestras, makes regular guest appearances with the New York PO, the Philadelphia Orchestra and the Los Angeles PO. She also frequently conducts major European orchestras, including the Royal Concertgebouw Orchestra, Zürich Tonhalle, Orchestre de Paris, Munich PO, and La Scala Milan, and she is one of the few conductors to perform every season with both the London SO and London PO. In 2005 she became the first, and so far only, conductor named a MacArthur Foundation Fellow. Among her other numerous and prestigious awards on both sides of the Atlantic are *Gramophone*'s "Artist of the Year" (2003), the Royal Philharmonic Society's Conductor's Award (2003), Classical Brit Award for Best Female Artist (2005), European Women of Achievement Award (2007), American Academy of Arts and Sciences Fellow (2008), *Musical America*'s Conductor of the Year (2009), and Classical Music Hall of Fame (2010).

During the past two decades both Alsop and the orchestras she has headed have grown in technical skill and artistic depth. Her performances are praised for their musical insights—pacing and architectural clarity

Marin Alsop, 2008. (T.Martinot/Lebrecht Music & Arts)

as well as nuanced phrasing and timbral detail. Although sometimes most closely associated with contemporary American music, her insights also create compelling musical performances of 19th-century central European repertoire. She is acknowledged for her rapport with players and superb communication with audiences, and also promotes accessibility through educational initiatives and outreach programs. Her commitment to works by contemporary composers is evident in her large discography with acclaimed recordings of works by Samuel Barber (complete orchestral works in six volumes, Naxos) with the Royal Scottish National Orchestra; works by Béla Bartók, Bernstein, Torū Takemitsu, and Kurt Weill with the Bournemouth Symphony; and performances by the Colorado Symphony Orchestra of American composers such as John Adams, Libby Larsen, Joan Tower, Michael Daugherty, and Christopher Rouse. Especially noteworthy recordings of traditional repertoire are the Brahms symphonies with the London Philharmonic Orchestra and a Dvořák symphony cycle with the Baltimore Symphony.

As the first woman music director of a major full-time American orchestra—one of many "firsts" on her resume—Alsop's work has received considerable attention, and she has acknowledged the opportunity of this and her responsibility to assist future generations of women conductors. Already in 2002 she had established the Taki Concordia Conducting Fellowship, which supports one exceptional woman each year for mentoring and professional conducting opportunities with Alsop.

BIBLIOGRAPHY

J.M. Edwards: "Women on the Podium," *Cambridge Companion to Conducting*, ed. J. Bowen (Cambridge, 2003), 220–36

A. Tommasini: "A One-Woman Vanguard," *New York Times* (11 Nov 2007)

A. Ross: "Maestra: Marin Alsop Leads the Baltimore Symphony," *New Yorker* (17 Jan 2008)

J. MICHELE EDWARDS

Alston, Lettie Beckon (*b* Detroit, MI, 13 April 1953). Composer and pianist. As a teenager, she studied piano with Pearl Roberts McCullom. She received bachelor and master's degrees in music composition at Wayne State University, studying with James Hartway. In 1983, she became the first female African American composer to receive the DMA in composition from the University of Michigan, where she studied with WILLIAM BOLCOM, Eugene Kurtz and LESLIE BASSETT. She also worked in electronic music with George Wilson for several years.

Alston taught briefly at Wayne State University (1983), Oakland University (1987), and Eastern Michigan University (1988). In 1991, she rejoined the faculty at Oakland University, where she is an associate professor in music composition. Her music has been performed in the United States and abroad. Alston's *Four Moods for Piano* and *Three Rhapsodies for Piano* were selected for New York premieres by the North/South Consonance Ensemble. *Memories*, for violin, violoncello, and piano, was premiered by Il Trio della Musica in Salzburg, Austria. Alston's *Four Short Pieces* for soprano and piano were performed at the National Black Arts Festival in Atlanta and by the Contemporary Music Forum in Washington, DC. In June 2005, *Conquest of Jericho* for SATB, narrator, piano, and string orchestra received its New York premiere by the Bronx Singers and Bronx Singers Chamber Orchestra. Alston is a recipient of the ASCAP Standard Award, 2001–7. Her music has been recorded on the Albany, Leonarda, Videmus, Patterson, and Calvin College labels.

WORKS

(*selective list*)

Energico, vn, vc, pf, 1981; Conquest of Jericho, SATB, nar, pf, str orch, 1990; Four Moods, pf, 1993; Pulsations, vn, 1993; Three Rhapsodies, pf, 1994; Anxiety, orch, 1994; Rhapsody No.4 "Keyboard Maniac," pf, 1996; Journey: The Longest Mile, pf, 2000; Sonata of the Day, pf, 2000; Done Made My Vow, 2001 [arr.]; Four Short Pieces, S, pf, 2005

Principal publishers: MMB, Vivace, Hildegard, Willis C. Patterson, Rhapsody Music

ELDONNA L. MAY

Altamont Festival. A free outdoor music festival organized and headlined by the Rolling Stones that took place on 6 December 1969. Goaded by the music press to put on a free show in the wake of the recent Woodstock festival and unprecedentedly high ticket prices for their own shows, the group quickly and haphazardly arranged the festival. The remote Altamont Speedway in the scrubland northeast of San Francisco was used after attempts to hold it at more congenial spots fell through. Possibly at the suggestion of the Grateful Dead's manager, the Stones hired some members of San Francisco Hells Angels, the notorious motorcycle gang, to work security. Over 300,000 people flocked to the desolate place on a wintry day. Violence, primarily attacks by the Hells Angels on audience members and musicians, began almost immediately, and culminated in the murder of a young African American man, Meredith Hunter. Documentarians Albert and David Maysles captured Hunter's knifing at the hands of a Hells Angel, and the rest of the day's dysfunction and violence in their film *Gimme Shelter*. The film has become the official record of the event, a vivid reminder that nothing, not even rock and roll or the Woodstock generation, was immune from the violence and disorder of the late 1960s. Altamont has come to signify "the end of the 1960s" as well as to the end of idealistic dreams that youth culture, abetted by and its rock and roll soundtrack, could build a new society based on peace, love, and music rather than war and violence.

NORMA COATES

Alter, Martha (*b* New Bloomfield, PA, 8 Feb 1904; *d* Newport, PA, 3 June 1976). Composer, pianist, and teacher. She studied at Vassar College (AB 1925), Columbia University (AM in musicology, 1931), and the Eastman School of Music (MM in composition, 1932). Her teachers included ERNEST HUTCHESON (piano, 1925–6), RUBIN GOLDMARK (composition, 1926–7), and, at Eastman, HOWARD HANSON and BERNARD ROGERS. She taught at Vassar from 1929 to 1931 and between 1938 and 1942. In 1942 she joined the faculty of Connecticut College for Women, teaching composition, theory, history, and the piano.

She became a full professor in 1956 and department chair in 1963.

Alter began to compose while at college and continued until she retired from teaching in 1969. While at Eastman she composed large works with orchestra which Hanson conducted; these included a staged ballet *Anthony Comstock* at the Festival of American Music in 1934. At that time a reviewer called her "a distinguished talent," one who wrote "in a clear-cut manner, with force, sentiment, and humor." Alter's later works were heard primarily in universities in the northeastern United States and on radio. Her music is tonal with varying amounts of added dissonance. She used a lyrical and rhythmically energetic style and clear structures to create music of immediate communicative power. Some of the piano works and pieces on American themes incorporate irony, whimsy, or wit.

WORKS
(selective list)

Stage: Groceries and Notions (operetta, 3, K.K. Doughtie), 1931 (1931); Anthony Comstock, or, A Puritan's Progress (ballet, Alter and G. McGarrahan), 1934; A Dimensional Fantasy (ballet, N. Noyes), 1946

Vocal: The Voice (R. Brooke), Bar, pf, 1927; 3 Epigrams (S. Crane), medium v, pf, 1931, arr. chbr orch by D. Diamond; Bill George: March and Song (M. Cowley), Bar, 21 insts, 1931, arr. Bar, orch, 1932 (1940); Factory Windows (V. Lindsay), Bar, pf, 1931; Simon Legree: a Negro Sermon (Lindsay), Bar, 2 pf, 1937; 2 Songs (no.2, Lindsay), medium v, pf, 1938; Blackout (E. Horn), dramatic chbr work, Bar, 2 tpt, jazz perc, pf, 1941; 2 Songs (Horn), Bar, pf, 1941; 6 Songs from Time and Eternity (E. Dickinson), S, pf, 1948; Prayers of Kierkegaard, 1v, pf, 1957; On the Other Side of the Moon (Alter), 1v, pf, 1959

Choral: Peace (Bacchylides), women's vv, pf, 1940; 2 Plato Settings, women's vv, fl, pf, 1942 (New York, 1943); Let God be Magnified (cant., Pss), women's vv, pf/org, 1947; Pennsylvania Dutch Songs (W.J. Meter), male vv, pf, 1953; A Prayer for my Daughter (W.B. Yeats), S, women's vv, pf, 1961; Ideas from Actuelles (A. Camus, trans. J. O'Brion), women's vv, org, 1964; God be Merciful (Ps lxvii), women's vv, kbd, 1965; Whispers of Heavenly Death (W. Whitman), women's vv, org, 1965

Orch and chbr: Pf Trio, 1925; Trio, cl, vc, pf, 1926; Suite of 3 Dances, vn, pf, jazz perc, 1928; Rhythmic Dance, orch, 1931; Sinfonietta (Ov.), 1932; Sextet for Wind Insts, 1933; Suite from Anthony Comstock, 1934; Wedding Music, ob, vc, pf, 1937; Pastorale, va, pf, 1943; The Trial of the Dog (Aristophanes, trans. G. Allen), S, Bar, B, spkr, pf, 1951; Sarabande, vn, pf

Kbd (pf unless otherwise stated): Sonata, 1927; Telegraph Poles, suite, 1929–32; Etudes, 1930–46; Bric-a-Brac Suite, pf/hpd, 1931; Jig, 1931 [from Anthony Comstock]; Nocturne, 1931; Suite of Songs and Dances, 2 pf, 1936; Sonata, hpd, 1941; Americana Pieces, hpd, 1941; Elegy and Alert, 1941–2; 4 Lyric Moods, 1945; 4 Pieces for Children, 1945; A Jig Sonatine, 1949; Biblical Sonata: the Story of Daniel, org, 1955; Festive March, org, 1962

Unpubd. MSS in Connecticut College Archives

BIBLIOGRAPHY

Anderson2

A. Hooker: "Rochester Sees 'Anthony Comstock'," *MM*, xi (1933–4), 218–21

KAREN AHLQUIST

Alternative country. The term "alternative country" refers to Country music of the late 20th century that existed outside of mainstream country (as represented by Nashville and contemporary country radio) and incorporated country music with aspects of punk, rock and roll, and roots influences. During the 1990s, alternative country identified with a punk rock do-it-yourself ethos and a connection to indie-rock fans and scenes, with live venues and independent record labels playing a crucial role in its emergence. Further, the term owes much to the success of underground rock bands like R.E.M. and Nirvana that became commercially successful, marketed as "alternative."

The mythologized origins of alternative country begins in 1990, when the Belleville, Illinois band Uncle Tupelo released their debut album, *No Depression* (Rockville Records, 1990), which featured a collection of punk-influence rock songs and ballads with a country influence, including the title track, an edgy cover of the Carter Family tune "No Depression in Heaven." The album led to a discussion folder on America Online, also named "No Depression," which in turn led to a bimonthly magazine of the same name. Although Uncle Tupelo disbanded in 1994, they gave rise to Wilco and Son Volt, both of which continued to produce music that blended country, punk, and rock. Other alternative country bands demonstrated similarities to Uncle Tupelo, such as the Jayhawks and Whiskeytown, while others, such as Freakwater, Will Oldham's musical projects, and Gillian Welch, tended toward a more traditional country style. Others were more eclectic, such as the Waco Brothers, Lucinda Williams, the Bottle Rockets, Alejandro Escovedo, and Robbie Fulks.

Alternative country embraced a deep sense of history and found roots in oppositional approaches to country music, revering artists such as Gram Parsons and the Nitty Gritty Dirt Band who blended elements of country and rock and mainstream "outlaw" country artists such as Waylon Jennings and Willie Nelson. It also identified with the southern California punk scene that flourished in the 1980s and produced a wide variety of "cowpunk" bands that claimed a punk identity but played country music or incorporated country music into their own punk musical style, including Rank and File, X, and the Knitters.

A wide-reaching category, alternative country has been referred to by a variety of nicknames, including alt.country (perhaps owing to the online community associated with the music), No Depression, insurgent country (coined by Chicago's Bloodshot Records, which released several acclaimed alternative country compilations), y'alternative, and the widely used Americana. Alternative country also claimed a variety of aging country performers and legends that have maintained an outsider identity or were no longer commercially viable in mainstream country music, including Johnny Cash, George Jones, Loretta Lynn, and Merle Haggard.

BIBLIOGRAPHY

D. Goodman: *Modern Twang: an Alternative Country Music Guide and Directory* (Nashville, TN, 1999)

K. Wolff: "Settin' the Woods on Fire: Alternative Country in the 1990s," *Country Music: the Rough Guide*, ed. O. Duane (London, 2000), 549–91

G. Alden and P. Blackstock, eds.: *The Best of No Depression: Writing about American Music* (Austin, TX, 2005)

P. Fox and B. Ching: *Old Roots New Routes: the Cultural Politics of Alt. country Music* (Ann Arbor, MI, 2008)

NANCY P. RILEY

AlterNATIVE music [alter-Native]. AlterNATIVE music combines elements of Western culture with traditional Native American musics and storytelling, including use of western and Native American instruments, Native languages, socio-political and cultural issues, and Native regalia. The origin of the term is attributed to both KEITH SECOLA (Anishinabe) and Jim Boyd (Colville).

BIBLIOGRAPHY

B. Burton: *Moving Within the Circle: Contemporary Native American Music and Dance* (Danbury, CT, 2/2008), 117–23

BRYAN BURTON

Alternative rock. The label was applied to rock artists who met one or more of the following criteria: they recorded and performed on independent ("indie") networks of record companies and venues; they subverted rock and pop conventions musically in some way; or their stylistic pedigree could be traced back to PUNK. A largely underground sector of rock in the 1980s, a few alternative groups became commercially successful (Jane's Addiction, R.E.M.). College radio and venues were particularly important for alternative rock's promotion. By the early 1990s, alternative subgenres (indie, GRUNGE, punk-funk) were embraced by mainstream rock audiences, especially following Nirvana's 1991 breakthrough. Since the mid-1990s, alternative rock has been synonymous with modern and mainstream rock, and the sounds of grunge, indie, and British alternative rock (especially Radiohead) remain important stylistic touchstones.

CHRIS McDONALD

Althouse, Monroe A. (*b* Centre Township, nr Reading, PA, 26 May 1853; *d* Reading, PA, 12 Oct 1924). Conductor and composer. After playing violin and, later, trombone in local organizations, he decided on a musical career and left Reading, touring with various bands, one of which accompanied Buffalo Bill's Wild West Show. In 1872 he returned to Reading, worked in a hat factory, and played with local bands and orchestras. In 1886 he organized a ten-piece pit orchestra at the Reading Academy of Music, later renamed the Rajah Theater; for the next 20 years this ensemble accompanied all the legitimate theatrical productions there. He revived the Germania Orchestra, and in 1887 organized the Germania Band, which achieved some popularity and an excellent reputation. He assumed leadership of the Ringgold Band of Reading on the death of its bandmaster in 1900. The Germania Band was then effectively dissolved, its members joining the Ringgold Band; under Althouse's direction (until 1922) the band expanded its activities, giving regular summer concerts in Reading, as well as performances across the country. Althouse was associated with many of the important performers of his time, including Sousa, who became his close friend.

Althouse composed about 150 works, of which the best known are his marches; they are effective, inspiring "street" marches, somewhat simple in structure. Many of his works are recorded in the Heritage of the March series compiled by Robert Hoe (26, BB, TT, TTT, DDDD, and HHHH). In 1961 his *Tall Cedars* was made the official march of the Tall Cedars of Lebanon of North America, a Masonic organization.

BIBLIOGRAPHY

R. Hoe Jr., ed.: "Brief Biographies of Famous March Composers," *Journal of Band Research*, xv/2 (1980), 53

G.M. Meiser: "Monroe Althouse: Reading's 'March King'," *Reading Eagle* (3 Nov 1982); R: *Woodwind, Brass & Percussion*, xxiv/2 (1985), 19–20

W.H. Rehrig: *The Heritage Encyclopedia of Band Music* (Westerville, OH, 1991, suppl. 1996); CD-ROM (Oskaloosa, IA, 2005)

N.E. Smith: *Program Notes for Band* (Lake Charles, LA, 2000), 12–13

RAOUL F. CAMUS

Althouse, Paul (Shearer) (*b* Reading, PA, 2 Dec 1889; *d* New York, NY, 6 Feb 1954). Tenor. Educated at Bucknell University, he studied with P.D. Aldrich in Philadelphia and Oscar Saenger and P.R. Stevens in New York. The first American tenor without European experience to sing at the Metropolitan Opera, he made his debut there as Grigory in the American premiere of *Boris Godunov* under Toscanini (1913); between then and 1920 he participated in its first productions of Giordano's *Madame Sans-Gêne*, Herbert's *Madeleine*, De Koven's *Canterbury Pilgrims*, Cadman's *Shanewis*, and Breil's *The Legend*. His voice was described as a "lyric tenor of the more robust Italian type." During part of the 1920s he devoted himself exclusively to concerts, but after a visit to Bayreuth, he decided to retrain as a Heldentenor. In 1933 he sang Tristan in San Francisco, and returned to the Metropolitan as Siegmund, which he repeated in 1935 at Flagstad's debut. Until the 1939–40 season he shared the principal Wagner roles at the Metropolitan with Melchior. After a final appearance as Loge in 1941, he devoted himself to teaching; among his pupils were RICHARD TUCKER, ELEANOR STEBER, Léopold Simoneau, and IRENE DALIS.

BIBLIOGRAPHY

J.E. Heyl: *The Career and Teaching of Paul Althouse* (diss., University of Iowa, 1995)

PHILIP L. MILLER

Alton, Robert [Robert Alton Hart] (*b* Bennington, VT, 28 Jan 1897; *d* Los Angeles, PA, 12 June 1957). Choreographer and musical theater director. He fell in love with show business at an early age. When his hopes of becoming a circus contortionist were dashed by his parents, he began seriously studying dance and eventually made his professional début with Mikhail Mordkin's ballet company. He spent the early 1920s dancing in Broadway musicals and on the vaudeville stage in a duo act with his wife. When she left to have a baby, he began staging dance numbers for a St. Louis movie theater and teaching dance in a local school.

Alton's early success as a dance director led to a choreographic career that encompassed most of the major Broadway hits of the 1930s and 1940s. He learned stagecraft from working with innovative director John Murray Anderson and developed his instinctive musicality through collaborating with composers such as

Cole Porter and Richard Rodgers. He revolutionized Broadway show dancing by replacing the precision routines of the chorus line with dances for soloists and small groups, always elegantly staged and with unusual attention to stylistic details. Among the many shows for which he staged dances are *Anything Goes* (1934), *Leave It to Me* (1938), *Dubarry Was a Lady* (1939), *Panama Hattie* (1940), *Pal Joey* (1940), *By Jupiter* (1941), and *Laffing Room Only* (1944). He won a Tony award for directing a revival of *Pal Joey* in 1952.

In 1936 Samuel Goldwyn summoned Alton to Hollywood to stage the dances in *Strike Me Pink*, starring Eddie Cantor and Ethel Merman with music by Harold Arlen. Working with famed cinematographer Gregg Toland set Alton on a firm course as a director of movie musicals. His next film was *Two-Faced Woman* (1941), in which he appears as Greta Garbo's dance partner in a nightclub rumba. This was followed by many of the biggest hits of Hollywood's "golden age of the movie musical." Among them are *Till the Clouds Roll By* (1946), based on the life of composer Jerome Kern; *Good News* (1947), highlighted by June Allyson and Peter Lawford dancing "The Varsity Drag"; *Easter Parade* (1948), one of several collaborations with Fred Astaire; and *There's No Business Like Show Business* (1954), with Ethel Merman, again.

BIBLIOGRAPHY

J. Kobal: *Gotta Sing, Gotta Dance: a History of Movie Musicals* (New York, rev. 1983)

R. Kisland: *Hoofing on Broadway: a History of Show Dancing* (New York, 1987)

L. Billman: *Film Choreographers and Dance Directors* (Jefferson, NC, 1997)

CLAUDE CONYERS

Aluli, Irmgard Farden (*b* Lahaina, HI, 7 Oct, 1911; *d* Honolulu, HI, 4 Oct 2001). Hawaiian songwriter and performer. She was largely self-taught as a musician but was nurtured by a large family of active and well-known musicians. She played guitar, ukulele, bass, and piano. She began performing professionally while still a teenager, and continued playing and singing until near her death. She wrote her first songs in 1935 and composed her first hit, "Puamana," in 1937. The song recalls her childhood home in Lahaina on the island of Maui. Like many in her generation, she was not fluent in the Hawaiian language, and so collaborated with others to compose lyrics in Hawaiian. Her songs spoke of themes important in island life, such as family and place, and her repertoire also included religious and children's songs. Notable compositions include "E Maliu Mai," "The Boy from Laupahoehoe," and "Baby Kalai." Estimates of her output range from 100 to 400 songs, though she never maintained detailed records. Many of these have been recorded and performed by Hawaii's top artists.

She formed the group Puamana with her sister Diana and Thelma Anahu in the late 1960s. In later years, the group consisted of Aluli, two of her daughters, Mihana and Aima, and a niece, Luana. The quartet performed regularly at the Willows restaurant in Mo'ili'ili and on the mainland until the late 1990s, when Aluli retired from active performance. She won a composition award from the Hawaii Academy of Recording Arts (1986), as well as the Lifetime Achievement Award (1999). She was inducted into the Hawaiian Music Hall of Fame in 1998.

BIBLIOGRAPHY

"Aluli, Irmgard Keali'iwahinealohanohokahaopuamana Farden," *Hawaiian Music and Musicians: Illustrated History*, ed. G. Kanahele (Honolulu, 1979), 16–18

I. Aluli and A. Sinesky: *Irmgard Farden Aluli* (Honolulu, HI, 1987)

M.C. Richards: *Sweet Voices of Lahaina: Life Story of Maui's Fabulous Fardens* (Aiea, HI, 1990)

PAULA J. BISHOP

Álvarez, Luis Manuel (*b* Yabucoa, PR, 31 March 1939). Puerto Rican composer and guitarist. He studied guitar under Moisés Rodríguez and later received the BA from the University of Puerto Rico and the BM from the Puerto Rico Conservatory of Music. In 1970, he earned a master's degree in composition from Indiana University. He studied composition with Héctor Tosar, ROQUE CORDERO, JUAN ORREGO-SALAS, Bernard Hayden, Iannis Xenakis, and JOHN EATON. He teaches guitar and composition at the University of Puerto Rico at Río Piedras. His teaching also includes the production of radio and television programs. In addition, he investigates and publishes on Puerto Rican traditional music.

The music of Álvarez employs avant-garde techniques. In addition to an orchestra and narrator, his *La creación* (1974) exploits the use of electronic tape. In *Sueños de colores* (1975), he utilizes aleatoric (chance) procedures with soprano and traditional Puerto Rican instruments. He uses serial techniques for the construction of the melodies and two-part fugues in *Seis piezas breves* for flute and clarinet (1977). Beginning in 1975, he initiated an ongoing series of solo works for guitar as well as piano, which he refers to as *Alvaradas*, a term that combines his last name with the dawn song *alborada*.

BIBLIOGRAPHY

K. Degláns and L.E. Pabón Roca: *Catálogo de música clásica contemporánea de Puerto Rico* (Río Piedras, PR, 1989)

W. Ortiz: "A Panoramic View of Puerto Rican New Music," *New World Music Magazine* 6 (1996), 73–80

MARK E. PERRY

Amacher, Maryanne (*b* Kane, PA, 25 Feb 1938; *d* Rhinebeck, NY, 22 Oct 2009). Composer, performer, and multimedia artist. She studied composition with GEORGE ROCHBERG at the University of Pennsylvania (BFA 1964) and with Stockhausen. A concern for physical space pervades her music, best exemplified by three ongoing multimedia installation projects. In *City Links #1–22* (1967–), she transmits sounds picked up by microphones placed throughout a city to mixing facilities at a central location. The resulting sound collages are broadcast at "live" performances or over the radio. Locations for this project have included Boston, Chicago, New York, and, in the Netherlands, Groningen. In *Music for Sound-Joined Rooms* (1980–), careful loudspeaker placement within a multiroom space creates "structure-borne" sound that travels through walls and floors rather than through air. As the listener walks through a site, he or she experiences multiple sonic viewpoints arranged by Amacher to produce dramatic or narrative effects. The result is electronic music theater designed according to the architectural features of a particular building. In *Mini-Sound Series* (1985–), Amacher presents a chronological as well as a spatial sound-narrative that evolves at a site over a period of several days or weeks. Such installations have been created in galleries and halls throughout Europe, the United States, and Japan. She also collaborated with John Cage, providing sonic environments on electronic tape to accompany his readings (*Close-Up* for Cage's *Empty Words*, 1979). She composed similar works for Merce Cunningham's dance ensemble.

WORKS

Multimedia installations (all works in progress): City-Links nos.1–22, 1967–; Music for Sound-Joined Rooms, 1980–; Mini-Sound Series, 1985–

Dance scores (all choreog. M. Cunningham): Everything in Air, tape, 1974; Events 100, 101, tape, 1975; Labyrinth Gives Way to Skin, tape, 1975; Remainder, tape, 1976

Other works (for tape, unless otherwise stated): Presence, 1975; Music for Sweet Bird of Youth, 1976; Lecture on the Weather, 1976 [collab. J. Cage]; Empty Words/Close Up, 1979 [collab. Cage]; Petra, 2 pf, 1991

BIBLIOGRAPHY

T. Johnson: "Maryanne Amacher: Acoustics Joins Electronics," *Village Voice* (15 Dec 1975)

J. Rosen: "Composers Speaking for Themselves: An Electronic Music Panel Discussion," *The Musical Woman: an Interdisciplinary Perspective*, ii (1987), 280–312

L. Durner: "Maryanne Amacher: Architect of Aural Design," *Ear*, xiii/ Feb (1989), 28–34

G. Borchert: "American Women in Electronic Music, 1984–94," *CMR*, xvi/1–2 (1997), 89–97

GAVIN BORCHERT

Amato, Pasquale (*b* Naples, Italy, 21 March 1878; *d* Jackson Heights, NY, 12 Aug 1942). Italian baritone. He studied in Naples and made his debut there in 1900. Soon in much demand, he sang at Covent Garden (1904) and at La Scala under Toscanini (1907–8) before making his debut at the Metropolitan Opera as Germont in *La traviata* on 20 November 1908. He established himself quickly as an indispensable member of the New York company, and was on its roster for all but one season until 1921. He sang there all the principal roles of the Italian repertory, as well as Valentin (Gounod's *Faust*), Escamillo (*Carmen*), and many other parts in French, and Wagner's Kurwenal (*Tristan und Isolde*) and Amfortas (*Parsifal*) in German. Amato often sang with Caruso, notably in the role of Jack Rance in the premiere of Puccini's *La fanciulla del West* (1910). After his retirement from the Metropolitan, he made sporadic appearances with smaller opera companies elsewhere in the United States, then became a voice teacher at Louisiana State University as well as privately in New York. On the 25th anniversary of his Metropolitan debut he emerged from retirement to sing the same role (Germont) to an audience of 5000 at the New York Hippodrome.

Amato's voice was of splendid quality and extensive range, with brilliant resonance in the upper register. During his New York years he became an exceptionally reliable and complete artist, with impeccable enunciation, classical purity of style, and strong dramatic powers. These and other qualities, including pathos and humor, are best shown in a long series of admirable recordings made for Victor (1911–15), among which the *Pagliacci* Prologue, Figaro's "Largo al factotum," and several duets with Caruso, Gadski, and Hempel may be called exemplary.

BIBLIOGRAPHY

P. Kenyon and C. Williams: "Pasquale Amato," *Record Collector*, xxi (1973–4), 3–47 [with discography]

D. Ewen: *Musicians since 1900* (New York, 1978)

DESMOND SHAWE-TAYLOR/R

Amberg, Gustav (*b* Prague, Bohemia [now Czech Republic], 1844; *d* New York, NY, 22 May 1921). Theater manager and producer. He immigrated at the age of 20 to the United States, in the midst of the Civil War, and within two years was managing German-language theaters in Detroit and Cincinnati. In 1879, along with Mathilde Cottrelly and Heinrich Conried, Amberg refurbished the historic old Bowery Theatre in New York, renamed it the Thalia, and presented there what George C. Odell one historian has called "the most brilliant sequence of stars and plays ever given here in German" (*Annals of the New York Stage*, xiv, 319). Amberg made regular trips to Europe in the 1880s and early 1890s in search of the best actors and musicians. His theaters gave the American premieres of many contemporary Berlin and Viennese operettas and also presented such great German performers as Marie Geistinger, Antoine Janisch, Heinrich Bötel, Ernst Possart, and Gertrud Giers. In 1888 he built the Amberg Theatre (later the Irving Palace) on the Lower East Side of Manhattan, but a succession of poorly attended seasons cost him the house. His last active years were spent working for the Shuberts, studying the European market and procuring plays he thought suitable for the American market.

BIBLIOGRAPHY

Obituary, *New York Times* (24 May 1921)

H. Rothfuss: "Gustav Amberg, German-American Theater Promoter," *Monatshefte*, xliv/7 (1952), 357–65

J. Koegel: *Music in German Immigrant Theater: New York City, 1840–1940* (Rochester, NY, 2009)

BONNIE ELIZABETH FLEMING

Ambient music. Term associated with BRIAN ENO that describes a type of ENVIRONMENTAL MUSIC.

America. A national song of the United States, also known by the words of its first line, "My country, 'tis of thee"; *see* PATRIOTIC MUSIC.

Americana. *See* ALTERNATIVE COUNTRY.

American Academy in Rome [AAR]. Artists colony. The AAR was founded by Charles F. McKim in 1894 for architects and classicists. In 1920, the AAR added composers, urged by Edward MacDowell before his death and administered from 1920–40 by Felix Lamond. The AAR is modeled on the French Academy that awards the Prix de Rome (to Hector Berlioz and Claude Debussy, for example). The Rome Prize is awarded through a national juried competition. Winning Fellows, 30 American artists and scholars, are given a year in Rome supported by a stipend, room, board, travel expenses, and a studio at the 11-building complex atop the Janiculum hill. The Academy's mission is "to foster the pursuit of advanced research and independent study in the fine arts and humanities." Resident and Visiting Artists and Scholars also contribute to the interactive artists' colony atmosphere, which includes communal living, eating, and traveling, and twice weekly trips with AAR members lecturing on the history, archeology, or architectural or art history of various Roman, Vatican, and nearby sites.

The majority of music Fellows have had a profound impact on music life in the United States. Among them are, in chronological order: Leo Sowerby, Howard Hanson, Randall Thompson, Roger Sessions, Normand Lockwood, Werner Janssen, Hunter Johnson, Vittorio Giannini, Samuel Barber, Kent Kennan, David Diamond, Alexei Haieff, Andrew Imbrie, Jack Beeson, George Rochberg, Lucas Foss, Ulysses Kay, Elliott Carter, Yehudi Wyner, Salvatore Martirano, John Eaton, Leslie Bassett, Ezra Laderman, Stephen Albert, Richard Trythall, Morris Cotel, Barbara Kolb, Daniel Perlongo, Tison Street, George Edwards, Martin Bresnick, Chester Biscardi, Robert Beaser, Stephen Jaffe, Larry Bell, Tamar Diesendruck, Aaron Jay Kernis, Paul Moravec, Rand Steiger, Kamran Ince, Kathryn Alexander, Lee Hyla, David Lang, Stephen Hartke, Sebastian Currier, Nathan Currier, Christopher Theofanidis, Michael Hersch, Derek Bermel, Kevin Puts, Mason Bates, Harold Meltzer, Steven Burke, Susan Botti, Charles Mason, Andrew Norman, and Ken Ueno.

BIBLIOGRAPHY

L. Valentine and A. Valentine: *The American Academy in Rome: 1894–1969* (Charlottesville, VA, 1973)

B.G. Koh, W.A. Linker, and B.S. Kavelman, eds.: *The Centennial Directory of The American Academy in Rome* (New York and Rome, 1995)

M. Brody, ed.: *Music and Composition at the American Academy in Rome* (Rochester, NY, forthcoming)

American Academy in Rome, official website, <http://www.aarome.org>

ANDREA OLMSTEAD

American Academy of Arts and Letters. Organization of American writers, artists, architects, and composers. The National Institute of Arts and Letters, founded in 1898 by the American Social Sciences Association, formed the American Academy of Arts and Letters in 1904 to confer further distinction on 50 of its 250 members. In 1976 the two organizations merged under a single board of directors, although they continued to function as separate bodies. In 1993, the two organizations combined to form one organization of 250 members, called the American Academy of Arts and Letters. Its headquarters is in New York.

The Academy has encouraged the advancement of music in the United States by presenting concerts of American works and by giving financial assistance to composers through the administration of awards and prizes. Among the musicians elected to the academy have been John Adams, Samuel Barber, Leonard Bernstein, Cage, Elliott Carter, Copland, Henry Cowell, Ellington, Gideon, Charles Ives, Piston, Rochberg, Schuman, Sessions, Stravinsky, Thomson, Tower, and Zwilich. At an annual ceremony, new members are inducted, honorary membership is bestowed on foreign artists (such as Benjamin Britten and Pierre Boulez), and various awards are presented (*see* AWARDS). The institute's *Proceedings* (1909–) are published annually.

JOHN SHEPARD/R

American Academy of Music. One of the finest opera houses built in the United States in the 19th century; *see* PHILADELPHIA.

American Association for Music Therapy. *See* AMERICAN MUSIC THERAPY ASSOCIATION (AMTA).

American Ballet. Company derived from the School of American Ballet, which opened in New York City in January 1934. Directed by george Balanchine and supported by lincoln Kirstein and E.M.M. Warburg, the company was short-lived (1934–8).

CLAUDE CONYERS

American Ballet Company. Troupe founded by choreographer eliot Feld in New York City in 1969. After a debut season at the Festival of Two Worlds in Spoleto, Italy, and appearances in New York, the company was disbanded in 1971.

CLAUDE CONYERS

American Ballet Theatre [American Ballet Theater]. Company founded by Richard Pleasant in 1939, originally named Ballet Theatre. Under the direction of lucia Chase and designer Oliver Smith from 1945, the company built a large repertory of short ballets by leading choreographers, including some especially commissioned American works.

See also BALLET.

CLAUDE CONYERS

American Ballroom Theater Company. Theatrical ballroom dance company founded by Pierre Dulaine and Yvonne Marceau in New York City in 1984. The company was disbanded in 1989 when the founding directors joined the cast of the Broadway musical *Grand Hotel*.

CLAUDE CONYERS

American Bandmasters Association [ABA]. Professional organization founded in 1929 in New York by Edwin Franko Goldman (who also became its first president) and a group of eminent bandmasters from the United States and Canada. John Philip Sousa served as its first honorary life president. The objectives of the ABA are to honor (by invitation to membership) outstanding achievement in the area of the concert band and its music; to encourage prominent composers of all countries to write for the concert band; and by example and leadership to enhance the cultural standing of bands. Associate Membership may be attained by firms in the music industry or related fields who wish to identify themselves with the objectives and activities of the association. The association sponsors the Ostwald Band Composition Award, and has published the biannual *Journal of Band Research* since 1964. The American Bandmasters Association Foundation, affiliated with the ABA but not under its control, provides funds for the Ostwald Band Composition Award, commissions symphonic band music, and partially funds the ABA Research Center at the University of Maryland.

BIBLIOGRAPHY

P. Yoder: "The Early History of the American Bandmasters Association," *Journal of Band Research*, i/1 (1964), 1–9; i/2 (1965), 1–5; ii/1 (1966), 4–8; iii/1 (1966), 39–45

A.L. Davis: *A History of the American Bandmasters Association* (diss., Arizona State U., 1987)

RAOUL F. CAMUS

American Bandstand. Television program. *Bandstand* premiered in Philadelphia in September 1952, hosted by Bob Horn. DICK CLARK became host and producer in July 1956. The show achieved a nationwide audience when it was picked up by the American Broadcasting Company (ABC) and retitled *American Bandstand* in 1957. ABC moved it to Los Angeles in 1964 and carried the show until 1987. Syndicated broadcasts continued until September 1989.

American Bandstand, which featured teenagers dancing to the top rock and roll and rhythm and blues tunes of the day, brought popular music and dance into millions of households each weekday afternoon. In a popular feature called "Rate-a-Record," Clark often asked the participants to evaluate the songs, giving rise to the phrase "I'll give it a 95 because it has a great beat and it's easy to dance to." *American Bandstand* also included dance contests, and each program featured appearances by at least one popular musical act. The artists, who appeared, lip-synching to their latest hits, represented the most popular performers of the era. Although exclusively white in its early years, many of the artists popularized African American music and dance forms. For 37 years, teenagers watching the show absorbed a myriad of the latest dance crazes, including the twist, the locomotion, the stroll, the hustle, the mashed potato, the fish, the madison, disco, and the hand jive. Although virtually every urban area had an imitation show, including *Bandstand Matinee* (Chicago), *Time Out for Teens* (Madison City, Iowa), *Spotlight on Youth* (Los Angeles), and the all-black *Mitch Thomas Show* (Philadelphia), *American Bandstand* remains the program that set the standard.

BIBLIOGRAPHY

J. Jackson: *American Bandstand: Dick Clark and the Making of a Rock 'n' Roll Empire* (New York and Oxford, 1997)

J. Malnig: *Ballroom, Boogie, Shimmy Sham Shake: A Social and Popular Dance*, (Champaign, IL, 2009)

ELIZABETH ALDRICH

American Baroque. Instrumental ensemble. Founded in 1986 in San Francisco by Stephen Schultz (principal flutist with Philharmonia Baroque Orchestra and Musica Angelica), its members include Gonzalo X. Ruiz (oboe), Elizabeth Blumenstock (violin), Roy Whelden (viola da gamba), and Katherine Shao (harpsichord). The ensemble has performed in Europe and America, and been featured on National Public Radio. The group's repertory includes 18th-century music and new works by American composers. American Baroque has recorded 14 CDs, beginning with quartets by Telemann—the "Paris" and Fourth Book sets (Amon Ra, 1989/Koch, 1990). In 1991, the group issued *French Cantatas of the 18th Century*, with soprano Julianne Baird, also on Koch. *Galax* (New Albion, 1993) followed, with music by Whelden (*Quartet After Abel/Gamba Quartet*), and Carl Friedrich Abel. Another collaboration with Whelden yielded *Like a Passing River* (1995), featuring poet/reader Rudy Rucker, on the same label. After albums of sonatas by Boismortier and Telemann (Naxos 1995, 1998/Dorian 2000), American Baroque collaborated with Jonathan Berger on *Of Hammered Gold* (featuring digital bird organ), at Stanford (2000). The ensemble recorded eight pieces by the Common Sense Composers' Collective (*The Shock of the Old*, Santa Fe Music Group, 2001), and a theatrical/multimedia *The Death of Anton Webern*, with music by Whelden, and text and direction by Shao (*The Path to the New Music—Webern Album*, 2002). A CD of *Mozart Quartets* (Music and Arts) appeared in 2003, as did *Solace/Circa* on Belinda Reynolds' *Cover* (Innova) in 2006.

MARK ALBURGER

American Brass Quintet. Brass quintet, formed by trombonists Arnold Fromme and Gilbert Cohen in 1960; its present members are Kevin Cobb and Raymond Mase, trumpets; David Wakefield, horn; Michael Powell, tenor trombone; and John D. Rojak, bass trombone. The group gave its first public performance at the 92nd Street Y and made its official New York debut at Carnegie Recital Hall in 1962. At that time the brass quintet was little heard in the concert hall, and the ensemble played a major part in introducing audiences to brass instruments in the chamber context. Its commitment to the expansion of the brass chamber literature and its renowned virtuosity, precision, and stylistic accuracy have resulted in the composition of more than 100 new works by such composers as Bolcom, Carter, Thomson, Druckman, Ewazen, Plog, Sampson, Schuller, Schuman, Starer, and Tower. The group's concerts usually include premieres and the performance of "rediscovered" older pieces. The quintet has also explored performance practice on older instruments, and its many recordings include two of 19th-century American brass music played on period instruments. Since becoming the ensemble-in-residence at the Aspen Music Festival in 1970 and at Juilliard in 1987, the group has played a key role in training members of other prominent brass ensembles, including the Meridian Arts Ensemble, Manhattan Brass Quintet, and Urban Brass Quintet.

BIBLIOGRAPHY

M. Shakespeare: "The American Brass Quintet: Still Shining (from Sea to Sea) after Thirty Years," *Chamber Music* viii/1 (1983), 18–21

R. Darke: "The American Brass Quintet on Musical and Professional Accountability," *ITG Journal* xxxiv/2 (2010), 37–8

C. Lane: "The Commissioners," *Chamber Music* xxvii/6 (2010), 36–41

ELLEN HIGHSTEIN/NATHAN PLATTE

American Choral Directors Association [ACDA]. Professional organization founded in 1959. A group of 35 attendees at the biennial conference of the Music Teachers National Association in Kansas City, Missouri, formed this organization. A steering committee consisting of J. Clark Rhodes, Elwood Keister, Curt Hansen, Harry Robert Wilson, R. Wayne Hugoboom, Warner Imig, and Archie N. Jones created a working philosophy called the original ten purposes. The first purpose states: "To foster and promote choral singing which will provide artistic, cultural, and spiritual experiences for the participants." The first national convention, held the following year in Atlantic City, New Jersey, in conjunction with a convention of the Music Educators National Conference (MENC), featured five concerts, reading and interest sessions, and panel discussions, a model that continues to the present day. During its first decade the ACDA formed division and state chapters following the MENC model. R. Wayne Hugoboom was appointed the first executive secretary (1964) on a part-time basis, and the first national office was in his home in Tampa, Florida. The ACDA held its first independent division conventions in 1970, followed in 1971 by the first independent national convention in Kansas City, Missouri. After Hugoboom's death in 1977, Gene Brooks was appointed executive secretary and the national office was moved to Lawton, Oklahoma, where the McMahon Foundation funded construction of a modern facility on the campus of Cameron University (1979). The ACDA grew from 111 charter members to 10,000 members in 1978 and an all-time high of 21,000 members in 2003. In 2004 the ACDA moved its national office from Lawton to Oklahoma City, Oklahoma, again with the financial support of the McMahon Foundation.

Since its inception the ACDA has been involved with choral organizations worldwide by inviting outstanding international choirs to perform on national conventions, and it is a founding member of the International Federation for Choral Music (1982). The ACDA has established several awards to encourage excellence in choral music, notably: The Julius Herford Dissertation Award (1983), The Robert Shaw Award (1991), The Raymond W. Brock Choral Composition Commissions (1991), and undergraduate and graduate conducting awards. *The Choral Journal*, ACDA's peer-reviewed journal, started in 1959 as a newsletter and has been published continuously since. Gene Brooks died in 2007 after serving for 30 years as executive secretary, and was followed by Tim Sharp (2008). The 2009 ACDA biennial national convention in Oklahoma City commemorated the organization's 50th anniversary.

BIBLIOGRAPHY

N.R. De Journett: *The History and Development of the American Choral Directors Association, 1957–1970* (diss., Florida State U., 1970)

R. Mathis: "ACDA's Forty Year Journey," *Choral Journal*, xl/4 (1999), 9–25

C. Zamer: *Gene Brooks and His Contributions to the American Choral Directors Association* (diss., Florida State U., 2007)

J. Haberlen and R. Mathis: "The ACDA Presidency: a Snapshot," *Choral Journal*, xlix/7 (2009), 9–19

DEBRA L. SPURGEON

American Composers Alliance [ACA]. Organization of composers. It was founded in 1937 by Aaron Copland, Virgil Thomson, Wallingford Riegger, and others to promote the interests of American composers of serious concert music. The Composers Facsimile Edition was established for the ACA in 1952 by Roger Goeb to make copies of members' works more accessible in the interim between composition and publication, and the American Composers Edition was created in 1972 to publish members' compositions. Composers whose work is published by the ACA retain copyright of their work. By 2011 the catalog contained more than 12,000 titles. Approximately 9000 titles are on deposit at the American Composers Alliance Collection, Special Collections in Performing Arts (SCPA), University of Maryland in College Park, Maryland. As of 2011, roughly 3500 titles, primarily representing work by longtime custodial and active members, have been digitized; since 2008, active members have been depositing their work in PDF format. The organization draws on both the digital collection and printed masters held at SCPA for its print-on-demand service. There is also a collection of composer history files on more than 500 past and current members that, as of 2011, were being processed for research access at SCPA. Perusal copies of some smaller works, once held at the American Music Center (AMC), are now part of the non-circulating AMC collection at the New York Public Library. The ACA founded the record label Composers Recordings, Inc. in 1954 and the American Composers Orchestra in 1977, though both organizations became independent entities shortly after their inception. The ACA was associated with BMI as early as 1944, and became an official publisher-affiliate in 1972. The *American Composers Alliance Bulletin* was published in 1938 and again between 1952 and 1965. The ACA's Laurel Leaf Award (since 1951) recognizes achievement in the encouragement of American music, while Friends of American Composers, an offshoot of the ACA, promoted outreach programs. The ACA became a nonprofit corporation in 2007, and had approximately 160 members in 2011.

BIBLIOGRAPHY

ACAB, xi/2–4 (1963) [25th anniversary issue]

F. Thorne: "The ACA Story," *BMI: the Many Worlds of Music* (1984), no.1, 32–3

E. Good: "'The Composers Organize': Fifty Years of the American Composers Alliance," *Institute for Studies in American Music: Newsletter*, xvii/1 (1987–8), 1–2, 15

S. Neff: "Some Comments for the Fiftieth Anniversary of the American Composers Alliance," *Sonneck Society Bulletin*, xiv (1988), 121–5

S. Richardson: *Defining a Place for Composers: the Early Histories of the American Composers Alliance and the American Music Center, 1937–1950* (diss., Indiana U., 1997)

RITA H. MEAD/FRANCES BARULICH/MICHAEL BOYD

American Composers' Concerts. Concerts consisting exclusively of works by American composers. The practice of promoting American composers by segregating their music has recurred often since the middle of the 19th century and was especially in vogue in the late 1880s, during World War II, and in the years around the Bicentennial of American independence in 1976.

1. The 19th century. The American Music Association was founded in 1855 by C.J. Hopkins to counter the assertion that American composers had not written enough compositions to present an entire concert. It presented ten concerts of works by native composers and resident foreigners in three seasons before succumbing to the financial panic of 1857. In May 1877, Russian pianist Annette Essipoff performed American Composers' Concerts in Boston and New York on stages decked with red, white and blue.

The fad for American Composers' Concerts in the 1880s was a reaction to inequities in the copyright laws of the era. Because the United States did not have an international copyright agreement, publishers could reprint foreign works without paying royalties. Even the best American composers—who were entitled to royalties—found it difficult to compete against cheaply produced foreign compositions flooding the American market. In addition to lobbying for copyright protection, composers and performers were determined to introduce their works to the public through performances.

At the 1884 convention of the Music Teachers' National Association (MTNA), pianist Calixa Lavallée presented a concert of works by 15 American composers. The event touched a chord with the leadership of the organization, and at the next six annual conferences, the MTNA presented increasingly more lavish concerts of American orchestral and choral works. These concerts became the primary focus of the organization, and their exorbitant costs nearly bankrupted the association. Many of the state MTAs also staged such concerts, notably the Ohio MTA and the Illinois MTA, both of which presented annual concerts featuring composers from their respective states.

Other organizations followed suit, with amateur and professional groups eager to show their solidarity with the movement. Among the noteworthy series of concerts were five concerts by Lavallée in Boston in 1885 and 1886, and a festival of five concerts presented by Frank Van der Stucken in New York's Chickering Hall in November 1887. American Composers' Concerts in Paris (Frank Van der Stucken in conjunction with the Exposition Universelle, 1889) and various German cities (Franz Xavier Arens, 1891 and 1892) were met with mixed reviews from European critics. Theodore Thomas planned to include an ambitious series of American Composers' Concerts in his programs for the World's Columbian Exposition (Chicago World's Fair) in 1893, but he resigned midway through the season, leaving the official music program in disarray.

An important result of the movement was the formation of Manuscript Societies in Boston, New York, Chicago, and Philadelphia. These organizations were founded and run by composers in order to hear unpublished works by members. The Manuscript Society of New York and the Manuscript Society of Chicago were particularly active throughout the 1890s, presenting American Composers' Concerts after other organizations had abandoned the practice.

In 1888, composer Wilson G. Smith characterized the movement with the statement, "A tidal wave of encouragement is sweeping over the land, and will assuredly bear upon its crest some native talent capable of and anxious to do honor to his profession and native land." Only two years later, Henry Krehbiel opined, "The American composer...after long suffering neglect, now seems to be in imminent danger of being coddled to death." The demise of the vogue is attributable in part to an overabundance of such concerts and in part to the adoption of an international copyright law in 1891. Also significant was the opposition of Edward MacDowell, who believed they were detrimental to unbiased assessment of American music.

2. After 1900. In the early years of the new century, attention shifted away from American concerts (termed conceptual Americanism by Barbara Zuck) to the use of American thematic elements in composition (compositional Americanism). Both the Indianist movement spearheaded by Arthur Farwell and the growth of art music based on African American styles reflected this new direction. The search for stylistic Americanism is perhaps best exemplified by the vigorous efforts of Aaron Copland, Roy Harris, and others to create a body of art music based on American folk elements in the 1930s and 1940s.

Conceptual Americanism did not die, however, as individuals and organizations periodically strove to support the cause of American music through American Composers' Concerts. The American Music Society was founded by Farwell and Henry Gilbert in 1905, expanding to stage American Composers' Concerts at 20 centers nationwide by 1910. The American music guild (1921–4) promoted the cause of serious American music by presenting concerts in New York. Howard Hanson presented American Composers' Concerts at the Eastman School of Music from 1925 to 1971, premiering numerous works by contemporary American composers. The American composers alliance, founded in 1938 by Copland, Virgil Thomson, and Wallingford Riegger, sought to promote the interests of American composers through performances and facsimile publications of new works. The American music center, founded in 1940 by composers Copland, Hanson, Marion Bauer, Otto Luening, and Quincy Porter to encourage the creation, performance, publication, and distribution of American music, was named the official American music information center by the National Music Council in 1947. All of these organizations pursued a similar strategy to their 19th-century predecessors by using the tool of all-American concerts to promote the cause of American music.

The 20th century also spawned new means of promoting American music, notably through series of publications (such as Farwell's Wa-Wan Press, 1901–12, and the Society for the Publication of American Music, 1919–69) and recordings (such as New World Records, which released over 100 recordings of American music for free distribution after its founding in 1975 with the support of a Rockefeller Foundation grant, and has subsequently brought the total to over 400 recordings). A scholarly society devoted exclusively to the study of American music was the Sonneck Society, founded in 1975 to serve as a corrective to Eurocentric music scholarship and renamed the SOCIETY FOR AMERICAN MUSIC in 1999. The journal, bulletin, and annual conferences of this organization are dedicated to the study, performance, and dissemination of American music and music in America, the definitions of which have been broadened since the organization's founding.

BIBLIOGRAPHY

W. G. Smith: "American Compositions in the Class and Concert Room," *The Etude*, vi/8 (1888), 129

H.E. Krehbiel: "The Manuscript Society," *New York Daily Tribune* (12 Dec 1890)

S.N. Penfield: *Historical Handbook of the Music Teachers' National Association, 1876–1893* (n.p., [1893])

S. Salter: "Early Encouragements to American Composers," *MQ*, xviii (1932), 76–105

V.B. Lawrence, ed.: *The Wa-Wan Press, 1901–1911* (New York, 1970)

M.M. Lowens: *The New York Years of Edward MacDowell* (diss., U of Michigan, 1971)

W.M. Holman: *A History of the Society for the Publication of American Music, 1919–1969* (diss., U. of Iowa, 1977)

B. Zuck: *A History of Musical Americanism* (Ann Arbor, MI, 1980)

E.D. Bomberger: *"A Tidal Wave of Encouragement": American Composers' Concerts in the Gilded Age* (Westport, CT, 2002)

A.S. Kalyn: *Constructing a Nation's Music: Howard Hanson's American Composers' Concerts and Festivals of American Music, 1925–1971* (diss., Eastman School of Music, U. of Rochester, 2002)

E. DOUGLAS BOMBERGER

American Composers Orchestra. American orchestra. Founded in 1977 by composer FRANCIS THORNE and conductor DENNIS RUSSELL DAVIES, the American Composers Orchestra is devoted exclusively to performing and promoting 20th- and 21st-century American music. Based in New York City, it maintains a subscription series at Carnegie Hall. Its artistic leadership results from a collaboration of composers and conductors. As of the 2010–11 season, the leadership included composers Robert Beasor and Derek Bermel, founding conductor Davies (1977–2002), his successor Steven Sloane (2002–06), and the orchestra's third conductor, George Manahan (2010–). Distinguished by ASCAP as "the orchestra that has done the most for new American music in the United States," the American Composers Orchestra has sought to link the American past and present by regularly commissioning new works, reviving neglected repertory and programming forgotten classics. By 2010 it had performed the work of more than 600 American composers. It had also commissioned more works by American composers than any other orchestra in the world, including the first orchestral commissions of Ellen Taaffe Zwilich and Joseph Schwantner, both of which won the Pulitzer Prize. Through a number of innovative programs over the years, the orchestra has helped identify and support the creativity of emerging composers, provided opportunities for audiences to hear cutting-edge orchestral music, encouraged the continual redefinition of American concert music through experimentation—most recently with new technology, multimedia, and multidisciplinary collaborations—and investigated influences, such as the music of Latin America, on the soundscape of the 20th and 21st centuries. To date, the orchestra has issued more than 20 recordings, including the music of Cage, Elliott Carter, Lou Harrison, McPhee, and Sessions. Recordings of select live programs can be heard free of charge through the Internet. Since its founding, the American Composers Orchestra has maintained an eclectic aesthetic and given some of the best performances of contemporary American orchestral music in New York City.

BIBLIOGRAPHY

R.M. Braun: "Presenting an Orchestra for the American Composer," *New York Times* (4 Dec 1977)

F. Thorne: "An Orchestra is Born: the Story of the American Composers Orchestra," *A Celebration of American Music: Words and Music in Honor of H. Wiley Hitchcock*, ed. R.A. Crawford and others (Ann Arbor, 1990), 487–91

M. Kriesberg: "When Composers Take Control of the Orchestra," *New York Times* (14 April 2002)

A. Tommasini: "An Anniversary with a Forward Look," *New York Times* (28 March 2007)

LEON BOTSTEIN

American Conservatory of Music. Conservatory founded in Chicago in 1886. *See* CHICAGO (i).

American Contemporary Music Ensemble [ACME]. Ensemble founded in 2004 by the cellist Clarice Jensen, the conductor Donato Cabrera, and the manager Christina Jensen. Cabrera left in 2005 for a post with the San Francisco Opera. The group made its debut on 7 November 2004, at the Tenri Cultural Institute in New York. In 2008 ACME performed a month-long residency at the Whitney Museum of American Art, New York, and in March 2009 it appeared at Carnegie Hall for the first time, performing the premiere of Timothy Andres's *Senior* with the New York Youth SO. The following year the ensemble toured with the pianist Simone Dinnerstein playing chamber arrangements of J.S. Bach's keyboard concertos BWV 1052 and 1056, and participated in Louis Andriessen's Carnegie Hall residency. It has also programmed and presented Composer Portraits at the Miller Theater, Columbia University. Through 2010, ACME had given 75 public concerts, performing music by John Adams, John Cage, Elliott Carter, George Crumb, Charles Ives, Phil Kline, Steve Reich, Neil Rolnick, Frederic Rzewski, Arnold Schoenberg, Toru Takemitsu, Kevin Volans, and Iannis Xenakis. The group's repertoire, which also includes music by Henryk Górecki and John Luther Adams, suits their musical artistry, precision, and flexibility; this last enables them to break down into a separate, highly capable string quartet. Members through 2010 have included the violinists

Miranda Cuckson, Ben Russell, and Caleb Burhans, the viola player Nadia Sirota, and the pianist Eric Huebner. ACME has collaborated with musicians in various genres, including the pop group Grizzly Bear, the electronica duo Matmos, the composer Jefferson Friedman and the rock singer Craig Wedren (the song cycle *On in Love*), and the composer–performers Jóhann Jóhannsson and Max Richter.

GEORGE J. GRELLA JR.

American Dance Festival. American dance organization. The American Dance Festival is a nonprofit organization, based in Durham, North Carolina, committed to serving the needs of dance, dancers, and choreographers, and professionals in dance-related fields. Its mission is to present dance works, assist in the creation of new works, preserve the heritage of modern dance, build wider audiences and enhance the appreciation and understanding of dance, and provide training and education for dancers and choreographers. Each summer, it presents a six and a half week festival of modern dance performances, classes, workshops, and a variety of community programs. Additional year round programming includes educational and professional programs, national and international projects, humanities and media projects, and community outreach.

The American Dance Festival traces its origins to the Bennington School of Dance, founded in 1934 in Bennington, Vermont by several notable figures in the emerging art of modern dance: Martha Graham, Hanya Holm, Doris Humphrey, and Charles Weidman. The school, led by Martha Hill, allowed choreographers to experiment and teach dance techniques. A performance series, held in conjunction with the school, provided the choreographers with opportunities to present their newly created works. For one season, in 1939, the festival was held at Mills College in Oakland, California, but returned to Bennington the following year. Beginning in 1947, the festival was held at Connecticut College, and in 1977, the decision was made to move it to Duke University in Durham, North Carolina.

Courses of instruction in modern dance and performances by professional dance companies have remained at the heart of the festival. The school's curriculum includes, among others, classes in modern, jazz, and ballet techniques, composition, improvisation, repertory, voice and gesture, dance videography, and African dance. Notable attendees of the school include choreographers Anna Halprin, Merce Cunningham, Alwin Nikolais, Paul Taylor, Lar Lubovitch, Lucinda Childs, Martha Clarke, Meredith Monk, Trisha Brown, Doug Varone, and lighting designer Jennifer Tipton.

Performances at the American Dance Festival have included nearly every notable choreographer and performing company since the advent of modern dance. Perhaps its greatest value to the world of dance is the critical role it has played in increasing the repertoires of American modern dance companies. The ADF has been the site of over 600 premieres, with more than half of those being commissioned by the organization.

DEAN JEFFREY

American Federation of Musicians. Trade union founded in 1896 for professional musicians. Membership was extended to Canadian musicians in 1900, when "of the United States and Canada" was added to its title. Affiliated with the AFL-CIO in the United States and with the Central Labor Council in Canada, in 1996 it had 130,000 members in 300 local affiliates, which have jurisdiction over local areas of employment, while the international union has exclusive jurisdiction over recordings, film, and network broadcasting. The history of the organization is extensive, with changes in policies reflecting the needs of AFM's members. Especially important have been issues involving venues, performance techniques, and technology. In the 1980s, for example, the advent of music video required new rules governing musician's rights. Music for videogames became a focus in 2007, when the organization pressed the industry to allow for a stronger presence of AFM musicians. Concerns with piracy and audio downloading were major issues in 2009. Advocacy, lobbying, and a close relationship with the business side of the music industry have all been important activities of the union. A highlight of the organization's activities in the 21st century was the creation of the Musician's Disaster Relief Fund (a response to Hurricane Katrina) in 2005. The federation publishes the *International Musician* (1901–), which appears monthly.

BIBLIOGRAPHY

G. Seltzer: *Music Matters: The Performer and the American Federation of Musicians* (Metuchen, NJ, 1989)

RITA H. MEAD/JONAS WESTOVER

American Festival of Microtonal Music [AFMM]. Founded in 1981 by New York-based composer, theorist, bassoonist, and author Johnny Reinhard (*b* 1956), the American Festival of Microtonal Music, otherwise referred to as AFMM (<http://www.afmm.org>) provides an international forum for composers, theorists, and performers whose work is concerned with just intonation and microtonality. Originally founded as an outlet for Reinhard's in-depth studies in microtonality, the AFMM has gone on to produce an ongoing concert series that presents a vast array of music from contemporary composers. Programming has broadened to include works of composers such as Partch, Cage, Varèse, and Charles Ives. The AFMM also presents works of J.S. Bach, Andreas Werckmeister and others performed in historical tunings and temperaments. The AFMM has produced many significant and successful premieres including a realization of Ives's *Universe Symphony* (1996). Their concerts have featured solo and chamber works, including the loosely connected American Festival of Microtonal Music ensemble. The AFMM has archived these concerts since around 1985. Additionally, it has produced lectures on topics ranging from historical temperaments through modern uses of microtonality. The AFMM is the publisher of *PITCH For The International Microtonalist*, a four-issue publication (1986–90) that serves as a resource for information, fingering charts, and tuning tables related to microtonality. *PITCH*

(<http://pitch.xentonic.org>) has expanded to produce and release recordings of varied music, early through contemporary, all microtonal in nature.

See also TUNING SYSTEMS.

PAUL R. WEST

American Folklife Center. Government agency and archive. The American Folklife Center at the LIBRARY OF CONGRESS was created by the US Congress in 1976 to "preserve and present American Folklife," the first time US federal law mandated the conservation of folk culture. The Center soon acquired the Archive of Folk Culture, which had been established by the Library of Congress's music division in 1928. Through the efforts of such leaders as Robert W. Gordon, John Lomax, Alan Lomax, and Joe Hickerson, the archive had acquired thousands of hours of field recordings, and provided access to them in a public reading room as well as through books and record albums. By 1978, when it became part of AFC, it was already the largest ethnographic archive in the United States, as well as the source for many popular pieces of music, including Aaron Copland's *Hoedown*, Johnny Cash's "Rock Island Line," and the Kingston Trio's "Tom Dooley."

ALAN JABBOUR, the AFC's first director, focused on field collecting, and published the results on LP records and CDs. In 1999, Peggy A. Bulger succeeded Jabbour. AFC shifted focus to the acquisition of existing field collections, including institutional collections from organizations such as the National Council for Traditional Arts, private collections from folk music luminaries such as Jean Ritchie, and the massive Alan Lomax Collection, containing more than ten thousand hours of sound recordings and more than ten thousand other documents. AFC's activities also include regular concerts, lectures, and symposia, an extensive website with rich musical collections freely available online, and a publications program including a quarterly newsletter. AFC is also a significant oral history archive, including the Veterans History Project and the Civil Rights History Project among its congressionally mandated activities.

STEPHEN D. WINICK

American Guild of Musical Artists [AGMA]. Labor guild affiliated with the Associated Actors and Artistes of America and the AFL-CIO, serving the interests of concert and opera soloists, as well as members of opera and ballet companies.

Lawrence Tibbett, Jascha Heifetz, and Efrem Zimbalist founded the American Guild of Musical Artists, Inc. on 11 March 1936 to protect the interests of artists who made their living on the stage. As originally conceived, the guild represented two groups: instrumentalists and vocalists who appeared in recital or concert accompanied by a pianist or orchestra, and vocalists who performed solo operatic roles. The guild restricted its sphere of influence to opera companies operating within the United States.

By 1941 the group had merged with the Grand Opera Artists Association and the Grand Opera Choral Alliance. They then began negotiating bargaining agreements with all major companies including the Metropolitan Opera. The guild also organized the previously un-represented ballet artists and members of independent choral organizations. During this time instrumental performers were subsumed into the AMERICAN FEDERATION OF MUSICIANS.

Throughout its history the guild has served its members not only through its negotiations, but also through lobbying activities aimed at increasing federal support for the arts. AGMA membership now includes singers and dancers from the major opera houses and ballet companies, as well as production personnel. The national office administers collective bargaining agreements with companies across the United States, provides relief benefits for its members and represents its members in disputes with employers. Guild records are held in the Robert F. Wagner Labor Archives, Tamiment Library, New York University.

KAREN M. BRYAN

American Guild of Organists. An educational and service organization for organists, clergy, and choral conductors. The guild was founded in New York in 1896 by over 100 of the leading organists and clergy, including John Knowles Paine and George Chadwick, and chartered by the New York State Board of Regents. Dudley Buck served as the first honorary president. Its goals are to promote the organ, encourage excellence in the performance of organ and choral music, to support education and certification of Guild members, and to set and maintain standards of artistic excellence among its members. The Guild sponsors competitions in organ performance, improvisation, and in organ and choral composition, as well as national and regional conventions. The Guild also conducts examinations in organ playing and choir training, awarding successful candidates certificates and designating them as fellows, associates, or choirmasters. Monthly since 1967 it has published the *American Organist*, the most widely read journal devoted to organ and choral music in the world. With some 20,000 members in 322 chapters in all 50 states, Panama, and Europe, the Guild is one of the world's largest organizations of musicians specializing in a single instrument.

BIBLIOGRAPHY

"The AGO Chronicles 1896" *The American Organist*, xxix (1995), no.1, pp.74–75; no.2, pp.79–80; no.3, pp.84–7; no.4, pp.80–88

RITA H. MEAD/N. LEE ORR

American Harp Society. Organization founded in New York in 1962. Its archetype was the National Association of Harpists (established in 1919 by William Place Jr.), active between 1920 and 1933 under president Carlos Salzedo. During the interim between its dissolution and the founding of the American Harp Society, the Northern California Harpists Association (which evolved from the Northern California Chapter of the National Association of Harpists) published *Harp News* (1950–66), an immediate forerunner to the American Harp Society's*American Harp Journal* (since 1967). Under Marcel Grandjany, chairman of the founding committee, the American Harp Society (<http://www.harpsociety.org/>) was established to function as a clearinghouse for information related to the harp. Its stated mission is "to foster the appreciation of the harp as a musical instrument, to encourage the composition of music for the harp and to improve the quality of performance of harpists." The society has over 3000 members from all 50 states and 20 countries. Membership elects a board to oversee its activities: including a biennial national conference (concerts, lectures and workshops combined with a general meeting), a biennial Summer Institute (with biennial AHS National and Lyon & Healy Awards Competitions), administration of the Concert Artist Program, and an endowment fund to support conferences, competitions, institutes, harp literature, education programs, audiovisual, and archives/research collections. A separate support organization, the AHS Foundation (established in 1993), houses donations held for specific educational projects and funds. The society has a harp repository at the Library of Congress (since 1980) and AHS Archives (1997–) at Brigham Young University.

BIBLIOGRAPHY

"The AHS Collection," *American Harp Journal*, xvi/4 (1998), 41–6

R. Rensch: *Harps and Harpists* (Bloomington, IN, 1989, rev. and expanded 2/2007)

MARTHA WOODWARD/SUZANNE L. MOULTON-GERTIG

American Idol. Television show. Developed by the music executive Simon Fuller of 19 Entertainment, *American Idol* is one of more than 40 "Idol" programs that have been televised around the world, each designed for a particular nation or region. The show was first broadcast on British television as *Pop Idol* in 2001, before airing in the United States on the Fox Network the following year. *American Idol* itself has been broadcast in more than half of all sovereign states.

Its format draws on forerunners including *Major Bowes' Amateur Hour*, *Star Search*, *Popstars*, and *The Eurovision Song Contest* and invites viewers to vote, typically by telephone or text message, in the election of a new pop star. Candidates vying for a recording contract are chosen by producers through a series of open auditions. When the voting episodes begin, contestants' live weekly performances are critiqued by a panel of judges. Simon Cowell, Randy Jackson, and Paula Abdul served as the initial panel of judges for *American Idol* in 2002. Kara DioGuardi judged in 2009 and 2010, and Ellen DeGeneres replaced Abdul in 2010. Changes in late 2010 resulted in a new panel comprising Jackson, Jennifer Lopez, and Steven Tyler. Further changes were announced in 2012. Ryan Seacrest has hosted the show solo since 2003.

American Idol debuted on the Fox Network on 11 June 2002, exactly nine months after 9/11, during a period of crisis when the familiar American dream narratives, American identities, and music performed on the show found an especially eager audience. Contestants were required to perform in a range of commercial genres from big band to disco to 21st-century chart-toppers. An emphasis in the show's early years on classic soul yielded to the promotion of country, rock, and alternative genres in later seasons. *American Idol* has also featured guest judges or mentors, including Ashford and Simpson, Randy Travis, and Harry Connick Jr., who have often corresponded with a designated theme, such as Motown, Grand Ole Opry, or Frank Sinatra songs. Later seasons have also included performances by established artists promoting their own work. The show has also presented backstage footage, interviews, and short biographical segments characteristic of reality television.

While its total impact on the US entertainment industry has yet been calculated, *American Idol* has produced several commercial and Broadway stars—although not all of them have won the title—and popularized the idea of the public vote as an application of consumer choice. Despite slowly slipping ratings and the frequent criticism of Cowell's harsh judgments, the broadcast humiliation of auditioning hopefuls, and the melismatic style of vocals favored by many contestants, *American Idol* achieved network television's highest viewership and continued to do so into the 2010s.

BIBLIOGRAPHY

S. Holmes: "'Reality Goes Pop!' Reality TV, Popular Music, and Narratives of Stardom in *Pop Idol*," *Television & News Media*, v (2004), 147–72

M. Stahl: "A Moment like This:*American Idol* and Narratives of Meritocracy," *Bad Music*, ed. C. Washburne and M. Derno (London, 2004), 212–32

H. Jenkins: "Buying into *American Idol*: How we are being Sold on Reality Television," *Convergence Culture: Where Old and New Media Collide* (New York, 2006)

K. Meizel: *Idolized: Music, Media, and Identity in* American Idol (Bloomington, 2010)

KATHERINE MEIZEL

American Indian Dance Theatre. Dance company. It was co-founded in 1987 in Colorado Springs by Kiowa/Delaware playwright, director and educator Hanay Geiogamah and New York concert and theatrical producer Barbara Schwei. The first professional all-Native American company of dancers, singers and musicians, it comprises roughly 20 members drawn from tribes across the United States and Canada. It has presented various styles of Native American and First Nations dancing—including the Zuñi Buffalo Dance, Eagle Dance, and Apache Crown Dance—without altering the basic structure of the dances. It has performed in all 50 states and has toured Europe, North Africa, the Middle East, and Australia. The troupe has also performed on television specials, in documentaries, at the Gathering of the Tribes music festivals held in Los Angeles and San Francisco, and as part of Ban the Dam Jam in New York City. Through benefit performances it has supported Native community agencies and foundations such as the American Indian College Fund and the American Indian Culture Center and Museum in San Diego. In 2006 it joined the "Cultural Roundtable," a multicultural consortium at the Los Angeles Theatre Center.

BIBLIOGRAPHY

S. Malinowski and S. Glickman, eds.: "Hanay Geiogamah," *Native North American Biography* (Detroit, MI, 1996), 140–43

H. Geiogamah: "American Indian Tribes in the Media Age," *The Native North American Almanac*, ed. D. Champagne (Farmington Hills, MI, 2/2001), 859–63

PAULA J. CONLON

American Indians. *See* NATIVE AMERICAN MUSIC.

American Musical Fund Society. Benevolent organization for musicians, founded in Philadelphia in 1849; *see* UNIONS, MUSICIANS'.

American Musical Instrument Society. Organization founded in New York in 1971 "to promote study of the history, design, and use of musical instruments in all cultures and from all periods." In 2011 it had some 500 members, including museum curators, collectors, performers, instrument makers, scholars, and institutions, both in the United States and abroad. The society holds annual meetings devoted to performances, panel discussions, the presentation of papers, and visits to collections. It awards subventions and annual prizes for research that furthers the society's goals: these include the Curt Sachs Award (for lifetime achievement), the Frances Densmore Prize (for the most significant article in English), and the Nicholas Bessaraboff Prize (for the most distinguished book-length work in English). Its *Journal* (published annually since 1974) and *Newsletter* (three per year from 1971, biannually since 2009) contain articles, reviews, bibliographies, acquisition lists, and news of interest to members. The Society also sponsors occasional publications. It maintains a website (http://www.amis.org) with information on its activities and links to other sites of interest. An account of the society's first ten years appears in Carolyn Bryant, " 'In the Beginning': the Early Days of the American Musical Instrument Society," *JAMIS*, xxxiii (2007), 162–239.

JOHN SHEPARD/JANET K. PAGE

American Music Center. Organization founded in 1939 by composers Marion Bauer, Aaron Copland, Howard Hanson, Otto Luening, Quincy Porter, and Harrison Kerr. By bringing together composers, performers, and presenting organizations, AMC (<http://www.amc.net/>) encourages the creation, performance, publication and distribution of new American music. In 1947 it was named the official American music information center by the National Music Council. During the 1970s MEET THE COMPOSER, a funding program for composers, was based at AMC. In May 1999 with American composer Frank J. Oteri as its editor, AMC started its online magazine, NewMusicBox (<http://www.newmusicbox.org/>), which promotes the music of American composers through articles, detailed profiles, and news. In 2001 AMC transferred its previously circulating library of scores and tapes to the New York Public Library for the Performing Arts; the following year it introduced an extensive and searchable database, now called AMC Online Library, containing 50,000 works by more than 6000 American composers. AMC Online Library includes detailed information about contemporary American repertoire and access to hundreds of scores and streaming audio samples. In March 2007 AMC launched Counterstream, an internet radio station directed by Molly Sheridan, which provides access to AMC's extensive library of recorded American music. Since 1964, AMC has issued annual Letters of Distinction to a person or organization that has made a significant contribution to American music. Over the years recipients have included Virgil Thomson, American Composers Orchestra, Milton Babbitt, Chanticleer, Oral History of American Music at Yale University (Vivian Perlis), and Meredith Monk. Other awards presented by AMC include the Founders Awards, Trailblazers Awards, and Educator's Awards. In addition, AMC administers three grant programs: Composers Assistance Program, Live Music for Dance Program, and the CAP Recording Grant. In 2010 AMC had nearly 2400 members in the United States and other countries. In April 2011, AMC and Meet the Composer announced their decision to merge into a new advocacy and service organization, NEW MUSIC USA. Under the leadership of Ed Harsh, current president of Meet the Composer, the focus of the new organization will be grant making and media programs.

MARGARET F. JORY/ANNA E. KIJAS

American Music Guild. Organization formed in New York in 1921 to encourage serious efforts in composition by American composers. Its founding members, Marion Bauer, Louis Gruenberg, Sandor Harmati, Charles Haubiel, Frederick Jacobi, A. Walter Kramer, Harold Morris, Albert Stoessel, and Deems Taylor, first met informally to listen to each other's works and offer criticism. From 1922 until 1924 they presented public and private concerts, performing their own works as well as those of Carpenter, Griffes, Loeffler, Daniel Gregory Mason, John Powell, Sowerby, and others.

BIBLIOGRAPHY

C.D. McNaughton: *Albert Stoessel, American Musician* (diss., New York U., 1957) [contains list of programs given by the guild]

C.J. Oja: *Making Music Modern: New York in the 1920s* (New York, 2000)

A.M. Lien: *Against the Grain: Modernism and the American Art Song, 1900–1950* (diss., U. of California, Davis, 2002)

R. ALLEN LOTT/R

American Musicological Society. Academic society founded in 1934 to advance scholarly research in the various fields of music as a branch of learning and scholarship. The genesis of the American Musicological Society (AMS) may be traced to the rise of musicology as a scholarly discipline. European societies with similar aims, as well as American societies for other scholarly disciplines, provided ample exemplars: the Royal Musical Association (1874; Great Britain), the Internationale Musikgesellschaft (1899), and the Société Française de Musicologie (1917; France) laid foundations for the discipline of musicology in the first decades of the 20th century, and the American Council of Learned Societies (ACLS), a federation of 13 organizations, was formed in 1919. A group of American musicologists led by Oscar Sonneck, Music Division chief at the Library of Congress, formed the American Section of the Internationale Musikgesellschaft in 1907. It grew to nearly a hundred members by 1911, but World War I led to the demise of both the parent and child organizations. This notwithstanding, *The Musical Quarterly*, the first journal published in America to contain significant musicological research, was established (with Sonneck as its editor) in 1915. In the 1920s, musicologists gathered regularly at meetings of the Music Teachers National Association, and in 1929 the ACLS sponsored an exploratory Committee on Musicology under the direction of Oliver Strunk. In the early 1930s a group of scholars formed the New York Musicological Society, with the express wish that it serve as the nucleus of a national society. On 3 June 1934, George Dickinson, Carl Engel, Gustave Reese, Helen Heffron Roberts, Joseph Schillinger, Charles Louis Seeger, Harold Spivacke, Oliver Strunk, and Joseph Yasser met in New York, disbanded the New York Musicological Society, and formed the "American Musicological Association," nominating as its first president Otto Kinkeldey. A constitution and bylaws were prepared by the end of the year, at which time its current name was established.

Unlike its European counterparts, however, the AMS did not at first pursue the history of music in its homeland, but rather oriented itself to a broad spectrum of musical studies: in addition to historical research in European music, papers on acoustics, ethnomusicology, systematic musicology, bibliography, theory, composition, and aesthetics may be found in its early publications. The research interests of the first members indicate that the society was formed primarily as a forum for music scholarship in higher education. Indeed, in 1930 Otto Kinkeldey received the first professorship in musicology in America (Cornell University), and of the 36 people who have served as the society's president, only two (Carl Engel, 1937–8, and Carleton Sprague Smith, 1939–40) did not hold prominent university posts.

In the late 1930s, a number of European musicologists came to America and played important roles in the society. Two (Curt Sachs, 1949–50; Karl Geiringer, 1955–6) served as president; others (including Manfred Bukofzer, Alfred Einstein, Paul Henry Lang, Hugo Leichtentritt, and Albert Riemanschneider) served as officers or board members. In September 1939, an International Congress of the American Musicological Society was held in New York, with over 750 participants in the week-long program of papers and concerts: a sign that the AMS was well established.

The growth of American academe following World War II was mirrored in the growth of the AMS, from 850 members in 1948 to over 3500 in 2012 During this period, specialized subdisciplines and its applications also grew, leading to the rise of parallel independent scholarly societies which separated from the AMS: the College Music Association (later the College Music Society, 1947), the Society for Ethnomusicology (1955), the Sonneck Society (later the Society for American Music, 1975), and the Society for Music Theory (1977).

In 1948, the society's *Journal of the American Musicological Society* was established. The *Journal* was preceded by the *Annual Bulletin* (1936–47) and *Papers* (1936–41). Further publication projects appeared in the series *Studies and Documents*, which contains seven volumes published between 1948 and 1992, including the collected works of Johannes Ockeghem, the complete works of John Dunstable, and books by Joseph Kerman, Edward R. Reilly, and Edgar H. Sparks. The AMS turned its financial resources towards providing support to publishers in 1965, and currently devotes much of its publishing efforts in this direction. Since 1965 it has awarded grants to over 130 scholarly projects. Other notable publications of the AMS include *The Complete Works of William Billings* (ed. K. Kroeger, H. Nathan and others, Charlottesville, VA, and Boston, 1977–90), and, supported with funding from the National Endowment for the Humanities, the series *Music of the United States of America* (including Marion Cook's *In Dahomey*, works by Ruth Crawford, Irving Berlin, Amy Beach, Daniel Read, Timothy Swan, Edward Harrigan and David Braham, Lou Harrison, Harry Partch, Thomas "Fats" Waller, Charles Ives, Leo Ornstein, Dudley Buck, Earl "Fatha" Hines, David Michael, Charles Hommann, Virgil Thomson, and Florence Price; 19 vols. to date; 1993–). In 2002 the AMS established the series *AMS Studies in Music*, which includes six volumes to date. The AMS also supports the *RISM* and *RILM* bibliographic projects and the internet database *Doctoral Dissertations in Musicology* (<http://www.ams-net.org/ddm/>).

In 1967 the AMS began to recognize outstanding scholarship through annual awards for outstanding books and articles. Its awards program expanded significantly in the early 2000s; currently 11 awards are given annually. In 1986 the AMS began to award annual fellowships to graduate students, and has given more than a hundred such fellowships to date.

AMS annual meetings attract numerous scholars from North America and abroad, and consist of presentations, panels, and concerts, as well as meetings of related societies. More than two hundred presentations and meetings are scheduled over a four-day period each fall. The annual meeting abstracts are published each year.

BIBLIOGRAPHY

O. Strunk: "State and Resources of Musicology in the United States," *ACLS Bulletin*, xix (1932) [whole vol.]

A. Mendel, C. Sachs, and C.C. Pratt: *Some Aspects of Musicology* (New York, 1957)

B.S. Brook, ed.: *American Musicological Society, Greater New York Chapter: a Programmatic History 1935–1965* (New York, c1965)

W.J. Mitchell: "A Hitherto Unknown—or a Recently Discovered...," *Musicology and the Computer*, ed. B.S. Brook (New York, 1970), 1–8

H. Woodward: "Annals of the College Music Society, I," *College Music Symposium*, xvii (1977), 121–34

D.K. Holoman and C.V. Palisca, eds.: *Musicology in the 1980s: Methods, Goals, Opportunities* (New York, 1982) [whole vol.]

R. Crawford: *The American Musicological Society 1934–1984: An Anniversary Essay* (Philadelphia, 1984) <http:// www.ams-net.org/resources>

C.E. Steinzor, ed.: *American Musicologists, c. 1890–1945* (New York, 1989)

R. Crawford: "Sonneck and American Musical Historiography," *Essays in Musicology: A Tribute to Alvin Johnson*, ed. L. Lockwood and E. Roesner (Philadelphia, 1990), 266–83

AMS Newsletter (semiannual, 1970–) <http://www.ams-net.org/newsletter>

AMS Directory (annual, 1979–)

Celebrating the American Musicological Society at Seventy-Five (Brunswick, Maine, 2011) <http://www.ams-net.org/resources>

ROBERT JUDD

American Music Therapy Association [AMTA]. National professional association for music therapy. AMTA was founded in 1998 as a result of the unification of the National Association for Music Therapy (founded 1950) and the American Association for Music Therapy (founded 1971). AMTA's mission is to increase public awareness of the benefits of music therapy and to increase access to quality music therapy services throughout the United States and the world. This mission has evolved from a shared vision that every person who can benefit from music therapy, irrespective of economic status, severity of disability, or ethnic background, should have access to music therapy services of the highest quality.

The association holds annual conferences and is governed by a 15-member Board of Directors consisting of elected and appointed officers. Policy responsibility lies with an Assembly of Delegates composed of representatives from each of the association's seven regional chapters. Association documents include: Standards of Clinical Practice, Professional Competencies, Advanced Competencies, Education and Clinical Training Standards, and a Code of Ethics for Music Therapists. The eight membership categories include: professional, associate, student, inactive, retired, affiliate, patron, and honorary life.

Credentialing music therapists is the responsibility of the Certification Board for Music Therapists (CBMT). CBMT administers a national music therapy certification examination that is officially recognized by the National Commission on Certifying Agencies. The examination measures the individual's skills, knowledge, and ability to engage in professional music therapy practice. Qualified individuals who pass the national music therapy certification examination earn the credential "Music Therapist-Board Certified" (MT-BC). The National Music Therapy Registry (NMTR) serves qualified music therapy professionals with the following designations: Registered Music Therapist (RMT), Certified Music Therapist (CMT), and Advanced Certified Music Therapist (ACMT).

AMTA publications include the *Journal of Music Therapy*, a quarterly research-oriented journal; *Music Therapy Perspectives*, a semi-annual practice-oriented journal; *Music Therapy Matters*, a quarterly newsletter; and a variety of other monographs, bibliographies, and brochures. AMTA holds organizational membership in various coalitions including the Consortium for Citizens with Disabilities, the National Alliance of Pupil Services Organizations, National Coalition of Creative Arts Therapies Associations, the Commission on Accreditation of Rehabilitation Facilities, the Joint Commission Coalition of Rehabilitation Therapy Organizations, and the National Rehabilitation Caucus.

AMTA is composed of 3,529 members (2009) and is a 501(c)3 non-profit organization funded by annual membership dues, sales of publications, charitable contributions, and other revenue producing activities.

BIBLIOGRAPHY

W.B. Davis, K.E. Gfeller, and M.H. Thaut: *An Introduction to Music Therapy: Theory and Practice* (Dubuque, IA, 1/1992)

ALAN L. SOLOMON

American Opera Company. Opera company. It was founded in 1885 by Jeannette Thurber, whose policy was to engage competent, if unknown, American singers for productions of grand opera sung in English. Thurber appointed a board of eminent directors with ANDREW CARNEGIE as president, and engaged THEODORE THOMAS, who had his own touring orchestra, as music director. Among the fully staged operas presented by the troupe were W.A. Mozart's *The Magic Flute*, C.W. Gluck's *Orpheus and Euridice*, Richard Wagner's *Lohengrin* and *The Flying Dutchman*, Victor Massé's *Galatea*, Verdi's *Aida*, Karl Goldmark's *Queen of Sheba*, and the American premiere of Anton Rubinstein's *Nero*; the repertory also included the ballets *Sylvia* and *Coppélia* by Léo Delibes. The first season opened on 4 January 1886 at the Brooklyn Academy of Music, and the company's ensuing six-month tour of the United States (mainly the Northeast) was hailed as an artistic success and a commendable effort in spite of poor management. After the first season, the company was reincorporated: Thomas became president, and it began its second season in November 1886 as the National Opera Company, with performances at the Metropolitan Opera House and the Brooklyn Academy of Music. Lacking adequate financial support, the enterprise eventually failed when the company was performing on tour in Buffalo in June 1887, and Thomas left the group. After a few performances during the 1887–8 season under different directors, it soon collapsed altogether. Programs for the years 1886–8 are preserved in *NYpl*.

BIBLIOGRAPHY

T. Thomas: *A Musical Autobiography*, ed. G.P. Upton (Chicago, 1905/*R*)

E. Rubin: "Jeannette Meyer Thurber (1850–1946): Music for a Democracy," *Cultivating Music in America*, ed. R.P. Locke and C. Barr (Berkeley, 1997), 134–63

DEE BAILY/R

American Orff-Schulwerk Association [AOSA]. Professional organization for Orff Schulwerk teachers. The organization promotes the artistic and pedagogical principles of Bavarian composer and educator CARL ORFF (1895–82) and his colleague Gunild Keetman (1904–90). Orff Schulwerk (schoolwork) uses children's poems, rhymes, games, songs, and dances as examples and basic materials. The non-competitive approach emphasizes creativity through music and movement. Specially designed Orff instruments are a part of the approach. The American Orff-Schulwerk Association was founded in Muncie, Indiana, in 1968 when educators who had studied Orff Schulwerk convened a meeting. The organization holds annual conferences and oversees guidelines for Orff teacher training courses. There are almost 120 regional chapters that sponsor teacher education workshops. The organization's journal, the *Orff Echo*, is published quarterly. The membership elects a board of directors representing each region of the country. AOSA is the largest of many Orff organizations internationally that look to the Orff Institute of the University Mozarteum in Salzburg as the center of the Orff movement. AOSA members and other Orff-trained teachers use various materials published by Orff and Keetman, most prominently the multi-volume set *Music für Kinder* (Music for Children) (1950–54), as models for their teaching.

ALAN L. SPURGEON

American Piano Co. *See* AEOLIAN.

American Samoa. *See* SAMOA, AMERICAN.

American School Band Directors Association (ASBDA). Professional association of band directors teaching at the elementary- or secondary-school level. Established in 1953, its objectives were to represent school band directors in the academic and business communities; to foster the exchange of ideas and methods that will advance the standards of musical and educational achievement; to stress the importance of the school band in the educational process and establish bands as a basic course in the school curriculum; to maintain a program for the improvement of school bands through research and experimentation; and to cooperate with existing associations that share the aim of promoting the band as a worthwhile medium of musical expression. Membership (by invitation) is open to active school band directors with a minimum of five years' teaching experience who command the respect of their colleagues for the standard of performance and musicianship achieved by their bands. The association presents two biennial awards, the A. Austin Harding Award to individuals for valuable and dedicated service to the bands of America, and the Edwin Franko Goldman Award as a measure of appreciation for outstanding personal contributions to the school band movement.

RAOUL F. CAMUS

American Society for Jewish Music. Organization founded in New York in 1974, a successor to the Mailamm (active 1931–9), the Jewish Music Forum (1939–63), and the Jewish Liturgical Music Society of America (1963–74). Membership includes libraries, synagogues, cantors, composers, educators, musicologists, ethnologists, historians, performers, and lay members who are active or interested in Jewish liturgical and secular music. The society maintains relationships with similar organizations throughout the world. It presents a variety of public programs each season, often with the American Jewish Historical Society, its host at the Center for Jewish History. The organization publishes scholarly works relevant to Jewish music, notably the multilingual journal *Musica judaica* (since 1975). It also sponsors the Jewish Music Forum, which hosts academic seminars, events, and forums to promote awareness and dialogue about Jewish music. It awards prizes for new Jewish works and schedules to have them performed. Albert Weisser served as its first president.

ISRAEL J. KATZ/R

American Society of Ancient Instruments. Chamber ensemble formed in Philadelphia in 1925 by Ben Stad. *See* EARLY-MUSIC REVIVAL.

American Society of Composers, Authors and Publishers [ASCAP]. The oldest performing rights organization in the United States (founded 1914), and the largest in terms of revenue and distribution of royalties to its membership, which comprises more than 400,000 composers, lyricists, and music publishers. The society licenses almost every kind of composition to radio stations, television stations, new media firms, and other music users (*see* PERFORMING RIGHTS SOCIETIES), and, in addition to the royalties it distributes from such uses, makes financial awards in popular music and other fields to composers whose works are performed in the media outside its traditional domain. ASCAP has a number of awards and programs to help new composers and encourage the growth of music in the United States; these include, among many others, the Rudolf Nissim Award (grants to composers for new or previously unperformed orchestral works), the ASCAP Foundation Grants to Young Composers, orchestra awards for adventurous programming of contemporary music, the Deems Taylor Award for excellence in writing about music (*See also* AWARDS), songwriter workshops, and educational music programs for inner-city youth.

BIBLIOGRAPHY

R. Hubbell: *The Story of ASCAP by a Founder* (MS, c1937, NNC)

B.L. DeWhitt: *The American Society of Composers, Authors and Publishers, 1914–1938* (diss., Emory U., 1977)

J. Ryan: *The Production Of Culture in the Music Industry: The ASCAP-BMI Controversy* (Lanham, MD, 1985)

For further bibliography *see* COPYRIGHT; PERFORMING RIGHTS SOCIETIES.

KAREN SHERRY/R

American Society of University Composers. *See* SOCIETY OF COMPOSERS, INC.

American Spiritual Ensemble, the. Founded by Everett McCorvey in 1995, the ensemble defines its mission as the preservation of the spiritual tradition. McCorvey, a native of Montgomery, Alabama, and Professor of Voice and Director of Opera at the University of Kentucky, founded the group because he felt that the arranged spiritual tradition was not being celebrated in the same manner as other forms of African American sacred music, especially gospel music. The group's membership, which ranges from 25 to 50 performers depending on the performance requirements, consists of singers who have performed on the stages of the Metropolitan Opera, the Houston Grand Opera, and concert halls throughout Europe. Although he traveled the world as a tenor soloist and has served as artist faculty at the American Institute of Musical Study in Graz, Austria,

McCorvey has made a considerable contribution to the American concert tradition through the group. The group's repertory includes not only arranged spirituals in the ensemble and art song format, but also jazz and Broadway tunes. It has traveled extensively around the world. In 2007 the American Spiritual Ensemble produced the documentary *The Spirituals* for PBS and they have released four CDs: *On My Journey Now—The American Spiritual Ensemble on Tour* (American Spiritual Ensemble, 1997), *Ol' Time Religion* (American Spiritual Ensemble, 2001), *Lilly of the Valley* (American Spiritual Ensemble, 2002), and *The Spirit of the Holidays* (American Spiritual Ensemble, 2009).

TAMMY L. KERNODLE

American String Quartet. Chamber ensemble formed in 1974 by students at the Juilliard School. Its current members are violinists Peter Winograd (*b* New York, NY, 5 Feb 1960) and Laurie Carney (*b* Englewood, NJ, 28 Sept 1956), violist Daniel Avshalomov (*b* Portland, OR, 23 May 1953), son of the composer JACOB AVSHALOMOV, and cellist Wolfram Koessel (*b* Madison, WI, 5 July 1966). In 1990, Winograd replaced Mitchell Stern, who had replaced the original first violinist, Martin Foster, in 1980. Avshalomov replaced Robert Becker, the original violist, in 1976, and Koessel replaced the original cellist David Geber in 2006. After performing at the Aspen Music Festival in 1974, the quartet made its New York debut at Alice Tully Hall in 1975 and won the Coleman Competition and the Naumburg Award the same year.

Based in New York, the ensemble's tours have taken it to prominent halls and festivals around the world, including China's Great Wall International Music Academy in the summer of 2010. With a sound that is polished and exceptionally well balanced, and a style at once authoritative and unmannered, the ensemble has earned acclaim for its performances of the complete quartets of Beethoven, Schubert, Schoenberg, Bartok, and Mozart. Its recordings of the complete Mozart string quartets on a matched set of Stradivarius instruments are widely admired. In the field of new music, the American String Quartet has commissioned and premiered works by composers Claus Adam, Richard Danielpour, Lester Trimble, Kenneth Fuchs, Giampaolo Bracali, Curt Cacioppo, Tobias Picker, Glen Cortese, and George Tsontakis. Its extensive discography includes works by Adam, Corigliano, Danielpour, Dvořák, Kenneth Fuchs, Sergey Prokofiev, Schoenberg, Alban Berg, Anton Webern, and Tsontakis. The ensemble has also recorded both of Prokofiev's quartets and those of Adam, Barkin, and Corigliano. Since 1974, the ensemble has served as quartet-in-residence and taught at the Aspen Music Festival; since 1984, it has been quartet-in-residence and taught at the Manhattan School of Music.

SUSAN FEDER/JAMES BASH

American String Teachers Association [ASTA]. National professional organization for string music education. ASTA was founded in 1946 to encourage student performance of bowed instruments; to foster study and research on the pedagogy of string playing; and to facilitate the continuing education of string teachers. It was organized partly in reaction to the proliferation of wind bands in the public schools. The association's activities have included special study of violin pedagogy (beginning in 1966), workshops for school orchestra directors who are not string specialists (1971–), and an international workshop with the European String Teachers Association held in Exeter, Great Britain (1975). ASTA also grants annual awards to artist-teachers and for distinguished service to the string teaching profession. In addition to various monographs and bulletins, the association has published the (now quarterly) *American String Teacher* since 1951. Its 11,500 members are string teachers and performers from all 50 states. Its current headquarters opened in Reston, Virginia, in 1996, and an executive director position was created in the mid-1990s. Formerly affiliated with the Music Educators National Conference, ASTA became an independent association in 1998. It sponsors an annual national teaching conference, an annual orchestra festival, and a biennial national high school honors orchestra.

BIBLIOGRAPHY

R.A. Ritsema: *History of the American String Teachers Association* (Bryn Mawr, PA, 1972)

ROBERT GILLESPIE

American Symphony Orchestra League. *See* LEAGUE OF COMPOSERS.

American Theatre Organ Society. An educational and service organization for organists and theater organ enthusiasts, founded in 1955. Its goals are to preserve and promote the organs that were originally designed to accompany silent movies in the motion picture palaces of the 1920s. In addition, the society works to preserve, restore, maintain, and promote the theater pipe organ in places ranging from original motion picture palaces to skating rinks, schools, colleges and universities, pizza restaurants, and even private homes. To encourage young musicians to become proficient theater organists the ATOS sponsors an annual Young Organist Competition as well as annual scholarships for aspiring young organ students. The society has more than 3500 members in approximately 75 chapters across the United States, Great Britain, and Australia. The organization and the various chapters sponsor an annual convention, concerts, screening of silent films, and educational and technical programs (including a youth camp for young organists), and publish a bimonthly journal, *Theatre Organ*.

N. LEE ORR

American Tract Society. An interdenominational Protestant organization devoted to the publication and distribution of religious literature. It was founded in Massachusetts in 1814 by Ebenezer Porter, a Congregational minister, and adopted the name American Tract Society in 1823. In 1825 it merged with a similar group, the New York Religious Tract Society, and the resulting national organization operated for many years from headquarters in New York. In 1978, the society relocated to Garland, Texas. The society was especially influential during the 30 years before the Civil War, after which newer religious agencies became more active. In addition to publishing millions of copies of tracts, the society issued a number of hymn and tune collections, aiming for the broadest possible circulation among middle- and working-class families. These collections became progressively less Calvinist and more evangelical in outlook, and they provide an interesting and useful record of changing tastes in American hymnody, their contents ranging from traditional 18th-century melodies through hymn tunes of the Mason–Hastings reform movement and popular sacred songs in the style of Bradbury and the Methodist revivalists to early gospel hymns. The society's most important publications were *The Family Choir*, edited by S.S. Arnold and E. Colman (1837), Hastings's *Sacred Songs for Family and Social Worship* (1842, rev. and enlarged with Lowell Mason 2/1855) and *Songs of Zion* (1851, enlarged 2/1864), and three anonymously compiled collections—*Hymns and Tunes for the Army and Navy* (*c*1861), *Happy Voices* (1865), and *Gems for the Prayer-meeting* (*c*1868).

BIBLIOGRAPHY

Brief History of the American Tract Society (New York, 1855)
The American Tract Society documents, 1824–1925 (New York, 1972)

PAUL C. ECHOLS/R

American Women Composers. *See* INTERNATIONAL ALLIANCE FOR WOMEN IN MUSIC [IAWM].

Amerindian. *See* NATIVE AMERICAN MUSIC.

Ames, Charles (*b* Pasadena, CA, 1 March 1955). Composer, theorist and computer programmer. He studied at Pomona College (mathematics and music composition, BA 1977) and SUNY, Buffalo (MA 1979, PhD 1984); his teachers included MORTON FELDMAN, LEJAREN HILLER, KARL KOHN, Włodzimierz Kotoński, John Steele Ritter, and Dorrance Stalvey. In 1995 he was appointed Senior Programmer Analyst with Client Logic Corporation (also known as the Softbank Services Group, UCA&L and Upgrade Corporation of America). He has also served as a visiting instructor for numerous courses in computer music, automated composition, and systematic compositional procedures at SUNY, Buffalo; the New England Conservatory; and the Kurzweil Foundation.

Ames is most noted for his work in systematic approaches to music composition. His use of computers in the composition of works for acoustic instruments has been influenced by techniques originated by Iannis Xenakis, Gottfried Michael Koenig, and Hiller. His interests range from music cognition and hierarchical structures in music to computer-verified modeling of musical styles. His computer music programs, most notably Cybernetic Composer (1986–8, designed for jazz, rock, and ragtime composition), Markov (1988), and Compose (1989) are inexorably intertwined with his compositional style. Psychology is only one of many fields that Ames has mined to find models for his musical forms; for his piece, *Concurrence* (violin, 1986), the composer used Gestalt psychology to develop the structure for the work. Since the 1990s, Ames has been fascinated by the interaction between artificial intelligence and human creativity, and his musical output has often addressed this topic.

WORKS
(selective list)

Crystals, orch, 1980; Peripheries, 6 perc, 1980; Protocol, pf, 1981; Gradient, pf, 1982; Undulant, 7 inst, 1983; Artifacts, amp gui, 1984; 11 Demonstrations, cl, 1984; Excursion, amp gui, 1984; Maze, vn, 1985; Concurrence, vn, 1986; Interplay, perc, 1988; 12 Variants, Kurzweil 250 synth, 1990; Metaplex, fl, 1993, collab. N. Bobbitt

WRITINGS

"Automated Composition in Retrospect: 1956 to 1986," *Leonardo Music Journal*, xx (1987), 169–85
"The Markov Process as a Compositional Model," *Leonardo Music Journal*, xxii (1989), 175–88
"Statistics and Compositional Balance," *PNM*, xxvii (1990), 80–111
"A Catalog of Statistical Distributions: Techniques for Transforming Random, Determinate and Chaotic Sequences," *Leonardo Music Journal*, i (1991), 55–70

KRISTINE H. BURNS/JONAS WESTOVER

Amfitheatrof [Amfitheatrov; Amfiteatrov], **Daniele (Alexandrovich)** (*b* St Petersburg, Russia, 16/29 Oct 1901; *d* Rome, Italy, 7 June 1983). Italian composer and conductor of Russian origin. A grandson of the composer Nikolay Sokolov and a brother of the cellist Massimo Amfitheatrof, he studied with Vītols in St. Petersburg and Křička in Prague, but the greater part of his training was undertaken in Rome, where he studied composition with Respighi at the Conservatorio di S Cecilia (diploma 1924) and the organ at the Pontifical Academy of Sacred Music. He was engaged as a pianist, organist, and chorus assistant at the Augusteo (1924–9), also conducting the orchestra under Molinari's supervision. Thereafter he was artistic director of the Genoa and Trieste radio stations and conductor and manager for Italian radio in Turin; he also conducted elsewhere in Europe. In 1937 he went to the United States as associate conductor of the Minneapolis SO, and in 1939 he settled in Hollywood as a film composer, becoming an American citizen in 1944. He moved to New York in the 1950s and then to Venice.

Most of Amfitheatrof's works are in a Respighi-like Romantic-Impressionist style marked by vivid orchestral coloring. His more than 70 film scores are occasionally experimental in their instrumentation, and, though lacking in personality, reveal considerable versatility. Amfitheatrof worked with such directors as Max Ophüls, Fritz Lang, Henry Hathaway, Anthony Mann, Sidney Lumet, George Cukor, and Sam Peckinpah, gaining Academy Award nominations for *Guest Wife* (1945) and *Song of the South* (1946). He did not, however, adjust to the profound linguistic changes in film music of the 1970s, and this led to his prematurely cutting short his work.

WORKS
(selective list)

Op: The Staring Match (J. McNeely), 1965

Orch: Poema del mare, 1925; Il miracolo delle rose, 1927; Italia, 1929; Panorama americano, 1933; Pf Conc., 1937–46

Choral: De profundis, 1944; Requiem, perf. 1962

Chbr: Sonata, vc, pf, 1930; Pf Trio, 1932

Film scores (directors' names in parentheses): La signora di tutti (M. Ophüls), 1934; Lassie Come Home (F.M. Wilcox), 1943; Days of Glory (J. Tourneur), 1944; Guest Wife (S. Wood), 1945; I'll be Seeing You (W. Dieterle), 1945; Song of the South (H. Foster and W. Jackson), 1946; The Beginning or the End (N. Taurog), 1947; The Lost Moment (M. Gabel), 1947; Letter from an Unknown Woman (M. Ophüls), 1948; Another Part of the Forest (M. Gordon), 1948; Rogue's Regiment (R. Florey), 1948; The Fan (O. Preminger), 1949; House of Strangers (J.L. Mankiewicz), 1949; The Damned Don't Cry (V. Sherman), 1950; The Desert Fox (H. Hathaway), 1951; Devil's Canyon (A. Werker), 1953; Salome (W. Dieterle), 1953; Human Desire (F. Lang), 1954; The Naked Jungle (B. Haskin), 1954, The Mountain (E. Dmytryk), 1956; Trial (M. Robson), 1956; The Unholy Wife (J. Farrow), 1957; From Hell to Texas (H. Hathaway), 1958; That Kind of Woman (S. Lumet), 1960; Heller in Pink Tights (G. Cukor), 1960; Major Dundee (S. Peckinpah), 1965

Principal publisher: Ricordi

BIBLIOGRAPHY

M. Tibaldi Chiesa: "Daniel Amfitheatrof," *L'Ambrosiano* (27 May 1933), 3

D. Amfitheatrof: "La musica per film negli Stati Uniti d'America," *La musica nel film*, ed. E. Masetti (Rome, 1950), 118–28

C. McCarty: *Film Composers in America: Checklist of their Works* (Glendale, CA, 1953/*R*)

M. Evans: *Soundtrack: the Music of the Movies* (New York, 1975)

G. Tintori, *Duecento anni di Teatro alla Scala. Cronologia opere-balletti-concerti 1778–1977*, (Bergamo, 1979)

S. Miceli, *Musica per film. Storia, Estetica-Analisi, Tipologie* (Milan–Lucca, 2009)

CHRISTOPHER PALMER/SERGIO MICELI

Amigo, Cristian (*b* Santiago, Chile, 2 Jan 1963). Composer, guitarist, ethnomusicologist, educator, and producer of Chilean birth. He immigrated to the United States as a child and studied guitar with Joseph Torello, Vincent Bredice, Lou Mowad, and George Aguiar. Amigo enrolled at Florida State University (1980) where he studied classical guitar with Bruce Holzman and William Carter and was active as a performer of popular music. In 1986, he moved to Los Angeles, earning a degree in political science from California State University, Northridge (BA 1995) and degrees in ethnomusicology (MA 1988, PhD 2003) from the University of Calfornia, Los Angeles. He studied in Los Angeles with KENNY BURRELL, Gary Pratt, Harihar Rao, and WADADA LEO SMITH. Amigo also performed with African, Arabic, funk, hard rock, free jazz, jazz, and reggae groups, and worked as a session guitarist for Hans Zimmer, Mark Mancina, Jay Rifkin, and Les Hooper, among others.

As a guitarist, improviser, and experimentalist, Amigo explores the musical and social spaces between traditional Western art music, jazz, and various musics from around the world. In this regard he has collaborated with artists such as Afro-Peruvian guitarist Carlos Hayre, David Ornette Cherry, the JACK Quartet, Spontaneous River Orchestra, ARK Guitar Trio, Surrealestate, and the Electric Eel Multimedia Ensemble. In 2003 he moved to New York City where he continued performing and improvising, and has taught courses in Latin American music at New York University and world music at the College of Staten Island (City University of New York). He has lectured and published on topics such as jazz, Andean music and dance, and contemporary Chilean music. As a composer and independent music producer Amigo has worked in the fields of dance, theater, film, radio, and television, including commercial advertising. His compositions often draw on his heritage and his musical experiences. While his operatic and orchestral music displays aspects of traditional processes, other works reflect an eclectic, multi-cultural synthesis of traditional and non-traditional methodologies, a variety of musical languages (acoustic, electronic, and environmental sounds), and hybrid, innovative formal structures. The results of these variegated combinations create, as the composer has stated, compositions that are "betwixt and between." Works such as *The Buzzy Garden*, *Kingdom of Jones*, and *Echoes of Latin America* manipulate elements of blues, jazz, rock, funk, hip-hop, and electronic sounds into a complex and highly improvisational sound fabric.

Amigo's many awards include: fellowships in composition from the Sundance Filmakers Labs (1999), the Durfee Foundation (2002), a Meet the Composer Van Lier Fellowship (2003), the Raw Impressions Music Theatre in New York City (2004), the Guggenheim Foundations (2006), and the Brooklyn Philharmonic (2006); an American Composers Forum Subito performance award (2003); and grants from the Danish Arts Council (2006), the New York State Music Fund (2008), and the National Endowment for the Arts (2009). Amigo was an artist-in residence at the American Lyric Theater (2007–8) and composer-in-residence at the INTAR theatre in New York City (2010).

WORKS
(selective)

Opera: Nylons (1, E. Conbere), 2008; Notes on the Balinese Cockfight, (4, R. Rosaldo after C. Geertz), 2010; Picasso: Payaso, (5, A. Vallega), in progress

Orch: Brooklyn Dances, 2007

Chbr: Craig Wright's Grace, str qt, 2005; Impressions of Energy, vc, gui, 2005; Monk Sketches, elec. jazz ens, 2005; ABC Identity Songs, pf, vn, cl, 2 perc, 2007; Henrik Ibsen's Rosmersholm, prep gui, elecs, 2007; Jon Fosse's deathvariations, prep str, 2007; Str Qt No.1, 2007; Gui Qt No.1, 2008; Str Qt No.2 "Ambiguous Dog," 2009; 66 Americana Songs, vv, lead sheet, 2010; Three Truths, elecs, 2010; Five Rasas, gui, found perc, 2011; The Buzzy Garden, str, perc, sound manipulations, field recordings, sound-scapes, 2011; f=ma, vc, cl, b cl, soundscapes, 2011

Vocal: SPEAK, vv, funk-rock band, 1997; The Upside Down Boy, vv, Latin jazz ens, 2004; Echoes of Latin America, vv, samples, loops, Latin/African perc, 2006; Han Ong's Swooney Planet, vv, gui, 2006; Music for Juan Felipe Herrera's Salsalandia, vv, samples, beats, guis, theremin, perc, 2007; Killing Play, vv, R&B band, 2007; Song Suite from David Anzuelo's Minotaur, vv, alternative country band, 2008; Kingdom of Jones, prep guis, elec/ac guis, perc, soundscapes, field recordings, 2008; Western Spaces, vv, elec. guis, perc, 2009

Principal recording companies: BA Records, Innova

ROBERT PAUL KOLT

Amirkhanian, Charles (Benjamin) (*b* Fresno, CA, 19 Jan 1945). Composer and administrator. He studied at Fresno State University (BA in English 1967), San Francisco State University (MA in interdisciplinary creative arts 1969) and Mills College (MFA in electronic music and recording media 1980), where his teachers included DAVID BEHRMAN, ROBERT ASHLEY, and Paul de Marinis. He has served as music director for KPFA Radio (Berkeley, CA, 1969–92), executive director of the Djerassi Artists Program (1993–7), and both artistic (from 1993) and executive director (from 1998) of the Other Minds Festival (San Francisco). His honors include ASCAP's Deems Taylor Award for innovative musical programming (1989) and residencies at the Tyrone Guthrie Centre, Ireland (1997), and the Bellagio Study and Conference Centre, Italy (1997); he won the first Ella Walker Fellowship from the Rockefeller Foundation, including a residency on Lake Como, Italy (1999–2000).

Amirkhanian's experiences as a percussionist and radio presenter have informed all of his works. Between 1961 and 1969 he wrote many pieces for live performance, often involving percussion or tape. In 1965 he began to compose tape pieces using the spoken voice and ambient sounds, sources he continued to employ in later music. His vocal settings, the texts of which are sometimes drawn from literature, take words out of context and exploit them for their rhythmic and timbral qualities. Works such as *Seatbelt Seatbelt* (1973) and *Dutiful Ducks* (1977), made up largely of the words in their titles, display a laconic, affectionate humor and a taste for surreal combinations. He has also created *Hörspiele* that process both abstract and representational sounds; these include *Metropolis San Francisco* (1985–6), *Walking Tune 'A Room-Music for Percy Grainger'* (1986–7), and *Pas de voix* (1987). Among his other works are homages to Nicolas Slonimsky and Lou Harrison and, reflecting his Armenian descent, compositions that refer to American and Armenian culture. He has devoted much of his career to publicizing and producing the works of other composers, and to administrative work in new music; he is a central figure in the network of West Coast artists and musicians, which has involved numerous retrospectives and recordings of work by earlier experimental composers.

WORKS
(selective list)

LIVE PERFORMANCE

Genesis 28 Four Speakers, 4 spkrs, 1965; Sym. no.1, 2 solo perc, perc duo, amp perc, tpt trio, trbn, pf/cl, va, 1965; Composition nos.1–5, amp ratchet, 1965–7; Ode to Gravity (theater piece), graphic score, any medium, 1967; Serenade II 'Jance Wentworth', graphic score, any medium, 1967, collab. T. Greer; Egusquiza to Falsetto (theater piece), chbr orch, tape, 1979, collab. M. Fisher; Spoilt Music (theater piece), 1v, tape, 1979; collab. C. Law; His Anxious Hours, chbr ens, tape, 1987; Octet, 8 ratchets, 1998; Rippling the Lamp, vn, tape, 2006–7; many other works

TEXT-SOUND (TAPE)

Words, 1969; Oratora konkurso rezulto: autoro de la jaro (Portrait of Lou Harrison), 1970; Radii, 1970, rev. 1972; If In Is, 1971; Dzarin bess ga khorim, 1972; Just, 1972; Sound Nutrition, 1972, rev. 1972; Heavy Aspirations (Portrait of Nicolas Slonimsky), 1973; Mugic, 1973; Seatbelt Seatbelt, 1973; Much-Rooms, 1974; RAY MAN RAY, 1974; she she and she, 1974; Mahogany Ball Park, 1976; Dutiful Ducks, 1977; Dreams Freud Dreamed, 1979; Church Car, 1980; Dot Bunch, 1981; History of Collage, 1981; Hypothetical Moments (in the Intellectual Life of Southern California), 1981; Andas, 1982; Dog of Stravinsky, 1982; Gold and Spirit, 1983; Metropolis San Francisco, 1985–6; Dumbek Bookache, 1986; Walking Tune (A Room-Music for Percy Grainger), 1986–7; Pas de voix (Portrait of Samuel Beckett), 1987; Politics as Usual (1988); Bajanoom, 1990; Im Frühling (1990); Loudspeakers (for Morton Feldman), 1990; Vers les anges (for Nicolas Slonimsky), 1990; Chu Lu Lu, 1992; Miatsoom, 1994–7; Ka himeni hehena, 1997; Marathon, 1997; Son of Metropolis San Francisco, 1997; Varsity Pewter, 1998; Hymenoptera in the 4th Dimension, 1999; Pianola (Pas de mains), 1997–2000; Mqsical Lou, 2003; many other works

Recorded interviews in *NHob*
Principle publisher: Arts Plural Publishing (BMI)
Principle recording company: Starkland

BIBLIOGRAPHY

GroveA (J. Adams) [incl. further bibliography]
M. Summer, M. Sumner and K. Burch, eds.: *The Guests Go in to Supper* (Oakland, CA, 1987) [incl. interview and text compositions]
"Pâte de *Pas de voix*," *PNM*, xxvi/2 (1988), 32–43
G. Smith and N.W. Smith: *New Voices: American Composers Talk about their Music* (Portland, OR, 1995)
M. Alburger: "Dinner in the Loop with Charles Amirkhanian," *20CM*, iv/5 (1997), 10–26
N. Zurbrugg: "Charles Amirkhanian," *Art, performance, media: 31 interviews* (Minneapolis, 2004), 17–24

PAUL ATTINELLO

Amish and Mennonite music. The Protestant denominations of the Amish (249,000 in North America in 2010) and the Mennonites (1.6 million in 56 countries worldwide and 524,000 in North America in 2009) have a common source in the Anabaptist movement of 16th-century Europe. Emerging in the 1520s, the Swiss Brethren separated from the early Reformers and the Roman Catholics for reasons more radical than those of Luther or Zwingli: believers' baptism (thus Anabaptists, or "Rebaptizers"), priesthood of all believers, separation of church and state, and commitment to discipleship of Christ to the point of rejecting participation in war. Within the next decade, Anabaptists emerged in Bohemia, southern Germany, and the Netherlands.

Known as Mennonites after their Dutch leader Menno Simons (*d* 1561), Anabaptists have divided numerous times over issues related to both lifestyle and theology. Lifestyle issues often centered on the degree of "separation from the world" envisioned by such groups as the Amish, Hutterites, and Old Colony Mennonites, and which was expressed through practices such as strict modes of dress and resistance to contemporary technologies. Theological issues have entailed modes of baptism, the exercise of the ban (or shunning), and interpretations of eschatology. Historically, music has also been a defining feature of Mennonite denominational separations, with a focus on tensions between traditional and contemporary repertoire, selection of hymnals, the use of musical instruments, the style of musical leadership, congregational song versus choral performance in worship, historic versus inclusive-language hymn texts, and philosophies of musical education.

Although a few early 16th-century Anabaptist leaders followed Zwingli's example in advocating the total elimination of music from church services, other Anabaptists of that era, such as Balthasar Hubmaier, encouraged singing from the heart and with the spirit. Persecuted for their faith, Anabaptists soon produced a distinctive hymnody, borrowing tunes of popular songs,

Lutheran and Reformed hymns, and ancient Roman Catholic chants. Their first publication, *Etlicher schöner christlicher Geseng* (1564), was a collection of 53 hymn texts composed by Anabaptist prisoners at Passau between 1535 and 1540. It was followed by *Ausbund, das ist etliche schöne christliche Lieder* (1583), its first part consisting of 80 Anabaptist hymns from as early as 1524 and the second, 52 hymns from the 1564 collection.

During successive migrations to North America beginning in the late 17th century, groups of Anabaptists brought along their various hymnals. The South German and Swiss congregations brought the *Ausbund* in 1683, while the north German Mennonites also brought psalters and German Lutheran hymnals. The Amish, who had broken away from the Mennonites in Europe in 1693 under the leadership of the Swiss bishop Jakob Ammann, similarly brought the *Ausbund* when they began migrating in 1720. This book appeared in 11 known European editions by 1838 and had at least 32 further editions and reprints in America between 1742 and 1980. The *Ausbund* is still the most frequently used hymnal of the Old Order Amish, and its continuous use for more than 400 years is unique in Protestant hymnody.

Mennonites who have adhered to a lifestyle intentionally separated from the rest of society have also developed a distinctive style of church singing. Thus, among groups such as the Amish, Hutterites, Old Colony, and Old Order Mennonites, there has historically been only congregational song in Sunday morning church services, which are attended primarily by adults. Their singing is characteristically monophonic, melismatic, unaccompanied, nonmetrical, and extremely slow. It often uses a nasalized vocal style and is usually led by a *Vorsänger* (cantor) or group of cantors. Yet, youth in these traditions may gather for weekday singings of livelier, albeit mostly religious, music.

In contrast to the conserving groups, American Mennonites of Swiss-German background slowly but continuously adopted new musical repertoire and singing styles. By the 18th century they were singing Reformed Psalms and Lutheran chorales, and by the early 19th century they were using two German hymnals: *Die kleine geistliche Harfe der Kinder Zions* (1803), published by the descendants of the Germantown settlers, and *Ein unpartheyisches Gesang-Buch* (1804). These retained 64 *Ausbund* songs but added German hymns and French Calvinist psalms in Ambrosius Lobwasser's translation.

The American Mennonites' transition from German to English hymnody, as well as from unison to part-singing, was facilitated by the singing schools organized by Joseph Funk (1778–1862). The publication of Funk's *Compilation of Genuine Church Music* in 1832, revised in 1876 as *New Harmonia Sacra,* offered Mennonites "the most appropriate tunes of the different meters, for public worship": English psalm tunes, American hymn tunes, and revival melodies of the early 19th century. Funk also notated some oral folktunes and incorporated early American anthems which are still used in Mennonite congregations. The book's oblong format, characteristic of singing-school books, and its didactic function paralleled similar American books such as Ananias Davisson's *Kentucky Harmony* (1816). Funk, possibly aided by Davisson, prefaced the book with the rudiments of music and music-reading in the four shapes (*fa, sol, la,* and *mi*) of W. Little and W. Smith's *The Easy Instructor* (1801; *See also* SHAPE-NOTE HYMNODY). Part-singing—initially in three parts, with the melody in the middle, and later in four parts from the 12th (1866) edition onward—probably entered American Mennonite worship as a result of Funk's influence.

The first American Mennonite hymnal published in English was *A Selection of Psalms, Hymns, and Spiritual Songs* (1847). It consisted only of texts, so the editors specified that *Genuine Church Music* be used as the companion tunebook and recommended specific text-tune combinations. *Hymns and Tunes for Public and Private Worship, and Sunday School Songs Compiled by a Committee* (1890) was the first American Mennonite hymnal with music. It was not until 1902, however that a fully official hymnal of the American Mennonites, *Church and Sunday School Hymnal with Supplement,* was published.

The transition to English-language hymnody, however, was not continuous. Instead, successive immigrations of German-speaking Mennonites from Prussia and Russia influenced the General Conference Mennonite Church (GCM), organized in Iowa in 1860, to continue singing in German. These immigrants brought to America their hymnal, *Gesangbuch in welchem eine Sammlung geistreicher,* published in Russia in 1844 but based on the Prussian *Geistreiches Gesangbuch* of 1767. In 1873, the GCM republished a hymnal from south Germany, *Gesangbuch zum gottesdienstlichen und häuslichen Gebrauch* (1856), to accommodate these newcomers. This hymnal allowed the immigrants to revive and strengthen the chorale and hymn traditions borrowed from the German Lutherans and Pietists. Later, in 1890 the General Conference Mennonites published another German hymnal, *Gesangbuch mit Noten* (16/1936), which combined various German hymn traditions. Because it contained both text and four-part harmony, it fostered part-singing. When the GCM also needed an English-language hymnal in 1894, they turned to a mainline Protestant book, *Many Voices.*

While American Mennonites made significant changes to their language and hymn repertoire in the mid-19th century, many Canadian Mennonites made similar adjustments but considerably later. In 1874–5, German-speaking Mennonites from Russia, like their American counterparts, retained the *Gesangbuch in welchem eine Sammlung geistreicher Lieder...* (1844), a book still used by Old Colony Mennonites, who now live in locales such as western Canada, Texas, Mexico, and Bolivia. Whereas these late 19th-century immigrants maintained a conserving musical style of melismatic unison singing, those who came after 1923, who had learned to read *Ziffern* (numeral notation) and to sing in four-part harmony in their Mennonite school system in Russia, brought new repertoire, singing styles, and musical expectations. In particular, the Mennonite Brethren, who had separated from the mainstream and developed their own musical practices in Russia after 1860, brought along their livelier gospel songs, many of them German translations of American hymns, and a church choir tradition. The GCM, meanwhile, focused more on traditional congregational song.

Periodic musical cooperation between the Canadian Mennonites lasted during the pioneering years of the 1920s to 30s, but during the early 1940s the Mennonite Brethren became more institutionalized and founded colleges and bible schools to emphasize their own doctrine and history. This increasing denominational focus was expressed in the 1940 GCM publication *The Mennonite Hymnary* with the observation that hymns are "one of the most effective means of knitting together more closely its scattered membership." Mennonite Brethren and General Conference Mennonites both published German denominational hymnals in mid-century, the former in 1952 and the latter in 1965, but soon followed this with English denominational hymnals to reflect both language and repertoire changes among their primarily ethnic German membership at the time.

Mid-20th-century changes in Mennonite church music are exemplified by the changing practices of Canadian Mennonite Brethren. Here musical transitions occurred in the wake of postwar affluence, rising consumerism, increasing urbanization, improved travel options, and new communications media. Regional choral conductors' workshops gave way to church college music programs, the church choir lost its function as a primary source of musical training and social outlet for the youth, staff notation replaced *Ziffern* in order to accommodate more sophisticated choral repertoire, women gained access to more public church ministries as accompanists and conductors of children's and women's choirs, German-speaking churches began English-language outreach radio programs, gospel songbooks were abandoned for worship music and denominational hymnals, Sunday clothing was covered by matching choir robes, pump organs were replaced by electronic organs, and choir and congregational music-making was supplemented with instrumental and vocal solos.

Since the mid-20th century, music among North American Mennonites has been characterized by high levels of professional performance fostered by Mennonite educational institutions, periodic interdenominational cooperation, greater diversity of musical styles, and increasing musical expression of the multicultural and international nature of the Mennonites.

Increasing institutional Mennonite ecumenism is evident in hymnals compiled during the latter half of the 20th century. In 1969 the (Old) Mennonite Church and the General Conference Mennonite Church joined in publishing *The Mennonite Hymnal* in round- and shape-note editions. It drew together their historical strands and also incorporated songs from the Moody-Sankey revival. When musical needs changed in the mid-1980s, the Church of the Brethren joined these two Mennonite denominations to compile *Hymnal: a Worship Book*, published in 1992. The book's 202 worship resources exemplify greater attention to liturgical format, and its 658 hymns contain a broader range of inclusive language and Mennonite ethnicities, encompassing Asian, Latin and Native American, and African cultures. The multi-lingual, international songbooks prepared for the 1978 and 1990 Mennonite World Conferences had already created a growing awareness that most Mennonites live in the global south, although the publication of David Graber's *Tsese-Ma Heonenemeotôtse Cheyenne Spiritual Songs* in 1982 also revealed the increasing ethnic diversity among North American Mennonites. Publications related to the 1992 hymnal also indicate new trends. An accompaniment book demonstrates that those from historic a cappella traditions were moving toward instrumental accompaniment, while supplementary books, namely *Sing the Journey* (2005) and *Sing the Story* (2007), similarly demonstrate that church music is constantly changing, balancing historical with contemporary musical expression.

No single textual or musical style characterizes 21st-century Mennonite and Anabaptist music. Instead, it could just as easily entail a solemn procession while singing a Cheyenne spiritual song (1982) as it could the lively singing of a contemporary worship song text beamed onto a screen and accompanied by a band. Or it might be a family singing a grace before a meal, a group of 30-year-olds reviving Russian Mennonite singing circle games or Swiss Mennonite singing school traditions, a group singing songs of social criticism in Low German, Amish youth enjoying English gospel songs and hymns at a Sunday evening singing, Hutterite choirs singing gospel music and four-part anthems in Manitoba, Old Colony youth singing gospel music at a Low German Mennonite gathering, a children's choir singing at an international event, or multilingual singing by evangelical, charismatic Mennonites in northern Mexico. Although the practices differ, there is a common thread: commitment to fostering community and a more peaceful world through music.

BIBLIOGRAPHY

R. Wolkan: *Die Lieder der Wiedertäufer* (Berlin, 1903/*R*)

"The Mennonites and Dunkers, their Emigration and Hymnody," *Church Music and Musical Life in Pennsylvania*, ed. Committee on Historical Research of the Colonial Dames of America, ii (Philadelphia, 1927)

H.S. Bender: "The First Edition of the Ausbund," *Mennonite Quarterly Review*, iii (1929), 147–50

J. Umble: "The Old Order Amish, their Hymns and Hymn Tunes," *Journal of American Folklore*, lii (1939), 82–95

J. Umble: "Amish Service Manuals," *Mennonite Quarterly Review*, xv (1941), 26–32

G.P. Jackson: "The Strange Music of the Old Order Amish," *MQ*, xxxi (1945), 275–88

C. Burkhart: "The Music of the Old Order Amish and the Old Colony Mennonites: a Contemporary Monodic Practice," *Mennonite Quarterly Review*, xxvii (1953), 34–54

C. Krahn, ed.: "Amish Division," "Ausbund," "Hymnology of the American Mennonites," "Hymnology of the Mennonites of West and East Prussia, Danzig, and Russia," "Music, Church," "Old Order Amish," *Mennonite Encyclopedia* (Scottdale, PA, 1955–9)

R.R. Duerksen: "The Ausbund," *The Hymn*, viii (1957), 82–90

H.A. Brunk: *History of the Mennonites in Virginia* (Staunton, VA, 1959)

J.A. Hostetler: *Amish Society* (Baltimore, 1963, 3/1980)
P.M. Yoder and others: *Four Hundred Years with the Ausbund* (Scottdale, PA, 1964)
H.L. Eskew: *Shape-Note Hymnody in the Shenandoah Valley* (diss., Tulane U., 1966)
A. Kadelbach: *Die Hymnodie der Mennoniten in Nordamerika (1742–1860): eine Studie zur Verpflanzung, Bewahrung und Umformung europäischer Kirchenliedtradition* (Mainz, 1971)
M.E. Ressler: *A Bibliography of Mennonite Hymnals and Songsbooks 1742–1972* (Quarryville, PA, 1973)
A. Kadelbach: "Hymns written by American Mennonites," *Mennonite Quarterly Review*, xlviii (1974), 343–70
P.W. Wohlgemuth: "Singing the New Song," in J.A. Toews: *History of the Mennonite Brethren Church*, ed. A.J. Klassen (Fresno, CA, 1975), 239–53
M.E. Ressler: "A History of Mennonite Hymnody," *Journal of Church Music*, xxiii/6 (1976), 2–5
M.E. Ressler: "Hymnbooks Used by the Old Order Amish," *The Hymn*, xxviii/1 (1977), 11–16
M. Oyer: *Exploring the Mennonite Hymnal: Essays* (Newton, KS, 1981)
O. Schmidt: *Church Music and Worship among the Mennonites* (Newton, KS, 1981)
D. Graber: *Tsese-Ma Heonenemeototse Cheyenne Spiritual Songs* (Newton, KS, 1982)
D. Friesen: *The Development of Church Music in the Mennonite Brethren Churches* (Fresno, CA, 1983)
A. Loewen and others: *Exploring the Mennonite Hymnal: Handbook* (Newton, KS, 1983)
W. Berg: *From Russia with Music: a Study of the Mennonite Choral Singing Tradition in Canada* (Winnipeg, MB, 1985)
C. Hiebert: "The Making of a New Mennonite Brethren Hymnal," *Direction: a Mennonite Brethren Forum*, ii (1993), 60–71
D.H. Klassen: "From 'Getting the Words Out' to 'Enjoying the Music': Musical Transitions among Canadian Mennonite Brethren," *Bridging Troubled Waters: Mennonite Brethren at Mid-century*, ed. P. Toews (Fresno, CA, 1995), 227–46
J. Dueck: "From Whom is the Voice Coming? Mennonites, First Nations People and Appropriation of Voice," *Journal of Mennonite Studies*, xix (2001), 144–57
M. Kropf and K. Nafziger: *Singing: a Mennonite Voice* (Scottdale, PA, 2001)
D.H. Klassen: "To Improve Congregational Singing: Music in the Church," *For everything a season: Mennonite Brethren in North America, 1874*–2002, ed. P. Toews and K. Enns-Rempel (Fresno, CA, 2002), 121–36
J. Dueck: "The State of the Art in Studies of Mennonite Music: Worship Wars, World Music, and Menno-Nots," *Journal of Mennonite Studies*, xxiii (2005), 131–45
M. Epp and C.A. Weaver, eds: *Sound in the Land* (Kitchener, ON, 2005)
J. Rempel: "Mennonite Worship: a Multitude of Practices Looking for a Theology," *Mennonite Life*, lv/3 (2000), <http://www.bethelks.edu/mennonitelife/2000sept/rempel_john_manifesto.html>
J. Dueck: "Binding and loosing in song: Conflict, identity and Canadian Mennonite music," lv *EthM* (2011), 229–54

MARY OYER/DOREEN HELEN KLASSEN

Ammons, Albert (C.) (*b* Chicago, IL, 23 Sept 1907; *d* Chicago, IL, 2 Dec 1949). Jazz pianist. He was one of the most important figures in the popularization of boogie-woogie. Ammons began playing professionally as a teenager and performed in jazz bands and on the rent party circuit in Chicago. By the late 1920s he was working regularly as the pianist in several small bands, including those of Francis Moseley, William Barbee, and Louis D. Banks. It was with the last of these that he first recorded, in 1934. Around the same time Ammons formed his own six-piece band, the Rhythm Kings, with whom he recorded for Decca in 1936. A seminal event in Ammons' career was his participation in the "From Spirituals to Swing" concert in Carnegie Hall in 1938 as a member of a boogie-woogie piano trio with Pete Johnson and Meade "Lux" Lewis (the latter had been a close friend and musical influence since childhood). There followed a series of successful solo and small band recordings for the fledgling labels Solo Art and Blue Note that consolidated his reputation among the jazz public. Ammons continued to perform and record in the 1940s and made an important series of more than 30 recordings with the Rhythm Kings for Mercury between 1945 and 1949. Ammons was stylistically flexible, equally at home with the driving approach of Chicago boogie-woogie as with stride. His later recorded work is distinctive and displays a stylistic maturity that anticipates rhythm and blues.

SELECTED RECORDINGS

As unaccompanied soloist: *Shout for Joy* (1939, Voc.); *Boogie Woogie Stomp/Boogie Woogie Blues* (1939, BN); *Suitcase Blues/Bass Goin' Crazy* (1939, BN); *Mecca Flat Blues* (1939, Solo Art)
Duos with P. Johnson: *Foot Pedal Boogie/Movin' the Boogie* (1941, Vic.)
As leader: *Nagasaki/Boogie Woogie Stomp* (1936, Decca); *Swanee River Boogie* (1946, Mer.); *Ammons Stomp* (1949, Mer.)

BIBLIOGRAPHY

Y. Bruynoghe: "Albert Ammons," *Jazz Era: the Forties*, ed. S. Dance (London, 1961), 48
C. Page: *Boogie-Woogie Stomp: Albert Ammons and his Music* (Cleveland, 1997)
P.J. Silvester: *The Story of Boogie-Woogie: a Left Hand like God* (Lanham, MD, 2009)

PETER C. MUIR

Ammons, Gene [Eugene; Jug] (*b* Chicago, IL, 14 April 1925; *d* Chicago, IL, 6 Aug 1974). Jazz tenor saxophonist and bandleader, son of ALBERT AMMONS. He studied music under Captain Walter Dyett at Du Sable High School and was influenced by Lester Young and Coleman Hawkins. After touring with the trumpeter King Kolax in 1943, he was a member of Billy Eckstine's seminal big band from 1944 to 1947—Eckstine is said to have given him the nickname Jug, referring to his hat size—and was also a member of Woody Herman's Second Herd in 1949. Ammons began leading his own small groups in 1947 and had a hit with "Red Top" (named after his wife) that year. In the early 1950s he co-led a popular two-tenor band with Sonny Stitt and in the early 1960s he took part in successful collaborations in a soul-jazz idiom with several organists, including Jack McDuff and Johnny Smith. He served prison sentences for drug offences (1958–60 and 1962–9), but resumed performing and recording after his release; he made his comeback in 1969 with a two-week engagement at the Plugged Nickel in Chicago leading a band that included King Kolax. Later projects before his death from cancer included collaborations with Dexter Gordon, Cannonball Adderley, and Stitt. Ammons was a prolific recording artist. He worked principally for Prestige, but also for Mercury, Chess, Decca and Verve, among others. His powerful, emotionally direct style had a broad appeal and combined the harmonic complexity of bebop with more commercial influences from blues and rhythm and blues.

BIBLIOGRAPHY

M. Crawford: "Jug ain't Changed," *DB*, xxviii/17 (1961), 24

L. Feather: "The Rebirth of Gene Ammons," *DB*, xxxvii/12 (1970), 12

KENNY MATHIESON

Amos, Tori [Myra Ellen] (*b* Newton, NC, 22 Aug 1963). Alternative-rock singer-songwriter, pianist, and record producer. She emerged in the early 1990s amid a resurgence of female singer-songwriters and has been one of the few well known alternative-rock artists to use the piano as her primary instrument. She attended the preparatory division of the prestigious Peabody Conservatory but left the school at the age of 11. She began to play her own music in nightclubs at 14, chaperoned by her father, who was a preacher. After Amos moved to Los Angeles in her late teens to pursue a recording career, her band Y Kant Tori Read released a self-titled album (Atl., 1987). Although this was unsuccessful, Atlantic Records retained her six-album contract.

Amos's debut solo album, *Little Earthquakes* (Atl., 1992), earned her critical acclaim for her vocal expressivity, pianistic virtuosity, and fearless exploration of a wide range of personal themes, notably female sexuality, personal relationships, religion, sexual violence, and coming of age. The album *Under the Pink* (Atl., 1994) was an acoustic piano-based album which sold more than one million copies, and Amos toured in support of it performing on her Bösendorfer concert grand. Recorded at a number of interesting recording venues, *Boys for Pele* (Atl., 1996) included tracks on which Amos played harpsichord and clavichord as well as piano and explored rich, dark sounds while still featuring her signature whimsical lyricism. *From the Choirgirl Hotel* (Atl., 1998) was the first album recorded at Amos's studio Martian Engineering in Cornwall, England, and the first to explore a full band sound with emphasis on dance beats, thanks to a new collaboration with the drummer Matt Chamberlain. The double album *To Venus and Back* (Atl., 1999) was supported by a concert tour with Alanis Morissette, and *Strange Little Girls* (Atl., 2001) was a covers project for which Amos interpreted songs written by men to offer a female perspective. *Scarlet's Walk* (Epic, 2002) was a musical and lyrical narrative of a cross-country tour and explored American and Native American history and values. This album explicitly developed a subjective persona, Scarlet, as Amos's alter ego. In *American Doll Posse* (Epic, 2007) Amos developed five female personae which projected different modes of female identity and subjectivity. Amos turned to a prestigious classical label for her twelfth studio album (*Night of Hunters,* Deutsche Grammophon, 2011), collaborating with a quartet of wind players and the string quartet Apollon Musagète, in a set of 14 songs that are compositionally based on a range of classical works. This album marked the recording debut of Amos's own daughter, Natashya Hawley, whose voice contributes an intriguing texture to the complex lyrical narrative of the album.

Amos also oversaw the production of a five-disc box set, *A Piano: the Collection* (Rhino, 2006); this exploration of her career to date included material from her previous albums as well as unissued songs, alternate versions, demos, and B-sides. Amos has also been involved in the production, presentation, publication (via her company Sword and Stone), and dissemination of her music. Throughout her career, she has explored themes of gender, sexuality, race, and class, as well as American history, religion, and politics. Drawing upon themes and symbols from mythology as well as contemporary representations of women, she has confronted misogyny and pornography and celebrated female agency and power.

LORI BURNS, JADA WATSON

Amram, David (Werner) (*b* Philadelphia, PA, 17 Nov 1930). Composer, horn player, and conductor. As a youth he played the piano, trumpet, and horn, developing a strong interest in jazz as well as classical music. After a year at Oberlin Conservatory (1948), where he studied the horn, he attended George Washington University (BA in history, 1952). He was engaged as a horn player with the National SO, Washington, DC (1951–2), and then played with the Seventh Army SO in Europe; during his three years there he also toured as a soloist, performed with chamber ensembles, and in Paris took part in jazz sessions. He returned to the United States in 1955 and enrolled in the Manhattan School, where he studied with DIMITRI MITROPOULOS, VITTORIO GIANNINI, and GUNTHER SCHULLER; he was also a member of the Manhattan Woodwind Quintet. He was awarded honorary degrees from Moravian College, Bethlehem, Pennsylvania (1979), and St. Lawrence University (1994).

In 1956 Amram began a long association with Joseph Papp, producer for the New York Shakespeare Festival, who commissioned incidental music for *Titus Andronicus*; during the period 1956–67 Amram composed scores for 25 Shakespeare productions at the festival, and in 1968 completed his comic opera *Twelfth Night*. Among his many subsequent commissions for television, jazz bands, films and the theatre is the incidental music for Archibald MacLeish's *J.B.*, which won a Pulitzer Prize in 1959. Amram formed friendships with Jack Kerouac and Allen Ginsberg and other writers of the "Beat Generation," and provided notable film scores for *Pull my Daisy* (1959), narrated by Kerouac, *Splendour in the Grass* (1961) and *The Manchurian Candidate* (1962). Amram was the first composer-in-residence with the New York PO (1966–7), and in 1972 he was appointed conductor of the Brooklyn Philharmonia's youth concerts. In 1968 Amram published his first memoir, entitled *Vibrations: the Adventures and Musical Times of David Amram (New York).* He has also undertaken several State Department tours: he visited Brazil in 1969 (an experience that was to affect his compositional style), Kenya in 1975 (with the World Council of Churches), Cuba in 1977 with Dizzy Gillespie, Stan Getz, and Earl Hines, and the Middle East in 1978. He became music director of the International Jewish Arts Festival in 1982. In 2008 he served as the Democratic National Convention's "Composer in Residence for Public Events." Amram's works reflect his love of music of all cultures; they are romantic, dramatic, and colorful, and are marked by rhythmic and improvisatory characteristics of jazz. In recent years Amram has continued to write about his musical experiences, publishing a book on his work with Kerouac in the 1960s, and an episodic collection of life stories in 2007.

WORKS

Dramatic: The Final Ingredient (TV op, A. Weinstein, after R. Rose), 1965; Twelfth Night (op, J. Papp, after W. Shakespeare), 1965–8; incid music, incl. The Beaux Stratagem, J.B., The Family Reunion, Caligula, Peer Gynt, Lysistrata, The Passion of Josef D., 25 Shakespeare scores; numerous film scores

Orch: Autobiography, str, 1959; Shakespearean Conc., ob, hn, str, 1959; The American Bell, nar, orch, 1962; King Lear Variations, wind band, 1965; Hn Conc., wind ens/orch/pf, 1965; Triple Conc., ww qnt, brass qnt, jazz qnt, orch, 1970; Elegy, vn, orch, 1970; Bn Conc., 1971; Vn Conc., 1972; Brazilian Memories, gui, orch, 1973; Fanfare, brass, perc, 1974; En memoria de Chano Pozo, fl, elec b gui, pf, orch/wind band, 1977; Ov., brass, perc, 1977; Ode to Lord Buckley, a sax, orch/sym. band, 1980; Aya Zehn, ob/tpt, orch, 1982; Honor Song, vc, orch, 1983; Across the Wide Missouri: a Musical Tribute to Harry S. Truman, 1984; Andante and Variations on a Theme for Macbeth, sym. band, 1984; Fox Hunt, 1984; Travels, tpt, orch, 1985; American Dance Suite, 1986; Songs of the Soul (Shiray Neshama), 1986; Celebration Suite, 1992; Theme and Variations on Red River Valley, fl, str, 1992; Retratos de Mexico, 1993; A Little Rebellion: Letters of Jefferson, nar, orch, 1995; Kokopelli, 1997; Giants of the Night, fl, orch, 2000; Symphonic Variations on a Song by Woody Guthrie, 2007; Three Songs, pf conc., 2009; works for jazz qnt, orch

Inst: over 20 chbr works for 1–5 insts, incl. Trio, t sax, bn, hn, 1958;; Pf Sonata, 1960; Sonata, vn, pf, 1960; Str Qt, 1961; 3 Songs for Marlboro, hn, vc, 1962; Dirge and Variations, pf trio, 1962; The Wind and the Rain, vn, pf, 1963; Fanfare and Processional, brass qnt, 1966; Wind Qnt, 1968; Zohar, fl/a rec, 1974; Native American Portraits, vn, perc, pf, 1977; Portraits, pf qt, 1979; Landscapes, perc qt, 1980; Blues and Variations for Monk, hn, 1982; Conversations, fl, str trio, pf, 1988; Duets, 2 fl, 1990; Trombone Alone, 1996; works for jazz ens

Vocal: Friday Evening Service, T, SATB, org, 1960; A Year in our Land (cant., J. Baldwin, J. Dos Passos, J. Kerouac, J. Steinbeck, T. Wolfe, W. Whitman), S, A, T, B, SATB, orch/pf, 1964; Let us Remember (cant., L. Hughes), solo vv, SATB, orch, 1965; The Trail of Beauty (American Indian texts), Mez, ob, orch, 1976; other sacred choral works; songs, incl. 3 Songs for America, B, wind qnt, str qnt, 1969; 3 Songs for Young People, 1–3 vv, perc, 1991; Journals of Kerouac, 1v, chbr orch, 1995

Principal publishers: C.F. Peters, Remsen

WRITINGS

Vibrations: the Adventures and Musical Times of David Amram (New York, 1968)

Offbeat: Collaborating with Kerouac (New York, 2002)

Upbeat: Nine Lives of a Musical Cat (Boulder, CO, 2007)

BIBLIOGRAPHY

EwenD

"Amram, David (Werner)," *CBY 1969*

"Music and Survival in the World Today," *Newsletter*, Society of Composers, Iowa City, IA, xxvi/2 (1996), 1

E. Caprioglio: "Daring to Improvise: Talking with David Amram," *Peters Notes*, i/2 (1996), 1

BARBARA A. PETERSEN/DON C. GILLESPIE/HILARY BAKER

Amusement parks. An amusement park is a commercially-operated, outdoor venue that offers games, rides, and other types of entertainment, including music. The amusement park concept originated in the pleasure gardens of 17th-century Europe, which were originally large landscaped outdoor spaces primary devoted to games with a few refreshment stands. Dances and social and instrumental concerts became commonly integrated into these pleasure gardens in the 18th century. (*See* Pleasure garden.) Another important part of early amusement park soundscapes was the mechanical organ, which was used by street performers as early as the 18th century and was frequently built into carousel rides by the end of the 19th century. Over the course of the 19th century, the popularity of amusement parks skyrocketed, especially in the United States, where large tracts of land were available for development. Bandstands and pavilions devoted explicitly to musical performances were common in the 19th century, in part influenced by the popular World's Fairs, which were industrial and cultural expositions that featured specific stages devoted to performers from around the world. A change came with the 1893 Chicago World's columbian exposition, the first to feature a "midway," or specific area devoted to rides, games, and entertainment stages away from exhibition houses. Throughout the early 20th century, the most popular kinds of musical entertainment in amusement parks were vaudeville-type variety shows, brass bands, and performances featuring exotic dancers, such as Fahreda Mahzar ("Little Egypt") of Coney Island in New York. With the introduction of loudspeakers to most parks in the 1910s, music could be broadcast throughout the grounds, adding to the pervasive noise from crowds, sideshows, and penny arcade sound effects.

Although amusement parks experienced an economic decline during the interwar period, the introduction of the first commercially-successful theme park—Disneyland, established in Anaheim, California, in 1955—revived the amusement park as a popular entertainment venue while simultaneously changing the paradigm for amusement park operation. Unlike older amusement parks, Disneyland was built around planned areas featuring themes prominent in the Walt Disney films—including the frontier, fantasy, and the future. Like the Walt Disney animated and live action films, this amusement park (and later Disney parks built around the world) draws heavily on music to create its different "lands." Music became a central organizing feature for attractions, composed specifically by Disney film composers for rides such as Walt Disney's Enchanted Tiki Room, the Pirates of the Caribbean, and It's a Small World. To facilitate the aural relationship between moving rides, animatronic figures, and park visitors, composers timed their works precisely to be broadcast over the complex systems of speakers installed throughout the rides and later throughout the park to create immersive soundscapes. The Disney parks additionally draw from older amusement park and World Fair models by providing daily staged and parade performances of brass bands, orchestras, vocalists performing Disney film songs, and themed musical entertainment. This theme park musical model served as an industry leader for a number of subsequent amusement parks.

Today, both background music and live performances are integral to the amusement park experience at the more than 20,000 amusement parks currently operating within the United States. Many parks also offer opportunities for primary and secondary schoolchildren to show off their musical talent; these include the Six Flags

Music Festival in St. Louis, Missouri; the Universal Orlando Stars Program in Orlando, Florida; Hersheypark in Hershey, Pennsylvania; Cedar Point in Sandusky, Ohio; and Disney World and Disneyland. Some amusement parks market themselves specifically around music. Opryland USA, in operation from 1972 to 1997 in Nashville, Tennessee, was built as an amusement park offshoot of the famous Grand Ole Opry performance venue. Billed as "Home of American Music" and "America's Musical Showplace," the park hosted nightly concerts within the park and at the adjacent Grand Ole Opry House, attracting top country and other popular music stars. Dollywood (established in 1986), a park owned by Dolly Parton in Pigeon Forge, Tennessee, includes regular concerts by Parton herself, traditional Smokey Mountains musicians, and performance artists from around the world.

Although generally touted as an important and positive contribution to amusement parks, recent scholarship (Carson, Nooshin) has critiqued the illusion that music creates within theme park experiences, citing concerns about representation, Orientalism, authenticity, and a manufactured sense of nostalgia. While the moral impact of music in amusement parks may be debated, there is no doubt that music is a vital part of the overall amusement park experience.

BIBLIOGRAPHY

G. Kyriazi: *The Great American Amusement Parks: a Pictoral History* (Secaucus, New Jersey, 1976)

C. Carson: "'Whole New Worlds': Music and the Disney Theme Park Experience," *Ethnomusicology Forum*, xiii/2 (2004), 228–35

L. Nooshin: "Circumnavigation with a Difference? Music, Representation and the Disney Experience: It's a Small, Small World," *Ethnomusicology Forum*, xiii/2 (2004), 236–51

A. Fauser: *Musical Encounters at the 1889 Paris World's Fair* (Rochester, 2005)

J. Kurtti: *Walt Disney's Legends of Imagineering and the Genesis of the Disney Theme Park* (New York, 2006)

ELIZABETH A. CLENDINNING

Analysis. *See* MUSICOLOGY; THEORY.

Anchorage. City in ALASKA.

Anderson, Beth [Barbara Elizabeth] (*b* Lexington, KY, 3 Jan 1950). Composer. She studied at the University of Kentucky, the University of California, Davis (BA 1971), where she was a pupil of LARRY AUSTIN, JOHN CAGE, and RICHARD SWIFT, and Mills College (MFA 1973, MA 1974), where her teachers included ROBERT ASHLEY and TERRY RILEY. In 1974 she completed the oratorio *Joan* as a commission for the Cabrillo Music Festival. Active as a writer and editor, Anderson was co-editor of *Ear* (1973–9), and one of its principal contributors. On moving to New York in 1975 she founded *Ear Magazine*; her criticism has also appeared in the *Soho Weekly News*, *Heresies* and *Intermedia*. She teaches college music courses and accompanies dancers at the Martha Graham School of Dance and the American Dance Studio, among others.

By the early 1970s Anderson had composed graphic scores (*Music for Charlemagne Palestine*, 1973), text-sound pieces (*Torero Piece*, 1973), and tape works (*Tulip Clause*, 1973). Later in the decade her music became more conventional in orientation, exhibiting greater rhythmic regularity and an overtly romantic style. She described this turn toward "beauty" as revolutionary in a musical context defined by conceptualism and noise. By the late 1980s, Anderson was composing almost entirely for instrumental forces. She often adopted a principled arbitrariness in composing, determining pitches through code transfer of a linguistic or numerical pattern. She has also shown consistent interest in feminist imagery and history and is particularly fond of music as theatrical entertainment. Since 1984 she has characterized her compositions as "swales," compilations of diverse newly composed music.

WORKS
(*selective list*)

STAGE

Queen Christina (op, Anderson), 1973; Soap Tuning (theater piece, Anderson), 1976; Zen Piece (theater piece, Anderson), 1976; Nirvana Manor (musical, J. Morely), 1981; Elizabeth Rex (The Well-Bred Mother goes to Camp) (musical, J. Kreston), 1983; Avon (musical, S.P. Miller), 1990; The Fat Opera (musical, Kreston), 1991

INSTRUMENTAL

Ens: Lullaby of the Eighth Ancestor, fl, pf, 1979–80; Skater's Suite, 4 insts, 1980, arr. as Skate Suite; Trio: Dream, D, fl, vc, pf, 1980; Ov., band, 1981; Revelation, orch, 1981, rev. chbr orch as Revel, 1984; Suite, wind, perc, 1981; Pennyroyal Swale, str qt, 1985; Rosemary Swale, str qt, 1986; Brass Swale, brass qt, 1989; Saturday/Sunday Swale, brass qnt, 1991; Gui Swale, 2 guis, 1993; Minnesota Swale, orch, 1994; New Mexico Swale, fl, vn, va, vc, perc, 1995; Pf Conc., pf, perc, str orch, 1997; Three Swales (Kentucky, Bluebell, and March), str orch, 2000; March Swale (new arr.), str qt, 2000; August Swale (new arr.), fl, ob, cl, bn, hn, 2003; Jasmine Swale, vn, va, vc, 2005

Solo: Preparation for the Dominant: Outrunning the Inevitable, fl/vn/ocarina, 1979; Manos inquietas, pts. 1–3, pf, 1982; Quilt Music, pf, 1982; Taking Sides, pf, 1983; Belgian Tango, pf/(vn, accdn, pf), 1984; New Work, pf, 1984; Flute Swale, 1995; May Swale, va, 1995; Rhode Island Swale, hpd, 1996; Sept Swale, hpd, 1996

VOCAL
(*texts by Anderson unless otherwise stated)*

A Day, Mez, pf, 1967; WomanRite (A. Perez), C, pf, 1972; Music of Myself, 1v, vib, pf, 1973; She Wrote (G. Stein, K. Acker), Mez, 2 vn, tape, 1973; Torero Piece, 2vv, 1973; Joan (orat.), 1974; Incline Thine Ear to Me (*Bible*), chant, 1975; The People Rumble Louder, 1v, tape, 1975; Black/White, chant, 1976; I Can't Stand It, 1v, perc, 1976; Beauty Runs Faster, Mez, pf, 1978; Yes Sir Ree, 1v, perc, 1978; In Six, Mez, pf, 1979; Knots (R.D. Laing), Mez, pf, 1981; Dreaming Fields (E. Field), Mez, pf, 1987; The Angel (H.C. Andersen, A. Calabrese), S, 2 vn, va, vc, hp, cel, 1988; Precious Memories (J. Krestan and B. Anderson), SATBB, 1996; Harlem Songs, Bar, str bass, pf, 1999; Cat Songs, Bar, pf, 2000; Dark Songs, S, A, pf, 2004; Swimmers on the Shore (D. Mason), Bar, pf, 2004

ELECTRO-ACOUSTIC AND MULTIMEDIA

Tape: Tower of Power, org, tape, 1973; Tulip Clause, chbr ens, tape, 1973; Good-Bye Bridget Bardot (Hello Charlotte Moorman), vc, tape, 1974; They Did It, pf, tape, 1975–6; Ode, 1976; Joan, 1977; German Swale, 1990; several other works

Multimedia: Music for Charlemagne Palestine, graphic score, 2 str insts, lighting, 1973; Peachy Keen-O, vv, org, elec gui, vib, perc, tape, dancers, lighting, 1973; Morning View & Maiden Spring, spkr, tape, slide projections, lighting, 1978

Other: Hallophone, musical environment, 1973; film score, 1980

MSS in *NYp*; recorded interviews in *NHob*

CHARLES SHERE/BENJAMIN PIEKUT

Anderson, Bill [William James] (*b* Columbia, SC, 1 Nov 1937). Country music singer-songwriter, recording artist, and television host. He received his journalism degree from the University of Georgia, but turned to music after Ray Price scored a hit with his song "City Lights" in 1958. Anderson signed with Decca Records in 1958 and joined the Grand Ole Opry in 1961. Known as "Whisperin' Bill" for his distinctive delivery, he composed many of his hits: "Mama sang a song" (Decca, 1962), "Still" (Decca, 1963), "For Loving You" (with Jan Howard; Decca, 1967), and "Sometimes" (with Mary Lou Turner; MCA, 1975), among others, all reached the number one position in *Billboard*'s "Hot Country Singles" chart. He also crafted Lefty Frizzell's "Saginaw, Michigan" (Columbia, 1964), Connie Smith's career-making "Once a Day" (RCA Victor, 1964), and Jean Shepard's "Slippin' Away" (United Artists, 1973), among many others.

Tall, handsome, and poised, Anderson hosted his self-titled syndicated television series (1965–73) and the game shows *The Better Sex* (ABC, 1977–8) and *Fandango* (TNN, 1983–9). He co-hosted TNN's *The Opry Backstage* and later launched *Bill Anderson Visits with the Legends* on SiriusXM Radio in 2006.

Anderson charted his last recording in 1978 and exited Decca/MCA in 1982; subsequently he has recorded mainly for independent labels. Since the mid-1990s, however, he has been quite successful as a songwriter, co-writing such hits as Vince Gill's "Which Bridge to Cross (Which Bridge to Burn)" (MCA, 1995), Kenny Chesney's "A Lot of Things Different" (BNA, 2002), the Brad Paisley–Alison Krauss duet "Whiskey Lullaby" (Arista Nashville, 2005), and George Strait's "Give it away" (MCA Nashville, 2006). Anderson was elected to the Country Music Hall of Fame in 2001.

BIBLIOGRAPHY

B. Anderson: *Whisperin' Bill: an Autobiography* (Athens, GA, 1989)

JOHN W. RUMBLE

Anderson, Cat [William Alonzo] (*b* Greenville, SC, 12 Sept 1916; *d* Norwalk, CA, 29 April 1981). Jazz trumpeter. Orphaned when he was four, he grew up at the Jenkins Orphanage in South Carolina. He took up trombone at the age of seven but switched to trumpet in 1929, and learned music theory as a member of the school's band. In 1932 Anderson and a group of students left the school and formed the Carolina Cotton Pickers. He was a member of the group until 1935, after which he had stints with the orchestras of Claude Hopkins, Doc Wheeler, Lucky Millinder, Erskine Hawkins, Lionel Hampton, and Sabby Lewis, and joined Duke Ellington in 1944. Although he left Ellington's group in 1947, he returned to work with him again during the periods 1950–59 and 1961–71. He was subsequently based in Los Angeles, playing in the studios and with big bands led by Bill Berry and Louis Bellson. Anderson was a high note specialist, often hitting pitches in the upper register during the climax of pieces; on a recording of "Satin Doll" he made with Ellington in 1969 for the Solid State label, the lowest note in his chorus is c''''. While his mastery of the trumpet in this range was largely unparalleled. he was also skilled with the plunger mute, half valve effects, and in his lower register.

BIBLIOGRAPHY

S. Dance: *The World of Duke Ellington* (New York, 1970), 144ff

E. Lambert: "Cat Anderson: a Resumé of his Recorded Work," *JJI*, xxxv/6 (1982), 16

SCOTT YANOW

Anderson, Ernestine (Irene) (*b* Houston, TX, 11 Nov 1928). Jazz and blues singer. At the age of twelve, she won a talent contest held at the El Dorado Ballroom in Houston by improvising new melodies to popular songs and in 1941 began performing with Russell Jacquet. In an attempt to remove Anderson from the nightclub scene and improve her academic standing, her family moved to Seattle in 1944. However, this was just as the jazz scene began to thrive there, and Anderson subsequently performed in bands under Bumps Blackwell, Ray Charles, Johnny Otis, and Lionel Hampton. She also recorded with Gigi Gryce (*Nica's Tempo*, 1955, Savoy) and toured Scandinavia with Rolf Ericsen (1956). While in Sweden, she recorded her debut album *Hot Cargo* (1956, Met.). This album, coupled with performances championed by Ralph J. Gleason, made Anderson a sensation. However, a legal dispute with Mercury, which prevented her from recording for around five years, then derailed her career. Anderson's popularity was revived by a celebrated performance at the Concord Jazz Festival in 1976. This led to a string of recordings for Concord, including *Never make your move too soon* (1981) and *Big City* (1983), that achieved commercial success. She has received four Grammy nominations and was awarded the IMPACT Award by the Pacific Northwest Chapter of the Recording Academy in 2004.

BIBLIOGRAPHY

W.R. Stokes: "Ernestine Anderson: 'Feeling Good!'," *JT* (1987), Sept, 13

F. Bouchard: "Ernestine Anderson," *JT* (1990), Nov, 13

CHADWICK JENKINS

Anderson, Gillian (Bunshaft) (*b* Brookline, MA, 28 Nov 1943). Conductor, musicologist, and music librarian. Anderson attended Bryn Mawr (BA 1965), the University of Illinois (MM 1969), and the University of Maryland (MLS 1989). Anderson was a Music Librarian at the Library of Congress from 1978 to 1995 before resigning to pursue an independent career as a conductor, specializing in the conducting of music to accompany the showings of silent films. Her interest in this area began in the late 1970s while working on the score for Carl Dreyer's *The Passion of Joan of Arc*. Her conducting is informed by scholarly work; whenever possible her performances use the music for its original release; lacking that, she compiles a score using material which might have been used during the film's first showings. A good example of her work is the 1922 film *Häxan* (now on Criterion Collection DVD 134).

Anderson served as President of the Sonneck Society for American Music (now Society for American Music) between 1993 and 1995. In 1972 she founded the Colonial Singers and Players in Washington, DC, dedicated to performing American music of the 17th and 18th centuries. She has published several scholarly editions of colonial American music. In 1997 she founded the group Cinemusica Viva. She also co-founded, with Ronald Sadoff, the journal *Music and the Moving Image*, which began publication in 2008.

WRITINGS

Freedom's Voice in Poetry and Song (Wilmington, DE, 1977)

"'The Temple of Minerva" and Francis Hopkinson: a Reappraisal of America's First Poet-Composer," *Proceedings of the American Philosophical Society*, cxx/3 (1979), 166–77.

Music for Silent Films, 1894–1929: A Guide (Washington DC, 1988)

"Putting the Experience of the World at the Nation's Command: Music at the Library of Congress, 1800–1917," *JAMS*, xlii/1 (1989), 108–49

WAYNE D. SHIRLEY

Anderson, Ivie (Marie) [Johnson, Ivie (Marie); Ivy] (*b* Gilroy, CA, 10 July 1905; *d* Los Angeles, CA, 28 Dec 1949). Jazz singer. She traveled abroad as Ivie Marie Johnson on two occasions; it is unknown whether Johnson was her married name or her given name at birth. She studied singing at a local convent and then for two years with Sara Ritt in Washington, DC. After returning to California, she worked with Curtis Mosby, Paul Howard, and Sonny Clay, and sang and danced in the vaudeville revues *Fanchon and Marco* and *Shuffle Along*. She toured Australia with Clay in 1928 before organizing her own show in the United States. After Duke Ellington heard her perform with Earl Hines, she worked with him from February 1931. Ellington thought highly of Anderson, and many critics consider her to be the finest singer to work in Ellington's band. Certainly her vivacious sense of rhythm and dramatic delivery mark several noted Ellington recordings of the 1930s and early 1940s, including "It don't mean a thing" (1932, Bruns.); "Solitude" (1940, Col.); and "I got it bad and that ain't good" (1941, Vic.). Anderson appeared in several films and shorts, often with Ellington's band. She sings a wonderful rendition of "Stormy Weather" in *Bundle of Blues* (1933) and plays Ellington's jilted lover in the short *I got it bad and that ain't good* (1941). She also appeared in films without Ellington, notably *Hit Parade of 1937* and *A Day at the Races* (1937). Chronic asthma forced Anderson to retire from performing with Ellington in August 1942, after which she moved back to California, opened Ivie's Chicken Shack, and sang in local nightclubs. Following the continuted deterioration of her health, she gave up performing altogether in the late 1940s.

BIBLIOGRAPHY

P.E. Miller: "Ivie Joined the Duke for Four Weeks, Stays with Band for 12 Years," *DB*, ix/14 (1942), 31

S. Placksin: *American Women in Jazz, 1900 to the Present: their Words, Lives, and Music* (New York, 1982, London, 1985 as *Jazzwomen, 1900 to the Present: their Words, Lives, and Music*)

CHADWICK JENKINS

Anderson, John Murray (*b* St. John's, NF, 20 Sept 1886; *d* New York, NY, 30 Jan 1954). Impresario, producer, and director of Canadian birth. Rivalled only by Florenz Ziegfeld for his lavish revues, Murray Anderson produced *The Ziegfeld Follies* in 1934, 1936, and 1943, *Life Begins at 8:40* (1934), and eponymous *Almanac* revues in 1929 and 1953. His *Greenwich Village Follies* (1919–24) were billed as offering "intellectual beauty," though they showcased nudity on a reduced budget from non-Equity performers (complemented by a handful of class acts). Still, their popularity and quality (of Murray Anderson's sketches, if not the music) propelled them on to Broadway by 1921. He also produced or directed other key shows, including *Dearest Enemy* (1925) and Billy Rose's *Jumbo* (1935). In Hollywood he was involved with *King of Jazz* (1930), *Bathing Beauty* (1944), *The Great Ziegfeld* (1946), and *The Greatest Show on Earth* (1952). He ran an acting school in New York in the 1920s and 1930s, where a number of later stars trained, including Bette Davis, with whom he maintained a lifelong friendship. He also worked as a songwriter, designer, and actor, and some of the more sensational elements of shows like the *Music Box Revue* (1924) included his designs.

DOMINIC SYMONDS

Anderson, June (*b* Boston, MA, 30 Dec 1952). Soprano. She studied at Yale University, studied with Robert Leonard in New York City, and made her debut in 1978 as the Queen of Night at the New York City Opera, where she also sang Rosina, Gilda, Olympia (*Les contes d'Hoffmann*), and Lora (*Die Feen*). In 1982 she made her European debut at the Rome Opera in *Semiramide*. Building a spectacular career in Europe, she performed in a wide array of *bel canto* roles at La Scala and many other key European venues. In the United States she has sung in Chicago and San Francisco, among other cities, and first appeared at the Metropolitan Opera in 1989, as Gilda. She made her British debut in 1984 with the WNO as Violetta, disclosing her dramatic talents, and first sang at Covent Garden in 1986 in a concert performance of *Semiramide*, returning as Lucia, Gilda, and Elvira (*I puritani*, 1992), roles that are peculiarly well suited to her vocal gifts of plangent tone and technical flexibility, and her sincere and eloquent acting. She has sung Rossini's Desdemona, Anna (*Maometto II*), Zoraid, and Armida; Bellini's Amina, Juliet, Elvira, and Beatrice; Donizetti's Marie (*La fille du régiment*), Verdi's Lida (*La battaglia di Legnano*), and Gulnara (*Il corsaro*). Her extensive recording career chronicles her wide-ranging skills, especially in the Italian and French repertory. She has received a particularly fond embrace from the French government, which elevated her to "Commandeur" of the Order des Arts et des Lettres in 2008.

ELIZABETH FORBES/ALAN BLYTH/R

Anderson, Laurie (*b* Chicago, IL, 5 June 1947). Performance artist, composer, and musician. Although Anderson played the violin from childhood, she received her formal training in art history and the visual arts (Barnard College, BA 1969; Columbia University, MFA 1972). Anderson has pioneered a type of multimedia performance art that bridges the gap between music and art: combining age-old storytelling techniques with futuristic, electronically produced images and sounds, telling tales and creating purely instrumental music. Since the 1970s Anderson has created a broad range of works:

books, films, videos, photographs, mixed-media installations, large-scale performances, records, and an interactive CD-ROM. By 1976 her work was featured prominently in museums and concert venues across Europe and North America.

The first phase of Anderson's career culminated in her magnum opus, *United States I–IV*, performed at the Brooklyn Academy of Music in 1983. Hailed by critics as a captivating portrait of American life in the late 20th century, the work was regarded as thematizing the contradictions and tensions of late-capitalist society. Lasting over seven hours and involving 11 other performers, *United States I–IV* was staged on two separate nights, incorporating electronically enhanced violins, slide projection, film, music and recitation of Anderson's own witty, yet disturbing stories loosely related to four major themes: transportation, politics, love, and money. Typical of much of her work, Anderson expresses her ideas about alienation produced by contemporary culture while at the same time self-consciously relying on the very technological mediation she appears to lament.

In 1981 Anderson's single "O Superman (For Massenet)" reached number two on the British pop charts with its eerie mix of purring stringed instruments, chattering saxophones and sinister angel chorus. Until then music had been only one of the media employed in her work. As a performance artist, she had been reluctant to release recorded fragments of live concerts. The unlikely success of "O Superman," however, offered new audiences and new directions for artistic experimentation. In 1982 she recorded her first full-length commercial project *Big Science*, an album made up of works originally designed for live performance. A second album, *Mister Heartbreak* (1984), announced her willingness to privilege sound over other components in her work; together with Peter Gabriel she composed new songs and revised earlier ones so that they could stand as independent musical entities. Although some critics regarded *Mister Heartbreak* as a violation of her performance-art principles, the album secured her crossover to a mainstream audience. A feature-length film, *Home of the Brave* (1986), presented her in concert performances to an even larger audience. In 1987 the unusual name-recognition she had acquired through these popular successes allowed her (with her male clone) to host "Live from Off Center," a weekly showcase of avant-garde art on American public television.

Subsequent albums, if not as successful as *Mister Heartbreak*, continued to engage the attention of both popular-music and avant-garde audiences. She published several books of texts and visual imagery and continued to perform in concert. Although her work has occasionally highlighted the fact that she is a woman (for example, *Langue d'amour* on *Mister Heartbreak*; her use of the vocoder to make her voice sound like that of a smug patriarch), much of it maintains an androgynous stance.

In 2010, with *Homeland*, Anderson continued to create works that meditate on modern existence. The centerpiece of *Homeland* is a ten-minute track featuring a spoken-word monologue by her alter ego, Fenway Bergamot, who appears on the album cover, with his greasepaint mustache and eyebrows. On "Another Day in America," he expounds on punctuation, God, Kierkegaard, and the vagaries of life in the 21st century. *Homeland* achieved critical acclaim, making NPR's list of the Five Best Genre-Defying Albums of 2010. "Flow," the haunting final track, was nominated for a Grammy Award for Best Pop Instrumental Performance. Recognized as a pioneer in the use of technology in the arts, Anderson has invented several instruments, such as the tape-bow violin used for *Duets on Ice* (1974) and her talking stick from *Songs and Stories from Moby Dick* (1999); she received the 2011 SEAMUS (Society for Electro-Acoustic Music in the United States) Lifetime Achievement Award.

Laurie Anderson, 2001. (Markus Stuecklin/Associated Press)

As a composer, Anderson has contributed musical scores to films by Wim Wenders and Jonathan Demme; dance pieces by Bill. T. Jones and Trisha Brown; pieces for National Public radio and the BBC; musical collaborations with Philip Glass, Brian Eno, Fred Frith, Nona Hendryx, Frank Zappa, Bobby McFerrin, and Lou Reed; and worked with poets William S. Burroughs and John Giorno, and even with comedian Andy Kaufman in the late 1970s. She also holds the unique position as the first and only artist-in-residence at NASA. Her orchestra work *Songs for A.E.* was premiered at Carnegie Hall in 2000, performed by the American Composers Orchestra, and later toured Europe with the Stuttgart Chamber Orchestra. Anderson has achieved greater visibility than most composers of her generation, in part because of her originality: coming to music from the visual arts, she was free to manipulate sounds as she liked. Her unexpected crossover into the popular domain brought her a degree of fame usually unavailable to avant-garde artists, making her one of the most influential women composers of her time.

WORKS

Performances: Automotive, 1972; Institutional Dream Series, 1972; O-RANGE, 1973; As: If, 1974; Duets on Ice, 1974; In the Nick of Time, 1974; Out of the Blue, 1974; Tales from the Vienna Woods, 1974; Songs and Stories for the Insomniac, 1975; For Instants 3

'Refried Beans', 1976; Stereo Stories, 1976; Audio Talk, 1977; On Dit, 1977; Some Songs, 1977; Stereo Decoy, 1977; That's Not the Way I Heard It, 1977; Down Here, 1978; Like a Stream, 1978; Suspended Sentences, 1978; Americans on the Move, 1979; Blue Horn File, 1979; Born, Never Asked, 1980; It's Cold Outside, 1981; United States I–IV, 1983; Mister Heartbreak, 1984; Natural History, 1986; Talk Normal, 1987; Empty Places, 1989; Voices from the Beyond, 1991; Halcyon Days: Stories from the Nerve Bible, 1992; The Speed of Darkness, 1996; Songs and Stories from Moby Dick, 1999; Happiness, 2001; The End of the Moon, 2005; Homeland, 2007; Burning Leaves, 2009; Amelia Earhart, 2010; Delusion, 2010

Film, Video, Multimedia: Laurie Anderson: Collected Videos (1990); Home of the Brave: a Film by Laurie Anderson (1986); What You Mean We (1987); Puppet Motel Multimedia, CD-ROM (Anderson with Hsin-Chien Huang, 1995)

RECORDINGS

You're the Guy I Want to Share my Money With (with W.S. Burroughs and J. Giorno) (1981, Giorno Poetry Systems); *Big Science* (1982, Warner Bros., BSK 3674); *Mister Heartbreak* (1984, Warner Bros., 9 25077-1); *United States Live* (1984, Warner Bros., 9 25192-1); *Home of the Brave* (soundtrack album), (1986, Warner Bros., 9 25400-1); *Strange Angels* (featuring B. McFerrin) (1989, Warner Bros., 9 25900-1); *Bright Red* (1994, Warner Bros., 9 45534-1); *The Ugly One with the Jewels and Other Stories* (1995, Warner Bros., 9 45857-2); *Talk Normal: the Laurie Anderson Anthology* (2000, Rhino., B00004Y-LIR); *Life on a String* (2001, Nonesuch, B000050K9A); *Live in New York* (2002, Nonesuch, B0000668N9); *Homeland* (2010, Nonesuch, B003905M2O)

WRITINGS

United States (New York, 1984)
Home of the Brave (New York, 1986)
Postcard Book (New York, 1990)
Empty Places (New York, 1991)
Stores from the Nerve Bible: A Retrospective 1972–1992 (New York, 1994)
Night Life (2007)

BIBLIOGRAPHY

P. Stewart: "Laurie Anderson: With a Song in My Art," *Art in America*, lxix (1979), 110–13

M. Gordon: "Laurie Anderson: Performance Artist," *Drama Review*, xxiv (1980), 51–64

C. Owens: "Amplifications: Laurie Anderson," *Art in America*, lxix/3 (1981), 120–33

J. Kardon, ed.: *Laurie Anderson: Works from 1969–1983*, Institute of Contemporary Art, 15 Oct–4 Dec 1983 (Philadelphia, 1983) [exhibition catalog]

J. Rockwell: "Laurie Anderson: Women Composers, Performance Art and the Perils of Fashion," *All American Music: Composition in the Late Twentieth Century* (New York, 1983), 123–32

J. Apple: "Commerce on the Edge: The Convergence of Art and Entertainment," *High Performance*, ix/2 (1986), 34–8

J. Mowitt: "Performance Theory as the Work of Laurie Anderson," *Discourse*, xii/2 (1990), 48–65

S. McClary: "This is Not a Story my People Tell: Musical Time and Space According to Laurie Anderson," *Feminine Endings* (Minneapolis, 1991), 132–47

J. Howell: *Laurie Anderson* (New York, 1992)

W. Duckworth: *Talking Music: Conversations with John Cage, Philip Glass, Laurie Anderson and Five Generations of American Experimental Composers* (New York and London, 1995)

R. Goldberg: *Laurie Anderson* (New York, 2000)

J. McGuire: *The Language of Laurie Anderson* (diss., Indiana U., 2002)

The Record of Time: Sound in the Work of Laurie Anderson, Musée d'Art Contemporain de Lyon (Lyon, 2002) [exhibition catalog]

SUSAN McCLARY/JULIE McGUIRE

Anderson, Leroy (*b* Cambridge, MA, 29 June 1908; *d* Woodbury, CT, 18 May 1975). Composer, arranger, and conductor. He studied piano and organ with his mother and Henry Gideon, and double bass with Gaston Dufresne. He also worked with Albert Spalding (theory), Edward Ballantine (counterpoint), Clifford Heilman (fugue), and Walter Piston and George Enescu (composition) at Harvard, receiving his bachelor's degree in 1929 and master's in 1930. As he pursued studies in German and Scandinavian languages at Harvard (1930–34), he tutored at Radcliffe College (1930–32) and conducted and arranged music for the Harvard University Band as well as dance bands. In 1936 he composed an arrangement of Harvard songs for the conductor of the Boston Pops, Arthur Fiedler, who subsequently performed two original pieces, *Jazz Pizzicato* (1938) and *Jazz Legato* (1939). While serving in the military (1942–6), Anderson continued writing music for Fiedler and, after World War II, he became an arranger for the Boston Pops in addition to providing them with a series of short orchestral novelties, often with picturesque titles.

In the early 1950s his fame spread with CBS's selection of *Syncopated Clock* (1945) as the theme song for "The Late Show," and Anderson's hit recording of *Blue Tango* (1951), which sold over a million copies. The concurrent growth of Pops concerts around the nation and a contract with Decca allowing him to conduct and record his own music consolidated his popularity, and a 1953 study named him the American composer most frequently performed by native orchestras. In that same year he composed the Concerto in C for piano and orchestra, his only extended orchestral work. In 1958 his one musical comedy, *Goldilocks*, opened in New York. A romantic farce set against the early days of the motion picture industry, it enjoyed only a short run, though some of the show's numbers had continued success when arranged for orchestra. In collaboration with Mitchell Parish, he also adapted some of his orchestral music to make songs, including "Sleigh Ride," which became a Christmas perennial, although Anderson intended it simply as a winter landscape. In 1988 he was elected posthumously to the Songwriters Hall of Fame.

Distinguished by careful workmanship and an ingratiating whimsy, Anderson's music derived largely from Gershwin and other popular song composers. He orchestrated vividly (see, for example, the use of whip, sleigh bells, and trumpet "horse whinny" effect in *Sleigh Ride*, 1948), and on two occasions (*The Typewriter*, 1950, and *Sandpaper Ballet*, 1954) he featured nontraditional instruments. Anderson raised the prominence of the popular orchestral miniature, and such music proved useful not only to pops concerts, but to radio, television and Muzak, making his music familiar to millions who would not necessarily recognize his name. The music, which often stylishly adapted popular dance forms, also attracted dancers, most notably choreographer Mark Morris, whose *Sandpaper Ballet*, set to 11 Anderson miniatures, premiered in 1999.

WORKS
(selective list)

Stage: Goldilocks (musical, 2, J. Ford, J. and W. Kerr), New York, Lunt-Fontanne, 11 Oct 1958

Orch: Jazz Pizzicato, str, 1938; Harvard Sketches, 1939, rev. as Alma Mater, 1954; Jazz Legato, str, 1939; Promenade, 1945; The Syncopated Clock, 1945 [as song with M. Parish, 1950]; Fiddle-Faddle, str, 1947; Serenata, 1947 [as song with Parish, 1950]; Governor Bradford March, 1948; Saraband, 1948; Sleigh Ride, 1948 [as song with Parish, 1950]; A Trumpeter's Lullaby, 1949; The Typewriter, 1950; The Waltzing Cat, 1950 [as song with Parish, 1951]; Belle of the Ball, 1951 [as song with Parish, 1953]; Blue Tango, 1951 [as song with Parish, 1952]; China Doll, 1951; Horse and Buggy, 1951; The Penny-Whistle Song, 1951; The Phantom Regiment, 1951; Plink, Plank, Plunk!, str, 1951

Conc. in C, pf, orch, 1953; The Girl in Satin, 1953; Song of the Bells, 1953; Summer Skies, 1953; Bugler's Holiday, 1954; The First Day of Spring, 1954; Forgotten Dreams, 1954 [as song with Parish, 1962]; Sandpaper Ballet, 1954; Arietta, 1962; Balladette, 1962; The Captains and the Kings, 1962; Clarinet Candy, 1962; The Golden Years, 1962; Home Stretch, 1962; Lullaby of the Drums, 1970; March of the Two Left Feet, 1969; Waltz Around the Scale, 1970

Marching band: Ticonderoga March, 1945

Arrs: Harvard Fantasy, 1936, rev. as A Harvard Festival, 1969; Carousel [from R. Rodgers], 1946; Chicken Reel, 1946; Annie Get Your Gun [from I. Berlin], 1947; Buttons and Bows [from J. Livingston and R. Evans], 1947; Irish Suite, 1947, addl. 2 movts, 1949; Old Macdonald had a Farm, 1947; Richard Rodgers Waltzes, 1947; Brigadoon [from F. Loewe], 1948; Kiss Me, Kate [from C. Porter], 1949; A Christmas Festival, 1950; Classical Jukebox [from B. Baum and S. Weiss], 1950; South Pacific [from Rodgers], 1950

Song of Jupiter [from G.F. Handel], orch, 1951; The Bluebells of Scotland, 1954; Turn Ye to Me, 1954; Suite of Carols, brass choir, 1955; Suite of Carols, str, 1955; Suite of Carols, ww ens, 1955; 76 Trombones [from M. Willson], 1957; Birthday Party [from P. Hill and M. Hill], orch, opt. chorus, 1970; Second Regiment Connecticut National Guard March [from D.W. Reeves], 1973; Girl Crazy [from Gershwin], 1974

Principal publishers: Mills, Woodbury Music

BIBLIOGRAPHY

L.W. Gilbert: "Salute to a 'Popular' Master," *MJ*, xii/11 (1954), 25 only

"The 'Syncopated Clock' Still Ticks," *MJ*, xxvi/9 (1968), 30–31

G.W. Briggs Jr: "Leroy Anderson on Broadway: Behind-the-Scene Accounts of the Musical 'Goldilocks'," *AM*, iii/3 (1985), 329–36

F. Fennell: "Music by Leroy Anderson," *The Instrumentalist*, lxiv/9 (1989–90), 26–31

H. Pollack: *Harvard Composers* (Metuchen, NJ, 1992)

E. Spalding: "Leroy Anderson," *Harvard Magazine*, cxvi/6 (1992–3), 38, 40

A. Tommasini: "Tuneful Gems from a Master of a Lost Art," *New York Times* (10 March 1996)

B. Speed, E. Anderson, and S. Metcalf: Leroy Anderson: a Bio-Bibliography (Westport, CT, 2004)

HOWARD POLLACK

Anderson, Marian (*b* Philadelphia, PA, 27 Feb 1897; *d* Portland, OR, 8 April 1993). Contralto. After graduating from South Philadelphia High School, she studied in her native city with Giuseppe Boghetti but was refused entry as an African American applicant to the Philadelphia Music Academy on racial grounds. With the support of pianist Joseph Pasternack, Anderson was the first to record Negro spirituals with a major American record label, the Victor Talking Machine Company (later RCA Victor), in 1923. Having won first prize in a competition sponsored by the New York Philharmonic, she appeared as a soloist with the orchestra at Lewisohn Stadium on 27 August 1925. After further study with Frank La Forge, she made a number of concert appearances in the United States, and her European debut took place at the Wigmore Hall, London, in 1930. She was subsequently lionized throughout Europe, winning from Toscanini the reported tribute: "A voice like yours is heard only once in a hundred years," a description that followed her throughout her entire career. By then a mature artist, Anderson gained high critical acclaim for her appearance at Town Hall in New York (1935) and then undertook further tours, across the United States and in Europe. Because of a lack of stage experience—and therefore confidence—she refused offers to sing in opera, but such best-selling discs as Delilah's "Softly awakes my heart" show what might have been. On account of her race, the Daughters of the American Revolution denied Anderson the use of Constitution Hall in Washington, DC, for a concert in 1939; with the support of then First Lady Eleanor Roosevelt and the US Department of the Interior, she gave a concert at the Lincoln Memorial (9 April 1939), which drew an audience of some 75,000 people. At the invitation of Rudolf Bing, she made a belated debut at the Metropolitan Opera in New York as Ulrica in *Un ballo in maschera* in 1955. Although her voice was no longer at its best and she was understandably affected by the emotion of the moment, as the first black singer on the company's roster she paved the way for her successors.

Marian Anderson with Rudolf Bing, general manager of the Metropolitan Opera Company, 1950. (Lebrecht Music & Arts)

After leaving the Metropolitan in 1956, Anderson continued her concert career, making a farewell tour in 1965. Her voice was a rich, vibrant contralto of intrinsic beauty. She left recordings covering every aspect of her repertory. Her lieder, though hardly idiomatic, are deeply felt, while in spirituals she is compelling. Her autobiography, *My Lord, What a Morning*, was published in New York in 1956.

BIBLIOGRAPHY

K. Vehanen: *Marian Anderson: a Portrait* (New York, 1941/*R*)

M. Anderson: *My Lord, What a Morning* (New York, 1956/*R* Urbana, IL, 2002 with intro. by J.A. DePriest)

J.L. Sims: *Marian Anderson: an Annotated Bibliography and Discography* (Westport, CT, 1981)

N.M. Westlake and O.E. Albrecht: *Marian Anderson: a Catalogue of the Collection at the University of Pennsylvania* (Philadelphia, 1982)
R. Story: *And So I Sing: African American Divas of Opera and Concert* (New York, 1993)
J.B. Steane: *Singers of the Century* (London, 1996), 46–50
A. Keiler: *Marian Anderson: a Singer's Journey* (New York, 2000)
R. Arsenault: *The Sound of Freedom: Marian Anderson, The Lincoln Memorial, and the Concert that Awakened America* (New York, 2010)

MAX DE SCHAUENSEE/MARTI NEWLAND

Anderson, Maxwell (*b* Atlantic, PA, 15 Dec 1888; *d* Stamford, CT, 28 Feb 1959). Playwright. After studies at the University of North Dakota and at Stanford University he taught in North Dakota and California. In 1918 he moved to New York, where he worked for several years as a journalist before establishing himself as a playwright. His writings include several verse dramas, radio plays, film scripts, music dramas, essays, and one volume of poetry.

Anderson had a lifelong interest in the musical stage. For many years he was associated closely with Kurt Weill, with whom he collaborated on *Knickerbocker Holiday* and *Lost in the Stars*, a dramatization of Alan Paton's novel *Cry, the Beloved Country*. Uncompleted works with Weill include *Ulysses Africanus* (whose leading role was intended for Paul Robeson) and *Raft on the River*, a musical adaptation of Twain's *Adventures of Huckleberry Finn*. Weill and Anderson also collaborated on a scenic cantata, *The Ballad of Magna Carta*, and Anderson translated Brecht's *Der Jasager* for Weill's school opera.

Other uncompleted music dramas are *Hell On Wheels* (with John Jacob Niles and Douglas S. Moore), *Devil's Hornpipe* (with Allie Wrubel), and *Art of Love*, for which Anderson found no collaborator. One of the few Anderson poems set to music is *St. Agnes' Morning* by Henry Cowell, a friend of the author. Other adaptations include *A Christmas Carol*, a version of Dickens's story with music by Bernard Herrmann, and a musical adaptation for television of Anderson's play *High Tor*, with music by Arthur Schwartz.

See also Irving, Washington.

BIBILIOGRAPHY

M. Anderson: "Assembling the Parts for a Musical Play," *New York Herald Tribune* (30 Oct 1949)
M. Anderson: "Kurt Weill," *Theatre Arts*, xxxiv (1950), 58–88
M. Anderson: "Inside Story of a Musical: from Book to Broadway," *New York Herald Tribune* (29 Oct 1951)
L.G. Avery: *A Catalogue of the Maxwell Anderson Collection at the University of Texas* (Austin, 1968)
L.G. Avery: "Maxwell Anderson and *Both your Houses,*" *North Dakota Quarterly*, xxxviii (1970), 5–24
M. Matlaw: "Alan Paton's *Cry, the Beloved Country* and Maxwell Anderson's/Kurt Weill's *Lost in the Stars*: a Consideration of Genres," *Arcadia*, x (1975), 260–72
L.G. Avery, ed.: *Dramatist in America: Letters of Maxwell Anderson, 1912–1958* (Chapel Hill, NC, 1977)
R. Sanders: *The Days Grow Short: the Life and Music of Kurt Weill* (New York, 1980)
M.A. Hovland: *Musical Settings of American Poetry: a Bibliography* (Westport, CT, 1986) [incl. list of settings]
E. Juchem: *Kurt Weill und Maxwell Anderson: Neue Wege zu einem amerikanischen Musiktheater, 1938–1950* (Stuttgart and Weimar, 1999)

MICHAEL HOVLAND/R

Anderson, R(obert) Alex (*b* Honolulu, HI, 6 June 1894; *d* Honolulu, HI, 30 May 1995). Composer, musician, and record producer. Anderson's parents were socially prominent in Honolulu, and he was educated in Honolulu and at Cornell University. Soon after graduation, he joined the Air Force and was sent into air combat in France during World War I. Shot down and captured, he led a daring escape across German lines into Holland by speaking the limited French and German he had learned in high school. Eventually, his exploits were turned into *The Dawn Patrol* (1930), a film starring Richard Barthelmess. Anderson married Peggy Center, a high school classmate, and began a successful Hawaii-based career in business and service to the community. Although he had no formal musical training, and played the piano by ear, his talent for clever lyrics and songwriting flourished as well.

Anderson wrote more than 200 songs during his lifetime, which spanned most of the 20th century. Anderson lived to see not only the birth of hapa haole music, but witnessed every step in its evolution through ragtime, big band swing, and Hawaiian style hula, earning him the title of "The Godfather of Hapa Haole Music." Anderson's hapa haole compositions (songs with predominantly English lyrics with some references to Hawaii and the Hawaiian language) may be among the most distinctively Hawaiian music ever recorded. His songs collectively share the Hawaii of his birth, with its unique people, places, and elements. Among his most famous compositions, which have been recorded countless times, are "Haole Hula," "Lovely Hula Hands," "White Ginger Blossoms," "On a Coconut Island," "Malihini Mele," "The Cockeyed Mayor of Kaunakai," "I'll weave a lei of stars for you," and the premiere Hawaiian Christmas song, "Mele Kalikimaka."

BIBLIOGRAPHY

T. Todaro: *The Golden Years of Hawaiian Entertainment, 1874–1974* (Honolulu, 1974)
G.S. Kanahele: *Hawaiian Music and Musicians: an Illustrated History* (Honolulu, 1979)
C.S. Stone: *Joyful Heart: the Life and Music of R. Alex Anderson* (Honolulu, 2001)

HARRY B. SORIA JR.

Anderson, Robert (i) (*b* Anguilla, MS, 21 March 1919; *d* Hazel Crest, IL, 15 June, 1995). Gospel director, singer, composer, and publisher. Anderson established a career forming and training gospel groups in Chicago. His formative years were spent as one of the original Roberta Martin Singers, one of the premiere gospel groups of the 1930s and 1940s. He left briefly, between 1939 and 1941, to form the first of his many ensembles, the Knowles and Anderson Singers with R.L. Knowles. He rejoined Martin, but ultimately resigned because of the travel demands. In 1947 he formed Robert Anderson and his Gospel Caravan, but after several members left in 1952, he formed a new set of singers that recorded and performed under the name the Robert Anderson Singers through the mid-1950s. Throughout his career, Anderson recorded on a multitude of labels including Miracle and United with

Robert Anderson and the Caravans; and later with the Robert Anderson Singers, on Apollo. Anderson wrote, and often sang lead on, many of the songs his groups performed, including "Why should I worry" (1945). "Prayer changes things" (1947) and "Oh Lord, is it I?" (1953) demonstrate Anderson's resonant baritone voice and fondness for the slow gospel ballad format. His characteristic delivery, commonly compared to popular crooners, had a sense of formality that evoked his training with ROBERTA MARTIN. A roster of gospel notables also performed Anderson's songs including Mahalia Jackson and James Cleveland. In 1942 Anderson established the Good Shepherd Music House in Gary, Indiana. Anderson also served as choir director at a number of churches that included Greater Harvest Baptist Church, Chicago; Opportunity Baptist Church in Los Angeles, and Hertzell United Methodist Church, Chicago.

BIBLIOGRAPHY

H.C. Boyer: *How Sweet the Sound: the Golden Age of Gospel* (Washington, DC, 1995)

A. Heilbut: *The Gospel Sound: Good News and Bad Times* (New York, 1971, rev. and updated, 6/2002)

ROXANNE R. REED

Anderson, Robert (Theodore) (ii) (*b* Chicago, IL, 5 Oct 1934; *d* Honolulu, HI, 29 May 2009). Educator and organist. He attended Illinois Wesleyan University and Union Theological Seminary (MSM 1957, DSM 1961), studying organ with Lillian McCord, ROBERT BAKER, and, as winner of a Fulbright grant for two years, Helmut Walcha in Frankfurt, Germany. An exacting, demanding, and colorful organ teacher, Anderson spent his entire career (1960–98) in the Meadows School of the Arts at Southern Methodist University, Dallas, where he mentored a large number of prize-winning organists, served as organist of the school's Chapel, and was honored with the highest academic rank, University Distinguished Professor. Three recordings for the Aeolian-Skinner Organ Company's *King of Instruments* series organized as three separate programs, one each of 18th-, 19th-, and 20th-century organ music, illustrate a brilliant stylistic command of organ repertory spanning all periods from the earliest to the most contemporary. Holder of the highest certificate from the American Guild of Organists (FAGO), Anderson served that organization as National Councilor for Education and was program chair for two national conventions of the Guild in Dallas. He toured widely as a recitalist in the United States and Europe and was frequently employed as a competition adjudicator and organ consultant.

LARRY PALMER

Anderson, (Evelyn) Ruth (*b* Kalispell, MT, 21 Mar 1928). Composer, flutist and orchestrator. She studied flute (BA 1949) and composition (MA 1951) at the University of Washington. Postgraduate work at the Columbia-Princeton Electronic Music Center and at Princeton University followed, along with private study in composition with EMILE BOULANGER and DARIUS MILHAUD and in flute with JOHN WUMMER and JEAN-PIERRE RAMPAL while in Paris on two Fulbright scholarships (1958–60). Initially, she worked as a flutist in the Totenberg Instrumental Ensemble (1951–58) and as principal of the Boston Pops (1958). Her career branched out into orchestration, working at NBC (1960–66) and Lincoln Center Theater (1966). She wrote that after her exposure to tape manipulation she became open to the potential of, "all sounds...as material for music" and her career then focused on electronic music composition, for which she is best known. She designed and became the director of the first electronic music studio at CUNY Hunter College, where she taught composition and theory (1966–89). She had several residencies at the MacDowell Colony (1957–73) and Yaddo (1969, 1982) and has received numerous grants to support her work. She retired from Hunter College in 1989 and divides her time between New York and Montana.

Anderson views sound as energy that has the power to effect one's state of being. Keenly interested in the healing, restorative powers of music, she attempts to foster wholeness of self and unity with others as central ideals in all her work. Those concepts are prevalent in her two sonic meditations, *Points* (1974), which uses sine waves, and *I come out of your sleep* (1979), which is constructed from sounds in Louise Bogan's poem "Little Lobelia," set as canonic, electronically elongated whispered vowel sounds. *Centering* (1979) is a performance piece for a dancer and four observers whose reactions to the dance are translated into sound by oscillators, via galvanic skin resistance sensors, to which the dancer then responds. Her later works, such as SUM (State of the Union Message), are sonic collage pieces, incorporating sound clips intricately interwoven to create a complex tapestry of sound.

WORKS

(selective list)

El-ac: The Pregnant Dream (M. Swenson), 1968; ES II, 1969; DUMP, 1970; SUM (State of the Union Message), 1973; Conversations, 1974; Points, 1974; Tuneable Hopscotch, 1975; Dress Rehearsal, 1976; Centering, 1979; I come out of your sleep (L. Bogan), 1979; Resolutions, 1984; Time and Tempo, 1984

Text pieces: Naming, 1975; A Long Sound, 1976; Sound Portraits I–II, 1977; Silent Sound, 1978; Greetings from the Right Hemisphere, 1979; Communications, 1980

Other: Fugue, pf/str, 1948; The Merchant's Song (P. Coombs), C, pf, 1951; Two Pieces, str, 1957; Two Movts, str, 1958

Scores and tape recordings in: *NYamc, NYp*

BIBLIOGRAPHY

A.C. McGinnis: "Music and Healing," *Heresies*, iii/2 (1980), 12

A.I. Cohen: *International Encyclopedia of Women Composers* (New York, 1981, 2/1987)

B. Grigsby: "Women Composers of Electronic Music," *The Musical Woman: an International Perspective*, i (1984), 173–5

J. Rosen, ed.: "Composers Speaking for Themselves: an Electronic Music Panel Discussion," *The Musical Woman: an International Perspective*, ii (1987), 308–12

E. Hinkle-Turner: *Women Composers and Music Technology in the United States* (London, 2006), 29

BARBARA A. PETERSEN/JUDITH ROSEN/BONNIE E. FLEMING

Anderson, T(homas) J(efferson) (*b* Coatesville, PA, 17 Aug 1928). Composer. Born into a musical family, he began piano study with his mother at the age of five and formed his first touring jazz ensemble at the age of 13. He studied at West Virginia State College (BMus 1950), Pennsylvania State University (MMEd, 1951), the Cincinnati Conservatory (summer 1954) and the University of Iowa (PhD 1958). His teachers included Edward Lewis, Ted Phillips, P. Ahmed Williams, George Ceiga, SCOTT HUSTON, PHILIP BEZANSON, and RICHARD B. HERVIG, among others. He also attended the Aspen Music School (summer 1964), where he studied with DARIUS MILHAUD. He taught at the North Carolina public schools and at West Virginia State College (1955–6), Langston University (1958–63), and Tennessee State University, Nashville (1963–9). From 1969 to 1971 he served as the first African-American composer-in-residence of the Atlanta SO. He was appointed professor at Tufts University in 1972, a position he held until his retirement in 1990. His honors include fellowships from the MacDowell Colony and Fromm Foundation, seven honorary doctorates, and commissions from the Berkshire Music Center, Yo Yo Ma, and Bill T. Jones/Arnie Zane Dance Company, among others. In 2005, Anderson was elected to the American Academy of Arts and Letters.

Anderson's music constitutes a poignant mixture of traditions, from tonal and avant-garde jazz, blues, and spirituals to the music of Ives and Berg. His predilection for rhythmic complexity and his imaginative use of instrumental color are particularly notable. His orchestration of the score for Scott Joplin's opera *Treemonisha* facilitated its premiere in Atlanta in 1972. His own one-act chamber opera *Walker* (1992) is a musical meditation on slavery explored through the life of 19th-century black abolitionist David Walker. Several of Anderson's works have been recorded including *Squares* (1964), the Chamber Symphony (1968), *Songs of Illumination* (1990), *Spirit Songs* for cello and piano (1993), and *Words My Mother Taught Me* (2000).

WORKS

Dramatic: The Shell Fairy (operetta, S. Beattie, after C.M. Pierce), 4 solo vv, chorus, dancers, chbr orch, 1976–7; Re-creation (L. Forrest), 3 spkrs, dancer, tpt, a sax, drums, vn, vc, pf, 1978; Soldier Boy, Soldier (op, Forrest), 5 solo vv, chorus, jazz combo, orch, 1982; Thomas Jefferson's Orbiting Minstrels and Contraband: a 21st Century Celebration of 19th Century Form (multimedia), S, dancer, ww qnt, str qt, jazz sextet, synth, cptr, visuals, 1984; Walker (chbr op), 1992; Slip Knot (op), 2000; orch of Joplin: Treemonisha (op), 1972

Orch: Pyknon Ov., 1958; Introduction and Allegro, 1959; New Dances, chbr orch, 1960; Classical Sym., 1961; 6 Pieces, cl, chbr orch, 1962; Squares, essay, orch, 1964; Sym. in 3 Movts, 1964; Chbr Sym., 1968; Intervals, 1970–71; Messages, a Creole Fantasy, 1979; Chbr Conc. (Remembrances), 1988; Conc., 2 vn, chbr orch, 1988; early works

Chbr and solo inst: Str Qt no.1, 1958; 5 Bagatelles, ob, vn, hpd, 1963; 5 Etudes and a Fancy, ww qnt, 1964; 5 Portraitures of 2 People, pf 4 hands, 1965; Connections, 2 vn, 2 va, vc, 1966; Transitions, fantasy, 10 insts, 1971; Watermelon, pf, 1971; Swing Set, cl, pf, 1972; 5 Easy Pieces, vn, pf, jew's harp, 1974; Minstrel Man, b trbn, perc, 1977; Street Song, pf, 1977; Play me Something, pf, 1979; Vocalise, vn, hp, 1980; Call and Response pf, 1982; Intermezzi, cl, a sax, pf, 1983; Spirit songs, vc, pf, 1993; Grace, str qt, 1994; Broke Baroque, vn, pf, 1996; b Bop in 2, a sax, 2 rec, 1998; Game Play, fl, va, vc, hp, 2001; Gospel Ghost, fl, pf, 2003; Jazz Overtones, ten sax, hp, perc, 2008; other works

Vocal: Personals (cant., A. Bontemps), nar, chorus, brass septet, 1966; Variations on a Theme by M.B. Tolson, cant., S, a sax, tpt, trbn, vn, vc, pf (1969); This House, male vv, 4 pitch pipes, 1971; Block Songs (P.C. Lomax), S, pitch pipe, jack-in-the-box, musical busy box, 1972; Beyond Silence (P. Hanson), T, cl, trbn, va, vc, pf, 1973; In Memoriam Malcolm X (R. Hayden), S, orch, 1974; Spirituals (Hayden), T, nar, children's vv, chorus, jazz qt, orch, 1979; Jonestown, children's chorus, pf, 1982; Thomas Jefferson's Minstrels (T.J. Anderson), Bar, male chorus, jazz band, 1982; Dear John, Dear Coltrane, SATB, 1989; The Suit, male chorus, 1998; Words My Mother Taught Me (A.T. Anderson), sop, pf, 2000; Slavery Documents (cant.), 2002; A Sonic Language, sop, pf, 2005; Bird Songs for Soprano and Rock Band (T.J. Anderson), 2008; other choral and solo vocal works

Band: Trio Concertante, cl, tpt, trbn, band, 1960; Rotations, 1967; In Memoriam Zach Walker, 1968; Fanfare, tpt, 4 small bands, 1976

Principal publishers: ACA, Bote & Bock, Fischer, Peters

BIBLIOGRAPHY

EwenD

GroveA (E. Southern, incl. further bibliography)

SouthernB

D.-R. de Lerma, ed.: *A Birthday Offering to T.J. Anderson* (Baltimore, 1978)

B. A. Thompson: "The Influence and Use of Jazz and Blues in the Music of T.J. Anderson," *Jazz Research*, xix (1987), 157–75

G.A. Steinke: "T.J. Anderson," *International Dictionary of Black Composers*, ed. S.A. Floyd (Chicago, 1999)

GUTHRIE P. RAMSEY JR./ELIZABETH PERTEN

Anderson, Walter F. [Andy] (*b* Zanesville, OH, 12 May 1915; *d* Washington, DC, 24 Nov 2003). Educator, pianist, composer, and arts administrator. The grandson of former slaves, Anderson was a musical prodigy, playing piano and organ professionally while in elementary school. He attended Oberlin College where he studied composition with HERBERT ELWELL, followed by studies at the Berkshire Music Center with PAUL HINDEMITH and at the Cleveland Institute of Music. Anderson received the equivalent of a doctoral degree in 1952 as a fellow of the American Guild of Organists (AAGO and FAGO), and in the 1970s he was awarded four honorary doctorates.

Early in his professional career he taught at the Kentucky State College for Negroes (1939–42), became chairman of the Wilberforce University music department, and directed music programs at Karamu House, a neighborhood arts center for underprivileged residents of the east side of Cleveland, Ohio. He also began a 30-year career as a concert pianist, performing throughout the United States and Europe. Anderson's appointment as chair of the music department at Antioch College in 1946 was revolutionary, as he was the first African American hired to chair a department outside the nation's historically black colleges. Anderson not only taught musical technique but viewed music as a catalyst for social change. One of his most famous pupils was Coretta Scott King, who he encouraged to apply to the New England Conservatory of Music in Boston.

Anderson left Antioch College in 1968 to join the National Endowment for the Arts, where he served as director of music programs for a decade, retiring in 1983. In addition to his work to sustain a broad variety of music and musicians, he established a challenge grant concept used to stimulate and foster private sector support for the arts. In 1993, the American Symphony Orchestra League recognized his efforts in support of American orchestras, one of several tributes he garnered. Anderson also served as a founding member of the organization now known as the Association of Performing Arts Presenters and a board member of Theater Chamber Players of Washington and Young Concert Artists of New York and Washington.

As a composer, Anderson wrote works for orchestra, chorus, and string quartet. Among them was Fantasy for Harmonica and Orchestra (1947), commissioned by harmonica virtuoso John Sebastian for a performance with the Cleveland Orchestra. Another was a commission by the Rosenwald Foundation, at the suggestion of first lady Eleanor Roosevelt, titled D-Day Prayer Cantata, which was performed during a CBS telecast in 1950.

BIBLIOGRAPHY

C.E. Claghorn: *Biographical Dictionary of American Music* (New York, 1973)

H. Roach: *Black American Music: Past and Present. Vol. II* (Miami, 1985)

A. Horn: *Brass Music of Black Composers: a Bibliography* (Westport, CT, 1996)

J. Horn: *Playing On All the Keys: the Life of Walter F. Anderson*, ed. J. Baker (Yellow Springs, OH, 2008)

ELDONNA L. MAY

Andover. Organ building firm. It was founded in 1955 by Thomas W. Byers of Andover, Massachusetts. Byers was shortly joined by Charles B. Fisk, and the company moved to a larger workshop in Methuen, Massachusetts. When Fisk relocated to Gloucester, Massachusetts in 1961, two former employees, Leo Constantineau (*b* Lawrence, MA, 1 Nov 1924; *d* North Andover, MA 1 Feb 1979) and Robert J. Reich (*b* Urbana, IL, 15 Dec 1929), reorganized under the Andover name. Beginning with rebuilding and restoration work, the company soon began to attract contracts for new organs, one of its first instruments being completed in 1965 for St. John's Lutheran Church, Northfield, Minnesota. As the firm grew, it eventually became a multiple partnership, and in addition to building new organs has a special department dedicated to the restoration of mechanical action organs as well as an extensive service department that maintains over 300 organs in several states. Among significant restoration projects is the large 1876 Hook & Hastings organ in St. Joseph's Cathedral, Buffalo, restored in 2000. In 1997 Donald H. Olson, a Wisconsin native who first came to work for the company after graduating from St. Olaf College in 1962, succeeded Robert J. Reich as President, and Robert Newton, a Vermont native who joined the company in 1963, became Tonal Director, later succeeded by John Morlock. In 2012 Olson retired, and Benjamin Mague, a Maine native who joined the firm in 1975, became president. Significant examples of Andover's work include organs built for the Lawrenceville School, Lawrenceville, New Jersey (1968), Church of Epiphany, Danville, Virginia (1978), Phillips Academy, Andover, Massachusetts (1981), Westminster Presbyterian Church, Clinton, South Carolina (1990), Christ Lutheran Church, Baltimore, Maryland (2007), and Christ Episcopal Church, Charlottesville, Virginia (2012). Andover has also built several small practice and continuo organs.

BIBLIOGRAPHY

G. Bozeman: "The Andover Organ Co. of Methuen, Mass.," *Art of the Organ*, i/4 (1971), 25

U. Pape: *The Tracker Organ Revival in America* (Berlin, 1977)

D. H. Olson: "Christ Lutheran Church, Baltimore, Maryland. Andover Organ Company. *The American Organist*, 47/1 (2013), 50.

BARBARA OWEN

Andres, Timothy (*b* Palo Alto, CA, 10 Oct 1985). Composer and pianist. After studying composition during high school at Juilliard's Pre-College division, he attended Yale, where he studied composition with MARTIN BRESNICK, INGRAM D. MARSHALL, AARON JAY KERNIS, and Chris Theofanidis (BA 2007, MM 2009). He studied piano for many years with Eleanor Marshall, then later with Frederic Chiu. Andres had a notable debut with his CD, *The Shy and the Mighty*, released on Nonesuch in 2010. It is a recording of ten interrelated pieces, by Andres, for two pianos, played by the composer and David Kaplan. The piece is both a survey of the ideas of the piano literature from the Baroque era to 20th-century minimalism, and also a personal and distinctive synthesis of the legacy of that history. Andres incorporates the processes of minimalism as well as the elegant, song-form harmonic structure and motion of Schubert. He writes skillfully for the two pianos, each sounding distinctively in the overall texture. Sections of the piece have been performed by Brad Mehldau at Zankel Hall (2011). Among his commissions are *It takes a long time to become a good composer*, a companion suite to Schumann's *Kreisleriana*; original left hand parts and cadenzas to the Mozart Piano Concerto No.26; a piece for the ACME String Quartet; a chamber orchestra work for the Los Angeles Philharmonic; and music for singer-composer Gabriel Kahane. As a pianist, Andres has given solo concerts at the Strathmore Performing Arts Center and for the Wordless Music Series at Miller Theater, Columbia University. While dedicated to contemporary music, he has also performed works by Mozart and by Charles Ives, including the *Concord Sonata*. He has received awards from the American Academy of Arts and Letters, BMI, and ASCAP, and grants from Meet The Composer and the American Music Center.

GEORGE J. GRELLA JR.

Andress, Barbara (Collier) (*b* Herrington, KS, 4 June 1929). Music educator, author, and illustrator. She obtained two degrees from the same institution, Arizona State College (BA 1951), later Arizona State University (MA 1961). She was a teacher and music supervisor in the public schools of Arizona (1951–72), where she became known for her energy, leadership, and creativity. She then taught at Arizona State University (1972–90), during which time she was a consultant for school music series textbooks and the principal author of several other series, all published by Holt, Rinehart and Winston. Andress also served on and chaired numerous state- and national-level committees; made over 250 teaching and workshop presentations, including some internationally for US Department of Defense Dependency Schools; and published two books on early childhood music education. She served as president of the Arizona Music Educators Association

(1967–9), was named its Arizona Music Educator of the Year (1968), and received its Distinguished Service Award (1989). She has remained professionally active since retiring, and was inducted into the Music Educators Hall of Fame in 2002.

WRITINGS

with B. Landis and E. Boardman: *Exploring Music, Grades K-5* (New York, 1975)
with E. Boardman: *Holt Individualized Music Program, Grades 1–3* (New York, 1978)
Music Experiences in Early Childhood (New York, 1980)
with E. Boardman: *The Music Book, Grades K-8* (New York, 1981)
with E.B. Meske, M. Pautz, and F. Willman: *Holt Music, Grades K-8* (New York, 1988)
Music for Young Children (Fort Worth, 1998)

BIBLIOGRAPHY

J.D. Harriott: *Barbara Andress: Her Career and Contributions to Early Childhood Music Education* (diss., U. of Oklahoma, 1999)

JERE T. HUMPHREYS

Andrews, Dwight (*b* Detroit, MI, 24 Sept 1951). Composer, theorist, and jazz saxophonist. He attended public schools in Detroit, including Cass Technical High School, where he studied jazz and led his own band, the Seven Sounds. He continued his education at the University of Michigan (BMEd 1973, MA 1974) and at Yale University (MDiv 1977, PhD music theory 1993). Andrews was ordained as a minister in 1978, serving as Yale University campus chaplain and as faculty member in the Music Department and Department of African American Studies for more than a decade. During that period he met Lloyd Richards, director of the Yale Repertory Theatre, and playwright August Wilson. Andrews became resident music director (1979–86) for the company and contributed original music scores to a number of Wilson's plays, including *Ma Rainey's Black Bottom*, *Joe Turner's Come and Gone*, *Fences*, *The Piano Lesson*, and *Seven Guitars*. He was musical director for the Broadway revival of *Ma Rainey* (2003) and composed music for the revival of Lorraine Hansberry's *A Raisin in the Sun* (2004). He scored a number of documentary films and television dramas, including PBS Hollywood's *The Old Settler* and Louis Massiah's film biographies of W.E.B. Du Bois and Louise Alone Thompson.

As a woodwind player, Andrews has been featured on more than 25 jazz and new music recordings with Anthony Braxton, Anthony Davis, James Newton, Wadada Leo Smith, Jay Hoggard, Geri Allen, and others. He is fluent in a wide range of styles, ranging from the experimental to the broader heritage of African American music embraced in his Jazz Vespers services.

In 1994 Andrews became Associate Professor of Music Theory at Emory University in Atlanta, Georgia; he was also called to minister at First Congregational Church. In addition to receiving Emory University's Distinguished Teacher Award, he was awarded a number of prestigious fellowships and residencies. He inaugurated the Quincy Jones Professorship of African American Music at Harvard University (1997) and was Guest Visiting Professor of Composition at the Yale School of Music (2003). In 2004 he gave the Alain Locke Lectures at Harvard University.

LAWRENCE SCHENBECK

Andrews, George W(hitfield) (*b* Wayne, OH, 19 Jan 1862; *d* Honolulu, HI, 18 Aug 1932). Organist, conductor, teacher, and composer. His family moved to Oberlin when Andrews was six; two years later he began study at what was then a department of music of Oberlin College. He graduated from what had become a Conservatory of Music in 1879 and only three years later joined its faculty, where he spent the rest of his career until retirement in 1931. He took two leaves for further study in Leipzig, Munich, and Paris and eventually became a nationally known organ recitalist. He was a founding member of the American Guild of Organists and later an honorary president of that organization. He was named organist and later director of Oberlin's Musical Union and also of the Conservatory Orchestra, serving the former for 30 years, the latter for two decades. He also conducted choruses in Akron and elsewhere in northern Ohio. Oberlin conferred an honorary Master of Arts degree on Andrews in 1900, an honorary doctorate three years later, and a bachelor of music degree in 1906. He published many articles and composed a considerable body of literature for the organ (including six sonatas and four suites), much of it unpublished and apparently lost, as well as solo vocal pieces, chamber music, an orchestral Suite in C played by the Chicago Symphony under Frederick Stock at the 1910 Oberlin May Festival, and *Lincoln, Song of Democracy* for chorus and orchestra.

WILLIAM OSBORNE

Andrews, Dame Julie [Julia Elizabeth Wells] (*b* Walton-on-Thames, England, 1 Oct 1935). British singer and actress. Her prodigious talents as singer and dancer were recognized early on by her mother (Barbara Morris Wells, a pianist), and stepfather (Ted Andrews, a Canadian vaudeville performer). After vocal lessons with Lilian Stiles-Allen and sporadic appearances in her parents' act, she made her solo debut at the age of 12 in the *Starlight Roof* revue (1947), singing "Je suis Titania" from Ambroise Thomas' *Mignon*. In 1948 she repeated this feat at the Royal Command Performance.

Following engagements on radio (*Educating Archie*, BBC, 1950–52) and in Christmas pantomimes, she was asked to play the female lead in the Broadway production of Sandy Wilson's West End musical *The Boy Friend* (1954). This led to her portrayal of Eliza Doolittle in *My Fair Lady* (1956), a role she repeated in London (1958) and which confirmed her pre-eminence as a singing actress on both sides of the Atlantic. Her performance in *Camelot* (1960) was also highly praised, as were her television appearances in Maxwell Anderson's *High Tor* (1957, with Bing Crosby), *Rodgers and Hammerstein's Cinderella* (1957), and *Julie and Carol at Carnegie Hall* (1962, with Carol Burnett), in which her boisterous duets with Burnett went some ways towards deflating her image as a prim, perfect Englishwoman and allowed her to show off her comedic timing. Nevertheless, the screen musicals *Mary Poppins* (1964; Academy Award for Best Actress) and *The Sound of Music* (1965), both of which featured her as an angelic governess, made her an international icon of purity and goodness, and, less fortunately, a victim of typecasting and critical backlash.

Her next screen musical, the 1920s homage *Thoroughly Modern Millie* (1967) was at least a financial success; *Star!* (1968), a biopic of Gertrude Lawrence, and *Darling Lili* (1970), a World War I spy farce, were complete flops. The last was the first of many collaborations with director and second husband Blake Edwards, whom she married in 1969, after divorcing her first husband, set designer Tony Walton. After this she concentrated on dramatic roles, television work, concerts, and recordings. Her last screen musical was *Victor/Victoria* (1980); an acclaimed return to the New York stage (off-Broadway) in Stephen Sondheim's revue *Putting it Together* (1993) paved the way for a staged version of *Victor/Victoria* (1995). Rising above its second-rate material, Andrews subsequently made headlines when she refused a Tony nomination for her work, protesting the show's absence from other award categories. Towards the end of the show's run, Andrews underwent an operation to remove vocal cord nodules that left her with only a fraction of her previous range. Undaunted, she took starring roles in Disney's *Princess Diaries* films, lent her voice to several of the *Shrek* series of animated films, and, in 2010, returned to the London stage for a concert of "speak-singing." In 2000 she was named a Dame Commander of the Order of the British Empire, while in 2003 she directed a revival of *The Boy Friend* that later toured nationally. She has authored several children's books and the first volume of her memoirs was published in 2008.

In her prime, Andrews was the best-known example of the operetta-rooted Broadway soprano; her voice is basically light, with head voice often used throughout her range, although she can use chest voice for dramatic effect, and in general, her lower register has a pleasing edge. An excellent sense of pitch, clear diction, and conversational phrasing made her one of the most distinctive Broadway/Hollywood singers.

BIBLIOGRAPHY

R. Windeler: *Julie Andrews* (New York, 1970, 2/1983)
L. Spindle: *Julie Andrews: a Bio-Bibliography*, (Westport, CT, 1989)
R. Windeler: *Julie Andrews: a Life on Stage and Screen* (New York, 1997)
J. Andrews: *Home: a Memoir of My Early Years* (New York, 2008)
R. Stirling: *Julie Andrews: an Intimate Biography* (New York, 2008)

HOWARD GOLDSTEIN

Andrews Boggess, Mildred (*b* Hominy, OK, 25 Sept 1915; *d* Norman, OK, 10 Aug 1987). Organist, teacher, and clinician. Andrews Boggess received her BM degree from the University of Oklahoma and a MFA degree from the University of Michigan. She was a member of Phi Beta Kappa. She did additional graduate work at Union Theological Seminary in New York. Her teachers included ARTHUR WILLIAMS POISTER, DAVID MCK. WILLIAMS, PALMER CHRISTIAN, CARL WEINRICH, and Marcel Dupré. She served as organist/choirmaster of St John's Episcopal Church in Norman, Oklahoma (1936–62). She taught at the University of Oklahoma from 1938 until her retirement in 1976, at which time she was named the David Ross Boyd Professor Emeritus of Music. She received every award given by the University of Oklahoma, including Outstanding Young Woman Faculty Member (1948), Outstanding Professor (1952), and the Distinguished Service Citation (1976). She was inducted into the Oklahoma Hall of Fame in 1971. She was awarded the University of Michigan School of Music Alumni Society Citation of Merit in 1986. She was the National Founder and for many years Director of Guild Student Groups, American Guild of Organists. She was the teacher of many prominent organists including 14 Fulbright fellows and 20 national or regional competition winners. She co-authored, with her former student Pauline Riddle, *Church Organ Method* (New York, 1973). After her retirement she continued to give masterclasses and workshops for several years. The University of Michigan School of Music Alumni Society Citation of Merit reads in part: "Throughout your career, you have influenced students through your teaching and scholarship, and thereby have created the standard of excellence now being practiced in the field of organ performance."

BIBLIOGRAPHY

"Mildred Andrews Boggess University of Michigan Award," *The American Organist* (July 1987), 43
Obituary: *The American Organist* (Nov 1987), 56
L.J. Herrmann: "Mildred Andrews Boggess, An Appreciation," *The Diapason* (Oct 1987), 2

SARAH L. MARTIN

Andrews Sisters. Vocal trio. It was formed in 1932 by the sisters LaVerne (*b* Minneapolis, MN, 6 July 1911; *d* Brentwood, CA, 8 May 1967), Maxene (Maxine) (*b* Minneapolis, MN, 3 Jan 1916; *d* Hyannis, MA, 21 Oct 1995), and Patti (Patricia) (*b* Minneapolis, MN, 16 Feb 1918) Andrews. They began performing in vaudeville houses in the Midwest with the Larry Rich Orchestra in 1932, and first achieved national prominence with a version of "Bei mir bist du schön" in 1937. They made frequent radio appearances in the late 1930s and 40s, including regular performances with the Glenn Miller Orchestra; they acted in 15 films (1940–48), often cast as themselves; they made nationwide tours; and they produced a steady stream of popular song recordings, some with Bing Crosby and Guy Lombardo. Among the most popular of their recordings were "Beer Barrel Polka" (1939), "In Apple Blossom Time" (1940), "Boogie Woogie Bugle Boy" (1941), "Don't Sit Under the Apple Tree" (1942), and "Rum and Coca-Cola" (1944). The best-selling female vocal group of their era, the Andrews Sisters are estimated to have sold over 75 million records.

The Andrews Sisters began by emulating their idols the Boswell Sisters of New Orleans and first achieved success with settings in close harmony that had a Dixieland flavor; Patti sang lead soprano, Maxene second soprano, and LaVerne alto. They went on to embrace all the current strains of popular song—the ballad of the swing era, boogie woogie, South American dance songs, and novelty songs. Their singing presented a generally sweet and optimistic mood and exhibited a strong sense of ensemble and swing; improvisation played only a small role and was usually confined to Patti's solos.

The retirement of the Andrews Sisters in the mid-1950s, caused by the changing temper of popular music and Patti's attempt at a solo career, was short-lived, and from the late 1950s until LaVerne's death in 1967 they performed in night clubs. Bette Midler's unabashed imitation of "Boogie Woogie Bugle Boy" in 1973 sparked a renewal of interest in their recordings, and Patti and Maxene, with a substitute for LaVerne, starred in the nostalgic Broadway musical "Over There" (1974). Many of their recordings have been remastered, rereleased, and continue to be enjoyed and licensed for new uses in advertising, television, and film.

BIBLIOGRAPHY

M. Andrews and B. Gilbert: *Over Here, Over There: The Andrews Sisters and the USO Stars in World War II* (New York, 1993)
J. Sforza: *Swing It! The Andrews Sisters Story* (Lexington, KY, 2000)
A.H. Nimmo: *The Andrews Sisters: a Biography and Career Record* (Jefferson, NC, 2004)

MICHAEL J. BUDDS

Angelic Gospel Singers, the [Angelics, the]. Gospel ensemble. The Angelic Gospel Singers, or the Angelics, were an African American female gospel quartet based in Philadelphia. Founder, lead singer, and pianist Margaret Allison (1921–2008) a native of McCormick, South Carolina, moved with her family to Philadelphia as a youth. Allison joined the Spiritual Echoes in 1942 and learned vocal arranging, composition, and accompanying techniques. Allison's family was affiliated with the Pentecostal Church, but stylistically her gospel sound was closer to that of the southern Baptist church and gospel tradition. Allison left the Spiritual Echoes in 1944 to form the Angelics. Joining her were fellow former Spiritual Echoes members Lucille Shird and Ella Mae Norris. The third member was Allison's sister Josephine MacDowell. The quartet's sound mimicked that of popular male quartets such as the Fairfield Four and the Dixie Hummingbirds with controlled harmonies and simple accompaniment. The Angelic Gospel Singers commonly performed with the Hummingbirds. As a group, the Angelics performed primarily on the Pentecostal Church circuit. Their rendition of Lucie Campbell's "Touch Me, Lord Jesus" (1941) gained widespread popularity, becoming the standard rendition of the song. The ensemble later recorded under the Nashboro label. In the early 1980s, they signed with Malaco Records. Other personnel shifts occurred throughout 1950s, with Bernice Cole joining the group, and in the early 1960s the first male voice was added.

RECORDINGS
(selected)

The Best of the Angelic Gospel Singers, Vol. I (1967 Nashboro, NASH 4509-2)
The Best of the Angelic Gospel Singers, Vol. II (1980 Nashboro, NASH 4531)

BIBLIOGRAPHY

H. Boyer: *How Sweet the Sound: The Golden Age of Gospel* (Washington, DC, 1995)
A. Heilbut: *The Gospel Sound: Good News and Bad Times* (New York, 1971, updated and rev. 6/2002)

ROXANNE R. REED

Angelou, Maya [née Marguerite Annie Johnson] (*b* St. Louis, MO, 4 Apr 1928). Poet, novelist, playwright, actor, and educator. Angelou was educated at Stamps, AR, and the Labor School in San Francisco. Her early career focused on dance and drama. In 1959 she moved to New York, where she joined the Harlem Writers Guild. Exploring various kinds of oppression (economic, racial, and sexual), she has published more than ten books of poetry, six autobiographies, of which *I Know Why the Caged Bird Sings* (1969) is the best known, numerous plays, and librettos for musicals, as well as scripts for film and television. The reading of her commissioned poem "On the Pulse of Morning" at the inauguration of President William Jefferson Clinton (20 January 1993) brought her national recognition. Other texts by this celebrated African American poet have been set to music by Bolcom, Danielpour, Garner, Deon Nielson Price, and Judith Weir. Among her honors are two nominations for the Pulitzer Prize, three Grammy Awards (1994, 1996, 2003), and more than 30 honorary doctorate degrees. Since 1991 she has held the first lifetime Reynolds Professorship of American Studies at Wake Forest University (Winston-Salem, NC).

BIBLIOGRAPHY

C. Tate, ed.: *Black Women Writers At Work* (New York, 1983)
M.J. Lupton: *Maya Angelou: a Critical Companion. Critical Companions to Popular Contemporary Writers*, ed. K.G. Klein (Westport, CT, 1998)
T.M. Hawthorne: "Angelou, Maya," *Black Women in America*, ed. D.C. Hine (New York, 2/2005)
K.E. Clifton: *Recent American Art Song: A Guide* (Lanham, MD, 2008)

JOSEPHINE WRIGHT

Anievas, Agustin (*b* New York City, NY, 11 June 1934). Pianist. He first performed at the age of four in a recital of his mother's students. At ten, he was the first child to perform at the palace of Fine Arts in Mexico City. He later enrolled at the Juilliard School of Music, where he studied with EDWARD STEUERMANN, OLGA SAMAROFF, and ADELE MARCUS. He made his debut as soloist with the Little Orchestra Society of New York at the age of 18. In 1959, he won the Concert Artists Guild Award, followed by first prize in a number of important competitions in Europe and the United States, including the Dimitri Mitropoulos Competition in 1961. Since that time, he has toured widely in the United States, South America, Europe, South Africa, Australia, and the Far East. Anievas settled in Belgium for ten years, but in 1974 returned to New York, where he became a piano professor at Brooklyn College Conservatory of Music until his retirement in 1999, after which he continued to perform. He has appeared as soloist with the New York PO; the London PO, the BBC SO, the Hong Kong PO, and the Chicago, Los Angeles, and Brussels orchestras. His repertoire features 19th- and 20th-century music and includes the concertos of Béla Bartók and Sergey Prokofiev. He has recorded all of Rachmaninoff's concertos, the complete impromptus of Franz Schubert, works by Franz Liszt and Johannes Brahms, and the complete waltzes, études, ballades, and impromptus of Fryderyk Chopin. He has recorded mainly on the EMI label.

RONALD KINLOCH ANDERSON JR./ANYA LAURENCE

Animal dances. Popular name for a group of ragtime dances and dance steps named after various animals and birds. The group includes the bunny hug, the camel walk, the eagle rock, the grizzly bear, and the turkey trot. The Foxtrot originated as a ragtime dance but was not named for a fox (*see* RAGTIME DANCE.)

CLAUDE CONYERS

Anka, Paul (Albert) (*b* Ottawa, ON, 30 July 1941). Canadian singer-songwriter, naturalized American. He was singing for amateur shows and local radio stations by the age of ten and formed the Bobby Soxers vocal trio while still in high school. At 15 he recorded one of his own songs in Hollywood and in 1957 signed a songwriting and recording contract with ABC-Paramount in New York. His first single, "Diana" (EMI Columbia, 1957), was a number one hit and became one of the best-selling records in pop music history. Other hits followed, including "You are my destiny" (ABC-Paramount, 1958), "Lonely Boy" (ABC-Paramount, 1959), and "Put your head on my shoulder" (EMI Columbia, 1959). He also has more than 400 songs to his credit, many of which have been covered by other artists, among them, Buddy Holly, Johnny Mathis, Patti Page, Elvis Presley, Sammy Davis Jr., Barbra Streisand, and Michael Bublé. "My Way" (Reprise, 1969; with lyrics by Anka) and "She's a lady" (Decca, 1971; music and lyrics by Anka) were major successes for Frank Sinatra and Tom Jones respectively, and Anka's theme music for Johnny Carson's "The Tonight Show" (on NBC) was performed an estimated 1.4 million times, earning him far more than $1 million in royalties. He has recorded over 900 songs in five languages on more than 120 discs and has collaborated with numerous artists, including such songwriters as Michael Jackson, David Foster, and Sammy Cahn, and such singers as Céline Dion, Ricky Martin, and Julio Iglesias. Anka's songs have also been used in films and television shows.

S. TIMOTHY MALONEY

Annapolis Brass Quintet. Brass quintet. The group was founded in 1971 and disbanded in 1993. David Cran (trumpet) and Robert Posten (bass trombone) remained with the group for the duration through various personnel changes. It was the first American brass quintet to serve as the full-time and exclusive professional occupation of its members. The group toured extensively in the United States (New York debut, 21 January 1984), Canada, Europe, and Asia; they also became mainstays at music festivals and music camps worldwide. The group played a major role in developing brass quintet literature through editions of Renaissance and Baroque music and an active commissioning program; it gave over 75 premieres, including works by George Walker, Robert Starer, Lawrence Moss, and Jiri LaBurda. In 1979 the ensemble organized the Brass Chamber Music Society of Annapolis, and in 1980 it established the International Brass Quintet Festival in Baltimore, to bring together professionals from both Europe and the United States with student ensembles for brass performance and study.

JOANNE SHEEHY HOOVER/R

Ann Arbor. City in Michigan (pop. 113,934; 2010 US Census). It was founded in 1824 by John Allen and Elisha Rumsey, then chartered as a city in 1851. When the new city charter arrived by train at the Ann Arbor depot in 1851, performances from the local German Brass Band heightened the awaiting crowd's celebratory mood. From the time of that inaugural event, Ann Arbor's musical life has continued as a sonic expression of the city's people, institutions, and spaces.

The UNIVERSITY OF MICHIGAN and University Musical Society (UMS) have long played a vital role. In 1879 a group of community members led by university professors Henry Frieze and Calvin Cady formed the Choral Union to perform choruses from Handel's *Messiah*. The UMS formed the following year to support additional Choral Union concerts and attract visiting artists. The Ann Arbor School of Music—which has since become the University's School of Music, Theatre, and Dance—also formed in 1880 under the aegis of the UMS. In 1894, UMS hosted the Boston Festival Orchestra for Ann Arbor's first May Festival, a concert series that recurred each spring until 1995. During and beyond this period, UMS expanded its regular concert offerings to include performers, ensembles, and troupes representing a diverse range of nationalities and artistic genres. Alongside the efforts of the UMS, the university's faculty, students, and alumni fostered myriad musical initiatives in Ann Arbor, including the university's bands program (1906–), the avant-garde ONCE Festival (1961–6), the student-run radio station (WCBN-FM, 1972–), the Center for World Performance Studies (2000–), and the Collage Concert (1978–), a virtuosic showcase for the university's ensembles and performers.

Performing spaces have also shaped the city's music scene. Many of the earliest documented concerts were held in local churches, some of which continue to present concerts. George D. Hill's Opera House opened in 1871 to become one of Ann Arbor's first venues specifically designed for musical entertainments; the building closed in 1952. Hill Auditorium, designed by the firm Kahn and Wilby and named in honor of University Regent Arthur Hill, opened in 1913. Renowned for its acoustics, it regularly hosts local and touring orchestras, soloists, and choirs. When the Michigan Theater opened in 1928, it featured both a lavish Barton Theater organ and a live orchestra for silent film and vaudeville. Since 1984 it has hosted the Ann Arbor Symphony Orchestra (established in 1928). Occupying a structure built before 1860, the Kerrytown Concert House opened in 1984 and offers an intimate performance space for ensembles of all types. The Concert House also hosts the improvisation-themed Edgefest (1997–). The Ann

Arbor Ark (established in 1965) rose to national prominence as a folk music venue and began hosting the Ann Arbor Folk Festival in 1977. Live jazz and blues have thrived at the Bird of Paradise (1985–2004), the Firefly (2000–9), and in the Ann Arbor Blues and Jazz Festivals (1969–74, 1992–2006), though economic pressures have prompted their respective closure and disbanding. The Blind Pig (1971–) originally served coffee by day and blues at night before transforming to a live rock club in the 1980s. In the 21st century, continuing support for local music education and community ensembles, which range from temple choirs such as Kol Halev to student-run orchestras, help keep Ann Arbor's music diverse, eclectic, and connected to the city's past.

NATHAN PLATTE

Anonymous 4. A cappella vocal quartet, based in New York. The quartet has been a resident ensemble at St. Michael's Episcopal Church in New York City since its formation in 1986. The founding members include New York natives, Johanna Marie Rose, Susan Hellauer, Marsha Genensky, and Ruth Cunningham. In 1998, Cunningham left the group and was replaced by Jacqueline Horner-Kwaitek, a native of Northern Ireland. Although the group announced its retirement as a full-time group in 2005, with the return of Cunningham (replacing Rose) in 2007, it continues to record and tour.

The group's name is borrowed from the most important of the unsigned 13th-century treatises on music. This treatise describes the compositional styles and practices at the Cathedral of Notre Dame in Paris in the early part of the 13th century, and attributes works to master composers, Leoninus and Perotinus of the Notre Dame School. Upon formation, the group's repertoire consisted of sacred and secular polyphonic music of the 11th to 14th centuries. Over the years it has expanded to include Renaissance music, which they often perform with the six-man vocal ensemble Lionheart; contemporary music; traditional music from the British Isles; and, more recently, American shape-note tunes, gospel songs, and folk songs.

The quartet has recorded more than 20 albums, beginning with *An English Ladymass* (1992). Several have made the Billboard classical top ten charts, including *Gloryland* (2006), *Cherry Tree* (2010), and *American Angels* (2004). Anonymous 4 has commissioned and performed new works, including Richard Einhorn's oratorio *Voices of Light* (1995) and *A Carnival of Miracles* (2002), Steve Reich's *Know What Is Above You* (2002), John Tavener's *The Bridegroom* (1999), and Peter Maxwell Davies' *A Calendar of Kings* (2002).

ANNA E. KIJAS

Anschütz, Karl (*b* Koblenz, Germany, Feb 1913; *d* New York, NY, 30 Dec, 1870). Conductor and composer of German birth. He studied with his father in Koblenz and Frederick Schneider in Dessau. He conducted in Koblenz at the Royal Musical Institution before moving to Nuremberg in 1848 to conduct its orchestra. He took a position in 1849 conducting the German opera at Amsterdam and traveled to London with a German opera troupe the same year. By 1857 Anschütz had become a conductor of great renown throughout the British Isles, and he traveled with Bernard Ullman's Italian opera troupe to the United States. He conducted this group from 1857 through 1860, bringing Italian opera to American audiences while establishing himself as the most respected conductor in America during this era. In 1862 he founded the German Opera Company in New York. He also played an active role in establishing the New York Conservatory of Music. In addition to his conducting career, Anschütz composed noteworthy music of his own and transcribed Beethoven's nine symphonies into arrangements for brass band.

BIBLIOGRAPHY

"Anschütz, Karl," *Appletons' Cyclopedia of American Biography* (New York, 1900)

J. Koegel: *Music in German Immigrant Theater: New York City, 1840–1940* (Rochester, NY, 2009)

BONNIE ELIZABETH FLEMING

Antes, John (*b* Frederick, PA, 24 March 1740; *d* Bristol, England, 17 Dec 1811). Composer. His father, Henry Antes, a member of the Reformed Church, worked to bring about unity among the various Christian denominations in Pennsylvania. After Henry Antes became disillusioned with the Reformed Church and joined the Moravians, John was baptized in 1746 by Augustus Gottlieb Spangenberg. He was educated at the Moravian boys' school at Bethlehem; among his early teachers was musician Johann Christoph Pyrlaeus (1713–85). In 1759, he crafted one of the first violins made in British North America. In 1762, he opened an instrument-making shop in Bethlehem. Congregational records refer to six bowed stringed instruments constructed by Antes (two "basses," actually celli; two violas; two violins), and a violin and viola are in museums in Nazareth and Lititz, Pennsylvania. He is thought to have also made several keyboard instruments, for following a complaint from organ builder David Tannenberg that Antes's new business would infringe on his own trade, in 1762 the congregation elders directed Antes not to undertake any new keyboard construction.

In 1764, he was invited by Bishop Spangenberg to come to Europe, where he undertook several kinds of business with little success. Called to serve as a missionary in Egypt beginning in 1769, he survived many adventures both in travel and in his work there. He was tortured and nearly killed by followers of Osman Bey, a local official of the Ottoman Empire. Antes published an account of his Egyptian travels: *Observations on the Manners and Customs of the Egyptians, the Overflowing of the Nile and Its Effects* (London, 1800; also published in German in 1801). It was sometime during this Egyptian period of his life that Antes wrote the Three Trios for two violins and violoncello, identified as Opus 3. These were signed "Giovanni A-T-S, Dilletante Americano," and were published in England by John Bland prior to 1795. These trios, the earliest known chamber music by a North American-born composer, demonstrate his considerable compositional talent and lively imagination, and facility in writing for string instruments. Also dating from this period is a set of missing string quartets, which he sent to Benjamin Franklin with a letter dated 10 July 1779. This letter illuminates another side of Antes: he interceded for the American Moravians in their hardships during the American Revolution.

Antes was recalled to Germany in 1782, and served as business manager for the unmarried Moravian brothers in Neuwied. Beginning in 1785, he served as a business manager of the Fulneck Moravian congregation in Yorkshire, England. He became acquainted with Joseph Haydn's London impresario, Johann Peter Salomon, and Antes's nephew, composer Christian Latrobe, was an acquaintance of Haydn. Antes's music shows the influence of Haydn as well as other composers of the time.

Antes's composition of sacred concerted vocal works began during the 1780s. Ten of his vocal works are found in the Moravian Archives in Herrnhut, Germany, presumably composed for use in Herrnhut and Neuwied. It is likely that most of the rest of his 31 anthems and 59 chorale tunes were composed during his tenure at Fulneck, since they have only English texts. These were preserved not in Moravian archives in England but in America, where the Moravians of the 1790s and early 1800s were seeking vocal works in English; they were therefore brought from England, copied in Bethlehem, and sent on to Salem (now Winston-Salem, NC). His compositions span a wide variety of themes from various occasions of the church year and the life of the congregations. His anthems are primarily for SATB voicing, unlike the more usual Moravian SSAB voicing of the time. His vocal writing is lyrical, but often disjunct and less facile than his more skillful writing for strings, and is marked by long vocal lines, high tessituras, and wide ranges. His music is published by Boosey & Hawkes, H.W. Gray, and the Moravian Music Foundation

Antes continued his interest in mechanical inventions, and published a summary of his experiments for improving piano hammers, the violin tuning mechanism, and violin bows (*AMZ* viii, 1806, 657), and invented a page turning mechanism for use with a music stand.

BIBLIOGRAPHY

"Lebenslauf des Bruders John Antes," *Nachrichten aus der Brüder-Gemeine* ii (1845), 249–311 (The Lebenslauf in Moravian tradition is a spiritual autobiography.)

D. McCorkle: *John Antes, "American Dilettante"* (Winston-Salem, NC, 1956)

W.J. Smith: *A Style Critical Study of John Antes' String Trios in Relation to Contemporary Stylistic Trends* (thesis, SUNY, Binghamton, 1974)

K.M. Stolba: "From John Antes to Benjamin Franklin: a Musical Connection," *Moravian Music Foundation Bulletin*, xxv/2 (1980), 5–9

K. Kroeger: "John Antes at Fulneck," *Moravian Music Journal*, xxx/1 (1985), 12–18

W.P. Flannagan: *A Performing Edition and Study of the Unpublished Concerted Anthems of John Antes (1740–1811)* (diss., Catholic U. of America, 1995)

K. Kroeger, "What Happened to the Antes String Quartets?" *Moravian Music Journal*, xli/1 (1996), 23–26

C.D. Crews: *John Antes* (Winston-Salem, NC, 1997)

N.R. Knouse: *The Music of the Moravian Church in America* (Rochester, NY, 2008)

KARL KROEGER/NOLA REED KNOUSE

Antheil, George [Georg] (Carl Johann) (*b* Trenton, NJ, 8 July 1900; *d* New York, NY, 12 Feb 1959). Composer and pianist.

1. Revolution: up to 1925. 2. Reaction: 1925–59.

1. Revolution: up to 1925. Antheil began piano lessons when he was six and from the age of 16 traveled regularly to Philadelphia for theory and composition lessons with constantin Sternberg. On the advice of Sternberg, Antheil went to New York in 1919 to study composition with ernest Bloch. In 1920 while studying with Bloch, Antheil began his first major work, the Symphonie no.1 "Zingareska"; it is interesting for the jazz rhythms in the last movement. After leaving Bloch's tutelage in 1921, Antheil returned to Philadelphia, where financial problems forced him to look for a patron. With Sternberg's help he gained the support of mary louise curtis Bok; although she disapproved of Antheil's music, she continued her financial assistance for the next 19 years.

With Bok's support, Antheil went to Europe on 30 May 1922 to pursue a career as a concert pianist. After presenting his first recital on 22 June 1922 at the Wigmore Hall in London, he settled in Berlin and from there made a successful tour of central Europe, often with recitals of his own music. In Berlin Antheil met Stravinsky, who exercised the single most important influence on his compositional style during the 1920s. The American's admiration of the Russian's anti-Romantic, machine-like, rhythmically propulsive style is reflected in the piano compositions *Airplane Sonata*, *Mechanisms*, *Sonata Sauvage*, *Death of Machines*, and *Jazz Sonata*. The *Airplane Sonata* exemplifies Antheil's preoccupation with machines and time-space theories in the early 1920s. It is constructed out of the addition and manipulation of rhythmically activated blocks, each delineated by a different ostinato pattern. Stuckenschmidt (1923) summarized the style of Antheil's Berlin piano pieces as "a most lively polyrhythmical homophony."

Antheil moved from Berlin to Paris in June 1923. His notoriety was ensured by the riotous reception of his performance of his piano pieces at the Théâtre des Champs-Elysées on 4 October 1923, and he was championed and befriended by Joyce, Pound, Yeats, Satie, Picasso, and other artists, including the violinist Olga Rudge. Applauded as a genius by the Parisian literary community, he became the musical spokesman for their "modernist" ideas. Pound wrote a book and numerous articles in praise of Antheil's music, and, together with Rudge, he commissioned two violin sonatas which were first performed on 11 December 1923 at the Salle du Conservatoire with Antheil accompanying Rudge; they performed them throughout Europe in the next few years. These sonatas, together with a third violin sonata (1924) and a string quartet (1924), illustrate Antheil's musical discourse of this period: an abstract juxtaposition of musical blocks on a time canvas, similar to the arrangements of objects in a Cubist painting. Summarizing the formal procedures of these chamber pieces is the massive *Ballet mécanique*, dating from the same period; it is a comprehensive statement of the composer's mechanistic outlook and time-space formulae modeled after Stravinsky's *The Wedding*. (Antheil sought to accompany this large-scale synthesis of his formal ideas with a motion picture. The problems of coordinating the film with the music, scored for 16 pianolas, xylophones, drums, and other percussion, proved, however, insurmountable and both works became autonomous.) *Ballet mécanique* was first performed publicly on 19 June 1926 in a reduced version for one pianola with amplifier, two pianos, three xylophones, electric bells, small wood propeller, large wood propeller, metal propeller, tam-tam, four bass drums, and siren. A milestone in the literature for percussion ensemble, the *Ballet mécanique* is more tightly unified than Antheil's other Paris works.

2. Reaction: 1925–59. With the enthusiastic reception of the *Ballet mécanique*, Antheil felt that he had become the leading young composer in Paris. He also believed that the *Ballet* had been a summary, and he consciously chose to change his compositional style in the *Symphonie en fa* (1925–6) and the Piano Concerto (1926), compositions which in 1936 he labeled neo-classic. The *Symphonie en fa* was well received when first performed with the *Ballet mécanique* (19 June 1926), but the Piano Concerto, given its premiere on 12 March 1927, was criticized as being a mere imitation of Stravinsky's neo-classicism and an abandonment of the earlier iconoclastic mechanistic style. Antheil's prominent position in Parisian musical life began to erode. The decline was cemented on the other side of the Atlantic by the disastrous American premiere of the *Ballet mécanique* on 10 April 1927 in Carnegie Hall, a carnival presentation by the over-eager promoter Donald Friede that alienated many.

Antheil's rejection in Paris and then New York in 1927 caused him to approach a new musical genre; attracted by the operatic "renaissance" in Germany, he moved to Vienna in 1928 to complete *Transatlantic*, an opera whose plot centers on an American presidential election and presents a wild caricature of American life. Its premiere in Frankfurt am Main on 25 May 1930 was a modest success, as was its American premiere more than 50 years later (Trenton, NJ, 1981). Antheil electrifies the drama with fast cinematographic staging: the final act is played on an arrangement of four stages and a screen that allows quick cuts between scenes. Musically, the modular structure, jazz-inspired rhythms, and parody of popular tunes reinforce the pace of the plot and underline the satirical tone of the opera.

While Antheil was preparing for the production of this opera, he also worked on his second large-scale opera *Helen Retires*, which proved to be critically unsuccessful. From 1929 to 1933 he divided his time between Europe and America. In the two non-dramatic orchestral works *Capriccio* and *Morceau* Antheil solidified what he called "a fundamentally American style," one that had appeared in embryo form in *Transatlantic* and would be strengthened by his study of symphonic form in the late 1930s and 40s, culminating in the Fourth Symphony. In both these works Antheil made a conscious effort to be "popular," using a synthesis of American folk-like material that appears in almost all of his later compositions.

Before returning permanently to the United States in August 1933, Antheil completed *La femme 100 têtes*, a collection of 44 preludes and a concluding "Percussion Dance" for piano after the surrealist collage novel of etchings by the painter Max Ernst; it presents the mechanistic style of Antheil's early Paris years within a controlled framework. Once home, Antheil continued to write works for musical theater, a genre he believed could broaden the public's support for modern music. In New York he became a part of what he identified as "a new theater movement—musical ballet-opera theatre," and wrote ballet scores for Balanchine and Martha Graham as well as several film scores for Ben Hecht and Charles MacArthur's Astoria production company.

Antheil settled in Hollywood in August 1936. He viewed Hollywood as "the Mecca of young American composers," a place that offered him the opportunity of becoming financially independent. He became a respected film composer, completing 33 scores for such noted directors as Cecil B. DeMille and Nicholas Ray. His score for a documentary film for the 1939 World's Fair World's Communications Building is notable for its return to a bitonal machine aesthetic. In some 12 columns on film music published in *Modern*

George Antheil, 1927. (George and Boske Antheil Papers, Music Division, Library of Congress)

Music he articulated his belief that film music, like music theater, provided composers with a means to educate and attract a large audience. His activities also included devising SEE-note, a tablature notation for piano, and writing articles on topics from endocriminology to romance. By 1941, following the death of his brother, he felt he had reached the low point of his career.

In 1942, however, with the acceptance by Boosey & Hawkes of his Fourth Symphony Antheil recovered momentum and embarked on the most creative period of his life. The Fourth Symphony marks Antheil's turn to a Romantic spirit in music, embodies the preoccupation with symphonic form that had governed his musical philosophy for two decades, and reflects his admiration of Shostakovich's music. Its four programmatic movements are cast in traditional forms, and the entire cycle is unified through the transformation of thematic contours and intervallic patterns. Written to appeal to the public, the work's success is due to the infectious and "schmaltzy" melodies, similar in character to those of *Capriccio* and *Morceau*. After the premiere by the NBC SO under Stokowski on 13 February 1944, the symphony was described in *Time* magazine as "the loudest and liveliest symphonic composition to turn up in years" (xliii/9, 1944).

Antheil's embrace of a new Romanticism is most evident in his Symphony no.5 "Joyous" (this work is not the "Tragic" Fifth Symphony discussed in his autobiography). It crystallizes the formal, stylistic, and emotional principles of the Symphony no.4 and epitomizes his preoccupation with Beethoven and obsession with form dating from the mid-1920s. The Symphony no.5 was regarded by Virgil Thomson as Antheil's most skillfully crafted work. After 1942 Antheil wrote other compositions of a similar expressive intent with varying degrees of success. The best of the later works include the Serenade for String Orchestra, Violin Sonatina, Violin Sonata no.4, Piano Sonata no.4, *Songs of Experience,* and *Eight Fragments from Shelley*.

In 1949 Antheil revived his interest in music drama with the opera *Volpone*, the most successful of a set of four operas completed in the early 1950s. The libretto is farcical, fast-moving, and singable, and the music not only supports but, in the manner of Antheil's film music, expertly enhances the comedy. The heterogeneous harmonic language, the thematic versatility, the rhythmic continuum, the mosaic construction, and the colorfully programmatic timbres all combine to reinforce the plot dramatically. Antheil's talent for satire and caricature also promotes the spirit of his last ballet *Capital of the World*. It attracts, as does the best in all Antheil's music, because of its rhythmic vitality, harmonic pungency and melodic vigor.

WORKS

(projected and incomplete works not listed; for a fuller list see Whitesitt [1983])

STAGE

Transatlantic (op, 3, Antheil), 1927–8, Frankfurt am Main, 25 May 1930
Oedipus Rex (incid music, Sophocles), 1928, lost, Berlin, 4 Jan 1929
U.S.A. with Music (incid music, W. Lowenfels), 1928, lost
Fighting the Waves (incid music, W.B. Yeats), female v, chorus, small orch, 1929, Dublin, 13 Aug 1929
Flight (Ivan the Terrible) (op-ballet, 1, G. and B. Antheil), 1927–30, arr. Str orch as Crucifixion Juan Miro, 1927, lost
Helen Retires (op, 3, J. Erskine), 1930–31, New York, 28 Feb 1934
Dance in Four Parts (ballet, M. Graham), *c*1933–4, lost, New York, 11 Nov 1934 [based on pf work La femme 100 têtes, 1933]
Eyes of Gutne (ballet, G. Balanchine), *c*1934, lost
The Seasons (ballet, Balanchine), *c*1934, lost
Dreams (ballet, Balanchine), 1934–5, New York, 5 March 1935
Course (ballet, Graham), 5 insts, 1935, lost
The Cave Within (ballet), arr. Of pf pieces, *c*1948, lost
Capital of the World (ballet, after E. Hemingway), 1952, arr. Orch suite, *c*1955, TV broadcast, 6 Dec 1953
Volpone (op, 3, A. Perry, after B. Jonson), 1949–52, Los Angeles, 9 Jan 1953
The Brothers (op, 1, Antheil), 1954, Denver, 28 July 1954
Venus in Africa (op, 1, M. Dyne), 1954, Denver, 24 May 1957
The Wish (op, 4 scenes, Antheil), 1954, Louisville, 2 April 1955
Tongue of Silver (incid music, M. Dyne), *c*1955–9, lost

ORCHESTRAL

Conc. For Pf (Conc. No.1), 1922; Symphonie no.1 "Zingareska," 1920–22, rev. 1923; Ballet mécanique, large perc ens, 1923–5, rev. 1952–3, Paris, 19 June 1926; A Jazz Sym., 1925, rev. 1955; Symphonie en fa, 1925–6; Pf Conc., 1926; Suite for Orch, 1926; Capriccio, 1930; Sym. No.2, 1931–8, rev. 1943; Morceau (The Creole), 1932; Archipelago "Rhumba" [3rd movt of Sym. No.2], 1935; Sym. No.3 "American," 1936–9, rev. 1946; The Golden Spike [2nd movt of Sym. No.3], 1939; Sym. No.4 "1942," 1942

Water-Music for 4th-of-July Evening, str, 1942–3; Decatur at Algiers, 1943; Heroes of Today [1st movt of Sym. No.6], 1945; Over the Plains, 1945; Sym. No.5 "Tragic," 1945–6; Vn Conc., 1946; Spectre of the Rose Waltz, 1946–7 [from film, 1946]; Autumn Song "An Andante for Orch," 1947; Sym. No.5 "Joyous," 1947–8; Sym. No.6 "after Delacroix," 1947–8, rev. 1949–50; American Dance Suite no.1, 1948; McKonkeys Ferry Ov., 1948; Serenade, str, 1948; Serenade II, chbr orch, 1949; Tom Sawyer, 1949; Accdn Dance, 1951; Nocturne in Skyrockets, 1951

VOCAL

Choral: Election (Antheil), *c*1927, lost [from op Transatlantic]; Merry-go-round from "Candide," 1v, unison chorus, pf, 1932 [from inc. musical play after Voltaire]; 8 Fragments from Shelley, chorus, pf, 1951, 3 movts orchd 1951; Cabeza de vaca (cant., A. Dowling, after A. Nuñez), mixed chorus, 1955–6, orchd E. Gold, 1959

Songs (1v, pf, unless otherwise stated): 5 Songs (A. Crapsey): November Night, Triad, Suzanna and the Elders, Fate Defied, The Warning, 1919–20; 5 Lieder, 1922; You are Old Father William (L. Carroll), 1924; Turtle Soup (Carroll), 1924; Nightpiece (J. Joyce), 1930; 6 Songs: The Vision of Love (G. Russell), Down by the Sally Gardens (W.B. Yeats), The Sorrow of Love (Yeats), Lightning (D.H. Lawrence), I Hear an Army (Joyce), An End Piece (F.M. Ford), 1933; Frankie and Johnny [arr.], 1936; Songs of Experience (W. Blake): The Garden of Love, A Poison Tree, The School Boy, The Sick Rose, The Little Vagabond, I Told my Love, I Laid me Down upon a Bank, Infant Sorrow, The Tyger, 1948; Sighs and Grones (G. Herbert), 1956; The Ballade of Jessie James, n.d.; Bequest (M. Shelton), n.d.; Madonna of the Evening Flowers (A. Lowell), n.d.; Song of Spring, n.d.; In Time of Death (Lowell), n.d.

CHAMBER

Sym. For 5 Insts, fl, bn, tpt, trbn, va, 1st version, 1922–3, 2nd version, 1923; Sonata no.1, vn, pf, 1923; Sonata no.2, vn, pf, drums, 1923; Sonata no.3, vn, pf, 1924; Str Qt, 1st version, 1924, 2nd version, 1925; Str Qt no.2, 1927, rev. 1943; Concertino, fl, bn, pf, 1930; 6 Little Pieces, str qt, 1931; Concert, wind qnt, dbn/db, tpt, trbn, 1932; Sonatina, vn, vc/pf, 1932; Sonatina, vn, pf, 1945; Sonata no.4 (no.2), vn, pf, 1947–8; Str Qt no.3, 1948; 2 Odes (J. Keats): Ode to a Nightingale, Ode on a Grecian Urn, spkr, pf, 1950; Sonata, fl, pf, 1951; Sonata, tpt, pf, 1951; Bohemian Grove at Night, fl, ob/eng hn, cl, b cl, bn, 1952

PIANO

Fireworks and the Profane Waltzers, 1919, part lost; Golden Bird, 1921, orchd c1921; 4-hand Suite, 1922, rev. 1939; Airplane Sonata (Sonata no.2), 1921; Sonata Sauvage (Sonata no.1), 1922 or 1923; Death of Machines (Sonata no.3), 1923; Jazz Sonata (Sonata no.4), 1922 or 1923; Sonata no.5, 1923, part lost; Sonata, 1923; Woman Sonata (Sonata no.6), c1923, lost; The Perfect Modernist, c1923, lost; Mechanisms, pianola, 1923 or 1924, lost

Habañera, Tarantelle, Serenata, 2 pf, 1924; Sonatina für Radio, 1929; Tango, arr. A. Steinbrecher, c1930 [from op Transatlantic]; La femme 100 têtes, 44 preludes and Perc Dance, 1933; La vie Parisienne, 1939; Suite, pedagogical, 1941; The Ben Hecht Valses, 1943; Musical Picture of a Friend, 1946; Sonata no.3, 1947; Prelude, d, *c*1948; Sonata no.4, 1948; 2 Toccatas, 1948; Valentine Waltzes, 1949; Sonata no.5, 1950; Waltzes from Volpone, 1955 [from op]; Piano Pastels, pedagogical, 1956

FILM, TELEVISION, AND RADIO SCORES

Ballet mécanique [music never synchronized with film; see under ORCHESTRAL]; Harlem Picture, 1934 or 1935; Once in a Blue Moon, 1935; The Scoundrel, 1935, lost; The Plainsman, 1936; Make Way for Tomorrow, 1937, lost; The Buccaneer, 1938, lost; Music to a World's Fair, film for World's Communications Building, 1939; Angels Over Broadway, 1940; Orchids for Charlie, 1941; The Plainsman and the Lady, 1946; Spectre of the Rose, 1946; That Brennan Girl, 1946; Repeat Performance, 1947; The Fighting Kentuckian, 1949; Knock on any Door, 1949; Tokyo Joe, 1949; We Were Strangers, 1949

House by the River, 1950; In a Lonely Place, 1950; Sirocco, 1951; Actors and Sin, 1952, lost; The Juggler, 1952; The Sniper, 1952; Conquest of the Air, 1955, lost; Dementia, 1955; Hunters of the Deep, 1955; Not as a Stranger, 1955; Target Ploesti, 1955, lost; The Pride and the Passion, 1957; The Young Don't Cry, 1957, only 2 songs extant; Woman Without Shadow (CBS TV), 1957; The Twentieth Century Series, 10 CBS TV documentaries, 1957–8; 2 Edward R. Murrow programmes, 1959, lost; Rough Sketch; Airpower (TV score); The Path and the Door (radio score)

MSS in *ATS, LAum, LOu, PHci, R, Wcg*

Principal publishers: Antheil Press, Boosey & Hawkes, Leeds, Schirmer, Universal, Weintraub

BIBLIOGRAPHY

EwenD; *GroveA* (L. Whitesitt, C. Amirkhanian); *KdG* (N. Grosch)

H. Stuckenschmidt: "Umschau: Ausblick in die Musik," *Das Kunstblatt*, vii (1923), 221–2

M. Lee: "George Antheil: Europe's American Composer," *The Reviewer*, iv/4 (1924), 267–75

E. Pound: *Antheil and the Treatise on Harmony with Supplementary Notes* (Paris, 1924, 2/1927/*R* 1968)

E. Pound: "George Antheil," *Criterion: a Quarterly Review*, ii/7 (1924), 321–33

W. Atheling [E. Pound]: "Notes for Performers," *Transatlantic Review*, i/2 (1924), 111, i/5 (1924), 370, ii/2 (1924), 222–5 [with marginalia by Antheil]

E. Pound: "Treatise on Harmony," *Transatlantic Review*, i/3 (1924), 77–81

A. Copland: "George Antheil," *League of Composers Review*, ii/1 (1925), 26–8

E. Walsh, ed.: Antheil suppl. to *This Quarter*, i/2 (1925)

A. Copland: "America's Young Men of Promise," *MM*, iii/3 (1926), 13–20

E. Pound: "Antheil, 1924–1926," *New Criterion*, iv (1926), 695–9

R. Hammond: "Ballyhoo," *MM*, iv/4 (1927), 30–33

A. Lincoln Gillespie Jr.: "Antheil & Stravinski," *Transition*, xiii (1928), 142–4

L. Zukofsky: "Critique of Antheil," *The Exile*, iv (1928), 81–4

T. Wiesengrund-Adorno: "Transatlantic," *MM*, vii/4 (1930), 38–41

R. Thompson: "American Composers: V George Antheil," *MM*, viii/4 (1931), 17–28

A. Copland: "Our Younger Generation Ten Years Later," *MM*, xiii/4 (1936), 3–11

G. Antheil: *Bad Boy of Music* (Garden City, NY, 1945/*R*) [autobiography]

D. Friede: *The Mechanical Angel: his Adventures and Enterprises in the Glittering 1920's* (New York, 1948)

L. Morton: "An Interview with George Antheil," *Film Music Notes*, x/11 (1950), 4–7

H. Stoddard: "Stop Looking—and Listen! An Interview with George Antheil," *International Musician*, xliv/5 (1950), 24–5, 33 only

R. Sabin: "George Antheil: Sixth Symphony," *Notes*, xiii (1955–6), 145–6

W. Hoffa: "Ezra Pound and George Antheil: Vorticist Music and the *Cantos*," *American Literature*, xliv/1 (1972), 52–73

C. Amirkhanian: "An Introduction to George Antheil," *Soundings*, vii–viii (1973), 176–81

E. Schönberger: "The Nightmare of George 'Bad Boy of Music' Antheil," trans. K. Freeman, *Key Notes*, iv/2 (1976), 48–51

D. Albee: *George Antheil's "La femme 100 têtes": a Study of the Piano Preludes* (diss., U. of Texas, Austin, 1977)

W. Shirley: "Another American in Paris: George Antheil's Correspondence with Mary Curtis Bok," *Quarterly Journal of the Library of Congress*, xxxiv (1977), 2–22

H. Heinsheimer: "My Friend George: Composer Antheil Remembered," *ON*, xlv/8 (1980–81), 32–4

A. Henderson: *Pound and Music: the Paris and Early Rapallo Years* (diss., UCLA, 1983) [incl. bibliography of Antheil's writings]

L. Whitesitt: *The Life and Music of George Antheil: 1900–1959* (Ann Arbor, MI, 1983) [incl. complete catalog of works, discography, and full bibliography]

G. Wehmeyer: "Der Pianist ist bewaffnet: George Antheil, das Enfant terrible der Neuen Musik," *NZM*, Jg.146, no.6 (1985), 14–18

H. Ford: *Four Lives in Paris* (San Francisco, 1986)

C. McCarty: "Revising George Antheil's Filmography," *The Cue Sheet*, vi/4 (1989), 139–42

S.C. Cook: "George Antheil's *Transatlantic*: an American in the Weimar Republic," *JM*, ix (1991), 498–520

G.D. Goss: "George Antheil, Carol Robinson, and the Moderns," *American Music*, x (1992), 468–85

K.A. Cochrane: *George Antheil's Music to a World's Fair Film* (diss., U. of Northern Colorado, 1994)

C. Oja: *Making Music Modern: New York in the 1920s.* (New York, 2000)

J. Schmidt-Pirro: *George Antheils Ballet Mécanique: auf der Suche nach einer amerikanischen Musik.* (Frankfort am Main, 2000)

J. Schmidt-Pirro: "Bad Boy of Music: zum 100. Geburtstag des amerikanischen Komponisten George Antheil," *NZM clxi*/5 (2000), 53–55

L. Garafola: "George Antheil and the Dance," *Ballet Review* xxix/3 (2001), 82–95

G. Livingston and E. Dubielzig: "Der Mann hinter dem Mythos: George Antheils amerikanische Kindheit," *NZM clxii*/5 (2001), 18–21

M. Piccinini: "'Non più andrai farfallone rumoroso': 'You Will Go No More, Noisy Butterfly': Joyce and Antheil," *J Modern Literature xxvi*/1 (2002), 73–89.

M.C. Schildt: *Music for Film by American Composers During the Great Depression: Analysis and Stylistic Comparison of Film Scores, 1936–1940, by Aaron Copland, Virgil Thomson, George Antheil, and Marc Blitzstein* (diss., Kent State U., 2005)

E.E. Templeton: "Dear EzzROAR,' 'Dear Anthill': Ezra Pound, George Antheil and the Complications of Patronage," ed. R. McParland, *Music and Literary Modernism: Critical Essays and Comparative Studies* (Newcastle, 2006), 66–86

S.I. Statham: *Contemporary Music and the Publishing Industry in America from 1938 to 1965 as Represented in Letters and Documents of the Displaced Universal Edition Composers and Their Publishing Agents* (diss., CUNY, 2009) [includes previously unpublished collection of letters]

LINDA WHITESITT, CHARLES AMIRKHANIAN/SUSAN C. COOK

Anthem. A Protestant sacred choral composition, of 16th-century British origin, usually a setting of English prose from the Scriptures. It was adopted by 18th-century Americans and became the most elaborate composition of the first New England School of composers (*see also* PSALMODY). The Second New England School took up this genre in the 19th century, adopting the European musical style and organ accompaniment. During the 20th century the definition of the genre expanded both musically and textually, but it remains an important part of Protestant church services to the present day.

1. To 1800. 2. The 19th century. 3. The 20th century. 4. After 2000.

1. To 1800. The models for the American anthem were English works composed for rural Anglican parishes or nonconformist congregations. They were known from the collections of church music brought by immigrants or imported from England, and they appeared in American publications after about 1760. The most important English collections were William Tans'ur's *The Royal Melody Compleat* (1754–5) and Aaron Williams's *The Universal Psalmodist* (1763); the first American publication to include a significant number of English anthems was James Lyon's *Urania* (1761), but two other Americans, Josiah Flagg of Boston and Daniel Bayley of Newburyport, Massachusetts, were more influential in the introduction of the anthem to British North America. Flagg issued *Sixteen Anthems* (1766), and Bayley was responsible for printing and distributing Tans'ur's collection as well as his own *New Universal Harmony* (1773), which contained 20 anthems by English composers, including John Arnold, William Knapp, Joseph Stephenson, and Aaron Williams. Bayley also published John Stickney's *The Gentleman and Lady's Musical Companion* (1774), the largest collection of English anthems compiled in America during the 18th century. Among the most popular anthems taken from English sources were Tans'ur's *O Clap Your Hands* and *O Give Ye Thanks unto the Lord*, Knapp's *The Beauty of Israel is Slain* and *Give the King Thy Judgments*, Williams's *Arise, Shine, O Zion* and *O Lord God of Israel*, and Arnold's *The Beauty of Israel*. English composers such as William Tuckey and William Selby were also influential when they emigrated to the colonies and established themselves as leaders of the musical communities in New York and Boston.

The earliest American anthems were the longest and most elaborate works written by the first native composers; they were also the most demanding music sung by budding church choirs and singing school students. Stylistically they are similar to the hymn tunes, fuging tunes, and set pieces from the period. They were typically unaccompanied works for four-part mixed chorus with variations in texture, often including sectional solos and duets. Each line of the text often served as the basis of an independent section. Composers followed the rules of consonant counterpoint, and works often remained in one key and lacked harmonic direction.

After Independence, works by native composers quickly outnumbered English ones in American publications. Of about 7000 sacred compositions published in the United States up to 1810, about 100 are anthems by Americans. The inclusion of at least one anthem became the norm in the tunebooks of singing-school masters. They were performed in singing-school "assemblies" (concerts), as well as in worship services, where they were sung for Thanksgiving, Christmas, Easter, Fast Day, and at funerals.

The center of anthem composition during the 18th century was New England, where the leading composer was William Billings. Among the best-known of his 47 anthems is his Easter Anthem, *The Lord Is Ris'n Indeed* (1787). It remains popular to this day and may be Billings's most enduring work with over 150 printings before the mid 1980s. About 60 composers from the First New England School wrote anthems. Among the most prolific were Oliver Holden, Jacob French, Amos Bull, Samuel Holyoke, Daniel Read, and Timothy Swan.

Outside the mainstream were the German-speaking immigrants, most notably the Moravians, who settled in Pennsylvania and North Carolina (*see* MORAVIAN CHURCH). Chief among them were Johannes Herbst, John Antes, and Johann Friedrich Peter. Herbst composed more than 115 anthems during the 15 years of his residence in the United States (1787–1812), among them the moving chorale-anthem for chorus and orchestra *O Haupt voll Blut und Wunden*. Antes's best-known anthem is *Go, Congregation, Go!—Surely He Has Borne Our Griefs* (1795) for vocal solo and chorus. No Moravian anthems were printed in 19th-century American collections, and most were not known outside Moravian communities. Unlike the English imports or the New England examples, many call for string and organ accompaniment and some require obbligato instruments. By the turn of the century, instrumental participation in anthems was gaining ground generally, and most included at least organ or piano accompaniment. Daniel Read included an optional instrumental bass part in his *O Be Joyful in the Lord (Columbian Harmonist No.3*, 1795), and Benjamin Carr prescribed an organ accompaniment for the *Anthem for Christmas* (1805).

2. THE 19TH CENTURY. During the beginning of the 19th century, reform of sacred music shifted the focus back to British and Continental models, although New England remained the most active center geographically. Early in the century anthems were composed with tonal chord progressions and more harmonic direction, and modulations to the dominant or relative major/minor were common. Immigrants, such as George K. Jackson and Benjamin Carr, continued to set the standard for the new generation of native composers. The most significant American composer was Lowell Mason. Beginning with *The Boston Handel and Haydn Society Collection of Church Music* (1822), which included about a dozen anthems to music by Mozart, Madan, and others, Mason established a formula adopted by many of his contemporaries and successors—the adaptation of European works, both vocal and instrumental, to English words for publication as anthems. Composers such as George Webb, Nathaniel Gould, and Thomas Hastings followed Mason's example by publishing collections that included such anthems alongside original works. Although he was better known for his hymns, Mason also composed anthems,

such as *Thanksgiving Anthem* (1840) and *I was glad when they said unto me* (1842).

During the second half of the 19th century, the European influence on American anthems intensified, because a large number of American composers studied both harmony and organ in Europe, especially in Germany. Late in the century, more complex chromatic harmonies were introduced. Numerous anthems were published; they were widespread because the market was large. Most influential among the European-trained Americans were organist-composers Dudley Buck and Horatio Parker. Buck spent four years in Leipzig and Paris before returning to serve as organist and choirmaster in several American cities; he composed 55 anthems, a number of them for the "quartet choir" of professionally trained soloists that had become increasingly fashionable in city churches as a replacement for or supplement to volunteer choirs. Buck composed verse anthems, often in ABA form, with substantial organ accompaniments that became popular in Episcopal, Presbyterian, and Methodist churches. His *Sing, Alleluia Forth* (1901), dating from the early 20th century, is notable.

Later composers such as George Whitefield Chadwick also developed a large following among church musicians, particularly for their anthems. Chadwick's style is representative of the Second New England School of composers, for example with his *Three Sacred Anthems*, op.6 (1882). Other turn-of-the-century anthem composers include Harry Rowe Shelley and William H. Neidlinger. Shelley's *The king of love my shepherd is* (1886) and Neidlinger's *The Silent Sea* (1908) and *The Birthday of a King* (1890) remained popular for more than half a century. The rise of the hymn-anthem, a straightforward choral piece based on a familiar text and melody, dates from this period; many representative examples of the genre were composed by P.A. Schnecker (*My faith looks up to thee*) and George B. Nevin (*Jesus, My Saviour! Look on me*, 1899). Horatio Parker was perhaps the most important American choral composer of the 19th century. A student of Chadwick and as Yale University's first professor of music the teacher of Charles Ives, Parker served churches in New York and Boston before moving to New Haven, Connecticut. Parker composed about 25 anthems, among which is *The Lord is my light* (1890), an especially effective, well-crafted work in three-part structure.

3. The 20th century. Ives continued Parker's legacy by composing anthems as a young church musician at the turn of the century. Among his most notable anthems are *Psalm 67* (*c*1898–9) and *Psalm 90* (1923–4), although Ives is noted more for his use of hymn tune melodies in his secular pieces than for his sacred works. In contrast, Leo Sowerby's most famous works are sacred choral compositions, especially his cantatas. He composed about 120 anthems for the Episcopal Church, including *Great is the Lord* (*c*1933). Randall Thompson and Jean Berger were also active during the middle of the century. Thompson's *Alleluia* (1940) and Berger's *Brazilian Psalm* (*c*1941) became standards and remain popular. Ned Rorem is known for his vocal music (especially his songs), but he also composed anthems such as *Christ the Lord is ris'n today* (1955). Organist and church musician Daniel Pinkham expanded the definition of the genre in the 1970s by introducing styles from the concert hall and by setting a wider variety of texts. Pinkham set not only English texts (*Evergreen*, *c*1974), but also texts in Latin and Hebrew. His *The Lament of David* (1974) is an example of an anthem with tape accompaniment. Also during this period anthem composers introduced elements from vernacular styles, including gospel, rock, and folk music. Alice Parker, known for her more traditional arrangements of folk and hymn tunes, worked as the arranger for the Robert Shaw Chorus from the 1940s through the 1960s and composed many anthems; *Jesus, Whom Every Saint Adores* (1972) is one of her most popular works in this genre. Examples from the 1980s include René Clausen's *All that hath life and breath, praise ye the Lord!* (1981) and Paul Manz's *E'en so, Lord Jesus, quickly come* (1987).

Many major 20th-century American composers have occasionally set religious, spiritual, or moral texts in a wide range of musical styles including more complex harmonies and rhythms that, in some churches, have served as anthems. Among these are Leonard Bernstein, Norman Dello Joio, Howard Hanson, Alan Hovhaness, and Vincent Persichetti. John Harbison is a major American composer who has written relatively little for chorus, but his anthem *Nunc dimittis* (1982) in English is noteworthy. One of the major American choral composers of the late 20th and early 21st century is Morten Lauridsen. Although he does not define any of his music as anthems, Lauridsen has composed psalm settings that are sometimes used as such. Likewise, his *O Magnum Mysterium* (1994), properly a motet, is also used in some churches as an anthem.

4. After 2000. Trends from the late 20th century continue; anthems are composed by both church musicians and choral composers and sometimes include complex chord structures, striking dissonances, and even aleatoric sections. Lauridsen's music continues to be popular as does the music of another leading choral composer, Eric Whitacre. Like Lauridsen, Whitacre has not composed anthems in the strictest definition. However, his *Lux Aurumque* (2000) and "I thank you God for most this amazing day" from *Three Songs of Faith* (2009) are both sometimes used in Protestant church services as anthems. Other recent examples include Kinley Lange's *Esto les digo* (2001), Gwyneth Walker's *Dazzling as the Sun* (2004), and Z. Randall Stroope's *Come dwell in Solomon's walls* (2006).

BIBLIOGRAPHY

R.T. Daniel: *The Anthem in New England before 1800* (Evanston, IL, 1966/*R*)

E.A. Wienandt and R.H. Young: *The Anthem in England and America* (New York, 1970)

T.L. Fansler: *The Anthem in America: 1900–1950* (diss., North Texas State U., 1982)

K. Kroeger: "William Billings's 'Anthem for Easter': The Persistence of an Early American 'Hit,'" *Proceedings of the American Antiquarian Society*, xcvii (1987), 105–28
A.P. Britton, I. Lowens, and R. Crawford: *American Sacred Music Imprints, 1698–1810: A Bibliography* (Worcester, MA, 1990)
B.A. Gerlach: *A Critical Study of Selected Anthems, Published 1961–1991, by Twentieth-century American and British Composers* (diss., Southern Baptist Theological Seminary, 1992)
D.P. DeVenney: *Varied Carols: A Survey of American Choral Literature* (Westport, CT, 1999)
K. Kroeger: *Early American Anthems*, i, ii (Madison, WI, 2000)
J. Ogasapian: *Church Music in America, 1620–2000* (Macon, GA, 2007)
N.R. Knouse, ed.: *The Music of the Moravian Church in America* (Rochester, NY, 2008)

RALPH T. DANIEL/ELWYN A. WIENANDT/LAURIE J. SAMPSEL

Anthony, Jacob (*b* Germany, 1736; *d* Philadelphia, PA, 29 Dec 1804). Woodwind instrument maker of German birth. Jacob was one of the earliest woodwind makers to take his skills to the New World. He arrived in Philadelphia in about 1764 and continued in business as a turner and musical instrument maker until his death in 1804. Three of his instruments are in the Dayton C. Miller collection at the Library of Congress. One of these is an excellent ebony flute with three graduated upper joints, a foot extension to *c*′, and five silver keys. Although this instrument has a *c*′ key there is no key for *c*♯′. The other instruments are a four-key cane flute and a five-key clarinet. Anthony's business was continued by his son Jacob Anthony Jr. until 1811.

BIBLIOGRAPHY

WaterhouseLangwillI
L.P. Farrar: *Newsletter of the American Musical Instrument Society*, xviii/1 (1989)

ROBERT E. ELIASON

Anthony, Marc. *See* MARC ANTHONY.

Antone, Clifford Jamal (*b* Port Arthur, TX, 27 Oct 1949; *d* Austin, TX, 23 May 2006). Nightclub owner, promoter, and producer. The son of Lebanese immigrants, he briefly attended the University of Texas at Austin (summer 1969), then opened an imported food and clothing store. Its backroom became a place for informal jam sessions, often with Antone playing bass. On 15 July 1975 he opened Antone's. Although not the first or only club in Austin to book blues musicians, it became significant for both its relevance to the Austin music scene and the opportunities allowed for young musicians to share the stage with blues legends. In 1987 he launched recording label Antone's Record and Tapes and opened Antone's Records Shop. After serving two drug-related prison terms (1985–6; 1999–2002), Antone began an annual fundraiser for troubled youth. During the last two years of his life, he taught a course on the blues at both the University of Texas at Austin and Texas State University-San Marcos. A recipient of the National Blues Foundation Lifetime Achievement Award, he was inducted into the Blues Hall of Fame in 2009.

BIBLIOGRAPHY

R. Draper, "Clifford's Blues," *Texas Monthly* (Oct 1997), <http://www.texasmonthly.com/1997-10-01/feature8-4.php>
Obituary, *New York Times* (25 May 2006)
Antone's Home of the Blues, DVD, dir. D. Karlok, Silver Star Entertainment (Port Washington, NY, 2006)

KEVIN E. MOONEY

Antoniou, Theodore (*b* Athens, 10 Feb 1935). Greek composer. He studied the violin, singing, and composition at the National Conservatory, Athens (1947–58); he also studied composition with Papaioannou at the Hellenic Conservatory, Athens (1956–61). His studies were continued with Günther Bialas at the Munich Musikhochschule, where he gained his first experience in electronic music. He made a tour of the United States in 1966 and spent the year 1968 in Berlin. In 1967 he founded the Hellenic Group of Contemporary Music in Athens. He taught composition and orchestration at the universities of Stanford (1969–70)—where he founded the "Alea II" ensemble—and Utah (1970), at the Philadelphia College of the Performing Arts as professor (1970–78), and at Tanglewood (1974–85), where he was also assistant director of contemporary activities. In 1979 he was appointed professor of composition at the University of Boston and in 1989 became president of the Union of Greek Composers. Since then he has divided his time between the United States and Greece, conducting many contemporary works, particularly by younger Greek composers. Awards made to him include the Richard Strauss Prize of the City of Munich (1964), the City of Stuttgart Prize (1966) for his Violin Concerto, the Steghi Grammaton Prize for his *Miniatures*, the Spanish television Premio Ondas for *Cassandra* in 1970, and two US National Endowment for the Arts grants (1975, 1977).

An enormously prolific composer, Antoniou's music hesitated at first between a simple atonality (Violin Sonatina, 1959) and an engaging Bartókian folklorism (Trio, 1961). Later he adapted serial procedures in writing pieces in elegantly constructed small forms; he has continued to favor such designs. The influences of Christou, Zimmermann, and Penderecki and the use of other advanced techniques became evident in the large-scale works of the early 1970s. However, he always maintained his distance from avant-garde excesses, and has developed a highly practical "synthetic" notation, which represents complex sound structures in an easily assimilable fashion. Describing himself as "essentially a dramatic composer [of] abstract programme music," he has adopted a shrewd eclecticism, even on occasion mixing serial techniques with folk elements. In his opera *Bacchae* (1992), distant echoes of Orff, Stravinsky, and Bernstein are combined with an extensive use of irregular rhythmic patterns. Meanwhile *Oedipus at Colonus* (1998), a somber and tightly woven score, represents one of Antoniou's more mature achievements.

WORKS

STAGE

(selective list)

Epirus (ballet), 1964; Noh-Musik (music theatre), 4 pfms, 1964; Rhinoceros (ballet, after E. Ionesco), 5 insts, tape, 1964; Clytaemnestra (sound-action), actresses, dancers, orch, tape, 1967; Cassandra (sound-action for TV), mixed media, 1969; Protest I, actors, tape, 1970; Protest II, mixed media, 1971; Aftosyngentrossi-peirama

[Meditation-Experiment], mixed media, 1972; Chorochronos I, mixed media, 1973; Parastasis II, dancer AD lib, perc, tape, 10 insts, 1978; Periander (mixed media op, 2, G. Christodoulakis), 1977–9, Munich, Am Gärtnerplatz, 6 Feb 1983; Bacchae (ballet, 1, after Euripides), 1980; The Imaginary Cosmos (ballet, 1, S. Lambert), 1984; Bacchae (op, 2, K. Botsford), 1992, Athens, Herod of Atticus, 17 Aug 1995; Monodrama, actor, fl, cl, bn, hn, tpt, trbn, 2 perc, pf, vn, vc, db, 1992; Oedipus at Colonus (op, 1, Y. Michaïlidis, after Sophocles), 1997–8, Athens, Friends of Music Hall, 9 May 1998

Incid. music for 52 plays (1960–95), 8 film scores (1962–94)

ORCHESTRAL

Suite, chbr orch, 1959; Conc., cl, tpt, vn, orch, 1960; Ov., 1961; Antitheses, 1962; Pf Concertino, 1962; Jeux, vc, str, 1963; Mikrographies, 1964; Vn Conc., 1965; Kinesis ABCD, 2 str orch, 1966; Op Ov., orch, tape, 1966; Events I, vn, pf, orch, 1967–8, II, 1969, III, small orch, tape, slides, 1969; Threnos, wind, pf, perc, db, 1972; Fluxus I, 1974–5; Fluxus II, pf, chbr orch, mid-1970s; Double Conc., perc, chbr orch, 1977; The GBYSO Music, 1982; Skolion, 1986; Paean, 1989; Conc., str, 2 perc AD lib, 1992; Celebration (I), 1994; Cadenza for Leonidas, conc., vn, str, 1995

VOCAL

Choral: Griechische Volkslieder, SATB, 1961; Epirus [after folksongs], 1962; Kontakion (Romanos the Melode), S, Mez, T, B, chorus, str, 1965; 10 School Songs, 1965–6; Nenikikamen [We Are Victorious] (T. Tolia), Mez, Bar, nar, chorus, orch, 1971; Verleih uns Frieden [after H. Schütz], 3 choruses, 1971–2; Die weisse Rose (T. Tolia and others), Bar, 3 nars, children's chorus, chorus, orch, 1974–5; Circle of Thanatos and Genesis (cant., Takis Antoniou), nar, T, mixed chorus, orch, 1977–8; Revolution der Toten (cant., Takis Antoniou), S, A, T, B, mixed chorus, orch, 1981; Prometheus (cant., after Aeschylus: *Prometheus Bound*), nar, Bar, mixed chorus, orch, 1983; Thalassa tou proiou I, II, [Morning Sea] (C. Cavafy), mixed chorus, 1983; Kriti, oneiro méga [Crete, the Great Dream] (D. Kakavelakis), S, T, nar, ob, cl, tpt, perc, va, vc, db, 1984; Colossus Epigram (ancient Gk.), mixed chorus, 1985; Oraseis opsondai [They will See Visions] (Bible: *Joel*), mixed chorus, nar AD lib, fl, 4 tpt, 4 hn, 3 trbn, tuba, 2 perc, 1988; Eros I (Sappho, Alcaeus, Plato, Archilochus, Ibycus), mixed chorus, fl, cl, 2 hn, tpt, trbn, tuba, 2 perc, pf, 2 vc, db, 1990; Agape (Bible: *Corinthians*), mixed chorus, fl, 4 hn, 4 tpt, 3 trbn, tuba, 2 perc, 1990; 3 Children's Songs (Gk. folk texts), children's chorus, chorus, 1992; 3 Canons (Aeschylus, Sophocles, Euripides), male vv, female vv, mixed chorus, 1993

Solo vocal: Melos (Sappho), Mez/Bar, orch, 1962; Epilogue (Homer: *Odyssey*), Mez, nar, 6 insts, 1963; Klima apoussias [Climate of Absence] (O. Elytis), Bar, chbr orch, 1968; Moirologia for Jani Christou, Mez/Bar, pf, 1970; Parodies (H. Ball), 1v, pf, 1970; Chorochronos II, 1v, orch, 1973; Chorochronos III, Bar, pf, perc, tape, 1975; Epigrams (Antoniou), S, chbr orch, 1982; 11 Aphighiseis [Narrations] (Cavafy), medium v, pf, 1983, arr. chbr orch, 1984; "For Ernst," S, fl, tpt, trbn, perc, pf, vn, vc, db, 1985; Salome (anon.), S, pf, 1985; Paravasis I (ancient Gk.), 1v, tape, any solo inst, 1987; Westwinds (Chin., ancient Gk. texts), S, pic, perc, hp, pf, 2 vn, va, vc, 1991; Paravasis II (ancient Gk.), 1v, tape, any solo inst, 1992; Ode (A. Kalvos), S, fl + pic, hp, pf, mandolin, vc, 1992

OTHER INSTRUMENTAL AND TAPE

Large ens: Concertino, pf, 9 wind, perc, 1963; Katharsis, fl, ens, tape, lights, 1968; Cheironomiai [Gestures], at least 8 performers, 1971; Synthesis, ob, elec org, perc, db, 4 synth, 1971; Circle of Accusation, 16 insts, 1975; Suite, ob, cl, bn, hn, tpt, perc, pf, db, 1960; The Do Quintet, 2 tpt, hn, trbn, tuba, 1978; Afiérosis [Dedication], fl, cl, pf, vn, vc, 1984; Octet, fl, ob, cl, bn, 2 vn, va, vc, 1986; Ertnos, fl, ob, bn, hn, tpt, trbn, tuba, hp, perc, 1987; Conc., tambura, small orch, 1988; Conc./Fantasia, v, 16 insts, 1989; Dexiotechnika Idiomela, fl, ob, 2 cl, 2 bn, 2 hn, tpt, 1989; North/South, pf, chbr orch, 1990; Palermo, Maggio 23, 1992, lament and improvisation, solo fl, fl, cl, bn, tpt, 2 perc, pf, vn, va, vc, 1992; Hania, pf, 2 vn, 2 va, 2 vc, dv, 1992; Suite, brass qnt, org AD lib, perc, 1993; East/West, a fl, cl, pf, 2 vn, va, vc, tape, 1993; Celebration II, 6 tpt, 4 hn, 4 trbn, euphonium, tuba, org, 1994

2–4 insts: Sonatina, vn, pf, 1959; Str Qt, 1960; Trio, fl, va, vc, 1961; Dialogues, fl, gui, 1962; Quartetto giocoso, ob, pf trio, 1965; Lyrics, vn, pf, 1967; Stychomythia, fl, gui, 1976; Commos, vc, pf, 1989; Epigramma II, vn, hp, 1993; For Va and Pf, 1993–4; 10 Miniatures, 2 gui, 1994

Solo inst: Aquarelles, pf, 1958; Pf Sonata, 1959; Vn Sonata, 1961; Music for hp, 1965; Sil-ben, pf, 1965; 6 Likes, tuba, 1967; 5 Likes, ob, 1969; 4 Likes, vn, 1972; 3 Likes, cl, 1973; 2 Likes, db, 1976; Stichomythia II, gui, 1977; Parastasis (I) [Performance], perc, tape, 1977; Prelude and Toccata, pf, 1982; Entrata, pf, 1983; Lament, fl, 1988; Suite, gui, 1994–5

Tape: Gravity, video, 1966; Heterophony, 1966; Telemusic, 1970

Principal publishers: Antoniou, Bärenreiter, Gerig, Gunmor, Modern, Orlando

GEORGE LEOTSAKOS

Antony [Hegarty, Antony] (*b* Chichester, England, 1971). Singer-songwriter and pianist. After the Hegarty family moved to San Jose, California, in 1981, Antony studied experimental theater at New York University, formed a performance collective with Johanna Constantine, and collaborated with filmmaker William Basinski (Life on Mars, 1997) and rock icon Lou Reed (*The Raven*, Sire, 2003; *Animal Serenade*, RCA, 2004). Antony has become the world's most famous transgender musician. Male-bodied and feminine-identified, Antony retains his birth name and uses masculine pronouns professionally. His band, Antony and the Johnsons (formed in 1996), is named after the murdered African American transgender activist Marsha P. Johnson.

Antony's vocal depth, resonance, and melismatic grace evoke African American musical traditions. His tremulous vibrato and seemingly self-imposed limitations (also evident in his amateurish piano playing) express the grave earthly burdens of his lyrics. His eclectic work has been influenced by the AIDS-ravaged New York art scene (Peter Hujar), British synth-pop (Marc Almond), soul (Nina Simone, Boy George), and experimental underground music (Diamanda Galás). His band includes vocals, piano, drums, guitar, bass, cello, violin, and horns, he regularly appears with an orchestra, and he released an album of live symphonic performances with the Danish National Chamber Orchestra featuring arrangements by Nico Muhly, Rob Moose, Maxim Moston, and himself (*Cut the World*, Rough Trade, 2012). He sang on the acclaimed single "Blind" released on the disco revival album *Hercules and Love Affair* (DFA, 2008). Among many guest appearances include Rufus Wainwright (*Want Two*, Geffen, 2004), Yoko Ono (*Yes, I'm a witch*, Caroline Astralwerks, 2007), Björk (*Volta*, One Little Indian, 2007), Laurie Anderson (Homeland, Nonesuch/Elektra, 2010) and CocoRosie (*Noah's Ark*, Touch and Go, 2005; *We Are on Fire*, 2012).

Antony's star-studded album *I am a bird now* (Secretly Canadian, 2005), which addressed themes of gender transformation, death, and family archetypes, won the Mercury Prize and was named Album of the Year by *Mojo*. In 2004 Secretly Canadian re-released the band's performance art and cabaret-influenced debut album (*Antony and the Johnsons*, Durtro, 1998). Antony collaborated with the video artist Charles Atlas in a touring performance piece about transfemininity called *TURNING* (Rebis/Kobalt, 2006). Subsequent work includes the album, *The Crying Light* dedicated to Butoh originator Kazuo Ohno (Secretly Canadian, 2009), the album and visual art monograph, *Swanlights* which voiced opposition to environmental destruction (Secretly Canadian, 2010, performance commissioned by the Museum of Modern Art in 2012), a biographical performance piece, *The Life and Death of Marina Ambramović* (2011) with the director Robert Wilson, and curation of the 2012 Meltdown Festival.

BIBLIOGRAPHY

R. Middleton: "Mum's the Word: Men's Singing and Maternal law," *Oh Boy! Masculinities and Popular Music*, ed. F. Jarman-Ivens (New York, 2007), 103–124

S. Goldin-Perschbacher: *Sexuality, Listening, and Intimacy: Gender Transgression in Popular Music, 1993–2008* (diss., U. of Virginia, 2008), 148–190

E. Hayward: "More Lessons from a Starfish: Prefixial Flesh and Transspeciated Selves," *Women's Studies Quarterly*, xxxvi/3–4 (2008), 64–85

SHANA GOLDIN-PERSCHBACHER

Aoki, Tatsu(yuki) (*b* Tokyo, Japan, 19 Sept 1957). Composer, double bass player, *taiko* drummer, *shamisen* player, filmmaker, and educator of Japanese birth. He learned *shamisen* and *taiko* as a child, then turned to double bass, on which he performed as a teenager in Tokyo jazz clubs, before moving to the United States in 1977. Interested in various creative arts, he studied filmmaking at Ohio University and the Art Institute of Chicago (BA 1983, MA 1985), where he began teaching film production and history in 1995. Aoki's musical interests have ranged from jazz to pop and traditional Japanese music to experimental music. He has played electric guitar in rock bands and created music in which his bass is accompanied by sounds made with soda bottles and chopsticks. Performing jazz, he has worked as an unaccompanied soloist, a leader (of Power Trio and other ensembles), and a sideman, alongside Fred Anderson, Glenn Horiuchi, and Jon Jang, among others. Aoki has become a key figure in Chicago's music scene and a leader in ASIAN AMERICAN JAZZ, integrating the sounds of Asian instruments within more conventional jazz ensembles and founding the Chicago Asian-American Jazz Festival, which premiered in 1996. In his role as executive director of Asian Improv aRts Midwest, he has promoted a variety of Asian American cultural and educational programs. He has made more than 60 recordings and 30 experimental films.

CHARLES HIROSHI GARRETT

Apache. Native Americans of northwestern, north-central, and southeastern New Mexico, southeastern Arizona, the southern Plains, and northern Mexico. Numbering about 53,330 (according to the 1990 census), they are divided into six tribes, all southern Athapaskan: Jicarilla, Lipan, Kiowa-Apache, Mescalero, Chiricahua, and Western Apache (of whom four internal subdivisions are recognized: White Mountain, San Carlos, Cibecue, and Tonto groups). All speak Apachean dialects closely related to the Athapaskan language of the NAVAJO, and, more distantly, to Athapaskan languages in Oregon, California, and Canada. In many respects the Apache culture is a conservative form of the way of life of their Navajo neighbors. This similarity extends in some respects to their music.

Like that of almost all Native Americans, the traditional music of the Apache is almost entirely vocal, often with rattle or drum accompaniment. A chorus–verse–chorus alternation, an old Athapaskan musical form, is found in most Apache traditional music, both popular and sacred. The Apache vocal style is strikingly nasal and rises to falsetto in some of the highly melodic choruses. The verses, more like chants, are sung with a choppy, almost parlando delivery. Some syllables are sharply emphasized and others suddenly muffled or swallowed. The tonal system very often incorporates major or minor triads. Choruses utilize triadic shapes as well as octave leaps. When singing together, the ensemble is loosely unison, with much individual variation allowed.

A focal point in traditional Apache culture is the girls' puberty rite, which is considered to support the life of the whole tribe. A five-day, four-night ceremony accompanied by many songs celebrates the life story of White Painted Woman (*ʔisdzanatlʔeesh*), the principal deity, in her role as creator and source of fertility. There may be one or several young girls honored in the ceremony, where they are identified with the goddess. The puberty rite is often combined with the dance of the Mountain Spirits—masked dancers wearing headdresses of crown-like wooden slats in carved and painted designs. Their strong, straddling steps and repetitive owl and turkey calls are thought to bring special power to the occasion. The singers for the girls' puberty rite accompany themselves with fawn-hoof rattles, holding a gentle one-pulse rhythm throughout. The Mountain Spirits dance around a large bonfire and are accompanied by multiple water drums as well as the loud singing of a group of men standing on the periphery of the dance circle. The women dance in clan clusters around the edge of the dance circle and the music of the conjoined ceremonies often is heard simultaneously.

Other curing ceremonies reenact other aspects of the Apache creation story. Deities such as Monster Slayer, White God, and Black God, and various forces of nature such as wind, lightning, and prototypical birds and animals, are invoked in song and prayer for help in curing those for whom the ceremonies are performed. Designs in colored pigments may be laid out on the floor of the ceremonial shelter to depict the powers being appealed to and some of these designs are the same as those painted on the bodies of the Mountain Spirit dancers (known in various past literature as "Crown Dancers," "Devil Dancers," and "Fire Dancers"). Ghost-chasing rituals are sung for those who have died. (Apaches traditionally destroy the homes and belongings of the dead.) Like the Navajos, the Apaches have many songs that honor horses, which were of tremendous importance in their cultures. The following text from Opler was used to help treat someone injured by a horse:

> The sun's horse is a yellow stallion;
> His nose, the place above his nose, is of haze,
> His ears, of the small lightning, are moving back and forth;
> He has come to us.

The sun's horse is a yellow stallion,
A blue stallion, a black stallion;
The sun's horse has come out to us.

Besides the ritual music, the traditional Apache repertory includes social dance-songs, songs honoring great warriors of the past, and joking songs to accompany small drinking parties as well as the "forty-niner" songs sung on many reservations in part to mock the White Man. Moccasin Game songs accompany a form of gambling in which tokens are concealed by one side and their location is guessed by the other. These songs mention humorous incidents from the creation story to confuse the guessers. Paul Ortega has recorded one of these ("Moccasin Game") on his album *Two Worlds/Three Worlds*.

The Apache fiddle, which has one or two strings stretched on a length of century-plant stalk, is one of the few Native American string instruments (*see* TSLI'EDO'A'TL). Most fiddle tunes derive from the drinking-song repertory and the instrument is now rarely seen in use. Another Apache musical instrument is a flageolet made of river cane with three stops tuned approximately to the first, third, fourth, and fifth degrees of a diatonic major scale. Short repetitive melodies are played with a breathy over-blowing technique and a wide vibrato. The drum, used in most ceremonial music, is made of a large iron pot with water inside and wet buckskin stretched over the mouth. Two or three drummers play in unison on the same instrument, producing a deep, booming accompaniment for the voice.

New musics of the Apache include the songs of the Native American Church (Peyote religion) and of other recent movements such as the Silas John religion and the various Christian denominations on the reservations. Records and tapes of powwow music in Plains Indian style are prized, and country and rock music are also popular. Philip Cassadore and his sister Patsy of the San Carlos reservation have recorded ritual music, somewhat revised, as well as traditional social songs and love-songs. Mescalero singer and healer, A. Paul Ortega has invented a hybrid music with his own vocables and instrumental accompaniments; his lyrics stress Apache values, such as friendship and an understanding of nature and some of them use the song forms and tunes of ritual songs.

Recordings of Apache music are in the holdings of the Wesleyan University Archive of World Music, Middletown, Connecticut; the Indiana University Archives of Traditional Music, Bloomington, Indiana; the Archive of Folk Culture, Library of Congress, Washington, DC; and the Peabody Museum, Harvard University.

See also NATIVE AMERICAN MUSIC and NATIVE AMERICAN FLUTE.

DISCOGRAPHY (SELECTIVE)

Music of the American Indian, Vol. 9: Apache, ed. W. Rhodes, Library of Congress (1954)
Music of the Pueblos, Apache, and Navaho, ed. D. McAllester, Taylor Museum, Colorado Springs R61–1317 (1961)
P. Cassadore: *Apache Songs in the Authentic Rhythms and Language*, Can. ARP6056 (1968)
Philip Cassadore Sings Apache Songs, Can. (1968)
P. Cassadore, R. Cassadore, and W. Hinton: *The Apache Day in Song*, AmW-101380 (1980)
J. Shenandoah and A.P. Ortega: *Loving Ways*, Can. (1994)
P. Cassadore: *Apache: Apache Traditional Songs*, Can. (1998)
A.P. Ortega: *Two Worlds/Three Worlds*, Can. (2006)

BIBLIOGRAPHY

M.E. Opler: *An Apache Life Way* (Chicago, 1941/*R*)
D.P. McAllester: "The Role of Music in Western Apache Culture," *Men and Cultures: Selected Papers of the Fifth International Congress of Anthropological and Ethnological Sciences: Philadelphia, 1956*, ed. A.F.C. Wallace (Philadelphia, 1960)
D.P. Clark: *They Sang for Horses, The Impact of the Horse on Navajo and Apache Folklore* (Boulder, CO, 1966/R2001)
C.R. Farrer: "Singing for Life: the Mescalero Apache Girls Puberty Ceremony," *Southwestern Indian Ritual Drama*, ed. C.J. Frisbie (Albuquerque, 1980), 125–59
A.D. Shapiro and I. Talamantez: "The Mescalero Girls' Puberty Ceremony, the Role of Music in Structuring Ritual Time," *Yearbook of the International Council for Traditional Music*, xviii (1986)
I. Talamantez: "The Presence of Isanaklesh: A Native American Goddess and the Path of Pollen," *Unspoken Worlds: Women's Religious Lives*, ed. N.A. Falk and R. Gross (Belmont, 1989), 246–56
C.R. Ganteaume: "White Mountain Apache Dance: Expressions of Spirituality," *Native American Dance: Ceremonies and Social Traditions*, ed. C. Heth (Golden, 1992), 65–81
T.L. Larson: *Gaan/Gahe: the Art and Performance of the Apache Mountain Spirit Dancers* (diss., U. of California, Santa Barbara, 1996)
A.D. McLucas: "The Music of the Mescalero Apache Girls' Puberty Ceremony," *Music in Indigenous Religious Traditions*, ed. K. O'Keefe and G. Harvey (Aldershot, 2000), 198–209
D.W. Samuels: *Putting a Song on Top of It: Expression and identity on the San Carlos Apache Reservation* (Tucson, 2004)
A.D. McLucas: "Silent Music: The Apache Transformation of a Girl to a Woman," *Musical Childhoods and the cultures of Youth*, ed. S. Boynton and R. Kok (Middletown, CT, 2006), 49–67
T.C. Aplin: "'This is Our Dance' The Fire Dance of the Fort Sill Chiricahua Warm Spring Apache," *Music of the First Nations: Tradition and Innovation in Native North America*, ed. T. Browner (Urbana, 2009), 97–112

DAVID P. McALLESTER/ANNE DHU McLUCAS

Apaka, Alfred (Aholo) [Afat, Alfred Aiu] (*b* Honolulu, HI, 19 Mar 1919; *d* Honolulu, HI, 30 Jan 1960). Hawaiian pop singer. In many ways, Apaka was the first modern pop star in Hawaiian music. His warm baritone reflected the enormous impact of Bing Crosby's crooning in Hawaii during the 1930s, but also evoked comparisons with Elvis Presley and Marty Robbins a generation later, especially when they sang Hawaiian repertoire. Apaka's good looks, trademark red carnation lei and easygoing charm attracted mainstream media, and he was one of the few Hawaiian artists to appear regularly on national programs in the 1950s. Romantic ballads were Apaka's forte, especially hapa haole songs such as "Beyond the Reef" and "Lovely Hula Hands." Much of his Hawaiian-language repertoire was similarly *nahenahe* (sweet) though he also performed up-tempo songs and novelties. Instrumental support tended to reflect the then-thriving Waikiki lounge scene with amplified steel guitar, ukulele, rhythm guitar, string bass and sometimes vibraphone and percussion.

Born Alfred Aiu Afat, Apaka grew up in Honolulu in a musical family. Don McDirmid, Sr., bandleader at the Royal Hawaiian Hotel, hired Apaka as lead singer in 1938. In 1940, Apaka joined Ray Kinney at the Hawaiian Room of the Hotel Lexington in New York and made his first record with Kinney's group for Decca. In 1943, Apaka formed his own group. With support from Webley Edwards, he joined the "Hawaii Calls" radio program in 1947 and began headlining clubs around Waikiki. Comedian Bob Hope saw Apaka there in 1952, which led to offers to sing on a number of national radio and television programs. In 1955, industrialist Henry Kaiser opened the Tapa Room at the Hawaiian Village, installing Apaka as the headliner. Apaka recorded for Decca, Capitol, and other multinational labels. In 1957, he appeared twice on Ed Sullivan's "Talk of the Town" variety show. At the height of his fame, with his own TV pilot in the works, Apaka died of a heart attack at age 40.

JAY W. JUNKER

Aparicio, Frances R (*b* Santurce, San Juan, PR, 11 Dec 1955). Literary scholar. She studied Spanish and Comparative Literature at Indiana University (BA 1978), and earned the MA (1980) and PhD (1983) in Spanish from Harvard University. Aparicio's research focuses on languages, cultural hybridity, and transnationalism in Latino and Latina culture. She examines the role of popular music in defining the cultural changes, hybridity and cultural politics in Latin American popular culture. She is the author of *Listening to Salsa* (1998), co-editor of two volumes of essays: *Musical Migrations* (New York, 2003) and *Tropicalizations* (Hanover, NY, 1997), and has published many articles. She received the Modern Languages Association's Katherine Kovac Singer Award for the best book in Hispanic Studies and the Best Book Award from the International Association for the Study of Popular Music for *Listening to Salsa*. Aparicio has taught at Stanford University, University of Arizona, University of Michigan, and University of Illinois at Chicago, and currently holds the position of professor of Spanish and Portuguese and director of the Latina and Latino Studies Program at Northwestern University.

WRITINGS
(selective)

Versiones, interpretaciones, creaciones: Instancias de la traducción literaria en Hispanoamérica en el siglo veinte (Gaithersburg, MD, 1991)

ed. with S. C. Silverman: *Tropicalizations: Transcultural Representations of Latinidad*. Re-Encountering Colonialisms Series (Hanover, NY, 1997)

Listening to Salsa: Gender, Latin Popular Music, and Puerto Rican Cultures. Music/Culture Series (Hanover, NH, 1998)

"The Blackness of Sugar: Celia Cruz and the Performance of (Trans) Nationalism," *Cultural Studies*, xiii/2 (1999), 223–36

"Reading the 'Latino' in Latino Studies: Toward Reimagining our Academic Location," *Discourse: Studies in Media and Culture*, xxi/3 (1999), 3–18

ed. with C. Jáquez: *Musical Migrations: Transnationalism and Cultural Hybridity in the Americas* (New York, 2003)

MARYSOL QUEVEDO

Apollo Theater. Theater in New York. Located at 253 West 125th Street, the Apollo Theater is situated in the heart of Harlem. Benjamin Hurtig and Harry Seamon originally owned the building and operated it as the New Burlesque Theater until Sidney Cohen purchased the establishment in 1934, reopening it as the 125th Street Apollo Theater. Frank Schiffman and Leo Brecher bought the building soon thereafter, and the theater flourished under their direction for more than 30 years. Schiffman achieved a reputation for programming entertainment intended to attract sizeable African American audiences and for employing African American musicians, dancers, comedians, and stagehands. He used a vaudeville-style variety format to organize the shows, also called revues, which allowed multiple acts to perform in a single evening. A similar approach was employed for "Amateur Night at the Apollo," which began in the 1930s, quickly became popular with audiences and talents scouts, and evolved into a long-standing Apollo tradition. Winning Amateur Night helped launch the careers of many black musicians and entertainers, among them Ella Fitzgerald, Sarah Vaughan, Dionne Warwick, James Brown, Gladys Knight, and Jimi Hendrix. Throughout the years, the Apollo became a symbol of musical innovation, embracing new styles of music from swing, bebop, and rhythm-and-blues during the 1930s through 1950s to soul music, Motown, and experimental jazz in the decades that followed. In the 1970s and 1980s the Apollo suffered from financial difficulties and intermittent closings until it became a city and state landmark in 1983, thereby securing its continued presence in Harlem.

BIBLIOGRAPHY

J. Schiffman: *Uptown: The Story of Harlem's Apollo Theatre* (New York, 1971)

T. Fox: *Showtime at the Apollo* (New York, 1983)

R. Carlin and K. Conwill: *Ain't Nothing Like the Real Thing: How the Apollo Theater Shaped American Entertainment* (Washington, DC, 2010)

JENNIFER L. CAMPBELL

Aponte Ledée, (José) Rafael (*b* Guayama, PR, 15 Oct 1938). Puerto Rican composer. Aponte Ledée received a degree in composition in 1964 from the Conservatorio Real de Madrid, where his professors included Enrique Massó, Emilio López, Cales Otero, and Cristóbal Halffter. With a scholarship from the Latin American Center for Higher Musical Studies he continued his graduate studies with Alberto Ginastera and Gerardo Gandini in Buenos Aires at the Instituto Torcuato di Tella. Aponte Ledée belongs to the generation following self-proclaimed nationalist composers such as Campos Parsi and Amaury Veray. He and other Puerto Rican composers of his generation privilege the use of avant-garde compositional techniques. Although he adheres to Puerto Rican nationalist ideals Aponte Ledée does not search intentionally to express a national identity through music. In his compositions, he has experimented with serialism, aleatoric music, indeterminacy, electronic music, atonalism, pointillism, and extended instrumental techniques with string, woodwind, and brass instruments. When using popular music rhythms and melodies, he employs quotation as a technique that intends to challenge musical stereotypes. In 1967 he founded Fluxus Group of Puerto Rico, along with Francis Schwartz, with the purpose of disseminating contemporary music. Both composers have been instrumental in promoting avant-garde music in the island and throughout the Caribbean. In 1978 Aponte Ledée organized the first biennial of the Sociedad Puertorriqueña de Música Contemporánea. He has been a music theory and composition professor at the Universidad de Puerto Rico and at the Conservatory of Music of Puerto Rico (1968–73).

WORKS

Pf: Tema y seis diferencias, 1963; Volúmenes, 1971

Chbr: Elejía, chbr orch, 1965; Dialogantes, fl, viol, 1965 Epíthasis, T, B, 3 ob, 2 trbn, 3 perc, 1967; Dialogantes 2, T, 3 fl, 3 trbn, 3 cl, 1968; La ventana abierta, 3 Mez, 3 fl, cl, hn, tpt, pf/celest, 2 perc, str qt, 1968; Aquí presente!, 5 tpt, 1969; Tentativas, vn, chbr orch, 1970; SSSSSS, db, 3 fl, tpt, perc, 1971; Los huevos de Pandora, cl, tape, 1974; Bagatelles, gui, 1988; El otro cielo, fl, eng hn, hn, 1996

Orch: Elejía, str, 1967; Impulsos…in memoriam Julia de Burgos, 1967; Cantos de Daniel Santos, 1995; In Memoriam Salvador Allende, orch, tape

Tape and narrator: Presagio de pájaros, 1966; Estravagario, 1973; Cuídense de los ángeles que caen, 1974

Other works: Divertimento, orch; Estas lágrimas tan bellas; Los huevos de Pandora, cl; Impulsos, 1967; Intemperancia, 1971; Lema y seis diferencias; Streptomicina, 1970; Un pájaro de papel en el pecho dice que el tiempo de los besos no ha llegado, 1969; Asiento en el paraíso; Cantata; Amorous, 1970

BIBLIOGRAPHY

Compositors de América/Composers of the Americas, ed. Pan American Union, xix (Washington, DC, 1971), 23–6

D. Thompson: "La música contemporánea en Puerto Rico," *RMC,* xxxviii (1984), 110–17

E. Díaz Díaz: "Puerto Rican affirmation and denial of musical nationalism: The cases of Campos Parsi and Aponte Ledée," *Latin American Music Review,* xvii (1996), 1–20

C. Toro Vargas: *Diccionario biográfico de compositores puertorriqueños* (Ponce, PR, 2003)

MARYSOL QUEVEDO

Appalachia. Appalachia is the inextricable union of a place and a people bound in a vibrant but invisible web of culture specific to the Appalachian Mountains. While there is the physical reality of a mountain range, the concept of "Appalachia" as a region is a synthetic construct that developed towards the end of the 19th century. The borders of this region are fluid and subject to continuous interpretation and negotiation. Mountains are not constrained by political boundaries; identity is engendered by geography and culture. A highly inclusive definition based on economics formulated by the Appalachian Regional Commission in 1965 included 410 "economically distressed" counties scattered through 13 states. A more focused definition envisions a core "Southern Appalachian Region" consisting of eastern Kentucky, eastern Tennessee, western North Carolina, western Virginia, and the entire state of West Virginia. Small portions of Ohio, Pennsylvania, Georgia, Alabama, Maryland, and South Carolina are generally considered an extension of this Southern Appalachian hearth.

1. INTRODUCTION. Conceiving an accurate and inclusive cultural landscape for the music of Appalachia is just as problematic as creation of the geographic entity. There is a vast spectrum of musical activity in the region spanning nearly every style, repertoire, and genre found in the United States and the world beyond. While Appalachia is commonly associated with rural vernacular styles, such as bluegrass and country, the region embraces a diverse range of musical practices including Buddhist chant, symphony orchestras, hip hop, and cathedral choirs. To provide clarity it is useful to construct a dichotomy between music *in* Appalachia and Appalachian music.

While there is a constant dialogue of music that is both internal and external to the region, the musical idioms that are most characteristic and emblematic of the Southern Appalachia consist of balladry, dance tunes, and lyric folk song, as well as sacred expression in the shape-note hymnody, the Old Regular/Primitive Baptist church, and Pentecostalism. The rise of late-19th-century industrialization, particularly coal and timber extraction and the changes effected by the Tennessee Valley Authority increasingly altered the traditional subsistence agricultural lifestyle. Consequently, rural, vernacular styles altered by automobiles, radio, and recording technology were commodified into more commercial styles including hillbilly, country, bluegrass, and Southern gospel. Industrialization also sparked a direct musical response in the form of work songs, such as "John Henry," and labor songs by union activists such as Aunt Molly Jackson.

The history of Appalachian music can be interpreted as the transformation of a traditional, localized, vernacular style cultivated within oral tradition by early immigrants (especially from the British Isles and Germany) to more national popular styles cultivated by an increasingly diverse immigrant base (including African Americans and Eastern Europeans). Several waves of folk revivalism preserved facets of traditional music expression even as the expansion of popular culture nurtured diverse forms of musical expression in the region.

2. BALLADS AND SONGS. Balladry provided a narrative voice within traditional Appalachian culture. The Child ballads, stanzaic poetry coupled with monophonic vocal melodies imported from the British Isles, served as entertainment, but more importantly, they also forged community through a common lineage of shared stories, and myths that inculcated societal values. (*See* CHILD BALLADS.) Because of the process of oral transmission, over time, Child ballads developed distinctively Appalachian versions and variants. A Scottish version of "Barbara Allen" sings: "He's turned his face unto the wa'/And death was with him dealin.'" In Appalachia, that same line was transformed into: "He turned his deathbed plumb to the wall/He busted out to crying." The stories remain constant while the mode of expression and the tune may vary considerably.

Over time, Americans created original narrative songs modeled after the Child ballads. Known as native American ballads, these songs told the stories of American experiences and events, such as train wrecks or life as a cowboy. These circulated widely throughout Appalachia, and many were based on historical events in the region including a quantity of gruesome murder ballads, such as "Omie Wise" and "Tom Dula." Lyric songs, such as "Pretty Saro," provided another form of expression marked by emotional content and subjective expression rather than narrative structure. While these song forms are closely identified with the region's identity, they also engendered stereotyping that fostered an ideology of Anglo-Saxonism and nativism.

3. Instrumental music. The earliest instrumental music, often performed by solo fiddle, was frequently used to accompany dances, such as reels, hornpipes, quicksteps, waltzes, and schottisches, but there were also airs and marches intended as entertainment (*see* Fiddling). The foundational repertoire consisted of tunes imported from the old world, primarily of British origin, but musical influences peculiar to the Appalachian mountains and the growing popularity of square dances soon created a large, distinctive body of music that can be broadly characterized as modal, built on gapped scales, often performed in "open tunings," with regular 4-bar phrase length and a repeated binary structure. Fiddle tunes could also be "crooked" (irregular number of beats) or consist of odd numbers of sections and repeats because a "caller" shouted out dance figures and instructions as the dance unfolded; the structure of the dance was not tied to the architecture of the tune (*see* Square dance).

By the mid-19th century the combination of fiddle and banjo was common; the clawhammer or frailed technique and tunings were gleaned directly from African American slaves living on small farms in the mountains. The introduction of the guitar by the late nineteenth century altered the character of tunes because the guitar's frets facilitated three-chord I–IV–V harmony. Beginning in 1894, the guitar's popularity continued to grow as mail order catalogs, such as those published by Sears, Roebuck, and Company, began offering inexpensive instruments to people living in remote rural areas. The expanded concept of a String band featuring mandolin, guitar, string bass (or cello), banjo, and fiddles developed in the 1920s concurrent with the rise of hillbilly recordings.

4. Sacred music. Religion has long been an important force in Appalachia, but collective worship was challenging because of the sparse, diffused population and the difficulty of travel through the mountains. In response, "circuit riding" preachers covered a network of rural churches of various independent denominations such as Old Regular or Primitive Baptist. Music in these churches was strictly vocal and unaccompanied; the most usual performance practice was "lining out" in which a leader would chant a line of text read from a text-only hymnal. The congregation then would respond with that same line of text sung in a heavily ornamented form of choral heterophony.

In response, a style of singing that developed in the eastern seaboard during the late 18th century as a replacement for lined-out singing, began to spread westward through the Shenandoah Valley and down along the Ohio River in the early 19th century. Singing school masters such as Ananais Davisson and Joseph Funk instructed classes using a shape-note solfège system and published instructional books with hymns collected and arranged in a very linear style of three- or four-part harmony. Shape-note tunebooks compiled and circulating in Appalachia bore increasing numbers of folk-like hymn tunes and added repetitive-chorus forms adapted from camp meetings, such as Cane Ridge, Kentucky in 1801.

5. Hillbilly music. During the 1920s the nascent recording industry began recording performances of traditional Appalachian fiddle tunes and songs—what came to be marketed as Hillbilly music—at the same time as African-American musical expression was being commodified in the form of "race records." The first hillbilly recording is generally credited to Eck Robertson who recorded the fiddle tune "Sally Gooden" on 20 June 1922. In making the transition from live performance at a community dance to remote performances on radio and recordings, string bands began to devise entertainment strategies, such as creating skits that interspersed music and comic dialogue in settings that recreated a traditional context such as "A Fiddler's Convention in North Georgia" by the Skillet Lickers.

The "Bristol Sessions" recordings made in 1927–8 by Ralph Peer for the Victor Talking Machine Company drew musicians from all over Appalachia to record, and in the process, regional hillbilly style moved toward the national popular music known as country music. The recordings featured pioneers such as the Carter family from rugged Scott County, Virginia and gospel musicians including Ernest Phipps's Holiness Quartet of Corbin, Kentucky.

6. Country music. Country music developed as the country was drawn to the city. Because of the inhospitable terrain, there were few large cities anywhere in the mountains. Bristol was chosen for the site of the Victor recordings because it (along with nearby Johnson City and Kingsport) was the largest population center in the mountains. The country radio and recording industry soon moved to the fringes of the region, situating themselves in Atlanta and Nashville. As various waves of out-migration from the region spread Appalachian people to northern cities, the audience and the performers retained a nostalgic bond with mountain culture, but were increasingly influenced by the northern and urban environments. Country remains the dominant popular music in the region and many of its performers, including Dolly Parton, Loretta Lynn, and Patty Loveless are strongly identified with Appalachia.

7. Bluegrass. The origins of Bluegrass music are centered in western Kentucky where the Monroe Brothers first created the improvisational mix that fused elements of string band tradition influenced by Arnold Schultz's African American "thumb picking" guitar style

wedded to vocals that combined aspects of balladry and the harmonic texture of Southern gospel. Bluegrass is strongly associated with the Appalachian region; many performers, such as the STANLEY BROTHERS, were from the mountains and the Appalachian experience itself is distilled in the "high lonesome" sound and the mountain narrative of outmigration inscribed in the lyrics. In recent years, bluegrass has been incorporated within the curriculum of academic institutions in Appalachia such as East Tennessee State University and Berea College.

8. SOUTHERN GOSPEL. Building on the foundation of shape-note singing schools, Southern gospel developed in the 1920s through mass conventions and traveling vocal quartets that performed original sacred songs through a network of evangelical churches and singing events. Publishing firms, such as the Shenandoah Valley's Ruebush-Keiffer Company, circulated this repertoire through inexpensive hymnals printed in 7-shape notation. The style was further spread by bluegrass bands that regularly embraced gospel songs, such as "I'll fly away" in their performances.

9. FOLK REVIVALISM. In the first few decades of the 20th century, folk collectors, such as Cecil Sharp, traveled through the Appalachian mountains, focusing attention on Anglo-American balladry and leading to an initial wave of FOLK REVIVAL performers, such as JOHN JACOB NILES, who presented the repertoire—though not necessarily the style—to a national audience. In the 1960s another wave of revivalism sparked by the NEW LOST CITY RAMBLERS rediscovered traditional music through 1920s-era recordings and surviving tradition bearers, and presented songs in versions that were informed by authentic performance style. Finally, the revival of string band tradition in the 1970s led by bands such as Hollow Rock and the Highwoods String Band nurtured a genre of OLD-TIME MUSIC that was celebrated in Appalachian festivals, such as those at Galax, Virginia and Cliff Top, West Virginia, and disseminated through workshops including Swannanoa Gathering and the Augusta Heritage Center. While revivalism insured the survival of traditional forms of Appalachian music, a rich and diverse current of contemporary musical expression continues to flourish in the region today.

BIBLIOGRAPHY

C. Sharp: *English Folksongs from the Southern Appalachians* (London 1917, 2/1932)

A. Green: *Only a Miner: Studies in Recorded Coal-Mining Songs* (Urbana, IL, 1972)

C. Wolfe: *Tennessee Strings* (Knoxville, TN, 1977)

B. Malone: *Southern Music—American Music* (Lexington, KY, 1979)

C. Wolfe: *Kentucky Country* (Lexington, KY, 1982)

C. Conway: *African Banjo Echoes in Appalachia* (Knoxville, TN, 1995)

D. Davidson: *Big Ballad Jamboree* (Jackson, MS, 1996)

C. Wolfe: *Devil's Box* (Nashville, TN 1996)

B. Filene: *Romancing the Folk: Public Memory and American Roots Music* (Chapel Hill, NC, 2000)

M. McGee: *Traditional Musicians of the Central Blue Ridge* (Jefferson, NC, 2000)

RON PEN

Appalachian dulcimer [lap dulcimer, mountain dulcimer, Kentucky dulcimer, plucked dulcimer]. A fretted zither traditional to the southern Appalachian mountains of the eastern United States consisting of a narrow fingerboard attached to a larger soundbox underneath. Variant names include "delcumer," "dulcymore," "harmonium," "hog fiddle," "music box," and "harmony box." Long found only in scattered pockets of tradition, the dulcimer has since the 1950s gained popularity outside the mountains; at the beginning of the 21st century it was being widely used by both amateur and professional musicians in folk-based repertories.

1. History. 2. Construction, technique, and repertory.

1. HISTORY. The organological development of the Appalachian dulcimer divides into three periods: transitional (1700 to the mid-1800s), traditional (mid-1800s to 1940) and revival or contemporary (after 1940). During the transitional period the dulcimer developed in the Shenandoah River Valley region of southwestern Pennsylvania through the blending of British (predominantly Scottish) musical traditions with those of other immigrants, who brought with them the German *Scheitholt* and possibly the Swedish *hummel*, the Norwegian *langeleik* or the French *épinette des Vosges*. In the traditional period the dulcimer solidified into its present shape. Two makers were probably responsible for the dissemination of the instrument within Appalachia. J. Edward Thomas of Knott County, Kentucky, had connections with the Hindman Settlement School in eastern Kentucky and made dulcimers between 1871 and 1930, many of which he peddled from a mulecart. C.P. Pritchard of Huntington, West Virginia, manufactured what he termed an "American dulcimer" and offered strings by mail order. Both made instruments in hourglass form with three strings.

Towards the end of the 19th century the Settlement School and crafts movements brought the dulcimer to the attention of outsiders, and the interpretation of Appalachia as the home of America's "Elizabethan ancestors" encouraged a romanticized view of the instrument as emblematic of an imagined Appalachian culture. This attention encouraged mountain residents to preserve the dulcimer but also discouraged them from developing it any further. In the early 1900s it was taken up by scholars, notably I.G. Greer, and folk music enthusiasts, such as Andrew Rowan Sumner, Mellinger Henry, Maurice Matteson, and John Jacob Niles.

Around the middle of the 20th century the dulcimer entered the urban northeast folk revival scene, largely due to the Kentucky-born musician Jean Ritchie, who performed and recorded extensively and published the first important instruction book (1963). The recordings and performances of revivalist (Richard Fariña, Paul Clayton, Howie Mitchell, Betty Smith, Ann Grimes) and traditional players (Frank Proffitt, Frank Proffitt Jr., the Melton and Russell families of Galax, Virginia, the Presnell and Hicks families of Beech Mountain, North Carolina, the Ritchie family of eastern Kentucky) introduced the dulcimer to a wide audience and dulcimer making became a hobby and cottage industry throughout the United States. Makers refined the instrument and developed new variants: a cardboard dulcimer, a "backpacker's dulcimer" or dulcerine (a fretboard without soundbox) and an electric dulcimer. A magazine, *Dulcimer Players News*, was founded in 1975.

2. Construction, technique, and repertory. The instrument is usually 75 to 90 cm long, its width varying according to the shape of the soundbox, commonly hourglass or teardrop, although oval, diamond, rectangular, and other shapes are found. There are many variants, including a child-sized one and a larger one for concerts. The dulcimer has three strings, usually of metal, sometimes with one (the melody string) or more doubled. Contemporary dulcimers frequently add a fourth string, either doubling the melody string or equidistant between the melody and middle strings. The fingerboard is divided by metal frets into two and half to three octaves of the diatonic scale, rendering the dulcimer a modal instrument; the two most common modes seem to have been Ionian (the major scale) and Mixolydian. Two common Ionian tunings have melody and middle strings at the same pitch with the bass string a 5th or an octave below. Other tunings have melody and bass strings an octave apart with the middle string a 5th above the bass, or strings tuned to create a chord. Some contemporary instruments have extra, chromatic, frets, and players have devised more tunings and adopted the *capo tasto* to change key without retuning. On earlier dulcimers the frets were under the first two strings only, but on contemporary instruments they extend the full width of the fingerboard, allowing all strings to be used for the melody or chords.

The instrument was usually placed horizontally across a table or the player's lap. The right hand sounded the strings by plucking with the fingers or a plectrum made from wood or quill (or, occasionally, bowing) while the left hand played a melody by pressing on the fretboard with a noter (a wooden rod used as a slide) or the fingers. Melodies were usually played on the first string only, the others acting as drones. Techniques for using all the strings for melody, for playing chords and for fingerpicking have been developed by both traditional and contemporary players. The traditional repertory included British ballads and hymns, dance tunes, play party songs, minstrel show tunes, sentimental popular songs, gospel, blues, and commercial hillbilly music. The older British-derived repertory was emphasized by the romanticists of the instrument and the dulcimer was still associated with those styles at the end of the 20th century, although contemporary players had expanded the repertory enormously. Because of its soft volume, the dulcimer is thought to have been used to accompany singing or for instrumental solos, but it was also in string bands and instrumental duets, where it sometimes played the melody and sometimes provided harmony or a rhythmic accompaniment through the slapping of the pick against the strings. At the start of the 21st century, numerous clubs and workshops for playing and making the instrument were common throughout the United States.

BIBLIOGRAPHY

C. Seeger: "The Appalachian Dulcimer," *Journal of American Folklore*, lxxi (1958), 40–51

J. Ritchie: *The Dulcimer Book* (New York, 1963/*R*)

Dulcimer Players News (Winchester, VA, 1975–)

J. Ritchie: *Jean Ritchie's Dulcimer People* (New York, 1975)

M. Murphy: *The Appalachian Dulcimer Book* (St Clairsville, OH, 1976)

L.A. Smith: "Toward a Reconstruction of the Development of the Appalachian Dulcimer: what the Instruments Suggest," *Journal of American Folklore*, xciii (1980), 385–96

L.A. Smith: *A Catalogue of Pre-Revival Appalachian Dulcimers* (Columbia, MO, 1983)

L.M. Long: *The Negotiation of Tradition: Collectors, Community, and the Appalachian Dulcimer in Beech Mountain, North Carolina* (diss., U. of Pennsylvania, 1995)

R.L. Smith: *American Dulcimer Traditions* (Lanham, MD, 1997, 2/2002)

M. Voloshin: "The Appalachian Dulcimer: an Essay and Bibliography," *Music Reference Services Quarterly*, viii/1 (2001), 79–88

For further bibliography *see* Zither, fretted.

LUCY M. LONG/R

Appel, Toby (*b* Elmer, NJ, 22 Nov 1952). Violist and violinist. Born into a family of amateur musicians, he began his studies with Max Aronoff, first at the New School of Music in Philadelphia then at the Curtis Institute, and with Joseph Di Pasquale. He was the winner of the Young Concert Artists International Auditions. By the age of 15 he was playing engagements ranging from popular music and church concerts to solo appearances with the Philadelphia Orchestra. He became assistant principal violist with the St. Louis Symphony Orchestra in 1970 and the following year made his Carnegie Hall recital début. From 1975 to 1977 he was a member of the Lenox Quartet and was on the faculty of SUNY, Binghamton, NY, from 1972 to 1979. He also taught at the Virginia Polytechnic Institute, the University of New Mexico and Carnegie Mellon University.

Appel has given recitals at Alice Tully Hall and the Metropolitan Museum of Art, and has appeared at the Marlboro Festival in Vermont. In demand as a chamber musician he is a regular guest artist with Tashi. He is interested in many different areas of music and gave the world première of Ezra Lademan's *Other Voices*, for three violas, in 1977 on a CBS television special, playing all the parts himself (live and on tape). Having taken up the violin, in part for the sake of its larger repertoire, he served briefly as first violinist of the Audubon Quartet (1983–4). He has given recitals on both instruments and in 1983–4 toured Europe and Japan with Chick Corea. In 1990 he was appointed to the faculty of the Juilliard School.

ELLEN HIGHSTEIN/ANYA LAURENCE

Applebaum, Louis (*b* Toronto, ON, 3 April 1918, *d* Toronto, ON, 20 April 2000). Canadian composer and arts administrator. He studied the piano with Boris Berlin, and theory and composition with Healey Willan, Ernest MacMillan, and Leonard B. Smith, before continuing composition studies with Roy Harris and Bernard Wagenaar in New York (1940–41). For the next eight years, Applebaum worked for the National Film Board of Canada, producing some 250 film scores. During this period he became increasingly concerned with improving the position of professional musicians in Canada. His combined interests in creative and socioeconomic development led to a career that influenced every aspect of Canadian music. During the 1960s he served as consultant for CBC television and chair of the planning committee for the National Arts Centre, Ottawa. His 1965 *Proposal for the Musical Development of the Capital Region* led to the formation of the National Arts Centre Orchestra and the University of Ottawa music department. Throughout the 1970s he served as executive director of the Ontario Arts Council and in 1980 became co-chair of the Federal Cultural Review Committee.

Applebaum has composed incidental music for more than 50 productions of the Stratford (Ontario) Shakespearean Festival (1953–90) and written fanfares to announce performances at the Festival Theatre. In 1955, partly to supplement the work of theater musicians, he founded the music wing of the festival, which consists of concerts, opera workshops, and conferences. In addition to a steady stream of theater music (including four ballets) as well as film and television scores, he wrote many instrumental and vocal works. His numerous honors include the Canadian Centennial Medal (1967) and appointment to the Order of Canada (1995). In 1998, in celebration of his 80th birthday, a concert of his works was performed in Toronto.

WORKS
(selective list)

Vocal: City of the Prophet (Bible: *Jeremiah*), Bar, pf, 1952; A Folio of Shakespearean Songs, medium v, pf, 1954–87; Cherry Tree Carol (trad.), SATB, 1958; King Herod, SATB, 1958; Algoma Central "In the Tracks of the Black Bear," S, fl, hp, 1976; Inunit, 1v, orch, 1977; Of Love and High Times, S, SATB, opt. fl, opt. hn, opt. perc, 1979; The Last Words of David, cantor, SATB, 1980; Ode to a Birthday City: 1834/Toronto/1984 (L. Sinclair), spkr, solo vv, SATB, orch, 1984; 2 Nostalgic Yiddish Folk Songs (trad.), SATB, 1987; Play On, solo vv, SATB, vn, cl, 2 pf, orch, 1987

Orch: Suite of Miniature Dances, 1953; Action Stations, 1962; Revival Meeting and Finale from "Barbara Allen," 1964; Suite of Miniature Dances, band, 1964; Concertante, 1967; Fanfare and Anthem, 1969; Homage, 1969; Place Setting, 1973; Dialogue with Footnotes, jazz band, orch, 1984; Celebration York, band, 1985; High Spirits, ov., band, 1986; Passacaglia & Toccata, band, 1986; Balletic Ov., 1987

Hundreds of film scores as composer or music director, including Call for Volunteers (1941), The Story of G.I. Joe (1945), Farewell to Yesterday (1950), Operation A-Bomb (1952), Oedipus Rex (1957), Paddle to the Sea (1966), and Karsh: The Searching Eye (1986)

Chbr and solo inst: 3 Stratford Fanfares, brass, perc, 1953; Essay, fl, 1971; 2 Ceremonial Fanfares, 5–6 tpt, c1984; 4 Dances in a 19th-Century Style, brass qnt, opt. perc, 1987; The Harper of Stones (ghost story, R. Davies), nar, chbr ens, 1987

BIBLIOGRAPHY

W. Pitman: Louis Applebaum: a Passion for Culture (Toronto, 2002)

KENNETH WINTERS/R

Applebaum, Mark (*b* Chicago, IL, 13 Oct 1967). Composer, pianist, and educator. Applebaum grew up in a musical family in Chicago. His father, Bob Applebaum, a high school physics teacher, studied classical music and composes. Applebaum graduated from Carleton College (BM 1989); his senior thesis took him to Mexico City to interview Conlon Nancarrow. He received his Masters (1992) and his Doctorate (1996) in composition from the University of California at San Diego (UCSD), studying with Brian Ferneyhough, Joji Yuasa, Rand Steiger, and Roger Reynolds. He taught at USCD, Mississippi State University, and Carleton College before his current faculty position at Stanford University, where he also serves as the founding director of the Stanford Improvisation Collective.

Applebaum's solo, chamber, choral, orchestral, operatic, and electro-acoustic work has been performed throughout the United States, Europe, South America, Africa, and Asia at numerous new music festivals. His music is mercurial, highly detailed, disciplined, and exacting, but it also features improvisational and whimsical aspects. As such, he is considered as much in the experimentalist camp exemplified by composers such as Cage and Zappa as part of the European modernist lineage represented by his principal teacher Brian Ferneyhough. He has drawn inspiration from jazz pioneers and maverick composers such as Nancarrow and Partch, who found it necessary to use or invent unusual instruments to realize their artistic visions.

Since 1990 Applebaum has built unique electroacoustic instruments from a variety of objects for use as both compositional and improvisational tools. For example, his "Mouseketier" consists of threaded rods, nails, combs, doorstops, springs, squeaky wheels, ratchets, a toilet tank flotation bulb, and other unlikely objects, which are plucked, scratched, bowed, and modified by a battery of live electronics. *Mousetrap Music* (Innova, 1996) features a recording of sound-sculpture improvisations, while *The Bible without God* (Innova, 2006) includes a 2005 collaboration with the Merce Cunningham Dance Company. Hybrid pieces featuring both acoustic and electronic instrumentation can be heard on *Intellectual Property* (Innova, 2003).

Visual and theatrical elements abound in Applebaum's work. Pieces like *Echolalia* comprise the rapid execution of 22 dadaist rituals; *Straitjacket* includes performers drawing on amplified easels; *Aphasia* requires its performer to synchronize choreographed hand gestures to tape; and *Tlön* is a work for three conductors and no players. Applebaum's *Sock Monkey* album, released in 2008, shows off his absurdist side with pieces such as "Magnetic North" in which performers are asked to stand for no apparent reason.

Some of the scores that convey Applebaum's music are unique creations in themselves. For example, *Wristwatch: Geology* (2004) appears on the face of custom-made wristwatches, its players responding musically as the second hand passes over various glyphs. His score for *The Metaphysics of Notation* (2008) consists of a series of symbols and images that extend over very long sheets of scroll-like paper. Film-maker Robert Arnold's documentary on the project appears on Applebaum's *The Metaphysics of Notation* (Innova DVD, 2010).

Applebaum has received commissions from individuals, foundations, festivals, and ensembles, including philanthropist Betty Freeman, the Merce Cunningham Dance Company, the Vienna Modern Festival, the Fromm Foundation, and the Paul Dresher Ensemble.

In 1997 he received the American Music Center's Stephen Albert Award. Among the new music ensembles that have performed his music are the Arditti String Quartet, Speculum Musicae, Zeitgeist, The Meridian Arts Ensemble, and Beta Collide. He has been especially prolific as a composer of percussion music, writing numerous pieces for virtuoso percussionist Steven Schick. Performances of his chamber music can be heard on *Catfish* (Tzadik, 2003) and *56 1/2 ft* and *Asylum* (Innova, both 2006). His orchestral works appear on the *Martian Anthropology* (Innova, 2006), and solo acoustic works appear on the *Disciplines* (Innova, 2004). He has engaged in numerous intermedia collaborations, including with neural artists, film-makers, animators, architects, choreographers, and laptop DJs.

As a jazz pianist, Applebaum has performed around the world, including a solo recital in Ouagadougou, Burkina Faso that was sponsored by the American Embassy. In 1994 he received the jazz prize of the Southern California Jazz Society. At present he performs with his father in the Applebaum Jazz Piano Duo, which has performed widely, including in Tunisia and Singapore. Their first studio recording, *The Apple Doesn't Fall Far from the Tree* (2002), is also available on Innova.

BIBLIOGRAPHY

B. Campbell: "Heard This One?," *Stanford Magazine* (May/June 2008), <http://www.stanfordalumni.org/news/magazine/2008/mayjun/features/applebaum.html>

R. Wallace: "A musical puzzle," *Palo Alto Weekly* (22 May 2009), <http://www.paloaltoonline.com/weekly/story.php?story_id = 11003>

JAMES BASH

Appleton, Jon (Howard) (*b* Los Angeles, CA, 4 Jan 1939). Composer. Born to a family of musicians, he studied piano and began composing as a child. He attended Reed College (BA 1961), studied privately in Berkeley, California, with ANDREW IMBRIE (1961–2), and then taught music at a private school in Arizona (1962–3). While at the University of Oregon (MA 1965) he studied under Homer Keller and began composing electronic music, an interest that led to further study at the Columbia-Princeton Center for Electronic Music (1965–6), principally under VLADIMIR USSACHEVSKY, MARIO DAVIDOVSKY, and WILLIAM MITCHELL. He taught for a year at Oakland University, Rochester, Michigan, before joining the faculty of Dartmouth College in 1967, where he founded and directed the Bregman Electronic Music Studio and in 1979 received an endowed chair. Since 1968 Appleton has worked periodically in Sweden and in 1976 he directed the Stiftelsen Elektronmusikstudion, Stockholm (EMS). In 1973 in Tonga and in 1979 in Ponape and Truk he took part in projects to record and broadcast traditional Polynesian and Micronesian musics. He received Guggenheim and Fulbright fellowships (1970) and two NEA awards (1976). In writings for popular and scholarly publications he has dealt with the social role, aesthetics, theory, and technology of electronic music, and with Perera has edited *The Development and Practice of Electronic Music* (Englewood Cliffs, NJ, 1975).

Appleton's electronic compositions are tonally based and his compositional techniques remain those traditional to Western music, but they are worked out using 20th-century technology—for example, musical ideas, including those based on timbre, are developed by electronic manipulation. Although much of his electronic music is synthesized, between 1967 and 1973 Appleton extended the earlier technique of *musique concrète*, often combining *concrète* and synthesized sounds. In some of his *concrète* works he exploits the tension between extramusical allusions of *concrète* sounds and their purely musical development.

In the 1970s, concerned that electronic music was functioning primarily as a "studio" rather than a "performing" art, Appleton collaborated with the engineer Sydney Alonso and the software specialist Cameron Jones to develop the SYNCLAVIER, a polyphonic digital synthesizer that can be used for live performance. Based on the Dartmouth Digital Synthesizer designed by the same team between 1972 and 1974 for use at the Bregman Electronic Music Studio, the Synclavier was the first such instrument to utilize microcomputers and the first to be manufactured commercially. In 1980 it was updated as the Synclavier II, and further developments were incorporated in 1981–2 (*see* ELECTROACOUSTIC MUSIC).

In the 1980s, Appleton continued to compose computer and live-electronic music that enjoyed many performances both in the United States and abroad. During this decade he became a founding member of the International Confederation for Electro-Acoustic Music and also help found the Society for Electro-Acoustic Music in the United States (SEAMUS) and served a time as its president. In 1984 he helped the late Moses Asch, founder of Folkways Records, to release their first recordings of electro-acoustic music, which continue to remain in print under Smithsonian/Folkways auspices.

The 1990s saw Appleton traveling abroad extensively with time spent in Japan and Russia, where he helped encourage the establishment of the Theremin Center at the Moscow Conservatory. This period saw him return to the composition of instrumental and choral music and the completion of two full-length operas. He also continued teaching in the graduate program in electro-acoustic music at Dartmouth College in a program he co-founded with composer David Evan Jones in 1989 that combines the study of composition, acoustics, computer-science, and music cognition. Although he retired from Dartmouth in 2009 he believes this program and its students to be his greatest contribution. Since leaving Dartmouth, he has taught occasionally at the University of California, Santa Cruz, and continues to pursue his composition activities.

WORKS

(sync—synclavier)

DRAMATIC

Film scores: Nobody Knows Everything, 1965; Anuszkiewicz, 1968; Computer Graphics at 110 Baud, 1969; Scene Unobserved, 1969, collab. W. Wadham, P. Payne, J. Mellquist; Charlie Item and Double X, 1970; Glory! Glory!, 1971; Arriflex 16SR, 1978; Hay Fever, 1988; Rassias in China, 1991

Incid music: The Ghost Sonata, 1969; Subject to Fits, 1978; Death Takes a Holiday, 1987; Aunt Dan and Lemon, 1988

Dance scores: Pilobolus, 1971; Anaendrom, 1972; Aubade, 1972; Cameo, 1972; Spyrogyra, 1972; Ciona, 1974–7; Otahiti, 1978; The Sydsing Camklang, 1978; Prelude, 1979; Beginnings, 1980; Nukuoro, 1980; The Tale of William Mariner, 1980

INSTRUMENTAL

Ens: 2 Movts, ww qnt, 1963; 4 Explorations, vn, pf, 1964; 6 Movts, ww qnt, 1964; After "Nude Descending a Staircase," orch, 1965; 4 Inventions, 2 fl, 1965; The Bremen Town Musicians, 12 toy insts, toy pf, 1971; Winesburg, Ohio, fl, cl, vn, vc, pf, 1972; Str Qt, 1976; Soviet-American Dances, fl, cl, vn, va, vc, perc, sync, 1984; Duo for Oscar, pf, sync, 1985; The Endless Melody, cl, sync, 1986; Fanfare for a New President, brass qnt, 1987; ...to the Islands, vn, sax, db, accdn, 1989; Duobatoni, 2 pf, 1994; Quatre regards sur le Parc du Roy d'Espagne, pf 4 hands, 1995; Eight Hands, 2 pf 8 hands, 1996; The Turkina Sonata, 2 pf, 1998; Ilya Andrevich Smirnov, theremin, vn, fl, cl, vc, 2005; Concerto, pf, str, 2006; Fantasy, vc, str, 2007; Concerto Grosso, vn, vc, pf, str, 2008

Scarlatti Doubles, 2008; 5 Easy Pieces, vn, cl/theremin, pf, 2010; The Alexandra Trio, vn, vc, pf, 2011; Sonata No.2, 2 pf, 2011

Solo: 3 Lyrics, pf, 1963; Pf Sonata no.2, 1968; The Day Jesus Kissed Me, hp, 1986; A Summer's Lullaby for Molly, pf, 1991; The Turkina Suite, pf, 1995; Nihon no omide (Japanese Memories), vn, 1996; Julia, 9 pieces, pf, 2001

VOCAL

2 Songs (B. Brecht, J.B. Friedman), 1v, pf, 1964; The Dying Christian to His Soul, 1v, pf, 1965; The American Songs (E. Dickinson, H. Crane), T, orch, 1966 [arr. T, pf, 1966]; A Swedish Love Song, 1v, sync, 1985; 3 canciones Cubanas, 1991; Canciones Latinas, 1991; The Green Wave (E. Baker), SATB, 1964; Ballad of the Soldier (Brecht), TTBB, 1974; This is America (C. Watson), SATB, 1976; Sonaria (Appleton), 4vv, sync, 1978; Le dernier voyage, nar, children's chorus, sync, 1989; Our Voyage to America, SATB, 1992; HOPI: La naissance du désert, children's chorus, orch, 1993; Vocalise for Voice and Piano, 2003

ELECTRO-ACOUSTIC AND MULTIMEDIA

Georganna's Fancy, 1966; Infantasy, 1966; Chef d'oeuvre, 1967; Spuyten duyvil, 1967; Nyckelharpen, 1968; Second Scene Unobserved, 1968; Boghosian's Piece, a.k.a. Hommage to Orpheus, 1969; Burdock Birds, 1969; C.C.C.P., In memoriam Anatoly Kuznetsov, 1969; Newark Airport Rock, 1969; Scenes Unobserved, wind, str, perc, pf, tape, film, 1969; Times Square Times Ten, 1969; Apolliana, 1970; Hommage to G.R.M., 1970; Double Structure, 1971, collab. C. Wolff; Dr Quisling in Stockholm, 1971; Kungsgatan 8, 1971; Nevsehir, 1971; Sones de son blas, 1972; Stereopticon, 1972; Ofa atu Tonga, 1973; Otahiti, 1973; Rodluvan, 1973; Zoetrope, 1974; Georganna's Farewell, 1975; Mussems Song, 1976; The Sydsing Camklang, 1976; In deserto, 1977; Syntrophia, 1977; In medias res, 1978; Prelude, live elec, 1978; Kapingamarangi, live elec, 1979; Nukuoro, live elec, 1979; [Untitled], live elec, 1979; The Tale of William Mariner, live elec, 1980; Vava'u, live elec, 1980; Sashasonjon, live elec, 1981; The Snow Queen, live elec, 1981; The Sweet Dreams of Miss Pamela Beach, 1981; Boum Sha Boom, 1983; Degitaru ongaku, live elec, 1983; Kamuela, Return to Waimea, 1983; The Lament of Kamuela, Hawaiian singer, Jap. classical singer, SATB, rock band, tape, film, video, 1983; Oskuldens drøm, 1985; Brush Canyon, live elec, 1986; Eros ex machina, live elec, 1987; Homenaje à Milanes, 1987; Borrego Springs, live elec, 1988; Happening USA 1968, dancers, mime, tape, live elec, 1988; A Summer's Lullaby, live elec, 1989; Ce que signifie la déclaration des droits de l'homme et du citoyen de 1789 pour les hommes et les citoyens des îles Marquises, 1989; Sudden Death, 1989; Pacific Rimbómbo, live elec, 1991; Dva Interview, 1993, collab. S. Kossenko; 'Uha 'amata 'atou i te himene, 1996; Yamanotesen to ko, 1997; Ko To Yamanotesen, 1998; Marco Polo Revisited, turntables, processed v, 2000; JJ Pop, 2000; *Quiff, 2001; Narita Airport Rock, 2003; Solitude, 2011

BIBLIOGRAPHY

D. Walley and P. Kennely: "Electronic Composers," *Jazz & Pop,* viii/12 (1969), 26

P. Wienecke: "Music for Synclavier and other Digital Systems," *Computer Music Journal,* iii/1 (1979), 7

N. Slonimsky: *Baker's Biographical Dictionary of Twentieth-Century Classical Musicians,* ed. L. Kuhn, assoc ed. D. McIntire (New York, 1997)

GENEVIEVE VAUGHN/GREG A. STEINKE

Appleton, Thomas (*b* Boston, MA, 26 Dec 1785; *d* Reading, MA 11 July 1872). Organ builder. The son of a housewright, he was apprenticed to a cabinetmaker, entering the employment of Boston organ builder William M. Goodrich at the age of 20. In 1811 he became a partner in the firm of Hayts, Babcock, and Appleton, makers of pianos, chamber organs, and claviorgans; in 1820 this firm dissolved and Appleton became an independent organ builder, quickly gaining a reputation for fine workmanship and securing important commissions. Some of his earliest organs were voiced by William Goodrich's brother Ebenezer, and Henry Corrie, an Englishman trained in the Elliot workshop. Between 1847 and 1850 Thomas D. Warren, who had been in his employ for several years, became his partner under the firm name of Appleton & Warren. In 1851 he moved to a new workshop in Reading, Massachusetts, built for him by his son Edward, a railway developer. In 1856 another longtime employee, Horatio Davis, was briefly in partnership with him. Appleton's output after moving to Reading was not as great as it had been in Boston, and he eventually retired in 1868 at the age of 83. His most important work was carried out before the move to Reading, and included organs for Beneficent Church, Providence, Rhode Island (1826), Bowdoin Street Church, Boston, where Lowell Mason was organist (1831), the Boston Handel & Haydn Society (1832), Center Church, Hartford, Connecticut (1835), First Unitarian Church, New Bedford, Massachusetts (1841), Church of the Pilgrims, Brooklyn, New York (1846), and St. Luke's Episcopal Church, Rochester, New York (1850). Appleton's work is characterized by meticulous craftsmanship, refined tonal quality, and, during his Boston period, strikingly handsome casework, notably in the Greek Revival style, and often executed in mahogany with decorative carved pipe shades.

BIBLIOGRAPHY

W.H. Clarke: "Thomas Appleton," *The Organ,* i/2 (1892), 29

B. Owen: "The Goodriches and Thomas Appleton," *The Tracker,* iv/1 (1959), 2

B. Owen: *The Organ in New England* (Raleigh, NC, 1979)

L. Libin: "Thomas Appleton and his Organ at the Metropolitan Museum of Art," *The Tracker,* 27/4 (1983)

BARBARA OWEN

Appo, William (*b* Philadelphia, PA, *c*1808; *d* New York State, after 1871). Composer, French horn player, pianist, and conductor. Of Santo Domingan descent, he was one of black America's earliest published composers. He began his career playing horn in Philadelphia's Walnut Street Theatre Orchestra (1826). Around 1830 he opened a music studio and taught piano in New York, Philadelphia, and occasionally Baltimore for more than 20 years. In 1837 he joined his brother-in-law Frank Johnson's band and toured with this group to England in November giving concerts. Appo was widely sought after as a conductor, and he directed concerts in Philadelphia and throughout New York State. He presented the first performance of instrumental music in Philadelphia's African Methodist Episcopal Mother Bethel Church (1848) and was described by Bishop Alexander Payne as "the most learned musician of the race." His best-known compositions are the anthem *Sing unto God* and *John Tyler's Lamentation*, commissioned by the Utica (New York) Glee Club, probably with reference to the US presidential election campaign of 1844. His daughter, future activist Helen Appo (Cook), inherited his talent and played organ, according to Martin R. Delany, for Philadelphia's Central Presbyterian Church at age 14.

BIBLIOGRAPHY

SouthernB

M.R. Delany: *The Condition, Elevation, Emigration, and Destiny of the Colored People of the United States* (Philadelphia, 1852/R New York, 1968), 125–6

J. Trotter: *Music and Some Highly Musical People* (Boston, 1881/*R*)

E. Southern: "A Portfolio of Music: the Philadelphia Afro-American School," *BPiM*, iv (1976), 238–56

J. Winch: *A Gentleman of Color: The Life of James Forten* (New York, 2002), 118

RECORDINGS

"John Tyler's Lamentation," *Hail to the Chief*, CD SonyB0000029QW (1996)

DORIS EVANS McGINTY/JOSEPHINE WRIGHT

Apsara Ensemble. Cambodian music ensemble. Named for the female celestial figures that adorn Angkor Wat, this music and dance ensemble has featured performances of Cambodian music for audiences in the United States since 1986. Dr. Sam-Ang Sam—a master musician who studied with court and village master musicians in Siem Reap and Phnom Penh and who was named a 1994 MacArthur Fellow—established the ensemble with his wife, Chan Moly Sam, a master dancer trained to portray both male (*neay rong*) and female (*neang*) dance roles. The artists met in Cambodia and studied at the University of Fine Arts before the rise of the Khmer Rouge. Later, he studied with José Maceda at the University of the Philippines. The couple immigrated to the United States in 1977. They formed the ensemble while he completed his doctoral dissertation on the *pinn peat* (court music ensemble) at Wesleyan University. Afterward, the ensemble moved to Washington, DC, and partnered with the Cambodian-American Heritage Troupe directed by Sam-Oeun Tes, a master dancer who studied with the Cambodian Royal Ballet before moving the United States in 1971 and who also joined the ensemble. In 1998, the ensemble received the NEA National Heritage Fellowship and soon after relocated to Seattle, where Chan Moly Sam continues to lead performances accompanied by her students. Performances of the ensemble feature royal court dance and folk-influenced performances developed at the University of Fine Arts in Phnom Penh, as well as educational demonstrations of dance styles and instruments.

ALEXANDER MICHAEL CANNON

Apthorp, William Foster (*b* Boston, MA, 24 Oct 1848; *d* Vevey, Switzerland, 19 Feb 1913). Critic and writer on music. In 1869 he graduated from Harvard College, where he studied music with John Knowles Paine. He taught at the New England Conservatory of Music (1873–86). After contributing to the *Atlantic Monthly*, *Dwight's Journal of Music*, and *Scribner's Magazine*, he became music critic of the *Boston Evening Transcript* (1881–1903) and program annotator for the Boston SO (1892–1901). Apthorp sought to raise standards of performance and of informed understanding. He believed that the role of the critic was not to judge; rather, he was "to set people thinking" as an interpreter between the composer or performer and the public. Apthorp avowed an open spirit in communicating about controversial newer compositional approaches. He translated and published *Hector Berlioz: Selections from His Letters* (New York, 1879/R) and compiled a catalog of Wagner's published works appearing in E.L. Burlingame, ed., *Art Life and Theories of Richard Wagner* (New York, 1875). Apthorp was author of *Musicians and Music Lovers* (New York, 1894/R), *By the Way, being a Collection of Short Essays about Music and Art in General* (Boston, 1898), and *The Opera, Past and Present* (New York, 1901/R). He co-edited, with John D. Champlin, *Scribner's Cyclopaedia of Music and Musicians* (New York, 1888–90) and edited Robert Franz, *Fifty Songs* (Boston, 1903).

BIBLIOGRAPHY

R.B. Nelson: *The Commentaries and Criticism of William Foster Apthorp* (diss., U. of Florida, 1991)

M.N. Grant: *Maestros of the Pen* (Boston, 1998)

O.F. Saloman: "Apthorp, William Foster," *American National Biography*, ed. J.A. Garraty and M.C. Carnes (New York and Oxford, 1999, 1/567–8)

RICHARD ALDRICH/ORA FRISHBERG SALOMAN

Arab American music. Having come to *Amrīkā* (or *Amērikā*) from every Arabic-speaking society, Arab Americans have sought liberty and opportunity like their newfound compatriots hailing from elsewhere in the world. With roots stretching from Morocco to Iraq and from Syria to Yemen, they have brought a rich musical heritage that involves wide-ranging musical practices and that includes some of the oldest continuously performed art music in the world. They also have played formative roles in the development of American popular music and in the multilateral exchange of music culture between Arab and American societies.

1. Diverse backgrounds and shared heritage. 2. Musical features: (i) Instrumental configurations and textures (ii) Melodic modes and neutral tones (iii) Metric modes and additive rhythms (iv) Genres and suite form. 3. Immigration patterns. 4. Music making and cross-cultural exchange.

1. Diverse backgrounds and shared heritage. Arabs have immigrated to the United States from widespread geographical and socio-political environments. Their motivations to leave home for a land halfway around the world have included fleeing political persecution, seeking greater economic prosperity, and following loved ones who preceded them. Immigrants typically have sent money "back home" in support of immediate and

extended families while any hope of eventually returning themselves has often given way to an acceptance or an embrace of the United States as their new and permanent home.

Americans of Arab ancestry total at least 3.5 million in number and reside in every state, with about one third of the total living in California, New York, and Michigan. While Lebanese Americans represent the highest percentage of Arab Americans in most states, Egyptian Americans are the largest number in New Jersey, Iraqi Americans in Tennessee, and Palestinian Americans in Illinois. About 94% of Arab Americans live in metropolitan areas, with the highest concentrations in the vicinities of Los Angeles, Detroit, New York, Chicago, and Washington, DC. About one-third of the population of Dearborn, Michigan, home to the Arab American National Museum, is of Arab ancestry. The proximity of Arab American musicians of different backgrounds to one another, and to a greater degree than normally found within their nations of origin, has led to collaboration in response to various combinations of necessity, convenience, opportunity, and desire.

Straddling the continents of Asia and Africa, the countries and attendant cultural milieus of origin are wide-ranging and are 22 in number, as measured by membership in the Arab League: Algeria, Bahrain, Comoros, Djibouti, Egypt, Iraq, Jordan, Kuwait, Lebanon, Libya, Mauritania, Morocco, Oman, Palestine, Qatar, Saudi Arabia, Somalia, Sudan, Syria, Tunisia, United Arab Emirates, and Yemen. The individual geographies, histories, politics, customs, and musical practices of these countries vary widely. Arabic-speaking inhabitants include adherents of many religions, including Islam, Christianity, and Judaism, as well as numerous respective sects. Many other distinct ethnic groups have contributed greatly to the development of Arab music and culture more generally, including Armenians, Berbers, Kurds, Nubians, and Roma (Gypsies).

Generally speaking, Arabs are those whose native language is Arabic. To this definition we may add that such people consider themselves to be Arab or Arabic, which may entail other aspects of heritage with which Arabs identify (including values, religion, music, literature, art, dress, food, and politics).

Relationships between Arab American music and the Arabic language can be quite complex due both to cultural diversity in general and to intricacies of the language itself. A linguistic complexity stems from the fact that Arabic is diglossic—two contrasting registers of the language regularly function together. On the one hand, fluent Arabic speakers understand formal Arabic (*fuṣḥā*). Even if a person does not speak the formal register well, it is unavoidably found in public speaking, broadcasting, publications, scriptures (whether originally in Arabic or translated), and other formal communications. Regardless of geographic and ethnic background, all Arabic speakers are generally able to comprehend formal Arabic and lyrics in this register.

On the other hand, Arabic speakers also use colloquial Arabic (*'āmmiyya*), or a dialect rooted in their home region. These dialects can differ greatly. While each dialect can vary further in terms of accent from locality to locality, there are five general regions commonly identified with major corresponding dialects: the Maghreb (North Africa not including Egypt), Egypt, the Arabian Peninsula, the Levant (Syria, Lebanon, Palestine, Israel, and Jordan), and Iraq. While certain characteristics of music making generally follow a similar geo-linguistic pattern, the Levant and Egypt have a particularly closely shared tradition of art music.

The significance of the interconnection of distant social groups with the rise of Islam in the seventh century and the attendant establishment of Arabic as the lingua franca in Southwest Asia and North Africa continues to the present. The lasting impact on music and the arts more generally can be seen in a great way in the shared heritage (*turāth*) of music making across Arab society and in Arab America. A component of this heritage is *ṭarab*, which can refer both to the feeling of enchantment or ecstasy produced by captivating music and to such music itself. While *ṭarab* ties to musical experience, it is also mutually reinforced in an active performer–audience dynamic, where performers express themselves musically and audience members respond in affirming ways. Audience participation can be lively and include vocal acclamations of delight, such as "Allah!" (God!) and "*Yā salām!*" (Oh, peace!). Of course, the combination of music and language can be especially powerful for Arab Americans in relation to personal and social identity, and in processes of remembrance and nostalgia.

2. Musical features. The music of Arab Americans ranges from traditional Arab art music to modern American popular music. Historically in Arab societies, art, religious, folk, and popular music cultures have significantly influenced each other and have benefited from substantive contributions of interconnected social groups including men and women of diverse backgrounds. Arab musical culture also has connected historically to neighboring cultures of the larger region including those of Iranian (Persian) and Turkish (Ottoman) music. Like the larger region, musical features that are generally shared across Arab society and that have migrated to the United States include a special import attributed to the human voice, instrumentation, heterophonic and drone textures, melodic modes, neutral tones or quartertones, metric modes, improvisation, and suite form.

(i) Instrumental configurations and textures. Performance configurations range from a solo format to a chamber ensemble to a large orchestra, with a certain value placed on contrasting instrumental color in group formats. The multiple unique attributes of the voice, including its range of expressivity and ability to convey rich Arabic poetic texts, tend to accord it a special status when present, whether as soloist or in a group. Correspondingly, the most endeared icons of Arab art and popular music over the last century both have been female vocalists, Umm Kulthum (*c*1904–1975) and Fairuz (*b* 1935). An utmost facility with the techniques of Arab art song and an uncanny capacity to bring

poetic texts to life characterize both of their markedly different styles. Accordingly, the repertoire of these two performers has figured prominently in the music of Arab Americans, and their work has set a lofty standard for singers who have followed.

By the late 19th century, the instrumentation of the chamber ensemble (*takht*) typically included some three to five performers playing a combination of *ʿūd*, *qānūn*, *kamanja*, *nāy*, and *riqq* or *daff* in heterophonic textures with or without vocals. Often instrumentalists would also provide a drone for another's improvisation, and during improvised vocal passages in particular, an instrumentalist typically would shadow the underlying melody by following the vocalist in a relatively soft streamlined way. Traditionally a leading instrument in compositional and performance practice, the *ʿūd* is a short-necked, fretless, plucked lute that usually has five pairs of strings tuned in unisons and often has a single bass string below them for a total of six courses. A development in recent decades of Arab music making has been to eliminate the single bass string, shift the other five courses in position, and add another pair of strings in unison in the highest register. However, Arab American *ʿūd* players have largely eschewed this decrease in the lower range and extension of the upper range of the instrument, preferring traditional configurations to more modern ones. The *qānūn* is a trapezoidal plucked zither that usually has some 78 strings arranged in sets of three per course. Each course is tuned in unison and is fitted with multiple levers for changing modality. The *kamanja* (or *kamanjā* or *kamān*) is a violin, which Arabs assimilated from Europeans in the 19th century. Adaptation of the instrument included retuning the two highest strings (to produce *g-d′-g′-d″* from lowest to highest string) thereby better suiting the Arab melodic modal system. The *nāy* is the lone aerophone in the traditional *takht*. It is an end-blown reed flute that features a relatively breathy tone and has long evoked certain spiritual associations. The *riqq* or *daff* is a tambourine that typically has a head made of fish skin and ten pairs of finger cymbals that are arranged to play one pair against another at five evenly spaced locations around the rim.

Although the traditional configuration of the *takht* has been particularly prominent in the performance of Arab art music in the United States, the larger and differently configured *firqa* has played an important role as well. A development of the 20th century, the *firqa* includes the instruments of the *takht*, increases the number of violins to create a section, and typically adds cello, contrabass, and *darabukka* or *ṭabla*, a popular goblet-shaped hand drum. Depending on the ensemble, several other instruments might be present, including accordion, electric guitar, and electronic keyboard. To play the neutral tones of Arab music, the reeds of the accordion are modified to generate the notes necessary for the melodic modal system through performance techniques that involve a combined control of octave along with expansion and contraction of the bellows. Depending on design specifications, for example, a particular "B♭" on the keyboard might produce B♭ with inward movement and B-half-♭ with outward movement, whereas another "B♭" key might do the opposite or always produce B♭. The rise of the *firqa* also paralleled an increased use of adapted five-line-staff notation, which in part moved the traditionally aurally-based tradition closer to a literate one and also brought about increasingly monophonic textures in place of customarily heterophonic ones.

In their diasporic context, there has been some tendency among musicians to lean toward the older format of the *takht*. This may be a result of both a scarcity of performers to constitute a *firqa* in a given locale as well as a certain value placed on rooting musical performance in tradition rather than embracing modernization. While bringing new sounds to the New World, the instruments of Arab immigrants also helped them to maintain a sonic connection to their heritage. Even in relatively Americanized families, such instruments may be brought out on special occasions to invoke ancestry and for enjoyment. At Christmas or Ramadan celebrations, for example, musical instruments like the *ʿūd* or *darabukka* can articulate ethnic identity in ways that words cannot.

(ii) Melodic modes and neutral tones. Arab immigrants brought with them music that features deeply rooted systems of modality in terms of pitch and rhythm, and generally speaking each melodic and metric mode has its own particular character. The system of melodic modes or *maqāmāt* (singular: *maqām*) is traditionally realized in heterophonic textures that sometimes include passing or contrasting points of monophony, polyphony, or harmony. Ornamentation owing to an individual *maqām*, instrument, and performer can be valued highly and differ from performance to performance. Examples of the underlying scales associated with ten of the main *maqāmāt* are shown in ex.1. The C-based modes appear with the E-half-♭ mode to show their interconnection based on the shared final of C and the ascending neutral third of C to E-half-♭ (containing seven quartertones) that links *Rāst* and *Sīkāh* in a "relative" type of relationship. Likewise, the D-based modes appear with the B♭ mode to show their interrelation via the shared final of D and the descending major third of D to B♭ that connects *Bayyātī* to *ʿAjam*. Integral to the melodic modal system are four types of steps—half, three-quarter, whole, and augmented, the three-quarter step being a neutral second (or a quartertone larger than a minor second). While the scales show a tendency for B to be raised in ascent and lowered in descent, compositional and stylistic considerations as well as characteristics of particular *maqāmāt* can mitigate this and dictate otherwise. The systemic relationship between the two groups of modes can be seen in part by intervallic relationships between them. For example, with 2/4 representing a half step, 3/4 a three-quarter step, and 4/4 a whole step, the stepwise intervallic content of *Rāst* in ascent is 4/4–3/4–3/4–4/4–4/4–3/4–3/4. With *Bayyātī* based on the next note higher, the stepwise content in ascent is 3/4–3/4–4/4–4/4–3/4–3/4–4/4. In other words, the intervallic content of *Rāst* and

Ex.1 Examples of scales of *maqāmāt*

a. Examples of scales for C and E-Half-♭ melodic modes

b. Examples of scales for D and B♭ melodic modes

Bayyātī

Ṣabā

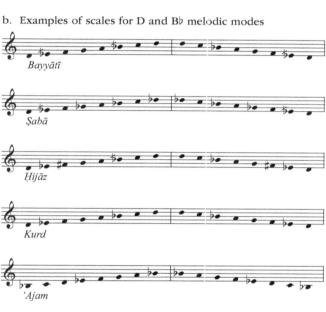

Ḥijāz

Kurd

'Ajam

Bayyātī as shown in the scales is equivalent except that the fundamental resting point of the two modes differs by the whole step C–D.

(iii) Metric modes and additive rhythms. The system of metric modes or rhythmic modes—*īqā'āt* (singular: *īqā'*), *awzān* (singular: *wazn*), or *ḍurūb* (singular: *ḍarb*)—is based on groupings of low- and high-sounding percussion strokes, the low sound called *dumm* and the high sound called *takk*. The *īqā'āt* commonly range from short two-beat patterns to longer configurations of 10 to 14 beats, and less often, to 32 beats or more. The *dumm* and *takk* can occur on the beat or be syncopated in the pattern, and multiple *īqā'āt* can comprise the same number of beats, as shown in ex.2, where a down stem indicates a *dumm* and an up stem indicates a *takk*. Further, *īqā'āt* that vary dramatically in

Ex.2 Examples of rhythmic patterns of *īqā'āt*

a. Examples of rhythmic patterns for contrasting metric modes with same number of beats

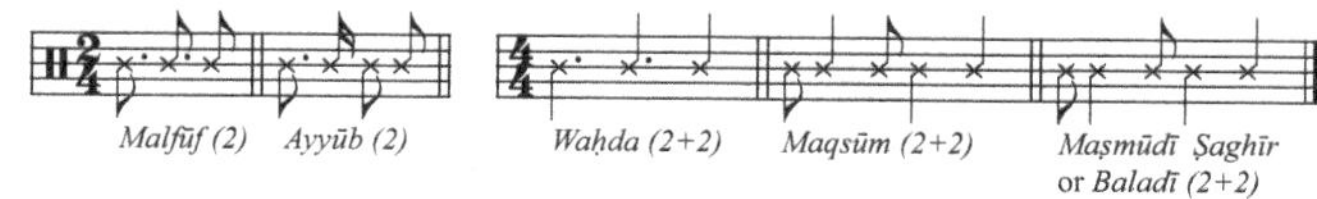

b. Examples of rhythmic patterns for increasingly longer metric modes

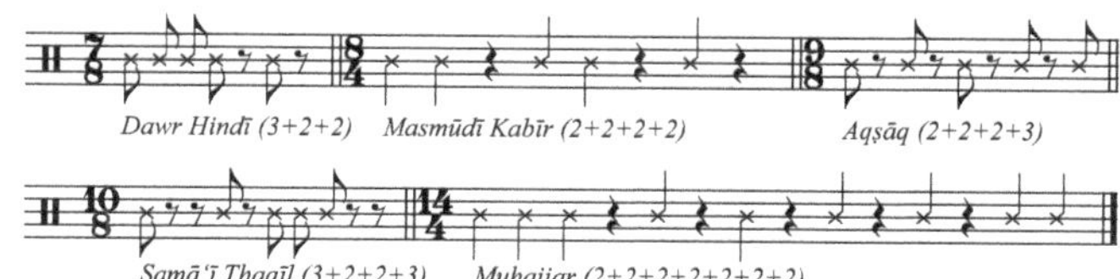

tempo and character can feature a certain equivalence of underlying rhythmic organization, as shown in the examples of *malfūf* and *waḥda*, and again in *maṣmūdī ṣaghīr* and *maṣmūdī kabīr*. There sometimes also can be closely related alternate patterns for the same *īqā'*, and in the case of *waḥda*, which conveys a meaning of being one or single, the mode can be realized in a number of ways, though the single *dumm*, on beat one, always maintains a prevailing metrical significance. The additive quality of the *īqā'āt* yields internal organizations that form some combination of two and/or three beats, as shown in both the shorter and increasingly longer examples in ex.2. Ornamentation of the main underlying patterns of the *īqā'āt* is a vital part of realizing them in performance and depends on the sensibilities and capabilities of the percussionist.

(iv) Genres and suite form. The art music of Arab immigrants features many traditional formal genres both composed and improvised, and proficiency in both areas is expected of professionals. Improvisation, in particular, for singers as well as instrumentalists represents an opportunity to demonstrate depth and virtuosity as a serious performer. Attributes of great improvisers include their individual creativity, idiomatic expertise, and technical prowess. Some of the genre types that were brought by the first major wave of immigrants to the United States and that continue to be performed and composed among Arab Americans include:

- *Dūlāb*: A short composed instrumental genre that is introductory in nature.
- *Fāṣil* or *Waṣla*: A compound or suite form that generally includes a combination of compositions and improvisations that are unified by a particular melodic mode.
- *Layālī*: An improvised vocal genre that is non-metric and uses the words *yā layl* ("oh night") as vocables for melodic improvisation.
- *Mawwāl*: An improvised vocal genre that is non-metric and that typically interprets a poetic text in a stirring fashion.

- *Muwashshaḥ*: A composed vocal genre that historically traces to medieval Andalusia and often features a vocal soloist and a chorus as well as lyrics in formal Arabic.
- *Qaṣīda*: A composed solo vocal genre based on a poem in formal Arabic.
- *Samāʿī*: A composed instrumental genre that features a refrain or *taslīm* alternating with contrasting episodes or *khānāt* (singular: *khāna*) and that typically modulates from the main metric mode of *samāʿī thaqīl* to a triple or compound mode in the final *khāna* before returning to the concluding *taslīm*.
- *Taqsīm*: An improvised instrumental genre that can be rhythmically free, metered, or a combination of the two.

3. Immigration patterns. While the earliest recorded Arab American was a Moroccan slave who arrived in the United States in the 16th century, significant numbers of Arabic-speaking immigrants started coming to the United States in the middle 1870s with the first major wave of Arab American immigration beginning in the 1880s. Christians were more numerous than Muslims, Druze, and Jews in this migration, and while men outnumbered women at first, by 1919 the numbers of women and men were about even. Fleeing persecution and seeking opportunity, these immigrants came especially from Greater Syria or the Levant. Making a living and learning English were priorities, street vending was common upon arrival, and Palestinian Americans and others from the region found an American market for crafts from the Holy Land and nearby places. While many immigrants came from the area of Mount Lebanon, they commonly described themselves by the broader appellation of Syrian. Coming from the Ottoman Empire, with its Turkish governance and with modern state borders in the region yet to be drawn, these immigrants might have been considered Turks or others as readily as Syrians or Arabs at the US border. Addressing their misidentification as Turks, the United States Bureau of Immigration added the classification of Syrian to its records in 1899.

The quota legislation that emerged from World War I quashed the flow of Arab immigrants to the United States, with the Immigration Act of 1924 marking the passing of the first wave of Arab immigration. Subsequent immigration patterns reflected prevailing political circumstances in both Arab and American societies. Fleeing the turmoil stemming from the rise of the Zionist movement in the British mandate of Palestine, Palestinian immigrants to the United States outnumbered Syrians and Lebanese for the first time in 1936. The second wave of Arab immigration to the United States came in the aftermath of World War II, with the establishment of Israel in 1948, the associated generation of over 700,000 Palestinian refugees, and ongoing regional distress. This group exhibited more balance in numbers between Muslims and Christians, a higher percentage of college students and educated professionals, and more equitable representation from countries of origin. With the ending of immigration restrictions based on national origins, the Immigration Act of 1965 led to the third wave of Arab immigration. This group has been the most diverse in terms of place of origin, religious background, and economic status, and has included many refugees and those fleeing socio-political problems.

Arabic Music Retreat, c2010. (George and Boske Antheil Papers, Music Division, Library of Congress)

Casey Kasem, 2003. (AP Photo/David G. Massey)

4. Music making and cross-cultural exchange. The Arabic singing and musical instruments brought by first-wave immigrants quickly came to play in their home lives, worship services, and community activities. Lebanese, Palestinian, and Syrian American social clubs and cultural associations soon began emerging, such as *Zahrat Lubnān* (The Flower of Lebanon), founded in 1890 in Allentown, New York, and the Palestinian Association and Syrian Club, both formed in Chicago in the wake of the World's Columbian Exposition of 1893, where Arab merchants came with others from around the world to sell their wares and in some cases remained to settle in the United States. Arabic-language newspapers, magazines, and other periodicals also quickly were established, such as *Kawkab Amērikā* (The Star of America), the newspaper that began weekly publication in New York in 1892, and by the time it became a daily in 1898, had a circulation of perhaps 10,000 in the United States, of some 5000 in Latin American countries, and among Arabic speakers who had not emigrated as well. These clubs, associations, and publications factored formatively in the lives of Arab Americans and, in turn, also influenced Arab society through personal, cultural, and professional ties.

The remarkable association of Arabic writers, *Al-Rābiṭa Al-Qalamiyya* (The Pen League), was formed in New York in 1915, and then revived in 1920 by one of the most famous Arab Americans, Kahlil Gibran (1883–1931), along with his compatriot who also was from Mount Lebanon, Mikhail Naimy (1889–1988), and their colleagues. Keen on the interconnection of the arts and on the significance of the arts to spirituality and to life in general, Gibran penned his extended poem *Al-Mawākib* (Processions) from which would be extracted *A'ṭinī al-Nāy* (Give me the flute), which would have an enduring impact on music. Gibran's continuing appeal in Lebanon led in the 1970s to the setting of *A'ṭinī al-Nāy* to music by Najib Hankash with arrangement and orchestration by the Rahbani Brothers and vocals by Fairuz. In formal Arabic, it begins:

a'ṭinī al-nāya wa ghanni	Give me the flute and sing
fa-al-ghinā sirru al-khulūd	For singing is the secret of eternity
wa anīnu al-nāyi yabqā	And the lament of the flute remains
ba'da an yafnā al-wujūd	Even after existence passes away

In a dynamic reciprocal flow of culture often characteristic of diasporic contexts, Gibran's poem gave rise to one of the most popular songs across Arab society, which by extension became greatly admired among Arab American musicians and audiences.

Traditions of musical expression that first-wave immigrants transplanted from Arab to American society and that continue to the present include the use of Arabic hymnody and language, often juxtaposed with English, in Arab American churches. Similarly, immigrants transferred the context of a traditional evening gathering (*sahra*) at the home of friends, which might produce music of exceptionally high quality in accordance with the caliber of the musicians and the artistic atmosphere, thereby enabling serious musicians to make music together, exchange ideas, and perhaps connect with important artists in other fields. The larger and more formal framework of a concert (*ḥafla*) often takes place at clubs and gathering halls, and has served as a vital performance context for professional musicians. Audience members may stay for hours enjoying dancing and elaborate presentations of Arabic food in addition to the music. The still larger setting of a festival (*mahrajān*) provides a professional performance venue in tandem with many other forms of artistic and cultural expression generally over the span of a full day or weekend. Festivals often serve as big events of cultural identification with some willing to travel a significant distance to a metropolitan center in order to attend. Likewise, artists of regional stature may perform in addition to local talent. Well established examples that draw especially large audiences and program artists ranging from traditional Arab music genres to Arab American hip hop include the Arab American Cultural Festival in Florida, the Arab American Day Festival in California, and the Arab International Festival in Michigan.

By the early 20th century Arab Americans were working with major record labels like Columbia, Victor, and His Master's Voice as the music industry grew increasingly interested in "ethnic" music at home and abroad. These musicians often brought their Arab musical sensibilities to bear on work in American idioms as well. Early examples include Syrian immigrant Naim Karakand, who was playing violin and recording in the United States by 1915 and continued performing into the 1960s, and Alexander Maloof, who emigrated from Greater Syria and became a successful pianist, composer, orchestra leader, publisher, and record producer during the 1920s and 1930s. In the 1920s Arab Americans began establishing their own small studios and tending to their own business needs with labels such as

Abdel Ahad, Al-Chark/Orient, Arabphon, Cleopatra, Golden Angel, Macksoud, Maloof, Metrophon, Nilephon, and Star of the East. The engagement of technology brought an adaptation of tradition in both American and Arab societies as recordings could not really capture the live audience dynamic that was a vibrant part of Arab music making, and neither could the 78-rpm records accommodate the long performances. While much research remains to be conducted on the music of early Arab immigrants, the compilation of early recordings on compact disc, *The Music of Arab Americans: a Retrospective Collection* (Rasmussen 1997), provides an excellent look into Arab American music starting at about the second decade of the 20th century.

Arab immigrants who put their musical skills to work in the United States sometimes left or could not return to their homelands as a result of political strife. The war in Palestine caused Amer and Sana Khadaj, who sang together as children in Lebanon before performing regularly for the Near East Radio Station in Palestine, to remain in the United States after both their home and the radio station were destroyed while they were on tour in 1947. Palestinian *ʿūd* player, violinist, and composer Jalil Azouz also worked at the Near East Radio Station before traveling to the United States for a music tour and settling. Hanan Harouni, who began her singing career in Lebanon where she worked with the young Fairuz, also immigrated to the United States in the wake of World War II, as did Lebanese *ʿūd* player, composer, and actor Mohammed El Bakkar. Iraqi American singer, *ʿūd* player, and percussionist Saadoun Al-Bayati, who as a young man substituted for his neighborhood muezzin in Baghdad, immigrated in 1956 and continues to be a leading proponent of Iraqi music in the United States. Following the 1967 War, Syrian American singer Youssef Kassab in 1970 moved to the United States from Syria, where he had performed as a vocalist with the Syrian Radio Orchestra. The social ravages of the Gulf War and attendant sanctions against Iraq in the 1990s caused *ʿūd* player and composer Rahim Alhaj to flee Baghdad and eventually relocate to the United States in 2000.

Immigrants who have played vital roles in music education at academic institutions include Lebanese American multi-instrumentalist and composer Ali Jihad Racy, who is a professor of ethnomusicology at the University of California, Los Angeles (UCLA). One of his roles at UCLA has been direction of the Near Eastern Music Ensemble through which he has taught the performance of Arab music to a generation of students. Although primarily known for his postcolonial scholarship and his long tenure as a Columbia University professor, Christian Palestinian American Edward Said also was a pianist and music critic. His work with Jewish Israeli pianist and conductor Daniel Barenboim in creating the West-Eastern Divan Orchestra brought together Israeli, Palestinian, and other Arab musicians of the Muslim, Christian, and Jewish faiths.

Immigrants involved with music education in the way of community ensembles include Jordanian American multi-instrumentalist Wael Kakish, who directs the Los Angeles based Kan Zaman Community Ensemble, formed in 1994. Palestinian American multi-instrumentalist and composer Nabil Azzam, trained in both Arab and Euro-American art music, similarly conducts the Los Angeles based Multi Ethnic Star Orchestra, established in 2001. Lebanese American multi-instrumentalist and composer Bassam Saba, also trained in Arab and Euro-American art music, has worked with a wide range of superstars including Fairuz, Marcel Khalife, Ziad Rahbani, Yo-Yo Ma, Simon Shaheen, Wadi Al-Safi, Paul Simon, Alicia Keys, Sting, Santana, Herbie Hancock, and Quincy Jones, and is the director of the New York Arabic Orchestra, which was founded in 2007.

These educators, along with many others of the best-known Arab American musicians, work together in various professional configurations from one project to another. A foremost talent on the *ʿūd* and violin, Palestinian American composer and conductor SIMON SHAHEEN focuses on traditional Arab music in his Near Eastern Music Ensemble and on Arab jazz in Qantara. He also directs the Annual Arabic Music Retreat (with Racy as Associate Director), which has set the standard for summer programs in Arab music. His brothers Najib and William Shaheen also are accomplished *ʿūd* players who teach at the retreat, as have Lebanese American Jamal Sinno on *qanūn* and violinist Georges Lammam, who is Lebanese American of Palestinian descent. Lammam similarly comes from a musical family and performs with his brothers Elias on accordion and Tony (Antoine) on percussion. Michel Merhej Baklouk, a Lebanese American *riqq* player of Palestinian origin who also has taught at the retreat, has worked with many of the greatest figures in Arab music including Mohamed Abdel-Wahab and Abdel-Halim Hafez. He is best known as the main percussionist for Fairuz, with whom he worked since nearly the beginning of her career in the late 1940s. A student of Baklouk, Egyptian American percussionist Karim Nagi directs the Sharq Ensemble, which has featured Moroccan American multi-instrumentalists and singers Rachid Halihal and Boujemaa Razgui as well as Syrian American singer Aboud Agha and Syrian American *ʿūd* player, guitarist, and composer Kareem Roustom. Additional distinguished musicians include Jordanian American *ʿūd* player, singer, and composer Naser Musa of Palestinian descent, Lebanese American percussionist Souhail Kaspar, and Syrian American percussionist Faisal Zedan.

Some of these performers manufacture instruments as well, such as *nāy* maker Boujemaa Razgui and *ʿūd* maker Najib Shaheen. In particular, Viken Najarian, who was born into the Armenian diaspora of Lebanon before moving to the United States, began playing the *ʿūd* in the tutelage of his grandfather, Dikran, himself a famous *ʿūd* maker. Najarian was an early designer of the electric *ʿūd*, and some of his largest customers for electric instruments are distributors in the Arabian Peninsula, though most Arab American musicians appear more interested in maintaining tradition with acoustic instruments than in taking up modern electric ones.

On the retail side of the music business, Albert Rashid emigrated from Syria in 1920 and became a forerunner in Arab music distribution in the United States. His groundbreaking company Rashid Music Sales dates to 1934 in Detroit and became a major retailer of Arab records and musical products with his move to New York following World War II. Rashid's sons, Ray and Stan, took over management and further cultivated the establishment through several stages of technological development in music retailing, including the transition to online operation of the company, which began in 1995 and has continued since closing the storefront in 2010. Indicative of the times, Bashar Barazi is a third-generation Lebanese American who bypassed the opening of a store altogether and became a major retailer of Arab music through his online company, Maqam.

Children of immigrants have frequently worked in some combination of Arab and American musical traditions, and shown attachment to their heritage in different ways and to differing degrees. While Syrian American Tony (Anton) Abdel Ahad enjoyed a successful career from the 1940s to the 1970s playing *ʿūd* and singing songs in formal and colloquial Arabic, he likely did not grow up studying formal Arabic or fully understand the lyrics that he sang in this register. At the same time, Lebanese American Philip Soloman enjoyed a reputation as a violinist performing traditional Arab music as well as Euro-American art music in the Rhode Island Philharmonic Orchestra. Ensconced in American popular culture, Lebanese American Danny Thomas (Amos Yakhoob) was known primarily as a popular comedian and actor as well as the founder of St. Jude Children's Research Hospital, though he also sang and recorded an album of Arabic folksongs. Becoming an icon of American pop radio, Lebanese American voice actor and radio personality Casey (Kemal) Kasem hosted the nationally syndicated countdown show *American Top 40*, which he created with producer Don Bustany, who also was born in Detroit to Lebanese parents. Born in San Francisco to Lebanese and Palestinian parents, Dawn Elder became a concert promoter, artist and event manager, composer, producer, and director who has worked with artists in styles ranging from traditional Arab music to American popular music including Fairuz, Kazem Al-Sahir, Khaled, Simon Shaheen, Bassam Saba, Quincy Jones, Stevie Wonder, Paul McCartney, the Beach Boys, Sting, Grover Washington, George Clinton, and Santana. Lebanese American DICK DALE (Richard Monsour) was born in Boston and pioneered instrumental surf rock in the early 1960s bringing to bear the influences of the Levantine and Mediterranean music that he grew up hearing and that would have an impact more generally within the genre. More recently, Arab American hip-hop artists whose politically conscious songs in English and in Arabic are informed by Arab American concerns include DJ Khaled (Palestinian American Khaled bin Abdul Khaled, born in New Orleans), Iron Sheik (Palestinian American Will Youmans, born in Dearborn), The Narcicyst (Iraqi American Yassin Alsalman, born in the United Arab Emirates), Omar Offendum (Syrian American Omar Chakaki, born in Saudi Arabia), and Ragtop (Palestinian American Nizar Wattad, born in Palestine).

Cross-cultural exchange between Arab and American cultures and across Arab nationalities has been a prominent part of Arab American musical life since its beginnings. The diasporic context of the United States further has led to collaboration among Arab American musicians of different national backgrounds in ways that would have been difficult or impossible from within the associated state borders of their respective homelands. In this sense, a kind of transnational exchange has taken place within American borders. At the same time, a certain nostalgia can be seen in preferences to maintain tradition rather than to innovate and readily depart from it. While some Arabs have immigrated to the United States as active musicians, others have learned Arab music in their diasporic context specifically because music and culture elicit ethnic identity. In either case, Arab American musicians have shared deeply rooted repositories of music culture among each other and with larger American society. Accordingly, they might echo the sentiment of Kahlil Gibran in his address to the next generation of Arab Americans in the first issue of *Syrian World Magazine* (1926): "I believe that you have inherited from your forefathers an ancient dream, a song, a prophecy, which you can proudly lay as a gift of gratitude upon the lap of America."

See also DETROIT; ISLAM.

BIBLIOGRAPHY

K. Gibran: "Young Americans of Syrian Origin," *Syrian World Magazine*, no.1 (July 1926)
R. D'Erlanger: *La musique arabe* (Paris, 1930–59/*R*)
E. Hagopian and A. Paden, eds.: *The Arab-Americans: Studies in Assimilation* (Wilmette, IL, 1969)
A. Bulos: *Handbook of Arabic Music* (Beirut, 1971)
T. Grame: "The Symbolism of the 'Ud," *Asian Music*, iii/1 (1972), 25–34
B. Aswad, ed.: *Arabic Speaking Communities in American Cities* (Staten Island, 1974)
G. Atiyeh, ed.: *Arab and American Cultures* (Washington, DC, 1977)
L. Al-Faruqi: *An Annotated Glossary of Arabic Musical Terms* (Westport, CT, 1981)
A. Shiloah: "The Arabic Concept of Mode," *JAMS*, xxxiv (1981), 19–42
S. Abraham and N. Abraham, eds.: *Arabs in the New World: Studies on Arab-American Communities* (Detroit, 1983)
A. Naff: *Becoming American: The Early Arab Immigrant Experience* (Carbondale, IL, 1985)
E. Hooglund, ed.: *Crossing the Waters: Arabic-Speaking Immigrants to the United States Before 1940* (Washington, DC, 1987)
A. Naff: *The Arab Americans* (New York, 1988)
A. Rasmussen: "'An Evening in the Orient:' The Middle Eastern Nightclub in America," *Asian Music*, xxiii/2 (1992), 63–88
E. McCarus: *The Development of Arab-American Identity* (Ann Arbor, 1994)
A. Rasmussen: "Theory and Practice at the 'Arabic Org': Digital Technology in Contemporary Arab Music Performance," *Popular Music*, xv (1996), 345–65
H. Touma: *The Music of the Arabs* (Portland, OR, 1996)
A. Rasmussen: liner notes, *The Music of Arab Americans: a Retrospective Collection*, Rounder CD 1122 (1997)
A. Rasmussen: "The Music of Arab Detroit: a Musical Mecca in the Midwest," *Musics of Multicultural America: a Study of Twelve Musical Communities*, ed. K. Lornell and A. Rasmussen (New York, 1997), 73–100
S. Zuhur, ed.: *Images of Enchantment: Visual and Performing Arts of the Middle East* (Cairo, 1998)
M. Suleiman: *Arabs in America: Building a New Future* (Philadelphia, 1999)

N. Abraham and A. Shryock, eds.: *Arab Detroit: From Margin to Mainstream* (Detroit, 2000)
S. Zuhur, ed.: *Colors of Enchantment: Theater, Dance, Music and the Visual Arts of the Middle East* (Cairo, 2001)
K. Benson and P. Kayal, eds.: *A Community of Many Worlds: Arab Americans in New York City* (New York, 2002)
P. Kesting: "A Community of Arab Music," *Aramco World*, liii/5 (2002), 28–33
S. Maalouf: *History of Arabic Music Theory: Change and Continuity in the Tone Systems, Genres, and Scales* (Kaslik, Lebanon, 2002)
E. Boosahda: *Arab-American Faces and Voices: the Origins of an Immigrant Community* (Austin, TX, 2003)
A.J. Racy: *Making Music in the Arab World: The Culture and Artistry of Tarab* (Cambridge, 2003)
B. Eyre: "Becoming the Thing," *Aramco World*, lv/2 (2004), 36–9
T. Swedenburg: "The 'Arab Wave' in World Music after 9/11," *Anthropologica*, xlvi (2004), 177–88
O. Bloechl: "Orientalism and Hyperreality in 'Desert Rose,'" *Journal of Popular Music Studies*, xvii/2 (2005), 133–61
A. Malek: *A Country Called Amreeka: Arab Roots, American Stories* (New York, 2009)
J. Haiek, ed.: *Arab American Almanac: the Most Comprehensive Reference Source on Arab Americans* (Glendale, CA, 6/2010)

KENNETH S. HABIB

Arapaho. Native American tribe of the central part of the western Plains. They speak an Algonquian language closely related to Cheyenne and Blackfoot and more distantly to many of the Indian languages of eastern North America. In late prehistoric times they were probably agriculturalists in the area that is now Minnesota, but by the 19th century they had moved westward and established the nomadic, buffalo-hunting culture typical of Plains peoples. Although they were among the smaller tribes of the area (in the 19th century the population was estimated at *c*2000), the Arapaho were central in developing the Plains culture type. After 1850 they suffered great deprivation and were eventually divided into three groups. The Gros Ventres or Atsina moved to Canada and gained independent status in association with the Blackfoot; a group of Arapaho were assigned in 1867 to Oklahoma, where they shared land and eventually culture traits with the Cheyenne; and in 1876 the remainder were placed on the Wind River Reservation in Wyoming, which they share with Shoshone people.

The traditional characteristics of Arapaho musical life are typical of Plains culture. The music is largely vocal. Religious music dominates and includes songs of the main public ceremony, the Sun Dance, which is thought to have become most complex among the Arapaho and possibly to have originated with them. Also important is music for the religious ceremony of the "flat pipe," the tribe's chief ritual object, as well as ceremonial songs of age-grade societies, songs preceding and following war parties, personal songs received by individuals from guardian spirits in visions, and curing songs. Social dances include the Owl, Rabbit, Snake, Wolf, Round, and Grass dances, all introduced after 1850 by neighboring tribes. There are also hunting songs, love-songs, and many songs to accompany gambling in a hiding game still widely played. Instruments include duct flutes, many types of container and strung rattles, frame drums, large drums played by several singers at a time, bullroarers, and bone buzzers.

The style of the Arapaho repertory is typical of the Plains. Songs have sharply descending melodic contours, complex but strictly maintained rhythmic divisions, drumming off the melodic beat, an ambitus of an octave or a 9th, and pentatonic and tetratonic scales. The form usually consists of a short section sung by a soloist and repeated by a second singer, followed by several phrases sung by the group and then repeated by the group (*AA BCD BCD*). The manner of singing is harsh and tense with pulsation on the longer tones. Song texts are short, taking up only part of a melody, and are surrounded and sometimes interrupted by nonlexical vocables.

The Arapaho were among the most prominent participants in the Ghost dance religion of the 1880s and had many dozens of songs of this sect with a characteristic small ambitus and paired-phrase form. In the 20th century the Peyote religion (Native American Church) was introduced, and a large repertory of these musically distinctive songs developed through borrowing and indigenous composition. In this century also the Arapaho began to participate in the pan-Indian musical culture of the Plains, in which many songs with texts consisting only of vocables and some with words in English were used. By the 1950s the total repertory had great diversity. In the 1970s, tribal authorities in Oklahoma established an archive for collecting recordings and other documents for preservation and study of the musical culture. The contemporary musician Thomas Duran Jr. (Northern Arapaho) has recorded Peyote songs in a traditional style on *Life Giver* (Can., 2002).

See also Peyote drum; Peyote rattle

BIBLIOGRAPHY

J. Mooney: *The Ghost-dance Religion and the Sioux Outbreak of 1890* (Washington, DC. 1896, 2/1965)
A.L. Kroeber: *The Arapaho* (New York, 1902)
F. Densmore: *Cheyenne and Arapaho Music* (Los Angeles, 1936)
B. Nettl: "Musical Culture of the Arapaho," *MQ*, xli (1955), 325

BRUNO NETTL/R

Araújo, João Gomes de (*b* Pindamonhangaba, Brazil, 5 Aug 1846; *d* São Paulo, Brazil, 8 Sept 1943). Brazilian composer. He began his musical studies with Benedito Gomes de Araújo, his father, and João Baptista de Oliveira, his uncle. In 1861, he moved to Rio de Janeiro, where he enrolled at the Conservatory and studied composition with Francisco Manuel da Silva and Gioacchino Giannini.

Returning to Pindamonhangaba, he founded a conservatory with clarinetist José Maria Leite in November 1863. He also established an orchestra and conducted the local military band. In 1884 favorable reviews for his *Missa de São Sebastião* led him to meet Emperor Pedro II, who rewarded him financially and helped him secure a grant to study with Cesare Dominiceti at the Royal Conservatory in Milan. For his graduation he composed the opera *Edmea* (1886). He based his next opera, *Carmosina* (1888), on a comedy by Alfred de Musset. It opened on 1 May 1888 at the Dal Verme in Milan. Araújo returned to Brazil later that year, and went on to found the Conservatory of Drama and Music of São Paulo (with Pedro Augusto Gomes Cardim). He composed four operas, six symphonies, 12 orchestral masses, several marches for orchestra and military band, valses and polkas for the piano, and more than 60 songs and choral pieces.

BIBLIOGRAPHY

GMO (R. Stevenson)

L.H. Corrêa de Azevedo: *Relação das óperas de autores brasileiros* (Rio de Janeiro, 1938), 49–50

E.C.G. de Araújo: *João Gomes de Araújo, sua vida e suas obras* (São Paulo, 1972)

M. Marcondes, ed.: *Enciclopédia da música brasileira* (São Paulo, 1977, 2/1998)

ROGERIO BUDASZ

Arbuckle, Matthew (*b* Lochside, Scotland, 1828; *d* New York, NY, 23 May 1883). Bandmaster and cornetist of Scottish origin. He joined the 26th Regiment of the British Army, known as the Cameronians, at 13; he served in India and China, returned to Britain, then went to Canada with a military band. He reportedly deserted his regiment to assume the leadership of a band in Troy, New York, where he remained for six months before accepting a similar position in Worcester, Massachusetts. Three years later, in 1860, he joined the Gilmore Band, which in 1861 became attached to the 24th Massachusetts Infantry Regiment; he served with the band during the Civil War. Arbuckle was an outstanding cornet soloist, who was admired for his beautiful, cantabile style of playing. He was a soloist at the National Peace Jubilee of 1869 and the World Peace Jubilee of 1872, both of which were organized by Gilmore. In 1873, when Gilmore was appointed leader of the 22nd Regiment Band in New York, Arbuckle went with him and became the cornet soloist with the band, which acquired a national reputation and toured throughout the United States. In New York, where he settled, he also performed under such well-known bandmasters as Carlo Cappa and David L. Downing. In 1880 he became bandmaster of the Ninth Regiment of the New York Militia and in 1883 organized a band under his own name; he died shortly before embarking on a tour with the new ensemble.

BIBLIOGRAPHY

Obituaries: *Musical Herald*, iv (1883), 157; *New York Times* (24 May 1883)

F.O. Jones, ed.: *A Handbook of American Music and Musicians* (Canaseraga, NY, 1886/*R*)

A. Roe: *The Twenty-fourth Massachusetts Volunteers 1861–66, "New England Guard Regiment"* (Worcester, MA, 1907)

G.D. Bridges: *Pioneers in Brass* (Detroit, 1965); CD-ROM (Coupeville, WA, 2000)

FRANK J. CIPOLLA

Arcade Fire. Canadian indie rock band. With captivating live performances and acclaimed recordings, the Montreal-based multi-instrumentalist group stood at the forefront of indie rock's ascendency in the 2000s, growing from internet fanbase to festival-headlining slots over the decade. Often augmented by friends and touring members live, the core band consists of husband and wife Win Butler and Régine Chassagne, with Will Butler, Richard Reed Parry, Tim Kingsbury, Sarah Neufeld, and Jeremy Gara.

Formed in 2001 in Montreal, Quebec—where the Texas-born Butler brothers attended school and met Chassagne, the daughter of Haitian immigrants—Arcade Fire quickly earned a local cult following that exploded upon the release of *Funeral*, its 2004 debut (Merge Records). An ecstatic review on the popular music website *Pitchfork* is often cited as the catalyst, though the band capitalized on that enthusiasm with its theatrical live show. Soaring melodies and anthemic, singalong hooks earned the album endorsements from David Bowie, David Byrne, and U2, all of whom have since performed with the band.

The follow-up, *Neon Bible*, recorded in a church that the band transformed into a recording studio, earned similar acclaim in 2007, and 2010's *The Suburbs* proved the band's big breakthrough; topping the *Billboard* album chart upon its release, its sprawling sound led to headline shows at the Coachella and Bonnaroo festivals, sell-out shows at Madison Square Garden, and Grammy and Juno Awards for Album of the Year. Though the band ranked among the world's most popular alternative bands, its members continued to operate with a DIY model, owning their recordings and rarely licensing their music out to commercial endeavors except to explicitly support charitable work, most notably relief efforts following the 2010 earthquake in Haiti.

BIBLIOGRAPHY

D. Frey: "One Very, Very Indie Band," *New York Times Magazine* (4 Mar 2007)

D. Fricke: "The Unstoppable Ambition of Arcade Fire," *Rolling Stone* (Aug 2010), 52–84

J. Wray: "The View from the Top," *Spin Magazine* (Oct 2010), 44–50

RYAN R. McNUTT

Archer, Frederick [Frederic] (*b* Oxford, England, 16 June 1838; *d* Pittsburgh, PA, 22 Oct 1901). English organist, conductor, and composer. He became organist of Merton College, Oxford, and in 1873 was appointed to Alexandra Palace in London, where he afterwards became conductor, a post he held until 1880. In 1881 he visited the United States, giving organ recitals in several cities, and later the same year returned to become organist first at Henry Ward Beecher's church in Brooklyn and then at the Church of the Incarnation in New York. In 1883 he founded the illustrated weekly *The Keynote*, which he edited for a year. He moved to Boston in 1887 to become conductor of the Boston Oratorio Society, and subsequently to Chicago where he was organist of St. James's Church.

When Andrew Carnegie established the Carnegie Institute and Library in Pittsburgh, he instituted weekly free organ recitals there; Archer was engaged as organist and inaugurated the series on 7 November 1895. The institute's music hall also served the new Pittsburgh Orchestra, which Archer conducted from its first concert on 27 February 1896 until 28 January 1898, when he was succeeded by Victor Herbert. He continued as organist until his death, however, and also worked as organist of the Church of the Ascension.

Archer composed many works for the organ, piano pieces, songs, and a cantata, King Witlaf's Drinking-Horn. He wrote several instructional manuals and also compiled anthologies of organ pieces.

BIBLIOGRAPHY

DAB (C.N. Boyd)

"Archer, Frederic," *The Cyclopedia of Music and Musicians*, ed. J.D. Champlin jr. and W.F. Apthorp (New York, 1888) [autobiographical article]

Obituary, *MT*, xlii (1901), 827

H.C. Lahee: *The Organ and its Masters* (Boston, 1903/R, rev. 2/1927)

R. Wolfe: *A Short History of the Pittsburgh Orchestra* (diss., Carnegie Library School, Carnegie Institute of Technology, 1954)

F. Dorian and J. Meibach: "A Short History of the Pittsburgh Symphony Orchestra," *Carnegie Magazine* (1986), Jan–Feb, 6–20; Mar–Apr, 18–30

R. Schmalz: "Personalities, Politics and Prophecy: Frederic Archer and the Birth of the Pittsburgh Symphony Orchestra," *American Music*, v/3 (1987), 305–16

ALEXIS CHITTY/BRUCE CARR

Archives, sound recording and moving image. Repositories for the permanent retention, preservation, and access of sound recordings (e.g., CDs, LPs, audio cassettes, cylinders, digital audio files) and moving image media (e.g., motion-picture film, kinescope, videotape, digital video files); often included alongside of these collections are the mechanical playback devices for such media. The history of archives of this kind in the United States reveals trends towards the amalgamation of sound and moving image materials into single units based either on format (e.g., Library of Congress's Motion Picture Broadcasting and Recorded Sound Division) or academic discipline (UCLA Ethnomusicology Archive). Traditionally the distinction between a library and an archive is essentially one of purpose and a material's publication status: whereas libraries collect published materials for use by general patrons within and outside the library, archives generally accession and preserve unpublished materials, allowing restricted access for research purposes. However, with the development of the Internet, digitization technologies, and online modes of distribution, the distinction between library- and archive-hosted sound recording and moving image collections has become more fluid with both kinds of institutions posting published and unpublished audio and video files online with varying degrees of accessibility. Parallel advances in preservation technologies that enable archivists to digitize analog sound recordings and moving image recordings are thought to ensure long-term, if not permanent, access to the content housed on the original analog carriers.

1. Early technologies. 2. Sound recording archives. 3. Ethnomusicology and folklore archives. 4. Moving image archives. 5. Professional organizations. 6. Early 21st century archives.

1. Early technologies. In 1857 French inventor Édouard-Léon Scott de Martinville devised and patented the phonautograph, a device that could record (but not play back) ambient sound etched by the vibrations of a bristle on a sheet of soot-covered paper (in 2008 researchers at the University of California optically scanned several phonautographs and successfully converted the images into playable digital audio file). In 1877, influenced by this and other early sound recording inventions, Thomas Edison invented and patented a phonograph with a rotating cylinder that was capable of both recording and playing back sound. His device was a commercial success. In 1878 English photographer Eadweard Muybridge used 24 cameras to produce a series of stereoscopic images of a galloping horse. Influenced by Muybridge and Étienne Jules Marey (an even earlier moving image pioneer), Edison in 1891 invented the kinetoscope, a device that is widely regarded as the first motion picture, or moving image, exhibition device.

Josephine and Aurora Gonzalez, Pearl Manchaco, Lia Trujillo, and Adela Flores sing for a Library of Congress recording collected by Alan Lomax, San Antonio, Texas, 1934. (Library of Congress, Prints & Photographs Division, Lomax Collection, LC-DIG--ppmsc-00277)

Both the inventors and scientific writers of the period foresaw the importance of these new tools for the collection and dissemination of data long before librarians, archivists, and educators were aware of their potential uses. In a June 1878 issue of the *North American Review*, Edison predicted that his recent invention of the phonograph would benefit mankind in ten ways, including educational ones such as "preserving the explanations made by a teacher so that the pupil can refer to them at any moment, [and aiding] the teaching of elocution and phonographic books." In December 1877, the editors of *Scientific American* wrote: "the voices of such singers as Parepa and Titiens will not die with them, but will remain as long as the metal in which they may be embodied will last." Similar predictions were made for moving image media some years later, as noted by Edison's co-inventor W.K.L. Dickson in the June 1894 edition of *The Century Illustrated Monthly Magazine*: "The advance to students and historians will be immeasurable. Instead of dry and misleading accounts, tinged with the exaggerations of the chroniclers' minds, our archives will be enriched by the vitalized pictures of great national scenes, instinct with all the glowing personalities which characterized them."

Despite the inventors' prescience for these devices' cultural and historical import, only sporadic attempts by researchers and archivists to collect and provide access to these materials existed in the late 19th and early 20th centuries. With minor exceptions, such as the copyright deposit of several kinographic records by W.K.L. Dickson (on behalf of the Edison Company) in 1893 and 1894, and the gift of a cylinder recording to the Library of Congress made by Kaiser Wilhelm II of Prussia in 1904, publicly accessible libraries and archives did not begin to systematically collect these materials until well into the 20th century.

2. Sound recording archives. Specialized archives for sound materials were first established in Europe. Both the Vienna *Phonogramm-Archiv* and the Berlin *Phonogramm-Archiv*—founded 1899 and 1900, respectively—were established for the dedicated purposes of collecting, preserving, and providing limited access to unique ethnomusicological sound recordings. Although dedicated sound recording archives did not exist until the late in 1920s in the United States, a handful of sporadic sound recordings collections were established in historical societies and natural history museums in late 19th and early 20th Centuries. In March 1890, Jesse Walter Fewkes made the first field recording of Native American music (Passamaquoddy songs, tales, and vocabulary, sung and spoken by Noel Josephs and Peter Selmore) at Calais, Maine. He deposited this and other field recordings at the Peabody Museum of Archaeology and Ethnology at Harvard University during that decade (since transferred to the Library of Congress in 1970). In 1894, a small collection of unique oral history cylinder recordings was established at the Kansas Historical Society. Between 1895 and 1912, Charles F. Lummis made more than 700 cylinder recordings of Mexican American and Native American music in the Southern California area. He deposited these and hundreds of other unique recordings into his Southwest Museum in 1903 (the Southwest Museum was merged into the Autry National Center in 2003).

Among the earliest collections of published sound recordings owned by a publicly accessible library in the United States was the one owned by the St Paul Public Library. It began actively collecting sound recordings for its users in 1913. It was not until the following year that a library publication, the *Public Library*, openly advocated the acceptance of sound recordings in libraries. In an issue of *Library Journal* published in August 1915 and devoted entirely to music libraries, it is mentioned that five libraries had sound recordings in their collections. *Pierre Key's International Music Year Book* of 1928 lists 12 (out of 53) academic institutions maintaining sound recordings in their libraries. Some of the schools with music holdings that did not collect recordings at the time were Yale, Oberlin, Northwestern, Illinois, Columbia, Vassar, and Eastman. The first evidence of widespread acceptance of sound recordings in libraries was the success of the discs and printed materials distributed free of charge by the Carnegie Corporation of New York to 371 universities and colleges, beginning in 1927. It is interesting to note, however, that only one of the more prominent sound archives today, the Diane and Arthur Belfer Audio Laboratory and Archive at Syracuse University, traces its beginning to these College Music Sets recordings.

The Library of Congress has played a significant role in the creation of archival collections of sound recordings in the United States. Its plan to establish a collection of this kind was announced in an issue of the *Library Journal* in August 1907. But with the exception of mechanical devices (such as piano rolls and music-box discs) acquired in 1900 and 1901 and the cylinder donated by Kaiser Wilhelm II in 1904, it was not until 1923 that the Library of Congress began to actively accumulate sound materials—and even then it was only when phonorecord companies gave the Library promotional copies of their records. In 1928, the Library established the Archives of Folk Song (AFS), the institution's first systematic and concerted effort to establish a sound archive; the first dedicated folklore archive in the United States. In an effort to build the AFS, folksong collector John A. Lomax (1867–1948, *see* Lomax family) began working at the Library in 1933, accompanied by his son Alan Lomax (1915–2002, *see* Lomax family). In 1936, Alan Lomax made field recordings on behalf of the Library and produced a series entitled "Folk Music of the United States." Among the recorded were legendary performers Jelly Roll Morton, Lead Belly (Huddie William Ledbetter), and Woody Guthrie. The AFS was originally established with the intent to collect and preserve American music. However, beginning in 1935 when Alan Lomax made a recording expedition to the Bahamas, the AFS quickly acquired a multinational scope. The Archive of Folk Culture, as it is now called, is administered by the American Folklife Center at the Library of Congress.

In 1940, a grant from the Carnegie Corporation established the Library of Congress's Recording Laboratory. Later, technological advances in the post-war years—the LP in 1948, and later the tape recorder—boosted the Library's sound recordings collections. Recordings were included in the *National Union Catalog* for the first time in the 1950s, the first full-time recordings specialist was appointed in 1960, and a special unit with responsibility for the collection and maintenance of such media across the entire Library was established in 1962. The Library's audio collections are now the largest in the United States and among the most comprehensive in the world. NBC Radio's broadcast discs (1935–70) at the Library includes radio coverage of the Depression, World War II, post-war recovery, and a rich mine of radio drama and comedy. Armed Forces Radio, the WOR-AM collection, United Nations recordings, and the Library's own concerts and literary recordings further broaden the collections. The Library's collections reflect the entire history of sound technology, from the first wax cylinders, through LPs and tape, to the latest 24bit/96kHz BWAV digital audio files.

By the second half of the 20th century, other archival sound recordings collections in the United States had grown considerably. Stanford and Tulane universities established audio archives in 1958. Following this, many institutions established notable sound recording collections, including those at the Boston and New York public libraries and the universities of Bowling Green, Indiana, Michigan State, Rutgers, Syracuse, Kansas, Maryland, North Carolina (Chapel Hill), Texas (Austin), Yale, California (Los Angeles and Santa Barbara), and Washington (Seattle).

Copyright deposit, the means by which the Library of Congress now acquires much of its physical collections, specifically excluded sound recordings as copyrightable objects until 1976. In 1906, in an effort to determine the legal status of its recordings, the Victor Talking Machine Company attempted to register a sound recording with the Library's Copyright Office but the Office noted that recorded sound was "non-copyrightable matter." It was not until a rider in February 1972 that protection was extended to include sound recordings, and the 1976 revision of the law was the first attempt at the federal level to deal with the particular problems of the registration of sound materials. In 2009, the National Recording Preservation Board (established November 2000) at the Library of Congress published a ten-state analysis of how laws pertaining to pre-1972 sound recordings affect preservation of and access to audio recordings. In 2010 Congress directed the US Copyright Office to conduct a study on the desirability and means of bringing sound recordings fixed before 15 February 1972 under federal jurisdiction. As of June 2011, this study had not concluded (*see* Copyright).

3. Ethnomusicology and folklore archives. As described above, European and American ethnologists and ethnomusicologists created the earliest sound recording collections. These researchers saw early on the utility of sound recording technologies as they offered an accurate means of preserving and studying spoken folklore, languages, and music. With music, in particular, sound recording technologies enabled early comparative musicologists to capture and then study the rhythmic, melodic, and harmonic expressions that defied accurate registration by conventional Western notation. Ethnomusicology and folklore archives are fundamentally similar to other types of sound archive in their common mission of collecting, preserving, and providing access to historical materials, but differ from other materials in the kinds of material they contain. In general, such archives include recorded, written, and photographic documents pertaining to musical and oral traditions of groups and classes of people whose visions of the world are not usually found in assembled letters, diaries, and memoirs, or in institutions devoted to the culture of the occidental elite. Ethnomusicological and folk archives, for example, often have collections of African American, American Indian, Asian American, and other ethnically diverse groups who may have been colonized, marginalized, and/or exploited by European nations, the United States, and other colonial powers. These archives often focus on the so-called non-Western music and a great variety of other kinds of traditional (and increasingly popular) music played in the United States.

The distinction between various kinds of archives of traditional music in terms of their holdings has become less clear in recent years. In general, ethnomusicology archives contain recordings of music, as well as some oral data (myths, stories, anecdotes, interviews, and so on) and some written documentation. Usually they include both instantaneous recordings (e.g., unique materials recorded in the field, radio broadcasts, and tape collections of recording companies), which are preserved on wax cylinders, discs, wire spools, magnetic tapes, videotapes, and born digital files, and those that have been produced for commercial purposes. Most folklore archives, on the other hand, collect written transcriptions of oral data and contain some recordings. Oral history archives generally collect interviews, and language archives specialize in languages and speech forms.

Pioneering archives of this kind in the United States were established in 1928 (the Archive of Folksong at the Library of Congress), and in 1936 (the Archives of Folk and Primitive Music at Columbia University, now moved to Indiana University and called the Archives of Traditional Music). Ethnomusicology and folklore archives are found in a variety of institutional settings. Some are associated with university departments (University of Washington, Ethnomusicology Archives, 1963), others serve a particular region (Bishop Museum Audio Recording Collections, Hawaii, 1967), musical style (Rock and Roll Hall of Fame and Museum's Library and Archives, 2007), genre (Flanders Ballad Collection at Middlebury College, 1941; Archive of American Popular Beliefs and Superstitions at UCLA, 1944–2005), or ethnic group (the many archives devoted to Native American music). An extensive listing of sound recording, moving image, and other archives is available at UNESCO's Archives Portal: <http://www.unesco-ci.org/cgi-bin/portals/archives/page.cgi>. Most folk and ethnomusicology archives have specialized catalogs and listening facilities; some provide copies of recordings and written documents for the researcher. Archives of these kinds face the same challenges of preservation, space, and access to their collections as other kinds of sound archive, but they have a singular importance because of their rich holdings of recordings and documents (many of which, if not unique, are difficult to obtain elsewhere) of people whose culture cannot be preserved solely in books or other written materials.

4. Moving image archives. Motion pictures were legally recognized and registered for the first time in 1912,

although, as with sound, some materials had been given to the Library of Congress earlier. In 1883 W.K.L. Dickson, on behalf of the Edison Company, made the first moving image copyright deposit at the Library of Congress with several kinographic records (unfortunately they were destroyed due to the difficulty of safely storing flammable nitrate film). Between 1894 and 1912 moving-picture images on paper strips were deposited as sequential photographs under the provisions of the 1865 copyright law, since there was no provision for their registration as projectable motion-picture film. The 1912 revision allowing the deposit of actual motion-picture film was a major landmark in the development of moving image collections, yet even this did not mean that moving image materials were immediately accepted into the collections of the Library of Congress (though it was eventually the first library in the world to begin building a collection of this kind). Until the deposit and acquisition of film began in 1937, the Library of Congress acquired only written descriptive materials on moving image copyright deposit. It was not until the late 1950s, due in part to the highly unstable and flammable nature of nitrate film, that the library began systematically building a moving image collection.

As was the case with sound recordings collections, many of the earliest archival moving image collections in the United States were stored in natural history museums. Filmmaking equipment was taken into the field by American Museum of Natural History (AMNH) ornithologist Frank Chapman in 1908 and by explorer and taxidermist Carl Akeley in 1909. As of 2011, AMNH's Archival Film Collection included 291 titles, most of which were created during museum-sponsored expeditions of the 1920s and 30s. The Smithsonian Institution's National Museum of Natural History, Department of Anthropology, Human Studies Film Archive (HSFA), has moving image collections from the late 1920s, including the Kodak Cinegraph Films and Department of Agriculture Films made in New Guinea. The HSFA has more than eight million feet of original film and video materials. The University of Pennsylvania Museum of Archaeology and Anthropology also holds a significant collection of early moving image materials, including documentary footage from Watson Kintner and his travels to Guatemala, Guyana, Ecuador, Morocco, Pakistan, India, Indonesia, Nigeria, Australia, Iran, and Ethiopia (all filmed with a 16mm camera between 1933 and 1969).

The Museum of Modern Art in New York (MoMA) established a seminal moving image archive in 1935. Its aim was to "trace, catalog, assemble, exhibit and circulate a library of film programs so that the motion picture may be studied and enjoyed as any one of the arts is studied and enjoyed." MoMA film curator Iris Barry traveled to Hollywood in 1935, and through Europe and the Soviet Union in 1936, persuading filmmakers (such as Sergei Eisenstein) to donate prints to the Museum. So successful was this initial assembling of the collection that in 1937 the Academy of Motion Pictures Arts and Sciences commended the Museum with an award "for its significant work in collecting films...and for the first time making available to the public the means of studying the historical and aesthetic development of the motion picture as one of the major arts." As of 2011, MoMA's archive contained 25,000 moving image items and was housed at the Museum's Celeste Bartos Film Preservation Center (opened in 1996).

MoMA's early moving image collection development efforts influenced the Library of Congress to do the same. In the early 1940s, MoMA and the LC entered into a cooperative agreement for the acquisition of these materials. Among the results of this pact was the creation in 1943 of the first separate Motion Picture Section at the Library of Congress, the goal of which was the creation of a national film archive. This section was upgraded to a division in 1946, but the success of the project was short-lived, and the new division and its staff were disbanded in July 1947. Despite this organizational setback, the Library continued to collect moving image material and, in 1949, also began to collect films made for television.

Nearly three decades later, in carrying out the mandate of the 1976 Copyright Act to establish an American Television and Radio Archives, the Librarian of Congress reviewed the status of all of the Library's broadcast media (both sound recordings and moving image materials) and decided that it was more efficient to combine all visual, audio, and broadcast holdings into a single administrative unit. This resulted in the establishing of the Motion Picture, Broadcasting, and Recorded Sound (MBRS) Division in 1978. The MBRS is responsible for the acquisition, cataloging, and preservation of the motion picture and television collections. The Division also operates the Motion Picture and Television Reading Room to provide access and information services to an international community of film and television professionals, archivists, scholars, and researchers. In 2011, the Library's holdings included 1.1 million film, television, and video items, as well as 3.5 million sound recordings. The collections are stored on 90 miles of shelving at the Library's Packard Campus of the National Audio-Visual Conservation Center, in Culpepper, Virginia.

Even though radio and, to a lesser degree, television recordings have been collected for decades, particularly by the major broadcasting companies, the National Archives, and the Library of Congress, much of the early period of broadcasting history has been lost or destroyed by broadcast companies. What has been retained, however, is significant. The ABC Radio Network has transferred its collections to the National Archives; NBC Radio has given some 175,000 16-inch acetate discs to the Museum of Broadcasting in New York (founded 1975), and the Library of Congress; National Public Radio is transferring its collection to the National Archives and the Library of Congress on a five-year delay basis; the news talk radio station WOR and the Mutual Broadcasting System, known for its radio dramas, have given their remaining archives to the Library of Congress. Other great collections, such as the broadcasts of the Voice of America, the Armed Forces

Radio and Television Services, the Office of War Information, and the American Broadcasting Station in Europe can be found in the holdings of the Country Music Foundation, the Museum of Broadcasting, UCLA, the Library of Congress, and the Institute of Jazz Studies at Rutgers, among others. CBS destroyed its instantaneous collection many years ago (the only major network to have done so) and transferred its commercial discs to the Library of Congress, but fortunately many of its great shows have survived in other collections.

The New York Public Library (NYPL) founded its Jerome Robbins Dance Division in 1944. It is one of the largest archives devoted to the subject of dance, and contains thousands of moving image recordings (both on film and video). Its aim is to chronicle "the art of dance in all its manifestations—ballet, ethnic, modern, social, and folk." In 1953, NYPL also began collecting 16mm films produced by independent filmmakers, formally establishing a library for these materials in 1958. As of 2011 this film collection contained over 6000 titles (8650 prints) and is located at the Library for the Performing Arts at Lincoln Center. The Library also houses the Theatre on Film and Tape Archive (TOFT), a collection of approximately 6000 unique videos documenting Broadway musical performances. Established in 1970, TOFT materials are only accessible within the library.

In 1965, UCLA's Theater Arts Department partnered with the Academy of Television Arts and Sciences (ATAS) to create the ATAS/UCLA Television Library. In 1968, the UCLA Film Department founded the UCLA Film Archive. The two were merged in 1976 to create the UCLA Film and Television Archive. With over 300,000 films and television programs, and 27 million feet of newsreel footage, the UCLA Film & Television Archive is the world's largest university-held collection of moving image materials and second largest archive of moving image materials in the United States after the Library of Congress. Its collections include material dating back to the 1890s. Important acquisitions include the Hearst Metrotone News collection, films from American Film Institute and the Academy of Motion Picture Arts and Sciences, as well as materials from all the major US studios: Warner Brothers, Columbia Pictures, 20th Century Fox, and Republic Pictures. The archive also holds a collection of sound recordings, a significant portion of which contains radio programming on 16-inch transcription discs.

The National Archives was established in 1934 and was renamed the National Archives and Records Administration (NARA) in 1984. While its primary focus is on collecting paper documents, it is nonetheless important in the history of sound recording and moving image archives as it was the first archive to place both materials into the same administrative unit. Even with this provision in its charter, it was well into the 1950s before NARA began systematically to develop either film or audio collections. NARA's concept of grouping these materials into a single archive has come to fruition in many other collections, such as the Rodgers and Hammerstein Archives of Recorded Sound (NYPL) and the Country Music Hall of Fame and Museum's Frist Library and Archive.

5. Professional organizations. Developments in the archival collection of media materials have given rise to professional organizations. The Association for recorded sound collections was established in 1966 to collect and disseminate information concerning the preservation and distribution of sound recordings. The Association of Moving Image Archivists was established in 1990 to advance the field of moving image archiving. Some professional organizations with specific research interests, such as the Society for Ethnomusicology (founded 1955), maintain archival interest groups and committees focus on such issues as preservation and access to sound recordings and moving image media. A growing national concern for the preservation of media resulted in the establishment of the National Film Preservation Board (NFPB). In 2000 it did the same for sound recordings by establishing the National Recording Preservation Board (NRPB). The NFPB and the NRPB advise the Librarian of Congress in the annual selection of films and recordings for the National Film Registry and the National Recording Registry respectively. Further, they have developed a national preservation planning policy for moving image and sound recordings. In addition, the NRPB commissioned the report *The State of Recorded Sound Preservation in the United States: a National Legacy at Risk in the Digital Age* in 2010.

6. Early 21st century archives. With the development of the Internet and digitization technologies, numerous sound recording and moving image collections have been digitized and subsequently disseminated online. Significant online archival sound recordings collections include 8000 cylinder recordings online at the University of California, Santa Barbara; 6000 cylinder recordings online at Syracuse University; and 30,000 78 rpm recordings online at the UCLA (copyright concerns resulted in limited off-campus access). The Library of Congress's National Jukebox, at its launch in 2011, included more than 10,000 recordings made by the Victor Talking Machine Company between 1901 and 1925, and is expected to grow significantly with recordings from other Sony-owned US labels—including Columbia and its subsidiary OKeh—being added in the near term. The Library of Congress also hosts the American Memory Project, which has provided free and open access to numerous documents pertinent to American history, including spoken-word and music sound recordings since 1990. Some publicly-funded institutions have partnered with for-profit companies to make their sound recording archives available online, such as Smithsonian Global Sound, while a new breed of nonprofit archival organization, such as the Internet Archive, host institutional and individual users' sound and moving images collections.

Several significant archival moving image collections have also been distributed online. The Library of Congress has uploaded many historical films to both its American Memory site and its YouTube channel. In

2006 NARA partnered with Google Inc. to digitize and host a selection of historic newsreels and films on Google Video, which ceased in 2011. The University of Pennsylvania Museum of Archaeology and Anthropology has distributed dozens of early ethnographic moving image titles on the Internet Archive. Folkstream.net, a non-profit organization supported by the Southern Folklife Collection at the University of North Carolina, provides free and open access to folkloric films, including dozens about music and dance. For-profit corporations, such as Alexander Street Press, also provide subscribers access to music and dance moving image materials (e.g., Dance in Video, Ethnographic Video Online). The EVIA Digital Archive Project, a collaborative project of Indiana University and the University of Michigan, is an effort to establish a repository of ethnographic video recordings and an infrastructure of tools and systems supporting scholars in the ethnographic disciplines. EVIA is being made available to university IP ranges. In addition to increased access, digitization technologies led to a preservation revolution in the early 21st century. Up until the late 1990s, archival preservation practice was to copy sound recordings to analog reel-to-reel tape. With the rise of reliable and affordable analog-to-digital audio conversion hardware and digital audio editing software, and the increasing obsolescence of reliable analog playback equipment, digitization became the de facto means of preserving analog sound recording content. Sound recording digital preservation best practices were published by the International Association of Sound and Audiovisual Archivists (IASA) in 2004, and by Indiana University and Harvard University in 2007 (a partnership called Sound Directions). Moving image archives have been slower to adopt digitization as the standard preservation practice. Many moving image archivists argue that motion-picture film (more so than video) is a stable media and has a long shelf life. Additionally, unlike digital files, film does not need to be continually migrated into different generations of digital storage system to ensure longevity.

For information about important sound collections not mentioned above, *see* Libraries and collections, including, under *California*, Palo Alto (Stanford University Archive of Recorded Sound); *Missouri*, Kansas City (University of Missouri's Marr Sound Archives); *Massachusetts*, Cambridge (Harvard University's Archive of World Music Collection); *New Jersey*, Newark (Rutgers University's Institute of Jazz Studies); and *North Carolina*, Chapel Hill (Southern Folklife Collection at the University of North Carolina at Chapel Hill).

Other notable sound archives not mentioned above or in the Libraries and collections entry include the ARChive of Contemporary Music, New York City; American Radio Archives and Museum; Edison National Historic Site; Library of American Broadcasting; Paley Center for Media; Queens College, Louis Armstrong Archives; Center for Popular Music at Middle Tennessee State University; and the G. Robert Vincent National Voice Library at Michigan State University.

BIBLIOGRAPHY

PRINTED MATERIALS

Catalogue of the College Music Set, ed. Carnegie Corporation (New York, 1933, rev. 2/1938 as *A List of 953 Records…in the Sets of…Material for Use in Colleges*)

Folklore and Folk Music Archivist (1958–68)

The National Union Catalog: Music and Phonorecords (Ann Arbor, MI, later Washington, DC, 1958–)

J.N. Moore: "The Historical Sound Recordings Program at Yale University," *Notes*, xix (1961–2), 283

A. Briegleb: *Directory of Ethnomusicological Sound Recording Collections in the U.S. and Canada* (Ann Arbor, MI, 1971)

D.L. Leavitt: "Recorded Sound in the Library of Congress," *Library Trends*, xxi/1 (1972), 53

Catalog of Copyright Entries, ser.3, pt xiv: *Sound Recordings*, ed. US Copyright Office (Washington, DC, 1972–7; as ser.4, pt vii, 1980– [coinciding with the implementation of the copyright act of 1976])

K. Berger: "The Yale Collection of Historical Sound Recordings," *Journal* [Association for Recorded Sound Collections], vi/1 (1974), 13

A Catalog of Phonorecordings of Music and Oral Data held by the Archives of Traditional Music, ed. Archives of Traditional Music, Folklore Institute, Indiana U. (Boston, 1975)

C.J. Frisbie: *Music and Dance Research of Southwestern United States Indians* (Detroit, 1977) [lists recordings]

Sibley Music Library Catalog of Sound Recordings, ed. Eastman School (Boston, 1977)

G. Koch: *Directory of Member Archives* (London, 1978, 2/1982) [International Association of Sound Archives]

E.A. Davis: *Index to the New World Recorded Anthology of American Music* (New York, 1981)

Dictionary Catalog of the Rodgers and Hammerstein Archives of Recorded Sound (Boston, 1981)

W. Crutchfield: "Grooves of Academe," *Opera News*, xlviii/2 (1983), 26 [Yale collection]

J. Hickerson, S. LoCurto, and G. Parsons: *Folklife and Ethnomusicology Archives and Related Collections in the United States and Canada* (Washington, DC, 1984)

INTERNET RESOURCES

Alexander Street Press, *Belfer Cylinders Digital Connection*, Syracuse University, <http://library.syr.edu/digital/splash/cylinders/>

Internet Archive, <http://www.archive.org>

National Jukebox, Library of Congress, <http://www.loc.gov/jukebox/>

Sound Directions: Best Practices for Audio Preservation, <http://www.dlib.indiana.edu/projects/sounddirections/papersPresent/index.shtml>

The Strachwitz Frontera Collection of Mexican and Mexican American Recordings, <http://frontera.library.ucla.edu/>

UCSB Cylinder Preservation and Digitization Project, <http://cylinders.library.ucsb.edu/>

United Nation's Educational, Scientific, and Cultural Organization (UNESCO) <http://www.unesco.org/new/en/media-services/multi-media/film-and-radio-collection> [extensive listing of sound recording and moving images]

JOHN VALLIER

Archives and Manuscripts. Archives and manuscripts constitute the "raw materials" of music history, since the foundation of much humanistic scholarship is based on the interpretation and re-interpretation of primary and secondary sources. Music archival collections and manuscripts may be found both within and outside musical organizations, such as conservatories, academic institutions, libraries, historical societies, museums, businesses, performing arts organizations, research centers, radio and television stations, government archives, and church archives.

This article will cover the single manuscript and paper-based archival traditions in the United States. For media-based archives, *see* Archives, sound recording and

MOVING IMAGE. For details of specific collections *see* LIBRARIES AND COLLECTIONS; for jazz archives *see* "Libraries and archives" in *GroveJ*.

1. Archives, definition. 2. Types of archives. 3. History of archives in the United States. 4. Manuscripts 5. Access in the digital era. 6. Archival research.

1. ARCHIVES, DEFINITION. Archives are defined as groups of documents produced by an institution, an organization, an individual, or a family in the course of daily activity, and preserved for enduring value. They are typically kept together as organized bodies of records and are maintained in their original order. The term archive also refers to the repository where archives are located; it is often also used to describe a specialized collection.

2. TYPES OF ARCHIVES. Archives generally fall into three broad categories. The first type, organizational or corporate archives, contains records created by an organization, institution, government, corporation, foundation, or society as a routine part of conducting affairs. Thus, the National Archives contain the records of the US federal government, while the archives of a music publisher may contain contracts, records of copyrights, royalties, other legal and financial papers, back files of published music, correspondence, manuscript scores, and corrected proofs. Organizational archives may be public or private. They may be located in-house or transferred to a library or other archival repository for long-term protection and public access. For example, the previously private archives of the performance rights organization ASCAP have been transferred to the Library of Congress, including their non-current business and legal records, music manuscripts, lead sheets, photos, and letters.

Personal papers of individuals or families, the second category of archives, document the lives and careers of individuals. While personal archives are private unless declared otherwise, it became standard during the 20th century for prominent musical figures or their families to be involved with the disposition of their papers—depositing or selling them to institutions, libraries, or research centers—thereby making them available for research.

The third type of archive contains materials of various provenance gathered in support of a particular subject. This type of collection is sometimes referred to as an "artificial" archive. For example, the Smithsonian Archives Center gathers collections that document American popular music and performance traditions, particularly in the areas of jazz, gospel, and folk musics, for its American Music Collections.

Other collections with materials not generally defined as 'archival' are sometimes considered as such, for example those containing published materials that are ephemeral or unique, like the African-American Sheet Music Collection at Brown University, comprised of rare publications from the 19th and early 20th centuries. Collections of photographic reproductions of primary source materials represent another kind of archive altogether, such as the Toscanini Archives at the New York Public Library, which contains microfilms of composer autograph scores and sketches.

3. HISTORY OF ARCHIVES IN THE UNITED STATES. The development of music-related archives in the United States is intertwined with the establishment of archives in general, as well as with the development of music as a field of study. In colonial times it was generally recognized that keeping documents and records was a community responsibility, both at the local and colony level. Historical societies, emerging at the end of the 18th century, functioned as another sort of public archive. However, the centralized National Archives, keepers of records of the federal government, was only officially organized in 1934, whereas most European national archives were established in the late 18th or 19th centuries. American archivists adopted practices from European models, including basic principles dictating that papers of the same provenance should be kept together and maintained in their original order, thus preserving relationships between documents.

The creation of most archival institutions located in the United States took place during the 20th century, especially in the second half; by 2000, there were over 5000 archives in the United States. During the late 20th century numerous archives were formally installed in institutions that had been long producing and retaining records. To name a few, the Metropolitan Opera, founded in 1883, only began to organize its archives in the 1950s, while the Boston Symphony Orchestra, founded in 1881, established their archives in 1990–91.

The systematic collection of American music primary resources has followed the acceptance of American music as a scholarly discipline in academic institutions. However, the Library of Congress, under Oscar Sonneck, was one of the first with an aggressive program for collecting Americana before the rise of American music studies. With over 500 named collections, LC holds the personal papers and manuscripts of major composers, performers, conductors, scholars, as well as papers from musical organizations. The Yale University Music Library has amassed archives of American composers and performers of classical music, jazz, and musical theatre, beginning with the Charles Ives Papers in 1956. Numerous other research centers devoted to American musics have been established during the second half of the 20th century, including the William Ransom Hogan Jazz Archive at Tulane University (1958); the Center for Black Music Research (Chicago, 1983); the Southern Folklife Collection (North Carolina, 1986); and the Center for American Music (Pittsburgh, 1996).

4. MANUSCRIPTS. Manuscripts are documents that are handwritten or hand-notated; manuscript collections often also include typewritten documents, known as typescripts. Manuscripts are highly valued, not only because they are unique, but also because they have much to reveal about compositional and creative process, as well as performance practice, dissemination, the development of musical style, and details about a manuscript's

creator, recipient, and its intended function. Manuscripts are primarily held in academic or public libraries, or in private collections. There are many European manuscripts in the United States largely because musical scholarship privileged European composers until the late 20th century. Thus, Otto Albrecht's 1953 survey of music manuscripts in the United States was limited to the autograph scores of European composers.

Building significant manuscript collections has depended largely upon donors and foundations, in part because manuscripts, especially holographs, are rare, valuable, and usually costly. As a result, they have tended to be sold and acquired separately. In the early part of the 20th century, significant collections of music manuscripts in private hands were purchased or donated intact to institutions and formed the nucleus of their music collections. Notable examples include the Joseph W. Drexel Collection at the New York Public Library, the Lowell Mason Collection at Yale, and the Allen A. Brown Collection at the Boston Public Library. Public research libraries, especially NYPL and LC, developed significant holdings of manuscript collections during the early decades of the 20th century, particularly through bequests and foundations. LC has assembled an especially rich and extensive collection of manuscripts, in part due to the establishment in 1923 of the Elizabeth Sprague Coolidge Foundation (the commissions of which brought autographs of many American composers) and the Gertrude Clark Whittall Foundation in 1941. The private manuscript collections of Mary Flagler Cary, and Dannie and Hettie Heineman were donated to the Pierpont Morgan Library, and the collection of Robert Owen Lehman placed on deposit, making the library one of the world's major repositories of music manuscripts. Other more recent musical benefactors include Hans Moldenhauer, who distributed a substantial portion of his collection of autograph music manuscripts and correspondence in nine American and European institutions, and Bruce Kovner, who donated his manuscript collection to Juilliard in 2006.

The growth of music manuscript collections within universities has been intertwined with the expansion of musicology as a field of study after World War II. In the post war years many European collections were dispersed, and manuscripts, even autographs, were available on the antiquarian market at prices unimaginably low by early 21st-century standards; buyers were frequently American antiquarian dealers, universities, or private collectors. The Music Library at the University of California Berkeley, under Vincent Duckles, augmented its music manuscript collection through extended European buying trips in the 1950s and 60s. Ruth Watanabe undertook similar buying trips on behalf of the Sibley Library, as did David Wood for the University of Washington. As academic programs broadened to encompass American music, ethnomusicology, and jazz, popular, and other musics as fields of study, libraries expanded their collecting parameters and added manuscripts from these traditions to their collections. Auctions devoted to jazz materials or Broadway productions, as well as autograph manuscripts of American composers, have helped to develop markets for American music memorabilia.

5. Access in the digital era. The rapid development of digitization since the 1990s has had an extraordinary impact on conducting research with primary sources and has improved access both to information about primary sources, as well as to the sources themselves. There are many published guides to repositories and collections; however, as of 2011 there is no comprehensive guide to music archives. The *National Union Catalog of Manuscript Collections* (NUCMC) provides detailed catalog records online via OCLC. There are also commercially available databases such as *Archive Finder* and *ArchiveGrid*, which provide partial coverage of archival records. The publications of RISM are important access tools for locating individual music manuscripts, especially those from before 1800.

There are generally two levels of access to archival collections: cataloging records, which provide information about a particular collection as a whole, and finding aids, which provide an inventory of the contents at the folder or item level, as well as contextual information. Since the establishment of the online Encoded Archival Description (EAD) standard at Berkeley (mid-1990s), finding aids are increasingly available online. Many institutions have created their own finding aid union catalogs, such as the Online Archive of California.

In response to growing demand for remote access to copies of primary source materials, many repositories have begun to digitize their archival materials and make them available online. The Library of Congress's American Memory project, initiated in the early 1990s, was one of the first; it includes a wide variety of the library's music-related collections as well as those of other institutions. Launched in 2010, the Music Treasures Consortium provides open digital access to unique music resources held by participating institutions. The founding members are LC, Harvard, the British Library, Juilliard, and the Morgan Library. New models for access to archives continue to emerge, some presenting materials from dispersed locations in one virtual space, enabling the discovery of previously hidden connections that the simultaneous search of large quantities of data provides. Most digital projects intend that preservation be an additional outcome. Not only does the use of digital surrogates protect fragile originals from frequent handling, but digital re-formatting can provide a sustainable means of providing long-term reliable access as long as archival-quality protocols and standards, such those from the Open Archives Initiative (OAI), are used.

6. Archival research. Scholars have long consulted primary documents to obtain detailed and accurate information on musicians, compositions, organizations, and societies, as well as to study music in its historical and social context. The broadening of the discipline in the late 20th century, incorporating new areas of scholarly inquiry, has renewed interest in archival work. The definition of what is considered a primary source has

expanded as a result. In order to study music in a wider culture, contemporary sources that have not traditionally been considered archival (such as newspapers, broadsides, leaflets, directories, and ephemera) are now viewed as primary sources for the historical context they provide. This expanded view of archives has encouraged fresh approaches to traditional source studies.

The landscape of archival research is evolving as resources become more widely available online; however, preserving the past in the digital era poses significant challenges due to rapid changes in technology. Furthermore, the methodologies of archival research will continue to change as digital-born materials replace paper-based materials.

BIBLIOGRAPHY

O.E. Albrecht: *A Census of Autograph Music Manuscripts of European Composers in American Libraries* (Philadelphia, 1953)

C. Wade: "The Music Division of the Library of Congress," *FAM*, xvi (1969), 109–12

M.E. Peltz: "The Metropolitan Opera Archives," *FAM*, xxx (1967), 471–75

F. Lesure: "Archival Research: Necessity and Opportunity," *Perspectives in Musicology*, ed. B.S. Brook, E.O.D. Downes and S. Van Solema (New York, 1972), 56–79

P.L. Miller and F.C. Campbell: "How the Music Division of the New York Public Library Grew: A Memoir," *Notes*, xxxv (1979), 537–55

D.W. Krummel: *Resources of American Music History: a Directory of Source Materials from Colonial Times to World War II* (Urbana, 1981)

R.C. Berner: *Archival Theory and Practice in the United States: a Historical Analysis* (Seattle, 1983)

S. Grigg: "Archival Practice and the Foundations of Historical Method," *Journal of American History*, lxxviii (1991), 228–39

A. Wathey: "Musicology, Archives, and Historiography," *Musicology and Archival Research: Brussels 1993*, 3–26

R.C. Wegman: "Elaborating Themes: the Collaboration between Archivists and Historians," *Musicology and Archival Research: Brussels 1993*, 27–35

H.E. Samuel: "Rare Resources in the Yale Music Library," *The Library Quarterly*, lxiv (1994), 61–72

J.H. Roberts: "The Music Library, University of California, Berkeley," *The Library Quarterly*, lxiv (1994), 73–84

J.B. Howard: "The Eda Kuhn Loeb Music Library at Harvard University," *The Library Quarterly*, lxiv (1994), 163–76

M.W. Davidson: "The Research Collections of the Sibley Music Library of the Eastman School of Music, University of Rochester," *The Library Quarterly*, lxiv (1994), 177–94

V.H. Duckles and I. Reed: *Music Reference and Research materials: an Annotated Bibliography* (New York, 5/1997)

J. Newsom and A. Mann, ed.: *The Rosaleen Moldenhauer Memorial: Music History from Primary Sources: a Guide to the Moldenhauer Archives* (Washington, DC, 2000)

D. Farneth: "Valuing Composers' Archives: How One Institution Encourages International Study, Performance, and Publication," *Their Championship Seasons: Acquiring, Processing and Using Performing Arts Archives*, Performing Arts Resources, xxii (New York, 2001), 117–42

M. Hassen: "The Early Development of American Music Libraries Serving Academic Departments of Music," *FAM*, xlviii (2001), 342–52

J.R. Turner: "Music Collections at the Pierpont Morgan Library," *FAM*, xlviii (2001), 367–71

P. Hall and F. Sallis, eds.: *A Handbook to Twentieth-century Musical Sketches* (Cambridge, 2004)

H. Bloch: *Directory of Conductors Archives in American Institutions* (Lanham, MD, 2006)

J. M. O'Toole and R.J. Cox: *Understanding Archives & Manuscripts* (Chicago, 2006)

M. Van Wingen and A. Bass: "Reappraising Archival Practice in Light of the New Social History," *Library Hi Tech*, xxvi (2008), 575–85

SARAH ADAMS

Arden, Jann [Richards, Jann (Arden Anne)] (*b* Springbank, AB, 27 March 1962). Canadian singer-songwriter. Her songs are characterized by a lyrical emphasis on heartbreak and introspection, set to seamless pop and rock arrangements featuring smooth vocals and catchy rhythmic riffs. She began writing songs at the age of 13 and released her debut single "Never Love a Sailor" as Jann Richards in 1980. Arden busked and performed with rock bands in clubs and at festivals before signing with A&M Records and releasing her debut album *Time for Mercy* (A&M, 1993), which included the single "I would die for you." The album garnered her a Juno Award for Best New Solo Artist in 1994 and she subsequently received two more, for Songwriter of the Year, in 1995 and 2002.

Arden's success continued with *Living under June* (A&M, 1994), which featured three of her biggest singles "Insensitive," "Could I be your Girl," and "Good Mother." Arden has continued to release studio albums as well as a greatest hits album (*Greatest Hurts*, Universal Canada, 2001) and a recording of a performance with the Vancouver SO (Universal Canada, 2002). She has profited from a number of collaborations, including participating in the traveling music festival Lilith Fair, regular appearances on the CBC television show "The Rick Mercer Report," and a performance with Michael Bublé in the Olympic torch ceremony in Vancouver the 2010. With Bublé, Arden co-wrote "Lost," which was featured on Bublé's album *Call me Irresponsible* (143 Records, 2007) and released as a video, and then included on Arden's own album *Free* (Universal Canada, 2009). Her recording *Uncover Me* (Universal Canada, 2007) was well received and the song choices reveal some of her most important influences: Cat Stevens' "Peace Train," Carly Simon's "You're so Vain," Pat Benatar's "Love is a Battlefield," and Janis Ian's "Seventeen." This collection of covers was so successful that she released a second collection (*Uncover Me 2*, Universal Canada, 2011), featuring a greater range of songs, from Doris Day's "Que Sera Sera" to The Beach Boys' "In My Room" to Fleetwood Mac's "Dreams." Her live album *Spotlight* (2010), included a documentary DVD and Arden's complete music video collection to that date.

Arden has written two books of poetry and personal reflections (*If I Knew, Don't You Think I'd Tell You*, Insomniac Press, 2002, and *I'll Tell You One Damn Thing and That's All I Know*, Insomniac Press, 2004), as well as an autobiography (*Falling Backwards*, Alfred A. Knopf, 2011). She has also worked as a restaurateur, and acted on film and television.

LORI BURNS, JADA WATSON

Arden, Victor [Fuiks, Lewis John] (*b* Wenona, IL, 8 March 1893; *d* New York, NY, 31 July 1962). Pianist, best known for his work in a duo with PHIL W. OHMAN.

Ardévol (Gimbernat), José (*b* Barcelona, Spain, 13 March 1911; *d* Havana, Cuba 9 Jan 1981). Cuban composer and conductor of Spanish descent. He studied piano, conducting, and composition with his father, and when only twelve he composed the *Sonatina* and *Capricho* for piano. He graduated from the Instituto Musical de Barcelona in 1929, and the following year studied orchestral conducting with Scherchen in Paris. In 1930 he completed the degree in humanities at Barcelona University, and formed the Beethoven Trio, which was short-lived as he moved to Havana the same year. In Cuba he became the friend and colleague of Amadeo Roldán and Alejandro García Caturla, and quickly involved himself in musical life. He founded and conducted the Orquesta de Cámara de La Habana (1934–52) with whom he performed a wide range of music, from 17th- and 18th-century works to contemporary compositions, including some by Cuban composers. He was musical director of the Ballet de la Sociedad Pro-Arte Musical (1941–3), whose orchestra he also led; among other pieces he conducted the Cuban premieres of Stravinsky's ballets *Petrushka* and *Apollon musagète*, *Icaro* by Harold Gramatges, *Antes del Alba* by Hilario González, and his own *Forma*.

From 1936 onward he was professor of music history and aesthetics at the Conservatorio Municipal de La Habana, and two years later he replaced Amadeo Roldán as professor of harmony and composition. Ardévol's composition class at the conservatory gave birth to the Grupo de Renovación Musical (1942–8), whose members included Gramatges, Martín, Gisela Hernández, Pró, Argeliers León, Hilario González, Orbón, and Virginia Fleites. Atonality (though not dodecaphony), polytonality, polyrhythm, the superimposition of different harmonies, modalism, and above all neo-classicism constituted the basis of Ardévol's strict teaching regime. He warned his students against the limitations of nationalism, although he did not completely ignore the possibilities afforded by folk music. He worked as a music critic for various newspapers and journals, sometimes writing also on theater and cinema. Some of his reviews and other essays appear in his book *Música y revolución* (1966).

After the victory of the Cuban Revolution in 1959, he took part in cultural reorganization and management and in the planning of music education at different levels. He was the national director for music, a delegate of the Ministro de Educación to the Instituto Cubano de Derechos Musicales (1960–5), and in 1965 resumed his professional activity at the conservatory. From 1968 onward he worked for the establishment of advanced musical studies, subsequently organizing the first advanced courses, at the Escuela Nacional de Arte. On the foundation of the Instituto Superior de Arte in 1976 he was named dean of the music faculty and chair of composition. He was professor of the summer schools at the universities of Havana and Oriente and gave lectures on Cuban music at a number of universities, including Harvard, Columbia, and Rochester, and to composers' unions in various countries. He belonged to various international institutions, such as the Instituto Interamericano de Musicología, and was a permanent member of the Pan American Association of Composers; he presided for more than eight years over the Comité Nacional Cubano de la Música. In 1971 he was elected president of the music section of the Unión de Escritores y Artistas de Cuba (UNEAC). He received various national and international prizes for his music.

Ardévol wrote over 130 works, covering all genres except opera. His early pieces (1924–30) show the influence of Debussy, Stravinsky, and the keyboard writing of Scarlatti. From 1930 his music assumed an expressionist atonality, and became at once more experimental and more systematic in a quasi-serialist manner. His *Tres ricercari* (1936) mark to an extent a turning-point between this period and a move toward a neo-classical style with nationalist tendencies that incorporated both Spanish and Cuban elements. It was a style which prevailed uninterrupted until the 1960s. After 1965, Ardévol incorporated techniques of the postwar period, although not electro-acoustics; for example, in *Noneto*, the cantata *Che comandante,* and *Ninfra*, he took up atonality again and touched on serialism and post-serialism.

In general, Ardévol's work is rigorous in its construction, austere, and occasionally rather arid. He creates tension through the repeated use of dissonant seconds and his consistent use of counterpoint, and he often superimposes classical forms on contemporary material. In the manner of Stravinsky, he was an avid defender of what he considered to be musical "objectivity."

WORKS

(selective list)

Orch: 3 ricercari, str, 1936; Conc., 3 pf, orch, 1938; Sym. no.2 "Homenaje a Falla," 1945; Sym. no.3, 1946; Suites cubanas nos.1–2, 1947, 1949; Sym. Variations, vc, orch, 1951; El son, vn, orch, 1952; Música, chbr orch, 1957; Música, gui, chbr orch, 1967; Movimientos sinfónicos nos.1–2, 1967, 1969; Pf Conc., 1975; Caturliana, pf, orch, 1976 [based on a theme by A. Caturla]

Vocal: Burla de Don Pedro a caballo (cant., F. García Lorca), 3 solo vv, chorus, orch, 1943; Versos sencillos (J. Martí), 1v, orch, 1952; Cantos de la Revolución, chorus, 1962; La victoria de Playa Girón (cant., F. Jamis), 4 solo vv, chorus, orch, 1967; Che comandante (cant., N. Guillén), 3 solo vv, chorus, orch, 1968; Lenin (V.I. Lenin, F.P. Rodríguez), 6 solo vv, chorus, orch, 1970; Chile: compañero presidente (cant., S. Allende, Guillén, P. Neruda, F. de Rojas), 5 solo vv, reciter, chorus, orch, 1974

Chbr and solo inst: Study in the Form of a Prelude and Fugue, perc, 1933; Suite, perc, 1934; Música da camera, 6 insts, 1936; Sonate a 3 nos.1–5, 1937, 1938, 1942, 1942, 1943; Conc., pf, wind, perc, 1944; Pf Sonatas nos.1–3, 1944; Sonate a 3 no.6, 1946; Sonata, vc, pf, 1948; Sonata, gui, 1948; Sonatina, vc, pf, 1950; Wind Qnt, 1957; Str Qt no.3, 1958; 3 Short Pieces, vn/vc, pf, 1965; Noneto, 1966; Ninfra, fantasia, 2 pf, 1968; Tensiones, pf left hand, 1968; Música a 6, fl, cl, small ens, 1976; Música, 9 perc, 1978; Música, ob, ens, 1979

Principal publishers: Empresa de Grabaciones y Ediciones Musicales, Editora Musical de Cuba, Music for Percussion (New York), Pan American Union, Southern

WRITINGS

Música y revolución (Havana, 1966)

Introducción a Cuba: la música (Havana, 1969)

"Entrevista," *Unión* [Havana], x/4 (1971), 103–36

BIBLIOGRAPHY

A. Carpentier: La música en CubaLa música en Cuba (Mexico City, 1946, 2/1979)

O. Mayer-Serra: *Música y músicos de Latinoamérica* (Mexico, 1947)
E. Martin: *Panorama histórico de la música en Cuba* (Havana, 1971)
M.I. Ardévol Muñoz: "Los Ardévol, Fernando y José: dos músicos olvidados," *D'Art*, xi (Universitat de Barcelona, 1985), 285–300
Diccionario de la música española e hispano-americana, ed. E. Casares Rodicio, J. López-Calo, I. Fernandez de la Cuesta, vol. 1 (Madrid, 1999), 618–21
J. Ardévol: *Correspondencia cruzada*. Selección, introducción y notas C. Díaz (La Habana, 2004)
R. Giró: *Diccionario enciclopédico de la música en Cuba*, vol. 1 (Havana, 2007), 67–69

VICTORIA ELI RODRÍGUEZ

Arditi, Luigi (*b* Crescentino, Italy, 16 July 1822; *d* Hove, England, 1 May 1903). Italian conductor and composer. After studying and working in Milan until 1846, he went with Giovanni Bottesini to Havana, where he conducted the Havana Italian Opera Company and produced his own one-act opera, *Il corsaro*. In the summer months he performed in the United States and conducted the Havana company in New York in 1847 and 1850. From 1851 to 1856 he was the conductor for various opera troupes in New York, including Maretzek's company (1851), and toured with Marietta Alboni. He conducted the concert for the opening of the Academy of Music (2 October 1854), where his opera *La spia*, based on James Fenimore Cooper's novel *The Spy*, was given its first performance on 24 March 1856. The *New York Courier and Enquirer* opined:

> Written by an Italian, to Italian words, in the Italian style, for Italian singers, there is not even the shadow of a ground for calling La Spia an American work. Let us not deceive ourselves. It is well for the arts to flourish here; but it is not well for us to be deluded with the idea that we have American Art, when we have no such thing, but are cultivating an exotic.…But when music in this country does assume a character of its own, we can only wish the composer of the first American opera the good fortune to meet with a manager so ready to encourage him and bring him advantageously before the public as the present director of the affairs of the Academy of Music.

After leaving New York, Arditi settled in London in 1858 as conductor at Her Majesty's Theatre, where he remained for 11 years. He continued to compose, mostly occasional orchestral music, popular songs, and ballads; the vocal waltz *Il bacio* was renowned. He also conducted operas and promenade concerts at Covent Garden and made many tours in the provinces and Europe, chiefly with Italian opera companies. From 1878 to 1886 he conducted Mapleson's annual opera tours of the United States. Several of these were with Adelina Patti, as were all his remaining American tours, the last of which took place in 1893–4.

BIBLIOGRAPHY

Grove7 (Nigel Burton and Keith Horner)
"First Performance of Signor Arditi's Opera, 'La Spia'," *New York Courier and Enquirer* (25 March 1856), 203 [repr. in *Dwight's Journal of Music* (29 March 1856)]
"Luigi Arditi," *Brainard's Musical World* (Dec 1881); repr. in *Brainard's Biographies of American Musicians*, ed. E. Douglas Bomberger (Westport, CT, 1999)
The Mapleson Memoirs (London, 1888, 2/1966)
L. Arditi: *My Reminiscences* (New York, 1896/*R*1977)
J.F. Cone: *First Rival of the Metropolitan Opera* (New York, 1983)
J. Dizikes: *Opera in America: A Cultural History* (New Haven, CT, 1993)

KEITH HORNER/R. ALLEN LOTT/E. DOUGLAS BOMBERGER

Ardoin, Alphonse "Bois Sec" (*b* L'Anse des Prien Noir, near Duralde, LA, 16 Nov 1915; *d* Eunice, LA, 18 May 2007). Creole accordionist, vocalist, and songwriter. A cousin of the legendary Creole accordionist Amédé Ardoin, Alphonse became interested in the Creole "la-la" music of his community, learning to play on his older brother's accordion. In the late 1940s, he teamed up with his long-time partner, Creole fiddler Canray Fontenot. Together they were the core of the Duralde Ramblers, performing at local dance halls and house dances. In 1964, they were recorded by Ralph Rinzler, who was doing fieldwork for the Newport Folk Festival. They were invited to perform at Newport in 1966 and recorded their first album, *Les blues du bayou*, on the way home. By the 1970s, Ardoin and Fontenot were performing with the Ardoin Family Band, featuring several of Ardoin's sons. With this band, Ardoin and Fontenot took their pre-zydeco Creole music to many parts of the country, becoming fixtures on the folk festival circuit. Ardoin tried to retire in the early 1970s, passing the torch to his son Gustave, but he rejoined the group when Gustave died in 1974. He and Fontenot were awarded National Endowment for the Arts National Heritage Fellowships in 1986. Together they were featured in several documentary films, including Les Blank's *Dry Wood* (1973), André Gladu's *Les Créoles* (1976) and *Zarico* (1984), Nick Spitzer's *Zydeco* (1986), and Les Blank, Chris Strachwitz, and Maureen Gosling's *J'ai été au bal* (1989). Despite his musical success, he supported himself throughout his life by working as a hand in nearby ricefields and on his own family farm.

BIBLIOGRAPHY

A.A. Savoy: *Cajun Music: a Reflection of a People* (Eunice, LA, 1984)
B.J. Ancelet and E. Morgan Jr.: *Cajun and Creole Music Makers* (Jackson, MS, 1984/*R*)
M. Tisserand: *The Kingdom of Zydeco* (New York, 1998)
R. Brasseaux and K. Fontenot, eds.: *Accordions, Fiddles, Two Steps and Swing* (Lafayette, LA, 2006)

BARRY JEAN ANCELET

Ardoin, Amédé (*b* L'Anse des Rougeau, near Basile, LA, 11 March 1898; *d* Pineville, LA, 4 Nov 1941). Creole accordionist, vocalist, and songwriter. Ardoin was influenced as a child by Adam Fontenot, father of Creole fiddler Canray Fontenot. He eventually became a locally popular accordionist and vocalist who in turn influenced many Cajun, Creole, and zydeco musicians. Alone or with his occasional partner, Cajun fiddler Dennis McGee, he recorded a total of 31 songs, many of which were eventually adopted and adapted by musicians such as Nathan Abshire, Austin Pitre, and especially Iry Lejeune, and later Dewey Balfa and Michael Doucet; these songs have become an important part of the core repertoire of Cajun and Creole music. His original 78s were collected and re-released by Arhoolie records, first on an LP and later on CD, and remain influential. Stylistically, he also influenced the development of zydeco with his highly syncopated, improvisational, complex accordion playing. His soulful, soaring vocal style and poetics influence both Cajun and Creole singers to this day. Stories concerning his death vary; some claim that he died as the result of venereal disease, others maintain that he died as the result of a racist-motivated beating he received after performing near Crowley, while still others say that he was poisoned by a jealous musician. His death certificate indicates only that he died 4 November 1941, of general paresis, and was buried in an unmarked grave on the grounds of the Louisiana State Hospital at Pineville.

BIBLIOGRAPHY

A.A. Savoy: *Cajun Music: a Reflection of a People* (Eunice, LA, 1984)

B.J. Ancelet: "Zarico/Zydeco: the Term and the Tradition," *Creoles of Color of the Gulf South*, ed. J.H. Dormon (Knoxville, TN, 1996)

M. Tisserand: *The Kingdom of Zydeco* (New York, 1998)

R. Brasseaux and K. Fontenot, eds.: *Accordions, Fiddles, Two Steps and Swing* (Lafayette, LA, 2006)

BARRY JEAN ANCELET

Ardoin, John (*b* Alexandria, LA, 8 Jan 1935; *d* San José, Costa Rica, 16 March 2001). Music critic. Ardoin studied composition and music theory at North Texas State College, the University of Texas at Austin, the University of Oklahoma, and at Michigan State University. After completing army service in Germany, he began his professional career in New York City as an editor for *Musical America* and Philharmonic Hall, where he was responsible for program books. Before relocating to Dallas, he also contributed to *The Saturday Review* and *The Times* of London. In 1966 he became the music critic for *The Dallas Morning News*, a position he held until his retirement in 1998. Ardoin's passion was opera: he contributed regularly to the Metropolitan Opera's radio broadcasts and wrote four books about Maria Callas, among them a survey of her recordings (*The Callas Legacy*, 1977) and a reflection upon her teaching (*Callas at Juilliard: the Master Classes*, 1987), which was the inspiration for Terence McNally's Tony Award-winning play *Master Class*. Across his writings, Ardoin delighted in and profiled the soloists, conductors, and composers who populated classical music star culture. He received an honorary doctorate from the University of North Texas in 1987.

ANDREA F. BOHLMAN

A-R Editions. Firm of music publishers. It was founded in New Haven in 1962 by Gary J.N. Aamodt and Clyde Rykken to provide modern critical editions of music of historical interest and artistic integrity for scholars, students, and performers of Western art music. The "Recent Researches" series were launched in 1964 with volumes of music from the Renaissance and Baroque periods; it has since expanded to span the history of Western music. Another series is dedicated to oral traditions in music. The series Recent Researches in American Music was initiated in 1977 in collaboration with the Institute for Studies in American Music. In 1968 the firm moved to Madison, Wisconsin, and the same year took over the production and distribution of the Yale University Collegium Musicum series of historical editions. Starting in 1988, the company has served as publisher for Music of the United States of America (MUSA), a set of scholarly editions, in collaboration with the American Musicological Society and with support from the National Endowment for the Humanities. Other projects have included A-R Special Publications (for performers) and a three book series co-published with the Music Library Assocation.

JEAN M. BONIN/R

Areíto [areyto]. The term variously refers to a large-scale ceremonial/celebratory event, the music-dance practices performed on these occasions, and a "song" based on the recitation or singing of ancient histories (e.g., genealogies), laws, and possibly specific song lyrics. The tradition was practiced by the Taíno (Arawak) peoples living in the Greater Antilles prior to and shortly after the Spanish *Conquista* (Conquest). Our knowledge of *areíto* is very limited, based primarily on the accounts of early European chroniclers (namely Pané, Las Casas, and Oviedo) and archaeological evidence. While no documentation of the specific poetic and musical practices exist today, *areíto* likely involved the use of specific musical instruments and sound makers (such as the *mayohuacán* [a slit-drum], rattles, and perhaps maraca), musical techniques (e.g., antiphonal singing) and dance routines. As a community-based group activity, *areíto* is variously described as a ceremony, celebration, funerary rite, or form of recreation, or as serving specific pedagogical functions.

SEAN BELLAVITI

Arel, Bülent (*b* Istanbul, Turkey, 23 April 1919; *d* Stony Brook, NY, 24 Nov 1990). Composer of Turkish birth. He graduated from the Ankara State Conservatory with a diploma in composition, conducting, and piano performance (1947). In 1951 he studied sound engineering in Ankara with Joze Bernard and Willfried Garret of Radio Diffusion Française. He co-founded the Helikon Society of Contemporary Arts and was the first music director of Radio Ankara's Western music programs (1951–9). With his 1957 work, *Music for String Quartet and Tape*, Arel became a pioneer in the world of electro-acoustic composition. A grant from the Rockefeller Foundation (1959) enabled him to work at the Columbia-Princeton Electronic Music Center, New York, where his compositions and teachings greatly influenced the development of electronic music. In 1965, after establishing Yale University's first electronic music studio (1962), he became a professor at Yale. He went on to found the Electronic Music Studio at SUNY, Stony Brook (1971), where he taught until 1988. Also a painter and sculptor, his artwork is in the permanent collection of the National Gallery.

WORKS

(selective list)

El-ac: Music for Str Qt and Tape, 1957, rev. 1962; Elec Music no.1, tape, 1960; Stereo Elec Music no.1, tape, 1961; Deserts, 1962, collab. Varèse; Mimiana I (dance score), tape, 1968; Capriccio for TV, tape, 1969, collab. J. Seawright; Mimiana II (dance score), tape, 1969; Stereo Elec music no.2, tape, 1970; Out of Into (animated film score), 1971, collab. D. Semegen; Mimiana III (dance score), tape, 1973; Fantasy and Dance, 5 viols, tape, 1974; Rounding (dance score), 1985

Other: Masques, wind, str, 1949; Music for Vn and Pf, 1966

BIBLIOGRAPHY

R. Teitelbaum: "Son-Nova 1988: Electronic Music by Bülent Arel, Mario Davidovsky and Vladimir Ussachevsky," *PNM*, iii/1 (1964), 127 only

A. Shields: *Pioneers of Electronic Music*, Composers Recordings, Inc. CD 611 (1991), [disc notes]

F. Ali: *Elektronik müziğin öncüsü: Bülent Arel* (Istanbul, 2002)

A. Shields: *Columbia-Princeton Electronic Music Center 1961–1973*, New World Records, CD 80521-2 (1998), [disc notes]

DARIA SEMEGEN

Arena rock. A genre of recorded music and performance that peaked in the 1970s. After a decade of the music's development, the label stabilized in critical discourse around 1977. It describes a subset of rock music either designed for, or to evoke, performance in large venues, delivered chiefly by American groups backed by powerful conglomerate record companies. As a marker of its wide popularity, the genre drew the scorn of rockist critics but the adoration of unabashed entertainment seekers. Typical songs are either anthemic, encouraging the vocal and visceral participation of audiences, or of a ballad type, providing moments of repose. Instrumental solo features also figure prominently, showcasing drummer proficiency and reinforcing the ideals of guitar-hero culture. Designed for live performance, these songs also succeed as sonic artifacts, since recordings that include pre-recorded audience noise and rhythmic hand claps frequently give the illusion of concerts. Although recordings are equally deserving of the term, more illumination derives from an examination of its performance history.

In Britain and North America, rock-and-roll concerts in large stadiums were made fashionable by the Beatles during the mid-1960s. Concert promoters subsequently labored to attract crowds in the tens of thousands, while performing in such contexts became the aspiration of rock musicians. The rock festival, itself an outgrowth of folk-music gatherings, maximized rock audiences at a time when the Rolling Stones, Led Zeppelin, and various other British groups held court. As festival culture waned, arena concerts proliferated and the first cadre of leading American arena rock groups came to prominence in the mid-1970s. These groups, which included Aerosmith, Kiss, Styx, Cheap Trick, Journey, and Boston, toured exhaustively in support of their recorded material, catalyzing an informal network of arena rock venues. Their lone American predecessor in this respect was the short-lived and demonstrably less polished trio Grand Funk Railroad.

As against recorded artifacts, live arena rock owes its distinction to its physical setting and to the rapidly improving technological capabilities of the industry, which in combination sharpened the dramatic effects of interiority. Public address speakers grew in number, wattage, and quality to produce an overwhelming potential for amplification. Meanwhile stage lighting, pyrotechnics, smoke machines, and other effects contributed arresting non-aural stimuli. Yet the most elaborate hydraulic mechanisms and props drew the strongest reprobation of critics, who considered such camp especially detractive of musical efforts.

The genesis of the arena rock industry intertwined in two important ways with other facets of American culture. First, it originated at the end of a nationwide renaissance in stadium construction, precipitated by the financial successes of the professional sports trade. Taking its place alongside sports, the genre manifestly contributed to the conversion of arenas into spaces of family entertainment. Thus it provided an opulent and commercial background against which punk rock communities construed themselves. Second, it marked the development of the arena as a regulatory public apparatus, channeling counter-cultural energies in a new age of surveillance away from the expansive festival paradigm toward restricted seating arrangements, more manageable scheduling, and the interchangeability characteristic of high capitalism.

BIBLIOGRAPHY

M. Ethen: *A Spatial History of Arena Rock, 1964–1979* (diss., McGill U., 2011)

MICHAEL ETHEN

Arens, Franz Xavier (*b* Neef, Rheinland, 28 Oct 1856; *d* Los Angeles, CA, 28 Jan 1932). Conductor, composer, and voice teacher of German birth. He was brought to America at age eleven, received his first musical training from his father, Clemens Arens, and later studied with John Singenberger at the Normal College in St. Francis, Wisconsin. After further studies with Joseph Rheinberger in Munich 1881–3 and with Franz Wüllner in Dresden 1883–4, where he earned a Preiszeugnis (one of six in a student body of 734), he settled in Cleveland as conductor of the Cleveland Philharmonic Society and the Cleveland Gesangverein.

He returned to Europe around 1890 to study vocal pedagogy with Julius Hey in Berlin. In 1891 and 1892 he conducted American Composers' Concerts with orchestras in Berlin, Dresden, Leipzig, Weimar, Hamburg, and Sondershausen, concluding his tour with an appearance at the Vienna Musical and Theatrical Exhibition on 5 July 1892. His performances earned mixed reviews from European critics who were unreceptive to American orchestral music, and they stirred a controversy in the United States over the advisability of such "missionary" efforts.

He was director of the Metropolitan School of Music in Indianapolis 1892–6 and was a voice teacher and conductor in New York City from 1896 until his retirement to California in 1920. He was an active member of the Manuscript Society of New York, serving as conductor in 1898 and as president 1908–16. In 1900 he founded the People's Symphony Orchestra, which presented orchestral concerts at affordable prices for students and workers. During World War I the concerts were downsized to chamber music, continuing to the present day thanks to a substantial bequest from Annie Louise Cary (Raymond) in 1921.

Arens was a skillful conductor and committed advocate of American music. He was most productive as a composer during his student years and the early part of his career. His symphonic fantasy, "Aus meines Lebens

Frühlingszeit" [Life's Springtide], op. 12, was performed often under his baton. James Huneker wrote of the première in 1887: "The Orchestral novelty was a Symphonic Fantasie, by F. X. Arens, of Cleveland, an ardent disciple of the new school, who has lots of ideas, knows how to clothe them with the proper orchestral garb, but has much to learn in moderation and self control. The work, however, as a whole, impresses one as the production of a gifted and poetic mind." The manuscripts of this and other unpublished works by Arens have not been located.

WORKS
(selective list)

Chbr: Str Qt, a, 1884

Choral: Salve Regina, 1884; Missa Exultate Deo (New York, 1890); The Lotus Flower, TTBB (Boston, 1905)

Orch: Symphonic Fantasie "Aus meines Lebens Frühlingszeit," op. 12, 1884; Ov., before 1892

Org: Canon and Fugue

Solo vocal: Oh Eyes so Blue and Tender, ?1886; Serenade (New York, 1887); Sendung, before 1892

WRITINGS

My Vocal Method (New York, 1903)

BIBLIOGRAPHY

"The Boston 'Musical Herald' and Mr. Arens," *Musical Courier*, xxv/5 (1892), 7 only

"F. X. Arens," *Musical Courier*, xxv/6 (1892), 7–8

E.D. Bomberger: "A Tidal Wave of Encouragement": *American Composers' Concerts in the Gilded Age* (Westport, CT, 2002)

E. DOUGLAS BOMBERGER

Arévalo, Miguel Santiago (*b* Guadalajara, Mexico, 5 July 1843; *d* Los Angeles, CA, 28 June 1900). Guitarist, composer, and music teacher of Mexican birth. He began his musical studies at the age of 15 in Guadalajara, where he was active in musical circles and where he also probably helped establish the Sociedad Filarmónica Jalisciense (founded 1869). Arévalo left Mexico for San Francisco in 1870, moving permanently to Los Angeles the next year. He became the preeminent guitarist in Los Angeles and Southern California, and was active there through the 1890s. Arévalo was also a teacher of guitar, voice, and piano, and a composer for the guitar. He played in many recitals, society musicales, club events, and other contexts throughout Southern California, and the Spanish- and English-language press frequently mentioned him and favorably reviewed his performances. At least two of his students achieved prominence, including guitarist Luis Toribio Romero and pianist María Pruneda. Arévalo's guitar works are in the standard European and American salon styles of the day, though he also wrote "Latin-tinged" pieces (e.g. his guitar duet *La súplica*, a "danza habanera"). He died in Los Angeles in straightened circumstances. Like guitarist-composer Manuel Ferrer in San Francisco, Arévalo "successfully upheld Mexican cultural prestige against the floodtide of German and Anglo musical immigrants who engulfed Los Angeles in the 1880s" (Stevenson, 60). His published and manuscript works are held at the International Guitar Archive, California State University, Northridge, Vahdah Olcott Bickford Collection.

BIBLIOGRAPHY

R. Stevenson: "Music in Southern California: A Tale of Two Cities," *Inter-American Music Review*, x/1 (1988), 39–111

J. Koegel: "Manuel Y. Ferrer and Miguel S. Arévalo: Premier Guitarist-Composers in Nineteenth-Century California," *Inter-American Music Review*, xvi/2 (2000), 45–66

J. Noonan: *The Guitar in American Banjo, Mandolin and Guitar Periodicals, 1882–1933* (Madison,WI: A-R Editions, 2009)

JOHN KOEGEL

Argento, Dominick (*b* York, PA, 27 Oct 1927). Composer. The son of Sicilian immigrants, he showed early interest in music and began his early education reading Gershwin's biography, writings by Stravinsky, and Rimsky-Korsakov's book on orchestration. Self-taught in theory and analysis, he began piano lessons at age 16. In 1945 he was drafted into the army, and served as a cryptographer in North Africa during World War II. Following the war he entered the Peabody Conservatory in Baltimore as a pianist on the GI Bill of Rights. His harmony teacher, NICOLAS NABOKOV, urged him to focus on composition, and through this influence as well as contact with the Baltimore composer HUGO WEISGALL, Argento's pronounced gift for vocal writing was furthered. It was also during this period that Argento met Carolyn Bailey, a soprano who premiered many of his early compositions, and later became his wife. After graduation from Peabody (BM 1951) he went, on a Fulbright grant, to study in Florence with Luigi Dallapiccola at the Cherubini Conservatory; this altered Argento's previous rejection of dodecaphonic composition. Returning to Peabody (MM 1954), he studied with HENRY COWELL and became musical director of a summer-stock opera company organized by Weisgall, the Hilltop Musical Company, a position which afforded him a practical foundation in opera. The group's stage director, John Scrymgeour, was to be Argento's librettist for seven operatic collaborations and was to co-found with him the Center Opera Company (1963), now Minnesota Opera. Their one-act *The Boor*, after Chekhov, was completed and produced while Argento was at the Eastman School (PhD 1957), where his teachers were RICHARD RODGERS, ALAN HOVHANESS, and HOWARD HANSON.

In 1958 Argento began teaching music theory and composition at the University of Minnesota, Minneapolis; he was appointed Regents' Professor in 1979 and retired in 1997. He was also Composer Laureate for the Minnesota Orchestra. Argento received commissions from nearly every kind of performing organization in Minnesota. It is clear that these influences were essential to his development, yet also evident that the upper midwest is indebted to him, as he clearly helped to further the Twin Cities' recognition on an international stage.

He was awarded the Pulitzer Prize in 1975 for the song cycle *From the Diary of Virginia Woolf*, and was honored by the American Academy and Institute of Arts and Letters in 1976 and elected to membership in 1980. Other awards include the National Music Theatre Award (1986 for his opera *Casanova's Homecoming*), a Grammy Award nomination (1991, Philip Brunelle's recording of his *Te Deum*), an Award for Achievement from Opera America (1993), the Peabody Medal from Johns Hopkins University (1993), the Founders Award from Chorus America (1994), the McKnight Foundation Distinguished Artist Award (1998), an honorary degree from St. Olaf College (2003), the Grammy Award for Classical Contemporary Composition (2004, von Stade's performance of his song cycle *Casa Guidi*), another Grammy Award nomination (2004 for The Dale Warland Singers recording of his choral works *I hate and I love*, *A Toccata of Galuppi's*, and *Walden Pond*), and the World of Song Award from the Music Teachers National Association (2006). He also returned to Florence on two Guggenheim fellowships (1957–8, 1964–5) and has used the city as his base for composition almost every summer since the mid-1960s.

While Argento has written music in every significant 20th-century genre, he is best known for his vocal compositions. In 1963 the establishment in Minneapolis of the Tyrone Guthrie Theatre led to incidental music for Shaw's *St Joan* and Jonson's *Volpone*, 1964, as well as fruitful discussions about the stage. In that same year, *The Masque of Angels* inaugurated the Center Opera Company. It contains some of his finest choral writing before the *Te Deum*; and, as in many of his works, a discreet serialism co-exists with a rich harmonic palette and eclectic musical references, such as chant-like vocal contours which match the libretto in which a group of angels promotes mortal romance in the face of contemporary defeatism.

Argento's compositional output in the 1970s is dominated by opera, and it is through his work in this genre that he attained significant national reputation. Works from this period include the abstract *Postcard from Morocco* (1971); the one-act monodrama *A Water Bird Talk* (1974–6), on Argento's own libretto after Audubon and Chekhov; the full-length *The Voyage of Edgar Allan Poe* (1975–6); and the New York City Opera commission *Miss Havisham's Fire* (1977–8). Although sometimes grouped with American Neo-Romantics, Argento's idiom is more varied than this might suggest. In these operas, and up to *Casanova's Homecoming* (1980–4), he achieved his stated intention to create a distinctly different vocal idiom for each work, which would override harmonic considerations in distinguishing the piece. In *Casanova's Homecoming*, again a work to his own libretto, the second scene of Act 1 is set in an opera house during an 18th-century performance, and material from Jommelli's *Demofoonte* is overlaid with modern sonorities, illustrating Argento's awareness of operatic tradition.

In writing the libretto for his opera *The Aspern Papers* (1988), Argento moved Henry James's setting from Venice to the shores of Lake Como in order to recreate the ambience of 19th-century operatic life as experienced by the artists who resided there. Most significantly, the papers sought by a scholar after the death of the hero, Aspern, are not love letters but an opera manuscript composed by Aspern and suppressed by his mistress. In flashbacks to the 1830s, Argento establishes but quickly dissolves period bel canto musical references. Though greater seamlessness characterizes the works of the 1980s and 1990s, Argento remained capable of juxtaposing stylistic elements as in the multimedia opera *The Dream of Valentino* (1993). The orchestral work *Valentino Dances*, drawn from the opera, captures the lush nuances of American film scoring in material that surrounds a central tango and creates a paean to the genre of film music.

Argento's contribution to the art song repertory is marked by the frequent choice of prose texts and the creation of epistolary song cycles. *Letters from Composers* (1968) is based on the words of seven composers including Chopin, Mozart, and Bach. *From the Diary of Virginia Woolf* (1974), written for Janet Baker, traces Woolf's emotional life to the brink of suicide through eight songs drawn from lines in her journal entries. *The Andrée Expedition* (1982), composed for Håkon Hagegård, is based on the notebooks and diary entries of three ill-fated Swedish explorers who attempted to reach the north pole in a hydrogen balloon, and *Casa Guidi* (1983), for Frederica von Stade, consists of five songs with texts taken from ten different letters which Elizabeth Barrett Browning wrote to her sister Henrietta between 1846 and 1859. *Miss Manners on Music* (1998) is a song cycle in which Argento sets seven different pairs of letters and responses, each consisting of a question posed by a reader regarding etiquette at a musical event, and a humorous response by Judith Martin (Miss Manners), nationally syndicated columnist for *The Washington Post*. In the latter four of the preceding five cycles, Argento uses 12-tone material and occasional polytonality, all within the framework of a harmonic language that is consistently rich, tonal, and accessible.

Though perhaps less known than his operatic and solo vocal works, Argento's choral music comprises the largest category within his oeuvre, and consists of pieces which vary from short, unaccompanied motets to multi-movement works with orchestra. *The Revelation of St John the Divine* (1966) and *Jonah and the Whale* (1973) are two works wherein Argento's instrumentation and musical language are largely symbolic in design, based on the textual themes. Argento approaches *Peter Quince at the Clavier* (1981) and *A Toccata of Galuppi's* (1989) in similar ways, paying homage to the title characters in each work; in *Peter Quince*, he sets the work for chorus and piano, literally seating the title character at the instrument and in *A Toccata of Galuppi's* he brings Browning's evocative text to life by juxtaposing 12-tone serialism with keyboard music by Baldassare Galuppi. *Evensong: Of Love and Angels* (2007) was written as a memorial to his wife Carolyn Bailey Argento, who died in 2006 of a neurological disorder. One of the principal unifying motives consists of a repeating three note pattern, his wife's initials, C–B–A.

Of Argento's choral works, the extended *Te Deum (Verba Domini cum verbis populi)* (1987) for chorus and orchestra and *Walden Pond* (1996) for chorus, harp, and three violoncellos stand as his foremost achievements. In the *Te Deum*, liturgical prayer is paired with the *verbis populi*, anonymous Middle English texts.

This juxtaposition of macaronic texts, a device which also structures his *Spirituals and Swedish Chorales* (1994), allows for varying musical approaches; the solemn, learned cast of the music in the Latin portions, such as the fugal Sanctus in the opening movement, contrasts with vigorous outbursts using full orchestral resources, as in the third movement's vivid refrain. One of Argento's most tonally grounded scores, the *Te Deum*'s religious symbolism is founded on the unifying circle of fifths. In *Walden Pond*, scoring plays an evocative role, in which three cellos and harp support and illustrate the water images in the settings of text compiled by Argento from Thoreau's *Walden*. Much of the structure for this work comes as a result of the composer's use of repeated themes, further unified by recurring sonorities based on the circle of fifths.

While Argento's vocal music is often described as eclectic, several characteristics recur as unifying hallmarks. The theme of self-discovery permeates his entire output. Further, Argento claims his compositional technique exists only in so far as it allows him to effectively communicate text and subtext, resulting in a uniquely intimate relationship between the text and his music.

WORKS

OPERAS

Sicilian Limes (1, J. Olon-Scrymgeour [pseud. of J. Scrymgeour] after L. Pirandello), 1953, Baltimore, Peabody Conservatory, spr. 1954, withdrawn

The Boor (ob, 1, J. Olon [Scrymgeour], after A. Chekhov: *The Bear*), 1957, Rochester, NY, Eastman School of Music, 6 May 1957, vs (New York, 1960)

Colonel Jonathan the Saint (comic op, 4, Olon-Scrymgeour), 1958–61, Denver, Loretto Heights College, 31 Dec 1971

Christopher Sly (comic op, 2 scenes, J. Manlove, after W. Shakespeare: *The Taming of the Shrew*), 1962–3, Minneapolis, U. of Minnesota, 31 May 1963, vs (New York 1968)

The Masque of Angels (1, Olon-Scrymgeour), 1963, Minneapolis, Tyrone Guthrie, 9 Jan 1964, vs (New York, 1964)

The Shoemaker's Holiday (ballad op, 2, Olon-Scrymgeour, after T. Dekker), 1967, Minneapolis, Tyrone Guthrie, 1 June 1967, vs (New York, 1971)

Postcard from Morocco (1, J. Donahue), 1971, Minneapolis, Cedar Village, 14 Oct 1971, vs (New York, 1972)

A Water Bird Talk (monodrama, 1, Argento, after Chekhov and J.J. Audubon), 1974–6, Brooklyn Academy of Music, 19 May 1977, vs (New York, 1980)

The Voyage of Edgar Allan Poe (2, C. Nolte), 1975–6, St Paul, O'Shaughnessy Auditorium, 24 April 1976, vs (New York, 1979)

Miss Havisham's Fire (2, Olon-Scrymgeour, after Dickens), 1977–9, New York, New York State, 22 March 1979, revised again in 1995

Miss Havisham's Wedding Night (monodrama, 1, Olon-Scrymgeour, after C. Dickens: *Great Expectations*), 1977–81, Minneapolis, Tyrone Guthrie, 1 May 1981, vs (New York, 1981)

Casanova's Homecoming (ob, 3, Argento, after J. Casanova: *L'histoire de ma vie*), 1980–4, St Paul, Ordway, 12 April 1985, vs (New York, 1985)

The Aspern Papers (2, Argento, after H. James), 1987, Dallas, Fair Park Music Hall, 19 Nov 1988, vs (1991)

The Dream of Valentino (2, C. Nolte), 1993, Washington DC, Kennedy Center, 15 Jan 1994

OTHER STAGE

The Resurrection of Don Juan (ballet, 1), 1955, Karlsruhe, 24 May 1959, arr. orch suite, 1956; Royal Invitation (Homage to the Queen of Tonga) (ballet, 5 parts), 1964, St Paul, 22 March 1964, arr. orch suite, 1964; St Joan (incid music, G.B. Shaw), 1964; Volpone (incid music, B. Jonson), 1964; S. S. Glencairn (incid music, E. O'Neill), 1966; The House of Atreus (incid music, after Aeschylus: *Oresteia*), 1967

SOLO VOCAL

Songs about Spring (e.e. cummings), 5 songs, S, pf, 1950–55, arr. S, chbr orch, 1960; Ode to the West Wind (conc., P.B. Shelley) S, large orch, 1956; 6 Elizabethan Songs, high v, pf, 1957, arr. high v, baroque ens, 1962; Letters from Composers (F. Chopin, W. Mozart, F. Schubert, J.S. Bach, C. Debussy, G. Puccini, R. Schumann), 7 songs, T, gui, 1968; To be Sung upon the Water (W. Wordsworth), song cycle, high v, cl, pf, 1973; From the Diary of Virginia Woolf (Woolf), song cycle, Mez, pf, 1974; The Andrée Expedition (Journals of Andrée), song cycle, Bar, pf, 1982; Casa Guidi (5 songs, E.B. Browning), Mez, orch, 1983, arr. Mez, pf; A Few Words About Chekhov (A. Chekhov, O. Knipper), Mez, Bar, pf, 1996; Miss Manners on Music (song cycle, J. Martin), Mez, pf, 1998; The Bremen Town Musicians (Argento, after Brothers Grimm), nar, chbr orch, 1999; Three Sonnets of Petrarch (Petrarch, trans Argento) Bar, pf, 2007; Three Meditations (Whitman, de la Mare, Lewis) solo S, 2008

CHORAL

Gloria, SATB, pf/org, 1963, arr. SATB, org, perc, hp, str [from op The Masque of Angels, 1964]; Sanctus, SSAATTBB, pf/org, 1963 [from op The Masque of Angels, 1964]; The Revelation of St John the Divine, rhapsody, T, male chorus, brass, perc, 1966; A Nation of Cowslips (7 bagatelles, J. Keats), SATB, 1968; Tria Carmina Paschalia (Easter cant.) SSA, hp, gui/hpd, 1970; Jonah and the Whale (orat, medieval Eng.), T, B, nar, SATB, small ens, 1973; A Thanksgiving to God, for His House (R. Herrick), SATB, 1979; Let All the World in Every Corner Sing (G. Herbert) SATB, brass qt, timp, org, 1980; Peter Quince at the Clavier (sonatina, W. Stevens), SATB, pf, 1981; I Hate and I Love (Odi et Amo) (song cycle, Catullus), SATB, perc, 1982; Te Deum (Verba Domini cum verbis populi) (Latin Te Deum, anon middle Eng.), SATB, orch, 1987; Easter Day (R. Crashaw), SATB, 1988; A Toccata of Galuppi's (R. Browning), chbr choir, hpd, str qt, 1989; Everyone Sang (S. Sassoon), SSAATTBB, 1991; To God (Herrick), SATB, tpt, 1994; Spirituals and Swedish Chorales, SATB, 1994; Walden Pond (choral cycle, H. Thoreau), SATB, 3 vc, hp, 1996; The Bell-Man (Herrick) SATB, bells, 1998; The Vision (motet, after Dante), chorus, str qt, 1999; Sonnet 64 (In memoriam 9/11/01) (Shakespeare), SATB, 2001; Orpheus (O. Sitwell), SSA, 2002; Four Seascapes (Melville, Wilder, James, Twain), SATB, orch, 2004; Brother Sun, Sister Moon (Argento trans. after St. Francis of Assisi), SATB, organ, 2004; Dover Beach Revisited (Arnold), SATB, pf, 2004; Apollo in Cambridge (Lowell, Holmes, Wadsworth) male chorus, pf, 2005; Evensong: Of Love and Angels (Argento, Biblical) solo treble, S, reader, SATB, orch, 2007; Cenotaph (Sassoon, Binyon, Ecclesiastes, Teasdale) SATB, orch, 2008;The Choir Invisible (Eliot) SATB, 2009; The Choirmaster's Burial (Hardy) SATB, 2009

ORCHESTRAL

Divertimento, pf, str, 1954; The Resurrection of Don Juan, suite, 1955 [based on ballet]; Ov., 1957 [from op The Boor]; Royal Invitation (Homage to the Queen of Tonga), suite, chbr orch, 1964 [based on ballet];

Variations for Orch (The Mask of Night), S [last mvt only], orch, 1965; Bravo Mozart "an Imaginary Biography," vn, ob, hn, orch, 1969; A Ring of Time "Preludes and Pageants for Orch and Bells," 1972; In Praise of Music, 7 songs, 1977; Fire Variations, 8 variations and finale, 1982; Le tombeau d'Edgar Poe, suite, 1985 [based on op The Voyage of Edgar Allan Poe, 1975–6]; Capriccio "Rossini in Paris," cl, orch, 1985; Valentino Dances, 1994 [from op The Dream of Valentino, 1993]; Valse triste, hp, str, 1996; Reverie (Reflections on a Hymn Tune), 1997: see choral [Te Deum, 1987; Four Seascapes, 2004; Evensong, 2007; Cenotaph, 2008] and solo vocal [Ode to the West Wind, 1956; Songs about Spring, arr. 1960; Casa Guidi, 1983; The Bremen-Town Musicians, 1998]

CHAMBER AND SOLO INSTRUMENTAL

Str Qt, 1956; From the Album of Allegra Harper, 2 pf, 1962 [arr. of dance suite from comic op Colonel Jonathan the Saint, 1958–61]; Prelude for Easter Dawning, org, 1982; The Angel Israfil, 2 hp, 1989; Valentino Dances, arr. 2 pf, 1994

Principal publisher: Boosey & Hawkes

BIBLIOGRAPHY

D. Argento: "The Composer and the Singer" *The Nats Bulletin*, xxxiii/3 (1977), 18–31

T.M. Sabatino: *A Performer's Commentary on To be Sung Upon the Water by Dominick Argento* (Ohio State U., 1980)

T.A. Brewer: *Characterization in Dominick Argento's Opera "The Boor"* (diss., U. of Texas, Austin, 1981)

H.F. Sigal: *The Concert Vocal Works of Dominick Argento Performance Analysis* (diss., New York U., 1983)

L.E. Swales: *Characterization in Dominick Argento's Opera "Postcard from Morocco": a Director's Guide* (diss., U. of Iowa, 1983)

E.W. Garton: *Dominick Argento's From the Diary of Virginia Woolf: Elements of Tonality in Twelve Tone Composition* (thesis, Duquesne U., 1986)

D. Argento: "The Matter of Text," *The NATS Journal*, xliv/4 (1987), 6–10

S. Meredith: *Casa Guidi by Dominick Argento: A Musical Discussion* (diss., U. of Iowa, 1987)

C.R. Johnson: *An Examination of Dominick Argento's Te Deum (Verba Domini cum Verbis Populi)* (diss., U. of Cincinnati, 1989)

V. Saya: *The Current Climate for American Musical Eclecticism as Reflected in the Operas of Dominick Argento* (diss., U. of Cincinnati, 1989)

D.P. Ellefson: *The Choral Music of Dominick Argento* (diss., Arizona State U., 1990)

C.L. Gonzalez: *An Analysis of Dominick Argento's "Peter Quince at the Clavier": The Music and its Relationship to the Text* (thesis, U. of North Texas, 1990)

D. Vars: *The Choral Music of Dominick Argento* (diss., U. of Washington, 1991)

D. Argento: "A Contemporary Composer and Sacred Music," *The American Organist*, xxvi/12 (1992), 24–9

W.D. Stevens: *Dominick Argento's Six Elizabethan Songs* (diss., U. of Texas, Austin, 1994)

A.R. Tintner: "*The Aspern Papers*: Dominick Argento's Opera and Henry James's Tale," *Opera Journal*, xxvii/1 (1994), 23–32

N. Woods: *Reflections of a Life: Biographical Perspectives of Virginia Woolf Illuminated by the Music and Drama of Dominick Argento's Song Cycle, From the Diary of Virginia Woolf* (diss., Ohio State U., 1996)

M.A. Paxson: *A Performer's Guide to the Text and Music of Dominick Argento's The Andrée Expedition* (diss., Ohio State U., 1997)

M.R. Smashey: *The Relationship of the Piano Accompaniments to the Texts and Vocal Lines in Dominick Argento's From the Diary of Virginia Woolf* (diss., U. of Missouri, Kansas City, 1997)

J. Stevens: *Notes on the Mono-Opera A Water Bird Talk by Dominick Argento* (diss., Arizona State U., 1997)

J.H. Dowell: *The Monodrama, As Represented by Dominick Argento's A Water Bird Talk* (treatise, The U. of Texas at Austin, 1999)

H.K. Hwang: *Performance Practice Issues in Dominick Argento's Six Elizabethan Songs* (diss., U. of California, Los Angeles, 1999)

L.B. Hanson: *Dominick Argento's Jonah and the Whale: A Study of the Oratorio and Comparison to Representative Twentieth-Century Oratorios* (diss., U. of Cincinnati, Cincinnati, 2001)

S. Savage-Day: *Miss Havisham's Wedding Night: Dominick Argento and the Mad Scene Tradition* (diss., U. of Wisconsin-Madison, 2001)

K.J. Qualls: *Miss Manners on Music: a New Prose Song Cycle for Mezzo-Soprano and Piano by Dominick Argento* (diss., Florida State U., 2002)

B.A. Ray: *Dominick Argento's Casa Guidi: A Character and Musical Study* (diss., U. of Texas, Austin, 2002)

D. Argento: *Catalogue Raisonné as Memoir: a Composer's Life* (Minneapolis, 2004)

R. Blackburn: *Musical Characterization in Dominick Argento's The Andrée Expedition* (diss., Indiana U., 2005)

C.J. Ratner: *Chicago Opera Theatre: Standard Bearer for American Opera, 1976–2001* (diss., Northwestern U., 2005)

H. Wrensch: *Giving Voice to Virginia Woolf: Finding the Musical Coalescence of Dominick Argento's From the Diary of Virginia Woolf* (U. of Kansas, 2005)

E.E. Colwitz: *Dominick Argento's A Toccata of Galuppi's: A Critical Analysis and Its Relationship to the Text* (treatise, U. of Southern California, 2007)

J.G. Lassetter: *Dominick Argento's The Andrée Expedition: A Performer's Musical and Dramatic Analysis* (diss., U. of Cincinnati, 2008)

R.A. Salter: *Dominick Argento's Songs about Spring and Miss Manners on Music: A comparative analysis of compositional styles in poetry versus prose* (diss., U. of Oklahoma, 2009)

M.C. McGaghie: *Macaronic things: Thornton Wilder and the late choral music of Dominick Argento* (diss., Boston U., 2010)

J.D. Mott: *A performer's analysis of Dominick Argento's Miss Havisham's Wedding Night* (U. of North Texas, 2010)

R.D. Hughes: *Textual-Musical Relationships in Three Choral Works by Dominick Argento: Walden Pond, The Vision and Sonnet LXIV (In Memoriam 9/11/01)* (diss., U. of Illinois, 2012)

VIRGINIA SAYA/R. DANIEL HUGHES JR.

Arhoolie. Record company. It was originally established in Los Gatos, California, in 1960 by record collector Chris Strachwitz. The label's first release was bluesman Mance Lipscomb's *Texas Sharecropper and Songster*, of which 250 copies were originally produced. Strachwitz held down a day job as a high school teacher for the first two years of the label's existence, supplementing his income with sales of collectible 78s. In exchange for engineering the recording session at which Country Joe McDonald first recorded "I-Feel-Like-I'm-Fixin'-to-Die Rag," Strachwitz was awarded the publishing rights to the song, which was featured in the *Woodstock* concert documentary film and album, and which brought Arhoolie its "first real money."

While Arhoolie is best known as a blues label, with a roster that includes Big Mama Thornton, Bukka White, Mississippi Fred McDowell, and others, Arhoolie maintains an extensive catalog of Cajun and Zydeco music, featuring artists such as Clifton Chenier, Beausoleil, and Canray Fontenot. The label also has released a wide-ranging collection of Mexican regional and Tejano music from artists such as Freddy Fender, Flaco Jimenez, and others. Arhoolie is the sole American importer of the Dutch world music label Pan and the Austrian blues and gospel label Document, and retains ownership of a retail outlet, Down Home Music Store, located in El Cerrito, California.

THANE TIERNEY

Arista. Record company. It was formally established in New York, New York, by former Columbia Records chief CLIVE DAVIS in June 1974. A year to the day after having been fired from Columbia, Davis signed a deal with Columbia Pictures Industries (unrelated to his former label) to organize their music businesses, which at that time consisted mainly of the Bell label and Screen Gems Music, a publishing company. Other labels owned by the company at the time, but largely dormant, were Colgems (the successor to Colpix) and SGC.

When Davis debuted the newly-organized Arista Records (named for the New York City high school honor society of which he was once a member) in November 1974, its front-line artists included a few holdovers from the Bell era, such as Suzi Quatro, Gryphon, and Tony Orlando and Dawn, plus new signings including Gil Scott-Heron. Surprisingly, it was some of their less-heralded artists—Melissa Manchester, Barry Manilow, and the Outlaws—that would bring the label some of its biggest early successes.

In August 1979, the label was sold to Ariola-Eurodisc GmbH, a division of the German publisher Bertelsmann, at which point the label's distribution was switched from independents to RCA. In 1983, RCA purchased half the label from Ariola, but by 1986, after RCA Records' parent company had been bought by General Electric, Bertelsmann purchased RCA's music business (and, in the process, re-acquired 100% of Arista). During this time, the label achieved major success with Whitney Houston, Aretha Franklin, the Thompson Twins, and Ray Parker Jr. In 1989, Arista established a presence in country music with their Arista Nashville imprint. The following year, Arista found itself in the middle of a scandal after it was disclosed that their Best New Artist Grammy winner, Milli Vanilli, actually hadn't performed on the multi-million-selling album that won them their acclaim.

In 2000, Davis was replaced by Antonio "L.A." Reid, who maintained the label's hitmaking streak with the likes of Avril Lavigne, Usher, OutKast, and P!nk. Reid was forced out in 2004, and the label was subsequently merged with Clive Davis's new venture, J Records, which put Davis back at the helm of the label he'd started more than 30 years earlier. In 2008, Bertelsmann sold out its remaining music business to Sony, and Arista continues to function as part of Sony Music Entertainment's RCA Music Group.

BIBLIOGRAPHY

F. Dannen: *Hit Men: Power Brokers and Fast Money Inside the Music Business* (New York, 1990), 101–7

N. Strauss: "A Salute to Clive Davis, Ousted at Arista Records," *New York Times* (12 April 2000)

THANE TIERNEY

Arizona, University of. The University of Arizona was established as the territory's land grant institution in 1885. The School of Music—an independent entity within the five-unit College of Fine Arts—began as a Department of Music (1893) and took its current name in 1926. In 2009, under director Peter McAllister, the 60-member faculty serviced approximately 550 students. Degrees offered include the BA in music; the BM in composition, jazz studies, music education, and performance; the MM in composition, conducting, ethnomusicology, music education, musicology, music theory, and performance; the DMA in composition, conducting, and performance; and the PhD in music education and music theory. The Fine Arts Library houses collections for the College of Fine Arts and College of Architecture, with notable music collections such as the National Flute Association Library, Conley Choral Library, Frank Simon Band Library, Hill and Phillips Collections of popular sheet music, and the Nelson Riddle and Artie Shaw Collections.

SHELLY C. COOPER

Arlen, Harold [Arluck, Hyman] (*b* Buffalo, NY, 15 Feb 1905; *d* New York, NY 23 April 1986). Composer. Arlen was the son of a cantor and sang in his father's synagogue, but his attraction to popular music soon led him to become a pianist for local bands and silent movies. In 1925 he went to New York to work as arranger for Fletcher Henderson and as a rehearsal pianist in radio. He began his compositional career by writing cabaret numbers and interpolations for Broadway revues. Arlen's first success was the song "Get Happy" for *9:15 Revue* (1930). Introduced by Ruth Etting, the number has a lyric by Ted Koehler and remains one of Arlen's best-known songs.

He continued to work as a pianist and composer, writing several Harlem Cotton Club revues with Koehler, one of which included "Stormy Weather," a song Ethel Waters made into an American standard. He contributed material to the *Earl Carroll Vanities* (1930), *You Said It* (1931), *George White's Music Hall Varieties*, and *Americana* (1932). *Life Begins at 8:40* (1934) was something of a turning point: on this show, he collaborated with E.Y. Harburg and Ira Gershwin, as well as stars Ray Bolger and Bert Lahr. Arlen's next show, *Hooray for What!* (1937), was a star vehicle for Ed Wynn and once more had lyrics by Harburg.

He then left for Hollywood, where his prolific work included *Let's Fall in Love* (1934), *The Singing Kid* (1936), *Gold Diggers of 1937* (1936), and *Love Affair* (1939). The score for which Arlen enjoys by far the greatest renown is *The Wizard of Oz* (1939), which includes the Oscar-winning song "Over the Rainbow." Working with lyricist Harburg and star Judy Garland on this film proved to be inspirational for Arlen, and *Oz* is widely considered to be amongst the greatest movie musicals of all time. Subsequent film scores included *The sky's the limit* (1943) for Fred Astaire and the remake of *A star is born* (1954), starring Garland and with lyrics by Ira Gershwin. The highlight of *A star is born* was the torch song "The man that got away." The film was the climax of Arlen's Hollywood career, though he later wrote songs for the cartoon *Gay Purr-ee* (1962) and the title song for *I could go on singing* (1963), both of which involved Garland and Harburg.

The composer's later Broadway career was less high profile and did not include any long-running hits, but the quality of his work remained consistently high. Arlen joined forces with Harburg for *Bloomer Girl* (1944) and with Johnny Mercer on *St. Louis Woman* (1946). Artistic success continued with *House of Flowers* (1954); Arlen wrote the lyrics in collaboration with author Truman Capote. He then returned to Harburg for *Jamaica* (1957) and to Mercer for the unsuccessful *Saratoga* (1959). The same year, he also created a "blues opera," *Free and Easy*, based on *St. Louis Woman*; after performances in Amsterdam and Paris, it disappeared. In later years he worked on two unproduced musicals: one for television, *Clippity Clop and Clementine* (1973), to his own lyrics, and the stage show *Softly* (1966), with words by Martin Charnin. Arlen was also a performer of some renown and appeared as a vocalist on several recordings, including albums by Barbra Streisand and Duke Ellington.

Arlen is something of a connoisseur's composer, someone whose name is somehow held in greater esteem by those inside the music industry—Sondheim has often spoken of his regard for Arlen's music—than by the public at large. In his later years, he became a recluse and shunned the wider recognition that he could have pursued. Yet the best of his music has many distinctive qualities, the most important of which is a strong African American influence. He combined the structure of the popular 32-bar song form with the harmonic and gestural aspects of commercialized jazz forms, especially blues. Though he worked with numerous lyricists, his prolific work with Mercer and Harburg is surely the most potent and important, not least because these writers were also able to assimilate black and colloquial aspects into their words in the same way that Arlen did in his music.

WORKS

STAGE

(All are musicals and all dates are those of first New York performance, unless otherwise stated. Librettists and lyricists are listed in that order in parentheses.)

You Said It (J. Yellen, S. Silvers; Yellen, T. Koehler), orchd H. Jackson, 19 Jan 1931 [incl. Sweet and Hot, While You are Young, It's Different with Me, Learn to Croon, If He Really Loves Me]

Life Begins at 8:40 (revue, D. Freedman, H.I. Phillips, A. Baxter, H.C. Smith, F. Gabrielson; I. Gershwin, E.Y. Harburg), orchd H. Spialek, 27 Aug 1934 [incl. You're a Builder-Upper, Fun to be Fooled, Let's Take a Walk Around the Block, I Couldn't Hold My Man, What Can You Say in a Love Song?]

Hooray for What? (H. Lindsay, R. Crouse; Harburg), orchd D. Walker, 1 Dec 1937 [incl. God's Country, Moanin' in the Mornin', Down with Love, In the Shade of the New Apple Tree, Buds Won't Bud, I've Gone Romantic on You]

Bloomer Girl (F. Saidy, S. Herzig; Harburg), orchd R.R. Bennett, T. Royal, 5 Oct 1944 [incl. The Eagle and Me, Right as the Rain, It was Good Enough for Grandma, Evelina, Sunday in Cicero Falls]

St. Louis Woman (A. Bontemps, C.P. Cullen; J. Mercer), orchd Royal, A. Small, M. Salta, W. Paul, 30 Mar 1946; rev. as Free and Easy (addl lyrics, Koehler), orchd Q. Jones, B. Byers, Amsterdam, Netherlands, 17 Dec 1959 [incl. Come Rain or Come Shine, Any Place I Hang my Hat is Home, I had Myself a True Love, Legalize my Name, I Wonder what Became of Me]

House of Flowers (T. Capote; Capote, Arlen), orchd Royal, 30 Dec 1954 [incl. A Sleepin' Bee, Two Ladies in de Shade of de Banana Tree, Bamboo Cage, I'm Gonna Leave Off Wearin' my Shoes, I Never has Seen Snow, Don't like Goodbyes]

Jamaica (Harburg, Saidy; Harburg), orchd P.J. Lang, 31 Oct 1957 [incl. Pretty to Walk With, Push de Button, Cocoanut Sweet, Take it Slow Joe, Leave the Atom Alone]

Saratoga (M. DaCosta; Mercer), orchd Lang, 7 Dec 1959 [incl. Petticoat High, Love Held Lightly, Goose Never be a Peacock, You or No One]

FILMS

Let's Fall in Love (Koehler), 1934; Gold Diggers of 1937 (Harburg), 1936; The Singing Kid (Harburg), 1936; Stage Struck (Harburg), 1936; Strike me Pink (L. Brown), 1936; At the Circus (Harburg), 1939; The Wizard of Oz (Harburg), orchd H. Stothart, 1939 [incl. Over the Rainbow]; Blues in the Night (Mercer), 1941 [incl. Blues in the Night, This Time the Dream's on Me]; Star Spangled Rhythm (Mercer), 1942 [incl. That Old Black Magic]; The Sky's the Limit (Mercer), 1943 [incl. One for my Baby, My Shining Hour]

Here Come the Waves (Mercer), 1944 [incl. Ac-cent-tchu-ate the Positive]; Kismet (Harburg), 1944; Up in Arms (Koehler), 1944; Casbah (L. Robin), 1948 [incl. For Every Man there's a Woman, What's Good about Goodbye?]; My Blue Heaven (R. Blane, Arlen), 1950; The Petty Girl (Mercer), 1950; Mr. Imperium (D. Fields), 1951; Down Among the Sheltering Palms (Blane, Arlen), 1953; The Farmer Takes a Wife (Fields), 1953; The Country Girl (Gershwin), 1954; A Star is Born (Gershwin), 1954 [incl. The Man that Got Away]; Gay Purr-ee (Harburg), 1962; I Could Go on Singing (Harburg), 1963

SONGS

(selective list; except for films, all dates are those of first New York performance.)

The Album of my Dreams (L. Davis), 1929; Get Happy (Koehler), in 9:15 Revue, 1930; Out of a Clear Blue Sky (Koehler), in Earl Carroll Vanities, 1930; Linda, Song of the Gigolo (Koehler), in Brown Sugar, 1930; I Love a Parade, Between the Devil and the Deep Blue Sea (Koehler), in Rhythmania, 1931; I Gotta Right to Sing the Blues (Koehler), in Earl Carroll Vanities, 1932; Satan's Li'l Lamb (Harburg, Mercer), in Americana, 1932; I've got the World on a String (Koehler), in Cotton Club Parade, 1932

Cabin in the Cotton (I. Caesar, G. White), Two Feet in Two Four Time (Caesar), in George White's Music Hall Varieties, 1932; It's Only a Paper Moon (B. Rose, Harburg), in The Great Magoo, 1932; Stormy Weather (Koehler), in Cotton Club Parade, 1933; Ill Wind (Koehler), in Cotton Club Parade, 1934; Last Night when We were Young (Harburg), 1935; How's by You?, Song of the Woodman (Harburg), in The Show is On, 1936; Happiness is a Thing Called Joe (Harburg), in Cabin in the Sky (film), 1943

INSTRUMENTAL

(selective list)

Minor Gaff, blues fantasy, pf, collab. D. George, 1926; Rhythmic Moments, pf, 1928; Mood in Six Minutes, orchd R.R. Bennett, 1935; American Minuet, orch, 1939; Americanegro Suite (Koehler), vv, pf, 1941

BIBLIOGRAPHY

E. Jablonski: *Harold Arlen: Happy With the Blues* (Garden City, NY, 1961; reprint New York, 1985)

E. Jablonski: *Harold Arlen: Rhythm, Rainbows and Blues* (Boston, 1996)

DOMINIC McHUGH

Armenian American music. *See* EUROPEAN AMERICAN MUSIC.

Armenteros, Alfredo [Chocolate] (*b* Ranchuelo, Las Villas, Cuba, 4 April 1928). Cuban trumpet player. Known for his uniquely traditional Cuban style, Armenteros began playing trumpet in the youth municipal band of Ranchuelo. After moving to Havana in 1949, he made his first recordings with René Álvarez y Su Conjunto titled "Llegó María La 'O" and "Jovenes del muelle." He later became a member of Arsenio Rodríguez y Su Conjunto and the Beny Moré orchestra, performing on Cuban radio as well as recordings. Armenteros performed in New York for the first time in 1956 as a member of Fajardo y Sus Estrellas. Soon afterward he moved there, performing and recording with Machito and His Afro-Cubans, La Sonora Matancera, Larry Harlow, Moncho Leña, Charlie Palmieri, Eddie Palmieri, Grupo Folklórico y Experimental Nuevayorquino, and many others through the 1970s. Since then he has recorded with Cachao, John Santos, and Poncho Sanchez, as well as leading his own recording projects totaling more than eight albums. His ongoing performance and recording career encompasses seven decades. Recordings of his playing demonstrate the idiomatic markers of Cuban trumpet playing and music, including *son*, *comparsa*, *guajira*, bolero, and *guaguancó*.

BIBLIOGRAPHY

R. Davies: *Trompeta: Chappottín, Chocolate, and the Afro-Cuban Trumpet Style* (Lanham, MD, 2003)

DAVID F. GARCIA

Armer, Elinor (Florence) (*b* Oakland, CA, 6 Oct 1939). Composer, pianist, and educator. She studied composition at Mills College (BA 1961), the University of California, Berkeley (1966–8), and California State University, San Francisco (MA 1972). Her teachers included ROGER NIXON, DARIUS MILHAUD, and LEON KIRCHNER (composition), and Alexander Libermann (piano). In 1976 she began teaching at San Francisco Conservatory of Music, where she founded the composition department and, as its head (1985–96), built a program with a high international profile that attracted gifted composers and significant endowments. She continues to teach composition there part-time. Eschewing such directions as serial writing and minimalism, she has developed an individual voice that draws together diverse materials through strong articulation of phrasing and gesture. Her compositions are often programmatic yet avoid musical literalism. Even with her recent focus on instrumental works, Armer often generates compositions using unidentified programmatic or visual elements. Typical of her compositions, *Lockerbones/Airbones* melds strong metrical, dance-like rhythms with ambiguous temporal treatment, created with shifting subdivisions as well as indeterminate notation. Developed in collaboration with author Ursula K. Le Guin, *Uses of Music in Uttermost Parts* is an imaginative cycle of eight separate works for various forces, all of which were released on a two-CD set (Koch 3-7331-2). In this fantasy journey through an archipelago, each island puts music to extraordinary uses, for example as food, aphrodisiac, weaving, geology, or as a means of survival. The first piece in this cycle, *The Great Instrument of the Geggerets*, employs a variety of styles, producing a wide range of expression: dense textures of sound mass occur alongside extended instrumental techniques, a tuneful waltz, and allusions to ragtime. *Open and Shut*, the fifth work in the cycle, exemplifies her successful mix of playful and abstract elements. Her rich harmonic vocabulary is atonal—but not exclusively—and her scoring is imaginative and vivid. Armer has made notable contributions with her percussion ensemble works, and her skillful treatment of percussion is also evident in Concerto for Piano and Orchestra (2008), one of her most significant works. She is the recipient of numerous commissions, awards, and fellowships. Her manuscripts and sketches are archived at the UC Berkeley Library.

WORKS

(selective list)

Orch: Pearl, 1986; The Great Instrument of the Geggerets (U.K. Le Guin), nar, orch, 1989 [Uses of Music in Uttermost Parts no.1]; Call of the West, 2006; Concerto for Piano and Orchestra, 2008

Chbr and solo inst: Thaw, pf, 1974; Are You Sleeping?, 5 perc, cel, 1976; Recollections and Revel, vc, pf, 1978; Str Qt, 1983; The Seasons of Oling (Le Guin), nar, va, vc, pf, perc, 1987 [Uses of Music no.3]; Open and Shut (Le Guin), reader, ob/eng hn, cl/b cl, vn, vc, db, 1991 [Uses of Music no.5]; Sailing among the Pheromones, gui, mar, hp, tape, 1991 [Uses of Music no.6]; Mirror, Mirror, pf 4 hands, 1993; Oasis, hp, 1996; Open & Shut, ob, cl, vn, vc, db, nar, 2001; Ringing In, 4 perc, 2006; Trout Surviving, 3 perc, 2007; Tidepool, pf, hpd, 2008; String Quartet 2011

Vocal: Spin, Earth (J.R. Baughan), mixed vv, pf/org, 1970; Lockerbones/Airbones (Le Guin), Mez, fl, vn, pf, perc, 1983; Eating with the Hoi (Le Guin), S, nar, chorus, perc, 1986 [Uses of Music no.4]; A Season of Grief (A. Tennyson and W. Bynner), Mez/Bar, pf, 1987; Anithaca (Le Guin), girls' vv, 1990 [Uses of Music no.2]; Island Earth (Le Guin), chorus, orch, 1993 [Uses of Music no.8]; She-Who Apple Songs (Judy Grahn), 3 S, wws/pf, 1999; Eve's Apologie (Amelia Lanier, also spelled Lanyer), 3 S, hpd, 2004; Eine Kleine Snailmusik (May Sarton), Mez, pf, 2005

MSS in BE

Principal publishers: J.B. Elkus & Sons, Fallen Leaf, Lawson-Gould, MMB, Peters

BIBLIOGRAPHY

E. Armer: "A Conversation with Vivian Fine Two Composers Talk Shop," *Strings*, v/5 (1991), 73–8

P. Moor: "Armer: Uses of Music in Uttermost Parts," *Audio*, lxxx/7 (July 1996), 75

A.P. Matson: *An Organic Program: Uses of Music in Uttermost Parts*, i (diss., UCLA, 1997)

G. Raps: "Creative Collaboration: Elinor Armer and Ursula Le Guin. An Interview," *Persimmontree* 15 (Fall 2010), <http://www.persimmontree.org/articles/Issue15/articles/GenaRaps_CreativeCollaboration.php>

J. MICHELE EDWARDS

Armonica. An improved form of musical glasses invented by BENJAMIN FRANKLIN in 1761, in which a row of glass bowls, nested within one another concentrically, is mounted on a horizontal axle which is turned with a pedal.

Armstrong, Anton (Eugene) (*b* West Hempstead, NY, 26 April 1956). Music educator, choral arranger, editor, and conductor. He was a member of the American Boychoir (1969–71), and received degrees from St Olaf College (BM 1978), the University of Illinois at Urbana–Champaign (MM 1980), and Michigan State University (DMA 1987). He was on the summer faculty of the American Boychoir School and now serves on the Board of Trustees. He taught at Calvin College (1980–90) before becoming the fourth conductor of the St Olaf Choir and the Harry R. and Thora H. Tosdal Endowed Professor of Music (1990–). Armstrong is the editor for *Earthsongs* publications and co-editor of the *St. Olaf Choir Series*. He chronicled the history of the St Olaf Choir in his doctoral dissertation. He is featured on an instructional video for adolescent singers, *Body, Mind, Spirit, Voice* (2002), and is a contributing author for *Teaching Music through Performance in Choir* (2005) and the founding conductor of the Oregon Bach Festival Stangeland Family Youth Choral Academy (1998). He received the Robert Foster Cherry Award for Great Teaching from Baylor University (2006), and is recognized for his expertise in the area of youth and children's choral music.

BIBLIOGRAPHY

J.M. Shaw: *The St. Olaf Choir: a Narrative* (Northfield, MN, 1997)

GREG A. HANDEL

Armstrong, (William) Howard (Taft) (*b* Dayton, TN, 4 March 1909; *d* Boston, MA, 30 July 2003). Fiddler and mandolinist. Armstrong was born in Dayton, the county seat of Rhea County in East Tennessee and raised in Lafollette in Campbell County. He was a multi-faceted instrumentalist who was not only a great fiddler and mandolinist, but also played 20 other instruments, spoke seven languages, and was a talented, imaginative painter. When Armstrong was a young boy, his father moved the family to Lafollette, north of Knoxville, Tennessee. Around this time Armstrong began playing fiddle and mandolin in a family band with his brothers. In 1930 he took part in a now-historic recording session for Vocalion Records, playing fiddle with the Tennessee Chocolate Drops, an African American string band that included the guitarist Carl Martin, the mandolinist Ted Bogan, and Martin's step-brother the bass player Roland Martin. With Martin and Bogan, Armstrong became a traveling musician, moving from the southern Appalachian Mountains to the Midwest. The trio settled in Chicago where they played in taverns and appeared at the World's Fair in 1933. Armstrong worked as a sign painter and an automobile factory worker in Detroit from 1944 until 1971.

Having been rediscovered in 1971, Martin, Bogan, and Armstrong renewed their careers as recording and performing artists. Armstrong received a National Heritage Fellowship from the National Endowment for the Arts in 1990. He was the subject of two PBS television documentary programs, "Louie Bluie" (1985) and "Sweet Old Song" (2002).

RICHARD BLAUSTEIN

Armstrong, Karan (*b* Havre, MT, 14 Dec 1941) Soprano and director. As a child she studied piano and clarinet; later she received the BA from Concordia College in Minnesota and studied singing privately with a number of teachers including LOTTE LEHMANN in Santa Barbara. She sang Elvira (in Rossini's *L'italiana in Algeri*) for her debut with the San Francisco Opera in 1966, and a year later she sang for the first time at the Metropolitan Opera as the Dew Fairy in Engelbert Humperdinck's *Hänsel und Gretel*. She appeared at Santa Fe (1968) and the Caramoor Festival (1974), and was a member of the New York City Opera from 1975 to 1978. Her European career has included a very successful Salome at Strasbourg (1976), a role she repeated in Munich, Vienna, and elsewhere. She made her debut at Bayreuth as Elsa (in Wagner's *Lohengrin*) in 1979 and at Covent Garden in the title role of Berg's *Lulu* in 1981.

Over the next decade she came to be known for her involvement in opera premieres in which her strong voice, striking appearance, and acting ability were found particularly effective for contemporary music, earning her the nickname "prima donna of modern music." These included the role of Death in Gottfried von Einem's *Jesu Hochzeit* in Vienna (1980), Giuseppe Sinopoli's *Lou Salomé* (1981), Luciano Berio's *Un re in ascolto* (1984), York Höller's *Maître et Marguerite* (1989), and Siegfried Matthus's *Desdemona und ihre Schwestern* (1991). As her voice has matured and darkened, she has expanded her repertoire to include character and dramatic roles such as Leonore (*Fidelio*), Klytaemnestra (*Elektra*), the Old Lady (*Candide*), and Ortrud (*Lohengrin*). Her appearances on video include a performance as Alice Ford in Verdi's *Falstaff* under Georg Solti's direction and as Elsa in Wagner's *Lohengrin* under Woldemar Nelsson. In 2009 she made her debut as a director in a new production of Verdi's *La Traviata* at the Vjoldkstheater Rostack. In 1985, she was awarded the title of *Kammersängerin* in Baden-Württemberg and in 1994 she received the same title in Berlin.

BIBLIOGRAPHY

R.R. Reif: *Karan Armstrong: Das Mädchen aus dem goldenen Westen* (Langen, 1995)

ELIZABETH FORBES/JOSEPH E. MORGAN

Armstrong [née Hardin], **Lil(lian)** (*b* Memphis, TN, 3 Feb 1898; *d* Chicago, IL, 27 Aug 1971). Jazz pianist, singer, bandleader, and composer. She studied keyboard privately from an early age and had hopes of becoming a concert pianist. While she was enrolled at Fisk University, her mother and stepfather moved to Chicago, where in 1917 she took a job as a sheet music demonstrator, which led to her joining the Original Creole Jazz Band as its pianist. It was her first job playing jazz and she decided not to return to Fisk. She subsequently worked with several bands, including King Oliver's Creole Jazz Band, with which she performed in San Francisco in 1921 and made her recording debut in 1923. By this time the band included LOUIS ARMSTRONG, whom she married in 1924. Armstrong's place in jazz history was assured by her participation on Oliver's Gennett recordings and Louis's Hot Five sessions for Okeh. She played an important role in Louis's move into a brighter spotlight before their separation in 1931. For the next two decades Armstrong toured with her own bands, billed early on as "Mrs Louis Armstrong and her Orchestra." In the late 1930s she recorded for Decca and eventually became the label's house pianist. In the 1940s she attended and graduated from a school for men's tailoring, but soon returned to music. Armstrong worked as a solo act and with small groups in the United States and Europe throughout the 1950s. She recorded occasionally during the same period and made her last, in Chicago, in 1961, although she contined to perform for another ten years. Armstrong's compositions include "Struttin' with some barbecue," a Louis Armstrong classic that became a Dixieland perennial, and "Just for a Thrill," which Ray Charles revived and turned into a hit in 1959.

SELECTED RECORDINGS

As a leader: *Lil Hardin Armstrong* (1961, Fantasy OJCCD)
As a sideman with Louis Armstrong: *Hot Fives and Sevens* (1925, JSP)

BIBLIOGRAPHY

L.H. Armstrong and R.S. Greene: "Satchmo and Me," *American Music*, xxv/1 (2007), 106–18

J.J. Taylor: "With Lovie and Lil: Rediscovering Two Chicago pianists of the 1920s," *Big Ears: Listening for Gender in Jazz Studies*, eds. N.T. Rustin and S. Tucker (Durham, NC, 2008), 48–63

<http://stomp-off.blogspot.com/2009/08/new-orleans-creole-jazz-band.htm>

<http://stomp-off.blogspot.com/2009/11/as-we-return-to-lil-armstrongs.html>

<http://stomp-off.blogspot.com/2010/08/lil-armstrong-interview-1-of-2.html>

<http://stomp-off.blogspot.com/2010/09/lil-poses-for-me-with-louis-old-trumpet.html>

CHRIS ALBERTSON

Armstrong, Louis [Dippermouth; Papa Dip; Pops; Satchelmouth; Satchmo] (*b* New Orleans, LA, 4 Aug 1901; *d* New York, NY, 6 July 1971). Trumpeter, singer, and entertainer.

1. Life. 2. Recordings. 3. Compositions. 4 Films and shows. 5. Legacy.

1. Life. Despite his lifelong claim of 4 July 1900 as his birthday, Armstrong was actually born on 4 August 1901 as recorded on a baptismal certificate discovered after his death. Although calling himself "Louis Daniel Armstrong" in his 1954 autobiography, he denied knowledge of his middle name or its origin. Nevertheless, evidence of "Daniel" being a family name is strong: Armstrong's paternal great-great-grandfather, a third generation slave brought from Tidewater Virginia for sale in New Orleans in 1818, was named Daniel Walker, as was his son, Armstrong's great-grandfather. The latter's wife, Catherine Walker, sponsored her great-grandson's baptism at the family's home parish, the Sacred Heart of Jesus Catholic Church on Canal Street.

Armstrong's mother, Mary ("Mayann") Albert (1885–1927), a recent arrival in New Orleans from rural Boutte, Louisiana, was living with relatives "back o' town" on Jane Alley when she met Catherine and Daniel Walker's grandson, William Armstrong (1880–1933), residing just around the corner on South Dupree. William abandoned the family soon after his son's birth but a short-lived reconciliation with Mayann produced a second child, Beatrice ("Mama Lucy") two years later.

Initially, Louis stayed with his paternal grandmother, Josephine, while his mother, working as a domestic and part-time prostitute, came and went. Around age five, he joined his mother, sister, and a parade of "step-fathers" at a dilapidated tenement on Perdido Street in the colored red-light district. From here he attended Fisk School nearby, "wailed" enthusiastically at the sanctified Baptist church across the street, "second-lined" marching brass bands, and absorbed the proto-jazz mixture of ragtime and blues pouring from surrounding honky-tonks, brothels, and saloons.

Before age ten Armstrong began contributing to the family income by selling newspapers, delivering coal, or collecting junk by day and singing with a quartet on the street by night. On New Year's Eve 1912, he was arrested for firing his "step-father's" pistol in public and, as a "repeat offender," remanded to the Colored Waif's Home on the edge of the city. The Home, a military reform school for boys run by ex-cavalry officer Joseph Jones, provided Armstrong with a daily routine, regular meals, and his instruction on the cornet from band director Peter Davis. Soon appointed leader of the school band, which often paraded and performed in and around the city, he was unhappy to leave the Home when released to his father's custody after 18 months.

William Armstrong, a "charcoal man" at a turpentine company whose wife was expecting her third child, had petitioned the court to release Louis to cook for his family and mind his young boys. When his extra mouth

Louis Armstrong, c1930. (Private Collection/ Peter Newark American Pictures/The Bridgeman Art Library)

proved too expensive for his father's household after a few months, Louis rejoined Mayann and Mama Lucy, resumed delivering coal or selling newspapers, and obtained his first job as a professional musician, playing the blues for pimps and prostitutes at a local tavern. Upon his cousin Flora's death, 14-year-old Armstrong "adopted" her illegitimate son, Clarence (1915–1998). This child, who later suffered brain damage from a fall, remained in Armstrong's care for the rest of his life, putting a strain on more than one of the trumpeter's four marriages.

Armstrong idolized King Oliver, reputedly the best cornetist in the city, who reciprocated by giving the boy lessons and recommending him for gigs. Oliver left New Orleans for Chicago in early 1919, ceding his place in the highly regarded Kid Ory Band to his protégé. That summer, Armstrong, newly but unhappily married to prostitute Daisy Parker (*c*1897–1950), joined Fate Marable's riverboat band in which he played through 1921, taking odd jobs in New Orleans during the off-season. Since bands on the river played for dancing from stock arrangements, Armstrong, tutored by Marable and fellow bandsman David Jones, learned to read music for the first time. Armstrong claimed to have met and subsequently to have been influenced by Bix Beiderbecke. On a trip upriver to Davenport, Iowa from St. Louis, the riverboats' summer hub.

In late summer 1922 Oliver summoned Armstrong to join his Creole Jazz Band at the Royal Gardens cabaret in Chicago. Here the cornetist played second to Oliver's lead, intriguing audience and musicians alike by his faultless harmony on "improvised" duet breaks. While with Oliver, Armstrong met, wooed and (after a quickie divorce) married Lillian (Lil) Hardin (1898–1971), the Creole Band's pianist, in 1924. Lil encouraged her husband to leave Oliver and establish his own career with Fletcher Henderson in New York City. Armstrong spent a little over a year with Henderson as the band's "hot" soloist before being lured back to Chicago in late 1925 by his wife, who negotiated an "unheard-of salary" for him as the "World's Greatest Jazz Cornetist" in her new band at the Dreamland cabaret on the South Side. Simultaneously Armstrong began recording a now historic series of small-group sides, collectively known as the Hot Fives and Hot Sevens, which extended through 1928. One of these recordings, "Heebie Jeebies," forever identified Armstrong with scat singing.

Shortly after his return to Chicago, Armstrong began doubling with Erskine Tate's Orchestra, playing for silent films at the Vendome Theater a few blocks from the Dreamland. Having alternated between trumpet with Henderson and cornet on small-group recordings in New York, he now switched permanently from the latter instrument to the former. His high-register playing and dramatic solos on operatic numbers with Tate attracted crowds as well as the attention of Alpha Smith (1907–43), who would become his third wife. When the Dreamland closed for liquor violations in 1926, Armstrong doubled from the Vendome to the Sunset Café four blocks away, whose band included pianist Earl Hines. At the Sunset, a black-and-tan dance hall that also staged elaborate floor shows, Louis honed his entertainment skills by adding mugging, dancing, and singing to his act, all of which he had been discouraged from doing with Oliver and Henderson.

The year 1927 was one of professional and personal instability for Armstrong. Early that year the leader of the Sunset Café Band, Carroll Dickerson, was fired and the group reborn as Armstrong's Stompers. The publication of Armstrong's transcribed "hot choruses" and jazz breaks in the middle of the year testified to the trumpeter's growing popularity but was marred by the death of his mother, which, notwithstanding her apparent shortcomings as a parent, left her son disconsolate. By year's end the Sunset had closed, Armstrong's attempts to operate his own dance hall with Hines and drummer Zutty Singleton had failed, and, having earlier left the Vendome, he returned to being the "feature man" in a movie theater orchestra.

Armstrong spent most of his final two years in Chicago fronting the reunited Sunset Café Band under Dickerson (but minus Hines) at the new Savoy Ballroom. Financial difficulties at the Savoy in 1929 prompted him to take the band to New York City, where his record-producer manager, Tommy Rockwell, eventually found them work in Harlem substituting for the house band at Connie's Inn. Connie's band was then on Broadway accompanying Fats Waller and Andy Razaf's *Hot Chocolates,* in which Armstrong's cameo appearance on "Ain't Misbehavin'" caused a sensation and introduced him to a sizable white audience.

Fired from Connie's Inn in early 1930 after the close of "Hot Chocolates," Armstrong broke up his band, briefly reconciled with Lil and traveled with her to Los Angeles where he had been hired to front the Sebastian's New Cotton Club Orchestra, which included Lionel Hampton. A recording with country singer Jimmie Rodgers earned Louis and Lil early crossover credit, and an appearance in *Ex-Flame* (of which no trace survives) inaugurated Armstrong's movie career. Regarding the West Coast as his new home, Armstrong canceled his contract with Rockwell, who wanted him back at Connie's Inn. But a tip to the police by a rival club owner got Armstrong arrested for smoking marijuana, a drug which he used with apparent impunity for the rest of his life. After serving minimal jail time in March 1931, he fled to the Midwest where his new manager, Johnny Collins, booked him into a Chicago club. When a feud with Rockwell over his client's services appeared to threaten the trumpeter's safety, Collins found Armstrong a summer residency at the white Suburban Gardens dance hall in New Orleans.

On his first trip home since leaving nine years earlier, the black community greeted "Little Louie" with a hot jazz band and carried him on their shoulders down Canal Street. Before the large crowd gathered at the Suburban Gardens for the band's first performance, the white radio announcer could not bring himself to "announce that nigger" (Jones and Chilton, 148). Unfazed, Armstrong took the microphone and introduced himself—something unprecedented in Jim Crow New Orleans. With dancers thronging the Gardens nightly, Louis enjoyed his three-month stay in the Crescent City. He organized a baseball team (the Armstrong Nine), which played conservatively to avoid soiling their new uniforms, and paid well publicized visits to relatives, old haunts, and the Colored Waif's Home. Racism, though, probably instigated the precipitous cancellation of a farewell concert for his black fans and unquestionably caused the band's arrest and temporary imprisonment in Memphis during their subsequent tour of southern states.

In mid-1932 before settling out of court with Rockwell, Collins sent Armstrong on a four-month tour of England, where the performer's exuberant onstage demeanor and altissimo playing both shocked and fascinated skeptical British audiences. A year later Armstrong was greeted tumultuously by crowds on an 18-month tour of Europe, although he had to curtail his playing for a large portion of the trip because of lip problems. Recuperating in Paris, he jammed with gypsy guitarist Django Reinhardt, who, inspired by these sessions, founded (with Stephane Grappelli) the first European jazz band of significance. Armstrong returned to New York in early 1935 with his finances in disarray. Having fired Collins in Europe, he decided to hire the tough, disreputable former manager of the Sunset Café, Joe Glaser, as his manager. Armstrong cared only to perform and wanted nothing to do with the business aspects of his career. Settled by a handshake, the agreement of a 50–50 split of the trumpeter's revenues with his manager lasted for life and made millionaires of them both.

Glaser put Armstrong back on the road fronting a big band at increasingly profitable venues and had him in the recording studio constantly. Glaser arranged for articles in *Vanity Fair*, and in 1936 negotiated Armstrong's appearance in the film *Pennies From Heaven*, which initiated a long professional and personal relationship between the trumpeter and the film's star, Bing Crosby. In 1937 Armstrong became the first African American to host a national radio program, the *Fleischman's Yeast Hour*, and in 1938 Lil finally agreed to a divorce, freeing him to marry Alpha Smith. During WWII he performed on military bases, cut V-discs during the 1942–4 American Federation of Musicians' recording ban, continued making films, and won the first *Esquire* jazz poll.

The decline of the big-band era in the mid-forties combined with Armstrong's appearance in the film *New Orleans*, in which he led a small band of Crescent City jazz legends, radically altered his career. Leonard Feather, producer of the film's recording sessions, arranged for Armstrong to appear with Edmond Hall's New Orleans revivalist band at Carnegie Hall in early 1947, which, in turn, led to the now-famous Town Hall concert in May with a select group of performers impulsively billed as the All Stars. From then until shortly before his death Armstrong was typically on the road with this band, now officially known as Louis Armstrong's All Stars, for ten months of the year. Time off was spent at home in Queens, NY, with fourth wife, Lucille Wilson (1914–83), whom he married in 1942.

An outspoken opponent of bebop with a stage persona regarded in the 1940s and 50s as vaudevillian or, worse, smacking of "Uncle Tom," Armstrong was dismissed by many younger musicians of his race (e.g., Dizzy Gillespie) as old-fashioned, out-of-touch, or a sell-out. Others (e.g., Miles Davis) respected his playing but hated his "clowning," while still others (e.g., Sammy Davis Jr.) condemned him for his silence on civil rights and his performances for segregated audiences. Armstrong responded to the criticism by making clear that his audience came first: "...coming out all chesty, making faces, the jive with the audience clapping, aw, it's all in fun. People expect it of me; they know I'm there in the cause of happiness. What you're there for is to please the people. I mean the best way you can. Those few moments belong to them." (Meryman, 97).

Even so, Armstrong could not contain his outrage during the 1957 "Little Rock Nine" incident, which provoked him to write President Eisenhower a heated letter denouncing the treatment of "his people" and to cancel a scheduled government-sponsored tour of the Soviet Union. Before the passage of the Civil Rights Act, his anger extended as well to his home state, where he refused to perform with his All Stars because Louisiana prohibited integrated bands. Dizzy Gillespie, for one, would later recant his judgment of Armstrong and even became his neighbor in Queens, New York.

Such musical and political issues failed to resonate with the general public, for Armstrong, by adding TV spots to his movie and recording work, had already became a cultural icon. In 1956, for example, he was featured by the prestigious Newport Jazz Festival, the Royal Philharmonic in London, Leonard Bernstein and the New York Philharmonic, and CBS as the subject of an autobiographical documentary, *Satchmo the Great*. The US State Department continued to offer him tours abroad, enabling "Ambassador Satch" to spread the gospel of jazz worldwide.

Notable accomplishments besides those mentioned above include being the first jazz musician to publish an autobiography (*Swing That Music*, New York, 1936/*R*), the first jazz musician to appear on the cover of *Time* (1949), and the first honoree in *Down Beat*'s Jazz Hall of Fame (1952). In 1964 Armstrong's recording of "Hello Dolly" displaced the Beatles as number one on the pop charts, where it remained for six weeks. At age 63 he was the oldest musician to attain this milestone.

After several bouts of heart disease, Armstrong died at his home, one of the most widely-known and best-loved personalities in the world. The Armstrong Archive opened on the campus of Queens College, Queens, New York in 1994, and the Armstrong House in Corona, Queens, a designated New York City landmark, opened as a museum in 2003. Posthumous recognition includes a Grammy Lifetime Achievement Award in 1972, a statue unveiled in New Orleans' Louis Armstrong Park in 1980, the issuance of a commemorative stamp in 1995, and the identification as one of *Variety*'s Top 100 Entertainers of the Twentieth Century in 1999.

2. Recordings. Armstrong recorded almost 1500 tracks (excluding alternate takes) in studios or at live concerts, and at least an equal number of tracks on air checks, film soundtracks, and television performances. His earliest recordings were with King Oliver, whose 35 sides in 1923 represent the first significant body of black recorded jazz. The two choruses of "Chimes Blues," Armstrong's first recorded solo, display a full, rich tone and contain the stylistic trademarks of a rip to a high note on a weak beat, the neighboring function of the raised second scale degree (*d*♯) and an ascending triplet followed by a descending arpeggio (ex.1). Consisting of repeated arpeggios that suggest clarinet passage work (Harker, 2003, 143), the solo's melodic redundancy is relieved harmonically and rhythmically by the passing diminished chord (*f*♯–*a*–*c*) and metric displacement (quarter-note triplets across the bar line).

Although Armstrong's solos on the Creole Jazz Band's recordings of "Riverside Blues" are even more formulaic than that of "Chimes Blues," his series of breaks on "Tears" foreshadow the brilliant stop-time solos of "Cornet Chop Suey" with the Hot Five in 1926 and "Potato Head Blues" with the Hot Seven (the Hot Five plus tuba and drums) in 1927. In "Tears" (ex.2) each pair of breaks forms a "call-and-response" pattern in which the second "answers" the first with motivic correspondences. The series concludes with an accelerated group of breaks that sums up the whole, while the eighth-note triplet figure unifies the sequence. This kind of coherent structure, dubbed the "correlated chorus" by the Bix Beiderbecke circle, typifies many of Armstrong's solos in the 1920s and distinguishes his improvisations from those of his contemporaries.

Virtually inaudible on most of his acoustically recorded sides with Oliver, Armstrong's second cornet work, when clearly heard (e.g., the duet on the OKeh version of "Mabel's Dream" [1923]), demonstrates a flair

Ex.1 Armstrong's Solo in "Chimes Blues"

for counterpoint, a sensitivity to harmony, and a sure sense of swing. The latter quality—a combination of uneven eighth notes, pervasive syncopation, irregular phrasing and playing around rather than on top of the beat—conveys a sense of forward motion that characterizes Armstrong's approach to rhythm and that would become the prototype for music of the Swing Era.

In 1924–5 Armstrong recorded over one hundred sides with Fletcher Henderson, Clarence Williams's Blue Five, the Red Onion Jazz Babies, and various blues singers, including Bessie Smith and Ma Rainey. Capable of improvising equally inventive but entirely different solos on alternate takes of the same piece (e.g., "Stomp Off, Let's Go" [1926] with Erskine Tate), multiple takes of Armstrong's recordings show that he tended, rather, to refine his ideas from one take to the next than totally rethink each one. His overall approach to improvisation consists of melodic paraphrase varying from the literal (a virtual duplication of the melody) to the abstract (a virtually new melody based on salient features of the old). As Armstrong put it, "The first chorus I plays the melody. The second chorus I plays the melody round the melody, and the third chorus I routines" (Sudhalter-Evans, 192).

Liberated from the constraints of the eight- or sixteen-bar solos with Henderson, Armstrong's New York small-group sides disclose a more relaxed, expansive and virtuosic style on "Cold in Hand Blues" [1925] with Bessie Smith, "Railroad Blues" [1925] with Trixie Smith, "I Ain't Gonna Play No Second Fiddle" [1925] with Perry Bradford's Jazz Phools, and "Cake Walking Babies From Home" [1925] with Sidney Bechet in Clarence Williams' Blue Five. His 1925 accompaniment of Bessie Smith on "St Louis Blues" is considered a classic interpretation of W.C. Handy's best-known composition.

Epitomizing the change from an emphasis on the ensemble represented by Oliver's Creole Jazz Band to an emphasis on the soloist, Armstrong's early Hot Fives have long been regarded a watershed of jazz history. The stylistic shift transpires during the course of the band's 33 recordings from November 1925 through December 1927 in which Armstrong dominates the proceedings with a solo-like lead and a steadily increasing number of instrumental and/or vocal solos. Although the band's members (except for Lil) and its repertoire hailed from New Orleans, the innovative harmony, melody, and form of "Savoy Blues," [1927] the final number recorded by the group, leaves Crescent City blues far behind.

The relaxed tempo of "Savoy Blues" (ex.3) enables Armstrong to stretch out melodically. Swooping and gliding in undulating streams of fluid eighth notes, he blurs phrase beginnings and endings with expanded pick-ups or lengthy extensions and enriches his harmonic vocabulary with 7ths, 9ths, 11ths, and 13ths in almost every bar. Particularly striking is the C major seventh (C–E–G–B) he plays against the accompanying D seventh (D–F♯–A–C) harmony in bars 57–58 and 69–70. By means of skillful voice-leading from above

Ex.2 Armstrong's Breaks in "Tears"

Ex.3 Armstrong's Solo in "Savoy Blues"

and below, Armstrong employs the resulting dissonance to converge convincingly on the G major tonic harmony in bars 59 and 71 (Anderson, 2007, 186–87).

Armstrong's dilemma as a soloist at this point in his career was to integrate break-like passages and melodic paraphrase into a "unified solo style" (Harker, 1999, 58). He achieved this synthesis to varying degrees in several early Hot Fives, but most successfully in "Big Butter and Egg Man," [1926] a structural masterpiece that seamlessly integrates melodic and rhythmic ideas. The golden proportions of "King of the Zulus" [1926]; correlated choruses of "Yes! I'm in the barrel" [1925], "Cornet Chop Suey" [1936], and "Once in a While" [1927]; motivic relationships of "Hotter Than That" [1927], "Skid-Dat-De-Dat" [1926], and "Put 'Em Down Blues" [1927]; and the balance of melodic and harmonic improvisatory impulses in "Struttin' with Some Barbecue" [1927] further exemplify Armstrong's intuitive preoccupation with form. The early Hot Fives confirm Armstrong's singular ability to internalize the harmonic and melodic possibilities of a tune, which, when coupled with imaginative phrasing, mastery of rhythm, avoidance of stock figures, and the capacity to conceive the work as a whole, encapsulates his genius.

Armstrong's last small-group recordings before the 1940s were made with members of Carroll Dickerson's Orchestra under the names Hot Five, Savoy Ballroom Five, and Louis Armstrong's Orchestra. Of the several noteworthy sides in this batch, "West End Blues" [1928] and "Weather Bird" [1928] stand far above the rest. The opening cadenza of the first became Armstrong's most heralded solo and the dazzling musical dialogue between the piano (Hines) and trumpet of the second became, in the view of many critics, "one of the all-time masterpieces of recorded jazz" (Miller, 107–8).

With few exceptions, Armstrong recorded exclusively with big bands from mid-1929 to mid-1947. Some of these groups preexisted, like Luis Russell's, Les Hite's, and Chick Webb's, while others, like Zilner Randolph's, formed only to back up the soloist. Armstrong seemed unaffected by their uneven quality of support and recorded some the of the best sides of his career during these years, e.g., "I can't give you anything but love" (1929), "Sweethearts on Parade" (1930), "Stardust" (1931), "Between the Devil and the Deep Blue Sea" (1932), "Basin Street Blues" (1933), "I've got my fingers crossed" (1935), and "Jubilee" (1938).

Stylistically, Armstrong refined the synthesis of melodic paraphrase with elements of rhythm and harmony achieved on some of the early Hot Fives. Now he more often forsook the original tune and extended coherence over multiple choruses by means of recurring rhythmic and melodic motives combined with a systematic heightening of register from one chorus to the next. Unfailingly announced by a rip or glissando, the climax on the final or "shout" chorus frequently highlighted a lengthy held note, as on "Mahogany Hall Stomp" (1929 and 1933) or rhythmically varied repeated pitches, as on "Swing That Music" (1936). His further adoption of a "leaner," less florid, and more rhythmically dependent style might have been stimulated by the *AABA* form of his pop song repertoire, in which the need for contrast between sections could have encouraged an economy of note selection and greater reliance on rhythmic manipulation.

The primacy of rhythm especially characterizes his vocals, which are usually minimalistic, speech-like distillations of the melody with melodic interpolations between phrases. For Armstrong, a lyric's meaning ranked second to the timbral possibilities of its words, to which he applied bends, elisions, and smears or replaced entirely with scat. These techniques premiered on the early Hot Fives and persisted in 1931 on "All of Me" and "Lazy River" and on almost all other vocal solos thereafter. Upon returning from his second European trip in 1935, however, Armstrong occasionally modified the raspy texture of his voice to reveal "crooning" capabilities on songs like "Solitude" and "Ev'ntide."

Armstrong's style of performance evolved little after 1932 and his repertoire progressively narrowed to popular hits. Concerts and recordings by the All Stars fell into a predictable routine: invariably opening with "Indiana," the program continued with a string of Dixieland, New Orleans, or pop favorites and closed with "When It's Sleepy Time Down South," Armstrong's theme song since 1931. In the final two decades of his career Armstrong's ravaged lip curtailed or precluded forays into the trumpet's high register, encouraging him, ever more extensively, to showcase his inimitable voice. Thus, thanks to his countless live and recorded renditions of "Blueberry Hill" (1949), "Mack the Knife" (1955), "Hello Dolly" (1964), and "What A Wonderful World." (1967), Armstrong's singing concluded his celebrity as it had begun in New Orleans a half-century earlier.

3. Compositions. Armstrong began composing in New Orleans. When he replaced Oliver in Ory's band, the leader asked him to work up a number that featured him playing, singing, and dancing. One night when performing the bawdy tune he called "Get off Katie's head," Louis saw Clarence Williams writing it down. Afterwards Williams offered him $50 for the song, which Armstrong said he never received. Copyrighted by Creole society bandleader, A.J. Piron, as "I wish I could shimmy like my sister Kate," the song became a hit for the Williams-Piron Publishing Company in 1919.

In Chicago with Oliver, Louis and Lil used to sit on her back steps and write "five or six songs a day" which they sold outright to the OKeh Record Company (*Louis Armstrong in His Own Words*, 132). Three of these ("Weather Bird Rag," "Where did you stay last night?" and "Tears") were recorded by the Creole Jazz Band, two ("Yes! I'm in the barrel" and "Cornet Chop Suey") were recorded by the early Hot Five and one ("Coal Cart Blues") was recorded by Armstrong with Clarence Williams' Blue Five.

Although not identified on the copyright deposit, Armstrong shared composer credit with Oliver on the record sleeves of the Creole Band's "Canal Street Blues" and "Dippermouth Blues." Other Hot Five or Hot Seven tunes assigned to him by copyright are "Gully Low Blues," "Gut Bucket Blues" and "Potato Head Blues." "Don't jive me," "I'm not rough," and "Jazz Lips," named Armstrong as composer on the record sleeve but credited Lil Hardin or Lil Armstrong on the copyright deposit. Record sleeves of "Put 'Em Down Blues" "S.O.L. Blues" and "Keyhole Blues," for which copyright deposits are no longer extant, also listed Armstrong as the composer (Chevan, 257–60). In addition, Louis claimed to have written the Hot Five's "Muskrat Ramble" (Williams, 211), copyrighted by Kid Ory, and "Struttin' With Some Barbecue," attributed solely to Lil after she filed suit in the 1930s.

In all, Armstrong applied for more than 80 copyrights registered at the Library of Congress (Berrett, 1992, 239). His most recorded compositions after the 1920s are "Back 'O Town Blues" (with Luis Russell); "Pretty Little Missy" (with Billy Kyle); "Velma's Blues" (with Velma Middleton); "Swing That Music" (with Horace Gerlach), which appeared in connection with his 1936 autobiography; and "Someday you'll be sorry," which came to him in a dream while touring frigid North Dakota in 1947. None of Armstrong's tunes have jazz standards.

4. Films and shows. Armstrong's first Broadway opportunity fizzled but his second triumphed. In 1929 when he surprised his manager by showing up in New York with his band in tow rather than alone, Rockwell had already secured him the position of lead trumpet in the pit orchestra for Vincent Youman's *Great Day*. Demoted to second trumpet then fired for "not [being] adapted to show business" during previews in Philadelphia (*New York Age*, 8 June 1929), Armstrong returned to New York to appear in *Hot Chocolates*. The overwhelming response to his performance of "Ain't Misbehavin'" between acts quickly earned him a larger role on stage and sent him to the studio to record the show's hits. By the end of the musical's six-month run, Armstrong, already famous among blacks, had become a star among whites as well. Two later theatrical ventures met with less acclaim, however. In 1939, *Swingin' the Dream*, a jazz *Midsummer Night's Dream*, in which Armstrong played Bottom, lasted only 13 performances on Broadway, and in 1961, Dave Brubeck's *The Real Ambassadors*, a jazz oratorio about race relations featuring Armstrong, yielded a recording and only one live performance.

Armstrong made 22 American feature films (not counting the lost *Ex-Flame*), six foreign feature films, eight documentaries or concerts, three movie shorts, two cartoons, and four soundies for coin-operated viewing machines. In features he played versions of himself in bit parts that seldom interacted with the main characters or had much to do with the plot. He usually managed to transcend racial or demeaning stereotypes common to movies of the day, such as being draped in a leopard skin surrounded by soap bubbles in *Rhapsody in Black and Blue* (1932) or serenading a racehorse in *Going Places* (1938). Armstrong's most memorable Hollywood moments occurred in *New Orleans* (1947) with Billie Holiday and in *High Society* (1956) with Bing Crosby. *A Man Called Adam* (1966) starring Sammy Davis Jr., in which Armstrong played a washed-up jazz musician, afforded him his largest scope as an actor and second-billing on the marquee.

5. Legacy. According to assessments by Kenney, Hersch, and Brothers (2006), Armstrong had no desire to assimilate with white culture but was driven by forces of the marketplace. To please white audiences, he donned the "minstrel mask" in accordance with W.E.B. Du Bois's notion of "double consciousness." Some critics argue that Armstrong's "tomming," instead of denigrating his race, actually celebrated black vernacular culture by "signifying" upon racism. His stage behavior, moreover, was crucial to his success as a jazz ambassador. Armstrong, to a greater extent than any other early jazz musician, transformed a regional folk music into an international art form through the virtuosity of his playing as the first great jazz soloist and through the force of his charismatic personality, which disdained pretense, eschewed hypocrisy, honored life, and projected a genuine confidence in music's power to transcend cultural and racial differences.

RECORDINGS

(selective)

(The following lists supplements the annotated list of Armstrong's recordings supplied in Meckna, 2004)

Chronological Louis Armstrong (1989–2008, Classics Records); *Complete Decca Master Takes 1935–39* (2001, Definitive Records);

Complete Decca Master Takes 1940–49 (2001, Definitive Records); *Complete Louis Armstrong and Fletcher Henderson* (1993, Kings of Jazz) *Fleischmann's Yeast Show and Louis' Home Recorded Tapes* (2008, Jazz Heritage Society);
Intégrale Louis Armstrong, vols. 1–8 (*2006–10, Frémeaux & Associés*); *King Oliver: The Complete 1923 Jazz Band Recordings* (2006, Off the Record); *Let's Do It, Best of the Verve Years* (1995, Verve); *Louis Armstrong,* Columbia Jazz Masterpieces Series, vols. 1–7 (1988–93, Columbia Legacy); *Louis Armstrong Complete Edition,* Masters of Jazz Series, vols. 1–8 (1991–99, Media 7)

BIBLIOGRAPHY

L. Armstrong: *Swing That Music* (New York, 1936/*R*)
L. Armstrong: *Louis Satchmo Armstrong's Immortal Trumpet Solos,* transcr. L. Castle [Castaldo] (New York, 1947)
L. Armstrong: *Satchmo: My Life in New Orleans* (New York, 1954/*R*)
R. Meryman: "An Interview with Louis Armstrong," *Life* (15 April 1966)
M. Williams: *Jazz Masters of New Orleans* (New York, 1967/*R*)
G. Schuller: *Early Jazz: Its Roots and Early Development* (New York, 1968)
M. Jones and J. Chilton: *Louis: The Louis Armstrong Story 1900–1971* (Boston, 1971/R)
R.M. Sudhalter and P.R. Evans: *Bix: Man & Legend* (New Rochelle, NY, 1974)
L. Armstrong: "Weather Bird," *Schirmer Scores: a Repertory of Western Music*, ed. J. Godwin (New York, 1975), 414–22
J.L. Collier: *Louis Armstrong, An American Genius* (New York, 1983)
G. Giddins: *Satchmo* (New York, 1988)
W.H. Kenney: "'Going to Meet the Man': Louis Armstrong's Autobiographies," *MELUS*, xv/2 (1988), 27–46
G. Schuller: *The Swing Era: the Development of Jazz, 1930–1945* (New York, 1989)
E. Anderson: "Louis Armstrong, a Personal Memoir," *Storyville* (1 Dec 1991)
L. Armstrong: *A Louis Armstrong Study Album*, transcr. L. Grigson (London, 1992)
J. Berrett: "Louis Armstrong and Opera," *MQ*, lxxvi (1992), 216–41
L. Grigson: *A Louis Armstrong Study Album* (London, 1992)
M. Miller, ed.: *Louis Armstrong: a Cultural Legacy* (Seattle, 1994)
L. Armstrong: *Great Trumpet Solos*, transcr. P. Ecklund (New York, 1995)
S. Zenni: *Louis Armstrong–Satchmo: Oltre il mito del jazz* (Viterbo, 1995)
G. Anderson: "Blues for You Johnny: Johnny Dodds and His 'Wild Man Blues' Recordings of 1927 and 1928," *Annual Review of Jazz Studies*, viii (1996), 39–62
L. Bergreen: *Louis Armstrong: an Extravagant Life* (New York, 1997)
D. Chevan: *Written Music in Early Jazz* (diss., CUNY, 1997)
B. Harker: *The Early Musical Development of Louis Armstrong, 1901–1928*, (diss., Columbia U., 1997)
L. Gushee: "The Improvisation of Louis Armstrong," *In the Course of Performance: Studies in the World of Musical Improvisation*, ed. B. Nettl (Chicago, 1998), 291–334
J. Taylor: "Louis Armstrong, Earl Hines, and 'Weather Bird,'" *MQ*, lxxxiii (1998), 1–40
L. Armstrong: *Louis Armstrong, In His Own Words*, ed. T. Brothers (New York, 1999)
J. Berrett, ed.: *The Louis Armstrong Companion* (New York, 1999)
B. Harker: "'Telling A Story': Louis Armstrong and Coherence in Early Jazz," *CM*, no.63 (1999), 46–83
L. Armstrong: *Cornet Chop Suey As Recorded By Louis Armstrong and His Hot Five*, transcr. R. Sandke, Essential Jazz Editions Set, ii (Washington, DC, 2000)
L. Armstrong: *Potato Head Blues As Recorded By Louis Armstrong and His Hot Seven,* transcr. D. Vappie, Essential Jazz Editions Set, i (Washington, DC, 2000)
L. Armstrong and L. Hardin: *Hotter Than That As Recorded By Louis Armstrong and His Hot Five*, transcr. R. Sandke, Essential Jazz Editions Set, ii (Washington, DC, 2000)
E. Brooks: *Influence and Assimilation in Louis Armstrong's Cornet and Trumpet Work, 1923–1928* (Lewiston, NY, 2000)
L. Curl: *Tight Like This as Recorded by Louis Armstrong and His Savoy Ballroom Five*, transcr. R. Sandke, Essential Jazz Editions Set #2 (Washington, DC, 2000)
J. Oliver and C. Williams: *West End Blues as Recorded by Louis Armstrong and His Hot Five*, transcr. R. Sandke, Essential Jazz Editions Set, ii (Washington, DC, 2000)
S. Williams: *Mahogany Hall Stomp As Recorded By Louis Armstrong and His Savoy Ballroom Five, 1929*, transcr. R. Sandke, Essential Jazz Editions Set, ii (Washington, DC, 2000)
J. Berrett: "'West End Blues' Revisited," *Musica Oggi: Louis Armstrong verso il ventunesimo secolo* 21 (2001), 35–41
T. Brothers: "Louis Armstrong: The 'Saints' and the 'Boys,'" *Musica Oggi: Louis Armstrong verso il ventunesimo secolo* 21 (2001), 5–21
L. Gushee: "Modes of Reception/Influence: The Influence of Louis Armstrong," *Musica Oggi: Louis Armstrong verso il ventunesimo secolo* 21 (2001), 22–7
E. Brooks: *The Young Louis Armstrong on Records: a Critical Survey of the Early Recording, 1923–1928* (Lanham, MD, 2002)
B.H. Edwards: "Louis Armstrong and the Syntax of Scat," *Critical Inquiry*, xxviii (2002), 618–49
C. Hersch: "Poisoning Their Coffee: Louis Armstrong and Civil Rights," *Polity*, xxxiv (2002), 371–92
M. Cogswell: *Louis Armstrong: the Offstage Story of Satchmo* (Portland, OR, 2003)
B. Harker: "Louis Armstrong and the Clarinet," *American Music*, xxi/2 (2003), 137–58
J. Berrett: *Louis Armstrong and Paul Whiteman: Two Kings of Jazz* (New Haven, CT, 2004)
M. Meckna: *Satchmo: the Louis Armstrong Encyclopedia* (Westport, CT, 2004)
B. Givan: "Duets for One: Louis Armstrong's Vocal Recordings," *MQ*, lxxxvii (2005), 188–218
J. Magee: *The Uncrowned King of Swing: Fletcher Henderson and Big Band Jazz* (New York, 2005)
T. Brothers: *Louis Armstrong's New Orleans* (New York, 2006)
J. Willems: *All of Me: the Complete Discography of Louis Armstrong* (Lanham, MD, 2006)
G. Anderson: *The Original Hot Five Recordings of Louis Armstrong* (Hillsdale, NY, 2007)
C.H. Garrett: *Struggling to Define a Nation: American Music and the Twentieth Century* (Berkeley, 2008)
B. Harker: "Louis Armstrong, Eccentric Dance, and the Evolution of Jazz on the Eve of Swing," *JAMS*, lxi (2008), 67–121
T. Teachout: *Pops: a Life of Louis Armstrong* (New York, 2009)
B. Harker: *Louis Armstrong's Hot Five and Hot Seven Recordings* (New York, 2011)
R. Riccardi: *What a Wonderful World: the Magic of Louis Armstrong's Later Years* (New York, 2011)

GENE H. ANDERSON

Armstrong, Vanessa Bell (*b* Detroit, MI, 2 Oct 1953). Gospel singer. She was raised as a member of the Church of God in Christ (COGIC) for which her father served as an elder and a pastor. At the age of 13, she entered the tutelage of MATTIE MOSS CLARK, the influential president of the COGIC's music department. A performance during the Gospel Music Workshop of America led to Armstrong making the recordings *Peace be still* (1983, Muscle Shoals), which featured Thomas Whitfield's iconic arrangement of the title song, *Chosen* (1984, Muscle Shoals), and *Following Jesus* (1986, Muscle Shoals). "Nobody but Jesus" and "God So Loved the World" are among the classics recorded during this period. From 1987 to 2001, Armstrong recorded for Verity, Tommy Boy, and Jive Records. With the last label she made four albums, notably *Vanessa Bell Armstrong* (1987, Jive) that included the radio singles "You bring out the best in me" and "Pressing On." Subsequent recordings have included *Walking Miracle* (2007, EMI

Gospel) and *The Experience* (2009, EMI Gospel), the latter featuring the popular song "Good News." Armstrong performed the theme for the 1980s TV sitcom "A-men"; she also sang in such productions as the Broadway show *Don't get God started* (1987) and the made-for TV movie *The Women of Brewster Place* (1989). A recipient of a Soul Train Award, she has been nominated for seven Grammys and received the Ambassador Bobby Jones Legend Award at the Stellar Awards in 2009.

BIBLIOGRAPHY

B. Carpenter: *Uncloudy Days: The Gospel Music Encyclopedia* (San Francisco, 2005)

W.K. McNeil, ed.: *Encyclopedia of American Gospel Music* (New York, 2005)

DEBORAH SMITH POLLARD

Armstrong, William D(awson) (*b* Alton, IL, 11 Feb 1868; *d* Alton, IL, 9 July 1936). Organist and teacher. He trained in St Louis and later in Chicago under CLARENCE EDDY. In 1890 he returned to Alton, serving as organist of the First Baptist Church, St Paul's and during 1894–8 at the Church of the Redeemer. Armstrong then held a decade-long appointment at the Church of the Unity in St Louis. He joined the faculty of the Forest Park University for Women in St Louis in 1891 and the following year became music director and chair of the newly founded music department of Shurtleff College and the Western Military Academy, both in Upper Alton. Although he relinquished his administrative duties in 1908 or 1909, he continued to teach there for several more years, resigning to found the Armstrong School of Music in Alton. He served as organist of the St Louis Exposition in 1904, as vice president of the Music Teachers National Association in 1905–06 and in 1914 was offered but refused a position as director of a new school of music at what was then Illinois State University in Champaign. Armstrong composed an opera, *The Spectre Bridegroom* (1899, after Washington Irving), orchestral and choral works (including two masses [1899 and 1908] and two complete services), as well as chamber music, keyboard pieces and songs, a total of at least 129 opus numbers. He was the author of *Rudiments of Musical Notation* (New York, 1900), *The Pianoforte Pedals* (1911) and *The Romantic World of Music* (Freeport, NY, 1922/R), a series of entertaining biographical sketches.

BIBLIOGRAPHY

W.T. Norton: *William Dawson Armstrong, American Composer* (New York, 1916)

WILLIAM OSBORNE

Arnaz (y de Acha III), Desi [Desiderio Alberto] (*b* Santiago de Cuba, 2 March 1917; *d* San Diego, CA, 2 Dec 1986). Entertainer, bandleader, and television producer of Cuban birth. Arnaz left Santiago for the United States when his father, the mayor, was exiled upon the fall of the Machado government in 1933. Arnaz began his career as a singer in Miami and joined the internationally famous Xavier Cugat orchestra in the late 1930s. He started his own band, which recorded with Columbia in 1941 and Victor from 1946 through 1951. While Arnaz was the leader and featured singer, the band also recorded with prominent American singers, including the Andrews Sisters and Jane Harvey. Arnaz also appeared in the Broadway and film versions of *Too Many Girls* in 1939 and 1940, respectively. He married the film actress Lucille Ball, and the couple eventually starred in and produced their classic television show, *I Love Lucy* (featuring Arnaz as a bandleader), from 1951 to 1959. The cofounder (along with Ball) of Desilu Productions, Arnaz was revered more as an innovator of television production than music. Yet he played a significant role in popularizing Latin music on Broadway, film, and television.

DAVID F. GARCIA

Arndt, Felix (*b* New York, NY, 20 May 1889; *d* Harmon, NY, 10 Oct 1918). Composer and pianist. After studying the piano at the National Conservatory of Music in America and taking private lessons with Alexander Lambert, he pursued a varied career in New York, writing material for vaudeville entertainers, serving as a staff pianist for various publishers, and recording extensively both on piano rolls (Duo-Art, QRS) and discs (Victor). Arndt's compositions combine salon gentility with occasional ragtime syncopation, foreshadowing the novelty-piano works of the 1920s by such composers as Confrey and Bargy. They include *Clover Club*, *Desecration*, *Love in June*, *Marionette*, and the well-known *Nola* (1916).

RONALD RIDDLE

Arnold, David (*b* Luton, UK, 23 Jan 1962). British film, television, video game, and popular music composer and producer. Best known for his scores for James Bond films of the late 1990s and 2000s, Arnold began his career scoring the student films of director Danny Cannon, leading to their professional collaboration on *The Young Americans* (1993). For this film, Arnold cowrote the song "Play Dead" with Icelandic singer Björk. This project brought Arnold to the attention of producer Roland Emmerich, who hired him to compose the music for *Stargate* (1994). He worked with Emmerich again on two more films (*Independence Day* (1996) and *Godzilla* (1998)), composing large, brass-heavy orchestral scores that matched the over-the-top quality of these blockbusters. During the 2000s, Arnold also developed a professional relationship with director John Singleton, scoring four of his films, beginning with *Shaft* (2000), incorporating more popular music and in general a more electronic sound palate for these films. After producing *Shaken and Stirred: The David Arnold James Bond Project*, a collection of James Bond theme songs covered by a variety of popular artists, Arnold came to the attention of John Barry, the longtime Bond composer who recommended Arnold for *Tomorrow Never Dies*. In addition to a 1997 James Bond videogame, he also scored the next four Bond films. Arnold also scored a music library for the British television series, *Little Britain*, returning for subsequent seasons and specials to contribute additional cues. In 2001, Arnold arranged the theme for the long-running British television program *Doctor Who* for use in CD-only audio adventures from Big Finish Productions. In addition to his film and television composing, he continues to produce recordings for many popular artists.

WORKS

FILM

The Young Americans, 1993; Stargate, 1994; Last of the Dogmen, 1995; Independence Day, 1996; A Life Less Ordinary, 1997; Tomorrow Never Dies, 1997; Godzilla, 1998; The World Is Not Enough, 1999; Shaft, 2000; Baby Boy, 2001; The Musketeer, 2001; Zoolander, 2001; Changing Lanes, 2002; Die Another Day, 2002; Enough, 2002; 2 Fast 2 Furious, 2003; The Stepford Wives, 2004; Four Brothers, 2005; Stoned, 2005; Amazing Grace, 2006; Casino Royale, 2006; Hot Fuzz, 2007; Agent Crush, 2008; How to Lose Friends and Alienate People, 2008; Quantum of Solace, 2008; Made in Dagenham, 2010; The Chronicles of Narnia: the Voyage of the Dawn Treader, 2010; Morning Glory, 2010Television

UC: Undercover, 2001; Little Britain, 2003–6; Crooked House, 2008; Little Britain USA, 2008; Free Agents, 2009; Sherlock, 2010

VIDEOGAMES

Guinness World Records 2005, 2004; GoldenEye 007, 2010

LOUIS NIEBUR

Arnold, Eddy [Richard Edward] (*b* Henderson, TN, 15 May 1918; *d* Brentwood, TN, 8 May 2008). Country-music recording artist and television performer. He personified country music's commercial expansion during the period 1940–70. His father died when Arnold was 11, and the family became sharecroppers on the farm they had owned in Chester County, Tennessee. By 1936 he had begun working on radio programs and in beer joints, first in Jackson, Tennessee, and then in Memphis and St. Louis. Becoming the featured vocalist of the band led by Pee Wee King on the radio program *Grand Ole Opry* in 1940 heightened his profile. Arnold began to perform under his own name in 1943 and subsequently headlined the show's segment broadcast over the Mutual Network. He made his first recordings for RCA Victor in 1944.

Between 1945 and 1955 Arnold scored 66 top-ten country hits; 21 reached number one including "That's how much I love you" (RCA, 1946), "I'll hold you in my heart (till I can hold you in my arms)" (RCA, 1947), and "Bouquet of Roses" (RCA, 1948). Typical sales of 400,000 copies or more indicate that his smooth baritone voice won wider audiences than was usual for country music; indeed, Arnold estimated the number of singles and albums that he sold during his lifetime at more than 85 million. Supported by widely distributed, syndicated radio programs, Arnold left the *Grand Ole Opry* in 1948 to maximize his income from personal appearances. His manager, the shrewd "Colonel" Tom Parker, negotiated guest spots on network radio and pioneering roles on television, notably summer replacement shows for Perry Como (1952) and Dinah Shore (1953). His own syndicated television series (1955) and ABC-TV program (1956) followed.

After a slump in late 1950s, Arnold's career witnessed a resurgence in the late 1960s as he dropped Roy Wiggins's steel guitar and added strings on his records, thus redefining himself as a suave purveyor of the country-pop style known as the Nashville Sound, typified by his popular crossover hit "Make the World Go Away" (1965). Trading his Tennessee Plowboy image for an uptown, tuxedoed look further broadened his fan base (especially on network television) and helped secure his election to the Country Music Hall of Fame in 1966, although by this point his music leaned more toward pop than country. Arnold appeared with symphony orchestras and played in show rooms in Nevada into 1999. He released his 100th, and final, album in 2005.

BIBLIOGRAPHY

E. Arnold: *It's a Long Way from Chester County* (New York, 1969)

M. Streissguth: *Eddy Arnold: Pioneer of the Nashville Sound* (New York, 1997)

BILL C. MALONE/JOHN W. RUMBLE

Arnold, Kokomo [James; Gitfiddle Jim] (*b* Lovejoy, GA, 15 Feb 1901; *d* Chicago, IL, 8 Nov 1968). Blues singer and guitarist. He grew up on a farm in Georgia, learning to play guitar at the age of ten, and was an accomplished musician by the time he settled in Buffalo at the age of 18. In the 1920s he performed in local clubs and traveled with other singers as far south as Mississippi. Arnold played a steel-bodied guitar laid horizontally across his lap, stroking the strings with a glass flask to produce a wailing sound. Although his natural voice was low, the singing on many of his records is high pitched; he often employed a buzzing tone as a drone to accompany guitar solos. As Gitfiddle Jim he recorded "Paddlin' Blues" (1930, Vic.), an instrumental tour de force, in Memphis, but despite his dazzling technique, Victor did not record him again. In 1934 his recording "Old Original Kokomo Blues" (Decca) was an immediate success. In the next four years he made more than 80 titles as Kokomo Arnold and several more with the pianist Peetie Wheatstraw, including "Set down gal" (1937, Decca), a fine example of their barrelhouse duets. The solo "Policy Wheel Blues" (1935, Decca) was typical of his lyrically original blues, while "Twelves" (1935, Decca), a version of "The Dirty Dozen," demonstrated his use of traditional themes as a vehicle for his own performance style. In 1936 Arnold began working in a steel mill and eventually gave up music altogether. His song "Milk Cow Blues" has been covered regularly, by artists as diverse as Robert Johnson, Willie Nelson, and Aerosmith.

BIBLIOGRAPHY

P. Oliver: "Kokomo Arnold," *Jazz Monthly*, viii/3 (1962), 10

J. Parsons: "Kokomo Arnold Discography," *Jazz Monthly*, viii (1962), no. 3, p.16; no. 4, p.15

J. Demêtre: "Kokomo Arnold," *Soul Bag*, no.148 (1997), 28–33

PAUL OLIVER/R

Arnold, Maurice [Strothotte, Maurice Arnold] (*b* St. Louis, MO, 19 Jan 1865; *d* New York, NY, 23 Oct 1937). Composer and conductor. At first, he was known professionally by his full name but eventually dropped his surname and went by Maurice Arnold. He studied music with his mother, a prominent pianist. At 15, he enrolled in the College of Music in Cincinnati Ohio, then travelled to Germany, attending the Friedrich

Wilhelm Gymnasium (Berlin) and the Cologne Conservatory of Music, where his first piano sonata was written and performed. Arnold subsequently went to Breslau where, under the instruction of Max Bruch, he wrote one of his first major works, a cantata, *The Wild Chase*. Upon his return to St. Louis he worked as a violinist, educator, opera conductor, and composer. Arnold attended the newly-established National Conservatory of Music in New York City (1892–95), where he studied with ANTONÍN DVOŘÁK and eventually became an instructor of harmony. He subsequently toured Europe (1902, 1907), often conducting his own works, and served as music director of the Princess Theatre in London. Along with other African American composers influenced by Dvořák, he sought to apply (in non-rigid fashion) the aesthetic nuances of Creole folk music, spirituals, plantation work songs, and popular tunes as the basis for a new American music, evident in works such as his four-movement suite, *American Plantation Dances*, and *Minstrel Serenade* for violin and piano. Other works include his *Dramatic Overture*, *Danse de la Midway Plaisance, Tarantelle*, and an unpublished symphony for orchestra, two comic operas (*The Merry Benedicts* and *Cleopatra*), the *Violin Sonata in E Minor*, various chamber compositions, piano pieces, and songs.

BIBLIOGRAPHY

R. Hughes: *Famous American Composers* (Boston, 1900), 135

T.L. Riis: "Dvořák and His Black Students," *Rethinking Dvořák: Views from Five Countries*, ed. D. R. Beveridge (New York, 1996), 265–73

ROBERT PAUL KOLT

Aronson, Rudolph (*b* New York, NY, 8 April 1856; *d* New York, NY, 4 Feb 1919). Theater manager, conductor, and composer. After studying harmony and composition with Emile Durand at the Paris Conservatoire (1874–7), Aronson returned to New York as a young manager and conductor at the Metropolitan Hall. He encountered his greatest success as founder of the Casino Theatre in Manhattan, a building celebrated for its "Moorish" architecture and its roof garden (the first of its kind). Opening on 21 October 1882 with a performance of *The Queen's Lace Handkerchief*, the Casino quickly became the major venue for comic opera performances in New York, featuring sumptuously designed performances of the works of J. Strauss, Sullivan, Offenbach, and Millöcker, among others. Though he considered the production inferior to his other work, Aronson's most successful run at the Casino was Jakobowski's *Erminie* (1256 performances). Throughout his career, Aronson maintained strong European connections, managing theater houses abroad and contracting American tours of major European musicians, including Leoncavallo.

As a composer, Aronson completed over 150 works, including comic operas such as the poorly-received *Rainmaker of Syria* (1893), marches for Presidents T. Roosevelt and Taft, and many waltzes in the style of Strauss (an early influence, as acknowledged in his memoir); the most famous of these waltzes is "Sweet Sixteen," composed for the cornet virtuoso Jules Levy in 1880.

BIBLIOGRAPHY

R. Aronson: *Theatrical and Musical Memoirs* (New York, 1913)

F. Wilson: *Francis Wilson's Life of Himself* (Boston and New York, 1924)

S.B. Johnson: *The Roof Gardens of Broadway Theatres, 1883–1942* (Ann Arbor, MI, 1985)

BLAKE HOWE

ARP. Firm of synthesizer manufacturers. It was founded as ARP Instruments by Alan R. Pearlman (and named from his initials) in Newton, near Boston, in 1970. Pearlman had previously founded a company that marketed operational amplifiers; this experience gave him the expertise to design what were at that time exceptionally stable temperature-controlled oscillators for the ARP synthesizers. The company employed musicians, including Roger Powell and Thomas Piggott, in different roles. Besides Pearlman, designers included David Friend, Dennis Colin, Jeremy Hill, and Philip Dodds.

The ARP synthesizer was one of the principal "second-generation" synthesizers, which profited from the greatly increased availability of integrated circuits in the five or six years that had elapsed since the first generation. ARP marketed modular synthesizers in several sizes as the 2000 series, the most successful of which was the ARP 2500 (1970). This was designed primarily for electronic music studios, but it found some concert applications. In 1971 the 2600 model was introduced, followed later that year by the Odyssey (a direct rival to the R.A. Moog Company's Minimoog, introduced in 1970), and about 1973 by the three-octave Pro-Soloist, which could be used in conjunction with an electronic organ.

During the second half of the 1970s ARP's sales were the highest of any synthesizer company, capturing 39% of the American market. Models produced by the company included the Explorer, Pro/DGX (developed from the Pro-Soloist), Solus and Axxe, and the Avatar, a guitar synthesizer marketed in 1978 and based in part on the Odyssey (it was a comparative failure, from which ARP did not recover). The company's first polyphonic synthesizer, the Quadra (*c*1980), was followed by the digital Chroma (developed though not manufactured by ARP), which included a microcomputer programmed from a touch panel. From about 1974 ARP also manufactured the Solina string synthesizer, under license from the Dutch Solina company, and subsequently developed its own models, the Omni (1975, the best-seller of the ARP range) and the Quartet (*c*1980, manufactured for ARP in Italy), which included brass, organ, and piano sections. In spite of its success, ARP ceased to operate in 1981, owing to "corporate mismanagement." After its demise the Chroma and two electronic pianos were taken over by CBS Musical Instruments and marketed by its Rhodes division.

Important innovations from ARP included the use of PROMs (Programmable Read Only Memory) in the Pro-Soloist in 1972. The use of jacks for patching prewired functions on the ARP 2600 was a major ergonomic advancement, making live and studio use much easier, while still retaining the capabilities of a fully modular instrument. The change of the keyboard for the 2600, which added an extra low frequency oscillator, better bending capabilities, octave switching, and an upper voice control voltage exemplifies ARP's forward thinking. ARP also provided additional expressive controls and capabilities to its synthesizers, by using aftertouch on the Soloist, Pro-Soloist, and Quadra, and introducing Proportional Pitch Control (PPC) on later models of the monophonic Axxe and the polyphonic Odyssey.

Perhaps the most important innovation was in the Chroma, a multi-timbral synthesizer designed around a proprietary bus system that allowed the synthesizer to interface with a home computer. This is a normal design practice now, but at the time it was quite revolutionary.

See also SYNTHESIZER.

BIBLIOGRAPHY

D. Friend: "The Super-Stable ARP Precision Voltage Controlled Oscillator," *Synthesis* (1970) no.1, 9

D. Friend, A.R. Pearlman, and E. Maltzman: *Lessons in Electronic Music* (Milwaukee, 1974)

D. Friend, A.R. Pearlman, and T.D. Piggott: *Learning Music with Synthesizers* (Milwaukee, 1974)

B.L. Gardner: *The Development and Testing of a Basic Self-Instructional Program for the ARP 2600 Portable Electronic Synthesizer and Effects on Attitudes toward Electronic Music* (diss., Michigan State U., 1978)

D.T. Horn: *Electronic Music Synthesizers* (Blue Ridge Summit, PA, 1980), 59

Devarahi: *The Complete Guide to Synthesizers* (Englewood Cliffs, NJ, 1982), 177

R. Powell: "ARP: the Early Years," *Keyboard*, viii/5 (1982), 58

C.R. Waters: "Raiders of the Lost ARP," *Inc.* (Nov 1982); rev. as "The Rise & Fall of ARP Instruments," *Keyboard*, ix/4 (1983), 16

HUGH DAVIES/JOHN LEIMSEIDER

Arpino, Gerald [Gennaro, Peter] (*b* Staten Island, NY, 14 Jan 1923; *d* Chicago, IL, 29 Oct 2008). Dancer, choreographer, teacher, and ballet company director. He began to study dance after meeting Robert Joffrey while on military service in Seattle, and continued this study in New York at the School of American Ballet and with the modern dancers May O'Donnell and Gertrude Shurr. He became a founding member of the faculty of Joffrey's school, the American Dance Center, and of Joffrey's first dance group, which later became the Joffrey Ballet. He also performed on Broadway and with New York City Opera. After retiring as a performer in 1964, he focused on the choreographic work he had begun in 1961 with the ballet *Ropes*, to music by Charles Ives. As chief choreographer of the Joffrey Ballet, he created ballets that celebrated the company's youthful verve and vitality, frequently utilizing scores by American contemporary composers. Among his most popular ballets were *Olympics* (1966; Toshiro Mayuzumi), danced by an all-male ensemble; *Trinity* (1970; Alan Raph and Lee Holdridge), a tribute to the counterculture of the 1960s; and *Light Rain* (1981; Douglas Adams and Russ Gauthier). In 1984 he created *Jamboree* (music by Teo Macero), the first ballet commissioned by an American city, San Antonio. After Joffrey's death in 1988 Arpino was appointed artistic director of the company, a position he held in the face of many tribulations until 2007, after the company's relocation from New York to Chicago. His last completed ballet was *The Pantages and the Palace Present Two-a-Day* (1989; Rebekah Harkness and Elliot Kaplan), the first choreography commissioned in honor of the Office of the American Presidency.

BIBLIOGRAPHY

International Dictionary of Ballet (Detroit, 1993)

S. Anawalt: *The Joffrey Ballet: Robert Joffrey and the Making of an American Dance Company* (New York, 1996)

International Encyclopedia of Dance (New York, 1998)

SUSAN AU

Arranger. The creator of a musical arrangement, which typically comprises decisions of instrumentation, chord voicing, formal routine (the placement of verses, interludes, modulations, etc.), or genre characteristics (bluegrass, mambo, punk, etc.) applied to a composition for performance.

Many common aural performance practices, such as fixed-interval vocal harmonizing, the improvised interpretation of jazz standards, or DJ record "sampling," may be broadly defined as an arrangement. In this regard, performers, conductors, and producers frequently take on the duties of an arranger in rehearsal or performance.

More narrowly, the work of an arranger reflects the print music publishing tradition of marketing a composition for popular formats such as four-hand piano, SATB choir, marching band, ukulele and voice, or dance orchestra. During the mid-20th century, a thriving music performance industry supported the careers of thousands of full-time arrangers employed by music publishers, film studios, television and radio stations, record companies, theaters, and advertising agencies, taking part in an assembly line process between the contributions of a composer or musical director and an orchestrator or music copyist. But many jobs—especially in the freelance market—require arrangers to also serve as composer, director, orchestrator, copyist, conductor, or editor.

Early American music arrangers were often publishers themselves, such as the 18th-century hymnal editor John Wesley. During the mid-19th century, a growing parlor music culture fueled demand for secular music arranged in "leadsheet" format, an arrangement that indicates a composition's melody, lyrics, and optional harmonic accompaniment; leadsheet publications of Stephen Foster compositions enjoyed influential success. By the early 20th century, the popularity of both ragtime music and marching band performances offered markets for ragtime band arrangements such as those by E.J. Stark. Successful tours of the Fisk Jubilee Singers likewise precipitated published choir arrangements of African American spirituals, including those by Harry T. Burleigh; interest in other American folk idioms are reflected in published "transcriptions," such as the ballad and cowboy song arrangements of JOHN LOMAX III. Other arranging trends through the 20th century include the Tin Pan Alley marketing of Broadway "show tunes" during the 1910s and 20s, the distribution of swing dance band "stock" arrangements during the 1930s and 40s, and Brill Building publications supporting jukebox singles of the 1950s and 60s. Since the 1950s, arrangers such as QUINCY JONES, MITCH MILLER, and PHIL SPECTOR have expanded arranging into the realm of studio recording technique and production. More recently, digital synthesizer programming (or "sequencing") and interactive computer music software provide additional media for arranging work.

Arrangers apply a wide range of strategies in their art. In addition to the assignment of instrumentation appropriate to available musicians, an arranger may make adaptations in response to the requests or reputation of a particular client, or even a personal arranging style. A technically demanding work may be simplified for less skilled performers, or reinterpreted through systems such as guitar tablature. New harmonic accompaniment may be assigned to a familiar melody to create a "reharmonization" (e.g. Gil Evans's arrangement of "St. Louis Blues," 1958). Another approach is the alteration of a composition's form, meter, or rhythmic values to reference a specific genre, practices especially common in popular dance music (e.g. Walter Murphy's disco arrangement "A Fifth of Beethoven," 1976).

American pop arrangements frequently combine characteristics from different genres or styles; iconic examples include Ferde Grofé's setting of *Rhapsody in Blue* for Paul Whiteman's orchestra (1924), Jerry Gray's arrangement of "St. Louis Blues March" for Glenn Miller (1943), and Jimi Hendrix's solo guitar rendition of "The Star-Spangled Banner" (1969). Efforts such as the Boston Pops Orchestra's symphonic settings of popular hits may reflect the work of arrangers within the tradition of the "cover": one performer's use of repertoire associated with that of another, and often including stylistic alterations or updates to the original arrangement, whether by necessity or design. In some instances, an arrangement may be considered to be as important as the original composition in the successful marketing of a song (e.g. Carlos Santana's arrangement of Tito Puente's "Oye como va," 1971). Historically, arrangements are not protected under copyright (unless the source work lies in the public domain), and many professional arrangers are paid on a "work for hire" basis.

Although few arrangers achieve celebrity status, their musical legacy remains as widely influential as it is stylistically varied. Just a few notable figures include Broadway stage arrangers Robert Russell Bennett and WILL VODERY, Hollywood film arrangers HENRY MANCINI and Conrad Salinger, recording studio arrangers Richard Evans, Arthur Lange, and NELSON RIDDLE, and jazz arrangers DON REDMAN, Maria Schneider, and Billy Strayhorn.

BIBLIOGRAPHY

D. Sebesky: *The Contemporary Arranger* (New York, 1975, rev. 2/1984)

G. Schuller: *The Swing Era: the Development of Jazz, 1930–1945* (New York, 1989)

W. Everett, ed.: *Expression in Pop-Rock Music: Critical and Analytical Essays* (New York, 2000, 2/2008)

G. Lees: *Arranging the Score: Portraits of the Great Arrangers* (New York, 2000)

J. Howland: *Ellington Uptown: Duke Ellington, James P. Johnson, and the Birth of Concert Jazz* (Ann Arbor, 2009)

S. Suskin: *The Sound of Broadway Music: A Book of Orchestrators and Orchestrations* (New York, 2009)

JOHN WRIGGLE

Arrau, Claudio (*b* Chillán, Chile, 6 Feb 1903; *d* Mürzzuschlag, Austria, 9 June 1991). Chilean pianist, naturalized American. A child prodigy, he gave his first public recital at the age of five in Santiago. After studying with Paoli for two years, he was sent, with the support of the Chilean government, to study at the Stern Conservatory in Berlin, where he was a pupil of Martin Krause from 1912 to 1918. He never went to another teacher. During this period he won many awards including the Ibach Prize and the Gustav Holländer Medal. He gave his first recital in Berlin in 1914, followed by extensive tours of Germany and Scandinavia, and a European tour in 1918. At this time he played with many of the leading orchestras of Europe under conductors including Nikisch, Muck, Mengelberg, and Furtwängler. In 1921 he returned for the first time to South America, where he gave successful concerts in Argentina and Chile. He first played in London in 1922, in a concert shared with Melba and Huberman, and this was followed a year later by a tour of the United States, where he made his Carnegie Hall debut and appeared with the Boston SO and the Chicago SO.

In 1924 Arrau joined the staff of the Stern Conservatory, where he taught until 1940, and in 1927 he further enhanced his international reputation by winning the Grand Prix International des Pianistes in Geneva. Notable among his European concerts before World War II was a series of 12 recitals in Berlin in 1935, in which he played the entire keyboard works of Bach. However, he gave up playing Bach in public, after deciding that his music could not be performed satisfactorily on the piano. In 1940 he left Berlin, returning to Chile to found a piano school in Santiago. A year later, after a further tour of the United States (which was greeted with the highest critical acclaim), he and his family settled in New York. Highlights of his subsequent international career included complete performances of Beethoven's piano sonatas in London, New York, and elsewhere, including a broadcast of the cycle by the BBC in 1952, and world tours in 1968 and 1974–5. Reducing the number of concerts he gave annually (from as many as 100 to about 70) as he approached his ninth decade, he toured Europe, North America, Brazil, and Japan in 1981–2. After a 17-year absence he made an emotional tour of Chile in May 1984, having been awarded the Chilean National Arts Prize the previous year.

Arrau acquired a special reputation for his interpretations of Brahms, Schumann, Liszt, Chopin, and, above all, Beethoven, a reputation which is reflected by his many recordings. He had the technique of a virtuoso, but was one of the least ostentatious of pianists. His tempos were sometimes unusually broad, and even when they were not he gave the impression of having considered deeply the character and shape of each phrase. He could give performances so thorough in their consideration of detail that they seemed lacking in spontaneity and momentum. However, at its best his grand, rich-toned and thoughtful playing conveyed exceptional intellectual power and depth of feeling.

BIBLIOGRAPHY

N. Boyle: "Claudio Arrau," *Gramophone Record Review*, nos.73–84 (1959–60), 195–6 [with discography by F.F. Clough and G.J. Cuming]

J. Kaiser: *Grosse Pianisten in unserer Zeit* (Munich, 1965, 5/1982; Eng. trans., 1971)

C. Arrau: "A Performer Looks at Psychoanalysis," *High Fidelity/Musical America*, xvii/2 (1967), 50–54

R. Osborne: "Keyboard Oracle: Claudio Arrau in Conversation," *Records and Recording*, xvi/1 (1972–3), 26–9

B. Morrison: "Arrau at 75," *Music and Musicians*, xxvi/8 (1977–8), 32–4

R. Osborne: "Claudio Arrau at 75," *Gramophone*, lv (1977–8), 1385–6

J. Horowitz: *Conversations with Arrau* (New York, 1982)

A. Snedden: "The Interpretive Vision of Claudio Arrau," *The Journal of the American Liszt Society*, 36 (July–Dec 1994), 54-78

C. Öhm-Kühnle and D. Ballek: *Die Klaviertechnik in der Tradition von Claudio Arrau: Freier Bewegungsfluss als Grundlage von Tongestaltung und Virtuosität* (Köln-Rheinkassel, 2005)

ROBERT PHILIP/R

Arrested Development. Hip hop group. Formed in Atlanta, Georgia, in 1987 by the rapper Speech (Todd Thomas; *b* Milwaukee, WI, 25 Oct 1968), they have combined social commentary and sample-based production with a non-aggressive stance. Other members have included Rasadon (drums), Headliner (DJ), DJ Kemit, Nadirah Shakoor (lead vocals), Za (bass), One Love (vocals), JJ Boogie (guitar), Dionne Farris (vocals), Aerle Teree (poetry and vocals), Ajile and Montsho Eshe (both dance and vocals), and Baba Oje (spiritual adviser). Arrested Development first achieved fame with their debut album, *3 Years, 5 Months and 2 Days in the Life of...* (Chrysalis, 1992), the title of which referred to the length of time it took them to get a record contract. The album won Grammy awards for Best New Artist and Best Rap Performance by a Duo or Group in 1993 and has sold more than four million copies. The album's main hit "Tennessee" is a spiritually themed track about reclaiming Southern black traditions amid a history of racism. Other notable songs from the album include "Mr. Wendal," which drew attention to the plight of the homeless, and "People Everyday," which reworked Sly and the Family Stone's "Everyday People." Their mixture of rapped verses and soulfully sung choruses prefigured music by groups such as the Fugees. Arrested Development's success furthered a stream of intelligent, gentle, and commercially viable Afrocentric hip hop which was begun by De La Soul's album *3 Feet High and Rising* (1989), and they were one of many alternative rap groups to emerge in the 1990s along with the Pharcyde, A Tribe Called Quest, the Fugees, and the Roots.

In 1993 Arrested Development demonstrated the appeal of their live performances with the release of the album *Unplugged* (Chrysalis). Adopting a different approach for the album *Zingalamaduni* (Chrysalis, 1994), which was named after the Swahili word for "beehive of culture," Speech chose to increase the group's use of African vocals. In 1994 the group performed in South Africa before Nelson Mandela, but by the following year they had disbanded. In 1996 Speech released an eponymous solo album, but did not reproduce his earlier success. The band reunited in a different form in 2000 and has continued to make albums. This material has been particularly popular in Japan, where the group scored a top ten hit with "The World is Changing"(Vagabond Records & Tapes) in 2010.

IAN PEEL/JUSTIN A. WILLIAMS

Arrillaga, Santiago [y Ansola] (*b* Tolosa, Guipúzcoa, Spain, 25 July 1847; *d* Oakland, CA, 27 Jan 1915). Spanish-Basque composer, pianist, organist, and music teacher. Born into a family connected to the manufacture of berets, he studied solfège with the director of the Tolosa municipal band, and began piano and organ lessons with his parish organist. Arrillaga later studied at the Real Conservatorio de Música in Madrid—solfège with Hilarión Eslava (author of the famous solfège method), harmony with Rafael Hernando, and piano with Manuel Mendizábal. After receiving gold medals at the Madrid Conservatory for harmony and piano in July 1867, presented to him by Queen Isabel II, later in 1867 he began piano studies with Antoine-François Marmontel at the Paris Conservatoire. Around 1869, he traveled throughout Latin America, performing and teaching in San José, Costa Rica from 1870 to 1875. He moved to California in 1875, first to Los Angeles, and then soon thereafter permanently to San Francisco. He was noted for his work as a piano accompanist, performing with musicians such as singer Carlotta Patti and San Francisco guitarist-composer Manuel Ferrer. Arrillaga composed numerous instrumental and vocal works, including several for piano on Spanish themes (e.g., "Zortzico" and *El paseo por España* for piano and orchestra), as well as Catholic sacred music. He served for several decades as choirmaster and organist for the Spanish-speaking parish at the Church of Our Lady of Guadalupe. In 1910, he established the Arrillaga Musical College at his home, which he expanded and remodeled to accommodate teaching studios and a recital hall with an impressive Johnson organ. At least six of his children became musicians: Elena, Graziela, and Cecilia (piano); Leo and Amelia (voice); and Vincent (music teacher, organist, composer). After Arrillaga's death, Vincent assumed the directorship of his father's school, until its closure in 1940. Basque writers include Santiago and Vincent Arrillaga in their histories of illustrious Basques in Spain and the United States, and Santiago was noted as a representative of Spanish culture in the Bay area. The San Francisco Public Library has some of his scores and other materials related to his career.

WORKS

(*selective list*)

Rizos de oro, "Spanish dance," pf, 1880; Un beso, mazurka, pf, 1883; O Salutaris, 1v, pf, vn, 1884; Ave Maria, S, A, chorus, pf /org, 1890; 2 Spanish Characteristic Pieces: Zortzico, Graziela, pf, 1912; Paseo por España, pf, orch; Villancico, 4 vv, chorus, orch; other Catholic sacred music including masses and motets, and many piano works

Principal San Francisco publishers: Matthias Gray, Pacific Music Co., Sherman Clay, Waldteufel

BIBLIOGRAPHY

W.S.B. Mathews: *A Hundred Years of Music in America* (Philadelphia, PA, 1900), 574, 576

I. Linazasoro: "Los Arrillaga, una dinastía de músicos vasco-californianos. Santiago Arrillaga Ansola, un emigrante tolosano," *Euskor: Euskadiko Orkestra Sinfonikoaren boletin albistaria/Boletín informativo de la Orquesta Sinfónica de Euskadi*, xiii (1986)

R. M. Stevenson: "Spain's Musical Emissary in San Francisco: Santiago Arrillaga (1847-1915)," in *De musica hispana et aliis: Miscelanea en honor al Prof. Dr. Jose Lopez-Calo, S.J., en su 65° cumpleanos*, 2 (Santiago de Compostela, 1990) 287–306

L. E. Miller: *Music and Politics in San Francisco: From the 1906 Quake to the Second World War* (Berkeley, CA, 2011)

JOHN KOEGEL

Arrow Music Press. Music publishing firm. It was founded in New York in 1938 by Marc Blitzstein, Aaron Copland, Lehman Engel, and Virgil Thomson to encourage the composition, publication, and distribution of contemporary American music. In addition to leasing the catalog of the Cos Cob Press, it published works by Carter, Cowell, Diamond, Ray Green, Harris, Ives, Piston, Schuman, and Sessions as well as its founders. Its catalog was acquired by Boosey & Hawkes in 1956, but with the provision that composers could withdraw their works for placement elsewhere.

R. ALLEN LOTT

Arroyo, Martina (*b* New York, NY, 2 Feb 1937). Soprano. She studied at Hunter College, New York, and (with Grace Bumbry) won the 1958 Metropolitan Opera Auditions. That year she sang in the American premiere of Pizzetti's *L'assassino nella cattedrale* at Carnegie Hall. After taking minor roles at the Metropolitan, she went to Europe for major roles at Vienna, Düsseldorf, Berlin, Frankfurt, and Zürich (where she was under contract from 1963 to 1968). In 1965 she was a substitute Aïda for Birgit Nilsson at the Metropolitan; she sang all the major Verdi parts that formed the basis of her repertory with the Metropolitan, as well as Donna Anna, Cio-Cio-San, Liù, Santuzza, Gioconda, and Elsa. She made her London debut as Valentine at a concert performance of *Les Huguenots* in 1968—the year of her first Covent Garden appearance as Aïda. Her rich, powerfully projected voice, heard to greatest advantage in the Verdi *spinto* roles, was flexible enough for Mozart (she recorded Donna Elvira with Böhm and Donna Anna with Colin Davis). In the United States she has often sung in oratorio and recital—she was the first performer of Barber's concert scena, *Andromache's Farewell* (April 1963). Arroyo's most admired recordings include Hélène (*Les vêpres siciliennes*), Amelia (*Un ballo in maschera*), Leonora (*La forza del destino*), and Aïda.

Arroyo served on the National Endowment for the Arts (beginning in 1976), as a Trustee Emerita of the Hunter College Foundation, and as artistic adviser of the Harlem School for the Arts. She taught at the University of California in Los Angeles, Louisiana State University, and is Distinguished Professor of Music Emerita at Indiana University. In 2003 she founded the Martina Arroyo Foundation, coaching emerging singers on role preparation. In 2002 she was inducted as a Fellow into the American Academy of Arts and Sciences and in 2010 she was named an NEA Opera Honoree.

BIBLIOGRAPHY

J.B. Steane: *The Grand Tradition* (London, 1974/R), 413ff

ALAN BLYTH/KAREN M. BRYAN

Arroyo de la Cuesta, Felipe (*b* Cubo de Bureba, Burgos, Spain, 29 Apr 1780; *d* Mission Santa Inés, CA, 20 Sept 1840). Spanish musician and Franciscan missionary to Alta California. He entered the Franciscan order in Burgos in 1796, and in 1804 was ordained to the priesthood. He sailed for New Spain in September 1804, and, from 1804 to 1807, was assigned to the Colegio de San Fernando in Mexico City, the Franciscan missionary college that supplied priests for Alta California. In 1807, Arroyo de la Cuesta departed for Alta California, arriving in Monterey in 1808. He managed temporal, spiritual, and musical matters at Mission San Juan Bautista (about 30 miles from Monterey) from 1808 to 1833, when ill health forced him to retire from active missionary life. His superiors lauded his merit, ability, and zeal as a missionary, as well as his skill in teaching music to native musicians. His contemporaries noted his linguistic abilities, as a master of California Indian languages. To his detailed *Vocabulary and Phrase Book of the Mutsun Language*, he appended musical transcriptions of several California Indian social dance songs. He wrote out masses and hymns and also sang well. In 1829 he reported the acquisition of a barrel organ brought to California by Captain George Vancouver that contained 30 songs, including "Spanish Waltz" and "Go to the Devil." In 1833 he was sent to Mission San Luis Obispo, and later was at Missions San Miguel, Purísima, and Santa Inés.

BIBLIOGRAPHY

O.F. da Silva, ed.: *Mission Music of California: A Collection of Old California Mission Hymns and Masses* (Los Angeles, CA, 1941)

M. Geiger: Franciscan Missionaries in Hispanic California 1769–1848 (San Marino, CA, 1969), 19–24

C.H. Russell: *From Serra to Sancho: Music and Pageantry in the California Missions* (New York, 2009)

MARGARET CAYWARD

ARSC. *See* Association for Recorded Sound Collections (ARSC).

Art Ensemble of Chicago [AEC]. Avant-garde jazz and new-music ensemble formed in Paris in 1969 by the trumpeter Lester Bowie (*b* Frederick, MD, 11 Oct 1941; *d* New York, NY, 9 Nov 1999), the saxophonists Roscoe Mitchell (*b* Chicago, IL, 3 Aug 1940) and Joseph Jarman (*b* Pine Bluff, AR, 14 Sept 1937), and the bass player Malachi Favors (*b* Lexington, MS, 22 Aug 1927; *d* Chicago, IL, 30 Jan 2004). The drummer Famoudou Don Moye (*b* Rochester, NY, 23 May 1946) joined the following year. Having collaborated in the Experimental Band (formed in 1961) and its successor the Association for the Advancement of Creative Musicians (1965), Mitchell, Jarman, and Favors founded the Roscoe Mitchell Sextet

(1966), which they renamed the Roscoe Mitchell Art Ensemble (1967) and finally the AEC during an 18-month tenure in France (1969–71). While based in Paris they recorded 11 albums and three film scores, made numerous radio and television appearances, and gave many government-sponsored concerts throughout Western Europe. The AEC founded its own record label, AECO, in 1974 and signed contracts with ECM in 1978 and the Japanese label DIW in 1982. The group's popularity rose in the early 1980s, and they made extensive tours of the United States in 1980 and 1984, performing at large concert halls, jazz festivals, and university venues. Jarman left the group between 1993 and 2003, during which time it continued as a quartet and then, after Bowie's death from liver cancer in 1999, as a trio. Following Favors' death from pancreatic cancer, his and Bowie's positions were filled in late 2004 by the trumpeter Corey Wilkes and the bass player Jaribu Shahid. Although it performed less frequently from 2000, the group continued to tour and record until 2006.

Having grown out of a distinct free-jazz aesthetic, the AEC incorporated influences from blues, gospel, rock and roll, early New Orleans jazz, vaudeville, waltz, and the marching band tradition in order to abide by their motto "Great Black Music—Ancient to Modern." They realized their eclectic mix of contradictory musical styles in both original compositions and collective improvisations, preferring free and large-scale forms. All members of the AEC vocalized during their performances, but were also multi-instrumentalists. Mitchell and Jarman played reed instruments, vibraphone, and marimba as well as various unusual wind instruments such as whistles and conch shells; Bowie played brass instruments, harmonica, celeste, and kelp horn; Favors played double bass, zither, melodica, and banjo; and Don Moye played "sun percussion." In addition, they frequently used what they called little instruments, including drums from several continents, cymbals, gongs, bells, woodblocks, wind chimes, sirens, bicycle horns, whistles, kazoos, and cooking utensils. The group's performances had a ritualistic, theatrical character as part of what they described as a search for their African roots. Jarman and Favors wore costumes and face paintings, and frequently engaged in dances, pantomimes, comedy, and parody acts. Such visual and aural spectacles were primarily intended to raise social and political consciousness among the audience.

BIBLIOGRAPHY

J. Solothurnmann: "Insights and Views of the Art Ensemble of Chicago," *JF* [intl edn], no.49 (1977), 28–33

L. Birnbaum: "Art Ensemble of Chicago: 15 Years of Great Black Music," *DB*, xlvi/9 (1979), 15–17, 39–40, 42

P. Kemper: "Zur Funktion des Mythos im Jazz der 70er Jahre: Soziokulturelle Aspekte eines musikalischen Phänomens dargestellt an der ästhetischen Konzeption des Art Ensemble of Chicago," *Jf*, xiii (1981), 45–78

E. Janssens and H. de Craen: *Art Ensemble of Chicago Discography: Unit and Members* (Brussels, 1983) [incl. list of compositions]

J. Rockwell: "The Art Ensemble of Chicago: Jazz, Group Improvisation, Race and Racism," *All American Music: Composition in the Late Twentieth Century* (New York, 1983/R), 164–75

M. Pfleiderer: "Der kollektive Improvisationsstil des Art Ensemble of Chicago: ein Beitrag zur musikalischen Analyse in der Popularmusikforschung," *Grundlagen, Theorien, Perspektiven* (Baden-Baden, 1994), 47–62

Lenox Avenue: a Journal of Interartistic Inquiry, no.3 (1997) [includes essays on the ensemble by R. Kelley, B. Tucker, and M. J. Budds]

M. Pfleiderer: "Das Art Ensemble of Chicago in Paris, Sommer 1969: Annäherungen an den Improvisationsstil eines Musikerkollektivs," *Jf*, xxix (1997), 87–157

S. Lehmann: "'I Love You with an Asterisk': African-American Experimental Music and the French Jazz Press, 1970–1980," *Critical Studies in Improvisation*, i/2 (2005), 38–53

P. Steinbeck: "'Area by Area the Machine Unfolds': the Improvisational Performance Practice of the Art Ensemble of Chicago," *JSAM*, ii (2008), 397–427

P. Steinbeck: *Urban Magic: The Art Ensemble of Chicago's Great Black Music* (diss., Columbia U., 2008)

MICHAEL BAUMGARTNER

Arthur, Alfred F. (*b* Pittsburgh, PA, 8 Oct 1844; *d* Lakewood, OH, 20 Nov 1918). Tenor, educator, conductor, and composer. Arthur moved throughout the United States as a young man, studying in Ashland, Ohio, as well as the Boston Music School. After additional studies in Europe, Arthur fought in the Civil War before moving to Cleveland in 1871. Within two years, he founded the Cleveland Vocal Society, which he conducted for 29 seasons; the group was good enough to win first prize at the world choral competition of the World's Columbian Exposition in 1893. He conducted an orchestra at Brainard's Piano Warerooms beginning in 1872, performing classical music and popular dances that represented the first sustained orchestral presence in Cleveland. Arthur also opened a voice studio that eventually became the Cleveland School of Music in 1875.

Arthur wrote three operas: *The Water Carrier* (1875), *The Roundheads and Cavaliers* (1878), and *Adaline* (1879). The first was produced at the Euclid Avenue Opera House in Cleveland but never published. Vocal works and their performance were a specialty of Arthur, and he wrote several songs and put together two hymnals and one collection of choral works. His Seventy Lessons in Voice Training was published in 1892 and remained in use well into the 20th century.

BIBLIOGRAPHY

W.S.B. Mathews, ed.: *A Hundred Years of Music in America* (Chicago, 1889/*R*)

W. Osborne: *Music in Ohio* (Kent, OH, 2004)

JONAS WESTOVER

Art music. One of three categories in a contemporary taxonomy that typically includes folk, art, and popular musics. The viability of any of these categories depends upon its perceived distinctiveness from the others, although insisting upon too rigorous a separation of types runs the risk of ignoring their intersections and overlaps, and denying their numerous commonalities. While the application of such a taxonomy to Western music prior to the late 18th century is largely inappropriate, by the mid-19th century the categories had become well established and served a number of purposes, especially among those seeking to separate "good" music from the rest. The terms continue to circulate into the 21st century, although with increasingly less clarity regarding their differences, meaning, purpose, or usefulness. (*See also* Folk music and Popular music.)

It had been assumed by many 19th- and early 20th-century Euro-Americans that art music was a predominantly Western musical type composed by specially trained individuals, the most gifted of whom were considered geniuses; construed as uniquely reflective of natural laws; universal because of its transcendence; intrinsically interesting without recourse to programmatic explanations; unparalleled in its complexity, expressivity, originality, and thus meaning (Becker). The term "art music," if considered a viable category at all today, is now more often understood to refer to a kind of music found across cultures that is defined not by any particular or exclusively musical qualities but instead by its origins (Gelbart), its systems of support and transmission (Booth and Kuhn), and its primarily literate dissemination. Insistence upon literate dissemination as a criterion for art music status is, however, increasingly contested given the ubiquity of electronic media used to create, preserve, and disseminate music.

Newer conceptions of what constitutes art music reflect increased awareness, understanding, and valuation of non-Western musics and their modes of transmission; recognize the possibility of individual musical works inhabiting multiple categories simultaneously and/or successively; realize the role played by technology in all aspects of music production; acknowledge a range of forms of patronage and subsidy (Brooks) that support and promote the repertoire and its makers and practitioners; and admit the socially-constructed origins and functions of all categorical distinctions. Contemporary discussions of art music as a distinct category also engage with questions regarding ethnocentricism, canonicity, economics, education, class, race, gender, and hierarchical formulations of all kinds. That the term "art music" has shaped the thinking and perceptions of composers, performers, scholars, audience members, and funding agencies since its first uses and continues to do so today argues for understanding the concept as it has emerged, evolved, and been applied in American musical culture despite doubts regarding its continuing relevance or that of its many semantic equivalents: good music, classical music, serious music, cultivated music, scientific music, or high-art music.

The idea of distinguishing a "higher" type of music from other more folkish idioms gained traction in Germany in the last decades of the 18th century before establishing a foothold in the United States. The close relationship between a nascent American musical culture and large numbers of German immigrant musicians, especially in the first half of the 19th century, explains in part the ease with which Old World categorical thinking and repertoire entered New World discourse. That the first works assigned to this category in the United States were of the then contemporary Austro-Germanic tradition explains the musical criteria that would be insisted upon for subsequent admission of works to this class.

In Colonial and early Federal America the idea of art music was virtually nonexistent. Outside of church, music was considered to be entertainment, and even though the value of visual arts was recognized, by the founding of institutions such as the Charleston Museum in 1773 and the Boston Athenaeum in 1807, and literature enjoyed a position of prestige, music was not deemed worthy of serious study or consideration. In 1832 students at Harvard College petitioned to have music introduced as part of the curriculum. Even though President Josiah Quincy looked upon their petition favorably, the faculty overwhelmingly voted the idea down. The notion that certain types of music could be perceived as more than entertainment, as either aesthetically or morally superior to other types of music, grew only gradually through the 19th century. Such music was described in different ways and with different terms, and the concept of "art music" evolved, although it typically embraced a core set of values.

The first attempt to apply an aesthetic hierarchy to music came from the hymnodic reformers of the early 19th century, particularly Thomas Hastings and Lowell Mason. (*See also* Hymnody.) They sought a type of church music that was more decorous and more suitable for worship. John Hubbard had published his *Essays on Church Music* in 1808 followed by Hastings more substantial *Dissertation of Musical Taste* in 1822. That same year Mason published the *Boston Handel and Haydn Society Collection of Church Music*, one of the most influential anthologies of the 19th century. It went through 18 editions, selling more than 50,000 copies.

Mason and Hastings had two specific goals for church music: to eliminate the borrowing of secular popular songs, and to bring harmonizations more in line with European practice. Music that followed European models was referred to as "scientific." Mason in particular also began to draw upon European concert music as a source for tunes. Yet neither purging the repertoire from popular influences nor adopting European classical models was strictly carried out for musical or aesthetic reasons. Mason felt that secular songs familiar to the congregation would call to mind too many profane associations; European sources were useful precisely because local congregations were unfamiliar with them. He was especially concerned with the unrestrained emotionalism of Western revivalism, and believed that his hymnodic practices espoused restraint, decorum and dignity. It was only a small step to apply these conceits to European and scientific music.

Originally as an extension of hymnodic reform many choral societies appeared in Federal America, including the Providence Psallonian Society, the Beethoven Society of Portland Maine, and several Handel and Haydn Societies. While choirs were organized initially to improve music in regular church services, such choral societies also programmed more substantial works from European composers: Handel's *Messiah*, Haydn's *Creation*, and Beethoven's *Christ am Oldberg*. Announcing its formation, Boston's Handel and Haydn Society explained its purpose: "cultivating and improving a correct taste in the performance of Sacred Music, and also to introduce into more general practice, the works of Handel, Haydn and other eminent composers." Three concepts that would later define art music are present in this statement: the idea of taste, the importance of cultivation, and the presence of select composers who occupy a special place in the musical pantheon. That this further occurred through choral music is also emblematic of musical practice in Federal America: while choral societies had little prestige in the overall musical landscape on the European continent, they were the one type of organization in which idealistic views of music were recognized in the United States.

The notion that secular instrumental music could be edifying and morally uplifting came soon after. John Rowe Parker, who founded the most important early music journal, *Euterpiad* (1820–23), was one of the first to recognize that such music could go beyond entertainment: "the only Music by which the mind is ever truly gratified, is such as has a direct and powerful tendency, either to enliven, soften, or to elevate the feelings." Parker proposed the addition of another element to the concept of art music, that it appealed to the mind as well as the emotions, but his views fell mostly on deaf ears. In 1839, Theodore Hach, a recent immigrant from Germany, founded the *Musical Magazine*. In it he espoused the German Romantic view of music, and specifically referred to music as art. Responding to critics who found his standards too high, Hach explained: "The art [music] is infinite, and our conception of it will ever soar higher than our earthly means of representation will enable us to bring before the outward senses.... he [the critic] must have art, pure art, alone in view, as the ultimate object of what falls under his notice."

Hach was writing on the eve of two events that would have a major impact on the characterization of music as art: the founding of orchestras in Boston and New York. The Boston Academy of Music gave its first predominantly orchestral concert on 14 November 1840, and the Philharmonic Society of New York, which later became The New York Philharmonic, on 7 December 1842. In origin and organization the two orchestras were significantly different, but both shared similar goals. The New York orchestra was organized by musicians as a cooperative society, and existed as such until financial exigencies in the early 20th century forced a reorganization. The Boston orchestra was the brainchild of Samuel Atkins Eliot, Mayor of Boston, and a member of the socioeconomic elite. He wrested control of the Academy from Mason in 1835, and immediately began to transfer it from a choral to an orchestral organization. Under Eliot symphony replaced psalmody.

Although earlier orchestras existed in both cities, none had the impact of these ensembles, largely through their performances of Beethoven symphonies. Throughout the 1840s both orchestras programmed more Beethoven orchestral works than those of any other composer. Writers in Boston and New York heard these pieces as new and distinctive. Of the Fifth Symphony, Margaret Fuller wrote, "we seem to have something offered us, not only more, but different, and not only different from another work of his, but different from anything we know." She associated it with creation itself: "all is present now, and the secret of creation is read. This, not Haydn's is '*the* Creation.'" In New York, George Templeton Strong, admitted, "I expected to enjoy that Symphony, but I did not suppose it possible that it could be the transcendent affair it is." He also saw music as a special art, its source mysterious and unfathomable. After hearing the *Eroica* he wrote: "The other arts reproduce visible objects;...Even where they rise into a transcendent beauty above Nature, we can conceive how they reach it. But where and what is the standard, the source, the parallel of a sublime musical thought?...The 'harmonies and melodies' of Nature don't answer – they do not even hint at some reply. Yet somewhere in creation it must be."

No one had more impact on defining art music in the 19th century than JOHN SULLIVAN DWIGHT. Both Dwight and Fuller, his counterpart in Boston, were Transcendentalists whose writings about music in the 1840s appeared in the Transcendental magazines *The Dial* and the *Harbinger*. Transcendentalism, the American philosophical movement that emerged the previous decade, was indebted to German Romanticism but overlaid with values particular to America at the time. Important among them was the pantheistic association of God with and in nature. To Dwight not only was music sacred, it was also the very voice of God: "It [music] is God's alphabet, and not man's. It is the inbreathing of God, who is love." He then singled out Beethoven's music: "Perhaps no music ever stirred profounder depths in the hearer's religious consciousness, than some great orchestral symphonies, say those of Beethoven."

With the Transcendentalists music was thoroughly sacralized. When Dwight reviewed the string quartet concerts of the Harvard Musical Association in 1844 he described the event as more a religious assembly than a musical event. To Dwight that which qualified as pure music was sacred by definition. Popular music, minstrel songs, and any other types of music for entertainment were simply not worthy of discussion. According to Dwight there was a clear musical hierarchy, regardless of whether he identified what he valued as "art music" *per se*.

Soon after the establishment of orchestras in Boston and New York European traveling virtuosos began to arrive in the United States, among them Ole Bull in 1843, Henri Vieuxtemps in1844, and Leopold de Meyer in 1845. The Germania Orchestra, a chamber orchestra whose ensemble abilities far exceeded what most Americans were accustomed to hearing toured the nation and many of the musicians opted to remain. And then there was the Jenny Lind craze of 1850. It is not coincidental that virtuosos arrived just as railroad lines were being laid across the country; railroad travel made such touring physically and economically feasible.

Although advocates of art music in the United States later would react to virtuoso performance with ambivalence and even contempt—believing it represented shallow and empty showmanship—the first appearances of

European virtuosos did much to advance the cause of art music. Initially, Dwight was profoundly moved by Vieuxtemps's "divine solos" and described Bull's performance as "the most glorious sensation I ever had." In New York George Templeton Strong described Bull's playing as "transcendent," and the *New York Herald* critic called it "heavenly" and "beyond the power of language." Early touring virtuosos thus demonstrated to Americans that musical instruments well known to them contained potential that few had suspected. This realization further elevated concert music played by trained professionals to a level far above that which could be achieved by most amateur players and separated it from more popular and folk styles.

Thus by mid-century certain types of music had been recognized as special, defined by taste, transcendence, and emotional power, whose source remained mysterious. Music as art was distinguished from music as entertainment, an attitude often accompanied with an elitist tone. In describing the Harvard Musical Association's concerts Dwight argued that the audience must be "small and select," purged from "incongruous and unsympathetic elements." He also associated taste with "men of education and intellect," that is those of the upper class. Although he would become a troglodyte, unable to change with the musical world and to see the widening appeal of new orchestral music, Dwight, more than any other person, defined the notion of art music for the 19th-century nation.

Prior to 1860 two figures dedicated to the composition of art music stand out: ANTHONY PHILIP HEINRICH (1781–1861) and WILLIAM HENRY FRY (1813–64). Both wrote grandiose programmatic orchestral works, although Fry was best known for his operas and his music journalism. Heinrich, an Austrian merchant, stranded in the United States because of a series of financial misfortunes, turned to music, first as violinist, then as a self-taught composer. While living in Lexington, Kentucky, he published *The Dawning of Music in Kentucky* (1821), a collection that ranged from songs to elaborate chamber works. He became known as "The Log Cabin Composer," and John Rowe Parker, in the *Euterpeiad*, dubbed him "The Beethoven of America." Heinrich spent the rest of his life playing in orchestras (Boston, Philadelphia, New York, briefly London), and composing large programmatic pieces, often with unusual chromatic harmony. His most well-known piece was *The Ornithological Combat of Kings, or The Condor of the Andes and the Eagle of the Cordilleras*. Most of his compositions were beyond the capabilities of American orchestras at that time. Fry's orchestral works, like Heinrich's, put unusual demands on an orchestra; his *Niagara Symphony*, for instance, called for eleven timpani. Fry's and Heinrich's instrumental compositions—Romantic in their conception and purpose, and often programmatic—were later critiqued by Dwight, who advocated in *Dwight's Journal of Music* an art music that was European in style if not in origin, classical and abstract.

Fry articulated his own personal view of instrumental music. He became involved in journalism through his father's newspaper, the Philadelphia *National Gazette*, and was later music editor of the *New York Tribune* (1852–64). He recognized the elevated nature of abstract instrumental music, although his view differed considerably from Dwight's. Fry did not stress the emotional power or sacred quality of music. "Pure music," Fry's term, demanded cultivation, which would lead it to take its place "as a first class intellectual science; along with Astronomy, or Chemistry, or the science of growing rich."

Fry's principal contribution as a composer was in opera, a genre that complicated the definition of art music in the 19th century. Fry himself composed several operas, his most important being *Leonora* (1858), the first grand opera by an American composer to be staged in the United States. Earlier in the century bel canto arias from Italian operas had the status of popular songs, and opera's close association with the theater made it socially suspect. It was rowdy, considered unfit for ladies, and prostitutes often plied their wares in boxes. European operas were freely adapted, often with popular songs replacing original arias. The role of opera in American society would soon depend as much on its performance venue as its musical quality.

A number of short-lived attempts were made early in the 19th century in New York City to interest the elite in opera in its original form. In 1825 Manuel Garcia brought an Italian opera troupe to New York for the first presentation of opera in Italian. In 1833 a group of wealthy New Yorkers formed the Italian Opera Association, and built a grandiose opera house, with opulent boxes, the first of several attempts to separate opera from the theater. In 1847 Astor Place Opera House opened. All three of these ventures, however, lasted only briefly.

The Academy of Music opened in New York in 1854. It survived until 1886 as a residence for opera, although it was used for other entertainment until 1929. Its demise was precipitated by the opening of the rival Metropolitan Opera (The Met) in 1883. Insufficient numbers of box seats at the Academy—estimates run between 18 and 28 boxes—to accommodate the newly prominent Gilded Age families in the city were one factor in the founding of the Met. Even though the Academy hall was gigantic, at one point seating 4600 in comparison to 3,000 at the Met, opera was defined by the elite, who saw it as an important social occasion and a chance to be seen. The Met housed 122 boxes.

The appeal of opera extended beyond the elite, however. In 1851, when San Francisco was still a rough mining town, the Pelligrini troupe scored a hit with Bellini's *La Sonnambula*. In 1855 Tom McGuire, an illiterate brawling bar keeper, built his first opera house, although he did not engage a residential opera troupe until 1859. Altogether McGuire built 12 opera houses in California, although he went bankrupt several times. He continued to underwrite his passion with profits from his saloon and gambling halls. Maguire epitomized the enthusiasm for opera that many outside the elite boxes of New York felt.

THEODORE THOMAS, a violinist and conductor, did much to advocate the idea of art music and to establish the symphony orchestras as the prime symbol of high art. He conducted several orchestras in New York beginning in 1862, and from 1891 until his death in 1905 was the conductor of the Chicago Symphony. What made him one of the most visible musicians in America was a series of tours that he took with his orchestra between 1869 to 1888. The tours visited dozens of cities, large and small, and at least two (1883 and 1885) were from coast to coast. Later his tour route would be dubbed the Thomas Highway. Unlike other ensembles who would supplement a core of musicians with local talent Thomas insisted on traveling with his entire orchestra. His presence in so many towns and cities went far to foster an interest in art music and the symphony orchestra in particular. It also set a standard that could discourage some from participating in amateur music making. Without intending to, Thomas's actions created another kind of divide between art music and other kinds of music involving who was qualified to participate.

Although early on Thomas could be flexible in his programming, and in his first conducting ventures purposely programmed lighter works to increase the size of his audiences, he believed thoroughly in a sacralized art music. He called his concerts "sermons in tones." He avoided personal activities such as reading immoral books or using vulgar talk that might compromise his character because he believed that "a musician must keep his heart pure and his mind clean if he wishes to elevate, instead of debase his art."

By the end of the 19th century the notion that some music had a special, sacrosanct quality, and was in essence art, was firmly entrenched in the American psyche. Symphony orchestras had been formed in many cities. Concert programs seldom mixed high and low musical selections. Leopold de Meyer's and Sigismund Thalberg's tours of the 1840s and 50s had featured fantasias on popular operas, and they often shared the stage with singers and other performers. In contrast Anton Rubinstein and Hans von Bülow, who toured in the 1870s, played programs that focused on the classical repertoire—Beethoven, Mendelssohn, Chopin, Schumann, Schubert, Wagner, and Liszt. Thomas became less receptive to lighter pieces in his later tours. The sense of a high-low division that had been growing throughout the 19th century was captured by Johann Friedrich Ludwig "Fritz" Scheel, founding conductor of the Philadelphia Orchestra. Asked by the Board of Directors to lighten his programs, he replied, "I stand for art; as long as I am conductor of the Philadelphia Orchestra waltzes will not be played on a symphony program."

By the end of the 19th century the boundaries between what was art music and what was other music (folk and popular musics) had simultaneously solidified and become more porous. Claims that orchestral music (that is, art music) could act as a force for character development and uplift continued in the opening decades of the 20th century, advanced by American musical taste-makers as diverse as Daniel Gregory Mason, Walter Damrosch, and Charles Seeger. In the 1930s Seeger would attribute similar moral potential to America's folk music suggesting not only the mutability of the qualities that supposedly distinguished the categories, but also the vulnerability of the entire taxonomy to personal interpretation and social exigencies.

Venues such as the Academy of Music in Philadelphia (established in 1857), Carnegie Hall in New York (1891), Symphony Hall in Boston (1900), and the Auditorium Building (1889) and then later Orchestra Hall (1904) in Chicago made visible the aspirations of art music and the classes who supported it. Their European-inspired designs and décor, function as home to resident symphony orchestras featuring ritualistic performances and old world masterworks programming, and identification as must-play stops for touring virtuosos provided appropriately elaborate sites for the physical institutionalization of art music. The sacralized mission of American concert halls was evident in numerous references to the various sites as temples for music.

The overwhelming influence of German music and musicians continued apace in the late 19th century even though efforts by groups of proximate composers—including members of the Second New England School such as JOHN KNOWLES PAINE, GEORGE WHITEFIELD CHADWICK, ARTHUR FOOTE, HORATIO PARKER, and AMY MARCY BEACH—suggested the possibility that identifiably American art music was imminent. The number of these composers holding first-ever academic positions as Professors of Music in the United States (Paine at Harvard, Chadwick at the New England Conservatory, and Parker at Yale), announced its institutionalization in yet another venue: the academy. Gradually conservatories and universities became essential patrons of art music, although the predominance of German-trained faculty in American music education, starting with Paine, Chadwick, and Parker and continuing well into the 20th century, meant that students were taught and then perpetuated the old-world values and practices of their teachers. The steady pilgrimage of musicians to Germany in the closing decades of the 19th century and then to France starting in the 1920s and continuing until World War II for training in composition, conducting, and instrumental study compromised the possibility of an American musical culture free of its European yoke and delayed its commencement. That complete independence was desirable or attainable remained open to debate given the make-up of the nation's citizenry and its deep roots in a variety of European practices. While Beach never trained in Germany, she studied the scores of the high-art masters (Beethoven and Brahms especially) and modeled many of her works upon them; she aspired to the creation of art music according to their standards as did most of her contemporaries. All would be judged against the accomplishments of European composers.

In the last decade of the 19th century American composers reacted to ANTONIN DVOŘÁK's directive to claim their own nation's indigenous music for the raw materials of a distinctive cultivated art. Folk music was valorized primarily because of its usefulness to a perceived loftier enterprise, that of creating art music. It became a valuable aesthetic commodity even if it underwent significant modification in the process of integration. Like their nationalist colleagues in Europe, American composers tilled widely-varied, music-historic fields in search of identifiably national roots. Rejecting Dvořák's assessment that the most authentic American music belonged exclusively to African or Native Americans, Beach turned toward her own British Isles heritage for source materials. Her *Gaelic Symphony*, which used four melodies published in *The Citizen*, a short-lived Irish nationalist magazine, seemingly ennobled the folk tunes by folding them into the most respected art music genre, the symphony. A number of her keyboard works also referenced Scottish and Irish folk tunes, and in one set of character pieces, *Eskimos*, she engaged with Inuit music. Folk materials found a welcome home in Beach's compositions. EDWARD MACDOWELL turned to Native American sources for his *Indian Suite*, ostensibly demonstrating his commitment to an authentic American musical culture, even if the materials were taken from a vanquished, indigenous people. In both cases, the music of Beach and MacDowell was thoroughly informed by German musical romanticism. While Beach soon lost prominence in part because of societal restrictions regarding a woman composer's place in the professional musical world, which confined her to what was dismissed as the amateur domain of the parlor and its female patrons, MacDowell was broadly championed as the most skilled and representative American art music composer of his day. He was appointed the first Professor of Music at Columbia University in 1896, thus continuing the tradition of German-trained composer/musicians as leaders of American university music programs.

Folk materials, regardless of their level of purity, did not compromise the supposed integrity of Beach's and MacDowell's music, which synthesized highly valued forms and genres and featured a thoroughly European, late-Romantic harmonic idiom. That the specific folk tunes were virtually unknown and could only be identified by a few partisans allowed them to function as acceptable representatives of a type, as abstractions, similar to the newly created, original, "absolute" music surrounding them. In this way they functioned for modern audiences much like the folk tunes that Haydn regularly used in his symphonies, quartets, and sonatas. Unknown, they posed no threat to the idea of transcendent "art music."

Within two decades, however, the autonomy of such a category as art music was directly contested by the works of composers as varied as CHARLES IVES, FERDE GROFÉ, WILLIAM GRANT STILL, and GEORGE GERSHWIN, each of whom imported thoroughly familiar materials taken from popular and folk styles of music clearly outside the boundaries of the high art category, and most importantly recognized as such. Although Ives wrote songs, sonatas, string quartets, concerti, and symphonies, and thus worked within the genres most valued by 19th-century art music standard bearers, his use of widely known Protestant hymns, familiar Civil War songs, and popular tunes of the day as essential compositional materials upon which entire pieces were built challenged and, some argued, compromised the distinctiveness, seriousness, and sanctity of the art music endeavor. Should listeners be tapping their toes to a popular rag when contemplating an orchestral work such as Ives's *Central Park in the Dark*? Do the numerous extra-musical effects, along with the simulation of clip-clopping hooves, in Grofé's *Grand Canyon Suite* undermine its claim to seriousness? Still's *Afro-American Symphony* threatened assumptions regarding acceptable orchestral instruments and the inviolability of antecedent-consequent phrases when he included a banjo in his symphony score and used a 12-bar blues pattern, which upset expectations for periodic structure and harmonic behavior. Quite aside from the aesthetic challenges such music presented, how did programmatic works so clearly anchored in the mundane (and non-elite) reconcile themselves with art music's aspiration for transcendence?

Gershwin may have pushed the boundaries of categorical autonomy further than any of the others with his bold hybridized aesthetic. Tin Pan Alley, jazz, blues, folk, and art music (as well as car horns) came together in pieces such as *Rhapsody in Blue*, Piano Concerto in F, *American in Paris*, and *Porgy and Bess*. At home on Broadway as well as in Carnegie Hall Gershwin's music resisted confinement within established categories or venues. It would seem that the further American composers moved away from 19th-century notions of taxonomic purity, the closer they moved toward a nationally identifiable music. Their insistence upon an American music rooted in distinctly American materials was at odds with essential aspirations traditionally associated with "art music": inspiration, elevation, transcendence, and moral uplift. It was not that they rejected these goals for their music but rather that they denied such goals were the exclusive property of any single type of music or that all music had to embody such aspirations. With their crossbred creations these American composers defied narrow readings of music's function and purpose and critiqued a taxonomy that denied the multiplicity of meanings inherent in basic materials regardless of their source. They expanded ownership of the nation's musical culture as they insisted upon a broader reading of what counted as "good" music.

Simultaneously with the efforts of Ives, Grofé, Still, and Gershwin, the first decades of the 20th century saw a number of formal initiatives aimed at establishing a high-art national musical culture that could compete with the best of Europe. In 1915 *The Musical Quarterly* published its first issue. Its editor, OSCAR G. T. SONNECK, long a partisan of American music, remained at the helm until his death in 1928. *Musical Quarterly* would testify to the seriousness of the nation's musical thinking. In 1921 AARON COPLAND went abroad to study with NADIA BOULANGER in the first group of composers to train at the Conservatoire Américain at Fontainebleau, an institution whose original conception grew out of World War I political alliances and which offered systematic musical education that was decidedly non-German. The Franco-American initiative was the brainchild of Walter Damrosch and Robert Casadesus, among others, who sought to continue war-time music education efforts (originally directed at band conductors) through a newly conceived summer program now aimed at aspiring American composers. Over the years Boulanger, a close and deeply admired associate of Damrosch, became the pedagogue of choice for a steady stream of musical Americans studying abroad, including Marc Blitzstein, Elliott Carter, David Diamond, Philip Glass, Roy Harris, Quincy Jones, Douglass Moore, Walter Piston, Roger Sessions, Elie Siegmeister, Louise Talma, and Virgil Thomson, to name only some of her most prominent students. While an argument could be made that the United States simply substituted one European parent for another, the variety of personal styles present in the aforementioned list of composers suggests Boulanger's respect for a nascent individualistic American musical culture despite her rigorous, Paris Conservatoire-derived training methods. Her rejection of George Gershwin as a student was rooted in the belief that such training might compromise his already fully-formed and distinctive musical voice. Her decision may also be construed as reflecting her respect for Gershwin's absorption and mastery of indigenous American styles, in particular jazz.

Starting in the 1920s an even greater impact on the nation's music culture involved the emergence of radio, which could disseminate music of all kinds to thousands of listeners in a single evening. In the early years of the decade stations were launched in cities such as Pittsburgh, New York, San Jose, and Detroit carrying a variety of programming, including sportscasts, religious services, and live theater productions. Specialty programs, such as that broadcast from Chicago's KYW, catered to opera lovers; it transmitted only opera six days a week. While families and friends gathered around the radio to listen to their favorite shows—advertisements stressed the social advantages of owning a prominently placed attractive machine—the explosion of stations and the variety of broadcasts meant that there was less incentive to leave home to experience musical culture, especially if a live concert was programmed on radio. Democratized access challenged the elite status that had been attached to art music and threatened the need for the temple-like halls that had been, heretofore, the exclusive home to its performance. Radio guaranteed that no single musical style would speak to or for the nation's increasingly diverse population who came to the country with musical cultures, values, and preferences of their own. Conductors in the tradition of Theodore Thomas and Fritz Scheel, who had been intent on improving American culture through the performance of predominantly German music and who brooked no opposition when it came to determining the repertoire they programmed for the Chicago and Philadelphia orchestras in the first decade of the century, could be silenced with the simple twist of the dial by listeners unwilling to be "uplifted" according to someone else's standards, or uplifted at all.

But champions of a 19th-century belief in the superiority and edifying possibilities of art music did not give up without attempting again to "raise" the nation's musical literacy and taste. Embracing the very medium that had the potential to undermine the dominion of high-art music Walter DAMROSCH hosted the NBC *Music Appreciation Hour* (1928–42) with the goal of educating a broad range of audiences from elementary school children to high school, college, and community groups. Unsurprisingly Damrosch primarily discussed German and Austrian composers and their masterworks. French music placed a distant second. With his decided distaste for dissonant music, Damrosch did not program contemporary composers of a more modernist bent. In 1959, another German-born American, Karl Haas, picked up the mantle of radio-host-in-residence with *Adventures in Good Music*, a program designed to disseminate art music. It was carried by stations across the nation until 2005 and endeared both Haas and his program to the millions who regularly tuned in. The 1950s saw the charismatic LEONARD BERNSTEIN, recently appointed conductor of the New York Philharmonic, use the new medium of television to disseminate musical knowledge to a broad public. Bernstein's easy-going style, all-embracing musical aesthetic, dramatic flair, and palpable engagement with the music, however, meant that the *Young People's Concerts* (broadcast live from Carnegie Hall starting in 1958) were not as mired in 19th-century notions of music's exclusive, serious, and elevating purpose. Indeed, Bernstein's all-American training resulted in his programming and recording much American music throughout his tenure with the NYPO and in the years afterward. As video recordings of the *Young People's Concerts* demonstrate, Bernstein encouraged laughter in the hallowed halls of Carnegie.

At the same time that radio emerged on the scene American composers organized themselves into societies and guilds to promote new music. In 1921 Edgard Varèse and Carlos Salzedo founded the first of these groups located in New York: the INTERNATIONAL COMPOSERS' GUILD gave the premieres of a number of important works at their concerts and then disbanded in 1927. In 1923 the LEAGUE OF COMPOSERS came together, sponsored its own concerts, and a year later published the *League of Composers Review*. The journal changed its name to *Modern Music* in 1925 and continued publication until 1946. In 1928 the Pan-American Association of Composers reached across the border to engage with composers in Mexico and South America and promote a musical aesthetic that was American in the largest sense of the term. They remained a formal organization until 1934. In 1925 HENRY COWELL launched the New Music Society of California, the west-coast affiliate of the ICG, and championed performances of ultra-modern music. Two years later Cowell began *New Music,* a quarterly journal dedicated to the publication of scores of recently composed works that had little commercial appeal, but that represented the most advanced musical thinking of the time. A partial list of composers published in the earliest years of *New Music* suggests the reach of Cowell's efforts to encourage American music: Ruggles, Rudhyar, Ornstein, Imre Weisshaus, Chávez, Ruth Crawford, Ives, Adolph Weiss, Copland, Slonimsky, John Becker, Riegger, and McPhee. In time *New*

Music would also publish Edgard Varèse, Arnold Schoenberg, and Anton Webern. Cowell found a friend and champion in Ives, whose financing of the journal and then later of the *New Music Quarterly Recordings*, made the dissemination of a wide range of contemporary music possible. In all cases the societies and their publications threw their support to a group of composers whose music was not embraced by either radio programmers or music education specialists, or regularly heard in large, established concert halls. New music would find its home elsewhere.

The emergence of sound film eventually attracted composers such as VIRGIL THOMSON, who took advantage of the opportunity to include hymn tunes, popular music, and cowboy songs in his 1936 score to Pare Lorentz's New Deal documentary *The Plow that Broke the Plains*; he followed it with *The River* in 1937, which drew from folk music and jazz. Both films were sponsored by the US Government, which unintentionally endorsed this new taxonomically-hybridized musical score. Inspired by Thomson's work and an idea from Lorentz, Copland scored a documentary film for the 1939 New York World's Fair. In *The City* Copland paired the sight of a traffic jam with the sound of dance music. The wholly American film scores of Thomson and Copland provided a clear contrast to the Wagnerian-inspired soundtracks of Austrian émigré composers Erich Korngold and Max Steiner. Thomson's and Copland's corpus of Hollywood scores would be recognized with multiple awards and inspire generations of early American film composers. The Federal Music Project of the Works Progress Administration provided another site for developing the nation's music culture. Between 1935 and 1938 the FMP, under the direction of Nikolai Sokoloff, sponsored hundreds of orchestral concerts that included works by dozens of American composers with the aim of educating and entertaining an economically depressed citizenry.

Sensitive to the volatile economic and political climate of the interwar years and eager to reach larger audiences, Copland turned away from the abstract and architectural style present in the *Piano Variations* and *Short Symphony* to compose pieces whose subject matter and musical language drew from and evoked American pastoral tradition and western mythology. This is nowhere more evident than in his three famous ballets. With their storylines, settings, costumes, dances, and music *Billy the Kid* (1938), *Rodeo* (1942), and *Appalachian Spring* (1943–4) made a unique American contribution to ballet repertoire. Not comfortable importing a European classical dance aesthetic to tell American stories, these works demanded that choreographer and composer reconsider the genre and what was acceptable as source material and choreographic movement. With their American spirit and sensibility, which recalled the instrumental works of Ives, Grofé, Still, and Gershwin, these works challenged existing boundaries that separated what was considered folk, popular, or high art music.

The influx of émigrés before and during World War II brought composers as diverse as Kurt Weill, Igor Stravinsky, Ernst Krenek, Béla Bartók, Arnold Schoenberg, Stefan Wolpe, and Paul Hindemith among others to the United States. Once again, large numbers of European-trained musicians found themselves in positions of power and influence, but now they entered a more mature musical culture than had greeted them a century earlier, one that was less vulnerable to the imposition of a foreign aesthetic. In fairness, the exiled composers did not share or propagate a single set of musical values. Categorical thinking that had once separated art from popular and folk musics and that had insisted upon a qualitative difference between the types held little sway over composers such as Weill, Krenek, Stravinsky, and Bartók, whose music drew from multiple sources. While Damrosch might have recoiled at the dissonances and pounding (primitive) rhythms of Stravinsky's *Rite of Spring*, there was no denying the ballet's seriousness of purpose. That Bartók's quartets, concerti, operas, and various chamber and keyboard works were thoroughly imbued with folk tunes or Bartók's own inspired imitations of folk songs and dances could not keep his works from the concert hall. If European masters had provided the original archetypes for the nation's aspiring art-music culture, newer European composers presented different models that regularly traversed categories. It is possible that their works, combined with the undeniable popularity of pieces by Gershwin and Grofé, challenged the sanctity of the term "art music" or at least expanded its usage. If the term "art music" had not disappeared, it meant something quite different in the 1940s than it had when it first gained currency.

Commercial recordings of art music, along with a very wide range of additional musical styles, had become increasingly available to consumers during the first half of the 20th century. With the advent of the LP record in 1948, audiophiles found reason to purchase more advanced sound systems to enjoy longer recorded works in higher fidelity. As with the case of radio, the recording industry presented substantial challenges to established concert-going practices, but at the same time the commercial potential, the artistic possibilities, and the manifold uses of audio recordings attracted performers and audiences new and old.

The years immediately following the war also saw an expansion of music programs in American universities across the country. Schoenberg, Hindemith, Wolpe, and Krenek were appointed to faculty positions and thus the tradition of Austro-German musical training at American educational institutions that had begun in the late 19th century continued well into the second half of the 20th century. They were joined by American composer colleagues including Sessions, Piston, Schuman, Howard Hanson, Finney, and Babbitt, whose eclectic training both stateside and abroad guaranteed that American students would experience a more balanced and enlarged vision of musical possibilities. An increase in academic offerings in music appreciation promoted the idea of a canon of "classical" European masterworks at the same time that musicology programs with courses devoted to American music slowly proliferated. Important histories of American music also emerged (*see* Histories), including the first editions of Gilbert Chase's seminal study *America's Music, from the Pilgrims to the Present* (New York, 1955) and H. Wiley Hitchcock's *Music in the United States: a Historical Introduction* (Englewood Cliffs, NJ, 1969). Hitchcock adopted the terms "cultivated" and "vernacular" from John Kouwenhoven's work on American design and the arts (*Made in America*, 1948) and codified their use to describe two broad categories of musical types found in the United States. Hitchcock's concepts continue to circulate and impact today's formulations of the nation's musical culture.

Of more importance, perhaps, than the widely expanded training available to American students was the support that educational institutions provided for artistic experimentation; faculty composers could now create without worry of being rejected by a conservative symphony board that refused to program their works, failing to sell out an oversized concert hall, or having to appeal to a wide audience. Rather than respond to charges of elitism through nationally broadcast radio programs that were designed to "raise" listeners' musical literacy and increase audience size, as had been done in the past, a new breed of university composers simply acknowledged the reality that their audience would likely be a small one comprised of audacious amateurs and trained specialists.

Babbitt's now-infamous 1958 article originally titled "The Composer as Specialist," but provocatively renamed "Who Cares If You Listen?" by a *High Fidelity* editor, captured the situation. Freed from the constraints of writing for anyone but themselves, many university composers guaranteed their insulation and passively accepted charges of elitism. In many cases their music achieved levels of complexity that were beyond human recreation or comprehension. Questions regarding serious music's purported purpose of universality, transcendence, and expressivity were circumvented completely. While the sounds produced by electronic instruments pushed beyond the boundaries of what qualified as music for some listeners, the highly complex works drove a deeper wedge between such composers' creations and popular and folk musics.

The composer John Cage took things in a different direction by questioning essential Western assumptions regarding music as an inspired autonomous creation and the composer as its genius creator. Uninterested in composing transcending masterpieces according to old paradigms or hyper-organized and electronic works according to new ones Cage acted more the role of host than artist when he invited listeners to engage the world of ambient sound and embrace the results of willful unintention. His breakthrough work *4' 33"*, a "silent" piece that premiered in 1952, questioned every facet of musical thinking that had held sway in Western practice. There were no taxonomies in Cage's world, only sound and silence, and the latter was debatable. What had been described as ultra-modern music in the 1920s became known as experimental music in the post war decades as Tudor, Earle Brown, and Morton Feldman joined Cage in a vibrant, newly elite, if occasionally playful, musical scene.

Although classical music lost a significant share of the mainstream American music audience during the middle decades of the century to popular genres such as swing and, later, rock and roll, the postwar period saw a number of developments that helped to bolster art music in the United States. Large private foundations such as the Carnegie, Rockefeller, and Ford Foundations offered increased institutional funding (*see* Foundations), while smaller organizations—including the Fromm, Guggenheim, and Elizabeth Sprague Coolidge Foundations, and the MacDowell Colony—continued to support the commissioning and performance of new works and/or to fund residencies. Substantial government support was established in 1965 with the creation of the National Foundation on the Arts and Humanities, funded by Congressional appropriations and managed by the National Endowment for the Arts (NEA) and the National Endowment for the Humanities (NEH). Over the next 30 years, the NEA made over one thousand grants to individual composers; since 1995, funds for individual composers have been directed through re-granting authorities such as state arts councils and organizations such as American Composers Forum, Meet the Composer, and the American Music Center. The three latter organizations also assist composers through programs for commissioning, performing, and recording their work. Art music composers also have gained honor, prestige, and financial support through various institutions—including the Pulitzer Prizes and the Grawemeyer Awards—that grant awards for excellence in music (*see* Awards). The formation of scholarly organizations devoted to individual composers, including the Charles Ives Society (which became active in 1973), has also prompted further concerts, conferences, festivals, and critical editions. The success of the Lincoln Center for the Performing Arts in New York (which opened in stages beginning in the early 1960s)—a centralized consortium of cultural institutions including the Metropolitan Opera, New York Philharmonic, The Juilliard School, and the New York City Ballet among others—demonstrates how much American audiences continue to treasure these musical traditions.

At the same time, new challenges to notions of "art music" emerged. The 1960s saw the spread of an interdisciplinary genre commonly referred to as Performance art. Composers, choreographers, instrumental and vocal performers, artists, writers, and creative types of all kinds worked between and across the borders of their disciplines. Artists such as Laurie Anderson and Meredith Monk, each of whom was accomplished in multiple fields, confused critics with works that defied categorization. Questions regarding to what taxonomy the music part of their multi-disciplinary works belonged seemed incidental if not downright irrelevant. This period also gave birth to Minimalism, a musical style growing out of the Eastern-inflected experimental thinking of Cage and characterized by its limited materials, if not limited durations. Its earliest exponents included LA MONTE YOUNG, TERRY RILEY, STEVE REICH and PHILIP GLASS. JOHN ADAMS, born in 1947, a decade after Glass, adapted basic tenets of the style but greatly expanded the timbral palette in his works and employed dynamic schemes and more narrative structures that negated the hypnotic effect often achieved in the music of the original four. Materializing first in San Francisco and New York, minimalism was among the most important movements to emerge in the second half of the 20th century; it is recognized as an original American contribution to Western musical culture. That its originators were broadly influenced by jazz, popular, and global musical practices as much as by their classical high-art training, that some of its practitioners have achieved virtual celebrity status, and that their crossover music is heard today variously in prestigious concert halls, film soundtracks, and commercial advertisements, challenges the viability of taxonomies such as "art" (or "classical"), "folk," and "popular" when discussing this repertoire.

In the late 19th century the terms "art" and "classical" referred to the same repertoire and writers on music had a clear sense of what they meant when they described a work as "classical." In 1895 William Mason explained it was "music which through prolonged usage has proved its possession of those qualities which entitle it to be taken as a standard of excellence, and which has come to be acknowledged... as representing the highest expression of musical taste and hence authoritative as a model." In the same year George F. Root described classical music as "a model of excellence that possesses that mysterious vitality which makes it outlive its companions," music that by "common consensus of musical opinion... belongs to the first rank." From their perspectives excellence, taste, authority, mystery, and hierarchy all belonged to "classical" or "art music" alone. That such music was European went without saying.

At the opening of the second decade of the 21st century America's "art music" culture embraces a variety of styles, culled from many eras and traditions, and reflecting a range of aesthetic values pulled from across the globe. Performances of Beethoven symphonies by the New York Philharmonic, cross-cultural collaborations organized by the Kronos Quartet or Yo-Yo Ma, and experimental pieces by the new music ensemble eighth blackbird offer clear proof of the breadth of art music today. These musicians all may aspire to make "good" music, but "good" no longer carries the moral imperative of 19th-century taste-makers who endeavored to lift up a nation using a model repertoire that they felt was superior to all others. Likewise, American colleges and universities, which for decades had focused their music curriculum primarily on Western art music, now offer full programs in subjects ranging from jazz studies to musical theater as well as courses in popular music, world music, and much more. The clanging of a gamelan ensemble is just as likely to be heard alongside the strains of European classics being practiced on traditional orchestral instruments, while sounds of Irish fiddles, Caribbean pans, Chinese zheng, and African drums course through the modern music school soundscape.

Contemporary composers often work at their laptops or digital audio workstations, influenced by myriad styles from around the world, source material that is instantly downloadable at the touch of a button. Their richly hybridized works may freely incorporate traditional, found, and synthesized instruments as well as sampled sounds. A new predominantly tonal, neoromantic idiom thrives in the works of composers such as LIBBY LARSEN, PAUL MORAVEC, JOAN TOWER, and ELLEN TAAFFE ZWILICH. Environmental consciousness finds a place in the music of JOHN LUTHER ADAMS and Emily Doolittle who engage animal vocalizations and the earth's resonance in their compositions. A continuing fascination with the ritualistic potential of music is heard in the music of GEORGE CRUMB with its eclectic mix of strange and familiar sounds, which continue to provoke and inspire. PAULINE OLIVEROS has entered her ninth decade with an intensified commitment to Deep Listening, which grew out of her early electronic work in the 1950s and 1960s, and continues to question the roles of composer and performer much like fellow traveler Cage.

Today the terms "art music" and "classical music" frequently appear in quotes, one indication of their fraught status. While classical radio stations continue to cultivate audiences whose listeners they identify as more refined, the repertoire they play is significantly broader and more eclectic than what Mason or Root had in mind, even as the notion of its excellence and durability persists. With jazz now fully ensconced in Lincoln Center—and many of its pieces and purveyors broadly acknowledged as "classics" or "masters"—the idea of distinguishing a clearly bounded "art music" grows increasingly untenable. The diminishing market share of classical music and the recognition of the economic power of popular music culture mean that partisans of "art music" have been forced to acknowledge the existence of a variety of types and idioms comprising a rich and complex musical culture of which "art music" is merely a part. As much as it remains meaningful to and cherished by contemporary audiences, the category will never again be the standard against which all other musical expressions are measured.

BIBLIOGRAPHY

GEWM, viii ("History of European Art Music," D. Schulenberg)

G.F. Root: "What is Classic Music?" *Music, a Monthly Magazine, Devoted to the Art, Science, Technic and Literature of Music*, 7 (January 1895), 281 only

W. Mason: "What is Classical Music?" *Music, a Monthly Magazine, Devoted to the Art, Science, Technic and Literature of Music*, 7 (March 1895), 520 only

W. Damrosch: *My Musical Life* (New York, 1930)

L. Sabaneev and S.W. Pring: "Light Music," *MT*, lxxix (1938), 496–98

J. Kouwenhoven: *Made in America* (Garden City, NY, 1948)

W.T. Upton: *William Henry Fry: American Journalist and Composer-Critic* (New York, 1954/*R*)

G. Chase: *America's Music, from the Pilgrims to the Present* (New York, 1955, 3/1987)

L. Crickmore: "Third Stream or Third Programme?" *MT*, cii (1961), 701–2

W. Mellers: *Music in a New Found Land* (London, 1964)

J.T. Howard: *Our American Music: a Comprehensive History from 1620 to the Present* (New York, 1965)
B. Szabolcsi: "Folk Music, Art Music, History of Music," *SMH*, xxi/4 (1965) 171–9
H.W. Hitchcock: *Music in the United States: a Historical Introduction* (Englewood Cliffs, NJ, 1969, 4/2000)
H. Roach: *Black American Music: Past and Present* (Boston, 1973)
W. Brooks: "On Being Tasteless," *Popular Music*, ii (1982), 9–18
C. Hamm: *Music in the New World* (New York, 1983)
E. Southern: *The Music of Black Americans: a History* (New York, 2/1983)
J. Parakilas: "Classical Music as Popular Music," *JM*, iii (1984), 1–18
C. Pemberton: *Lowell Mason, His Life and Work* (Ann Arbor, MI, 1985)
J. Becker: "Is Western art music superior?" *MQ*, lxxii (1986), 341–59
V.B. Lawrence: *Strong on Music: the New York Music Scene in the Days of George Templeton Strong, 1836–1875*, i (New York, 1988)
L.W. Levine: *Highbrow/Lowbrow: the Emergence of Cultural Hierarchy in America* (Cambridge, MA, 1988)
R. Qureshi and others: "From Composer to Audience: the Production of 'Serious' Music in Canada," *Canadian University Music Review*, ix (1989), 117–37
G.D. Booth and T.L. Kuhn: "Economic and Transmission Factors as Essential Elements in the Definition of Folk, Art, and Pop Music," *MQ*, lxxiv (1990), 411–38
M. Broyles: *"Music of the Highest Class": Elitism and Populism in Antebellum Boston* (New Haven, CT, 1992)
D. Brackett: "Economics and Aesthetics in Contemporary Art Music," *Stanford Humanities Review*, iii/2 (1993), 49–59
M. Citron: *Gender and the Musical Canon* (Cambridge, 1993)
J. Dizikes: *Opera in America: a Cultural History* (New Haven, CT, 1993)
A.F. Block: *Amy Beach: Passionate Victorian* (New York, 1998)
J. Dunbar: "Art Music on the Radio, 1927–1937: Conflicting Views of Composers and Educators," *The Bulletin of Historical Research in Music Education*, xix (1998), 165–76
J. Horowitz: "'Sermons in Tones': Sacralization as a Theme in American Classical Music," *American Music*, xvi (1998), 311–40
D. Nicholls, ed.: *The Cambridge History of American Music* (Cambridge, 1998)
B. Nettl: "The Role of History in Contemporary European Art-Music Culture," *The Garland Encyclopedia of World Music VIII: Europe* (New York, 2000)
C. Oja: *Making Music Modern: New York in the 1920s* (New York, 2000)
R. Crawford: *America's Musical Life: a History* (New York, 2001)
R.A. Lott: *From Paris to Peoria: How European Piano Virtuosos Brought Classical Music to the American Heartland* (New York, 2003)
M. Gelbart: *The Invention of "Folk Music" and "Art Music": Emerging Categories from Ossian to Wagner* (Cambridge, 2007)
V. Agnew: Review of Matthew Gilbert: *The Invention of "Folk Music" and "Art Music": Emerging Categories from Ossian to Wagner* (Cambridge, 2007), *JAMS*, lxiii (2010), 155–9
M. Broyles: "Bourgeois Appropriation of Music: Challenging Ethnicity, Class, and Gender," *The American Bourgeosie: Distinction and Identity in the Nineteenth Century*, ed. S. Beckert and J.B. Rosenbaum (New York, 2010), 233–46
E. Drott: "Fraudulence and the Gift Economy of Music," *JMT*, liv (2010), 61–74

DENISE VON GLAHN, MICHAEL BROYLES

Art rock. Art rock is a contested term referring to British progressive rock influenced by classical music, as well as rock music made by musicians whose creative experience and training was drawn more from visual art than music. Many musicians of the latter group attended art schools, where they developed familiarity with the techniques and theory of contemporary art. Emphasis was placed on postmodern, eclectic, and avant-garde approaches. This stream of art rock had a significant influence on the development of punk, new wave, and related styles in the United States.

Early cross-fertilization of rock and contemporary art in the United States was evident in Andy Warhol's collaboration with the Velvet Underground in 1966. His multi-media events, called the Exploding Plastic Inevitable, combined his films with the band's rock music, which was overlaid with minimalist features, including drones. Warhol's goal of using rock as part of a larger, interdisciplinary-art work based around performance was influential on later incarnations of art rock. Frank Zappa's work from the same era sat ambiguously between rock, avant-garde composition, and *musique concrète*, with similar avenues explored by Captain Beefheart.

In Britain the term art rock most often described groups in the late 1960s and early 1970s that fused Western art music with rock, including the Nice, King Crimson, Yes, Jethro Tull, Genesis, Gentle Giant, and Emerson, Lake and Palmer. While some of these groups, especially Genesis, came close to generating interdisciplinary performance art at times, the art in this genre derived mainly from classical techniques and forms in their music and literary references in their lyrics. In the United States the genre was commonly referred to as PROGRESSIVE ROCK, rather than art rock.

During the 1970s groups experimenting with the style of minimalism pioneered by the Velvet Underground and garage-rock primitivism developed as PUNK; these included Iggy Pop and the Stooges and the Ramones. Commentators have compared punk to shock-art movements like Dada, which were interdisciplinary and not specifically music focused. Performers like Roxy Music, David Bowie, and the New York Dolls, with distinctly camp and androgynous visual presentations, accompanied by experimental musical approaches, used rock as a medium for arty stylizations. Some new-wave performers, like Pere Ubu and Talking Heads, brought expressionist and postmodern sensibilities to bear in their work. Much post-punk art rock attempted to erase or question distinctions between art and commodity as a key creative strategy.

The use of rock and pop as part of PERFORMANCE ART is notable in the work of Laurie Anderson and Diamanda Galás, as well as that of such singer-songwriters as Kate Bush, Peter Gabriel, and Tori Amos. Some art-rock performers, notably David Sylvian, Joni Mitchell, and Brian Eno, worked simultaneously in art media to develop their profiles as multifaceted artists.

Some alternative rock draws from similar aesthetics to its post-punk art rock predecessors, exemplified in Sonic Youth's experiments with dissonance, non-tempered guitar tunings, and associations with the avant-garde composer Glenn Branca. In the 1990s and 2000s the surprising commercial success of Radiohead's studio experimentation and subversions of pop song aesthetics suggest that fusions of avant-garde art ideas and rock music still had a niche.

BIBLIOGRAPHY

J. Rockwell: "Art Rock," *The Rolling Stone Illustrated History of Rock & Roll*, ed. J. Miller (New York, 1976, 2/1980), 347–52; rev. as "The Emergence of Art Rock," *The Rolling Stone Illustrated History of*

Rock & Roll, A. DeCurtis, J. Henke, and H. George-Warren (New York, 3/1992), 492–9
P. Stump: *The Music's all that Matters: a History of Progressive Rock* (London, 1998)
K. Holm-Hudson, ed.: *Progressive Rock Reconsidered* (New York, 2002)
S. Baker, ed.: *New York Noise: Art and Music of the New York Underground 1978–88* (London, 2007)

CHRIS McDONALD

Arts administration. The field of managing the business side of an arts organization. In today's music world, most of these positions are with not-for-profit 501(c)(3) organizations. Professional arts administrators are responsible for facilitating an organization's day-to-day operations as well as the strategic long-range planning necessary to fulfill the organization's mission. Not-for-profit music organizations include but are not limited to: professional and community symphony orchestras and bands, choirs and chorales, chamber orchestras, music ensembles, opera companies, university music societies, presenters, music festivals and jazz bands and ensembles. General duties of an arts administrator can include human resource management, marketing, accounting and financial management, public relations, fundraising, program development and evaluation, strategic planning, and board development and relations.

The role of the arts administrator has grown organically from its original artist/manager model. Ureli Corelli Hill (1802–75), founder and president of the New York Philharmonic in 1842, is an excellent example of an early artist/manager combining the roles of volunteer, administrator, and artist. For American businessman Henry Lee Higginson (1834–1919) and volunteer philanthropist, it was music appreciation, rather than avocation, that led him to found the Boston Symphony Orchestra. Arthur Judson (1881–1975) was one of the earliest professional arts administrators in the field of music. Judson worked with both established orchestras and individual artists. He was president of the Columbia Concerts Corporation (now Columbia Artists Management) and manager of both the Philadelphia Orchestra and the New York Philharmonic. As programming for these early cultural organizations grew, so did the need for formal business management, and thus a separate arts administrator role developed.

Need for arts administrators expanded when in 1913 the 16th Amendment to the US Constitution established the income tax, thus affecting the flow of disposable income from wealthy philanthropists to cultural organizations. Soon after, the Revenue Act of 1918 offered a tax deduction for charity. The Revenue Act of 1943 required all not-for-profit organizations to file an annual 990 form with the IRS, increasing the need for fiscal management of these organizations. The Revenue Act of 1954 would establish the not-for-profit 501(c) tax code we use today.

The National endowment for the arts (NEA), founded by the Johnson administration in 1965, expanded the reach of not-for-profit cultural organizations throughout the United States and further professionalized the field of arts administration. The current trend to decrease NEA appropriations began in 1989 when a political debate over artistic content of government-funded projects began. Declines in NEA funding through the 1990s encouraged organizations to diversify their sources of money to become more sustainable, again shifting the role of the administrator toward revenue development.

Today the arts administrator focuses on strategic planning and a more comprehensive approach to arts advocacy, beyond the NEA. This has enhanced an understanding of the positive and essential impact arts and culture have on our communities. Not-for-profit music organizations outside of the classical traditions, such as the Rock and Roll Hall of Fame, the Experience Music Project, and Jazz at Lincoln Center, depend on this community/cultural organization relationship. Although most symphony orchestras were created during the later 19th century/early 20th century, many regional cultural organizations were founded with initial support from the NEA. The sustained institutional leadership of these organizations is a critical issue in arts administration today, since many founders are now retiring. In addition, not-for-profit arts organizations are beginning to question their own lasting legacies, often overtly affected by changes in the broader national economy, audience taste, and trends and impacts of human resource management.

Formal training programs in arts administration were developed in the mid-1960s. The Association of Arts Administration Educators (AAAE) has supported the development of this field since its founding in 1975. AAAE members currently include 16 undergraduate and 37 graduate programs in the United States. Founded in 1969, the Bolz Center for Arts Administration at the University of Wisconsin Madison is often noted as the first multidisciplinary program in the country.

Today, art administrators spend much of their efforts focused on the balance of contributed to earned income. The growing role of planned giving and endowment funds have allowed many larger orchestras and opera companies to become more financially secure. Earned income streams continue to take on an entrepreneurial focus with new initiatives including expanded food and beverage service and retail outlets for audiences, in addition to educational services for K-12 students, teacher professional development, and adult and elder educational programming. Trends since the development of the Internet and the use of social media have created audiences less interested in purchasing a full season of programming months in advance, and instead prefer making entertainment decisions much closer to events. This has created challenges for pre-season planning and suggests a need to look beyond traditional event marketing toward the importance of new media development even for established cultural institutions.

BIBLIOGRAPHY

R.H. Bremmer: *American Philanthropy* (Chicago, 1988)
K.V. Mulcahy, and M.J. Wyszomirski: *America's Commitment to Culture: Government and the Arts* (Boulder, CO, 1995)
National Endowment for the Arts: *A Legacy of Leadership in America's Living Cultural Heritage Since 1965* (Washington, DC, 2000)

P. Korza, M. Brown, and C. Dreeszen: *Fundamentals of Arts Management* (Amherst, MA, 2007)
M.M. Kaiser: *The Art of the Turnaround: Creating and Maintaining Healthy Arts Organizations* (Hanover, PA, 2008)
W.J. Byrnes: *Management and the Arts* (Amsterdam, 2009)
Association of Arts Administration Educators, <http://www.artsadministration.org>

SUSAN BADGER BOOTH

Arts Enterprise [AE]. Nonprofit organization dedicated to educating, promoting, and supporting emerging leaders by exploring the intersection between the arts and business to promote social growth and entrepreneurial thinking. The organization was founded in 2006 at the University of Michigan, Ann Arbor, by an interdisciplinary team of students and faculty, including Chris Genteel, Kelly Dylla, Nathaniel Zeisler, and Mark Clague. Operating first as a student group, AE soon expanded to other colleges and universities, including Bowling Green State University, University of Wisconsin, University of Missouri at Kansas City, University of Iowa, and Claremont Graduate University. Chapters operate independently, advocating on behalf of AE's mission while engaging the broader student body through skills-based workshops, performances, consulting projects, and service programs. To account for the movement's continued growth, a national support organization was formed in 2008 to offer professional development resources and empower student leadership through action-based learning. Since 2009 Arts Enterprise has produced an annual summit, which includes keynote addresses from industry leaders and a case competition for new student businesses.

MICHAEL MAUSKAPF

Arts management [music management]. This article addresses the history of individuals and organizations devoted to the management of musical artists and their careers in the United States.

1. To 1900. 2. 1900 and after.

1. To 1900. Musicians who toured the United States during the first half of the 19th century relied on individuals to manage their tours. Some of the most important early impresarios included William Brough, MAX MARETZEK, BERNARD ULLMAN, and MAURICE STRAKOSCH. These men travelled the musicians' routes, sometimes with the performers and sometimes a week or two ahead, and were responsible for renting a performance venue, arranging publicity, and engaging supporting musicians and needed instruments. Managers also made travel arrangements, secured lodging, and negotiated terms with the managers of local theaters or halls. Some of these managers were themselves performers; the pianist Strakosch frequently toured with singers, and Maretzek was the conductor for his opera companies. This style of management essentially replicated the *modus operandi* of itinerant theatrical stars. (*See* OPERA COMPANIES, ITINERANT.)

During the second half of the century many solo performers, ensembles, and opera companies continued to rely on individuals for their management needs and to plan tours on what was essentially the theatrical circuit. The Strakosches (Max, Maurice, Edgar, Robert, Ferdinand, Karl) continued to manage both opera companies and individual performers, Ullman organized an American tour by Hans von Bülow, and the Graus (Jacob, Robert, and Maurice; *see* GRAU, MAURICE) and many others oversaw tours by opera companies, singers, and instrumentalists. During this period, however, musical management began to change in response to population growth, expansion of the transportation and communication systems, and an insatiable postwar American appetite for entertainment. Organizing a tour grew increasingly complex not only because of the sheer geographical breadth of the country (which now included the West and the Pacific Coast) and an exponential growth in the population, but also because of the increased number of ensembles, opera troupes, and solo performers that competed for audiences.

The complexity of the emerging American entertainment industry led inevitably to the development of arts agencies that could coordinate activities from a central location. The first such management firms appeared in the late 1860s as outgrowths of the American LYCEUM. Lyceums had emerged in the 1820s and 30s in New England as local lecture series designed to provide morally uplifting education and social interaction. This idea eventually spread to the entire nation, and by the 1850s some 400,000 Americans attended these public lectures each week. After the Civil War, the orientation of the lyceum series (now called "star courses") shifted from education to entertainment; each local series of 10 or 12 events now included concerts (by solo instrumentalists, singers, opera companies, orchestras, and bands) in addition to lectures. But as individual lyceums all over the country attempted to engage performers and lecturers of national reputation, the organizational structure broke down. In the late 1860s, in response to the resulting chaos, two national lyceum booking agencies emerged: the Boston (later the Redpath) Lyceum Bureau and the American Literary Bureau of New York. Both agencies engaged musicians and musical ensembles as well as speakers and actors, and served as clearing houses, greatly facilitating the organization of local "star courses." The agencies also provided musicians with a new method for organizing tours or securing performance engagements. The earliest known American concert management agency emerged from this background. The Roberts Musical Agency was established in Boston in 1875 by Effie Hinkley Ober, who had worked at the Boston branch of the American Literary Bureau. Through this agency she managed concert tours and performances by American singers Adelaide Phillips, Annie Louise Cary, and Caroline Richings, Theodore Thomas's Orchestra, the Temple Quartet of Boston, and other musicians and ensembles. In 1879 Ober organized the Boston Ideal Opera Company around singers she represented; she managed this company quite successfully until 1885. Similar agencies were organized in Boston, New York, Chicago, and elsewhere. This development in musical management—which paralleled similar changes in management of the American theater—would become the norm in the 20th century.

2. 1900 AND AFTER. Since 1900 individual arts managers as well as large management organizations have performed many functions. In addition to recruiting and cultivating artistic talent, managers arrange concert bookings, negotiate artist fees, organize tours, and market their clients to performing arts organizations and presenters. Managers are compensated either via retainer fee or a percentage of their client's earnings, typically 10 or 20%. The field has become increasingly professionalized, leading to the formation of multi-million dollar agencies with thousands of clients. Today, artist management is a business-to-business operation, in which managers rarely interact with audiences and instead work directly with presenters to book artists. This process can take place as many as two or three years in advance of a scheduled concert, with some artists receiving a portion of their fee prior to performance.

The major developments in arts management since 1900 can be traced through the careers of several enterprising men (and later women) and the growth of their companies. Two of the first professional arts managers were SOL HUROK (1888–1974) and Charles Ellis. Hurok, a Russian impresario who managed Marian Anderson, Arthur Rubinstein, and Isaac Stern, among others, became known for his larger-than-life personality, often billing himself more forcefully than his clients. Ellis, while often recognized for his work as the first manager of the Boston SO, became one of the most sought after artist representatives. His dual career as artist buyer and seller resulted in a significant conflict of interest, a type of challenge which reached new heights during the career of ARTHUR JUDSON (1881–1975). A dynamic businessman who simultaneously managed the New York Philharmonic and the Philadelphia Orchestra, Judson also represented many of the world's most prominent soloists and conductors, including Leopold Stokowski, Eugene Ormandy, and Leonard Bernstein.

In 1930 Judson purchased the Wolfsohn Musical Bureau, the oldest artist-management firm (est. 1884) in the United States, and formed Columbia Concerts Corporation. As a major stakeholder of Columbia Broadcasting System (CBS), he continued to acquire smaller management agencies, including Community Concerts, which was largely responsible for bringing classical music to smaller regional venues across the United States. As Judson's power grew, he was pressured by government regulators to cut ties with CBS, resulting in the independent formation of Columbia Artists Management, Inc., or CAMI, in 1948. Although Judson semi-retired in 1961, CAMI continued to grow into the country's preeminent artist management agency, expanding its purview under long-time CEO Ronald A. Wilford (*b* 1927), who later hired current general manager of the Metropolitan Opera Peter Gelb and represented Herbert von Karajan, Claudio Abbado, Riccardo Muti, and James Levine, among others.

Although CAMI became one of the largest artist management companies in the world, other agencies established themselves as competitors by paying more personal attention to artists, especially those in the early part of their careers. Hurok's legacy led to the 1975 formation of International Creative Management (ICM) and later Opus 3 Artists (2006). In 1961, Young Concert Artists, Inc. began offering international performance opportunities to up-and-coming musicians. In recent years, the arts management field has become increasingly globalized. Media mogul Mark McCormack bought a small New York–based agency run by Charles Hamlen and Edna Landau in the 1980s to form IMG Artists (1984), formerly affiliated with International Management Group and now with offices in London, New York, and Los Angeles. Landau served as managing director for 23 years before leaving in 2007. The success of superstar popular artists such as Dave Matthews and Lady Gaga has drawn LIVE NATION (founded 2005) and other media conglomerates into the arts management field, threatening the livelihood of some smaller agencies. Despite these developments, however, a new generation of musicians seem to be reacting against efforts to commodify their art by either managing their own careers with the assistance of the Internet or hiring smaller scale, independent managers.

BIBLIOGRAPHY

A.L. Bernheim et al.: *The Business of the Theatre; Prepared on Behalf of the Actors' Equity Association by Alfred L. Bernheim, Assisted by Sara Harding and the Staff of the Labor Bureau, Inc.* (New York, 1932)

C. Bode: *The American Lyceum, Town Meeting of the Mind* (New York, 1956)

P. Hart: *Orpheus in the New World: The Symphony Orchestra as an American Cultural Institution—its Past, Present, and Future* (New York, 1973), 71–95

D.M. Scott: "The Popular Lecture and the Creation of a Public in Mid-Nineteenth-Century America," *The Journal of American History*, lxvi (1980), 791–809

R.A. Lott: "Bernard Ullman: Nineteenth-Century American Impresario," *A Celebration of American Music. Words and Music in Honor of H. Wiley Hitchcock*, eds R. Crawford, R.A. Lott, and C. Oja (Ann Arbor, 1990), 174–91

N. Lebrecht: *Who Killed Classical Music?: Maestros, Managers, and Corporate Politics* (New York, 1997)

R.A. Lott: *From Paris to Peoria. How European Piano Virtuosos Brought Classical Music to the American Heartland* (New York, 2003)

R. Henderson: "A Confluence of Moravian Impresarios. Max Maretzek, the Strakosches, and the Graus," *European Music & Musicians in New York City, 1830–1890*, ed. J. Graziano (Rochester, NY, 2006), 235–52

K.K. Preston: "'Dear Miss Ober.' Music Management and the Interconnections of Musical Culture in the United States, 1876–1883," *European Music & Musicians in New York City, 1830–1890*, ed. J. Graziano (Rochester, 2006), 273–98

K.K. Preston: "To the Opera House? The Trials and Tribulations of Operatic Production in Nineteenth Century America," *Opera Quarterly*, xxiii/1 (2008), 39–65

J.R. McKivigan: *Forgotten Firebrand: James Redpath and the Making of Nineteenth-Century America* (Ithaca, NY, 2008)

KATHERINE K. PRESTON (1), MICHAEL MAUSKAPF (2)

Art song. A short vocal piece of serious artistic purpose. During the 18th century "art song" came to have its predominant modern meaning of secular solo song with an independent keyboard accompaniment; for a discussion of songs for more than one voice (or partsongs) *see* CHORAL MUSIC. The subject of this article is the development of the art song tradition in the United States. Other types of song (discussed elsewhere in this dictionary) include theater songs, popular songs, ragtime and jazz songs, folksongs, and work songs.

1. *c*1750–*c*1850. 2. *c*1850 to World War II. 3. After World War II.

1. *c*1750–*c*1850. The earliest extant American art songs, signed "F. H.," are contained (along with some 100 mid-18th-century English songs) in a manuscript copied out by Francis Hopkinson, an amateur musician from Philadelphia. The first of these to appear in the manuscript is "My days have been so wondrous free," dated 1759 and long regarded as the first American secular song; the others initialed by Hopkinson—"The Garland, Oh come to Mason Borough's grave," and "With pleasure I have past my days"—may be contemporaneous. Like the songs in Hopkinson's later published collection, *Seven Songs for the Harpsichord or Forte Piano* (1788), dedicated to George Washington and in fact containing eight songs, the pieces in the manuscript are in the style of English songs written by such composers as Thomas Arne, Stephen Storace, William Shield, and James Hook for performance in pleasure gardens or to be inserted in light operas.

English songs provided the models for American songs throughout the colonial and federal periods; indeed, Hopkinson's most notable successors were British immigrants. Benjamin Carr, also of Philadelphia, published many of his 61 songs in two serial anthologies, *Musical Journal for the Piano Forte* (1800–04) and *Carr's Musical Miscellany in Occasional Numbers* (1812–25). Also among Carr's songs are several sets of ballads, including *Six Ballads…from The Lady of the Lake* op.7, published in the same year (1810) as the poem by Sir Walter Scott on which they are based; the set contains the *Hymn to the Virgin* ("Ave Maria"), which is especially notable for its harp-like arpeggiated accompaniment. Carr's most popular song was "The Little Sailor Boy" (1798). James Hewitt, who immigrated in 1792, was second only to Carr in his success as a composer of songs: "The Wounded Hussar" (*c*1880) went through 12 printings, as did "Primroses" (or "The Primrose Girl," *c*1793). Oliver Shaw, the first native American to make a mark as a composer of songs, was best known for his settings of texts by Thomas Moore, such as "Mary's Tears" (1812) and "There's nothing true but heav'n" (1816), both on poems from Moore's *Sacred Melodies*.

In the period between the War of 1812 and the Civil War American art song moved away from the English style and began to reflect the influence of various musical genres and styles in a way that became typical of American artistic expression. John Hill Hewitt, the son of James Hewitt, composed more than 300 songs, beginning with the successful "The minstrel's return'd from the war" (?1828), which was written in the manner of his father's songs; later he incorporated elements of Italian opera arias, Alpine yodeling songs (which were performed in the United States by visiting singers from Switzerland and Austria), and minstrel songs. Anthony Philip Heinrich, an immigrant from Bohemia who became known as "the Beethoven of America," began to compose after his arrival in the United States. Heinrich's songs, many of which are occasional pieces (such as the *Visit to Philadelphia*, 1820), are less audacious than his keyboard works; nevertheless, the vocal lines often combine a mellifluous Viennese charm with surprising outbursts of coloratura and are supported by elaborate accompaniments. The cadenza of the *Prologue Song* which opens *The Dawning of Music in Kentucky* op.1 (1820), an extensive collection of songs and instrumental pieces, extends over more than two octaves; his setting of Robert Burns's "From thee Eliza I must go," has a similar range and exploits abrupt harmonic contrasts between tonic major and minor keys.

The most gifted song composer of the era was Stephen Foster. Foster was well acquainted with the various song styles of his day, and this knowledge is evident in his own songs, of which there are approximately 200. "Open thy lattice, love" (1844), his first published song, is in the English tradition. But echoes of Italian opera arias by Rossini, Bellini, and Donizetti can be heard in "The Voice of By Gone Days" and "Ah! may the red rose live always" (both 1850) and "Beautiful dreamer" (1864), among others. And Foster, of Irish ancestry himself, readily absorbed the style of Thomas Moore's popular *A Selection of Irish Melodies* (1808–34), as is demonstrated in such songs as "Jeanie with the Light Brown Hair" (1854) and "Gentle Annie" (1856). Some of his songs for minstrel shows—perhaps especially "Nelly was a lady" (1849), "Old Folks at Home" (1851), "My old Kentucky home, good night" (1853), and "Old Black Joe" (1860)—transcend that genre in sensitivity of expression. In the period immediately before, during, and after the Civil War, the songs of George Frederick Root and Henry Clay Work addressed popular causes, and rivaled Foster's songs in public acceptance.

2. *c*1850 TO WORLD WAR II. Before the Civil War the aim of both popular and art songs was usually to express common emotions, but thereafter some American composers became artistically more ambitious, and the distinction between the popular song and the "serious" art song became greater. An increasing number of American composers chose to study in Europe, where they found in the German lied and the French *mélodie* new ways of enhancing the relationship between lyric poetry and music. As early as 1846, in "Thine eye hath seen the spot," George F. Bristow extended the range of modulation, anticipating the sophistication of such composers as Amy Beach, George W. Chadwick, Edward MacDowell, and Ethelbert Nevin, who were a generation younger. Beach passionately embraced the chromatic styles of Chopin and Liszt in songs such as "Ah, love, but a day" (1900). The same skill is evident in *A Flower Cycle* (1892) and *Lyrics from Told in the Gate* (1897), two sets of songs by Chadwick, although the texts of these songs, by Arlo Bates, are less impressive than the music. The 42 songs by MacDowell are equally well crafted, but they too are limited by their texts, which for the

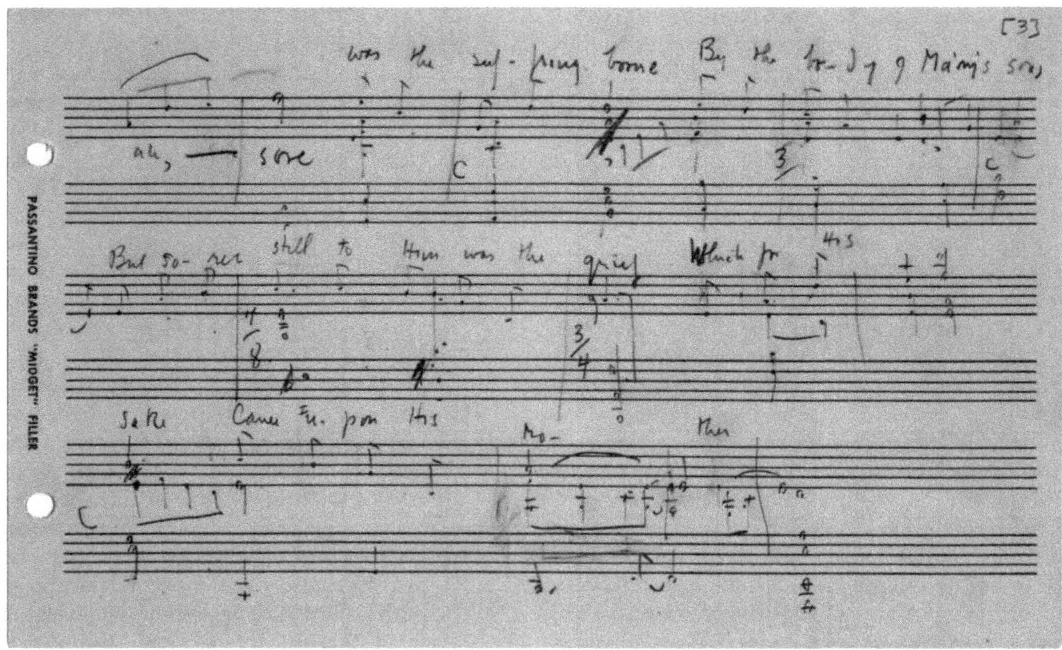

A sketch for "The Crucifixion" from Hermit Songs *by Samuel Barber. (Library of Congress/G. Schirmer, Inc.)*

most part are MacDowell's own. Many other composers wrote songs in this period, but few are as polished as the early ones by Nevin, and none had the success of his "The Rosary" (1898).

The growing interest of American composers in French songs is apparent in many songs of the first two decades of the 20th century, including several cycles by John Alden Carpenter, such as *Water-colors* (1916) and the widely performed *Gitanjali* (1913). Carpenter's "Serenade" (1920) imitates Debussy in its use of Spanish elements. Early in his career Charles T. Griffes composed settings of both German and French texts; later he reconciled the two strands of influence in such strikingly original works as *Three Poems of Fiona MacLeod* (1918), the orchestral version of which reflects his knowledge of the music of Richard Strauss, and "Sorrow of Mydath" (1917), the second of two settings of poems by John Masefield.

The indigenous influences parodied in minstrel shows early in the century entered the recital hall in the form of folk music arranged for voice and piano. Arthur Farwell was one of many composers who used American Indian melodies. (Farwell also set many texts by Emily Dickinson, the first as early as 1907.) Charles Wakefield Cadman wrote over 300 songs; his adaptations of tribal melodies, especially "From the Land of the Sky-blue Water" (1909) and "At Dawning" (1906), became favorite recital pieces and were extensively recorded. Other composers turned to arrangements of black spirituals for voice and piano. Those by H.T. Burleigh are especially noteworthy; the composer himself sang them for Dvořák, and they have been performed internationally by many singers.

Charles Ives, the first American composer of international stature, made particularly important contributions to the song repertory. His heterogeneous output of about 150 songs includes a wide range of styles and subjects and forms a kind of musical diary of his composing career. Like some of his piano studies and parodies, the songs adumbrate many distinctive Ivesian techniques and effects: interval control in "The Cage" (1906) and "Soliloquy" (1907); Victorian potpourri in "He is there!," "The Things our Father Loved," and "In Flanders Fields" (all 1917); rhythmic and harmonic disruption of pre-existing music in the hymns "Watchman" (1913) and "At the River" (?1916), and in "The Sideshow" (1921), based on a popular song by Pat Rooney; microtonal sliding in "Like a Sick Eagle" (?1913); rhythmic speech in Charlie Rutlage (1920/21); and the capturing of popular culture in "The Circus Band" and "Waltz" (both ?1894).

Some of Ives's songs are reductions of works for larger forces, while others are sketches intended to be incorporated into larger works. Ives wrote no song cycles, though he suggested some groupings of songs for performance without voice as instrumental pieces. He wrote early songs to German and French texts, trivial comedies for the salon, and such intensely dissonant works as "Majority" (1921), the first piece in the collection *114 Songs* which he printed privately in 1922. The tone-clusters of "Majority" are characteristic, as is the use of quotation (from the "Dead March" in Handel's *Saul*) in "Slow March" (?1887) for the funeral of a family pet. Generations of singers have used the ungainly but powerful "General William Booth Enters into Heaven" (1914), on a poem by Vachel Lindsay, almost as a campaign song to gain recognition for the uncompromising—and uncompromisingly American—Ives.

It is difficult to generalize about the nature of American art song between the world wars. The major composers of the period were occupied with work in other genres, and the few songs they wrote exemplify their personal styles rather than any general aesthetic trends. Early and concentrated atonality, for example, appears in "Toys" (1919) by Carl Ruggles. A mellow neoclassicism informs two songs of 1943 by Elliott Carter: "Voyage" (to a text by Hart Crane) and "Warble for Lilac-time" (Walt Whitman). Roger Sessions produced only one song with piano accompaniment, "On the Beach at Fontana" (1930; James Joyce). The prolific Henry Cowell wrote but a handful of songs and no song cycles.

Of the generation of song composers born around 1900, John Duke was the most prolific, composing more than 250 examples, including a well-known setting of A.E. Housman's *Loveliest of Trees*. Although Aaron Copland came to song writing somewhat late, his *Twelve Poems of Emily Dickinson* (1949–50) may be considered the first truly distinguished American cycle. Another important Copland group is the *Old American Songs* (1950, 1952), arrangements that transcend their origins as folk and minstrel tunes. The songs of Samuel Barber are of uniformly high quality, featuring sensitive vocal writing and challenging, evocative accompaniments. Barber was steeped in the vocal idiom, being a singer himself and the nephew of the opera singer Louise Homer. Barber's *Hermit Songs* (1952–3), set to anonymous and at times ribald late medieval Irish texts, were written for and first performed by soprano Leontyne Price. His *Three Songs* to texts by Joyce (1936) are among the most atmospherically effective settings of the poems concerned.

3. After World War II. Four factors had an important impact on the composition of art songs after 1945: the development of modern American poetry, which provided composers with a new kind of text; the influence of the expressionistic, serial music of Schoenberg and Webern, a style that came to dominate progressive American music after 1950; a growing interest in the expressive and structural possibilities of sonority, which led composers to seek alternatives to the traditional piano accompaniment; and the growing acceptance of popular music and jazz as source material for classical song.

By the mid-20th century American composers could benefit from the rich maturity of their country's literature. The personality of the poet, now treated as an equal partner in the creative process, emerges clearly in songs of differing musical styles. Two poets, Gertrude Stein and e.e. cummings, have been especially influential. It was in response to Stein's poetry that Virgil Thomson developed his distinctive approach in the 1930s, characterized by simplicity and a concern for natural text setting. His large output includes several cycles, including *Five Songs to Poems of William Blake* (1951) and *Praises and Prayers* (1963). The influence of Stein is also evident in the works of John Cage, who set her poems in the early *Three Songs* (1932), and in Gunther Schuller's *Meditations* (1960) and William Brooks's *Medley* (1978), an anthology which makes use of various American song styles. Texts by cummings have been set by Cage and Copland, as well as Morton Feldman, Salvatore Martirano, Marc Blitzstein, David Diamond, William Bergsma, Celius Dougherty, and John Duke, among many others.

After 1945 there emerged a distinction between composers specializing in songs of a traditional sort and those with wider interests. Eminent among the former is Ned Rorem, whose more than 500 songs cover a range of subjects almost as wide as Ives's. His cycle *Poems of Love and the Rain* (1963) is especially notable for its ingenious form: each poem is set twice, and the cycle is ordered palindromically. *War Scenes* (1969), composed in the midst of the Vietnam War, features evocative settings of texts by Walt Whitman. Rorem's *Evidence of Things Not Seen* (1997) is the largest song cycle yet written by an American, spanning nearly 40 songs by 24 different authors. Theodore Chanler and Paul Bowles are two of the many composers of songs who have adopted conservative, tonal styles; Chanler's cycle *The Children* (1945) approaches the diatonic insouciance of Poulenc, and Bowles is fearlessly nostalgic in setting such texts as his own *Once a Lady was Here* (1946). Dominick Argento, also one of America's most important opera composers, has made major contributions to song. His cycle *From the Diary of Virginia Woolf*, first performed by mezzo-soprano Janet Baker, won the 1975 Pulitzer Prize in music.

A large group of postwar composers has written in a more dissonant idiom, using the serial techniques developed by Schoenberg and Webern. This group includes Milton Babbitt, Ruth Crawford, Wallingford Riegger, Ernst Krenek, George Rochberg, and George Perle, whose *13 Dickinson Songs* (1979) were written for the soprano Bethany Beardslee. The most adventurous composers have experimented with new treatments of both text and accompaniments. The piano parts for Cage's early *Five Songs* (1938) are fully notated, but carry no dynamic markings; the piano is closed in the accompaniment to *The Wonderful Widow of Eighteen Springs* (1942); and in later works such as *Aria* (1958) and the *Song Books* (1970) the voice is unaccompanied. Babbitt's *Sounds and Words* (1960) has an abstract phonetic text, influenced perhaps by the verbal experiments of cummings. And Babbitt is one of many composers who have combined voice and electronic tape, notably in works such as *Vision and Prayer* (1961) and *Philomel* (1964).

While the popularity of the art song in its traditional guise declined in the later 20th century among more progressive circles, several composers have turned to an eclectic, neo-tonal approach. One of the most important is David Del Tredici, whose cycle *Chana's Story* (2000) weds contemporary poetry to complex yet accessible music. Lee Hoiby's songs include the Broadway-tinged "Where the Music Comes From" (1974/rev. 1986) and the bluesy "Three Ages of Woman" (1990). Richard Hundley favors a lyrical idiom in works such as "Come Ready and See Me" (1971) and "Waterbird" (1988), both to poems by James Purdy. William Bolcom's *Cabaret Songs* (1978,

1983) to texts by Arnold Weinstein, reflect a contemporary reaction to earlier cabaret collections by Schoenberg and Britten. The broad musical styles range from atonality ("Thius King of Orf") to torch song ("George").

Women composers—including Libby Larsen, Ruth Schonthal, Elizabeth Vercoe, Joelle Wallach, and Judith Lang Zaimont—have made significant contributions to a genre previously dominated by men. Larsen's *Love After 1950* (2000) uses elements of Latin dance (including the tango) to comment on the status of modern relationships. Lori Laitman's prolific song output features the Sondheimesque *Metropolitan Tower* (1997) and the witty, childlike *Men with Small Heads* (2002). Influenced by pioneers such as Burleigh, African American composers have also made their mark, as in H. Leslie Adams's numerous examples and T.J. Anderson's *Songs of Illumination* (1989), which features a conflation of styles drawn from classical, jazz, and hip hop.

A milestone in American song history took place in 1992 with the premiere of the *AIDS Quilt Songbook* at New York's Alice Tully Hall. Organized by baritone William Parker—who openly stated that classical singers has been largely silent about AIDS when compared to artists in other fields—the work features intense musical responses to the disease by 18 different composers. Daron Aric Hagen's *Muldoon Songs* (1989) and *Figments* (2002), with texts by Alice Wirth Gray, reflect thoughtful settings of the texts. Jake Heggie's introspective approach and gentle dissonances suits the evocative poetry of Gavin Geoffrey Dillon and Gini Savage in the three-volume collection titled *The Faces of Love* (1995–2000). The songs of Ricky Ian Gordon highlight the intimacy of Emily Dickinson's *Will There Really be a Morning?* (1983)—also set by Laitman, Ernst Bacon, Vincent Persichetti, and André Previn—and the campy insouciance of Frank O'Hara's *Poem (Lana Turner Has Collapsed!)* (1985). O'Hara has proven a strong influence on the song output of several recent composers, especially Christopher Berg, whose musical theater style mirrors aspects of gay urban experience in *Autobiographia Literaria* (1991).

Since about 2000, composers have often evoked or cited earlier music, including Ben Moore, whose "Sexy Lady" (2002), written for mezzo-soprano Susan Graham, references Mozart and Richard Strauss. Tom Cipullo quotes classical masterpieces, popular music, and film scores in several of his nearly 200 songs; the poignant cycle *Another Reason Why I Don't Keep A Gun in the House* (2000), featuring poetry by Billy Collins, quotes music by Beethoven.

Contemporary American art song is undergoing a welcome renaissance. Poetic topics previously ignored or considered off-limits for musical setting (for example, certain aspects of gender, sexuality, and race) are now more frequent. At the same time, composers are responding to texts with diverse musical styles that transcend earlier boundaries. The genre as a whole is more vibrant today than it has been in at least a generation, which bodes well for its future.

BIBLIOGRAPHY

O.G.T. Sonneck: *Early Concert-life in America (1731–1800)* (Leipzig, Germany, 1907/*R*)

W.T. Upton: *Art-song in America* (Boston, 1930/*R*1969 with suppl. 1938)

H. Nathan: "United States of America," *A History of Song*, ed. D. Stevens (New York, 1960), 408–60

B. Middaugh: "The Songs of Ned Rorem: Aspects of Musical Style," *The NATS Bulletin*, xxiv (1968), 443–7

G.D. Yerbury: *Song in America, from Early Times to about 1850* (Metuchen, NJ, 1971)

P.L. Miller: "The American Art Song, 1900–1940," *When I have Sung my Songs*, NW 247 (1976) [liner notes]

D. Argento: "The Composer and the Singer," *The NATS Bulletin*, xxxiii/3 (1977), 18–25

H.W. Hitchcock: *Ives* (London, 1977, 3/1988)

R.C. Friedberg: "The Recent Songs of John Duke," *The NATS Bulletin*, xxxvi/1 (1979), 31–6

C. Hamm: *Yesterdays: Popular Song in America* (New York, 1979)

K.W. Keller and C. Rabson, eds.: *The National Tune Index: 18th-century Secular Music* (New York, 1980)

J.L. Kreiling: *The Songs of Samuel Barber: a Study in Literary Taste and Text Setting* (diss., U. of North Carolina, 1986)

J. Manning: *New Vocal Repertory* (Houndsmills, 1986)

W.W. Austin: *"Susanna," "Jeanie," and "The Old Folks at Home": The Songs of Stephen C. Foster from His Time to Ours*, (Urbana, IL and Chicago, 2/1987)

R.C. Friedberg: *American Art Song and American Poetry* (Metuchen, NJ, 1981–7)

V.E. Villamil: *A Singer's Guide to the American Art Song, 1870–1980* (Lanham, MD, 1993)

J.P. Burkholder: *All Made of Tunes: Charles Ives and His Use of Musical Borrowing* (New Haven, CT, 1995)

R. Platt: "Artful Simplicity: The Art Songs of Daron Hagen," *Journal of Singing*, lv:i (1998), 3–11

S.A. Floyd Jr., *ed.: International Dictionary of Black Composers* (Chicago, 1999)

L.A. Cellucci: *An Examination of Selected Songs by Richard Hundley* (diss., U. of Cincinnati, 2000)

J.E. Carman and others: *Art-song in the United States, 1801–1976: an Annotated Bibliography* (Lanham, 3/2001) [incl. G. Myers: "Art-song in the United States 1759–1811"]

K.H. Burns: *Women and Music in America Since 1900: an Encyclopedia* (Westport, CT, 2002)

S. Mabry: *Exploring Twentieth-Century Vocal Music: a Practical Guide to Innovations in Performance and Repertoire* (Oxford, 2002)

L. Starr: *The Dickinson Songs of Aaron Copland* (Hillsdale, 2002)

C.J. Bradley: *Index to Poetry in Music: a Guide to the Poetry Set as Solo Songs by 125 Major Song Composers* (New York, 2003)

K.S. Todd: "Cabaret as Musical Montage: The Cabaret Songs of William Bolcom," *Blue: The Complete Cabaret Songs of William Bolcom and Arnold Weinstein*, Summit 361 (2003) [liner notes]

C. Kimball: *Song: a Guide to Art Song Style and Literature* (Milwaukee, rev. 2/2005)

C.F. Lines: "The Songs of Lori Laitman," *Journal of Singing*, lxiv/1 (2007), 31–46

K.E. Clifton: *Recent American Art Song: a Guide* (Lanham, MD, 2008)

PETER DICKINSON, H. WILEY HITCHCOCK/KEITH E. CLIFTON

Artzt, Alice (Josephine) (*b* Philadelphia, PA, 16 Mar 1943). Guitarist. She started playing classical guitar at the age of 13, studying in France with Ida Presti and Alexandre Lagoya, and graduated from Columbia University (BA 1967). Her debut (London, 1969) was followed by concert tours of Europe and North America; later tours took her around the world. She was one of the leading woman guitarists worldwide in the 1970s and 80s. She recorded albums featuring the work of individual composers or of certain periods (e.g. *Guitar Music by Fernando Sor*, 1978; *English Guitar Music*, 1979; *Guitar Music by Francisco Tárrega*, 1979; *20th*

Century Guitar Music, 1980) at a time when other guitarists often recorded mixed programs. She is the author of *Guitar: the Art of Practising* (London, 1978) and *Rhythmic Mastery: an Imaginative Guide for Guitarists* (Pacific, 1997) and has contributed articles and reviews to guitar magazines. She taught at Mannes College (1966–9) and Trenton State College, New Jersey (1977–80) and was on the board of directors of the Guitar Foundation of America (1978–91). Artzt also played chamber music, mostly guitar duos and trios (Alice Artzt Guitar Trio), and with the harpsichordist Igor Kipnis.

BIBLIOGRAPHY

M.J. Summerfield, *The Classical Guitar* (Blaydon on Tyne, 2002), 38–39 [with discogr. and bibliogr.]

THOMAS F. HECK/JÖRG JEWANSKI

ASCAP. *See* AMERICAN SOCIETY OF COMPOSERS, AUTHORS AND PUBLISHERS.

Asch, Moe [Moses] (*b* Warsaw, Poland, 2 Dec 1905; *d* New York, NY, 19 Oct 1986). Record producer of Polish birth. He founded the label Asch in New York in 1939, initially to release local Jewish music. He soon expanded to jazz and American vernacular music releasing records by such musicians as Mary Lou Williams, James P. Johnson, Woody Guthrie, Lead Belly, and Pete Seeger, who subsequently gained widespread acclaim. He then founded Disc (1945), Cub Records (1948), and Folkways Records and Service Corporation (1948).

It was Asch's goal with Folkways to create an encyclopedia of the sounds of the 20th century. He did not take anything out of print, regardless of sales, using the rationale that one does not take "Q" out of the alphabet and leave "P" simply because "Q" is not used as much as "P." During his career he released 2168 albums, the equivalent of about one a week. As well as folk music, his catalog included spoken word, recordings of natural and manmade sounds, jazz, blues, children's music, political speeches, and non-Western musics from around the world.

Asch believed that an electorate in a democratic society needed to have access to information from which to learn. His records always came with a thick booklet and were prized by teachers and libraries. He spent much of his time attending library and educational conventions displaying his wares. Throughout his career he released records by performers whom he felt had something to say, often passing on someone who later became a star and instead signing someone whose lyrics he liked better. He preferred to sell small numbers of all his many titles than 100,000 of one.

As he reached the end of his life he was worried that whoever took over Folkways would only keep the best sellers and discard the rest, thereby destroying his encyclopedia. At the time of his death negotiations were underway for the Smithsonian Institution to take on the Folkways catalog with the stipulation that everything remain in print. The deal was finalized 1987.

BIBLIOGRAPHY

P.D. Goldsmith: *Making People's Music: Moe Asch and Folkways Records* (Washington DC, 2000)

R. Carlin: *Worlds of Sound: the Story of Smithsonian Folkways* (Washington DC, 2008)

JEFF PLACE

Ashborn, James (*b* England, *c*1816; *d* Wolcottville [now Torrington], CT, 7 Dec 1876). Guitar, banjo, and string manufacturer, and inventor, of English birth. He established America's first guitar factory, producing approximately 11,000 instruments from 1842–64, triple that of his competitor C.F. Martin. Immigrating to New York sometime before 1840, Ashborn evidently became associated with wholesaler/retailer Firth, Hall, and Pond's Fluteville woodwind factory (acquired from Asa Hopkins and Jabez Camp) on the Naugatuck River near Litchfield, Connecticut. From 1842–7 this facility produced guitars characterized by Spanish design elements (body shape, fan bracing, and tie-bridges), apparently informed by an imported Panormo guitar they sold a decade earlier. Following their separation into William Hall & Son and Firth, Pond & Co., in 1848 Ashborn started his own two-story, 16-room guitar factory eight miles upriver in Daytonville (now Torrington) adjacent to Arvid Dayton's reed organ factory, selling guitars exclusively to these two firms (and their 1863–4 permutations), stamped with their brand names and shipped via the newly built Naugatuck Railroad. Employing waterwheel powered machinery and seven to ten specialized workers (including a son), Ashborn made uniformly sized guitars in various woods and ornamentation, featuring exotically veneered backs, necks and headstocks. He manufactured their elegant tuners (machined of brass from the foundry owned by his original business partner's father) and elaborately cloth-lined cases inhouse. Ashborn patented a moveable guitar capo (1850) and improved friction tuning pegs (1852). America's first known manufacturer of guitar strings, he shipped 14,000 annually according to his extant ledger (1851–6). He capitalized on minstrelsy, making very high quality banjos now prized by collectors. Elected to the Connecticut State Legislature in 1863, Ashborn rented his building in 1864 and sold it in 1866, his guitar output never resuming in comparable quantity. Ashborn, an owner of several properties, died in 1876 following years of ill health.

BIBLIOGRAPHY

P.F. Gura: *Manufacturing Guitars for the American Parlor: James Ashborn's Wolcottville, Connecticut, Factory, 1851–56* (Worcester, MA, 1994)

P. Szego and G. Wunderlich: "Art and Craft of the Early Banjo," *The Birth of the Banjo* (Katonah, NY, 2003), 36–51

P.F. Gura: "Ashborn, Tilton, and the Battle for New York, 1852–1861," *C.F. Martin and His Guitars 1796–1873* (Chapel Hill, NC, 2003), 109–42

DAVID GANSZ

Ashby [née Thompson], **Dorothy (Jeanne)** (*b* Detroit, MI, 6 Aug 1932; *d* Santa Monica, CA, 13 April 1986). Jazz harpist and bandleader, daughter of the jazz guitarist Wiley Thompson. She attended Cass Technical

High School with Donald Byrd and Kenny Burrell, and took up piano, double bass, saxophone, and, eventually, harp. She then studied piano and music education at Wayne State University. Although she performed on piano in nightclubs, she had settled on harp as her primary instrument by 1952. She also formed a trio in which her husband, John Ashby, played drums. During the 1960s, Ashby presented her own radio show and, with her husband, formed the Ashby Players, an African American theater group. *Down Beat* included her on its poll of best jazz performers in 1962, and by the late 1960s, she was in demand as a studio musician, in which capacity she recorded with Stevie Wonder, Barry Manilow, and Diana Ross, among others, and on movie soundtracks. Ashby's most celebrated albums include *Afro-Harping* (1968) and *The Rubaiyat of Dorothy Ashby* (1970); on the latter she performs on Japanese koto and eletrified harp. Her performances blend elements of bebop language with deep, often funk-derived grooves. Samples from her recorded performances have often been used in hip-hop recordings, including Rahzel's "All I Know" (1999).

BIBLIOGRAPHY

S. Placksin: *American Women in Jazz, 1900 to the Present: their Words, Lives, and Music* (New York, 1982, London, 1985 as *Jazzwomen, 1900 to the Present: their Words, Lives, and Music*), 239

CHADWICK JENKINS

Asheville. City in North Carolina (pop. 83,318; metropolitan area 417,012; 2010 US Census). Situated in the Blue Ridge Mountains of western North Carolina, at the crossing of early livestock drover roads, Asheville was incorporated in 1797. Since the early 1800s, when visitors arrived by stagecoach, this small Appalachian mountain city has been promoted as a tourist destination ("The Land of the Sky") for those seeking the beauty and cooler temperatures of the Southern Highlands. As a result, Asheville has never been culturally deprived. In 1876, residents were enjoying performances ranging from vaudeville to opera in an opera hall on the third floor the county courthouse. During the decade following the completion of the railroad in 1880, the city's population quadrupled, and Asheville was transformed with the construction of dozens of resort hotels and George W. Vanderbilt's Biltmore House (completed in 1895). During the summer months, dance orchestras played the latest waltzes and polkas in the hotel ballrooms every night of the week.

While the city of Asheville sought sophistication and modernity, a rich tradition of folk music continued to thrive in the rural mountain communities. In 1916, English folksong collector, CECIL SHARP visited Asheville in search of British ballads and folksongs, and in nearby Madison County, he collected variants of 500 "love songs" from 281 singers. The film *Songcatcher* (2000), filmed in the Asheville region, is loosely based on Sharp and other early ballad collectors.

Some of the first country musicians to be recorded lived in the Asheville area. In 1924, Samantha Bumgarner of Jackson County became the first old-time banjo player ever recorded, and the following year, Ralph Peer recorded banjo player and singer Bascom Lamar Lunsford and others for Okeh Records at a session in Asheville. This was two years before Peer's historic recording sessions at Bristol, Tennessee.

In 1928, in an effort to promote tourism in western North Carolina, the Asheville Chamber of Commerce enlisted Bascom Lunsford to arrange a program featuring the region's traditional music and dance as part of the city's Rhododendron Festival. Lunsford invited Bumgarner and other musicians and dancers from the region to perform at what became the Mountain Dance and Folk Festival, the first and oldest continuously running folk festival in the United States. It was at this festival, that folksinger Pete Seeger, as a young man in the 1930s, was first inspired to learn to play the five-string banjo. It was also at the Mountain Dance and Folk Festival that square dancing evolved into the modern dance form known as clogging.

Today, with a population over 80,000, Asheville supports a rich and varied music scene, and many musicians make it their home. The Asheville Symphony Orchestra (established 1960), the Asheville Choral Society (1977), the Asheville Symphony Chorus (1991), and the Asheville Lyric Opera (1999), as well as touring companies perform throughout the year. The region's many music venues host local as well as nationally known touring musicians, and outdoor music festivals are held from April to October. The largest of these is Bele Chere, a street festival that has taken place each July since 1979. Others include the African American Goombay Festival (August) and the Lake Eden Arts Festival in nearby Black Mountain (May and October). The Mountain Dance and Folk Festival still takes place every August, and on Saturday nights during the summer, thousands of spectators enjoy performances of traditional old-time and bluegrass music and clogging at Shindig-on-the-Green on the Bascom Lamar Lunsford stage at the newly-completed Pack Square Park. The revitalization of downtown in recent years has encouraged numerous street performers, and every Friday night a drum circle forms at Pritchard Park. Asheville's vibrant music scene supports an equally active dance scene, including swing dances, salsa dances, contra dances, square dances, and clogging.

Undergraduate degrees in music and music education are offered at several colleges in the Asheville region (University of North Carolina at Asheville, Mars Hill College, Brevard College, and Western Carolina University). In addition, each summer, music workshops held at Warren Wilson College (The Swannanoa Gathering) and Mars Hill College (Blue Ridge Old-Time Music Week) attract folk musicians from across the country and around the world to learn the traditional music of the southern mountains.

BIBLIOGRAPHY

L. Jones: *Minstrel of the Appalachians: The Story of Bascom Lamar Lunsford* (Lexington, KY, 2002)

N.K. Chase: *Asheville: a History* (Jefferson, NC, 2007)

PHILIP A. JAMISON

Ashford and Simpson. Soul duo and songwriting and production team. Nickolas Ashford (*b* Fairfield, Hilton Head Island, SC, 4 May 1942; *d* New York, NY, 22 Aug 2011) and Valerie Simpson (*b* Bronx, NY, 26 Aug 1946) met in 1963; their first successful songwriting collaboration was "Let's go get stoned" which, in a recording by Ray Charles (ABC, 1966), reached no.31 on the pop chart. They became staff writers and producers for Motown, where they worked with such performers as Marvin Gaye and Tammi Terrell ("You're all I need to get by," Motown, 1968, and "Ain't nothing like the real thing," Motown, 1968) and Diana Ross ("Ain't no mountain high enough," Motown, 1970). Ashford produced two albums that Simpson recorded under her own name (*Exposed!*, Motown, 1971, and *Valerie Simpson*, Motown, 1972). After leaving Motown, they released their first album together for Warner Bros., *Gimme something real*, in 1973 and married in 1974. Ashford and Simpson continued to make recordings through the 1970s and into the 1980s, and produced albums for Diana Ross (*The Boss*, Motown, 1979) and Gladys Knight and the Pips (*About Love*, Columbia, 1980), among others. As recording artists their best work, delivered at the peak of their career in hits such as "Solid" (Capitol, 1984) and "Real Love" (Capitol, 1986), employs a pop-gospel style, distinguished by Simpson's wide-ranging melodies and Ashford's inspirational love lyrics. Although they seldom recorded during the 1990s and 2000s, they remained active as songwriters and occasionally performed together until Ashford's death from throat cancer in 2011.

STEPHEN HOLDEN/R

Ashforth, Alden (Banning) (*b* New York, NY, 13 May 1933). Composer, jazz researcher, and teacher. He studied composition with EDWARD BURLINGAME HILL and Richard Hoffmann at Oberlin College (BA 1958, BM 1958) and with ROGER SESSIONS, EARL KIM, and MILTON BABBITT at Princeton University (MFA 1960, PhD 1971). He began his teaching career at Princeton (1961) and held positions at Oberlin (1961–5) and several other schools before joining the faculty of UCLA in 1967, where he taught until his retirement in 1994. In 1969 he became coordinator of the UCLA electronic music studio and in 1980 he was made a full professor. Since 1952 he has been active as a producer of New Orleans jazz recordings. His writings include contributions to Perspectives of New Music (on Schoenberg), *The Music Review* (on Beethoven), and *The New Grove Dictionary of Jazz*. Ashforth has received particular notice for his electronic works. *Byzantia: Two Journeys after Yeats* (1971–3) is panoramic in dramatic effect, with mosaic-like juxtapositions of electronic, acoustic (voice, traditional instruments), and natural (flowing water, bird calls) sounds.

WORKS

Inst: Pf Sonata, 1955; Sonata, fl, hpd, 1956; 2 Pf Pieces, 1957; Variations, orch, 1958; Fantasy-variations, vn, pf, 1959; Episodes, chbr conc., 8 insts, 1962–8; Big Bang, pf 4 hands, 1970; Pas seul, fl, 1974; The Flowers of Orcus (Intavolatura), gui, 1976; Sentimental Waltz, pf, 1977; St Bride's Suite, hpd, 1983; The Miraculous Bugle, flugelhorn, perc, 1989; Palimpsests, org, 1997

Vocal: The Unquiet Heart (Tanka Songs), S, chbr orch/pf, 1959–68; 4 Lyric Songs, high v, pf, 1961; Our Lady's Song, A, va, hpd, 1961; Aspects of Love, T/S, pf, 1978; Christmas Motets, chorus, 1980

Elec: Vocalise, 1965; Cycles, 1965; Mixed Brew, 1968; Byzantia: Two Journeys after Yeats, tape/(org, tape), 1971–3

Principal publishers: E.C. Schirmer, C.F. Peters

KATHERINE K. PRESTON/BARRY SCHRADER/R

Ashley, Lowell Edwin (*b* Christianburg, VA, 4 April 1942). Music librarian. He studied music and English at Emory and Henry College, Emory, Virginia (BA 1963) and received his graduate degree in library science (MLS 1973) from George Peabody College for Teachers (now part of Vanderbilt University) in Nashville, Tennessee. He did additional graduate work in music at Yale University as a Woodrow Wilson Fellow and at Indiana University. Following three years of service in the US Army in Vietnam and Italy, he studied Italian at the Università Italiana per Stranieri, Perugia, Italy, 1969–70. After holding various library positions at James Madison University from 1973 to 1984, he served as principal cataloger and music cataloger at Virginia Tech University from 1984 to 1997, when he joined the staff of the Smithsonian Institution Libraries, where he currently serves as Head of the Original Cataloging Section of the Cataloging Services Department.

Ashley has been active in the Music Library Association, Online Audiovisual Catalogers (OLAC), and the Association for Library Collections and Technical Services (ALCTS), a division of the American Library Association. He led an MLA working group that formulated important fundamental principles and established guidelines for cataloging audiovisual materials with music content, drafting and editing Cataloging Musical Moving Image Material. In 1999 he received the MLA Special Achievement Award in recognition of his contributions to the bibliographic control of videorecordings.

WRITINGS

ed.: *Cataloging Musical Moving Image Material: a Guide to the Bibliographic Control of Videorecordings and Films of Musical Performances and other Music-Related Moving Image Material: with Examples in MARC Format* (Canton, MA, 1996)

MARK McKNIGHT

Ashley, Robert (Reynolds) (*b* Ann Arbor, MI, 28 March 1930). Composer and performer. He studied music theory at the University of Michigan (1948–52) and piano and composition at the Manhattan School of Music (MS 1953); he then returned to Ann Arbor to study acoustics and composition (1957–60). His teachers in composition included WALLINGFORD RIEGGER, ROSS LEE FINNEY, LESLIE BASSETT, and Gerhard. As a composer and performer Ashley was active in Milton Cohen's Space Theater (1957–64), the ONCE festivals and ONCE Group (*c*1958–69), and the SONIC ARTS UNION (1966–76); with each of these groups he toured the Americas and Europe. From 1969 to 1981 he directed the Center for Contemporary Music at Mills College, Oakland, California, where he organized an important public-access music and media facility. Subsequently he moved to New York, where he has become best known for a complex, interlocking series of highly unconventional operas for television, including *Perfect Lives*, *Atalanta*, and the tetralogy *Now Eleanor's Idea*.

Ashley realized his early electro-acoustic pieces while working with Cohen, a painter and sculptor. Like the other Sonic Arts Union composers, Mumma, Lucier, and Behrman, he invented electronic devices for the live generation, manipulation, and deployment of sounds. The group was less interested in polished electronic compositions, however, than in conceptual processes whose details were often left to chance. Unlike the others, Ashley was inexorably drawn toward the theater, and his works rarely had as much to do with sounds as with theatrical situations. In this he was also influenced by filmmaker George Manupelli, the artist Mary Ashley (Ashley's wife), and the pianist "Blue" Gene Tyranny, who has had a major presence in Ashley's works.

From 1959 to 1963 Ashley wrote instrumental works, such as *Fives* (1962), which explore improvisatory freedom. A 1963 quartet of *In memoriam* pieces—*In memoriam... Crazy Horse (Symphony)*, *In memoriam... Esteban Gomez (Quartet)*, *In memoriam... John Smith (Concerto)*, and *In memoriam... Kit Carson (Opera)*—apply the widest possible latitude to the genres parenthesized in their titles and provide the performers with graphics that allow for a variety of potential definitions. In *Kit Carson*, for example, the performers use geometric symbols to chart the nature of and relations between groups, events, and time.

Soon, however, working with Manupelli on multiple-projection films, Ashley moved in the direction of mixed-media performance art. In 1964 he took a provocative move into his own personal theater with *The Wolfman*. In this seminal work of the 1960s, Ashley played as background a tape collage of sounds recorded at a backyard party. He then walked onto the stage and began to project long vocal sounds, each duration consisting of one full breath. As one review (*Source*, no.3) described it:

> Gradually the relatively articulate collage is transformed into an inchoate mass of electronic sound, the voice overcoming the holocaust of feedback in the circuit and becoming more and more indistinguishable from the tape. The volume level is extremely high; the audience is literally surrounded by a wall of sound that is comparable to and even surpassing that of today's rock music.

In another, equally provocative nightclub-ambience piece, *Purposeful Lady Slow Afternoon* (1968), a woman hesitantly describes a sexual act over an accompaniment of bells.

About 1978 Ashley came to much wider public attention with his opera *Perfect Lives* (originally entitled *Private Parts*; 1977–83). Convinced that he suffered a mild form of Tourette's syndrome, which can compel automatic speech, he began to record his spells of compulsive speaking, and to use the results in electronic collage works such as *Automatic Writing* (1979). Employing similar methods, he also generated texts that have eventually grown into a series of operatic works, in which one opera derives from the plot and characters of another. The first, *Perfect Lives*, was developed in stages, the composer originally performing it as a solo text with piano and tape, and later with other singers and video. In this, as in subsequent operas, the work is created by slowly piling layer upon layer of text and music, sometimes achieving indecipherability and information overload.

In addition to internal interrelation, the operas draw on a wide range of literary sources: *Perfect Lives* is structured after the *Tibetan Book of the Dead*; *Improvement* is based on Frances Yates's books on Neoplatonism; *Now Eleanor's Idea* draws letters from *Low Rider* magazine (about customized cars); *eL/Aficionado* (a series derived from *Now Eleanor's Idea*) uses material from *Forbes* magazine and the business section of the *New York Times*; *Foreign Experiences* is an homage to and parody of the novels of Carlos Castaneda.

All Ashley's operas are collaborative, the composer's contribution sometimes consisting largely of the text and the rhythmic structure. Others who have provided elements of the music and video images include the singers Thomas Buckner, Jacqueline Humbert, Sam Ashley (the composer's son), and Joan La Barbara, the video producer John Sanborn, the rock musicians Peter Gordon and Jill Kroesen, the percussionist and performance artist David Van Tiegham, and the sound designer Tom Hamilton.

Despite this multiple input and an overriding sense of freedom the operas remain highly structured. *Improvement*, for example, for its 88-minute length, is a passacaglia based on a 24-note row over two chords, B♭ minor resolving to F minor; the length to which each central pitch is sustained varies with the intensity of the main character's situation at the moment in question. Likewise, *eL/Aficionado* is structured over a 16-note ostinato, and each scene is defined by a modal structure within which the soloist improvises on the text. *Atalanta (Acts of God)* is an immense text divided into 27 scenes, of which nine are chosen for any individual performance, so that in a multi-night run the text can differ from evening to evening. The whole opera is held together, though, with a passacaglia of six recurring chords.

Ashley's operas had always drawn heavily on autobiographical anecdote, but in his 70s his operatic production, as ambitious as ever, became even more directly self-referential. Two operas, *Dust* and *Concrete*, consist largely of stories about Ashley's youth, even though the premise in *Dust* is that they are told by homeless people living in Tribeca Park, across the street from Ashley's apartment. *Celestial Excursions* is a more whimsical fantasia on the subject of old age, with a meditation on Samuel Beckett and a sonnet from Giordano Bruno, a rare Ashley setting of another writer's words. *Quicksand* is a climactically complex opera based on the detective fiction genre. Though intended for television, the daring and unconventional nature of Ashley's operas has meant that, with the exception of *Perfect Lives*, none has yet been broadcast.

WORKS

OPERAS

(all composed for television and unless otherwise stated with librettos by Ashley)

That Morning Thing (stage op), 1967, Ann Arbor, 8 Feb 1968
Music with Roots in the Aether, 1976, Paris, 1976

Perfect Lives (Private Parts), 1977–83, Channel 4 TV, 1984
The Lessons, 1981, New York, 1981 [may be perf. as part of Perfect Lives (Private Parts)]
Music Word Fire and I would Do it Again Coo Coo, 1981
Atalanta (Acts of God), 1982, Paris, 1982
Atalanta Strategy, 1984
Improvement (Don Leaves Linda), 1984–5
eL/Aficionado, 1987
Yellow Man with Heart with Wings, 1990
Now Eleanor's Idea, 1993
Foreign Experiences, 1994
The Immortality Songs, 1994–20108
Balseros (M. Fornes), 1997
Your Money My Life Goodbye, 1998
Dust, 1998
Celestial Excursions, 2003
Concrete, 2006
Quicksand, 2008
Many other works derived from the operas

ELECTRONIC MUSIC THEATER

#+ Heat, pfmr, tape, 1961, Ann Arbor, Dec 1962
Public Opinion Descends upon the Demonstrators (Ashley), 1961, Ann Arbor, 18 Feb 1962
Boxing, sound-producing dance, 1963, Detroit, 9 April 1964
Combination Wedding and Funeral (Ashley), 1964, New York, 9 May 1965
Interludes for the Space Theater, sound-producing dance, 1964, Cleveland, 4 May 1965
Kittyhawk (An Antigravity Piece) (Ashley), 1964, St. Louis, 21 March 1965
The Lecture Series (Ashley), 1964, collab. M. Ashley, New York, 9 May 1965
The Wolfman, 1964
The Wolfman Motorcity Revue (Ashley), 1964
Morton Feldman Says, 1965, rev. 1970
Night Train (Ashley), 1966, collab. M. Ashley, Brandeis U., Waltham, MA, 7 Jan 1967
Orange Dessert (Ashley), 1965, Ann Arbor, 9 April 1966
Unmarked Interchange (Ashley), 1965, collab. ONCE Group, Ann Arbor, 17 Sept 1965
Four Ways, 1967 [from op That Morning Thing]
Frogs, 1967 [from op That Morning Thing]
Purposeful Lady Slow Afternoon, 1967, New York, 1968 [from op That Morning Thing]
She was a Visitor, 1967 [from op That Morning Thing]
The Trial of Anne Opie Wehrer and Unknown Accomplices for Crimes against Humanity (Ashley), 1968, Sheboygan, WI, 30 April 1968
Fancy Free (It's There) (Ashley), 1970, Brussels, April 1970
Illusion Models, hypothetical computer tasks, 1970
Night Sport, simultaneous monologues, 1975, L'Aquila, Italy, April 1975
Over the Telephone, remote/live audio installations, 1975, New York, March 1975
Automatic Writing, 1979
Tap Dancing in the Sand, 1982
Genezzano, 1983
The City of Kleist (Berlin), 1984
Susie Visits Arlington (Paris), 1985

INSTRUMENTAL AND VOCAL

Pf Sonata (Christopher Columbus crosses to the New World in the Niña, the Pinta and the Santa Maria using only dead reckoning and a crude astrolabe), pf, 1959, rev. pf, elecs, 1979; Maneuvers for Small Hands, pf, 1961; Fives, 2 pf, 2 perc, str qnt, 1962; Details, pf 4-hands, 1962; In memoriam... Crazy Horse (Sym.), 20 or more str/wind/other sustaining insts, 1963; In memoriam... Esteban Gomez (Quartet), 4 players, 1963; In memoriam... John Smith (Conc.), 3 players, assistants, 1963; In memoriam... Kit Carson (Opera), 8-part ens, 1963; Trios (White on White), any sustaining insts, 1963; Waiting Room (Quartet), any wind/str, 1965, rev. 1978; The Entrance, elec org, 1965; Revised, Finally, for Gordon Mumma, gong-like insts in pairs, 1973; Odalisque, 1v, chorus, 24 insts, 1985; Basic 10, snare drum, 1988; Superior Seven, fl, chorus, orch insts, 1988; Outcome Inevitable, chbr orch (8 or more insts), 1991; Van Cao's Meditation, pf, 1991; Tract, (1v, 4 str/str orch)/(1v, 2 kbd), 1992; When Famous Last Words Fail You, voice, chorus, and orchestra, 1997; Tap Dancing in the Sand, alto voice and 8 instruments, 2004; Hidden Similarities, voices and 8 instruments, 2005

OTHER ELECTRONIC

The 4th of July, tape, 1960; Something for Clarinet, Pianos and Tape, 1961; Complete with Heat, orch insts, tape, 1962; Detroit Divided, tape, 1962; Heat, tape, 1962; Big Danger in 5 Parts, tape, 1962; The Wolfman Tape, 1964 [with opt. amp v as The Wolfman]; Untitled Mixes, jazz trio, tape, 1965, collab. Bob Jones Trio; Str Qt Describing the Motions of Large Real Bodies, str qt, elecs, 1972; How can I Tell the Difference, vn/va, elecs, tape, 1974; Interiors without Flash, tape, 1979; Factory Preset, tape, 1993; Late at Night the Artist Works on his Piano Concerto, Oblivious of the Noise, tape, 1994
Discs: In Sate, Mencken, Christ, and Beethoven these were Men and Women (J.B. Wolgamot), 1v, elecs, 1972 (Cramps 6103, 1974); Automatic Writing, 1v, elecs, 1979 (Vital 1002, 1979)

FILMS AND VIDEOTAPES

Films (collab. G. Manupelli unless otherwise stated): The Image in Time, 1957; Bottleman, 1960; The House, 1961; Jenny and the Poet, 1964; My May, 1965; Overdrive, 1967; Dr. Chicago, 1968–70; Portraits, Selfportraits, and Still Lifes, 1969, collab. Manupelli and "Blue" Gene Tyranny; Battery Davis, 1970, collab. P. Makanna
Videotapes: The Great Northern Automobile Presence, lighting accompaniments for other people's music, 1975; What she Thinks, 1976
Recorded interview in *NHob*
Principal publisher: Visibility

WRITINGS

"The ONCE Group," *Arts in Society*, v (1968), 86–9
"The ONCE Group," *Source*, no.3 (1968), 19–22
"And So it Goes, Depending (1980): About Perfect Lives, an Opera for Television (1983)," *Words and Spaces: an Anthology of Twentieth Century Musical Experiments in Language and Sonic Environments*, ed. S.S. Smith and T. DeLio (Lanham, MD, 1989), 3–32
R. Ashley: Perfect Lives: An Opera (1991, Santa Fe, NM)
"The ONCE Group: Three Pieces," *Happenings and Other Acts*, ed. M.B. Sandford (New York, 1995), 182–94
"From Foreign Experience," *Conjuctions*, no.28, ed. T. Field (New York, 1997), 144–79
Music with Roots in the Aether (2000, Cologne, Germany)
Outside of Time: Ideas About Music (2009, Cologne, Germany)
Atalanta (Acts of God) (2010, Santa Fe, NM)

BIBLIOGRAPHY

H.W. Hitchcock: "Current Chronicle," *MQ*, xlviii (1962), 245–8
G. Mumma: "The ONCE Festival and How it Happened," *Arts in Society*, iv (1967), 381–98
W. Zimmermann: *Desert Plants: Conversations with 23 American Musicians* (Vancouver, BC, 1976), 121–35
N. Osterreich: "Music with Roots in the Aether," *PNM*, xvi/1 (1977), 214–28
J. Howell: "Robert Ashley's Perfect Lives (Private Parts)," *Live: Performance Art*, iii (1980), 3–7
C. Gagne and T. Crass: "Robert Ashley," *Soundpieces: Interviews with American Composers* (Metuchen, NJ, 1982), 15–34
J. Rockwell: "Post-Cageian Experimentation and New Kinds of Collaboration: Robert Ashley," *All American Music: Composition in the Late Twentieth Century* (New York, 1983), 96–108
T. DeLio: "Structural Pluralism," *Circumscribing the Open Universe: Essays on Cage, Feldman, Wolff, Ashley and Lucier* (Lanham, MD, 1984), 69–88
M. Sumner, K. Burch and M. Sumner, eds.: *The Guests Go In to Supper: Texts, Scores and Ideas of Seven American Composers: Ashley, Ono, Gage, Anderson, Amirkhanian, Peppe, Atchley* (Oakland, CA, 1986)
G. Smith and N.W. Smith: *American Originals: Interviews with 25 Contemporary Composers* (London, 1994)
K. Gann: *American Music in the 20th Century* (New York, 1997)

C. Herold: "The Other Side of Echo: the Adventures of a Dyke-Mestiza-Chicana-Marimacha Ranchera Singer in (Robert) Ashleyland," *Women & Performance*, xviii (1998)
L. Miller: "ONCE and Again: The Evolution of a Legendary Festival," liner notes to *Music from the ONCE Festival 1961–66*, New World Records 2003
K. Gann: Music Downtown (2006, Berkeley and Los Angeles, CA)

RICHARD S. JAMES/KYLE GANN

Ashley, Thomas C. [Ashley, Clarence Tom; Ashley, Clarence; McCurry, Clarence Earl; Tom] (*b* Bristol, VA, 29 Sept 1895; *d* Winston-Salem, NC, 2 June 1967). Banjoist, guitarist, and singer. His career as a performer spanned nearly 56 years, although he seldom earned his entire living from music and was largely inactive from 1943 to 1960. He was the child of a short-lived marriage between Rosie Belle Ashley and George McCurry. He was raised primarily by his maternal grandparents and adopted their surname as his own. Ashley took up banjo when he was eight years old and learned from two maternal aunts. He began his professional career at the age of 16 performing blackface comedy with a traveling medicine show. This gave him the opportunity to meet and play with many of the best musicians in the region, including G.B. Grayson and Hobart Smith. He made numerous 78 rpm recordings for the hillbilly market in the late 1920s and early 1930s, both as a soloist and as a member of the Carolina Tar Heels, and Byrd Moore & his Hot Shots. The Great Depression had a big impact on Ashley's musical activities, as it did for many other southern rural musicians, and he was often forced to find other means of making a living. Ashley quit medicine shows for good in 1943, and a subsequent injury to his left hand caused him to abandon performing for several years. He continued to stay in touch with musician friends and to attend regional events such as the annual fiddle contest in Union Grove, NC. In 1952 three of Ashley's 78 rpm recordings were included in the *Anthology of American Folk Music* on Folkways Records. This influential reissue project brought Ashley's music to the attention of northern urban audiences. In 1960 the folklorist, musician, and promoter Ralph Rinzler traveled to the Union Grove contest looking for old-time musicians, including Ashley. Through Rinzler's efforts Ashley was subsequently able to pursue an entirely new avenue of performing. During the final years of his life he played at many folk festivals, performed in cities such as New York (including at Carnegie Hall), Los Angeles, Chicago, and Minneapolis, and also toured England. Many of his songs were recorded by bluegrass, folk revival, and even rock musicians.

BIBLIOGRAPHY

A.M. Manning, M.M. Miller: "Tom Ashley," *Tom Ashley, Sam McGee, Bukka White: Tennessee Traditional Singers*, ed. T.G. Burton (Knoxville, TN, 1981/*R*/1996 as *Tom Ashley, Sam McGee, Bukka White*), 9–59

PAUL F. WELLS

Ashman, Howard (Elliot) (*b* Baltimore, MD, 17 May 1950; *d* New York, NY, 14 Mar 1991). Lyricist. Ashman studied the performing arts at Boston University and Goddard College, and earned his MFA from Indiana University. A lyricist for both stage and screen, Ashman is best known for his collaborations with composer ALAN MENKEN. In 1982, they created *Little Shop of Horrors* off-Broadway, where it ran for five years and led to the 1986 film version, for which the duo slightly reworked the score and oversaw the production. It reached Broadway in 2003. In 1986 Ashman provided the book, lyrics, and direction for Broadway's short-lived *Smile*, with music by Marvin Hamlisch. Ashman and Menken composed the songs for the Disney animated film musical *The Little Mermaid* in 1989, and the success of this project (the song "Under the Sea" won an Oscar) led to the pair's second Disney film, *Beauty and the Beast* (1991). Ashman and Menken had not completed their work on their third Disney animated musical, *Aladdin* (1992), when Ashman died from AIDS complications; lyricist Tim Rice completed the work. Both *The Little Mermaid* and *Beauty and the Beast* reached Broadway in reworked live-action form; *Beauty and the Beast* enjoyed an extremely successful 13-year run beginning in 1994, and *The Little Mermaid* ran for just over a year and a half beginning in 2008.

Ashman's style as a lyricist is perhaps best understood as clever, humorous, and sometimes unexpected in its rhymes or jokes. Both the dark, socially pointed commentary in *Little Shop of Horrors* and the family-friendly lyrics of the Disney films abound in surprising wit and frequent cultural references.

BIBLIOGRAPHY

S. Holden: "For Alan Menken, A Partnership Ends But the Song Plays On," *New York Times* (15 Mar 1992)
S. Holden: "To Its Creators, 'Smile' Was Always A Beauty," *New York Times* (23 Nov 1986)

JESSICA STERNFELD

Asia, Daniel (Issac) (*b* Seattle, WA, 27 June 1953). Composer and conductor. He studied composition with Stephen Albert, RONALD PERERA, and Randall McClellan at Hampshire College (BA 1975). His teachers at Yale University (MM 1977) included JACOB DRUCKMAN and MacCombie (composition), and ARTHUR WEISBERG (conducting). He also studied composition with GUNTHER SCHULLER at the Berkshire Music Center (1979) and with Yun at the Berlin Hochschule für Musik (1980). He served on the faculty of the Oberlin Conservatory from 1980 to 1986. A UK Fulbright Arts Fellowship and a Guggenheim Fellowship (1987–8) enabled him to work in London from 1986 to 1988, where he was a visiting lecturer at City University. He joined the faculty of the University of Arizona in 1988. He has conducted the university-based Arizona Contemporary Ensemble, co-founded and directed the New York contemporary music ensemble Musical Elements (1977-1990), and served as composer-in-residence for the Phoenix SO (1991–4). His awards include grants from the NEA (1978, 1985, 1993), the Fromm Foundation (1986), the Koussevitzky Foundation (1989), Meet the Composer (1994), the Aaron Copland Fund (1994), the Barlow Endowment and Arizona Friends of Chamber Music (for Nonet, 2010), and the Academy Award from the American Academy of Arts and Letters (2010). His works have been commissioned by the Seattle SO (Symphony no.1, 1987), the American Composers Orchestra (*Black Light*, 1990), and the Cincinnati SO (*Gateways*, 1993) among others.

Asia's music of the 1970s, particularly *Miles Mix* (1976) and *Sand II* (1978), experiments with vernacular influences. Later works, especially the symphonies and the Piano Concerto, are more indebted to the music of Barber, Bernstein, and Copland.

WORKS

Orch: Rivalries, chbr orch, 1980–81; 3 Movts, tpt, orch, 1984; Sym. no.1, 1987; Black Light, 1990; Sym. no.2 "Celebration" (Khagiga: In Memoriam Leonard Bernstein), 1990; At the Far Edge, 1991; Sym. no.3, 1992; Gateways, 1993 (arr wind ens, 2003); Sym. no.4, 1993; Pf Conc., 1994; Vc Conc., 1997 ; Then Something Happened (A Languid Dance), 1999; Once Again, 1999; Bear Down Arizona, 2002; What About It, 2003; Why (?) Jacob, 2007; Sym. no.5, 2008

Vocal: Sound Shapes, SSAATTBB, pitch pipes, 1973; On the Surface (Mass. Daily Collegian), S, pf, hp, vc, perc, 1974–5; Sand II (G. Snyder), Mez, chbr ens, 1978; Why (?) Jacob (D. Asia), SSAATTBB, pf, 1979 (arr orch 2007); Ossabaw Island Dream (P. Pines), Mez, chbr orch, 1981–2, arr sym orch, 1986; She (Pines), SATB, 1981–2; Pines Songs (Pines), S, pf, 1983, arr. S, ww qnt, pf, 1983–4, arr. Bar, ob, pf, 1985; V'shamru, Bar, chbr orch, 1985; Ps 30, Bar, vn, pf, 1986; Songs from the Page of Swords (Pines), Bar, ob, pf/chbr ens, 1986; Celebration, Bar, SATB, brass qnt, org, 1988; 2 Sacred Songs (*Kaddish*, Ps xcvi), S, fl, gui, vc, 1989 (arr S, fl, vc, pf, 2003); Fanfare, 1993; Breath in a Ram's Horn (Pines), 1v, pf, 1995; Purer than the Purest Pure (E.E. Cummings), SATB, 1996; Out of More (Cummings), SATB, 1996; Summer is Over (Cummings), SATB, 1997; An E.E. Cummings Songbook, 1v, pf, 1998; Pines Songs II, T, pf, 2002; Breath in a Ram's Horn (Pines), T, chbr ens, 2003; Songs From Adrift on Blinding Light (Pines), T, pf, 2004; The Tin Angel (Pines), opera, 2011

Chbr and solo inst: Dream Sequence I, amp trbn, 1975; Pf Set I, 1975, Pf Set II, 2 pf, 1976; Str Qt no.1, 1976; Plum-DS II, fl, tape, 1977; Sand I, fl, hn, db, 1977; Line Images, ww ens, 1978; Orange, va, 1979; Mar music, 1983; Music for tpt and org, 1983; Why Jacob?, pf, 1983; Str Qt no.2, 1985; Scherzo Sonata, pf, 1987; B for J, fl, b cl, trbn, vib, elec org, vn, va, vc, 1988; Pf Qt, 1989; Your Cry will be a Whisper, gui, 1992; Five Images, fl, bn, 1994; The Alex Set, ob, 1995; Embers, fl, gui, 1995; Piano Trio, vn, vc, pf, 1996; Piano Variations, pf, 1998; Guitar Set I, gui, 1998; Woodwind Quintet, fl, ob, cl, hn, bn, 1998; Songs of Transcendence, gui, 1999; Momentary Lapses, vn, gui, 2000; Sonata, vn, pf, 2001; A Lament, vc, pf, 2001; Brass Quintet, 2001; Unicorns are Fireproof, fl, 2002; Cello Suite, vc, 2002; New Set, gui, vn, 2004; No Time, pf, 2004; Ragflections, pf or org, 2004; Str Qt no.3, 2007; Shuffle and Blues, vn, vc, pf, 2009; Nonet, chbr ens, 2010

Tape: Shtay, 1975; Miles Mix, 1976; As Above (film score), 1977

Principal publisher: Presser

JAMES CHUTE

Asian American jazz. The boundaries of Asian American jazz are debatable. Its practioners could be said to extend from the popular fusion group Hiroshima to Filipino Americans playing in the early New Orleans jazz scene. The term, however, has had the greatest resonance with a cohort of musicians and activists that has come together since early in the 1980s to organize its musical activities around racial issues. These include Anthony Brown, Jeff Chan, Glenn Horiuchi, Fred Ho, Jason Kao Hwang, Vijay Iyer, Mark Izu, Jon Jang, Miya Masaoka, Hafez Modirzadeh, and Francis Wong.

Confronting a lack of interest in their work by mainstream outlets, these musicians used "Asian American" as a rubric to promote, present, document, and distribute their work. They have consequently established a nationwide network of artists and organizations with nodes in major US metropolitan areas. For example, in 1981 Paul Yamazaki, George Leong, and Izu co-founded the San Francisco Asian American Jazz Festival. Similar festivals have since been established in Chicago, Los Angeles, and New York. Asian American musicians produced their own recordings as a way to maintain creative control and reach target audiences. Jon Jang's first were released on RPM Records, an independent label created to record the avant-garde Afro-Asian group United Front co-led by Brown, Izu, Lewis Jordan, and George Sams. In 1987 Jang and Wong founded the nonprofit Asian Improv Records and Asian Improv Arts, which has since recorded numerous albums by Asian American musicians and their collaborators. In New York, Ho's Big Red Media has served as a platform for a number of musical projects and stage productions that take a strong stance against racism, sexism, and economic oppression.

The development of Asian American jazz coincided with the Asian American movement of the 1970s and 1980s that sought an official apology and financial compensation for the Japanese Americans who suffered preemptive incarceration during World War II. The issue of redress as well as cases of anti-Asian violence such as the Vincent Chin incident energized Asian American activists and encouraged them to form a variety of coalitions. Reflecting the demographic of the activists, the first wave of Asian American jazz musicians were mainly Chinese and Japanese Americans born in the 1950s. They saw their work as an integral part of the political movement, and many early performances and recordings, such as Horiuchi's *Manzanar Voices* (1989), Ho's *Tomorrow is now!* (1985), and Jang's *Are you Chinese or Charlie Chan?* (1983), addressed the same issues.

Rather than create a separate music that was uniquely Asian, however, these musicians drew upon what Lisa Lowe has called the hybridity of Asian American culture: the growing together of cultural practices that resulted from the intersection of Asian American and African American artistic traditions. Many Asian American jazz musicians studied texts such as *The Autobiography of Malcolm X* and the poetry and essays of Amiri Baraka; they listened closely to "freedom jazz" albums such as Max Roach and Abbey Lincoln's *We Insist! Freedom Now Suite* (1960); and they collaborated with African American musicians. In 1982 Ho founded the interracial Afro-Asian Music Ensemble in New York. Similarly Jang's Pan-Asian Arkestra was a multi-racial affair, inspired by the Pan African People's Arkestra led by Horace Tapscott. In San Diego and Los Angeles Horiuchi worked with the African American bass player M'Chaka Uba, who had previously lived in Chicago and was a member of the AACM.

Although many of the musicians above experimented with combining traditional Asian music and improvised jazz, their music is stylistically varied and cannot be defined by formal considerations alone. Despite the many changes in political and musical outlook that have occurred since the 1980s, Asian American jazz is most accurately described as a rallying point. Younger musicians, most of whom did not participate in the movement of the 1980s, have benefited from uniting as Asian Americans. What they share with first-wave musicians is the awareness that, as racially distinct outsiders to the jazz tradition, they confront similar challenges. In the 1990s and 2000s a diverse crop of musicians, including Tatsu Aoki, Jeff Chan, Vijay Iyer, Kuni Mikami, Hafez Modirzadeh, and Jeff Song, produced their own recordings on Asian Improv. By deliberately identifying themselves as Asian American, they distinguished themselves from others such as Gerald Oshita, Russel Baba, and Toshiko Akiyoshi who have also played jazz while inserting Asian elements.

BIBLIOGRAPHY

D. Wong: *Speak it Louder: Asian Americans Making Music* (New York, 2004)

S.M. Asai: "Cultural Politics: the African American Connection in Asian American Jazz-based Music," *Asian Music*, xxxvi/1 (2005), 87–108

K. Fellezs: "Silenced but not Silent: Asian Americans and Jazz," *Alien Encounters: Popular Culture in Asian America*, eds. M.T. Nguyen and T.L.N. Tu (Durham, NC, 2007), 69–110

L. Kajikawa: "The Sound of Struggle: Black Nationalism and Asian American Jazz in the 1980s," *Jazz/Not Jazz: the Music and its Boundaries*, eds. D. Ake, C.H. Garrett and D. Goldmark (Berkeley, 2012), 190–218

LOREN KAJIKAWA

Asian American music.

1. Introduction. 2. East Asian American music. (i) Chinese American music. (a) Traditional instrumental ensembles. (b) Chinese opera and traditional vocal music. (c) Concert music and crossovers. (d) Popular music/jazz. (ii) Japanese American music. (iii) Korean American music. 3. South Asian American music. (i) Mainland Southeast Asian American music. (a) Laotian. (b) Cambodian. (c) Vietnamese. (ii) Filipino American music.

1. Introduction. Although Filipino sailors established fishing villages in the Louisiana bayous in the 1760s, sustained Asian immigration to the United States and Hawaii did not begin until the 1830s. Over the next century, hundreds of thousands of Chinese, Japanese and Filipinos—and smaller numbers of Koreans and immigrants from South Asia—arrived on American and Hawaiian soil to work on plantations and railroads, and in goldmines and factories. Racial tension and outright hostility, often generated by white laborers who feared for their jobs, greeted these early Asian immigrants, and they became frequent targets of mob violence and lynchings. Discrimination and race-based crimes encouraged the growth of ethnic enclaves, which aided the development of distinct micro-musical cultures. "Yellow Peril" fears fueled the passage of the 1882 Chinese Exclusion Act, which expanded into the 1924 Asian Exclusion Act. These bills effectively halted the first wave of Chinese, and later, most Asian immigration to the United States. This extended history of racial bigotry and intolerance against all Asians ultimately sparked the formation of a pan-ethnic "Asian American movement" in the 1960s.

Although the 1943 Magnuson Act repealed the Asian Exclusion Act, the second major wave of Asian immigration began only after the passage of the 1965 Immigration and Nationality Act. Compared to earlier immigrants, who were primarily working-class and from a small number of geographic areas, the most recent arrivals are much more diverse. While some came for educational and economic opportunities, others immigrated to reunite with family members or to escape political persecution. Starting in the late 1970s, numerous refugees from Southeast Asia have immigrated to the United States. According to the 2010 Census, there are 17.3 million people of Asian descent (including 2.6 million who identify as multiracial) in the United States (5.6% of the total population). Between 2000 and 2010, the Asian population in the United States grew by 43%, making it the fastest growing racial group in the country. The 2008 Census Bureau Population Projection estimated that, by 2050, the Asian population in the United States would exceed 40 million (9.2% of the total population).

Since Asian Americans have diverse backgrounds and dissimilar knowledge of and interest in Asian cultures, they participate in many different forms of musicking. It is, however, important to recognize that "Asian American music" is a highly contested term. While some apply the label to any music made by Asian Americans, others only use the designation for Asian American–made music that is about the Asian American experience.

In pre-1965 ethnic enclaves, first-generation immigrants tended to play and listen to the folk, classical and popular music of their homelands. In the late 19th and early 20th centuries, many Chinese Americans kept abreast of recent developments in Cantonese opera by sponsoring tours by well-known troupes. At the same time, many immigrants have adapted Asian traditions. When singing *muyu*, a narrative song tradition from Taishan, Chinese Americans often used new texts that reflect the immigrant experience. In performances of Cantonese opera, they have sometimes used mixed-gender troupes, an innovative practice that ultimately influenced performance practice in Asia. Meanwhile, second- and third-generation immigrants often preferred American and European musical traditions. During the forced internment of 110,000 Americans of Japanese descent in the American West and South during World War II, many Japanese Americans displayed their American-ness by playing and listening to jazz. This resulted in the formation of many high-quality big bands. When the war ended, several of these musicians moved to Japan and helped to establish jazz scenes there.

Three major developments affected Asian American music after 1965. One is the emergence of Asian American jazz (or creative music), an experimental genre that is rooted in jazz, but uses elements that reflect the musicians' Asian heritages and their experiences as Asian Americans. This genre is closely associated with the Asian American movement and progressive politics. The second is the great diversity of new immigrants. Unlike first wavers, many post-1965 immigrants have limited knowledge of and interest in traditional and classical music of their native countries. They are just as likely to be interested in popular music (either from their homeland or from the United States) and Western classical music—the latter is a genre where

Asian Americans are particularly visible. That said, numerous virtuosos of Asian classical musics are now based in the United States. They perform classical and fusion music at prestigious venues, and teach in both universities and their own ethnic communities. The third development is the pop stardom recently achieved by several Asian Americans in Asia. Rochester-raised singer Wang Leehom has won four Taiwan Golden Melody Awards (the Taiwanese "Grammy"), and the Korean American rapper Tiger JK is considered a pioneer of the Seoul hip hop scene.

As the experiences of Asian Americans become even more diverse and transnational, their musical activities undoubtedly will become even more varied in the future.

2. East Asian American music.

(i) Chinese American music. The large-scale immigration of Chinese to the United States began in the mid-19th century; by 1882 over 300,000 had arrived. Early immigrants were attracted by the California gold rush; they later came to build railroads, develop agriculture and fisheries along the Pacific Coast, as well as operate laundries and build the export/import trade business. Initially, Chinese immigrants, protected by the Burlingame Treaty (1868), entered the United States with few restrictions, but labor competition fueled anti-Chinese sentiment and racial discrimination intensified. Eventually Chinese exclusion laws (1882–1943) barred Chinese laborers from entering the United States and admitted only merchants and their families, teachers, students, diplomats, and tourists. A dark Exclusion Era ensued, codifying Chinese as a racial "other," unwanted and ineligible for citizenship. In the 1930s, as China waged a war against Japanese imperialism, discrimination against Chinese Americans grew less intense, helped by sympathetic portrayals of Chinese circulating in popular culture through authors such as Pearl Buck. During World War II America found an important ally in China, and congress repealed the Chinese Exclusion laws in 1943 and allotted China an annual quota of 105 immigrants. A second wave of immigration began with the passing of the Immigration and Nationality Act in 1965, in which the US government put Chinese immigration on an equal par with all other countries and set separate quotas for the People's Republic of China, Republic of China (Taiwan), and Hong Kong. Periodically, however, cold war politics placed Chinese Americans again under a cloud of suspicion as potential communist spies. The 1980s saw a third wave of immigration, prompted by Chinese economic reforms beginning in 1978, the normalization of diplomatic relations between China, and the United States and extraordinary economic growth in Taiwan and Hong Kong. The

Parade, Festival of Mountain and Plain, Denver, c1900. (Denver Public Library, Western History Collection, James B. Brown, X-18263)

Yo-Yo Ma performs with members of the Silk Road Ensemble, 2002. (AP Photo/Osamu Honda)

population of Chinese Americans in 1990 doubled from the previous decade to 1,645,472, a figure that doubled again only 15 years later.

Most Chinese migrants of the 19th century came from the Pearl River Delta of Guangdong Province, and were speakers of Cantonese, Taishanese, and Hakka Chinese dialects. In the United States, they concentrated in mining communities, railroad construction camps, rural farms, or fishing villages. The rise of anti-Chinese riots, as well as the completion of the railroad, drove them to urban areas, forming Chinatowns. Such ethnic enclaves, though helping to reinforce cultural ties and shield the populace from racial hostility, did not always arise by choice: during exclusion many restrictive covenants prevented Chinese and other Asians from living elsewhere. Due to exclusion laws that discouraged the immigration of Chinese women, Chinatowns were also populated mostly by men. Many Chinese also moved to eastern and midwestern cities and to the South, where they could find work and where their presence was better tolerated. Starting in the 1970s, the Chinese population diversifed, with immigrations from various regions and ethnic groups in China. Mandarin and Fujian dialects gained prominence. Many new migrants and their families, who came with better economic means and education, or became professionals, settled in suburbs throughout the United States. Many also continue to maintain, over however extended a period, a transnational existence.

When Chinese Americans established communities across the continent, they found both old and new ways to establish institutions for various social functions. Music groups formed prominent cultural institutions (theaters and associations). The exclusion laws, however, barred Chinese musicians from entering the United Sates, causing performances to decline. The operation of prominent Chinese American music spaces became severely restricted. Situations were improved when in the post–World War II and early Cold War period cultural pluralist ideologies began to gain traction, and when virtuoso performers, as well as diverse music traditions, arrived with the second wave of Chinese immigration. In addition, music performance by native-born Chinese Americans emerged in the early 20th century, flourished over the course of the century and became by turns more diversified, hybridized and distinctively individual. Various performing groups, new genres and fusions have developed, partly in response to new patterns of American multiculturalism since the 1970s and partly due to the weakening of Chinese identity as a social boundary for the second generation. Collectively they comprise articulations of ethnicity in popular culture and in the public sphere of American society.

(a) Traditional instrumental ensembles. Traditional Chinese instrumental performers and their ensembles were popular among Chinese immigrants from the beginning. Images of Chinese performers holding traditional instruments are ubiquitous in depictions of Chinese immigrants' lives in US popular magazines of the 19th century. The instruments depicted are those commonly found in traditional Guangdong ensembles. As evidenced by many drawings and newspaper accounts, the primary instruments in the traditional ensemble include the *erhu* (a two-string bowed vertical fiddle),

sanxian (a plucked three-string lute), *yueqin* (a plucked four-string lute, also known as a moon-zither or moon-guitar), *pipa* (a plucked pear-shaped vertical fretted lute with four strings), *dizi* (a transverse bamboo flute with finger holes), *yangqin* (a hammered dulcimer), and *guban* (a drum and wooden clapper), while outdoor instruments often included the *suona* (a double-reed wind instrument with a flaring metal bell), Chinese gongs, drums, and cymbals. The *erhu* is frequently used as a solo instrument. Played sitting down, its sound box is placed on the top of the left thigh and the neck held vertically, while the bow, its hair between the two strings, is played with an underhand grip. The *pipa*, another virtuoso instrument, is positioned with the wooden body held between two arms, and played generally with one hand holding the neck and the other plucking with all five finger nails. These two instruments were ubiquitous, and both were featured in "The Living Chinese Family" exhibit by Phineas Barnum in the Chinese Museum of the 1850s, the earliest extant iconographical material related to the music of the Chinese in America.

Traditional music was regularly played, and instrumental ensembles of various combinations continued well into the 20th century. Large Chinatown communities tended to have music organizations that provided performances for various social functions, including holiday celebrations, charity events, or the ceremonies and banquets of groups such as the Chinese Consolidated Benevolent Association, and district or family clan associations. Amateur music clubs were also formed to educate both the community and the students of Chinese schools.

To the larger American society of the 19th and early 20th centuries, Chinese instrumental music was often part of the spectacles in public space, and was seen in holiday parades, Chinese New Year celebrations, funeral processions, and (together with Chinese theaters) prominent world fairs. The penetrating sound of the *suona* was particularly suitable for processions, and the large Chinese gong was nearly ubiquitous in Chinese parades, while drums, cymbals and gongs continue to be inseparable from popular lion dances. Historical photographs of Chinese parades document the existence of Chinese instruments in rural towns such as Boise, Idaho, and Denver, Colorado, and in urban streets of San Francisco and Seattle. San Francisco's Cathay Club (1911–62), associated with funerals and parades, involved a band primarily of Western instruments, but also including a smaller group of Chinese instruments, which played a key role in the community's music life.

The second wave of immigration brought both virtuoso musicians and new performance practices influenced by recent changes in musical tradition in China. Among them was the larger Chinese ensemble, modeled after the Western orchestra, that incorporated substantial wind and string sections. The Chinese Music Ensemble of New York, established in 1961, became the largest such ensemble in the United States. The arrival of professional musicians with the third wave further enhanced the level of performance. In addition to *erhu* and *pipa*, *guzheng* (16–26 stringed zither with movable bridges) and *dizi* also became popular solo instruments. Virtuoso performances could be heard both in concerts and at social functions. Music from China, a small ensemble established in 1986, has promoted both traditional and new repertoire with annual competitions and concerts and has been featured frequently in festivals and symposia. Notably, instrumental performing groups were sustained by strong interest, helped by the absence of a linguistic barrier and the ease with which they have become integrated with other cultural traditions and performance media.

(b) Chinese opera and traditional vocal music. Cantonese opera performance was the first known staged Chinese opera in the United States. Since their arrival in 1852, Cantonese opera troupes and performers had constituted the most important musical entertainment for Chinese immigrants until the beginning of the second wave of Chinese immigration in the 1960s. Cantonese opera theaters, remaining resilient through periods of wax and wane, were themselves prominent cultural institutions, sometimes functioning as Chinatown residents' surrogate family. They enjoyed a first golden period in the 1870s, and a renaissance in the 1920s (after shrewdly circumventing exclusion laws) with powerhouse establishments like the Mandarin Theater and Great China Theater. With 750–950 seats each, their audiences cut across economic, class, and occupational boundaries and the theaters held leading roles in community initiatives. In addition, since the 1920s, prominent Cantonese opera clubs were formed, not only to educate the cultural heritage and to produce opera performances, but also to stage opera for benevolent purposes such as fundraising for charitable or social service organizations. In the 1970s San Francisco boasted six singing clubs, and the Nam Chung Music Association (1925–) remains the largest; New York City in 1990 could claim eight Cantonese opera clubs. The opera has been enjoyed in multiple ways, including recordings (most imported, but also produced by two short-lived local record companies, Gold Star and Oriental Records), but also via radio and opera films. For 40 years until 1979, the San Francisco community enjoyed the daily radio program "The Chinese Hour," featuring opera performances by the theaters and opera clubs. In recent decades, as Chinese Americans have been dispersed into the suburbs of major cities, a significant virtual Chinatown community has coalesced by means of stage productions by amateur Cantonese opera clubs from satellite, suburban Chinatowns. (*See* MUSICAL THEATER §13: CHINESE AMERICAN MUSICAL THEATER)

Peking opera and Kunqu exist mainly through amateur opera clubs, often emblematic of the Chinese *literati* tradition, although visiting troupes tended to be the focus of larger community events. The most significant of these was the performing tour of Peking opera star Mei Lanfang in 1930. This remains a notable event in American music history, because the enthusiasm for Mei spurred the interest in Chinese opera in general, and his performance had an indelible effect on American ultra-modern music and modern theaters. In the 1990s, Peking and Kunqu amateur clubs received a boost from a large number of newly-arrived virtuosi from mainland China, giving rise to quasi-professional performing groups. In the folk music tradition, a little known genre, *muyu* songs (a southern-China ballad tradition), constituted an important musical tradition for Chinese Americans. A genre popular among immigrants since as early as the mid-19th century, the tradition of *muyu* songs involves narrative songs whose texts range from romances and folk tales to the sentiment and predicament of early immigrants, in collections such as that compiled in *Songs of Golden Mountain*.

(c) Concert music and crossovers. Since the mid 20th century, Chinese Americans have gradually and steadily established themselves on the Western classical music scene, as performers, composers, and collaborators. Yo Yo Ma, Chia Liang Lin, Wu Han, Hao Jiang Tian, Xian Zhang, and Lang Lang are just a few of a long list of concert musicians of Chinese descent in the United States. As advocates for new music, Margaret Leng Tan is a leading exponent of John Cage's music and toy piano, and Jenny Lin is an expert in virtuosic contemporary piano work. In composition, Chou Wen Chung led the way, followed by Bun-Ching Lam in the late 1970s. Composers of the so called "1978 class," Tan Dun, Zhou Long, Chen Yi, Bright Sheng, and many others moved to New York City from China in the 1980s. With an aesthetic shaped importantly by the social-cultural milieu in New York, by early 2000 they had established themselves as leading voices of contemporary concert music in America, giving new meaning to the term émigré composers. Whether for their craftsmanship, striking imagination, innovative ideas, or multimedia visions, these composers have received the highest acclaim, and their works evince multi-accented articulations. The Metropolitan Opera House's commission and premiere of Tan's epic opera, *The First Emperor* (2006), and the Pulitzer Prize awarded to Zhou's opera *Madame White Snake* (2010) are two historical landmarks in Chinese American music. Gabriela Lena Frank's rich work explores her multi-cultural heritage (Jewish-Peruvian-Chinese). Furthermore, in response to the new pattern of cultural fusion in music making, masters of Chinese traditional music have become key collaborators with contemporary music groups and productions, including the collaboration between *pipa* virtuoso Wu Man and the Kronos Quartet on repertoire ranging from Lou Harrison to jazz improvisation; the collaboration between Chinese opera singer and director Chen Shi Zheng and composer Stewart Wallace on the opera *The Bonesetter's Daughter*, with a libretto by Amy Tan; or many others' participation in the 20-country collaborative Silk Road Project (1998–). At the cusp of China's emergence as a global economic power, many such cultural fusions in contemporary music are considered cosmopolitan and are active in the transnational terrain.

(d) Popular music/jazz. With a few exceptions, Chinese American popular music has developed primarily in the hands of the second generation, who found new means of claiming a public identity nearly unthinkable for their parents. California-born Lee Tung Foo, the first Chinese American singer on the vaudeville stage, debuted in 1905. Chung Hwa Four (1912–26) was the first Chinese barbershop quartet. Many female singers and dancers were also active on stages, in night clubs and in films in the first half of the century, such as vaudevillians Jue Quon Tai, Anna Chang, Chee Toy, Helen Jean Wong, and Lady Tsen Mei, screen star and vaudevillian Anna May Wong, cabaret performers Rose Yuen Ow and Li Tei Ming, and swing singer Beatrice Fung Oye. Their repertoire comprises familiar songs from Tin Pan Alley, occasionally sung in Cantonese. While Chinese American nightclubs can be traced back to Shanghai Low in 1913, a golden era began with the World War II era. More than a dozen opened in San Francisco alone. Charlie Low's "Forbidden City" (San Francisco, 1938–1961) was a pre-eminent performing venue and housed a company of over 100 singers and dancers. Since the beginning of American musical theater, many titles based on Chinese topics have featured yellowface performers, yet *Flower Drum Song* (1958) was the first to focus on Chinese Americans, and as a musical film (1961) has proved the only major Hollywood film to star an all-Asian American cast. Playing a showgirl in the film of the musical, Nancy Kwan's performance of "I enjoy being a girl" became an iconic moment of Asian femininity in the 60s. In Hawaii, many songs by Kui Lee, including "I'll remember you," were made famous by Don Ho and Elvis Presley. The Asian American Movement of the 1970s spurred the development of Asian american jazz, and Chinese American jazz musicians, including Jon Jang, Jason Kao Hwang, Fred Ho, and Francis Wong, introduced a new form of jazz that grapples in various ways with Chinese American experience and heritage, sometimes incorporating Chinese instruments and musical practices. Popular musicians also show divergent use of Chinese tradition: Winston Tong is known both for his collaborations with art rock group Tuxedomoon (1977–83, 2005) and for solo albums such as *Theoretically China* (1984); Chinese American musicians of the 21st century expressed themselves in a wide range of genres, including indie rock (Eric Hsu), rap (Jin), R&B/soul (Kelis), electronica (Dave Liang), R&B/pop (Ne-Yo), experimental (Jen Shyu), indie folk (Vienna Teng), and film music (Christopher Tin).

(ii) Japanese American music. Japanese American music is an expression of ethnic identity, a hybrid genre drawing on the idiomatic playing styles of traditional Japanese instruments and use of pentatonic melodies, rhythms, forms, stylistic and aesthetic elements from Japanese folk or classical traditions. The incorporation of these traditional elements in Western or American music has resulted in a transculturated music with varying degrees of experimentation and success.

Kinnara Taiko, Los Angeles, c1990. (Ed Ikuta)

Japanese American music has developed primarily in the hands of *sansei*, third generation immigrants who were born after World War II. A number of *sansei* musician-composers, taking their cues from African American culture and the Black Power movement, write in a jazz-based idiom as a vehicle for their artistry and in some cases politics. The improvisational nature of jazz allows great freedom of expression in form, rhythm, melody, and timbre. For some Japanese American musicians, the pioneering improvisational dimension of free jazz proffers thematic development of melodies rather than harmonic variation, employing drums to add color and texture, using pedal points and ostinatos in creating static harmonic environments, executing angular, jagged intervals to express abstraction, and performing modal scales, collective improvisation, and polyrhythms. Japanese American musicians consider the openness and spirit of jazz to be conducive for synthesizing Japanese and Asian musical elements and ideas in their compositions. (*See* Asian American jazz)

The internment of Japanese Americans during World War II and the redress and reparations movement in the 1980s serve as themes for several *sansei* jazz-based compositions: Glenn Horiuchi's *Poston Sonata* for *shamisen* (three-string plucked lute), alto saxophone, tenor saxophone, bass clarinet, bass, percussion, and piano, Sumi Tonooka's *Out from the Silence* (inspired by her mother's internment experience) for *koto* (13-string board zither), *shakuhachi* (end-blown bamboo flute), violin, clarinet, trumpet, tenor saxophone, trombone, vibes, rhythm section, and voice; and Anthony Brown's *E.O. 9066 (Truth be Told)* for piano, bass, drum set and percussion, *sheng* (Chinese mouth organ), *di* (Chinese transverse bamboo flute), *suona* (shawm), tenor saxophone, clarinet and *taiko* (Japanese barrel drum). The *sansei* Key Kool and his partner Rhettmatic also address internment in their rap song "Reconcentrated" for voice, turntable, DJ mixer, and other "scratching" resources. The expressive range of these compositions, from anger to reconciliation, speak to the injustices and humiliation of the internment experience and its aftermath.

The greatest concentration of Japanese American musical activity is in California, particularly in the urban areas of San Francisco and Los Angeles. The Asian American creative music scene in San Francisco is home to a number of *sansei* musician-composers, many of whom study or have studied Japanese court music (*gagaku*). The San Francisco Gagaku Society, which was active in the 1970s and 80s, attracted many Japanese American musicians who received training under the tutelage of Suenobu Togi, former Imperial Japanese court dancer and musician and instructor at UCLA. *Gagaku*'s tripartite *jo-ha-kyū* form and aesthetic concept of *ma* (silent beat) are examples of musical features that broaden the musical landscape for *sansei*s in their own work.

Other forms of traditional music from which *sansei* musician-composers draw include Japanese *taiko* drumming, folksongs, and the repertories of the *koto*, *shamisen*, and *shakuhachi*. This music is combined with a wide spectrum of contemporary musical styles. Nobuko Miyamoto, with the assistance of Reverend Masao Kodani of the Senshin Buddhist Church in Los Angeles, composed two Japanese folksongs set to English-language lyrics, *Yuiyo Bon Odori* and *Tanpopo*, intended for use at O-Bon festivals of the dead. Among fusion bands, the well-known Los Angeles–based group Hiroshima was first to incorporate the *koto*, *shakuhachi*, *taiko*, and *shamisen* in popular music. The spectrum of Hiroshima's music fuses elements of rock, rhythm and blues, jazz, pop, and Latin with the pentatonic stylings of the *koto*.

Taiko drumming continues to be the most pervasive and popular Japanese American genre. It is an ensemble drumming style based on the *kumi daiko* style created by Daihachi Oguchi in 1951 in Japan. Combining music and choreographed movement, it reached the United States in 1968 through the music of the San Francisco Taiko Dojo led by Seiichi Tanaka. In 1969, *sansei* Reverend Kodani and George Abe formed Kinnara Taiko, the first *taiko* group to emerge from the Japanese American community. Both groups came into being as *sansei* began to seek cultural ties to their heritage, an awareness spawned by the growing Asian American movement.

A *taiko* ensemble consists of five to 30 or more performers, and includes drums of various sizes (most of which are made by the drummers themselves), *atarigane* (small bronze gong), *hōragai* (conch-shell trumpet), and *takebue* (Japanese bamboo transverse flute). Contexts for *taiko* drumming include sacred events, such as Buddhist festivals, including summer O-Bon celebrations throughout the United States, as well as secular celebrations—the Cherry Blossom Festivals of San Francisco, New York and Washington, DC, the Asian-Pacific American Heritage Festival in New York and elsewhere, and cultural festivals and various community events. Although *taiko* drumming continues to serve as an emblem of a Japanese American identity, ensembles now include non-Japanese American members who uphold its cultural meaning and enjoy its dynamism.

(iii) Korean American music. Before the Immigration and Nationality Act of 1965, Koreans in the United States constituted a small population mainly concentrated in Hawaii and California. Since then, the increase in Korean immigrants to the United States has given rise to thriving Korean American communities in urban areas, particularly in greater metropolitan Los Angeles and New York. In Korean American societies, music is the main emblem for high culture, an indispensable vehicle for social and religious functions and a favored medium for the expression of Korean identity. As such, Korean American music embraces diverse categories ranging from Korean traditional performing arts and the Western musical canon to Christian evangelical music and recent popular idioms.

The Christian church serves as perhaps the most important social institution within Korean American communities. According to studies from the 1980s and 90s, as many as 70–80% of Korean Americans and recent Korean immigrants were church members. Although membership in Korean churches has diminished drastically among second-generation Korean American adults, the majority of the population have grown up attending churches; as a result, old Protestant hymns, sacred classical music, and contemporary Christian music comprise musical knowledge common to the majority of Korean Americans. Indeed, music of various styles plays a vital role for both worship services and community building. Even in small churches, choirs attempt challenging repertory and strive to achieve professional-quality performances, and the musical director and worship accompanist are treated as highly valued leaders within most churches. Korean churches also serve as cultural institutions, often sponsoring concerts by church members or visiting artists.

Most visibly within the mainstream musical culture of the United States, Korean Americans perform and create music of the Western classical canon. Not only do many Korean and Korean American students occupy the violin sections and piano classes of the leading musical conservatories, but Korean Americans have founded and participate in their own organizations, such as the Los Angeles Korean Philharmonic Orchestra, and sponsor musical events at prestigious concert halls throughout the country. These events typically feature Korean and Korean American artists performing virtuosic and lyrical repertories of 19th-century Europe or new works by Korean composers.

Just as the preservation, performance, and dissemination of *gugak* (Korean traditional performing arts) figure prominently in the nationalist discourse of modern Republic of Korea, *gugak* is of prime importance to Korean immigrants and Korean Americans for the preservation and representation of ethnic identity within the United States. Koreans in the United States have founded several cultural centers devoted to *gugak* including the Halla Pai Huhm Studio in Hawaii, the Korean Classical Music and Dance Company in Los Angeles, and the Korean Traditional Music and Dance Institute and Korean Traditional Performing Arts Association in New York. Moreover, the Korean American communities enthusiastically support the programs of cultural institutions operated by the South Korean government within the United States (e.g., Korean Cultural Center in Los Angeles and Korean Cultural Service in New York). During the past decade, many universities and colleges throughout the United States have started to incorporate Korean music into their curricula, providing yet another avenue for Korean Americans (and non-Koreans) to explore and disseminate Korean culture.

The awakening of political consciousness among Korean Americans in the late 1980s and 90s has led younger generations to take up *pungmul*, the traditional farmers' dance music popularized by the group SamulNori. As a musical idiom prominently performed by student and labour groups in Korea during the anti-government protests of the 1980s and 90s, *pungmul* became a Korean symbol of populist struggle against oppression. Young Korean Americans in the United States drew upon *pungmul*'s newly created political associations and adopted this powerful and communal percussion music to give sound and visibility to their ethnic identity and to bring attention to the socio-political obstacles facing Korean Americans. The 1992 Los Angeles riots (*Sa-I-Gu*) and the general socio-political powerlessness felt by Korean American communities in the late 1980s and early 1990s caused many Korean Americans and Korean immigrants in the United States to reexamine their passive acceptance of the "American Dream" and to work actively toward political and cultural representation within American society. Throughout the 1990s, Korean American students at numerous colleges (e.g. University of California schools, Yale, Cornell, Stanford, and so on) took part in that political and cultural work by organizing Korean drumming ensembles on their campuses in conjunction with their campaigns for the establishment of Korean Studies courses. Korean American community centers in cities like New York, Los Angeles, Oakland, and Baltimore also started offering *pungmul* workshops. Although the association of *pungmul* with political activism has abated in recent years, the Korean American drumming groups formed during the activist era of the 1990s continue to exist as socio-cultural organizations enabling younger generations in the United States to connect with their Korean heritage.

Korean American musical expressions also extend to popular music genres, particularly hip hop. Rap artists such as Fists of Fury and Jamez Chang, who self-consciously reject the ideologically fraught "model minority" image and identify instead with their African American counterparts, embrace this "African American" musical form to perform their own racialized Korean American identities and to protest racism within the United States. Other musicians such as Sooyoung Park have pursued careers in indie rock. In 1995, Park put together a compilation album of Asian American performers, *Ear of the Dragon*, and its subsequent tour, seeking to show that Korean and Asian Americans can "rock and roll" and defy the stereotype of the meek Asian American.

Finally, the flow of musical culture between Koreans and Korean Americans in the United States and Korea point to the increasingly transnational character of Korean American communities. Internationally famous classical musicians like Sarah Chang have always traveled back and forth easily between the two nations, and American popular culture has flowed into Korea since the days of Japanese colonialism. What has changed in the past 20 years is that Korean Americans now listen to popular music from Korea and disseminate K-pop among their Korean and non-Korean peers, and Korean Americans such as Tiger JK travel back to Korea to participate in its bourgeoning media industry. Thus, even as Koreans in the United States create a uniquely Korean American identity through the performance and consumption of music and other cultural forms, these expressions of identity become increasingly linked to contemporary culture in the "old country" of Korea.

3. South Asian American music. The term South Asian American refers to Americans who trace their heritage to Bangladesh, India, Nepal, Pakistan, Sri Lanka, or to South Asian diasporic communities in the UK, the Caribbean, and elsewhere. Indian Americans form by far the largest subgroup, numbering over 2.8 million in 2010 (0.9% of the total US population), and are currently the fastest growing Asian American immigrant population, having increased almost 70% since 2000. The first significant wave of South Asian immigrants came from the Punjab in the early 20th century to work as migrant farm laborers in California. Since the 1965 Immigration and Naturalization Act, which abolished the restrictive national origins quota system, large numbers of South Asians have sought economic opportunities in the United States, especially educated professionals in the fields of medicine, engineering, and technology. Many South Asian Americans now live in large metropolitan areas including New York, Los Angeles, Chicago, Dallas-Fort Worth, and Washington DC. For both foreign-born immigrants and American-born second and third generation South Asians, music has been an integral part of social life. Communities have formed socio-cultural and religious organizations to support, promote, and transmit their South Asian heritage, including language, cuisine, and music and dance. Performances of South Asian music take place in ethnic festivals, concert halls, universities, and schools. From the 1990s, South Asian American youth in particular have created their own hybrid music and dance forms that serve to negotiate and transform their cultural identity distinct from that of their parents' generation.

Madurai T.N. Seshagopalan at Cleveland Thyagaraja Festival, 2010. (Gopi Sundaram, Aradhana Committee)

Musical performance is tied to the cultural, social, and religious organization of South Asian Americans. Tamil, Bengali, and Gujarati Associations, for example, celebrate sacred and cultural festivals with live and recorded songs sung in their respective languages. Weddings, anniversary celebrations, and music parties likewise provide contexts for social bonding and live music making. Among the early post-1965 immigrants, small groups of musicians would perform on such occasions, accompanying themselves on harmonium and tabla or other traditional instruments. In more recent years, DJs commonly host music and dance entertainment, playing recordings of Bollywood songs, bhangra, and other South Asian popular music as well as American music. For weddings and other special occasions, families may hire and transport popular bands from other American cities or even from South Asia.

The classical music and dance traditions of India are preserved and promoted in both South Asian American and broader American contexts. Indian classical music and dance associations in many major US cities present Hindustani and Karnatak music concerts by visiting and local artists. University music departments and South Asian student groups likewise organize classical concerts for the general public, and some universities, including the University of Texas at Austin and the University of Pennsylvania, offer classes in sitar and other Indian instruments. One of the oldest and most prestigious institutions for North Indian classical music is the Ali Akbar College of Music in San Rafael, California, which began in 1967 and offers instruction in performance and theory up to the highest level. Among South Asian American communities nationwide, music teachers in private studios and schools of Indian music and dance offer vocal and instrumental lessons, as well as performance opportunities in talent shows and community events. Students are for the most part children from South Asian families who are strongly encouraged by their parents to balance Indian music and dance classes with sports and other mainstream after-school activities.

For many South Asian Americans, the temple, church, and synagogue are central locations for religious and social activities that include musical performance. The first South Asian religious center established in the United States was a Sikh gurdwara in Stockton, California, in 1915. Since the 1970s, Hindu, Jain, and Sikh communities have built temples in many American cities where they hold regular worship services in both South Asian and English languages and organize gatherings for the communal singing of *bhajans* and *kirtans* (devotional songs). The annual Tyagaraja festival in Cleveland, Ohio, is the largest of its kind in America celebrating the death anniversary of the South Indian 18th–19th century Hindu saint-composer, and combines sacred and secular music. The ten-day festival, centered in the Siva Vishnu Temple of Greater Cleveland, includes participatory *bhajan* singing in praise of the Hindu deity Rama, professional concerts of Karnatak (South Indian classical) music by world-renowned artists, local music recitals, and competitive music events, all of which serve to celebrate, promote, and transmit Indian cultural traditions within and beyond the South Asian American population. Christian groups, in contrast, frequently share worship spaces with non–South Asian Americans, as do many Muslims and Buddhists. Some Christian congregations, however, are sufficiently large to support independent worship centers. The Church of South India Malayalam Congregation of Greater New York and St. Basil's Syriac Orthodox Church in Boston, for example, hold daily and weekly services in their sanctuaries with hymn singing in Malayalam and English. For South Asian American Muslims, while prayer sessions in mosques focus on spoken recitation, Sufi gatherings include the chanting of religious poetry and rhythmic invocations to Allah and the prophet Muhammad. Performances of qawwali (Sufi devotional songs) take place in both sacred and secular contexts. In 1992–3, the world-renowned Pakistani qawwal singer, Nusrat Fateh Ali Khan (*d* 1997) performed and taught at the University of Washington, Seattle. The genre of Sufi rock music, pioneered by the Pakistani band Junoon in 1990, combines lyrics based on the Sufi poetry of Rumi, Iqbal, Hafez, and other major Sufi poets, with classic rock guitars, South Asian tabla drums, and raga-inspired melodies. Labeled "the U2 of Pakistan" by the *New York Times*, Junoon first toured the United States in the late 1990s, and has since inspired both music bands and youths around the globe. The band's founder, songwriter, and lead guitarist Salman Ahmad has now moved to New York.

Among South Asian American young adults and college students, a new hybrid genre of music known as "urban desi" is popular in the party scene and club culture. The Sanskrit term *desi* refers to regional music and dance forms in India, and in modern usage the word refers to the peoples and cultures of South Asia, particularly those in the diaspora. Urban desi describes the fusion of popular South Asian music (including Bollywood songs, Hindi pop, Gujarati *raas garba*, and bhangra) with Western urban contemporary music (hip hop/rap, R&B, pop, techno, reggae, and Latin). The growing demand for South Asian remix songs and DJs spinning urban desi fusions led to the launch of MTV Desi in July 2005, an American network channel promoting music videos and shows from India and the United States. Urban desi music has furthermore attracted the attention of African American hip hop artists. In 2003 Jay-Z released a remix version of British Indian artist Panjabi MC's song "Mundian to bach ke" titled "Beware of the Boys," and Snoop Dogg appeared in the 2008 Bollywood film *Singh Is Kinng*, collaborating in the title song with Bollywood star Akshay Kumar. With such syncretic music, young American desis distance themselves from their South Asian-born parents and self-consciously express and assert their own ethnic and cultural identity, one that distinguishes this American-born generation within the global network of young diasporic South Asians.

(i) Mainland Southeast Asian American music. Beginning in 1975, many refugees from Laos, Cambodia, and Vietnam were given asylum in the United States, and by

the end of the century over one million immigrants from these countries had been admitted; over a third of them settled in California, and there are large population clusters in several other states. Representing virtually all segments of mainland Southeast Asian society, they continue their traditional musical practices. In addition, they are developing innovative as well as imitative cultural forms that reflect the new elements of their ethnic and social identity created by their radically changed environment.

(a) Laotian. Laotians in the United States include both Lao-speaking lowland villagers and urban dwellers, and members of non-Lao-speaking tribal groups from mountain villages. Of their several musical traditions the best-known is the court music, which is Khmer and Thai in origin but has been established in Laos for many centuries. The two major Lao classical music traditions are derived from the court, that of the orchestra and dance ensemble of the royal palace in Luang Prabang, and that of the more Thai-influenced and modernized Lao Natassin (National School of Fine Arts) in Vientiane; both are practiced in the United States. Using imported masks, costumes, and musical instruments, immigrants continue to perform the most important items of the repertory in concerts and community festivals such as the Lao New Year. These presentations include parts of the *Rāmāyaṇa* story as well as other tales and dances related to religious themes. Many are accompanied by the *pī phāt* orchestra of xylophones (*lanat*), gong-chimes (*khǫng wong*), flutes (*khoui*), drums, and cymbals.

Lao Buddhist ritual forms, which include chanting and sermons, are practiced at religious festivals, other rites and wakes by Lao monks now living in the United States. The musical content of these rituals ranges from near-monotone recitations of Pali texts to highly ornate cantillation of scriptures.

The lowland village traditions featuring the national instrument, the *khene*, a free-reed bamboo mouth organ, also continue in many American Lao communities. The solo repertory for this instrument includes both metred and unmetred polyphonic compositions; the instrument is also used to accompany the memorized or extemporized verses sung by one *mohlam* ("song expert") or several. Singers and instrumentalists alike may incorporate dance movements in these performances. Since Lao is a tonal language, the melodic contours of the songs are generated, in part, by speech tone. The texts of the songs are usually romantic but often contain philosophical, poetic, and humorous comments on current events. Social circle-dancing (*lam vong*) may also take place during *mohlam* performances or may be performed to modernized folksong renditions played by Lao rock bands.

Modern urban forms are particularly prominent among the Lao communities in the United States. Local Lao pop and rock bands, often deriving some of their material from the large repertory of South east and East Asian popular songs, commonly perform at major festivals and communitiy events. Stylistic elements of this music are derived from both Asian and Western popular music.

Laotian tribal groups in the United States include the Hmong (Miao, Meo), Tai Dam, Kmhmu, Mien (Yao), and others. The Hmong are the largest group in the United States and in Laos, and have continued the unique and rich musical traditions of their homeland. These include over 30 genres of sung poetry. Among their instruments, always played individually, are the *gaeng* (*qeej*), a free-reed mouth organ, the *ja* (*raj nplaim*), a transverse free-reed bamboo aerophone, and the *nja* (*ncas*), a jaw harp. The melodic contours follow speech tones and may function to some extent as "speech surrogate" systems. Ritual performances involving music still accompany life-cycle rites, although some forms are also heard at New Year festivals. The mouth organ is characteristic of funerals, at which the tones and rhythms of its music represent sacred texts, and the player's dance movements are ritually meaningful. Some of the traditional Hmong sung poetry has been incorporated into Catholic masses and pageants. As among other Southeast Asian communities, pop, rock, and hip-hop groups (with lyrics in the native language) are prominent participants at Hmong festivals, dances, and community events.

(b) Cambodian. Cambodian musical traditions have much in common with those of Laos and Thailand. In the United States the court orchestra (*pin peat*) is sometimes augmented by aerophones and chordophones from the folk orchestra (*mohori*). The combined ensemble may include xylophones (*roneat*), tuned gong-chimes (*khǫng wong*), flutes (*khloy*), oboes (*sralai*), two-string fiddles (*tror*), struck zithers (*khim*), plucked zithers (*krapeu*), drums (*skor*), wooden clappers (*krap*), and finger cymbals (*ching*). A chorus (*chamrieng*) sings poetic texts that narrate the classical dance dramas, such as the *Rāmāyaṇa* story, as well as other dances of religious significance. The wedding orchestra (*phleng kar*), considered to be the most characteristically Khmer ensemble, performs at Cambodian weddings and festival occasions. It may include a hammered dulcimer (*chin*), a two-string spike fiddle (*tror*), plucked lute (*takkei*, *krapeu*), drums, and voices.

Many Cambodian American communities also have youth groups devoted to folk traditions, whose dances depict the cultural forms of various Khmer village and tribal groups; they perform chiefly at Cambodian New Year. Like the other South east Asian groups, Cambodian American youths also enjoy their own versions of pop, rock, hip hop, and other contemporary genres.

Cambodian Buddhist forms, such as the chanting of Pali scriptures by Khmer monks, are maintained at Cambodian temples in the United States. Congregational singing of contemporary Khmer devotional poetry, following classical rhyme-tune formulae, can also be heard.

(c) Vietnamese. The most popular classical solo instrument for both study and listening among Vietnamese Americans is the 16-string board zither (*đàn tranh*), the

metal strings of which are particularly well suited to ornamentation and arpeggiation; other popular solo instruments include the four-string pear-shaped lute (*đàn tỳ bà*), moon-shaped lute (*đàn nguyệt*), and the plucked single-string box zither (*đàn bầu*), which is uniquely Vietnamese; its delicate tone is produced from harmonics and by manual variations in string tension. Many of these instruments are played in the United States at Tết (Vietnamese New Year); also presented are excerpts from classical theater (*hát bội*), folk theater (*hát chèo*), and "modernized" theater (*hát cải lu'o'ng*), folkdances, nightclub routines, and at least one performance of the aria *Vọng cổ*. This aria, sometimes called *Nostalgia for the Past*, is the most widely known piece of south Vietnamese music and can be sung to virtually any suitable text. It allows the singer extensive opportunities to express feelings, either in the song or in the unmetred prelude (*rao*); a few string instruments supply a freely heterophonic accompaniment, the improvised ornaments and melodic contours of which create new polyphonic strata and textures in each performance.

(ii) Filipino American music. The earliest Filipino American community consisted of 19th-century settlers in Louisiana. Migration during American colonization of the Philippines (1898–1935) brought a large number of agricultural laborers to Hawaii and California and cannery workers to the Pacific Northwest, while *pensionados* (students supported by the US government) attended college in various states. As with any immigrant group, Filipinos brought music from their homeland. Settlers assembled their own versions of instrumental ensembles popular in the Philippines—including Rondalla, wind bands, and popular music groups—playing and singing primarily within their own communities. During both World Wars, Filipinos joined the US Navy, and some participated in military bands. Others served as musicians on international cruise ships. After World War II, Filipino and Filipino American musicians found employment throughout the United States playing popular tunes in hotels and nightclubs. Filipino Americans continue to participate widely in popular music bands, jazz ensembles, and orchestras. The Los Angeles-based Filipino-American Symphony Orchestra, the first of its kind, made its debut in 2009.

Second and third-generation Filipino Americans utilize traditional Filipino music as a part of establishing their ethnic identity in a multicultural society. Community groups and student organizations that cultivate traditional music and dance have flourished throughout the United States; however, the ability to perform live music lags behind dance, due to a lack of qualified teachers and the inherent difficulty of teaching the many varied instruments required for folkloric productions. These instruments may include gongs from the northern highlands of the Philippines, jaw harps, stamping tubes, buzzers, bamboo flutes, and the instruments of *rondalla* and Kulintang. Learning to perform live music often is based on recordings and sometimes the teachings of performers from the Philippines—particularly those from the national folk dance company, Bayanihan, as well as the Ramon Obusan Folkloric Group—and may include singing in Filipino languages.

Beyond folkloric music used to accompany dance performances, the most prevalent musical practices related to those found in the Philippines are solo vocal (including art music and karaoke), choral singing, *kulintang*, and *rondalla*. Most ensembles are community-based, though *kulintang* and *rondalla* are taught either regularly or periodically as classes or in clubs at institutions such as the University of Hawaii at Manoa, the University of Washington, the University of California, Los Angeles, the University of California, Riverside, Cornell University, and the University of Michigan. Filipino American musicians also experiment with neo-traditional music that uses traditional instruments in popular music idioms. For instance, Eleanor Academia recorded *kulintang* with rock music instruments on her album *Oracle of the Black Swan* (1998).

Filipino Americans support popular musicians from the Philippines, some of whom have entered the American mainstream. Lea Salonga played Kim in *Miss Saigon* and Éponine in *Les Misérables* on Broadway. She also sang in the animated films *Aladdin* (1992), *Mulan* (1998), and *Mulan II* (2004). In 2007, the Filipino vocalist Arnel Pineda became the lead singer of the popular music group Journey. Additionally, Filipino teenager Charice Pempengco became a phenomenon after appearing on television in *Ellen*, *The Oprah Winfrey Show*, *Glee*, and at pre-inaugural events for President Barack Obama. Several Filipino Americans have also appeared as finalists on the popular televised singing contests, *American Idol* and *The Voice*.

Musical artists of all or partial Filipino descent have attracted audiences over the years, including Joe Bataan (best known for his Latin soul and Latin R&B songs of the 1970s), Kirk Hammett (lead guitarist of Metallica), Jocelyn Enriquez, Enrique Iglesias, Tia Carrere, Chad Hugo (of the Neptunes production duo), Vanessa Hudgens (from Disney's *High School Musical* series), Nicole Scherzinger (lead singer of the Pussycat Dolls), and Allen Pineda Lindo Jr. (apl.de.ap of the Black Eyed Peas). Notably, Filipino Americans have achieved great success in the genre of hip hop, particularly as DJs. Prominent artists include Mix Master Mike (Michael Schwartz), DJ Qbert (Richard Quitevis), DJ Babu (Chris Oroc), DJ Kuttin Kandi (Candice Custodio), and DJ Enferno (Eric Jao).

BIBLIOGRAPHY
(and other resources)

GENERAL

Asian Music in North America, ed. N. A. Jairazbhoy and S.C. De Vale, *Selected Reports in Ethnomusicology*, vi (1985)

W. Wei: *The Asian American Movement* (Philadelphia, 1993)

Y. Terada, ed.: *Transcending Boundaries: Asian Musics in North America* (Osaka, 2001)

O. Wang: "Between the notes: Finding Asian America in Popular Music," *American Music*, xix (2001), 439–65

D. Wong: *Speak it Louder: Asian Americans Making Music* (New York, 2004)

E.K. Lee: "Between the Personal and the Universal: Asian American Solo Performance from the 1970s to the 1990s," *Journal of Asian American Studies*, vi (2003), 289–312
E. Hisama: "'We're All Asian Really': Hip-hop's Afro-Asian Crossings," *Critical Minded: New Approaches to Hip Hop Studies* (Brooklyn, 2005), 1–21
M.T. Nguyen and T.L.N. Tu, eds.: *Alien Encounters: Popular Culture in Asian America* (Durham, NC, 2007)
M. Yoshihara: *Musicians from a Different Shore: Asians and Asian Americans in Classical Music* (Philadelphia, 2007)

CHINESE AMERICAN MUSIC
P. Chu and others, eds.: *Chinese Theaters in America* (Washington, DC, 1936)
R. Riddle: *Flying Dragons, Flowing Streams: Music in the Life of San Francisco's Chinese* (Westport, CT, 1983)
T.W. Chinn: *Bridging the Pacific: San Francisco Chinatown and its People* (San Francisco, 1989)
H.J. Wong: "Playing the Palace Theatre: A Chinese American's Recollections of Vaudeville," *Chinese America: History and Perspectives*, no.3 (1989), 111–16
Forbidden City, U.S.A., DVD, dir. A. Dong (Los Angeles, 1989)
L. Dong: "The Forbidden City Legacy and Its Chinese American Women," *Chinese America: History and Perspectives*, vi (1992), 124–48
W.H. Zhang: *The Musical Activities of the Chinese American Communities in the San Francisco Bay Area: A Social and Cultural Study* (diss., U. of California, Berkeley, 1994)
A. Bonner: *Alas! What Brought Thee Hither?: The Chinese in New York, 1800–1950* (Madison, NJ, 1997)
J.K.W. Tchen: *New York before Chinatown: Orientalism and the Shaping of American Culture, 1776–1882* (Baltimore, 1999)
Y. Chen: *Chinese San Francisco, 1850–1943* (Stanford, CA, 2000)
N. Rao: "Racial Essence and Historical Invisibility: Chinese Opera in New York, 1930." *COJ*, xii (2000), 135–62
A. Lee: *Picturing Chinatown: Art and Orientalism in San Francisco* (Berkeley, 2001)
N. Rao: "Songs of the Exclusion Era: New York's Cantonese Opera Theaters in the 1920s," *American Music*, xx (2002), 399–444
E. Lee: *At America's Gates: Chinese Immigration During the Exclusion Era, 1882–1943* (Chapel Hill, NC, 2003)
S. Metzger, "Charles Parsloe's Chinese Fetish: An Example of Yellowface Performance in Nineteenth-Century American Melodrama," *Theatre Journal*, lvi (2004), 627–51
K. Moon: *Yellowface: Creating the Chinese in American Popular Music and Performance, 1850s–1920s* (New Brunswick, NJ, 2005)
D. Lei: *Operatic China: Staging Chinese Identity across the Pacific* (New York, 2006)
F. Ho: *Wicked Theory, Naked Practice: Collected Political, Cultural and Creative Writings* (Minneapolis, 2007)
E. Hung: "Performing 'Chineseness' on the Western Concert Stage: The Case of Lang Lang," *AsM*, xl/1 (2009), 131–48
S. Zheng: *Claiming Diaspora: Music, Transnationalism, and Cultural Politics in Asian/Chinese America* (New York, 2010)
S. Kwan: "Performing a Geography of Asian America: The Chop Suey Circuit," *The Drama Review*, lv/1 (2011), 120–36
N. Rao: "The Public Face of Chinatown: Actresses, Actors, Playwrights, and Audiences of Chinatown Theaters in San Francisco of the 1920s," *Journal of Society for American Music*, v (2011), 235–70
K. Moon: "The Rise of Asians and Asian Americans in Vaudeville, 1880s–1930s," Asian Pacific American Collective History Project, <http://www.sscnet.ucla.edu/history/faculty/henryyu/APACHP/teacher/research/moon.htm>

JAPANESE AMERICAN MUSIC
K. Onishi: "'Bon' and 'Bon odori' in Hawaii," *Social Process in Hawaii*, iv (1938), 49
M. Kodani: *Hōraku* (Los Angeles, 1979)
S. Asai: "Hōraku: a Buddhist Tradition of Performing Arts and the Development of Taiko Drumming in the United States," *Asian Music in North America: Los Angeles 1984* [*Selected Reports in Ethnomusicology*, vi (1985)], 163–72
S. Asai: "Transformations of Tradition: Three Generations of Japanese American Music Making," *MQ*, vxxix (1995), 429–53
S. Asai: "Sansei Voices in the Community: Japanese American Musicians in California," *Musics of Multicultural America: a Study of Twelve Musical Communities*, ed. K. Lornell and A.K. Rasmussen (New York, 1997), 257–85
S. Asai: "Cultural Politics: The African American Connection in Asian American Jazz-based Music," *AsM*, xxxvi/1 (2005), 87–108
Rolling Thunder Taiko Resource, <http://www.taiko.com/taiko_resource/history.html>

KOREAN AMERICAN MUSIC
R. Riddle: "Korean Musical Culture in Los Angeles," *Asian Music in North America: Los Angeles 1984 [Selected Reports in Ethnomusicology, vi (1985)]*, 189–96
R.A. Sutton: "Korean Music in Hawaii," *AsM*, xix (1987), 99–120
M. Dilling: "Kumdori Born Again in Boston: the Life Cycle of Music by a Korean American," *Korean Culture*, xv (1994), 14–25
P. Myo-Young Choy: "Korean Music and Dance," *The Asian American Encyclopedia*, ed. F. Ng (New York, 1995), 914–20
O. Hwang: "Korean Music," *Garland Encyclopedia of World Music Volume 3: United States and Canada*, ed. E. Koskoff (New York, 2000), 975–79
H. Gweon (D. Kwon): "The Roots and Routes of Pungmul in the United States" (in Korean), *Eumak gwa munhwa/Music and Culture*, v (2001), 39–65
M.K. Seo: "Korean Americans and Their Music: Transcending Ethnic and Geographic Boundaries," *Transcending Boundaries: Asian Musics in North America* (Osaka, Japan, 2001), 79–112
J. Van Zile: *Perspectives on Korean Dance* (Middletown, Connecticut, 2001)
P. Yoon: *Christian Identity, Ethnic Identity: Music Making and Prayer Practices among 1.5- and Second-Generation Korean-American Christians* (diss., Columbia U., 2005)
Y. Yu: *Musical Performance of Korean Identities in North Korea, South Korea, Japan, and the United States* (diss, UCLA, 2007)
L.O. Bryant: "Performing race and place in Asian America: Korean American adoptees, musical theatre, and the land of 10,000 lakes," *AsM*, xl/i (2009), 4–30

SOUTH ASIAN AMERICAN MUSIC
G. Farrell: *Indian Music and the West* (Oxford, 1997)
P. Kurien: "Becoming American By Becoming Hindu: Indian Americans Take Their Place at the Multicultural Table," *Gatherings in Diaspora: Religious Communities and the New Immigration*, ed. R.S. Warner and J. Wittner (Philadelphia, 1998), 37–70
S. Maira: "Identity Dub: The Paradoxes of an Indian American Youth Subculture (New York Mix)," *Cultural Anthropology*, xiv/1 (1999), 29–60
A. Arnold: "Indian and Pakistani Music," *The Garland Encyclopedia of World Music, Vol.3: The United States and Canada*, ed. E. Koskoff (New York, 2001), 980–87
C. Martin: "*Snapshot:* "The Tyagaraja Festival in Cleveland, Ohio," *The Garland Encyclopedia of World Music*, iii, *The United States and Canada*, ed. E. Koskoff (New York, 2001), 988–992
A. Punathambekar: "Bollywood in the Indian-American Diaspora: Mediating a Transitive Logic of Cultural Citizenship," *International Journal of Cultural Studies*, viii/2 (2005), 151–73
G. Rajan and S. Sharma, ed.: *New Cosmopolitanisms: South Asians in the US* (Stanford, California, 2006)
S. Maira: *Desis in the House: Indian American Youth Culture in New York City* (Philadelphia, 2002)
P. Kvetko: "When the East is in the House: The Emergence of Dance Club Culture among Indian-American Youth," *The Subcontinental*, ii/2 (2004), <http://www.thesubcontinental.org/public/journal/issue2.2.jsp>
A. Dawson: "Desi Remix: The Plural Dance Cultures of New York's South Asian Diaspora" (2009), <http://ashleyjdawson.files.wordpress.com/2009/12/desi-remix.pdf>
A. Kavoori and C. Joseph: "Bollyculture: Ethnograph of Identity, Media and Performance," *Global Media and Communication*, vii/1 (2011), 17–32

SOUTHEAST ASIAN AMERICAN MUSIC
P. Duy: *Musics of Vietnam* (Carbondale, IL, 1975)
A. Catlin: *Music of the Hmong: Singing Voices and Talking Reeds* (Providence, RI, 1981)

B.T. Downing and D.P. Olney, eds.: *The Hmong in the West: Observations and Reports* (Minneapolis, MN, 1982)
T. Miller: "The Survival of Lao Traditional Music in America," *Selected Reports in Ethnomusicology*, vi (1985), 99–109
R. Trimillos: "Music and Ethnic Identity: Strategies Among Overseas Filipino Identity." *Yearbook for Traditional Music*, xviii (1986), 9–20
G. Giuriati: *Khmer Traditional Music in Washington, DC* (diss., U. of Maryland, 1988)
Sam Sam-Ang: *The Pin Peat Ensemble: its History, Music and Context* (diss., Wesleyan U., 1988)
U. Cadar: "The Maranao Kolintang Music and its Journey in America," *AsM*, xxvii/2 (1996), 131–48
Hmong Musicians in America, videotape, dir. A. Catlin APSARA Media for Intercultural Education (Van Nuys, CA, 1997)
J.P. Leary, ed. and trans.: "Joua Bee Xiong, Hmong musician," *Wisconsin Folklore* (Madison, 1998), 292–304
M. Talusan: *Reconstructing Identity: Appropriation and Representation of Kulintang Music in the United States* (thesis, U. of California, Los Angeles, 1999)
B. Gaerlan: "In the Court of the Sultan: Orientalism, Nationalism, and Modernity in Philippine and Filipino American Dance," *Journal of Asian American Studies*, ii (1999), 251–87
S. Parnes: *A History of Filipino* Rondalla *Music and Musicians in Southern California* (diss., U. of California, Los Angeles, 1999)
J.T. Pecore: *Sounding the spirit of Cambodia: The living tradition of Khmer music and dance-drama in a Washington, D.C. community* (diss., U. of Maryland, 2004)
P. Costes: *TUNOG PiL-AM: Creating and Reinventing the Sound of the Filipino Natives of America* (diss., U. of Washington, 2005)
T. Gonzalves, ed.: *Stage Presence: Conversations with Filipino American Performing Artists* (San Francisco, 2007)
A.S. Shiu: "Styl(us): Asian North America, Turntablism, Relation," *CR: The New Centennial Review*, vii/1 (2007), 81–106
R. Devitt: "Lost in Translation: Filipino Diaspora(s), Postcolonial Hip Hop, and the Problems of Keeping It Real for the 'Contentless' Black Eyed Peas," *AsM*, xxxix/1 (2008), 108–34
C.-A. Castro: "Subjectivity and Hybridity in the Age of Interactive Internet Media: The Musical Performances of Charice Pempengco and Arnel Pineda," *Humanities Diliman*, vii/1 (2010), 1–23

ERIC HUNG (1), NANCY YUNHWA RAO (2(i)), SUSAN MIYO ASAI (2(ii)), YOU YOUNG KANG (2(iii)), ALISON ARNOLD (3), AMY R. CATLIN/R (3(i)), CHRISTI-ANNE CASTRO (3(ii))

Asian American Orchestra. Ensemble founded by ANTHONY BROWN.

Asian Improv Records. Record label based in San Francisco, California. Founded by Jon Jang and Francis Wong in 1987, it was inspired by African American musicians, including Charles Mingus, Max Roach, Sun Ra, and members of Chicago's AACM, who turned to self-production as a way to maintain creative control of their work. With its name derived from the phrase "Asian American Improvised Music," the label initially functioned as an outlet for recordings by Jang and pianist Glenn Horiuchi, two early leaders in ASIAN AMERICAN JAZZ. In 1988, Jang and Wong created Asian Improv Arts, a nonprofit organization promoting performances by Asian American artists, many of whom record with the label.

Early Asian Improv releases reflect the concerns of the Asian American consciousness movement, such as combating anti-Asian violence and gaining redress and reparations for Japanese Americans incarcerated during World War II. In the 1990s, however, the label began broadening its roster to reflect a greater diversity of artistic and ethnic viewpoints, including a greater engagement with music and musicians from Asian countries. Although primarily devoted to creating space in the recording industry for Asian American voices, the record label has fostered collaboration across racial lines. For example, African American musicians Fred Anderson, Joseph Jarman, James Newton, Max Roach, and numerous others have released recordings with Asian Improv or appeared on recordings by its artists.

LOREN KAJIKAWA

Asleep at the Wheel. Western-swing band. The group was established in Paw Paw, West Virginia, in 1970 and became one of the leading participants in the western swing revival centered around Austin, Texas, during the 1970s. The group's personnel has frequently been in flux, but the best-known combination consisted of the bandleader, singer, guitarist, and songwriter Ray Benson (Seifert), the singer, songwriter, drummer, and guitarist Leroy Preston, the singer and guitarist Chris O'Connell, the steel guitarist Lucky Oceans (Ruben Gosfield), and the pianist Floyd Domino (James Haber).

In 1971 the group moved from West Virginia to Berkeley, California, at the recommendation of the rockabilly musician Commander Cody and the entertainer Wavy Gravy. For the following two years the group toured as the backup band for the country singers Stoney Edwards, Freddie Hart, and Connie Smith. In early 1973 they moved to Austin, where they met the former members of the Texas Playboys Jesse Ashlock and Al Stricklin and became one of the leading acts in the city's progressive country-music scene. In 1975 Benson's composition "The Letter that Johnny Walker Read" reached number ten on the *Billboard* Hot Country Singles chart, the group's only major hit recording.

As members of the original lineup began to depart around 1978, Benson took on the responsibilities of bandleader, maintaining the group without a break for more than three decades. Under his direction Asleep at the Wheel has served as a training ground for young musicians and earned nine Grammy awards. The band has consisted of as many as 13 musicians simultaneously, and more than 60, most of them fiddlers and wind players, have been associated with it in total. An avid record collector and music historian Benson has also supported the older generation of western-swing musicians and organized concerts and television specials for the Texas Playboys following the incapacitation and subsequent death of its leader, Bob Wills, in 1975. His advocacy for western swing has also extended into the realm of musical theater in the critically acclaimed *A Ride with Bob*, which he wrote with the screenwriter Anne Wrap in 2005.

RECORDINGS
(selective list)

Comin' Right at Ya (UA, 1973); *Texas Gold* (Cap., 1975); *Ride with Bob* (Dream Works, 1999); with W. Nelson: *Willie and the Wheel* (Bismeaux, 2009)

BIBLIOGRAPHY

J. Morthland: "Asleep at the Wheel," *Country Music*, v/10 (1977), 28
T. Stimeling: *Cosmic Cowboys and New Hicks: the Countercultural Sounds of Austin's Progressive Country Music Scene* (New York, 2011)

JOHN MORTHLAND/TRAVIS D. STIMELING

Aspen Music Festival and School. An annual summer music festival, comprising hundreds of concerts and training courses, held in Aspen, Colorado. It grew out of the Goethe Bicentennial Convocation and Music Festival of 1949; concerts have been presented by faculty members, students of the music school, and guest artists since 1950. The festival includes performances by student orchestras and guest artists as well as concerts of chamber, choral, and contemporary music. The music school program includes the Aspen Opera Theater Center, the Edgar Stanton Audio Recording Institute, individual lessons, and master classes; the Center for Advanced Quartet Studies, founded by Claus Adam, provides opportunities for students to work with renowned ensembles. The Conference on Contemporary Music, founded by Darius Milhaud in 1951, enabled students to attend lectures and seminars given by one or more composers-in-residence; today's budding composers study at the Susan and Ford Schumann Center for Composition Studies. Each summer, the school enrolls approximately 750 students, and the festival is attended by more than 100,000 people.

RITA H. MEAD/R

Assad, Clarice (*b* Rio de Janeiro, Brazil, 9 Feb 1978). Brazilian composer, arranger, pianist, and vocalist. Clarice Assad is a member of one of Brazil's most acclaimed musical families. Daughter of guitarist and composer Sergio Assad, and niece of Odair and Badi Assad, she began performing with her family when she was seven years old. Assad skillfully traverses the worlds of jazz and classical music in her performances and compositions. As a composer and arranger, she has written commissioned works and arrangements for violin, symphony orchestra, string quartets, and guitar quartets. She has also written original compositions for the ballet *Step to Grace* by Lou Fancher and the play *The Anatomy Lesson* by Carlus Mathus. Some of her notable compositions include *Pole to Pole*, *O Curupira*, *Bluezilian*, and *Ratchenitsa*. As a pianist, she performs her own compositions and also arranges popular Brazilian songs and jazz standards. As a vocalist, Assad sings in Portuguese, French, Italian, and English, and is known for her precise intonation, even when performing improvised scatting.

Assad studied piano in Brazil with Sheily Zagury, Natalie Fortin, and Leandro Braga, and in the United States with Ed Bedner and Bruce Berr. She has studied composition with Ilya Levinson, Stacy Garrop, David Rakowski, Michael Daugherty, and Claude Baker. She has been awarded the Aaron Copland Award, the Franklin Honor Society Award, and ASCAP's Morton Gould Young Composer Award.

DAN SHARP

Assad, Sérgio (Simão) (*b* Mococa, São Paulo, Brazil, 26 Dec 1952). Brazilian guitarist, arranger, and composer. He is internationally known as part of the Assad Duo with his brother, Odair. He received his first music lessons from his father, an amateur guitar and mandolin player; in 1969 he went on to study with guitarist Monina Távora for seven years. Later he graduated from the Escola National de Música in Rio de Janeiro with a degree in composition and conducting. The Assad Duo was a prizewinner in the 1979 Bratislava International Rostrum of Young Interpreters, a competition that launched their international career. Since then they have collaborated on several projects with Yo-Yo Ma, Gidon Kremer, and Nadja Salerno-Sonnenberg, among others. Demonstrating impeccable technique, precise articulation of musical ideas, and cohesive ensemble, their recordings have received numerous awards, including the 2002 Latin Grammy for best tango album. As a composer, Sérgio synthesizes elements of Brazilian popular music with contemporary techniques and jazz idioms. His catalog of works includes compositions written mostly for guitar, solo or with larger ensembles, and numerous arrangements of works from various periods and styles, many of which are now part of the standard guitar repertoire. He has conducted master classes around the world and has taught at the San Francisco Conservatory since 2009.

BIBLIOGRAPHY

J.E. Szydlowski: Review of works by Assad, *Notes*, xl/3 (2004), 804–8

J.P. Figueiroa da Cruz: *An Annotated Bibliography of Works by the Brazilian Composer Sérgio Assad* (diss., Florida State U., 2008)

SILVIO J. DOS SANTOS

Associated Music Publishers [AMP]. Firm of music publishers. It was founded in 1927 by Paul Heinicke, originally as the sole American agency for leading European music publishing houses, including Bote & Bock, Breitkopf & Härtel, Doblinger, Eschig, Schott, Simrock, Union Musical Español, and Universal Edition. The firm began publishing in its own right and built up an important catalog of American composers, including John Adams, Elliott Carter, Cowell, Dello Joio, John Harbison, Harris, Husa, Ives, Kirchner, Peter Lieberson, Piston, Riegger, Schuller, Surinach, Tower, and Wilder. In 1964 it was acquired by Schirmer.

ALAN PAGE/R

Association for Recorded Sound Collections [ARSC]. US-based organization, founded in 1966 to promote the preservation and study of historical recordings in all areas of music and the spoken word. ARSC is unusual among scholarly organizations in that it brings together private collectors and scholars interested in using historical sound materials with professional archivists and libraries charged with preserving those materials. Its membership is drawn about equally from the user and holder groups, represents 23 countries, and numbers approximately 1000. The association has local chapters and holds an annual national conference that provides a forum for presentations and panel discussions in all aspects of recorded sound research. ARSC also publishes a biannual journal which includes major research articles, technical developments, discographies, record and book reviews, and bibliographies; a newsletter which contains information about member activities, meetings and events; and a membership directory, which lists all ARSC members, their collecting interests and research projects. Among its major projects have been *Rules for Archival Cataloging of Sound Recordings* (Albuquerque, 1980, 2/1995), *Audio Preservation: a Planning Study* (Silver Spring, MD, 1988), the *Rigler and Deutsch Record Index* (Syracuse, NY and Rochester, NY, 1983–6), which inventoried the 78 rpm holdings of five major sound archives, and founding the Historical Recording Coalition for Access and Preservation (2008), which advocates for reform in US copyright laws to allow preservation of and access to historical sound materials. ARSC annually awards grants for researchers in the field of recorded sound as well as awards for excellence in historical sound research.

See also ARCHIVES, SOUND RECORDING AND MOVING IMAGE.

BIBLIOGRAPHY

T. Brooks: "Association for Recorded Sound Collections: an Unusual Organization," *Goldmine*, no.81 (1983), 22–3

E. McKee: "ARSC/AAA: Fifteen Years of Cooperative Research," *ARSC Journal*, no.1 (1988–9), 3–13 <http://www.arsc-audio.org>

Historical Recording Coalition for Access and Preservation: <http://www.recordingcopyright.org>

SARA VELEZ/TIM BROOKS

Association for the Advancement of Creative Musicians [AACM]. A nonprofit organization devoted to African American avant-garde music. It was founded in Chicago's South Side on 8 May 1965 by members of Muhal Richard Abrams' free-jazz ensemble the Experimental Band. As well as Abrams, who was its first president, the AACM's original members were Fred Anderson, Roscoe Mitchell, Amina Claudine Myers, Malachi Favors, Thurman Barker, Joseph Jarman, and Maurice McIntyre. Its main objectives have been to organize concerts for the public and workshops for its members, and since the foundation of the AACM School of Music in 1969 to conduct free training programs for young musicians. In addition it has aimed "to set an example of high moral standards for musicians." Its primary intention was to provide an alternative to the established art institutions in order to promote the music of young, independent, experimental African American musicians. With the postulate to move towards a multicultural and multiethnic outlook, each member created "original music"—notated, improvised, or both—by striving beyond the set boundaries of jazz to explore a stylistic hybridity. Its musicians broke new ground by making use of extended techniques, interactivity, experimental forms and notation, invented acoustic instruments, installations, and kinetic sculptures.

Between 1966 and 1969 the AACM's founder members performed at the Abraham Lincoln Center and the University of Chicago. During that period they were joined by Lester Bowie (who became its second president), Leo Smith, John Stubblefield, Henry Threadgill, Anthony Braxton, Mchaka Uba, and Leroy Jenkins. In order to enlarge the organization's audience, from 1969 until the early 1970s Jenkins, Smith, Braxton, and the members of the Art Ensemble of Chicago were based in Paris, where they were well received by audiences and critics. In the early 1970s another wave of musicians joined the AACM, among them Chico Freeman, Douglas Ewart, Malachi Thompson, George Lewis, and Adegoke Steve Colson. Several members moved to New York where they took part in the city's downtown scene. The AACM organized a festival in 1977 and established a New York chapter in 1982, out of which emerged the M-BASE collective. In Chicago the main branch gave concerts to celebrate the organization's 25th, 30th, 35th, and 40th anniversaries.

BIBLIOGRAPHY

Jb, nos.356–7 (1978–9) [AACM issue]

R.M. Radano: "Jazzin' the Classics: the AACM's Challenge to Mainstream Aesthetics," *Black Music Research Journal*, xii/1 (1992), 79–95

N.T. De Jong: *Chosen Identities and Musical Symbols: the Curaçaoan Jazz Community and the Association for the Advancement of Creative Musicians* (diss., U. of Michigan, 1997)

A. Cromwell: *Jazz Mecca: an Ethnographic Study of Chicago's South Side Jazz Community* (diss., Ohio U., 1998)

G. Lewis: "Singing Omar's Song: a (Re)construction of Great Black Music," *Lenox Avenue: a Journal of Interarts Inquiry*, no.4 (1998), 69–92

L. Smith: "Creative Music and the AACM," *Keeping Time: Readings in Jazz History*, ed. R. Walser (New York, 1999), 315–24

G. Lewis: "Experimental Music in Black and White: the AACM in New York, 1970–1985," *Current Musicology*, no.71–3 (2001), 100–57

T.A. Newsome: *"It's after the end of the world! Don't you know that yet?" Black Creative Musicians in Chicago (1946–1976)* (diss., U. of North Carolina, 2001)

D.P. Brown: *Noise Orders: Jazz, Improvisation, and Architecture* (Minneapolis, 2006)

N.T. De Jong: "Women of the Association for the Advancement of Creative Musicians: Four Narratives," *Black Women and Music: More than the Blues* (Urbana, IL, 2007), 134–52

G. Lewis: *A Power Stronger than Itself: the Association for the Advancement of Creative Musicians* (Chicago, 2008)

MICHAEL BAUMGARTNER

Association of Concert Bands (ACB). Professional organization designed to serve the particular interests of adult band musicians, rather than those of school or college groups. Founded in 1977, its purpose is to encourage and foster adult concert community, municipal, and civic bands and to promote the performance of the highest quality traditional and contemporary literature for band. It holds annual conventions where directors, band members, managers, industry leaders, administrators, and board members assemble to exchange personal views, share experiences, and benefit from educational seminars and musical performances. The *Journal of the Association of Concert Bands*, published three times per year, carries informative articles, programs, reviews, as well as general membership information.

RAOUL F. CAMUS

Astaire [Austerlitz], **Fred(erick)** (*b* Omaha, NE, 10 May 1899; *d* Beverly Hills, CA, 22 June 1987). Dancer, singer, choreographer, and actor. He began performing at the age of seven with his sister Adele. As a duo they worked in vaudeville from 1906 to 1916 and moved to Broadway in 1917. Starring roles in *The Bunch and Judy* (1922) and *For Goodness Sake* (1923) led to *Lady, be good!* (1924), which marked their arrival as top Broadway stars. During the 1920s several of the Astaires' successful shows appeared in the West End in London, where the pair enjoyed a cult-like following. After *The*

Band Wagon (1931) Adele retired from the stage to marry an English aristocrat. Astaire appeared in *Gay Divorce* in New York (1932) and London (1933), before signing a contract with RKO, the smallest major film studio in Hollywood.

Astaire's first RKO picture, *Flying Down to Rio* (1933), initiated his partnership with GINGER ROGERS. The pair made nine films between 1933 and 1939, most including three or four partner routines and a solo feature for Astaire. *Top Hat* (1935), *Swing Time* (1936), and *Shall We Dance* (1937) typify the Astaire-Rogers cycle of dance-oriented musicals. After his partnership with Rogers ended Astaire embarked on an unusual freelance career in Hollywood which lasted to the end of the studio era. He worked at all the musical-making studios apart from Warner Bros. and danced with almost all the major musical stars of the time, including Eleanor Powell, Vera-Ellen, Judy Garland, and Cyd Charisse at MGM, Rita Hayworth at Columbia, Betty Hutton at Paramount, and Leslie Caron at 20th Century Fox. He made two of his most commercially successful films, *Holiday Inn* (1942) and *Blue Skies* (1946), with Bing Crosby at Paramount.

After the musical production units in Hollywood closed in the late 1950s, Astaire made a seamless transition to television variety shows. He produced and starred in four television specials (1958, 1959, 1960, and 1968) and guest hosted "The Hollywood Palace" numerous times (1965–6). With Barrie Chase, who was 34 years his junior, Astaire explored the rhythms and social-dance styles of the rock-and-roll era. He regularly invited African American jazz musicians onto his specials at a time when interracial performance was uncommon on television, dancing solos accompanied by the trumpeter Jonah Jones, the organist Jimmy Smith, and Count Basie and his Orchestra.

Astaire's career benefited from his relationships with almost all the major songwriters of his time. George and Ira Gershwin and Cole Porter wrote for him on Broadway and in Hollywood. Irving Berlin and Johnny Mercer were his most important Hollywood collaborators, and Jerome Kern also contributed important songs. Many of the songs Astaire introduced on film endured as popular and jazz standards. In 1952 he recorded an album of his signature songs with the Jazz at the Philharmonic All Stars led by the pianist Oscar Peterson for Norman Granz's label Clef.

Astaire crafted his own dance routines working with various assistants, including Hermes Pan, his most frequent dance director. Rehearsal pianists, among them Hal Borne, were also essential creative partners. On most of his film dances, Astaire exercised creative control over the choice of song, its structure and orchestration, as well as the costuming—usually his own clothes—camera angles, dubbing of foot sounds, and editing. In a few instances he earned a composer credit for the music as well.

Astaire played piano in four of his film routines, and when seen playing on screen he is always also heard on the soundtrack. He also played drums on screen and at home, a hobby he often highlighted in interviews. He described himself as a frustrated songwriter, and his tune "I'm building up to an awful letdown" (lyrics by Mercer) was a hit in 1936.

SELECTED RECORDINGS

The Astaire Story (1952, Clef)

BIBLIOGRAPHY

F. Astaire: *Steps in Time* (New York, 1959/*R*)
A. Croce: *The Fred Astaire and Ginger Rogers Book* (New York, 1972/*R*)
J. Mueller: *Astaire Dancing: the Musical Films* (New York, 1985, 2/2010)
L. Billman: *Fred Astaire: a Bio-Bibliography* (Westport, CT, 1997)
P. Levinson: *Puttin' on the Ritz: Fred Astaire and the Fine Art of Panache* (New York, 2009)
T. Decker: *Music Makes Me: Fred Astaire and Jazz* (Berkeley, 2011)
K. Riley: *The Astaires: Fred and Adele* (New York, 2012)
J. Franceschina: *Hermes Pan: the Man Who Danced with Fred Astaire* (New York: 2012)

TODD DECKER

Astin-Weight Piano. Firm of piano makers. It was founded by Edwin R. Astin (*b* Burnley, England, 1918), Raymond Astin (*b* Accrington, England, 1941), and Donald Weight (*b* Salt Lake City, UT, 1930) in Salt Lake City in 1956. It began production in 1959 and was incorporated in 1971. The company is known for differences in design from other makers. In its upright pianos the most obvious innovation is the absence of wooden posts at the back of the case, which the company claims prevents destabilizing reactions to humidity changes. A more massive cast-iron frame controls stability. The soundboard is heavier than standard, and the pinblock is not set at one end but is mounted in front of the soundboard, allowing more vibrating surface.

The company makes a grand piano of about 5 ft. 9 in. long, with a symmetrical case and with the lid hinged on the treble side. Inside, the bridges are repositioned, which allows longer bass strings than the standard. The symmetrical case permits a soundboard about 45% larger than usual in that size of grand.

The company suffered extensive storm damage to its factory in 2004, and its production has been seriously limited into the 2010s. One of very few piano companies still active in the United States, Astin-Weight's location makes noticeable the dispersal of manufacturing from such centers as New York.

EDWIN M. GOOD

Aston Magna Foundation for Music and the Humanities. Musical organization. It was founded in 1972 under the name of the Aston Magna Foundation for Music by the harpsichordist Albert Fuller (1926–2007) and Lee Elman. In September of that year the foundation initiated the Aston Magna Festival, the first professional summer festival of music on period instruments in the United States. The foundation's early educational activities took place on Elman's estate "Aston Magna" in Great Barrington, Massachusetts. In 1973 the summer festival under artistic director Albert Fuller found a permanent home at St James's Church in Great Barrington, after initial misgivings by the local townspeople.

Aston Magna quickly became a leading force of the early music movement in the United States, presenting concerts on instruments played with techniques known to the composers and offering educational programs on music and its relation to the other arts and society. In 1977 Aston Magna gave the first US public performances in modern times of the complete Bach Brandenburg Concertos on period instruments, and in 1978 presented the first American performances of Mozart symphonies on original instruments. The same year, with funding from the NEH, Aston Magna launched its cross-disciplinary academy program under the direction of harpsichordist and musicologist Raymond Erickson. The three-week academy was originally held at Simon's Rock of Bard College in Great Barrington. Subsequent academies were held at Rutgers University in New Brunswick, New Jersey and at Yale University. The academy brought together scholars in the humanities and musicians to explore particular moments in Western culture, from the end of the Renaissance to the early Romantic period.

A dispute with the foundation board led to Fuller's resignation as artistic director in 1983. He was succeeded by the viola da gamba player John Hsu, who served as artistic director from 1984 to 1990. The violinist Daniel Stepner was appointed artistic director in 1990.

In 1989 to reflect the high level of its cross-disciplinary educational activities, the foundation changed its name to the Aston Magna Foundation for Music and the Humanities. From 1986–92, with significant funding from the NEH, the foundation undertook a series of Outreach Academies, shorter programs geared to general audiences, at colleges, libraries, and museums throughout the United States. The entire academy program concluded in 1997, and the foundation subsequently initiated a publication series that same year beginning with *Schubert's Vienna* (New Haven, CT, 1997), a volume of essays by academy faculty edited by Raymond Erickson and published by Yale University Press. A second publication, *The Worlds of Johann Sebastian Bach* (New York, 2009), also edited by Erickson, was published by Amadeus Press.

In 2005, the festival moved its Great Barrington concerts to the Daniel Arts Center on the campus of Bard College at Simon's Rock. Additional summer concerts are held annually at Bard College in Annandale-on-Hudson, New York. In 2010, the festival also added a series of concerts on the campus of Brandeis University in Waltham, Massachusetts.

Music from Aston Magna touring concerts have taken the group across the United States. European tours have included concerts in the Czech Republic, German, and Italy.

The foundation's executive offices are in Danbury, Connecticut. Its website is <http://www.astonmagna.org>.

SALLY SANFORD

Astor, John [Johann] **Jacob** (*b* Waldorf [now Walldorf], nr Heidelberg, Germany, 1763; *d* New York, NY, 29/30 March 1848). Instrument maker and importer. He went to London to join his brother George [Georg] Astor (*b* Waldorf, *c*1760), who had gone to England about 1778; together they started business as flute makers, their firm operating as George & John Astor from 1782 to 1797 or 1798. In 1783 John Jacob came to the United States with a small consignment of flutes, visiting another brother who had settled in Baltimore. The value of his stock of flutes is said to have been only about £5, but on advice given him by a fellow voyager he invested the proceeds of his sales in furs and by selling these in England made a handsome profit. He returned to the United States and quickly profited by fur trading and by the sale of musical instruments sent to him from England. By 1786 he had opened a music shop in his mother-in-law's house at 81 Queen Street, New York. His merchandise, most of which was imported from London, included pianos, spinets, guitars, violins, flutes, clarinets, oboes, fifes, music books, paper, and strings. He relinquished the business to Michael and John Paff in 1802, but continued to import instruments as late as 1807. In 1809 Astor established a fur-trading company, and by this and the purchase of land in the Bowery laid the foundations of the Astor wealth. Some of the instruments that Astor had brought to the United States when visiting Baltimore in 1783 were purchased by Samuel W. Hildebrandt of 19 North Liberty Street, Baltimore, a maker of brass instruments; they remained in the firm's possession well into the 20th century.

BIBLIOGRAPHY

DAB (W.J. Ghent)

J. Parton: *Life of John Jacob Astor, to which is Appended a Copy of his Last Will* (New York, 1865)

"Astor: Musical Instrument Maker," *Musical Courier*, xxxix/6 (1899), 15

A.D.H. Smith: *John Jacob Astor: Landlord of New York* (Philadelphia, 1929)

K.W. Porters: *John Jacob Astor, Business Man* (Cambridge, MA, 1931)

A. Baines: *The Bate Collection of Historical Wind Instruments* (Oxford, 1976)

FRANK KIDSON/H.G. FARMER/R

Asylum. Record company. David Geffen and partner Elliot Roberts founded Asylum in 1971, signing Jackson Browne as their first artist. With Atlantic handling distribution, Asylum focused on building a roster of singer-songwriters and country-rock artists, which eventually included artists such as Linda Ronstadt, Joni Mitchell, the Eagles, Tom Waits, Warren Zevon, and Bob Dylan. In 1972, Atlantic's parent company, Warner Communications, acquired Asylum and merged it with Elektra, forming Elektra/Asylum. The pair split in the late 1980s, with Asylum regrouping as a country label for much of the 1990s; a division of Asylum joined in 2003 with Curb Records, a prominent country label. In 2004, Asylum Records was relaunched as a label specializing primarily in hip hop and R&B. David Geffen, who stayed with Asylum until 1975, founded Geffen records in 1980 and steadily established himself as one of the leading figures in the entertainment industry.

CHARLES HIROSHI GARRETT

Ataneli, Lado (*b* Tilfis, Georgia). Baritone of Georgian birth. He is considered one of the world's leading interpreters of Puccini and Verdi's music. He made his debut in 1989 as Renato in Verdi's *Un Ballo in maschera* at the Tilfis National Theater. In the following three years, Ataneli received several major awards, including first prize and the Grand Prix at the International Francisco-Vinas Competition in Barcelona (1991), and first prize at the "I Cestelli" Competition. He has appeared across the world, including with the Vienna State Opera, the Deutsche Oper Berlin, the Hamburg State Opera, and the Bavarian State Opera. His relationship with the Metropolitan Opera blossomed in the 21st century, as Tonio in *I Pagliacci* in 2006, *Macbeth* (under the direction of James Levine) in 2007–8, and *Rigoletto* in 2010. He also has been active as a performer in concert and on television and radio. His tremendously powerful voice has engaged audiences worldwide, and his skill is featured on numerous recordings and DVD releases.

JONAS WESTOVER

Athapaskan. Native-American language family; *see* Apache and Navajo.

Atherton, James (Peyton, Jr.) (*b* Montgomery, AL, 27 April 1943; *d* St. Louis, MO, 20 Nov 1987). Tenor and director. He studied at the Peabody Conservatory, chiefly with Martial Singher but also with Rosa Ponselle, and made his debut with the San Francisco Opera in 1971 as Goro. With the Santa Fe Opera from 1973 he sang Sir Philip Wingrave in the American stage premiere of Britten's *Owen Wingrave*, as well as Janáček's Schoolmaster, Fenton, Jo (*The Mother of Us All*), Monsieur Triquet, Antonio (Oliver's *Duchess of Malfi*), Leukippos (*Daphne*), and Pluto (*Orphée aux enfers*). He sang with the Canadian Opera Company in 1976 as Fritz in Offenbach's *La Grande-duchesse de Gérolstein* and with the Metropolitan in 1977 as the Holy Fool in *Boris Godunov*, returning in more than a dozen other roles; he made his English debut at Glyndebourne in 1979 in Haydn's *La fedeltà premiata*. He appeared at Dallas, Miami, Toronto, Houston, Philadelphia, and other cities. From 1977 he also worked as a director of opera. His flexible vocal technique and dramatic abilities made him highly respected as a character performer, and he was equally successful in lyrical roles.

JAMES WIERZBICKI, ELIZABETH FORBES/R

Atkins, Chet [Chester Burton] (*b* nr Luttrell, TN, 20 June 1924, *d* Nashville, TN, 30 June 2001). Country-music guitarist and recording company executive. Although the first instrument he played professionally was the fiddle, he became internationally famous as a guitarist. Developed while he was in high school, his guitar style was influenced by Merle Travis, Les Paul, Django Reinhardt, and George Barnes and was characterized by the use of the thumb to establish a rhythm on the lower strings and multiple fingers to play melodic or improvisational passages on the higher strings, sometimes with complex voicings. In the early 1940s Atkins toured with Archie Campbell and Bill Carlisle playing both fiddle and guitar, and appeared with them on WNOX radio in Knoxville. He then toured with the second generation Carter Family as a sideman and in 1946 joined Red Foley. After beginning his association with the "Grand Ole Opry" he settled in Nashville in 1950. In the early 1950s he began playing electric guitar, an instrument he was chiefly responsible for popularizing as a solo instrument in country music. He also participated in numerous recording sessions in Nashville and made his first recording under his own name, *Chet Atkins' Gallopin' Guitar* (RCA Victor, 1953).

Atkins became an assistant to Steve Sholes in RCA Victor's artists and repertory department in 1952 and was later manager of its studio in Nashville. In 1960 he became the label's artists and repertory manager and in 1968 its vice-president. He produced successful recordings by such singers as Jim Reeves, Hank Snow, and Waylon Jennings and played an important role in the resurgence of country music in the 1950s and 1960s and the creation of the pop-influenced Nashville sound. His own recordings generally emphasized instrumental interpretations of pop and jazz standards. In the 1960s he toured with the saxophonist Boots Randolph and the pianist Floyd Cramer and became interested in classical guitar playing. After he retired from RCA in 1982, he signed a recording contract with CBS, where he focused on jazz as often as country. In the 1970s he recorded with guitarists Jerry Reed and Les Paul, in the 1980s with Mark Knopfler, and in the 1990s with Tommy Emmanuel. He was elected to the Country Music Hall of Fame in 1973, received a Grammy Lifetime Achievement Award in 1993, and was elected to the Rock and Roll Hall of Fame, posthumously, in 2002.

BIBLIOGRAPHY

C. Atkins and B. Neely: *Country Gentleman* (Chicago, 1974)

W. Ivey: "Chet Atkins," *Stars of Country Music*, ed. B.C. Malone and J. McCulloh (Urbana, IL, 1975), 274

C. Atkins and R. Cochran: *Chet Atkins: Me and my Guitars* (Milwaukee, 2003)

BILL C. MALONE/BARRY MAZOR

Atkinson, (Justin) Brooks (*b* Melrose, MA, 28 Nov 1894; *d* Huntsville, AL, 13 Jan 1984). Theater critic and author. Upon graduating from Harvard University in 1917, Atkinson taught English at Dartmouth College and worked at the *Springfield Daily News* and the *Boston Evening Transcript* before joining the *New York Times* as its *Book Review* editor in 1922. He held the post of drama critic at the *Times* from 1925 to 1960, with the exception of a wartime stint as a foreign correspondent. After retiring as drama critic, Atkinson wrote a Critic at Large column for the *New York Times* until 1965.

Arguably the most influential theater critic of his time, Atkinson was respected for his integrity as well as incisive, literate reviews. He reviewed such well-known and now canonical plays and musicals as *Our Town*, *South Pacific*, *The Crucible*, and *West Side Story*, but he was also known for his instrumental attention to Off Broadway during its emergence as a separate institution. Although Atkinson purposefully kept some distance from theater society during his tenure as critic, the theater world showed its appreciation upon his retirement. He received both Obie and Tony Award special citations as well as an honorary lifetime membership to Actors' Equity. Atkinson was also a Pulitzer Prize winner, having earned the correspondence award in 1947 for his series of articles on Moscow, and the recipient of numerous honorary degrees. In 1960, the Mansfield Theatre was renamed the Brooks Atkinson Theatre in his honor.

In addition to his writings on theater, Atkinson's published works span a range of topics, including personal essays, travel and nature, and the writings of Henry David Thoreau and Ralph Waldo Emerson. His papers are held by the Billy Rose Theatre Division of the New York Public Library for the Performing Arts.

WRITINGS
(selective)

Broadway Scrapbook (New York, 1947)
Tuesdays and Fridays (New York, 1963)
Brief Chronicles (New York, 1966)
Broadway (New York, 1970)
with A. Hirschfeld: *The Lively Years, 1920–1973* (New York, 1973)

BIBLIOGRAPHY

J.C. McNeely: *The Criticism and Reviewing of Brooks Atkinson* (diss., U. of Wisconsin, 1956)

ELIZABETH TITRINGTON CRAFT

Atlanta. Capital city of Georgia (pop. 420,000; metropolitan area 5,268,860; 2010 US Census). Concert life in Atlanta probably began in February 1858 when European virtuoso pianist Sigismond Thalberg, assisted by violinist Henry Vieuxtemps, brought his Grand Concert to the recently completed Athaeneum Theater. Opera appeared for the first time in October 1866 when Max Strakosch's Ghioni and Sussini Grand Italian Opera Company opened the Bell-Johnson Hall (cap. 600) with *Il trovatore*, *Norma*, and *Il barbiere di Siviglia*. The next month the Grover Opera Troupe staged an operatic concert, and in 1868 Maurice Grau's German Opera Company presented operatic excerpts, followed by the McCulloch Opera Troupe with performances of *Il barbiere di Siviglia* and *Don Pasquale*. Demand for a better theatre prompted Belgian Consul Laurent DeGive to build DeGive's Opera House (cap. 2000 in 1873). In February 1872 conductor Theodore Thomas brought his orchestra to the city for the first time, and the next year Ferdinand Wurm organized the city's first serious instrumental ensemble.

During the 1870s Italian opera performances dwindled, supplanted by a succession of British companies that presented a few Italian favorites in English. Atlanta's first performance of an English operetta, Eichberg's *The Doctor of Alcantara*, took place in 1877, and in 1879 William Gilbert and Arthur Sullivan's *H.M.S. Pinafore* enjoyed its Atlanta premiere. Several concert organizations were founded during this period, most importantly the Mozart Club (1867), the Beethoven Society (1872), and the Rossini Club (1876). The city gained its first professional musician when Italian pianist ALFREDO BARILI moved there in 1880. He started teaching at Mrs. Ballard's School and introduced many standard works, including Beethoven's piano sonatas and later Charles Gounod's *Messe solennelle de Sainte Cecile*. Barili organized Atlanta's first music festival in the autumn of 1883, overseeing the city's premiere of five major European symphonic works during the three-day event.

The last years of the century saw the Emma Abbott Grand English Opera, Grau's English Opera Company, and Ford's Opera Company make multiple appearances. In February 1889 Atlanta presented its first week-long operatic festival when the Abbott company staged eight operas, including *Faust*, *Norma*, *Il trovatore*, and *Martha*. Famous concert artists also visited the city, including the century's most notable soprano, Adelina Patti (Barili's aunt), whose performance in January 1894 filled DeGive's. The next year, the African American soprano Sissieretta Jones (known as "Black Patti") performed. Also in 1895 Victor Herbert conducted Patrick Gilmore's Twenty-Second Regiment Band at the Cotton States and International Exposition, and in November performances by the popular band of John Philip Sousa rescued the festival financially.

The year 1901 brought Atlanta's first visit by the touring company of the Metropolitan Opera House, including conductor Walter Damrosch, soprano Emma Eames, and contralto Ernestine Schumann-Heink. In 1905 the Atlanta Music Festival Association was established; in 1907 and 1909 it organized a series of five concerts, featuring such famous opera singers as Enrico Caruso (who failed to appear), Geraldine Farrar, and Olive Fremsted, along with concerts by the Dresden Philharmonic Orchestra from Germany. Listeners were brought by special railroad excursions from neighboring cities. The Association also supported construction of a city auditorium and the installation of a 77-stop Austin organ, which was inaugurated under Edwin H. Lemare for an audience of 7,000. These successes resulted in annual tours by the Metropolitan Opera, beginning in 1910 and featuring such stars as Caruso, Farrar, and Louise Homer. From 1911 to 1923 Atlanta was the only city outside the Northeast to which the Metropolitan toured, with breaks occurring only during the Great Depression and World War II. The annual visits continued, with a few interruptions, until the company ceased national tours after the 1986 season.

The Atlanta Music Club was formed in 1915 to enrich the city's musical life by sponsoring noted artists in recitals. Primarily a women's organization, the club continues its vital role of supporting the community's artistic life. It was instrumental in the establishment of the Atlanta SO, the Choral Guild of Atlanta (1940) and other groups, as well as providing music scholarships for talented young people.

Early attempts to establish a professional symphony orchestra proved frustrating. In 1923 the first organization to bear the title the Atlanta SO was formed, with 60 players drawn from the Howard and Metropolitan theater orchestras under the direction of Enrico Leide. In 1944 the Atlanta Music Club founded the Atlanta Youth SO, merging two school orchestras under Chicago conductor Henry Sopkin. Two years later the group began adding professional players and changed its name to the Atlanta SO. Sopkin gradually built the group into a competent semi-professional ensemble until his retirement in 1966.

A plane crash in Paris on 3 June 1962 took the lives of more than 100 of Atlanta's leading art patrons, who were commemorated with the construction of the Memorial Arts Center (opened 1968, and in 1982 renamed to honor Robert W. Woodruff). The largest of its four performance halls is Symphony Hall (cap. 1762), the first permanent home of the Atlanta SO; the complex also houses the Savannah College of Art and the Alliance Theater. Civic leaders upgraded the orchestra to full professional status in 1967, engaging ROBERT SHAW as music director to lead 87 musicians. In 1970 Shaw founded the Atlanta SO Chorus, which grew to 200 volunteer members; the elite ASO Chamber Chorus numbers between 40 and 60 voices debuted in 1967. Under Shaw's direction the orchestra and chorus grew into one of the nation's finest, winning numerous Grammy Awards. From two concerts of the 1944–5 season, the ASO progressed to giving well over 200 annual performances by the 1980s. When Shaw retired in 1988, Yoel Levi took over, directing the ensemble from 1988 to 2000. In 2001 ROBERT SPANO became music director, working in tandem with the symphony's new principal guest conductor, Donald Runnicles.

Opera in Atlanta experienced similar difficulties establishing itself. Memorial Arts Center opera productions began in 1968. Unfortunately, the city's first resident professional company collapsed through financial mismanagement after its opening performances of Henry Purcell's *King Arthur.* Two ambitious professional companies emerged in the mid-1970s: the Atlanta Lyric Opera (1976) and the Music Theater Guild of Atlanta (1974), which became Georgia Opera in 1977 and moved to the Woodruff Arts Center. In 1979, after periods of financial difficulty, the two companies merged to form the Atlanta Civic Opera. Struggling financially and artistically, the Civic Opera ceased performing in 1983. The following year the company reorganized with William Fred Scott as artistic director; he served until 2005. Since then, Atlanta Opera has become the largest operatic organization in the Southeast. The city also boasts two remarkable early music groups—the Atlanta Baroque Orchestra (founded 1997) and the New Trinity Baroque (founded in London in 1998).

Atlanta continues its thriving choral and organ traditions, mainly in its many churches, which contain notable organs, especially the Rosales organ at St Bartholomew's Episcopal (completed 2003), the magnificent Flentrop organ at St Anne's Episcopal (built 1966), and the large Aeolian-Skinner (built 1962) at St Philip's Cathedral.

Popular music continues to prosper in Atlanta as well, notably rhythm and blues, southern rock, and hip-hop. Several performers began their careers in the city, notably MA RAINEY, LITTLE RICHARD, Willie Lee "Piano Red" Perryman, RAY CHARLES, and "BLIND" WILLIE MCTELL, for whom an Atlanta blues club is named. Many of these and other local musicians had their careers enhanced by the opportunity to perform for an emerging audience by Zenas "Daddy" Sears, owner of WAOK (on air beginning 1954), the first radio station with an all R&B format.

Atlanta native Joe South came to the music scene in the 1950s. He played on recordings of many popular singers and composed songs for The Tams, Billy Joe Royla, Johnny Rivers, Deep Purple, and Lynn Anderson. In 1969, he received two Grammy awards for "Games People Play." His career, along with other contemporary musicians was helped along by producer/publisher Bill Lowery, often referred to as "Mr. Atlanta Music." Lowery's efforts dominated the Atlanta popular music scene from the 1950s until the end of the 20th century. He was one of the first two individuals inducted into the Georgia Music Hall of Fame along with Ray Charles.

In 1972, a group of Atlanta-area studio musicians formed the Atlanta Rhythm Section, playing SOUTHERN ROCK. Unlike other groups, the ARS had a softer, more sophisticated sound found in such hits as "Georgia Rhythm" and "So Into You." As southern rock declined in the early 1980s, so did the ARS. Their last song on *Billboard's* Top 40 was "Alien" in 1981.

The 1990s saw the emergence in Atlanta of the "Dirty South," a widely influential style of southern hip hop; well known local figures include songwriter/producer Jermaine Dupri and the rap artists Kris Kross, OutKast, and Ludacris.

Virtually all of Atlanta's universities, colleges, and junior colleges provide some musical instruction. Most important is Georgia State University (founded 1913, 32,000 students), where the School of Music has 450 majors taught by a faculty of nearly 70. Its Rialto Theater (cap. 1200) has become the finest medium-sized concert hall in the area. Emory University also contributes to Atlanta's concert life with its Flora Glenn Candler Concert Series. Two predominantly black colleges, Spelman and Morehouse, provide advanced music training programs. The Georgia Academy of Music (founded 1973), a private institution, has enjoyed noteworthy success in teaching music to children. Other prominent musical groups include the Atlanta Boy Choir (since 1946), the Georgia Boy Choir (established 2009), the Pro-Mozart Society of Atlanta (founded 1964), and the Festival Singers of Atlanta (founded 1981). Several chamber groups enjoy widespread recognition, notably the Atlanta Chamber Players (founded 1976), neoPhonia (since 1995), Bent Frequency (since 2003), and Sonic Generator (founded 2006), all of which specialize in contemporary music.

Celebrating such a vibrant popular music heritage, several Atlanta institutions preserve the city's and state's music, making their considerable archives available to researchers, including Georgia State University, Emory University, Atlanta History Center, and the Audubon Avenue Research Library.

BIBLIOGRAPHY

J.A. Mussulman: *Dear People... Robert Shaw: a Biography* (Bloomington, IN, 1979/*R*)

K. Graham: "Atlanta's Music Man," *Atlanta Constitution* (7 Aug 1988)

W.W. Daniel: *Pickin' on Peachtree: A History of Country Music in Atlanta* (Urbana, IL, 1990)

N.L. Orr: *Alfredo Barili and the Rise of Classical Music in Atlanta* (Atlanta, GA, 1996)
Z. Miller: *They Heard Georgia Singing* (Macon, GA, 1996)
S. Goodson: *Highbrows, Hillbillies, and Hellfire: Public Entertainment in Atlanta, 1880–1930* (Athens, GA, 2002)
K. Powell: "Bill Lowery: Pop Music Impresario," *Atlanta Journal-Constitution* (9 June 2004)
New Georgia Encyclopedia, <http://www.georgiaencyclopedia.org>

N. LEE ORR, JUDI CALDWELL

Atlanta Ballet. The first regional ballet company in the United States, founded in 1929 by DOROTHY ALEXANDER. Closely allied with the Atlanta Ballet School, the Dorothy Alexander Concert Group changed its name to Atlanta Civic Ballet in 1940 and to Atlanta Ballet in 1967.

CLAUDE CONYERS

Atlantic. American record company. It was founded in New York by Herb Abramson and Ahmet Ertegun (1923–2006; *see* ERTEGUN), both jazz and blues enthusiasts, in 1947, primarily to issue African American music; it achieved considerable commercial success with recordings of musicians whose work encompassed jazz, blues, and rhythm-and-blues. Ertegun's brother Nesuhi (1917–89) joined the organization in 1955, and supervised artists and repertory for the LP catalog; around the same time the company established a new label, Atco, which was chiefly devoted to popular music. During the late 1950s and early 1960s the company made significant recordings marking the emergence of the free jazz style, but by the middle of the decade it was primarily known for soul music; in 1966, at the height of the company's success in this field, it founded the Vortex label for the release of jazz records. During this period Atlantic and its subsidiaries recorded many significant artists: the singers Lavern Baker, Ray Charles, Ben E. King, Esther Phillips, Wilson Pickett, and Otis Redding; the vocal groups the Coasters and the Drifters; and the jazz musicians Lennie Tristano, Lee Konitz, Charles Mingus, the Modern Jazz Quartet, John Coltrane, Ornette Coleman, Keith Jarrett, and Chick Corea. It also presented gospel groups and important white popular musicians, including Bobby Darin and Sonny and Cher.

In 1967 the company was bought by Warner Bros., which in turn was purchased two years later by the Kinney Corp.; Ahmet and Nesuhi Ertegun, however, continued to direct Atlantic. With the emergence of Aretha Franklin, further recordings by Redding and Pickett and such new artists as King Curtis, Roberta Flack, and the Temptations, Atlantic became one of the most significant labels in soul music. It also gained a huge presence in rock with recordings by international groups including the Bee Gees, Buffalo Springfield, Cream, Crosby, Stills and Nash (and Young), Led Zeppelin, the Rolling Stones, Yes, Genesis, and AC/DC. Its prominent jazz artists included Keith Jarrett, the Modern Jazz Quartet, and Manhattan Transfer. While Ahmet Ertegun remained directly in charge of Atlantic, Nesuhi moved in 1971 into the position of president and chief executive officer of the conglomerate WEA (Warner Brothers-Elektra-Atlantic); in 1985 he became its chairman and co-chief executive.

Atlantic remained a leading popular music label in the 1990s through such singer-songwriters as Tori Amos and Jewel and rock groups including Stone Temple Pilots and Hootie & the Blowfish. Corporate reorganization also gave Atlantic a presence in classical music when it took over US distribution of the European labels Teldec, Erato, and Finlandia with recordings by Nikolaus Harnoncourt, Daniel Barenboim, and others. In country music, an Atlantic Nashville division was set up in 1991 with a roster including Rickie Skaggs and John Michael Montgomery. The label became less prominent in producing African American music, although it issued recordings by Anita Baker and the gospel star Bebe Winans.

BIBLIOGRAPHY

C. Gillett: *Making Tracks: Atlantic Records and the Growth of a Multi-Billion-Dollar Industry* (London, 1975)
M. Ruppli: *Atlantic Records: a Discography* (Westport, CT, and London, 1979)
J. Picardie and D. Wade: *Atlantic and the Godfathers of Rock 'n Roll* (London, 1993)
G. Marsh and G. Callingham, eds.: *East Coasting: the Cover Art of New York's Prestige, Riverside and Atlantic Records* (Zürich, 1993)
A. Ertegun: *"What'd I say?" The Atlantic Story: 50 Years of Music* (London, 1998)

BARRY KERNFELD, HOWARD RYE, DAVE LAING/R

A Tribe Called Quest. Rap group. Formed in Queens, New York City, in 1988, and signed with Jive Records in 1989, A Tribe Called Quest included producer/DJ Ali Shaheed Muhammad, MC/producer Q-Tip (Jonathan Davis), and MCs Phife (Malik Taylor) and Jarobi (the latter appearing only on the group's first album). They were part of the Native Tongues, a loose collective of New York City–based groups, including the Jungle Brothers and De La Soul, whose Afrocentric lyrics often recalled the political and social consciousness of 1960s and 1970s America. Yet their eclecticism in both lyrical topics and musical styles almost always included an element of humor, allowing them to engage critically, but playfully, with a variety of themes, ranging from love to the music industry, from date rape to domestic abuse, from religion to the use of the word "nigger."

A Tribe Called Quest's first album, *People's Instinctive Travels and the Paths of Rhythm* (1990), featured a number of jazz samples, which helped to position them as a "jazz" or "alternative" rap group. Their second album, *The Low End Theory,* was more overt in its use of jazz samples and even featured a collaboration between the group and jazz bassist Ron Carter for the song "Verses from the Abstract." The group's third album *Midnight Marauders* (1993) also has been celebrated as a hip-hop classic. Popular singles from their first three albums included "Can I kick it?," "I left my wallet in El Segundo," "Bonita Applebum," "Scenario," "Check the Rhime," "Jazz (We've Got)," "Award Tour," and "Electric Relaxation."

The group's remaining albums were also highly successful, full of positivity amid the dominance of West Coast gangsta rap, and would continue to solidify their associations with an alternative rap subgenre, influencing other more recent alternative acts such as Common,

Erykah Badu, and the Roots. The group dissolved following their album *The Love Movement* in 1998, and the members have since pursued a host of independent projects. Q-Tip has had the most successful solo career of the three, working as both a producer and MC. In the late 2000s, the band began to perform reunion sets, but have not released any new studio material.

BIBLIOGRAPHY

J. Wood: "Native Tongues: A Family Affair," *The Vibe History of Hip Hop,* ed. A. Light, (New York, 1999), 187–99

S. Taylor: *People's Instinctive Travels and the Paths of Rhythm* (New York, 2007)

J. Williams: "The Construction of Jazz Rap as High Art in Hip-hop Music." *JM*, xxvii (2010), 435–59

JUSTIN A. WILLIAMS

Atteridge, Harold R. (*b* Chicago, IL, 1887; *d* Lynbrook, NY, 15 Jan 1938). Librettist, lyricist, and producer. He was the driving force behind many musicals that took place under the auspices of the Shubert brothers in New York from 1911 until his death in 1938. He was born and educated in Chicago, where he first honed his theatrical skills as a scriptwriter and lyricist. After moving to New York (September 1910) he worked first at the Folies Bergere and a year later was hired by the Shuberts to write the script and the lyrics for *Vera Violetta* (1911), which starred Al Jolson. Atteridge and Jolson continued to work together closely for many years thereafter. Atteridge shaped what became known as Winter Garden revues, musicals that took place seasonally at the Winter Garden theater well into the 1930s. The most significant of these was *The Passing Show* series, which began in 1912. Atteridge's most popular song is "By the Beautiful Sea" (1914), the music of which was written by Harry Carroll. He married the actress Laura Hamilton in 1914. Hundreds of unpublished songs and dozens of scripts by Atteridge are housed at the Shubert Archive in New York.

BIBLIOGRAPHY

"Harold Atteridge: a Rapid-fire Librettist," *New York Times* (14 June 1914), X8

J. Westover: *A Study and Reconstruction of The Passing Show of 1914: the American Musical Revue and its Development in the Early Twentieth Century* (diss., City U. of New York, 2010)

JONAS WESTOVER

Atwill, J(oseph) F(airfield (*b* Boston, MA, 4 June 1811; *d* Oakland, CA, 29 Nov 1891). Proprietor of music stores and sheet music publisher. From 1833 to 1849, Atwill operated a "Music Saloon" music store and publishing business on Broadway in New York City, using printing plates of the Thomas Birch Company. He married Eliza Dugliss in 1834. After suffering financial setbacks, the business was taken over by Samuel C. Jollie, and Atwill left his family to travel to San Francisco. He arrived penniless on 28 October 1849 but hit paydirt in the gold fields. Unlike many miners who sent paper money drafts home, Atwill sent about $75,000 in gold dust to New York. He brought his wife and daughters to California in 1854. Atwill moved his East Coast stock to California and established California's first music store, a tiny metal-constructed building at 158 Washington Street that withstood San Francisco's many firestorms. In New York, Atwill published Vincenzo Belini's *La Sonnambula*; it was also the first opera performed in California by Pellegrini's Opera Troupe on 12 February 1851. Atwill revitalized his publishing enterprise in 1852 with the song "The California Pioneers," which claims on the cover to be "The First Piece of Music Pubd. in Cala." In mid-1854, Mrs. C.W. Hunt established a dance studio above Atwill's Music Store. Atwill & Co was sold to Mathias Grey in 1860, who later sold the business to Sherman Clay & Co.

BIBLIOGRAPHY

F. Soule, J.H. Gihon, and J. Nisbet, *Annals of San Francisco* (New York, 1854)

H. Dichter and E. Shapiro: *Early American Sheet Music* (New York, 1941/*R*)

M.K. Duggan, "Music Publishing and Printing in San Francisco Before the Earthquake and Fire of 1906," *Kemble Occasional*, no.24 (1980), esp. 3f

Biographical Files of Society of California Pioneers, San Francisco

Frederick R. Sherman Music Collection, Society of California Pioneers, San Francisco

BARBARA TURCHIN/MEREDITH M. ELIASSEN

Atwood, Ethel [Atwood-Grant, Lizzie Ethel] (*b* Fairfield, ME, 12 Sept 1866; *d* Los Angeles, CA, 9 April 1948). Violinist and co-founder and business manager of the Fadette Ladies' Orchestra. Atwood, the daughter of a farmer/merchant father and a milliner mother, began violin lessons at age eight in Fairfield, Maine, but moved to Boston as a teenager to further her study. In October 1888 she and Caroline B. Nichols (1864–1939) founded the Fadette Ladies' Orchestra, which became one of the best-known women's orchestras in the country. Atwood became the organization's principal second violin and its first business manager; she played with the Fadettes from 1888 to 1895. In 1895 the Fadettes incorporated, but Atwood copyrighted the group's name. When Atwood left the Fadettes shortly before her 1896 marriage, she sold the name to Mary Messer, who attempted to use it to start another ladies' orchestra. Messer sued the Fadettes for continuing to perform under a name she had purchased, but the Massachusetts Supreme Court sided with the Fadettes. Beginning in the 1890s, Atwood also worked as a prompter and was, reportedly, the only woman prompter in the United States. By 1903, Atwood was working as a programmer for the Portland, Oregon-based Northwest Theatrical Association.

BIBLIOGRAPHY

F.E. Willard and M.A.R. Livermore, eds.: *A Woman of the Century: Fourteen Hundred Seventy Biographical Sketches Accompanied by Portraits of Leading American Women in All Walks of Life* (Buffalo, NY, 1893), 34–5

ANNA-LISE P. SANTELLA

Auberjonois, René (*b* New York City, NY, 1 June 1940). Performer. As a child, he met Alan Jay Lerner while working for him as a babysitter. With the help of mentor John Houseman, he became an apprentice at a Connecticut theater when he was 16. He studied theater at

Carnegie-Mellon University, and taught acting at Juilliard. Although he never received formal training as a singer, his relationship with Lerner led to his first role in a musical, playing Sebastian Bay in *Coco* (1969). He later performed in the musicals *Tricks* (1973), *The Good Doctor* (1974), *Big River* (1985), *City of Angels* (1989), and *Dance of the Vampires* (2002), and went on to a successful film and television career. He was nominated for a number of awards, and won a Tony Award for *Coco* and a Drama Desk Award for *Big River*. His success as a character actor with a versatile, baritone singing voice is showcased especially in roles like the Duke in *Big River* and Louis the chef in Disney's *The Little Mermaid* (1989).

BIBLIOGRAPHY

D. McGovern and D.G. Winer: *Sing Out, Louise!: 150 Stars of the Musical Theatre Remember 50 Years on Broadway* (New York, 1993)

PETER PURIN

Auden, W(ystan) H(ugh) (*b* York, England, 21 Feb 1907; *d* Vienna, Austria, 29 Sept 1973). English poet, naturalized American. Of all the mid-20th-century poets, Auden was the most actively concerned with music; the third part of his *Collected Poems* (New York, 1945) consists of 38 "songs and other musical pieces," including the five lyrics set in Britten's cycle *On this Island* (1938), his *Song for St Cecilia's Day* (1941), and arias from his "choral operetta" *Paul Bunyan* (1941). With Britten he collaborated on films (*Coal Face*, 1935; *Night Mail*, 1936), broadcasts (*Hadrian's Wall*, 1937; *The Dark Valley*, 1940), plays (*The Ascent of F.6*, 1937; *On the Frontier*, 1938), the "symphonic cycle" *Our Hunting Fathers* (1936), and cabaret songs for Hedli Anderson (1938). Two quotations from the *St Cecilia* poem show how well Auden wrote words for music. The opening lines:

In a garden shady this holy lady
With reverent cadence and subtle psalm,
Like a black swan as death came on
Poured forth her song in perfect calm

demonstrate his command of cantabile, of rhythm, and of vowel pattern, while the subsequent scherzo section is prompted by the lilt of:

I cannot grow;
I have no shadow
To run away from,
I only play.

In 1948, Auden declared himself an "opera addict"; his friend Chester Kallman "was the person who was responsible for arousing my interest in opera, about which previously, as you can see from *Paul Bunyan*, I knew little or nothing." In that year Kallman and Auden collaborated on the libretto for Stravinsky's *The Rake's Progress*. In 1953 they published *Delia*, a delicate masque, written for Stravinsky but unset. Thereafter for Henze they produced two librettos, *Elegy for Young Lovers* and *The Bassarids*, and for Nabokov adapted *Love's Labour's Lost*. Their last libretto, *The Entertainment of the Senses*, was an antimasque for insertion into the Gibbons-Locke *Cupid and Death* (1653, 1659). It was posted to its composer, John Gardner, a few days before Auden's death. About half of *The Rake's Progress* and, by Auden's account, "about 75%" of *Elegy* has been credited to Kallman—though, in a joint essay, the collaborators described themselves as a "corporate personality." Auden's theories about opera (among them: "a good libretto plot is a melodrama in both the strict and the conventional sense of the word; it offers as many opportunities as possible for the characters to be swept off their feet by placing them in situations which are too tragic or too fantastic for 'words'") were set out in several essays; his practice produced the most elegantly wrought librettos of the day. *Elegy*, for example, opens with full-voiced pentameters, linked by patterns of alliteration and internal rhyme:

At dawn by the window in the wan light of today
My bridegroom of the night, nude as the sun, with a brave
Open sweep of his wonderful Samson-like hand

and, among its variety of carefully planned forms, includes simple songs:

On yonder lofty mountain
a lofty castle stands
where dwell three lovely maidens,
the fairest in the land

and scherzo patter:

Blood-pressure drops,
Invention stops;
Upset tum,
No images come

as well as conversational exchanges for recitative, conventional declarations of love, and a chorale. Despite his preference for opera in the original, Auden was also drawn to fit words to existing scores, and with Kallman he made translations of operas by Mozart (*Die Zauberflöte*, 1956; *Don Giovanni*, 1960), Weill (*Die sieben Todsünden*, 1958; *Aufstieg und Fall der Stadt Mahagonny*, 1960), and Dittersdorf (*Arcifanfano*, 1965). These are mellifluous, elegant, and better poetry than anything else of the kind, but on occasion they stray far from the original—quite deliberately so, since "a too-literal translation of the original text may sometimes prove to be a falsification."

Many composers have been attracted to set Auden's poetry, among them Berkeley (*Night Covers Up the Rigid Land* and *Five Poems*) and Maw (in his *Nocturne*); the "Christmas oratorio" *For the Time Being* attracted settings from both Marvin David Levy and (of the first section, "Advent") Thea Musgrave. Auden's poetry has also inspired purely instrumental works such as Berio's orchestral *Nones* (1954) and Bernstein's Symphony no.2, subtitled "The Age of Anxiety" (1949). Later poems written specifically for musical setting include two translations in Barber's *Hermit Songs* (1953), Stravinsky's *Elegy for J.F.K.* (1964), and Walton's *The Twelve* (1965). Auden and Kallman were the text editors of *An Elizabethan Song Book* (Garden City, NY, 1955), whose music editor was Noah Greenberg, and in 1957 Auden wrote the narratives for Greenberg's performing edition of *The Play of Daniel*. A recent choral setting, "He is the way," by Richard Webster, is based on a text from Auden's Christmas Oratorio.

WRITINGS

Librettos: *Paul Bunyan*, Britten, 1941; *Moralities*, Henze, 1969

with C. Kallman: *The Rake's Progress*, Stravinsky, 1951; *Elegy for Young Lovers*, Henze, 1961; *The Bassarids*, Henze, 1966; *Love's Labour's Lost*, Nabokov, 1973; *The Entertainment of the Senses*, John Gardner, 1974

Essays: "Opera on an American Legend: Problems of Putting the Story of Paul Bunyan on the Stage," New York Times (4 May 1941); Introduction to *An Elizabethan Song Book* (Garden City, NY, 1955); "A Public Art," *Opera*, xii (1961), 12–15; [with C. Kallman: "Genesis of a Libretto," *Elegy for Young Lovers* (Mainz, 1961); *The Dyer's Hand* (New York, 1962), 463–527 [incl. "Notes on Music and Opera," "Cav & Pag," "Translating Opera Libretti" (with Kallman), "Music in Shakespeare"]; "The World of Opera," *Secondary Worlds* (London, 1969)

BIBLIOGRAPHY

GroveA; *GMO*

N. Miller: "Prosperos Insel: W.H. Auden und die Musik," *Beziehungszauber: Musik in der modernen Dichtung* (Munich and Vienna, 1988), 105–28

P. Reed: "A Rejected Love Song from Paul Bunyan," *MT*, cxxix (1988), 283–8

J.-M. Vaccaro, ed.: *The Rake's Progress: Un opéra de W. Hogarth, W.H. Auden, C. Kallman, et I. Stravinsky; une réalisation de J. Cox et D. Hockney* (Paris, 1990)

K. Rugoff: "Auden and Opera: The Poet's Magic Flute," *Ars Lyrica*, vi (1992) 63–71

G. Chew: "Pastoral and Neoclassicism: a Reinterpretation of Auden's and Stravinsky's *Rake's Progress*," *COJ*, v (1993), 239–63

E. Mendelson, ed.: *W.H. Auden and Chester Kallman: Libretti and Other Dramatic Writings, 1939–1973* (Princeton, 1993) [incl. critical texts of all libretti and of trans. of *Die Zauberflöte*]

W. Bernhart: "Prekäre angewandte Opernästhetik: Audens 'sekundäre Welt' und Hans Werner Henzes *Elegie für junge Liebende*," Die Semantik der musiko-literarischen Gattungen: Methodik und Analyse: ein Festgabe für Ulrich Weisstein (Tübingen, 1994), 233–46

A. Schwartz: "Prospero's Isle and the Sirens' Rock," *COJ*, xv (2003), 83–106

ANDREW PORTER/MICHAEL HOVLAND

Audsley, George Ashdown (*b* Elgin, Scotland, 6 Sept 1838; *d* Bloomfield, NJ, 21 June, 1925). Organ designer, architect, author and art expert of Scottish birth. After working as an architect in England, he immigrated to New York City in 1892, where he worked for a short time with his brother William in the architectural firm of W. & G. Audsley. His interests were widespread, and he wrote several books on architecture, oriental art, and religious symbolism. One of his major interests, however, was the organ. He consulted on various church organ projects, had an organ in his home built to his own design, and was instrumental in the design of the five-manual organ built in 1904 by the Los Angeles Art Organ Company for Festival Hall at the World's Fair in St. Louis, upon which the noted French organist Alexandre Guilmant performed 40 recitals. This organ was later purchased by John Wanamaker, and became the foundation of the large organ in Wanamaker's Philadelphia department store. Audsley was the author of four influential works on organ design: *The Art of Organ-building* (2 vols., 1905), *The Organ of the Twentieth Century* (1919), *Organ-stops and their Artistic Registration* (1921), and *The Temple of Tone* (1925). These are lavishly illustrated with prints of organ-cases and Audsley's own meticulous drawings of pipes and mechanisms. He was also an early advocate for the standardization of organ consoles, subsequently adopted by the American Guild of Organists. Audsley's approach to organ design and tonal structure was conservative, providing a much-needed balance to some of the excesses of the early 20th century. Although he generally favored an eclectic approach to tonal design, he also espoused some of the prevalent orchestral concepts which emphasized string tone and imitative stops, and he believed that all the divisions of an organ should be enclosed in expression boxes.

BIBLIOGRAPHY

"George Ashdown Audsley" [obituary], *The Diapason*, (July 1925), 1

F.R. Webber: "The St. Louis Exposition Organ," *The Tracker*, iii/3 (April 1959), 5

E.W. Flint: "The Works of George Ashdown Audsley," *Art of the Organ*, ii/2 (June 1972)

O. Ochse: *The History of the Organ in the United States* (Bloomington, IN, 1975)

D.H. Fox: *George Ashdown Audsley* (1995)

BARBARA OWEN

Audubon Quartet. String quartet formed in 1974 by Gregory Fulkerson, Janet Brady, Larry Bradford, and Clyde Thomas Shaw. After several changes of membership, it consisted, in 2009, of Ellen Jewett, Akemi Takayama, Doris Lederer, and Shaw. The group was quartet-in-residence at Marywood College, Scranton, Pennsylvania, between 1974 and 1979, and at the Virginia Polytechnic Institute and State University, Blacksburg, from 1979 to 2001; it was quartet-in-residence at the Shenandoah Conservatory from 2007 to 2011, at which point the group disbanded, giving its final concert on 8 August 2011. The Audubon has toured extensively and was the first American string quartet to perform in mainland China (1981–2). In 1977 it won first prizes in the Villa-Lobos International String Quartet Competition in Rio de Janeiro and in the contemporary music category at the Evian Festival. Equally adept at the Classical and contemporary repertories, the Audubon gave many world premieres, including those of Laderman's String Quartet no.6 (1981), which is named after it, and Schickele's String Quartet no.1 (1984), which it commissioned. In 2009–10 the group performed the complete Beethoven string quartet cycle (2009–10).

DAVID HUNTER/LAURA E. KENNEDY

Auer, Leopold (von) (*b* Veszprém, Hungary, 7 June 1845; *d* Loschwitz, nr Dresden, Germany, 15 July 1930). Hungarian violinist and teacher. From 1868–1917, he taught violin at the St. Petersburg Conservatory, where his pupils included Jascha Heifetz, Nathan Milstein, Mischa Elman and Efrem Zimbalist. He helped to establish the Russian school of violin playing that included use of the "Russian bow hold" in which the middle of the index finger presses into the stick resulting in a noticeably high wrist posture. He famously rejected the original dedication of Tchaikovsky's Violin Concerto and only played the work after his own revisions to the solo part in 1893.

Auer left Russia in 1918 due to the revolution and settled in New York. He quickly scheduled a Carnegie Hall recital and was welcomed into the social circles of musicians such as Franz Kneisel and Donald Lambert. During the 1920s he taught at both the Institute of

Musical Art (Juilliard) in New York and the Curtis Institute in Philadelphia. His teaching career was an important link in the lineage of violin pedagogy extending back to Joachim. Auer also published an autobiography and two instruction manuals of which *Violin Playing As I Teach It* (1921) is still in wide circulation.

BIBLIOGRAPHY

GMO (B. Schwarz)

L. Auer: *My Long Life in Music* (New York, 1923)

G. Kosloski: *The Teaching and Influence of Leopold Auer* (diss., Indiana U., 1977)

B. Schwarz: *Great Masters of the Violin* (New York, 1983)

EDWARD EANES

Aufderheide, May F(rances) (*b* Indianapolis, IN, 21 May 1888; *d* Pasadena, CA, 1 Sept 1972). Composer and pianist. She was born into a musical family: her father, John Henry Aufderheide (1865–1941), was a semi-professional violinist and his sister, May Kolmer, was a noted pianist who performed with the Indianapolis SO and taught at the Metropolitan School of Music. Aufderheide learned classical piano with Kolmer, but showed more interest in popular music. While a teenager in finishing school in New York, she composed her first rag, "Dusty Rag" (1908), which was arranged by Paul Pratt and published initially by an acquaintance from Indianapolis, Cecil Duane Crabb. Following several months completing her education in Europe, in the spring of 1908 Aufderheide returned to Indiana, married Thomas M. Kaufman, and settled in Richmond, Indiana. "Dusty Rag" had not sold well in her absence owing to Crabb's limited distribution, so when Aufderheide produced several more after her return, her father, a prominent banker, used his considerable resources to establish J.H. Aufderheide & Company to publish her works. He reissued "Dusty Rag" with greater success and in the three years that followed published roughly a dozen of his daughter's rags, waltzes, and songs in addition to works by such other regional composers as Gladys Yelvington, Julia Lee Niebergall, Paul Pratt, and Crabb. Several of Aufderheide's more popular piano rags were given lyrics and published in song form. Her career as a pianist and composer was brief, spanning just four years. Despite the commercial and critical success of her compositions "The Richmond Rag," "The Thriller!," "Buzzer Rag," and "Blue Ribbon Rag," by the age of 23 she had ceased composing. She and her husband adopted a daughter in 1922, and in the mid-1940s the family moved to Pasadena, CA, where she died at the age of 84.

Aufderheide was among the most prolific female composers of piano ragtime, with seven published rags and nine waltzes and songs to her credit. Her rags feature clear, moderately syncopated melodic lines over regular oom-pah bass patterns, but Aufderheide typically eschewed the standard AABBACCDD rag form in favor of three-strain compositions that repeat either the A, B, or C section at the end.

BIBLIOGRAPHY

AGrove

M. Morath: "May Aufderheide and the Ragtime Women," *Ragtime: its History, Composers, and Music*, ed. J.E. Hasse (New York, 1985), 154–65

D. Jasen and G. Jones: *That American Rag* (New York, 2000)

N. Bostick and N. Hulse: "Ragtime's Women Composers," *The Ragtime Ephemeralist Number 3* (Oak Park, IL, 2002), 106–35

BRYAN S. WRIGHT

Augér, Arleen (*b* Long Beach, CA, 13 Sept 1939; *d* Leusden, Netherlands, 10 June 1993). Soprano. As a girl she sang in a church choir and studied the piano and violin. She studied singing and the violin at the University of California, later took singing lessons in Chicago with Ralph Errolle, and won a scholarship to Vienna in 1967. At her audition she so impressed the conductor Josef Krips that he engaged her for the Staatsoper, with the role of the Queen of Night in *Die Zauberflöte* for her debut. Another powerful admirer at this time was Böhm, with whom she sang, and also recorded, a notable Konstanze in *Die Entführung aus dem Serail*. Appearances at the Vienna Volksoper included Marie in Donizetti's *La fille du régiment*. Her reputation as a coloratura soprano grew with debuts at the New York City Opera (1969) and Salzburg (1970), both as the Queen of Night.

With her move to Frankfurt in 1974 Augér turned more to lyric roles in opera and to the development of her career as a concert singer. She toured Japan in programs of Bach and Handel, and worked extensively with the pianist Irwin Gage in the lieder repertory. In 1975 she sang as Fire in *L'enfant et les sortilèges* at La Scala, and in 1978 made her debut at the Metropolitan Opera as Marzelline in *Fidelio*. She was greatly admired in Britain, where she gave many recitals and sang in memorable performances of *Alcina* and *L'incoronazione di Poppea* (both of which she recorded) at Spitalfields in the City of London Festival. In 1986 her singing of Mozart's *Exsultate, jubilate* at the wedding of Prince Andrew and Sarah Ferguson in Westminster Abbey was heard by millions worldwide on television. Augér's many recordings show her as a delightful singer of Bach, Haydn, Mozart, Schubert, and Richard Strauss, to whose *Vier letzte Lieder* she brought a fresh voice and mature understanding in a performance with Previn. Among her last recordings were a distinguished contribution to Graham Johnson's Complete Schubert Song Edition and *Sonnets from the Portuguese*, written for her by Libby Larsen. Her voice was of a gentle character with impressive reserves of power: her singing was unfailingly musical, and her death, after operations for a brain tumor, was deeply mourned.

BIBLIOGRAPHY

J.B. Steane: *Singers of the Century* (London, 1996), 181–5

L. Holmes: "A conversation with Arleen Auger," *Journal of singing*, lxii/3 (2006), 337–42

B. Kellow: "Something Cool," *Opera News*, lxxi/1 (2006), 34–37

J.B. STEANE/R

Augustin, Frisner (*b* Port-au-Prince, Haiti, 1 March 1948; *d* Port-au-Prince, Haiti, 28 Feb 2012). Haitian master drummer. After learning his craft in the oral tradition, he came to New York City in 1972 and established himself as a teacher of Haitian traditional drumming and as a performer. In 1981 he became Artistic Director of La Troupe Makandal. Over the next three decades he recorded, taught, and performed with Makandal in the United States, Europe, and Asia. The recordings, including *Èzili* and *Prepare*, featured his arrangements of mostly sacred Afro-Haitian songs with drumming and percussion. Jazz artists Kip Hanrahan and Andrew Cyrille recorded with him as well, and he contributed to a soundtrack by filmmaker Jonathan Demme. In 1999 the National Endowment for the Arts awarded him its National Heritage Fellowship. Listeners know his style as dynamic, with an exceptionally broad tonal palette, and his drum breaks rivaled the most far-reaching jazz improvisations. As a senior drummer in his tradition, he performed a variety of tonal-rhythmic styles rarely heard in the work of younger Haitian drummers. While developing his public career, he privately maintained his devotion to his spiritual roots as a master drummer for the rites of Vodou, an Afro-Haitian religion.

LOIS WILCKEN

Austin. Capital city of Texas (pop. 790,390; metropolitan area 1,716,291; 2010 US Census) situated on the Colorado River in the central area of the state. First settled in 1835, the city was incorporated in 1839. Music in the city has grown from that predominantly associated with 19th-century German singing societies to an internationally recognized music industry fed by nearly 200 live music venues, about 2,000 bands and performing artists living in and around the city, annual music festivals featuring a mix of local, national, and international artists, radio stations promoting local music, a recording industry, a flagship university, and state and local government offices with the specific charge to promote the state's and city's music. In 1991 the State Legislature declared Austin "The Live Music Capital of the World" and since has used the slogan to promote the city and its music.

Evening concerts were given on the grounds of the state capitol beginning in 1846. Around 1850 a German singing society was formed; this lasted nearly 70 years. By the late 1800s, the city of 15,000 had three opera halls and a municipal band. The Austin Musical Union, organized in 1886, gave opera and concert performances, chiefly at Scholz Garden; other concerts were held at Tips Hall, Turner Hall, and the Jones Library. The Austin SO was incorporated in 1911 with a concert at the Hancock Opera House conducted by Hans Harthans; the orchestra remained loosely organized until 1938, when it was more formally established under the direction of Henrik J. Buytendorf. Later conductors have included Ezra Rachlin, Maurice Peress, Akira Endo, Sung Kwak, and Peter Bay (1998–). Other performing arts ensembles and organizations include Chorus Austin founded as the Austin Civic Chorus (1965–); Austin Civic Wind Ensemble (1975–); Austin Civic Orchestra (1977–); La Follia Austin Baroque (1980–); Austin Symphonic Band (1981–); Austin Vocal Arts Ensemble founded as the Austin Handel-Haydn Society in 1985; Austin Lyric Opera (1986–); Texas Early Music Project (1987–); Istanpitta (1994–), performing music of the Middle Ages; Mundi (2004–), a folk, classical, and rock ensemble; and many others.

The Sarah and Ernest Butler School of Music at the University of Texas at Austin presents some 500 concerts, recitals, operas, and other special musical events annually. The 700-seat Bates Recital Hall contains the Visser-Rowland Tracker Organ of 5313 pipes and 4 manuals. The university's Humanities Research Center houses the largest collection in existence of manuscripts by modern French composers; the University String Project, founded by Phyllis Young, brings local public-school students to the campus for private and group lessons and has been a model for similar programs throughout the country. The Fine Arts Library contains the art and music collections and most of the University of Texas Libraries' theater and dance materials. Latin American music, literature, and archives are collected at the Benson Latin American Collection. The University is equipped with a 24-track professional recording studio and is home to the Center for Music Learning, Butler Opera Center, Center for American Music, and Center for Sacred Music.

Huston-Tillotson College and Concordia University Texas offer BA degrees in music and music education; Austin Community College offers an Associate of Arts Degree in Music and a Commercial Music Management degree; and music courses are also given at St. Edwards University.

Among Austin's concert halls are the Long Center for the Performing Arts, the Paramount Theater for the Performing Arts, and the Moody Theater, which as of 2011 also serves as the home of the KLRU-TV produced PBS program AUSTIN CITY LIMITS, the longest running music series in American television history. The campus of the University of Texas offers many concert facilities, including Jessen Auditorium, Bates Recital Hall, and Hogg Memorial Auditorium. Concerts are also given at Huston-Tillotson College, St. Edwards University, Concordia University Texas, Austin Community College, the Presbyterian and Episcopal seminaries, and at local churches; outdoor performances are held at Zilker Park and Auditorium Shores.

By 2011 there were about 120 music study, appreciation, and performance societies and organizations in the Austin metropolitan area, including Wednesday Morning Music Club (1923–), Austin Friends of Traditional Music (1974–), DiverseArts Production Group (1994–), The Cipher, Austin's Hip-Hop Project (1999–), New Music Co-op (2001–), and Austin Tejano Music Coalition (2005–), to name only a few.

While there is a long history of music-making in Austin, the birth of the "Austin music scene" is typically traced to the 1960s at Threadgill's (1932–74 and 1981–), a venue that welcomed traditional blues, folk, and country singers, and University of Texas student folksingers. The 1960s also saw an increase of live music opportunities, local independent recording studios, a vibrant fraternity party and club scene, and the success of several Austin artists on a national level. The scene grew with help from venues such as the Jade Room and the New Orleans Club (rock music upstairs; jazz downstairs), the Split Rail and the Broken Spoke (country), the Chequered Flag (folk music), and such East Austin clubs as the Victory Grill, Charlie's Playhouse, and Ernie's Chicken Shack (rhythm and blues). Local recording studio Sonobeat (est. 1967) recorded such Austin bands as Shiva's Headband, the Sweetarts, the Conqueroo, the Afro-Caravan, and Lavender Hill Express.

By the mid-1970s Austin was recognized nationally as home to an alternative music industry (to Nashville, New York, and Los Angeles). The Armadillo World Headquarters (1970–80), an old armory converted into a concert hall and community arts center, featured not only such progressive country artists as Willie Nelson, Michael Martin Murphey, and Jerry Jeff Walker, but also blues and rock musicians, monthly ballets, and folkloric groups from around the world. Soap Creek Saloon (1973–85) offered another venue for both singer songwriters and Austin bands from a variety of music genres. Antone's Blues Club (1975–) enabled Jimmie Vaughan and Stevie Ray Vaughan, Kim Wilson, and other local white blues musicians to share the stage with such touring legends as Muddy Waters, Albert King, and Hubert Sumlin.

In the 1980s punk and alternative rock emerged at such venues as Raul's, Club Foot, and Club 29, at the same time that local bands such as the Fabulous Thunderbirds, Christopher Cross, and Stevie Ray Vaughan achieved international fame. The first issue of *The Austin Chronicle* (1981–), an alternative newspaper with articles focusing on Austin music in addition to writings on theater, art, and cinema, was published on 4 September 1981. In 1985 the Texas Legislature identified music as an industry in need of state government recognition and assistance and created the Texas Music Commission—the first law passed by a state legislature in the United States creating an office promoting commercial music business. In 1986 oil prices plummeted, local banks collapsed, and by 1987 Austin's downtown had the highest vacancy rate of any city in the country. In the late 1980s, however, the Austin music scene received growing national and international attention with the *South by Southwest Music and Media Conference* (SXSW) (1987–), which has steadily grown from showcasing 177 artists in 1987 to 1978 in 2010.

Austin's economy recovered in the 1990s, and the commodification of its music went into full swing, with continued help from the legislature. The Texas Music Office (TMO) opened on 20 January 1990. In September 1994 the Texas Chapter of the National Academy of Recording Arts and Sciences opened its doors in Austin, the first new chapter in 22 years. (By 2007, 13 city and state music promotion offices were in operation.) By the end of the 1990s the scene had expanded beyond an arguably centralized Sixth Street and East Austin to Red River Street, the Warehouse District, Fourth Street, and South Lamar.

Originating in 2000, "Keep Austin Weird" became the unofficial motto for a city experiencing rapid growth, and the first decade of the 21st century witnessed an even greater emphasis on the diversity of the city's music. The Austin Latino Music Association (ALMA) (2001–) produces a variety of music programs, the longest running series of which is "Sonidos de Barrio," featuring a broad array of Latino musical styles. In 2005, co-sponsored by the City of Austin, ALMA launched "Sabor Latino," a Friday noon-concert series during the month of May, which as of 2006 has been designated Latino Music Month, the last weekend of which is specifically Latin Jazz Weekend. In 2006 the Austin City Council led an initiative called The Trail of Tejano Legends, a re-naming of five East Side facilities/areas, three of which were designated to receive public art, in commemoration of the lives and contributions of significant musicians in Austin's Tejano and Hispanic communities. This project provided recognition to several local Latino musicians who were an integral part of Austin's music scene in the 1940s and 50s: Roy Montelongo, Nash Hernandez, Matias Velasquez, Johnny Degollado, Manuel "Cowboy" Donley, and the Perez-Ramos families. Launched in 2009 the *Austin Vida: Latino Lifestyle and Culture Magazine* is an English-language online publication, covering the local Latino music scene as well as touring Latin music acts playing in Austin. As of 2010 there were eight Latin or Tejano music radio stations broadcasting from Austin.

The first annual Austin City Limits Festival was held in 2002, featuring local, regional, national, and international performers. Catering specifically to the city's African American community, the Urban Music Festival (2006–) is an annual weekend music and cultural event. By 2010 the diversity, pervasiveness, and history of the Austin music scene are enthusiastically embraced and vigorously marketed by the leaders in the industry.

BIBLIOGRAPHY

L.M. Spell: *Music in Texas* (Austin, 1936)
M.O. James-Reed: *Music in Austin, 1900–1956* (Austin, 1957)
M.S. Barkley: *History of Travis County and Austin, 1839–1899* (Waco, TX, 1963)
J. Reid: *The Improbable Rise of Redneck Rock* (Austin, 1974/*R*)
T. Holland: *Texas Genesis: a Wild Ride Through Texas Progressive Country Music 1963–78, with Digressions* (Austin, 1978)
A. Green: "Austin's Cosmic Cowboys: Words in Collision," *And Other Neighborly Names*, ed. R. Bauman and R. Abrahams (Austin, 1982), 152–94
H.C. Sparks: *Stylistic Development and Compositional Processes of Selected Solo Singer/Songwriters in Austin, Texas* (diss., U. of Texas, Austin, 1984)
L. Willoughby: *Texas Rhythm Texas Rhyme: A Pictorial History of Texas Music* (Austin, 1984)
B. Shank: *Dissonant Identities: The Rock "n" Roll Scene In Austin, Texas* (Hanover, NH, 1994)
A. C. Turley: *Music in the City: A History of Austin Music* (Cedar Park, 2000)
B. Wilson with J. Ortman: *The Austin Music Scene Through the Lens of Burton Wilson, 1965–1994* (Austin, 2001)
G. Hartman: *The History of Texas Music* (College Station, 2008)
J.D. Melard: *Cosmic Cowboys, Armadillos, and Outlaws: The Cultural Politics of Texan Identity in the 1970s* (Ph.D. diss., U. of Texas, Austin, 2009)
J. Long: *Weird City: Sense of Place and Creative Resistance in Austin, Texas* (Austin, 2010)
A. Powell and D. Freeman: *The Austin Chronicle: Music Anthology* (Austin, 2011)
P. Blackstock, J. Cohen and A. Smith, eds.: *SXSW Scrapbook: People and Things that Went Before* (Austin, 2011)
T. Stimeling: *Cosmic Cowboys and New Hicks: The Countercultural Sounds of Austin's Progressive Country Music Scene* (New York, 2011)
C.D. Hillis: *The Austin Music Scene in the 1970s: Songs and Songwriters* (diss., U. of Texas, Austin, 2011)

HUGH CULLEN SPARKS/KEVIN E. MOONEY

Austin, Elizabeth (*b* Leicester, England, c1800; *d* after 1835). English singer. Her performances in Dublin in 1821 led to engagements at the Theatre Royal, Drury Lane (debut on 23 November 1822), and the English Opera House. On 10 December 1827 she made her American debut at William Warren's Chestnut Street Theatre, Philadelphia, in Arne's comic opera *Love in a Village*; her New York debut was at the Park Theater on 2 January 1828. For the next six years, managed by F.H.F. Berkeley, she became America's reigning prima donna, touring with Charles Edward Horn and other singers to New York, Boston, Providence, Philadelphia, Baltimore, and Washington, among other cities. Her repertory ranged widely, from 18th-century English ballad operas to contemporary English adaptations of Italian works. She received praise for her performances in Gay's *The Beggar's Opera* and an adaptation of Weber's *Der Freischütz*; she was most closely identified, however, with Rossini's *Cenerentola* (adapted by M.R. Lacy), which she introduced to the United States on 24 January 1831 at the Park Theater. Descriptions of her voice attest to its full soprano resonance, extensive range, and flexibility, but remark that its most distinguishing attribute remained an equality and evenness of tone. A considerable beauty, Austin's vocal expertise was only diminished by her limited acting ability. Her prestige began to decline after the arrival in the United States of Mary Anne Paton Wood in late 1833; in May 1835 she and Berkeley returned to England and retired from the stage.

BIBLIOGRAPHY

"Mrs. Austin," *The Euterpeiad: An Album of Music, Poetry & Prose*, i (Boston, MA, 1830), 147

"Mrs. Austin," *American Musical Journal* (April 1835), 114–5

F.C. Wemyss: *Twenty-Six Years of the Life of an Actor and Manager* (New York, 1847)

K.K. Preston: *Opera on the Road: Traveling Opera Troupes in the United States, 1825–60* (Urbana, 1993)

J. Graziano, ed.: *Italian Opera in English: "Cinderella" (1831), Adapted by M. Rophino Lacy from Gioacchino Rossini's "La Cenerentola"* (New York, 1994)

S.W. Rogers: "The Tremont Theatre and the Rise of Opera in Boston, 1827–1847," *OQ*, xvi/3 (2000), 363–96

WILLIAM BROOKS/KATHERINE K. PRESTON/KIMBERLY GREENE

Austin, Gene [Lucas, Lemuel Eugene] (*b* Gainesville, TX, 24 June 1900; *d* Palm Springs, CA, 24 Jan 1972). Singer, composer, and pianist. He received his stage name from his stepfather. He began his career by joining the circus at the age of 15 and soon thereafter reached New Orleans where he played piano in parlor houses. After military service in World War I, he met Roy Bergere, with whom he subsequently toured in a vaudeville duo. Austin began writing songs and moved on to work for Mills Music in New York as a demo singer. After he made his first recording for Victor Records (1924), his crooning style, influenced by African American work songs and cowboy singers, came to the attention of the producer Nat Shilkret, who teamed him with Aileen Stanley for a duet, "When my Sugar Walks down the Street" (Vic., 1925). Within months Austin became a star in his own right with hit songs such as "Ain't she sweet" and "Five Foot Two, Eyes of Blue," and continued this streak throughout the 1920s with "My Blue Heaven" and "Girl of My Dreams," among others. Austin then started his own music company, recorded with Fats Waller, and performed extensively on radio and in concert. In the early 1930s he also appeared in several Hollywood films as a singing cowboy. His singing style soon became outdated, and he began other ventures, including starting nightclubs in New Orleans, Hollywood, and Las Vegas, as well as traveling shows. He revived his singing career in the 1950s, when he appeared on television and in nightclubs. Austin composed or copyrighted 85 songs. His last appearance was at a New Year's Eve concert in Miami in 1972.

BIBLIOGRAPHY

M.R. Pitts and F. Hoffman: *The Rise of the Crooners* (Lanham, MD, 2002)

JEFFEREY WANSER

Austin, John Turnell (*b* Podington, Bedfordshire, UK, 16 May 1869; *d* Hartford, CT, 17 Sept 1948). Organ builder of English birth. His father, Jonathan, was a gentleman farmer who is also credited with having built three small organs, one of which is still in use in a church in Denton, England. J.T. Austin immigrated to the United States in 1889, and was employed by the organ firm of Farrand & Votey in Detroit, where he soon became foreman. There he first conceived a radically different system of organ construction called the "universal windchest" system, which consisted of an individual pipe-valve chest, the lower portion of which was a walk-in air chamber with a regulator. Pipe valves were attached to thin wooden trace for each note, operated by a small pneumatic motor. Stop action was first by means of sliders; later a pivoting fulcrum affecting the valves was utilized. Farrand & Votey appear to have shown no interest in Austin's design, and in 1893, joined by his brother Basil G. (1874–1958), he moved to the Clough & Warren firm in Detroit, where the first organ was built to his new design (patented the same year), followed by several others. In 1898 a three-manual organ, built to Austin's design, was installed in the Fourth Congregational Church of Hartford, CT, which attracted the interest of some prominent organists. The following year the Clough & Warren factory burned down, and Austin briefly moved to Boston to complete one of their organs there. However, encouraged by some local businessmen, he removed to Hartford, where the Austin Organ Company was established in 1900.

Business thrived there, and Austin patented his all-electric console in 1913, followed by a self-player mechanism in 1914. His mechanical ingenuity was not limited to organ mechanisms; he also designed many labor-saving machines for his factory. During this early period some notable organs were built, including that in City Hall Auditorium, Portland, ME (1912), the "outdoor" organ in Balboa Park, San Diego, CA (1914), Eastman Theatre, Rochester, NY (1919), and Bushnell Memorial Hall, Hartford, CT (1929). In 1937 John T. Austin retired; the firm was reorganized as Austin

Organs, Inc., and his nephew Frederic B. Austin became president. In 1949 Richard J. Piper, a voicer from the Willis firm of London, joined Austin as Vice President and Tonal Director, bringing a more progressive tonal outlook to the firm's work. One of his first projects was the organ in St. John's Episcopal Church, West Hartford, CT (1950), given in memory of John T. Austin. During the 1960s, several large organs were built for New York City, including that for Fifth Avenue Presbyterian Church (1961). In 1973 Frederic retired, and was succeeded by his son Donald B. Austin. Among innovations in this period was the introduction of a series of small unified organs. David A.J. Broome, formerly of the British Walker firm, was Tonal Director from 1978 to 1999, and from 1998 to 2005 Kimberlee Austin was president. Notable organs of the later 20th century include those for Trinity College, Hartford, Connecticut (1972), Holy Family Cathedral, Tulsa, Oklahoma (1984) and Forbidden City Concert Hall, Beijing, China (2000). The company closed for a short time in 2005, but resumed operation in 2006 after being purchased by Richard Taylor and Michael Fazio.

BIBLIOGRAPHY

"American Organ Builders of Today: Austin Organ Company," *Diapason*, xvi/1 (1924), 6

"John Turnell Austin and His Contribution to the Modern Organ," *Diapason*, xxxiv/8 (1943), 6

W.H. Barnes: *The Contemporary American Organ* (Glen Rock, NJ, 8/1964)

R.E. Coleberd: "John Turnell Austin: Mechanical Genius of the Pipe Organ," *The American Organist*, xlix/9 (1966), 14

O. Ochse: *Austin Organs* (Richmond, VA, 2001)

"Austin Organ Milestones," *Diapason*, xcviii/2 (2007), 1

BARBARA OWEN

Austin, Larry (Don) (*b* Duncan, OK, 12 Sept 1930). Composer. A talented trumpet player from Vernon, Texas, Austin played jazz in the first One O'clock Lab Band at North Texas State University, and later served in the Fourth US Army Band based in San Antonio. He studied with Violet Archer (North Texas State University), DARIUS MILHAUD (Mills College) and ANDREW IMBRIE (University of California, Berkeley). Austin's 38-year academic career included positions at University of California-Berkeley, University of California, Davis, University of South Florida, and the University of North Texas (formerly NTSU). He taught composition and other subjects as diverse as marching band and advanced computer music research.

In the 1960s he was associated with Karlheinz Stockhausen and David Tudor, and also formed an extended association and friendship with John Cage. While a member of the faculty at UC Davis, he co-founded, edited, and published the journal *SOURCE: Music of the Avant Garde*. He first gained recognition as a composer through a television broadcast of his *Improvisations for Orchestra and Jazz Soloists* (1961), presented by Leonard Bernstein and the New York Philharmonic. Since that time, Austin's works have been performed and recorded by the Boston SO, National SO, and many other North American and European ensembles. He also held many residencies (Rome, Bellagio, Birmingham, and York in the UK, Tokyo, MacDowell Colony) and received numerous commissions.

He founded and directed experimental music centers at the University of South Florida (System Complex for Studio and Performing Arts, 1972–8) and the University of North Texas (Center for Experimental Music and Intermedia, 1978–96), and co-founded and served as president of the Consortium to Distribute Computer Music. He also served as President of the International Computer Music Association (1990–94).

Austin's works from the 1960s embrace an "open style" reflecting a fascination with group improvisation. Several of his works are based on studies of Ives's compositional sketches, including his complete realization of Ives's *Universe Symphony*, recorded in 1994. Later compositions employ a combination of acoustic and digital sound sources, octophonic sound diffusion, and intricate compositional algorithms, such as fractals. In 1996 Austin was the first American to be awarded the *Magistère* title at the International Electroacoustic Music Competition, Bourges, France, for his composition *Blues Ax* and honoring his 30 years of leadership in electro-acoustic music. After his academic retirement that same year, he continued an active composing career.

WORKS

(*selective list*)

Orch and large ens: Fantasy on a Theme by Berg, jazz orch, 1960; Improvisations for Orchestra and Jazz Soloists, 1961; In Memoriam JFK, sym. wind ens, 1964; Catharsis: Open Style, large and small improvisation ens, tape, cond., 1965; Open Style, pf, orch, 1965; Agape Set, jazz orch, 1971; Quadrants: Event/Complex No.1, sym. wind ens, tape, 1972; Protoforms: Fractals for 'Cello Choir and Computer Band, 13 vc, tape, 1981; Life Pulse Prelude, 20 perc, 1984; Clarini!, 20 tpt, 1985; Sinfonia Concertante: A Mozartean Episode, chbr orch, recorded narrative, tape, 1986; C. Ives: Universe Symphony [realized and completed from Ives's sketches], orch, 21 perc, 1993

Chbr and solo inst: Homecoming, cant., S, tpt, t sax, pf, db, drum set, 1959; Pf Variations, 1960; A Broken Consort, fl, cl, tpt, hn, pf, db, drum set, 1962; Qt in Open Style, str qt, 1964; Current, cl, pf, 1964; Pf Set in Open Style, 1964; Continuum: Open Style for a Number of Instruments, various insts, 1964; Second Fantasy on Ives's Universe Symphony "The Heavens," cl, va, pf/cel, perc, tape, 1976; Charley's Cornet, cornet, pf, 1976; Canadian Coastlines: Canonic Fractals for Musicians and Computer Band, tape, str, wind, perc, kbds, vv, 1981; art is self-alteration is Cage is…, 4 db, 1982; Beachcombers, 4 perf, live elecs, tape, 1983; Tango Violento, pf, 1984; Violet's Invention, pf, 1988; Variations…beyond Pierrot, S, fl/pic, cl/b cl, vn, vc, pf, elecs/tape, 1995; Ottuplo!, real and virtual str qts, 2000

Solo with tape or elecs: Changes: Open Style, trbn, tape, 1965; Quadrants: Event/Complex Nos. 3–4, 6–11, tape, one or more from vn, pf, vc, fl, va, perc, trbn, db, 1973–7; Catalogo Sonoro—"Narcisso," va, tape, 1978; Sonata Concertante, pf, tape, 1984; Montage: Themes and Variations, vn, tape, 1985; La Barbara: The Name/The Sounds/The Music, 1v, cptr, 1991; AccidentsTwo: Sound Projections, pf, tape/elecs, 1992; Quadrants: Event/Complex No. 4, pf, Yamaha Disclavier, tape/elecs, 1972, rev. 1994; BluesAx, s/a sax, tape/elecs, 1995; Singing!…the music of my own time, Bar., cptr, 1996–8; ¡Tárogató!, tárogató (opt. cl/s sax/b cl), dancer(s), tape, 1998; Threnos, 1/2/4/8 b cl, virtual b cl, cptr, 2002; Tableaux: Convolutions on a Theme, a sax, cptr, 2003; Adagio: Convolutions on a Theme by Mozart, cl, cptr, 2005; Les Flûtes de Pan: Hommage à Debussy, fl/pic, cptr, op. dancers, 2006; Redux, vn, cptr, 2007; ReduxTwo, pf, cptr, 2008

Tape or cptr music: Caritas, 1969; Quartet Three, 1971; Quartet Four, 1971; Primal Hybrid, 1972; Quadrants, 1972; Nineteen seventy-six, 1973; Phoenix, 1974; Protoforms: Fractals for Computer Band, 1980;

*Stars, 1982; SoundPoemSet: Pauline Oliveros/Jerry Hunt/Morton Subotnick/David Tudor, 1991; ¡Rompido!, 1993; Shin-Edo: CityscapeSet, 1996; Djuro's Tree, cptr, 1997; Williams [re]Mix[ed], cptr, 2000; John Explains, cptr, 2007

Vocal: Quadrants: Event/Complex No.2, chorus, tape, 1972; Catalogo Voce, B-Bar., tape, slides, 1979; Ceremony, S/T, org, 1980; Euphonia: A Tale of the Future (op, T. Holliday, based on Berlioz: *Evenings with the Orchestra*), 1982; Euphonia 2344 (intermezzo, 5 scenes, T. Holliday), 1988; Transmission Two: The Great Excursion, chorus, vc, pf/kbd, perc, tape, 1990

Music theatre and multimedia: Roma: A Theater Piece in Open Style, improvisation ens, tape, 1965; Bass: A Theater Piece in Open Style, db, tape, film, 1966; The Maze: A Theater Piece in Open Style, 3 perc, dancer, tapes, machines, projections, 1966; Accidents, theater piece, electronically prepared pf, 1967; Prelude and Postlude to Plastic Surgery, pf/ kbd, film, tape, 1971; Tableaux Vivants, 4–6 perf, tape, slides, 1973, rev. 1981; Roma-Due: Sounds and Movements, improvisation ens, dancers, tape, 1965, rev. 1997; First Fantasy on Ives's Universe Symphony, "The Earth," 4 tpt, 2 hn, 4 trbn, 2 tuba, nar, tape, 1975; Ludus Fractalis, video, 1984

Principal publishers: Borik Press; Composer Performer (Source); Larry Austin Music; MJQ; Peer-Southern

WRITINGS

with T. Clark: *Learning to Compose: Modes, Materials, and Models of Musical Invention* (Dubuque, IA, 1989)

"The Realization and First Complete Performances of Ives's Universe Symphony," *Ives Studies*, ed. P. Lambert (Cambridge, UK, 1998), 179–232

BIBLIOGRAPHY

CC (T. Clark); *EwenD*; *VintonD*

A. Kennedy: "Sound-Script Relations and the New Notation," *Artform*, xii/1 (1973), 38–44

D. Ernst: *The Evolution of Electronic Music* (New York, 1976)

W. Zimmermann: *Desert Plants: Conversations with 23 American Musicians* (Vancouver, 1976)

T. Clark: "Duality of Process and Drama," *PNM*, xxiii (1984), 112–25

T. Clark: "Coasts: on the Creative Edge," *Computer Music Journal*, xiii/1 (1989), 21–35

Z. Lyman: "Completing Ives's Universe symphony: an interview with Larry Austin," *American Music*, xxvi/4 (2008), 442–73

THOMAS CLARK

Austin, Lovie [Calhoun, Cora] (*b* Chattanooga, TN, 19 Sept 1887; *d* Chicago, IL, 10 July 1972). Jazz and blues pianist, composer, bandleader, arranger, and music director. After studying at Roger Williams University (Nashville) and Knoxville College, she performed on the TOBA circuit and toured accompanying her second husband Buster Austin. In the early 1920s Austin moved to Chicago, where for almost 20 years she directed shows for touring stage performers as the music director and bandleader at the Monogram and Joyland theaters. From 1923 to 1926 she also led the house band at Paramount Records, accompanying blues singers and making instrumental recordings featuring such jazz musicians as Tommy Ladnier, Al Wynn, Johnny Dodds, and Jimmy O'Bryant. After working in a defense plant during World War II, Austin returned to music, working in dancing schools. Her final recording, in 1961 for Riverside Records, was a reunion with her friend Alberta Hunter and several musicians she had previously worked with in Chicago.

As an African American woman respected not only for her organizational and arranging abilities but also for her piano playing, Austin was remarkable for her time. Mary Lou Williams cited her as a prime influence and singers such as Ma Rainey, Ida Cox, and Hunter profited by her direction in the studio as well as her ability to transcribe their original songs and get them copyrighted and published. Her own songs "Downhearted Blues" (composed with Hunter and recorded by Hunter and Bessie Smith) and "Bleeding Heart Blues" (recorded by Smith) are excellent examples of classic blues.

BIBLIOGRAPHY

S. Placksin: *American Women in Jazz: 1900 to the Present: their Words, Lives, and Music* (New York, 1982, London, 1985 as *Jazzwomen, 1900 to the Present: their Words, Lives, and Music*)

L. Dahl: *Stormy Weather: the Music and Lives of a Century of Jazz Women* (New York, 1984)

JOHN L. CLARK JR.

Austin, William W(eaver) (*b* Lawton, OK, 18 Jan 1920, *d* Ithaca, NY, 15 March 2000). Musicologist. He was educated at Harvard University, where he received the BA in 1939, the MA in 1940, and the PhD in 1951; his professors included WALTER PISTON, A.T. DAVISON, and A. Tillman Merritt. Austin began his teaching career at the University of Virginia (1945–7). He taught at Cornell University from 1947 until his retirement in 1990; in 1969 he was elected a Fellow of the American Academy of Arts and Sciences. He was a visiting professor at Princeton University during the academic year 1957–8. In 1970 he became a member of the Gesellschaft für Musikforschung.

Austin specialized in the music of Russia and the United States in the 19th century, and in the history of 20th-century music. With *Music in the 20th Century* (1966) he contributed a broad yet comprehensive survey of music from 1900 to 1950. The book deals with stylistic and technical developments, aesthetic trends and music as a facet of cultural history. Although his evaluations have been debated, Austin avoided the use of "isms" and similar labeling often used by writers attempting to come to grips with the musical developments of the past 75 years, and he was the first scholar to elevate jazz to a position of first-rank importance in a serious historical study. *"Susanna," "Jeanie," and "The Old Folks at Home"* (1975) is not only a concentrated analysis of Stephen Foster's songs but a highly original and perceptive inquiry into the reasons for their unique durability in American culture from Foster's time to the mid-1970s.

WRITINGS

Harmonic Rhythm in Twentieth-Century Music (diss., Harvard U., 1951)

"Piston's Fourth Symphony: an Analysis," *MR*, xvi (1955), 121–237

"The Music of Robert Palmer," *MQ*, xlii (1956), 35–50

Music in the 20th Century (New York, 1966)

"Susanna," "Jeanie," and "The Old Folks at Home": the Songs of Stephen C. Foster from His Time to Ours (New York, 1975, 2/1987/*R)*

PAULA MORGAN/R

Austin City Limits [ACL]. Syndicated music television program. It is the longest-running music performance television program in broadcast history. Recorded at the public station KLRU in Austin, Texas, and housed at the University of Texas, ACL aired its pilot episode, featuring Willie Nelson, in 1975. Nelson's rise to iconic status during the same era ensured the show's auspicious beginning. During more than three decades ACL has evolved from its original focus on Austin's progressive country scene to an eclectic mix of musical genres. In some ways its growing prominence mirrors that of Austin itself, particularly the reputation of its music scene.

The station executive Bill Arhos founded ACL and produced its first few seasons. In its fourth season he turned production over to Terry Lickona, whose musical vision has continued to shape each season. Under the latter's guidance ACL has maintained an artful balance between local acts and musicians from further afield. High quality musicianship and production values have remained constant threads throughout changing trends in programming, notably mainstream country in the 1980s and Americana in the 1990s. Early seasons included performances by Taj Mahal and Tom Waits. Guests during the 1980s ranged from B.B. King to Bonnie Raitt, and Flaco Jimenez to Queen Ida. Los Lobos and the Dirty Dozen Brass Band appeared in the 1990s, as did Nanci Griffith and John Prine. In the 2010s ACL featured a wide variety of styles, from Coldplay to Damian Marley, the Gourds to Miranda Lambert, the Decemberists to K'Naan.

In 2001 KLRU joined with the Austin-based company Capital Sports & Entertainment to create the ACL Music Festival. This successful three-day event spawned C3 Presents, an outdoor event company that now licenses the name and logo from the station. Another new era for ACL began in February 2011, with the opening of ACL Live at the Moody Theater in downtown Austin, the site for television recordings and dozens of concerts each year.

TRACEY E.W. LAIRD

Autoharp. A box zither of German origin, popular in the United States from the late 19th century. The player strums the strings with fingers, a fingerpick or a plectrum; damper bars controlled by buttons damp all the strings except those that sound the required chord. The basis of the instrument is a box, about 12" long, 18" broad and 1.2" deep. The strings, which are graded in thickness, are attached to wrest-pins; they number between 15 and 50, or even more, and the range is between two and four octaves (*C–c‴*). Some instruments are diatonic, others partly or fully chromatic. A 15-string instrument is likely to have only three bars, giving the tonic, the subdominant and the dominant 7th of C major. A nine-bar instrument may offer a selection of chords, including these basic chords in two keys and a range of related chords. Autoharps used for folk music may offer fewer chords per key, but a wider range of keys. Some manufacturers supply spare, blank bars for the player to fit as desired. The circle of 5ths, normal on other extended diatonic instruments such as the accordion, the zither, and the dulcimer, is unusual on the autoharp. Examples of autoharps that are fully chromatic or include frets have also been manufactured.

According to Sachs, the autoharp was invented by C.A. Gütter of Markneukirchen. The first American patent was granted in 1882 to Charles F. Zimmermann, a German who had immigrated to Philadelphia in 1865. He had already devised a new system of musical notation using "tone numbering" for use with the accordion, and the development of the autoharp was a logical step. He began production in 1885 and sold 50,000 instruments within three years (see Moore). He offered a wide range of models, from one with 21 strings and three bars to a "concert harp" with 49 strings, six bars, slides and levers, enabling it to produce 72 different chords. Zimmermann sold his controlling interest in the company in 1892 to Alfred Dolge, who moved the factory to Dolgeville, New York; by the mid-1890s Dolge was manufacturing 3000 autoharps each week, which were sold by door-to-door salesmen and through sale catalogs as well as by local music shops. He produced nearly half a million instruments, but the advent of the gramophone and commercial factors led to the firm's failure in 1898. The instrument was also known in Britain.

Instruction manuals and collections of music for the autoharp (e.g. *Collection of Popular Figure Music for C.F. Zimmermann's Miniature Autoharp*) were commercially distributed as early as 1885 and helped to promote the instrument as a means of providing rhythmic accompaniment to a simple melody or to singing. In this style of playing, the autoharp was laid flat on a table or stand, and a melody plucked with the first finger while chords were strummed with the thumb and first finger. This method required little musical or technical skill and the autoharp thus became known as the "idiot zither." A playing style which emphasized the melodic capabilities of the instrument was developed in the mid-1890s and introduced to the public by Aldis Gery, who toured with the Victor Herbert Band. At about the same time, the instrument was introduced to the southern Appalachian mountain region through mail-order catalogs, traveling salesmen and "home" missionaries.

Around 1910, the autoharp enjoyed a further phase of popularity in the United States, when it came to be used in social gatherings, by travelling preachers, and for therapy by hospital workers. The Pianoharp Company of Boston obtained the right to manufacture autoharps in 1910; in 1926, this company merged with Oscar Schmidt International, of Jersey City. Schmidt's instruments were modeled on Zimmermann's less complex ones. Fretted Industries, of Illinois, bought the firm of Oscar Schmidt in 1978, and continues to manufacture the instruments, as do a number of German firms. The autoharp is still used, especially in schools, for the teaching of rudimentary harmony.

A tradition of using the autoharp for folk music developed, largely independently of the popular tradition, in the Appalachian mountains at the turn of the century. The early style used for folk music was similar to the popular style of the 1880s in that the instrument was laid on the lap or on a table. A noted exponent was Ernest ("Pop") Stoneman, who made the first recording of the instrument in 1924, and developed a style consisting of short strokes in strict rhythm rather than long strokes in free rhythm, bringing forefinger and thumb together in a pinching action; this style allowed for greater agility. The lap playing style was further disseminated in the southern mountain tradition and in early recordings of country music by Sara Carter (of the celebrated Carter family singing group), who used the autoharp for rhythmic accompaniment. Maybelle Carter developed a third style of playing in the 1950s, plucking the strings in the middle instead of close to the hitchpins, and playing erect, holding the instrument vertically against her chest, thus permitting greater flexibility in the use of microphones and in plucking styles. In the popular style, where melodic movement is slow, the player arpeggiates upwards from the bass note, finishing on the melody note; in the folk style, where dance music, fiddle tunes and fast moving songs may be performed, the arpeggiation is downwards from the melody note (the bass may be provided by a supporting instrument or even omitted). The folksong revival of the 1960s inspired players to use the autoharp for harmonic and rhythmic accompaniment or as a melody instrument. Since then, innovations in tuning, playing styles, and repertory have resulted in the expansion of the instrument's versatility and increased its musical potential. Recent techniques include the use of metal or plastic plectra or metal thimbles. The instrument has been used in rhythm-and-blues, folk-rock, Caribbean, flamenco, jazz, Celtic, and New Age styles. Electric autoharps have also been made.

In the 1980s a network of autoharp aficionados developed through magazines and newsletters, including *Autoharpoholic* (1980–93), *Autoharp Teachers Digest*, *Autoharp Quarterly* (1989–) and *Autoharp Clearinghouse* (1989–2000). Competitions, clubs, and festivals provide public venues for performance on the autoharp, and there are many workshops on old-time and American folk music where instruction on the instrument is offered.

BIBLIOGRAPHY

C. Sachs: *Real-Lexicon der Musikinstrumente* (Berlin, 1913/*R*, 2/1964)

M. Seeger: disc notes, *Mountain Music Played on the Autoharp*, Folkways FA 2365 (1962)

A.D. Moore: "The Autoharp: its Origin and Development from a Popular to a Folk Instrument," *New York Folklore Quarterly*, xix (1963), 261–74

H. Taussig: *Folkstyle Autoharp* (New York, 1967)

B. Blackley: *The Autoharp Book* (Brisbane, CA, 1983)

T. Schroeder: "In the Beginning: Five Year Review," *Autoharpoholic*, xii (1991), 6

I. Stiles: "The True History of the Autoharp," *Autoharp Quarterly*, iii (1991), 3–6

DAVID KETTLEWELL/LUCY M. LONG/R

Autry, Gene [Orvon Grover] (*b* Tioga, TX, 29 Sept 1907; *d* Los Angeles, CA, 2 Oct 1998). Country-music and popular singer, songwriter, and actor. He began his career singing on the radio station KVOO in Tulsa, while working as a relief telegraph operator for the Frisco Railroad. In October 1929 he went to New York to make his first recordings, which were much in the style of Jimmie Rodgers, for RCA Victor and several small independent labels; these were released under the name Gene Autry and led to a contract with the American Record Corporation, which was later taken over by the Columbia Broadcasting System; Autry's recordings would then be issued by the Columbia Recording Co. In 1931 Autry had his first hit with "Silver Haired Daddy of Mine." He moved to Chicago in 1932 to star on radio station WLS. There his singing-cowboy persona was developed on the *National Barn Dance* and his own radio program, as well as through his songbooks and personal appearances. In 1933 he began to focus on cowboy songs like "The Last Round-Up" and "Tumbling Tumbleweeds." On the strength of his radio popularity, he went to Hollywood in 1934, where he became the first fully fledged singing cowboy. He appeared in 93 films, including the first feature-length musical western, *Tumbling Tumbleweeds* (1935). From 1940 to 1956 he was the host of a popular CBS radio show *Melody Ranch*. After serving in the army air corps during World War II, Autry started his own film production company, Flying A Pictures, with distribution by Columbia. In 1950 he was the first major Hollywood star to create his own television program, *The Gene Autry Show*. He began recording seasonal and children's songs, including the original version of "Rudolph the Red-nosed Reindeer" (Columbia, 1949).

Autry developed a number of business interests, including music-publishing companies; a chain of radio and television stations; two record companies, Champion and Republic; and an American League baseball team, the California Angels. By giving country music the image of the singing cowboy to replace the less popular hillbilly stereotype, he did more than any other singer to introduce the genre to a national audience. He was elected to the Country Music Hall of Fame in 1969 and received a Grammy Lifetime Achievement Award in 2009. He is the only person on the Hollywood Walk of Fame with five stars, honoring his success in movies, radio, recording, television, and personal appearances. In 1984 in Los Angeles, he established (building finished in 1988, when it opened) the Museum of Western Heritage, which later expanded and was renamed the Autry National Center of the American West.

BIBLIOGRAPHY

D.B. Green: "Gene Autry," *Singing in the Saddle* (Nashville, 2002), 120

H. George-Warren: *Public Cowboy No. 1: the Life and Times of Gene Autry* (New York, 2007)

HOLLY GEORGE-WARREN

Avalon, Frankie [Avallone, Francis Thomas] (*b* Philadelphia, PA, 8 Sept 1940). Pop vocalist of Italian descent. His career spanned music, film, and television, helping to define the image of the post-war TEEN IDOL. A virtuoso trumpeter, Avalon released instrumental singles early in his career and led a jazz group, Rocco and the Saints, based in Philadelphia. Chancellor Records signed Avalon as a vocalist, aiming to capitalize on his boyish looks. Avalon's singles for Chancellor include "Venus," which spent five weeks at number one on the *Billboard* charts in 1959, and its follow-up, "Why." The smooth vocals and reverberant textures of these recordings defined Avalon's sound. He was first and foremost a ballad singer, and his recordings positioned him as a tame alternative to rock and roll, while his charm and boy-next-door appeal propelled him to fame with middle-class teenage girls.

Avalon made frequent appearances on Dick Clark's television show *American Bandstand* and his first film role was alongside Clark in *Jamboree* (1957). He went on to co-star opposite Annette Funicello in a film franchise produced by American International Pictures that began with *Beach Party* in 1963. Playing on the youthful appeal of Avalon and Funicello, these films were marketed to young audiences and showcased the vocal talents of their two co-stars, as well as those of other guest musical acts, including Dick Dale and the Deltones and Stevie Wonder.

In 1978 Avalon played the Teen Angel in the film *Grease*, a caricature of the teen idol archetype that he helped to create. He has continued to tour and perform teen pop music associated with the 1960s.

BIBLIOGRAPHY

J.R. Parish and M.R. Pitts: *Hollywood Songsters, Singers who Act and Actors who Sing: a Biographical Dictionary* (New York, 2003 [2nd edn of *Hollywood Songsters*])

J. Lanza: *Vanilla Pop: Sweet Sounds from Frankie Avalon to ABBA* (Chicago, 2005)

ALEXANDRA M. APOLLONI

Avant-garde jazz. A term applied to a range of progressive jazz styles originating in the 1950s and early 1960s. Though initially synonymous with Free jazz, much of the music was distinct from that style, engaging structure and organization through composed melodies; predetermined, if shifting, meters and tonalities; and distinctions between soloists and accompanists. Harmonic contexts avoided traditional jazz conventions, and improvisers similarly broke with bebop and post-bop expectations in favor of increasingly blurred divisions between the written and spontaneous. Early proponents, in the mid- to late 1950s, included Cecil Taylor, Lennie Tristano, Jimmy Giuffre, Sun Ra, and Ornette Coleman. John Coltrane's growing body of experimental work became a major influence during the 1960s as the movement acquired momentum and broader awareness. Other advocates during this period included his wife, Alice Coltrane, fellow saxophonists Archie Shepp, Pharoah Sanders, and Albert Ayler, and emerging European improvisers such as Derek Bailey and Evan Parker. Jazz's avant-garde drew parallels with counterparts from the Western art tradition as well as the Black Arts literary movement. The poet Amiri Baraka, in particular, championed its importance and made two politically controversial, spoken word tracks, with the New York Art Quartet ("Black Dada Nihilismus," 1964, ESP) and Sonny Murray ("Black Art," 1965, Jihad). Members of the Association for the Advancement of Creative Musicians, including Anthony Braxton, Muhal Richard Abrams, Roscoe Mitchell, Lester Bowie, and the Art Ensemble of Chicago, were proponents and exerted a significant influence through a prolific schedule of recordings and performances. Avant-garde jazz has continued to influence modern musicians.

BIBLIOGRAPHY

E. Jost: *Free Jazz* (Graz, Austria, 1974)

V. Wilmer: *As Serious as your Life: the Story of the New Jazz* (London, 1977, 2/1992)

E. Porter: *What is this thing called jazz?* (Berkeley and Los Angeles, 2002), 191–239

I. Anderson: *This is our Music: Free Jazz, the Sixties, and American Culture* (Philadelphia, 2007)

G. Lewis: *A Power Stronger than itself: the AACM and American Experimental Music* (Chicago, 2009)

MARK C. GRIDLEY/BARRY LONG

Avian, Bob [Avedisian, Robert] (*b* New York, NY, 26 Dec 1937). Dancer, choreographer, producer, and director. After simultaneous study at Boston University and the Boston School of Ballet, Avian appeared in a touring production of *West Side Story*. He met Michael Bennett during the show's European tour; they became friends and long-time artistic and business partners. Avian was in *West Side Story* (1960) on Broadway, followed by *Funny Girl* (1964). He was assistant stage manager for *I do! I do!* (1966), then performed in *Henry, Sweet Henry* (1967). Avian collaborated with Bennett for two decades on a remarkable succession of shows. He was assistant choreographer to Bennett for *Promises, Promises* (1968), associate choreographer for *Coco* (1969), *Company* (1970), and *Follies* (1971), and production assistant for the play *Twigs* (1971), which Bennett directed. Avian served as associate choreographer for *Seesaw*, and then as assistant director under Bennett for the play *God's Favorite* (1974). They co-choreographed *A Chorus Line* (1975), for which they won a Tony. Avian played a similar role in Bennett's *Ballroom* (1978, another Tony-winning effort), but also co-produced, and then Avian produced *Dreamgirls* (1981). After Bennett's death in 1987, Avian worked in London as choreographer for *Follies* (1987) and musical stager for *Miss Saigon* (1989) and *Sunset Boulevard* (1993), performing the same role for the latter two shows in New York (1991, 1994). He won an Olivier Award in London for his musical staging of *Martin Guerre* (1996), and later on Broadway did the musical staging for *Putting It Together* (1999) and directed a revival of *A Chorus Line* (2006). After many years of work with Bennett, Avian cannot be noted for a strong personal style, but he has played an important role as a choreographer for major Broadway shows.

BIBLIOGRAPHY

R. Viagas, B. Lee, and T. Walsh: *On The Line: the Creation of* A Chorus Line (New York, 1990)

PAUL R. LAIRD

Avshalomov, Jacob (David) (*b* Tsingtao, China, 28 March 1919). Composer and conductor of Chinese birth; naturalized American; son of the composer Aaron Avshalomov. In 1937 he came to the United States, where he studied in Los Angeles with Ernst Toch, at the Eastman School of Music (MA 1942) with Bernard Rogers, among others, and at Tanglewood with AARON COPLAND (1947). He became a naturalized American citizen in 1944, and from 1946 to 1954 he taught at Columbia University, where he conducted the university chorus and orchestra in the American premieres of Bruckner's Mass in D minor, Tippett's *A Child of our Time* and Handel's *The Triumph of Time and Truth*. In 1954 he began a 41-year tenure as conductor of the Portland (Oregon) Junior SO (later the Portland Youth PO), the nation's first youth orchestra. A number of recordings, six international tours, and praise from New York and European audiences followed. He served on the National Council of the Humanities (1968–74), the NEA's Music Planning Section (1974–9), and the Pro Musicis Foundation (1986–92). His compositional style embraces Asian sonorities, Renaissance counterpoint, and Ivesian allusions to American folk music. He has identified *Inscriptions at the City of Brass* (1957) as his most significant work. He received a Guggenheim Fellowship (1951), a New York Music Critic's Circle Award (1953) for *Tom O'Bedlam*, a Naumburg Recording Award (1956) for his *Sinfonietta*, and a Ditson Conductor's Award (1965).

WORKS

Orch: The Taking of T'ung Kuan, *c*1943; Slow Dance, *c*1945; Sinfonietta, *c*1946; Suite from the Plywood Age, unison vv, orch; Phases of the Great Land, *c*1958; Sym. "The Oregon," 1962; The 13 Clocks, 2 nar, orch, 1973; Raptures for Orch on Madrigals of Gesualdo, vv, orch, 1975; Open Sesame!, 1984; Sym. of Songs, 1992; Seasons' Greetings 2009

Choral: How Long, O Lord, cant., A, chorus, orch, *c*1948; Prophecy, SATB, cantor, org, 1948; Tom O'Bedlam (anon. 17th-cent.), SATB, ob, tabor, jingles, *c*1953; Make a Joyful Noise unto the Lord, SATB, (cl, tpt, 2 hn, b trbn, perc)/(org, perc); City upon a Hill (Blake), nar, chorus, liberty bell, orch, *c*1964; Glorious th'Assembled Fires (Sym. no.3), chorus, orch, 1994; Songs in Season, SATB, db, pf, *c*1994; His Fluid Aria, SATB, b cl, *c*2001; Arcana, SATB, tpt, bn, hn, trbn, *c*2006; more than 30 songs for 1v, pf, incl. Songs for Alyce (Dickinson, M. Swenson), 1976

Chamber: 2 Bagatelles, cl, pf; Cues from the Little Clay Cart, chbr ens, arr. orch; Disconsolate Muse, fl, pf; Sonatine, va, pf, *c*1943; Evocations, cl/va, pf, *c*1947, arr. cl, chbr orch; Quodlibet Montagna, tpt, 4 hn, trbn; 3 kbd pieces; Up at Timberline, 16 wind and brass, db, 3 perc, *c*1987; Chintimini Turns, fl, cl, str qt, 2008

MSS in *NYp*

Principal publishers: E.C. Schirmer, Southern

Principal recording companies: CRI, Albany

BIBLIOGRAPHY

EwenD

W. Bergsma: "The Music of Jacob Avshalomov," *ACAB*, iii/3 (1956), 3 [incl. list of works]

C.H. Encell: *Jacob Avshalomov's Works for Chorus and Orchestra: Aspects of Style* (diss., U. of Washington, 1983)

J. Avshalomov and A. Avshalomov: *Avshalomovs' Winding Way* (2002) [incl. list of works]

DAVID STABLER/JAMES BASH

Awards. Prizes for excellence in music can be loosely divided into two categories: honors, for which an individual must be nominated, and competitive awards, for which he or she must apply or in some other way compete. Some awards, such as medals, citations, or membership in certain organizations, are honorary. Others are monetary gifts in the form of grants, fellowships for particular study programs, commissions, promotional funding (management, concert performances, etc.), and similar kinds of subsidy. The following list of honors and competitive awards is selective and with few exceptions includes only those awards that were made on a regular basis in 2010. For other commissioning projects, *see* COOLIDGE, ELIZABETH SPRAGUE; FOUNDATIONS, MUSIC; FREEMAN, BETTY; FROMM MUSIC FOUNDATION; KOUSSEVITZKY FOUNDATIONS; LOUISVILLE ORCHESTRA COMMISSIONING PROJECT; PATRONAGE; and ROCKEFELLER, MARTHA BAIRD.

1. Honors. 2. Competitive awards. (i) Composers. (ii) Performers. (iii) Scholars.

1. HONORS. The honors listed below are ordered alphabetically according to the name of the award or the organization that sponsors it. Date of founding, frequency of presentation, the nature and purpose of the award and categories in which it is given are listed whenever possible; the names of recipients (and in some cases the compositions for which they have been honored) are also listed for some of the more important prizes.

ACADEMY AWARDS, Academy of Motion Picture Arts and Sciences (annually in various categories; music awards 1934–); for achievements in motion pictures. Categories in music include original score and original song, as well as sound editing, and sound mixing. <http://www.oscars.org/>

ACADEMY OF COUNTRY MUSIC AWARDS (annually in various categories, 1964–). Categories include entertainer, female vocalist, male vocalist, vocal group, vocal duo, album, single, song, and video. <http://www.acmcountry.com/home/index.php>

ALICE M. DITSON FUND OF COLUMBIA UNIVERSITY (1940–); Supports performances, recordings, and publications of works by younger American composers and those older American composers who are not widely known.

AMERICAN ACADEMY OF ARTS AND LETTERS. The American Academy of Arts and Letters, founded in 1904 by the National Institute of Arts and Letters (founded 1898), merged with the parent organization in 1976 to form the American Academy and Institute of Arts and Letters. In 1993 the merger was completed with a name change to the American Academy of Arts and Letters; election to the prestigious Academy is by nomination only, and is one of the highest honors accorded for artistic achievement. In 2010, 45 of the 250 members were composers, including J. Adams, S. Adler, T.J. Anderson, D. Argento, M. Babbitt, L. Bassett, R. Beaser, W. Bolcom, M. Bresnick, E. Carter, W. Chou, O. Coleman, J. Corigliano, G. Crumb, M. Davidovsky, D. Del Tredici, C. Floyd, P. Glass, J. Harbison, S. Hartke, K. Husa, B. Jolas, E. Laderman, T. León, F. Lerdahl, P. Lieberson, S.Ran, B. Rands, S. Reich, N. Rorem, C. Rouse, F. Rzewski, G. Schuller, J. Schwantner, S. Sondheim, S. Stucky, A. Read Thomas, F. Thorne, J. Tower, G. Walker, R. Ward, O. Wilson. C. Wuorinen, Y. Wyner, and E.T. Zwilich. With the exception of the Richard Rodgers Awards, all of the music awards listed below are by nomination only. <http://www.artsandletters.org/about.php>

Academy Awards in Music: Four awards of $7500 each given annually to composers, plus another $7500 subsidy for a recording of one work.

Mark Blitzstein Award (established 1965): Award of $5000 given periodically to a composer, lyricist, or librettist for musical theater or operatic works.

Benjamin H. Danks Award (established 2003): Annual prize of $20,000 in rotation to a composer of ensemble works, a playwright, or a writer.

Gold Medal (two annually in rotating categories: music awards 1919–): Recipients in music: M. Babbitt, S. Barber, L. Bernstein, J.A. Carpenter, E. Carter, G.W. Chadwick, A. Copland, W. Damrosch, L. Foss, L. Kirchner, C.M. Loeffler, N. Rorem, G. Schuller, W. Schuman, R. Sessions, S. Sondheim, I. Stravinsky, V. Thomson, H. Weisgall.

Walter Hinrichsen Award (1984–): Established by the C.F. Peters Corporation for publication of a work by a mid-career American composer.

Charles E. Ives Awards, established by Harmony Twichell (Mrs. Charles) Ives for scholarships to young composers. Six scholarships of $7500 and two fellowships of $15,000 are given annually. In 1998, the Academy inaugurated the Charles Ives Living, which gives an American composer $75,000 a year for three years. In 2008, the Academy awarded the inaugural Charles Ives Opera Prize of $50,000, to be given to a composer and a librettist for a recently produced work.

Wladimir and Rhoda Lakon Award (established 1987): Annual award of $5000 to either a composition student or an experienced composer.

Goddard Lieberson Fellowships (one or more annually, 1979–): Established by the CBS Foundation to young composers of "extraordinary gifts." $15,000.

See also Richard Rodgers Production Award under §II, 1 Competitive awards: Composers.

AMERICAN COMPOSERS ALLIANCE LAUREL LEAF AWARD (generally one annually, 1951–): Presented to individuals and organizations in recognition of "distinguished achievement in fostering and encouraging American music." Recipients have included the Juilliard String Quartet, American Music Center, Leonard Slatkin, Minnesota Composers Forum (now known as American Composers Forum), and the Los Angeles Philharmonic New Music Group.

AMERICAN MUSICOLOGICAL SOCIETY http://www.ams.net>.

Alfred Einstein Award (annually, 1967–): Given to a young scholar who is a member of AMS for a musicological article of exceptional merit.

Otto Kinkeldey Award (annually, 1967–): Honors a musicological book of exceptional merit published during the previous year by a scholar who is past the early stages of his or her career.

Lewis Lockwood Award (annually, 2005–): Honors a musicological book of exceptional merit by a scholar in the early stages of his or her career.

Music in American Culture Award (annually, 2009–): Honors a book of exceptional merit that both illuminates some important aspect of the music of the United States and places that music in a rich cultural context.

Claude V. Palisca Award (annually, 2005–): Honors a scholarly edition or translation in the field of musicology deemed to "best exemplify the highest qualities of originality, interpretation, logic and clarity of thought, and communication."

Paul A. Pisk Prize (annually, 1991–): Recognizes the most outstanding scholarly paper read by a graduate student at the AMS annual meeting.

H. Colin Slim Award (annually, 2005–): Recognizes an outstanding musicological article published in the previous year by a scholar beyond the early stages of her or his career.

Ruth A. Solie Award (annually, 2007–): Recognizes a collection of musicological essays of exceptional merit.

Robert M. Stevenson Award (annually, 2004–): Recognizes outstanding scholarship in Iberian music.

Philip Brett Award (annually, 1997–; administered by the LGBTQ Study Group of AMS): Recognizes exceptional musicological work in the field of gay, lesbian, bisexual, transgender/transsexual studies.

See also Noah Greenberg Award under §II, 2 Competitive awards: Performers.

ASCAP: *see* Deems Taylor Awards.

AVERY FISHER ARTIST PROGRAM

Avery Fisher Career Grants (up to five annually): Awarded to talented instrumentalists; since 2004 chamber ensembles are also considered. $25,000.

Avery Fisher Prize, established by Avery Fisher (one or two annually, 1975–): Awarded to an outstanding American instrumentalist nominated by a recommendation board, $75,000; since 2004 chamber ensembles are also considered.

COUNTRY MUSIC ASSOCIATION AWARDS (annually, 1967–): Categories include entertainer, single, album, song, female vocalist, male vocalist, vocal group, vocal duo, instrumental group or band, and instrumentalist. <http://www.cmaawards.com/>

COUNTRY MUSIC HALL OF FAME (1961–): Founded by the Country Music Association and administered since 1964 by the Country Music Foundation to "recognize significant contributions to the advancement of country music by individuals in both the creative and business communities." Plaque and portrait in the Country Music Hall of Fame and Museum (opened in 1967). <http://www.countrymusichalloffame.com/>

DITSON CONDUCTORS AWARD (1945–); Honors conductors for their support of American Music. Recipients have included Howard Hanson, Leonard Bernstein, Eugene Ormandy, Leopold Stokowski, David Zinman, James DePreist, David Robertson, and Robert Spano.

DITSON FUND: *see* Alice M. Ditson Fund of Columbia University.

EDWARD MacDOWELL MEDAL (annually in rotating categories, 1960–): Established to commemorate the 100th anniversary of MacDowell's birth. Medal to a composer, visual artist, or writer.

GERSHWIN PRIZE FOR POPULAR SONG (Library of Congress): "Celebrates the work of an artist whose career reflects lifetime achievement in promoting song as a vehicle of musical expression and cultural understanding." Recipients (to 2010): Paul Simon, Stevie Wonder, and Paul McCartney. <http://www.loc.gov/about/awardshonors/gershwin/>

GILMORE ARTIST AWARD (quadrennially); GILMORE YOUNG ARTIST AWARD (biennially) (established 1989): Pianists of any age are eligible for the former; pianists under the age of 22 for the latter. Nominations are received from anonymous judges for both awards; there is no formal competition. Gilmore Artist award includes cash prize of $300,000; Young Artist Award includes cash prize of $15,000. <http://www.thegilmore.org>

GRAMMY AWARDS: *see* National Academy of Recording Arts and Sciences.

GRAWEMEYER AWARD FOR MUSIC COMPOSITION, administered by the University of Louisville (annually, 1985–): For a work in a large genre (e.g. choral, orchestral, chamber, song cycle, dance, opera, musical theater, extended solo), $100,000.

Winners: 1985: W. Lutosławski (Symphony no.3); 1986: G. Ligeti (*Etudes*); 1987: H. Birtwistle (*Mask of Orpheus*); 1989: C. Ung (*Inner Voices*); 1990: J. Tower (*Silver Ladder*); 1991: J. Corigliano (Symphony no.1); 1992: K. Penderecki (*Adagio*); 1993: K. Husa (Cello Concerto); 1994: T. Takemtisu (*Fantasma/Cantos*); 1995: J. Adams (Violin Concerto); 1996: I. Tcherpenin (Double Concerto); 1997: S. Bainbridge (*Ad Ora Incerta*); 1998: T. Dun (*Marco Polo*); 2000: T. Adès (*Asyla*); 2001: P. Boulez (*Sur Incises*); 2002: A.J. Kernis (*Colored Field*); 2003: K. Saariaho (*L'amour de loin*); 2004: U. Chin (Violin Concerto); 2005: G. Tsontakis (Violin Concerto no.2); 2006: G. Kurtág (*... concertante... op.42*; 2007: S. Currier (*Static*); 2008: P. Lieberson (*Neruda Songs*); 2009: B. Dean (*The Art of Letter Writing*). <http://www.grawemeyer.org/music/>

KENNEDY CENTER HONORS (annually, 1978–): Honorary awards to outstanding artists. Recipients in music include R. Rodgers, M. Anderson, A. Rubinstein (1978); E. Fitzgerald, A. Copland (1979); L. Bernstein, L. Price (1980); Count Basie, R. Serkin (1981); B. Goodman, E. Ormandy (1982); F. Sinatra, V. Thomson (1983); L. Horne, G. C. Menotti, I. Stern (1984), F. Loewe, B. Sills (1985); Y. Menuhin, R. Charles (1986); P. Como, N. Milstein (1987); A Schneider (1988); H. Belafonte, W. Schuman (1989); D. Gillespie, J. Styne, R. Stevens (1990); R. Acuff, R. Shaw (1991); L. Hampton, M. Rostropovich (1992); S. Sondheim, G. Solti, M. Williams (1993); A. Franklin, P. Seeger (1994); B.B. King, M. Horne (1995); B. Carter, J. Cash (1996); B. Dylan, J. Norman (1997); J. Kander, W. Nelson, A. Previn (1998); V. Borge, S. Wonder (1999); C. Berry, P. Domingo (2000); V. Cliburn, Q. Jones, L. Pavarotti (2001); J. Levine, C. Rivera, P. Simon (2002); J. Brown, L. Lynn, I. Perlman (2003); E. John, J. Sutherland, J. Williams (2004); T. Bennett, T. Turner (2005); A.L. Webber, Z. Mehta, D. Parton, S. Robinson (2006); D. Ross, L. Fleischer, B. Wilson (2007); G. Jones, B. Streisand, R. Daltrey, P. Townsend (2008); D. Brubeck, G. Bumbry, B. Springsteen (2009); J. Herman, P. McCartney, (2010). <http://www.kennedy-center.org/programs/specialevents/honors/index.cfm>

LAUREL LEAF AWARD: *see* American Composers Alliance Laurel Leaf Award.

LIEBERSON FELLOWSHIP: *see* American Academy of Arts and Letters, Goddard Lieberson Fellowship.

MacARTHUR FELLOWS PROGRAM, John D. and Catherine D. MacArthur Foundation (1981–): "Awards unrestricted fellowships to talented individuals who have shown extraordinary originality and dedication in their creative pursuits and a marked capacity for self-direction. There are three criteria for selection of Fellows: exceptional creativity, promise for important future advances based on a track record of significant accomplishment, and potential for the fellowship to facilitate subsequent creative work." currently $500,000 to cover a period of five years. <http://www.macfound.org/>

MacDOWELL MEDAL: see Edward MacDowell Medal.

MUSIC LIBRARY ASSOCIATION: <http://www.musiclibraryassoc.org/awards.aspx?id=83>

Publication Prizes (annually, 1977–): Vincent H. Duckles Award for best book-length bibliography or other research tool in music; Richard S. Hill Award for best article-length bibliography, article on music librarianship, or similar work; and Eva Judd O'Meara Award for best book or music review published in *Notes*.

MLA Citation. Awarded for distinguished service in music librarianship over the course of a career.

Special Achievement Award. Recognizes extraordinary service to the profession of music librarianship over a relatively short period of time.

See also §II, 3 Competitive awards: Scholars

NASHVILLE SONGWRITERS HALL OF FAME (annually, 1968–): Certificate of achievements, etc., to songwriters. Inducts a minimum of three new members each year. <http://www.nashvillesongwriters-foundation.com/home.aspx>

NATIONAL ACADEMY OF RECORDING ARTS AND SCIENCES: <http://www.grammy.com>

Grammy Awards (annually in numerous categories, 1958–): Nominations solicited from Academy members (singers, songwriters, producers, and others active in the recording field) and record companies. Categories include record, album, song, new artist, classical album, and opera recording.

Grammy Legend Award (1990–): Recognizes individuals or groups for ongoing contributions and influence in the recording field.

Lifetime Achievement Awards: Recognizes performers "whose achievements with the recording field over a period of many years have been deemed exceptionally outstanding."

Grammy Hall of Fame Award (1973–): Recognizes recordings of "lasting, qualitative or historical significance" released before the inauguration of the Grammy Awards.

Technical Grammy Award: Recognizes individuals and/or companies who have made contributions of outstanding technical significance to the recording field.

Trustees Awards: Recognizes "individuals who, during their careers in music, have made significant contributions, other than performance, to the field of recording."

Latin Grammy Awards (2000–): Recognizes artistic and technical achievements in recordings of Latin music.

Latin Grammy Hall of Fame Award (2001–): Honors "early recordings of lasting qualitative or historical significance that were released more than 25 years ago."

NATIONAL MEDAL OF ARTS: *see* National Endowment for the Arts, National Medal of Arts

NATIONAL ENDOWMENT FOR THE ARTS (NEA)

Jazz Masters Fellowships (established 1982), sponsored by the NEA: to honor "living legends who have made exceptional contributions to the advancement of jazz." <http://www.nea.gov/honors/jazz/index.html>

National Medal of Arts: Established by Congress in 1984, upon the recommendation of President Ronald Reagan and the President's Committee on the Arts and the Humanities for the purpose of honoring artists and patrons of the arts. The Congress authorized the President to award no more than 12 medals each year "to individuals or groups who, in the President's judgment, are deserving of special recognition by reason of their outstanding contributions to the excellence, growth, support and availability of the arts in the United States." <http://www.nea.gov/honors/medals/medalists_year.html>

NEA Opera Honors (2008–): Honors "visionary creators, performers, and other interpreters who have made a lasting impact..." Recipients have included J. Adams, F. Corsaro, C. Floyd, M. Horne, L. Price, J. Rudel, and J. Levine.

OSCARS *see* Academy Awards.

PULITZER PRIZE, Columbia University (annually, 1943–; originally the Pulitzer Prize Music Scholarship, 1917–42, established by Joseph Pulitzer): To an American composer for a "distinguished musical composition...in any of the larger forms, including chamber, orchestral, choral, opera, song, dance, or other forms of musical theater, which has had its first performance in the United States during the previous year," $10,000. Nominations are evaluated by juries in each field. Recipients: W. Schuman (*A Free Song*, 1943), H. Hanson (Symphony no.4, 1944), A. Copland (*Appalachian Spring*, 1945), L. Sowerby (*Canticle of the Sun*, 1946), C. Ives (Symphony no.3, 1947), W. Piston (Symphony no.3, 1948), V. Thomson (*Louisiana Story*, film score, 1949), G.C. Menotti (*The Consul*, musical drama, 1950), D. Moore (*Giants in the Earth*, opera, 1951), G. Kubik (Symphony concertante, 1952), Q. Porter (Concerto concertante, 1954), Menotti (*The Saint of Bleecker Street*, opera, 1955), E. Toch (Symphony no.3, 1956), N. Dello Joio (*Meditations on Ecclesiastes*, 1957), S. Barber (*Vanessa*, opera, 1958), J. La Montaine (Piano Concerto, 1959), E. Carter (String Quartet no.2, 1960), W. Piston (Symphony no.7, 1961), R. Ward (*The Crucible*, opera, 1962), S. Barber (Piano Concerto, 1963), L. Bassett (Variations, orch, 1966), L. Kirchner (String Quartet no.3, 1967), G. Crumb (*Echoes of Time and the River*, 1968), K. Husa (String Quartet no.3, 1969), C. Wuorinen (*Time's Encomium*, 1970), M. Davidovsky (*Synchronisms*, no.6, 1971), J. Druckman (*Windows*, 1972), E. Carter (String Quartet no.3, 1973), D. Martino (*Notturno*, 1974), D. Argento (*From the Diary of Virginia Woolf*, 1975), N. Rorem (*Air Music*, 1976), R. Wernick (*Visions of Wonder and Terror*, 1977), M. Colgrass (*Déjà vu*, 1978), J. Schwantner (*Aftertones of Infinity*, 1979), D. Del Tredici (*In Memory of a Summer Day*, 1980), R. Sessions (Concerto for Orchestra, 1982), E.T. Zwilich (Three Movements for Orchestra, 1983), B. Rands (*Canti del sole*, 1984), S. Albert (*RiverRun*, 1985); G. Perle (*Wind Quintet IV*, 1986); J. Harbison (*The Flight Into Egypt*, 1987); W. Bolcom (*12 New Etudes for Piano*, 1988); R. Reynolds (*Whispers Out of Time*, 1989); M. Powell (*Duplicates*, 1990); S. Ran (Symphony, 1991); W. Peterson (*The Face of the Night, the Heart of the Dark*, 1992); C. Rouse (Trombone Concerto, 1993); G. Schuller (*Of Reminiscences and Reflections*, 1994); M. Gould (*Stringmusic*, 1995); G. Walker (*Lilacs*, 1996); W. Marsalis (*Blood on the Fields*, 1997); A.J. Kernis (String Quartet no. 2 'musica instrumentalis', 1998); M. Wagner (Concerto for Flute, Strings, and Percussion, 1999); L. Spratlan (*Life is a Dream*, opera, act 2, concert version, 2000); J. Corigliano (Symphony no.2, 2001); H. Brant (*Ice Field*, 2002); J. Adams (*On the Transmigration of Souls*, 2003); P. Moravec (*Tempest Fantasy*, 2004); S. Stucky (Second Concerto for Orchestra, 2005); Y. Wyner (Piano Concerto "Chiavi in Mano," 2006); O. Coleman (*Sound Grammar*, 2007); D. Lang (*The Little Match Girl Passion*, 2008); S. Reich (*Double Sextet*, 2009); J. Higdon (Violin Concerto, 2010). Special awards and citations to R. Sessions (1974), S. Joplin (1976), M. Babbitt (1982), W. Schuman (1985), G. Gershwin (1998), D. Ellington (1999), T. Monk (2006), J. Coltrane (2007), B. Dylan (2008), and H. Williams (2010). <http://www.pulitzer.org>

SCHUMAN AWARD: *see* William Schuman Award.

SOCIETY FOR AMERICAN MUSIC <http://www.american-music.org/>

Irving Lowens Memorial Book Award (annually, 1983–): Recognizes outstanding book in the field of American music published in prior year.

Irving Lowens Memorial Article Award (annually, 1991–): Recognizes articles deemed to make an outstanding contribution to the study of American music.

Wiley Housewright Dissertation Award (1995–): Recognizes an outstanding dissertation on American music.

Mark Tucker Award for Outstanding Student Paper Presented at Annual Conference (annually, 2002–): Recognizes an outstanding paper delivered by a student at the society's annual conference.

Honorary Membership: (annually, 1979–): Recognizes prominent individuals who have made important contributions to the field of American music.

Lifetime Achievement Award (1991–): Recognizes significant and substantial lifetime achievement in scholarship, performance, teaching, and/or support of American music.

Distinguished Service Citations (1989–): Honors individual members of the Society who have provided exemplary service to the organization and its mission. <http://american-music.org/awards/AwardInformation.php>

SOCIETY FOR ETHNOMUSICOLOGY <http://webdb.iu.edu/sem/scripts/home.cfm>

Awards that recognize scholarly publications in various categories (selected list):

Jaap Kunst Prize (annually): Recognizes the most significant article in ethnomusicology written by a member of the SEM.

Alan Merriam Prize (annually): Recognizes a distinguished English-language monograph in the field of ethnomusicology.

Charles Seeger Prize (annually): Recognizes the most distinguished student paper presented at the SEM Annual Meeting.

Robert M. Stevenson Prize (annually): Honors ethnomusicologists who are also composers by encouraging research, and recognizing a book, dissertation, or paper (published or unpublished), on their compositional oeuvre.

Klaus P. Wachsmann Prize for Advanced and Critical Essays in Organology (biennially): Recognizes a major publication that advances the field of organology through the presentation of new data and by using innovative methods in the study of musical instruments.

WILLIAM SCHUMAN AWARD, Bydale Foundation, administered by the School of the Arts, Columbia University (quadrennially, 1981–): Named for its first recipient William Schuman, the award, in the form of a direct, unrestricted grant of $50,000, is one of the largest to an American composer. In the language of the gift establishing the prize, the purpose of the William Schuman Award is "to recognize the lifetime achievement of an American composer whose works have been widely performed and generally acknowledged to be of lasting significance." Winners have included Schuman, D. Diamond, G. Schuller, M. Babbitt, H. Weisgall, S. Reich, J. Zorn and P. Oliveros.

2. Competitive awards. All the cash prizes in the following selective list of awards to composers, performers, and scholars are of $1000 or more.

(i) Composers.

AMERICAN BANDMASTERS ASSOCIATION SOUSA/OSTWALD AWARD (annually): $5000 prize for new works for concert band.

AMERICAN ACADEMY IN ROME

Residents Program: Program under which distinguished artists and scholars are invited to reside at the academy and serve as advisors to Rome Prize recipients

Rome Prize Fellowships (25–30 annually in various fields including music composition): Stipend and expenses to American composers with a BA degree or the equivalent to enable them to study at the academy. http://www.aarome.org/index.php

ASCAP

ASCAP Foundation Morton Gould Young Composers Award (annually, 1978): Cash awards to American citizens or permanent residents 30 years of age or under.

ASCAP Foundation Rudolf Nissim Prize (annually, 1982–): Cash award to a member of ASCAP for an orchestral work, and sponsorship of the first performance by a major orchestra.

SCI/ASCAP Student composition competition. Sponsored by Society of Composers, Inc. (SCI) and ASCAP (annually): Awards commissions to two student composers. Winners will receive a premiere performance of their work at the SCI National Conference and placement in the SCI CD series.

ASCAP/Lotte Lehmann Foundation Art Song Composition Contest (2005–): Recognizes talented young composers who write for the voice. First Prize is $3500 commission to compose a song cycle for voice and piano, to be published by E.C. Schirmer, and performed in three major American cities. Second Prize ($1000) and Third Prize ($500) will be awarded a commission to compose an art song for voice and piano. Fourth Prize, *The Damien Top Prize* will be a $500 commission to set a poem by Andrée Brunin to be premiered at the 2010 Albert Roussel International Festival in France.

ASCAP/CBDNA Frederick Fennell Prize for The Best Original Score for Concert Band (biennially): ASCAP and the College Band Directors National Association (CBDNA) seek to recognize talented young composers who write music for concert band. The winning composer receives $5,000, and the score is performed at the ensuing CBDNA National Conference.

The ASCAP Foundation Young Jazz Composer Awards. (annually, 2002–): Encourages talented young jazz composers, under the age of 30. Program is supported by The Gibson Foundation and The ASCAP Foundation Bart Howard Fund.

BEARNS PRIZE: *see* Joseph H. Bearns Prize in Music.

BMI FOUNDATION: <http://www.bmifoundation.org/>

BMI Awards to Student Composers (annually, 1951–): Cash awards to American citizens or permanent residents of the Western hemisphere under 26 years of age enrolled in an accredited school or studying with an established teacher, for a musical composition of any instrumentation, style, or length.

Charlie Parker Jazz Composition Prize (annually): Awarded to best new work created in the BMI Jazz Composers Workshop. Winner receives $3000 commission for new work to be performed the following year.

John Lennon Scholarships (1997–): Established by Yoko Ono in memory of John Lennon, and administered in conjunction with the National Association for Music Education/MENC: Provides scholarship support to songwriters and composers between the ages of 15 and 24.

Peermusic Latin Scholarship (annually, 2003–): For songwriters and composers of Latin music between the ages of 16 and 24. Offers $5000 scholarship for the best song or instrumental work in a Latin music genre.

See also Thelonious Monk International Jazz Composers Competition.

DELTA OMICRON INTERNATIONAL MUSIC FRATERNITY TRIENNIAL COMPOSITION COMPETITION (triennially in rotating categories): Cash award to composer for a previously unpublished and unperformed work, and sponsorship of the first performance.

FROMM MUSIC FOUNDATION AT HARVARD UNIVERSITY (established 1972, annually): Commissions young as well as established composers. Also sponsors annual Fromm Music Foundation at Harvard Concert Series, as well as premieres of works supported by their commissioning program.

GUGGENHEIM FELLOWSHIPS, John Simon Guggenheim Memorial Foundation (annually, 1925–): Grants to composers and scholars 30–45 years of age who propose research into the history or theory of music. Categories: citizens and residents of the United States and Canada, and citizens and residents of other countries in the Western hemisphere. <http://www.gf.org>

JOSEPH H. BEARNS PRIZE IN MUSIC, Columbia University (two annually, 1928–): Cash awards to American composers 18–25 years of age. Categories: a large-scale work and a composition in a smaller form. <http://music.columbia.edu/awards/bearns>

NATIONAL ENDOWMENT FOR THE ARTS: *see* NEA.

WALTER W. NAUMBURG FOUNDATION. <http://www.naumburg.org>

Naumburg Competition for Composers. Open to American composers under the age of 40. Two winning composers receive $5000 cash award as a commission to write a chamber music work which will be performed by a leading chamber music ensemble. Instrumentation to be decided by the Naumburg Jury.

See also Walter W. Naumburg Foundation under §II, 2 Competitive awards: Performers.

NISSIM COMPETITION: *see* ASCAP.

RICHARD RODGERS PRODUCTION AWARD, established by Richard Rodgers and administered by the American Academy and Institute of Arts and Letters (1978–): subsidy to a composer or lyricist for the production in New York by a nonprofit theater organization of a previously unproduced music theater work "to encourage the development of the musical theatre."

ROME PRIZE FELLOWSHIPS: *see* American Academy in Rome.

RUDOLF NISSIM COMPOSER COMPETITION: *see* ASCAP.

THELONIOUS MONK INTERNATIONAL JAZZ COMPOSERS COMPETITION (annually, 1993–). Sponsored by BMI, and held in conjunction with the Thelonious Monk International Jazz Competition, the competition awards $10,000 to a composer "who best demonstrates originality, creativity, and excellence in jazz composition." <http://www.monkinstitute.org/competition>

See also Thelonious Monk International Jazz Competition under §II, 2 Competitive awards: Performers.

(ii) Performers.

AMERICAN NATIONAL CHOPIN COMPETITION (quinquennially, 1975–): Chopin Foundation of the United States: cash awards (first prize also includes transportation costs to the International Chopin Competition in Warsaw and sponsorship of performances) to American pianists 17–28 years of age. <http://www.chopin.org>

BACHAUER INTERNATIONAL PIANO COMPETITION: *see* Gina Bachauer International Piano Competition.

CASADESUS INTERNATIONAL PIANO COMPETITION: *see* Robert Casadesus International Piano Competition.

CLEVELAND INTERNATIONAL PIANO COMPETITION (biennially): Cash awards and promotional support to pianists 18–30 years old. Founded at the Cleveland Institute of Music in 1975 as the Robert Casadesus International Piano Competition and renamed in 1995. First prize winner receives $50,000 and sponsorship of performances. <http://www.clevelandpiano.org>

CLIBURN INTERNATIONAL PIANO COMPETITION: *see* Van Cliburn International Piano Competition.

COLEMAN CHAMBER ENSEMBLE COMPETITION (annually, 1947–): Cash prizes for string, brass, and wind chamber ensembles with players under the age of 26. <http://coleman.caltech.edu/competition.shtml>

CONCERT ARTISTS GUILD VICTOR ELMALEH INTERNATIONAL COMPETITION (annually): Open to instrumentalists, singers, and chamber ensembles under the age of 35, performing classical and non-traditional repertoire. All winners receive: management contract with Concert Artists Guild, and a New York Recital. Other prizes include Victor and Sono Elmaleh Award of $5000, BMI Commissioning Prize, Naxos Recording Prize, and performances with leading orchestras, concert series, and festivals. <http://www.concertartists.org>

DRANOFF INTERNATIONAL TWO PIANO COMPETITION (biennially, established 1987): Cash prizes to two-piano teams between the ages of 21 and 33. The Dranoff Foundation also administers the Alvin Coleman Commission of new compositions for performance by finalist teams. <http://www.dranoff2piano.org/>

FISCHOFF NATIONAL CHAMBER MUSIC COMPETITION (annually in two divisions, 1973–): Cash awards to chamber ensembles of three to five players with no more than one vocalist. Categories: senior (30 years of age and under), junior (18 years of age and under). <http://www.fischoff.org>

GEORGE LONDON FOUNDATION FOR SINGERS AWARDS (annually). Cash awards to American or Canadian singers under age 35. <http://www.georgelondon.org/>

GINA BACHAUER INTERNATIONAL PIANO COMPETITION, sponsored from 1980 by the Utah SO (annually in different categories, 1976–): Cash awards and concert engagements. *Artists Competition*: pianists ages 19–32; *Junior & Young Artists Competition*: pianists ages 14–18 and 11–13 respectively. <http://www.bachauer.com>

GREENBERG AWARD: *see* Noah Greenberg Award.

HILTON HEAD INTERNATIONAL PIANO COMPETITION (biennially, 1996–): For pianists aged 18–30, alternating with "Young Artists Competition" for pianists aged 13–17. Prizes include cash awards and sponsorship of performances. <http://www.hhipc.org/>

INTERNATIONAL VIOLIN COMPETITION OF INDIANAPOLIS (quadrennial): Cash awards, and sponsorship of recordings and concert appearances throughout the United States and Europe to a violinist 16–29 years of age. <http://www.violin.org>

WILLIAM KAPELL INTERNATIONAL PIANO COMPETITION (quadriennal): For pianists between 18 and 33 years old. Cash prizes.

KURT WEILL AWARDS IN PERFORMANCE: Sponsored by the Kurt Weill Foundation for Music, Inc. to encourage high standards of music theater performance. <http://www.kwf.org>

See also Kurt Weill Foundation Prize under §II, 3 Competitive Awards: Scholars.

LIEDERKRANZ FOUNDATION ANNUAL COMPETITIONS FOR VOICE: Cash awards. Categories: vocalists 18–35 years of age, Wagnerian singers, 25–45 years of age.<http://www.liederkranznycity.org/vcompetition.asp>

METROPOLITAN OPERA NATIONAL COUNCIL REGIONAL AUDITIONS PROGRAM (annually, 1952–): Cash awards and other educational funding to singers; the purpose of the auditions is "to discover new talent for the Metropolitan Opera and to find, assist and encourage young singers in preparation for their careers." Auditions at the district, semifinal, and final levels. <http://www.metoperafamily.org/metopera/auditions/national/>

NATIONAL ENDOWMENT FOR THE ARTS: *see* NEA.

NAUMBURG FOUNDATION: *see* Walter W. Naumburg Foundation.

NEA. National Endowment for the Arts (NEA) programs currently offer support to music performing organizations and presenting ensembles in the following categories; the agency does not offer outright funding to individual artists or composers.

Access to Artistic Excellence: "To encourage and support artistic excellence, preserve our cultural heritage, and provide access to the arts for all Americans."

Challenge America Fast-Track: "To support projects that extend the reach of the arts to underserved populations."

Learning in the Arts for Children and Youth: "To advance arts education for children and youth in school-based or community-based settings."

See also National Endowment for the Arts (NEA) under §I Honors.

NOAH GREENBERG AWARD, established by the New York Pro Musica and presented by the American Musicological Society (annually, 1978–): Cash awards to performers and scholars "for a distinguished contribution to the study and performance of early music."

ORATORIO SOCIETY OF NEW YORK LYNDON WOODSIDE SOLO COMPETITION FOR SINGERS (annually, 1975–): Cash award and possible performance contract to singers 40 years of age or under who have not yet made a formal New York oratorio debut in a reviewed New York concert. <http://www.oratoriosocietyofny.org/solo.html>

PEABODY-MASON MUSIC FOUNDATION SPONSORSHIP FOR PIANISTS: Cash prizes and piano recital in Boston area.

ROBERT CASADESUS INTERNATIONAL PIANO COMPETITION *see* Cleveland International Piano Competition.

SAN FRANCISCO OPERA. MEROLA OPERA PROGRAM (annually): Offers specialized operatic training program to approximately 20 singers, four apprentice coaches, and one apprentice stage director. Participants receive classes in acting, languages, and stage movement, as well as individual coaching and masterclasses with international artists and directors. "For five years after leaving Merola, alumni may be eligible, with Merola's approval, to receive up to a total of $10,000 in career grants, with a maximum of $5000 in any single year." <http://sfopera.com/merola.asp>

SPHINX COMPETITION FOR YOUNG BLACK & LATINO STRING PLAYERS (annually): Open to junior high school and high school Black and Latino string players. Winners receive cash prizes, as well as performances and promotional opportunities. The program's goal is to "encourage, develop and recognize classical music talent in the Black and Latino communities." <http://www.sphinx.org>

THELONIOUS MONK INTERNATIONAL JAZZ COMPETITION (annually, 1987–): Competition sponsored by the Thelonious Monk Institute of Jazz. Awards cash prizes and scholarships to talented young jazz artists; instruments (including a vocal competition) rotate annually. Judges have included B. Marsalis, P. Metheny, H. Hancock, C. Terry, D. Brubeck, M. McPartland, Q. Jones, and D. Krall. *See also* Thelonious Monk International Jazz Composers Competition under §II, 1 Competitive awards: Composers. <http://www.monkinstitute.org/competition>

VAN CLIBURN INTERNATIONAL PIANO COMPETITION (quadrennially, 1962–): Cash awards (first prize also includes sponsorship of a recital in Carnegie Hall, first appearances with major orchestras, and a European concert tour; other prizes include performances as well) to pianists 18–30 years of age. <http://www.cliburn.org>

Amateur competition (1999–): Open to pianists ages 35 and older who consider themselves amateurs. Prizes include cash awards.

WALTER W. NAUMBURG FOUNDATION

Naumburg International Competition (annually in rotating categories): cash award (first prize also includes sponsorship of two recitals in Alice Tully Hall, other performances, and a recording). Categories: piano, violin, voice. <http://www.naumburg.org>

See also Naumburg Competition for Composers under §II, 1 Competitive awards: Composers. (*See also* NAUMBURG, WALTER WEHLE)

YOUNG CONCERT ARTISTS INTERNATIONAL AUDITIONS (any number annually, 1961–): sponsorship of recitals in New York, Boston, and Washington, DC, and management services of Young Concert Artists for three of more years. <http://www.yca.org>

(iii) Scholars.

AMERICAN ACADEMY IN ROME *see* §II, 1 Competitive Awards: Composers.

AMERICAN ASSOCIATION OF UNIVERSITY WOMEN EDUCATIONAL FOUNDATION (1882–): Fellowships to American women for scholarly research in all disciplines. <http://www.aauw.org/index.cfm>

AMERICAN COUNCIL OF LEARNED SOCIETIES (1975–): Fellowships for humanistic research to scholars at the doctoral and post-doctoral levels. <http://www.acls.org/grants/default.aspx?id=354>

AMERICAN MUSICOLOGICAL SOCIETY (AMS): Selective list. <http://www.ams.net>

AMS Subventions for Publications: Funds to assist with various aspects of publication expenses.

AMS 75 PAYS Subventions: Provides support up to $5000 for the publication of first books by scholars in the early stages of their career.

M. Elizabeth Bartlett Fund for Research in France (annually): To one or more graduate students to conduct doctoral or postdoctoral work in France.

Thomas Hampson Fund Supporting Research and Publication on Classic Song (established 2009): "The fund is dedicated to fostering editions and scholarship on classic song in all its contexts, as well as new and innovative technologies for promoting and understanding classic song via interactive media and the Internet."

Jan LaRue Travel Fund for Research Travel to Europe: Supports travel to Europe to carry out doctoral or postdoctoral research.

Harold Powers World Travel Fund for Research in Music: Supports travel anywhere in the world for doctoral or postdoctoral research.

See also American Musicological Society under §I Honors.

ASCAP DEEMS TAYLOR AWARD COMPETITION (annually, 1967–): Cash awards for excellence in writing about music (popular and serious, for books, articles, liner notes, broadcasts, and websites on the subject of music).

INSTITUTE OF INTERNATIONAL EDUCATION: Fulbright and other fellowships to American citizens with BA degrees for graduate study outside the United States. <http://www.iie.org>

KURT WEILL PRIZE (biennial, 1994–): Sponsored by the Kurt Weill Foundation for Music, Inc., to recognize scholarship focusing on musical theater in the 20th century.

See also Kurt Weill Award in Performance under "Competitive Awards – Performers." <http://www.kwf.org>

MUSIC LIBRARY ASSOCIATION (MLA)

Dena Epstein Award for Archival and Library Research in American Music (1996–; annual): Supports research in libraries in the United States and abroad on any aspect of American music.

Carol June Bradley Award for Historical Research in Music Librarianship (2004–): Supports research in the history of music libraries or music librarianship.

NATIONAL ENDOWMENT FOR THE HUMANITIES (NEH) FELLOWSHIPS. Grants for full-time independent study and research. <http://www.neh.gov>

NOAH GREENBERG AWARD: *see* §II, 2 Competitive Awards, Performers.

SOCIETY FOR AMERICAN MUSIC (SAM) <http://www.american-music.org/>

H. Earle Johnson Bequest for Book Publication Subvention: Supports the costs of the publication of a significant monograph on an important topic in American Music; application must come from publisher.

Sight and Sound Fund: subventions for publication of non-print materials.

See also Society for American Music under §I Honors.

BIBLIOGRAPHY

Musical America...International Directory of the Performing Arts (New York, 1960–) [annual pubn]

Foundation Grants to Individuals (New York, 1977–) [biennial pubn]

The Grants Register: The Complete Guide to Postgraduate Funding Worldwide [annual pubn]

Concert Artists Guild: *Guide to Competitions* (New York, 1987–2005)

G. Alink: *International Piano Competitions* (The Hague, 1990)

K. Little: *Grawemeyer Award for Music Composition: The First Twenty Years* (Lanham, MD, 2007)

H.-D. Fischer, ed.: *The Pulitzer Prize Winner for Music: Composer Biographies, Programs, and Jury Reports* (Frankfurt am Main, 2010)

World Federation of International Music Competitions <http://www.wfimc.org/>

JANE GOTTLIEB

Aweau, Nathan. *See* HAPA.

Ax, Emanuel (*b* L'viv, Poland, 8 June 1949). Pianist of Polish birth. His first teacher was his father, Joachim Ax, a coach at the L'viv Opera. The family immigrated to Canada in 1959, settling in Winnipeg, then moved to New York in 1961. Ax began seven years of study with Mieczysław Munz at the Juilliard School of Music in 1966 and also attended Columbia University (BA 1970). He had already won honors in the Chopin competition, Warsaw, the Vianna da Motta Competition, Lisbon, and the Queen Elisabeth of Belgium Competition, and had made his New York debut (Alice Tully Hall, 1973) when he won the first Artur Rubinstein International Piano Competition in 1974, which also enabled him to study with Rubinstein. The next year he received the Young Concert Artists' Michaels Award, and in 1979 he won the Avery Fisher Prize. Ax has performed with many leading orchestras, including the Boston SO, the Philadelphia Orchestra, the New York PO, the Los Angeles PO, and the Cleveland Orchestra. In 1991 he made his debut at the Proms in London, performing Brahms's First Piano Concerto. He has taken part in numerous chamber music and recital series, including performances by the Chamber Music Society of Lincoln Center, the Mostly Mozart Festival, and a three-concert series entitled "Emanuel Ax Invites" at Alice Tully Hall. In 1980 he formed a trio with the violinist Young Uck Kim and the cellist Yo-Yo Ma; he and Ma continue to frequently perform and record together. Their recordings of Beethoven and Brahms sonatas have won several Grammy awards, as have Ax's recordings of the Haydn Piano Sonatas. Other recordings by Ax include the concertos of Beethoven (with the Cleveland Orchestra), Brahms (with the Chicago SO), Chopin (with the Orchestra of the Age of Enlightenment), Liszt (Philharmonia Orchestra), Mozart, and Schoenberg. Although he has recorded chamber music by Prokofiev, Rachmaninoff, and Shostakovich (typically with Ma), his repertoire tends to focus on European common practice period composers. Since 1990, however, he has commissioned and performed important additions to the piano and orchestral repertoire, including John Adams' *Century Rolls*, 1997 (which he also recorded with the Cleveland Orchestra); Christopher Rouse's *Seeing*, 1998 (with the New York Philharmonic) and Bright Sheng's *Red Silk Dance*, 1999 (with the Boston SO). He has also premiered works by Stephen Prutsman, Peter Lieberson, Tomas Ades, Krzysztof Penderecki, Osvaldo Golijov, and Melinda Wagner. A Fellow of the American Academy of Arts and Letters and recipient of Yale University's Sanford Medal, Ax belongs in the top rank of American pianists. As a chamber musician, he is a collaborator of uncommon flexibility, musical insight, and intuition. His solo performances are often lauded both for their poetic nature and analytical clarity.

JAMES CHUTE/R

Axt, William L. (*b* New York, NY, 19 April 1888; *d* Ukiah, CA, 13 Feb 1959). Composer and conductor. After private music study in Berlin, he conducted for Oscar Hammerstein's Manhattan Opera Company, which closed in 1910, and then for productions on Broadway. By 1921 he had become an assistant conductor at the Capitol Theater, where silent films were presented with full orchestral accompaniment; in 1923, in partnership with David Mendoza, he replaced Erno Rapée as principal conductor. In addition to conducting, he composed incidental film music for the Capitol as needed, including 57 pieces published in the *Capitol Photoplay Series* (New York, 1923–7). From 1925 to 1929 he collaborated with Mendoza in New York on compilation scores for at least 20 MGM films, beginning with *The Big Parade*. Their collaboration continued with the music for *Don Juan* (1926), the first feature film score to be presented using the Vitaphone process, which mechanically synchronized the playback of music recorded on wax discs with the projection of the film. In 1929 or 1930 he moved to Hollywood, where he played a key role in the MGM music department. He continued to work for MGM, providing music for numerous films, until his retirement in the early 1940s.

Neither in the collaborations with Mendoza, nor in the MGM films is a distinctive Axt style easily discernible; his works of the 1920s, however, serve as excellent examples of the compilation score. In the music for *The Big Parade*, principal themes exhibit clear expressive content and undergo simple, skillful transformations; new music is interwoven with arrangements of pre-existent pieces to create a smooth pastiche. The scores of the 1930s are often sparse, consisting mainly of modest mood pieces and source music. Many of these are polished examples of MGM's star-centered style, in which the craftsmanship of the composer was subordinated to the effect of the whole. Axt's contributions to *Grand Hotel* (1932), however, were singled out by contemporary critics as an early and effective demonstration of orchestral music's dramatic potency in sound film.

WORKS

(*selective list*)

Film scores (collab. D. Mendoza): Ben-Hur, 1925; The Big Parade, 1925; La Bohème, 1926; Don Juan, 1926; A Woman of Affairs, 1928; Our Dancing Daughters, 1928; White Shadows in the South Seas, 1928; The Kiss, 1929; The Single Standard, 1929

Other film scores: Smilin' Through, 1932; Broadway to Hollywood, 1933; Dinner at Eight, 1933; The Thin Man, 1934; Pursuit, 1935; Libeled Lady, 1936; The Last of Mrs Cheney, 1937

BIBLIOGRAPHY

GroveA (M. Marks) [incl. further bibliography]

Musical Courier (27 Dec 1923)

E.J. Lewis: "The Archive Collection of Film Music at the University of Wyoming," *Cue Sheet*, vi (1989), no.3, pp.89–99; no.4, pp.143–60

D. James: "Performing with Silent Films," *Film Music I*, ed. C. McCarty (1989), 61–79

MARTIN MARKS/R

Axton, Hoyt (Wayne) (*b* Duncan, OK, 25 March 1938; *d* nr Victor, MT, 26 Oct 1999). Singer-songwriter and actor. He took lessons in classical piano as a child and began playing guitar in his teens. His mother, Mae Boren Axton, co-wrote "Heartbreak Hotel," which was a hit for Elvis Presley in 1956. Axton attended Oklahoma State University, where he excelled in football before leaving to serve in the navy. His music career began in the early 1960s, when he began performing as a singer-songwriter in the folk clubs of southern California. "Greenback Dollar," a song he co-wrote with Ken Ramsey, became a hit for the Kingston Trio. In 1962 Axton signed with Horizon Records, which released his first album *The Balladeer* (Horizon, 1962), recorded live at the Troubadour in Hollywood, followed by *Thunder'n Lightnin'* and *Saturday's Child* (both Horizon, 1963). From 1964 to 1971 he was associated with several labels, including Vee-Jay, Surrey, Exodus, Columbia, and Capitol. His albums with A&M – *Life Machine* (A&M, 1974), *Southbound* (A&M, 1975), and *Fearless* (A&M, 1976) – all reached the top 30 of the *Billboard* "Country Albums" chart. His single "Boney Fingers" (A&M, 1974) reached the top ten of the "Hot Country Singles" chart, and duets with Linda Ronstadt, "When the Morning Comes" (1974) and "Lion in Winter" (1975), were widely acclaimed. After recording two albums with MCA, Axton started his own label, Jeremiah Records, in 1979. Both "Della and the Dealer" (1979) and "A Rusty Old Halo"

(1979) became top 20 country hits. A talented songwriter, Axton wrote or co-wrote several songs that were successful for other artists including Steppenwolf ("The Pusher" and "Snowblind Friend"), Three Dog Night ("Joy to the World" and "Never Been to Spain"), and Ringo Starr ("No No Song"). In addition to singing and songwriting, Axton had a significant career as an actor, making several appearances on television and in movies (*The Black Stallion*, 1979 and *Gremlins*, 1984).

LINDA J. DANIEL

Ayala, Pedro (*b* General Terán, Nuevo León, México, 29 June 1911; *d* Donna, TX, 1 Dec 1990). Mexican accordionist, songwriter, and composer, active in the United States. Ayala was born into a musical family: his father played clarinet and accordion, his sisters played violin, and his brothers played accordion and guitar. In order to make a living, the Ayalas crossed the border to live in Donna, Texas, working in agriculture. Ayala accompanied his father at the age of ten on the *tambora* (small hand drum) playing polkas and *huapangos* in traditional Mexican *tamborliero* (drum and clarinet ensemble) style. He briefly played guitar in a local *orquesta* and with popular accordionist, Chon Alanis. Greatly influenced by Alanis, he switched to the accordion in the mid-1930s. Though he played professionally in the Rio Grande Valley region, he did not record until 1947, more than ten years after his contemporaries Narciso Martínez and Santiago Jiménez. His first recordings were made for an early Mexican American record label, Mira, which eventually became Falcón Records. His recordings earned him the title "El monarca del acordeón" (the Monarch of the Accordion) for his rapid-fire, uniquely syncopated playing style and eloquent articulation. He is also recognized for following Jiménez's lead by featuring the *tololoche* (double bass) on his recordings, thus solidifying the instrument (alongside the accordion and *bajo sexto* in the Texas Mexican *conjunto* and norteña styles.

CATHY RAGLAND

Ayala, Ramón [Garza, Ramón Covarrubias] (*b* Monterrey, Nuevo León, Mexico, 8 Dec 1945). Mexican accordionist, singer, and bandleader. Born in Monterrey and raised in Reynosa, Tamaulipas, Ramón Ayala has been the foremost figure in norteño music along the Gulf Coast and Texas border region since the 1970s. He first became famous in the 1960s as the accordionist and coleader of Los Relámpagos del Norte, with the singer-songwriter Cornelio Reyna; then formed his own band, Los Bravos del Norte, in 1971. In Mexico, Ayala is regarded as part of a great generation of border bandleaders, along with Carlos y José and Los Cadetes de Linares. North of the border, though, he has far outstripped his peers, and only California's Los Tigres del Norte rival his ongoing popularity. Unlike the Tigres, who have consistently pushed norteño in new directions, Ayala is a traditionalist, and his success is due as much to his image as a hard-working, old-fashioned bearer of the classic tradition as to his intricate accordion passages and his keen eye for good material, from gunfighter corridos to romantically mournful *rancheras* and perky cumbias. His gritty, working-class persona has made him a particular favorite not only in the countryside but in the tougher barrios of Houston and Los Angeles, and this street credibility has led to his work being sampled and remixed by Chicano hip-hop artists.

ELIJAH WALD

Ayers, Roy (E.) (*b* Los Angeles, CA, 10 Sept 1940). Vibraphonist. He grew up in a musical family and learned other instruments before taking up vibraphone at the age of 17, despite being given a pair of vibraphone mallets by Lionel Hampton as a child. In the 1960s he worked mainly in Los Angeles and was hired as the music director of Herbie Mann's group after performing with the flutist in 1966. He recorded several successful albums with Mann, including *Memphis Underground* (1968, Atl.). After moving to New York, Ayers founded the ensemble Ubiquity (1970), which featured a line-up of musicians—veterans as well as newcomers—that changed regularly and a repertoire that drew from jazz, soul, pop, blues, and funk. Ayers found success among mainstream pop and disco audiences, notably with "Everybody loves the sunshine" (1976). After touring Nigeria with Fela Kuti in 1979, he was inspired to address social issues, and such themes subsequently shaped his album *Africa, Center of the World* (Pol., 1981). In 1982 he founded Uno Melodic records through which he has since produced other musicians' work. During the late 1980s Ayers's group served as the house band at Ronnie Scott's club in London and produced several live albums. He was later a featured guest on the album *Nu Yorican Soul* (Blue Thumb, 1997). Ayers's music has resurfaced in the popular market through sampling and the acid jazz movement, leading to collaborations with Erykah Badu and Talib Kweli.

MARK LOMANNO

Ayler, Albert (*b* Cleveland, OH, 13 July 1936; *d* ?New York, NY, between 5 and 25 Nov 1970). Jazz tenor saxophonist and bandleader. He began on alto saxophone and was playing professionally in rhythm-and-blues bands by his mid-teens. While serving in army concert bands, he switched to tenor saxophone. He occasionally played in Paris clubs while stationed in France from 1959 to 1961. After his discharge, he remained in Europe, leading a bop trio for eight months in Sweden and playing with Cecil Taylor in Copenhagen (1962–3). In 1963 he moved to New York, and the following year he formed a quartet with Don Cherry, Gary Peacock and Sunny Murray.

Ayler was never able to find a steady audience for his radical music—his group performed perhaps only three times in 1965—and although his albums were well received by the critics, he had trouble landing gigs. He made no effort to clarify his music for listeners, discouraging musical interpretations of his recordings and instead stressing their social and spiritual themes; the inconsistent and confusing titles to his pieces further obscured his work. Nevertheless, in studios, New York clubs (1965–8), and for college concerts he was able to assemble faithful sidemen. His groups included his brother, the trumpeter Donald Ayler; one or two double bass players, such as Peacock and Henry Grimes; the drummers Murray, Milford Graves, and Beaver Harris, and Cal Cobbs, who played piano and harpsichord. Cobbs continued to work with Ayler after the saxophonist returned to playing rhythm-and-blues in 1969. On 5 November 1970, shortly after returning from a tour of Europe with his quintet, Ayler was reported missing in New York; his body was found in the East River on 25 November.

Ayler's extraordinary and original music of the mid-1960s rejected most of the conventions of the prevailing bop and free-jazz styles. According to Jost, Ayler often replaced tempered melody with sweeping flourishes; he combined these with sudden low-pitched honks and a wide, sentimental vibrato. Peacock and Murray provided sympathetic accompaniments, and the recordings they made with Ayler in 1964 juxtapose complex collective improvisation with his simple, rhythmically square, frequently tonal themes. Sometimes these two factors are interrelated, as in the gradual deformation of the folk-like melody in several versions of "Ghosts" (1964, including one on the album *Spiritual Unity*, ESP). More often, however, the brief themes serve as foils for lengthy improvisations in which the group, avoiding predictable sounds, achieves varied textures and rhythms.

Soon after recording the album *Bells* in May 1965 (ESP), the balance of Ayler's music shifted from improvisation to composition. Three tracks on *Spirits Rejoice* (1965, ESP) emphasize thematic material. This striving for simplicity, augmented by pressure from the record company Impulse! to increase his sales, led Ayler to return to rhythm-and-blues in the late 1960s, although he achieved little success.

RECORDINGS
(selective list)

My Name is Albert Ayler (1963, Debut 140); *Spirits* (1964, Debut 146); *Spiritual Unity* (1964, ESP 1002); *New York Eye and Ear Control* (1964, ESP 1016); *Ghosts* (1964, Debut 144); *Bells* (1965, ESP 1010); *Spirits Rejoice* (1965, ESP 1020); *Lörrach/Paris* (1966, Hat Hut 3500); *In Greenwich Village* (1966–7, Imp. 9155); *Love Cry* (1967, Imp. 9165); *New Grass* (1968, Imp. 9175); *Music is the Healing Force of the Universe* (1969, Imp. 9191)

BIBLIOGRAPHY

N. Hentoff: "The Truth is Marching in," *Down Beat*, xxxiii/23 (1966), 16–18, 40 [interview]
V. Wilmer: "Albert and Don Ayler," *JazzM*, xii/10 (1966), 11–13
E. Jost: "Albert Ayler," *Free Jazz* (Graz, 1974, 3/1994), 121–32
V. Wilmer: "Albert Ayler: Spiritual Unity," *As Serious as your Life: the Story of the New Jazz* (London, 1977, 2/1980), 92–111
J. Litweiler: "Albert Ayler," *Down Beat*, xlix/2 (1982), 45–6
M. Hames: *Albert Ayler, Sunny Murray, Cecil Taylor, Byard Lancaster, and Kenneth Terroade on Disc and Tape* (Ferndown, Dorset, 1983)
E.G. Price, III: *Free Jazz and the Black Arts Movement*, 1958–1967 (diss., U. of Pittsburgh, 2000)
F. Moten: *In the Break: the Aesthetics of the Black Radical Tradition* (Minneapolis, 2003)

BARRY KERNFELD/R

Aylmer, Jennifer (*b* Oceanside, NY, 21 June 1972). Soprano. After graduating from the Eastman School of Music she studied at the Juilliard Opera Center. She then joined the Houston Grand Opera Studio, where she sang the role of Amy in the world premiere of Adamo's *Little Women* in 1998. She has subsequently sung a wide range of lyric soprano roles, including Mozart's Susanna and Pamina, Norina (*Don Pasquale*), Sophie (*Der Rosenkavalier*), Helena (*A Midsummer Night's Dream*), and the Governess (*The Turn of the Screw*), in companies throughout the United States. With Austin Lyric Opera, Aylmer has performed Gilda in *Rigoletto* and Stella in Previn's *A Streetcar Named Desire*. She sang Cynthia Read in the world premiere of Rands's *Belladonna* at Aspen in 1999, and in 2005 created the role of Bella in Picker's *An American Tragedy* in her Metropolitan Opera debut. She returned to the Metropolitan, as Papagena, the following season. In 2001 she made her New York recital debut in the Alice Tully Hall. Aylmer's bright, silvery timbre has also been admired in Baroque repertory, including Handel's *Orlando*, *Flavio*, and *Acis and Galatea*, and on the concert platform in works such as Mozart's *Exsultate, jubilate* and Mahler's Fourth Symphony. She has also performed recitals featuring American Tin Pan Alley songs.

RICHARD WIGMORE/R

Ayres (Johnson), Frederic (*b* Binghamton, NY, 17 March 1876; *d* Colorado Springs, CO, 23 Nov 1926). Composer. After studying engineering at Cornell University (1892–3) he worked designing electric motors. He studied composition with EDGAR STILLMAN KELLEY (1897–1901) and FOOTE (summer 1899) "to perfect...what I believed to be my proper work." Because of ill health (tuberculosis) he moved to Las Cruces, New Mexico (1901), and then to Colorado Springs (1902), where he lived for the rest of his life composing and teaching theory privately. In 1926 he was awarded an honorary doctorate by the Cincinnati Conservatory of Music. His earlier output occasionally drew on thematic material evocative of Amerindian music, but the late works, for instance the Trio in D minor and the Violin Sonata in B minor, discard those influences in favor of a more abstract lyricism.

WORKS
(printed works published in New York unless otherwise stated)

Songs: 3 Songs (R. Browning, M. Fuller), op.2 (Berlin, 1906); 3 Songs (W. Shakespeare), op.3 (Newton Centre, MA, 1906–7), ed. Lawrence (1970); 2 Songs (Shakespeare), op.4: no.1 (Berlin, 1907), no.2 (Newton Centre, MA, 1907), ed. Lawrence (1970); 2 Songs (anon., Shakespeare), op.5 (1918); 3 Songs (Shakespeare, H. van Dyke, M.T. Ritter) op.6: no.1 (1915), no.2 (Newton Centre, MA, 1911), ed. Lawrence (1970), no.3 (1923); Mother Goose Melodies, op.7 (1919); Sunset Wings (D.G. Rossetti), op.8 (1918); The Seeonee Wolves (song cycle, R. Kipling), op.10, unpubd; 3 Songs (Kipling, H.C. Bunner, W.V. Moody) (1921); My Love in her Attire (anon.) (1924); 2 Songs (Kipling, C. Roberts) (1924); Christmas Eve at Sea (J. Masefield) (1925); Sappho (1927); 19 other unpubd songs

Orch: From the Plains, ov., op.14, unpubd

Chbr: Pf Trio, op.13 (Berlin, 1914); Sonata, op.15, vn, pf (Berlin, 1914); Str Qt, op.16, rev. 1916, unpubd; Pf Trio, d (1925); Elegy, vc, pf, unpubd; Str Qt no.2, unpubd; Sonata, vc, pf, unpubd; Sonata, b, vn, pf, unpubd

Pf solo: 2 Fugues, op.9 (Berlin, 1910); The Open Road, intermezzo, op.11 (1916); 3 Compositions, op.12: no.1 (Newton Centre, MA, 1910), ed. V.B. Lawrence (1970), no.2 (1917), no.3, unpubd; Pf

Preludes, b, e♭, unpubd; The West Wind and the Daughter of Nokomis, unpubd

MSS in *Wc*

Principal publishers: G. Schirmer, Stahl (Berlin), Wa-Wan Press

BIBLIOGRAPHY

A.G. Farwell: "Frederic Ayres," *Wa-Wan Press Monthly*, vi (1907), April; repr. in *The Wa-Wan Press, 1901–1911*, iv, ed. V.B. Lawrence (New York, 1970), 44

W.T. Upton: "Frederic Ayres," *MQ*, xviii (1932), 39–59 [incl. full list of works]

J.P. Perkins: *An Examination of the Solo Piano Music Published by the Wa-Wan Press* (diss., Boston U., 1969)

BARNEY CHILDS

Azerrad, Michael (*b* New York, NY, 1961). Music critic and musician. He graduated from Columbia University in 1983. In the 1980s, he was a contributing editor for *Rolling Stone*, writing hundreds of pieces for the magazine. His success as a critic corresponded with the rise of "alternative" rock in the early 1990s, and he wrote cover articles on Nirvana and the B-52s during that period. Azerrad has published two books, *Come As You Are: the Story of Nirvana* (New York, 1993) and *Our Band Could Be Your Life: Scenes from the American Indie Underground (1981–1991)* (Boston, 2002). *Come As You Are* was the first book about Nirvana and Kurt Cobain, written with the support of the band and published before Cobain's death. *Our Band Could Be Your Life* is a collection of essays about 13 of the best-remembered underground bands from the 1980s and 1990s, and includes new interviews and archival research. *The Guardian* and the *Los Angeles Times* are among the publications to issue high praise for *Our Band Could Be Your Life*. Azzerrad's other projects include the Kurt Cobain documentary *Kurt Cobain: About a Son* and editing Hüsker Dü leader Bob Mould's autobiography.

CAROLINE POLK O'MEARA

Azoff, Irving (*b* Danville, IL, 13 Dec 1947). Entertainment executive. One of the most powerful businessmen in entertainment, Irving Azoff has led a successful career for more than four decades. He began promoting concerts in his hometown while still in high school. In the early 1970s, he moved to Los Angeles with client Joe Walsh and joined the management team connected to David Geffen's Asylum Records. There, Azoff began working with the country-rock band the Eagles, and was soon joined by Walsh. When Geffen sold Asylum, Azoff co-founded Front Line Management in 1974, taking on the Eagles as his clients. He earned a reputation as one of the most feared managers in the business for both his temper and his political savvy, negotiating lucrative deals for a high-powered pop roster that also included Steely Dan, Stevie Nicks, and Chicago. In 1983, Azoff became president of MCA Records, expanding his interests into video and merchandise distribution, as well as the film industry. In 2008, he sold Front Line to Ticketmaster Entertainment Inc. and became Ticketmaster's new CEO. He became Executive Chairman of Live Nation when the two concert promotion giants merged in 2010. He has continued to manage pop stars, including Christina Aguilera.

BIBLIOGRAPHY

F. Dannen: *Hit Men* (New York, 1990)

JESSE JARNOW

Azpiazú, Don (*b* Santa Clara, Cuba, 11 Feb 1893; *d* Havana, Cuba, 20 Jan 1943). Cuban pianist and bandleader. As the leader of the Havana Casino Orchestra he is best known for having launched the "El manicero" ("Peanut Vendor") craze in the United States after his band performed this number at New York's Palace Theater on 26 April 1930. Written by Moises Simon, the song became an instant hit, and within a year popular jazz artists such as Louis Armstrong and Duke Ellington had recorded versions of the tune. Expanding upon the traditional Cuban *conjunto* (sextet or septet), Azpiazú's band was a 14-piece dance orchestra with trumpets, saxophones, trombone, tuba, piano, bass, and Cuban percussion. Although Latin bands already existed in New York, his was the first group to be successful with the non-Latino public, helping to catalyze the rhumba dance craze that lasted throughout the decade. The Havana Casino Orchestra recorded popular versions of other tunes such as "Mama Inéz," "Aquellos ojos verdes," "Siboney," and "Amapola," and also appeared in many short and feature-length movies. Significantly, Azpiazú is remembered for forming the first racially integrated popular dance band in Cuba, also breaking the color barrier in the United States. After a successful European tour, he went back to Cuba in 1932, returning regularly to New York's ballrooms through the late 1930s and early 40s. A stubborn man who rejected ethnic stereotypes, he reputedly lost a job at the Rainbow Room for playing American tunes and refusing to stick to Cuban numbers. See also J.S Roberts: *The Latin Tinge: the Impact of Latin American Music on the United States* (New York, 1979, 2/1999).

LISE WAXER

B

Babbitt, Milton (Byron) (*b* Philadelphia, PA, 10 May 1916; *d* Princeton, NJ, 29 Jan 2011). Composer and theorist. He contributed extensively to the understanding and extension of 12-tone compositional theory and practice and was one of the most influential composers and teachers in the United States since World War II.

1. Life. 2. Works. (i) Serial theory and practice to 1970. (ii) Electronic works.

1. Life. Brought up in Jackson, Mississippi, he started playing the violin at the age of four and several years later also studied clarinet and saxophone. He graduated from high school in 1931, having already demonstrated considerable skills in jazz ensemble performance and the composition of popular songs. His father's professional involvement with mathematics (as an actuary) was influential in shaping Babbitt's intellectual environment. In 1931 Babbitt entered the University of Pennsylvania with the intention of becoming a mathematician, but he soon transferred to New York University, concentrating on music under Marion Bauer and Philip James. He received the BA in music in 1935. As a student and during the ensuing years, Babbitt immersed himself in the intellectual milieu of New York, encountering influential philosophers such as Sidney Hook and James Wheelright, developing a life-long engagement with analytical philosophy, and reading widely in rapidly emerging and sometimes short-lived journals such as *Symposium* and *Politics*. His early attraction to the music of Varèse and Stravinsky soon gave way to an absorption in that of Schoenberg, Alban Berg, and Anton Webern—particularly significant at a time when 12-tone music was unknown to many and viewed with skepticism by others.

After graduation Babbitt studied privately with Roger Sessions, wrote criticism for the *Musical Leader*, and then enrolled for graduate work at Princeton University, where he continued his association with Sessions. In 1938, aged 22, he joined the Princeton music faculty and in 1942 received one of Princeton's first MFAs in music. His *Composition for String Orchestra*, a straightforward 12-tone work, was completed in 1940.

During World War II Babbitt divided his time between Washington, DC, where he was engaged in mathematical research, and Princeton, as a member of the mathematics faculty (1943–5). Musically, these were years of thought and discovery, rather than of actual composition; they resulted in 1946 in a highly technical work entitled *The Function of Set Structure in the Twelve-Tone System*, which was the first formal and systematic investigation of Schoenberg's compositional method. Babbitt submitted this paper for the degree of PhD. Although lauded by mathematics professor John Tukey, the dissertation was rejected by the music department who, at that time, only offered higher degrees in historical musicology. Between 1946 and 1948, shuttling between Jackson and New York, he once again directed his energies to composition, writing some film scores and an unsuccessful Broadway musical.

In 1948 Babbitt rejoined the music faculty at Princeton, eventually succeeding Roger Sessions as the William Shubael Conant Professor of Music in 1965; in 1973 he became a member of the composition faculty of the Juilliard School. He also taught at the Salzburg Seminar in American Studies, the Berkshire Music Center, the New England Conservatory of Music, and the summer courses in new music at Darmstadt, Germany. In 1992, 46 years after Princeton's music department rejected Babbitt's dissertation, his colleagues Paul Lansky and Claudio Spies resubmitted the work on his behalf. On review the dissertation was accepted. The Dean of Princeton's graduate school at the time, Theodore Ziolkowski, explained that Babbitt's "dissertation was so far ahead of its time it couldn't be properly evaluated at the time." Babbitt's earned doctorate was granted one year after he had been awarded an honorary doctorate also from Princeton. He won the Joseph Bearns Prize (for *Music for the Mass I* in 1942), New York Music Critics' Circle citations (for *Composition for Four Instruments* in 1949 and for *Philomel* in 1964), a National Institute of Arts and Letters Award (1959) for demonstrating a "penetrating grasp of musical order that has influenced younger composers," a Guggenheim Fellowship (1960–61), membership in the National

Institute (1965), a Brandeis University Gold Medal (1970), a special Pulitzer Prize citation "for his life's work as a distinguished and seminal American composer" (1982), a MacArthur Fellowship (1986), and the Gold Medal of the American Academy and Institute of Arts and Letters (1988). In 1974 he became a fellow of the American Academy of Arts and Sciences, and in 2000 he became a National Patron of Delta Omicron.

Throughout his career, he was actively involved in contemporary music organizations, including the ISCM (he was president of the American section, 1951–2), the American Music Center, *Perspectives of New Music* (as a member of its editorial board), the Columbia-Princeton Electronic Music Center (from 1985), and the BMI Student Composer Awards (he was the chairman from 1985 until his death in 2011). Articles, reviews, and interviews by him have appeared in many music publications; he traveled widely, speaking on issues of current musical thought. His 1983 Madison lectures are published under the title *Words about Music*. Babbitt was a remarkably successful lecturer; perceptive and adept at logical extemporization, he continually stimulated and provoked his audiences. He was also an inveterate follower of popular sports, a raconteur and punster, and an omnivorous reader.

In a controversial article published in *High Fidelity* magazine in 1958, Babbitt claimed that serious music required an educated audience. He urged the informed musician to "re-examine and probe the very foundations of his art." Babbitt was displeased with the published title of the article, "Who Cares if You Listen?" which had been added by the magazine editor without his agreement (the original title was "The Composer as Specialist"). "Now obviously," he told the *Princeton Alumni Weekly* in 2006, "I care very deeply if you listen. From a purely practical point of view, if nobody listens and nobody cares, you're not going to be writing music for very long. But I care how you listen."

During his lifetime Babbitt was revered as an artistic mentor whose students produced music and scholarly work that spanned the music discipline from the avant-garde to Broadway musicals. He loved popular music and had an encyclopedic knowledge of Tin Pan Alley songs. In a 2001 interview with *NewMusicBox* he commented: "If you know anybody who knows more popular music of the '20s or '30s than I do, I want to know who it is." Babbitt's students, many of whom called him "Uncle Milton," included MARIO DAVIDOVSKY, PAUL LANSKY, JOHN C. EATON, and STEPHEN SONDHEIM. His work in serialism influenced major European composers such as Luigi Nono, Pierre Boulez, and Karlheinz Stockhausen.

2. WORKS.

(i) Serial theory and practice to 1970. Babbitt's early fascination with 12-tone practice, particularly in its formal aspects, developed into a total reconsideration of musical relations. Throughout his compositional career he was occupied with the extension of techniques related to Schoenberg's (and Webern's) "combinatorial" sets; with the investigation of sets that have great flexibility and potential for long-range association; and with an exploration of the structuring of non-pitch components "determined by the operations of the [12-tone] system and uniquely analogous to the specific structuring of the pitch components of the individual work, and thus, utterly nonseparable" (Babbitt, 1955, p.61). He was a pioneer in his ways of talking and thinking about music, invoking terms from other disciplines, such as philosophy, linguistics, mathematics, and the physical sciences.

Babbitt revealed and formalized many of the most salient aspects of 12-tone compositional technique in several important essays. In "Some Aspects of Twelve-Tone Composition" (1955), "Twelve-Tone Invariants as Compositional Determinants" (1960), and "Set Structure as a Compositional Determinant" (1961), he systematically investigated the compositional potential of the 12 pitch class set, introducing such terms (derived from mathematics) as "source set," "combinatoriality," "aggregate," "secondary set," and "derived set." These terms facilitate the classification of the various types of pitch class set and contribute to the description of diverse procedures for the compositional projection of such sets. A secondary set, for example, results when a "new" set of 12 pitch classes emerges from the linear linking of segments of two forms of a 12-tone series, as shown in Table 1. Similarly, an "aggregate can be thought of as a simultaneous statement of…parts [of a 12-tone set]…it is not a set, inasmuch as it is not totally ordered, because only the elements within the component parts are ordered, but not the relationship between or among the parts themselves" (Babbitt, 1955, p.57). 12-tone sets that yield such aggregate and secondary set formations are called "combinatorial." (Further distinctions between various types of combinatorial sets—that is, semi- and all-combinatorial sets, the first-, second-, third-, and fourth-order all-combinatoriality—are discussed in the same essay.) The nomenclature that Babbitt introduced in his prose writings has become widely adopted and is the basis for much theoretical work and composition. Moreover, in his compositions he demonstrated the efficacy of his theories. Thus Babbitt extended the notion of compositional creativity to

TABLE 1

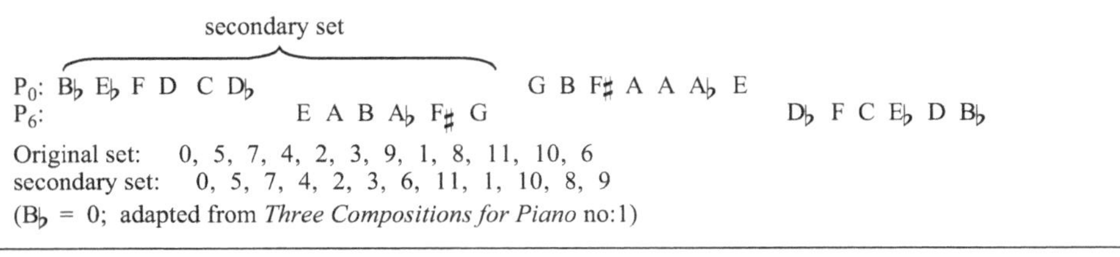

secondary set

P_0: B♭ E♭ F D C D♭ G B F♯ A A A♭ E
P_6: E A B A♭ F♯ G D♭ F C E♭ D B♭

Original set: 0, 5, 7, 4, 2, 3, 9, 1, 8, 11, 10, 6
secondary set: 0, 5, 7, 4, 2, 3, 6, 11, 1, 10, 8, 9
(B♭ = 0; adapted from *Three Compositions for Piano* no:1)

encompass the development of musical systems themselves, as well as specific compositional achievements within such systems. He also persistently explored the relationships between set transformation and derivation procedures, and virtually all other aspects of musical structure, such as grouping and form, large- and small-scale rhythm, texture and register, instrumentation, and timbre.

In "Twelve-Tone Rhythmic Structure and the Electronic Medium" (1962) Babbitt demonstrates a number of methods for interpreting the structures of pitch class sets in the temporal domain. By positing an analogy between the octave (in pitch structure) and the bar (in rhythmic and metrical structure), and by dividing the bar into 12 equal units (each of which can be musically articulated by individual points of attack), Babbitt provides a basis for mapping pitch class sets onto "time-point sets." Thus an uninterpreted set of integers (for example, 0, 11, 6, 7, 5, 1, 10, 2, 9, 3, 4, 8) may be interpreted as a specific instance of a pitch class set (ex.1) or as a specific instance of a time-point set (ex.2). (The time-point of a particular point of attack is a measure of its position within the bar.) In ex.2 the metrical unit is a demisemiquaver, a 12th of the whole bar; time-point 0 therefore occurs on the first demisemiquaver of the bar, time-point 1 on the next, and so on. In this example the 12 available points of attack within a bar are ordered according to the numerical set given above. Ex.1 and 2 each represent only one of the possible interpretations of the numerical set given above; pitch classes may be presented in various registers, just as time-points may be displaced to subsequent bars, as long as the same order of presentation (of pitches or points of articulation) is preserved. Furthermore, a time-point set and a pitch class set determined by the same set of integers may unfold at different speeds: in the first four bars of the second violin part of Babbitt's String Quartet no.3 (1969–70), the first six notes may be understood as a realization in terms of pitch of the first five integers in the set indicated above (ex.3). Also, the three *forte* markings in this passage articulate the time-points that correspond to the first and third entities of the same numerical set (time-point 0 is reiterated in bar 2 before the third time-point, 6, is articulated in bar 4). The second time-point of this set is presented in a different instrumental line, the last note of violin 1 in bar 3 (ex.4). Each of the eight dynamic gradations from *ppp* to *fff* inclusive is employed in the String Quartet no.3 to articulate a particular layer of the time-point structure, and each of these layers is analogous to one of eight layers of pitch class sets simultaneously presented in the work; the eight layers of pitch class sets are differentiated by distinctions of instrumentation, register, and mode of sound production (for example, the use of pizzicato and arco) throughout the work. This brief discussion of a musical fragment may serve as an indication of the extraordinary richness of structural relationships that are projected in Babbitt's music.

An earlier example of Babbitt's approach may be seen in his *Three Compositions for Piano* (1947), one of his first consistent attempts to extend Schoenbergian 12-tone procedures. The surface of the music is, in some respects, reminiscent of Schoenberg: registrally dispersed lines alternate with thickly clustered chordal

Ex.1

Ex.2

0 11 6 7 5 1 10 2 9 3 4 8

Ex.3

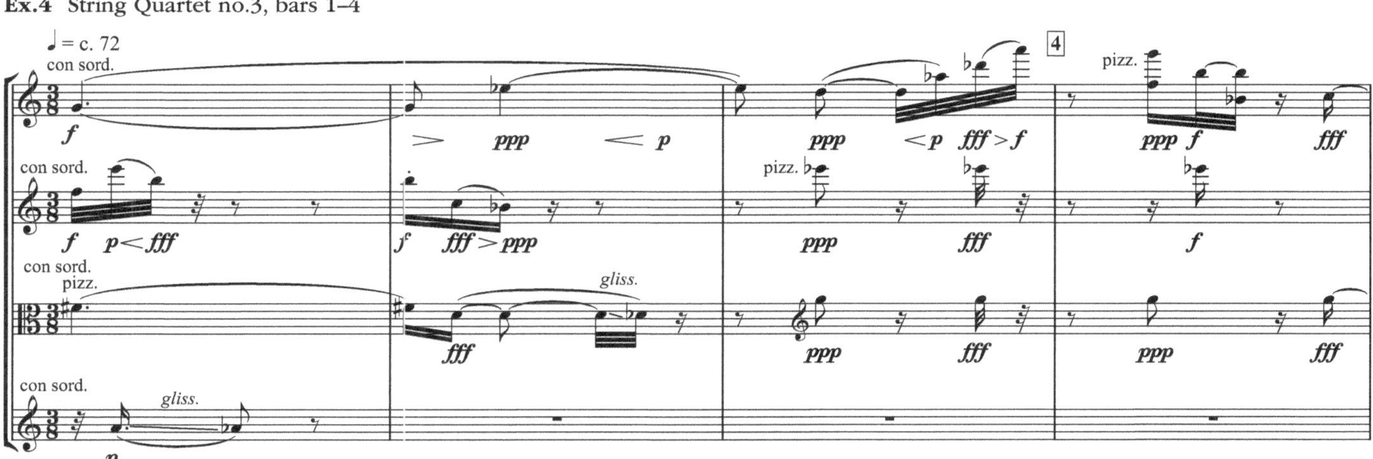

Ex.4 String Quartet no.3, bars 1–4

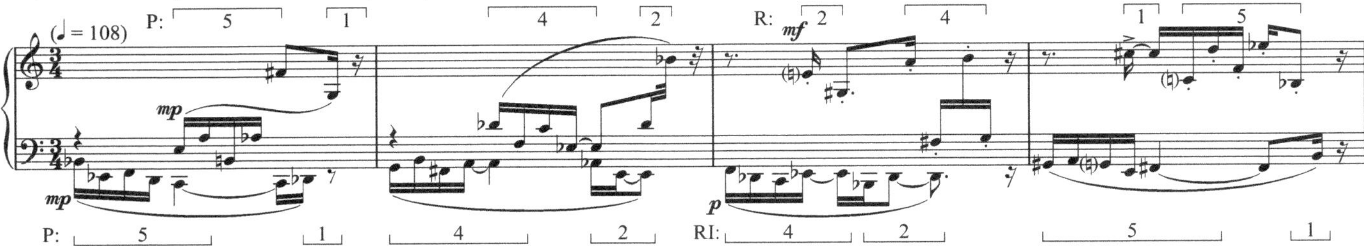

Ex.5 Three Compositions for Piano, no.1, bars 1–4

attacks (in the framework of a quasi-ternary structure), yet the absence of expressive indications and the reliance on metronome markings would seem to reveal a Stravinskian concern for a clear, undistracted projection of the temporal domain. Some of the innovative aspects of the work reside in the conjunction of the structuring of pitch and other domains, resulting in an early example of "totally serialized" music. Points of articulation made by the superimposition of lines and the number of consecutive attacks within a contrapuntal line are determined by a set (whose prime form is 5, 1, 4, 2). In the first four bars of the work, this set is presented twice in its prime form (P), once in retrograde (R), and once in retrograde inversion (RI; ex.5). There is also a correspondence between dynamics and pitch set forms.

Babbitt's *Composition for Four Instruments* and *Composition for Twelve Instruments* (both of which were written in 1948) go a step further towards a structuring of rhythm isomorphic with 12-tone pitch structuring. In the 12-instrument work a set of 12 durations emerges and operates throughout. It is transformed by "classical" serial operations: transposition (addition of a constant to each duration number of the set), inversion (the complementation of the duration numbers), retrogression (the complementation of the order numbers of the set) and retrograde inversion. The ending of each of the three major sections of the work is articulated by the completion of a rhythmic set. The presentation of the rhythmic sets is often complex—various instruments characteristically participate in the presentation of a single rhythmic set, and more than one rhythmic set may be presented simultaneously. Nonetheless, the surface characteristics of the work delineate a simple process. Beginning with sparsely textured single events (which can be considered an extension of Webern's sound world) and slowly becoming more compact (with regard to aggregate completions), the work concludes with thicker textures and sustained sonorities, unfolding newly shaped but familiar harmonic environments.

Babbitt was profoundly involved in the clarification and extension of the systematic aspects of 12-tone composition, but his music is in no sense rigidly determined by precompositional schemes. Within the constraints of serial techniques, he used a great range of expressive possibilities and contextually varied structures. A work such as *Partitions* (1957) demonstrates numerous precompositional constraints (such as the projection of an all-interval set, a polyphonic texture in which distinct transformations of 12-tone pitch sets are unfolded in each line, and aggregates formed by various vertical partitionings of segments of these lines). In the first four bars a hexachord is presented in each of four different registers (ex.6). The hexachords in the lower two registers (E♭ A♭ F♯ F C♯ E; C G A B♭ D B) are complementary and are, respectively, the retrogrades of the hexachords presented in the higher two registers. There are 49 different ways in which the pitches presented in these hexachords might be partitioned to form aggregates. (For example, each hexachord might be divided 3 + 3; or the hexachords might be divided alternately 2 + 4 and 4 + 2, etc.) The actual partitioning of pitches (1 + 5 in the highest register, 3 + 3 in the next highest register, 5 + 1 in the next register, and 3 + 3 in the lowest register) contributes to a rich pattern of interval and pitch associations and echoes. Such partitioning establishes a specific rate of movement through the pitch class sets in each register and also suggests possibilities for hierarchical distinctions among the pitch classes that constitute the sets involved. Each registral line has its own rhythm of movement through its pitch class sets, and these characteristic rhythms are varied contextually throughout the work.

The commitment to systematic precompositional planning is maintained in works with dramatic, poetic or other associative aspects. In *Du* (1951), a song cycle for soprano and piano (which represented the United States at the 1953 ISCM Festival), there is continual interplay between the text and the vocal and piano lines. Phoneme, syllable, word, and line are carefully contoured, subtly and imaginatively set to music: the pitch, durational, dynamic, and registral schemata, themselves transformed from poem to poem, are allied with the verbal elements and indeed help to project the many delicate nuances of the text. These lyrical, imagist tendencies were most fully realized in *Philomel* (1964) but are also evident in *All Set* (1957), for small jazz ensemble, with its conjunction of 12-tone structure (based on an all-combinatorial set) and what Babbitt calls "jazz-like properties…the use of percussion, the Chicago jazz-like juxtapositions of solos and ensembles recalling certain characteristics of group improvisation."

Babbitt took a novel serial approach to handling the sonic resources of a large orchestra in *Relata I* (1965). Here timbral "families" are correlated with set structure,

Ex.6 *Partitions*, bars 1–4

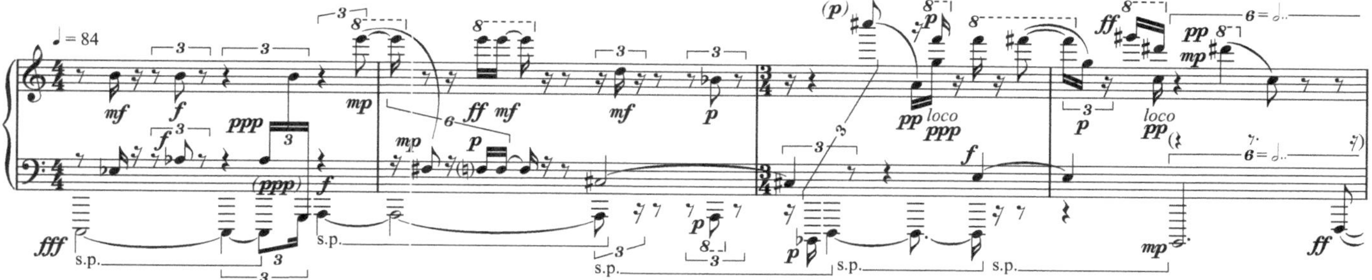

with woodwind instruments as four trios, brass as three quartets, and string instruments as two sextets (one bowed, the other plucked). The work is insistently polyphonic (with as many as 48 instrumental lines), framed at both ends by massive sonorities and filled with constantly changing and recombined textures and colors. While parts of the work are analogous to other parts, there is no simple repetition: all aspects undergo reinterpretation, rearrangement and "resurfacing." In the more timbrally homogeneous works of the late 1960s (*Sextets*, *Post-Partitions*, parts of *Correspondences*, the String Quartets nos.3 and 4), the handling of timbre and tone-color seems even more refined. Sonorously embodied successions of relations are projected in ever varying contexts, producing changes of "atmosphere" from the most rarefied to the most dense, with every conceivable gradation. The complexity of Babbitt's orchestral music created difficulties for some ensembles, with the New York Philharmonic, in 1969, and the Philadelphia Orchestra, in 1989, postponing their premieres of his work when the rehearsal periods were not adequate.

(ii) Electronic works. Another concern of Babbitt's was electronic sound synthesis. In his 1960 essay "Electronic Music: the Revolution in Sound" he wrote "Electronic music is just what its name suggests: music produced by means of 'instructed' electronic oscillations. To produce it electrically should be no more alarming than producing it with that oddly shaped wooden box equipped with taut strings which we call a violin." At the time of the first instrumental film soundtrack, in the late 1930s, he had already recognized the enormous compositional potential of such synthesis. Two decades later, in the mid-1950s, when he was invited by RCA to be a composer-consultant, he became the first composer to work with its newly improved and developed synthesizer, the Mark II (see illustration). The Mark II became the focus of the Columbia-Princeton Electronic Music Center from 1959. Babbitt, alongside Roger Sessions, Vladimir Ussachevsky, and Otto Luening, was one of the center's first directors.

Babbitt was attracted by the convenience of composing for electronic means, explaining in 1969 to the *New York Times* that "the medium provides a kind of full satisfaction for the composer. I love going to the studio with my work in my head, realizing it while I am there and walking out with the tape under my arm. I can then send it anywhere in the world, knowing exactly how it will sound." *Composition for Synthesizer* (1961) was Babbitt's first totally synthesized work. It was followed soon after by *Vision and Prayer* for soprano and synthesizer (1961) and *Ensembles for Synthesizer* (1962–4). His basic compositional attitudes and approaches underwent little change with the new resource; rather, with the availability and flexibility of the synthesizer's programming control they were now realizable to a degree of precision previously unattainable in live performances of his music. Babbitt's interest in synthesis was not concerned with the invention of new sounds per se but with the control of all aspects of events, particularly the timing and rate of change of timbre, texture, and intensity. (His Woodwind Quartet (1953) and String Quartet no.2 (1954) had already given some indication of the rapidity of dynamic change he wished to achieve, on both single and consecutive pitches.) The electronic medium allowed him to project time-point sets however he liked, without regard to the demands made on live performers.

Though the lucidity of his conceptual world finally became manifest under the ideal performance conditions provided by sound synthesis, Babbitt nevertheless retained his interest in live performance, and carried over to it several structural procedures from the electronic medium. Perhaps the most appealing work combining live performance with tape is *Philomel*, written in conjunction with the poet John Hollander for the soprano Bethany Beardslee. It is based on Ovid's interpretation of the Greek legend of Philomela, the ravished, speechless maiden who is transformed into a nightingale. New ways of combining musical and verbal expressiveness were devised by composer and poet: music is as articulate as language; language (Philomela's thoughts) is transformed into music (the nightingale's song). The work is an almost inexhaustible repertory of speech-song similitudes and differentiations, and resonant word-music puns (unrealizable without the resources of the synthesizer). Babbitt stopped writing music with electronic components after the Columbia-Princeton studio was vandalized in the late 1970s.

(iii) Later serial developments. During the 1970s and early 1980s Babbitt was increasingly prolific. The fecundity of his compositional thought was revealed in such diverse combinations as female chorus, double brass sextet, orchestra and tape, and guitar duo. He continued

Milton Babbitt, 1986. (Marion Kalter/Lebrecht Music & Arts)

to explore the potential, and to refine the procedures of, 12-tone composition, always discovering new ways of extending and interpreting principles of combinatoriality and correlating the various dimensions of his musical universe.

In works such as *Arie da capo* (1973–4), Babbitt incorporates "weighted aggregates"—transformations (by inversion) of pitch class arrays (abstract, precompositional designs made up of combinatorially related rows) in which at least one pitch class appears more than once (see Babbitt, 1973–4). *Arie da capo* also employs an "all-partition array" that systematically uses all the possible partitionings of the structural elements that comprise an aggregate (in this case, all the possible partitionings of 12-tone sets into as many as six parts). All-partition arrays are found in much of Babbitt's music after 1960. Each of the sections of *Arie da capo* may be construed as an "aria" for one of the five instruments; but the conception of the aria is reimagined so that "the central instrument dominates less quantitatively than relationally, in that its music is the immediate source of, and is complemented and counterpointed by, the music of the 'accompanying' instruments." "Da capo" repetitions of set forms recur throughout the arias, both on the musical surface and as non-consecutive pitches associated by register, articulation or instrumentation.

A Solo Requiem for soprano and two pianos (1976–7) is Babbitt's most extended composition for voice. This magisterial work (a memorial to the composer Godfrey Winham) incorporates a wide range of vocal techniques and reveals the extraordinary range and sensitivity of Babbitt's response to a variety of dramatic and lyrical poetic texts. In *My Complements to Roger*, one of several short works of the late 1970s and early 1980s for solo piano, Babbitt succinctly demonstrated a number of methods for associating pitch and rhythmic structures. The partitioning of metrical units and pitch class sets is correlated in each bar to form aggregates. Often in the piece the grouping of a string of pitches extracted from the abstract pitch class array is articulated on the musical surface by presenting the pitch string within a single beat, subdivided into the same number of parts as there are pitches in the string (see Mead, 1983).

Babbitt continued in the 1980s to expand the 12-tone universe. He explored the premise of the "superarray," the combination of individual arrays to form larger and more intricate 12-tone structures. These very large arrays of pitch class structure have inspired ever more inventive musical textures. For example, in *Transfigured Notes* for string orchestra (1986), Babbitt divided each of four instrumental groups (1st and 2nd violins, violas and cellos) into two sub-groups and then distinguished between three separate registers in each group in order to articulate 24 distinct areas. These instrumental groupings are then recombined to project the structural counterpoint which comprises one interpretation of the abstract superarray.

The world that Babbitt's music evokes is not simple. He once said "I want a piece of music to be literally as much as possible." While some critics felt that such an attitude has resulted in a body of inaccessible music, others praised his pioneering approach, involving as it has a systematic and comprehensive exploration of the 12-tone compositional universe. Babbitt liked to merge serious music with light-hearted and humorous titles, such as "The Joy of More Sextets," "Four Play," and "Sheer Pluck." His emphasis on the relationship between practice and theory, his insistence on the composer's assumption of responsibility for every musical event in a work, and his reinterpretation of the constituent elements of the Western musical tradition have had a vital influence on the thinking and music of numerous younger composers.

See also THEORY; TWELVE-TONE MUSIC.

WORKS

all published unless otherwise stated

INSTRUMENTAL

Orch: Generatrix, 1935, inc., withdrawn; Composition for Str Orch, 1940, withdrawn; Sym., 1941, inc., withdrawn; Into the Good Ground, film score, 1949, inc., withdrawn; Relata I, 1965; Relata II, 1968; Ars combinatoria, small orch, 1981; Conc. for Pf and Orch, 1985; Transfigured Notes, str orch, 1986; Conc. no.2, pf, orch, 1998; Concerti for Orchestra, 2004

Chbr: Str Trio, 1941, withdrawn; Composition for 4 Insts, fl, cl, vn, vc, 1948; Composition for 12 Insts, wind qnt, tpt, hp, cel, str trio, db, 1948, rev. 1954; Str Qt no.1, 1948, withdrawn; Composition for Va and Pf, 1950; Ww Qt, 1953; Str Qt no.2, 1954; All Set, a sax, t sax, tpt, trbn, db, pf, vib, perc, 1957; Sextets, vn, pf, 1966; Str Qt no.3, 1969–70; Str Qt no.4, 1970; Arie da capo, fl, cl + b cl, pf, vn, vc, 1973–4; Paraphrases, fl, ob + eng hn, cl, b cl, bn, hn, tpt, trbn, tuba, pf, 1979

Dual, vc, pf, 1980; Str Qt no.5, 1982; Groupwise, pic + fl + a fl, vn, va, vc, pf, 1983; Four Play, cl, vn, vc, pf, 1984; The Joy of More Sextets, vn, pf, 1986; Fanfare, 4 hn, 4 tpt, 3 trbn, tuba, 1987; Souper, spkr, fl, cl, vn, vc, pf, 1987; Whirled Series, a sax, pf, 1987; The Crowded Air, fl, ob, cl, bn, pf, mar, gui, vn, va, vc, db, 1988; Consortini, fl, pf, vib, mar, vc, 1989; Soli e Duettini, 2 gui, 1989; Soli e Duettini, fl, gui, 1989; Soli e Duettini, vn, va, 1990; Little Goes a Long Way, vn, pf, 2000; Swan Song no. 1, fl, ob, vn, vc, 2 gui, 2003; An Encore, vn, pf, 2006

Counterparts, 2 tpt, hn, trbn, tuba, 1992; Septet, but Equal, 2 cl, cl + b cl, vn, va, vc, pf, 1992; Fanfare for All, 2 tpt, hn, trbn, tuba, 1993; Str Qt no.6, 1993; Accompanied Recitative, s sax, pf, 1994; Arrivals and Departures, 2 vn, 1994; Triad, cl, va, pf, 1994; Bicenquinquagenary Fanfare, 2 tpt, hn, trbn, tuba, 1995; Pf Qt, 1995; Qnt, cl, 2 vn, va, vc, 1996; When Shall We Three Meet Again?, fl, cl, vib, 1996

Pf: 3 Compositions for Pf, 1947; Duet, 1956; Semi-Simple Variations, 1956; Partitions, 1957; Post-Partitions, 1966; Tableaux, 1972; Minute Waltz (3/4 ± 1/8), 1977; Playing for Time, 1977; My Complements to Roger, 1978; About Time, 1982; Don, pf 4 hands, 1981; Canonical Form, 1983; Playing for Time, 1983; It Takes Twelve to Tango, 1984; Lagniappe, 1985; Overtime, 1987; In his Own Words, spkr, pf, 1988; Emblems (Ars Emblematica), 1989; Envoi, pf 4 hands, 1990; Preludes, Interludes and Postlude, 1991; Tutte le corde, 1994; The Old Order Changeth, 1998; Allegro Penseroso, 1999; More Melismata, vc, 2005–6

Other solo inst: My Ends are my Beginnings, cl, 1978; Melismata, vn, 1982; Sheer Pluck (Composition for Gui), 1984; Homily, snare drum, 1987; Beaten Paths, mar, 1988; Play it Again Sam, va, 1989; None but the Lonely Flute, fl, 1991; Around the Horn, hn, 1993; Manifold Music, org, 1995; Composition for One Inst, celesta, 1999; Conc. Piccolino, vibr, 1999

VOCAL

Dramatic: Fabulous Voyage (musical, R. Childs, R. Koch, Babbitt), 1946

Choral: Music for the Mass I, SATB, 1940, withdrawn; Music for the Mass II, SATB, 1941, withdrawn; 4 Canons, female chorus, 1968 [after Schoenberg]; More Phonemena, 12vv, 1978; An Elizabethan Sextette, female chorus 6vv, 1979; Glosses, boys' choir, 1988

Solo vocal: Three Theatrical Songs, 1v, pf, 1946 [from musical Fabulous Voyage]; The Widow's Lament in Springtime (W.C. Williams), S, pf, 1950; Du (Stramm), song cycle, S, pf, 1951; Vision and Prayer, S, pf, 1954, unpubd, unperf.; 2 Sonnets (G.M. Hopkins), Bar, cl, va, vc, 1955; Composition for Tenor and 6 Insts, T, fl, ob, vn, va, vc, hpd, 1960; Sounds and Words, S, pf, 1960

Phonemena, S, pf, 1969–70; A Solo Requiem (W. Shakespeare, Hopkins, G. Meredith, Stramm, J. Dryden), S, 2 pf, 1976–7; The Head of the Bed (J. Hollander), S, fl, cl, vn, vc, 1982; The Virginal Book, C, pf, 1988; 4 Cavalier Settings (R. Herrick, T. Carew), T, gui, 1991; Mehr "Du" (Stramm), Mez, va, pf, 1991; Quatrains, S, 2 cl, 1993; No Longer Very Clear, S, fl, cl, vn, vc, 1994; Pantuns, S, pf, 2000; From the Psalter, S, str, 2002; Now Evening After Evening (D. Walcott), S, pf, 2002; A Waltzer in the House (S. Kunitz), S, vib, 2003; Autobiography of the Eye (P. Auster), S, vc, 2004

WORKS WITH TAPE

Composition for Synth, 4-track tape, 1961; Vision and Prayer (D. Thomas), S, 4-track tape, 1961; Ensembles for Synth, 4-track tape, 1962–4; Philomel (Hollander), S, 4-track tape, 1964; Correspondences, str orch, tape, 1967; Occasional Variations, 4-track tape, 1971; Concerti, vn, small orch, tape, 1974–6; Phonemena, S, tape, 1975; Reflections, pf, tape, 1975; Images, sax, tape, 1979

Recorded interviews in *Nhob*

Principal publishers: Associated, Boelke-Bomart, Peters

WRITINGS

(for fuller list see Mead, 1994)

The Function of Set Structure in the Twelve-Tone System (unpubd paper, 1946; diss., Princeton U., 1992)

"The String Quartets of Bartók," *MQ*, xxxv (1949), 377–85

"Some Aspects of Twelve-Tone Composition," *The Score*, no.12 (1955), 53–61

"Who Cares if You Listen?," *High Fidelity*, viii/2 (1958), 38–40; repr. in *The American Composer Speaks*, ed. G. Chase (Baton Rouge, LA, 1966), 234–44; repr. in *Contemporary Composers on Contemporary Music*, ed. E. Schwartz and B. Childs (New York, 1967), 243–50

"Electronic Music: the Revolution in Sound," *Columbia University Magazine* (1960), spr., 4–8; rev. as "The Revolution in Sound: Electronic Music," *MJ*, xviii/7 (1965), 34–7

"Twelve-Tone Invariants as Compositional Determinants," *MQ*, xlvi (1960), 246–59; repr. in *Problems of Modern Music*, ed. P.H. Lang (New York, 1960), 108–21

"Past and Present Concepts of the Nature and Limits of Music," *IMSCR VIII: New York 1961*, 398–403; repr. in *Perspectives on Contemporary Music Theory*, ed. B. Boretz and E.T. Cone (New York, 1972), 3–9

"Set Structure as a Compositional Determinant," *JMT*, v (1961), 72–94; repr. in *Perspectives on Contemporary Music Theory*, ed. B. Boretz and E.T. Cone (New York, 1972), 129–47

"Twelve-Tone Rhythmic Structure and the Electronic Medium," *PNM*, i/1 (1962), 49–79; repr. in *Perspectives on Contemporary Music Theory*, ed. B. Boretz and E.T. Cone (New York, 1972), 148–79

"Remarks on the Recent Stravinsky," *PNM*, ii/2 (1963–4), 35–55; repr. in *Perspectives on Schoenberg and Stravinsky*, ed. B. Boretz and E.T. Cone (Princeton, NJ, 1968, 2/1972/*R*), 165–85

"An Introduction to the RCA Synthesizer," *JMT*, viii (1964), 251–65

"The Synthesis, Perception and Specification of Musical Time," *JIFMC*, xvi (1964), 92–5

"The Use of Computers in Musicological Research," *PNM*, iii/2 (1964–5), 74–83

"The Structure and Functions of Music Theory I," *College Music Symposium*, v (1965), 49–60; repr. in *Perspectives on Contemporary Music Theory*, ed. B. Boretz and E.T. Cone (New York, 1972), 10–21

"Edgard Varèse: a Few Observations of his Music," *PNM*, iv/2 (1965–6), 14–22; repr. in *Perspectives on American Composers*, ed. B. Boretz and E.T. Cone (New York, 1971), 40–48

"Three Essays on Schoenberg," *Perspectives on Schoenberg and Stravinsky*, ed. B. Boretz and E.T. Cone (Princeton, NJ, 1968, 2/1972/*R*), 47–60

"Relata I," *The Orchestral Composer's Point of View*, ed. R.S. Hines (Norman, OK, 1970), 11–38; repr. as "On Relata I," *PNM*, ix/1 (1970–71), 1–22

"Contemporary Music Composition and Music Theory as Contemporary Intellectual History," *Perspectives in Musicology*, ed. B.S. Brook, E.O.D. Downes and S.J. Van Solkema (New York, 1972), 151–84

"Since Schoenberg," *PNM*, xii/1–2 (1973–4), 3–28

"Responses: a First Approximation," *PNM*, xiv/2 (1975–6), 3–23

"The Next Thirty Years," *High Fidelity/Musical America*, xxxi/4 (1981), 51–66

Words about Music, ed. S. Dembski and J.N. Straus (Madison, WI, 1987)

"Stravinsky's Verticals and (Schoenberg's) Diagonals: a Twist of Fate," *Stravinsky Retrospectives*, ed. E. Haimo and P. Johnson (Lincoln, NE, 1988), 15–35

"On Having Been and Still Being an American Composer," *PNM*, xxvii/1 (1989), 106–12

with others: "Brave New Worlds: Leading Composers Offer their Anniversary Predications and Speculations," *MT*, cxxxv (1994), 330–37

S. Peles and others, eds.: *The Collected Essays of Milton Babbitt* (Princeton, 2003)

BIBLIOGRAPHY

CBY 1962; *VintonD* (B. Boretz)

G. Perle: *Serial Composition and Atonality* (Berkeley, CA, 1962, 6/1991)

R. French: "Current Chronicle: New York," *MQ*, l (1964), 382–8 [on Philomel]

P. Westergaard: "Some Problems Raised by the Rhythmic Procedures in Milton Babbitt's *Composition for Twelve Instruments*," *PNM*, iv/1 (1965), 109–18

E. Barkin: "A Simple Approach to Milton Babbitt's 'Semi-Simple Variations,'" *MR*, xxviii (1967), 316–22

J. Hollander: "Notes on the Text of *Philomel*," *PNM*, vi/1 (1967), 134–41

R. Kostelanetz: "The Two Extremes of Avant-Garde Music," *New York Times Magazine* (15 Jan 1967)

E. Salzman: "Babbitt and Serialism," *Twentieth-Century Music: an Introduction* (Englewood Cliffs, NJ, 1967, 3/1988), 154–5, 158

"An Interview with Milton Babbitt," *MEJ*, lv/3 (1968–9), 56 only

S. Arnold and G. Hair: "Champion of Serialism," *Music and Musicians*, xvii/10 (1969), 46–7
H.W. Hitchcock: "Systematic Serial Composition," *Music in the United States* (Englewood Cliffs, NJ, 1969, 3/1988), 252–9
P. Lieberson, E. Lundborg, and J. Peel: "Conversation with Milton Babbitt," *Contemporary Music Newsletter*, viii (1974), no.1, pp.2–3; no.2, pp.2–3; no.3, pp.2–4
J. Peel: "Milton Babbitt: String Quartet no.3," *Contemporary Music Newsletter*, viii/1 (1974), 1–2
PNM, xiv/2–xv/1 (1976) [double issue, 3–23]
B. Benward: "The Widow's Lament in Springtime," *Music in Theory and Practice*, ii (Dubuque, IA, 1977, 2/1981), 483–96
R. Gauldin: "A Pedagogical Introduction to Set Theory," *Theory and Practice*, iii/2 (1978), 3–14
H. Wilcox and P. Escot: "A Musical Set Theory," *Theory and Practice*, iv/2 (1979), 17–37
M. Capalbo: "Charts," *PNM*, xix/1–2 (1981–2), 310–31
C. Gagne and T. Caras: "Milton Babbitt," *Soundpieces: Interviews with American Composers* (Metuchen, NJ, 1982), 35–52
A. Mead: "Detail and the Array in Milton Babbitt's *My Complements to Roger*," *Music Theory Spectrum*, v (1983), 89–109
J. Rockwell: "The Northeastern Academic Establishment and the Romance of Science," *All American Music: Composition in the Late Twentieth Century* (New York, 1983), 25–36
A. Mead: "Recent Developments in the Music of Milton Babbitt," *MQ*, lxx (1984), 310–31
P. Lieberson: *Milton Babbitt's "Post-Partitions"* (diss., Brandeis U., 1985)
P. Swartz: "Milton Babbitt on Milton Babbitt (Interview with the Composer)," *AM*, iii/4 (1985), 467–73
S. Blaustein and M. Brody: "Criteria for Grouping in Milton Babbitt's *Minute* Waltz (or) 3/4 ± 1/8," *PNM*, xxiv/2 (1986), 30–79
W. Lake: "The Architecture of a Superarray Composition: Milton Babbitt's String Quartet no.5," *PNM*, xxiv/2 (1986), 88–111
J.N. Straus: "Listening to Babbitt," *PNM*, xxiv/2 (1986), 10–24
R. Taub: "An Appreciation of Milton Babbitt's Piano Music," *PNM*, xxiv/2 (1986), 26–9
A. Mead: "About *About Time*'s Time: a Survey of Milton Babbitt's Recent Rhythmic Practice," *PNM*, xxv/1–2 (1987), 182–235
J. Peel and C. Cramer: "Correspondences and Associations in Milton Babbitt's Reflections," *PNM*, xxvi/1 (1988), 144–207
J. Dubiel: "Three Essays on Milton Babbitt," *PNM*, xxviii/2 (1990), 216–61; xxix/1 (1991), 90–123; xxx/1 (1992), 82–131
A. Mead: *An Introduction to the Music of Milton Babbitt* (Princeton, NJ, 1994) [incl. further bibliography]
M. Brody: "'Music for the Masses': Milton Babbitt's Cold War Music Theory," *MQ*, lxxvii/2 (1993), 161–92
D. Lewin: "Generalized Interval Systems for Babbitt's Lists and for Schoenberg's String Trio," *Music Theory Spectrum*, xvii/1 (1995), 81–118
Milton Babbitt, videotaped interview, Brandeis University Archive of Electro-Acoustic Music (1997)
PNM, xxxv/2 (summer 1997) [special issue, "A Symposium in Honor of Milton Babbitt"]
Babbitt: Portrait of a Serial Composer, documentary film, dir. R. Hilferty (1998)
F.J. Oteri: "Milton Babbitt: A Discussion in 12 Parts," *NewMusicBox* (1 Dec 2001) <http://www.newmusicbox.org/article.nmbx?id=1545>
G. Zuckerman and M. Babbitt, "An Interview with Milton Babbitt," *American Mavericks* (American Public Media, July 2002) <http://musicmavericks.publicradio.org/features/interview_babbitt>
Obituaries, *New York Times* (29 Jan 2011), *Washington Post* (30 Jan 2011), *Guardian* (30 Jan 2011), *Gramophone* (2 Feb 2011), *Los Angeles Times* (2 Feb 2011)

ELAINE BARKIN/MARTIN BRODY/JUDITH CRISPIN

Babcock, Alpheus (*b* Dorchester, MA, 11 Sept 1785; *d* Boston, MA, 3 April 1842). Piano maker. He began his career as an apprentice to BENJAMIN CREHORE, as did his brother Lewis (*b* 13 Feb 1779; *d* Milton, MA, 14 Jan 1814); the brothers had their own firm from 1809 to 1811. Alpheus Babcock worked for, supplied pianos for, or was a partner in the following firms: Babcock, Appleton & Babcock (Boston, 1811–4); Hayts, Babcock & Appleton (Boston, 1814–5); J.A. Dickson (Boston); Christopher Hall (Norfolk, Virginia); John, Ruth and G.D. Mackay (Boston, 1822–9); J.G. Klemm (Philadelphia, 1830–32); William Swift (Philadelphia, 1832–7); and Chickering (Boston, 1837–42). His most significant contribution to the evolution of the piano was his invention of a one-piece cast-iron frame including hitch-pin plate, for which he received a patent on 17 December 1825. This invention is regarded as the basis for subsequent piano frame development. His patents for "cross-stringing" (24 May 1830), improved action (31 December 1833), and improvement in the jack or "grasshopper" (31 October 1839) were not of lasting importance. Many historians erroneously credit Babcock with having invented or advocated the overstrung scale. This conclusion undoubtedly results from the equation of overstringing with cross-stringing. Babcock's "cross-stringing" patent concerns itself with unison double-strung piano strings (formed from a single wire which crosses over itself when looped over either hitch-pin or hook), not with bass strings running diagonally above the others. Babcock's instruments were acclaimed for their superb craftsmanship, and all known examples are of the square variety, patterned after English pianos of the period with a range of either five and a half or six octaves (F' to c'''' or F' to f''''). Recent research has shown that stamped numerals on his pianos from the 1820s are probably cumulative serial numbers. Representative instruments are at the Smithsonian Institution, Yale University, and the Museum of Fine Arts, Boston.

See also PIANO.

BIBLIOGRAPHY

D. Spillane: *History of the American Pianoforte* (New York, 1890/R1969, with a new introduction by Rita Benton)
C.M. Ayars: *Contributions to the Art of Music in America by the Music Industries of Boston, 1640 to 1936* (New York, 1937/R)
H.E. Johnson: *Musical Interludes in Boston, 1795–1830* (New York, 1943/R)
K.G. Grafing: *Alpheus Babcock, American Pianoforte Maker (1785–1842): his Life, Instruments, and Patents* (diss., U. of Missouri, Kansas City, 1972)
K.G. Grafing: "Alpheus Babcock's Cast-iron Piano Frames," *GSJ*, xxvii (1974), 118–24

KEITH G. GRAFING/DARCY KURONEN

Babcock, Samuel (*b* Milton, MA, 18 Feb 1760; *d* French Mills, NY, 23 Nov 1813). Composer, singing master, singer, and tunebook compiler. Babcock lived most of his life in Watertown, MA, where he worked as a hatter. As a teenager he fought in the Revolutionary War, and he died while enlisted in the army during the War of 1812. He was active primarily as a psalmodist during the period from 1790 to 1810. Babcock was the choir leader at the Watertown Congregational church, sang at and composed music for town events, and taught singing schools there in 1798 and 1804. He may also have been an itinerant singing master in the Boston area. Babcock composed 75 extant pieces, including anthems, set pieces, fuging tunes, psalm, and hymn tunes. Most of his music was first published in his own tunebook, *Middlesex Harmony*, which was published in two editions (1795 and 1803) by Thomas and Andrews in Boston. His was the only single-composer tunebook issued by publishers between 1789 and 1803 to have a second edition. First printings of his works also appeared in tunebooks compiled by Oliver Holden, Daniel Belknap, and Abijah Forbush.

Babcock's music was strongly influenced by British Methodist-style psalmody, demonstrating primarily three-part, treble dominated textures, florid melodies, and faster tempi. Other composers who adopted this "modern" style of psalmody include Oliver Holden, Samuel Holyoke, Jacob Kimball, and Timothy Olmsted. Babcock chose relatively unusual sacred texts to set and paid careful attention to setting them expressively through the use of a variety of word painting techniques. As a result, he composed more set pieces than many of his contemporaries. Striking examples in this genre include "Caledonia" and "Needham". Babcock's musical style links him with the reform of sacred music at the turn of the 19th century that favored European models over the music of the First New England School of composers. A handful of works have ambiguous attributions in contemporary sources; these are most likely by Samuel's fourth cousin, Lemuel Babcock (1748–1835). Other musical Babcocks include Lemuel's sons, Alpheus and Lewis, who were piano makers.

WORKS

EDITIONS

Middlesex Harmony: Being an Original Composition of Sacred Music, in Three and Four Parts (Boston, 1795, 2/1803)

Samuel Babcock (ca. 1760–1813): the Collected Works, ed. L. Sampsel (New York, 1999)

PSALM AND HYMN TUNES

Andover; Babel; Cana; China; Crete; Crucifixion; Dissolution; Doxology; Elim; Elim [ii]; Ephratah; Flanders; Florence; Gihon; Horeb; Humility; Immanuel; Lexington; Lima; Medford; Minorca; Morning hymn; Morning hymn [ii]; Nativity; Newton; North-Kingston; Omicron; Placentia; Pomfret; Quincy; Rama; Randolph; Roxbury; Sabbath; Spring; Stow; Stratton; Triumph; Truro; Vernon; Waltham; Weston; Wilmington

FUGING-TUNES

Decision [Resolution II]; Dorchester; Elevation; Gratitude; Lubec; Palmer; Resolution; Sunday; Vienna

ANTHEMS, SET-PIECES, AND OCCASIONAL PIECES

Ashford; Auspicious Morn; Caledonia; Cambridge; Cambridge [ii]; Charity; Christian's Hope; Christmas; Comfort Ye, My People; Consecration; Delaware; Hamburg; Harvard; Intercession; Lord, Thou Hast Been Our Dwelling Place; Menotomy; Milton; Needham; Norfolk; O Come Let Us Sing Unto The Lord; Palmyra; Pretorium; Remember Now Thy Creator; Resignation; Smyrna; Song for the Anniversary of St. John the Baptist; Watertown

LOST WORKS

Elegant Tribute

DOUBTFUL WORKS

Attributed to "Babcock" in contemporary sources, probably by Lemuel Babcock: Admiration; Admonition [Admiration ii]; Springfield; Springfield [ii]; Warren; Westborough; Wrentham

BIBLIOGRAPHY

L. Sampsel: "Samuel Babcock: A New England Psalmodist Suspended between Tradition and Reform," *American Music Research Center Journal*, vi (1996), 109–46

L. Sampsel: *Samuel Babcock (1760–1813), Archetypal Psalmodist of the First New England School of Composers* (diss., U. of Pittsburgh, 2009)

LAURIE J. SAMPSEL

Babin, Victor (*b* Moscow, Russia, 30 Nov/13 Dec 1908; *d* Cleveland, OH, 1 March 1972). Pianist and composer of Russian birth. He studied at Riga, in 1928 moving to Berlin to study composition with Franz Schreker and piano with ARTUR SCHNABEL at the Hochschule für Musik. In 1933 he married another of Schnabel's pupils, Vitya (Victoria) Vronsky (1909–92), and his career as a player thereafter was almost exclusively that of a duo-pianist with his wife. Vronsky and Babin quickly established themselves in Europe, then moved to the United States in 1937. Babin taught at the Aspen Music School (where he was director, 1951–4, and member of the Festival Quartet along with Szymon Goldberg, William Primrose, and Nikolay Graudan), at the Berkshire Music Center, Tanglewood, at the Cleveland Institute of Music (where he was director from 1961 until his death), and at Case Western Reserve University, also in Cleveland. His compositions, in a conservative, post-Romantic language, include two concertos for two pianos and orchestra, other compositions for one and two pianos, chamber music, and many songs, including a cycle, *Beloved Stranger*, on texts by Witter Bynner.

MICHAEL STEINBERG/R

Baca (de la Colina), Susana (Esther) (*b* Chorrillos, Lima, Peru, 24 May 1944). Peruvian singer, composer, and music researcher. Although brought up in a family with close connections to criollo and Afro-Peruvian musical traditions, from early in her career Baca was attracted to vanguardist poetry. Since then she has explored various ways of setting poems to music, drawing from Afro-Peruvian traditions and also from *nueva canción*, jazz, and world music. She and her husband, Ricardo Pereira, are also known for their efforts in researching and promoting Afro-Peruvian musical traditions. Until recently, the experimental character of her music was not favored by Peruvian audiences so she mainly pursued a performing career abroad. In 1995 her inclusion in the David Byrne compilation *The Soul of Black Peru* launched Baca into the international spotlight. While outside of Peru her sound has become synonymous with that of Afro-Peruvian music, it is only since Baca won a Latin Grammy in 2002 that her music has become more widely recognized in Peru. Baca is also known for her support of various humanitarian causes and has received awards and appointments from the Peruvian, French, and German governments as well as from Amnesty International, Oxfam, and UNICEF.

JAVIER F. LEÓN

Baccaloni, Salvatore (*b* Rome, 14 April 1900; *d* New York, NY, 31 Dec 1969). Italian bass. He studied with Giuseppe Kaschmann and made his debut at the Teatro Adriano, Rome, in 1922 as Dr. Bartolo in *Il barbiere di Siviglia*. In 1926 he was engaged at La Scala, where he sang regularly until 1940. He made his North American debut in Chicago in 1930 as Melitone. In 1940 he joined the Metropolitan Opera, making his debut, again as Dr. Bartolo, on 3 December 1940. He sang there regularly until 1962, giving 297 performances, mostly in the Italian *buffo* repertory. He appeared often with the San Francisco Opera, and made numerous tours of the United States. Portly in build and good-humored, Baccaloni had a communicative gift for comedy and was noted for his musicianship; in his early years he displayed a rare vocal quality in his *buffo* roles. He had a particularly large repertory, consisting of some 150 roles in many languages. He also appeared in several films, including *Full of Life* with Judy Holliday (1957) and *Fanny* (1961).

FRANCIS D. PERKINS/ALAN BLYTH/R

Bach, Jan (Morris) (*b* Forrest, IL, 11 Dec 1937). Composer. He studied with KENNETH LOUIS GABURO and Robert Kelly (University of Illinois, BM 1959, DMA 1971), DONALD MARTINO (Yale University, 1960), AARON COPLAND and Roberto Gerhard (Tanglewood, 1961), and THEA MUSGRAVE (Aldeburgh and London, 1974). The recipient of many honors, including a Koussevitzky Award (1961), he taught at the University of Tampa (Florida; 1965–6) before joining the music department at Northern Illinois University.

Bach's accessible style combines traditional and contemporary musical elements. A predominant aspect of his work is his charming and inexhaustible sense of humor. *Four Two-Bit Contraptions* (1964), for example, is a study in musical caricature cast in the form of rags, waltzes, and other dances. Later works, such as *Rounds and Dances* (1980), are more eclectic in nature, employing playful and teasing thematic materials, but making more strenuous demands on the performer. His operatic works, the most frequently performed being *The Student from Salamanca*, exhibit an ingenious use of ensembles; contrapuntal textures are a primary feature. In all genres, Bach's works display both structural clarity and a subtle use of instrumental timbre.

WORKS

(selective list)

Ops: The System (1, Bach), New York, 5 March 1974; The Student from Salamanca (1, Bach), New York, 9 Oct 1980

Orch: Toccata, 1959; Dionysia, band, 1964; Burgundy Variations, 1968; Pf Conc., 1975; The Eve of St Agnes, band, 1976; Praetorius Suite, band, 1977; Hn Conc., 1983; Escapade, 1984; Dompes and Jompes, str, 1986; Hp Conc., 1986; Conc., tpt, wind, 1987; Euphonium Conc., 1990; Steel Drum Conc., 1994

Vocal: 3 Shakespeare Songs, chorus, 1960; 3 Choral Dances, female vv, 1969; 3 Sonnets on Woman, T, hpd, 1972; Hair Today, chorus, 1977; 5 Sylvan Songs, Bar, str qt, 1981; With Tpt and Drum, 16vv, pf, 1991; People of Note, vv, insts, 1993

Chbr: Str Trio, 1956; Str Qt, 1957; Four Two-Bit Contraptions, fl, hn, 1964; Laudes, brass qnt, 1971; Concert Variations, euphonium, pf, 1977; Qnt, tuba, str, 1978; Rounds and Dances, brass qnt, 1980; 8 Duetudes, fl, bn, 1983; Helix, a sax, fl, cl, bn, hn, tpt, trbn, 2 perc, 1983; Anachronisms, str, 1991

BIBLIOGRAPHY

Anderson2; *Baker7*

K.E. Shrum: *An Analytical Commentary on the Euphonium and Tuba Music of Jan Bach* (diss., Arizona State U., 1989)

R.H. Kornick: *Recent American Opera: a Production Guide* (New York, 1991), 36–9

D.S. Bristol: *The Composition and Analysis of a New Fantasy for Euphonium and Orchestra with Analysis of Jan Bach's Concerto for Euphonium and Orchestra* (diss., U. of Northern Colorado, 2002)

J.S. Tuinstra: *The Tuba in Twentieth-century Brass Quintet Repertoire: a Pedagogical Discussion of Excerpts from Selected Compositions* (diss., U. of Wisconsin, Madison, 2003) [on Laudes and Rounds for brass quintet]

JAMES P. CASSARO

Bach, Vincent [Schrottenbach, Vinzenz] (*b* Baden, nr Vienna, Austria, 24 March 1890; *d* New York, NY, 8 Jan 1976). Brass instrument maker of Austrian birth; naturalized American. He played violin as a child and studied trumpet (cornet) with Josef Weiss and Georg Stellwagen. In 1910 he earned a degree in mechanical engineering at the Maschinenbauschule in Wiener Neustadt. After a year as an Austrian navy bandsman, he studied the solo cornet repertory with Fritz Werner in Wiesbaden (1911–12), then toured as a cornet virtuoso in Europe and England, arriving in New York in September 1914. While continuing his solo career in the United States, he played one season each as assistant first trumpet with the Boston SO (1914–15) and as first trumpet with Sergey Diaghilev's ballet orchestra at the Met (1915–16). In 1916–18 he was bandmaster of the 306th Field Artillery Regiment. He became an American citizen in 1925.

On 1 April 1919 Bach set up a shop at 204 East 85th Street in New York, mainly for the purpose of making mouthpieces for his own use. In 1922 he moved to 241 East 41st Street, where he had ten employees; the manufacture of cornets and trumpets was started there in 1924. From 1928 to 1952 he was at 621 East 216th Street, with 50 employees, and began the manufacture of tenor and bass trombones. In 1953 he built a factory in Mount Vernon, New York. He sold his business to the H. & A. SELMER Co. in September 1961; four years later the firm moved to Elkhart, Indiana. The Selmer Co. became a division of Steinway Musical Instruments in 1995–6, and in 2003 merged with UMI (which Steinway had acquired in 2000) to form Conn-Selmer. As of the 2010s Steinway Musical Instruments had two divisions: Conn-Selmer, for some 20 brands of band and percussion instruments (including Bach), and Steinway & Sons for pianos.

In combining his musical proficiency with his engineering training, Bach succeeded in establishing the most exacting standards of brass instrument design and construction. His point of departure, as with Elden Benge, was the French Besson B♭ trumpet; unlike Benge, however, who desired more flexible intonation, Bach strove to give his instruments a secure "feel" for each note in the scale. Bach was also the first to set up a system for duplicating mouthpieces exactly. His instruments, especially trumpets, are employed more widely than any others. They are prized for their full and yet compact tone, with a solid core.

BIBLIOGRAPHY

V. Bach: *The Art of Trumpet Playing* (New York 1916, R/Elkhart, IN, 1969)

G. Fladmoe: *The Contributions to Brass Instrument Manufacturing of Vincent Bach, Carl Geyer and Renold Schilke* (diss., U. of Illinois, 1975)

A. Smith: "The Life and Work of Vincent Bach," *Journal of the International Trumpet Guild*, xix/2 (1994–5), 5–35; xix/3 (1994–5), 4–34

EDWARD H. TARR

Bacharach, Burt (F.) (*b* Kansas City, MO, 12 May 1928). Composer and pianist. He learned cello, drums, and piano from an early age and developed a particular interest in jazz. He played as a night club pianist, and then served in the army, touring as a pianist (1950–52). He went on to study music at the Mannes College of Music, New York, the New School of Social Research, McGill University, Montreal, and gained a scholarship to the Music Academy of the West, Santa Barbara, California. His composition teachers included DARIUS MILHAUD, BOHUSLAV MARTINŮ, and HENRY COWELL. Bacharach became an accompanist for Vic Damone, subsequently working with such performers as Polly Bergen, Steve Lawrence, the Ames Brothers, and Paula Stewart, to whom he was married from 1953 to 1958. From 1958 to 1961 he toured internationally with Marlene Dietrich. Bacharach began writing arrangements and composing songs in the mid-1950s, working at the Brill Building and collaborating with lyricist HAL DAVID, the brother of lyricist Mack David, on a large number of popular songs, including "The Story of my Life" (1957), "Magic Moments" (1958), "Anyone who Had a Heart" (1963), "Walk on by" (1964), and "(There's) Always something there to remind me" (1964). Some 60 of their songs were recorded by their protégée Dionne Warwick and these, along with recordings by Dusty Springfield (notably "I just don't know what to do with myself" and "The Look of Love"), have remained among the best interpretations of the Bacharach–David repertory. Such songs, in addition to the Broadway musical *Promises, Promises* (1968), which was also staged to great success in Australia and Europe, made them one of the most successful songwriting teams in American music history.

Bacharach's style, though eclectic, is well defined and accessible; its heterogeneous elements include variable meter, irregular phrasing, pandiatonic and jazz harmonies, rhythmic ostinatos from various sources, including African American styles. Many of his melodies—for example, "Do you know the way to San Jose?"—exhibit an internal momentum, created by the repetition of short, syncopated rhythmic patterns, which complements David's clever, colloquial lyrics. Bacharach has written a number of film scores, and won two Academy Awards for *Butch Cassidy and the Sundance Kid* (1969), for best score and best song ("Raindrops keep fallin' on my head"). He has also contributed to other films including the title song to *Alfie* (1966), and collaborated with Carole Bayer Sager on the song "Arthur's Theme" for *Arthur* (1981), which won an Academy Award. He married Sager in 1982.

A revival of interest in "lounge" music and EASY LISTENING in the early 1990s brought Bacharach back to international prominence, and his work has since been covered by such artists as Adele, Jamie Cullum, R.E.M., Rufus Wainwright, and Oasis. He has continued to perform regularly in concert, sometimes with Dionne Warwick (for whom he wrote a new song, "Sunny Weather Love" in 1993), collaborated with Elvis Costello on the song "God give me strength" (1995) and the album *Painted from Memory* (1998), and released a new solo album, *At this Time* (2005).

WORKS

(selective list)

lyrics by H. David unless otherwise stated

Stage, writers shown as (lyricist; book authors): Promises, Promises (musical, 2, H. David; N. Simon after B. Wilder and I.A.L. Diamond: *The Apartment*), Schubert, New York, 1 Dec 1968 [incl. I'll never fall in love again; Promises, Promises; Whoever you are I love you]

Film scores and songs: What's New, Pussycat?, 1965 [incl. Here I am, My Little Red Book]; Casino Royale, 1968 [incl. the Look of Love]; Butch Cassidy and the Sundance Kid, 1969 [incl. Raindrops keep fallin' on my head, Come touch the sun]; Lost Horizon (musical), 1973 [incl. Question me an answer, Reflections, The world is a circle]; Night Shift (C.B. Sager), 1982 [incl. That's what friends are for]; Arthur 2: On the Rocks (Sager), 1988 [incl. Love is my decision]

Many popular songs, incl. Magic Moments, 1957; The Story of my Life, 1958; I just don't know what to do with myself, 1962; Make it easy on yourself, 1962; (The Man who Shot) Liberty Valance, 1962; Close to You, 1963; Twenty-Four Hours from Tulsa, 1963; Wishin' and Hopin', 1963; Everyone needs someone to love, 1964; (There's) Always something there to remind me, 1964; Walk on by, 1964; Don't go breaking my heart, 1965; Trains and Boats and Planes, 1965; What the world needs now is love, 1965; Alfie, 1966; Made in Paris, 1966; Do you know the way to San Jose?, 1967; This guy's in love with you, 1968; The Hurtin' Kind, 1970; Arthur's Theme (Sager, C. Cross and P. Allen), 1981; Sunny Weather Love, 1993; God give me strength (E. Costello), 1995

Principal publishers: Blue Seas, Jac, US Songs

BIBLIOGRAPHY

CBY 1970

D. Ewen: *Popular American Composers* (New York, 1972)

B.A. Lohof: "The Bacharach Phenomenon: a Study of Popular Heroism," *Popular Music and Society*, i (1972), 73–82

R. Prendegast: *A Neglected Art: a Critical Study in Films* (New York, 1978)

J. Fitzgerald: "When the Brill Building Met Lennon-McCartney: Continuity and Change in the Early Evolution of the Mainstream Pop," *Popular Music and Society*, xix (1995), 59–77

R. Platts: "Anyone who had a Heart: the Songs of Burt Bacharach and Hal David," *Discoveries* (Dec 1997)

R.L. Doerschuk and H. Kubernik: "The Harmony of Opposites: Elvis Costello and Burt Bacharach Explore the Art of Unlikely Collaboration on *Painted from Memory*," *Musician*, no.242 (1999), 30–40 [interview]

R. Platts: *Burt Bacharach & Hal David: What the World Needs now* (Burlington, Canada, 2003)

M. Cucos: "A few Points about Burt Bacharach . . . ," *PNM*, xliii/1 (2005), 198–211

K. Emerson: *Always Magic in the Air: the Bomp and Brilliance of the Brill Building era* (New York, 2005)

MICHAEL J. BUDDS/R

Bachata. Dominican musical genre and dance. *Bachata* developed out of earlier rural string musics, principally bolero but also *son*, *merengue*, and *ranchera*. The term originally applied to the informal rural parties where such music was played. In the 1960s, as peasants moved to the cities, *bachata* developed as part of the urban underworld and changed from a romantic serenade style to one associated with brothels and harsh lyrics. At that time, it was known as *musica de amargue* (bitter music) or *musica de guardia* (military-man music, reflecting its audience) and was widely despised for its low-class connotations and explicit double entendres, although it received heavy airplay on Santo Domingo's Radio Guarachita.

In the 1980s Blas Durán's experiments with electric guitar and the development of a unique dance style began to expand *bachata*'s audience, while the so-called *technoamargue* by 1990s artists like Víctor Víctor, Luis Díaz, Sonia Silvestre, and particularly Juan Luis Guerra led to its widespread acceptance across social classes. Today, *bachata* is played with two electroacoustic guitars, electric bass, *güira*, and bongos, and *bachateros* play both the bolero-like rhythm associated with the term and the northwestern border-area *merengue* popularized by early *bachatero* Eladio Romero Santos. Modern artists like the bilingual New York group Aventura use influences from rock and rhythm and blues, while northwestern-border artists like Antony Santos and Luis Vargas remain popular.

BIBLIOGRAPHY

D. Pacini Hernández: *Bachata: A Social History of a Dominican Popular Music* (Philadelphia, 1995)

L.M. Brito Ureña: *El merengue y la realidad existencial del hombre dominicano: bachata y nueva canción* (Moca, Dominican Republic 1997)

D.C. Wayne: "*The History of Bachata*" <http://www.iasorecords.com/bachata.cfm>

SYDNEY HUTCHINSON

Bachman, Harold B. (*b* Atlanta, IL, 2 Sept 1892; *d* 10 April 1972). Conductor and author. Bachman's career included leadership positions of college, military, and professional bands. He received his academic training at the North Dakota Agricultural College (1914–16) where he led the student cadet band. At this time, he toured with several professional bands as cornetist, including Bohumir Kryl's Concert Band. During World War I, Bachman served as bandleader of the 116th Engineer Band. After the war he organized and conducted a professional concert band, Bachman's Million Dollar Band. Between 1928 and 1942, the band had headquarters in Chicago and toured extensively each year. He was director of bands at the University of Chicago from 1935 to 1942. In 1942, Bachman was recalled to military duty as the head of band music in the Pacific Theater, retiring as lieutenant colonel after the war. He was appointed director of bands at the University of Florida, serving from 1948 until 1958. He was a prolific writer with two books and over seventy articles to his credit. Bachman was president of the American Bandmasters Association (1950). His papers are held at the University of Florida; his World War II papers are at the ABA Archives at the University of Maryland.

BIBLIOGRAPHY

H.B. Bachman: *The Million Dollar Band* (Chicago, 1962)

H.B. Bachman: *The Biggest Boom in Dixie* (Gainesville, FL, 1968)

A.W. Tipps: *Harold B. Bachman, American Bandmaster: his Contributions and Influence* (diss., U. of Michigan, 1974)

WILLIAM BERZ

Bachmann, Maria (*b* Chester, PA, 9 Sept 1960). Violinist. While a student of IVAN GALAMIAN and SZYMON GOLDBERG at the Curtis Institute of Music in Philadelphia in the 1980s, Bachmann was also awarded a scholarship by The Tuesday Musical Club to study composition with GEORGE ROCHBERG. After winning first prize at the Fritz Kreisler International Violin Competition in Vienna, she made her professional debut in 1987 at Town Hall in New York, quickly followed by debuts with the St. Louis Symphony under Leonard Slatkin, the National Symphony at the Kennedy Center with Robert Spano, and with the Pacific Symphony in Los Angeles under Marin Alsop. She has won the Concert Artists Guild Competition in New York and the Pro Musicis Foundation Award. Of Hungarian descent, she is noted for her interpretation of the music of Béla Bartók. A champion of new music, Bachmann has premiered and recorded works by many composers, including Philip Glass, John Corigliano, William Bolcom, Lou Harrison, Leon Kirchner, George Rochberg, Arvo Pärt, Paul Chihara, Alfred Schnittke, Paul Moravec, Daniel Bernard Roumain (DBR), Derek Bermel, James MacMillan, Sebastian Currier, Paul Dresher, and Robert Beaser. She has recorded and presented numerous acclaimed performances with her piano trio, Trio Solisti (Bachmann, cellist Alexis Gerlach, and pianist Jon Klibonoff). Bachmann is the Artistic Director of Telluride MusicFest in Colorado, an annual festival where Trio Solisti is the resident ensemble. Bachmann performs on a 1782 violin made by Nicolo Gagliano.

ELAINE L. PETERSON

Bachman-Turner Overdrive [BTO]. Canadian rock band formed in Winnipeg, Manitoba, in 1971. They had significant success in the early 1970s, notably in October 1974 when three of their albums were in the Billboard album chart: *Not Fragile* (no.1), *Bachman-Turner Overdrive II* (no.26), and *Bachman-Turner Overdrive* (no.127). Originally called Brave Belt before signing with Mercury Records, BTO was led by Randy Bachman (*b* Winnipeg, MB, 27 Sept 1943; electric guitar and vocals) and featured the brothers Robbie (*b* Winnipeg, MB, 18 Feb 1953; drums) and Tim Bachman (*b* Winnipeg, MB, 1 Aug 1951; electric guitar and vocals) and Fred Turner (*b* Winnipeg, MB, 16 Oct 1943; bass guitar and vocals). Blair Thornton (*b* Vancouver, BC, 23 July 1950) replaced Tim Bachman in 1974 and subsequent lineup changes ensued. The band's name, inspired by a trucking magazine, its logo, a cog emblazoned with the band's initials, and many of their songs suggest the power of industrial machinery and the freedom associated with the open highway. Combined with their rugged, burly image, this formula attracted a large, predominantly male following. The band's sound, described as "heavy duty rock" by Turner, featured robust guitars, driving drums, and Turner's low, growling voice. Unapologetically geared for commercial success, BTO embraced basic song structures with straightforward lyrics addressing accessible themes, which, along with their catchy riffs, strong hooks, high production values, and professionalism, align them with so-called corporate rock. Their major hits, including "Taking Care of Business," "Hey You," "Roll on Down the Highway," and

"Let it Ride," remain stalwarts of classic and album-oriented rock radio and are used frequently for advertisements and sporting events.

STEVEN BAUR

Backbeat. Percussive accents on nominal weak beats, typically played on the snare drum on the second and fourth beats in 4/4 meter. The term came into common usage in the early 1950s in connection with rock 'n' roll music (also known then as "beat music" or the "big beat"), although the backbeat originated in earlier American musics. It remains one of the most common and distinctive features of post-1950 popular music. Significant early precursors include the weak beat accents common in ragtime music and the rhythmic clapping and body percussion common in African American work songs and gospel traditions.

The emergence of the backbeat as a central feature of contemporary popular music depended on the development of the drum kit during the 1910s and 1920s, which brought the disparate components of a band percussion section (bass drum, snare drum, cymbals, toms/woodblocks) under the control of one player. The drum kit developed alongside so-called Dixieland jazz, which often featured a "shout chorus" wherein the rhythm section (banjo or guitar, piano, and/or drums) played emphatic accents on the weak beats. For instance, drummer Andrew Hilaire plays what we now recognize as a backbeat during the last two choruses of "Black Bottom Stomp," recorded with Jelly Roll Morton's Red Hot Peppers in 1926. Early rock-and-roll session drummer Earl Palmer identified the Dixieland shout chorus as the inspiration for his use of the backbeat on Fats Domino's seminal 1949 hit "The Fat Man."

Swing and big band drummers of the 1930s and 1940s occasionally played backbeats, but rarely throughout an entire piece (one exception being "Back Beat Boogie" recorded by Harry James and His Orchestra in 1939), and the central component of jazz drumming remained the swing or shuffle cymbal pattern rather than the backbeat. Slap-back upright bass, present in some swing (and later Western swing and rockabilly) recordings, occasionally functions as a backbeat with percussive accents on nominal weak beats.

Numerous recordings released under the "hillbilly" and "race" categories during the 1920s and 1930s featured guitar or piano accompaniments that consistently emphasized weak beats, most importantly stride piano, boogie-woogie, and the blues. While drum backbeats were not common in these genres, a remarkable 1936 session by blues guitarist Memphis Minnie yielded six songs, including "Bad Luck Woman," all of which feature consistent, emphatic backbeats played by an unidentified drummer, arguably qualifying them as early exemplars of rhythm-and-blues. During the mid-1940s, Chicago session drummers—most notably Judge Riley, who recorded with Muddy Waters, Arthur "Big Boy" Crudup, Big Bill Broonzy, and Memphis Minnie starting in 1946—consistently employed a backbeat, which became a common feature of subsequent rhythm-and-blues music.

Before the 1950s, the backbeat almost always occurs in conjunction with swing or shuffle rhythms (based on the triple subdivision of the pulse); however, influential recordings by Little Richard (with Earl Palmer drumming) and other early rock-and-roll artists feature the backbeat in the context of straight eighth-note rhythms (with duple subdivision of the pulse), which remains the convention in numerous post-rock 'n' roll styles. The backbeat is often varied, as in the 1960s "girl-group" beat in which every other backbeat is doubled, or in the common funk practice of displacing the occasional backbeat by an eighth note. It is also commonly embellished by additional snare drum accents or grace notes.

The backbeat garnered controversy when it was introduced with rock 'n' roll to the American mainstream in the 1950s. Critics charged that it was "primitive" or "barbaric," entranced and seduced young people into delinquency, and replicated the rhythms of sex. More recently, John Mowitt has theorized modern American society as a "percussive field" wherein the emergence of the backbeat during the Civil Rights era signifies a "beating back" of marginalized groups against a history of violent oppression.

BIBLIOGRAPHY

G. Tamlyn: *The Big Beat: Origins and Development of Snare Backbeat and other Accompanimental Rhythms in Rock 'n' Roll* (diss., U. of Liverpool, 1998)

J. Mowitt: *Percussion: Drumming, Beating, Striking* (Durham, NC, and London, 2002)

STEVEN BAUR

Background music. *See* ENVIRONMENTAL MUSIC.

Backstreet Boys. Boy band formed in Orlando, FL, in 1993. Founded by the teen-pop aficionado Lou Pearlman, the group became part of a hugely successful teen-pop movement in the late 1990s. Its best-known lineup was Nick Carter (*b* Jamestown, NY, 28 Jan 1980), Howie Dorough (*b* Orlando, FL, 22 Aug 1973), Brian Littrell (*b* Lexington, KY, 20 Feb 1975), A(lexander) J(ames) McLean (*b* Palm Beach, FL, 9 Jan 1978) and, until 2006, Kevin Richardson (*b* Lexington, 3 Oct 1971). Their albums include *Backstreet Boys* (Jive Records, 1996), *Backstreet's Back* (Jive Records, 1997), *Millennium* (Jive Records, 1999), *Black & Blue* (Jive Records, 2000), *Never Gone* (Jive Records, 2005), *Unbreakable* (Jive Records, 2007), and *This is Us* (Jive Records, 2009). The band was widely known and celebrated in Europe, Asia, and Canada before becoming popular in the United States. By the 2010s they had sold more than 130 million records worldwide and were considered the most successful boy band of all time. The Backstreet Boys have been recognized internationally with awards from MTV Europe (1996, 1997, and 1999), MTV (1998 and 1999), the Teen Choice Awards (1999), the American Music Awards (2000 and 2001), and the People's Choice Awards (2000), among others. In 2010 they toured with the pop group New Kids on the Block. The group and its individual members have brought lawsuits concerning the group's earnings against Pearlman and his company Trans Continental, as well as against Zomba Music Group (owners of Jive Label Group). Although popular media representations of the Backstreet Boys depict their fan base as adolescent heterosexual females, subcultural fan communities challenge this notion, notably with the appropriation of Backstreet Boys imagery and music in queer drag communities.

BIBLIOGRAPHY

C. Taylor: "Backstreet Boys View their Teen Act Origins as just the Start of a Career," *Billboard* (23 May 1998)
G. Wald: "I Want it that Way," *Genders*, no.35 (2002)
J. Halberstam: *In a Queer Time & Place: Transgender Bodies, Subcultural Lives* (New York, 2005)

CRAIG JENNEX

Backus, John (Graham) (*b* Portland, OR, 29 April 1911; *d* Los Angeles, CA, 28 Oct 1988). Acoustician. After studying at Reed College, Portland (BA 1932), he undertook postgraduate study at the University of California in Berkeley (MA 1936, PhD 1940). His early research work was in nuclear physics, working under the supervision of Ernest Lawrence in the Radiation Laboratory at Berkeley. In 1945 he was appointed professor of physics at the University of Southern California, and he continued in that post until his retirement in 1980. An accomplished performer on piano and bassoon, Backus was awarded the degree of MMus in conducting by the University of Southern California in 1959. In the later stages of his research career he made major contributions to the study of the acoustics of woodwind instruments, brass instruments, and organ pipes. In 1969 the first edition of *The Acoustical Foundations of Music* was published; this became one of the most popular and successful introductory textbooks in musical acoustics. He was awarded the Silver Medal of the Acoustical Society of America in 1986.

WRITINGS

"Small-Vibration Theory of the Clarinet," *JASA*, xxxv (1963), 305–13
with T.C. Hundley: "Wall Vibrations in Flue Organ Pipes and their Effect on Tone," *JASA*, xxxix (1966), 936–45
The Acoustical Foundations of Music (New York, 1969, 2/1977)
"Input Impedance Curves for the Reed Woodwind Instruments," *JASA*, lvi (1974), 1266–79
"Input Impedance Curves for the Brass Instruments," *JASA*, lx (1976), 470–80
"The Effect of the Player's Vocal Tract on Woodwind Instrument Tone," *JASA*, lxxviii (1985), 17–20

MURRAY CAMPBELL

Bacon, Denise (*b* Newton, MA, 20 March 1920). Music educator. A leader in the American Kodály movement, she attended the Dana Hall School in Wellesley, Massachusetts, and the New England Conservatory (BM 1952, MM 1954). She taught in the former school before becoming founding director of its music unit, the Dana School of Music (1957). With encouragement from ZOLTÁN KODÁLY and support from a Braitmayer Fellowship, Bacon earned a Kodály method teaching diploma from the Franz Liszt Academy in Budapest (1968). She founded the Kodály Musical Training Institute (KMTI) (1969) with a Ford Foundation Grant, and established the Kodály Center of America (KCA) (1977), both in Wellesley, for the purpose of developing model schools, training teachers, and conducting research. A demonstration in Hungary of her adaptation of the Kodály approach by her first KMTI class (1970), which included a film entitled *Let's Sing Together*, led to Hungarian collaboration in the development of Kodály-based curriculum in the United States during the 1970s. She published method books, videos, articles, choral compositions, and a chamber opera. She received two Hungarian government medals (1983, 1989) and the Lifetime Achievement Award from the Organization of American Kodály Educators (2000). Since retiring (1995) Bacon has worked to establish the KCA/KMTI Archives at the University of Maryland, College Park.

JUI-CHING WANG

Bacon, Ernst (*b* Chicago, IL, 26 May 1898; *d* Orinda, CA, 16 March 1990). Composer and pianist. He studied at Northwestern University (1915–18), the University of Chicago (1919–20) and the University of California (MA 1935). Among his teachers were Alexander Raab and GLENN DILLARD GUNN (piano), KARL WEIGL and ERNEST BLOCH (composition), and sir EUGENE GOOSSENS (conducting), under whom he was assistant conductor of the Rochester Opera Company. He taught at the Eastman School (1925–8) and the San Francisco Conservatory (1928–30); in 1935 he instituted and conducted the Carmel Bach Festival in California, and the next year he was supervisor of the WPA Federal Music Project in San Francisco and conductor of its orchestra. Subsequent teaching appointments took him to Converse College, Spartanburg, South Carolina, as dean and professor of piano (1938–45), and to Syracuse University as director of the school of music and professor (1945–63, professor emeritus from 1964). Among the awards he received were a Pulitzer Prize (1932, for the Symphony no.1) and two Guggenheim Fellowships.

As a composer Bacon is best known for his songs, which show unusual sensitivity to the color and inflection of words, and a masterly use of syncopation to give the impression of natural speech. His settings of texts by Emily Dickinson and Walt Whitman are considered by many to be among the finest examples of 20th-century American art song. He made many folksong arrangements, and a number of his works on American subjects, such as the folk opera *A Tree on the Plains* (1942) and the orchestral suite *From these States* (1951), draw on various types of indigenous music, including African American and Appalachian tunes, hymns, spirituals, and jazz. His music favors clear melodic contours, vigorous contrapuntal energy, and strong rhythms that allude occasionally to ragtime and other dance idioms. Though he made use of non-diatonic scales, such as the octatonic, Bacon's harmony remained fundamentally tonal, with an emphasis on open, diatonic intervals.

In addition to composing, Bacon performed as a pianist in Europe and the United States. His published writings include two books, *Words on Music* (Syracuse, NY, 1960/*R*) and *Notes on the Piano* (Syracuse, NY, 1963/*R*). His article "Our Musical Idiom," published in *The Monist* in October 1917, represents one of the earliest attempts at a systematic classification of all possible harmonies within the 12-tone system.

WORKS
(selective list)

Dramatic: Take your Choice (musical comedy), collab. P. Mathias and R. Stoll, San Francisco, 1936; A Tree on the Plains (musical play, 2, P. Horgan), Spartanburg, SC, 1942; A Drumlin Legend (children's op, H. Carus), New York, 1949; Dr. Franklin (musical play, C. Lengyel), 1976; ballets

Orch: Sym. no.1, d, 1932; Bearwalla, pf, str, 1936; Country Roads, Unpaved, suite, 1936; Sym. no.2, 1937; Ford's Theater, 1946; From these States, suite, 1951; Fables (Bacon, J. Edmunds), nar, orch, 1953; Great River (Sym. no.3), 1956; Conc. grosso, 1957; Elegy, ob, str, 1957; Erie Waters, suite, 1961; Riolama (Pf Conc. no.1), 1963; Over the Waters, ov., 1976; Pf Conc. no.2, 1982; Remembering Ansel Adams, cl, str, 1985; band works; songs with orch

Chbr: Coal Scuttle Blues, 2 pfs (1942); Buncombe County, vn, pf, 1943; Sonata, vc, pf, 1948; Qnt, str qt, db, 1950; Peterborough, suite, va, pf, perf. 1952; A Life, suite, vc, pf, 1966–81; Old Airs from Many Countries, wind ens, 1968; Pf Trio no.1, 1978; Tumbleweeds, cycle, vn, pf, 1979; Sonata, vn, pf, 1982; Pf Trio no.2, 1986; Sonata, va, pf, 1987; pieces for pf, pf 4 hands, and org; other works for various insts

Choral: Ecclesiastes, cant., S, B, SATB, orch, 1936; From Emily's Diary (E. Dickinson), women's chorus, pf/small orch, 1947; By Blue Ontario (W. Whitman), cant., A, B, SATB, orch, 1958; Requiem "The Last Invocation" (Dickinson, Whitman), B, chorus, orch, 1968–71; 3 Carols for Christmas, SATB (published 2004); Let me be your Friend (n.d.), unison children's chor. and pf (published 2004); orats; choral folksong arrs, hymns, and anthems

Songs, 1v, pf: Songs at Parting (Whitman) (1930); 6 Songs (C. Sandburg, Whitman, Dickinson) (1942); The Erie Canal (Amer.) (1942); 5 Poems (Dickinson) (1943, 2/1998 with other Dickinson song settings); Along Unpaved Roads (Amer.), 8 songs (1944); Is there such a thing as day? (Dickinson) (1944); Buffalo Gals (Amer.) (1946); The Grass (Dickinson) (1946); O Friend (Dickinson) (1946); 4 Songs (W. Shakespeare, J. Lewis, E. Millay) (1946); The Commonplace (Whitman) (1946); The Red Rose (R. Burns) (1947); Velvet People (Dickinson) (1948); over 200 others

Principal publishers: Associated, Birchard, Broude, Chappell, Lawson-Gould, Leeds, E.B. Marks, Mercury, G. Schirmer, Shawnee, Southern, Syracuse UP, Peters, L. Webster

BIBLIOGRAPHY

EwenD; *VintonD*

J. St. Edmunds: "The Songs of Ernst Bacon," *Shawnee Review* (Oct 1941)

W. Fleming: "Ernst Bacon," *MusAm*, lxix/36 (1949), 8, 28

E. Bacon: *Ernst Bacon* (Orinda, CA, ?1974) [incl. bibliography, discography, and P. Horgan: "A Contemporary Tribute"]

R.C. Friedberg: *American Art Song and American Poetry*, i (Metuchen, NJ, 1981)

S. Neff: "An American Precursor of Non-tonal Theory: Ernst Bacon," *CMc*, no.48 (1991), 5–26

P. Griffths: "Tribute to a Neglected Composer," *New York Times* (17 Sept 1998)

PHILIP L. MILLER/MICHAEL SAFFLE

Bacon, Fred(erick J.) (*b* Holyoke, MA, 17 Jan 1871; *d* Newfane, VT, 18 Nov 1948). Banjoist and banjo maker. He began his career playing with a medicine show and a Wild West show, then from 1890 to 1915 performed in a vaudeville act with his wife. He studied with ALFRED A. FARLAND in the mid- 1890s and about 1897 organized the Bacon Banjo Quintette. He toured with the Bacon Trio in 1905–6, and made another very successful tour in 1908 with "The Big Three," consisting of himself, the guitarist William Foden, and the mandolinist Guiseppe Pettine. Bacon continued to play into the 1940s and his few recordings attest to his virtuoso performances; contemporary reviewers praised his tone, his great technique, and the expressiveness of his playing. He taught, published several method books, and wrote many arrangements and compositions for five-string banjo. Bacon also designed banjos, bringing out his first instrument in 1905 in Forest Dale Vermont and opening his own factory in Groton, Connecticut, not long after; the famous "Silver Bell" model, produced with David L. Day, was introduced in 1923. Although his company produced instruments under different monikers, the most common name was the Fred Bacon Manufacturing Company or the Bacon Banjo Company. Bacon's particular interest was the development of a new tailpiece for the instrument wherein each string could be individually tuned. His banjos are still prized for their power and tone.

BIBLIOGRAPHY

E. Kaufman and M. Kaufman: "Fred Bacon," *The 5-stringer*, no.120 (1975), 1, 10; no.121 (1976), 1, 3, 9

K. Linn: *That Half-barbaric Twang: The Banjo In American Culture* (Urbana, IL, 1994)

ROBERT B. WINANS/JONAS WESTOVER

Bacon, Leonard (*b* Detroit, MI, 19 Feb 1803; *d* New Haven, CT, 23 Dec 1881). Author of hymn texts and hymnbook compiler. The son of a missionary to the Native Americans, he was educated at Yale University and Andover Theological Seminary. While at Andover he compiled a small pamphlet containing 101 missionary hymns, three of them his own: entitled *Hymns and Sacred Songs; for the Monthly Concert* (Andover, MA, 1823), it was intended for use at missionary prayer meetings and was the first such collection to be published in the United States. In 1825 Bacon was ordained and became pastor of the Center Church, New Haven, where he served until he joined the faculty of the Yale Divinity School in 1866. In 1833 he published in New Haven a revision of Timothy Dwight's edition of Isaac Watts's *Psalms and Hymns*, to which he appended the collection *Additional Hymns, Designed as a Supplement to Dwight's Psalms & Hymns* (2/1837); it included four of his own texts. He also supervised the preparation of a new Connecticut Congregational hymnal, *Psalms and Hymns, for Christian Use and Worship* (1845), which contained five of his texts. He is best known for his hymn "O God, beneath thy guiding hand," written for New Haven's bicentennial celebration in 1833, and since sung generally to John Hatton's tune "Duke Street."

BIBLIOGRAPHY

F.M. Bird: "Bacon, Leonard," *A Dictionary of Hymnology*, ed. J. Julian (New York, 1892, 2/1907/*R*)

T.D. Bacon: *Leonard Bacon, a Statesman in the Church* (New Haven, 1931)

C.W. Hughes: *American Hymns Old and New: Notes on the Hymns* (New York, 1980), 174, 265

PAUL C. ECHOLS

Bacon, Thomas (i) (*b* Isle of Man, *c*1700; *d* Frederick, MD, 24 May 1768). Violinist and composer. Bacon spent his early years in Ireland, where he was engaged in various occupations from overseeing a coal depot and running a coffee house to editing his own newspaper in Dublin. In 1743, he abandoned these pursuits to enter the priestly orders of the Church of England, where he was ordained the following year. In 1745 he immigrated to America and settled in Oxford, Maryland, where he was appointed rector of St. Peter's Church. In addition to composing hymns and anthems, by 1750 he had organized the Eastern Shore Triumvirate, a musical club with a membership of local merchants, which regularly presented concerts; Bacon played violin, viola da gamba, lute, and keyboard. His plans for establishing the first charity school in Maryland led to a series of benefit concerts in Maryland and Virginia from 1750 to 1754. Bacon was also an honorary member of the Tuesday Club, an organization attended chiefly by clerics and professional men in Annapolis, Maryland that was the center of scientific inquiry. He wrote an *Anniversary Ode of the Tuesday Club* in 1750, the earliest-known extant piece of chamber music composed in the United States, as well as other similar works. In 1758, he moved to Frederick, Maryland, where he was appointed rector of All Saints Church in 1762. He spent his later years working on educational projects, and he published a compilation of the laws of Maryland (1766).

BIBLIOGRAPHY

W.B. Sprague: *Annals of the American Episcopal Pulpit or Commemorative Notices of Distinguished Clergymen of the Episcopal Church in the United States from the Early Settlement of the Country to the Close of Eighteen-hundred and Fifty-five* (New York, 1859), 118–21

E. Allen: "Rev. Thomas Bacon," *American Quarterly Church Review and Ecclesiastical Register*, xvii/3 (October 1865), 430–51

W.E. Deibert: "Thomas Bacon, Colonial Clergyman," *Maryland Historical Magazine*, lxxiii (1978), 79–85

J.B. Talley: *Secular Music in Colonial Annapolis: the Tuesday Club, 1745–1756* (Urbana, IL, 1988)

P. Johnson: *A History of the American People* (New York, 1999), 98–99

J. Ogasapian: *Music of the Colonial and Revolutionary Era, American History through Music* (Westport, CT, 2004), 63, 65

E.G. Breslaw: *Dr. Alexander Hamilton and Provincial America: Expanding the Orbit of Scottish Culture* (Baton Rouge, LA, 2008), 224–37

JAMES R. HEINTZE/KIMBERLY GREENE

Bacon, Thomas (ii) (*b* Chicago, IL, 31 Oct 1946). Horn player. Bacon began playing piano at age four, trumpet at age 11, and the horn at age 14. His teachers included Max Pottag, Frank Brouk, Rudy Macciochi, Marvin Howe, VERNE REYNOLDS, RAY STILL (chamber music), and Robert McDowell (piano). He has served as first horn of the Chicago Civic Orchestra (1964–6) and the Syracuse SO (1966–8), assistant principal and acting principal of the Detroit SO (1968–73), solo horn of the Berlin RS (1975–8), and principal of the Houston SO (1978–88), Houston Grand Opera (1990–92), and the Houston Ballet Orchestra (2000–09). Exploring other musical expressions, Bacon was a member from 1969 to 1974 of Metamorphosis, a rock group comprising Detroit SO musicians. His long involvement with chamber music includes roles as founding member of the Summit Brass (1985–present), the Chamber Orchestra of Arizona (1992–3), the Opus 90 chamber ensemble (1990–present), and the Golden Horn chamber ensemble (1994–present), and member of the St. Louis Brass Quintet (1997–present). In addition, he has taught at Rice University (1978–91) and Arizona State (1991–2000). His discography features 11 solo recordings (1983–2006) and 22 recordings with other various ensembles (1968–2006). His wide-ranging experience has led him to author and edit numerous publications.

GERALD E. WOOD

Bacon Banjo Company, Inc., The. Banjo manufacturer. It was founded in 1921 in Groton, Connecticut, by FRED BACON, a 5-string banjo performer, inventor, and publisher. The company is best known for the instruments developed after David L. Day, a veteran of the Fairbanks and Vega companies, joined Bacon's firm in Sept 1922. Their flagship B&D Silver Bell, introduced in June 1923, is still considered one of the most desirable banjos of the Jazz Age. Day standardized Bacon's quality control and further modularized banjo construction, so that any neck would fit any rim—with only minor adjustments. This allowed "just-in-time" assembly, to fill orders more efficiently.

During the 1920s the Silver Bell line was expanded with the lavish ebony and ivory "Ne Plus Ultra" models. Bacon's endorsers included top stars of Vaudeville, dance orchestras, radio, and recordings: Ray "Montana" Coleman, Roy Smeck, Perry Bechtel, Eddie Connors, and many others. The Depression required the company to lower costs. The use of celluloid overlays increasingly replaced wood and pearl inlays. Notable 1930s models were the Senorita, Serenader, Sultana, Symphonie, and Montana.

In 1932, Rudolf and Farny Wurlitzer joined the board of directors, Fred Bacon retired to Vermont, and D.L. Day became president. Bacon began selling their B&D and Bacon brands through large distributors, and also manufactured private label models, including Lyric (Wurlitzer), Gordon (Progressive), and Rhythm King (CMI). Bacon commissioned B&D- and Bacon-branded guitars from the Regal Co. of Chicago to capitalize on changing musical tastes.

The Bacon Banjo Company filed for bankruptcy in 1939 following flood damage to their factory in the Great Hurricane of 21 Sept 1938. Day contracted with the Gretsch Co. to finish any undamaged work-in-progress, and assemble banjos with any useable parts. Gretsch ultimately purchased Bacon's trade names, designs, and patents in 1940. After WWII, the Gretsch Co. made Bacon and B&D banjos of a lesser quality than those from the Groton factory. These brands were discontinued in 1970, after Baldwin purchased Gretsch.

EDMUND J. BRITT

Bad Boy Entertainment. Record company. Bad Boy Entertainment is a label specializing in hip hop and R&B. It was founded in 1993 in New York City by Sean "Puffy" Combs who had been A&R man for Andre Harrell's Uptown Records. Once Combs secured a deal with Clive Davis's Arista Records, he released Craig Mack's *Project: Funk the World* and The Notorious B.I.G.'s *Ready to Die* on 1 September 1994. The massive success of The Notorious B.I.G.'s (aka Biggie Smalls or Biggie) debut brought national attention to Bad Boy and its founder, spearheading a revival in East Coast hip hop at a time when the West Coast had dominated the rap scene for two years (most notably the acts on Dr. Dre and Suge Knight's Death Row Records). This led to a media-enhanced rivalry between Death Row Records and Bad Boy Entertainment, which some believe fuelled the still-unsolved murders of Death Row's Tupac Shakur (*d* 13 Sept 1996) and Bad Boy's Notorious B.I.G. (*d* 9 March 1997).

Combs, under the artist name "Puff Daddy," produced a number of successful solo albums after Biggie's death, including *No Way Out* with the tribute "I'll be Missing You" (featuring B.I.G.'s widow, Faith Evans), and produced The Notorious B.I.G. posthumous releases *Life After Death, Born Again* and *Duets: the Final Chapter.* The label's musical style in the 1990s consisted of borrowing large portions of earlier R&B and pop hits, a strategy which drew criticism from some quarters. Other successful Bad Boy Artists in the 1990s included 112, Faith Evans, The L.O.X., Total, and Mase. The label was bought by Warner Music Group in 2005 and has since distributed music by a number of successful artists including Yung Joc, Cassie, and Danity Kane.

BIBLIOGRAPHY

A. Light, ed.: *The Vibe History of Hip Hop* (New York, 1999)

JUSTIN A. WILLIAMS

Bad Brains. Hardcore punk rock group. Formed in Washington, DC in 1977, its classic lineup includes guitarist Dr. Know (Gary Miller), bassist Darryl Jenifer, drummer Earl Hudson, and vocalist H.R. (Earl's brother, Paul D. Hudson). The group remained active into 2011, despite various breakups, departures, and reunions. Originally formed as a jazz fusion group, but inspired by punk rock and reggae, Bad Brains pioneered the extremely fast and loud style that became known as HARDCORE, influencing bands such as Minor Threat and Black Flag. Integrating reggae songs, complex rhythms, heavy metal and jazz-influenced guitar solos, and unison riffs—all unusual in hardcore—Bad Brains remains highly distinctive. Its lyrics often explore themes of Rastafarianism and social-political consciousness.

Although one of the definitive 1980s hardcore bands, the group's popularity was hampered by erratic touring and poor distribution of its recordings. Nevertheless, its influence has been acknowledged by subsequent groups such as the Beastie Boys, Rage Against The Machine, Red Hot Chili Peppers, and Living Colour.

LUKAS PEARSE

Badea, Christian (*b* Bucharest, Romania, 10 Dec 1947). Conductor of Romanian birth. He studied violin at the conservatory in Bucharest and later became a répétiteur at the Bucharest Opera, playing piano and coaching singers at rehearsals. After leaving Romania (1970), he studied conducting in Brussels, the Mozarteum in Salzburg, and the Juilliard School. He became music director of the Spoleto Festival (1978), which he directed in both Italy and later in Charleston, South Carolina (1980–86), conducting a variety of operas by Mozart, Verdi, Menotti, Prokofiev, and Shostakovich. He has conducted at the Royal Opera House at Covent Garden, the Bayerische Staatsoper, Vienna State Opera, the Grand Theatre in Geneva, the Teatro Regio in Torino, the Teatro Comunale in Bologna, the Opera National de Lyon, and, in North America, the opera companies of Houston, Dallas, Toronto, Montreal, and the Metropolitan Opera, where he is a regular guest. Also an orchestral conductor, Badea has appeared with the Royal Philharmonic, the BBC Symphony, the Residentie Orchestra, the Beethovenhalle Orchestra, the Orchestre National de Lyon, the RAI Orchestra in Torino, the Santa Cecilia Orchestra in Rome, the Maggio Musicale Orchestra in Florence, the Tokyo Philharmonic, and, in the United States, the symphony orchestras of Pittsburgh, Atlanta, Detroit, and Baltimore. He was music director of the Savannah SO (1983–91) and music director of the Columbus SO in Ohio. He received a Grammy Award in 1985 for his recording of Samuel Barber's *Anthony and Cleopatra* at the American Spoleto Festival. Badea is noted for his dramatic vitality and secure command of phrasing and balance.

ROBERT PAUL KOLT

Badger, Alfred G. (*b* Connecticut, 1814 or 1815; *d* Brooklyn, NY, 8 Nov 1892). Flute maker. Badger was a major advocate for and maker of the Boehm system flute in the United States. He described himself as having an early interest in flute making and in 1834 apprenticed in flute making with Ball & Douglass in Utica, New York. In 1838 he moved to Buffalo, where he made simple system flutes and was partner in a music store with John R. Nickels. Sometime after 1843 Badger moved to Newark, New Jersey; by 1848 he had moved his manufactory to Manhattan, where his shop was located at several addresses on Broadway until his death.

Throughout his career, Badger's work was characterized by an innovative approach and a high level of craftsmanship. He recognized the superiority of the Boehm system flute and became an early proponent for its adoption in the United States, making his first commercial Boehm system flute in 1846. The earliest ones were of the conical ring-keyed 1832 Boehm system, likely copied from one made by Godfroy. In 1851, Badger made cylindrical flutes according to the Boehm 1847 system; these were exhibited in London and later Paris. The flutes were constructed of ebonite tubing from Charles Goodyear. Badger was the first to use this material for flute making and acquired the patent for this use from Goodyear in 1859. Some of his early metal flutes explored the use of metal alloys that were silver plated, though many of his later flutes were of solid coin silver. Badger experimented with tone hole position and size to improve the scale, including graduated tone holes on some of his later flutes. His metalwork was frequently elaborately engraved and included a gold cartouche with his name and New York location affixed to the head joint or barrel of his silver flutes. His ring-keyed conical and early cylindrical flutes were pitched near $a'=440$, but his later instruments were often of higher pitch ($a'=450$ or higher). A tireless promoter of the Boehm system flute, Badger published broadsides, enlisted testimony of the best flute players of the day (e.g. Philip Ernst and John Kyle) and published four editions of his *An Illustrated History of the Flute* (New York, 1853, 4/1875). The fate of the Badger flute manufactory after his death is unknown. His wife, who was said to have taken over the business, actually predeceased him by three years. Gustav Behrle and William S. Richards have been mentioned as successors to Badger, but few flutes by these makers survive.

BIBLIOGRAPHY

WaterhouseLangwillI

M.J. Simpson: *Alfred G. Badger (1815–1892), Nineteenth-century Flute-maker: his Art, Innovations, and Influence on Flute Construction, Performance and Composition, 1845–1895* (diss., U. of Maryland, 1982)

S. Berdahl: *The First Hundred Years of the Boehm Flute in the United States, 1845–1945: a Biographical Dictionary of American Boehm Flutemakers* (diss., U. of Minnesota, 1985)

N. Groce: *Musical Instrument Makers of New York: a Directory of Eighteenth- and Nineteenth-century Urban Craftsmen* (Stuyvesant, NY, 1991)

DAVID W. THOMAS

Badu, Erykah [Wright, Erica Abi] (*b* Dallas, TX, 26 Feb 1971). Singer, songwriter, and producer. She was singing for audiences by the age of four and cultivated her skills at the Booker T. Washington High School for the Performing and Visual Arts. She briefly attended Grambling State University, but left to develop her music career and soon landed a contract with Universal Records. She became an immediate sensation; her first recording, *Baduizm* (Universal, 1997), reached number two on the *Billboard* charts, while its top single "On and On" received widespread attention and airplay. Her dark, breathy vocal style, reminiscent of jazz and soul singing, earned her two Grammy Awards and four nominations. She went on to release a live album, *Erykah Badu Live* (Universal, 1997), and to work on a number of side projects with other artists, notably providing the hook for the Roots' song "You got me." After a brief respite she returned with *Mama's Gun* (Universal, 2000); the single "Bag Lady" remained at the top of the Billboard R&B chart for seven weeks. After a period of what she described as writer's block, Badu made the album *Worldwide Underground* (Universal, 2003). She has continued to tour and record, often writing powerful and controversial material, including the recording *New Amerykah Part Two: Return of the Ankh* (Universal, 2010).

JONAS WESTOVER

Baermann, Carl [Bärmann, Karl] (*b* Munich, Germany, 9 July 1839; *d* Newton, MA, 17 Jan 1913). Pianist, teacher, and composer of German birth. His father, Carl Bärmann (1810–85), and his grandfather, Heinrich Joseph

Erykah Badu, 2008. (JM Charlotte/Landov)

Bärmann (1784–1847), were both renowned clarinetists; the latter was an intimate friend of Weber and Mendelssohn, both of whom composed works for him. Carl Baermann studied in Munich with Franz Lachner and Peter Cornelius and later became a pupil and close friend of Franz Liszt. He taught for many years at the Königliche Musikschule in Munich, becoming a professor in 1876, then in 1881 came to the United States. He made a successful debut as pianist in Boston (22 December 1881). Having decided to remain, he became prominent there as a performer, playing Beethoven's "Emperor" concerto with the Boston Symphony Orchestra during its first season in 1882. He was also highly esteemed as a teacher: AMY BEACH and FREDERICK SHEPHERD CONVERSE were among his pupils, and Olin Downes and George Chadwick both gave addresses at a memorial service held after his death. Baermann wrote a *Festival March* for orchestra and a number of piano compositions. Among the few published works are a set of 12 *Etüden*, op.4 (1877) and a stylish *Polonaise pathétique* (1914).

His correspondence with his pupil Lee Pattison is held in *Bc*.

BIBLIOGRAPHY

J.P. Brown: "Carl Baermann," *Musical Record and Review*, no.481 (1902), 40

L.C. Elson: *The History of American Music* (New York, 1904, enlarged 3/1925/*R*)

"Carl Baermann," *New England Conservatory Review*, ii/1 (1912), 1

JOHN GILLESPIE/LAURA MOORE PRUETT

Baez, Joan (Chandos) (*b* Staten Island, NY, 9 Jan 1941). Folk singer, songwriter, and activist. She was born to a Mexican father and Scottish mother. A self-taught singer and guitarist, she began performing informally for classmates as a way to make friends. She became enthralled with folk music as a high school student in Cambridge, Massachusetts. Her polished soprano voice and deft finger-picking style gained her local attention, and a guest performance at the Newport Folk Festival in 1959 was her first major professional success. After a short time attending Boston University Baez left to pursue her music career, which proceeded rapidly. She released six successful albums with Vanguard Records in the first half of the 1960s and toured widely. Her repertoire in these years consisted principally of traditional songs, but subsequently included new folk songs written by such contemporaries as Phil Ochs ("There but for Fortune") and Bob Dylan ("It ain't me babe" and "Farewell, Angelina"). Dylan's songs became a staple for Baez, and the two had a high-profile but short romance. Baez was a bona fide folk star and used her celebrity to advocate for civil rights and protest against the Vietnam War. She was married to the anti-war activist David Harris from 1968 to 1971, with whom she had her only son, Gabriel.

Baez's successful career continued in the 1970s, beginning with her rendition of "The Night they Drove old Dixie Down" (*Blessed Are…*, Vanguard, 1971), her greatest chart success. As America's musical tastes changed beyond folk, she had begun to incorporate contemporary styles such as country and pop into her work. With her albums *Come from the Shadows* (A&M, 1972) and *Diamonds and Rust* (A&M, 1974) Baez began writing her own songs. "Diamonds

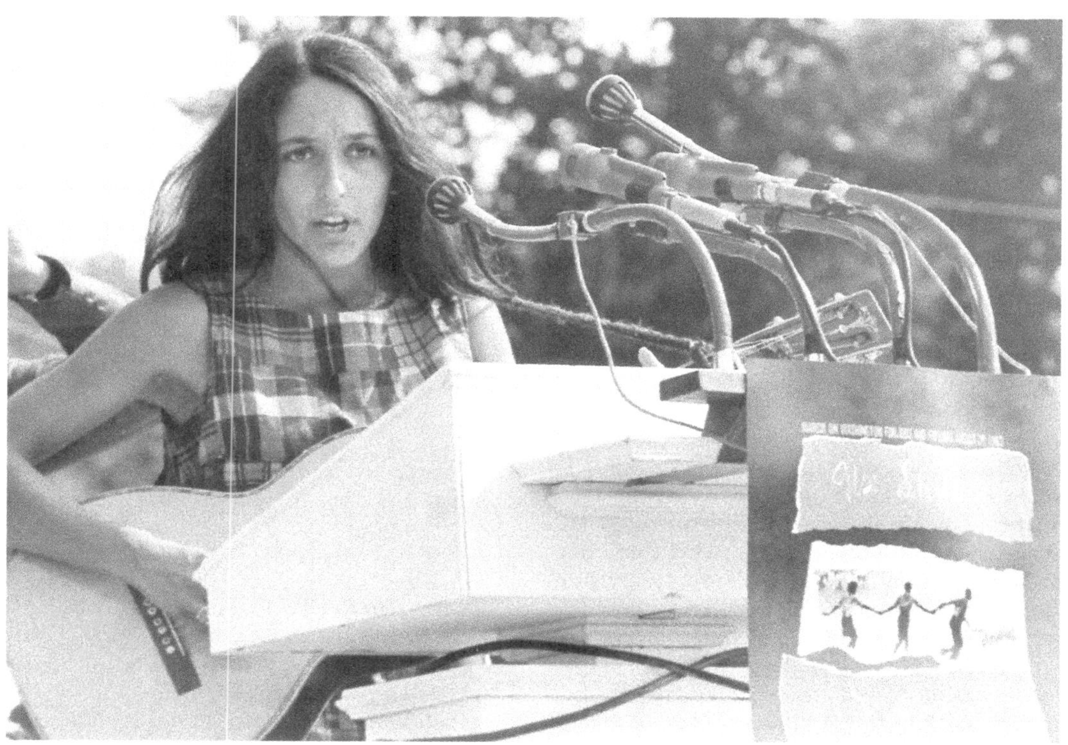

Joan Baez at the Civil Rights March on Washington, DC, 1963. (National Archives)

and Rust" remembers her time with Dylan a decade earlier and along with "Rider, Please Pass By" is one of her best-known originals. Although Baez had recorded Spanish songs as early as 1960, the album *Gracias a la Vida* (1974) was sung entirely in Spanish, highlighting her Hispanic heritage. Baez's prolific pace in the studio slowed after 1979. Prominent performances at such events as Live Aid (1985) and the publication of her autobiography, *And a Voice to Sing With* (1987), reinforced her profile and humanitarianism. She has continued to perform to large and appreciative audiences. Her album *Day after Tomorrow* (Proper, 2008) was a conscious attempt to return to her folk beginnings.

Baez has remained a folk icon of her generation. In her heyday she embodied the image of the folk troubadour, both in her beautifully simple, self-accompanied performance, and her activism. As a result of her family's Quaker roots and the influence of Martin Luther King, her music delivered messages of nonviolence, pathos, and hope. She tended towards ballads of loneliness ("Lonesome Road") and songs of hope ("We shall Overcome"). This made her music more accessible to broader audiences than that of such folk protest singers as Ochs, whose lyrics were more aggressive. Although she is acknowledged as a songwriter, her musical legacy inevitably lies in her consummate interpretations of others' songs.

BIBLIOGRAPHY

[J. McPhee:] "Sibyl with Guitar," *Time* (23 Nov 1962), 54–60

J.L. Rodnitzky: *Minstrels of the Dawn: the Folk-protest Singer as a Cultural Hero* (Chicago, 1976)

J. Baez: *And a Voice to Sing With: a Memoir* (New York, 1987/*R*)

C.J. Fuss: *Joan Baez: a Bio-bibliography* (Westport, CT, 1996)

D. Hajdu: *Positively 4th Street: the Lives and Times of Joan Baez, Bob Dylan, Mimi Baez Fariña, and Richard Fariña* (New York, 2001)

MARK C. SAMPLES

Bagley, Edwin Eugene (*b* Craftsbury, VT, 29 May 1857; *d* Keene, NH, 29 Jan 1922). Composer and performer. One of America's best-known composers of military marches, Bagley is legendary for his *National Emblem*, with its quotation of *The Star Spangled Banner*, which is still frequently performed. A self-trained musician, he was a professional performer as a vocalist and comedian with Leavitt's Bellringers, a company of entertainers that toured many of the larger cities of the United States. Having learned the cornet he toured for six years with the Swiss Bellringers, after which time he joined Blaisdell's Orchestra of Concord, New Hampshire. In 1880 he came to Boston as a solo cornetist at the Park Theater and he also traveled for nine years with the Bostonians, an opera company. While with this company, he played the trombone and subsequently performed with the Germania Band of Boston and the Boston Symphony Orchestra. He was the composer of a number of marches, including *Front Section*, *The Imperial*, *The Ambassador*, and *America Victorious*, but none found the popularity of his *National Emblem*. Anumber of his works are recorded in Robert Hoe's *Heritage of the March* series (18).

BIBLIOGRAPHY

W.H. Rehrig: *The Heritage Encyclopedia of Band Music* (Westerville, OH, 1991, suppl. 1996); CD-ROM (Oskaloosa, IA, 2005) [includes selective list of works]

DAVID WHITWELL

Bailes Brothers. Country music group. Its principal members were four brothers: Kyle (Otis) Bailes (*b* Enoch, WV, 7 May 1915; *d* 3 March 1996), Johnnie (John Jacob) Bailes (*b* St. Albans, WV, 24 June 1918; *d* 21 Dec 1989), Walter (Butler) Bailes (*b* North Charleston, WV, 17 Jan 1920; *d* Sevierville, TN, 27 Nov 2000), and Homer (Vernon) Bailes (*b* North Charleston, WV, 8 May 1922); at different times various combinations of the brothers and other musicians made up the group. Brought up by a widowed mother during the Depression, the brothers formed a group called the Hymn Singers to earn their living. Among the performers who influenced their style were Hank and Slim Newman and the Holden Brothers. The Bailes Brothers worked on various West Virginia radio stations, where their colleagues included Molly O'Day (then known as Dixie Lee) and Little Jimmy Dickens, billed by Johnnie as the Singing Midget. During World War II, while Homer was in military service, Johnnie and Walter performed as a duo on the "Grand Ole Opry," having secured the booking through their friendship with Roy Acuff. In the mid- 1940s the group made its most successful recordings, mostly of songs written by Walter, for Columbia; at that time it was known as the West Virginia Home Folks. In 1946 the brothers moved to Shreveport, Louisiana, to perform on the radio station KWKH; with Dean Upson, formerly a commercial manager at WSM, Nashville, they founded the program *Louisiana Hayride* in April 1948, which helped to launch the careers of Hank Williams and Webb Pierce. Walter left the group in 1947 to become a minister and it disbanded in 1949, but two pairs of brothers (Walter and Johnnie, and Kyle and Homer) continued to perform and record intermittently as late as the mid-1970s.

The Bailes Brothers were among the most popular performers on the *Grand Ole Opry* and *Louisiana Hayride*. Their style was a unique mixture of old-time secular duet singing and gospel intensity, and they sang both secular and sacred repertory. Many of their songs were recorded by other country and bluegrass artists, for example, "Dust on the Bible" by the Blue Sky Boys and "Give Mother my Crown" by Flatt and Scruggs.

BIBLIOGRAPHY

I.M. Tribe: "The Bailes Brothers," *Bluegrass Unlimited*, ix/8 (1975), 8–14

I.M. Tribe: *Mountaineer Jamboree: Country Music in West Virginia* (Lexington, KY, 1996)

RONNIE PUGH/R

Bailey, Buster [William C.] (*b* Memphis, TN, 19 July 1902; *d* New York, NY, 12 April 1967). Jazz clarinetist. As a teenager he played in W.C. Handy's orchestra, and in 1919 he moved to Chicago, where he studied with Franz Schoepp and performed and recorded with Erskine Tate, Mamie Smith, and King Oliver. In 1924 he moved to New York to join Fletcher Henderson's group, in which he worked until 1929 and then again in the mid-1930s. Bailey's technical facility earned him a role as a soloist on several of Henderson's notable recordings. He also played with Noble Sissle (early 1930s) and the Mills Blue Rhythm Band (1934–5). In 1934 he made the first of many recordings alongside Henry "Red" Allen, in both the Henderson and Mills orchestras. In 1937 Bailey joined a group that soon took shape as John Kirby's sextet. His classical training served him well in this "chamber jazz" setting, as the group favored intricate arrangements and precise ensemble coordination. He recorded frequently with Kirby and remained with the group until 1946. After a stint with Wilbur de Paris, Bailey spent much of the 1950s with Allen's band, which held a residency at the Metropole from 1954. He later worked with Wild Bill Davison (1961–3) and Louis Armstrong's All Stars (1965–7). Never an overtly passionate blues player, Bailey instead brought a graceful fluency to his solos throughout his long careeer. His pure, smooth tone and nimble finger technique are heard to best advantage in his work with Kirby, on such tunes as "Dizzy Debutante" (1937, Var.) and "Man with a horn goes berserk" (1938, Voc.).

BIBLIOGRAPHY

W.C. Allen: *Hendersonia: the Music of Fletcher Henderson and his Musicians: a Bio-discography* (Highland Park, NJ, 1973)

J. Chilton: *Who's Who of Jazz: Storyville to Swing Street* (London, 1970, rev. and enlarged 4/1985)

G. Schuller: *The Swing Era: the Development of Jazz, 1930–1945* (New York, 1968, 2/1989)

CHARLES E. KINZER

Bailey, DeFord (*b* Smith County, TN, 14 Dec 1899; *d* Nashville, TN, 2 July 1982). Country-blues harmonica player. He was one of the early stars of the radio show *Grand Ole Opry*. He began playing the harmonica at age three when he was bedridden with polio and made his first radio performance on the Nashville radio station WDAD in September 1925. Thanks to Dr. Humphrey Bate, Bailey soon began performing on WSM's show "Barn Dance." George D. Hay called him the Harmonica Wizard and credited him with inspiring the naming of the "Grand Ole Opry." In 1928 Bailey recorded eight tunes for Victor Records in the first recording session in Nashville. Except for a brief time when he lived in Knoxville and played on WNOX radio, he performed on WSM every Saturday night from 1926 until 1941. He was included in many WSM touring groups during the 1930s. Uncle Dave Macon, the Delmore Brothers, Roy Acuff, and Bill Monroe, among others, wanted him on the tour because of his strong draw with the audience of the *Grand Ole Opry*. As an African American performer, Bailey encountered difficulties on the road involving lodging and food, but received an enthusiastic reception from white audiences. He left the Opry in 1941 at the height of a licensing battle between ASCAP and BMI. Bailey was posthumously inducted into the Country Music Hall of Fame in 2005. His signature tune, "Pan American Blues" (Victor, 1928), was inducted into the Grammy Hall of Fame in 2007.

BIBLIOGRAPHY

D.C. Morton (with C.K. Wolfe): *DeFord Bailey: a Black Star in Early Country Music* (Knoxville, TN, 1991)

DAVID C. MORTON

Bailey [née Rinker], **Mildred** (*b* Tekoa, WA, 27 Feb 1903; *d* Poughkeepsie, NY, 12 Dec 1951). Jazz singer of Coeur d'Alene heritage. In her youth she was influenced by tribal song, vaudeville, and blues. She sang in West Coast speakeasies until she was introduced to Paul Whiteman by her brother Al Rinker and his friend Bing Crosby. Hired by Whiteman in 1929, Bailey became the first significant female big band vocalist. In the 1930s and 40s she made more than 200 recordings with some of the top jazz musicians of the time. She also toured with her husband, the xylophone player RED NORVO (1936–8). Although they never achieved great commercial success, their subtle swing was widely admired in jazz circles, and his delicate mallet work complemented her clear, sweet tone and refined phrasing, pitch, and diction. They worked closely with the classically trained arranger Eddie Sauter and the composers Hoagy Carmichael, Johnny Mercer, Willard Robison, and Alec Wilder. The influence of the Bailey–Norvo partnership resonated widely: in 1933 they introduced the producer John Hammond to the young Billie Holiday and in 1935 they hosted Benny Goodman as he formed his first small group at their house in Queens.

Bailey's fame evaporated following her death at the dawn of the LP era. However, a few of her recordings have remained popular: "Darn that Dream" (with Goodman), "Ghost of a Chance" (with Norvo), and Carmichael's "Rockin' Chair." Those who professed her influence—including Crosby, Frank Sinatra, Rosemary Clooney, and Tony Bennett—sustained her reputation as a singer's singer.

BIBLIOGRAPHY

R. Sudhalter: *Lost Chords: White Musicians and their Contributions to Jazz, 1915–1945* (Oxford, 1999)

G. Giddins: "Mrs. Swing," *Village Voice Jazz Supplement* (June 2000)

W. Friedwald: *The Complete Columbia Recordings of Mildred Bailey*, Mosaic (2000) [disc notes]

TINA SPENCER DREISBACH

Bailey, Pearl (Mae) (*b* Newport News, VA, 29 March 1918; *d* Philadelphia, PA, 17 Aug 1990). Jazz and popular singer. She sang with Noble Sissle's band in the mid-1930s and with Cootie Williams and Count Basie in the early 1940s. She made her solo debut in New York at the Village Vanguard in 1941. By the middle of the decade, she was working with Cab Calloway and his band, with whom she developed a comical, offhand style of performance, which included a patter of droll asides. She made her Broadway debut in Harold Arlen's musical *St. Louis Woman* (1946), for which she won a Donaldson Award. She later starred in Arlen's *House of Flowers* (1954) and in an African American version of Jerry Herman's *Hello, Dolly!* (1967), which earned her a Special Tony Award (1968). Among her film roles, Bailey is best remembered for her appearances in *Carmen Jones* (1954), *That Certain Feeling*

(1956, with Bob Hope), *St. Louis Blues* (1958), and *Porgy and Bess* (1959). Her first hit recording was "Tired" (1946, Col.) and her most successful the comic song "Takes Two to Tango" (1952, Coral). Although she announced her retirement in 1976 to serve as a member of the American delegation to the United Nations, she later resumed television and concert appearances, frequently performing with the band led by the jazz drummer Louis Bellson, whom she had married in 1952.

BIBLIOGRAPHY

P. Bailey: *The Raw Pearl* (New York, 1968/*R*)
P. Bailey: *Talking to Myself* (New York, 1971/*R*)
J.S. Wilson: Obituary, *New York Times* (19 Aug 1990)

ARNOLD SHAW/R

Bain, Wilfred (Conwell) (*b* Shawville, PQ, Canada, 20 Jan 1908; *d* Bloomington, IN, 7 March 1997). Music educator and administrator of Canadian birth. He was educated at Houghton College (BA 1929), Westminster Choir College (BMus 1931), and New York University (MA 1936, EdD 1938). He was head of the Music Department at Wesleyan Methodist College in Central, South Carolina (1929–30), head of voice and choral music at Houghton College (1931–8), dean of the School of Music at North Texas State University (1938–47), and dean of the School of Music at Indiana University (1947–73). After retiring he became artistic director of the Opera Theater at Indiana University. The eminence of the Indiana University School of Music, especially its excellent facilities for operatic production, is largely due to his efforts, and he was instrumental in enticing professional artists to join the faculty, including the mezzo-soprano Margaret Harshaw and cellist János Starker. He was also active in music education nationally, and was a chairman of the US Information Agency Music Advisory Panel.

BIBLIOGRAPHY

E. Williams: "Wilfred C. Bain: A Reminiscence in Memoriam," *College Music Symposium*, xxxviii (1998), 1–5
G.M. Logan: *The Indiana University School of Music: a History* (Bloomington, IN, 2000)

PATRICK J. SMITH/KEITH COCHRAN

Bainum, Glenn Cliffe (Rusty) (*b* Olney, IL, 6 Jan 1888; *d* Evanston, IL, 4 Oct 1974). Conductor and arranger. Bainum began his study of music at age ten playing trombone and alto horn. He attended the University of Illinois, studying English and engineering, and played bass drum in the band under A.A. Harding. After teaching high school for a year, he became director of music at Southern Illinois Normal University (1914–22). Bainum worked toward completing a BA in music while serving as Harding's first assistant director (1922–4), then became director of music for the Grand Rapids (MI) public schools (1924–6). In 1926 he was appointed director of bands at Northwestern University, a position he held until his retirement in 1953. From 1942 to 1945, Bainum was Chief of the United States Army Overseas Music Branch of Special Services, responsible for music in the European theater.

Many of his band arrangements are widely performed, *Australian Up-Country Tune* (Grainger) and the Finale from Symphony no.1 (V. Kalinnikov) among the most popular. He was elected President (1947) and Honorary Life president (1971) of the American Bandmasters Association. His scrapbooks, papers and photographs are in the Northwestern University Archives.

BIBLIOGRAPHY

C.C. Burford: *We're Loyal to You, Illinois* (Danville, IL, 1953), 355–67
J.P. Paynter: "Glenn Cliffe Bainum," *NBA Journal*, xv/2 (1974), 2–3

WILLIAM BERZ

Baiocchi, Regina Harris (*b* Chicago, IL, 16 July 1956). Composer and writer. She studied at Roosevelt and De Paul universities, where her teachers included Robert Lombardo and GEORGE FLYNN. She has also studied jazz piano with Alan Swain and composition with HALE SMITH. Her music reveals an eclectic mixture of idioms and techniques, from serialism to black American folk music. Jazz is seldom far from the surface in *Sketches* (1992) and *Gbeldahoven: No One's Child* (1996), an opera based on the lives of Harlem Renaissance writers Zora Neale Hurston and Langston Hughes that includes numbers inspired by African chant, spirituals, blues, jazz, gospel, work songs, and rap music. The aria "How It Feels to Be Colored Me" shares motivic material with the final movement of the brass quintet *QFX* (1993); both are based on a 12 tone series she describes as her "stand-by tone row," as well as on black American harmonies and rhythms. Her African heritage also provides sounds for *African Hands* (1997), a concerto for African drummer and orchestra. Works showing a strong influence of jazz include *Miles Per Hour* for trumpet (1990), which recalls the style of Miles Davis, and *Friday Night* (1995) for jazz singer and ensemble.

Baiocchi has written fiction and non-fiction works and poetry, and has worked in public relations and as a composer-in-residence for Mostly Music, a Chicago organization that sponsors children's music programs. She has taught at East-West University (2000–04) and Columbia College (2005–06), both in Chicago.

WORKS

(selective list)

Op: Gbeldahoven: No One's Child, 1996

Inst: Equipoise by Intersection, pf, 1978; Miles Per Hour, tpt, 1990; Orch Suite, 1992; Sketches, vn, vc, pf, 1992; QFX, brass qnt, 1993; After the Rain, sax, pf, perc, 1994; Deborah, pf, perc, 1994; Liszten, My Husband Is Not a Hat, pf, 1994; Kidstuff, chbr ens, 1995; African Hands, African drummer, orch, 1997; Message to My Muse, pf, 1997; Communion, mar, str, 1999, rev. 2009; Azuretta, pf, 2000; HB4A, pf, b, perc, sax, 2005; Karibu, cl, 2007; Concerto, cl, str, 2010; Triptych, cl, vc, perc, 2010

Vocal: Black Voices, rap singers, perc, 1992; Best Friends, S, B, pf, 1993; Friday Night, 1v, jazz ens, 1995; Ask Him, 1v, jazz trio, 1999; Cycles, 1v, jazz trio, 1999; Lovers and Friends, 1v, jazz trio, 1999; Psalm Cat, 1v, b, sax, 2000; Litany of Saints, SATB, 2001; Three Love Lyrics, S, pf, 2008; ETHS Fanfare, SATB, orch, 2009; 2 Swahili Poems, SATB, orch (also arr. S, pf), 2008–9; e.e. cummings Songbook, S, pf, 2009–10

MSS in Center for Black Music Research, Chicago; Indiana University Center for Black Music Research, Tulane University

BIBLIOGRAPHY

H. Walker-Hill: *Piano Music by Black Women Composers: a Catalog of Solo and Ensemble Works* (New York, 1992)

H. Walker-Hill: *Music by Black Women Composers* (Chicago, 1995)

S.A. Floyd Jr.: *International Dictionary of Black Composers* (London, 1999)

W.C. Banfield: *Musical Landscapes in Color: Conversations with Black American Composers* (Lanham, MD, 2003)

H. Walker-Hill: *From Spirituals to Symphonies: African American Women Composers and Their Music* (Westport, CT, 2003)

KARIN PENDLE

Baird, Julianne (*b* Statesville, NC, 10 Dec 1952). Soprano. She attended the Eastman School (BA 1973, MA 1976), where she studied singing with Masako Ono Toribara, and Stanford University, where she completed a dissertation on P.F. Tosi (PhD 1991). Baird also studied with Walter Berry and Nicolas Harnoncourt and at the Salzburg Mozarteum, where she earned a Diploma in Performance Practice in 1977. She began her singing career in New York as a member of the Waverly Consort and Concert Royal, with which she made her stage debut in 1980 in *Il pastor fido*. Baird has since sung in many operas by Marc-Antoine Charpentier, Marco da Gagliano, Gluck, Mozart, Purcell, and others, in Los Angeles, Philadelphia, Santa Fe, Washington, DC, Chicago, and elsewhere. Her international appearances include performances in London, Leipzig, and Warsaw. Baird has appeared as soloist with several prominent symphony orchestras, including the New York Philharmonic, the Philadelphia Orchestra, and the Cleveland Orchestra.

Recordings of *Amadis de Gaule*, *Imeneo*, *Orfeo* (Monteverdi), and *La serva padrona* are among her nearly 100 releases. Baird's world premiere performance of Reich's *Tehillim* (1983) accompanied by the New York Philharmonic has been included in the ten-CD set celebrating the Philharmonic's best performances of 20th-century composers. Her performances are distinguished by pristine vocalism, fluent coloratura, and expressive, imaginative ornamentation founded in serious scholarship.

A respected specialist in Baroque vocal music, Baird has taught at Rutgers University since 1989. Her publications include articles in *Continuo* (1984) and *Early Music* (1987), as well as an annotated translation of Johann Friedrich Agricola's 18th-century treatise *Introduction to the Art of Singing* (Cambridge, UK, 1995).

CORI ELLISON/ELIZABETH PERTEN

Bajo sexto. Twelve-string instrument sharing some similarities with an acoustic guitar. Although its exact origins are unclear, the *bajo sexto* appeared in Mexico during the late 1800s and has gained popularity since that time. The instrument is tuned lower than a typical acoustic guitar, hence the *bajo* part of the name; the *sexto*, or six, refers to the original number of strings. Changes to the instrument were made to increase its volume, including an expansion of the body (to around 30% larger than an acoustic guitar), a larger bridge, a widened neck, an increase to seven frets, and the doubling of strings to 12, or six double courses. The highest three strings are typically tuned in unison; the lower three strings in octaves, which offers great resonance and depth. The husky, hoarse sound of the refashioned *bajo sexto* is capable of both bass rhythm and harmony, allowing greater flexibility for other instruments, such as the accordion, in various ensembles. Once it gained popularity, the *bajo sexto* began to be manufactured in the Mexican States of Aguascalientes, Morelos, Puebla, Oaxaca, Tlaxcala, and Distrito Federal. The *bajo sexto* now plays an especially significant role in *conjunto* and *norteño* music, and it represents a key contribution by Mexican instrument makers to local traditions and, increasingly, international musical practices.

RAMÓN HERNÁNDEZ

Baker. Family of singers who between 1844 and the 1880s formed various differently constituted groups under the family name. A vocal quartet named the Baker Family was first formed around 1844 and consisted of by siblings John C. Baker, George E. Baker, Sophia M. Baker, and Henry F. Baker in Salisbury, New Hampshire. They followed the example of the Hutchinson Family in style, repertory, and presentation, and became one of the most popular ensembles of this type. The group, sometimes with the addition of other family members including Jaspar and Emilie, toured widely in the mid- and late 1840s, especially to smaller cities and towns. In 1851 some of the family moved to Waukegan, Illinois, from where the newly named Baker Vocalists made periodic tours to the West until the 1880s. Although the bass George had the most impressive voice, it was John who was the leading member of the group. A Baker Family concert often consisted only of his glees, choruses, and ballads; among his 35 published pieces, "Where can the soul find rest?" (1845), "The Burman Lover" (1845), and "My Trundle Bed" (1860) achieved significant popularity. He also wrote a cantata, *Esther*, and an oratorio, *The Great Feast of Babylon*. *The Baker Vocalists: Book of Words* was published in 1862. Dartmouth College, Hanover, New Hampshire, and the New Hampshire Historical Society, Concord, have collections of music and papers relating to the family.

BIBLIOGRAPHY

J.T. Howard: *Our American Music* (New York, 1931), 182–3

DALE COCKRELL

Baker, Anita (*b* Toledo, OH, 26 Jan 1958). R&B singer and songwriter. After moving to Detroit and achieving some success with the group Chapter 8, she began her own career with the album *The Songstress* (1983). Although she only found moderate success at first, her second album, *Rapture* (1985–6), contained several hits that rocketed her to stardom on both the R&B and pop music charts, especially the song "Sweet Love," which she co-wrote with Gary Bias and Louis Johnson. Baker remained a fixture on the charts throughout the 1980s and early 90s with such songs as "Giving you the best that I got" (from *Giving you the Best that I Got*, 1988), for which she is best known. By 2010 Baker had won eight Grammy Awards and four of her albums had reached platinum status. Using her exceptional range and powerful voice, she has mixed soul, gospel, and

R&B in an adult contemporary style, which some critics have called romantic soul. She has toured extensively, especially during the early 1990s and the mid-2000s. In 2004 she signed an exclusive contract with Blue Note Records. Over the course of her career she has recorded a number of duets, including "Witchcraft" (1993, with Frank Sinatra), "Like you used to Do" (2004, with Babyface), and "Give me your Love (Love Song)" (2010, with Snoop Dogg).

JONAS WESTOVER

Baker, Arthur (*b* Boston, MA, 22 April 1955). Record producer and DJ. A club DJ in Boston, he ventured into dance music production by borrowing money from relatives. After producing a number of obscure dance singles he moved to New York and got involved with the early rap recording scene. He worked for the label Tommy Boy Records, engineering and producing its second release, "Jazzy Sensation" by the Jazzy Five. He also produced the next single, "Planet Rock" (1982) by Afrika Bambaataa and Soul Sonic Force. This track, which was influenced by the electronic music of Kraftwerk, Yellow Magic Orchestra, and Gary Numan, changed the sound of Hip hop. Baker's association with futuristic dance music, known as Electro, led to more than two decades of production work for New Order (including the hit "Confusion"), along with further Afrika Bambaataa releases such as "Looking for the Perfect Beat" and "Renegades of Funk." Launching a label of his own, Streetwise, he released New Edition's *Candy Girl* (1983). Later production and remix work included singles or albums by Bruce Springsteen, Cyndi Lauper, Hall & Oates, Bob Dylan, the Stylistics, Al Green, and Diana Ross. After many years of mainstream work, Baker returned to producing club dance records. As of the early 2010s he was living in London, where he also worked and owned a chain of successful bars.

DAVID TOOP/R

Baker, Benjamin Franklin (*b* Wenham, MA, 10 July 1811; *d* Boston, MA, 11 March 1889). Teacher, singer, and composer. He sang, directed choirs, and taught music in Salem, Massachusetts, and in 1833 toured the country with a concert company. He then settled in Bangor, Maine, as a businessman, but moved to Boston in 1837 to study music with John Paddon. He was director of music at W.E. Channing's church for eight years, and succeeded Lowell Mason as superintendent of musical instruction in the Boston public schools in 1841. Also in that year he began holding "musical conventions," which led to many appearances as soloist with the Handel and Haydn Society, of which he later became vice-president. He founded the Boston Music School and served as principal and head of the singing department until 1868, when he retired and the school closed. He was editor of the *Boston Musical Journal* for several years. Baker collaborated in compiling over 25 collections of songs, hymns, anthems, and glees, including *The Boston Musical Education Society's Collection of Church Music* (with Isaac B. Woodbury, Boston, 1842) and *Baker's Church Music* (Boston, 1855). He wrote two harmony textbooks (1847 and 1870), and composed vocal music, including three secular cantatas: *The Storm King* (1856), *The Burning Ship* (1858), and *Camillus, the Roman Conqueror* (1865).

BIBLIOGRAPHY

DAB

F.O. Jones, ed.: *A Handbook of American Music and Musicians* (Canaseraga, NY, 1886/*R* 1971), 10 only

WILLIAM E. BOSWELL

Baker, Chet [Chesney Henry] (*b* Yale, OK, 23 Dec 1929; *d* Amsterdam, Netherlands, 13 May 1988). Jazz trumpeter, flugelhorn player, and singer. He was almost entirely self-taught; he never obtained more than a rudimentry knowledge of music theory and thus had to improvise by ear. Baker played in army bands sporadically from 1946 to 1951. While stationed in Berlin in 1946, he started listening to modern jazz and thereafter blossomed as a jazz player. In 1952 he was hired by Charlie Parker, and later that year joined the Gerry Mulligan Quartet. Mulligan's pianoless group had a relaxed, pleasant sound that appealed to a broad audience, and it was in this context that Baker achieved national fame. In 1953 Baker began leading his own groups and in the mid-1950s made a series of recordings as a singer that showcased the distinctive, intimate quality of his voice.

Baker led an erratic lifestyle due to drug addiction, and in 1956 he served a prison sentence for possession of drugs. He subsequently spent 16 months in an Italian prison, also for drug-related offenses, during a five-year period in Europe (1959–64). When he returned to the United States, jazz was becoming less fashionable, so he recorded a series of commercial albums with Herb Alpert–like brass groups and popular songs with strings. Baker's career was interrupted when his upper teeth were replaced by dentures in 1968; one of the causes being an attack in 1966, after which his teeth deteriorated. He made a comeback in New York in 1973. From the 1970s, on, he spent increasing amounts of time in Europe, where he regained his confidence and found a new audience, which adored his lyrical approach, adventurous improvisations, and tender sound. He also performed skillfully as a scat singer. This later period has often been ignored in the jazz literature as a result of Baker's limited visibility in the United States.

Baker died from a fall or jump from his room on the third floor of a hotel in Amsterdam. The police ruled out murder, as the trumpeter had locked his hotel door from the inside and there were no traces of a struggle or any involvement of a second person. Baker's life as a drug addict is documented in Bruce Weber's film *Let's Get Lost* (1988) and James Gavin's biography *Deep in a Dream* (New York, 2002).

SELECTED RECORDINGS

As leader: *The Best of Chet Baker Sings* (1953–6, PJ); *Chet is Back* (1962, Bb); *Baby Breeze* (1964, Verve); *She was too good to me* (1974, CTI/Epic); *The Sesjun Radio Shows* (1976–85, T2 Entertainment); *You can't go home again* (1977, A & M/Verve); *Chet's Choice* (1985, Criss Cross); *Live from the Moonlight* (1985, Philology); *Chet Baker in Tokyo* (1987, Evidence); *The Last Great Concert* (1988, Enja)

As sideman with G. Mulligan: *The Complete Pacific Jazz Recordings of the Gerry Mulligan Quartet with Chet Baker* (1952–7, PJ)

BIBLIOGRAPHY

J. de Valk: *Chet Baker: Herinneringen aan een Lyrisch Trompettist* (Amsterdam, 1989; enlarged 2/2007)
S. Sjogren: *Chet: a Discography by Thorbjorn Sjogren* (Copenhagen, 1993)
I. Wulff, ed.: *Chet Baker in Europe* (Kiel, Germany, 1993)
C. Baker: *As though I had Wings* (New York, 1997)
J. de Valk: *Chet Baker: his Life and Music* (Berkeley, CA, 2000)

JEROEN DE VALK

Baker, Claude (*b* Lenoir, NC, 12 April 1948). Composer and educator. He began his musical training with his junior high school band, playing first the euphonium, and later switching to trombone, which became his principal instrument. After graduating from East Carolina University (BM, 1970), Baker studied composition with SAMUEL ADLER and WARREN BENSON at the Eastman School of Music where he received his masters in 1973 and doctorate in 1975. Baker taught music at the University of Georgia (1974–6) and the University of Louisville (1976–88) before joining the faculty of the Jacobs School of Music at Indiana University in 1988. In 2007, he was appointed to the rank of Chancellor's Professor at Indiana University.

At age 21, he wrote his first composition, a duo for flute and clarinet. Since that time he has received numerous commissions from around the world, but he is chiefly noted for his orchestral works. From 1991 to 1999, Baker served as the composer-in-residence for the St. Louis Symphony Orchestra, when Leonard Slatkin was its music director. During that period, he composed five large-scale works for the orchestra and two occasional pieces.

In 1996 the National Symphony Orchestra commissioned and premiered Baker's song cycle for soprano and orchestra, *Into the Sun*. His "Märchenbilder" (Fairy Tale Images) was premiered by the Indianapolis Symphony in May, 2005. Important compositions for orchestra include *The Glass Bead Game* (1982, rev. 1983), *Shadows: Four Dirge-Nocturnes* (1990), *The Mystic Trumpeter* (1999), and *Aus Schwanengesang* (2002). Other noted works are the Three Pieces for Five Timpani, Five Roto-toms and Wind Ensemble (1990), *Awaking the Winds* for chamber orchestra (1993), and *Three Phantasy Pieces* for viola and percussion (2003, rev. 2005). Orchestras that have performed his music include the St. Louis, San Francisco, Atlanta, Pittsburgh, Indianapolis and Louisville as well as the New York Philharmonic, the National Symphony Orchestra, the Orquesta Nacional de España, and the Musikkollegium Winterthur. His works have been published by Lauren Keiser Music and Carl Fischer and are recorded on the ACA, Gasparo, TNC, and Louisville First Edition labels.

In 2008–09, he was the Paul Fromm Composer-in-Residence at the American Academy in Rome. He has also received an Academy Award in Music from the American Academy of Arts and Letters; two Kennedy Center Friedheim Awards; the Eastman-Leonard and George Eastman Prizes; a "Manuel de Falla" Prize (Madrid); BMI-SCA and ASCAP awards; a commission from the Fromm Music Foundation; and fellowships from the John Simon Guggenheim Memorial Foundation, the National Endowment for the Arts, the Rockefeller Foundation, the Bogliasco Foundation, and the state arts councils of Indiana, Kentucky, and New York. In recognition of the educational outreach programs that he developed with for the St. Louis Symphony, the University of Missouri-St. Louis awarded him an honorary doctorate in 1999.

BIBLIOGRAPHY

A. McCutchan: *The Muse that Sings: Composers Speak about the Creative Process* (London, 1999)

JAMES BASH

Baker, David (Nathaniel) (*b* Indianapolis, IN, 21 Dec 1931). Composer and jazz cellist. He received both the BME (1953) and MME (1954) degrees from Indiana University and studied privately with J.J. JOHNSON, BOB BROOKMEYER, GEORGE RUSSELL, JANOS STARKER, JOHN LEWIS, and GUNTHER SCHULLER, among others. Unable to play the trombone professionally following a 1953 accident, Baker turned exclusively to the cello and pioneered the use of that instrument in jazz with such artists as Maynard Ferguson, Quincy Jones, George Russell, John Montgomery, and Lionel Hampton. He has taught at Lincoln University in Jefferson City, Missouri, at Indiana Central University, Indianapolis, and in the Indianapolis public schools. In 1966 he joined the faculty of Indiana University, where he now serves as Distinguished Professor of Music and Chairperson of the Jazz Department. At IU, he established the 21st-Century Bebop Band, a student group dedicated to the preservation of bebop literature. He has received honorary doctorates from Wabash College, Oberlin College, and the New England Conservatory of Music. In 2007 Baker was honored by the John F. Kennedy Center for the Performing Arts with their Living Jazz Legend Award. Baker continues to serve as the conductor and musical and artistic director of the Smithsonian Jazz Masterworks Orchestra.

Baker also has toured as a lecturer, conducted workshops, and written over 400 articles and 70 books on jazz and African American music. He has served in a wide-range of music organizations, such as the National Council on the Arts, and as chair of the Jazz Advisory Panel to the Kennedy Center and Jazz/Folk/Ethnic Panel of the NEA. He has also served as president for the International Association of Jazz Education and the National Jazz Service Organization. Baker has received numerous awards, including a 1973 Pulitzer Prize nomination (*Levels*) and a nomination for a Grammy Award in 1979. He was honored by *Down Beat Magazine*, as a trombonist, for lifetime achievement, and in 1994 he was inducted to their Jazz Education Hall of Fame. Other awards include the National Association of Jazz Educators Hall of Fame Award (1981), the Arts Midwest Jazz Masters Award (1990), the Governor's Arts Award of the State of Indiana (1991), the Indiana Historical Society's Living Legend Award (2001), the James Smithson Medal from the Smithsonian Institution (2002), the American Jazz Masters

Award from the National Endowment for the Arts (2000), and an Emmy Award (2003) for his score for the PBS documentary *For Gold and Glory*.

His compositions are often cited as examples of third-stream jazz, although they range from traditional jazz compositions to through-composed symphonic works.

Baker has acknowledged Ives and Bartók as principal influences. Over the course of his career, Baker has composed more than 2000 works, among which 500 compositions were commissioned for ensembles and individuals, including Janos Starker, the New York Philharmonic, the Beaux Arts Trio, the Fisk Jubilee Singers, the Indianapolis Symphony, and many others.

WORKS
(selective list)

Levels, conc., db, jazz band, fl qt, hn qt, str qt, 1973; Sonata, cl, pf, 1974; Vc Conc., 1975; The Soul of '76, jazz ens, 1975; Ethnic Variations on a Theme of Paganini, 1976; Ellingtones: a Fantasy, sax, orch, 1987, rev. 1988; Images, Shadows and Dreams: Five Vignettes, 1993; Concertino, cell phones, orch, 2006; Dancing Shadows, 2007

TIMOTHY M. CRAIN

Baker [née Reid], **Etta (Lucille)** (*b* Caldwell County, NC, 31 March 1913; *d* 23 Sept 2006, Fairfax, VA). Guitarist and banjoist. She began guitar studies with her father, Boone Reid, at the age of three. Baker, who specialized in the Piedmont blues style, was known only in her home region of North Carolina until she was discovered by the folksinger Paul Clayton, who made a recording of her that appeared as part of the 1956 release Instrumental Music of the Southern Appalachians. Although this recording brought Baker considerable attention, she initially declined to pursue music professionally, opting in favor of family life and her job at a local textile company. Her career as a professional musician began in the 1970s, after her husband Lee Baker had died and her children had grown to adulthood. Baker and several of her family members recorded the album *Music From the Hills of Caldwell County*, which was released in 1975. Baker's high-profile public performances included the National Folk Festival at Wolf Trap (1980) and the World's Fair in Knoxville (1982). She made a series of home recordings with her sister Cora Phillips between 1988 and 1990; these were later released under the title *Carolina Breakdown*. Her first solo album was *One-dime Blues* (Rounder, 1991). Baker's other recordings (aside from her inclusion on various anthologies) are Railroad Bill (Music Maker, 1999), *Etta Baker with Taj Mahal* (Music Maker, 2004), and the posthumously released *Banjo* (Music Maker, 2009). She was named a National Endowment for the Arts National Heritage Fellow in 1991. Baker's repertoire consisted primarily of her own solo guitar arrangements of traditional folk, blues, and country music in addition to original compositions. She played the guitar with a thumb and finger right-hand technique strongly associated with her native region.

BIBLIOGRAPHY

B. Bastin: Red River *Blues: the Blues Tradition in the Southeast* (Champaign, IL, 1986)

C. Signorelli: "Piedmont Blueswoman Etta Baker: One-diming it with the Hands of Time," *Sing Out*, xli/4 (1997), 34–41

T. Olson: *Blue Ridge Folklife* (Jackson, MS, 1998)

M. Freed: "Preliminary Bibliography of Best-known Black Appalachian Musicians," *Black Music Research Journal*, xxiv/1 (2004), 91–169

LARS HELGERT

Baker, Israel (*b* Chicago, IL, 11 Feb 1921). Violinist. He studied first at the American Conservatory, Chicago, and made his debut at Orchestra Hall in Chicago at the age of six. After further periods of study with Louis Persinger at the Juilliard School and with Jacques Gordon and Bronisław Huberman, he developed a considerable reputation as a chamber musician, orchestral leader, and soloist. Much of Baker's career was spent in California, where he was the regular second violinist in the Heifetz–Piatigorsky Chamber Concerts and leader in the long series of recordings by Stravinsky and by Bruno Walter. As a soloist he had particular success with such works as Schoenberg's Concerto and *Phantasy* and Berg's Chamber Concerto; his recordings of those pieces combine stylistic acumen with the advantages of a thorough grounding in the Viennese Romantic tradition. Both as a soloist and as a member of the Pacific Art Trio, Baker performed and recorded works by Antheil, Ives, Korngold, Vernon Duke, and Gail Kubik. Beyond the concert stage, he contributed to many popular music recordings, working with artists such as Barbra Streisand, Frank Sinatra, Nina Simone, Celine Dion, and Ella Fitzgerald. He also played on several film soundtracks, including *The Man with the Golden Arm*, *Indiana Jones and the Temple of Doom*, and *The Color Purple*, among others.

BERNARD JACOBSON/MEGAN E. HILL

Baker [née McDonald], **(Freda) Josephine** (*b* St. Louis, MO, 3 June 1906; *d* Paris, France, 12 April 1975). Dancer and singer, naturalized French. She started out dancing on the streets of St. Louis with the Jones Family Band, a vaudeville troupe. After touring the South with the Dixie Steppers, she gained attention in the touring company of *Shuffle Along* (1921), the most important African American show of the decade. A member of the female dancing chorus, Baker stood out by making faces and embellishing dance moves, mixing comedy with the erotic persona of the black chorus girl. After appearing on Broadway in *The Chocolate Dandies* (1924) as That Comedy Chorus Girl, Baker traveled to Paris with *La revue nègre* (1925), a nightclub revue that introduced the new black performance styles of Broadway to French audiences. Her pas de deux "Danse Sauvage," which she performed with her partner Joe Alex, introduced an explicit eroticism and exuberant physicality which marked Baker's initial renown. Famously appearing at times with little more than a string of bananas around her waist, she made an impact on French popular culture that was immediate and enduring.

After performing at the Folies-Bergère and the Casino de Paris, Baker later ran her own nightclub, Chez Josephine. She appeared in only one musical stage work, a revival of Offenbach's *La créole* (1934). A natural subject for the new medium of sound film, she starred in three feature films in France early in her career: *La sirène des tropiques* (1927), *Zou Zou* (1934), and *Princess Tam Tam* (1935). The films capture Baker's unrestrained and joyful persona, her abilities as a physical comedian, and her strikingly personal dancing style. Baker spent the war years working for the French Resistance and performing for Allied troops in North Africa. She was twice decorated by the French president Charles de Gaulle. Her periodic trips to the United States were not always successful. In the *Ziegfeld Follies of 1936*, she shared headliner status with Fannie Brice and appeared in three elaborately staged numbers, including "5 am," choreographed by George Balanchine. Baker used an American tour of her nightclub act in 1951 to push for racial integration. Her appearance at Copa City was attended by the first integrated audience in Miami. She returned to Broadway twice in later decades: *Josephine Baker and her Company* (1964, 40 performances) and *An Evening with Josephine Baker* (1973, seven performances).

Although her voice was powerful and her act, particularly after 1936, increasingly centered on singing, Baker's appeal was primarily visual. Her loose-limbed dancing and free, angular body style helped define the visual vocabulary of the jazz age, particularly for photographers and visual artists who took her as an ideal subject. Baker's now-iconic personae were wide ranging, from the smiling, nearly naked African "savage" to the inscrutable black Venus; her costumes were equally diverse, from exquisite haute couture gowns to the top hat, white tie, and tails usually worn by men. Later in life Baker appeared in public as both a decorated war hero—she wore her French military uniform on the dais with Martin Luther King at the March on Washington in 1963—and a welcoming mother, surrounded by the members of her multi-racial family, what she described as her Rainbow Tribe, 13 children she adopted and raised in a chateau in Dordogne from 1956 to 1969. She recorded with Odeon starting in 1926, typically with small jazz ensembles. Her recordings include English- and French-language songs, in which her voice varies as much as her costumes did, shifting from a light, well-articulated middle register to a growling lower range and a hooting upper register often used for wordless flights of melodic play. Baker died after making 14 performances of *Josephine '75*, a show in Paris that celebrated her career.

BIBLIOGRAPHY

B. Rust (with A.G. Debus): *The Complete Entertainment Discography: from the mid-1890s to 1942* (New Rochelle, 1973) [Baker's English-language records only]

J. Baker and J. Bouillon: *Josephine* (New York, 1977/*R*)

L. Haney: *Naked at the Feast: a Biography of Josephine Baker* (New York, 1981, 2/2002)

P. Rose: *Jazz Cleopatra: Josephine Baker in her Time* (London, 1987/*R*)

B. Hammond and P. O'Connor: *Josephine Baker* (Boston, 1991)

E. Wood: *The Josephine Baker Story* (London, 2000, 2/2002)

B. Jules-Rosette: *Josephine Baker in Art and Life: the Icon and the Image* (Urbana, 2007)

O. Lahs-Gonzales: *Josephine Baker: Image and Icon* (St. Louis, 2006)

TODD DECKER

Baker, Julius (*b* Cleveland, OH, 23 Sep 1915; *d* Brewster, NY, 6 Aug 2003). Flutist and teacher. Baker studied with William Kincaid before serving as principal flutist with the Pittsburgh SO (1941–3), CBS SO (1943–50), Chicago SO (1951–3), and New York PO (1964–83). He taught at the Juilliard School (1954–81) and Curtis Institute (1980–2003). Upon his retirement from the New York PO he concertized and taught throughout the United States, Europe, and Asia, conducting more than two dozen master classes. His students included Paula Robison, Jeffrey Khaner, Eugenia Zukerman, Gary Schocker, and Jeanne Baxtresser. Baker performed with the Bach Aria Group (1946–64), developing an affinity for Baroque music that resulted in a published collection of flute solos from Bach's cantatas, oratorios, and Passions (1972). His recordings include the complete works for flute by Bach and Handel, as well as the Mozart flute concertos.

KAREN MONSON/KAREN M. BRYAN

Baker, Kenny [Kenneth Clayton] (*b* Burdine, KY, 26 June 1926; *d* Gallatin, TN, 8 July 2011). Fiddler. His artistry spanned multiple styles, but his extensive career in bluegrass and long association with Bill Monroe led to his reputation as America's quintessential bluegrass fiddler. Although he came from generations of old-time fiddle players, he played mostly guitar as a youth, accompanying his father's fiddle playing at local dances. During naval service in World War II he began playing fiddle for troop events and decided to concentrate on the instrument. In addition to country fiddlers, Baker listened to the jazz and swing styles of Stephane Grappelli, Bob Wills, and Marion Sumner.

For years Baker worked in eastern Kentucky's coalmines with interruptions to play professionally. From 1953 to 1957 he played with Don Gibson. In the late 1950s he started performing periodically as a member of Monroe's Blue Grass Boys; this collaboration led to a now-historic stint that lasted from 1967 to 1984 and included more than 230 recordings. Baker was Monroe's closest musical partner, serving as a creative collaborator and vessel for many of the bandleader's signature instrumental compositions, including "Jerusalem Ridge." While working for Monroe he recorded a string of influential fiddle albums, including *Portrait of a Bluegrass Fiddler* (County, 1969) and *Kenny Baker Plays Bill Monroe* (County, 1976), which showcase his characteristic smooth, long bowing style as well as his compositional talents. After his association with Monroe, Baker continued performing and releasing his own recordings, the last of which came in 2002. He also had an enduring musical relationship with the dobro player Josh Graves that produced multiple albums, notably *Something Different* (Puritan, 1972) and *Bucktime* (Puritan, 1974), and lasted until shortly before Graves's death in 2006.

BIBLIOGRAPHY

A. Foster: "Kenny Baker," *Bluegrass Unlimited*, iii/6 (1968), 8–11

B. Devan: "Kenny Baker: One of the Masters," *Bluegrass Unlimited*, xxv/8 (1991), 20–24

R. Michel: "Kenny Baker: a Week with a Bluegrass Legend," *Fiddler Magazine*, i/4 (1994), 4–12

RONNIE PUGH/KEVIN KEHRBERG

Baker, LaVern [Little Miss Sharecropper; Bea Baker] (*b* Chicago, IL, 11 Nov 1929; *d* New York, NY, 10 March 1997). Rhythm and blues singer. Research by Chip Deffaa suggests that references to her birth name as Dolores (or Delores) Williams may be in error. She was a niece of blues singer Merline Johnson and a distant relative of Memphis Minnie. As a teenager she sang in Chicago nightclubs. She performed and recorded for the National label as Little Miss Sharecropper, and as Bea Baker for Okeh. In 1953 she began an 11-year association with Atlantic Records, for which she sang the hit versions of "Tweedle Dee" (1955), "Bop-Ting-A-Ling" (1955), "Still" (1956), "Jim Dandy" (1956), and "I Cried A Tear" (1959). During the same period, rock-and-roll DJ Alan Freed featured her on his touring shows and in his movies.

After a stint with Brunswick Records (1965–6), she embarked on a performing tour in Vietnam for American soldiers; while there, Baker became ill and was advised to rest. She spent the next two decades in the Philippines, performing and managing entertainment at the American military base in Subic Bay. She returned stateside in 1988 for Atlantic Records' 40th-anniversary celebration at Madison Square Garden. She continued singing to the end of her life, even after losing to diabetes both legs below the knees in 1995.

BIBLIOGRAPHY

C. Deffaa: "LaVern Baker: 'Where Ya Been So Long?'" *Blue Rhythm* (Urbana, 1996), 174–216

B. Dahl: "LaVern Baker," *Living Blues*, no.133 (1997), 37–8

EDWARD KOMARA

Baker, Robert S(tevens) (*b* Pontiac, IL, 7 July 1916; *d* Hamden, CT, 24 Jan 2005). Organist and teacher. He graduated from Illinois Wesleyan University in 1938 and received the DSM degree from the Union Theological Seminary School of Sacred Music, New York, in 1944. His teachers included CLARENCE DICKINSON, T. TERTIUS NOBLE, FREDERICK STOCK, and DAVID MCK. WILLIAMS. He taught at the school from 1946. After a 1947 debut at the national convention of the American Guild of Organists in St Louis, he quickly established himself as an outstanding recitalist. In 1957 he gave the opening recital in the First International Congress of Organists at Temple Church in London; and in 1966 he was one of two American organists to play during the 900th anniversary celebration season at Westminster Abbey. He served as organist and choirmaster at various churches including Fifth Avenue Presbyterian, Temple Emanu-El, St James' Episcopal, and First Presbyterian in New York. He was dean of the School of Sacred Music at Union Seminary from 1961 to 1973, when the school was closed. It was immediately re-established as the Yale Institute of Sacred Music at Yale University, with Baker as director. After three years in that position, he returned to that which he loved most—teaching and church music.

BIBLIOGRAPHY

"Nunc Dimittus [Robert Baker]," *The Diapason*, xcvi/3 (2005), 8

T. Murray: "In Memoriam: Robert Baker," *The Diapason*, xcvi/4 (2005), 23

VERNON GOTWALS/JUDI CALDWELL

Baker, Theodore (*b* New York, NY, 3 June 1851; *d* Dresden, Germany, 13 Oct 1934). Music scholar and lexicographer. Trained as a young man for a career in business, he decided to pursue the field of music instead. For a time he was an organist in Concord, Massachusetts; but in 1874 he moved to Germany to study music with Oskar Paul at the University of Leipzig, where he took the PhD in 1882 with a dissertation based on field studies among the Seneca Native Americans in New York state which included numerous transcriptions. This, the first serious work on Native American music, was shown to Edward MacDowell by Henry Gilbert, and provided themes for MacDowell's Second ("Indian") Suite for orchestra.

Baker returned to the United States in 1891 and became literary editor and translator for the music publishing firm of Schirmer, Inc. (1892), a post he held until his retirement in 1926, when he returned to Germany. Besides translating into English many books, librettos, and articles, some published in *Musical Quarterly*, he also compiled a useful and widely used *Dictionary of Musical Terms* (1895) and the *Biographical Dictionary of Musicians* (1900), the work for which he is best known. Within this work Baker included numerous musicians that had never before been mentioned in a reference volume. The dictionary has remained an important work for scholars and has been expanded in subsequent editions by various scholars. The ninth edition, published in 2001, consists of six volumes and broadened the work's scope to include jazz and popular musicians.

WRITINGS

Dictionary of Musical Terms (New York, 1895/*R*, 23/1923/*R*)

[*Baker's*] *Biographical Dictionary of Musicians* (New York, 1900, 2/1905; rev., enlarged 3/1919 by A. Remy; rev. 4/1940 by C. Engel; rev. 5/1958, suppl. 1971, rev. 6/1978, 7/1984, 8/1992, by N. Slonimsky; 9/2001 by L. Kuhn and N. Slonimsky)

A Pronouncing Pocket Manual of Musical Terms (New York, 1905, 2/1947)

Beethoven: a Critical Biography (New York, 1913/*R*) [trans. of V. d'Indy: *Beethoven*, Paris, 1911]

H. WILEY HITCHCOCK/JOHN B. VALLIER

Baker, Thomas (*b* England, *c*1820, *d* Brooklyn, NY, 10 Dec 1888). Composer, conductor, arranger, and violinist of English birth. The date and specific location of his birth remain unknown, but Baker's youth was spent in England. By age seven he showed enough promise on the violin to merit the attention of Princess Augusta, who secured him a place at the Royal Academy of Music in London. There he studied violin under the tutelage of Francois Cramer and Paolo Spagnoletti. Baker also learned piano, composition, and harmony with Thomas Attwood, with whom Baker claimed to have studied many of Mozart's manuscripts. As a violinist, Baker made his debut at the Theatre Royal, Covent Garden, on 4 June 1832, while his conducting career began in 1840 with a concert at the Queen's Concert Rooms, London. Shortly afterwards, he performed as concertmaster and violin soloist with the orchestra of Philippe Musard. Baker would reprise these two roles under the direction of Louis Jullien, for whom he also arranged several pieces of music. During this period, Baker had begun to compose, and Jullien himself published some of his earliest works. Though the start date of Baker's contract with Jullien is not clear, he was still working with the conductor on his tour to the United States in the spring of 1850; Baker found a warm reception in this country and soon made New York City his permanent residence.

In the United States, Baker was highly regarded as a conductor, and his first engagement was as the director of English Opera at Niblo's Garden in New York City. He then took a position as the conductor at Laura Keene's Theater, and subsequently worked at a variety of theaters, including the Cremorne Garden, the Olympic, and Wallack's. Baker made the claim—though it is has not been substantiated—that he introduced the baton to the United States.

As a composer, Baker wrote in a variety of genres, including songs, ballads, quadrilles, and works for piano. While still in England, Baker wrote *The Modern Pianoforte Tutor*, used by the Royal Conservatory of Music. He is best known, however, for his compositions for the theater, from pantomimes and melodramas to larger extravaganzas. *The Seven Sisters* (1861) and *Under the Palms* (1864) were both successful stage productions with music by Baker. The most famous work by Baker is the original production of *The Black Crook* (1866), which is considered by many the precursor to the modern American musical.

BIBLIOGRAPHY

"Dramatic and Other Sketches: Thomas Baker," *New York Clipper* (12 Dec 1863), 277

T.A. Brown: *A History of the New York Stage from the First Performance in 1732 to 1901* (New York, 1903)

D.L. Root: *American Popular Stage Music, 1860–1880* (Ann Arbor, MI, 1981)

D.L. Root: "Music Research in Nineteenth-Century Theater: or, The Case of a Burlesquer, a Baker, and a Pantomime Maker," *Vistas of American Music: Essays and Compositions in Honor of William K. Kearns* (Warren, MI, 1999)

JONAS WESTOVER

Bakersfield sound. A country music style that originated in San Joaquin Valley, California, in the 1950s. While the coeval NASHVILLE SOUND gentrified country music by featuring soft crooning, lush string and chorus sections, and clinical studio craftsmanship, Bakersfield distinguished itself by exaggerating the exciting immediacy of honky-tonk and live bands and at times echoing the abandon of rock and roll. Its heyday lasted to the 1970s, since when the style has influenced country rock, outlaw country, new traditionalist country, alternative country, and Americana.

Immigration from the Southwest during the Dust Bowl era resulted in a ready audience for country music in central California, with the city of Bakersfield as a hub. Honky-tonks and large dance halls entertained displaced Okies, Arkies, and Texans with familiar musical sounds, delivered by regional and traveling acts. Early local musicians included Bill Woods, Billy Mize, Herb Henson, Oscar Whittington, Tommy Collins, Lewis Talley, Fuzzy Owen, Dallas Frazier, and Jean Shepard; others such as Ferlin Husky, the Maddox Brothers and Rose, Buck and Bonnie Owens, Roy Nichols, Ralph Mooney, and Joe Maphis moved from elsewhere, using the fecund scene as a launching pad. Henson's television show the *Trading Post* on Bakersfield's KERO-TV fostered the homegrown sound, as did the local radio station KUZZ, Tally Records, and Owen Publishing. Ken Nelson, head of country music at Capitol Records in Los Angeles, helped launch it nationally.

Although distinctions were not always hard and fast, the increasingly honeyed sounds of Nashville offset the immediacy of the Bakersfield music. Local artists such as Wynn Stewart also incorporated rock-and-roll influences on some material, notably twangy electric guitars and driving, emphatic rhythms, and in doing so distinguished the sound from other kinds of honky-tonk. After serving apprenticeships in local bands Buck Owens and Merle Haggard eventually achieved international success and established distinctive versions of the sound in the mainstream; Red Simpson also achieved widespread recognition, in the truck-driving country subgenre.

Grittier songwriting and vocals accompanied by distinctive Telecaster and steel-guitar hooks endeared the music not only to national and international audiences but also to musicians in other places and times. Nashville underground and outlaw country, country rock, southern rock, progressive country, new traditionalist country, Bakersfield revival, alternative country, and Americana have all found their inspiration in the uncompromising, hard country sound of Bakersfield.

BIBLIOGRAPHY

G. Haslam: *Workin' Man Blues: Country Music in California*. (Berkeley, 1999)

B. Ching: *Wrong's what I do Best: Hard Country Music and Contemporary Culture* (New York, 2001)

P. LaChapelle: *Proud to Be an Okie: Cultural Politics, Country Music, and Migration to Southern California* (Berkeley, 2007)

AJAY KALRA

Baklanov [Bakkis], **Georgy (Andreyevich)** (*b* Riga, Latvia, 23 Dec 1880/4 Jan 1881; *d* Basle, Switzerland, 6 Dec 1938). Russian baritone of Latvian birth. He studied with Pets in Kiev, Ippolit Pryanishnikov in St. Petersburg, and Vittorio Vanza in Milan. He made his debut (1903, Kiev) as Anton Rubinstein's Demon, sang with the Zimin Private Opera in Moscow, and was engaged in 1905 by the Bol'shoy, creating the Baron in Serge Rachmaninoff's *The Miserly Knight* (1906) and remaining until 1909, when he sang Barnaba (*La Gioconda*) at the inaugural performance of the Boston Opera House. At Covent Garden he appeared as Rigoletto (debut, 1910), Scarpia, and Amonasro, repeating the first two roles at the Komische Oper, Berlin in 1911. He sang in Boston (1915–18), then with Chicago Opera (1917–26), and in New York, where he later became a mainstay of the Russian Opera Company. Baklanov's repertory included Yevgeny Onegin, Hamlet, Boris, Méphistophélès (*Faust*), the Father (*Louise*), Golaud (*Pelléas et Mélisande*), Telramund, and Wotan. He was greatly admired for his dramatic talents, and his voice was rich and vibrant, particularly in the middle and upper registers. Between 1910 and 1930 he made a number of recordings. Further notes on his career can be found in M. Scott: *The Record of Singing*, ii (London, 1979), 12–4.

HAROLD BARNES, KATHERINE K. PRESTON

Baksa, Robert Frank (*b* New York, NY, 7 Feb 1938). Composer. He grew up in Tucson, Arizona, and studied composition with Henry Johnson and ROBERT MCBRIDE at the University of Arizona (BA 1969) and LUKAS FOSS at the Berkshire Music Center. From 1962, he has lived in New York and has worked as a composer and music copyist. He serves as New Music Coordinator and Composer in Residence for the Pleshakov Music Center. He has composed over 600 works, including two operas, choral pieces, song settings of Shakespeare, Housman, Bierce, and Dickinson, over 70 chamber works for various instrumentation, sonatas for most major instruments, and numerous works for keyboard. He has received commissions from the Metropolitan Opera Studio, Harpsichord Unlimited, and the American Accordion Association. In his music, Baksa seeks to achieve harmonic and structural clarity based on coherent melodic expressivity, achieved through established methods of formal architecture rather than experimentation.

WORKS

(selective list)

Stage: Aria da capo (op, 1, after E. St. Vincent Millay), 1966, rev. 1978; Red Carnations (op, 1, after L. Hughes), 1969

Large ens: Conc. for Ob and Str; Sinfonia for Str, 1964; other works for large ens

Choral: Housman Songs, SATB, *c*1981; Madrigals from the Japanese, SSATB, *c*2004; other choral works

Inst: Alto Sax Sonata, 1993; Hp Sonata, 1994; numerous other works

Kbd: Antica nova: Suite no.1 for Hpd, 1987–96; Org Sonata, 1997; Spring Games, pf four hands, 2002; numerous other works

Principal publisher: Presser

BIBLIOGRAPHY

R. Friedberg: *American Art Song and American Poetry*, iii (Metuchen, NJ, 1981)

V. Villamil: *A Singer's Guide to American Art Song, 1879–1980* (Lanham, MD, 1993)

ROBERT PAUL KOLT

Balada. Spanish-language variant of the international pop music ballad. A hybrid of Mexican *bolero*, Italian and French orchestrated love songs, and early rock and roll ballads, balada emerged simultaneously in Spain and throughout the Americas in the late 1960s. Lyrics are invariably about love and purposely lack references to socio-political issues or local events to maximize potential target audiences. Most often performed by a solo singer, early balada moves at a slow to moderate tempo, and the musical accompaniment, by either a rock ensemble or a studio orchestra, is secondary to the voice. Early baladistas include Mexicans Carlos Lico and Armando Manzanero, Cuban American La Lupe, Spaniards Raphael and Julio Iglesias, Brazilian Roberto Carlos, Argentines Leonardo Favio and Sandro, and Chilean band Los Ángeles Negros.

During the 1970s, the genre's golden age, balada featured sophisticated orchestral arrangements and lavish studio production, a trend developed in Spain by producer Rafael Trabucchelli and arranger Waldo de los Ríos. In the 1980s, Miami became the most important balada production center, as the city grew into the main hub for United States marketing and distribution in Latin America. The Miami-based balada industry served as a gateway for Latin American artists hoping to extend their popularity beyond their country of origin to the rest of Latin America and the United States. Balada albums produced in Miami are not limited to slow romantic ballads, but also include up-tempo, dance-oriented songs. During its golden age, the majority of balada singers were males, who targeted a mostly female audience by appearing sensitive and vulnerable. Baladas were regularly featured in Latin American soap opera soundtracks, and many baladistas, such as José Luis Rodríguez, Chayanne, and Daniela Romo, starred in soap operas.

BIBLIOGRAPHY

D.K. Stigberg: "Foreign currents during the 60s and 70s in Mexican popular music: Rock and Roll, the Romantic Ballad and the Cumbia," *Studies in Latin American Popular Culture*, iv (1985), 170–84

S. Araújo: "Brega: Music and Conflict in Urban Brazil," *LAMR*, ix/1 (1988), 50–89

M. Tupinambá de Ulhôa: "Música romântica in Montes Claros: inter-gender relations in Brazilian popular song," *British Journal of Ethnomusicology*, ix/1 (2000), 11–40

D. Party: "The Miamization of Latin American pop music," *Postnational Musical Identities: Cultural Production, Distribution and Consumption in a Globalized Scenario*, ed. I. Corona and A.L. Madrid (Lexington, NY, 2008), 65–80

DANIEL PARTY

Balada(-Ibáñez), Leonardo (*b* Barcelona, Spain, 22 Sept 1933). Composer and teacher of Spanish birth. He began his musical studies at the Conservatorio del Liceu during the 1950s. In 1956, he won a scholarship to travel to New York to continue his musical education at the Juilliard School where he studied conducting with Igor Markevitch and composition with AARON COPLAND, NORMAN DELLO JOIO, and VINCENT PERSICHETTI. After finishing his studies in 1960, he collaborated with painter Salvador Dalí in New York on a film satire about painter Piet Mondrian, which was realized for US television. Balada also developed his career as a teacher, accepting posts at the Walden School and the United Nations International School. In 1970, he accepted the position at Carnegie Mellon University as a professor of composition. Balada's compositional style went through several stages throughout his career, influenced by experimental styles, folklore, drama, and the plastic arts. His works during the late 1960s follow a dramatic avant-garde style, exemplified in *Guernica* (1966), his first orchestral work to receive international acclaim and *Sinfonía en negro: Homage to Martin Luther King* (1968). During the 1970s, he continued to produce works that were not programmatic, but exhibited elements of drama. His well-known work *Steel Symphony* (1972) suggested the sounds of a steel mill through tone clusters and complex rhythms. During this period Balada also incorporated influences of Catalan music and traditional music of Spain into his works, such as his *Homage a Casals, Homenaje a Sarasate* (1975). His attraction to folkloric topics extended into three prominent operas: *Hangman, Hangman!* (1982), a one-act opera in Catalan about an American cowboy; *Zapata* (1984), an opera in two acts about the Mexican Revolutionary leader; and *Cristóbal Colón* (1986), a two-act work about the explorer which was an international success.

WORKS

Stage: Maria Sabina (C.J. Cela), nars, chorus, orch, 1969; No-Res (J. Paris), nars, chorus, orch, 1974, rev. 1997; Hangman! Hangman! (chbr op, 1, Balada), 1982; Zapata (op, 2, T. Capobianco and G. Roepke), 1982–4; Cristóbal Colón (grand op, 2, A. Gala), 1989; Thunderous Scenes (Balada), cant., 1v, chorus, orch, 1992; Thunderous Scenes (cant., Balada), solo vv, chorus, orch, 1992; Death of Columbus (op, 2, Balada), 1996; The Town of Greed (chbr op, 1, Balada), 1997

Orch: Musica tranquila, str, 1960; Pf Conc. no.1, 1964; Gui Conc. no.1, 1965; Guernica, 1966; Sinfonia en negro: Homage to Martin Luther King, 1968; Bandoneon Conc., 1970; Cumbres, band, 1972; Persistencies (Sinfonia concertante), gui, orch, 1972; Steel Sym., 1972; Auroris, 1973; Ponce de Leon, nar, orch, 1973; Conc. no.2, pf, wind, perc, 1974; Homage to Casals, 1975; Homage to Sarasate, 1975; Conc., 4 gui, orch, 1976; 3 Anecdotes, castanets/wood perc, orch, 1977; Sardana: Dance of Catalonia, 1979; Quasi un pasodoble, 1981; Quasi Adelita, wind band, 1982; Vn Conc., 1982; Zapata: Images for Orch, 1987; Fantasias sonoras, 1987; Alegrias, 1987; Columbus: Images for Orch, 1991; Divertimentos, str, 1991; Celebration, 1992; Sym. no.4 "Lausanne," chbr orch, 1992; Song and Dance, wind ens, 1992; Music for Ob and Orch (Lament from the Cradle of Earth), 1993; Union of the Oceans, band, 1993; Morning Music, fl, orch, 1994; Concierto magico (Conc. no.2), gui, orch, 1997; Folk Dreams, suite, 1995–8; Shadows, Line and Thunder, Echoes; Pf Conc. no.2, 1999; Reflejos, fl, str, 1999 [from chbr work]; Music for Fl and Orch, 2000; Passacaglia, 2000

Vocal: 4 canciones de la Provincia de Madrid, song cycle, 1v, pf, 1962; 3 Cervantinas, song cycle, 1v, pf, 1967; 3 epitafios de Quevedo, song cycle, 1v, pf, 1967; Las moradas (S. Teresa de Avila), chorus, 7 insts, 1970; Voices no.1, 1972; Torquemada (Balada), B/Bar, 14 insts, chorus, 1980; En la era, song cycle, 1v, pf, 1989

Chbr and solo inst: Musica en 4 tiempos, pf, 1959; Sonata, vn, pf, 1960; Conc., vc, 9 insts, 1962; The Seven Last Words, org, 1963; Geometrias: no.1, fl, ob, cl, bn, tpt, perc, 1966; no.2, str qt, 1967; no.3, bandoneon, 1968; Cuatris, 4 insts, 1969; Minis, bandoneon, 1969; End and beginning, rock ens, 1970; Mosaico, brass qnt, 1970; Elementalis, org, 1972; Tresis, fl/vn, gui, vc, 1973; 3 Transparencies of a Bach Prelude, vc, pf, 1976; Transparency of Chopin's First Ballade, pf, 1977; Persistencies, pf, 1978; Preludis obstinants, pf, 1979; Sonata, 10 wind, 1980; Reflejos, fl, str, insts, 1987; Diary of Dreams, vn, vc, pf, 1995

Gui: Lento with Variation, 1960; Suite no.1, 1961; 3 Divagaciones, 1962; Analogias, 1967; Apuntes (Sketches), 4 gui, 1974; Minis, 1975; 4 Catalan Melodies, 1978; Persistencies, 1979

Principal publishers: Belwin-Mills, Beteca Music, General, G. Schirmer

BIBLIOGRAPHY

P.E. Stone: "Leonardo Balada's First Half Century," *Symphony* (1983), 85–9

M. Cureses: "Leonardo Balada Ibáñez," *Diccionario de la Música Española e Hispanoamericana*, ed. E. Casares (Mexico, 1999)

JACQUELINE AVILA, DAVID WRIGHT (Works)

Balanchine [Balanchin, Balanchivadze], **George** [Gyorgy Melitonovich] (*b* St. Petersburg, Russia, 22 Jan 1904; *d* New York, NY, 30 April 1983). Dancer, choreographer, teacher, and ballet company director of Russian birth. He was trained at the Imperial Ballet School in St. Petersburg, where he created his first choreography. He also studied piano and music theory at the Petrograd Conservatory of Music, gaining a firm musical foundation. After graduating in 1921, he danced in the ballet company of the State Theater of Opera and Ballet, and choreographed for his own ensemble, the Young Ballet. In 1924 he left Russia for western Europe, where he joined Diaghilev's Ballets Russes. After the company disbanded following Diaghilev's death in 1929, he worked in Europe until 1933, when he came to the United States at the invitation of Lincoln Kirstein. The two founded the School of American Ballet in New York in 1934, and together formed four successive companies with the dancers trained there: the American Ballet (1935–8), American Ballet Caravan (1941), Ballet Society (1946–8), and New York City Ballet (1948–83), for which he served as ballet master and chief choreographer until his death.

Over the course of his life he created more than four hundred dance works, including choreography for musicals, operas, films, and television as well as ballets. His long collaboration with Stravinsky produced masterworks such as the "Greek trilogy" of *Apollo* (1928), *Orpheus* (1948), and *Agon* (1957). American music and themes interested him from the beginning of his life in the United States, inspiring such works as *Ivesiana* (1954; Ives), *Western Symphony* (1954; Kay), *Stars and Stripes* (1958; Sousa, adapted and orchestrated by Kay), and *Who Cares?* (1970; Gershwin). With memories of the evening-length story ballets of his youth, he created *The Nutcracker* (1954; Tchaikovsky), *A Midsummer Night's Dream* (1962; Mendelssohn), and *Coppelia* (1974; Delibes). His work for the musical theater included *On Your Toes* (1936; Rodgers and Hart), considered the first musical to integrate dance with dramatic action.

Balanchine is generally credited with extending and revitalizing the classical ballet. Many of his works dispensed with what he saw as nonessentials—extravagant stage dressing, elaborate costumes, complicated libretti—in order to focus the audience's attention on dance and music. In keeping with his view that music is "the floor for dancing," he gave it primacy of place in the credits on his company's programs, and often titled his ballets after their musical scores. His dancers often performed in leotards and tights, formerly considered practice clothes, as a matter of artistic choice rather than economic necessity. Although he did not invent the plotless ballet, he made it popular by demonstrating how riveting pure dance could be—even for the course of a full-length ballet, as in *Jewels* (1967; Fauré, Stravinsky, Tchaikovsky). His works are still performed today by ballet companies around the world.

WRITINGS

with F. Mason: *Balanchine's Complete Stories of the Great Ballets* (Garden City, NY, 1954, enlarged 2/1977)

ed. T. Schoff: *By George Balanchine* (New York, 1984)

BIBLIOGRAPHY

GMO

"George Balanchine," *Dance Index*, iv (1945)

B. Taper: *Balanchine: a Biography* (New York, 1963, enlarged 2/1984)
D. McDonagh: *George Balanchine* (Boston, 1983)
N. Reynolds, ed.: *Choreography by George Balanchine: a Catalogue of Works* (New York, 1984)
S. Volkov, trans. A.W. Bouis: *Balanchine's Tchaikovsky: Interviews with George Balanchine* (New York, 1985)
F. Mason, ed.: *I Remember Balanchine: Recollections of the Ballet-Master by Those Who Knew Him* (New York, 1991)
"Balanchine, George," *International Dictionary of Ballet*, ed. M. Bremser (Detroit, 1993)
"Balanchine, George," *International Encyclopedia of Dance*, ed. S.J. Cohen (New York, 1998)
R. Buckle in collaboration with J. Taras: *George Balanchine, Ballet Master: a Biography* (New York, 1998)
C.M. Joseph: *Stravinsky & Balanchine: a Journey of Invention* (New Haven, 2002)
R. Gottlieb: *George Balanchine: the Ballet Maker* (New York, 2004)
A. Hogan, ed.: *Balanchine Then and Now* (Paris, 2008)

SUSAN AU

Balatka, Hans (*b* Hoffnungsthal, nr Olmütz [now Olomouc, Czech Republic], ?26 Feb 1825; *d* Chicago, IL, 17 April 1899). Moravian conductor and composer. He studied music at Hoffnungsthal and later at the gymnasium and university in Olomouc, where he was a choirboy at the cathedral. From 1845 he studied music (under Simon Sechter and Heinrich Proch) and law at the University of Vienna, where he worked as a music copyist and a tutor. During the 1848 revolution he sided with the Academic Legion, and following its defeat he fled Europe. He arrived in New York in 1849 and went via Chicago to Milwaukee, where he organized a male chorus (1849) and a string quartet (1850). From 1850 to 1860 he was musical director of the Milwaukee Musical Society (Musikverein) and conducted its first concert (May 1850) and its first oratorio, Haydn's *The Creation* (July 1851, in German), and directed and sang in its first opera, Lortzing's *Zar und Zimmermann* (April 1853). He also founded a singing school and served as musical director of the German theater (1855–60). Because of his reputation with the Milwaukee Musical Society he was asked to conduct music festivals in Cleveland, Cincinnati, Detroit, and Chicago. His performance of Mozart's Requiem for the Northwest Sängerfest (Chicago, 1860) led to his appointment as director of the Chicago Philharmonic Society (1860–69). His first concert on 19 November included Beethoven's second symphony and a chorus from *Tannhäuser*. While in Chicago he also conducted the Musical Union, the Oratorio Society, and other singing groups. In 1871–2 he again conducted the Milwaukee Musical Society, but returned in 1876 to Chicago, where he remained except for a short stay in St. Louis (1877). In 1879 he founded the Balatka Academy of Musical Art, which was important to music education in Chicago in the late 19th and early 20th centuries. During his later residence in Chicago he directed the Mozart Club and the Germania Society. He was also active as a journalist and regularly contributed columns on music to the Chicago newspaper *Daheim*.

Balatka wrote several orchestral fantasies, a piano quartet, and other piano music; his vocal works include about 30 songs, pieces for chorus such as *The Power of Song* (1856) for double male chorus, and a *Festival Cantata* (1869) for soprano and orchestra. Balatka's significance nevertheless involved his conducting and educational activities, and he was one of the first important figures for the development of music in the Midwest.

BIBLIOGRAPHY

The National Cyclopedia of American Biography, x (New York, 1900), 197
J.J. Schlicher: "Hans Balatka and the Milwaukee Musical Society," *Wisconsin Magazine of History*, xxvii (1943–4), 40–55
J.J. Schlicher: "The Milwaukee Musical Society in Times of Stress," *Wisconsin Magazine of History*, xxvii (1943–4), 178–93
Dictionary of Wisconsin Biography (Madison, 1960), 23
T.H. Schleis: *Opera in Milwaukee: 1850–1900* (diss., U. of Wisconsin, 1974)
J. Deaville: "The Origins of Music Journalism in Chicago: Criticism as a Reflection of Musical Life," *American Musical Life in Context and Practice to 1865*, ed. J.R. Heintze (New York, 1994), 301–66

THOMAS H. SCHLEIS

Baldwin. Firm of instrument makers, predominantly of pianos and organs. It was founded in Cincinnati in 1862 by Dwight Hamilton Baldwin (1821–99). He attended the preparatory department of Oberlin College (1840–42) and was then a minister and school singing teacher in Kentucky and Ohio. Moving to Cincinnati in 1857 to teach music in schools, he also became in 1862 or 1863 a retailer of pianos and organs. D.H. Baldwin & Co. was formed in June 1873 when Lucien Wulsin (1845–1912), a clerk in Baldwin's firm since 1866, became partner. Robert A. Johnson (1838–84) opened a Louisville branch in 1877 and became a partner in 1880. Three more partners joined in 1884: Albert A. van Buren, George W. Armstrong, Jr. (1857–1932), and Clarence Wulsin (1855–97), who ran an Indianapolis branch. Until the late 1880s the firm was one of the largest dealers in keyboard instruments in the Midwest as agent for such makers as Decker, Estey, J. & C. Fischer, and Steinway.

In 1889, a subsidiary, the Hamilton Organ Co., Chicago, began to manufacture reed organs, and by 1891 the Baldwin Piano Co., a subsidiary in Cincinnati, was making upright pianos. The company acquired the Ellington Piano Co. (1893) and the Valley Gem (originally the Ohio Valley) Piano Co., founded in 1871 in Ripley, Ohio. John Warren Macy led in the early manufacture, developing a piano that won the Grand Prix at the Paris Exhibition in 1900. Baldwin's death caused some upheaval, ultimately solved when Lucien Wulsin and George Armstrong bought control in July 1903. Wulsin was president until 1912, Armstrong from 1912 to 1926, and Lucien Wulsin, Jr. (1889–1964) from 1926 to 1964.

In the late 1920s, in collaboration with the physics department of the University of Cincinnati, the company began a research program in electronics that resulted in the introduction of an electronic organ in 1947 (*see* BALDWIN ORGAN). Baldwin's director of electronic research, Dr. Winston E. Kock, designed the original models, some of which were intended for use in churches. Most Baldwin organs are smaller instruments for the home, many of them "spinet" organs with two staggered manuals.

In 1965 the firm introduced the model SD-10, a concert grand piano newly designed by Harold Conklin. By the 1970s the parent company, by then under the chairmanship of the founding partner's grandson, Lucien Wulsin (1916–2009), had expanded into Baldwin United, a large corporation. The music subsidiary, Baldwin Piano & Organ Co., continued to manufacture pianos and electronic organs at factories in Mississippi and Arkansas. In 1963 Baldwin bought Bechstein of Berlin, which retained its own identity and continued to make pianos in its own style.

An experimental concert grand piano with electronically enhanced sound served as a prototype for later, more successful electronic and computerized instruments. After 1960 the company extended its range of electronic instruments to harpsichords, guitars, and pianos. Several manufacturing operations, including Gretsch (guitars, drums, and amplifiers) and Ode (banjos), were sold in 1980 to Charles Roy of Nashville, Tennessee.

In 1983 Baldwin United filed for bankruptcy after sustaining heavy losses in its insurance business. Baldwin Piano & Organ Co. was bought the following year by some of the company's executives, including Harold Smith, who became president, and R.S. Harrison, who became chairman. Baldwin sold Bechstein in 1987 and in the following year purchased the Wurlitzer Company, which owned the Chickering name. Baldwin, which produced around 20,000 instruments annually, sold mid-range grands under the name Chickering and lower-priced instruments under Wurlitzer. The company also produced a digital reproducing player system, the ConcertMaster, housed in a grand piano. In 2001, Baldwin filed for bankruptcy and was acquired by the Gibson Guitar Co. Although it has downsized operations, Baldwin has continued to manufacture a wide range of pianos as a division of Gibson into the 2010s.

CYNTHIA ADAMS HOOVER/EDWIN M. GOOD/R

Baldwin, Dalton (*b* Summit, NY, 19 Dec 1931). Pianist. He began his formal musical training at the Juilliard School of Music but gained the BM from the Oberlin College Conservatory. He continued his studies in Paris with Emile Boulanger and Madeleine Lipatti and in 1954 began his long and successful partnership with the baritone Gérard Souzay. Concentrating primarily on the song repertory, Baldwin was coached by such composers as Francis Poulenc, Jean Sibelius, Frank Martin, and Samuel Barber. Baldwin has participated in a number of first performances (notably of Ned Rorem's *War Scenes* in 1969, with Souzay as soloist) and has accompanied such other eminent singers as Elly Ameling, Jessye Norman, Arleen Augér, Marilyn Horne, and Frederica von Stade. Perhaps his finest achievements have been his recordings of the complete songs of Cluade Debussy, Gabriel Fauré, Poulenc, Maurice Ravel, and Albert Roussel. Baldwin's playing is characterized by a softness of touch and superb legato, which allow him to phrase with the singer; he is supportive without being too subdued. He has also trained a new generation of collaborative pianists by serving as professor of accompanying and coaching at Westminster Choir College of Rider University.

RICHARD LESUEUR/R

Baldwin, Ralph L(yman) (*b* Easthampton, MA, 27 March 1872; *d* Canaan, NH, 30 Sept 1943). Composer, organist, conductor, and music educator. He graduated from Williston Seminary in Northampton, Massachusetts (1890), and studied music in Boston with GEORGE WHITEFIELD CHADWICK and others (1890–93). He then returned to Northampton and became a church musician, recitalist, school music supervisor (beginning in 1899), and director of the Vocal Club of Northampton (1894–1904). In 1900 he took over the Institute of Music Pedagogy, a summer program for training school music supervisors. In 1904 he became a church music director, organist, and school music supervisor in Hartford, Connecticut, eventually moving to the Immanuel Congregational Church of Hartford (1917). He also founded and directed the all-male Choral Club of Hartford (1907–37), and directed the Mendelssohn Glee Club of New York City (1923–34). He received honorary degrees from Trinity College in Hartford (BA 1915) and Ithaca College (MusD 1943). In addition to composing and arranging numerous songs and organ and choral works, Baldwin authored and co-authored several series of classroom music textbooks and anthologies (1910–38).

WRITINGS

"The Evolution of Public School Music in the United States: From the Civil War to 1900: Settling the Problem of Reading," *Music Supervisors Journal*, x/2 (1923), 8–57

BIBLIOGRAPHY

International Who's Who in Music 1918, ed. C. Saerchinger (New York, 1918)

J.F. Hall: *Musical Memories of Hartford: Drawn from Records Public and Private* (Hartford, CT, 1931)

M.A. Flaherty: *Ralph Lyman Baldwin (1872–1943): Musician and Educator* (thesis, Catholic U. of America, 1960)

E.B. Birge: *History of Public School Music in the United States* (Reston, VA, 1966), 139, 165, 213, 233, 238, 250, 272, 280, 285, 287

RICHARD R. BUNBURY

Baldwin, Samuel A(tkinson) (*b* Lake City, MN, 25 Jan 1862; *d* New York, 15 Sept 1949). Organist and composer. He studied the organ in St Paul and while still a teenager served as organist of the House of Hope Presbyterian Church in that city. Early in the 1880s he went to Germany to study with Gustav Merkel at the Royal Conservatory of Dresden, graduating in 1884. Baldwin then returned and held positions as a church organist in Chicago, St Paul and Minneapolis, where he also directed choral societies. In 1895 he became organist of the Church of the Intercession in New York, and seven years later succeeded Dudley Buck at Holy Trinity Church in Brooklyn, a position he held until 1911.

In 1907 Baldwin was appointed to the new chair of music at the City College of New York (later becoming head of the department) and on 11 February 1908 presented an inaugural recital on the 84-stop Skinner organ in CCNY's Great Hall, an instrument he had designed.

This was the first of 1362 Sunday and Wednesday afternoon programs which he played over a span of twenty-four years; it was estimated that as many as 70,000 people heard him perform each season. His repertory, comprising about 2000 works, ranging from Bach, Mendelssohn, Rheinberger, and Widor to transcriptions (particularly of Wagner) as well as new pieces by American contemporaries Homer N. Bartlett, Arthur Foote, Edwin Lemare, James H. Rogers, and W. Eugene Thayer. Baldwin presented recitals throughout the Northeast and also performed at expositions in Chicago (1893), St. Louis (1904), and San Francisco (1915). A Founder and Fellow of the American Guild of Organists, he wrote in 1946 a history of the organization commemorating the fiftieth anniversary of its founding. Baldwin's compositions include organ pieces, a Symphony in C minor, concert overtures and an orchestral suite, chamber works, several large-scale choral works, songs, and church music. The New York Public Library holds a collection of his scores.

WILLIAM OSBORNE

Baldwin organ. An electronic organ, many models of which were manufactured by the BALDWIN Piano & Organ Co. beginning in 1946. The original models were designed by Dr. Winston E. Kock (1909–82), the company's director of electronic research from 1936. Baldwin organs normally have two manuals and pedals; the earlier models were mostly church, cinema, and concert organs, but the company has subsequently manufactured a wide range of instruments, including many for home use, especially "spinet" organs in which two shorter manuals are staggered by one octave. Advances in electronic technology around 1970 made possible several new devices that soon became widespread: rhythm and "walking bass" units, arpeggiators, memories, and a choice of chord systems. Baldwin introduced microcomputer organs around 1981, and their Pianovelle digital pianos were based on sampled timbres. In 2001, Baldwin was acquired by Guitar Gibson Corp., which no longer manufactures electronic organs.

HUGH DAVIES/R

Baldwin-Wallace Bach Festival. Music festival. The oldest collegiate and second-oldest Bach festival in the United States, the Baldwin-Wallace Bach Festival is an annual three-day celebration of the works of J.S. Bach held at Baldwin-Wallace College in Berea, Ohio. Founded by former Baldwin-Wallace professor ALBERT RIEMENSCHNEIDER and his wife Selma, the first festival took place in June 1933 and was organized to encourage artistic and community development in northeastern Ohio through exposure to the works of the famous composer. Since 1936, the festival has featured a four-year rotation cycle of Bach's B minor Mass, *St. Matthew Passion*, *St. John Passion*, and the *Christmas Oratorio*, so that each student at the Baldwin-Wallace Conservatory has the opportunity to perform these major choral works.

Throughout its development, the festival has continued to grow in both quality and prestige. Each festival annually features internationally renowned soloists and Bach lecturers. Since its inception, the festival has included performances of over 300 works by J.S. Bach, as well as works by more than 50 other composers. From 1975 the festival has featured a smaller ensemble size, more closely resembling forces used during Bach's lifetime, and all vocal works are sung in the original language. The Riemenschneider original vision of Bach performance is supplemented today by the work of the Riemenschneider Bach Institute, a world-renowned collection of Bach-related materials housed at the college since 1969 and frequent presenter of conferences devoted to his music and legacy.

BIBLIOGRAPHY

E. Barber: "Albert Riemenschneider: A Portrait of the Founder of Baldwin-Wallace College's Conservatory on the Occasion of its 100th Anniversary," *Bach: Journal of the Riemenschneider Bach Institute*, xxix/2 (1998), 1–7

T. Riemenschneider and M. Unger: "History of the Bach Legacy at Baldwin-Wallace," *75th Baldwin-Wallace Bach Festival Annotated Program* (2007), 17–21; available online at <http://www.bw.edu/academics/libraries/bach/festivals/bachfest/about/BFEST07booklet.pdf>

M. Assad: *Baldwin-Wallace College* (Charleston, SC, 2008)

DANIELLE M. KUNTZ

Bales, Richard (Henry Horner) (*b* Alexandria, VA, 3 Feb 1915; *d* Washington, DC, 25 June 1998). Composer and conductor. He graduated in 1936 from the Eastman School, where HOWARD HANSON was a decisive influence in shaping his interest in American music, and continued studies at the Juilliard School (1939–41) and with SERGE KOUSSEVITZKY at the Berkshire Music Center (summer 1940). His musical activities centered on the National Gallery of Art (Washington, DC), where he became the first music director in 1942 and founder and conductor of the National Gallery Orchestra the following year; in this position, which was like that of an 18th-century Kapellmeister, he organized the National Gallery's Sunday evening concerts—most of which were free—and contributed to them both as conductor and composer. During his tenure at this post, he conducted a total of 1786 concerts at the museum's Garden Courts location. His promotion of American music, particularly through the annual American Music Festival which he initiated at the Gallery in the spring of 1944, provided opportunities for performers and composers from all over the country. Most of his compositions, characterized by pleasant melodies and a clear tonal idiom, were written for presentation at the Gallery; over 35 of his works remain extant. The topics of his most famous pieces are the American Revolution and the Civil War; his three cantatas are based on 18th- and 19th-century American music, including patriotic and Civil War songs. One of these, *The Republic*, has been performed at every presidential inauguration since 1955. Bales retired from the National Gallery position on 3 August 1985. Bales donated his papers to the Special Collections Division of the Alexandria Library; the collection contains clippings, correspondence, compositions, writings, and recordings of interviews and performances. The manuscripts of most of his music are housed at the Library of Congress.

WORKS

Orch: National Gallery Suites, no.1, 1943, no.2, 1944, no.3 "American Design," 1957, no.4 "American Chronicle," 1965; The Spirit of Engineering, suite, 1983–4; other works

Vocal: 3 cantatas : The Confederacy, 1953, The Republic, 1955, The Union, 1956; A Set of Jade (ancient Chin.), song cycle, 1v, pf, 1964, orchd, 1968; several songs and choral pieces

Chbr: Str Qt, 1944; pf suite, 1963; To Elmira with Love, pf suite, 1972, orch 1983; Diary Pages, 2 pf, 1978

Transcrs., arrs., most for orch

8 documentary film scores

Principal publisher: Peer-Southern

BIBLIOGRAPHY

"Bales, Richard," *Compositores de América/Composers of the Americas*, ed. Pan American Union, xv (Washington, DC, 1969)

M. Hunter: "A Music Maker for Sunday Nights," *New York Times* (6 Oct 1984)

JOANNE SHEEHY HOOVER/JONAS WESTOVER

Baley, Virko (*b* Radekhov, Ukraine, 21 Oct 1938). Composer and conductor of Ukrainian birth. Having worked as farm laborers in Slovakia during the German invasion, his family immigrated to Los Angeles in 1949. He studied at the Los Angeles Conservatory of Music and Art (BA 1960, MM 1962; later the California Institute of the Arts), where his teachers included Earle Voorhies and Morris Ruger; he also studied piano with ROSINA LHÉVINNE and composition with DONALD ERB and MARIO DAVIDOVSKY. Baley joined the music department at the University of Nevada, Las Vegas, in 1970. He has also served as founder-conductor of the Nevada SO (1980–95), music director of the Las Vegas Opera Company (1983–8), and principal guest conductor and music adviser of the Kiev Camerata (from 1995). His scholarly work has established him as an authority on Soviet music, and in 1996 he was awarded the Shevchenko Prize for Music by the Ukranian government.

Although Baley's music frequently refers to Ukrainian sources, his style became increasingly Americanized after 1980. The First Violin Concerto (1987) includes Ukrainian folk elements and exhibits a European polish and mood, but its unusual orchestral textures, rippling with celeste, vibraphone, and harpsichord, seem American, as does the energetic drumming of the second movement "Dies irae" and the muted jazz trumpet of the final "Agon." His gradual move away from a mournful, Eastern European, somewhat neoclassical idiom climaxed in *Dreamtime* (1993–5), which includes a Ukrainian *kolomïyka* dance but reflects new world styles in its ensemble unisons, tuned water goblets, and dream-like suspension of time. He has frequently reworked earlier material into later pieces; for example, his Symphony no.1 is partly based on the earlier soliloquy *Duma* and *Dreamtime* reuses material from the wind quintet *Adam's Apple*. Mostly tonal though chromatic, his music occasionally approaches the "holy minimalist" style of Arvo Pärt or Henryk Górecki, particularly in the cycle of pieces called *Treny* (Laments) for cellos and soprano, but is in general more given than theirs to ambiguity, textural layering, and catharsis.

WORKS

Op: Hunger (1, B. Boychuk), 1985–97

Orch: Woodcuts, str, 1971, rev. 1997; Duma, soliloquy, 1985, rev. 1988; Sym. no.1 "Sacred Monuments," 1985, rev. 1997–9; Vn Conc. no.1 "Quasi una fantasia," 1987, arr. vn, chbr orch; Vn Conc. no.2 "Favola in musica," 1988, rev. 1989; Pf Conc. no.1, 1990–93; Adam's Apple, wind qnt, 1989, arr. prelude, 1991, arr. str qt, 1997; Orpheus Singing, ob, str, 1994, arr. ob, pf/str qt; Partita, concerto grosso, tpt, trbn, violect [5-str elec vn], orch, elecs, 1995; Dreamtime suite no.4, 1999–2000; Sym. no.2 "Red Earth," 2004

Vocal: 2 Songs in Olden Style (W. Wordsworth, J. Joyce), S, pf, 1960; Edge (S. Plath), Mez, fl + a fl, tpt, vc, pf + synth, elecs, 1977, rev. 1997; Treny, S, 2 vc, 1996–7; Klytemnestra (O. Zabuzhko), Mez, cl, pf trio, 1998; A Journey after Loves (Boychuk), Bar, pf, 1999; The Emily Dickinson Songbook Vol. I, S, pf, 2001–2; Uniforms of Snow, S, chamber orch, 2002–3; The Emily Dickinson Songbook Vol. II, S, pf, 2003–4

Chbr and solo inst: Partita no.1, 3 trbn, 3 pf, 1970–76; Jurassic Bird, vc, perc, pf, 1978, rev. 2001; Duo-Concertante, vc, pf, 1971, rev. 1990; Sculptured Birds, cl, pf, 1978–84; ...Figments (Etudes tableaux, bk I), vn, 10 vn/tape, 1981–92; Partita no.2, bn, pf, 1991–2, rev. 1997; Dreamtime Suite no.1, cl, vn, pf, 1993–4; Dreamtime (masque), fl, cl, vn, vc, kbd, 2 perc, 1993–5; Stamping Dance, b cl, 1995 [from Dreamtime]; Dreamtime Suite no.2, vn, vc, pf, 1996; Lament I, bn, 1996 [from Treny]; Lament Ia, dbn, 1996 [from Treny]; Shadows, fl, pf, 1996; Partita no.3, 2 vn, pf, 1996–7; Persona I, ob, 1997; Persona II, cl, 1997; ...à trois, ob, bn, pf, 1998; Songs Without Words, vn (or va, vc, cl), 2002–4; Dreams of Phantom Battlements, 6 perc, 2004; Et lux perpetua, vc, pf, 2004, arr, str orch

Pf: Nocturnal no.1 "Mirrors," 1958; 2 Dumas, 1959; Nocturnal no.2 "Tears," 1960; Nocturnal no.3, 3 pf, 1970; Nocturnal no.4, 1971–87; Nocturnal no.5, 1980; Nocturnal no.6, 1988; Pajarillo (from Cante Hondo), 2002; Et lux perpetua, 2004

Principal publisher: Troppe Note (ASCAP)

KYLE GANN

Balfa Family. Family of Cajun musicians. They are some of the most influential musicians in Cajun music. The principal members were Dewey Balfa (*b* Bayou Grand Louis, near Mamou, LA, 20 March 1927; *d* Eunice, LA, 17 June 1992), his older brother (and godfather) Will Bolfa (his preferred spelling, *b* Bayou Grand Louis, 1917; *d* near Mamou, 6 Feb 1979) and younger brother Rodney Balfa (*b* Bayou Grand Louis, 24 May 1934; *d* Mamou, 6 Feb 1979). They learned to play and sing from their family, including father, Charles, who played fiddle. Just after World War II, the brothers formed a Cajun group called the Musical Brothers (later, the Balfa Brothers), first as a string band and later with an accordion player. Brothers Harry and Burkman occasionally joined, and Rodney's son Tony eventually became a regular member. They played music in addition to regular day jobs. In 1964, they were recorded by Newport Folk Festival fieldworkers including Ralph Rinzler and Mike Seeger. Dewey was invited to play guitar at Newport that same year, with a band that also included Gladdy Thibodeaux on accordion and Louis "Vinesse" Lejeune on fiddle. Dewey was deeply affected (and surprised) by the enthusiastic response they received, since at that time, Cajun music was considered raucous and uncouth by many in Louisiana. Dewey returned to Louisiana committed to spreading the message that Cajun music was appreciated by outsiders.

Dewey and his brothers were soon featured at festivals throughout the United States, Canada, and France. They appeared in several documentary films, including

Les Blank's *Spend It All* (1972), Jean-Pierre Bruneau's *Dedans le sud de la Louisiane* (1974), Yasha Aginsky's *Blues de Balfa* (1983), and Paul Goldsmith's *The Good Times Are Killing Me* (1975). Dewey appeared in several feature films, including *Southern Comfort* (1981) and *The Big Easy* (1986). The Balfa Brothers produced many recordings, often featuring guest musicians such as Nathan Abshire, Marc Savoy, Hadley Fontenot, and Ally Young. They brought young musicians into the band, including Robert Jardell, Steve Riley, Jamie Barzas, and Jason Frey. They also performed and recorded with Creole musicians such as the Ardoin Family Band and Rockin' Dopsie and the Twisters. They recorded and performed regularly with Nathan Abshire as members of his Pine Grove Boys.

The Balfa brothers influenced many young musicians. Dewey obtained a grant from the National Endowment for the Arts to present workshops and performances in schools throughout South Louisiana. He hosted a weekly Cajun and Creole radio show on KEUN, and helped plan and organize the first Tribute to Cajun Music concert in 1974, produced by the Council for the Development of French in Louisiana, which evolved into the annual Festivals Acadiens in Lafayette.

In 1979, Will and Rodney were killed in an automobile accident. Dewey continued to perform and teach until his death. In 1982, NEA awarded him a National Heritage Fellowship, and in 1987, he was appointed Adjunct Professor of Cajun Music by the University of Louisiana at Lafayette. After Dewey's death, his daughter Christine (*b* Basile, LA, 31 Dec 1969) took up the family torch, forming the group Balfa Toujours, which has also occasionally featured daughter Nelda. Christine worked with the organization Louisiana Folk Roots to found and organize an annual Cajun and Creole music camp, and also performs with the group Bonsoir Catin.

BIBLIOGRAPHY

J. Broven: *South to Louisiana: The Music of the Cajun Bayous* (Gretna, LA, 1983)

B.J. Ancelet and E. Morgan Jr.: *Cajun and Creole Music Makers* (Jackson, MS, 1984/*R*)

A.A. Savoy: *Cajun Music: a Reflection of a People* (Eunice, LA, 1984)

R. Brasseaux and K. Fontenot, eds.: *Accordions, Fiddles, Two Steps and Swing* (Lafayette, LA, 2006)

BARRY JEAN ANCELET

Ball, Ernest R(oland) (*b* Cleveland, OH, 21 July 1878; *d* Santa Ana, CA, 3 May 1927). Composer and singer. After studying music at the Cleveland Conservatory he went to New York, where he became a pianist in vaudeville theaters and a founding member of ASCAP. From 1907 to 1927 he was a staff pianist and composer at M. Witmark and Sons. His first success came with the ballad "Will you love me in December as you do in May?," written in 1905 to lyrics by Jimmy Walker. Many of his most popular songs thereafter were composed for the Irish tenors John McCormack and Chauncey Olcott, with whom he also collaborated. Ball composed some 400 songs, including such standards as "Mother Machree" (1910), "When Irish Eyes are Smiling" (1913), and "A Little Bit of Heaven" (1914). Much of the last decade of his life was spent performing in vaudeville. His film biography, *When Irish Eyes are Smiling* (1944), starred Dick Haymes.

BIBLIOGRAPHY

J. Burton: "Honor Roll of Popular Songwriters: Ernest R. Ball," *Billboard*, lxi (14 May 1949), 38

R. Kinkle: *The Complete Encyclopedia of Popular Music and Jazz, 1900–1950* (New Rochelle, NY, 1974)

P. Gammond: *The Oxford Companion to Popular Music* (New York, 1991), 34

D. Jasen: *Tin Pan Alley: an Encyclopedia of the Golden Age of American Song* (New York, 2003), 22

DALE COCKRELL

Ball, Marcia (*b* Orange, TX, 20 March 1949). Blues singer and pianist. Ball began playing piano at age five, one in a long line of female pianists in her family. Her earliest influences were Tin Pan Alley songs, but as a young teenager she became interested in soul and blues music. Inspired by the music of Irma Thomas, Ball continued to play, attended Louisiana State University and performed with the blues/rock band Gum. She decided to leave the area in 1970, but only made it as far as Austin, Texas, where she put together a band named Freda and the Firedogs. Ball began songwriting in earnest around the same time, feeling a kindred spirit in the music of Professor Longhair. She was signed to Capitol Records in 1974, and launched her solo career with the album *Circuit Queen* (1978). In the next two decades, she would release six records on Rounder Records while working on her personal sound, which has been described as a mix between "Texas stomp-rock" and "Louisiana swamp blues." One of her most successful albums was *Dreams Come True* (1990), and in 1998, she was able to work with Irma Thomas on the record *Sing It!*, which was nominated for a Grammy Award. She has been nominated for several Grammys and has won over six Blues Music Awards. After moving to Alligator Records in 2001, Ball has released six more records. She continues to be a mainstay of the Austin music scene and has appeared on numerous television programs and films, including *New Orleans Music in Exile* (2006).

JONAS WESTOVER

Ballad. A short popular song that often features a narrative element. The word often signifies a slow-tempo love song, and ballads became especially important to jazz repertory and Tin Pan Alley song. In recent decades, ballads have been performed frequently by modern-day crooners, jazz singers, pop superstars, and hard rock groups ("power ballads").

Ballad opera. A form of popular musical theater (*opéra comique*) current in the early 18th century, in which spoken dialogue, usually of a humorous or satirical nature, alternated with sung parodies based on preexisting lyrics to known melodies. John Gay's *The Beggar's Opera* (1728) was the first such piece in English, capitalizing on Thomas D'Urfey's widely popular output of political and personal satire set to popular tunes of the day, both traditional and newly composed. As these songs were used and reused, they carried the original satire with them in the minds of the audiences; thus the selection of tunes was carefully made to enhance each dramatic situation. In England, the genre was first used with considerable success for two purposes: to lampoon Walpole's government and to mock the popularity of Italian opera among the upper class. With the Licensing Act of 1737, much of this bitter satire disappeared, and after that time the genre became pasticcio musical theater in which previously used songs, parodies of older lyrics and newly composed pieces were interpolated into the dialogue. With familiar music and librettos in English, it became the most popular type of theater.

The first ballad opera known to have been performed in America was *Flora, or Hob in the Well* (1729), which was presented in Charleston on 18 February 1735. By 1752 several other English ballad operas had become popular in America, including *Damon and Phillida* (1729), *The Devil to Pay* (1731), *The Honest Yorkshireman* (1735), *The Mock Doctor* (1732), *The Virgin Unmasked* (1735), and, most frequently performed, *The Beggar's Opera*. Such works continued to dominate the American musical stage until the Revolution, though a number of newer forms had been performed in America by 1772. These included ballad-burlettas, in which spoken dialogue was replaced by rhymed recitation; concerted pieces in imitation of light Italian comic opera and brought from England--as in *Midas* (1760), the pasticcio that used music from the works of named composers, usually English—alongside traditional songs, as in *Love in a Village* (1762), *Maid of the Mill* (1765), and *Lionel and Clarissa* (1768); and operas written by a single composer, such as Charles Dibdin's *The Padlock* (1768).

The first American-born author to produce a ballad opera was James Ralph (*b* 1695 or 1705; *d* 1762), who wrote *The Fashionable Lady* in 1730 after moving to London. In 1767 the *Philadelphia Gazette* announced the performance of a full-length comic opera called *The Disappointment, or The Force of Credulity* (ed. in RRAM, iii–iv, 1976). The author's name, Andrew Barton, was a pseudonym taken from a Scottish pirate (*d* 1511) who had been immortalized in ballads. Four days before the opening, the performance was suppressed as "unfit for the stage" because of the personal "reflections" in the script.

Based on fact, *The Disappointment* was a social satire in which several prominent Philadelphians were made to look foolish in a treasure-hunting scheme. It was a true ballad opera in the original sense and played on the continuing popularity of *The Beggar's Opera*. No 18th-century performance has been documented, but the libretto was immediately published and a second edition followed in 1796. Tunes are indicated for 18 airs and a dance. Of these at least 13 are ballad tunes (most had previously been used in other operas) and at least four are contemporary popular songs. The tunes range in complexity from the simple bawdy jig called "Black Joke" to Thomas Arne's pastoral air "My fond shepherds." While *The Disappointment* is often cited as including the earliest example of "Yankee Doodle," this identification is in error. The intended tune for Air IV, sung by the German character called Raccoon, is "Doodle do," a melody associated with the Raree Show tradition and commonly used for satires by German or French men speaking heavily accented English.

Although theatrical entertainment was discouraged in America during the Revolution, British soldiers in New York between 1776 and 1783 regularly presented shows, including ballad operas, for loyalist inhabitants and occupying troops. *The Blockheads, or Fortunate Contractor*, published in London in 1782 but described as "performed in New York," was probably part of their repertory. The author of this work is unknown, but the subject matter and the political sentiments expressed point to a loyalist or even a British soldier. Sixteen songs are indicated, but no titles or first lines are provided; it is probable, to judge from the statement "composed by several of the most eminent masters in Europe" on the title page, that the work was a pasticcio.

Theater was gradually reestablished after the Revolution, but by then pure ballad opera had long been succeeded by the pasticcio. For the most part the music was still simple and unpretentious, but occasionally pieces in the more cultivated and ornate *galant* style were used. Royall Tyler's comic opera *May Day in Town, or New-York in an Uproar* was performed on 19 May 1787; neither libretto nor songs are extant, but the music was "compiled from the most eminent masters."

Another pasticcio, *The Better Sort, or The Girl of Spirit*, probably by William Hill Brown, was published in Boston in 1789, but only the prologue was performed. The plot is thin, but provides opportunities for the principal characters to discuss various social and political questions. Of its 18 songs only seven carry an indication of the tunes to be used for them (one song is furnished with an alternative tune). Since theatrical presentations were prohibited in Boston until 1792, there was little chance that the work would be performed and the author probably felt it unnecessary to supply tunes for all the songs. Of the eight tunes given, two are from popular songs and three have ballad origins; five had already appeared in other contemporary stage works.

William Dunlap's one-act afterpiece *Darby's Return* was first performed in New York on 24 November 1789. It was was written as a sequel to *The Poor Soldier* (1783), probably the most popular opera in the United States at that time. *The Poor Soldier* was a conservative work, about two-thirds of its music having been taken from ballad sources, mostly Irish. Dunlap's text is entirely in verse, and his musical choices are also conservative; the songs that open and close the work are both from folk sources—in fact the opening tune is also that of the finale of *The Poor Soldier. Darby's Return* was moderately successful, largely owing to the performance of Thomas Wignell in the role of Darby.

Peter Markoe's *The Reconciliation, or The Triumph of Nature* (Philadelphia, 1790) was accepted by the Old

American Company but never staged. Three airs, one with music (the tune is from Arne's *Artaxerxes*, 1762), were printed in the *Universal Asylum and Columbian Magazine* in June 1790, the first printing of music from any American opera. The same magazine gave a critical report of the opera, concluding that "the want of humour, of variety in the dialogue, and the length of some of the soliloquies, render it less fit for the stage than for the closet" (that is, to be read privately). All 11 songs in the work use tunes that were widely available in published sources; five are ballads, and nine had appeared in other 18th-century operas. The influence of the *galant* style is very clear in the choice of music.

During the last decade of the 18th century both ballad operas and pasticcios were superseded by operas in which the majority of the music was newly written by a single composer. Pelissier, Reinagle, Benjamin Carr, and James Hewitt, for example, wrote new music for works performed in their respective theaters. An occasional reference to the use of pasticcio techniques is found in newspaper descriptions: *Little Yankee Sailor* was presented in Philadelphia in 1795 with music "selected from William Shield, James Hook, Rayner Taylor, Charles Dibdin, etc.," and arranged by George Gillingham. The most popular English ballad operas continued to be performed into the early 19th century, but no American ballad opera or pasticcio achieved lasting success. The genre's importance, however, lies in its contribution to the establishment of a musical tradition in the American theater.

See also Musical theater; Opera; *and* Popular music.

BIBLIOGRAPHY

O.G.T. Sonneck: "Early American Operas," *SIMG*, vi (1904–5), 428–95
O.G.T. Sonneck: *Early Opera in America* (New York, 1915/*R*)
M.C. Diebels: *Peter Markoe (1752?–1792): a Philadelphia Writer* (Washington, DC, 1944)
T. Ridgway: "Ballad Opera in Philadelphia in the Eighteenth Century," *Church Music and Musical Life in Pennsylvania*, iii (Philadelphia, 1947), 371–426
H.G. Moss: *Ballad-Opera Songs: a Record of the Ideas Set to Music, 1728–1733* (diss., U. of Michigan, 1970)
E.I. Zimmerman: *American Opera Librettos, 1767–1825: the Manifestation and Result of the Imitative Principle in American Literary Form* (diss., U. of Tennessee, 1972)
R. Fiske: *English Theatre Music in the Eighteenth Century* (New York, 1973)
W. Rubsamen, ed.: *The Ballad Opera: a Collection of 171 Original Texts of Musical Plays Printed in Photo-facsimile* (New York, 1974)
J. Layng: "America's First Opera," *Opera Journal*, ix/3 (1976), 3–7
D. McKay: "*The Fashionable Lady*: the First Opera by an American," *MQ*, lxv/3 (1979), 360–67
P.H. Virga: *The American Opera to 1790* (Ann Arbor, MI, 1982)
C. Rabson: "*Disappointment* Revisited: Unweaving the Tangled Web," *AM*, i/1 (1983), 12–35; ii/1 (1984), 1–28
S. Porter: *With an Air Debonair: Musical Theatre in America, 1785–1815* (Washington, DC, 1991)
Ballad Operas Online <http://www.odl.ox.ac.uk/balladoperas/>

SUSAN L. PORTER/KATE VAN WINKLE KELLER

Ballanta(-Taylor), Nicholas George Julius (*b* Kissy, nr Freetown, Sierra Leone, 14 March 1893; *d* ?Sierra Leone, 1961). African ethnomusicologist and composer. Missionaries changed Ballanta, the grandfather's African surname, to Taylor. Nicholas George's father, Gustavus, hyphenated the name, under which the son published. He sang and played the organ at St. Patrick's Chapel, Kissy, as a youth. In 1917 he passed the intermediary examination for the BM degree at Fourah Bay College, Freetown, an affiliate of the University of Durham, UK, but he could not complete this degree because of travel requirements that the final examination be taken in England. Between 1918 and 1919, he participated in a Freetown choral society, for which he wrote the oratorio *Belshazzar's Feast*. He spent the winter of 1921 in Boston, sponsored by an American patron, where he conducted his *African Rhapsody* at Symphony Hall and studied orchestration privately. In 1922 he matriculated at the New York Institute of Music Art (now Juilliard School of Music), where he obtained his diploma (1924).

Ballanta emerged as one the earliest trained African musicians to adopt ethnomusicological approaches and write about the linkages between the traditional music of black America and Africa in the early 20th century. Under sponsorship from the Penn Normal Industrial School in St. Helena, South Carolina, he toured the southern United States collecting African American folk songs, which he ultimately published as *Negro Spirituals of Helena's Island* (New York, 1925). He conducted similar studies of folk songs throughout West Africa with support of two Guggenheim Fellowships (1925, 1927).

WORKS

(selective list)

Belshazzar's Feast, solo vv, chorus, str, org, pf, 1919; African Rhapsody, ?1921; String Quartet, 1923; The Music of Africa, orch, 1924

WRITINGS

"Jazz Music and Its Relation to African Music," *Musical Courier*, lxxxiv (1922), 51 only; repr. in *Keeping Time, Readings in Jazz History*, ed. R. Walser (New York, 1999), 36–8
"Gathering Folk Tunes in the African Country," *MusAm*, xliv (1923), 3–11
"Music of the African Races," *Negro Year Book, 1931–1932* (Tuskegee, AL, 1931), 441–4

EDITIONS

St. Helena's Island Spirituals (New York, 1925)

BIBLIOGRAPHY

"American Jazz Is Not African," *New York Times* (19 Sept 1926); repr. in *Metronome*, xlii (1 Oct 1927), 21 only; repr. in *Jazz in Print (1866–1929): an Anthology of Selected Early Readings*, ed. K. Koenig (Hillsdale, NY, 2002), 483–4
C.C. White: "Ballanta: African Musician," *New York Amsterdam News* (4 May 1927); repr. in *Pittsburgh Courier* (20 April 1927)
M.C. Hare: *Negro Musicians and Their Music* (Washington, DC, 1936/*R*), 347–8
J.H. Kwabena Nketia: "*The Scholarly Study of African Music: a Historical Review*," *Africa: the Garland Encyclopedia of World Music*, ed. R.M. Stone, i (New York, 1998), 19–22

JOSEPHINE WRIGHT

Ballantine, Edward (*b* Oberlin, OH, 6 Aug 1886; *d* Oak Bluffs, MA, 2 July 1971). Composer. He studied at Harvard University (BA 1907) with Walter Spalding and Frederick Converse, then went to Berlin, where he was a student of Artur Schnabel, Rudolf Ganz, and Philippe

Rüfer (1907–9). In 1912 he was appointed to the music faculty of Harvard, and he remained there until his retirement in 1947. His music, cast in a post-Romantic, tonal, and accessible style, is often marked by humor, occasionally by a satirical eclecticism. These traits are most apparent in his best-known pieces, two sets of piano variations on *Mary Had a Little Lamb* (1924, 1943), in which each variation is in the style of a different composer, and the *Four Lyrical Satires* for voice and piano.

WORKS
(selective list)

Stage: The Lotus Eaters (masque, D.W. Streeter), 1907

Orch: Prelude to "The Delectable Forest," 1914; The Eve of St Agnes, 1917; By a Lake in Russia, 1922; From the Garden of Hellas, 1923

Chbr and solo inst: Morning, pf, 1913; Sonata, vn, pf; Mary had a little lamb, variations, pf: ser. 1, 1924; ser. 2, 1943

Vocal: Retrospect (Ballantine), 1913; Four Lyrical Satires, v, pf; Song for a Future (T. Spencer), mixed vv (New York, 1945); Lake Werna's Water (E. Bronte), SSAA (New York, 1946); other choruses and songs

Principal publishers: O. Ditson, G. Schirmer, A.P. Schmidt

BIBLIOGRAPHY

Obituary, *New York Times* (4 July 1971)

S. Arzuni: "An American Jester," *Keyboard Classics*, xiv/5 (1994), 54–6

H. WILEY HITCHCOCK/MICHAEL MECKNA

Ballard, Hank [Kendricks, John Henry] (*b* Detroit, MI, 18 Nov 1927; *d* Los Angeles, CA, 2 March 2003). Rhythm and blues singer and songwriter. He began his career with the Detroit-based group the Royals. His first success came with the song "Work with me, Annie" (Federal, 1954), which was a hit on the R&B chart. By 1958 the Royals had changed their name to Hank Ballard and the Midnighters, reflecting the influence and success of Ballard as its lead singer and songwriter. By 1961, when Ballard left the group to perform under his own name, he had 22 singles on the R&B charts with three different labels, Federal, Vee-Jay, and King. Before his retirement in the early 1970s, two more of his songs were listed on the R&B charts.

Undoubtedly his best and most successful song was "The Twist," which he wrote in 1958. Dick Clark, when asked what he considered the most significant song in rock-and-roll history, said, "That's easy; it was 'The Twist'," explaining that the song represented "the first time that parents and their kids could freely admit they liked rock and roll." Although Ballard claimed that he always believed the song would be a hit—"just for the lyric 'the twist',"—it was Chubby Checker's version that achieved the most success, reaching the top of the charts in 1960 and again in 1962. Ballard reformed the Midnighters in the mid-1970s and continued to perform under his own name until the mid-1990s. In 1990 he was inducted into the Rock and Roll Hall of Fame.

RECORDINGS
(selective list)

The Very Best of Hank Ballard and the Midnighters (Collectables, 2001); *Hank Ballard and the Midnighters: 1952–1954* (Classic R & B, 2005); *Hank Ballard and the Midnighters: all 20 of their Chart Hits* (King, 2005)

BIBLIOGRAPHY

B. Bracken: *Hot Rods, Pink-Bellies and Hank Ballard* (Frederick, MD, 2008)

RANDOLPH LOVE

Ballard, James (*fl* 1830–55). Music teacher and writer. He taught music in New York during the 1840s; advertisements in Edgar Allan Poe's *Broadway Journal* (1845–6) describe him as "a professor of the guitar, singing and the flute," with a studio at 135 (later 15) Spring Street. The third (and earliest known) edition of his work *The Elements of Guitar-playing* appeared in 1838. Largely inspired by Fernando Sor's *Method for the Spanish Guitar* (in Merrick's English edition of 1832) from which he occasionally quotes directly, its unusually detailed text contains much valuable information about guitar technique of the period. A unique feature is Ballard's theory of teaching chords and their inversions through "chord positions," an attempt to relate diatonic harmony directly to the fingerboard of the instrument. A second method, Ballard's *Guitar Preceptor*, is actually an abridged edition of his *Elements* published about the same time. Ballard also composed numerous arrangements for the instrument. He wrote *A History of the Guitar, from the Earliest Antiquity to the Present Time* for the William B. Tilton Co. in 1855, which, despite its ambitious title, is largely an endorsement of two Tilton guitar patents.

BIBLIOGRAPHY

P. Danner: "A Noteworthy Early American Guitar Treatise: James Ballard's 'Element' of 1838," *Soundboard*, ix (1981), 270 only

J.W. Stallings: *James Ballard's The Elements of Guitar Playing* (diss., Arizona State U., 2005)

PETER DANNER

Ballard, Louis W(ayne) [Honganózhe] (*b* Devil's Promenade, OK, 8 July 1931; *d* Santa Fe, NM, 9 Feb 2007). Composer and music educator of Cherokee Indian, Quapaw Indian, French, and Scottish descent. (Honganózhe is a Quapaw name that means "Grand Eagle.") As a child, he studied piano with his mother and took voice and piano lessons at a local Baptist mission school. He gained certification as an artist at Bacone College in Muskogee, Oklahoma, and studied at the University of Tulsa (BME 1954, BFA 1954, MM 1962), becoming the first Native American to obtain a graduate degree in composition. He also had private composition lessons with DARIUS MILHAUD, MARIO CASTELNUOVO-TEDESCO, CARLOS SURINACH, and FELIX LABUNSKI. After teaching in Oklahoma public schools and serving as music director at local churches (1954–8), he was appointed director of music and performing arts at the Institute of American Indian Arts, Santa Fe (1962–9). Subsequently, as National Curriculum Specialist for the Bureau of Indian Affairs (1969–79), he developed a bicultural music education program that earned him a Distinguished Service Award from the Central Office of Education and a citation in the Congressional Record (1975). Ballard held numerous university appointments and appeared internationally as a guest conductor and lecturer. Among his other honors are National Indian Achievement Awards

(1972, 1973, 1976), an honorary doctorate from the College of Santa Fe (1973) and William Jewel College (2001), the first MacDowell Award for American chamber music (1969), and grants from the Rockefeller Foundation (1969), Ford Foundation (1970) and NEA (1967, 1973, 1977, 1982, 1989). He received a Lifetime Musical Achievement Award by First Americans in the Arts (1997) and the Cherokee Medal of Honor (2002).

Ballard's compositional style fuses 20th-century techniques with diverse Native American influences. For his woodwind quintet *Ritmo Indio* (1969), he added a Lakota flute in the second movement, which features incomplete repetition and also pairs instruments playing the melody at the octave, evoking certain elements of Plains vocal style. His compositions have been performed by such prominent organizations as the St. Paul Chamber Orchestra, the American Composers Orchestra, the Los Angeles PO, the Tulsa PO, and the Harkness Ballet. In 1989 he became the first American composer to have an entire program dedicated to his music in the newly constructed Beethovenhalle, Bonn. He was the first composer of Native heritage to introduce Western audiences to various aspects of Native American music within the Western art music idiom.

WORKS

DRAMATIC

Jijogweh, the WitchWater Gull (ballet, after Iroquois Indian myth), 1960, unperf.
Koshare (ballet, choreog. D. Sadler), 1964, Barcelona, 17 May 1966
The Four Moons (ballet, choreog. G. Skibine, R. Jasinski, M. Terekhov, R. Hightower), 1967, Tulsa, OK, 28 Oct 1967
Sacred Ground (film score, dir. R. Jacobs), 1976
The Maid of the Mist and the Thunderbeings (dance score, choreog. R. Trujillo, L. Smith), 1991, Buffalo, NY, 18 Oct 1991
Moontide (The Man who Hated Money) (rock op, 1, L. Ballard), 1992, Norden, 11 April 1994

INSTRUMENTAL

Orch: Fantasy Aborigine no.1 "Sipapu," 1963; Scenes from Indian Life, 1963, arr. concert band, 1970; Why the Duck has a Short Tail (Ballard, R. Dore), nar, orch, 1968; Devil's Promenade, 1972; Incident at Wounded Knee, chbr orch, opt. perc, 1973; Ishi (America's Last Civilized Man), 1975; Fantasy Aborigine: no.2 "Tsiyako," str, 1976, no.3 "Kokopelli," 1977, no.4 "Xactee'oyan, Companion of Talking God," 1982, no.5 "Naniwaya," 1988, no.6 "Niagara," 1991; Feast Day, sketch, 1994
Band: Siouxiana, ww, 1973; Wamus 77 (Indian Heroes, History and Heritage), marching band, 1977; Nighthawk Keetowah Dances, 1978; Ocotillo Festival Ov., 1978
Chbr: Str Trio, 1959; Perc Ego, perc, pf, 1962; Rhapsody, 4 bn, 1963; Cacega Ayuwipi, 5 perc, 1969; Katcina Dances, vc, pf, 1969; Ritmo Indio, ww qnt, 1969; Desert Trilogy, 8 insts, 1970; Midwinter Fires, Amerindian fl, cl, pf, 1970; Pan Indian Dance Rhythms, 4 perc, 1970; Rio Grande Sonata, vn, pf, 1976; Music for the Earth and the Sky, amp cel, 5 perc, 1986; Bellum atramentum, ob, vn, vc, 1988; Capientur a nullo, va, vc, db, 1988; The Lonely Sentinel, fl, ob, tpt, hn, trbn, tuba, 1993; The Fire Moon, str qt, 1997
Solo: 4 American Indian Pf Preludes, 1963; A City of Silver, pf, 1981; A City of Fire, pf, 1984; A City of Light, pf, 1986; Awakening of Love, org, 1992; Quetzalcoatl's Coattails, gui, 1992

VOCAL

Choral: Espiritu di Santiago (Ballard), SATB, fl, gui, pf, 1963; The Gods will Hear (L.H. New), SATB (perc, pf)/orch, 1964; Mojave Bird Dance Song, SATB, 1964; Portrait of Will Rogers (Ballard, W. Rogers), nar, SATB, pf/orch, 1971; Thus Spake Abraham (cant., Ballard), solo vv, SATB, pf, 1977; Dialogue differentia (orat, Ballard), chorus, orch, 1989; 4 American Indian Christian Hymns, SATB, pf, 1990; Live on, Heart of My Nation (Ballard, M.C. Fry), nar, SATB, chbr orch/pf, 1990
Solo: The Spider Rock (J. Miami), T, pf, 1966 [composed under pseud. Joe Miami]; Gado Dajvyadvhneli Jisa (trad.), Bar, pf, 1990; Mi Cinski, Hec'ela T'ankalake K'uniyaye (Ballard), Mez, pf, 1997

EDITIONS AND TEACHING MATERIALS

The American Indian Sings (Santa Fe, 1970)
Oklahoma Indian Chants for the Classroom (Santa Fe, 1972)
American Indian Music for the Classroom, Canyon C-3001 to 3004 (1973) [incl. teachers' guide and other materials]
My Music Reaches to the Sky: Native American Indian Instruments (Santa Fe, 1973)
Music of North American Indians (Morristown, NJ, 1975)

Principal publishers: New Southwest, Bourne, Presser

WRITINGS

"Cultural Differences: a Major Theme in Cultural Enrichment," *Indian Historian*, ii/1 (1969), 4–7
"Put American Indian Music in the Classroom," *MEJ*, lvi/7 (1969–70), 38–44
Native American Music of the Western Hemisphere (Santa Fe, 1974)
"Toward Another (Musical) Aesthetic," *Minority Voices*, i/1 (1977), 29–34
'Two Ogàxpa Sacred Robes Visit Home," *Public Historian*, xviii/4 (1996), 193–7

BIBLIOGRAPHY

J. Katz, ed.: "Louis Ballard: Quapaw/Cherokee Composer," *This Song Remembers: Self Portraits of Native Americans in the Arts* (Boston, 1980), 132–8
R. Dore: "Louis Ballard: Music for the Earth and the Sky," *Artspace*, xii/4 (1988), 25–7
R. Luce: "Louis Ballard, Composer," *Santa Fean Magazine* (Jan–Feb, 1990), 24–5
T. Browner: *Transposing Cultures: the Appropriation of Native North Amer. Musics, 1890–1990* (diss., U. of Michigan, 1995), 164–82
S. Malinowski and S. Glickman, ed.: "Louis W. Ballard," *Native North American Biography* (Detroit, MI, 1996), 21–3
C. Crappell: *Native American Influence in the Piano Music of Louis W. Ballard* (diss., U. of Oklahoma, 2008)

CHARLOTTE J. FRISBIE/PAULA J. CONLON

Ballet. The early history of ballet in America is primarily a record of visits of European artists and performances of European ballets. Companies of dancers visited the American colonies as early as 1735, when an English company headed by Henry Holt performed several ballet-pantomimes, including *The Adventures of Harlequin and Scaramouche* and *The Burgo'master Trick'd*, in Charles Towne, the principal seat of government of the royal colony of South Carolina. After the American Revolution, the French acrobat Alexandre Placide and dancer Suzanne Théodore Vaillande, billed as his wife, also appeared in Charleston, in 1791, in a "dancing ballot" entitled *The Bird Catcher*. The following year they presented a full season of ballets in New York City, offering *The Bird Catcher*, *The Return of the Labourers*, and *The Two Philosophers, or The Merry Girl*. Appearing in their company was JOHN DURANG, America's first professional dancer and said to be George Washington's favorite entertainer. Suzanne Vaillande (later Douvillier) eventually became *première danseuse* of the Théâtre de Nouvelle-Orléans, where she was, in effect, America's first female choreographer and set designer.

Following the success of Placide's New York season, various European dancers presented performances in New York, Philadelphia, Boston, and other American cities. In the 1820s, a number of French artists brought ballets that featured a new, virtuosic style of dancing that delighted their growing audiences. Paul Hazard and his wife, former members of the Paris Opéra Ballet, opened the first American school of ballet in Philadelphia around 1835 and trained several American dancers who became well known, including ballerinas Mary Ann Lee (?1823–99) and Augusta Maywood (1825–76). Another Philadelphia native, George Washington Smith (?1820–99), originally a clog and hornpipe dancer, joined the company of the famous Austrian ballerina Fanny Elssler during her American tours in 1840–42 and was given ballet training, in which he excelled. He became Elssler's partner in classical ballets such as *Giselle* and is thus acknowledged as the first American *premier danseur.* In 1845, he formed a small troupe with Mary Ann Lee, and they toured the United States for two years as the first American couple to dance leading roles as partners in classical ballets. Lee retired in 1847 and was succeeded by Julia Turnbull (1822–87), also an American protégée of Elssler, as the country's leading ballerina.

Meanwhile, Elssler and her company enjoyed enormous success in America. President Martin Van Buren and members of his cabinet attended the third of the company's five performances in Washington in July 1840, and the president was so enchanted that he invited the ballerina to a private audience at the White House the following morning. On the evenings of her final two performances, the business of the House of Representatives was interrupted because so many members preferred to occupy seats at the theater rather than their seats in the House. In 1857 the Cecchetti family, including young son Enrico, also toured the United States, and the Ravel family spent more than 30 years on the road with a repertory of original ballets, pantomimes, and circus acts. Soon after the Civil War, the production of *The Black Crook,* a theatrical extravaganza, sparked a new wave of interest in theatrical dance, thanks largely to the performance of Italian ballerina Maria Bonfanti. It opened at Niblo's Garden in New York City in 1866 and had an almost uninterrupted run there and on tour until 1909, during which time it introduced new generations of Americans to the art of ballet. (*See* Musical theater.)

During the early years of the 20th century American audiences were again inspired by visits of dancers from foreign troupes. In 1908, the Danish ballerina Adeline Genée, star of London's Empire Theatre, appeared to great acclaim in *The Soul Kiss,* a spectacular mélange of musical comedy, burlesque, and elaborate production numbers staged by Florenz Ziegfeld at the Chestnut Street Opera House in Philadelphia. After a trial run there, the show opened in New York, where Genée was greeted with equal enthusiasm. In 1910, Russian dancers Anna Pavlova and Mikhail Mordkin appeared at the Metropolitan Opera House in *Coppélia,* set to the fine score by Léo Delibes, and their success was little short of sensational. New York audiences also applauded Pavlova and Mordkin in other works, including *Valse Caprice, The Legend of Azyiade,* and, especially, *Bacchanale,* set by Mordkin to the Autumn section of Aleksandr Glazunov's ballet *The Seasons.* Subsequently, Pavlova and her company toured extensively in the United States and contributed greatly to the popularization of ballet. Topping the acclamation given to these great ballet stars was that awarded to the performances of Ballets Russes de Sergei Diaghilev, which toured America in 1916–17. Despite the national preoccupation with the course of World War I, American critics and audiences in 16 cities were dazzled by the Diaghilev company's repertory of innovative modern ballets choreographed by Michel Fokine, Léonide Massine, and Vaslav Nijinsky. Besides the dancing of such artists as Nijinsky, Lydia Lopokova, Vera Nemchinova, and Adolf Bolm, the company offered stunning décors and costumes designed by Léon Bakst and Alexandre Benois and wonderful Russian music by Igor Stravinsky, Nikolai Rimsky-Korsakov, and Aleksandr Borodin.

During all these years American dancers were being trained by visiting foreign artists, and some had begun to make professional careers for themselves. In 1909, the Metropolitan Opera Association invited Italian ballerina Malvina Cavalazzi to return to the opera house as director of a school of ballet for the dancers in its company. She and teachers elsewhere in the country trained their students in the ballet techniques of the French, Italian, and Russian schools in which they themselves had been trained. It was not until 1934, with the foundation of the School of American Ballet in New York City by George Balanchine and Lincoln Kirstein that the concept of ballet as an American art form was first put forth.

With students from this school, Balanchine and Kirstein formed, as opportunity and funding allowed, a succession of companies, including the American Ballet, Ballet Caravan, American Ballet Caravan, and Ballet Society, that aimed to present a new, American kind of classical dance. These companies introduced American subjects for ballets and engaged the participation of American choreographers, American composers, and a growing number of quick-footed American dancers trained by Balanchine. For the American Ballet, Balanchine himself choreographed one of the first ballets on an American subject, *Alma Mater* (1935; music by Kay Swift, orchestrated by Morton Gould), a humorous account of football-mad college boys and their girlfriends. For Ballet Caravan, Lew Christensen, the youngest of the three dancing Christensen brothers, created *Pocohontas* (1936; music by Elliott Carter) and *Filling Station* (1938; music by Virgil Thompson), and Eugene Loring made *Yankee Clipper* (1937; music by Paul Bowles) and *Billy the Kid* (1938; music by Aaron Copland), which has proved to be the most enduring of all these early American ballets. Ballet Society, formed in 1946, was in due course invited to make its home at New York City Center, where it became the foundation of the New York City Ballet, now resident at the David H. Koch

Dancers from the Alvin Ailey American Dance Theater performing "Revelations" on the television program Lamp Unto My Feet, *1961. (CBS/Landov)*

Theater at Lincoln Center. Since the death of Balanchine in 1983, the company has been directed by Peter Martins, formerly a principal dancer with the company and Balanchine's chosen successor.

During his first decade in the United States, Balanchine created a large body of musical theater dances for Broadway shows and Hollywood films. Among those including classical ballet numbers are *On Your* Toes (1936) and *I Married an Angel* (1938), both with music by Richard Rodgers; *Louisiana Purchase* (1940), with music by Irving Berlin; and *Song of Norway* (1944), with music and lyrics by Robert Wright and George Forrest based on the music of Edvard Grieg. For the all-black musical *Cabin in the Sky* (1940), with music by Vernon Duke, Balanchine collaborated on the choreography with KATHERINE DUNHAM, creating dances combining classical ballet technique with Dunham's own highly developed dance technique. This show, starring Ethel Waters, had an imaginative book based on fantastic stories from African American folklore. A similar show, although less well known, was *Courtin' Time* (1951), with music and lyrics by Don Walker and Jack Lawrence. It dealt with the folklore of rural Maine and included a fantastic Balanchine ballet about a weather vane and some Down East pixies, "Johnny and the Puckwudgies."

On the ballet stage, Balanchine choreographed works in the distinctive style that had come to be called "neoclassical," first clearly evident in his *Apollon Musagète* (1928; music by Stravinsky), created for the Diaghilev company. For his works made for New York City Ballet, he continued to prefer the music of European composers. (He is said to have considered most American ballet music to be "non-balletic.") Nevertheless, he used American music for some of his best-loved ballets, including *Western Symphony* (1954; music by Hershy Kay), *Ivesiana* (1954; music by Charles Ives), *Stars and Stripes* (1958; music by John Philip Sousa, adapted and orchestrated by Kay), *Tarantella* (1964; music by Louis Moreau Gottschalk, reconstructed and orchestrated by Kay), and *Who Cares?* (1970; music by George Gershwin, orchestrated by Kay). All these works remain in the active repertory of New York City Ballet.

Other major ballet companies that helped establish the classical tradition in the United States include the San Francisco Ballet, Ballet Russe de Monte Carlo, and American Ballet Theatre. Founded in 1933, San Francisco Ballet has the distinction of being known as the oldest professional ballet company in America. Its original purpose was to train dancers to appear in opera productions, but with the arrival in 1938 of

Willam Christensen as ballet master the company started to present independent productions. Christensen, the eldest of the three dancing Christensen brothers, staged the first full-length productions of *Coppélia*, *Swan Lake*, and *The Nutcracker* in America, in 1939, 1940, and 1944, respectively. The company enjoyed artistic success under Christensen, but tottered under subsequent administrations until finding firm financial footing in the mid-1970s. Now directed by Helgi Tomasson, a former principal dancer of New York City Ballet, it gives regular seasons in its home city and makes occasional national and international tours. Its repertory remains rooted in the classics and has not been particularly welcoming of works set to American music.

Ballet Russe de Monte Carlo was founded in the aftermath of a 1938 lawsuit between Colonel Wassily de Basil and René Blum over performing rights to the "Russian ballets" of the Diaghilev repertory. Upon settlement of the suit, the companies of de Basil and Blum went their separate ways, and a third company, under the direction of Sergei Denham, was established in the United States, where it flourished until 1962. Although it bore a foreign name and was devoted to a cosmopolitan style of dancing, it was an essentially American company. Through its indefatigable touring of cities and towns large and small, it was perhaps the company most responsible for popularizing ballet in America. Led by *prima ballerina* Alexandra Danilova and *premier danseur* Frederick Franklin, the company included many fine dancers and offered an eclectic repertory. Notable works on American themes were Léonide Massine's *The New Yorker* (1940; music by Gershwin), Agnes de Mille's *Rodeo* (1942; music by Copland), Ruth Page and Bentley Stone's Frankie *and Johnny* (1945; music by Jerome Moross), Valerie Bettis's *Virginia Sampler* (1947; music by Leo Smit), and Ruth Page's hilarious *Billy Sunday* (1948; music by Remi Gassman). The works by AGNES DE MILLE and RUTH PAGE are considered classics of Americana.

In 1939, today's American Ballet Theatre, originally named simply Ballet Theatre, was founded by Richard Pleasant on the remains of the Mordkin Ballet. Its stated aim was to build a repertory of the best ballets from the past and to encourage the creation of new works by gifted young choreographers, especially Americans. The company gave its first performance on 11 January 1940 at the Center Theater in New York's Rockefeller Center. True to its statement of purpose, the novelty ballet on the program was *The Great American Goof*, choreographed by Eugene Loring to music by Henry Brant and a scenario and script by William Saroyan. (In the cast was LUCIA CHASE, who would become a co-director of the company in 1945.) Sadly, this bit of Americana fell almost immediately into the dustbin of history. Ballets made by JEROME ROBBINS and Agnes de Mille proved much more durable. Robbins created two now-classic works in the mid-1940s, *Fancy Free* (1944; music by Bernstein) and *Interplay* (1945; music by Gould), and de Mille added more than a dozen works over the years, including *Fall River Legend* (1948; music by Gould) and *The Harvest According* (1952; music by Thompson). In 1957 the company changed its name to American Ballet Theatre, thus emphasizing its original stated aim. It continued to expand its repertory of masterworks by Balanchine, Fokine, Antony Tudor, Birgit Cullberg, Robbins, and de Mille by adding works by younger choreographers, including the Americans ALVIN AILEY, TWYLA THARP, and MARK MORRIS. Ailey's *The River* (1970; music by Duke Ellington), Tharp's *Push Comes to Shove* (1976), and Morris's *Drink to Me Only with Thine Eyes* (1988; music by Thompson) were significant additions. Under the direction of Kevin McKenzie since 1992, the company now has a roster of international stars and a bifurcated repertory, with one part devoted to full-length classical ballets such as *Swan Lake*, *Le Corsaire*, *Don Quixote*, and *Giselle* and one part devoted to the one-act ballets that characterized its early years as an American dance theater.

Smaller ballet companies in various cities in the United States have also played a significant part in popularizing ballet in America. The Atlanta Ballet, founded in 1929 by DOROTHY ALEXANDER, was the first regional ballet company in the country and is, in fact, the oldest continuously operating ballet company in America (*pace* the claim of San Francisco Ballet). The Boston Ballet, founded in 1963 by E. VIRGINIA WILLIAMS, is the principal classical company in New England, and in opposite corners of the country are two fine companies under the direction of former principal dancers in New York City Ballet: Peter Boal is now artistic director of Pacific Northwest Ballet, based in Seattle, and Edward Villella has for some years been highly successful as artistic director of Miami City Ballet. All three of these companies have had close connection to and been influenced by the works of George Balanchine. Other notable companies include the Joffrey Ballet, founded by Robert Joffrey and Gerald Arpino in 1956 in New York but relocated to Chicago in 1995. It is now directed by Ashley C. Wheater. The Southwest can boast of Ballet West, founded in 1963 by Willam Christensen in Salt Lake City, and the Huston Ballet, founded in 1965, directed for many years by Ben Stevenson, and now flourishing under the direction of Stanton Welch.

From the 1950s onward, ballet schools and companies of varying standards proliferated in cities and towns across America. Today there is hardly any American city of moderate size that does not have one or more schools of classical ballet and a resident ballet company that gives occasional performances and offers the inevitable production of *The Nutcracker* at Christmastime. The continued popularity of local and regional ballet companies is undisputed evidence that ballet has become a truly American art form.

BIBLIOGRAPHY

G. Amberg: *Ballet in America: the Emergence of an American Art* (New York, 1949)

L. Moore: "Some Early American Dancers," *Dancing Times* (Aug 1950), 668–71

A. de Mille: *Dance to the Piper* (Boston, 1952)

L. Moore: "New York's First Ballet Season, 1792," *Bulletin of the New York Public Library* (Sept 1960)
D. Hering: "'A Kind of Oneness': Regional Ballet and Its Festivals, What Do They Mean to American Dance?" *Dance Magazine* (Oct 1970), 48–61
L. Kirstein: *Movement and Metaphor: Four Centuries of Ballet* (New York, 1970)
C. Payne and others: *American Ballet Theatre* (New York, 1977)
J. Anderson: *The One and Only: the Ballet Russe de Monte Carlo* (New York, 1981)
Choreography by George Balanchine: a Catalogue of Works (New York, 1983)
C. Steinberg: *San Francisco Ballet: the First Fifty Years* (San Francisco, 1983)
A. Danilova: *Choura: the Memoirs of Alexandra Danilova* (New York, 1986)
L. Garafola: *Diaghilev's Ballets Russes* (New York, 1989)
S. Anawalt: *The Joffrey Ballet: Robert Joffrey and the Making of an American Dance Company* (New York, 1996)
S.J. Cohen and others, eds.: *International Encyclopedia of Dance* (New York, 1998)
L. Garafola with E. Foner, eds.: *Dance for a City: Fifty Years of the New York City Ballet* (NewYork, 1999)
J. Fisher: *Nutcracker Nation: How an Old World Ballet Became a Christmas Tradition in the New World* (New Haven, CT, 2003)
N. Reynolds and M. McCormick: *No Fixed Points: Dance in the Twentieth Century* (New Haven, CT, 2003)
C. Conyers: *Popular Balanchine*. A research project of the George Balanchine Foundation, 2004 <http://www.balanchine.org>
J. Ross: *San Francisco Ballet at Seventy-Five* (San Francisco, 2007)
M. Schierman and N. Reynolds, dirs.: *Balanchine Catalogue*. A project of the George Balanchine Foundation, 2007 <http://www.balanchine.org>
A.C. Ewing: *Bravura!: Lucia Chase and the American Ballet Theatre* (Gainesville, FL, 2009)

CLAUDE CONYERS

Ballet Caravan. Company founded by Lincoln Kirstein in New York City in 1936 to foster work by young American choreographers. Its repertory included works by Lew Christensen and Eugene Loring set to music by Elliott Carter, Virgil Thompson, Paul Bowles, and Aaron Copland. Later called American Ballet Caravan, the company was disbanded in 1941.

CLAUDE CONYERS

Ballet Folklórico. A generic term since the 1950s for dance groups that merge theatrical elements of classical ballet with Mexican folk dances. The use of the term was primarily modeled on the famous Ballet Folclórico de México, founded in 1952 by Amalia Hernández (1917–2000). Mexican dance companies had begun to incorporate regional folk dances into their modern dance and classical ballet theatrical productions by the 1920s, as part of the postrevolutionary Mexican nationalist movement in the arts. By the 1950s, such "staged spectacles" were founded on anthropological and historical research and reflected a "revolutionary nationalism" that celebrated and highlighted the importance of music and dance in Mexican identity. No doubt this was partly in response to increasing anti-Mexican sentiment in the United States. Regional Mexican folk dances have always been practiced by Mexican American immigrant communities in the United States. With the Chicano social and artistic movement that followed the Civil Rights Movement of the 1960s, *folklórico* swept the United States, with prominent Mexican teachers like Rafael Zamarripa invited to teach courses in Mexican dance subsequently offered at universities with strong Mexican American student populations through the 1970s, and the emergence of many local troupes and teachers, many still active in 2013.

BIBLIOGRAPHY

S. Hutchinson: "The Ballet Folklórico de México and the Construction of the Mexican Nation through Dance," *Dancing across Borders: Danzas y bailes mexicanos*, ed. O. Nájera-Ramírez, N.E. Cantú, and B.M. Romero (Chicago, 2009), 206–36
O. Nájera-Ramírez: "Staging Authenticity: Theorizing the Development of Mexican *Folklórico* Dance," *Dancing across Borders: Danzas y bailes mexicanos*, ed. O. Nájera-Ramírez, N.E. Cantú, and B.M. Romero (Chicago, 2009), 277–317
O. Nájera-Ramírez: *Danza Folklórica Escénica: El Sello Artístico de Rafael Zamarripa/Mexican Folkloric Dance: Rafael Zamarripa's Artistic Trademark*. DVD. 2011.

BRENDA M. ROMERO

Ballets: USA. Company formed by Jerome Robbins in 1958 to perform at the Festival of Two Worlds in Spoleto, Italy, and the Brussels World's Fair. Programs were planned to show the variety of American techniques and styles in dance. After successful tours of Europe in 1959 and 1961, the company was disbanded.

CLAUDE CONYERS

Ballet West. Ballet company founded on the Utah Civic Ballet and established as a professional company based at the University of Utah in Salt Lake City in 1963, with Willam Christensen as artistic director and chief choreographer.

See CHRISTENSEN BROTHERS.

CLAUDE CONYERS

Balliett, Whitney (Lyon) (*b* New York, NY, 17 April 1926; *d* New York, 1 Feb 2007). Jazz writer. An eminent figure in jazz journalism, he is best known as a long-time columnist for the *New Yorker*. As a young man, he studied at the Philips Exeter Academy in New Hampshire, where he played drums and wrote his earliest essays on jazz. He continued this activity at Cornell University (BA 1951), where he published pieces in the *Cornell Daily Sun* and the *Widow*. After graduation, he joined the staff of the *New Yorker*, initially working as a proofreader, poet, and fiction writer. His first widely circulated jazz pieces appeared in the *Saturday Review* (1953–7). These caught the attention of *New Yorker* editor William Shawn, who asked him to begin writing a jazz column for the magazine in 1957. That same year, Balliett conceived the idea and was adviser for the television special *The Sound of Jazz*, broadcast live by CBS on 8 December. The show was a landmark in jazz broadcasting, presenting historic performances by Billie Holiday, Count Basie, Lester Young, Thelonious Monk, and a host of others.

Balliett would continue writing for the *New Yorker* until 1998, publishing over 550 pieces in the magazine. His prose is known for its eloquent and highly evocative style, aimed at vividly capturing the details of jazz performance—what he famously dubbed "the sound of surprise." English poet Philip Larkin referred to him as "a master of language," and his writing employs a range of metaphors, similes, and other devices in order to capture its subjects. Where some jazz writers shied away from the term impressionist, Balliett embraced it, citing his goal of conveying as much of the musical atmosphere as possible. His extended profiles of musicians, which he began writing in 1962, present intimate and dignified portraits of musicians' lives both on and off the bandstand. After leaving the *New Yorker*, Balliett continued writing for the *New York Review of Books* in the late 1990s and 2000s.

WRITINGS

(all collections of previously published articles and reviews)

The Sound of Surprise (New York, 1959/*R*)
Dinosaurs in the Morning (Philadelphia, 1962/*R*)
Such Sweet Thunder (Indianapolis, 1966)
Ecstasy at the Onion (Indianapolis, 1971/*R*)
Alec Wilder and his Friends (Boston, 1974/*R*)
American Singers: Twenty-Seven Portraits in Song (New York, 1979, enlarged 2/1988)
Jelly Roll, Jabbo and Fats: Nineteen Portraits in Jazz (New York, 1983)
American Musicians: Fifty-Six Portraits in Jazz (New York, 1986)
Barney, Bradley and Max: Sixteen Portraits in Jazz (New York, 1989)
American Musicians II: Seventy-One Portraits in Jazz (New York, 1996)
Collected Works: a Journal of Jazz, 1954–2000 (New York, 2000)
New York Voices: Fourteen Portraits (Jackson, MS, 2006)

BIBLIOGRAPHY

W. Balliett: "Introduction," *Collected Works: a Journal of Jazz, 1954–2000* (New York, 2000), vi–viii
P. Larkin: "Crows and Daws," *American Scholar*, li/2 (1982), 288–91
Obituary, *The Guardian*, 5 Feb 2007

BARRY KERNFELD/MICHAEL C. HELLER

Ballin' the jack. A theatrical and social dance of African American origin, thought to have originated in Sea Island, Georgia. The name comes from the vocabulary of African Americans working on railroad tracks in the 1890s. "Jack" was a colloquial term for locomotive, and "balling" was a hand signal used to notify the engineer to "highball" the engine. The term thus means not so much "start the train" as "move faster," "get going," and "have fun." During the early 1900s amateur black dancers developed steps that would eventually be incorporated into a recognized dance, and patent records indicate that a song called "Ballin' the Jack" was recorded in 1909.

The dance was introduced to New York theater audiences in *The Darktown Follies* (1913), which played at the Lafayette Theater in Harlem. Set to music by dancer-composer Chris Smith, the lyrics by Jim Burris describe the movements:

First you put your two knees close up tight,
Then you sway 'em to the left, then you sway 'em to the right.
Step around the floor kind of nice and light,
Then you twis' around and twis' around with all your might.
Stretch your lovin' arms straight out in space,
Then you do the Eagle Rock with style and grace.
Swing your foot way 'round, then bring it back,
Now that's what I call "Ballin' the Jack."

Such movements seem innocent enough, but Burris's descriptions hardly do justice to what was actually exhibited on stage, which was a sensual, suggestive dance punctuated with pelvic thrusts and gyrations—in other words, bumps and grinds. Notorious in its day, ballin' the jack was performed during the 1910s and 1920s both as a solo dance in a serpentine pattern and by couples dancing to swing music. It became a dance fad across America and was danced everywhere by both blacks and whites. When it was merged with the Lindy hop in the 1930s, it lost most of its original form and became simply a variant of swing dance.

"Ballin' the Jack" has been recorded by many musical groups and artists, notably Eddie Condon, Buck Clayton, Jelly Roll Morton, Duke Ellington, Johnny Maddox, Ken Colyer, and even Pérez Prado. Vocalists who have favored the song include Pearl Bailey, Georgia Gibbs, Danny Kaye, Chubby Checker, Fats Domino, and the Chordettes. In the movies, the number is performed in *For Me and My Gal* (1942) by a young Judy Garland and Gene Kelly, making his Hollywood debut. The dance they do bears virtually no resemblance to the original.

BIBLIOGRAPHY

M. and J. Stearns: *Jazz Dance: the Story of American Vernacular Dance* (New York, 1968)
L.F. Emery: *Black Dance in the United States from 1619 to 1970* (Palo Alto, 1972)
G. Jones and D.A. Jasen: *Spreadin' Rhythm Around: Black Popular Songwriters, 1880–1930* (New York, 1998)

CLAUDE CONYERS

Ballou, Esther (Williamson) (*b* Elmira, NY, 17 July 1915; *d* Chichester, England, 12 March 1973). Composer, pianist, and educator. She studied piano and organ as a child and graduated from Bennington College, Vermont (1937), Mills College (1938), and the Juilliard School (1943); at Bennington she took composition lessons from OTTO LUENING, and at Juilliard from BERNARD WAGENAAR and privately from WALLINGFORD RIEGGER. While in California she composed ballets for Louise Kloepper and José Limón and toured nationally as a pianist with various dance companies. During the 1940s she taught at Juilliard and from 1955 at the American University, Washington, DC. During her subsequent career as an educator she put forward experimental methods for theory teaching at the college level. Her music, according to her own description, "tends towards classicism in that it stresses clarity of design and directness of expression." Among a broad range of compositions are her *Accompaniments for Modern Dance Technique* (1933–7), which were used by such pioneers of the modern dance movement as Martha Hill, Doris Humphrey, and Bessie Schoenberg. In 1963 she became the first American woman composer to have a work (the *Capriccio* for violin and piano) given its first performance at the White House, and in 1964 she received the honorary doctorate from Hood College, Maryland. Her manuscripts, which include a pedagogical text, *Creative Explorations of Musical Elements* (1971), are in the Special Collections Department of the American University Library, Washington, DC.

WORKS
(selective list)

Orch: Suite, chbr orch, 1939; Blues, 1944; Pf Conc. no.1, 1945; Prelude and Allegro, pf, str, 1951; Concertino, ob, str, 1953; Adagio, bn, str, 1960; In memoriam, ob, str, 1960; Gui Conc., 1964; Pf Conc. no.2, 1964

Choral: Bag of Tricks (I. Orgel), SSAA, 1956; The Beatitudes, SATB, org, 1957; A babe is born (15th century), SATB, 1959; May the words of my mouth (Ps xix), SATB, 1965; I will lift up mine eyes (Ps cxxi), S, SATB, org, 1965; O the sun comes up-up-up in the opening sky (E.E. Cummings), SSA, 1966; Hear us!, SATB, brass, perc, 1967

Other vocal: 4 Songs (A.E. Housman), S, vc, pf, 1937; What if a much of a which of a wind (Cummings), S, Bar, B, wind qnt, 1959; Street Scenes (H. Champers), S, pf, 1960; 5–4–3 (Cummings), Mez, va, hp, 1966

Chbr: Impertinence, cl, pf, 1936; In Blues Tempo, cl, pf, 1937; Nocturne, str qt, 1937; Pf Trio, 1955, rev. 1957; Divertimento, str qt, 1958; Sonata, vn, pf, 1959; A Passing Word, fl, vc, pf, ob, 1960; Capriccio, vn, pf, 1963; Prism, str trio, 1969; Romanza, vn, pf, 1969

Kbd: Dance Suite, pf, 1937; Sonatina, pf, 1941; Sonata, 2 pf, 1943; Beguine, pf, 8 hands, 1950, arr. 2 pf, 1957, arr. orch, 1960; Music for the Theatre, 2 pf, 1952; Pf Sonata, 1955; Sonata no.2, 2 pf, 1958; Rondino, hpd, 1961; Sonatina [no.2], pf, 1964; Impromptu, org, 1968

Principal publisher: ACA

BIBLIOGRAPHY

E.W. Ballou: "Theory with a Thrust," *MEJ*, lv/1 (1968–9), 56–8; lv/5 (1968–9), 55–7

J.R. Heintze: *Esther Williamson Ballou: a Bio-Bibliography* (New York, 1987)

L.A. Wallace: *The Educational Experiences of American Composer Esther Williamson Ballou* (diss., U. of Wisconsin, Milwaukee, 1995)

JAMES R. HEINTZE/R

Ballroom dance. A broad category of SOCIAL DANCE in which two people dance as partners, one leading and one following, to popular music, independent of other couples on the dance floor. The term came into general use in the 20th century with two meanings: (1) social dances for partnered couples done for recreation and personal pleasure or (2) specific sets of couple dances performed in national and international competitions. Ballroom dances are also often performed in a theatrical context and are enjoyed as entertainment on stage, in films, and on television.

1. Modern ballroom dance. 2. Competitive ballroom dance. 3. Exhibition ballroom dancing. 4. Ballroom dance on film and video.

1. MODERN BALLROOM DANCE. Early in the 20th century, modern ballroom dance firmly took root America. Primarily, this was due to the increasing trend away from sequence dances and toward dances where couples moved independently, such as the WALTZ and the TWO-STEP, a kind of quick march with a skip in each step. A second important development came with a wave of new popular music, such as ragtime and jazz, much of which was based on the ideas of African American musicians. Since dance is to a large extent tied to music, this led to a burst of newly invented social dances during the period 1910–30. (*See* RAGTIME DANCE.)

Prior to World War I, interest in ballroom dance was boosted by the celebrity of exhibition dancers VERNON AND IRENE CASTLE. Their good manners, decorum, and charm as well as their lightfooted dancing helped to popularize the ONE-STEP, the CASTLE WALK, the MAXIXE, the hesitation waltz, the American TANGO (i), and the FOXTROT. The Castles also opened studios for dance instruction, realizing that, if popular dance was to flourish, participants had to learn basic movements that they could confidently perform with any partner they might meet. One of the Castles' students and early employees was ARTHUR MURRAY. In 1924, he opened a school in New York City and began to develop an effective business plan for teaching ballroom dance. As a leader of dance professionals who analyzed, codified, published, and taught a number of standard dances, Murray eventually became the proprietor of a worldwide chain of dance studios and the most successful dance instructor of all time. Today, the curriculum at the Murray studios includes the classic ballroom dances—foxtrot, waltz, tango, Viennese waltz, and QUICKSTEP (ii)—as well as SWING DANCES such as LINDY HOP and east coast swing; rhythm and Latin dances such as the HUSTLE, RUMBA (ii), CHA-CHA, MAMBO, PASO DOBLE, BOLERO, and SAMBA; COUNTRY-WESTERN DANCE; and specialty dances such as the POLKA (ii) and the Argentine tango.

Another chain of dance studios, stretching across America, was founded in the 1950s in the name of movie star FRED ASTAIRE, with a curriculum similar to the Murray studios. Astaire's influence on ballroom dancing came, however, from his movie roles. His on-screen pairing with GINGER ROGERS in their movies of the 1930s set ideal standards of ballroom dancing around the world. Although carefully choreographed, staged, and rehearsed, their filmed dance sequences have iconic status as the epitome of elegance, grace, and high style in ballroom dance.

2. COMPETITIVE BALLROOM DANCE. Traditionally, ballroom dancing has been a recreational pastime for privileged social classes, but in recent decades it has become a competitive activity akin to sport, popular in developed countries around the world. Sometimes referred to as dancesport, competitions range from world championships, regulated by the World Dance Council, to national championships to contests at various lower levels of proficiency. Most competitions are organized into professional and amateur divisions, although "pro-am" competitions are sometimes held in the United States. In America, amateur dance proficiency levels are defined by USA Dance, formerly the United States Amateur Ballroom Dance Association.

At the international level, there are ten competitive dances, designated International Standard (slow waltz, tango, Viennese waltz, slow foxtrot, quickstep) and International Latin (cha-cha, samba, rumba, paso doble, jive). In the United States, there are nine competitive dances, organized in two divisions, American Smooth (waltz, tango, foxtrot, Viennese waltz) and American Rhythm (cha-cha, rumba, east coast swing, bolero, mambo). The PEABODY was once included in the American Smooth division but has now been dropped. In Standard and Smooth divisions, the music is normally popular music from the mid-20th century. In competition, couples usually wear formal attire—ball gowns for ladies, tailcoats or tuxedos for gentlemen—and dance counter-clockwise around a rectangular floor following the line of dance. In Latin and Rhythm divisions, dances are performed to contemporary Latin American music. In competition, women often wear revealing, short-skirted outfits and men wear tight-fitting shirts and trousers, so as to emphasize leg action and body movements. With the exception of traveling dances such as the samba and the paso doble, couples perform their routines more or less in one spot on the dance floor.

3. Exhibition ballroom dancing. Also known as show-dance, adagio dance, and cabaret dance, exhibition ballroom dancing as a theatrical form of entertainment arose in the early 20th century when the French team of Maurice Mouvet and Madeleine d'Arville introduced their combative, acrobatic *danse apache* and an authentic tango at the Café de Paris in New York in 1911. Around the same time, Vernon and Irene Castle began a series of appearances in hotels and nightclubs to publicize their schools of ballroom dance. Although they performed many different social dances, perhaps their most popular was the cheerful Castle walk, a one-step danced first to "Trés Moutarde" ("Too Much Mustard," 1911) by English composer Cecil Macklin and subsequently to "The Castle Walk" (1914) by James Reese Europe and Fred T. Dabney.

In the wake of the Castles came Frank Veloz and Yolanda Casazza who, as Veloz and Yolanda, became a celebrated exhibition dance team of the 1930s and 1940s. Among their most popular numbers were those danced to "Darktown Strutters' Ball" (1917) by Shelton Brooks, "I'm Just Wild about Harry" (1921) by Eubie Blake, "The Charleston" (1923) by James P. Johnson, "Black Bottom"(1926) by Perry Bradford, and "Jeepers Creepers" (1938) by Harry Warren. Tony and Sally de Marco were also well known in the 1940s for their exhibitions of the waltz, acrobatic adagio numbers, and various Latin dances. Even more famous in later years were Marge and Gower Champion, who began performing a cabaret act in hotel ballrooms and nightclub floorshows and went on to become stars of the Broadway stage and Hollywood films. Inheriting the mantle of all these teams are Pierre Dulaine and Yvonne Marceau, founders of American Ballroom Theater.

4. Ballroom dance on film and video. The earliest film record of exhibition ballroom dancing may be the nightclub scene of *Four Horsemen of the Apocalypse* (1921), in which Rudolph Valentino and Beatrice Dominguez dance an Americanized version of the Argentine tango. Although the film is silent, Valentino's musicality is clearly evident. His pantherine dancing and sultry masculinity catapulted him to stardom and created a national fad for the tango. A few years later, the advent of sound in motion pictures ushered in the age of the Hollywood musical film, featuring song and dance. Certainly the best-known films depicting ballroom dancing are those of Fred Astaire and Ginger Rogers. Of the ten films in which they dance together, *The Story of Vernon and Irene Castle* (1939) is an homage to the pioneers of exhibition ballroom dancing in America.

Other remarkable movies featuring ballroom settings include *Queen of the Stardust Ballroom* (1975), starring Maureen Stapleton and Charles Durning, and *Roseland* (1977), a Merchant-Ivory film anthology of three stories that all have the same theme: finding the right partner at the fabled Manhattan ballroom. *Shall We Dance?* (2004), starring Richard Gere and Jennifer Lopez, is a remake of a 1996 Japanese film known by the same English title. Because of inept casting and heavy-handed direction, it lacks the charm and artistry of the Japanese original, which depicts learning ballroom dancing as a life-affirming, life-altering experience.

More successful are two films dealing with competitive ballroom dancing: *Strictly Ballroom* (1992) and *Mad Hot Ballroom* (2005). The former, written and directed by Australian movie-maker Baz Luhrmann, is a mock documentary about an accomplished male ballroom dancer who selects a frumpy girl to be his partner and sets out to win a championship competition by "doing his own steps." Defying competition regulations leads to some hilarious situations and an exhibition of a triumphant paso doble. Similarly informative and entertaining is *Mad Hot Ballroom,* a true documentary of children from several New York City elementary schools who learn various ballroom dances in order to enter a city-wide competition.

Various kinds of dance competitions have also been shown on television and, since the 1990s, have proved to be among the most popular of the "reality shows" that have won millions of viewers in numerous countries around the globe. In the United States, *Dancing with the Stars*, a competition pairing celebrities of varying degrees of fame with professional ballroom dancers, has attracted a huge television audience for many seasons. It does not, however, represent a high level of ballroom dancing: the "stars" are often inept, despite weeks of training; the costuming is usually blatantly provocative; the music is often rhythmically inappropriate; and the choreographed routines are often tawdry and/or acrobatic, more suitable to a cabaret than to a ballroom.

BIBLIOGRAPHY

R.M. Stephenson and J. Iaccarino: *The Complete Book of Ballroom Dancing* (New York, 1980)

B. Quirey: *May I Have the Pleasure? The Story of Popular Dancing* (London, 1987)

J. Malnig: *Dancing till Dawn: a Century of Exhibition Ballroom Dance* (Westport, CT, 1992)

K. Van Winkle Keller: *If the Company Can Do It! Technique in Eighteenth-Century American Social Dance* (Sandy Hook, CT, 1992)

V. Silvester: *Modern Ballroom Dancing,* 3d rev. ed. (North Pomfret, VT, 2005)

American Memory. An American Ballroom Companion: Dance Instruction Manuals, ca. 1490–1920. Library of Congress, 2006 <http://memory.loc.gov/ammem/dihtml/dihome.html>

J. McMains: *Glamour Addiction: Inside the American Ballroom Industry* (Middletown, CT, 2006)

C.J. Picart: *From Ballroom to Dancesport: Aesthetics, Athletics, and Body Culture* (Albany, NY, 2006)

J. Malnig, ed.: *Ballroom, Boogie, Shimmy Sham, Shake: a Social and Popular Dance Reader* (Urbana, 2009)

CLAUDE CONYERS

Ball State University. State university in Muncie, Indiana, founded in 1918. Its music courses began to flourish during the 1930s. In 2009, under director Meryl Mantione, the School of Music enrolled approximately 500 students, of whom about 400 were undergraduates, served by a faculty of more than 70. BA, BM, BS, MA, MM, and DA degrees are offered in performance, theory-composition, music education, and music history.

WILLIAM McCLELLAN/KEITH COCHRAN

Balmer, Charles (*b* Mühlhausen, Germany, 21 Sept 1817; *d* St. Louis, MO, 15 Dec 1892). Organist, conductor, composer, and publisher, of German birth. A child prodigy, he studied at the Göttingen Conservatory of Music and was assistant conductor there in 1833. He immigrated to the United States in 1836, settling in St. Louis in 1839. The following year he conducted the orchestra of the Jesuit College and was instrumental conductor of the St. Louis Sacred Music Society; he founded the St. Louis Oratorio Society in 1846 and served as its director until it ceased activities. He was organist at Christ Episcopal Church for 46 years. In 1848 he founded the BALMER & WEBER MUSIC HOUSE with Carl Heinrich Weber. He composed a large number of piano pieces, songs, organ works, and choral works, using a number of pseudonyms, including Charles Remlab, T. van Berg, Alphonse Leduc, Charles Lange, Henry Werner, August Schumann, T. Meyer, and F.B. Rider. In 1865 Balmer conducted the music at Lincoln's funeral in Springfield, Illinois.

BIBLIOGRAPHY

E.C. Krohn: *Missouri Music* (New York, 1971)

E.C. Krohn: *Music Publishing in the Middle Western States before the Civil War* (Detroit, 1972)

JAMES M. BURK

Balmer & Weber Music House. Firm of music publishers. Charles Balmer (*b* Mühlhausen, Germany, 21 Sept 1817; *d* St. Louis, MO, 15 Dec 1892) and Carl Heinrich Weber (*b* Koblenz, Germany, 3 March 1819; *d* Denver, CO, 6 Sept 1892) left Germany for the United States in the 1830s; Balmer became an organist and conductor, Weber a cellist, and their early compositions were published in the eastern United States. In 1848 they entered into partnership and opened a shop in St. Louis, publishing a variety of popular marches and various piano pieces including Balmer's own arrangements of popular titles. Balmer was so prolific that he adopted a number of pseudonyms, including Charles Remlab, T. van Berg, Alphonse Leduc, Charles Lange, Henry Werner, August Schumann, T. Mayer, and F.B. Rider. Gradually the firm absorbed most of its competitors including Nathaniel Phillips, James & J.R. Phillips, H.A. Sherburne, H. Pilcher & Sons, W.M. Harlow, Cardella & Co., and Compton & Doan; by the end of the century it had an exceptionally large and flourishing business.

After the death of the partners, the business was managed by a company in which the Balmer family predominated. Lack of efficient direction and the rise of Kunkel Brothers, Shattinger, and Thiebes-Stierlin caused the business to deteriorate, and in 1907 the catalog was sold to Leo Feist of New York. He attempted to ship the sheet music to New York down the Mississippi, but the vessel foundered off the coast of New Jersey and its cargo sank.

BIBLIOGRAPHY

E.C. Krohn: *A Century of Missouri Music* (St. Louis, 1924); repr. as *Missouri Music* (New York, 1971)

E.C. Krohn: *Music Publishing in the Middle Western States before the Civil War* (Detroit, 1972), 27–8

E.C. Krohn: *Music Publishing in St. Louis* (Warren, MI, 1988), 43

ERNST C. KROHN

Balsam, Artur (*b* Warsaw, Poland, 8 Feb 1906; *d* New York, NY, 1 Sept 1994). Pianist of Polish birth. He studied in Łódź, where he made his debut at the age of 12, and at the Hochschule für Musik in Berlin. He received first prize in the International Piano Competition in Berlin in 1930, and won the Mendelssohn prize for chamber music with violinist Roman Totenberg in 1931. In 1932, he first toured North America with the 14-year old violinist Yehudi Menuhin, and settled there after Hitler came to power in 1933. He also married the pianist Ruth Miller (1906–99) in 1933. He gave numerous solo recitals and made many appearances with orchestras (including a series of Mozart Concertos for the BBC during the 1956 Mozart bicentenary), but he was most celebrated as an ensemble pianist who combined sensibility and a capacity for listening with strength of personality. In 1960, he joined the Albeneri Trio (which later became the Balsam-Kroft-Heifetz Trio) in place of pianist Erich Itor Kahn. He also toured extensively with the violinist Nathan Milstein. He was a distinguished teacher at the Eastman School of Music; Boston University; the Manhattan School of Music, and the Philadelphia Academy of Music. He led summer courses from 1956 to 1992 at Kneisel Hall in Blue Hill, Maine. The celebrated pianist MURRAY PERAHIA was one of his students.

Balsam recorded about 250 works in the solo and chamber literature, including all the solo piano works of Haydn and Mozart; all Mozart's sonatas for violin and piano with Oscar Shumsky and all of Beethoven's sonatas for violin and cello, with Joseph Fuchs and Zara Nelsova. His partners in concert, and often on recordings, also included Francescatti, Goldberg, Rostropovich, Szigeti, Totenberg, Milstein, David Oistrakh, and Leonid Kogan. The recording *Artur Balsam in Concert at the Manhattan School of Music* (2007) features works by Haydn, Beethoven, Brahms, Mendelssohn, and Chopin. The Manhattan School of Music holds the *Artur Balsam Competition for Duos* in his honor.

MICHAEL STEINBERG/ANYA LAURENCE

Balthrop, Carmen Arlen (*b* Washington, DC, 14 May 1948). Soprano. Balthrop studied at the University of Maryland, College Park (where she serves as Professor of Voice) and at the Catholic University of America. She made her professional debut in 1973 as Virtue (*L'incoronazione di Poppea*) with Washington National Opera, where in 1974 she sang Minerva in the United States premiere of *Il ritorno d'Ulisse*. In 1975 she sang the title role of Joplin's *Treemonisha* with Houston

Grand Opera and later on Broadway. Having won the 1975 Metropolitan Opera National Council Auditions, she made her debut with the company as Pamina in April 1977, then sang Climene in Cavalli's *Egisto* at Wolf Trap Opera. In 1978 she sang the first Mermaid (*Oberon*) and Ruggiero (*Tancredi*) with Opera Orchestra of New York at Carnegie Hall. She sang Monteverdi's Poppea at Spoleto (1979), Innsbruck (1980), and Santa Fe (1986), and Gluck's Eurydice (1982) and Poppaea in Handel's *Agrippina* (1983) in Venice at the Teatro La Fenice. Among her other roles are Bess in *Porgy and Bess*, Micaëla in *Carmen*, and the title role in Carlisle Floyd's *Susannah*. Her discography includes *Treemonisha*, *L'Incoronazione di Poppea*, *Agrippina*, and John Knowles Paine's *Mass*, and she has given the premieres of several 21st-century works, including Leslie Burrs's *Vanqui* and Frank Proto's *The Profanation of Hubert J. Fort*, *The Tuner*, and *Shadowboxer*. Of diminutive stature, she has been praised for a fresh, pleasing voice, a refined style, and an alluring stage presence.

ELIZABETH FORBES/RYAN EBRIGHT

Baltic American music. *See* European American music.

Baltimore. Largest city in Maryland (pop. 620,961; metropolitan area: 2,799,226; 2010 US Census). First settled in 1662, Baltimore became a town in 1730. A prominent port of entry for immigrants, Baltimore's sizable harbor facilitated the growth of the city's population and economy, the latter of which was fueled by its shipping and manufacturing industries. By 1800 its population was larger than that of the state's capital, Annapolis. As early as 1784 concerts in the city were advertised in the press. These early programs were of great diversity, including works by Bach, Carl Ditters von Dittersdorf, Joseph Haydn, František Kočžwara, Ignace Joseph Pleyel, Giovanni Battista Viotti and Johann Baptist Vanhal, as well as by immigrant musicians Alexander Reinagle and Raynor Taylor, who resided in Baltimore.

In 1794, a year after establishing a music shop in Philadelphia, Joseph Carr and his sons Thomas and Benjamin inaugurated a similar enterprise in Baltimore. Although instructional tunebooks were published as early as 1792 (*Baltimore Collection of Sacred Music*), most Baltimore tunebooks, including John Cole's *Beauties of Psalmody* and *The Divine Harmonist*, were produced after 1800, in part due to an effort to reform congregational singing that had been pejoratively influenced by the sacred settings and fuguing tunes of New England composers. The first printing of "The Star-Spangled Banner" in sheet music form was by Thomas Carr in November 1814. Following the demise of Thomas Carr's business in 1821, other publications, notably by the firms of Arthur Clifton (*fl* ?1823), George Willig (1823–1910), John Cole (1821–38), Frederick Benteen (1839–55), Miller and Beecham (1853–73), James Boswell (1835–59), Samuel Carusi (1839–44), W.C. Peters (1844–52), and G. Fred Kranz (1910–*c*1960), made Baltimore a major center of music publishing. A significant factor in the success of a number of these firms was the presence in Baltimore of the early American lithography firm of A. Hoen & Co., which supplied illustrated covers for many Baltimore imprints. Several Baltimore music publishing firms were taken over by the Boston firm of Oliver Ditson in the late 1800s. In the 19th century, Baltimore was also home to a number of instrument manufacturers, including the piano builders William Knabe and Charles Steiff and the brass and woodwind maker Heinrich Christian Eisenbrandt.

1. Opera. 2. Educational institutions, libraries. 3. Concert organizations, halls. 4. Orchestras. 5. Popular music.

1. Opera. Music theater in Baltimore traces its beginnings from 1772 with a performance by Lewis Hallam's traveling American Company of Milton's *Comus* in a stable. The first resident theatrical company, Thomas Wall and Adam Lindsay's Maryland Company of Comedians, built Baltimore's first theater (New Theatre) in 1781 and performed there until 1785. A resurgence of Hallam's Old American Company and a series of local companies provided sporadic theatrical, musical, and circus entertainment during the 1780s and early 1790s. Thomas Wignell's and Alexander Reinagle's Philadelphia Company dominated the last decade of the 18th century, offering substantial seasons of plays, interludes, and afterpieces in their newly constructed Holliday Street Theater (opened 1795). From the turn of the century to the Civil War, Baltimore hosted a variety of resident and touring companies in both the Holliday Street Theater and the Front Street Theatre. After the Civil War, a new "theater district" sprang up, including the Concordia Opera House (1865–91), Ford's Grand Opera House (1871–1964), and the Academy of Music (1875–1927). Each featured a variety of theatrical entertainments, with Ford's hosting at least 24 opera companies performing over 90 different works. With the rise of the New York Theatrical Syndicate around 1900, Baltimore faded as a major stop for touring opera troupes. Local efforts to establish an opera company resulted in the creation of Eugene Martinet's Baltimore Civic Opera Company in 1932. As early as the 1940–41 season, Martinet was able to enlist the help of soprano Rosa Ponselle, who served as artistic director until 1979. In 1970 the company was renamed the Baltimore Opera Company and operated until its 2009 bankruptcy. Several smaller companies, including Baltimore Opera Theater, Baltimore Concert Opera, Lyric Opera Baltimore, Baltimore Rock Opera Society, and the English-language Opera Vivente, continue to meet the city's demand for music theater.

2. Educational institutions, libraries. Formal, institutional music education in Baltimore began with the 1789 opening of Ishmael Spicer's singing school, which operated for several years. With the establishment in the 1830s of Ruel Shaw's Academy and John Hewitt and William Stoddard's Musical Institute, music instruction broadened to include secular music. The growth in interest in choral societies led to the introduction of vocal music into the public school curriculum in 1843.

Peabody Institute, Baltimore, c1902. (Library of Congress, Prints & Photographs Division, Detroit Publishing Company Collection, LC-DIG-det-4a09471)

The Peabody Conservatory, founded on 12 February 1857, is technically the oldest music conservatory in the United States, although it did not actually offer instruction until 1868. As part of the Peabody Institute of the City of Baltimore, the conservatory was endowed by George Peabody, one of America's earliest philanthropists. The Institute included provision for an extensive library, a gallery of art, and an Academy of Music (which became the Peabody Conservatory of Music in 1872). In 1977 Peabody Conservatory affiliated with Johns Hopkins University and in 1983 became a school of the university. It is now known as the Peabody Institute of the Johns Hopkins University.

There are about two dozen other institutions of higher education in Baltimore and its environs. Goucher College, Morgan State University, and Towson State University are among those that offer not only music courses but also distinguished concert series. Important research collections include Baltimore's Arthur Friedheim Library and the archives of the Peabody Institute and the Maryland Historical Society. Both collections offer extensive primary source materials for the study of Baltimore's musical life. The Lester S. Levy Collection at Johns Hopkins's Milton S. Eisenhower Library boasts one of the most important collections of American sheet music in approximately 40,000 items.

3. Concert organizations, halls. With many residents of British and German extraction, Baltimore has enjoyed a rich choral tradition. 19th-century choral organizations included the Liederkranz (1836–1900), Germania Männerchor (1856–1929), and Baltimore Oratorio Society (1881–1900). In the 20th century the Handel Society (est. 1933), Choral Arts Society (est. 1965), Concert Artists of Baltimore (est. 1987), Bach Concert Series (est. 1988), and Baltimore Symphony Chorus (1969–2002) maintained this tradition. Most of these organizations continue to give distinguished readings of choral classics, and the Choral Arts Society encourages the creation of new choral works with an annual competition. In the 1970s, the Chamber Music Society of Baltimore, the most prominent of the city's chamber music groups, sponsored a controversial series of concerts consisting almost entirely of 20th-century music. Founded in 1950 by composer Hugo Weisgall and subsequently overseen by philanthropist Randolph Rothschild, the society commissioned important works from Milton Babbitt, Ernst Krenek, Ross Lee Finney, Charles Wuorinen, and other prominent composers before dissolving in 1997. Since the 1990s and 2000s, organizations such as the Evolution Contemporary Music Series and Baltimore Composers Forum have continued to promote the creation and performance of new music.

Baltimore has six outstanding concert halls, all aesthetically pleasing and acoustically effective. The Lyric, constructed in 1894, is modeled on the Neues Gewandhaus in Leipzig, and serves as the city's primary venue for grand opera. After extensive renovation in 1980–81, the theater (cap. 2683) was reopened in 1982, and during further renovations in 2010 was renamed the Patricia and Arthur Modell Performing Arts Center at the Lyric. In 1982, Joseph Meyerhoff Symphony Hall (cap. 2467) was opened as the permanent home of the Baltimore SO. Designed by Pietro Belluschi, the hall is named after one of the city's most generous philanthropists. A second hall named after Meyerhoff, the Joseph and Rebecca Meyerhoff Auditorium (cap. 363), opened in 1982 at the Baltimore Museum of Art and was the home of the Chamber Music Society of Baltimore concerts. Kraushaar Auditorium at Goucher College, again designed by Belluschi, opened in 1962 (cap. 995). Shriver Hall (cap. 1100) of the Johns Hopkins University is the site of a distinguished chamber music series. Opened in 1866, the Miriam A. Friedberg Concert Hall (cap. 800) at the Peabody Institute is the oldest of the existing halls; it underwent extensive renovation in 1983.

4. Orchestras. The first orchestra of professional musicians in Baltimore was the Peabody Orchestra in 1866. Under the direction of James Monroe Deems, Lucian Southard, and Asger Hamerik the orchestra gave the premieres of works by American composers and the American premieres of numerous European works, especially those from Hamerik's native Denmark. The Peabody Orchestra ceased operations in 1896. Ross Jungnickel organized the first Baltimore Symphony Orchestra, which gave its opening season of three concerts in 1890.

Following the demise of Jungnickel's orchestra in 1899, the Florestan Club, an elite group of local musicians and music lovers (including H.L. Mencken), made plans to found the city's first resident orchestra. In 1916 Baltimore became the first city in the United States to found an orchestra on a municipal appropriation. The first conductor of the new Baltimore SO, Gustav Strube, remained in the post until 1930. Subsequent directors included George Siemonn (1930–35), Ernest Schelling (1935–7), Werner Janssen (1937–9), and Howard Barlow (1939–42). This orchestra played its last concert in 1942. The same year, conductor Reginald Stewart, also director of the Peabody Conservatory, devised a plan for the reorganization of the Baltimore SO as a private institution. Stewart attracted superior musicians by offering them faculty appointments at the Conservatory, an arrangement based on Felix Mendelssohn's linkage of the Leipzig Conservatory to the Gewandhaus Orchestra. Although Stewart was the only one to have held both positions, the relationship between the Baltimore SO and the Peabody Conservatory faculty remains strong. Subsequent conductors have included Massimo Freccia (1952–9), Peter Herman Adler (1959–68), Brian Priestman (1968–9), Sergiu Comissiona (1968–84), David Zinman (1985–98), and Yuri Temirkanov (1999–2006). With the appointment of Marin Alsop in 2007, the Baltimore SO became the first major US orchestra to be led by a female music director, and under her leadership has seen an emphasis on performing works of American composers. Since Alsop's appointment, the orchestra has launched a number of outreach initiatives that have become industry models, such as the year-round after-school program OrchKids (modeled after Venezuela's El Sistema), the in-school music education workshop BSO on the Go, and various broadcasts.

Under the inspiration of A. Jack Thomas, conductors Charles L. Harris and later W. Llewellyn Wilson led the Baltimore Colored SO and Chorus in concerts from 1929 until a bitter musicians' strike in 1939 closed the orchestra. The Baltimore Women's String SO played from 1936 to 1940 under the direction of Stephen Deak and Wolfgang Martin.

5. Popular music. The history of popular music in Baltimore is intricately tied to its large population of free blacks during the period of American slavery as well as its past as a highly segregated city. In the 19th century, choral and instrumental music flourished in Baltimore's many black churches, with musical practices spreading freely between denominations. Racial segregation in the mid-20th century helped give rise to early African American rhythm and blues vocal groups, like the Orioles, Swallows, and Cardinals. The Orioles, modeling themselves on The Ink Spots and the Ravens, rose to national prominence in 1948 with their hit "It's Too Soon to Know" and became a model for subsequent vocal harmony ("doo-wop") groups.

Baltimore also fostered a dynamic jazz scene in the early and mid-20th century and was home to several prominent musicians, including Cab Calloway, Chick Webb, Billie Holiday, and ragtime artists Eubie Blake and Noble Sissle. The arrival of jazz in the city was documented by the *Baltimore Afro-American* newspaper in 1917, and through the 1960s the most important jazz venues, including the Royal Theatre, Club Tijuana, and the Jazz Closet, were found on Pennsylvania Avenue and attracted nationally-renowned musicians while fostering local jazz talent such as Ethel Ennis. 1954 saw the founding of the short-lived Interracial Jazz Society, which sought to promote both jazz and racial integration. One month after the passage of the Civil Rights Act in 1964, the Left Bank Jazz Society began offering Sunday concerts, primarily at the Famous Ballroom on Charles Street. Co-founder Vernon Welsh recorded hundreds of the Society's performances; these recordings, now housed at Morgan State University, include performances by renowned artists such as Stan Getz, Count Basie, Dave Brubeck, Dizzy Gillespie, Duke Ellington, John Coltrane, Sun Ra, Charles Mingus, and Maynard Ferguson. Since the late 1980s, jazz has occupied a smaller role in the city's musical life, in part due to limited venues and the growth of other musical styles.

Much of Baltimore's popular music is performed at small venues in the Fells Point and Federal Hill neighborhoods. Despite a thriving mix of popular music styles (punk, rock, soul), few of Baltimore's bands or artists have achieved national prominence, with the notable exception of the R&B singing group Dru Hill. The city can lay claim, however, to a unique blend of hip hop and electronic dance music known as BALTIMORE CLUB music, which developed in the 1990s and achieved widespread exposure following its use on the television series *The Wire* and the national distribution of Baltimore DJ Rod Lee's 2005 album *Vol. 5: The Official.*

BIBLIOGRAPHY

O.G. Sonneck: *Early Concert-Life in America (1731–1800)* (Leipzig, 1907/*R*, 3/1959)

S.E. Lafferty: *Names of Music Teachers, Musicians, Music Dealers, Engravers, Printers and Publishers of Music, Conservatories of Music, Music Academies, Manufacturers of Pianos, Organs, and other Musical Instruments appearing in the Baltimore City Directories from 1796–1900, BApi*, 1937

L. Keefer: *Baltimore's Music: the Haven of the American Composer* (Baltimore, 1962)

J.L. Fisher: "The Roots of Music Education in Baltimore," *JRME*, xxi/3 (1973), 214–24

R.A. Disharoon: *A History of Municipal Music in Baltimore, 1914–1947* (diss., U. of Maryland, 1980)

D. Ritchey, ed.: *A Guide to the Baltimore Stage in the Eighteenth Century* (Westport, CT, 1982)

H. Weems: *The History of the Women's String Symphony Orchestra of Baltimore Inc* (diss., Peabody Institute, Johns Hopkins U., 1990)

E. Lawrence: *Music at Ford's Grand Opera House, 1871–1894* (diss., Peabody Institute, Johns Hopkins U., 1991)

W. Spencer: *The Baltimore Symphony Orchestra, 1965–1982: the Meyerhoff Years* (Peabody Institute, Johns Hopkins U., 1993)

S.L. Goosman: *Group Harmony: the Black Urban Roots of Rhythm & Blues* (Philadelphia, 2005)

A. Devereaux: "'What Chew Know about Down the Hill?': Baltimore Club Music, Subgenre Crossover, and the New Subcultural Capital of Race and Space," *Journal of Popular Music Studies*, xix (2007), 311–41

M. Osteen and F. Graziano, eds.: *Music at the Crossroads: Lives and Legacies of Baltimore Jazz* (Baltimore, 2010)

ELLIOTT W. GALKIN/N. QUIST/RYAN EBRIGHT

Baltimore club [Bmore club, club music]. A style of house music influenced by hip hop that originated in Baltimore in the late 1980s. During that decade house and hip-house from Chicago and New York were popular in Baltimore's clubs, leading to several local productions. Early club tracks, notably Scottie B's "I got the Rhythm" (1991) and Frank Ski's "Whores in this House" (1993), show a marked influence from British breakbeat hardcore. Perhaps due to this lineage, Baltimore club is noticeably more sample based than similarly inspired genres such as ghettotech and ghetto house and has a characteristic breakbeat shuffle built using samples from Lynn Collins's "Think" (1972). Producers incorporate recognizable snippets from television themes and pop songs, and frequently punctuate tracks with sampled gun shots, horns, and shouts. DJ Rod Lee pioneered a more song-based style of club, in which he sang and chanted over his beats; his album *The Official* (2005) was the first Baltimore club record with national distribution.

In the mid-2000s Baltimore club became increasingly popular with tastemaking artists like Diplo and M.I.A., both of whom have worked extensively with Baltimore DJs and producers. Baltimore rhythms and sampling sensibility appeared in DJ sets worldwide, as well as in remixes of songs by rappers and indie bands alike. The Baltimore rappers Labtekwon and Young Leek also released hip-hop tracks with a strong club element. Baltimore club received a further boost in profile from the television show *The Wire*, which featured tracks by Lee and DJ Technics. It has exercised a strong influence along the East Coast, notably in Philadelphia, New Jersey, and Virginia.

GAVIN MUELLER

Bambaataa, Afrika. *See* AFRIKA BAMBAATAA.

Bampton, Rose (Elizabeth) (*b* Lakewood, nr Cleveland, OH, 28 Nov 1907; *d* Bryn Mawr, PA, 21 Aug 2007). Mezzo-soprano, later soprano. She studied at the Curtis Institute of Music with QUEENA MARIO. Originally a soprano, her teachers pushed her toward the mezzo-soprano range after she suffered a bout with laryngitis. Brampton made her debut in 1929 at Chatauqua as Siébel in Gounod's *Faust*, and then sang secondary roles with the Philadelphia Grand Opera. She introduced the role of Wood-Dove in the American premiere of Schoenberg's *Gurrelieder*, garnering critical acclaim. Bampton made her Metropolitan debut in November 1932 as Laura in *La Gioconda*. She married Met conductor Wilfred Pelletier (who had earlier been married to Mario) in 1937. She soon returned to a soprano repertory, making her soprano debut as Leonora in *Il trovatore*; her other soprano roles included Aida and Amneris (in the same season), Donna Anna, Alcestis, Elisabeth, Elsa, Sieglinde, and Kundry, continuing until 1950. Bampton appeared at Covent Garden (1937) as Amneris; in Chicago (1937–46), where her roles included Maddalena de Coigny; and at the Teatro Colón, Buenos Aires (1942–8), where she performed the Marschallin, and Daphne in the South American premiere of Richard Strauss's opera. Prior to retiring in 1950, she appeared in San Francisco. Bampton had a strong, finely polished voice, and a svelte, statuesque figure. Toscanini admired her elegant musicianship, working with her Leonore in a recording of *Fidelio*. Many of her Metropolitan broadcasts are preserved on recordings, notably an exciting Donna Anna under Bruno Walter in 1942 (see P. Jackson: *Saturday Afternoons at the Old Met*, New York, 1992), as is a performance of *Gurrelieder* with Stokowski. Bampton taught at Juilliard from 1974 to 1991.

BIBLIOGRAPHY

Obituaries: *New York Times* (23 Aug 2007); *ON*, lxxii/5 (2007), 74 only

MAX DE SCHAUENSEE, ALAN BLYTH/MEREDITH ELIASSEN

Band. A musical ensemble consisting of the standard woodwind, brass, and percussion instruments. Adjectives, such as circus, college, concert, military, parade, symphonic, or town denote specific functions, often implying instrumental combinations and usages; this article deals mainly with the history of such ensembles in the United States (*see also* CIRCUS MUSIC; MILITARY MUSIC; and WIND ENSEMBLE.) In its more general sense, the term "band" is used to describe other vernacular ensembles, such as banjo, dance, jazz, jug, mummers, rock, steel, string, and theater bands. For information on such groups see COUNTRY MUSIC; FOLK MUSIC; JAZZ; POP; and ROCK.

The terms "band" and "orchestra" were often used interchangeably in the past but have become increasingly distinct. Bands, descended from the medieval "high" (loud) instruments, the human Marsyas in Greek mythology, the waits, and *Stadtpfeifer*, generally performed outdoors, therefore requiring a predominance of the louder brass and percussion instruments. They were mobile, usually associated with a military organization and therefore uniformed, had a vernacular appeal, and generally gave free performances of lighter forms of music for the mass public. Orchestras, on the other hand, are descended from the medieval "low" (soft) instruments, the god Apollo, and the concept of chamber music. The musicians normally performed indoors using predominantly strings and the softer wind instruments; were stationary and usually associated with the church or nobility; and appealed to a sophisticated audience with more serious music for which audiences paid. Until the early 20th century professional musicians were expected to be "double-handed": competent on both string and wind instruments. The function therefore determined the ensemble's instrumentation, the performers forming a wind band for outdoor occasions or an orchestra for indoor concerts and entertainments.

The colonists brought European musical customs and traditions to North America. A distinction was made in military organizations between "field music" and the "band of music." The former denoted the assembled company musicians who provided the camp duty calls that regulated the field or garrison with snare drums, fifes, trumpets, bugles, or bagpipes (*see* MILITARY MUSIC and MILITARY SIGNALS). The band of music, on the other hand, served ceremonial and social functions.

1. The Band of Musick: hautboys, harmonies, and janissaries. 2. Brass bands. 3. The Golden Age of bands. 4. The academic band movement. 5. The postwar era. 6. The contemporary wind band scene. (i) Professional bands. (ii) Educational ensembles. (iii) Marching bands. (iv) Community bands.

1. THE BAND OF MUSICK: HAUTBOYS, HARMONIES, AND JANISSARIES. The French army of Louis XIV developed bands usually consisting of drums, three oboes, and either a bass oboe or bassoon; British regiments had such bands by the end of the 17th century. The earliest reference to a band in North America is a newspaper account of the celebrations for the accession of George I of England in New York in 1714 where it is stated that the governor and the regular forces marched "with Hoboys and Trumpets before them." By the 1750s the term "band of musick" appears frequently in connection with parades and civic ceremonies. In 1756 Benjamin Franklin, the commander of a militia regiment, was preceded on parade by the "Hautboys and Fifes in Ranks." It may be assumed that the term "hautboys," following European practice, referred to the military musicians in general, and that Franklin had a band typical of the time. Other major American cities no doubt had similar ensembles, particularly in the militia units then being formed, as did the British regiments serving in America during the Seven Years' or French and Indian War.

Meanwhile, to reinforce the inner voices and add a new timbre, two french horns had been added to the European band. Clarinets were introduced shortly after, and the instrumentation became standardized into what is today referred to as *Harmoniemusik*. The ideal band consisted of pairs of oboes, clarinets, bassoons, and horns, though the music might range from five to eight parts. Such bands had no drums; as signaling instruments, these remained with the field music. The many serenades, nocturnes, cassations, partitas and divertimentos composed for this combination by Mozart, Haydn, Pleyel, and countless others are accordingly the repertoire of the 18th-century band.

British regimental bands gave concerts in New York, Boston, and Philadelphia before the Revolution, and residents quickly formed bands of their own. Both British and American regiments supported bands during the Revolutionary War, and performances were frequent and notable. The 3rd and 4th Continental artillery regiments had bands as early as 1777; both served until the end of the war and achieved reputations of excellence surpassing any other musical group, civilian or military, in existence at the time, and may alone serve as sufficient basis for the establishment of an American band tradition.

Colonel Crane's 3rd Artillery Regiment Band, later known as the Massachusetts Band, continued to give concerts following demobilization and is believed to be the ancestor of Gilmore's Boston Brigade Band. There were other bands active in post–Revolutionary America as well: bands welcomed Washington in almost every village and city that he visited on his grand tour in 1789. Taverns, coffee houses, theaters, and pleasure gardens all attracted customers with bands performing selections of popular stage works, medleys, battle pieces, transcriptions of orchestral works, original compositions, marches, and patriotic songs (for examples of the music, see Camus, 1992).

The Militia Act of 1792, by which every able-bodied adult white male was required to perform military service for at least two "muster days" each year, greatly promoted the development of bands. The regular meetings for drill and ceremonies of elite organizations supplied a further impetus. No military, civic, festive, or holiday occasion was complete without music, and bands were organized to provide it. Usually attached to militia units, the bandsmen were normally uniformed, a tradition that remains to the present. Tutors such as Timothy Olmstead's *Martial Music* (1807) began to appear in print. (For tutors and music of the period, see Camus, 1989, and Keller, 2002.) Other Revolutionary War bandmasters active into the Federal period included Philip Roth and John Hiwell, the former Inspector of Music in the Continental Army. New leaders, such as Peter von Hagen, James Hewitt, and Gottlieb Graupner, came from Europe.

Widespread interest in Turkish (janissary) music at the beginning of the 19th century brought the bass drum, cymbals, triangle, tambourine, Turkish crescent

(Jingling Johnnie), and single kettledrum into the band. The more exotic instruments soon fell into disuse, but the bass drum, frequently with mounted cymbal, became standard in American bands and field music. Combined performances of the two groups became more frequent, and the snare drum soon became an integral part of the band. Further changes to Harmoniemusik in the Federal period included new keys on the woodwind instruments, and the addition of the piccolo, bass clarinet, trombone, bass horn, and serpent. William Webb's *Grand Military Divertimentos* (*c*1828) were published for such a combination (*see* Table 1, 1828).

Another new instrument, the Kent or keyed–bugle, was patented by Joseph Halliday of Dublin in 1810. Applying keys to the regulation bugle, it permitted a fully chromatic brass instrument (*see* Keyed bugle). It was popularized in New York through the performances of Richard Willis, who within a year of his arrival from Dublin in 1816 became the first teacher of music and leader of the band at the US Military Academy at West Point. Other virtuosi on the keyed bugle included Frank [Francis] Johnson in Philadelphia and Edward [Ned] Kendall in Boston. Keyed bass horns and ophicleides were developed, and bands continued to increase in size. By 1832 US Army infantry regiments had bands consisting of 15 to 24 members, a size emulated by militia bands. In that year, however, General Order 31 limited infantry bands to ten privates and a chief musician, a drastic reduction that led to the elimination of woodwinds in favor of the new valved brass instruments, and thus to the next phase in the history of American bands.

2. Brass bands. In the early 1830s many American bands, among them the Boston and Providence Brass Bands and Thomas Dodworth's City Band of New York (later the Dodworth Band), changed to all-brass instrumentation. Such bands included keyed and valved instruments, posthorns, bugles, trombones, and ophicleides. Over the next two decades manufacturers such as Thomas D. Paine, John F. Stratton, Isaac Fiske, Samuel Graves, J. Lathrop Allen, and E.G. Wright produced a family of conical-bore valved bugles with deep-cupped mouthpieces similar to those developed by Adolph Sax in Paris; the new design permitted ease of execution and accurate intonation, and produced an even, mellow timbre throughout from soprano to contrabass. This homogeneous brass family soon supplanted mixed woodwind and heterogeneous brass groups. The change to all-brass instrumentation was so swift and complete that by 1856 the editor of *Dwight's Journal of Music* complained that “all is brass now-a-days—nothing but brass.” Besides bell-front and bell-upward instruments, a valved over-the shoulder family was developed. Allen Dodworth claimed that his family first introduced these instruments in 1838; he explained that they were intended for military bands “as they throw all the tone to those who are marching to it,” but for general purposes those with their bells upward were “most convenient.” He also advised “care should be taken to have all the bells one way.”

Allen Dodworth, with his father and three brothers, had established a band in the mid-1830s. For many years the Dodworth Band was considered the finest in America. The Dodworths were a very enterprising family: all were composers proficient on more than one instrument. Harvey was a brilliant soloist and proprietor of the Dodworth music store and publishing company, and Allen became a very successful teacher of ballroom dancing. The Dodworths were also influential in establishing the New York Philharmonic Orchestra Society in 1842: four Dodworths played in the orchestra, and, in addition to being a member of the violin section, Allen became its first treasurer (*see* Dodworth). Some of the band's members who later developed reputations as leaders of their own organizations included Theodore Thomas, Alessandro Liberati, Carlo Cappa, and D.L. Downing.

After the reduction of US Army infantry bands to ten privates and a chief musician in 1832 these bands became all-brass. In 1845 the regulations authorized an increase to 16 musicians, and since most civilian bands were associated with militia organizations patterned on army models, this change had a significant impact on the size of these bands as well.

Brass bands flourished in the 1850s: one writer estimated there were some 3000 bands with more than 60,000 members in existence in the years preceding the Civil War (Felts, 1967). While musicianship in amateur groups varied widely, many professional bands performed at the highest level. The American Band (Providence, RI, 1837) led by Joseph Green, the Salem (MA) Brass Band, led in the 1850s by Kendall and later by Patrick S. Gilmore, the Boston Brass Band, led by Eben Flagg were highly reputed. Russel Munger's Great Western Band of St. Paul and Christopher Bach's Band of Milwaukee were well known among the many bands organized in the newly settled midwestern states. Agrand festival concert, a benefit for the American Musical Fund Society, was held at Castle Garden (NY) on 4 September 1852, and 11 outstanding bands performed, including the Dodworth Cornet Band, the Boston Brigade Brass Band and Joseph Noll's 7th Regiment Band. The program, including dances, marches, overtures and potpourris from popular operas, solos and duets, is typical of the time.

Little printed band music from this period is extant; most bands played from manuscript. Published piano music frequently included the statement “as performed by [some famous band]” to increase sales, and often a note stating that parts for military band—presumably manuscript—were available from the publisher. In 1846 E.K. Eaton published *Twelve Pieces of Harmony for Military Brass Bands*, an excellent compilation for 17-piece ensemble that demanded advanced technical facility not only from the player of the high E♭ bugle but from the entire group (Table 1, 1846). To meet the “increasing demand for such a work, caused by the rapid advancement of the brass bands of our country,” Allen Dodworth published his *Brass Band School* in 1853. Besides the rudiments of music, he provided fingering charts; advice on rehearsing and choosing an instrument; and military regulations, tactics, and camp duties. He also included 11 popular airs and marches arranged for a band of 12 players, with drums and cymbals (ex.1). The music may

Table 1: Comparative band instrumentation

	1828	*1846*	*1863*	*1878*	*1900*	*1918*	*1926*	*1944*	*1946*	*1948*	*1952*	*1960*	*1983*	*1985*	*2011*
Flute/piccolo	3		1	4	4	2	1/1/2	3	4	12	3	6		3	16
Oboe/eng. hn				2	2	2	-/1/2	1	2	8	3	3		3	
Heckelphone										1					
Bassoon	2			2	2	2	-/1/2	1	2	6	2	2		2	
Contrabassoon				1	1					1	1				
Contrab. Sarrus.						1	-/-/1								
A♭ clarinet				1											
E♭ clarinet				3	2	1	1/1/2	1	1		1	1		1	
B♭ clarinet	2		1	16	16	10	6/8/10	12	19	29	8	18		9	28
Alto clarinet				1	2	2	-/-/2	1		4	1	6			
Bass clarinet				1	2	2	-/-/2	1	1	5	1	3		1	
Contraalto cl														1	
Contrabass cl										3		2			
Soprano sax				1			-/1/-					1			
Alto sax				1	2	1	1/1/1	4	1	3	2	1		2	24
Tenor sax				1	2	1	1/1/1	2	1	3	1	1		1	12
Baritone sax				1	1	1	1/1/1	1	1	1	1	1		1	
Bass sax										1		1			
E♭ cornet		1	2	1								1	1		
B♭ cornet			2	4	4		2/2/2		4	7	3	3	8–10		
E♭ trumpet		2													
B♭ trumpet	1			2	2	4	4/4/4	10	3	4	2	3		6	70
B♭ flugelhorn		2		2	2	2				2			1		
Bugle/posthorn	1	1													12
French horn	2	2		4	4	4	3/4/4	4	4	9	4	4		5	
Alto horn			2	2									3		28
Alto ophicleide		2													
Tenor horn			2	2											
Trombone	1	3		3	4	4	3/3/4	6	6	9	3	4	3	3	60
B♭ baritone													2		
Euphonium			1	2	2	2	1/2/2	2	2	6	2	3	2	2	28
Bass ophicleide		2													
Serpent	1														
Bass			3	5	4	4	2/3/4	5	4	8	2	3	4	2	36
String bass									1	3	1			1	
Percussion		2	2	4	3	3	2/2/2	2	3	9	3	5	2–4	5	36
Piano/keyboard														1	
Harp									1	2	1			1	
Total	13	17	16	66	61	48	28/36/48	56	60	136	45	72	26–30	50	350

1828: W. Webb, *Grand Military Divertimentos*. (Philadelphia: George E. Blake, [c1828])
1846: E.K. Eaton, *Twelve Pieces of Harmony for Military Brass Bands*. (New York: Firth and Hall, 1846)
1863: 3rd New Hampshire (Port Royal) band books, 1863–5 (Library of Congress)
1878: Gilmore's 22nd Regiment Band (R.F. Goldman, *The Wind Band*, pp.59, 62)
1900: Sousa Band, 1st European Tour, 1900 (Bierley, p.148)
1918: US Army Regimental Band authorization
1926: Instrumentation of 28-, 36-, and 48-piece army bands, 1926 TR 130–35, 1926
1944: US Army Division Band authorization
1946: The Goldman Band (R.F. Goldman, *The Concert Band*, pp.78–9)
1948: The University of Illinois Symphonic Band under Albert Austin Harding
1952: Frederick Fennell, Eastman Wind Ensemble, 1952
1960: College Band Directors National Association "Ideal Balanced Band," (R.F. Goldman, *The Wind Band*, p.167)
1983: NABBA British brass band
1985: Dallas Wind Symphony founded
2011: Texas A&M University Fightin' Texas Aggie Band

107th United States Colored Infantry Band, 1865. (Library of Congress, Prints & Photographs Division, LC-DIG-cwpb-04279)

be played by as few as six, or, with doubling, as many as 21. In 1854 G.W.E. Friederich published his *Brass Band Journal*, a collection of 24 pieces with similar instrumentation, and in 1859 W.C. Peters & Sons published *Peters' Sax-Horn Journal*. These collections consisted principally of patriotic and sentimental songs, popular airs, operatic excerpts, waltzes, polkas, schottisches, and marches. Aimed at a mass market, these arrangements are generally less technically demanding, and therefore not representative of the better professional bands, which normally had extensive manuscript collections.

General Order 15 (4 May 1861) called for the raising of 40 volunteer regiments for the Union (39 of infantry, one of cavalry). Each infantry regiment was authorized "2 principal musicians, 24 musicians for band" (2 and 16 for the cavalry) in addition two field musicians per company. Confederate regulations authorized a chief musician and 16 privates to act as musicians. General Order 16 extended the same organization to the regular army, and later calls did so to additional volunteer regiments. Many civilian and militia bands enlisted as a body in the new volunteer regiments. While most conformed to regulations, some exceeded the authorized strength; supported, as in the past, by the officers, some were dressed in elaborate uniforms. The 24th Massachusetts Volunteer Infantry had 20 drummers, 12 buglers, and a 36-piece mixed wind band led by Patrick S. Gilmore. Greene's American Brass Band of Providence enlisted as a unit in the 1st Rhode Island Regiment. Other famous civilian bandmasters who answered the call with their men included Claudio S. Grafulla, Harvey Dodworth, E.B. Flagg, Thomas Coates, and Walter Dignam. Gustavus W. Ingalls enlisted 22 men for the 3rd New Hampshire Regiment, and their "Port Royal Band Books" constitute a primary source for research into the instrumentation and repertoire of the period (Table 1, 1863). Eight members of the Salem Brass Band enlisted in the 26th North Carolina Regiment; their story (Hall 2006) is typical of the experiences of many bands serving on both sides of the conflict. Bufkin (1973) estimates conservatively that the Union Army, with a strength of over two and a half million men, had 500 bands and 9000 players in addition to the two field musicians per company.

Civil War bands served not only to provide music for military and civilian ceremonies, but to promote esprit de corps through informal entertainments as well; bandsmen also served as medical assistants during battle. Nevertheless, there were those in Congress who felt that too much money was spent on bands; in 1861 a moratorium was placed on new bands and filling vacancies in existing ones, and General Order 91 (1862) directed that all volunteer regimental bands be mustered out of service. One brigade band of 16 musicians was authorized instead of the four regimental bands. In an army this large, however, it was difficult to enforce every regulation uniformly, and some regimental, militia, and post bands continued to serve until the end of the war. The band of the 107th US Colored Infantry,

Ex.1 "Gift Polka" by Allen Dodworth, from his *Brass Band School* (New York, 1853)

while typical in size and instrumentation to the many white and black brigade bands in service, is nevertheless a regimental band (Figure 1).

The 26th North Carolina and 1st Wisconsin Brigade bands were resurrected in the early 1960s for the Civil War Centennial; other reconstituted bands include the Federal City Brass Band, the Great Western Band of St. Paul and the 4th Cavalry Regiment Band.

Even during this heyday of all-brass bands, some retained woodwind instruments. Dodworth's concerts included works for mixed wind bands as early as 1852. In that same year the 7th Regiment (NY) Band was reformed as a 42-piece woodwind and brass group. It soon achieved a reputation of excellence under Joseph Noll, and then Claudio Grafulla, surpassed only by the Dodworth Band. Emigrant bandmasters, especially Italians, favored reed instruments as an important part of their musical heritage. Francis Scala, a virtuoso clarinetist, maintained the Italian woodwind tradition while leader of the Marine Band (1855–71). Gilmore had five reed instruments in 1862, and may have had them as early as 1859. These were all large and exceptional bands, and not representative of the typical Civil War band. They were, however, the precursors of the next great period in American band history.

3. The Golden Age of bands. A flamboyant and jovial Irishman with seemingly boundless energy and enthusiasm may rightfully be considered the father of the modern American symphonic band. Arriving in America in 1849, Patrick S. Gilmore soon became leader of the Salem Brass Band. In 1859, with his reputation secure, he established Gilmore's Band, personally assuming all financial and business responsibilities for the organization. After a brief period of Civil War service with the 24th Massachusetts Infantry, Gilmore was placed in charge of organizing and training all of that state's bands. It was in this capacity that he assembled a band of 500 and a chorus of 6000 for the ceremonies inaugurating the governor of Louisiana in 1864. The National Peace Jubilee of 1869 and the World Peace Jubilee of 1872, both held in Boston and each doubling the previous in the number of performers, scope, and imagination, brought him international attention and fame. In 1873 he assumed the leadership of New York's 22nd Regiment Band, and soon established it as the finest professional band in America. A skilled promoter, he attracted large audiences by adept programming and by engaging such outstanding soloists as the cornetists Matthew Arbuckle, Herman Bellstedt, Alessandro Liberati, and Jules Levy; the saxophonist E.A. Lefèbre; the

trombonist Frederick Neil Innes; the euphonium player Michael Raffayolo; and the sopranos Emma Thursby, Eugenie Pappenheim, and Lillian Nordica.

Gilmore treated his people honestly and fairly, and paid them well. Far exceeding military regulations of the time, his 22nd Regiment Band normally had a complement of 66 musicians (Table 1, 1878). The band made an American tour in 1876, followed by a successful European tour two years later. During the 1880s they worked year-round: summers at Manhattan Beach, winters at Gilmore's Garden (P.T. Barnum's Hippodrome) and the 22d Regiment armory, fall and spring on tour. Since at this time there were only four major professional symphony orchestras, none of which had a full season, the very finest musicians applied to Gilmore for employment. Considered the finest in the land, his band was an inspiration to bands all over America to reintroduce the woodwind instruments and to raise the level of performance and repertoire. He aspired to the establishment of a permanent band of 100 musicians, but his death in 1892 aborted the venture.

While none toured as extensively or reached Gilmore's fame and reputation, there were others active at the time. Claudio S. Grafulla, of Civil War fame, continued to conduct the 7th Regiment (NY) Band until his death in 1880. He was succeeded by Carlo A. Cappa, a trombonist who had left Ned Kendall's band to serve under Grafulla. Cappa also appeared as soloist with the Dodworth Band, and for many years was first trombonist with Theodore Thomas's Orchestra. David Wallis Reeves, another Dodworth soloist, had taken over the American Band of Providence in 1866. Reeves added woodwinds and created a professional ensemble. Gilmore soloists Matthew Arbuckle and Alessandro Liberati formed bands of their own. Robert B. Hall, one of the finest cornet soloists in the northeast, directed bands in Maine from 1882 until a stroke in 1902 left him partially paralyzed. Fred Weldon, Jean M. Missud, and Mace Gay are only some of the many other bandmasters who developed fine local reputations of excellence with their bands.

Unquestionably, the towering figure of the Golden Age, perhaps of American music in general, was JOHN PHILIP SOUSA. He had assumed the leadership of the Unites States Marine Band in 1880; by 1891 he had brought the ensemble to a high level of professionalism, and with it undertook an American tour. The manager of that tour, David Blakely, had been Gilmore's manager for many years, and in 1892 he persuaded Sousa to resign from the Marine Corps and form his own band. Preparations were under way for the first concert when word was received that Gilmore had passed away. Sousa quickly scheduled as his opening selection Gilmore's own *The Voice of a Departing Soul* in tribute. Even though D.W. Reeves, and Victor Herbert after him, tried to keep the Gilmore band intact, it was Sousa's band that dominated the scene. Several of Gilmore's major soloists joined with Sousa, who was also able to obtain many of Gilmore's unfilled engagements.

An astute showman, fine composer, and excellent musician, Sousa treated his performers kindly and fairly, paid them well, and demanded the utmost in musical achievement. He engaged the finest available players for each position, and attracted such outstanding soloists as cornetists Herman Bellstedt, Herbert L. Clarke, John Dolan, Bohumir Kryl, Alessandro Liberati, Walter Rogers, and Frank Simon; trombonist Arthur Pryor; euphonium soloists Simone Mantia and Joseph DeLuca; violinists Maud Powell, Florence Hardeman, and Nicoline Zedeler; and sopranos Estelle Liebling and Marjorie Moody. He experimented with instrumentation, beginning with a group of 46 similar to the Marine Band, gradually adding until he averaged between 66 and 70 performers (Table 1, 1900). He toured regularly from 1892 until his death in 1932, including European tours in 1900, 1901, and 1903, and a world tour, 1910–11.

The typical Sousa program usually listed nine compositions, ranging from his own suites, selections, and marches, to novelty numbers and solos, to orchestral transcriptions and opera arias and the most recent contemporary music such as selections from *Parsifal* a decade before its Metropolitan Opera premiere. His printed programs are deceiving, however: after each listed title Sousa would normally add one or two encores, so that a program with nine selections might actually contain as many as 30. The encores were always spontaneous, and usually consisted of his own marches. In addition to the ever popular marches, he wrote over 200 original band compositions, 15 operettas, 70 songs, educational materials, over 300 arrangements, three novels, an autobiography, and numerous articles. He was an active champion for musicians' and composers' rights, and was a charter member of ASCAP. His influence on the American musical scene was immense, and no musician ever received as many honors, medals, trophies, honorary degrees, memberships, and tokens of respect from an adoring public.

Many Sousa alumni went on to develop significant careers of their own: bandmasters Bellstedt, Clarke, Kryl, Eugene LaBarre, Liberati, Mantia, Pryor, and Simon; Broadway composer, conductor, and author Meredith Willson; musical instrument maker Frank Holton; and orchestral musicians and educators William Bell, Jaroslav Cimera, John J. Heney, Anton Horner, Ernest S. Williams, and many others. Other major figures of the period included such veterans as Monroe Althouse, Thomas Brooke, Cappa, Francesco Fanciulli, Missud, and Victor Herbert; and bandmasters such as Giuseppe Creatore, Patrick Conway, Edwin Franko Goldman, and Innes who organized new professional ensembles. Since women were not admitted to the professional bands except as violin, soprano or harp soloists, they formed bands of their own. Helen May Butler's Ladies Military Brass Band was only one such professional band.

In addition to the professional bands there were other bands as well: an 1889 article in *Harper's Weekly* estimated there were more than 10,000 military bands active in the United States. At a time when there were few orchestras, a band was seen as a status symbol: "it is a fact not to be denied that the existence of a good brass band in any town or community is at once an indication of enterprise among its people, and an evidence that a certain spirit of taste and refinement pervades the masses" (Patton). W.H. Dana wrote: "a town without its brass band is as much in need of sympathy as a church without a choir. The spirit of a place is recognized in its band." ("Brass Band" by this time had become a generic term implying a brass section core, but with woodwinds added where possible.) There were municipal, town, or civic bands, many dating back to ante bellum times, such as the Allentown Band (Pennsylvania, 1828), the Repasz Band (Williamsport, Pennsylvania, 1831), the Barrington Band (New Hampshire, 1832), the American Band (Rhode Island, 1837), the Stonewall Brigade Band (Staunton, Virginia, 1845), the Ringgold Band (Reading, Pennsylvania, 1852), and the Naperville Band (Illinois, 1859), to name just a few. Several states passed "band laws," whereby special taxes could be levied for use in providing free band concerts "upon occasions of public importance." The association with the military remained: a "band" is one that is composed "of such musical instruments as are recognized in the standard instrumentation established for the use of U.S. army bands." In many western communities the only music available was that provided by the local military post band. While most were unknown outside their own areas, some had famous directors, such as the Fort Dodge (Iowa) Military Band, led for 38 years by Karl L. King, and the Long Beach (California) Municipal Band led by Herbert L. Clarke, then J.J. Richards. There were fraternal and sororal organizations such as the many Shrine bands led by Henry Fillmore, Fred Jewell, Ned Mahoney, and others, and, following World War I, the many American Legion and Veterans of Foreign Wars bands. Many Salvation Army bands maintained the brass band tradition. There were industrial bands, whose primary purpose was to provide a recreational activity for the employees, but at the same time serving a community relations and advertising function for the employer. The Armco Band, led by former Sousa soloist Frank Simon, the Arma Band, led by Erik Leidzén, the Philco Band, led by Herbert N. Johnston, and the Metropolitan Life Insurance Company Band, led by George F. Briegel, are just a few of the many. The directors frequently had multiple positions: Briegel, for example, in addition to the Metropolitan Band, also directed the 22nd Regiment (New York) Band (Gilmore's organization), the New York City Fire Department Band, and the Kismet Temple Band, with many of his musicians playing in more than one of the groups. To train musicians for all these bands, a number of schools were established, such as Hale A. VanderCook's College of Music (Chicago, 1909), Frank H. Losey's Military Band School (Erie, Pennsylvania, 1914), Ernest S. Williams's School of Music (Brooklyn, New York, 1922), Patrick Conway's Military Band School (Ithaca, New York, 1922), and Frederick N. Innes's Conn National School of Music (Chicago, 1923).

Many bands were associated with local militia units, and though uniformed, retained their civilian status. Most were similar in size and instrumentation to the army bands, which in 1926 consisted of three sizes (Table 1, 1926). Professional and amateur bands appeared at military ceremonies, parades, civilian celebrations, concerts, amusement parks, seaside resorts, county and state fairs, and national and international expositions. They entertained their public, and they were ubiquitous. Their repertoires ranged from the ever-popular marches, songs, waltzes, and novelty numbers to the classical standards of the day. Most Americans had their first, and in many instances only, exposure to Mozart, Beethoven, Rossini, and Verdi, and such moderns as Liszt and Wagner, and even staged grand opera through these bands. Marches were extremely popular, followed by operatic selections and variations performed by the great soloists. European marches usually consisted of a melody with rhythmic accompaniment. D.W. Reeves is generally credited with being the first to add a countermelody and develop a style that served as a model. His *2d Regiment Connecticut N.G. March* was a favorite of Charles Ives, who quoted it in his *Decoration Day* (1912).

While large bands were conducted, the solo cornet player frequently led the smaller ones, as in the days of brass bands. Consequently the solo cornet part in printed arrangements usually served as the conductor's cue sheet. Carl Fischer of New York was one of the first to publish band music with printed parts for each instrument, and to include a two- or three-line conductor's score. The firm engaged many outstanding editors, among them Louis-Philippe Laurendeau, Frank H. Losey, Vincent F. Safranek, Theodore Moses Tobani, and Mayhew Lester Lake, many of whose arrangements are still performed. Thomas H. Rollinson prepared many arrangements during his 40 years with Ditson. Later important publishers of band music included Charles L. Barnhouse, John Church, Harry Coleman, Henry Fillmore, George F. Briegel, and several bandmasters who issued their own music, such as Missud, Fred Jewell, and Karl L. King.

In a world of their own were many professional musicians who followed the circus. With traditions dating back to the 18th century, and for a while influenced by the popularity of minstrel bands, circus bands held a unique position in American life. The elaborate circus parades, led by colorfully decorated bandwagons, heightened the feeling of joyous expectation when the circus came to town. Circus bandmasters and musicians, such as Russell Alexander, Carl Clair, Charles E. Duble, Fillmore, Jewell, King, Perry G. Lowery, and Joseph J. Richards developed a repertoire and style of their own. Providing the music for such memory-evoking shows as Barnum and Bailey, Ringling Brothers, Forepaugh-Sells Brothers, Sells-Floto, Wallace and Hagenbeck, and others, they invariably played everything at a much faster "circus" tempo (*see* Circus music, March).

Another separate world was that of the New Orleans Brass Band. Descended from the brass bands of the

Civil War, but with a mixed African American and Creole heritage, these developed a repertoire and a style of their own. Often associated with benevolent societies, these bands provided music for club functions and funerals. Since at least the 18th century bands traditionally played a solemn march on their way to the cemetery, but a brisk quickstep, usually "Merry Men Home from the Grave" on their return. The New Orleans musicians began improvising on tunes (such as the spiritual "When the saints go marching in"), developing an early form of jazz. There were many permanent black ensembles at the end of the 19th century, including the Excelsior, Eureka, Onward, Tuxedo, and St. Bernard brass bands, and many leading jazz instrumentalists gained their first experiences in these groups. As bandmasters of the 350th and 369th US Infantry Regiment Bands serving in France during World War I, Tim Brymn and James Reese Europe brought jazz to European audiences for the first time. Forces that were to affect the decline of the Golden Age were already in motion, even as these times seemed brightest. The competition of radio, the phonograph, and motion pictures was a major factor. The automobile contributed to the demise of amusement parks, which had featured bands prominently. The jazz band provided music for dancing, and staples of the band repertoire, such as the polka, waltz, and schottische, were out of fashion. Sousa continued to draw enthusiastic crowds, but other professional bandmasters, such as Creatore and Kryl, had to be satisfied with fairs, expositions, and Chautauquas. The Great Depression was the final blow, and when John Philip Sousa died in 1932, there was no major figure to take his place. The scene had changed from the professional bandmaster to the educator.

4. The academic band movement. Through the 19th century, instrumental music in schools and colleges was primarily an extracurricular activity. Music education in the schools was typically devoted to vocal music. Participation in musical ensembles at the college level remained extracurricular even after John Knowles Paine's promotion to full professor at Harvard University in 1875 marked the acceptance of music theory, history, and composition as academic disciplines. It would be some years, however, before performing groups would similarly be recognized as curricular activities.

Will Earhart is usually given credit for being the first to organize a successful instrumental program in American schools (Richmond, Indiana, 1898). Osbourne McConathy established the precedent of granting school credit for private study under outside teachers (Chelsea, Massachusetts, 1906). The period just before World War I is widely claimed as the beginning of the school band movement, a time when Otto Miessner was working in Connersville (Indiana), A.R. McAllister in Joliet (Illinois), and Glen Woods in Oakland (California). While pioneers, they were not alone, nor perhaps even the first, but by the latter end of the 19th century there were bands all over America.

Harvard and Yale had bands by about 1827, and other universities soon followed their example. The Morrill Act of 1862, which granted public lands for the establishment of educational institutions, required land grant colleges to offer courses in military training. Military ceremonies required music, and there are records of bands at practically all institutions following the Civil War. Associated with and trained by the military, the bands were uniformed and organized according to army regulations, which authorized a 16-piece brass band with a leader and an assistant. The leaders were usually students with previous town band experiences, and the instrumentation in many cases was fully balanced according to brass band principles. Members received military but not academic credit for their work. Military ceremonies, political rallies, parades, dedications, outdoor festivities, and sports events were all enlivened by the presence of bands performing music ranging from popular overtures and medleys to spirited marches and school songs.

The participation of bands at sporting events became increasingly important, and by the end of the century pre-game and half-time football performances were common. With the addition of woodwind instruments, the bands increased in size and were organized more often like professional rather than military ensembles. Professional bandmasters, such as Conway at Cornell University (1895–1908) and Gustav Bruder at Ohio State University (1896–1929), soon replaced student directors on a part-time basis. Paul Spotts Emrick began his almost 50 years' service at Purdue in 1905, the same year that Oregon State engaged Harry L. Beard and Albert Austin Harding became director of the University of Illinois Band. Harding, a personal friend of Sousa and greatly influenced by him, believed that the band should play music of the same importance and as competently as the symphony orchestra, and that its indoor performances should be equally as pleasing to the audience. Seeing that the Illinois Military Band was far from the level of the professional bands of the time, it is the college band movement's good fortune that he resolved to do something about it. By making greater use of alto and bass flutes and clarinets, oboes, bassoons, contrabassoon, the full saxophone family, flugelhorns, and horns instead of altos, Harding developed a truly symphonic sound. Since arrangements for such a band did not exist, he made almost 150 transcriptions of orchestral works, including compositions by Ernő Dohnányi, Jacques Ibert, Zoltán Kodály, Sergey Prokofiev, Dmitri Shostakovich, Richard Strauss, and other moderns. The artistic standard of the University of Illinois Band soon equaled that of the best professional bands, and Harding's work was widely emulated.

World War I brought a renewed interest in military bands, and mobilization fostered an expanded musical instrument industry. A school for army bandleaders at Fort Jay (NY), directed by Arthur A. Clappé, had been organized through the efforts of Frank Damrosch in 1911. Walter Damrosch organized a similar school at Chaumont, France, in 1918. Comparing unfavorably with European bands in size and instrumentation, American regimental bands were increased from 20 to

48 (Table 1, 1918), and greater emphasis was placed on thorough musical training. When these men returned to civilian life, they brought with them their enthusiasm as well as their skill and experience, and many became instrumental directors in the public schools. Joseph E. Maddy, generally credited with being the first Supervisor of Instrumental Music in America (Rochester, NY, 1918), commented that class instruction in band and orchestra instruments was beginning to receive support from school officials by the close of the World War, and that the real era of public school class instruction in instrumental music dates from about this time. The emphasis was primarily on orchestral groups, however, as seen in a report of a joint committee of the National Education Association, the Music Teacher's National Association, and the Music Supervisors' National Conference in 1919: of the 359 cities in 36 states that responded, only 88 reported having bands, while 278 had orchestras. Since no note was taken of extra-curricular and non-school bands, the report is probably misleading: a 1973 report found ten times as many bands as orchestras.

Musical instrument manufacturers welcomed the new interest in instrumental music education, for the decrease in professional bands following World War I led to a declining market. To stimulate demand, they organized the first national school band contest, in Chicago in June 1923. Though many of the 25 bands that competed were local, the results were considered spectacular. To avoid future criticism, the manufacturers asked the National Bureau for the Advancement of Music to sponsor the contests. The Committee on Instrumental Affairs of the Music Supervisors' National Conference, with funds supplied by the manufacturers, developed state contests to achieve greater participation. Response was so great that by 1937 the National School Band Association, organized in 1926 to administer the contests, had formed ten separate regions. By 1941 there were 562 bands (33,398 students) participating, besides the many bands eliminated at district level.

While the contests unquestionably fostered the growth of the symphonic band, marching bands benefited from the popularity of intercollegiate football. Larger bands were needed to fill the huge stadiums built between the two world wars. Separated from the Officers Training Corps, bands were liberated from the tradition of marching on and off the field in military formation at halftime. The University of Illinois Band under Harding is generally credited with being the first to play opening fanfares from the goal line, and to form a block "I" while marching down the field, though many others soon followed. In 1936 Eugene J. Weigel had his 120-piece Ohio State University Marching Band form the word "Ohio" in script, beginning a tradition that has remained to the present (*see* Figure 2).

During this period measures were taken to raise the musicianship of symphonic and marching bands. In 1928 Joseph E. Maddy founded the National Music Camp at Interlochen, Michigan, the most famous of the many summer music schools. As early as 1919 Harding had invited school band directors to observe his rehearsals at the University of Illinois and to discuss specific problems and repertoire. In 1930 he began a series of band clinics that became so successful and influential that Harding may rightfully be called the "Dean of University Band Directors." When the American Bandmasters Association was organized in 1929, Harding was the only educator included among the service and professional band directors. By 1941 it was felt that an organization devoted to the professional concerns of the college band was needed, and William D. Revelli, director of bands at the University of Michigan, founded the College Band Directors National Association. (CBDNA). Its aims included acoustical and tonal research, better musicianship among college band directors, and the development of a standard instrumentation (Table 1, 1960), a concept later rejected as too restrictive. Another aim was the commissioning of original band music, especially from composers already recognized in other media, a project effectively begun by Edwin Franko Goldman some years earlier. But World War II had taken away most of the bandsmen, and music, like the other arts, joined the war effort.

5. The postwar era. World War II curtailed the school band movement, but returning veterans inspired a second golden age. In 1946 Kappa Kappa Psi, the national honorary band fraternity (founded 1919), entered into a cooperative arrangement with Tau Beta Sigma, its sororal counterpart (founded 1939; *see* Fraternities and sororities). New professional organizations were formed, such as the National Association of College Wind and Percussion Instructors (1951), the American School Band Directors Association (1953), the National Catholic Bandmasters Association (1953), the National Band Association (1960), Women Band Directors National Association (1969), and the Association of Concert Bands (1977).

Bands grew larger and more numerous: a 1973 survey counted some 50,000 secondary-school bands in the United States, with 2000 at institutions of higher education. Harding's University of Illinois Band expanded to 136 members (Table 1, 1948) and some of the marching bands fielded over 200. In reaction to these larger ensembles, Frederick Fennell formed the Eastman Symphonic Wind Ensemble in 1952 (Table 1, 1952). With flexible composer-determined instrumentation, it stressed the concept of individual performers as in chamber music, with no doubling except where indicated by the composer. Repertoire ranged from Renaissance wind music to avant-garde compositions: works by Gabrieli and Pezel to Piston, Riegger, Schoenberg, and Varèse, wind serenades of Mozart and Richard Strauss and wind symphonies by Hindemith and Stravinsky. Fennell's work at Eastman was carried on by Donald Hunsberger (1965–2002) and then Mark Scatterday. (*See* Wind ensemble.) The success of this concept can be measured from the fact that there are wind ensembles in virtually every major university and most colleges. Robert A. Boudreau founded the American Wind Symphony in 1957, and has commissioned over 400 works from contemporary composers.

The professional band had not completely disappeared: Richard Franko Goldman, who assumed leadership of the Goldman band on the death of his father, E.F. Goldman, in 1956, continued the tradition of free outdoor concerts begun in 1911 (Table 1, 1946). Through the League of Composers, and later the American Bandmasters Association, the Goldmans commissioned and gave first performances of original works by Robert Russell Bennett, William Bergsma, Paul Creston, Bainbridge Crist, Vittorio Giannini, Morton Gould, Percy Grainger, Howard Hanson, Henry Hadley, D.G. Mason, Peter Mennin, Douglas Moore, Vincent Persichetti, Walter Piston, Ottorino Respighi, Albert Roussel, Leo Sowerby, Virgil Thomson, Jaromir Weinberger, and C.C. White. In 1946 Leonard Smith took the daring step of organizing a new professional band, the Detroit Concert Band, which made a successful series of recordings of Golden Age band music, including orchestral transcriptions, virtuoso solos, novelty pieces and stirring marches (*Gems of the Concert Band*). While many of the old circuses are no more, Merle Evans, bandmaster of the Ringling Brothers Barnum & Bailey Circus, entertained more than 165,000,000 people in his 50 years under the big top until his retirement in 1969. In the military, reductions in the number and size of bands continued. The World War II division band of 56 players (Table 1, 1944) replaced as many as ten regimental bands; the division or post band of the 1980s was a 40-piece multipurpose musical unit.

In 1956 the Ostwald Uniform Company established an award in memory of Ernest Ostwald for the best band composition submitted each year to a jury of the American Bandmasters Association; winners have included James Barnes, John Barnes Chance, James Curnow, Donald Grantham, David Holsinger, Robert Jager, Joseph Willcox Jenkins, John Mackey, Timothy Mahr, Ron Nelson, Roger Nixon, Fisher Tull, Dan Welcher, and Clifton Williams. CBDNA continued its commissioning project as well: Leslie Bassett, Ingolf Dahl, Howard Hanson, John Harbison Ernst Krenek, David Maslanka, and Joseph Schwantner, among others.

6. The contemporary wind band scene. There appear to be four distinct aspects, with considerable overlapping: (i) professional bands, (ii) educational ensembles, (iii) marching bands and (iv) community bands, each with distinctive characteristics, repertoire, audiences, and levels of musicianship.

(i) Professional bands. The only full-time professional bands remaining in America are those of the armed services. In 2010 Army bands were reorganized into smaller "music performance teams." The 39-piece band, for example, can support concurrent missions by one large or two small popular music ensembles (jazz, rock, country), three brass quintets, and a woodwind quintet, all easily transported by helicopter. The special bands have set a standard for school and college bands to emulate by their high level of artistic achievement and their many CDs available for educational use (for the organization of service bands in 2011, *see* Military music). Some part-time ensembles, such as the Allentown Band, the New Sousa Band, and the Dallas Wind Symphony (Table 1, 1985) perform on a highly professional level.

(ii) Educational ensembles. That same professional level is evident in many educational institutions. Many universities have multiple bands, separating traditional activities into several distinct units with differing purposes and performance levels. The Department of Bands at Indiana University, for example, has three music-major concert ensembles: Wind Ensemble, Symphonic Band, Concert Band; the members also form various chamber ensembles. All students may participate in an All-Campus Band, a 280-member "Marching Hundred," the Big Red Basketball Band and the Crabb Pep Bands (men's and women's soccer, women's volleyball and women's basketball). There is little overlap of membership in the various groups, and all, except for the pep bands, may be taken for credit. There is also a Summer Music Clinic for high school instrumentalists. The department includes four full-time directors, a full-time secretary and six graduate assistants. Repertoire depends upon the level of achievement of the specific group, the taste of the conductor, and the audience or occasion for which the group performs.

There are symphonic bands and wind ensembles in the junior and senior high schools, the colleges, and the universities. The wind ensemble normally has the most proficient players, although some schools ignore the chamber music concept and use the term to indicate their premier group. Normally performing in concert halls and auditoriums, their repertoire is more serious, with major original works including symphonies by Copland, Hindemith, Gustav Holst, Husa, Vittorio Giannini, Grainger, Persichetti, Schoenberg, Schuller, Schwantner, and Ralph Vaughan Williams. Contemporary composers, such as the many Ostwald and CBDNA winners, Warren Benson, Mark Camphouse, Thomas Duffy, David Gillingham, and Frank Ticheli, have composed major works, intrigued that a band composition may have hundreds of performances while an orchestral work may wait for a repeat performance.

Because education is a state responsibility, there is great variety in the way instrumental music is organized in the schools. The National Association for Music Education (MENC) has developed Standards for Music Education, and most districts require certified instrumental music teachers. Some districts provide released-time homogeneous classes as early as the 3rd grade, while others offer heterogeneous classes somewhere between the 4th and 7th grades. Publishers currently offer a tremendous amount of music, including original as well as simplified arrangements of standard works, using a grading system designed to help directors determine which compositions their groups can effectively perform. While there is some variety among publishers, the American Band College's "Music Grading Chart" is increasingly accepted as standard. Works

The Ohio State University Marching Band, 1978. (Marvin Fong/The Plain Dealer/Landov)

are graded according to meter, key signature, tempo, rhythm, articulation, and instrument range: elementary (1–2), intermediate (3–4), advanced (4–6). John Edmondson, Frank Erickson, John Kinyon, Anne McGinty, Paul Murtha, John O'Reilly, Robert Sheldon, Michael Story, and Michael Sweeney are a few of the many who have artistically composed for the lower grades. Modern technology, including DVDs and CDs, is used to motivate the students with music to which they can easily relate. Depending on the level, there is an exciting variety of activities, with students involved in marching and concert performances, festivals, national and international tours, and composer-in-residence programs.

The clinics started by Harding in 1930 to help young band directors inspired the formation of the Mid-West Band Clinic in 1946 (now the Midwest Clinic). The aim is still pedagogical: to provide an opportunity for directors to hear new music, showcase outstanding ensembles and present clinics by model teachers. The 64th Clinic (2010) featured 39 performing organizations, 63 clinics, 361 exhibitors of music, musical instruments and accessories, and over 14,000 attendees.

(iii) Marching bands. In contrast to the seated concert bands, marching bands are obviously mobile, just as their forerunners were. Whether a civic parade or an elaborate half-time show, the musicians must be able to move, and the music loud enough to be heard outdoors. Instrumentation is accordingly determined by the occasion and the venue, just as in earlier periods. Marches are naturally a major part of their repertoire, but football halftime shows have become elaborate pageants; directors aim for the unusual, the exotic, and the spectacular. Bands may reach immense proportions, and are increasingly brass and percussion. The "drumline" has become especially important: the snare, tenor (or timp toms), and bass drums provide an underlying cadence. Some bands include a stationary pit section, with timpani, xylophones, bells, vibraphones, marimbas, gongs, guitars, and synthesizers (*see* Drum corps). Military precision marching may give way to ever higher, more unusual, and faster steps. William Foster combined jazz, rock, and African American elements in his routines at Florida A&M University: his band danced and gyrated down the field at a cadence of 320 steps per minute. Drill teams, color guards, and dance lines have become increasingly popular. So too with competitions: Music for All (founded 1976) and the US Scholastic Band Association (USSBA, formed 1988) organize events with over 700 high school bands participating. Asserting that athletic bands are purveyors of school tradition, pageantry, and pride on campus, CBDNA has developed a set of guidelines. In order to support these activities, many schools organize band camps during the summer, usually in August; basic fundamentals are taught, music distributed for memorization, and sectional rehearsals held for one or two weeks before the semester begins.

The Fightin' Texas Aggie Band of Texas A&M University is one of the largest marching bands in the world. Note the preponderance of brass instruments in its instrumentation (Table 1, 2011). The Aggie Band, whose 350 (sometimes as many as 450) musicians are all ROTC cadets, operates under strict military guidelines as an integral part of the Corps of Cadets. The director, Timothy Rhea, has a full-time staff of five assistants; he is also director of the University's elite wind symphony.

(iv) Community bands. According to the Association of Concert Bands, an organization devoted to fostering adult concert bands, the number of such civic groups continues to increase. Their primary aim is entertainment,

both for the musical gratification of the members and the enjoyment of the audiences. Many of the more than 5000 part-time bands, such as the Indiana Wind Symphony and the Virginia Grand Military Band, have achieved professional levels. The more proficient bands perform serious music by the composers mentioned in section (i) above, along with exceptional works, some commissioned by these groups, by John Barnes Chance, James Curnow, Robert Jager, W. Francis McBeth, Roger Nixon, Alfred Reed, and William Schuman. As in the Golden Age, marches, novelty numbers, transcriptions of orchestral works, potpourris, and dances are ever popular, although the dances will be modern and the selections most often from Broadway shows, films and folk songs by such established composers/arrangers as Warren Barker, Robert Russell Bennett, Jerry Brubaker, James Christensen, and Clare Grundman. Lucien Cailliet, Mark Hindsley, Donald Hunsberger, and Erik Leidzén have made excellent transcriptions that closely adhere to the orchestral originals.

Perry Watson was influential in founding the North American Brass Band Association (NABBA) in 1983 to "foster, promote, and otherwise encourage the establishment, growth, and development of amateur and professional British-style brass bands throughout the United States and Canada." NABBA adopted the basic British instrumentation (Table 1, 1983), holds yearly graded competitions (Youth through advanced Championship level), and publishes an online journal-newsletter, *Brass Band Bridge*.

In 1938 R.F. Goldman stated that the primary purpose of bands was "to entertain rather than to educate or elevate." In 1961 he felt that the purpose was "to educate." One can only be reminded of Sousa's comment: "[Theodore] Thomas had a highly organized symphony orchestra, with a traditional instrumentation; I a highly organized wind band with an instrumentation without precedent. Each of us was reaching an end, but through different methods. He gave Wagner, Liszt, and Tchaikovsky in the belief that he was educating his public; I gave Wagner, Liszt, and Tchaikovsky with the hope that I was entertaining my public."

While not thought of as bands in the military or symphonic sense, Dixieland, swing, bop, rock, and fusion bands carry on traditions established many years ago. (It is worth noting that the innovative Beatles LP *Sgt. Pepper's Lonely Hearts Club Band* showed the performers in uniform.) Jazz is now an accepted curriculum in most colleges, and the period of the "Big Bands," meaning the Swing era, has been considered worthy of historical research. Dissertations relating to bands are increasingly accepted, and scholarly articles are being published not only in the *Journal of Band Research* but also the NBA, MENC, and WASBE journals and IGEB's *Alta Musica* series. IGEB has established a biennial Thelen Prize for the best dissertation on wind music research. Clearly, wind music is no longer only associated with marches, entertainment music, and amateur performers.

BIBLIOGRAPHY

E. Howe: *First Part of the Musician's Companion* (Boston, 1844)

E.K. Eaton: *Twelve Pieces of Harmony for Military Brass Bands* (New York, 1846)

A. Dodworth: *Dodworth's Brass Band School* (New York, 1853/*R*)

G.W.E. Friederich: *Brass Band Journal* (New York, 1853–4) [music; some parts repr. as *American Brass Band Journal*]

W.C. Peters & Sons: *Peters' Sax-Horn Journal* (Cincinnati, 1859)

G.F. Patton: *A Practical Guide to the Arrangement of Band Music* (Leipzig, 1875/*R*)

W.H. Dana: *J. W. Pepper's Practical Guide and Study to the Secret of Arranging Band Music, or The Amateur's Guide* (Philadelphia, 1878)

A.A. Clappé: *The Wind-band and its Instruments* (New York, 1911/*R*)

E.F. Goldman: *Band Betterment* (New York, 1934)

R.F. Dvorak: *The Band on Parade* (New York, 1937)

R.F. Goldman: *The Band's Music* (New York, 1938)

C.B. Righter: *Gridiron Pageantry: the Story of the Marching Band for Bandsmen, Directors and Football Fans* (New York, 1941)

R.F. Goldman: *The Concert Band* (New York, 1946)

F. Fennell: *Time and the Winds* (Kenosha, WI, 1954)

F.N. Mayer: *A History of Scoring for Band* (diss., U. of Minnesota, 1957)

H.W. Schwartz: *Bands of America* (Garden City, NY, 1957/*R*)

Band Music Guide (Evanston, IL, 1959, 9/1989)

K. Berger: *Band Encyclopedia* (Evansville, IN, 1960)

J. Wagner: *Band Scoring* (New York, 1960)

R.F. Goldman: *The Wind Band* (Boston, 1961/*R*)

J. Felts: "Some Aspects of the Rise and Development of the Wind Band during the Civil War," *Journal of Band Research*, iii/2 (1967), 29–33

H.H. Hall: *The Moravian Wind Ensemble: Distinctive Chapter in America's Music* (diss., George Peabody College for Teachers, 1967)

G. Grose: "Patrick S. Gilmore's Influence on the Development of the American Concert Band," *Journal of Band Research*, vi/1 (1970), 11–16

A.G. Wright and S. Newcomb: *Bands of the World* (Evanston, IL, 1970)

J.T. Haynie: *The Changing Role of the Band in American Colleges and Universities, 1900 to 1968* (diss., George Peabody College for Teachers, 1971)

L.K. McCarrell: *A Historical Review of the College Band Movement from 1875 to 1969* (diss., Florida State U., 1971)

C.H. Tiede: *The Development of Minnesota Community Bands during the Nineteenth Century* (diss., U. of Minnesota, 1971)

D. Whitwell: A *New History of Wind Music* (Evanston, IL, 1972)

W.A. Bufkin: *Union Bands of the Civil War (1862–65): Instrumentation and Score Analysis* (diss., Louisiana State U., 1973)

C. Bryant: *And the Band Played On* (Washington, DC, 1975)

L. Smith: *A Study of Historical Development of Selected Black College and University Bands as a Curricular and Aesthetic Entity* (diss., Kansas State U., 1976)

F.M. Marciniak: "The American Band of Providence," *Journal of Band Research*, xiii/1 (1977), 7–9

D. Whitwell and A. Ostling, Jr., eds.: *The College and University Band* (Reston, VA, 1977)

F.J. Cipolla: "Annotated Guide for the Study and Performance of Nineteenth Century Band Music in the United States," *Journal of Band Research*, xiv/1 (1978), 22–40

F.J. Cipolla: "A Bibliography of Dissertations Relative to the Study of Bands and Band Music," *Journal of Band Research*, xv/1 (1979), 1–31; xvi/1 (1980), 29–36

J. Newsom: "The American Brass Band Movement," *Quarterly Journal of the Library of Congress*, xxxvi (1979), 114–39

K.E. Olson: *Music and Musket: Bands and Bandsmen of the American Civil War* (Westport, CT, 1981)

J.P. Watson: *Starting a British Band* (Grand Rapids, MI, 1982/*R*)

D. Whitwell: *The History and Literature of the Wind Band and Wind Ensemble* (Northridge, CA, 1982)

M. Good: "A Selected Bibliography for Original Concert Band Music," *Journal of Band Research*, xviii/2 (1983), 12–35; xix/1 (1983), 26–51

P.J. Martin: *A Status Study of Community Bands in the United States* (diss., Northwestern U., 1983)

D. Eiland: "A Bibliography of Histories of College and University Bands," *Journal of Band Research*, xxix (1984), 31–8
R. Garofalo and M. Elrod: *A Pictorial History of Civil War Era Musical Instruments & Military Bands* (Charleston, WV, 1985)
P. Watson: *The Care and Feeding of a Community British Brass Band* (Farmingdale, NY 1986)
N.E. Smith: *March Music Notes* (Lake Charles, LA, 1986)
M.H. and R.M. Hazen: *The Music Men: an Illustrated History of the Brass Bands in America, 1800–1920* (Washington, DC, 1987)
R.M. Rasmussen: *Recorded Concert Band Music, 1950–1987: a Selected, Annotated Listing* (Jefferson, NC, 1988)
R.F. Camus: "Early American Wind and Ceremonial Music 1636–1836," *The National Tune Index*, phase 2 (New York, 1989) [incorporated into Keller, 2002]
J.T. Humphreys: "An Overview of American Public School Bands and Orchestras before World War II," *Bulletin of the Council for Research in Music Education*, no.101 (1989), 50–60
K. Kreitner: *Discoursing Sweet Music: Town Bands and Community Life in Turn-of-the-Century Pennsylvania* (Urbana, IL, 1990)
W.H. Rehrig: *The Heritage Encyclopedia of Band Music* (Westerville, OH, 1991, suppl., 1996); CD-ROM (Oskaloosa, IA, 2005)
R.F. Camus: *American Wind and Percussion Music* (Boston, 1992)
N.M. Hosler: *The Brass Band Movement in North America: a Survey of Brass Bands in the United States and Canada* (diss., Ohio State U., 1992)
R.F. Camus: "The early American Wind Band: Hautboys, Harmonies, and Janissaries," *The Wind Ensemble and its Repertoire*, ed. F. J. Cipolla and D. Hunsberger (Rochester, 1994), 57–76
J. Newsom: "The American Brass Band Movement in the Mid-Nineteenth Century," *The Wind Ensemble and its Repertoire*, ed. F.J. Cipolla and D. Hunsberger (Rochester, NY, 1994), 77–94
D.B. and M.J. Powell: *The Fightin' Texas Aggie Band* (College Station, TX, 1994)
F. Battisti: *The Twentieth Century American Wind Band/Ensemble: History, Development and Literature* (Fort Lauderdale, FL, 1995)
J.T. Humphreys: "Instrumental Music in American Education: in Service of Many Masters," *Journal of Band Research*, xxx/2 (1995), 39–70
J. Manfredo: *Influences on the Development of the Instrumentation of the American Collegiate Wind Band and Attempts for Standardization of the Instrumentation from 1905–1941* (Tutzing, 1995)
E.C. Koehler: *Banda Minichini: an Italian Band in America* (diss., John Hopkins U., 1996)
M.D. Martin: "Band Schools in the United States: A Historical Overview," *Journal of Historical Research in Music Education*, xxi/1 (1999), 41–61
R.J. Meaux: "A Selected Bibliography of the Marching Band: 1980–1998," *Journal of Band Research*, xxxv/2 (2000), 75–92
R.M. Keller, R.F. Camus, K.V.W. Keller, and S. Cifaldi, eds.: *Early American Secular Music and Its European Sources, 1589–1839: an Index* (Annapolis, 2002) [available at <http://www.colonialdancing.org/Easmes/index.html>]
R. Demkee: *The Band Plays On! The Allentown Band's 175th Anniversary* (Yardley, PA, 2003)
R.K. Hansen: *The American Wind Band: a Cultural History* (Chicago, 2005)
H.H. Hall: *A Johnny Reb Band from Salem: the Pride of Tarheelia* (Raleigh, 2/2006)
R.W. Holz: *Brass Bands of the Salvation Army: their Mission and Music* (Stotfold, UK, 2006, 2007)
F.J. Cipolla and D. Hunsberger, eds.: *The Wind Band in and Around New York ca. 1830–1950*. (Van Nuys, CA, 2007)
D. Herak: *NABBA: 25-years of NABBA History* (Columbus, OH, 2007)
R.W. Holz: *The Proclaimers: A History of the New York Staff Band [1887–2007]* (New York, 2007)
M.D. Moss: *Concert Band Music by African-American Composers: 1927–1998* (Tutzing, 2009)

RAOUL F. CAMUS

Band, the. Canadian rock group. It comprised ROBBIE ROBERTSON (*b* Toronto, ON, 5 July 1943; electric guitar and songwriting), Levon Helm (*b* Elaine, AR, 26 May 1940; *d* Woodstock, NY, 19 April 2012; drums), Richard Manuel (*b* Stratford, ON, 3 April 1943; *d* Winter Park, FL, 4 March 1986; piano and songwriting), Rick Danko (*b* Simcoe, ON, 29 Dec 1942; *d* Hurley, NY, 10 Dec 1999; bass guitar, fiddle, mandolin, and songwriting), and Garth Hudson (*b* Windsor, ON, 2 Aug 1937; organ, accordion, woodwind, and brass). All except Hudson also sang.

Following a move to Toronto in 1958, the Arkansas rockabilly performer RONNIE HAWKINS hired a backing group that later became the Band. Helm was the original drummer, but other positions in the group changed for three years, until Robertson, Manuel, Danko, and Hudson were established as permanent members. In 1964 the group left Hawkins and performed first as the Levon Helm Sextet, then Levon Helm and the Hawks, and finally as the Band. The group was hired by Bob Dylan to back him on his first electric rock tour (1965) and its well-honed skills in rock and roll, blues, and country helped Dylan define his sound as a rock performer. Dylan and the Band's year-long sojourn in a house near Woodstock, New York, in 1967 resulted in a series of innovative songwriting and recording experiments, documented in Dylan's album *The Basement Tapes* (CBS, 1975).

The Band's first recording in their own right was the album *Music from Big Pink* (Cap., 1968), which established the group as eclectic performers, drawing rock, country, folk, blues, and Cajun music into a blend that suggested a deep affection for the music of the American South. Their second album, *The Band* (Cap., 1969), featured "Up on Cripple Creek," the group's only top 40 single, as well as "The Night they Drove Old Dixie Down," a song reflecting on the loss of the Civil War from a poor white Southerner's perspective, which became a top five hit for Joan Baez in 1971. The title track of their third album, *Stage Fright* (Cap., 1970), chronicled the group's mixed feelings about their roles as rock performers. *Cahoots* (Cap., 1971) featured songs written around the theme of small town and rural America's decline and the loss of communities and livelihoods in the face of modernization. The group explored new musical directions on this recording, including brass arrangements by Allen Toussaint. Its live album, *Rock of Ages* (1972), has received widespread acclaim and was followed by a collection of early rock and rhythm-and-blues covers, *Moondog Matinee* (Cap., 1973), which revisited the roots of their sound and capitalized on nostalgia in the 1970s for 1950s' rock and roll.

The group worked again with Dylan in the period 1973–4, performing on his album *Planet Waves* and touring with him. They then returned to the studio for the album *Northern Lights–Southern Cross* (Cap., 1975), which featured longer songs and re-established the group's lyrical interest in the myths and stories of North American history. This is well illustrated in such songs as "Acadian Driftwood," which recounted the exile of Canada's Acadian French from Nova Scotia to Louisiana. The group stopped working together in 1976 and released another live album and a final studio recording, *Islands* (Cap., 1977). In 1978 the director Martin Scorsese released *The Last Waltz*, a highly acclaimed documentary of a performance given on 25 November 1976 by the Band and a number of high-profile guests. Each of the group's members subsequently worked at solo careers, although the group never formally broke up. However, when the other members tried to rekindle the Band in the early 1980s, Robertson declined to join them. Manuel's suicide in 1986 halted their efforts until the mid-1990s, when Hudson, Danko, and Helm reformed the group and made three more albums. Further collaboration was halted by Danko's death in 1999.

Through their spare but imaginative musicianship, as well as the small town, working class and often historical narratives explored in their lyrics, the Band carved a unique and unexpected niche in rock's history. They frequently referenced the past and carefully cultivated a seemingly anti-modern sound, steeped in various sorts of traditional music from the American South. Songs portraying small-town lives and scenes from a vanishing rural Americana supported this ethos, further underscored by the group's imagery—members sometimes dressed like 19th-century Southern American gentlemen.

However, the Band was not restricted to these conceits and sometimes made use of contemporary grooves and technology to augment their sound. Hudson's timbral experiments with the Lowrey organ were influential, and the group's vocal harmonies, which stress the members' individual vocal timbres over a more blended sound, is recognized as one of its signature features.

RECORDINGS
(selective list)

Music from Big Pink (Cap., 1968); *The Band* (Cap., 1969); *Stage Fright* (Cap., 1970); *Caboots* (Cap., 1971); *Rock of Ages* (Cap., 1972); *Moondog Matinee* (Cap., 1973); *Northern Lights—Southern Cross* (Cap., 1975); *Islands* (Cap., 1977); *The Last Waltz* (WB, 1978); *Jericho* (Pyramid, 1993)

BIBLIOGRAPHY

D. Emblidge: "Down Home with the Band: Country-Western Music and Rock," *EthM*, xx (1976), 542–52

G. Marcus: *Mystery Train: Images of America in Rock 'n' Roll Music* (New York, 1982)

N. Minturn: *The Last Waltz of the Band* (Hillsdale, NY, 2005)

CHRIS MCDONALD

Banda [Banda Sinaloense]. *Banda* (band) is a generic Spanish term for a variety of ensembles consisting of brass, woodwind, and percussion instruments found throughout Latin America. Introduced in the mid-1800s, brass bands were a fixture of Mexico's musical life in the late 19th century and flourished in both rural and urban areas. With the revolutionary movement (1910–20) *bandas populares* (popular bands) developed pronounced regional characteristics, and the lineup in regional bands became increasingly more standardized.

Among the many regional bands, *banda sinaloense* (Sinaloan banda) stands out, as this type gained a reputation in the international popular music market at the close of the 20th century. The ensemble dates back to the military bands of European colonists and to the brass music of German immigrants to Mexico's northern Pacific coast in the mid-19th century. After its consolidation in the early 20th century, band membership in Sinaloa averaged from nine to 12 musicians playing clarinets, cornets or trumpets, trombones with valves, saxhorns, tubas, snare drums (*tarola*), and a double-headed bass drum with attached cymbals (*tambora*). While the drums were manufactured locally, all wind instruments were imported from Europe.

Bandas performed at various outdoor celebrations. Like the military bands of that time, they played an eclectic repertory of marches, operatic selections, and popular pieces. Although brass band music had long served as one of the educated class's favorite pastimes, *bandas* eventually became associated with lower-class music, rejected by the elite as a crude imitation of their venerable military bands by ignorant peasants who could do no better. *Banda* musicians' low social status was related to the alleged low quality of their music and to the rather disreputable locales where some of them found work. Urbanization, capitalism, and eventually the culture industry altered Sinaloa's society, lifestyles, habits, and popular musical tastes, but *bandas* remained popular among the rural population and the lower-class urbanites throughout the 20th century.

In the 1950s and 1960s some of the urban popular bands became involved with the newer technological media of radio and recordings. Entrepreneurial bandleaders began to modify the makeup of the traditional band by incorporating Cuban percussion instruments, slide trombones, and saxophones, which allowed them to perform a more cosmopolitan repertory of mainstream dance music and popular international pieces, such as big band mambo—yet with an unmistaken *sabor sinaloense* (Sinaloan flavor). This distinct Sinaloan character resulted from the contrast of wood and brass timbres, a dynamic alternation between the whole band and the individual instrument groups of the front line (trumpets, trombones, and clarinets), and the improvisation of countermelodies by one of the frontline musicians, a technique often used while accompanying vocalists.

The main appeal of *banda* was, and continues to be, its danceable rhythms ranging from the local *son*, *guaracha*, polka, waltz, and schottische to the international fox trot, Cuban *danzón*, bolero, mambo, and cha-cha. Early 21st-century transnational and commercially oriented Sinaloan bandas such as Banda El Recodo and Banda La Costeña furthermore began to emphasize the visual and the verbal and shifted their musical repertory toward the more universally appealing danceable *cumbia* and the romantic *balada*.

BIBLIOGRAPHY

H. Simonett: *Banda: Mexican Musical Life across Borders* (Middletown, CT, 2001)

H. Simonett: *En Sinaloa nací: Historia de la música de banda* (Mazatlán, Mexico, 2004)

HELENA SIMONETT

Banda El Recodo (de Cruz Lizárraga). Internationally renowned Mexican *banda*, originally from the village of El Recodo, some 30 miles from Mazatlán, Sinaloa. Clarinetist Cruz Lizárraga (*b* El Recodo, 1918; *d* Mazatlán, 1995), who led the band starting in 1938, secured a recording session with RCA-Victor in Mexico City in 1954 which helped to establish the band's name beyond its regional confines. Its key to success was the musicians' ability to accommodate their *ranchera* (country) music to an urban audience of the upper social strata by adopting international popular dance styles from fox trot and Cuban *danzón* to mambo and *cumbia*. Due to the band's professional accomplishments, Lizárraga was always able to recruit the best performers out of a large pool of regional musicians. Although Banda El Recodo recorded with famous ranchera singers such as José Alfredo Jiménez in 1968, it was not until the early 1990s, when Sinaloan *banda* entered a new phase of international commercialization, that it began to integrate vocalists into the hitherto purely instrumental makeup. After Lizárraga's death, his sons resumed leadership of the band. Nowadays, Banda El Recodo is one of Sinaloa's commercially oriented, high-profile touring bands that perform styles increasingly defined by the transnational music market.

BIBLIOGRAPHY

H. Simonett: *Banda: Mexican Musical Life across Borders* (Middletown, CT, 2001)

HELENA SIMONETT

Bandmaster. The master, leader, or director of a band.

See Band, Military music, §3.

Band organ. A mechanical organ (known as "fairground organ" in Europe) used to provide music for merry-go-rounds and in amusement parks, circuses, and skating rinks in Europe and the United States. The instrument originated in Europe as an outdoor version of the Orchestrion, voiced to sound above the hurly-burly of the fairground. Initially it was put near the entrance in order to attract attention. It was usually built in an elaborately carved and colourfully painted case which sometimes incorporated moving figures in its façade. All but the very largest instruments were designed to be portable, robust enough to travel around the country on rough roads. With the coming of bioscope (moving picture) theaters, the organ sometimes became the front of the show-tent, its façade incorporating entry and exit doors.

The earliest band organs, developed during the 18th century, were essentially barrel organs: they had a wooden cylinder or barrel covered with metal pins that formed a musical program. By about 1880 such instruments were being produced in large sizes containing several hundred pipes and a variety of percussion effects. These large models were powered by steam or water engines and later by electric motors. In the United States Eugene DeKleist of North Tonawanda, New York, was an important builder of barrel-operated band

Steam calliope drawn by six elephants, color lithograph, 1857. (Collection of the New-York Historical Society, USA/ The Bridgeman Art Library)

organs. In 1892 Gavioli of Paris developed a new mechanism for playing organs in which a series of perforated cardboard sheets were hinged together to form a continuous strip. As this was drawn across the keyframe by rubber-covered rollers, the music was read by a row of small metal keys which extended through the perforations and caused the appropriate pipe to speak via a responsive pneumatic mechanism. Other keys operated percussion effects or could turn ranks of pipes on and off. Barrel organ manufacture declined after 1900, and the cheaper and more versatile "book music" system came to be used extensively by European builders such as Gasparini, Limonaire, and Marenghi (all in Paris); Hooghuys (Geraadsbergen, Belgium); Mortier (Antwerp); Wrede (Hanover); Ruth and Bruder (both Waldkirch); Wellershaus (Mülheim an der Ruhr); and Frati (Berlin).

Shortly after 1900 the German organ-building business of Gebrüder Bruder adopted the perforated paper-roll playing action. As with the player piano, the musical program was arranged as a series of perforations in a roll of paper that was passed over a tracker bar (initially of wood but later of brass) containing a single row of openings along its length. When a hole in the tracker bar was uncovered by a perforation passing over it, air was sucked into the hole and thus triggered a pneumatic mechanism to sound a note or operate an organ function. This system was later taken up in America by the Rudolph Wurlitzer Manufacturing Co. of North Tonawanda, which was the manufacturing agent for many European musical instruments and eventually had its own factories. Most instruments made in the United States employing this system used vacuum (negative pressure) to read the rolls; European organs used positive pressure, but in Europe the paper-roll system was never widely adopted for organs, and Gebrüder Bruder remained the principle manufacturer of this system. As with book music, the choice of tunes available on rolls was unlimited; selections ranged from classical pieces to the popular songs of the day.

The pipework in fairground organs consisted of both flue and reed pipes voiced on 203 to 304 mm of water-gauge pressure. Flue pipes were the organ's equivalent of flutes, piccolos, violins, and cellos; reed pipes imitated trumpets, clarinets, baritones, and trombones. Pipes were usually made of wood, but in the earlier organs the reed pipes had polished brass resonators arranged symmetrically in the façade. Organs ranged in compass from 35 to 112 notes. The pipework was divided into bass, accompaniment, melody, and counter-melody sections. On a small organ a typical distribution of notes in each section might be 5, 9, 14, and 13; on a large instrument it could be 21, 16, 21, and 38. Only in very large instruments were these sections chromatic. Certain notes of the scale were omitted in smaller organs in order to keep the physical size of the instrument to a minimum; this permitted them to be played only in certain keys, precluding the correct performance of many pieces; arrangers would often modify the music to fit a given organ scale.

For many years the American manufacture of band organs was centered in North Tonawanda. In 1893 DeKleist formed the North Tonawanda Barrel Organ Works to produce barrel-operated organs and pianos; the firm became a supplier to the Rudolph Wurlitzer Company in 1897, at which time it became the DeKleist Musical Instrument Manufacturing Co. Wurlitzer purchased the company in 1908, and continued to manufacture band organs in large quantities through the 1920s; production then declined and ended in 1939. Two other firms of band-organ makers that were formed in North Tonawanda by former employees of DeKleist were the North Tonawanda Musical Instrument Works, active from about 1906 to 1918, and Artizan Factories, which operated from 1922 through the late 1920s. In Brooklyn, New York, the B.A.B. Organ Company was in business from the 1920s to 1957; this firm manufactured folding cardboard music books and paper music rolls, and converted many band organs of other types to systems that used these devices.

The economic conditions of the 1930s caused the failure of most band organ companies, though a small number of craftsmen still build instruments and restore original organs. A rich postwar revival has resulted in the building of a number of new instruments.

BIBLIOGRAPHY

R. de Waard: *Van speeldoos tot pierement* (Haarlem, 1964; Eng. trans., 1967)

F. Wieffering: *Glorieuze orgeldagen* (Utrecht, 1965)

E.V. Cockayne: *The Fairground Organ: its Music, Mechanism and History* (Newton Abbot, 1970)

R. de Waard: *Het draaiorgel* (Alkmaar, 1971/*R*)

Q.D. Bowers: *Encyclopedia of Automatic Musical Instruments* (New York, 1972)

A.W.J.G. Ord-Hume: *Barrel Organ* (London, 1978)

A.A. Reblitz and Q.D. Bowers: *Treasures of Mechanical Music* (New York, 1981)

H. Jüttemann: *Waldkircher Dreh- und Jahrmarkt-Orgeln* (Waldkirch, 1993)

DURWARD R. CENTER/ARTHUR W.J.G. ORD-HUME/R

Bang, Billy [Walker, William Vincent] (*b* Mobile, AL, 20 Sept 1947; *d* Harlem, NY, 11 April 2011). Jazz violinist and composer. He moved with his mother to the Bronx as a young child and attended school in Harlem where he played the conga. Bang took up violin at the age of 12 and played it in his school orchestra. After studying with a scholarship at the Stockbridge School, MA (1961–3), he served a tour of combat duty in the Vietnam War and subsequently joined the anti-war movement. Bang was inspired to take up violin again by the records of Ornette Coleman and Leroy Jenkins. He purchased an instrument at a pawnshop in 1968 and was playing professionally by 1972 after studying with Jenkins and practicing with Eric Dolphy records. He was active in the New York avant-garde loft scene, leading the Survival Ensemble and playing with Sam Rivers and Frank Lowe, and in 1977 he formed the critically acclaimed String Trio of New York with James Emery and John Lindberg, a collaboration that lasted until 1986. He also played with Dennis Charles and Ronald

Shannon Jackson's Decoding Society, and alongside Sonny Sharrock in Bill Laswell's Material. During the early 1980s Bang performed with Marilyn Crispell in various contexts and in a collective with Andrew Cyrille. In the early 1990s he collaborated with Rashied Ali, Sun Ra, and William Parker, and during the following decade he recorded two albums, *Vietnam: the Aftermath* (2001, Justin Time) and *Vietnam Reflections* (2005, Justin Time), that were inspired by his experience of the Vietnam War. Bang's playing strikes a balance between blues inflected foundations and the creative freedom espoused by Coleman and the AACM.

BIBLIOGRAPHY

B. Rusch: "Billy Bang: Interview," *Cadence*, vi/11 (1980), 5
L. Jeske: "Billy Bang," *DB*, xlviii/9 (1981), 26 [incl. discography]
K. Whitehead: "String Trio of New York: a Decade of Perserverance," *DB*, liv/11 (1987), 26 [incl. discography]
G. Lock: "Strings can really hang you up the most," *Wire*, no. 57 (1988), 26
F. Jung: "A Fireside Chat with Billy Bang" <http://www.allaboutjazz.com/php/article.php?id=711>

BARRY LONG

Bang on a Can. Musical collective based in New York. Bang on a Can encompasses a yearly new-music marathon concert, a touring ensemble, a commissioning fund for new works, a summer music institute, a recording label, and a loosely-based compositional aesthetic. In 1987 fellow Yale composition alumni MICHAEL GORDON, DAVID LANG, and JULIA WOLFE staged the First Annual Bang on a Can Music Marathon, a 12-hour event held at a downtown New York art gallery. The concert, which featured performances by local musicians, showcased not only recent compositions by the organizers and their peers, but also a wide array of "revolutionary classics" such as Steve Reich's *Four Organs* (1970) and Milton Babbitt's *Vision and Prayer* (1961). A key goal of the concert was to question boundaries drawn between different compositional camps. Since its founding, the yearly show has grown to incorporate works by non-Western ensembles, jazz artists, and avant-garde rock musicians.

In 1992 Gordon, Lang, and Wolfe established the Bang on a Can All-Stars, a touring ensemble designed to showcase highlights from the marathon concert. An amplified group originally composed of cellist Maya Beiser, double bassist ROBERT BLACK, pianist Lisa Moore, percussionist Steven Schick, electric guitarist Mark Stewart, and clarinetist/saxophonist EVAN ZIPORYN, the ensemble's eclectic instrumentation allowed the All-Stars to perform pieces from a number of different musical styles and traditions. In 1995 they released *Industry*, a CD on Sony Classical featuring music by Gordon, Lang, Wolfe, and Louis Andriessen. After putting out recordings on Nonesuch and Point Music, the All-Stars found a new home on Cantaloupe Music, a label set up in 2000 by the Bang on a Can founders.

Bang on a Can has been involved in a number of grassroots endeavors designed to nurture the contemporary music community. In 1997 they formed the People's Commissioning Fund, a program which pools donations from individuals to support the creation and performance of new works by emerging composers, many of whom blend classical and popular styles. Bang on a Can's Summer Institute of Music, launched in 2002 at MASS MoCA (the Massachusetts Museum of Contemporary Art), targets young composers and musicians. Through mentorships under seasoned composers such as Terry Riley, masterclasses, music business seminars, and Balinese gamelan workshops students gain a deeper understanding of how to operate within the new music realm.

Music critics, pointing to the types of works presented on Bang on a Can's concerts and recordings, often label the collective's signature sound as post-minimalist in character. Like the music of minimalists Steve Reich and Philip Glass, many of the compositions by the Bang on a Can founders, as well as featured artists such as Annie Gosfield and Arnold Dreyblatt, revolve around the repetition of short rhythmic and melodic motives. At the same time, Bang on a Can compositions differ markedly from Reich and Glass in their incorporation of harmonic dissonance, use of thematic contrast, and approach to compositional processes.

RECORDINGS
(selected)

Bang on a Can Live Volume 1, CRI, CD 628 (1992); *Bang on a Can Live Volume 2*, CRI, CD 646 (1993); *Bang on a Can Live Volume 3*, CRI, CD 672 (1994); *Industry*, Sony Classical, CD SK 66483 (1995); *Cheating, Lying, Stealing*, Sony Classical, CD SK 62254 (1996); *Music for Airports—Brian Eno*, Point Music, CD 314 563 847–2 (1998); *Renegade Heaven*, Cantaloupe, CD CA21001 (2000); *Terry Riley In C*, Cantaloupe, CD CA21004 (2001); *Classics*, Cantaloupe, CD CA21010 (2002)

BIBLIOGRAPHY

E. Ziporyn: "Who Listens If You Care?" *New Observations*, lxxxvi (1991), 25–8
K. Gann: "The Rhythms of Totalism: Rhys Chatham, Mikel Rouse, Michael Gordon, Kyle Gann, Larry Polansky, Ben Neill," *CMR*, x (1993), 33–50
A. McCutchan: "David Lang," *The Muse that Sings: Composers Speak about the Creative Process* (New York, 1999), 219–27
F. Richard, R. Kessler, and F.J. Oteri: "Interview with Bang on a Can," *New Music Box* (1 May 1999) <http://www.newmusicbox.org/page.nmbx?id=01fp00>
M. Alburger: "Bang on an Ear: An Interview with David Lang," *21st-century Music*, vii/9 (2000), 1–14
K. Gann: "Minimal Music, Maximal Impact," *New Music Box* (1 Nov 2001) <http://www.newmusicbox.org/page.nmbx?id=31tp00>
R. Fink: "(Post-)minimalisms, 1970–2000: the Search for a New Mainstream," *The Cambridge History of Twentieth-century Music* (Cambridge, UK, 2004), 539–56
C. Sun: "Resisting the Airport: Bang on a Can Performs Brian Eno," *Musicology Australia*, xxix (2007), 135–59

MARGARET MARTIN

Bangs, Lester [Conway] (*b* Escondido, CA, 13 Dec 1948; *d* New York, NY, 30 April 1982). Rock critic. Bangs's parents were devout Jehovah's Witnesses; he was raised mostly by his mother after his father died in a house fire in 1955. Bangs began writing freelance reviews for *Rolling Stone* magazine in 1969, and would go on to write for *Creem*, *The Village Voice*, *Penthouse*, *Playboy*, *New Musical Express*, and many others. He wrote a 1980 book on the new-wave act Blondie and co-authored, with Paul Nelson, a biography of Rod Stewart, but the published works for which he is best known remain the two posthumous anthologies of his rock criticism: *Psychotic Reactions and Carburetor Dung* (New York, 1987), edited by Greil Marcus; and *Mainlines, Blood Feasts, and Bad Taste* (New York, 2003), edited by John Morthland.

Bangs was inspired by the drug-fueled stream-of-consciousness style of Beat poets like William S. Burroughs and the confrontational, subjective New Journalism of Hunter S. Thompson and Tom Wolfe. Alongside John Mendelssohn, Nick Tosches, and Richard Meltzer, Bangs was grouped into the subset of early rock critics dubbed "the Noise Boys," whose wild, digressive, slang-filled style contrasted with the more sober, academic approach of Greil Marcus and Robert Christgau. Bangs was an advocate of what would come to be called "punk rock," celebrating its return to the raw, amateur spirit that defined the earliest rock 'n' roll. He wrote critical pieces on many of the scene's seminal acts, including The Ramones, Iggy and the Stooges, and the Velvet Underground. "I finally realized that grossness was the truest criterion for rock 'n' roll, the cruder the clang and grind the more fun and longer listened-to the album would be," Bangs wrote, and his prose aspired towards the same energy. Bangs died from respiratory and pulmonary complications related to the ingestion of Darvon.

BIBLIOGRAPHY

J. DeRogatis: *Let it Blurt: The Life and Times of Lester Bangs* (London, 2001)

JAYSON GREENE

Banjo. A plucked string instrument with a long guitar-like neck and a circular soundtable, usually called the "head," of tautly stretched parchment or skin (now usually plastic), against which the bridge is pressed by the strings. The banjo and its variants, classified as plucked lute chordophones, have had long and widespread popularity as folk, parlor, and professional entertainers' instruments. It used to be speculated that the name of the instrument probably derived from the Portuguese or Spanish bandore, but another possibility, at least as likely, comes out of recent research into West African plucked lute traditions, which has identified at least six traditional plucked lutes whose necks are made from a thick stalk of papyrus, known throughout the Senegambian region by the Mande term "bang" (also "bangoe," "bangjolo," "bangjulo," "bung," "bungo").

1. Structure. 2. History.

1. Structure. The modern five-string banjo is normally fitted with raised frets and strung with steel wire strings. It is tuned *g′–c–g–b–d′* (C tuning) or *g′–d–g–b–d′* (G tuning), but many other tuning patterns, such as *g′–c–g–c′–d′*, *g′–d–g–c′–d′*, and *g′–d–g–a–d′*, are used to facilitate the playing of particular tunes/songs. Usually 24 or more screw-tightening brackets (for adjusting the head tension) are attached to the outer side of a tambourine-like rim of laminated wood about 28 cm in diameter. In banjos of high quality the upper edge over which the head is stretched is often of complicated design (usually involving a "tone ring"), as in an early (1920s) "Mastertone" system of O.H. Gibson, or the "Electric" design of A.C. Fairbanks. A pan-shaped wooden "resonator" is often attached to the lower side of the otherwise open-backed body and serves to reflect outward the sound emitted by the underside of the head. The "thumb string" (sometimes known in older literature as "chanterelle"), the short fifth string, is placed adjacent to the lowest-pitched string and secured by a peg inserted into the side of the neck at the fifth fret position.

Until the early 20th century banjos were normally strung with gut strings, and these or nylon strings are still used by "minstrel" and "classic" banjoists. Raised frets were advocated by James Buckley in *Buckley's New Banjo Method* (1860) but did not become common until the 1880s. Mid-19th-century banjos tended to be larger than modern ones. The earliest documented tuning was *c′–f–c–e–g*, quickly raised to *d′–g–d–f♯–a*, and then (by 1958) to *e′–a–e–g♯–b*. By the mid-1880s most banjos were of modern proportions and commonly tuned to the modern C tuning (*g′–c–g–b–d′*). All of these tunings maintain the same interval relationship. In the United States, at the point the banjo was pitched in C, it became a transposing instrument with music still written in "A notation," a situation that continued until 1909 when the American Guild of Banjoists, Mandolinists, and Guitarists voted to abandon the old A notation and write the music in C or "English notation." In England both the written and tuning pitch were fixed at the modern level by the 1880s.

A number of hybrid and specialized banjos were developed during the late 19th and early 20th centuries, including cello and piccolo banjos (tuned an octave below and above the regular banjo), banjeurines (tuned a 4th above the regular banjo), and "ladies" and "pony" banjos (slightly smaller than a regular banjo), all of the above being five-string instruments; guitar, mandolin and ukulele banjos (strung and tuned like their parent instruments); and plectrum banjos (in structure and tuning like the regular banjo but lacking the fifth string). The tenor banjo (tuned *c–g–d′–a′*) is similar to the regular banjo but has a shorter neck and no fifth string. Like the plectrum banjo it was developed for use in jazz and dance orchestras and is played with a plectrum. It has been widely adopted by players of traditional music in Ireland and England.

In England and Australia banjos with six or more strings were common during the late 19th century, the additional strings serving to extend the compass downwards. Another English type, the "zither banjo," never adopted in the United States although invented by and brought to England by an American, Alfred Cammeyer, in the late 1880s, had first, second, and fifth strings made of wire (the others were gut or wire-wound silk), frets, geared tuning machines instead of the more usual friction pegs, and a fifth string that was tunneled from the fifth fret to the peghead. It also had an integral closed back, functioning much like a modern resonator, very similar to the closed back on banjos made by the

American makers Henry Dobson and George Teed of New York.

2. History. The development of the modern banjo began in the second quarter of the 19th century as an increasingly commercial adaptation of an instrument used by enslaved West Africans in the New World, specifically in the Caribbean, as early as the 17th century. The earliest evidence of plucked lutes comes from Mesopotamia around 6000 years ago; this instrument type gradually moved west into Egypt in the time of the Pharaohs, and from there across North Africa and then across the Sahara to West Africa, where a vast array of distinct plucked lutes evolved.

Recent research in West African music has revealed more than 60 plucked lute instruments, all of which, to a lesser or greater degree, show some resemblance to the banjo, and therefore could perhaps be conceived, collectively, to be precursors to the banjo. Prior to around 2000, the favored candidates as antecedents to the banjo were the Malian Bamana *ngoni* and Senegalese Wolof *xalam* type of semi-spike, wood-bodied lutes of the griots. However, another category of more recently investigated West African plucked lutes bears the greatest resemblance to the early New World banjo: full-spike, gourd-bodied, folk/artisan (i.e. non-griot) plucked lutes from the Greater Senegambian region. "Full-spike" means that the round stick neck goes fully through, or over the rim of, the body of the instrument and projects out the tail-end, to which the strings are attached. Other characteristics of these instruments include a body made from a gourd or a calabash over which is stretched an animal skin, a floating bridge (a carved, two-footed piece that sits on the skin "head," held in place by the tension of the strings), and, most commonly, three strings (two long, one short) that are tied to sliding rings on the neck. Examples of such West African plucked lutes include the Jola (Diola) *ekonting/akonting* (Gambia/Senegal/Guinea-Bissau), the Manjago (Manjak) *bunchundo/buchundo* (Gambia/Guinea-Bissau), and the Papel *busunde* (Guinea-Bissau). While semi-spike (neck ending before reaching the tail-end of the body, with a fan-shaped bridge attached to the end of that neck through a hole in the skin head), wood-bodied griot lutes differ in structure from the full-spike, gourd, non-griot lutes, they share the skin head, round stick neck, sliding rings for tuning, and, most importantly, the short drone string plucked with the thumb, which is a defining feature of both the early New World banjos and the modern five-string banjo.

West African plucked lutes are generally played with two fingers (thumb and either index or middle finger), either up-picking or down-picking (or, much more rarely, with a plectrum). Semi-spike, wood-bodied griot lutes are overwhelmingly played in an up-picking manner, while full-spike, gourd-bodied folk/artisan lutes are most commonly played in a down-picking manner. The prevailing down-picking style of the latter type of West African lutes looks and sounds astonishingly like the earliest documented playing style of the banjo, the minstrel era "stroke" style, as well as the folk styles known as frailing or clawhammer.

Dena Epstein, in her *Sinful Tunes and Spirituals; Black Folk Music to the Civil War*, stated that "the *banza* or banjo, seems to have been the most widely reported and longest lived of all the African instruments in the New World." The earliest New World reference to enslaved West Africans playing instruments apparently similar to the gourd-bodied West African lutes just described dates from 1627 in the Caribbean, instruments that may or may not have been early banjos. By the late 17th century, what may be called the "early gourd banjo" had emerged in the Caribbean.

The first definitive description of an early gourd banjo comes from Sir Hans Sloane, an English physician visiting Jamaica, who called this Afro-Caribbean instrument a "strum strump" in a 1687 journal entry. Between this time and the middle of the 19th century 35 Caribbean references to banjo-like instruments played by enslaved Africans and their descendants have been uncovered. Few offer any description of the instrument; those that do mention only a gourd or calabash body, a skin head, and a long neck. However, illustrations—in Sloane's *A Voyage to the Islands of Madeira, Barbados, Nieves, S. Christopher and Jamaica* (London, 1707) and John Stedman's *Narrative of a Five-year's Expedition Against the Revolted Negroes of Surinam from the Year 1772 to 1777* (1796, 2/1806/*R*)—and extant instruments—the "Stedman Creole-Bania" (*c*1770s) in the Rijksmuseum voor Volkenkunde, Leiden, and the recently rediscovered "Haiti banza" (*c*1840) in the Musée de la Musique, Paris—show that these instruments differ from their African antecedents by having flat necks rather than a rounded stick neck and having pegs for mounting and tuning strings rather than leather thong rings. These new features represent a process of creolization: gourd body with drum head, full-spike neck, short drone string from West Africa, and flat neck/fingerboard with peghead and tuning pegs from Europe, the latter most likely inspired by Spanish and Portuguese plucked lutes encountered in the Caribbean, such as the vihuela de mano, guitar, tiple, and cavaquinho. By 1708 and into the early 19th century, this instrument is referred to by some version of the word "banjo" (19 different spellings, from "banza" to "bonjoe").

The first image of this creolized early gourd banjo in North America is a watercolor, "The Old Plantation" (1785–90), in the Abby Aldrich Rockefeller Folk Art Museum, Williamsburg, showing a group of slaves in South Carolina dancing to the music of a stick-played drum and a gourd-bodied banjo with all of the characteristics just noted. Taking this image together with the Sloane and Stedman images, the extant Suriname and Haiti instruments, and the most detailed of the Caribbean textual descriptions, one can state that the most common form of the early gourd banjo throughout the New World had four strings: three long strings of equal length and a short top "thumb string."

The earliest reference to the banjo in North America appeared in 1736 in John Peter Zenger's *The New-York*

Weekly Journal. He published an anonymous letter which described blacks playing the "Banger" at a fair held in a "Field, little Way out a Town" to mark an unspecified holiday (perhaps Pinkster). Further references to black banjo players in the 18th century are found in runaway slave advertisements in newspapers. Between 1748 and 1799, 18 runways were identified as banjo players in Maryland (6), Virginia (5), Delaware (2), North Carolina (1), South Carolina (1), New York (1), New Jersey (1), and Pennsylvania (1). As in the Caribbean references, the instrument's name had multiple spellings, but in no case did the writers see a need to describe it. Dena Epstein presents another eight references to black banjo playing, to accompany singing and dancing, in the 18th century, almost all of them from Virginia and Maryland, with more variant spellings. The most well-known of these references is that by Thomas Jefferson, who, in his *Notes on the State of Virginia* (Paris, 1784), stated of the negroes: "The instrument proper to them is the Banjar…its chords [strings] being precisely the four lower chords of the guitar." The common English guitar of the period was tuned *C–e–g–c′–e′–g′*; hence the banjar would have been tuned either *C–e–g–c′*, if by "lower" Jefferson meant "lower in pitch," or else *g–c′–e′–g′*, if he meant "lower in position when held by the player." The former interpretation gives a traditional tuning pattern still sometimes used for the banjo's four full-length strings; the latter gives the pattern of the modern G tuning.

As of this writing, no evidence has been found to document the playing of the banjo in the 18th century by white persons. Because of close contact between enslaved African Americans and white indentured servants, some have speculated, not illogically but without documentation, that at least a few whites must have taken up the banjo from an early date. The earliest evidence of whites playing the banjo occurs concurrently, in the 1820s and 30s, with the growth of blackface performances by whites, on stage and in the circus, of songs, dances, and skits supposedly based on rural slave life. These performances did not initially involve the banjo, but apparently created the conditions leading some whites to learn, from African Americans, to play it. The most important of these, by far, was JOEL WALKER SWEENEY of Appomattox, Virginia.

In the past, Sweeney has been credited, incorrectly, with adding the short fifth string to the banjo and also the thin bent-wood, open-back rim. As noted above, the short drone string had been a feature of the instrument going back to Africa. And the bent-wood frame construction appears to have been an alternate to the gourd body type among African Americans by the early 19th century. Sweeney may have added a bass string, extending downward the range of the instrument. He certainly may be credited with popularizing the kind of banjo he played, the frame-bodied, five-string banjo, and, if not with being the first white person to play the instrument, then the first professional banjoist in the public record, and the one who brought the banjo into blackface minstrelsy in 1836. Through the influence of Sweeney, Dan Emmett and many other popular minstrel-show banjoists, many of whom probably learned from black banjo players, the banjo was rapidly introduced to white urban culture.

The wood-frame banjo was better suited to commercial mass-production, and by the 1840s and 50s banjos were being produced by the first known commercial maker, William Boucher of Baltimore (by 1845), and James Ashborn of Wolcottville, Connecticut (by 1850). Banjo-related patents began in 1850, with one granted to Ashborn. About 45 of Boucher's banjos are known to be extant. Over time, hundreds of manufacturers built instruments to supply the burgeoning popularity of the banjo.

By around 1860, and possibly earlier, the banjo had also taken root among traditional white musicians of the rural South, who, like Sweeney, had learned about it from direct contact with African American musicians, as well as touring minstrel shows, medicine shows, and circuses. The banjo had joined the fiddle to initiate a tradition of what is now called "old-time string band music," and was also played as a solo instrument for dancing and to accompany songs. The black tradition remained fairly strong in the rural South through the 1930s, but by the 1990s few black players remained. Until the latter decades of the 20th century, interplay between the black and white traditions was common.

Two general classes of playing styles, each with many variations, have developed. No detailed descriptions or notations of playing style are known before the 1850s, when the first minstrel banjo tutors were published. The "stroke" style they teach produces a sound similar to that described in many of the earlier accounts. It is similar to the earliest style of rural southern white banjo players, today known as "clawhammer" or "frailing," in which patterns of downward strikes by the index or middle fingernail are combined with downward strokes of the thumb against the fifth string. More complex patterns may be produced by the thumb dropping further down to pick individual notes on the full length strings. The other major family of styles, "finger-picking," combines upward plucking by the first, and sometimes second and third fingers, with downward plucks of the fifth and other strings by the thumb. In both styles the fingers of the left hand, in addition to merely stopping strings at particular fret positions, pluck, hammer, and slide on individual strings to contribute additional notes and rhythmic accents.

Finger-picking is first mentioned in the *Briggs' Banjo Instructor* (1855) as an alternate, guitar-like way to accompany songs (called "guitar style" at first), and is more fully described in an 1865 tutor by Frank B. Converse, who credited the Buckley family with being the first to play it. By the 1890s it had become the dominant style on the minstrel, vaudeville, and concert stages and for amateur urban musicians, but the down-stroking styles remained popular in many rural areas until well into the 20th century. Finger-style playing became increasingly well established after 1900 in the rural folk tradition, both black and white. At first, folk finger styles were primarily two-finger picking (i.e. thumb and index finger), but a three-finger style (adding the middle finger) was popularized in the 1920s by the North Carolina banjo player Charlie Poole, and somewhat later by Dewitt "Snuffy" Jenkins and others from the region. In the 1940s it was further developed by Earl Scruggs into "bluegrass picking," the most widely heard style today.

After the 1850s the banjo was increasingly used in the United States and England as a genteel parlor instrument for the performance of popular music. During the last quarter of the century S.S. STEWART of Philadelphia, and other banjo popularizers, sought to upgrade the instrument's social standing by downplaying its black origins and disparaging the "old-fashioned" stroke style in favor of the more "elevated" finger-picking style. Their marketing campaigns were successful, and the period from 1890 to 1930 saw a vast expansion in the production of banjos and great elaboration in their design and decoration, by makers such as Stewart, the Dobsons (New York and Boston) and A.C. Fairbanks (Boston). Besides making regular banjos, these makers (primarily Stewart) created a set of banjo orchestra instruments, all with five strings but of different sizes and pitches. From about 1890 to 1920 there was a craze for banjo, mandolin, and guitar clubs and orchestras; by the turn of the century most good-sized cities and colleges had such organizations. In this period specialized journals and great quantities of marches, rags, and transcriptions of popular and light classical music were published for banjo by Stewart, Walter Jacobs of Boston, Clifford Essex of London, and others.

The banjo's important relationship to popular music at that time is well illustrated in the case of RAGTIME. Nathan (1962) finds in some minstrel-show banjo tunes the earliest examples of the kinds of syncopation that later appear in the genre. Banjo pieces such as George Lansing's *The Darkie's Dream* (1887) are among the precursors of ragtime; ragtime itself immediately entered the banjo repertory, and banjo compositions from the mid-1890s onwards were heavily influenced by ragtime. The recorded output of the greatest turn-of-the-century banjo recording artists, VESS OSSMAN and FRED VAN EPS, includes many rags, and banjo recordings of ragtime (available long before ragtime piano recordings were issued) were influential in increasing its popularity. Other important concert banjo virtuosos of the time included Parke Hunter, Alfred A. Farland, and Fred Bacon.

By the 1920s the popularity of the five-string banjo was rapidly declining among urban players. It was displaced by the four-string tenor and plectrum banjos, which were favored as rhythm instruments in the jazz and dance orchestras of the day, largely because a pick-played banjo was louder and better suited to the music for the fast, rhythmic new dance steps. The first true tenor banjo (with four strings, 10–11 inch rim, *c–g–d′–a′* tuning, 17 frets, and called a "tenor banjo") was advertised by the Vega Company in 1912, but Vega had been making these instruments on a custom basis since 1908. Such an instrument found ready acceptance among mandolinists and violinists, whose original instruments did not adapt well to the new music. Regular banjoists converted more easily to the plectrum banjo. Once introduced, these instruments did not long remain as mere accompanying rhythm instruments; solo styles developed, as did virtuoso soloists such as Eddie Peabody and Harry Reser. The "Jazz Age" created a new society craze for the banjo, this time in its four-string versions. By the 1940s, however, the four-string banjo was being replaced by the guitar, especially the electric guitar, as the rhythm instrument of choice; and by then the five-string banjo had also been abandoned by many rural musicians, either in favor of the guitar, or because of the decline in home music-making.

The five-string banjo regained something of its former popularity after World War II, largely because of the influence of the American banjoists PETE R. SEEGER, who popularized traditional rural southern styles among urban players as one aspect of the folksong revival, and Earl Scruggs (*see* FLATT AND SCRUGGS), who became famous as the developer of the "bluegrass" style of banjo playing (*see* BLUEGRASS MUSIC). It has also regained some popularity as a newgrass and jazz instrument through the virtuosity of such performers as Bela Fleck. The revival of frailing or clawhammer banjo playing is still strong among old-time musicians, and recent years have seen an active revival of the minstrel stroke style (and the manufacture of appropriate period reproduction banjos) and, among African American musicians, a growing movement to recapture the banjo as part of their musical heritage.

In the southeast United States, many white traditional country musicians still played banjos through the 20th century; their many tunings, playing techniques, and repertory include survivals of 19th-century practice. The Archive of Folk Culture, Library of Congress, Washington, DC, has a good collection of field recordings of such music, as does the Southern Folk-Life Collection (Wilson Library, University of North Carolina, Chapel Hill, NC). In the United States the American Banjo Fraternity promotes classic banjo playing and holds biannual conventions. Among the few composers to score for the instrument are Weill (*Mahagonny*, 1927), Krenek (*Kleine Sinfonie*, op.58, 1928) and Peter Maxwell Davies (*The Boy Friend*, 1971).

Public instrument collections possessing banjos include the Smithsonian Institution, Washington, DC; the Metropolitan Museum of Art, New York; the Stearns Collection of Musical Instruments, University of Michigan, Ann Arbor; and the Victoria and Albert Museum, London.

BIBLIOGRAPHY

T.F. Briggs: *Briggs' Banjo Instructor, Containing the Elementary Principles of Music* (Boston, 1855/*R*)
The Cadenza (1894–1924)
The Crescendo (1908–33)
P. Seeger: *How to Play the 5-String Banjo* (New York, 1948, 3/1962)
H. Nathan: *Dan Emmet and the Rise of Early Negro Minstrelsy* (Norman, OK, 1962, 2/1977)
D.J. Epstein: "Slave Music in the United States before 1860: a Survey of Sources," *Notes*, xx (1962–3), 195–212, 377–90
B.C. Malone: *Country Music U.S.A.: a Fifty-Year History* (Austin, TX, 1968, 2/1985)
A. Rosenbaum: *Old-Time Mountain Banjo: an Instruction Method* (New York, 1968)

C.P. Heaton: "The Five-String Banjo in North Carolina," *Southern Folklore Quarterly*, xxxv (1971), 62–82

T. Adler: "The Physical Development of the Banjo," *New York Folklore Quarterly*, xxviii (1972), 187–208

D.J. Epstein: "African Music in British and French America," *MQ*, lix (1973), 61–91

R.C. Toll: *Blacking Up: the Minstrel Show in Nineteenth-Century America* (New York, 1974)

D.J. Epstein: "The Folk Banjo: a Documentary History," *EthM*, xix (1975), 347–71

R.L. Webb: "Banjos on their Saddle Horns," *American History Illustrated*, xi/2 (1976), 11–20

R.B Winans: "The Folk, the Stage, and the Five-String Banjo in the Nineteenth Century," *Journal of American Folklore*, lxxxix (1976), 407–37

D.J. Epstein: *Sinful Tunes and Spirituals: Black Folk Music to the Civil War* (Urbana, IL, 1977)

R.B. Winans: "The Black Banjo-Playing Tradition in Virginia and West Virginia," *Journal of the Virginia Folklore Society*, i (1979), 7–30

R.B. Winans: "Black Instrumental Music Traditions in the Ex-Slave Narratives," *Black Music Research Newsletter*, v/2 (1982), 2–5

S. Cohen: "Banjo Makers and Manufacturers," *Mugwumps*, vii (1983), 10–16

R.L. Webb: *Ring the Banjar! The Banjo in America from Folklore to Factory* (Cambridge, MA, 1984)

U. Wegner: *Afrikanische Saiteninstrumente* (Berlin, 1984)

R.B. Winans: "Early Minstrel Show Music, 1843–1852," *Musical Theatre in America*, ed. G. Loney (Westport, CT, 1984), 71–97

N.V. Rosenberg: *Bluegrass: a History* (Urbana, 1985)

G. Kubik: "The Southern Periphery: Banjo Traditions in Zambia and Malawi," *World of Music*, xxxi/1 (1989), 3–29

R.B. Winans: "Black Instrumental Music Traditions in the Ex-Slave Narratives," *Black Music Research Journal*, x (1990), 43–53

M.T. Coolen: "Senegambian Influences on Afro-American Musical Culture," *Black Music Research Journal*, xi (1991), 1–18

M. Hendler: *Altwelticbe Wurzeln eines neuweltlichen Musikinstruments: Verschuttete Spuren zur Vor- und Fruhgeschichte der Saiteninstrumente* (Göttingen, 1991)

K.E. Linn: *That Half-Barbaric Twang: the Banjo in American Popular Culture* (Urbana, IL, 1991)

G. Gruhn and W. Carter: *Acoustic Guitars and Other Fretted Instruments: a Photographic History* (San Francisco, 1993)

U. Heier and R.E. Lotz, eds: *The Banjo on Record: a Bio-Discography* (Westport, CT, 1993)

A. Tsumura: *1001 Banjos* (New York, 1993)

P.F. Gura: "Manufacturing Guitars for the American Parlor: James Ashborn's Wolcottville, Connecticut, Factory, 1851–56," *Journal of the American Antiquarian Society* (1994), 117–56

R.B. Winans and E. Kaufman: "Minstrel and Classic Banjo: American and English Connections," *AM*, xii/1 (1994), 1–30

C. Conway: *African Banjo Echoes in Appalachia: a Study of Folk Traditions* (Knoxville, TN, 1995)

P.F. Gura and J.F. Bollman: *America's Instrument: the Banjo in the Nineteenth Century* (Chapel Hill, NC, 1999)

B. Carlin: *The Birth of the Banjo: Joel Walker Sweeney and Early Minstrelsy* (Jefferson, NC, 2007)

W.R. Dobbins: *Tambourines, Bone Castanets, and Banjos Meet Jump Jim Crow: a History of Blackfaced Minstrelsy in America from 1828 to 1898: a Forgotten Heirloom in American Entertainment* (Parker, CO, 2011)

JAY SCOTT ODELL, ROBERT B. WINANS

Banjo, Mandolin, Guitar movement. A loose association of instrument manufacturers, music publishers, professional performers, teachers, and amateur players dedicated to promoting the banjo, mandolin, and guitar (BMG) as solo and ensemble instruments for the concert hall. The movement coincided with the spread of mass production and mail-order magazines in the music industry and remained closely tied to music publishers and instrument manufacturers. Rooted in the activities of Samuel Swaim Stewart, a banjo manufacturer, music publisher, and creator of *Stewart's Banjo and Guitar Journal* (1882–1901), the movement coalesced as other publishers and manufacturers imitated him with magazines promoting the fretted instruments. While early manufacturers and magazines focused on the banjo, the mandolin eventually became the principal instrument of the movement. The guitar generally played a supporting role in BMG ensembles. BMG magazines supported the industry with promotional reviews and direct access to consumers while the industry supported the magazines with advertising. Initially centered in the northeast, the BMG movement expanded nationally and internationally.

Instrument technology loomed large in the movement, and design changes to the five-string banjo drove early BMG advocates like Stewart. Early BMG proponents created professional, semi-professional, and student ensembles of banjos and guitars to perform popular dance tunes and occasional light classical numbers. The Boston Ideals were a top professional BMG ensembles of the late 19th century, touring widely in the Northeast. Reflecting strong commercial ties, publishers produced works for these ensembles, while manufacturers developed new instruments aimed at them. By the early years of the 20th century, the mandolin superseded the banjo, and manufacturers created a family of mandolins, imitating the sized instruments of the standard string ensemble. Mandolin orchestras, sometimes comprising 100 or more plucked instruments (often augmented by standard orchestral instruments), became the performance focal point of the movement. While many ensembles played popular tunes, some performed light classics and a few attempted more sophisticated works by Haydn, Mozart, Beethoven, Liszt, and Wagner.

The BMG cause was promoted (and documented) in BMG magazines like *Cadenza*, *Crescendo*, *American Music Journal*, *Allegro*, and others. While some publications were little more than advertising sheets, other magazines featured technical and pedagogical articles, concert and product reviews, biographies of historical and contemporaneous performers, and musical scores of solo and ensemble works. In 1901, East Coast BMG leaders created the American Guild of Banjoists, Mandolinists and Guitarists, an official association dedicated to advancing the three instruments and their music. Publishers Clarence Partee, Walter Jacobs, H.F. Odell, and the Gibson Mandolin-Guitar Company vigorously promoted the movement and the Guild.

Important members of the BMG movement included banjoists Alfred Farland and Frederick Bacon, mandolinists Giuseppe Pettine and Samuel Siegel, and guitarists William Foden and Vahdah Olcott Bickford. The most important BMG magazines ceased publication by 1935, and formal mandolin orchestras gave way to ensembles performing popular and novelty numbers with tenor banjos, saxophones, Hawaiian guitars, percussion, and eventually electric guitars. While the Guild persisted into the 1950s, the movement splintered as new musics and new instruments dominated America's musical culture.

BIBLIOGRAPHY

S. Hambly: *Mandolins in the United States Since 1880: an Industrial and Sociological History* (diss., U. of Pennsylvania, 1977)

P. Ruppa: *The Mandolin in America after 1880 and the History of Mandolin Orchestras in Milwaukee, Wisconsin* (diss., U. of Wisconsin-Milwaukee, 1988)

P.F. Gura and J.F. Bollman: *America's Instrument: the Banjo in the Nineteenth Century* (Chapel Hill and London, 1999)

J. Noonan: *The Guitar in America as Reflected in Topical Periodicals, 1882–1933* (diss., Washington U. in St. Louis, 2004)

J. Noonan: *The Guitar in America: Victorian Era to Jazz Age* (Jackson, MS, 2008)

J. Noonan: "Highbrow, Lowbrow and Middlebrow: an Introduction to America's Progressive Era Mandolin Orchestra," *Musique/Images/Instruments: Revue française d'organologie et d'iconographie musicale*, 12 (2010), 171–189

JEFFREY J. NOONAN

Banks, Brian Robert (*b* Seattle, WA, 5 March 1964). Composer. He holds degrees from the Peabody Institute of Music (BA 1986), the San Francisco Conservatory (MM 1998), and University of California at Berkeley (PhD 1995). He studied under Morris Moshe Cotel, ANDREW IMBRIE, RICHARD FELCIANO, and OLLY W. WILSON JR. In 1996, Banks received a Fulbright Scholarship for research and instructing in Mexico, where he has continued to teach at the Universidad de las Américas Puebla.

Banks's music is often scale-based, often featuring octatonic and pentatonic scales. Some of his works display a rich interaction between popular musical idioms (jazz, blues, klezmer, rock, and danzón), and contemporary techniques, as in the Serenata no.1 (*Legados imaginarios*). An interest in improvisation has led him to include controlled improvisatory sections (Piano Sonatas nos.1, 3, and 4, the Second Violin Sonata, and the Suite for cello and piano). His early vocal music reflected both aleatoric rhythms and the use of quotation from medieval and Renaissance music. An avid reader of poetry, Banks has set to music texts by Sor Juana Inés de la Cruz, Emily Dickinson, and William Stafford. His music is commissioned and performed both in Mexico and in the United States.

ANA R. ALONSO-MINUTTI

Bannock. Native American group of the Great Basin area. *See* PAIUTE.

Baptist Churches. The first Baptist church in America was founded by English immigrants at Providence, Rhode Island, in 1639, and by 1700 there were at least 24 congregations. From these modest beginnings the denomination has grown into the largest Protestant Christian body in the United States, including dozens of distinct subgroups as well as numerous independent churches that are not part of conventions or associations. As suggested by their name, believers' baptism by immersion is one of the hallmark doctrines of the church. Other beliefs generally held include the priesthood of the believer, a symbolic view of the Lord's Supper, the authority of the Bible as a guide to faith and practice, and the autonomy of the local church.

While some 17th-century English Baptists objected to congregational singing in worship, most of the early American churches apparently practiced psalm singing, probably using texts and tunes from Thomas Sternhold and John Hopkins's *Whole Book of Psalms* or from Henry Ainsworth's *Book of Psalms Englished both in Prose and Metre*. In some cases singing was abandoned when large numbers of non-singing English Baptists immigrated to America and joined these churches. Objections to singing in Baptist worship began to die out during the 18th century, and by mid-century many non-singing congregations had adopted or reintroduced psalmody, while newly formed churches sang from their inception. Like other early American denominations with Puritan leanings, Baptists generally lined out the psalms and sang without accompaniment during the 17th and 18th centuries.

The congregational song collections used by Baptists in America during the 18th and early 19th centuries were usually of English origin. In addition to or as a successor to Sternhold and Hopkins, some 18th-century Baptist churches sang from Tate and Brady's *New Version of the Psalms*. This was succeeded during the second half of the century by various editions of ISAAC WATTS's psalms and hymns, frequently supplemented by Englishman John Rippon's *A Selection of Hymns* (London, 1787, repr. New York and Elizabethtown, 1792). Earlier editions of Watts were replaced in common use by the *Psalms and Hymns of Dr. Watts Arranged by Dr. Rippon* (London, 1801/*R*), often known as "Rippon's Watts."

The first Baptist hymnal compiled in America, *Hymns and Spiritual Songs* (the "Newport Collection"), was issued anonymously at Newport, Rhode Island, in 1766. This contained mainly hymns by Watts and the English Baptist writer Joseph Stennett, but does not appear to have been widely used. In 1790 the Philadelphia Association—at that time the largest Baptist denominational body in the United States—put forth *A Selection of Psalms and Hymns*; this was the first authorized hymnal published by any Baptist group in America. However, it was not until the publication of James Winchell's *An Arrangement of the Psalms, Hymns, and Spiritual Songs of the Rev. Isaac Watts* (Boston, 1818), with its supplement of "more than three hundred hymns," that an American compilation seriously rivaled British collections among Baptists, especially in New England. "Rippon's Watts" continued in use in the Middle Atlantic States until both it and "Winchell's Watts" were superseded by Baron Stow and Samuel F. Smith's *The Psalmist* (Boston, 1843). In addition to its popularity, *The Psalmist* was significant because it was the first Baptist hymnal to be given a national denominational imprimatur in the United States. It also marked a turning away from "Watts entire" and from collections that were merely supplemental to Watts. Smith, the author of "My Country, 'Tis of Thee," was the most important Baptist hymn text writer of the 19th century until the development of the gospel song.

A volume that was somewhat outside the mainstream of Baptist hymnody in the North was Joshua Smith's *Divine Hymns* (Portsmouth, 1791). This collection was one of the first American hymnals to contain a large number of vernacular hymn texts and was widely used in rural areas, reaching at least 24 editions or reprints. Though *Divine Hymns* seemingly had little direct impact on standard Baptist hymnals in the North, it did serve as a significant source of texts for tunebooks compiled by the non-Baptists Samuel Holyoke (*The Christian Harmonist*, Salem, MA, 1804) and Jeremiah Ingalls (*The Christian Harmony*, Exeter, NH, 1805).

The denomination also counted several important composers among its members, including Oliver Holden—the composer of "Coronation," the oldest American tune still in common use—and Oliver Shaw, both of whom wrote music specifically for Baptist churches as well as for other communions. Holyoke's *The Christian Harmonist* was the first tunebook published specifically for Baptists in America, but it was not authorized or adopted by any denominational organization and apparently saw little use.

During the 18th century, Baptists in all parts of the country generally shared the same hymn texts and tunes. After 1800, however, Baptists of the South relied increasingly on regional and vernacular words and music. The first Baptist hymnal published in the South was *Collection of Sacred Ballads* (n.p., 1790) by the Virginians Richard and Andrew Broaddus. A. Broaddus's later hymnals *The Dover Selection of Spiritual Songs* (Richmond, VA, 1828) and *The Virginia Selection of Psalms, Hymns, and Spiritual Songs* (Richmond, 1836) were both recommended by the Dover Baptist Association of Virginia. The most popular southern collections (all words-only) included JESSE MERCER's *The Cluster of Spiritual Songs* (Augusta, GA, 1810), Starke Dupuy's *Hymns and Spiritual Songs* (Frankfort, KY, 1811), William Dossey's *The Choice* (Philadelphia, 1820), and Staunton S. Burdett's *Baptist Harmony* (Philadelphia, 1834). A number of congregations, especially in urban areas, adopted Stow and Smith's *The Psalmist* when it was published in 1843. Three widely used southern shapenote tunebooks, heavily influenced by camp-meeting and folk melodies, were compiled by Baptists: William Walker's *The Southern Harmony* (New Haven, CT, 1835), B.F. White and E.J. King's *The Sacred Harp* (Philadelphia, 1844), and John G. McCurry's *The Social Harp* (Philadelphia, 1855).

Controversies among Baptists caused a division of the denomination into Northern and Southern Baptist Conventions in 1845. Dissatisfaction with the absence from *The Psalmist* of some of the most popular hymns among Southern Baptists led two prominent pastors, Richard Fuller and J.B. Jeter, to compile a supplement to it in 1847. While this helped increase circulation of *The Psalmist* in the South, pressure was building for the publication of a regional collection. The *Baptist Psalmody* (Charleston, SC, 1850) of Basil Manly and Basil Manly, Jr., was the first hymnal to be officially sanctioned by the Southern Baptist Convention and gained rapid acceptance in the South, holding much the same place that *The Psalmist* did in the North.

The most important influence on late 19th-century Baptist hymnody was the emergence of the Sunday school song and the gospel song. Many prominent Sunday school and gospel songwriters were Northern Baptists, for example, WILLIAM BATCHELDER BRADBURY (composer of "Jesus Loves Me"), ROBERT LOWRY (author/composer of "Shall We Gather at the River"), WILLIAM H. DOANE (composer of "To God be the Glory"), and GEORGE C. STEBBINS (composer of "Woodworth"). A few individuals advocated the adoption of English liturgical hymnody among Baptists in the North, including E.H. Johnson, whose *Sursum corda* (Philadelphia, 1898) was not widely used but provided this type of material for the churches that wanted it. *The Baptist Hymnal* (Philadelphia, 1883)—for which Doane served as musical editor and Johnson as associate musical editor—as well as similar collections that attempted to balance liturgical hymnody with the gospel song were more widely accepted.

The New Baptist Hymnal, produced jointly by Northern and Southern Baptists in 1926, became popular in the North but found less favor in the South. Northern Baptists (who renamed themselves the American Baptist Convention in 1950 and the American Baptist Churches USA in 1972) published the hymnals *Christian Worship* (Philadelphia, 1941) and *Hymnbook for Christian Worship* (Valley Forge, PA, 1970), both jointly compiled with the Disciples of Christ. Arthur N. Wake prepared a handbook for the latter collection titled *Companion to Hymnbook for Christian Worship* (St. Louis, MO, 1970). The Northern convention has not published a hymnal since 1970.

Late 19th-century Southern Baptists wholeheartedly embraced gospel songs, which became the new basis of their congregational singing. This emphasis on the gospel song continued well into the 20th century in such books as Robert H. Coleman's independently produced *The Modern Hymnal* (Dallas, TX, 1926) and *The American Hymnal* (Dallas, 1933) and the denominational collection *The Broadman Hymnal* (Nashville, TN, 1940). The last-named—one of the best-selling American hymnals of all time, with more than ten million copies distributed—was edited by B.B. McKinney, the Southern Baptists' most popular gospel song writer and the music editor for a number of Coleman's books. A more eclectic approach was taken in three books issued by the Southern Baptist Sunday School Board during the second half of the century, each named *Baptist Hymnal* (Nashville, 1956, 1975, 1991); the last two of these were distinctive for the large number of texts and tunes by Baptists they contained. Companions for the 1956 and 1975 hymnals (*Hymns of Our Faith*, Nashville, 1964; *Companion to Baptist Hymnal*, Nashville, 1976) were prepared by William J. Reynolds, who had served as editor of the latter book, and a team of nine Baptist writers did the same for the 1991 volume (*Handbook to the Baptist Hymnal*, Nashville, 1992). A fourth recent denominational collection with the title *Baptist Hymnal* (Nashville, 2008) accentuates popular Christian music styles, while an independently produced book designed for both Baptist and ecumenical use, *Celebrating Grace* (Macon, GA, 2010), emphasizes contemporary hymns in more traditional styles.

Other bodies among the larger Baptist groups include Free Will Baptists, Seventh-Day Baptists, Primitive Baptists, and Regular Baptists. The hymnals of Free

Will Baptists—so-called because of their doctrine of free grace—range from John Buzzell's *Psalms, Hymns and Spiritual Songs* of 1823 (Kennebunk, ME) to Vernon Whaley (ed.), *Rejoice: The Free Will Baptist Hymn Book* (Nashville, 1988). Seventh-Day Baptists, who worship on Saturday rather than Sunday, issued *A New Selection of Psalms and Hymns* (Schenectady, NY, 1826), *Christian Psalmody* (New York, 1847), and *The Seventh-Day Baptist Praise Book* (Westerly, RI, 1879). Among Primitive Baptists, Benjamin Lloyd's *The Primitive Hymns* (Wetumpka, AL, 1841) has continued in use to the present day, as have John R. Daily and E.W. Thomas's *Primitive Baptist Hymn and Tune Book* (Luray, VA/Danville, IN, 1902), C.H. Cayce's *The Good Old Songs* (Thornton, AR, 1913), and J.A. Monsees and J. Harvey Daily's *The Old School Hymnal* (Luray, VA/Atlanta, GA, 1920). Some Regular Baptist churches continue the practice of lining out folk hymns, while others sing gospel-style hymns and have dispensed with lining out.

African American Baptists are organized into three main denominational entities. The National Baptist Convention, USA, issued *The National Baptist Hymnal* (Nashville, 1903), *Gospel Pearls* (Nashville, 1921, a significant collection of standard hymns, gospel songs, and African American spirituals), and *The Baptist Standard Hymnal* (Nashville, 1924), the last-named continuing in use into the 21st century. *The New National Baptist Hymnal* (Nashville, 1977) and its *21st Century Edition* (Nashville, 2001) were important collections from the National Baptist Convention of America, while the Progressive National Baptist Convention published the *Progressive Baptist Hymnal* (Washington, DC, 1976) and *The New Progressive Baptist Hymnal* (Washington, DC, 1982), both revisions of earlier hymnals from other groups.

Baptist churches are free to make use of any hymnal or none at all, and in the late 20th and early 21st centuries some churches have made use of collections from other denominations or from independent publishers, while others have abandoned hymns and hymnals altogether in favor of choruses and contemporary Christian music sung from song sheets or electronic projection. Most churches have sought some sort of balance between hymns, gospel songs, and contemporary Christian music, either by providing multiple worship services or by combining the various types in a single service.

Like other dissenting denominations in America, Baptists rejected the use of choirs and musical instruments in worship until the late 18th century. The earliest record of choral singing dates from the year 1771, when a choir was formed at the First Baptist Church of Boston. A few other urban churches in the North imitated this practice, and by 1820 many of the larger churches had instituted choirs. Some churches in the South formed choral ensembles in the early 19th century, but even as late as 1868 certain Southern Baptist churches were struggling with the propriety of admitting choirs. Early Baptist choirs were generally composed of volunteers who sat in the balcony facing the pulpit. In the late 19th and early 20th centuries the influence of English liturgical movements prompted many Baptist churches to vest their choirs, place them in full view of the congregation, and begin singing calls-to-worship and responses. In recent years some churches have replaced or supplemented choirs with a "praise team," a small group of singers that performs popular style Christian music.

Despite considerable opposition to instruments, the bass viol began appearing in Baptist churches of the North shortly after 1800, largely through the influence of the singing school and the practices of other denominations. Some churches made use of a "gallery orchestra" consisting of a variety of instruments. About 1819 an organ was installed in the Baptist church at Pawtucket, Rhode Island, and the older, better-established New England Baptist churches soon began acquiring organs. Lingering objections to instruments prevented the majority of Baptist churches in the South from acquiring organs until after 1850. Most churches of the major Baptist denominational branches in the United States today use some sort of instrument or instrumental group—organ, piano, orchestra, or "praise band"—in their worship. However, certain groups, most notably Regular Baptists and Primitive Baptists, have maintained an a cappella tradition.

Beginning in the 1940s music programs in many Baptist churches began expanding rapidly, and over the course of the next several decades the larger Baptist congregations hired full-time ministers of music to lead the church's entire music program. These persons direct or supervise separate choirs and ensembles for different age groups and various types of instrumental ensembles and lead congregational singing. In smaller churches the music director is frequently a part-time or volunteer worker with more limited responsibilities.

The Southern Baptist Sunday School Board inaugurated a Church Music Department in 1941 to provide sacred music literature and consulting services for the churches. Baptist musicians have formed two professional organizations, the Southern Baptist Church Music Conference (1957) and the Fellowship of American Baptist Musicians (1964), both of which sponsor an annual conference.

BIBLIOGRAPHY

H.S. Burrage: *Baptist Hymn Writers and their Hymns* (Portland, ME, 1888)

G.P. Jackson: *White Spirituals in the Southern Uplands* (Chapel Hill, 1933/*R*)

H.W. Foote: *Three Centuries of American Hymnody* (Cambridge, MA, 1940/*R*)

G.P. Jackson: *White and Negro Spirituals* (New York, 1943/*R*)

C.R. Brewster: *The Cluster of Jesse Mercer* (Macon, GA, 1983)

"Church Music in Baptist History," *Baptist History and Heritage*, xix (1984) [complete issue]

H. Dorgan: *Giving Glory to God in Appalachia: Worship Practices of Six Baptist Subdenominations* (Knoxville, TN, 1987)

R.P. Drummond: *A Portion for the Singers: a History of Music among Primitive Baptists since 1800* (Atwood, TN, 1989)

J.V. Adams, ed.: *Handbook to the Baptist Hymnal* (Nashville, TN, 1992)

J.M. Spencer: *Black Hymnody: a Hymnological History of the African-American Church* (Knoxville, TN, 1992)

H. Eskew, D.W. Music, and P.A. Richardson: *Singing Baptists: Studies in Baptist Hymnody in America* (Nashville, TN, 1994)

B.B. Patterson: *The Sound of the Dove: Singing in Appalachian Primitive Baptist Churches* (Urbana, IL, 1995)
D.W. Music, ed.: *We'll Shout and Sing Hosanna: Essays on Church Music in Honor of William J. Reynolds* (Fort Worth, TX, 1998)
J.H. Cauthen, ed.: *Benjamin Lloyd's Hymn Book: A Primitive Baptist Song Tradition* (Montgomery, AL, 1999)
K. Norton: *Baptist Offspring, Southern Midwife: Jesse Mercer's Cluster of Spiritual Songs (1810)* (Warren, MI, 2002)
J.M. Raley and D.C. Loftis: *Minds and Hearts in Praise of God: Hymns and Essays in Church Music in Honor of Hugh T. McElrath* (Franklin, TN, 2006)
D.W. Music and P.A. Richardson: *"I Will Sing the Wondrous Story": a History of Baptist Hymnody in North America* (Macon, GA, 2008)

DAVID W. MUSIC

Barab, Seymour (*b* Chicago, IL, 9 Jan 1921). Composer and cellist. At the age of 13 he performed as a church organist in Chicago. Later he studied cello with GREGOR PIATIGORSKY and Edmund Kurtz and between 1940 and 1960 played in several major orchestras, including those of Indianapolis, Cleveland, Portland (Oregon), and San Francisco. Among the chamber ensembles he helped to organize are the Composers Quartet, and the New York Pro Musica, in which he played viola da gamba. During the 1960s Barab taught at Rutgers, the State University of New Jersey, and at the New England Conservatory.

A sojourn in Paris in 1952 fostered Barab's interest in composition; while there he wrote more than 200 art songs, and he continues to write mainly vocal works. He has written dozens of operas, most of which are in one act. Of these the most frequently performed are *Chanticleer* (libretto by M.C. Richards, after Chaucer; first performed in Aspen, 4 August 1956), *A Game of Chance* (E. Manacher; Rock Island, Illinois, 11 January 1957), *Little Red Riding Hood* (Barab, after J. and W. Grimm; New York, 13 October 1962), and *The Toy Shop* (Barab; New York, 3 June 1978). His more recent operas include *A Piece of String* (after G. de Maupassant; Greeley, Colorado, May 1985), and *The Maker of Illusions* (Barab; New York, 21 April 1985). Barab has also composed orchestral works, chamber pieces, and choruses; among his song settings are *The Child's Garden of Verses* and *Songs of Perfect Propriety*, both of which have been recorded. His full-length opera *Philip Marshall* (1974) was nominated for the Pulitzer Prize, but he is equally well regarded for his comic one-act operas and his music for young audiences. In 1998, he was presented with a Lifetime Achievement Award by the National Opera Association.

BIBLIOGRAPHY

M.L. Malone: *Opera for American Youth: a Practical and Analytical Study* (diss., U. of Cincinnati, 1994)
W. McCrary: *The Fairy Tale Operas of Seymour Barab* (diss., U. of Northern Colorado, 1997)
J.K. Moore: *The Songs of Seymour Barab* (diss., U. of Washington, 2000)

Baraka, Amiri [Jones, (Everett) LeRoi] (*b* Newark, NJ, 7 Oct 1934). Writer. He studied piano, drums, and trumpet privately and attended Howard University (BA 1954). In the early 1960s he achieved wide recognition for his poetry and plays and for his writings about jazz, which included articles for *Down Beat*, *Jazz*, and *Jazz Review*; a selection of his writings, many from *Down Beat*, was published in 1967 as *Black Music*. His book *Blues People* (1963), the first full-length study of jazz by a black writer, is both a sociological inquiry, using blues and jazz as a means of understanding how African Americans became assimilated into American culture, and a superb discussion of the cultural context of the music in the United States. Besides his activities as a writer, Baraka has been involved in many black cultural and community projects. He was a founder of the Black Arts Repertory Theater-School, which was in existence from 1964 to 1965, and taught at various distinguished institutions, including the State University of New York at Stony Brook, where he retired as professor emeritus. He received the American Academy of Arts and Letters Award and the James Weldon Johnson Medal, and served as Poet Laureate of New Jersey.

Baraka has had a profound influence on jazz criticism, ranging beyond its conventional boundaries to examine such topics as the relationship to jazz and the blues of black nationalism and Marxism. In addition to his works on jazz his published writings include more than 20 plays (of which the best known is *Dutchman*, New York, 1964) and 12 volumes of poetry.

WRITINGS

Blues People: Negro Music in White America (New York, 1963/*R*)
Black Music (New York, 1967/*R*)
The Autobiography of Leroi Jones (New York, 1984, 2/1997)
with A. Baraka: *The Music: Reflections on Jazz and Blues* (New York, 1987)
Digging: The Afro-American Soul of American Classical Music (Berkeley, CA, 2009)

BIBLIOGRAPHY

K.W. Benston: *Baraka: the Renegade and the Mask* (New Haven, CT, 1976)
K.W. Benston, ed.: *Imamu Amiri Baraka (LeRoi Jones): a Collection of Critical Essays* (Englewood Cliffs, NJ, 1978)
L.W. Brown: *Amiri Baraka* (Boston, 1980)
L. Thomas: "Ascension: Music and the Black Arts Movement," *Jazz among the Discourses*, ed. K. Gabbard (Durham, NC, 1995), 256–74
J. Gennari: *Blowin' Hot and Cool: Jazz and its Critics* (Chicago, 2006)

DANIEL ZAGER/R

Barati, George [Gyorgy Braunstein] (*b* Györ, Hungary, 3 April 1913; *d* San Jose, CA, 22 June 1996). Composer, conductor, and cellist of Hungarian birth. He took classes from Zoltán Kodály and studied composition with Leo Weiner at the Liszt Academy of Music in Budapest (1932–8), and he became well known as a cellist in Hungary. As a chamber musician, he made his mark through performances with the Pro Ideale Quartet, of which he was a founding member. He came to the United States shortly before World War II. From 1939 until 1943 he studied composition at Princeton University with ROGER SESSIONS and taught there as a cellist. He played cello with the San Francisco SO from 1946 to 1950, and continued performing chamber music in California. During this time, he also began composing regularly. An important move to Hawaii gave him the opportunity to conduct the Honolulu SO from 1950 to 1967. Beginning in the 1960s, Barati concentrated on composing and conducting, leading over 85 orchestras around the world. He composed more than 50 works, which show the influence of Bartók and Kodály and, by his own assessment, his time living in Hawaii and touring in East Asia. He received a Naumburg Award in 1959 and a Guggenheim Fellowship in composition in 1965. His extensive papers, including several manuscripts, are held at the George Barati Archives at the University of California, Santa Cruz.

WORKS
(selective list)

Str Qt no.1, 1944; Chamber Conc., 1952; Vc Conc., 1957; The Dragon and the Phoenix, orch, 1960; Str Qt no.2, 1962; Polarization, orch, 1965; Baroque Qt Conc., 1969; Pf Conc., 1973; Conc., gui, small orch, 1976, rev. 1982; Branches of Time, 2 pf, orch, 1981; Confluence, orch, 1982; The Ugly Duckling, film score, 1982, arr. orch suite, 1982; Indiana Triptych, 1983; Chant to Pele, fl, 1983; B. U. D. Pf Sonata, 1984

Principal publishers: ACA, Peters

KATHLEEN HAEFLIGER/JONAS WESTOVER

Barbecue Bob [Hicks, Robert] (*b* Walnut Grove, GA, 11 Sept 1902; *d* Lithonia, GA, 21 Oct 1931). Blues singer and guitarist. As a youth he worked on a farm before moving to Atlanta, where he was employed first at a hotel and later as a cook in Tidwell's Barbecue Place in the wealthy suburb of Buckhead—a job that earned him his nickname. His characteristic vocal range and the ringing notes of his 12-string guitar, which he played with a slide, were demonstrated on his first recording, "Barbecue Blues" (1927, Col.), which was a bestseller. Barbecue Bob experimented with various blues forms, was continually inventive in his themes, and played occasional dance or comic songs such as "The Monkey and the Baboon" (1930, Col.). He became the central figure of a school of blues singers working in and around Atlanta, a group that included his elder brother Laughing Charlie Hicks, Curley Weaver, and several lesser-known musicians. He made a couple of recordings with his brother, who also recorded solo under the name Charlie Lincoln. Within three years Barbecue Bob had performed on more than 70 recordings. His last were with the Georgia Cotton Pickers, which included Weaver on guitar and Buddy Moss on harmonica, an outstanding example being "She's coming back some cold rainy day" (1930, Col.). Shortly afterwards he contracted influenza and subsequently pneumonia, from which he died at the age of 28.

BIBLIOGRAPHY

P. Oliver: "Barbecue Bob," *Music Mirror*, v/8 (1958), 6

P. Lowry: "Some Cold Rainy Day," *Blues Unlimited*, no.104 (1973), 15

PAUL OLIVER/R

Barber, Lesley (*b* Guelph, ON, 23 June 1968). Canadian film and television composer, orchestrator, conductor, pianist, and producer. Barber began composing at the age of ten and was an award winner in Canada's SOCAN National Competition for Young Composers. She studied music at the University of Western Ontario (BM 1985) and composition at the University of Toronto (MA 1988), where she worked with composers Gustav Ciamaga and Lothar Klein. She has composed music for various CBC radio dramas, made her film debut with her score for Patricia Rozema's award-winning film *When Night Is Falling* (1995), and has written scores for Miramax, New Line, Focus Features, Nickelodeon, Warner Brothers, and Home Box Office.

Barber has also composed music for the more than 20 theater productions of Canadian plays, including *Unidentified Human Remains* and *The True Nature of Love* (Brad Fraser), *Love and Anger* (George F. Walker), *Nothing Sacred* (George F. Walker), *The Warriors* (Michel Garneau) and *Escape from Happiness* (George F. Walker). The latter two of these received Canadian Dora Awards for Outstanding Original Score. As a composer of new music for the concert hall her commissions include works for the Canadian Electronic Ensemble, Hemispheres, harpist Erica Goodman, percussionist Beverly Johnston, and pianist Eve Egoyan.

WORKS

Film: When Night Is Falling, 1995; What's His Face, 1995; Turning April, 1996; Bach Cello Suite no.6: Six Gestures, 1997; Los Locos, 1997; A Price Above Rubies, 1998; Luminous Motion, 1998; Mansfield Park, 1999; You Can Count on Me, 2000; This Might Be Good, 2000; The Little Bear Movie, 2001; Marion Bridge, 2002; Uptown Girls, 2003; Comeback Season, 2006; A Thousand Years of Good Prayers, 2007; Death in Love, 2008; Victoria Day, 2009

TV: Maurice Sendak's Little Bear, 1995; Yo-Yo Ma Inspired by Bach, series, 1997; Hysterical Blindness, 2002; The Real Jane Austen, 2002; Seven Little Monsters, series, 2000–3

Concert works: Shapes of Light, Shapes of Thunder, 1989; 5 Pieces, vn, cl, bn, pf, 1991; Rhythmic Voodoo, perc, elecs, 1992; Long White Line, orch, 1993; Marshland, str qt, 1996; Music for a Lonely Zamboni, pf trio, 2001

BIBLIOGRAPHY

"Lesley Barber," Canadian Music Center website: <http://www.musiccentre.ca>

E. Lumley: "Barber, Lesley," *Canadian Who's Who 2003* (Toronto, 2003)

JEANNIE GAYLE POOL

Barber, Patricia (*b* Lisle, IL, 8 Nov 1955). Singer, pianist, composer, and bandleader. Her father played with the Glenn Miller band and her mother was a professional blues singer. After studying psychology and classical piano at the University of Iowa, Barber returned to Chicago and began playing five nights a week at the Gold Star Sardine Bar, where she attracted varying critical attention for her husky voice and the inclusion of pop songs, including "Black Magic Woman" and "A Taste of Honey," in her repertoire. She recorded her first album, *Split* (Floyd), in 1989 and her second album, *A Distortion of Love* (Antilles) in 1991. She subsequently moved to the independent label Premonition, which was bought by Blue Note in 1998. In 2003 Barber became the first songwriter to be awarded a Guggenheim Fellowship. Under its aegis she composed a song cycle based on Ovid's *Metamorphoses*. She is the subject of a documentary, *Patricia Barber Quartet: Live in France*, and is currently on the faculty of the University of Illinois at Chicago.

BIBLIOGRAPHY

N.A. Lee: "Hearsay: Patricia Barber," *JT*, xxv/1 (1995), 15

J. Seiz: "Patricia Barber," *Jazz News* (15 April 2005) <http://home.nestor.minsk.by/jazz/articles/2005/04/0001.html>

CHADWICK JENKINS

Barber, Samuel (Osmond) (*b* West Chester, PA, 9 March 1910; *d* New York, NY, 23 Jan 1981). Composer. One of the most honored and most frequently performed American composers in Europe and the Americas during the mid-20th century, Barber pursued, throughout his career, a path marked by a vocally inspired lyricism and a commitment to the tonal language and many of the forms of late 19th-century music. Almost all of his published works—including at least one composition in nearly every genre—entered the repertory soon after he wrote them and many continue to be widely performed today.

1. Life. 2. Works and style.

1. Life. From the age of seven, Barber displayed a prodigious talent for composing both vocal and instrumental music, writing an operetta, *The Rose Tree*, when he was ten to a libretto by the family's Irish cook. His musical studies were encouraged by his aunt and uncle—the contralto Louise Homer and the composer Sidney Homer, who, as his nephew's mentor for more than 25 years, profoundly influenced Barber's aesthetic principles. Early piano lessons were with William Hatton Green. At 14 he entered the newly founded Curtis Institute of Music, where he studied the piano with George Frederick Boyle and then with Isabelle Vengerova, singing with Emilio de Gogorza and composition with Rosario Scalero. Also at the institute in 1928, he met Gian Carlo Menotti, an encounter which led to a lifelong personal and professional relationship. In 1934, shortly before his graduation, the founder of the Curtis Institute, Mary Curtis Bok, began to take a special interest in Barber; beyond providing financial help, she actively promoted his career.

Early travels and extended stays in Europe, Italy in particular, solidified his affinity with European culture and intensified his Romantic orientation. In Vienna in 1934, he studied conducting and singing with John Braun. After his graduation from Curtis he had a brief career as a baritone, performing on the NBC Music Guild series; in 1935 he won a contract for a series of weekly song broadcasts. His recording of his own setting of Arnold's *Dover Beach* was hailed as having "singular charm and beauty," "intelligently sung by a naturally beautiful voice." First-hand experience as a singer and an intuitive empathy with the voice would find expression in the large legacy of songs that occupy some two-thirds of his output.

Barber gained early recognition as a composer, winning two Bearns awards—for a violin sonata (1928), of which only the third movement is extant, and for the Overture to *The School for Scandal* (1931), his first published large-scale orchestral work. A Rome Prize enabled him to spend two years at the American Academy (1935–7), where he completed the Symphony in One Movement (1936), which received immediate performances in Rome, Cleveland, and New York. Rodzinski conducted it at the opening concert of the Salzburg Festival in 1937, the first performance at the festival of a symphonic work by an American composer. His international stature was confirmed in 1938, when Toscanini and the NBC SO broadcast his *Essay* (no.1) and the *Adagio for Strings* (an arrangement of the second movement of the String Quartet). After that point, nearly all of Barber's works were composed on commission for prominent performers or ensembles.

He returned to the Curtis Institute in 1939 where he taught composition until 1942, though he was not really attracted to teaching and did not accept another position. In 1943 Mary Bok enabled Barber and Menotti to purchase "Capricorn," the house in Mount Kisco, New York, which (until 1973) was the hermitage of Barber's most productive years, as well as a gathering place for many artists and intellectuals. In the same year he completed his Second Symphony, a commission from the US Army Airforces (in which he served from 1942 to 1945). The work was given its premiere by the Boston SO, as was the Cello Concerto, written for Raya Garbousova, and the orchestral song *Knoxville: Summer of 1915*, commissioned by the soprano Eleanor Steber. His ballet score *Medea* (1946) was composed for Martha Graham; it was subsequently reworked both as an orchestral suite and as a separate orchestral tone poem, *Medea's Meditation and Dance of Vengeance*. The Piano Sonata (1949), commissioned by Irving Berlin and Richard Rodgers to celebrate the 25th anniversary of the League of Composers, was first performed by Horowitz. Its instant critical success was followed by numerous performances in America and Europe within the first year of its premiere; it retains a secure place in the repertory.

Barber had studied conducting with Fritz Reiner at the Curtis Institute and later with Nikolai Malko, who in 1951 coached him in preparation for the recordings of the Second Symphony, the Cello Concerto, and the *Medea* ballet suite. Later that year he also conducted concerts of his Violin Concerto, the Second Symphony, and *Medea* in Berlin and Frankfurt. But though he had ambitions as a conductor in the 1950s, these were to be short-lived.

While few think of Barber as a prominent standard-bearer for American music, he was more than once chosen to represent the United States: at an international music festival in Prague in 1946, as vice-president of the International Music Council in 1952, and as the first American composer to attend the biennial Congress of Soviet Composers in Moscow in 1962. He won the first of two Pulitzer Prizes in 1958 for *Vanessa*, staged initially by the Metropolitan Opera (1958) and later that year as the first American opera produced at the Salzburg Festival. Among the many other awards he received were the Henry Hadley Medal (1958) for his exceptional services to American music, nomination to the American Academy of Arts and Letters (1958), and the Gold Medal for Music at the American Academy and Institute of Arts and Letters (1976).

At the peak of his career, Barber was commissioned to write three works for the opening of Lincoln Center: the Piano Concerto, commissioned for the inaugural week of Philharmonic Hall (1962), which won him the Pulitzer Prize; *Andromache's Farewell* (1962), a concert

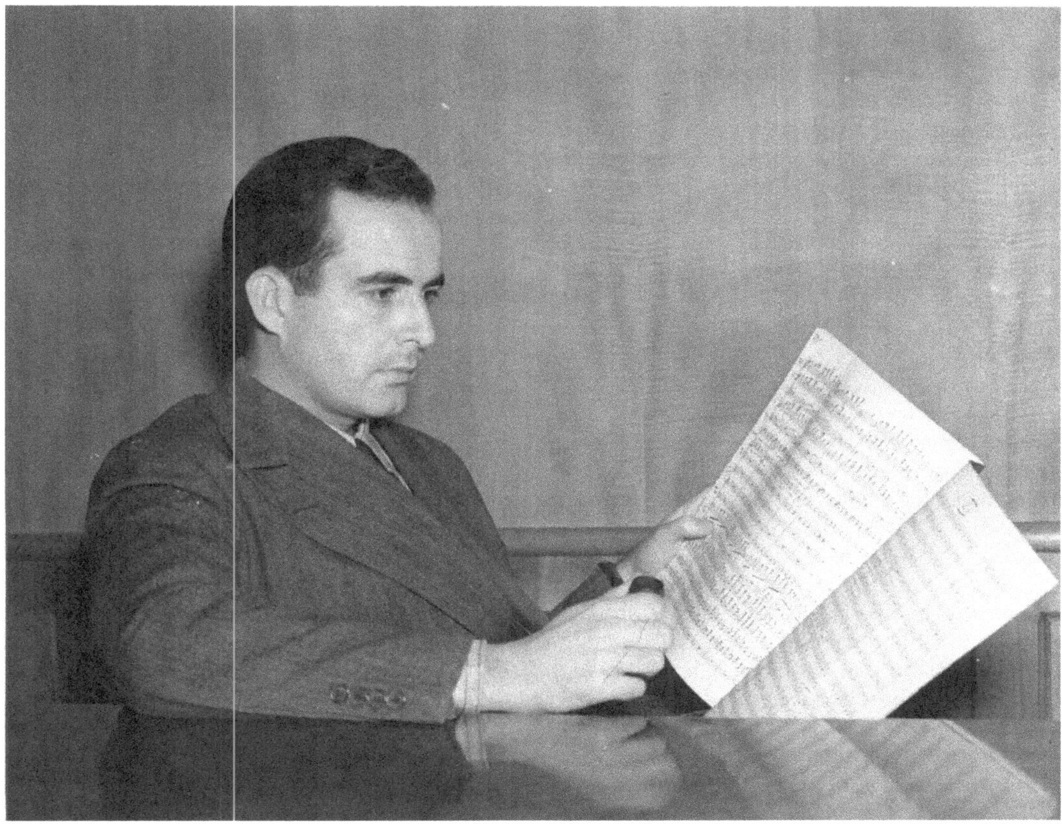

Samuel Barber, 1938. (Musical America Archives/Lebrecht Music & Arts)

scene for soprano and orchestra based on Euripides; and the opera *Antony and Cleopatra* (1966), written for the opening of the new Metropolitan Opera House. But the third commission, in principle one of the greatest tributes to his work, turned out to be his nemesis. Prompted by a conviction that, in spite of the vitriolic reviews, the opera contained some of his best work, Barber directed much of his energy towards its revision over the following decade.

After 1966 he divided his time between Santa Cristina in Italy and New York. He struggled with depression, alcoholism, and creative blocks that profoundly affected his productivity. Yet he continued to concentrate on what had always been for him the gratifying task of writing vocal music in short forms, as well as fulfilling a few commissions for larger works, including the cantata *The Lovers*. From 1978 to the end of his life, Barber was intermittently hospitalized for the treatment of cancer. His last composition, an oboe concerto of which only the second movement was completed, was published posthumously as *Canzone* for oboe and string orchestra.

2. Works and style. Unlike many of his contemporaries whose careers came to maturity between the two world wars, Barber rarely responded to the experimental trends that infiltrated music in the 1920s and again after World War II. Instead he continued to write expressive, lyrical music, using conventional formal models and the tonal language of the 19th century. Nine years of rigorous training in composition under Scalero, a student of Eusebius Mandyczewski, helped to preserve Barber's connection to the 19th-century tradition. That classical heritage was also reinforced by the personal guidance he received from Sidney Homer, who held up the European masters of the 19th century as role models, while at the same time directing Barber to trust the validity of his "inner voice."

Elements of modernism incorporated into his work after 1940—increased dissonance and chromaticism (*Medea's Meditation and Dance of Vengeance* and the Cello Concerto), tonal ambiguity and a limited use of serialism (movements 1, 2, and 3 of the Piano Sonata, the *Nocturne*, and *Prayers of Kierkegaard*)—were only of use in so far as they allowed him to pursue without compromise principles of tonality and lyrical expression. The 12-tone rows in the Piano Sonata, for example, are not used as part of a rigid technique of organization. Their presence in melodic lines or accompaniment is rarely in conflict with—indeed often reinforces—the tonal structure. Barber's propensity for writing elegiac, long-lined melodies is exemplified by two of his best-known works, the justifiably admired *Adagio for Strings* and the Violin Concerto. These and such large-scale orchestral works as the three *Essays* from the early, middle, and late stages of his career employ a rich orchestral palette and are characterized by well-crafted formal design, fluent counterpoint, and haunting themes—often assigned to solo woodwind instruments—that reflect a strong vocal orientation. The finale of the Violin Concerto and subsequent works from the 1940s, in particular the Second Symphony, *Medea's Meditation and Dance of Vengeance*, *Capricorn Concerto* (a 20th-century concerto grosso), and the Cello Concerto, show an increasing use of dissonance and syncopated rhythms, displaying some influence of Stravinsky.

A prolific composer of songs that are grateful to the voice as well as the ear, Barber favored lyrical and nostalgic texts by European, often Celtic, poets. He set Joyce, Stephens, Graves, Spender, and Rilke (in French) as well as the American poets Agee, Rothke, and Dickinson. Arroyo, Bampton, Dietrich Fischer-Dieskau, and Steber, among others, have introduced his vocal works. *Sure on this shining night*, op.13, no.3—with its long, seamlessly lyrical canonic lines—is one of the most frequently performed of his songs. The cycle *Hermit Songs*, op.29, commissioned by Elizabeth Sprague Coolidge and first sung by Leontyne Price, is a major work. The ten songs, based on comments written on the margins of medieval manuscripts by Irish monks, are infused with a modal harmonic language of great stylistic integrity; they led Schuman to hail Barber as an unmatched art-song composer. The intellectually and vocally challenging late cycle *Despite and Still*, op.41, written for Price, has profound biographical significance, probing themes of loneliness, lost love, and isolation—themes which call for a more dissonant harmonic language characterized by tonal ambiguity, tritones, a frequent use of the complete chromatic, conflicting triads, and whole-tone segments directed towards vivid expression of textual imagery.

Unaccompanied choral works written between 1930 and 1940 include a setting of Emily Dickinson's "Let down the bars, O Death," a precursor of the sensitivity to textual expression that would come to characterize Barber's later choral compositions. His settings of three poems from *Reincarnations* reflect the exuberance, wit, and melancholy of James Stephens's reinterpreted Gaelic texts through a wide variety of musical nuance, ranging from the rapid parlando rhythms of *Mary Hynes* to the chilling dirge *Anthony O'Daly*, its theme intensified by archaic-sounding open fifths over an E pedal. The large-scale *Prayers of Kierkegaard* (1954), composed at the peak of Barber's maturity, fuses 20th-century, Baroque, and medieval musical practice and stands unequivocally as one of the great spiritual works of the contemporary genre.

Barber's long-awaited first opera, *Vanessa* (1956), with a libretto by Menotti inspired by Isak Dinesen's *Seven Gothic Tales*, is in the grand operatic tradition. Eleanor Steber, in one of the great challenges of her career, took the title role. With set-piece arias, love duets, a glimpsed ball scene requiring a waltz, a folkdance ballet (reminiscent of *Yevgeny Onegin*), and a coloratura skating aria (cut from the revised version), it was described by Paul Henry Lang as "remarkable and second to none on the Salzburg–Milan axis"; Sargeant extolled it as "by far the finest and most truly 'operatic' opera ever written by an American, as well as one of the most impressive things of its sort to appear anywhere since Richard Strauss's more vigorous days." Predominantly neo-Romantic, the music highlights many of Barber's compositional strengths: metric flexibility that supports the natural rhythms of the text, a fluid use of harmonic color to underscore the bittersweet poetry, and an abundance of accessible melody.

A second opera, *Antony and Cleopatra*, contains some of Barber's most dramatic vocal writing, but initial appreciation was eclipsed by the inflated Zeffirelli production with its problematic technical apparatus and gaudy costumes, and a press preoccupied with the social glitter of the occasion. Some of the most sensuous and soaring lyrical passages were composed especially with the voice of Price in mind, who created the role of Cleopatra. Revised by Barber and restaged by Menotti, the work subsequently received critical accolade with performances at the American Opera Center at the Juilliard School in New York in 1975, the Spoleto festivals in Charleston and Italy in 1984, and the Lyric Opera of Chicago in 1992.

While he shared the concern of his generation for writing music accessible to a broadly based audience, unlike Copland, Harris, Blitzstein, and Thomson, who searched for a music with national identity, Barber rarely incorporated popular, jazz, and folk idioms into his compositions. Of his works that do include native elements, *Knoxville: Summer of 1915* is considered the most American. A reverie of childhood in a small Southern town, on a text by James Agee, it is a palpable evocation of folklore in a quasi-pastoral style, with frequent word-painting, hints of the blues, rich orchestral color, and freely varied meter. Diamond claimed *Knoxville* was "the pinnacle beyond which many a composer will find it impossible to go." Barber's few instrumental works that draw on the vernacular include *Excursions* (1941–2), a set of stylized piano pieces based on American idioms (a boogie-woogie, a blues, a barn dance and a Latin American popular dance), the Piano Sonata (1949), with its paradigmatic contemporary fugue, and the Piano Concerto (1962), which makes use of motoric jazz rhythms.

Though deemed conservative by contemporary critics, Barber's lasting strength comes precisely from his conservation of a post-Straussian chromaticism along with a typically American directness and simplicity. The international recognition accorded him throughout most of his life and the new significance his works have gained since the arrival of the "new romanticism" is testimony to the vitality and enduring viability of his extended tonal language and melodic invention.

WORKS

(all published during Barber's lifetime unless otherwise stated)

STAGE

op.

– The Rose Tree (opera, A.S. Brosius), 1920, inc., unpubd; West Chester, PA

– One Day of Spring (incid music, M. Kennedy), 1v, str, 1935, unlocated; Winter Park, FL, 24 Jan 1935

23 Medea (Serpent Heart) (ballet, M. Graham), 1946, New York, 10 May 1946; rev. as The Cave of the Heart, New York, 27 Feb 1947; arr. as orch suite, 1947, Philadelphia, 5 Dec 1947, Philadelphia Orchestra, cond. E. Ormandy; arr as tone poem: Medea's Meditation and Dance of Vengeance, op.23a, 1953, New York, 2 Feb 1956, New York PO, cond. D. Mitropoulos (ballet, John Butler, 1955)

28 Souvenirs (ballet, T. Bolender), 1952, New York, 15 Nov 1955; arr. as suite, pf 4 hands, 1952, NBC TV, July 1952; suite, orch, 1952, Chicago, 12 Nov 1953, Chicago SO, cond. F. Reiner; suite, solo pf, 1954

32 Vanessa (opera, 4, G.C. Menotti), 1956–7, New York, Met, 15 Jan 1958, cond. Mitropoulos; rev. 1964

35 A Hand of Bridge (opera, 1, Menotti), 4 solo vv, chbr orch, 1959, Spoleto, 17 June 1959

40 Antony and Cleopatra (op, 3, F. Zeffirelli, after W. Shakespeare), 1966, New York, Met, 16 Sept 1966, cond. T. Schippers; rev. 1974, New York, 6 Feb 1975, cond. Conlon

ORCHESTRAL

1 Serenade for string orchestra, 1928
5 Overture to *The School for Scandal*, 1931
7 Music for a Scene from Shelley, 1933
9 Symphony no.1, 1936
11 Adagio for Strings, 1936 [arr. of 2nd movt of Str Qt]
12 [First] Essay for Orchestra, 1937
14 Violin Concerto, 1939
17 Second Essay, 1942
– Funeral March, 1943 [based on Army Air Corps Song], unpubd
– Commando March, band, 1943
19 Symphony no.2, 1944, rev. 1947; 2nd movt rev. as Night Flight, op.19a, 1964
21 Capricorn Concerto, fl, ob, tpt, str, 1944
22 Cello Concerto, 1945
– Horizon, *c*1945 pubd posth, 2011
– Adventure, fl, cl, hn, hp, "exotic" insts, 1954, unpubd
23 Medea, orch suite from ballet, 1947
23a Medea's Meditation and Dance of Vengeance, 1955
32 arr. Intermezzo from *Vanessa*, 1957
36 Toccata Festiva, org, orch, 1960
37 Die Natali, chorale preludes for Christmas, 1960
38 Piano Concerto, 1962; 2nd movt transcr., fl, pf, 1961
– Mutations from Bach, brass choir, timp, 1967
44 Fadograph of a Yestern Scene (after J. Joyce: *Finnegans Wake*), 1971
47 Third Essay, 1978
48 posth. Canzonetta, ob, str, orchd C. Turner, 1977–8

CHORAL

XIII Christmas Eve: a Trio with Solos, 2 solo vv, SAA, org, c1924, unpubd

– Thirteen Rounds: A Lament (P.B. Shelley), To Electra (R. Herrick), Farewell (anon.), Dirge (unknown), Not I (R.L. Stevenson), Of a Rose Is Al Myn Song (anon.), Sunset (Stevenson), The Moon (Shelley), Sun of the Sleepless (Byron), The Throstle (A. Tennyson), Late, Late, So Late (Tennyson), When Day is Gone (R.Burns), The Moon (pf acc), 3 vv, 1927, ed. as Twelve Rounds in *Complete Choral Music* (New York, 2/2010)

– Duett: Summer is coming (A Tennyson), 1927

– Motetto on Words from the Book of Job (Bible: *Job*), SATB and double chorus (4vv, 8vv), *c*1930, ed. in *Complete Choral Music* (New York, 2/2010)

8/1–2 The Virgin Martyrs (Sigebert of Gembloux, trans. H. Waddell), SSAA, 1935; Let down the bars, O Death (E. Dickinson), SATB, 1936

– God's Grandeur (G.M. Hopkins), double chorus (ea SATB), 1938, ed. in *Complete Choral Music* (New York, 2/2010)

– Peggy Mitchell (J. Stephens), inc., 4vv, c1939, unpubd

– Ave Maria (arr from Josquin), SATB, 1940, ed. in *Complete Choral Music* (New York, 2/2010)

15 A Stopwatch and an Ordnance Map (S. Spender), male vv, 3 kettle-drums, 1940

16 Reincarnations (Stephens), 4vv, 1937–40: Mary Hynes, Anthony O'Daly, The Coolin

– Ave Maria (after Josquin Des Prez), 4vv, c1940, ed. in *Complete Choral Music* (New York, 2/2010)

– Ad "Bibinem" cum me regaret ad cenam (V. Fortunatus), 4vv unacc., 1943, ed. in *Complete Choral Music* (New York, 2/2010)

– Long Live Louise and Sidney Homer, canon, 1944, unpubd

30 Prayers of Kierkegaard (S. Kierkegaard), S, A ad lib, T ad lib, chorus, orch, 1954

– Under the Willow Tree, 1v, SATB, pf, 1956 [from *Vanessa*]

– Heaven-Haven (A Nun Takes the Veil), SATB/SSAA, 1961 [from op.13 no.1]

– Sure on this shining night, SATB, pf, 1961 [from op.13, no.3]

– Chorale for Ascension Day (Easter Chorale) (P. Browning), chorus, brass, timp, org ad lib, 1964

11 Agnus Dei, chorus, org/pf, 1967 [arr. of 2nd movt of Str Qt]

– The Monk and his Cat, SATB, pf, 1967 [from *Hermit Songs*, op.29]

– Two Choruses: On the Death of Antony, SSA, pf; On the Death of Cleopatra, SATB, pf, 1968 [from *Antony and Cleopatra*]

42 Twelfth Night (L. Lee), To be Sung on the Water (L. Bogan), 4 vv unacc., 1968

43 The Lovers (P. Neruda), Bar, chorus, orch, 1971

CHAMBER

– Fantasie, 2 pf, 1924, ed. in *Early Piano Music* (New York, 2/2010)
XVI Sonata in Modern Form, 2 pf, c1925, unpubd
1 Serenade, str qt/str orch, 1928
4 Violin Sonata, f, 1928, I and II unlocated; III, pubd in *Music for Violin and Piano*, 2010
6 Cello Sonata, 1932
11 String Quartet, 1936 [arrs. for str and chorus, org, see op.11, ORCHESTRAL and CHORAL]
– Commemorative March, vn, vc, pf [pubd, 2010]
31 Summer Music, wind qnt, 1955
38a Canzone (Elegy), fl, pf, 1961 [reworked as 2nd mov't of Pf Conc; also transcr for vn, pf.]

SOLO INSTRUMENTAL

(– facs. pubd in R. Walters, ed.: Early Piano Music (New York, 2/2010))*

– Sadness, pf, 1917*
I/3 Melody in F, pf, 1917*
I/4 Largo, pf, 1918*
I/5 War Song, pf, 1918*
III/1 At Twilight, pf, 1919*
III/2 Lullaby, pf, 1919*
X/2 Themes, pf, *c*1923*
– 3 Sketches, pf, 1923–4: Love Song (to Mother), To my Steinway (to Number 220601), Minuet (to Sara) [=Themes: movt 1]
– Petite Berceuse (to Jean), pf, *c*1924*
– Prelude to a Tragic Drama, pf, 1925*
– To Longwood Gardens, org, 1925*
– Fresh from West Chester (Some Jazzings): Poison Ivy, a Country Dance, 1925; Let's Sit it out, I'd rather watch (I Sam Barber did it with my little hatchet, a walls [sic]), 1926*
– To Aunt Mamie on Her Birthday, pf, 1926*
– 3 Essays, pf, 1926*
– 4 Canons, kbd, 1926—27, ed. in *Complete Piano Music* (New York, 2/2010)
– 2 Chorale Preludes, kbd, 1927, unpubd
– 4 Partitas, kbd, 1927, ed. in *Complete Piano Music* (New York, 2/2010)
– 5 Fugues, pf, 1927, ed. in *Complete Piano Music* (New York, 2/2010)
– Prelude and Fugue, b, org, 1927, ed. in *Music for Organ* (New York, 2/2010)

– Pieces for Carillon: Round, Allegro, Legend, 1930–31, unpubd
– Suite for Carillon, 4 pieces, 1932, ed. in *Music for Organ* (New York, 2/2010)
– 2 Interludes (Intermezzi), pf, 1931–2, ed. in *Early Piano Music* (New York, 2/2010)
– Chorale for a New Organ, 1936, ed. in *Music for Organ* (New York, 2/2010)
20 Excursions, pf, 1942–4
26 Sonata, pf, 1949
34 Wondrous Love, variations on a shape-note hymn, org, 1958
33 Nocturne (Homage to John Field), pf, 1959
– After the Concert, pf, *c*1968, ed. in *Complete Piano Music* (New York, 2/2010)
– Variations on Happy Birthday [to Eugene Ormandy], 1970
46 Ballade, pf, 1977

SONGS

** – facs. pubd in R. Walters, P. Wittke, eds.: 65 Songs (New York, 2010) (1v, pf, unless otherwise stated)*

– Sometime (to Mother), Mez, 1917, unpubd
– Why Not (K. Parsons), 1917, unpubd
II/3 In the Firelight, 1918, unpubd
II/4 Isabel (J.G. Whittier), 1919, unpubd
– The Wanderer, 1920, unpubd
– An Old Song (C. Kingsley), 1921*
– Hunting Song (J. Bennett), Bar, pf, cornet, *c*1921, unpubd
– Prayer, 1921, unpubd
V/2 Thy Will be Done (3 verses from *The Wanderer*), *c*1921, unpubd
VII 7 Nursery Songs (to Sara), S, 1920–22, unpubd [I Do Not like Thee, Dr. Fell*]
– October Weather (Barber), S, *c*1923*
– Minuet, S, A, pf, c1923, unpubd—Dere Two Fella Joe, high v, 1924*
XIV My Fairyland (R.T. Kerlin), 1924, unpubd
– Summer is Coming (after A. Tennyson), 2 solo vv, pf, *c*1924, unpubd
– 2 Poems of the Wind (F. Macleod), 1924: Little Children of the Wind, Longing [pubd in 65 Songs, 2010]
– A Slumber Song of the Madonna (A. Noyes), 1v, org, 1925 [pubd in *Ten Early Songs,* 1995]
– Fantasy in Purple (L. Hughes), 1925, ed. in *65 Songs* (New York, 2010)
– Three Songs, The Words from Old England: Lady when I Behold the Roses (anon.), 1925; An Earnest Suit to his Unkind Mistress not to Forsake him (Sir T. Wyatt),1926; Hey Nonny No (Christ Church MS), 1926, ed. in *65 Songs* (New York, 2010)
– La nuit (A. Meurath), 1925, ed. in *65 Songs* (New York, 2010)
– Music, when soft voices die (P.B. Shelley), *c*1925, ed. in *65 Songs* (New York, 2010)
– 2 Songs of Youth, 1925: I Never Thought that Youth would Go (J.B. Rittenhouse), Invocation to Youth (L. Binyon), ed. in *65 Songs* (New York, 2010)
– Ask me to Rest (E.H.S. Terry), 1926, ed. in *65 Songs* (New York, 2010)
– Au clair de la lune, 1926, ed. in *65 Songs* (New York, 2010)
– Man (H. Wolfe), 1926, ed. in *65 Songs* (New York, 2010)
– Thy Love (E. Browning), 1926, ed. in *65 Songs* (New York, 2010)
– Watchers (D. Cornwell), 1926, ed. in *65 Songs* (New York, 2010)
– Dance (J. Stephens), 1927, unlocated
– An Evening Falls (J. Stephens), 1927, unlocated
– The Piper (J. Stephens), 1927, unlocated
– Shame (J. Stephens), 1927, unlocated
– The Watcher (J. Stephens), 1927, unlocated
– The End of the Road (J. Stephens), 1927, unlocated
– Mother I cannot mind my wheel (W.S. Landor), 1927, ed. in *65 Songs* (New York, 2010)
– Only of Thee and Me (L. Untermeyer), *c*1927, unlocated
– Rounds, 3vv, pf, 1927, ed. in *65 Songs* (New York, 2010): A Lament (Shelley); To Electra (R. Herrick); Dirge: Weep for the World's Wrong; Farewell; Not I (R.L. Stevenson); Of a Rose is al myn Song (anon., 1350); Sunset (Stevenson); The Moon (Shelley); Sun of the Sleepless (Byron); The Throstle (Tennyson); When Day is Gone (R. Burns); Late, Late, so Late (Tennyson: *Guinevere*)
– There's Nae Lark (A. Swinburne), 1927, ed. in *Ten Early Songs* (New York, 1995)
2 3 Songs: The Daisies (Stephens), 1927, With Rue my Heart is Laden (A.E. Housman), 1928, Bessie Bobtail (Stephens), 1934
– The Shepherd to his Love and the Nymph's Reply, 1928, unpubd
3 Dover Beach (M. Arnold), Mez/Bar, str qt, 1931
– Addio di Orfeo (C. Monteverdi), 1934, arr. 1v, str, hpd, unpubd
– Love at the Door (from Meleager, trans. J.A. Symonds), 1934, ed. in *Ten Early Songs* (New York, 1995)
– Serenader (G. Dillon), 1934, ed. in *Ten Early Songs* (New York, 1995)
– Love's Caution (W.H. Davies), 1935, ed. in *Ten Early Songs* (New York, 1995)
– Night Wanderers (Davies), 1935, ed. in *Ten Early Songs* (New York, 1995)
– Of that so sweet imprisonment (J. Joyce), 1935, ed. in *Ten Early Songs* (New York, 1995)
– Peace (from Bhartirihari, trans. P.E. More), 1935, ed. in *65 Songs* (New York, 2010)
– Stopping by Woods on a Snowy Evening (R. Frost), 1935, ed. in *65 Songs* (New York, 2010)
– Strings in the earth and air (Joyce), 1935, ed. in *Ten Early Songs* (New York, 1995)
10 3 Songs (Joyce: *Chamber Music*), 1936, arr. 1v, orch: Rain has fallen, Sleep now, 1935; I hear an army, 1936
– The Beggar's Song (W.H. Davies), 1936, ed. in *Ten Early Songs* (New York, 1995)
– In the dark pinewood (Joyce), 1937, ed. in *Ten Early Songs* (New York, 1995)
13 4 Songs: A Nun Takes the Veil (G.M. Hopkins), 1937, arr. SATB/SSAA; The Secrets of the Old (W.B. Yeats), 1938; Sure on this shining night (J. Agee), 1938, arr. 1v, orch, and chorus, pf; Nocturne (F. Prokosch), 1940, arr. 1v, orch
– Song for a New House (Shakespeare), 1v, fl, pf, 1940, unpubd
– Between Dark and Dark (K. Chapin), 1942, lost
– Who carries corn and crown (R. Horan), *c*1942, ed. in *65 Songs* (New York, 2010)
18 2 Songs: The Queen's Face on a Summery Coin (R. Horan), 1942; Monks and Raisins (J.G. Villa), 1943
24 Knoxville: Summer of 1915 (Agee), high v, orch, 1947, unpubd, rev. 1v, chbr orch, 1950
25 Nuvoletta (from Joyce: *Finnegans Wake*), 1947
27 Mélodies passagères (R.M. Rilke), 1950–51: Puisque tout passe, Un cygne, Tombeau dans un parc, Le clocher chante, Départ
29 Hermit Songs (Irish texts of 8th–13th centuries), 1952–3: At Saint Patrick's Purgatory (trans. S. O'Faolain); Church Bells at Night (trans. H. Mumford Jones); Saint Ita's Vision (trans. C. Kallman); The Heavenly Banquet (trans. O'Faolain); The Crucifixion (anon., from *The Speckled Book*, trans. Mumford Jones); Sea-Snatch (trans. K. Jackson), arr. SATB, pf (1954); Promiscuity (trans. Jackson); The Monk and his Cat (trans. W.H. Auden); The Praises of God (trans. Auden); The Desire for Hermitage (trans. O'Faolain)
39 Andromache's Farewell (from Euripides: *The Trojan Women*, trans. J.P. Creagh), S, orch, 1962
41 Despite and Still: A Last Song (R. Graves), My Lizard (T. Rilke), In the Wilderness (Graves), Solitary Hotel (from Joyce: *Ulysses*), Despite and Still (Graves), 1968–9
45 3 Songs, 1972: Now have I fed and eaten up the rose (G. Keller, trans. Joyce), A Green Lowland of Pianos (J. Harasymowicz, trans. C. Milosz), O Boundless, Boundless Evening (G. Heym, trans. C. Middleton)

MSS in *Wcg*
Principal publisher: G. Schirmer

BIBLIOGRAPHY

A. Copland: "From the '20s to the '40s and Beyond," *MM*, xx (1942–3), 78–82

R. Horan: "Samuel Barber," *MM*, xx (1942–3), 161–9

"Barber, Samuel," *CBY 1944*

N. Broder: "The Music of Samuel Barber," *MQ*, xxxiv (1948), 325–35

H. Dexter: "Samuel Barber and his Music," *MO*, lxxii (1948–9), 285–7

N. Broder: "Current Chronicle: New York," *MQ*, xxxvi (1950), 276–82

H. Tischler: "Barber's Piano Sonata opus 26," *ML*, xxxiii (1952), 352–4

N. Broder: *Samuel Barber* (New York, 1954/*R*)

R. Friedewald: *A Formal and Stylistic Analysis of the Published Music of Samuel Barber* (diss., U. of Iowa, 1957)

C. Turner: "The Music of Samuel Barber," *ON*, xxii/13 (1957–8), 7, 32–3

"Classified Chronological Catalog of Works by the United States Composer Samuel Barber," *Inter-American Music Bulletin*, no.13 (1959), 22–8

Compositores de América/Composers of the Americas, v (Washington, DC, 1959), 14–21 [pubn of the Pan American Union]

L.S. Wathen: *Dissonance Treatment in the Instrumental Music of Samuel Barber* (diss., Northwestern U., 1960)

B. Rands: "Samuel Barber: a Belief in Tradition," *MO*, lxxxiv (1960–61), 353 only

J. Briggs: "Samuel Barber," *International Musician*, lx/6 (1961–2), 20–23

"Barber, Samuel," *CBY 1963*

W.A. Dailey: *Techniques of Composition Used in Contemporary Works for Chorus and Orchestra on Religious Texts as Important Representative Works of the Period from 1952 through 1962* (diss., Catholic U. of America, 1965)

E. Salzman: "Samuel Barber," *Hi Fi/Stereo Review*, xvii/4 (1966), 77–89

J.E. Albertson: *A Study of Stylistic Elements of Samuel Barber's "Hermit Songs" and Franz Schubert's "Die Winterreise"* (diss., U. of Missouri, Kansas City, 1969)

R.L. Larsen: *A Study and Comparison of Samuel Barber's "Vanessa," Robert Ward's "The Crucible," and Gunther Schuller's "The Visitation"* (diss., Indiana U., 1971)

L.L. Rhoades: *Theme and Variation in Twentieth-century Organ Literature: Analyses of Variations by Alain, Barber, Distler, Dupré, Duruflé, and Sowerby* (diss., Ohio State U., 1973)

S.L. Carter: *The Piano Music of Samuel Barber* (diss., Texas Tech U., 1980)

H. Gleason and W. Becker: "Samuel Barber," *20th-Century American Composers*, Music Literature Outlines, iv (Bloomington, IN, rev. 2/1980) [incl. further bibliography]

H. Heinsheimer: "Samuel Barber: Maverick Composer," *Keynote*, iv/1 (1980), 7

J. Sifferman: *Samuel Barber's Works for Solo Piano* (diss., U. of Texas, Austin, 1982)

D.A. Hennessee: *Samuel Barber: a Bio-bibliography* (Westport, CT, 1985)

J.L. Kreiling: *The Songs of Samuel Barber: A Study in Literary Taste and Text-Setting* (diss., U. of North Carolina, 1986)

B.B. Heyman: *Samuel Barber: a Documentary Study of his Works* (diss., CUNY, 1989)

B.B. Heyman: "The Second Time Around: Barber's 'Antony and Cleopatra', *ON*, lvi/6 (1991–2), 56–7

B.B. Heyman: *Samuel Barber: the Composer and His Music* (New York, 1992/R)

P. Wittke: *Samuel Barber: an Improvisatory Portrait* (New York, 1994)

H. Pollack: "Samuel Barber, Jean Sibelius, and the Making of an American Romantic," *MQ*, lxxxiv (2000), 175–205

R.C. Carlson: "As We Were Born Today: Characterization and Transformation in Samuel Barber's Vanessa," *OQ*, xvii (2001), 235–49

W.C. Wentzel: *Samuel Barber: a Guide to Research* (New York, 2001/R)

S. Poxon: *From Sketches to Stage: the Genesis of Samuel Barber's "Vanessa"* (diss., Catholic U. of America, 2005)

L. Howard: "The Popular Reception of Samuel Barber's Adagio for Strings," *AM*, xxv/1 (2007), 50–80

W. Simmons: *Voices in the Wilderness: Six American Neo-Romantic Composers* (New York, 2007)

P. Dickinson: *Samuel Barber Remembered: a Centenary Tribute* (Rochester, NY, 2010)

B.B. Heyman: *Samuel Barber: a Thematic Catalogue of the Complete Works* (New York, 2011)

BARBARA B. HEYMAN

Barbershop Harmony Society, the. A society founded by Owen C. Cash in Oklahoma in 1938 as the Society for the Preservation and Encouragement of Barber Shop Quartet Singing in America (SPEBSQSA). The organization was the first to promote and preserve barbershop as an art form. Its goal was to promote barbershop singing among men of all ages. The society "perpetuates and celebrates harmony in the barbershop style; promotes fellowship and friendship among men of good will; provides the opportunity to experience the joy of four-part a cappella singing; and introduces and sustains music in the lives of people everywhere." In 2010 the Barbershop Harmony Society, with national headquarters in Nashville, Tennessee, had approximately 30,000 members in the United States and Canada. The society sponsors district, collegiate, and national competitions, provides resources for educators, and awards scholarships to vocal students. It also sponsors an annual "Harmony University" for singers, directors, and music educators.

JOHN SHEPARD/KAREN M. BRYAN

Barbershop quartet singing. Barbershop quartet singing is characterized by homophonic, close-harmony, four-part arrangements, either improvised or prepared in advance, with the melody performed by the second tenor, or "lead." Harmonies emphasize circle of fifth progressions, often with added sevenths. Modern performers use just intonation, allowing the overtones produced by the singers to reinforce one another, creating chords that "ring" or "expand." Both arrangements and performance practices favor the prolonging, or "worship," of such chords. To vary the homophonic texture of their arrangements and create novel harmonies, barbershop groups often add "snakes" or "swipes" in which one or more non-melody voices change pitch, thereby altering the chord. The style emerged in 1880s and was popular among diverse amateur and professional groups across the United States between 1890 and 1910.

The core barbershop repertory was composed during the Tin Pan Alley era (1890–1930). Lyrics in these songs address, often nostalgically, the social norms and iconic places of Victorian America, including Victorian courtship rituals, same-sex camaraderie, fashions, inventions, small towns, and street corners.

The origins of barbershop singing have yet to be located precisely. The style likely emerged amid a thriving tradition of African American recreational quartet singing in the 1880s that drew on commercial influences from blackface minstrelsy, various professional touring quartets, ragtime, and the sheet music industry.

Professional touring quartets, variety shows, early recordings, and sheet music publications popularized the style. By the turn of the 20th century barbershop was among the most popular and widespread musical styles in America; it thrived in vaudeville acts, early recordings, Tin Pan Alley arrangements, fraternal society gatherings, and among diverse amateur groups, especially in masculine social spaces. The term "barbershop," originally a pejorative label, was widely applied to the style in a positive sense after the song "Play that Barbershop Chord" by Lewis F. Muir and William Tracey (1910) became a hit on Vaudeville circuits.

As radio and recordings eroded participatory musical traditions in the 1920s, jazz, syncopated dance music, and other genres eclipsed barbershop in popularity. A series of nostalgic revivals in the late 1920s and 1930s led to the formal definition of the style, creation of the barbershop canon, and the founding of THE BARBERSHOP HARMONY SOCIETY (formerly the Society for the Preservation and Encouragement of Barber Shop Quartet Singing in America) in 1938. This revival movement also constructed a narrative of barbershop's origins as amateur, rural, and primarily white, thus obscuring the importance of African American groups and musical practices, commercial quartets, and recordings for the development of the style.

The Barbershop Harmony Society organized contests for quartets and, beginning in 1943, choruses, an ensemble type not previously affiliated with the style. These innovations generated lively debate within the Society over the authenticity of judging criteria and the merits of written arrangements, debates that have continued into the 21st century. Along with concerns about sex- and race-based membership restrictions and musical style, these debates led to the formation of three separate societies, including the Ancient Harmonious Society of Woodshedders, SWEET ADELINES INTERNATIONAL, and Harmony, Incorporated. Today the Barbershop Harmony Society boasts approximately 30,000 members and affiliate organizations in nine countries. Barbershop singing remains a powerful symbol of Victorian America and male camaraderie.

BIBLIOGRAPHY

V. Hicks: *Heritage of Harmony* (Kenosha, WI, 1988)

L. Abbott: "'Play That Barbershop Chord': a Case for the African American Origin of Barbershop Harmony," *AM*, x (1992), 289–325

M. Kaplan, ed.: *Barbershopping: Musical and Social Harmony* (Rutherford, NJ, 1993)

R. Stebbins: *The Barbershop Singer: Inside the Social World of a Musical Hobby* (Toronto, 1996)

G. Averill: *Four Parts, No Waiting: a Social History of American Barbershop Harmony* (New York, 2003)

L. Garnett: *The British Barbershopper: a Study in Socio-Musical Values* (Aldershot, 2005)

R. Mook: "White Masculinity in Barbershop Quartet Singing," *JSAM*, i/4 (2007), 453–83

RICHARD MOOK

Barbirolli, Sir John [Giovanni Battista] (*b* London, England, 2 Dec 1899; *d* London, 29 July 1970). English conductor and cellist of French-Italian descent. He won scholarships to Trinity College (1911–12) and the Royal Academy of Music (1912–17), London, and made his debut as a cellist at the age of 11. He played in orchestras and ensembles in London and began his conducting career in the late 1920s, working with numerous orchestras including those at Covent Garden and Sadler's Wells. Starting in 1933, he became the conductor of the Scottish Orchestra and was considered a promising talent when he was invited by the New York PO to serve as its guest conductor for ten weeks during the 1936–7 season.

In his American debut on 5 November 1936, Barbirolli's program consisted of works by Berlioz, Bax, Mozart, and Brahms. During this trial period, he conducted Charles Martin Loeffler's tone-poem *Memories of My Childhood*, a symphony by Anis Fuleihan, Philip James's *Bret Harte Overture*, and Serge Koussevitzky's Double Bass Concerto. He made such a favorable impression that he was offered a three-year contract as principal conductor, to succeed Toscanini. The contract was renewed for two years through 1941–2, the orchestra's centenary season, when the conducting was shared with Toscanini and other eminent colleagues. During holiday periods Barbirolli conducted in other cities across the country.

During his period in New York, Barbirolli gave the world premieres of Walton's second *Façade Suite* and Britten's Violin Concerto (1940) and *Sinfonia da Requiem* (1941). He also introduced pieces by Jacques Ibert, Eugene Goossens, and Arthur Bliss, and by many American composers including Samuel Barber, Deems Taylor, and Daniel Gregory Mason. His core repertoire, however, was the late-Romantic symphonists of northern Europe, notably Ralph Vaughan Williams, Edward Elgar, and Jean Sibelius. Barbirolli refused to take American citizenship in order to join the American Musicians' Union and conducted through the 1942–3 season, making his final appearance as a regular conductor of the NYPO in March of 1943. In April, he was appointed permanent conductor of the Hallé Orchestra, Manchester, England, with which he was associated for the rest of his life. He also worked with the Berlin PO.

Barbirolli's New York years were plagued by critic Olin Downes who wanted a native conductor and by composer-critic Virgil Thomson who was still under the spell of Toscanini. His manner was much more restrained than Toscanini's, and New York audiences, accustomed to a more virtuoso style, were lukewarm in their reaction to him. Yet Barbirolli reached a vast listening public through regular broadcasts of NYPO's concerts on NBC radio. He also took the NYPO on several major tours across the United States and guest-conducted, to great acclaim, orchestras in Chicago, Los Angeles, Seattle, Cincinnati, and Vancouver, British Columbia. He was warmly welcomed back to the NYPO podium to guest conduct concerts in 1959 and 1962. His final performance with the NYPO in 1968 featured works by Alan Rawsthorne, Vaughan Williams, and Dvořák. In 1960, he was appointed music director of the Houston SO, succeeding Stokowski, and built that ensemble to 90, adding six string players. When he resigned in 1967, he was named conductor emeritus. Barbirolli was much honored in England, and also received awards from the governments of Italy and Finland.

BIBLIOGRAPHY

B. Shore: *The Orchestra Speaks* (London, 1938)

D. Bicknell and K. Anderson: "Sir John Barbirolli, C.H.," *Gramophone*, xlviii (1970–71), 401–2

M. Kennedy: *Barbirolli, Conductor Laureate* (London, 1971/*R*) [with discography by M. Walker]

C. Reid: *John Barbirolli* (New York, 1971)

H. Shanet: *Philharmonic: a History of New York's Orchestra* (Garden City, NY, 1975)

M. Kennedy: *The Hallé, 1858–1983: a History of the Orchestra* (Manchester, 1982)

E. Barbirolli: *Life with Glorious John: a Portrait of Sir John* (London, 2003)

KATHERINE K. PRESTON/JAMES BASH

Barbosa-Lima, Carlos (*b* São Paulo, Brazil, 17 Dec 1944). Brazilian guitarist, arranger, and teacher. Barbosa-Lima has been performing for over 50 years in important venues around the world. He started playing the guitar at age 7 and two years later began studying with Isaías Sávio, one of the foremost guitar teachers in Brazil. His concert career started with his debut in São Paulo and Rio de Janeiro at age 13. After his successful 1967 concert tour in the United States, he received scholarships to participate in Andrés Segovia's 1968 masterclasses in Santiago de Compostela, Spain. He has produced more than 40 recordings, with a repertoire ranging from classical and contemporary music to jazz and Brazilian popular music, and has published books on guitar techniques and repertoires in collaboration with John Griggs. He has also published and recorded works dedicated to him by composers such as Guido Santórsola, Francisco Mignone, and Alberto Ginastera. His transcriptions and performances of works by Domenico Scarlatti, Claude Debussy, George Gershwin, Antônio Carlos Jobim, Scott Joplin, and Stephen Sondheim are remarkable for their clarity of textures, where the melody and bass lines are clearly distinguished from countermelodies and harmonies. Formerly a member of the guitar faculty at the Manhattan School of Music, he still conducts masterclasses throughout the world. He has published several books on guitar techniques and repertoires in collaboration with John Griggs.

BIBLIOGRAPHY

Grove7 (Ronald C. Purcell)

W.M. Appleby: "Carlos Barbosa-Lima," *Guitar News*, no.42 (1958), 45 only; no.48 (1959), 78 only; no.99 (1968), 104 only

P. Danner: "How I Came to the Guitar," *Soundboard*, xxi/1 (1994), 5–10

L. Del Casale: "Carlos Barbosa-Lima," *Classical Guitar*, xxiv/10 (2006), 11–16

L. Del Casale:: "50 Years of Performing: Carlos Barbosa-Lima, Legendary Guitarist," *Classical Guitar*, xxvi/7 (2008), 20–21

SILVIO J. DOS SANTOS

Barbour, J(ames) Murray (*b* Chambersburg, PA, 31 March 1897; *d* Homestead, PA, 4 Jan 1970). Acoustician, musicologist, and composer. He taught himself piano and organ and studied at Dickinson College, Pennsylvania (1914–18); after graduating he worked as organist and mathematics teacher at the Haverford School in Pennsylvania (1919–21, 1922–6) while continuing his studies at Dickinson College (MA 1920) and Temple University (MusB 1924). He subsequently taught music theory as assistant professor at Wells College, New York (1926–9), leaving with a fellowship to the universities of Cologne and Berlin. After studies at Cornell University under OTTO KINKELDEY (1931–2) he gained the doctorate in 1932 with a dissertation on the history of equal temperament from Ramis de Pareia to Jean-Philippe Rameau. He taught at Ithaca College, New York (1932–9), while working for the MusD of the University of Toronto (1936). The rest of his career (1939–64) was spent teaching at Michigan State College (later University), as professor from 1954. He was president of the American Musicological Society (1957–8), and Temple University awarded him an honorary doctorate in 1965.

His book *Tuning and Temperament: a Historical Survey* is widely accepted as the most authoritative study of the history and theory of temperaments, to which he applied his talents as mathematician, historian, and musician. His scholarly articles appeared in mathematical as well as musical journals and were marked by precision, clarity, and conciseness. With Fritz A. Kuttner he issued three gramophone records concerning the history of tuning systems. His compositions include a Requiem, the symphonic poem *Childe Rowland*, solo and choral songs, works for the organ and piano, and some chamber music.

WRITINGS

Equal Temperament: its History from Ramis (1482) to Rameau (1737) (diss., Cornell U., 1932)

"Nierop's Hackebort," *MQ*, xx (1934), 312–9

"Just Intonation Confuted," *ML*, xix (1938), 48–60

"Allgemeine Musikalische Zeitung: Prototype of Contemporary Music Journalism," *Notes*, v (1947–8), 325–37

"Musical Scales and their Classification," *JASA*, xxi (1949), 586–9

Tuning and Temperament: a Historical Survey (East Lansing, MI, 1951/*R*, 2/1953)

"Franz Krommer and his Writing for Brass," *Brass Quarterly*, i (1957–8), 1–9

"Unusual Brass Notation in the Eighteenth Century," *Brass Quarterly*, ii (1958–9), 139–46

"The Principles of Greek Notation," *JAMS*, xiii (1960), 1–17

The Church Music of William Billings (East Lansing, MI, 1960)

"Pokorny Vindicated," *MQ*, xlix (1963), 38–58

"Missverständnisse über die Stimmung des Javanischen Gamelans," *Mf*, xvi (1963), 315–23

Trumpets, Horns and Music (East Lansing, MI, 1964)

R. Smith, ed.: *Harmonica, or the Philosophy of Musical Sounds (1749)* (New York, 1966)

"The "Unpartheyisches Gesang-Buch," *Cantors at the Crossroads: Essays on Church Music in Honor of Walter E. Buszin*, ed. J. Riedel (St Louis, 1967), 87–94

BIBLIOGRAPHY

F.A. Kuttner: "J. Murray Barbour (1897–1970)," *JAMS*, xxiii (1970), 542–3

JON NEWSOM

Bare, Bobby (Robert Joseph) (*b* Ironton, OH, 7 April 1935). Country music singer-songwriter. An eclectic artist known for his wit and storytelling abilities, he has blurred boundaries between country, pop, and folk, earning crossover success in each of these genres. In addition to his distinctive performing style, his associations and collaborations with and promotion of a diverse range of acclaimed songwriters have made him an icon of country music.

Raised on a farm in southern Ohio, Bare was performing with a local band in Springfield by his teenage years. After moving to Los Angeles in 1955, he signed with Capitol Records and later the small label Challenge. His first hit, "All American Boy" (Fraternity, 1958), was recorded under the name Bill Parsons who was credited as both the singer and writer. Although the song reached number two on the pop charts, Bare received neither credit nor royalties because of his previous contractual obligations.

Following army service, Bare was signed to RCA Records by the producer Chet Atkins in 1962; his recordings for the label included a string of top ten hits, notably "Shame on Me" (RCA, 1962), "Detroit City" (RCA, 1963), "500 Miles Away from Home" (RCA, 1963), and "Four Strong Winds" (RCA, 1964). Bare recorded prolifically through the 1960s, often straddling the line between folk and country with his gravitation towards narrative songs and folk material. Following a brief period with Mercury Records (1970–72), Bare returned to RCA and began collaborating with the songwriter Shel Silverstein. Their efforts produced the concept albums *Lullabies, Legends, and Lies* (RCA, 1973), *Singin' in the Kitchen* (RCA, 1974), and *Hard Time Hungrys* (RCA, 1975), all of which became popular with country and rock audiences and anticipated the outlaw-country movement. In 1977 Bare achieved more crossover success through associations with the concert promoter Bill Graham. In the same year he signed with Columbia Records, for which he recorded *Bare* (1978) and *Sleep Wherever I Fall* (1978); the latter included songs by Rodney Crowell, the Byrds, and the Rolling Stones. In 1980 Bare released *Down and Dirty*, another collaboration with Silverstein that featured the top 30 hit "Tequila Sheila." The following year the album *As Is* included material by a diverse selection of songwriters including J.J. Cale, Townes Van Zandt, and Guy Clark. In 1998 he released *Old Dogs* with Jerry Reed, Mel Tillis, and Waylon Jennings, and in 2005 he was coaxed out of retirement to record *The Moon Was Blue* (Bluetone).

JOHN STANISLAWSKI

Barenaked Ladies. Canadian rock group. Steven Page (*b* Toronto, ON, 22 June 1970; vocals) and Ed Robertson (*b* Toronto, 25 Oct 1970; guitar) began performing as a duo in 1988, developing a folk-rock style based on satirical songs and droll stage banter. After adopting the name Barenaked Ladies, they performed on the college circuit and built up a fan base. They added further backup musicians in 1991, including Jim Creegan (*b* Toronto, 12 Feb 1970; bass guitar), Andy Creegan (*b* Toronto, 4 July 1971; keyboards), and Tyler Stewart (*b* 21 Sept 1967; drums). The group sold independently produced cassettes at live shows. As their notoriety grew, one of these, *The Yellow Tape* (1991), became a runaway hit, achieving platinum-level sales in Canada, leading to a deal with Reprise Records. The band's first album, *Gordon* (Rep., 1992), achieved high sales and acclaim in Canada. "If I had $1,000,000" and "Be my Yoko Ono" became signature hits. Creegan was replaced by Kevin Hearn (*b* Grimsby, ON, 3 July 1969; various instruments) in 1995.

With its fourth album, *Stunt* (1998), Barenaked Ladies achieved recognition in the United States and worldwide on the strength of the single "One Week," which topped the *Billboard* singles chart. Reprise did not renew the group's contract following the release of *Everything to Everyone* (Rep., 2003) as sales declined. The band became an independent act again, and a Christmas album and children's album followed, although the latter was marred by Page's arrest in the United States on drug charges. Following Page's departure in 2009, the remaining quartet has continued to tour and record.

RECORDINGS
(selective list)

Gordon (Rep., 1992); *Maybe you should Drive* (Rep., 1994); *Born on a Pirate Ship* (Rep., 1996); *Stunt* (Rep., 1998); *Maroon* (Rep., 2000); *Everything to Everyone* (Rep., 2003); *Barenaked for the Holidays* (Desperation, 2004); *Barenaked Ladies are Men* (Desperation, 2007); *Snacktime!* (Desperation, 2008); *All in Good Time* (Raisin', 2010)

CHRIS MCDONALD

Barenboim, Daniel (*b* Buenos Aires, Argentina, 15 Nov 1942). Israeli pianist and conductor. He was first taught by his parents, and made his debut as a pianist in Buenos Aires when he was seven. In 1951 the family moved to Europe where he played at the Salzburg Mozarteum, and thence to Israel. Back in Salzburg in 1954, he met Edwin Fischer and Furtwängler, both major influences on his future career. He made his first recording the same year. Studies at the Accademia di S Cecilia in Rome and with NADIA BOULANGER completed his education.

Barenboim made his British debut as a soloist in 1955 and his American debut two years later, and first conducted, in Israel, in 1962. From 1964 he worked for some years with the English Chamber Orchestra as conductor and pianist. Meanwhile he began an international career as a conductor. He directed the South Bank Summer Festival in London (1968–70) in company with a group of musicians that included Zukerman, Perlman, and Jacqueline Du Pré, whom he had married in 1967.

He was chief conductor of the Orchestre de Paris from 1975 to 1989, and served as music director of the Chicago SO (succeeding Solti) from 1991 to 2006. While concentrating on the central Classical and Romantic repertory, he has also been a firm advocate of new music, giving premieres of works by Berio, Boulez, Carter, Goehr, and Henze, among others. Barenboim has been equally active as an opera conductor, beginning at the Edinburgh Festival in 1973 with *Don Giovanni*. In 1981 he was invited to the Bayreuth Festival, and he continued to conduct there throughout the 1990s. In 1992 he was appointed music director of the Berlin Staatsoper, where he has conducted an especially wide repertory, most notably of German works. In recent years he has also moved into popular and crossover repertory, with a recording of Argentine tango, a tribute to Duke Ellington, and an album of Brazilian popular music.

His interpretations of both opera and the orchestral repertory give emphasis to freedom of expression, allowing for many changes in tempo and a careful disclosure of detail. His recordings, as a pianist, of the Mozart and Beethoven concertos and the complete Beethoven sonatas, all made when he was young, are distinguished by their flexibility, spontaneity, and quick sensitivity. To promote communication between Israel and neighboring countries, Barenboim and Edward Said founded in 1999 the West-Eastern Divan Orchestra, a student orchestra trained by professional musicians. In July 2001 Barenboim provoked an outcry in Israel by defying the country's ban on Wagner and playing the Prelude from *Tristan und Isolde* with the Berlin Staatskapelle as an encore in concert at the Israel Festival. In addition to his other posts, he has served since 2006 as principal guest conductor of La Scala opera house in Milan.

ALAN BLYTH/CHRISTI L. COREY

Barere [Barer], **Simon** (*b* Odessa, Ukraine, 20 Aug/1 Sept 1896; *d* New York, NY, 2 April 1951). Pianist of Ukrainian birth. He received his early musical instruction at the hands of two of his elder brothers and later from a neighbor. By the age of 11, after the death of his father, he was able to help support his family by playing for silent films, nightclubs, and restaurants.

At 16 he was accepted at the St Petersburg conservatory, studying first with Anna Yesipova and later with HAROLD BLUMENFELD. Barere graduated in 1919 and was awarded the Rubinstein Prize. His development led Glazunov to observe that "Barere is Franz Liszt in one hand and Anton Rubinstein in the other." Barere's progress was all the more remarkable in that his personal circumstances (he still supported his family by playing in restaurants) permitted him relatively little time for practice.

After graduation he combined the career of a traveling virtuoso with that of professor of piano at the Kiev Conservatory. In 1932 he moved with his young son and his wife, fellow St Petersburg student Helen Vlashek, whom he had married in 1920, to Berlin. After initial successes the growing persecution of the Jewish community forced him to flee from there to Sweden. In 1934, Barere signed a recording contract in London with HMV, for whom he recorded many works with which his name was to become closely associated, including Liszt's *Réminiscences de Don Juan* and *Rhapsodie espagnole*, Balakirev's *Islamey*, Blumenfeld's *Etude for the Left Hand*. As well as demonstrating Barere's astonishing virtuosity, these recordings testify to his extraordinary delicacy and the consistent tonal beauty of his playing throughout a wide dynamic range. Equally, his playing of works by Chopin evidences breathtaking technical command together with rare poetic nobility.

After an acclaimed American debut in November 1936, Barere and his family moved to the United States, which was to remain his base. Tours of Australia, New Zealand, and South America, as well as his successes in the States, served to consolidate his reputation as one of the foremost artists of the day. He died suddenly as a result of a cerebral hemorrhage during his first performance of the Grieg Piano Concerto in a concert at Carnegie Hall.

CHARLES HOPKINS/R

Bargy, Roy F(rederick) (*b* Newaygo, MI, 31 July 1894; *d* Vista, CA, 16 Jan 1974). Composer and pianist. He spent his formative years in Toledo, Ohio, where he began piano lessons at the age of five. By the time he was 17 he had discarded his ambitions to become a concert pianist, having become fascinated with the ragtime pianists in Toledo's red-light district. He played piano and organ professionally in cinemas and organized his own local dance orchestra. Following a five-month stint in the army in 1918, he returned to Toledo and then moved to Chicago where he auditioned for Charley Straight, a notable ragtime composer and pianist then acting as a production manager at the Imperial Player Roll Company. Although Bargy had virtually no formal training in composition or arranging, Straight hired him in 1919 to edit, arrange, compose, and record for Imperial. During his tenure at Imperial, Bargy composed *Piano Syncopations*, a set of novelty rags for solo piano which achieved widespread popularity and included "Slipova," "Justin-Tyme," "Sunshine Capers," "Jim Jams," "Pianoflage," and "Behave Yourself." In 1920 Straight recommended Bargy to the cellist and agent Edgar Benson, who was organizing a band. For the next two years Bargy served as the pianist and director of the Benson Orchestra of Chicago, making dozens of recordings for the label Victor, both with the band and as an unaccompanied soloist. Following creative conflicts with Benson, Bargy left the group to lead his own band and then worked with Isham Jones's orchestra for two years. From 1928 he maintained a 12-year association with Paul Whiteman's orchestra, serving as its pianist, arranger, and assistant conductor, in which capacities he helped to popularize George Gershwin's *Rhapsody in Blue*. Later he served as a conductor and arranger for Lanny Ross's radio show, and from 1943 until his retirement in 1963 he worked as a music director for Jimmy Durante.

Bargy is best known for his contribution to the ragtime-based style of NOVELTY PIANO. Like the work of his contemporary Zez Confrey, his compositions may be viewed as advanced rags: he routinely employed tenths in the bass (a feature more readily associated with early jazz than ragtime), but favored right-hand patterns found in ragtime of the 1910s, recalling at times the work of Straight and the classic ragtime composer James Scott. Although Bargy's works are not as ambitious or imaginative as Confrey's, they represent a charming recasting of the language of Midwestern ragtime in the more vivacious mode of the late 1910s and 20s.

BIBLIOGRAPHY
D. Jasen and T.J. Tichenor: *Rags and Ragtime: a Musical History* (New York, 1978)
D. Jasen and G. Jones: *That American Rag* (New York, 2000)
B. Wright: *Charley Straight: That's what I Call Keen* (Lynchburg, VA, 2010)

DAVID THOMAS ROBERTS/BRYAN S. WRIGHT

Barilari, Elbio Rodríguez (*b* Montevideo, Uruguay, 13 Dec 1953). Uruguayan composer, writer, and teacher, active in the United States. He studied in Montevideo with Coriún Aharonian and Héctor Tosar before pursuing his education in Brazil and Germany. Since he relocated to the United States in 1998, his work has been commissioned and performed by numerous groups in Chicago, including the Lyric Opera of Chicago, the Grant Park Festival Orchestra, the Civic Orchestra of Chicago, and the Concertante di Chicago.

Barilari's classical compositions draw on a diversity of Latin American musical traditions and are often inspired by literature or historical figures. In 2002, as part of a tribute to Argentinian tango composer Astor Piazzolla, Barilari premiered a concerto for bandoneon at Chicago's Grant Park Music Festival. His *Heights of Machu Picchu* (2005), incorporates Andean scales and rhythms, while his *Canyengue* (2006) features the distinctive rhythms of the *milongon* and the *candombe*—Afro-Uruguayan styles typical of his native Montevideo. His work for soprano, choir, and orchestra, *Los Cantos*, was premiered at the Lyric Opera of Chicago in 2007. Like much of his work, his *Lincolniana* (2008) represents a unique blending, combining jazz, texts by Walt Whitman and Carl Sandburg, and a *corrido* sung in Spanish to tell the story of the friendship between American President Abraham Lincoln and Mexican President Benito Juárez. This piece commemorated Lincoln's bicentennial and premiered at the Ravinia Festival.

In addition to his musical output, Barilari is an active writer and educator. He has lectured at the University of Chicago and the Instituto Cervantes of Chicago, and teaches at the University of Illinois at Chicago.

RUTH E. ROSENBERG

Barili, Alfredo (*b* Florence, Italy, 2 Aug 1854; *d* Atlanta, GA, 17 Nov 1935). Pianist, conductor, and teacher. He was born into one of the leading musical families in 19th-century America, which included Adelina Patti, and made his debut as a pianist on 7 April 1865 in New York. His family soon moved to Philadelphia, where he studied piano with Carl Wolfsohn before embarking for the Cologne Conservatory in 1872. Barili settled in Atlanta in 1880 and became the city's first professional musician, introducing many standard works, including Ludwig van Beethoven's sonatas and later Charles Gounod's *Messe solennelle de Sainte Cécile*. In 1883 he planned the first Atlanta Music Festival, which included a chorus of 300 accompanied by Carl Sentz's orchestra from Philadelphia. During that one weekend Barili introduced symphonies by Franz Schubert (no.8), Joseph Haydn, and Beethoven, as well as a number of Felix Mendelssohn's and Giuseppe Verdi's overtures. That same year he conducted the chorus for Theodore Thomas and his orchestra. Barili developed a reputation as one of the finest teachers in the South, and many of his pupils achieved successful musical careers. His pioneering work in Atlanta laid the foundation for many of the city's musical institutions.

See also Atlanta.

BIBLIOGRAPHY
N.L. Orr: *Alfredo Barili and the Rise of Classical Music in Atlanta* (Atlanta, GA, 1996)

N. LEE ORR

Barker, Danny [Daniel Moses] (*b* New Orleans, LA, 13 Jan 1909; *d* New Orleans, LA, 13 March 1994). Guitarist, banjoist, singer, composer, and writer, husband of the singer Blue Lu Barker. His great-uncle Louis Arthidore was a clarinet virtuoso who played with the Onward Brass Band and his grandfather Isidore Barbarin played alto horn; on the latter's advice he studied clarinet (with Barney Bigard) and ukulele, banjo, and guitar (with Bernard Addison). He also learned drums with Louis and Paul Barbarin. Barker performed professionally in the 1920s in Mississippi and Florida, before moving in 1930 to New York, where he played guitar in the groups of James P. Johnson, Albert Nicholas, Sidney Bechet, and Henry "Red" Allen and in the swing orchestras of Lucky Millinder, Benny Carter, and Cab Calloway. In the 1940s he switched to six-string banjo and took part in the Dixieland revival. During the same period he worked with West Indian musicians and recorded for Spotlite with Sir Charles Thompson and Charlie Parker. Before returning to New Orleans in 1965, he worked as a freelance, performing with Wilbur De Paris, Billie Holiday, Eubie Blake, and his uncle Paul Barbarin, among others, and recording in California with Albert Nicholas. In New Orleans he continued to perform regularly and became the master of ceremonies of the Onward Brass Band and the New Orleans Jazz & Heritage Festival. He also founded the Fairview Baptist Church Brass Band, an ensemble for young people whose members subsequently included Wynton and Brandford Marsalis and Nicholas Payton and which later became the Dirty Dozen Brass Band. During his career Barker recorded as a leader and sideman for many labels, including Decca, Columbia, Riverside, Atlantic, Esp-Disk, Apollo, Bethlehem, Swingsville, and Circle. His instrumental style was admired in both harmonic and melodic terms; his approach to rhythm guitar was conventional, and his banjo playing contributed a danceable feeling to the music.

As well as performing and recording, Barker served as assistant curator of the New Orleans Jazz Museum and wrote three books on early jazz. Collections of his papers and writings are held in the Hogan Jazz Archive and the Amistad Research Center (both at Tulane University) and at the Louisiana State Museum, New Orleans. He appears in the films *Minnie the Moocher* and *The Sound of Jazz*.

BIBLIOGRAPHY
GroveJ
N. Shapiro and N. Hentoff: *Hear me Talkin' to Ya: the Story of Jazz by the Man who Made it* (New York and London 1955, 2/1966)

D. Barker (with J.V. Buerkle): *Bourbon Street Black: the New Orleans Black Jazzman* (New York, 1973)

D. Barker: *A Life in Jazz*, ed. A. Shipton (London and New York, 1986)

D. Barker: *Buddy Bolden and the Last Days of Storyville*, ed. A. Shipton (London, 1998)

LUCA CERCHIARI

Barker, Sister (Ruth) Mildred (*b* Providence, RI, 3 Feb 1897; *d* Sabbathday Lake, New Gloucester, ME, 25 Jan 1990). Shaker singer and songleader. After her father died, when she was seven, she lived with the Shaker Society in Alfred, Maine; she later became a member of the society and lived there until it disbanded in 1931. With other members she moved to the Shaker Society at Sabbathday Lake, New Gloucester, Maine, where for many years she tended to young people and from 1947 was a trustee; she became the spiritual leader of the community in 1972. She learned by ear several hundred spirituals and gospel hymns in the traditional Shaker repertory, and also studied piano; her excellent singing voice and reliable memory enabled her to become the songleader in Shaker services. She wrote several commentaries on early songs, as well as biographical, historical, and devotional articles and poems for the *Shaker Quarterly*; she also cooperated in the filming of song performances and in the production of recordings by scholars. She received a National Heritage Fellowship from the NEA in 1983.

BIBLIOGRAPHY

D.W. Patterson: *The Shaker Spiritual* (Princeton, NJ, 1979)

D.W. Patterson: "Sister Mildred Barker and the Maine Song Tradition," *Shaker Quarterly*, xxii (1994), 192–202

DANIEL W. PATTERSON

Barker, Warren (*b* Oakland, CA, 16 April 1923; *d* Greenville, SC, 3 Aug 2006). Composer and conductor. Barker attended the University of California, Los Angeles, and studied composition with MARIO CASTELNUOVO-TEDESCO and Henri Pensis. Following service in the Army Air Corps during World War II, he returned to Los Angeles and became chief arranger for NBC radio's *The Railroad Hour* (1947–53). He was staff director for Warner Brothers Records for 12 years, leaving in 1960 to focus on television work for 20th Century Fox, Columbia, and MGM studios as a composer, arranger and conductor. His television credits include more than thirty series, including *77 Sunset Strip*, *Daktari*, *That Girl*, *Hawaiian Eye*, *The Flying Nun*, and most notably *Bewitched*. He composed the theme song for the *Donny and Marie Osmond Show* and won an Emmy in 1970 for his original music for the series *My World and Welcome to It*. Barker wrote scores for the films *Strange Lovers* and the *Zebra in the Kitchen* and was on the arranging staff for the Oscar-winning movie *Hello Dolly!* He also arranged songs for Frank Sinatra. A member of the American Bandmasters Association, Phi Mu Alpha Sinfonia Fraternity, Broadcast Music, Inc., and the National Band Association, he received numerous commissions for concert band and wind ensemble works.

BIBLIOGRAPHY

W.H. Rehrig: *The Heritage Encyclopedia of Band Music* (Westerville, OH, 1991, suppl. 1996); CD-ROM (Oskaloosa, IA, 2005) [includes selective list of works]

N.E. Smith: *Program Notes for Band* (Lake Charles, LA, 2000), 35–6

THOMAS E. CANEVA

Barkin [née Radoff], **Elaine** (*b* Bronx, NY, 15 Dec 1932). Composer, writer, and performer. She earned the BA (1954) from Queens College where she studied composition with KAROL RATHAUS. At Brandeis University (MFA 1956, PhD 1971) she studied composition with IRVING FINE, HAROLD SHAPERO, and ARTHUR BERGER and at the Berlin Hochschule für Musik (1956–7) with Boris Blacher. She taught at various colleges in New York and at the University of Michigan (1970–74), before joining the composition and theory faculty at UCLA (1974–97). For four decades she has been a major contributor to and co-editor (1972–82) of *Perspectives of New Music*; she has written extensively on 20th-century music in a variety of journals, publishing more than 80 articles, 36 of which are reprinted in *e: an anthology. music texts & graphics (1975–1995)*. In 1989, Barkin, Benjamin Boretz, and Jim Randall founded the OPEN SPACE publications series. In her compositions, writings, and presentations she has given attention to women and gender issues along with her primary focus on new music and the very problem of writing about music at all.

In about 1975 Barkin turned from idiosyncratic serial techniques to a freer and more eclectic approach to pitch and design choices. In the early 1980s she began to explore compositional processes involving collaboration, interactive performance, and improvisation. In notes written about her 1989 piece for basset-horn and tape, *...out of the air...*, she outlined her aesthetic: "to foster the potentials of collaborative participation; to enable possibilities for the performer, ranging from the most traditional to the most far-out liberated; to relinquish authority albeit not responsibility; and to minimize my role as proprietary instruction-giver." Her search for non-hierarchical socio-musical environments led to her interest in Javanese and Balinese gamelan. She was involved with gamelan as a player and composer from 1987–2000 and during five study trips to Bali compiled interviews, led improvisation workshops, and produced audio and video tapes about new music in Bali. In fall 1996 she was invited to join the Institute for Shipboard Education's Semester at Sea, where she taught Gamelan Angklung and traditional and intercultural World Music.

Barkin's "texts"—whether for print medium, live performance, or tape collage—often blur the distinction between text and music or between essay and poetry. Some works also merge theoretical commentary with the creative process in the form of poetic-graphic explications of music by other composers. Her compositions invoke extensive verbal and gestural interplay, as in the chamber opera *De Amore* (1980) and other mixed media pieces; later works integrate timbral and conceptual influences from non-Western sources, especially gamelan. In 2004 Barkin began using her iMAC-G5 for composing and performance. A variety of sound samples have enabled her to design novel instrumentation, such as: dulcimer, sitar, three gamelan instruments, chimes, harp, and piano in *Faygele's Footsteps* (2006).

WRITINGS

"A view of Schoenberg's op.23/1," *PNM*, xii (1973–4), 99–127

"Questionnaire [about being a woman composer in the US]," *PNM*, xix/1–2 (1980–81), 460–62; continued as "In Response," xx/2 (1981–2), 288–329

e: an anthology: music texts & graphics (1975–1995) (Red Hook, NY, 1997)

E. Barkin and L. Hammesley, eds.: *Audible Traces: Gender, Identity, and Music* (Zürich, 1999)

"A text on the Music of Harry Partch taken from Notes and Commentaries on Notes made during and after Auditions of the Music of Harry Partch," *Harry Partch: an Anthology of Critical Perspectives*, ed. D. Dunn (Amsterdam, 2000), 71–8

"reexperiencing [Benjamin Boretz's] *Language, as a music* revisited," *PNM*, xxxviii/1 (2000), 223–45

"Colloquy and Review," *The OPEN SPACE Magazine*, no.3 (2001), 202–23

"Cross-cultural Collaboration: Composing a work for Balinese Gamelan and Basso Bongo with I Nyoman Wenten," *Intercultural Music*, v (2003), 85–101

Review of P. Ramey: *Irving Fine: An American Composer in his Time*, *The OPEN SPACE Magazine*, no.8 (2006), 209–18

Review of Hollis Taylor: *post impressions: an Australian travel book for tragic intellectuals*, *The OPEN SPACE Magazine*, nos.12–13 (2011), 156–66

WORKS

Stage (incl. text-pieces and tape collages): De amore (chbr mini-op, after A. Capellanus and 12th–20th-century love texts), 8 vv, va, gui, hp, db, slide projection, 1980; Media Speak, 9 spkrs, sax, slide projection, 1981;...to piety more prone..., 4 female spkrs, tape, 1983, rev. 1985; Anonymous was a Woman (tape collage for dancers), 1984; Out Back (tape collage for dancers),1984; on the way to becoming (tape collage, Barkin), 1985; Past is Part of (tape collage, Barkin), 1985

Orch: Essay, 1957; Plus ça change, str, 3 perc (incl. mar, vib, xyl), 1971 [also version for tape, arr. S. Beck, 1987]; Poem for Symphonic Wind and Perc Ens, 1999

Chbr and solo inst: Brandeis 1955 (Cambridge, Natick, Waltham, Lenox), pf, 1955; Refrains, fl, cl, cel, str trio, 1967; 6 Compositions, pf, 1968; Str Qt, 1969; Inward & Outward Bound, fl + pic, cl + b cl, bn, hn, tpt, trbn, tuba, vn, va, vc, db, 2 perc (incl. vib, mar, timp), 1975; Mixed Modes, b cl, vn, va, vc, pf, 1975; Plein chant, a fl, 1977;...in its surrendering..., tuba, 1980; 3 Rhapsodies, pic + fl, cl + a fl, 1986; [Be]Coming Together Apart, vn, mar, 1987; Encore, Javanese gamelan, 1988;...out of the air..., basset hn, graphics, tape, 1989; Legong Dreams, ob, 1990; exploring the rigors of in between, fl, hn, vn, va, vc, 1991; Gamelange, hp, mixed gamelan, 1992; Lagu Kapal Kuning, Balinese gamelan angklung, 1996; touching all bases/ di mana-mana, elec db, perc, Balinese gamelan, 1997, collab. I. Nyoman Wenten; Song for Sarah, vn, 2001; Ballade, 1v, vc, 2002–4; Tambellan Suite, giant mar, 2004; Inti Sari, gamelan angklung, 2005; 3 Violin Duets, 2 vn, 2007; Violin Duo, 2 vn, 2007–8; 6 Pieces (Blanc, Holding On, Spirals, Sarabande, Blanc et Noir, Postlude), pf, 2008

Vocal: 2 Dickinson Choruses, SATB, 1977;...the supple suitor...(set to 12 poems of E. Dickinson), Mez, fl, ob, vc, vib + bells, hpd + pf, 1978;...the sky...(E.E. Cummings), SSA, pf, 1978;...for my friends' pleasure...(Sappho, Dickinson, hooks, deVale, and Santal girl), S, hp, 1995

Computer with Sibelius: Purnama, 2004; Cut Short, 2005; From the Abbeys, 2005; Step by Step, 2005; Barely There, 2006; Faygele's Footsteps, 2006; ShadowPlay, 2007; Whorl, 2007; End Piece, 2008; When the Wind Blows, 2008; Faygele and Friends, 2010; XTET: Last Dance for Milton, 6 Midi instruments (2 pf, cel, hpd, org, drum set), 2011

Principal publishers: Association for the Promotion of New Music, Mobart, Open Space, Yelton Rhodes Music

Principal recording companies: CRI, Open Space

BIBLIOGRAPHY

E. Cory: "Barkin's String Quartet," *MQ*, lxii (1976), 616–20

J. Rahn: "New Research Paradigms," *Music Theory Spectrum*, xi/1 (1989), 84–94

J.M. Edwards: "North America since 1920," *Women and Music: A History*, ed. K. Pendle (Bloomington, IN, 1991, 2/2001), 314–85, esp. 356

S. McClary: "A Response to Elaine Barkin," *PNM*, xxx/2 (1992), 234–8

B. Boretz: "A ((P)Re)View of Elaine Barkin's Twenty-Year Retrospective Collection of Her Works for Print," *PNM*, xxxiv/2 (1996), 224–32

J.W. Sobaskie: Review of *OS* CDs 3, 4, 5, *Computer Music Journal*, xxv/1 (2001), 79–81

J. MICHELE EDWARDS

Barlow, Harold (*b* Boston, MA, 15 May 1915; *d* Manhasset, Long Island, NY, 15 Feb 1993). Writer on music and composer. He graduated from the Boston University College of Music (BM 1937), where he studied the violin. He later became a big band leader, conducting one with fellow servicemen during World War II. As a violinist, he played with such conductors as Arthur Fiedler and Fabien Savitsky. With Sam Morgenstern he compiled two indexes, *A Dictionary of Musical Themes* (New York, 1948) and *A Dictionary of Vocal Themes* (New York, 1950): both employ an alphabetic system, devised by Barlow, for identifying a theme when only the melody is known. As a composer, Barlow is perhaps best known for his 1949 song "I've got tears in my ears (From lyin' on my back in my bed while I cry over you)," for which he wrote both the words and the music. However, he also wrote or co-wrote a variety of lesser-known tunes, including the Connie Francis hit "Mama" (1960) and "The Things I Love" (1941), which was recorded by Harry James and later Dizzy Gillespie. He also frequently acted as an expert witness in criminal cases involving music, usually concerning plagiarism. One famous example was a trial that pitted George Harrison's "My Sweet Love" against the Chiffon's "He's So Fine," where Barlow acted in favor of Harrison, who eventually lost the lawsuit.

PAULA MORGAN/JONAS WESTOVER

Barlow, Samuel L(atham) M(itchell) (*b* New York, NY, 1 June 1892; *d* Wyndmoor, PA, 19 Sept 1982). Composer and administrator. He studied at Harvard University (BA 1914), then in New York with PERCY GOETSCHIUS and Franklin Robinson, in Paris with Isidor Philipp, and in Rome with Ottorino Respighi (orchestration, 1923). Before World War I, and for two decades thereafter, he was active in New York civic and professional groups formed to promote music, and in liberal political action groups. He was the first chairman of the New York Community Chorus, chairman of the Independent Citizens Committee for the Arts, Sciences, and Professions, governor of the ACA, chairman of the American Committee for the Arts, director of the China Aid Council, and vice-president of the American Committee for Spanish Freedom. In addition, he taught in various settlement schools and was a frequent contributor to *Modern Music*.

Barlow's opera *Mon ami Pierrot*, to a libretto by Sacha Guitry on the life of Jean-Baptiste Lully and purporting to show the origin of the French children's song "Au clair de la lune," was the first by an American to be performed at the Opéra-Comique in Paris (11 January 1935); his "symphonic concerto for magic lantern," *Babar* (after Jean de Brunoff's picture books), uses slide projections. Despite such novelties, Barlow's style was relatively conservative: he admitted that "tunes which wouldn't shock Papa Brahms keep sticking their necks out."

WORKS
(selective list)

Stage: Ballo sardo, ballet, 1928; Mon ami Pierrot (op, S. Guitry), 1934; Amanda, op, 1936; Amphitryon 38 (incid music, J. Giraudoux), 12 orch pieces, 1937

Orch: Vocalise, 1926; Alba, sym. poem, orch/chbr orch, 1927; Circus Ov., 1930, rev. 1960; Pf Conc., 1931; Biedermeier Waltzes, 1935; Babar, sym. conc., slide projection, 1936; Leda, 1939; Sousa ad Parnassum, 1939

Chbr and solo inst.: Ballad, Scherzo, str qt, 1933; Spanish Quarter, pf suite, 1933; Conversation with Tchekhov, pf trio, 1940; Jardin de Le Nôtre, pf suite

Vocal: choruses and songs, incl. 3 Songs from the Chinese, T, 7 insts, 1924

Principal publishers: Choudens, Joubert, G. Schirmer

BIBLIOGRAPHY

S.L.M. Barlow: *The Astonished Muse* (New York, 1961) [autobiography]

Obituary, *New York Times* (21 Sept 1982)

M. Lederman: *The Life and Death of a Small Magazine (Modern Music, 1924–1946)* (Brooklyn, NY, 1983)

H. WILEY HITCHCOCK

Barlow, Wayne (Brewster) (*b* Elyria, OH, 6 Sept 1912; *d* Rochester, NY, 17 Dec 1996). Composer and teacher. He studied composition with Edward Royce, BERNARD ROGERS, and HOWARD HANSON at the Eastman School (1930–37), where he received the MMus and the PhD degrees, and with ARNOLD SCHOENBERG at the University of Southern California (1935). In 1937 he joined the faculty of the Eastman School, eventually becoming chairman of the composition department, director of the electronic music studio (1968), and dean of graduate studies (1973); in 1978 he was named professor emeritus. He received two Fulbright scholarships (1955–6, 1964–5) and numerous commissions, and traveled widely as lecturer, guest composer, and conductor of his own works. He also served as organist and choirmaster at two churches in Rochester, St. Thomas Episcopal (1946–76) and Christ Episcopal (1976–8). He was a prolific composer in an eclectic, tonal, free 12-tone style.

WORKS

Dramatic: 3 Moods for Dancing (ballet), 1940

Orch: De Profundis, prelude, 1934; False Faces, ballet suite, 1935; Sinfonietta, C, 1936; The Winter's Passed, rhapsody, ob, str/pf, 1938; Lyrical Piece, cl, str/pf, 1943; Nocturne, chbr orch, 1946; Rondo-Ov., 1947; Sinfonietta, C, 1950; Lento and Allegro, 1955; Night Song, 1957; Intrada, Fugue and Postlude, brass ens, 1959; Rota, chbr orch, 1959; Images, hp, orch, 1961; Sinfonia da Camera, chbr orch, 1962; Vistas, 1963; Conc., sax, band, 1970; Hampton Beach, ov., 1971; Soundscapes, orch, tape, 1972; Divertissement, fl, chbr orch, 1980; Frontiers, band, 1982

Vocal: Zion in Exile (cant.), S, A, T, B, chorus, orch, 1937; Songs from The Silence of Amor, S, orch, 1939; Madrigal for a Bright Morning (J.R. Slater), chorus, 1942; Ps xxiii, chorus, org/orch, 1944; 3 Songs (W. Shakespeare), 1948; Mass, G, chorus, orch, 1951; Poems for Music (R. Hillyer, Shakespeare), S, orch, 1958; Missa Sancti Thomae, chorus, org, 1959; Diversify the Abyss (H. Plutzik), male chorus, 1964; We all Believe in One True God, chorus, brass qt, org, 1965; Wait for the Promise of the Father, T, Bar, chorus, small orch, 1968; Voices of Faith (cant.), spkr, S, chorus, orch, 1974; Voices of Darkness, spkr, pf, perc, tape, 1975; What Wondrous Love, chorus, org, gui, 1976; Out of the Cradle Endlessly Rocking, T, chorus, cl, va, pf, tape, 1978; 7 Seals of Revelation (cant.), S, A, T, B, chorus, orch, 1989

Chbr: Prelude, Air and Variation, bn, str qt, pf, 1949; Pf Qnt, 1951; Triptych, str qt, 1953; Trio, ob, va, pf, 1964; Elegy, va, pf/orch, 1968; Duo, hp, tape, 1969; Vocalise and Canon, tuba, pf, 1976; Intermezzo, va, hp, 1980; Sonatina for 4, fl, cl, vc, hp, 1984

Kbd: Pf Sonata, 1948; Hymn Voluntaries for the Church Year, org, 1963–81; Dynamisms, 2 pf, 1966; 2 Inventions, pf, 1968; 3 Voluntaries, org, 1970; 4 Chorale Voluntaries, org, 1979–80; Pange lingua, org, 1980; Preludes on Darwell's 148th, Gott sei Dank, Knickerbocker, Austria, org, 1983

Tape: Study in Electronic Sound, 1965; Moonflight, 1970; Soundprints in Concrete, 1975

Principal publishers: Concordia, C. Fischer, J. Fischer, Gray, Presser

WRITINGS

"Contemporary Music: an Orientation," *MJ*, xi/6 (1953), 26–7, 33–5

Foundations of Music (New York, 1953)

"Crisis!," *MJ*, xx/2 (1962), 26–7, 74

"Of Choral Music for the Church," *Choral Journal*, vi (1963–4), 13–4

"Electronic Music and Music Education," *Electronic Music Review*, vi (1968), 40–3; repr. as "Electronic Music: Challenge to Music Education," *MEJ*, lv/3 (1968), 66–9

W. THOMAS MARROCCO/MARY WALLACE DAVIDSON

Barnabee, Henry Clay (*b* Portsmouth, NH, 14 Nov 1833; *d* Jamaica Plains, MA, 16 Dec 1917). Actor and singer. He began performing in amateur theatricals and concerts while working as a clerk in a dry-goods store. He became professional in 1865 but did not gain widespread recognition until he was recruited by the BOSTON IDEAL OPERA COMPANY in 1879 (he was one of its original members). When the group was later reorganized as the Bostonians, Barnabee was elected one of its officers; he remained with the company for the rest of its existence and the rest of his career. His most celebrated role was the Sheriff of Nottingham, which he created in the operetta *Robin Hood* by De Koven and H.B. Smith (1891), and which he sang more than 2000 times. His other notable roles included Sir Joseph Porter in Gilbert and Sullivan's *H.M.S. Pinafore*, Izzet Pasha in Franz von Suppé's *Fatinitza*, and Lord Allcash in Daniel Auber's *Fra Diavolo*. He was admired for his excellent bass-baritone voice and restrained but deft comedy. He wrote a volume of reminiscences, *My Wanderings* (1913).

GERALD BORDMAN

Barn dance. Originally a rural meeting for dancing held in a barn or similar large building. From the 1920s the term was used to designate variety radio programs of rural, folk-like entertainment, although artists frequently performed a wide range of musics from old-time fiddling and ballads to contemporary popular songs and blues. The first program so described was broadcast on the radio station WBAP in Fort Worth, Texas, in 1923, although many Southern radio stations had presented similar programs the previous year. The most important of the broadcast barn dances were the

WLS Barn Dance (later National barn dance, Chicago, 1924–70) and the *WSM Barn Dance* (Nashville, from 1925), which as the Grand ole opry became the longest-running radio program in the United States; both were started by George D. Hay. Other programs included the *Renfro Valley Barn Dance* (WLW, Cincinnati, from 1937), the *Tennessee Barn Dance* (WNOX, Knoxville, TN, from 1942), the *Old Dominion Barn Dance* (WRVA, Richmond, VA, from 1946), and the *WHN (New York) Barn Dance*. Similar programs that used different titles were the Louisiana hayride (KWKH, Shreveport, LA, from 1948), the *Midwestern Hayride* (WLW, Cincinnati, from 1937), the *Big D Jamboree* (KRLD, Dallas, TX, from 1924), and the *World's Original WWVA Jamboree* (Wheeling, WV, from 1926). By 1949 around 650 radio stations were broadcasting live country music performances, but by the mid-1950s such shows had nearly disappeared, with the notable exception of the *Grand Ole Opry*, which benefited from the growth of the country music industry in Nashville.

See also Country music.

BIBLIOGRAPHY

G.C. Biggar: "The WLS National Barn Dance Story: the Early Years," *JEMF Quarterly*, vii/23 (1971), 105–12

T.A. Patterson: "Hillbilly Music among the Flatlanders: Early Midwestern Radio Barn Dances," *Journal of Country Music*, vi/1 (1975), 12–18

P. Stamper: *It all Happened in Renfro Valley* (Lexington, KY, 1999)

M.A. Williams: *Staging Tradition: John Lair and Sarah Gertrude Knott* (Urbana, IL, 2006)

K.M. McCusker: *Lonesome Cowgirls and Honky-Tonk Angels: the Women of Barn Dance Radio* (Urbana, IL, 2008)

P. Fox: *Natural Acts: Gender, Race, and Rusticity in Country Music* (Ann Arbor, MI, 2009)

TRAVIS STIMELING

Barnes, James Charles (*b* Hobart, OK, 9 Sept 1949). Composer, educator, and conductor. He earned degrees in music at the University of Kansas (BM 1974, MM 1975), where he has been a faculty member since 1976, and is currently Division Director for Music Theory and Composition. His compositions include six symphonies, many overtures and several works for solo winds with band. He has twice received the American Bandmasters Association Ostwald Award as well as the Kappa Kappa Psi Distinguished Service to Music Medal and the Bohumil Makovsky Award for Outstanding College Band Conductors.

Barnes is known as an expert orchestrator; his trademarks include the integration of tuned percussion, piano, and harp into the band texture, and the extensive melodic and solo use of low brass and woodwind instruments. Among the most performed of his more than 100 published works are Third Symphony (1996), *Fantasy Variations on a Theme of Niccolo Paganini* (1989) and *Yorkshire Ballad* (1985).

As a conductor he has recorded three CDs of his works with the Tokyo Kosei Wind Orchestra. He is a member of ASCAP and the American Bandmasters Association. His works are published by Southern Music.

BIBLIOGRAPHY

W.H. Rehrig: *The Heritage Encyclopedia of Band Music* (Westerville, OH, 1991, suppl. 1996); CD-ROM (Oskaloosa, IA, 2005) [includes selective list of works]

J.C. Barnes: "James Barnes," *Composers on Composing for Band*, ed. M. Camphouse (Chicago, 2002), i, 1–42

CHARLES CONRAD

Barnet, Charlie [Charles Daly] (*b* New York, NY, 26 Oct 1913; *d* San Diego, CA, 4 Sept 1991). Bandleader and tenor saxophonist. Born to a wealthy New York family, he began studying saxophone and immersing himself in New York's jazz scene while in his early teens. He achieved commercial success as a bandleader, beginning in 1939 with the release of a hard-swinging version of Ray Noble's "Cherokee" (1939, Bb). Subsequent recordings, including "Pompton Turnpike" (1940, Bb) and "Skyliner" (1944, Decca), confirmed his position as the leader of one of the era's hottest swing bands.

At the height of its popularity, the Barnet Orchestra was frequently compared to the Duke Ellington band. Although the influence of Count Basie as well as Ellington is clear, Barnet's group had a distinctive sound shaped by his easygoing direction, Andy Gibson's and Billy May's dynamic charts, and the band's virtuosic soloists, notably guitarist Bus Etri, pianist Dodo Marmaroso, and trumpeter Peanuts Holland. Along with Benny Goodman, Barnet was an important force for interracial musical collaboration, and he invited such African American musicians as Benny Carter, Andy Gibson, Lena Horne, Holland, and Frankie Newton to play with and write for his band. Like Woody Herman and Stan Kenton, Barnet was open to the sounds of bebop and incorporated some of its musical practises into his orchestra's performances. With the decline of the dance bands, however, Barnet was forced to disband his group in the late 1940s, although he reunited it several times during the next few decades. As well as tenor saxophone, he also occasionally played the soprano instrument.

BIBLIOGRAPHY

C. Garrod: *Charlie Barnet and his Orchestra* (Spotswood, NJ, and Zephyrhills, FL, 1973, 4/1999 as *Charlie Barnet and his Orchestra, 1933–1973*) [discography]

C. Barnet and S. Dance: *Those Swinging Years: the Autobiography of Charlie Barnet* (Baton Rouge, LA, 1984, 2/1992) [incl. discography]

D. Mather: *Charlie Barnet: an Illustrated Biography and Discography* (Jefferson, NC, 2002)

Oral history material in *NEij*

ANDREW BERISH

Barnett, Alice (Ray) (*b* Lewiston, IL, 26 May 1886; *d* San Diego, CA, 28 Aug 1975). Composer, teacher, and patron. She studied with Rudolf Ganz and Felix Borowski at the Chicago Musical College (BM 1906) and with Heniot Levy and Adolf Weidig at the American Conservatory, Chicago; she also studied composition in Chicago with Wilhelm Middleschulte and in Berlin with Hugo Kaun (1909–10). From 1917 to 1926 she taught music at the San Diego High School. A respected and influential leader of musical life in San Diego, she helped to found the San Diego Opera Guild and the San Diego Civic SO (of which she was chairwoman for

14 years). Barnett wrote some 60 art songs, 49 of which were published by G. Schirmer and Summy between 1906 and 1932. They display a lyrical gift, sure tonal sense, and, despite her German training, strong French harmonic influence. They are often exotic and colorful, especially "Chanson of the Bells of Oseney" (1924) and the Browning cycle *In a Gondola* (1920), which is also dramatic; others of her songs are "Panels from a Chinese Screen" (1924), "Harbor Lights" (1927), and "Nirvana" (1932). She also wrote instrumental music, including a piano trio (1920) and *Effective Violin Solos* (1924). Although Barnett stopped composing in the late 1930s, she maintained her musical activities in San Diego. Her manuscripts and papers are at the San Diego Historical Society.

BIBLIOGRAPHY

W.T. Upton: "Some Recent Representative American Song-Composers," *MQ*, xi (1925), 383–417, esp. 398–417

W.T. Upton: *Art-Song in America* (Boston, 1930), 214–24

A.F. Block and C. Neuls-Bates: *Women in American Music: a Bibliography of Music and Literature* (Westport, CT, 1979)

C.K. Smith: *The Art Songs of Alice Barnett* (diss., U. of Northern Colorado, 1996)

ADRIENNE FRIED BLOCK

Barnett, Carol E(dith Anderson) (*b* Dubuque, IA, 23 May 1949). Composer. As a child she studied the piano, the violin, and the flute, and performed in various choral and instrumental ensembles. At the University of Minnesota (BA 1972, MA 1976) she studied composition with DOMINICK ARGENTO and Paul Fetler, the piano with Bernhard Weiser, and the flute with Emil Niosi. From 1992 through 2001 she was appointed composer-in-residence for the Dale Warland Singers, and she has created several works for the Twin Cities chorus Vocal Essence. Her instrumental works have been performed by the Minnesota Orchestra and the St Paul Chamber Orchestra. In 2003 her as yet unperformed opera *Snow* won the Nancy Van de Vate International Composition Prize in Opera, and in 2005 she received a McKnight Fellowship in composition. She currently teaches at Augsburg College in Minneapolis and plays flute in the Minneapolis Civic Orchestra.

Barnett's harmonic idiom is flexibly chromatic and freely dissonant within a context that includes references to tonality. She tends to work with small, striking musical ideas, repeating them within various textures and timbres that shift effortlessly from one to the next. Barnett is particularly distinguished for her choral music. The cycle *An Elizabethan Garland* (1994) features deftly managed textures that range from imitation and dialogue among the voices to streams of closely positioned chords over a deep bass. Her lyricism is wide-ranging, creating a singing quality in even disjunct melodic lines. *The World Beloved: a Bluegrass Mass* (2006), described by one reviewer as "profoundly moving," has received several performances and is available on CD. She says of her style: "While writing accessibly, I try to find something unusual to say, something unique, magic, that bypasses intellect and goes straight to the heart."

WORKS

(selective list)

Opera: Snow, 1992

Band: Cyprian Suite, 2002; Tirana, 2005; Prelude and Romp, 2008

Orch: Adon Olam Variations, 1976; Hn Conc., 1985; Carnival, 2 pf, orch, 1990; Ov. to a Greek Drama, 1994; Remembering Khachaturian, 1996

Vocal (SATB, unless otherwise stated): 5 poemas de Bécquer (G.A. Bécquer), 1979; Requiem (liturgical texts), SSA, 1981; Voices (N. Cox), S, gui, 1983; Epigrams, Epitaphs (various authors), 1986; 2 canti meridionali (M. Ferraguti), S, pf, 1989; Let it Go (M. Estok), S, pf, 1992; The King of Yellow Butterflies (V. Lindsay), 1993; An Elizabethan Garland (J. Fletcher, S. Daniel, 2 anon. texts), 1994; Children'songs (E.St.V. Millay, L. Carroll, C. Sandburg, W. Welles), SA, cl, pf, 1996; A Spiritual Journey (trad. spirituals), orch., 1997; The Mystic Trumpeter (W. Whitman), 1997; Meeting at Seneca Falls, S, Mez, B, pf, perc, 1998, rev. 2006; An American Thanksgiving, 2003; Veni Sancte Spiritus (Lat.), 2005; Music for Heroines, S, hp (J. Nikpay), 2006; The World Beloved: a Bluegrass Mass (M. Chamberlain, trad.), SATB, fiddle, mand, banjo, gui, bass, 2006; Sappho Fragments, S, sax, vib, bass, 2007; Lilacs (Whitman), 2009.

Chbr and solo inst: Sonata, hn, pf, 1973; 4 Chorale Meditations, vn, 1982; Str Qt no.1 "Jewish Folk Fantasies," 1986; Mythical Journeys, fl, gui, 1991; Russian Sketches, str, 1995; Cyprus: First Impressions, va, vc, db, 2000; Vignettes, after Pierides, fl, vc, pf, 2001; Among Friends, cl, vn, vc, pf, 2004; Praise, org, perc, 2007; Variations, Oh Yes!, cl, pf, 2008

MSS in *PHf*

Principal publishers: earthsongs, Boosey & Hawkes, Walton, Thompson, Colla Voce, Alliance, Augsburg Fortress

BIBLIOGRAPHY

P. Berg: "Composer Profile," *Minnesota Women's Press* (28 Dec 1994)

K. Conlin: "Soprano, Tenor, Alto...Banjo!," *Sounding Board*, xxxiv/4 (2007), 5–6

K. Gehrke, "Carol Barnett writes music for real life heroines," *Minnesota Public Radio News Quarterly* (7 Apr 2006)

K. Pendle: "For the Theatre: Opera, Dance and Theatre Piece," *CMR*, xvi (1997), 69–80

KARIN PENDLE

Barnhouse, Charles Lloyd (*b* Grafton, WV, 20 March 1865; *d* Oskaloosa, IA, 18 Nov 1929). Music publisher, bandmaster, and composer. As a child, he was given cornet lessons by his uncles. He became a proficient soloist, and by the age of 16 was director of the Grafton Band. He then toured for several years with musical comedy companies. In 1886 he moved to Mount Pleasant, Iowa, where he directed the local band and set up a music publishing business. He moved his family and business first to Burlington, Iowa, in 1888, and then to Oskaloosa in 1891. For many years he directed the Iowa Brigade Band, for which he provided a rehearsal hall. He published more than 100 of his own band compositions, including cornet solos, marches, galops, waltzes, and dirges; some works appeared under the pseudonyms Jim Fisk and A.M. Laurens. A number of his marches are recorded in the Heritage of the March series compiled by Robert Hoe, Jr. (6, A, G, O, FF, ZZ, RRR). His publishing business flourished, becoming one of the largest in the country. In addition to his own compositions, he published the works of such important composers as Fred Jewell, J.J. Richards, Karl King, Russell Alexander, and Walter English. The company bearing his name continues to publish band music of high quality.

BIBLIOGRAPHY

A. Suppan: *Repertorium der Märsche für Blasorchester* (Tutzing, 1982) [incl. selective list of marches]

W.H. Rehrig: *The Heritage Encyclopedia of Band Music* (Westerville, OH, 1991, suppl. 1996); CD-ROM (Oskaloosa, IA, 2005) [incl. extensive works list]

N.E. Smith: *Program Notes for Band* (Lake Charles, LA, 2000), 38–9

RAOUL F. CAMUS

Barnum, P(hineas) T(aylor) (*b* Bethel, CT, 5 July 1810; *d* Bridgeport, CT, 7 April 1891). Impresario, author, publisher, philanthropist, and politician/reformer. He produced theatrical matinées, blackface minstrelsy, melodramas, circus tours (the first to own private trains), farces, baby and beauty contests, and temperance lectures. After an early success exhibiting Joyce Heth (advertised as George Washington's 160-year-old nurse) in 1835, he capitalized on the enthusiasm for Tyrolean acts by introducing the often parodied "Swiss Bell Ringers" in 1844. His management of such novelties as the celebrated midget Tom Thumb had established him as America's leading showman, and the lecture hall at the Museum became an early venue for "family" minstrelsy and variety. Barnum's greatest triumph, however, was a tour by soprano JENNY LIND (1850–51); under his management she gave 95 concerts in 19 cities, attracting unprecedented receipts of $712,161.34 (*see also* BAYARD TAYLOR). This was the first major tour in the United States to be managed by a nonperformer, marking the rise of a separate class of agents and promoters. He also sponsored the Irish soprano Catherine Hayes on a tour of California (1852). Barnum purchased a moribund collection of curiosities and several museums, including Peale's Museum (Philadelphia Museum). By relentless promotion he made Barnum's Museum one of New York's central attractions. In 1853, he launched the pictorial weekly *Illustrated News* and built the "Moral Lecture Room," one of New York's largest and most modern theaters, whose official motto was "We study to please." As president of the New York Crystal Palace he played an important role in Jullien's "Grand Musical Congress" (1854). His much revised autobiography sold more than one million copies. Barnum excelled in self-promotion through mass publication. Although his wealth and public stance were in decline by 1856, after years of litigation and humiliation he reestablished himself and his success continued to grow after 1860. Barnum changed the public attitude towards mass entertainment and popular stage culture with novel methods that influenced popular entertainers and impresarios such as Max Maretzek and the Strakosch brothers. His impact on America's music industry was lasting and profound; to this day, he is regarded as an American icon.

BIBLIOGRAPHY

P.T. Barnum: *The Life of P. T. Barnum, Written by Himself* (New York, 1855/*R*; rev. as *Struggles and Triumphs*, 1869); ed. G.S. Bryan as *Struggles and Triumphs, or The Life of P.T. Barnum, Written by Himself* (New York, 1927)

N. Harris: *Humbug: the Art of P.T. Barnum* (Boston, 1973)

W.P. Ware and T.C. Lockard, Jr.: *P.T. Barnum Presents Jenny Lind: the American Tour of the Swedish Nightingale* (Baton Rouge, LA, 1980)

A.H. Saxon, ed.: *Selected Letters of P.T. Barnum* (New York, 1983)

A.H. Saxon, ed.: *P.T. Barnum: the Legend and the Man* (New York, 1995)

WILLIAM BROOKS/DENIZ ERTAN

Baron, Joey [Bernard Joseph] (*b* Richmond, VA, 26 June 1955). Jazz drummer. He learned to play drums by listening to and imitating recordings and first worked professionally in Dixieland and rock-and-roll bands. He briefly attended the Berklee College of Music before moving to Los Angeles, where he worked as a studio musician and played with, among others, Chet Baker, Stan Getz, Dizzy Gillespie, Carmen McRae, and Helen Merrill. After moving to New York in 1982, he worked with Toshiko Akiyoshi, Fred Hersch, Red Rodney, and Toots Thielmans and began a ten-year working relationship with Bill Frisell, during which he recorded seven albums. In the late 1980s he performed as a soloist and with the band Miniature. Known for his ability to combine music from many traditions, including klezmer, jazz, and blues, Baron played a prominent part in the neo-bop movement of the early 1990s, leading a trio, Baron Down, from 1991, in which Ellery Eskelin and Steve Swell were sidemen. He later formed the Down Home Band with Frisell, Ron Carter, and Arthur Blythe and worked in John Zorn's bands, including Naked City and Masada, performing a combination of Hebraic folk music and free jazz. Baron is a creative, versatile drummer, specializing in an avant-garde style. Renowned for humor, melody, liveliness, and spontaneity in his playing, he relishes musical intrigue and excitement.

BIBLIOGRAPHY

GroveJ2

K. Micallef: "Avant-jazz's Joey Baron: Inside the Mind of One of Drumming's Most Creative Thinkers," *Modern Drummer*, xx/7 (1996), 48

S. Vickery: "Joey Baron: my Approach is Always to keep Thinking," *Coda*, no.274 (1997), 20

A. Budofsky, ed.: *The Drummer: 100 Years of Rhythmic Power and Invention* (Cedar Grove, 2006)

GARETH DYLAN SMITH

Baron, Samuel (*b* Brooklyn, NY, 27 April 1925; *d* New York, NY, 16 May 1997). Flutist and conductor. He studied at Brooklyn College (1940–45), and at the Juilliard School (1942–8) with GEORGES BARRÈRE, Arthur Lora (flute), and Edgar Schenkman (conducting). He gained orchestral experience with the New York SO, the New York City Opera, and the Minneapolis SO (principal flute), and in 1949 was a founder-member of the New York Woodwind Quintet, with which he played regularly (1949–69, and again from 1980), making many notable recordings and giving many first performances. In the mid-1950s he turned increasingly to chamber music and until 1965 was associated successively with the American Chamber Orchestra, the New York Chamber Soloists, and the Contemporary Chamber Ensemble. In that year, he joined the Bach Aria Group, of which he became music director in 1980. As a soloist his repertory is large, and he has given many first performances.

A distinguished teacher, Baron served on the staff of the Yale School of Music (1965–7), Mannes College

(1969–72), SUNY, Stony Brook (beginning in 1966), and the Juilliard School (beginning in 1971). He was founder and conductor, in 1948, of the New York Brass Ensemble, which he directed in many recordings. He edited Bach's Flute Sonata in A BWV 1032 (1974) with a reconstruction of the first movement, and his arrangement of the *Art of Fugue*, for string quartet and five wind instruments, though unpublished, has been recorded. Baron wrote *Chamber Music for Winds* (1969). In 1996 he received the Lifetime Achievement Award from the National Flute Association.

PHILIP BATE/R

Barone, (J.) Michael (*b* Kingston, PA, 1946). Radio personality and producer. Barone is a nationally recognized radio personality heard via Minnesota Public Radio (MPR)/American Public Media (APM) as host and executive producer of the nationally syndicated series, *Pipedreams*, a 120-minute weekly program devoted to organ music. He served a similar function for national broadcasts of *The Saint Paul Chamber Orchestra* from 1983 to 2005. Barone joined MPR in 1968 following graduation from the Oberlin Conservatory in Ohio with a BM degree in music history, with organ as principal applied instrument. From 1968 to 1992 he was network music director for MPR, and is currently senior executive producer. *Pipedreams,* in continuous production since 1982, is the longest-running and only nationally distributed weekly program devoted to the pipe organ in US radio history. Awards and honors include the American Guild of Organists President's Award (1996), the Distinguished Service Award of the Organ Historical Society (1997), the ASCAP Deems Taylor Award (2001), and induction into the Minnesota Music Hall of Fame (2002). He has served on the Minnesota State Arts Council, is co-founder of the Chamber Music Society of Saint Cloud, and frequently serves as guest speaker at organists' meetings across the country. He was named adviser to the Fred J. Cooper Memorial Organ for the Kimmel Center in Philadelphia.

BIBLIOGRAPHY

M.A. Dodd: "Pipedreams at Twenty: a Milestone Observed, a Glance Backward, and a Look to the Future." *The American Organist*, xxxvi/2 (February 2002), 74–77

WILLIAM F. COSCARELLI

Barrelhouse. A style of piano playing that originated among African American blues musicians in the early 20th century. It was first practiced in the makeshift saloons of lumber camps in the South and is related to Boogie-woogie (i), which it may have preceded as a blues piano style. Barrelhouse was played in regular 4/4 meter, whereas boogie developed as fast music largely of eight beats to the bar. Ragtime bass figures or the heavy left-hand vamp known as "stomping" were often employed with occasional walking-bass variations. Characteristic early recordings are "Barrel House Man" (1927, Para.) by Texas pianist Will Ezell, "The Dirty Dozen" by Speckled Red (Rufus Perryman) (1929, Bruns.), and "Soon this Morning" by Charlie Spand (1929, Para.); Perryman and Spand worked in Detroit after leaving the South. "Diggin' my Potatoes" (1939, Bb), by Washboard Sam with Joshua Altheimer on piano, and "Shack Bully Stomp" (1938, Decca), by Peetie Wheatstraw, are examples of the persistence of the style. Many barrelhouse themes became standards and were played by blues pianists after other styles had superseded the form. The term barrelhouse was also used to mean rough or crude, as in "Mooch" Richardson's "Low Down Barrel House Blues" (1928, OK), and several blues singers, among them Nolan Welch, Buck McFarland, and Bukka White, were known by this nickname.

BIBLIOGRAPHY

S. Calt, J. Epstein, and N. Perls: liner notes, *Barrelhouse Blues, 1927–1936*, Yazoo 1028 (1971)
E. Kriss: *Barrelhouse and Boogie Piano* (New York, 1974)
P. Oliver: "Piano Blues and Barrelhouse," *Blues off the Record* (Tunbridge Wells and New York, 1984)
C. Lornell: "Barrelhouse Singers and Sanctified Preachers," *Saints and Sinners: Religion, Blues and (D)evil in African-American Music and Literature*, ed. R. Sacré (Liége, 1996), 115–34

PAUL OLIVER/R

Barrère, Georges (*b* Bordeaux, France, 31 Oct 1876; *d* New York, NY, 14 June 1944). French flutist. Trained at the Paris Conservatoire, first with Henri Altès under whom he made slow progress, then under Paul Taffanel, Barrère was one of the most brilliant pupils to win a *premier prix*. His studies completed, he filled a number of important posts leading to the Opéra and Colonne orchestras. In 1895 he formed the Société Moderne des Instruments à Vent, which replaced Taffanel's group, disbanded in 1893; during this period Barrère contributed a flute section to Charles Marie Widor's continuation of Hector Berlioz's treatise on orchestration. In 1905 Walter Damrosch invited Barrère to join the New York SO, with which he played, with only one break, for the rest of his life. As an exponent of the French style of flute playing, Barrère's influence was profound, and it is sad to realize that, in spite of his kindly and generous nature, his success led to the eclipse of Carl Wehner, Boehm's pupil and the doyen of flute teachers in New York. In the United States, as in France, Barrère founded small instrumental groups: in 1910 the Barrère Ensemble of Wind Instruments, and in 1915 the Little Symphony chamber orchestra. These activities continued until his death.

BIBLIOGRAPHY

S. Nelson: "Georges Barrère," *ARSCJ*, xxiv/1 (1993), 4–48
N. Toff: *Monarch of the Flute: the Life of Georges Barrère* (New York, 2005)

PHILIP BATE/R

Barrett, "Sweet" Emma (*b* New Orleans, LA, 25 March 1897; *d* New Orleans, 28 Jan 1983). Pianist, singer, and bandleader. The daughter of the Civil War veteran and Louisiana state senator W.B. Barrett, she learned piano by ear as a child and was playing professionally by her early teens. She never learned to read music and worked almost exclusively in New Orleans. During the 1920s Barrett played with many of the uptown New Orleans groups, including those led by Papa Celestin, Armand Piron, and John Robichaux. In the following decade she worked most often with Bebe Ridgley, with whom she developed a local following that subsequently brought her success at the Happy Landing from 1949 and the Paddock Lounge during the late 1950s. It was at this time that she became known as Sweet Emma the Bell Gal because of her habit of wearing garters with bells attached that created a tambourine-like effect as she played. In 1961 she became one of the first performers to be featured at Preservation Hall, appearing there with a group of local musicians that became known as the Preservation Hall Jazz Band. This ensemble can be seen in the Norman Jewison film *Cincinnati Kid* (1965). Barrett suffered a stroke and temporarily retired in 1967, after which she continued to play in a reduced capacity, but rarely left New Orleans due to her fear of flying.

BIBLIOGRAPHY

M. Unterbrink: *Jazz Women at the Keyboard* (New York, 1983)

C. Bottsford: "Sweet Emma's 1968 Interview," *Jazzbeat* (1990–91), Fall–Winter,

JOHN L. CLARK, JR.

Barretto, Ray (*b* Brooklyn, NY, 29 April 1929; *d* Hackensack, NJ, 17 Feb 2006). Conga player, bandleader, and producer of Puerto Rican descent. He began playing percussion informally during time in Germany as part of the US occupation army (1946–9). Returning to New York City in 1949, he participated in the lively jam-session scene in Harlem, playing bongos in sessions with Charlie Parker and Dizzy Gillespie. In 1957, he replaced Mongo Santamaría in Tito Puente's band. By 1960, he became the house percussionist for various jazz labels (Blue Note, Prestige, Riverside), recording his first album as leader for Riverside in 1961. The Charanga La Moderna was his first full-fledged Latin dance band, beginning in 1962. In 1963, his song "El Watusi" became the first Latin tune to enter the Billboard Top 20. By 1990, his salsa career stagnant, he formed a small, jazz-influenced sextet, New World Spirit, recording a number of Grammy-nominated albums.

Barretto's style, at once elastic and hard-driving, influenced more jazz recordings than that of any other conga player. His musical flexibility enabled him to record with artists as diverse as Crosby, Stills & Nash, the Average White Band, the Bee Gees, Gilberto Gil, Judy Collins, Edgar Winter, and Bernard Lavilliers. As a bandleader, he was characteristically progressive. In 1999, Barretto was inducted into the Latin Music Hall of Fame, and in 2006, one month before his death, he received the National Endowment for the Arts Jazz Masters Award, the first ever received by a US-born Latin musician.

BIBLIOGRAPHY

A.J. Smith: "Ray Barretto's Crossover Crisis," *DB*, xliii (1976), 17–18

P. Guzman: "Riffs: Ray Barretto's Salsa Revival," *The Village Voice*, xxvii (1982), 68–9

R. Mangual: "Ray Barretto: Living by the Beat of the Drum (interview)," *Latin Beat*, xiii (2003), 20–3

J. Brody: "Ray ou la salsa *Piquante* (1981 interview with Ray Barretto)," *Jm* (2006), 34–5

J. Murphy: "Percussionist Ray Barretto Dies (obituary)," *DB*, lxxiii (2006), 24

J. Varela: "Ray Lives! In Memory of Ray Barretto," *Latin Beat*, xvi (2006), 20–3

E. Álvarez Peraza: "A Posthumous Tribute to Ray Barretto," *Latin Beat*, xvi (2006/2007), 6–7

J. Moreno: "La salsa y sus muertes," *El son y la salsa en la identidad del Caribe; memorias del II Congreso Internacional Identidad y Cultura en el Caribe* (Santiago de los Caballeros, República Dominicana, 2008), 473–9

JAIRO MORENO

Barrett Sisters, the [Delois Barrett and the Barrett Sisters]. Gospel trio. Its members were Delores [Delois] (soprano), Billie (alto), and Rhodessa (high soprano) Barrett. Hailing from the Southside of Chicago, they grew up with seven other siblings and were members of the Morning Star Baptist Church where they sang in a choir directed by their aunt. As the Barrett–Hudson Singers, Delores and Billie had performed in a group with a cousin, whom Rhodessa later replaced to form the Barrett Sisters. Delores, the eldest and the group's leader, started singing at the age of six. Her professional career began in earnest after graduating from Englewood High School, when she became the first female to join the Roberta Martin Singers (1944; *see* MARTIN, ROBERTA). Billie and Rhodessa received some formal training, but it was through the Roberta Martin Singers that Delores learned technique and honed her individual style, along with the unique ensemble quality known as the Roberta Martin sound. Delores continued to sing with Martin from time to time, even as the Barrett Sisters took shape. Getting their start as an African American gospel trio, the Barrett Sisters first recorded with the label Savoy (1964). Their debut album, *Delores Barrett and her Sisters*, contains such songs as "You'll never walk alone" and "Somebody Bigger than you and I." The concertized nature of the Barrett's sound established a repertoire that included renditions of hymns and popular standards, including "What a Wonderful World" and "Count your Blessings." The Barrett Sisters appear in the documentary film *Say Amen, Somebody* (1984). In addition to making several European tours, they continued to perform in and around Chicago into the late 1990s. They have appeared on television and in concert with numerous popular and gospel artists and have received substantial recognition for their contributions to gospel.

BIBLIOGRAPHY

H.C. Boyer: *How Sweet the Sound: the Golden Age of Gospel* (Washington DC, 1995)

A. Heilbut: *The Gospel Sound: Good News and Bad Times* (New York, 1971, 6/2002)

ROXANNE R. REED

Barron, Bebe [née Charlotte Wind] (*b* Minneapolis, MN, 16 June 1927; *d* Los Angeles, CA, 20 April 2008). Composer. She and her husband LOUIS BARRON were pioneers in the field of electro-acoustic music. She received the MA in political science from the University of Minnesota, where she studied composition with Cordero, and she also spent a year studying composition at the University of Mexico. In 1947 she moved to New York and, while working as a researcher for *Time-Life*, studied composition with WALLINGFORD RIEGGER and HENRY COWELL. Married that year, the Barrons began their experiments with taped electronic sounds; in 1948 in New York they established one of the earliest electro-acoustic music studios. It contained both disc and tape equipment with sine- and square-wave oscillators, mixers and filters, and four synchronous projectors used for the manipulation of sound on optical tracks. Their experiments led the Barrons to use and develop characteristics of individual circuits to create different types of sound events, each of which was considered a Gestalt, and they eventually constructed a large collection of cybernetic circuits for compositional use. When they collaborated on a composition, Louis designed and built the electronic circuits for sound generation while Bebe searched the taped material for its musical potential and proposed the application of particular processing and compositional techniques.

Their first fully realized work was *Heavenly Menagerie* (1951–2). During 1952 and 1953 their studio was used by John Cage for the preparation of his first tape works. In 1956 they composed the music for *Forbidden Planet*, one of the first electronic scores written for a commercial film, and an influential work in the development of electronic music. In 1962 the Barrons moved to Los Angeles, where, although divorced in 1970, they continued to collaborate on compositional projects. Bebe became the first Secretary of the Society for Electro-Acoustic Music in the United States in 1985 and also served on the board of directors. In 1997 she was presented with an award from the Society for Electro-Acoustic Music in the United States for the Barrons' joint lifetime achievement in electro-acoustic music.

WORKS

(all electro-acoustic, composed with Louis Barron)

Dramatic: Legend (American Mime Theatre), 1955; Ballet (P. Feigay), 1958; incid music for 4 plays, 1957–62

Tape: Heavenly Menagerie, 1951–2; For an Electronic Nervous System, 1954; Music of Tomorrow, 1960; Spaceboy, 1971; The Circe Circuit, 1982; Elegy for a Dying Planet, 1982

Film scores: Bells of Atlantis (I. Hugo), 1952; Miramagic (W. Lewisohn), 1954; Forbidden Planet (F.M. Wilcox), 1956; Jazz of Lights (Hugo), 1956; Bridges (S. Clarke), 1959; Crystal Growing (Western Electric), 1959; The Computer Age (IBM), 1968; Spaceboy (R. Druks), 1973 [arr. of 1971 tape piece]; More than Human (A. Singer), 1974; Cannabis (Computer Graphics), 1975

BIBLIOGRAPHY

GroveW (B. Schrader) [incl. further bibliography]

L. Barron and B. Barron: "Forbidden Planet," *Film Music*, xv/5 (1956), 18

S. Rubin: "Retrospect: Forbidden Planet," *Cinefantastique*, iv/1 (1975), 4–13

J. Brockman: "The First Electronic Filmscore: Forbidden Planet," *The Score*, vii/3 (1992), 5–13

V. Vale and A. Juno: *Incredibly Strange Music no.2* (San Francisco, 1994), 194–202

M. Burman: "Making Music for Forbidden Planet," *Projections* 7, ed. J. Boorman and W. Donohue (London, 1997), 252–63

J. Wierzbicki: *Louis and Bebe Barron's Forbidden Planet: a Film Score Guide* (Lanham, MD, 2005)

J. Barham: "Scoring Incredible Futures: Science-Fiction Screen Music, and 'Postmodernism' as Romantic Ephiphany," *MQ*, xci/3–4 (2008), 240–74

BARRY SCHRADER

Barron, Louis (*b* Minneapolis, MN, 23 April 1920; *d* Los Angeles, CA, 1 Nov 1989). Composer. He and his wife Bebe wrote pioneering works in the field of electro-acoustic music. He studied the piano and wrote jazz criticism while a student at the University of Minnesota. He then worked for the Gallup organization as a social psychologist. Married in 1947, the Barrons established one of the earliest electro-acoustic music studios, in which Louis's knowledge of electronics allowed him to design and build so-called behavioral circuits, based on Norbert Wiener's science of cybernetics.

A fuller discussion of the Barrons' compositional techniques, with a list of their collaborative works and a bibliography, can be found under BEBE BARRON.

BARRY SCHRADER

Barron, Ronald (*b* Harrisburg, PA, 31 Oct 1946). Trombonist. He grew up in Greenville, South Carolina, and Fort Worth, Texas, and studied at the Cincinnati College-Conservatory of Music. Before joining the Boston Symphony as second trombonist in 1970, he toured with the American Wind Symphony and served one season as Principal Trombonist in the Montreal Symphony Orchestra. In 1975, Barron became principal trombone in Boston and also served 13 seasons with the Boston Pops. In 1974, he shared the top prize of the Munich International Solo Competition and performed Frank Martin's *Ballade* with the Bavarian State Radio Orchestra. Barron has performed and recorded with the Canadian Brass, Empire Brass, and Summit Brass, appeared numerous times as a soloist with the Boston Pops, released nine recordings of solo literature, and commissioned new works. He has been a member of the faculties of the New England Conservatory of Music, Boston University, and Tanglewood Music Center. In 2005 the International Trombone Association honored him with the prestigious ITA Award for his distinguished career and contributions to trombone performance. Since his retirement in 2008, after 38 seasons as a member of the Boston Symphony Orchestra, Barron has toured extensively as a soloist and continues to record.

BIBLIOGRAPHY

International Trombone Association: "Ronald Baron" <http://www.trombone.net/about/bio.cfm?id=60>

BRUCE TYCHINSKI

Barrows, Cliff(ord) (*b* Ceres, CA, 6 April 1923). Evangelical music director, media personality, and administrator. Barrows studied sacred music and Shakespearean drama at Bob Jones University (BA 1944) and was ordained a minister in the Baptist church. He became a full-time worker with Youth For Christ in the immediate postwar years, and in 1945 joined the Billy Graham Evangelistic Association as music director. In 1950, Barrows became the host and crusade choir director for Graham's *Hour of Decision* radio (and later television) program, a post which he still held in 2011. From 1965–70, Barrows was the president of World Wide Pictures, Graham's film production company. He appeared in the film *His Land* (1970) alongside pop star Cliff Richard. Barrows has also edited many collections of gospel music for Graham's Association. For his significant contributions to the field of music, he was inducted into the Gospel Music Hall of Fame in 1988, and was also inducted into the Religious Broadcasting Hall of Fame in 1996. His papers are held at the Billy Graham Center Archives in Wheaton, Illinois.

JONAS WESTOVER

Barrows, John (*b* Glendale, CA, 12 Feb 1913; *d* Madison, WI, 11 Jan 1974). Horn player. He studied at the Eastman School of Music (1930–32), San Diego State Teachers College (1933–4), and at Yale University (1934–8). He played horn with the Minneapolis SO (1938–42) and with the orchestras of the New York City Opera (1946–9) and the New York City Ballet (1952–5). Barrows was best known for the reliable virtuosity he exhibited with the New York Woodwind Quintet, an ensemble that he co-founded in 1952 and performed with until 1961. He taught at Yale (1957–61) and at New York University (1958–61); in 1961 he was appointed professor at the University of Wisconsin, Madison, where he remained until his death. He composed two string quartets, a wind quintet, and a string trio, and made many arrangements of orchestral works that are among the staples of the concert band repertory.

JAMES WIERZBICKI

Barrueco, Manuel (*b* Santiago de Cuba, 16 Dec 1952). Guitarist of Cuban birth. He studied at the Esteban Salas Conservatory in Santiago de Cuba and with Aaron Shearer at the Peabody Conservatory. He won first prize in the Concert Artists Guild Competition in 1974, and that year made his debut at Carnegie Hall. In 1986 he gave the first American performance of Takemitsu's concerto *To the Edge of Dream* with the Tulsa PO under Bernard Rubenstein. He was also soloist in the world premiere of Takemitsu's *Spectral Canticle*, a double concerto for guitar, violin, and orchestra, with violinist Franz Peter Zimmerman at the Schleswig-Holstein Music Festival, Kiel, in 1995. Barrueco has made several recordings, notably of Albéniz and Granados, and has arranged works for the guitar including transcriptions of J.S. Bach's Three Violin Sonatas. He helped establish the guitar department at the Manhattan School of Music, and currently teaches at the Peabody Conservatory.

BIBLIOGRAPHY

S. Cosentino: "A Conversation with Manuel Barrueco," *Guitar Review*, no.104 (1996), 21–7

J. Ferguson: "Manuel Barrueco and David Tanenbaum," *Guitar Player*, xxix/6 (1996), 35–9

D. Reynolds: "Manuel Barrueco: the Baltimore Interview," *Guitar Review*, no.114 (1998), 22–8

A. Sigurdardottir and others: "Manuel Barrueco. I," *Classical Guitar*, xxv/8 (2007), 11–16

A. Sigurdardottir and others: "Manuel Barrueco. II," *Classical Guitar*, xxv/9 (2007), 20, 22–4

THOMAS F. HECK/R

Barry, Flora Elizabeth (*b* Paris, ME, 18 Sept 1836; *d* after 1920). Contralto and teacher. Barry descended from old New England stock dating back to the early Puritans. She began her vocal studies early, and her first public appearances in 1863 were in Boston with the Mendelssohn Quintette Club and the Handel and Haydn Society. She later studied with Luigi Vannucini in Florence, Italy. Barry had significant success as a singer, performing operatic roles and singing oratorios throughout the United States and in Canada and Mexico. Married twice, Barry's first husband was John S. Cary, brother of the singer Annie Louise Cary. Her second marriage to artist Charles A. Barry in 1868 ended in a sensational divorce in 1873. From 1877, Barry concentrated her musical career on teaching. She continued to be known and respected as a voice teacher in Boston well into her 80s.

BIBLIOGRAPHY

G.T. Edwards: *Music and Musicians of Maine* (New York, 1928)

F.E. Willard and M.A. Livermore, eds.: *Woman of the Century: Fourteen Hundred-Seventy Biographical Sketches Accompanied by Portraits of Leading Women in All Walks of Life* (Buffalo, NY, 1893)

LAURIE BLUNSOM

Barry, John [Prendergast, John Barry] (*b* York, England, 3 Nov 1933; *d* Oyster Bay, NY, 30 Jan 2011). English composer. As a boy he worked at his father's theater chain in the north of England and listened to such established Hollywood composers as Steiner, Korngold, and Waxman. He contemplated a career as a film composer and left school to study music with Francis Jackson, then the Master of Music at York Minster. During his national service (1952–5) he studied jazz arranging and orchestration by mail with Stan Kenton's famous arranger William Russo.

In 1957 he formed the John Barry Seven, a jazz-rock group, and was music director for the singer Adam Faith on several hit songs, including "What do you Want" (1959, Parlophone). The Seven's recording "Hit and Miss" (1960, EMI) was adopted as the theme for the BBC's popular television show *Juke Box Jury*. Around this time Barry wrote, performed, and recorded pop music, appearing with his group on such influential shows as *Six-Five Special* and *Drumbeat*. He later worked as a music director for EMI and Ember Records.

Following his first film score, for *Beat Girl* (1960, with Faith), Barry gained fame for his fusion of jazz, pop, and orchestral sounds in the James Bond films, beginning with his arrangement of Monty Norman's *James Bond Theme* for *Dr. No* (1962) and concluding with his music for *The Living Daylights* (1987). His soundtrack for the 007 film *Goldfinger* (1964) displaced the Beatles at the top of the American charts; his title songs for *Thunderball* (1965), *You Only Live Twice* (1967), *Octopussy* (1983), and *A View to a Kill* (1985) also charted.

While the Bond films attracted most of the attention, Barry also scored a wide variety of other British films including *Zulu* (1964); six Bryan Forbes films including *King Rat* (1965), *The Whisperers* (1967), and *Deadfall*

(1968), in which Barry appears conducting the London PO performing his single-movement guitar concerto; the cimbalom-flavored *The Ipcress File* and the hip *The Knack… and how to get it* (both 1965); and the African lion adventure *Born Free* (1966), which won Oscars for his score and title song. He added choir to his lavish orchestral scores for the period films *The Lion in Winter* (1968, another Oscar winner), *The Last Valley* (1971), and *Mary, Queen of Scots* (1971).

Barry gradually developed a more lush, romantic style that suited such movies as the romantic fantasy *Somewhere in Time* (1980), *Out of Africa* (1985), and the Western *Dances with Wolves* (1990), the last two of which won him further Academy Awards. He revisited his earlier, jazzy style in the concept album *Americans* (1976) and in his scores for *Body Heat* (1981), *The Cotton Club* (1984), and *Playing by Heart* (1998).

Barry achieved sporadic success with stage musicals. He had West End hits with *Passion Flower Hotel* (1965) and *Billy* (1974, starring Michael Crawford) and Broadway failures with *Lolita, My Love* (1971, with lyrics by Alan Jay Lerner) and *The Little Prince and the Aviator* (1981), both of which closed during previews. *Brighton Rock* (2004, based on the Graham Greene novel) played briefly in London. For *Billy*, *The Little Prince*, and *Brighton Rock*, Barry collaborated with the lyricist Don Black, with whom he had worked on songs from the mid-1960s.

Barry's television themes also proved popular, notably those for *The Persuaders!* (1971), *The Adventurer* (1972), and *Orson Welles' Great Mysteries* (1973). He was profiled on American television in *Great Performances* (1993) and on the British program *Omnibus* (2000). He moved to America in 1975 and, late in his career, turned his attention to such reflective orchestral concept albums as *The Beyondness of Things* and *Eternal Echoes*. He was named an Officer of the British Empire in 1999, received an honorary doctorate from the University of York in 2001, and became the first composer to receive the British Academy of Film and Television Arts Fellowship in 2008.

WORKS

Film scores: Beat Girl, 1960; Never Let Go, 1960; Mix me a Person, 1962; The Amorous Prawn, 1962; From Russia with Love, 1963; Goldfinger, 1964; Man in the Middle, 1964; Séance on a Wet Afternoon, 1964; They all Died Laughing, 1964; Zulu, 1964; Four in the Morning, 1965; The Ipcress File, 1965; King Rat, 1965; The Knack… and how to get it, 1965; Mister Moses, 1965; The Party's Over, 1965; Thunderball, 1965; Born Free, 1966; The Chase, 1966; The Quiller Memorandum, 1966; The Wrong Box, 1966; Dutchman, 1967; The Whisperers, 1967; You Only Live Twice, 1967; Boom!, 1968; Deadfall, 1968; The Lion in Winter, 1968; Petulia, 1968; The Appointment, 1969; Midnight Cowboy, 1969 On her Majesty's Secret Service, 1969

Monte Walsh, 1970; Diamonds are Forever, 1971; The Last Valley, 1971; Mary, Queen of Scots, 1971; Murphy's War, 1971; They might be Giants, 1971; Walkabout, 1971; Alice's Adventures in Wonderland, 1972; Follow me, 1972; A Doll's House, 1973; The Dove, 1974; The Man with the Golden Gun, 1974; The Tamarind Seed, 1974; The Day of the Locust, 1975; King Kong, 1976; Robin and Marian, 1976; The Deep, 1977; First Love, 1977; The White Buffalo, 1977; The Betsy, 1978; Game of Death, 1978; Moonraker, 1979; The Black Hole, 1979; Hanover Street, 1979; Starcrash, 1979

Inside Moves, 1980; Night Games, 1980; Raise the Titanic!, 1980; Somewhere in Time, 1980; Touched by Love, 1980; Body Heat, 1981; The Legend of the Lone Ranger, 1981; Frances, 1982; Hammett, 1982; Murder by Phone, 1982; The Golden Seal, 1983; High Road to China, 1983; Octopussy, 1983; The Cotton Club, 1984; Mike's Murder, 1984; Until September, 1984; Jagged Edge, 1985; Out of Africa, 1985; A View to a Kill, 1985; The Golden Child, 1986; Howard the Duck, 1986; A Killing Affair, 1986; Peggy Sue got Married, 1986; Hearts of Fire, 1987; The Living Daylights, 1987; Masquerade, 1988

Dances with Wolves, 1990; Chaplin, 1992; Indecent Proposal, 1993; My Life, 1993; Ruby Cairo, 1993; The Specialist, 1994; Across the Sea of Time, 1995; Cry the Beloved Country, 1995; The Scarlet Letter, 1995; Swept from the Sea, 1997; Mercury Rising, 1998; Playing by Heart, 1998; Enigma, 2001

Television scores (selected): Elizabeth Taylor in London, 1963; Sophia Loren in Rome, 1964; The Glass Menagerie, 1973; Love among the Ruins, 1975; Eleanor and Franklin, 1976; Eleanor and Franklin: the White House Years, 1977; The Gathering, 1977; The War between the Tates, 1977; Young Joe: the Forgotten Kennedy, 1977; Willa, 1979; The Corn is Green, 1979; Svengali, 1983

Orch: Americans, 1976; The Beyondness of Things, 1999; Eternal Echoes, 2001

BIBLIOGRAPHY

R.S. Brown: *Overtones and Undertones: Reading Film Music* (Los Angeles, 1994)

E. Fiegel: *John Barry: a Sixties Theme, from James Bond to Midnight Cowboy* (London, 1998)

B. Stanley: "Some Like it Cool: a Tale of Sex, Spies, Success and Cimbalons," *Mojo* (2001), Dec, 67–74

G. Leonard, P. Walker, and G. Bramley: *John Barry: the Man with the Midas Touch* (Bristol, 2008)

J. Burlingame: "Billion Dollar Composer: John Barry," *Daily Variety* (3 Nov 2008), A1–A6

B. Handy: "The Man who Knew the Score," *Vanity Fair* <http://www.vanityfair.com/culture/features/2009/02/john-barry200902> (2009)

JON BURLINGAME

Barry, Phillips (*b* Boston, MA,1880; *d* Framingham, MA, 1937). Ballad scholar. He studied folklore, theology, and classical and medieval literature at Harvard, and was probably self-taught in music. He founded the Folk-Song Society of the North-East and edited its *Bulletin* from 1930 until his death. His academic training combined with his later fieldwork allowed him to develop a broad yet penetrating view of ballad creation, and he was the first North American scholar to investigate folksong in terms of text, tune, performance, and transmission. His idea of "individual invention plus communal re-creation," which was similar to Cecil Sharp's theory, proposed that a folksong was creatively re-made within the community each time it was sung; this view replaced prevailing theories of a communal origin of the folksong by means of group improvisation. He collected mainly in New England and collaborated with scholars in Vermont and Maine. Through his efforts, research methods used in ballad studies changed from scholarship based on library sources, as in the work of Child and Kittredge, to the study of traditional performers and a more complete analysis of folksong as a genre. His essay "The Part of the Folksinger" (1961) was particularly influential.

WRITINGS

"Irish Come-All-Ye's," *Journal of American Folklore*, xxii (1909), 374–88; see also "Irish Folk-Song," *Journal of American Folklore*, xxiv (1911), 332–43

"The Origin of Folk-Melodies," "A Garland of Ballads," *Journal of American Folklore*, xxiii (1910), 440–45, 446–54
"Some Aspects of Folk-Song," *Journal of American Folklore*, xxv (1912), 274–83
with F.H. Eckstorm and M.W. Smyth: "The Music of the Ballads," *British Ballads from Maine* (New Haven, CT, 1929), xxi–xxxvii
"Notes on the Songs and Music of the Shakers," *Bulletin of the Folk-Song Society of the North-East*, no.1 (1930), 5–7
"Communal Recreation," *Bulletin of the Folk-Song Society of the North-East*, no.5 (1933), 4–6; see also "On the Psychopathology of Ballad-Singing," *Bulletin of the Folk-Song Society of the North-East*, no.11 (1936), 16–18
"American Folk Music," *Southern Folklore Quarterly*, i/2 (1937), 29–47
"Notes on the Ways of Folk-Singers with Folk-Tunes," *Bulletin of the Folk-Song Society of the North-East*, no.12 (1937), 2–6
Folk Music in America (New York, 1939)
"The Part of the Folk Singer in the Making of Folk Balladry," *The Critics and the Ballad*, ed. M. Leach and T.P. Coffin (Carbondale, IL, 1961), 59–76

EDITIONS

The Maine Woods Songster: Fifty Songs for Singing (Cambridge, MA, 1939)
with others: *The New Green Mountain Songster* (New Haven, CT, 1939)

BIBLIOGRAPHY

G. Herzog: "Phillips Barry," *Journal of American Folklore*, li (1938), 439–41
R.G. Alvey: "Phillips Barry and Anglo-American Folksong Scholarship," *Journal of the Folklore Institute*, x (1973), 67–95

JAMES PORTER

Barth, Hans (*b* Leipzig, Germany, 25 June 1897; *d* Jacksonville, FL, 8 Dec 1956). Composer and pianist of German birth; naturalized American. As a child he attended the Leipzig Conservatory, studying under Carl Reinecke. He moved to the United States with his family in 1907 and made his New York recital debut the next year. He became a US citizen in 1912. Busoni inspired him to experiment with new scales, and Barth helped to invent a portable quarter-tone piano in 1928, for which he composed numerous works; he was acquainted with Ives and may have rekindled that composer's interest in quarter-tone music. Barth performed in the United States and Europe on the harpsichord, piano, and quarter-tone piano, and was a soloist with orchestras in Cincinnati, Havana, and Philadelphia; with the Philadelphia Orchestra he served for five years under Stokowski, and performed his Concerto for quarter-tone piano on 28 March 1930. He was a MacDowell Fellow, directed the Institute of Musical Art (Yonkers, New York) and the National School for Musical Culture (New York), and taught piano at the Mannes School and the Jacksonville College of Music (1948–56).

WORKS

Stage: *Miriagia* (operetta), op.2, 1938; Save me the Waltz (incid. music, B. Bernier)
Orch: Pf Conc., 1928; Conc., ¼-tone str, ¼-tone pf, op.11, 1930; Conc., quarter-tone pf, str, op.15, 1930; Drama Sym., 1940; Sym. "Prince of Peace," op.25, 1940; 10 Etudes, ¼-tone pf, orch, 1942–4
Chbr: Pf Sonata, op.7, 14, 1929; Qnt, ¼-tone pf, str, 1930; Suite, ¼-tone str, brass, timp, 1930; Pf Sonata no.2, op.14, 1932; Suite, pf, op.20, 1938; Suite no.2, pf, op.23, 1941
Many songs
Principal publishers: Associated, Axelrod, Mills

BIBLIOGRAPHY

EwenD
"Barth at Miami Conservatory," *Musical Courier*, cxxxix (1 Jan 1949), 33

KATHERINE K. PRESTON

Bartholomew, Dave (*b* Edgard, LA, 24 Dec 1920). Trumpeter, arranger, producer, songwriter, bandleader, and singer. He started his career as a trumpeter playing with established bands led by, among others, Papa Celestin, Joe Robichaux, and Claiborne Williams before joining Fats Pichon's ensemble, considered one of the top groups in New Orleans, in 1939. During World War II he played in the 196th AGF (Army Ground Forces) Band, where he met Abraham Malone, who taught him how to write and arrange. After the war, he formed his own band in New Orleans, which made its debut at the Dew Drop Inn and later performed at Sam Simoneaux's club Graystone where many of the city's top instrumental players, including the drummer Earl Palmer and the saxophonists Lee Allen and Red Tyler, were showcased.

Bartholomew is best known for his talents as an arranger and songwriter. In the 1950s and 60s he worked with many of the biggest stars of the day, including Smiley Lewis, Lloyd Price, Shirley and Lee, and Joe Turner. By the 1970s he had associations with some of rock and roll's most established talents, including Paul McCartney, Elton John, and the Rolling Stones. His most productive association was with FATS DOMINO, whom he met through Lew Chudd, the owner of Imperial Records, where he worked as a house arranger, an A&R man and an in-house bandleader. From 1949 to 1963 Bartholomew co-wrote more than 70 hit songs with Domino, including "Blue Monday" and "I'm Walkin'." His contributions in solidifying the "big beat" of New Orleans with the rock and roll of the 1950s are significant and uncontested.

SELECTED RECORDINGS

Dave Bartholomew & Maryland Ja (GHB, 1995); *In the Alley* (SFM, 2001); *The Chronological Dave Bartholomew: 1947–1950* (CLRB, 2001); *The Chronological Dave Bartholomew: 1950–1952* (CLRB, 2003); *Dave Bartholomew: the King Sides* (Collectables, 2004)

BIBLIOGRAPHY

F.P. Miller, A.F. Vandome, and J. McBrewster: *Dave Bartholomew* (Beau Bassin, 2010)

RANDOLPH LOVE

Bartholomew, Marshall (Moore) (*b* Belleville, IL, 3 March 1885; *d* Guilford, CT, 16 April 1978). Choral conductor. He studied at the University of Pennsylvania (BM 1909) and the Hochschule für Musik in Berlin with HORATIO PARKER, Engelbert Humperdinck, and Albert Coates. During World War I he organized singing activities among war prisoners and directed the Music Bureau of the National War Council. Bartholomew taught at Yale University (1921–53), where he directed the Yale Glee Club and achieved international renown. He also established and directed the University Glee Club of New Haven (1924–48). He founded the International Student Music Council in 1931 to promote international goodwill through singing, and during World War II he served on the Joint Army and Navy Committee on Welfare and Recreation. He composed and arranged works for choirs, edited a Yale songbook, and published articles and books on singing. His last major project researched the history of music at Yale. Yale awarded him an honorary degree (MA 1953) and the Yale Medal (1955). To celebrate his 90th birthday, he conducted 2000 former members of the Yale Glee Club. Bartholomew composed a number of vocal works including *Song in the Night*, *April Song*, and *Call of Spring*; he was also an arranger and editor. His papers are held at *NH*.

BIBLIOGRAPHY

M. Kaplan: Obituary, *New York Times* (18 April 1978)

SORAB MODI/PATRICE MADURA WARD-STEINMAN

Bartlett, Daniel B. Instrument dealer and maker, active in Concord, New Hampshire, during the 1840s in partnership with DAVID M. DEARBORN.

Bartlett, Homer N(ewton) (*b* Olive, NY, 28 Dec 1846; *d* Hoboken, NJ, 3 April 1920). Organist and composer. Bartlett studied piano, organ, and composition in New York, where he began a career as a church organist at age 14. He spent 12 years in that capacity at the Marble Collegiate Church and then almost 35 years at the Madison Avenue Baptist Church, retiring in 1912. A founding member of the American Guild of Organists, he was also active in the rival National Association of Organists (president, 1910–11) and the Manuscript Society of New York.

Bartlett was a prolific composer whose published opus numbers reached 277. Some of his early salon pieces for the piano, for example the *Grande polka de concert*, op.1 (1867), reflect the influence of Liszt and Gottschalk and were popular enough to be published in several editions. Other works include a three-act opera *La vallière* (1887), the operetta *Magic Hours* (1910), the oratorio *Samuel*, the cantata *The Last Chieftain*, violin and cello concertos, and the symphonic poem *Apollo* (1911). He also wrote anthems, secular part songs, organ music, character pieces for the piano (many obviously Chopinesque), and some 80 solo songs. Piano pieces such as *Kuma saka* (1907), *Japanese Revery* [*sic*] (1908), and *Dondon-bushi* (1918) manifest a fascination in his later career with Japanese themes, although they reflect no real understanding of Japanese music.

BIBLIOGRAPHY

DAB (S. Salter)
R. Hughes: *Contemporary American Composers* (Boston, 1900), 317–23
J. Gillespie: "Nineteenth-Century American Piano Music," *Sonneck Society Newsletter*, xii/3 (1986), 81–4

WILLIAM OSBORNE

Bartlett, James Carroll [J.C.] (*b* Harmony, ME, 14 June 1850; *d* Medfield, MA, 30 Nov 1929). Tenor, composer, voice teacher, and organist. By 1860 Bartlett was studying singing in Boston with excellent teachers and later in London with William Shakespeare. This launched a very successful career as tenor when he returned to the United States. Bartlett served as soloist in the Arlington Street Church in Boston (25 years), the Harvard Church in Brookline, and the Plymouth Church in Worcester. He also sang in quartets (Lotus Male Quartet, Albion Quartette), in operas and operettas (touring the country with the Booth-Barrett Company and playing the leading role in *H.M.S. Pinafore*), and with touring concert companies (Camilla Urso, 1875–6, Sauret-Carreño in the early 1870s, and Barnabee in 1878). He was regarded as one of the leading teachers in Boston for 30 years (1896–1926), Worcester (*c*1901–18), and Medfield, MA, where he married Alice Hamant Austin and lived the last 33 years of his life as a composer, singer, conductor, gentleman farmer, and highly respected citizen. One of the numerous prolific American art-song composers of his time, he also wrote sacred solo and choral music, part songs, and cantatas. His most successful piece was *A Dream*, with words by Charles Cory, published by Oliver Ditson in 1895. It became a national favorite, heard on the radio in vocal and instrumental versions, and recorded by such masters as Enrico Caruso and John McCormack.

WORKS
(selective list)

Art songs: A Christmas Lullaby; Come to Me, Sweetheart; A Dream; Fair Phyllis; Ma Pale-brown Lady Sue; Memories; With Fingers Weary and Worn

Sacred: Come Jesus, Redeemer (1927), adaptation of *A Dream*; Grass and Roses (*Gulistan of Saudi*); The Day Is Ended: An Evening Hymn; various sacred duets

Cant.: From Death to Life

BIBLIOGRAPHY

Grove2, Amer. suppl.
R. Hughes: *American Composers* (Boston, 1914)
O. Downes: *The Lure of Music* (New York, 1922)
Obituaries, *Boston Evening Transcript* (2 Dec 1929); *Dedham Transcript* (6 Dec 1929)
W. T. Upton: *The Art Song in America: a Study in the Development of American Music* (Boston, MA, 1930)
R. DeSorgher: *The History of the Town of Medfield, Massachusetts, 1887–1925* (Medfield, MA, 1999)

MARILYNN J. SMILEY

Bartók, Béla (*b* Nagyszentmiklós [now Sînnicolau Mare, Romania], 25 March 1881; *d* New York, NY, 26 Sept 1945). Hungarian composer, ethnomusicologist, and pianist. Although he earned his living mainly from teaching and playing the piano and was a relentless collector and analyst of folk music, Bartók is recognized today principally as a composer. He lived in the United States during his last five years.

1. Life and works. 2. Posthumous significance in the United States.

1. LIFE AND WORKS. Bartók studied piano and composition at the Budapest Academy of Music (1899–1903), and was influenced at a young age by the works of Wagner, Liszt, and Richard Strauss. In 1903–4 he appeared in concerts outside of Hungary for the first time. In 1904, he made his first transcription of a Hungarian

peasant song—a response to increasing national sentiment in Hungary. As he wrote to his sister in December 1904: "Now I have a new plan: to collect the finest Hungarian folksongs and to raise them, adding the best possible piano accompaniments, to the level of art-song." In 1905 he met Zoltán Kodály, and the two began a lifelong collaboration in folksong research. Bartók taught piano at the Budapest Academy from 1906 to 1934, which gave him enough financial security to extend his folksong research to other nationalities. In his own compositions he began to synthesize art music and peasant song in the 14 Bagatelles op.6 (1908), the First String Quartet op.7 (1908–9), and the Two Pictures op.10 (1910) for orchestra. By 1918 he had collected over 9000 folksongs, all the while composing intensively, notably the one-act opera *Bluebeard's Castle* (1911). His first popular success was *The Wooden Prince* (1917); he was striving for concise effects in the Piano Suite op.14 (1916) and the Second String Quartet op.17 (1914–17). Within several years Bartók was making regular recital tours through Europe, which resulted in the composition of a number of piano works, neoclassical in style, to fulfill his needs as a performer: two piano concertos (1926, 1930–31), the Sonata (1926), and the suite *Out of Doors* (1926).

Between December 1927 and February 1928 Bartók made a tour of the United States. After his American debut (in New York on 22 December 1927, playing the Rhapsody op.1 with the New York PO under Willem Mengelberg), he made 25 appearances, many of them lecture-recitals on new Hungarian national music (including Kodály's), sponsored by the Pro-Musica Society. Among the cities he visited were San Francisco, Los Angeles, Portland, Seattle, Denver, Kansas City, Chicago, and St. Paul; he was also soloist in orchestral concerts in Cincinnati, Philadelphia, and New York again before his return to Budapest. The next few years were among his most prolific; he completed the two rhapsodies for violin and piano (and arrangements of both for violin and orchestra and of the first for cello and piano) and the Fourth String Quartet (all 1928), the *Cantata profana* (1930) and other choral works, the Second Piano Concerto (1931), and the 44 Violin Duos (1931).

In 1934 Bartók was relieved of his formal teaching duties and accepted a commission from the Hungarian Academy of Sciences to prepare the publication of his Hungarian folksong collection; but his teaching efforts continued in lectures on folk music and in the composition of *Mikrokosmos* (1926, 1932–9), a set of six volumes (153 pieces) of progressive piano studies. His important compositions of the 1930s were written to commission: the Fifth String Quartet (1934) was composed for Elizabeth Sprague Coolidge, the Music for Strings, Percussion, and Celesta (1936) and the Divertimento (1939) for Paul Sacher (conductor of the Basle Chamber Orchestra), the Sonata for two pianos and percussion (1937) for the Basle ISCM chapter, the Violin Concerto (1937–8) for the violinist Zoltán Székely, and *Contrasts* (1938), commissioned by Benny Goodman, for Goodman and Joseph Szigeti. These works display many of the metrical and rhythmic characteristics—and

Béla Bartók with hurdy-gurdy, Budapest, 1908. (Lebrecht Music & Arts)

especially the palindromic form—that are perhaps the most original features of Bartók's style.

Bartók's anti-fascist views and actions resulted in attacks against him in the Hungarian and Romanian newspapers. He became concerned for the safety of his manuscripts and sent them abroad for safekeeping, and he began to consider emigrating, especially after the annexation of Austria by Nazi Germany in 1938. He made a second American tour (11 April to 18 May 1940), during which he gave a concert with Szigeti in the Library of Congress, recorded *Contrasts* in New York with Szigeti and Goodman, and lectured on folk music. He learned then too of the existence at Harvard University of the Milman Parry collection of some 2600 discs of Serbo-Croatian folk music. With help from members of the music faculty at Columbia University a research grant to enable him to work in the collection was made available from the Alice M. Ditson Fund; under the grant he received a music assistantship at Columbia for the period from March 1941 through December 1942. He returned home to settle his affairs and in autumn 1940, with his second wife, the pianist Ditta Pásztory, left Hungary forever; they disembarked in New York on 30 October. Bartók's last significant European composition had been the Sixth String Quartet (1939), a lament punctuated by "scenes from life."

Soon after arriving in the United States, where he lived for the remainder of his life, Bartók was awarded an honorary doctorate by Columbia University and during 1941–2 he held a research appointment there, working on Parry's Serbo-Croatian collection, which was on loan from Harvard. That work eventually resulted in the volume *Serbo-Croatian Folk Songs* (New York, 1951), of which Bartók completed the musical parts and Lord the textual. He settled into a familiar routine of regular ethnomusicological work and occasional concert tours. Bartók worked on the final forms of his volumes of Romanian instrumental and vocal melodies, which were essentially complete by December 1942, and of Romanian folk texts, which took until late 1944. He also revised and polished his Turkish volume, which was finished in late 1943. Without prospect of publication for either, Bartók deposited them in the music library at Columbia, to be available "to those few persons (very few indeed) who may be interested in them." These Romanian volumes were published in 1967, the Turkish in 1976.

As a composer his American output was initially meager. The orchestral version of the Sonata was made in 1940 and the arrangement of his Second Suite, as the Suite for Two Pianos op.4b BB122, in 1941. But he did not engage in any original composition until the spring of 1942, when some ideas emerged perhaps for a suggested concerto for "combinations of solo instruments and string orchestra." From April 1942, however, chronic illness intervened and Bartók put this work aside. On 21 January 1943 he performed for the last time in public, playing with his wife in the American premiere of the Concerto for Two Pianos at a New York PO concert under Reiner. Bartók decided to go ahead with a visiting appointment at Harvard for the spring semester of 1943. There his duties were to present one recital and two lecture series on recent Hungarian music, principally his own and that of Kodály, and on folksong and ethnomusicological procedure. While Bartók only managed to present three of the first series' lectures and to draft a fourth, these Harvard lectures provide the most candid and detailed explanation of his compositional techniques. He was then hospitalized, with a tentative diagnosis of blood (polycythemia) and lung (tuberculosis) disorders. The American Society of Composers, Authors and Publishers (ASCAP), of which Bartók was not a member, decided to underwrite the costs of his medical treatment and recuperation. For the following three summers recovery took him to Saranac Lake in New York State, and for the 1943–4 winter to a sanatorium in Asheville, North Carolina. It was while on these rest cures away from New York that Bartók's final compositions were written.

The Concerto for Orchestra BB123 was commissioned by the Koussevitzky Music Foundation in May 1943. The various folk-music and art-music components of its style are also less integrated than in his music of the 1930s. First performed in Boston on 1 December 1944, the Concerto for Orchestra proved immediately attractive to the American public, although Bartók was soon persuaded to write a second, less abrupt ending to the finale. Whether, or how much, Bartók's new accessibility betrayed his longer-term creative directions became a frequent point of debate after his death. On Menuhin's suggestion of a commission, Bartók had by 14 March 1944 written the four-movement Sonata for solo violin BB124, a work of overt homage to Bach, in particular Bach's solo Sonata in C, which Bartók had heard Menuhin perform. While writing the sonata Bartók's health again declined. During the summer of 1944 ethnomusicological demands largely took over from composition, but Bartók also regained his enthusiasm for performance, even to the extent of wanting to make new recordings of his own works. Bartók's final two substantial compositions were both concertos. While in Saranac during July–August 1945 he worked intensively on the Third Piano Concerto BB127, intended for his wife to perform, in tandem with the Viola Concerto BB128, commissioned by William Primrose. The idea of a new piano concerto grew from Bartók's realization that his wife could not master some of the more challenging sections of his previous one.

Bartók died in New York on 26 September 1945, after a month-long relapse in health. During his final weeks he managed to complete the Third Piano Concerto, except for the scoring of the final 17 bars, which his colleague Tibor Serly quickly accomplished. His Viola Concerto, however, only remained in sketch; since 1945 several attempts have been made to complete the concerto, either for viola or cello.

2. Posthumous significance in the United States. Bartók's music enjoyed immense popularity in the United States in the years shortly after his death. A Hungarian diaspora of conductors (Reiner, Doráti), violinists (Székely, Szigeti), and pianists (Kentner, Sándor) energetically spread his music around the world, as did recent commissioners of his works (Sacher, Koussevitzky, Menuhin, and Primrose). Already in 1948–9 American orchestras played works by Bartók more often than those by any other 20th-century composer except Strauss and Prokofiev. For a time, younger American composers were strongly attracted to Bartók's music and influenced by it, especially its formal, rhythmic, and contrapuntal techniques. Even adherents of 12-tone composition found the intellectual rigor and protoserialism of some of the works worthy of their attention. Ultimately, however, Bartók's language and his aesthetics proved to be too personal (perhaps too national) and resistant to adaptation; no "Bartók school" crystallized in the United States. Moreover, in the 1950s, a complex dispute arose concerning the estates which Bartók had left, by different wills, in Hungary and America. Lasting into the 1980s, this dispute perpetuated a "cold war" attitude of musical and scholarly noncooperation between the two countries of his residence, and resulted in the slow dissemination of many important primary-source materials as well as distinctly different research traditions and repertory focuses. The greatest legacy of Bartók's folk-music studies undoubtedly lies in his own compositions. It was exactly those ethnomusicological fascinations with musical detail and subtle observations of variant forms which fed his greatest creative strengths. Many of Bartók's writings have been published as ***Béla Bartók Essays*** (ed. B. Suchoff, 1976).

BIBLIOGRAPHY

Grove7 (M. Gillies) [incl. writings and works list]
M. Babbitt: "The String Quartets of Bartók," *MQ*, xxxv (1949), 377–85

H. Stevens: *The Life and Music of Béla Bartók* (New York, 1953, 2/1964)
A. Fassett: *Béla Bartók's American Years: the Naked Face of Genius* (Boston, 1958)
A. Forte: "Bartók's Serial Composition," *MQ*, xlvi (1960), 233–45
V. Bator: *The Béla Bartók Archives: History and Catalogue* (New York, 1963)
J. Vinton: "Bartók on his own Music," *JAMS*, xix (1966), 232–43
E. Lendvai: *Béla Bartók: an Analysis of his Music* (London, 1971)
J. McCabe: *Bartók Orchestral Music* (London, 1974)
D. Dalton: "The Genesis of Bartók's Viola Concerto," *ML*, lvii (1976), 117–29
B. Suchoff: "Bartók in America," *MT*, cxvii (1976), 123–4
G. Perle: "The String Quartets of Béla Bartók," *A Musical Offering: Essays in Honor of Martin Bernstein*, ed. E.H. Clinkscale and C. Brook (New York, 1977), 193–210
H.G. Miskin: "Bartók at Amherst," *Amherst* (1978), 14
S. Kovacs: "Reexamining the Bartók/Serly Viola Concerto," *Studia musicologica Academiae scientiarum hungaricae*, xxiii (1981), 295–322
M. Gillies: "Bartók's Last Works: a Theory of Tonality and Modality," *Musicology*, vii (1982), 120–30
E. Antokoletz: *The Works of Béla Bartók: a Study of Tonality and Progression in Twentieth-century Music* (Berkeley, CA, 1984)
P. Griffiths: *Bartók* (London, 1984)
L. Somfai and V. Lampert: "Bela Bartók," *Modern Masters*, The New Grove Composer Biography Series (New York, 1984), 1–101 [incl. full list of works]
Y. Lenoir: *Folklore et transcendance dans l'oeuvre américaine de Béla Bartók (1940–1945)* (Louvain-la-Neuve, 1986)
B. Suchoff: "Ethnomusicological Roots of Béla Bartók's Musical Language," *World of Music*, xxix/1 (1987), 43–65
M. Gillies: "Bartók as Pedagogue," *Studies in Music*, xxiv (1990), 64–86
P. Wilson: *The Music of Béla Bartók* (New Haven, CT, 1992)
M. Gillies, ed.: *The Bartók Companion* (London, 1993)
P. Laki, ed.: *Bartók and his World* (Princeton, NJ, 1995)
A. Bayley: *Cambridge Companion to Bartók* (Cambridge, UK, 2001)
D. Fosler-Lussier: *Music Divided: Bartok's Legacy in Cold War Culture* (Berkeley, CA, 2007)

VERA LAMPERT, LÁSZLÓ SOMFAI/
H. WILEY HITCHCOCK/MALCOLM GILLIES/R

Bartz, Gary (Lee) (*b* Baltimore, MD, 26 Sept 1940). Jazz alto and soprano saxophonist, bandleader, composer, and vocalist. He began playing in Baltimore, where his father owned the well-known club the North End Lounge. He attended the Juilliard School between 1957 and 1958 and then studied at the Peabody Conservatory. After moving to New York he worked with Charles Mingus (1962–4) and Max Roach (1964 and 1968–9, when he traveled to Europe and the Middle East). He also performed and recorded with Art Blakey's Jazz Messengers (1965–6) and Miles Davis (1970–71). Between 1969 and 1974 Bartz led his own ensemble, Ntu Troop, which recorded six albums blending African music and funk with jazz. In the late 1970s and 1980s, he worked occasionally with Woody Shaw's group as well as with McCoy Tyner. After playing with Kenny Barron (1990s), Bartz was a member of the ensemble Sphere (1999–2003), in which he replaced the late Charlie Rouse, and performed in Europe and America with Tyner. He is a member of the faculty of Oberlin Conservatory.

Bartz's recordings as a leader are uneven, with exceptional examples such as *Another Earth* (1968, Mlst.), *Home!* (1969), and *I've Known Rivers and Other Bodies* (1973) offset by weak commercial efforts in the mid-1970s and 1980s. From the end of the latter decade, however, he recorded a number of excellent albums on a variety of independent labels. As a sideman he has performed on more than 100 albums, with artists including Norman Connors, Shirley Horn, and Roy Hargrove, and won two Grammy Awards (1997 with Roy Hargrove and 2004 with McCoy Tyner).

BIBLIOGRAPHY

D.C. Hunt: "Gary Bartz," *Jazz & Pop*, ix/4 (1970), 26–7
H. Nolan: "Gary Bartz: Music is my Religion!" *DB*, xl/12 (1973), 14–15, 32
B. Rusch: "Gary Bartz: Interview," *Cadence*, x/2 (1984), 5–8
A. Nahigian and E. Enright: "Take Back the Music," *DB*, lxv/9 (1998), 24–7

MICHAEL FITZGERALD

Barzin, Leon (Eugene) (*b* Brussels, Belgium, 27 Nov 1900; *d* Naples, FL, 29 April 1999). Conductor and educator of Belgian birth. Barzin immigrated with his family to the United States in 1902 and was naturalized in 1924. He initially studied violin and viola with his father Leon Joseph, who played violin with the Pittsburgh SO and was principal viola in the Metropolitan Opera Orchestra. He later studied with Edouard Deru, Pierre Henrotte, Eugène Meergerhin, and EUGÈNE YSAŸE. He also studied composition with ABRAHAM WOLF LILIENTHAL before joining the salon orchestra at the Hotel Astor in New York in 1917. By 1919 Barzin had moved to the second violin section of the National SO, shortly before it merged with the New York PO; he became first viola in the New York PO (1925–9). On Toscanini's advice he left this post to become assistant conductor of the American Orchestral Society, which he reorganized in 1930 as the National Orchestral Association with himself as music director (1930–59 and 1969–76). Barzin was music director of the New York City Ballet (1948–58), where he collaborated with George Balanchine and Jerome Robbins. Barzin devoted the bulk of his career to teaching and training young orchestral musicians. His National Orchestral Association, which is today a multifaceted arts organization, began as a semi-professional training group. Barzin led the group in successful radio broadcasts, and the association became the training ground for thousands of musicians who went on to play in professional orchestras. He moved for a few years to Paris, where he conducted the Orchestre Pasdeloup (1958–60) and taught at the Schola Cantorum. In 1969, Barzin joined the faculty of the New England Conservatory as conductor and head of orchestral training. He retired from the National Orchestral Association in 1976 to devote himself to private teaching, and remained active in education until the end of his life. Barzin received the Columbia University Ditson Award and the Gold Medal of Lebanon, and was made a member of the Légion d'Honneur.

BIBLIOGRAPHY

National Orchestral Association: *So Practical a Contribution, 1930–1940* (New York, 1940)
J.C. Voois: *Leon Barzin, America's Pioneer Orchestra Trainer: a Survey of His Career; a Chronicle with Historical Perspective of His Tenure at the National Orchestral Association and the New York City Ballet* (diss., Johns Hopkins U., 1986)

JOSÉ A. BOWEN/DAVID ATKINSON WELLS

Barzun, Jacques (*b* Créteil, France, 30 Nov 1907; *d* San Antonio, TX, 25 October 2012). Cultural historian, critic, and teacher of French birth. Born into the artistic environs of French modernism, he wrote widely on Western culture and its documents, founding the discipline of cultural history at Columbia University, where he spent his academic career.

After leaving France for America in 1920, he attended Columbia University (BA 1927, PhD 1932) where he lectured on contemporary civilization from 1927, becoming assistant professor (1937), professor (1945), Seth Low Professor of History (1955), Provost (1958–67), and University Professor (1967–75). He also served as president of the American Academy of Arts (1972–5, 1977–8), and was made an Extraordinary Fellow of Churchill College, Cambridge University in 1960.

Barzun regarded culture as a fabric of interwoven ideas which historians should trace through time, and between which exist a series of links: "because culture is a web of many strands; none is spun by itself, nor is any cut off at a fixed date." He viewed music through the prism of a broader culture, typified in the scope of *Darwin, Marx, Wagner: Critique of a Heritage* (Boston, MA, 1941/*R*, 2/1958/*R*). His major publications in music focus on Hector Berlioz, including *Berlioz and the Romantic Century* (Boston, MA, 1950, rev. abridged 2/1965/*R* as *Berlioz and his Century*, rev. 3/1969 under original title), an edited volume of letters (New York, 1954/*R*), and a translation of *Les soirées de l'orchestre* (New York, 1956). As a literary critic he believed that "music begins to speak to us at the point where words stop" (*Critical Questions*) and reflected on the role of music in society (*Music in American Life*).

As a public intellectual he promoted the Columbia model of liberal humanities through direct engagement with the major texts of Western literature. His body of publications outside music, the vast majority, focuses on culture and education, culminating in *From Dawn to Decadence* (2000) which traces the last 500 years of Western culture.

WRITINGS
(selective list)

ed.: *The Pleasures of Music* (New York, 1951, 2/1977)
Music into Words (Washington, DC, 1953); repr. in *Lectures on the History and Art of Music: the Louis Charles Elson Memorial Lectures at the Library of Congress, 1946–1963* (New York, 1968), 65–93
Music in American Life (Garden City, NY, 1956)
B. Friedland, ed.: *Critical Questions on Music and Letters, Culture and Biography, 1940–1980* (Chicago, 1982)

BIBLIOGRAPHY

Grove7 (H. Macdonald) [includes more writings]
D.B. Weiner and W.R. Keylor, eds.: *From Parnassus: Essays in Honor of Jacques Barzun* (New York, 1976)

DAVID TRIPPETT

Basart, Ann (Phillips) [Todd Mayfield, Ann; Todd, Ann E.] (*b* Denver, CO, 26 Aug 1931). Music librarian, editor, and publisher. Daughter of composer Burrill Phillips and Alberta Phillips, and wife of composer ROBERT BASART, she was raised by her maternal grandparents who named her Ann Todd Mayfield. As Ann E. Todd, she was a child actress featured in more than 20 films such as *Intermezzo*, *All This, and Heaven Too*, and *Three Daring Daughters*. In 1953 she graduated from University of California, Los Angeles, in Music History and continued her studies at the University of California, Berkeley, earning an MLS in 1958 and MA in 1960. She had a distinguished career as reference librarian at the UC Berkeley Music Library from 1960 to 1961 and from 1970 to 1990, during which time she founded and edited the library's newsletter, *Cum Notis Variorum*, which gained a national audience. It contained news, reviews, and substantial articles, including bibliographies, checklists, and indexes on various topics and sources. Basart also wrote numerous reviews for *Notes*, the journal of the Music Library Association, and served as its Music Review and Book Review Editors. She taught at the San Francisco College for Women and University of California, Berkeley, and began Fallen Leaf Press, which published music reference books and contemporary American music, from 1984 to 1999. In 1993 she was recognized by the Music Library Association with its Citation, the Association's tribute for lifetime achievement.

WRITINGS

Serial Music: a Classified Bibliography of Writings on Twelve-tone and Electronic Music (Berkeley, CA, 1961)
with R. Crocker: *Listening to Music* (New York, 1971)
Perspectives of New Music, an Index, 1962–1982 (Berkeley, CA, 1984)
The Sound of the Fortepiano: a Discography of Recordings on Early Pianos (Berkeley, CA, 1985)
"Music Bibliography: The American Contribution," *Modern Music Librarianship: Essays in Honor of Ruth Watanabe*, ed. Alfred Mann (Stuyvesant, NY, 1989), 185–92
"Reference Lacunae: Results of an Informal Survey of What Librarians Want," *Foundations in Music Bibliography*, ed. R. Greene (Stuyvesant, NY, 1993), 365–84

MIMI TASHIRO

Basart, Robert (*b* Watertown, SD, 17 Nov 1926; *d* Berkeley, CA, 7 Feb 1993). Composer. After a stint in the US Navy, he studied at the University of Colorado, Stanford University, and the University of California, Berkeley, where he earned a PhD. His works for chorus, chamber ensemble, orchestra, and other media have been noted for their clarity, lyricism, and fantasy. Among his compositions are *Imaginary Song* (1981), for string quartet, *Kansas City Dump* (1964), for chamber ensemble and tape, *The Round Ocean and the Living Air* (1984), for chamber ensemble, and a piano trio, *Stem, Leaf, Leaves, Small Flower* (1977). He taught composition and theory at San Francisco State University and California State University, Hayward. His honors included the Norman Fromm Composer's Award, residencies at Yaddo, Briarcombe, and Villa Montalvo, an Alfred Hertz Fellowship to Paris, and grants from the National Endowment for the Arts and the Martha Baird Rockefeller Foundation. His music was published by Salabert and Fallen Leaf Press, recorded by Composers' Recordings, Inc., and performed by various groups, including the Lenox Quartet, the Francesco Trio, and the San Francisco Contemporary Chamber Players.

ANN BASART

Bashell, Louis (*b* Milwaukee, WI, 1 July 1914; Milwaukee, 17 Dec 2008). Polka band leader. He is best remembered as "Milwaukee's Polka King." Bashell was born into a musical family and began playing the accordion at the age of seven, and soon after was playing at his father's bar, Bashell's Tavern; he subsequently studied with Tony Martinsek. He made a career of playing Slovenian-style polka in the tradition of his family, forming a trio in the mid-1930s and playing in bars in the south side of Milwaukee, such as the Muskego Beach Ballroom and the Blue Canary. He added two members to his group in the middle of the next decade and they released a local record of the Slovenian folksong, "Zidana Marela" ("The Silk Umbrella") that sold as fast as the record could be produced by the Pfau label. Its success brought the group attention, and they were signed onto RCA Records for eight years. Bashell's reluctance to tour with his band tempered his success on a national level, but he remained very active on the local scene, playing throughout the area for over 50 years. Acting as a mentor for a slew of younger performers, Bashell became one of the most influential performers of polka music in America. He garnered a variety of awards for his dedication and musical prowess, including a National Heritage Fellowship Grant from the NEA in 1987 and a lifetime achievement award from the National Cleveland-Style Polka Hall of Fame.

JONAS WESTOVER

Basie, Count [Bill; William] (*b* Red Bank, NJ, 21 Aug 1904; *d* Hollywood, CA, 26 April 1984). Jazz pianist and bandleader. After taking piano lessons as a child, he was soon playing ragtime and show tunes at local dance events and performing for silent movies. In 1924 he worked with the singer and dancer Katy Krippen with whom he also toured. In the mid-1920s he met Fats Waller, who introduced him to the sound of the pipe organ, after which he was always fascinated by the instrument. He played in several bands in New York and in 1926 he embarked on a tour with Gonzelle White, during which he heard Walter Page's band, the Blue Devils, in the Midwest. Basie left White's group in Kansas City, worked as a silent movie organist, and was active on the city's lively music scene. He heard many of the so-called territory bands, played for a while with Page's Blue Devils, and then became a member of the Bennie Moten Orchestra, first as an arranger and then as a pianist.

With Moten, Basie made his first recordings. His solos on "Toby" and "Prince of Wails" (both 1932, Victor) show a pianist with drive and attack who was fluent in the Harlem stride style which he had learned from Waller and James P. Johnson. One of the most advanced ensembles in Kansas City, Moten's band visited New York and other cities on the East Coast. After the leader's death in 1935, Basie took over the band which then included Jimmy Rushing, the bass player Walter Page, the drummer Jo Jones, and the saxophonists Buster Smith and Lester Young. The impresario John Hammond heard the band on a live radio broadcast and signed them for Decca for which they started recording in 1936. With a small band called Smith Jones Inc. Basie recorded "Shoe Shine Boy" and "Oh! Lady be Good" with Young, Page, Jones, and the trumpeter Joe Smith, making an immediate impact on the jazz world. His big band, billed as the Count Basie Orchestra, mingling a relaxed and swinging atmosphere with clear roots in the blues, produced a sound distinctive from that of other bands of the swing era.

In 1936 the guitarist Freddie Green joined Green, Page, and Jones in the orchestra's rhythm section, which subsequently became known as the All American Rhythm Section because of its reliable swing. They placed their accents around the beat in a way that achieved a driving dynamic, which for many embodied the epitome of swing. Basie's big band recordings sold well, and pieces such as "Topsy," "Good Morning Blues" (with Rushing), "Swingin' at the Daisy Chain," and "One o'Clock Jump" became commercial hits. Many of these were head arrangements with simple riff themes setting the instrumental sections against each other.

In late 1936 the band moved to New York where it performed in all of the big dance halls and for radio broadcasts, and caught the attention of the national media. In 1938 Benny Goodman invited some of Basie's musicians including the bandleader himself to participate in a jam session at Carnegie Hall on "Honeysuckle Rose." Basie subsequently performed with a small band announced as the Kansas City Six in a series of concerts known as Spirituals to Swing organized by Hammond at the same venue. When Goodman formed a sextet for recordings in the early 1940s to replace his successful small group from the 1930s, he often included Basie in the lineup.

Count Basie. (Lebrecht Music & Arts)

For a short period Basie's band featured Billie Holiday as a second vocalist (after Rushing); she was replaced by Helen Humes, who remained for four years. Basie's music always relied on a specific Kansas City tradition, the instrumental battle of the after-hours clubs in which competing musicians traded solos. Basie made sure always to have two tenor saxophonists who could fill this competitive spot in the arrangements: Lester Young and Herschel Evans, for example, or Buddy Tate and Don Byas, Lucky Thompson, Illinois Jacquet, or Paul Gonsalves. He had excellent soloists in the other sections as well, including Buck Clayton, Harry Edison, Al Killian, and Joe Newman on trumpet, and Dicky Wells, Vic Dickenson, and briefly J.J. Johnson on trombone. The band played at the Famous Door (one of the hippest New York clubs), toured the country, recorded extensively, and was regularly featured on the radio.

As a pianist Basie with his own band had developed the stride idiom into a sparse, reductionist variant in which sometimes the bass is only implied and melodic phrases of the right hand are reduced to a few single notes or a poignantly placed chord. This reductionist approach contrasted with the powerful roar of the brass section and made it sound as if he could make the whole orchestra swing with one finger.

By the mid-1940s the swing era was over commercially and bebop had taken over aesthetically. Basie's style, strongly rooted in the blues, was compatible with the up-and-coming popular music, early rhythm-and-blues. Even jump bands of the time, such as Louis Jordan's, clearly reflected Basie's influence. In the late 1940s Basie himself tried to reach younger listeners by catering to the R&B audience. Yet, instead of enjoying long engagements at clubs he had to play one-night stands. In the early 1950s he decided to disband the orchestra and instead formed a group whose personnel varied between six and nine members and included Clark Terry, Buddy DeFranco, Charlie Rouse, Wardell Gray, and Paul Quinichette, plus a rhythm section with Green, Gene Ramey, and Buddy Rich. This instrumentation offered Basie the possibility to adapt his basic musical concept and become more modern. Most of his soloists now had a bebop background; the common ground between them and him was mainly the blues.

In 1952 Basie formed a new big band, which contrasted starkly with his previous one. The musicians were younger and more modern in their conception, the arrangements were cleaner, and the band had more power and precision. Basie kept the proven concept, though: he focused on solos, he always had extraordinary saxophonists in his band—notably Frank Wess and Frank Foster—to maintain a spirit of friendly competition, and he bolstered his music with a swinging rhythm section (Basie, Green, Eddie Jones, and Gus Johnson). Both Foster and the trumpeter Thad Jones wrote arrangements for the band, as did the arrangers Ernie Wilkins, Quincy Jones, and Neal Hefti. Instrumental pieces like "Lil' Darling," "Cute," and Foster's "Shiny Stockings" redefined big band jazz. Joe Williams proved a successful successor to Rushing, projecting a clear, deep voice reminiscent of Billy Eckstine's that was ideally suited for elegant blues and ballads. Williams's version of "Every day I have the blues" became one of the band's biggest hits.

The new Basie band toured all over the world. It recorded for the labels Verve and Roulette, performed on TV and in Las Vegas, played a command performance in front of Queen Elizabeth II, and apart from the Duke Ellington Orchestra was the only big band from the swing era to keep busy while updating its basic sound. In the 1960s the band suffered the same fate as his 1940s orchestra when jazz once again lost popular appeal and failed to attract younger listeners. Basie tried to compensate by recording Beatles songs and playing arrangements better suited to an easy-listening audience.

Through such adjustments the band initially lost some of its distinctive style, but in the late 1960s the arranger Sammy Nestico succeeded in fashioning a new, third Basie sound. His arrangements were the focus of the ensemble in the 1970s, which featured soloists such as Sonny Cohn, Al Grey, Eric Dixon, and Jimmy Forrest. Nestico used the precision of the Basie sections to come in right on point like no other band, and he contrasted the full band with the Basie's spare piano style, in which musical accents were increasingly reduced to pronounced "plink plinks."

In the 1970s Basie became an elder statesman of jazz. He recorded for the label Pablo, performed with Ella Fitzgerald, and made some noteworthy trio albums with Ray Brown and Louie Bellson on which for the first time in more than 40 years he was not accompanied by Green's guitar. He also recorded two albums with the pianist Oscar Peterson, whose virtuosic style contrasted with, but nevertheless complemented, Basie's. Other studio recordings featured small bands in 1930s style that were issued under "Kansas City" titles. After his death Basie's orchestra has continued as a "ghost band" led by Thad Jones, Frank Foster, Grover Mitchell, and Bill Hughes.

RECORDINGS

*(selective list; *– recorded with a small group)*

Good Morning Blues (1937, Decca); One o'Clock Jump (1937, Decca); Swingin' at the Daisy Chain/Roseland Shuffle (1937, Decca); Topsy (1937, Decca); Jumpin' at the Woodside (1938, Decca); Taxi War Dance (1939, Voc.); Tickle-toe (1940, Col.); *Dance Sessions* (1952–4, Clef); *Count Basie Swings and Joe Williams Sings* (1955, Clef), incl. Every day I have the blues; *April in Paris* (1955–6, Verve 8012); *Atomic Basie* (1957, Roulette), incl. Lil' Darling; *Basie Plays Hefti* (1958, Roul.); *Basie at Birdland* (1961, Roul.); *Ella and Basie* (1963, Verve); *Straight Ahead* (1968, Dot); **For the First Time* (1974, Pablo); *Basie Big Band* (1975, Pablo); **Count Basie Jam Session* (1975, Pablo); **Count Basie Meets Oscar Peterson* (1978, Pablo); **Kansas City 7* (1980, Pablo)

As sideman: B. Moten: Prince of Wails (1932, Vic.); B Moten: Toby (1932, Vic.); Smith Jones Inc.: Oh! Lady be good (1936, Voc.); Smith Jones Inc.: Shoe Shine Boy (1936, Voc.); B. Goodman: Honeysuckle Rose (1938, Col.)

TRANSCRIPTIONS

F. Paparelli: *Count Basie Boogie Woogie Blues* (New York, 1944)

W.L. Fritsch, ed.: *Count Basie und seine Welterfolge* (Hamburg, 1960)

The Basie Style (London, 1977)

Blues by Basie (London, 1979)

Count Basie Collection (Milwaukee, 2004)

BIBLIOGRAPHY

B. Bach: "You gotta swing! Says the Count: Bill Basie tells Bob Bach a thing or two about swing and such and the present state of his band," *Metronome*, lxiii/5 (1947), 19, 46 only

J. Hammond: "Twenty Years of Count Basie," *Eddie Condon's Treasury of Jazz*, ed. E. Condon and R. Gehman (New York, 1956)

R. Horricks: *Count Basie and his Orchestra: its Music and its Musicians* (London, 1957)

B.J. Gardner: "Count Basie: Portrait of a Band," *DB*, xxvii/9 (1960), 30–32, 53

H.W. Shih: "Portrait of the Count," *DB*, xxxii/9 (1965), 23–4, 27–9

B. Sherman and C.A. Hällström: *A Discography of Count Basie, 1929–1950* (Copenhagen, 1969)

R. Russell: *Jazz Style in Kansas City and the Southwest* (Berkeley, 1971)

H.W. Shih: "Count Basie," *Jazz Masters of the Thirties*, ed. R. Stewart (New York, 1972), 195–206

S. Dance: *The World of Count Basie* (New York, 1980)

A. Morgan: *Count Basie* (Tunbridge Wells, England, 1984)

C. Basie and A. Murray: *Good Morning Blues: the Autobiography of Count Basie* (New York, 1985)

M. Tucker: "Count Basie and the Piano that Swings the Band," *Popular Music*, v (1985), 45–79

M. Williams: "Count Basie in the 1950s: Horses in Midstream," *Jazz Heritage* (New York, 1985)

C. Sheridan: *Count Basie: a Bio-Discography* (Westport, CT, 1986)

G. Schuller: *The Swing Era: the Development of Jazz, 1930–1945* (New York, 1989), 222–62

D. Helland: "The Count Basie Orchestra: Keeping the Spirit in a Ghost Band," *DB*, lvii/6 (1990), 21–3

D.H. Daniels: *One o'Clock Jump: the Unforgettable History of the Oklahoma City Blue Devils* (Boston, 2006)

WOLFRAM KNAUER

Baskerville, Priscilla (*b* Brooklyn, NY, 1962). Soprano. Baskerville pursued vocal studies at the institution now known as the LaGuardia High School of Music & Art and Performing Arts, where she serves on the vocal faculty. She is a graduate of the Manhattan School of Music and was a finalist in the National Vocal Competition for Young Opera Singers in 1979.

Baskerville is highly regarded as both a jazz vocalist and operatic lead. As a jazz vocalist she appeared in the original Broadway production of *Sophisticated Ladies* in 1981, a revue celebrating the music of Duke Ellington, and sang "Creole Love Call" in *The Cotton Club*, a 1984 blockbuster film. She made her Metropolitan Opera House debut in 1985 with the role of Lily in Gershwin's *Porgy and Bess*. In the 1989 remounting of the production she starred as Bess, earning favorable reviews for her expressive vocal nuances. In 1987 she was Musetta in a run of Met performances of Puccini's *La bohème*. She has won acclaim, both in the United States and abroad, for singing the title role in Verdi's *Aida*, which she first performed at the Met in 1991. In 1986 she created the roles of Louise Little, Queen Mother, and Betty Shabazz in Anthony Davis's *X, the Life and Times of Malcolm X*, an opera comprising a series of vignettes dramatizing pivotal moments in the life of the African American activist. She was the Music Director of the Girls Choir of Harlem prior to its disbanding in 2007.

JESSICA PAYETTE

Basquin, Peter (John) (*b* New York, NY, 19 June 1943). Pianist. He studied at Carleton College (Minnesota) under William Nelson (BA 1963), and at the Manhattan School of Music under Dora Zaslavsky (MM 1967). In 1971 he won second prize (the highest awarded) in the Montreal International Music Competition and on 8 March made his concert debut at Alice Tully Hall, New York. Since then he has been soloist with the Boston Symphony Orchestra, the Minnesota Orchestra, and the Montreal Symphony Orchestra, and has performed in venues including Carnegie Hall and the Kennedy Center. An accomplished chamber musician, he was a founder-member of the American Chamber Trio in 1972 and began an association with the Aeolian Chamber Players in 1981. He is known particularly for his performances of neglected 19th-century works (he has played a number of programs of such pieces at the Newport Music Festival) and of the music of contemporary American composers; his recordings include sonatas by Karel Husa and Marga Richter, and chamber works by Roy Harris and David Diamond. Basquin has served on the faculty of the City University of New York (Hunter College and the Graduate Center) since 1970 and teaches at the Bowdoin International Music Festival during the summer. He is a co-author, with Gerald Pincess, Marlies Danziger, and Wayne Dynes, of *Explorations in the Arts* (1984), and holds the Francis Thorne Piano Chair of the American Composers Orchestra.

KAREN MONSON/ELIZABETH N. MORGAN

Bass. *See* DOUBLE BASS.

Bassett, Leslie (Raymond) (*b* Hanford, CA, 22 Jan 1923). Composer. He studied at the University of Michigan with ROSS LEE FINNEY, by whose teaching he was particularly influenced, and also had lessons with NADIA BOULANGER and Arthur Honegger (1950–51), Roberto Gerhard (1960) and MARIO DAVIDOVSKY (electronic music, 1964). In 1952 he joined the faculty of the University of Michigan, becoming head of the composition department in 1970 and Albert A. Stanley Professor in 1977; he was also a founder-member of the university's electronic studio and directed the Contemporary Directions Performance Project until he retired in 1991. Among the awards he has received are the Rome Prize (which took him to the American Academy in Rome, 1961–3), a Pulitzer Prize (1966, for the Variations for orchestra), Guggenheim Fellowships (1973–4, 1980–81), a Naumburg Foundation recording award for the Sextet for piano and strings (1974) and a Rockefeller Foundation grant (1988); his *Echoes from an Invisible World* was commissioned by the Philadelphia Orchestra for the Bicentennial. In 1976 he was elected a member of the Institute of the American Academy and Institute of Arts and Letters. Bassett's music is carefully structured, its formal processes clear; conventional pitch materials are frequently deployed in an original manner. Even his writing for voices is instrumental in character, a quality he uses to advantage in the choral works, where voices and instruments are cohesively combined. A dozen doctoral dissertations focus on various aspects of Bassett's music.

WORKS

ORCHESTRAL

5 Movts, 1961; Variations, 1963; Designs, Images and Textures, band, 1964; Colloquy, 1969; Forces, vn, vc, pf, orch, 1972; Echoes from an Invisible World, 1975; Conc., 2 pf, orch, 1976; Sounds, Shapes and Symbols, band, 1977; Conc. grosso, brass qnt, wind, perc, 1982; Conc. lirico, trbn, orch, 1983; Colors and Contours, band, 1984; From a Source Evolving, 1985; Lullaby, band, 1985; Fantasy, cl, wind ens, 1986; Conc. for Orch, 1991; Thoughts that Sing, Breathe and Burn, 1995

CHAMBER

Trbn Qt, 1949; Sonata, hn, pf, 1952; Brass Trio, tpt, hn, trbn, 1953; Trio, va, cl, pf, 1953; Qnt, str qt, db, 1954; Sonata, trbn, pf, 1954; Cl Duets, 1955; Sonata, va, pf, 1956; 5 Pieces, str qt, 1957; Suite, trbn, 1957; Ww Qnt, 1958; Sonata, vn, pf, 1959; Vc Duets, 1959; Pf Qnt, 1962; Str Qt no.3, 1962; Music for Vc and Pf, 1966; Nonet, wind qnt, tpt, trbn, tuba, pf, 1967; Music for Sax and Pf, 1968; Sextet, pf, 2 vn, 2 va, vc, 1971

Sounds Remembered, vn, pf, 1972; Music for 4 Hns, 1974; 12 Duos, 2/4 trbn, 1974; Wind Music, fl, ob, cl, a sax, bn, hn, 1975; Soliloquies, cl, 1976; Str Qt no.4, 1978; Sextet, fl, a fl, cl, b cl, vc, db, 1979; Temperaments, gui, 1979–83; A Masque of Bells, carillon, 1980; Trio, vn, cl, pf, 1980; Conc. da camera, fl, cl, tpt, vn, vc, pf, perc, 1981; Duo Concertante, a sax, pf, 1984; Salute, 5 tpt, 1985; Dialogues, ob, pf, 1987; Duo-Inventions, 2 vc, 1988; Brass Qnt, 1988, Illuminations, fl, pf, 1989; Metamorphoses, bn, 1990; Arias, cl, pf, 1992; Narratives, 4 gui, 1993; Song and Dance, tuba, pf, 1993; 3 Equale, 4 trbn, 1996; Trio-Inventions, 3 vc, 1996

CHORAL

The Lamb (W. Blake), SATB, pf, 1952; Out of the Depths (Ps cxxx), SATB, org, 1957; For City, Nation, World (cant.), T, SATB, children's chorus ad lib, congregation, 4 trbn, org, 1959; Moonrise (D.H. Lawrence), SSA, 9 insts, 1960; Remembrance (H. Rupert), SATB, org, 1960; Eclogue, Encomium and Evocation (Bible: *Song of Solomon*), SSA, pf, hp, 2 perc, 1962; Follow Now that Bright Star (carol), SATB, 1962; Prayers for Divine Service (Lat.), TTBB, org, 1965; Hear my Prayer, O Lord (Ps lxiv), SA, org, 1965; Notes in the Silence (D. Hammarskjöld), SATB, pf, 1966

Collect, SATB, tape, 1969; Moon Canticle, S, amp nar, SATB, vc, 1969; Celebration: in Praise of Earth, amp nar, SATB, orch, 1970; Of Wind and Earth (P.B. Shelley, W.C. Bryant, St. Francis), SATB, pf, 1973; A Ring of Emeralds (Irish poets), SATB, pf, 1979; Sing to the Lord (Ps xcv), SATB, org, 1981; Lord, who hast formed me (G. Herbert), SATB, org, 1981; Whoe'er She Be (R. Crashaw), SSA, pf, 1986; Almighty, Eternal (Bassett), SATB, org, 1990; Maker of Our Being (Bassett), SATB, org, 1993

OTHER WORKS

Kbd: 6 Pf Pieces, 1951; Toccata, org, 1955; Voluntaries, org, 1958; Mobile, pf, 1961; 4 Statements, org, 1964; Elaborations, pf, 1966; Liturgies, org, 1980; 7 Preludes, pf, 1984; Configurations, pf, 1987

Solo vocal: 4 Songs (W. Blake, G. Herbert, E.A. Robinson), S, pf, 1953; Easter Triptych (Bible), T, wind ens, 1958; To Music (B. Jonson, R. Herrick, W. Billings), 3 songs, S/T, pf, 1962; The Jade Garden (oriental), S, pf, 1973; Time and Beyond (R.W. Emerson, R. Tagore, M. Van Doren), B, cl, vc, pf, 1973; Love Songs (Gk. anon., W.S. Landor, A. Brodstreet, Emerson, H. Harrington), S, pf, 1975; Pierrot Songs (A. Giraud, Ger. trans. O. Hartleben), S, fl, cl, vn, vc, pf, 1988

Elec: 3 Studies in Elec Sound, 1965; Triform, 1966

*c*20 works now withdrawn, incl. 2 syms., 1949, 1956, 2 str qts, 1949, 1951

Principal publishers: ACA, King, Merion, Peters

BIBLIOGRAPHY

EwenD

A. Brown: "Leslie Bassett," *Asterisk*, ii/2 (1976), 8–15 [incl. list of works]

E.S. Johnson: *Leslie Bassett: a Bio-bibliography* (Westport, CT, 1994)

C.C. Chapman: *Leslie Bassett: a Composer's Insight; Thoughts, Analysis, and Commentary on Contemporary Masterpieces for Wind Band* (Galesville, MD, 2003)

J. Martin: *Leslie Bassett: a Biography and Study of Selected Works for Trombone* (diss., U. of Northern Colorado, 2004)

EDITH BORROFF/MICHAEL MECKNA

Bassford, William Kipp (*b* New York, 23 April 1839; *d* New York, 22 Dec 1902). Pianist, organist, and composer. Unlike many American composers of his time, Bassford did not study in Europe. Rather, he pursued his musical education solely within the United States, under the tutelage of Samuel Jackson. He started his career as a pianist with a concert troupe, touring extensively, but after deciding that the life of a touring concert pianist was not to his liking, he settled in New York. There he was engaged as an organist at several churches, including the Madison Square Presbyterian Church and Calvary Church in East Orange, NJ, his last position. He also taught piano and composition, training many notable musicians. His compositions include a Mass in E♭ (1875), which enjoyed much popularity in his time, many character and salon piano pieces, and a two-act opera, *Cassilda*. He was also commissioned by the widow of William Vincent Wallace to finish the composer's opera *Estrella*, which he completed before his death in 1902.

BIBLIOGRAPHY

"Bassford, W.K.," *Brainard's Musical World* (Feb 1881); repr. in *Brainard's Biographies of American Musicians*, ed. E.D. Bomberger (Westport, CT, 1999)

JOSEPH A. BOMBERGER

Bassman, George (*b* New York, NY, 7 Feb 1914; *d* Los Angeles, CA, 26 June 1997). Composer, arranger, and songwriter. The son of Russian-Jewish immigrants, Bassman studied at the Boston Conservatory of Music. From 1931 to 1934 he arranged for big bands, including those led by Duke Ellington and Benny Goodman. During this period he composed (with lyricist Ned Washington) the Tommy Dorsey theme "I'm Getting Sentimental Over You." From 1934 to 1936 he was key arranger for conductor André Kostelanetz's radio show. In 1936 he moved to Hollywood, where he joined MGM as arranger, composer, and general music/vocal director. He worked on many of the studio's early classic and lesser-known musicals, including *The Wizard of Oz* (1939), for which he composed some of the cyclone music, *Honolulu* (1939), *As Thousands Cheer* (1943), and *Cabin in the Sky* (1943). He also composed dramatic underscores for *The Clock* (1945) and *The Postman Always Rings Twice* (1946).

In 1947 Bassman was a victim of the HUAC blacklistings. Returning to New York he worked in television and on Broadway, where he orchestrated Frank Loesser's *Guys and Dolls*. He later returned to scoring small features such as *The Joe Louis Story* (1953) and the sleeper hit *Marty* (1955). Bassman returned to MGM for Sam Peckinpah's *Ride the High Country* (1962), creating an epic yet intimate Americana sound that exemplified the scaled-down shift in Hollywood scoring that had occurred in the 1950s. He later adapted this music for his last film, *Mail Order Bride* (1964). When his scores for later films (including *Bonnie and Clyde*,

1967) were rejected Bassman retired from Hollywood and died, reportedly in obscurity, in Los Angeles in 1997.

WORKS

Film scores: Suzy, 1936; Conquest, 1937; A Damsel in Distress, 1937; The Last Gangster, 1937; Bulldog Drummond's Peril, 1938; A Day at the Beach, 1938; Everybody Sing, 1938; Marie Antoinette, 1938; Sweethearts, 1938; At the Circus, 1939; Babes in Arms, 1939; Broadway Serenade, 1939; Gulliver's Travels, 1939; Honolulu, 1939; The Ice Follies of 1939; Lady of the Tropics, 1939; The Wizard of Oz, 1939; Broadway Melody of 1940, 1940; Go West, 1940; I Take This Woman, 1940; Little Nellie Kelly, 1940; Babes on Broadway, 1941; Lady Be Good, 1941; Ziegfeld Girl, 1941; Cairo, 1942; For Me and My Gal, 1942; Her Cardboard Lover, 1942; Panama Hattie, 1942; Ship Ahoy, 1942; Tortilla Flat, 1942; As Thousands Cheer, 1943; Best Foot Forward, 1943; Cabin in the Sky, 1943; Du Barry Was a Lady, 1943; Girl Crazy, 1943; Presenting Lily Mars, 1943; Bud Abbott and Lou Costello in Hollywood, 1945; The Clock, 1945; The Postman Always Rings Twice, 1946; Two Smart People, 1946; The Romance of Rosy Ridge, 1947; A Slight Case of Larceny, 1953; Big Leaguer, 1953; The Joe Louis Story, 1953; Marty, 1955; Mayerling TV, 1957; The Great Chase, 1962; Ride the High Country, 1962; Mail Order Bride, 1964

BIBLIOGRAPHY

A. Harmetz: *The Making of The Wizard of Oz* (New York, 1977), 92–5, 98

C. Goldman: "George Bassman: Rhapsody In Black," *Film Score Monthly*, ix/6 (2004), 14–16, 44

ROSS CARE

Bassoon. The *bajón*, an early, one-piece bassoon, was brought into the southwestern United States during the 17th century by Jesuit and Franciscan missionaries seeking to convert the native peoples. In 1625–6 the packing list for a Franciscan expedition into what is now New Mexico included a *bajón*, while a supply contract of 1631 required that every five Franciscan friars there receive a set of *chirimías* (shawms) and *bajónes*. The administrator Fray Alonso de Benavides reported in 1634 that natives were taught music in eight or more missions, and that *bajónes* and *chirmías* accompanied polyphonic music in sacred services. *Bajónes* were documented in New Mexican missions at Ácoma Pueblo and Socorro (both 1672) and Cochiti (1776). The Jesuit mission of San Juan Bautista in Alta California in 1792 had a bassoon of some description, as did the Franciscan mission at Tumacacori (Arizona), built in 1800.

The four-piece Baroque bassoon was imported into the eastern colonies by English settlers by the mid-18th century. In Anglican or Episcopal churches, it was sometimes used to support congregational singing. A bassoon was used by 1800 in the Collegium Musicum of Bethlehem, Pennsylvania, founded by Moravian immigrants. In 1753 a "musician from London" named Charles Love advertised himself in New York as a teacher of bassoon and other instruments; a Virginia plantation owner alleged in 1757 that Love had stolen "a very good bassoon" by Schuchart (a firm of London makers). Resident bassoon makers included Gottlieb (David) Wohlhaupter (New York, 1761–70) and Joshua Collins, described as "an immigrant from Manchester" (Annapolis, 1773). Bassoon playing was documented in Charleston (by 1765), Boston (1775), Providence (1784), Philadelphia (1786), Savannah (1796), and New Orleans (1811). In 1807 three multi-instrument tutors including identical instructions for six-key bassoon were published in Exeter, New Hampshire, and Dedham, Massachusetts, while in Providence, Oliver Shaw published a collection of instrumental music containing scorings for bassoon, along with flute and two clarinets.

During the Revolutionary War, both British and Hessian bands provided a model for later military and civilian *Harmoniemusik* ensembles that included clarinets, horns, and bassoons, usually in pairs. The US Marine Band in 1800 reportedly included one bassoon. At its founding in 1815 the US Military Academy Band included two bassoons. During the 1820s an African American band led by Francis Johnson in Philadelphia included one or two bassoons.

American makers of bassoons included John Meacham (*fl* Albany, NY, 1810–32), William Whiteley (*fl* Utica, NY, 1810–54), H.G. Guetter (*fl* Bethlehem, PA, *c*1824–47), and George Catlin (*fl* Hartford, CT, 1799–1815; Philadelphia, PA, 1816–50). Relatively expensive and troublesome to produce, bassoons were often imported from Europe, sometimes receiving the stencil or stamp of an American woodwind maker or dealer.

When the New York Philharmonic Society was established in 1842, the two bassoonists were immigrants from England and Germany. The New York Philharmonic was long dominated by bassoonists of German background, as were the Chicago SO and the Philadelphia Orchestra. Auguste Mesnard, imported by Walter Damrosch for his New York SO in 1905 along with other French-trained woodwind players, began to teach the French-system bassoon at the New York Institute of Musical Art. The Buffet or Conservatoire system bassoon was favored in the New York and Boston SOs during the early 20th century, but it decisively fell from use with the retirement of Raymond Allard from the Boston SO in 1953, and the French-system bassoon is rarely seen in American use. Instead an "American school of wind playing" has prevailed, employing the German or Heckel-system bassoon with its quite different technique, in conjunction with principles of phrasing and tone production traceable to French wind players. During the middle third of the 20th century this approach was notably taught at the Curtis Institute of Music in Philadelphia. American bassoon makers of the 20th century included H. Bettoney (Boston); C.G. Conn, Linton, Lesher, Armstrong, and Selmer, all of Elkhart, Indiana; and Fox (South Whitley, Indiana; also contrabassoons).

The bassoon, heard in jazz recordings as early as the 1920s, has continued in sporadic use in jazz, now often aided by amplification. The International Double Reed Society counted more than 3000 bassoon-playing members in the United States in the years 2005–9; the number of active US bassoonists was several times that number.

BIBLIOGRAPHY

WaterhouseLangwillI, *Grove7* (W. Waterhouse), *GroveJ* (L. Porter)

J.T. Scharf and T. Wescott: *History of Philadelphia, 1609–1884* (Philadelphia, 1884), ii

W. Dietz: "A Conversation with Sol Schoenbach," *The Double Reed*, x/3 (1987), 48–51

C. Shive: "Harmoniemusik and the Early Wind Band in the United States," *Kongressbericht, Internationale Ges. zur Erforschung und Förderung der Blasmusik*, ed. W. Suppan (Tutzing, 1996), 158–79
R. Starner: "The Introduction of Double Reeds to New Mexico, 1624–1633," *The Double Reed*, xxiii/2 (2000)
J. Koegel: "Spanish and French Mission Music in Colonial North America," *Journal of the Royal Musical Society*, cxxvi/1 (2001), 1–53
D. Mendoza de Arce: *Music in North American and the West Indies from the Discovery to 1850* (Lanham, MD, 2006)

JAMES B. KOPP

Bass viol a bowed string instrument. Although in modern usage the term refers to a six- or seven-string instrument of the viol family often called viola da gamba, in the 18th and 19th centuries in the United States and occasionally in Britain "bass viol" meant a four-string instrument tuned in fifths like a cello. It was probably a shortened version of the term "bass violin." Such instruments were of two kinds: the first like a cello except for certain local constructional details, the second of larger body size but with the same string length and fingerboard as a cello, with a short neck (accommodating playing only up to the second position without recourse to thumb positions). Instruments of both kinds were occasionally made with five strings, but no contemporary instruction book refers to the practice or indicates the tuning. The large-sized instruments are called "church basses." Certain archaisms in construction reflect earlier European building techniques, the most common being an f-hole in which small connecting bridges of wood are left at the turns, a groove or channel routed in the wood of the back and belly into which the ribs are fitted and glued, and the use of a foot-like extension of the neck block (almost always integral with the neck itself) projecting into the body and fixed to the wood of the back by a butted glue joint and a screw. A peculiarly American feature is the use of plank-sawn wood in the belly and back, giving the instruments a curious florid appearance; but the best makers used quarter-sawn wood according to traditional European practice.

From the late 18th up to the mid-19th century there was an active American industry in the manufacture of these instruments, probably created partly by the demand for bass instruments to accompany the church choirs which had been relieved of their Puritan obligation to perform unaccompanied. By the 1830s there were makers specializing in the production of bass viols; over 35 are known to have been working in New England in this period. The earliest known maker was Crehore of Boston, who is reported to have made his first bass for a local music master in 1785; he made basses of both sizes. The most prominent and prolific was ABRAHAM PRESCOTT, who made his first instrument in 1809. The popularity of the instrument declined around the time of the Civil War, partly because the pipe or reed organ had superseded it in church music.

BIBLIOGRAPHY

F.R. Selch: "Some Moravian Makers of Bowed Stringed Instruments," *JAMIS*, xix (1993), 38–64

FREDERICK R. SELCH

Bates, Leon (*b* Philadelphia, PA, 3 Nov 1949). Pianist and teacher. He began his studies of piano and violin at the age of six and gave his first piano recital in his native city at seven. He studied with Irene Beck at the Settlement Music School (1962–67) and with NATALIE HINDERAS at the Esther Boyer College of Music, Temple University in Philadelphia. A prominent African American figure on the concert scene, he has maintained an intense performance schedule since the 1970s with major symphony orchestras in the United States and has performed at prestigious venues in Europe and Africa. In 1992 Leon Bates premiered Adolphus Cunningham Hailstork's Piano Concerto. He has composed pieces for beginning piano students employing a progressive method (*Piano Discoveries*, 2001, in collaboration with Janet Vogt). Bates's large repertoire, released on Orion, Performance Records, and Naxos, ranges from the classics to contemporary works, with particular interest in Ravel, Gershwin, Barber, Corea, Brahms, Rachmaninoff, and African American women composers. He has also received awards for his extensive work in the field of music education.

DANIELE BUCCIO

Bates, Mason (*b* Philadelphia, PA, 23 Jan 1977). Composer and DJ. He grew up in Richmond, studying piano and composition, and received his first commission while in high school. He enrolled in the Columbia-Juilliard program, where he worked with JOHN CORIGLIANO (ii), DAVID DEL TREDICI, and SAMUEL ADLER, and earned Bachelor's degrees in music composition and English literature. He is in the doctoral program at the University of California, Berkeley, where he studies with Edmund Campion at the Center for New Music and Audio Technologies.

Active as a performer and as a composer, Bates has earned acclaim in classical concert music and "electronica," a term that he has used to encompass a variety of techno music. The Los Angeles Philharmonic's Green Umbrella Series at Disney Hall in 2004 premiered his *Omnivorous Furniture* for sinfonietta and electronica. *From Amber Frozen* for string quartet, commissioned by the Naumburg Foundation for the Biava Quartet, received its premiere in 2004 at Alice Tully Hall. *Rusty Air in Carolina* (2006), composed for the Winston-Salem Symphony Orchestra, explored the combination of orchestral sonorities and the white noise of insects. *Digital Loom*, an electro-acoustic work was commissioned in 2006 by the Juilliard School to celebrate its 100th anniversary. Bates composed *Liquid Interface* for the National Symphony Orchestra, which gave its world premiere in 2007, under Leonard Slatkin, at the Kennedy Center in Washington, DC, and its New York premiere at Carnegie Hall in 2008. In 2009, the San Francisco Symphony, under Michael Tilson Thomas, premiered *The B-Siders*.

As a disc jockey of trip-hop and electronica, Bates appears regularly in clubs and lounges in San Francisco and Berlin under the pseudonym "Masonic." He has also performed as soloist in his Concerto for Synthesizer and Orchestra with the orchestras of Atlanta and

Phoenix. His compositions for purely acoustic forces, for electronic ones, and for combinations of various kinds have been performed in Europe, Australia, Canada, and throughout the United States. His works include song cycles, piano pieces, theatrical works, and a music-drama for one actor and five musicians called *Trout Fishing in America*, which premiered at Lincoln Center's Clark Theater in 1997. His solo piano piece *White Lies for Lomax* was performed by all of the finalists in the Van Cliburn 2009 International Piano Competition. His film score for *The Locrian Mode* (2005, dir. E. Lodal) was played by the Dryden String Quartet, and his opera *California Fictions* (2006) was presented by the New York City Opera annual VOX Showcase.

Bates has received many awards, including an American Academy in Berlin Fellowship, a Rome Prize from the American Academy in Rome, a Guggenheim Fellowship, a fellowship from the American Academy of Arts and Letters, the Jacob Druckman Memorial Prize from Aspen Music Festival, ASCAP and BMI awards, and a fellowship from the Tanglewood Music Center. He was also chosen as composer-in-residence by Young Concert Artists in 2000 and has served composer residencies with the California Symphony and the Mobile Symphony.

BIBLIOGRAPHY

D. Perlmutter: "Concerto for two universes," *Los Angeles Times* (31 Oct 2004) <http://articles.latimes.com/2004/oct/31/entertainment/ca-bates31>

J. Kosman: "Composer charts new territory with marriage of classical and trip-hop," *San Francisco Chronicle* (22 Mar 2006) <http://www.sfgate.com/cgi-bin/article.cgi?f=/c/a/2006/03/22/DDG7RHRC461.DTL>

JAMES BASH

Báthory-Kitsz, Dennis (*b* Plainfield, NJ, 14 March 1949). Composer, engraver, author, and editor. Báthory-Kitsz has written under a wide array of aliases, including Kalvos Gesamte, Grey Shadé, D.B. Cowell, Brady Kynans, and Kalvos Zondrios. He is a self-proclaimed humanist and believes strongly in the power of everyday people to create and perform music. He has also advocated for locally-centered performances and has been a tremendous force in the creative life of Vermont, where he has made his home. While Báthory-Kitsz remains a highly prolific composer, penning over one thousand works since the late 1960s, he is also recognized as an important writer, both on music and on other topics, such as computers and Vermont country stores. Báthory-Kitsz's commitment to the life of music reaches out from his own compositions, which he allows people to download and perform for free, and also to his advocacy for the performance of contemporary music, seen especially in his involvement with several festivals and projects that keep "modern" music in the forefront. He has served on the board, directed, and founded many of these events himself. He was the director and founder of Dashuki Music Theater (1975–83), the head of Malted/Media Arts Publications (from 1978 onward), and co-founder of the Vermont Composer's Consortium (from 1988 onward). He served on the Vermont Contemporary Music Ensemble board (since 1994) and was the creative force behind *Kalvos and Damian's New Music Bazaar*, a cybercast and radio show, since 1995. Some of his projects include the "We Are All Mozart" campaign, where Báthory-Kitsz challenged himself to write a piece a day in 2007. He has also served as a music teacher at numerous locations, including Johnson State College.

Many of Báthory-Kitsz's musical works are referred to by the composer as "contemporary 'nonpop' music." They frequently take the form of installations, using non-conventional instruments or traditional instruments in unusual ways. Several of his works are also theatrically based. An example of this is *Echo: a Performance Ritual in Four Parts* (1985), which mixes performance art, dance, new instruments, and specific costuming. *In Bocca Al Lupo* (1986) was a "sound and sculptural environment." His work *Wolf5 at Traveler's Rest* (1991) was written for a specific vacant field, complete with choreography and musical performance. Several of his pieces are operas, including *Plasm over Ocean: a Chamber Opera in Three Scenes* (1977) and *Erzsébet* (2010), about the vampire Countess Báthory. The bulk of Báthory-Kitsz's music, however, is for small instrumental groups, frequently using computers, electronic tape, video, playback, and even exotic elements like "ice" and "aromas." His works are commissioned by a wide range of organizations and have had premieres throughout the world.

WORKS
(selective list)

Opera/Theatrical/Installations: Plasm over ocean, op., 1977; Echo: A Performance Ritual, 1985; Beepers, cabaret, 1986; In Bocca Al Lupo, installation, 1986; Wolf5 and Traveler's Rest, 1991; Detritus of Mating, installation, 1997;

Orchestra and band: The Lily and the Thorn, orch, 1990; Softening Cries, orch, 1991; Sourian Slide, str, 1999; Mountain Dawn Fanfare, orch, 2000; Mirrored Birds, fl conc., 2001; Icecut, orch, 2004; Jameo y el Delfin Mareado, orch, 2005; Autumn Dig, orch, 2008; Crosscut, pf, band, 2009

Vocal: Hypertunes, Baby, 1v, tape, 1994; Spammung, extended v, playback, 2003; By Still Waters, 1v, drone, 2004

Chbr: Construction on "nix rest...in china," trbn, tape, 1972; Somnambula, rec, elec sound, 1975; Mass, chbr ens, 1978; Rando's Poetic License, elecs, cptr, vv, inst, 1978; Mantra Canon, large ens, 1986; Variations on Amanda; 3 str, hpd, 1989; A Time Machine, 1v, chbr ens, cptr, 1990; Yçuré, 2 chbr ens, 1990; The Pretty Songs, 1v, sax, 1991; Binky Plays Marbles, va, db, 1992; Emerald Canticles, Below, small ens, 1993; Llama Butter, tuba, tape, 1993; Build, Make, Do, small ens, 1994; Gardens, eng hn, str qt, 1996; xirx, tape, ice, aromas, 1996; zéyu, quânh & sweeh, playback, 1996; Into the Morning Rain, small ens, 1998; Zonule Glaes II, elec str qt, 1999; Low Birds, small ens, 1999; Quince and Fog Falls; chbr ens, 2000; RatGeyser, MalletKat, playback, 2000; The Sub-Aether Bande, fl, perc, 2000; HighBirds, Prime, 2 elec gui, playback, 2001; Fuliginous Quadrant, chbr ens, 2001; The Key of Locust, chbr trio, 2001; Bales, Barrels, & Cones: Antebellum/Antibellum, drumkit, playback, 2002; LiquidBirds, theremins, video, playback, 2003; Rose Quartz Crystal Radio, sax, perc, 2005; L'Estampie du Chevalier, str qt, 2005; Clouds of Endless Summer, pf trio, 2006;

Solo: Rough Edges, pf, 1987; Csárdás, pf, 1989; Tïrkïinistrá: 25 Landscape Preludes, pf, 2002; Northsea Balletic Spicebush, db, 2003; Shahmat, fl, 2003; Sweet Ovals, hn, 2005; Yer Attention, Please, org, 2006; Lunar Cascade in Serial Time, t gui, 2007; Compound Refractions, fl, 2007; Framing the Sum of Three, pf, 2007

Principal publisher: Westleaf Edition.

JONAS WESTOVER

Baton Rouge. City in Louisiana (pop. 229,553; metropolitan area 802,484; 2010 US Census). The capital city of Louisiana, it was founded about 1699 and colonized successively by French, Spanish, and US settlers, accompanied by African American slaves. The city is located on the first of a series of bluffs north of the Mississippi River Delta. It was incorporated as a town in 1817. Located near areas of 18th-century Cajun and German settlement, it became the state's capital in 1849. Like its larger neighbor New Orleans, its rich mix of ethnicities and the wealth derived from river trade and the plantation economy led to a relatively advanced musical life despite its initially small size.

Records of Creole and early American Baton Rouge reveal a musical life centered on church, family, secular benevolent organizations, and seasonal celebrations like Mardi Gras. Pike's Hall, or Opera House, opened shortly after the Battle of Baton Rouge (1862). Two sources for the growth of economic and cultural life of the city's white population in the 20th century were wealth from the oil refining and petrochemical industries (from 1909), and higher education—reflected by the opening of Southern University (1914), the opening of the present campus of Louisiana State University (LSU, 1926), and the opening of the LSU School of Music (1931). The Baton Rouge SO began its first season in 1947. LSU's opera program dates from the 1930s; L'Opéra Louisiane has served as the civic venue for opera performance. The LSU Festival of Contemporary Music began in 1945. In 1976 Centaur Records began issuing recordings of classical and avant-garde music from its Baton Rouge studios.

Baton Rouge's African American population made the city a regional center of blues and rock and roll: Lightnin' Slim (1913–74), Slim Harpo (1924–70), Buddy Guy (*b* 1936), Tabby Thomas (*b* 1929), Raful Neal (1936–2004), and Chris Thomas King have lived, worked, and/or recorded in Baton Rouge since the 1940s. Venues associated with their music include the Texas Club, Tabby's Blues Box, and Buddy Stewart's Rock Shop. From 1954 to 1965 J.D. Miller, who had recorded a number of Cajun and "hillbilly" recordings in his small studio in Crowley, Louisiana, began recording Baton Rouge artists for the Nashboro label of Nashville, Tennessee. Recording of Baton Rouge blues artists continued on other small labels into the 1970s. The Baton Rouge Blues Festival began in 1980.

From 1957 Dr. Harry Oster of LSU documented the African American and vernacular music of Baton Rouge and the surrounding area in books and recordings. He also conducted field research at the Angola state prison farm north of the city as well as in the city's African American social clubs. Although segregation barred most African Americans from participation in concert music, McKinley High School, the sole area high school open to African Americans prior to desegregation, has launched musical careers of all types of artists, including the opera singer Lenora Lafayette, since its founding in 1907.

The Louisiana tradition of street festivals provides live music of all genres throughout the year, while Baton Rouge's River Center serves as the largest performing arts venue in the region, with 1900 seats.

BIBLIOGRAPHY

J. Beyer: *Baton Rouge Blues: a Guide to the Baton Rouge Bluesmen and their Music* (Baton Rouge, LA, 1980)

S.K. Bernard: *Swamp Pop: Cajun and Creole Rhythm and Blues* (Oxford, MS, 1996)

JEFF PERRY

Batson [Bergen], **Flora** (*b* Washington, DC, 16 April 1864; *d* Philadelphia, PA, 1 Dec 1906). Soprano. She grew up in Providence, singing in public there and in Boston while still quite young. She first appeared in New York (at Steinway Hall) and Philadelphia in 1885, at which time she became a member of James Bergen's Star Concert Company, replacing Nellie Brown. She married Bergen in 1887. During the years 1887–96 she toured internationally, singing before Pope Leo XIII and the royal families of Hawaii and Great Britain, and in New Zealand and Africa; her later tours with the bass Gerard Millar included a visit to Australia in 1899. She also sang in opera excerpts with the South Before the War Company, as well as at Boston's Music Hall. Her repertory was much like that of other traveling singers of her time, and included both ballads and arias, mostly from operas by Bellini, Donizetti, and Rossini.

BIBLIOGRAPHY

SouthernB

M.C. Hare: *Negro Musicians and their Music* (Washington, DC, 1936/*R*), 219

T.L. Riis: "Concert singers, prima donnas, and entertainers: the Changing Status of Black Women Vocalists in nineteenth-century America," *Music and Culture in America, 1861–1918*, ed. M. Saffle (New York, 1998), 53–78

DOMINIQUE-RENÉ DE LERMA

Battisti, Frank Leon (*b* Ithaca, NY, 27 June 1931). Conductor, author, and educator. Battisti studied at Ithaca College under Walter Beeler and joined the music staff of the Ithaca Public Schools in 1953. He became director of the Ithaca HS band in 1955, and from 1958 to 1967 led the band in commissioning 24 works by composers including Bassett, Husa, Benson, Chavez, Persichetti, Schuller, Wilder, and Childs. Prominent featured guests included Benny Goodman, Donald Sinta, William D. Revelli, Frederick Fennell, and "Doc" Severinson. In 1967 Battisti moved to Baldwin-Wallace College and then to the New England Conservatory where he founded the NEC Wind Ensemble, highly recognized as one of the premiere wind ensembles in the United States and throughout the world. He again led commissioning projects including Tippett, Colgrass, and Lutosławski. In 1971 he founded the National Wind Ensemble Conference and in 1981 the foundation for the World Association for Symphonic Bands and Wind Ensembles. He has appeared as guest conductor/clinician throughout the United States, UK, Europe, Middle East, Scandinavia, China, Taiwan, South America, and the former USSR, among other countries and regions. A past president of the College Band Directors National Association and a member of the American Bandmasters Association, Battisti has written several books and has contributed numerous articles to professional journals.

WRITINGS

with R. Garofalo: *Guide to Score Study for the Wind Band Conductor* (Fort Lauderdale, FL, 1990)

The Twentieth Century American Wind Band/Ensemble (Fort Lauderdale, FL, 2000)

The Winds of Change: the Evolution of the Contemporary American Wind Band/Ensemble and its Conductor (Galesville, MD, 2002)

On Becoming a Conductor: Lessons and Meditations on the Art of Conducting (Galesville, MD, 2007)

BIBLIOGRAPHY

B.H. Norcross: *One Band that Took a Chance: the Ithaca High School Band from 1955 to 1967 Directed by Frank Battisti* (Fort Lauderdale, FL, 1994)

DONALD HUNSBERGER

Battle, Kathleen (*b* Portsmouth, OH, 13 Aug 1948). Soprano. Possessing a distinctive, light, nimble voice, Battle has won international acclaim for soubrette opera roles, recital performances, and award-winning recordings. Her mother and her father, a steel worker, were active musicians in the African Methodist Episcopal church. After winning a National Merit Scholarship for her achievement in math, Battle studied with Franklin Bens and Italo Tajos at the University of Cincinnati College-Conservatory of Music, and graduated with bachelor's and master's degrees in music education. While teaching in the Cincinnati public school system, Battle launched her career with a successful audition for Thomas Shippers, then director of the Cincinnati Symphony Orchestra. She has since become one of the world's most accomplished coloratura sopranos and one of the most recognized African American opera singers. Shippers contracted her to sing in the 1972 Brahms's Requiem in Spoleto, Italy, and in 1974 James Levine hired Battle to sing in Mahler's Eighth Symphony at the Cincinnati May Festival. She made her New York debut in 1976 as Susanna with New York City Opera. In 1977 she made her Metropolitan debut as the Shepherd in *Tannhäuser*, subsequently singing Rosina, Despina, Zerlina, Blonde, Pamina, Zdenka, Strauss and Massenet's Sophie, and Handel's Cleopatra. She made her British debut in 1979 at Glyndebourne as Nerina (Haydn's *La fedeltà premiata*) and sang Adina at Zürich in 1980. At Salzburg she has sung Despina, Susanna, and Zerlina. She made her Covent Garden debut in 1985 as Zerbinetta and was the first American to be awarded the Laurence Olivier Award for best performance in a new opera production.

Battle has won five Grammy Awards for her wide-ranging recordings, including opera (Zerlina, Blonde, Zerbinetta, Semele), Fauré and Brahms Requiems, solo recital recordings with James Levine and Margo Garrett, and collaborative recordings with trumpeter Wynton Marsalis, guitarist Christopher Parkening, violinist Itzhak Perlman, and flautist Jean-Pierre Rampal. She is a sensitive interpreter of spirituals, notably recorded in the 1990 *Spirituals in Concert* album with Jessye Norman. In 1992 Battle commissioned the song cycle *Honey and Rue*, with music by André Previn and text by Toni Morrison. Battle remains committed to nonclassical music genres, recording a crossover album, *So Many Stars*, and performing with popular music artists such as James Ingram and Alicia Keys. Despite her reputation as a temperamental artist, Battle continues to govern her singing with technical finesse and thrill audiences with her attractive stage presence and the sheer beauty of her voice.

BIBLIOGRAPHY

"Fortune's Favorite: A Conversation with Kathleen Battle," *ON*, xlvi/15 (1982)

P. Hoban: "Battle Mania," *New York Magazine* (12 July 1993)

R. Story: *And So I Sing: African American Divas of Opera and Concert* (New York, 1993)

C. McCants: *American Opera Singers and their Recordings* (Jefferson, NC, 2004), 30–38 [includes discography]

RICHARD DYER/MARTI NEWLAND

Battle Hymn of the Republic. Title of a poem written to the melody "Glory hallelujah" during the Civil War, and by extension the title of the resulting national song; *see* PATRIOTIC MUSIC.

Battle music. Program music depicting battles. While such works as Ludwig van Beethoven's *Wellington's Victory* are usually regarded as lacking in taste, this important genre was as ubiquitous as the more exalted sonata in the 19th century. Compositions commemorating famous land or naval battles normally appeared shortly after the event to take advantage of the public's interest. Louis-Emmanuel Jadin's *La Grande Bataille d'Austerliz* was published in Philadelphia less than two years after Napoleon Bonaparte's famous 1805 victory. Alphonse Leduc published his dance quadrilles commemorating battles of the Crimean War in Paris and London within months of the event. With no copyright laws, publishers apparently did not hesitate to recycle other works. In 1797 James Hewitt published *The Battle of Trenton*, celebrating George Washington's victory in 1776. Taking Natale Corri's *Siege and Surrender of Valenciennes* published in Edinburgh around 1792, Hewitt changed the programmatic references, substituted *Washington's March* for Corri's general march, *Yankee Doodle* instead of "An Original Austrian Quick March," and *Roslyn Castle*, the standard American funeral march, for the lamentation section. The anonymous *Battle of Copenhagen*, commemorating the British victory in 1807, was published in London the next year with basically the same music as Jadin's *Grande Bataille d'Austerlitz* but with different programmatic captions, reversing the roles of the opponents, a French victory now celebrating a British one. The "Triumphant March" in both appears as "General Bulow's March" in Jonathan Blewitt's *Battle of Waterloo*, published in Philadelphia in 1816.

Already popular in the Renaissance, by the 18th century battle pieces usually displayed the same general programmatic form. While mainly for piano, some had violin, cello, or drum accompaniments; other pieces were composed for full orchestra or band. An introduction depicting a peaceful scene was followed by trumpet, bugle, or drum signals and the call to arms. The combatants were introduced, and the conflict begun. The composer's imagination was shown in the battle section, characterized by special keyboard and compositional techniques: extended tremolos, persistent diminished seventh chords, expansive scales and arpeggios, and unusual harmonic progressions and modulations. A special feature, to imitate cannon shots or gun-fire, was a cluster of keys in the bass, played by one or both hands and designated by a special sign such as ⊗ (used by Bernard Viguerie and Peter Ricksecker among others) or a fermata. Percussion stops were available on some pianos, and Denis-Germain Etienne specified two of them in his *Battle of New Orleans* (1816). The next musical section depicted the cries of the wounded or lamentation for the slain, represented by a slow tempo and chromaticism. This was normally followed by shouts of victory or trumpet fanfares introducing the final celebratory section, usually a fast dance, march, or patriotic melody such as "God Save the King," "La Marseillaise," "Yankee Doodle," "Hail Columbia," and even variations on "The Star-Spangled Banner."

American battle music was modeled on European works, in particular František Kocžwara's *The Battle of Prague* (*c*1788), which was published in the United States from about 1793 throughout the 19th century. Other very popular perennial works include Bernard Viguerie's *The Battle of Maringo* [1802] and Ogilvy's *The Battle of Waterloo* (1818); the latter ends with a triumphal chorus instead of the usual dance or march and was usually published under the name of the original arranger for piano, "G. Anderson."

Other popular early battle pieces include Benjamin Carr's *The Siege of Tripoli* (1804), Francesco Masi's *The Battles of Lake Champlain and Plattsburg* (1815), where the American army is represented in the right hand with sixteenth-notes, and the slower British in the left with eighth- and quarter-notes (1815; *see* illustration), and Peter Ricksecker's *The Battle of New Orleans* (1816). Many featured the fife and drum, and most printed editions included program captions. Some had illustrated covers; two works by Peter Weldon, *The Battle of Baylen* (1809) and *The Siege of Gerona* (1810–12), have particularly elaborate engravings depicting the battle and the military leaders.

The most prolific 19th-century composer of battle pieces in the United States was Charles Grobe, who from the late 1840s on wrote no fewer than 12 "descriptive fantasies," as well as other pieces, on battles of the Mexican and Civil wars. *The Battle of Manassas* (about the Battle of Bull Run in Virginia) by Thomas Bethune (Blind Tom) was played many times by the composer and became a best-selling publication. The pianist is to imitate a train by saying "chu-chu" and whistling; otherwise the piece consists mainly of relevant popular tunes and marches, though it also inexplicably includes *The Marseillaise*.

Other 19th-century American composers of battle pieces include James C. Beckel, Francis Buck, Louis-Moreau Gottschalk, and William Striby. Among 20th-century examples are the battle pieces of E.T. Paull, published between 1905 and 1922 with elaborate lithographed covers in five colors. Famous battle pieces composed for band include John Philip Sousa's *Sheridan's Ride* (1891), Albert C. Sweet's *Battle of San Juan Hill* (1909), and C.L. Barnhouse's rousing circus march *The Battle of Shiloh* (1927).

BIBLIOGRAPHY

J.A. Hennig: *Battle Pieces for the Pianoforte Composed and Published in the United States between 1795 and 1820* (diss., Boston U., 1968)

M. Hinson, ed.: *Piano Music in Nineteenth Century America* (Chapel Hill, NC, 1975)

J.B. Clark: "European and American Keyboard Battles, 1793–1818," *The Sonneck Society Newsletter*, xi (1985), 47, 53, 85 [incl. worklist of selected battle pieces]

J.B. Clark: "European and American Keyboard Battles," *The Dawning of American Keyboard Music* (Westport, CT, 1988)

J. BUNKER CLARK/RAOUL F. CAMUS

Bauer, Harold (*b* Kingston-upon-Thames, England, 28 April 1873; *d* Miami, FL, 12 March 1951). Pianist of English birth; naturalized American. He gave his first concerts as a violinist by the time he was ten. At 15 he appeared in recital playing both the violin and the piano and was advised to concentrate on only one instrument. Ignacy Jan Paderewski arranged for him to play in Russia and advised him to study intensively in order to pursue a career as a pianist. In 1899 he made highly successful appearances in Scandinavia and the Netherlands and played with the Vienna PO under Hans Richter, and in 1900 he made his American debut with the Boston SO in Johannes Brahms's D minor Concerto. Over the following years he became especially associated with the works of Ludwig van Beethoven, Robert Schumann, and Brahms, and in addition to his tours of the United States and Europe he also visited Australia and Asia, becoming highly respected for the seriousness of his approach and his lack of mannerism. Bauer was also drawn to the music of the French school, introducing Maurice Ravel's G major Concerto in New York.

Bauer took American citizenship in 1917; two years later he founded the Beethoven Society of New York. He later became president of the Friends of Music of the Library of Congress and was associated with various educational establishments, most notably the Manhattan School of Music, where he was head of the piano department, continuing on its advisory board until his death. In the intellectuality of his approach and his lack of egocentricity, Bauer represented a more modern outlook than that of many of his contemporaries. He was also highly inventive in his use of coloristic pedal effects, which he developed through his study of French music. He wrote *Harold Bauer, his Book* (New York, 1948). Many of his papers are held by the Library of Congress.

CHARLES HOPKINS/R

Bauer, Marion (Eugénie) (*b* Walla Walla, WA, 15 Aug 1882; *d* South Hadley, MA, 9 Aug 1955). Composer, teacher, and writer on music. Throughout her adult life, Bauer gave her year of birth as 1887, and 1884 appears on her tombstone; however, Susan Pickett located a newspaper birth announcement and census documents that confirm 1882 as the correct date. She studied in Portland, Oregon, and in Paris and Berlin, her teachers including NADIA BOULANGER, André Gédalge, HENRY HOLDEN HUSS, and Raoul Pugno. During 12 summers between 1919 and 1944 she visited the MacDowell Colony where she produced many of her compositions and met other important women composers including Amy Beach, Mabel Daniels, Miriam Gideon, and Ruth Crawford. Bauer taught music history and composition at New York University (1926–51), was affiliated with the Juilliard School of Music from 1940 until her death, and lectured widely. Open to various styles, she was a champion of American music and modern composers, as evidenced by her participation in many organizations, for example, founding member of the American Music Guild (1921), the Society of American Women Composers (1925), the ACA (1937), and the AMC (1939). She was secretary and then vice president for the Society for the Publication of American Music, and a board member for the League of Composers, International Society for Contemporary Music, and the ACA. Frequently she was the only woman in a position of leadership in these associations. Bauer also played an active role with the weekly concerts of the New York Composers' Forum, supported by the Federal Music Project and the WPA (1935–40).

Like many women of her generation, she focused her initial compositional activity on songs and piano solos. Her works of the 1930s and 40s were larger and more significant. Despite brief experiments with 12-tone writing in the 1940s and 50s, her music rarely ventured beyond extended tonality, emphasizing coloristic harmony and diatonic dissonance. Her compositions remained melodic in focus and grounded in third-based harmony and periodic rhythm even when functional tonality was blurred. On occasion energetic rhythm propelled her works. In the 1920s her music had been seen as that of a left-wing modernist, but by the 1940s it was deemed conservative yet well-crafted. During her lifetime her music received many performances, including the 1947 premiere of *Sun Splendor* by the New York Philharmonic conducted by Stokowski and a 1951 Town Hall concert devoted to her compositions. In reviewing the latter concert, Olin Downes described her music as "concentrated," "prevailingly contrapuntal," and commented that "dissonance is not absent. Yet the fundamental conception is melodic, the thinking clear and logical" (*New York Times*, 9 May 1951). Like many of her works, *Sun Splendor* shows evidence of Impressionism and her study in France. Also recognized were her influence as a music critic and her intellectual approach to new music, demonstrated in writings such as *Twentieth Century Music* (New York, 1933, 2/1947). Addressing general readers as well as music specialists, her writings were widely published in journals; she also wrote a number of other books, and was editor of the *Musical Leader*.

WRITINGS

with E. Peyser: *How Music Grew: from Prehistoric Times to the Present Day* (New York, 1925, rev. 1939)

with E. Peyser: *Music through the Ages: a Narrative for Student and Layman* (New York, 1932, enlarged 3/1967 by E. Rogers as *Music through the Ages: an Introduction to Music History*)

Twentieth Century Music (New York, 1933/*R*; 2/1947)

Musical Questions and Quizzes: a Digest of Information about Music (New York, 1941)

"Darius Milhaud," *MQ*, xxviii/2 (1942), 139–59

"The Music Educator's Obligation to Study Contemporary Trends," *MJ*, i/4 (1943), 8, 29, 46

with E. Peyser: *How Opera Grew: from Ancient Greece to the Present Day* (New York, 1956)

WORKS

(selective list)

INSTRUMENTAL

Orch: Indian Pipes, op.12, no.2a, 1927–8; Sym. Suite, op.34, str, 1940; Pf Conc. "American Youth," op.36, 1943, arr. 2 pf (New York, 1946); Sun Splendor, 1934/46 orchd pf work (1926), perf. edn by N.T. Sutton, ii (diss., UCLA, 2000); Prelude and Fugue, op.43, fl, str/pf, 1948 or 1949; Sym. no.1, op.45, 1945–50

Chbr: Up the Ocklawaha, op.6, vn, pf, 1912 (Boston, 1913); Sonata no.1, lost, op.14, vn, pf, 1921 or 1922; Fantasia quasi una sonata, op.18, vn, pf, 1925; Str Qt, op.20, 1925; Sonata, op.22, va/cl, pf, 1932; Suite (Duo), op.25, ob, cl, 1932; Concertino, op.32b, ob, cl, str qt/str orch, 1939, rev. 1943; Trio Sonata no.1, op.40, fl, vc, pf (New York, 1944); 5 Pieces (Patterns, also: Paterns), op.41 nos.1–5, str qt, 1946–9, orig. pf, no.2 arr. double ww qnt, db, 1948; Aquarelle, op.39 no.2[a], double ww qnt, 2 db, 1948, orig. pf; Prelude and Fugue, op.43, fl, pf/str orch, 1948, new edn Bryn Mawr, PA, 2009; Trio Sonata no.2, op.47, fl, vc, pf, 1951; Qnt for Wws, op.48, fl, ob, cl, bn, hn (New York, 1956)

Kbd (pf solo unless otherwise stated): Arabesque (Cincinnati, 1904); Élégie (Cincinnati, 1904); From the New Hampshire Woods, op.12 nos.1–3, 1921; 3 Preludettes, 1921; 6 Preludes, op.15, 1922; Turbulence, op.17 no.2 [1924?]; Sun Splendor (lost), 1926, arr. 2 pf, 1930; A Fancy, 1927; 4 Pf Pieces, op.21, 1930; Dance Sonata, op.24, 1935; Aquarelle [I], op.39 no.1, 1942? (Providence, RI, 1944); Aquarelle II, 1945?, arr. double ww qnt, 2 db; Moods (3 Moods for Dance), op.46, 1950–54; Anagrams, op.48, 1950; Meditation and Toccata, org, 1951

Other inst: Prometheus Bound (incid music, Aeschylus), 2 fl, 2 pf, 1930; Pan and Syrinx (choreog. sketch for film), op.31, fl, ob, cl, pf, vn, va, vc (New York, 1937)

VOCAL

Choral: Wenn ich rufe an dich, Herr, mein Gott (Ps xxviii), op.3, S, women's chorus, org/pf, 1903; Light (F.W. Bourdillon), 1v, pf, 1907–8; Fair Daffodils (R. Herrick), women's chorus, pf (Boston, 1914); The Lay of the Four Winds (C.Y. Rice), op.8, men's chorus, pf (Boston, 1915); 3 Noëls (L.I. Guiney, trad.), op.22 nos.1–3, A, women's chorus (Boston, 1930; new edn Chapel Hill, NC, 2003); Here at High Morning (M. Lewis), op.27, men's chorus, 1931; The Thinker, op.35, mixed chorus, 1938; China (B. Todrin), op.38, mixed chorus, orch/pf, 1943; At the New Year (K. Patchen), op.42, mixed chorus, pf, 1947; Death Spreads his Gentle Wings (E.P. Crain), op.44?, mixed chorus, 1949 or 1951 (New York, 1952); A Foreigner Comes to Earth on Boston Common (H. Gregory), op.49, S, T, mixed chorus, pf, 1953

Other vocal: Coyote Song (J.S. Reed), Bar/A, pf (Boston, 1912); Send Me a Dream (Intuition) (E.F. Bauer), 1v, pf (Boston, 1912); The Red Man's Requiem (E.F. Bauer), 1v, pf (Boston, 1912); Phillis (C.R. Defresny), 1v, pf (Boston, 1914); Orientale. Fair Goes the Dancing (Sir E. Arnold), S, orch, 1914?, orchd 1932; By the Indus (C.Y. Rice), 1v, pf (1st perf. 1916); Lad and Lass (C.Y. Rice), 1v, pf, [c 1917?], new edn *Women Composers: Music Through the Ages*, vii (New Haven, CT, 2003); My Faun (O. Wilde), 1v, pf, 1919, new edn *Women Composers: Music Through the Ages*, vii (New Haven, CT, 2003); Night in the Woods (E.R. Sill), med v, pf (New York, 1921); The Epitaph of a Butterfly (T. Walsh), 1v, pf (Boston, 1921); A Parable: The Blade of

Grass (S. Crane), 1v, pf (New York, 1922); 4 Poems (J.G. Fletcher), op.16, high v, pf (New York, 1924); How Doth the Little Crocodile (from *Through the Looking Glass*, L. Carroll), 1v, pf, 1928, new edn *Women Composers: Music Through the Ages*, vii (New Haven, CT, 2003); When the Shy Star Goes Forth (J. Joyce), 1v, pf, 1931, new edn *Women Composers: Music Through the Ages*, vii (New Haven, CT, 2003); To Losers (F. Frost), 1v, pf, 1932, new edn *Women Composers: Music Through the Ages*, vii (New Haven, CT, 2003); Faun Song, A, chbr orch, 1934; 4 Songs (Suite) (A. Kreymborg), op.30 nos.1–4 [no.1 lost?], S, str qt, no.2 1933, completed 1936?; Songs in the Night (M.M.H. Ayers), 1v, pf (New York, 1943); The Harp (E.C. Bailey), 1v, pf (New York, 1947); Swan (Bailey), 1v, pf (New York, 1947); Here Alone, Unknown (C. Aitken), 1v, pf (radio perf 7 Nov 1954), new edn *Women Composers: Music Through the Ages*, vii (New Haven, CT, 2003)

MSS in *NYamc*, *NYgo*, *NYp*, *Wc*, American Composers Alliance, Mount Holyoke College

Principal publishers: Composers Facsimile Edition/ACA, G. Schirmer, A.P. Schmidt

BIBLIOGRAPHY

EwenD; *GroveA* (B.H. Renton); *GroveW* (J.M. Edwards)

O. Downes: "Miss Bauer's Work Makes Up Concert," *New York Times* (9 May 1951), 41

M. Goss: *Modern Music Makers* (New York, 1952)

Obituary. *New York Times* (11 Aug 1955)

Obituary. *Musical Leader*, lxxxvii/9 (Sept 1955), 14, 18

A.F. Block and C. Neuls-Bates: *Women in American Music: a Bibliography of Music and Literature* (Westport, CT, 1979)

A.F. Block: "Arthur P. Schmidt, Music Publisher and Champion of American Women Composers," *The Musical Woman: an International Perspective*, ii, ed. J.L. Zaimont and others (New York, 1987)

P.A. Horrocks: *The Solo Vocal Repertoire of Marion Bauer* (diss., U. of Nebraska, 1994)

J.M. Edwards: "Bauer, Marion Eugénie," *Jewish Women in America: an Historical Encyclopedia*, ed. P.E. Hyman and D.D. Moore (New York, 1997), 128–30 <http://jwa.org/encyclopedia/article/bauer-marion-eugenie>

E.M. Hisama: *Gendering Musical Modernism: the Music of Ruth Crawford, Marion Bauer, and Miriam Gideon* (Cambridge, UK, 2001)

P.A. Holloway: "Marion Bauer," *Women Composers: Music Through the Ages*, vii, ed. S. Glickman and M.F. Schleifer (New Haven, CT, 2003), 672–99

S. Pickett: "Marion Bauer: from the Wild West to New York Modernism," *The Maud Powell Signature, Women in Music*, ii/2 (June 2008), 31–45

Marion Eugenie Bauer Papers 1936–1951, New York University Archives <http://dlib.nyu.edu/findingaids/html/archives/bauer_content.html>

J. MICHELE EDWARDS

Bauer, Ross (*b* Ithaca, NY, 19 Dec 1951). Composer and conductor. He studied at the New England Conservatory (BM 1975) with John Heiss and Ernst Oster and at Brandeis University (PhD 1984) with MARTIN BOYKAN, ARTHUR BERGER, and SEYMOUR SHIFRIN. During the summer of 1982 he was a fellow at Tanglewood, where he worked with LUCIANO BERIO. He has taught at Brandeis University (1981–5), Stanford University (1986–8), where he directed the ensemble Alea II, and the University of California, Davis (1988–), where he has founded and directed the Empyrean Ensemble. He also served as a founding member and chair of the Griffin Music Ensemble, Boston (1985–92). His honors include the American Academy & Institute of Arts and Letters Walter Hinrichsen Award (1984), a Guggenheim Fellowship (1988), a prize in the ISCM National Composers Competition (1989), and commissions from the Fromm and Koussevitzky foundations (1991, 1994). He was a MacDowell Colony fellow in 1996. In 2001, Bauer was the guest composer for the Wellesley Composer's Conference. One of his most prominent moments of recognition came in 2005, when Bauer received an award in music from the American Academy of Arts and Letters. Bauer's music derives its structure, pitch succession, and pitch centricity from relationships between hexachords and the collections of intervals and chords they comprise. An inventive and subtle manipulation of timbre is also characteristic of his work.

WORKS
(selective list)

Orch: Pf Conc., 1990; Halcyon Birds, chbr orch, 1993; Romanza, vn, orch, 1996; Icons, bn, orch, 1997; Dusk, orch, 2002

Chbr and solo inst: Hang Time, cl, vn, pf, 1984; Chimera, fl, cl, hn, vn, va, vc, perc, hp, pf, 1987; Chin Music, va, pf, 1989; Birthday Bagatelles, pf, 1990–93; Anaphora, fl, vn, va, vc, pf, 1991; Tributaries, vc, perf, pf, 1992; Aplomb, vn, pf, 1993; Octet, cl, bn, hn, str qt, db, 1994; Stone Soup, fl, cl, vn, vc, pf, 1995; Motion, vn, vc, pf, 1998; Pulse, cl, va, vc, 1999; Fast and Loose, fl, orch, 2001; This, That, and the Other, sax, perc, chbr orch, 2001; Thin Ice, vc, orch, 2006; Dirge–Elegy, pf, 2007; Implicit Memory, 2006; Leda, pf trio, 2008; Bust a Flame, sax, gui, pf, perc, 2009; Symboisis, cl, bsn, fh, va, vc, 2009; Pas de Deux, va, vc, 2009

Vocal: 4 Honig Songs (E. Honig), S, pf, 1989; Eskimo Songs (trans. J. Houston and L. Millman), Mez, fl, vc, pf, 1992–6; Ritual Frags. (Amerindian), S, fl, cl, vn, vc, perc, pf, 1995

Principal publisher: Peters

RICHARD SWIFT/JONAS WESTOVER

Baur, Clara (*b* Württemberg, Germany, 1835; *d* Cincinnati, OH, 1912). Music educator and administrator of German birth. She studied piano in Stuttgart before joining her two brothers in Cincinnati, Ohio, in 1849, where she studied piano with Caroline Rivé and taught private piano and voice. After studying again in Europe in 1867, she returned to the United States and founded the Cincinnati Conservatory of Music in 1868. The faculty included Baur, Rivé, cellist Michael Brand, and pianist Henry Andres. Housed in Clara Nourse's School for Young Ladies, enrollment was predominantly female. The Conservatory offered one of the first summer music programs in the United States. Studies included all the arts, literature, foreign languages, and health. Baur's goals were to prepare students for professional music careers and instill values she believed would enable them to become positive influences on society. Local citizens who disagreed with the Conservatory's curriculum established the College of Music of Cincinnati in 1878. With greater resources, the College soon outdistanced the Conservatory, which rallied through philanthropic support. Bertha Baur, a faculty member and administrative assistant, succeeded her aunt as director of the Conservatory upon Clara Baur's death in 1912. The two institutions merged in 1955 to form the Cincinnati College-Conservatory of Music.

BIBLIOGRAPHY

B. Shifflet: *A History of Ten Influential Women in Music Education, 1885–1997* (thesis, Bowling Green State U., 2007)

CAROLYN LIVINGSTON

Bauzá, Mario (*b* Havana, Cuba, 28 April 1911; *d* New York, NY, 11 July 1993). Cuban trumpeter. He learned clarinet, oboe, and flute before studying trumpet with Lazaro Herrera and subsequently played with the groups of Antonio Maria Romeu, Domingo Corbacho, and Belisario Lopez, among others. In 1930 he moved to New York, where he performed from 1932 to 1939 with the orchestras of Noble Sissle, Chick Webb, Sam Wooding, and Don Redman. A meeting with John Bartee, Cab Calloway's arranger, inspired him to develop a synthesis of the cuban clave and the latest jazz, which became known as Afro-Cuban jazz. Bauzá subsequently began working with the percussionist Frank Grillo (later known as Machito) to integrate jazz elements into Cuban dance music. After that collaboration finished, he joined the Cab Calloway orchestra in 1939, brought Dizzy Gillespie into the band, and encouraged him to explore Afro-Cuban music. From 1940 he was music director of Machito's re-formed Afro-Cubans for nearly 35 years. In 1943 Bauzà composed his first important tune, *Tanga*, which has become a staple of Latin jazz. With the Afro-Cubans, he also worked on Afro-Cuban jazz recordings, with Charlie Parker, Chico O'Farrill, Harry Edison, and the producer Norman Granz. In his later years, he formed a group with Victor Paz on trumpet and Jesus "Chuco" Valdés on conga. He also performed with the singer Graciela Grillo (Machito's sister) in a big band that made some recordings and toured in Europe and the United States.

BIBLIOGRAPHY

J. Conzo: *Mucho Macho*, Pablo 2625712 (1978) [disc notes]
Obituary, *New York Times* (12 July 1993)
T. Pérémarti: "Mario Bauzá," *Jb*, no.496 (1993), 24

LUCA CERCHIARI

Baxter, J(esse) R(andall Jr.) (*b* Lebanon, AL, 8 Dec 1887; *d* Dallas, TX, 21 Jan 1960). Publisher and composer of gospel songs. He attended singing schools of Thomas B. Mosley and Anthony J. Showalter and became proficient in writing both words and music of gospel songs, probably composing more convention songs than any other gospel music publisher of his time. A compilation of his songs, *Precious Abiding Peace*, was published in 1960. He was an outstanding singing school teacher and conducted his own schools until 1922, after which he managed the Showalter office in Texarkana, Texas. In 1926 Baxter joined with Virgil O. Stamps in establishing the Stamps-Baxter Music Company in Jacksonville, Texas. When the company moved to Dallas in 1929, Baxter opened a branch office in Chattanooga, Tennessee. Stamps-Baxter became the foremost publisher of gospel music in seven-shape notation. Following Stamps's death in 1940, Baxter moved to Dallas and became president of the firm. By 1940 this firm, now the Stamps-Baxter Music and Printing Company, was printing books for more than a dozen denominational publishing houses in addition to their own books, and sponsoring gospel radio programs featuring Stamps quartets. In 1949 an article in *Time* likened the company to a gospel Tin Pan Alley. At that time the firm employed 50 people and its journal, *Gospel Music News*, had a circulation of 20,000. After Baxter's death his widow, Clarice Baxter, operated the firm until her death in 1972. Stamps-Baxter was sold to the Zondervan Corporation in 1974. Both Baxters were inducted into the Southern Gospel Music Hall of Fame.

BIBLIOGRAPHY

C. Baxter and V. Polk: *Gospel Song Writers Biography* (Dallas, 1971)
S.L. Beary: *The Stamps-Baxter Music and Printing Company: a Continuing Tradition, 1926–1976* (diss., Southwestern Baptist Theological Seminary, 1977)
J. Fresne: *Schools of the Stamps-Baxter Music and Printing Company: a History from 1926 to 1964* (diss., Arizona State U., 2004)

SHIRLEY BEARY/HARRY ESKEW

Baxter, Les(lie T.) (*b* Mexia, TX, 14 March 1922; *d* Palm Springs, CA, 15 Jan 1996). Composer, conductor, and arranger. His family moved to Michigan, where he studied piano at the Detroit Conservatory. They later moved to Los Angeles, where Baxter continued his studies at Pepperdine University. After attempting to become a concert pianist, Baxter decided to focus his career elsewhere in the recording industry and joined Mel Tormé and his Mel-Tones as a vocalist and arranger in 1945. Two years later he collaborated with theremin player Dr. Samuel Hoffman and composer Harry Revel to make his first recording, *Music out of the Moon*, which established Baxter's place in the genre of Exotica. By 1950 he had signed a contract with Capitol Records as a conductor and arranger and helped to produce such recordings as Nat "King" Cole's "Mona Lisa" and "Too Young," both of which became hits. In the same year he also produced the album *Voice of the Xtabay* by Peruvian singer Yma Sumac. In 1951 Baxter produced *Le sacre du sauvage*, which contained the hit "Quiet Village," after Capitol Records gave him license to compose his own concept album. As an arranger with his own orchestra Baxter achieved chart-topping success with his versions of "Unchained Melody" (1955) and "The Poor People of Paris" (1956). Although he was included to write exotica, Baxter pursued diverse interests. He composed for *The Bob Hope Show* and *Abbott and Costello*, and in 1963 he formed a folk-based group called the Balladeers, which featured David Crosby. Throughout the 1950s and continuing to the end of his life, he worked as a film composer, ultimately contributing to more than 100 movies. Along with many science fiction and horror films, the *Dr. Goldfoot* series and Roger Corman's Edgar Allan Poe films are his most notable. His music utilized the full range of hi-fidelity sound. As a composer Baxter is noted for his unusual timbral effects, the bright and shimmering colors in his orchestral arrangements, and his affinity for whistling and birdcalls in his songs. In 1951 he married Los Angeles socialite Patricia Constance Fitzmaurice. He lived in Palm Springs in later years and died from kidney failure in 1996.

SELECTED RECORDINGS

As leader: *Baxter's Best* (Cap., 1996); *Mondo Exotica* (Cap., 1996); *Space Capades* (Cap., 1996)

BIBLIOGRAPHY

P. Hayward, ed.: *Widening the Horizon: Exoticism in Post-war Popular Music* (Sydney, 1999)

D. Toop: *Exotica: Fabricated Soundscapes in a Real World* (London, 1999)

F. Adinolfi: *Mondo Exotica: Sounds, Visions, Obsessions, of the Cocktail Generation* (Durham, NC, 2008)

MONICA F. AMBALAL

Bayard, Samuel Preston (*b* Pittsburgh, PA, 10 April 1908; *d* Pittsburgh, 10 Jan 1997). Ethnomusicologist. He studied folklore and comparative literature with Kittredge at Harvard (MA 1936) and in 1945 was appointed instructor at Pennsylvania State University, where he was later professor of English and comparative literature; he also served as president of the American Folklore Society, 1965–6. He collected folksongs in Pennsylvania and West Virginia between 1928 and 1963, usually in the summer months, and documented fiddle and fife melodies in his editions *Hill Country Tunes: Instrumental Folk Music of Southwestern Pennsylvania* (Philadelphia, 1944) and *Dance to the Fiddle, March to the Fife: Instrumental Folk Tunes in Pennsylvania* (University Park, PA, and London, 1982). He also made an important contribution to the theory of tune relationships, identifying three central factors in such relationships: contour, important scale degrees, and stereotypical motifs. Building on the work of G.P. Jackson he identified a number of Tune families (varying from 35 to 55) in British-American folk tradition; his findings resulted in a series of articles begun in 1939, of which the best-known were published in 1950.

WRITINGS

"Aspects of Melodic Kinship and Variation in British-American Folk-Tunes," *PAMS* (1939), 122–9

"Prolegomena to a Study of the Principal Melodic Families of Folk-song," *Journal of American Folklore*, lxiii (1950), 1–44

"Principal Versions of an International Folk Tune," *JIFMC*, iii (1951), 44–50

"American Folksongs and their Music," *Southern Folklore Quarterly*, xvii (1953), 122–39

"Two Representative Tune Families of British Tradition," *Midwest Folklore*, iv (1953), 13–34

"A Miscellany of Tune Notes," *Studies in Folklore: in Honor of Distinguished Service Professor Stith Thompson*, ed. W.E. Richmond (Bloomington, IN, 1957), 151–76

"Decline and 'Revival' of Anglo-American Folk Music," *Folklore in Action and Essays for Discussion in Honor of MacEdward Leach*, ed. H.P. Beck (Philadelphia, 1962), 21–9

"Scales and Ranges in Anglo-American Fiddle Tunes: Report on a Desultory Experiment," *Two Penny Ballads and Four Dollar Whisky: a Pennsylvania Folklore Miscellany*, ed. K.S. Goldstein and R.E. Byington (Hatboro, PA, 1966), 51–60

BIBLIOGRAPHY

R. Blaustein: "Samuel Preston Bayard," *Journal of American Folklore*, cx (1997), 415–17

C. Rahkonen: "An essential resource of American music: the Samuel Bayard Collection at the Pennsylvania State University," *ARSC Journal*, xxxv/1 (2004), 90–94

JAMES PORTER/R

Bayes [Goldberg], **Nora** [Dora; Leonora; Eleanor] (*b* Milwaukee, WI, or Joliet, IL, 1880; *d* Brooklyn, NY, 19 March 1928). Actress and singer. Her birth name is variously given as Dora, Leonora, and Eleanor. Little is known of Bayes's early years before she moved to Chicago at the age of 17. There she began performing in the Chicago Opera House between acts. After a short stint in the Fisher Stock Company in San Francisco, Bayes began appearing in vaudeville and in 1901 made her Broadway debut in *The Rogers Brothers in Washington*. Her first musical hit came the following year with "Down where the Wurzburger Flows." Between 1904 and 1907 Bayes toured England and Europe, performing in variety acts and musical comedies, before returning to the United States to star in the first production of the *Ziegfeld Follies* (1907). The following year she returned to the *Follies* with her new husband, Jack Norworth, where they introduced the show's most popular song, "Shine on, Harvest Moon." After divorcing Norworth in 1913, Bayes toured Europe and the United States billed as the Greatest Single Woman Singing Comedienne in the World. An international favorite with her deep contralto voice and one of the foremost pre-World War I hit-makers, Bayes recorded prolifically between 1910 and 1923, memorializing such songs as "Turn off your light, Mr. Moon Man," (Victor, 1910) "Anybody here Seen Kelly?," (Victor, 1910) ""Over there," (Victor, 1917) "How Ya Gonna Keep 'em Down on the Farm (After They've Seen Paree)?" (Columbia, 1918), "Prohibition Blues," (Columbia, 1919) "Japanese Sandman," (Columbia, 1920) and Her Broadway credits include *Maid in America* (1915), *Ladies First* (1918), *Her Family Tree* (1920), and *Queen o' Hearts* (1922).

GERALD BORDMAN/MARIA PURCIELLO

Bayley, Daniel (*b* Rowley, MA, 27 June 1729; *d* Newburyport, MA, 29 Feb 1792). Tunebook compiler and publisher. He moved to Newburyport with his family as a boy, and by 1761 he was proprietor of a pottery shop. He identified himself in some publications as "Chorister of St. Paul's Church, Newburyport," and though no surviving records confirm that he held that title, he did receive the church's thanks in 1775 "for his Services as Clerk for sundry years past." His son, Daniel Bayley Jr. (1755–99), with whom he has sometimes been confused, played the organ at St. Paul's from 1776.

Bayley's publications borrow heavily from the works of others. He began his prolific career as a compiler by bringing out *A New and Complete Introduction* (Newburyport, 1764), drawn from successful works by Thomas Walter of Massachusetts and the Englishman William Tans'ur. In 1768 he issued Tans'ur's *The Royal Melody Complete* (first published in London in 1754, in Boston in 1767); he then combined it with Aaron Williams's *Universal Psalmodist* (1763) under the title *The American Harmony*, several editions of which were published between 1769 and 1774. Bayley's earlier works had been printed in Boston; by 1769, however, he had acquired a press, and from that time his collections were issued from Newburyport. Publications of the early 1770s included *The Essex Harmony* (1770–2), a tune supplement for metrical psalters; *The New Universal Harmony* and *A New Royal Harmony* (1773), both devoted mostly to anthems and set-pieces; and John Stickney's *The Gentleman and Lady's Musical Companion*

(1774), a large compendium printed mostly from plates engraved for *The American Harmony*. After the War of Independence, Bayley pirated the title and part of the contents of Andrew Law's successful *Select Harmony* (1779), despite Law's vigorous protests. His last tunebooks, *The Essex Harmony* (1785) and *The New Harmony of Zion* (1788), are eclectic mixtures of British and American pieces, following the model introduced by Law.

In the decade preceding the war, Bayley was by far the most active American compiler and publisher, accounting for some two-thirds of the 21 sacred music collections that survive from the years 1764–74. His tunebooks introduced to New England a large repertory of mid-century British sacred music, including several works that came to be standard favorites.

BIBLIOGRAPHY

F.J. Metcalf: *American Writers and Compilers of Sacred Music* (New York, 1925/*R*), 23–9

I. Lowens: "The Origins of the American Fuging Tune," *JAMS*, vi (1953), 43–52

I. Lowens and A.P. Britton: "Daniel Bayley's 'The American Harmony': a Bibliographical Study," *Papers of the Bibliographical Society of America*, xlix (1955), 340

R.T. Daniel: "English Models for the First American Anthems," *JAMS*, xii (1959), 49–58

I. Lowens: *Music and Musicians in Early America* (New York, 1964), 58–72

R. Crawford: *Andrew Law, American Psalmodist* (Evanston, IL, 1968/*R*), 19–22, 23n

I.F. Auger: *Music in Newburyport: Daniel Bayley* (thesis, Brown U., 1970)

RICHARD CRAWFORD/KIMBERLY GREENE

Baylor University. University located in Waco, Texas. It was chartered by the Republic of Texas in 1845 (in Independence, Texas) and sponsored by the Texas Union Baptist Association (from 1848 the Baptist State Convention). In 1886 it merged with Waco University and moved to its present site. A college of fine arts offering courses in music and expression was organized in 1919 but was replaced in 1921 by the School of Music. Today, the School of Music enrolls nearly 400 students and has a full-time faculty of more than 60. It offers BM and MM degrees, with emphasis on performance, piano pedagogy, collaborative piano, church music, music history and literature, and music theory and composition. The school also offers the BMEd and MMEd degrees (music education), a dual Master of Divinity/Master of Music in Church Music degree, and an Advanced Performer's Certificate (non-degree). The Crouch Music Library, which is especially strong in sacred music, contains approximately 75,000 music scores and 50,000 books on the arts.

WARREN HENRY

Bay Psalm Book. The name by which the first American metrical psalter, *The Whole Booke of Psalmes Faithfully Translated into English Metre* (Cambridge, MA, 1640), is commonly known.

See Psalms, metrical; Psalmody; *and* Printing and publishing.

Bazelon, Irwin (Allen) (*b* Evanston, IL, 4 June 1922; *d* New York, NY, 2 Aug 1995). Composer. After graduating from DePaul University (BA 1944, MA 1945), he studied with Darius Milhaud at Mills College (1946–8) and then settled in New York in 1948, where he received numerous fellowships, honors, and commissions. His music is in the tradition of urban American expressionism, with audible antecedents in the works of Varèse and Ruggles but with a distinctive angular simplicity, characterized by dramatic alternations between violence and tenderness. Bazelon's language, while influenced by serialism, borrows the jabbing brass and percussion chords and the propulsive rhythms of big-band jazz. This driving energy is contrasted with moments of relative repose in which orchestral colors are subtly varied.

Bazelon's ten symphonies (1962–92) form the heart of his musical output. The immediacy of these works derives from their spare textures, which often feature one or two contrapuntal lines presented in striking instrumental combinations; characteristic passages are harmonically and timbrally static, treating sound as a sculptural object. A free use of serial techniques combined with an undercurrent of jazz creates a dark sense of New York, reminiscent of *film noir*. The influence of a lighter jazz style, reflecting the manic side of life in New York, dominates such works as the chamber concerto *Churchill Downs* (1971): it features electronic instruments more typically employed in rock and pop music.

Bazelon's vocal works set texts from the modernist tradition of American poetry (i.e. Hart Crane, Wallace Stevens, etc.) in a highly charged, chromatic style, more dramatic than lyrical, with striking and uncluttered accompaniments. Also notable are percussion works such as *Propulsions* (1974), with their emphasis on rhythmic invention, dramatic structure, and the exploration of timbre. Several film scores, as well as music for television, number among his other compositions. He is the author of *Knowing the Score: Notes on Film Music* (New York, 1975).

WORKS

(selective list)

ORCHESTRAL

10 syms.: no.1, 1961; no.2 "Testament to a Big City," 1961; no.3, brass, str sextet, perc, pf, 1962; no.4, 1965; no.5, 1967; no.6, 1969; no.7 (ballet), 1980; no.8, str, 1986; no.8 1/2, 1988; no.9 "Sunday Silence," 1992

Other: Adagio and Fugue, str, 1947; Concert Ov., 1951, rev. 1961; Suite, small orch, 1953, rev. 1960; Centauri 17 (ballet), 1959; Ov. to Shakespeare's "The Taming of the Shrew," 1960; Suite from Shakespeare's "The Merry Wives of Windsor," 1960; Dramatic Movt, 1965; Excursion, 1965; Sym. concertante, cl, tpt, mar, orch, 1968; Dramatic Fanfare, brass, perc, 1970; A Quiet Piece for a Violent Time, chbr orch, 1975; De-Tonations, brass qnt, orch, 1976; Spirits of the Night, 1976; Memories of a Winter Childhood, 1981; Spires, tpt, small orch, 1981; For Tuba with Str Attached, tuba, str/str qt, 1982; Tides, cl, orch, 1982; Fusions, chbr orch, 1983; Pf Conc., 1983; Trajectories, pf conc., 1985; Motivations, trbn, orch, 1986; Fourscore + 2, perc qt, orch, 1987; Midnight Music, wind, 1990; The Bridge (H. Crane), Prelude, str, 1991; Entre nous, vc, orch, 1992; Fire and Smoke, timp, winds, 1994

CHAMBER

4 or more insts: Str Qt no.2, 1946; Movimento da camera, fl, bn, hn, hpd, 1954, rev. 1960; Chbr Conc. no.1, pic + fl, E♭ cl + cl, tpt, tuba, vn, pf, perc, 1957; Brass Qnt, 1963; Early American Suite, ww qnt, hpd, 1965; Churchill Downs (Chbr Conc. no.2), brass, str septet,

perc, 1971; Propulsions, perc ens, 1974; Ww qnt, 1975; Concatenations, va, perc qt, 1976; Sound Dreams, fl, cl, va, vc, pf, perc, 1977; Triple Play, 2 trbn, perc, 1977; Cross Currents, brass qnt, perc, 1978; Fusions, chbr ens, 1983; Quintessentials, fl, cl, mar, perc, db, 1983; Fourscore, perc qt, 1985; Fairy Tale, va, chbr ens, 1989

1–3 inst: Suite, cl, vc, pf, 1947; 5 Pieces, vc, pf, 1950; Duo, va, pf, 1963, rev. 1970; Double Crossings, tpt, perc, 1976; 3 Men on a Dis-Course, cl, vc, perc, 1979; Partnership, timp, mar, 1980; Suite, mar, 1983; Alliances, vc, pf, 1989; Bazz Ma Tazz, trbn, perc, 1992

KEYBOARD

(for piano unless otherwise stated)

Sonata no.1, 1947, rev. 1952; Sonata no.2, 1949, rev. 1952; Suite for Young People, 1950; 5 Pieces, 1952; Sonatina, 1952; Sonata no.3, 1953; Vignette, hpd, 1975; Imprints…on Ivory and Strings, 1978; Re-Percussions, 2 pf, 1982; Sunday Silence, 1989

VOCAL

Phenomena (syllabic text), S, chbr ens, 1972; Junctures (syllabic text), S, orch, 1979; Legends and Love Letters (H. Crane), S, chbr ens, 1987; Four…Parts of the World (W. Stevens), S, pf, 1991

Principal publishers: Presser, Boosey & Hawkes

BIBLIOGRAPHY

CC1 (R.R. Bennett)

D.H. Cox: "A World of Violent Silence: a Note on Irwin Bazelon," *MT*, cxxiii/Oct (1982), 683–5

D.H. Cox: *Irwin Bazelon: a Bio-bibliography* (Westport, CT, 2000)

SCOTT WHEELER

Bazin, James Amireaux (*b* Boston, MA, 29 March 1798; *d* Canton, MA, 5 Jan 1883). Instrument maker. The son of French Huguenots, he designed a variety of free-reed musical instruments. They had limited influence on later manufacturers, but are among the earliest of their type made in the United States. About 1821, Bazin developed an adjustable pitch pipe with a sliding bar that pressed against the reed to create multiple pitches. Soon after that time he began to create various mouth-blown instruments with multiple reeds. The most elaborate, made in 1824, was a "reed trumpet" with a chromatic range of three octaves, in which the reeds rotated past a fixed mouthpiece. He developed a diatonic harmonica around 1830 and an accordion in 1836.

Bazin's most successful instrument, first made in 1831, was a melodeon (lap organ) with a chromatic button keyboard and bellows operated by rocking the body back and forth. By 1833 they were sold in Boston, and by 1837 Abraham Prescott and other New England makers were copying the design, sometimes with a normal keyboard. Bazin developed various other reed organs, some with unusual button keyboards to facilitate simplified fingering. Later designs have regular keyboards, such as those patented on 22 June 1842 and on 2 August 1853. These have stirrup pedals that move forward and backward, a pressure system of winding, and shifting keyboards for transposition. An advocate of meantone temperament, Bazin's 1853 patent contains a complex system of switching between meantone and equal temperament. The complexity of many of Bazin's instruments apparently prohibited them from being commercially successful.

BIBLIOGRAPHY

G.W. Chase: "History of Reed Instruments in the United States," *The Musical World and Times* (9 April 1853)

J.A. Bazin: "First Reed Organs in America," *The Musical and Sewing Machine Gazette* (14 Feb 1880)

R.F. Gellerman: *The American Reed Organ and the Harmonium* (Vestal, NY, 1996), 9–16

D. Kuronen: "James A. Bazin and the Development of Free-Reed Instruments in America," *JAMIS*, xxxi (2005), 133–82

DARCY KURONEN

B-boying/b-girling. *See* Breakdancing, Hip-hop dance.

Beach [née Cheney], **Amy Marcy** [Mrs H.H.A. Beach] (*b* Henniker, NH, 5 Sept 1867; *d* New York, NY, 27 Dec 1944). Composer and pianist. She was the first American woman to succeed as a composer of large-scale art music and was celebrated during her lifetime as the foremost woman composer of the United States. A descendant of a distinguished New England family, she was the only child of Charles Abbott Cheney, a paper manufacturer and importer, and Clara Imogene (Marcy) Cheney, a talented amateur singer and pianist. At the age of one she could sing 40 tunes accurately and always in the same key; before the age of two she improvised alto lines against her mother's soprano melodies; at three she taught herself to read; and at four she mentally composed her first piano pieces and later played them, and could play by ear whatever music she heard, including hymns in four-part harmony. The Cheneys moved to Chelsea, Massachusetts, about 1871. Amy's mother agreed to teach her the piano when she was six, and at seven she gave her first public recitals, playing works by George Frideric Handel, Ludwig van Beethoven, and Fryderyk Chopin, and her own pieces. In 1875 the family moved to Boston, where her parents were advised that she could enter a European conservatory; but they decided on local training, engaging Ernst Perabo and later Carl Baermann as piano teachers. Her development as a pianist was monitored by a circle including Louis C. Elson, Percy Goetschius, H.W. Longfellow, Oliver Wendell Holmes, William Mason, and Henry Harris Aubrey Beach (1843–1910), a physician who lectured on anatomy at Harvard University and was an amateur singer; she married him in 1885.

At her successful debut in Boston (24 October 1883) she played Chopin's Rondo in E and Ignaz Moscheles's G minor Concerto, conducted by Adolf Neuendorff; at her debut with the Boston SO (28 March 1885), the first of several appearances with that orchestra, she played Chopin's F minor Concerto with Wilhelm Gericke conducting. After her marriage to Dr. Beach, and in respect of his wishes, she curtailed her performances, giving only annual recitals, with proceeds donated to charity. Most significantly, following her husband's wishes, her focus changed to composition.

Beach's training in composition was limited to one year of harmony and counterpoint with Junius W. Hill. In 1884 she sought a composition teacher, consulting Gericke, who prescribed a course of independent study using the masters as models. Following his advice, and for the next ten years, she taught herself fugue, double fugue, composition, and orchestration, using a range of theory texts, and translating treatises by Hector Berlioz and François-Auguste Gevaert. During that time, she

Amy Marcy Beach. (T.P./Lebrecht Music & Arts)

also produced a substantial body of work including her Mass in E op.5, an 85-minute work for chorus and orchestra. Almost all of her compositions were performed (in particular her songs and choral pieces), and were published by Arthur P. Schmidt, her exclusive publisher from 1885 to 1910. Several of her songs were recorded by Emma Eames and other soloists after the turn of the century.

Though largely removed from the polemics of her day, Beach was counted among the composers known as the Second New England School. Her Boston colleague G.W. Chadwick famously wrote to her after the premiere of her "Gaelic" Symphony op.32 (1896): "I always feel a thrill of pride myself whenever I hear a fine new work by any one of us, and as such you will have to be counted in, whether you will or not—one of the boys." This work may be heard as a response to Antonín Dvořák's call to American composers to draw on native materials. She chose to base the work on themes from the British Isles, which in her view most accurately reflected her Anglo-American heritage.

Beach's first published work, composed in 1880 and issued in 1883, was *The Rainy Day*, a setting of Longfellow's poem. Her major works during the period 1885–1910 include the Mass, the Symphony op.32, the Violin Sonata op.34, the Piano Concerto op.45, the *Variations on Balkan Themes* op.60, and the Piano Quintet op.67—introduced by such ensembles as the Boston Handel and Haydn Society, the Kneisel Quartet, and the Boston SO. Eminent singers of the time, such as Eames and Marcella Sembrich, presented her songs on recital programs. Two of her many songs, "Ecstasy" op.19 no.2 and "The Year's at the Spring" op.44 no.1, sold many thousands of copies. Among her commissioned works were the *Festival Jubilate* op.17, written for the dedication (1 May 1893) of the Women's Building of the World's Columbian Exposition, Chicago, *Eilende Wolken* op.18, given its premiere by the Symphony Society of New York (2 December 1892), and the *Song of Welcome* op.42, for the Trans-Mississippi Exposition, Omaha (1898); others were the *Panama Hymn* op.74, for the international Panama Pacific Exposition in San Francisco (1915), and the Theme and Variations for Flute and String Quartet op.80, for the San Francisco Chamber Music Society.

After her husband's death in 1910 and her mother's in 1911, Beach went to Europe (sailing on 5 September 1911), determined to establish a reputation there as both performer and composer and to promote the sale of her own works. Beginning in autumn 1912 she gave recitals in German cities, playing her sonata and quintet and accompanying her songs; her symphony was given in Leipzig and Hamburg, and her concerto in those two cities and in Berlin. The reviews were favorable: one journal stated that Beach was the leading American composer, and critic Ferdinand Pfohl called Beach a "virtuoso pianist" who had, as a composer, "a musical nature tinged with genius."

At the outbreak of World War I Beach returned to the United States, with 30 concerts already scheduled in the East and Midwest, and in 1915 moved briefly to New York and San Francisco, settling in Hillsborough, New Hampshire, in 1916. Thereafter she spent winters on tour and summers practicing and composing in Hillsborough; in Centerville on Cape Cod, Massachusetts, where she owned land purchased with the proceeds of her song *Ecstasy*; and from 1921 as a fellow at the MacDowell Colony where almost all her later works were composed. Outstanding among them are the String Quartet op.89, the two *Hermit Thrush* pieces op.92, *From Grandmother's Garden* op.97, *Rendezvous* op.120, *The Canticle of the Sun* op.123, Three Piano Pieces op.128, and the chamber opera *Cabildo* op.149. She made several trips abroad, including one to Rome (1929), where she finished her String Quartet. In 1942, to celebrate Beach's 75th birthday, Elena de Sayn, a violinist and critic from Washington, DC, organized two retrospective concerts of her music.

A highly disciplined composer, capable of producing large-scale works in a few days, Beach was also energetic in the promotion of her compositions, arranging for performances as soon as works were completed. As a pianist, she had a virtuoso technique and an extraordinary memory. She was interested in philosophy and science, and was fluent in German and French. Deeply religious, she later became virtual composer-in-residence at St. Bartholomew's Episcopal Church, New York. She was generous, using her status as dean of American women composers to further the careers of many young musicians. She served as leader of several organizations, including the Music Teachers National Association and the Music Educators National Conference, and was co-founder in 1925 and the first president of the Society of American Women Composers. Heart disease caused her retirement in 1940 and her death in 1944. Her will assigned her royalties to the MacDowell Colony.

Beach's earliest works demonstrate her ability to create a long line and her sensitivity to relationships between music and text. Song is at the core of her style—she used some of her songs as themes in her instrumental works (e.g. the Symphony, the Piano Concerto op.45, and the Piano Trio op.150)—but her remarkable ear for harmony and harmonic color is also apparent from the beginning. Like the early Romantics, Beach emphasized modal degrees and used mixed modes. Her perfect pitch and association of keys with colors and by extension with moods resulted in the expressive use of modulation (e.g. the song "Die vier Brüder" from op.1). Piano textures in her works draw especially from the techniques of Johannes Brahms, for instance in the rich chordal sonorities of the *Variations on Balkan Themes*, op.60 (1904).

Her mature style, characterized by increasing chromaticism, use of long-held and overlapping appoggiaturas, seventh and augmented-sixth chords, modulation by thirds, and avoidance of the dominant, shows her debt to the late Romantics, as well to the use of Scottish, Irish, American, and European folk music in some 30 compositions. However, she was acutely aware of the stylistic changes in music from the 1910s, and a significant number of her late works depart from the previously lush harmonies. The song "The Lotos Isles," op.76 no.2 (1914) and the two *Hermit Thrush* pieces for piano, op.92 (1921) make extensive use of impressionistic techniques. The String Quartet (1929), which quotes three simple Inuit melodies, displays lean textures and contrapuntally driven, unresolved dissonances. *From Grandmother's Garden*, whose title may suggest a retrospective style, moves further away from tonality. Her most adventurous pieces verge on atonality itself: the first of the op.128 set of three pieces for piano, "Scherzino: a Peterborough Chipmunk," begins with a series of arpeggiated seventh chords without tonal implications, while the *Improvisation*, op.148 no.1, employs whole-tone arpeggios arranged in chromatic wedges.

Beach first made her reputation as a composer of art songs. But it was her large-scale works beginning with the Mass and the Symphony that won her acceptance first by her Boston colleagues then nationally and internationally. Her most popular works in addition to the songs were the Symphony, which had dozens of performances by leading orchestras, the Violin Sonata, the Piano Quintet, the Theme and Variations for flute quintet, the *Hermit Thrush* pieces for piano, and, among the secular choral works, *The Chambered Nautilus*. Her sacred works, in particular the anthem *Let this mind be in you* and the expressionist *The Canticle of the Sun*, remained in the repertory of church choirs for years after her death when her other works were no longer heard. Many of her works have returned to the concert stage and about two-thirds of a total of 300 have been recorded. The years since 1990 have produced a significant number of dissertations and theses on her works, along with scholarly editions from multiple publishers. Scholarly conferences devoted to her works were held at the University of New Hampshire in October 1998 and the Mannes College of Music in December 1999.

WORKS

(printed works published in Boston unless otherwise stated; fs: full score; os: organ score; ps: piano score; for index to vocal works see GroveA*)*

OPERA

op.	
149	Cabildo (1, N.B. Stephens), solo vv, chorus, spkr, vn, vc, pf, 1932, (Athens, GA, 27 Feb 1945)

ORCHESTRAL, VOCAL-ORCHESTRAL

18	Eilende Wolken, Segler die Lüfte (F. von Schiller), A, orch, 1892, vs (1892)
22	Bal masque, perf. 1893, version for pf (1894)
32	"Gaelic" Symphony, e, 1894–6, fs (1897)
45	Piano Concerto, c, 1899, arr. 2 pf (1900)
53	Jephthah's Daughter (Mollevaut, after Bible: *Judges* xi.38, It. trans., I. Martinez, Eng. trans., A.M. Beach), S, orch, vs (1903)

CHAMBER

23	Romance, vn, pf (1893)
34	Vn Sonata, a, 1896 (1899), transcr. va, pf, transcr. fl, pf
40/1–3	Three Compositions, vn, pf (1898), arr. vc (1903): La captive, Berceuse, Mazurka
55	Invocation, vn, pf/org, vc obbl (1904)
67	Piano Quintet, f, 1907
80	Theme and Variations, fl, str qt, 1916 (1920), ed. J. Graziano, *American Chamber Music*, Three Centuries of American Music, viii (1991)
—	Caprice, The Water Sprites, fl, vc, pf, 1921, The Water Sprites arr. pf
89	String Quartet, 1 movt, 1929, ed. A.F. Block, Music of the United States of America, iii (Madison, WI, 1994)
90	Pastorale, fl, vc, pf, 1921, arr. vc, org, arr. vc, pf
—	Prelude, vn, vc, pf, 1931 [frag.]
125	Lento espressivo, vn, pf
150	Piano Trio, 1938 (1939)
151	Pastorale, ww qnt (1942)

KEYBOARD

(for pf unless otherwise stated)

3	Cadenza to Beethoven: Piano Concerto no.3, op.37, 1st movt (1888)
4	Valse-caprice (1889)
6	Ballad (1894), G
15/1–4	Four Sketches (1892): In Autumn, Phantoms, Dreaming, arr. vc, pf, Fireflies
—	Untitled, 3 movts, pf 4 hands, before 1893
22	Bal masque (1894)
25	Children's Carnival (1894)
28/1–3	Trois morceaux caractéristiques (1894): Barcarolle, rev. 1937, arr. vn, pf, 1937; Minuet italien; Danse des fleurs
36/1–5	Children's Album (1897): Minuet, Gavotte, Waltz, March, Polka
47	Summer Dreams, pf 4 hands (1901)
54/1–2	Scottish Legend, Gavotte fantastique (1903)
60	Variations on Balkan Themes, 1904 (1906), orchd 1906, rev. (1936), arr. 2 pf (1937)
64/1–4	Eskimos: Four Characteristic Pieces (1907), rev. (1943): Arctic Night, The Returning Hunter, Exiles, With Dog Teams
65/1–5	Suite française (1907): Les rêves de Columbine, La fée de la fontaine, Le prince gracieux, Valse étoiles, Danse d'Arlequin
70	Iverniana, 2 pf, 1910, lost
81	Prelude and Fugue, 1917 (1918)
83	From Blackbird Hills (1922)
87	Fantasia fugata (1923)
91	The Fair Hills of Eire, pf/org (1922), rev. as Prelude on an Old Folk Tune, org (1943)
92/1–2	Hermit Thrush at Eve, Hermit Thrush at Morn, 1921 (1922)

97/1–5 From Grandmother's Garden (1922) Morning Glories, Heartsease, Mignonette, Rosemary and Rue, Honeysuckle
102/1–2 Piano Compositions (1924): Farewell Summer, Dancing Leaves
104 Suite for Two Pianos Founded upon Old Irish Melodies (1924)
106 Old Chapel by Moonlight (1924)
107 Nocturne (1924)
108 A Cradle Song of the Lonely Mother (1924)
111 From Olden Times
114 By the Still Waters (1925)
116 Tyrolean Valse-fantaisie (1926)
119 From Six to Twelve (1927)
— A Bit of Cairo (1928)
— A September Forest, 1930
128/1–3 Three Pf Pieces (1932): Scherzino: a Peterborough Chipmunk, Young Birches, A Humming Bird
130 Out of the Depths (1932)
148 Five Improvisations, 1934 (1938)

SACRED CHORAL

(for 4vv and org unless otherwise stated)

5 Mass, E, 4vv, orch, 1890, os (1890)
— Graduale (Thou Glory of Jerusalem), T, orch, ps (1892) [addition to Mass, op.5]
7 O praise the Lord, all ye nations (Ps cxvii) (1891)
8/1–3 Choral Responses (1891): Nunc dimittis (Bible: *Luke* ii.29), With prayer and supplication (Bible: *Philippians* iv.6–7), Peace I leave with you (Bible: *John* iv.27)
17 Festival Jubilate (Ps c), D, 7vv, orch, 1891, ps (1892)
24 Bethlehem (G.C. Hugg) (1893)
27 Alleluia, Christ is risen (after M. Weisse, C.F. Gellert, T. Scott, T. Gibbons) (1895), arr. with vn obbl (1904)
33 Teach me thy way (Ps lxxxvi.11–12), 1895
38 Peace on earth (E.H. Sears) (1897)
50 Help us, O God (Pss lxxix.9, 5; xlv.6; xliv.26), 5vv (1903)
52 A Hymn of Freedom: America (S.F. Smith), 4vv, org/pf (1903), rev. with text O Lord our God arise (1944)
63 Service in A, S, A, T, B, 4vv, org: Te Deum, Benedictus (1905), rev. omitting Gloria, 1934; Jubilate Deo; Magnificat; Nunc dimittis (1906)
74 All hail the power of Jesus' name (E. Perronet), 4vv, org/pf, 1914 (1915)
76 Thou knowest, Lord (J. Borthwick), T, B, 4vv, org (1915)
78/1–4 Canticles (1916): Bonum est, confiteri (Ps xcii. 1–4), S, 4vv, org; Deus misereatur (Ps lxvii); Cantate Domino (Ps xcviii); Benedic, anima mea (Ps ciii)
84 Te Deum, f, T, male chorus 3vv, org, 1921 (1922)
95 Constant Christmas (P. Brooks), S, A, 4vv, org (1922)
96 The Lord is my shepherd (Ps xxiii), female chorus 3vv, org (1923)
98 I will lift up mine eyes (Ps cxxi), 4vv (1923)
103/1–2 Benedictus es, Domine, Benedictus (Bible: *Luke* i.67–81), B, 4vv, org (1924)
105 Let this mind be in you (Bible: *Philippians* ii.5–11), S, B, 4vv, org (1924)
109 Lord of the worlds above (I. Watts), S, T, B, 4vv, org (1925)
115 Around the Manger (R. Davis), 4vv, org/pf (1925), version for 1v, pf/org (1925); rev. female chorus 3vv, org/pf (1925), rev. female chorus 4vv, org/pf (1929)
121 Benedicite omnia opera Domini (Bible: *Daniel* iii.56–8) (1928)
122 Communion Responses: Kyrie, Gloria tibi, Sursum corda, Sanctus, Agnus Dei, Gloria, S, A, T, B, 4vv, org (1928)
— Agnus Dei, SA, chorus, org/pf (1936) [suppl. to op.122]
123 The Canticle of the Sun (St Francis), S, Mez, T, B, 4vv, orch, 1924, os (1928)
125/2 Evening Hymn: The shadows of the evening hours (A. Procter), S, A, 4vv, 1934 (1936)
132 Christ in the universe (A. Meynell), A, T, 4vv, orch, os (1931)
133 Four Choral Responses (J. Fischer) (1932)
134 God is our stronghold (E. Wordsworth), S, 4vv, org
139 Hearken unto me (Bible: *Isaiah* li.1, 3; xliii.1–3; xl.28, 31), S, A, T, B, 4vv, orch, os (1934)
141 O Lord, God of Israel (Bible: *1 Kings* viii.23, 27–30, 34), S, A, B, 4vv, 1935
146 Lord of all being (O.W. Holmes) (1938)
147 I will give thanks (Ps cxi), S, 4vv, org (1939)
— Hymn: O God of love, O King of peace (H.W. Baker), 4vv, 1941 (1942)
— Pax nobiscum (E. Marlatt) (female chorus 3vv)/(male chorus 3vv/4vv), org (1944)

SECULAR CHORAL

9 The Little Brown Bee (M. Eytinge), female chorus 4vv (1891)
— Singing Joyfully (J.W. Chadwick), children's chorus 2vv, pf
16 The Minstrel and the King: Rudolph von Hapsburg (F. von Schiller), T, B, male chorus 4vv, orch, ps (1890)
26/4 Wouldn't that be queer (E.J. Cooley), female chorus 3vv, pf (1919) [arr. of song]
— An Indian Lullaby (anon.), female chorus 4vv (1895)
30 The Rose of Avon-Town (C. Mischka), S, A, female chorus 4vv, orch, ps (1896)
31/1–3 Three Flower Songs (M. Deland), female chorus 4vv, pf (1896): The Clover, The Yellow Daisy, The Bluebell
37/3 Fairy Lullaby (W. Shakespeare), female chorus 4vv (1907)
39/1–3 Three Shakespeare Choruses, female chorus 4vv, pf (1897): Over hill, over dale, Come unto these yellow sands, Through the house give glimmering light
42 Song of Welcome (H.M. Blossom), 4vv, orch, os (1898)
43/4 Far Awa' (R. Burns), female chorus 3vv, pf (1918) [arr. of song]
44/1–2 The year's at the spring (R. Browning), female chorus 4vv, pf (1909); Ah, love, but a day (Browning), female chorus 4vv, pf (1927)
46 Sylvania: a Wedding Cantata (F.W. Bancroft, after W. Bloem), S, S, A, T, B, 8vv, orch, ps (1901)
49 A Song of Liberty (F.L. Stanton), 4vv, orch, 1902, ps (1902), arr. male chorus 4vv, pf (1917)
51/3 Juni (E. Jensen), 4vv, pf (1931), version for female chorus 3vv (1931) [arr. of song]
56/4 Shena Van (W. Black), female chorus 3vv/male chorus 4vv (1917) [arr. of song]
57/1–3 Only a Song (A.L. Hughes), One Summer Day (Hughes), female chorus 4vv (1904)
59 The Sea-Fairies (A. Tennyson), S, A, female chorus 2vv, orch, org ad lib, 1904, ps (1904), acc. arr. hp, pf
66 The Chambered Nautilus (Holmes), S, A, female chorus 4vv, orch, org ad lib, ps (1907), ed. A.F. Block (Bryn Mawr, PA, 1994)
74 Panama Hymn (W.P. Stafford), 4vv, orch, arr. 4vv, org/pf (1915)
75/1, 3 The Candy Lion (A.F. Brown), Dolladine (W.B. Rands), female chorus 4vv (1915) [arrs. of songs]
— Friends (Brown), children's chorus 2vv (1917)
— Balloons (L.A. Garnett) children's chorus (1916)
82 Dusk in June (S. Teasdale), female chorus 4vv (1917)
86 May Eve, 4vv, pf, 1921 (1933)
94 Three School Songs, 4vv (1933)
101 Peter Pan (J. Andrews), female chorus 3vv, pf (1923)
110 The Greenwood (W.L. Bowles), 4vv (1925)
118/1–2 The Moonboat (E.D. Watkins), children's chorus (1938), Who has seen the wind (C. Rossetti), children's chorus 2vv (1938)
126/1–2 Sea Fever (J. Masefield), The Last Prayer, male chorus 4vv, pf (1931)
127 When the last sea is sailed (Masefield), male chorus 4vv (1931)
129 Drowsy Dream Town (R. Norwood), S, female chorus 3vv, pf (1932)
140 We who sing have walked in glory (A.S. Bridgman), 1934 (1934)
144 This morning very early (P.L. Hills), female chorus 3vv, pf, 1935 (1937)
— The Ballad of the P.E.O. (R.C. Mitchell) female chorus, 1944

SONGS

(for 1v and pf unless otherwise stated)

1/1–4 Four Songs: With violets (K. Vannah) (1885), Die vier Brüder (F. von Schiller) (1887), Jeune fille et jeune fleur (F.R. Chateaubriand) (1887), Ariette (P.B. Shelley) (1886)

2/1–3 Three Songs: Twilight (A.M. Beach) (1887), When far from her (H.H.A. Beach) (1889), Empress of night (H.H.A. Beach) (1891)

10/1–3 Songs of the Sea (1890): A Canadian Boat Song (T. Moore), S, B, pf; The Night Sea (H.P. Spofford), S, S, pf; Sea Song (W.E. Channing), S, S, pf

11/1–3 Three Songs (W.E. Henley): Dark is the night (1890), The Western Wind (1889), The Blackbird (1889)

12/1–3 Three Songs (R. Burns): Wilt thou be my dearie? (1889) Ye banks and braes o' bonnie doon (1891), My luve is like a red, red rose, 1887 (1889)

13 Hymn of Trust (O.W. Holmes) (1891), rev. with vn obbl (1901)

14/1–4 Four Songs, 1890 (1891): The Summer Wind (W. Learned), Le secret (J. de Resseguier), Sweetheart, sigh no more (T.B. Aldrich), The Thrush (E.R. Sill); nos.2–3 rev. (1901)

19/1–3 Three Songs (1893): For me the jasmine buds unfold (F.E. Coates), Ecstasy (A.M. Beach), 1v, pf, vn obbl, Golden Gates

20 (Villanelle) Across the World (E.M. Thomas) (1894), arr. 1v, vc obbl

21/1–3 Three Songs (1893): Chanson d'amour (V. Hugo), arr. 1v, orch, arr. 1v, vc obbl (1899), Extase (Hugo), Elle et moi (F. Bovet)

26/1–4 Four Songs (1894): My Star (C. Fabbri), Just for this (Fabbri), Spring (Fabbri), Wouldn't that be queer (E.J. Cooley); no.4 arr. chorus (1919)

29/1–4 Four Songs, 1894 (1895): Within thy heart (A.M. Beach), The Wandering Knight (anon., Eng. trans., J.G. Lockhart), Sleep, little darling (Spofford), Haste, O beloved (W.A. Sparrow)

35/1–4 Four Songs, 1896 (1897): Nachts (C.F. Scherenberg), Allein! (H. Heine), Nähe des Geliebten (J.W. von Goethe), Forget-me-not (H.H.A. Beach)

37/1–3 Three Shakespeare Songs (1897): O mistress mine, Take, O take those lips away, Fairy Lullaby; no.3 arr. chorus (1907)

41/1–3 Three Songs (1898): Anita (Fabbri), Thy beauty (Spofford), Forgotten (Fabbri)

43/1–5 Five Burns Songs (1899): Dearie, Scottish Cradle Song, Oh were my love yon lilac fair!, Far awa', My lassie; no.3 arr. 2 S, pf (1918); no.4 arr. chorus (1918), arr. 2vv (1918), arr. female vv (1918), arr. org, 1936, arr. pf, 1936

44/1–3 Three [R.] Browning Songs (1900): The year's at the spring, Ah, love but a day, I send my heart up to thee; no.1 arr. S, A, pf (1900), arr. chorus (1928), arr. female vv (1928), arr. 1v, pf, vn (1900), arr. male chorus, pf (1933); no.2 arr. A, B, pf (1917), arr. S, T, pf (1917), arr. 1v, pf, vn (1920), arr. chorus by H. Norden (1949), nos.1–2 arr. chorus (1927)

48/1–4 Four Songs (1902): Come, ah come (H.H.A. Beach), Good Morning (A.H. Lockhart), Good Night (Lockhart), Canzonetta (A. Sylvestre)

51/1–4 Four Songs (1903): Ich sagete nicht (E. Wissman); Wir drei (H. Eschelbach), Juni (E. Jansen), Je demande à l'oiseau (Sylvestre); no.3 arr. v, pf, vn (1903), arr. 1v, orch, arr. chorus (1931)

56/1–4 Four Songs, 1903–4 (1904): Autumn Song (H.H.A. Beach), Go not too far (F.E. Coates), I know not how to find the spring (Coates), Shena Van (W. Black); no.4 arr. chorus (1917), arr. with vn obbl (1919)

61 Give me not love (Coates), S, T, pf (1905)

62 When soul is joined to soul (E.B. Browning) (1905)

68 After (Coates) (1909), arr. vn, vc, arr. A, chorus, 1936, arr. S, A, chorus, org, 1936

69/1–2 Two Mother Songs (1908): Baby (G. MacDonald), Hush, baby dear (A.L. Hughes)

71/1–3 Three Songs (1910): A Prelude (A.M. Beach), O sweet content (T. Dekker), An Old Love-Story (B.L. Stathem)

72/1–2 Two Songs (1914): Ein altes Gebet, perf. 1914, Deine Blumen (L. Zacharias)

73/1–2 Two Songs (Zacharias) (1914): Grossmütterchen, Der Totenkranz

75/1–4 The Candy Lion (A.F. Brown), A Thanksgiving Fable (D. Herford), Dolladine (W.B. Rands), Prayer of a Tired Child (Brown) (1914); nos.1, 3 arr. female chorus (1915)

76/1–2 Two Songs (1914): Separation (J.L. Stoddard), The Lotos Isles (Tennyson)

77/1–2 Two Songs (1916): I (C. Fanning), Wind o' the Westland (D. Burnett)

78/1–3 Three Songs (1917): Meadowlarks (I. Coolbrith), Night Song at Amalfi (Teasdale), In Blossom Time (Coolbrith)

— A Song for Little May (E.H. Miller), 1922

— The Arrow and the Song (H.W. Longfellow), 1922

— Clouds (F.D. Sherman), 1922

85 In the Twilight (Longfellow) (1922)

88 Spirit Divine (A. Read), S, T, org (1922)

93 Message (Teasdale) (1922)

99/1–4 Four Songs (1923): When Mama Sings (A.M. Beach), Little Brown-Eyed Laddie (A.D.O. Greenwood), The Moonpath (K. Adams), The Artless Maid (L. Barili)

100/1–2 Two Songs (1924): A Mirage (B. Ochsner); Stella viatoris (J.H. Nettleton), S, vn, vc, pf

112 Jesus my Saviour (A. Elliott) (1925)

113 Mine be the lips (L. Speyer) (1921)

115 Around the Manger (Davis), 1v, pf/org (1925), also version for chorus

117/1–3 Three Songs (M. Lee) (1925): The Singer, The Host, Song in the Hills

— Birth (E.L. Knowles), 1926

120 Rendezvous (Speyer), 1v, vn obbl (1928)

— Mignonnette (1929)

124 Springtime (S.M. Heywood) (1929)

125/1–2 Two Sacred Songs: Spirit of Mercy (anon.) (1930), Evening Hymn: The shadows of the evening hours (A. Procter) (1934); no.2 arr. chorus (1936)

131 Dark Garden (Speyer) (1932)

135 To one I love (1932)

136 Fire and Flame (A.A. Moody), 1932 (1933)

137/1–2 Baby (S.R. Quick); May Flowers (Moody); 1932 (1933)

— Evening song, 1934

— April Dreams (K.W. Harding), 1935

— The Deep Sea Pearl (E.M. Thomas), 1935

142 I sought the Lord (anon.), 1v, org, 1936 (1937)

143 I shall be brave (Adams) (1932)

145 Dreams

152 Though I Take the Wings of Morning (R.N. Spencer), 1v, org/pf (1941)

— The heart that melts

— The Icicle Lesson

— If women will not be inclined

— Time has wings and swiftly flies

— Whither (W. Müller) [after Chopin: Trois nouvelles études, no.3]

— Du sieh'st, B, pf [frag.]

OTHER WORKS

— Arr.: Beethoven: Piano Concerto no.1, 2nd movt, pf 4 hands, 1887

— St John the Baptist (Bible: *Matthew*, *Luke*), lib, 1889

— Arr.: Berlioz: Les Troyens, Act 1 scene iii, 1v, pf, 1896

— Serenade, pf (1902) [transcr. of R. Strauss: Ständchen]

— Arr.: On a hill: Negro melody (trad.), 1v, pf (1929)

JUVENILIA

Air and Variations, pf, 1877; Mamma's Waltz, pf, 1877; Menuetto, pf, 1877; Romanza, pf, 1877; Petite valse, pf, 1878; The Rainy Day (H. Longfellow), 1v, pf, 1880 (1883); Allegro appassionata, Moderato, Allegro con fuoco, pf 4 hands, pubd as Three Movements for Piano Four-Hands (1998)

4 Chorales: Come ye faithful (J. Hupton); Come to me (C. Elliott); O Lord, how happy should we be (J. Anstice); To heav'n I lift my waiting eyes, 4vv, 1882
The Rainy Day (Longfellow), 1v, pf, 1880

MSS and other sources in University of New Hampshire, Durham; *US-Bc*, *KC*, *PHf*, *Wc*
Principal publishers: A-R Editions, Classical Vocal Reprint, Ditson, Hildegard, Masters Music, Presser, Recital, G. Schirmer, Schmidt, Walton

WRITINGS

"Cristofori redivivus," *Music*, xvi/May (1899), 1–5
"Why I Chose my Profession: the Autobiography of a Woman Composer," *Mother's Magazine*, xi/Feb (1914), 7–8
"The Outlook for the Young American Composer," *The Etude*, xxxiii (1915), 13–4
"Music's Ten Commandments as given for Young Composers," *Los Angeles Examiner* (28 June 1915)
"Common Sense in Pianoforte Touch and Technic," *The Etude*, xxxiv (1916), 701–2
"To the Girl who Wants to Compose," *The Etude*, xxxv (1918), 695
"Work out your own Salvation," *The Etude*, xxxvi (1918), 11–2
"Emotion Versus Intellect in Music," *Studies in Musical Education, History, and Aesthetics*, xxvi (1932), 17–9
"The Twenty-Fifth Anniversary of a Vision," *Studies in Musical Education, History, and Aesthetics*, xxvii (1933), 45–8
"A Plea for Mercy," *Studies in Musical Education, History, and Aesthetics*, xxx (1936), 163–5
"The Mission of the Present Day Composer," *Triangle of Mu Phi Epsilon*, xxxvi/Feb (1942), 71–2
"How Music is Made," *Keyboard*, iv (1942), 11, 38
"The 'How' of Creative Composition," *The Etude*, lxi (1943), 151, 206, 208–9
"The World Cries out for Harmony," *The Etude*, lxvii (1944), 11
"Los Angeles "Fairyland" Marks an Epoch in American Music," in H. Parker: *"Fairyland" Scrapbook, NH*

BIBLIOGRAPHY

EwenD; *NAW*; *SchmidlD*
"Mrs H.H.A. Beach," *Musikliterarische Blätter*, i (Vienna, 1904), 1 only
L.C. Elson: *The History of American Music* (New York, 1904, 2/1915, enlarged 3/1925 by A. Elson), 294–305
P. Goetschius: *Mrs H.H.A. Beach* (Boston, 1906) [incl. analytical sketch of Sym. op.32 and list of works]
G. Cowen: "Mrs H.H.A. Beach, the Celebrated Composer," *Musical Courier* (8 June 1910)
"Mrs. Beach's Compositions," *Musical Courier* (24 March 1915)
H. Brower: *Piano Mastery* (New York, 1917), 179–87
B.C. Tuthill: "Mrs H.H.A. Beach," *MQ*, xxvi (1940), 297–310
E.L. Merrill: *Mrs H.H.A. Beach: her Life and Music* (diss., U. of Rochester, 1963)
M.G. Eden: *Anna Hyatt Huntington, Sculptor, and Mrs H.H.A. Beach, Composer* (diss., Syracuse U., 1977) [incl. list of works]
A.F. Block: *Introduction to Amy Beach: Quintet in f op.67* (New York, 1979)
C. Ammer: *Unsung: a History of Women in American Music* (Westport, CT, 1980)
B. Sicherman and others, eds.: *Notable American Women*, iv (Cambridge, MA, 1980)
A.F. Block: "Why Amy Beach Succeeded as a Composer: the Early Years," *CMc*, no.36 (1983), 41–59
A.F. Block: "Arthur P. Schmidt, Publisher and Champion of Women Composers," *Musical Woman*, ii (1984–5), 145–76
M.S. Miles: *The Solo Piano Works of Mrs. H.H.A. Beach* (diss., Peabody Institute, Johns Hopkins U., 1985)
L. Petteys: "*Cabildo* by Amy Marcy Beach," *Opera Journal*, xxii/1 (1989), 10–9
A.F. Block: "Amy Beach's Music on Native American Themes," *AM*, viii (1990), 141–66
A.F. Block: "Dvořák, Beach and American Music," *A Celebration of American Music: Words and Music in Honor of H. Wiley Hitchcock*, ed. R. Crawford, R. Allen Lott and C.J. Oja (Ann Arbor, MI, 1990), 256–80
E.D. Bomberger: "Motivic Development in Amy Beach's *Variations on Balkan Themes*, op.60," *AM*, x/3 (1992), 326–47
M.K. Kelton: *The Songs of Mrs H.H.A. Beach* (diss., U. of Texas, 1992)
A.F. Block: "Communications: on Beach's *Variations on Balkan Themes*, op.60," *AM*, xi/3 (1993) 368–71
A.F. Block: "Amy Beach's Quartet on Inuit Themes: toward a Modernist Style," preface to Amy Beach: *Quartet for Strings (in One Movement) opus 89* (Madison, WI, 1994), xi–xxxi
A.F. Block: "A 'Veritable Autobiography'? Amy Beach's Piano Concerto in C-Sharp Minor, op.45," *MQ*, lxxviii (1994), 394–416
R.C. Brittain: *Festival Jubilate, op. 17 by Amy Beach (1867–1944): a Performing Edition* (diss., U. of North Carolina at Greensboro, 1994)
J.W. Brown: *Amy Beach and her Chamber Music: Biography, Documents, Style* (Metuchen, NJ, 1994)
W.S. Jenkins: *The Remarkable Mrs. Beach: American Composer*, ed. J.H. Baron (Warren, MI, 1994)
R. Schempf: *The New England Character Piece: a Comparative Study of Four Representative Composers* (diss., Manhattan School of Music, 1995)
D.E.C. Clark: *Pedagogical Analysis and Sequencing of Selected Intermediate-Level Solo Piano Compositions of Amy Beach* (diss., U. of South Carolina, 1996)
B.J. Reigles: *The Choral Music of Amy Beach* (diss., Texas Tech U., 1996)
A.F. Block: *Amy Beach, Passionate Victorian: an American Composer's Life and Work* (New York, 1998)
P. Zerkle: *A Study of Amy Beach's Grand Mass in E-flat Major, op. 5* (diss., Indiana U., 1998)
A.F. Block: "Amy Beach as Teacher," *American Music Teacher*, xlviii (April/May 1999), 22–5
L. Blunsom: *Gender, Genre and Professionalism: the Songs of Clara Rogers, Helen Hopekirk, Amy Beach, Margaret Lang, and Mabel Daniels, 1880–1925* (diss., Brandeis U., 1999)
E.D. Bomberger: "Amy Marcy Cheney Beach," *Women Composers: Music Through the Ages*, vi, *Composers born 1800–1899: Keyboard Music*, ed. S. Glickman and M.F. Schleifer (New York, 1999), 351–70
C.M. Treybig: *Amy Beach: an Investigation and Analysis of the Theme and Variations for Flute and String Quartet, op. 80* (diss., U. of Texas, 1999)
L.H. Ledeen: "Remembering Amy Beach: a conversation with David Buxbaum (son of singer Lillian Buxbaum, longtime collaborator with Beach)," *IAWM Journal*, vi/1–2 (2000), 17 only
K.C. Rushing: *Amy Beach's Concerto for Piano and Orchestra in C-sharp Minor, op. 45: a Historical, Stylistic, and Analytical Study* (diss., Louisiana State U., 2000)
B. Buchanan: "Connection: a Medieval text and Twentieth-Century Expressionism in 'Canticle of the Sun,' by Amy Beach," *Choral Journal*, xli (May 2001), 9–19
J. Radell: "Sphere of Influence, Clara Kathleen Rogers and Amy Beach," *Essays on Music and Culture in Honor of Herbert Kallman*, ed. B.H. Haggh (Paris, 2001), 503–17
T.L. Walker: *The Quintet for Piano and Strings, op. 67 by Amy Beach: An Historical and Analytical Investigation* (diss., U. of Illinois at Urbana-Champaign, 2001)
A.F. Block: "An Amy Beach discography," *Institute for Studies in American Music Newsletter*, xxxi (Spring 2002), 10 only
Y.H.J. Hung: *The Violin Sonata of Amy Beach* (diss., Louisiana State U., 2005)
C.J. Song: *Pianism in Selected Partsong Accompaniments and Chamber Music of the Second New England School (Amy Beach, Arthur Foote, George Whitefield Chadwick, and Horatio Parker), 1880–1930* (diss., Ball State U., 2005)
S. Llewellyn: *Amy Beach and Judith Lang Zaimont: a Comparative Study of their Lives and Songs* (diss., Arizona State U., 2008)
K.A. Kuby: *Analysis of Amy Cheney Beach's 'Gaelic Symphony,' op.32* (diss., U. of Connecticut, 2011)
H. Tsou: "Unpublished Song by Amy Beach Discovered," *Society for American Music Bulletin*, xxxvii/1 (2011), 1–4

ADRIENNE FRIED BLOCK/E. DOUGLAS BOMBERGER

Beach, Frank A(mbrose) (*b* Weedsport, NY, 20 Sept 1871; *d* Emporia, KS, 21 Jan 1935). Music educator. He studied at the School of Fine Arts, Syracuse University (1890–93) and the University of Michigan (BA 1895). Beach also studied singing at the Juliana School of Opera in Paris (from 1905) and became chair of music education at Kansas State Normal School in Emporia (now Emporia State University) in 1908 and then chair of its music department (1913–35). Under his leadership the school maintained one of the nation's most prominent music education programs. Beach was a pioneer in using recorded listening lessons in public schools. He organized the first state-wide music contests in the nation at Emporia in 1915, which became a model for contests in other states. He developed the first standardized test of musical achievement (1920) and in 1929 devised a music contest rating system still in use in American competitions. He continued his research on music tests and measurements until his death. He served as president of the Music Supervisors National Conference (now Music Educators National Conference) in 1922, and was active in many other professional organizations. He was inducted into the Music Educators Hall of Fame in 1992.

BIBLIOGRAPHY

M.K. Kastendieck: *Frank Ambrose Beach: His Life and Career in the Music Educators National Conference* (thesis, U. of Kansas, 1985)

GEORGE N. HELLER/ALAN L. SPURGEON

Beach, John Parsons (*b* Gloversville, NY, 11 Oct 1877; *d* Pasadena, CA, 6 Nov 1953). Composer. A pupil of GEORGE WHITEFIELD CHADWICK, he studied piano at the New England Conservatory, Boston. In 1900 he obtained a position as a piano teacher at the Northwestern Conservatory, Minneapolis, and from 1904 to 1910 taught first in New Orleans and afterwards in Boston. He then went to Europe, where he studied with André Gédalge (composition) and HAROLD BAUER (piano) in Paris, and with Gian Francesco Malipiero in Venice. On returning to Boston he took further composition lessons with CHARLES MARTIN LOEFFLER. He finally settled in Pasadena. Beach's opera *Pippa's Holiday* (after Browning) was staged in Paris in 1915, and a ballet, *Phantom Satyr*, was performed in Asolo, Italy, in 1925; another ballet, *Mardi Gras*, was performed in New Orleans in 1926. His orchestral works include *Asolani* (performed in Minneapolis, 1926), *New Orleans Street Cries* (Philadelphia, 1927; Stokowski conducting), and *Angelo's Letter*, for tenor and chamber orchestra (New York, 1929). Beach also composed a number of chamber works and many songs and piano pieces. His music favors the rich sonorities of late Romanticism and almost invariably has programmatic associations.

ELIZABETH A. WRIGHT

Beach Boys, the. Rock band. It was formed in 1961 in Hawthorne, California, by the brothers Brian (Douglas) Wilson (*b* Hawthorne, CA, 20 June 1942; vocals, piano, and bass guitar), Dennis (Carl) Wilson (*b* Hawthorne, 4 Dec 1944; *d* Marina del Ray, CA, 28 Dec 1983; vocals and drums) and Carl (Dean) Wilson (*b* Hawthorne, 21 Dec 1946; *d* Los Angeles, CA, 6 Feb 1998; vocals and guitar), their cousin Mike (Michael Edward) Love (*b* Baldwin Hills, CA, 15 March 1941; vocals and drums), and Al(an Charles) Jardine (*b* Lima, OH, 3 Sept 1942; vocals and guitar). Bruce Arthur Johnston (Billy Baldwin; *b* Peoria, IL, 27 June 1944) joined the group in 1965. For most of the 1960s they were the most successful and important American band, turning out a series of impressive hit singles, which addressed mostly teenage and youth culture sensibilities, and albums of increasing musical and technical sophistication culminating in their most celebrated effort, *Pet Sounds* (Cap., 1966).

Until he suffered from a nervous breakdown in 1965, when he was replaced by Glen Campbell and then Johnston, BRIAN WILSON was the creative force behind the group. He had ceased touring with the band in 1964, and thereafter reduced his role to writing, arranging, recording, and producing the songs and albums that secured the Beach Boys' international success. Although his style had a unique quality and evolved rapidly in response to fierce competition from other bands, particularly those associated with the British invasion, several early influences left a lasting impact on his work: the vocal harmonies of the Four Freshmen, which he had learned from records as a teenager; the light-spirited, high-energy style of southern Californian surf music, including that of Jan and Dean, with whom Brian had regularly collaborated in the early 1960s; and the famous "wall of sound" style of instrumental arrangement developed by Phil Spector, as well as the latter's artistic vision as a studio producer.

Brian assimilated these influences and transformed them into a new idiom. Even in the group's early songs, which celebrate the US male teenage lifestyle preoccupied with surfing, cars, and girls, several of the features for which the band later became famous are recognizable: unconventional and arresting harmonic

Cover of the Beach Boys' single "409" from the album Surfin' Safari, *Capitol Records, 1962. (Photofest/Lebrecht Music & Arts)*

progressions ("The Warmth of the Sun," Cap., 1964); a tendency to experiment with new sounds and recording techniques, including vocal overdubbing, which gave the group's vocal timbre an almost luminescent brilliance ("Surfin' USA," Cap., 1963); and a disarming and soulful quality of intimacy, vulnerability, and introspection ("She knows me too well," Cap., 1964, and "Please let me wonder," Cap., 1965). These trends culminated first in the superbly polished and sophisticated album *The Beach Boys Today!* (Cap., 1965) and then in the masterpiece *Pet Sounds*, an album whose exquisitely colorful orchestration, breathtakingly original harmonies, and intensely poignant expression have won the acclaim of critics since it was released. Brian attempted to surpass the album with an even more innovative effort in collaboration with the lyricist Van Dyke Parks. Entitled *Smile*, it ran aground in 1967 due mainly to a combination of psychological trauma and internal tensions within the band. A full re-recording version of the album was eventually released under Brian Wilson's name on Nonesuch in 2004. In 2011 a box-set containing original recording and outtakes was issued.

After his breakdown Brian continued to be involved on an irregular basis, allowing other band members, especially Carl and Bruce Johnston, to develop their talents in composition, arrangement, and production. Although the band produced several fine later albums, including *Friends* (Cap., 1968) and *Surf's Up* (Brother, 1971), and continued to tour into the 21st century, their position in the history of rock is based chiefly on their influential contributions during the period 1962–7.

BIBLIOGRAPHY

B. Golden: *The Beach Boys: Southern California Pastoral* (San Bernadino, CA, 1976)

D. Leaf: *The Beach Boys and the California Myth* (New York, 1979)

B. Elliott: *Surf's Up! The Beach Boys on Record, 1961–1981* (Ann Arbor, MI, 1984)

T. White: *The Nearest Faraway Place: Brian Wilson, the Beach Boys, and the Southern California Experience* (New York, 1994/*R*)

K. Abbott, ed.: *Back to the Beach: a Brian Wilson and the Beach Boys Reader* (London, 1997, 2/2003)

P. Williams: *Brian Wilson & the Beach Boys: how Deep is the Ocean?* (London, 1997/*R*)

C.L. Granata: *Wouldn't it be nice: Brian Wilson and the Making of the Beach Boys'* Pet Sounds (Chicago, 2003)

A.G. Doe and J. Tobler: *Brian Wilson and the Beach Boys: the Complete Guide to their Music* (London, 2004)

P. Lambert: *Inside the Music of Brian Wilson: the Songs, Sounds, and Influences of the Beach Boys' Founding Genius* (New York, 2007)

ROB C. WEGMAN/R

Beamer. Hawaiian family of musicians. The Beamer family has produced significant performers, composers, and teachers across the spectrum of Hawaiian music genres, from chant and hula to art song, falsetto singing, and slack key. They trace their musical lineage back to the 15th century when *mele oli* (a cappella chant) and *mele hula kahiko* (chant with percussion and choreography tied to the text) constituted Hawaiian musical expression. In the early 19th century chant and hula were suppressed and the Beamers were among those who helped reintroduce them into the mainstream. Members of the family have also been innovators, open to new musical ideas that reinforce core Hawaiian concepts or functions.

Helen Desha "Sweetheart Grandma" Beamer (1882–1952) composed songs that combine Hawaiian poetic sensibility with Western ideas of melody and harmony. Many have become standards such as "Kimo Hula" composed to honor a friend, "Na Kuahiwi 'Elima," about five mountains she observed on a trip near her home, and "Kawohikukapulani," created for her youngest daughter's wedding. She also taught hula and chant. Not only were her husband Carl and five children musical but she also musically trained her 18 grandchildren, all of whom became accomplished performers. Two established themselves as leading figures of their generation.

Winona "Auntie Nona" Beamer (1923–2007), granddaughter of Helen Desha Beamer, was a chanter, dancer, composer, and storyteller, but is best known as a teacher. In 1949 she established Hawaiian culture classes at Kamehameha Schools, a groundbreaking event that marked a turning point in local attitudes. She taught at Kamehameha for 40 years and was also active in the public sphere, participating in numerous workshops, forums, and media projects. In 2000 she helped establish the Hula Preservation Society, administered by her *hanai* (adopted) daughter Maile Loo.

Edwin "Uncle Mahi" Beamer (*b* 1928), grandson of Helen Desha Beamer, attended the Juilliard School of Music in the late 1940s. He returned to Hawaii and worked in Waikiki as a pianist, hula dancer, and singer, specializing in *leo ki'eki'e* (Hawaiian falsetto). In 1959 the recordings *Hawaii's Mahi Beamer* and *More Authentic Island Songs* established Mahi as a leading vocalist who was both traditional and urbane. In the 1960s he performed in Las Vegas at the Stardust Hotel. Since returning home in 1974 he has focused on keyboards, often performing with Nina Kealiiwahamana and others.

Keolamaikalani "Keola" Beamer (*b* 1951), son of Winona Beamer, is an influential composer, singer, and slack key guitarist. He received his early training from family members and released his first album in 1972, *In the Real Old Style*, based on the teachings of his grandfather Pono Beamer and other elders.

In 1975 Keola and younger brother Kaponomalamalani "Kapono" Beamer (*b* 1952), son of Winona Beamer, formed a highly successful duo that performed a diverse mix of Hawaiian standards, slack key instrumentals, and originals. Their biggest hit, "Honolulu City Lights," written by Keola, seamlessly blends elements of the *mele pana* (place song) with the modern pop ballad. Keola and Kapono recorded six best-selling albums and toured throughout Polynesia.

Since 1982 both have pursued separate, high-profile careers. Keola has recorded as a soloist and a group leader as well as in collaborations with artists outside of Hawaiian music, such as Kenny Rankin, R. Carlos Nakai, George Winston, and Geoffery Keezer, and with Hawaiian artists, such as Raiatea Helm. Keola worked closely with his mother on numerous projects, including the annual Aloha Music Camp. He tours internationally with his wife Moana weaving hula, Hawaiian percussion, *'ohe hano ihu* (nose flute), and chant into his carefully arranged, guitar-based music.

Kapono has also recorded extensively in Hawaii as well as Europe. In 1996 his single "Sunny Holiday" was released in 28 countries. In 1999 his award-winning album *Great Grandmother, Great Grandson* refashioned 13 songs by Helen Desha Beamer as guitar instrumentals. He has also worked with prominent singer and kumu hula Keali'i Reichel and Dave Jenkins of Pablo Cruise. His son Kamana (*b* 1972) performs in the group Kamau.

JAY W. JUNKER

Beardslee, Bethany (*b* Lansing, MI, 25 Dec 1927). Soprano. After studying at Michigan State University and the Juilliard School, Beardslee made her New York debut in December 1949. At Juilliard she met composer Jacques-Louis Monod, whom she later married. With Monod, she presented premieres of a number of American works, becoming known as a specialist in 20th-century music, and giving the first American performances of works by Schoenberg, Stravinsky, Krenek, and Alban Berg. In 1956 she remarried, to composer Godfrey Winham. The American Composers Alliance awarded her its 1962 Laurel Leaf "for distinguished achievement in fostering and encouraging American music." With a 1964 Ford Foundation grant, she commissioned and performed Babbitt's *Philomel* for soprano and recorded tape. Her wide range, accuracy, and silvery lyric soprano have also proved effective in early music with New York Pro Musica (1957–60), in Bach, and in recordings of Haydn and Pergolesi. In 1972 she performed *Pierrot lunaire* (earlier recorded under Robert Craft) with Boulez and members of the Cleveland Orchestra. Her recordings of American music include works by Babbitt, Perle, Sessions, Randall, Mel Powell, Robert Helps, and Malcolm Peyton. In 1981 she began a partnership with Richard Goode in recitals of lieder. Although she officially retired from singing in 1984, she continued to perform through the mid-1990s. Beardslee taught at Westminster Choir College (from 1976) and was professor of singing at the University of Texas, Austin (1981–2); on leaving Austin she spent a year as performer-in-residence at the University of California, Davis, and in 1983 began to teach at Brooklyn College, CUNY. She was awarded an honorary doctorate at Princeton University in 1977, and continues her advocacy of contemporary music.

MARTIN BERNHEIMER/STEPHANIE JENSEN-MOULTON

Bear Family. German record company. It was established in a farmhouse just outside of Bremen in the former West Germany by musicologist/collector Richard Weize in 1975. The company's name and logo were taken from an engraving Weize found in a 1898 encyclopedia. While the first record released on the imprint was *Going Back to Dixie* by bluegrass legend Bill Clifton, the label soon branched out into the reissue field, where it made a name for itself with definitive compilations of individual artists, labels, genres, and eras, all accompanied by meticulously-crafted liner notes and superior sound. Owner Weize claims he has never sold more than 3000 units of any Bear Family title, but any shortfall is offset by his successful music mail-order business, which distributes product from other labels.

Perhaps the label's level of commitment is best demonstrated by their seven-CD set *Lily Marleen: an allen Fronten ein Lied geht um die Welt*, which collects 195 versions of the song "Lili Marleen." Releases from the imprint continue to be conspicuously eclectic, both in terms of genre and era. Notable artists include the likes of Roy Acuff, Harry Belafonte, Johnny Cash, Nat "King" Cole, Doris Day, Lonnie Donegan, Bill Haley and the Comets, Howlin' Wolf, the Louvin Bros, Dean Martin, Ricky Nelson, Carl Perkins, Marty Robbins, Del Shannon, Sons of the Pioneers, Rufus Thomas, Allen Toussaint, Ernest Tubb, Billy Vaughn, the Weavers, Hank Williams, and Bob Wills, plus a wide variety of German-speaking artists.

THANE TIERNEY

Beaser, Robert (*b* Boston, MA, 29 May 1954). Composer. A percussionist with the Greater Boston Youth SO, he conducted the orchestra in the premiere performance of his first orchestral work, *Antigone* (1972). He studied composition with Arnold Franchetti before entering Yale University, where his teachers included Jacob Druckman, Toru Takemitsu, Earle Brown, and Yehudi Wyner (BA 1976, MMA 1981, DMA 1985). He also studied composition with Goffredo Petrassi in Rome and Betsy Jolas at Tanglewood. His conducting teachers included Otto-Werner Mueller, Arthur Weisberg, and William Steinberg. He served as co-director of the New York ensemble Contemporary Elements (1978–89) and composer-in-residence of the American Composers Orchestra (1988–93), before becoming artistic adviser, and then artistic director of the American Composers Orchestra (2000–). He joined the composition department at the Juilliard School in 1993, becoming department chair in 1994. Among his awards are the Prix de Rome (1977), Guggenheim and Fulbright foundation fellowships, a 1988 Grammy nomination (*Mountain Songs*, 1985), and a lifetime achievement award from the American Academy of Arts and Letters (1995). His works have been commissioned by the St. Paul Chamber Orchestra (*Song of the Bells*, 1987), St. Louis SO (Piano Concerto, 1989), Chicago SO (*Double Chorus*, 1990), Baltimore SO (*The Heavenly Feast*, 1994), the New York PO (*Manhattan Roll*, 1998), the New York City Opera/Glimmerglass Opera/WNET (*The Food of Love*, 1999), the Albany Symphony and guitarist Eliot Fisk (Guitar Concerto, 2009), and the Seattle Symphony (*Ground "O,"* 2011).

Beaser's music from the late 1970s onwards embraces both the American vernacular tradition and the tenets of Romanticism in its epic scale, use of programmatic elements, and tonal foundation, and he is often included among a group of American composers considered by some critics as the "new tonalists." His melodic gift and finely developed sense of irony, however, elevate his compositions above mere exercises in nostalgia. Thematic variation and transformation is central to the structure of many of his works, particularly the set of variations that forms the second movement of the Piano Concerto. While the concerto quotes material from Beethoven to Bernstein, a subtle incorporation of his musical influences is more characteristic of Beaser's style.

WORKS

Orch: Song of the Bells, fl, orch, 1987; Pf Conc., 1988; Double Chorus, 1991; Chorale Variations, 1992; Sexigessimal Chorus, 1996; Folk Songs, 2007; Evening Prayer, 2008; Gui Conc., 2009; Ground "O," 2011

Vocal-orch: Sym. (E.E. Cummings, W.B. Yeats, J. Fowles), S, orch, 1977; The Seven Deadly Sins (A. Hecht), Bar, orch, 1984 (arr Bar or T, pf, 1984); Heavenly Feast (G. Schnackenberg), S, orch, 1994; Manhattan Roll, 1998 (arr wind ens 2010); Food of Love (Opera in One Act; T. MacNally), voices, orch, 1999

Other vocal: Silently Spring (Cummings), S, chbr ens, 1973; Quicksilver (D.M. Epstein), T, pf, 1978; The Seven Deadly Sins (Hecht), B/T, pf, 1979; Teach Me, O Lord (Ps cxix), S, A, T, B, SSAATTBB, brass qnt ad lib, 1983; Songs from "The Occasions" (E. Montale), T, chbr ens, 1985; The Old Men Admiring Themselves in the Water (Yeats), 1v, pf, 1986 [also version for fl, pf]; A Martial Law Carol (J. Brodsky), S, pf, 1994; I Dwell in Possibility (E. Dickenson), S, pf, 1994; Ps, cl, SATB, pf/org, 1995; Prayer for Peace (R. Beaser), 1v, children's chorus, pf, 1996; Adam, T, pf, 2001; Four Dickinson Songs, S, pf, 2002; Follower (S. Heanery), T, pf, 2003

Chbr and solo inst: Trasparenza, vc, 1971; Canti notturni, gui, 1974; Str Qt, 1975–6; Shadow and Light, ww qnt, 1978–80; Notes on a Southern Sky, gui, 1980; Variations, fl, pf, 1982; Il est ne le divin enfant, fl, gui, 1982; Mountain Songs, fl, gui, 1985; Landscape with Bells, pf, 1986; Minimal Waltz, fl, pf, 1986; Shenandoah, gui, 1995; Brass Qnt, 1996; Manhattan Roll, wind ens, perc, 2010

Recorded interviews in *NHob*
Principal publisher: Helicon

JAMES CHUTE

Beastie Boys. Rap group. Critically acclaimed and commercially popular, the Beastie Boys are arguably the most successful white group in rap music history. Having sold in excess of 40 million albums worldwide, they are known for groundbreaking music videos and for incorporating a wide range of influences, including rock, funk, punk, and R&B into their overall sound.

Originally formed as a hardcore punk band at New York University, the Beastie Boys recorded singles in a variety of styles before signing to Def Jam Recordings. With a group comprising MCA (Adam Yauch; *b* Brooklyn, NY, 5 Aug 1965; *d* New York, NY, 4 May 2012), Mike D (Michael Diamond; *b* New York, 20 Nov 1965) and Ad-Rock (Adam Horowitz; *b* New York, 31 Oct 1966), their album *Licensed to Ill* (Def Jam, 1986) became CBS's fastest-selling debut album. It was also the first full-length hip-hop album to debut at the top position on the *Billboard* 200 album charts. Hit singles such as "(You Gotta) Fight for Your Right (To Party!)" crossed the racial divisions within popular music, appealing to fans of hip-hop and rock music. Controversy also followed the band in the wake of its riotous live performances.

Disagreements between the Beastie Boys and Def Jam led to a three-year hiatus which ended with the excellent and influential, though commercially unsuccessful, album *Paul's Boutique* (Cap., 1989). Relocated in California, the band launched a record label, studio, and magazine under the name Grand Royal. In 1992, they released the highly acclaimed album *Check Your Head* (Cap., 1992), which continued the band's experimental nature, fusing elements of rock, hardcore, and funk. Their next album, *Ill Communication* (Cap., 1994) debuted at number one on the *Billboard* 200 and catapulted the group to the forefront of the popular music world. The album, which featured turntablist Mix Master Mike. charted several songs including "Sure Shot" and "Sabotage." The latter inspired one of the most memorable videos of the 1990s, with Spike Jonze in the director's chair.

The group toured heavily in support of *Ill Communication*, headlining events such as Lollapalooza in 1994. They released the punk inspired EP *Aglio e Olio* in late 1995 and the following year released the instrumental funk album *The Sound in From Way Out!*. The group returned to the success of *Ill Communication* with the 1998 release *Hello Nasty*. Selling close to 700,000 copies in its first week, the album won two Grammy Awards. After much anticipation and a six-year drought between releases, 2004's *To the 5 Boroughs* became their third album in a row to debut at number 1 on the *Billboard* 200. They followed this release with another instrumental album, *The Mix-Up* in 2007. They delayed the release of their *Hot Sauce Committee* series of releases for over two years as bandmate Adam Yauch battled cancer. *Hot Sauce Committee Pt. 2* (Cap., 2011) finally came out in 2011, along with plans to release the material produced for *Hot Sauce Committee Pt. 1* sometime in the near future.

DAVID TOOP/JARED PAULEY

Beatlemania. The term refers to the extraordinary zealotry of Beatles fans during the Liverpool band's first flush of international fame, initially appearing in British newspapers in late 1963. It was soon adopted in North America as well to refer to fans' seemingly insatiable desire for Beatles products—records (both 45s and LPs), concert tickets, fan magazines, or objects imprinted with the Beatles' logo or images of the performers. This was exceeded only by fans' demand for personal contact with the performers; typically, highly demonstrative crowds would cluster around the stage door of concert venues, television studios, and radio stations wherever and whenever the band was expected. The Beatles were also greeted by hordes of ardent fans at airports around the world, notably at JFK Airport in February of 1964 (their US arrival) and 1965 concerts at Shea Stadium and the Hollywood Bowl. Their fans' behavior, especially that of their female fans, was characterized by incessant screaming, crying, and even fainting, satirized in the film *A Hard Day's Night*. The type of fan obsession depicted in the film has become a staple of documentary films on 1960s popular culture and a cornerstone of the Beatles legend. Beatlemania was a major reason for the band's decision to stop touring in 1966.

Beatlemania, aided crucially by two key socioeconomic conditions, raised serious fandom to a new,

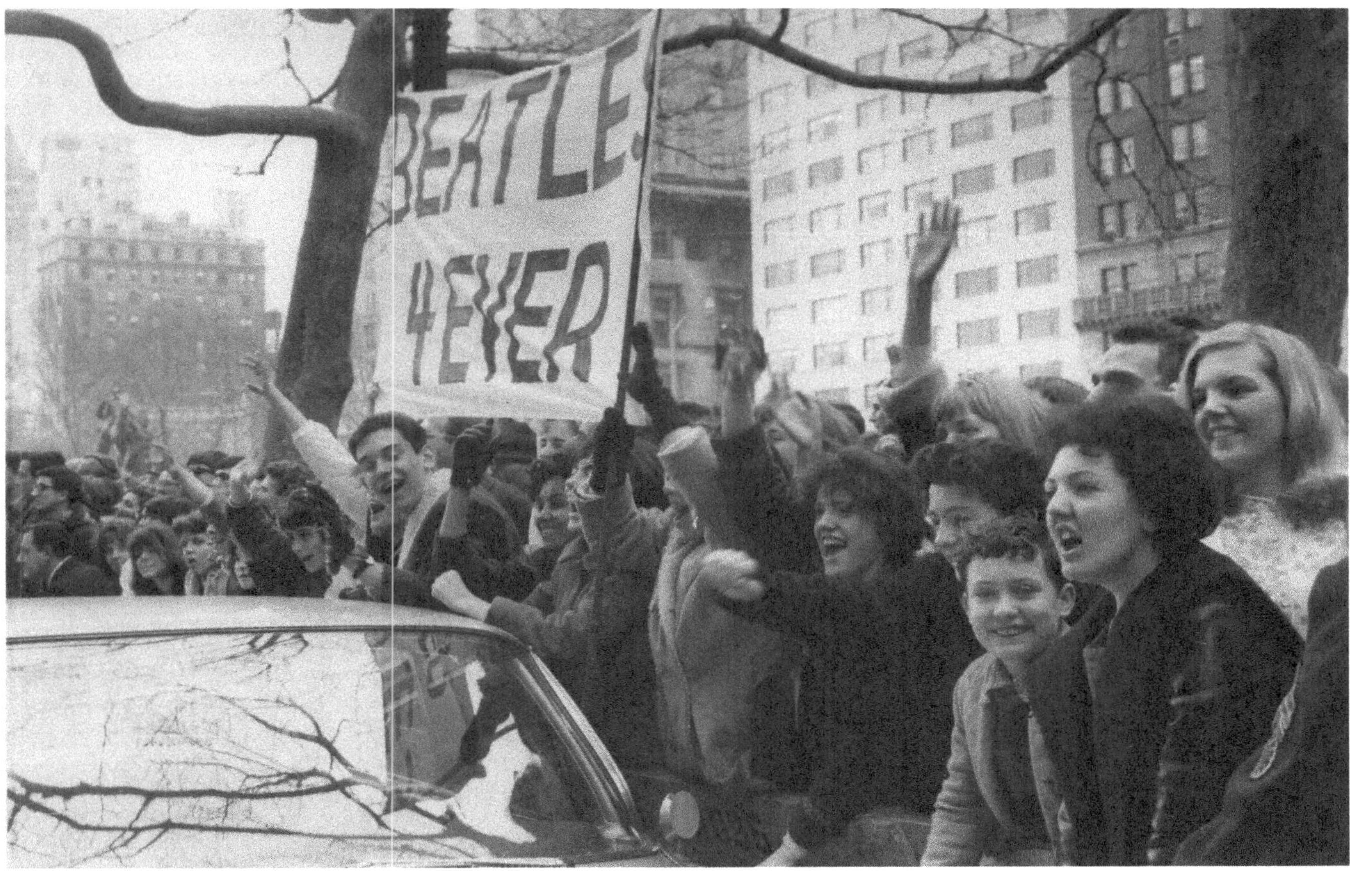

Beatles fans outside the Plaza Hotel, New York, 1964. (AP Photo)

international level. First, British-produced records and media appearances could be distributed throughout the Anglophone world, in ready-made markets comprising the then-current and former British Commonwealth countries—Canada, Australia, India, Hong Kong, the Caribbean, and several other nations with British ties in Africa and Asia. Second, postwar social, economic, and demographic conditions gave greater amounts of disposable income and leisure time to the population bubble known as the "baby boom" (consumers born after 1945). Dramatically, and for the first time, adolescents and teenagers in the developed world demonstrated their enormous spending power and made the Beatles among the best selling bands, worldwide, of all time. Beatlemania spearheaded the so-called "British Invasion" of the United States in 1963 during which numerous British performers achieved varying levels of success in North American and world markets.

BIBLIOGRAPHY

B. Ehrenreich, E. Hess and G. Jacobs: "Beatlemania: Girls Just Want to Have Fun," *The Adoring Audience: Fan Culture and Popular Media*, ed. L. Lewis (New York, 1992), 84–107

M. Frontani: *The Beatles: Image and the Media* (Jackson, MS, 2007)

ANNIE J. RANDALL

Beatles, the. English pop group. George Harrison (*b* Liverpool, England, 25 Feb 1943; *d* Los Angeles, CA, 29 Nov 2001), John Lennon (John Winston (Ono) Lennon; *b* Liverpool, 9 Oct 1940; *d* New York, NY, 8 Dec 1980), Paul McCartney (James Paul McCartney; *b* Liverpool, 18 June 1942), and Ringo Starr (Richard Starkey; *b* 7 July 1940). They were the world's most popular musical force from 1964 through their 1970 break-up, and their legacy has continued to be highly influential for subsequent artists, the entertainment industry, baby-boom culture and beyond. This article outlines the inspiration taken by the Beatles from American sources, and the group's appearances and reception in America; for a general introduction to their career and extensive bibliography, see *Grove7*.

1. American influences. 2. The Beatles in America.

1. American influences. Whereas the Beatles' early sound was partly based on British folk and popular forms—including skiffle and music-hall styles—American rock 'n' roll was by far their dominant resource. The group began by covering, and then borrowing stylistic traits from American performers, principally Elvis Presley (particularly his expressive vocal embellishments), Chuck Berry (reciting-tone vocals with witty rhymes, extended guitar sonorities, rhythm chording, melodic blues riffs, and bass ostinati), Little Richard (vocal falsetto and bluesy pentatonicism), Bo Diddley (mixolydian chords, direct simplicity), Carl Perkins (rockabilly

picking), Jerry Lee Lewis (keyboard pounding, raw energy), Buddy Holly (major-mode melody), and the Everly Brothers (descant vocal arrangements). In the few years surrounding the late-1962 launch of their recording career, the group drew variously from American male R&B figures (the Isley Brothers, the Coasters, the Drifters, Larry Williams, Arthur Alexander, Barrett Strong, the Miracles), female vocal groups (the Teddy Bears, the Shirelles, the Marvelettes, the Cookies) and pop singers (Del Shannon, Roy Orbison). Many traits taken from these sources remained at the musicians' core even as they continued to borrow American ideas: the group used Caribbean models for their first two B-sides, and based their fourth single, "She Loves You"/"I'll Get You" (1963), on harmonic twists found in records by Bobby Rydell and Joan Baez, respectively. The introspective beat poetry of Bob Dylan and blues guitar leads by B.B. King affected their work in 1964–5, and traces of bass lines by James Jamerson, vocal harmonies by the Beach Boys and the Byrds, guitar stylings of Jimi Hendrix, and avant-garde approaches to incongruous juxtapositions can be heard through much of their releases of 1965–9.

In these later years, the Beatles also incorporated American culture more generally in their work: aspects of the San Francisco hippie scene had a bearing on *Sgt. Pepper's Lonely Hearts Club Band* (1967); their pursuit of the spiritual aspect of the American experimentation with LSD (followed by an embrace of Indian mysticism and music) made an imaginative imprint on their art; their 1968 eponymous two-record set (usually referred to as the "White" Album) included both McCartney's paean to the American civil rights struggle ("Blackbird") and Lennon's dual referencing of the popular comic strip, "Peanuts," and America's fascination with violence in "Happiness is a Warm Gun." Their last-recorded album, *Abbey Road* (1969), includes several uses of the Moog synthesizer, which Harrison first heard in California in late 1968, but also recalls the band's roots in Chuck Berry and Fats Domino as well as contributions from American keyboardist Billy Preston, whom they had first met in 1962. The Beatles' last album to be released, *Let It Be* (1970), was mixed (with additions of obtrusive orchestral and choral parts) by legendary Los Angeles-based producer Phil Spector.

2. The Beatles in America. Despite topping the British album charts every week for a full year beginning in May 1963 and gaining light radio exposure in Chicago and Philadelphia markets that summer, the Beatles remained largely unknown in America until November, 1963, when their management secured a contract to release recordings through Capitol Records. Capitol's huge promotional budget resulted in sales in the multiple millions and chart domination beginning immediately with "I Want to Hold Your Hand." They were booked for February 1964 performances in Carnegie Hall and Washington, DC, and on "The Ed Sullivan Show," which attracted 73 million viewers to one telecast (see Beatlemania). The Beatles toured 32 cities in the United States and Canada in the summers of 1964–6, presenting 67 shows in theaters, coliseums, and stadiums. Their audience peaked at 55,600 fans in the August 1965 Shea Stadium concert, which was filmed for a televised documentary. Many of these shows were broadcast live, and later appeared on unauthorized discs; Capitol recorded the 1964 and 1965 Hollywood Bowl performances, releasing their highlights in 1977.

The group's adoration for the music produced in the Motown studios of Detroit and the Stax studio of Memphis led them to consider recording there in early 1966 to the point of commissioning compositions by Motown writers, but plans were scrapped as impracticable. As adviser for the Monterey Pop Festival of 1967, McCartney contributed both to the launching of Jimi Hendrix's and Janis Joplin's careers and to the primary antecedent for the Woodstock Music and Art Fair two years hence. In separate 1969 visits, Lennon moved towards a solo career by recording "Give Peace a Chance" at his Montreal "Bed-In," performing alongside several of his early rock 'n' roll heroes at Toronto's Peace Festival, and taking an audience with Canadian Prime Minister Pierre Trudeau in Ottawa to discuss efforts aimed at world peace.

Capitol Records subjected the Beatles' American releases to sonic alteration and revised track listings. The artists supported this schedule initially, even recording new tracks specifically intended to fill out one US-only album, *Beatles VI* (1965), but—particularly after such tampering diminished the integrity of more consciously artistic projects *Rubber Soul* (1965) and *Revolver* (1966)—the Beatles reacted by submitting the "Butcher" cover photo for the US release *"Yesterday"...and Today* (1966). This allegorical depiction of violence created trouble for American marketing, and along with the group's denouncing of US involvement in Vietnam and, especially, a controversy erupting from the reprinting of John Lennon's statement that the Beatles were "more popular than Jesus," a backlash against the group erupted in the Southern states in the summer of 1966, contributing to their decision later that year to discontinue live concerts. This move resulted in a greatly enhanced focus on the resources of the recording studio in popular music, and the production of promotional videos as substitutes for live performances.

Lennon, a New York resident from 1971, was murdered there in 1980; Harrison died in a friend's Los Angeles home in 2001, following a long illness. McCartney and Starr own homes in the United States and regularly tour the country with their respective bands.

BIBLIOGRAPHY

Grove7 (I. MacDonald)
G. Martin: *All You Need Is Ears* (New York, 1982)
The Beatles: Complete Scores (Chicago, 1993)
B. Spizer: *Beatles Records on Vee-Jay* (New Orleans, 1998)
W. Everett: *The Beatles as Musicians:* Revolver *through* The Anthology (New York, 1999)
The Beatles: Anthology (San Francisco, 2000)
B. Spizer: *The Beatles' Story on Capitol Records* (New Orleans, 2000)
A. Babiuk: *Beatles Gear* (London, 2001)
W. Everett: *The Beatles as Musicians: The Quarry Men through* Rubber Soul (New York, 2001)
D. Pedler: *The Songwriting Secrets of the Beatles* (London, 2003)

B. Spizer: *The Beatles on Apple Records* (New Orleans, 2003)
J.C. Winn: *That Magic Feeling: the Beatles' Recorded Legacy, 1966–1970* (Sharon, VT, 2003)
J.C. Winn: *Way Beyond Compare: the Beatles' Recorded Legacy, 1957–1965* (Sharon, VT, 2003)
B. Spizer: *The Beatles Swan Song* (New Orleans, 2007)

WALTER EVERETT

Beat-making. A colloquial term synonymous with Hip hop production, referring to the creation of musical and rhythmic tracks or "beats" in hip-hop music. Whereas in other musical genres the figure of "the producer" often refers more to an overseer and coordinator of the larger recording process, in hip hop the producer/beat-maker is generally presumed to create, compose, and/or arrange the music for a recording. Throughout its history, beat-making has inherently reflected adaptations to technological innovations—including the Drum machine, the Sampler or Sequencer, and the Digital audio workstation—that empowered individuals or small groups of collaborators to create musical tracks without the assistance of studio bands or related personnel.

1. Pre-history. 2. The drum machine era. 3. Sampling. 4. Sampling and copyright. 5. "Beat digging." 6. Synthesizers and Digital Audio Workstations. 7. Current trends.

1. Pre-history. Although the term "beat-making" was not used until the large-scale adoption of drum machines and samplers, hip-hop production pre-dates the era of digital reproduction. The earliest rap producers in the late 1970s and early 1980s were holdovers from the R&B industry, directing studio musicians during taping sessions. The most famous example is that of Sugar Hill Records' Sylvia Robinson instructing members of the Positive Force band to replay portions, including the prominent bass line, of Chic's "Good Times" as the rhythmic bed for what would become the Sugarhill Gang's "Rapper's Delight," the first hit rap record from 1979.

From the late 1970s through early 1980s—the so-called "old school" era—the notion of hip-hop production was in a state of constant flux and competing aesthetics. On the one hand, much rap production of the time reflected the origins of rapping in flashy disco parties, where MCs toasted crowds with rhymes while DJs played popular disco and funk hits. The success of "Rapper's Delight" led many other competitors to rework the same formula of interpolating melodies and riffs from other disco hits.

In contrast, one of the distinguishing features of Grandmaster Flash and the Furious Five's "The Message" (1982) was how Sugar Hill producers Ed "Duke Bootee" Fletcher and Clifton "Jiggs" Chase created an original track, which was distinctively slower in tempo and included a spacey synthesizer melody sharing little in common with other rap songs based on disco hits. "The Message," along with Afrika Bambaataa and Soul Sonic Force's "Planet Rock," were among the first hip-hop singles to help establish an emergent, hip-hop aesthetic less beholden to previous genres and more unique unto itself. Much of that aesthetic drew inspiration from the sounds of technology, anticipating how advancements in production equipment (aka "gear") would come to shape rap music's sonic identity.

2. The drum machine era. One moment when a "beat-making" mode began in hip-hop production was 1982's "Planet Rock," produced by Bambaataa, Arthur Baker, Tony Silverman, and John Robie. This team attempted to actualize the science fiction theme of the track's title with an array of futuristic sounds, beginning with the interpolation of the highly mechanized and electronic rhythms of Kraftwerk's 1977 hit "Trans Europe Express." However, one significant departure from Kraftwerk's original was the addition of a dramatic orchestral chord (ORCH5) that the "Planet Rock" team discovered in the pre-loaded sound library of a Fairlight CMI, one of the earliest commercial synthesizers to replay digital samples. In what would become a common recurrence in hip hop, "Planet Rock" created a distinct sonic palette from the "found sounds" of audio equipment.

An example would be the Roland tr-808 Rhythm Composer, besides the Fairlight one of the other major devices used on "Planet Rock" and the source of the song's dense and burbling percussion. Originally debuted in 1980, the TR-808 (colloquially known as the "808") initially sold poorly, partially because its programmed drum sounds sounded too obviously artificial to attract the interest of conventional rock artists. By 1983, Roland had replaced the 808, but in doing so inadvertently spurred a brisk secondary market for the now-discounted model. It soon became one of the most popular and important drum machines in the history of popular music, fueled in large part by its adoption among budding rap producers.

In hindsight, those same attributes of the 808 that others disliked were part of its selling point for beat-makers trying to carve out a sonically distinct genre. The 808's most notable drum sounds simply could not be replicated by conventional acoustic drums: its thick-bottomed kick drum, its sharp handclaps, its strange but memorable cowbell "doink." The 808 was not the first drum machine to be used by rap artists—Joseph "Grandmaster Flash" Sadler's famous "beat box" routine from the late 1970s used a lo-fi Vox Percussion King—but it took another half-decade until the proliferation of drum machines radically altered rap's beat-making aesthetic. The 808 was not a sampler—its pre-loaded drum sounds couldn't be altered or added to—but it had a built-in step sequencer that allowed producers to "program" overlaying percussive tracks that would be difficult, even humanly impossible, to play on a drum kit. This empowered drum machine programmers to experiment with different rhythmic patterns and combinations, giving birth to the idea of "beat-making," with the image of a solitary producer pressing buttons on a box to create his/her rhythm tracks.

Appropriately, the song that marked the old school's end—Run DMC's "Sucker MCs" (1983)—made full use of the drum machine. Producer Larry Smith, an old school veteran who once played bass for rapper Kurtis Blow, created the rhythm track for "Sucker MCs" using an Oberheim DMX—one of the 808's main competitors—to program the song's distinctive flurries of handclaps and kick drums. The success of "Sucker MCs" in turn inspired Def Jam co-founder Rick Rubin to learn to use the 808, resulting in T La Rock's "It's Yours" (1983) and then LL Cool J's "I Need a Beat" (1984), both key singles marking the rise of a "new school" aesthetic.

Drum machines heralded the first "home grown" generation of hip-hop producers because their relative affordability and simplicity freed individuals from the cost and complications of managing studio musicians or equipment; an artist could nearly create a hit single with the device alone. This empowered the emergence of not just new rap artists but entire hip hop scenes. Many American cities outside of New York saw a generation of rap artists rise in the mid-1980s, thanks to the popularity of drum machine-derived beats, but no scene shared a deeper connection to the device than in Florida, where the Miami bass sound referenced the booming low end of the TR-808 kick drum.

One early Miami bass hit was the Dynamix II's "Give the DJ a Break" (1987), produced by "Eric G." Griffin. Although the song heavily features a drum machine track, Griffin created the song's multi-tonal bass line using a newly emerging tool—E-Mu's SP-12 digital sampler—signaling a coming sea change within beat-making techniques and technologies.

3. Sampling. The concept of sampling—that is, the idea of borrowing musical sections from recorded material for use within new musical compositions—existed since hip hop's earliest days, both as a live performance where DJs would "loop" breakbeats using two copies of the same record and as the studio practice discussed above where bands would replay portions of popular bass lines and melodies. However, the dawn of the "sampling era" within hip hop only began with the increased use of digital samplers; that is, electronic devices capable of converting an analog source into a digital format where it can then be manipulated and replayed.

The creative potential of this technology cannot be overstated. As powerful and influential as the 808 was, it and similar drum machines had fundamental limitations. For one, their sound banks could not be added to. If producers did not like the sound of the 808's snare drum, their only choice was to experiment with an entirely different drum machine, an expensive and inefficient alternative. However, as Marlon "Marley Marl" Williams discovered—likely around 1983–4—with a sampler, he could digitize the snare drum from a James Brown record and add that to his sound banks for later use.

Secondly, as a purely percussive device, the drum machine's sonic palette wasn't only limited, but its rhythms locked into a mechanical rigidity that didn't always mesh well with other forms of instrumentation. By comparison, the sampler's potential wasn't limited to percussion sounds; as samplers improved their clarity and extended their recording time, producers could digitize chords, loops, and riffs, allowing beats to swing. Especially before copyright litigation chilled the practice, producers could draw from as many sources as they wished, in whatever combinations they wanted. Hip-hop beats could be collages, drawn from multiple genres, time periods, and geographies.

One of the first major singles built primarily from samples was Eric B and Rakim's 1986 song, "Eric B Is President." Using an E-Mu SP-12 sampler-sequencer (the predecessor to the more powerful and popular SP-1200), Marley Marl assembled the song's track by layering different samples, including James Brown's "Funky President" drums, a scream from the Mohawks' "Champ," and a vocal snippet from Mountain's "Long Red." On top of that, he used a Casio keyboard to replay a bass line from Fonda Rae's "Over Like a Fat Rat." Marl thus built a single rap song from at least four different sources, a harbinger for the kind of creative possibilities that would soon follow.

Notably, Marl did not receive a producer's credit on the song; that went to DJ "Eric B" Barrier, who explained that while Marl had engineered the song's assembly, the musical ideas were Barrier's. In this instance, Barrier's definition of a "producer" was similar to that within older music styles: the producer brings the ideas and helps direct, but is not necessarily expected to do the technical, studio work. Especially in this era, where sampling helped transform hip-hop aesthetics, it was often engineers—who had access to sampling equipment through their studios—who possessed the technical know-how to put beats together even if it was the rap artists who brought the ideas—and in many cases, the records to be sampled. Many engineers did much of the production work for artists and groups without receiving credit, including "Paul C" McNasty and Ivan "Doc" Rodriguez.

As sampler prices fell, however, this separation faded, and increasingly the title "producer" became synonymous with the person handling both the concept and crafting of rap beats. The main device that ushered this change was the SP-1200, first introduced in 1987. By modern standards, the SP-1200 (colloquially known as the "SP") was severely limited. Although E-Mu claimed it possessed 10 seconds of sampling time, that total was actually subdivided into four 2.5-second blocks. The unit also lacked an internal hard drive, so all compositions had to be saved to 3.5-inch floppy disks. Despite these limitations, the SP-1200 included several notable functions, including the ability to retune samples, giving users the ability to re-pitch a single sample using eight trigger buttons to form an octave. Features such as these empowered producers to create original compositions even if their source material drew from pre-existing recordings. The SP-1200 also processed its samples in a distinctive way, largely owing to its limited, 12-bit resolution: samples came out sounding grittier or, as producers liked to say, "crunchier," and for many major producers, especially Robert "RZA" Diggs of the Wu-Tang Clan and Cash Money's Byron "Mannie Fresh" Thomas, that unmistakably "dirty" sound is why they kept using the SP-1200 even after far more powerful and higher-resolution samplers were available.

Between 1987 and 1991, the pace of sampling in hip hop increased rapidly and any number of intrepid beat-makers began to make names for themselves, including Cedric "Ced Gee" Miller, Mark "The 45 King" James, Howard "Hitman Howie Tee" Thompson, and, most famously, the Long Island-based Bomb Squad, a production team that included Hank and Keith Shocklee, Eric "Vietnam" Salder, and Carlton "Chuck D" Ridenhour, the lead rapper for the group Public Enemy. The Bomb Squad's production aesthetic was unfettered sampling at its zenith: they would stack short sample snippets on top of one another, creating remarkable collages of squawking, noisy rhythms that ostensibly drew heavily from James Brown and Parliament–Funkadelic, but reassembled them in ways that barely made the source material recognizable.

As the Bomb Squad explored sampling's potential through their sonic collages, another set of Long Islanders—Paul "Prince Paul" Houston and the group De La Soul—expanded the musical palette of hip hop through their eclectic taste in samples. Though their major 1989 hit, "Me, Myself and I" liberally used Funkadelic's "(Not Just) Knee Deep," other parts of De La Soul's debut album, *3 Feet High and Rising*, drew from 1970s jazz-rockers Steely Dan, 1980s pop stars Hall and Oates, and 1960s doo-woppers the Jarmels. However, it was the group's 12-second sample of the Turtles' 1969 song, "You Showed Me" that resulted in one of the landmark lawsuits that would alter the use of samples in hip hop.

4. Sampling and copyright. Prior to the early 1990s, Copyright law pertaining to sampling was ambiguous at best, but in 1991 two cases created formal and informal precedents that established common practice. In the first, the Turtles filed a multi-million dollar lawsuit against De La Soul, alleging that their use of "You Showed Me" on the rap song "Transmitting Live from Mars" constituted a violation of copyright. The two parties eventually settled out of court for $1.7 million. Though De La Soul avoided accepting liability, in essence the Turtles "won," putting producers on notice that their actions could have expensive consequences.

The same year, the copyright owners of Gilbert O'Sullivan's catalog successfully sued Biz Markie for sampling portions of Sullivan's "Alone Again (Naturally)" for Markie's song by the same name. (In a tongue-in-cheek response, Biz Markie titled his 1993 album, *All Samples Cleared*.) Importantly, this and other similar rulings established that the length of a given sample made little difference; even something as short as a horn stab, theoretically, could be the basis of a successful suit, thus shifting power to copyright holders.

Although these cases did not put an end to sampling, they established new parameters for practical use. The Bomb Squad approach of layering dozens of samples together was no longer tenable, at least not economically. Especially for artists on major labels, the bureaucratic and financial costs of sample clearance became part of the price of the creative process: songs unable to gain clearance could simply be mothballed. (Artists on independent labels sometimes gambled by skipping clearance, believing that more limitedly distributed work wouldn't garner litigation attention.) As the catalogs of more established artists—such as James Brown or George Clinton—became more expensive to sample from, producers began turning to more obscure sources, giving rise to an informal, competitive practice of sample one-upmanship among producers.

5. "Beat digging." The term "digging in the crates" came from a 1992 song of the same name by the Bronx duo of producer Rodney "Showbiz" Lemay and MC Andre "A.G." Barnes. "Crate digging," or "beat digging," refers to the practice of searching through used records for hitherto unused sample material. Beat digging could be seen as a reaction to the legal limitations being put on sampling—the more obscure a sample, the less likely it would attract copyright attention—but it seems more likely that this was an ancillary benefit rather than the driving force. Instead, the beat digging ethic merits comparison to previous hip-hop traditions, especially from the late 1970s, when DJs accrued cultural capital by being the first to "break" a record at a party, thereby claiming informal "ownership" over that song.

Among rap producers, bragging rights went to those who were the first to successfully introduce a new sample. Under certain circumstances, especially if the source material was sufficiently unexpected, other producers would be deterred from using the same source. In other cases, producers wishing to use the same source would find alternative ways of incorporating the sample, thus distinguishing their use from that of others. One reason why producer Sean "Puffy" Combs earned the scorn of certain rap consumers in the late 1990s was his minimal alterations while reusing samples made popular by previous artists. Critics deemed this an uncreative form of copying, a somewhat ironic critique given how rap songs, generally, were based on samples of other artists' music to begin with.

The beat digging aesthetic was especially prominent with a newer generation of producers, including Joseph "Diamond D" Kirkland, Kamaal "Q-Tip" Fareed, "Pete Rock" Phillips, and Chris "DJ Premier" Martin, all of whom came to the fore in the early 1990s. Their rise coincided with a shift in technology as newer devices offered higher quality sound processing, longer sampling time, and more powerful features than the venerable (but still highly popular) SP-1200. The most prominent of these newer competitors was Akai's MPC samplers, first introduced with the MPC60 in 1988.

The MPC60, like the SP-1200, featured only 12-bit resolution. Yet if the SP processed samples to sound more "crunchy," the MPC was known for its warmth, making it a popular sampler among producers working with jazz samples who wanted to maintain the sonic feel of acoustic bass lines and electric piano. The MPC also featured a 4×4 array of velocity-sensitive trigger pads that allowed producers to "play" the MPC like an instrument in real time. Borrowing a technique—"chopping"—made famous by Marley Marl, producers could dissect samples into small, component bits and then use the device's trigger pads to reconstitute them into new melodies, chord progressions, and drum patterns.

Sampling's rise paralleled hip hop's so-called "golden era" (roughly 1986–94) as the music and culture's critical and commercial stature grew dramatically. Sample-based production techniques were certainly a contributing factor to hip hop's growing acclaim: they were a new, innovative approach to music making that impacted many styles of popular music, including R&B, rock, and jazz. However, rather than lionizing sample-based techniques as the sole "authentic" method in hip-hop beat-making, it is better to understand them as among several approaches that have held sway in the music's history. By the latter half of the 1990s, the diversity in techniques and approaches to hip-hop beat-making became more apparent as different regional scenes began to challenge the dominance of New York as hip hop's aesthetic center.

6. Synthesizers and Digital Audio Workstations. Prior to his 1992 solo debut *The Chronic*, Andre "Dr. Dre" Young had worked in practically every major production style up to that point: live instruments and turntables, drum machine programming, and sample-based styles. However, the enduring sound on *The Chronic* became the snaking synthesizers on the album's two main singles, "Let Me Ride" and "Nuthin' But a 'G' Thing." In an era where jazz-influenced, sample-based hip hop was the norm, especially that originating in New York, Dre's synthesizer-heavy songs hearkened back to the lush funk and R&B styles of the 1970s, marking an alternative aesthetic path for rap artists on the West Coast that helped fuel regional rivalries.

Many production equipment manufacturers already created sampling equipment in a keyboard format, including the popular Akai "S" series and Ensoniq's ASR-10, both of which were among the first sampling synthesizers to offer superior 16-bit resolution. However, because these were also synthesizers, producers could also experiment with the banks of pre-installed sounds with which they came. As with previous eras of production equipment—the distinctive drum sounds of the TR-808 or the warmth of the MPC's processor, for example—what producers discovered among those stock banks often became the basis for their own production style and, thus, new directions in beat-making.

For example, few synthesizers in hip hop have been as popular as Korg's Triton series, first introduced in 1999. As producer Kasseem "Swizz Beatz" Dean discovered, even though the Triton featured powerful sampling capabilities, it was the keyboard's own stock sounds that became the basis for a series of top-charting rap singles he produced at the turn of the century. Using the Triton, the signature Swizz Beatz production could be described as "shiny" and "hyper-real" in its texture; in essence, the opposite of the gritty, dirty sound of the SP-1200.

As much of an impact as synthesizer-based hip hop had at the turn of the century, within a few short years computer-integrated audio systems could now do the work of all these previous stand-alone devices. Digidesign's industry-standard Pro Tools led the way towards incorporating Digital Audio Workstations (DAW) into beat-making. Not only could Pro Tools' massive suite of software plug-ins replicate an entire room full of equipment—from drum machines to synthesizers to samplers—but its high-end audio processing enabled home producers to engineer songs with a sound that rivaled professional studios.

In the early 2000s, more accomplished producers, including Timothy "Timbaland" Mosely and the Neptunes (Pharrell Williams and Chad Hugo), tended to assemble large arrays of older synthesizers, samplers, drum machines, and acoustic instruments in addition to a DAW system. However, as DAWs became cheaper and easier to learn, artists with limited capital and/or technical skills could still find ways of minting hits from a single piece of software alone. The most famous example of the mid-2000s was that of a teenage Soulja Boy, who created his 2007 hit "Crank That" using a laptop and the built-in sounds he discovered in the DAW package known as FruityLoops (later renamed to FL Studios).

7. Current trends. As hip hop aged into its fourth decade, the beat-making repertoire was as expansive as ever, not the least because previous styles remain in constant circulation. 808 drum sounds can still be heard regularly on contemporary rap songs, and although sample-based hip hop may not dominate the record charts as it once did, many producers (and their fans) remain passionate about the quest to find new samples and new ways to create beats from them. As hip hop increasingly shifted to European-style dance music by the end of the 2000s, synthesizers remained an important device in a producer's toolbox. Added to these technologies, any number of competing DAW systems helped even technological neophytes begin beat-making out of the literal box.

An exemplar of hip hop's production past and possible future has been Kanye West, who began his career in the early 2000s as a soul-influenced, sample-based producer. However, as he embarked on his own solo career mid-decade, West increasingly shifted into any number of different approaches, including an entire album using the faddish vocal alteration technique known as "auto-tune," and his sample sourcing went from 1970s R&B stars such as the Persuaders to contemporary dance groups like Daft Punk. By the time West released his critically-acclaimed fifth studio album in 2010, *My Beautiful Dark Twisted Fantasy*, his productions were elaborately baroque, with long, noodling arrangements more familiar to prog-rock and jazz than conventional hip hop. If West's experimentations are any indication, the beat-making tradition in hip hop could continue to embrace past styles while pushing forward into new realms of sonic play.

BIBLIOGRAPHY

J.G. Schloss: *Making Beats: the Art of Sample-based Hip Hop* (Middleton, CT, 2002)

J. Chang: *Can't Stop, Won't Stop: a History of the Hip-hop Generation* (New York, 2005)

D. Charnas: *The Big Payback: the History of the Business of Hip Hop* (New York, 2011)
K. McLeod: *Creative License: the Law and Culture of Digital Sampling* (Durham, NC, 2011)

OLIVER WANG

Beattie, John W(alter) (*b* Norwalk, OH, 26 Nov 1885; Evanston, IL, 22 Nov 1962). Music educator and administrator. He obtained a degree in history from Denison University (BA 1907), where he directed the glee club, studied voice, and was a founding member of the band. He also attended a Ginn and Company music textbook summer school in Chicago (1907). He was music supervisor in the Xenia, Ohio, public schools (1907–11), and a music teacher (1911–12) and supervisor in Grand Rapids, Michigan (1912–24), where he hosted the conference of the Music Supervisors National Conference (MSNC) in 1917. He was a song leader with the YMCA (attached to the US Army) in France (1917–19), MSNC president (1920–21), and member of the MSNC Research Council (1923–31) and editorial committee of the *Music Educators Journal* (1932–62). He obtained a degree in educational administration (MA 1923) and a superintendent's diploma from Teachers College, Columbia University (1923), and was the first state supervisor of music in Michigan (1924–5). He was music supervisor for the Evanston, Illinois, schools and a professor of music education (both 1925–50) and dean of music (1933–50) at Northwestern University. He was a visiting (summer) professor at several institutions, co-author and compiler of numerous school and community song books, and a composer/collector of more than 400 songs for children. Beattie was inducted into the Music Educators Hall of Fame in 1986.

BIBLIOGRAPHY

L.W. Curtis: "The Versatile John Beattie," *MEJ*, xliii/2 (1956), 22–24, 26
"Obituary: John W. Beattie," *The Instrumentalist*, xvii/5 (1963), 81 only
L.W. Edwards: *John Walter Beattie, 1885–1962: Pragmatic Music Educator* (diss., U. Michigan, 1971)
L.W. Edwards: "John Walter Beattie, 1885–1962: Pragmatic Music Education," *Bulletin of Historical Research in Music Education*, vi/2 (1985), 45–79

JERE T. HUMPHREYS

Beatty, Talley (*b* Cedar Grove, LA, 22 Dec 1918; *d* New York, NY, 29 April 1995). Dancer, choreographer, teacher, and company director. Having begun formal dance training with KATHERINE DUNHAM in Chicago, he made his first appearance on stage in Ruth Page's 1934 production of *La Guiablesse* (The Devil Woman, 1933), with Dunham in the title role. He later performed as a soloist in Dunham's company and continued his training with Martha Graham and with various ballet teachers in New York City. Recognized as a charismatic dancer in several companies, he formed his own troupe in 1947 and toured widely with a revue entitled *Tropicana* (1950–55). For this show he made his first significant work, *Southern Landscape* (1949; music, traditional spirituals), which launched his reputation as a brilliant choreographer. In later years he choreographed more than 50 ballets, some of which, centering on social issues and experiences of African Americans, became classics of the modern dance repertory. Among them are *The Road of the Phoebe Snow* (1959; music by Duke Ellington and Billy Strayhorn), *Come and Get the Beauty of It Hot* (1960; music by Charles Mingus, Miles Davis, and Lalo Schifrin), *The Black* Belt (1967; music by Ellington), *The Stack-Up* (1983; music by various artists), and *Ellingtonia* (1994). He also collaborated with Ellington on two television specials. His Broadway choreographic credits include *Ari* (1971; music by Walt Smith), *Don't Bother Me, I Can't Cope* (1972; music by Micki Grant), *Your Arm's Too Short to Box with God* (1976; music by Alex Bradford and Micki Grant), and *But Never Jam Today* (1979; music by Bert Keyes and Bob Larimer).

BIBLIOGRAPHY

R.A. Long: *The Black Tradition in American Dance* (London, 1989)
E. Thorpe: *Black Dance* (Woodstock, NY, 1990)
T.D. Ellison: "Beatty, Talley," *International Dictionary of Modern Dance*, ed. T. Benbow-Pfalzgraf (Detroit, 1998)
J. Perpener: *African-American Concert Dance: the Harlem Renaissance and Beyond* (Champaign, IL, 2001)

CLAUDE CONYERS

Beaux Arts String Quartet. String quartet founded in 1955.

See TARACK, GERALD.

Beaux Arts Trio. Piano trio. It was formed in New York in 1955 by the pianist Menahem Pressler (*b* Magdeburg, Germany, 16 Dec 1923), the violinist Daniel Guilet (*b* Rostov, Russia, 10 Jan 1899; *d* New York, NY, 14 Oct 1990), and the cellist Bernard Greenhouse (*b* Newark, NJ, 3 Jan 1916; *d* Wellfleet, MA, 13 May 2011). Encouraged by Robert Casadesus, in whose house they rehearsed, the three made a sensational debut at the Berkshire Music Festival in Tanglewood; and in autumn 1955 they made their first nationwide tour. Guilet (under his original name Guilevitch) had been a member of the Calvet Quartet of Paris for a decade before the war and had led the Opéra-Comique Orchestra; after immigrating to the United States in 1941, he had led his own quartet and Toscanini's NBC SO. His style of playing, grounded in Franco-Belgian traditions, strongly colored the trio's early performances and recordings, the latter including works by Haydn, Mendelssohn, Dvořák, Fauré, and Ravel, as well as outstanding Mozart, Beethoven, and Schubert cycles. His younger colleagues, who counted Egon Petri and Pablo Casals among their teachers, played with refulgent tone and deep musicality but—under his influence—always with a light touch. For a time all three taught at the University of Indiana School of Music. When Guilet retired in 1969 he was replaced by Isidore Cohen, a former member of the Schneider and Juilliard Quartets.

This formation of the ensemble toured indefatigably and recorded a vast range of music, including all the trios of Haydn and the Mozart and Brahms piano quartets (with Bruno Giuranna and Walter Trampler respectively). The Mozart, Beethoven, and Schubert trios were re-recorded, confirming the impression gained in the concert hall that the group's style had broadened and deepened, but also coarsened to a degree. Its saving grace was the wit it brought to many of its performances, for instance in Charles Ives's Trio. In 1987, on Greenhouse's retirement, Peter Wiley came into the group. In 1990 George Rochberg's *Summer 1990* received its premiere by the Beaux Arts Trio, followed in 1991 by Ned Rorem's *Spring Music* and then by David Baker's *Roots II*. In 1992 Cohen retired, his replacement being Ida Kavafian. This formation proved to have a more combustible chemistry; in the recording studio, it was commemorated by an excellent disc of trios by Hummel. In 1998 both string players withdrew and Pressler was joined by the violinist Young Uck Kim and the cellist Antonio Meneses. The group made a final evolution in 2002 when Kim was replaced by British violinist Daniel Hope. The trio re-recorded Dvořák's "Dumky" Trio and Mendelssohn's Trio no.1 in 2004, and released their final disc in 2006, joined by soprano Joan Rodgers.

The Beaux Arts Trio played their last American concert at Tanglewood, where they debuted, in August 2008; they disbanded after their concert that September in Luzern, Switzerland. Only one of the founder-members, Pressler, remained for the 53 year duration of the ensemble's existence. Much of the trio's ability to renew itself across several generations owed to his sparkling technique, wholehearted involvement, and sense of style. The group has been vastly influential and has raised the profile of the piano trio as a form but has left the repertory more or less as it found it.

BIBLIOGRAPHY

H. Waleson: "Beaux Arts Trio an Enduring Sound," *New York Times Magazine* (18 Nov 1984), 76

N. Delbanco: *The Beaux Arts Trio: a Portrait* (New York, 1985)

B.L. Sand: "The Beautiful Art of the Trio," *The Strad,* cvi (1995), 686–91

TULLY POTTER/MEGAN E. HILL

Bebop. *See* Bop.

Bechet, Sidney (Joseph) (*b* New Orleans, LA, 14 May 1897; *d* Paris, France, 14 May 1959). Jazz clarinetist and soprano saxophonist.

1. Life. 2. Music.

1. Life. He was an Afro-French Creole, descended from free people of color residing in Tremé, an early hotbed of jazz activity. As a boy he emulated his older brothers who worked semi-professionally as musicians and played in a family band, the Silver Bells. "Big Eye" Louis Nelson and George Baquet were his primary teachers. Nelson remembered Bechet resisting formal instruction ("He wouldn't learn notes, but he was my best scholar"), and the latter never became musically literate. Like many younger Creoles, Bechet rejected traditional Creole proprieties and gravitated to African American vernacular culture, particularly the blues as expressed by Buddy Bolden. By 1910 he was sitting in with bands such as the Eagle, and by 1915 he was being praised as a prodigy by musicians who frequented the Piron and Williams music publishing company on Tulane Avenue. Peter Bocage recalled, "He didn't know what key he was playing in, but you couldn't lose him." In the fall of 1916 Bechet went with Clarence Williams to Galveston, Texas, a trip that landed him in jail. Undeterred, in 1917 he traveled to Chicago with the Bruce & Bruce stock company after a stint playing alongside King Oliver in Kid Ory's band, and he was with Lawrence Duhé's group when Oliver arrived there in 1918. The following year Will Marion Cook recruited Bechet for a tour of England with his Southern Syncopated Orchestra. When the Swiss conductor Ernest Ansermet heard Bechet performing "Characteristic Blues" (a pastiche of New Orleans standards such as "Shake it and Break it"), he declared him "an extraordinary clarinet virtuoso…this artist of genius" who must "follow his own way." Bechet often did so, and he abandoned Cook to work with the drummer Benny Peyton in England and France. He was deported from England after a woman he claimed was a prostitute brought charges of battery against him, but not before he had acquired a soprano saxophone, an instrument that enabled him to challenge trumpet players for command of the ensemble.

A return to New York in 1922 led to his first recordings, beginning in July 1923 with Clarence Williams's Blue Five and culminating in two extraordinary duels with Louis Armstrong on the out-choruses of separate versions of "Cakewalking Babies from Home," one with the Blue Five in December 1924 and the other with the Red Onion Jazz Babies (essentially the same group) in January 1925. Most critics believe that Bechet won the first of these duels, but that Armstrong took the rematch. The clarinetist soon came to the attention of Duke Ellington, who saw him vanquish Coleman Hawkins in a "cutting contest" and then hired him. It was not

Sidney Bechet, 1947. (William P. Gottlieb/Ira and Leonore S. Gershwin Fund Collection, Music Division, Library of Congress)

a happy union: Ellington dismissed him after Bechet missed several engagements, offering the excuse that he had been lost in a taxi "for three days." Yet, as he was wont, Ellington found a way around the problem. In July 1925 Bechet invested in a nightclub scheme, Club Basha, where a protégé, Johnny Hodges, rose to prominence. Ellington hired Hodges, at once fulfilling his desire to have a kindred presence in the band, while also foregoing the inconvenience of contending with Bechet's unpredictability and authority issues. Meanwhile, Club Basha lost money, and Bechet fled to France with *La revue nègre*, which featured Josephine Baker. From his base in Paris he made various forays in Europe, including a trip to Moscow, where he met trumpeter Tommy Ladnier. He returned to Paris to work with Noble Sissle in the summer of 1928 but in December was involved in a shooting incident with guitarist Mike McKendrick, who had insulted him. Bechet wounded three people (including pianist Glover Compton) and spent 11 months in prison before being deported to Germany, where he appeared in the film *Einbrecher* in 1930.

After returning to the United States, in 1932 Bechet recorded as a leader with the New Orleans Feetwarmers for RCA Victor, with Ladnier as his mainstay. The records were mesmerizing in their intensity and virtuosity, but they failed to sell, and the pair lapsed into spot jobs with Sissle, while also managing a tailor's shop. During the 1940s the New Orleans revival brought Bechet opportunities and complications. Thanks to his exemplary contributions to Jelly Roll Morton's recordings for RCA Victor in September 1939, Bechet was offered a contract that was supposed to feature him with the label's top big bands. Instead, he was given novelty projects such as his "one-man-band" recordings (1941), directed at the revival market. (He did better with Blue Note and H.R.S. before going with RCA.) In 1949 Charles Delaunay hired Bechet for the first Paris Jazz Festival, where he triumphed at the expense of Charlie Parker, who was making his European debut. Bechet took the message to heart and spent his last decade there, living parallel lives with a wife and a mistress and soaking up the adulation of French teenagers, who fought pitched battles to get into his concerts.

2. Music. Bechet was one of the first jazz musicians to transcend collective improvisation and concentrate on solo improvisation, although he remained a gifted ensemble player, when so inclined. While his signature vibrato occasionally masked deficiencies, it also became emblematic of his passion, rhythmic intensity, and lyricism. Like many New Orleans musicians, Bechet readily combined entertainment with artistry, indulging in devices such as circular breathing to achieve dramatic effects. He remained dedicated to the original New Orleans ideal of jazz as continuous experimentation and variegation, apparent in projects ranging from his Haitian Band rumbas in 1939 to duets with modernist pianist Martial Solal in 1957. According to his student Bob Wilber, Bechet often prepared variations for his solos in advance, selecting them like an archer plucking arrows from a quiver, but he had an uncanny ability to make the right choices, from the wild exuberance of "Shag" (1932, Vic.) to the haunting melancholy of "Blue Horizon" (1944, BN). More than 50 years after his death he was still revered for the sheer brilliance and sincerity of his playing.

SELECTED RECORDINGS

As leader: Summertime (1939, BN); China Boy (1940, HRS); Make me a Pallet on the Floor (1940, Bb); Blue Horizon (1944, BN); *Sidney Bechet avec Claude Luter et son orchestre* (1949, Vogue)

As sideman: C. Williams: Texas Moaner Blues (1924, OK), Mandy make up your mind (1924, OK); Red Onion Jazz Babies: Cake Walking Babies (1924, Gen.); New Orleans Feetwarmers: Sweetie Dear/ Maple Leaf Rag (1932, Vic.)

BIBLIOGRAPHY

SouthernB

E. Ansermet: "Bechet and Jazz Visit Europe, 1919," *Frontiers of Jazz*, ed. R. de Toledano (New York, 1947, 3/1994), 2

H. Lyttelton: *I Play as I Please* (London, 1954)

R. Mouly: *Sidney Bechet: notre ami* (Paris, 1959)

S. Bechet: *Treat it Gentle* (New York, 1960, 2/1975)

M. Williams: *Jazz Masters of New Orleans* (New York, 1967)

G. Schuller: *Early Jazz: its Roots and Musical Development* (New York, 1968)

H.J. Mauerer: *A Discography of Sidney Bechet* (Copenhagen, 1969)

J.-R. Hippenmeyer: *Sidney Bechet* (Geneva, 1980)

B. Priestley: "Blues to Bechet," *The Wire*, iii (1983), 14

M. Hazeldine: "Dear Wynne: a Review of the Events of 1945–6, concerning Bunk Johnson, Sidney Bechet, Boston and Beyond" *Footnote*, xv/5 (1984), 4

J. Chilton: *Sidney Bechet:the Wizard of Jazz* (London and New York, 1987)

B.B. Raeburn: "King Oliver, Jelly Roll Morton, and Sidney Bechet: Ménage à Trois, New Orleans Style," *The Oxford Companion to Jazz*, ed. B. Kirchner (Oxford, 2000), 88

BRUCE BOYD RAEBURN

Bechler, Johann Christian (*b* Baltic island of Oesel [now Saaremaa], 7 Jan 1784; *d* Herrnhut, Germany, 18 April 1857). German composer, organist, and pastor. Son of a Moravian minister, he was educated at Moravian schools in Niesky and Barby, Germany. Music was his favorite subject, and he wrote in his memoir that he "devoted every moment of time left by other duties, to the acquisition of the various branches of this charming art with the greatest delight, learning to sing, to play various stringed instruments, but more particularly the piano and the organ."

At the completion of his studies he taught organ at Barby and in 1806 accepted a call to America, where he became one of the first professors at Moravian Theological Seminary. His interest in music continued during this time, and he may have studied with David Moritz Michael. He served as minister to the Moravian congregations of Philadelphia; Staten Island, New York; Lititz, Pennsylvania; and Salem, North Carolina. In 1836, shortly after his consecration as bishop, he went to serve the congregation in Sarepta, Russia. In 1849 he retired to Herrnhut, the center of the Moravian Church in Germany.

Bechler's musical compositions include some 30 anthems with orchestral accompaniment, settings of liturgical texts, hymns, ariettas with keyboard accompaniment, and a suite for woodwinds. His choral anthems are marked by a variety of styles, ranging from the lyrical to the bombastic; some of his longer anthems include sections in contrasting styles and tempos. Bechler's orchestration, using woodwinds, trumpets, and horns in pairs, as well as strings, is varied and quite effective in his use of tone colors. He is not known to have composed music either before coming to America in 1806 or after his return to Europe.

BIBLIOGRAPHY

J.C. Bechler: "Memoir of the Rt. Rev. John C. Bechler," *The Moravian* (26 June 1857)

N.R. Knouse: *The Music of the Moravian Church in America* (Rochester, NY, 2008)

C.D. Crews: *Johann Christian Bechler* (Winston-Salem, NC, 2011)

NOLA REED KNOUSE

Beck [Campbell, Bek David; Hansen, Beck] (*b* Los Angeles, CA, 8 July 1970). Rock singer, songwriter, guitarist, and producer. He has recorded and performed songs in a wide range of genres including folk, country, bluegrass, grunge, indie, metal, rock, lounge, Latino, and noise. An obvious contributing factor to his eclectic tastes is his artistic and performer-laden family. His father, David Campbell, is a string player and arranger who has worked on string parts for some of his son's more recent albums. His mother, Bibbe Hansen, worked with Andy Warhol at the artist's studio the Factory in New York at an early age and was involved in the West Coast punk scene during the 1980s. His grandfather Al Hansen was an artist and performer involved in the Fluxus movement. Beck grew up around rockers and in various ethnic neighborhoods which all contributed to his music education. After spending time at the end of the 1980s involved with New York's anti-folk scene he returned west and began performing as often and wherever he could. These gigs involved him using a leaf-blower on stage, telling stories, setting fire to his acoustic guitar, and rocking out with a boom-box backing tape. His breakthrough came in 1994 with the single "Loser," which combined a looped guitar riff, hip-hop vocals, and a catchy chorus. The subsequent album, *Mellow Gold*, attracted attention around the world. In 1996 his first recording for a major label, *Odelay*, established his reputation as the coolest American singer of the mid-1990s and included such singles as "Where it's at," "Devil's Haircut," and "The New Pollution." Other albums of this period include the multi-genre *Stereopathetic Soulmanure* and the folksy *One Foot in the Grave*. To follow up the mainstream acceptance of *Odelay* Beck turned away from rock music with the downbeat album *Mutations*. In 1999 *Midnite Vultures* was more upbeat but patchy. Subsequent albums have tended to be more laid back, especially the introspective *Sea Change* and *Modern Guilt*, although *Guero* and *The Information* included a diverse range of genres. In 2009 Beck began the Record Club, an Internet-only series of cover-version albums recorded with friends and posted with videos on his website.

Beck, 1997. (AP Photo/Chris Pizzello)

SELECTED RECORDINGS

Golden Feelings (Sonic Enemy, 1993); *Stereopathetic Soulmanure* (Flipside, 1994); *Mellow Gold* (DGC, 1994); *One Foot in the Grave* (K, 1994); *Odelay* (DGC, 1996); *Mutations* (DGC, 1998); *Midnite Vultures* (DGC, 1999); *Sea Change* (Geffen, 2002); *Guero* (Interscope, 2005); *The Information* (Interscope, 2006); *Modern Guilt* (Interscope, 2008)

BIBLIOGRAPHY

R. Jovanovic: *Beck! On a Backwards River* (New York, 2001)

ROB JOVANOVIC

Beck, Carl (*b* Ilmeneau, Thuringia, 16 April 1850; *d* San Antonio, TX, 2 Oct 1920). Conductor of German birth. Perhaps the "Father of the Orchestra in Texas," Beck was conductor of the Beethoven Männerchor in San Antonio (1884–1904; 1919–20). Statewide he established orchestras for the Texas Sängerfests (1885–1904), conducting the largest repertoire of orchestral music performed in the state to that time. He established an orchestra in San Antonio by 1889, which became the nucleus of the city's first professional orchestra (1905). Beck left San Antonio in 1905, becoming an itinerant bandmaster in Odessa and Pecos before retiring to Kingsville during World War I.

BIBLIOGRAPHY

R. Barkley, ed.: *The Handbook of Texas Music* (Austin, 2003)

L. Clayton and J.W. Specht, eds.: *The Roots of Texas Music* (College Station, 2003)

LARRY WOLZ

Beck, Christophe [Chris] (*b* Montreal, QC, Canada, 6 Jan 1969). Canadian composer of television and film scores. After taking private music lessons and playing with rock bands, he attended Yale University (BA 1992) where he studied music composition and wrote two musicals and an opera. He then studied at the University of Southern California's film scoring program (1992–3) where his teachers included JERRY GOLDSMITH. After getting his first television scoring assignment with the Canadian series *White Fang*, Beck went on to score multiple episodes of the critically acclaimed cult television series *Buffy the Vampire Slayer*. As a series regular for most of seasons two, three, and four, Beck introduced a number of recurring and continually developing melodic motifs that enhanced the narrative and dramatic power of the ironic show. His work on *Buffy* earned him an Emmy award in 1998 for best music composition in a series; after leaving regular composition duties for the series after season five, he made notable returns for the episodes "The Gift," the episode marking the end of *Buffy's* run on the WB network, and "Once More, with Feeling," a musical episode of the series for which Beck arranged and orchestrated songs written by series creator Joss Whedon. Beck's *Buffy* scores employed heavily processed electronic sounds and samples of orchestral instruments, creating virtual orchestras that he occasionally augmented with a small number of live performers.

Since 1999 he has composed mainly for feature films, where his deft ability to write in a number of musical styles—from experimental timbres and throbbing techno to delicate orchestral and piano passages—has made him a sought-after composer associated with many big budget and high-grossing films from the first decade of the 21st century.

WORKS

White Fang (TV series) (1993); Past Perfect (1996); Buffy the Vampire Slayer (TV series) (1997–2001); Angel (TV series) (1999–2000); Guinevere (1999); Let the Devil Wear Black (1999); The Practice (TV series) (1999–2000); Bring It On (2000); The Tuxedo (2002); Stealing Harvard (2002); Confidence (2003); Under the Tuscan Sun (2003); Cheaper by the Dozen (2003); Just Married (2003); A Cinderella Story (2004); The Event (2004); Garfield: The Movie (2004); Saved! (2004); Without a Paddle (2004); Elektra (2005); The Pink Panther (2006); We Are Marshall (2006); Drillbit Taylor (2008); The Hangover (2009); Waiting for "Superman" (2010); Hot Tub Time Machine (2010); Death at a Funeral (2010); Red (2010); Burlesque (2010); Cedar Rapids (2011)

BIBLIOGRAPHY

N. Holder: *The Watcher's Guide*, ii (New York, 2000), 433–7

J. Bond: "Elektra-fied (Christophe Beck scores *Elektra*)," *Film Score Monthly*, ix (2004), 20–21

R. Haskins: "Variations on Themes for Geeks and Heroes: Leitmotif, Style and the Musico-dramatic Moment," *Music, Sound and Silence in* Buffy the Vampire Slayer, ed. P Attinello, J.K. Halfyard and V. Knights (Surrey, England, 2010), 45–60

A. Cox and R. Fülöp: "'What rhymes with lungs?': When Music Speaks Louder than Words," *Music, Sound and Silence in* Buffy the Vampire Slayer, ed. P. Attinello, J.K. Halfyard and V. Knights (Surrey, England, 2010), 61–78

NEIL LERNER

Beck, Joe [Joseph Arnold] (*b* Philadelphia, PA, 29 July 1945; *d* Woodbury, CT, 22 July 2008). Guitarist, composer, and producer. After graduating from high school, he moved to New York and played with a jazz trio in the club Chuck's Compository. He also worked as a studio musician and jingle writer, which eventually led to collaborations with Gil Evans. Beck was among the first jazz guitarists to incorporate rock guitar techniques, including the use of a distorted tone, into his playing. He was also a key figure in the fusion movement of the 1970s, along with the Brecker Brothers and David Sanborn. In 1967 he participated in recording sessions with Miles Davis's second quintet (alongside Ron Carter, Herbie Hancock, Wayne Shorter, and Tony Williams). Although the music from this session was not immediately released, it influenced Davis's later fusion of jazz and rock on such albums as *Bitches Brew*. From the 1970s through the 2000s, Beck recorded and performed with many notable jazz musicians, including Woody Herman, Larry Coryell, Kai Winding, Don Grolnick, Sanborn, Atilla Zoeller, Red Mitchell, and John Abercrombie. He also invented and performed on an instrument he called the alto guitar. Beck remained an in-demand session guitarist throughout his life, performing on albums by popular musicians including James Brown and Paul Simon. He also founded and ran the company Code Works, which specialized in creating jingles and songs for television and radio commercials.

BIBLIOGRAPHY

G. Cole: *The Last Miles: the Music of Miles Davis, 1980–1991* (Ann Arbor, 2007)

Obituary: *JT*, xxxix (2009), 34; also available at <http://jazztimes.com/articles/21268-joe-beck>

JOHN BASS

Beck, Johann H(einrich) (*b* Cleveland, OH, 12 Sept 1856; *d* Cleveland, OH, 26 May 1924). Conductor, composer, and violinist. He studied at the Leipzig Conservatory from 1879 to 1882, and made his European debut as a violinist at the Leipzig Gewandhaus in his own String Quartet in C minor. On his return to Cleveland he continued activity with the Schubert String Quartet, which he organized in 1877, and the Beck String Quartet, giving frequent concerts during the 1880s and 1890s. After 1878 he was active as a conductor. He directed the Detroit SO (1895–6) and local Cleveland orchestras during the early years of the 20th century, and appeared frequently with major orchestras in other cities. He conducted his own works with much success and numerous contemporary articles and reviews give him high praise. Only his *Elegiac Song* op.4 no.1 seems to have been published. Beck was active in the Music Teachers National Association and the Ohio Music Teachers' Association. An extensive collection of his manuscripts and memorabilia is in the Cleveland Public Library.

WORKS

Stage: Salammbo (J.H. Beck), begun 1887, inc.

Vocal: 6 sym. poems, 1v, orch, 1877–89, incl. Elegiac Song, arr. 1v, vn, pf, op.4 no.1 (Cleveland, 1877), 2 inc.; Deukalion (B. Taylor), 4 solo vv, chorus, orch, ?1877, inc.; Wie schön bist du, T, orch; Meeresabend (M. Strachwitz, trans. Beck), Mez/T, orch, ?1908; Salvum fac regem, 4vv, pf; partsongs; songs

Orch: Sym. ("Sindbad"), op.1, *c*1875–7, inc.; 4 ovs., 1875–85; Skirnismael, cycle of 5 sym. poems, *c*1887–93, 3 inc.; 2 scherzos, 1885–95, 1889; Aus meinem Leben, sym. poem, 1917
Chbr: 4 str qts, 1877–80; Str Sextet, 1885–6; Sonata, vn, pf, inc.; piece for fl, pf; other works
Pf: Sonata, inc.; Canone all'ottave, 1875; variations; other works

BIBLIOGRAPHY

DAB (W.T. Upton)
"Biographies of Noted American Musicians Johann H. Beck," *Brainard's Musical World*, xxiv (1887), 364; xxviii (1891), 174
"American Composers Johann H. Beck," *The Musician*, ii (1897), 1
R. Hughes: *Contemporary American Composers* (Boston, 1900), 406–411
M.H. Osburn: *Ohio Composers and Musical Authors* (Columbus, OH, 1942) 28–9
J.H. Alexander: *It Must be Heard: a Survey of the Musical Life of Cleveland, 1836–1918* (Cleveland, 1981)
Encyclopedia of Cleveland History (Bloomington, IN, 1987), 84–5

J.H. ALEXANDER

Beck, Sydney (*b* New York, NY, 2 Sept 1906; *d* Brattleboro, VT, 7 April 2001). Music scholar and librarian. He was educated at the College of the City of New York, New York University, the Institute of Musical Art, and the Mannes College of Music; his studies included the violin and chamber music with Louis Sveçenski, composition with BERNARD WAGENAAR and Hans Weisse, and musicology with Curt Sachs and Gustave Reese. From 1931 to 1968 he worked in the music division of the New York Public Library as head of the Rare Book and Manuscript Collections, editor of music publications and curator of the Toscanini Memorial Archives; from 1950 to 1968 he taught at the Mannes College of Music. In 1968 he became director of libraries and a member of the faculty at the New England Conservatory of Music in Boston. He retired in 1976.

Beck's principal fields of study were early string techniques and performing practice, textual analyses and criticism (see his *Music in Prints*, New York, 1965, with E. Roth), and instrumental teaching and study, with an emphasis on English Renaissance music. He appeared as director and performer with various concert groups. During the 1930s and 40s Beck edited many music publications issued by the New York Public Library from manuscript and printed materials; this was reproduced by the Federal Music Project and included composers from the 16th to the 20th centuries, such as Coprario, Locke, Bach, Grétry, Gossec, and John Knowles Paine.

PAULA MORGAN

Beckel, James Cox (*b* Philadelphia, PA, Dec 1811; *d* Philadelphia, 7 Feb 1905). Organist and composer. From the age of 13 he assisted his father, also an organist. Beckel worked in several Philadelphia churches including the Clinton Street Emanuel Church (Presbyterian) for over 50 years beginning in 1829. He edited the *Musical Clipper*, a music, art, and literature journal. Beckel, a Mason, lived in the Philadelphia Masonic Home when he became elderly, playing the organ there and composing music for special occasions. A prolific composer, Beckel wrote music commemorating the Civil War, including "The Battle of Gettysburg," a programmatic work with special effects in which he altered the outcome of the battle. His works are held in collections including *PHf*, *NYpl*, and *Wc*. Other publications include *Amateur's School for the Piano*, *New and Improved Operatic Instruction-Book for the Pianoforte*, *Amateur's Organ School*, *The Psalter, a Collection of Sacred Music*, and *Philadelphia Anthem Book*. His *Amateur's School for the Melodeon* (Philadelphia, 1855) included the popular "What Is Home Without a Mother" by Alice Hawthorne.

BIBLIOGRAPHY

J.D. Brown: *Biographical Dictionary of Musicians* (London, 1886)
F.O. Jones: *Handbook of American Music and Musicians* (Canaseraga, NY, 1886)
Obituary, *Philadelphia Inquirer* (8 Feb 1905)
B.C. Kelly and M.A. Snell: *Bugle Resounding, Music and Musicians of the Civil War Era* (Columbia, MO, 2004)

MARTHA FURMAN SCHLEIFER

Becker. Family of violin makers. Carl G. Becker (*b* Chicago, IL, 20 Sept 1887; *d* Chicago, 6 Aug 1975) was the son of a prominent violinist and teacher, and his maternal grandfather, Herman Macklett, had been a violin maker. He began as a craftsman in 1901, and a year later joined the firm of Lyon & Healy, where he worked under John Hornsteiner until 1908. When Hornsteiner left to start his own business Becker went with him, staying as an assistant until 1923. By 1924 he had become an outstanding violin maker, repairer, and connoisseur, and he took a position with William Lewis & Son, another Chicago firm; before 1924 he had already made about 100 violins in his spare time. After he joined Lewis he spent at least three summer months doing new work at Pickerel, Wisconsin; from 1925 to 1947 he made 389 new violins, violas, and cellos, each with its serial number (100–488). For the rest of each year he supervised the repair workshop of Lewis & Son, or accompanied the president of the firm on his journeys in search of old instruments.

His son, Carl F. Becker (*b* Chicago, 16 Dec 1919), inherited his father's great ability, and worked with him from 1936. Between them they developed the art of violin restoration to a high level, introducing a number of important innovations and technical improvements. Carl F. Becker's particular speciality is varnish restoration. From 1948 to 1967 new instruments (nos.489–726) were produced by father and son in Wisconsin in association with Lewis & Son. By 1968 the Beckers' rare understanding of their craft and their perfectionism had become incompatible with the increasing pace of big business, and they left Lewis & Son to work on their own account. Both new work (now over 750 instruments) and restoration continue to the same very high standard. In the years before the elder Becker's death they each made a few instruments individually. Carl F. Becker continued to make violins into his 90s.

Carl F. Becker's children have also become violin makers and restorers. Jennifer Becker-Glows Brightly (*b* Chicago, 14 Aug 1955), his daughter, began working with her father at the age of 11, finishing her first violin in 1970. She began to work full time at the age of 16. Following her first marriage she moved to Minneapolis in 1978, maintaining her association with the family business; in 1986 she opened her own shop in that city, which in recent years was moved to Lakeville, Minnesota. Her brother Paul Becker (*b* Chicago, 21 Dec 1958) began making violins in 1974, working full time after 1976. He later opened his own business in cabinet making, in which he also excelled, pursuing this craft from 1988 to 1992 while simultaneously working in the family business. He returned to the family business in that year where he has been active as a violin maker. The firm has since opened an affiliate office in Taipei, Taiwan, and in 2010 moved their workshop and showroom from Belmont Street to Adams Street in downtown Chicago.

CHARLES BEARE/PHILIP J. KASS

Becker, Dan (*b* Cleveland, OH, 1 May 1960). Composer. Becker, whose grandfather was a professional big band trumpeter, grew up in Los Angeles with his father from age six. He played clarinet and saxophone at ten, and became a classical and music theater enthusiast. Becker studied at the University of California at San Diego, and California State University, Northridge, and became familiar with the music of Béla Bartók and Joseph Schwantner. He received a BM from San Francisco Conservatory, where his principal teacher was ELINOR ARMER. At an artistic crossroad, Becker turned his focus towards concert music. He earned three degrees (MM, MMA, and DMA) in Composition from Yale University, where his teachers included Poul Ruders, JACOB DRUCKMAN, and MARTIN BRESNICK, and subsequently studied with Louis Andriessen and TERRY RILEY. Becker met his future wife, composer BELINDA REYNOLDS, at the festival June in Buffalo, and the two founded, with four other Yale composers and one each from Harvard University and Columbia University, the Common Sense Composers' Collective, for which Becker has served as Artistic Director. The group has continued with its original members as a San Francisco/New York-based consortium that has collaborated with such organizations as American Baroque, the Dogs of Desire, Meridian Arts, New Millennium, and Twisted Tutu—recording three CDs of their projects, available on CRI, Santa Fe New Music, and Albany. After returning to San Francisco with Reynolds, the two produced five OPUS415 Bay Area New Music Marathons, the final two presented by Charles Amirkhanian's Other Minds organization. Becker has received awards and grants from the American Academy of Arts and Letters (2001), Meet the Composer (2002 and 2008), the Mary Flagler Cary Charitable Trust (2003), the America Composers Forum (2004), American Music Center (2006), and Live Music for Dance (2006). His music—energetic, rhythmic, and always expertly crafted—has been performed across the United States, including at the Norfolk Summer Festival, Chicago Arts Series, the Other Minds Festival, Bang on a Can Summer Festival, and many others. He served on the board of directors of the American Music Center from 2001 to 2009 and has served as Chairman of the Composition Department at San Francisco Conservatory.

WORKS

Orch: Perchance to Dream, 1988; Fanfare, 1991; Steve & Jerry, 1997; Ragged Time, 1999; UpRising, 1999

Mixed ens: Don't Make Me Go Back To LA, kbd, elec b, 1992; Freeze Dried Music, 2 sax, tpt, trbn, 1992; Gridlock, 10 instr,1994; S.T.I.C., fl, cl, vn, vc, pf, 1995; Tamper Resistant, Baroque fl, ob, vn, va da gamba, hpd, 1996; Droned, brass qnt, perc, 1998; Gravity Planet, nar, fl, cl, vn, vc, pf, 2001; Dream of Waking, vn, pf, 2003; Fade, fl, vib, vc, pf, 2003; Rates of Exchange, fl, sheng, bn, 2005; Keeping Time, vn, vc, b cl, pf, vib, 2008; Better Late, 2 b cl, 2008

Str qt: Points, Lines, and Planes, 1989; Vanishing Point, 2002; Time Rising, 2009; Lockdown, 2010

Pf: Point of Balance, 1988

Electroacoustic: 5 Re-Inventions, disklavier, 1993; HappyKat Eclipse, elecs, kbds, 1997

MARK ALBURGER

Becker, John J(oseph) (*b* Henderson, KY, 22 Jan 1886; *d* Wilmette, IL, 21 Jan 1961). Composer. He belongs, together with Ives, Ruggles, Cowell, and Riegger, to the group named the "American Five" of avant-garde music. Over several decades he served as the group's militant crusader for new music in the American Midwest, seeking to establish a national music with experimental tendencies drawn from the American experience rather than from Europe.

Becker graduated from the Cincinnati Conservatory in 1905 and received the doctorate in composition from the Wisconsin Conservatory in 1923. His principal teachers were Alexander von Fielitz, CARL BUSCH, and the noted contrapuntist WILHELM MIDDELSCHULTE. He taught the piano and theory at the North Texas College Kidd-Key Conservatory in Sherman, Texas, from 1906 until about 1914, an otherwise obscure period in his life. In 1917 he began a long career of teaching and administration in Midwestern Catholic institutions, among them the University of Notre Dame (1917–27), the College of St. Thomas, St. Paul, Minnesota (1929–33), and Barat College, Lake Forest, Illinois (1943–57). After meeting Cowell in 1928, he became an energetic member of the newly organized Pan American Association of Composers. In addition to lecturing and writing (his writings include articles on 20th-century composers, the aesthetics of music, and music education), he conducted Midwestern premieres of works by Ives, Ruggles, and Riegger in the early 1930s. His warm friendship with Ives, documented in a remarkable correspondence between the two men (1931–54), resulted in his orchestration of Ives's *General William Booth Enters into Heaven* for baritone, male chorus, and small orchestra (1934). From 1935 to 1941 he was the controversial director of the Federal Music Project in Minnesota and was associate editor of the *New Music Quarterly*. A devout Catholic, he was chosen as the American musical representative to the First International Congress of Catholic Artists in Rome in 1950. His musical activity slackened somewhat in his later years because of declining health and the continual neglect of his music.

Becker's early symphonies and songs reveal the influence of German Romanticism and, to a lesser extent, French Impressionism. In the late 1920s his musical style underwent a radical change, leading to the highly dissonant yet lyrical *Symphonia brevis* of 1929. His creativity culminated in the 1930s in such works as *Abongo*, the Horn Concerto, *Concertino pastorale*, and a unique series of "Soundpieces," abstract chamber works of diversified instrumentation. His most significant contributions were large-scale stage works fusing dance, color, mime, stage design, and music into shapes prophetic of "mixed-media" theater. He considered his masterpiece to be his Stagework no.3: *A Marriage with Space* (1935), written in collaboration with the Chicago poet Mark Turbyfill. Becker favored such contrapuntal forms and procedures as chorale, fugue, and canon and preferred a dissonant, atonal counterpoint reminiscent of 16th-century polyphony in its even flow. His music employs rhythmic polytonal patterns and large chordal outbursts featuring overtones calculated to blend with and transform the basic sonority. An unusually clear orchestration is characterized by strongly contrasting colors and much use of percussion. The swift change of moods, from violent to darkly tragic, is most clearly revealed in the brilliant Violin Concerto (1948), Becker's last completed orchestral composition. His work, although occasionally gentle and serene, is frequently satirical and forcefully expressive of social protest. At a time when neo-classicism and a return to folk sources dominated American music, Becker insisted on the responsibility of the composer to "add new resources, evolve new techniques, develop new sound patterns."

WORKS

(unpubd unless otherwise stated; list excludes most lost and unfinished works; for details see GroveA)

STAGE

The Season of Pan (ballet suite), small ens, *c*1910; Dance Figure: Stagework no.1 (ballet, E. Pound), S, orch, 1932 [incl. music from unfinished cinema op Salome]; Abongo, a Primitive Dance: Stagework no.2 (ballet), wordless vv, 29 perc, 1933, pubd, New York, 16 May 1963; A Marriage with Space: Stagework no.3 (ballet, after M. Turbyfill), speaking chorus, orch, 1935, pubd [incl. music from Sym. no.3], arr. as Sym. no.4 "Dramatic Episodes," 1940; Nostalgic Songs of Earth (ballet), pf, 1938, Northfield, MN, 12 Dec 1938; Vigilante 1938 (ballet), pf, perc, 1938, Northfield, MN, 12 Dec 1938; Privilege and Privation: Stagework no.5c (op, 1, A. Kreymborg), 1939, pubd, Amsterdam, 22 June 1982; Rain down Death: Stagework no.5a (incid music, Kreymborg), chbr orch, 1939, earlier orch version, A Prelude to Shakespeare, 1937, rev. as Orch Suite no.1, 1939; When the Willow Nods: Stagework no.5b (incid music, Kreymborg), spkr, chbr orch, 1940 [incl. music from 4 Dances, pf, and Nostalgic Songs of Earth], rev. as Orch Suite no.2, 1940, pubd; Antigone (incid music, Sophocles), orch, 1940–44; Deirdre: Stagework no.6 (op, 1, Becker, after J.M. Synge), 1945, unorchd; Julius Caesar (film score, W. Shakespeare), brass, perc, 1949; Faust (TV op, J.W. von Goethe, trans. B. Taylor), T, pf, 1951, pubd, Los Angeles, 8 April 1985; Madeleine et Judas (incid music, R.L. Bruckberger), orch, 1958, Paris radio broadcast, 25 March 1959

ORCHESTRAL

A Tartar Song, *c*1912; 2 Orch Sketches (Cossack Sketches), 1912, 2nd movt arr. of The Mountains; Sym. no.1 "Etude primitive," 1912, last movt arr. as Sym. Movt "Americana," pf, *c*1912 arr. as Sonate American, vn, pf, *c*1925; Sym. no.2 "Fantasia tragica," 1920, lost, rev. *c*1937 [incl. music from Pf Sonata]; Sym. no.3 "Symphonia brevis," 1929, arr. pf, 1929, both pubd

Conc. arabesque, pf, 12 insts/small orch, 1930, pubd; Concertino pastorale: a Forest Rhapsodie, 2 fl, orch, 1933; Hn Conc., 1933, pubd; Mockery, scherzo, pf, dance orch, 1933; A Prelude to Shakespeare, 1937 [arr. of pt of Rain down Death]; Va Conc., 1937; Pf Conc. no.2 "Satirico," 1938 [incl. music from Mockery]; Orch Suite no.1, 1939 [from incid music from Rain down Death]; Orch Suite no.2, 1940, pubd [from incid music from When the Willow Nods]; Sym. no.5 "Homage to Mozart," 1942; Victory March, 1942 [from Sym. no.6]; The Snow Goose: a Legend of the Second World War, after P. Gallico, 1944; Vn Conc., 1948, pubd

Orch of Ives: General William Booth Enters into Heaven, B, male vv, chbr orch, 1934–5, pubd

For Sym. no.4 see under STAGE, for syms. nos.6–7 see under CHORAL

CHORAL

Rouge bouquet (J. Kilmer), T, male vv, tpt, pf, 1917; Jesu dulcis memoria (offertory), male vv, org ad lib, 1919; Martin of Tours (C.L. O'Donnell), T/B, male vv, org, pf, 1919; The Pool (H. Doolittle), 1923, arr. female vv, pf, *c*1947; Out of the Cradle Endlessly Rocking (cant., W. Whitman), spkr, S, T, chorus, orch, 1929

Missa symphonica, male vv, 1933; Pater noster, unacc., 1935; Sym. no.6 "Out of Bondage" (A. Kreymborg, A. Lincoln), spkr, chorus, orch, 1942; Mass in Honor of the Sacred Heart, 3 equal vv, 1943; A Little Easter Cycle (J.B. Tabb), S, female vv, 1944; Mater admirabilis (offertory), female vv, 1944; Song of the Cedar Tree (anon.), female vv/ (unison chorus, pf), 1944

Moments from the Passion (cant., Goday, trans. McLaren), solo vv, chorus, org, 1945, pubd; Nunc sancte nobis spiritus (St Ambrose), *c*1945; Morning Song (H.P. Horne), double chorus, 1946; Tantum ergo, female vv, 1946; Unison Mass in Honor of St. Madeleine Sophie Barat, female vv, pf, 1946; Ecce sacerdos, female vv, 1947

O domina mea, female vv, 1947; The Seven Last Words, female vv/male vv, 1947; Moments from the Liturgical Year (G. von Le Fort, trans. M. Chanler), spkr, speaking chorus, 1v, chorus of 3 equal vv, 1948; Mass in Honor of St Viator (unison chorus, org)/2vv, 1949; Sym. no.7 (Becker, Bible: *Beatitudes*, Dante), speaking chorus, female vv, orch, 1954, unfinished

CHAMBER

Pf Sonata "The Modern Man I Sing," *c*1910; The Mountains, pf, *c*1912; 2 Architectural Impressions, pf, 1924; My Little Son, 18 Months Old: Studies in Child Psychology, pf, 1924; 2 Chinese Miniatures, pf, 1925, pubd [arr. R.F. Kraner, orch, 1928]; Soundpiece [no.1], pf, str qt, 1932, arr. as no.1a, pf, str qnt, 1935; arr. as no.1b, pf, str, 1935; Soundpiece no.2a "Homage to Haydn": Str Qt no.1, 1936, arr. as no.2b, str, 1936, both pubd, Soundpiece no.3: Vn Sonata, 1936, pubd; Soundpiece no.4: Str Qt no.2, 1937, pubd; Soundpiece no.5: Pf Sonata, 1937, pubd; 4 Dances, pf, 1938; Soundpiece no.6: Sonata, fl, cl, 1942, pubd; Soundpiece no.7, 2 pf, 1949; Soundpiece no.8: Str Qt no.3, 1959, unfinished; Improvisation, org, 1960; kbd arrs. of orch works, incl. Fantasia tragica, org, 1920, pubd

SONGS

(for solo voice and piano)

John Becker's Songbook (A. Austin, F. Stanton, A. Upson, M.F. Robinson, H. Heine), 1907–9; 2 Simple Songs (H.A. Waithman, M. O'Neil), *c*1917; 4 Songs (C. Doris, J. Keats, P.B. Shelley, H. Cook), 1918–20, nos.2–3 arr. S, str qt, 1919; Little Sleeper (Hāfiz, trans. P. le Gallienne), S , str qt, 1919; 2 Songs (G. O'Neil), 1921; 2 Songs (C.P. Baudelaire, trans. Symons, G.B. Hallowell), 1923; 2 Songs from H.D., 1923; 2 Songs (J. Joyce, E.W. McCourt), 1923; A Heine Songs Cycle (Heine, trans. J. Thompson), 1924–5; 2 Poem of Departure (Rihaku, trans. E. Pound), 1927; 4 Songs from the Japanese (Matsuo Bashō, trans. C.H. Page), 1933; The Lark (Schubert) (A. Kreymborg), 1934; Psalms of Love (P. Baum, trans. J. Bitchell), 1935; 3 Songs to Poems by Mary Cecilia Becker, 1935; The Stars about the Lovely Moon (Sappho, trans. E. Arnold), 1943; At Dieppe (A. Symons), 1959

MSS in *NYp*

Principal publishers: Peters, Presser

BIBLIOGRAPHY

GroveA (D.C. Gillespie) [incl. further bibliography]

H. Cowell: "John Becker," *American Composers on American Music* (Stanford, CA, 1933/*R*1962), 82–4

E.M. Becker: *John J. Becker: American Composer* (MS, *Wc*, 1958)
W. Riegger: "John J. Becker," *American Composers Alliance Bulletin*, ix/1 (1959), 2–7
D.C. Gillespie: *John Becker: Midwestern Musical Crusader* (diss., U. of North Carolina, 1977)
D.C. Gillespie: "John Becker's Correspondence with Ezra Pound: the Origins of a Musical Crusader," *Bulletin of Research in the Humanities*, lxxxiii (1980), 163–71
K. Gann: "The Percussion Music of John J. Becker," *Percussive Notes*, xxii/3 (1984), 26–41
L. Crawford: *Harmonic and Melodic Organization in the Later Works of John J. Becker* (diss., Catholic U. of America, 1988)

DON C. GILLESPIE

Beddoe, Dan (*b* Aberaman, Wales, 16 March 1863; *d* New York, NY, 26 Dec 1937). Welsh tenor. Though he won an Eisteddfod gold medal when only 19, his career as a singer made little headway until 1903. He had immigrated to the United States, living in Pittsburgh and Cleveland, where he worked in a steel factory and sang with choirs and in oratorio. He had a remarkable voice, however, and attracted the attention of Walter Damrosch in New York. He was engaged first to sing the solo part in Berlioz's Requiem as part of the centenary celebrations of 1903, and was then heard in a concert performance of *Parsifal*. Many important occasions followed, such as the New York premiere of Strauss's *Taillefer*, some of the first performances in the United States of Mahler's *Das Lied von der Erde*, and a performance of Beethoven's Ninth Symphony with Mahler himself conducting. The Cincinnati Festival heard him first in 1910 and for the last time in 1927. He continued to sing with a wonderfully well-preserved voice as late as 1934 when he was tenor soloist in *Messiah* at New York. He never sang on the operatic stage, but concert versions of *Die Meistersinger*, *Aida*, and *Samson et Dalila* were in his repertory. He returned occasionally to England and Wales, his last concerts there being given in 1924. He died after an automobile accident in 1937. His highly prized recordings include some made in 1928 when, at the age of 65, the beauty, evenness, and power of his voice seem scarcely to have diminished. Peculiarities of pronunciation and sometimes a shortness of breath prevent his earlier recordings from being completely acceptable as models of their kind, but they make quite credible the story that Caruso himself once attended one of Beddoe's concerts to learn from his art.

J.B. STEANE/R

Bedient, Gene R. (*b* Alliance, NE, 23 Aug 1944). Organ builder. After graduating from the University of Nebraska, he apprenticed with Charles McManis of Kansas City, and in 1969 established his own firm in Lincoln, Nebraska. In 1971 he received his master's degree from University of Nebraska. Bedient's organs usually have mechanical key action, are tonally influenced by historic north German and French models, and are often tuned in unequal temperaments. In addition to larger custom-designed organs, Bedient has also developed a series of instruments for small churches and home practice. Some representative organs include those for Ripon College, Ripon, Wisconsin (1984), St. Mark's Episcopal Church, Grand Rapids, Michigan (1985), Queens College, Flushing, New York (1991), and First Congregational Church, Sioux Falls, South Dakota (2008).

BIBLIOGRAPHY

U. Pape: *The Tracker Organ Revival in America* (Berlin, 1977)
M. Beech and C. Cramer: "Bedient Company Celebrates 20 Years," *The American Organist*, xxiv/4 (April 1990)
L. Edwards, ed.: *The Historical Organ in America* (Hadley, MA, 1992)
B. Jones: "The Organs of Gene Bedient," *Choir and Organ* (June/July 1995)

BARBARA OWEN

Bee, Tom (*b* Gallup, NM, 8 Nov 1947). Native American (Dakota) producer, vocalist, songwriter, and record label owner. During the 1970s and 80s he was founder, manager, and featured artist with XIT, the first commercially successful Native American rock band. Although his albums and performances were highly successful in Europe and among young Native Americans, the political nature of Bee's lyrics prevented the group from achieving star status among mainstream audiences in the United States. Songs from albums such as *Plight of the Redman* (1972) and *Silent Warrior* (1973) presented the Native viewpoint about social and political issues using a combination of traditional chant and languages and Western rock. This early work led to an artist, writer, and producer contract with Motown Record's Rare Earth label for Bee, where he wrote for artists including the Jackson Five, Michael Jackson, and Smokey Robinson as well as XIT. In 1989 Bee formed Sound of America Records (SOAR), which specializes in traditional and contemporary Native American music; he later expanded SOAR, adding a distribution company that served other independent labels and artists that produced Native music. In addition to releasing a solo album, *Color me Red*, in 1994, Bee has narrated and produced several audio books written by author Paul Goble. Bee has received many awards, including the Eagle Spirit in 1994 from the American Film Institute and the Will Sampson Award in 1996 from the First Americans in the Arts. In 1998 Bee received the Producer of the Year Award from the First Annual Native American Music Awards (NAMMY's). The following year he received the NAMMY's Lifetime Achievement Award (1999). Bee received a Grammy as Producer for Best Native American Music Album in 2001 and 2004.

BIBLIOGRAPHY

B. Burton: *Moving Within the Circle: Contemporary Native American Music and Dance* (Danbury, CT, 2/2008), 118–21
Sound of America Records <http://www.soundofamerica.com>

J. BRYAN BURTON

Beecham, Sir Thomas (*b* St Helens, Lancashire, England, 29 April 1879; *d* London, England, 8 March 1961). English conductor and impresario. He was educated at Rossall School and Wadham College, Oxford. He was mostly self-taught as a conductor and founded the New SO in 1910. With the backing of his father, the industrialist Sir Joseph Beecham, he mounted opera seasons at Covent Garden and other houses, and founded the Beecham SO in 1909, the Beecham Opera Company in

1915, and the London PO in 1932. After World War II began, he left in the spring of 1940 to tour Australia and then came to the United States, where he became the music director of the Seattle SO (1941–3). His volatile and domineering personality caused him to spar with the audience, music critics, and Seattle in general, which he labeled a cultural "dustbin," a viewpoint that he never relinquished, even when he returned to conduct concerts in 1960. Overall, though, his concerts often sold out and he left the organization in the black. Some recordings from the 1943 season, taken from broadcasts, have been re-mastered and made available on CD. In 1942 he joined the Metropolitan Opera as joint senior conductor with his former assistant Bruno Walter. He began with his own adaptation of Johann Sebastian Bach's comic cantata *Phoebus and Pan*, followed by *Le Coq d'Or*. His main repertoire during his time at the Met (1942–4) was French: *Carmen*, *Louise* (with Grace Moore), *Manon*, *Faust*, *Mignon*, and *The Tales of Hoffmann*, but he also conducted other operas such as *Falstaff* and *Tristan und Isolde* (with Lauritz Melchior and Helen Traubel). In addition to his Seattle and New York posts, Beecham guest-conducted 18 American orchestras.

BIBLIOGRAPHY

Grove7 (R. Crichton and J. Lucas)

N. Cardus: *Sir Thomas Beecham: a Memoir* (London, 1961)

C. Reid: *Beecham: an Independent Biography* (London, 1961)

J.D. Gilmore, ed.: *Sir Thomas Beecham: the Seattle Years, 1941–1943* (Aberdeen, WA, 1978)

J.D. Gilmore, ed.: *Sir Thomas Beecham: the North American Tour, 1950* (Ocean Shores, WA, 1979)

A. Blackwood: *Sir Thomas Beecham: the Man and the Music* (London, 1994)

J. Lucas: *Thomas Beecham: an Obsession with Music* (Woodbridge, Suffolk, 2008)

JAMES BASH

Beecher. Family of clergymen, authors, and reformers active in the 19th century. Lyman Beecher (1775–1863), a Presbyterian minister and renowned evangelical leader, was a strong advocate of reform in church music and congregational singing. He was pastor of the Hanover Street Church, Boston, where he helped Lowell Mason in his career as a musical reformer; Mason served as Beecher's music director from 1827 to 1832. Beecher then moved to Cincinnati, where his music director was Mason's brother Timothy. Three of Beecher's 13 children were of importance in the development of American hymnody. Henry Ward Beecher (1813–87), who was pastor of Plymouth Church, Brooklyn, from 1847, edited the *Plymouth Collection* (New York, 1851, 2/1855), an influential hymnal which included two hymns by his brother Charles Beecher (1815–1900), also a minister and one of the music editors for the hymnal (*see* HYMNODY). Their sister Harriet Beecher Stowe (1811–96), who wrote the novel *Uncle Tom's Cabin* (1855), contributed three hymns to the collection, and published other hymns in her *Religious Poems* (1867). Her most popular hymn text, "Knock, knocking, who is there," was adapted and set to music by G.F. Root; it became widely sung as a gospel song after its inclusion by Sankey and Bliss in their first collection, *Gospel Hymns and Sacred Songs* (1875).

BIBLIOGRAPHY

J. Julian, ed.: *A Dictionary of Hymnology* (New York, 1892, 2/1907/*R*)

L.F. Benson: *The English Hymn* (New York, 1915/*R*), 473

PAUL C. ECHOLS

Bee Gees, the. Australian pop group formed by Barry (*b* Douglas, Isle of Man, 1 Sept 1946), Robin (*b* Douglas, Isle of Man, 22 Dec 1949; *d* London, England, 20 May 2012), and Maurice Gibb (*b* Douglas, Isle of Man, 22 Dec 1949; *d* Miami Beach, FL, 12 Jan 2003). They were raised in Manchester, England, until 1958, when the family moved to Brisbane, Australia, where the brothers formed a trio called the Rattlesnakes. They soon began writing their own music, often composed by Barry, and attracting media attention. In 1963 the group signed a deal to record singles as the Bee Gees with Festival Records and two years later released their first album. After moving to Polydor Records, they released two songs, "New York Mining Disaster 1941" and "To Love Somebody," which became hit singles. Both were included on the album *Bee Gees 1st* (Polydor, 1967), which found an international audience. In the late 1960s the group had a string of hits, mostly ballads, but it took another decade for them to achieve superstar status. After moving to a disco-influenced style and working with new producers, their popularity exploded with the release in 1977 of the soundtrack (Polydor) to the film *Saturday Night Fever*. Three of its singles, "How Deep Is your Love," "Stayin' Alive," and "Night Fever," all reached number one and the double-album, which included many songs written by the Gibbs and performed by other artists, stayed at the top of the charts for 25 weeks in 1978. The following album, *Spirits Having Flown* (WB, 1979), included three more number one hit singles. Although their popularity evaporated with the decline of disco, the Bee Gees defined the sound of a brief period. Although the band continued to perform and record into the 21st century, they never enjoyed another phase of widespread success. In 2009 Barry and Robin emerged from a hiatus to perform again following Maurice's death in 2003.

BIBLIOGRAPHY

M. Bilyeu, H. Cook, and A.M. Hughes: *The Bee Gees: Tales of the Brothers Gibb* (London, 2000, 2/2003)

JONAS WESTOVER

Beeson, Jack (Hamilton) (*b* Muncie, IN, 15 July 1921). Composer and teacher. He attended the Eastman School (BM 1942, MM 1943) as a pupil of BURRILL PHILLIPS, BERNARD ROGERS, and HOWARD HANSON, and had private lessons with BÉLA BARTÓK in New York (1944–5). From 1945 to 1948 he did graduate work in conducting and musicology at Columbia University, where he was an accompanist and conductor for the opera workshop; this apprenticeship strengthened the leaning towards opera which he had had from childhood. In 1945 he began to teach at Columbia, becoming MacDowell

Professor of Music in 1967 and serving as chairman of the music department (1968–72); meanwhile he also taught at the Juilliard School (1961–3) and lectured at various universities in the United States. Among the awards he has received are a Rome Prize, a Fulbright Fellowship, a Guggenheim Fellowship, the Marc Blitzstein Award for the Musical Theater, and the Gold Medal of the National Arts Club. He has held office in many music organizations, including the AMC, the American Composers Forum, the American Academy of Arts and Letters, and ASCAP.

Beeson's operas may be considered to continue some of the qualities of those of Douglas Moore, one of his predecessors at Columbia. Though his style is of a later generation, it shares with Moore's a feeling for lyrical line, occasionally suggesting an American folk idiom; and Beeson, like Moore, has shaped successful opera subjects from American life and literature. In *Captain Jinks of the Horse Marines* (1975) he exploits the period charm of traditional operatic forms, as he did earlier with that of evangelical hymns and flapper dances in *The Sweet Bye and Bye* (1956). Beeson borrows from a variety of sources (popular songs, European Expressionism, folksong and dance, jazz, and Italian opera) to enrich the musical dramatic background; any theatrical work that lasts for two hours, Beeson has said, should have a range of styles (Johns). Beeson's symphonic music is notable for its expert orchestration and effective use of polyphony.

WORKS

(all published unless otherwise stated)

OPERAS

Jonah (2 or 3, Beeson, after P. Goodman), 1950

Hello out There (chbr op, 1, Beeson, after W. Saroyan), 1954, New York, Brander Matthews, 27 May 1954

The Sweet Bye and Bye (2, K. Elmslie), 1956, New York, Juilliard Concert Hall, 21 Nov 1957

Lizzie Borden (family portrait, 3, Elmslie), 1965, New York, City Center of Music and Drama, 25 March 1965

My Heart's in the Highlands (chbr op, 2 or 3, Beeson, after Saroyan), 1969; NET, 17 March 1970

Captain Jinks of the Horse Marines (romantic comedy, 3, S. Harnick, after C. Fitch), 1975, Kansas City, Lyric, 20 Sept 1975

Dr. Heidegger's Fountain of Youth (chbr op, 1, Harnick, after N. Hawthorne), 1978, New York, National Arts Club, 17 Nov 1978

Cyrano (heroic comedy, 3, Harnick, after E. Rostand), 1990, Hagen, 10 Sept 1994

Sorry, Wrong Number (chbr op, 1, Beeson, after L. Fletcher), 1996, New York, Kaye Playhouse, 25 May 1999

Practice in the Art of Elocution (chbr operina, 1, Beeson), 1998, New York, Merkin Hall, 12 May 1998

CHORAL

A Round for Christmas (Bible: *John*), chorus, 1942, rev. 1951; Boys and Girls Together (anon.), chorus, 1965; Greener Pastures (anon.), chorus, 1965; Homer's Woe (anon. nursery rhymes), Tr vv, 1966; In Praise of the Bloomers (anon., from *Mrs. Partington's Carpetbag of Fun*), male chorus, 1969; To a Lady Who Asked for a Cypher (anon., from *Mrs. Partington's Carpetbag of Fun*), chorus, 1969; Everyman's Handyman (Beeson, after E.W. Smith), male chorus, 1970; The Model Housekeeper (Smith), female chorus, 1970; Knots: Jack and Jill for Grown-ups (R.D. Laing), 1979; Hinx, Minx (trad. nursery rhyme), 1980; Magicke Pieces (R. Herrick and others), chorus, 3 wind, 2 bells, 1991; Epitaphs (anon.), 1993; Summer Rounds and Canons (anon.), chorus, 2002; other shorter choral pieces

SOLO VOCAL

4 Crazy Jane Songs (W.B. Yeats), A, pf, 1944, rev. 1959, 1992; 3 Songs (W. Blake), T, pf, 1945, rev. 1951, 1995; 5 Songs (F. Quarles), S, pf, 1946, rev. 1950; Piazza Piece (J.C. Ransom), S, T, pf, 1951; 2 Songs (J. Betjeman), Bar, pf, 1952; 6 Lyrics (Eng. and Amer. poets), high v, pf, 1952, rev. 1959, 1995; 2 Concert Arias, S, orch: The Elephant (D.H. Lawrence), 1953, The Hippopotamus (T.S. Eliot), orig. for S, pf, 1951, rev. and orchd, 1952, 1995; Indiana Homecoming (A. Lincoln), Bar, pf, 1956; Leda (A. Huxley), spkr, pf, 1957, rev. 1995; Against Idleness and Mischief and In Praise of Labor (I. Watts), high v, pf, 1959

A Creole Mystery (Beeson, after L. Hearn), Mez/Bar, str qt, 1970; To a Sinister Potato (P. Viereck), Bar, pf, 1970; The Day's no Rounder than its Angles Are (Viereck), Mez/Bar, str qt, 1971; Death by Owl-Eyes (R. Hughes), high v, pf, 1971; The You Should Have Done It Blues (Viereck), S, pf, 1971; From a Watchtower (W. Wordsworth, W.H. Auden, G.M. Hopkins, W. de la Mare), 5 songs, high v, pf, 1976; Cat (J. Keats), S, pf, 1979; Cowboy Song (C. Causley), Bar, pf, 1979; In the Public Gardens (J. Betjeman), T, pf, 1991; Inerludes and Arias from Cyrano, Bar, orch, 1997; The Daring Young Man on the Flying Trapeze (G. Leybourne and Beeson), Ct, chbr orch/pf, 1999; Ophelia Sings, Mez, ens, 2000; A Rupert Brooke Cycle (5 song cycle, R. Brooke, Beeson), B-Bar, pf, 2002; other songs

INSTRUMENTAL

Orch: Hymns and Dances, 1958 [from The Sweet Bye and Bye], arr. band, 1966; Sym. no.1, A, 1959; Transformations, 1959; Commemoration, band, chorus ad lib, 1960; Fanfare, brass, wind, perc, 1963

Chbr and solo inst: Song, fl, pf, 1945; Interlude, vn, pf, 1945, rev. 1951; Pf Sonata no.4, 1945, rev. 1951; Pf Sonata no.5, 1946, rev. 1951; Sonata, va, pf, 1953; 2 Diversions, pf, 1953, rev. of Pf Sonata no.3, 1944; Sketches in Black and White, pf, 1958; Round and Round, pf 4 hands, 1959; Sonata canonica, 2 a rec, 1966; 2 Pieces, ens, 1967 [for film, radio or TV]; Old Hundredth: Prelude and Doxology, org, 1972; Fantasy, Ditty and Fughettas, 2 Baroque/modern fl, 1992

45 works written before 1950

Principal publishers: Boosey & Hawkes, Presser

WRITINGS

"The Autobiography of Lizzie Borden," *OQ*, iv/1 (1986–7), 15–42

How Operas Are Created by Composers and Librettists: the Life of Jack Beeson, American Opera Composer (Lewiston, NY, 2008)

BIBLIOGRAPHY

Q. Eaton: *Opera Production: a Handbook* (St. Paul, MN, 1961–74) [entries on Hello out There, The Sweet Bye and Bye, Lizzie Borden, and My Heart's in the Highlands]

D. Johns: "Connections: an Interview with Jack Beeson," *MEJ*, lxvi/2 (1979–80), 44–9

HOWARD SHANET/R

Begian, Harry (*b* Pontiac, MI, 24 April 1921; *d* Alpena, MI, 26 July 2010). Conductor and music educator. The son of Armenian immigrants, his childhood was spent in Dearborn, Michigan. As a youth, he often observed conductors, such as Fritz Reiner and Serge Koussevitzky, rehearse the Detroit SO; by the time he was a senior in high school he was studying privately with the symphony's principal trumpet player, Leonard B. Smith. After studies at Wayne State University (BME 1943), Begian began teaching at Mackenzie HS in Detroit, then was drafted into the army. He returned to Wayne State after the war (MS 1947) and studied conducting at Tanglewood. He developed one of the finest high school bands in the country at Detroit's Cass Technical High School (1947–64) while studying with William Revelli at the University of Michigan (EdD 1964). His university band conducting career included appointments at Wayne State (1964), Michigan State

(1967) and the University of Illinois (1970–84), where he greatly expanded the band program and instituted a prestigious conducting internship program. During retirement, he conducted at Purdue University (1985–7) and made numerous guest-conducting appearances, including with the Detroit SO and Interlochen Center for Arts. He was widely regarded for his published articles on rehearsal and analysis.

DISCOGRAPHY

University of Illinois Symphonic Band: 43 recordings (1970–84). (UI 60–122; CD 1001–20]; *The Music of Karl King* (Golden Crest CRS 4096); [n.d.]. *A Salute to Henry Fillmore* (Golden Crest CRS 4112) [n.d.].

Cass Technical High School: 25 recordings in the Harry Begian Collection, *Wc* (1954–64)

BIBLIOGRAPHY
(and other resources)

C.L. Wallace: *The Life and Work of Harry Begian* (diss., Southern Baptist Theological Seminary, 1994)

A. LaBounty: "An Interview with Dr. Harry Begian: Special Remembrances and Candid Observations," *National Band Association Journal*, xlviii/3 (2008), 34–43

Master Conductors: Reflections on Life and the Podium: Dr. Harry Begian, DVD, dir. T. Lautzenheiser, interviewer, DVD-801 (GIA Publications, Chicago, 2009)

J.P. Nichols: "Michigan Musical Legends: Dr. Harry Begian," *Band Director* <http://www.banddirector.com/article/rl-history/feature0001> (n.d.)

JON CEANDER MITCHELL

Beglarian, Eve (Louise) (*b* Ann Arbor, MI, 22 July 1958). Composer. The daughter of the composer GRANT BEGLARIAN, she studied at Princeton University (BA 1980) and Columbia University (MA 1983), and was trained in intricate serial techniques by MILTON BABBITT and FRED LERDAHL. At Columbia, however, she came to view post-serialism as sterile and elitist and began to write pieces that incorporated rock elements and performance art. From 1991 on, she has had a strong presence in the downtown Manhattan scene, especially with the pianist Kathleen Supové, with whom she formed the electronic duo Twisted Tutu.

Beglarian's output is extremely diverse, including contrapuntal variations on medieval songs, computer-altered disco collages, post-minimal and numerically structured synthesizer pieces, songs of nonsense syllables, and electric theater pieces, notably *TypOpera*, based on Kurt Schwitters's *Ur Sonata*. Expert in sampling technology, she often uses noise samples in instrumental contexts; *FlamingO*, for example, combines chamber orchestra and samplers in such a way that the latter dominate, the orchestra emerging from an engulfing whirr of noise. In *Wonder-Counselor* for organ and tape, flurries of melody on the organ are laid over an ecstatic ebb and flow of a harmonic series and sampled accompaniment of ocean sounds, bird song, and a couple having orgasms. Feminist and uninhibited, Beglarian is not afraid to tackle subjects of sex, politics, and religion, though her music usually remains joyous and uplifting.

Beglarian's music is as often text-based as not, frequently collaborative, and it addresses issues of intercultural relations. Since 2001, many of her pieces have been part of a project titled *The Book of Days*, a series of 365 text-music-visual pieces for live and Internet performance. Starting in August, 2009, Beglarian took a ten-month pilgrimage down and up the Mississippi River, kayaking downstream and driving back, while collecting sound snippets, historical phenomena, and collaborators to inspire a set of new works about American identity.

WORKS
(selective list)

Inst: Making Hay, 2 pf, 1980; Quartettsatz, str qt, 1981; Music for Orch, 1981–2; 5 for Cl, 1982; Cl Qt, 1983; Spherical Music, 2 March 1985; Getting to Know the Weather, bar sax, 1986; Machaut in the Machine Age I, pf, perc, 1986, rev. fl, cl, vn, vc, pf, perc, 1990; Miranda's Kiss, pf, 1988; FlamingO, 3 chbr ens, 1995 (revised 2004); Play Nice, hp/toy pf, 1997; Elf Again, indeterminate ens, 1998; Atque Semper, fl, hn, gui, bs, pf, 2006; Night Psalm, pf, 2009

Inst with elecs: Uncle Wiggly, va, tape, 1980; Fresh Air, sax qt, tape, 1983; Michael's Spoon, 2 hn, tape, 1984; Making Sense of It, fl, cl, vn, vc, pf, perc, tape, 1987; Your Face Here, a sax, pf, vv, tape, 1988; Born Dancin', elec vc, drum machine, actor, 1989; Preciosilla, any single line inst, tape, 1990; Preciosilla (Margaret's Mix), fl, tape, 1992; Dive Maker, sampled perc, elecs, 1992; Machaut in the Machine Age II, b, MIDI perc, 1993; Wolf Chaser, vn, amp bowed cymbals, tape, 1995; Wonder Counselor, pipe org, elecs, 1996; Creating the World, vn, bn, gui, elec kbd, perc, drums, 1996; Boy Toy Toy Boy, 2 kbd, elecs, 1997; Father/Daughter Dance, accdn, elecs, 1998 ; The Continuous Life, orch, tape, 2000; Blazes, processed pf or gui, 2001; The Bus Driver Didn't Change His Mind, cl, gui, vc, cb, perc, pf, tape, 2002; All U Got 2 D0, org, electronics, 2003; Be/Hold, electronics, 2003; I Will Not Be Sad in This World, fl, electronics, 2006; Feed Forward, trom quartet, electronics, 2007; I'm Worried Now, but I Won't Be Worried Long, vn, electronics, 2010; Waiting for Billy Floyd, fl, cl, vn, vc, pf, perc, electronics, 2010; Early in the Morning, vn, gui, trom quartet, pf, electronics, 2010

Vocal: 3 Love Songs, Mez, cl, va, pf, 1981–2; Ps cxxxiii, SATB, 1983; Medea, 7 choral odes, 1985; Enough, S, pf, b, 1993; The Marriage of Heaven and Hell, 1v, fl, sax, ob, bn, va, db, pf, perc, 1994; Landscaping for Privacy, spkr, kbd, 1995; The Bacchae (incid music), male chorus, Chin. ens, 1996; My Feelings Now, 1v, pf, 1996; Non-Jew (E. Pound), 2 spkrs, 1998

Vocal with elecs: Overstepping, sampled vv, elecs, 1991; Machaut a Go Go, v, a sax, hn, trbn, elec gui, vc, elec b, hp, drums, 1991; YOursonate, 1v, perc, tape, 1993; typOpera, vv, elecs, 1994; No. You are Not Alone, vv, kbd, gui, b, drums, elecs, 1994; No Man's Land, 1v, amp hand drum, 2 elec kbd, 1995; Hildegurls, or The Play of the Virtues, 4vv, elecs, 1996; Written on the Body, 1v, kybds, elecs, 1999; Not Worth, 1v, 2 bs cl, va, vc, bs, 1999; Forgiveness, voices, pipa, piri, perc, elecs, 1998–2000; Just a Little More, 1v, 2 kybds, tape, 2000; Animal Magnetism, voices, vn, reeds, elecs, 1997–2000; All Ways, 1v, pf, 2001; Fireside, 1v, pf, 2001; Five Things, 1v, fl, bsn/bar sax, 2001; Lullaby, voices, pf, vib, 2002; Dust, 1v, elecs, 2003; The Story of B, voices, fl, kybds, bs, elecs, 2001–4 (with composer Phil Kline); I Am Writing to You from a Far-Off Country, 1v, vc, elecs, video, 2006; Making Hey, 1v, bs, pf, perc, 2006; It Happens Like This, 1v, vc, 2006; Osculati Furniture, 1v, prerecorded sitars, 2007; From Within and Outside a Bright Room, vv, perc, elecs, 2008; Machaut in the Machine Age VI: Liement Me Depart, chorus, harmonicas, 2009; I Am Really a Very Simple Person, mixed chorus, 2010; Kaimos, 1v, elecs, opt. vn, 2010

KYLE GANN

Beglarian, Grant (*b* Tbilisi, Georgia, 1 Dec 1927; *d* White Plains, NY, 5 July 2002). Music administrator and composer of Georgian birth. After immigrating to the United States in 1947, he studied composition with ROSS LEE FINNEY at the University of Michigan (BM 1950, MM 1951, DMA 1958). He then studied with AARON COPLAND at the Berkshire Music Center (1959–60), during which time he won the George Gershwin Memorial Award. In the course of his expansive career he was an editor at Prentice-Hall (1960–61), director of the Contemporary Music Project (1961–9), dean of the School of Performing Arts at the University of Southern California (1969–82), and president of the National Foundation for Advancement in the Arts (1982–91). An effective administrator, he explained that he "designed activities to demonstrate that the artist shapes cultural and social institutions." His compositional style reflects the influence of his principal teachers, Finney and Copland.

SELECTIVE WORKS

Violin Duets in Contemporary Style (1955); And All the Hills Echoed, Bar, chorus, timp, org (1968); A Hymn for Our Times, 3 bands (1969); Of Fables, Foibles, and Fancies, nar, vc (1971); Elegy, vc (1979); Partita, orch (1986)

BIBLIOGRAPHY

D.M. Bess: *A History of Comprehensive Musicianship in the Contemporary Music Project's Southern Division Institutes for Music in Contemporary Education* (diss., West Virginia U., 1988)

Contemporary Music Project Archives, Special Collections in Performing Arts, University of Maryland

KAREN MONSON/VINCENT J. NOVARA

Behrend, Jeanne (*b* Philadelphia, PA, 11 May 1911; *d* Philadelphia, 20 March 1988). Pianist and composer. She graduated from the Curtis Institute (1934), where she studied piano with JOSEF HOFMANN and composition with ROSARIO SCALERO. Recommended by Villa-Lobos, who called her a "heroine of the Americas," she was sponsored by the US State Department in a goodwill tour of South America in 1945–6. She founded and directed the Philadelphia Festival of Western Hemisphere Music (1959–60), which opened with her *Festival Fanfare: Prelude to the National Anthem*, performed by members of the Philadelphia Orchestra. Her other compositions include a string quartet, *Lamentation* for viola and piano, *Quiet Piece* and *Dance into Space* for piano, songs, and a cantata. She gave up composing in the late 1940s because she felt the opportunities for women in that field were too limited. She regularly performed as a pianist throughout the United States and in Latin America; in 1965 Behrend was awarded the Order of the Southern Cross from the Brazilian government for her services to Brazilian music. She taught piano at the Juilliard School, the Curtis Institute, and Western College (Oxford, Ohio), and gave courses in American music at Juilliard, the Philadelphia Conservatory, and Temple University. In 1969 she joined the piano faculty of the Philadelphia College of Performing Arts, and in 1974 instituted a course for adult beginners called "It Is Never Too Late!" She edited a selection of piano music by Gottschalk (1956) and songs by Foster (1964), Gottschalk's *Notes of a Pianist* (1964), and a volume of early American fuging tunes (1976). Behrend's first husband was pianist Alexander Kelberine, who died in 1940. Her papers and several of her manuscripts are held at the Free Library of Philadelphia.

BIBLIOGRAPHY

E.A. Hostetter: *Jeanne Behrend: Pioneer Performer of American Music, Pianist, Teacher, Musicologist, and Composer* (diss., Arizona State U., 1990)

JOHN G. DOYLE/JONAS WESTOVER

Behrman, David (*b* Salzburg, Austria, 16 Aug 1937). Composer of Austrian birth. The son of playwright S.N. Behrman and a nephew of Jascha Heifetz, he was brought up in New York, where he studied composition privately with WALLINGFORD RIEGGER. At Harvard University (BA 1959) he was a pupil of WALTER PISTON. He then went to Europe on a Paine Traveling Fellowship and studied with Henri Pousseur and Karlheinz Stockhausen. After returning to the United States he received an MA degree in music theory from Columbia University. He was from 1966 a member of the Sonic Arts Union, a cooperative of composers of electronic music, with which he toured extensively in the United States and Europe (1966–76). In the years 1965–70 he produced a notable series of recordings of experimental music ("Music of our Time" series) for Columbia Masterworks (including Terry Riley's *In C*). From 1970 to 1976 (and sporadically thereafter) he worked with John Cage, David Tudor, and Gordon Mumma for the Merce Cunningham Dance Company. Since 2004 Behrman has been a member, with Christian Wolff, John King, and Stephan Moore, of the Cunningham Company's Music Direction Committee. He has been artist-in-residence at several universities: Mills College (visiting professor, 1999), Oakland, California, where he served as co-director of the Center for Contemporary Music (1975–1980); Cal Arts, Rutgers University, Bard College, Ohio State University, Technical University in Berlin; member of the faculty, Milton Avery Graduate Arts Program at Bard College since 1998.

Other residencies have included the KGNM (Cologne Society for New Music), the Art Institute of Chicago, Harvestworks in New York, Stanford University in Palo Alto, California, and the Escola Superior de Musica de Catalunya in Barcelona. Behrman has received grants from the NEA, New York State Council of the Arts, and New York Foundation for the Arts, and residencies from the Japan–United States Friendship Commission and the DAAD (Berlin). From the Foundation for Contemporary Arts in New York he received two awards, an Artist's Award in 1995 and the John Cage Award in 2004. In 2005 he was a co-recipient, with Larry Polansky and Kristin Norderval, of the Henry Cowell Award from the American Music Center.

Behrman designed his first electronic circuitry in 1966; this resulted in *Runthrough* (1967). Since then homemade or home-adapted electronics systems that involve sound synthesizers, microcomputers, and video have been integral to his music: "The form of the music," he has said, is "a slow unfolding of the possibilities of the system." Many of Behrman's systems are pitch-responsive, in that a microcomputer responds to a pitch or pitch sequence improvised by the performers, answering them in pre-programmed ways. Subsequently he has created sound installations (often in collaboration with

Paul De Marinis), some of them interactive, with listeners able to play simple instruments and contribute to the audio-visual effect. No matter what electronics he has used, Behrman has written music that is prevailingly lyrical, even pastoral, and thus eloquently refutes the notion that electronic music must be futuristic and dehumanizing. His works have enjoyed performances worldwide for a number of years.

WORKS
(selective list)
cms: computer music system

Dance scores: For Nearly an Hour (choreog. M. Cunningham: *Walkaround Time*), 6-track tape, 3 pfmrs, 1968; Voice with Melody-Driven Elec (choreog. Cunningham: *Rebus*), 1975; Interspecies Smalltalk (choreog. Cunningham: *Pictures*), vn, elec kbd, cms, 1984

El-ac: Wave Train, 2 amp pf, 2–4 gui mic, 2–4 pfmrs, 1966; Runthrough, 4 pfmrs, 1967, rev. as Sinescreen, 1970; Questions from the Floor, loudspkrs, 1968, collab. S. Dienes, rev. as A New Team Takes Over, 1969; A New Team Takes Over, 2 spkrs, 4-track tape, elec, 1969; Runway, 3 pfmrs, tape, loudspkrs, tape delay; 1969, collab. G. Mumma; Sinescreen, 4 pfmrs, elec, 1970; Pools of Phase-Locked Loops, 1972, collab. K. Morton; Homemade Synth Music with Sliding Pitches, 1973; Vc with Melody-Driven Elec, 1974; Voice with Tpt and Melody-Driven Elec (I.F. Stone), 1974; Voice with Melody-Driven Elec, 1975; Figure in a Clearing, vc, synth, cptr, 1977; On the Other Ocean, pfmrs, cms, 1977; All Thumbs, fl, tpt, cms, 1986–9; Leapday Night (3 scenes), 2 tpt, 1986–8; Mbira Preserves, elec mbira, cms, 1986; A Traveller's Dream Journal, tape, cptr, 1988–90; Koto Kayak, 13- and 17-str koto ens, kbd, cms, 1990; Navigation and Astronomy, 21-str koto, cms, 1990; Refractive Light, kbd, cms, 1991; Unforeseen Events, 1991; QSRL, 1–2 wind/amp str, cms, 1994–7; My Dear Siegfried…(S. Sassoon, S.N. Behrman), 2vv, shakuhachi, trbn, kbd, cms, 1996; other works

Sound Installations: Cloud Music, synth, video, 1974–9, collab. R. Watts, B. Diamond; Sound Fountain, 4 gui, cms, 1982, collab. P. De Marinis; Algorithme et kalimba, 1 or more mbiras, cms, 1986, collab. G. Lewis; A Map of the Known World, 1 or more mbiras, cms, 1987, collab. Lewis; Keys to Your Music, 1 or more mbiras, cms, 1987–9; In Thin Air, pedals, light board, loudspkrs, cms, 1995–7, collab. J. Lo; Pen Light, 1998; other works

Principal recording companies: Lovely Music, Nova Era, New Tone, Classic Masters

WRITINGS

"What Indeterminate Notation Determines," *PNM*, iii/2 (1965), 58–73

"Designing Interactive Computer-Based Music Installations," *CMR*, vi/1 (1991)

BIBLIOGRAPHY

J. Huff: "An Interview with David Behrman," *Composer* [Hamilton, OH], iv/1 (1972), 29–32

J. Rockwell: "Electronic & Computer Music & the Humanist Reaction: David Behrman," *All American Music: Composition in the Late Twentieth Century* (New York, 1983), 133–44

H. Pollack: *Harvard Composers* (Metuchen, NJ, 1992), 370–96

JOHN ROCKWELL/GREG A. STEINKE

Beiderbecke, (Leon) Bix [Bismark] (*b* Davenport, IA, 10 March 1903; *d* New York, NY, 6 Aug 1931). Jazz cornetist. Researchers have debated whether he was originally named Leon Bix or Leon Bismark. As a boy he had a few piano lessons, but he was self-taught on cornet and developed an unorthodox technique by playing along with recordings. His family disapproved of his interest in jazz, and sent him in 1921 to Lake Forest Academy, but the opportunity to play and hear jazz in nearby Chicago caused frequent truancy and eventually his expulsion. After several months working for his father in Davenport he turned to a career in music. Based in Chicago, he became known through his playing and recordings with the Wolverines in 1924. In the same year he began a long association with Frankie Trumbauer, recording with him in New York under the pseudonym of the Sioux City Six; after working with Jean Goldkette's dance band (1924), he played with Trumbauer's group in St. Louis (1925–6). His association with Trumbauer broadened his musical experience and improved his music reading, in which, however, he was never to become adept. In late 1926 he and Trumbauer joined Goldkette, and were prominent members of his group in New York until it disbanded in September 1927. They then joined Paul Whiteman's band, with which, and with various groups under their own names, they made a series of influential recordings, notably *Singin' the Blues* and *Riverboat Shuffle* (both 1927, OK), issued under Trumbauer's leadership. Beiderbecke's alcoholism caused his health to deteriorate, and he was frequently unable to perform. He left Whiteman in September 1929 and his hopes of rejoining the group after recuperation were not realized. Until his death he worked in New York, in a radio series, with the Dorsey Brothers a few times, with the Casa Loma Orchestra, and with Benny Goodman.

From relatively undistinguished influences Beiderbecke developed a beautiful and original style. His distinctive, bell-like tone (his friend Hoagy Carmichael described it as resembling a chime struck by a mallet) achieved additional intensity through his unorthodox fingering, which often led him to play certain notes as higher partials in lower overtone series, imparting a slightly different timbre and intonation to successive pitches. With his basically unchanging tone as a foil, Beiderbecke relied for expressiveness on pitch choice, pacing, and rhythmic placement (as opposed to Louis Armstrong, who systematically used variety of timbre). Beiderbecke played and composed at the piano throughout his working life; *In a Mist*, *Flashes*, *Candlelights*, and *In the Dark* (his published piano compositions), in their use of pandiatonicism, whole-tone scales, and parallel seventh and ninth chords, reflect his interest in impressionist harmonic language. However, his work on cornet, nearly always in settings over which he had no control, had to conform to the harmonic usages of contemporary jazz and popular music. His playing was largely diatonic and made sparing use of non-diatonic ninths and 13ths as well as the lowered thirds and sevenths common in jazz. By avoiding harmonically functional chromatic pitches his improvisations often seemed to transcend the ordinary harmonic progressions of their accompaniment without contradicting them, as his solo on *Royal Garden Blues* (1927, OK) shows. This characteristic, together with his unique timbre, gave his work a restrained, introspective manner and often set his playing apart from its surroundings.

Beiderbecke's originality made him one of the first white jazz musicians to be admired by African American performers; Louis Armstrong recognized in him a kindred spirit, and Rex Stewart exactly reproduced some of his solos on recordings. Beiderbecke's influence on such white players as Red Nichols and Bunny Berigan was decisive. Although he was largely unknown to the general public at the time of his death, he acquired an almost legendary status among jazz musicians and enthusiasts; on account of such popularized accounts as Dorothy Baker's novel *Young Man with a Horn* (Boston, 1938), based very loosely on his life and career, he soon came to symbolize the "Roaring Twenties" in the popular imagination. Only towards the end of the 20th century did legend and fact become separated enough to put Beiderbecke's career and achievement into perspective.

BIBLIOGRAPHY

SchullerEJ

E. Nichols: "Bix Beiderbecke," *Jazzmen*, ed. F. Ramsey and C.E. Smith (New York, 1939, 3/1977), 143–60

N. Shapiro and N. Hentoff, eds.: *Hear me Talkin' to ya: the Story of Jazz by the Men who Made it* (New York, 1955, 2/1966), 140–64

B. James: *Bix Beiderbecke* (London, 1959), repr. in *Kings of Jazz*, ed. S. Green (South Brunswick, NJ, 1978), 41–73

B. Green: *The Reluctant Art: Five Studies in the Growth of Jazz* (London, 1962), 18

V. Castelli and others: *The Bix Bands: a Bix Beiderbecke Disco-Biography* (Milan, 1972)

J.P. Perhonis: *The Bix Beiderbecke Story: the Jazz Musician in Legend, Fiction, and Fact* (diss., U. of Minnesota, 1978)

R. Kelly: *Jelly Roll, Bix and Hoagy: Gennett Studios and the Birth of Recorded Jazz* (Bloomington, IN, 1994)

R.M. Sudhalter: *Lost Chords: White Musicians and their Contribution to Jazz, 1915–1945* (New York, 1999)

J.P. Lion: *Bix: the Definitive Biography of a Jazz Legend: Leon 'Bix' Beiderbecke (1903–1931)* (New York, 2005)

JAMES DAPOGNY/J. BRADFORD ROBINSON/R

Beissel [Beisel], **(Johann) Conrad** [Konrad] (*b* Eberbach, Germany, 1 March 1691; *d* Ephrata, PA, 6 July 1768). Composer and hymnodist of German birth. As a boy he was apprenticed to a baker (his father's trade) who was a musician, from whom he learned violin. Beissel converted to Pietism in 1715 and found himself in conflict with church authorities; he was later arrested and jailed. Following his release, he was held before the ecclesiastical court and banished from Mannheim and Heidelberg. After journeying to Schwarzenau and Crefeld, he came into contact with the German Baptist Brethren and the Inspirationists. In order to flee the religious persecution in the Palatinate, Beissel immigrated to America. He eventually found his way to Lancaster County, Pennsylvania, having first arrived in Boston in 1720.

In Germantown, near Philadelphia, Beissel found little demand for his trade as a baker, which led to his serving an apprenticeship to learn the weaver's trade with Peter Becker, a Dunker (Church of the Brethren) leader who baptized Beissel into the church. Eventually, Beissel served as elder of a congregation of believers known as the Conestoga Congregation; however, after serving for seven years, he began preaching of the evils of marriage and sexual intercourse and insisting on the observance of Saturday as the true Sabbath, which led to a schism with the parent church. Although the Dunkers repudiated Beissel's teaching, a few followers left with him in 1732. Shortly thereafter, Beissel established and administered a Protestant monastic society at Ephrata, Pennsylvania, basing it on austere self-denial, celibacy, and pious simplicity. (*See also* EPHRATA CLOISTER.)

Toward the end of the 1730s, both a singing and a writing school were instituted at Ephrata; they were established as mechanisms for religious self-improvement, creative involvement, and spiritual discipline. Beissel was a prolific writer with a literary style that was mystical, metaphorical, erotically symbolic, and filled with scriptural allusions. Benjamin Franklin published three of his hymn collections (1730, 1732, 1736), and Christopher Saur issued his *Zionitescher Weyrauchs Hügel*, a large collection of hymns and other poetry (including some by European authors), in Germantown. After a quarrel with Saur, Beissel obtained his own printing press, which became, next to Saur's, the most important colonial German American press. *Das Gesäng der einsamen und verlassenen Turtel-Taube* (The Song of the Solitary and Lonely Turtle Dove, 1747) was the first major hymnal from the Ephrata press; like earlier hymnals, it contains only texts, but whereas the earlier books listed standard European hymn tunes, this and subsequent Ephrata hymnals adopted Beissel's own melodies.

An untrained musician who played the violin by ear, Beissel developed his own method for singing and composition, and he trained his followers to compose hundreds of hymns and anthems according to his compositional system, in which text dominated music. His method is outlined in the "Verrede über die Sing-Arbeit" (Preface on the Art of Singing) to the *Das Gesäng der einsamen und verlassenen Turtel-Taube*, by one of his followers, Edward Blum. He took the tonic triad as the center of any given tonality, designating the tones of that triad as "masters" and the remaining tones of the scale as "servants"; accented or concluding syllables of verses usually fell on a "master" tone, unaccented ones on a "servant." Beissel's rules for harmonization take as their foundation the soprano line rather than the bass, which often results in extensive parallel movement; while dominant-tonic progressions are common at cadences, other chord progressions are random. Rhythms closely follow the accentuation of the words, but without establishing a set metrical relation between long and short notes, thus creating unusual metric flexibility.

The *Paradisisches Wunder-Spiel* (1754) is the only Ephrata publication to include music; since the community press lacked musical type, the notation was entered by hand. This collection contains 49 pieces, most of which are for four voices, though some are in as many as seven parts. (A second *Wunder-Spiel*, published in 1766, included only texts, taken primarily from earlier Ephrata hymnals.) Musical production at Ephrata ceased about 1762, and the community declined after Beissel's death in 1768. The unique nature of the music limited its performance almost exclusively to the community itself, and even the hymn texts by Beissel and his followers found only limited acceptance among Pennsylvania Germans. A few are in German tunebooks published by Joseph Doll (1810), Johannes Rothbaust (1821), and Michael Bentz (1827), and 43 are in the Harmony Society's *Gesangbuch* (1827), but not with the Ephrata tunes.

WORKS

Collection: *[10] Ephrata Cloister Chorales: a Collection of Hymns and Anthems*, ed. R.P. Getz (New York, 1971)

Das Gesäng der einsamen und verlassenen Turtel-Taube (Ephrata, PA, 1747)

Paradisisches Wunder-Spiel (Ephrata, 1754)

Hymns in: *Göttliche Liebes und Lobes gethöne* (Philadelphia, 1730); *Vorspiel der Neuen-Welt* (Philadelphia, 1732); *Jacobs Kampff- und Ritter-Platz* (Philadelphia, 1736); *Zionitischer Weyrauchs Hügel* (Germantown, PA, 1739); *Nachklang zum Gesäng der einsamen Turtel-Taube* (Ephrata, 1755); *Neuvermehrtes Gesäng der einsamen Turtel-Tuabe* (Ephrata, 1762)

BIBLIOGRAPHY

Grove7 ("Beissel, Conrad," R.P. Getz; "Ephrata Cloister," D.A. Seachrist)

W.C. Klein: *Johann Conrad Beissel, Mystic and Martinet* (Philadelphia, PA, 1942)

L.G. Blakely: "Johann Conrad Beissel and the Music of the Ephrata Cloister," *JRME*, xv/2 (1967), 120–38

O. Kilian: "Konrad Beisel (1691–1768): Founder of the Ephrata Cloister in Pennsylvania," *Bach: Journal of the Riemenschneider Bach Institute*, vii/3 (1976), 25–8; vii/4 (1976), 31–6; viii/1 (1977), 23–4

P.C. Erb: *Johann Conrad Beissel and the Ephrata Community, Mystical and Historical Texts* (Lewiston, NY, 1985)

D.A. Seachrist: "Snow Hill and the German Seventh-Day Baptists: Heirs to the Musical Traditions of Conrad Beissel's Ephrata Cloister" (diss., Kent State U., 1993)

D.P. DeVenney *Source Readings in American Choral Music* (Missoula, MT, 1995)

EDWARD C. WOLF/DENISE A. SEACHRIST

Belafonte, Harry [Belafonete, Harold George, Jr.] (*b* New York, NY, 1 March 1927). Popular singer, actor, and activist. As a child, he lived in Kingston, Jamaica, returning to New York in 1940. In 1945 he began a career as an actor, having studied in Erwin Piscator's drama workshop at the New School of Social Research. He experienced greater commercial success, however, as a popular singer, making his debut at the Royal Roost, New York, in 1949. The following year he began to sing traditional melodies from Africa, Asia, America, and the Caribbean, which he collected in folk music archives. Having secured an RCA recording contract in 1952, Belafonte went on to become the most popular "folk" singer in the United States. His interpretations of Trinidadian Calypso music between 1956 and 1959 won him his greatest success and marked the pinnacle of his career. His mass appeal through the 1950s, moreover, enabled him to resume his work as an actor, and he appeared in several films. During the 1960s and 70s his popularity waned, but he continued to record, and to perform in nightclubs and theaters for a predominantly white, middle-class audience. Until his last concert in 2003, he continued to perform his folk-inspired songs for large crowds of dedicated followers. He also became increasingly committed to social activist causes, ranging from his work for UNICEF to the anti-Apartheid songs that constituted his last studio album, *Paradise in Gazankalu* (1988). He received the Kennedy Center Honors in 1989 and a Grammy Lifetime Achievement Award in 2000.

BIBLIOGRAPHY

"Belafonte, Harry," *CBY* 1956

D. Cerulli: "Belafonte: the Responsibility of an Artist," *DB*, xxiv (1957), no.5, p. 17; no.6, p. 14; no.7, p. 17

H. Steirman: *Harry Belafonte: his Complete Life Story* (Washington DC, 1957)

A.J. Shaw: *Belafonte: an Unauthorized Biography* (New York, 1960)

M. Eldridge and H. Belafonte: "Remains of the Day-O: a Conversation with Harry Belafonte," *Transition*, no.92 (2002), 110–37

K. Beavers: *Lead Man Holler: Harry Belafonte and the Culture Industry* (diss., U. of Southern California, 2008)

RONALD M. RADANO/R

Belasco, David (*b* San Francisco, CA, 25 July 1853; *d* New York, NY, 15 May 1931). Director and playwright. Born into a theatrical family who had immigrated (*c*1850) from England to California at the time of the Gold Rush, he was educated by a Catholic priest, whose dress he affected all his life. At the age of 12 he had written his first play, *Jim Black, or The Regulator's Revenge*. From 1871 he was stage manager at various San Francisco theaters, adapting foreign plays and frequently appearing in them himself. He moved to New York in 1884 and achieved his first success as the author of *May Blossom*. Over the course of his career, he wrote over 50 plays and produced over 350 for theaters on Broadway and stock companies. Prolific in every genre from light comedy to historical melodrama, he specialized in plays with an exotic ambience, which he evoked with elaborate decor and cunningly devised lighting. *Adrea* (1904) is set on an Adriatic island in the fourth century; *Madame Butterfly* (1900) and *The Darling of the Gods* (1902, once considered his masterpiece) take place in Japan; and *The Girl I Left behind Me* (1893) and *The Heart of Maryland* (1895) are stage westerns. As a director Belasco could be called the Stanislavsky of his day, while the visual effects for which he was famous owe something to the early cinema. Indeed, in *Madame Butterfly* it was the scene of the heroine's silent vigil, during which the lighting portrays the passage of time from dusk to dawn, complete with birdsong, that first attracted Puccini to the drama. While visiting New York early in 1907 for the first performance of *Madama Butterfly* at the Metropolitan Opera, Puccini saw three of Belasco's plays in a search for a suitable operatic subject. These included *The Girl of the Golden West*, which had first been produced at Pittsburgh in 1905. Puccini decided to adapt it as *La fanciulla del West*, which received its world premiere at the Metropolitan in December 1910. Belasco published a two-volume autobiography, *My Life's Story*, in 1915.

BIBLIOGRAPHY

D. Belasco: *The Theatre through the Stage Door* (New York, 1918)

W. Winter: *The Life of David Belasco* (New York, 1919)

A.J. Randall and R.G. Davis: *Puccini & the Girl: History and Reception of* The Girl of the Golden West (Chicago, 2005)

JULIAN BUDDEN/R

Belcher, Supply (*b* Stoughton, MA, 29 March 1751; *d* Farmington, ME, 9 June 1836). Composer and tune-book compiler. He began a career as a merchant in Boston, but by 1776 he was back in his hometown, where he purchased a farm and operated a tavern; he was also a member of the Stoughton Musical Society. In 1785 he and his family moved to Maine and spent six years in Hallowell (now Augusta). In 1796 a local newspaper reported of a public ceremony marking the Hallowell Academy's first year of operation: "The exercises were enlivened by vocal and instrumental music under the direction of Mr. Belcher, the 'Handel of Maine.'" Belcher then settled in Farmington, where he spent the rest of his life. He played a leading role in the community, as town clerk, magistrate, representative to the state government, selectman, and schoolmaster, and was also known as a violinist and singer; he is said to have organized the town's first choir.

Almost all of Belcher's 60-odd published compositions appear in his tunebook *The Harmony of Maine* (Boston, 1794/*R*), devoted entirely to his own music. In 1797 he brought out a smaller work including the *Ordination Anthem* and "a number of other fuging pieces, never before published," but no copies have been located. His music is rooted in New England psalmody, yet shows other modern stylistic influences. Several of his pieces are in three rather than four voices and move the melody from the tenor to the treble voice. Several more set secular texts, often with copious melodic ornamentation and even appoggiaturas (for example, "Invitation"). Unusually frequent and precise performance directions ("Crescendo," "Divoto," "Vigoroso," "Pianissimo") suggest that Belcher was a demanding leader. He was a talented, communicative composer, though his music was not popular and was never widely reprinted.

BIBLIOGRAPHY

F. Butler: *History of Farmington, Franklin County, Maine* (Farmington, ME, 1885), 378–80

F.J. Metcalf: *American Writers and Compilers of Sacred Music* (New York, 1925/*R*), 83–5

R.T. Daniel: *The Anthem in New England before 1800* (Evanston, IL, 1966), 136

E. Owen: *The Life and Music of Supply Belcher (1751–1836), 'Handel of Maine'* (diss., Southern Baptist Theological Seminary, 1969)

A.P. Britton, I. Lowens, and R. Crawford: *American Sacred Music Imprints 1698–1810: a Bibliography* (Worcester, MA, 1990), 81–82, 155–56, 378–79

L.G. Davenport: *Divine Song on the Northeast Frontier: Maine's Sacred Tunebooks, 1800–1830* (Lanham, MD, 1995)

L.G. Davenport, ed.: *Supply Belcher (1751–1836): the Collected Works*, Music of the New American Nation: Sacred Music from 1780 to 1820, v (New York, 1997)

RICHARD CRAWFORD/R

Bel Geddes, Norman [Geddes, Norman] (*b* Adrian, MI, 27 April 1893; *d* New York, 8 May 1958). Stage designer. He studied briefly at the Cleveland School of Art, but had no formal education after the age of 16. His first wife, Helen Belle Sneider, became his collaborator, and "Norman-Bel-Geddes" was their nom de plume for articles on art and the theater, until their divorce in 1932. Notable designs for Montemezzi's *La nave* for Chicago Opera (1919) and Henry Hadley's *Cleopatra's Night* for the Metropolitan (1920) attracted Broadway attention, and his innovative approach was soon recognized. At an early stage of his career he discarded the proscenium arch and planned open-stage projects. For a commission in 1924 to design Vollmöller's morality play *The Miracle* with Humperdinck's music for Max Reinhardt, he converted the theater into a Gothic cathedral. His work for Broadway included Kurt Weill's *The Eternal Road* (1937), Gershwin's *Strike up the Band* (1927), Porter's *Fifty Million Frenchmen* (1929), and *The Seven Lively Arts* (1944, his last for Broadway): in all, he designed more than 200 theatrical productions. He later turned primarily to industrial design, but he also had a pivotal influence on the development of American theater. His archives, designs, and drawings were given to the University of Texas, Austin, in 1959.

BIBLIOGRAPHY

ES (L. Moore)

F. Bruguière: *The Divine Comedy* (New York, 1924)

N. Bel Geddes: *Horizons* (New York, 1932)

T. Komisarjevsky, T. Simonson, and L. Simonson: *Settings and Costumes of the Modern Stage* (New York, 1933)

T. Komisarjevsky, T. Simonson, and L. Simonson: *Miracle in the Evening* (New York, 1960)

D. Oenslager: *Stage Design: Four Centuries of Scenic Invention* (London, 1975)

DAVID J. HOUGH

Belknap, Daniel (*b* Framingham, MA, 9 Feb 1771; *d* Pawtucket, RI, 31 Oct 1815). Composer, tunebook compiler, and singing master. The son of Jeremiah Belknap Jr. and Hepzibah Stone, he grew up in Framingham, where he received a common-school education. He then worked as a farmer, mechanic, and militia captain, and taught singing-schools from the age of 18. Around 1800 he married Mary Parker, with whom he had five children by 1809. In 1812 he and his family moved to Pawtucket, where he died of a fever.

Most of his 86 known compositions were first printed in his own tunebooks, an exception being his most widely published piece, "Lena," which was introduced in *The Worcester Collection* (Boston, 5/1794). His ambitious Masonic ode, "A View of the Temple," was sung at the installation of the Middlesex Lodge of Framingham in 1795. Belknap's *The Harmonist's Companion* (Boston, 1797), a brief 32-page collection, contains only his own compositions, which are written in an American idiom untouched by European-inspired reform. His later compilations, *The Evangelical Harmony* (Boston, 1800), *The Middlesex Collection* (Boston, 1802), and *The Village Compilation* (Boston, 1806), are devoted almost entirely to American music; they include pieces by other Massachusetts composers such as Bartholomew Brown, Ezra Goff, Joseph Stone, and Abraham Wood, as well as many of his own pieces. Unlike many of his fellow psalmodists, Belknap also wrote secular music. His compilation *The Middlesex Songster* (Dedham, MA, 1809) contains "Belknap's March," his only known instrumental composition.

BIBLIOGRAPHY

T.W. Baldwin: *Vital Records of Framingham, Massachusetts to the Year 1850* (Boston, MA, 1911)

Vital Records of Carlisle, Massachusetts, to the End of the Year 1849 (Salem, MA, 1918), 41

F.J. Metcalf: *American Writers and Compilers of Sacred Music* (New York, 1925/*R*1967), 146
R.J. Wolfe: *Secular Music in America 1801–1825: a Bibliography* (New York, 1964)
A. Perdue Britton, I. Lowens, and R. Crawford: *American Sacred Music Imprints 1698–1810: a Bibliography* (Worcester, MA, 1990)
N. Cooke: *American Psalmodists in Contact and Collaboration, 1770–1820* (diss., U. of Michigan, 1990)
N. Cooke: "William Billings: Representative American Psalmodist?" *The Quarterly Journal of Music Teaching and Learning* vii/1 (1996), 47–64
D.W. Steel, ed.: *Daniel Belknap: the Collected Works* (New York, 1999)

RICHARD CRAWFORD/DAVID WARREN STEEL

Bell, Joshua (*b* Bloomington, IN, 9 Dec 1967). Violinist. He studied with Mimi Zweig (1975–80) and with Josef Gingold at the University of Indiana, Bloomington (1980–89). He made his solo debut with the Philadelphia Orchestra under Riccardo Muti in 1981, and has subsequently followed an international career as a soloist, appearing with many leading orchestras including the New York PO, the Boston SO, and the Los Angeles PO, as well as the LPO and the CBSO. In October 1993 he gave the first performance of Nicholas Maw's Violin Concerto, of which he is the dedicatee, with the Philharmonia conducted by Leonard Slatkin. Bell has made many recordings of the concerto repertory (including a multi-award-winning disc of Maw's concerto), and he has also recorded chamber music with the pianists Jean-Yves Thibaudet and Olli Mustonen, and with the Takács Quartet. In 1991 he formed a trio with Olli Mustonen and cellist Steven Isserlis, and in 1997 he established an annual chamber music festival at the Wigmore Hall, London. His 2004 recording *Romance of the Violin* was named the 2004 Classical CD of the year by *Billboard*, which also named him the Classical Artist of the Year. He has contributed to various Grammy-winning recordings, including the spoken word children's album *Listen to the Storyteller*, on which he collaborated with Wynton Marsalis, as well as Béla Fleck's *Perpetual Motion*. A prodigious prize-winner, Bell was awarded Germany's Echo Klassik for the recording of concertos by Jean Sibelius and Karl Goldmark (2000) with Esa-Pekka Salonen and the Los Angeles PO. He also received the Gramophone Award for his recording of Samuel Barber's and William Walton's violin concertos and Ernest Bloch's *Baal Shem* (2007).

Bell has been, as he has put it, keen to "escape from the classical mold" from time to time and includes among his many recordings a CD called *Gershwin Fantasy*, in collaboration with John Williams and the LSO; *West Side Story Suite*, a deconstruction of Leonard Bernstein's original score; and *Short Trip Home*, in which he teamed up with his former classmate Edgar Meyer for a recording of bluegrass music. He also starred in the soundtrack to the film *The Red Violin* and performed the violin solos for the films *Angels & Demons* and *Defiance*. Bell has combined a virtuoso technique with sweetness of tone and phrasing that is suave and musical. Earlier in his career, he played a 1732 Stradivari, the "Tom Taylor." In 2001 he acquired a 1713 Stradivari, the "Gibson ex Huberman," on which he has subsequently performed.

BIBLIOGRAPHY

H. Waleson: "Bel Canto," *The Strad*, xcix (1988), 391–3
J. Duchen: "High-Flying Adored," *The Strad*, cvii (1996), 564–71
Violin Virtuosos (San Anselmo, CA, 2000)

MARGARET CAMPBELL/MEGAN E. HILL

Bell, Larry Thomas (*b* Wilson, NC, 17 Jan 1952). Composer and pianist. After taking piano lessons and playing in a rock band, Bell attended East Carolina University and Appalachian State University in North Carolina (BM 1974) working at both with Gregory Kosteck. At The

Joshua Bell, 1990. (Suzie Maeder/Lebrecht Music & Arts)

Juilliard School (MM 1977, DMA 1982) he studied with VINCENT PERSICHETTI and ROGER SESSIONS. Influenced by Beethoven, Carter, and solfège pedagogue Renée Longy, Bell's modernist early music (1970s and 80s) emphasized thematic development, polyphony, and elaborate polyrhythmic structures. A Guggenheim Fellowship (1981), Rome Prize (1982–3), and Rockefeller grant (1985) took him to Italy, where he began a performing career as a pianist and reconnected with American folk hymnody. Both these choices led to a more tonal, melodically oriented, neo-Romantic style.

After teaching at the Juilliard Pre-College, Bell taught at the Boston Conservatory (1980–2005), the New England Conservatory (from 1992), and the Berklee College of Music (from 2007). His speed of composition and frequency of piano performances increased, resulting in multi-movement keyboard pieces in Baroque and classical forms, as well as works for orchestra and chorus, chamber, solo music, and song cycles. By 2010 he had produced 110 works with opus numbers, many released on CD. Bell's music has been performed by the Seattle SO and Atlanta SO and under conductors Gerard Schwarz, Jorge Mester, and Benjamin Zander; by the Juilliard and Borromeo String Quartets, and Speculum Musicae; cellists Eric Bartlett and Andrés Díaz; pianists Sara David Buechner and Jonathan Bass; and singers Robert Honeysucker, Matthew DiBattista, and D'Anna Fortunato.

All aspects of Bell's music are synthesized in his two-act opera *Holy Ghosts* (premiered 2009). Scored for a rock band, incorporating nine hymn tunes, and based on Romulus Linney's play, it combined his Pentecostal Holiness background with his keyboard, vocal writing, and conducting skills.

WORKS
(selective list)

Orch: The Idea of Order at Key West (W. Stevens), dbl conc., S, vn, orch, 1981; Sacred Symphonies, 1985; Pf Conc., 1989; Idumea Sym., 1996; The Sentimental Muse, bn conc., 1997; Short Sym. for Band, 1999; Songs of Innocence and Experience (W. Blake), children's chorus, orch, 2000; Hansel and Gretel (J. and W. Grimm), nar, orch, 2001; Dark Orange Conc, va, wind, 2005; Holy Ghosts (op, 2, A. Olmstead), 2007; Baroque Conc., a rec, hpd, vc, 2010

Stage: *Holy Ghosts* (R. Linney, A. Olmstead), op, 2, 2008

Chbr: Str Qt no.1, 1973; Str Qt no.2, 1982; Fantasia on an Imaginary Hymn, vc, va, 1983; River of Ponds, vc, pf, 1986; The Black Cat (E.A. Poe), nar, vc, pf, 1987; The Book of Moonlight, vn, pf, 1987; Conc., ob, pf, vn, va, vc, db, 1988; Quintessence, wind quintet, 1993; Pf Qt, pf, vn, va, vc, 1991; Mahler in Blue Light, a sax, vc, pf; arr. for cl, vc, pf, 1996; Tarab, 8 vc, 2003; Str Qt no.3, "Homage to Beethoven," 2004; Unchanging Love, brass quintet, org, 2007

Vocal: 4 Sacred Songs, S, pf, 1984; The Immortal Beloved (L. van Beethoven) Mez, pf, 1999; 4 Shakespeare Sonnets, T/S, pf, 2001; Songs of Time and Eternity (E. Dickinson), S, pf, 2002; Dream within a Dream (W. Whitman, W. Blake, E.A. Poe, E. Dickinson, M. Arnold), S, pf, 2006; The Seasons (E. Kirschner) cant., of 20 duets, T, hp; Mez, pf; Bar, hpd; S, gui, 2010

Kbd: Miniature Diversions, pf, 1983; Revivals, pf, 1984; Pf Sonata, 1990; Reminiscences and Reflections, 12 preludes and fugues, pf, 1998; Pf Sonata, "Tâla," 2002; 4 Chorale Preludes, pf, 2003; Liturgical Suite, org, 2004; Elegy, pf, 2005; Pf Sonata "Sonata Macabre," 2006; Music of the Spheres, pf, 2006; 15 2-Part Inventions, pf, 2008; Partita no.1, hpd, 2009; Partita no.2, hpd, 2010; 12 Piano Etudes, 2010

Principal publishers: Casa Rustica Publications, ECS

ANDREA OLMSTEAD

Bell, Thom(as Randolph) (*b* Kingston, Jamaica, 27 Jan 1943). Record producer, arranger, and songwriter of Jamaican birth. After spending his youth in Philadelphia he worked in the 1960s as a pianist for Cameo Records in Philadelphia and was a member of the group Kenny Gamble and the Romeos; Gamble later became Leon Huff's production partner, and Bell collaborated with them on a number of projects. Bell had his first success as an independent record producer with the Delfonics' "(La-La) means I love you" (Philly Groove, 1968) and two years later was responsible for another of their hits, "Didn't I blow your mind this time" (Bell, 1970). He went on to create the refined, silky pop-soul sound of the Stylistics, who like the Delfonics made prominent use of falsetto in crooning ballads such as "You are everything" (Avco, 1971) and "Betcha by golly, wow" (Avco, 1972). Bell's melodic style was heavily indebted to Burt Bacharach, and his sparkling orchestrations, using strings, woodwind, horns, and delicately scored percussion, were among the most ingenious quasi-symphonic, pop-soul arrangements of the 1970s. His equally fine work with the Spinners—including "I'll be around" (Atlantic, 1972), and "They just can't stop it" (Atlantic, 1975)—featured intricate vocal harmonies and a more sinewy sound. Bell continued making records into the early 1980s, notably writing and producing for Deniece Williams, but is best known for producing the quintessential Philly soul sound of the 1970s.

BIBLIOGRAPHY

J. Jackson: *House on Fire: the Rise and Fall of Philadelphia Soul* (New York, 2004)

STEPHEN HOLDEN/R

Bell, William (John) (*b* Creston, IA, 25 Dec 1902; *d* Perry, IA, 7 Aug 1971). Tuba player and teacher. He was known for his impeccable musicianship, pure tone quality, flawless technique, and exceptional intonation. At the age of 18, Bell was summoned by John Philip Sousa to be principal tuba in the Sousa Band (1921–4); by Fritz Reiner for the Cincinnati Symphony Orchestra (1924–37); by Arturo Toscanini, who considered Bell to be the world's greatest tuba player, for the NBC Symphony Orchestra (1937–43); and by the New York Philharmonic Orchestra (1943–61). In 1957 he performed the American premiere of the *Concerto for Tuba and Symphony Orchestra* by Ralph Vaughan Williams with the Little Orchestra Society of New York City. He was professor of tuba at the Cincinnati Conservatory of Music (1924–37); Columbia University Teachers College, the Juilliard School, and the Manhattan School of Music (1937–61); and the Indiana University School of Music (1961–71). He inspired TubaChristmas, a massed choir of tuba and euphonium players performing Christmas carols in honor of his December 25th birthday. The first TubaChristmas took place on December 22, 1974 on Rockefeller Plaza's ice rink in New York City. In 2008, 242 cities celebrated TubaChristmas.

PATRICE MADURA WARD-STEINMAN

Bellamann, Henry [Heinrich] **(Hauer)** (*b* Fulton, MO, 28 April 1882; *d* New York, NY, 16 June 1945). Author, pianist, and teacher. He attended Westminster College in Fulton (1899–1900) and the University of Denver (1900–03), and then continued his studies in London and New York, and in Paris, where he worked with ISIDORE PHILIPP (piano) and Charles Widor (organ and composition). He was dean of the School of Fine Arts at Chicora College for Women in Columbia, South Carolina (1907–24), where he developed a reputation as a pianist and expert on modern French music. He was chairman of the examining board of the Juilliard School (1924–6) and dean of the Curtis Institute (1931–2). Bellamann composed a piano concerto, chamber music, and choral works. His literary output includes several novels (*King's Row*, the most successful of them, was later adapted as a film), some volumes of poetry, and articles on music (in *Musical Quarterly* and other journals). He was one of the first to write and lecture on the music of Ives (Ives set two of Bellamann's poems, *Yellow Leaves* and *Peaks*).

BIBLIOGRAPHY

P. Pathun: "*Concord*, Charles Ives, and Henry Bellamann," *Student Musicologists at Minnesota*, vi (1975–6), 66–86

PAULA MORGAN

Bellamy Brothers. Country duo. For more than 35 years, Florida natives and University of Florida graduates, Howard (*b* Darby, FL, 2 Feb 1946) and David (*b* Darby, 16 Sept 1950) Bellamy have provided a hip crossover component to country music. They absorbed traditional country music influences from their father and pop and rock influences from sources such as the Beatles. Signed by Curb/Warner Brothers Records in 1975, the Bellamys helped reinforce and define the Outlaw, Urban Cowboy, and Countrypolitan eras of the 1970s and 1980s. Their music helped to broaden the sound and listenership of country music, projecting a laid-back, contemporary cowboy imagery reinforced by their Florida ranch lifestyle.

Their music, while reflecting changing times, remains relevant in the 21st century. "If I said you had a beautiful body would you hold it against me" (Warner/Curb, 1979) uses linguistic playfulness to address dynamics of heterosexual relationships valued by the country music audience. "You just ain't whistlin' dixie" (Warner/Curb, 1979) draws on traditional elements of southern lifestyle, geography, and history, mentioning fishing, alligators, pine trees, Southern states, the Confederacy, and Robert E. Lee. "Old Hippie"(Curb/MCA, 1985) comments on the aging process for 1960s-era counterculture activists trying to adjust to cultural changes. Similarly, "Get into Reggae Cowboy" (Elektra/Curb, 1982), which uses Caribbean music elements, and "Country Rap" (Curb/MCA, 1987), reflected new cultural developments in the form of emerging popular genres.

Still touring and recording on their own record label, the Bellamy Brothers have released some 49 albums, 71 singles, and 22 videos. Eleven of their singles have reached number one on *Billboard*'s "Hot Country Singles" chart. In 2009, a UK banking commercial featured "Let Your Love Flow" and the single reached number one on the UK charts some 34 years after becoming their first number one country hit. In recognition of their many contributions, the Bellamy Brothers have been nominated more than 20 times for awards given by the Country Music Association and the Academy of Country Music.

JAMES E. AKENSON

Bellini, Luiz (*b* Monte Azul Paulista, São Paulo State, Brazil, 25 Nov 1935). Violin maker of Brazilian birth. He moved to São Paulo City with his family at age five. There, in 1950, he began his training in woodcarving at the Escola Tecnica Getulio Vargas, studying under Vicente Policene. After completing his studies in 1954, his teacher showed him a violin, which he found highly interesting, and so early in 1955 he commenced studies in violin making, working under Guido Pascoli. He studied under Pascoli for five years, after which time it was suggested that he pursue wider horizons. Geraldo Modern, a friend of Pascoli's, contacted Rembert Wurlitzer in New York on his behalf, and he was invited to join their workshop. He arrived there on 21 November 1960 and began working in restoration; he soon worked directly under FERNANDO SACCONI's supervision, and Sacconi continued his instruction in both violin restoration and making. During this time he performed a restoration on the "Lord Wilton" Guarneri, a violin that he studied intently and which subsequently became his preferred model, although until 1981 he also made copies after the "Baron Knoop" Stradivari and "Kreisler" Guarneri.

In 1968, he went to work for Jacques Francais. While working for Francais, he kept his still-unvarnished copy of the "Lord Wilton" over his bench, where, thanks to good words from both Charles Beare and Michele de Luccia, it drew the attention of the concert violinist Ruggiero Ricci. Once it had been varnished, Ricci borrowed the violin, which he eventually purchased, and used it for many performances and recordings, and in the process created a flood of attention and interest in Bellini's craft. As a result, in 1975 he left the Francais shop to work on his own, concentrating exclusively on making.

While studying under Pascoli, Bellini made about 20 instruments, including a viola and cello, but since being in the United States he has made exclusively violins—as of this writing about 175. Created on the "Lord Wilton" model, he carefully imitates the appearance of age and wear to simulate the original. Earlier in his career he created about eight per year; in more recent times he has scaled back to about four per year. The copy he made for Ruggiero Ricci was illustrated in the 2010 *Strad* calendar and is currently in the collection of the Smithsonian Institution, to whom Mr. Ricci donated it after paring down his performance schedule.

PHILIP J. KASS

Bellison, Simeon (*b* Moscow, Russia, 4 Dec 1883; *d* New York, NY, 4 May 1953). Clarinetist, pedagogue, arranger, and author of Russian birth. Beginning at age nine, he received clarinet instruction from his father and performed in amateur and military bands. He studied with Joseph Friedrich at the Imperial Conservatory of Moscow (1894–1901), where he completed a BA degree with honors (1903). He was principal clarinetist in the Moscow Opera and Symphony Orchestra (1903–15) and the St. Petersburg Imperial Opera (1915), and served in the Russian Army during World War I. He organized and played in several touring ensembles, including the Moscow Quintet (1902) and Zimro (1918). While touring the United States with the Zimro ensemble (1919), he was offered the position of principal clarinetist in the New York Philharmonic, which he held from 1920 to 1948. He founded the first clarinet choir (1927), which included four B♭ clarinets, two basset horns, and two bass clarinets, and which by 1948 had grown to 75 members. Trained in the German School, Bellison played Oehler clarinets. His students included Leon Russianoff, Sidney Forrest, Kalman Bloch, and David Weber. He revised and expanded landmark pedagogical materials, particularly his 1946 edition of the *Klosé Clarinet Method* and method books by Lazarus and Kroepsch. He arranged many solo and chamber works for clarinet, including those by Bach, Mozart, Beethoven, Schubert, and Rimsky-Korsakov. He wrote numerous articles on clarinet pedagogy and advocated strongly against the use of vibrato. He collected, edited, and arranged Hebrew instrumental folk music and was an authority on Jewish music.

BIBLIOGRAPHY

GMO
Obituary, *The Clarinet*, i/11 (1953), 12–13
R.K. Weerts: "The Clarinet Choir," *JRME*, xii/3 (1964), 227–30
P. Weston: *More Clarinet Virtuosi of the Past* (London, 1977), 45–47

CHARLES P. SCHMIDT

Bellringing. Considerable evidence suggests that the use of tower bells in North America was somewhat widespread by at least the last quarter of the 17th century, if not before. The bells themselves, as well as the ringing traditions associated with them, were imported by European missionaries and settlers. The earliest bell founders working in this country were John Pass and John Stowe, whose first bell was the recasting of the "Liberty Bell" (originally by Whitechapel Foundry of London) in 1753 for the Commonwealth of Pennsylvania.

A basic division has always existed between the use tower bells as a signal for secular or sacred functions, with the former more customarily being hung stationary and the latter tending to be swinging bells. By the turn of the 17th century stationary civic bells and clock chimes had developed in the Low Countries into the art of the traditional carillon, while the swinging church bells found across continental Europe evolved in England into the practice of change ringing. Handbells, developed in the 18th century for practicing change ringing indoors, have found wide use and popularity as a musical art form quite apart from their original association with tower bells.

The carillon is a musical instrument consisting of at least two octaves of tuned (usually bronze) tower bells arranged in chromatic series and played from a keyboard that permits control of expression through variation of touch. A set of bells smaller than this is known as a "chime," and there were numerous examples to be found in the United States by the early 19th century. A set of carillon bells by Bollée of Le Mans, France, was installed in 1852 in the Basilica of Notre Dame, in Indiana. This instrument, however, was playable only by automatic drum and functioned strictly as a clock chime (until the mid-20th century). The first true carillon in the United States (with a keyboard for manual playing) is the 25-bell instrument from 1882 by van Aerschodt of Leuven, Belgium, for Holy Trinity Church in Philadelphia. The earliest carillon of American manufacture and tuning was produced in 1928 by Meneely and Company of Watervliet, New York, for St. James Church in Danbury, Connecticut.

By 2010 the number of carillons in the United States had reached 169, including the 72-bell carillon of the Riverside Church in New York City (the largest in the world by weight at 100 tons) and the 77-bell instrument at Kirk in the Hills Presbyterian Church of Bloomfield Hills, Michigan (the largest by number of bells). The Guild of Carillonneurs in North America was founded at Ottawa in 1936, and the University of Michigan began

The keyboard of the Baird Carillon at the University of Michigan, built in Loughborough, England, by the John Taylor Foundry, 1936. (Steven Ball)

a degree program in the Study of the Carillon and Campanology in 1939, adding a course in bell founding and tuning in 2010.

The peculiarly English art of change ringing is the most evolved and complex manner of sounding swinging bells. Normally, six to 12 bells in diatonic sequence are rung by a band of ringers in strict mathematical sequences or "changes." The first "ring" of bells in the United States was installed in Old North Church (Christ Church) in Boston in 1744; two other churches—Christ Church, Philadelphia, and St. Michael's, Charleston, South Carolina—installed rings of eight bells previous to the American Revolution. Not until 1850 was a full tower "peal" (5000 or more changes rung in sequence) achieved, at Christ Church, Philadelphia. In 1856 the firm of Meneeley in Troy, New York, produced a ring of bells for St. Paul's Episcopal Church, Buffalo, New York. Interest in change ringing declined after the Civil War, but was revived in the late 1890s by Arthur Nichols at Old North Church, Boston, and elsewhere. Another revival that started in the 1960s led to an increase in the number of towers with swinging bells. The North American Guild of Change Ringers was formed in 1971. In 2010 there were some 45 towers equipped for change ringing in the United States.

Handbell ringing was introduced to the United States in 1844 by P.T. Barnum, who engaged a group of British handbell ringers (called the "Swiss Bell Ringers") for an American tour. They attracted much attention in the United States, Canada, and Cuba, and were responsible for far reaching early popularization of the art. By 1866 an American manufacturer, Rowland H. Mayland, was producing handbells in Brooklyn, New York. An amateur team of handbell ringers was formed in Boston in 1895 by Nichols, and his daughter, Margaret Shurcliff, organized the Beacon Hill Ringers in 1923. She established the New England Guild in 1937 and was instrumental in the founding the American Guild of English Handbell Ringers in 1954 (more than 7000 members in 2010). In the 1940s Scott Parry and Doris Watson of Brick Presbyterian Church, New York, began to incorporate handbell ringing into services; American churches have since played a large part in spreading the popularity of handbell ringing. Many handbells were of British manufacture until the 20th century. American, Dutch, and French firms have in recent years made substantial contributions to the number and unique musical qualities of bells available.

More than 200 bell foundries are known to have operated in the United States at various times from the late 18th into the 20th century; some 13 supplied bells that are (or were) contained in carillons or chimes, and one produced some change ringing bells. Almost all closed by the 1950s; in the 21st century Meeks, Watson, & Company of Georgetown, Ohio, is the only firm currently producing carillon bells.

The firm of Schulmerich, in Sellersville, Pennsylvania, manufactures electronic carillons, which have a similar sound to that of the true instrument. Handbells (usually in two- to five-octave sets) are manufactured by Schulmerich and by Malmark (New Britain, Pennsylvania).

BIBLIOGRAPHY

Grove7 ("Carillon," L. Rombouts; also "Change ringing," W.G. Wilson and S. Coleman)
P.T. Barnum: *The Life of PT Barnum, Written by Himself* (New York, 1854); repr. with introduction by T. Whalen (Champaign, IL, 2000)
S.B. Parry: *The Story of Handbells* (Boston, MA, 1957)
W. Westcott: *Bells and Their Music* (New York, 1970)
L.E. Springer: *That Vanishing Sound* (New York, 1976)
R.J. Siegel: "A Survey of the History of Campanology in the Western Christian Cultural Tradition," *Sacred Music*, cxxii/4 (1995), 7–20
G.W. Williams: *Change Ringing in the Carolina Low-Country: a Record of Full-Circle Ringing from 1751 to 2000* (Charleston, SC, 1999)
J.M. Simpson, ed.: *There Was Life Before NAG* (Philadelphia, 2/2000)
J. Gouwens: *Playing the Carillon: an Introductory Method* (Culver, IN, 2002)
J.L. Kessell: *Spain in the Southwest: a Narrative History of Colonial New Mexico, Arizona, Texas, and California* (Norman, OK, 2003)
J. Johnston: *England's Child: the Carillon and the Casting of Big Bells* (San Francisco, 2008)
G.B. Nash: *The Liberty Bell* (New Haven, CT, 2010)

STEVEN BALL

Bellson, Louie [Balassoni, Luigi Paulino Alfredo Francisco Antonio] (*b* Rock Falls, IL, 6 July 1924; *d* Los Angeles, CA, 14 Feb 2009). Drummer, composer, arranger, and music director. He began learning drums with his father at the age of three and won the first annual Slingerland National Gene Krupa Drumming Contest when he was 17. He performed with, among others, Louis Armstrong, Count Basie, Sammy Davis Jr., Tommy Dorsey, Ella Fitzgerald, Dizzy Gillespie, Benny Goodman, Lionel Hampton, Woody Herman, Harry James, Oscar Peterson, Mel Tormé, Sarah Vaughan, and PEARL BAILEY, to whom he was married. He was a member of Duke Ellington's orchestra several times (1951–3, 1956, and 1965–6), and Ellington incorporated a number of Bellson's compositions into the band's repertoire, including the drum kit feature "Skin Deep." Bellson also led his own band almost uninterrupted for 40 years, and wrote more than 1000 compositions in a range of classical and jazz styles. An ambidextrous player, he pioneered the use of two bass drums that was subsequently emulated by numerous heavy metal drummers as well as others such as Billy Cobham, Jon Hiseman, and Ian Paice. He was awarded four doctorates, nominated for four Grammy Awards, named a Living Legend of Music by the Avedis Zildjian Company (2007), and inducted into the American Society of Composers, Authors and Publishers' Wall of Fame (2007). He also co-wrote with Gilbert Breines two of the most enduring educational music texts: *Modern Reading Text in 4/4* (Miami, 1963) and *Odd Time Reading Text* (ed. H. Adler, Miami, 1968). He was also noted for his work with charities, especially orphanages.

BIBLIOGRAPHY

R. Flans: "Louie Bellson," *Modern Drummer*, iv/5 (1980), 12–15.
R. Mattingly: "Louie Bellson," *Modern Drummer*, xv/1 (1991), 18–23
R. Spagnardi: *The Great Jazz Drummers* (Cedar Grove, 1992)

GARETH DYLAN SMITH

Bellstedt, Herman (*b* Bremen, Germany, 21 Feb 1858; *d* San Francisco, CA, 8 June 1926). Bandmaster, cornetist, composer, and arranger of German birth. He immigrated to the United States with his family in 1867, and settled in Cincinnati in 1872. He studied music with his father and Mylius Weigand, and was acclaimed as a prodigy when he first performed a cornet solo in public at the age of 15. A year later he joined the Cincinnati Reed Band, remaining with them until he assumed the post of cornet soloist with the Red Hussar Band at Manhattan Beach, NY, in 1879. He rejoined the Cincinnati Reed Band in 1883. From 1889 to 1891 he was soloist with the Gilmore Band; by this time his reputation equaled that of his contemporaries William Paris Chambers and Jules Levy. He returned once again to Cincinnati, and in 1892 founded the Bellstedt-Ballenger Band, with which he appeared as conductor and comet soloist. In 1904 he joined the Sousa Band, alternating as soloist with Herbert L. Clarke and Walter Rogers, but he left Sousa in 1906 to join Innes's Band as soloist and assistant conductor. He directed the Denver Municipal Band from 1909 to 1912. In 1913 he became professor of wind instruments at the Cincinnati Conservatory, where he won respect as a dedicated teacher and numbered among his students Frank Simon, who also played with Sousa. Bellstedt composed works for piano, violin, orchestra, and band, but is best known for his cornet solos *La Mandolinata* and *Napoli*. Several of his works were included in Robert Hoe's *Heritage of the March* series (31).

BIBLIOGRAPHY

F.R. Seltzer: "Famous Bandmasters in Brief," *Jacobs' Band Monthly*, iv/3 (1919), 14

G.D. Bridges: *Pioneers in Brass* (Detroit, 1965); CD-ROM (Coupeville, WA, 2000)

W.H. Rehrig: *The Heritage Encyclopedia of Band Music* (Westerville, OH, 1991, suppl. 1996); CD-ROM (Oskaloosa, IA, 2005) [incl. selective works list]

N.E. Smith: *Program Notes for Band* (Lake Charles, LA, 2000), 46–47

F. Simon: "A Glimpse into the Distinguished Career of Herman Bellstedt," *ACB Advance*, xix/3 (2001), 8–9

RAOUL F. CAMUS

Belmonts. Rock-and-roll vocal group led by DION.

Belt, Philip R(alph) (*b* Hagerstown, IN, 2 Jan 1927). Fortepiano maker. In 1959 he discovered and later copied an original German square piano by Christian Ernst Frederici (*c*1758) in Cambridge City, Indiana. In 1965 his copy of this instrument attracted the attention of Scott Odell, conservator of musical instruments at the Smithsonian Institution, who invited Belt to examine and make drawings of the Smithsonian's fortepiano built by Johann Lodewijk Dulcken (1795, formerly attributed to Johann Andreas Stein). That same year, after a short apprenticeship with WILLIAM DOWD, he became an apprentice of FRANK HUBBARD. Soon Belt started receiving commissions and relocated to New Hampshire, where he began making fortepianos based on the instrument at the Smithsonian. Harvard University professor Luise Vosgerchian purchased Belt's first fortepiano in 1967 and used it in a concert with violinist Robert Koff, including works by C.P.E. Bach, Wolfgang Amadeus Mozart, and Ludwig van Beethoven. This performance on a replica was unprecedented in the United States; Belt had broken ground in what would become a new era in historical keyboard performance. In 1969 Malcolm Bilson, an early proponent of the use of period instruments in 18th-century music, examined one of Belt's fortepianos and immediately ordered a copy.

In the late 1960s Belt restored a fortepiano by Johann Andreas Stein (1784) from the Toledo Museum of Art, and in 1972 he developed the first fortepiano kit. In 1973, after selling the kit business to Hubbard, he traveled to Europe with musicologist Maribel Meisel, his wife at the time. They visited instrument collections in six countries, taking measurements, making drawings of and photographing fortepianos, including Mozart's fortepiano by Anton Walter (1782) in the Mozart Museum, Salzburg. Belt's most sought-after instruments have been his copies of the Stein fortepiano (1781) from the Gothenburg City Museum (with modifications) and Mozart's Walter fortepiano. Between 1975 and 1979 he worked with David Way at Zuckermann and developed a kit of Mozart's Walter. In 1986 Belt remarried and moved to the Philippines, but the inaccessibility of quality wood, in addition to other circumstances, prompted him to return to the United States in 1993. With 45 instruments completed, Belt has been a pioneer in the building of period instruments. His work has influenced musicians, instrument builders, and the performance of 18th-century keyboard literature.

BIBLIOGRAPHY

T. Kunkel: "200 Years of Experience," *Hope Magazine* (May/June 1996), 54–61

P. O'Donnell: "Philip Belt—Fortepiano Maker," *Southeastern Historical Keyboard Society Newsletter* (Nov 1997), 6–7

L. Sanchez: "Philip Belt and the Revival of the Fortepiano," *Early Music America*, xvii/4 (2012), 24–8

LUIS SANCHEZ

Beltrán (Alcayaga), Lola [María Lucila] (*b* El Rosario, Sinaloa, Mexico, 7 March 1932; *d* Mexico City, 25 March 1996). Mexican singer. She was one of seven children born to a working-class family. She began singing at an early age for church services and at family celebrations. In 1953 she traveled to Mexico City to search for work in the secretarial field. As luck would have it, Beltrán was hired as member of the office staff at Radio XEW. Mariachi Vargas de Tecalitlán performed regularly on XEW, and after persistent requests, Beltrán was allowed to sing with them. As a result, her career path radically changed, and she became the most famous female mariachi singer of her generation.

Beltrán recorded works by the most notable Mexican songwriters of the era including Agustín Lara and José Alfredo Jiménez, and her interpretations of songs such as "Cucurrucucu paloma" and "Paloma negra" are classics within the mariachi repertory. As the premier *canción ranchera* singer of the 1950s through 70s, and first female superstar of mariachi, Beltrán was referred to as *La reina* (The Queen) by her loyal fans. Her performance of such songs as "Tres días," a ranchera about loneliness and separation, were particularly popular among Mexican migrants in the United States as well as Mexican American audiences.

BIBLIOGRAPHY
L. Richter: "Lola Beltrán: Mariachi's Queen Ignites Hope, Soothes Hardship for Multitudes," *New York Times* (10 Jan 1988)
Obituary, *New York Times* (26 March 1996)

DONALD A. HENRIQUES

Belwin-Mills. Firm of music publishers. Belwin, Inc., was founded in 1918 by Max Winkler, and Mills Music Publishers started a year later under the aegis of Jack and Irving Mills; the two organizations merged as the Belwin-Mills Publishing Corporation in 1969, with Martin Winkler as director. Formerly located in Melville, New York, the company is now based in Miami; it is one of the most important publishers of educational music, producing many widely-used piano series, a number of class band methods and material for teaching string instruments. The firm represents such composers as Creston, Crumb, Davidovsky, Dello Joio, Ellington, Vittorio Giannini, Gould, Gustav Holst, Menotti, Krzysztof Penderecki, Schuller, Sessions, Virgil Thomson, Toch and Villa-Lobos, and also issues popular music. In the 1970s, the company branched out to produce a few Broadway musicals, although this was a short-lived endeavor. Belwin-Mills became the primary distributor for E.B. Marks in 1973. In 1985 Belwin-Mills was acquired by Columbia Pictures, who divided the firm's printing and publishing concerns; during 1987–8 the printing arm was sold to Boston Ventures while the publishing company was purchased by the London-based Filmtracks firm (subsequently a subsidiary of EMI). Since 1988 the publishing company has been known as CPP/Belwin Inc., a name retained by Warner-Chappell Music, which purchased the company in 1994. The firm's catalog has continued to grow, expanding on the educational publications associated with the Belwin name. The firm changed hands again in 2005, when Alfred Music Publishing purchased the majority of Warner Bros. music publishing division.

BIBLIOGRAPHY
M. Winkler: *A Penny from Heaven* (New York, 1951)
M. Winkler: *From A to X: Reminiscences* (New York, 1957)
R. Sanjek and D. Sanjek: *American Popular Music Business in the 20th Century* (New York, 1991)

W. THOMAS MARROCCO, MARK JACOBS/
R. ALLEN LOTT, LESLIE A. TROUTMAN/JONAS WESTOVER

Benade, Arthur (Henry) (*b* Chicago, IL, 2 Jan 1925; *d* Cleveland, OH, 4 Aug 1987). Acoustician. His parents being missionaries, he spent much of his childhood in Lahore. After returning to the United States to study at Washington University, St. Louis (AB 1948, PhD 1952), Benade was appointed in 1952 to the physics faculty at Case Institute of Technology, Cleveland, which later became Case Western Reserve University. Promoted to a full professorship in 1969, he continued in that post until shortly before his death. A skilled woodwind player, he had an exceptional ability to relate the results of acoustical research to the practical requirements of musicians and musical instrument makers. Benade established a research program which made many fundamental contributions to the understanding of the operation of wind instruments. Also active in string instrument research, he was a founding member of the Catgut Acoustical Society and its president between 1969 and 1972. Through his technical papers, and through the hospitality which his laboratory afforded to foreign visitors, Benade was a major influence on a generation of music acousticians, and in popular articles and books he introduced a much larger public to the basic science of musical instruments. The Acoustical Society of America awarded him its Silver Medal in 1984 and its Gold Medal posthumously in 1988.

WRITINGS
Horns, Strings, and Harmony (New York, 1960/*R*)
"On the Mathematical Theory of Woodwind Finger Holes," *JASA*, xxxii (1960), 1591–608
"The Physics of Woodwinds," *Scientific American*, cciii/4 (1960), 144–54; repr. in *The Physics of Music*, ed. C.M. Hutchins (San Francisco, 1978)
"The Physics of Brasses," *Scientific American*, ccxxix/1 (1973), 24–35; repr. in *The Physics of Music*, ed. C.M. Hutchins (San Francisco, 1978)
Fundamentals of Musical Acoustics (New York, 1976, 2/1990)
with W.B. Richards: "Oboe Normal Mode Adjustment via Reed-Staple Proportioning," *JASA*, lxxiii (1983), 1794–803
with S.N. Kouzoupis: "The Clarinet Spectrum: Theory and Experiment," *JASA*, lxxxiii (1988), 292–304
"Woodwinds: the Evolutionary Path since 1700," *GSJ*, xlvii (1994), 63–110

MURRAY CAMPBELL

Benary, Barbara (*b* Bay Shore, NY, 7 April 1946). Composer, performer, instrument builder, and ethnomusicologist. She received the BA from Sarah Lawrence College, and the MA and PhD from Wesleyan University, where she studied Indonesian and Indian music. She has performed with the ensembles of Philip Glass, Jon Gibson, Alvin Lucier, Philip Corner, and Daniel Goode. In 1976 she co-founded, with Corner and Goode, the Gamelan Son of Lion, New York, a new music collective and repertory ensemble under her direction. In addition, she has built several Javanese-style iron gamelans, including the instruments used by the Gamelan Son of Lion and Gamelan Encantada, Albuquerque, New Mexico.

Benary's compositional output has been primarily in the areas of ensemble and chamber music, and music for the theater. She has described herself as a "part-time minimalist who also likes to write melody." Many of her works integrate world music forms, structures, and instruments with traditional Western materials. Her works for gamelan ensemble, which number more than 30, have been performed internationally. *Karna: a Shadow Puppet Opera* (1994) and *Wayang Esther* (2001) combine gamelan, vocal oratorio, and Javanese *wayang kulit* (leather shadow puppets). She has also written theater and dance scores for such companies as the New York Shakespeare Festival, Lenox Arts Theater, and the Bali-Java Dance Theatre. She describes her approach to music in D. Goode: "Braiding Hot-Rolled Steel: the Music of Barbara Benary," *Musicworks*, no.56 (1993), 14–23. Her improvisational structures are published in her book *System Pieces, 1971–1992* (Hanover, NH, 1992).

WORKS

(selective list)

The Only Jealousy of Emer (chbr op, W.B. Yeats), 1966; Systems, improvisations, 1973–93; Gamelan Works, vols.1–4, 1974–94; Hot-Rolled Steel, gamelan, 1985; Sun on Snow, vv, insts, 1985; Karna: a Shadow Puppet Opera (chbr op), vv, insts, gamelan, 1994; Downtown Steel, wind, perc, 1995; Tintinnalogia, vn, pf, perc, 1995; Aural Shoehorning, b cl, perc, Javanese gamelan, 1997

Principal publishers: Frog Peak, American Gamelan Institute

JODY DIAMOND

Benatar [née Andrzejewski], **Pat(ricia Mae)** (*b* Brooklyn, NY, 10 Jan 1953). Rock singer. She was initially taught to sing by her mother, an opera singer, but she eventually chose not to pursue a career in classical music. She married Dennis Benatar in 1972 and took health education courses at the State University of New York at Stony Brook with the intention of becoming a teacher. In 1973 she began working as a performing waitress at the Roaring Twenties Café in Enon, Virginia. She later returned to New York to pursue a professional music career and recruited Rick Newman as her manager; he took her to Chrysalis Records to front an all-male rock band. She subsequently married the band's leader, guitarist, and producer Neil Giraldo in 1982, having divorced her first husband in 1979.

In October 1979 Benatar's first album, *In the Heat of the Night*, established her position as a woman in rock and introduced what became her signature sound: tightly constructed pop song structures, Benatar's classically trained four-and-a-half octave vocal range, and Giraldo's distorted electric-guitar solos. In 1980 she released *Crimes of Passion*, which included the single "You Better Run," the first video by a female performer to be aired on MTV and only the second video in the music station's history. After EMI took over Chrysalis in 1989, Benatar produced two more albums (*True Love*, Chrysalis, 1991, and *Gravity's Rainbow*, Chrysalis, 1993) before releasing *Inamorata* (CMC International, 1997). In 2001 she and Giraldo founded their own record label called Bel Chiasso to release the album *Go* (2003).

Benatar has won four Grammy Awards for Best Rock Vocal Performance, Female (1980–83), sold more than 22 million copies of her albums, and produced 19 top 40 singles. She was inducted into the Long Island Music Hall of Fame in 2008.

BIBLIOGRAPHY

L.A. Lewis: *Gender Politics and MTV: Voicing the Difference* (Philadelphia, 1990)

P. Benatar and P. Bale Cox: *Between a Heart and a Rock Place: a Memoir* (New York, 2010)

JESSICA L. BROWN

Bendix, Max (*b* Detroit, MI, 28 March 1866; *d* Chicago, IL, 6 Dec 1945). Violinist, conductor, musical director, teacher, and composer. Bendix was born to Jewish parents who had emigrated from Germany. His father William was a music teacher. Bendix began formal study at the Cincinnati College of Music where, at the age of 12, he performed with the college orchestra, directed by Theodore Thomas. This began a long association between the two men, leading to Bendix's appointment as first violinist and concertmaster of the Theodore Thomas Orchestra in 1886. In August 1893 Thomas resigned his position as music director of the Chicago World's Columbian Exposition following a series of unsuccessful concerts. Bendix took Thomas's place as conductor of the Exposition orchestra. This created tension between the two men, and Bendix left the Thomas orchestra in 1896. He went on to serve as conductor at the Manhattan Opera House and to conduct orchestras for world fairs in St. Louis (1904) and Chicago (1933). From 1910–30 Bendix acted as musical director for several Broadway productions. He composed numerous songs, a violin concerto, and several other orchestral works, as well as incidental music and ballet music for plays.

BIBLIOGRAPHY

Baker4

E. Schabas: *Theodore Thomas: America's Conductor and Builder of Orchestras, 1835–1905* (Chicago, 1989)

KARA GARDNER

Ben-Dor [née Buka], **Gisèle (Ivonne)** (*b* Montevideo, Uruguay, 26 April 1955). Conductor of Uruguayan birth; naturalized American. Born to Polish immigrant parents, she began piano studies at age four, started conducting at 12, and at 14 was hired as music director of her school. She taught herself to play various instruments, including guitar, and also studied violin, clarinet, and cello. She immigrated to Israel in 1973, moved to the United States in 1980, and became a US citizen in 2000. A graduate from the Rubin Academy of Music, Tel Aviv (artist diploma in orchestral conducting 1980) and Yale University (MMA 1982), she made her conducting debut with the Israel Philharmonic in Igor Stravinsky's *Rite of Spring*. Her talent was recognized by Leonard Bernstein at Tanglewood and the Schleswig-Holstein Music Festival. Ben-Dor held long-term positions as music director with the Santa Barbara SO (1994–2006) and the Boston Pro Arte Chamber Orchestra (1991–2000)—a cooperative orchestra whose musicians elect conductors—and has continued these relationships, respectively, as conductor laureate and conductor emerita. She was also resident conductor of the Louisville Orchestra (1987–8) and Houston Symphony (1988–91) and music director of the Annapolis Symphony (1991–7). She has led the New York Philharmonic, LSO, BBC National Orchestra of Wales, Helsinki Philharmonic, Geneva Opera, New World Symphony, Rotterdam Philharmonic, Seoul and Hong Kong Philharmonics, National Orchestra of Taiwan, orchestras in France and Latin America, and all the main Israeli orchestras—the Israel PO, the Israeli Opera, and the Jerusalem SO. She has been an important champion of music by Latin American composers, including Alberto Ginastera, Silvestre Revueltas, Heitor Villa-Lobos, Luis Bacalov, and Ástor Piazzolla, in concerts, festivals, and acclaimed world premiere recordings for Delos, Koch, and Naxos. Especially noteworthy are Revueltas's ballet, *La Coronela* (Koch 1998), Villa-Lobos's large choral-orchestral Symphony no.10, *Amerindia* (Koch 2000), and ballets by Ginastera, including *Popol Vuh: the Mayan Creation* (Naxos 2010). In an interview with Lisa Hanson, Ben-Dor indicated that her recordings were among her proudest achievements because of her involvement with the entire process as well as their high quality. Reviews of Ben-Dor's conducting, including those of standard repertoire, often mention her charisma on the podium along with the spark and musicality she brings to performances.

BIBLIOGRAPHY

L. Hanson: "A Musician in Heart and Soul: a Conversation with Gisèle Ben-Dor," *Signature*, i/3 (1996), 9–12, 29–30

J. Reel: "A Conversation with Conductor Gisèle Ben-Dor," *Fanfare*, xxiv/2 (2000), 12, 14, 17–8

R.L. Sharpe: *Maestros in America: Conductors in the 21st Century* (Lanham, MD, 2008), 17–20

L.R. Bayley: "An Interview with Gisèle Ben-Dor," *Fanfare*, xxxiv/3 (2011), 16–8, 20, 22, 24

J. MICHELE EDWARDS

Benét, Stephen Vincent (*b* Bethlehem, PA, 22 July 1898; *d* New York, NY, 13 March 1943). Writer. He wrote poetry and prose with great facility, producing a wide variety of works: light verse, short stories, novels, essays, reviews, and long poems. Though their quality is uneven, they include several important works, notably the epic poem *John Brown's Body* (New York, 1928) for which he received a Pulitzer Prize. Many of Benét's subjects come from American history or folklore. Among the many American composers who have been drawn to his poetry are Randall Thompson, Leslie Bassett, Gail Kubik, and Douglas Moore (who also set poems by Benét's brother William Rose Benét, 1886–1950). Moore was a lifelong friend of Benét's, and the two worked closely together on the one-act opera *The Devil and Daniel Webster*. This tale first appeared in 1936 as a short story in the *Saturday Evening Post*. Its spectacle of bringing the dead to life and the drama of its final courtroom scene make it excellent material for the stage. The opera version, first produced in 1939 by the American Lyric Theater in New York, met with considerable popular and critical success.

Simplicity, directness, and strong poetic rhythm are the qualities that make much of Benét's verse well suited for musical setting, particularly in traditional musical styles. These qualities are most evident in *A Book of Americans* (New York, 1933), a collection of 55 short poems for children by Benét and his wife, Rosemary Carr Benét. Several composers, including Josef Alexander, Earl George, Kubik, and Arnold Shaw, have written sets of pieces using selections from this book.

BIBLIOGRAPHY

C.A. Fenton: *Stephen Vincent Benét* (New Haven, CT, 1958)

P. Stroud: *Stephen Vincent Benét* (New York, 1962)

M. Hovland: *Musical Settings of American Poetry: a Bibliography* (Westport, CT, 1986)

D.G. Izzo and L. Konkle, eds.: *Stephen Vincent Benét: Essays on His Life and Work* (Jefferson, NC, 2002)

HOWARD NIBLOCK/R

Benge, Elden (*b* Winterset, IA, 12 July 1904; *d* Burbank, CA, 12 Dec 1960). Trumpeter and trumpet manufacturer. He studied cornet with William Eby, Vladimir Drucker, and Harold Mitchell, and trained as first trumpet in the Chicago Civic Orchestra. He was first trumpeter with the Detroit Symphony Orchestra (1928–33) and with the Chicago Symphony Orchestra (1933–9), then with the Chicago Philharmonic (1939–49) and also with the WGN (radio) staff orchestra (1939–53). Around 1934 Benge started to experiment in his basement with trumpet construction. He sold his first trumpet in 1935; in 1953 he moved to Burbank, California, to devote himself exclusively to manufacturing.

On his death the business passed to his son Donald (1933–2007), who in 1970 sold it to Leisure Time Industries of Los Angeles. After that, the company changed hands rapidly: in 1972 to the H.N. White Co. (King), who moved it to Anaheim, also expanding the number of models, then to Eastlake, Ohio, in 1983; in 1985 to C.G. Conn and later that year to a Swedish conglomerate, the resulting company being named United Musical Instruments (UMI). In 2000, UMI was purchased by Steinway, the owner of Selmer, and the corporate name changed in 2003 to Conn-Selmer. Production of most Benge models was suspended in 2005; limited production was restored in 2008.

Under Donald the firm produced over 20 models of trumpet (in B♭, C, D/E♭, and piccolo B♭/A), cornet and flugelhorn. Like Vincent Bach, Benge took the French Besson B♭ trumpet as his point of departure, but sought a more brilliant tone and more flexible intonation. Benge trumpets (especially the older models) are widely used, particularly on the West Coast, by trumpeters in symphony orchestras as well as in commercial entertainment.

BIBLIOGRAPHY

J.P. Mathez: "The History of King and Benge," *Brass Bulletin*, no.104 (1998), 58–72

F. Keim: *Das grosse Buch der Trompete* (Mainz et al., 2005), 285

J.W. Lill: *Elden Benge and the Chicago Benge Trumpet* (diss., Northwestern U., 2007)

EDWARD H. TARR

Benitez, "Jellybean" [John] (*b* South Bronx, New York, 7 Nov 1957). Producer, songwriter, label manager, and DJ of Puerto-Rican descent. Although Benitez emerged from the disco and freestyle scenes of the late 1970s as an active DJ, his work as a producer and remixer spans many popular styles and genres, including house, pop, rock, and R&B. Benitez is known as an important producer, remixer, and romantic partner of Madonna during the early 1980s. On Madonna's eponymous debut album (1983), he produced one track ("Holiday") and provided several remixes ("Borderline," "Burning Up," "Lucky Star," "Physical Attraction"). The success of these projects led to remixes for the likes of Pat Benatar, Hall and Oates, Michael Jackson, Sheena Easton, Paul McCartney, and David Bowie. He also produced Whitney Houston's top-ten hit "Love Will Save the Day" from her sophomore album, *Whitney* (1987). He has released his own albums (*Wotupski!?!*, 1984; *Just Visiting this Planet*, 1987; *Spillin' the Beans*, 1991), although he rarely sings on his recordings, instead featuring other vocalists.

Benitez owns Jellybean Music Group (founded in 1984), which has produced soundtracks for film and television and manages several subsidiary recording labels. One of these labels, H.O.L.A. (House of Latin Artists), features hip-hop and R&B artists working in both English and Spanish.

LUIS-MANUEL GARCIA

Bennett (Di Figlia), Michael (*b* Buffalo, 8 April 1943; *d* Tucson, 2 July 1987). Dancer, choreographer, and musical theater director. He first appeared on stage at age two, in a dance recital in his hometown. As a youngster, he studied ballet, tap, jazz, and modern dance, appeared in summer stock, and had his first directorial experience with high school musicals. He dropped out of school in 1960 to dance the role of Baby John in a European touring production of *West Side Story*, with choreography by Jerome Robbins. After a year abroad, he went to New York and found work as a chorus boy in shows choreographed by Ron Field, Michael Kidd, and Peter Gennaro. All these innovative choreographers influenced Bennett's subsequent choreographic work, which included numerous television shows and summer stock productions.

On Broadway, Bennett's first solo assignments as choreographer were for *A Joyful Noise* (1966; music by Oscar Brand and Paul Nassau) and *Henry, Sweet Henry* (1967; music by Bob Merrill. Both shows were failures, but Bennett won Tony nominations for his dances as well as praise in the *New York Times* as "the most hopeful new name around Broadway dance." His third show proved the point. *Promises, Promises* (1968), with a book by Neil Simon, a score by Burt Bacharach and Hal David, and dances by Bennett, was a substantial Broadway hit. Next came *Coco* (1969; music by Alan Jay Lerner and André Previn), an expensive production starring Katherine Hepburn as Coco Chanel that was a major disappointment. Nevertheless, Bennett won another Tony nomination, his fourth. His fifth, sixth, and seventh came for two shows with music and lyrics by Stephen Sondheim, the brilliant *Company* (1970) and the spectacular *Follies* (1971). For *Follies,* featuring luminous performances by Alexis Smith, Dorothy Collins, and Yvonne DeCarlo, Bennett finally won two Tony Awards, one for choreography and one for co-direction. His third Tony came from his work on *Seesaw* (1973; music by Cy Coleman), which he had rescued from imminent disaster during out-of-town tryouts.

This success, coupled with experiences directing several non-musical shows, encouraged Bennett to develop *A Chorus Line* (1975). From a text based on two 12-hour talk sessions by a group of theatrical dancers, and with a score by Marvin Hamlisch and Edward Kleban, Bennett created a collage of dance, speech, and song that transformed stories of dancers seeking work into a metaphor for human striving and achievement. Once again, Bennett won two Tonys for his work on the show, one for choreography and one for direction.The show ran from 1975 to 1990 in New York and remained in production for years afterward in other cities around the world. Bennett's astonishing success with *A Chorus Line* was followed and almost repeated by *Dreamgirls* (1981; music by Henry Krieger), another seamlessly integrated, Tony Award-winning megahit.

BIBLIOGRAPHY

ANB (K. Grubb: "Bennett, Michael")
K. Kelly: *Our Singular Sensation: the Michael Bennett Story* (New York, 1990)
K. Mendelbaum: *A Chorus Line and the Musicals of Michael Bennett* (New York, 1990)
R.E. Long: *Broadway, the Golden Years: Jerome Robbins and the Great Choreographer-Directors, 1940 to the Present* (New York, 2001)

CLAUDE CONYERS

Bennett, Robert Russell (*b* Kansas City, MO, 15 June 1894; *d* New York, NY, 18 Aug 1981). Composer, orchestrator, and conductor. His early musical studies were directed by his parents and the composer and conductor Carl Busch. He went to New York in 1916, where he worked first at G. Schirmer and then at T.B. Harms. Employment as a copyist and arranger, interrupted briefly by Army service during World War I, led to his first theater orchestrations in 1920. Upon Frank Saddler's death Bennett became America's pre-eminent theater orchestrator, a position which he held for four decades; he developed especially close relationships with Oscar Hammerstein II, Jerome Kern, and George Gershwin. Bennett interrupted his commercial work for much of 1926–9 to study in Paris with Nadia Boulanger, funded in part by a Guggenheim fellowship. Prizewinning entries in composition competitions sponsored by *Musical America* magazine and Victor Records led to frequent performances of his orchestral pieces in the United States during the 1930s and 40s. Most of 1936–40 was spent in Hollywood, principally at RKO, providing both orchestrations and original scoring. He returned to New York to host and conduct WOR's network radio program "Russell Bennett's Notebook," which sparked his most prolific period as a composer. His extensive work for NBC television after World War II began with *Victory at Sea* (1952–3), which he scored using a dozen themes provided by Richard Rodgers; he went on to provide original music for about 35 of NBC's documentary telefilms. More than 30 wind-band scores were completed, and among them are his most-played compositions. His large-scale works include seven symphonies and the opera *Maria Malibran*, premiered at the Juilliard School.

Bennett provided arrangements for some 300 Broadway musicals. Renowned for both his phenomenal working speed and the effective use of the limited orchestral forces available to him, Bennett supplied tasteful and disciplined song accompaniments as well as underscoring, bridges, dance music, overtures, and exit music. His many published medleys remain exemplars of their type and have circulated widely. *Instrumentally Speaking* (Melville, NY, 1975), distilled from a lifetime's experience, remains an unmatched "how-to" study of American theater orchestration. Praised by Boulanger as "a true artist," Bennett stands apart from his theater-arranging colleagues for his sustained independent creativity and long-standing associations with the leading conductors and soloists of his day, and his success as a composer was pivotal in elevating the theater orchestrator's status in the United States. More recently, renewed interest in the performance and recording of original orchestrations has prompted a heightened appreciation of his work on Broadway.

Like his commercial orchestrations, Bennett's compositions are scored with masterful simplicity and clarity. Though the geniality of his best-known pieces has led to an under-appreciation of the more serious and expansive scores, Bennett's works in all genres are distinguished by their distinctive and personal tonal idiom, effortless counterpoint, and rhythmic vitality.

WORKS

(selective list)

STAGE

Endymion (ballet-operetta), 1927; Hold Your Horses (musical play), 1933; Maria Malibran (opera), 1934

Musicals (as sole or principal orchestrator): Wildflower (V. Youmans), 1923; Rose Marie (R. Friml and H. Stothart), 1924; Song of the Flame (Stothart and G. Gershwin), 1925; Show Boat (J. Kern), 1927; Girl Crazy (Gershwin), 1930; Of Thee I Sing (Gershwin), 1931; Anything Goes (C. Porter), 1934; Oklahoma! (R. Rodgers), 1943; Carmen Jones (after Bizet's Carmen), 1943; Annie Get Your Gun (I. Berlin), 1946; Kiss Me, Kate (Porter), 1948; South Pacific (Rodgers), 1949; The King and I (Rodgers), 1951; My Fair Lady (F. Loewe), 1956; Bells are Ringing (J. Styne), 1956; Flower Drum Song (Rodgers), 1958; The Sound of Music (Rodgers), 1959; Camelot (Loewe), 1960; On a Clear Day You Can See Forever (B. Lane), 1965

INSTRUMENTAL

Orch: Charleston Rhapsody, 1926; Sights and Sounds, 1929; Sym. "Abraham Lincoln," 1929; Eight Etudes, 1938; Vn Conc., 1941; Sym. "Four Freedoms," 1943; Ov. to an Imaginary Drama, 1946; Sym. no.7, 1962

Wind Band: Tone Poems, 1939–40 [for the NY World's Fair]; Suite of Old American Dances, 1949 (orch, 1950); Symphonic Songs for Band, 1957; Concerto Grosso, ww qt, wind orch, 1957

Chbr: Rondo Capriccioso, 4 fl, 1916, rev. 1962; Organ Sonata, 1929; Hexapoda, vn, pf, 1940; A Song Sonata, vn, pf, 1947

FILM SCORES

Orchestrated by (composer in parentheses): Show Boat (J. Kern), 1936; Born to Dance (C. Porter), 1936; Swing Time (Kern), 1936; Shall We Dance (G. Gershwin), 1937; A Damsel in Distress (Gershwin), 1937; Gunga Din (A. Newman), 1939; Hunchback of Notre Dame (Newman), 1939; Rebecca (F. Waxman), 1940; Lady in the Dark (K. Weill), 1944; Victory at Sea (R. Rodgers), 1954; Oklahoma! (Rodgers), 1955

As composer: Annabel Takes a Tour, 1938; Fugitives for a Night, 1938; Career, 1939; Fifth Avenue Girl, 1939; Pacific Liner, 1939; Stanley and Livingstone, 1939

MSS in *Eu*

WRITINGS

"Orchestrating for Broadway," *MM*, ix (1931–2), 148–52

"Orchestration of Theatre and Dance Music," *Music Lovers' Encyclopedia*, ed. R. Hughes, D. Taylor, and R. Kerr (Garden City, NY, 1939/R), 780–86

"All I Know about Arranging Music," *IM*, xlvii (1949), no.8, pp.9, 33; no.9, pp.16, 33, and April 1949)

"Another Chapter on Arranging Music," *IM*, xlvii/10 (1949), 13

Instrumentally Speaking (Melville, NY, 1975)

G.J. Ferencz, ed.: *The Broadway Sound: the Autobiography and Selected Essays of Robert Russell Bennett* (Rochester, NY, 1999)

BIBLIOGRAPHY

"The Boys that Make the Noise," *Time* (5 July 1943)

H.W. Wind: "Another Opening, Another Show," *New Yorker* (17 Nov 1951)

R.B. Hawkins: *The Life and Works of Robert Russell Bennett* (diss., Texas Tech U., 1989)

G.J. Ferencz: *Robert Russell Bennett: a Bio-bibliography* (Westport, CT, 1990)

T. Carter: *Oklahoma! The Making of an American Musical* (New Haven, 2007)

G.J. Ferencz: "*Porgy and Bess* on the Concert Stage: Gershwin's 1936 Suite (*Catfish Row*) and the 1942 Gershwin-Bennett *Symphonic Picture*," *MQ*, xciv (2011), 93–155

GEORGE J. FERENCZ

Bennett, Tony [Bari, Joe; Benedetto, Anthony Dominick] (*b* New York, NY, 3 Aug 1926). Popular singer. He sang with military bands during World War II and then studied singing with Miriam Spier at the American Theatre Wing school. He appeared on Arthur Godfrey's television shows *Talent Scouts* and *Songs for Sale* and was discovered by Bob Hope in 1950 while performing in a New York nightclub with Pearl Bailey; it was Hope who suggested he change his stage name from Joe Bari to Tony Bennett. Bennett signed a recording contract with Columbia Records in 1950 through its director of popular music Mitch Miller and had a series of hit singles that included "Boulevard of Broken Dreams" (Col., 1950), "Because of you" (Col., 1951), "Cold, Cold Heart" (Col., 1951), "Blue Velvet" (Col., 1951), and "Rags to Riches" (Col., 1953). In 1962, after a slump in his career attributable to the rise of rock-and-roll, Bennett returned to the charts with what became his signature song, "I left my heart in San Francisco"; this helped to establish him as a sophisticated, versatile popular stylist. He went on to perform with swing bands led by Count Basie and Duke Ellington, among others, and worked with popular orchestras, toured with small groups, and recorded with the jazz pianist Bill Evans. From the late 1960s to the early 1980s his career suffered again due to changing tastes; however, from the late 1980s and into the 2000s Bennett experienced a resurgence in popularity, thanks to listener nostalgia, increased interest in classic pop songs, savvy marketing to different generations, and a continuous stream of critically acclaimed recordings and performances. In addition to winning more than a dozen Grammy Awards, he has been named an NEA Jazz Master and is a recipient of the Kennedy Center Honors.

In his early career Bennett became one of the most popular male ballad singers in the romantic Italian American bel canto tradition of Frank Sinatra. But unlike the young Sinatra and Vic Damone, who exemplified the same tradition, he had a lyric baritone with a distinctively husky edge, which served him well as he matured into an increasingly jazz-oriented saloon singer. An admirer of classic jazz, he claims to have modeled his breathing and phrasing on the playing of the jazz pianist Art Tatum and his relaxed delivery on that of the singer Mildred Bailey.

BIBLIOGRAPHY

FriedwaldB

W. Conover and others: "20 Years with Tony," *Billboard*, lxxx (30 Nov 1968), 1–40 [incl. discography]

W. Balliett: "A Quality that Lets you in," *New Yorker*, xlix (7 Jan 1974), 33; repr. in Balliett: *American Singers: Twenty-seven Portraits in Song* (New York, 1988), 130

T. Bennett (with W. Friedwald): *The Good Life: the Autobiography of Tony Bennett* (New York, 1998/*R*)

STEPHEN HOLDEN/R

Bennington College. Liberal arts college located in Bennington, Vermont. From its opening in 1932 as a women's college, it has remained fervently committed to its founders' vision of an experimental approach to higher education which includes neither grades nor regimented program requirements. Music has figured prominently at Bennington since the 1934 arrival of composer Otto Luening, who followed Kurt Schindler's brief initial tenure as director of music. Under Luening students gave well-received performances at venues such as New York's Town Hall. Eschewing the requirement of PhDs for faculty, Bennington prefers noteworthy practitioners in various fields of endeavor. Although every student's academic program is self-designed, all music majors receive sustained encounters with performance, improvisation, original composition, and theoretical analysis. Men were admitted in 1969. Both the BA and MFA in music are offered. The college's annual Chamber Music Conference and Composers' Forum of the East is one of the longest-running summer festivals for amateur musicians.

BIBLIOGRAPHY

T.P. Brockway: *Bennington College in the Beginning* (Bennington, VT, 1981)

NINA DAVIS-MILLIS/DAVID G. TOVEY

Benny, Jack [Kubelsky, Benjamin] (*b* Chicago, IL, 14 Feb 1894; *d* Beverly Hills, CA, 26 Dec 1974). Entertainer, actor, and violinist. The son of Jewish immigrants from Poland and Lithuania, he began playing violin at age six and was considered a local prodigy. By age 17 he was playing in vaudeville pit orchestras and soon moved onto the stage. Benny paired up with a pianist—initially Cora Salisbury, then Lyman Wood—in his signature musical act of this time, "From Grand Opera to Ragtime." After brief service in the US Navy during World War I, Benny returned to vaudeville as a single in an act emphasizing comedy over music. He married Mary Livingstone (Sadye Marks) in 1927. She was an integral part of Benny's act for most of his career. Although a movie contract with MGM in 1929 led nowhere, Benny found his true medium on radio. His first radio appearance came on *The Ed Sullivan Show* in 1932.

Soon Benny had his own program, built around a group of regular characters and lasting from 1932 to 1955. The nascent situation comedy genre developed many of its fundamental contours in Benny's well-scripted and rehearsed programs. A self-reflexive show about a radio star, the cast included figures from the world of popular music: bandleader Phil Harris and boy singer Dennis Day performed on almost every episode. Benny's self-absorbed, cheapskate character—described by comedy writer Larry Gelbart as "a giant of pettiness"—allowed his co-stars to get laughs at his expense. The pregnant pause was Benny's most effective comic tool. Added to the cast in 1937, Eddie "Rochester" Anderson played Benny's African American valet. The NAACP, actively engaged with the task of improving depictions of black Americans in the media, never criticized Benny's and Anderson's 21-year relationship, which permitted Anderson to demonstrate impertinence towards his white boss. The act eliminated minstrel stereotypes after World War II. Benny encouraged Anderson's nearly equal co-stardom.

The Jack Benny Program moved to television in 1950 and ran through 1965. Benny's 30 films draw directly on his radio persona; *To Be or Not to Be* (1942) has remained the most lasting. While his radio and television character was a notoriously incompetent violinist, Benny was skilled enough to play large-scale benefit concerts during the final 18 years of his life. Beginning with a 1956 concert in Carnegie Hall with the New York Philharmonic under Alfred Wallenstein, Benny played major concert works—a bit under tempo and sometimes with pitch problems—with symphony orchestras across the nation, often to benefit musicians' pension funds or support struggling orchestras.

BIBLIOGRAPHY

M.L. Benny and H. Marks: *Jack Benny* (Garden City, NY, 1978)
J. Benny and J. Benny: *Sunday Nights at Seven: the Jack Benny Story* (New York, 1990)
G. Nachman: *Raised on Radio* (New York, 1998)
G. Giddins: *Natural Selection* (New York, 2006)
K.H. Marcus: "The Seriousness of Comedy: the Benefit Concerts of Jack Benny and Danny Kaye," *AM*, xxv/2 (2007), 137–68

TODD DECKER

Benoit, David (Bryan) (*b* Bakersfield, CA, 18 Aug 1953). Jazz pianist, composer, arranger, and producer. He studied piano and theory at El Camino College (1972), arranging and orchestration at Valley College (1973), and film scoring at UCLA (1981). His teachers included Abraham Fraser (piano), Donald Neligan, Heichiro Ohyama, Donald Ray, and Jan Robertson. In 1976 he became music director and conductor for the singer Lainie Kazan, followed by similar work for the singers Ann Margaret and Connie Stevens. From 1977 he has recorded his own smooth jazz albums; those from the 1980s, including *This Side Up* and *Every Step of the Way* (one of his many Grammy-nominated recordings), helped to define the genre. He has been involved in a wide range of projects, including working for ten years as a composer for "Peanuts" TV specials, with the GRP All-Star Big Band, and with such musicians as Kenny Loggins, Patti Austin, Kenny Rankin, and Faith Hill. He is also a film score composer and conductor; in the latter role he has worked with the Asia America Symphony Orchestra, which gave the first performance of his piano concerto *The Centaur and the Sphinx* with Frederic Chiu as soloist (2004). His symphonic tone poem *Kobe* was first performed by the Philippine Philharmonic in 2001. Among his many honors are the Oasis Smooth Jazz Awards Keyboardist of the Year (2000 and 2001), the Excellence in Music Education award from the Mr. Holland's Opus Foundation (2001), and American Smooth Jazz's Lifetime Achievement Award (2010).

JEFFREY HOLMES

Benson, George (*b* Pittsburgh, PA, 22 March 1943). Jazz guitarist, singer, composer, and producer. Born and raised in Hill District, a poor neighborhood of Pittsburgh, he was a child prodigy. He won a singing contest and performed on radio as Little Georgie Benson at four, danced and played ukulele at seven, appeared on weekends in an illicit nightclub at eight, released a single ("She makes me mad," Groove, 1954) at ten, performed with local rhythm-and-blues group the Altarrs, and led his own quintet as a teenager. He was influenced by the music of Charlie Christian, George Shearing, Nat "King" Cole, Charlie Parker, and Errol Garner. Guitarists Wes Montgomery, Tal Farlow, and Hank Garland sparked his interest in modern jazz, while blues singers Ray Charles, Charles Brown, and Little Willie John shaped his vocal style. In 1961 Benson began working with organist Jack McDuff, an important mentor who performed on his debut album *The New Boss Guitar of George Benson* (1964, Prestige). After recording several albums in a soul jazz and hard bop style for Columbia and Verve, and appearing as a sideman with Miles Davis, Herbie Hancock, and Jimmy Smith, he made a series of albums with the producer Creed Taylor for A&M and CTI. Mass popular appeal followed the release of the single "This Masquerade" from his first Warner Bros. recording, *Breezin'* (1976), a popular jazz album that launched a series of commercially successful pop-oriented albums produced by Tommy LiPuma. By the late 1980s Benson had returned to a more traditional jazz approach that emphasized his guitar playing. His influential guitar technique is fast but precise, and he is noted for the ability to accompany improvisations with scat vocals. A multiple Grammy winner and 2009 NEA Jazz Master, Benson has combined broad commercial appeal with artistic integrity to play a seminal role in exposing general audiences to jazz.

BIBLIOGRAPHY

S. Britt: *The Jazz Guitarists* (Poole, Dorset, England, 1984)
B. Blumenthal: "Pazz & Jop: George Benson and Russell Malone," *JT*, xxx/6 (2000), 34–40, 144–5
C. Chapman: "George Benson," *Interview with the Jazz Greats* (Pacific, MO, 2001, 17–9
A. Scott: "Rise," *Wax Poetics*, xlvi (2011), 56–70

THOMAS H. GREENLAND

Benson, Joan (*b* St. Paul, MN, 9 Oct 1929). Keyboard player. After attending the University of Illinois (BM, MM 1951) and Indiana University (1953), she studied in Europe with Edwin Fischer, OLIVIER MESSIAEN, Viola Thern, and Guido Agosti. Her growing interest in early music and the clavichord led to further work with Fritz Neumeyer, Ruggero Gerlin, and Macario Santiago Kastner before she returned to the United States in 1960 following a tour of the Middle East. After a highly successful recording in 1962, Benson began concert appearances on the clavichord and, in time, the fortepiano. Her debut on the clavichord was at the 1963 Carmel Bach Festival. Since 1965, she has made many concert and lecture tours of North America, Europe, and Asia, and has performed on instruments of most of the major music collections. After teaching at Stanford University (1968–76), she accepted an appointment in 1976 at the University of Oregon and also joined the faculty of the Aston Magna Festival in 1980. She left the concert stage for a decade to explore Buddhist meditation, then returned to perform once more. Benson has been praised for unusually sensitive and stylish interpretations in concert and on recordings of a repertory that spans keyboard music from the Renaissance to the Viennese Classics and includes also contemporary works, some of which have been written for her. Her work has been crucial in the revival of interest in the fortepiano and the music of C.P.E. Bach.

BIBLIOGRAPHY

M. Bargreen: "Profile: Joan Benson, Clavichordist," *Clavier*, xix/10 (1980), 42

HOWARD SCHOTT/R

Benson, Warren (Frank) (*b* Detroit, MI, 26 Jan 1924; *d* Rochester, NY, 6 Oct 2005). Composer. He studied music theory at the University of Michigan (BM 1949, MM 1951) but was essentially self-taught as a composer. He was timpanist with the Detroit SO in 1946. He conducted and taught composition at Anatolia College in Salonica, Greece (1950–52, as a Fulbright scholar), Mars Hill (North Carolina) College (1952–3), Ithaca (New York) College (1953–67), where he organized the Ithaca College Percussion Ensemble, and the Eastman School (1967–93); he was also active in the Contemporary Music Project from its inception, developing its first pilot project. As a composer he wrote especially successfully for percussion and wind ensembles and received numerous commissions and awards, including a Guggenheim Fellowship (1981–2). His music, as exemplified by the popular *Ginger Marmalade* (1978) and *The Solitary Dancer* (1966), is varied and selective in technique; lyricism is prominent, as is colorful instrumentation. He is the author of *Creative Projects in Musicianship* (Washington, DC, 1967) and *Compositional Processes and Writing Skills* (Washington, DC, 1974).

WORKS

Orch: A Delphic Serenade, 1953; 5 Brief Encounters, str, 1961; Theme and Excursions, str, 1963; Chants and Graces, str, pic, harp, perc, 1964; Bailando, 1965; Hn Conc., 1971; The Man with the Blue Guitar, 1980; Beyond Winter: Sweet Aftershowers, str, 1981; Concertino, fl, str, perc, 1983

Band: 8 works, incl. The Leaves are Falling, 1963; The Passing Bell, 1974; Sym. no.2 "Lost Songs," 1982

Wind ens: Concertino, a sax, wind, 1954; Sym., drums, wind orch, 1962; Recuerdo, ob/eng hn, wind, 1965; Star-edge, a sax, wind, 1965; Helix, tuba, wind, 1966; The Solitary Dancer, 1966; The Mask of Night, 1968; Shadow Wood (T. Williams), S, wind, 1971; The Beaded Leaf (A. Hecht), B, wind, 1974; Ginger Marmalade, 1978; Other Rivers, 1984; Wings, 1984; Dawn's Early Light, 1987: Meditation on "I Am for Peace" 1990; Danzón-Memory, 1991; Adagietto, 1992; Divertissement I, 1993; Daughter of the Stars, 1998; other works withdrawn or left in revision

Perc: Variations on a Handmade Theme, 8 handclappers, 1957; Perc Trio, 1957; 3 Pieces, perc qt, 1960; Streams, 7 perc, 1961; 3 Dances, 1962; Rondino, 8 handclappers, 1967; Winter Bittersweet, 6 perc, 1981; Thorgard's Song, hn, 4 perc, 1982 (1997)

Chamber: 15 pieces for solo inst, pf, 1951–66; Marche, ww qt, 1955; Qnt, ob/s sax, str, 1957; Wind Rose, sax qt, 1967; Str Qt, 1969; Capriccio, pf qt, 1972; The Dream Net, a sax, str qt, 1976; Largo Tah, b trbn, mar, 1977; Qnt, perc, str, 1984; Str Qt II: Hawk Music, 1986; Str Qt III: Cat's Cradle, 1995; other inst pieces

Choral: Psalm xxiv, SSAA, str, 1957; 27 pieces for SATB, incl. Songs of O, SATB, brass qnt, mar, 1974; Earth, Sky, Sea (K. Rexroth), SATB, fl, b trbn, mar, 1975; Meditation, Prayer and Sweet Hallelujah (E. Bullins), chorus, pf, 1979; A Song of Praise, SATB, 1983; The Singers (W.W. Longfellow), 1983 (1998) S(2)ATB; The Hearth Within (L. Latham), 1985 (1998), S(2)A(2)T(2)B(2); They Brought a Joyful Song (S. Teasdale), 1985, S(3)A(2)T(2)B(2); Sing and Rejoice, 1997, S(2) A(2)T(2)B(2); and others

Solo vocal: Nara (E. Birney), S, fl, pf, 2 perc, 1970; 5 Lyrics of Louise Bogan, Mez, fl, 1977; Songs for the End of the World (J. Gardner), Mez, eng hn, hn, vc, mar, 1980; Moon Rain and Memory Jane, song cycle, S, 2 vc, 1982; The Putcha Putcha Variations (Gardner), 1v, 1983; Moon Rain and Memory Jane (M. Swenson, J. Jerome, B. Dmitrova, S.K. Russell, R. Hayden, L.M.Rosenberg), 1984, S, 2vc; Dos Antifonas Lindas, S, Mez, va, 1985 (1996); and others

MSS in *NRU-Mus*

Principal publishers: C. Fischer, MCA, E.C. Schirmer, Presser

BIBLIOGRAPHY

EwenD; *GroveA*

R. Ricker: "Composer's Profile: Warren Benson," *Saxophone Symposium*, iv/1 (1979), 4–10

D. Hunsberger: "A Discussion with Warren Benson: *The Leaves are Falling*," *College Band Directors National Association Journal*, i/1 (1984), 7–17 [incl. list of wind compositions]

R.G. George: *An Analysis of the Compositional Techniques Used in Selected Works of Warren Benson* (diss., U. of Cincinnati, 1995)

A.D. Wagner: *A Bio-bibliography of Composer Warren Benson* (New York, 2005)

JERALD C. GRAUE/MICHAEL MECKNA

Bentley, Gladys (*b* Philadelphia, PA, 12 Aug 1907; *d* Los Angeles, CA, 18 Jan 1960). Blues singer and pianist. Born into poverty, she moved to New York when she was 16 and lived in Harlem during the Jazz Age. She was openly lesbian and began performing at racially mixed rent parties, buffet flats, and other gay venues. She subsequently worked in the well-known clubs of "Jungle Alley" including Harry Hansberry's Clam House, the Ubangi Club, and the Cotton Club. Bentley performed in tuxedo and top hat, accompanying herself on piano, pounding the floor, and alternating her powerful alto with trumpet-like scat singing. Several Harlem Renaissance novelists including Langston Hughes describe her all-night performances as unforgettable. She recorded for OKeh (eight blues titles), Victor, Excelsior, and Flame. Following the repeal of the prohibition act in 1933, she worked sporadically on the West Coast, notably at Mona's in San Francisco. She abandoned her drag act in the 1950s and appeared late in life at the Rose Room in Hollywood and twice on the Groucho Marx television show.

BIBLIOGRAPHY

E. Garber: "Gladys Bentley: the Bulldagger who Sang the Blues," *OUT/Look: National Lesbian & Gay Quarterly*, i/1 (1988), 52–61

E. Garber: "A Spectacle in Color: the Lesbian and Gay Subculture of Jazz Age Harlem," *Hidden from History: Reclaiming the Gay and Lesbian Past*, ed. M.B. Duberman, M. Vicinus, and G. Chauncey (New York, 1989), 318–31

TINA SPENCER DREISBACH

Benton, Brook [Peay, Benjamin Franklin] (*b* Camden, SC, 19 Sept 1931; *d* New York, NY, 9 April 1988). Singer and songwriter. Having started a black gospel singer, in the 1950s he co-wrote hits for artists including Nat "King" Cole ("Looking Back," with Clyde Otis) and Clyde McPhatter ("A Lover's Question," with Otis and Belford Hendricks). During the period 1959–63 the latter songwriting partnership provided a series of hits for Benton himself. With Hendricks's opulent string and choral arrangements, these included "It's a matter of time," "Thank you pretty baby," "So Many Ways" and "Endlessly"; Benton's resonant, ingratiating baritone showed the influence of Billy Eckstine and Cole. At the same time, Benton recorded arrangements of the traditional "Boll Weevil Song" and "Frankie and Johnny." One of his most effective recordings was an atmospheric version of Tony Joe White's "A Rainy Night in Georgia" (1970). Benton also sang with Dinah Washington on the standard "Babe you got what it takes" and the uptempo "A Rockin' Good Way," which was re-recorded in 1984 by the Welsh singers Bonnie Tyler and Shakin' Stevens.

DAVE LAING

Benton, Rita (*b* New York, NY, 28 June 1918; *d* Paris, France, 23 March 1980). Music librarian and musicologist. Benton received a diploma at the Juilliard School (1938), the BA at Hunter College (1939), and the MA (1951) in musicology at the University of Iowa. She began her career at the University of Iowa Libraries in 1952 as one of a team of faculty wives who worked to reclassify the library's collections from Dewey to Library Congress. She became the University's first music librarian in 1953, completed the PhD in musicology in 1961, and was appointed to the faculty of the School of Music in 1967. She was president of the MLA (1962–3), active in the International Association of Music Libraries, Archives, and Documentation Centres, and served as editor of its journal, *Fontes artis musicae*, from 1976 until her death. Among Benton's scholarly interests was French music of the late 18th century. She solved the difficult bibliographical problems associated with Ignace Pleyel and published a thematic catalog of his works, which earned MLA's award for best book-length bibliography for that year (1977). Her translation (1970) of Frits Noske's *La mélodie française de Berlioz à Duparc* has been praised for the fluidity of its English and fidelity to the author's literary style. Her four-volume *Directory of Music Research Libraries* provides a wealth of information about major library collections of music. Following her death, the University of Iowa honored her by naming the library the Rita Benton Music Library.

WRITINGS

Directory of Music Research Libraries (Iowa City, IA, 1967–75, 2/1979–85)

"The Music Library of the University of Iowa," *FAM*, xvi (1969), 124–9

French Song from Berlioz to Duparc (New York, 2/1970/*R*) [trans. of F. Noske: *La mélodie française de Berlioz à Duparc* (Amsterdam, 1954)]

"The Nature of Music and some Implications for the University Music Library," *FAM*, xxiii (1976), 53–60

Ignace Pleyel: a Thematic Catalogue of his Compositions (New York, 1977)

BIBLIOGRAPHY

Grove7 (P. Morgan)

PAULA MORGAN/RUTHANN B. MCTYRE

Beranek, Leo (Leroy) (*b* Solon, IA, 15 Sept 1914). Acoustician. After studying at Cornell College, Iowa (BA 1936), Beranek was awarded his doctorate in 1940 by Harvard University. During World War II he directed the Electro-Acoustic Laboratory at Harvard University and later taught at MIT. In 1948 he founded a company of acoustics consultants (Bolt, Beranek and Newman, Inc.), which quickly established an international reputation. Before writing his seminal book, *Music, Acoustics and Architecture* (New York, 1962), he traveled through 20 countries, listening and making measurements in many halls and consulting fellow acousticians and musical performers. Beranek has since been responsible for the acoustical design of a large number of major concert halls and opera houses, and through his writings has contributed greatly to the dissemination of good practice in the design and construction of buildings intended for musical use. Largely through his influence, the acoustical parameters used in scientific evaluation of concert hall acoustics have become much more sophisticated; he published a magisterial review (1996, R/2004) of many of the world's most important concert halls and opera houses, in which these parameters are tabulated and related to the subjective judgments of conductors and performers. Among Beranek's many honors are the Gold Medals of the Acoustical Society of America, the Audio Engineering Society, and the American Society of Mechanical Engineers. In 2003 he received the US Presidential National Medal of Science.

WRITINGS

Acoustic Measurements (New York, 1949)
Acoustics (New York, 1954)
Music, Acoustics and Architecture (New York, 1962)
"Concert Hall Acoustics," *JASA*, xcii (1992), 1–39
Concert and Opera Halls: How they Sound (Woodbury, NY, 1996; 2/2004 expanded and retitled as *Concert Halls and Opera Houses: Music, Acoustics, and Architecture*)

MURRAY CAMPBELL

Berberian, Ara (*b* Detroit, MI, 14 May 1930; *d* Boynton Beach, FL, 21 Feb 2005). Bass. He attended the University of Michigan where he was a member of the Men's Glee Club and *Novelaires Quartet* (with baritone Dick Frank). He made his debut in 1958 at the Turnau Opera in Woodstock, New York, in the role of Don Magnifico in Gioachino Rossini's *La Cenerentola*. He debuted with the Metropolitan Opera in Cleveland on their 1979 spring tour, playing Kecal in Smetana's opera *The Bartered Bride*. Later that year he appeared with the Met in New York as Zacharie in Giacomo Meyerbeer's *Le prophète*. Berberian also appeared with the New York City Opera, the San Francisco Opera, and the Michigan Opera Theatre. He performed over one hundred different roles in his career, most notably Osmin in Mozart's *Abduction from the Seraglio* and Sparafucile in Verdi's *Rigoletto*. Of Armenian ancestry, Berberian also sang and recorded music by Armenian and Armenian American composers such as Komitas Vardapet and Alan Hovhaness.

ANYA LAURENCE

Berberian, Cathy [Catherine] (*b* Attleboro, MA, 4 July 1925; *d* Rome, Italy, 6 March 1983). Singer. Varied training and early experience helped to equip this versatile artist: courses in mime, writing, and opera at Columbia and New York universities; Hindu and Spanish dancing; work as a soloist with an Armenian dance group and in summer repertory; and vocal study in Milan with Giorgina del Vigo. She made her debut in Naples in 1957, at an Incontri Musicali concert. The following year, at a John Cage concert in Rome, she sang his *Aria with Fontana Mix*. Her American debut was at Tanglewood, in 1960, with Luciano Berio's *Circles*. LUCIANO BERIO, to whom she was married from 1950 to 1966, in a series of works (notably *Circles*, *Sequenza III*, *Visage*, and *Recital I*) inspired by her vocal virtuosity, darting, witty intelligence, and vivid presence, in effect limned the voices, styles, and temperament of this remarkable performer. The long list of composers who wrote for her includes Stravinsky (*Elegy for JFK*), Henze, Haubenstock-Ramati, and Bussotti. Her repertory embraced 17th-century opera (she had a particular affinity with Monteverdi), folksong of all countries, and the salon *morceaux*—ranging from exquisite miniatures to such *trouvailles* as Griepenkerl's vocal version of the "Moonlight" Sonata—gathered in her recital "Une Soirée chez Mme Verdurin." Her compositions include *Stripsody* for solo voice (1966) and *Morsicat(h)y* for piano (1971).

BIBLIOGRAPHY

Symphonica, no.30 (Sept 1993) [Special issue on Berberian]
M. Vila: *Cathy Berberian Cant'actrice* (Paris, 2003)
D. Osmond-Smith: "The Tenth Oscillator: the Work of Cathy Berberian 1958–1966," *Tempo*, lviii/227 (2004), 2–13
J. Paull: *Cathy Berberian and Music's Muses* (Vouvry, Switzerland, 2007)

ANDREW PORTER/R

Berezowsky, Nikolai [Berezovsky, Nikolay Tikhonovich] (*b* St Petersburg, Russia, 17 May 1900; *d* New York, NY, 27 Aug 1953). Composer, conductor, and violinist of Russian birth, naturalized American. He studied at the court chapel in St. Petersburg (1908–16), where he performed regularly for royalty (and the notorious Rasputin) and played the violin at the Saratov opera (1917–19) and the Bolshoi (1919–20). Berezowsky held the position of musical director at the School of Modern Art in Moscow for a brief time, but in 1920 he left the USSR; he studied violin with Robert Pollack in Vienna and in 1922 reached New York, where he was a member of the New York PO (1923–9), and served in the first violin section. In 1927 he held a fellowship to study composition with RUBIN GOLDMARK and violin with Pawel Kochański at the Juilliard School; he also conducted the Atwater Kent Radio Concerts (1926–7). In 1928 he became an American citizen. The following year he left the United States to live in Europe, but returned after two years. From 1935 to 1940, he was a member of the Coolidge String Quartet; Berezowsky was also assistant conductor at CBS radio (1932–6 and 1941–6). Many of his recordings were for the Victor label. He received a grant from the National Institute of Arts and Letters (1944) and a Guggenheim Fellowship (1948). His style blended Russian folk melos, Rimsky-Korsakovian orchestral expertise, and mild dissonance. The palatable symphonies, championed by Koussevitzky, won immediate critical acclaim, as did the concertos introduced by Primrose and Piatigorsky. His children's opera *Babar the Elephant* was widely performed. Berezowsky's manuscript scores, many of his papers, and much of his correspondence is held at the Music Division of the New York Public Library. Berezowsky's suicide in 1953 ended what had promised to be an even more impressive career.

WORKS

(selective list; dates in parentheses are those of publication, others are those of first performance)

Orch: Introduction and Allegro, op.8, small orch (1945); Sym. no.1, op.12, 1931; Vn Conc., op.14, 1930; Sinfonietta, op.17, 1932; Sym. no.2, op.18, 1934; Conc. lirico, op.19, vc, orch, 1935; Sym. no.3, op.21, 1937; Sym. no.4, op.27, 1943; Va Conc., op.28, 1941; Cl Conc., op.29 (1941); Hp Conc., op.31, 1945; Passacaglia, theremin, orch, 1948

Vocal: Gilgamesh, cant., op.32, nar, solo vv, chorus, orch, 1947; Babar the Elephant (children's op., 1, D. Heyward), op.40, 1953

Chbr: Thème et variations, op.7, cl, str, pf, 1926; Str Qt, op.16 (1933); Duo, op.15, va, cl (1941); Suite, op.22, wind qnt (1941); Brass Suite, op.24, 7 brass (1942); Fantasy, op.9, 2 pf (1944); Sextet Conc., op.26, str (1951)

Principal publishers: Boosey & Hawkes, Edition Russe

BIBLIOGRAPHY

Baker8; *EwenD*

J.T. Howard: *Our Contemporary Composers* (New York, 1941), 184

A. Berezowsky: *Duet with Nicky* (Philadelphia, 1943)

N. Slominsky: *Music since 1900* (New York, 1937, 5/1994)

ROBERT STEVENSON/JONAS WESTOVER

Berg, Lillie P. (*b* New York, NY, *c*1845; *d* after 1896). Musician and teacher. Lillie Berg was born in New York City but spent her childhood in Germany, the native country of her father. She attended the Royal Conservatory of Music in Stuttgart, displaying an early talent at the piano and organ. She also studied voice, ultimately relocating to Milan to study with Francesco Lamperti. She worked with Lamperti for three years as a voice student and accompanist. By 1887, Berg had returned to New York where she became a sought-after singer at private musicales as well as a public performer in small-scale recitals. She also spent several seasons in London, gaining a reputation as a singer. In New York she established a teaching studio and by 1890 was known as "the most fashionable" singing teacher in the city. Her pedagogy centered on the Lamperti method, in which she was recognized as the nation's authority. Attracting a large number of students, Berg's studio engaged many teachers and trained students in voice, piano, elocution, and languages. In the 1890s, Berg took up conducting and formed the Lillie Berg Glee Club, which gave several performances of cantatas and operettas.

BIBLIOGRAPHY

"Lillie Berg," *Boston Herald* (March 1890) [NYpl Clipping File]

F.E. Willard and M.A. Livermore, eds.: *Woman of The Century: Fourteen Hundred-Seventy Biographical Sketches Accompanied by Portraits of Leading Women in All Walks of Life* (Buffalo, NY, 1893)

"Professional Notes," *The looker-on*, ii/2 (1896), 488–90

F.E. Willard and M.A. Livermore, eds.: *American Women: Fifteen Hundred Biographies with over 1,400 Portraits* (New York, 1897)

LAURIE BLUNSOM

Berger, Arthur (Victor) (*b* New York, NY, 15 May 1912; *d* Boston, MA, 7 Oct 2003). Composer and critic. He was a student at the Townsend Harris High School, the College of the City of New York, and New York University (BS 1934). During these years he espoused leftist politics and was a member—along with Bernard Herrmann, Jerome Moross, Israel Citkowitz, Vivian Fine, Elie Siegmeister, and others—of various radical composers' groups including the Young Composers Group that formed around Aaron Copland. He was a fellowship student in the newly formed Professional Division of the Longy School of Music (1935–7) concurrently with graduate studies at Harvard University (MA 1936), where he trained in musicology with Hugo Leichtentritt, aesthetics with D.W. Prall, and theory and analysis with Walter Piston. From 1937 to 1939 he studied theory with Nadia Boulanger in Paris. He taught at Mills College (1939–42), Brooklyn College (1942–3), and the Juilliard School, and then at Brandeis University from 1953 to 1978, and at New England Conservatory from 1979 to 1998.

From his high school years he was active as a music critic, starting as a stringer for the New York *Daily Mirror*; this was followed by more steady work as music critic for the *Boston Transcript* during his years at Harvard and Longy, and then at the *New York Sun* (1943–6) and the *New York Herald Tribune* (1947–53). He was editor of *Musical Mercury* (1934–7), and was the cofounder, with Benjamin Boretz, and the first editor of *Perspectives of New Music* (1962–3). He contributed articles to numerous journals, including *Modern Music*, *Saturday Review*, *Atlantic Monthly*, *High Fidelity*, *Score*, *The Boston Review*, *Musical Quarterly*, and *The New York Review of Books*. He also wrote a monograph on the music of Copland (New York, 1953) and a memoir, *Reflections of an American Composer* (Berkeley, 2002).

Among his awards were an American Council of Learned Societies grant (1936), a Fulbright Fellowship (1960), and a Guggenheim Fellowship (1975–6). He was a member of the American Academy of Arts and Sciences and of the Institute of the American Academy and Institute of Arts and Letters.

From his high school days Berger was passionately involved with modern music. One of the most powerful of his early experiences came at age 18 when he attended the New York staged premiere of *The Rite of Spring* in 1930 at the Metropolitan Opera House featuring Leopold Stokowski and the Philadelphia Orchestra, with Martha Graham as the chosen victim. It was not the work by Igor Stravinsky, however, but rather the other work on the program, Arnold Schoenberg's *Die glückliche Hand*, that affected him profoundly and caused him to determine the compositional path he wished to follow; his earliest surviving works, *Three Episodes for Piano* (1933) are from that period. However, the difficulty of reconciling a Schoenbergian style with his political conviction that "serious" music should be accessible to "the masses," and his lack of sympathy with the Germanic aesthetic, which he deemed inseparable from that musical language, left him uncertain how to proceed compositionally, so he ceased writing music and devoted his efforts to criticism (it was as spokesman that he was welcomed into the Young Composers Group) and to the study of theory and musicology. Eventually he found the neo-classical style of Stravinsky to be a path for returning to composition, and by the time he was appointed to the faculty of Mills College he had resumed composition. When Darius Milhaud joined the faculty at Mills, Berger, following the example of his colleague Charles Jones, began showing the older composer his work, and, in effect, became his student; it was through Milhaud's efforts that Berger received a commission for his *Woodwind Quartet in C* (1941), one of his best-known works, for members of the San Francisco Symphony.

During the early years of his career, Berger was generally thought of, along with his friends from Harvard (Irving Fine and Harold Shapero) and to a lesser extent with Alexei Haieff, Leo Smit, Louise Talma, Ingolf Dahl, John Lessard, Leonard Bernstein, and Lukas Foss, as being part of a group described variously as "The New Boston Classical School," "The Harvard Neoclassicists," or "The New England School." They were closely associated with Stravinsky and Copland, both personally and stylistically. Berger's music of this period was diatonic and aspired to a more or less traditional long line of continuity, reflecting aspects of sonata form, and was characterized by wide melodic leaps and a rhythmically fragmented texture of criss-crossing lines. By the 1950s he was writing works such as the *'Cello Duo* (1951) and *Polyphony* (1956), which seem to have a traditional surface and structure but are based on three-note diatonic cells, manipulated in various quasi-serial ways. It was this music, where tonality is a conceit produced largely by the use of diatonic pitch-class collections deployed in ways not completely congruent with tonal practices, that Milton Babbitt called "diatonic Webern." During the late 1950s Berger began to develop a more chromatic language, chiefly through working with what eventually became completely chromatic trichords (C–C♯–D, for instance), always presented not as clusters, but in widely spaced sonorities spread over two or three octaves, with variety achieved by using such traditional methods as chord inversions, as well as by changes in timbre among the groups of notes in fixed registers. A sense of tonal variety and contrast, analogous to key change, is achieved by a free use of hexachordal fields, loosely following Josef Matthias Hauer's principle of tropes. As Berger's music moved further from the sound of traditional tonal music, it also moved further from traditional modes of structural organization, characterized more and more by a discontinuous or fragmentary continuity, described by Berger as being "like a movie—or better, the slick night-time soap opera, where a number of different plots, ultimately related, constantly cut into one another without transition."

Although Berger did write 12-tone music for a short while—in *Chamber Music for Thirteen Players* (1956), String Quartet (1958), and the withdrawn Chamber Concerto of 1959—he eventually found serialism not to be congenial to his personal working methods, and he developed a more intuitive mode of composition. For a time he wrote works in which rigorous patterns set the boundaries for a sort of controlled, written-out improvisation: *Three Pieces for Two Pianos* (1961), *Five Piano Pieces* (finished in 1969), and the Septet (1966). Eventually he developed a looser form of construction which he thought of as "perpetual variation," described by him as "a form of ruminating over the same material, turning it this way and that, allowing it to fluctuate in mood and tempo within sections, and ultimately yielding, despite sectional breaks (mere pauses for breath), one relatively long movement."

In his later years, although he ceased to compose new works, Berger re-wrote, one might more accurately say re-imagined and re-composed, works he had already written. He considered these works to be collages, in the manner of the collages of his friend the visual artist Robert Motherwell. The idea of recomposing existing pieces began with his *Clarinet Duo* of 1957, which is closer to being an arrangement of the *Duo* for oboe and clarinet of 1952. The later works, however, sometimes re-order events, add completely new music to obliterate an earlier version of a particular passage (which he compared to placing a new piece of paper over an existing image), or overlay a line or several lines over existing music which then becomes an accompaniment to the new "tunes" (in manner similar to painting an image on top of some detail). *Perspectives II* (1985), for chamber orchestra, and *Perspectives III* (1982), for piano four hands, are, like the earlier *Duo,* closer to being revisions and reorchestrations of movements from the withdrawn Chamber Concerto of 1959, but *Diptych* (1990) and *Collage III* (1992) are drastic recompositions of *Quintet for Woodwinds* (1984) and *Composition for Piano Four Hands* (1976, rev. 1989), respectively. These recomposed works always involve a higher degree of instrumental color and variation than their originals.

Berger exerted considerable influence on contemporary music and on university compositional training in the United States during the second half of the 20th century as composer, teacher, critic, and author. His relatively small body of compositions combines a tireless and painstaking concern for artistic and musical operation and expression with what Virgil Thomson described as an "only slightly disguised sidewalks-of-New-York charm."

WORKS

Orch: Serenade Concertante, 1944, rev. 1951; Ideas of Order, 1952; Polyphony 1956; Chbr Conc., 1959, Perspectives II, 1985

Chbr: Qt in C, fl, ob, cl, bn, 1941; 3 Pieces, str qt, 1945; 5 Duos: vl, pf, 1944, vn, pf, 1950; vc, pf, 1951, ob, cl 1951; cl, pf, 1957; Chamber Music for 13 Players, 1956; St Qt, 1958; Septet, fl, cl, bn, vn, va, vc, pf, 1966; 2 Trios: gui, vn, pf, 1972, vn, vc, pf, 1980; Qnt, fl, cl, ob, hn, bn, 1984; Dyptich, fl, cl, vn, vc, pf, 1990; Collage III, fl, cl, vn, vc, perc, pf, 1992

Pf: 3 Episodes, 1933; Entertainment Piece ("Ballet for Piano"), 1940; Fantasy, 1942; Rondo, 1945; Capriccio, 1945; 3 Bagatelles, 1946; Partita, 1947; Intermezzo, 1948; 3 Two Part Inventions, 1948–9; 3 One Part Inventions, 1954; 3 Pieces for Two Pf, 1961; 5 Pieces, 1969; Improvisation for A. C. ("Birthday Piece for Aaron Copland"), 1981; For Elliott at 75, a study in 7ths and 9ths ("Birthday Piece for Elliott Carter"), 1983

Pf 4 hands: Composition, 1976, rev, 1989; Perspectives III, 1982; Suite [Capriccio, Aria, Rondo (Duet for H. S.)], 1999

Vocal: Words for Music Perhaps (3 Songs) (W.B. Yeats), S/Mez (fl, cl, vc)/pf, 1939–40, rev. 1987; Garlands (Asklepiades), Mez, pf, 1945; Tov l'Hodos ("Psalm 92"), SATB, 1946; When I Am Dead (C. Rossetti), 1978; Five Setting of European Poets (Horace, R.M. Rilke, P. Valéry, G.G. Belli, C. Rossetti) T, pf, 1978–79, O Love, Sweet Animal (D. Schwartz), SATB, pf 4 Hands, 1982; Ode of Ronsard, Mez, pf/fl,vc, pf, 1987, rev. 2001

Principal publishers: Associated, Boelk-Bomart, C.F. Peters, E.B. Marks, G. Schirmer, Lawson-Gould, Mercury, New Music

WRITINGS

"The Songs of Charles Ives," *Musical Mercury*, i (1934), 97–8

"Form is Feeling," *MM*, xxii (1944–5), 87–92

Aaron Copland (New York, 1953)

"Stravinsky and the Younger American Composers," *The Score*, xii (1955), 38–46; repr. in *The American Composer Speaks*, ed. G. Chase (Baton Rouge, LA, 1966), 201–15

"Aaron Copland's Piano Fantasy," *Juilliard Review*, v/1 (1957–8), 13–27

"Problems of Pitch Organization in Stravinsky," *PNM*, ii/1 (1963), 11–42; repr. in *Perspectives on Schoenberg and Stravinsky*, ed. B. Boretz and E.T. Cone (New York, 1972), 123–54

"Notes on the Plight of the American Composer," *Culture for the Milions? Mass Media in Modern Society*, ed. N. Jacobs (Boston, 1964), 111–9

"New Linguistic Modes and the New Theory," *PNM*, iii/1 (1964–5), 1–9; repr. in *Perspectives on Contemporary Music Theory*, ed. B. Boretz and E.T. Cone (New York, 1972), 11–30

"Some Notes on Babbitt and his Influence," *PNM*, xiv/2–xv/1 (1976), 32–6

"Music as Imitation," *Perspectives on Musical Aesthetics*, ed. J. Rahn (New York, 1994), 302–12

Reflections of an American Composer (Berkeley, 2002)

BIBLIOGRAPHY

P. Glanville-Hicks: "Arthur Berger," *ACA Bulletin*, iii/1 (1953), 2–5

J.M. Perkins: "Arthur Berger: the Composer as Mannerist," *PNM*, v/1 (1966–7), 75–92, repr. in *Perspectives on American Composers*, ed. B. Boretz and E.T. Cone (New York, 1971), 230–47

Festschrift for Berger, *PNM*, xvii/1 (1978), 1–91 [incl. interview by J. Coppeck; articles by E. Barkin, S. Silver, and others; bibliography of writings by P. Jones; and list of works]

E. Barkin: "Arthur Berger's Trio for Violin, Guitar and Piano," *Breaking the Sound Barrier*, ed. G. Battcock (New York, 1981), 215–20

B. Northcott: "Arthur Berger: an Introduction at 70," *MT*, cxxiii (1982), 323–9

P. Driver: "Arthur Berger and his Unmistakable Music," *Boston Globe* (28 Dec 1983)

P. Child: "A Glance Backward: Musical Activity in New England, c. 1930–1950: an Interview with Arthur Berger," *Essays in Modern Music*, iii/1–4 (1987), 11–22

R. Lister: "Arthur Berger: the Progress of a Method," *AM*, xiii/1 (1995), 56–95

R. Bauer: "An Interview with Arthur Berger," *Musically Incorrect*, ed. H. Biggs and S. Orzel (New York, 1998), 49–69

RODNEY LISTER

Berger, Henry [Heinrich Wilhelm] (*b* Berlin, Germany, 4 Aug 1844; *d* Honolulu, HI, 14 Oct 1929). Hawaiian bandmaster, composer, and arranger of Prussian birth. Berger studied music in Germany before joining the Prussian Army in 1862. He was a member of the combined Prussian music corps that won first prize at the 1867 Paris Exposition. After Paris, Berger began his military bandmaster training, likely at the Berlin Conservatory. In 1872 Kaiser Wilhelm sent him to Honolulu to fulfill a request by King Kamehameha V for a Prussian bandmaster. Berger assumed leadership of the Royal Hawaiian Band and led the band until his retirement in 1915. Over the course of his 43-year tenure as royal bandmaster, Berger is credited with conducting over 32,000 band concerts, arranging more than 1,000 Western musical compositions and 200 Hawaiian songs. He composed an estimated 75 Hawaiian melodies, supposedly more than 500 marches (mostly lost), and over 100 published compositions and arrangements. Berger helped to preserve numerous ancient *oli* (chants) and *mele* (songs) through his arrangements while helping to popularize European genres in Hawaii such as waltzes, polkas, and especially marches. Among his most popular compositions are the *Kohala March*, *Huki March*, and the music to "Hawai'i Ponoʻī," the kingdom's national anthem and now Hawaii's state song. He arranged Princess Liliʻuokalani's song "Aloha 'Oe" for band and introduced it in San Francisco in 1883, where it became very popular. On the occasion of his 70th birthday in 1914, Liliʻuokalani, the former queen of Hawaii, proclaimed Berger the "Father of Hawaiian Music."

BIBLIOGRAPHY

G.S. Kanahele: *Hawaiian Music and Musicians: an Illustrated History* (Honolulu, HI, 1979), 34 only

P. Hennessey: *Henry Berger: From Prussian Army Musician to "Father of Hawaiian Music," the Life and Legacy of Hawai'i's Bandmaster* (diss., U. of Hawaii, 2007)

PATRICK HENNESSEY

Berger, Jean [Schlossberg, Artur] (*b* Hamm, Germany, 27 Sept 1909; *d* Aurora, CO, 28 May 2002). Composer, musicologist, conductor, and pianist of German birth; naturalized American. Born Artur Schlossberg, he grew up in an orthodox Jewish family. After the Schlossbergs moved to Mannheim in 1919, he was introduced to German organ and choral literature by Arno Landmann, first Kantor (1911–43) of Christuskirche, and received piano instruction from Landmann's wife. With Mannheim's proximity to Strasbourg and Alsace-Lorraine, Schlossberg became fluent in French. Shortly after entering the University of Heidelberg in 1928, he applied for musicological studies with medievalist Heinrich Besseler. At the end of three years of intensive work, he submitted his doctoral dissertation (*Die italienische Sonate für mehrere Instrumente im 17ten Jahrhundert*, diss., U. of Heidelberg, 1932). Later that year he was engaged as a coach and conducting assistant to Hans Schmidt-Isserstedt at the Darmstadt Opera.

Beaten with guns by Adolf Hitler's Stormtroopers in early 1933, Schlossberg left Germany for Paris. Taking the name Jean Berger in 1934, he became a sought-after concert accompanist and vocal coach, founded and conducted a small chorus (Les Compagnons de la Marjolaine) and a workers theater (Les Blouses Bleues de

Bobigny), and joined a film production company as a staff pianist in 1938. Louis Aubert guided his early efforts as a composer. In 1937 his choral work *Le sang des autres* won first prize at an international competition in Zurich, prompting jurist Arthur Honneger to encourage him directly. Sensing the imminent outbreak of war, Berger immigrated to Rio de Janeiro in May 1939, where he worked as an opera coach at the Teatro Municipal, coached singers at the Conservatorio Brasileiro de Musica, concertized extensively, and composed—most notably, his *Four Sonnets* (L. de Camoens, 1939).

Berger entered the United States on 11 November 1940 as accompanist for a concert tour and officially immigrated in March 1941. Now able to incorporate Latin American styles and rhythms, he found an eager market in New York for the full range of his musical skills. In 1941 he composed *Brazilian Psalm* (the work that in 1950 established his reputation as a choral composer), *Caribbean Concerto* (commissioned by harmonica virtuoso Larry Adler), and the song cycle *Villanescas*. He arranged for CBS and NBC. Talents such as Eileen Farrell, Nan Merriman, Bidú Sayão, and Garfield Swift performed his songs. When America entered the war, Berger served first at the Office of War Information, then, after becoming a citizen in 1943, toured worldwide with USO Camp Shows (1944–6).

Berger's full-time academic career spanned 20 years: Middlebury College (1948–59), University of Illinois, Urbana (1959–61), and University of Colorado, Boulder (1961–8). His most significant contributions to musicology were centered on forgotten manuscripts (by G. Torelli, G.A. Perti, and others) housed at the basilica of San Petronio in Bologna. This coincided with his increasing output as a composer and steady rise to prominence in the field of choral music. For his almost two dozen choral works composed for the Lutheran Church in America, Pacific Lutheran University awarded him an honorary doctorate (1969). A MacDowell Colony fellow on four occasions, Berger founded John Sheppard Music Press (1964), devoted exclusively to the publication of his own music. Wanting "to inject new life into our stale choral presentations," he produced six "works for the staged chorus" between 1968 and 1975. From ages 55 to 90 he greatly expanded his publishing business; lectured on American choral music in the United States and abroad; led hundreds of clinics, workshops, and performances; accompanied singers in recitals of his songs; and, most significantly, added many song cycles and other works to his oeuvre, which ultimately totaled about 315 published and about 55 unpublished compositions.

A consummate and sophisticated craftsman, Berger readily assimilated musical influences but had no inclination to experiment with avant-garde procedures. He remained to the end of his life "unflinchingly tonal," yet decidedly contemporary. In his vocal music, which dominates his output, depending on the language—whether English, French, Spanish, Portuguese, Latin, Italian, or Hebrew—his music exquisitely supports the inflections and nuances of that language and echoes the musical styles of its culture(s). His "dance-based metabolism" impelled music that can be highly forceful, energetic, and rhythmic, incorporating mixed and asymmetrical meters. His approach to text-setting was generally non-polyphonic and often declamatory. Berger rarely tried to analyze or explain his idiom, except to say that it was necessarily "the result of the sum total of an integrated intuitive experience."

WORKS

(published unless otherwise noted)

Stage works (all with various combinations of soloists, mixed vv, actors, dancers, insts): The Pied Piper (play with music, after R. Browning), 1968; Birds of a Feather (entertainment in 1 act, C.P.S. Gilman), 1970; Yiphtah and his Daughter (arr. and trans. J. Berger), 1971; The Cherry Tree Carol (liturgical drama), 1974; 2 others pubd

Orch: Caribbean Conc., harmonica, orch, 1941; arr. 2 tpts, orch, n.d.; Concertino, pf, chbr orch, 1948; Sonata da Camera, ob, str/ob, pf, 1949; Sinfonia di San Petronio, 3 tpts, str, 1951; Short Sym., 4 movts in 1, orch, 1952; Short Ov., str, 1955; Divertissement, str, 1944 (inc., completed 1960); 6 others pubd

Instr: Suite for Fl. and Pf., 1947; Six Short Pieces, pf, ww qnt, 1948 (arr. ww qnt, 1959); Partita, pf, 1952, unpubd (arr. ww qnt, 1969); Divertimento, 3 tr insts, 1955; Intrada, brass qt, 1957; Three Dances, str qnt, 1977; Seven Inventions, pf/ hpd, 1980; Souvenirs de France (5), pf, 1981, unpubd; arr. vn, va, vc, *c*1984; Four Bagatelles, vn, va, 1981; Diversion for 3 Trbn, 1982; *c*20 others pubd

Choral (all SATB; solo vv and acc. insts noted): Le sang des autres (R. Arcos), 1936; Brazilian Psalm (J. de Lima), 1v, 1941; The Exiles (S. Funaroff), songs for Alto (no SATB), orch, 1943, unpubd; SATB, Bar, Mez, 2 pf, perc, 1970; Vision of Peace (Isaiah), 1948; Psalms of Penitence (Ps. 6, 31, 32, 51, 102), org/orch, 1953; Skelton Poems (J. Skelton), Bar, pf/org, 1955; Psalm 57 (3 movts), brass qt/org/pf, 1960; Devotional Songs (Penn. Dutch, trans. J. Berger), 1960; Magnificat, S, fl, perc, 1961; The Fiery Furnace (Book of Daniel), solo vv, 1962; How Lovely Are Thy Tabernacles (Ps. 84, 3 movts), double chorus, solo vv, 1963; A Song of Seasons (compiled J. Berger), solo vv, tr insts, perc, 1967; The Word of God (Bible, M. Luther), nar, solo vv, opt. insts, 1968; Ben Franklin's Wit and Wisdom (Poor Richard's Almanac), 1967 (inc., rev. with pf, 1989); Songs of Sadness and Gladness (16th- and 17th-century Eng.), solo vv, 1970; Of Life (cycle), fl, perc, 1973; Canticle of the Sun (St. Francis, trans. M. Arnold), va, perc, 1980; *c*213 other extended works, anthems, partsongs pubd

Songs (all for 1v; acc. insts noted): Four Sonnets (L. de Camoens), str qt, 1939 (arr. pf, *c*1970); Villanescas (E. Blanco-Amor), pf, 1941; Two Vocalises: Etude, 1v/vc, pf and Cantiga, 1v, pf, 1942; Four Songs (L. Hughes), pf, 1947; Five Songs (Mary Queen of Scots), fl, va, vc, 1948 (arr. pf, *c*1986); Six Rondeaux (C. d'Orleans), va, 1962; Diversion for Three (misc. Eng.), S, fl, pf, 1974; Five Shelley Poems, pf, 1975; Three Songs (J. Thomson), pf, 1982; Amoretti (16th- and 17th-cent. Eng.), pf, 1984; Epigrams, pf, 1987; Blame not my lute (T. Wyatt), pf, 1991; Chansons (Chansonnier) de femme (medieval Fr.), pf, *c*1992; 13 other sets, *c*10 individual songs pubd

Musical and personal papers at American Music Research Center and *BO*

Principal publishers: Augsburg, Broude Bros., N.A. Kjos, T. Presser, G. Schirmer, Shawnee, J. Sheppard

WRITINGS

"Notes on some 17th-century Compositions for Trumpets and Strings in Bologna," *MQ*, xxxvii/3 (1951), 354–67

"Our Choral Heritage," *The Choral Journal*, iii (1962), 18

"B on B," *The Diapason*, lviii/6 (1967), 42–3

"The Composer of Choral Music in Our Time," *RESPONSE*, viii/3 (1967), 138–45

"Interpretation of 20th-Century Choral Music," *The Choral Journal*, vii/4 (1967), 15–7

"Relations of Sound and Structure in Elizabethan Choral Music," *The Choral Journal*, xi (1971), 8–9

BIBLIOGRAPHY

W.D. Pritchard: "The Choral Style of Jean Berger," *American Choral Review*, viii/4 (1965), 4

M.J. Beachy: "*Birds of A Feather* by Jean Berger: Choral Performance: a New Dimension," *The Choral Journal*, xii/1 (1971), 22
P. Shuman: *A Stylistic Analysis of Selected Solo Works by Jean Berger* (diss., U. of Northern Colorado, 1989)
M. Smith: *Jean Berger: his Life and Musical Compositions for the Solo Voice: a Performance Project* (diss., U. of Maryland, 2001)
L. Giedl: "Jean Berger–1909–2002: a Biographical Chronology," *American Music Research Center Journal*, xviii (2010), 1

NED QUIST/LINDA L. GIEDL

Bergmann, Carl (*b* Ebersbach, Saxony, 12 April 1821; *d* New York, NY, 16 Aug 1876). Conductor and cellist of German birth. He studied with Adolph Zimmermann at Zittau and Adolf Friedrich Hesse at Breslau. Involved in the German Revolution of 1848, he immigrated to New York in 1849, having had orchestral experience in Breslau, Vienna, Pest, Warsaw, and Venice. He joined the Germania Musical Society, serving for a time as cellist, then as conductor until 1854. In 1852–4 he also conducted the concerts of the Boston Handel and Haydn Society. When the Germania Society disbanded in 1854, he settled in New York, becoming conductor of the Männergesangverein Arion, cellist of the Thomas chamber ensemble, and, in 1855, conductor (alternating with Eisfeld) of the New York Philharmonic Society orchestra. His surprising success in performances of the radical new music of Wagner (the overture to *Tannhäuser* on 21 April 1855, and other works later in the spring) led to his being appointed sole conductor for the 1855–6 and 1858–9 seasons of the Philharmonic. He then shared the conductorship with Eisfeld until the latter's retirement in 1865, after which he retained the post alone until failing health compelled his resignation in March 1876. He was also conductor for several years of the Brooklyn Philharmonic Society orchestra. One of his most noteworthy performances was that of *Tannhäuser* on 4 April 1859 at the New York Stadt Theater: it was the first hearing in America of a complete Wagner opera.

Among Bergmann's boldest New York ventures was a series of 11 concerts given in 1856 not by the Philharmonic but by his own smaller orchestra and including the American premieres of Schumann's Fourth Symphony and Berlioz's overture *Le carnaval romain*; but it was Wagner whom Bergmann championed above all, conducting, besides the 1859 *Tannhäuser*, the first known American Wagner performance (1852) and the first all-Wagner concert in the United States (1853). The best-known assessment of Bergmann's abilities is that of Theodore Thomas, in his autobiography: "He lacked most of the qualities of a first-rate conductor." Compared to Thomas, Bergmann was lazy, erratic, and insufficiently schooled. But he was not an innocuous podium presence. William Mason judged him "an excellent, though not a great, conductor."

BIBLIOGRAPHY

DAB (C.N. Boyd)
H.E. Krehbiel: *The Philharmonic Society of New York* (New York, 1892/*R*); ed. H. Shanet in *Early Histories of the New York Philharmonic* (New York, 1979)
H.E. Johnson: "The Germania Musical Society," *MQ*, xxxix (1953), 75–93
H. Shanet: *Philharmonic: a History of New York's Orchestra* (Garden City, NY, 1975)
J. Horowitz: *Wagner Nights: an American History* (Berkeley, 1994)
N. Newman: *Good Music for a Free People: the Germania Musical Society in Nineteenth-Century America* (Rochester, NY, 2010)

H. WILEY HITCHCOCK/JOSEPH HOROWITZ

Bergner, Frederic (*b* Donaueschingen, Germany, 1 Feb 1827; *d* New York, NY, 31 March 1907). Cellist of German birth. He studied with C.L. Böhm and Johann Kalliwoda before immigrating to New York in 1849. Bergner joined the New York Philharmonic Society in 1853. He was the orchestra's leading cellist for more than 40 years, made frequent solo appearances at Society concerts, and served on the board of directors almost continuously from 1864 to his retirement in 1901. He was elected an honorary member of the Society in 1900. Bergner was also active in New York's burgeoning chamber music scene in the 1850s and 1860s. He began playing with Theodore Eisfeld's quartet during the fifth season (1855) of the Eisfeld *soirées*, and from 1861 to its disbandment in 1868 he played with the Mason-Thomas Quartet, taking the position formerly held by Carl Bergmann. Bergner's reputation was such that he was often invited to perform alongside touring virtuosos, including Louis Moreau Gottschalk (1862), Anton Rubinstein and Henryk Wienawski (1872), and Hans von Bülow (1875–6). Throughout his career Bergner was one of the most sought-after assisting artists at New York concerts and also headlined his own annual concerts beginning in the mid-1860s.

BIBLIOGRAPHY

H.E. Krehbiel: *The Philharmonic Society of New York: A Memorial* (New York, 1892; repr. in *Early Histories of the New York Philharmonic*, New York, 1979)
G.C.D. Odell: *Annals of the New York Stage* (New York, 1927–49)
V.B. Lawrence, ed.: *Strong on Music: the New York Music Scene in the Days of George Templeton Strong* (New York, 1988 and Chicago, 1995 and 1999)

BETHANY GOLDBERG

Bergsma, William (Laurence) (*b* Oakland, CA, 1 April 1921; *d* Seattle, WA, 18 March 1994). Composer. He studied at Stanford University (1938–40) and at the Eastman School (1940–44, BA, MA), where his principal composition teachers were HOWARD HANSON and BERNARD ROGERS. After teaching composition at the Juilliard School (1946–63) he joined the school of music at the University of Washington, Seattle, where he later became professor emeritus. He received numerous awards including two Guggenheim fellowships (1946, 1951), an NEA fellowship (1976), and the American Academy of Arts and Letters Award (1965).

When other 20th-century composers were abandoning tonality in favor of serialism, Bergsma remained unwaveringly conservative in his compositional style. This conservatism should not be mistaken for conventionality, however, for he was very successful in blending several styles into a highly individual compositional language. Predominately lyrical in nature, his music is resourceful and imaginative, employing long lines and transparent textures. His instrumental music (e.g. the *Concerto for Wind Quintet*, 1958) successfully infuses traditional formal frameworks with a clearly 20th-century use of melody, harmony, rhythm, and meter. The early string quartets demonstrate the composer's skill as a contrapuntist. His two operas, *The Wife of Martin Guerre* (1956) and *The Murder of Comrade Sharik* (1973), deal with realistic issues and provide vivid social commentary. In later works, Bergsma explored elements of avant-garde compositional style, including aleatory techniques and a more dissonant harmonic language.

WORKS
(selective list)

Stage: Paul Bunyan (ballet), 1938, San Francisco, 22 June 1939, orch suite, 1938, rev. 1945; Gold and the Señor Commandante (ballet), 1941, Rochester, 1 May 1942; The Wife of Martin Guerre (op, 3, J. Lewis), 1956, New York, 15 Feb 1956; The Murder of Comrade Sharik (op, Bergsma, after M. Bulgakov), 1973

Orch: Dances from a New England Album, 1939, rev. 1969; Music on a Quiet Theme, 1943; The Fortunate Islands, str, 1947, rev. 1956; Sym. no.1, 1949; A Carol on 12th Night, 1954; March with Tpts, band, 1956; Chameleon Variations, 1960; In Celebration, 1963; Documentary 1 "Portrait of a City," 1963, rev. 1968; Serenade "To Await the Moon," chbr orch, 1965; Vn Conc., 1966; Documentary 2 "Billie's World," 1968; Changes, 1971; Sym. no.2 "Voyages," solo vv, chorus, orch, 1976; Sweet was the Song the Virgin Sung: Tristan Revisited, va, orch, 1978

Choral: In a Glass of Water Before Retiring (S.V. Benét), 1945; Black Salt, Black Provender (L. Bogan), 1946; On the Beach at Night (W. Whitman), 1946; Let True Love Among us be, 1948; Riddle Me This, 1957; Praise (G. Herbert), chorus, org, 1958; Confrontation (Bible: *Job*), chorus, kbd/orch, 1963, rev. 1966; The Sun, the Soaring Eagle, the Turquoise Prince, the God (Florentine MS), chorus, brass, perc, 1968; Wishes, Wonders, Portents, Charms, mixed vv, insts, 1974

Songs: 6 Songs (E.E. Cummings), 1944–5; Bethsabe, Bathing (G. Peele), 1961; 4 Songs (trad., Peele), medium v, cl, bn, pf, 1981

Chbr and solo inst: Suite, brass qt, 1940; Str Qt no.1, 1942; Pastorale and Scherzo, rec/fl, 2 va, 1943; 3 Fantasies, pf, 1943, rev. 1983; Str Qt no.2, 1944; Tangents, pf, 1951; Str Qt no.3, 1953; Conc., wind qnt, 1958; Fantastic Variations on a Theme from Tristan and Isolde, va, pf, 1961; Illegible Canons, cl, perc, 1969; Str Qt no.4, 1970; Clandestine Dialogues, vc, perc, 1976; Blatant Hypotheses, trbn, perc, 1977, Qnt, fl, str qt, 1980, rev. 1981; Four All, cl, trbn, perc, 1981; The Voice of Coelacanth, hn, vn, pf, 1981; Str Qt no.5, 1982; Symmetries, ob, bn, pf, 1982; Variations, pf, 1984

Principal publishers: C. Fischer, Galaxy, Hargail

BIBLIOGRAPHY

W. Bergsma: "Mechanics of Orchestral Notation," *MM*, xxiii/1 (1946), 27–30

R.F. Goldman: "Current Chronicle," *MQ*, xlii (1956), 390–95

A. Skulsky: "The Music of William Bergsma," *Juilliard Review*, iii/2 (1956), 12–26

W. Bergsma: "The Laboratory of Performance," *College Music Symposium*, ix (1969), 23–9

L.R. Wyatt: *The Mid-twentieth-century Orchestral Variation, 1953–1963: an Analysis and Comparison of Selected Works by Major Composers* (diss, U. of Rochester, 1974) [analysis of *Chameleon Variations*]

JAMES P. CASSARO

Berigan, Bunny [Rowland Bernard] (*b* Hilbert, WI, 2 Nov 1908; *d* New York, NY, 2 June 1942). Jazz trumpeter and bandleader. He played violin as a child but switched to trumpet as a teenager. Berigan played with local bands, including the University of Wisconsin's jazz ensemble, although he never went to college. In 1928 he auditioned for Hal Kemp's band but was turned down due to a weak tone. Two years of intense practicing resulted in Berigan developing a beautiful sound, a wide range, and impeccable musicianship. Inspired by Louis Armstrong and, to a lesser extent, Bix Beiderbecke, Berigan also developed his own, risk-taking solo style. After a second, successful audition with Kemp in 1930, he joined the band and subsequently made his recording debut and toured Europe. After returning to the United States in 1931, Berigan was a busy studio musician, performing on hundreds of recordings for both jazz groups and studio orchestras during the next five years. He often worked with the Fred Rich Orchestra, with which he made his only film appearance, performing a solo on "Until Today" in *Fred Rich & his Orchestra* in 1936. He worked with Paul Whiteman for a few months during the period 1932–3 and played a prominent role on recordings with the Dorsey Brothers and the Boswell Sisters.

In 1935 Berigan was persuaded to leave the studios to work with Benny Goodman's big band. During his three months with Goodman, Berigan experienced the band's success at the Palomar Ballroom and took solos on the clarinetist's first hit records "King Porter Stomp" and "Sometimes I'm Happy," which subsequently received acclaim. After leaving Goodman, Berigan returned to the studios, appearing regularly on the weekly series *Saturday Night Swing Club* for CBS, making guest appearances, and leading his own recording sessions. After recording the ballad "I can't get started" as a sideman with Red McKenzie on 3 April 1936, he recorded it with his own group ten days later. In 1937 he spent six weeks as the star soloist of the Tommy Dorsey Orchestra; his solos on hit versions of "Marie" and "Song of India" are famous. That year Berigan also launched his own big band. This group started well, with a record contract for Victor and a hit record with Berigan's third version of "I can't get started." However, Berigan was already an alcoholic and lacked the strength to succeed as a bandleader during the swing era. By the fall of 1938, the band included drummer Buddy Rich and tenor saxophonist Georgie Auld, and although it played to a high standard, it struggled commercially. In early 1940 Berigan declared bankruptcy and broke up the band. He rejoined the Tommy Dorsey Orchestra but his excessive drinking led to his being fired after six months. Berigan tried twice more to lead a big band but his health quickly declined and he died from pneumonia and other ailments in 1942.

SELECTED RECORDINGS

As leader: You took advantage of me/Chicken and Waffles (1935, Dec.); I can't get started (1936, Voc.); Blue Lou (1936, BR); Sobbin' Blues (1938, Vic.)

As sideman: Boswell Sisters: Everybody loves my baby (1932, Br); B. Goodman: King Porter Stomp/Sometimes I'm Happy (1935, Vic.); A Jam Session at Victor: Honeysuckle Rose/Blues (1937, Vic.); T. Dorsey: Marie/Song of India (1937, Vic.)

BIBLIOGRAPHY

G. Frazier: "Bunny Berigan," *Jam Session*, ed. R. Gleason (New York, 1958), 42

I. Crosbie: "Bunny Berigan," *JJ*, xxvii/9 (1974), 8

V. Danca: *Bunny* (Rockford, IL, 1978)

R. Dupuis: *Bunny Berigan: Elusive Legend of Jazz* (Baton Rouge, LA, 1993)

S. Yanow: *Trumpet Kings* (San Francisco, CA, 2001), 50–3

SCOTT YANOW

Berio, Luciano (*b* Oneglia, Imperia, Italy, 24 Oct 1925; *d* Rome, Italy, 2003). Italian composer. Berio's connection with the United States began in 1950 on his honeymoon with his American wife, CATHY BERBERIAN. He made a number of trips to the United States, moved there in 1962, and then returned to Europe in 1971.

By the time Berio moved to the United States at the age of 36, he had earned impressive credentials and was already a mature composer. He studied with Giulio Paribeni and Giorgio Federico Ghedini at the Milan conservatory, earning his diploma in 1950. In the summer of 1952 he attended the Berkshire Festival at Tanglewood, Massachusetts, on a Koussevitzky Foundation scholarship, where he studied with 12-tone composer and fellow Italian Luigi Dallapiccola (1904–75), who provided for Berio many points of reference. This year also marked Berio's first exposure to electronic music. He heard pieces by Luening and Ussachevsky at the museum of Modern Art in New York in a program that was the first to present electronic music in America. In 1953 or 1954, he attended the Darmstadt summer school, where he met and studied alongside contemporaries John Cage, Karlheinz Stockhausen, Pierre Boulez, Henri Pousseur, and others. By this time electronic music was one of Berio's main areas of interest, and in 1955 he and close friend Bruno Maderna founded the Studio di Fonologia Musicale at Milan Radio. Berio also honed his orchestral writing in Milan during the 1950s.

In the summer of 1960 he returned to the Berkshire Festival as a faculty member. Copland, who was also teaching there, commented in a letter to Bernstein that things were rather routine that summer except for Berio who was "stirring things up considerably." Later in the year Berio and his wife toured the United States with the help of new-found friend Leonard Stein, who helped to promote his music in many concerts. Most noteworthy at this time was *Circles* (1960), a piece for female voice, harp, and 2 percussionists, which features circular musical construction. Other pieces featured on these concerts included the electronic music piece *Thema (Omaggio a Joyce)* (1958), and *Différences* (1958–9). Both *Circles* and *Thema* featured Berberian, who became a leading figure in the performance of avant-garde vocal music. She was Berio's most important and most long-standing collaborator even after their marriage ended in 1964. Her importance to Berio's career cannot be overemphasized.

In 1961 Berio accepted an offer from Darius Milhaud to replace him for the spring semester, 1962, at Mills College. This temporary appointment began what David Osmond-Smith has called Berio's American Decade. This decade can be divided into two parts, the West Coast Years (1962–4), primarily based at Mills College, and the East Coast Years (1965–71), primarily at Juilliard. Berio wrote important works while at Mills College, including *Passaggio* (1963), his first large "musical action," *Sequenza II* for harp (1963), and *Folk Songs* (1963–4), and his stay there also provided him opportunities to present his earlier works to American audiences. *Folk Songs*, performed and largely inspired by Berberian, was commissioned by Mills College, and includes the arrangements of two songs by American folk musician John Jacob Niles. In 1963, Berio co-founded with Morton Subotnick the Mills Performing Group, an ensemble consisting of students and professionals dedicated to the performance of contemporary music.

Berio brought to America a unique voice and very open ears. He was independent-minded and refused to belong to any particular system of composing; rather, he believed strongly in using any style of composition that would help him create the music he wished to write. Although he emphatically disapproved of serialism and aleatorism, he nevertheless employed them when the occasion called for it. He also explored extending techniques for voice and instruments to discover new sonorities, as well as using electronic music, jazz, and proportional as well as graphic notation. Berio was fascinated with linguistics and had a propensity to write vocally and to incorporate theatrical elements in his music. He embraced complexity, filling many of his compositions with a multitude of interconnections and layers of meaning.

After completing the academic year of 1963–4 at Mills College, Berio moved east to Cambridge, Massachusetts. In 1966 he married his second wife Susan Oyama, a PhD student in psychology at Harvard. During the second period of his American decade, he taught composition at Juilliard, where he founded the Juilliard Ensemble, his second American group devoted to the performance of contemporary music. In 1966–7, in addition to his duties at Juilliard, he also held the position of Lauro de Bosis Lecturer on Music at Harvard, to which he later would return for the 1992–3 academic year as Norton Lecturer.

The 1960s were immensely important for Berio in continuing his *Sequenze*, a monumental series of fourteen works for solo instruments and voice. The five Sequenze composed during Berio's Juilliard period were *III* (female voice), *IV* (piano), *V* (trombone) (all 1966); *VI* (viola, 1967), and *VII* (oboe, 1969). These pieces were written for and performed extensively by internationally prominent virtuoso musicians, which also helped to elevate Berio's reputation both in the United States and in Europe. They have since become staples of the literature. His major work *Laborintus II*, written for the 700th birthday of Dante, and the revision of *Epifanie* were both completed in 1965. In 1968, he composed perhaps his most significant and most popular piece, *Sinfonia* (1968–9), establishing himself as an internationally renowned composer. Having an interest in the American civil rights movement, Berio incorporated within *Sinfonia* his piece "O King" as the second movement, a tribute to Martin Luther King, the text based on the phonemes of his name. In the third movement, Berio offered his outlook on the evolution of music. He did this by constructing a complex collage of musical quotations embedded within a musical current adopted from the scherzo of Mahler's Second Symphony. Interacting with Mahler, a narrative of Samuel Beckett's *The Unnamable* also weaves its way throughout the movement. In 1969, a fifth movement was added to the original four, and in 1970 this final version was premiered by the New York Philharmonic, for whom it was written, under the direction of Leonard Bernstein, to whom it was dedicated.

Toward the end of Berio's American years, his massive *Opera* (1970), a deconstruction of the genre, premiered in Santa Fe, New Mexico. In 1971, nearing the completion of another significant solo vocal theatrical work, *Recital I (for Cathy)* (1972), Berio, "feeling like a dentist" from teaching 14–15 hours of lessons every week at Juilliard, was watching his second marriage fall apart. It was time, he decided, to return to Italy.

BIBLIOGRAPHY

M. Donat: "Berio and his 'Circles,'" *MT*, cv (1964), 105–7

L. Berio: "Meditation on a Twelve-Tone Horse," *Christian Science Monitor* (1968), 8–9

D. Avron and J.-F. Lyotard: "'A few words to sing': Sequenza III," *Musique en jeu*, no.2 (1971), 28–44; Eng. trans. in J.-F. Lyotard: *Toward the Post-Modern* (NJ, 1996)

G.W. Flynn: "Listening to Berio's Music," *MQ*, lxi (1975), 388–421

D. Osmond-Smith: "Berio and the Art of Commentary," *MT*, cxvi (1975), 871–2

P. Altmann: *Sinfonia von Luciano Berio. Eine analytische Studie* (Vienna, 1977)

P. Schnaus: "Anmerkungen zu Luciano Berios *Circles*," *Musik und Bildung*, x (1978), 489–97

D. Osmond-Smith: *Playing on Words: a Guide to Luciano Berio's "Sinfonia"* (London, 1985)

A. Schultz: *Sequenze I–VII by Luciano Berio: Compositional Idea and Musical Action* (diss., U. of Queensland, Australia, 1986)

D. Osmond-Smith: *Berio* (Oxford, 1990)

J.K. Halfyard, ed.: *Berio's Sequenzas* (Hampshire, 2007)

J. Paull: *Cathy Berberian and Music's Muses* (Vouvry, 2007)

DAVID R. BUBSEY

Berkeley. City in California, part of the San Francisco Bay area. The University of California established a campus at Berkeley in 1868; the music department was founded 33 years later (*see* SAN FRANCISCO; CALIFORNIA, UNIVERSITY OF; and LIBRARIES AND COLLECTIONS).

Berkeley, Busby [Enos, William Berkeley] (*b* Los Angeles, CA, 29 Nov 1895; *d* Palm Springs, CA, 14 March 1976). Choreographer and film director. He is best known for producing lavish musical numbers, which led to the slang term *busby berkeley*, for any elaborate dance number. The son of theatrical parents, Berkeley made his stage debut at age five. In 1917 he enrolled in the US Army where parade drills may have influenced his later choreography. During the 1920s he choreographed over 20 Broadway productions and in 1930 began his first Hollywood work for a series of films featuring comedian Eddie Cantor. The making of these films, in which Berkeley developed his distinctive palette of cinematic devices for choreographing and filming dance numbers—including the "parade of faces" and the famous kaleidoscopic "top shot" (which he did not originate)—occurred during a slump in audience interest with musicals. However, the stunning sequence of musical numbers he choreographed for *42nd St.* (WB, 1933) contributed to reigniting audience interest in the genre and set the formula for the series of "backstage" musicals with which he is most associated, including *Gold Diggers of 1933*, *Footlight Parade* (1933), *Fashions of 1934*, and *Dames* (1934). In 1939 he began working at MGM, he directed one film for Fox in 1943, and then he returned to MGM to direct and choreograph a number of films, the last in 1962. The revival of interest in Art Deco in the late 1960s sparked a parallel interest in Berkeley's work, and in 1971 he was credited with supervising the successful Broadway revival of the musical *No, No, Nanette* from 1925. His creative achievement involved cinematically reconceptualizing the presentation of the regimented chorus formations of stage spectacle for the screen through creative camera work and editing to create extravagant—and many times surreal—musical narratives that, while ostensibly grounded in the conceits of a theatrical performance, were irreproducible on a proscenium stage.

BIBLIOGRAPHY

T. Thomas and J. Terry, with B. Berkeley: *The Busby Berkeley Book* (Greenwich, CT, 1973)

R. Hanley: "Busby Berkeley, the Dance Director, Dies," *New York Times* (15 March 1976)

M. Rubin: *Showstoppers: Busby Berkeley and the Tradition of Spectacle* (New York, 1993)

J. Spivak: *Buzz: the Life and Art of Busby Berkeley* (Lexington, KY, 2010)

GORDON HARAMAKI

Berklee College of Music. School of music founded in Boston in 1945; *see* BOSTON.

Berkshire Music Center. Former name of the Tanglewood Music Center, an educational institution in Lenox, Massachusetts.

See TANGLEWOOD.

Berl, Christine (*b* New York, NY, 22 July 1943). Composer of dual American and Italian citizenship. Her first music teacher was her father, Paul Berl, an accompanist for Victoria de Los Angeles and a founding member of the Mannes College of Music. Ernst Oster was also a primary influence. She studied at Mannes (1961–4) with NADIA REISENBERG (piano) and Carl Schachter (theory) among others, and at Queens College, CUNY (MA 1970), where her teachers included HUGO WEISGALL and GEORGE PERLE; she later studied privately with HENRY WEINBERG and YEHUDI WYNER. She has received commissions from the Chamber Music Society of Lincoln Center (1989), Peter Serkin (1990), and Pierre Amoyal (1991). From 1980 to 1997 she taught composition at Mannes.

Berl's style has been described as free of both modernist abstraction and neo-Romantic nostalgia. *Sonata quasi una fantasia* (1988), premiered by André-Michel Schub in 1990, is in a one-movement cyclical sonata form that evokes Ives's *Concord Sonata*. *The Violent Bear it Away* (1989), premiered by the Bay Area Women's Philharmonic under JoAnn Falletta in 1989, bases its phrase structure on the Southern Baptist hymn *I'm Going Thro', Jesus*. *Dark Summer* (1989), written for Frederica von Stade, treats the voice operatically. Indian metric and modal structures feature prominently in *Lord of the Dance* (1989), influences she attributed to her career as a Middle Eastern dancer in Morocco and

Europe (1988–96). In 1998, she published *The Classic Art of Viennese Pastry* (Hoboken, NJ) and taught as a pastry chef at the Culinary Institute of America. By 1999, she had destroyed most of her compositional files, taken the professional name of Touta and was pursuing the art of classical belly dancing.

WORKS
(selective list)

Vocal: Ab la dolchor (cant. H. Weinfield), S, chorus, orch, 1979, arr. Mez, cl, vn, pf, 1990; And How that a Life was but a Flower (Weinfield: *The Book of Sir Tristram*), unacc. chorus, 1979; Dark Summer (L. Bogan), Mez, str trio, pf, 1989

Inst: Elegy, pf, 1974; 3 Pieces, chbr ens, 1975; Sonata quasi una fantasia, pf, 1988; Lord of the Dance, pf, 1989; The Violent Bear it Away (after F. O'Connor), opt. chorus, orch, 1989, arr. opt. chorus, 2 pf, orch, 1990; Ballade, vc, pf, 1990; Masmoudi, vn, pf, 1991

BIBLIOGRAPHY

A. Kozinn: "A Composer and Some Celebrated Friends," *New York Times* (21 Oct 1990)

D. Smith: "Shimmying her Way Into a New Career," *New York Times* (31 July 1999)

JANELLE GELFAND

Berlin, Irving [Beilin, Israel; Baline, Israel] (*b* Russia, 1888, exact place and date uncertain but marked on 11 May; *d* New York, NY, 22 Sept 1989). Songwriter of Russian birth; naturalized American.

1. Life. 2. Songwriting.

1. Life. The youngest of eight children of Moses and Leah Beilin, Israel ("Izzy") Beilin immigrated to America with his family when he was five. Registered as the "Baline" family at the Ellis Island checkpoint on 13 September 1893, they settled on Manhattan's Lower East Side in a neighborhood densely packed with newcomers. Moses Baline, a cantor by profession in the Old World, took on work as a meat inspector and house painter while Leah earned money as a midwife. Izzy also worked as a newsboy and junk seller, and when his father died in 1901, he dropped out of school with hopes of increasing his income. He found his niche as a busker and singing waiter, jobs that proved foundational to his later success, for they satisfied his hunger for recognition as they afforded the chance to observe how song performance made its impact on a live audience. The work stoked his desire to write his own material, so with pianist Mike Nicholson he published his first song, "Marie from Sunny Italy," in 1907. The song made little impact but for the way the lyricist's surname appeared in the published sheet music: "I. Berlin."

Over the next decade Irving Berlin became a rare hybrid on Tin Pan Alley: a singer-songwriter equally known for performance and publication. A headliner on vaudeville, he enjoyed popularity as a performer of his own songs with a light, raspy tenor voice backed by an expressive face and hands. After a string of hits in 1909–10, he published "Alexander's Ragtime Band" in 1911, earning him international celebrity and the moniker "Ragtime King." The following year he married Dorothy Goetz, but she became ill on the honeymoon and died, inspiring Berlin's melancholy waltz "When I Lost You." After hearing Berlin perform his hit ragtime song in vaudeville, producer Charles Dillingham tapped Berlin to write the score for a "syncopated musical show" called *Watch Your Step* (1914) featuring the dance duo Irene and Vernon Castle. In a gesture almost unheard of in the world of musical comedy, Berlin published the show's piano vocal score. He had good reason. The year 1914 had also seen the formation of the American Society for Composers, Authors, and Publishers (ASCAP), with Berlin's help, so protecting his copyrights had assumed fresh importance.

Broadway now emerged as an increasingly crucial forum for Berlin's work. In 1918, he became a US citizen and promptly joined the army at Camp Upton in Yaphank, Long Island, where he created an all-soldier camp show called *Yip Yip Yaphank* that made it to Broadway. The crowd showered Berlin with applause when he sang his comic soldier's complaint "Oh! How I Hate to Get Up in the Morning." Meanwhile, Florenz Ziegfeld regularly interpolated Berlin songs into his annual *Follies* productions, leading to the 1919 edition, widely recognized as his best, with many Berlin numbers such as "A Pretty Girl Is Like a Melody" and "I'd Rather See a Minstrel Show."

These experiences stoked Berlin's ambition to produce his own revues, and so, with business partner Sam H. Harris, he built the Music Box Theatre on Manhattan's West 45th Street and developed an annual series called the *Music Box Revues*, of which four editions appeared from 1921 to 1924. The series featured the premieres of many Berlin hits, including the theme song "Say It with Music" and a song called "Everybody Step," widely construed as an exemplar of jazz in the 1920s.

The period was also filled with notable events in Berlin's personal life. His mother died in 1922, having witnessed her son's spectacular ascent. Joining the fabled Algonquin Round Table—a social group of writers, actors, and musicians—Berlin made important new connections with theater critic Alexander Woollcott, who wrote Berlin's first biography, and playwright George S. Kaufman, who would collaborate with Berlin on *The Cocoanuts* (1925), the first Broadway musical that featured the Marx Brothers, who would reprise their roles in the show's film version.

In this period, Berlin's budding romance with Ellin Mackay received as much public attention as his musical endeavors. Their marriage on 4 January 1926 over the strenuous objections of her father, the Postal Telegraph Cable tycoon Clarence Mackay, was page-one news in the *New York Times*. As a wedding present, Ellin received the copyright of "Always," a tender waltz about enduring love. Later that year, on Thanksgiving Day, Ellin bore the couple's first child, Mary Ellin, to whom Berlin dedicated his new song "Blue Skies." A son, Irving, Jr., followed in early December 1928, but he died in infancy, on Christmas Day. The Berlins had two more daughters: Linda (*b* 1932) and Elizabeth (*b* 1936).

Meanwhile, Berlin continued to write for the stage. In the early 1930s, he worked with George S. Kaufman's protégé and collaborator Moss Hart on two shows that skewered people and events in the news: *Face the*

Music (1932), dubbed a "musical comedy revue," and *As Thousands Cheer* (1933), a revue in which each comedy sketch and musical number reflected a newspaper headline. A critic described the Berlin-Hart style as "a lot of satin songs…with an acid, cruel sense of humor." The "satin songs" include the Depression-era Pollyanna song "Let's Have Another Cup of Coffee," the smooth ballad "Soft Lights and Sweet Music," and the perky holiday anthem "Easter Parade." *As Thousands Cheer* also included the wailing grief of a lynched man's widow in "Supper Time." To a few prominent critics, the number's tragic tone had no place in a revue.

By the mid-1930s, Berlin's career had shifted its center of gravity to Hollywood, where he participated vigorously in the burgeoning genre of film musicals. For RKO Pictures, he wrote songs featured in a series of films starring Fred Astaire and Ginger Rogers: *Top Hat* (1935), *Follow the Fleet* (1936), and *Carefree* (1938). For 20th Century Fox he wrote songs for *On the Avenue* (1937) and *Alexander's Ragtime Band* (1938), the latter a "cavalcade" musical with a plot stuffed with—and grown from—well-established hits in the Berlin catalog. Several other cavalcade films followed over the next two decades, all with themes and titles revolving around Berlin standards, including *Blue Skies* (1946), *Easter Parade* (1948), *White Christmas*, and *There's No Business Like Show Business* (both 1954). Yet another film, *Holiday Inn* (1942), remains notable for introducing "White Christmas" and won an Academy Award.

By the 1940s it had become commonplace for a stage success to be transformed into a screen musical, and many of Berlin's shows crossed over. *Louisiana Purchase* (1940) ran for over a year on Broadway before becoming a motion picture starring Bob Hope. In 1942, Berlin re-tooled his World War I revue for the new war and dubbed it *This Is the Army* (1942). That, too, became a Hollywood film (starring Ronald Reagan) and emerged as one of the top grossing films of the period. The film also included Kate Smith singing the song that she had made famous on radio in 1938: "God Bless America." Meanwhile, the stage version of *This Is the Army*, despite a short Broadway run, became a cultural phenomenon, touring the United States and the United Kingdom, where General Dwight D. Eisenhower saw the production and asked Berlin to take it to troops in Europe, Africa, the Middle East, and the South Pacific. Seen by millions of civilians and soldiers the show became for Berlin "the best thing I was ever connected with," and for it, Berlin earned the army's Medal for Merit. Yet his most successful stage musical was still to come. *Annie Get Your Gun* (1946) starred Ethel Merman as the expert sharpshooter Annie Oakley in Buffalo Bill's Wild West show and spawned many musical numbers that became song standards, including "They Say It's Wonderful," "I Got the Sun in the Morning," "Anything You Can Do," and "There's No Business Like Show Business." It ran for 1147 performances on Broadway, second only to Rodgers and Hammerstein's *Oklahoma!* in its time. A successful film once again ensued (1950), with Betty Hutton in the lead role. That same year, Berlin collaborated with playwrights Howard Lindsay and Russel Crouse on another Merman vehicle, *Call Me Madam,* with hits such as "The Hostes' with the Mostes'," "They Like Ike," and "I Wonder Why." This time, Merman also starred in the film version (1953).

The mid-to-late 1950s constitute a fallow period in Berlin's career, marked by severe depression and several unfinished projects. He would write one last Broadway show, however, aiming to capture the glamour of the White House and the ordinary appeal of its occupants. *Mr. President* (1962) had all the right ingredients, with a stellar team of collaborators including Lindsay and Crouse, director Joshua Logan, and producer Leland Hayward, and the largest advanced ticket sales in Broadway history—but it proved a "fiasco," as more than one writer would dub it. Yet Berlin kept working. The 1966 revival of *Annie Get Your Gun* sparked a show-stopping new counterpoint song called "Old Fashioned Wedding." Although his music well would soon dry, he continued to dictate lyrics over the next two decades as he lived an increasingly reclusive and private life. Berlin died at his townhouse on Beekman Place and was buried in Woodlawn Cemetery in the Bronx.

Berlin's life sustains two persistent and treasured American narrative archetypes: the rags-to-riches success story and the story of the untutored genius for whom hard work yields greater rewards than those enjoyed by the higher-born and better-educated. No wonder that nearly every generation has seen a new biography of Irving Berlin since Alexander Woollcott published the first in 1925.

2. Songwriting. Berlin came of age in a milieu that accepted songwriters with melodic and harmonic gifts who could not read or write music and therefore relied on assistants to fulfill their goals to publish sheet music. Thus Berlin's lifelong working method involved singing or picking out tunes on the piano while others wrote them down. Early on, he also acquired a transposing piano, called the "Buick," which could change keys with the shift of a lever, allowing Berlin to play in his favored key of F-sharp. Such facts inspired his first biographer Alexander Woollcott to dub him "a creative ignoramus." Yet first-hand testimony indicates that Berlin dictated and controlled every aspect of his songs, and that music gushed from his imagination.

Berlin's work manifests a commitment to Tin Pan Alley's conventional verse-refrain song form, in which a 32-bar refrain usually parses into eight-bar segments in *AABA* or *ABAC* patterns. Success in the music industry encouraged adherence to formal convention almost as rigidly as the requirements of a Shakespearean sonnet or the 12-bar blues.

And yet, he regularly discovered ways to treat convention with unexpected flexibility. "God Bless America" and "Always," to take two of his most enduring songs, remain memorably tuneful despite their nearly through-composed, non-repetitive melodies. In his early stage works he wrote many musical scenes that carried dialogue and action like opera, sometimes with pop songs embedded into the musical flow, as in the extended opening number and sumptuous "Dining Out" scene of his first *Music Box Revue*. In some films, he molded songs into unusual structures that matched the elegance of the performer for whom they were written: Fred Astaire. "Cheek to Cheek" comprises a 72-bar refrain with a *C* section (beginning "Dance with me") appearing after the bridge in a double-sized *AABA* form. "Let's Face the Music and Dance" deploys the *AABA* pattern as well but with variably sized *A* sections, each one longer than the preceding one, forming a ruminative musical monologue. Dramatic context could also extend a song's reach. For all of his great film songs, Berlin believed that the one that had been best spotted in a movie was the elegant ballad "Now It Can Be Told." Introduced in *Alexander's Ragtime Band,* it was woven into a ten-minute sequence that tracked the composition, rehearsal, and performance of the number as it accompanied the development of a love triangle among the film's principal characters played by Don Ameche, Alice Faye, and Tyrone Power.

In Berlin's early years Tin Pan Alley made a sharp distinction between the ballad and the ragtime song: one smooth and lyrical, the other animated by syncopation. Berlin exploited this contrast in two ways. First, he made a point of blending the styles into a hybrid that he dubbed the "syncopated ballad." He wrote such songs throughout his career, including "All By Myself," "How About Me?," "Be Careful, It's My Heart," "You Keep Coming Back Like a Song," and "Whisper It." In others, he juxtaposed lyricism and syncopation in adjoining passages, most famously in "Cheek to Cheek." Second, he developed the counterpoint song, which presents two complete melodies, one smooth and one syncopated, in succession and then together. Audiences greeted the first of them, "Simple Melody/Musical Demon," so enthusiastically in *Watch Your Step* that Berlin strove to incorporate a counterpoint song in almost every subsequent Broadway show he wrote up to the 1966 revival of *Annie Get Your Gun*, with "Old Fashioned Wedding."

The waltz occupies a special place in Berlin's ballad writing. The half-century that spans from "When I Lost You" (1912) to "Let's Go Back to the Waltz" (1962), includes many waltz ballads that became standards: "All Alone," "Always," "What'll I Do?," "Remember," "Russian Lullaby," and "The Girl That I Marry." For Berlin, the waltz was chiefly a medium for expressing old-fashioned values, domestic stability, and enduring love. "What'll I Do?" and "Russian Lullaby" conjure a melancholy mood by leaning on the minor mode. In "All Alone" Berlin spins through-composed tune from a concise rhythmic motif. Among the waltzes, however, "Always," whose copyright he gave to his wife, Ellin, as a wedding present, remains the most popular.

Generous with praise to songwriters he admired, Berlin likewise earned praise from his peers. George Gershwin called him "the greatest songwriter that has ever lived...America's Schubert." And Jerome Kern famously claimed that "Irving Berlin has no place in American music. He IS American music." Both statements were made when Berlin still had many song, stage, and screen successes ahead of him.

WORKS

STAGE

(works for which Berlin wrote all or much of the score; lyrics are by Berlin. Names of librettists are given in parentheses; dates are those of first New York performance.)

Watch Your Step (musical comedy, H.B. Smith), 8 Dec 1914 [incl. Play a simple melody]

Stop! Look! Listen! (musical comedy, Smith), 25 Dec 1915 [incl. The girl on the magazine cover, I love a piano]

The Century Girl (revue, collab. H. Blossom), collab. V. Herbert, 6 Nov 1916

The Cohan Revue of 1918, collab. G.M. Cohan, 31 Dec 1917

Yip, Yip, Yaphank (revue), 2 Sept 1918 [incl. Mandy; Oh! how I hate to get up in the morning]

Ziegfeld Follies of 1919 (revue), 16 June 1919 [incl. A pretty girl is like a melody, You'd be surprised, I'd rather see a minstrel show]

Ziegfeld Follies of 1920 (revue), 22 June 1920 [incl. Tell me, little gypsy]

Music Box Revue 1921–2, orchd F. Tours, M. DePackh, S. Jones, H. Akst, 22 Sept 1921 [incl. Say it with music, Everybody step]

Music Box Revue 1922–3, orchd Tours, DePackh, Jones, Akst, 23 Oct 1922 [incl. Lady of the evening, Crinoline days, Pack up your sins and go to the devil]

Music Box Revue 1923–4, orchd Tours, DePackh, Jones, Akst, 22 Sept 1923 [incl. When you walked out someone else walked right in, The waltz of long ago]

Music Box Revue 1924–5, orchd Tours, DePackh, Jones, Akst, 1 Dec 1924

The Cocoanuts (musical comedy, G.S. Kaufman), 8 Dec 1925; film, 1929 [incl. A little bungalow]

Ziegfeld Follies of 1927 (revue), 16 Aug 1927 [incl. Shaking the blues away]

Face the Music (musical comedy, M. Hart), 17 Feb 1932 [incl. Let's have another cup o' coffee, Soft lights and sweet music]

As Thousands Cheer (revue, Hart), orchd Tours, A. Deutsch, H. Kresa, 30 Sept 1933 [incl. Easter parade, Heat wave, How's chances, Supper time]

Louisiana Purchase (musical comedy, M. Ryskind), orchd D. Walker, 28 May 1940 [incl. It's a lovely day tomorrow]; film, 1942

This is the Army (revue), 4 July 1942 [incl. I left my heart at the stage door canteen; This is the army, Mr. Jones]; film, 1943

Annie Get your Gun (musical comedy, H. Fields, D. Fields), orchd P.J. Lang, R.R. Bennett, T. Royal, 16 May 1946 [incl. Anything you can do, Doin' what comes natur'lly, The girl that I marry, I got the sun in the morning, There's no business like show business, They say it's wonderful]; film, 1950

Miss Liberty (musical comedy, R. Sherwood), orchd Walker, 15 July 1949 [inc. Let's take an old-fashioned walk; Give me your tired, your poor]

Call me Madam (musical comedy, H. Lindsay, R. Crouse), orchd Walker, 12 Oct 1950 [incl. The best thing for you, The hostess with the mostes' on the ball, It's a lovely day today, Marrying for love, They like Ike, You're just in love]; film, 1953

Mr. President (musical comedy, Lindsay, Crouse), orchd Lang, 20 Oct 1962 [Let's go back to the waltz, The Washington twist, The secret service]

FILMS

(not all scores wholly by Berlin)

The Awakening, 1928 [incl. Marie]

Hallelujah, 1929

Puttin' on the Ritz, 1930 [incl. Puttin' on the ritz]

Mammy, 1930 [incl. Let me sing and I'm happy]

Reaching for the Moon, 1930

Kid Millions, 1934

Top Hat, 1935 [incl. Cheek to cheek; Isn't this a lovely day?; Piccolino; Top hat, white tie, and tails]

Follow the Fleet, 1936 [incl. Let yourself go; I'm putting all my eggs in one basket, Let's face the music and dance]

On the Avenue, 1937 [incl. I've got my love to keep me warm, This year's kisses]
Alexander's Ragtime Band, 1938 [incl. Now it can be told]
Carefree, 1938 [incl. Change partners]
Second Fiddle, 1939
Holiday Inn, 1942 [incl. Be careful, it's my heart; Happy holiday; White Christmas]
Blue Skies, 1946 [incl. You keep coming back like a song]
Easter Parade, 1948 [incl. Better luck next time, It only happens when I dance with you]
White Christmas, 1954 [incl. Sisters; The best things happen while you're dancing; Count your blessings; Love, you didn't do right by me]
There's No Business Like Show Business, 1954

OTHER SONGS
(selective list; lyrics by Berlin)

Marie from Sunny Italy (music M. Nicholson), 1907; Alexander's ragtime band, 1911; Everybody's doin' it, 1911; When I lost you, 1912; When the midnight choo choo leaves for Alabam', 1912; International rag, 1913; Snooky ookums, 1913; When I leave the world behind, 1914; Someone else may be there while I'm gone, 1917; I've got my captain working for me now, 1919; All by myself, 1921; Always, 1925; Remember, 1925; Blue skies, 1927; Russian lullaby, 1927; The song is ended, 1927; Say it isn't so, 1932, How deep is the ocean?, 1932; God bless America, 1938 [chorus written 1918]; Whisper it, 1963 (1996)

Principal publisher: Berlin

BIBLIOGRAPHY

A. Woollcott: *The Story of Irving Berlin* (New York, 1925)
A. Wilder: *American Popular Song: The Great Innovators, 1900–1950* (New York, 1972)
I. Whitcomb: *Irving Berlin and Ragtime America* (New York, 1988)
L. Bergreen: *As Thousands Cheer: the Life of Irving Berlin* (New York, 1990)
P. Furia: *The Poets of Tin Pan Alley* (New York, 1990)
C. Hamm: "Irving Berlin's Early Songs as Biographical Documents," *MQ*, vii (1993), 10–34
M.E. Barrett: *Irving Berlin: a Daughter's Memoir* (New York, 1994)
C. Hamm, ed.: *Irving Berlin: Early Songs, 1907–1914* (Madison, WI, 1994)
A. Forte: *The American Popular Ballad of the Golden Era, 1924–1950* (Princeton, 1995)
C. Hamm: *Putting Popular Music in Its Place* (Cambridge, UK, 1995)
C. Hamm: *Irving Berlin: Songs from the Melting Pot: The Formative Years, 1907–1914* (New York, 1997)
P. Furia: *Irving Berlin: A Life in Song* (New York, 1998)
D.C. Berry: "Dynamic Introductions: the Affective Role of Melodic Ascent and Other Linear Devices in Selected Song Verses of Irving Berlin," *Intégral*, xiii (1999), 1–62
E. Jablonski: *Irving Berlin: American Troubadour* (New York, 1999)
J. Melnick: *A Right to Sing the Blues: Jews, African Americans, and American Popular Song* (Cambridge, MA, 1999)
J. Magee: "Irving Berlin's 'Blue Skies': Ethnic Affiliations and Musical Transformations.," *MQ*, lxxxiv (2000), 537–80
D.C. Berry: "Gambling with Chromaticism? Extra-Diatonic Melodic Expression in the Songs of Irving Berlin," *Theory and Practice*, xxvi (2001), 21–85
R. Kimball and L. Emmet, eds.: *The Complete Lyrics of Irving Berlin* (New York, 2001)
G.F. Custen: "I hear music and…Darryl and Irving Write History with *Alexander's Ragtime Band*," *Authorship and Film*, ed. D.A. Gerstner and J. Staiger (New York, 2003), 77–95
A. Anderson: *The Songwriter Goes to War* (Pompton Plains, NJ, 2004)
C. Greenspan: "Irving Berlin in Hollywood: the Art of Plugging a Song in Film," *AM*, xxii (2004), 40–49
A. Most: *Making Americans: Jews and the Broadway Musical* (Cambridge, MA, 2004)
D. Leopold: *Irving Berlin's Show Business* (New York, 2005)
L. Bomback: "The Music of the *Music Box Revues*," *Musicological Explorations*, vii (2006), 51–88
J. Magee: "'Everybody Step': Irving Berlin, Jazz, and Broadway in the 1920s," *JAMS*, lix (2006), 597–632
J. Rosen: *White Christmas: the Story of an American Song* (New York, 2007)
A.O. van der Merwe: *The Ziegfeld Follies: a History in Song* (Lanham, MD, 2009)
T. Decker: *Music Makes Me: Fred Astaire and Jazz* (Berkeley and Los Angeles, 2011)
T. Decker: "On the Scenic Route to *Irving Berlin's Holiday Inn*," *J M*, xxviii (2011), 464–97
S.R. Kaskowitz: *As We Raise Our Voices: a Social History and Ethnography of "God Bless America," 1918–2010* (diss., Harvard U., 2011)
J. Magee: *Irving Berlin's American Musical Theater* (New York, 2012)
B. Sears: *The Irving Berlin Reader* (New York, 2012)

JEFFREY MAGEE

Berlin, Jeff(rey Arthur) (*b* Queens, NY, 17 Jan 1953). Jazz bass player. The son of musical parents, he played violin as a child but switched to bass in his early teens (influenced by Jack Bruce) and attended the Berklee College of Music for a time. Berlin's talent for performing jazz, fusion, and progressive rock came to prominence on a series of album projects with the drummer Bill Bruford's self-titled group. He has subsequently worked with Bill Frisell, Alan Holdsworth, Yes, John McLaughlin, Arturo Sandoval, Dave Liebman, and kd lang. Berlin has also made a number of recordings as a leader beginning with *Motherlode* (1985) and including the contemporary mainstream album *High Standards* (2010). Touring projects have involved his own band, featuring Randy Brecker, Danny Gottlieb, and Othello Molineaux, among others; the group Bx3 with the bass players Stuart Hamm and Billy Sheehan; and a trio with John Abercrombie and Adam Nussbaum in 2009. A pioneer of slap bass and two-handed tapping styles, Berlin is known for mixing innovative chordal and linear approaches that highlight the lyrical and technical capabilities of his instrument. He is a proponent of music education, a central idea that has underlined his columns for *Bass Player* and *Guitar Player* magazines and his founding of the Players School of Music in Clearwater, Florida. He has won several readers polls in *Guitar Player*.

JEFFREY HOLMES

Berliner, Emile [Emil] (*b* Hanover, Germany, 20 May 1851; *d* Washington, DC, 3 Aug 1929). Inventor of German birth. He graduated from the Samsonschule in Wolfenbüttel at age 14 and immigrated at 18 to the United States, working odd jobs in Washington, DC, Milwaukee, and New York City. Despite limited formal scientific education, Berliner pursued his interest in electricity and acoustics and in 1876 developed and patented an improved microphone for Bell's newly-invented telephone. For the next seven years, he worked as a research assistant for the American Bell Telephone Company before leaving to become a freelance researcher and inventor. Between 1883 and 1886 he obtained patents for acoustic tiles and floor coverings and experimented with a lightweight internal combustion engine for helicopters.

Berliner is best remembered for developing the gramophone in 1887, a variation of THOMAS EDISON's phonograph. Where the phonograph recorded sounds with a vertically-cut groove of varying depth on a rotating cylinder, Berliner's gramophone recorded sounds with a spiraling laterally-cut groove of constant depth on the surface of a flat disc. Unlike Edison, who viewed his phonograph primarily as a tool for dictation, Berliner envisioned the commercial appeal of the gramophone as a device for home entertainment. In 1891 he formed the American Gramophone Company, which issued the first commercial disc records in the United States the following year. Berliner was a pianist himself and reportedly played on some of his company's earliest issues. In 1901, he exited the burgeoning American record industry and transferred many of his rights and patents to Eldridge R. Johnson's newly-formed Victor Talking Machine Company. Berliner then moved for a time to Montreal where he established the Berliner Gramophone Company of Canada, Ltd. to issue recordings licensed from Victor.

See also RECORDED SOUND.

BIBLIOGRAPHY

R. Gelatt: *The Fabulous Phonograph* (New York, 1977)

K. Nauck and A. Sutton: *American Record Labels and Companies, 1891–1943* (Denver, CO, 2000)

BRYAN S. WRIGHT

Berlinski, Hermann (*b* Leipzig, Germany, 18 Aug 1910; *d* Washington, DC, 27 Sept 2001). Organist and composer, born in Germany. He studied piano and composition at the State Conservatory of Leipzig and attended the Ecole Normale de Musique in Paris, where he was a pupil of Cortot and Boulanger. He immigrated to the United States in 1941. At the Seminary College of Jewish Music in New York he studied organ and musicology with Joseph Yasser and was awarded the PhD. Berlinski was organist at the Temple Emanu-El in New York (1954–63) and minister of music at the Washington (DC) Hebrew Congregation (1963–77). He was a liturgical musician and composer, and his music contains historical Jewish materials. His principal works for the organ include twelve *Organ Sinfonias* (1954–2000), *The Burning Bush* (1957), and *The Glass Bead Game* (1974). His choral and chamber works include *Altar Tryptichon for Bonhoeffer* (1993), *Oratorio Job* (1993), and *CELAN* (2001). He was a gifted recitalist and his recordings reflect an international Jewish background coupled with brilliant technical achievement.

BIBLIOGRAPHY

M. Kayden: "The Music of Herman Berlinski," *ACAB*, vii/3 (1959), 2

K.S. Mervine: "Herman Berlinski after 'The Burning Bush': an Interview," *American Organist*, xvi/5 (1982), 46

"A Life in Music: Herman Berlinski Donates Collection to Library," *Library of Congress Information Bulletin*, lx/9 (2001)

VERNON GOTWALS/JUDI CALDWELL

Berman, Boris (*b* Moscow, Russia, 3 April 1948). Pianist of Russian birth. He studied at the Moscow Conservatory with Lev Oborin from 1965 to 1971, and took part in the Russian premieres of works by Ligeti, Berio, Stockhausen, and Cage, as well as the first performances of Denisov's *Ode* and Schnittke's *Serenade*. In 1973 he immigrated to Israel, and for six years taught at Tel Aviv University. After moving to the United States in 1979 he held various teaching posts, and from 1984 to 1997 was head of piano at Yale University, where he also directed the Yale Music Spectrum concert series. Among Berman's many recordings are the complete piano works of Prokofiev, which display his powerful but always clear, stylish, and intelligent playing.

BIBLIOGRAPHY

L. Gerber: "Conversation with Boris Berman," *Fanfare*, xiv/3 (1990–91), 435–9

H. Goldsmith: "Boris Berman: Balancing Intellect and Heart," *Clavier*, xxxi/7 (1992), 10–15 [interview]

DAVID FANNING

Bermel, Derek (*b* New York, NY, 14 Oct 1967). Composer and clarinetist. A native of New York City, Bermel as a youth studied clarinet with Ben Armato. He studied composition with Michael Tenzer at Yale University (BA 1989) and with WILLIAM BOLCOM and WILLIAM HUGH ALBRIGHT at the University of Michigan (DMA 1998). Later he worked with Louis Andriessen as a Fulbright Fellow in Amsterdam and Henri Dutilleux at the Tanglewood Music Center. He has also studied ethnomusicology and orchestration with André Hajdu in Jerusalem; Lobi xylophone (*gyil*) in Ghana; Thracian folk style with Nikola Iliev in Bulgaria; and *caxixi* in Brazil with Julio Góes.

In 1998 Bermel premiered his own clarinet concerto, *Voices*, in Carnegie Hall with the American Composers Orchestra under Tan Dun. He has since performed it with the Los Angeles Philharmonic as well as in London and Beijing. He was the founding clarinetist of Music from Copland House, the resident ensemble at Copland's New York home, which has been restored as a creative center for American music. He also performs with Brooklyn-based band Peace by Piece, for which he serves as bandleader, singer, and songwriter. The group has released two albums, *Peace by Piece* (2000) and *The Elements* (2004).

His compositions draw from a variety of musical genres, including classical, jazz, pop, rock, blues, folk, and gospel. In *Voices*, Bermel examines different facets of the vocal capabilities of the clarinet and orchestra. Through the use of tone clusters, glissandi, portamenti, mutes, and electric guitar wa-wa pedal, he makes sections and the entire orchestra imitate the sound of one voice. *Soul Garden* is an exploration of what Bermel calls the rub. This is achieved through the juxtaposition of the African pentatonic and European diatonic scales. He also uses notated glissandi and quarter-tones to capture the emotional and even sensual nature of gospel music. *Elixir* is a work that reflects Bermels eclectic musical influences. The composer calls it "a spectral love potion," reflecting influences as varied as Charles Ives, Gesualdo, John Lennon, and the Isley Brothers.

He has received numerous commissions from prestigious organizations, established ensembles and renowned performers, including the Music Society of Lincoln Center, Indianapolis SO, New Jersey SO, Pittsburgh SO, Saint Louis SO, eighth blackbird, the Guarneri Quartet, violinist Midori, cellist Fred Sherry, pianists Christopher Taylor and Andy Russo, and

Wynton Marsalis and Jazz at Lincoln Center Orchestra. Among his many awards are a Guggenheim Fellowship (1999), the Rome Prize from the American Academy in Rome (2001), the Koussevitzky Music Foundation Award (2008), and the Alpert Award in the Arts (2008). He has been appointed to creative residencies with the American Composers Orchestra (2006–9), the Los Angeles Chamber Orchestra (2009–12), and the Institute for Advanced Study of Princeton University (2009–13).

Bermel's music can be heard on *Soul Garden*, a full-length disc of his chamber music (CRI, now available from New World Records); the Grammy-Award nominated *Voices*, a full-length disc of his orchestral music with Boston Modern Orchestra Project on BMOP Sound; and a new release by the ensemble Alarm Will Sound including his compositions *Hot Zone*, *Three Rivers*, *Continental Divide*, *Natural Selection*, *At the End of the World*, and *Canzonas Americanas*.

WORKS
(selective list)

Voices, cl, orch 1998; Soul Garden, va, str qt, 2000; Natural Selection, Bar, ens, 2000; Thracian Echoes, orch, 2002; Slides, orch, 2003; Turning Variations, pf, orch, 2006; Migration Series, jazz ens, orch, 2006; The Good Life (text by W.S. Walters), 2 vv, chorus, orch, 2008; A Shout, a Whisper, and a Trace, orch, 2009; Canzonas Americanas, orch, 2010; Mar de Setembro, S, chbr orch, 2011

Principal publisher: Peer Classical New York, Faber Music

ELIOT GATTEGNO

Bernal, Paulino (*b* Raymondville, TX, 22 June 1939). Accordionist, songwriter, and producer. Texas-Mexican musician Paulino Bernal led the highly influential and innovative El Conjunto Bernal, formed in 1952 with his older brother Eloy on *bajo sexto*. The Kingsville-based group became one of the top *conjuntos* in South Texas. By 1955, they were making records for Ideal Records, accompanying many of its artists. Bernal was influenced by early recordings of accordion pioneers such as Narciso Martínez and Tony de la Rosa; however, he was also interested in Latin dance genres like the bolero, *son*, and cha cha cha played by *orquestas* and Mexican trios. Bernal had his conjunto perform in suits, rather than the typical western attire, and they began to set regional *rancheras* and *corridos* to these pan-Latin rhythms, showcasing rich, three-part harmonies and a versatile chromatic accordion. "Mi único camino" (My Only Path) was one of the most popular songs in this style. The new sound attracted upwardly-mobile Mexican Americans who had shunned traditional accordion-based conjuntos. In the 1960s, Bernal (with Víctor González) formed Bego Records and became a skilled producer. He added a second accordionist to the group, Oscar Hernandez, which allowed for more complex arrangements and expanded compositional possibilities. Bernal abandoned the label and his group in the 1970s and became an evangelical preacher, recording and performing only Christian music. In 2008, he returned to performing his popular songs, appearing at local festivals and community events.

CATHY RAGLAND

Bernal Jiménez, (José Ignacio) Miguel (*b* Morelia, Michoacán, Mexico, 16 Feb 1910; *d* León, Guanajuato, Mexico, 26 July 1956). Mexican composer, organist, conductor, and musicologist. A choirboy at the Morelia Cathedral, he studied organ, sacred composition, and Gregorian chant at the Escuela Superior de Música Sagrada, under Ignacio Mier Arriaga, Felipe Aguilera, and José María Villaseñor. He received diplomas *di licenza* and *di magistero* in organ, Gregorian chant, and sacred composition from the Pontificia Scuola Superiore di Musica Sacra in Rome, where he studied (1929–33) under Raffaele Manari, Raffaele Casimiri, Paolo M. Ferretti, Cesare Dobici, and Licinio Refice. In Morelia he was a professor and director of the Escuela Superior, founded the Coro de los Niños Cantores (1944), founded and directed the Conservatorio de las Rosas (1945), and founded and edited the periodical on sacred music and culture *Schola Cantorum* (1939–56). He was a professor and dean of the College of Music at Loyola University in New Orleans (1954–6). Bernal Jiménez was a pioneer of research on music of the viceroyal period (16th–18th centuries). He cataloged the archive of the 18th-century Colegio de Santa Rosa de Santa María de Valladolid, and transcribed and performed some of its pieces, including music by Antonio Sarrier and Ignacio Jerusalem. He toured in Mexico, Spain, and the United States as a concert organist, choral conductor, and lecturer. At a time of political and even armed conflict between the Catholic Church and the Mexican state, he was instrumental in creating a community of church musicians, institutions, and teachers throughout Mexico, and in implementing the reforms to sacred music promulgated in 1903 by Pope Pius X.

Among his sacred compositions are masses, villancicos, a Te Deum, religious anthems, matins, and incidental music for a religious play. Better known today is his secular music, which includes a symphonic drama, ballets, organ and piano pieces, a string quartet, a concertino for organ and orchestra, and several symphonies, symphonic poems, and suites, many of which remain in repertoire in Mexico. Bernal Jiménez believed that music for the church and concert stage should be modern, pious, and modest. Unlike his older contemporaries, Carlos Chávez and Silvestre Revueltas, who experimented with form, texture, and pitch collections, his modernism was moderate. His orchestration was colorful, his harmony mildly dissonant. He adhered to classical forms—which he nevertheless reinterpreted freely—and experimented with fusions of different genres within a single piece. He referenced Spanish culture, the church, and the life and landscapes of the Mexican provinces, in particular Michoacán. His reference to music of indigenous communities is almost diegetic within the programmatic intent of some of his compositions. He considered Western art music an inalienable part of the Mexican heritage and used his knowledge of early music styles, forms, and genres to make precise historical references in his music. He wrote music for five films, most of them on religious subjects.

WORKS
(selective list)

Stage: Tata Vasco (sym. drama, 5 scenes, M. Muñoz), 1941; Timgambato, ballet, 1943; El Chueco, 1951; Los Tres galanes de Juana, ballet, 1952

Orch: Michoacán: suite sinfónica, 1940; Noche en Morelia, sym. poem, 1941; Navidad en Pátzcuaro, sym. suite, 1941; Sinfonía-poema Mexico, 1946; Tres Cartas de México, 1946; Retablo medieval: concertino para órgano y orquesta, 1949; Sinfonía Hidalgo (chr), 1953

Chbr and inst: Cuarteto virreinal, str qt, 1937; Sonata de iglesia, org, 1941; Sonata de Navidad, org, 1942; Prelude and Fugue, org, *c*1944; Carteles, p, 1952; Antigua Valladolid, p, 1954

Sacred: Te Deum jubilar, org, chorus, 1938; Himno Fe, sangre y victoria (J.I. Padilla), 1940; Gran corrido a la Virgen de Guadalupe (D. Castañeda), 1941; Misa Aeterna Trinitatis, org, chorus, 1941; Misa guadalupana Juandieguito, 1945; Maitines de la Asunción, org, chorus, 1949; Himno catequístico nacional mexicano (M. Ponce), 1952; Himno misional mexicano (M. Ponce), 1952

Film: *Historia de un gran amor* (J. Bracho), 1942; *La Virgen que forjó una patria* (J. Bracho), 1942; *El padre Morelos* (M. Contreras), 1943; *El Rayo del sur* (M. Contreras), 1943; *María Magdalena* (M. Contreras), 1946.

Principal publishers: Fischer, Ediciones Mexicanas de Música, Schola Cantorum

WRITINGS

Morelia colonial. El archivo musical del Colegio de Santa Rosa de Santa María de Valladolid: siglo XVIII (Morelia, 1939)

La Disciplina coral (Morelia, 1947)

Cum Gregorio et Caecilia: viajando en pos de la música sacra (Morelia, 1948)

Las Tres etapas de la ejecución gregoriana (Morelia, 1949)

La Técnica de los compositores (Mexico City, 1950)

"La música en Valladolid de Michoacán," *Nuestra música*, vi (1951), 153–76; vii (1952), 5–16

"He hablado a Strawinsky," *Schola Cantorum*, ii (1940); *Pauta*, iv/16 (1985), 61–7

174 articles in *Schola Cantorum* (Morelia, 1939–1954)

BIBLIOGRAPHY

C. Seeger: "Music Education in the Americas," *MEJ*, xxx/6 (1944), 14–55

O. Mayer-Serra: *Música y músicos de Latinoamérica* (Mexico City, 1947), 105–9

R.M. Stevenson: *Music in Mexico* (New York, 1952/*R*)

Y. Moreno Rivas: *Rostros del nacionalismo mexicano: un ensayo de interpretación* (Mexico City, 1989)

L. Díaz Núñez: *Miguel Bernal Jiménez. Catálogo y otras fuentes documentales* (Mexico City, 2000)

L. Díaz Núñez: *Como un eco lejano: la vida de Miguel Bernal Jiménez* (Mexico City, 2003)

L. Saavedra: "Staging the Nation: Race, Religion and History in Mexican Opera of the 1940s," *Opera Quarterly*, xxiii/1 (2007), 1–21

LEONORA SAAVEDRA

Berne, Tim(othy Bruce) (*b* Syracuse, NY, 16 Oct 1954). Jazz alto and baritone saxophonist. He began playing while attending Lewis and Clark College in Oregon and was influenced by rhythm and blues and soul music as well as recordings by JULIUS HEMPHILL. In 1974 he moved to New York, where he studied with ANTHONY BRAXTON and Hemphill. A year after beginning lessons, he began writing his own music. Five years after beginning lessons, he established the record label Empire Productions for which he recorded his first album, *The Five Year Plan* (1979). Subsequent albums included *7X* (1980, Empire), *Spectres* (1981, Empire), *Songs and Rituals in Real Time* (1982, Empire), *The Ancestors* (1983, SN), *Mutant Variations* (1983, SN), *Fulton Street Maul* (1986, Col.), and *Sanctified Dreams* (1987, Col.). During the late 1980s he signed with JMT, for which he recorded *Fractured Fairy Tales* (1989, JMT) and a series of live performances in Paris by his ensemble Bloodcount (1994). After JMT was purchased by PolyGram and Berne's JMT catalog was deleted, he founded a second label, Screwgun, in 1996, for which he has made several recordings. Some of Berne's improvisatory pieces last more than 30 minutes and feature tempo and metric changes; they are nonetheless creative, energetic, and intriguing.

DANIEL JOHN CARROLL

Bernheimer, Martin (*b* Munich, Germany, 28 Sept 1936). Music critic of German birth. He studied at Brown University (BA 1958), the Hochschule für Musik in Munich (1958–9), and under Gustave Reese at New York University (MA 1961). He was on the music staff of the *New York Herald-Tribune* (1959–62), assistant to Irving Kolodin at the *Saturday Review* (1962–5), music critic for the *New York Post* (1961–5), and music critic of the *Los Angeles Times* (1965–1996). He won the Deems Taylor Award for music criticism in 1974 and 1978 and the Pulitzer Prize for criticism in 1982. Bernheimer is a widely respected and influential critic, who is particularly knowledgeable about opera and the voice. In addition to his activities as a journalist, he has taught criticism in various schools and universities, and has written about opera for various music journals, including *Opera News* and the *Financial Times* (London).

PATRICK J. SMITH/R

Bernstein, Elmer (*b* New York, NY, 4 April 1922; *d* Ojai, CA, 18 Aug 2004). Composer and conductor. He was trained as a pianist but also studied composition with ISRAEL CITKOWITZ, ROGER SESSIONS, Ivan Langstroth and STEFAN WOLPE. He attended New York University, then enlisted in the Army Air Corps (1942); he arranged and composed music for some 80 programs for the Armed Forces Radio Service and was a concert pianist for three years after his discharge. Norman Corwin then engaged him to score radio drama, which led to composition for films; Bernstein's third film, *Sudden Fear* (1952), attracted favorable attention. In 1955, despite suffering career difficulties due to McCarthyism (see Marmorstein), he rose to sudden prominence with his score for *The Man with the Golden Arm*. In this, as in several scores that followed (e.g. *Walk on the Wild Side*, 1962), he effectively blended jazz into a modern symphonic idiom to suit gritty stories and contemporary settings. He subsequently became known for his rousing scores for westerns and action films (notably *The Magnificent Seven*, 1960, and *The Great Escape*, 1963), and in the 1970s and 80s he showed a flair both for youth-market comedies such as *National Lampoon's Animal House* (1978) and for intimate adult dramas, including several Irish films.

Throughout a career of over 200 film and television scores, Bernstein crafted memorable themes, such as that for *To Kill a Mockingbird* (1963), and showed a fondness for thematic metamorphosis, lively rhythmic ostinatos and clean-cut, economical instrumental textures. In later years, he again blended jazz into his scores for period pieces such as *Devil in a Blue Dress* (1995), and from the 1980s made a point of using the ondes martenot. In the 1990s he worked with Martin Scorsese on a series of films, including a remake of *Cape Fear* (1991), for which he adapted Bernard Herrmann's score from the 1962 film. With his last film score, *Far From Heaven* (2002), Bernstein received his 14th Academy Award nomination. Bernstein also led efforts to secure screen composers' incomes and copyrights and promoted the appreciation of film music through his writing. He founded the Film Music Collection (1974–8), which published *Film Music Notebook* and released recordings, mostly by other eminent film composers and conducted by Bernstein.

WORKS
(selective list)

FILM SCORES
(director in parentheses)

Saturday's Hero (D. Miller), 1951; Sudden Fear (Miller), 1952; The View from Pompey's Head (P. Dunne), 1955; The Man with the Golden Arm (O. Preminger), 1955; The Ten Commandments (C.B. de Mille), 1956; Fear Strikes Out (R. Mulligan), 1957; Sweet Smell of Success (A. Mackendrick), 1957; Kings Go Forth (D. Daves), 1958; Desire under the Elms (D. Mann), 1958; God's Little Acre (Mann), 1958; Some Came Running (V. Minnelli), 1958; The Story on Page One (C. Odets), 1959; From the Terrace (M. Robson), 1960; The Magnificent Seven (J. Sturges), 1960; Summer and Smoke (P. Glenville), 1961; Birdman of Alcatraz (J. Frankenheimer), 1962; Walk on the Wild Side (E. Dmytryk), 1962

To Kill a Mockingbird (Mulligan), 1963; The Great Escape (Sturges), 1963; Love with the Proper Stranger (Mulligan), 1963; Baby the Rain Must Fall (Mulligan), 1964; The World of Henry Orient (G.R. Hill), 1964; The Hallelujah Trail (Sturges), 1965; The Sons of Katie Elder (H. Hathaway), 1965; Return of the Seven (B. Kennedy), 1966; Hawaii (Hill), 1966; Thoroughly Modern Millie (Hill), 1967; True Grit (Hathaway), 1969; The Bridge at Remagen (J. Guillermin), 1969; The Liberation of L. B. Jones (W. Wyler), 1970; Big Jake (G. Sherman), 1971; See No Evil (R. Fleischer), 1971; The Trial of Billy Jack (F. Laughlin), 1974

The Shootist (D. Siegel), 1976; From Noon Till Three (F.D. Gilroy), 1976; Slap Shot (Hill), 1977; National Lampoon's Animal House (J. Landis), 1978; The Great Santini (L.J. Carlino), 1979; Airplane! (J. Abrahams, D. Zucker, and J. Zucker), 1980; Stripes (I. Reitman), 1981; Heavy Metal (G. Potterton), 1981; An American Werewolf in London (Landis), 1981; The Chosen (J.P. Kagan), 1982; Trading Places (Landis), 1983; Ghostbusters (Reitman), 1984; The Black Cauldron (T. Berman), 1985; Spies Like Us (Landis), 1985; Da (M. Clark), 1988; My Left Foot (J. Sheridan), 1989

The Grifters (S. Frears), 1990; The Field (Sheridan), 1990; Rambling Rose (M. Coolidge), 1991; A Rage in Harlem (B. Duke), 1991; Cape Fear (M. Scorsese), 1991 [arr. of music by B. Herrmann]; The Babe (A. Hiller), 1992; Mad Dog and Glory (J. McNaughton), 1993; The Age of Innocence (Scorsese), 1993; Devil in a Blue Dress (C. Franklin), 1995; Frankie Starlight (M. Lindsay Hogg), 1995; Hoodlum (Duke), 1997; John Grisham's "The Rainmaker" (F. Coppola), 1997; Twilight (R. Benton), 1998; Wild Wild West (B. Sonnenfeld), 1999; Bringing Out the Dead (Scorsese), 1999; Far From Heaven (T. Haynes), 2002

Scores for documentary films, short subjects, television films and shows

OTHER WORKS

How Now, Dow Jones (musical, C. Leigh; M. Shulman), New York, 7 Dec 1967; Conc., gui, orch, 1999; 3 suites, orch; 2 song cycles; works for pf, va, and pf

BIBLIOGRAPHY

T. Thomas: *Music for the Movies* (South Brunswick, NJ, and New York, 1973), 185–94

I. Bazelon: Interview, *Knowing the Score: Notes on Film Music* (New York, 1975), 170–80

E. Bernstein: "Film composers vs. the Studios," *Film Music Notebook*, ii/1 (1976), 31–9

T. Thomas: "Elmer Bernstein," *Film Score: the View from the Podium* (South Brunswick, NJ, and New York, 1979, rev. 2/1991 as *Film Score: the Art and Craft of Movie Music*), 238–49

J. Macmillan: "A Filmography/Discography of Elmer Bernstein," *Soundtrack!* (Mechelen, Belgium), xiv/54 (1995), 23–41

G. Marmorstein: *Hollywood Rhapsody: Movie Music and its Makers* (New York, 1997), 136–41

Obituary, *New York Times* (20 Aug 2004)

CHRISTOPHER PALMER/CLIFFORD MCCARTY/
MARTIN MARKS/NATHAN PLATTE

Bernstein, Leonard [Louis] (*b* Lawrence, MA, 25 Aug 1918; *d* New York, NY, 14 Oct 1990). Conductor and composer. His accomplishments as a conductor, composer of musical theater and concert works, and musical educator through television mark Bernstein as an unusually versatile figure. Among his most lasting contributions are his tenure as music director of the New York Philharmonic and the score to the Broadway musical *West Side Story*.

1. Early life. 2. Education. 3. Early fame. 4. Conductor. 5. Educator and commentator. 6. Composer. 7. Dramatic works. 8. Symphonic works. 9. Smaller works. 10. Legacy

1. Early life. Bernstein's parents, Samuel Bernstein and Jennie Resnick, were Russian Jewish immigrants. Their family's faith played a major role in the young Bernstein's personal development and as a cultural and religious influence throughout his life. His father prospered in the barber and beauty supply business. Leonard was the eldest child; a sister and brother followed. (His mother's family insisted upon the name "Louis" after a recently-deceased grandfather, but his parents called him "Leonard" from the beginning, and he legally changed his name at 16.) There was little music in the background of either family; an aunt placed her piano in the Bernstein family home when Leonard was ten, piquing his interest. He began to study and made rapid progress, alternately arousing his father's pride (including playing piano on a radio show advertising his father's business) and concern as he saw his son drawn headlong into an uncertain career choice. Bernstein's first piano teacher of note was Helen Coates (assistant to Heinrich Gebhard, one of Boston's leading teachers), with whom he started to study at age 14; she later served as his assistant for most of his adult life. Bernstein attended Boston Latin School for his secondary education. His musical activities as a teenager included putting on summer productions of Bizet's *Carmen* (Bernstein played the title role and other major roles were also subject to gender reversals), *The Mikado*, and *H.M.S. Pinafore* with neighborhood friends, and playing piano wherever possible, including occasional gigs as a jazz pianist to help pay for lessons. Despite his father's objections to a musical career, he allowed Bernstein to major in music at Harvard and study piano with Heinrich Gebhard for those four years.

2. Education. Bernstein's time at Harvard was marked by several important events and the good fortune of

meeting major musical figures. His teachers included EDWARD BURLINGAME HILL, A. Tillman Merritt, and WALTER PISTON. Bernstein augmented his fine academic training through extracurricular activities. He wrote incidental music for productions of two plays by Aristophanes and organized a performance of Marc Blitzstein's *The Cradle Will Rock* attended by the impressed composer. Bernstein also met and was befriended by DIMITRI MITROPOULOS and Copland. The latter happened to attend the same dance recital that Bernstein did in New York. The former became a lifelong friend and mentor, and through informal lessons was Bernstein's most important compositional instructor.

Following his graduation from Harvard, Bernstein was accepted to the Curtis Institute, where he studied conducting with FRITZ REINER, piano with ISABELLE VENGEROVA, and transposition and sight-reading with Renée Longy-Miquelle. Reiner's economical gestures had no influence on Bernstein, but the student benefited from his teacher's disciplined approach. Bernstein attended the first summer of the new music school at the Berkshire Music Festival (Tanglewood) in 1940, where he studied conducting with SERGE KOUSSEVITZKY, who became one of Bernstein's primary mentors. Upon graduation from Curtis in 1941, he possessed solid conducting skills and was a fine pianist.

3. EARLY FAME. The position that changed Bernstein's life was as assistant conductor of the New York PO, offered to him by Artur Rodziński, the new music director, in August 1943. In the two years since his Curtis graduation, Bernstein lived in Boston in 1941–2 and New York in 1942–3. He worked briefly in the commercial music industry, composed his Symphony no.1 ("Jeremiah"), wrote his Sonata for Clarinet and Piano, and played piano with the Revuers, a Greenwich Village cabaret act that included Adolph Green (whom Bernstein already knew), Betty Comden, and Judy Holliday. (Comden and Green later collaborated with Bernstein on *On the Town* and *Wonderful Town*.)

Within 18 months of being hired by the Philharmonic, Bernstein was famous as a composer and conductor. He substituted at the last moment for an ill Bruno Walter on a 14 November 1943 concert that was broadcast nationally, and other conducting opportunities soon followed, meaning that his assistant conductorship of the New York PO lasted a single season.

Bernstein's compositional career took off in 1944. He conducted the "Jeremiah" Symphony in Pittsburgh in January 1944 and in Boston the next month. It won the New York Music Critics Circle prize for the season's best symphonic premiere. Choreographer Jerome Robbins commissioned Bernstein to write the score for his ballet *Fancy Free*, which the Ballet Theatre premiered in April at the Metropolitan Opera House, where it enjoyed a level of popularity unusual in the ballet world. The story of *Fancy Free* became the basis for the Broadway musical *On the Town*. That Bernstein managed to fulfill the expectations raised by his early debuts as a composer of various types of music and as a conductor, in addition to becoming the country's most important musical commentator and educator through the medium of television, bespeaks a most unusual life that can be dealt with best in separate areas of endeavor.

Leonard Bernstein giving children a music lesson, c1958. (RA/Lebrecht Music & Arts)

4. CONDUCTOR. Before Bernstein there were few American-born and trained conductors of international note. After his mentorship with Mitropoulos and study with Reiner and Koussevitzky, he had experienced varied temperaments and conducting styles. Like Mitropoulos, Bernstein was emotional and demonstrative on the podium and led piano concertos from the keyboard. Bernstein shared Koussevitzky's interest in contemporary music, and Boston's maestro was the conducting influence that Bernstein most often acknowledged. Bernstein became Koussevitzky's assistant in the Tanglewood conducting department in 1942, assuming the directorship after Koussevitzky's death in 1951. Between 1944 and 1957 Bernstein's conducting career was largely as a guest conductor, including work throughout the United States and Europe and extensively with the Israel PO. A tour he led with the orchestra during the Israeli War for Independence in October–November 1948, including concerts near the front, made Bernstein extremely popular in Israel. He served as the orchestra's musical adviser in 1948–9, conducted the premiere concert in their new hall in 1957, was again its musical adviser in 1988. He made a number of recordings with them. Between 1945 and 1948, he was

the part-time and uncompensated music director of the New York City Symphony, earning a reputation for daring programming with many contemporary and American works. In 1953 Bernstein led Cherubini's *Medea* at La Scala, starring Maria Callas, making him the first American to conduct at Milan's venerable opera house.

Bernstein's tenure with the New York PO was one of the most successful ever between an orchestra and a conductor. He was named co-conductor with Mitropoulos in 1957, and became the youngest music director ever to hold the position the following year. Bernstein served until 1969, when he was named Laureate Conductor for Life. The orchestra tripled its audience between the 1955–6 season and the late 1960s, added new series, became a year-round ensemble, and developed a regular television presence. Their broadcasts of Young People's Concerts, featuring Bernstein as the genial host, were cultural icons, and Bernstein also directed and narrated televised concerts for adults. He led the Philharmonic on some lengthy, well-publicized tours, including to South America in 1958 and to Europe, the Near East, and Soviet Union in 1959. Bernstein and the orchestra made hundreds of recordings for CBS Masterworks, many of which remain commercially available.

In addition to the Israel PO, Bernstein had lasting relationships as a guest conductor with other orchestras, perhaps most significantly the Vienna PO. Bernstein directed *Falstaff* at the Vienna State Opera in 1966 and *Fidelio* in 1970, and he returned there frequently in the last two decades of his life to conduct the Philharmonic, which is the orchestra of the Vienna State Opera. Bernstein made many recordings with the Vienna PO, included filming the complete Beethoven, Brahms, and Mahler symphonies, among other works. Other orchestras that Bernstein conducted with some regularity at various times in his career include the Boston SO, the Berkshire Music Center Orchestra (Tanglewood), the National SO, the Philadelphia Orchestra, the London SO, the Bavarian RSO, the Orchestre National de France, and the Orchestra dell' Accademia Nazionale di Santa Cecilia.

Many who saw Bernstein conduct remarked on the excitement of his programming and the inherent dramatic intensity of his work. He was always a demonstrative and fully-engaged conductor—some critics found his gestures excessively grand and his interpretations too emotional—but what kept him one of the most famous and highly-paid international conductors was his compelling, passionate music-making. Critics sometimes cited how they felt Bernstein bent the music out of shape or introduced questionable dynamics to clarify his own analysis of a work. His most strident critic during the Philharmonic years was Harold Schonberg of the *New York Times*, but even he admitted Bernstein's growth as a conductor upon his departure from the Philharmonic in 1969, stating that Bernstein had learned "to conduct the big works of the repertory in a way that had shape as well as color, structural integrity as well as freedom within the phrase." Bernstein's range was wide indeed, ranging from Haydn forward, and his interpretations of Mahler, most 20th-century works, and American music drew special praise. Bernstein was less sympathetic to 12-tone music and most avant-garde works. He recorded with Columbia Masterworks for years, but in 1972 entered into an exclusive agreement with Deutsche Grammophon. Bernstein also left an extensive video library of work with several orchestras.

5. Educator and commentator. Bernstein's lifelong interest in education manifested itself in his many television broadcasts, in teaching conducting to young practitioners, and sometimes working in the academic world. Bernstein was a gifted speaker about music who could make even those with little background feel as if they had learned something worthwhile about a sophisticated musical concept. This applied to both the children and adults who watched Bernstein on the network programs *Omnibus* (1954–61), *Lincoln Presents* (1958–9), *Ford Presents* (1959–62), *Young People's Concerts* (1958–72), and other broadcasts. The Young People's Concerts were hugely influential on an entire American generation, especially future musicians. Bernstein also turned his television scripts into popular books: *The Joy of Music* (New York, 1959), *The Infinite Variety of Music* (New York, 1967), and *Leonard Bernstein's Young People's Concerts* (New York, 1970).

In addition to his many years of teaching conducting at the Berkshire Music Center, Bernstein worked at the Los Angeles Philharmonic Institute in the early 1980s and in the late 1980s with the Schleswig-Holstein Music Festival Orchestra in Germany, two institutions that he helped found.

Bernstein was far too busy with other pursuits to hold a lifelong academic position, but he was inspired to teach briefly at Brandeis University because Koussevitzky had helped found the music program there. After the older conductor's death, Bernstein was appointed professor of music in 1951. He organized a notable Festival of the Creative Arts in June 1952 where his own *Trouble in Tahiti* and Blitzstein's English translation of *The Threepenny Opera* premiered, and then taught at Brandeis until 1954, including a memorable seminar where he discussed with composition students the choices he was making while working on *Candide*.

Bernstein served as the Charles Eliot Norton Professor of Poetry at Harvard in 1973, presenting six lectures that included filmed segments of him conducting the Boston Symphony. The lectures were later televised and released as recordings. Bernstein's major argument concerned the continued importance of tonality in contemporary music, which he defended tenaciously. Bernstein applied principles from linguist Noam Chomsky in his lectures, an approach that has been questioned by a number of music theorists, but Bernstein did provide interesting insights into the music that he considered. The lectures were published in book form as *The Unanswered Question* (Cambridge, MA, 1976).

6. Composer. As the collective memory of Bernstein the performer and teacher fades, it will be his compositions that form the most important part of his legacy. Bernstein made his most significant contributions in dramatic music, but there are also a number of concert works that have become fixtures in the repertory. His compositional style was based upon a potent mixture of vernacular elements—especially jazz rhythms and harmonies and the frequent use of blue notes—with his fondness for lyrical melodies often based on disjunct intervals, triadic harmonies with added tone chords, occasional bitonality, and shifting meters and time signatures based on unusual combinations of two- and three-note groups such as five or seven. The effectiveness with which Bernstein brought vernacular elements to his concert music makes a comparison to Gershwin seem appropriate. Bernstein accomplished the immediate appeal of his theatrical music through wide-ranging eclecticism, which appears in all of his music. He once said that he believed all of his works to be in some way theatrical. He took much from Copland, who critiqued a number of Bernstein's youthful efforts in the late 1930s and early 1940s, and one will also find moments in his music that smack of Blitzstein, Hindemith, Stravinsky, and other models, but his influences constantly shift. Although his taste ran strongly towards composing with a pitch center, Bernstein did use 12-tone rows and strong dissonances, usually for programmatic reasons whereby the resulting tension would be released by a pitch center and consonance. These stylistic choices exist in both his Broadway scores and his concert music, with the stronger dissonance more common in works of the latter category, but a recognizable Bernstein style resonates prominently in works intended for any venue.

7. Dramatic works. Bernstein's theatrical works include five Broadway scores, three ballets, two operas, incidental music for two plays, the "theater piece" *Mass*, and a film score. He offered excerpts from a number of these pieces as orchestral works, but here music written for these projects will be considered only in their dramatic contexts. As noted above, his first two dramatic works, both from 1944, were the ballet *Fancy Free* and the musical *On the Town*. The former was Bernstein's first collaboration with choreographer Jerome Robbins, with whom he later worked on two more ballets, *West Side Story*, and other projects. The scenario of *Fancy Free* involves three sailors on shore leave in New York. Robbins included social dances, which Bernstein reflected in the score with big band rhythms, some block scoring, and blues inflections, tied together with a Copland-like musical stance and neoclassicism heard in many concert works in the 1940s. Designer Oliver Smith suggested turning the story into a Broadway musical, and Bernstein brought his friends Comden and Green in as book writers and lyricists. When veteran Broadway director George Abbott joined the project, the necessary funding also appeared. Robbins infused the high-spirited show with ballets that were important to the plot, and Bernstein supplied a richly comic score with surprising sophistication. His use of jarring dissonance to portray the urban environment appears in the opening of "New York, New York," and his witty use of boogie-woogie, blues, and other types of commercial music adds much to "I Can Cook, Too" and "Come Up To My Place." The ballad "Lonely Town" shows Bernstein at his lyrical best, and "Carried Away" is an effective operatic send-up.

Bernstein's next collaboration with Robbins was the ballet *Facsimile* (1946), also for the Ballet Theatre. It was a major contrast to the light-hearted *Fancy Free*, involving three lonely people who meet on a beach and find physical passion, but no personal attachments. Bernstein's score featured a taut development of opening material and included his typical lyricism and rhythmic interest, but the reviews were mixed and the ballet is seldom performed.

Bernstein's busiest period for writing dramatic music was the 1950s, before he became music director of the New York PO. He wrote incidental music for a version of *Peter Pan* (1950) starring Boris Karloff and Jean Arthur, including seven songs (with Bernstein's own lyrics) and 13 instrumental segments. Brooks Atkinson in the *New York Times* praised his work as "a melodic, colorful and dramatic score that is not afraid to be simple in style." Bernstein's first opera, *Trouble in Tahiti*, as noted above, had its premiere at the Festival for the Creative Arts at Brandeis University in June 1952. Bernstein wrote his own libretto for the one-act work, which describes, in vignettes, the unhappy marriage between Sam and Dinah, names derived from Bernstein's family that make the work appear somewhat autobiographical. The opera includes a trio in a jazzy, commercial style with lyrics that suggests how ideal life should be in the suburbs. Bernstein's score demonstrated his ability to set lyrics to rhythms that approximate American speech, and the music is appropriate and dramatic, such as in Dinah's solo "What a movie!," which includes wickedly humorous moments as she lampoons the silly movie she just saw while being simultaneously consumed by the film's romance.

Bernstein joined the project that became *Wonderful Town* at the instigation of Comden and Green, brought aboard by director George Abbott when the first contracted team failed to produce a score. A vehicle for Hollywood star Rosalind Russell, *Wonderful Town* was based on the popular play *My Sister Eileen*, a story of two sisters from Columbus, Ohio, who move to New York City in the 1930s to seek their fortunes. Bernstein wrote the score with Comden and Green in about six weeks, producing a collection of ebullient songs that parodied the music of the Depression years and included moments of high comedy and effective character description. The song "Ohio" beautifully captures the sisters' ambivalent feelings on their first night in New York, and "Swing" is a brilliant evocation of 1930s jazz and its musical clichés. The finale, "Wrong Note Rag," combines vernacular rhythms with intentionally and comically dissonant harmonies.

Bernstein's sole film score (besides filmed versions of his musicals) was *On the Waterfront* (1954), an iconic depiction of corruption in a New Jersey dockworkers union, which starred Marlon Brando and was directed by Elia Kazan. Bernstein unified his score with two memorable motives and depicted the violent, urban story through gritty dissonance and irregular rhythms, choices that foreshadow the music he later used to depict the gang violence in *West Side Story*. The next year Bernstein wrote incidental music for *The Lark*, a French play about Joan of Arc by Jean Anouilh, translated into English by Lillian Hellman. The composer set three choruses with French texts and five Latin texts from the Roman Mass. He drew upon inspirations from early music while retaining an overall neo-classical feeling, with minimal percussion as the only accompaniment. Noah Greenberg and the New York Pro Musica Antiqua recorded the choruses for the Broadway production. Following a suggestion by Robert Shaw, Bernstein turned his score into a *Missa Brevis* (1988).

Bernstein concluded his dramatic music in the 1950s with two of his crowning achievements: *Candide* (1956) and *West Side Story* (1957). He worked on the scores simultaneously and the shows opened about nine months apart, meaning that ideas migrated between projects: music for the songs "One Hand, One Heart" and "Gee, Officer Krupke!," for example, originally appeared in the *Candide* score. The scores demonstrate Bernstein's large compositional range and ability to provide music for varied dramatic situations. *Candide* inspired him to write versions of European dance forms, such as the waltz, gavotte, and schottische, appropriate accompaniment to European characters galavanting around the globe seeking meaning in this "best of all possible worlds." For *West Side Story*, Bernstein fashioned a profoundly different concoction, combining the disturbing urban soundscape from *On the Waterfront* with a rich use of Latin rhythms, various types of jazz, and a fetching lyricism. Both scores are also approached symphonically with unifying gestures of recurring intervals and reprised musical ideas. In *Candide* the minor seventh sounds often at important moments; motives from "Candide's Lament" appear throughout the show. In *West Side Story* the tritone—perhaps symbolizing Tony and Maria and/or the story's inherent violence—appears in a number of songs and elsewhere in dramatically important places. The theme to "Somewhere" and other ideas also enhance musico-dramatic unification. These two shows had significantly different receptions. *Candide* ran for only 73 performances in its initial run, partly because Bernstein and book writer Lillian Hellman appeared never to agree what they were creating. Inspired by the hypocrisy of McCarthyism, Hellman wrote a bitter satire that suffered an irreconcilable contrast of mood with Bernstein's ebullient score. When some of the music was combined with a new book by Hugh Wheeler in a 1973 version directed by Hal Prince, audiences found the result far more palatable, although Bernstein's music was truncated. *West Side Story* ran for nearly two years, toured, and came back to Broadway for another seven months in 1960. The hugely popular film that premiered in 1961 helped turn *West Side Story* into one of the monuments of American culture.

Mass (1971) is one of Bernstein's most ambitious, original, and problematic works. Commissioned by Jacqueline Kennedy for the dedication of the John F. Kennedy Center for the Performing Arts in Washington, DC, Bernstein endeavored to set most of the Latin text from the Roman Catholic Mass with interpolated English "tropes" that provide modern commentary and reactions. The composer waited until it was almost too late to finish the piece, but his sister Shirley Bernstein, a theatrical agent, brought her client Stephen Schwartz to Bernstein's attention, and the young lyricist helped write the English texts and devise the work's loose plot. Bernstein re-used many musical segments originally conceived for other projects, and the score bears some of the widest eclecticism of his entire career with styles of concert music ranging from the simple and accessible to 12-tone movements and experimental, recorded cacophony. It also includes references to many vernacular styles: various types of rock, jazz, marching band music, blues, and Broadway ballads. Conceived for a cast of 200 singers, dancers, and instrumentalists, *Mass* approaches many contemporary problems and situations. Both moving and perplexing, it appears to be as close to Bernstein's spirit as any piece that he ever wrote.

Dybbuk (1974), commissioned by the New York City Ballet, was Bernstein's final completed collaboration with Robbins. It follows the story of the Jewish play *The Dybbuk* by Shlomo Ansky, which involves a Jewish marriage, cabalistic rites, and demonic possession. The 50-minute score includes tone rows derived from the Kabbalah, Hebrew texts sung by tenor and baritone soloists, and such Stravinskian devices as octatonicism. Public response was mixed, but this is an effective score by a mature Bernstein. His final completed Broadway musical was *1600 Pennsylvania Avenue* (1976) with book and lyrics by Alan Jay Lerner, a commercial disaster that closed after seven performances. The plot was unworkable, but the score included lively music from Bernstein and Lerner's typically stylish lyrics, which can be appreciated in *A White House Cantata* (1997), a concert version of the piece.

Bernstein returned to the story of his previous opera *Trouble in Tahiti* when he fulfilled a commission from three different opera companies with *A Quiet Place* in the early 1980s. The plot of the new work involves the same family 30 years later. Dinah has committed suicide and the family gathers for the funeral. The two children, one who is psychotic, do not get along with their father, but by the end of the work they have reached a minimal understanding. Stephen Wadsworth wrote the libretto, which includes parallels with the history of Bernstein's family. The new material was originally meant immediately to follow a performance of *Trouble in Tahiti*, but subsequent consideration placed the shorter first work as two flashbacks in Act 2 of *A Quiet Place*. It is a complex work in which Bernstein accesses his usual plethora of musical influences and places them at the service of the drama, but the most fascinating aspect of the score is the striking use of speech rhythms, which show a precision that one seldom finds in English-language operas. Unlike *Trouble in Tahiti*, *A Quiet Place* has not found a regular place in the repertory.

8. Symphonic works. Bernstein's symphonic works tend to be even more elusive in terms of genre designation than his dramatic works. Among Bernstein's three symphonies one has a lament as a finale, and the others might be called a piano concerto and a narrated oratorio. He wrote what became the finale of his Symphony no.1, "Jeremiah" in 1939, composing two more movements for a composition contest in 1942, creating an impressive first symphony from a young composer. Jack Gottlieb has shown that a number of the themes are based on Jewish liturgical melodies. The opening "Prophecy" is declamatory, displaying a rhythmic sense similar to that one hears in Copland, but the overall effect is more like Bloch's Jewish works. "Profanation" provides a strong contrast with its rapidly shifting meters and melodic content close to Bernstein's Broadway style. The closing "Lamentation," also declamatory, again carries the strong feeling of Bernstein's mentor Copland.

Bernstein's growth as a composer in the years before his Symphony no.2 ("The Age of Anxiety," after W.H. Auden's poem) premiered in 1949 was substantial. This is evident in the development of the opening material throughout the 14 variations of "The Seven Ages" and "The Seven Stages" and the symphonic jazz of "The Masque." The piano writing in "The Age of Anxiety" is soloistic, but in the original version Bernstein used the piano sparsely in "The Masque," an oversight corrected in the 1965 revision.

In the 1950s, a decade mostly devoted to composing dramatic music, Bernstein wrote his *Serenade* after Plato's *Symposium* for solo violin, strings, harp, and percussion. Like "The Age of Anxiety," the *Serenade* was a commission from the Koussevitzky Foundation. Bernstein wrote most of it in Europe during the summer of 1954 before its premiere in Venice with Isaac Stern as soloist. Despite the arcane program (the sincerity of which has been questioned by some commentators, who note that Bernstein's movement titles do not correspond to the order that the characters speak in Plato's text), Bernstein produced one of the more effective American violin concertos. The opening "Phaedrus: Pausanias" shows Bernstein's use of developing variations based on the cantabile opening melody, followed by the restrained "Aristophanes" and the impetuous "Eryximachus." "Agathon" is one of the composer's most sublime creations, a seraphic melody in the solo violin over undulating accompaniment. The finale, "Socrates, Alcibiades," opens with biting, ascetic dissonance (a gesture that Bernstein also uses to open the finale of *Chichester Psalms*), only to close with symphonic jazz.

Bernstein's compositional time was clearly limited during his tenure with the New York PO. The only two substantive works he completed were Symphony no.3 ("Kaddish," 1963) and the *Chichester Psalms* (1965), the latter written during a sabbatical. Bernstein's first two symphonies both addressed what he saw as the contemporary "crisis of faith." In "Kaddish," a modern oratorio for orchestra, mixed chorus, boys' choir, speaker, and soprano soloist, Bernstein addressed God directly, criticizing a lack of concern for human affairs and allowing such scourges as nuclear weapons. It was a controversial work that was one of Bernstein's most personal before *Mass*. Musically, Bernstein's feelings perhaps showed most strongly in his use of tone rows and extreme dissonance in the "Din-Torah," later resolved through tonal segments and typical lyrical writing. Bernstein extensively revised the symphony in 1977, toning down the narration, but the work remains somewhat problematic for audiences and is a huge commitment for an orchestra in terms of required forces. *Chichester Psalms* has proven to be one of Bernstein's most popular concert works. Based on a deleted song from *West Side Story* and music Bernstein had hoped to use in a musicalization of *The Skin of Our Teeth* that he abandoned in late 1964, this choral work with orchestra was commissioned by Chichester Cathedral. Each of the three movements includes the text of a full psalm and selections from another, all in Hebrew. A great deal of this extremely melodic and accessible piece sounds like the composer's Broadway music and the overall program resembles both "Kaddish" and *Mass*. It opens with a celebration of God, departs to strong contrast between the peaceful and violent in the second movement, and returns in peace for the final movement, the cathartic opening of which is reminiscent of *Serenade*'s finale.

Bernstein wrote four major works for orchestra in the last 15 years of his life. *Songfest* (1977) is a tribute to the American Bicentennial in 1976. He selected memorable texts by a diverse group of American poets and set them as a song cycle for soloists of six different voice types and orchestra. The solo and ensemble movements constitute an effective set that might have suffered from lack of performances because of the unusual forces, but the range of the work is exceptional, and perhaps Bernstein revealed his own homosexual leanings in his songlike setting of "To What You Said" by Walt Whitman. In *Divertimento for Orchestra* (1980), commissioned by the Boston SO for its centenary, Bernstein ties the movements together with the notes B and C ("Boston centennial") and based some of the work on his musical memories of growing up in Boston. The eight movements are primarily dances, including a cheeky but charming waltz in 7/8. *Halil, Nocturne* (1981) was composed in memory of a young Israeli flutist who died in the 1973 Arab–Israeli War (*halil* is Hebrew for "flute"). The accompanimental forces are reminiscent of the *Serenade*, but the work is quite different, opening with a 12-tone row and presenting a study of contrasts between tonality and atonality. The Concerto for Orchestra (1986–9) had a complicated history. Two of the four movements were premiered in Tel Aviv in 1986 during the 50th anniversary of the Israel Philharmonic, and the conglomerate varied, final version premiered three years later. The first movement includes improvisation and prerecorded tapes, and the second movement, "Mixed Doubles," was inspired by the "Play of the Couples" from Bartók's Concerto for Orchestra. "Diaspora Dances" parodies several dances, and in the "Benediction," a baritone intones a tranquil biblical text from the *Book of Numbers*.

9. Smaller works. Bernstein's output also includes a number of smaller works in various genres, some of which have become well known. His piano music includes the many brief *Anniversaries*, character pieces written throughout his career (from 1943 to 1988), and *Touches* (1981), a taut set of variations. The Sonata for Clarinet and Piano (1942) has been popular for decades. *Brass Music* (1948) and *Dance Suite* (1989) each include five movements for various combinations of brass instruments, some for soloists with piano accompaniment. The song cycles *I Hate Music* (1943), *La Bonne Cuisine* (1947), and *Arias and Barcarolles* (1988, for mezzo-soprano, baritone, and piano four-hands) form a useful body of recital literature. The *Prelude, Fugue, and Riffs* (1949) for jazz band, although not a major work, provides a look at Bernstein's musical style in microcosm because he convincingly combines a jazz persona (albeit without improvisation) with classical techniques.

10. Legacy. Bernstein lived an exceedingly full life, including many activities outside of music. His Jewish faith was important to him throughout and inspired a number of his works. Likewise, his interest in politics lasted his entire career. He lent his name to many left-wing groups early in his early years of fame, causing the FBI to amass a huge file on Bernstein over the decades. Questions about Bernstein's loyalties during the McCarthy years caused him to have trouble renewing his passport in 1953 and Barry Seldes has demonstrated that his career suffered some from a blacklist in the ensuing years, but Bernstein was back in favor by 1958 when he became music director of the New York PO. A later political controversy involved a party that Bernstein and his wife hosted to raise money for the legal defense of the Black Panthers in 1970.

Bernstein was one of many homosexual males associated with American concert music in the middle of the 20th century, and this was a major part of his life and personality. His sexual preference surely contributed to Bernstein's political problems in the 1950s, as was the case with many artists, and he pursued relationships with men throughout his life. All external evidence of Bernstein's marriage to Felicia Montealegre Cohn, an actress, indicates a sincere relationship until Bernstein left her briefly for a man in 1976. Not long afterwards he returned to her; she was diagnosed with lung cancer and died in 1978. Their union resulted in three children.

Bernstein's legacy looms large in each area that he worked. *West Side Story* remains his most important work, but his mastery of the Broadway idiom is just as clear in his other shows. *Mass* remains a powerful piece and is finding new audiences. Bernstein's concert music includes many enduring works, especially *Chichester Psalms*, and orchestral pieces based upon his popular shows also continue to be programmed. His fame as a conductor has barely diminished since his death, and many of his recordings remain critically and commercially popular. That he will also be remembered as one of America's most important musical educators seems certain.

WORKS

(all published unless otherwise stated)

DRAMATIC

The Birds (incid music, Aristophanes), 1938, unpubd; Cambridge, MA, 21 April 1939

The Peace (incid music, Aristophanes), 1940, unpubd; Cambridge, MA, 23 May 1941

Fancy Free (ballet, choreog. J. Robbins), 1944; New York, 18 April 1944

On the Town (musical, book and lyrics by B. Comden, A. Green, additional lyrics by Bernstein), orchd H. Kay, Bernstein, D. Walker, E. Jacoby, and T. Royal, 1944; Boston, 13 Dec 1944

Facsimile (ballet, choreog. Robbins), 1946; New York, 24 Oct 1946, cond. Bernstein

Peter Pan (incid music, lyrics by Bernstein, after J.M. Barrie), orchd Kay, 1950; New York, 24 April 1950, cond. B. Steinberg

Trouble in Tahiti (op, 1, libretto by Bernstein), 1951; Waltham, MA, 12 June 1952, cond. Bernstein

Wonderful Town (musical, book and lyrics by Comden and Green, after J.A. Fields and J. Chodorov: *My Sister Eileen*), orchd D. Walker, 1953; New Haven, CT, 19 Jan 1953

On the Waterfront (film score, dir. E. Kazan), 1954

The Lark (incid music, L. Hellman, after J. Anouilh), 1955; Boston, 28 Oct 1955

Salome (incid music, O. Wilde), 1955, unpubd

Candide (comic operetta, book by Hellman, lyrics by R. Wilbur, J. La Touche, D. Parker, Bernstein, after Voltaire), orchd Kay, Bernstein, 1956; Boston, 29 Oct 1956; rev. 1973 (lyrics by Wilbur, La Touche, S. Sondheim, Bernstein, book by H. Wheeler after Voltaire), Brooklyn, NY, 20 Dec 1973, cond. J. Mauceri

West Side Story (musical, lyrics by Sondheim and Bernstein, book by A. Laurents), orchd S. Ramin, I. Kostal, Bernstein, choreog. Robbins, 1957; Washington DC, 19 Aug 1957, cond. M. Goberman

The Firstborn (incid music, C. Fry), 1958, unpubd; New York, 20 April 1958

Mass (music theater piece, English lyrics by S. Schwartz and Bernstein), orchd J. Tunick, Kay, Bernstein, 1971, Washington DC, 8 Sept 1971, cond. M. Peress; arr. Ramin for chbr orch, Los Angeles, 26 Dec 1972, cond. Peress

Dybbuk (ballet, choreog. Robbins), 1974; New York, 16 May 1974, cond. Bernstein

By Bernstein (revue), 1975, withdrawn [based on unpubd and withdrawn theater songs]; New York, 23 Nov 1975

1600 Pennsylvania Avenue (musical, book and lyrics by A.J. Lerner), orchd Ramin, Kay, 1976; Philadelphia, 24 Feb 1976, cond. R. Gagnon, withdrawn; reworked as vocal-orch work White House Cant., 1997

A Quiet Place (op, 1, libretto by S. Wadsworth), 1983; Houston, 17 June 1983, cond. J. De Main; rev. 1984 in 3 acts, incl. Trouble in Tahiti

ORCHESTRAL

Fancy Free, suite, 1944 [based on ballet], withdrawn; 3 Dance Variations from Fancy Free, 1944; On the Town, 3 dance episodes, 1945 [based on musical], transcr. concert band; Facsimile, choreographic essay, 1946 [based on ballet]; Sym. no.2 'The Age of Anxiety', after W.H. Auden, pf, orch, 1949, rev. 1965; Prelude, Fugue and Riffs, cl, jazz ens, 1949; Serenade, vn, str, hp, perc, 1954 [after Plato: *Symposium*]; On the Waterfront, sym. suite, 1955 [based on film score]; West Side Story, sym. dances, 1960 [based on musical]; Fanfare I, 1961 [for inauguration of J.F. Kennedy], orchd Ramin; Fanfare II, 1961 [for 25th anniversary of the High School of Music and Art], orchd Ramin; 2 Meditations from Mass, 1971; Meditation III from Mass, 1972, withdrawn; Dybbuk Suite nos.1–2 (Dybbuk Variations), 1974 [based on ballet]; 3 Meditations from Mass, vc, orch, 1977, arr. vc, pf, 1978; Slava!, ov., 1977; CBS Music, 1977, withdrawn; Divertimento, 1980;

A Musical Toast, 1980; Halil, nocturne, fl, str, perc, 1981; Conc. for Orch, 1989; Suite, arr. Ramin, M.T. Thomas, 1991 [based on op A Quiet Place, 1983]

VOCAL-ORCHESTRAL

Sym. no.1 "Jeremiah" (Bible), Mez, orch, 1942; Hashkiveinu (Heb. liturgy), T, chorus, org, 1945; Afterthought, voice, orch, 1945 (study for Facsimile), Arr. of Reena (Heb. folksong), chorus, orch, 1947; Sym. no.3 "Kaddish" (Heb. liturgy, Bernstein), S, spkr, chorus, boys' chorus, orch, 1963; Chichester Psalms (Bible), Tr, chorus, orch, 1965; Songfest, 6 solo vv, orch, 1977: To the Poem (F. O'Hara), The Pennycandy Store beyond the El (L. Ferlinghetti), A Julia de Burgos (J. de Burgos), To What you Said (W. Whitman), I, too, Sing America (L. Hughes), Okay "Negroes" (J. Jordan), To my Dear and Loving Husband (A. Bradstreet), Storyette H.M. (G. Stein), if you can't eat you got to (e. e. cummings), Music I Heard with You (C. Aiken), Zizi's Lament (G. Corso), What Lips my Lips have Kissed (Millay), Israfel (E.A. Poe); Olympic Hymn (G. Kunert), chorus, orch, 1981; White House Cant., arr. C. Harmon, Ramin, 1997 [based on musical 1600 Pennsylvania Avenue, 1976]

OTHER VOCAL

Choral: Arr. of Simchu Na (Heb. folksong), SATB, pf, 1947; Yidgal (Heb. liturgy), chorus, pf, 1950; Harvard Choruses (Lerner), 1957, withdrawn; Dedication, Lonely Men of Harvard; Warm-Up, mixed chorus, 1970, incorporated into music theater piece Mass, 1971; A Little Norton Lecture (e.e. cummings), male vv, 1973, unpubd, arr. as Storyette H.M. in Songfest, 1977 [See vocal-orchestral]; Missa brevis (Ct, mixed chorus)/(7 sol vv), perc, 1988 [based on incid music The Lark, 1955]

Solo vocal (1 v, pf, unless otherwise stated): Psalm cxlviii, 1932; I Hate Music (Bernstein), song cycle, 1943: My Name is Barbara, Jupiter has Seven Moons, I Hate Music, A Big Indian and a Little Indian, I'm a Person Too; Lamentation, Mez, orch, 1943 [arr. of 3rd movt of Sym. no.1 "Jeremiah"]; Afterthought (Bernstein), 1945, withdrawn; La bonne cuisine (4 recipes, Bernstein), 1947: Plum Pudding, Queues de Boeuf, Tavouk Guenksis, Civet à Toute Vitesse; 2 Love Songs (R.M. Rilke), 1949: Extinguish my eyes, When my soul touches yours; Silhouette (Galilee) (Bernstein), 1951; On the Waterfront (La Touche), 1954, withdrawn; Get Hep! (Bernstein), 1955, withdrawn; So Pretty (Comden, Green), 1968; The Madwoman of Central Park West (Bernstein): My New Friends, Up! Up! Up!, 1979; Piccola serenata, 1979; Arias and Barcarolles (L. Bernstein, J. Bernstein, Y.Y. Segal), Mez, Bar, pf 4 hands, 1988: Prelude, Love Duet, Little Smary, The Love of My Life, Greeting, Oif Mayn Khas'neh, Mr. and Mrs. Webb Say Goodnight, Nachspiel; Vayomer Elohim, voice, pf, *c* 1989

CHAMBER

Pf Trio, 1937; Music for 2 Pf, 1937 [incl. in musical On the Town, 1944]; Pf Sonata, 1938; Music for the Dance, nos.1 and 2, 1938, unpubd [incl. in musical On the Town, 1944]; Scenes from the City of Sin, pf 4 hands, 1939, unpubd; Sonata, vn, pf, 1940, unpubd; 4 Studies, 2 cl, 2 bn, pf *c*1940, unpubd; Arr. of Copland: El salón Mexico, pf/2 pf, 1941; Sonata, cl, pf, 1941–2; 7 Anniversaries, pf, 1943; 4 Anniversaries, pf, 1948; Brass Music, tpt, hn, trbn, tuba, pf, 1948; 4 Sabras, pf, *c* 1950s, unpubd; 5 Anniversaries, pf, 1954; Bridal Suite, pf 4 hands, unpubd; Shivaree, brass, perc, 1969, incorporated into theater piece Mass, 1971; Touches, pf, 1981; 13 Anniversaries, 1988; Variations on an Octatonic Scale, rec, vc, 1989; Dance Suite, brass quintet, opt. perc, 1990

Recorded interviews in *NHob*

Principal publishers: Amberson, Harms, Jalni

BIBLIOGRAPHY

P. Gradenwitz: "Leonard Bernstein," *MR*, x (1949), 191–202

B. Atkinson: "First Night at the Theatre: Jean Arthur and Boris Karloff in an Excellent Version of Barrie's 'Peter Pan,'" *New York Times* (25 April 1950)

D. Drew: "Leonard Bernstein: *Wonderful Town*," *The Score*, no.12 (1955), 77–80

H. Keller: "On the Waterfront," *The Score*, no.12 (1955), 81–4

H.C. Schonberg: "New Job for the Protean Mr. Bernstein," *New York Times Magazine* (22 Dec 1957)

J. Briggs: *Leonard Bernstein, the Man, his Work, and his World* (Cleveland, OH, 1961)

A. Holde: *Leonard Bernstein* (Berlin, 1961)

J. Gottlieb: *The Music of Leonard Bernstein: a Study of Melodic Manipulations* (diss., U. of Illinois, 1964)

J. Gottlieb: "The Choral Music of Leonard Bernstein, Reflections of Theater and Liturgy," *American Choral Review*, x/2 (1967–8), 156–77

J. Gruen: *The Private World of Leonard Bernstein* (New York, 1968)

H.C. Schonberg: "End of His Formal Duties May Bring Busier Life," *New York Times* (19 May 1969)

E. Ames: *A Wind from the West: Bernstein and the New York Philharmonic Abroad* (Boston, MA, 1970)

J. Gruen: "In Love with the Stage," *ON*, xxxvii/3 (1972), 16–23

J.W. Weber: *Leonard Bernstein* (Utica, NY, 1975) [discography]

R. Chesterman: "Leonard Bernstein in Conversation with Robert Chesterman," *Conversations with Conductors* (Totowa, NJ, 1976), 53–60, 69–72

J. Ardoin: "Leonard Bernstein at Sixty," *High Fidelity/Musical America*, xxviii/8 (1978), 53–8

J. Gottlieb: *Leonard Bernstein: a Complete Catalogue of his Works* (New York, 1978, enlarged 2/1988)

A. Keiler: "Bernstein's The Unanswered Question and Problems of Musical Competence," *MQ*, lxiv (1978), 195–222

J. Gottlieb: "Symbols of Faith in the Music of Leonard Bernstein," *MQ*, lxvi (1980), 287–95

B. Bernstein: "Personal History: Family Matters," *New Yorker* (22–29 March 1982); repr. as *Family Matters* (New York, 1982)

H. Matheopoulos: *Maestro: Encounters with Conductors of Today* (London, 1982), 3

P. Robinson: *Bernstein* (New York, 1982)

L. Botstein: "The Tragedy of Leonard Bernstein," *Harper's*, cclxvi/May (1983), 38–40, 57–62

J. Peyser: *Bernstein: a Biography* (New York, 1983)

M. Freedland: *Leonard Bernstein* (London, 1987)

P. Gradenwitz: *Leonard Bernstein* (London, 1987)

P.S. Minear: *Death Set to Music: Masterworks by Bach, Brahms, Penderecki, Bernstein* (Atlanta, 1987)

J. Cott: "Leonard Bernstein," *RS* (29 November 1990)

J. Fluegel, ed.: *Bernstein Remembered* (New York, 1991)

S. Chapin: *Leonard Bernstein: Notes for a Friend* (New York, 1992)

H. Pollack: *Harvard Composers: Walter Piston and his Students from Elliott Carter to Frederic Rzewski* (Metuchen, NJ, 1992)

D. Schiff: "Re-hearing Bernstein," *Atlantic*, cclxxi/6 (1993), 55–8

H. Burton: *Leonard Bernstein* (New York, 1994)

M. Secrest: *Leonard Bernstein* (New York, 1994)

W. Burton: *Conversations about Bernstein* (New York, 1995)

G. Block: "*West Side Story*: the Very Model of a Major Musical," *Enchanted Evenings: the Broadway Musical from "Show Boat" to Sondheim* (New York, 1997), 245–73, 341–2

S.A. Gelleny: "Leonard Bernstein on Television: Bridging the Gap between Classical Music and Popular Culture," *Journal of Popular Music Studies*, xi–xii (1999–2000), 48–67

C.J. Page: *Leonard Bernstein and the Resurrection of Gustav Mahler* (diss., U. of California, Los Angeles, 2000)

P.R. Laird: "Choreographers, directors and the fully integrated musical," *The Cambridge Companion to the Musical*, ed. W.A. Everett and P.R. Laird (Cambridge, 2002, 2/2008), 220–34

P.R. Laird: *Leonard Bernstein: a Guide to Research* (New York and London, 2002)

b.d. mcclung and P.R. Laird: "Musical sophistication on Broadway: Kurt Weill and Leonard Bernstein," *The Cambridge Companion to the Musical*, ed. W.A. Everett and P.R. Laird (Cambridge, 2002, 2/2008), 190–201

Y.S. Ikach: *A Study of Selected Songs by Leonard Bernstein which Reflect his Contribution to the Evolution of Art Song in America* (diss., West Virginia U., 2003)

D. Schiller: *Bloch, Schoenberg, and Bernstein: Assimilating Jewish Music* (Oxford, 2003)

N. Hubbs: *The Queer Composition of America's Sound: Gay Modernists, American Music, and National Identity* (Berkeley, 2004)

E.L. Keathley: "Postwar Modernity and the Wife's Subjectivity: Bernstein's *Trouble in Tahiti*," *AM*, xxiii/2 (2005), 220–56

V. Perlis: "An Overview of the Friendship Between Copland and Bernstein and Selections from their Correspondence from the 1940s through 1980s," *Aaron Copland and his World*, ed. Carol J. Oja and Judith Tick (Princeton, NJ, 2005), 151–78
E.B. Crist: "Mutual Responses in the Midst of an Era: Aaron Copland's *The Tender Land* and Leonard Bernstein's *Candide*," *JM*, xxiii (2006), 485–527
H. Smith: "'Peter Grimes' and Leonard Bernstein: an English Fisherman and his Influence on an American Eclectic," *Tempo*, no.235 (2006), 22–30
A. Bushard: "He Could've Been a Contender: Thematic Integration in Leonard Bernstein's Score for *On the Waterfront* (1954)," *Journal of Film Music*, ii/1 (2007), 43–62
E.B. Crist: "The Best of All Possible Worlds: the Eldorado Episode in Leonard Bernstein's *Candide*," *COJ*, xix (2007), 223–48
B. Bernstein and B. Haws: *Leonard Bernstein: American Original: How a Modern Renaissance Man Transformed Music and the World during his New York Philharmonic Years, 1943–1976* (New York, 2008)
G. Block: "Bernstein's Senior Thesis at Harvard: the Roots of a Lifelong Search to Discover an American Identity," *College Music Symposium*, xlviii (2008), 52–68
L.E. Helgert: *Jazz Elements in Selected Concert Works of Leonard Bernstein: Sources, Reception, and Analysis* (diss., Catholic U. of America, 2008)
A. Ross: "The Legend of Lenny," *The New Yorker* (15 Dec 2008)
B. Seldes: *Leonard Bernstein: the Political Life of an American Musician* (Berkeley, CA, 2009)
N. Simeone: *Leonard Bernstein: West Side Story* (Farnham, 2009)
R.P. Bañagale: "'Each Man Kills the Thing He Loves': Bernstein's Formative Relationship with *Rhapsody in Blue*," *JSAM*, iii/1 (2009), 47–66
A. Bushard: "From *On the Waterfront* to *West Side Story*, or There's Nowhere Like Somewhere," *Studies in Musical Theatre*, iii/1 (2009), 61–75
W.A. Everett: "*Candide* and the tradition of American operetta," *Studies in Musical Theatre*, iii/1 (2009), 53–9
A. Giger: "Bernstein's *The Joy of Music* as Aesthetic Credo," *JSAM*, iii/3 (2009), 311–29
L. Helgert: "Songs from Leonard Bernstein's Stage Works as Jazz Repertoire," *AM*, xxvii/3 (2009), 356–68
N. Hubbs: "Bernstein: Homophobia, Historiography," *Women and Music*, xiii (2009), 24–42
S. Kaskowitz: "All in the Family: Brandeis University and Leonard Bernstein's 'Jewish Boston'," *JSAM*, iii/1 (2009), 85–100
D. Massey: "Leonard Bernstein and the Harvard Student Union: in Search of Political Origins," *JSAM*, iii/1 (2009), 67–84
E. Nash: "Understanding and Performing Bernstein's Chichester Psalms," *Choral Journal*, xxxxix/8 (2009), 8–31
C.J. Oja: "*West Side Story* and *The Music Man*: Whiteness, Immigration, and Race in the US during the late 1950s," *Studies in Musical Theatre*, iii/1 (2009), 13–30
J.D. Sarna: "Leonard Bernstein and the Boston Jewish Community of His Youth: the Influence of Solomon Braslavsky, Herman Rubenovitz, and Congregation Mishkan Tefila," *JSAM*, iii/1 (2009), 35–46
J. Gottlieb: *Working With Bernstein* (New York, 2010)
P.R. Laird: *Leonard Bernstein's Chichester Psalms* (Hillsdale, NY, 2010)
E.A. Wells: *West Side Story: Cultural Perspectives on an American Musical* (Lanham, MD, 2010)
H. Smith: *There's A Place for Us: the Musical Theatre Works of Leonard Bernstein* (Farnham, 2011)
Leonard Bernstein website (The Leonard Bernstein Office, Inc.) <www.leonardbernstein.com>
"The Leonard Bernstein Collection," *American Memory*, Library of Congress <http://memory.loc.gov/ammem/collections/bernstein/>

PAUL R. LAIRD (Text, Bibliography),
DAVID SCHIFF (Works)/R

Bernstein, Martin (*b* New York, NY, 14 Dec 1904; *d* 19 Dec 1999). Writer on music and music educator. Bernstein was an important figure in the establishment of musicology as a discipline in the early twentieth century. He studied with ALBERT STOESSEL at New York University (BS 1925, BMus 1927), where he began teaching in 1925. After working during World War II as an intelligence officer, he was appointed professor in 1947 and chairman of the music department in 1955. After his retirement in 1972 he was visiting professor at Harvard University in 1986; during the course of his career he was also a guest lecturer at many American universities, including Yale, Rutgers, and Indiana. Bernstein was known primarily for his dedication to teaching: he led graduate seminars (concentrating on Baroque performing practice, Bach, and Wagner), taught the survey course of Western music for over 30 years, wrote music textbooks (*Score Reading*, 1932/ *R*), and created an archive on music iconography of over 5000 slides. His success as a teacher was recognized in 1968 when he was the recipient of NYU's Great Teacher Award. He was also a lecturer on music in a weekly radio program for WCBS, New York (1955–7), and associate editor of the Reese Festschrift (1966). A collection of essays in his honor entitled *A Musical Offering* (ed. E.H. Clinkscale and C. Brook) was published in 1977. The subject matter ranged from music of the Middle Ages through the 20th century. As a performer, Bernstein played the double bass in the New York SO (1925) and the New York PO (1926–8) and was founder and conductor of the Washington Square Chorus and Orchestra, which introduced many lesser-known works of Purcell, J.S. Bach, and Handel to New York audiences. One of Bernstein's many influences on the world of music came in 1934, when he met Arnold Schoenberg in Chautauqua, New York, where Bernstein encouraged the composer to write the *Suite for String Orchestra* (1934).

WRITINGS

Introduction to Music (New York, 1937, 4/1972 with M. Picker)

PAULA MORGAN/JONAS WESTOVER

Bernstein, Steven (*b* Berkeley, CA, 8 Oct 1961). Jazz trumpeter, arranger, and composer. He took up trumpet at the age of 11 and, attracted to New York, chose to attend Columbia University. By the early 1980s he was regularly performing with a number of bands across a range of musical styles. He served as an arranger for the avant-garde group Spanish Flea in the early 1990s; its producer, Hal Willner, gave Bernstein many opportunities to compose and arrange, including a Leonard Cohen tribute and the music for Robert Altman's film *Kansas City* (1996). Bernstein has performed and collaborated with musicians as diverse as Mocean Worker, Linda Ronstadt, Digable Planets, and Sting. Some of his own albums have explored his Jewish heritage, notably *Diaspora Soul*, *Diaspora Blues*, *Diaspora Hollywood*, and *Diaspora Suite*, all of which have included contributions by John Zorn. From 1995 Bernstein's band Sex Mob has performed and recorded widely; its album *Sexotica* (2006) was nominated for a Grammy. Bernstein remains active in the recording studio, tours globally, collaborates, arranges, and composes for film and television.

BIBLIOGRAPHY

D. Ake: *Jazz Matters: Sound, Place and Time, Since Bebop* (Berkeley, 2010)

JONAS WESTOVER

Berry, Chu [Leon Brown] (*b* Wheeling, WV, 13 Sept 1908; *d* Conneaut, OH, 30 Oct 1941). Jazz tenor saxophonist. He grew up in a musical family and was inspired by Coleman Hawkins to take up saxophone. He played the alto instrument in high school and during his three years at West Virginia State College. He left college in 1929 after being offered his first important engagement, in Sammy Stewart's Chicago-based band. After moving to New York, he worked in various bands. While playing with Benny Carter (1932–3), he made his recording debut and participated in the now-famous Spike Hughes recording sessions (1933), in which he paired with Hawkins and held his own. (This was strictly a recording band, with many members of the Carter band participating.) Stints with Teddy Hill and Fletcher Henderson established Berry's reputation, and from 1937 until his death in a car accident he was the star soloist in Cab Calloway's band. From 1933 he was also a prolific freelance recording artist. Berry developed his own distinctive style and became prominent during Hawkins' absence from America (1934–9). Although his sound was not so voluptuous and his melodic imagination not as fertile as the older man's, he was his equal in terms of harmonic sophistication and perhaps his superior in term of rhythmic drive. He excelled performing at fast tempos, where his remarkable breath control, unerring sense of time, and evenness of phrasing stood out. His early ballad playing was a bit florid but a new maturity was evident in late recordings. He was an influence on the young Charlie Parker, who named his first son Leon.

SELECTED RECORDINGS

As leader: Indiana (1937, Var.); Sittin' in/Forty-Six West Fifty-Second Street (1938, Com.); Blowin' up a Breeze (1941, Com.)

As sideman: H. Allen: Rosetta (1935, Voc.); L. Hampton: Sweethearts on Parade (1939, Vic.); Shufflin' at the Hollywood (1939, Vic.); Hot Mallets (1939, Vic.);. C. Basie: Oh, Lady be Good (1939, Decca); C. Calloway: A Ghost of a Chance (1940, OK); Bye Bye Blues (1940; OK); Lonesome Nights (1940, OK)

BIBLIOGRAPHY

J. Evensmo: *The Tenor Saxophone of Chu Berry* (Hosle, Norway, 1976)

D. Chamberlain and R. Wilson, ed.: "The Otis Ferguson Reader," *December Magazine*, xxiv/1–2 (1982), 58–62

L. Schoenberg: *Classic Chu Berry Columbia and Victor Sessions*, Mosaic MD7-236(2007) [disc notes]

DAN MORGENSTERN

Berry, Chuck [Charles Edward Anderson] (*b* St. Louis, MO, 18 Oct 1926). Rock-and-roll singer, songwriter, and guitarist. He was one of the originators of rock and roll, forging it into a massively commercial, socially revolutionary musical force. A brilliant lyricist, inventive composer, innovative guitarist, and captivating performer, he was one of the genre's first black performers to appeal to a white mainstream audience. His national reputation, which began in the mid-1950s, lasted far longer than those of most other popular musicians; he enjoyed considerable success in 1964 at the height of the British invasion and continued to perform and record into the 21st century.

1. Life. Raised in St. Louis, he spent his childhood in comfortable, working-class circumstances. He attended Antioch Baptist Church, where his father was a bass in the choir. At Simmons Elementary School in St. Louis, he studied guitar with his music teacher, Julia Davis; later, while attending Sumner High School, he surprised the audience at a school program with a version of Jay McShann's "Confessin' the Blues." During World War II he was sent to a reform school for three years for attempted robbery; after he was released at the age of 21 he worked in a General Motors plant and studied cosmetology. He began his career as a performer with the Tommy Stevens Combo, but soon was drafted into a trio led by the pianist Johnnie Johnson. Berry assumed leadership of the group through a savvy business deal he made with the owner of the Cosmopolitan Club. There he refined his songwriting and stage presence and deliberately cultivated an act that was designed to have cross-racial appeal. Spurred by this local success, the group traveled to Chicago to audition for Leonard Chess, the owner of Chess Records, to whom Berry had been introduced by Muddy Waters. Their audition included some blues numbers, notably a song of which they were especially proud, "Wee Wee Hours," and a parodic rockabilly song, "Ida Red," which Chess suggested be retitled "Maybellene" and recorded with a "bigger beat."

Issued in 1955 and backed with "Wee Wee Hours," "Maybellene" became one of the first widely popular rock-and-roll recordings, and the first single to reach high positions on the pop, country, and rhythm-and-blues charts. During the next few years Berry wrote and recorded many memorable songs: "Thirty Days," "Roll over Beethoven" (also part of his Chess audition), "Havana Moon," "Brown-eyed Handsome Man," "School Day," "Rock and Roll Music," "Around and Around," "Johnny B. Goode," "Sweet Little Rock and Roller," "Sweet Little Sixteen," "Reelin' and Rockin'," "Back in the U.S.A.," "Memphis, Tennessee," "Little Queenie," and "Let it Rock." Throughout this period he toured constantly and made an ebullient impression in concert; he became well known for his stage deportment, in particular his "duck walk," which involved bending his knees and jerkily moving across the stage with his guitar poised away from his body in suggestive fashion. Berry's success also at times brought him face to face with racism: for example, when he arrived to play a show in Knoxville, Tennessee , following the release of "Maybellene," he was barred from performing after the promoter, who had been unaware of his race, saw the color of his skin.

In 1959 Berry was arrested for a violation of the Mann Act; he was convicted in 1961 and sent to the federal penitentiary in Terre Haute, Indiana. By the time of his

Chuck Berry, 1980. (AP Photo)

release in 1963 his nightclub had closed and his family had left him. He lived for a time in Wentzville, Missouri, where he developed an amusement park that bore his name. But he soon resumed his music career, encouraged by a number of English and American rock musicians who admired his work. In the face of the British invasion he made a triumphant return with songs like "Nadine" and "No Particular Place to Go" (both 1964), which rank with his best work. After this new flurry of success, however, Berry faded until 1972, when he recorded "My Ding-a-ling," a sexual novelty song that became his only recording to reach number one on the pop chart. He began to perform frequently on the nostalgia circuit, often as part of programs organized by the promoter Richard Nader. Although he usually played with hastily assembled backup bands, his performances rarely fell below a level of workmanlike professionalism. Berry's 60th birthday in 1986 became occasion for an opulent tribute concert at the Fox Theater in St. Louis spearheaded by the Rolling Stones' guitarist Keith Richards. Documented by the filmmaker Tayor Hackford in the film *Hail! Hail! Rock and Roll* (1987), the concert cemented Berry's stature as one of rock and roll's key architects, as did the publication of his autobiography (1987).

Berry's later life and career have been marked by legal travails. In 1979 he was convicted of income tax evasion, and a decade later he was sued for violating the privacy of a female employee at a restaurant he owned. In 2000 Johnson brought a suit against him to claim royalties and credit for his contributions to several songs attributed to Berry. The case was dismissed in 2002 on the grounds that too much time had passed before Johnson had filed his claim, but questions about the level of Johnson's creative input into Berry's music remained unresolved at the time of the pianist's death in 2005.

2. Style and influence. Berry is widely considered the leading pop-music poet of teenage life in the rock-and roll-era. His music combines the virtuoso guitar playing of country music and rockabilly with the rhythm-guitar riffs and 12-bar structure of blues and rhythm-and-blues. His lyrics, which celebrate cars, high school, girls, and the redemptive power of rock and roll, helped shape rock's themes for decades. His descriptions of teenage social rituals came just as the American youth movement began to change the repressive ambiance of the 1950s, and hence his was a key voice in the artistic articulation of that revolution.

St. Louis in the 1930s was a lively center for gospel, blues, and jazz, but many of Berry's primary influences came from farther afield. Among the guitarists who particularly influenced him were Charlie Christian, T-Bone Walker, and Carl Hogan (who played with Nat "King" Cole), all of whom were early exponents of the electric guitar's capacity for solo improvisations akin to the horn players of the day. The rhythm-and-blues singer Louis Jordan clearly left an imprint on Berry with his combination of rhythmic drive and a cutting sense of humor. Other influences extended beyond blues and jazz to include black and white pop singers of the day, especially Cole and Frank Sinatra. Even before he began to record, his songs constituted a tangled web of country and black influences; the confusion that led him to be prohibited from playing his own music in Knoxville stemmed from his sonic resemblance to white country singers.

The structural basis of Berry's songs is the blues, in formal variants ranging from eight to 24 bars, with a strong emphasis on the backbeat. He had an easy, conversational baritone, the inflections shorn of classic blues ornamentation, and crisp enunciation. As a guitarist he employed speeded-up blues and rhythm-and-blues licks, which he adapted to pop-song formats. He exploited the electric guitar's potential for rhythmic chording and ringing overtone effects in a way that has influenced rock guitarists ever since. A particular sonic signature was his tendency to introduce his songs with some unaccompanied melodic statement on his guitar, usually comprising a characteristic mix of single notes and double stops; the opening to "Johnny B. Goode" stands as a classic example.

Berry's lyrics treat cars as symbols of individual liberty, rock as an anthem to freedom and sexuality, and high school as a prison and microcosm. His songs portray the world of the typical teenager and achieve much of their impact from their wit and telling detail. His musical influences and themes varied widely. "Roll over Beethoven" is a humorous but explicit assertion of vernacular music over highbrow; "Havana Moon" is one of the first American pop-calypso songs; "Brown-eyed Handsome Man" is an early attestation of black pride;

"Sweet Little Sixteen" is an affectionate tribute to his fans.

While he never attained the legendary status in popular culture of Elvis Presley, Berry is perhaps the most critically acclaimed of the early rock-and-roll stars. In Marsh's words, "Chuck Berry is to rock what Louis Armstrong was to jazz." His enormous influence can be seen in the number of musicians who recorded his material. The Beach Boys' early hit, "Surfin' USA" (1963), was musically a copy of "Sweet Little Sixteen." Buddy Holly recorded his songs, as did the Beatles ("Roll over Beethoven" and "Rock and Roll Music)"; Mick Jagger and Keith Richards of the Rolling Stones met as teenagers when they discovered their common interest in Berry's music, and the Stones recorded many songs by and about him in their early years. Linda Ronstadt's album *Living in the USA* (1978) was inspired by Berry, and includes his song "Back in the USA," a song that had been covered in a very different style some years earlier by the American proto-punk band the MC5. In a more general, internalized way, innumerable rock musicians have borrowed his musical signatures and poetic themes, and emulated his mischievous, insouciant stage manner.

SELECTED RECORDINGS

Maybellene/Wee Wee Hours (Chess, 1955); Thirty Days/Together we will always be (Chess, 1955); Roll over Beethoven/Drifting Heart (Chess, 1956); Too much Monkey Business/Brown-eyed Handsome Man (Chess, 1956); You can't catch me/Havana Moon (Chess, 1956); School Day/Deep Feeling (Chess, 1957); *After School Session* (Chess, 1957); Rock and Roll Music/Blue Feeling (Chess, 1957); Sweet Little Sixteen/Reelin' and Rockin' (Chess, 1958); *One Dozen Berries* (Chess, 1958); Johnny B. Goode/Around and Around (Chess, 1958); Carol/Hey Pedro (Chess, 1958); Sweet Little Rock and Roller/Jo Jo Gunne (Chess, 1958); Back in the U.S.A./Memphis, Tennessee (Chess, 1959); Almost Grown/Little Queenie (Chess, 1959); *Berry is on Top* (Chess, 1959); Too Pooped to Pop/Let it Rock (Chess, 1960); *Rockin' at the Hops* (Chess, 1960); Nadine/O Rangutang (Chess, 1964); No Particular Place to Go/You Two (Chess, 1964); *St. Louis to Liverpool* (Chess, 1964); *Chuck Berry in Memphis* (Merc., 1967); *The London Chuck Berry Sessions* (Chess, 1972); "My Ding-a-ling" (Chess, 1972); *Rockit* (Atco, 1979); *Johnny B. Goode: his Complete '50s Chess Recordings* (Hip-O-Select, 2007); *You never can tell: the Complete Chess Recordings, 1960–1966* (Hip-O-Select, 2009); *Have Mercy: his Complete Chess Recordings 1969–1974* (Hip-O-Select, 2010)

BIBLIOGRAPHY

M. Lydon: "Chuck Berry," *Rock Folk: Portraits from the Rock 'n' Roll Pantheon* (New York, 1971, 2/1973/*R*), 1–24

R. Christgau: "Chuck Berry," *The Rolling Stone Illustrated History of Rock & Roll*, ed. J. Miller (New York, 1976, 3/1992), 60–66

D. Marsh: "Berry, Chuck," *The New Rolling Stone Record Guide*, ed. D. Marsh and J. Swenson (New York, 1979, 2/1983), 38

H. De Witt: *Chuck Berry: Rock 'n' Roll Music* (New York, 1981, 2/1985)

K. Reese: *Chuck Berry: Mr. Rock n' Roll* (New York, 1982)

C. Berry: *Chuck Berry: the Autobiography* (New York, 1987)

T. Wheeler: "Chuck Berry: the Story, the Interview, the Records," *GP*, xxii/3 (1988), 50–67

T. Taylor: "His Name was in Lights: Chuck Berry's 'Johnny B. Goode,'" *Popular Music*, xi/1 (1992), 27–40

B. Pegg: *Brown Eyed Handsome Man: the Life and Hard Times of Chuck Berry* (New York, 2002)

M. Reff: *The Chuck Berry International Directory*, i (York, 2008)

JOHN ROCKWELL/STEVE WAKSMAN

Berry, Wallace (Taft) (*b* La Crosse, WI, 10 Jan 1928; *d* Vancouver, BC, 16 Nov 1991). Theorist and composer. He studied at the Paris Conservatoire (1953–4) and at the University of Southern California (PhD 1956). In 1977, after teaching music theory at the University of Michigan (1956–76), he was appointed head of music at the University of British Columbia. Despite broad recognition as a composer, including a 1978 award from the American Academy and Institute of Arts and Letters, Berry largely reoriented himself mid-career toward theory. His books and contributions to teaching and administration made him a leader in the discipline. From 1982 to 1985 he served as President of the Society for Music Theory. The Society established an award in his name in 1993, given annually to a distinguished book on music theory by an author at any stage of his or her career.

Berry's music is in a freely dissonant, at times tonal idiom in a wide expressive range. His works are energetic and rhythmically complex yet precise in detail, and clear in phrase structure and formal outline. His theoretical work provides a balanced treatment of rhythm, texture and tonality. He views musical coherence as deriving from patterns of intensification ("progression") and détente ("recession"). While this perspective has precedents in the work of Ernst Kurth, among others, its originality lies in Berry's analysis of the concept of intensity in terms of concrete, measurable factors. He calls these "structural functions" and treats them hierarchically. Of special value are his essays linking analysis with performance that draw on his extensive professional experience as a pianist.

WORKS

(selective list)

Stage: The Admirable Bashville (chbr op, G.B. Shaw), 1954

Orch: 5 Pieces, small orch, 1961; Pf Conc., 1964; Canto elegiaco, 1968; Intonation: Victimis hominum inhumanitatem in memoriam, 1972; Acadian Images, 1977–8

Choral: No Man is an Island (J. Donne), 1959

Solo vocal: Limericks, 1v, pf, 1951; Paean from the Grave (S. Sassoon, P. Dehn, and A.E. Housman), 1v, pf, 1951; Spoon River (E.L. Masters), S, Bar, orch, 1952; Canticle on a Judaic Text, S/T, orch, 1953; 4 Songs of the Sea, 1v, pf, 1957; Des visages de France, S, Mez, ens, 1967; Credo in unam vitam, T, hn, vc, ens, 1969; Lover of the Moon Trembling Now at Twilight, S/T, ens, 1971; Of the Changeless Night and the Stark Ranges of Nothing (E. Birney), Mez, vc, pf, 1978–9; The Moment: Summer's Night (V. Woolf), Mez, pf, 1985

Inst: Variations, pf, 1952; 8 20th-Century Miniatures, pf, 1955; Canons, 2 cl, 1959; Str Qt no.1, 1960; Duo, vn, pf, 1961; Threnody, vn, 1963; Divertimento, wind qnt, pf, perc, 1964; Str Qt no.2, 1964; Canto lirico, va, pf, 1965; Str Qt no.3, 1966; Composition for Pf and Elec Sounds, 1967; Fantasy in 5 Statements, cl, pf, 1967; Duo, fl, pf, 1968; Pf Trio, 1970; 3 Anachronisms, vn, pf, 1973; 10 Pieces, tr inst, pf, 1973–4; Pf Sonata, 1975; Str Qt no.4, 1984

MSS in *CDN-Tcm, Vcm*

Principal publishers: Elkan-Vogel, Carl Fischer, Presser, Southern

WRITINGS

Form in Music (Englewood Cliffs, NJ, 1966, 2/1986)

Structural Functions in Music (Englewood Cliffs, NJ, 1975, 2/1987)

"Rhythmic Accelerations in Beethoven," *JMT*, xxii (1979), 177–236

"Symmetrical Interval Sets and Derivative Pitch Materials in Bartók's String Quartet no.3," *PNM*, xviii/1–2 (1979–80), 287–380

"On Structural Levels in Music," *Music Theory Spectrum*, ii (1980), 19–45

"Text and Music in the *Alto Rhapsody*," *JMT*, xxvii (1983), 239–53

"Metric and Rhythmic Articulation in Music," *Music Theory Spectrum*, vii (1985), 7–33
"Formal Process and Performance in the 'Eroica' Introductions," *Music Theory Spectrum*, x (1988), 3–18
Musical Structure and Performance (New Haven, CT, 1989)

WILLIAM BENJAMIN/MICHAEL BERRY

Berteling, Theodore (*b* Germany, 1826/7; *d* New York, NY, 1889). Maker of flutes, clarinets, and oboes of German birth. He began his career in Boston with E.G. Wright in 1849. During the next few years he worked successively with Graves & Co. and J. Lathrop Allen, setting up in business for himself in 1855. In 1857 he moved to New York, where his business continued until 1915. He was a member of the original Liederkranz Orchestra and of the Aschenbroedel Verein, in New York City.

In 1850 and again in 1856 he won silver medals for his instruments in exhibitions of the Massachusetts Charitable Mechanics' Association in Boston. US patents 76,389 of 1868 and 264,611 of 1882 were obtained by Berteling for improvements in his flutes. Berteling instruments are made of wood but make extensive use of metal linings, metal reinforcing at joints, and metal coverings. A piccolo at the Smithsonian Institution is entirely covered with nickel silver in addition to being lined with brass.

Most Berteling instruments have an elaborate key mechanism. His flutes often have foot extensions to B and B♭. Early Boehm system flutes with conical bore as well as cylindrical examples are among Berteling's instruments in the Dayton C. Miller collection at the Library of Congress. A Berteling oboe is in the collection of the Henry Ford Museum, Dearborn, Michigan.

BIBLIOGRAPHY

Obituary, *Music Trade Review* (5–20 Sept 1889)
N. Groce: *Musical Instrument Makers of New York: a Directory of Eighteenth- and Nineteenth-century Urban Craftsmen* (Stuyvesant, NY, 1991), 14–15

ROBERT E. ELIASON

Besoyan, Rick [Richard] **(Vaugh)** (*b* Alameda, CA, 1925; *d* Sayville, NY, 13 March 1970). Composer, lyricist, and librettist. Besoyan showed an early interest in music and studied at the University of California at Berkeley. After serving in the army he went to New York in 1946 to pursue a career as an actor and singer. For a while he toured with the Bredon-Savoy Light Opera Company performing operettas. Later Besoyan studied at the American Theatre Wing's school and became a musical coach at Stella Adler's Theatre School. He turned to writing and composing in the 1950s and, using his experience with light opera, wrote the book, music, and lyrics for *Little Mary Sunshine* (1959), one of the most popular off-Broadway musicals of the era and an enduring favorite with schools, summer theaters, and amateur groups. *Little Mary Sunshine* was a delicious spoof of *Rose-Marie* and other favorites of American operetta and the intimate production ran a surprising 1143 performances. Besoyan accurately captured the old style, playfully echoing the music of Romberg and Friml while satirizing the innocence of that era. Four years later Besoyan penned a similar parody, *The Student Gypsy, or the Prince of Liederkranz* (1963), based on *The Student Prince* and other European-set operettas, but the result was much less successful, opening in a Broadway theater but running for only 16 performances. He fared little better with his off-Broadway *Babes in the Woods* (1964). This musical version of Shakespeare's *A Midsummer Night's Dream* ran for 45 performances. Besoyan's output raises conjecture about his ability to compose beyond the level of parody, but there is an evident talent for lively and creative songwriting in his existing works.

WORKS

(dates are those of the first New York performance)

Little Mary Sunshine, 18 Nov 1959 [incl. Look for a Sky of Blue, Colorado Love Call]
The Student Gypsy, or The Prince of Liederkranz, 30 Sept 1963
Babes in the Woods, 28 Dec 1964

THOMAS S. HISCHAK

Bessaraboff, Nicholas [from 1945 Nicholas Bessaraboff Bodley] (*b* Voronezh, Russia, 12 Feb 1894; *d* New York, NY, 10 Nov 1973). Musicologist of Russian birth; naturalized American. Actively interested in music from childhood, he was trained as a mechanical engineer in St. Petersburg (1912–15). In 1915 he was sent to the United States to join a Russian Artillery Commission seeking to procure munitions. After the 1917 Revolution, Bessaraboff stayed in the United States, working as an engineer in Rochester, New York; it was there that he began the serious study of musical instruments. In 1927 he became a naturalized American citizen. Four years later he moved to Boston, where in 1935 he began a short catalog that grew into a general compendium of western European instruments, arranged in the form of a systematic classification of instruments. *Ancient European Musical Instruments: an Organological Study of the Musical Instruments in the Leslie Lindsey Mason Collection at the Museum of Fine Arts, Boston* was published in 1941, after which time Bessaraboff devoted himself mainly to his engineering career and to the study of prime numbers. For further information, see D.D. Boyden: "Nicholas Bessaraboff's *Ancient European Musical Instruments*," *Notes*, xxviii (1971–2), 21–7.

DAVID D. BOYDEN

Bethlehem Bach Festival. Annual festival featuring the music of J.S. Bach, inaugurated at Bethlehem, Pennsylvania, in 1900. It is presented by the Bach Choir of Bethlehem, the oldest Bach choir in the United States, founded as the Bethlehem Choral Union in 1882 by John Frederick Wolle, organist of the Central Moravian Church, and renamed in 1898. It is held at Packer Memorial Church, Lehigh University, on the second and third weekends of May. The origins of the festival are rooted in the religious traditions of the Moravians, who settled in the area in the 18th century. The festival itself was initiated on 27 March 1900 with the first American performance of Bach's B minor Mass, conducted by Wolle. Festivals were held in 1901, 1903, and 1905; after reorganization of the choir in 1911 they were resumed annually under Wolle (1912–32), whose successors include Ifor Jones (1939–69), Alfred Mann (1970–80), William Reese (1981–3), and Greg Funfgeld (from 1983). From 1912 to 1947 the orchestral ensemble was drawn from members of the Philadelphia Orchestra. Soloists have included such renowned artists as Rose Bampton, Helen Boatwright, Phyllis Curtin, Charles Bressler, and Phyllis Bryn-Julson. In 1976 the choir appeared in Germany at the 51st International Festival of the New Bach Society in Berlin and at the Thomaskirche, Leipzig. In 2000, the festival celebrated its centennial, which attracted more than 7000 listeners, with performances of the B minor Mass and the St. Matthew Passion.

BIBLIOGRAPHY

R. Walters: *The Bethlehem Bach Choir* (Boston, MA, 1918, 2/1923)
R. Walters: "Bach at Bethlehem, Pennsylvania," *MQ*, xxi (1935), 179
M.A.D. Howe: "'Venite in Bethlehem'—the Major Chord," *MQ*, xxviii (1942), 174–85

SARA VELEZ, RITA H. MEAD/MARK A. BOYLE

Bethune (Green), Thomas [Blind Tom] (*b* Columbus, GA, 25 May 1849; *d* Hoboken, NJ, 13 June 1908). Pianist and composer. He was blind from birth and was bought as a slave with his parents in 1850 by James N. Bethune, a journalist, lawyer, and politician in Columbus. He demonstrated musical aptitude and exceptional retentive skills by his fourth year and was given musical instruction by Bethune's daughter Mary. He was exhibited throughout the state by his master in 1857, and then hired out to Perry Oliver, a planter of Savannah, who took him on an extensive concert tour throughout the slaveholding states; this included a command performance at Willard Hall in Washington for visiting Japanese dignitaries. His programs included works by Johann Sebastian Bach, Ludwig van Beethoven, Frydryk Chopin, Franz Liszt, Sigismond Thalberg, and other European masters, improvisations on operatic tunes and popular ballads, and several of his own published and unpublished compositions. He could perform difficult pieces after one hearing, sing and recite poetry or prose in several languages, duplicate lengthy orations, and imitate the sounds of nature, machinery, and various musical instruments. On the outbreak of the Civil War, he was returned to the Bethunes, who continued to exhibit him in the South to raise money for the Confederacy. After the Bethunes were successful in a guardianship trial in July 1865, Tom was taken abroad, with W P. Howard of Atlanta as his musical tutor; he received testimonial letters from such musicians as Ignaz Moscheles and Charles Hallé. The Bethunes moved to Warrenton, Virginia, on their return, and Tom was shown throughout the United States and Canada; he studied with Joseph Poznanski in New York during the summers. In 1887 the widow of Bethune's son gained legal control over Tom, and continued to exhibit him in major concert halls and as a vaudeville attraction. His final appearances were on the Keith Circuit, in 1904–5.

Tom wrote more than 100 piano works which are typical examples of 19th-century parlor pieces; they include *The Rainstorm* (1865), *The Battle of Manassas* (1866), *March Timpani* (1880), *Cyclone Galop* (1887), *Blind Tom's Mazurka* (1888), and *Grand March Resurrection* (1901). His vocal compositions reveal a familiarity with revival hymns.

BIBLIOGRAPHY

SouthernB
Blind Tom: the Great Negro Pianist (Baltimore, 1867)
J. Becket: "Blind Tom as he is To-day," *Ladies' Home Journal*, xv/10 (1898), 13
A. Tutein: "The Phenomenon of 'Blind Tom,'" *The Etude*, xxxvii (1918), 91
E. Abbott: "The Miraculous Case of Blind Tom," *The Etude*, lviii (1940), 517
E.M. Thornton: "The Mystery of Blind Tom," *Georgia Review*, xv (1961), 395
N.T. Robinson: "Blind Tom: Musical Prodigy," *Georgia Historical Quarterly*, li (1967), 336
G.H. Southall: "Blind Tom: a Misrepresented and Neglected Composer-Pianist," *BPiM*, iii (1975), 141
G.H. Southall: *Blind Tom: the Post–Civil War Enslavement of a Black Musical Genius* (Minneapolis, 1979)
G.H. Southall: *The Continuing "Enslavement" of Blind Tom, 1865–1887* (Minneapolis, 1982)
J.R. Seawright: "Slavery Onstage," *Oxford American* (1998), 99–103 [Southern music issue no.2]
G.H. Southall: *Blind Tom, the Black Pianist Composer (1849–1908): Continually Enslaved* (Lanham, MD, 1999)

GENEVA H. SOUTHALL/R

Beversdorf, (Samuel) Thomas (*b* Yoakum, TX, 8 Aug 1924; *d* Bloomington, IN, 15 Feb 1981). Composer. He studied with KENT KENNAN at the University of Texas (BM 1945), with BERNARD ROGERS and HOWARD HANSON at the Eastman School (MM 1946, DMA 1957), and with AARON COPLAND and Arthur Honegger at the Berkshire Music Center (summer 1947). He taught at the University of Houston and was first trombonist with the Houston SO, 1946–8. From 1949 until his death, he was professor of music at Indiana University. He held the Hoblitzel Fellowship while a student at the University of Texas and in 1956 was awarded a Danforth Teaching Fellowship. He received a commission from the Cincinnati SO (for *Ode*, 1952) and one from the Houston SO (for *New Frontiers*, 1953). From 1944 to 1959, Beversdorf composed prolifically and rapidly, his music characterized by standard timbral combinations, but thereafter he worked more slowly, producing introspective compositions on a larger scale with more unusual instrumentation; all his works reflect sensitivity to the practical needs of a variety of ensembles and circumstances. He also wrote two opera librettos: *Metamorphosis* (after Kafka), 1955–66, and *Amphitryon 99, or I Hope it isn't a Cold Marble Couch* (after Plautus and Giraudoux), 1977–8.

WORKS

Stage: The Hooligan (op, 1, Beversdorf, after Chekhov: *The Boor*), 1964–9; Vision of Christ (mystery play, J. Wheatcroft, after Langland), 1971

Choral: 17 Antiphonal Responses, chorus, org, 1949; The Rock (orat., T.S. Eliot), 1958; Mini Motet from Micah, S, Bar, SATB, org, 1969; 2 Amen settings, chorus, org, 1969

Orch: 4 syms., 1946, 1950, 1954 rev. 1958, 1960, no.3, wind, perc; Mexican Portrait, small orch, 1948, rev. 1952; Conc. grosso, ob, chamber orch, 1948; Conc., 2 pf, orch, 1951; Ode, 1952; New Frontiers, 1953; Serenade, wind, perc, 1957; Vn Conc., 1959; Variations (Threnody), 1963; Murals, Tapestries, and Icons, wind, elec b gui, elec pf, 1975; La Petite Exposition, vn/cl, 11 stgs, 1976; other works

Brass: Hn Sonata, 1945; Cathedral Music, brass ens, 1950, brass qt, org, 1953; 3 Epitaphs, brass qt, 1955; Tuba Sonata, 1956; Tpt Sonata, 1962; Walruses, Cheesecake, and Morse Code, tuba, pf, 1973; Conc., tuba, wind, 1976

Inst: Suite on Baroque Themes, cl, vc, pf, 1947; 2 str qts, 1951, 1955; Vn Sonata, 1964–5; Fl Sonata, 1965–6; Divertimento da camera, fl + pic, ob + eng hn, db, hpd, 1968; Vc Sonata, 1968–9; Sonata, vn, harp, 1977; Corelliana Variations, fl + pic, fl + pic + a fl, vc, 1980; other works

Other: 6 pf works, incl. Pf Sonata, 1944, Toccata, 2 pf, 1953; 3 Songs (E.E. Cummings), S, pf, 1955; other songs

Principal publishers: Invention, G. Schirmer, Robert King, Seesaw Music Corp., Southern Music

BIBLIOGRAPHY

Baker8

D. Ewen: *American Composers: a Biographical Dictionary* (New York, 1982)

A. Beversdorf: Thomas Beversdorf website <http://beversdorf.com> [incl. complete bibliography and annotated list of works]

DAVID COPE/GREG A STEINKE

Bey, Andy [Andrew W.] (*b* Newark, NJ, 28 Oct 1939). Jazz singer and pianist. He played boogie-woogie from the age of three and launched his professional career with his siblings Salome and Geraldine. Their vocal trio, Andy and the Bey Sisters, was active from 1956 to 1967 and worked across Europe. Footage from their performance at a Parisian salon was included in the Chet Baker documentary *Let's Get Lost* (1989). After the group disbanded Bey worked with Max Roach, Horace Silver, and Stanley Clarke, as well as in big bands led by Howard McGhee and Thad Jones and Mel Lewis. Following a long period of the public eye, he worked again from the late 1980s, performing and recording alongside such musicians as Silver, McCoy Tyner, Lonnie Liston Smith, Eddie Harris, and Gary Bartz. In the 1990s he taught at the Universität für Musik und darstellende Kunst in Graz, Austria. During this period he also made public his ongoing battle with HIV/AIDS. Two solo albums, *Ballads, Blues & Bey* (1996) and *Shades of Bey* (1998), were critically acclaimed and established his reputation as an exceptional singer—both a honeyed, haunting balladeer and a robust bluesman. Bey follows in the tradition of velvet-voiced crooners such as Billy Eckstine and Johnny Hartman.

LARA PELLEGRINELLI

Beyer, Johanna (Magdalena) (*b* Leipzig, Germany, 11 July 1888; *d* New York, NY, 9 Jan 1944). Composer of German birth. She began her musical training in Germany, graduating from a German music conservatory in 1923, and continued her compositional studies in New York upon moving there the same year. By 1928 she had earned degrees from Mannes school of music and had begun composition studies with DANE RUDHYAR, CHARLES SEEGER, HENRY COWELL, and RUTH CRAWFORD. She held a scholarship at the New School for Social Research (1934–5), where she took Cowell's percussion class. She taught for the Federal Music Project at the Greenwich House Music School for a year, as well as at lower schools in the New York area, but earned her living predominantly by giving private lessons in piano and composition. She had close ties to the ultramodernist compositional circle, particularly Cowell, for whom she acted as administrative assistant while he was imprisoned at San Quentin. She advocated tirelessly on his behalf with conductors, musicians, and publishers. Beyer's letters to Cowell indicate an intimate, though troubled relationship between the two composers. The years from 1938 until her death in 1944 were marked by increasing debilitation from ALS (Lou Gehrig's Disease).

In the brief span of her compositional career (1932–43), Beyer wrote prolifically, composing works for percussion ensemble, chamber ensemble, orchestra, concert band, wind ensemble, solo piano, solo chamber instruments, solo voice, and chorus. The innovative and groundbreaking percussion music and the string quartets, particularly the first two, are significant contributions to 20th-century music literature. Despite writing over one hundred works, she was largely ignored as a composer, even by the experimental music community in New York. At the time of her death, Beyer's compositions had received few performances. Two concerts of her works in the New York Composers' Forum were negatively received. Cowell programmed her work on a New Music Society of California concert, and John Cage performed her percussion music on his tour of the Northwest. The only work published in her lifetime, *IV* (1936), appears in Cowell's *New Music Edition*.

Beyer's early works (1930–36) show an affinity with the ultramodernist style of Seeger, Crawford, and Cowell, particularly in the use of tone clusters, as in the *Movement for Two Pianos* (1936), and dissonant counterpoint, as in *Gebrauchs-Musik* (1934) and *Dissonant Counterpoint* (*c*1930). Her music is often characterized by wide-ranging, dissonant melodies and sometimes jagged lines with abrupt leaps, as in the String Quartet no.1 (1934) and *Quintet for Woodwinds* (1933), and by frequently changing meters and complex rhythms, as in *Dissonant Counterpoint* no.2. Several works in particular appear to have been influenced by Crawford's *String Quartet 1931* and *Piano Study in Mixed Accents*. These include the retrograde first movement of Beyer's Suite for Clarinet I (1932) and the second movement of her String Quartet no.2 (1936). The latter is reminiscent of the third movement of Crawford's Quartet, with a continual crescendo/decrescendo texture emphasizing timbre over melody, harmony, and rhythm. Yet the Second String Quartet also hints at her impending transition between a strictly ultramodernist style and a neoclassical style. The first movement, for instance, is in a steady 4/4 meter, with a tonal melody in the cello, quoting Papageno's first aria from Mozart's *Die Zauberflöte*. The other instrumental lines contrast starkly. Halfway through the movement, the other parts enter in canon with the cello's melody, adding small chromatic twists, almost Ivesian in nature. Beyer's music is often playful and quirky, at times revealing a romantic and lyrical side. Her later works show a continued commitment to experimental ideas, while also exhibiting elements of neo-classicism.

WORKS

Edition: *Selected Works*, ed. L. Polansky (Lebanon, NH, 1994–)

Orch: March, large ens, 1935; Cyrnab, chbr orch, 1937; Frag-MdG, chbr orch, 1937; Sym. Suite, 1937; Dance "Status quo," 1938; Elation, band, 1938; Reverence, wind, 1938; Sym. Movt no.1, 1939; Sym., op.3, 1939; Sym., op.5, 1940; Sym. Movt no.2, 1941

Choral: The Robin in the Rain, 1935; The Federal Music Project, 1936; The Composers' Forum Laboratory, 1937; The Main-Deep, 1937; The People, Yes, 1937

Chbr: Perc Suite, 1933; Str Qt no.1, 1933–4; Suite, cl, bn, 1933; Woodwind Qnt, 1933; IV, perc ens, 1935; Movt, db, pf, 1936; Movt, 2 pf, 1936; Sonata, cl, pf, 1936; Str Qt no.2, 1936; Suite, b cl, pf, ?1936; Suite, ob, bn, 1937; Suite, vn, pf, 1937; Movt "Dance," str qt, 1938; Movt, woodwind, 1938; Music of the Spheres 'Status quo', elec str ens, 1938; March, 30 perc, 1939; 3 Movts, perc ens, 1939; Perc, op.14, 1939; 6 Pieces, ob, pf, 1939; Waltz, perc ens, 1939; Trio, woodwind, *c*1940; Str Qt no.4, ?1943

Songs: Sky-Pieces (C. Sandberg), 1933; 3 Songs (Sandberg), S, perc, pf, 1933; Ballad of the Star-Eater (B. Wilkinson Overstreet), S, cl, 1934; 3 Songs (Beyer), S, cl, 1934; Have Faith! (Beyer), S, fl, 1936–7

Solo inst: Dissonant Counterpoint, pf, *c*1930; Suite no.1, cl, 1932; Gebrauchs-Musik, pf, 1934; Clusters (New York Waltzes), pf, 1936; Suite, pf, 1939

MSS in *NYp*

BIBLIOGRAPHY

L. Polansky and J. Kennedy: "Total Eclipse: the Music of Johanna Magdalena Beyer," *MQ,* xx (1996), 719–78

K. Reese: "Ruhelos: Annäherung an Johanna Magdalena Beyer," *Musiktexte: Zeitschrift für Neue Musik*, lxxxi–lxxxii (1999), 6–15

E. Hinkle-Turner: "Lady Ada's Offspring: Some Women Pioneers in Music Technology," *Frau Musica (nova): Komponieren heute/Composing today*, ed. M. Homma (Sinzig, 2000), 25–33

M.J. de Graaf: "Intersections of Gender and Modernism in the Music of Johanna Beyer," *Institute for the Study of American Music Newsletter*, 33/2 (2004), 8–9, 15

E. Hinkle-Turner: *Women Composers and Music Technology in the United States* (New York, 2006)

A. Beal: "How Johanna Beyer Spent Her Days," web-published essay draft (2007; rev. 2011), 1–46 <http://music.ucsc.edu/sites/default/files/BeyerEssayBeal.pdf>

M. Boland: "Experimentation and Process in the Music of Johanna Beyer," *Viva Voce*, lxxvi (2007) <http://mugi.hfmt-hamburg.de/A_materialsammlungen/beye1888/BeyerBoland.pdf>.

M.J. de Graaf: "'Never Call Us Lady Composers': Gendered Receptions in the New York Composers' Forum, 1935–1940," *AM*, xxvi (2008), 277–308

A. Beal: "'Her Whimsy and Originality Really Amount to Genius': New Biographical Research on Johanna Beyer," *American Music Review*, xxxviii (2008), 1, 4–5, 12–13

K. Hiser: *"An Enduring Cycle": Revaluing the Life and Music of Johanna Beyer* (diss., U. of Miami, 2009)

MELISSA DE GRAAF

Bezanson, Philip (Thomas) (*b* Athol, MA, 6 Jan 1916; *d* Hadley, MA, 11 March 1975). Composer and teacher. He studied at Yale University (BM 1940) and with PHILIP CLAPP at the University of Iowa (MA 1948, PhD 1951), where he joined the faculty in 1947 and succeeded Clapp as principal professor of composition in 1954. Ten years later he moved to the University of Massachusetts, Amherst, where he served as professor and head of the music department. Bezanson's honors include an award from the Fromm Foundation (1953) and a Guggenheim Fellowship (1971). Many of his pupils later achieved prominence as composers, among them T.J. ANDERSON, CHARLES DODGE, RICHARD FELCIANO, EDWIN LONDON, HARVEY SOLLBERGER, and OLLY W. WILSON, JR. His works fall within the mainstream of 20th-century music in the generation after Stravinsky, Bartók, and Hindemith. The style is rooted in diatonicism but has frequently changing scales and tonal centers; shifting major and minor thirds are common. Standard meters, often irregularly accented, predominate. Besides choral, orchestral, and chamber music he composed two operas: *Western Child* (3, P. Engle), first performed at the State University of Iowa (Iowa City) on 28 July 1959 and later revised as *Golden Child* (NBC television, 16 Dec 1960); and *Stranger in Eden* (1963), a three-act work to a libretto by William Reardon (never performed). In 1981 a Bezanson archive was established at the University of Massachusetts, Amherst.

WORKS

Operas: Western Child (3, P. Engle), 1959, U. of Iowa, 28 July 1959, rev. as Golden Child, NBC television, 16 Dec 1960; Stranger in Eden (3, W.A. Reardon), 1963

Vocal: Requiem for the University of Iowa Dead (Engle), chorus, orch, 1955; The Word of Love (Engle), song cycle, 1v, pf, 1956; Song of the Cedar (Engle), cant., chorus, orch, 1958; Songs of Innocence (W. Blake), song cycle, 1v, chbr orch/pf, 1959; Contrasts (R. Herrick, K. Gunderson, Blake), 1v, pf, 1966; Morning, Noon, Evening (J. Langland), chorus, 1966; That Time may Cease and Midnight never Come (C. Marlowe), Bar, orch, 1968, arr. Bar, pf; Dies Domini magnus (Bible), chorus, pf, 1971; St. Judas (N. Kazantzakis), oratorio, chorus, orch, 1973; Memory (A. Lincoln), chorus, chamber ens, 1975

Orch: 2 syms., 1946, 1950; Cyrano de Bergerac, ov., 1949; Dance Scherzo, small orch, 1950; Fantasy, Fugue and Finale, str, 1951; Pf Conc., 1952, rev. 1960; Rondo-prelude, 1954; Anniversary Ov., band, 1956; Capriccio concertante, 1967; Concertino, ob, str, 1968; Sinfonia concertante, 1971

Chbr and inst: Divertimento, 8 wind, 1947; 2 str qts, 1948, 1961; 2 vn sonatas, 1949, 1953; Pf Sonata, 1951; Str Trio, 1954; Cl Sonata, 1955; Sextet, 5 ww, pf, 1955; Homage to Great Americans, ww qnt, 1958; Prelude and Dance, 6 brass, 1958; Pf Trio, 1963; Divertimento, org, brass, timp, 1964; Trio, cl, hn, pf, 1966; Diversion, tpt, hn, trbn, 1967; Petite Suite, 7 ww, 1973; Brass Sextet, 1974; several inst duos, pf pieces

MSS in *IaU, MU*

Principal publisher: ACA

FREDERICK CRANE

B-52's [B-52s], **the**. Rock band. Its members have included Kate (Catherine Elizabeth) Pierson (*b* Weehawken, NJ, 27 April 1948; vocals and keyboards), Fred(erick William) Schneider (*b* Newark, NJ, 1 July 1951; vocals and novelty instruments), (Julian) Keith Strickland (*b* Athens, GA, 26 Oct 1953; percussion and electric guitar), Cindy (Cynthia Leigh) Wilson (*b* Athens, 28 Feb 1957; voice and bongos), and her brother Ricky (Helton) Wilson (*b* Athens, 19 March 1953; *d* New York, NY, 12 Oct 1985; electric guitar). From 2008 the group's name has appeared without an apostrophe.

From 1977 the B-52's were part of the music scene in Athens, Georgia , that nurtured R.E.M., Pylon, and Love Tractor. Soon thereafter the group performed in New York and in 1979 they released *The B-52's* (WB), a danceable and stylistically eclectic album now considered a classic of post-punk rock. Pitched instruments include Ricky Wilson's guitar, with non-standard tunings, and Pierson's electric organ. Cindy Wilson sings solo; the women sing together, in unison or unconventional counterpoint; Schneider's speech-song sometimes dominates, his camp delivery often depicting helpless exasperation. With each member's contribution distinctly audible, the B-52's emerge as a collaborative ensemble without hierarchy. The songs are sardonic, with deadpan delivery, some of them depicting sex acts, some reciting lists. Lyrics unfold over repeated riffs and draw on popular culture, including science fiction and beach movies.

The group's visual manner was in place by their first album. They wore outdated clothes, often with references to the 1960s; the women wore large wigs and the group's name comes from a slang term for the beehive hairstyle popular during that period. The women's styles had affinities with male drag and with feminist questioning of norms of beauty.

Wild Planet (WB) followed in 1980 in the style of the first album. A collaboration with David Byrne as producer led to an EP, in which the group's characteristic style is lost in over-elaborate production. The following two albums, *Whammy!* (WB, 1983) and *Bouncing off the Satellites* (WB, 1986), featured a more idiomatic style, integrating synthesizers and drum machines. Although the group failed to achieve the same degree of humor in their lyrics and edginess in their music as on their first two albums, these releases feature warm and charming songs, some revealing a new non-ironic beauty.

After Ricky Wilson died of an AIDS-related illness in 1985, the band took time off. Their next album *Cosmic Thing* (Rep., 1989) was its only mainstream hit and included the singles "Love Shack" and "Roam." It balances humor with the celebration of nature, conviviality, and sexuality. *Good Stuff* (Rep., 1992) suffered from the absence of Cindy Wilson, who was taking a break. In 2008 the group released *Funplex* (Astralwerks), skillfully produced and flavored with electronica, and in the 2010s they continued to perform regularly.

The B-52's have been known for their exhilarating performances in which a significant element of camp engages gender and sexuality productively. An egalitarian band consisting of women and gay men, they have provided a valuable model of friendship and collaboration, and in the context of AIDS their vigorous pro-sex stance has been politically significant.

BIBLIOGRAPHY

R.L. Brown: *Party out of Bounds: the B-52's, R.E.M., and the Kids who Rocked Athens, Georgia* (Atlanta, 1991/R)

M. Sexton: *The B-52's Universe: the Essential Guide to the World's Greatest Party Band* (Minneapolis, 2002)

FRED EVERETT MAUS

Bhangra. A contemporary music and dance form of the South Asian diaspora combining acoustic elements of the Punjabi folk genre of the same name with electronic elements of Western popular music. Traditional bhangra—a vibrant, celebratory style associated with the *Vaisakhi* harvest and solar new year festival celebrated by Punjabi Sikh farmers each spring—features vigorous male dancing accompanied by prominent, distinctive rhythms on the *dhol* drum, and sung verses with joyful lyrics. In the mid-1960s, amateur bhangra bands began to proliferate among Punjabi immigrant communities in the United Kingdom, performing at cultural, family, and religious functions. However, bhangra did not gain traction with British South Asian youth until the 1984 album *Teri Chunni de Sitare* by Southall, London-based group Alaap, which fused traditional Punjabi rhythms, melodies, and instruments with Western technologies such as drum machines and synthesizers. This innovation pioneered a new style of bhangra, sometimes called "bhangra beat" or "Southall beat."

This modern twist on bhangra spread quickly to North America, primarily through New York City and Toronto; however, whereas early UK-based bhangra typically focused on live performance and drew directly on Punjabi folk traditions, North American bhangra acts in the 1990s consisted mostly of underground DJs remixing recordings by British performers with samples from Western popular music genres such as reggae, hip hop, and techno, shifting the balance of elements within this hybrid style. The propagation of new musical combinations led to the rise of various subgenres, including bhangramuffin, influenced by Jamaican dancehall music and popularized by British Punjabi performer Apache Indian, and house bhangra, which draws on the Chicago club scene and emphasizes the repetitive beats of electronic dance music. The lyrical focus also shifted from celebratory to more everyday concerns, such as relationships, money, and parties. Bhangra today functions as a site of musical exchange among the disparate cultures of the South Asian diaspora and has made its way back to India, most notably in Bollywood film soundtracks.

BIBLIOGRAPHY

G. Diethrich: "Desi Music Vibes: the Performance of Indian Youth Culture in Chicago," *Asian Music*, xxxi/1 (1999), 35–61

J. Warwick: "'Make Way for the Indian': Bhangra Music and South Asian Presence in Toronto," *Popular Music and Society*, xxiv/2 (2000), 25–44

S.M. Maira: *Desis in the House: Indian American Culture in New York City* (Philadelphia, 2002)

MELISSA HOK CEE WONG

Bible, Frances L(illian) (*b* Sackets Harbor, NY, 26 Jan 1919; *d* Hemet, CA, 29 Jan 2001). Mezzo-soprano. Bible studied voice at Juilliard with Belle Julie Soudant and Queena Mario, where she gained wide attention as Dorabella in Mozart's *Così Fan Tutte* under the direction of Wilfred Pelletier. She made her professional debut at Chautauqua in Gilbert and Sullivan's *The Gondoliers* in 1948, then debuted as the Shepherd-boy in *Tosca* in 1948 at the New York City Opera. *Mademoiselle Magazine* named her "Young Woman of the Year" in 1950. She was particularly noted for her creamy voice, acting, and assured interpretations of trouser roles such as Cherubino, Hänsel, Nicklausse, Siébel, and Cherubino. She appeared as the last of these at Glyndebourne in 1955. Bible performed Monteverdi's Octavia with the NBC Opera Company during the 1956–7 season before joining the San Francisco Opera, where she was hailed as "the finest delineator of the part ever to be seen in the West." Bible created two important roles in American opera: Augusta Tabor Douglas Moore's *The Ballad of Baby Doe* with Central City

Opera in Colorado in 1956 and Elizabeth Proctor in Robert Ward's *The Crucible* in 1961. Bible made her concert debut at Lewisohn Stadium, New York, in 1961 and later performed as soloist with many American symphonies. She appeared in the New York premiere of David Tamkin's *Dybbuk* (New York City Opera, 1951) and the American premiere of William Walton's *Troilus and Cressida* with San Francisco Opera. Her repertory included Laura (*La Gioconda*), Cornelia (*Giulio Cesare*), Marina (*Boris Godunov*). Bible taught at Rice University from 1979 to 1982. Onstage, she excelled in roles demanding authority and both her performance in *Baby Doe* and *The Crucible* are preserved on commercial recordings.

BIBLIOGRAPHY

Obituaries: *New York Times* (7 Feb 2001); *ON*, lxv/11 (2001), 93; *American Record Guide* (1 May 2001)

RICHARD DYER, ELIZABETH FORBES/
MEREDITH ELIASSEN

Bibliographies. Music bibliography is the study and description of musical documents and of the literature about music. As a whole it entails two separate but interdependent areas of investigation. Analytical and descriptive bibliography are concerned with the study and identification of books as physical objects, and involve such matters as paper, design, typography or engraving, printing, and binding. Enumerative bibliography is concerned with access to information about musical materials and the literature of music and is usually embodied in lists that are known as "bibliographies." Since the mid 1990s, with the continued expansion of the Internet, online bibliographies have proliferated. This article is concerned exclusively with enumerative bibliographies that cover music materials published in or otherwise distinctive to the United States, as well as the study of bibliography.

1. Introduction. 2. Access by period. 3. Access by place. 4. Access by content. 5. Access by bibliographical form. 6. Study of bibliography

1. Introduction. The bibliographical record of American music has been described numerous times, notably in Guy Marco's *Information on Music* (1977) and G. Thomas Tanselle's *Guide to the Study of United States Imprints* (1971). It is discussed in terms of the historical period of the item in question, the geographical context, the content (artistic, intellectual, or as embodied in particular musical genres), and the physical form of the item in question (e.g. manuscript, broadside, etc.). These four dimensions are manifest in any single musical document and thus bibliographies inevitably overlap in coverage and emphasis. Even so, these dimensions are useful to readers, who are confronted by the vast and rapidly proliferating bibliographical record of American music, especially as presented via the Internet.

In addition, the Internet has opened access to the ephemeral, such as pathfinders or research guides, through LibGuides and other online platforms. Archival finding aids, previously considered local-access resources, are often presented in EAD (Encoded Archival Description) format. OCLC, the primary national bibliographic utility, and until recently available to the public only by subscription, now is easily accessible to all with online access, increasing the discoverability of music resources. Although it is relatively simple to publish web documents, maintaining those documents requires a commitment of time and effort that is all too often overlooked. Duke University's "DW3: Classical Music Resources" project was abandoned in 2005, and the "Worldwide Internet Music Resources" project at Indiana is no longer maintained actively. Powerful search engines may have been instrumental in moving efforts away from producing meta-lists. In addition, more libraries are including websites in their catalogs, providing systematic access. At the same time, the development of robust web-authoring tools, such as the LibGuides platform, have provided a mechanism to prepare online research aids tailored to the needs of the local user community.

2. Access by period. An important aspect of chronologically delimited lists is the inclusion or exclusion of sheet music; if such lists do not exclude it, they are overwhelmed by it. Sheet music may be defined negatively as any publication that cannot be defined as a book, that is, as the output of a book-trade publisher, or an item long and physically substantial enough to be bound; treatises, hymnals, songbooks, other anthologies, and books about music are normally listed in bibliographies from which sheet music is excluded. The lists that do include sheet music are generally directed towards performers, who need to know what repertory exists and where it can be found.

Materials from the earliest decades in American history are covered in two landmark bibliographies: for books in general, Charles Evans's *American Bibliography* (1903–34, extended in several later studies), and for music in particular, Oscar Sonneck's *Bibliography of Early Secular American Music* (1905), which has been essentially superseded by William Treat Upton's extensive revision of 1945. Evans excluded many forms of ephemera, and the largely undated sheet music included proved ill-suited to his annalistic arrangement. In the 1970 supplement, Roger Bristol included some sheet music on the basis of Upton's assigned datings in the Sonneck revision, but excluded the titles Upton had been unable to date. Most books cited in the Evans work are now accessible through online subscription. Evans also offered a listing of most tune-books and songsters, though these are better covered in Irving Lowens's songster bibliography (1976). The Sonneck–Upton work includes not only sheet music but also librettos, writings about music, and song anthologies.

Systematic attempts to chart the vast bibliographical map of American music published after 1800 have proliferated, modeled on the lists that cover the 18th century. Richard Wolfe's *Secular Music in America, 1801–1825* (1964) essentially continues the Sonneck–Upton bibliography in scope and conception, though the arrangement is by composer rather than title. The scope of the Evans work has been extended in the *American*

Bibliography, the continuation of Evans's annalistic arrangement, however, once again makes for curious placements of undated sheet music, especially in the volumes that were published before Wolfe's more authoritative work.

The burgeoning output of the American press in the middle of the 19th century has largely discouraged compilers interested in this important period. The list of copyright publications prepared in 1851 by Charles Coffin Jewett during his brief period at the Smithsonian Institution covers only a short time span. Other bibliographies, such as the two general ones by Orville Roorbach (1852–61) and James Kelly (1866–71), as well as the massive *Complete Catalogue of Sheet Music and Musical Works* issued in 1870 by the Board of Music Trade, are vast in scope but limited in publication details. Valuable unpublished records for this period do exist, in the district court copyright records (see Tanselle in *Studies in Bibliography*, xxii, 1969, pp.77–124). A few bibliographies of works written between 1826 and 1890 have been published (*see* §§3 and 4 below), but this period is essentially the darkest in American music bibliography. With the *American Catalogue of Books* issued by *Publishers Weekly* (1876–1910) and ostensibly limited to items in book format, the improvement in bibliographical controls began to be discernible.

The US Copyright Office began publishing its copyright registers in 1891; music entries have been collected separately since 1895. Varying entry practices during the early years, and a lack of good indexes, make the printed set very difficult to use. However, entries dating from 1 January 1978 are now accessible via online search; entries prior to that date must still be searched manually. For all its faults, the set of copyright registers remains the country's best attempt at a current national music bibliography. The improved format and highly selective approach to cataloguing begun in 1949 were unfortunately abandoned in 1956, partly in deference to the Library of Congress's improved music catalog, *Music and Phonorecords* (1953–72), followed by *Music, Books on Music, and Sound Recordings* (1973–89) which has been part of the *National Union Catalog* (*NUC*) program since the 1950s. In 1957 the Copyright Office reverted to its former practice of listing the basic data for new registrations.

Music coverage in the *NUC* was, until the 1970s, restricted by the arbitrary and awkwardly implemented exclusion of musical materials, which justified the catalog of printed music for 1953–72 compiled by the Music Library Association (1974) under Elizabeth Olmsted. Newly published music titles are listed in the copyright registers, national bibliographic utilities (primarily OCLC, which, in 2006 absorbed the RLIN catalog), and in music journals. The Music Library Association's journal *Notes*, which lists music submitted to it for review and books about music received at the Library of Congress, is an important source. Other journals also list new works of special interest to their particular readers, such as the *Journal of the American Musicological Society* (*JAMS*).

For critical evaluations of new publications, *Notes*, *JAMS*, and other journals include book and music reviews. Depending on the scope of the journal, the reviews vary in authority. Frequently, authoritative reviews, such as those appearing in society journals, appear well after publication, and although they are useful in establishing the critical reception of a work, do not supplant the need for colleagues' advice.

Currently available books about music have long been listed in the general lists of the book trade, such as the *Publisher's Trade List Annual* (1873–), and *Books in Print* (1948– in print; online from 2000) but successful attempts to produce lists devoted entirely to music in print did not occur until the 1960s and 1970s. The breakthrough came with Margaret Farish's *String Music in Print* (1965), ahead of the invaluable Music in Print series published by Musicdata from 1974 to 2000. In 2000, the series was taken over by emusicquest and converted to an online format. Publishers' catalogs and websites often provide essential information, although availability can change quickly.

In addition, there are lists designed to promote American music in particular historical periods. For example, bibliographies of early colonial American music were issued in connection with the US Bicentennial; among these are John Specht's list of early vocal music (1974), classified lists in the *Music Educators Journal* during the years 1975–6, James Heintze's *American Music before 1865* (1976), and Richard Jackson's bibliography of early music in editions published 1970–76 (1977). Current lists of the works of individual composers have been prepared by publishers, organizations (e.g., the American Composers Alliance), and performing rights societies, or as part of promotional projects for contemporary music in general. Groups of composers have also been promoted collectively through bibliographical lists, such as Alexander Janta's surveys of early 19th-century Polish American music (1961–5, 1982). Many publishers maintain websites devoted to the current composers they represent, and many current composers maintain their own websites, with lists of compositions and recordings.

3. Access by place. Local and regional imprint lists, as surveyed in Section A of Tanselle's *Guide* (1971), typically include writings about music and often songbooks, hymnals, and instruction books as well; rarely do they list any sheet music. Notable exceptions are the lists of Confederate music published by Richard Harwell in 1955 and 1957 and complemented by Frank Hoogerwerf's bibliography (1984), and Dena Epstein's survey of the Chicago music trade before the 1871 fire (1969). Some of the reasons for limited coverage of sheet music in regional bibliographies are discussed by Ralph Holibaugh and D.W. Krummel (1981).

Other regional lists describe the music of contemporary composers, ranging from modest pamphlets and biographical dictionaries (*see* Dictionaries and encyclopedias) to works such as the report of the Boston Composers Project coordinated by Linda Solow (1983). However, a great deal of the work of collecting titles pertaining to particular cities, states, and regions remains to be done.

4. Access by content. Bibliographies of specific kinds of music can be found in this dictionary (such as Band, Folk music, Jazz, and Orchestral music). Important repertory guides have been prepared by Judith Carman and her team on early art song (1976, suppl. 1978), Tom Goleeke on art songs in anthologies (1984, 2002), Marilou Kratzenstein (1980) and Prudence Curtis (1981) on organ music, John and Anna Gillespie on piano music (1984), and Jerome Landsman on violin music (1966). Other genre lists include Edith Boroff's checklist (1992), William Rehrig (1991) and Jeffrey Renshaw (1991) on band music, and the catalogs of ASCAP and BMI, both available online. Numerous other lists of international scope also include American works.

Genre lists are particularly suited to online guides. MLA's Midwest Chapter has prepared a meta-site, providing access to all LibGuides prepared by chapter members (<http://uiuc.libguides.com/mwmla>). The association maintains a bibliography of preservation-related resources (<http://committees.musiclibraryassoc.org/Preservation/General>), as well as a bibliography of materials related to music library construction (<http://facilities.musiclibraryassoc.org/>).

Folk and popular music are less adequately described in their notated forms partly because many of the repertories are more distinctively embodied in sound recordings (*see* Discography). Many of the major bibliographies are devoted to writings about the music. Notable among the general works are Charles Haywood's *A Bibliography of North American Folklore and Folksong* (1951), Larry Sandberg's and Dick Weissman's *The Folk Music Sourcebook* (1976, 1989), Mark Booth's *American Popular Music* (1983), and Paul Taylor's critical guide (1985). Ray Lawless (1965) covers the folk-music movement at one of its high points, Frank Hoffman's list (1981) is devoted to rock music, and Gargan and Sharma (1984, 1988) provide useful bibliographical access to current tunes. The first important compiler of a list for jazz was Jane Ganfield (1933), who was followed by Robert Reisner (1954), Alan Merriam and Robert Benford (1954, whose work is the most comprehensive in scope), Donald Kennington (1970), and Steven Winick (1974). The popular music series initiated by Nat Shapiro (1964–2004), covers popular song titles from 1920 to 2002. Its companion, edited by Barbara Cohen-Stratyner (1988), extends the coverage back to 1900–1919.

American sacred tunebooks are particularly well documented in bibliographies. The early 1800s are covered fairly comprehensively in works by James Warrington (1898), Frank Metcalf (1917), and Allen Britton (1949), all of which was superseded for the period to 1810 by Richard Crawford's tunebook bibliography (1990). Sacred music in later periods is surveyed only broadly, as for example by Waldo Selden Pratt in the *Grove American Supplement* (1920). The Hymn Society of America's *Bibliography* (1983) carries the list up to 1978, citing 7500 titles from both North and South America. Nicholas Temperley's *Index* (1998) includes English-language hymn tunes from 1535–1820. Katherine Diehl's index (1966) remains the best general source for locating standard hymns. Among the notable denominational bibliographies are Edward Wolf's list of Lutheran titles and the *Mennonite Bibliography* by Springer and Klassen (both 1977). Specialized repertory lists include those by Richard Stanislaw (1978) on four-shape tunebooks, Nicholas Temperley and Carl Manns (1983), Karl Kroeger (1994) on fuging-tunes, David W. Music (2001) on Christian hymnody, and Samuel J. Rogal (1983) on sacred collections for the young.

Bibliographies on other topics include lists of pedagogical books for string players by Jerome Landsman (1966) and Charles Sollinger (1974); Richmond Browne's listings of music theory (1977–8); the film music surveys of Clifford McCarty (1953), Win Sharples Jr. (1978), Martin Marks (1979–80), and Claudia Gorbman (1980); and choral music in Biblical order by James Laster (1983, 2/1996, suppl. 2002).

The bibliographical search for particular songs was difficult in the past, not only because the field is so vast and the collections were inadequately described, but because the information about the printed music is often incomplete. Various reference books, including chronologies and analytical indexes, were used in a complementary way, along with library catalogs and copyright registration records for easier access to song titles.

Chronologies are particularly valuable insofar as titles often prove to be distinctive to their periods (i.e. songs mentioning mother often date from the time of the Civil War, mock-Irish comic and coon songs from the early 20th century, big-band tunes and songs with nonsense titles from the 1930s and 40s). Fortunately, many libraries have adopted cataloging practices to include title-by-title contents listings for print anthologies and sound recordings and special projects on cataloging sheet music.

Duke University was one of the first to undertake a project to catalog sheet music, and provide online access to its extensive collection, including scanned images of public domain sheet music (<http://library.duke.edu/digitalcollections/hasm/>). The Sheet Music Consortium is a freely available, open archive of sheet music. Members of the consortium include the University of California-Los Angeles, Indiana University, Johns Hopkins University, and Duke University (<http://digital.library.ucla.edu/sheetmusic/>).

Among regional collections, an example is the University of Washington's Ashford Sheet Music Collection (<http://db.lib.washington.edu/sheetmusic/>), along with a subset of the collection, the Pacific Northwest Sheet Music Collection (<http://content.lib.washington.edu/smweb/>).

Through the 1980s, analytical indexes served both as reference books and as buying guides. The first of these to index song anthologies was Minnie Sears's *Song Index* (1926); among its successors, *Songs in Collections* by De Charms and Breed (1966) is the most respected. Coverage in these works and in the indexes by Robert Leigh (1964) and Patricia Havlice (1975, and supplements) extends to folksongs and foreign works as well; similarly, Florence Brunnings's *Folk Song Index* (1981) contains more than folk music. Several song indexes provide occasional subject groupings, and often, the first words of a song identify the subject as well.

Content bibliographies also include listings of the outputs of individual and groups of composers classified into large historical or geographical categories. Surveys of the works of African American composers include Helen Walker-Hill's *Black Women Composers* (2003) as well as Samuel Floyd's *International Dictionary of Black Composers* (1999), and the bibliographies of African American composers by Dominique-René De Lerma (1975 and 1981–4), choral music by Evelyn Davidson White (1981; 1996), traditions in music and art by Eileen Southern and Josephine Wright (1990), and spirituals by Kathleen Abromeit (1999).

Women composers are also surveyed by various reference guides, such as those compiled by Donald Hixon and Don Hennessee (1975, 1993), JoAnn Skowronski (1978), Adrienne Fried Block and Carol Neuls-Bates (1979), Aaron Cohen (1981, 1984, 1987), and Rose-Marie Johnson (1989). The annual listings in the winter issues of *Pan Pipes of Sigma Alpha Iota* serve to update the published work-lists of composers.

Bibliographies of other kinds of books about American music include David Horn's *The Literature of American Music* (1972), which includes unusual writings especially on popular music, but with no indication of scope of coverage; Richard Jackson's survey *United States Music* (1973) and Marco's *Information on Music* (1977); Tanselle's *Guide* (1971); Delli (1979); and *Resources of American Music History* (1981, 2/forthcoming). (For further bibliographies of music history books, *see* HISTORIES.) The few bibliographies of writings of and about American composers and musicians are cited in Section C of Tanselle's *Guide* (1971). Other distinguished bibliographies have been compiled by American scholars. Among those that include American coverage are the general surveys by Robert Darrell (1951), James Coover (1952), and Vincent Duckles (1964); the series indexes of Anna Harriet Heyer (1944, 1957); the ethnomusicology lists by Bruno Nettl (1961); the guides to criticism and analyses by Harold Diamond (1979, 1991); and the list of autobiographies by John Adams (1982). Many musical settings of texts by major American poets are cited in Tanselle's *Guide*, in Jacob Blanck's *Bibliography of American Literature* (1955–), and in Michael Hovland's *Musical Settings of American Poetry* (1986). Material of special interest to educators was summarized in 1968 by Thomas Clark Collins. An extensive survey of music therapy materials, *Music the Healer*, was published in 1970, and the field is described in *Music Therapy Index* (1976–84), *Music Psychology Index* (1978–84), George Heller's *Historical Research in Music Therapy* (1992), and James and Philip Parker's *Music Therapy* (2004). Various music aptitude and achievement tests have been surveyed by C.W. Flemming (1936) and P.R. Lehman (1969), among others.

5. ACCESS BY BIBLIOGRAPHICAL FORM. With regard to manuscripts, two surveys of early American handwritten documents, by James Fuld and Mary Wallace Davidson (1980) and Kate Van Winkle Keller (1981), overlap in that the former covers some of the items in the latter, but in greater detail. Although no comprehensive catalog of American musical manuscripts after 1801 has yet been published, locations of these materials appear in various resource materials on library collections (*see* ARCHIVES AND MANUSCRIPTS). In the area of printed ephemera, Gillian Anderson's *Freedom's Voice in Poetry and Song* (1977) covers song texts in newspapers from the Revolutionary War period; and mid-19th-century broadsides are listed in works by Earle Rudolph (1950) and Edwin Wolf (1963). Bibliographies of printed ephemera also include Lowens's list of songsters (1976), which normally contain no musical notation. Original American music source materials of all kinds are listed in *Resources of American Music History* (1981, 2/forthcoming).

American dissertations concerned specifically with music were first listed in 1932 by Oliver Strunk in a bulletin published by the American Council of Learned Societies. His list was updated by Daugherty, Ellinwood, and Hill in 1940 and continues with *Doctoral Dissertations in Musicology* (*DDM*), begun by the Music Teachers National Association and the American Musicological Society in 1952 and from 1977 to 1990 as a part of the international index by Adkins and Dickinson. The online version of *DDM*, available initially in 1996 and hosted by Indiana University, is managed by the American Musicological Society (<http://www.ams-net.org/ddm/index.php>). Among special subject lists are Kenneth Hartley's for sacred music (1966), Rita Mead's for American music topics in all areas (1974), and Frank Cipolla's for band music (1979–80); the lists by Dominique-René De Lerma (1970) and James Heintze (1985) enter the vast domain of master's theses in a highly selective way. With the exception of the specialized indexes, master's theses remain particularly difficult to identify, although some are included in the online *ProQuest Dissertations and Theses*.

Music periodicals, listed retrospectively by Charles Wunderlich (1962) and William Weichlein (1970), as well as elsewhere in this dictionary (*see* PERIODICALS), are also cited in several special bibliographies, including those prepared by Frank Campbell for choral conductors (1952). For several decades *Notes* has included occasional lists of new periodical titles. Indexes to music periodical literature have been prepared by Sheila Keats on American composers (1954), Hazel Kinscella on American music in the *Musical Quarterly* (1958), Dean and Nancy Tudor on popular music (1974), Joan Meggett (1978), and Thomas Warner on American music (1988). In addition, 83 music periodicals are included in JSTOR, and RIPM provides online and print access to historical periodicals, including 20 American titles. Music periodical indexes cover current writings: *RILM*

Abstracts (1967–) is devoted to scholarly writings. *Music Index* (1949–), although considerably less sophisticated than RILM in its indexing practices, includes a wider range of popular writings. RILM published print cumulations through 1999, while the online index includes the entirety of RILM's data; *Music Index* is available both in print and online, with the online index including citations from 1970 to the present.

Of the so-called "basic lists" that have been developed to aid small libraries in the selection of music collections, the earliest was begun in 1935 by the National Association of Schools of Music. The original list and a series of supplements were published in 1967 as *A Basic Music Library for Schools Offering Undergraduate Degrees in Music* (rev. 1977 by Michael Winesanker). *A Basic Music Library* (*BML*, 1978, 2/1983) was prepared by an MLA Committee, chaired by Pauline Bayne, J. Bunker, and Marilyn Clark (1969) for high school libraries, and Krummel (1976–7) for college libraries. Elizabeth Davis (1997) and Daniel Boomhower (2011) followed with the third and fourth editions of *BML*.

Catalogs of American music prepared for collectors are often valuable to scholars as well. In addition to codifying the corpus of recognized "collectors' items," *Early American Sheet Music* by Dichter and Shapiro (1941) provides an invaluable directory for the confirmation of publishers' names and the dating of editions. Dichter's three handbooks of the same repertory (1947–66), which are essentially sales catalogs, are still useful for their citations and pricing suggestions. James Fuld's 1955 study seeks to establish the first editions of the most popular music through a specification of the collector's "points" and illustrated covers; though international in scope, his book of 1966 (2/1971, 3/1985, 4/1995, 5/2000) includes many American works.

6. Study of bibliography. A course entitled Bibliography or Introduction to Research is common among graduate programs in the United States. Although many have credited Vincent Duckles with the first course in music research, beginning in 1949, Carol June Bradley (1990) refers to a 1931 course taught at Yale by Eva Judd O'Meara, as well as a similar course taught at Vassar by George Sherman Dickinson. Textbooks for such a course have been relatively uncommon, with many instructors relying on Keith Mixter's *Introduction to Library Resources for Music Research* (1963), Ruth Watanabe's *Introduction to Music Research* (1967), or Duckles's *Music Reference and Research Materials* (1964, 2/1967, 3/1974, 4/1988, 4a/1994, 5/1997). Others have used Richard Wingell's *Introduction to Research in Music* (2001). 2008 and 2009 saw the publication of three texts outlining courses of study in music research and bibliography: Bayne's *A Guide to Library Research in Music*, Laurie Sampsel's *Music Research: A Handbook*, and Jane Gottlieb's *Music Library and Research Skills*.

LIST

The following is a selective list of bibliographies of, and works about, American music. A number of important library catalogs have been included either for their extensive scope or for their comprehensive coverage in a particular area of music. (For other archival catalogs, *see* the bibliographies for the institutions concerned in Libraries and collections.)

"Appendix to the Librarian's Report: Copy-right Publications . . . Part II: List of Musical Compositions," *Fifth Annual Report of the Board of Regents*, ed. Smithsonian Institution (Washington, DC, 1851), 223–33, 186–322 [for 1846–50; 554 items, mostly from East Coast publishers; in the government publications serial set under "Senate, Special Session, March 1851: Miscellaneous"]

O.A. Roorbach: *Bibliotheca Americana, 1820–61* (New York, 1852–61/*R*), [occasional music references; indexed in master's papers prepared for Kent State U. by K. Dempsey, 1972, and M. J. Kuceyeski, 1975]

J. Kelly: *American Catalogue of Books Printed . . . from January 1861 to January 1871* (New York, 1866–71/*R*)

Complete Catalogue of Sheet Music and Musical Works, ed. Board of Music Trade (New York, 1870/*R*)

Publisher's Trade List Annual (New York, 1873–; author and title indexes 1948– as *Books in Print*)

American Catalogue of Books, ed. *Publishers Weekly* (New York, 1876–1910, repr. 1941), 21 vols. in 15 bks

Catalogue of Title Entries, later *Catalogue of Copyright Entries*, ed. US Copyright Office (Washington, DC, 1891–) [now issued biannually; from 1895 with separate music section]

O.G.T. Sonneck: *A Bibliography of Early Secular American Music* (Washington, DC, 1905, rev. and enlarged W.T. Upton 2/1945/*R*)

F.J. Metcalf: *American Psalmody, or Titles of Books Containing Tunes Printed in America from 1721 to 1820* (New York, 1917/*R*)

W.S. Pratt: "Tune Books," *Grove AS*, 385 [useful for mid-19th-century works]

M.E. Sears: *Song Index* (New York, 1926/*R*; suppl., 1934)

W. Gregory, ed.: *Union List of Serials in the Libraries of the United States and Canada* (New York, 1927, 2/1943, rev. E.B. Titus 3/1965; suppls., Washington, DC, 1973– as *New Serial Titles*, from 1982 in 3-month cumulations)

Periodicals Directory (New York, 1932–; from 1965/6 as *Ulrich's International Periodicals Directory*) [issued biennially]

O. Strunk: *State and Resources of Musicology in the United States* (Washington, DC, 1932) [includes lists]

J. Ganfield: *Books and Periodical Articles on Jazz in America from 1926–1932* (New York, 1933)

"A List of Books on Music," *National Association of Schools of Music Bulletin*, no.3 (1935; suppls., 1936–57) [see also 1967]

C.W. Flemming: *A Descriptive Bibliography of Prognostic and Achievement Tests in Music* (New York, 1936)

Microfilm Abstracts (Ann Arbor, MI, 1938–, from 1952 as *Dissertation Abstracts*, from 1969 as *Dissertation Abstracts International*)

D.H. Daugherty, L. Ellinwood, and R.S. Hill: *A Bibliography of Periodical Literature in Musicology and Allied Fields and a Record of Graduate Theses* (Washington, DC, 1940–43/*R*)

Bio-bibliographical Index of Musicians in the United States of America since Colonial Times, ed. Historical Record Survey (Washington, DC, 1941, 2/1956/*R*)

H. Dichter and E. Shapiro: *Early American Sheet Music: its Lure and its Lore, 1768–1889* (New York, 1941, 2/1977 as *Handbook of Early American Sheet Music*)

A Catalog of Books . . . to July 31; 1942, ed. Library of Congress (Ann Arbor, MI, 1942–6/*R*; suppl., 1948/*R* [1 Aug 1942 to 31 Dec 1947])

A.H. Heyer: *Check-list of Publications of Music* (Ann Arbor, MI, 1944)

Cumulative Catalog of Library of Congress Printed Cards [title varies], ed. Library of Congress (Washington, DC, 1947–55)

H. Dichter: *Handbook of American Sheet Music* (Philadelphia, 1947–66) [essentially antiquarian dealer's lists]

M.M. Mott: "A Bibliography of Song Sheets: Sports and Recreation in American Popular Songs," *Notes*, vi (1948–9), 379; vii (1949–50), 522–61; ix (1951–2), 33–62; continued by G.D. McDonald, xiv (1956–7), 325–52, 507–33

A.P. Britton: *Theoretical Introductions in American Tune-books to 1800* (diss., U. of Michigan, 1949)

The Music Index (1949–)

E.L. Rudolph: *Confederate Broadside Verse* (New Braunfels, TX, 1950)

R.D. Darrell: *Schirmer's Guide to Books on Music and Musicians: a Practical Bibliography* (New York, 1951)

C. Haywood: *A Bibliography of North American Folklore and Folksong* (New York, 1951, 2/1961)

F.C. Campbell: *A Critical Annotated Bibliography of Periodicals* (New York, 1952) [lists 44 periodicals on choral music]

J.B. Coover: *A Bibliography of Music Dictionaries* (Denver, CO, 1952, 3/1971 as *Music Lexicography, Including a Bibliography of Music Dictionaries*)

Doctoral Dissertations in Musicology, ed. Music Teachers National Association and American Musicological Society (Denton, TX, 1952; rev. H. Hewitt 2/1958; rev. C. Adkins 5/1971, 7/1984; suppls. in *JAMS* and *American Music Teacher*; new ser., 1984–)

J. Mattfeld: *Variety Music Cavalcade* (New York, 1952, 3/1971)

K. Berger: *Band Music Guide* (Evansville, IN, 1953, 8/1982)

A.P. Britton and I. Lowens: "Unlocated Titles in Early Sacred American Music," *Notes*, xi (1953–4), 33–48

Z.W. George: *A Guide to Negro Folk Music: an Annotated Bibliography of Negro Folk Music and Art Music by Negro Composers or Based on Negro Thematic Material* (diss., New York U., 1953)

Library of Congress Author Catalog: a Cumulative List of Works Represented by Library of Congress Printed Cards, 1948–1952 (Ann Arbor, MI, 1953)

C. McCarty: *Film Composers in America: a Checklist of their Work* (Glendale, CA, 1953/*R*)

S. Keats: "Reference Articles on American Composers: an Index," *Juilliard Review*, i/3 (1954), 21–34

A. Merriam and R. Benford: *A Bibliography of Jazz* (Philadelphia, 1954/*R*)

R. Reisner: *The Literature of Jazz* (New York, 1954, rev. and enlarged 2/1959)

J. Blanck and others.: *Bibliography of American Literature* (New Haven, CT, 1955–)

Compositores de América: datos biográficos y catálogos de sus obras/ Composers of the Americas: Biographical Data and Catalogs of their Works, ed. Pan American Union (Washington, DC, 1955–)

J.J. Fuld: *American Popular Music (Reference Book), 1875–1950* (Philadelphia, 1955; suppl., 1956)

R.B. Harwell: "Sheet Music," in M.L. Crandall: *Confederate Imprints: a Check List Based Principally on the Collection of the Boston Athenaeum*, ii (Boston, 1955), 561–669, 719–21 [suppl. in Crandall's *More Confederate Imprints* (Richmond, VA, 1957), 225, 250]

Library of Congress Catalog Books: Subjects (Ann Arbor, MI, 1955– [1950–])

J. Burton: *The Index of American Popular Music* (Watkins Glen, NY, 1957) [indexes songs in anthologies compiled by Burton]

A.H. Heyer: *Historical Sets, Collected Editions, and Monuments of Music: a Guide to their Contents* (Chicago, 1957, 3/1980) [see also G.R. Hill and N.L. Stephens]

H.G. Kinscella: "Americana Index to the Musical Quarterly, 1915–1957," *JRME*, vi/2 (1958), 1–144 [lists 7000 texts by or about Americans]

R.R. Shaw and R.H. Shoemaker: *American Bibliography: a Preliminary Checklist* (New York, 1958–63 [1801–19]; continued by Shoemaker, G. Cooper and others New York and Metuchen, NJ, 1964– [1820–] as *A Checklist of American Imprints*; indexes and suppls., 1965–6, 1972–3 [1801–29]) [continues Evans, 1903–34]

The National Union Catalog: a Cumulative Author List Representing Library of Congress Printed Cards and Titles Reported by Other American Libraries, ed. Library of Congress (Ann Arbor, MI, 1958–69 [1953–67]; suppl., 1961 [1952–5])

The National Union Catalog: Music and Phonorecords, ed. Library of Congress (Ann Arbor, MI, 1958 [1953–7]; New York, 1963 [1958–62]; Ann Arbor, 1969 [1963–7]; 1973 [1968–72]; Totowa, NJ, 1978 [1973–7]; Washington, DC, 1979– [1978–] as *Music, Books on Music, and Sound Recordings*)

ASCAP Symphonic Catalog, ed. ASCAP (New York, 1959, 3/1977)

J. Edmunds and G. Boelzner: *Some Twentieth-century American Composers: a Selective Bibliography* (New York, 1959–60)

A. Janta: "Early XIX Century American-Polish Music," *Polish Review*, vi/1–2 (1961), 73–105; x/2 (1965), 59–96

B. Nettl: *Reference Materials in Ethnomusicology* (Detroit, 1961, 2/1967)

R. Houser: *Catalogue of Chamber Music for Woodwind Instruments* (Bloomington, IN, 1962/*R*)

K.E. Mixter: *General Bibliography for Music Research* (Detroit, MI, 1962, 2/1975, 3/1996)

C. Wunderlich: *A History and Bibliography of Early American Musical Periodicals, 1782–1852* (diss., U. of Michigan, 1962; reprint, Ann Arbor, MI, 1963

A.P. Basart: *Serial Music: a Classified Bibliography of Writings on Twelve-tone and Electronic Music* (Berkeley and Los Angeles, 1963)

K.E. Mixter: *An Introduction to Library Resources for Music Research* (Columbus, OH, 1963)

Symphonic Catalogue, ed. BMI (New York, 1963, 2/1971)

E. Wolf, II: *American Song Sheets, Slip Ballads and Poetical Broadsides, 1850–1870* (Philadelphia, 1963)

S. Bull: *Index to Biographies of Contemporary Composers* (New York, 1964–74)

V. Duckles: *Music Reference and Research Materials: an Annotated Bibliography* (New York, 1964, 6/1997)

A. Eagon: *Catalog of Published Concert Music by American Composers* (Washington, DC, 1964, 2/1969; suppls., 1971–4)

Early American Periodicals Index to 1850 (New York, 1964)

R. Leigh: *Index to Song Books* (Stockton, CA, 1964/*R*)

N. Shapiro: *Popular Music: an Annotated Index of American Popular Songs* (New York, 1964–2004)

R.J. Wolfe: *Secular Music in America, 1801–1825: a Bibliography* (New York, 1964)

M.K. Farish: *String Music in Print* (New York, 1965, 2/1973/*R*; suppls., 1968–)

R.M. Lawless: *Folksingers and Folkways in America* (New York, 1965)

D. De Charms and P.F. Breed: *Songs in Collections: an Index* (Detroit, 1966) [index to 411 collections]

K.S. Diehl: *Hymns and Tunes: an Index* (New York, 1966)

J.J. Fuld: *The Book of World-Famous Music: Classical, Popular and Folk* (New York, 1966, 2/1971)

K.R. Hartley: *Bibliography of Theses and Dissertations in Sacred Music* (Detroit, 1966)

Song Catalogue, ed. BBC Music Library (London, 1966)

A Basic Music Library for Schools Offering Undergraduate Degrees in Music, ed. National Association of Schools of Music (Washington, DC, 1967; rev. 2/1977 by M. Winesanker as *A List of Books on Music*, 3/1979 as *Books on Music: a Classified List* 3/1979) [supersedes the association's lists, 1935–57; lists books, periodicals, and scores]

L.M. Cross: *A Bibliography of Electronic Music* (Toronto, 1967)

"Directory of American Contemporary Operas," *Central Opera Service Bulletin*, x/2 (1967)

RILM Abstracts (1967–)

The CMP Library, ed. Music Educators National Conference (Washington, DC, 1967–8, rev. 2/1969 by V.B. Lawrence)

D.L. Arlton: *American Piano Sonatas of the Twentieth Century: Selective Analysis and Annotated Index* (diss., Columbia U., 1968)

T.C. Collins: *Music Education Materials: a Selected Annotated Bibliography* (Washington, DC, 1968)

J.L. Landsman: *Annotated Catalogue of American Violin Music Composed between 1947–1961* (Urbana, IL, 1968)

J.B. Clark and M. Clark: "A Music Collection for the High School Student," *Notes*, xxv (1968–9), 685–691

The National Union Catalog, Pre-1956 Imprints: a Cumulative Author List, Representing Library of Congress Printed Cards and Titles Reported by Other American Libraries (London, 1968–80; suppls., 1980–81)

D.J. Epstein: *Music Publishing in Chicago before 1871: the Firm of Root & Cady, 1858–1871* (Detroit, 1969), 85–146

P.R. Lehman: "A Selected Bibliography of Works on Music Testing," *JRME*, xvii/4 (1969), 427–442

Library of Congress and National Union Catalog Author Lists, 1942–1962: a Master Cumulation, ed. Gale Research Company (Detroit, 1969–71)

E. B. Carlson: *A Bio-bibliographical Dictionary of Twelve-tone and Serial Composers* (Metuchen, NJ, 1970)

D.-R. De Lerma: *A Selective List of Masters' Theses in Musicology* (Bloomington, IN, 1970)

R.S. Denisoff: *American Protest Songs of War and Peace* (Los Angeles, 1970, rev. 1973 as *Songs of Protest, War & Peace*)

D.L. Hixon: *Music in Early America: a Bibliography of Music in Evans* (Metuchen, NJ, 1970)

D. Kennington: *The Literature of Jazz* (London, 1970, rev. 2/1980 with D.L. Read)

Music the Healer: a Bibliography, ed. Institutional Library Services, Washington State Library (Olympia, WA, 1970)

W.J. Weichlein: *A Checklist of American Music Periodicals, 1850–1900* (Detroit, 1970)

W.R. Ferris, Jr.: *Mississippi Black Folklore: a Research Bibliography and Discography* (Hattiesburg, MS, 1971)

D.W. Krummel: "The Facsimiliad," *Yearbook for Inter-American Music Research*, vii (1971), 135–160

H.B. Peters: *The Literature of the Woodwind Quintet* (Metuchen, NJ, 1971)

G.T. Tanselle: *Guide to the Study of United States Imprints* (Cambridge, MA, 1971) [analysis of music coverage, with addns by D.W. Krummel in *Yearbook for Inter-American Music Research*, viii (1972), 137–146

S.R. Charles: *A Handbook of Music and Music Literature in Sets and Series* (New York, 1972)

D. Daniels: *Orchestral Music: a Source Book* (Metuchen, NJ, 1972)

D. Horn: *The Literature of American Music* (Exeter, UK, 1972, 2/1977, as *The Literature of American Music in Books and Folk Music Collections*)

E.C. Krohn: *Music Publishing in the Middle Western States before the Civil War* (Detroit, 1972)

C.R. Arnold: *Organ Literature: a Comprehensive Survey* (Metuchen, NJ, 1973)

R. Jackson: *United States Music: Sources of Bibliography and Collective Biography* (Brooklyn, NY, 1973, 2/1976)

H. Voxman and L. Merriman: *Woodwind Ensemble Music Guide* (Evanston, IL, 1973)

R.K. Weerts: *Original Manuscript Music for Wind and Percussion Instruments* (Washington, DC, 1973)

S. Kostka: *A Bibliography of Computer Applications in Music* (Hackensack, NJ, 1974)

R.H. Mead: *Doctoral Dissertations in American Music: a Classified Bibliography* (Brooklyn, NY, 1974)

T.R. Nardone, J.H. Nye, and M. Resnick: *Choral Music in Print* (Philadelphia, 1974; suppl., 1976; Master Index, 1991)

E. Olmsted: *Music Library Association Catalog of Cards for Printed Music, 1953–1972* (Totowa, NJ, 1974)

D. Phillips: *A Selected Bibliography of Music Librarianship* (Urbana, IL, 1974)

C. Sollinger: *String Class Publications in the United States, 1851–1951* (Detroit, 1974)

R.J. Specht: *Early American Vocal Music in Modern Editions* (Albany, NY, 1974)

D. Tudor and N. Tudor: *Popular Music Periodicals Index* (Metuchen, NJ, 1974)

S. Winick: *Rhythm: an Annotated Bibliography* (Metuchen, NJ, 1974)

Folio-dex: Vocal, Piano, and Organ Music Finding List (Loomis, CA, 1974–)

Music in Print (Philadelphia, 1974–99; Master Composer Index, 1988, 3/1999; Master Title Index, 1990–) [series, see Nardone, Nye, and Resnik, 1974; Nardone, 1975; Nardone, 1976; Farish, 1978; Farish, 1979; Nardone, 1981; Nardone, 1982; Farish, 1984; Jape, 1989; Peters, 1997]

D.-R. De Lerma: *Black Concert and Recital Music: a Provisional Repertoire List* (Bloomington, IN, 1975)

J.G. Finell: *Catalog of Choral and Vocal Works* (New York, 1975) [lists works in the American Music Center; see also Famera, 1978]

P. Havlice: *Popular Song Index* (Metuchen, NJ, 1975; suppls., 1978, 1984)

P.S. Heard: *American Music, 1698–1800: an Annotated Bibliography* (Waco, TX, 1975)

D. Hixon and D. Hennessee: *Women in Music: a Biobibliography* (Metuchen, NJ, 1975, 2/1993) [lists dictionaries and encyclopedias containing biographies]

T.R. Nardone: *Organ Music in Print* (Philadelphia, 1975, rev. 2/1984 by W.A. Frankel; suppl. 1990 by F.M. Daugherty; suppl. 1997 by R.W. Cho; Master Index, 1997, by W.A. Frankel)

J. Voigt and R. Kane: *Jazz Music in Print* (Winthrop, MA, 1975, rev. 3/1982 as *Jazz Music in Print and Jazz Books in Print*)

"Selective List of American Music for the Bicentennial Celebration," *MEJ*, lx/8 (1975), 54–61; lxi/9 (1975), 48–52; lxii/2 (1975), 66–72; lxii/6 (1976), 55–63

American Music before 1865 in Print and on Records: a Biblio-discography (Brooklyn, NY, 1976, 2/1990)

J.E. Carman and others: *Art-song in the United States: an Annotated Bibliography* (New York, 1976; suppl. 1978)

I. Lowens: *A Bibliography of Songsters Printed in America before 1821* (Worcester, MA, 1976) [lists 649 books with song texts]

T.R. Nardone: *Classical Vocal Music in Print* (Philadelphia, 1976; suppl. 1985 by G.S. Eslinger; suppl. 1995 by F.M. Daugherty; Master Index, 1995)

L. Sandberg and D. Weissman: *The Folk Music Sourcebook* (New York, 1976, 2/1989)

Music Therapy Index (Lawrence, KS, 1976–)

D.W. Krummel: "Musical Editions: a Basic Collection," *Choice*, xiii (1976–7), 177–95

C. Adkins and A. Dickinson: *International Index of Dissertations and Musicological Works in Progress* (Philadelphia, 1977, 2/1984; American-Canadian suppl. 1979)

G. Anderson: *Freedom's Voice in Poetry and Song* (Wilmington, DE, 1977) [lists 1455 titles of political and patriotic lyrics in colonial newspapers, 1773–83]

R. Jackson: *U.S. Bicentennial Music* (Brooklyn, NY, 1977) [lists about 500 editions of early American music published 1970–76]

G.A. Marco: "The Americas," *Information on Music: a Handbook of Reference Sources in European Languages* (Littleton, CO, 1977)

N.P. Springer and A.J. Klassen: *Mennonite Bibliography, 1631–1961*, ii (Scottdale, PA, 1977), 285–97

E.C. Wolf: "Lutheran Hymnody and Music Published in America, 1700–1850: a Descriptive Bibliography," *Concordia Historical Institute Quarterly*, 1 (1977), 164–85

R. Browne: "Index of Music Theory in the United States, 1955–1970," *ITO*, iii/7–11 (1977–8)

A Basic Music Library (Chicago, 1978, 4/2011)

K.M. Famera: *Catalog of the American Music Center Library*, ii: *Chamber Music* (New York, 1978)

M.K. Farish: *Orchestral Music in Print: Educational Section* (Philadelphia, 1978)

J.M. Meggett: *Music Periodical Literature: an Annotated Bibliography of Indexes and Bibliographies* (Metuchen, NJ, 1978)

W. Sharples, Jr.: "A Selected and Annotated Bibliography of Books and Articles on Music in the Cinema," *Cinema Journal*, xvii/2 (1978), 36–67

J. Skowronski: *Women in Music: a Bibliography* (Metuchen, NJ, 1978)

R.J. Stanislaw: *A Checklist of Four-shape Shape-note Tunebooks* (Brooklyn, NY, 1978)

O. Williams: *American Black Women in the Arts and Social Sciences: a Bibliographic Survey* (Metuchen, NJ, 1978)

Music Psychology Index (Lawrence, KS, 1978–)

A.F. Block and C. Neuls-Bates: *Women in American Music: a Bibliography of Music and Literature* (Westport, CT, 1979)

F.J. Cipolla: "A Bibliography of Dissertations Relative to the Study of Bands and Band Music," *Journal of Band Research*, xv/1 (1979), 1–31; xvi/1 (1980), 29–36

B. Delli: "Music," *Arts in America: a Bibliography*, ed. B. Kappel (Washington, DC, 1979), vol. iii, sec. R.

H.J. Diamond: *Music Criticism: an Annotated Guide to the Literature* (Metuchen, NJ, 1979)

M.K. Farish: *Orchestral Music in Print* (Philadelphia, 1979; suppl. 1983, 1984; suppl. 1999 by R.W. Cho and R.W. Daugherty; Master Index, 1994, 2/1999)

I.V. Jackson: *Afro-American Religious Music: a Bibliography and a Catalogue of Gospel Music* (Westport, CT, 1979)

M. Marks: "Film Music: the Material, Literature, and Present State of Research," *Notes*, xxxvi (1979–80), 282–325

J.J. Fuld and M.W. Davidson: *Eighteenth-century American Secular Music Manuscripts: an Inventory* (Philadelphia, 1980)

C. Gorbman: "Bibliography on Sound in Film," *Yale French Studies*, no.60 (1980), 269–286

K. Van Winkle Keller: *Popular Secular Music in America through 1800: a Checklist of Manuscripts in Borth American Collections* (Philadelphia, 1980)

M. Kratzenstein: "The United States," *Survey of Organ Literature and Editions* (Ames, IA, 1980), 178–203

H. Sampson: *Blacks in Blackface: a Source Book on Early Black Musical Shows* (Metuchen, NJ, 1980), 131–327

R.C. Von Ende: *Church Music: an International Bibliography* (Metuchen, NJ, 1980)

Répertoire international de la presse musicale (RIPM) (Baltimore, MD, 1980–)

F.E. Brunnings: *Folk Song Index* (New York, 1981)
A.I. Cohen: *International Encyclopedia of Women Composers* (New York, 1981, 2/1987)
P.B. Curtis: *American Organ Music North of Philadelphia before 1860: Selected Problems and an Annotated Bibliography* (diss., Manhattan School of Music, 1981)
F. Hoffmann: *The Literature of Rock, 1954–1978* (Metuchen, NJ, 1981)
K. Van W. Keller: *Popular Secular Music in America through 1800: a Preliminary Checklist of Manuscripts in North American Collections* (Philadelphia, 1981)
D.W. Krummel and others, eds.: *Resources of American Music History* (Urbana, IL, 1981)
E. Meadows: *Jazz Reference and Research Materials: a Bibliography* (New York, 1981, 2/1995)
J.M. Meggett: *Keyboard Music by Women Composers: a Catalog and Bibliography* (Westport, CT, 1981)
N.K. Nardone: *Sacred Choral Music in Print: Supplement* (Philadelphia, 1981; rev. 2/1985 by G.S. Eslinger; suppl. 1988 by S.H. Simon; suppl. 1992, 1996 by F.M. Daugherty; Arranger Index, 1987; Master Index, 1992, 2/1996)
UTK Song Index (Knoxville, 1981)
E.D. White: *Choral Music by Afro-American Composers: a Selected, Annotated Bibliography* (Metuchen, NJ, 1981, 2/1996)
J.L. Zaimont and K. Famera: *Contemporary Concert Music by Women: a Directory of the Composers and their Works* (Westport, CT, 1981)
D.-R. De Lerma: *Bibliography of Black Music* (Westport, CT, 1981–) [vols. i–iv list black music, vi planned as a bibliography of writings on black music]
Garland Composer Resource Manuals (New York, 1981–2000; continued by *Routledge Music Bibliographies*, 2001–) [series, see Elliker, 1988; Ping-Robbins, 1998; Link, 2000]
J.L. Adams: *Musicians' Autobiographies: an Annotated Bibliography of Writings Available in English 1800 to 1980* (Jefferson, NC, 1982)
A. Janta: *A History of Nineteenth Century American-Polish Music* (New York, 1982)
N.K. Nardone: *Secular Choral Music in Print: Supplement* (Philadelphia, 1982; rev. 2/1987 by F.M. Daugherty; suppl. 1991, 1993 by F.M. Daugherty; suppl. 1996 by R.W. Cho; Arranger Index, 1987; Master Index, 1993, 2/1996)
D.B. Wilmeth: *Variety Entertainment and Outdoor Amusements: a Reference Guide* (Westport, CT, 1982)
Bibliography of American Hymnals, ed. Hymn Society of America (New York, 1983)
M. Booth: *American Popular Music: a Reference Guide* (Westport, CT, 1983)
S.A. Floyd and M.J. Reisser: *Black Music in the United States: an Annotated Bibliography of Selected Reference and Research Materials* (Millwood, NY, 1983)
J. Laster: *Catalogue of Choral Music Arranged in Biblical Order* (Metuchen, NJ, 1983, 2/1996, suppl., 2002)
M. Maguire: *American Indian and Eskimo Music: a Selected Bibliography through 1981* (Washington, DC, 1983)
S. Rogal: *The Children's Jubilee: a Bibliographical Survey of Hymnals for Infants, Youth, and Sunday Schools Published in Britain and America, 1655–1900* (Westport, CT, 1983)
L.I. Solow and others: *The Boston Composers Project: a Bibliography of Contemporary Music* (Cambridge, MA, 1983)
N. Temperley and C.G. Manns: *Fuging Tunes in the Eighteenth Century* (Detroit, 1983)
M.K. Farish: *String Music in Print: Supplement* (Philadelphia, 1984; suppl. 1998 by R.W. Cho, D.T. Reese, and F. James)
J. Gillespie and A. Gillespie: *A Bibliography of Nineteenth-century American Piano Music* (Westport, CT, 1984)
T. Goleeke: *Literature for Voice: An Index of Songs in Collections and Source Book for Teachers of Singing* (Metuchen, NJ, 1984, 2002)
J.R. Heintze: *American Music Studies: a Classified List of Master's Theses* (Detroit, 1984)
F.W. Hoogerwerf: *Confederate Sheet-music Imprints* (Brooklyn, NY, 1984) [lists 800 items published during the Confederacy]
W. Gargan and S. Sharma: *Find That Tune: an Index to Rock, Folk-rock, Disco, and Soul in Collections* (New York, 1984–8)
Bio-bibliographies in Music (Westport, CT, 1984–) [series, see Hennessee, 1985; Skowronski, 1985; Meckna, 1986; Carnovale, 1987; Heintze, 1987; Block, 1988; Deboer and Ahouse, 1988; Kreitner, 1988; Patterson and Patterson, 1988; Pemberton, 1988; McDonald, 1989; Tyler, 1989; Bailey and Bailey, 1990; Ferencz, 1990; Benser and Urrows, 1991; Hitchens, 1991; Perone, 1991; Stehman, 1991; Demsey and Prather, 1993; Bortin, 1993; Burbank, 1993; Doering, 1993; Perone, 1993; Hobson and Richardson, 1994; Johnson, 1994; O'Connor, 1994; Slomski, 1994; Sposato, 1995; Green, 1995; Dodd and Engquist, 1996; Green, 1996; Hitchens, 1996; Still, Dabrishus, and Quin, 1996; Adams, 1998; Faucett, 1998; Cohen, 1999; Hordan, 1999; Perone, 1999; Cox, 2000; Hixon, 2000; Perone, 2000; Cody, 2001; Hoek, 2001; Schlegel, 2001; Cohen, 2002; Perone, 2002; Martin, 2004; Ravas, 2004; Speed, Anderson, and Metcalf, 2004; Lehrman, 2005]
D.A. Hennessee: *Samuel Barber* (Westport, CT, 1985)
P. Lust: *American Vocal Chamber Music, 1945–1980: an Annotated Bibliography* (Westport, CT, 1985)
N. Shapiro and B. Pollock: *Popular Music, 1920–1979: a Revised Cumulation* (Detroit, 1985)
J. Skowronski: *Aaron Copland* (Westport, CT, 1985)
P. Taylor: *Popular Music since 1955: a Critical Guide to the Literature* (London, 1985)
M.A. Hovland: *Musical Settings of American Poetry: a Bibliography* (Westport, CT, 1986)
M. Meckna: *Virgil Thomson* (Westport, CT, 1986)
G. Anderson and N. Ratliff: *Music in New York During the American Revolution: an Inventory of Musical References in Rivington's* New York Gazette (Canton, MA, 1987)
J.H. Baron: *Chamber Music* (New York, 1987, 3/2010)
N. Carnovale: *Gunther Schuller* (Westport, CT, 1987)
D.P. DeVenney: *Nineteenth-century American Choral Music: an Annotated Guide* (Berkeley, CA, 1987)
J.R. Heintze: *Esther Williamson Ballou* (Westport, CT, 1987)
G. Block: *Charles Ives* (Westport, CT, 1988)
E. Brookhart: *Music in American Higher Education: an Annotated Bibliography* (Warren, MI, 1988)
B.N. Cohen-Stratyner: *Popular Music, 1900–1919: an Annotated Guide to American Popular Songs* (Detroit, MI, 1988)
K. Deboer and J.B. Ahouse: *Daniel Pinkham* (Westport, CT, 1988)
D.P. DeVenney: *Early American Choral Music: an Annotated Guide* (Berkeley, CA, 1988)
C. Elliker: *Stephen Foster* (New York, 1988)
K. Kreitner: *Robert Ward* (Westport, CT, 1988)
D.L. Patterson and J.L. Patterson: *Vincent Persichetti* (Westport, CT, 1988)
C.A. Pemberton: *Lowell Mason* (Westport, CT, 1988)
T.E. Warner: *Periodical Literature on American Music, 1620–1920: a Classified Bibliography with Annotations* (Warren, MI, 1988)
K. Graber: *William Mason (1829–1908): an Annotated Bibliography and Catalog of Works* (Warren, MI, 1989)
M. Jape: *Classical Guitar Music in Print* (Philadelphia, 1989; suppl. 1998 by D.T. Reese)
R.M. Johnson: *Violin Music by Women Composers: a Bio-bibliographical Guide* (New York, 1989)
A.L. McDonald: *Ned Rorem* (Westport, CT, 1989)
L.L. Tyler: *Edward Burlingame Hill* (Westport, CT, 1989)
W.B. Bailey and N.G. Bailey: *Radie Britain* (Westport, CT, 1990)
A.P. Britton, I. Lowens, and R. Crawford: *American Sacred Music Imprints, 1698–1810: a Bibliography* (Worcester, MA, 1990)
G.J. Ferencz: *Robert Russell Bennett* (Westport, CT, 1990)
J.R. Heintze: *Early American Music: a Research and Information Guide* (New York, 1990)
E. Southern and J. Wright: *African-American Traditions in Song, Sermon, Tale, and Dance, 1600s-1920: an Annotated Bibliography of Literature, Collections, and Artworks* (New York, 1990)
C.C. Benser and D.F. Urrows: *Randall Thompson* (Westport, CT, 1991)
S.H. Hitchens: *Karel Husa* (Westport, CT, 1991)
K.L. Perone: *Lukas Foss* (Westport, CT, 1991)
W.H. Rehrig: *The Heritage Encyclopedia of Band Music* (Westerville, OH, 1991, suppl. 1996); CD-ROM (Oskaloosa, IA, 2005)
J.H. Renshaw: *The American Wind Symphony Commissioning Project* (New York, 1991)
D. Stehman: *Roy Harris* (Westport, CT, 1991)
E. Boroff: *American Operas: a Checklist* (Warren, MI, 1992)
G.N. Heller: *Historical Research in Music Education: a Bibliography* (Lawrence, KS, 1989, 3/1995)

V. Bortin: *Elinor Remick Warren* (Westport, CT, 1993)
R.D. Burbank: *Charles Wuorinen* (Westport, CT, 1993)
D. Demsey and R. Prather: *Alec Wilder* (Westport, CT, 1993)
D.P. DeVenney: *American Choral Music Since 1920: an Annotated Guide* (Berkeley, CA, 1993)
W.T. Doering: *Elliott Carter* (Westport, CT, 1993)
J.E. Perone: *Howard Hanson* (Westport, CT, 1993)
C.T. Hobson and D.A. Richardson: *Ulysses Kay* (Westport, CT, 1994)
E.S. Johnson: *Leslie Bassett* (Westport, CT, 1994)
K. Kroeger: *American Fuging-Tunes, 1770–1820: a Descriptive Catalog* (Westport, CT, 1994)
J. O'Connor: *John Alden Carpenter* (Westport, CT, 1994)
M.J. Slomski: *Paul Creston* (Westport, CT, 1994)
D.P. DeVenney: *Source Readings in American Choral Music* (Missoula, MT, 1995)
J.D. Green: *Carl Ruggles* (Westport, CT, 1995)
J.E. Perone: *Musical Anthologies for Analytical Study: a Bibliography* (Westport, CT, 1995)
J.S. Sposato: *William Thomas McKinley* (Westport, CT, 1995)
M.A. Dodd and J.R. Engquist: *Gardner Read* (Westport, CT, 1996)
A. Green: *Allen Sapp* (Westport, CT, 1996)
S.H. Hitchens: *Ross Lee Finney* (Westport, CT, 1996)
J.E. Perone: *Orchestration Theory: a Bibliography* (Westport, CT, 1996)
J.A. Still, M.J. Dabrishus, and C.L. Quin: *William Grant Still* (Westport, CT, 1996)
S.L. Hettinger: *American Organ Music of the Twentieth Century* (Warren, MI, 1997)
G.R. Hill and N.L. Stephens: *Collected Editions, Historical Series & Sets & Monuments of Music: a Bibliography* (Berkeley, CA, 1997)
H.B. Peters: *Woodwind Music in Print* (Philadelphia, 1997)
K.G. Adams: *William Schuman* (Westport, CT, 1998)
B.F. Faucett: *George Whitefield Chadwick* (Westport, CT, 1998)
E. Luchinsky: *The Song Index of the Enoch Pratt Free Library* (New York, 1998)
N.R. Ping-Robbins: *Scott Joplin* (New York, 1998)
N. Temperley: *The Hymn Tune Index: a Census of English-language Hymn Tunes in Printed Sources from 1535–1820* (New York, 1998)
K.A. Abromeit: *An Index to African-American Spirituals for the Solo Voice* (Westport, CT, 1999)
D. Cohen: *Phil Ochs* (Westport, CT, 1999)
S.A. Floyd, Jr.: *International Dictionary of Black Composers* (Chicago, 1999)
D.M. Hordan: *Alfred Reed* (Westport, CT, 1999)
J.E. Perone: *Carole King* (Westport, CT, 1999)
D.H. Cox: *Irwin Bazelon* (Westport, CT, 2000)
D.L. Hixon: *Gian Carlo Menotti* (Westport, CT, 2000)
J.F. Link: *Elliott Carter* (New York, 2000)
J.E. Perone: *Paul Simon* (Westport, CT, 2000)
J. Cody: *Vivian Fine* (Westport, CT, 2001)
D.J. Hoek: *Steve Reich* (Westport, CT, 2001)
D.W. Music: *Christian Hymnody in Twentieth Century Britain and America: an Annotated Bibliography* (Westport, CT, 2001)
M. Robertson and R. Armstrong: *Aaron Copland* (New York, 2001)
E.G. Schlegel: *Emma Lou Diemer* (Westport, CT, 2001)
W.C. Wentzel: *Samuel Barber* (New York, 2001, 2/2010)
Routledge Music Bibliographies (New York, 2001–); continues *Garland Composer Resource Manuals* [series, see Baron, 1987; Wentzel, 2001; Robertson and Armstrong, 2001; Laird, 2002; Sharp and Floyd, 2002; Magee, 2002; Post, 2004; Pendle, 2005; Sharp, 2005; Bradley, 2005; Parker, 2005; Lindemann, 2006; Meadows, 2006; Comeau, 2009; Meadows, 2010]
D. Cohen: *George Crumb* (Westport, CT, 2002)
P.R. Laird: *Leonard Bernstein* (New York, 2002)
G.S. Magee: *Charles Ives* (New York, 2002, 2/2010)
J.E. Perone: *Louis Moreau Gottschalk* (Westport, CT, 2002)
A.T. Sharp and J.M. Floyd: *Choral Music* (New York, 2002)
S.V. Martin: *Henry F. Gilbert* (Westport, CT, 2004)
J.N. Parker and P.M. Parker: *Music Therapy: a Medical Dictionary, Bibliography, and Annotated Research Guide to Internet Resources* (San Diego, CA, 2004)
J.C. Post: *Ethnomusicology* (New York, 2004)
T. Ravas: *Peter Schickele* (Westport, CT, 2004)
B. Speed, E. Anderson, and S. Metcalf: *Leroy Anderson* (Westport, CT, 2004)
C.J. Bradley: *American Music Librarianship* (New York, 2005)
P. Danner: *Sousa at Illinois: the John Philip Sousa and Herbert L. Clarke Manuscript Collections at the University of Illinois at Urbana-Champaign* (Warren, MI, 2005)
L.J. Lehrman: *Marc Blitzstein* (Westport, CT, 2005)
M.E. Parker: *String Quartets* (New York, 2005, 2/2011)
K. Pendle: *Women in Music* (New York, 2005, 2/2010)
A.T. Sharp: *Church and Worship Music* (New York, 2005)
S.D. Lindeman: *The Concerto* (New York, 2006)
E.S. Meadows: *Jazz Scholarship and Pedagogy* (New York, 2006)
R.P. Smiraglia and J.B. Young: *Bibliographic Control of Music, 1897–2000* (Lanham, MD, 2006)
K.R. Little and J. Graepel: *Grawemeyer Award for Music Composition: the First Twenty Years* (Lanham, MD, 2007)
P.S. Bayne.: *A Guide to Library Research in Music* (Lanham, MD, 2008)
G. Comeau: *Piano Pedagogy* (New York, 2009)
J.E. Gottlieb.: *Music Library and Research Skills* (Upper Saddle River, NJ, 2009)
J.R. Heintze: *Music of the Fourth of July: a Year-by-year Chronicle of Performances and Works Composed for the Occasion, 1777–2008* (Jefferson, NC, 2009)
L.J. Sampsel: *Music Research: a Handbook* (New York, 2009)
J. Noonan: *The Guitar in American Banjo, Mandolin and Guitar Periodicals, 1882–1933* (Middleton, WI, 2009)
L. Lehrman and K.O. Boulton: *Elie Siegmeister, American Composer: a Bio-bibliography* (Lanham, MD 2010)
E.S. Meadows: *Blues, Funk, Rhythm and Blues, Soul, Hip Hop, and Rap* (New York, 2010)
K.C. Ward: *For the Parlor and the Concert Stage: a Guide to Recent Collection of American Piano Music from the Classic and Romantic Eras* (Hillsdale, NY, 2010)
J.L. McBride: *Douglas Moore: a Bio-bibliography* (Middleton, WI, 2011)

ONLINE RESOURCES

AMC Online Library, n.d. (New York, American Music Center) <http://amc.net/library/search.aspx>
Ashford Sheet Music Collection, n.d. (U. of Washington) <http://db.lib.washington.edu/sheetmusic/>
Historic American Sheet Music, n.d. (Duke U.) <http://library.duke.edu/digitalcollections/hasm/>
Pacific Northwest Sheet Music Collection, n.d. (U. of Washington) <http://content.lib.washington.edu/smweb/>
Sheet Music Consortium, n.d. (Sheet Music Consortium) <http://digital2.library.ucla.edu/sheetmusic/>
Répertoire International de Littérature Musicale (RILM), 1967– (Ipswich, MA, EBSCO; Ann Arbor, MI, ProQuest; Dublin, OH, OCLC) <http://rilm.org/>
Music Index, 1970– (Ipswich, MA, EBSCO) <http://www.ebscohost.com/public/music-index>
U.S. Copyright Office, 1978– (Washington, DC, Library of Congress) <http://www.copyright.gov/>
Répertoire international de la presse musicale (RIPM), 1980– (Ipswich, MA, EBSCO; Baltimore, MD, RIPM Publications) <http://www.ripm.org/>
JSTOR: the Scholarly Journal Archive (New York, 1995–) <http://www.jstor.org/>
Doctoral Dissertations in Musicology (DDM), 1996– (Brunswick, ME, American Musicological Society) <http://www.ams-net.org/ddm/>
International Index to Music Periodicals (IIMP), 1996– (Alexandria, VA, Chadwyck-Healey) <http://iimp.chadwyck.com/home.do>
emusicquest, 2000– (Lansdale, PA, emusicquest) <http://www.emusicquest.com/>
Index to Printed Music, 2004– (Ipswich, MA, EBSCO) <http://www.ebscohost.com/public/index-to-printed-music-ipm>
ProQuest Dissertations and Theses (Ann Arbor, MI, 2004–) <http://www.proquest.com/en-US/catalogs/databases/detail/pqdt.shtml>
General Preservation Resources (Preservation Committee, Music Library Association, 2008) <http://committees.musiclibraryassoc.org/Preservation/General>

Music Library Facilities Bibliography (Music Library Association, 2010) <http://www.musiclibraryassoc.org/association/committees/facilities/co_fac_bibchrono.htm>

MWMLA MetaGuide (Music Library Association—Midwest Chapter, 2011) <http://uiuc.libguides.com/mwmla>

Oxford Bibliographies Online: Music 2011– <http://www.oxfordbibliographies.com/obo/page/music>

BIBLIOGRAPHY

O.G. Sonneck: "The Bibliography of American Music," *Papers of the Bibliographical Society of America*, i (1904–6), 50–64

H. Dichter and E. Shapiro: *Early American Sheet Music: its Lure and its Lore, 1768–1889* (New York, 1941, rev. and enlarged 2/1977 as *Handbook of Early American Sheet Music*)

W.T. Upton: "Early American Publications in the Field of Music," *Music and Libraries*, ed. R.S. Hill (Washington, DC, 1943), 60–69

D.W. Krummel: "Graphic Analysis: its Application to Early American Sheet Music," *Notes*, xvi (1958–9), 213–33

D.W. Krummel and J.B. Coover: "Current National Bibliographies: their Music Coverage," *Notes*, xvii (1959–60), 375–88

G.T. Tanselle: "Copyright Records and the Bibliographer," *Studies in Bibliography*, xxii (1969), 77–124 [incl. inventory of district court copyright records, 1790–1870]

E.C. Krohn: "On Classifying Sheet Music," *Notes*, xxvi (1969–70), 473–78

D.W. Krummel, ed.: *Guide for Dating Early Published Music* (Hackensack, NJ, 1974), esp. 229ff; suppl. in *FAM*, xxiv (1977), 175–84

R.J. Wolfe: *Early American Music Engraving and Printing* (Urbana, IL, 1980)

R. Holibaugh and D.W. Krummel: "Documentation of Music Publishing in the U.S.A. in the Nineteenth Century," *FAM*, xxviii (1981), 94–97

C.J. Bradley: *American Music Librarianship: a Biographical and Historical Survey* (Westport, CT, 1990)

D. Hunter: "Two Half-Centuries of Music Bibliography," *Notes*, l (1993–4), 23–38

For further bibliography *see* PUBLISHING AND PRINTING OF MUSIC.

D.W. KRUMMEL/BONNA J. BOETTCHER

Bickford (Revere), Vahdah Olcott [née Olcott, Ethel Lucretia] (*b* Norwalk, OH, 17 Oct 1885; *d* Los Angeles, CA, 18 May 1980). Guitarist and teacher. She grew up in Los Angeles, where she received early guitar instruction from George Lindsey, the local distributor of C.F. Martin guitars. In 1903–4 she studied in Berkeley with MANUEL YGNACIO FERRER, who taught her the techniques of the European classical guitar and expanded her repertoire. She published her Opus 1 in 1905 (Fischer). In 1914 she moved to New York, where she played concerts, gave guitar lessons, and assisted Philip J. Bone in the publication of his book *The Guitar and Mandolin* (London, 1914). In 1915 she married Myron Bickford (1886–1971), a prominent mandolinist and teacher of the various fretted instruments. (They soon took the astrological names Vahdah and Zarh for numerological reasons.) Vahdah gave the American première of Mauro Giuliani's Concerto no.3 for guitar and string orchestra in Town Hall. Through her numerous published articles, Vahdah became perhaps the best-known American guitarist of her generation. She returned to Los Angeles in 1923 and was the founder of the Los Angeles (later the American) Guitar Society. She performed in and led various ensembles of fretted instruments in Los Angeles and taught guitar. Although she published more than 140 works (the majority of them arrangements), Bickford was best known for her *Guitar Method*, op.25, and her *Advanced Course*, op.116, published by Ditson, both of which influenced numerous guitarists. She consistently promoted the guitar as a chamber instrument, and remained active as a performer in ensembles at meetings of the American Guitar Society into the early 1970s. Her extensive collection of guitar music and voluminous correspondence is preserved in Special Collections, California State University, Northridge.

BIBLIOGRAPHY

P.J. Bone: *The Guitar and Mandolin* (London, 1914, 2/1954/*R*), 37 only

R. Purcell: "In memoriam Vahdah Olcott Bickford Revere," *Soundboard*, vii/3 (1980), 120 only

R. Purcell: "Vahdah Olcott-Bickford: *The International Guitar Research Archives*," *Guitar Review*, no.111 (1998), 1–9

THOMAS F. HECK/PETER DANNER

Biedermann, Edward J(ulius) (*b* Milwaukee, WI, 8 Nov 1849; *d* Freeport, NY, 26 Nov 1933). Organist and composer. He was the son of August Julius Biedermann, who had emigrated from Saxony in 1848 and settled in Milwaukee as a piano teacher. Little is known of Edward's career other than that he studied in Germany 1858–64 and then returned to become a church organist, first in Newburgh, New York, and then in New York City at Old Saint Mary's and later at St. Francis de Sales. Failing eyesight caused him to retire from active church work in 1918. For many years Biedermann worked as a prolific editor for the music publishing firm J. Fischer. He wrote four masses and other liturgical music, many songs and piano pieces, and also compiled collections of organ literature, anthologies of vocal duets (1914), and *The Most Popular Sacred Songs* (1913). Beaver College awarded him an honorary doctorate in 1906.

WILLIAM OSBORNE

Bielawa, Lisa (*b* San Francisco, CA, 30 Sept 1968). Composer, vocalist, and improviser; daughter of composer Herbert Bielawa and organist/scholar Sandra Soderlund. As a child she composed, sang, and played violin. She was a member of the San Francisco Girls Chorus and wrote some of her earliest compositions for the group. Bielawa studied literature at Yale, graduating in 1990, and soon moved to New York City. In 1992 she began singing and touring with the Philip Glass Ensemble and later sang with John Zorn. In 1997 she co-founded the MATA Festival, a concert series that presents the music of younger composers.

Bielawa's compositional output is extensive and includes orchestra works, music for voice and ensemble, and music for dance. Her musical language is rhapsodic, harmonically adventurous, and grounded in a propulsive energy. Her orchestrations are characterized by a warmly expressive range of timbres. Bielawa's musical oeuvre has been shaped by her close relationships with particular performers and their unique abilities. Her *Kafka Songs* (2001–3) for singing violinist were crafted for Carla Kihlstedt. Kihlstedt, along with violinist Colin Jacobsen, inspired Bielawa's *Double Concerto* (2008). Her desire to rethink the location of musical performance led Bielawa to develop her mobile-form piece *Chance Encounter* (2007) with soprano Susan Narucki. She has written for and improvised with cellist

Frances-Marie Uitti. Some of Bielawa's compositions were written for her own vocal performance, including *A Collective Cleansing* (1999–2000) for voice and digital audio and *unfinish'd sent* (1999–2000) for soprano and chamber orchestra.

From 2006 to 2009, Bielawa was composer-in-residence with the Boston Modern Orchestra Project for whom she composed her orchestral pieces *Double Concerto, In medias res* (2009), and *Synopses* (2006–9) for solo instruments. In 2009 she received the Rome Prize for music composition. She resides in New York City.

WRITINGS

L. Bielawa: "Where are we?—On Location," *Arcana II*, ed. J. Zorn (New York, 2007)

RYAN DOHONEY

Bierley, Paul Edmund (*b* Portsmouth, OH, 3 Feb 1926). Band researcher, author, and tuba player. He graduated from Ohio State University with a bachelor of engineering degree in 1953 and had a thirty-five year career as an aeronautical engineer, working primarily for Rockwell International in Columbus, Ohio. During this time he was also active as a professional tuba player in the Columbus Symphony Orchestra (1964–81), the Detroit Concert Band (1973–93), and the Brass Band of Columbus (1984–95). He is recognized as the foremost historian on the music, life, and band of John Philip Sousa. His more than forty years of meticulous research on Sousa led to three definitive publications, *John Philip Sousa: a Catalogue of His Works* (Urbana, IL, 1973); a biography, *John Philip Sousa: American Phenomenon* (Englewood Cliffs, NJ, 1973); and *The Incredible Band of John Philip Sousa* (Urbana, IL, 2006), an exhaustive documentation of the forty years of the Sousa Band, including tour routes, repertory lists, and personnel rosters. In addition, he published *Hallelujah Trombone! The Story of Henry Fillmore* (Columbus, OH, 1982) and was editor of *The Heritage Encyclopedia of Band Music* by William H. Rehrig (Westerville, OH, two vols., 1991, suppl., 1996). In recognition of his contributions, Ohio State University awarded Bierley an honorary doctorate in 2001.

GEORGE C. FOREMAN

Big & Rich. Country music duo. Big & Rich was formed in 2002 by Kenny Alphin (*b* Culpeper, VA, 1 Nov 1963) and John Rich (*b* Amarillo, TX, 7 Jan 1974). Both musicians performed in Nashville, Tennessee during the 1990s, Rich with the popular, middle-of-the-road country group Lonestar (formerly Texassee) (1993–8) and Alphin with his rock band Big Kenny and later luvjOi. After helping to found Nashville's MUZIKMAFIA in 2001, the two decided to join forces as Big & Rich in 2002, signing a recording contract later that year with Warner Bros.

Big & Rich's entrance into the country music industry brought surprising commercial success and considerable controversy, largely owing to their public flamboyancy and close association with the MuzikMafia, a collective of diverse artists who frequently referred to themselves as a "Freak Parade." Released in May 2004 and selling more than three million copies by April 2007, *Horse of a Different Color* (WB) included the duo's first significant hit "Save a Horse (Ride a Cowboy)" and the song "Rollin' (The Ballad of Big & Rich)," which featured a self-described "hick-hop" interlude by the black Texan rapper Cowboy Troy (Coleman). Their performances included national tours with Tim McGraw and Brooks and Dunn, and guest appearances on annual award shows for the Academy of Country Music and the Country Music Association. Big & Rich combined country music with rock, soul, funk, rap, blues, bluegrass, and Dixieland jazz to form their own witty, self-assured style. Their lyrics frequently addressed social issues such as rural life, veterans, violence against women, the music industry, and cultural diversity. Subsequent commercial album releases included *Comin' to Your City* (WB, 2005) and *Between Hell and Amazing Grace* (WB, 2007) and two DVD projects entitled *Big & Rich's Super Galactic Fan Pack, Vol. I* and *Vol. II* (WB, 2004 and 2008, respectively). The duo unofficially disbanded in 2008 to pursue separate solo careers.

BIBLIOGRAPHY

A. Rucker: *Big & Rich: Total Access* (Nashville, 2007)
D.B. Pruett: *MuzikMafia: from the Local Nashville Scene to the National Mainstream* (Jackson, MS, 2010)

DAVID B. PRUETT

Big apple. A lively and strenuous circle dance of African American origin, popular in the late 1930s. It was invented by patrons of the Big Apple Night Club, a black juke joint in Columbia, South Carolina, where it was observed by some white university students who copied it and named it after the club. Subsequently, the big apple was rearranged by dance instructor Arthur Murray into a ballroom favorite and was frequently performed to swing music.

The dance requires a caller to signal step changes, and it incorporates the most active jazz dance steps of the era, almost all of which are eight-count centered. Among them are apple jacks, the Suzie-Q, truckin' (with its shuffle step and waving index finger), the shag, the shout, spank the baby, tick tock, and the organ grinder. Interludes give individual dancers (or "shiners") a chance to exhibit their dancing prowess in the center of the circle, where they may perform such steps as the black bottom, the Lindy hop, the Shorty George, the Charleston, neckin', or pose and peck. All of the dancers get a chance to shine; in other words, everyone gets a slice of the big apple. The dance ends as all the dancers run to the middle of the circle and shout "Hallelujah!" while throwing their hands in the air from a bent-over posture.

Tin Pan Alley hit upon the craze almost immediately, and in 1937 two songs were copyrighted: "The Big Apple" by Bob Emmerich and Buddy Bernier, which was recorded by Tommy Dorsey's Clambake Seven, and "Big Apple" by Lee David and John Redmond. The dance was also commonly done to Tommy Dorsey's "Marie" and "The Dipsy Doodle." Its widespread popularity is attested in the classic Frank Capra film *You*

Can't Take It with You (1938), where the characters played by James Stewart and Jean Arthur are enticed by some children to learn the big apple upon payment of a dime.

By 1941, the big apple was a past fad that had been replaced by the Lindy hop. After decades of neglect, it was revived in the 1990s by Lance Benishek and Betty Wood, who had learned the dance in South Carolina in the 1930s. Gradually the dance regained popularity, so that in the first decade of the twenty-first century, big apple exhibitions, competitions, and open sessions were being held in ballrooms and dancesport venues in many American cities.

BIBLIOGRAPHY

N. Goodman: *The Big Apple: "The Latest Modern Dance"* (Newark, NJ, 1938)

A. Murray: *How to Become a Good Dancer* (New York, 1938)

K. Hazzard-Gordon: *Jookin': The Rise of Social Dance Formations in African-American Culture* (Philadelphia, 1990)

L. Benishek and C. Rudenick: "Historic Dance Ensemble Swaps Dances in South Carolina," *Dancing USA* (July–August 1993)

CLAUDE CONYERS

Bigard, Barney [Albany Leon] (*b* New Orleans, LA, 3 March 1906; *d* Culver City, CA, 27 June 1980). Jazz clarinetist. Born into a Creole family, he first learned to play E♭ clarinet, studying with Lorenzo Tio, Jr. and using an Albert system instrument. Discouraged on the clarinet, he adopted the tenor saxophone and late in 1922 joined Albert Nicholas's band, with which he traveled to Chicago late in 1924. There the two men joined King Oliver at the Plantation Café, playing with Oliver from February 1925 to March 1927. Bigard recorded with a contingent from Oliver's band and with Oliver.

As Oliver altered his band's personnel, Bigard was occasionally called on to play the clarinet, which soon became his principal instrument. He also recorded with Jelly Roll Morton and, in April 1927, with Johnny Dodds and Louis Armstrong. He joined Charlie Elgar's group in Milwaukee for the summer and then returned to New York, playing with Luis Russell for two months before joining Duke Ellington at the end of 1927 or the beginning of 1928.

Except for a brief absence in summer 1935, Bigard remained with Ellington until June 1942. During this period he perfected a highly individual clarinet style characterized by a warm tone in all registers, sweeping chromatic runs, and long, continuous glissandos. His quickly became a distinctive voice in the Ellington orchestra, and he was prominently featured on hundreds of recordings, most notably on "Clarinet Lament (Barney's Concerto)" (1936, Bruns.), which he wrote with Ellington (Bigard also collaborated on "Mood Indigo" [1930, Bruns.], "Ducky Wucky" [1932, Bruns.] and "Saturday Night Function" [1929, Vic.], among others). In addition he recorded with Morton in 1929.

After leaving Ellington, Bigard led his own groups in Los Angeles and New York. His work during the autumn of 1946 with Louis Armstrong in the film *New Orleans* led to his next important association, as the clarinetist with Armstrong's All Stars. During his long tenure with this group (1947–52, 1953–5, 1960–61) he toured the world. He went into semiretirement in 1962, but continued to play occasionally at concerts, for recording dates and television appearances, and at numerous jazz festivals, both in the United States and overseas.

RECORDINGS
(selective list)

As leader: *Barney Goin' Easy* (1939, Voc. 5378); *Step Steps Up/Step Steps Down* (1944, Signature 28114); *Rose Room/Coquette* (1945, Keynote 617); *Clarinet Gumbo* (1973, RCA APLI-1744)

As sideman with Duke Ellington: *Sweet Mama* (1928, Harmony 577-H); *Saturday Night Function* (1929, Vic. 38036); *Mood Indigo* (1930, Bruns. 4952); *Ducky Wucky* (1932, Bruns. 6432); *Clarinet Lament (Barney's Concerto)* (1936, Bruns. 7650); *Across the Track Blues* (1940, Vic. 27235)

As sideman with others: L. Russell: *29th and Dearborn/Sweet Mumtaz* (1926, Voc. 1010); King Oliver: *Too Bad* (1926, Voc. 1007); A. Wynn: *That Creole Band* (1926, OK 8350); J. Dodds: *Weary Blues* (1927, Voc. 15632); King Oliver: *Showboat Shuffle* (1927, Voc. 1114); J. Morton: *That's like it ought to be* (1929, Vic. 38601); L. Armstrong: *Tea for Two*, pts. i–ii (1947, Decca 9-28099–9-28100); *C Jam Blues* (1947, Decca 9-28102), *Just you, Just me* (1951, Decca 9-28175)

BIBLIOGRAPHY

Oral history material in *NEij, NORtu*

R. Stewart: "Illustrious Barney Bigard," *DB* (8 Sept 1966), 18–20; repr. in *Jazz Masters of the Thirties* (New York, 1972), 113–20

A. Judd: "Barney Goin' Easy," *JJc*, xx/9 (1967), 4 [interview]

S. Dance: "Barney Bigard [Clarinet]," *The World of Duke Ellington* (London, 1970/R), 77–87

D. Ellington: "Barney Bigard and Wellman Braud," *Music is my Mistress* (Garden City, NY, 1973), 114–15

D. Koechlin: *50 ans de jazz avec Barney Bigard* (n.p. [Darnetal], n.d. [1979])

B. Bigard: *With Louis and the Duke*, ed. B. Martyn (London, 1985)

M. Tucker, ed.: *The Duke Ellington Reader* (New York, 1993)

J. Krebs: "The Great 'Barney' Bigard (1906–1980)," *The Clarinet*, xxxv/3 (June 2008), 38–42

LEWIS PORTER

Big band. A type of dance band popular especially in the 1930s and 1940s, typically consisting of ten to 15 instruments, predominantly wind. A distinctive feature of the music played by such bands was the pitting against each other of the reed and brass sections.

See Jazz

Big Brother and the Holding Company. Blues and rock group formed in 1965 that included Janis Joplin among its members between 1966 and 1968.

Big Daddy Kane [Hardy, Antonio] (*b* Brooklyn, New York, 10 Sept 1968). Rapper. He began his solo career with the prominent Queens-based hip-hop collective the Juice Crew, which included members Marly Marl, Craig G, Kool G Rap, Biz Markie and Roxanne Shanté. The Juice Crew was one of the most popular and respected groups during the mid- to late-1980s. A gifted lyricist, Big Daddy Kane penned lines for other members of the group, playing a major role in their success. As an MC, Kane is heralded as one of the greatest of his time and is often cited as an inspiration by many who followed him. Known for his rapid yet cohesive delivery, his rhymes are intricately crafted and poetically sophisticated, but delivered with sharp rhythmic precision. In addition to his skills, Kane's smooth baritone voice and good looks helped him appeal to a larger female fan base than many other artists of his time. Kane seemed well aware of this fact, and he was one of the first MCs self-consciously to market himself as a "player" or pimp.

Kane's debut album, *Long Live the Kane* (1988), spurred a number of well-known songs including "Ain't No Half-Steppin,'" "The Bugged Tip," and "Set It Off." His largest successes, however, came during the late 1980s and early 1990s. In addition to making music, Kane dabbled in acting. Comfortable in front of the camera as well as behind the microphone, he appeared in *Playgirl* magazine and in Madonna's highly influential and controversial book *Sex*, along with supermodel Naomi Campbell. As a talented live performer, Kane also played a prominent role mentoring upcoming MC. For a time during the early 1990s, he employed a young Jay-Z as his hype man and was instrumental in exposing him to wider audiences, allowing the aspiring rapper to perform on stage during breaks. Since 2000, Kane has continued a variety of projects, but his output and popularity have decreased substantially in comparison to the previous two decades.

JARED PAULEY

Bigelow, Michael L. (*b* Annapolis, MD, 7 Dec 1946). Organ builder. A graduate of the University of Utah, where he majored in architecture, he apprenticed to organ builders Abbott & Sieker and JOHN BROMBAUGH before establishing his own business in 1978. In 1984 he moved to a larger workshop in American Fork, Utah, and the following year was joined by David Chamberlin (*b* Newport Beach, CA, 7 Nov 1956) as tonal director. His organs all employ mechanical action, and many of them feature Bigelow's "either/or" stop mechanism, a system whereby certain stops may be utilized on either one manual or the other, increasing registration options for the player. Some of Bigelow's significant organs include those in First Congregational Church, Oroville, California (1985); Victory Lutheran Church, Mesa, Arizona (1988); Conception Abbey, Conception, Missouri (1999); and St. Mark's Cathedral, Salt Lake City, Utah (2011).

BIBLIOGRAPHY

C. Cramer: "An Interview with Michael Bigelow." *The American Organist*, 20/10 (Oct 1986)

BARBARA OWEN

Biggs, E(dward George) Power (*b* Westcliff-on-Sea, Essex, England, 29 March 1906; *d* Boston, MA, 10 March 1977). Organist of English birth, naturalized American. He studied at the Royal Academy of Music in London. He began to play in the United States in 1930 and became an American citizen in 1937, pursuing a career as a recitalist, broadcaster, and recording artist that did much to popularize the concert organ and organ music as well as the artist. From 1942 to 1958 he broadcast weekly solo programs over a nationwide radio network. Originating in the Germanic (now Busch–Reisinger) Museum at Harvard, these recitals on an Aeolian-Skinner "classic style" organ brought the sound of organ mixtures, mutations, and Baroque reeds, as well as the music itself, to many listeners for the first time. Biggs was meanwhile an indefatigable public performer. A product of both activities was an extensive series of phonograph recordings, made in the United States and in many European cities, including "Historic Organs of England" and "The Glory of Gabrieli," the Handel organ concertos, various Bach projects; after 1958, when the Aeolian-Skinner instrument was replaced, his recordings from the Busch–Reisinger Museum were made on an organ by the Dutch builder Dirk Flentrop. Biggs published editions of early music and performed numerous new works. His career was marked by interest in organ music of all eras and in many kinds of organs most suitable to its interpretation and by unfailing energy in performance. He played with most major American orchestras, and in 1962 joined Catharine Crozier and Virgil Fox in inaugurating the organ at Philharmonic Hall, New York.

BIBLIOGRAPHY

"E. Power Biggs," *Music: The A.G.O. and R.C.C.O Magazine* XII/3 (1978), 23, 42 [includes 4 of Biggs's articles with list of edns. and discography]

B. Owen: *E Power Biggs. Concert Organist* (Bloomington, 1987)

VERNON GOTWALS/N. LEE ORR

Biggs, (William) Hayes (*b* Huntsville, AL, 5 May 1957). Composer. He studied at Southwestern (now Rhodes) College, Memphis (BM 1979), the Berkshire Music Center (1981), Southern Methodist University (MM 1982), and Columbia University (DMA 1992). His principal composition teachers included Don Freund, MARIO DAVIDOVSKY, JACK BEESON, DONALD ERB, FRED LERDAHL, and Marvin Lamb. Biggs first came to public attention in 1984 with the humorous song "Northeast Reservation Lines." In 1993 his *Mass for All Saints* was awarded second prize in the Fifth Concours International de Musique Sacrée, Festival de Musiques Sacrées de Fribourg. It was given its premiere there the following year by the NDR Chor. In 1995 he received a commission from the Fromm Music Foundation to write *When you are Reminded by the Instruments* (1997) for the Parnassus Ensemble, New York. He received a Guggenheim Fellowship in 1997 and was a resident at Copland House (2002). He started working as a faculty member at the Manhattan School of Music in 1992.

Biggs's experience as a vocal accompanist and choral singer has shaped his approach to text setting. His performances of Gregorian chant and Renaissance motets, in particular, have influenced the rhythmic and contrapuntal suppleness of his instrumental writing. Seeking to integrate tonal and nontonal elements by means of tight motivic unity, he has written music that also displays a concern for highly variegated and subtly shifting timbres.

WORKS

(selective list)

Inst: E.M. am Flügel, pf, 1992; God Hath Sent me to Sea for Pearls, va, pf, 1992; A Consuming Fire, fl + pic + a fl, ob + eng hn, pf, 1995; To Becalme his Fever, chbr orch, 1995; When you are Reminded by the Insts, ob + eng hn, cl + b cl, hn, str, 1997; Susan's Waltz (Valse sentimentale), pf, 2002; Pan-fare, 2 picc, 2 cl (2 + bcl), a sax + bar sax, t Sax, trp, tbn, tba, pf, 2 perc, 2007; String Quartet: O Sapientia/Steal Away, str qt, 2004; Sultry Air, Balmy Breezes, fl, vc, pf, hp, 2008; Symphonia brevis, 2 ob (+ eng hn), cl, 2 bn, 2 hn, 2 trpt, timp, str, 2010; Three Preludes on Hymn Tunes, org, 2010

Choral (unacc. SATB, unless otherwise stated): Introit: Requiem aeternam, S, SATB, orch, 1982; Phos hilaron (Book of Common Prayer), SATB, org, 1986; Der Gerechten Seelen sind in Gottes Hand (Apocrypha: *Wisdom of Solomon*), 1987; O sacrum convivium, 1989; O magnum mysterium, 1990; Vidi aquam, 1991; Mass for All Saints, 1993; Videntes stellam, S, SATB, 1994; O Sapientia, 1995; Quem vidistis pastores?, 1996; Cantate Domino, 1997; Miserere mei, Deus, T, TBarB, 1997; Wedding Motet: Tota pulchra es/Set me as a seal upon thine heart, mixed chorus, 1998; Funeral Motet: In the midst of life we are in death, SATB, fl + piccolo, fl + a fl, 2 va, vc, cb, 1998; Ochila laEil, SATB (div), org, hrn, 1999; From the Lamentations of Jeremiah the Prophet, 2 S, Mez, 2 A, T, B, SATB chorus, pf, four hands, and finger cymbals, 2002

Solo vocal: i carry your heart (e.e. cummings), med v, pf, 1977; 2 Poems from Chamber Music (J. Joyce), S, pf, 1977–8; Northeast Reservation Lines (J. Shore), S, pf, 1984; Songs from Water and Stone (A. Macleish, L. Glück, D. Levertov, L. Bogan), S, fl + pic + a fl, cl + b cl, vn, vc, pf, 1985; Ave formosissima (*Carmina Burana*), S + claves + tambourine, cl, vc, 1987; Child of the Ravenhair (C. Hebald), S, Mez, T, B-Bar, chbr orch, 1988; Sephestia's Song to her Child (R. Greene), S, pf, 1991; I pastori (G. d'Annunzio), S, 4 vc, 1994; Ps xxiii, S, pf, 1996; Jacob Wrestling, nar, S, Mez, cl + b cl, a sax + bar sax, t sax + s sax, perc, pf, 2004; Psalms, Hymns and Spiritual Songs, S, pf, 2011

Principal publisher: Association for the Promotion of New Music

BIBLIOGRAPHY

C. Carey, "Hayes Biggs," *Signal to Noise*, 48 (Winter 2008), 12

DON C. GILLESPIE/SARAH EYERLY

Biglow & Main. Firm of music publishers. A partnership was formed in New York in 1867 between Lucius Horatio Biglow (1833–*c*1910) and Sylvester Main (1819–73) in order to continue the publishing activities of WILLIAM BATCHELDER BRADBURY, who had become seriously ill during the previous year. Bradbury served the firm as music editor until his death in January 1868. Main had formerly been Bradbury's assistant, but it was his son Hubert Platt Main (1839–1925) who was responsible for shaping the editorial policy of the company and who built it into one of the foremost 19th-century firms of gospel-song publishers. Among the composers whose works he issued were Philip P. Bliss, William H. Doane, William J. Kirkpatrick, Robert Lowry, McGranahan, G.F. Root, Sankey, Sherwin, Stebbins, Sweney, and Whittle. Lowry succeeded Bradbury as music editor in 1868, and a number of other composers also had editorial relationships with the firm. The poet FANNY J. CROSBY worked closely with many of Biglow & Main's composers, contributing a total of almost 6000 texts; she formed a particularly successful collaboration with Doane.

Ira Sankey became president of the firm on the retirement of Biglow in 1895. On his death in 1908 he was succeeded by his son I. Allan Sankey (1874–1915), and for the next few years the firm was run by the Sankey family. Biglow & Main was purchased in 1922 by the HOPE PUBLISHING COMPANY, and merged in 1933 with the E.O. Excell Co.; the company's publications continue to be issued under its own imprint. Hubert Main's extensive collection of books concerning 19th-century American hymns and hymn writers is now in *Cn*.

CAROLINE RICHMOND

Bigsby, Paul (Adelburt) (*b* Elgin, IL, 12 Dec 1899; *d* Downey, Los Angeles, CA, 7 June 1968). Maker of fretted stringed instruments. He created electric lap steel, Spanish, and pedal steel guitars that became influential because of their novel designs and their use by mid-20th century Western swing musicians. His signature Bigbsy tremolo tailpiece, patented in 1953, was included as standard equipment on guitars by major American manufacturers, including Gibson, Gretsch, Fender, and Epiphone.

Bigsby moved with his family to Los Angeles in the early 1910s and began his career as a patternmaker in a machine shop. He achieved early success as a motorcycle racer and a designer at Crocker Motorcycle Company. Bigsby also performed with Western swing groups on guitar and upright bass in the 1940s, and saw opportunities to improve the design of the instruments. He built his first instrument, a double-eight-string lap steel guitar, for Joaquin Murphy, slide guitarist for Spade Cooley, in 1944. This was followed by a triple-eight-string console steel for Murphy in 1946. Bigsby's first true pedal steel was made for Wesley Webb "Speedy" West in 1948, and was the instrument he used early in his famous collaboration with Jimmy West. In this period, Bigsby also experimented with new designs for electric Spanish guitars, which were most frequently sold as hollow-body archtops with electromagnetic pickups in the 1930s and 40s. In 1948, he created an electric Spanish guitar for Merle Travis with a thin maple body with concealed hollow chambers on the interior, and no soundholes. This guitar, which also featured a peghead with all six tuners on one side, influenced the design of Leo Fender's successful Telecaster and Stratocaster guitars. Its body shape was echoed in Gibson's Les Paul model. Bigsby utilized his machining skills to create his own pickups; he was also successful at manufacturing volume and tone pedals, tremolo tailpieces, and the Bigsby brand of strings.

In 1965, Ted McCarty purchased the Bigsby brand and the following year moved production of guitar accessories to Kalamazoo, Michigan. After regaining control of the Gretsch name, Fred W. Gretsch III acquired Bigsby from McCarty in 1999.

BIBLIOGRAPHY

A. Babiuk: *The Story of Paul A. Bigsby: the Father of the Modern Electric Solidbody Guitar* (Milwaukee, 2009)

ARIAN SHEETS

Big Star. Rock band formed in Memphis, Tennessee, in 1970 by Christopher Bell (*b* Memphis, 12 Jan 1951; *d* Memphis, 27 Dec 1978), Alex Chilton (*b* Memphis, 28 Dec 1978; *d* New Orleans, LA, 17 March 2010), Andrew Hummel (*b* Valley Forge, PA, 26 Jan 1951; *d* Weatherford, TX, 19 July 2010), and Jody Stephens (*b* Memphis, 4 Oct 1952). Heavily influenced by the British invasion and the Beach Boys, Bell and Chilton conceived the band as a studio venture. This lineup played less than a dozen shows in and around Memphis. Under the eye of John Fry, the owner of the studio Ardent, they recorded *#1 Record* and had started work on *Radio City* when Bell quit after the debut album's commercial failure. Hummel left soon afterwards and was replaced by John Lightman (*b* Memphis, 31 Oct 1949) before he too quit. The producer Jim Dickinson then worked with Chilton and Stephens on a collection of brooding songs issued as the album *Third*, but few people were interested and the band split up. After numerous bands, including R.E.M. and Wilco, cited Big Star as an influence, its albums were re-issued and the group reformed in 1993. Chilton and Stephens added the Posies' Jonathan Auer (*b* Bellingham, WA, 29 Sept 1969) and Ken Stringfellow (*b* Hollywood, CA, 30 Oct 1968) for a one-off show in Missouri, after which the group toured on a semi-regular basis for the next 17 years. The album *In Space* (Rykodisc, 2005) failed to capture the magic of the original recordings. An album of Bell's own material, *I am the Cosmos*, was released by Rykodisc in 1992.

SELECTED RECORDINGS

#1 Record (Ardent, 1972); *Radio City* (Ardent, 1973); *Third/Sister Lovers* (PVC, 1978); *Big Star Live* (Rykodisc, 1992); *Columbia* (Rykodisc, 1993); *In Space* (Rykodisc, 2005); *Keep an Eye on the Sky* (Rhino, 2009)

BIBLIOGRAPHY

R. Jovanovic: *Big Star: the Short Life, Painful Death and Unexpected Resurrection of the Kings of Power Pop* (Chicago, 2005)

ROB JOVANOVIC

Big 3 Music Corporation. Firm of music publishers. It was formed in 1939 by Metro-Goldwyn-Mayer, which acquired three major publishers of popular music, Robbins Music Corporation, Leo Feist, Inc., and Miller Music, in order to gain control of copyrights for music used in films. The resulting company, the Big 3 Music Corporation, expanded its catalog with popular music, film scores, and television theme music; among its successes were "You don't have to say you love me," "*Batman*'s Theme," "The shadow of your smile," and "Somewhere my love." It also publishes arrangements of such tunes for use by schools in editions for chorus and for marching band. In 1973 MGM sold Big 3 to United Artists, and in 1990, it was acquired by EMI.

FRANCES BARULICH/R

Bikel, Theodore (*b* Vienna, Austria, 2 May 1924). American and Israeli actor and singer. Born into a Jewish family, he spent his youth in Austria. Following the Nazi occupation the Bikel family escaped to Palestine, where he made his stage debut in 1943. Moving to London to study at the Royal Academy of Dramatic Art, he began his acting career in 1948 in *A Streetcar Named Desire*. In 1954 he immigrated to the United States and, in 1961, became a naturalized American. He made his concert debut at Carnegie Recital Hall, New York, in 1956 with a program of folk songs. In 1959 he was cast as Georg von Trapp in the Rodgers and Hammerstein musical *The Sound of Music*. During his long career Bikel has appeared in numerous films, plays, and musicals, from the lead in *Zorba* to over 2000 performances as the penniless milkman Tevye in *Fiddler on the Roof*, becoming closely identified with the song "If I Were a Rich Man." His 33 film credits include *Goldfinger* (1964), *My Fair Lady* (1964), and *Fiddler on the Roof* (1967). He has also made many television appearances, in programs as diverse as *Gunsmoke* and *Star Trek: the Next Generation*. He has been active in theater guilds and liberal politics, opposing the anti-communist blacklist in the 1950s, working for voting rights for African Americans in Mississippi in the 1960s, and promoting Arab–Israeli reconciliation. A noted raconteur and renaissance man, he developed an international reputation as a singer of ethnic folk music, exploiting his strong baritone voice and guitar skills. His keen sense of humor, scholarly approach, and knowledge of many languages created authentic, zestful performances. His recordings cover a wide range of folk material from four continents, though most of his repertory derives from Europe, Israel, and the United States. Bikel is perhaps best known for his interpretations of Russian folk and gypsy songs, for which he has a particular affinity. Along with Harry Belafonte and Miriam Makeba, he helped introduce American audiences to much music from outside the Anglo-American tradition. Of his 36 albums, perhaps the most significant are *Israeli Folk Songs* (1955), *An Actor's Holiday* (1958), *Songs of a Russian Gypsy* (1958), *Bravo Bikel* (1959), *The Best of Bikel* (1962), and *A Folksinger's Choice* (1964). In addition to performing at many folk festivals, he opened the first folk music coffeehouse in Los Angles in 1957, and presented his own folk-music radio program from 1957 to 1962. In 1960 he published the book *Folksongs & Footnotes*, containing songs from around the world, and in 1994 his autobiography, *Theo*. In 2009, a Carnegie Hall concert headlined by Alan Alda, Arlo Guthrie, Tom Paxton, Noel Paul Stookey, and Peter Yarrow celebrated his illustrious career.

BIBLIOGRAPHY

K. Baggelaar and D. Milton: *Folk Music: More than a Song* (New York, 1976)

T. Bikel: *Theo: the Autobiography of Theodore Bikel* (New York, 1994)

D. Hadju: *Positively 4th Street* (New York, 2001)

CRAIG A. LOCKARD

Bikini Kill. Rock band formed in Olympia, Washington, in 1990. They were celebrated for their role in promoting the RIOT GRRRL movement from the early 1990s. Named after a zine produced by its members, the group comprised Kathleen Hanna (*b* Portland, OR, 12 Nov 1968; vocals), Billy Karren (AKA Billy Boredom, *b* Memphis, TN, 10 March 1965; guitarist), Kathi Wilcox (*b* Vancouver, WA, 19 Nov 1969; bass guitar), and Tobi Vail (*b* Auburn, WA, 20 July 1969; drums). Vail had previously performed in the bands Doris and Go Team before she met Hanna who had been impressed by her fanzine *Jigsaw*. The band became known for their advocacy of feminist politics with many of their songs dealing directly with gender issues. The track "Rebel Girl" became a key riot grrrl recording with its chugging distorted guitar, screamed vocals, and anthemic punk-style chorus. During the group's live shows they encouraged female audience members to occupy the normally male dominated area directly in front of the stage and frequently passed the microphone to these women in order to involve them in the performance. In 1993 they collaborated with the English riot grrrl band Huggy Bear; the groups completed a tour of the UK together and released a joint vinyl album with each band featuring separately on either side of the recording. The band's last studio album, *Reject all American*, was released in 1996. Bikini Kill eventually split in 1998, after which each of the members pursued other projects; a retrospective compilation of the band's singles was released in the same year. In 1997 Hanna released a solo recording under the name of Julie Ruin and the following year began a new collaboration which became the electronic music group Le Tigre. In 2012 Bikini Kill announced the establishment of Bikini Kill Records, a record label set up to reissue records and rare material from the catalog of the band.

RECORDINGS
(selective list)

New Radio/Rebel Girl (Kill Rock Stars, 1993); *Pussy Whipped* (Kill Rock Stars, 1993); *Yeah, Yeah, Yeah, Yeah* (Kill Rock Stars/Catcall, 1993, with Huggy Bear: *Our Troubled Youth*); *Reject all American* (Kill Rock Stars, 1996); *The Singles* (Kill Rock Stars, 1998)

MARION LEONARD

Billings, William (*b* Boston, MA, 7 Oct 1746; *d* Boston, 26 Sept 1800). Composer and singing teacher. He exerted a strong influence on the development of church music in New England during the 1770s and 80s, and subsequently throughout the United States, where his tunes and anthems were widely sung in churches, singing-schools, and at social gatherings. The contemporary diarist William Bentley described him as "the father of our New England music."

1. Life. 2. Works.

1. Life. Little is known of Billings's early life, but he probably had only a rudimentary formal education. In 1760 after the death of his father, a Boston shopkeeper, he was apprenticed to a tanner, a trade at which he seems to have worked off and on for much of his life. His musical education is undocumented, but he most likely attended singing schools in Boston and may also have participated in informal choral societies that met for the recreational singing of Psalmody. Lindstrom claimed, without presenting evidence, that Billings studied with the Boston singing master John Barry. He may also have received some instruction from Josiah Flagg and William Selby, though this was probably only occasional advice and criticism of his early compositions. Billings is thought to have been largely self-taught in music, gaining his knowledge from the study of the compositions and theoretical writings of such English psalmodists as William Tans'ur, Aaron Williams, John Arnold, and Uriah Davenport.

Billings began teaching Singing-school by 1769. Most of his activities were centered in and around Boston, although he taught briefly in Providence, Rhode Island, in 1774. In the same year he taught a school in Stoughton, Massachusetts, where one of his pupils was Lucy Swan, whom he married on 26 July 1774. The couple had nine children. Bentley described Billings as "a singular man, of moderate size, short of one leg, with one eye, without any address, and with an uncommon negligence of person. Still he spake and sung and thought as a man above the common abilities." Nathaniel D. Gould added that he had "a stentorian voice," one arm that was somewhat withered, and a propensity for taking large quantities of snuff (*Church Music in America*, 1853/*R*1972). In spite of his physical handicaps, Billings was a very successful singing master, teaching at fashionable Boston churches, including Brattle Street Church, Old South Church, First Church, and Stone Chapel. By 1780 he was affluent enough to purchase a house at 89 Newbury Street, and was a pew holder at the Hollis Street Church.

During the Revolutionary War, Billings was an active supporter of and advocate for the patriot cause, befriended by such revolutionaries as Samuel Adams, Rev. Samuel Cooper, and Paul Revere. The full extent of his activities is undocumented, but his support is affirmed by his patriotic compositions, such as the anthems *Lamentation over Boston* and *Independence* (both SMA) and psalm tunes like "Chester" (NEPS and SMA).

In the late 1780s, Billings's fortunes declined, and he accepted a succession of minor municipal appointments—scavenger, hogreeve, and sealer of leather. In 1790 a public concert was held for his benefit, the advertisement assuring the public that his "distress is real." Soon afterwards Billings mortgaged his house and tried to sell the rights to his music to the publishing firm of Thomas & Andrews. That firm did issue Billings's final tunebook in 1794, not as the business venture Billings proposed, but as a charitable enterprise sponsored by several musical societies in Boston and paid for by subscription. Billings's wife died in March 1795, leaving him with six children under the age of 18. He continued his activities as a singing master and retained the post of sealer of leather until 1796. On his death he left an estate valued after the payment of debts at slightly more than $800 (mostly the value of his house), and he was buried in an unmarked grave, probably in the Boston Common.

2. Works. Billings wrote over 340 compositions: mostly psalm and hymn tunes, but also 51 fuging tunes, four canons, and 52 anthems and set-pieces. All his music is for four-voice unaccompanied chorus, although he included parts for unspecified instruments in two of his anthems; such instruments as flute, clarinet, bassoon, violin, viola, and cello could double the vocal parts. The principal melody in his psalm and hymn tunes was assigned to the tenor voice, but Billings expressed the wish that some treble voices should double the tenor an octave higher, and vice versa, producing a full choral sound in which the tenor and treble lines are closely intertwined and vie for the listener's attention. Billings employed an additive compositional technique, in which the tenor melody was composed first, then the

Frontispiece engraving, William Billings' The New-England Psalm-Singer, *Boston, 1770. (Library of Congress, Performing Arts Encyclopedia)*

bass according to rules of consonant counterpoint, then the treble to provide a countermelody to the tenor, and finally the counter (or alto). All parts often share common musical motifs, but each usually maintains a good deal of rhythmic and melodic independence. The harmony is contrapuntally derived and, while related to functional tonality (particularly at cadences), it does not usually follow common 18th-century European harmonic formulas, but employs techniques similar to Renaissance polyphony.

The New-England Psalm-Singer (1770) was the first of Billings's six tunebooks, and the first published collection to be devoted exclusively to American compositions and to the music of a single American composer. The variety of its contents, ranging from psalm tunes of stark simplicity to florid hymn tunes and fairly complex polyphonic anthems, suggests that Billings had been composing for a number of years; the announcement in its preface that a second volume of music "consisting chiefly of Anthems, Fuges, and Chorus's" would be published if the first met "with Encouragement" supports this hypothesis. (The publication of the second volume was delayed by the political events of the 1770s, appearing only in part and undoubtedly greatly revised, as *The Psalm-Singer's Amusement* in 1781.) Paul Revere engraved the frontispiece for *The New-England Psalm-Singer*, which shows a group of gentlemen sitting around a table singing from several open tunebooks. There is no evidence to support the popular belief that Revere engraved the music in the book; that task was probably undertaken by Billings himself using Josiah Flagg's engraving tools. The volume includes a lengthy essay "On the Nature and Properties of Sound" by Charles Stockbridge, and Billings's own somewhat discursive but informative theoretical introduction, in which he states: "I don't think myself confined to any Rules for Composition laid down by any that went before me," and "it is best for every *Composer* to be his own *Carver*." These remarks have been considered by some writers to be Billings's declaration of musical independence, but they do not seem so radical when read in context. Although Billings surpassed in talent and esteem most other American psalmodists of his day, he did not attempt to forge a new style or create new modes of expression. He accepted the forms and techniques passed on to him by earlier church composers, adapting them to his needs through his own unique abilities.

The music of *The New-England Psalm-Singer* is uneven in inspiration and insecure in technique. Some psalm tunes and all the anthems have prosodical problems, causing conflicts between the accents of the words and the music, but the collection includes some of Billings's most popular tunes, such as "Amherst,"

"Brookfield," "Chester," and "Lebanon." Billings denounced the contents in 1778, saying that "many of the pieces in that Book were never worth my printing, or your inspection," but the volume remains one of the most important American musical documents, setting the tone for and giving direction to American psalmody for 30 or 40 years following its publication.

In 1772 Billings received legislative approval of copyright for *The New-England Psalm-Singer*, but the governor of Massachusetts, for reasons undisclosed, refused to sign the act to bring it into law. Only one piece by Billings appeared before his next collection: the fuging-tune "Lanesborough," printed anonymously in John Stickney's *The Gentleman and Lady's Musical Companion* (1774). "Lanesborough" already shows significant musical growth.

Billings's second tunebook, *The Singing Master's Assistant* (1778), was published for use in his singing schools and clearly shows the extent of his development during the intervening years. Not only are problems of prosody completely eliminated, but the texts are set more imaginatively and with greater attention to musical effect; the melodies are more fluid and the counterpoint more deftly handled. Popularly known as "Billings's Best," *The Singing Master's Assistant* went through four editions between 1778 and 1789. Billings characterized it as "An Abridgement of the New-England Psalm-Singer," but over two-thirds of its contents were newly published pieces; he thoroughly revised tunes reprinted from *The New-England Psalm-Singer* and provided a better-organized, more succinct theoretical introduction. To increase its utility as a textbook, it was organized (apart from the first two pieces) to move progressively from simple to more complex pieces. The music clearly shows the various sides of Billings's personality: the conscientious and capable singing master, the ardent patriot, and the humorous wag. Among the patriotic pieces, already mentioned above, is "Chester," reprinted with four new verses by Billings including the line: "And gen'rals yield to beardless boys." Billings's sense of humor is shown in his literary satire in the introduction ("An Historical Account of G. Gamut") and mock dedication ("To the Goddess of Discord"), and in his musical joke, "Jargon," in which he deliberately misapplied the rules of composition to produce a work of unresolved dissonance. *The Singing Master's Assistant* also includes a variety of music in other moods, such as the lyrical anthem "I Am the Rose of Sharon"; the majestic psalm tune "Majesty" ("The Lord descended from above"); the touching set-piece *David's Lamentation* ("David, the king, was grieved and moved"); the somber *Funeral Anthem* ("I heard a great voice from heav'n"); and the madrigalistic fuging-tune "Dunstable" ("With earnest longings of the mind"). The collection richly deserved its high reputation and served later tunebook compilers as a major source for Billings's music, which (because it was not protected by copyright) was reprinted without permission of or compensation to the composer.

Music in Miniature (1779), designed to be bound with a metrical psalter and directed towards the congregational singer, is quite different from Billings's other tunebooks in that it contained only psalm tunes. Nearly half its 72 pieces were reprinted from *The Singing Master's Assistant* or *The New-England Psalm-Singer*, and Billings also included ten standard English psalm tunes in his own arrangements, the only instance of his publishing music other than his own. The music was printed without text, facilitating the singing of a tune to any psalm or hymn text that matched the meter of the music.

The Psalm-Singer's Amusement (1781), according to Billings "not for Learners," was issued to meet the needs of musical society and more advanced singers. In the variety of its settings and the virtuosity of its contents it holds a unique position in 18th-century psalmody. It is the smallest of Billings's tunebooks, containing only 24 works, but nearly half of these are substantial anthems and set pieces. In his brief prefatory remarks Billings stated that "This work is a Part of the Book of Anthems, which I have so LONG promised." Although it cannot be determined precisely when any of Billings's pieces were composed—it is known that he held some works back for years before publishing them while others were never printed—it seems certain that any music in *The Psalm-Singer's Amusement* dating from early in his career was thoroughly revised. There is no evidence of technical weakness in any of the pieces; in choice of keys, text setting, fugal counterpoint, musical structure, and variety of effect, Billings may have reached his apex as a composer.

Among the noteworthy works in *The Psalm-Singer's Amusement* are two concert pieces, *Modern Musick* and *Consonance*, each describing the experience of attending a choral concert such as often closed a singing-school session. Several anthems make use of unusual keys, for example "And I Saw a Mighty Angel" (B major) and *Euroclydon* ("They that go down to the sea"; F♯ major)—both almost unknown in parish church psalmody. Others, such as "Who is This That Cometh," present an advanced complex of musical and textual imagery. The fuging-tune "Rutland" is unusual in that, from a beginning in A minor, it makes a modulation (uncommon in parish church psalmody) to D minor, then ends in C major.

In *The Suffolk Harmony* (1786) Billings seems to have been working towards a more refined style based on tuneful melody, greater variety of texture, closer integration of words and music, and a less flamboyant and more controlled musical language. Unlike his earlier tunebooks, *The Suffolk Harmony* does not seem to have been directed towards a particular group of users; it contains three anthems, four fuging-tunes, and 25 psalm and hymn tunes. A unique feature are 18 settings of Particular Meter texts by the English Universalist poets James and John Relly, which may have been intended for use by the Universalist Church in Boston. These settings, along with several by Watts and Billings's own Christmas hymn "Shiloh," have been described as "lovely part-songs on religious texts" rather than standard hymn tunes. *The Suffolk Harmony* was Billings's first collection to enjoy copyright protection (limited to the state of Massachusetts, however), and perhaps because of this and the intimate nature of the music, few pieces were reprinted by later tunebook compilers. Only "Jordan" enjoyed a popularity commensurate with some of Billings's earlier pieces.

The Continental Harmony (1794), published as a charitable act when the composer was in financial distress, appears to be a collection of pieces which Billings had composed at various times during his career. "Cobham" and "Victory," for example, are found in a manuscript dating from the early 1780s. The anthem "I Charge You, O Ye Daughters" is so close in style to "I Am the Rose of Sharon" (in *The Singing Master's Assistant*) that it is difficult not to conclude that they were composed at the same time. The fuging-tune "Great Plain" has prosodical problems not found in any piece by Billings outside *The New-England Psalm-Singer*, and the *Anthem for Ordination* ("O thou to whom all creatures bow") contains whole sections of music that had been published earlier in *Retrospect* ("Was not the day," in *The Singing Master's Assistant*) and *Peace* ("God is the king," *c*1783). Other tunes, such as "Adams," "Cross Street," "Hopkinton," and "Sudbury," and anthems, including *An Anthem for Thanksgiving* ("O clap your hands"), *Deliverance* ("I will love thee"), seem to tread stylistic paths laid out in *The Suffolk Harmony*. The anthem *Variety without Method* ("O God, thou hast been displeased") breaks new ground by introducing extensive changes of key into Billings's music, and seems, as the title hints at, to be an experiment in modulation techniques. Although the theoretical introduction to *The Singing Master's Assistant* was reprinted in *The Continental Harmony*, Billings supplemented it with an extended commentary on the rules of music in the form of a dialogue between a master and a scholar. This commentary provides many insights into Billings's thought and style and clearly indicates that he was familiar with a wide range of historical and theoretical literature on music.

In addition to his six collections Billings published a small number of pieces independently during the 1780s and 90s. These include *An Anthem for Easter* ("The Lord is ris'n indeed"; 1787, rev. 1795), which remains the most popular anthem by an 18th-century American composer, probably never having been completely out of print to the present day. He seems also have allowed a few of his unpublished tunes to be issued by others: for example, "Union" appeared in *The Worcester Collection* (2/1788) and "Mansfield" in *The Boston Collection* (*c*1799). Billings's last-known composition was *A Piece on the Death of Washington* (1799), mentioned in a list of his works drawn up after his death by Nahum Mitchell. Billings probably died before the work could be published, and it does not appear to have survived in manuscript. Some of his unpublished tunes—not in his hand, however—are found in manuscripts at the University of Michigan, Ann Arbor; the Massachusetts Historical Society; the Watkinson Library at Trinity College, Hartford; the Music Division, New York Public Library for the Performing Arts; and the private collection of Mrs. Dorothy Waterhouse of Boston. These manuscripts also contain tunes that are rhythmic, melodic, or structural variants of published pieces, suggesting the recycling of old works.

Billings also engaged in literary activity and was a poet of imagination if not distinction. Each of his tunebooks (apart from *Music in Miniature*) includes some of his poetry and prose; "Shiloh" (in *The Suffolk Harmony*) is perhaps the most successful of his texts. The words for most of his anthems were selected from various biblical and poetical verses, but Billings frequently altered them, supplying new words and phrases to create a stronger image, a more definite mood, or to provide opportunities for musical development. In 1783 he edited one issue of the *Boston Magazine* that so upset Boston's gentlemen that he was relieved of the editorship. The following year he published a satire on Puritan hypocrisy entitled *The Porcupine, Alias the Hedge-hog, or Fox Turned Preacher*. He may have issued other literary pamphlets that have not survived or are anonymous.

Billings's music reached the height of its popularity in the 1780s and 90s when it was reprinted and performed throughout the United States. In 1786 the publisher Isaiah Thomas wrote: "For the progress of Psalmody in this country the Publick are in a great measure indebted to the musical abilities of Mr. WILLIAM BILLINGS, of Boston." In 1788 a Philadelphia critic posed Billings as "the rival of Handel," predicting that "the English will pay proper tribute to his merits as soon as they are acquainted with his productions." A small step toward that acquaintance came the following year when Thomas Williams included two of Billing's tunes, "Marshfield" and "New England" (i.e. "Hartford"), in his *Psalmodia Evangelica* and about five years later John Rippon included "Spillman" (i.e. "Consolation") in his *Selection of Psalm and Hymn Tunes* (*c*1795). These are among the few American pieces to find a place in English tunebooks.

See also Psalmody.

WORKS

Edition: *The Complete Works of William Billings*, ed. K. Kroeger and H. Nathan, 4v. (Charlottesville, VA, and Boston, 1977–90)

Catalog: K. Kroeger, *Catalog of the Musical Works of William Billings*, Music Reference Collection, 32 (Westport, CT, 1991)

Collections: *The New-England Psalm-singer* (Boston, 1770) [NEPS]

The Singing Master's Assistant, or Key to Practical Music (Boston, 1778/*R*, 4/1786–9/*R*) [SMA]

Music in Miniature (Boston, 1779) [MM]

The Psalm-singer's Amusement (Boston, 1781/*R*1974) [PSA]

The Suffolk Harmony (Boston, 1786) [SH]

The Continental Harmony (Boston, 1794/*R*1961) [CH]

Waterhouse MS, private collection of D. Waterhouse, Boston [W]

PSALM AND HYMN TUNES

(—version with fuging chorus listed under "Fuging-tunes")*

Adams, CH; Africa, NEPS, rev. SMA, MM; Albany, NEPS; America, NEPS, rev. SMA, MM; Amherst, NEPS, rev. SMA, MM; Andover (i), NEPS; Ashford, NEPS; Ashham, SMA; Asia (i), NEPS; Asia (ii), MM; Attleborough, NEPS; *Aurora, MM

Baltimore, SMA; Baptism, SH; Barre, NEPS; Bedford, in *Sacred Harmony* (Boston, *c*1788) [variant of Waltham]; Bellingham, CH; Beneficence, SH; Bennington, W [variant of Friendship]; Berlin, PSA; *Bethlehem, MM; Bolton, SMA; Boston, NEPS, rev. SMA; Bradford, W [variant of Consolation]; Braintree, NEPS; Brattle Square, SH; Brattle

Street, NEPS; Brest, MM; Bridgwater, NEPS; Brookfield, NEPS, rev. SMA, MM; Brookline, NEPS, rev. MM; Brunswick, SMA; Burlington, SH

Calvary, MM, rev. CH as St. Thomas; Cambridge, NEPS, rev. SMA, MM; Camden, SH; Charlston, NEPS; Chelsea (i), NEPS; Chelsea (ii), SH; Chester, NEPS, rev. SMA, MM; Chesterfield, NEPS; Chocksett, SMA, MM; Claremont, CH; Cobham (Raynham), CH; Columbia, SMA, MM; Concord, NEPS; Connection, SMA, MM, CH; Conquest, SH; Consolation, SMA; Corsica, NEPS; *Creation, MM; Cross Street, CH; *Crucifiction, MM; Cumberland, NEPS

Danbury, MM; Dedham (i), NEPS; Deerfield, see Thomas-town; Delaware, MM; Dickinson, NEPS; Dighton, NEPS; Dorchester, NEPS, rev. SMA; Dublin, MM; Dudley, MM; Dunstable (i), *MHi* [variant of Saybrook]; *Dunstable (ii), MM; Duxborough, NEPS, rev. SMA, MM

Eastham, NEPS; East Sudbury, CH; Easttown, NEPS; Eden, SH; Effingham, in *Massachusetts Harmony* (Boston, 1784) [variant of Dickinson (NEPS)]; The 18th Psalm, NEPS; Election, SH; Emanuel, PSA; Emmaus, SMA, MM; Essex, NEPS; *Europe, MM; Exeter, SMA

Fairfield, NEPS; Fitchburgh, MM; *Framingham, MM; Franklin, MM; Freedom, NEPS; Friendship, NEPS

Georgia (i), NEPS; Georgia (ii), MM; Germantown, *MHi*; Gloucester, SH; Golgotha, PSA; Gospel Pool, in J. Ingalls: *Christian Harmony* (Exeter, NH, 1805) [excerpt from Was Not the Day, see "Anthems and Set-Pieces"]; Greenland, NEPS

Hacker's Hall, W; Halifax, SMA, MM; Hampshire (i), NEPS; Hampshire (ii), MM; Hamton, NEPS; Hanover, NEPS; Hanover New, NEPS; Hartford, PSA, SH; Harvard, NEPS; Hatfield, first pubd in posth. edn of PSA (n.p., *c*1804); Haverill, NEPS; Hebron (i), NEPS, rev. SMA, MM; Hingham, NEPS; Holden, NEPS; Hollis, NEPS; Hollis Street, NEPS, rev. SMA; Hull, SH

Ipswich, NEPS

Jamaica (i), NEPS; Jamaica (ii), MM; Jargon, SMA; Jerusalem, SH; Jordan, SH; Judea, SMA

Lancaster (Shirley), NEPS; The Lark (Boston, 1790); Lebanon, NEPS, rev. SMA, MM; Lewis-town, CH; Lexington, NEPS; Liberty, NEPS; Lincoln, NEPS; Lynn, NEPS

Madrid, MM, SH; Majesty, SMA; Malden, NEPS; *Manchester, MM; Mansfield (i), MM; Mansfield (ii), in *The Boston Collection* (Boston, *c*1799); Marblehead, NEPS, rev. SMA; Marshfield, NEPS, rev. SMA, MM; *Maryland, MM; Massachusetts, NEPS; Medfield, NEPS, rev. SMA; Medford, NEPS; Mendom, PSA, SH; Middlesex, NEPS; Middletown, NEPS; Moravia, SH; Moriah, SH; *Morpheus, MM; Morriston, W [variant of Medfield]

Nantasket, NEPS; Nantucket, NEPS; Nazareth, MM; New Boston, NEPS; Newburn, MM; New-castle, MM; New Haven, W [variant of Duxborough]; New Hingham, NEPS, rev. SMA, MM [variant of Hingham]; New North, NEPS, rev. SMA, MM; Newport, NEPS; New South, NEPS, rev. SMA, MM; New Town, NEPS; Norfolk, CH; North River, NEPS; no.45, NEPS; Nutfield, NEPS; Old Brick, NEPS; Old North, NEPS

Old South, NEPS; Orange Street, NEPS; Orleans, NEPS; Oxford, MM

Paris, MM; Pembroke, NEPS; Pembroke New, NEPS; Petersburgh, SH; *Philadelphia, MM; Philanthropy, SH; Phoebus, SMA; Pitt, NEPS; Plainfield, NEPS; Pleasant Street, NEPS; Plymouth New, in J. French; *Harmony of Harmony* (Northampton, MA, 1802); Plymton, NEPS; Pomfret, NEPS; Pownall, NEPS; Princetown, NEPS, rev. SMA, MM; Providence, NEPS; Pumpily, NEPS, rev. SMA, MM; Purchase Street (i), NEPS; Purchase Street (ii), MM

Queen Street, NEPS

Raleigh, in A. Maxim: *Northern Harmony* (Hollowell, ME, 1819), [doubtful]; Raynham, see Cobham; Resignation, PSA; Restoration, SH; Resurrection (Boston, 1787); *Revelation, MM; Richmond, SMA, SH; Rochester, CH; Roxbury (i), NEPS; Roxbury (ii), SMA, MM

St. Elisha's, NEPS; St. John's, CH; St. Peter's, in A. Pilsbury: *United States Sacred Harmony* (Boston, 1799) [variant of Savannah]; St. Thomas, CH [rev. of Calvary]; St. Vincent's, in *Sacred Harmony* (Boston, *c*1788) [variant of Concord]; Sappho, NEPS, rev. SMA; Savannah, SMA; Saybrook, MM; Scituate, NEPS; Sharon, SMA; Sherburne, SMA, MM; Shiloh, SH; Shirley, see Lancaster; Sinai, SH; Smithfield, NEPS; South-Boston, CH; Spain, SMA, MM; Spencer, W [variant of Bolton]; Stockbridge, SMA; Stoughton, NEPS; Sturbridge, MM; Sudbury (i), NEPS; Sudbury (ii), CH; Suffolk, NEPS, rev. SMA, MM; Sullivan, SMA; Summer Street, NEPS; Sunday, SMA; Swanzey, NEPS

Thomas-town (Deerfield), CH; Tower Hill, NEPS; Trinity-New, MM

Union (i), NEPS; Union (ii), in *The Worcester Collection* (Worcester, MA, 2/1788); Unity, NEPS; Uxbridge, NEPS

Vermont, SMA; Victory, CH

Waltham, NEPS, rev. SMA, MM; *Wareham, MM; Warren, SMA; Water Town, NEPS; Wellfleet, NEPS; West Boston, SH; Westfield, NEPS; West-Sudbury, CH; Wheeler's Point, NEPS; Wilks, NEPS; Williamsburgh, NEPS; Worcester, SMA; Wrentham, SMA, MM

FUGING TUNES

(—version without fuging chorus listed under "Psalm and hymn tunes")*

Adoration, PSA; Andover (ii), PSA; Assurance, PSA; *Aurora, SMA;

Benevolence, SMA; *Bethlehem, SMA; The Bird (Boston, 1790); Brattle Street, SH; Broad Cove, CH;

Cohasset, CH; *Creation, CH; *Crucifiction (Boston, 1787);

Dartmouth, W [variant of New North, see "Psalm and hymn tunes"]; Dedham (ii), CH; *Dunstable, SMA;

Egypt, CH; *Europe, NEPS;

*Framingham, PSA;

Gilead, CH; Great Plain, CH;

Hadley, *CtHT-W* [variant of opening section of Hark, hark, Hear You Not, see "Anthems and Set-pieces"]; Heath, SMA; Hebron (ii), in A. Pilsbury: *United States Sacred Harmony* (Boston, 1799) [variant of Northborough]; Hopkinton, CH;

Invocation, CH; Kittery, SH;

Lanesborough, in J. Stickney: *The Gentleman and Lady's Musical Companion* (Newburyport, MA, 1774);

*Manchester, PSA; *Maryland, SMA; Medway, SMA; Milton, NEPS; Morning-hymn, CH; *Morpheus, W;

New Plymouth, CH; Northborough, SH [variant of Lanesborough]; North Providence, SMA; Paria, in *Massachusetts Harmony* (Boston, 1874); *Philadelphia, SMA;

Redemption, PSA, *Revelation, CH; Rocky Nook, CH; Rutland, PSA

St. Andrew's, CH; St. Enoch, CH; Sheffield, in J. Huntington: *Apollo Harmony* (Northampton, MA, 1807)

Taunton, NEPS

*Wareham, PSA; Washington, SMA; Washington Street, CH; Weymouth, CH; Wheeler's Point, SH

ANTHEMS AND SET-PIECES

And I Saw a Mighty Angel, PSA; As the Hart Panteth, NEPS;

The Beauty of Israel, PSA; Behold How Good and Joyful (Union), SH; Blessed Is He That Considereth (i), NEPS; Blessed Is He That Considereth (ii), PSA; By the Rivers of Watertown (Lamentation over Boston), SMA

David, the King, Was Grieved and Moved (David's Lamentation), SMA; Down Steers the Bass (Consonance), PSA

Except the Lord Build the House (Boston, *c*1787–90)

God Is the King (Peace) (Boston, *c*1783)

Hark, Hark, Hear You Not (Anthem for Christmas), CH; Have Pity on Me, *MHi* [variant of Samuel the Priest]; Hear, Hear, O Heav'ns (Anthem for Fast Day), CH; Hear My Prayer, O Lord (i) (Anthem for Fast Day), NEPS; Hear My Prayer, O Lord (ii), SMA; The Heavens Declare (Sublimity), CH

I Am Come into My Garden, CH; I Am the Rose of Sharon, SMA; I Charge You, O Ye Daughters, CH; I Heard a Great Voice from Heav'n (Funeral Anthem), SMA; I Love the Lord (Gratitude), SMA; I Will Love Thee (Deliverance), CH; Is Any Afflicted, SMA

Let Ev'ry Mortal Ear Attend, PSA; Lift Up Your Eyes, SH; The Lord Descended From Above, NEPS; The Lord is King, NEPS; The Lord Is Ris'n Indeed (Anthem for Easter) (Boston, 1787), rev. pub 1795, lost, repr. in *The Village Harmony* (Exeter, NH, 5/1800); Mourn, Mourn, Mourn (Anthem for Fast Day), CH; My Friends I Am Going (The Dying Christian's Last Farewell), CH

O Clap Your Hands (Anthem for Thanksgiving) (Boston, *c*1787–90); O God, My Heart is Fixed, CH; O God, Thou Hast Been Displeased (Variety without Method), CH; O Praise God (Universal Praise), CH; O Praise the Lord of Heaven (Anthem for Thanksgiving), CH; O Thou to Whom All Creatures Bow (Anthem for Ordination), CH

Praise the Lord, O My Soul, *NN-L*;

Samuel the Priest (Funeral Anthem), SH; Sanctify a Fast, CH; Sing Praises to the Lord (Anthem for Thanksgiving Day Morning), CH; Sing Ye Merrily, SMA; The States, O Lord (Independence), SMA

They That Go Down to the Sea (Euroclydon), PSA; Thou, O God, Art Praised, PSA
Vital Spark of Heav'nly Flame (The Dying Christian to his Soul), PSA
Was Not the Day (Retrospect), SMA; We Are Met for a Concert (Modern Musick), PSA; We Have Heard with Our Ears, CH; When the Lord Turned Again, CH; Who Is This That Cometh from Edom?, PSA

CANONS
(all in NEPS)

Thus Saith the High, the Lofty One; Wake Ev'ry Breath; When Jesus Wept; Canon 4 in 1 [no text]

LOST WORKS

I Was Glad When They Said Unto Me, anthem, perf. Boston, 13 March 1785; A Piece on the Death of Washington, 1799, listed by Mitchell

WRITINGS

ed.: *The Boston Magazine* (Oct 1783)
The Porcupine, Alias the Hedge-hog, or Fox Turned Preacher (Boston, 1784)

BIBLIOGRAPHY

"An Account of Two Americans of Extraordinary Genius in Poetry and Music," *Columbian Magazine*, ii (1788), 211
N. Mitchell: "William Billings," *Musical Reporter*, i (1841), 297
F.J. Metcalf: *American Writers and Compilers of Sacred Music* (New York, 1925/R 1967)
C. Lindstrom: "William Billings and His Times," *MQ*, xxv/4 (1939), 479–97
R. Morin: "William Billings: Pioneer in American Music," *New England Quarterly*, xiv/1 (1941), 25–33
A. Garrett: *The Works of William Billings* (diss., U. of North Carolina, 1952)
J.M. Barbour: *The Church Music of William Billings* (East Lansing, MI, 1960)
H. Nathan: Introduction to facs. of W. Billings: *The Continental Harmony* (1794) (Cambridge, MA, 1961)
J.M. Barbour: "Billings and the Barline," *American Choral Review*, v/2 (1963), 1–5
H.W. Hitchcock: "William Billings and the Yankee Tunesmiths," *Hi Fi/Stereo Review*, xvi/2 (1966), 55
R. Crawford and D. McKay: "The Performance of William Billings' Music," *JRME*, xxi/4 (1973), 318–30
D. McKay: "William Billings and the Colonial Music 'Patent,'" *Old-Time New England*, lxiii (1973), 100–07
H. Nathan: "William Billings: a Bibliography," *Notes*, xxix/4 (1973), 658–69
R. Crawford and D McKay: "Music in Manuscript: a Manuscript Tunebook of 1782," *Proceedings of the American Antiquarian Society*, lxxxiv (1974), 43–64
G.B. Anderson: "'Samuel the Priest Gave up the Ghost' and *The Temple of Minerva*: Two Broadsides," *Notes*, xxxi/3 (1975), 493–516
D.P. McKay and R. Crawford: *William Billings of Boston: Eighteenth-century Composer* (Princeton, NJ, 1975)
H. Nathan: *William Billings: Data and Documents* (Detroit, 1976)
S. Gryc: "Explicating William Billings's 'Jargon,'" *In Theory Only*, iii/1 (1977), 22–8
G. Anderson: "Eighteenth-century Evaluations of William Billings: a Reappraisal," *Quarterly Journal of the Library of Congress*, xxxv (1978), 48–58
K. Kroeger: "William Billings's Music in Manuscript Copy and Some Notes on Variant Versions of His Pieces," *Notes*, xxxix/2 (1982), 316–45
M.G. De Jong: "'Both Pleasure and Profit': William Billings and the Uses of Music," *William and Mary Quarterly*, xlii/1 (1985), 104–16
K. Kroeger: "William Billings and the Hymn Tune," *The Hymn*, xxxvii (1986), 19–26
K. Kroeger: "William Billings's 'Anthem for Easter': The Persistence of an Early American 'Hit,'" *Proceedings of the American Antiquarian Society*, xcvii/1 (1987), 105–28
K. Kroeger: "Word Painting in the Music of William Billings," *AM*, vi/1 (1988), 41–64
A. Schrader: "'Wilks,' 'No.45,' and Mr. Billings," *AM*, vii/4 (1989), 412–29
N. Cooke: "William Billings in the District of Maine," *AM*, ix/3 (1991), 243–59
K. Kroeger: "William Tans'ur's Influence on William Billings," *Inter-American Music Review*, xi/2 (1991), 1–12
K. Kroeger: "William Billings and the Puritan Musical Ideal," *Studies in Puritan American Spirituality*, ii (1992), 31
R. Crawford: *The American Musical Landscape* (Berkeley, CA, 1993)
N. Cooke: "William Billings: Representative American Psalmodist?" *The Quarterly Journal of Music Teaching and Learning*, vii/1 (1996), 47–64
M. Fawcett-Yeske: "Stylistic Development in the Fuging Tunes of William Billings," *The Quarterly Journal of Music Teaching and Learning*, vii (1996), 32–46
G.N. Heller: "William Billings (1746–1800): Sources and Resources," *Bulletin of Historical Research in Music Education*, xviii/1 (1996), 49–70
K. Kroeger: "William Billings Sets the Tune," *The Hymn*, xlvii/4 (1996), 8–13
K. Kroeger: "William Billings's *The Singing Master's Assistant* as a Pedagogical Aid for Singing Schools," *The Quarterly Journal of Music Teaching and Learning*, vii/1 (1996), 18–29
K. Kroeger: "Two Unknown Billings Compositions in John Norman's *The Massachusetts Harmony* (1784)," *The Hymn*, xlvii (1996), 44
D. Music: "William Billings in the Southern Fasola Tunebooks, 1816–1853," *The Hymn*, xlvii (1996), 14
M. Fonder: "William Billings: A Patriot's Life?" *Journal of Historical Research in Music Education*, xix/1 (1997), 1–9
S. Howe: "The Tune Books of William Billings: Music Education in the Eighteenth Century," *Journal of Historical Research in Music Education*, xx/1 (1998), 43–55
E.S. Miller: "'Every Composer His Own Carver': the Manliness of William Billings," *Historical Journal of Massachusetts*, xxvii (1999), 117–39
E. Crist: "'Ye Sons of Harmony': Politics, Masculinity, and the Music of William Billings in Revolutionary Boston," *William and Mary Quarterly*, lx/2 (2003), 333–54
M. Broyles: *Mavericks and Other Traditions in American Music* (New Haven, 2004)
K. Kroeger: "William Billings: Nordamerikas förste kompositör av vikt," *Tidig Musik*, no.2 (2011), 9–12

KARL KROEGER

Billy Ward and His Dominoes. Vocal group. It was formed in 1950 by Billy Ward (*b* Robert L. Williams, Savannah, GA, 19 Sept 1921; *d* Inglewood, CA, 16 Feb 2002) along with a number of his vocal students. Initially the African American group performed at a number of New York talent shows, including those that were regularly held at the Apollo Theater, until they were signed to Federal Records and released their first single "Do Something for Me." It was quickly followed by the widely successful "Sixty Minute Man," which made both the R&B and pop charts in 1951 and is sometimes cited as an early example of rock and roll. The group had continued success throughout the 1950s with hits such as "Have Mercy Baby," "St. Therese of the Roses," and "Stardust," though none of these records met with the same level of success as "Sixty Minute Man."

The group's legacy is important to R&B and the early history of rock and roll. Their hit "Sixty Minute Man" was extremely popular with both black and white audiences and pushed the boundary for acceptable lyrics with its overtly sexual language. The single was initially banned by a number of radio stations, but it grew in popularity and was eventually covered by a number of white artists. The group also is known for helping launch the careers of successful R&B singers CLYDE MCPHATTER and JACKIE WILSON.

BIBLIOGRAPHY

D. Carter: *The Black Elvis: Jackie Wilson* (Berkeley, CA, 1998)

J. Miller: *Flowers in the Dustbin: the Rise of Rock and Roll, 1947–1977* (Whitby, ON, 2000)

RYAN KIRK

Bilson, Malcolm (*b* Los Angeles, CA, 24 Oct 1935). Pianist and fortepianist. After receiving his BA from Bard College in 1957, Bilson studied with Grete Hinterhofer at the Akademie für Musik und Darstellende Kunst in Berlin, with Reine Gianoli at the Ecole Normale de Musique in Paris, and with Stanley Fletcher and WEBSTER AITKEN at the University of Illinois (DMA 1968). In 1991, he received an honorary doctorate from Bard College. Appointed to the faculty of Cornell University in 1968, Bilson became a full professor in 1976 and the Frederick J. Whiton Professor of Music in 1990. In 1969 he purchased one of the first five-octave fortepianos by Philip Belt, based on a Louis Dulcken original in the Smithsonian Institution, and in 1977 he acquired a copy by Belt of Wolfgang Amadeus Mozart's Walter concert instrument. Bilson was one of the first artists to make a persuasive case for the use of period instruments in Viennese Classical music. He achieved this through stylish and imaginative performances that took the idiomatic capabilities of the fortepiano as their starting point. In the 1980s, Bilson recorded a pioneering cycle of Mozart's complete piano concertos with John Eliot Gardiner and the English Baroque Soloists. In 1994, he and six former students gave the world's first period-instrument performance of all of Beethoven's piano sonatas. Other recordings include all of Mozart's sonatas for piano and violin (with Sergiu Luca), Ludwig van Beethoven's sonatas for piano and cello (with Anner Bylsma), and Franz Schubert's piano sonatas. Bilson's interest in interpreting notation within the parameters of the performance practices of its time resulted in his pedagogical DVD *Knowing the Score* (2005).

ROBERT WINTER/CECILIA SUN

Bimboni, Alberto (*b* Florence, Italy, 24 Aug 1882; *d* New York, NY, 18 June 1960). Composer of Italian birth. He studied at the Cherubini Conservatory in Florence and began his career there as a conductor. As an accompanist he later worked with Enrico Caruso, Eugene Ysaÿe, and John McCormack; he was also active as an organist. In 1911 he immigrated to the United States, where he toured as a conductor with the Henry Savage Opera Company; he also conducted the Century Opera Company and later appeared at the Havana Opera House. He taught at the Curtis Institute and at the University of Pennsylvania and for 20 years was conductor of the Chautauqua Opera Association. For the last 26 years of his life he coached French and Italian at the Juilliard School.

Bimboni composed six operas, of which the most important is *Winona*, first performed by the American Grand Opera Company in Portland, Oregon, in 1926. Basing the opera on a Sioux-Dakota legend, Bimboni incorporated melodies that he had either collected from Minnesota Indians or obtained from the Smithsonian collection; overall, however, the opera's music may be likened to the idealized "Indian style" of his contemporary Charles Wakefield Cadman. Bimboni was awarded the David Bispham Memorial Medal when the opera was revived in Minneapolis in 1928. He also composed songs, including the collection *Songs of the American Indians* (1917). Further information is given in E.E. Hipsher: "Alberto Bimboni," *American Opera and its Composers* (Philadelphia, *c*1934); repr. with introduction by H. Earle Johnson (New York, 1978), 72–6.

WORKS

DRAMATIC

Calandrino (The Fire Worshippers), 1902 (1, after G. Boccaccio), ?unperf.

Fiaschi?! Delitto perpetrato dagli studenti W.C. e Costanzo Arrigoni (operetta-ballo, 3), Florence, 1903

Winona (3, P. Williams), Portland, OR, 11 Nov 1926

Karin, 1929–30 (3, C.W. Stork), unperf.

Il cancelleto d'oro (The Gilded Gate; There was a Gilded Gate) (1, A. Romano), New York, 11 March 1936

In the Name of Culture (1, N.F. Stolzenbach), Rochester, NY, 9 May 1949

OTHER WORKS

Lovelights, 1v, pf (1900); Preludio e fuga, org (1915); Red Day, 1v, pf (1917); Your Voices Raise, SATB; Mass "Cor Jesu, fons vitae" (1942)

THOMAS WARBURTON

Bing, Sir Rudolf (Franz Joseph) (*b* Vienna, Austria, 9 Jan 1902; *d* New York, NY, 2 Sept 1997). British impresario of Austrian birth. The son of an iron and steel magnate, he began his career in a Viennese bookshop whose proprietor soon branched out as an impresario of artistic events. In the 1920s Bing worked in Berlin before becoming assistant to Carl Ebert at the Hessisches Staatstheater in Darmstadt (1928–30), assistant to the Intendant of the Charlottenburg Opera, Berlin (1930–33), and general manager of the Glyndebourne Opera (1936–49), which he helped found. In 1946 he took British nationality and helped to found the Edinburgh Festival, of which he was artistic director from 1947 to 1949.

In 1950 Bing became general manager of the Metropolitan Opera, New York. His tenure (until 1972) was the second longest in its history. He had a great influence on both the company and American opera in the 1950s and 60s, his autocratic manner serving to improve standards of performance and direction. His emphasis on scenic design and imaginative direction reflected his European experience. During Bing's tenure, Marian Anderson became the first black performer to sing at the house, and he hired a number of other African American singers and dancers. He also extended the season to fill the whole year and supervised the move to Lincoln Center. In later years, however, like his predecessor Gatti-Casazza, he failed to develop strategies for coping with the economic and artistic climates of the period. In 1973 he was appointed Consultant for Special Projects by Columbia Artists Management. His *5000 Nights at the Opera* (New York, 1972) and *A Knight at the Opera* (New York, 1981) relate some of the many vicissitudes of his career. He was knighted in 1971.

PATRICK J. SMITH/MARIDA RIZZUTI

Bingham, Seth Daniels (*b* Bloomfield, NJ, 16 April 1882; *d* New York, NY, 21 June 1972). Organist and composer. He studied under HORATIO PARKER at Yale (BA 1904; BMus 1908) and in Paris with Vincent D'Indy, Charles-Marie Widor, Alexandre Guilmant, and HARRY BENJAMIN JEPSON (1906–7). After teaching at Yale from 1908 until 1919, he was a member of the music faculty of Columbia University until his retirement in 1954; he also held classes in advanced composition at the Union Theological Seminary and was for 35 years organist and music director at the Madison Avenue Presbyterian Church. Bingham was a prolific composer, whose rhythmic vitality, quasi-modal lines, and mildly chromatic contrapuntal textures can best be heard in his liturgical choral and organ works. Bingham also wrote numerous concertos, suites, and sonatas in a conservative, lyrical vein; perhaps his best-known secular work is the Concerto for brass, snare drum, and organ.

WORKS

Opera: La charelzenn, 1917

Chorus: Let God Arise, male vv, 1916; The Strife is O'er, 1916; Come thou Mighty King, 1916; Wilderness Stone, nar, solo vv, chorus, orch, 1933; Canticle of the Sun, chorus, orch, 1942; Perfect through Suffering, chorus, org, 1971; many other sacred choral works

Orch: Wall Street Fantasy, 1916; Passacaglia, 1918; Memories of France, 1920; Pioneer America, 1925; The Breton Cadence, 1928; Org Conc., 1946; Conc., brass, snare drum, org, 1954

Chamber: Suite, 9 wind, 1915; Str Qt, 1916; Tame Animal Tunes, 18 insts, 1918; Connecticut Suite, org, str, 1953; sonatas, suites

Org: Roulade, 1920–23; Suite, 1923; Pioneer America, 1926; Harmonies of Florence, 1928; Carillon de Château-Thierry, 1936; Pastoral Psalms, 1937; 12 Hymn-preludes, 1942; Baroques, suite, 1943; Variation Studies, 1950; 36 Hymn and Carol Canons, 1952; many other org pieces

Pubd songs, incl. An Old Song (1908), Brahma, The 4-way Lodge, 2 Japanese Songs

Principal publishers: J. Fischer, Gray, Peters, G. Schirmer

BIBLIOGRAPHY

P.J. Basch: "Seth Daniels Bingham: a Tribute," *Music: the AGO and RCCO Magazine*, vi/4 (1972), 32–3, 58–9 [incl. list of works]

M.S. Wright: "Seth Daniels Bingham: 100th Anniversary," *American Organist*, xvi/6 (1982), 40–43

H. WILEY HITCHCOCK/MICHAEL MECKNA

Binkerd, Gordon (Ware) (*b* Lynch, NE, 22 May 1916; *d* Urbana, IL, 5 Sept 2003). Composer. He studied the piano at Dakota Wesleyan University (BMus 1937), where Russell Danburg and GAIL KUBIK helped shape his musical thinking. After teaching in Kansas and Indiana, he pursued further training at the Eastman School of Music (MMus 1941). Following service in the US Navy during World War II, he entered Harvard University (MA 1952), where he studied with WALTER PISTON, IRVING FINE, OTTO KINKELDEY, and A.T. DAVISON, among others. From 1949 to 1971 he taught at the University of Illinois, Urbana-Champaign. His numerous honors include a Guggenheim Fellowship (1959), an award from the National Institute of Arts and Letters (1964), and commissions from the St. Louis SO, the Fromm and Ford foundations, and the McKim Fund of the Library of Congress. In 1996 a week-long series of concerts was organized at the University of Rhode Island and Brown University in celebration of his 80th birthday.

Binkerd's harmonic style developed from conventional tonality (in the early works, later withdrawn), through serialism (forsaken between the second and third movements of the First Symphony) and highly chromatic tonality (from the mid-1950s to the early 1980s), to simple but unconventional tonality (from the early 1980s). A deft handling of counterpoint is common to all of his compositions. In 1980 he began to concentrate on works for solo piano, an instrument he dubbed the "sonic machine," and on works for solo voice and piano. Also notable are his penetrating choral settings.

WORKS

(selective list)

Inst: Sonata, vc, pf, 1952; Sonata no.1, pf, 1955; Sym. no.1, orch, 1955; Trio, cl, va, vc, 1955; Service, org, 1957; Sym. no.2, orch, 1957; Str Qt no.1, 1958; Sym. no.3, orch, 1959; 3 Canzonas, brass, 1960; Entertainments, pf, 1960; Str Qt no.2, 1961; Concert Set, pf, 1969; Miscellany, pf, 1969; A Part of Heaven (2 Romances), vn, orch, 1972; The Battle, brass, perc, 1972 [after Frescobaldi]; Movt, orch, rev. 1972; Sonata, vn, pf, 1977; Str Trio, 1979; Sonata no.2, pf, 1981; Sonata no.3, pf, 1982; Sonata no.4, pf, 1983; short pf pieces; org works [several transcrs. orch, wind ens]; other chbr works

Choral: Autumn Flower (J. Very), 1968; To Electra (R. Herrick), 9 choruses, 1968–73; In a Whispering Gallery (T. Hardy), 1969; Nocturne (W.C. Williams), chorus, vc, 1969; A Christmas Carol (Herrick), 1970; A Scotch Mist (R. Burns), male vv, 3 choruses, 1976; Choral Strands (S. Freud, A. Tennyson), 4 choruses, 1976; Sung under the Silver Umbrella (G.K. Chesterton, W. Blake, J. Stephens, S. Mead, T. Moore), Tr vv, 6 choruses, pf, 1977; Requiem for Soldiers Lost in Ocean Transports (H. Melville), 1983–4; Houses at Dusk (H.W. Longfellow, H. Belloc, F.-G. Halleck, trad.), male vv, 4 choruses, pf, 1984; Dakota Day (Tennyson), mixed vv, fl, ob, cl, hp, 1985; *c*90 other choral works

Songs: Music I Heard with You (C. Aiken), 1v, pf, 1937; Shut out that Moon (Hardy), S/T, pf, 1968; 3 Songs (Herrick, A. Crapsey), Mez, str qt, 1971; Portrait intérieur (R.M. Rilke), 1v, vn, vc, 1972; 4 Songs, 1976; Secret-Love (J. Dryden), Mez, vc, hp, 1977; Shut out…Heart Songs (Burns), T, pf, 1980; 3 Songs from the Temple (G. Herbert), 1v, pf, 1985; Things Near and Far (4 Folk Songs of Wales), 1v, pf, 1987; 3 Dorset Songs (W. Barnes), S, pf, 1995; many other songs, 1v, pf

MSS in *R*

Principal publishers: Associated, Boosey & Hawkes, Peters, Samizdat

BIBLIOGRAPHY

GroveA (R.A. Monaco) [incl. further bibliography]

H. Pollack: "The Center Holding: Gordon Binkerd," *Harvard Composers* (Metuchen, NJ, 1992), 254–72

T. Duda: *What Sweeter Music: an Examination of Selected Later Songs of Gordon Binkerd with Suggestions for Performance* (diss., U. of Illinois, Urbana-Champaign, 1995)

D. Saladino: "An Interview with Gordon Binkerd," *Choral Journal*, xxxv/9 (1995), 33–41

THEODOR DUDA

Biography. An interpretive, historically informed account, usually of an individual or family, but also potentially of an object, association, building, institution, nation, or company whose creation, growth, development, and identity-formation invite analogies with living organisms. Scholarly biographies draw upon a range of sources including private and public documents and papers, correspondence, journals, memoirs, video footage and interview transcriptions, iconographic objects, previously written accounts, and, in the case of composers and performers, upon sketch materials, scores, reviews, and recordings. If the subject of the study is also the author, the work is called an autobiography.

While autobiographies may present information about a subject unknown to an autonomous author, they are also susceptible to a subject's limited perspective and desire to historicize himself or herself in specific ways. While "objectivity" may be desirable, it remains an elusive goal. Of late, bio-bibliographies have simplified the task of many scholars by combining a brief biographical sketch with a systematic annotated survey of relevant sources within the confines of a single book. The number of composers and musicians subject to this treatment continues to grow.

The earliest biographical studies of American musicians reflect a national culture that was home to sacred and secular, high-art and vernacular traditions. George Hood's 1846 pocketbook *A History of Music in New England with Biographical Sketches of Reformers and Psalmists* contains brief entries on 17 17th- and 18th-century clergymen for whom psalm singing was a common concern. Hood obtained his information from scant existing documents and letters and conversations with his subjects. In many cases the entries show Hood's respect, regard, and affection for his subjects. The first book-length biographical work dedicated to the study of a single family of American musicians may be Asa B. Hutchinson's 1852 work chronicling the experiences of his glee-singing siblings, *The Book of Brothers: History of the Hutchinson Family*. It was followed in 1874 and 1896 by other family members' accounts, offering additional perspectives.

Biographical studies can focus on one phase of a life or take the form of collections of letters or memoirs. In 1854 Lowell Mason published *Musical Letters from Abroad*, which was, in fact, a blend of his and his wife Abigail's writings. Although Mason was among the most highly regarded and influential musicians of the 19th century, and while numerous articles about him appeared regularly starting in the late 1870s, a free-standing biography would have to wait until Carol A. Pemberton's 1971 *Lowell Mason: his Life and Work*. Earlier books by Theodore F. Seward and Arthur L. Rich focused specifically upon Mason's work in music education.

Correspondence of two 19th-century pianists enjoyed wide circulation. Letters written by Amy Fay to her family detailing her experiences studying piano in Europe (1869–75) became *Music Study in Germany*. First published in 1880 with the help of Henry Wadsworth Longfellow, and printed 21 times in the United States alone prior to World War I, it inspired thousands of students to travel to Europe for music study. Although many writings about Louis Moreau Gottschalk had been published in monthly magazines in France and the United States during the composer/pianist's lifetime, keeping his name, music, and travels in the forefront of readers' minds, in 1881, 12 years after his death, *Notes of a Pianist* appeared. Given the popularity of traveling piano virtuosos and the importance of the instrument in domestic music-making, it comes as no surprise that the first free-standing biography of an African American musician is about the slave/pianist "Blind Tom" (Thomas Green Bethune), who was the subject of a booklet-length biography written in 1868 titled *The Marvelous Musical Prodigy, Blind Tom, the Negro Boy*. Beginning in the late 1930s biographies of African American jazz musicians began to appear with Louis Armstrong being among the first subjects treated in multiple studies.

Although 19th-century writers had begun to show interest in contemporary musicians, biographical writings that explored the lives of earlier American musicians were confined to relatively brief studies that appeared in surveys of American music or biographical dictionaries. In 1883 Frédéric Louis Ritter devoted the entire third chapter and parts of the fourth and fifth chapters of *Music in America* to a study of William Billings and his contemporaries. Additional editions of the book appeared in 1890 and 1900. Thomas Hastings, Lowell Mason, and Nathaniel D. Gould also received some attention. Perhaps striking given our current understanding of 19th-century American musical culture is the complete absence in Ritter's history of another influential early musician, Anthony Philip Heinrich. But while the Bohemian "American Beethoven" was forgotten or completely unknown by most national chroniclers until early in the 20th century, he did receive biographical attention as early as 1843 in Prague, where over a period of 14 years two books were published that chronicled his life and achievements. Such works fit into an established European biographical tradition. William Henry Fry and George Frederich Bristow, the century's two most celebrated native symphonists among scholars today, receive scant attention by Ritter or anyone else.

In 1889 W.S.B. Mathews published *A Hundred Years of Music in America: an Account of Music Effort in America*, a landmark book because of its size, breadth of coverage, and inclusion of graphics. It drew upon Ritter's book, and one written by F.O. Jones in 1886, *A Handbook of American Music and Musicians containing biographies of American Musicians and Histories of the Principal Musical Institutions, Firms, and Societies*. Mathews's 715 pages provided studies of over 500 men and women engaged in all aspects of the nation's music culture. He included native-born musicians and those whose careers brought them to the United States for extended periods of time. Brief references to the physical appearances of the subjects are enhanced with drawings, paintings, and photographs of many individuals as well as images of Oberlin College and the New England Conservatory of Music two of the first institutions dedicated to cultivating the nation's musical culture. Mathews drew upon materials provided by the subjects themselves "or their immediate representatives," resulting in considerable variation in the type and tone of information provided. Among subjects receiving relatively extensive coverage by Mathews are Lowell Mason and Stephen Foster. Foster became the sole subject of *Biography, Songs and Musical Compositions of Stephen Collins Foster* written by his brother Morrison in 1896. This highly selective and sympathetic portrayal of Foster went largely unchallenged for several generations until biographies by William Austin, Charles Hamm, and Ken Emerson presented more balanced readings of the composer.

Efforts to distinguish American musical life from its European forebears ramped up at the turn of the century as biographers strove to emphasize the uniqueness of the nation's culture through the subjects of their studies, who often portrayed themselves as free of influences or predecessors. In 1900 Rupert Hughes published *Famous American Composers: Being a Study of the Music of this Country, and of Its Future, with Biographies of the Leading Composers of the Present Time.* Hughes is unstintingly patriotic in his advocacy of American music and on multiple occasions emphasizes the unfortunate impact European, mostly German, practices and traditions had on the nation developing its own musical culture. Hughes's subjects are all American-born and he is the first to dedicate an entire section of a book to "The Women Composers" where Amy Beach and Margaret Ruthven Lang receive significant attention and approbation.

In 1905, Oscar G.T. Sonneck, the first prominent scholar and bibliographer dedicated to the study of American music, and the person who during his tenure as Chief of the Music Division at the Library of Congress secured and organized the complete works of Anthony Philip Heinrich among many others for that collection, published *Francis Hopkinson, the First American Poet-Composer (1737–1791) and James Lyon, Patriot, Preacher, Psalmodist (1735–1794).* With this composite monograph, Sonneck focused upon the two men often celebrated as the nation's original native composers. Their selection allowed him to address both the secular and sacred streams of American music that he recognized as central to the nation's culture. Sonneck's plan to write a biography on Heinrich, whom he regarded as "the most commanding figure as a composer in America before 1860," never came to pass.

In the 20th century biographies of American musicians continued to reflect the variety and range of the nation's musical culture and the porosity of boundaries between art and other types of music. The first two decades of the 20th century saw biographical studies on musicians as diverse as minstrel entertainers in Edward LeRoy Rice's 1909 *1000 men of minstrelsy and 1 woman which will include George Washington, John Adams, and Thomas Jefferson*, and the futurist Russian American pianist-composer Leo Ornstein in Frederick H. Martens's 1918 *Leo Ornstein, the Man, His Ideas, His Work,* written when Ornstein was just 25 years old. The 1930s and 40s saw the appearance of a variety of works focused upon earlier musicians: among these is John Tasker Howard's *Stephen Foster: America's Troubadour* (1934), H. Earle Johnson's 1943 *Musical Interludes in Boston, 1795–1830,* with its chapters devoted to the Von Hagen and Graupner families and the work of organist-composer George K. Jackson, and William Treat Upton's biography *Anthony Philip Heinrich: a Nineteenth-century Composer in America* published in 1939.

The publication of Henry and Sidney Cowell's hagiographic biography *Charles Ives and his Music* in 1955 signaled a trend toward the study of more recent musical figures, and Ives became the focus of extraordinary attention. Bicentennial fervor in the mid-1970s ignited many additional biographical projects of American musicians and Ives was among the chief beneficiaries. In 1975 Frank L. Rossiter published the first scholarly biography on the composer, *Charles Ives and His America.* Since that time the Connecticut composer has been the regular recipient of attention in numerous additional biographies, musical studies, essay collections, editions, reference guides, dissertations, and a steady stream of conference papers and journal articles.

The championing of Ives encouraged American music scholars' recovery efforts regarding a host of other composers, musicians, and music activists unknown to many in the musical community. Judith Tick's *Ruth Crawford Seeger: a Composer's Search for American Music* (1997), Adrienne Fried Block's *Amy Beach: Passionate Victorian* (1998), and Cyrilla Barr's *Elizabeth Sprague Coolidge: American Patron of Music* (1998) brought the achievements of three American women to the forefront of musicological studies. Since then biographies of Meredith Monk by Deborah Jowitt (1997) and Pauline Oliveros by Martha Mockus (2007), and carefully researched studies of women patrons and performers have expanded the understanding of women's interactions with and contributions to the nation's music culture. In the past 30 years many biographical works on musicians from across the spectrum of American music culture have appeared. Within art music, Aaron Copland, Lou Harrison, Harry Partch, William Grant Still, and Henry Cowell have been treated multiple times. Jazz musicians have also become the focus of biographies with Duke Ellington, Billie Holiday, Thelonious Monk, Miles Davis, John Coltrane, and Mary Lou Williams having numerous studies. Scholarly biographies of Leonard Bernstein, Johnny Cash, John Philip Sousa, John Lomax, Bill Monroe, Elvis Presley, and Stephen Sondheim reinforce the idea that American musical culture is high-art and popular, vernacular, and cultivated. University presses are among the greatest disseminators of American music scholarship. Independent presses have played an important role in publishing journalistic biographies of popular artists and musicians, although academics from cultural studies programs in literature and history have written some of the more insightful and compelling biographies of popular, country, and rock artists. Interest in American musical biography has grown so much that individual presses have launched specialized series focusing on particular genres such as the Yale University Press Broadway Musical Masters Series, with its volumes on George Gershwin, John Kander and Fred Ebb, Jerome Kern, Frank Loesser, Richard Rodgers, and Sigmund Romberg. Such an initiative has validated American musicals as a subject worthy of serious scholarly attention.

As a number of national musical institutions and associations have celebrated significant anniversaries, scholars have written biography-like accounts to mark the occasions. Studies on Carnegie Hall, the MacDowell Colony, the Juilliard School, the New York Philharmonic, the Auditorium Theater Building in Chicago, the John Simon Guggenheim Foundation, and the American

Musicological Society, among others, testify to the impact of collective action on American musical culture. The most recent biographies of American musicians acknowledge that diversity continues to be an essential quality of the nation's musical life. As postmodernism has challenged hierarchical thinking and contested the notion of who is biography-worthy, publishers have responded with biographical studies of people previously left out of conventional narratives. These studies are often of a decidedly non-hagiographic bent. While honoring "great men" continues to generate monographic studies, an increasing number of biographies devoted to individuals and groups of people who enjoy roles in American musical culture beyond that of composer, conductor, or performer appears to signal a trend toward the recognition of the depth and complexity of national identity as it is reflected in its music and musicians most broadly defined.

BIBLIOGRAPHY

G. Hood: *A History of Music in New England with Biographical Sketches of Reformers and Psalmists* (New York, 1846/*R*)
G. Hood: *History of the Hutchinson Family* (New York, 1852)
L. Mason: *Musical Letters from Abroad: Including Detailed Accounts of the Birmingham, Norwich, and Dusseldorf Musical Festivals of 1852* (New York, 1854)
A.B. Hutchinson: *Book of Words of the Hutchinson Family: to which is Added the Book of Brothers* (Boston, MA, 1857)
J. Hutchinson: *A Brief Narrative of the Hutchinson Family: Sixteen Sons and Daughters of the "Tribe of Jesse"* (Boston, MA, 1874)
A. Fay: *Music-Study in Germany: a Classic Memoir of the Romantic Era* (Chicago, 1880/*R*1965)
L.M. Gottschalk: *Notes of a Pianist: During his professional tours in the United States, Canada, the Antilles and South America: Preceded by a short biographical sketch with contemporaneous criticisms*, ed. C. Gottschalk, transl. R. E. Peterson (Philadelphia, PA, 1881/*R*1964)
T.F. Seward and A.W. Thayer: *The Educational Work of Dr. Lowell Mason* (?1885)
F.O. Jones: *A Handbook of American Music and Musicians, Containing Biographies of American Musicians, and Histories of the Principal Musical Institutions, Firms and Societies* (New York, 1886)
W.S.B. Mathews: *A Hundred Years of Music in America: an Account of Musical Effort in America* (Chicago, 1889)
M. Foster: *Biography, Songs and Musical Compositions of Stephen Collins Foster* (Pittsburgh, PA, 1896)
J.W. Hutchinson: *Story of the Hutchinsons (Tribe of Jesse)* (Boston, MA, 1896/*R*)
R. Hughes: *Famous American Composers: Being a Study of the Music of this Country, and of Its Future, with Biographies of the Leading Composers of the Present Time* (Boston, MA, 1900)
F.L. Ritter: *Music in America* (New York, 1900)
O.G.T. Sonneck: *Francis Hopkinson, the First American Poet-Composer (1737–1791) and James Lyon, Patriot, Preacher, Psalmodist (1735–1794): Two Studies in Early American Music* (Washington, DC, 1905)
E.L. Rice: *1000 Men of Minstrelsy and 1 Woman which Will Include George Washington, John Adams, and Thomas Jefferson* (New York, 1909)
F.H. Martens: *Leo Ornstein, the Man, His ideas, His Work* (New York, 1918)
J.T. Howard: *Stephen Foster: America's Troubadour* (Indianapolis, 1934)
H.E. Johnson: *Musical Interludes in Boston, 1795–1830* (New York, 1943)
A.L. Rich: *Lowell Mason: "The Father of Singing Among the Children"* (Chapel Hill, NC, 1946)
H. Cowell and S. Cowell: *Charles Ives and His Music* (London, 1955)
J.M. Barbour: *The Church Music of William Billings* (East Lansing, MI, 1960)
W.T. Upton: *Anthony Philip Heinrich: a Nineteenth-Century Composer in America* (New York, 1967)
C.A. Pemberton: *Lowell Mason: his Life and Work* (Ann Arbor, MI, 1971)
D.P. McKay and R. Crawford: *William Billings of Boston: Eighteenth-century Composer* (Princeton, NJ, 1975)
F.R. Rossiter: *Charles Ives & His America* (New York, 1975)
C. Hamm: *Yesterdays: Popular Song in America* (New York, 1979)
W.W. Austin: *"Susanna," "Jeanie," and "The Old Folks at Home": the Songs of Stephen Foster from His Time to Ours* (Urbana, IL, 1987)
C.A. Pemberton: *Lowell Mason: a Bio-bibliography* (New York, 1988)
K. Emerson: *Doo-dah! Stephen Foster and the Rise of American Popular Culture* (New York, 1997)
D. Jowitt, ed.: *Meredith Monk* (Baltimore, MD, 1997)
R.P. Locke and C. Barr: *Cultivating Music in America: Women Patrons and Activists Since 1860* (Berkeley, CA, 1997)
J. Tick: *Ruth Crawford Seeger: a Composer's Search for American Music* (New York, 1997)
C. Barr: *Elizabeth Sprague Coolidge: American Patron of Music* (New York, 1998)
A.F. Block: *Amy Beach, Passionate Victorian: the Life and Work of an American Composer, 1867–1944* (New York, 1998)
M. Mockus: *Sounding Out: Pauline Oliveros and Lesbian Musicality* (New Jersey, 2007)

DENISE VON GLAHN

Birchard, C(larence) C. (*b* Cambridge Springs, PA, 13 July 1866; *d* Carlisle, MA, 27 Feb 1946). Music publisher and music educator. Son of a Pennsylvania physician, Birchard taught music in public schools and managed summer schools for music songbook publishers in the 1890s. In 1901 he became founder and president of C.C. Birchard and Co., specializing in the publication of school music and the works of American composers. His school series, *The Laurel Song Book* (1901), was highly successful and set new standards in music selection and graphics. He promoted American composers, including Ives, Still, Hanson, and Copland, and encouraged Arthur Farwell to organize the Wa-Wan Press (1901) to stimulate American composition. He was one of the founders (at Keokuk, Iowa, 1907) of the Music Supervisors National Conference (MSNC). He took advantage of the community singing movement, the patriotic fervor of World War I, and the Americanization drive of the 1910s and published several collections of which the *Twice 55 Community Songs*, compiled by the MSNC, was his most successful. It sold millions of copies in its various editions. Birchard also promoted the use of the saxophone and published several pioneering orchestra and band method books. He was inducted into the Music Educators Hall of Fame in 1986.

BIBLIOGRAPHY

C.C. Birchard: "What About the Saxophone?" *Music Supervisors Journal*, xii/1 (1925), 56–7
"Clarence C. Birchard: Founder, President of Music and Textbook Publishing Firm," *New York Times* (28 Feb 1946) [obituary]
P.W. Dykema: "Clarence C. Birchard," *MEJ*, xxii/4 (1946), 30 only
N.M. Jansky: "On the Top Floor of the Old Pope Bicycle Building," *MEJ*, lx/1 (1973), 50–94
P.S. Foy: "A Brief Look at the Community Song Movement," *MEJ*, lxxvi/5 (1990), 26–7

WILLIAM R. LEE

Bird, Andrew (Wegman) (*b* Lake Bluff, IL, 11 July 1973). Singer, songwriter, and violinist. He is known for his eclectic sound recordings and dynamic live performances that draw on jazz, blues, folk, and art rock. He learned the violin from the age of four by the Suzuki method and attended Northwestern University, where he received a degree in violin performance (BM 1996). After releasing an album under his own name, *Music of Hair* (Grimsey Records, 1996), he recorded and performed with the swing band Squirrel Nut Zippers (1996–8). He subsequently formed his own group, Andrew Bird's Bowl of Fire, with which he released three albums, *Thrills* (Rykodisc, 1998), *Oh! The Grandeur* (Rykodisc, 1999), and *The Swimming Hour* (Rykodisc, 2001). Bird was also a member of Kevin O'Donnell's group Quality Six, in which he was the singer and violinist and contributed to songwriting on two albums released on Delmark Records.

After Bowl of Fire broke up, Bird began to establish himself as an artist in his own right particularly through his performances. He released two albums, *Weather Systems* (2003) and *The Mysterious Production of Eggs* (2005), on Righteous Babe Records, owned by the folk musician Ani DiFranco. In 2006 he signed to Fat Possum Records and released the album *Armchair Apocrypha* (Fat Possum, 2007), which received critical acclaim. He released his fifth album *Noble Beast* (Fat Possum Records, 2009) in 2009. Bird has also released a series of live recordings, *Fingerlings* (Grimsey Records, 2002), *Fingerlings 2* (Grimsey Records, 2004), *Fingerlings 3* (Grimsey, 2006), *Fingerlings 4* (Wegawam Music, 2010), and *Live in Montreal* (Bella Union, 2008). While best known for his exquisite violin playing, he is also an accomplished guitarist and whistler. His performances highlight his ability to provide an accompaniment for himself by looping sounds from his violin; he sometimes performs on his own and at others with Martin Dosh (percussion, looping, and keyboards) and Jeremy Ylvisaker.

MATTHEW A. DONAHUE

Bird, Arthur H. (*b* Belmont, MA, 23 July 1856; *d* Berlin, Germany, 22 Dec 1923). Composer and pianist. He received his early training from his father and uncle, who were composers and compilers of hymn tunes. He showed a particular talent for improvisation, and in 1875 was admitted to the Berlin Hochschule, where he became a pupil of K.A. Haupt, A. Loeschhorn and E. Rohde. In 1877 he returned to the United States and was appointed organist at St. Matthew's, Halifax, Nova Scotia; he also taught piano at the Young Ladies' Academy and the Mount St. Vincent Academy, and founded the Arion Club, a men's chorus. During his second stay in Germany (1881–6) he studied composition under H. Urban and became a close friend and disciple of Liszt. At the invitation of the North American Saengerbund he returned to the United States in 1886 to direct the Milwaukee Musical Festival, where his compositions were favorably received. He then returned permanently to Berlin to live the life of an American expatriate who—like Templeton Strong Jr. and other contemporaries—found European culture more hospitable to his muse. He became the Berlin correspondent for the Chicago journal *Musical Leader* and also wrote for other musical magazines such as *The Etude* and *The Musician*. Bird's music was well known in Germany, and most of it was published there, but after about 1895 he composed relatively little. Contemporary critics agreed that his works, late Romantic in style, were pleasing and melodious, and that he was an excellent contrapuntist. He was elected to the National Institute of Arts and Letters in 1898.

WORKS

STAGE

Daphne, or The Pipes of Arcadia (operetta, 3), New York, private perf., 13 Dec 1897; Volksfest (ballet), op.13, 1886, perf. 1887, lost [also version for pf 4 hands]; Rübezahl (ballet), Berlin, 1886, pf score pubd

ORCHESTRAL

Serenade, str, 1882; Suite, E, str, op.1, 1882 [incl. Gavotte, op.7]; Concert Ov., D, 1884; Eine Carneval Szene, op.5, 1884 (Wrocław, 1887); First Little Suite, 1884, lost [also version for pf 4 hands]; Second Little Suite, op.6, 1884–5; Sym., A, op.8, 1885 (Wrocław, 1886); Melody and Spanish Dance, vn, chamber orch, op.9, 1885; 3 Characteristic Marches, op.11, 1885; [Piece], g, vc, chbr orch, 1885; Introduction and Fugue, d, org, orch, op.16, 1886; Oriental Scene and Caprice, fl, chbr orch, op.17, 1887; 2 Episodes, 1887–8; 2 Poems, op.25, 1888; 2 Pieces, str, op.28, 1888;

Third Little Suite (Souvenirs of Summer Saturdays), C, op.32, 1890 (Boston, MA, 1892); Romance, vn, chbr orch, 1890; Variations on an American Folksong, fl, chbr orch, op.34, 1891; Galop, band, *c*1909; Symphonic Suite, E♭, *c*1910, rev. *c*1918

CHAMBER

Andante and Allegro, vn, pf, 1878; Adagio, fl, vn, vc, pf, 1879; Nonet (Marche miniature), ww, 1887; Suite, D, 10 wind insts, 1889; Mazurka, vn; Melody and Tarantella, vn, pf, op.38, 1896; Serenade, 10 wind insts, op.40, 1898; transcrs.

KEYBOARD

Pf: 3 Pieces, op.2, 1882; Sonata, 1883; Allegro con moto, 1883; Gavotte, Album Leaf, and Lullaby, op.3, 1883; Rondo Humoreske, 1883; 6 Sketches, 1883; 2 Pieces, 1883–4; Sonatina, 1885; 4 Pieces, op.10, 1886; 3 Waltzes, op.12, 1886; 8 Sketches, op.15, 1886; Gavotte, Waltz, and Minuet, op.18, 1887; 5 Puppet Dances, op.19, 1887; 7 Pieces, op.20, 1887; 3 Pieces, op.21, 1887; Piano Pieces for 4 Children, op.22, 1887; 4 Album Leaves, op.24, 1888; 4 Pieces, op.26, 1888; Theme and Variations, op.27, 1889; 4 Romances, op.29, 1889; 3 Pieces, op.31, 1890; 4 Pieces, op.33, 1890; Album Leaf and Scherzando, op.35, 1891; 3 Pieces, 1896; 2 Clog Dances and an Album Leaf, 1905; 4 Pieces, op.46, 1910; The Springlet, Elegiac Waltz, and a Fragment, op.49, 1911; 3 Miniature Poems (after Longfellow), op.50, 1912

Pf 4 hands: French Ov., 1878; 3 Marches, 1881; Waltz; Fantastic Caprice, 1883; First Little Suite, op.4, 1884 [also version for orch]; Volksfest, 1886 [also version for orch]; 3 Characteristic Waltzes, op.14, 1886; American Melodies, op.23, 1887

Org: Fugue on A.H., 1881; 4 Fugues and a Canon Trio, 1881; 4 Sonatas, 1882; 3 Oriental Sketches, op.42, 1898 (New York, 1903); Marcia, 1902; Concert Fantasia, 1904; Toccatina, 1905

Reed org: 10 Pieces, op.37, 1897; 3 Pieces, op.39, 1898; Tempo di minuetto and Spring, op.41, 1898; 4 Pieces, op.44, 1902; 3 Sketches, op.45, 1903; Prelude and Fuga, a, 1907; Prelude and Fuga, C, 1907; Postlude, 1909

VOCAL

The passions are at peace within, T, org, 1878; Lied, B, pf; The World's Wanderers (P.B. Shelley), B; 3 Quartettes (Shelley, G.E. Lessing), male vv; 4 Quartets, male vv, 1885; Frau Holde (R. Baumbach), song cycle, male vv, pf; Wanderlieder (R. Hammerling), male vv, pf, op.30, 1891; 5 Songs, female vv, pf, op.36, 1896; Hush, my child, and slumber (Wisby), S, pf, 1898; All the Summer Long (D. von Liliencron), Bar, reed org, 1903

MSS in *DLC*

BIBLIOGRAPHY

EwenD
DAB (W.T. Upton)
L.C. Elson: *The History of American Music* (New York, 1904, enlarged 2/1915)
W.C. Loring, Jr.: "Arthur Bird, American," *MQ*, xxix (1943), 78–91
W.C. Loring, Jr.: *The Music of Arthur Bird* (Atlanta, GA, 2/1974)
E.D. Bomberger: *The German Musical Training of American Students, 1850–1900* (diss., U. of Maryland, 1991)
A. Wodehouse: "Arthur Bird's 'Opus 37': Pieces for the American harmonium," *The American Organist*, xl/4 (2006), 62–63

W. THOMAS MARROCCO/E. DOUGLAS BOMBERGER

Birge, Edward Bailey (*b* Northampton, MA, 12 June 1868; *d* Bloomington, IN, 16 July 1952). Music educator. He attended Brown University (BA 1891) and taught music in public schools and teacher-training schools in New England before becoming public school music director in Indianapolis (1901–21). There he made instruction in music available to all elementary school students, organized bands and orchestras, and introduced courses in music theory and literature. During these years he also taught at the Jordan College of Music and the American Institute of Normal Methods. From 1921 to 1938 he headed the public school music department and directed the university chorus at Indiana University. Birge wrote 45 articles for professional publications and edited or co-edited six major series on school music; his *History of Public School Music in the United States* (Philadelphia, 1928, rev. 1937/*R*1966) is still widely used. He was a founder of the Music Supervisors National Conference and edited its journal (1930–44). He was also an officer of the National Education Association and the Music Teachers National Association. He was inducted into the Music Educators Hall of Fame in 1986.

BIBLIOGRAPHY

J.W. Beattie: "Appreciation of a Colleague," *MEJ*, xxv/1 (1938), 16 only
W. Earhart: "A Tribute to a Colleague," *MEJ*, xxx/6 (1944), 13, 59
C.F. Schwartz, Jr.: *Edward Bailey Birge: his Life and Contributions to Music Education* (diss., Indiana U., 1966)

GEORGE N. HELLER/R

Birmingham. City in Alabama (pop. 212, 237; metropolitan area 1,128,047). Founded in 1871, Birmingham grew rapidly as a steel-producing center and by World War II had become the industrial, economic, and cultural heart of the state. As early as 1874 the city fathers considered establishing a music department in the Free Public School, but the plan was abandoned because of lack of funds. A city brass band active in the 1870s and a Mendelssohn Glee Club (organized in 1887 and renamed the Mendelssohn Society in 1890) were among the earliest musical organizations. In 1895 Benjamin Guckenberger founded the Birmingham Conservatory of Music. The Conservatory was led by directors William Gussen (1903–20), Edna Gockel-Gussen (1920–30), and Dorsey Whittington (1930–1939) until it moved onto the campus of Birmingham-Southern College in 1939, and merged with the college in 1953.

The Birmingham SO was founded in 1933 but was not in continuous operation until 1946. Its first conductor and music director was Dorsey Whittington (1933–48), succeeded by Arthur Bennett Lipkin (1948–60), Arthur Winograd (1960–64), and Amerigo Marino (1964–85), during whose tenure the orchestra's name was changed to the Alabama SO (1976). Paul Polivnick served as conductor and music director for the next eight years. In 1993 the ASO declared bankruptcy, however, with considerable public and private support the orchestra was revived four years later. Since 1997 the orchestra has been directed by Mark Gibson (1997), Richard Westerfield (1997–2004), Christopher Confessore (2004–5), and Justin Brown (2006–12). Located on the campus of the University of Alabama at Birmingham (UAB), the beautiful Alys Robinson Stephens Performing Arts Center serves as official venue for the orchestra.

Opera Birmingham, the city's only professional opera company, began in 1955 as the Birmingham Civic Opera Association; its first production was Smetana's *The Bartered Bride*. In 1986 the company merged with Southern Regional Opera, and was renamed the Birmingham Opera Theater in 1987, and as Opera Birmingham in 1996. The company mounts two productions per year at Samford University's newly renovated Leslie Stephen Wright Fine Arts Center. The community also supports a variety of music organizations, performance ensembles, and festivals. Alabama Operaworks, the Birmingham Art Music Alliance, the Birmingham Chamber Music Society, and the Birmingham Music Club each organize a yearly concert series, and choral music is well-represented by the Birmingham Boys Choir, Birmingham Concert Chorale, the Birmingham Community Gospel Choir, the Magic City Choral Society, and Sursum Corda. The Birmingham International Festival (founded in 1951 as the Birmingham Festival of the Arts) salutes a different country each spring with a program of arts and educational events.

Established in 1968, the Alabama School of Fine Arts offers musical training for students in grades 7–12. Colleges in the Birmingham metropolitan area that offer baccalaureate and masters degrees in music include Birmingham-Southern College, Samford University, UAB, Miles College, and the University of Montevallo. The Birmingham Public Library and Samford University maintain extensive holdings and collections of local musical memorabilia, as well as collections of printed music, sound recordings, and personal correspondence of notable local musical figures.

Located west of Birmingham, the neighborhood of Ensley played an important part in the history of jazz. Nicknamed "Tuxedo Junction," the area was the cultural and social nerve center for the Birmingham African American community, and served as an important tour stop for jazz musicians during the 1930s and 40s. Birmingham has been the home to many influential jazz musicians, including John T. "Fess" Whatley, Erskine Hawkins, Sun Ra, Lionel Hampton, "Papa" Jo Jones, Cleveland Eaton, and Johnny Smith. The Alabama Jazz Hall of Fame Museum, established in 1978, continues its mission to honor and promote the contributions Alabama and its citizens have made to jazz.

Religious music has played a significant role throughout the city's history. During the early to mid-1900s, the city and its surrounding neighborhoods produced some of the country's most prominent black a cappella gospel quartets. Groups as such the Birmingham Jubilee Singers, the Famous Blue Jay Gospel Singers, and the Sterling Jubilee Singers helped shape a distinctly regional sound that featured close, blended harmonies and blue-note-laden melodies. During the 1950s and 60s, "Professor" Alex Bradford produced a string of national hits for Specialty Records, and Dorothy Love Coates and the Gospel Harmonettes recorded several songs that confronted racial inequality and the struggle for civil rights. Established in 1980, the National Sacred Harp Singing Convention is held in Birmingham every June.

Among the notable musicians who have made the Birmingham area their home include composer Hugh Martin, rhythm-and-blues singer Hank Ballard, soul singers Dennis Edwards, Eddie Kendricks, Eddie Levert, and Paul Williams, folk singer Odetta (Holmes), fiddler Tommy Jackson, and country singer-songwriter Emmylou Harris.

BIBLIOGRAPHY

GroveA (R.J. Nicolosi)

J.R. Hornady: *The Book of Birmingham* (New York, 1921)

M. Thomas: *Musical Alabama* (Montgomery, AL, 1925)

C.E. Roebuck: *The History of Birmingham from 1871 to 1890* (thesis, U. of Alabama, 1931)

M.C. McMillan: *Yesterday's Birmingham*, xviii (Miami, 1975)

D. Seroff: "On the Battlefield: Gospel Quartets in Jefferson County, Alabama," *Repercussions: a Celebration of African-American Music*, ed. G. Haydon and D. Marks (London, 1985), 30–53

J.P. Fairleigh: "Alabama Symphony Orchestra," *Symphony Orchestras of the United States: Selected Profiles*, ed. R.R. Craven (Westport, CT, 1986), 2–3

W. Fallin, Jr.: *The African American Church in Birmingham, Alabama, 1815–1963: a Shelter in the Storm* (New York, 1997)

C.S. Fuqua: *Music Fell on Alabama* (Montgomery, AL, 2008)

D.B. Fleming and M.A. Haynie: *Ensley and Tuxedo Junction* (Charleston, SC, 2011)

ROBERT J. NICOLOSI/WILLIAM PRICE

Biscardi, Chester (*b* Kenosha, WI, 19 Oct 1948). Composer. He earned the BA in English literature (1970) and the MA in Italian literature (1972) from the University of Wisconsin, Madison, before studying composition with Les Thimmig and electronic music with Bert Levy, receiving the MM in composition, also from the University of Wisconsin, Madison, in 1974. He spent the summers of 1974 and 1975 studying with MARIO DAVIDOVSKY at the Composers' Conference (Johnson, Vermont) and studied with ROBERT MORRIS, Krzysztof Penderecki, Toru Takemitsu, and YEHUDI WYNER at Yale University (MMA 1976, DMA 1980). In 1977 he joined the faculty at Sarah Lawrence College (Bronxville, New York), where he was the first recipient of the William Schuman Chair in Music. His many awards include the Rome Prize (1976–7), a Guggenheim Fellowship (1979–80), the Academy Award from the American Academy of Arts and Letters (2007), and numerous grants and commissions.

Timbral and spatial concerns play an important role in Biscardi's early works. Often a single word or poetic phrase generates the central idea of a composition, though his works are seldom overtly programmatic. The Italian *tenzone* (dialogue) inspired *Tenzone* (1975), while T.S. Eliot's "Burnt Norton," with its interplay of form and time, evoked *At the Still Point* (1977). In the 1985 opera *Tight-Rope* and the song cycle *The Gift of Life* (1990–93) Biscardi's lyrical impulses, pervasive in his later works, are more pronounced. *Resisting Stillness* (1996), an intimate, strikingly spare work, has autobiographical aspects, which are also a characteristic element of his mature music. His Piano Quintet (2004), written in memory of his father, uses elements from *The Odyssey*, Schumann's Piano Quintet in E♭ Major, op.44, and several of his own earlier works, all of which, in the composer's words, "explore the passage of time, loss, recovery, and transcendence."

WORKS

STAGE

Music for the Duchess of Malfi (incid music, J. Webster), v, fl, cl, tpt, hn, 2 vn, vc, perc, pf, 1976; Music for Witch Dance (dance, A. Gamson, after M. Wigman), 2 perc, 1983; Tight-Rope (op, 9 scenes, H. Butler), 1985; Music for NASDAQ, fl, hn, vn, vc, perc, pf, 1999

INSTRUMENTAL

Ens: Tartini, vn, pf, 1972; Chartres, ob, cl, s sax, vn, vc, 2 perc, pf, 1973; Orpha, str qt, mar, vib, 1974; Tenzone, 2 fl, pf, 1975; They had Ceased to Talk, vn, va, hn, pf, 1975; Trio, vn, vc, pf, 1976; At the Still Point, orch, 1977; Trasumanar, 12 perc, pf, 1980; Di vivere, cl, fl, vn, vc, pf/cl, pf, 1981; Pf Conc., pf, orch, 1983; Traverso, fl, pf, 1987; Netori, ob, cl, hn, vn, vc, pf, 1990; Companion Piece (for Morton Feldman), db, pf, 1989, arr. pf, 1991; Music for an Occasion, brass, perc, pf, 1992, rev. 2003; Incitation to Desire (Tango), cl, hn, vn, vc, perc, pf, 1993 [see Solo]; Nel giardinetto della villa, pf 4 hands, 1994; Resisting Stillness, 2 gui, 1996; Chbr Fanfare, fl, hn, vn, vc, perc, pf, 1999; Piano Quintet, pf, 2 vn, va, vc, 2004, arr as Recognition, pf, vn, str orch, 2007; The Viola Had Suddenly Become a Voice, va, pf, 2005

Solo: Mestiere, pf, 1979; Incitation to Desire (Tango), pf, 1984, arr. chbr ens 1993, arr. mar, 2006; Pf Sonata, 1986, rev. 1987; No Feeling Is the Same as Before, s sax, 1988; Companion Piece (for Morton Feldman), pf, 1991; In Time's Unfolding, pf, 2000

VOCAL

Choral: Heabakes: 5 Sapphic Lyrics (Sappho), 2 S, A, SATB, perc, 1974; Indovinello (Indovinello veronese), 12 vv, 1974; Eurydice (H.D.), SSAA, chbr orch, 1978; Good-bye My Fancy! (M. D'Alessio, from W. Whitman), nar, SATB, 1982; The Child Comes Every Winter, SATB, pf, 1999

Solo: Turning (C. Biscardi), S, vn, str trio, 1973; Trusting Lightness (J. Anderson), S, pf, 1975; Chez Vous (S. Harnick), S, pf, 1983, rev 2007; "Poet's Aria" (from Tight-Rope, H. Butler), Bar/T, pf, 1985, The Gift of Life (E. Dickinson, D. Levertov, T. Wilder), S, pf, 1990–93; Baby Song of the Four Winds (C. Sandburg), S/Mez, pf, 1994; Guru (A. Ginsberg), 1v, pf, 1995; Modern Love Songs (W. Zinsser), 1v, pf, 1997–2002 (What a Coincidence, 1997; I Wouldn't Know about That, 1997; Someone New, 1999; Now You See It, Now You Don't, 1998; At Any Given Moment, 2002); Prayers of Steel (Sandberg), Bar, pf, 1998; The Child Comes Every Winter (Zinsser), S, pf, 1999; Recovering (M. Rukeyser), 1v, pf, 2000; Sailors and Dreamers (S. Kaplan), 1v, pf, also arr 1v, chbr ens, 2007–2010 (You've Been on my Mind, 2007; Play me a Song, 2008; Seven O'Clock at the Cedar (Ode to Kline / de Kooning), 2008; It's Time to Feel Alright Now, 2009; Do you Remember?, 2010; I Dance the Tango, 2010; Falling Fast, 2010).

Principal publishers: Presser, Peters, Biscardi Music Press

JAMES CHUTE

Bischoff, John (Lee) (*b* San Francisco, CA, 7 Dec 1949). Composer and performer. He studied at the San Francisco Conservatory (1968–70) with ROBERT MORAN, ROBERT HELPS, and Ivan Tcherepnin (*see* TCHEREPNIN family (3)), at the California Institute of the Arts (BFA 1971), where his teachers included JAMES TENNEY and MORTON SUBOTNICK, and at Mills College (MFA 1973) with ROBERT ASHLEY, "BLUE" GENE TYRANNY, and DAVID TUDOR, among others. In 1978 he co-founded, with Jim Horton and Rich Gold, the League of Automatic Music Composers, the world's first computer network band. He was also a founding member of the computer network band The Hub in 1985. In 1989 with Chris Brown and Tim Perkis, he co-founded Artifact Recordings, a label specializing in experimental electronic and computer music. He was appointed studio coordinator at the Center for Contemporary Music and lecturer in computer music at Mills College in 1992. A composer of live electronic and computer music, he has created software instruments with rich and somewhat unpredictable sonic behaviors. He interacts with these in performance within predefined structures that leave room for exploration. The quirks and challenges of the devices he creates are incorporated into his music.

WORKS
(selective list)

Piece, pf, 1968; Sign Angle Side, cl, vc, gui, hp, 1970; Terrain, any insts, 1970; Summer Network, live elecs, 1973; Pf Social, live elecs, 1975; Three Manners of Attachment, pf, toy pf, tape, 1975; Silhouette, live elecs, 1977; Audio Wave, cptr, 1978; Next Tone, Please, cptr, 1983; Artificial Horizon, cptr, tape, 1985; Space Detail, tape, 1985; The Curve Behind the Line, cptr, 1987; The Industrial Revolution, cptr, 1990; The Glass Hand, cptr, 1991; Drift, cptr, 1993; Silent Theater, cptr, 1993; Surface 11–5–2, cptr, 1995; The Curve Behind the Line, pf, 1998; Variable Tranist, cptr, 1998; Piano 7hz, cptr, 2002; Local Color, cptr, 2003

WRITINGS

with J. Horton and R. Gold: "Microcomputer Network Music," *Foundations of Computer Music* (Cambridge, MA, 1985), 588–600
with C. Brown and T. Perkis: "Bringing Digital Music to Life," *Computer Music Journal*, xx/2 (1996), 28–32

BIBLIOGRAPHY

D. Cope: *New Directions in Music* (Dubuque, IA, 1971, 6/1993), 313–14
C. Roads: *The Computer Music Tutorial* (Cambridge, MA, 1996), 684–5
D. Kahn: "A Musical Technography of John Bischoff," *Leonardo Music Journal*, xiv (2004), 74–9

DISCOGRAPHY
(selective list)

The Glass Hand, Artifact (Recordings ART 1014, 1996)
Aperture (23Five 006 CD, 2003)
The League of Automatic Music Composers: 1978–1983 (New World 80671–2, 2007)
Boundary Layer: the Hub (Tzadik TZ8050–3, 2008)

CARTER SCHOLZ/BENJAMIN PIEKUT

Bisexual music. *See* LESBIAN, GAY, BISEXUAL, TRANSGENDER, AND QUEER MUSIC.

Bish, Diane (Joyce) (*b* Wichita, KS, May 1941). Concert organist. At age five she started piano lessons and at age eleven, after hearing Alexander Schreiner play the Mormon Tabernacle organ, she began organ studies. Bish studied organ with Dorothy Addy, Era Wilder Peniston, MILDRED ANDREWS BOGGESS, and Marie-Claire Alain, studied harpsichord with Gustav Leonhardt, and attended classes with NADIA BOULANGER. In 1982 she began her own television series *The Joy of Music*, which continues to reach a vast worldwide audience every week. She also served as organist at the Coral Ridge Presbyterian Church in Fort Lauderdale, Florida for 20 years.

Bish has won several performance competitions and has been the recipient of prestigious awards. In 1963, while a student at the University of Oklahoma, she won the Mu Phi Epsilon student performance competition and later went on to be a national Mu Phi composition winner. In 1989 she was awarded the National Citation by the National Federation of Music Clubs of America. In 2006 she was one of four organists selected to be an Artists, Composers, Musicologists, and Educators honoree by Mu Phi Epsilon. Reviewers praise her prodigious technique, effervescent personality, and diversity of programming.

BIBLIOGRAPHY

D. Lamb: "A Silver Jubilee of Sparkling Joy," *American Organist*, xli/4 (2007), 44–6
W.L. Woodruff: *Diane Bish: First Lady of the Organ* (Atlanta, 1993)

WILLIAM F. COSCARELLI

Bishop [née Riviere], **Anna** (*b* London, England, 9 Jan 1810; *d* New York, NY, 18 or 19 March 1884). English soprano. She studied singing with Henry Bishop and made her professional debut in London on 20 April 1831, shortly before her marriage to Bishop on 9 July. Her reputation grew over the decade through various tours and performances with her husband and the harpist NICHOLAS BOCHSA. In 1839, she eloped with Bochsa (leaving her husband and three children) and began a long tour of Europe. For the rest of her life "Madame Bishop," as she was now universally known, traveled almost incessantly, first with Bochsa and, after his death, alone.

In 1847, she and Bochsa arrived in New York, where she made her public debut in Donizetti's *Linda di Chamounix* at the Park Theater on 4 August. A long tour with Bochsa followed, with engagements in Mexico, Cuba, and California; in 1850 she was back in New York, where on 1 November 1852 she produced and sang in the first American performance of Flotow's *Martha*, at Niblo's Garden. In 1854 she was in San Francisco. She made several world tours: on one, in 1856, Bochsa died in Australia and on another, in 1866, she was shipwrecked on a coral reef with her second husband, Martin Schultz (whom she had married in 1858). The indomitable singer continued her tour in Hong Kong, Singapore, and India. She made her last public appearance in New York on 22 April 1883.

Anna Bishop was one of the most popular singers of her generation. Her high soprano voice was brilliant, her technique masterly, but she lacked the expressive power of Jenny Lind or Clara Novello.

BIBLIOGRAPHY

GMO (Nicholas Temperley); *DNB* (W.B. Squire)
Scrapbook of concerts by Bochsa and Anna Bishop, 1839–45 (MS, *Bp* 446.109)

Travels of Anna Bishop in Mexico, 1849 (Philadelphia, 1852)
G.G. Foster: *Biography of Madame Anna Bishop* (Sydney, 1855)
Obituaries: *American Art Journal*, xl (1884), 356 only; *MT*, xxv (1884), 212 only
R. Davis: *Anna Bishop: the Adventures of an Intrepid Prima Donna* (Canberra, 1996)

NICHOLAS TEMPERLEY/R

Bispham, David (Scull) (*b* Philadelphia, PA, 5 Jan 1857; *d* New York, NY, 2 Oct 1921). Baritone. He studied in Milan (1886–9) with Luigi Vannuccini and Francesco Lamperti, and then in London with William Shakespeare and Albert Randegger. He made his operatic debut in 1891 as Longueville in Messager's *La basoche* at the English Opera House, where his comic acting ability and singing brought him immediate success. He sang Kurwenal (*Tristan und Isolde*) the following year at Drury Lane, and later sang at Covent Garden as well. He made his debut at the Metropolitan Opera as Beckmesser in 1896 and remained with the company until 1903. Much in demand in England and the United States in opera and oratorio and on the recital stage for several decades, he excelled in the Wagnerian roles, of which he considered Kurwenal and Beckmesser to be his best. He sang at the premiere of Walter Damrosch's *The Scarlet Letter* (1896, Boston), and his repertory also included Masetto, Pizarro, Escamillo, Alfio, Peter (*Hänsel und Gretel*), Iago, Falstaff, and Urok in Paderewski's *Manru*. His voice was powerful and of fine quality, though with a tendency to excessive nasal resonance.

Bispham was ardently in favor of using the English language in operas and songs, and to this end helped to form the Society of American Singers in 1917, which presented comic operas in English using American casts; he toured with the troupe for several years both as singer and administrator. He also gave lecture-recitals, in which he promoted the works of English and American composers. The American Opera Society of Chicago awards the David Bispham Medal to motivate the composition and performance of American opera.

A highly skilled actor, Bispham appeared as Beethoven in Hugo Müller's play *Adelaide* (1898) in both England and America. In his later years he developed a repertory of monologues of poetry and prose which he performed to musical accompaniment, often provided by famous groups of the day. From 1902 he was also an influential teacher in Philadelphia. Bispham's musical memorabilia are in the New York Public Library (*NYp*).

BIBLIOGRAPHY

DAB (F.H. Martens); *GV* (J.B. Richards)
D. Bispham: *A Quaker Singer's Recollections* (New York, 1921/*R*)
Obituary, *MusAm*, xxxiv/24 (1921), 1 only
O. Thompson: "David Bispham," *The American Singer* (New York, 1937/*R*), 204 only
J. Dennis: "David Bispham," *Record Collector*, vi (1951), 5 [with discography]

RICHARD ALDRICH/DEE BAILY/R

Bitgood [Wiersma], **Roberta** (*b* New London, CT, 15 Jan 1908; *d* New London, CT, 15 April 2007). Composer, organist, and choral director. After graduation from Connecticut College for Women (BA 1928), she pursued theory and organ at the Guilmant Organ School (1930), studied music education at Teachers College, Columbia University (MA 1932) and was the first woman to take the doctorate at the School of Sacred Music, Union Theological Seminary (MSM 1935; DSM 1945). Her principal composition teachers included John Lawrence Erb, Howard Murphy, Edwin Stringham (1933–5), T. Tertius Noble (1943–5), and Wayne Bohrnsted (1957–60). During her career as organist and director of music she held positions in Protestant churches and temples in New Jersey, California, Connecticut, New York, and Michigan. She was the first woman president of the American Guild of Organists (1975–81) and received the AGO President's Award in 1998. Although she retired from full-time employment in 1976, and returned to her family home in Connecticut, Bitgood continued serving as a professional musician in local churches and synagogues until 1999. As a composer she has focused exclusively on church music, writing many anthems for young people and giving special attention to practicable works for small church choirs (e.g. *Hosanna*, 1935). Her style is triadic, using seventh chords, but often avoiding dominant sevenths. The harmonic motion and part-writing of her music are influenced by organ playing, with frequent common-note progressions, planing, and pedal points, as in "The Greatest of These Is Love" (1934) and "Be Still and know That I Am God" (1940), two of her most popular works. Modulations are frequent and generally move to the sixth or flattened third degree of the scale, producing false relations, for example in the Chorale Prelude on "Jewels" (1942) and in "Ye Works of the Lord." A substantial collection of her papers, music, and manuscripts is housed in the Special Collections Department, Charles E. Sham Library, at her alma mater, Connecticut College.

WORKS
(selective list)

Choral: Hosanna (Moravian liturgical texts), children's chorus, mixed chorus, org, 1935; Rosa Mystica, S, mixed chorus, 1935; Prayer Is the Soul's Sincere Desire, mixed chorus, 1939; Give Me a Faith (C.L. Reynolds), S, Bar, mixed chorus, org, 1945, arr. v, pf, 1950; Job (cant., Bible, D. ben Judah, trans. N. Mann), S, 2 T, B, chorus, org, 1945; Joseph (cant., Bible, Rev. N. Selnecker), S, A, 2T, Bar, mixed chorus, org, 1962?; Let There Be Light (cant., M.L. Kerr), children's SA chorus, org, 1965; Ye Works of the Lord (Bible, W. Blake), chorus, org, 1993; *c*75 other sacred works

Other vocal: The Greatest of These is Love (Bible: *1 Corinthians*), v, pf/org, 1934, arr. women's or mixed chorus, arr. (S, A)/(T, B); Be Still and Know That I Am God (Bible), 1v, pf/org, 1940, arr. mixed chorus

Org: Chorale Prelude on "Jewels," 1942; On an Ancient Alleluia, 1962; Offertories from Afar, 7 pieces based on folk melodies, 1964; Meditation on "Kingsfold," 1976

Principal publishers: H.W. Gray, Flammer, Choristers Guild, Westminster

BIBLIOGRAPHY

A.F. Block and C. Neuls-Bates: *Women in American Music: a Bibliography of Music and Literature* (Westport, CT, 1979)
A. Armstrong: "A Conversation with Roberta Bitgood," *American Organist*, xxx/4 (1996), 63–6; xxx/5 (1996), 70–72
B. Harbach: "Roberta Bitgood: Active Octogenarian," *Women of Note Quarterly*, iv/2 (1996), 1–10
R. Bitgood with J. Goodfellow: *Swell to Great: a Backward Look from My Organ Loft* (Salem, CT, 2000)

K. Thomerson: "[Review of] *Swell to Great: A Backward Look from My Organ Loft*," *American Organist*, xxxv/9 (2001), 82
Obituary, *Hartford Courant* (19 April 2007)
A.D. McNeely & M.B. Miller: "Roberta Bitgood Tribute," *American Organist*, xli/7 (2007), 70–71
M. Williams: "Roberta Bitgood," *Pan Pipes*, xcix/4 (2007), 6, 8–9

J. MICHELE EDWARDS

Biz Markie [Hall, Marcel Theo] (*b* Harlem, New York; 8 April 1964). Rapper, beatboxer, MC, DJ, and actor. He began his career in 1985 as a beatboxer for Roxanne Shanté of the Juice Crew. In 1988, he signed with Cold Chillin' Records and released his first solo album, *Goin' Off*. His second album, *The Biz Never Sleeps* (1989), went gold and included his first top ten hit, "Just a Friend," which peaked at number nine on *Billboard's* Pop Singles chart. The single, Markie's biggest hit to-date, features the self-deprecating and satirical humor that won him the title "Clown Prince of Hip Hop." Besides "Just a Friend," he is also well known for the controversy surrounding a 1991 lawsuit leveled against him by singer-songwriter Gilbert O'Sullivan. Markie's song "Alone Again," from his album *I Need a Haircut* (1991), featured an unauthorized sample of O'Sullivan's "Alone Again (Naturally)." The case featured the first federal decision regarding music sampling and had a profound effect on hip hop, requiring prior approval of samples on future recordings. An injunction was issued against the sale of *I Need a Haircut* and all copies were recalled from stores. The title of Markie's 1993 comeback album, *All Samples Cleared,* sarcastically referenced the lawsuit. His most recent album, *Ultimate Diabolical*, was released in 2007. Although his recording career never recovered after the lawsuit, he remains a hip hop and pop culture icon, extensively touring and appearing on other rap artists' albums. He was featured on VH1's *Celebrity Fit Club*, as well as the popular children's show *Yo Gabba Gabba*.

LAUREN JOINER

Björk [Gudmundsdottír, Björk] (*b* Reykjavik, Iceland, 21 Nov 1965). Icelandic singer and songwriter. She is best known for her distinctive vocal style and for bringing the challenging textures and stylistic elements of techno and post-rave electronica into the mainstream. Having achieved a degree of fame in Iceland at a young age, she first came to wider prominence as the lead singer of the Sugarcubes, an indie post-punk band based in Reykjavik. In the late 1980s she became increasingly interested in the electronic music emerging from the British acid house scene, and her subsequent solo projects adapted this dance sound to the dictates of album-centered pop. In her music Björk assembles a catholic range of sounds, drawing upon big-band jazz, Western chamber music, hip-hop drum programming, microhouse glitch production, and elements from global musical traditions. Throughout her career she has developed a singular approach as a singer, incorporating breathy murmurs, shouted growls, and dramatic emotional shifts into song forms built around modal structures and irregular, asymmetrical phrases.

Alongside her own collaborations with figures as diverse as Howie B, Nellee Hooper, Graham Massey, Rahzel, John Tavener, Timbaland, and Tricky, Björk's music has also been subjected to extensive remixing and "versioning" by well-known producers. She undertook a powerful acting role in Lars von Trier's film *Dancer in the Dark* (2000), for which she also produced the music.

SELECTED RECORDINGS

Debut (One Little Indian, 1993); *Post* (One Little Indian, 1995); *Homogenic* (One Little Indian, 1997); *Selmasongs* (One Little Indian, 2000); *Vespertine* (One Little Indian, 2001); *Medúlla* (One Little Indian, 2004); *Volta* (One Little Indian, 2007)

BIBLIOGRAPHY

A. Mattíasson: *Sykurmolarnir* [The Sugarcubes] (Reykjavík, 1992)
D. Grimley: "Hidden Places: Hyper-realism in Björk's *Vespertine* and *Dancer in the Dark*," *twentieth-century music*, ii/1 (2005), 37–51
S.K. Iitti: "Björk metsästäjänä ja naisellisuuden naamiot [Björk as a hunter and the masks of femininity]," *Musiikin suunta*, xxix/4 (2007), 66–74
V. Malawey: *Temporal Process, Repetition, and Voice in Björk's Medúlla* (diss., Indiana U., 2007)
N. Dibben: *Björk* (Bloomington, IN, 2009)

DALE E. CHAPMAN

Björling, Jussi [Johan] **(Jonaton)** (*b* Stora Tuna, Sweden, 5 Feb 1911; *d* Stockholm, Sweden, 9 Sept 1960). Swedish tenor. He was first taught by his father, David Björling (1873–1926), a professional tenor, and from 1916 made many concert tours with his father and two brothers as a treble in the Björling Male Quartet. In 1928 he entered the Stockholm Conservatory; two years later he made his debut with the Royal Swedish Opera. Until 1938 he was a regular member of the Stockholm Opera, as demand grew for him in the leading European operatic centers. He debuted at Chicago in *Rigoletto* (8 December 1937), in New York in *La bohème* (24 November 1938), and at San Francisco in *La bohème* (18 October 1940). In the United States he became an indispensable favorite, returning regularly to the Metropolitan and other houses except during the war years of 1941–5, which he spent in Sweden.

Although Björling's repertory had by this time become almost entirely Italian, the purity and restraint of his style may perhaps have disconcerted a public used to a more overt and impassioned display. His voice was a true tenor of velvety smoothness, though capable also of ringing high notes; admirably schooled, it showed remarkable consistency from top to bottom of his register and throughout the 30 years of his career. To the end, the glowing tone and impeccable musicianship provided ample compensation for a stage presence that was rather a matter of deportment than of acting. His smooth legato and plangent tone adapted well to recording, and he made a large number of delightful and valuable records, including many complete operas. He published a volume of memoirs, *Med bagaget i strupen* [Travels with my larynx] (Stockholm, 1945).

BIBLIOGRAPHY

GMO [includes additional bibliography]
A.-L. Björling and A. Farkas: *Jussi* (Portland, OR, 1996)

A.-L. Björling and A. Farkas: "Jussi Björling's Début at the Met," *OQ*, xiii/2 (1996–7), 78–88

DESMOND SHAWE-TAYLOR/ALAN BLYTH/R

Black, Clint [Patrick] (*b* Long Branch, NJ, 4 Feb 1962). Country recording artist. Despite the fact that Clint Black entered the country music mainstream in the late 1980s, he is frequently grouped with the "hat acts" of the early 1990s such as Garth Brooks, Tim McGraw, and Alan Jackson. However, it was his distinctive mix of Texan honky-tonk and pop rock, combined with his talents as a songwriter, entertainer, multi-instrumentalist, actor, and director, that paved the way for the artists who later overshadowed him throughout the 1990s and beyond.

Born in New Jersey and raised in Houston, Texas, Black spent his formative years as an ironworker, fishing guide, and bar room musician; he dropped out of high school in 1978 to perform in his brother's band, which brought him considerable local success over the next few years. Black eventually caught the attention of RCA, which in 1987 offered him a recording contract. His debut album, *Killin' Time* (RCA, 1989), was a commercial success, charting four number-one hits, including "Better Man" and "Nobody's Home," selling over two million copies within a year, and earning him the Academy of Country Music's awards for Album of the Year, Single of the Year, and Top Male Vocalist in 1989. His follow-up album, *Put Yourself in My Shoes* (RCA, 1990), was equally successful, yielding two number-one hits, "Loving Blind" and "Where Are you Now," and selling over three million copies by 1997. Black is also known for the many collaborations he recorded in throughout the 1990s with artists such as George Jones, Steve Wariner, and Martina McBride, the latter with whom he shared a Grammy Award in 1998 for Best Country Collaboration with Vocals for "Still Holding On." In 2003, Black stepped back from his performing career to found his own record label Equity Music that dissolved in late 2008, but not before releasing albums by artists such as Little Big Town, Shannon Lawson, and Mark Willis.

DAVID B. PRUETT

Black, Frank J. (*b* Philadelphia, PA, 29 Nov 1894; *d* Atlanta, GA, 29 Jan 1968). Conductor and composer. At Haverford College he studied piano and chemistry. He began the serious study of music with Rafael Joseffy, and wrote songs for vaudeville. He was conductor at the Fox Theater in Philadelphia from 1923, having started as assistant to Erno Rapee. In 1928 he was appointed music director of NBC, and served as general music director from 1932 to 1948. Active in recording studios, he accompanied such artists as Leonard Warren and Bidú Sayão; with Oscar Levant he recorded Gershwin's *Rhapsody in Blue*. His recordings with the NBC orchestra include works by C.P.E. Bach, Johannes Brahms, Albert Roussel, Jean Sibelius, and others. In the 1930s he coached the Revelers, a popular vocal quartet. Among Black's compositions are *Bells at Eventide* and *A Sea Tale*. He scored Edna St. Vincent Millay's *The Murder of Lidice* and Alice Duer Miller's *The White Cliffs of Dover*, and also made arrangements of works by Bach and Beethoven.

BIBLIOGRAPHY

W.G. King: "About Frank Black, Guest Conductor of the NBC Symphony: at the Stadium," *New York Sun* (22 July 1939)
D. Ewen: *Dictators of the Baton* (Chicago and New York, 1943, rev. and enlarged 2/1948), 273
J. Holmes: *Conductors on Record* (Westport, CT, 1982)

SORAB MODI

Blass, Robert (*b* New York, 27 Oct 1867; *d* Berlin, 3 Dec 1930). Bass. Educated in New York public schools, Blass entered the Leipzig Conservatory in 1887, planning violin study with Hans Sitt. Found to have an excellent singing voice, he continued instead under Gustav Ewald and then in Frankfurt with Julius Stockhausen. In 1895 Blass debuted at Weimar as Heinrich in *Lohengrin*, leading to engagements in Germany and at Covent Garden. In 1900 he debuted with the Metropolitan Opera as Herrmann in *Tannhäuser*. His sole season at Bayreuth was in 1901. Blass sang frequently at the Metropolitan until 1910; he participated in the American premiere of *Parsifal* (24 December 1903), the infamous New York premiere (22 January 1907) of *Salome*, and Mahler's debut (1 January 1908; *Tristan und Isolde*). Blass later sang at the Deutsche Oper, Berlin (1913–9), and again with the Metropolitan, singing German opera in English (1920–22). He subsequently retired to Berlin to teach.

Though familiar with French and Italian repertoire, Blass sang chiefly German repertoire in London and New York. Considering the roles he most often sang – Herrmann; Heinrich; Marke in *Tristan und Isolde*; Pogner in *Die Meistersinger*; Fasolt, Fafner, Hunding and Hagen in *Der Ring*; and Gurnemanz in *Parsifal* – Blass clearly possessed an instrument of considerable power and depth, as his extant recordings (Mapleson cylinders, Edison and Victor) also suggest.

BIBLIOGRAPHY

GroveO (J.B. Steane)
"Robert Blass Dies; Once in Opera Here," *New York Times* (10 Dec 1930) [obituary]

SCOTT ALAN SOUTHARD

Black American music. *See* African american music.

Black Artists Group [BAG]. Community artists' organization founded in St. Louis in 1968. Headed by the free-jazz proponents Oliver Lake, Julius Hemphill, Hamiet Blueitt, and Lester Bowie, this multi-arts collective produced poetry, dance, theater, and visual arts. Musicians frequently collaborated with others from the Chicago-based Association for the advancement of creative musicians, which provided a model for the BAG's activities, including free performances, lectures, and demonstrations at public schools. The BAG's free education program was directed towards St. Louis's low-income areas and its African American youth. The organization was heavily supported, with funding contributions from the Inner City Arts Project of St. Louis, the Rockefeller

Foundation, and the Danforth Foundation. With ties to the Black Arts and Black Power movements, the BAG focused on cultural and artistic autonomy for the African American community through collective self-determination. It fostered the careers of numerous musicians, poets, dance and drum ensembles, acting ensembles, entertainers, filmmakers, and TV producers; several performing arts centres were founded by BAG members. Although it was disbanded in October 1972, some of its members continued to promote its values in a number of notable groups including the BAG ensemble, based in Paris from 1972 to 1974, and the World Saxophone Quartet which was formed in 1976.

BIBLIOGRAPHY

B. Looker: *"Point from which Creation Begins": the Black Artists' Group of St. Louis* (St. Louis, 2004)

T. Perkins: "St. Louis Symposium Salutes BAG," *DB*, lxxiii/5 (2006), 13

RYAN D.W. BRUCE

Black Arts Movement. The Black Arts Movement is most commonly referred to as the artistic arm of the Black Power Movement. Although it has largely been referred to as a literary movement—due in large part to the impact of writers such as AMIRI BARAKA (LeRoi Jones), Larry Neal, and Nikki Giovanni—the movement's goals were also advanced by musicians, painters, photographers and filmmakers. Aesthetically and philosophically the movement and its leaders sought to articulate and represent, through various forms of artistic expression, the diverse cultural and historical phenomenon that have shaped the African American experience. Its beginnings can be traced to the assassination of Malcolm X (El Hajj Malik El-Shabazz) in 1965. Jones and Neal, both black nationalists, called out to artists to join the black liberation movement and work toward creating a decidedly "black" art that would appeal both to the masses and those within the academy by drawing heavily from an Afrocentric cultural tradition. Many avant-garde jazz artists, including John Coltrane, Albert Ayler, and Archie Shepp, among others, embraced the tenets of the movement. A 1965 concert by Sun Ra and his Arkestra at the Village Gate marked the opening of the Black Arts Repertory Theater/School (BART/S), the cultural "center" of the movement in Harlem. The movement helped inspire the creation of the Association for the Advancement of Creative Musicians (AACM) in Chicago, the Black Arts Group in St. Louis, the Jazz Composers Orchestra and Detroit's Creative Musicians Association. The impact of the Black Arts Movement can also be heard in the soundtracks that accompanied blaxploitation films of the 1970. The movement's end is often tied to the larger dismantling of the Black Power Movement during the mid-to-late 1970s.

BIBLIOGRAPHY

M.J. Gladney: "The Black Arts Movement and Hip-hop," *African American Review*, xxix (1995), 291–301

E.G. Price, III: *Free Jazz and the Black Arts Movement, 1958–1967* (diss., U. of Pittsburgh, 2000)

F. Ho: "An Asian American tribute to the Black Arts Movement," *Wicked Theory, Naked Practice: a Fred Ho Reader*, ed. D. Fujino (Minneapolis, 2009), 161–210

TAMMY L. KERNODLE

Black bottom [black shuffle]. A quick-tempo social dance performed in the 1920s to the music of the big bands. It is thought to have originated in the early 1900s in the "juke" joints of the "Bottoms," the African American quarter of Nashville. The movements of the dance are described in Perry Bradford's song "The Original Black Bottom Dance" (1919) thus:

> Hop down front and then you Doodle back
> Mooch to your left and then you Mooch to your right,
> Hands on your hips and do the Mess Around,
> Break a Leg until you're near the ground.
> Now that's the Old Black Bottom Dance.

The "doodle" was a slide, and the "break a leg" referred to a hobbling step. The dance also involved a twisting motion of the body (similar to the shimmy), hops forward and back, side turns, stamps, a skating glide performed with deep knee bends, and, according to Marshall and Jean Stearns, "a genteel slapping of the backside"; as a theatrical dance, it included kicks and high leaps. The popularity of the black bottom and other related dances, such as the Charleston (*see* CHARLESTON (ii)), developed from the success of the black revue *Shuffle Along* (1921). The first theatrical adaptation of the black bottom occurred in the show *Dinah* (1924), produced by Irving C. Miller in Harlem, but it was Ann Pennington's performance of the dance to the song "Black Bottom" (music by Ray Henderson, lyrics by Buddy DeSylva and Lew Brown) in *George White's Scandals of 1926* that led to its widespread popularity.

BIBLIOGRAPHY

M. Stearns and J. Stearns: *Jazz Dance: the Story of American Vernacular Dance* (New York, 1968)

L.F. Emery: *Black Dance in the United States from 1619 to 1970* (Palo Alto, CA, 1970)

P. Oliver: *The Meaning of the Blues* (New York, 1972)

B. Cohen-Stratyner: "'A Thousand Raggy, Draggy Dances': Social Dance in Broadway Musical Comedy in the 1920s," *Ballroom, Boogie, Shimmy Sham, Shake: a Social and Popular Dance Reader* (Urbana, IL, 2009), 217–33

PAULINE NORTON/R

Black Eyed Peas, the. Hip-hop group. It was formed in 1995 in Los Angeles by will.i.am (William James Adams, Jr.; *b* Inglewood, CA, 15 March 1975; rapping, vocals, various instruments), apl.de.ap (Allan Pineda Lindo Jr.; *b* Angeles City, Philippines, 28 November 1975; rapping, drums), and Taboo (Jaime Luis Gómez; *b* Los Angeles, CA, 14 July 1975; rapping, keyboard). The group grew out of Atban Klann (1991–5), a Los Angeles-based group signed for a time to Eazy-E's Ruthless Records. The Black Eyed Peas developed an approach that fused elements of global pop, jazz-rock, funk, soul, noise music, and a variety of hip-hop styles. Initially considered somewhat of an underground phenomenon, the Black Eyed Peas achieved worldwide commercial success after being joined by Fergie (Stacy Ann Ferguson; *b* Hacienda Heights, CA, 27 March 1975; rapping, vocals) in 2003. The group's third and fourth albums, *Elephunk* (2003) and *Monkey Business* (2005), feature her voice prominently and exhibit new levels of stylistic eclecticism, with Fergie alternating between rapping and singing often to accentuate the verse-chorus form of their songs. Their fifth album, *The E. N. D.* (2009), incorporates elements of electronic dance music, foregrounding the sound of synthesizer strings and bass over four-to-the-floor drum tracks. Benefitting from the success of two of the album's hit singles, "Boom Boom Pow" and "I Gotta Feeling," the group stayed on top of the *Billboard Hot 100* chart for a record-breaking 26-week period in 2009. In 2010, they released *The Beginning*, another commercially successful album.

AKITSUGU KAWAMOTO

Blackface minstrelsy. *See* MINSTRELSY.

Black Flag. Hardcore punk band founded in Hermosa Beach, California, in 1976 by the guitarist and songwriter Greg Ginn (*b* 8 June 1954). Key members included the singers Keith Morris, Dez Cadena, and notably HENRY ROLLINS (1981–6); the bass players Chuck Dukowski and Kira Roessler; and the drummers Robo and Bill Stevenson. One of the definitive hardcore bands of its era, Black Flag toured extensively and helped to establish the alternative rock circuit. Their strong DIY ethos inspired countless other bands, as did their forming the record label SST, which despite legal difficulties, released albums by important bands including Sonic Youth, Hüsker Dü, and Dinosaur Jr. The band's name and its distinctive visual imagery were provided by Ginn's brother, the artist Raymond Pettibon, helping to establish the trend of hardcore bands adopting easily copied symbols.

Until the band broke up in 1986, Ginn remained its main songwriter but its music evolved with changes in membership. Punk simplicity and confrontational vocals collided with stridently atonal guitar solos and frequent tempo changes. Like much punk, Ginn's lyrics express anti-authoritarian sentiments and explore themes of personal alienation. Early songs often featured a faster tempo than their hardcore contemporaries, but the group began to favor slower songs, reflecting the influence of heavy metal, as heard on the album *My War* (1984). The slower pace alienated many early fans but the new sound profoundly influenced the development of grunge.

BIBLIOGRAPHY

D. Grad: "Black Flag: an Oral history," *We Owe you Nothing: Punk Planet, the Collected Interviews*, ed. D. Sinker (New York, 2001), 76–93

R.M. Moore: *Sells like Teen Spirit: Music, Youth culture, and Social Crisis* (New York, 2010)

LUKAS PEARSE

Blackfoot (i) [Siksika]. Native Americans of a northern Plains culture, now primarily in Montana and southern Canada; they are distributed among three groups distinguished in name as the PIEGAN, BLOOD (Kainah), and NORTHERN BLACKFOOT. The amount of music and the association of musical performances with other activities in Blackfoot culture indicate that music fulfills a generalized role (although perhaps less now than in the late 19th century). Songs, both religious and secular, are symbols of real events and do not exist for their own sake; the main function of song is to serve as an authenticating device for ceremonial acts and as a statement of tribal identity.

The Blackfoot view the origin of songs as supernatural: songs are learned in dreams or visions, though modern songs may be borrowed from other cultures. When a song is performed, credit is normally given to the person who dreamed it or the tribe from which it is borrowed. The prescribed learning technique is not a phrase-by-phrase repetition but careful listening to the song in its entirety; recording equipment (whether in the form of cassettes or MP3s) is valuable for the dissemination of songs, especially those sung on the powwow circuit. Songs have special significance to the Blackfoot, and there is a traditional scale of values for songs according to the degree to which they fulfill their function. The most highly valued are those relating to ceremonies, but within each ceremony some are more powerful than others. Since the mid-20th century some songs seem to be valued for purely aesthetic reasons. The age of a song is considered important in determining its value, old songs being held in high esteem. Traditionally the knowledge of powerful songs was considered more important than technical ability, but now, perhaps through exposure to European musical values, a "good voice" has become a more important element of good singing. Various performance rules have also changed over the last 100 years. The rule requiring performance of songs at the "right time only" has been relaxed except among a few traditionalists, and the restriction of repetitions to the sacred number of four has changed to repetition for as long as the singers (or dancers) may desire.

Songs may be either ceremonial or social. Ceremonial songs include those related to the Sun Dance, medicine bundles (collections of ceremonial objects wrapped in cloth or skins, especially those objects associated with the beaver and horse cults), men's societies (seven age-grade societies), and healing. For both individual and group entertainment, song genres include riding songs, songs associated with sports (horse races and hand games), and various social dances (such as the Grass Dance, the Rabbit Dance, and the Forty-niner Dance, popular throughout the Plains area). In general the Blackfoot musical style conforms to that of other Plains cultures. An old and a new repertory, with some stylistic differences, can be distinguished. The old is derived from the music of older ceremonial practices, such as the Sun Dance and medicine bundle ceremonies. Fairly complex and varied, this material is often sung solo in a chest voice with typical Plains-style pulsations. Song texts generally are lexical. The new repertory conforms to the intertribal powwow style established in the 1940s. It consists of songs with sharply descending melodic contours, using scales of four or five tones in which the intervals of a minor third and major second occur frequently; tessitura is generally high and vocal delivery tense. The typical form consists of a short section sung by a soloist and repeated by a second singer, followed by several phrases sung by the group and then repeated by the group (*AABCA′ BCA′*, in which *A′* represents an octave displacement of *A*).

Blackfoot Indian powwow, c1893. (Minnesota Historical Society)

Instruments are less prominent among the Blackfoot than among other Indian cultures. In the 19th century the Blackfoot had two kinds of drum, a large double-headed drum and a smaller single-headed frame drum. The larger, used for the Sun Dance, was made from a hollowed-out tree trunk covered with two skin heads; as a result of contact with Whites a large washtub covered with a single head was often substituted, as later was the bass drum. The smaller drum, a hoop covered with one head, was used for various ceremonies. In the 1950s small double-headed drums also became common. The container rattle, usually made from rawhide, is the most varied and important instrument, though the importance of many of them is derived from their ceremonial usage. Musically their function is to provide a percussive accompaniment like that of the drum. However, unlike drums, rattles are used in more intimate contexts such as the various bundle ceremonies in which medicine bundles are unwrapped while prescribed songs are sung. Certain types of rattles, pertaining to men's societies and medicine cults, are rarely played today. The eagle-bone whistle is also a ceremonial object among the Blackfoot; as with other Plains tribes, this instrument is used almost exclusively for the Sun Dance and is played simultaneously with the drum. The flute is rare; its appearance and use may be a borrowing from other Plains tribes.

Contact with non-Blackfoot peoples has always had an influence on music in Blackfoot culture. The practice of "borrowing" individual songs from neighboring Indian cultures is documented in the 19th century, and today entire groups of songs may be "borrowed" by performers traveling thousands of miles a year on the powwow circuit. Another major outside influence has been the music of various Anglo groups: religious, educational, and popular. Performance of this so-called "white music" by Blackfoot musicians began in the early 20th century, reached a peak in the 1920s, then nearly disappeared before being revived in the 1950s In recent decades there have been dozens of groups, formal and informal, performing religious songs, band music, and (among the-young) country, rock, and gospel music. The practitioners of this "white music" normally do not perform traditional Blackfoot songs, though the audience for both may often be the same.

Recordings of Blackfoot music made in the field are in the holdings of the Archives of Traditional Music at Indiana University, Bloomington, and the American Museum of Natural History, New York.

DISCOGRAPHY

Indian Music of the Canadian Plains, 1955, FW P464 [with liner notes by K. Peacock]

Twelve Blackfoot Songs, 1965, Indian Records 220

Blackfoot A-l Club Singers, 1973, IH 4001–2

From the Land of the Blackfoot, 1973, Can. C6095

Blackfoot A-l Singers, 1975, Can. C6132

Songs from the Blood Reserve: Kai-Spai Singers, 1975, Can. C6133

An Historical Album of Blackfoot Indian Music, 1979, FW FE34001 [with liner notes by B. Nettl]

Kicking Woman Singers Pow-wow Songs, v.8, 1994, Can. CR6253
Oyate Ta Olowan: Songs of the People vol. 2, 1998, Lee Productions
Siksika Singers: Owl Dance of the Siksika Nation, 2001, Can. CR6332
Blackfoot Confederacy: Confederacy Style, 2006, Can. CR6405

BIBLIOGRAPHY

C. Wissler: *Social Organization and Ritualistic Ceremonies of the Blackfoot Indian* (New York, 1912)
A. Nevin: "Two Summers with the Blackfeet Indians of Montana," *MQ*, ii (1916), 257–70
J. Ewers: *The Blackfoot: Raiders on the Northwestern Plains* (Norman, OK, 1958)
B. Nettl: "Blackfoot Music in Browning, 1965, Functions and Attitudes," *Festschrift fur Walter Wiora* (Kassel, Germany, 1967), 593–98
B. Nettl: "Studies in Blackfoot Indian Musical Culture," *EM*, xi (1967), 141, 293; xii (1968), 11–48, 192
B. Nettl: "Biography of a Blackfoot Indian Singer," *MQ*, liv (1968), 199–207
R.E. Witmer: *The Musical Culture of the Blood Indians* (thesis, U. of Illinois, 1970)
R.E. Witmer: "Recent Change in the Musical Culture of the Blood Indians of Alberta, Canada," *Yearbook for Inter-American Musical Research*, ix (1973), 64–94
B. Nettl: *Blackfoot Musical Thought: Comparative Perspectives* (Kent, OH, 1989)
T. Browner: "Breathing the Indian Spirit: Thoughts on musical borrowing and the 'Indianist' movement in American Music," *AM*, xv (1997), 265–84

J. RICHARD HAEFER

Blackfoot (ii) [Sihasapa]. Native Americans belonging to the Teton subgroup of the SIOUX. They are unrelated to the Blackfoot (i) Indians.

Blackman, Cindy [Cynthia Regina] (*b* Yellow Springs, OH, 18 Nov 1959). Drummer. She was raised in Connecticut among a family of eclectic musicians and music-lovers. At the age of eight she decided to become a drummer. She played in school ensembles and a local fife-and-drum corps before studying classical percussion at the University of Hartford and jazz at the Berklee College of Music. From 1982 she moved to New York and befriended jazz drummers including Max Roach, Elvin Jones, Art Blakey, Roy Haynes, and Philly Joe Jones. Around the same time, she played with, among others, George Braith, Joe Henderson, Freddie Hubbard, Jackie McLean, Don Pullen, Esther Thomas, and Sam Rivers's Big Band. From 1987 she has led her own groups and performed with them around the world; her sidemen have included Wallace Roney, Gary Bartz, Gary Thomas, Antoine Roney, Marc Copland, Jacky Terrasson, Charnett Moffett, Clarence Seay, and Ugonna Okegwo. As a freelancer she has also worked with Ravi Coltrane, Roney, Rachel Z, and Michael Marcus. Blackman dismisses the notion of the drums as a man's instrument, maintaining positions in the top tier of both rock and jazz musics internationally. Her high profile as a drummer is matched among women only by Sheila E and is due mostly to a 14-year stint with the rock musician Lenny Kravitz (1993–2007). She has been influenced by the energetic, experimental, and technically advanced approach of musicians in the late 1960s, especially that of the drummer Tony Williams, after whose jazz-rock group her album *Another Lifetime* (Four Quarters 2010) was named. Referring to her intense approach to playing the drums, she says that when she plays she is the Terminator.

BIBLIOGRAPHY

R. Macdonald: "Present Intense," *Rhythm* (Jan 1993), 50–56
L. King: "A League of her Own," *Rhythm* (Dec 1999), 48–54
K. Micallef: "Cindy Blackman: the Lady Comes to Play," *Modern Drummer* (2008), June, 60–71

GARETH DYLAN SMITH

Blackmar, A(rmand) E(dward) (*b* Bennington, VT, 30 May 1826; *d* New Orleans, LA, 28 Oct 1888). Music publisher and dealer. After graduating from Western Reserve College, he worked as a music teacher in Huntsville, Alabama (1845–52), and Jackson, Louisiana (1852–5). In 1858 he joined E.D. Patton's music shop in Vicksburg, Mississippi, which he bought out the following year with his younger brother Henry. They moved to New Orleans in 1860, where they operated publishing firms and music shops jointly, separately, and often with others. From 1862 to 1865 Henry also ran a shop in Augusta, Georgia. Armand was imprisoned briefly in 1862 by the Union Army for his espousal of the southern cause; he issued more Confederate music than any other publisher in New Orleans, including one of the earliest editions of "Dixie" (1861), and "The Bonnie Blue Flag" (1861) and "Maryland! My Maryland!" (1862). He frequently arranged or composed music under the pseudonym A. Noir. Blackmar was in San Francisco between 1877 and 1880, but was publishing again in New Orleans from 1881 to 1888.

BIBLIOGRAPHY

R.B. Harwell: *Confederate Music* (Chapel Hill, NC, 1950)
P.C. Boudreaux: *Music Publishing in New Orleans in the 19th Century* (thesis, Louisiana State U., 1977)
R. Powell: *A Study of A.E. Blackmar and Bro., Music Publishers of New Orleans, Louisiana, and Augusta, Georgia, with a Checklist of Imprints in Louisiana Collections* (thesis, Louisiana State U., 1978)
F.W. Hoogerwerf: *Confederate Sheet-Music Imprints* (Brooklyn, NY, 1984)

JOHN H. BARON/R

Black music. *See* AFRICAN AMERICAN MUSIC.

Black Patti. *See* JONES, SISSIERETTA.

Black Rock Coalition [BRC]. Arts organization founded in New York in October 1985 and in Los Angeles in 1989. It was formed by African American musicians, artists, and music industry professionals based in New York in response to the race-based assumptions about music-making that dominated the 1980s. The BRC addresses the racial segregation of music in the recording industry and provides an outlet for African American rock musicians to develop and promote their craft. Its co-founders were the guitarist Vernon Reid, the writer Greg Tate, and the artist manager Konda Mason. A nonprofit organization run by volunteers, it stages concerts, sponsors panel discussions, produces recordings, and hosts a radio show in order to draw attention to the breadth of musical sounds and styles engaged by African American musicians.

The BRC argues against the recording industry's practice of limiting African American musicians to rhythm-and-blues and dance music. A primary reason for the formation of the BRC was to support Reid's efforts to win a recording contract for his hard-rock band Living Colour. To address the common view held by black and white recording industry executives and music fans that black people were not interested in rock and that rock was white music, BRC members invoked a historical argument that recalled the African American roots of rock and roll. Articulating their position in the *BRC Manifesto*, the organization's founding document, the members asserted, "Rock music is black music and we are its heirs."

Over the years, the BRC has offered a support network and performance opportunities for African American musicians. The BRC showcases black rock bands in concerts and through compilation recordings including *The History of our Future* (Rykodisc, 1991), *Blacker than that* (BRC, 1993), *The Bronze Buckaroo Rides Again* (BRC, 2000), and *Rock 'n' Roll Reparations, Vol. 1* (BRC, 2005), and *Rock 'n' Roll Reparations, Vol. 2* (BRC, 2010).

The BRC Orchestra has performed in Europe and the United States, presenting shows celebrating such artists as Otis Blackwell, Jimi Hendrix, Prince, Stevie Wonder, Nina Simone, and Gil Scott-Heron whose music epitomizes the creative freedom the organization seeks for its musicians. BRC members work in a range of musical styles including funk, punk, hard rock, metal, electronica, and jazz. Artists who have been affiliated with the organization include Kelvyn Bell, Jean-Paul Bourelly, Burnt Sugar, the BusBoys, Don Byron, Chocolate Genius, Eye and I, the Family Stand, Dave Fiuczynski, Follow for Now, Melvin Gibbs, Nona Hendryx, Living Colour, Michael Hill's Blues Mob, Meshell Ndegeocello, Sophia Ramos, Screaming Headless Torsos, Sekou Sundiata, 24–7 Spyz, and Bernie Worrell.

BIBLIOGRAPHY

K. Crazy Horse, ed.: *Rip it Up: the Black Experience in Rock 'n' Roll* (New York, 2004)

M. Mahon: *Right to Rock: the Black Rock Coalition and the Cultural Politics of Race* (Durham, NC, 2004)

MAUREEN MAHON

Blackstone, Tsianina Redfeather [Evans, Florence Tsianina] (*b* Eufaula, OK, 13 Dec 1882; *d* San Diego, CA, 10 Jan 1985). Mezzo-soprano of Cherokee and Creek descent, though often misidentified as Choctaw or Omaha. She attended the Eufaula, Oklahoma Government Indian School, where she learned to play the piano. Although she was frequently billed as "Princess Tsianina," there is no indication that Tsianina's family held any leadership role in their community. At the urging of school officials, 16-year-old Tsianina was sent to Denver to study piano with Edward Fleck. She also studied voice with John Wilcox, who introduced her to composer CHARLES WAKEFIELD CADMAN. Wilcox believed that the teenaged Tsianina was the perfect performer and "interpreter" of Cadman's Indianist compositions, and convinced Cadman to audition her for a national tour.

Tsianina and Cadman gave approximately 400 performances over the course of 14 years, performing at chautauquas, expositions, and in independent concerts. During World War I, Tsianina traveled to Europe to entertain the American army. After the war, she resumed her collaboration with Cadman, performing on the commercial chautauqua circuits. Cadman's opera *Shanewis, or The Robin Woman*, was loosely based on Tsianina's life. Tsianina was in the audience at the 1918 Metropolitan Opera premiere and sang the role of Shanewis in her operatic debut at a performance in Denver in 1924. Tsianina also appeared as a soloist with the US Indian Band (formerly the Carlisle Indian Band) on its 1924 tour, and in several operas on Native American subjects in the late 1920s. She sang the role of Shanewis again in 1926, in an elaborate production at the Hollywood Bowl. Tsianina retired from public performance in the 1930s and devoted her remaining years to activism on behalf of Native Americans.

BIBLIOGRAPHY

A.D. Palmer: "Tsianina Blackstone: a Chapter in the History of the American Indian in Opera," *Liberal Arts Review*, no.7 (1979), 40–51

T. Blackstone: *Where Trails have Led Me* (Santa Fe, 3/1982)

J. Troutman: *"Indian Blues": American Indians and the Politics of Music, 1890–1935* (diss., U. of Texas, 2004)

A. DEAN PALMER/PAIGE CLARK LUSH

Black Swan. Record label. It was launched in Harlem in 1921 by the Pace Phonograph Corp. (later renamed the Black Swan Phonograph Co.), whose principal Harry H. Pace (1884–1943) sought to make a phonograph record company a vehicle for social, political, and economic uplift for African Americans. The company aimed to issue high-quality records by African Americans in all styles of music—not just blues and popular genres, but also opera, concert music, and religious works. This catholicity, Pace believed, would undermine racial and cultural stereotypes about African Americans, on the one hand, and promote African Americans' own cultural development, on the other. At the same time, the company sought to be an archetype of economic development, both a model and symbol of African American capital accumulation and economic self-determination. The venture grew out of Pace's diverse background in music, business, and political activism: he was a former songwriting partner of W.C. Handy, with whom he established the Pace and Handy Music Publishing Co.; he had worked for important black-owned banking and insurance companies; and he had been a protégé of W.E.B. Du Bois, whom Pace recruited to sit on Black Swan's board of directors. The name of the label was inspired by the 19th-century African American concert singer Elizabeth Taylor Greenfield, whose sobriquet was "the Black Swan." (Although Black Swan is often cited as the first black-owned record company, this distinction apparently belongs to Broome Records, established in Boston in 1918.)

Despite receiving considerable support in the black press, the company struggled commercially, its competitive standing weakened by growing competition in the "race" market, Black Swan's halting commitment to blues records, and the growing popularity of radio. In three years of activity, however, the company issued nearly 200 recordings (including at least 45 sides of "serious" music), sold hundreds of thousands of discs, and distributed its products around the country and abroad. Black Swan helped launch the careers of Fletcher Henderson (leader of the house orchestra), William Grant Still (house arranger), Ethel Waters, Alberta Hunter, and Trixie Smith, and made the only known recordings of several notable figures from African American musical theater. Although Black Swan claimed in advertisements to market only records made by black musicians, straitened financial circumstances led the company to issue numerous records by white artists whose identities were hidden behind generic pseudonyms; this deception was later revealed by collectors and researchers, apparently having gone undetected at the time. Black Swan issued its last record in July 1923. The following year, Pace entered into a leasing agreement with Paramount Records to continue to sell Black Swan recordings, but this arrangement lasted little more than a year. As a label name, "Black Swan" has also been used by Jazzology, since 1987, for its series of Paramount reissues; by Island Records, to issue Jamaican music in the 1960s and 70s; and by Trojan Records, in the early 1970s, for its release of early reggae records.

BIBLIOGRAPHY

R. Ottley and W.J. Weatherby, eds.: *The Negro in New York: an Informal Social History* (New York, 1967), 232–5

H. Thygesen, M. Berresford, and R. Shor: *Black Swan: The Record Label of the Harlem Renaissance* (Nottingham, 1996)

D. Suisman: "Co-Workers in the Kingdom of Culture: Black Swan Records and the Political Economy of African American Music," *Journal of American History*, xc (2004), 1295–1324

DAVID SUISMAN

Blackwell, Ed(ward Joseph) (*b* New Orleans, LA, 10 Oct 1929; *d* Hartford, CT, 7 Oct 1992). Jazz drummer and educator. He grew up in a musical family in New Orleans. During the 1950s he was a member of the American Jazz Quintet, which included Ellis Marsalis, Alvin Battiste, Harold Battiste, and, for a time, Ornette Coleman. He also worked irregularly with Coleman between 1949 and 1956 in New Orleans and Los Angeles, toured with Ray Charles in 1957. In 1960 Blackwell moved to New York to become the drummer with Coleman's quartet at the Five Spot club, a position previously held by Billy Higgins, and both Higgins and Blackwell performed as members of the double quartets on Coleman's album *Free Jazz: a Collective Improvisation* (1960, Atl.). He became influential in the emerging free-jazz scene, performing and recording with, among others, Coleman (*This is our Music*, 1960, Atl., and *Ornette on Tenor*, 1961, Atl.), Don Cherry (*Complete Communion*, 1965, BN), and Eric Dolphy (*Eric Dolphy at the Five Spot*, 1961, New Jazz). After suffering from kidney failure in 1973, he resumed work with Cherry and founded the Old and New Dreams quartet with Dewey Redman (*Old and New Dreams*, 1979, ECM). In the 1980s he worked with Cherry, Dolphy, and Anthony Braxton.

Blackwell's style was well suited to free-jazz. His use of elements from New Orleans second-line parade, African, and Afro-Cuban musics moved the emphasis away from the swing sound associated with bebop, and his adeptness at shifting meters and tempos allowed the rhythmic structure of free jazz to be as mobile as the melodic structures created by Coleman, Cherry, and others. In contrast to most jazz drummers of the time, he also emphasised the drums more than the cymbals, and his playing was relatively sparse, which allowed for more agile transitions in tempo and less collision between the drums and the increasingly complicated bass techniques pioneered by Charlie Haden and Scott LaFaro. Blackwell worked at Wesleyan University as an artist-in-residence in the period 1971–2 and remained associated with the university from 1974 until his death from kidney disease in 1992.

BIBLIOGRAPHY

D.J. Schmalenberger: *Stylistic Evolution of Jazz Drummer Ed Blackwell: the Cultural Intersection of New Orleans and West Africa* (diss., West Virginia U., 2000)

T.S. Jenkins: *Free Jazz and Free Improvisation: an Encyclopedia* (Santa Barbara, CA, 2004)

L. Feather and I. Gitler: *The Biographical Encyclopedia of Jazz* (New York, 2007)

JOHN BASS

Blackwell, Otis (*b* Brooklyn, NY, 16 Feb 1932; *d* Nashville, TN, 6 May 2002). Rhythm-and-blues songwriter and singer. His list of over 900 songs includes several of Elvis Presley's best-known hits. Blackwell's earliest success as an African American songwriter came with "Fever," written for the singer Little Willie John in 1956; this sensual ballad was later taken up by the cabaret star Peggy Lee, who added new lyrics. In a different vein, Blackwell composed the gospel-tinged "Daddy Rolling Stone," which became a favorite of English rock groups such as the Who. For Presley, Blackwell wrote the pulsating "All Shook Up," "Don't be cruel," "Paralysed," and the quirky ballad "Return to Sender." As part of the publishing contract, Presley was credited as co-author of the songs, although he did not contribute to their composition. Blackwell also composed the tempestuous "Great Balls of Fire" and "Breathless" for another rock and roll star, Jerry Lee Lewis; like "All Shook Up," these songs built up tension through sudden breaks in the flow of the song. During the early 1960s Blackwell also wrote the song "Handy Man" for Jimmy Jones, "Nine Times out of Ten" for Cliff Richard, and "Hey Little Girl" for Dee Clark. He recorded his own versions of his best songs on the album *These are my Songs* (Inner City, 1978).

DAVE LAING/R

Blackwood, Easley (*b* Indianapolis, IN, 21 April 1933). Composer and pianist. He studied with Olivier Messiaen at the Berkshire Music Center (1949), with Paul Hindemith at Yale (1950–54), and, on a Fulbright scholarship, with Nadia Boulanger in Paris (1954–7). From 1958 to 1997, he taught theory and composition at the University of Chicago where, as of 2011, he serves as Professor Emeritus.

He has received a first prize from the Koussevitzky Foundation (1958), the Brandeis Creative Arts Award (1968), and commissions from the Chicago SO and the Library of Congress. In the late 1970s he received a grant from the NEH to investigate the harmonic and modal properties of microtonal tunings. Blackwood's 1986 book *The Structure of Recognizable Diatonic Tunings* is a great resource on these harmonic and modal properties, as well as the mathematics involved in tuning theory. As a pianist he has distinguished himself as an interpreter of the contemporary repertory, notably the second sonatas of Ives and Boulez and the solo works of Schoenberg, Berg, and Webern.

After early works in a modernist idiom (dating from 1946), Blackwood adopted in the 1950s a more conservative style, best represented in his First Symphony. During the 1960s and 70s he returned to an atonal language involving complex counterpoint. This phase culminated in works such as his *Twelve Microtonal Etudes* (1980) (*see* TUNING SYSTEMS), *Fanfare* (1981), and the Sonata for guitar (1983). In the early 1980s his style again became conservative with the adoption of forms and a harmonic language more commonly associated with the 19th century. Works from this period include his Fifth Symphony (1990), which has a conventional sonata-form first movement, developmental sections, and clear harmonic progressions, and his *A King James Magnificat* (2004), which subtly incorporates ten different keys over the course of its ten verses.

WORKS

Orch: Sym. no.1, op.3, 1955; Sym. no.2, op.9, 1960; Cl Conc., op.13, 1964; Sym. no.3, op.14, 1964; Sym. Fantasy, op.17, 1965; Ob Conc., op.19, 1965; Vn Conc., op.21, chbr orch, 1967; Fl Conc., op.23, str, 1968; Pf Conc., op.24, 1970; Sym. no.4, 1977; Sym. no.5, op.34, 1990

Vocal: Un voyage à Cythère (C. Baudelaire), op.20, S, wind, 1966; 4 Letter Scenes from Gulliver, op.25, Mez, Bar, tape, 1972; A King James Magnificat, op.44, chorus, 2004

Chbr and solo inst: Sonata, op.1, va, pf, 1953; Chbr Sym., op.2, 14 wind, 1954; Str Qt no.1, op.4, 1957; Concertino, op.5, 5 insts, 1959; Str Qt no.2, op.6, 1959; Sonata, op.7, vn, pf, 1960; Fantasy, op.8, vc, pf, 1960; Chaconne, op.10, carillon, 1961; Pastorale and Variations, op.11, wind qnt, 1961; Sonata, op.12, fl, hpd, 1962; Fantasy, op.15, fl, cl, pf, 1965; 3 Short Fantasies, op.16, pf, 1965; Sym. Movt, op.18, org, 1966; Pf Trio, op.22, 1967; Sonata no.1, op.26, vn, pf, 1973; Sonata no.2, op.27, vn, pf, 1975; Sonata, op.29, gui, 1983; 5 Concert Etudes, op.30, pf, 1984; Sonata, op.31, vc, pf, 1985; Sonata, op.32, vn, 1986; Suite, op.33, gui in 15-note equal tuning, 1987; Rondo Caprice, op.35, fl, gui, 1992; 7 Bagatelles, op.36, pf, 1993; Sonata, a, op.37, cl, pf, 1994; Sonatina, F, op.38, cl, pf, 1994; Sonatina, op.39, carillon, 1996; Sonata, op.40, pf, 1996; 2 Nocturnes, op.41, pf, 1996; Str Qt no.3, op.42, 1998; Sonata, op.43, va, pf, 2001

El-ac: 12 Microtonal Etudes, op.28, synth, 1980; Fanfare, op.28a, elec music media in 19-note equal tuning, 1981

Principal publisher: G. Schirmer
Principal recording company: Cedille

BIBLIOGRAPHY

D. Keislar: "Six American Composers on Nonstandard Tunings," *PNM*, xxix (1991), 176–211

P. Rapoport: "Just Inton(ot)ation," *1/1, the Journal of the Just Intonation Network*, vii/1 (1991), 1, 12–14

B. Duffie: "Easley Blackwood: the Composer in Conversation with Bruce Duffie" <http://www.bruceduffie.com/blackwood.html>

JAMES R. MCKAY/CHARLES COREY

Blade, Brian (*b* Shreveport, LA, 25 July 1970). Jazz drummer, bandleader, and composer. During his early years he became acquainted with gospel and soul music, studied violin, recorder and melodic percussion and eventually began playing drums in his father's church. While in high school he began listening to John Coltrane, Charlie Parker and other jazz musicians and worked with the Polyphonics, a jazz group led by Dorsey Summerfield Jr. After moving to New Orleans in 1988 to attend Loyola University, Blade studied and played with several local jazz musicians including Ellis Marsalis, John Mahoney, Harry Connick Jr., and Alvin Red Tyler. In 1997 he formed a trio with Joshua Redman and Christian McBride and later performed in another trio with Larry Grenadier and Pat Metheney. In 1998 Blade and Jon Cowherd started recording together as leaders of the group Fellowship; its first album was *Brian Blade Fellowship* (1998, BN). From 2000 Blade has been a member of the Wayne Shorter quartet. He has also worked with such pop musicians as Emmylou Harris and Bob Dylan. Blade has performed and written in various musical styles. Some of his work for Fellowship combines jazz with the sounds of pygmy chants and American folk music in addition to the exotic sounds of the steel guitar. His album *Mama Rosa* (2009, Verve) uses elements of rock, folk, and jazz.

DANIEL JOHN CARROLL

Blades [Bellido de Luna], **Rubén** (*b* Panama City, Panama, 16 July 1946). Panamanian singer, songwriter, actor, and activist. His musical projects are mostly defined by his commitment to social justice and civil rights. The US military occupation of the Canal Zone and riots of 1964, and the military coup of 1968 impacted young Blades's consciousness and artistry. Afro-Caribbean music of the 1970s to 80s, the *Nueva Canción* movement of the 1960–70s, and regional political events shaped his songs, which search for an urban sound and tell everyday life stories. His musical career started in Panama, performing with local bands while attending Law School. In 1969, Blades traveled to New York, when his university closed temporarily as a consequence of political instability. After recording *From Panamá to New York: Pete Rodríguez Presents Rubén Blades*, he returned to Panama and graduated in 1972. Opposed to the military regime, Blades moved back to New York, NY, debuted with Ray Barretto in 1975, and joined Willie Colón in 1976. Together, they recorded some of the most successful salsa albums in history for the Fania label, among them *Siembra* (1978). In 1982 Blades started a new project with his own group Seis del Solar, later Son del Solar. With a different sound (Afro-Caribbean drums, synthesizers, piano, and bass-drum set), Blades music prominently featured the voice and lyrics, including lyrics translated into several languages for the countries in which his albums were sold; *Buscando América* (1984), *Escenas* (1985), and *Antecedente* (1989) were recorded during this period. With *La rosa de los vientos,* recorded in Panama with songs written by Panamanian songwriters (1995), Blades entered a new musical phase that privileged collaborations with musicians from different countries. *Tiempos* (1999) and *Mundo* (2002), with Costa Rican world music band Editus, and *Cantares del subdesarrollo* (2003, released in 2010) with Costa Rican musician and producer Walter Flores were highlights of this period. His recordings have received numerous Grammy Awards. Along with his musical career Blades is active as an actor and politician; he ran for the presidency of Panama in 1994, and served as its Minister of Tourism (2004–8). Blades continues creating spaces for social and political awareness in his international tours, as he did when he broke into the New York dancing scene in the 1970s.

TANIA CAMACHO-AZOFEIFA

Blaine, Hal [Belsky, Harold Simon] (*b* Holyoke, MA, 5 Feb 1929). Drummer. He is best known for playing on pop, rock, and country recordings during the 1960s and 70s with such successful artists as Herb Albert, America, the Association, the Beach Boys, the Byrds, the Carpenters, Petula Clark, Sam Cooke, John Denver, Neil Diamond, the Fifth Dimension, Connie Francis, Lesley Gore, Jan and Dean, the Mamas and the Papas, Henry Mancini, Dean Martin, the Monkees, Roy Orbison, Elvis Presley, the Ronettes, Simon and Garfunkel, Frank Sinatra, Nancy Sinatra, Sonny and Cher, Barbara Streisand, the Supremes, and Tanya Tucker. Between 1959 and 1981 he played on more than 150 recordings that reached the *Billboard* top ten, 39 of which were number-one hits. Part of a group of in-demand session musicians in Los Angeles informally known as THE WRECKING CREW, Blaine worked frequently with the influential producer Phil Spector and is the drummer most responsible for the compelling drumming that undergirds Spector's celebrated "wall of sound," as heard on the Ronettes' "Be my Baby" and the Crystals' "Da doo ron ron," for example. A graduate of the Roy C. Knapp School of Percussion in Chicago, he also recorded drum and percussion parts for numerous television and film soundtracks and commercial jingles, and toured with Denver, Patti Page, Tommy Sands, and Nancy Sinatra.

STEVEN BAUR

Blaisdell, Frances (*b* Tellico Plains, TN, 5 Jan 1912; *d* Portola Valley, CA, 11 March 2009). Flutist. A pupil of Ernest Wagner and GEORGES BARRÈRE, she graduated from the Juilliard School, having won the concerto competition at the age of 18, and studied in France with Marcel Moyse. She played in New York on Broadway, with the Phil Spitalny All Girls' Band, and as accompanist to Lily Pons. In 1938 she formed the Blaisdell Wind Quintet with Bruno Labate (oboe), Alexander Williams (clarinet), Benjamin Cohen (bassoon), and Richard Moore (horn); active until 1941, the group played mainly on the radio and was often heard on the CBS and NBC networks. One of the first women to become a member of an orchestra, Blaisdell was first flutist with the National Orchestra Association and, for 15 years, with the New York City Ballet. She appeared as a soloist with the New York PO, the National Orchestra Association, and the New York SO; in Radio City Music Hall, Madison Square Garden, and major American cities; and on BBC radio. Blaisdell has been on the faculties of the Manhattan School of Music, New York University, and Mannes College, and in 1973 began teaching at Stanford University, where she taught for more than three decades. Blaisdell's playing combined the full tone and musical phrasing of the French school with her own vigorous rhythmic interpretation and an individual use of tone color. She was among the first women to achieve fame as a professional flutist.

BIBLIOGRAPHY

D. Martin: Obituary, *New York Times* (31 Mar 2009)

MARTHA WOODWARD/R

Blake, Blind [Arthur] (*b* Newport News, VA, 1896; *d* Milwaukee, WI, 1 Dec 1934). Songster, blues singer, and guitarist. He is known to have played extensively in Florida and was well known as a songster and guitarist in Georgia and the eastern states. Although he was blind, he traveled as far as Tennessee and Detroit. Between 1926 and 1932 he made some 80 recordings, including a number of instrumental pieces, among which "Blind Arthur's Breakdown" (1929, Para.) demonstrates his unparalleled technique. His playing, which was light and flowing, showed a strong ragtime influence in common with eastern guitarists. Many of his songs were ideal for dancing, while others clearly derived from the medicine show repertory, for example "He's in the jail house now" (1927, Para.). In Detroit Blake formed a partnership with the boogie-woogie pianist Charlie Spand, with whom he made several recordings. He had a melancholy voice that was particularly effective on such blues recordings as "Search Warrant Blues" (1928, Para.) and "Cold Hearted Mama Blues" (1928, Para.). He also accompanied other singers, including Bertha Henderson and Leola B. Wilson, and influenced later singers, Blind Boy Fuller and the songster Bill Williams among them.

BIBLIOGRAPHY

SouthernB
S. Charters: "Blind Blake," *Sweet as the Showers of Rain* (New York, 1977)
P. Oliver: *Songsters and Saints: Vocal Traditions on Race Records* (New York, 1984)
J. Obrecht: "The King of Ragtime Guitar: Blind Blake & his Piano-sounding Guitar" <http://www.gracyk.com/blake1.shtml> (2011)

PAUL OLIVER/R

Blake, Charles Dupee (*b* Walpole, MA, 13 Sept 1847; *d* Brookline, MA, 24 Nov 1903). Composer. He studied piano and composition from an early age with JOHN KNOWLES PAINE and J.C.D. PARKER, among others. He entered into an exclusive contract with White-Smith in Boston to publish his compositions; this arrangement lasted until 1888 when Blake began to publish his work himself. He may have written as many as 5000 works, many of which are for the piano but which also include songs and a light opera, *The Light-Keeper's Daughter* (1882). He published under ten or more different pseudonyms. "Rock-a-bye Baby" and "Waves of the Ocean" are probably his best-known songs today, although "Clayton's March" might have claimed that distinction in the 19th century. The style throughout is a simple one, fitted to the skills of most amateur pianists and vocalists; as his contemporaries realized, Blake aimed "at producing music for the masses, in which he [was] successful to an unusual degree" (Jones).

BIBLIOGRAPHY

EwenD

F.O. Jones, ed.: *A Handbook of American Music and Musicians* (Canaserga, NY, 1886/R 1971)

W.S.B. Mathews, ed.: *A Hundred Years of Music in America* (Chicago, 1889/*R* 1970)

W.H. Rehrig: *The Heritage Encyclopedia of Band Music* (Westerville, OH, 1991, suppl. 1996); CD-ROM (Oskaloosa IA, 2005)

DALE COCKRELL

Blake, Eubie [James Hubert] (*b* Baltimore, MD, 7 Feb 1883; *d* New York, NY, 12 Feb 1983). Ragtime pianist and composer. When he was six years old his parents, who had been slaves, purchased a home organ and arranged for him to have lessons. Later he studied music theory with a local musician, Llewelyn Wilson. Despite the disapproval of his mother, an extremely religious woman, Blake began to play professionally in a Baltimore nightclub at the age of 15, and in 1899 he wrote his first piano rag, "Charleston Rag." In 1915 he met the singer NOBLE SISSLE. The two men formed a songwriting partnership and had an immediate success with "It's all your Fault," performed by Sophie Tucker. Blake and Sissle went to New York and joined James Reese Europe's Society Orchestra, and after World War I they formed the Dixie Duo, a vaudeville act. In 1921 they produced an extremely successful musical, *Shuffle Along*, which ran for more than 14 months on Broadway and subsequently went on tour. Blake continued to write songs with Sissle and other lyricists for several Broadway and London shows during the 1920s and 30s and toured as musical director for United Service Organizations productions during World War II. He first made recordings in 1917 and continued to record as a soloist, including piano rolls, and with his orchestra into the 1930s. He retired in 1946 and returned to the study of composition at New York University, completing the Schillinger system of courses three years later. During the ensuing years he spent much time notating many of his compositions.

Eubie Blake, 1973. (JazzSign/Lebrecht Music & Arts)

A ragtime revival in the 1950s focused attention on Blake as the nation's foremost rag pianist and launched him on a new career as a touring player and lecturer. He returned to recording in 1969 with the album *The Eighty-six Years of Eubie Blake* (Col.), and in 1972 he established his own publishing and record company, Eubie Blake Music. He also made piano rolls for the QRS Company (1973). Blake became a legendary figure, constantly performing on television and at jazz festivals in the United States and abroad. He received awards from the music and theater industries and from civic and professional organizations; he was awarded the Presidential Medal of Freedom (1981) and honorary degrees from Brooklyn College (1973), Dartmouth College (1974), Rutgers University (1974), the New England Conservatory (1974), and the University of Maryland (1979). His life was celebrated in documentary films and on Broadway in such shows as *Eubie* (1978).

Blake's music is distinguished by an enormous diversity, reflecting tastes in popular music in the early and middle decades of the 20th century. Many of his more than 300 songs are infused with the syncopated ragtime rhythms that swept Tin Pan Alley between 1900 and 1920. His tunes tend to have a large melodic range and exhibit disjunct motion, while his harmonic language includes many altered blues chords and chromatic progressions. The broad range of Blake's music can be seen in his ethnic songs ("If You've Never been Vamped by a Brownskin"), which derive from the coon song, in musical theater ballads ("Love will Find a Way"), in spiritual songs ("Roll, Jordan"), and in novelty songs with double entendre ("My Handyman Ain't Handy any More"). His piano music, which consists mostly of rags, displays many of the melodic, harmonic, and rhythmic characteristics of the songs. With their use of broken-octave basses, highly embellished melodies, and arpeggiated figurations, they give a good indication of Blake's own virtuosity at the keyboard. His rags, along with works written in the 1920s by composers such as Fats Waller and James P. Johnson, had a direct influence on the development of the Harlem stride-piano school of the following decade.

WORKS

(selective list)

STAGE

(Musicals unless otherwise stated; some music written in collaboration with N. Sissle; writers shown as (lyricists; book author); dates are those of first New York performance)

Shuffle Along (N. Sissle; F.E. Miller and A. Lyles), 23 May 1921 [incl. Everything Reminds me of You, If You've Never been Vamped by a Brownskin, I'm just wild about Harry, Love will Find a Way]
Elsie (Sissle; C.W. Bell), 2 April 1923
The Chocolate Dandies (orig. title In Bamville) (Sissle; L. Payton and Sissle), 1 Sept 1924 [incl. That Charleston Dance, Bandanaland, Jazz-time Baby, The Sons of Old Black Joe]
Lew Leslie's Blackbirds (revue, A. Razaf; Miller and Razaf), 22 Oct 1930 [incl. Memories of You, My Handyman Ain't Handy any More, Who Said Blackbirds Are Blue?, Roll, Jordan]
Shuffle Along of 1933 (Miller; Sissle), 26 Dec 1932 [incl. Harlem Moon]
Swing It (C. Mack), 22 July 1937 [incl. Ain't we got Love]
Tan Manhattan (revue, Razaf), 1940 [incl. Tan Manhattan, We Are Americans Too, Weary]
Shuffle Along of 1952 (Sissle, Miller, and J. Scholl; Miller and P.G. Smith)
Others, unperf.
Contribs. to revues in London, incl. London Calling!, 4 Sept 1923 [incl. You Were Meant for Me]; Cochran's Revue of 1924, 1924; Charlot's Revue, 30 March 1925; Cochran's Revue (1926), 29 April 1926

SONGS

(Some associated with Broadway shows; unless otherwise stated, all lyrics by Sissle)

It's all your Fault, 1915; At the Pullman Porter's full dress Ball, 1916; Floradora Girls, 1920; Vision Girl, in Midnight Rounders, 1920; Serenade Blues, 1922; When the Lord Created Adam (Razaf), 1931; Blues—Why don't you Let me Alone? (A. Porter), 1937

PIANO

Charleston Rag (orig. title Sounds of Africa), 1899; Corner of Chestnut and Low (In Baltimo'), 1903; Tricky Fingers, 1904, rev. 1969; The Baltimore Todalo, 1908; The Chevy Chase, 1914; Just a simple little old Blues (Blue Rag in 12 Keys), 1919; Tickle the Ivories, 1928; Eubie's Boogie, 1942; Dicty's on 7th Avenue, 1955; Eubie's Classical Rag, 1972; Eubie Dubie, 1972; The High Muck de Mucks, 1972

BIBLIOGRAPHY

R. Blesh: "Little Hubie," Combo: USA; Eight Lives in Jazz (Philadelphia, 1971/*R*), 187–217
R. Blesh and H. Janis: *They All Played Ragtime* (New York, 1950, 4/1971)
E. Southern: *The Music of Black Americans: a History* (New York, 1971, 2/1983)
W. Bolcom and R. Kimball: *Reminiscing with Sissle and Blake* (New York, 1973/*R*2000) [incl. work-list, discography]
B. King: "A Legend in his own Lifetime," *BPiM*, i (1973), 151–6
W.J. Schafer and J. Riedel: *The Art of Ragtime* (Baton Rouge, LA, 1973/*R*)
E. Southern: "A Legend in his own Lifetime: Conversation with Eubie Blake," *BPiM*, i (1973), 50–5
D.A. Jasen and T.J. Tichenor: *Rags and Ragtime: a Musical History* (New York, 1978)
L. Carter: *Eubie Blake: Keys of Memory* (Detroit, 1979)
A. Rose: *Eubie Blake* (New York, 1979)
E.A. Berlin: *Ragtime: a Musical and Cultural History* (Berkeley, 1980/*R*1984 with addenda)
D.A. Jansen and G. Jones: "'If You've Never been Vamped by a Brown Skin': Black Theatre Composers of the 1920s," *Spreadin' Rhythm Around: Black Popular Songwriters, 1880–1930* (New York, 1998), 335–60
D.A. Jasen and G. Jones: *Black Bottom Stomp: Eight Masters of Ragtime and early Jazz* (New York, 2002)
T. Brooks: *Lost Sounds: Blacks and the Birth of the Recording Industry (1890–1919)* (Urbana, IL, 2004)

EILEEN SOUTHERN, JOHN GRAZIANO

Blake, George E. (*b* England, ?1775; *d* Philadelphia, PA, 20 Feb 1871). Music engraver and publisher. He immigrated to the United States before 1793 and in 1794 began teaching the flute and clarinet. In 1802 he acquired the piano manufactory of John I. Hawkins in Philadelphia, and soon after began to publish and to operate a circulating music library. His production included many American compositions (*c*1808) and political songs (*c*1813); an early piracy of Thomas Moore's *Irish Melodies* (1808–*c*1825); a serial, *Musical Miscellany* (from 1815); and the first American edition of *Messiah* (*c*1830), along with other major vocal works by George Frideric Handel. Most numerous among his output, however, were songs of the Philadelphia theater, based on London publications. Blake also issued typeset opera librettos and engraved tunebooks. He remained active throughout the 1830s, in later years issuing minstrel music and excerpts from Italian opera. At the height of his career (*c*1810–30) he was America's most prolific music publisher.

BIBLIOGRAPHY

WolfeMEP
Obituary, *Philadelphia Evening Transcript* (21 Feb 1871)
J.C. White: *Music Printing and Publishing in Philadelphia, 1729–1840* (thesis, Columbia U., 1949)
D.W. Krummel: *Philadelphia Music Engraving and Publishing, 1800–1820: a Study in Bibliography and Cultural History* (diss., U. of Michigan, 1958)
R.J. Wolfe: "Index of Publishers, Engravers and Printers," "Publishers' Plate and Publication Numbering Systems," *Secular Music in America, 1801–1825: a Bibliography*, iii (New York, 1964), 1133–1200

DONALD W. KRUMMEL

Blake, Norman (*b* Chattanooga, TN, 10 March 1938). Multi-instrumentalist and singer. Blake has had a long and varied career playing many different genres of country music, but focusing on older styles and material. He is best known as a guitarist, but is also skilled on mandolin, fiddle, banjo, and dobro. Blake played in a number of regional bands and came to wide attention through his work as a Nashville studio musician and sideman. He was a member of June Carter's road band, played on Bob Dylan's *Nashville Skyline* LP, and was a member of the house band on *The Johnny Cash Show* (1969–71). He began a solo career in the early 1970s. His first solo LP, *Home in Sulphur Springs* (Rounder, 1972), and his appearance on the seminal *Will the Circle Be Unbroken?*, the collaboration between the Nitty Gritty Dirt Band and a cadre of Nashville musicians, did much to establish his reputation. In 1974 he formed a partnership with Nancy Short, a cellist from Independence, Missouri; the couple married in 1975. Blake has continued to perform and record extensively, both solo and with Nancy, and has also collaborated frequently with other musicians.

RECORDINGS

(selective list)

Home in Sulphur Springs (Rounder, 1972); *Whiskey before Breakfast* (Rounder, 1976); *Full Moon on the Farm* (with Nancy Blake and James Bryan) (Rounder, 1981); *Just Gimme Somethin' I'm Used To* (with Nancy Blake) (Shanachie, 1992); *Far Away, Down on a Georgia Farm* (Shanachie, 1999); *Morning Glory Ramblers* (with Nancy Blake) (Plectrafone, 2004); *Back Home in Sulphur Springs* (with Nancy Blake) (Plectrafone, 2005)

BIBLIOGRAPHY

K. Maffitt: "Norman Blake," *Bluegrass Unlimited*, xvii (1982), 10–12

PAUL F. WELLS

Blake, Ran (*b* Springfield, MA, 20 April 1935). Jazz pianist and educator. His earliest work grew out of his studies in music at Bard College (1956–60) and his concurrent enrollment at the Lenox School of Jazz. He studied with various pianists, including MARY LOU WILLIAMS, Mal Waldron, and OSCAR PETERSON, and became a proponent of THIRD STREAM after working with Gunther Schuller in 1959. Since his first recording as a leader, with the vocalist Jeanne Lee (*The Newest Sound Around*, 1961, RCA), Blake has worked mostly as a soloist. He has won numerous awards, including the Guggenheim Fellowship in Music Composition (1982 and 1988) and a MacArthur Foundation Fellowship (1988). Influenced by vocalists from various genres, film noir, and the pianist Thelonious Monk, his performances often feature recomposed jazz standards, incorporating elements of gospel, Greek, and contemporary classical music. Blake was a founding member of the Third Stream department at the New England Conservatory during the period 1972–3 and was its chair from its inception until 2005, after which he has continued teaching there. His philosophy of music education advocates aural training and is described in his book *Primacy of the Ear* (Brookline, MA, 2010).

BIBLIOGRAPHY

F. Davis: *Outcasts: Jazz Composers, Instrumentalists, and Singers* (New York, 1990)

B. Shoemaker: "Overdue Ovation: Ran Blake," *JT*, xxxii/1 (2002), 36–8

RYAN D.W. BRUCE

Blakey, Art [Buhaina, Abdullah Ibn] (*b* Pittsburgh, PA, 11 Oct 1919; *d* New York, NY, 16 Oct 1990). Jazz drummer and bandleader. He received some piano lessons at school and by seventh grade was playing music full-time, leading a commercial band. Shortly afterward he switched to drums, on which he taught himself to play in the aggressive swing style of Chick Webb, Sid Catlett, and Ray Bauduc. In autumn 1942 he joined Mary Lou Williams for an engagement at Kelly's Stables in New York. He then played with the Fletcher Henderson Orchestra (1943–4), including a long tour of the South. After leaving Henderson, Blakey briefly led a big band in Boston before joining Billy Eckstine's new band in St. Louis. During his years with Eckstine (1944–7) Blakey became associated with the modern jazz movement, together with fellow band members Miles Davis, Dexter Gordon, Fats Navarro, and others.

When Eckstine disbanded his group in 1947, Blakey organized the Seventeen Messengers, a rehearsal band, and recorded with an octet called the Jazz Messengers, the first of his many groups bearing this name. He then reputedly traveled in Africa, perhaps for more than a year, to learn about Islamic culture. In the early 1950s he performed and broadcast with such musicians as Charlie Parker, Miles Davis, and Clifford Brown, and particularly with the pianist Horace Silver, his kindred musical spirit during this period. After making several recordings together, in 1955 Blakey and Silver formed a cooperative group with Hank Mobley and Kenny Dorham, retaining the name Jazz Messengers. When Silver left the following year, the leadership of this important group passed to Blakey, with whom it has been associated ever since. It became the archetypal "hard bop" combo of the late 1950s, playing a driving, aggressive extension of bop with pronounced blues roots. Over the years the Jazz Messengers served as a launch pad for young jazz musicians such as Donald Byrd, Johnny Griffin, Wayne Shorter, Freddie Hubbard, Keith Jarrett, Chuck Mangione, Woody Shaw, JoAnne Brackeen, and Wynton Marsalis. In addition to his numerous tours and recordings with the Messengers, Blakey also made a world tour in 1971–2 with the Giants of Jazz (with Dizzy Gillespie and Thelonious Monk) and frequently appeared as a soloist at the Newport Jazz Festival in New York, most memorably in a drum battle with Max Roach, Buddy Rich, and Elvin Jones (1974).

Blakey was a major figure in modern jazz and an important stylist on his instrument. From his earliest recording sessions with Eckstine and particularly with Thelonious Monk, in historic sessions from 1947, Blakey exuded power and originality, creating a dark cymbal sound punctuated by frequent loud snare- and bass-drum accents in triplets or cross-rhythms. Although he discouraged comparison of his own music with African drumming, Blakey adopted several African devices after his alleged visit in 1948–9, including rapping on the side of the drum and using his elbow on the tom-tom to alter the pitch. Later he organized recording sessions with multiple drummers, incorporating some African musicians and pieces. His much-imitated trademark, the forceful closing of the hi-hat on every second and fourth beat, became part of his style around 1950–51 (not, as is often assumed, earlier than that). A loud and domineering drummer, Blakey also listened and responded to his soloists. His contribution to jazz as a discoverer and molder of young talent over three decades is no less significant than his very considerable innovations on his instrument.

RECORDINGS

(selective list)

As leader: Message from Kenya/Nothing but Soul (1953, BN 1626); *A Night at Birdland*, i–iii (1954, BN 5037–9); *Drum Suite* (1956–7, Col. CL1002); *A Message from Blakey: Holiday for Skins* (1958, BN 4004); *Des femmes disparaissent* (1958, Fontana, 660224); *The Freedom Rider* (1961, BN 84156); *Buttercorn Lady* (1966, Lml. 86034); *Jazz Messengers '70* (1970, Catalyst 7902); *Anthenagin* (1973, Prst. 10076); *Recorded Live at Bubba's* (1980, Who's Who in Jazz 21019); *Album of the Year* (1981, Timeless 155)

As sideman: B. Eckstine: Blowin' the Blues Away (1944, De Luxe 2001), Mister Chips, on *Together!* (1945, Spotlite 100), I Love the Rhythm in a Riff (1945, National 9014); T. Monk: Who Knows (1947, BN 1565); M. Davis: Weirdo (1954, BN 45-1650)

BIBLIOGRAPHY

H. Frost: "Art Blakey in St. Louis," *Metronome*, lxiii/2 (1947), 26

H. Lovett: "Art Blakey," *Metronome*, lxxii/6 (1956), 17

J. Tynan: "The Jazz Message," *DB*, xxiv/21 (1957), 15 only

Z. Carno: "Art Blakey," *Jazz Review*, iii/1 (1960), 6–10

J. Cooke: "Art Blakey and the Jazz Messengers," *Jazz M*, vi (1960), no.3, pp.4–7, 31; no.8, pp.4–8

J. Goldberg: *Jazz Masters of the Fifties* (New York, 1965/*R*1980), 45–61

A. Taylor: *Notes and Tones: Musician to Musician Interviews* (Liège, Belgium, 1973/*R*), 251–68

J. Litweiler: "Bu's Delights and Laments," *DB*, xliii/6 (1976), 15

"Art Blakey and the Jazz Messengers," *Swing Journal*, xxxiii (Feb 1979), 224 [discography]
I. Gitler: "Art Blakey Speaks his Mind," *Jazz Magazine*, iv/1 (1979), 40
H. Nolan: "New Message from Art Blakey," *DB*, xlvi/17 (1979), 19
P. Danson: "Art Blakey," *Coda*, no.173 (1980), 14
M. Paudras: "Art Blakey: le message," *Jazz Hot*, nos.374–5 (1980), 16
B. Rusch: "Art Blakey: Interview," *Cadence*, vii (1981), no.7, p.8; no.9, p.12
C. Stern: "Art Blakey," *Modern Drummer*, viii/9 (1984), 8–13
D.H. Rosenthal: "Conversation with Art Blakey: the Big Beat!," *BPM*, xiv (1986), 267–90
K. Whitehead: "Art Blakey: Class Action," *DB*, lv/12 (1988), 16 [discography]
H. Giese: *Art Blakey: sein Leben, seine Musik, seine Schallplatten* (Schaftlach, Germany, 1990)
W. Enstice and P. Rubin: *Jazz Spoken Here: Conversations with Twenty-two Musicians* (Baton Rouge, LA, and London, 1992), 16
J. Ramsay: *Art Blakey's Jazz Messengers* (Miami, 1994) [incl. transcrs.]
A. Goldsher: *Hard Bop Academy: the Sidemen of Art Blakey and the Jazz Messengers* (Milwaukee, 2002)
I. Monson: "Art Blakey's African Diaspora," *The African Diaspora: a Musical Perspective*, ed. I. Monson (New York, 2003), 324–47

LEWIS PORTER

Blanchard, Terence (Oliver) (*b* New Orleans, LA, 13 March 1962). Trumpeter and film composer. He began piano lessons at the age of five and switched to trumpet in 1970. While enrolled at the New Orleans Center for Creative Arts (from 1978), he met the saxophonist Donald Harrison. In 1980 he won a music scholarship to Rutgers University and toured with Lionel Hampton's Orchestra. Two years later he and Harrison replaced Wynton and Branford Marsalis in Art Blakey's Jazz Messengers. Following the success of their joint album *New York Second Line* (1984, Concord), they left the group in 1986. Blanchard began collaborating with the filmmaker Spike Lee when he was invited to play on the soundtrack of *School Daze* in 1988, and he subsequently performed on *Do the Right Thing* in 1989. That year Blanchard curtailed his recording and performing in order to develop a new embouchure. After composing the score for Lee's *Jungle Fever* (1991), he has provided the soundtracks for most of the director's films. His scores are rooted in African American popular traditions and combine influences from world music and electronica as well as jazz. In 1992 Blanchard composed a score for Lee's film *Malcom X* that received critical acclaim and subsequently arranged the music into a suite for his quintet. *When the Levees Broke* (2006) is an outstanding example among Blanchard's documentary film scores. His album based on this score, entitled *Tale of God's Will (A Requiem for Katrina)* (2007, BN), won a Grammy for Best Large Jazz Ensemble Album. Among his other albums, *Bounce* (2003, BN) merged hard bop with afro-pop and *Flow* (2005, BN) verged towards electronic fusion. *Choices* (2009, Concord) was inspired by the empowerment of African Americans in post-Katrina New Orleans and included quotations from an interview with Cornel West. Blanchard has maintained a strong commitment to jazz education and mentorship, and was appointed the artistic director of the Thelonious Monk Institute of Jazz in 2000. Motivated by his commitment to the revitalization of his hometown, in 2007 the Monk Institute moved from Los Angeles to New Orleans, where it was hosted at Loyola University.

BIBLIOGRAPHY

K. Gabbard: "Signifyin(g) the Phallus: Representations of the Jazz Trumpet," *Jammin' at the Margins: Jazz and the American Cinema* (Chicago, 1996), 138–59
M. Schelle: *The Score: Interviews with Film Composers* (Los Angeles, 1999)
A. Margo: *Contemporary Cat: Terence Blanchard with Special Guests* (Lanham, MD, 2002)
M. Thomas: "Jazz in Documentary Film," *Dynamic Canons* (diss., U. of Southern California, 2011)

MATTHEW ALAN THOMAS

Bland, Bobby "Blue" [Robert Calvin] (*b* Rosemark, TN, 27 Jan 1930; *d* Germantown, TN, 23 June 2013). Blues singer. He moved to Memphis as a teenager and began his career as a gospel singer in the group the Miniatures before joining the Beale Streeters, a vocal group that included B.B. King, Little Junior Parker, Johnny Ace, and Roscoe Gordon. In the early 1950s he signed with Duke Records and recorded several singles that were released on three different R&B labels, but did not amount to any success. After being discharged from the US Army in 1954, he began touring as Junior Parker's valet and opening act. By this time Duke had been purchased by the Houston businessman Don Robey who teamed Bland with the Memphis-based Bill Harvey Orchestra. Together they recorded "It's my Life, Baby" (Duke, 1955), which became Bland's first number one hit. During the 1960s Bland's relationship with Duke produced dozens of records, many of which performed well in the R&B market. Many of his hits were written by Joe Scott, the bandleader and arranger who helped to create Bland's big band sound. The horns were complemented by the guitar playing of Wayne Bennett who blended his jazz-influenced solos with Bland's smooth vocals. Bland was blessed with the ability to tell a convincing story as he sang, and his unique vocal style mixed gospel, blues, and soul with the big band sound. He neither composed nor played an instrument, which set him apart from most blues artists. Throughout the 1970s and 80s he recorded several contemporary blues and soul albums for the labels ABC-Dunhill and Malaco that were both successful and critically acclaimed. One of the finest singers in postwar blues, he has been credited by dozens of blues, R&B, and rock vocalists as a primary influence. He was inducted into the Blues Hall of Fame in 1981 and the Rock and Roll Hall of Fame in 1992. In 1997 he received the Grammy Lifetime Achievement Award. He continued to perform regularly, often with King, until his death.

BIBLIOGRAPHY

C. Keil: *Urban Blues* (Chicago, 1966/*R*)
P. Guralnick: *Lost Highway: Journeys and Arrivals of American Musicians* (Boston, 1979/*R*)
G. Gart and R.C. Ames (with R. Funk, R. Bowman, and D. Booth): *Duke/Peacock Records: an Illustrated History with Discography* (Milford, NH, 1990)

DINA M. BENNETT

Bland, James A(llen) (*b* Flushing, NY, 22 Oct 1854; *d* Philadelphia, PA, 5 May 1911). Minstrel performer and songwriter. He was educated in Washington, DC, where he enrolled in the law department of Howard University

Portrait of James Bland on the cover of "3 Great Songs," 1879. (Library of Congress, Music Division)

but left at the end of his second year owing to lack of interest. He was deeply moved by the spirituals and the rhythm and harmony of the work songs of laborers on the university campus. He learned to play the banjo, taught himself the rudiments of harmony, and began composing songs. He organized musical groups, becoming active in the Manhattan Club (a group of musically gifted young African Americans employed in government), and performed at various social functions, where he soon became known as a versatile entertainer. He found the perfect outlet for his musical and theatrical talents in the minstrel show and joined the Original Black Diamonds of Boston as a leading performer in 1875. A year later he became a member of the Bohee Minstrels, later joining of Sprague's Georgia Minstrels. In order to overcome racial discrimination by white concert-hall owners, this group was sold to George B. Callender (becoming Callender's Original Georgia Minstrels), and went on to achieve nationwide success and fame. It was then taken over by Jack Haverly to become Haverly's Genuine Colored Minstrels, later Haverly's Colossal Carnival and Genuine Colored Minstrels.

Haverly took his group to London, opening at Her Majesty's Theatre on 30 July 1881. Bland was a star performer and became famous for his rendition of "Oh, dem golden Slippers" with a special comic routine at the end; another favorite with his audiences was "The Colored Hop." He also displayed his varied talents in "An Ethiopian Specialty," which consisted of singing, dancing, and acrobatic stunts. The show met with huge success and, when the company sailed for New York on 5 August 1882, Bland and a few others remained in London; there he became a member of English companies for a short time but achieved his greatest success as a solo performer.

Bland returned to the United States in 1890 at the peak of his career and fame, touring with W.S. Cleveland's Colossal Colored Carnival Minstrels; Bland and Tom McIntosh were advertised as "the Two Greatest Comedians of their Race." He remained with this company for about a year, but his subsequent appearances became fewer and his itinerary is unclear. In his autobiography, *Father of the Blues* (New York, 1941), W.C. Handy states that he met Bland in Louisville in 1897, but Bland was no longer such a dazzling entertainer. A year later he sang for a short time with Black Patti's Troubadours, but the black minstrel era was nearing its end, and another musical theater was developing. Bland tried to meet the new challenge by writing a musical comedy, *The Sporting Girl*, but it was a failure. Eventually he returned to Philadelphia, where, penniless and ill, he died of tuberculosis. He was buried in an unmarked grave in the Colored Cemetery in Merion, Philadelphia; a gravestone was not erected until 15 July 1946.

Only ten percent of the 600 songs that are repeatedly claimed for him are verifiably by him. He wrote his songs and dances for specific performances, shaping the melodies, texts, and rhythms to suit the situation and the character. They range from sentimental ballads to vigorous dances and sturdy marches. His musical inspiration was drawn from African American spirituals, gospel hymns, and work songs, with their rhythmic pulse and leader-response elements. Bland's most famous song, "Carry me back to old Virginny," was adopted by the State of Virginia in 1940 as its official song.

WORKS

(Unless otherwise indicated, all works are minstrel songs with texts by Bland and all were published in Boston)

Edition: *J.A. Bland: Album of Outstanding Songs*, ed. C. Haywood (New York, 1946)

The Farmer's Daughter, 1874; Carry me back to old Virginny 1878; Close dem Windows 1879; Fascinating Coon, New York, 1879; Father's Growing Old, 1879; Flowers will Come in May, 1879; In the Morning by the Bright Light, 1879; Lucy, the Pride of the South, 1879; My old Home in Mississippi, 1879; Oh, dem golden Slippers, 1879; Old Homestead, 1879; Old Plantation Lonely, 1879; Pretty Little South Carolina Rose, 1879; Rambling through the Clover, 1879; Silver Slippers, 1879; Take good Care of Mother, 1879; Uncle Joe, or The Cabin by the Sea, 1879; Whisper softly, Baby's Dying, 1879

Dancing on the Kitchen Floor, 1880; Darkey's Request, New York, 1880; Darkie's Jubilee, 1880; Dashing Harry May, New York, 1880; De Angels am a Coming, New York, 1880; De golden Wedding, 1880; In the Evening by the Moonlight, New York, 1880; Keep dem golden Gates wide Open, New York, 1880; Kiss me Goodnight, Mother, 1880; Listen to the silver trumpets, 1880; Oh, my Brother!, 1880; Sister Hannah (n.p., 1880; Sons of Ham, New York, 1880; Way up Yonder, 1880; Won't we Have a jolly Time?, New York, 1880; The Colored Hop, Philadelphia, 1881; Come along, Sister Mary, n.p., 1881; Dandy black Brigade, New York, 1881; Darkie's Moonlight Picnic, New York, 1881; Gabriel's Band, New York, 1881; I'll Name the Boy Dinnes, or no Name at All, n.p., 1881; Mid'st Pretty Violets, 1881; My own Sweet Wife to Be, n.p., 1881

Oh, Lucinda!, Philadelphia, 1881; Oh, why Was I so soon Forgotten?, n.p., 1881; The old fashioned Cottage, n.p., 1881; Only to Hear her Voice, n.p., 1881; Rose Pachoula, n.p., 1881; Taddy, please, Scare me Again, n.p., 1881; Tell all de Children Good Bye, Philadelphia, 1881; Tell 'em I'll Be There, New York, 1881; Traveling back to Alabama, n.p., 1881; You could have been True, New York, 1881; Christmas Dinner, 1889; Tapioca, n.p., 1891; Happy Darkies, New York, 1892

Climbing up the golden Stairs, lost; Kingdom Coming; The Missouri Hound Dog; The old Log Cabin in the Dell

The Sporting Girl (musical comedy), *c*1900

Principal publishers: B.W. Hitchcock, J.F. Perry, Pauline Lieder

BIBLIOGRAPHY

SouthernB

C. Haywood, James A. Bland: *Prince of the colored Songwriters* (Flushing, NY, 1944)

C. Haywood, James A. Bland: *A Bibliography of North American Folklore and Folksong* (New York, 1951, 2/1961)

T. Fletcher: *100 Years of the Negro in Show Business* (New York, 1954)

J.B. Bland: *James Allen Bland, Negro Composer: a Study of his Life* (diss., Howard U., 1968)

E. Southern: *The Music of Black Americans: a History* (New York, 1971, 2/1983)

I. Simond: *Old Slack's Reminisences and pocket History of the colored Profession from 1865 to 1891* (Bowling Green, OH, 1974)

R.C. Toll: *On with the Show* (New York, 1976)

C. Hamm: *Yesterdays: Popular Song in America* (New York, 1979)

CHARLES HAYWOOD/R

Blane, Ralph [Hunsecker, Ralph Uriah] (*b* Broken Arrow, OK, 26 July 1914; *d* Broken Arrow, 13 Nov 1995). Songwriter, composer, lyricist, arranger, and singer. He began his career as a singer, appearing in such Broadway musicals as *New Faces of 1936* (1936), *Hooray for What!* (1937), and *Louisiana Purchase* (1940). In 1940, with his friend Hugh Martin, he formed a vocal quartet, the Martins, which performed in night clubs and for radio. With each partner contributing both words and music, Blane and Martin wrote the campus musical comedy *Best Foot Forward* (1941) which became a Broadway hit. The pair subsequently moved to Hollywood for MGM's film version (1943). Their next film became their best known work, the MGM musical *Meet me in St. Louis* (1944) featuring Judy Garland. Their score included "The Trolley Song" (for which they received an Academy Award nomination for Best Original Song), "Have yourself a Merry Little Christmas," and "The Boy Next Door." In 1948 Blane, Martin, and Roger Edens were nominated for Best Original Song for "Pass that Peace Pipe" from *Good News* (1947). Blane also collaborated with Harry Warren in *Summer Holiday* (1948) and *My Dream is Yours* (1949), and with Harold Arlen in *My Blue Heaven* (1950).

SELECTED RECORDING

with H. Martin: *Martin & Blane Sing Martin and Blane* (DRG, 1994)

BIBLIOGRAPHY

P. Furia and M. Lasser: *America's Songs: the Stories Behind the Songs of Broadway, Hollywood, and Tin Pan Alley* (New York, 2006)

"Ralph Blane: Biography" <http://songwritershalloffame.org/index.php/exhibits/bio/C36> (25 Aug 2012)

IAN BROOKES

Blank, Allan (*b* New York, NY, 27 Dec 1925). Composer, violinist, and educator. As a youth, Blank studied violin and attended the High School of Music and Arts in New York where he became interested in composition and conducting. He went on to study at the Juilliard School (1945–7) where he held a fellowship in conducting, and at Washington Square College (New York University) where he received his Bachelor of Arts degree in 1948. Two years later Blank earned his Master of Arts degree in composition at the University of Minnesota. He also studied at the Columbia Teachers College and the University of Iowa. From 1950 to 1952 he was a violinist with the Pittsburgh Symphony Orchestra, and from 1956 to 1965 taught instrumental music in New York high schools. Blank then moved to Western Illinois University at Macomb (1966–8) where he taught theory and composition, followed by a two-year appointment at Paterson State College (New Jersey). From 1970 to 1977 Blank taught at Lehman College (City University of New York) and in 1978 became an associate professor at Virginia Commonwealth University in Richmond, Virginia, where he was director of the New Music Ensemble. He retired as emeritus professor of composition in 1996. Blank has received numerous grants, awards, and honors for his compositions, including a composer's grant from the National Endowment for the Arts for his one-act opera, *The Magic Bonbons* (1985). That same year, Blank received a commission from the New York State Council on the Arts' Presenting Organization to write a clarinet quintet for the Roxburg Chamber Players and was also awarded first prize in the George Eastman Competition for his *Duo for Bassoon and Piano*. In 1988 he won the Eric Satie Mostly Tonal Award for his string trio, *Fantasy on Cantillation Motives*, and the annual choral competition of the Chautauqua Chamber Singers for his setting of *Poor Richard's Almanacs*. In 1989 Blank won the Lind Solo Competition sponsored by Cornell University, and in 1990 he was awarded a grant from the Virginia Commission of the Arts for his *Concerto for Clarinet and String Orchestra*. He also received four separate commissions from the Virginia Music Teachers Association (1979, 1988, 1991, 2007). Blank's dramatic works include incidental music for two plays including Shakespeare's *Measure for Measure* written on commission from the Virginia Shakespeare Festival, Williamsburg, Virginia. His output of more than 100 works encompasses a broad range of genres that display expressive and idiomatic qualities including vocal works, chamber music, concert and stage pieces, and music for small, mixed ensembles, large wind ensembles, and orchestra. Blank's music, especially the chamber works, can be characterized as displaying a tendency towards soloistic emphasis in which flowing, arabesque-like melodic constructions combine to create sonorous, polyphonic textures with each voice remaining distinct.

WORKS

Stage: Aria da capo (chbr op, E. St. Vincent Millay), 1958–60; Excitement at the Circus (children's play, I. Leitne), vv, pf, 1968; The Magic Bonbons (8 scenes, A. Blank, after L. G. Baum), 1980–83; incid. music for 2 plays

Large ens: Concert Piece, band, 1960–63; Music for Orch, 1964–7; 6 Miniatures and a Fantasia, orch, 1972; 6 Significant Landscapes, chbr orch, 1972–4; Divertimento, tuba, band, 1979; Kreutzer March, band, 1981; Concertino, bn, str, 1984, Conc., cl, str, 1990

Chbr: Wind Qnt, 1968–70; Bicinium II, cl, bn, 1974; Coalitions, 2 cl, trbn, pf, 2 perc, 1975; Trio, tpt, hn, trbn, 1975; An American Medley, brass qnt, fl, perc, 1976; Coalitions II, sax qt, 1976; Paganini Caprices, 4 hn, 3 tpt, 3 trbn, tuba, 1976; Ceremonies, tpt, perc, 1977; Duo, bn, pf, 1978; 4 Inventions, bn, pf, 1979; Introduction and Rondo Fantastico, bn, pf, 1979; Str Qt, 1981; Fantasy on Cantillation Motives, vn, va, vc, 1983; Trio, fl, vc, pf, 1983; Duo, bn, pf, 1985; other works incl. 3 wind qnts

Solo inst: Rotation, pf, 1959–60; A Song of Ascents, va, 1968; 3 Pieces, tpt, 1969; 3 Novelties, a sax, 1971; Music for Vn, 1972; 2 Studies, cl, 1972; Restatement of Romance, pf, 1973

Vocal: Buy me an ounce & I'll sell you a pound (e.e. cummings), SATB, pf, 1956; Poem (cummings), S, cl, vc, harp, 1963; 2 Ferlinghetti Songs, S, bn, 1964; 2 Parables by Franz Kafka, S, vn, va, 1964; 13 Ways of Looking at a Blackbird (W. Stevens), S, fl + pic, cl + b cl, pf, vn + va, vc, 1964–5; Esther's Monologue (M. Blank), cantata, S, ob, va, vc, 1970; Lines from Proverbs, SATB, 1973; American Folio (trad.), SATB, pf/insts, 1976; 2 Holy Sonnets (J. Donne), A, ob + eng hn, va, harp, 1977; Some Funnies and Poems (O. Nash, E. Lear, cummings, M. Blank, A. Blank), nar, pf, 1982; 11 other works

Principal publishers: APNM, Associated, Boosey & Hawkes, CFE, Dorn, Falls House, Fischer, Frank Warren, International Opus, Music for Percussion, Northeastern, Smith, Presser, Seesaw, Nichols, Roncorp

Principal recording companies: Advance, Centaur, CRI, CRS, Open Loop, Orion

MARTIN BRODY/ROBERT PAUL KOLT

Blanton, Jimmy [Jimmie] (*b* Chattanooga, TN, 5 Oct 1918; *d* Monrovia, CA, 30 July 1942). Jazz double bass player. Growing up in a musical home, he played violin from a young age. Blanton later switched to the bass and had early professional experiences playing in bands led by his mother who was a pianist. While attending Tennessee State University, he performed with the Tennessee State Collegians and, during the summer, Fate Marable's riverboat band. Blanton then worked in territory bands based in St. Louis and in 1937 joined the Jeters–Pillars Orchestra, with which he remained until the autumn of 1939, when Duke Ellington heard him performing and immediately hired him for his jazz orchestra. During Blanton's stint with Ellington (1939 to early 1942), the band had some of its greatest success, thanks in part to Blanton's buoyant walking-bass style and the addition of the tenor saxophonist Ben Webster. This configuration of Ellington's group is commonly referred to as the Blanton–Webster band. Its recordings made for RCA Victor between 1940 and 1942, including "Ko-Ko," "Jack the Bear," "Harlem Air Shaft," and "In a Mellotone," display not only Blanton's impeccable time-keeping, but also his groundbreaking work as a bass soloist. This ability is further illustrated on a series of duet recordings that Blanton made with Ellington in 1941. That same year, Blanton was diagnosed with tuberculosis and forced to retire to a sanitarium in California, where he died in 1942.

Blanton is widely considered the first double bass player to incorporate melodic soloing into his playing using pizzicato (plucking the strings). While there are extant recordings of earlier jazz bass players performing in this way, the credit given to Blanton is likely the result of the proliferation and prominence of the Ellington band's recordings. Blanton's agile technique and penchant for harmonic exploration allowed him to fit in comfortably at several Minton's Playhouse jam sessions, which along with his Ellington band recordings influenced bebop bass playing for years. His walking style is melodically and rhythmically expressive, not necessarily limited to marking the roots of the harmonies or the downbeats. While Blanton had an immediate influence on swing and bebop bass players including Ray Brown and Charles Mingus, the double bass tradition that he is credited with continues to shape the way jazz musicians approach the instrument.

BIBLIOGRAPHY

D. Chevan: "The Double Bass as a Solo Instrument in Early Jazz," *BPM*, xvii/1–2 (1989), 73–92

G. Schuller: *The Swing Era: the Development of Jazz, 1930–1945* (New York, 1968, 2/1989)

D. Dicaire: *Jazz Musicians of the Early Years, to 1945* (Jefferson, NC, 2003)

S. Pollard: "Remembering Jimmy Blanton" <http://www.allaboutjazz.com/php/article.php?id=26536&pg=1> (2007)

DAVID CHEVAN

Blass, Robert (*b* New York, NY, 27 Oct 1867; *d* Berlin, Germany, 3 Dec 1930). Bass. Educated in New York public schools, Blass entered the Leipzig Conservatory in 1887, planning violin study with Hans Sitt. Found to have an excellent singing voice, he continued instead under Gustav Ewald and then in Frankfurt with Julius Stockhausen. In 1895 Blass debuted at Weimar as Heinrich in *Lohengrin*, leading to engagements in Germany and at Covent Garden. In 1900 he debuted with the Metropolitan Opera as Hermann in *Tannhäuser*. His sole season at Bayreuth was in 1901. Blass sang frequently at the Metropolitan until 1910; he participated in the American première of *Parsifal* (24 December 1903), the infamous New York premiere (22 January 1907) of *Salome*, and Mahler's debut (1 January 1908; *Tristan und Isolde*). Blass later sang at the Deutsche Oper, Berlin (1913–19), and again with the Metropolitan, singing German opera in English (1920–22). He subsequently retired to Berlin to teach.

Though familiar with French and Italian repertoire, Blass sang chiefly German repertoire in London and New York. Considering the roles he most often sang—Herrmann; Heinrich; Marke in *Tristan und Isolde*; Pogner in *Die Meistersinger*; Fasolt, Fafner, Hunding and Hagen in *Der Ring*; and Gurnemanz in *Parsifal*—Blass clearly possessed an instrument of considerable power and depth, as his extant recordings (Mapleson cylinders, Edison and Victor) also suggest.

BIBLIOGRAPHY

GroveO (J.B. Steane)

"Robert Blass Dies; Once in Opera Here," *New York Times* (10 Dec 1930) [obituary]

SCOTT ALAN SOUTHARD

Blaustein, Susan Morton (*b* Palo Alto, CA, 22 March 1953). Composer. She studied the piano and composition with Karl Kohn at Pomona College (BA 1975) and composition with Henri Pousseur at the Liège Conservatory in Belgium, with Seymour Shifrin at Brandeis University, and with Jacob Druckman and Betsy Jolas at Yale University (MM 1979, MMA 1980,

DMA in composition 1986), where she subsequently lectured. She was a junior fellow at Harvard University and an assistant professor of music at Columbia University (1985–90). She has received commissions from the Schoenberg Institute, the Koussevitsky Foundation, and the Fromm Foundation, and she was awarded a Guggenheim Fellowship in 1988, enabling her to live in Southeast Asia for a time. As a scholar, she joined with Martin Brody for an article on musical grouping in Milton Babbitt's "Minute Waltz." Her review of books by Thomas Delio sparked a brief debate. She also received the Charles Ives Scholarship from the American Academy of Art and Letters, as well as awards from the NEA and from the League of Composers–ISCM.

Her music is freely atonal with a lyric element. *Commedia* (1980), composed for the tenth anniversary of the group Speculum Musicae, blends the dramatic convention of the *commedia dell'arte* with 20th-century musical techniques. In 1981 her *Due Madrigali di Torquato Tasso* won the League of Composers–ISCM National Composers' Competition and received a Carnegie Hall premiere. The same year, her string quartet *Ricercae* received praise. Blaustein noted that the piece uses Schoenberg's String Quartet no.1 as inspiration. Her Sextet (1983), commissioned by New York New Music Ensemble under the direction of Robert Black, demonstrates her mastery of the chamber idiom. Since the 1990s, Blaustein has directed her attention to world issues through her work for the Millennium Cities Initiative at the Earth Institute at Columbia University.

WORKS

(selective list)

Orch and chbr: Commedia, 8 players, 1980; Str Qt no.1, "Ricercae," 1981; Sextet, fl, cl, pf, vn, vc, perc, 1983; Conc., vc, chbr orch, 1984

Pf: La espoza de Don Garcia, 1980; Fantasia 1980

Vocal: The Moon Has Nothing to be Excited About, canzona, 1977; The Moon Has Nothing to be Sad About, 6 poems (S. Plath); 2 Madrigals (T. Tasso), 1v, perc, ens, 1979; To Orpheus (R.M. Rilke), 4 sonnets, SATB, 1982; Song of Songs, Mez, T, orch, 1985

Principal publisher: BMI

SARA JOBIN/ALYSON PAYNE

Blazonczyk [Bell], **Eddie** [Eddy], Sr. (*b* Chicago, IL, 1941). Polka bandleader, singer, and bass player. He is best known as the leader of his band, the Versatones. The son of two Polish immigrant musicians, he grew up in northern Wisconsin and formed a rock and roll band, which played backup for such stars as Buddy Holly and Gene Vincent. Under the name of Eddie (or Eddy) Bell, he recorded "Hi-Yo Silver" and other songs on the Mercury label. The Lucky Four label released his well-liked novelty song "The Great Great Pumpkin." At the insistence of his good friend and fellow musician Chet Kowalkowski, he moved back to Chicago and joined Versatones in 1963, a six-piece polka band that played both traditional and modernized repertoire. The result ended up changing the polka world, and they were quickly invited to record. Their first disc was *Polka Parade* (1963), and they have released an album—sometimes two—almost every year since that time. They have toured widely across the United States, giving more than 6000 performances, and their recordings have been highly successful, garnering more than 18 Grammy nominations for Best Polka Album, winning the honor for *Another Polka Celebration* (1986). Blazonczyk received the National Heritage Fellowship Award from the NEA in 1998. After Eddie Sr. retired in 2002, the band continued to perform under the auspices of Eddie Jr., who grew up playing the accordion with his father's ensemble.

JONAS WESTOVER

Bledsoe, Jules [Julius] (*b* Waco, TX, 29 Dec 1897; *d* Hollywood, CA, 14 July 1943). Baritone. He studied at Central Texas College, Bishop and Virginia Union College, and then at Columbia University Medical School, but abandoned the idea of a career in medicine. He made his debut at the Aeolian Hall, New York, in April 1924. He appeared in W. Frank Harling's hybrid opera *Deep River* and Louis Gruenberg's *The Creation* and *In Abraham's Bosom*, and then in 1927 created the role of Joe in Jerome Kern's *Show Boat*, a role he also sang in the first film version in 1929. He toured Europe as a recitalist in 1931. Later roles in opera included the Voodoo Man in Shirley Graham du Bois's *Tom-Tom* and Amonasro in Aida, and the title roles in *Boris Godunov* and Gruenberg's *The Emperor Jones*. He was one of the first African American singers to appear in opera in the United States. His final appearance was in the film *Drums of the Congo* (1942).

BIBLIOGRAPHY

SouthernB

M.C. Hare: *Negro Musicians and their Music* (Washington, DC, 1936)

L.G. Geary: "Jules Bledsoe: the Original 'Ol' Man River,'" *BPiM*, xvii/1–2 (1989), 27–54

DOMINIQUE-RENÉ DE LERMA/R

Blegen, Judith (*b* Missoula, MT, 27 April 1941). Soprano. She studied singing with Euphemia Gregory at the Curtis Institute from 1959. After an apprenticeship at the Santa Fe Opera Festival (to which she later returned as a principal), she was engaged for concerts at Spoleto in 1963. She studied further in Italy and in 1964 went to Nuremberg, where during two years she sang such varied roles as Lucia, Susanna, and Zerbinetta. Engagements followed in Vienna, Salzburg, and the major American houses; her debut role of Papagena at the Metropolitan (1970) led to performances as Marcellina, Mélisande, Ascanius, and Sophie in *Werther*. She made her Covent Garden debut in 1975, as Despina, and her debut at the Opéra in 1977, as Sophie in *Der Rosenkavalier*. She was also a trained violinist and played that instrument in the role of Emily in Menotti's *Help, Help, the Globolinks!*. Her performances can be seen on videos of *Un ballo in maschera*, *L'elisir d'amore*, *Der Rosenkavalier*, and *Hänsel und Gretel*. She has also recorded *La bohème* with Sir Georg Solti, *Le nozze di Figaro* with Daniel Barenboim, *A Midsummer Night's Dream* with James Levine, and Fauré's Requiem with Robert Shaw, which won a Grammy. After retiring in 1991, she joined the boards of the "Symphony of the Americas" in Fort Lauderdale and Opera Naples.

MARTIN BERNHEIMER/KATHLEEN SEWRIGHT

Blesh, Rudi [Rudolph] **(Pickett)** (*b* Guthrie, OK, 21 Jan 1899; *d* Gilmanton, NH, 25 Aug 1985). Writer on music. He attended Dartmouth College and earned the BS in architecture from the University of California, Berkeley. In the 1940s he served as jazz critic for the *San Francisco Chronicle* and the *New York Herald Tribune*. He wrote a pioneering serious history of jazz, *Shining Trumpets* (New York, 1946) and with Harriet Janis was co-author of the first history of ragtime, *They All Played Ragtime* (New York, 1950). The latter work established him as the leading authority in this field and eventually prompted a revival of the music. Also with Janis, he founded Circle Records, a small but significant jazz label that became the first to issue the Library of Congress recordings of Jelly Roll Morton. In 1953 they sold the label—apart from the Morton recordings—to Jazzology Records. From 1947 to 1950, and again in 1964, Blesh wrote and narrated radio programs on jazz and American folk music. From 1956 he taught jazz history at Queens College, CUNY, and New York University, and in the 1970s he contributed disc notes to numerous ragtime recordings. Blesh also edited ragtime piano music and wrote about modern art and the cinema.

WRITINGS

This Is Jazz: a Series of Lectures Given at the San Francisco Museum of Art (San Francisco, 1943)
Shining Trumpets: a History of Jazz (New York, 1946/*R*, enlarged 2/1958/*R*)
with H. Janis: *They All Played Ragtime* (New York, 1950, 4/1971)
Combo: USA; Eight Lives in Jazz (Philadelphia, 1971/*R*)
"Scott Joplin: Black-American Classicist," *The Complete Works of Scott Joplin*, ii, ed. V.B. Lawrence (New York, 1981), xiii–xl [2d edn of *Ragtime Revival: the Collected Works of Scott Joplin*) (1971)]

BIBLIOGRAPHY

J.E. Hasse: "Rudi Blesh and the Ragtime Revivalists," *Ragtime: its History, Composers, and Music* (New York, 1985), 178–86
S. Holden: Obituary, *New York Times* (28 Aug 1985)

JOHN EDWARD HASSE

Bley, Carla [Borg, Lovella May] (*b* Oakland, CA, 11 May 1936). Jazz composer, arranger, bandleader, pianist, and organist. She is best known for her idiosyncratic multi-genre compositions for large ensembles and her sense of humor, omnipresent throughout her oeuvre. Her harmonic language and rich chordal structures are inspired by Duke Ellington, Charles Mingus, and Gil Evans, then infused with rock, tango, Indian music, and the music of European composers, including Kurt Weill and Eric Satie, often in the form of parody and satire. Her experimentalism is widespread and ranges from avant-garde jazz to big band, small formats, chamber music, and soundtracks. During the 1960s she was at the center of the free jazz movement and was instrumental in co-creating independent musicians' collectives, labels, and distribution services.

Except for music lessons from her father, a church musician who taught her piano from age three, she was largely self-taught. In her teens, she went to New York to immerse herself in the music she admired. She listened nightly to first-rate jazz, working at the Birdland jazz club, where she met the pianist Paul Bley, who encouraged her to compose. They married in 1957, and soon Paul and others such as George Russell and Jimmy Giuffre started to perform and record her compositions. In 1967 Gary Burton recorded her first work for large ensemble, *A Genuine Tong Funeral* (RCA). Two years later Charlie Haden commissioned her to arrange music for his album *Liberation Music Orchestra* (1969, Imp.), and she subsequently arranged for all of the group's future albums. The first performance of her best-known work, the genre-bending avant-garde jazz opera *Escalator over the Hill* (1971, with lyrics by Paul Haines), featured a huge cast that included Jack Bruce, Linda Ronstadt, Don Cherry, and John McLaughlin.

In 1964 Bley helped to organize the Jazz Composer's Guild. The next year, with Michael Mantler, she co-founded the JAZZ COMPOSER'S ORCHESTRA ASSOCIATION, a non-profit organization that promoted the commission, performance, and recording of new compositions. In 1973 Mantler and Bley founded their own record company WATT Works, the subsidiary XtraWATT, and the New Music Distribution Service, which supported a number of independent labels. The couple divorced in 1992. Throughout her career, Bley has worked with a number of different groups. Best known are her duos with the bass player Steve Swallow, the octet 4X4 (1999) and the quartet and quintet the Lost Chords (from 2003).

An innovative composer, Bley has received commissions from the Grenoble Jazz Festival, the Carnegie Hall Jazz Band, the Houston SO, and Ursula Oppens, among others. In 1997 she recorded an album of chamber pieces *Fancy Chamber Music*. Her piece for piano and orchestra entitled *3/4* has been performed by Oppens, Keith Jarrett, and Uri Caine. She has received numerous awards for her work, among them the Oscar du Disque de Jazz (1971, for *Escalator over the Hill*), a Guggenheim Fellowship for composition (1972), the Prix Jazz Moderne (for *The Very Big Carla Bley Band*), and a Jazz Journalist's award for best album of 2008 (*Appearing Nightly*).

SELECTED RECORDINGS

Duos with S. Swallow: *Duets* (1988, Watt); *Go Together* (1993, Watt)
As leader: *Escalator over the Hill* (1968–71, JCOA); *Tropic Appetites* (1974, ECM); *Dinner Music* (1977, Watt); *Musique Mecanique* (1979, ECM); *Heavy Heart* (1984, ECM); *Carla* (1987, ECM); *The Very Big Carla Bley Band* (1991, Watt); *Big Band Theory* (1993, ECM); *Fancy Chamber Music* (1998, ECM); *Looking for America* (2003, ECM); *The Lost Chords* (2004, ECM); *Appearing Nightly* (2008, ECM)

BIBLIOGRAPHY

B. Primack: "Carla Bley: First Lady of the Avant-garde," *Contemporary Keyboard*, v/2 (1979), 9–11, 46, 48
L. Dahl: *Stormy Weather: the Music and Lives of a Century of Jazzwomen* (New York, 1984, 4/1999)
F. Oteri: "Carla Bley: on her Own" <http://www.newmusicbox.org/articles/on-her-own-carla-bley/> (2003)
A.C. Beal: *Carla Bley* (Champaign, 2011)

URSEL SCHLICHT

Bley, Paul (*b* Montreal, QC, 10 Nov 1932). Canadian jazz pianist, composer, record producer, and bandleader. He was established by the age of 17, when Oscar Peterson recommended him as his replacement for the last year of an engagement at the Alberta Lounge in Montreal.

After moving to New York to attend the Juilliard School (1950–54), he became part of the traditional and modern music scenes and recorded his first album as leader, with Charles Mingus and Art Blakey among his sidemen (*Introducing Paul Bley*, 1953, Debut). He also played with other notable musicians such as Ben Webster, Lester Young, Roy Eldridge, and Charlie Parker during the 1950s. In 1957 he moved to Los Angeles where he performed at the Hillcrest Club. His quintet, which included Charlie Haden, Billy Higgins, Don Cherry, and Ornette Coleman, became Coleman's quartet when Bley left for New York in 1959. During the early 1960s he again played with Mingus, as well as with George Russell, Jimmy Giuffre, and Sonny Rollins. As a founding member of the Jazz Composers Guild (from 1964), Bley performed and recorded with other leading avant-garde jazz musicians from New York. Although his playing draws on traditional jazz, his improvisations incorporate free interaction that is not confined by meter or chorus length; his work in the 1960s thus places him as a transitional pianist between the styles of Bill Evans and the avant-garde. His wife at the time, CARLA BLEY, is among his most important influences—many of her compositions were central to his repertoire. In 1969 he took up synthesizer and toured with his second wife, Annette Peacock (1969–72). Playing electric piano, he also performed with Dave Holland, Pat Metheny, and Jaco Pastorius in the 1970s. With his third wife, Carol Goss, Bley stared a record label in 1974 called Improvising Artists Inc. From the 1980s he has played acoustic piano exclusively and worked with more traditional forms; however, he has retained an open approach to improvising. His extensive discography includes longstanding collaborations with Giuffre, Steve Swallow, Gary Peacock, and Paul Motian. In 2008 Bley became a Member of the Order of Canada.

BIBLIOGRAPHY

GroveJ

P. Bley and D. Lee: *Stopping Time: Paul Bley and the Transformation of Jazz* (Montreal, 1999)

N. Meehan: *Time will Tell: Conversations with Paul Bley* (Berkeley, 2003)

A. Cappelletti: *Paul Bley: la logica del caso* (Palermo, 2004; Eng. trans., Montreal, 2010)

H. Mandel: "I can't play any other way," *DB*, lxxv/1 (2008), 40–43

RYAN D.W. BRUCE

Blige, Mary J(ane) (*b* New York, NY, 11 Jan 1971). Singer, songwriter, and actress. She began singing at the age of four and soon afterwards began performing regularly at her family's Pentacostal church in Georgia, where she spent part of her childhood. Her career in popular music began after she had recorded an Anita Baker song on a machine in a shopping mall that made video recordings; the tape found its way to the top executive of Uptown Records, who quickly signed Blige to the label. After working as a backup singer, Blige released her debut album, *What's the 411?* (Uptown, 1992), produced by Sean Combs. Several songs from the album released as singles appeared on the *Billboard* R&B charts, including "Real Love" (which peaked at number one), "You Remind Me," and "Sweet Thing." Blige's second album, *My Life* (1994), included several of her own songs, the lyrics of which were based on her own experiences. It became a triple-platinum selling crossover success, solidifying Blige's financial and artistic status. In 1996 Blige received a Grammy Award for a duet with Method Man, "I'll be there for you/You're all I need to get by." Despite addictions to drugs and alcohol, she was able to release the album *Share my World* (1997), which contained five top-selling singles including "Love is all we need," and led to her first global tour. During the 2000s she remained one of the top-selling female recording artists in the United States, releasing new material and winning additional awards, including eight more Grammys. Her combination of soul and hip hop has inspired many other artists, and her confident, powerful, and accurate voice remains instantly recognizable.

JONAS WESTOVER

Blind Boys of Alabama [Happy Land Jubilee Singers]. Gospel quintet. It was formed by students at the Talladega Institute for the Deaf and Blind in Alabama in 1939 to sing black religious quartet music. The original members were Clarence Fountain, Johnny Fields, George Scott, Olice Thomas, and Velma Bozman Traylor. Influenced by the Golden Gate Jubilee Quartet, it began as a jubilee style quartet, singing mostly Negro spirituals and standard Protestant hymns, and emphasizing barbershop style harmony. It was called the Happy Land Jubilee Singers until a concert promoter suggested the group change its name in 1948 in anticipation of a double bill concert with the already successful Five Blind Boys of Mississippi. Tours with the two groups followed and the Alabama-based group, influenced by the impassioned, lead-driven sound of the Mississippi-based group, gradually evolved into a gospel style quartet with Fountain emerging as a hard-singing lead. It began recording for Coleman Records in 1948. The group's career waned in the 1970s but was reenergized when it appeared in the successful off-Broadway musical *Gospel at Colonus* in 1983. Several successful recordings followed on Peter Gabriel's Real World Records beginning in 2001, marking a transition to the contemporary gospel style that began influencing traditional quartets decades earlier. Their rendition of "Way Down in the Hole" brought them new fans when it was adopted in 2002 as the theme song of the HBO television show *The Wire*. Since signing with Real World Records, the group has won several Grammy Awards and was inducted into the Gospel Music Hall of Fame in 2003. By mid-2005, Fountain was the only original group member.

SELECTED RECORDINGS

Greatest Gospel Gems (Specialty SPCD-7206-2, 1991); *Spirit of the Century* (Real World Records 7243 8 12793 2 8, 2001)

BIBLIOGRAPHY

H.C. Boyer: *How Sweet the Sound: the Golden Age of Gospel* (Washington, DC, 1995)

R. Darden: *People Get Ready! A New History of Black Gospel Music* (New York, 2004)

CEDRIC DENT

Blind Tom. *See* Bethune, Thomas.

Bliss, Anthony A(ddison) (*b* New York, NY, 19 April 1913; *d* Prince Edward Island, 10 Aug 1991). Music administrator and lawyer. After attending Harvard University (BA 1936), he pursued graduate studies at Columbia University (1936–8) and law at the University of Virginia (LlB 1940); he practiced law in New York. In 1949 he became a member of the board of directors of the Metropolitan Opera Association, and served as its president (1956–7), executive director (1974–81), and general manager (1981–5). Among the changes Bliss initiated in the Metropolitan's operations, the expanding of its season and the introduction of sounder financing were especially important. He has also held administrative or board positions with a number of arts organizations, including the Joffrey Ballet in New York, the American Arts Alliance, Lincoln Center, the NEA (music and dance panels), and the New York Foundation of the Arts.

BIBLIOGRAPHY

CBY 1979

J. Rockwell: "Bliss Looks Back on Years at Met," *New York Times* (29 July 1985)

WILLIAM MCCLELLAN/R

Bliss, Philip P[aul] (*b* Huston Township area, Clearfield County, PA, 9 July 1838; *d* near Ashtabula, OH, 29 Dec 1876). Teacher, composer, songbook compiler, singer, and revival music leader. Despite his own limited opportunity for formal education, Bliss became a school teacher at the age of 18. He received his musical training at the Susquehanna Collegiate Institute and in singing and normal schools. He taught his first singing school about 1858, and in 1864 he sold his first secular song, "Lora Vale," to Root and Cady of Chicago. He joined the firm in 1865 as a member of a male quartet, "Yankee Boys," that sang primarily at patriotic meetings. Though the ensemble soon disbanded, Bliss stayed on with Root and Cady for four more years, representing the company at musical conventions and concerts and writing articles for its magazine. In 1870, he became music and Sunday school director at Chicago's prosperous First Congregational Church, all the while continuing his work in conventions, normal schools, and concerts. In 1874, after much encouragement by D.L. Moody (whom he had met in 1869), he became music director for the evangelistic meetings of D.W. Whittle, principally in the Midwest and South. In 1876, he and his wife were killed in a train wreck on their way to a meeting at D.L. Moody's Tabernacle in Chicago.

Bliss compiled his first songbook, *The Charm*, for Sunday school use in 1871 (Chicago/Cincinnati/New York). This volume was followed by similar collections of secular, Sunday school, and singing school/convention songs. His first publication for evangelistic meetings, *Gospel Songs* (Chicago/Cincinnati, 1874), is often said to have given the name to this important genre of late 19th-century revival music. Bliss joined with Ira D. Sankey to publish the first two volumes of the influential *Gospel Hymns* series (Chicago/Cincinnati/New York, 1875, 1876).

Bliss wrote the words and/or music for nearly 400 songs, more than 300 of which have sacred texts. His gospel song "Hold the Fort" was the most popular hymn of Moody's and Sankey's early revivals but has fallen from congregational use, perhaps due to its Civil War connections and later uses as a political and labor song. Several of Bliss's gospel hymns rank among this genre's most widely-sung and reprinted in hymnals, including the text of "I Will Sing of My Redeemer," the words and music of "Hallelujah! What a Savior" and "Wonderful Words of Life," and, above all, his tune for Horatio Spafford's "It Is Well with My Soul." The last-named, set to a text of glorious trust in the work of Christ despite life's storms, also remains one of the most frequently arranged and recorded gospel hymns—instrumentally, chorally, and by solo artists—featuring Bliss's lyrical musical setting with anthem-like chorus which captures both the serenity and radiant hope expressed in the text.

BIBLIOGRAPHY

G.C. Stebbins: *Reminiscences and Gospel Hymn Stories* (New York, 1924), 188–98

P.J. Scheips: *Hold the Fort! The Story of a Song from the Sawdust Trail to the Picket Line* (Washington, DC, 1971)

B.J. Neil: *Philip P. Bliss (1838–1876): Gospel Hymn Composer and Compiler* (diss., New Orleans Baptist Theological Seminary, 1977)

M.R. Wilhoit: *A Guide to the Principal Authors and Composers of Gospel Song of the Nineteenth Century* (diss., Southern Baptist Theological Seminary, 1982), 25–41

DAVID W. MUSIC

Blitzstein, Marc [Marcus] **(Samuel)** (*b* Philadelphia, PA, 2 March 1905; *d* Fort-de-France, Martinique, 22 Jan 1964). Composer. His early works reflect his admiration for the craft of musical composition, an aesthetic encouraged by both of his otherwise antipodal teachers in Europe, Nadia Boulanger and Arnold Schoenberg. Thereafter, his style changed from an abstract neo-classicism, in which form and structure were primary, to a more functional agit-prop style, crystallized in his stage works. Well-known examples such as *The Cradle Will Rock* bring together blues, pop, speech patter, parody, and satire (often involving quotation or other referential material). His skillful use of American vernacular speech patterns is perhaps his crowning achievement.

As a child, Blitzstein, whose parents were of Russian Jewish heritage, was sent to the Ethical Culture Sunday School and to programs sponsored by the Socialist Literary Society. At the age of seven he gave his first public performance, a reading of Mozart's "Coronation" Concerto K537 with his teacher, Constantin Sternberg, at the second piano. By the age of nine he had skipped two years at school, his academic precocity paralleling his remarkable musical talent. Following the separation of his parents, he moved with his mother and sister to Venice, California, where he continued his piano studies with Katherine Montreville Cocke and Julian Pascal, performed at charitable concerts, and basked in the attention of society writers. The family's return to Philadelphia early in 1917 enabled Blitzstein to re-establish a warm relationship with his father, with whom he attended the theater and concerts.

At the age of 16, Blitzstein enrolled at the University of Pennsylvania. After his scholarship was rescinded because of poor progress in physical education, however, he began a three-year period of study with Alexander Siloti, commuting to New York for lessons. In 1924, after a brief affair with Alexander Smallens, he entered the newly formed Curtis Institute of Music, where he studied composition with ROSARIO SCALERO. His works from this period include salon-style piano pieces and songs to texts by A.E. Housman and Walt Whitman. In 1926, shortly before leaving Europe, he performed as solo pianist with the Philadelphia Orchestra under Henry Hadley. While studying with Boulanger in Paris, he completed two more songs on Whitman texts: "O Hymen! O Hymenee!," a foray into bitonality, and "Gods," a tonal work featuring frequent changes in meter, key, and rhythm. He went on to Berlin, where he enrolled in a course with Schoenberg at the Akademie der Künste. As he immersed himself in the principles of 12-tone composition, he grew increasingly antipathetic toward what he came to view as a sterile approach to musical creation. His own compositions, which he later came to call *Songs for a Coon Shouter*, continued to consist of theatrical settings of Whitman texts. He returned to Philadelphia in 1927.

While resident at the MacDowell Colony during the summer of 1928, Blitzstein met the novelist and critic Eva Goldbeck, whom, despite his homosexuality, he later married. That same year he began writing articles in *Modern Music*, a journal to which he regularly contributed until 1940. As a composer, his fascination with Whitman texts continued. The blues harmonies employed in songs such as "I am He" and "Ages and Ages" suggest a commonality between jazz and primal sexuality. These were given their premiere in 1928, together with "O Hymen! O Hymenee!" and "As Adam," by the African American baritone Benjohn Ragsdale at a Copland-Sessions Concert in New York. The Piano Sonata (1927) was performed several times in 1929, and *Percussion Music for Piano* (1929) was introduced; the latter gained notoriety for its slapping, shutting, and opening of the piano lid. During the same year, *Triple-Sec* (1928), a one-act opera containing a love scene between a black man and a white woman, was first performed in Philadelphia. Blitzstein's association with both advanced musical circles and leftist political ideology was solidified through these challenges to public sensibility.

For the next several years, Blitzstein traveled in Europe and America, composing works in diverse styles. *Parabola and Circula* (1929), for example, although set in a cubist formal world and based on a story replete with symbolic abstraction, contains music that is melodious, conservative, and suggestive of the style of Les Six. The ballet *Cain* (1930) is modal and mildly dissonant, featuring moments best described as polytonal. *The Harpies* (1931), with its Thracian setting, satirization of Gluckian, Wagnerian, and Mozartian mythology, and Broadway theatricality, suggests the influence of neo-classicism. *The Condemned* (1932), an opera based on the Sacco and Vanzetti trial, broke new ground in employing a chorus for each of the four dramatic roles. "Jimmie's got a goil" (1935), and other songs set to texts by e.e. cummings, offered audiences musical amusement. The "Italian" String Quartet (1930), the *Romantic Piece* for orchestra (1930), the Piano Concerto (1931), and the *Serenade* for string quartet (1932) were designed to prove his compositional ability in the genres of absolute music.

If the early 1930s marked a period in which Blitzstein was searching for an appropriate musical language, they were also characterized by his yearning to understand the personal demons and political-social issues that so consumed him and his wife. Their marriage survived in part because of a shared support for the Communist movement and a shared concern about how best to express that support while continuing to enhance their careers. After Eva's untimely death from anorexia in 1936, Blitzstein became more open about his homosexuality. Hanns Eisler's lectures at the New School for Social Research, New York (1935), pushed him to agitate for music that would address social concerns, attack social enemies and, most important, convey its message in an accessible, vernacular musical language. To fulfill these objectives, he turned to tonality, popular song, sardonic references to earlier styles, and parodies of art music. He also wrote for "red" journals such as *New Masses* (1936–46), worked for leftist groups such as the Composers Collective, New York, and adhered to a belief that the composer must join and fight for the people, rather than live as a parasite on society's beneficence.

The intended premiere of *The Cradle Will Rock* (1936–7) was canceled by the Federal Theater Project when the work's anti-establishment, pro-union theme was deemed too controversial. It was later produced independently by John Houseman and Orson Welles at the Mercury Theater, New York. With its satirical quotations of Bach and Beethoven, conjoined with stylistic elements taken from patter, jazz, and the musical revue, the work has come to symbolize the musical equivalent of Brecht's "epic theater." *I've Got the Tune* (1937), a radio song-play, made Blitzstein the composer par excellence of the Communist movement. *No for an Answer* (1937–40), which followed, deals with hardships faced by unemployed and non-unionized Greek immigrants; the films *Valley Town* (1940) and *Native Land* (1940–41), for which Blitzstein wrote scores, are concerned with unemployment and fascistic elements in capitalist society. His reputation became so politicized that the FBI under J. Edgar Hoover (1895–1972) began a serious investigation of his ties to the American Communist Party.

In 1942 Blitzstein joined the war effort, becoming attached to the Eighth Air Force in London. With the breaking of the Hitler–Stalin pact in 1941 and the addition of the USSR as an ally, he felt the war had become entirely just. His works from this period, including *Freedom Morning* for orchestra and chorus of black enlistees (1943, when blacks were still segregated in the US armed services), the *Airborne Symphony* (1944–6), commissioned by the air force, and a film score for Garson Kanin's documentary *The True Glory* (1945–6), were pleasing both to the military and to his own social conscience.

After the war Blitzstein returned to writing for the stage. *Regina* (1946–8), a character study of the mores of the American South at the turn of the 19th century, melded together the diverse styles of the spiritual, ragtime, blues. and traditional opera. The work 's focus on the struggle of African Americans for equality reflected Blitzstein's continuing concern for minority issues. In *Reuben, Reuben* (1955) and *Juno* (1957–9) he continued his role as a social critic. It was his translation and adaptation of *Die Dreigroschenoper* by Bertolt Brecht and Kurt Weill, however, that brought him the long-elusive fame he had sought: the seven-year run of the production also brought him a financial bounty he could not have envisioned.

In 1959 Blitzstein was honored with membership in the National Institute of Arts and Letters. Despite his reputation as an advocate of leftist causes, he also gained a commission from the Ford Foundation to write an opera. Returning to the subject of his early work *The Condemned*, the Sacco–Vanzetti trial, he incurred the wrath of right-wing journalists such as George E. Sikolsky. He took time away from composition in 1962 to serve as the John Golden Professor of Playwrighting at Bennington College. While there, he established a friendship with Bernard Malamud and began to set the writer's short stories *The Magic Barrel* and *Idiots First*. In November 1963 he went to Martinique to work and rest. In January 1964, after a beating at the hands of three sailors he had met in a waterfront bar, he died in a hospital in Fort-de-France.

WORKS

DRAMATIC

Triple-Sec (op-farce, 1, R. Jeans), 1928, Philadelphia, 6 May 1929; Parabola and Circula (op-ballet, 1, G. Whitsett), 1929, unperf.; Cain (ballet), 1930; The Harpies (op, 1, Blitzstein), 1931, New York, 25 May 1953; The Condemned (choral op, 1, Blitzstein), 1932, unperf.; Send for the Militia (theater sketch, Blitzstein), 1v, pf, 1935; The Cradle will Rock (play in music, 10 scenes, Blitzstein), 1936–7, New York, 16 June 1937; I've Got the Tune (radio song-play, 1, Blitzstein), 1937, New York, 24 Oct 1937; No for an Answer (op, 2, Blitzstein), 1937–40, New York, 5 Jan 1941; Plowed Under (theater sketch, Blitzstein), 1937

Labor for Victory (radio series, Blitzstein), 1942; Galoopchik (musical play, Blitzstein), 1945, unfinished; Show (ballet), 1946; Regina (op, 3, L. Hellman and Blitzstein), 1946–8, New York, 31 Oct 1949, rev. 1953, 1958; The Guests (ballet), 1948; Reuben, Reuben (musical play, 2, Blitzstein), 1955, Boston, 10 Oct 1955; Juno (musical play, 2, J. Stein and Blitzstein, after S. O'Casey), 1957–9, New York, 9 March 1959; Sacco and Vanzetti (op, Blitzstein), 1959–64, unfinished; Idiots First (op, 1, B. Malamud and Blitzstein), 1963, completed L.J. Lehrman; The Magic Barrel (op, 1, Malamud and Blitzstein), 1963, unfinished

Incid music: Julius Caesar (W. Shakespeare), 1937; Danton's Death (G. Büchner), 1938; Androcles and the Lion (G.B. Shaw), 1946; Another Part of the Forest (Hellman), 1946; King Lear (Shakespeare), 2 versions: 1950, 1955; Volpone (B. Jonson), 1956; A Midsummer Night's Dream (Shakespeare), 1958; A Winter's Tale (Shakespeare), 1958; Toys in the Attic (Hellman), 1960

Film scores: Hände, 1928; Surf and Seaweed (R. Steiner), 1931; War Department Manual, 1935; Chesapeake Bay Retriever, 1936; The Spanish Earth (J. Ivens), 1936–7, collab. V. Thomson; Valley Town, 1940; Native Land (L. Hurwitz and P. Strand), 1940–41; Night Shift (J. Chambers), op, 1942; The True Glory (C. Reed and G. Kanin), 1945–6

VOCAL

After the Dazzle of Day (W. Whitman), 1v, pf, 1925; As if a Phantom Caress'd Me (Whitman), 1v, pf, 1925; Into my Heart an Air (A.E. Housman), 1v, pf, 1925; Gods (Whitman), Mez, str, 1926; 4 Whitman Songs, Bar, pf, 1928; Is Five (e.e. cummings), S, pf, 1929; Cantatina, female chorus, perc, 1930; Children's Cantata, chorus, 1935; Jimmie's Got a Goil (Cummings), 1v, pf, 1935

A Child Writes a Letter, Bar, pf, 1936; Invitation to Bitterness (Blitzstein), ATB, 1938; The Airborne Sym. (Blitzstein), nar, T, B, male chorus, orch, 1944–6; Displaced (Blitzstein), 1v, pf, 1946; This Is the Garden (Blitzstein), chorus, orch, 1957; 6 Elizabethan Songs (Shakespeare), 1v, pf, 1958; From Marion's Book (Cummings), 1v, pf, 1960; songs

INSTRUMENTAL

Orch: Sarabande, 1926; Romantic Piece, 1930; Pf Conc., 1931; Surf and Seaweed, suite, 1933; Variations, 1934; Freedom Morning, sym. poem, male chorus, orch, 1943; Native Land, suite, 1946; Lear: a Study, 1958

Chbr and solo: Sonata, pf, 1927; Perc Music, pf, 1929; Scherzo, pf, 1930; Str Qt "Italian," 1930; Serenade, str qt, 1932; Discourse, cl, vc, pf, 1933; Suite, pf, 1933; Le monde libre, march, pf, 1944; The Guests, suite, pf, 1949; Show, suite, pf, 1947

MSS in *MAu*

Principal publisher: Chappell

BIBLIOGRAPHY

GroveO (E. Gordon, "Blitzstein, Marc," "Regina")
E. Goldbeck: "Principles of 'Educational' Theater," *New Masses* (31 Dec 1935)
H. Brant: "Marc Blitzstein," *MM*, xxiii (1946), 170–75
J.O. Hunter: "Marc Blitzstein's 'The Cradle Will Rock' as a Document of America, 1937," *American Quarterly*, xvi (1964), 227–33
M. Lederman: "Memories of Marc Blitzstein, Music's Angry Man," *Show*, iv (1964), 18–24
W.H. Mellers: *Music in a New Found Land* (New York, 1964/*R*)
P.M. Talley: *Social Criticism in the Theatre Librettos of Marc Blitzstein* (diss., U. of Wisconsin, 1965)
J. Peyser: "The Troubled Time of Marc Blitzstein," *Columbia University Forum*, ix/1 (1966), 32–7
J. Gruen: *Close-Up* (New York, 1968)
R.J. Dietz: "Marc Blitzstein and the 'Agit-Prop' Theatre of the 1930s," *Yearbook of the Inter-American Institute for Musical Research*, vi (1970), 51–6
R.J. Dietz: *The Operatic Style of Marc Blitzstein* (diss., U. of Iowa, 1970)
J. Houseman: *Run-Through: a Memoir* (New York, 1972)
C. Davis: *The Sun in Mid-Career* (New York, 1975)
J. Lehrman: *A Musical Analysis of "Idiots First"* (thesis, Cornell U., 1975)
E. Gordon: "Of the People: Marc Blitzstein Remembered," *ON*, xliv/19 (1979–80), 26–8, 30
E. Gordon: "The Roots of 'Regina,'" *Performing Arts*, iii/8 (1980), 6
E. Gordon: *Mark the Music: the Life and Work of Marc Blitzstein* (New York, 1989)
C. Oja: "The Cradle Will Rock and Mass-Song Style of the 1930s," *MQ*, lxxiii (1989), 445–75
D.Z. Kushner: "Marc Blitzstein: Musical Propagandist," *Opera Journal*, xxvi/2 (1993), 2–20
D. Metzer: "Reclaiming Walt: Marc Blitzstein's Whitman Settings," *JAMS*, lxviii/2 (1995), 240–71
G. Block: "The Cradle Will Rock: a Labor Musical for Art's Sake," *Enchanted Evenings: the Broadway Musical from Show Boat to* Sondheim (Oxford, 1997), 115–32
The Marc Blitzstein Songbook, i, ed. L. Lehrman (New York, 1999)
The Marc Blitzstein Songbook, ii, ed. L. Lehrman (New York, 2001)
L. Lehrman: *Marc Blitzstein: A Bio-bibliography* (Westport, CT, 2005)

DAVID Z. KUSHNER

Blizard, Ralph (*b* Kingsport, TN, 5 Dec 1918; *d* Blountville, TN, Dec 2004). Old-time fiddler. He was born in the industrial city of Kingsport in Sullivan County, Tennessee, and grew up in a musical family. His father, an accomplished fiddler, taught him to play. The Blizard family's visitors and friends included the Carter Family from Maces Springs in neighboring Scott County, Virginia. Notable East Tennessee fiddlers such as Charlie Bowman from Gray Station in Washington County, and Dudley Vance from Chinquapin Grove in Sullivan County, also came to play with Blizard's father. Fiddlin' Arthur Smith's records and radio broadcasts strongly influenced young Blizard in the development of his smooth, bluesy long bow fiddling style. At the age of 12 he formed his first string band, the Southern Ramblers, and began playing on area radio stations.

After serving in World War II, Blizard married Mildred Bowman. He worked for the Tennessee Eastman Company in Kingsport until he retired in 1980. After laying his fiddle aside for 25 years, Blizard began attending fiddle contests and old time music festivals in the Southeast. He started playing with the New Southern Ramblers, a group that included younger musicians such as John Lilly, Gordy Hinner, Phil Jamison, John Hermann, and Meredith McIntosh. He also became an old time fiddle instructor at Warren Wilson College's annual Swannanoa Gathering

In 2002 he received a National Heritage Fellowship from the National Endowment for the Arts. In 2003 Blizard and the New Southern Ramblers performed at the Smithsonian Folklife Festival in Washington, DC. That same year, he received a Tennessee Folklife Heritage Award from the Tennessee Arts Commission.

RICHARD BLAUSTEIN

Bloch, Ernest (*b* Geneva, Switzerland, 24 July 1880; *d* Portland, OR, 15 July 1959). Composer and teacher of Swiss origin.

1. Life. 2. Works.

1. Life. He studied in Geneva with Albert Goss and Louis Etienne-Reyer (violin) and Emile Jaques-Dalcroze (solfège and composition) before leaving, at the suggestion of Martin Marsick, to study in Brussels. There he took lessons from Eugène Ysaÿe (violin), François Rasse (composition) and Franz Schörg (violin and chamber music), at whose home he lived from 1896 to 1899. He then went to study in Frankfurt with Ivan Knorr (1899–1901) and in Munich with Ludwig Thuille (1901–3). After a year in Paris (1903–4), during which time he absorbed the French Impressionistic style, he returned to Geneva, married Margarethe Augusta Schneider, and entered his father's business as a bookkeeper and salesman of Swiss tourist goods. Meanwhile, he kept his hand in music by composing in piecemeal fashion, conducting orchestral concerts in Neuchâtel and Lausanne (1909–10) and lecturing on aesthetics at the Geneva Conservatory (1911–15). A high point of this period was the premiere of his lyric drama *Macbeth* at the Opéra-Comique, Paris, on 30 November 1910.

Bloch went to the United States in 1916 with the encouragement of Alfred Pochon, second violinist of the Flonzaley Quartet, as conductor for a tour by Maud Allan's dance company. When the tour collapsed, he accepted a position at the newly formed David Mannes College of Music in New York, teaching theory and composition there and also privately (1917–20). He was thus able to bring his wife and three children, Suzanne, Lucienne, and Ivan, to America. The successful premiere of his String Quartet no.1 by the Flonzaley Quartet on 31 December 1916 led to performances of his orchestral works in Boston, New York, and Philadelphia. He conducted his *Trois poèmes juifs* with the Boston SO in March 1917 and *Schelomo*, with Kindler as the cello soloist, at a concert sponsored by the Society of the Friends of Music in New York in May of the same year. Following additional successes in Philadelphia, where he conducted a program of his "Jewish" works with the Philadelphia Orchestra in January 1918, he signed a contract with G. Schirmer, who published these compositions with what was to become a trademark logo—the six-pointed Star of David with the initials E.B. in the center; it was an imprimatur, which firmly established for Bloch a Jewish identity in the public mind.

Bloch expanded his contact with American life by conducting Renaissance choral music with amateur singers at the Manhattan Trade School, teaching the fundamentals of music to children in Joanne Bird Shaw's experimental summer school in Peterboro, New Hampshire, and discussing art and life with such figures as Julius Hartt. In 1919 his *Suite* for viola and piano (or orchestra) won the Coolidge Prize, quickly earning a place in the viola repertory.

Bloch served as founding director of the Cleveland Institute of Music (1920–25), where he conducted the student orchestra, taught composition, established master classes and courses for the general public, and proposed such radical reforms as the abandonment of examinations and textbooks in favor of direct musical experience, with study rooted in the scores of the great masters. However, the trustees continued to favor a practical curriculum and a more traditional approach to music education, and this, among other factors, eventually led him to resign. (It was in Cleveland, in 1924, that he became a naturalized US citizen.) He then accepted the directorship of the San Francisco Conservatory of Music (1925–30), during which time he was awarded the Carolyn Beebe Prize of the New York Chamber Music Society for his *Four Episodes* for chamber orchestra (1926), the first prize in a contest sponsored by *Musical America* for his epic rhapsody in three parts, *America*, and a shared RCA Victor Award for his homage to his native land, *Helvetia*.

During the 1930s Bloch lived mainly in Switzerland, composing such works as *Voice in the Wilderness*, the Piano Sonata, *Evocations* for orchestra, the Violin Concerto and, most importantly, the *Sacred Service*, with which he began his second European period. He conducted his works in various European cities, and returned briefly to the United States to conduct the *Sacred*

Ernest Bloch. (Lebrecht Music & Arts)

Service in New York in 1934. Major festivals of his works were held in London in 1934 and 1937, the latter in connection with the founding of an Ernest Bloch Society, with Albert Einstein as honorary president, and Alex Cohen as secretary. *Macbeth* was revived in Naples in Italian translation in March 1938, but only three performances were given owing to Mussolini's deference to a visit from Hitler. Because of growing anti-Semitism and also because he wished to retain his American citizenship, Bloch returned to the United States and, in 1940, assumed a professorship at the University of California at Berkeley, where he taught summer courses until his retirement in 1952. The Berkeley duties fulfilled an obligation he owed the institution, which, in conjunction with a grant from the Stern family had enabled him to compose in Europe from 1930 to 1939 freed from the responsibilities of teaching.

In his later years, during which he lived reclusively at Agate Beach, Oregon, he was the recipient of numerous honors, including the first Gold Medal in Music (String Quartet no.2), from the American Academy of Arts and Sciences (1947) and the Henry Hadley Medal of the National Association for American Composers and Conductors (1957). He continued to compose in a wide variety of genres, and to pursue his lifelong hobbies of photography and mushroom collecting, and his newer interest in collecting and polishing agates. In 1958, suffering from cancer, he underwent unsuccessful surgery and died a year later. In 1967 an Ernest Bloch Society was formed in the United States through the efforts of the composer's children, each of them now deceased. The Society, which flourished until 1991, published a bulletin as a means by which to provide information about performances and publications relative to Bloch and to disseminate material drawn from his letters, notes, and pedagogical writings. The Ernest Bloch Music Festival, held from 1990 to 2006 and based in Newport, Oregon, continued that state's tradition of honoring the artist who resided in their midst during his final 18 years. In 2007, the multi-pronged Ernest Bloch Legacy Project was formed there, and, in 2008, an International Ernest Bloch Society was established in London.

2. Works. Bloch's student compositions are diverse and derivative, ranging from the sprawling *Symphonie orientale* (1896) to the Romantically effusive *Vivre–aimer* (1900). The periods in Munich and Paris produced two major efforts, the extravagantly orchestrated Symphony in C♯ minor, a four-movement formally conceived work despite a broad program (a fugue opens the fourth movement), revealing the influence of Richard Strauss with regard to melody, harmony, and orchestration, and the pair of symphonic poems, *Hiver–Printemps*, with Impressionistically colored instrumentation, notable in the harp and woodwind solos, and in the closing reflective coda. *Macbeth*, the only published operatic venture by Bloch, established his credentials as a dramatic composer. In this work, he synthesized elements from the Wagnerian music drama, from Debussy's *Pelléas et Mélisande*, and from Musorgsky's *Boris Godunov* with his own emerging originality. Certain characteristics associated with the composer's later works appear in *Macbeth*: frequent changes of meter, tempo, and tonality, melodic use of the perfect fourth and augmented second at crucial moments, modal flavoring, dark instrumentation, repeated-note patterns, ostinatos and pedal points, and ever-present cyclic formal procedures (the last refined through study with Rasse, a pupil of Franck).

Bloch's search for his own musical identity found fulfillment in a series of highly charged epics on a broad scale, biblical in inspiration and known as the "Jewish Cycle." In these deeply emotive utterances, which include settings of Psalms cxxxvii and cxiv for soprano and orchestra (1912–14), Psalm xxii for baritone and orchestra (1914), the symphony *Israel* with five solo voices (1912–16), and *Schelomo* (1915–16), a Hebraic rhapsody for cello and orchestra (including the use of quarter-tones for the first time in his output), he painted sweeping musical canvases with a rich orchestral palette. Their "oriental" or quasi-Hebraic character is intensified by the augmented intervals, melismatic treatment of melody, and large, coloristic orchestra. The Scotch-snap rhythm and its variants is so pervasive that it has come to be known as the "Bloch rhythm." Authentic Hebrew material is rare (exceptions are quotations from the *Song of Songs* in *Israel* and a *gemora nigun* in *Schelomo*); however, certain of Bloch's compositional traits take on a new meaning in the context of the "Jewish Cycle." The repeated-note patterns and the augmented and perfect fourth intervals in the Psalms and

Schelomo, for example, evoke the call of the *shofar* as it is sounded in the synagogue on the High Holy Days (*Rosh ha-Shanah* and *Yom Kippur*); the unfettered rhythmic flow suggests the melismas of Hebrew chant. Additionally, the frequent accents on the final or penultimate beat of a bar have analogies in the Hebrew language.

Following the "Jewish" works, Bloch moved, in part, towards a neo-classical aesthetic as exemplified, to varying degrees, in his two sonatas for violin and piano, the First Piano Quintet (with effective use of quartertones in the first and third movements), and the first Concerto Grosso (with a powerful closing fugue). Even in these "abstract" works, however, certain referential associations are revealed, for example to the Gregorian mass *Kyrie "Fons bonitatis"* in the Second Violin Sonata, or the "Dirge" and "Pastorale and Rustic Dances" movements of the Concerto Grosso. And, in the same period, there is still a residue of overt Judaic expression, as in *Baal Shem* for violin and piano and *From Jewish Life* for cello and piano (albeit an expression more akin to the Jew of the eastern European ghetto than that of the Bible); Bloch's propensity to eclecticism is further seen in the piano cycle, *Poems of the Sea (inspired by the verses of Walt Whitman)*, in which there is a mixture of Impressionism, modality, and Hebrew *shtaygers*.

With his move to San Francisco, Bloch produced a series of widely varied works, including *America: an Epic Rhapsody*, a three-movement program symphony unified by a recurring motto and containing ample quotations from Amerindian melodies, English shanties, American Civil War tunes, and Negro spirituals, and references to the mechanization of 20th-century America (e.g., factory noises, car horns). A closing anthem is intended to be sung by the audience. The *Four Episodes* for chamber orchestra conjures another slice of American life, that of San Francisco's Chinatown, while *Helvetia*, replete with folksong quotations and other Alpine suggestions, pays homage to his native land.

In the 1930s Bloch returned to his roots and, in his retreat at Roveredo-Capriasca, Ticino, produced his monumental *Avodath ha-Kodesh* ("Sacred Service"), based on texts drawn from the Reform Jewish prayer book. His other music from that European decade is mostly large in scale and diverse in inspiration and subject matter. *Voice in the Wilderness*, an orchestral work with obbligato cello, is, essentially, a series of meditations but without a specific subject and decidedly not Jewish in intent (as opposed to *Schelomo*); a piano setting of the orchestral expositions of the first five sections is titled *Visions and Prophecies. The* orchestral *Evocations* has a quasi-"oriental" atmosphere, as in the second movement, "Houang-Ti," with its pentatonic and exotic scales, and the inclusion of harp, piano, and celesta, while the Violin Concerto, despite its Amerindian motto used structurally to unify the work, reverts to well-practiced traits, that is, cyclic procedures, the "Bloch rhythm," and open fourths and fifths.

The substantial body of music after 1941 is, in the main, less subjective than that of earlier years. The Concerto Grosso no.2 and the String Quartets nos.2–5, with their formal design and abstract quality, fall into the neo-classical category. Similarly, the passacaglias and fugues of the *Suite symphonique* and the String Quartets nos.2–4 cement a return to principles associated with early masters whose technical polish Bloch admired. The *Concerto symphonique*, on the other hand, is a large-gestured Romantic piano concerto, while the *Sinfonia breve* may be described as both tightly compressed and expressionistic. Twelve-tone themes and implications are commonly featured in the late works regardless of their style (as in the Symphony in E♭ major, *Sinfonia breve* and String Quartets nos.2–5), while Jewish associations are still occasionally noticed (e.g., in the Symphony for trombone and orchestra and the *Suite hébraïque* for violin or viola and orchestra or piano). Earlier pictorialism is largely absent; indeed the kaleidoscopic and sometimes rhetorical features of the "Jewish Cycle" have been supplanted by objectivity, balance, and control.

Bloch attracted many distinguished students (among them ROGER SESSIONS, DOUGLAS S. MOORE, BERNARD ROGERS, THEODORE CHANLER, FREDERICK JACOBI, QUINCY PORTER, and HERBERT ELWELL), whom he taught to develop and create according to their individual temperaments and talents, an approach he adopted from his teacher, Knorr. He neither founded any school nor blazed new trails; he molded into a distinctive style the ingredients he found already in use. He also attracted many lovers (more than two dozen according to his wife Marguerite), the letters to some of whom provide insights into his personal and professional life.

The passion, fervor and colorful florid writing of Bloch's "Jewish Cycle" are perhaps most characteristic, though in retrospect even these works are guided by an acute sense of form. However, unlike the late string quartets and suites for solo string instruments, the biblically inspired works, with their luxurious waves of phantasmagoria, engage the listener more emotionally than intellectually. Patriotic or nationalistic efforts such as *America* and *Helvetia*, though somewhat self-conscious, are meritorious as *pièces d'occasion*. But in his best work, the expression of his firm faith in the spirituality of mankind always shows through. Bloch was, and continues to be, a singular figure in the music of the 20th century.

See also JEWISH MUSIC.

WORKS

STAGE

Macbeth (op, 3, E. Fleg), 1904–9, Paris, Opéra-Comique, 30 Nov 1910

ORCHESTRAL

Helvetia, 1900–29, Chicago, 18 Feb 1932
Symphony in c♯, 1901–2, Geneva, 8 Jan 1910
Hiver—Printemps, sym. poems, 1904–5, Geneva, 27 Jan 1906
Three Jewish Poems, 1913, Boston, 23 March 1917
Israel, symph., 5 solo voices, 1912–14, 3 May 1917
Schelomo, vc, orch, 1915–16, New York, 3 May 1917
Suite, va, orch, 1919, Washington, 5 Nov 1920
In the Night, 1922
Concerto Grosso no.1, str, pf obbl, 1924–5, Cleveland, 1 June 1925
Four Episodes, chbr orch, 1926, New York, 20 March 1927
America, an Epic Rhapsody, sym., closing choral anthem, 1926, 20 Dec 1928

Voice in the Wilderness, orch, vc obbl, 1936, Los Angeles, 21 Jan 1937
Evocations, 1937, San Francisco, 11 Feb 1938
Violin Concerto, 1937–8, Cleveland, 15 Dec 1938
Suite symphonique, 1944, Philadelphia, 26 Oct 1945
Variation no.10 "Solemne," 1944, Cincinnati, 23 March 1945 [from the multi-composer *Variations on a Theme by Eugene Goossens*]
Concerto symphonique, pf, orch, 1947–8, Edinburgh, 3 Sept 1949
Scherzo fantasque, pf, orch, 1948, Chicago, 2 Dec 1950
Concertino, fl, va, str, 1950, New York, 8 Dec 1950
Suite hébraïque, va/vn, orch, 1951, Chicago, 1 Jan 1953
Concerto Grosso no.2, str qt, str, 1952, London, 11 April 1953
In Memoriam, 1952
Sinfonia breve, 1952, London, 11 April 1953
Symphony, trbn, orch, 1954, Houston, 4 April 1956
Symphony in E♭ major, 1954–5, London, 15 Feb 1956
Proclamation, tpt, orch, 1955, New York, 18 Nov 1957
Suite modale, fl, str, 1957;, New York, 6 Dec 1959
Two Last Poems, fl, orch, 1958, Naples, 5 Oct 1958

VOCAL

Choral: America: an Epic Rhapsody, chorus, orch, 1926; Avodath hakodesh [Sacred Service], Bar, chorus, orch, 1930–33
Other works: Historiettes au crépuscule, 1v, pf, 1904; Poèmes d'automne, Mez, orch, 1906; Prelude and 2 Psalms 137, 114, S, orch, 1912–14; Israel, 5 solo vv, orch, 1912–16; Psalm xxii, A/Bar, orch, 1914

CHAMBER AND SOLO INSTRUMENTAL

3–5 insts: Str Qt no.1, 1916; Pf Qnt no.1, 1921–3; 3 Nocturnes, pf trio, 1924; In the Mountains, str qt, 1925; Night, str qt, 1925; Paysages, str qt, 1925; Prelude, str qt, 1925; 2 Pieces, str qt, 1938–50; Str Qt no.2, 1945; Str Qt no.3, 1952; Str Qt no.4, 1953; Str Qt no.5, 1956; Pf Qnt no.2, 1957
Solo str: Suite, va, pf, 1919; Sonata no.1, vn, pf, 1920; Baal Shem, vn, pf, 1923, orchd 1939; From Jewish Life, vc. pf, 1924; Méditation hébraïque, vc, pf, 1924; Nuit exotique, vn, pf, 1924; Sonata no.2 (Poème mystique), vn, pf, 1924; Abodah, vn, pf, 1929; Melody, vn, pf, 1929; 2 Pieces, va, pf, 1951; Suite modale. fl.pf.1956; 3 suites, vc, 1956, 1956, 1957; Suite, va (unfin.), 1958; 2 suites, vn, 1958
Pf: Ex-voto, 1914; 4 Circus Pieces, 1922; In the Night, 1922; Poems of the Sea, 1922, orchd; Danse sacrée, 1923; Enfantines, 1923; Nirvana, 1923; Sonata, 1935; Visions and Prophecies, 1936
Org: 6 Preludes, 1949; 4 Wedding Marches, 1950

JUVENILIA 1895–1900
(all unpublished)

Symphonie orientale; Vivre—Aimer, sym. poem; Str Qt; Orientale, orch; Vn Conc.; Sonata, vc, pf; Poème concertante, vn, orch; Fantaisie, Pastorale, vn; songs incl. Là-bas, Larmes d'automne, Musette, Près de la mer

MSS in *Wc* [juvenilia], *BEm*, *R*, *Hbc*, *ATs*, Western Jewish History Center, Berkeley, CA
Principal publishers: Boosey & Hawkes, Broude, Carisch, Eschig, Fischer, Leuckart, Mills, G. Schirmer, Suvini Zerboni

WRITINGS

"Gustave Mahler et la Deuxième Symphonie," *Courrier musical*, vii (1904), 408–11; Eng. trans., *Ernest Bloch Society Bulletin* (1984), 5–12
"Man and Music," *The Seven Arts*, ii (1917), 493–502; repr. in *MQ*, xix (1933), 374–81
"Ernest Bloch Surveys the Problem of Music Education," *Musical America*, xxxiv/4 (1921), 3, 40
"Music," *A School in Action: a Symposium* (New York, 1922), 145–234
"Proper Music Education," *Woman's Forum* [Akron, OH] (15 March 1922)
"The Pitfalls of Memorizing," *The Musician*, xxviii (1923), 11–12
"Securing the Best Results from Piano Study," *The Etude*, xli (1923), 59 only
"How and When to Begin Musical Training," *The Musician*, xxiv (1924), 29 only
Biography and Comment (San Francisco, 1925) [privately printed]
"Musical Education," *Women's City Club Magazine of San Francisco* (1927), Nov, 7–8
"Thoughts at 70," *The Etude*, lxix (1951), 9–10, 57 only

BIBLIOGRAPHY

GroveO ("Macbeth (iii)," D.Z. Kushner)
P. Lalo: "*Macbeth* de M. Ernest Bloch," *Revue musicale de Lyon*, nos.12–13 (1911), 388–92
O. Downes: "Ernest Bloch, the Swiss Composer, on the Influence of Race in Composition," *Musical Observer*, xv (1917), 11–12
G. Gatti: "Ernest Bloch," *Critica musicale*, iii (1920); Eng. trans., in *MQ*, vii (1921), 20–38
G. Gatti: "*Schelomo* di Ernest Bloch," *RMI*, xvii (1920), 372–7
G. Gatti: "Two *Macbeths*: Verdi-Bloch," *MQ*, xii (1926), 22–31
Search-Light [W.D. Frank]: "Ernest Bloch, Madness, and Music," *Time Exposures* (New York, 1926), 79–84
R.H. Sessions: "Ernest Bloch," *MM*, v/1 (1927–8), 3–11
M. Tibaldi-Chiesa: "Ernest Bloch," *Rassegna Mensile di Israel*, vi/9–10 (1932), 403–30
M. Tibaldi-Chiesa: *Ernest Bloch* (Turin, 1933)
R. Hall: "The *Macbeth* of Bloch," *MM*, xv (1937–8), 209–15
G. Sharp: "Ernest Bloch's Violin Concerto," *MR*, i (1940), 72–78
D.L. Schorr: "Ernest Bloch at 60," *New York Times* (11 Aug 1940)
J. Chissel: "Style in Bloch's Chamber Music," *ML*, xxiv (1943), 30–35
H.S. Minsky: *Ernest Bloch and his Music* (diss., George Peabody College for Teachers, Nashville, TN, 1945)
L. Stein: "The Problem of Ernest Bloch," *Chicago Jewish Forum*, v/1 (1946), 27–33; repr. in *Mid-Century*, ed. H.U. Ribalow (New York, 1955), 406–16
D. Newlin: "The Later Works of Ernest Bloch," *MQ*, xxxiii (1947), 443–59
J. Hastings: "Ernest Bloch and Modern Music," *Menorah Journal*, xxxvi (1948), 195–215; repr. in *MR*, x (1949), 115–27, and in *The Menorah Treasury*, ed. L. Schwarz (Philadelphia, 1964), 769–87
H. Cowell: "Current Chronicle: New York," *MQ*, xl (1954), 235–43
E. Chapman: "Ernest Bloch at 75," *Tempo*, no.35 (1955), 6–12
F.B. Blanks: "Ernest Bloch, 1880–1959," *Canon*, xii/12 (1959), 381–3
W.M. Jones: *The Music of Ernest Bloch* (diss., Indiana U., 1963)
W.M. Jones: "Ernest Bloch's Five String Quartets," *MR*, xxviii (1967), 112–21
D.Z. Kushner: *Ernest Bloch and his Symphonic Works* (diss., U. of Michigan, 1967)
D.Z. Kushner: "A Singular Ernest Bloch," *Musical Journal*, xxviii/1 (1970), 40, 51, 53
Y.E. Guibbory: *Thematic Treatment in the String Quartets of Ernest Bloch* (diss., West Virginia U., 1970)
E. Johnson: "A Composer's Vision: Photographs by Ernest Bloch": *Aperture*, xvi/3 (1972), 20–34
E. Raditz: *An Analytical Study of the Violin and Piano Works of Ernest Bloch* (diss., New York U., 1975)
S. Bloch and I. Heskes: *Ernest Bloch, Creative Spirit* (New York, 1976)
E. Johnson: "Ernest Bloch," *Camera*, l/2 (1976), 5, 6–17, 27, 37
C.L. Wheeler: *The Solo Piano Music of Ernest Bloch* (diss., U. of Oregon, 1976)
R. Rafael: "Ernest Bloch at the San Francisco Conservatory of Music," *Western States Jewish Historical Quarterly*, ix/3 (1977), 195–215
R. Strassburg: *Ernest Bloch, Voice in the Wilderness* (Los Angeles, 1977)
A. Knapp: "Bloch: a Reassessment," *RCM Magazine*, lxxiv (1978), 85–91
M. Schwager: "A Contribution to the Biography of Ernest Bloch: Letters at the University of Hartford," *CM*, no.28 (1978), 41–53
D. Sorani: "Ernest Bloch: un compositore Ebraico?," *Rassegna mensile di Israel*, xlv (1979), 379–84
A. Knapp: "The Life and Music of Ernest Bloch," *Jewish Quarterly*, xxviii (1980), 26–30
D.Z. Kushner: "Ernest Bloch: a Retrospective on the Centenary of his Birth," *College Music Symposium*, xx/2 (1980), 77–86
C. Tappolet, ed.: *Lettres de compositeurs Genèvois à Ernest Ansermet (1908–1966)* (Geneva, 1981), 37–99
E. Brody: "Romain Rolland and Ernest Bloch," *MQ*, lxviii (1982), 60–79
D.Z. Kushner: "Ernest Bloch's *Enfantines*," *College Music Symposium*, xxiii/2 (1983), 103–12
D.Z. Kushner: "Ernest Bloch: Music Educator," *International Journal of Music Education*, iv (1984), 37–40
J.-F. Tappy, ed.: *Ernest Bloch/Romain Rolland Lettres (1911–1933)* (Lausanne, 1984)

J.-M. Fauquet: "Les quatuors à cordes d'Ernest Bloch," *Revue musicale Suisse Romande* (1985), 22–30
D.Z. Kushner: "The Jewish Works of Ernest Bloch," *Journal of Synagogue Music*, xiv/1 (1985), 28–41
D.L. Sills: "Bloch Manuscripts at the University of California," *Notes*, xlii (1985), 7–21
M.D. Nott: *Ernest Bloch's Pedagogical Writings: a Didactic Legacy of Twentieth-Century America* (diss., U. of Rochester, 1986)
D.L. Sills: "Bloch Manuscripts at the Library of Congress," *Notes*, xlii (1986), 726–53
N. Uscher: "Zara Nelsova and Ernest Bloch: The Story of a Friendship and a Musical Partnership," *Strings*, ii/4 (1988), 20–25
D.Z. Kushner: *Ernest Bloch: a Guide to Research* (New York, 1988)
A. Knapp: "Helvetia—Israel—*America*: Identity in Bloch's Life and Music," *Journal of Synagogue Music*, xix/2 (1989), pp. 5–16
D.Z. Kushner: "Ernest Bloch, Daniel Gregory Mason, and the Jewish Question," *American Music Teacher*, xxxviii/6 (1989), 16–19
K.E. Stirzaker: *Structure and Form in Two Works for Flute and Orchestra by Ernest Bloch (1880–1959): Suite modale (1956) and Two Last Poems (Maybe…) (1958)* (diss., U. of North Texas, 1992)
D.Z. Kushner: "Ernest Bloch's *America*," *Currents in Musical Thought*, ii (1993), 125–41
Z. Plavin: *Ernest Bloch (1880–1959) and a Comparative Analysis of His Jewish-Titled and General Compositions* (diss., U. of Jerusalem, 1997)
C. Brotman: "The Winner Loses: Ernest Bloch and His America," *AM*, xvi/4 (1998), 417–47
K. Moricz: "Sensuous Pagans and Righteous Jews: Changing Concepts of Jewish Identity in Ernest Bloch's Jezabel and Schelomo," *JAMS*, liv (2001), 439–91
D.M. Schiller: *Bloch, Schoenberg, and Bernstein: Assimilating Jewish Music* (New York, 2003)
D.Z. Kushner: "Religious Ambiguity in the Life and Works of Ernest Bloch," *Min-Ad*, iii (2004), 1–15
W. Simmons: *Voices in the Wilderness: Six American Neo-Romantic Composers* (Lanham, MD, 2004)
J. Lewinski and E. Dijon: *Ernest Bloch (1880–1959): sa vie et sa pensée* (Geneva, 2005)
K. Moricz: "Sealed Documents and Open Lives: Ernest Bloch's Private Correspondence," *Notes*, lxii (2005), 74–86
K. Moricz: *Jewish Identities: Nationalism, Racism, and Utopianism in Twentieth-Century Music* (Berkeley and Los Angeles, 2008)
H.J. Kintner: *The Ernest Bloch I Knew: the Agate Beach Years* (Eugene, OR, 2009)
D.Z. Kushner, "Ernest Bloch: the Cleveland Years (1920–1925)," *Min-Ad*, viii/2 (2010), 175–200

DAVID Z. KUSHNER

Bloch, Kalman (*b* New York, NY, 30 May 1913; *d* Los Angeles, CA, 12 March 2009). Clarinetist and teacher. Bloch attended New York University and took lessons from New York Philharmonic principal clarinetist SIMEON BELLISON. Although Bloch initially planned on a career in dentistry, Bellison encouraged him to pursue music. The Los Angeles Philharmonic invited him to audition for Otto Klemperer and appointed him principal clarinetist in 1937, a position he occupied until 1981. His experience as principal involved working with numerous noted conductors, including Giulini, Stokowski, Barbirolli, Zubin Mehta, and Bruno Walter. Bloch's daughter, Michele Zukovsky, was appointed co-principal in 1961, sharing the chair with her father until his retirement. She remains principal clarinetist. Bloch's artistry also may be heard on many film soundtracks, including *North by Northwest*, *The Wizard of Oz*, and *Gone with the Wind*. He recorded frequently with the Columbia Symphony Orchestra and is credited with several solo and chamber music recordings of his own, including the première recording of Arnold Schoenberg's *Pierrot lunaire*, conducted by the composer. Bloch was a member of the Los Feliz Woodwind Ensemble, a founding member of the Pacific Symphony, and a teacher at Pomona College and California State University, Fullerton. His former students include Joaquín Valdepeñas and Tim Paradise. He produced three volumes of orchestral excerpt books entitled *The Orchestral Clarinet*.

BIBLIOGRAPHY

S.M. Rochford: "Kalman Bloch: a Tribute," *The Clarinet*, xxxi/2 (2004), 52–7
D. Gilman: "In Memoriam: Kalman Bloch, 1913–2009," *The Clarinet*, xxxvi/3 (2009), 26 only

JONATHAN HOLDEN

Block, Adrienne Fried (*b* New York, NY, 11 March 1921; *d* New York, 5 April 2009). Musicologist. She received the PhD from CUNY (1978). Block was a leading scholar in American music studies and a pioneering contributor to feminist studies in music. Her biography of the pianist and composer Amy Beach helped secure a foundation for the revival of interest in a major American composer whom few took seriously and whose music was not well known. The biography won numerous awards—among them the Irving Lowens Award (Society for American Music [SAM], 1998)—and widespread recognition for its significance, originality, methodological richness, and literary quality.

Block began her career as a choral director in New York (1964–9) and turned to musicological studies in 1969. After writing a dissertation on French medieval music, Block invested herself in the burgeoning field of American music studies. There she found ways to link her passion for social justice with the women's history movement, especially in relation to American musical life. With her coeditor Carol Neuls-Bates, she published a major bibliography on women in American music; support by an unprecedented grant from the NEH helped this newly-emerging field. In the 1970s and 1980s Block also published important sociological profiles of the status of academic women in music.

In the last several years of her life, Block codirected the "Music in Gotham" project with John Graziano at the Graduate Center at CUNY, which focused on documenting the musical life of New York City in the 1860s. The project turned into a leadership site for research in aspects of 19th-century American music history. SAM honored her with a Lifetime Achievement Award (2004) and again, with a fellowship named for her.

WRITINGS

with C. Neuls-Bates, ed.: *Women in American Music: a Bibliography of Music and Literature* (Westport, CT, 1979)
"Arthur P. Schmidt, Publisher and Champion of Women Composers," *The Musical Woman*, vol. 2, ed. Judith L. Zaimont and others (Westport, CT, 1987)
"The Status of Women in College Music: A Statistical Study, 1976–1986," *Women's Studies/Women's Status. CMS Report v.* (Boulder, CO, 1989)
"Dvořák's Long American Reach," *Dvořák in America*, ed. J.C. Tibbetts (Portland, OR, 1993), 157–81
Amy Beach, Quartet for Strings in One Movement, Op. 89, ed. with an intro. by A.F. Block, *Music in the United States of America (MUSA)* iii (Madison, WI, 1994)

Amy Beach. Passionate Victorian. The Life and Work of an American Composer 1867–1944 (New York, 1998)
"New York's Orchestras and the 'American' Composer: A Nineteenth-Century View," *European Music and Musicians in New York City, 1840–1900*, ed. John Graziano (Rochester, NY, 2006), 114–34
"Matinee Mania, or the Regendering of Nineteenth-Century Audiences in New York City," *19CM*, xxxi/3 (Spring 2008), 193–216

JUDITH TICK

Block, Geoffrey (Holden) (*b* Oakland, CA, 7 May 1948). Musicologist. He received the BA in music history and literature from the University of California at Los Angeles in 1970. He studied music history and theory at Harvard University (MA 1973, PhD 1979). His dissertation, on compositional process in Beethoven's first and second piano concertos, was aided by manuscript research in Germany as a Fulbright Fellow (1975–6). He joined the faculty of the University of Puget Sound in 1980, attaining the rank of Professor in 1993, and was named Distinguished Professor of Music History in 2008.

A prolific and wide-ranging scholar, Block has published extensively on American musical theater, particularly the life and work of Richard Rodgers, and on the music of Charles Ives. He was the first to publish research on the compositional process of Broadway musicals ("Frank Loesser's Sketchbooks" and *Enchanted Evenings*). He has served as General Editor of the Yale Broadway Masters Series since 1998, and Series Editor of Oxford's Broadway Legacies Series since 2008. He is the composer of four full-length musicals.

WRITINGS

Charles Ives: a Bio-Bibliography (New York, 1988)
"Frank Loesser's Sketchbooks for *The Most Happy Fella*," *MQ*, lxxiii (1989), 60–78
"The Broadway Canon from *Show Boat* to *West Side Story* and the European Operatic Ideal," *JM*, xi (1993), 528–47
ed., with P. Burkholder: *Charles Ives and the Classical Tradition* (New Haven, 1996)
Ives: Piano Sonata no.2 ("Concord, Mass., 1840–1860") (Cambridge, UK, 1996)
"Remembrance of Dissonances Past: the Two Published Editions of *Concord Sonata*," *Ives Studies*, ed. P. Lambert (Cambridge, UK, 1998), 27–50
Richard Rodgers (New Haven, CT, 2003)
"The Melody (and the Words) Linger On: Musical Comedies of the 1920s and 1930s," *The Cambridge Companion to the Musical*, ed. W. Everett and P. Laird (Cambridge, UK, 2002), 77–97
Enchanted Evenings: the Broadway Musical from "Show Boat" to Sondheim and Lloyd Webber (New York, 2003/*R*)
"Revisiting the Glorious and Problematic Legacy of the Jazz age and Depression Musical," *Studies in Musical Theatre*, ii (2008), 127–46

GWYNNE KUHNER BROWN

Blodgett, Benjamin Colman (*b* Boston, MA, 12 March 1838; *d* Seattle, WA, 22 Sept 1925). Organist, pianist, composer, and teacher. At age 12, Blodgett began playing organ at churches in Boston, studying with James Hooton. He continued his training at the University and Conservatory of Music, Leipzig, where his teachers included Ignaz Moscheles and Moritz Hauptmann; later, he received his doctorate from Oxford University. Upon returning to the United States, he taught music at the Maplewood Institute in Pittsfield, Massachusetts (1865–78), then moved to Northampton, where he served as Professor of Music at Smith College for 25 years (1879–1903). He later became the first principal of Smith's School of Music, but in 1903 the college's board voted for the school's closure. Invited by Jane Stanford to join the staff of the newly-constructed Memorial Church at Stanford University, Blodgett then moved west and served as the organist and choir director. When the earthquake of 1906 severely damaged the church, Blodgett took a leave of absence and retired from the position the following year. He composed two oratorios—*The Prodigal Son* (1895) and *A Representation of the Book of Job* (1889, for the commencement at Smith)—and several pieces for piano, chorus, and chamber ensembles. His many lectures and writings on the role of music in contemporary Christian liturgy reveal his belief in music's transcendent properties.

BLAKE HOWE

Blomstedt, Herbert (Thorson) (*b* Springfield, MA, 11 July 1927). Swedish conductor. After early lessons in conducting at the Swedish Royal College of Music (1945–50) under Tor Mann and in musicology at the University of Uppsala (1948–52) under Carl-Allan Moberg, Blomstedt studied contemporary music with John Cage at Darmstadt and Renaissance and Baroque performance practice at the Schola Cantorum in Basle. He subsequently studied conducting with Igor Markevitch at the Salzburg Mozarteum (1950–55), with Jean Morel at the Juilliard School of Music (1953), and with Leonard Bernstein at Tanglewood (1953), winning the Koussevitzky Prize that year. Blomstedt made his professional debut with the Stockholm PO in 1954. He has subsequently held numerous musical directorships, including the Norrköping SO (1954–62), Oslo PO (1962–8), Danish RSO (1967–77), Dresden Staatskapelle (1975–85), and Swedish RSO (1977–82). In 1984 he first appeared with the San Francisco SO, and a year later he was appointed its music director, holding that position until 1995, and was thereafter named conductor laureate. He significantly strengthened the musical and analytical rigor of the orchestra, and gave premieres of works by Elliott Carter, Richard Danielpour, John Harbison, George Perle, and Charles Wuorinen, winning Columbia University's Ditson Award for distinguished service to American music in 1992. Blomstedt served as principal conductor of the North German RSO from 1996 to 1998 and of the Leipzig Gewandhaus Orchestra from 1998 to 2005.

He has remained a lifelong champion of Scandinavian composers, among them Sven-Erik Bäck, Erik Jørgensen, Ingvar Lidholm, Per Nørgård, Ib Nørholm, and Allan Pettersson. He has also been an admired exponent of Béla Bartók, Franz Berwald (editing the *Sinfonie singulière* for Bärenreiter in 1965), Paul Hindemith, Carl Nielsen, Jean Sibelius, and Richard Strauss, and has recorded cycles of symphonies by Ludwig van Beethoven, Nielsen, Franz Schubert, and Sibelius. He recorded more than 130 works with the Dresden Staatskapelle alone. His conducting is distinguished by rhythmic clarity and control, structural insight, and a powerful sense of drama. Blomstedt's years in San Francisco seem to have induced a deeper warmth and a more eloquent sense of phrase in his music making.

CHARLES BARBER

Blondie. New-wave band. It was formed in New York by Debbie [Deborah] Harry (*b* Miami, FL, 1 July 1945; vocals) and Chris(topher) Stein (*b* Brooklyn, NY, 5 Jan 1950; guitar), who met in the band the Stilettos in 1974. In 1975 they recruited Jimmy Destri (James Mollica; *b* Brooklyn, NY, 13 April 1954; organ and keyboards), Clem(ent) Burke (*b* Bayonne, NJ, 24 Nov 1954; drums), and Gary Valentine (*b* Bayonne, NJ, 24 Dec 1955; bass) to join them. The band regularly performed at CBGB, a club important to New York's punk and new-wave music scenes. Their music was defined by Harry's charismatic and seductive vocals (*see* DEBBIE HARRY) and their accessible dance-inspired sound, while their image was synonymous with Harry's own and dominated by her sex appeal. Throughout their career as a band, Blondie frequently found fans mistakenly identifying Harry as Blondie and hence began using the slogan "Blondie is the name of the band." In 1976 Blondie recorded their first single, "X Offender," which attracted the attention and business of the record label Private Stock. They released their first album, *Blondie*, later that same year, and although it wasn't very successful in the United States, it was well received overseas and resulted in Chrysalis Records buying out Blondie's contract with Private Stock for future recordings.

While Blondie were recording their second album (*Plastic Letters*, Chrysalis, 1977), the bass player Nigel Harrison replaced Valentine and the guitarist Frank Infante joined. Their next album, *Parallel Lines* (Chrysalis, 1978), was a tour de force and included the international hit "Heart of Glass"; propelled by a disco remix, it reached number one on the *Billboard* charts and led to album sales of more than 20 million copies worldwide. Blondie released three more albums with Chrysalis and reached number one again with their rap-influenced hit "Rapture" (Chrysalis, 1981), before breaking up in 1982. The band reunited in 1998 for a tour with the original five members, and subsequently began recording again without Valentine. In 1999 they released the album *No Exit*, which featured the successful single "Maria." They followed it up with *The Curse of Blondie* (2003) and a live album recorded from a concert in Toronto (2006). In 2006 Blondie were one of the last acts to perform at CBGB before its closing and were inducted into the Rock and Roll Hall of Fame.

BIBLIOGRAPHY

L. Bangs: *Blondie* (New York, 1980)

D. Harry, C. Stein, and V. Bockris: *Making Tracks: the Rise of Blondie* (New York, 1982/*R*)

A. Metz, ed.: *Blondie, from Punk to the Present: a Pictorial History* (Springfield, MO, 2002)

G. Valentine: *New York Rocker: my Life in the Blank Generation, with Blondie, Iggy Pop, and others, 1974–1981* (London, 2002)

JESSICA L. BROWN

Blood [Kainah]. Native American tribe of Montana, and Alberta, Canada; *see* BLACKFOOT (i).

Blood, Sweat and Tears. Jazz-rock group. Emanating from the late 1960s melting pot, it was one of the earliest bands to characterize the jazz-rock idiom. Formed in 1967 by Al Kooper (Alan Peter Kuperschmidt, *b* 5 Feb 1944, Brooklyn, NY; vocals and keyboards), Steve Katz (*b* 9 May 1945; guitar), and Bobby Colomby (*b* 20 Dec 1944; drums), the group blended original composition with its own stylized arrangements of jazz, country, rock, and rhythm-and-blues material. The band played jazz standards such as Billie Holiday's "God bless the child" and Herbie Hancock's "Maiden Voyage," as well as versions of songs by Laura Nyro ("And When I Die," "He's a runner"), Brenda Holloway ("You've made me so very happy"), John Lennon and Paul McCartney ("Got to get you into my life"), and Mick Jagger and Keith Richards ("Sympathy for the Devil"). Much of the original material framing these came from Katz and the band's second and longest-serving singer, the Canadian David Clayton-Thomas, who joined for the second, best-selling and Grammy Award-winning album *Blood, Sweat and Tears* (Col., 1968). Thomas is the writer of the much-covered "Spinning Wheel" from this album, as well as the fiery "Lucretia MacEvil" and "Go down gamblin."

Blood, Sweat and Tears produced arrangements enriched with jazz solos, which in turn often signaled a change in tempo or feel, creating multi-sectioned pieces rather than just straightforward songs. "Spinning Wheel" is a fine example of this, as is the group's version of Joe Cocker's "Something's coming on" from *Blood, Sweat and Tears 3* (Col., 1970). Discussing the overall style of Blood, Sweat and Tears, Thomas said that the band took works from other genres and "turned them over to Juilliard and Berkeley trained jazz arrangers and came up with this hybrid—this child of many worlds."

These arrangers were largely the horn players. As a section, the horns underwent something of a revolution with Blood, Sweat and Tears. Following the simple homophonic stabs in the soul bands of James Brown and Otis Redding, theirs was like a big-band sound in miniature with jazzy, contrapuntal lines both backing the vocals and featuring as melodic interludes. From an ever-changing personnel, which has involved upward of 130 performers over more than four decades, prominent members have included Randy Brecker (trumpet), Lew Soloff (trumpet), and Tom Malone (trombone), as well as the rhythm players Larry Willis (keyboards), Mike Stern (guitar), and Don Alias (percussion).

Diminished sales heralded the end of a nine-album partnership with Columbia in 1976. The band effectively split after *Brand New Day* (ABC, 1977), although Thomas has fronted Blood, Sweat and Tears intermittently and Colomby continues to direct new incarnations of the group.

BIBLIOGRAPHY

A. Kooper: *Backstage Passes & Backstabbing Bastards: Memoirs of a Rock 'n' Roll Survivor* (New York, 1998)

GEORGE DOUBLE/R

Bloom, Jane Ira (*b* Boston, MA, 12 Jan 1955). Soprano saxophonist, composer, and bandleader. She began playing piano, took up alto saxophone at the age of eight, and switched to the soprano instrument in her early teens. She studied with Herb Pomeroy before attending Yale University (BA 1976, MM 1977). After moving to New York, she studied with George Coleman. In addition to collaborating with such artists as David Friedman, Ed Blackwell, Charlie Haden, Bob Brookmeyer, Jay Clayton, Fred Hersch, and Kenny Wheeler, she has performed and recorded with various trios, quartets, quintets, and sextets, alongside Wheeler, Julian Priester, Mark Dresser, and Bobby Previte, among others. Her critically acclaimed recordings, which number more than a dozen, are at once contemporary, mainstream, and exploratory. Bloom has also composed for film and television, and for the American Composers Orchestra, St Luke's Chamber Ensemble, and the Pilobolus, Paradigm, and Philadanco dance companies. She has been granted two Chamber Music America artist fellowships, a Guggenheim Fellowship, a commission by the NASA Art Program, and the Charlie Parker Fellowship for Jazz Innovation. Among her many other honors are four Jazz Journalist awards, the *Downbeat* Critics Poll award for soprano saxophone, the Mary Lou Williams Women in Jazz award, and the International Women in Jazz Masters awards. Her musical voice has been fueled by a vigorous involvement with the visual arts and dance. Her well regarded work on the soprano saxophone sometimes incorporates live electronic effects. From 1989 she has worked as a full-time professor at the New School for Jazz and Contemporary Music and continued to perform with her quartet.

BIBLIOGRAPHY

S. Placksin: *American Women in Jazz, 1900 to the Present: their Words, Lives, and Music* (New York, 1982, London, 1985, as *Jazzwomen, 1900 to the Present: their Words, Lives, and Music*), 281

F. Bouchard: "Jane Ira Bloom: Sonic Bloom," *DB*, lviii/7 (1991), 25

L. Gourse: *Madame Jazz: Contemporary Women Instrumentalists* (New York, 1995), 124

JEFFREY HOLMES

Bloom, Robert (*b* Pittsburgh, PA, 3 May 1908; *d* Cincinnati, OH, 13 Feb 1994). Oboist. From the age of 19 he studied with the founder of the American school of oboe playing, MARCEL TABUTEAU, at the Curtis Institute, Philadelphia. Bloom was one of the most important of the first generation of American-born and -trained oboists. In 1930 he received his first appointment as assistant principal, and later solo, english horn with the Philadelphia Orchestra under Leopold Stokowski. After a short period as principal oboist in the Rochester Philharmonic, in 1937 Bloom was invited as a founding member of the NBC SO, where he played principal oboe under Toscanini. As a core member of the Bach Aria Group from its foundation by William Scheide in 1946 until 1980, Bloom played an important part in the revival of Baroque music in postwar America, and is remembered above all for his poised performances of Bach and tasteful ornamentation. Bloom was also eager to explore new oboe music; he played in an early US performance of Schoenberg's Wind Quintet and inspired numerous compositions, including Quincy Porter's Quintet for oboe and strings (1967) and *Winter's Past* by Wayne Barlow (1940). He was awarded an honorary MMus from Yale University in 1971. Bloom composed a number of short works for oboe, and taught at several of America's leading educational institutions, including Yale University (1957–76), the Hartt (1967–75) and Juilliard Schools (1973–81), and the Philadelphia University of the Arts (1978–85). His pupils included Bert Lucarelli, RAY STILL, and Allan Vogel. Bloom trained his wife Sara Lambert Bloom, who has edited a complete collection of her husband's compositions, recordings, and editions of oboe music as well as a biography and a set of writings, including his book *The Oboe, a Musical Instrument*.

BIBLIOGRAPHY

S. Bloom: "A Tribute to Robert Bloom," *Double Reed*, xi/3 (1988), 11–21; repr. in *The Robert Bloom Collection* (New Haven, CT, 1998)

R. Woodhams: "Robert Bloom, Eminent American Oboist," *The Instrumentalist*, xliv/4 (1989–90), 24–30

S. Bloom: *Robert Bloom: the Story of a Working Musician including his book on pedagogy dictated in 1975–1976*, The Oboe, a Musical Instrument (New Haven, CT, 2009)

GEOFFREY BURGESS

Bloom, Rube (*b* New York, NY, 24 April 1902; *d* New York, 30 March 1976). Pianist, composer, and songwriter. Although self-taught, he became an excellent pianist at an early age and in 1919 began work as an accompanist for vaudeville shows. He worked in dance bands and jazz groups throughout the 1920s, recording with such major artists as Bix Beiderbecke, the Dorsey brothers, Red Nichols, Frankie Trumbauer, Miff Mole, Noble Sissle, and Ethel Waters. In 1928 he was awarded first prize in the Victor Company's contest for his "Song of the Bayou." He arranged songs for numerous publishing companies during the 1920s and recorded his piano pieces for Victor, Okeh, Harmony, and Cameo. Bloom's best piano music comprises some of the most original work in the novelty-piano idiom. His brilliant "Spring Fever" (1926) is still performed by pianists interested in this repertory. An archive of his materials is held by the American Heritage Center at the University of Wyoming.

WORKS

(selective list)

all printed works published in New York

Pf: The Futuristic Rag, 1923; Soliloquy, 1926; Spring Fever, 1926; Silhouette, 1927; Jumping Jack (collab. B. Seaman and M. Smoley), 1928; Aunt Jemima's Birthday, 1931; One-finger Joe, 1931; Southern Charms, 1931

Songs: Song of the Bayou (Bloom), 1929; Truckin' (T. Koehler), 1935; Day in, day out (J. Mercer), 1939; Don't worry 'bout me (Koehler), 1939; Fools rush in (Mercer), 1940; Give me the simple life (H. Ruby), 1945; Lost in a dream (E. Leslie), 1949; Here's to my lady (Mercer), 1952

Principal publishers: Mills, Robbins, Triangle

BIBLIOGRAPHY

D.A. Jasen: *Recorded Ragtime, 1897–1958* (Hamden, CT, 1973)

D.A. Jasen and T.J. Tichenor: *Rags and Ragtime: a Musical History* (New York, 1978)

DAVID THOMAS ROBERTS/R

Bloom, Sol (*b* Pekin, Tazewell County, IL, ?9 March 1870; *d* Washington, DC, 7 March 1949). Publisher, real estate developer, and politician. Born into poverty, he began working as a child in a San Francisco vacuum cleaner brush factory, and soon began picking up odd jobs at local theaters. By 15, he was assistant treasurer at the Alcazar Theater, and he had become wealthy by 18. After traveling abroad, he settled in Chicago, and was in charge of the Midway Plaisance during the 1893 World's Fair. He claimed to have composed the well-known "snake charmer's" tune, or "Hoochie Coochie Dance" while there. Following the Fair, Bloom's past connections in San Francisco brought him into association with the Witmark family and his first experience in music publishing. By 1895, Rothschild's department store turned their sheet music department over to him. The next year he started his own company, publishing the hit "The Heroes Who Sank with the Maine" (1898). Increasingly frequent trips to New York led to his permanent relocation there by 1905, where his name became synonymous with the sale of Victor Talking Machines. Active for years in local politics, Bloom retired from music in 1910, first becoming a real estate developer and then elected a US Congressman in 1923. A far cry from his "Hoochie Coochie Dance," he assisted in the writing of the United Nations charter, famously contributing the line, "We, the Peoples of the United Nations."

BIBLIOGRAPHY

GMO (C. Conyers, "Hootchy-kootchy")

S. Bloom: *The Autobiography of Sol Bloom* (New York, 1948)

MARISTELLA FEUSTLE

Bloomfield, Theodore (Robert) (*b* Cleveland, OH, 14 June 1923; *d* Warrenton, OR, 1 April 1998). Conductor. After studying conducting (with Maurice Kessler) and piano at the Oberlin College conservatory (BM 1944), he attended the Juilliard Graduate School, where he studied conducting with Edgar Schenkman; further study followed with CLAUDIO ARRAU and CLAUDE MONTEUX. He made his debut on 9 September 1945 conducting the New York Little SO in Carnegie Recital hall and was apprentice conductor to Szell for the Cleveland Orchestra's 1946–7 season. He made his European debut in Como, Italy in 1952 and was appointed music director of the Portland (Oregon) SO in 1955. From 1959 to 1963, he was the music director of the Rochester PO; he then went to Germany and became the principal conductor of the Hamburg Staatsoper. After three seasons as music director of the Frankfurt am Main Opera (1966–8) and several years guest conducting in Europe, he became chief conductor of the Berlin SO (1975–82), winning the Berlin Critics Circle music prize in 1977. He retired to the Oregon coast in 1990, where he hosted a weekly classical music program. His final conducting engagement was with the Oregon Symphony in 1996, during the orchestra's centennial season. Bloomfield conducted the premieres of works by Bernard Rogers, Ron Nelson, Frank Martin, and Goffredo Petrassi, and the first European performances of works by Avshalomov, Mennin, and Kubik. He was committed to introducing rarely performed works by American composers to European audiences.

ANDERS TOBIASON

Bloomfield Zeisler [née Blumenfeld], **Fannie** (*b* Bielitz, Austria, 16 July 1863; *d* Chicago, IL, 20 Aug 1927). Pianist and pedagogue of Austrian birth. Bloomfield Zeisler rose to prominence in the 1890s following highly acclaimed European tours and remained a leading concert artist to about 1920. A brilliant performer who was dubbed "America's greatest virtuoso," she consistently impressed critics with her crystalline technique and power, nuanced tonal beauty, sensitive expression, and fiery, magnetic intensity. Through her popular success and artistic example she contributed significantly to rising standards of American pianism and changing identities of women pianists.

Bloomfield Zeisler began piano lessons with her brother Maurice by 1870, after her family's 1867 emigration from Bielitz, Austrian Silesia, to Appleton, Wisconsin, and moves to Milwaukee and Chicago; these whetted her appetite for formal study, first with Bernhard Ziehn (1870–73) and then CARL WOLFSOHN (1873–8). Wolfsohn, founder of Chicago's Beethoven Society, under whose auspices she debuted in February 1875, figured strongly in her early development, but the renowned pedagogue Theodor Leschetizky proved the greatest influence on her artistry. Prompted to study in Vienna by a successful 1877 audition with the Russian virtuoso Annette Essipoff, she endured a disappointing year at the Vienna Conservatory (1878–9) before undergoing rigorous training with Leschetizky from 1879 to 1883 and again in 1888.

In 1883, following her "graduation" from Leschetizky's studio, Bloomfield Zeisler returned to America, secured Henry Wolfsohn as agent, made her New York debut on 31 January 1885 with the Frank van der Stücken Symphony, and performed with the New York Symphony Society and Boston Symphony Orchestra in the same season. In the following years, she appeared at the Columbian Exposition (1893), toured Europe (1893 to 1895; 1898, 1902, 1912), the West Coast (1896, 1901), and Canada (1909), and performed frequently in American urban centers and small towns. She accrued 23 appearances with the Boston Symphony and at least 19 with the Chicago Orchestra, and she concertized with such prominent conductors as Theodore Thomas, Arthur Nikisch, and Richard Strauss. Her "staggering repertoire" (as noted by Harold Schonberg) centered on Romantic character pieces, virtuosic solo works, and concertos, along with a handful of Baroque compositions, early to late Beethoven sonatas, and contemporaneous works.

Bloomfield Zeisler balanced 50-concert seasons with teaching (in a private studio and at Chicago's Bush Temple of Music), family responsibilities, and participation in musical, literary, and women's organizations, and the hosting of a Chicago salon. On 18 October 1885 she married Sigmund Zeisler (1860–1931), a lawyer known for his defense of the infamous Haymarket Riot "anarchists," with whom she had three sons. After years of declining health, she died of a heart attack at age 64. Her papers are held at *CIhc*, *Cn*, and *NYpl*.

DISCOGRAPHY

Ampico and Welte-Mignon piano rolls (1908, 1912, 1924)

"Fannie Bloomfield Zeisler," *Caswell Collection*, iii, Pierian 0003/4 (2000)

WRITINGS

"Woman in Music," *American Art Journal*, lviii (1891), 1–3

"Appearing in Public," *Great Pianists on Piano Playing*, ed. J.F. Cooke (Philadelphia, 1913), 80–94

"Public to Blame for Blind Worship of European Fetish," *Musical America*, xvii/10 (1914)

"The Scope of Piano Technic," in H. Brower *Piano Mastery: Talks with Master Pianists and Teachers* (New York, 1915), 180–97; repr. in *The Harriette Brower Interviews*, ed. J. Johnson (Mineola, NY, 2003)

[with A. Jonás and others]: *Master School of Modern Piano Playing and Virtuosity: a Universal Method Embracing All the Technical, Esthetic and Artistic Features Required for the Highest Pianistic Virtuosity* (New York, 3/1929)

BIBLIOGRAPHY

A. Fay: "Fannie Bloomfi[e]ld-Zeisler," *Music*, ix (1895), 224–5

W.S.B. Mathews: "A Great Pianist at Home," *Music*, ix (1895), 1–10

W. Armstrong: "Mrs. Bloomfield Zeisler on Study and Repertory," *Etude*, xxiii/2 (1905), 51–2

G.M. Wilson: "Fannie Bloomfield-Zeisler, with a Study of Her Hands," *Musician*, xix/1 (1914), 1, 12

P. Allais, E.S. Gara, N. Killiam, R.H. Mergentheim and E. Moeller: *Fannie Bloomfield Zeisler Appreciation* (Chicago, 1927)

R. Cole: "Fannie Bloomfield Zeisler," *Studies in Musical Education, History and Aesthetics: Music Teachers' National Association Proceedings*, xii (1927), 26–38

T. Troendle: "How Fannie Bloomfield-Zeisler Taught," *Etude*, xxxxvii/11 (1929), 799–800

H.C. Schonberg: *The Great Pianists* (New York, 1963)

C. Ammer: *Unsung: a History of Women in American Music* (Westport, CT, 1980)

D. Hallman: *The Pianist Fannie Bloomfield Zeisler in American Music and Society* (thesis, U. of Maryland, 1983)

D. Hallman: "Fannie Bloomfield Zeisler," *Encyclopedia of American Jewish Women* (New York and London, 1997)

B. Macleod: *Women Performing Music: the Emergence of American Women as Instrumentalists and Conductors* (Jefferson, NC, and London, 2001)

DIANA R. HALLMAN

Bloomquist, Kenneth G. (*b* Boxholm, IA, 29 Dec 1931). Conductor and teacher. Bloomquist attended the University of Illinois (BM 1953, MM 1957), his enrollment interrupted by service in the United States Army as first sergeant and acting band leader of the 6th Armored Division Band. He joined the faculty at the University of Kansas in 1958, initially as assistant director of bands and professor of trumpet, then as director of bands starting in 1968. He became director of bands at Michigan State University in 1970, a post he held until his retirement in 1993 with the exception of 1978–88 when he was director of the School of Music. He has appeared as guest conductor, clinician, and adjudicator throughout North America, Europe, Asia, and Australia, including conductor-in-residence at the Musashino Academia Musicae in Tokyo, Japan, on four occasions. Bloomquist was president of the American Bandmasters Association (1995) and the National Band Association (1980–82), and has received numerous awards, including membership in the NBA Hall of Fame, the Midwest Clinic Medal of Honor, and the Phi Mu Alpha Sinfonia Orpheus Award. He has authored articles on band and trumpet pedagogy.

WILLIAM BERZ

Blossom, Henry (*b* St. Louis, MO, 10 May 1866; *d* New York, NY, 23 March 1919). Librettist and lyricist. The son of a St. Louis insurance salesman, Blossom started his career as a novelist. He contributed lyrics for the musical comedies *Sally in Our Alley* (1902) and *The Wizard of Oz* (1903) before gaining fame with a dramatization of his novel *Checkers* in 1903. He then turned to writing operettas and musical comedies, frequently collaborating with composer VICTOR HERBERT. Their first effort, *Mlle. Modiste* (1905), featured Fritzi Scheff and scored an immediate hit with her solo "Kiss Me Again." Blossom's libretto displayed a depth of characterization and social consciousness unusual for the time. He and Herbert continued their collaboration with seven more musicals, including *The Red Mill* (1906), *The Only Girl* (1914), and *Eileen* (1917), and their partnership led many critics to declare Blossom as Herbert's best lyricist. Partly through his successes with Herbert, Blossom gained a reputation as a thoughtful dramatist whose innate sense of storytelling, coupled with a knack for tight dramatic construction, created a fulfilling theatrical experience. He is often compared against Harry B. Smith, an extremely prolific lyricist who failed to make a lasting artistic impression due to the speed with which he wrote. Blossom's smaller but meatier contributions have earned him positive critical recognition from musical theater historians.

BIBLIOGRAPHY

G. Bordman and T. Hischak: *The Oxford Companion to American Theatre* (Oxford, 3/2007)

N. Gould: *Victor Herbert: a Theatrical Life* (New York, 2008)

ELLEN MARIE PECK

Blossoms, the. Female vocal group based in Los Angeles. Its principal members included Fanita James [Barrett], Jean King, Gloria Jones, Gracia Nitzsche, and Darlene Love [Wright]. Primarily backing vocalists for recordings and television broadcasts, the group worked with artists including Gene Pitney, Patty Duke, Shelley Fabares, Marvin Gaye, James Brown, and Buck Owens.

They began as the Dreamers in 1954 and were soon known as versatile singers and working in studios backing up other artists. After an executive at Capitol Records noticed their different skin tones and said they looked like a bouquet, they were re-named the Blossoms. In 1958 the 17-year-old Wright joined as the group's lead singer, but chart success was elusive until the producer Phil Spector recorded them performing a tune by the singer-songwriter Gene Pitney. Spector then used the Blossoms to record a song that was credited to the New York-based girl group the Crystals. "He's a Rebel" turned out to be a monster hit, building Spector's status as an independent producer, but the Blossoms only received a session fee. Over the next three years, the group were favored singers on all of Spector's California sessions.

By 1964 the Blossoms had become a trio, of Love, James, and King. This lineup worked as the house backing group on the weekly music television program *Shindig!* (1964–6), despite concerns from the network about featuring non-white performers so prominently. The Blossoms used their versatility to sing in various styles behind a range of artists, in addition to performing versions of popular songs of the day. The group, however, never achieved mainstream success. Love left in 1974, and subsequently appeared in the stage show "Leader of the Pack" (1983) and in the *Lethal Weapon* movie series.

BIBLIOGRAPHY

J. Clemente: *Girl Groups: Fabulous Females that Rocked the World* (Iola, WI, 2000)

J. Warwick: "'And the Colored Girls Sing…': Backup Singers and the Case of the Blossoms," *Musicological Identities: Essays in Honor of Susan McClary*, ed. S. Baur, R. Knapp, and J. Warwick (Aldershot, 2008), 63–76

JOHN CLEMENTE

Blow, Kurtis [Walker, Kurtis] (b Harlem, NY, 9 Aug 1959). Rapper. He was the first solo artist to achieve mainstream success in the genre. In 1979, Blow landed the first major label record deal granted to a rapper, signing with Mercury Records. Soon after he recorded the novelty single "Christmas Rappin'," a song co-written by his manager, Russell Simmons. A second single, "The Breaks" (1980), became only the second 12″ single in history to be certified gold. Kurtis Blow, the first full-length rap album, was released that same year. On the strength of these achievements, Blow became the first rapper to tour nationally and internationally.

Blow's subsequent albums did not attract the same level of interest or commercial success, but his influence on the genre has been profound. His songs have been covered by Run-DMC ("Hard Times") and Nas ("If I Ruled the World"). In 1997, Rhino Records invited him to compile and annotate *The History of Hip-hop*, a three-volume retrospective of rap's early years. Blow became a radio host in 1995, working first for Power 106 in Los Angeles, and later for Sirius Satellite Radio. He is also a licensed minister and founder of the Hip-Hop Church.

MICHAEL BERRY

Bluebird. Record label. A budget subsidiary of RCA Victor that released race records from 1932 to 1950. It is well regarded for jazz releases by musicians such as Jelly Roll Morton, Earl Hines, and Fats Waller. The label name has been revived occasionally to repackage reissues and present new jazz recordings.

Blue-eyed soul. A term popularized in the 1960s to describe rhythm-and-blues and soul music performed by white artists. First credited to Georgie Woods, a radio DJ based in Philadelphia, it recognized a wave of white artists and groups performing music similar to that which was being produced by the labels Motown and Stax. Unlike in the 1950s, when white artists often directly covered black artists' singles, most blue-eyed soul singers performed original material in the style of popular soul and R&B.

The American duo the Righteous Brothers were among the most famous of these groups—indeed, they named one of their albums *Some Blue-eyed Soul* (1964)—but many of the form's proponents were from the UK, including Dusty Springfield, Tom Jones, and the Small Faces. Accordingly blue-eyed soul experienced a cult revival in the UK during the 1990s as Northern soul and later inspired such popular retro-styled artists as Amy Winehouse and Adele.

BIBLIOGRAPHY

D. Brackett: "The Politics and Practice of 'Crossover' in American Popular Music, 1963 to 1965," *MQ*, lxxviii (1994), 774–97

B.L. Cooper: "Blue-Eyed Soul Performers before and after the Wicked Pickett and Lady Soul: a Bio-bibliography and Discography," *Popular Music and Society*, xxxiii (2010), 663–93

RYAN R. MCNUTT

Bluegrass Alliance. Bluegrass group. Based in Louisville, Kentucky from 1968–1978, Bluegrass Alliance included rock and pop material in its repertoire and coined the term Newgrass. Led by co-founder and fiddler Lonnie Peerce (Lonard W. Peerce; *b* 13 July 1923; *d* Louisville, KY, 31 May 1996), it provided a springboard to numerous musicians early in their careers. The lineup of Peerce, guitarist Dan Crary, mandolinist Danny Jones, banjoist Buddy Spurlock, and bassist Harry Shealor (Ebo Walker) released three LPs on the American Heritage label, including *Newgrass* (1970). In 1971, the lineup of Walker, mandolinist Sam Bush, guitarist and dobro player Curtis Burch, and banjoist Courtney Johnson recorded a cover of the Band's "The Night They Drove Old Dixie Down" (Plantation) before leaving Peerce to found New grass revival, while the entire 1976 lineup departed Peerce en masse to form the band Lazy River. Additional alumni from 1968 to 1978 include guitarists Tony Rice, Bob Hoban, Vince Gill, and Dennis White, mandolinists Chuck Nation, Glenn Lawson, and Tony Williamson, and banjoists Garland Shuping, Steve Cooley, and Bill Millet. After receiving permission from Peerce to use the name, Bluegrass Alliance re-formed under Nation's leadership in 1998, releasing *Re-Alliance* (Copper Creek, 2001) with early 1970s fiddler Hoot Hester returning as a guest.

DAVID ROYKO

Bluegrass music. A genre of American music that grew in the 1940s from the country music of Bill Monroe and his group, the Blue Grass Boys. Bluegrass includes traditional repertoire and acoustic instruments, values innovative and virtuosic performance techniques, enjoys varying degrees of commercial success, and has been embraced both by rural, working-class and urban, upper-class constituencies. Its definition is thus a matter of debate among bluegrass enthusiasts, and it blurs the categories of folk, popular, and classical music as much as any American genre. A bluegrass band typically consists of four to seven individuals who sing and accompany themselves on acoustic string instruments: two

Bill Monroe and his Blue Grass Boys on Austin City Limits, *1980s. (Photofest)*

rhythm instruments (guitar and double bass) and several melody instruments (fiddle, five-string banjo, mandolin, resonator guitar, and second guitar). Lead instrumentalists take solo breaks between verses of a song and provide a harmonic and rhythmic background often in a responsorial relationship to the vocal part. Instrumental works have alternating solos as in jazz. Notable performers who have initiated bluegrass instrumental techniques are Earl Scruggs (banjo) and Monroe (mandolin). The vocal range of bluegrass music is higher than most country music singing, often reaching *c″*. In vocal duets, the second (tenor) part lies above the melody, trios include a baritone part below the melody, and in religious songs a fourth (bass) part is added. Usually these parts are homophonic, but in duets and gospel quartets they can provide vocal counterpoint. The music is mostly in duple meter with rhythmic emphasis on the offbeats, and tempos are generally fast: an average slow song proceeds at around 160 beats per minute, a fast one 330.

The bluegrass repertory includes traditional folksongs but is dominated by newly composed music, and it includes sentimentally reminiscent secular songs, country blues, religious songs, revival hymns, and instrumental numbers. Recordings, originally in the form of 78-rpm phonographs, have always been important for disseminating the repertory and style. In the 1940s, most groups played on the radio and toured rural communities in the South, and the earliest forms of bluegrass existed as commercially successful country music: the 1940 incarnation of Bill Monroe and the Blue Grass Boys performed on the *Grand Ole Opry* and recorded for Bluebird (RCA Victor) Records. Bluegrass music emerged as such when bands in the late 1940s began imitating the sound of the Scruggs-era Blue Grass Boys (1945–8), and the term "bluegrass music" came into common usage by the mid-1950s. During this time, bands appeared on television and in "hillbilly bars" in the urban Northeast, and bluegrass music took a more definite shape in relation to rapidly evolving rock and roll and country music styles. Many former Blue Grass Boys, including Scruggs, Lester Flatt, Don Reno, Mac Wiseman, Jimmy Martin, and Sonny Osborne, established successful careers of their own, and Monroe's group, Flatt and Scruggs, and the Stanley Brothers created a principal foundation for traditional bluegrass.

In the 1960s, the folk revival opened up college concert halls, coffee houses, and folk festivals to bluegrass performers, and in 1965 Carlton Haney established the First Annual Blue Grass Festival in Fincastle, Virginia, the prototype for many such yearly events nationwide. By including parking-lot jam sessions and a variety of stages, these festivals relaxed the distinction between amateur and professional performance, and by including competitions on various instruments they would encourage the preservation of traditional styles and the development of novel and virtuosic instrumental techniques. The 1960s also witnessed the emergence of record labels, magazines, and instructional materials that focused on bluegrass: Rebel Records was founded in 1959, *Bluegrass Unlimited* began in 1966, and Earl Scruggs's influential banjo manual was issued in 1968. Mainstream visibility for bluegrass music increased when Flatt and Scruggs's "Foggy Mountain Breakdown" appeared in the 1967 film *Bonnie and Clyde*, prefiguring the later use of bluegrass in *Deliverance* (1972) and *O Brother, Where Art Thou?* (2000). Bluegrass continued as part of country music with acts such as the Osborne Brothers and Jim and Jesse, while it also expanded its demographic reach with the Country Gentlemen in Washington, DC, the Kentucky Colonels in Southern California, and Blue Grass Boys from the northeast such as Bill Keith.

During the 1970s, first-generation bluegrass artists maintained active performing and recording careers while younger groups broadened the stylistic possibilities for the music. Progressive acts including New Grass Revival, John Hartford, the Seldom Scene, and the David Grisman Quintet combined rock, folk, pop, and jazz repertoire and style with bluegrass instrumentation and performance techniques. J.D. Crowe and the New South, who played traditional and contemporary repertoire in a refined, precise style, made music that would later be a touchstone both for progressive groups such as Strength in Numbers and neotraditional ones such as Ricky Skaggs and Kentucky Thunder. Bluegrass gained institutional support with the establishment of the International Bluegrass Music Association in 1985, and festivals continued to mark regional bluegrass "scenes" such as the Bill Monroe-derived traditionalism of Indiana's Bean Blossom festival and the jam-oriented newgrass of the Telluride Bluegrass Festival (*see* New grass revival). Though bluegrass had largely been the music of white American men, it began to gain an international profile when several bands toured Japan in the early 1970s, and since the 1990s, bluegrass has changed significantly with the emergence of women including Alison Krauss and Rhonda Vincent as featured vocalists, instrumentalists, and bandleaders. The success of the *O Brother, Where Art Thou?* soundtrack accompanied a revival of traditional bluegrass, and since 2000 bluegrass has continued to function as a Southern heritage music, a string-based American chamber music, a suburban folk music, and a subgenre of country music.

BIBLIOGRAPHY

L.M. Smith: "An Introduction to Bluegrass," *Journal of American Folklore*, lxxviii/309 (1965), 245–56
E. Scruggs: *Earl Scruggs and the 5-String Banjo* (New York, 1968)
B. Artis: *Bluegrass* (New York, 1975)
R. Cantwell: *Bluegrass Breakdown* (Urbana, IL, 1984)
N.V. Rosenberg: *Bluegrass: a History* (Urbana, IL, 1985)
J. Wright: *Traveling the High Way Home: Ralph Stanley and the World of Traditional Bluegrass Music* (Urbana, IL, 1993)
M. Fenster: "Commercial (and/or?) Folk: the Bluegrass Industry and Bluegrass Traditions," in *Reading Country Music: Steel Guitars, Opry Stars, and Honky-Tonk Bars*, ed. Cecelia Tichi (Durham, NC, 1998), 74–97
A. Farmelo: "Another History of Bluegrass: the Segregation of Popular Music in the United States, 1820–1900," *Popular Music & Society*, xxv/1–2 (2001), 179–203
T. Goldsmith, ed.: *The Bluegrass Reader* (Urbana, IL, 2004)
N.V. Rosenberg and C. Wolfe: *The Music of Bill Monroe* (Urbana, IL, 2007)
J. Rockwell: "What is Bluegrass Anyway? Category Formation, Debate and the Framing of Musical Genre," *Popular Music*, xxxi/3 (2012), 363–81

NEIL V. ROSENBERG/JOTI ROCKWELL

Blue Jay Singers. Gospel quartet. It was organized in 1926 by Clarence Parnell, a pioneer figure in the black gospel-quartet tradition, and by the mid-1930s had become the most popular group of its type in the Deep South. Besides Parnell (bass), its original members were Silas Steele (lead), Jimmie Hollingsworth (tenor), and Charlie Beale (baritone). Steele in particular became a model for other gospel-quartet soloists. Although the group was known for its "sweet" style of singing, performing in close harmony in a style reminiscent of early barbershop quartets, towards the end of the 1930s it adopted a more aggressive manner; the singers are regarded as the progenitors of the "hard" gospel style in vogue among quartets by 1950. After moving to Chicago in the early 1940s, they helped to develop the Midwestern "clank-a-lanka" style of gospel music (named after a rhythmic quartet response to the leader's solo). The Blue Jay Singers flourished until the 1960s, including among its later members Nathaniel Edmonds, Charles Bridges, and Willie Rose.

BIBLIOGRAPHY

Black American Quartet Traditions (Washington, DC, 1981)
Liner notes, *Birmingham Quartet Anthology: Jefferson County, Alabama, 1926–1953*, Clanka Lanka CL-144 (1981)

HORACE CLARENCE BOYER

Blue note (i). A concept used by jazz critics and musicians from the early decades of the 20th century onwards to theorize African American music, notably in Blues and Jazz, to characterize pitch values perceived as deviating from the Western diatonic scale.

It was already observed in the 1920s that blues and jazz singers, as well as instrumentalists, tend to present the third and seventh, sometimes also the fifth degree in a diatonic framework by pitch values a semitone lower, often with microtonal fluctuations. Although its origin is unknown, by 1925 the term "blue note" was established in the literature (Niles, 1925–6). In contrast to this Western perspective, blues singers in the Deep South speak of "worrying" or "bending" the notes. Against the background of a strong central tonality, blues singers develop themes and melodic variations largely independent of the guitar chords used in the accompaniment. The intonation, often with glides and considerable melisma, sometimes deviates by microtonal values from the standard tunings of the guitar or the piano.

From a Western viewpoint, blue notes have been described in terms such as "deviations," "inflections" and "lowering," taking the Western tonal system as a yardstick. In search of underlying ideas, musicologists have systematized some of these deviations, proposing "blues scales" with ever-increasing numbers of notes; others suggest that blues musicians proceed from an awareness of "flexible pitch areas". Tonemic analysis of blues singers' concepts and behavior, in which all possible intonations together constitute the same toneme, has reconciled present-day ethnomusicological views with statements by blues singers (Kubik, 1999). If blue notes are considered intra-systemic as part of a non-Western tonal system, they vanish as separate entities and become those points where the deviations between western and non-Western systems of pitch are greatest. Thus, a non-Western analysis of the characteristic pitch-values prevalent in blues and jazz, described as "blue notes" in the literature, leads to results that diverge sharply from those obtained by any approach based on classical European music theory.

Despite many years of misunderstanding about its origins, reinterpretation of the blue note within the Western tonal system has become a prominent feature of much Western popular music, as well as some art music, such as *Rhapsody in Blue* by George Gershwin. Jazz harmony has largely placed the concept of blue notes within its own Western-oriented theoretical framework. Bebop harmony has incorporated elements of blues tonality as well as structural elements of harmonic parallelism in narrow intervals inherited from African tunings. Likewise, many of today's budding blues and jazz musicians continue to learn about "blue notes" and "blues scales" in relationship to the Western diatonic system.

BIBLIOGRAPHY

Grove6

A. Niles: "Blue Note," *The New Republic*, xlv (1925–6), 292–3

A. Niles: "The Story of the Blues," *Blues: an Anthology*, ed. W.C. Handy (New York, 1926, 2/1949 as *A Treasury of the Blues*, rev. 3/1972/*R* by J. Silverman under orig. title), 12–45

G. Schuller: *Early Jazz: its Roots and Musical Development* (New York, 1968), 43ff

W. Sargeant: *Jazz: Hot and Hybrid* (New York, 1938, 3/1975)

P. Oliver: *Savannah Syncopators: African Retentions in the Blues* (New York, 1970)

J.T. Titon: *Early Downhome Blues: a Musical and Cultural Analysis* (Urbana, IL, 1977, 2/1994 with new foreword by A. Trachtenberg)

T. Brothers: "Solo and Cycle in African-American Jazz," *MQ*, lxxviii (1994), 479–509

G. Kubik: *Africa and the Blues: Connections and Reconnections* (Jackson, MI, 1999)

GERHARD KUBIK/R

Blue Note (ii). Record company. It was established in New York in 1939 by jazz aficionado Alfred Lion, to record jazz; its earliest sessions produced records now acknowledged as classics, by such musicians as Sidney Bechet, Earl Hines, Albert Ammons, and Meade "Lux" Lewis. In the 1940s the company established a catalog of traditional jazz and swing, including recordings by James P. Johnson, Art Hodes, and Sidney Bechet; Blue Note was among the earliest to record bop musicians, notably items by Thelonious Monk.

In the LP era the company concentrated on styles that were then contemporary, with a close involvement with soul jazz and hard bop, represented by, among others, Horace Silver, Art Blakey, Lee Morgan, Jimmy Smith, and Ike Quebec. In 1963 Blue Note was purchased by Liberty; musicians recording for the company included Herbie Hancock and Wayne Shorter. Blue Note then began recording jazz-rock and more commercially oriented music; Donald Byrd's album *Black Byrd* (1973) became the company's best-selling album to date. In 1975 the systematic reissue of the back catalog began, and from the 1980s reissues appeared on Mosaic.

The connection with Liberty meant that Blue Note records were distributed by EMI. In 1979 EMI purchased Liberty's parent, United Artists Records, thus acquiring Blue Note, and the label's presence as an active unit was temporarily phased out. In 1984, EMI hired long-time record executive Bruce Lundvall away from his post at Elektra to re-launch the dormant Blue Note, and it began issuing albums again in 1985 as part of the Manhattan Records family of labels, a subsidiary of Capitol. In addition to a reissue program, the company began making new recordings again, including items by younger musicians as well as albums by established musicians, among them McCoy Tyner, Jackie McLean, and Freddie Hubbard. While the initial releases tended to follow the lead of founder Lion's vision, the label ultimately broadened its horizons beyond pure jazz, to substantial economic and artistic effect.

In 1989 EMI discontinued Manhattan and Blue Note became the umbrella company under which EMI's jazz activities were organized; in 1991 Manhattan was revived for releases in smooth jazz and pop-jazz styles. In 1993 Blue Note achieved its highest sales to date for a single disc when it crossed over from jazz into pop with the CD *Hand on the Torch* by the acid-jazz group Us3, which used samples from classic Blue Note sessions as a basis for a session of hip-hop dance music.

The Manhattan label was revived yet again in 2001 (ironically, as part of the Blue Note Label Group); the following year, singer Norah Jones' *Come Away With Me* garnered Blue Note more attention (and sales) than any album in the label's history, winning five Grammy Awards, including Album of the Year, Record of the Year, and Best New Artist. The current label roster includes such artists as Priscilla Ahn, Keren Ann, Amos Lee, Joe Lovano, Cassandra Wilson, and Jeff Bridges.

BIBLIOGRAPHY

M. Cuscuna and M. Ruppli: *The Blue Note Label: a Discography* (New York, 1988)

G. Marsh, G. Callingham, and F. Cromey, eds.: *The Cover Art of Blue Note Records* (Zürich, 1992)

F. Wolff: *The Blue Note Years: the Jazz Photography of Francis Wolff*, ed. M. Cuscuna, C. Lourie, and O. Schnider (New York, 1995)

R. Cook: *Blue Note Records: the Biography* (Boston, MA, 2004)

BARRY KERNFELD, HOWARD RYE/THANE TIERNEY

Blue Öyster Cult. Rock group. Despite various changes in lineup during a history that spans more than four decades, it has remained anchored by its original members Eric Bloom (singer, guitarist, and keyboard player) and Donald "Buck Dharma" Roeser (guitarist and singer). Its other original members included Albert Bouchard (drummer and singer), Joe Bouchard (bass guitarist), Allen Lanier (guitarist, keyboard player, and singer). The group settled on the name Blue Öyster Cult in 1971. Under the manager Sandy Pearlman and the producer Murray Krugman, the group made recordings that both epitomize and parody the mystical elements of rock and its occult pretensions through elaborate religious and military symbolism. The band members, as well as Pearlman, wrote most of the material, but they also used lyrics by the rock critic R. Meltzer and the rock singer Patti Smith. The albums *Blue Öyster Cult* (Col., 1972), *Tyranny and Mutation* (Col., 1973), and *Secret Treaties* (Col., 1974) are all characterized by Roeser's superior guitar playing, a heavy beat, vocal harmonies reminiscent of contemporary pop, and eerie, fantastic lyrics. *Agents of Fortune* (Col., 1976) was a commercial success and gave the group the hit single "Don't Fear the Reaper." Originally a band that appealed chiefly to critics, Blue Öyster Cult attracted a wide audience by the early 1980s as one of the most sophisticated heavy-metal bands of the time. Since the late 1980s they have released few albums and have spent most of their energy touring.

JOHN PICCARELLA/R

Blue Rodeo. Canadian country-rock band. Formed as the Hi-Fi's in Toronto in 1978, the group later changed their name to Fly to France and then Red Yellow Blue, while the band worked in New York from 1981 to 1984. After returning to Toronto in 1984, they became Blue Rodeo; at this time its members were Jim Cuddy (*b* 1955; vocals and electric guitar), Greg Keelor (*b* 1954; vocals and electric guitar), Bazil Donovan (bass guitar), Cleave Anderson (drums), and Bob Wiseman (piano). The band signed to the Warner Music Group in 1986 and released two albums, *Outskirts* (1987) and *Diamond Mine* (1989). Anderson was replaced by Mark French for the group's third album, *Casino* (1990). In the early 1990s James Gray replaced Wiseman, Glenn Milchem replaced French, and the pedal-steel guitarist Kim Deschamps was added to the band. This lineup remained intact throughout the 1990s, when the band released some of their most popular albums, including *Five Days in July* (1993). After the release of *Nowhere to Here* (1995) the band's music was deemed too eclectic for American radio formats, and they focused on the Canadian market. The pedal-steel guitarist Bob Egan, who had formerly played with Wilco, replaced Deschamps in 2000. Blue Rodeo developed small followings in the United States, Australia, and parts of Europe and gained immense popularity in Canada, partly as a result of their frequent touring to isolated towns. Their music blends country, rock, punk, folk, and pop, drawing on such influences as the Band, the Everly Brothers, Bob Dylan, and the Beatles. Known for Cuddy and Keelor's pleasing vocal harmonies and for lyrical references to Canadian places and history, the band has continued to record and perform into the 2010s.

SELECTED RECORDINGS

Outskirts (Warner Music Canada, 1987); *Diamond Mine* (Warner Music Canada, 1989); *Casino* (Warner Music Canada, 1990); *Lost Together* (Warner Music Canada, 1992); *Five Days in July* (Warner Music Canada, 1993); *Nowhere to Here* (Warner Music Canada, 1995); *Tremolo* (Warner Music Canada, 1997); *Just like a Vacation* (Warner Music Canada, 1999); *The Days in Between* (Warner Music Canada, 2000); *Palace of Gold* (Warner Music Canada, 2002); *Are you Ready* (Warner Music Canada, 2005); *Small Miracles* (Warner Music Canada, 2007); *The Things we Left Behind* (Warner Music Canada, 2009)

BIBLIOGRAPHY

M. Barclay, I.A.D. Jack, and J. Schneider: *Have not been the Same: the CanRock Renaissance* (Toronto, 2001)

A. Barris and T. Barris: *Making Music: Profiles from a Century of Canadian Music* (Toronto, 2001)

GILLIAN TURNBULL

Blues. A secular music with roots in African American folk forms, which arose in the Southern United States and became internationally popular in the 20th century. It has formed an integral part of jazz, R&B, rock, and to a lesser extent country music. The content and definitions of blues have changed to fit shifts in musical fashions, technologies, performance styles, and audiences, but it has maintained its own identity and evolutionary history. With its deep roots and broad influence, blues is widely regarded as the foundation for nearly all later American popular forms. (*See* African American music; Blues rock; Country; Jazz; Pop; Popular music; Rhythm-and-blues; Rock; Soul music.)

1. Definition. 2. Origins. 3. Early blues: publishing and recording. 4. Down home blues. 5. Pianists and urban blues. 6. The 1940s: swing, amplification, and jump blues. 7. Chicago, Memphis, and electric blues. 8. Rock 'n' roll, the blues revival, and blues-rock. 9. Soul and soul-blues. 10. Conclusion.

1. Definition. The most limited definition of blues is as a specific sequence of chords, the "12-bar blues," which consists of four measures of the tonic (I), two measures of the subdominant (IV), two of the tonic, one of the dominant seventh (V^7), one of the subdominant, and two of the tonic (*see* Blues progression). There are also 8- and 16-bar blues forms, which may have preceded the 12-bar pattern historically, and many blues songs follow none of these patterns. But the 12-bar form is what musicians mean if they simply agree to "play a blues."

A looser definition is based on mood: before the word was attached to a musical style, to have the blues or to feel blue designated a state of sadness or melancholy. This usage was widespread in the United States by the mid-1800s, and it continues to be part of many people's definition of the musical genre. It is not clear when or where the word became associated with certain kinds of songs or instrumental pieces, but the first 12-bar blues published as sheet music, in New Orleans in 1908, connected the music to the emotional state in its title: "I Got the Blues." Many blues songs and performances are upbeat and cheerful, but slow songs, whether mournful, soulful, or sexy, have continued to be considered the deepest, most representative form of blues.

A further definition involves West African tonal and rhythmic practices, which were retained with modifications by African American musicians. These include frequent use of slides between notes and microtones, especially hovering around the flatted third and seventh notes of the European major scale—the so-called "blue notes" (*see* Blue note (i)). These tonal particularities

Ma Rainey Georgia Jazz Band, c1924–5. (JazzSign/Lebrecht Music & Arts)

have often been described as giving the music a mournful sound, and hence at times overlap the emotional definition. Jazz musicians in all periods have been judged by their ability to convey a "blues feel," meaning both to comfortably execute these subtle tonal shadings and play "behind the beat" in a relaxed relationship to a song's rhythm, and also to give their listeners a powerful emotional experience. This ability has been connected by many musicians and scholars to an African American ethnic or cultural heritage, to the point that there have been acrimonious debates about the degree to which people who are not African American can convey a true blues feeling. The word has also been extended to non-musical forms, such as poetry or novels with a profound linguistic or cultural connection to African American traditions.

The final definition is the least satisfying to musicologists, but also by far the most widespread, and encompasses aspects of all the others. It is simply: whatever listeners, performers, and marketers have understood to be part of the genre. This definition has changed over the years, as styles and artists have been added to or dropped from the canon, and there is little agreement on exactly what music it comprises in any period. Conceptions of a typical blues performer have ranged from a black woman with a deep, rich voice, singing in front of a small jazz group to an old black man with an acoustic guitar growling rough lyrics on a dusty Southern street corner to a young white man playing a searing electric guitar solo in a rowdy Texas bar. Nonetheless, many historians now choose to use this cultural definition rather than insisting on precise musical qualities, and consider blues to be whatever a substantial audience understood the word to mean in any particular period or region.

2. Origins. Although there is no evidence that the word "blues" was applied to a musical style before the first decade of the 20th century, by the late 1800s there were songs being played throughout the Southern United States that most current historians would consider varieties of blues. Sometimes called pre-blues or proto-blues, these were adapted from earlier African American styles, including group work songs and the so-called moans or field hollers (*see* Work songs *and* Field holler). Work songs frequently used the "call-and-response" approach common in many African traditions, whereby one person sings a line and a group of singers respond, either echoing the same line or with a repetitive chorus. Though such singing became less common in secular contexts as machines replaced work gangs, call-and-response remained a staple of African American religious singing, which has always overlapped and influenced secular styles. In blues, the vocal call-and-response was reshaped into an interchange between a singer and an instrument, played either by the singer or by an accompanist. Bessie Smith's 1925 recording of "St. Louis Blues," accompanied

B.B. King, 1986. (Forum/Lebrecht Music & Arts)

by Louis Armstrong, is an example of how the standard 12-bar form and the most common blues lyric pattern (a line repeated twice and answered by a rhyming third line) are divided into three call-and-response phrases, each taking up four bars.

> Smith starts: "I hate to see the evening sun go down"; Armstrong plays a relaxed melodic response. Smith repeats, "I hate to see the evening sun go down"; Armstrong plays a series of slow, drawn-out notes. Smith completes the thought: "It makes me think I'm on my last go 'round"; Armstrong plays a final passage leading into the next verse.

The moans or hollers gave blues much of its tonal, timbral, and dynamic flavor. Sung a cappella and generally by a single singer, they were slow, free-form vocal improvisations without fixed melodies or measures, and often without words. Making frequent use of melisma and microtonal slides, hollers influenced both blues singing and instrumental performance. As a result most of the common blues instruments either do not have fixed pitches ("slide guitar," played by sliding a metal or glass bar along the strings) or allow an adept performer to bend notes (trumpet, saxophone, harmonica, guitar), capturing this vocal flavor, and blues pianists frequently use grace notes and "crunch" adjoining keys to create the illusion of slides and microtones.

Vocal styles were the strongest influence on blues, but African and European stringed instrument traditions also played a significant role. African slaves in the United States were generally forbidden to play drums, leading to the disappearance or dilution of the African drumming traditions, but slave owners permitted and even encouraged the playing of stringed instruments. West Africa has widespread stringed instrument traditions, including professional musicians such as the *jelli* or *griots*, who act as historians and social commentators in the more centralized societies, and herdsmen and village amateurs playing to amuse themselves or their friends. Slaves made banjos and fiddles based on models played in Africa, and also adapted African playing techniques to the European violin and later the guitar. Black musicians performed not only for their compatriots but also for European Americans—virtually all the music played for dances on southern plantations was played by slaves—and assimilated a wide repertoire of European instrumental music.

With the rise of minstrel shows in the 1840s, African American "plantation melodies" and banjo and fiddle techniques entered the popular music mainstream. Minstrel songs and styles developed by professional composers and entertainers, both Euro- and Afro-American, were also recycled back into black rural tradition, beginning a process of cultural and musical interchange that would continue into the early blues era and beyond.

Vernacular and rural music was rarely recorded before the 1920s, and folklorists were more interested in lyrics than in melodies, so much of the prehistory of blues is based on conjecture. Some historians consider it simplistic to view blues as a purely African American style, since the southern fiddle repertoire shows an intimate intermixing of tunes and techniques from Africa and the British Isles, and British ballads and early blues songs were widely sung by white and black southerners alike. However, African American vocal and instrumental performance retained distinctive characteristics that came to new prominence with the popularity of blues, and in the early 20th century blues songs and styles were universally viewed as coming from African American tradition.

The songs most commonly recalled as early or proto-blues included versions of "Make Me a Pallet on Your Floor," "Going Down the Road Feeling Bad," "Alabama Bound," and "Hesitation Blues." Only the last of these was a 12-bar blues, and such songs were not yet regarded as part of a separate musical genre. They were performed by singers, pianists, dance bands, guitarists, and fiddlers throughout the South, and depending on the setting might be thought of as ragtime, hoedowns, dance-hall tunes, or simply uncategorized songs and instrumental pieces. In retrospect, some historians have attempted to distinguish between "songsters" such as Henry "Ragtime Texas" Thomas and Mississippi John Hurt, who sang blues alongside a wide range of other material, and blues musicians (*see* SONGSTER (ii)). In practice, virtually all musicians until at least the 1940s played a variety of styles at live performances and this distinction may owe more to what survives on record than to broader patterns of musical performance.

3. EARLY BLUES: PUBLISHING AND RECORDING. In the fall of 1912 the publication of "Dallas Blues," "Baby Seals Blues," and "The Memphis Blues" brought the style to the attention of a broad national audience. The first two songs were already being performed in vaudeville shows (the latter by an African American song and dance man named Baby Seals), while "Memphis Blues" was the first publication by W.C. Handy, a Memphis bandleader. "Memphis Blues" became a major hit, in part due to its adoption by America's most famous dance instructors, Vernon and Irene Castle, who made it the accompaniment to their version of the foxtrot. Handy went on to write many blues hits, including "St. Louis Blues," and opened a publishing office in New York that specialized in blues numbers.

From 1913 to 1920 over 400 songs were published that had "blues" in their titles, and many more were associated with the blues style and performed by singers and bands in dance halls, vaudeville theaters, and cabarets. Interest increased in the later teens with the rise of jazz. The first article on jazz as a musical style, published by the *Chicago Tribune* in 1915, was titled "Blues Is Jazz and Jazz Is Blues," and the national jazz craze was sparked by the Original Dixieland Jazz Band's 1917 recording of "Livery Stable Blues," an instrumental using the 12-bar chord progression.

Much of the material published as blues in the teens could as easily be classified as ragtime, depending on the performance: the same song may be considered ragtime if played as a perky foxtrot by a northern dance band, but blues if sung by an artist like Bessie Smith. Since the only recordings of blues from this period were made by urban dance bands and white vaudeville singers, it is thus hard to get a clear sense of what proportion of blues before the 1920s would meet modern definitions of the genre.

The first significant blues record by an African American singer was Mamie Smith's "Crazy Blues," made for the OKeh company in August, 1920. Smith was a vaudeville performer who had not previously been associated with blues and she recorded the song at the behest of Perry Bradford, Handy's main rival as a blues composer and publisher. Its success inspired record manufacturers to present separate lines of material targeted at African American consumers, which became known as RACE RECORDS. For the next five years the overwhelming majority of these records featured female singers, often known as "blues queens." They were generally accompanied by a pianist or a small jazz group, and their style is sometimes known as "classic blues" in an analogy to European concert music, or as "vaudeville blues."

The first wave of blues queens included Ethel Waters, Lucille Hegamin, Alberta Hunter, and Edith Wilson. Although Waters was already known in black vaudeville for her blues work, these singers were versatile artists who were popular with northern audiences and recorded blues because that was what the record companies wanted. This focus shifted with the appearance of Bessie Smith's "Down Hearted Blues" in 1923. Smith was from Chattanooga, Tennessee, and her voice had the timbre and accent of the Deep South. She could sing other pop styles, but blues was her specialty, and she opened the door for a wave of southerners who shared her moaning, soulful sound, including Clara Smith (known as "the Queen of the Moaners," and no relation to Mamie or Bessie), Ida Cox, Sippie Wallace, and Ma Rainey. Rainey, known as "the Mother of the Blues," was the oldest of these singers, and claimed to have named the style in the first decade of the century. Both her musical approach and her material at times reflected rural sources, with banjo or guitar accompaniment and titles like "Bo-weevil Blues." In general, though, she performed in the mainstream vaudeville style, wearing elegant costumes and backed by jazz musicians. Indeed, the blues queens were the first major jazz singers, and influenced not only later vocalists but also brass and reed players.

4. DOWN HOME BLUES. In 1924 a New Orleans-born six-string banjo player named Papa Charlie Jackson became the first male singer successfully to challenge the recording monopoly of the blues queens. However, his records had a novelty, minstrel-show flavor, and self-accompanied men would not make a serious impact on the national blues market until Blind Lemon Jefferson began recording in 1926. Jefferson was a Dallas street singer with a huge voice and a quirkily virtuosic guitar technique. His repertoire consisted largely of 12-bar blues that mixed original lines with "floating verses" adapted and recycled by multiple singers, along with hollers, spirituals, and ragtime dance pieces. By vaudeville standards he sounded raw and unprofessional, but to a lot of listeners that rawness was an asset. His records were advertised with the rubric "down home," as the sound of the rural South, and set off a wave of what has come to be known as "country blues."

Jefferson's success surprised race record marketers, and for the next few years they combed the South for other unlikely stars, preserving a more varied and idiosyncratic range of artists than in any other period of blues. Most were singers accompanied by their own guitars, with sometimes an additional harmonica or fiddle. Though often classified as country blues artists, many were based in urban centers such as Dallas, Atlanta, and Memphis, and were professional entertainers, working as street musicians, at picnics and rural "juke joints," or with touring medicine shows. Their repertoires ranged from old rural songs to recent pop hits, but the record company scouts concentrated on their blues material and urged them to compose new pieces that fit the current blues trends. Later historians have tended to divide these artists into three regional categories: the Piedmont (the Carolinas, Georgia, East Tennessee, and Virginia), Mississippi (specifically the Delta region between Jackson and Memphis), and Texas.

The Piedmont was home to the South's oldest African American communities, and its players continued to perform a lot of pre-blues material and brought a ragtime flavor to their blues work. Popular Piedmont artists included Peg Leg Howell, who often worked with the fiddler Eddie Anthony; Barbecue Bob; and in the 1930s Josh White and Blind Boy Fuller. Blind Blake, reportedly born in Jacksonville, Florida, and based in Chicago, was the most influential Piedmont player, with a light, conversational singing voice and intricate guitar style related to ragtime piano, showcased on records such as 1927's "Wabash Rag." Atlanta's Blind Willie McTell recorded for multiple companies under various pseudonyms, preserving a varied repertoire including comic monologues, ragtime, gospel, and blues, with 12-string guitar accompaniments that ranged from infectious dance rhythms to haunting, holler-inflected slide lines.

Texas was largely populated by relatively recent immigrants from across the South, and as a result had no single unifying style, though many of its guitarists relied on a monotonic bass rather than the alternating bass notes favored by Piedmont players. Aside from Jefferson, the most prominent singer was Texas Alexander, who did not play an instrument and retained an exceptional degree of field holler phrasing, especially on free-form improvisations such as "Levee Camp Moan." Another prominent Texan, Blind Willie Johnson, sang only gospel music, but his records sold widely and his exceptionally fluid, voice-like slide style influenced blues guitarists across the South.

In Mississippi, Charlie Patton was the central figure of a group of distinctive players based in the central Delta region. Locally famed for his showy live performances, Patton sang in a gruff, dramatic voice and his guitar arrangements on recordings such as 1929's "Screamin' and Hollerin' the Blues" demonstrated an unsurpassed rhythmic control and complexity. Patton's partners and followers included Tommy Johnson, noted for his warm voice and swooping falsetto yodel; Son House, an awesome singer and the region's finest slide guitarist; and later players including Booker (Bukka) White, Robert Johnson, Tommy McClennan and Muddy Waters. Although these players had relatively little impact on the early race record market, their work formed the foundation of the electric Chicago style of the 1950s and was thus exceptionally influential on later blues and rock. In the 1920s and early 1930s, though, the region's most successful artists were the Mississippi Sheiks, who combined blues guitar and singing with country fiddling, and Bo Carter (brother of the Sheiks' fiddler Lonnie Chatmon), who made a specialty of double-entendre "party blues."

Many down-home blues recordings were also made in Memphis. Older artists such as Frank Stokes and Jim Jackson mixed blues and pre-blues styles, while the Memphis Jug Band and Cannon's Jug Stompers specialized in rowdy, good-time music. Such jug or washboard bands, featuring guitars, harmonicas, and various homemade instruments, had a vogue in the late 1920s and early 1930s that inspired imitators as far away as Chicago and New York (*see* Jug band *and* Washboard band).

5. Pianists and urban blues. Recordings are the best surviving guide to the music of the 1920s and 1930s, but they were less influential in this period than in later years and are not necessarily representative of what was being played in live venues. While the down-home recording trend favored guitarists, pianists were the most popular players in African American barrooms and honky-tonks throughout the South. Pianos were less common in rural areas than guitars and fiddles, so whereas guitarists generally mixed blues with older folk songs, pianists were more often influenced by urban ragtime and Tin Pan Alley styles.

With its loud volume, the piano was an ideal solo instrument for noisy barrooms or dances. The most rurally identified blues piano style was known as "barrelhouse," a reference to the makeshift lumber-camp saloons of Louisiana, Texas, and Mississippi where it thrived (*see* Barrelhouse). Barrelhouse players were not necessarily virtuosos, since their main function was to provide a powerful beat, but the best players combined intricate bass rhythms with bright treble riffs. Little Brother Montgomery and Roosevelt Sykes, who worked from New Orleans to Chicago and influenced many Mississippi pianists and guitarists, were known for pounding dance pieces and a distinctive slow blues arrangement that Montgomery recorded as "Vicksburg Blues" and Sykes as "44 Blues."

Among blues piano's most important contributions was its propulsive bass patterns. Charles "Cow Cow" Davenport's 1928 recording of "Cow Cow Blues" popularized a widespread barrelhouse theme that would be a key component of boogie-woogie, a style that seems to have acquired its name with the success of Pine Top Smith's 1929 record, "Pine Top's Boogie-Woogie" (*see* Boogie-woogie (i)). This approach was refined and expanded by players in Chicago and elsewhere in the urban Midwest, including Jimmy Yancey, Meade Lux Lewis, Albert Ammons, and Pete Johnson. Performing in speakeasies and at apartment "rent parties" where black urbanites circumvented the Prohibition-era liquor laws, they created distinctive, repetitive bass figures to back improvised right-hand riffs and melodies.

The period from the teens through the 1940s saw the "great migration" of African Americans out of the rural south, pushed by harsh conditions and the mechanization of agriculture and pulled by the promise of better jobs and a less racist social climate. Both hopeful emigrants in the South and new immigrants in the North turned increasingly to musical styles that reflected life in the black neighborhoods of northern cities. The trendsetting urban blues artist, Lonnie Johnson, was based in St. Louis and began recording in 1925, just before the wave of down-home singers. His sound was hip and urbane, featuring mellow, conversational vocals, guitar solos that earned him a reputation as the father of jazz guitar, and lyrics spiced with sexual double-entendres and references to gangsters and violence.

For a couple of years, Johnson had this style pretty much to himself, but in 1928 two records appeared that redefined the blues market. Leroy Carr's "How Long—How Long Blues" and "It's Tight Like That" by Tampa Red and Georgia Tom both featured light-voiced singers backed by piano and guitar, and defined the twin poles of the urban approach. Tampa Red was an innovative slide guitarist whose single-string leads were widely imitated, and Thomas "Georgia Tom" Dorsey had been Ma Rainey's bandleader and pianist and would become the pioneering composer in modern gospel music. But what made "It's Tight Like That" a hit was its slangy title, rollicking feel, and bawdy lyrics. Covered and copied by dozens of artists, it spawned a comic style known as "hokum," favored by Chicago studio bands like the Hokum Boys and the Harlem Hamfats.

Carr played his share of hokum, but had his greatest success as the defining master of the late-night blues ballad. Sensitively accompanied by the guitarist Scrapper Blackwell, he was a blues equivalent of pop crooners like Bing Crosby, taking advantage of the new intimacy provided by electronic microphones and phonographs. He was also an exceptional lyricist, and his introspective "Midnight Hour Blues" and "When the Sun Goes Down" became blues standards. Carr was by far the most widely imitated male blues singer of the era, influencing artists as disparate as Robert Johnson, the Ink Spots, and the gospel pioneer R.H. Harris, and inspired later generations of R&B and soul balladeers.

The stock market crash of 1929 and the ensuing Great Depression forced a drastic cut-back in recording. The race records market may have been less affected than mainstream pop, since it did not face similar competition from the virtually all-white programming available for free on radio, but both blues queens and down home players virtually ceased to be recorded. The new record stars were reliable studio performers in the hokum or ballad styles, mostly based in St. Louis and Chicago. The balladeers included Bumble Bee Slim, Walter Davis, and Peetie Wheatstraw, who was particularly appreciated for his rich voice and the raw lyrics that went with his nickname, "The Devil's Son-In-Law."

In Chicago, a shifting cast of musicians became studio regulars, backing one another and releasing the results under the name of whoever was singing. Big Bill Broonzy played guitar on hundreds of records, was equally comfortable singing hokum or ballads, and composed standards such as "Key to the Highway." Kokomo Arnold played frantically fast slide guitar and punctuated his vocals with a biting falsetto yodel, notably on his much-covered 1934 hit "Milk Cow Blues." John Lee "Sonny Boy" Williamson created a band-oriented harmonica style, playing horn-like riffs between his vocals on upbeat numbers like his 1937 debut, "Good Morning, Little School Girl." Casey Bill Weldon mixed blues slide guitar techniques with the shimmering vibrato of the Hawaiian style. Pianists Blind John Davis, Black Bob, and Memphis Slim created solid backgrounds, with the latter breaking out in the 1940s as an adept singer and composer. Though condemned by some rurally-oriented historians as overly commercial and formulaic, these artists shaped the blues combo approach that would form the foundation of later electric bands.

Though female singers no longer dominated the field, Memphis Minnie was one of the most successful Chicago artists, an excellent guitarist who brought sharp, nasal vocals and wryly hip humor to compositions like "Bumble Bee" and "Me and My Chauffeur." Lil Johnson and Georgia White also had success with hokum material.

The market for these artists expanded dramatically after the repeal of Prohibition in 1933. Thousands of new bars installed jukeboxes, and by the end of the decade some estimates suggest that more than half the records sold in the United States went into public machines. The rowdy boogies and late-night whiskey ballads of the urban blues artists were ideally suited to this market. In particular, black and white patrons alike turned to blues for rowdy party lyrics they could not hear on the radio. A Louisiana pianist and singer named Speckled Red had set a new standard for bawdy blues in 1929 with "The Dirty Dozens," Roosevelt Sykes followed with "Dirty Mother Fuyer," and by the mid-1930s a huge proportion of the blues market was devoted to such themes.

6. The 1940s: swing, amplification, and jump blues. Jazz and blues had drawn somewhat apart in the 1920s as dance orchestras expanded to suit the demands of the large Prohibition-era ballrooms and adopted a more arranged, classically-influenced approach. That changed in the 1930s, when a wave of swing bands turned to blues to reinvigorate the jazz repertoire. The most important figure in this renaissance was William "Count" Basie, whose Kansas City orchestra made its mark with 12-bar blues, including its riff-driven theme, "One O'Clock Jump," and slow numbers like "Goin' to Chicago Blues," featuring Jimmy Rushing's full-throated vocals. The Kansas City sound spread throughout the Midwest, then to both coasts, and the biggest blues hits of the later 1930s and 1940s tended to come from swing bands. Typical examples range from Earl Hines's "Jelly Jelly" with singer Jimmy Witherspoon and Eddie "Cleanhead" Vinson's "Cherry Red" with the Cootie Williams orchestra to Benny Goodman's "Why Don't You Do Right" with Peggy Lee and Tommy Dorsey's instrumental "Boogie Woogie."

The combination of blues singers with large orchestras was made possible by the new technology of electronic amplification. Though singers like Kansas City's Big Joe Turner were noted for their ability to shout over a full band, the microphone meant that anyone could make him- or herself heard, and many adopted the more intimate, lighter-voiced approaches pioneered by Ethel Waters and Leroy Carr. When Billie Holiday hit in 1939 with "Fine and Mellow," she inspired a new wave of blues queens including Dinah Washington, the most influential female blues stylist of the next two decades. Washington combined Holiday's intimacy and improvisational daring with a fuller, throatier vocal timbre developed as a teenaged church singer. Her first hits were hip swing numbers with Lionel Hampton's orchestra, but after going solo she increasingly brought gospel melisma and phrasing into her blues work, shaping an approach that would be adapted by later R&B and soul singers such as Ruth Brown, Ray Charles, and Aretha Franklin.

Jukeboxes and amplification both made it easier for small groups to compete with big bands, whether on records or at live appearances. As a result, there was an increasing overlap between what was played by swing orchestras and blues combos. Louis Jordan, an alto saxophonist with Chick Webb's Savoy Ballroom orchestra, formed a tight combo called the Tympany Five in the late 1930s and updated the hokum approach with sax and trumpet solos and hipster jive lyrics. Though not limited to blues, Jordan got his biggest hits with 12-bar numbers including "Caldonia" (1945) and "Choo-Choo Ch'Boogie" (1946), and his style, which became known as "jump blues," evolved into the hard-driving rhythm and blues of the early 1950s.

As World War II brought a mass migration of young African Americans to the West Coast to work in the ship-building industry, Los Angeles became the center of a new urban blues movement. Nat "King" Cole and his trio set the pattern for the local style in 1941 with a 12-bar ballad, "That Ain't Right." Their combination of swinging piano, jazzily sophisticated electric guitar, and whispery vocals was picked up by Johnny Moore's Three Blazers, whose "Drifting Blues" in 1945 launched the career of the defining ballad singer of the rhythm-and-blues era, Charles Brown.

The West Coast artists tended to come from Texas and Oklahoma, and their urbane approach drew on a variety of southwestern influences, from the down home styles of the 1920s to Western swing, the first music to regularly feature electrically amplified guitars. T-Bone Walker, a smooth singer in the Leroy Carr mode, shaped a new vocabulary of blues guitar by combining jazz harmonies and phrasing with a gritty down-home tone, and became a national star with records such as the enduringly popular "Call It Stormy Monday." Walker can be considered the father of modern lead guitar, and was soon joined by Pee Wee Crayton and Oakland's Lowell Fulson, who added gospel-flavored vocals. The Los Angeles scene also nurtured the upbeat jump combos of brothers Joe and Jimmy Liggins, and pianist-singers including the smooth balladeer Ivory Joe Hunter and Amos Milburn, noted for wry drinking songs like 1950's "Bad, Bad Whiskey." The West Coast sound dominated the blues market of the late 1940s, and as it was picked up and adapted by eastern artists such as B.B. King, shaped the mainstream of later blues.

7. Chicago, Memphis, and electric blues. At the turn of the 1950s, popular music in the United States was in an unprecedented state of flux. The combined effects of wartime upheavals, a two-year recording strike by the American Federation of Musicians, the incursions of television, and the arrival of lighter, less breakable vinyl records encouraged entrepreneurs all over the country to start small "indie" record companies, challenging the dominance of the New York-based major labels. Many of the indies specialized in niche markets such as "hillbilly" and "race music," which in 1949 were given new genre labels by *Billboard* magazine: "country and western" and "rhythm-and-blues."

The small labels were looking for sounds that would give them an edge on the majors, and as a result were willing to take chances on artists who might otherwise have been considered too primitive or old-fashioned for the current blues market. The first to make a national impact were Lightnin' Hopkins in Houston and John Lee Hooker, a transplanted Mississippian living in Detroit, who were often accompanied only by their guitars, sang in deep southern accents, and kept "country time," expanding and contracting musical measures to fit the mood of the moment. In 1949, Hooker got a number one R&B hit with "Boogie Chillen," an unrhymed monologue spoken over a loping, repetitive guitar rhythm.

In Chicago, the Chess record label became a prime showcase for the new down-home sound. Its defining star, Muddy Waters, transformed the rural Delta style of Son House by amplifying his slide guitar to ferocious volume, then added the innovative harmonica player Little Walter and a full rhythm section of piano, bass, and drums. Waters's work was distinguished by his deep, soulful voice, uncanny control of tone and rhythm, and sure taste in sidemen, but the fusion of older styles with electricity was picked up across the South. Though they soon moved to Chicago, Elmore James had his first hit in 1951 while still in Jackson, Mississippi, with a slide-powered reworking of Robert Johnson's "Dust My Broom," and Howlin' Wolf first recorded in Memphis. Wolf eventually became Waters's main rival, known for his gruff voice, awesome stage presence, and primal, one-chord compositions like 1956's "Smokestack Lightnin'."

Little Walter was a generation younger than Waters and Wolf, and his harmonica style owed as much to Louis Jordan's saxophone riffs as to rural traditions. His "Juke," a chart-topping instrumental in 1952, revolutionized perceptions of the instrument, which had previously been regarded as a toy or novelty. Using amplification to expand the range of tones and techniques, Walter, Sonny Boy Williamson (born Aleck Miller, and not to be confused with the John Lee Williamson who recorded in the 1940s) and Big Walter Horton reshaped the harmonica into one of the most evocative and familiar blues instruments.

Though "Chicago blues" is often used as a generic term for the electric blues band style, the most influential artist in this format was B.B. King, a Mississippian based in Memphis. King mixed the grit and emotion of the down-home tradition with the melisma-heavy vocal style of the new gospel quartets, jump combo backing, and the jazz-inflected guitar innovations of the West Coast players, inspiring both Memphis-based peers like Bobby Bland, Albert King, and Little Milton and a younger generation of Chicagoans including Otis Rush, Buddy Guy, and Magic Sam. In 1965, King's *Live at the Regal* album brought this sound to a broader audience of jazz and rock fans, earning him the title, "Ambassador of the Blues," and his guitar approach has been echoed by virtually every major electric soloist since the 1960s.

8. Rock 'n' roll, the blues revival, and blues-rock. King and the down-home players primarily served an audience of African American adults, but by the mid-1950s white teenage fans were discovering R&B under the new marketing term "rock 'n' roll." Fats Domino, a young pianist and singer from New Orleans, became the biggest-selling African American artist of the decade, Ruth Brown and Etta James updated Dinah Washington's style with current dance rhythms, and the veteran Kansas City shouter Big Joe Turner hit in 1954 with "Shake, Rattle, and Roll," which was covered by a white hillbilly group from Pennsylvania, Bill Haley and the Comets. The transformation of "race music" into an interracial teen style was completed in 1956 with the television-fueled success of Elvis Presley. Rock 'n' roll was hailed as a new sound, but many of its defining songs were 12-bar blues, including Presley's "Hound Dog," Little Richard's "Tutti Frutti," Chuck Berry's "Johnny B. Goode," and the biggest dance hit of the early 1960s, "The Twist."

In the South, there was a long history of European Americans performing and listening to blues. Jimmie Rodgers, "the father of country music," built his reputation in the 1920s on blues songs punctuated with his trademark yodel. Both southeastern artists like the Delmore Brothers and westerners like Bob Wills and his Texas Playboys made blues a bedrock of their repertoires, and the most celebrated songwriter in the country genre, Hank Williams, learned guitar from an African American street musician and remained a dedicated blues stylist.

In the northeast, blues had generally reached white listeners in jazz or swing settings, but a few rural artists had also attracted limited attention. Huddie "Lead Belly" Ledbetter, a 12-string guitarist and singer from Louisiana, came to New York in 1935 with the folklorist John Lomax and remained on the local folk scene until his death in 1949. In 1938 the jazz enthusiast John Hammond presented a concert titled "From Spirituals to Swing" at Carnegie Hall that contrasted the blues styles of Big Bill Broonzy, the North Carolina harmonica player Sonny Terry, and a trio of boogie-woogie pianists with Sidney Bechet's New Orleans jazz group and the Count Basie Orchestra. And in the 1940s Josh White combined the blues repertoire that had made him a popular Piedmont recording artist with British ballads and a sophisticated nightclub style and won a devoted audience of white cabaret-goers and college students.

A small group of New Yorkers also began to collect and study the race records of the 1920s, and in 1959 Samuel Charters's book and companion LP, both titled *The Country Blues*, sparked a new interest in the early down home artists. Over the next few years, enthusiasts sought out long-forgotten players and presented them at festivals, clubs, and concert halls, in what came to be known as the "blues revival." Like the broader "folk revival," this movement favored country-sounding artists over performers whose work reflected urban pop trends. As a result, some previously underappreciated performers came to be seen as major figures. Mississippi John Hurt was valued for his gentle charm, varied repertoire, and flowing guitar arrangements. Skip James, a Mississippian who played uniquely idiosyncratic accompaniments on both guitar and piano, mesmerized young listeners with original compositions like "Devil Got My Woman," performed in a haunting falsetto.

Robert Johnson, whose early reputation had been limited to his Mississippi peers, became the most celebrated of all pre-war blues artists after Columbia records issued an LP of his work in 1961 as *King of the Delta Blues Singers*. Johnson recorded only 29 songs before his death in 1938, but his blend of the Delta style of Son House with the urban innovations of Leroy Carr and Peetie Wheatstraw and his superlative poetic skills provided a uniquely powerful summation of the early down home style. In the 1960s his lyrical imagery inspired Bob Dylan and his guitar arrangements were studied by Eric Clapton, Keith Richards, and a generation of players in Europe, the United States, and beyond.

On the folk scene of the late 1950s and early 1960s, Dave Van Ronk in New York and Eric Von Schmidt in Cambridge, Massachusetts, led a wave of young urban blues performers. A few, like John Koerner in Minneapolis, developed distinctively personal styles, but most tried to recreate the sound of older performers. They learned songs, vocal styles, and guitar techniques from LP reissues of early records and personal contact with "rediscovered" artists like Hurt, James, House, and the Reverend Gary Davis, a South Carolinian gospel singer who had moved to Harlem and taught young revivalists his virtuosic ragtime-blues guitar arrangements.

The folk-blues movement at first eschewed electric instruments, but in Europe an annual touring "American Folk-Blues Festival" presented House, James, and the duo of Sonny Terry and Brownie McGhee alongside the electric bands of Muddy Waters, Howlin' Wolf, and Buddy Guy. English performers were soon bridging the gap between older acoustic and modern electric styles on records like the Animals' "House of the Rising Sun." This fusion crossed the Atlantic with the British Invasion, and in 1965 Dylan teamed with members of Chicago's Paul Butterfield Blues Band for an electric set at the Newport Folk Festival. Soon the Rolling Stones, Cream, and Led Zeppelin were playing rock versions of songs learned from the records of Robert Johnson, Skip James, and Memphis Minnie, and John Hammond and Taj Mahal (the one African American to make an impact in the folk-blues movement) were alternating acoustic and electric albums.

Blues-rock became established as its own style in the later 1960s. Aside from Janis Joplin and Mick Jagger, its biggest stars tended to be guitarists, many playing extended solos that blended techniques learned from black players like B.B., Freddie, and Albert King with "psychedelic" effects inspired by marijuana and hallucinogens. This approach reached its apex with Jimi Hendrix, who had cut his teeth on the R&B scene, then moved to London and returned in 1967 as the ultimate psychedelic bluesman. Hendrix transformed the sound of the electric guitar with wa-wa and feedback, creating a vocabulary that was adopted by contemporaries such as Clapton and Jeff Beck, and later by Stevie Ray Vaughan.

9. Soul and soul-blues. While folk-blues and blues-rock were primarily marketed to white listeners, the association of blues with deep southern roots also attracted some black performers. In the 1940s Charlie Parker used the blues-based Kansas City approach as a basis for the harmonic innovations of bebop, but most boppers preferred more complex chord structures and rhythms. In the 1950s, some young African American jazz artists feared the music was losing its black audience, and turned to blues forms and tonalities in a movement known as Hard bop. With titles like "Work Song" and "Back at the Chicken Shack," Cannonball Adderley and Jimmy Smith emphasized their connection to southern black traditions, which they signified with the word "soul."

The high priest of soul was Ray Charles. After some minor hits as a West Coast blues pianist, by the mid-1950s Charles was mixing jazz, blues, and gospel styles, and he used the 12-bar progression for both hard bop instrumentals and hit singles like 1959's "What'd I Say," which mixed blues lyrics with a gospel call-and-response. In the 1960s this approach became the mainstream of R&B, with Ike and Tina Turner, Etta James, Aretha Franklin, and Wilson Pickett blending church shouts with blues themes. (*See* Soul music.)

A couple of down-home guitarist-singers managed to make an impact on the R&B charts: Jimmy Reed played loping Mississippi boogie shuffles and sang in a nasal, country style punctuated by his whining harmonica, and in the early 1960s his "Big Boss Man" was covered by rock and soul singers alike. Louisiana's Slim Harpo, another guitar and harmonica player, even created a fusion of down home blues and contemporary funk with his "Baby, Scratch My Back."

Many soul performers had mixed feelings about the word "blues," which they associated with slavery and the miseries of southern segregation. James Brown, the most influential figure in the evolution from R&B through soul to funk, insisted that he neither liked nor played blues, though the 1965 record that heralded his independence from older R&B conventions, "Papa's Got a Brand New Bag," used the classic 12-bar progression.

A few performers, notably B.B. King, Bobby Blue Bland, and Little Milton, continued to be known as blues singers while retaining an African American audience, but by the mid-1970s their style seemed to be on the way out. That changed to some extent in 1982 when Z.Z. Hill's "Down Home Blues" became an anthem for older listeners who were tired of disco and uninterested in rap. Southern soul singers such as Denise LaSalle, Johnny Taylor, and Latimore began to be advertised as blues performers, and although they attracted few European American fans and thus relatively little attention from critics and historians, they have maintained a thriving blues circuit in the South and Midwest.

10. Conclusion. Blues of one kind or another continues to be played and disseminated through recordings, concerts, and electronic media around the world, but since the 1960s it has tended to be presented in nostalgic terms, as a link to older artists, styles, and times. Some performers attempt to put their own twist on the classic patterns, but always with the consciousness that they are preserving an important heritage. When white alternative rockers like the White Stripes and black rappers like Goodie Mob and Nas explore and rework blues material, it is a way of keeping in touch with their musical or cultural roots.

As earlier blues artists have retired or died, people interested in connecting with those roots have increasingly depended on recordings. Whatever their own background, young fans are now more likely to explore the blues tradition by studying records than by listening to their relatives or neighbors, and to be particularly drawn to artists whose music suggests a different time and place. Such explorations have ranged from the jazz singer Cassandra Wilson's imaginative reworkings of Robert Johnson's Delta blues to the hip-hop artist Queen Latifah recording an album of Dinah Washington material backed by a 1940s-style band.

In the 1990s a new wave of African American players fused old rural blues with other styles: Keb' Mo' with contemporary singer-songwriter music, Alvin Youngblood Hart with hard rock, and Chris Thomas King and Corey Harris with hip hop and in the latter's case also reggae. In the 2000s, Otis Taylor and the Carolina Chocolate Drops have reached still further back, reviving pre-blues fiddle and banjo traditions.

In commercial terms, blues-rock remains the most popular style. Carried forward in the 1970s by Johnny Winter and given a new dose of soul in the early 1980s by Robert Cray, it found its dominant modern figure in 1983 when Stevie Ray Vaughan released his *Texas Flood* album. Inspired by Buddy Guy, Jimi Hendrix, and his brother Jimmie's Fabulous Thunderbirds, Vaughan was a one-man encyclopedia of blues lead guitar, and became the model for a new wave of bar bands. The 2000s brought a further blend of traditional blues with punk and alternative rock, most prominently in the work of the White Stripes and the Mississippi All-Stars.

Though its golden ages are in the past, blues remains a vital component of virtually all contemporary popular music. Any guitar-based band or soulful singer is building on the innovations of earlier blues artists. Delta slide guitar and wailing harmonica are ubiquitous in film soundtracks and television commercials, symbolizing everything from urban romance to the dusty plains of the old West. And rap has made a blues-rooted lyrical sensibility the core of modern street languages around the world. While retaining its deep association with African American tradition, blues has become an inextricable thread of global popular culture.

BIBLIOGRAPHY

A: DISCOGRAPHY AND BIOGRAPHY.

M. Leadbitter and N. Slaven: *Blues Records: January 1943 to December 1966* (London, 1968; enlarged 2/1987–94 as *Blues Records: 1943–1970*) [discography]

R.M.W. Dixon and J. Godrich: *Recording the Blues* (London, 1970)

S. Harris: *Blues Who's Who: a Biographical Dictionary of Blues Singers* (New Rochelle, NY, 1979/R)

R. Santelli: *The Big Book of Blues: a Biographical Encyclopedia* (London, 1994; rev. 2/2001)

R.M.W. Dixon, J. Godrich and H.W. Rye: *Blues and Gospel Records, 1892–1943* (Oxford, 1997) [discography]

T. Russell and C. Smith: *The Penguin Guide to Blues Recordings* (London, 2006)

B: HISTORICAL OVERVIEWS.

L. Jones (Amiri Baraka): *Blues People: Negro Music in White America* (New York, 1963)

P. Oliver: *The Story of the Blues* (London, 1969/R, 2/1997)

G. Oakley: *The Devil's Music: a History of the Blues* (London, 1976)

R. Palmer: *Deep Blues* (New York, 1981/R)

L. Cohn, ed: *Nothing but the Blues* (New York, 1993)

F. Davis: *The History of the Blues* (New York, 1995)

T. Russell: *The Blues, from Robert Johnson to Robert Cray* (London, 1997)

E. Wald: *Escaping the Delta: Robert Johnson and the Invention of the Blues* (New York, 2004)

C: PRE-BLUES, PROTO-BLUES.

H.W. Odum and G.B. Johnson: *The Negro and his Songs* (Chapel Hill, NC, 1925)

N.I. White: *American Negro Folk Songs* (Cambridge, MA, 1928)

P. Oliver: *Savannah Syncopators: African Retentions in the Blues* (London, 1970)

T. Russell: *Blacks, Whites and Blues* (London, 1970)

E. Southern: *The Music of Black Americans: a History* (New York, 1971)

L.E. Levine: *Black Culture and Black Consciousness* (Oxford, 1977/R)

P. Oliver: *Songsters and Saints: Vocal Traditions on Race Records* (London, 1984)

L. Abbott and D. Seroff: *Out of Sight: the Rise of African American Popular Music, 1889–1895* (Jackson, MS, 2003)

T. Brooks: *Lost Sounds: Blacks and the Birth of the Recording Industry, 1890–1919* (Urbana, IL, 2004)

L. Abbott and D. Seroff: *Ragged But Right: Black Travelling Shows, "Coon Songs," and the Dark Pathway to Blues and Jazz* (Jackson, MS, 2007)

D: EARLY HISTORY.

W.C. Handy: *Father of the Blues: an Autobiography* (New York, 1941)

W. Broonzy and Y. Bruynoghe: *Big Bill Blues* (London, 1955)

S. Charters: *The Country Blues* (New York, 1959/R)

S. Charters: *The Bluesmen* (New York, 1967–77/R1991 as *The Blues Makers*)

S. Charters: *Sweet as the Showers of Rain* (New York, 1977)

B. Bastin: *Red River Blues: the Blues Tradition in the Southeast* (Urbana, IL, 1986)

D.D. Harrison: *Black Pearls: Blues Queens of the 1920s* (New Brunswick, NJ, 1988)

W. Barlow: *Looking Up at Down: the Emergence of Blues Culture* (Philadelphia, 1989)

A. Lomax: *The Land Where the Blues Began* (London, 1993)

D. Edwards: *The World Don't Owe Me Nothing* (Chicago, 1997)

A. Davis: *Blues Legacies and Black Feminism: Gertrude "Ma" Rainey, Bessie Smith and Billie Holiday* (New York, 1998)

J.W. Work, L.W. Jones, and S.C. Adams: *Lost Delta Found* (Nashville, 2005)

P. Oliver: *Barrelhouse Blues: Location Recording and the Early Traditions of the Blues* (New York, 2009)

P.C. Muir: *Long Lost Blues: Popular Blues in America, 1850–1920* (Urbana, IL, 2010)

E: POSTWAR HISTORY.

P. Oliver: *Conversation with the Blues* (London, 1965, 2/1997)

C. Keil: *Urban Blues* (Chicago, 1966/R)

C. Gillett: *The Sound of the City: the Rise of Rock and Roll* (New York, 1970, 3/1996)

W. Ferris: *Blues from the Delta* (London, 1971)

J. Broven: *Walking to New Orleans: the Story of New Orleans Rhythm and Blues* (Bexhill-on-Sea, UK, 1974)

M. Haralambos: *Right On: from Blues to Soul in Black America* (London, 1974/R)

A. Shaw: *Honkers and Shouters: the Golden Years of Rhythm and Blues* (New York, 1978)

P. Guralnick: *Feel Like Going Home: Portraits in Blues and Rock 'n' Roll* (New York, 1981)

M. Rowe: *Chicago Blues: the City & the Music* (New York, 1981)

H.O. Dance: *Hard Bop: Jazz and Black Music, 1955–1965* (New York, 1993)

B.B. King with D. Ritz: *Blues All Around Me* (New York, 1996)

J. Obrecht: *Rollin' and Tumblin': the Postwar Blues Guitarists* (San Francisco, 2000)

E. Wald: *Josh White: Society Blues* (Amherst, MA, 2000)

R. Gordon: *Can't Be Satisfied: the Life and Times of Muddy Waters* (Boston, MA, 2002)

J. O'Neal and A. Van Singel: *The Voice of the Blues* (New York, 2002)

N. Cohodas: *Queen: the Life and Music of Dinah Washington* (New York, 2005)

F: CONTENT AND ANALYSIS.

P. Oliver: *Blues Fell this Morning: the Meaning of the Blues* (London, 1960, 2/1990)

P. Oliver: *Screening the Blues: Aspects of the Blues Tradition* (London, 1968/R)

H. Oster: *Living Country Blues* (Detroit, 1969)

P. Garon: *Blues and the Poetic Spirit* (London, 1975/R)

J.T. Titon: *Early Downhome Blues: a Musical and Cultural Analysis* (Urbana, IL, 1977)

D. Evans: *Big Road Blues: Tradition and Creativity in the Folk Blues* (Berkeley, CA, 1982)

S. Tracy: *Write Me a Few of Your Lines: a Blues Reader* (Amherst, MA, 1999)

ELIJAH WALD

Blue Sky Boys, the. Country music duo. Its members were William A. (Bill) Bolick (*b* Hickory, NC, 28 Oct 1917; *d* Hickory, 13 March 2008), who played mandolin and sang tenor harmony, and his brother Earl Alfred Bolick (*b* Hickory, 16 Nov 1919; *d* Suwanee, GA, 19 April 1998), who played guitar and sang lead. Their early radio appearances with fiddler Homer Sherrill included gigs in 1935 on WWNC in Asheville, North Carolina as the Good Coffee Boys and WGST in Atlanta as the Blue Ridge Hillbillies. At the Bolicks' first recording-session, for RCA Victor in Charlotte, North Carolina in June 1936, they changed their name to the Blue Sky Boys, in homage to the Blue Ridge Mountains and the nickname for western North Carolina ("Land of the Sky"). They made 90 recordings for RCA Victor in Charlotte, Rock Hill, South Carolina, and Atlanta through October 1940, including gospel numbers ("The Royal Telephone," Bluebird, 1939), ballads ("Down on the

Banks of the Ohio," Bluebird, 1936), sentimental parlor songs ("The East Bound Train," Bluebird, 1940), and songs of unrequited love ("Who Wouldn't Be Lonely," Bluebird, 1938). Following military service during World War II, the Bolicks reformed the Blue Sky Boys in 1946, adding a fiddler (Samuel "Curley" Parker) and a bassist; five more RCA recording-sessions followed through March 1950. The duo retired in 1951, but reunited in 1963 to record two Starday albums in Nashville; three additional recording sessions followed between 1965 and 1976, in addition to a 1964 live album recorded at the University of Illinois. The Bolicks' sweet harmony-singing, accompanied by Earl's steady guitar and Bill's non-chorded mandolin playing (frequently employing tremolo), influenced performers such as Jim and Jesse (McReynolds), Don Reno, the Louvin Brothers, Johnny and Jack, and the Everly Brothers.

BIBLIOGRAPHY

W.W. Daniel: "Bill and Earl Bolick Remember the Blue Sky Boys," *Bluegrass Unlimited*, xvi/3 (1981), 14–21

C.K. Wolfe: "The Blue Sky Boys," *Classic Country: Legends of Country Music* (New York, 2000), 97–102

B. Malone: [liner notes], *The Blue Sky Boys: the Sunny Side of Life*, Bear Family BCD 15951 (2003)

ANTHONY S. LIS

Blues progression. The underlying harmonic structure of the blues. In the broadest sense, the term can refer to the harmonic progression of any piece called a BLUES, including songs whose harmonies bear no relation to a typical blues progression. In the narrow sense, it refers to a flexible, cyclic 12-bar structure, consisting of three four-bar phrases with the chord pattern shown in ex.1. Many variants of this pattern are possible: frequently IV is used in place of I in bar 2 or in place of V in bar 10. Country blues guitarists characteristically vary the rhythms of the basic progression and sometimes maintain a tonic drone on the bass strings; in this case a blues harmonic progression may be intimated by the vocal and treble-string melodies. Early sheet music publications, studio recordings, and field recordings document a number of established variants from the standard blues pattern, making it impossible to establish an original form of the blues progression.

Ex.1 Basic harmonic structure of the 12-bar blues progression

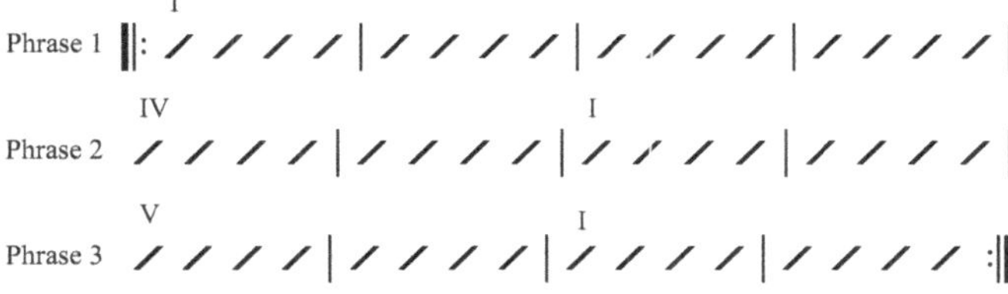

Jazz, particularly bop, musicians took advantage of the flexibility inherent in the simple 12-bar scheme and often presented it in new guises using a variety of passing and substitute harmonies. An extreme example is Charlie Parker's "Blues for Alice" (1951, on the EP *Charlie Parker*, 1951–3, Clef) which includes interpolated secondary dominant progressions. A minor-mode form of the blues progression also exists, which later became a common characteristic in soul jazz. Broadly speaking, the blues progression entered the repertory of rock musicians from two distinct sources: rock-and-roll and country and urban blues. It is found in its simplest form in Bill Haley's "Rock around the Clock" (1954) and across the spectrum of rock and roll, including Jerry Lee Lewis's "Whole Lotta Shakin' Goin' On" (1957) and Chuck Berry's "Johnny B. Goode" (1958). The 12-bar pattern and its variants entered the work of the Beach Boys ("Surfin' USA," 1963), the Beatles ("A Hard Day's Night," 1964), and the Rolling Stones ("19th Nervous Breakdown," 1966). By this point it had lost touch with the conventionalized *AAB* pattern of the blues lyric. In the later 1960s BLUES ROCK musicians took renewed inspiration from the recordings of such early blues musicians as Robert Johnson as well as the urban electric blues of Muddy Waters.

BARRY KERNFELD, ALLAN F. MOORE/R

Blues rock. A style of popular music derived from American derivatives of the blues that flowered in the 1960s when British guitarists emulated and expanded upon imported American ROCK AND ROLL and BLUES records. Typical instrumentation consists of electric guitars, electric bass, full drum kit, and, occasionally, keyboards. Driven by the timbre and the energy of 1950s rock and roll as well as the improvisatory character of blues and jazz, the sound of blues rock was that of a fast-paced virtuosic instrumental jam performed over standard blues progressions. Vocals often were of secondary importance; vocal delivery drew on rock and blues traditions, but lyrics were not consistently faithful to classic blues form.

Lonnie Mack, Howlin' Wolf, and Muddy Waters were among the many African American electric blues artists who contributed towards the crystallization of the genre. Their work influenced the early blues rock produced by admiring British acts such as the Savoy Brown Blues Band, Fleetwood Mac, Free, Cream, and Alexis Korner. Blues rock artists, predominantly white performers, were criticized, like many of their musical predecessors, for appropriating black music and capitalizing on its sale to white audiences. Yet these performers also helped to introduce American audiences to the richness of its blues heritage. Eventually such American musicians as Johnny Winters, Mike Bloomfield, Paul Butterfield, and Jimi Hendrix also thrived in the genre.

BIBLIOGRAPHY

P. Guralnick: *Feel like Going Home: Portraits in Blues and Rock 'n' Roll* (Boston, 1971/*R*)

S. McStravick and J. Roos, eds.: *Blues-Rock Explosion* (Mission Viejo, CA, 2001)

MICKEY VALLEE

Bluiett, Hamiet (*b* Lovejoy, nr East St. Louis, IL, 16 Sept 1940). Jazz baritone saxophonist. He grew up outside of St. Louis in a musical family. His aunt, a choir director, gave him piano lessons as a young child before he switched to trumpet and eventually clarinet at the age of nine. He briefly attended Southern Illinois University, studying flute and picking up baritone saxophone, before joining the navy in 1959. After serving his enlistment in military bands, Bluiett moved to St. Louis and began playing mostly baritone saxophone with Julius Hemphill, Oliver Lake, and Lester and Joseph Bowie. Together with Hemphill he founded the Black Artists Group, an interdisciplinary arts collective. After moving to New York (1969) he played with Olatunji, the Thad Jones–Mel Lewis Orchestra, Sam Rivers' large ensemble, and Charles Mingus' quintet (1972–4). While with Mingus he also worked with Abdullah Ibrahim's big band and recorded alongside Hemphill and Lake for Anthony Braxton (*New York, Fall 1974*, 1974, Ari.). Bluiett, Hemphill, and Lake added David Murray for a December 1976 quartet concert in New Orleans and became the critically acclaimed and highly influential World Saxophone Quartet, remaining at the forefront of improvised music for three decades and 20 albums. Additional activity as a leader and sideman includes work with Gil Evans, Randy Weston, Don Pullen, and James "Blood" Ulmer, among others. Equally comfortable anchoring a big band's reed section or exploring the avant-garde with the World Saxophone Quartet, Bluiett's creative voice finds no duplicate in modern jazz.

BIBLIOGRAPHY

C. Stern: "Stars on the Rise: Hamiet Bluiett," *DB*, xlv/15 (1978), 24

L. Van Trikt: "Hamiet Bluiett: Interview," *Cadence*, xii/5 (1986), 5

C. Allen: "Hamiet Bluiett" <http://www.allaboutjazz.com/php/article.php?id=1866> (2004)

BARRY LONG

Blumenfeld, Harold (*b* Seattle, WA, 15 Oct 1923). Composer and conductor. He was educated at the Eastman School (1941–3), Yale University (BM 1948, MM 1949), and the University of Zurich (1948); his principal teachers in composition were Bernard Rogers and Paul Hindemith. During several summers at the Berkshire Music Center (1949–52), he trained as a conductor with Robert Shaw and Leonard Bernstein and worked as stage director for Boris Goldovsky. Blumenfeld has held academic positions at Queens College, CUNY (1971–2) and Washington University, St. Louis (1950–89), where he was appointed professor emeritus upon his retirement. He has received awards from the Martha Baird Rockefeller Fund (1975), the American Academy and Institute of Arts and Letters (1977), and the NEA (1980), as well as a Missouri Composer Commission. During the 1960s, Blumenfeld devoted a major share of his energies to directing opera in St. Louis, where he campaigned for adequate production standards and cooperation within the local community. As director of the Opera Theatre of St. Louis (1962–6) and the Washington University Opera Studio (1960–71), he offered an innovative mixture of the standard repertory, Baroque opera, and 20th-century works.

Blumenfeld developed his early compositional style while under the influence of Hindemith, but later abandoned this course in favor of the approaches of such composers as Berio, Crumb, and Carter. About 1970, he began to relinquish his responsibilities as an opera director to concentrate on composing; all of his subsequent works focus on the declamation of texts, around which he weaves delicate, timbrally subtle accompaniments, often with chamber ensembles, percussion instruments, and extended techniques for piano. His music frequently employs contrapuntal textures and calls for the spatial separation of performance forces.

Blumenfeld was the first composer to devote himself exhaustively to the poetry of Arthur Rimbaud. In the 1980s and 1990s, he immersed himself in Rimbaud's poetry and writings and composed a variety of pieces that culminated with a two-act opera, *Seasons in Hell* (1996). The opera concentrates on the adventures of the adolescent *poèt maudit* and his later disastrous fortune-seeking escapades in Africa. His next opera, *Borgia Infami* (2001), is based on the German novelist Klabund's Borgia exposé and Victor Hugo's ultra-operatic drama *Lucrece Borgia*. With a libretto by Charles Kondrak, it dramatizes the obsessions and crimes of the infamous Spanish family, connecting their story to the present. The Gaylord Music Library at Washington University, St. Louis, holds a comprehensive collection of his materials, including correspondence and manuscripts. His music has been recorded on Centaur Records and Vox.

WORKS

(selective list)

Opera: Amphitryon 4 (3, after Molière), 1962, arr. orch, 1962; Fritzi (1, C. Kondek, after Molnar), 1979; Four-score: an Opera of Opposites (2, Kondek, after Nestroy: Haus der Temperamente), 1981–5; Seasons in Hell (after Rimbaud), 1996; Borgia Infami (Kondrak), 2001

Orch: Miniature Ov., 1958; Contrasts, 1961–2

Inst: Transformations, pf, 1963; Expansions, wind quintet, 1964; Movts, brass septet, 1965; Night Music, gui, 1973, withdrawn

Choral: See Here the Fallen, SATB, orch, 1943; 3 Scottish Poems, male vv, 1948–50; War Lament (S. Sassoon), SATB, gui, 1970; Song of Innocence (W. Blake), T, Mez, large chorus, chbr chorus, orch, 1973; other works

Vocal: Rilke, 3 songs, 1v, gui, 1975; Circle of the Eye (T. McKeown), song cycle, medium v, pf, 1975; Starfires (P. Hanson), Mez, T, orch, 1975; La vie antérieure (C. Baudelaire), cant., Bar, Mez, T, 13 insts, 1976; Voyages (H. Crane), cant., Bar, va, gui, 3 perc, 1977; Uščnost' [Essence] (O. Mandelstam), 9 songs, medium v, pf, 1979, retitled Silentium; La voix reconnue (P. Verlaine), cant., T, S, vc, pf, 1980; La face cendrée (A. Rimbaud), cant., S, vc, pf, 1981; other works

Principal publishers: Belwin-Mills, Galaxy

BIBLIOGRAPHY

EwenD

S. Jenkins, Jr.: "Waiting at the Gateway," *ON*, xxxii/26 (1968), 19

J. Wierzbicki: "Blumenfeld's Music," *St. Louis Globe-Democrat* (3–4 Feb 1979)

RICHARD S. JAMES/ANDERS TOBIASON

Blumenschein, W(illiam) L(eonard) (*b* Brensbach, Germany, 16 Dec 1849; *d* Dayton, OH, 27 March 1916). Conductor, organist, teacher, and composer of German origin. Blumenschein studied in Leipzig and after immigrating first settled in Pittsburgh. He moved to Ohio in 1876 to work briefly as an organist and choral conductor in the Ohio River towns of Portsmouth and Ironton. In 1878 he transferred to Dayton to become organist of the Third Presbyterian Church and from 1878 to

1907 conductor of the Dayton Philharmonic Society (as of 1913, the Dayton Choral Society), an ensemble of around 100 members that concentrated on presenting major works by Handel, Haydn, Mendelssohn, and others. He also conducted German singing societies in Indianapolis and Springfield, Ohio, as well as *Sängerfeste*, or regional gatherings of these German singing societies, in Dayton and Springfield. In addition he offered private lessons in piano and voice. He is supposed to have written about 150 pieces, although the highest opus number found is 127, a Polonaise for piano published in 1908. He also left church anthems (for example, *The Blessings*, op.21, for solo tenor, choir and organ [1893], and *My soul doth magnify the Lord*, op.60 [1895]), liturgical music, solo songs, and character pieces for the piano (for example, a *Coquette Gavotte*, op.41 [1891] and *Napolitana, Danse Caracteristque*, op.112 [1906]).

BIBLIOGRAPHY

H.W. Crew: *History of Dayton, Ohio. With Portraits and Biographical Sketches of Some of Its Pioneer and Prominent Citizens* (Dayton, OH, 1889)

F. Conover, ed.: *Centennial Portrait and Biographical Record of the City of Dayton and of Montgomery County, Ohio* (Chicago, 1897)

WILLIAM OSBORNE

Blye (Richardson), Birdice [Berdice, Birdie] (*b* Iowa, 1871; *d* Chicago, IL, 23 June 1935). Pianist. At a young age she toured Europe and the United States. In New York she studied piano with RAFAEL JOSEFFY and Edmund Neupert, and in London she attended the Royal Academy of Music. In Berlin she studied violin with Joseph Joachim at the Königliche Hochschule, piano with Ernst Rudorff, voice with Adolf Schulze, counterpoint and ensemble with Woldemar Bargiel, and musical form with Philipp Spitta, and with Hans von Bülow and ANTON RUBINSTEIN. In the 1890s she played with Anton Seidl's orchestra in New York. In Europe she performed in concerts, and privately, for the Baroness Rothschild, the Emperor Eugenie, and Princess Bismarck; in Washington, DC, she played in the White House on two occasions. Blye wrote her reminiscences of Rubinstein for the *Musical Courier*, and she lectured on the subject. In 1903 she published her "Impressions of the Great Musician" in the *Rosary Magazine*. She continued her performances until 1928: in 1903 and 1907 in New York, in 1906 with the Chicago Orchestra, in 1910 in Nashville, in 1922 in Monterey, and in 1928 in London for the Hyde Park Concerts. She favored Steinway pianos throughout her career.

BIBLIOGRAPHY

F.E. Willard and M.A. Rice Livermore: *A Woman of the Century* (Buffalo, 1893), 100 only

F. Ffrench, ed.: *Music and Musicians in Chicago* (New York, 1899/R), 73–4

VALERIA WENDEROTH

Blyth, Samuel (*b* Salem, MA, bap. 13 May 1744; bur. Salem, MA, 13 Jan 1795). Craftsman and organist. He worked all his life in Salem, where from 1766 to 1783 he occasionally played the organ at St. Peter's Church. He also ran a boarding school for girls, and is recorded in Salem account books as a painter of ships, carriages, carpets, and canisters; a gilder; and a maker of venetian blinds. Only one musical instrument by him is known: a spinet from about 1785, now in the Essex Institute, Salem. It is one of the few extant examples of 18th-century American plucked-string keyboard instruments, and is modeled on English types. The instrument has a range of *G/B* to f''' and has a mahogany case, with the painted inscription "Samuel Blyth SALEM Massachusetts Fecit" over the keyboard. A bill dated 7 February 1786 from Samuel Blyth to Mrs Margaret Barton "To making a Spinnett for her daughter—L 18 . . 0–0" is also in the Essex Institute.

BIBLIOGRAPHY

R. Russell: *The Harpsichord and Clavichord* (London, 1959, 2/1973)

N.F. Little: "The Blyths of Salem: Benjamin, Limner in Crayon and Oil, and Samuel, Painter and Cabinetmaker," *Essex Institute Historical Collections*, cviii (1972), 49–57

CYNTHIA ADAMS HOOVER

Blythe, Arthur (Murray) (*b* Los Angeles, CA, 7 May 1940). Alto saxophonist. He is known for his penetrating saxophone sound and ever-growing and changing musical style. His music is grounded in mainstream jazz, but he has also explored the avant garde. At the age of four or five, he moved with his family from Los Angeles to San Diego, where he began his musical training. His early experiences involved Mexican music as well as rhythm and blues. In his first professional engagement Blythe netted a profit of 13 cents. During this early stage of his career he played a mixture of songs from the mariachi and rhythm-and-blues traditions and his style reflected the influence of such saxophonists as Kirkland Bradford of the Jimmy Lunceford band. In the 1960s he moved back to Los Angeles and began to work in the pianist Horace Tapscott's ensemble, in which he performed the music of Duke Ellington, Charlie Parker, and John Coltrane. In the 1970s Blythe moved to New York and began working with Chico Hamilton and the Gil Evans Orchestra in addition to his own projects. He also performed in Europe with Evans, the Lester Bowie Quintet, and his own ensembles. From the mid-1990s he has lived in Farmdale, California, and continued to record as a leader. Among his most notable recordings are *Lenox Avenue Breakdown* (1979, Col.) and *Illusions* (1980, Col.).

E. RON HORTON

BMG [Bertelsmann Music Group]. German record and distribution company. It was formally established by Bertelsmann AG, a multinational media corporation, in 1987 with headquarters in Gütersloh, Germany. As an outgrowth of Bertelsmann's core publishing business, Ariola Records was formed in Germany in the late 1950s, backed by Bertelsmann investments; it subsequently spawned a host of international labels through the 1970s, including the short-lived Ariola America, which opened in 1975.

In August 1979, the Ariola-Eurodisc GmbH unit of Bertelsmann acquired Arista Records. In 1986, after RCA Records' parent company had been bought by

General Electric, Bertelsmann purchased RCA's music business, launching the Bertelsmann Music Group (BMG) in 1987, making it one of the so-called "Big Six" international record conglomerates. Its massive catalog holdings included recordings from Elvis Presley, Tommy Dorsey, Dolly Parton, Glenn Miller, Whitney Houston, Earl "Fatha" Hines, Jefferson Airplane, Henry Mancini, George Gershwin, and thousands more, as RCA and its associated labels had a history stretching back to the 1920s. The newly-formed corporation retired the RCA imprint, reissuing albums on and signing new artists to BMG.

The label's country division, BNA, was established in 1991 as a stand alone imprint that was acquired by Bertelsmann in 1993. In May 1992, BMG purchased 50% of acoustic music label Windham Hill, acquiring the remaining half in January 1996. In 2002, BMG completed its purchase of the Zomba Group, bringing with it the Jive Records label, then home to the likes of R. Kelly, Britney Spears, the Backstreet Boys, 'N Sync, and others.

Bertelsmann and Sony entered into a joint venture agreement in October of 2004 that meshed their distribution networks, resulting in a corporate streamlining and a new name: Sony BMG Music Entertainment. In August 2008, Sony Corp. bought out Bertelsmann's 50% stake in the joint venture, retired the BMG name and logo, and reactivated the old RCA Records imprint. The newly-merged enterprise was christened Sony Music Entertainment Inc., and comprises 15 main labels: Columbia, Columbia Nashville, Arista, BNA, Epic, Jive, J, Legacy, Masterworks, Provident, RCA, RCA Nashville, RocNation, Sony Music Latin, and Verity; it operates as a unit of Sony Corporation of America. Current artists of note include Avril Lavigne, Beyoncé, Christina Aguilera, Foo Fighters, Shakira, Pitbull, Kenny Chesney, Rod Stewart, Santana, Ke$ha, and others.

BIBLIOGRAPHY

F. Dannen: *Hit Men: Power Brokers and Fast Money Inside the Music Business* (New York, 1990)

J. Shepherd and others, eds.: *Continuum Encyclopedia Of Popular Music Of The World*, i, *Media, Industry, and Society* (New York, 2003)

THANE TIERNEY

BMI. *See* Broadcast music, inc.

Boardman (Meske), Eunice (Louise) (*b* Cordova, IL, 27 Jan 1926; *d* Bettendorf, IA, 5 May 2009). Music educator. She attended Cornell College in Mount Vernon, Iowa (BA 1947), Columbia University Teachers College (EdM 1951), and the University of Illinois (EdD 1964). She taught in the public schools of Postville (1947–9), Maquoketa (1949–51), Clinton (1951–2), and Grinnell (1952–6), Iowa, and in collegiate positions at Northern Illinois State University (1956–7), Wichita State University (1957–72), Illinois State University, Normal (1972–4), Roosevelt University (1973–5), University of Wisconsin, Madison (1975–88), and University of Illinois at Urbana-Champaign (1988–98). She held leadership positions for the University of Wisconsin School of Music (director, 1980–90), Society for Music Teacher Education of the Music Educators National Conference (chair, 1986–8), *Bulletin of the Council for Research in Music Education* (co-editor, 1993–9), and *International Journal of Education & the Arts* (editorial board, 1999–2009). She co-authored or edited several music textbooks and series, including *Musical Growth in the Elementary School* (1963, 6/1996), *The Music Book* (1980, 2/1984), *Dimensions of Musical Thinking* (1989), and *Dimensions of Musical Learning and Teaching* (2002). She was awarded a Distinguished Service Award from the Wisconsin Music Educators Association (1985) and inducted into the Music Educators Hall of Fame (2004).

BIBLIOGRAPHY

K.M. Baker: *Significant Experiences, Influences and Relationships in the Educational and Professional Development of Three Music Educators: Gretchen Hieronymus Beall, Eunice Louise Boardman, and Mary Henderson Palmer* (diss., U. of Illinois at Urbana-Champaign, 1992)

SHELLY C. COOPER

Board of Music Trade. Trade organization founded in New York in 1855 by 27 leading music publishers in reaction to steps taken by the New York firm William Hall & Sons to halve the list prices of non-copyrighted music. The member publishers of the group, which included Oliver Ditson in Boston, S. Brainard & Sons in Cleveland, and Horace Waters in New York, were able to reach a compromise whereby the prices for this music would be reduced by only 20%. The board issued a *Complete Catalogue of Sheet Music and Musical Works* (1870/*R*), a comprehensive list of all the works published by its members and the closest the industry had come to producing a list of music in print. After a slow decline, the board held its last meeting in 1895; it was succeeded in the same year by the Music publishers association of the united states. Any allusions to the Music Publishers' Association of the Music Publishers' Board of Trade in historical materials published before 1895 refer to the Board of Music Trade.

BIBLIOGRAPHY

D.J. Epstein: "Music Publishing in the Age of Piracy: the Board of Music Trade and its Catalogue," *Notes*, xxxi (1974–5), 7

DENA J. EPSTEIN

Boas, Franz (*b* Minden, Germany, 9 July 1858; *d* New York, NY, 21 Dec 1942). Anthropologist and ethnomusicologist of German birth. He was trained at Heidelberg, Berlin, and Kiel as a physicist and geographer (1877–81), and, having gone to Baffin Island, Canada, to do a survey of Cumberland Sound, he went on to compare Inuit perceptions of space with his own technical mapping. It was during his stay among the Inuits in 1883–4 that he formulated the anthropological perspectives and field methodology that were to shape the character of early 20th-century American anthropology. On his return to Berlin, he became interested in the methods used by Carl Stumpf, Hornbostel, and Herzog in the study of music in other cultures. In 1886 Boas returned to North America to work among the Bella Coola Indians of the Pacific Northwest coast; in 1888 he took a post teaching anthropology at Clark University and settled in the United States, having decided to make Native Americans the center of his anthropological work.

Boas was well acquainted with other pioneers in the study of Native American music, including Alice Cunningham Fletcher, J. Walter Fewkes, and Frances Densmore, with whom he was associated through the Bureau of American Ethnology. For some publications Boas and Fletcher shared the services of John Comfort Fillmore as transcriber for their recordings of indigenous melodies, and in 1893, while chief anthropological assistant at the World's Columbian Exposition in Chicago, Boas and Benjamin Ives Gilman simultaneously recorded a performance in the Kwakiutl exhibit.

Boas was professor of anthropology at Columbia University (1899–1936), and in his teaching he emphasized that music was vital to the integrated ethnological study of indigenous cultures. While curator of ethnology at the American Museum of Natural History (1901–5), he organized the Jesup North Pacific Expedition (1902–6), the first comprehensive anthropological survey of the north circumpolar region, during which he and his associates made sound and film recordings. He urged his students to collect music along with other ethnological data. He recorded much material among the Kwakiutl and neighboring tribes in British Columbia and among the Yoruba in Africa. His publications of the period 1887–1900 include many transcriptions: "The Central Eskimo" (1888) and "The Social Organization and the Secret Societies of the Kwakiutl Indians" (1897) served as models for later ethnological treatises that included music. After 1900 Boas developed a keen interest in linguistics and the closely linked oral arts and their accompanying forms (tale and myth, poetry, music, and dance), emphasizing the interrelationship of different aspects of culture within the whole cultural frame. His publications (more than 600 items) often included song texts with translations.

WRITINGS

"Poetry and Music of some North American Tribes," *Science*, ix (1887), 383–5

"The Central Eskimo," *Bureau of American Ethnology: Annual Report, 1884–1885*, vi (1888), 399–669; pubd separately (Lincoln, NE, 1964)

"Second General Report of the Indians of British Columbia," *Report of the British Association for the Advancement of Science*, lx (1891), 562–715

"Eskimo Tales and Songs," *Journal of American Folklore*, vii (1894), 45–50

"The Social Organization and the Secret Societies of the Kwakiutl Indians," *Report of the United States National Museum, 1895* (1897), 311–753

"The Mythology of the Bella Coola Indians," *Anthropological Papers of the American Museum of Natural History*, ii (1900), 25–127

Primitive Art (Oslo, 1927/*R*)

ed.: *General Anthropology* (New York, 1938/*R*) [incl. "Literature, Music and Dance," 589–608; "Music and Folk-Lore," 609–26]

ed.: *The Function of Dance in Human Society* (New York, 1944, 2/1972) [incl. "Dance and Music in the Life of the Northwest Coast Indians of North America (Kwakiutl)," 5–9]

ed. R.P. Rohner: *The Ethnography of Franz Boas* (Chicago, 1969) [diaries and letters, 1886–1931]

ed. G.W. Stocking: *The Shaping of American Anthropology, 1883–1911: a Franz Boas Reader* (New York, 1974/*R*)

ed. C.C. Knötsch: *Franz Boas bei den kanadischen Inuit im Jahre 1883–1884* (Bonn, 1992; Eng. trans., 1998) [diaries and letters]

ed. A. Jonaitis: *A Wealth of Thought: Franz Boas on Native American Art* (Seattle, 1995)

BIBLIOGRAPHY

B. Laufer, ed.: *Boas Anniversary Volume: Anthropological Papers Written in Honor of Franz Boas* (New York, 1906) [incl. list of pubns, 515–40]

"Franz Boas, 1858–1942," *American Anthropologist*, new ser., xlv/3, pt 2 [suppl.61] (1943) [memorial issue; incl. A.L. Kroeber: "Franz Boas: the Man," 5–26; R. Benedict: "Franz Boas as an Ethnologist," 27–34; G.A. Reichard: "Franz Boas and Folklore," 52–7; and complete list of writings, 67–109]

R.H. Lowie: "Biographical Memoir of Franz Boas, 1858–1942," *Biographical Memoirs* [National Academy of Sciences], xxiv (Washington, DC, 1947), 303–22

M.J. Herskovits: *Franz Boas: the Science of Man in the Making* (New York, 1953/*R*)

B. Nettl: *North American Indian Musical Styles* (Philadelphia, 1954)

L.A. White: *The Ethnography and Ethnology of Franz Boas* (Austin, 1963)

R. Darnell: *The Development of American Anthropology, 1879–1920: from the Bureau of American Ethnology to Franz Boas* (Philadelphia, 1969)

Guide to the Microfilm Collection of the Professional Papers of Franz Boas (Wilmington, DE, 1972)

M. Hyatt: *Franz Boas, Social Activist: the Dynamics of Ethnicity* (New York, 1990)

J.E. Liss: *The Cosmopolitan Imagination: Franz Boas and the Development of American Anthropology* (diss., U. of California, Berkeley, 1990)

M. Dürr: *Franz Boas: Ethnologe, Anthropologe, Sprachwissenschaftler*, Staatsbibliothek zu Berlin, 17 Dec 1992–6 March 1993 (Berlin, 1992) [exhibition catalog]

V. Rodekamp, ed.: *Franz Boas, 1858–1942: eine amerikanischer Anthropologe aus Minden* (Bielefeld, Germany, 1994)

SUE CAROLE DEVALE/R

Boatner, Edward Hammond (*b* New Orleans, LA, 13 Nov 1898; *d* New York, NY, 16 June 1981). Composer. The son of a traveling minister, he became familiar with African American religious folk music at an early age. He studied at Western University (1916), the Boston Conservatory (1921), and the Chicago College of Music (BM 1932). While in Boston, he studied composition with R. NATHANIEL DETT, who shared his interest in spirituals, and became a featured soloist in Dett's ensemble, the Hampton Institute Singers. In 1925 he moved to Chicago, where he was active as a singer, organist, and choral director, serving from 1925 to 1931 as music director for the National Baptist Convention. After teaching in Texas at Samuel Huston College and Wiley College, he moved to New York (1933), where he opened the Edward Boatner Studio.

Boatner's over 200 arrangements of African American spirituals are his primary musical legacy. Since the 1920s they have been performed by singers such as Marian Anderson, Roland Hayes, Leontyne Price, and Paul Robeson. In addition to his collection *Thirty Afro-American Choral Spirituals* (1971), he published several stage works and pedagogical manuals.

BIBLIOGRAPHY

SouthernB

E. Southern: *The Music of Black Americans: a History* (New York, 1971, 3/1997)

A. Tischler: *Fifteen Black American Composers: a Bibliography of their Works* (Detroit, 1981)

G. Glover: "The Life and Career of Edward Boatner and Inventory of the Boatner Papers at the Schomberg Center," *American Music Research Center Journal*, viii–ix (1998–9), 89–106

WILLIE STRONG/R

Boatwright, Howard (Leake) (*b* Newport News, VA, 16 March 1918; *d* Syracuse, NY, 20 Feb 1999). Composer, violinist, and musicologist. He was trained as a violinist in Norfolk, Virginia, by Israel Feldman, made his debut at New York Town Hall in 1942, and was assistant professor of violin at the University of Texas, Austin, from 1943 to 1945. At Yale University (BM 1947, MM 1948) he studied theory and composition and viola d'amore with PAUL HINDEMITH, at whose urging he stayed on as assistant professor of music theory. As music director at St. Thomas's Church, New Haven (1949–64), Boatwright established a reputation as a pioneer in the performance of early choral music. While in New Haven he also served as conductor of the Yale University Orchestra from 1952 to 1960 and was concertmaster of the New Haven SO (1950–62). He became dean of the school of music at Syracuse University in 1964, and from 1971 was professor of music in composition and theory. He was a Fulbright lecturer in India during the year 1959–60 and received a Fulbright grant to study in Romania, 1971–2. A pioneering scholar of Ives, he was elected to the board of directors of the Charles Ives Society in 1975.

He initially concentrated on sacred choral music and composed choral works as well as works for solo voice with piano or instruments. Of his instrumental works, the most notable are the Quartet for clarinet and strings, which received the award of the Society for the Publication of American Music in 1962, the Symphony, and String Quartet no.2. His earliest choral works are modal; subsequently the chamber works, in particular, were influenced by Hindemith's middle-period style. In 1966 Boatwright began to develop a style he described as "dodecaphonic, though not serial," in which he appropriated the total chromatic resource while exercising control over harmony, within the context of a layered, contrapuntal approach. This technique (described in *Chromaticism*, Fayetteville, NY, 1994) is demonstrated in String Quartet no.2, a work that is consistent in style but also impressive in its ability to project a wide variety of moods. A versatile and creative musician, Boatwright also demonstrated an unusually wide breadth of erudition as a scholar.

WRITINGS

Introduction to the Theory of Music (New York, 1956)

Indian Classical Music and the Western Listener (Bombay, 1960)

"Ives' Quarter-Tone Impressions," *PNM*, iii/2 (1964–5), 22–31

"Paul Hindemith's Performances of Old Music," *Hindemith-Jb 1973*, 39–62

Chromaticism: Theory and Practice (Fayetteville, NY, 1994)

WORKS

Orch: A Song for St Cecilia's Day, large str ens, 1948; Variations, small orch, 1949; Sym., 1976

Choral: The Women of Trachis (Sophocles, trans. E. Pound), 6 choruses, female vv, chbr orch, 1955; Mass, C, 1958; The Passion According to St Matthew, solo vv, SATB, org, 1962; Canticle of the Sun (St Francis of Assisi), S, SATB, orch, 1963; Music for Temple Service, Bar, SATB, org, 1969; A Song for St Cecilia's Day, S, SATB, orch, 1981; Nunc dimittis and Magnificat, SATB, org, 1997; over 20 other works incl. 4 masses, many choral partsongs

Chbr and solo inst: Str Qt no.1, 1947; Trio, 2 vn, va, 1948; Serenade, 2 str, 2 wind, 1952; Qt, cl, str, 1958; Str Qt no.2, 1974; 12 Pieces for Vn Alone, 1977; Sonata, cl, pf, 1980; other chbr and kbd works, incl. Orgelbuch, 8 preludes, org

Other vocal: The Ship of Death (D.H. Lawrence), S, A, T, B, str qt, 1966; The Lament of Mary Stuart (Carissimi cant. text), S, hpd/pf, opt vc, 1968; 6 Prayers of Kierkegaard (trans. P. LeFevre), S, pf, 1978; Prologue, Narrative and Lament (W. Whitman), T, str qt, 1987; From Joy to Fire (U. Vaughan Williams), Mez, pf, 1989; Adoration and Longing (Song of Solomon), S, str qt, 1991; 5 Poems of Sylvia Plath, S, pf, 1993; *c*50 songs

Principal publishers: Oxford UP, Walnut Grove

BIBLIOGRAPHY

EwenD

J. Knapp: "Howard Boatwright: an American Master of choral Music," *American Choral Review*, vi/1 (1963), 1

J.W. Sobaskie: "Associative Harmony: the Reciprocity of Ideas in musical Space," *ITO*, x/1–2 (1987), 31–64

A. Kozinn: "Howard Boatwright, Violinist, Composer and Professor, 80," *New York Times* (24 Feb 1999) [obituary]

J. Kay: *An Introduction to the Songs of Howard Boatwright: an Interpretive Approach* (diss., Boston U., 2008)

TERENCE J. O'GRADY/R

Boatwright, McHenry (*b* Tennille, GA, 29 Feb 1928; *d* New York, NY, 5 Nov 1994). Bass-baritone. He was educated at the New England Conservatory, where he obtained degrees in piano (BM 1950) and singing (BM 1954). During this time he won two Marian Anderson awards (1953 and 1954) and the Arthur Fiedler Voice Contest. His professional concert debut was at Jordan Hall, Boston, in February 1956, though he had earlier performed in a recording of Berlioz's *La Damnation de Faust* with the Boston SO conducted by Charles Munch. As a result of winning the National Federation of Music Clubs competition in 1957, he made his Town Hall debut in January, 1958. That year he also made his operatic debut, singing Arkel (*Pelléas et Mélisande*) with the New England Opera Theater. He was heard in opera, in concert, and with orchestras around the world. He created the central role in Schuller's opera *The Visitation* in Hamburg, Germany (12 October 1966), and he repeated the role when the Hamburg company made its American debut at the Metropolitan Opera House in 1967. Among his recorded performances is that of Crown in Gershwin's *Porgy and Bess*. He possessed strength and vibrancy in all registers, but it was as an interpreter that he was acclaimed, for fully projecting the inner drama, passion, and mood of the music he performed.

BIBLIOGRAPHY

SouthernB

D.J. Soria: "Artist Life," *HiFi/MusAm*, xvii/5 (1967), 5 only

THOR ECKERT JR./R

Bobo, Roger (*b* Los Angeles, CA, 8 June 1938). Tuba player and pedagogue. He studied from 1956 to 1961 with Donald Knaub, and EMORY REMINGTON at the Eastman School of Music, and subsequently with WILLIAM BELL and Robert Marsteller. He was a member of the Rochester PO (1956–62), Amsterdam's Royal

Concertgebouw Orchestra (1962–4), and the Los Angeles PO (1964–89). From 1965 to 1975 he was also a member of the Los Angeles Brass Quintet. During the 1970s and 80s Bobo played in studio orchestras for film soundtracks and commercial recordings.

As a pedagogue, Bobo has led master classes around the world, most notably at Domaine Forget in Quebec, Canada. In the 1990s, Bobo taught mainly in Europe at the Rotterdam Conservatory, Bern Conservatory, Fiesole School of Music, Lausanne Conservatory, and Royal Northern College of Music. Since 2006, Bobo has been on the faculty at the Musashino School of Music in Tokyo, Japan.

Bobo has made significant contributions as a soloist. In March 1961 he gave the first ever Carnegie Hall recital for solo tuba. About 100 solo pieces have been written for him, including concertos by William Kraft (1977) and Alexander Arutiunian (1992). He has given many performances of Ralph Vaughan William's Tuba Concerto with leading orchestras worldwide. He has made seven solo discs of tuba repertory, and has also written *Mastering the Tuba* (Bulle, 1993). He retired from performance in 2001, but remains active as a conductor and teacher.

BIBLIOGRAPHY

R. Hepola: "Roger Bobo Talks Tuba," *Instrumentalist*, xxxii (1977), 60–5

T. McCaslin: "Catching up with Roger Bobo," *ITEA Journal*, xxxv/4 (2008), 38–46

EDWARD H. TARR/NATHAN PLATTE

Bobri [Bobritsky], **Vladimir (Vassilievich)** (*b* Kharkiv, Ukraine, 13 May 1898; *d* Rosendale, NY, Nov 1986). Guitarist and editor of Ukrainian birth. His study of art at the Imperial Kharkiv Art School was halted by the Russian Revolution. He immigrated to the United States in 1922, and became successful in New York as a commercial artist. The classical guitar, to which Andrés Segovia first drew his attention in New York on a tour in 1928, captured Bobri's deep interest. He became president of the Society of the Classic Guitar in 1936 and editor of its publication *The Guitar Review* (*Guitar Review* from 1961) in 1946. His own guitar pieces, editions of guitar music, pedagogical publications, and contributions to *Guitar Review* for over 35 years attest to his devotion to the instrument. He wrote *The Segovia Technique* (New York, 1972) and compiled *A Musical Voyage with 2 Guitars* (New York 1974), a collection of arrangements and original music by himself and Carl Miller.

THOMAS F. HECK/R

Bocelli, Andrea (*b* Lajatico, Italy, 22 Sept 1958). Italian tenor. Blind from the age of 12, Bocelli is an extremely popular international classical crossover performer, whose career has benefited greatly from modern marketing strategies. He has recorded several complete operas and some 15 studio albums of both popular and classical music. The earnings from these commercial recordings have arguably made him the most successful solo artist in the history of classical music.

After working for a year as a lawyer, Bocelli decided to devote himself completely to singing, and took lessons privately. He first came to attention in 1992 when he sang the duet *Miserere* with the Italian rock singer Zucchero. This was to be the first of many such collaborations with well-known entertainers, including guitarist John Miles, Spanish singer Marta Sanchez, French singer Hélène Ségara, tenor Luciano Pavarotti, English soprano Sarah Brightman, Canadian pop diva Céline Dion, and American singers Natalie Cole and Mary J. Blige.

From 1999 on, Bocelli has sung in the United States mostly in large arena concert venues such as Madison Square Garden and the Hollywood Bowl, and in the television studio on programs such as *Sesame Street*, *The Today Show*, *The Oprah Winfrey Show*, *The Jay Leno Show*, and *Larry King Live*, where the limitations of his vocal technique can be overcome to some degree by careful electronic production and amplification. His few live stage appearances, including his 2011 Metropolitan Opera recital debut, have in general received negative reviews, with critics noting problems especially with his breath support and phrase shaping, and also a curious lack of emotional commitment to the music. This is certainly not the case, however, when he sings the repertory with which he is most comfortable and artistically successful, Italian popular song.

BIBLIOGRAPHY

A. Felix: *Andrea Bocelli: a Celebration* (London, 2000)

A. Bocelli: *The Music of Silence: a Memoir* (New York, 2001)

KATHLEEN SEWRIGHT

Bochsa, (Robert) Nicholas Charles (*b* Montmédy, France, 9 Aug 1789; *d* Sydney, Australia, 6 Jan 1856). French harpist, conductor, and composer. A large and imposing man who was among the greatest harpists of the 19th century, Bochsa was denoted by Fétis "as distinguished an artist as he was a miserable man." Bochsa fled France in 1817 to escape charges of forgery, contracted a bigamous marriage in England, declared bankruptcy in 1824, and eloped with the soprano Anna Bishop in 1839. The two toured Europe in the years following and traveled to New York in 1847. There Bishop's singing and Bochsa's playing triumphed over American moral outrage at their lifestyle, and the two achieved success on Broadway and in North American tours that took them to New Orleans in the south, Quebec in the north, and major cities in between. They toured Mexico from June 1849 to May 1850 and California in 1854 and 1855. When they traveled to Australia in the fall of 1855, Bochsa was already very sick; he died in Sydney after performing while so ill that he needed to be carried into the theater and propped up.

Bochsa played a crucial role in Anna Bishop's success. She featured his exquisite playing of the harp on her concerts and she used his versions of operas tailored to suit her strengths. He was a shrewd business manager who succeeded in arranging profitable tours in the New World where he had been less successful in Europe. Their story reflects the opportunities for reviving a career that drew many European musicians to America in the mid-19th century.

BIBLIOGRAPHY

FétisB

A. Pougin: "Un musicien voleur, faussaire et bigame," *Le ménestrel* (19 Jan 1907)

P. John: *Bochsa and the Biographical Dictionaries of Music and Musicians* (Houston, 1990)

K. Moon: *Robert Nicholas Bochsa (1789–1856): an Analysis of Selected Pedagogical Works for the Harp* (diss., UCLA, 1990)

K.K. Preston: *Opera on the road: Traveling Opera Troupes in the United States, 1825–60* (Urbana, IL, 1993)

R. Davis: *Anna Bishop: the Adventures of an Intrepid Prima Donna* (Sydney, 1997)

P. John: "Annals of the Harp: Bochsa's Ladies," *The American Harp Journal*, xx (2005), 42–3

E. DOUGLAS BOMBERGER

Bock, Jerry [Jerrold] **(Lewis)** (*b* New Haven, CT, 23 Nov 1928; *d* Mount Kisco, NY, 3 Nov 2010). Composer. He composed amateur shows in high school and while studying music at the University of Wisconsin (1945–9). After college he joined up with Larry Holofcener writing revues at Tamiment, an adult summer resort in Pennsylvania, where he met and worked with the Simon brothers, Danny and Neil. With the Simons and others he wrote songs and special material for television, most notably Sid Caesar's *Your Show of Shows*, and contributed songs for a failed revue, *Catch a Star* (1955). His only successes with Holofcener were two songs from the Sammy Davis Jr. vehicle *Mr. Wonderful*, the title song and "Too Close for Comfort." In 1958 Bock began a fruitful collaboration with lyricist Sheldon Harnick (*b* Chicago, IL, 30 April 1924), writing seven musicals in 12 years. An inauspicious but promising failure about a college-educated boxer, *The Body Beautiful* nonetheless created the opportunity that resulted in their first critical and popular success the following year. This second musical, *Fiorello!*, based on the life of former New York Mayor Fiorello La Guardia, received the Tony Award for Best Musical and the Pulitzer Prize for Drama (the third musical so honored). Their next collaboration, *Tenderloin* (1960), although it assembled many of the same illustrious creators and cast of *Fiorello!* and returned to New York City as its historical subject, was relatively unsuccessful critically and commercially, despite one of Bock's most highly regarded scores. In 1963 they produced another fine score for an intimate, modestly popular *She Loves Me* (1963; revived 1993), a story about two shy and tender pen pals who through most of the drama remain oblivious to the fact that they are acrimonious rivals in a Budapest parfumerie; although he had taken over the direction of John Kander and Fred Ebb's first Broadway musical *A Family Affair* the previous year, this was the first musical originally assigned to be directed by Harold Prince.

One year later Bock and Harnick's phenomenally successful and critically lauded musical realization of Sholem Aleichem's Yiddish stories set in the Russian village of Anatevka in 1905, *Fiddler on the Roof*, arrived on Broadway (1964; revived 1976, 1990, and 2004). Directed and choreographed by Jerome Robbins and produced by Prince, it ran for a record 3242 performances. Although both *The Apple Tree* (1966), a novel attempt to present three one-act musicals in a single evening, and *The Rothschilds* (1970), the story of the banker Meyer Rothschild and his five sons, ran for more than a year, neither show managed to capture the magic or popularity of Tevye the Dairyman and his five daughters in *Fiddler*. According to Harnick, a disagreement over whether to fire the director during the production of *The Rothschilds* led to the dissolution of this illustrious partnership (although they collaborated on a new song, "Topsy-Turvy," for the 2004 revival of *Fiddler*). Bock completed at least two musicals as his own lyricist, neither of which has been performed professionally, as well as several children's musicals, also without Harnick, for the Houston Children's Theatre Festival. In his most critically and popularly successful shows Bock was able to capture a convincing sound world for the subject at hand, including 1930s popular styles in *Fiorello!*, a pseudo-Hungarian style in *She Loves Me*, and, most effectively, Jewish vernacular musical idioms in *Fiddler*.

WORKS

(selective list)

(unless otherwise indicated, all are musicals, and dates are those of first New York performances; librettists and lyricists are listed in that order in parentheses)

Mr. Wonderful (J. Stein, W. Glickman; L. Holofcener, G. Weiss), 22 March 1956 (incl. "Mr. Wonderful"; "Too Close for Comfort")

Wonders of Manhattan (film score), 1956

The Body Beautiful (Stein, Glickman; S. Harnick), orchd T. Royal, 23 Jan 1958

Fiorello! (G. Abbott, J. Weidman; Harnick), orchd I. Kostal, 23 Nov 1959 (incl. "Little Tin Box," "'Til Tomorrow," "When Did I Fall in Love?," and "Politics and Poker")

Tenderloin (Abbott, Weidman; Harnick), orchd Kostal, 17 Oct 1960

Never Too Late (play by S.A. Long) (Harnick [one song]), 27 Nov 1962

Man in the Moon (marionette show) (A. Burns; Harnick), 11 April 1963

She Loves Me (J. Masteroff; Harnick, after Lubitsch film The Shop around the Corner), orchd. D. Walker, 23 April 1963 (incl. "Dear Friend," "Ice Cream," and "She Loves Me"); TV production, 1979

Fiddler on the Roof (J. Stein; Harnick, based on stories by S. Aleichem), orchd. Walker, 22 Sept 1964 (incl. "Matchmaker, Matchmaker," "If I Were a Rich Man," "To Life," and "Sunrise, Sunset"); film 1971

Generation (incid music to play by W. Goodhart), 6 Oct 1965

The Apple Tree (Bock, Harnick, J. Coopersmith, based on stories by M. Twain, F.R. Stockton, and J. Feiffer), orchd E. Sauter, 18 Oct 1966

The Canterville Ghost (TV musical, Harnick), 2 Nov 1966

The Rothschilds (S. Yellen; Harnick), orchd Walker, 19 Oct 1970

Songs in revues, incl. Catch a Star! (sketches by D. Simon and S. Simon; Holofcener), 6 Sept 1955; The Ziegfeld Follies of 1956, Boston, 16 April 1956

BIBLIOGRAPHY

S. Green: *The World of Musical Comedy* (New York, 1960, rev. and enlarged, 4/1980)

A. Kasha and J. Hirschhorn: *Notes on Broadway: Conversations with the Great Songwriters* (Chicago, 1985)

S. Suskin: *Show Tunes: the Songs, Shows and Careers of Broadway's Major Composers* (New York, 1992, rev. and enlarged, 4/2010)

J.R. Bryer and R.A. Davison, ed.: *The Art of the American Musical: Conversations with the Creators* (New Brunswick, NJ, 2005)

P. Lambert: *To Broadway, To Life!: The Musical Theater of Bock and Harnick* (New York, 2011)

GEOFFREY BLOCK

Bodanzky, Artur (*b* Vienna, Austria, 16 Dec 1877; *d* New York, NY, 23 Nov 1939). Austrian conductor, active in the United States. He studied the violin, and at 18 joined the orchestra of the Vienna Hofoper. In 1900 he made his debut conducting Sydney Jones's *The Geisha* with an 18-man orchestra in České Budějovice. In 1903 he returned to the Vienna Opera as Gustav Mahler's assistant, soon making his way rapidly in theaters and concert halls in Vienna, Berlin, Prague, and Mannheim. In 1914 he introduced *Die Fledermaus* to Paris and *Parsifal* to London, the latter making such an impression that he was named successor to Alfred Hertz at the Metropolitan Opera. He made his American debut conducting *Götterdämmerung* in 1915; from then his career was centered on New York, at the Metropolitan (with a brief break in 1928) until his death; with the New SO, which he took over in 1919 from Edgard Varèse, until its merger with the Philharmonic in 1922 and with the Society of the Friends of Music from 1921, as successor to Leopold Stokowski, until 1931 when the society was dissolved.

Best known as a Wagnerian, Bodanzky was anything other than a narrow specialist. He was on the rostrum for Enrico Caruso's last Metropolitan evening, which was Jacques Halévy's *La Juive*, and his repertory at the Metropolitan included Christoph Willibald Gluck, Richard Strauss, Pyotr Il'yich Tchaikovsky, Giacomo Meyerbeer, and Franz von Suppé, and he conducted the American premieres of Jaromir Weinberger's *Švanda the Bagpiper* and Ernst Krenek's *Jonny spielt auf*. At the Friends of Music his repertory ranged from *Dido and Aeneas* to Ildebrando Pizzetti and Alexander Zemlinsky, and his many American premieres included those of Mahler's *Das Lied von der Erde*, Arthur Honegger's *Le roi David*, and Leoš Janáček's Glagolitic Mass. Physically, Bodanzky was like a much taller Mahler, from whom his "the facts, not the show" attitude derived. The typical Bodanzky performance was fast, intense, and heavily cut (however, he gave as well as taking away, composing recitatives and other additions for *Oberon*, *Der Freischütz*, *Die Zauberflöte*, and *Fidelio*).

BIBLIOGRAPHY

J. Horowitz: *Classical Music in America: a History of its Rise and Fall* (New York, 2005), 361–9

MICHAEL STEINBERG/R

Bode, Harald (Emerich Walter) (*b* Hamburg, Germany, 19 Oct 1909; *d* ?North Tonawanda, NY, 15 Jan 1987). Designer of electronic instruments and equipment, of German birth. He studied at the University of Hamburg and the Heinrich-Hertz Institut of the Technische Hochschule in Berlin. He pioneered techniques that are now common in synthesizers and other electronic instruments, both to imitate existing instruments and to generate new sounds. He is credited with developing the first modular synthesizer/processor.

While in Germany, he designed the Warbo Formant-Orgel (1937), in which he introduced the "assignment" of notes on a partially polyphonic keyboard. Further developments were made in the Melodium (1938) and the monophonic Melochord (1947–53). He built a series of electronic organs beginning with the Polychord (1950) and the Bode organ (1951); the latter was the basis for the Polychord III (1951) and for electronic organs made in the United States by the Estey Organ Company from 1954. He immigrated to Brattleboro, Vermont, in 1954, to work as Estey's director of research and development and as vice-president. In 1960 he moved to North Tonawanda, New York, where between 1960 and 1963 he designed a new model of the Wurlitzer electric piano.

In 1959–60 Bode developed his "modular synthesizer and signal processor" and presented it at the 1960 convention of the Audio Engineering Society. This incorporated devices such as a ring modulator and elements of voltage control, and influenced the work of Robert Moog and others. In 1963–4 he devised a frequency shifter and ring modulator which were originally manufactured by the R.A. Moog Co. About 1964 Vladimir Ussachevsky commissioned from Bode a "Klangumwandler" (frequency shifter) for the Columbia-Princeton Electronic Music Center; this legendary device has been widely emulated in software. Bode continued to design sound-processing modules, in particular a vocoder (1977) and an infinite "barbershop" phaser; these and more recent models of the two earlier modules were manufactured by his company, Bode Sound, in North Tonawanda. During the 1970s he also composed electronic music on tape for concerts and television commercials. His instruments have been used by other composers from the classical avant garde to electro-pop and funk, in broadcast commercials and video art, and in academic and professional sound studios.

BIBLIOGRAPHY

Grove7 (H. Davies) [includes list of writings]

T. Rhea: "Harald Bode's Four-Voice Assignment Keyboard (1937)," *Contemporary Keyboard*, v/12 (1979), 89; repr. with the following in *The Art of Electronic Music*, ed. T. Darter and G. Armbruster (New York, 1984), 59–62

T. Rhea: "Bode's Melodium and Melochord," *Contemporary Keyboard*, vi/1 (1980), 68 only

T. Rhea: "Harald Bode's Frequency Shifters and Vocoders," *Contemporary Keyboard*, vi/2 (1980), 86 only

J. Lee: "Interview: Harald Bode," *Polyphony*, vii/Sept–Oct (1981–2), 14–17

H.A. Deutsch: *Electroacoustic Music: the First Century* (Miami, 1993), 17–19

HUGH DAVIES/R

Bo Diddley [Bates, Ellas Otha; McDaniel, Ellas] (*b* McComb, MS, 30 Dec 1928; *d* Archer, FL, 2 June 2008). Rock and roll singer. He was taken to Chicago at the age of five, and soon after began violin lessons, which he continued for 12 years. He grew up with black gospel music and the delta blues players of Chicago's South Side, but he was most strongly influenced by Nat "King" Cole, Louis Jordan, and John Lee Hooker, whose "Boogie Chillen" inspired him to play guitar. He formed a street-corner band, which attracted enough attention to be granted an audition with Chess Records in 1954. In early 1955 "Bo Diddley" (Checker) was released as a single and reached number one on the rhythm-and-blues chart. It had bragging, nonsense lyrics, like many of his later songs, but its chief appeal lay in its shimmering rumba rhythm and violent, primitive guitar playing. Diddley stood outside the mainstream of rock and roll of the 1950s; he recorded unusual jazz instrumental pieces with weird sound effects, doo-wop songs, blues, idiosyncratic rock and roll numbers, and rambling insult battles with Jerome Green, his maracas player. Many of his songs are based on a distinctive syncopated rhythm (ex.1).

Ex.1

Diddley had few pop hits (only "Say Man" reached the top 20 in the 1959 US pop chart), but his influence on such performers as Jimi Hendrix, the Rolling Stones, and the Yardbirds was considerable; cover versions of his songs were recorded by many American and English groups. In 1987, he was inducted into the Rock and Roll Hall of Fame; he also was granted Lifetime Achievement Awards by the Rhythm and Blues Foundation and the National Academy of Recording Arts and Sciences. His stage name is derived from the instrument known as a Diddley bow.

BIBLIOGRAPHY

SouthernB
N. Nite: *Rock On* (New York, 1974)
J. Miller, ed.: *The Rolling Stone Illustrated History of Rock & Roll* (New York, 1976, rev. 3/1992 by A. DeCurtis, J. Henke, and H. George-Warren)
R. Denyer: *The Guitar Handbook* (London, 1982)
G.R. White: *Bo Diddley, Living Legend* (Chessington, UK, 1995)
C. Hughes: Obituary, *Popular Music and Society*, xxxii/1 (2009), 113–15

JOSEPH MCEWEN/R

Bodky, Erwin (*b* Ragnit, East Prussia [now Neman, Belarus], 7 March 1896; *d* Lucerne, 6 Dec 1958). Pianist, harpsichordist, and musicologist of Prussian birth. He made his debut as a pianist at the age of 12. After attending the Gymnasium in Tilsit, he went to the Hochschule für Musik in Berline, where he studied with Ernő Dohnányi, Paul Juon, Robert Kahn, and others, graduating in 1920. He then continued his studies under FERRUCCIO BUSONI (piano) and Richard Strauss (composition), and performed as a solo pianist. During the 1920s he wrote a piano concerto, a symphony for chamber orchestra, works for solo piano, and chamber music. Until 1938 he occupied various teaching posts at music schools in Berlin and Amsterdam. In that year he came to the United States, where he taught first at the Longy School of Music in Cambridge, Massachusetts, and founded the Cambridge Collegium Musicum (later the Cambridge Society for Early Music) in 1942; in 1949 he received the first music appointment at Brandeis University, where he taught music history. He was primarily interested in methods of performance of early keyboard music: he played both harpsichord and clavichord, and explored ways of rendering certain harpsichord effects on the modern piano. He published three scholarly works connected with these interests. In 1955 he presented "Roads to Bach," one of the earliest programs on music seen on educational television.

WRITINGS

Der Vortrag alter Klaviermusik (Berlin, 1932)
Das Charakterstück (Berlin, 1933, 2/1960)
The Interpretation of Bach's Keyboard Works (Cambridge, MA, 2/1960, 1960/*R*)

BIBLIOGRAPHY

H.S. Slosberg, M.V. Ullman, and I.K. Whiting, eds.: *Erwin Bodky: a Memorial Tribute* (Waltham, MA, 1965)

WILLIAM D. GUDGER

Body, the. A loosely related set of methodological interests in analyzing the corporeal nature of music. Such interests are not new; at least since Plato's admonitions in *The Republic*, musical practices in the West have been seen as embodied not only in the creation but also in the reception and, potentially at least, in the analysis of music. Certain musical scholarship, particularly pedagogical literature and dance studies, has long examined the relationship of bodies to music, and a variety of analytical traditions over the centuries have attempted to quantify music's powers on the body. These traditions have never disappeared entirely, but 20th-century musical analysis was frequently concerned with more abstract procedures. One of the hallmarks of 21st-century scholarship on music on the body has been to recuperate those older traditions (Holsinger, Smart, Le Guin).

Recent analyses are often framed in reaction to the so-called "mind–body split"—symbolized for many by the famous Cartesian *cogito*, "I think therefore I am"—which seemed to privilege the mental over the physical. In contrast, modern phenomenology, especially the work of Maurice Merleau-Ponty in *Phenomenology of Perception* (1945), foregrounded the situated, embodied subject. A more socially-oriented approach to the body also emerged from France, thanks to French anthropologist Marcel Mauss and his influential 1934 lecture "Techniques of the Body." By comparing embodied practices ranging from military marching to styles of sitting and sleeping across a range of cultures, Mauss showed that these practices were, for the most part, learned behaviors situated historically and ideologically, and in fact one might view such embodiment as the heart of how cultural behavior is circulated.

While overlapping and not incompatible, these two strands of French scholarship represent a divide still recognizable today. Generalizing rather greatly, the more abstract and universalizing philosophical approach of Merleau-Ponty might be seen, on the one hand, as privileging the commonality of the human body shared by our species. George Lakoff and Mark Johnson, for instance, developed a theory of linguistics that emphasized the importance of bodily-based metaphors in language; for example, the privileging of terms resonating with meanings of "high" versus "low" might be seen as originating from our location of many sensory organs at the tops of our bodies (Lakoff and Johnson).

On the other hand, Mauss's approach was an important influence on those who emphasized historical and social contingency. The French historian-philosopher Michel Foucault focused attention on the historically changing role of embodiment in the circulation of power in such works as *Discipline and Punish* (1975) and the three-volume *History of Sexuality* (1976–84). Equally as sympathetic to Mauss were anthropologists, who had necessarily adopted a more holistic view of performance that resisted the tendency towards intellectual abstraction, and long taken seriously claims about the transformative power of music making, in much analysis of performance in the 20th century. Anthropological approaches to the body also informed the interdisciplinary field of Performance Studies, which has blended ethnographic analysis and performance with contemporary theater. Nor can the importance of performers to the analysis of embodiment be underestimated. Avant-garde artists in the 1960s and 1970s placed bodies, especially their own, at the heart of their craft, as in Meredith Monk's explorations of the human voice, the collaborations of Nam June Paik and Charlotte Moorman, and Alvin Lucier's experimental use of brain waves. Likewise, popular musicians of the same era advanced an embodied understanding of music, especially in dance-oriented genres such as R&B, funk, and disco.

Political claims have historically been at the heart of both of these strands of research, with a longstanding if somewhat romanticized notion that anti-Cartesian philosophy and holistic views of performance upset traditional orders of knowledge in politically constructive ways. In a recent formulation, Diana Taylor has useful contrasted the "archive" and the "repertoire" in the transmission of knowledge, the former depending on the written word and the latter on the corporeal knowledge, frequently dissident, that exists outside of such official and authorized circumstances. Such politics, however, have interesting repercussions, especially when disciplinarity relegates methodological procedures to certain genres and cultures. Despite longstanding traditions to the contrary, embodied musical analysis of the canonical Western tradition has lagged far behind such efforts as applied to other cultures or to popular music traditions. This may be inevitable given the centrality of racial discourse to both ethnomusicology and popular music studies, for the difference embodied in racialized phenotype has had very real social consequences. The carefully-cultivated invisibility—and thus, disembodiment—of whiteness, on the other hand, integrates well with the rhetoric of universality (and privilege) aspired to by classical styles. The mind–body duality has therefore often remained intact even as different disciplines and repertoires have privileged different sides of the binary.

Since the 1980s, such disciplinary and musical divides began to erode, largely thanks to the influence of several movements involving identity politics. Although largely originating outside of musicology, the influences of feminist theory, queer theory, and critical race studies made themselves felt in important ways. Feminist musicologists such as Susan McClary and Suzanne Cusick successfully wielded theories of philosophical embodiment to reconfigure the heart of the classical repertoire. Similarly, ethnomusicologists sought to complicate essentialized notions of racialized bodies, by both recuperating intellectual or otherwise "mind"-oriented approaches and allowing for the sort of individualized difference long afforded Western music.

Studying music and the body remains a widely divergent and only loosely organized field. Philosophical investigations indebted to Merleau-Ponty remain crucial today, and scholars such as Nicholas Cook and Philip Auslander have brought insights from Performance Studies into musicology. One particularly salutatory trend has been a deconstructive urge aimed not only at the mind-body duality, but at the terms themselves. Disability studies has questioned the normativizing tendencies inherent in much scholarship, asking what covert values lie behind what are often constructed as "normal" physical relationships with music. Sound studies, largely carried out by scholars outside of typical musical disciplines, have broadened our understanding not just of performance but of sound itself and our embodied relationships with its material reality. And music theorists have increasingly turned towards neuroscientific disciplines to lend detailed empirical grounding to an otherwise abstract discourse, reminding us that the mind is, after all, part of the body.

BIBLIOGRAPHY

G. Lakoff and M. Johnson: *Metaphors We Live By* (Chicago, 1980)

S. Cusick: "Feminist Theory, Music Theory, and the Mind/Body Problem," *PNM*, xxxii (1994), 8–27

S. McClary: "Music, the Pythagoreans, and the Body," *Choreographing History*, ed. S.L. Foster (Bloomington, IN, 1995), 82–104

P. Auslander: *Liveness: Performance in a Mediatized Culture* (New York, 1999)

D. Wong: "Ethnomusicology and Difference," *EthnM*, l (2000), 259–79

N. Cook: "Between Process and Product: Music and/as Performance," *Music Theory Online*, vii (2001) <http://www.mtosmt.org/issues/mto.01.7.2/mto.01.7.2.cook.html>

B. Holsinger: *Music, Body, and Desire in Medieval Culture* (Palo Alto, CA, 2001)

L. Zbikowski: *Conceptualizing Music: Cognitive Structure, Theory, and Analysis* (New York, 2002)

D. Taylor: *The Archive and the Repertoire: Performing Cultural Memory in the Americas* (Durham, 2003)

M. Smart: *Mimomania: Music and Gesture in Nineteenth-Century Opera* (Berkeley, CA, 2004)

E. Le Guin: *Boccherini's Body: an Essay in Carnal Musicology* (Berkeley, CA, 2006)

N. Lerner and S. Straus, eds.: *Sounding Off: Theorizing Disability in Music* (New York and London, 2006)

F. Dyson: *Sounding New Media: Immersion and Embodiment in the Arts and Culture* (Berkeley, CA, 2009)

PHILIP GENTRY

Boelke-Bomart. Firm of music publishers. It was founded by Margot and Walter R. Boelke (*b* 20 Jan 1905; *d* 25 Jan 1987) in New York in 1948 and incorporated in 1951. Affiliated to ASCAP, the firm specializes in the publication of contemporary music, and under the general editorship (1952–82) of Jacques-Louis Monod, who succeeded Kurt List, built up a small but important catalog. Among its composers are Arthur Berger, Lansky, Lerdahl, Perle, Roslawez, Schoenberg, Skrowaczewski, and Claudio Spies. In 1975 a sister company, Mobart Music Publications (an affiliate of BMI), was founded; its composers include Babbitt, Gideon, Ives, Leon Kirchner, Leibowitz, Monod, Pollock, Shifrin, Ben Weber, Webern, Zemlinsky, and Zwilich. The distributor for both companies in the United States and Canada is Jerona Music Corporation, part of the Music Associates of America.

BIBLIOGRAPHY

G. Sturm: "Encounters: Walter R. Boelke," *MadAminA! A Chronicle of Musical Catalogues*, iv/1 (1983), 9–10

"Walter R. Boelke," *MadAminA! A Chronicle of Musical Catalogues*, viii/1 (1987), 7 only [obituary]

ALAN POPE/R. ALLEN LOTT

Boelzner, Gordon (*b* Inglewood, CA, 1937; *d* New York, NY, 17 Aug 2005). Pianist, accompanist, conductor, and music adviser of New York City Ballet. Reared in a musical home, he began piano lessons at age eight and by 12 was accompanying his father's vocal students. He undertook advanced study at the Eastman School of Music in Rochester and at the Manhattan School of Music, where he earned a bachelor's degree. He later studied in Italy with Arturo Benedetto Michelangelo, on a scholarship, and in New York City with John Cage. To support himself, he took a job in 1959 as a class accompanist and rehearsal pianist at New York City Ballet, little thinking that he was beginning a lengthy and distinguished career with that organization. He soon became George Balanchine's choice to accompany his ballets set to solo piano works by Stravinsky as well as those set to music by Tchaikovsky, Gershwin, Hindemith, Schumann, and others. Jerome Robbins also favored him as accompanist for his ballets set to the piano music of Bach, Chopin, Gould, and Ravel. He served as the company's music director from 1990 to 2000, conducting numerous performances of the standard repertory. Renowned for his musicianship and instinctive sympathy for dance movement, he became the mentor and inspiration for a new generation of ballet musicians.

BIBLIOGRAPHY

R. Sealy: "Mr. Robbins, Mr. Balanchine, Mr. Boelzner," *Ballet Review*, iii/3 (1970), 16–22

J. Anderson: "Dance View: a Ballet Pianist May Equal Dancers in Importance," *New York Times* (29 June 1985)

L. Garafola and E. Foner, eds.: *Dance for a City: Fifty Years of the New York City Ballet* (New York, 1999)

CLAUDE CONYERS

Boggs, Dock [Moran Lee] (*b* near Norton, VA, 7 Feb 1898; *d* Needmore, VA, 7 Feb 1971.) Banjoist and singer. Boggs was born near the coal-mining town of Norton in Wise County in Southwest Virginia. He was only 12 years old when he began working in area coal mines; he began playing the banjo around the same time. Strongly influenced by local African American musicians, he learned to play banjo in an old time three-finger style and to sing the blues.

In 1927, Boggs auditioned for Brunswick Records in Bristol, Tennessee, and traveled to New York City where he recorded several classic songs. Among these were "Country Blues" and "Sugar Baby" that were reissued on the Folkways *Anthology of American Folk Music* in 1952 and again by Smithsonian Folkways Records in 1997. Boggs recorded again in 1929 but during the Great Depression, he gave up trying to make his living as a professional musician. Boggs was a full-time coal miner in southwest Virginia when folk music performer and collector Mike Seeger rediscovered him in 1963. Like other early old-time musicians and blues artists whose records had been reissued on the Folkways *Anthology*, Boggs enjoyed a new career as a performer and recording artist during the folk revival of the 1960s. He recorded for Folkways Records and appeared at concerts, clubs and festivals, including the Newport Folk Festival in 1966. His health failed in the early 1970s. Boggs was 73 years old when he died on his birthday in his home in Needmore, Virginia.

RICHARD BLAUSTEIN

Bohannon [Bohannon, Hamilton Frederick] (*b* Newman, GA, 7 March 1942). Drummer, bandleader, and producer. He received a BA in music education from Clark College in Atlanta and taught music in public schools. While in Atlanta, he met Jimi Hendrix, who became a major influence on his style. He began his professional performing career in 1965 as a drummer for Stevie Wonder. In 1967 he became the leader of the Motown's leading road band—known on radio as Bohannon and the Motown Sound—and spent the next five years on tour backing such acts as Gladys Knight and the Pips, the Temptations, Diana Ross and the Supremes, the Spinners, Smokey Robinson and the Miracles, and the Four Tops. When Motown moved its headquarters from Detroit to Los Angeles, Bohannon left the company and signed a contract with Dakar, a small label based in Chicago. There he began writing and arranging, and produced a series of disco albums, dominated by his percussion playing, which blended mellow funk with primitive, irrepressible rhythms. In 1975 his single "Footstompin' Music" reached the top 40 on the rhythm-and-blues chart; Bohannon then moved to Mercury and recorded the scintillating "Let's start the dance" (1978), which reached the rhythm-and-blues top ten. Later releases, however, such as "Let's start the dance again" (1981), had less success. Most of Bohannon's recordings are characterized by dominant percussion lines, simple guitar solos, and intermittent vocal passages. Its percolating beat has led many hip-hop artists to sample his tracks. Although no longer well known among a wide audience, he has remained an active and respected producer, arranger, and performer into the 2010s. His son, Hamilton Bohannon II, has recorded under his own name.

GARY THEROUX/R

Bohlman, Philip V(ilas) (*b* Boscobel, WI, 8 Aug 1952). Ethnomusicologist. He received the BM in piano at the University of Wisconsin-Madison in 1975, and the MM in 1980 and the PhD in 1984 in musicology and ethnomusicology at the University of Illinois at

Urbana-Champaign with BRUNO NETTL and Alexander Ringer; he also studied for two years at the Hebrew University of Jerusalem with Amnon Shiloah, 1980–82. He was assistant professor at MacMurray College (1982–4) and the University of Illinois at Chicago (1985–7) before joining the faculty at the University of Chicago, where he was appointed professor in 1999. He was visiting professor at the University of Vienna, 1995–6. In 1997 he was awarded the Dent medal.

Bohlman's work may be characterized as a sustained critique of modernity, canon-formation, and the monumentalization of 19th-century Austro-German musical practice through an ethnographic engagement with the "others" of Europe, whether on or within its margins. His earlier work investigated music making among immigrant Jews in early 20th-century Palestine; his later work brings ethnographic critique back to the center, exploring popular religious, street, and folk musics in Vienna and elsewhere in Central Europe. Other areas of research include immigrant and ethnic folk musics in America, music and religion, and the intellectual history of ethnomusicology.

WRITINGS

"Deutsch-amerikanische Musik in Wisconsin: Überleben im Melting Pot," *Jb für Volksliedforschung*, xxx (1985), 99–116

The Study of Folk Music in the Modern World (Bloomington, IN, 1988)

"Ernest Bloch's 'America': Aesthetic Dimensions of a Swiss-American Auswandererbericht," *Yearbook of German-American Studies*, xxv (1990), 35–54

ed., with B. Nettl: *Comparative Musicology and Anthropology of Music: Essays on the History of Ethnomusicology* (Chicago, 1991)

ed. with K.A. Bergeron: *Disciplining Music: Musicology and its Canons* (Chicago, 1992)

"Musicology as a Political Act," *Journal of Musicology*, xi (1993), 411–36

"Fieldwork in the Ethnomusicological Past," *Shadows in the Field: New Directions in Ethnomusicological Fieldwork*, ed. G.F. Barz and T. Cooley (New York, 1997), 139–62

ed. with O. Holzapfel: *Land Without Nightingales: Music in the Making of German-America* (Urbana, IL, 2002)

ed. with E. Blumhofer, M.M. Chow, and M.E. Marty: *Music in American Religious Experience* (New York, 2006)

ed.: *Jewish Musical Modernism, Old and New* (Chicago, 2008)

Jewish Music and Modernity (New York, 2008)

MARTIN STOKES/R

Bohmann, Joseph Frederich (*b* Prussia, 1848; *d* Chicago, IL, 26 March 1928). String instrument maker, merchant, and wholesaler. He and his family immigrated from Prussia to Illinois around 1864. He founded Bohmann's American Musical Industry in Chicago around 1876. After winning multiple World Exposition awards from 1889 to 1900, Bohmann became an American Academy of Violin Makers charter and committee member in 1914. Bohmann manufactured violin family instruments and accessories, mandolins, guitars, zithers, harp guitars, and banjos, but also rebranded other instruments, such as accordions, concertinas, brass instruments, and drums. Quality ranged from inexpensive student and wholesale merchandise to artist model violins and lavishly ornamented presentation-grade guitars and mandolins.

Bohmann invented or adapted features in the late 19th century that most other manufacturers did not standardize until well after the 1900s. Such novel aspects included shaded, sunburst finishes, guitar tops with single or double X-shaped, internal braces designed specifically for steel strings, and three-ply laminated sides and backs. Though his claim remains unconfirmed, Bohmann advertised that he built the first American-made mandolin, exemplifying his keen marketing instincts. Members of Carlos Curti's Spanish Students, a nationally popular 1880 mandolin ensemble, endorsed his instruments. His marketing—artful, bombastic, and inventive—challenged all makers, wagering up to $125,000 on his instruments' unmatchable sound quality.

Bohmann's largest harp guitar model was the gigantic "Contrabass Harp Guitar." Leading the market, his invention developed a market niche: a guitar loud enough to be heard above large mandolin orchestras. This plainly appointed, double-necked instrument was 19 inches wide, six inches deep, and had a 23-inch-long body. The main neck's six strings were tuned to standard pitch; the second neck held up to 12 additional sub-bass strings. Bohmann's six-string Contrabass was marketed as a solo instrument.

After 1900, Bohmann's habitual experimentation culminated in no less than six patents (PAF 1911–16) for his modern guitar and mandolin family design. These instruments featured arched, convex tops and backs; sloped (cutaway) upper bouts; palm rests; proprietary, geared tuners on unique headstock designs; and internal rods that vibrated sympathetically. Never mass-produced, nor of presentation grade, their size ranged from small mandolins to large harp guitars. Bohmann probably built few instruments after 1900. The factory closed down near the time of his death. Whether or not family continued to operate the business remains undocumented; the factory remained mothballed for some 40-odd years, holding over 3,000 instruments in various stages of completion. Factory inventory and effects were gradually sold off starting in the 1960s.

BIBLIOGRAPHY

J. Bohmann: *Catalog of the celebrated Jos. Bohmann Violins-Mandolins, Guitars, Zithers, and Banjos* (Chicago, IL, 1895)

R. Vannes: *Dictionnaire universel des luthiers* (Brussels, 1951–9)

G. Miner: "The Harp Guitars of Joseph Bohmann" <http://www.harpguitars.net/history/bohmann/bohmann1.htm>

BRUCE HAMMOND

Boise. City in Idaho (pop. 205,671; metropolitan area 616,500; 2010 US Census). It is the capital of Idaho and the state's largest city. The City of Trees bordering the Boise River grew in response to a gold rush that drew settlers from around North America and China to the Boise Basin in 1862. Immigrants from Germany developed the musical infrastructure, from wind bands and orchestras to theaters suitable for typical touring attractions of the late 1900s. The first Boise Philharmonic Association (1901) was primarily a choral society. Several incarnations of a civic symphony orchestra followed, but the title Boise Philharmonic Orchestra refers to an organization named in 1960 that became the core of professional music making in the region. Jacques Brourman was the first music director (1960–67);

current conductor Robert Franz leads the orchestra's eight pairs of subscription concerts and numerous outreach concerts. Boise Philharmonic Association, Inc. sponsors the Boise Philharmonic Youth Orchestra and has recently absorbed Boise Master Chorale.

From the late 19th century on, local amateurs staged operatic productions, including an unauthorized 1879 *H.M.S. Pinafore*. Growing out of the Boise Opera Workshop, the Boise Civic Opera was formed in 1973, and renamed Opera Idaho in 1997; the company has produced one to three full operas per season for 40 years. Classical and modern dance has been a stimulus for live music in Boise during the latter half of the 20th century. Ballet Idaho (formerly American Festival Ballet) and Idaho Dance Theatre have featured the Boise Philharmonic and other local musicians for decades.

In 1919, Eugene Farner, recently returned from the military's Liberty Chorus program, headed a postwar effort called Boise Music Week, involving numerous free performances by churches, schools, and music clubs. The first to be produced in the United States, Boise Music Week was not unique at this time, but is rare in its longevity. The community production of the musical *Oklahoma!* in 1959 changed the thrust of the project, but the week-long buffet of traditional Euro-American concert music continues, involving hundreds of city school children every May. The Boise Public School music program and those of nearby districts have a history of widespread success, with choral, band, and orchestral ensembles at their core.

Boise State University's department of music began in 1932 with the founding of Boise Junior College by Bishop Barnwell of St. Michael's Episcopal Cathedral. Barnwell shared the church's organist, James L. Strachan, with the college, where he taught organ, theory, and piano. Organist-composer C. Griffith Bratt, chair for the next 25 years, followed. As the college rapidly grew to a university of over 20,000, the music program developed the comprehensive degree offerings and expertise commensurate with an active state university. The Velma V. Morrison Center for the Performing Arts, completed in 1984, combined public and substantial private funding to house the music department as well as to offer its 2000-seat hall to the Boise Philharmonic and opera and dance companies. The Gene Harris Jazz Festival, originally led by the eponymous jazz pianist, is one of many campus outreach activities. The University has been the host of the Gilbert and Sullivan Archive, online since 1993.

BIBLIOGRAPHY

M.E. Stallcop: *Music in Boise, Idaho, 1863 to 1890* (thesis, U. of Montana, 1968)

E.B. Chaffee: *An Idea Grows...a History of Boise College* (Boise, ID, 1970)

G. Barrett: *Boise State University: Searching for Excellence; 1932–1984* (Boise State U., 1984)

A.A. Hart: *Life in Old Boise* (Boise, ID, 1989)

M. Wells and A.A. Hart: *Boise: an Illustrated History* (Sun Valley, ID, 2000/*R*)

Boise Philharmonic Orchestra, Inc.: "BPO History Panels Narrative Text" (Boise, ID, 2007)

JEANNE M. BELFY

Boise, Otis Bardwell (*b* Oberlin, OH, 13 Aug 1844; *d* Baltimore, MD, 2 Dec 1912). Composer and music educator. Boise's family moved to Cleveland when he was a child. He showed early musical aptitude, becoming organist at St Paul's Church when he was 14. From 1861–3, he studied in Germany at the Leipzig Conservatory, where his teachers included Ignaz Moscheles and Ernst Wenzel (general music), Moritz Hauptmann and Ernst Richter (composition), and Louis Plaidy (piano). He then studied piano under Theodor Kullak in Berlin for two years. He returned to Cleveland in 1865, working as an organist and teaching piano. He moved to New York City, teaching harmony and composition at the New York Conservatory of Music from 1870 to 1876, his most productive period as a composer. His Piano Concerto in G minor (1874) may be the earliest piano concerto by a native-born American composer. It was given its premiere by the Peabody Conservatory of Music symphony orchestra in Baltimore, directed by Asger Hamerik, which also performed Boise's Symphony in D "In Memoriam" (1875). From 1876 to 1878, Boise lived in Weimar and Wiesbaden, Germany. He visited Franz Liszt on many occasions, discussing composition and American music education, and playing through manuscripts. He also spent time with Joachim Raff. Boise resumed teaching in New York City in 1878, with Henry Huss as one of his pupils. Boise composed *Festival Overture* (1878) for orchestra and organ, *Three Contralto Songs* (1879), *Child's Requiem* (1879) for vocal quartet and organ, and *Christmas Overture*. Other works include *Romeo and Juliet Suite* (1881), a Christmas cantata, motet, and Psalm for chorus and orchestra. From 1888 to 1901, he lived in Berlin, teaching theory and composition to American students. Ernest Hutcheson, Howard Brockway, Arthur Nevin, and Edward Schneider were among his pupils. He wrote two books, *Harmony Made Practical: a Comprehensive Treatise* (Philadelphia, 1900) and *Music and Its Masters* (Philadelphia, 1901). He was an esteemed teacher of theory and composition at the Peabody Conservatory in Baltimore from 1901 to 1912.

BIBLIOGRAPHY

O.B. Boise: "An American Composer Visits Liszt," *MQ*, xliii (1957; written in 1876), 316–26

O.B. Boise: *Harmony Made Practical* (Philadelphia, 1906/*R* as CD-ROM)

JAMES DOBES REITZELL

Bojangles. (1) Nickname of Bill Robinson, a tap dancer and actor in musical theater, meaning "happy-go-lucky." He was called Bill Robinson or Bojangles or Mr. Bojangles; he was never called Bojangles Robinson. (2) Title of songs by various artists, including "Mr. Bojangles" (1968) by Jerry Jeff Walker and "Bojangles" (2006) by Pitbull.

CLAUDE CONYERS

Bok Zimbalist, Mary Louise Curtis (*b* Boston, MA, 6 Aug 1876; *d* Philadelphia, PA, 4 Jan 1970.) Writer and music patron. She was the only child of columnist Louisa Knapp Curtis and publisher Cyrus H.K. Curtis, the founder of *Ladies' Home Journal* and the *Saturday Evening Post*, as well as a major Philadelphia philanthropist. She married the Dutch-born Pulitzer Prize-winning author and editor Edward William Bok when she was 19.

She became an active supporter of the Settlement Music School (est. 1906) and provided $150,000 to establish its home on Queen Street in Philadelphia in 1917. In 1924, she purchased three mansions on Rittenhouse Square to create the Curtis Institute of Music in honor of her father and provided an unprecedented $12.5 million endowment. With artistic guidance from Josef Hofmann and Leopold Stokowski, she assembled a faculty of world-class performers, tapped former Symphony Club conductor Johann Grolle as its first director, and established a tuition-free, merit-based admission standard. She served on the board of the Philadelphia Orchestra until Stokowski's departure, sponsored Sunday evening chamber concerts at the Philadelphia Museum of Art that featured Curtis students, and served as board chairman to the Philadelphia Grand Opera Company from 1929 to 1934 in a partnership beneficial to Curtis students. Other significant ventures included a fellowship for the Maitland Art Center in Florida, her gift of the Annie Russell Theater to Rollins College in Winter Park, Florida, and a $175,000 organ to the Philadelphia Academy of Music. At age 66, she married violinist and Curtis director Efrem Zimbalist Sr.—widower of Alma Gluck and father of a famed actor. She served as president of the Curtis Institute until her death. Recognitions for her dedication to music included an honorary Doctor of Humane Letters from the University of Pennsylvania in 1932, an honorary Doctor of Music from Williams College in 1934, and the National Institute of Social Sciences Gold Medal in 1937.

BIBLIOGRAPHY

M.L.C. Bok: *The Curtis Institute of Music Catalogue, 1927–1928* (Philadelphia, 1927)

"Mrs. Efram Zimbalist Sr., Curtis Heiress is Dead," *New York Times* (6 Jan 1970)

E.A. Viles: *Mary Louise Curtis Bok Zimbalist: Founder of the Curtis Institute of Music and Patrons of American Arts* (diss. Bryn Mawr College, 1983)

M. Mender: *Extraordinary Women in Support of Music* (Lanham, MD, 1997)

GARY GALVÁN

Bolcom, William (Elden) (*b* Seattle, WA, 26 May 1938). Composer, pianist, and author. He began composition studies at age 11 with John Verrall at the University of Washington (he completed his BA there in 1958). His studies continued with Darius Milhaud at Mills College from 1958–61 (MA 1961) and with both Milhaud and Olivier Messiaen at the Paris Conservatoire. After working with Leland C. Smith at Stanford University (DMA 1964), he taught at the University of Washington (1965–6) and Queens College, CUNY (1966–8). While in New York he developed a style of playing ragtime that, through concerts and recordings, placed him in the forefront of the ragtime revival. He has also composed original rags, among them *Graceful Ghost*. From 1968 to 1970 he was composer-in-residence at the Yale University Drama School and the New York University School of the Arts. He taught at the University of Michigan from 1973 until his retirement in 2008. Bolcom was awarded the Pulitzer Prize for music in 1988 (for *12 New Etudes* for piano) and named to the American Academy of Arts and Letters in 1993.

In 1975 Bolcom married mezzo-soprano Joan Morris, with whom he began to develop programs on the history of American popular song. Their recitals and recordings of songs by Henry Russell, Henry Clay Work, and others have aroused much interest in parlor and music-hall songs of the 19th and early 20th centuries. Bolcom has also recorded solo albums of music by Gershwin, Milhaud, and himself. He is the author with Robert Kimball of *Reminiscing with Sissle and Blake* (New York, 1973) and has edited the collected writings of Rochberg, *The Aesthetics of Survival: a Composer's View of 20th-century Music* (Ann Arbor, MI, 1984, 2/2004).

Bolcom began his career composing in a serial idiom; he particularly admired the work of Boulez, Stockhausen, and Berio. In the 1960s, however, he gradually shed this academic approach in favor of a language that embraced a wider variety of musical styles. In most of his mature music he has sought to erase boundaries between popular and serious music. An intensely dramatic atonality may contrast with the song styles of World War I (as in the cabaret opera *Dynamite Tonite*), ragtime (*Black Host*), old popular tunes (*Whisper Moon*), or a waltz (Piano Quartet). He has cited Charles Ives as an important influence on his compositional style.

The dance suite *Seattle Slew* (1986), named after a famous racehorse, uses regular, formally predictable dances such as the tango, gavotte, and rag to evoke the old-fashioned atmosphere of a racetrack. The Fifth Symphony (1989) opens in a highly abstract, even expressionistic style, featuring angular melodies and dissonant harmonies. Later the music mixes these in a collage-like manner with popular tunes and quotations from works such as Wagner's *Tristan* prelude and Mahler's horn fanfares. Bolcom's ideology, rooted in the transcendentalism of William Blake, has inspired compositions concerned with momentous religious and philosophical themes. These concerns are expressed with intense, even flamboyant music of vivid illustrative power. Such qualities appear in *Frescoes*, for example, and most notably in the monumental setting of the 46 poems in Blake's *Songs of Innocence and of Experience*, a work that stands as a summation of Bolcom's achievements as a composer.

WORKS

(selective list)

DRAMATIC

Songs of Innocence and of Experience (musical illumination, W. Blake), 1956–81; Dynamite Tonite (cabaret op, 2, A. Weinstein), 1963, New York, 1963; Greatshot (cabaret op, 2, Weinstein), 1966, New Haven, CT, 1969; Theatre of the Absurd (paraphrase, Bolcom), 1970, San Francisco, 1979; Hester Street (film music, with H. Clarke), 1975; The Beggar's Opera (J. Gay), 1978, Minneapolis, 1979 [completion of adaptation begun by Milhaud, 1937]; Casino Paradise (music-theater op, 2, Weinstein), 1986–90, Philadelphia, 1990; McTeague (op, 2, Weinstein and R. Altman, after F. Norris), 1991–2, Chicago, 1992; Broken Glass (incid music, A. Miller), 1994; Illuminata (film score, with A. Black), 1998; A View from the Bridge (op, 2, Weinstein, after A. Miller), 1997–9, Chicago, 1999, rev. 2002, New York, 2002; A Wedding (op, 2, Weinstein and Altman), 2002–2004, Chicago, 2004; Lucrezia (op, 1, M. Campbell), New York, 2008

INSTRUMENTAL

Orch: Sym. no.1, 1957; Concertante, fl, ob, vn, orch, 1961; Conc. Serenade, vn, str, 1964; Sym. no.2 "Oracles," 1965; Fives, vn, pf, str, 1966; Commedia, chbr orch, 1971; Summer Divertimento, 1973; Pf Conc., 1976; Humoresk, org, orch, 1979; Sym. no.3, chbr orch, 1979; Broadside, ceremonial, wind, 1981; Ragomania, 1982; Vn Conc., 1983; Conc., D, vn, orch, 1984; Seattle Slew, dance suite, 1986; Sym. no.4 (T. Roethke), medium v, orch, 1986; MCMXC Tanglewood, 1990; Lyric Conc., fl, orch, 1993; A Whitman Triptych (W. Whitman), Mez, orch, 1995; Gaea, 2 pf LH, orch, 1996; Gala Variation, 1996; Molto adagio, 1996 [from Sym. no.6]; Sym. no.6, 1996–7; Fanfare for a New President, band, 1997; Concert-Suite, a sax, band, 1998; Song (for Band), 2000; Inventing Flight, 2003; A Seattle Overture, 2005; Serenata Notturna, ob, orch, 2005; Sym. no.8, 2005; Canciones de Lorca, T, orch, 2006; Prometheus, pf, orch, chorus, 2010

Chbr and solo inst: 7 str qts, 1950–61, Sonata no.1, vn, pf, 1956, rev. 1984; Concert Piece, cl, pf, 1958; Décalage, vc, pf, 1961; Pastorale, vn, pf, 1961; Octet, fl, cl, bn, vn, va, vc, db, pf, 1962; Scherzo-Fantasy, wind qnt, pf, 1962; Session I, 7 insts, 1965; Str Qt no.8, 1965; Dream Music no.2, hpd, 3 perc, 1966; Phrygia, hp, 1966; Black Host, org, perc, tape, 1967; Dark Music, vc, timp, 1969; Praeludium, org, vib, 1969; Fancy Tales, vn, pf, 1971; Duo Fantasy, vn, pf, 1973; Seasons, gui, 1974; Pf Qt, 1976; Short Lecture, cl, 1976; Sonata no.2, vn, pf, 1978; Graceful Ghost, concert variation, vn, pf, 1979; Capriccio, vc, pf, 1985; 3 Rags, str qt, 1989; Sonata, vc, pf, 1989; Celestial Dinner Music, fl, hp, 1996; Pf Qtrs. no.2, 1996; Spring Trio, pf trio, 1996; Suite, vn, vc, 1997; Pf Quintet, 2000; Str Qt no.11, 2002; Scherzino, sax qt, 2004; Chalumeau, cl, 2005; Octet: Double Qt, 2 str qt, 2007; Introduzione e Rondo: Haydn Go Seek, vn, vc, pf, 2008; Shakyamuni, pic, fl, Eö cl, cl, 2 vn, va, vc, db, pf, perc, 2009

Kbd (pf, unless otherwise stated): 12 Etudes, 1959–60; Romantic Pieces, 1959; Fantasy Sonata no.1, 1961; Interlude, 2 pf, 1963; Brass Knuckles, 1968; Chorale Prelude, org, 1970 [after Abide with me]; 3 Ghost Rags, 1970; Seabiscuits Rag, 1970; Abendmusik, 2 pf, 1973; 12 New Etudes, 1977–86; Fields of Flowers, 1978; Gospel Preludes, org, 1979–84; Monsterpieces (and Others), 1980; Cadenzas for Beethoven Conc. no.4, 1986; 3 Dance Portraits, 1986; Recuerdos, 2 pf, 1991; Dédicace: a Small Measure of Affection, pf 4 hands, 1992; Sonata, 2 pf, 1993; Collusions (with C. Curtis-Smith), 1998; Bird Spirits, 1999–2000; Borborygm (with W. Albright), org, 2001; New York Lights, 2003; Four Preludes on Jewish Melodies, org, 2005; Le Fantome du Clavecin, harpsichord, 2005; 9 New Bagatelles, 2006; Ballade, 2007; Knockout: A Rag, 2008

VOCAL

Choral: Satires (Bolcom), madrigal ens, 1970; Vocalise, SATB, 1977 [from Songs of Innocence and of Experience]; Simple Stories (D. Hall), S, SATB, fl, cl, hn, vc, pf, 1979–91; Carol (Neighbors on This Frosty Tide) (A. Weinstein after K. Graham), SATB, pf, 1981–82, collab. J. Morris; Alleluia, SATB, 1992; The Miracle (A. Weinstein after G. Pascoli), men's vv, ww quintet, perc, 1999; May-Day (Emerson), SATB, pf or org, 2002; The Rhodora (Emerson), SATB, org, 2002; Two Meditations (Herbert), SATB, org, 2006; Four Piedmont Choruses (Byer), SATB, pf, 2007; Lady Liberty (Weinstein), SATB, pf, 2008; A Song for St. Cecilia's Day (Dryden), SATB, org, 2008; Searchlight Soul, men's vv, pf, 2009

Other vocal: Cabaret Songs (Weinstein), medium v, pf, 1963–96; Morning and Evening Poems (W. Blake), C/T/Ct, a fl, va, hp, pf, perc, 1966; Open House (Roethke), T, chbr orch, 1975; Cabaret Songs (Weinstein), medium v, pf, 1977–85; 3 Irish Songs (T. Moore), medium v, fl, vn, va, vc, pf, 1978; Mary (Blake), medium v, pf, 1978; On the Beach at Night (Whitman), tenor v, 4 timpani, 1978, rev. 1988; 3 Songs (Hall), medium v, fl, cl, hn, vc, pf, 1979; Songs to Dance (G. Montgomery), dancer, medium v, pf, 1989; Villanelle (R. Tillinghast), medium v, pf, 1989; I Will Breathe a Mountain (Amer. women poets), medium v, pf, 1990; The Junction, On a Warm Afternoon (H. Nemerov), S, Mez, T, Bar, B, pf, 1990; Vaslav's Song (E. Eichelberger), Bar, pf, 1991; Camp Shadywillow (Tillinghast), Bar, pf, 1993; Tillinghast Duo, S, pf, 1993; Let Evening Come (M. Angelou, E. Dickinson, J. Kenyon), S, va, pf, 1994; Briefly it Enters (Kenyon), S, pf, 1996; Turbulence: a Romance (A. Fulton), S, Bar, pf, 1996; The Last Days of Mankind (McGuinness), medium v, pf, 1997; Ancient Cabaret (Weinstein), medium v, pf, 2001; Sonnet 29 (W. Shakespeare), v, pf, 2007; Minicabs (Weinstein), medium/low v, pf, 2009; The Hawthorne Tree, Mez, pf, fl, ob, va, db, 2010; Laura Sonnets (Petrarch), Bar, pf, 2010; see also ORCH [Sym. no.4, 1986; A Whitman Triptych, 1995; Canciones de Lorca, 2006]

Recorded interviews in *NHoh*

Principal publishers: Edward B. Marks, Presser

BIBLIOGRAPHY

J. Hiemenz: "Musician of the Month: William Bolcom," *High Fidelity/ Musical America*, xxvi/9 (1976), 4–5

M. Wait: "Meet the Composer-Pianist: William Bolcom," *Piano Quarterly*, no.142 (1988), 33–40

W. Bolcom: "Parallel Universes," *ON*, lviii/1 (1993), 34–7

B. Holland: "Composing a Kinship Between Classical and Pop," *New York Times* (18 Jan 1995)

A. McCutchan: *The Muse That Sings: Composers Speak About the Creative Process* (New York, 1999)

W. Bolcom: "The End of the Mannerist Century," *The Pleasure of Modernist Music: Listening, Meaning, Intention, Ideology*, ed. A. Ashby (Rochester, NY, 2004), 46–53

D. Herwitz: "Writing American Opera: William Bolcom on Music, Language, and Theatre," *OQ*, xxii (2006), 521–33

M. Shrude: "Teaching Composition in Twenty-first Century America: a Conversation with William Bolcom," *AM*, xxviii/2 (2010), 173–90

STEVEN JOHNSON/LARS HELGERT

Bolden, Buddy [Charles Joseph] (*b* New Orleans, LA, 6 Sept 1877; *d* Jackson, LA, 4 Nov 1931). Jazz cornetist and bandleader. Although he has been widely celebrated as an avatar of jazz origins in the literature, this characterization rests primarily on anecdotal information derived from interviews conducted from 1933 into the 1970s with informants such as Willie Cornish, Jelly Roll Morton, Bunk Johnson, George Baquet, Kid Ory, Sidney Bechet, and Peter Bocage. Accordingly, the subtitle "first man of jazz" to Don Marquis's biography of Bolden (supplied by the publisher rather than the author) and depictions of Bolden as the "first of the New Orleans cornet kings" rest on little tangible evidence, given that the apocryphal Bolden cylinder sought by "hot" record collectors from the 1930s to the 1950s has never surfaced. The first public notice of Bolden is an 1890 arrest record in the *Daily Picayune* for an armed robbery committed by him in his Central City neighborhood; E. Belfield Spriggins' account in *Louisiana Weekly* (April 1933) was the first historical perspective in print. Whether they approved of Bolden's music and behavior or not, the informants who offered observer-based testimony on the music he played gave a fairly consistent picture of his attributes as a musician, emphasizing his power and volume, predilection for improvising, and aversion to written scores (although he may have been a "speller," capable of reading a little), eclectic repertoire (including a substantial representation of blues, but also adding old-fashioned schottisches and waltzes), emotionally expressive execution, and rhythmic intensity.

Bolden began his professional career with Charley Galloway's string ensemble before venturing into leadership of his own band about 1895. His often-cited competition with the formally trained musicians who worked for the violinist John Robichaux probably dates from that early period, but the relocation of many of Robichaux's sidemen who served in Cuba during the Spanish–American War in 1899 gave an advantage to Bolden, who seems to have appreciated the desire of young dancers for the less polite and more suggestive musical fare that was already present in New Orleans. Although he did not perform in Storyville, the proliferation of saloons and liquor outlets that attended the district's rise from 1897 to 1913 provided opportunities for "sporting life" musicians of Bolden's ilk, and he apparently made the most of them, leading to a reputation as a "ladies man" of the first caliber. At "Funky Butt Hall" (Union Sons' Hall, alternating as a union hall, a dance hall, and a church) Bolden's band performed regularly for pimps, hustlers, prostitutes, and, increasingly, other musicians. He also performed outdoors at Johnson and Lincoln parks in the Carrollton section uptown, and for carnival balls associated with the Knights of Pleasure in Central City. In 1906 he had a breakdown while performing at a Labor Day street parade and was institutionalized at the state sanitarium in Jackson, Louisiana, in 1907, where he remained until his death.

BIBLIOGRAPHY

D.M. Marquis: *In Search of Buddy Bolden: First Man of Jazz* (Baton Rouge, LA, 1978)

C. Hersch: *Subversive Sounds: Race and the Birth of Jazz in New Orleans* (Chicago, 2007)

BRUCE BOYD RAEBURN

Bolero. An international genre of Latin American popular music. Bolero first developed in the late 19th century as part of the traditional *trova* style of Santiago de Cuba. A hybrid of *criollo* and Afro-Cuban music, early bolero was a strongly syncopated duple-meter dance song in binary form. It was performed in a troubadour-like style with two voices in thirds or sixths accompanied with two guitars. José Sánchez composed the first published bolero, "Un beso," in 1885.

Bolero first arrived in the Mexican province of Yucatán in the 1910s, where composers of the *trova yucateca* style, most notably GUTY CÁRDENAS, adopted it. In the early 1930s bolero became a staple in Mexico City's radio station XEW, where Cárdenas hosted a show. In Mexico City bolero was transformed into an urban and cosmopolitan style, particularly thanks to the work of composer and pianist AGUSTÍN LARA, arguably the most influential of bolero composers. Lara favored a slower 4/4 instead of the original 2/4 meter and the piano as the main instrumental accompaniment. Most importantly, Lara is responsible for bolero's emphasis on lovelorn lyrics, as many of his compositions present women as unapproachable femme fatales and dwell on unrequited love. His many recordings, film appearances, and concert tours played a key role in disseminating bolero throughout Latin America.

During bolero's Golden Age (1930–60), bolero songs were popular in a number of different arrangements. In the 1940s an ensemble of three singer-guitarists, known as the bolero trio, was ubiquitous throughout the Americas, largely due to the popularity of Trio Los Panchos (1944–93). Some of the most influential bolero singers, such as Puerto Rican Daniel Santos, Argentine Leo Marini, and Cuban Celia Cruz, recorded with the Cuban dance-oriented ensemble La Sonora Matancera in the 1950s. Boleros were also popular in recordings by crooners, such as Cuban Olga Guillot and Chilean Lucho Gatica, backed by lush orchestral arrangements.

BIBLIOGRAPHY

C. Monsiváis: "Bolero: A History," *Mexican Postcards*, ed. J. Kraniauskas (London and New York, 1997)

M. Pedelty: "The Bolero: the Birth, Life, and Decline of Mexican Modernity," *LAMR*, xx/1 (1999), 30–58

J. Rico Salazar: *Cien años de boleros: su historia, sus compositores, sus mejores intérpretes y 700 boleros inolvidables* (Bogotá, 2000)

T. Évora: *El libro del bolero* (Madrid, 2001)

DANIEL PARTY

Bolet, Jorge (*b* Havana, Cuba, 15 Nov 1914; *d* Mountain View, CA, 16 Oct 1990). Pianist of Cuban birth. He studied with his sister Maria before entering the Curtis Institute of Music in Philadelphia in 1927, where he worked principally with DAVID SAPERTON (Leopold Godowsky's son-in-law). During this time he also played for Godowsky, Josef Hofmann, and Moriz Rosenthal. In 1935 he spent nine months in Paris and London broadening his education before returning to the Curtis Institute to study conducting with Fritz Reiner. In 1937 Bolet won New York's Naumburg International Piano Competition; his official New York debut, given later that year, was attended by Serge Rachmaninoff, Vladimir Horowitz, Mischa Elman, Gregor Piatigorsky, and Godowsky. However, success followed slowly, and the 1940s and 50s were notably lean years supplemented by teaching as Rudolf Serkin's assistant at the Curtis Institute (1939–42) and Bloomington, Indiana (1968–77). In 1942 he was made military attaché for Cuba in Washington, DC, and in 1946, while serving in the US Army in Japan, he conducted the first Japanese performance of W.S. Gilbert and Arthur Sullivan's *Mikado*. During the 1970s he achieved greater recognition, beginning with his magisterial performances of Franz Liszt's transcriptions of *Rigoletto* and *Lucia di Lammermoor* at an International Piano Archive concert at New York's Hunter College in 1970. The following year Bolet played Liszt's *Totentanz* with the New York PO under Pierre Boulez to great critical success, and in 1974 his epic Carnegie Hall recital proved a turning point in his career. A 1976 recital at London's Queen Elizabeth Hall confirmed his stature; in the same year he signed an exclusive contract with Decca, with whom he recorded the cornerstones of his repertory, principally music by Fryderyk Chopin, Robert Schumann, and, above all, Liszt. Although he disliked working in the studio, missing the stimulus of an audience, he recorded extensively and in 1984 he won a Gramophone Award for his disc of the first (Swiss) book of Liszt's *Années de pèlerinage*. While his repertory was essentially orientated toward the Romantics, it was surprisingly wide, and included such works as John La Montaine's Piano Concerto, Norman Dello Joio's Third Sonata, and Joseph Marx's *Romantisches Klavier-Konzert*. Acclaim came late to Bolet, but his very personal mastery and refinement are widely held in awe and affection.

BRYCE MORRISON

Bolger, Ray [Raymond Wallace] (*b* Dorchester, MA, 10 Jan 1904; *d* Los Angeles, CA, 15 Jan 1987). Dancer and singer in musical theater and films. He claimed to be largely self-taught, although he did attend ballet and tap classes as a young man in Boston. In the early 1920s he began his professional career with a musical comedy repertory group and then spent some years on the vaudeville circuit. At first known as a rubber-legged, "eccentric dancer," he eventually built a reputation as an elegant tapper, a fine mime, actor, and satirist, and a passable singer. Beginning in 1926, he appeared in more than a dozen Broadway shows. In *On Your Toes* (1936; music by Richard Rodgers), he danced in the famous number "Slaughter on Tenth Avenue," choreographed by George Balanchine, and in *Where's Charley?* (1948), also staged by Balanchine, he memorably sang and danced to Frank Loesser's "Once in Love with Amy," winning a Tony Award for his performance. He also appeared in many Hollywood musicals, of which only one took full advantage of his many talents. That was the 1939 movie classic *The Wizard of Oz*, in which he appears as the lovable, loose-limbed Scarecrow, longing for a brain.

BIBLIOGRAPHY

ANB (M.E. Christoudia: "Bolger, Ray")
T. Thomas: *That's Dancing!* (New York, 1984)

CLAUDE CONYERS

Bollywood. The term Bollywood is used variously to refer to the mainstream Indian film industry, to Bombay (now Mumbai) Hindi cinema, to Hindi cinema from the 1990s onward, and most recently to an Indian culture industry encompassing Hindi films and related commercial products distributed via satellite and cable TV, radio, DVD and video, CD and MP3, and Internet websites. Some Indian film producers and actors consider the term pejorative, in referencing a Hollywood clone, but it gained currency when Indian popular cinema began to attract international attention. The deregulation of India's media industries in the 1990s encouraged Bollywood filmmakers to reach out to the large overseas Indian diasporic market.

The commercial Hindi film is typically a three-hour-long melodrama mixing romance, comedy, action, intrigue, and several elaborate song and dance sequences. Since the early 1990s Bollywood films have featured elements indicative of the new global orientation, including a greater use of English words and phrases, and foreign locations employed not merely as exotic song and dance contexts but as homelands in which Indian nationals reside. Producer Yash Chopra's 1995 blockbuster film *Dilwale Dulhania Le Jayenge* ("The True Heart Will Win the Bride") about a non-resident Indian (NRI) family living in London heralded this new Bollywood genre. The movie and its music earned enormous commercial success in the United States and UK, as well as in India. Producer-director Karan Johar's "NRI films," including *Kabhi Alvida Naa Kehna* ("Never Say Goodbye") (2006) set in New York City, and *My Name is Khan* (2010), filmed in the United States and India, have each broken all previous Bollywood overseas box-office records, the latter earning $19.2 million. Bollywood films provide a nostalgic fantasy world for first-generation immigrants in America, but they also signify the new global India, and in this respect they have a significant impact on second- and third-generation Indians and their understanding of cultural and diasporic identity.

Bollywood films reach audiences in America primarily via art cinemas, satellite TV channels, website downloads, and DVDs, and Bollywood film culture plays a significant role in South Asian American life. Community cultural events and celebrations host Bollywood song and dance performances, dance schools and fitness centers offer Bollywood dance and aerobics classes, and college and university campuses promote South Asian American youth dance groups that perform locally and nationally. In April 2010 the first "Bollywood America" event was held in Boston, where dance groups from around the country competed in the national "Filmi Fusion Championships." Furthermore, British film director Danny Boyle's Academy Award-winning *Slumdog Millionaire* (2008), which incorporated the Indian version of the TV quiz show "Who Wants to be a Millionaire," successfully introduced Bollywood cinematic elements to the larger American film-going public. Diasporic Indian directors Mira Nair (*Mississippi Masala*, *Monsoon Wedding*) and Gurinder Chadha (*Bend It Like Beckham*, *Bride & Prejudice*) have likewise referenced Bollywood in their films, albeit on a smaller scale, and such successful productions acknowledge a growing awareness of Bollywood cinema in mainstream American culture.

BIBLIOGRAPHY

A. Rajadhyaksha: "The 'Bollywoodization' of the Indian Cinema: Cultural Nationalism in a Global Arena," *Inter-Asia Cultural Studies*, iv/1 (2003), 25–39
J. Desai: "Planet Bollywood: Indian Cinema Abroad," *East Main Street: Asian American Popular Culture*, ed. S. Dave, L. Nishime, and T. Oren (New York and London, 2005), 55–71
S. Gopal and S. Moore, ed.: *Global Bollywood: Travels of Hindi Song and Dance.* (Minneapolis and London, 2008)
A. Kavoori and A. Punathambekar, ed.: *Global Bollywood* (New York and London, 2008)
R.B. Mehta and R. Pandharipande, ed.: *Bollywood and Globalization: Indian Popular Cinema, Nation, and Diaspora* (London and New York, 2010)

ALISON E. ARNOLD

Bolt, Beranek and Newman. Firm of acoustic consultants founded in 1948 by Leo L. Beranek.

Bolton, Guy [Reginald] (*b* Broxbourne, England, 23 Nov 1884; *d* London, England, 5 Sept 1979). Librettist of English birth. Bolton made his name writing the Princess Shows, intimate musical comedies written mainly with Jerome Kern and P.G. Wodehouse: *Nobody Home* (1915), *Have a Heart* (1917), *Oh, Boy!* (1917), *Leave it to Jane* (1917), *Miss 1917* (1917), *Oh, Lady! Lady!* (1918), and *Oh! My Dear* (1918). The formula was successful critically, though too small-scale commercially to enable the Princess to enjoy sustained popularity, even when *Oh, Boy!* ran for 463 performances. The Princess Shows, though seldom revived, remain well respected. When bigger producers up-scaled, the collaboration dissipated and Bolton instead wrote books for George Gershwin and his brother Ira: *Lady, Be Good* (1925), *Tip-Toes* (1926), *Oh, Kay!* (1926), and *Girl Crazy* (1930). Bolton's work in theater and film alongside many of the greats—Kern, Gershwin, Berlin, Porter, Chaplin, and Astaire—resulted in books for over 50 shows, including *Primrose* (1924) and *Anything Goes* (1935), and a number of film scripts, notably *Ziegfeld Follies* (1945), *Til The Clouds Roll By* (1946), and *Easter Parade* (1948). His contemporary characters and vernacular dialogue were popular for being up-to-date, though this also caused them to become easily outdated, and several key libretti, including *Anything Goes* and *Girl Crazy*, have subsequently been updated. Bolton's legacy has been overshadowed by later developments in integration, whose mythology dismisses earlier shows for their "flimsy" plots and stereotyped characters.

DOMINIC SYMONDS

Bomba. Puerto Rican traditional music and dance genre. This creole music and dance was practiced on plantations and in free Black communities throughout the coastal regions of the island, by some accounts, as early as the 17th century. Bomba is African-derived music that has deep roots in Congolese, West African, and Afro-French cultural expressions and European (colonial) dances. Song structures, or *seises*, dictate a distinct rhythm for the drummers and the dancers; some of these *seises* include *Sicá*, *Danué*, *Gracimá*, *Kalindá*, *Cuembé*, *Yubá*, *Leró*, *Holandé*, *Rulé*, *Paulé*, *Cocobalé*, *Corvé*, *Cunyá*, and *Bambulaé*, amongst others. Bomba is both the name of the genre and the name of the main instrument—a barrel-shaped drum. The lead drum, or the *subidor*, marks the movements of a dancer who is using his or her body, clothing, or another prop to interpret the constant rhythm; the second drum, or the *buleador*, maintains a steady rhythm. The two other necessary instruments are a shaker or *maraca* and two sticks called *cua* that are played on the side of the *buleador*.

After the abolition of slavery, Bomba continued as part of family and community practices. During the middle of the 20th century, Bomba was commercialized and simultaneously folklorized for broader consumption. In the wake of its mid-century folkloric period, Bomba was revolutionized in the 1990s by the "Bombazos," started by Hermanos Emmanuelli Náter of Puerto Rico, who took the genre off the stage and brought it back to the streets for communal participation. Since then, it has become widely popular both throughout Puerto Rico and the Puerto Rican diaspora.

See also PUERTO RICO.

BIBLIOGRAPHY

H. Barton: "The Challenges of Puerto Rican Bomba," *Caribbean Dance: From Abakuá to Zouk: How Movement Shapes Identity*, ed. S. Sloat (Gainesville, FL, 2003), 183–96

L.M. González García: *Elogio de la Bomba* (Loiza, PR, 2004)

S.E. Ferreras: *Solo Drumming in the Puerto Rican Bomba: an Analysis of Musical Processes and Improvisational Strategies* (diss., U. of British Columbia, 2005)

M. Maldonado: "Bomba Trigueña: Diluted Culture and (loss of) Female Agency in AfroPuerto Rican Music and Dance Performance," *Caribbean Without Borders*, ed. D. Smith, R. Puig, and I. Cortés Santiago (Newcastle, 2008), 95–117

MELANIE MALDONADO

Bomb Squad, the. Group of hip-hop producers. It was formed in the mid-1980s by Hank Shocklee (Henry Boxley; *b* 1958) and included Keith Shocklee (Keith Boxley), Eric Sadler (*b* 1961), and Chuck D (Carl Ryder; Carlton Ridenhour; *b* 1960). Evolving from the Spectrum City DJs (later Spectrum City), a Long Island DJ group led by brothers Hank and Keith Shocklee, the Bomb Squad is best known for creating the backing tracks for rap group Public Enemy. Although the group collectively produced music together as early as 1985, the name "Bomb Squad" did not appear on a label credit until 1990.

The Bomb Squad used samplers/sequencers, turntables, and drum machines to combine layers of atmospheric sounds drawn from recordings of sirens, speeches, and crowds with re-contextualized phrases and bursts of music from funk records. The resulting tracks sounded dense and aggressive, while retaining elements of funk and jazz. The Public Enemy album *It Takes A Nation of Millions to Hold Us Back* (Def Jam, 1988) exemplifies the group's unique musical aesthetic. Their style of layering multiple interlocking loops can be heard on Public Enemy's *Fear of a Black Planet* (Def Jam, 1990), particularly "Fight The Power" and "Welcome to the Terrordome," and this energetic sound matched and contributed to the intensity of Chuck D's militant lyrics. In addition to later albums by Public Enemy (in which additional producers joined the Bomb Squad), influential productions include Ice Cube's debut solo album *AmeriKKKa's Most Wanted* (Priority, 1989).

BIBLIOGRAPHY

R. Walser: "Rhythm, Rhyme, and Rhetoric in the Music of Public Enemy," *EthM*, xxxix (1995), 193–217

C. Keyes: *Rap Music and Street Consciousness* (Urbana, IL, 2002)

WILL FULTON

Bonade, Daniel (*b* Geneva, Switzerland, 4 April 1896; *d* Cannes, France, 11 Nov 1976). Clarinetist and teacher of Swiss birth. He studied clarinet with Ferdinand Cappelle, Henri Lefèbvre, and M. Mimart, and won the Premier Prix at the Paris Conservatoire (1913). He traveled to the United States with the Garde Républicaine Band (1915), and returned in 1916 to freelance with the Diaghilev Ballets Russes, Victor Herbert Orchestra, Sousa Band, and other groups. He was a member of the Philadelphia Orchestra (December 1916–22; 1924–30), Columbia Broadcasting Symphony Orchestra (1931–3), Cleveland Orchestra (1933–41), and several other groups. He contributed significantly to the development of the Philadelphia school of orchestral woodwind playing. He was also a founder of the American style of clarinet playing, marked by a tone quality that combined the depth and breadth of the German clarinet sound and clear tonal center and flexibility of the French sound. Bonade was a distinguished teacher, writer of articles, and editor of solo and orchestral repertoire for clarinet. He taught at the Curtis Institute of Music (1924–40), Cleveland Institute of Music (1933–42), and Juilliard School (1948–60). His students included Artie Shaw, Robert Marcellus, Mitchell Lurie, Bernard Portnoy, and Anthony Gigliotti, among many others. A preponderance of American symphony clarinetists have studied with Bonade or his students.

BIBLIOGRAPHY

C.A. Kycia: *Daniel Bonade: a Founder of the American Style of Clarinet Playing* (Captiva, FL, 1999)

S. Thompson: *A History of the Philadelphia School of Clarinet Playing* (diss., U. of Texas at Austin, 1998)

CHARLES P. SCHMIDT

Bonawitz, Johann Heinrich (*b* Dürkheim, Germany, 4 Dec 1839; *d* London, UK, 15 Aug 1917). German pianist, composer, and teacher. Bonawitz studied piano and composition at the Liège Conservatory and came to the United States in 1852. His life as a struggling immigrant musician in Philadelphia during the 1850s is vividly described in a lengthy article written by his childhood friend Karl Merz for *Brainard's Musical World*. He returned to Europe in 1861 for concert tours with Joseph Joachim, then taught in Wiesbaden, Paris and London. Following a failed concert series in New York, 1872–3, he successfully toured playing piano recitals later in 1873. A review in the *Cincinnati Daily Gazette* noted that in Paris his playing had been compared to that of Liszt and Rubinstein. Bonawitz produced two of his operas, *The Bride of Messina* and *Ostralenka*, in Philadelphia in 1874. Armstrong noted that the operas had musical, but not dramatic, merit. Bonawitz moved to Vienna in 1876, then spent the last 30 years of his life in London, where he founded the Mozart Society. The society presented an annual concert series. Bonawitz's known works include five operas, a Requiem, a Stabat Mater, a piano quintet, string quartet, trio, songs, and piano compositions.

BIBLIOGRAPHY

Grove2, Amer. suppl.

K. Merz: "Bonawitz, Johann Heinrich," *Brainard's Musical World* (Feb 1880); repr. in *Brainard's Biographies of American Musicians*, ed. E.D. Bomberger (Westport, CT, 1999), 39–43

W.G. Armstrong: *Record of the Opera in Philadelphia* (Philadelphia, 1884)

J. Bennett: *Forty Years of Music, 1865–1905* (London, 1908)

R.A. Gerson: *Music in Philadelphia* (Philadelphia, 1940)

MARTHA FURMAN SCHLEIFER

Bond [Jacobs-Bond], **Carrie** (*b* Janesville, WI, 11 Aug 1862; *d* Hollywood, CA, 28 Dec 1946). Composer and publisher. She showed early talent for improvising songs to her own words and in painting. Her only formal study was with local teachers and at 18 she married E.J. Smith, by whom she had one child. They separated in 1887 and in 1889 she married Frank Lewis Bond. She published her first songs in 1894. Frustrated by difficulties in getting further songs published, and displaying the enterprising spirit that characterized the rest of her life, she formed her own publishing company, Carrie Jacobs-Bond & Son. By performing her songs she cultivated influential contacts. The baritone David Bispham sang a recital exclusively of Bond songs in Chicago in 1901, and friends arranged for her to perform for President Roosevelt at the White House. She published about 175 songs, of which two were highly successful. "I Love you Truly" (1901) sold over a million copies, and "A Perfect Day" (1910) sold eight million copies of sheet music and over five million records. She designed her own music covers, and the wild rose was a prominent image. Her publishing company moved eight times in Chicago to accommodate the growing business, and in 1920 she moved it to Hollywood. In 1927 she published her autobiography, *The Roads of Melody*; in 1928 she stopped composing for a time after her son's suicide. Her last song, "Because of the Light," was copyrighted in 1944 when she was 82.

WORKS
(selective list)
(most works published in Chicago)

Songs (texts by Bond unless otherwise stated): 7 Songs as Unpretentious as the Wild Rose (1901); California, the Land of Blossoms (1902); 2 Songs for Contralto: His Lullaby (B. Healy), Longing (1907); Love and Sorrow (P.L. Dunbar) (1908); A Perfect Day (1910); Half Minute Songs (1910–11); A Cottage in God's Garden (1917); Roses are in Bloom (1926); Because of the Light (F. Carlton) (1944)

Arrs. (transcr. M. Gillen and O. Chalifoux): Negro Spirituals of the South (1918); Old Melodies of the South (1918)

Pf: The Chimney Swallows (1897); Memories of Versailles (1898); Reverie (1902); Betty's Music Box (1917)

Principal publisher: Boston Music Co.

BIBLIOGRAPHY

C. Jacobs Bond: "Music Composition as a Field for Women," *The Etude*, xxxviii (1920), 583–4

Obituary, *New York Times* (29 Dec 1946)

P.R. Bruce: *From Rags to Roses: the Life and Times of Carrie Jacobs Bond, an American Composer* (thesis, Wesleyan U., 1980)

M. Good: *Carrie Jacobs Bond: Her Life and Times* (thesis, Butler U., 1984)

S.P. Finger: *The Los Angeles Heritage: Four women composers, 1918–1939* (diss., U. of California, Los Angeles, 1986)

S. Leding Lawhorn: *A Performer's Guide to Selected Twentieth-century Sacred Solo Art Songs Composed by Women from the United States of America* (diss., Southern Baptist Theological Seminary, KY, 1993)

M. Morath: *Three Songs: a Study of Carrie Jacobs-Bond and her music* (thesis, Columbia U., 1996)

Carrie Jacobs Bond Collection <http://ucblibraries.colorado.edu/amrc/collection/bondGuide.htm>

PAMELA FOX/R

Bond, Victoria (Ellen) (*b* Los Angeles, CA, 6 May 1945). Composer and conductor. From a family of musicians, she played piano from a very early age and then studied in the preparatory program at the Mannes School of Music. Her conducting studies began as a teenager with Leonard Slatkin at Aspen, where she had gone to study voice. Bond studied at the University of Southern California (BMA 1968) with Ingolf Dahl and William Vennard (voice) and was then hired to assist film composer Paul

Glass in creating scores for Universal and Metromedia Studios. Her advanced study was at the Juilliard School (MM 1975, DMA 1977), where her teachers included ROGER SESSIONS, VINCENT PERSICHETTI, JEAN MOREL, and SIXTEN EHRLING; she was the first woman to be awarded the doctorate in orchestral conducting from Juilliard. During her Juilliard years she also worked with Pierre Boulez as assistant conductor for a contemporary music ensemble and took classes with Herbert von Karajan and Herbert Blomstedt. Under a fellowship from the Exxon/Arts Endowment Conductors Program (1978–80), Bond was assistant conductor with the Pittsburgh SO. She served as music or artistic director of the New Amsterdam SO (1978–80), the Roanoke (Virginia) SO (1986–95), the Bel Canto Opera Company, New York (1982–8), Opera Roanoke (1989–95), and the Harrisburg (Pennsylvania) Opera (1998–2003). In addition to appearances with US orchestras, she made her European debut with the RTÉ Orchestra, Dublin, in 1982; her Chinese debut with the Shanghai SO in 1993; and became Music Adviser of the Wuhan SO (China) in 1997.

Bond has worked consistently and at a high level as both conductor and composer throughout her career, simultaneously serving as music director for leading ensembles and receiving commissions from major organizations. Recently she has given more attention to composition by limiting her conducting to guest appearances. Dramatic elements play a strong role in Bond's compositions whether ballet scores for leading companies (*Equinox*; *Trio: Other Selves* for Jacob's Pillow Dance Festival); operas (*Travels*; *Mrs. President*, based on the life of Victoria Woodhull, the first woman to run for US president in 1872); or her transformations of thematic material in instrumental works (*Seduction and Sanctification*, a triple concerto based around Esther, Ruth, and Judith—biblical women who defied convention to save their people). Although she sometimes uses 12-tone technique, her harmonic language is tonally based, ranging from triadic consonance to spiky dissonance. Among stylistic influences, she identifies Béla Bartók ("with his rhythmic liveliness and sense of play") and Alban Berg (for "lush yet rigorously structured Romanticism") on her website (<http://victoriabond.com/about>). Although her catalog includes works in many genres, her chamber works are among her most widely performed. Especially important works include *Molly ManyBloom* for soprano with string quartet, setting Molly Bloom's monologue at the end of James Joyce's *Ulysses*; *Dreams of Flying* for string quartet; and *Frescoes and Ash*, inspired by art of Pompeii.

WORKS

(selective list)

Stage: Equinox (ballet), orch/pf, New York, 1977; Trio: Other Selves (ballet), vn, vc, pf, 1979, Lennox, MA, 21 Aug 1979; Sandburg Suite (ballet), pf, 1980, 16 Aug 1980; Great Galloping Gottschalk (ballet), pf, orch, arr. of 7 solo pf pieces by L.M. Gottschalk, 1981, Miami, 12 Jan 1982; The Frog Prince (musical fairy-tale, after J.L. and W.C. Grimm), Albany, NY, 1985; What's the Point of Counterpoint? (musical fable, V. Bond), nar, orch, Albany, NY, 1985; Everyone is Good for Something (musical for young audiences), Louisville, KY, 1986; Gulliver (after J. Swift: *Gulliver's Travels*), Louisville, KY, 17 March 1988, rev. as Travels, 1994, Roanoke, VA, 18 May 1995; Molly ManyBloom (monodrama), S, str qt, 1990, New York, 16 June 1991; Rage (ballet), pf, 1993, Erie, PA, 16 Oct 1993; Mrs. President (op, 2, Hilary Bell), 3 S, Mez, 2 T, B-Bar, SATB, orch, 2002; A More Perfect Union (op, Isaiah Sheffer), 2 S, Ct, 2 T, Bar, actor, fl, vn, va da gamba, hpd, perc, 2004, New York, 27 May 2004; Corn in the Rock (Mayan folktale for children, B. Sander), nar, 2 hn, 2 tpt, b trbn, perc, 2006; Instruments of Revelation (ballet about Tarot cards), vn, va, vc, cl, pf, 2011, Chicago, 27 Feb 2011; Clara: the Life and Loves of Clara Schumann (op, B.Z. Krieger), incomplete, scenes perf. Symphony Space, New York, 26 April 2010

Orch: Elegy, 1971; 4 Fragments, pf, str, perc, 1972; Sonata, 1972; White on Black, conc., sax qt, concert band, 1983; Frog Prince (V. Bond, B. McGrath, A.S. McGrath), nar, orch/chbr orch/ww qnt, 1984; Ringing, 1986; Black Light, conc., jazz pf, orch, 1988/rev 1997; Urban Bird, conc., a sax, orch, 1993; Dreams of Flying, str orch, 1994; Thinking Like a Mountain, nar, 1994; Variations on a Theme of Brahms, 1998; Ancient Keys, conc., pf, chbr orch; Pater Patriae: A Washington Portrait, nar, 2007; Seduction and Sanctification, conc., fl, va, hp, orch, 2007

Vocal: Aria (Bond), S, str qt, 1970; Suite aux troubadours, S, inst ens, 1970; Peter Quince at the Clavier (W. Stevens), S, pf, perc, 1978; Tarot, S, mixed chorus, perc ens (7), 1978; Margaret (G.M. Hopkins), S, fl, vn, vc, pf, 1984; Scat (II), S, tpt, 1984; Molly ManyBloom (J. Joyce), S, str qt, 1990; A Modest Proposal (J. Swift), T, orch, 1999; Art and Science (A. Einstein), Bar, pf, 2001; Let Us Sing the Soul in Every Name, Mez (Cantor), chorus, 2004; On the Way (H. Chen), Mez, vc, pf, 2006; Babies Can't Eat Kimchee! (N. Patz, S.L. Roth), children's chorus, pf, 2007

Chbr and solo inst: Qt, cl, vn, va, vc, 1967; Trio, hn, tpt, trbn, 1969; Recitative, eng hn, str qt, 1970; Ménage à trois, a fl, b cl, a sax, 1971; Sonata, vc, pf, 1971; C-A-G-E-D, str qnt, 1972; Conversation Piece, va, vib, 1975; Batucada, pf, 1985; Notes from Underground, a sax, pf, 1985; Old New Borrowed Blues (Variations on Flow my Tears), perc, hpd, db, vib, 1986; Shenblu, fl, 1987; Hot Air, wind qnt, 1991; Dreams of Flying, str qt, 1994; Moli hua (Jasmine Flower), va, 1999; Samba, fl, pf, 2002; Dancing on Glass, vn, va, vc, 2003; Peculiar Plants, hpd, opt. nar, 2004; Sacred Sisters, vn, hp, 2005; Binary, 2 pf, 2005; Bridges, cl, bcl, erhu, pipa, 2006; A New Light, vn, pf, perc, 2009; Oracles, vn, 2009; Frescoes and Ash, cl, 2 vn, va, vc, db, cl, pf, perc, 2009; There Isn't Time, Partch's homemade perc, str, kbd insts, 2010

Principal publishers: Theodore Presser, G. Schirmer, Subito Music, Southern Music and Protone Music

Principal recording companies: Koch International, Albany, GEGA, Leonarda, Protone, Family Classic

BIBLIOGRAPHY

C. Apone: "Victoria Bond: Composer, Conductor," *High Fidelity/Musical America*, xxix/4 (1979), 28–35

J.W. LePage: *Women Composers, Conductors, and Musicians of the Twentieth Century*, i (Metuchen, NJ, 1981)

N Herndon: "How a Small Virginia City Saved Its Withering Symphony," *Christian Science Monitor* (15 May 1989)

V. Bond: "The Making of an Opera. A Personal Recollection and Reflection on Victoria Woodhull. 'Mrs. Satan,'" *VivaVoce*, lxxiii (spring 2006), 4–9

W. Delacoma: "Two Music Lives Better than One for Conductor," *Chicago Sun-Times* (10 Oct 2008)

R.L. Sharpe: *Maestros in America: Conductors in the 21st Century* (Lanham, MD, 2008), 25–6

J. MICHELE EDWARDS

Bonds [Richardson], **Margaret Allison** (*b* Chicago, IL, 3 March 1913; *d* Los Angeles, CA, 26 April 1972). Composer, pianist, and teacher. She began musical studies with her mother, whose home was a gathering place for young black writers, artists, and musicians including Will Marion Cook, Lillian Evanti, Abbie Mitchell, and Florence Price. Bonds showed promise early, composing her first work, *Marquette Street Blues*, at the age of five. In high school Bonds studied piano and composition with

FLORENCE BEA PRICE and later with WILLIAM LEVI DAWSON; she received BM and MM degrees from Northwestern University (1933, 1934). She moved to New York in 1939 and in 1940 married Lawrence Richardson. At the Juilliard Graduate School she studied the piano with Djane Herz and composition with ROBERT STARER. Other teachers included ROY HARRIS, Emerson Harper, and Walter Gossett.

Bonds first came to public notice when she won the Wanamaker prize in 1932 for the song *Sea Ghost*; in 1933 she became the first African American soloist to appear with the Chicago SO, in a performance of Price's Piano Concerto at the World's Fair. During the 1930s Bonds taught piano (NED ROREM studied with her in 1933) and was active as a solo and duo pianist in Canada and the United States. In New York she taught and served as music director for musical theater institutions, and organized a chamber society to foster the work of black musicians and composers. She also established a sight-singing program at Mount Calvary Baptist Church in Harlem. Later, she taught at the Inner City Institute and worked with the Inner City Repertory Theater in Los Angeles.

Bonds's output consists largely of vocal music. Her best-known works are spirituals for solo voice and/or chorus, but she also wrote large musical theater works, notably *Shakespeare in Harlem*, *Romey and Julie*, and *U.S.A.* As a popular-song writer she collaborated with Andy Razaf, and Langston Hughes; the best known of their works are *Peachtree Street* and *Spring will be so Sad*. Her works for orchestra and for piano are programmatic and reflect her strong sense of ethnic identity in their use of spiritual materials, jazz harmonies, and social themes (e.g. *Montgomery Variations* for orchestra, dedicated to Martin Luther King and written at the time of the march on Montgomery in 1965). Her last major work, *Credo*, was partially performed the month after her death by the Los Angeles PO under Mehta. Some of her arrangements of spirituals were commissioned and recorded by Leontyne Price during the 1960s.

WORKS

Stage: Shakespeare in Harlem (music theater, L. Hughes), Westport, CT, 1959; Romey and Julie (music theater, R. Dunmore); U.S.A. (music theater, J. Dos Passos); The Migration (ballet), perf. 1964; Wings over Broadway (ballet); 4 other music-theater works

Orch: 4 works, incl. Montgomery Variations, 1965

Choral: The Ballad of the Brown King (Hughes), solo vv, chorus, orch, 1954; Mass, d, chorus, org, perf. 1959 [only Kyrie is extant; reconstructed score in Thomas, 1983]; Fields of Wonder (Hughes), song cycle, male chorus, pf, perf. 1964; Credo (W.E.B. Du Bois) S, Bar, chorus, orch, perf. 1972; many other sacred and secular works

Songs: 42, incl. Sea Ghost, 1932; The Negro Speaks of Rivers (Hughes), 1941; To a Brown Girl, Dead (Hughes), 1956; 3 Dream Portraits (Hughes), 1959; The Pasture (R. Frost), 1958; Stopping by the woods on a snowy evening (Frost), 1963

Popular songs: 14, incl. Peachtree Street, collab. A. Razaf, J. Davis, 1939; Georgia, collab. Razaf, Davis, *c*1939; Spring will be so sad when she comes this year, collab. H. Dickinson, 1940

Spirituals (all or most arrs.): 5 Spirituals, perf. 1942 (1964); Ezekiel saw the wheel, 1v, pf (1959), arr. orch, 1968; I got a home in that rock, 1v, orch/pf (1959), rev. 1968; Sing Aho, 1v, pf (1960); Go tell it on the mountain, 1v/chorus, pf (1962); This little light of mine, S, chorus, orch; Standin' in the need of prayer (1v, pf)/(S, chorus); He's got the whole world in his hands, 1v, pf (1963); Ev'ry time I feel the spirit, 1v, pf (1970); I wish I knew how it would feel to be free, S, chorus, orch; Sinner, please don't let this harvest pass (1v, pf)/(S, mixed chorus); 6 others

Pf: 4 works, incl. Spiritual Suite, Troubled Water, 1967

Principal publishers: Beekman Music, Dorsey, Sam Fox, W.C. Handy, Mutual Music Society, Ricordi, Hildegard

BIBLIOGRAPHY

SouthernB

C.C. Harris, Jr.: "Three Schools of Black Choral Composers and Arrangers 1900–1970," *Choral Journal*, xiv/8 (1974), 11ff

A. Tischler: *Fifteen Black American Composers with a Bibliography of their Works* (Detroit, 1981) [incl. list of works]

M.D. Green: *Black Women Composers: a Genesis* (Boston, 1983)

A.J. Thomas: *A Study of the Selected Masses of Twentieth-century Black Composers: Margaret Bonds, Robert Ray, George Walker and David Baker* (diss., U. of Illinois, 1983)

H. Walker-Hill: "Black Women Composers in Chicago: then and now," *Black Music Research Journal*, xii (1992), 1–23

D. Hawkins: "Bonds, Margaret," *International Dictionary of Black Composers*, ed. S.A. Floyd (Chicago, 1999)

H. Walker-Hill: *From Spirituals to Symphonies: African American Women Composers and Music* (Westport, CT, 2002)

BARBARA GARVEY JACKSON/DOMINIQUE-RENÉ DE LERMA

Bones. Concussion idiophones or clappers, of indefinite pitch. Instruments derived from the ancient use of animal ribs are commonly made of flat hardwood sticks, about 15 cm long and slightly curved. They are played in pairs (usually a pair in each hand); one "bone" is held between the first and second fingers, pressed to the base of the thumb, and the other, held between the second and third fingers, is clacked against the first with a rapid flicking of the wrist. The bones produce a castanet-like sound capable of great rhythmic complexity. The bones were played in China before 3000 BCE, in Egypt around that date, and in ancient Greece, ancient Rome, and medieval Europe. There are occasional references to bones (as "knicky-knackers") in 17th-century English sources. They are also known in sub-Saharan Africa. In the United States, they are associated primarily with African American musical traditions as well as the minstrel show. It has been suggested that when the use of drums by slaves was banned in the 18th century the bones were used as a substitute. Their use by African Americans before the 1840s is little documented. In the early minstrel shows, however, the bones were an essential rhythmic constituent in the ensemble (fiddle, banjo, tambourine, and bones); they were also played in solos, usually imitations of drums and horses. In recent decades there has been a minor revival of interest in playing the bones.

BIBLIOGRAPHY

O. Logan: "The Ancestry of Brudder Bones," *Harper's*, lviii (1878–9), 687–98

H. Nathan: *Dan Emmett and the Rise of Early Negro Minstrelsy* (Norman, OK, 1962/*R*)

S. Marcuse: *A Survey of Musical Instruments* (London, 1975)

D.J. Epstein: *Sinful Tunes and Spirituals: Black Folk Music to the Civil War* (Urbana, IL, 1977)

R.B. Winans: "Black Instrumental Music Traditions in the Ex-slave Narratives," *Black Music Research Newsletter*, v/5 (1982), 2–5

R.B. Winans: "Early Minstrel Show Music, 1843–1852," *Musical Theatre in America*, ed. G. Loney (Westport, CT, 1984), 71–97

ROBERT B. WINANS/R

Bongos [bongo drums]. A pair of Afro-Cuban single-headed drums with conical or cylindrical hardwood shells, joined together horizontally. The shells are of the same height but of different diameters; the drumheads (animal membrane or plastic) are generally screw-tensioned and tunable, usually tuned to high pitches at least an interval of a fourth apart. The bongos are usually played with the bare hands, the fingers striking the heads like drumsticks. Created in Cuba around 1900 to answer the needs of small ensembles, bongos remain integral instruments in Latin-American dance bands, rumba bands, and jazz and pop bands. Bongo players usually position the large drum on the right, a common practice in the history of drumming. Great virtuosity of playing technique is possible, the players obtaining subtle shades of timbre, as well as glissando effects, by varying the amount of pressure applied by the fingertips, flat fingers and butt of the hand.

While bongos have played a less important role in jazz than the conga, to which they are related, there have been some prominent bongo players in Afro-Cuban jazz: the conga player Chano Pozo played bongos occasionally in Dizzy Gillespie's orchestra (1947–8); the bandleaders Francisco "Machito" Grillo and Mongo Santamaria regularly included the bongos in their rhythm sections, and Santamaria also sometimes played them himself. Many composers have included bongos in their scores, including Edgard Varèse, *Ionisation* (1929–31); Carl Orff, *Astutuli* (1953); and Pierre Boulez, *Le marteau sans maître* (1953–5, rev. 1957). Part 1 of Steve Reich's *Drumming* (1971) is scored for four sets of precisely tuned bongos mounted on stands and played with timbale sticks.

JAMES BLADES/JAMES HOLLAND/THOMAS BRETT

Bon Jovi. Hard-rock band founded in early 1983 and led by John Bon Jovi (Bongiovi; *b* 2 March 1962; vocals and songwriting). It achieved prominence as part of the so-called hair metal or lite metal wing of the general heavy-metal movement during 1980s. The group's first two albums gradually built up its success, but Bon Jovi broke into the mainstream following the release of *Slippery when Wet* (Mercury, 1986), which featured finely honed production and contributions by the famous "hired-gun" songwriter Desmond Child. The group's energetic rock style engages with topics of romance and hedonism but nevertheless retains important connections to a set of working-class experiences in a manner popularized by Bruce Springsteen. Music videos for "You give love a bad name" and "Livin' on a Prayer," both of which became top ten singles, showcased a photogenic and non-threatening version of heavy metal quite at odds with that put forth by such groups as Metallica and Iron Maiden. "Wanted Dead or Alive" couched the travails of life on the road in the sentimental aesthetics of an acoustic power ballad. The group quickly followed with *New Jersey* (Mecury, 1988), an homage to the band's home state, and toured through 1990 before a series of solo albums and hiatuses largely subsumed the group's visibility during the 1990s. After reappearing in the 2000s, Bon Jovi aimed at a more crossover pop market, regularly releasing new albums that retained their familiar hard-rock edge and kept a core of fans satisfied.

GLENN T. PILLSBURY

Bonney, Barbara (*b* Montclair, NJ, 14 April 1956). Soprano. As a child, she learned how to play both cello and piano, continuing on the cello as part of the Portland Youth Symphony when her family moved to Maine. She studied at the University of New Hampshire with Patricia Stedry, then in Salzburg, where she sang with several choirs. In 1979 she joined Darmstadt Opera, making her debut as Anne Page (*Die lustigen Weiber von Windsor*), also singing Blonde, Cherubino, Adina, Gretel, Gilda, Ilia, Massenet's Manon, and Natalie (Henze's *Prinz von Homburg*). At Frankfurt (1983–4) she sang Aennchen (*Der Freischütz*), Norina, Marzelline, and Papagena. In 1984 she made her debuts in Munich and at Covent Garden as Sophie (*Der Rosenkavalier*), a role she has also sung at the Vienna State Opera (1994). She sang Pamina at La Scala (1985) and in Zürich (1986), where she returned in 1989 as Susanna. Meanwhile, Bonney made her Metropolitan debut in 1988 as Naiad (*Ariadne auf Naxos*), followed by Adèle (*Die Fledermaus*), Sophie, Nannetta (*Falstaff*), and Susanna. She sang Despina at San Diego (1991), Eurydice (Gluck's *Orfeo*) at Geneva (1995), and Alphise in Rameau's *Les Boréades* at the Salzburg Festival and the BBC Proms (1999). As a concert singer she has appeared in works such as Brahms's *German Requiem*, Haydn's *Creation*, Handel's *Acis and Galatea*, and Mahler's Fourth Symphony. She is also a fine lieder singer and has sung songs by Edvard Grieg, Felix Mendelssohn, W.A. Mozart, Henry Purcell, Richard Strauss, Hugo Wolf, and Alexander Zemlinsky. Born with perfect pitch, she has a beautiful, pure-toned voice, a charming personality and sings with an assured sense of style. Bonney has released more than 90 recordings, including several of her own solo recitals. She also teaches on the faculty at the Swedish Royal Academy of Music and at the Royal Academy of Music in England.

BIBLIOGRAPHY

J. Allison: "Barbara Bonney," *Opera*, l (1999), 905–14

ELIZABETH FORBES/JONAS WESTOVER

Bonny, Helen Lindquist (*b* Rockford, IL, 31 March 1921). Music therapy clinician, educator, and researcher. She received degrees from Oberlin College Conservatory (BM violin performance 1943), the University of Kansas (music therapy equivalency 1964, MME 1968), and Union Institute and College in Cincinnati, Ohio (PhD 1976). She is acknowledged as the first pioneer in humanistic/transpersonal music psychotherapy for the method she developed in 1970: Guided Imagery and Music (GIM), alternatively referred to as the "Bonny Method." GIM sessions combine a relaxation procedure with evocative classical music. A trained therapist assists the client in experiencing music as a vehicle for psychological and spiritual transformation. After developing GIM, Bonny was director of music therapy at

Catholic University (1975–9). She also disseminated her method and its adaptations through her Institute for Music and Consciousness in Baltimore, Maryland (1972–9), and at the Bonny Foundation for Music-centered Therapies in Salina, Kansas (1988–2000). She is recognized worldwide as the key figure in the acceptance of music therapy as a primary intervention in psychiatry. Bonny's principal contributions to music therapy theory, research, and practice are collected in *Music and Consciousness*.

WRITINGS

Music and Consciousness: the Evolution of Guided Imagery and Music, ed. L. Summer (Gilsum, NH, 2002)

LISA SUMMER

Bono, Sonny [Salvatore Phillip] (*b* Detroit, MI, 16 Feb 1935; *d* South Lake Tahoe, CA, 5 Jan 1998). Singer, composer, producer, actor, and politician. Bono began his career as a composer; one of his first songs, "Things You Do To Me," was recorded by Sam Cooke in 1957–8. He eventually made contact with Phil Spector, with whom he worked closely for several years. One of his first successes came in 1963, when his song "Needles and Pins" (co-written with Jack Nitzsche) was recorded by Jackie DeShannon and reached number one on the charts in Canada. The height of his musical career came in the 1960s and 1970s as part of the duo Sonny and Cher. He wrote, produced, and performed on many of their hits, including "I Got You Babe" and "The Beat Goes On." Success with Cher, to whom he was married from 1964 to 1975, led to many appearances on television, including *The Sonny and Cher Variety Hour*. After their divorce, Bono pursued other acting jobs and business ventures, eventually turning to politics and becoming the mayor of Palm Springs, California, in 1988. During the early 1990s, Bono championed revisions to copyright law, which resulted in the Sonny Bono Copyright Term Extension Act (1998), effectively lengthening the time period that copyrighted works can be protected. His unexpected death from a skiing accident came after a successful bid for US Representative in 1994.

BIBLIOGRAPHY

S. Bono: *And the Beat Goes On* (New York, 1991)

JONAS WESTOVER

Bonvin, Ludwig (*b* Sierre, Switzerland, 17 Feb 1850; *d* Buffalo, NY, 18 Feb 1939). Swiss composer, organist, and scholar. Born and trained in Europe, Bonvin served as organist and choirmaster for a German Jesuit order in Exaeten, the Netherlands. He came to the United States after being ordained as a priest in England in 1885. In 1887, Bonvin was sent by the Church to Buffalo, New York, where he lived for the remainder of his life. While there, he became a key figure in the musical life of Canisius College. He first established a choir, which he directed for nearly 20 years. He then founded and conducted the school's orchestra, beginning in 1881. In addition to his duties at the college, Bonvin worked with a local school, the Sacred Heart Academy, in 1922.

Very active as a composer, Bonvin wrote for a variety of ensembles, even though his specialty was in sacred vocal works. In addition to several works for piano and pieces for organ, Bonvin's catalog includes masses, motets, litanies, four children's operas, 11 song cycles, a symphony, six tone poems, and 17 works for chamber ensembles. His first orchestral composition was a short work entitled *In gehobener Stimmung* (1891); after this, Bonvin wrote several extensive tone poems. His work displays a firm technical mastery of post-Wagnerian harmony and counterpoint, with long, romantic lines, rich orchestral sonorities, and a fine sense of formal detail. He sometimes used the pseudonyms Georges De'Sierre, B. von Siders, and J.B. Rainer.

As a scholar, Bonvin wrote *Hosanna: Catholic Hymn Book* (St. Louis, 1910) as well as a wide range of articles on sacred music. Bonvin was a leading advocate, alongside Antoine Dechevrens and Alexander Fleury, for the application of mensural rhythm to Gregorian chant. He wrote a number of essays on the subject, including "On Syrian Liturgical Chant" (*MQ*, iv, 1918, p.593) and "The 'Measure' in Gregorian Music" (*MQ*, xv, 1929, p.16). He also recommended the admission of women to the congregational choir.

BIBLIOGRAPHY

L. Bonvin: *Verzeichnis sämtlicher Kompositionen und Schriften* (Leipzig, 1907)

L. Bonvin: "Liturgical Music from the Rhythmic Standpoint up to the Twelfth Century," *Studies in Musical Education History and Aesthetics: Proceedings of the Musical Teacher's National Association 37th Meeting* (Hartford, CT, 1916)

ARTHUR J. NESS/JONAS WESTOVER

Boogaloo. A social dance originating in New York and popular in the mid-1960s. Stepping diagonally, the dancer twisted each leg in alternation to the outside, bent the knee, and pointed the foot; with upturned hands, the arms were twirled from the elbows, which were pulled in and forward. Music for the boogaloo combined syncopated Latin bass and drum ostinatos with conventional soul songs. Hits during its brief vogue included Tom and Jerrico's "Boogaloo" (1965), Joe Cuba's "Bang, Bang" (1966), Hector Rivera's "At the Party" (1967), and Fantastic Johnny C.'s "Boogaloo Down Broadway" (1967).

BIBLIOGRAPHY

M. Stearns and J. Stearns: *Jazz Dance: the Story of American Vernacular Dance* (New York, 1968)

J.S. Roberts: *The Latin Tinge* (New York, 1979)

BARRY KERNFELD

Boogie-woogie (i). A style of piano blues characterized by the use of driving ostinati in the bass (left hand). The genre first emerged in the 1920s and acquired mainstream popularity in the late 1930s. Regarded as one of the most significant styles of instrumental blues to emerge before World War II, it has continued to enjoy currency and from the 1940s has been a major influence on the development of various styles of vernacular music.

The essence of the boogie-woogie idiom is the ostinati, which typically continue throughout a boogie-woogie performance except for occasional breaks (usually two or four bars in length), and which provide the music with a strong rhythmic impetus. A wide range of ostinati is used. The most common and harmonically simplest is split eighth-note octaves (ex.1a). A harmonically denser approach is shown in the chord-based ex.1b. Ex.1c is sparser and simpler, but its rhythmical variety allows for subtle polyrhythmic interplay with the right hand. In the fully developed boogie-woogie style the pianist's right hand makes frequent use of riffs, which play off against the left hand ostinati to create engaging polyrhythms, as well as other devices of blues piano-playing such as blue notes and tremolos (melodic or chordal). Boogie-woogie can be played at a variety of speeds, but is most commonly performed at a medium-fast or fast tempo. It is technically demanding, mainly because of the rhythmic independence required between the player's hands. Its harmonic basis is most commonly a 12-bar blues chord sequence, although other blues structures (for example, 16-bar forms) are frequently employed, and the style has been successfully adapted to non-blues-related material such as popular songs.

The quintessential example of the style is Clarence PineTop Smith's "Pinetop's Boogie Woogie," perhaps the most famous of all boogie-woogie compositions. Smith's recording (1928, Voc.) is also the earliest known usage of the term, which is of uncertain origin, although Smith's spoken comments which punctuate the recording make clear it was a type of dance, and there seems to be a connection with an earlier use of "boogie" meaning rent party.

The evidence overall suggests that the fully fledged boogie-woogie style was a product of the 1920s, although elements existed earlier. The characteristic split-octave pattern (ex.1a) is reported from as early as the 1890s, although its first surviving appearance is in William "Blind" Boone's "Southern Rag Medley, No. 2" from 1909. Its earliest known use in published blues is from 1915 (Artie Matthews: "Weary Blues"), although an unpublished manuscript in the Library of Congress from Texas dates from a year earlier (House and Patterson: "The Blues"). A key figure in the development of boogie-woogie seems to have been the pianist and composer George W. Thomas who used boogie-woogie ostinati in a succession of published blues compositions, beginning in 1916 with "New Orleans Hop Scop Blues." In particular, his song "The Rocks" (1922) seems to have directly influenced a number of early boogie-woogie players. By the early 1920s boogie-woogie-type ostinati were becoming more frequently used in piano blues-playing. The first blues piano recording to use such ostinati continuously is James Blythe's "Chicago Stomp" (1924, Para.), although it arguably lacks the characteristic drive of the fully evolved boogie-woogie style. Meade "Lux" Lewis's "Honky Tonk Train Blues," first recorded in 1927 (Para.) is a boogie-woogie in all but name, and, in fact, was to become a particularly popular example of the style.

Boogie-woogie remained largely unknown to the general public until the late 1930s. Key to the growth of its popularity was the producer John Hammond Jr., who, driven by a personal enthusiasm for the style, promoted and recorded leading players, notably Lewis and Albert Ammons. Particularly important was Hammond's 1938 "From Spirituals to Swing" concert in Carnegie Hall, which featured a boogie-woogie piano trio consisting of Lewis, Ammons, and Pete Johnson that made a deep impression with both critics and public. Other important boogie-woogie pianists recorded in the late 1930s include Jimmy Yancey and "Cripple" Clarence Lofton. By this time boogie-woogie had developed into a full-blown craze among mainstream listeners, as manifested in a succession of adaptations of boogie-woogie compositions for big band, such as the recording "Yancey Special" by Bob Crosby and his Orchestra (Decca, 1938), and the appearance of popular songs celebrating the genre, such as Raye and Prince's "Boogie Woogie Bugle Boy" (1941).

In the later 1940s the mass popularity of the genre began to ebb, yet boogie-woogie continued to shape the evolution of American vernacular music profoundly. In particular its characteristic ostinati and rhythmic drive had a major influence on the stylistic development of both rhythm and blues and rock and roll. It also became, and has remained, an integral element of blues piano style, as seen for instance in the recorded work of Memphis Slim and Champion Jack Dupree, as well as jazz pianists like Oscar Peterson and Monty Alexander. Following the turn of the 21st century, it has been performed as widely as ever, and while it has become part of the general language of jazz and other styles, there have remained specialist practitioners such as Bob Seeley in the United States and Axel Zwingelburger in Germany.

BIBLIOGRAPHY

W. Russell: "Boogie Woogie," *Jazzmen*, ed. F. Ramsey and C.E. Smith (New York, 1939)

E. Bornemann: "Boogie Woogie," *Just Jazz*, ed. S. Traill and G. Lascelles (Kingswood, Surrey, 1957)

P. Oliver: *The Story of the Blues* (London, 1969)

E. Kriss: *Barrelhouse and Boogie Piano* (New York, 1974)

E.H. Newberger: "Archetypes and Antecedents of Piano Blues & Boogie-Woogie Style," *JJS*, iv/2 (1977), 43–71
M. Rowe: "Piano Blues and Boogie Woogie," *The New Blackwell Guide to Recorded Blues*, ed. J. Cowley and P. Oliver (Oxford, 1996)
P.J. Silvester: *The Story of Boogie-Woogie: a Left Hand like God* (Lanham, MD, 2009)
P.C. Muir: *Long Lost Blues: Popular Blues in America, 1850–1920* (Urbana, IL, 2010)

PETER C. MUIR

Boogie-woogie (ii). Any social dance for couples performed to swing music. The term does not describe a specific dance, dance sequence, or dance step; rather, it refers to any of several dance forms performed to music written in the distinctive boogie-woogie style. The term achieved widespread use through the popularity of tunes such as Pine Top Smith's "Boogie Woogie" (1928), Jack Fina's "Bumble Bee Boogie" (1933), and Tommy Dorsey's "Boogie Woogie" (1938), "Boogie Woogie Bugle Boy of Company B" (1941), sung by the Andrews Sisters, and "Cow Cow Boogie" (1942), sung by Ella Mae Morse. *See* SWING DANCES.

CLAUDE CONYERS

Booker T. and the MGs. Instrumental soul group. The group formed in the summer of 1962 when the four original members, Booker T. Jones (*b* 12 Nov 1944, keyboards), Steve Cropper (*b* 21 Oct 1941, electric guitar), Al Jackson (27 Nov 1935, *d* 1 Oct 1975, drums) and bassist Lewie Steinberg (*b* 1933) were hired for a session at Stax records. That year they had their first hit with "Green Onions," which has since become the best-known soul instrumental of all time. With Donald "Duck" Dunn (*b* 24 Nov 1941) replacing Steinberg in 1964 they achieved success in the rhythm and blues and pop charts with such singles as "Bootleg" (Stax, 1965), "Groovin'" (Stax, 1967), "Hip hug-her" (Stax, 1967), "Soul Limbo" (Stax, 1968), "Hang 'em high" (Stax, 1968), and "Time is tight" (Stax, 1969). Until 1969 they served (with Isaac Hayes occasionally replacing Jones or acting as a second keyboard player) as the rhythm section for virtually every record made at the Memphis-based Stax. The group originally stopped working together in 1971 when Jones became disenchanted with the ownership of the label. The members reunited for an album and a tour in 1977 with former Bar-Kays and Isaac Hayes drummer Willie Hall and again with various drummers beginning in 1989. Three years later they were inducted into the Rock and Roll Hall of Fame and in 1994 they released a new album, *That's the Way it Should be* (Sony).

As the primary architects of the "Stax sound," they can be heard on such seminal soul recordings as Otis Redding's "(Sittin' on) The Dock of the Bay" (Volt, 1968), Rufus Thomas's "Walking the Dog" (Stax, 1963), Sam and Dave's "Soul Man" (Stax, 1967), Carla Thomas's "B-A-B-Y" (Stax, 1966), and Johnnie Taylor's "Who's making love" (Stax, 1968). Often doubling bass and guitar, keyboard and guitar, or keyboard and bass, Booker T. and the MGs were classicists who opted for a spare sound. To that end Jackson employed little cymbal work and rarely played fills when backing other artists. With Cropper, Jackson developed a characteristic groove in which both players would slightly delay the backbeat, one of the hallmarks of the Stax sound. Although Jones was accomplished on both piano and organ, with the MGs he generally preferred the Hammond B-3. Both he and Cropper were concerned with timbral coloration, employing a variety of complementary sounds from their instruments. While most bass players largely fulfilled rhythmic and harmonic functions, Dunn tended to play lines that also served as melodic counterpoint. In 1978, Steve Cropper and Duck Dunn joined the Blues Brothers, with whom they proceeded to have chart success for the next three years.

BIBLIOGRAPHY

G. Hirshey: *Nowhere to Run: the Story of Soul Music* (New York, 1984)
P. Guralnick: *Sweet Soul Music* (New York, 1986)
R. Bowman: "Stax Records: a Musicological Analysis," *Popular Music*, xiv (1995), 285–320
R. Bowman: *Soulsville U.S.A.: the Story of Stax Records* (New York, 1997)
R. Bowman: [disc notes] *Booker T. and the MGs: Time is Tight* (Berkeley, 1998)

ROB BOWMAN

Boone, Blind [John William] (*b* Miami, MO, 17 May 1864; *d* Warrensburg, MO, 4 Oct 1927). Pianist and composer. He was blind from infancy, but soon revealed musical abilities, and several prominent local families contributed funds to send him to the Missouri School for the Blind in St. Louis, where he could further develop his talents. Although he was later expelled from this school, he received some formal piano instruction and acquired a reputation as a prodigy. He earned his living as an itinerant musician until 1879, when he came to the attention of John Lange, Jr., a prominent black contractor in Columbia, Missouri, who took charge of the youth's musical career. Within five years Boone was giving regular concerts in a group with a banjoist, a violinist, and a child singer. They played an annual ten-month season from 1885 to 1915, performing six nights a week; by 1915 Boone had played 8400 concerts and traveled more than 200,000 miles.

During the years of his greatest success Boone published a number of compositions, including waltzes, coon songs, and classical character pieces. The best known of these are *Blind Boone's Southern Rag Medleys* nos. 1 and 2 (1908–9). His most spectacular composition, however, was apparently *Marshfield Tornado*, a musical depiction of a storm that struck this small Missouri town in the 1880s. Although Boone was reportedly offered thousands of dollars to reproduce this piece in sheet music or on a piano roll, he always refused, claiming that he wanted to reserve the work solely for his own use. In 1916 Lange died, and Boone's career began an inevitable decline that was hastened by his aversion to jazz. By the time of his final performance in the little town of Virden, Illinois, on 31 May 1927, much of his former enthusiasm and flamboyant manner had disappeared. His works were rediscovered during the ragtime revival of the 1970s, however. One of his instruments, an ornate Chickering grand piano, is displayed by the Boone County Historical Society in the Maplewood Mansion, Nifong Memorial Park, Columbia.

W.K. MCNEIL

WORKS
(selective list)
(all printed works published in Columbia, MO, unless otherwise stated)

Pf: Caprice de concert (sur thèmes nègres) nos.1–2 (St. Louis, 1893); Old Folks at Home (St. Louis, 1894); Sparks (St. Louis, 1894); Dance des nègres (Caprice de concert no.3) (St. Louis, 1902); Blind Boone's Aurora Waltz (1907); Blind Boone's Southern Rag Medley no.1 (1908; repr. in *Ragtime Rarities*, ed. T.J. Tichenor, New York, 1975); Blind Boone's Southern Rag Medley no.2 (1909; repr. in *Ragtime Rarities*, ed. T.J. Tichenor, New York, 1975); Last Dream (1909); Love Feast (1913); Grand valse de concert, op.13 (Kansas City, MO, 1923)

Songs: What shill we go when de great day comes (New York, 1892); When I meet dat coon tonight (New York, 1892); Dinah's Barbeque (St. Louis, 1893); You can't go to gloria that a'way (St. Louis, 1893); That little German band (St. Louis, 1894); Melons Cool and Green (St. Louis, 1894); Dat morning in de sky (Kansas City, MO, 1899); Georgia Melon (1908)

Principal publishers: Allen, Kunkel

JAMES M. BURK

BIBLIOGRAPHY

SouthernB

M. Fuell: *Blind Boone: his Early Life and his Achievements* (Kansas City, MO, 1915)

N.T. Gentry: "Blind Boone and John Lange Jr.," *Missouri Historical Review*, xxxiv (1940), 232

G.T. Ashley: *Reminiscences of a Circuit Rider* (Hollywood, CA, 1941), 115

R. Blesh and H. Janis: *They All Played Ragtime* (New York, 1950, 4/1971)

R. Darch: "Blind Boone: a Sensational Missouri Musician Forgotten," *Bulletin of the Missouri Historical Society*, xvii (1961), 245

M. Harrah: "The Incomparable Blind Boone," *Ragtimer* (July–Aug 1969), 9

M. Harrah: "Wayne B. Allen: 'Blind' Boone's Last Manager," *Ragtimer* (Sept–Oct 1969), 10

W. Parrish: "'Blind' Boone's Ragtime," *Missouri Life*, vii/5 (1979), 17

J. Batterson: *Blind Boone: Missouri's Ragtime Pioneer* (Columbia, MO, 1998)

W.K. MCNEIL/R

Boone, Charles (*b* Cleveland, OH, 21 June 1939). Composer. Boone studied at the Academy of Music in Vienna (1960–61), the University of Southern California (BM, theory, 1963), and San Francisco State College (MZ, composition, 1968). Among his composition teachers were Karl Schiske, ADOLPH WEISS, and ERNST KRENEK. In the 1960s he served as chair of the San Francisco Composer's Forum and coordinator of the Mills College Performing Group and Tape Music Center. In 1971 Boone founded the Bring Your Own Pillow concert series, which evolved into the San Francisco Contemporary Music Players; and he was composer-in-residence at the Deutscher Akademischer Austauschdienst in Berlin (1975–7). Boone taught at the California College of Arts and Crafts and is currently an associate professor at the San Francisco Art Institute, where he teaches studio and history courses that relate sound and music to other art forms. He has been awarded three grants from the National Endowment for the Arts (1968, 1975, 1983). Overall, Boone's music can be described as atonal modernism in that it is freely atonal and avoids allegiances to any specific serial or narrative method. His early works, inspired by contemporary Polish music and pointillism, utilized static, slowly evolving sound blocks, which continued as a feature of his later compositions. Initial use of bright instrumental colors eventually gave way to a more monochromatic palette. His self-described "complex simplicity" exploits complex juxtapositions of relatively simple formal and sonic structures expressed through timbral relationships and changing textures. It also seeks classical balance and tonal relationships of the kind found in the music of Anton Webern, György Ligeti, and Witold Lutosławski.

WORKS

Inst: Oblique Formation, fl, pf, 1965; Starfish, fl, cl, 2 vn, pf, 2 perc, 1966; The Edge of Land, orch, 1968; Qt, vn, cl, vc, pf, 1970; Vermilion, ob, 1970; Zephyrus, ob, pf, 1970; First Landscape, orch, 1971; Second Landscape, chbr orch, 1973, arr. orch, 1979; Raspberries, 3 perc, 1974; Linea meridiana, chbr ens, 1975; San Zeno/Verona, chbr ens, 1976; Shunt, 3 perc, 1978; Str Piece, str orch, 1978; Little Fl Pieces, 1979; Streaming, fl, 1979; Springtime, ob, 1980; Trace, fl, 10 pfmrs, 1981–3; The Watts Towers, perc, 1981; Weft, 6 perc, 1982; Drum Bug, mechanical woodblocks, 1983; Drift, octet, 1984–5; 3 Pieces, perc, 1989: Lightfall; Last Gleaming; Twenty-Seven Lines; Morphosis, 6 perc, 1997

Vocal: 3 Motets (e.e. cummings), SATB, 1962–5; Chinese Texts (trans. K. Rexroth), S, orch, 1971; Vocalise, S, 1972

El-ac: A Cool Glow of Radiation, fl, tape, 1966; The Khaju Bridge, S, tpt, db, elec org, perc, tape, 1984–6; Ellipse, vc, elecs, 1997

Principal publisher: Salabert

CHARLES SHERE/ROBERT PAUL KOLT

Boone, Pat [Charles Eugene] (*b* 1 June 1934, Jacksonville, FL). Singer, actor, and author. He is best known for his success during the 1950s and 60s, when he delivered old-fashioned sounds with a wholesome image and was seen a safe antidote to the African American artists who were performing R&B and rock 'n' roll. His success was due in part to his choice to cover many of their songs in his own fashion. These were targeted specifically to middle-class white teenagers and resulted in 38 top 40 hits. Boone began recording in 1954 for Republic Records, where he covered music by Fats Domino, Little Richard, Nat "King" Cole, and the El Dorados. Second only to Elvis Presley in terms of album sales during the 1950s, he branched out as an actor, appearing on television in *Arthur Godfrey and his Friends* and *Ozark Jubilee*. From 1957 he hosted his own program, *The Pat Boone Chevy Showroom*, in which he served as a spokesman for the car company and pitched his music. Among his most popular hits are "Ain't that a Shame" (1956), "I almost lost my mind" (1956), and "April Love" (1957). By the mid-1960s Boone had turned almost exclusively to acting and changed his musical style to reflect his deepening interest in Christianity. After acting in the film *The Greatest Story Ever Told* (1965), he wrote several books on Christianity and right-wing American ideals. He became a gospel singer in the mid-1960s and started his own recording label, Lion and Lamb Records, in the early 1970s. In 1997 he surprised fans with the album *In a Metal Mood: No More Mr. Nice Guy*, which features covers of heavy metal songs in a big-band style.

BIBLIOGRAPHY

P. Boone: *Twixt Twelve and Twenty: Pat Talks to Teenagers* (Upper Saddler River, NJ, 1958)

P. Boone: *Pat Boone's America: 50 Years* (Nashville, 2006)

JONAS WESTOVER

Boosey & Hawkes, Inc. Firm of music publishers and dealers in musical instruments. Based in New York, it is a subsidiary of Boosey & Hawkes Ltd. of London. The London firm was established in 1930 as the result of a merger between Boosey & Co. and Hawkes & Co. It has grown into a major international publishing house with branches throughout the world. Besides the standard repertory, it publishes much 20th-century music and represents, among others, Stravinsky, Bartók, Kodály, Strauss, Britten, Prokofiev, Peter Maxwell Davies, and Nicholas Maw. The New York firm was first established as a branch of Boosey & Co. in 1892 and became Boosey & Hawkes, Inc., in 1930. Under Ralph Hawkes and his successors as president, it has developed its own catalog, which emphasizes the works of American composers, including Carter, Copland, Piston, Argento, Del Tredici, Kolb, Rorem, Floyd, and Lees. In 1979 a musical instrument division was created for the sale of instruments manufactured by the London firm; it was sold in 2003. Boosey & Hawkes has remained committed to publishing contemporary music into the 21st century, signing Reich, Carter, and Adams, among others. Its catalog also features music by jazz artists and by television and film composers.

BIBLIOGRAPHY

H. Wallace: *Boosey & Hawkes: the Publishing Story* (London, 2007)

FRANCES BARULICH/JONAS WESTOVER

Bootleg. An unauthorized copy of a recording of a concert or live broadcast. More recently the term has come to encompass recordings of rehearsals and demo sessions. Music industry organizations distinguish between bootlegs, counterfeit recordings which are manufactured to resemble legitimate discs and tapes, and pirate copies which make no attempt to duplicate the packaging of legitimate releases. In all cases, the recordings are issued without the permission of the copyright owners of the music or the performance. The earliest bootleg recordings were said to have been made at the Metropolitan Opera in New York in 1901–3 and many subsequent bootleg discs were circulated in the United States before Congress granted copyright protection to sound recordings in 1951. Elsewhere, ineffective copyright laws in Italy (which protected performances for only 20 years) enabled the manufacture and export of numerous bootleg recordings of opera performances and radio broadcasts given by Maria Callas and other stars. In popular music, fanatical followers of such artists as Bob Dylan, David Bowie, and Led Zeppelin have made recordings of hundreds of concerts and circulated them in a semi-clandestine manner. Some groups, notably the Grateful Dead, have actively encouraged audience members to make recordings of their concerts. With the adoption of digital media and Internet distribution since the late 1990s, bootlegs have circulated even more widely among fans; some contemporary artists have responded by distributing originally bootlegged recordings in the form of official releases.

BIBLIOGRAPHY

C. Heylin: *The Great White Wonders: a History of Rock Bootlegs* (London, 1994)

C. Heylin: *Bootleg! The Rise & Fall of the Secret Recording Industry* (London, 2003)

L. Marshall: "For and against the Record Industry: an Introduction to Bootleg Collectors and Tape Traders," *Popular Music*, xxii/1 (2003), 57–72

DAVE LAING

Bootsy's Rubber Band. Rhythm-and-blues group led by BOOTSY COLLINS.

Boott, Francis (*b* Boston, MA, 24 June 1813; *d* Cambridge, MA, 1 March 1904). Composer. He graduated from Harvard in 1831. Following the death of his wife, Boott took his young daughter Elizabeth [Lizzie] (1846–88) to Florence, Italy, where he studied harmony with Luigi Picchianti, and Lizzie was soon recognized as a talented artist, eventually marrying one of her teachers, Frank Duveneck. Boott became an honorary professor in the Academy of Fine Arts in Florence, and was friends with others in the Anglo-American community there, including Henry and William James, the Brownings, Isa Blagden and Constance Fenimore Woolson. The Bootts lived at the Villa Castellani in the Bellosguardo heights. His compositions include a Mass, Te Deum, and a cantata, "The Song of Zechariah," all for soloists, chorus, and orchestra, *Miserere* a cappella, anthems, string quartets, and many songs, including "Ave Maria," "Aftermath," and "Kyrie Eleison" (H.W. Longfellow), "Break, Break" (A. Tennyson), "Laus Deo" (J.G. Whittier), "Lethe," (M.A. Barr), "Here's a health to King Charles," "Rose upon the Balcony" (W.M. Thackeray), "Sands of Dee" (A. Locke), "Serenade" (F. Locker-Lampson), "Through the long days" (J. Hay), "We Two" (J. Ingelow), "When Sylvia sings" (S.P. Duffield), and "Maria Mater" (from *Memento Rerum Conditor*). Boott bequeathed $10,000 to Harvard to establish an annual prize for the best four-part vocal work written by a Harvard student.

BIBLIOGRAPHY

Grove2, Amer. suppl.

"Boott, Francis," *Cyclopedia of Music and Musicians*, i, ed. J.D. Champlin, Jr. (New York, 1888), 215

Obituary, *New York Times* (2 March 1904)

Recollections of Francis Boott for his Grandson F.B.D. (Boston, 1912)

W. James: "Francis Boott: Obituary (1904)," *Essays, Comments, and Reviews* (Cambridge, 1987), 97–8

JOHN C. SCHMIDT

Bop [bebop, rebop]. One of the main styles of jazz, generally considered to be the foundation for modern jazz. It was developed in the early to mid-1940s by musicians such as CHARLIE PARKER, DIZZY GILLESPIE, Thelonious Monk, and Bud Powell. By the mid-1950s, it was used more generally to describe the musical language underlying various substyles, such as COOL JAZZ, HARD BOP, SOUL JAZZ, and POSTBOP.

The word "bop" derives from the syllables "re-bop" or "be-bop," an onomatopoeic reference to a two-note rhythm created by the alternation of snare drum and bass drum accents found in the drumming of KENNY CLARKE (immortalized in his nickname "Klook-mop"). While the syllables had long been commonly used in scat singing, their specific connection to bop emerged in 1944 with Gillespie's composition *Be-bop* (first recorded in 1945). Critics such as Leonard Feather, who chronicled the style for the jazz press, found the term a convenient way to refer to new jazz styles.

Bebop's first innovations began with the rhythm section. Before bebop, the large swing orchestras relied on the piano, acoustic guitar, bass, and drums playing in tandem to create a solid, danceable four-beat rhythmic foundation. In the late 1930s, Clarke developed a new style of drumming that shifted time-keeping from the bass drum to the ride cymbal. The drummer's other hand and feet were now free to interact with the rest of the ensemble through spontaneous accents ("dropping bombs") on the snare drum, bass drum, or tom-toms. While such playing was discouraged on the bandstand by swing bandleaders, it was admired and widely imitated at Minton's Playhouse, where Clarke was hired in 1940, and in after-hours clubs such as Monroe's Uptown House that featured jam sessions. Younger, more progressive soloists tested their skills improvising alongside the polyrhythmic drummers, as one can hear on a recording from Minton's in 1941 that pairs Clarke with the electric guitarist Charlie Christian. By the time bebop emerged publicly in the mid-1940s, timekeeping was pared down to the drummer's steady ride-cymbal pattern and the four-beat walking bass line of the string bass. Pianists learned to add their own rhythmic layer by playing their accompanying chords in a rhythmically unpredictable manner, or comping.

Bop built upon and extended the chromatic harmony of the more progressive artists of swing. Throughout the 1930s and 40s, composers and pianists used increasingly complex chords, featuring chromatically altered extensions such as ninths and 13ths. Improvisers worked with this harmonic landscape, often adding new chords to the original progression. Perhaps the most popular chromatic alteration was the tritone substitution, which replaced the root of a dominant chord with a root a tritone away, for example, substituting a D7 for an A♭7, as Coleman Hawkins had done on "Body and Soul" (1939, Bb). Other substitutions increased the harmonic rhythm by adding chromatic passing chords. Through jam sessions, which placed improvisers with unfamiliar rhythm sections and challenged them with harmonic obstacles, this more flexible approach to chromaticism spread through the jazz community. In this way, both rhythm sections and improvisers became comfortable playing fluently with the new chords.

For soloists, bop demanded a startling leap in technical virtuosity. Throughout the swing era, gifted young musicians competing for positions in the top big bands set higher and higher standards for range, speed, and the ability to improvise over complex chord progressions. In the front of the pack were Parker and Gillespie, each of whom had independently developed an intricate method of improvising before meeting one another in 1942. Gillespie, who had been prominently featured with national big bands since 1937 including a lengthy stint with Cab Calloway, had learned to play elaborate 16th-note runs in the trumpet's highest register. Parker fused his equally complex rhythms with a bluesy sensibility honed in his hometown of Kansas City.

Even as Parker and Gillespie pursued their careers as big-band soloists (they performed together in Earl Hines's band in 1942 and Billy Eckstine's band in 1944), broader social and economic factors pushed the music toward the small-combo format. One was racial segregation. Throughout the 1930s and 40s, African American swing musicians endured Jim Crow segregation while touring throughout the South. In the North the bands that employed them were barred from commercially sponsored radio programs as well as engagements as house bands in major New York hotels (which offered free broadcasting as well as an opportunity to rest from touring). Another factor was a growth in the audience for small-combo jazz, including jam sessions. Under pressure from the musicians' union, which refused to tolerate unpaid performances by its members, these small-group performances became an alternative source for income for the most gifted musicians. While many, especially Gillespie, pushed to adapt the idiom to large jazz orchestras, bop ultimately became known as a small group style.

The first engagements by bop bands began in late 1944 in clubs on New York's 52nd Street, with recordings following in 1945 by small companies including Savoy, Guild, Manor, and Dial. The repertory of these bands was based on the blues as well as popular songs favored in jam sessions. Rejecting the melody and lyrics, which were protected by copyright, musicians composed new melodies on these familiar chord progressions, startling audiences with their intricate rhythms, pungent dissonance, and off-putting titles such as "Anthropology," "Salt Peanuts," and "Ko-Ko".

Bebop reached a peak in popularity from 1947 to 1949. During those years Gillespie and Parker were featured at Carnegie Hall, and new nightclubs in New York such as Bop City and Birdland cited the music in their names. This brief flurry did little to sustain bebop commercially, but the new style steadily gained ground among young musicians as diverse as Max Roach, Miles Davis, Dexter Gordon, Fats Navarro, Tadd Dameron, J.J. Johnson, Sonny Stitt, Jackie McLean, Sonny Rollins, Stan Getz, Art Blakey, and Gerry Mulligan. The rapid acceptance of bebop as the basic style by an entire generation of musicians helped pull jazz away from its previous reliance on contemporary popular song, dance music, and entertainment and toward a new sense of the music as an autonomous art.

As the novelty of bebop faded, its fundamental principles became the foundation for later jazz styles. The experimentalism of cool jazz moved well beyond bebop in areas such as instrumentation, meter, and form, while softening the music's impact through less interactive rhythm sections. By contrast hard bop insisted on retaining bebop's jam-session instrumental format, as well as its repertory of blues and pop-song forms. Bebop retreated from the vanguard in the 1960s when increasingly chromatic harmonies weakened or dissolved the tonal framework and the widespread use of modal improvisation directly attacked the harmonic foundation. Yet bebop has retained a central position in jazz education, where mastery of its core repertory has often been seen as a minimum standard of competence.

BIBLIOGRAPHY

I. Kolodin: "The Dance Band Business: a Study in Black and White," *Harper's* (1941), June, 74–9, 82
I. Kolodin: "Life Goes to a Party: Bebop" *Life* (1948), 138–42
L. Feather: *Inside Bebop* (New York, 1949, rev. 2/1977 as *Inside Jazz*)
M.W. Stearns: *The Story of Jazz* (New York, 1956, enlarged 2/1970), 155–72
R. Russell: "Bebop," *The Art of Jazz: Essays on the Nature and Development of Jazz*, ed. M. Williams (New York, 1959), 187–214
R. Ellison: "The Golden Age, Times Past," *Shadow and Act* (New York, 1964), 198–210
I. Gitler: *Jazz Masters of the Forties* (New York, 1966)
D. Gillespie: *To Be, or Not... To Bop: Memoirs* (New York, 1979)
J. Patrick: "Al Tinney, Monroe's Uptown House and the Emergence of Modern Jazz in Harlem," *ARJS*, ii (1983), 150–79
I. Gitler: *Swing to Bop: an Oral History of Jazz in the 1940s* (New York, 1985)
S. DeVeaux: "Conversations with Howard McGhee: Jazz in the Forties," *BPiM*, xv/1 (1987), 64–78
G. Giddins: *Celebrating Bird: the Triumph of Charlie Parker* (New York, 1987)
S. DeVeaux: "Bebop and the Recording Industry: the 1942 AFM Recording Ban Reconsidered," *JAMS*, xvi/1 (1988), 126–65
E. Lott: "Double V, Double Time: Bebop's Politics of Style," *Callaloo*, no.36 (1988), 597–605
M. Davis with Q. Troup: *Miles: the Autobiography* (New York, 1989)
P. Berliner: *Thinking in Jazz: the Infinite Art of Improvisation* (Chicago, 1994)
B. Gendron: "A Short Stay in the Sun: the Reception of Bebop, 1944–1950," *The Bebop Revolution in Words and Music*, ed. D. Oliphant (Austin, TX, 1994), 137–59
T. Owens: *Bebop: the Music and its Players* (New York, 1995)
S. DeVeaux: *The Birth of Bebop: a Social and Musical History* (Berkeley, 1997)
A. Shipton: *Groovin' High: the Life of Dizzy Gillespie* (New York, 1999)
P. Burke: *Come in and Hear the Truth: Jazz and Race on 52nd Street* (Chicago, 2008)

SCOTT DEVEAUX

Borda, Deborah (*b* New York, NY, 15 July 1949). Orchestra executive. As a child she played the violin, later switching to the viola with the intention of pursuing a performance career. After studying for one semester at the New England Conservatory, Borda graduated from Bennington College in Vermont with a BA in music (1977). She pursued graduate studies at the Royal College of Music, but chose instead to go into administration after working for the Marlboro Music Festival. Her first permanent position was with the Handel and Haydn Society of Boston, but she quickly was named artistic administrator and later general manager of the San Francisco Symphony. In 1986 she was appointed the president and managing director of the Saint Paul Chamber Orchestra. Three years later she moved to the Detroit SO, and in 1991 was named executive director of the New York Philharmonic, establishing her reputation as a formidable orchestral manager.

While in New York Borda successfully blended innovative artistic initiatives with fiscal constraint. Despite her reputation as a strong-willed administrator, she became a vocal advocate for musicians' rights and an effective negotiator with the union. In 2000 she was appointed the executive director of the Los Angeles Philharmonic, where she oversaw the design and construction of the Frank Gehry-designed Walt Disney Concert Hall and worked closely with music director Esa-Pekka Salonen to transform the orchestra into one of the world's best. After being promoted to president and CEO, Borda hired the Venezuelan phenom Gustavo Dudamel to succeed Salonen as music director in 2009. She has also chaired the Music Panel of the National Endowment for the Arts.

MICHAEL MAUSKAPF

Borden, David (Russell) (*b* Boston, MA, 25 Dec 1938). Composer and keyboard player. He studied composition with LOUIS MENNINI, BERNARD ROGERS, and HOWARD HANSON at the Eastman School (BM 1961, MM 1962) and with BILLY JIM LAYTON, LEON KIRCHNER, and RANDALL THOMPSON at Harvard University (MA 1965). He also studied at the Berkshire Music Center with Wolfgang Fortner (1961) and GUNTHER SCHULLER (1966); on a Fulbright fellowship with Boris Blacher at the Berlin Hochschule für Musik (1965–6); privately with jazz artists JIMMY GIUFFRE and JAKI BYARD; and with ROBERT A. MOOG, inventor of the Moog synthesizer and other electronic instruments. After serving as the Ford Foundation's composer-in-residence for the Ithaca, New York, public school system (1966–8), he became composer and pianist in the dance department of Cornell University, where he later founded and assumed the directorship of the Digital Music Program. He is perhaps best known for his work with Mother Mallard's Portable Masterpiece Co., a performing group comprising electronic keyboard instruments, synthesizers, and voices (1969–91), the first synthesizer ensemble of its kind.

From 1967 Borden has used synthesizers in live performances, and, through the use of solo improvisations, wave-form manipulation and multi-track tape techniques, he has developed a personal polyphonic style. His music from the early 1980s is minimalist, characterized by a steady rhythmic pulse and running lines of quavers accompanied by melodic counterpoint. Borden's interest in counterpoint culminated into one of his best-known works, *The Continuing Story of Counterpoint*, which he composed over the course of 12 years (1976–87). Combining high-energy electronics, classical concepts and forms, strict counterpoint, and dense musical textures, this piece consists of 12 parts lasting for three hours and was released on three CDs containing four parts each. Later works comment on history by using an entire work by another composer as a cantus firmus. *Notes From Vienna* (1993–4), for example, borrows movements from Haydn and Beethoven's cello works.

WORKS
(selective list)

Orch: Trbn Concertino, 1960; The Force, S, chbr orch, 1962; Cairn for JFK, orch, tape, 1965; All-American, Teenage, Lovesongs, wind ens, tape, 1967; Trudymusic, pf, orch, 1967; Variations, wind ens, tape,

1968; Notes from Vienna, elec gui, wind, 1993–4; Silent Stars, 2 pf, chbr orch, 1995; Infinity Variations, 2 pf, chbr orch, 1995

Chbr: 3 Pieces, wind qnt, 1958; 15 Dialogues, trbn, tpt, 1959–62; Short Trio, pf trio, 1964; Flatland Music, vc, elec gui, pf, perc, 1965; Pentacle & Epitaph, ob, va, hp, 1966; Omnidirectional Halo III, 2 S, 2 hpd, 2 vc, 1974; Counterpoint, fl, vc, hp, 1978; The Vermeer Variations, fl, ob, vc, hpd, 1985; Double Portrait, 2 pf, 1986; Gary McFarland (Boston Elegies), fl, ens, synth, 1986; Unjust Malaise, 2 pf, 1991

Synth ens: Cloudscape for Peggy, 1970; Easter, synth ens, tape, 1970; Endocrine Dot Pattern, synth ens, 2 brass, 1970; A. Art, synth ens, tape, 1971; Frank (i.e. Sin), synth ens, tape, 1971; Tetrahedron, 1971; All Set, 1972; Music, synth ens, tape, 1972; The Omnidirectional Halo, synth ens, wind ens, 1972; C-A-G-E, pts I–III, 1973–5; The Continuing Story of Counterpoint, pts 1–12, 1976–87; Anas platyrhynchos, 1977; Enfield in Winter, 1978; True Leaps, with 1v, wind, 1986; Dick Twardzik (Boston Elegies), with sax, 1987; Trains, 1v, cl, synth ens, 1987; Cayuga Night Music, S, wind, synth ens, 1988–90; The Satan Aria, Bar, synth ens, 1988; Angels, vv, wind, synth ens, 1989–90; Her Inner Lock, with b cl, 1989; Earth Journeys, synths, 1990–2010; Variations on a Theme of Philip Glass, 1991; Birthday Variations, elec gui, sequencer, synth ens, 1993; Perilous Night Companion, synth ens, chbr ens, 1997; K216.01a, elec vn, synth, 2003; A Tin Haiku (anagram of Kia-Hui Tan), vn, synth, 2005; Smart Hubris (anagram of Ritsu Brahm), elec vn, synth, 2006; Viola Farber in 7 Movements, 4 kbds, synth, live digital video, 2009; Dreams of Jimmy, 2 synth, elec gui, 2010

Other elec: Technique, Good Taste and Hard Work, 3 tapes, 1969; Esty Point, Summer 1978, elec pf, 4 synth, opt. s sax, 1981; Anatidae, 1984: I, s sax, elec pf, 2 synth, tape; II, bar sax, elec gui, 2 synth, tape; Enfield in Summer, elec pf, 3 synth, 1984; The Heurtgen Forest, Germany, Jan 22 1945, elec pf, 3 synth, 1984; Infinity Variations 2, 2 amp pf, tape, 1994; Heaven-Kept Soul (anagram of Kathleen Supové), 2 kbd, pf, 2007; "Third Sunset/The Dawns/Denishawn" (anagrams of Ruth St. Denis and Ted Shawn), 4 kbd, elec perc, elec gui, digital video, 2007

Principal publishers: Lameduck
Principal recording companies: Cuneiform, Earthquack, Red

JOAN LA BARBARA/ELIZABETH PERTEN

Border music. The 2000-mile border between Mexico and the United States is among the longest and most significant found in the world. The border that separates these two countries—sometimes in sand, other times in water—is also perceived as an imaginary line that separates "America" from Latin America, rich from poor, brown indigenous people of the South from the white settlers of the North; there may not be another border in the world of such stark distinctions from one side to the other. Contemporary views of borders, however, also suggest that these geo-political contact zones are as much locations of historical connection and continuity as they are locations of difference. The transnational movement of capital, labor, and media, however, are now more responsive to the realities of globalization than the borders of nation-states. The music cultures that exist along the border are largely ethnic Mexican but are also defined by indigenous nations that reside in the region, as well as a diversity of other ethnic groups that have made the border home over the past 200 years and more, reflecting both sides of the border in traditional and modern ways. As a region, the Mexico–US border is now, arguably, as much a distinct cultural area as it is the meeting point between two nation-states.

In a seminal overview on the subject, anthropologist Robert R. Alvarez (1995) notes that the predominant approaches to the study of society and culture on the Mexico–US border "represented the juncture between the literal and the conceptual." "Literalists" focused on the actual problems of life on the border (e.g., migration, environment, labor, policy); "conceptualists" focused on the metaphorical understanding of life within cultural contact zones (social boundaries, shifting identities, cultural hybridity). Border music can similarly be understood within this framework as both locating specific music cultures and practices that historically exist within the border region, and those music cultures and practices that emerge out of a border experience that reflects cultural contact and conflict.

1. Mexican musics. 2. Waila. 3. Popular musics.

1. Mexican musics. While the border between the countries of Mexico and the United States is often perceived in terms of the political and economic dominance of the United States, everyday cultural life along the border is exceedingly Mexican. A history of border music correspondingly demonstrates a predominance of Mexican forms and styles. As the creation of the border itself was born out of an act of conquest, it is of no surprise that the earliest—and most durable—musical form is that of the Corrido. The *corrido* is a narrative ballad recounting meaningful stories of the popular classes, stories that would not otherwise be "officially" recorded, or remembered from the perspective of the masses. They are forms of popular memory, stories that need remembering in order to be re-told again and again. Topics include acts of violence, such as a battle or conflicts between individuals or groups, a tragic event (such as an accident), or an injustice from the state or the upper classes. They may also address the deeds of an important individual or the significance or commemoration of a place.

Early *corridos* of the Texas–Mexico border (mid-to-late 19th through the early 20th century) have been found to speak directly to the intercultural conflict between socially subordinate Texas Mexicans and dominant Anglos. As one of the few, if only, avenues to mediate the social and cultural conflict, *corridos* of this era often reversed the social order by narrating stories with the Mexican protagonist in the position of dominant hero. In the years after World War II, with the rise of the civil rights era, *corridos* of intercultural conflict shifted emphasis away from hero *corridos* to narratives of victimization based the experience of discrimination and second-class citizenship (Peña 1982).

The *corrido* of intercultural conflict is not the only theme to be found on the Mexican–US border. As a border that exhibits extremes of power and class from one side to the other, other subgenres have come to prominence, such as the Narcocorrido—*corridos* about narcotics trafficking across the border—and those that chronicle the experience of undocumented migrants. The aura of transgression and illegality that both of these topics suggest have made them popular to Mexican populations on either side of the border.

Along with the *corrido*, the accordion-based music of the *conjunto norteño* is also synonymous with the

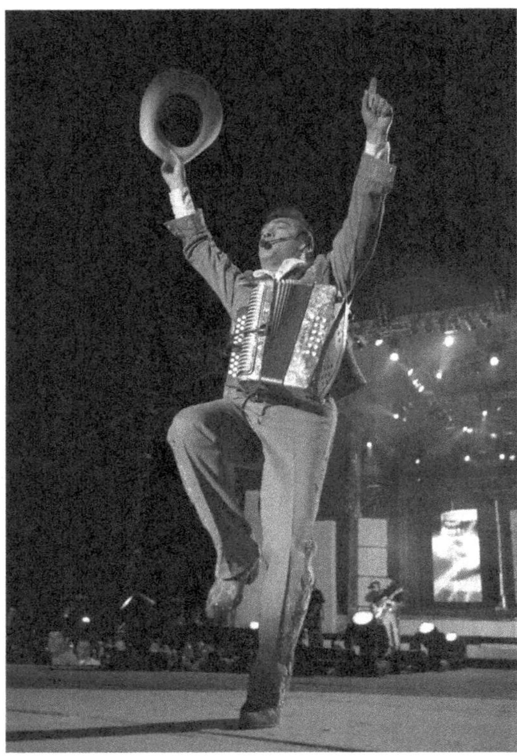

Los Tigres del Norte, 2007. (TOMAS BRAVO/Reuters /Landov)

Mexican border experience. Deriving from the music of German and Czech immigrants to the Texas and Mexican border region in the 19th century, *conjunto norteño* is currently the predominant music style of a larger category—REGIONAL MEXICAN MUSIC—that is the single most commercially successful category for Spanish-language music sold in the United States.

The border itself plays a role in the stylistic development of the *conjunto norteño* as the style that emerged north of the border in Texas is known as CONJUNTO (or *conjunto tejano*) and the style south of the border is considered *norteño* (*see* NORTEÑA MUSIC). Both ensembles are based on the three-row button accordion accompanied by the BAJO SEXTO, a bass-heavy 12-string Mexican folk guitar, as well as the contemporary complement of electric bass and trap drum set. By the early to-mid-20th century, Mexican musicians from both sides of the border had taken the button accordion and European salon dances (e.g. polka, waltz, redova, schottische, mazurka) and transformed them, making them Mexican through performance techniques on the accordion, the use of the *bajo sexto*, the incorporation of a then new vocal genre, the *canción ranchera*, all through the aesthetic world of the Mexican popular classes on either side of the border. (*See* RANCHERA MUSIC.)

Through the mid-century, there were more stylistic continuities within *conjunto norteño* on either side of the border than there were differences. Increasing commercialization of the style by Mexican artists, such as Los Relámpagos del Norte, after the 1960s led to its increasing popularity within Mexico as well as with growing migrant communities in the United States. This, coupled with stylistic experimentation of Texas-Mexican artists, such as Esteban Jordan and Flaco Jiménez, began to highlight the differences between practices on either side of the border; these differences, however, are admittedly subtle to outsiders of the music culture.

2. WAILA. Accordion-based music practices along the Mexico–US border are not confined to ethnic Mexican groups. The TOHONO O'ODHAM Nation (formerly known as the Papago Indians) straddles the border in southern Arizona and northern Sonora. The long history of contact with Mexico has influenced music cultures of the Tohono O'odham, along with neighboring YAQUI communities. *Waila* is an O'odham word related to the Spanish word *baile*, or dance; *waila* refers to social dances that occur within O'odham communities that serve as occasions people convene as a community around music making and dance. Another name for *waila* is "chicken scratch," but the latter term is not universally used. (*See* CHICKEN SCRATCH)

Instrumentally, contemporary *waila* ensembles owe much to the *conjunto norteño*: button accordion, electric bass, and trap drum set. In place of the *bajo sexto*, O'odham musicians use the electric guitar and typically also use one or two saxophones, sometimes in place of the accordion. Earlier *waila* groups were string-based groups with one or two violins accompanied by one or more guitars and sometimes percussion in the form of snare and bass drums. This style of *waila* is still active, as is the string-based music for another dance, the *kwariya*, an O'odham couples circular promenade. *Waila* repertoire is largely instrumental; the word refers not only to a social dance but also to the specific genre of the polka. The polka, along with the *chotis* (Spanish for schottische) or two-step, and increasingly the Mexicanized *cumbia* (of Colombian origin), are the main music and dance genres heard within *waila* music.

Within Yaqui communities are found Yaqui-based *norteño* groups. The Yaqui historically originated in southern Sonora but moved north to escape persecution around the turn of the 20th century. Yaqui *norteño* music is closely related to mainstream *norteño*, including Spanish lyrics, although there are some groups that compose songs in the Yaqui language (Griffith 1997).

3. POPULAR MUSICS. By definition, border areas are zones of cultural contact resulting in the blending of disparate cultural elements, often creating new forms or even styles of cultural expression, organization, and meaning; these processes take place both at the geo-political boundary between countries as well as locations—near or far from international borders—where cultural groups have historically encountered other groups. In the history of music along the Mexico–US border, commercially popular music has been the primary terrain where musicians from both sides of the border have exchanged musical ideas in both the development and creation of new styles and genres, as well as border identities themselves.

As the population existing in between the cultures of Mexico and the United States, Mexican Americans—or Chicanos—have experienced for generations the social meaning of the border. In turn, their expressive culture is full of cultural mixing, demonstrating intimate knowledge of cultural expressions from both countries. These expressions are often stylistically distinct from either Mexican or American inventions and thus Chicanos have carved out a cultural niche particular to their own border experience. Musically these expressions run the gamut of mainstream styles: rock, jazz, and rap or hip hop. In tandem with Mexican migrant communities within the United States, Chicanos have also been active within mainstream Mexican musical forms operating across the border, such as MARIACHI, BANDA, and SON JAROCHO.

Just as within Chicano culture, indigenous communities along the border also have felt the power of cross-cultural inter-relations, with *waila* and *norteño* being two powerful musical examples. Mainstream music styles, such as rock, hip hop, country-western, and reggae are important expressive avenues for indigenous communities to both national and international socio-cultural currents relevant to their experience, and their own feeling of being Hopi, Navajo, or Apache. Indigenous connections to and expressions of popular musics are examples of the complex articulations of border identities that defy standard categorization.

The continuities of the metaphorical concept of border music resonate in the city of Tijuana. While there are numerous sister cities all along the 2000-mile-long border, the Tijuana–San Diego greater metropolitan area is the largest and most important along the border and among the most significant border crossings in the world. With its proximity to Southern California, Tijuana is an emergent center in the production of popular culture in Mexico, the greater border region, and beyond. While many of the above-mentioned popular music styles flourish in the city, its most celebrated contribution to popular music is in the area of electronic dance music, *nortec*. As represented in the name—a combination of *norteño* and techno—*nortec* is a hybrid of tradition and modernity: the sounds of accordions, the brass instruments of the banda sinaloense, and the booming *tambora* drum blended with modern computer technology and DJ mixing techniques resulting in a new sound signifying the border on multiple levels.

Music along the Mexico–US border reflects the diversity of peoples that have inhabited these lands for many generations, the history of conflict within and between groups, and the potential for the medium of music to make connections between seemingly disparate populations. The music also reflects the innovative site the border has become though the work of artists who have lived in the region itself or whose ancestry has been shaped by the lived experience of the border.

See also CHICANO MOVEMENT MUSIC; LATINO MUSIC; TEJANO MUSIC; and SOUTHWEST.

BIBLIOGRAPHY

A. Paredes: *"With His Pistol in his Hand": a Border Ballad and its Hero* (Austin, TX, 1958)

A. Paredes: *A Texas-Mexican Cancionero: Folksongs of the Lower Border* (Austin, TX, 1976/*R*)

M.H. Peña: "Música fronteriza/Border Music," *Aztlán*, xxi/1–2 (1992–6), 191–225

R.R. Alvarez Jr.: "The Mexico–US Border: the Making of an Anthropology of Borderlands," *Annual Review of Anthropology*, xxiv (1995), 447–70

G. Béhague: "Boundaries and Borders in the Study of Music in Latin America: A Conceptual Re-Mapping," *LAMR*, xxi/1 (2000), 16–30

R. Pérez-Torres: "Mestizaje in the Mix: Chicano Identity, Cultural Politics, and Postmodern Music," *Music and the Racial Imagination*, ed. R. Radano and P.V. Bohlmann (Chicago, 2000), 206–30

F.R. Aparicio and C.F. Jáquez, eds.: *Musical Migrations: Transnationalism and Cultural Hybridity in Latin/o America* (New York, 2003)

A.L. Madrid: *Nor-Tec Rifa!: Electronic Dance Music from Tijuana to the World* (New York, 2008)

A.L. Madrid, ed.: *Transnational Encounters: Music and Performance at the U.S.-Mexico Border* (New York, 2011)

ESTEVAN CÉSAR AZCONA

Bordman, Gerald M(artin) (*b* Philadelphia, PA, 18 Sept 1931; *d* Wynnewood, PA, 9 May 2011). Writer on musical theater. He graduated from Lafayette College (BA) in 1952, then undertook graduate studies at the University of Pennsylvania (MA 1953, PhD 1956). Although he has written on English folklore, his main work has been in the field of the American theater, particularly the American musical. His *American Musical Theatre: a Chronicle* (1978, 2/1992, 3/2001, 4/2011) is an extensive and exhaustive summary from the origins of the form to 2000, and displays his characteristic chronicling of detail and thorough examination of narrative history. Consequently, his publications have proved invaluable in the early establishment of what is still a developing field of academic study. He has also published biographies of Jerome Kern and Vincent Youmans.

WRITINGS

American Musical Theatre: a Chronicle (New York, 1978, 4/2011)

Jerome Kern: his Life and Music (New York, 1980)

American Operetta: from H.M.S. Pinafore to Sweeney Todd (New York, 1981)

American Musical Comedy: from Adonis to Dreamgirls (New York, 1982)

Days to be Happy, Years to be Sad: the Life and Music of Vincent Youmans (New York, 1982)

The Oxford Companion to American Theatre (New York, 1984)

American Musical Revue: from the Passing Show to Sugar Babies (New York, 1985)

The Concise Oxford Companion to American Theatre (New York, 1987)

American Theatre: a Chronicle of Comedy and Drama, 1869–1914 (New York, 1994); *1914–1930* (New York, 1995); *1930–1969* (New York, 1996)

PAULA MORGAN/R

Boretz, Benjamin (*b* Brooklyn, NY, 3 Oct 1934). Composer and theorist. He began composing at an early age and studied philosophy as well as music in high school and at Brooklyn College (BA 1954). He received an MFA in composition from Brandeis University (1957), where he was a pupil of ARTHUR BERGER and IRVING FINE. He also studied with LUKAS FOSS at UCLA and DARIUS MILHAUD at Aspen. In 1970 he received his PhD from Princeton, where he had been a pupil of ROGER SESSIONS and

MILTON BABBITT. From 1973 to 1998 he taught at Bard College, Annandale-on-Hudson, New York, and he has also taught at Columbia University, Evergreen College, the University of Michigan, and UC Berkeley, among others. His awards include the Fromm Composition Prize (1956), a Fulbright scholarship (1970–71, during which he taught at the University of Southhampton), and a Princeton University Council of the Humanities fellowship (1971–2).

His early work demonstrates concern for systematic design and the realization of complex and multiple networks of nested musical relationships. Later he explored contexts for improvisatory music making: scenarios and texts for group interaction, notational and gestural stimuli for performance, and so-called soundscores—taped sound intended as a "text" for performance. Beginning in 1980 he taped many hundreds of episodes of "solo and collaborative soundmaking expression." An important ongoing project at Bard College was Music Program Zero, which Boretz described as "a continuing experiment in holistic development and inter-arts exploration," and which brought together composers, performers, visual artists, filmmakers, and more to experiment with and critically examine music and sound as they relate to other artistic media as well as politics, philosophy, and the environment.

Boretz's work as a writer and editor has had a particularly great impact. He was music critic for the *Nation*, 1962–9, and with Arthur Berger founded the journal *Perspectives of New Music* in 1962, of which he remained a co-editor (with Berger, Edward T. Cone, and Elaine Barkin, in succession) until 1982; he then resumed, with Robert Morris and John Rahn, in 1999. The lengthiest of his writings, *Meta-Variations: Studies in the Foundation of Musical Thought*, which appeared in that journal in installments (1969–73) and was subsequently published by Open Space Publications in 1995, applies principles of relativist philosophy in examining the possibility of discourse about musical cognition and composition. *Meta-Variations* engages a wide array of music-theoretical and philosophical models, and has become required reading in music-theoretical circles. Among the important positions that Boretz takes in *Meta-Variations* is a radical close examination of what a discourse about music should be like, especially in regard to the experiential relationship to the music that that discourse engages. In later writings, including perhaps most notably "Language, as a Music," he investigates varieties of musical-verbal discourse in which the sonority of language, changes in narrative voice, and the graphic presentation of the text play a fundamental role. In his later work, Boretz is concerned with the relationship between structure or design and meaning or communication, including issues that subtend personal and interpersonal communicative languages, and many of his written works occupy a space that encompasses both rigorous, formalist, analytic prose and highly experimental poetic expression. Boretz's theoretical epistemology resonates strongly in the work of theorists Joseph Dubiel, Marianne Kielian-Gilbert, Jay Rahn (whose *A Theory for All Music* explicitly applies the methodological thrust of *Meta-Variations* to a multi-ethnographic terrain), John Rahn, Martin Scherzinger, and many others.

Boretz has published articles in *Perspectives of New Music*, *Musical Quarterly*, *Harper's*, *Journal of Philosophy*, *Journal of Music Theory*, and more. In 1988 he founded Open Space Publications with Elaine Barkin and J.K. Randall, which in 1999 began publishing (with additional support from Mary Lee Roberts and Tildy Bayar) *The Open Space* magazine, the latter as a forum "for texts which, in one way or another, might feel somewhat marginal—or too 'under construction'—for other, kindred publications." Most of his shorter writings, including "Nelson Goodman's Languages of Art from a Musical Perspective," "in Quest of the Rhythmic Genius," "What Lingers On (, when the Song is Ended)," "Interface I–VII," and many ruminations, notes, reviews, and "text compositions" have been compiled in the two-volume anthology *Being About Music: Textworks, 1960–2003*. *Being About Music* also includes contemporaneous writings of his long-time friend and colleague J.K. Randall. A double-issue festschrift was released by *Perspectives of New Music* in 2005 in honor of Boretz's 70th birthday, which included tributes, analytic essays, and philosophical ruminations written by a wide cross-section of friends, colleagues, and former students.

WORKS

(selective list)

Concerto grosso, str, 1954; Partita, pf, 1955; Divertimento, ens, 1956; Vn Conc., 1956; Str Qt, 1957–8; 3 Donne Songs, S, pf, 1959–60; Brass Qnt, 1961–3; Group Variations I, chbr orch, 1964–7, II, tape, 1968–71; Liebeslied, pf, 1974; ("…my chart shines high where the blue milks upset…"), pf, 1976; Language, as a Music: Six Marginal Pretexts for Composition, spkr, pf, tape, 1978; Soliloquy II, pf, 1979; Forming, tape-recorded improvisations, 1980; Soliloquy III, kbd, 1980; Musics for Two Composers, perfs, 1981; Soliloquy IV, pf, 1981; Soliloquy V, elec b gui, 1982; Midnight Music, perfs, 1982; forM (a music), tape, 1986; Lament for Sarah, pf, 1989; music/consciousness/gender, live and recorded speakers, prerecorded music, video images, 1994; Black/Noise I, cptr, 1998; Black/Noise III, video images, cptr, 1998; Music, as a Music, spkr and video, 1998; UN(-), chbr orch, 1999; O, pf, 2001; Ainu Dream, pf, 2002; Downtime, pf, elecs, 2005; Is Every Entity a Being?, Str Qt, 2007–8; The Memory of All That: a Holy Sonnet of John Donne for Milton Babbitt (1916–2011), 2011

BIBLIOGRAPHY

F.E. Maus: "Recent Ideas and Activities of James K. Randall and Benjamin Boretz: A New Social Role for Music," *PNM*, xxvi/2 (1988), 214–22

M. Scherzinger: "Feminine/Feminist? In Quest of Names with No Experiences (Yet)," *Postmodern Music/Postmodern Thought*, ed. J. Auner and J. Lochhead (New York, 2002)

E. Barkin: "Reexperiencing *Language, as a Music* Revisited." *PNM*, xxxviii/1 (2000), 223–45

S. Gleason, M. Scherzinger, J. Rahn, eds.: "Special Double Issue: Perspectives On and Around Ben Boretz at 70," *PNM*, xliv/1–2 (2005–6)

D. Hanninen: "'What is about, is also of/also is': Words, Musical Organization, and Boretz's *Language, as a music*, 'Thesis'." *PNM*, xxiv/2 (2006), 14–65

MARTIN BRODY/CHRIS STOVER

Borge, Victor [Rosenbaum, Børge] (*b* Copenhagen, Denmark, 3 Jan 1909; *d* Greenwich, CT, 23 Dec 2000). Pianist and musical humorist of Danish birth. Borge was born into a family of musicians. His father played in the Royal Danish Orchestra, and Victor began his study of music at the age of two. He attended the Royal Danish Academy of Music and studied with Frederic Lamond and EGON PETRI in Berlin. During the 1930s, Borge performed satirical revues in which he began blending classical music and jokes. Borge immigrated to America in 1940 but did not learn English until he arrived in the United States; he picked it up easily by watching American films.

In New York he began to appear regularly on Bing Crosby's *Kraft Music Hall* radio series in 1940, and in 1941 changed his name to Victor Borge. He was soon given his own radio show with NBC, and starting in 1953, gave hundreds of daily recitals under the title *Comedy in Music* at the Golden Theater on Broadway. Borge also traveled internationally, performing his solo routines and with major symphony orchestras well into old age.

Borge's routines were partly improvised and mixed verbal and musical humor. His elaborate musical jokes included playing sheet music upside down, repeatedly falling off the piano bench only to produce a seatbelt and buckle himself in, and veering off into popular tunes while performing classical numbers. Borge commonly embodied the role of music educator in his routines and responded to the dichotomy of high and low culture firmly entrenched in American minds at that time. Within the tradition of music recitals he mocked the pretentions of classical music culture by maintaining a serious façade while absent-mindedly forgetting what he was to play or breaching what was then considered good concert behavior by criticizing members of his audience for their lateness or distinctive laughs ("Excuse me, madam, but did you just lay an egg?").

Sometimes Borge's acts included other musicians like singer Marilyn Mulvey and pianist Şahan Arzruni in which the guest artist would try to perform in spite of comical interjections from Borge. Other routines emphasized Borge's play with words and language, such as his famous presentations of "Phonetic Punctuation" and "Inflationary Language." He wrote two books, *My Favorite Intermissions* (New York, 1971) and *My Favorite Comedies in Music* (New York, 1980), made several recordings, and appeared in films and on numerous television specials. Among his many honors were knighthoods conferred by Denmark, Norway, Sweden, and Finland.

BIBLIOGRAPHY
(and other resources)

R. King: "Victor Borge, Comedy's Music Man," *MJ*, xxxv/10 (1977), 4–7

B. Wechsler: "Victor Borge: Conductor and Concert Pianist," *MJ*, xxxviii/4 (1980), 35–6

J. Wagner: "Victor Borge: Clown Prince of Music," *Clavier*, xx/6 (1981), 15–17

V. Borge and N.-J. Kaiser: *Smilet er den korteste afstand: erindringer.* (Copenhagen, Denmark, 2001) [Borge's autobiography]

Victor Borge Classic Collection [Questar Entertainment, QD3816] (Chicago, 2008)

KAREN MONSON/JOHN MACINNIS

Bori, Lucrezia [Borja y Gonzáles de Riancho, Lucrecia] (*b* Valencia, Spain, 24 Dec 1887; *d* New York, NY, 14 May 1960). Spanish soprano. She studied first in Spain and then in Milan with Melchiorre Vidal and made her debut in 1908 at the Teatro Adriano, Rome, as Micaëla. She gave a guest performance of Puccini's Manon during the Metropolitan's visit to Paris in 1910 at the Théâtre du Châtelet, and repeated the role in 1912 at her official Metropolitan debut in New York. Between 1911 and 1914 she appeared at La Scala, notably as Octavian in the first Italian performance of *Der Rosenkavalier* and as Nannetta under Toscanini in the Verdi centenary performances of *Falstaff*, and at the Colón, Buenos Aires. She stopped singing in 1915 because of vocal problems but resumed her career in 1919. Except for the years 1916 to 1920, she continued to appear at the Metropolitan until 1936. Throughout the 1930s, she was an influential force in "Save the Met" campaigns, and in 1935 she was elected a member of the Metropolitan board of directors; in 1942, she became chairman of the Metropolitan Opera Guild. The Lucrezia Bori Foundation, established through Bori's estate, supported the development of young artists in the decade following her death.

Endowed with a voice of modest size, rather limited in the upper register, Bori used its clear and delicate timbre to draw characters of pathetic fragility (Mimì, Manon, Juliet); she imbued them with intense and passionate feeling and, in the comic repertory, with gentle and stylized charm. She may be considered a modern version of the "sentimental" 18th-century prima donna.

DISCOGRAPHY

Lucrezia Bori, the Victor Recordings, 1914–25 and 1825–37, Romophone 81016-2 and 81017-2 (1995)

BIBLIOGRAPHY

G. Gatti-Casazza: *Memories of Opera* (New York, 1941)

J.B. Richards: 'Lucrezia Bori', *Record Collector*, iii (1948), 161–6; iv (1949), 2–12, 98–9; ix (1954), 104–23; xxi (1973–4), 147–74 [with discography by H.M. Barnes and J.B. Richards]

M. de Schauensee: "Lucrezia Bori," *ON*, xxv/1 (1960), 26 only

J.F. Marion: *Lucrezia Bori of the Metropolitan Opera* (New York, 1962)

L. Rasponi: *The Last Prima Donnas* (London, 1982), 433–46

RODOLFO CELLETTI/VALERIA PREGLIASCO GUALERZI/ KATIE BUEHNER

Borneman, Ernest [Bornemann, Ernst Wilhelm Julius] (*b* Berlin, Germany, 12 April 1915; *d* Scharten, Austria, 4 June 1995). German writer on jazz. As a teenager in Berlin, he studied with the comparative musicologist Erich von Hornbostel, who first introduced him to jazz. In 1933, he fled to London for political reasons. While there, he volunteered for the BBC, wrote radio and television scripts, worked as a dance band musician, studied social anthropology with Bronisław Malinowski, and completed an unpublished work on the origins of jazz. In 1940, he was interned as an enemy alien before being released to work for Canada's National Film Board. He then continued his studies with Melville Herskovits and Richard A. Waterman at Northwestern University and began writing for *Melody Maker* and *Record*

Changer, among other periodicals. His book *A Critic Looks at Jazz* (London, 1946) draws from his 1944 column in *Record Changer*. Borneman's writings on jazz were unique in their anthropological orientation, given the period during which they were published. Later, Borneman headed UNESCO's film division in Paris, worked for Orson Welles on a screenplay for *The Iliad* and *The Odyssey*, worked for the BBC, and taught and published in the field of sexology.

WRITINGS

A Critic Looks at Jazz (London, 1946)

"The Roots of Jazz," *Jazz: New Perspectives on the History of Jazz by Twelve of the World's Foremost Jazz Critics and Scholars*, ed. N. Hentoff and A.J. McCarthy (New York, 1959), 1–20

BIBLIOGRAPHY

Grove7 (W. Grünzweig)

C. McCabe [Borneman, E.]: "Afterword," *The Face on the Cutting-Room Floor* (Boston, 2/1981/*R*), 247–71

ALEX HARRIS STEIN

Bornschein, Franz (Carl) (*b* Baltimore, MD, 10 Feb 1879; *d* Baltimore, MD, 8 June 1948). Composer. The son of a German-born violist and sometime orchestra leader, he studied violin in Baltimore with Lawrence Rosenberger and Julius Zech (*see* ZECH). He started to compose at the age of eight; in 1895 he entered Peabody Conservatory, where he studied violin with Joan C. Van Hulsteyn and harmony with Phillip L. Kahmer and Otis B. Boise (diploma 1902). He joined the faculty of the Peabody preparatory department in 1905 and also became Baltimore correspondent for *Musical America*. From 1910 to 1913 he served as music critic for the Baltimore *Sun* and from 1919 until his death taught violin, conducting, and composition at Peabody.

As a composer, Bornschein is known chiefly for his many choral works, of which *The Djinns*, *Onowa*, *Joy*, and *Conqueror Worm* were the most popular (for some of these he wrote his own texts under the pseudonym Frank Fairfield). He also wrote several well-received orchestral tone poems on American themes, including *Moon over Taos* and *The Earth Sings*, which were given their premieres by Werner Janssen and Reginald Stewart, respectively. Bornschein was for many years active as a conductor of orchestras and choral groups in Baltimore.

WORKS

Stage: Mother Goose's Goslings (children's operetta, Bornschein), 1918; Willow Plate (operetta, D. Rose), 1932; Song of Songs (lyric op, F. Coutts, Bornschein), 1934; 2 other operettas

Orch: Southern Nights, 1935; Leif Erikson, 1939; Moon over Taos, 1939; The Earth Sings, 1939; The Mission Road, 1939; Ode to the Brave, 1944; 9 other sym. poems; 2 vn concs., g, E; many suites for youth orch

Inst: Str Qt, 1900; Pf Qnt, 1904; Pan Dances (Prankish Pan), fl, str, 1933; Appalachian Legend, vc, pf, 1940; The Sprite, hp, 1945; 22 duos, vn, pf; 3 other duos, vc, pf; kbd works; arrs.; juvenilia for 1–2 insts

Vocal: over 80 choruses, incl. Wet-Sheet and Flowing Sea (A. Cunningham), 1906, The Djinns (V. Hugo), 1913, Onowa (F.H. Martens), 1915, Four Winds (C. Luders), 1921, The Sea (J. McLeod), 1923, The Knight of Bethlehem (S. Maugham), 1924; 7 cants., incl. Zorah (F.H. Martens), 1914, Conquerer Worm (Poe), 1939, Joy (The Mystic Trumpeter) (W. Whitman), 1942; Deodate (Bible), orat.; 27 anthems; many choral arrs.; 30 songs; 10 recitations, lv, pf

MSS in *MdHi*, *MdBPC*

Principal publishers: Ditson, J. Fischer, G. Schirmer

BIBLIOGRAPHY

Choral Compositions by Franz Bornschein (Baltimore, 1940s) [copy in *MdBPC*]

E.M. Daniels: "A Checklist of the Bornschein Collection at the Maryland Historical Society" (MS, *MdHi, MdBPC*)

J. M. Gingerich: "Index of the Franz C. Bornschein Scrapbooks in the Peabody Conservatory Library" (MS, *MdBPC*)

NED QUIST

Borowski, Felix (*b* Burton-in-Kendal, Cumbria, England, 10 March 1872; *d* Chicago, IL, 6 Sept 1956). Composer, teacher, and critic of British birth. He was educated in London and Cologne and began his career in Aberdeen. In 1897 he joined the Chicago Musical College as teacher of the violin, composition, and history. He became president of the college (1916–25) and then moved to Northwestern University, first as special lecturer in history and form, then as professor of musicology (1937–42). His books *The Standard Operas* (Chicago, 1928) and *The Standard Concert Guide* (Chicago, 1932), republished together in 1936, were expansions of works by George P. Upton, whose role as Chicago's leading music critic (for the *Chicago Tribune*) Borowski inherited. He was also responsible for building the music collection of the Newberry Library, beginning soon after his arrival in Chicago and continuing as a part-time staff member (1920–56).

WORKS

(selective list)

Stage: Boudour (ballet), 1919; A Century of the Dance (ballet), 1934; Fernando del Nonsensico (op), 1935

Orch: Pf Conc., 1914; Allegro de concert, org, orch, 1915; Elégie symphonique, 1917; 3 peintures, 1918; Le printemps passionné, 1920; Youth, 1922; Ecce homo, 1923; Semiramis, 1924; 3 syms., 1931, 1933, 1938; The Mirror, 1953

Other works: 3 str qts, 1897, 1928, 1944; 3 org sonatas; short vn pieces, incl. Adoration; short vocal and pf pieces

DONALD W. KRUMMEL

Borowsky, Alexander [Aleksandr] (*b* Mitau [now Jelgava, Latvia], 6/18 March 1889; *d* Waban, MA, 27 April 1968). Pianist of Russian birth. He received his first instruction from his mother, an accomplished pianist who had been a pupil of Safonov. Subsequently he pursued studies in law before entering the St. Petersburg Conservatory, where he studied with Anna Esipova. In 1912 he was awarded the Rubinstein Prize and began his career as a soloist performing throughout Russia. Between 1915 and 1920 he taught masterclasses at the Moscow Conservatory, after which he toured extensively in Europe appearing as recitalist and soloist with most of the major symphony orchestras and conductors. In 1941 he settled in the United States, becoming professor of piano at Boston University in 1956.

Borowsky's repertory was wide and unusually eclectic, ranging from 18th-century music (Bach remained a special preoccupation) to works by Hindemith, Schoenberg, Szymanowski, Stravinsky, as well as contemporary French composers. Throughout his career he maintained a keen interest in new developments, giving the premiere of Lopatnikoff's Sonata in E op.29 in 1944 and often featuring works by Messiaen in his programs. Ironically, his most extended series of recordings features the first 15 Hungarian rhapsodies of Liszt, a composer whose works he played comparatively rarely. The taste and refinement for which he was renowned, however, are evident here, as well as a distinctive tonal warmth and clarity of articulation.

CHARLES HOPKINS

Borroff, Edith (*b* New York, NY, 2 Aug 1925). Musicologist and composer. The daughter of pianist Marie Bergersen and (Albert) Ramon Borroff, a tenor who sold carillons by trade, she was raised in a home of extraordinary musical and artistic talent. At the age of 16 she entered the American Conservatory of Music, Chicago (MusB 1946, MusM 1948), where she studied the piano with Louise Robyn and composition with IRWIN FISCHER. In 1958 she earned a PhD in music history from the University of Michigan. She was a visiting professor at the University of North Carolina, Chapel Hill, in 1972–3 and in 1973 joined the faculty of SUNY, Binghamton, where she taught until her retirement in 1992. Noted for her work in early music, Borroff has also championed American music, women in music, and liberal arts in the 20th century. She is the author of more than 15 books, including the comprehensive *Music in Europe and the United States: a History* (Englewood Cliffs, NJ, 1971/*R*), and more than 100 articles on wide-ranging historical and theoretical topics. Her well-crafted compositions, which span a career of over 70 years, are marked by diverse compositional styles.

WORKS

(selective list)

STAGE

Spring over Brooklyn (musical), 1952; Pygmalion (incid music, G.B. Shaw), S, chbr chorus, ww qnt, 2 perc, 1955; La folle de chaillot (J. Giraudoux), S, perc, pf, 1960; The Sun and the Wind: a Musical Fable (op, 3 scenes, E. Borroff), 1977

INSTRUMENTAL

4 or more insts: Str Qt, *c*1942; Grande rondo, str qt, *c*1943; Str Trio, 1944, rev. 1952; Theme and Variations, vc, pf, *c*1944; Qnt, cl, str, 1945; Str Qt no.3, e, 1945; Minuet, str orch, 1946; Ww Qnt, D, *c*1947; Ww Qnt, C, 1948; Vorspiel über das Thema "In dulci jubilo," 2 fl, 2 hn, pf, 1951; Variations for Band, 1965; Chance Encounter (Romp or Rehearsal?), str qt, 1974; Game Pieces, suite, ww qnt, 1980; Mar Conc., 1981; Suite: 8 Canons for 6 Players, perc, 1984; Mottoes, suite, 8 sax, 1989; 2 Pieces from the Old Rag Bag, sax qt, 1989

2–3 insts: Berceuse, rec, vc, pf, 1944; Song Without Words, va/vc, pf, 1944; Sonata, vc, pf, *c*1946; Sonatina giocosa, va, pf, 1952; Sonata, hn, pf, 1954; Variations and Theme, ob, pf, 1956; Voices in Exile: 3 Canons, fl, va, 1962; Ions: 14 Pieces in the Form of a Sonnet, fl, pf, 1968; Trio, t sax, perc, pf, 1982; Trio, vn, vc, pf, 1983; The Elements, sonata, vn, vc, 1987; Comic Miniatures, suite, vn, pf, 1988; 5 Pieces, va, pf, 1989; An Historical Anagram: 11 Duets, 2 rec, 1991; 32 Variations in the Form of a Sonata, cl, pf, 1991; Rondelay, 2 vn, 1992; Sonata, vc, pf, 1993; Sonata no.2, vn, vc, pf, 1995; Interactions, suite, 2 ob, 1996

Solo: Passacaglia, org, 1946; A Suite for Drukka, pf, 1948; Org Prelude, D, 1950; Rag no.1, pf, 1952; Rag no.2, pf, 1972; Divertimento, fl, 1980; 3 Chorale Preludes, 1981; Variations on 2 American Tunes, org, 1982; An American Olio, org, 1983; Sonata, gui, 1983; Diptych, org, 1985; Fantasy, 2 pf, 1985; Honors for His Name: a Celebration of Praises, org, 1985; Variations on a Trill, pf, 1985; Meditation and Toccata, org, 1989; Wings of Love, sonata, org, 1989 [Amer. hymn tunes]; Figures of Speech, hpd, 1990; Aria, org, 1993; International Suite: a Quodlibet, pf, 1994

VOCAL

Choral: 3 Madrigals (E. Borroff, M. Borroff), female chorus, 1953; A Psalm of Praise, SATB, 1972; The Poet (W. Shakespeare), tr vv, pf, 1973; Choral Trilogy (J. Rinka), SSAATTBB, 1983; Light in Dark Places (19th-century black women), SATB, pf, 1988; Love and Law (Pss, Bible: *1 John*), anthem, TBB, 1990; A Holy Thing (T. Moore), TBB, 1991; A Joyful Noise (Bible, T. Moore), vv soloists, SATB, 3 tpt, pf, 1991

Songs: Summum Bonum (R. Browning), 1949; Feed my Sheep (M.B. Eddy), 1953; 7 Early Songs, 1957; Truth (Pss), 1973; Goodbye, Baby! (E. Borroff), rock song, 1978; Modern Love (song-cycle, J. Keats, P.B. Shelley), 7 lyrics, S, pf, 1979; A House of Love (G. Meyers), 5 songs, 1986; Food and Gladness (F. Farmer), 7 songs, 1986; The Querulous Music Teacher (Meyers), 1987; A Love Song of the 80s (E. Borroff), 1989; Changeling (F.B. Jacobs), S, ob, bn, pf, 1990; 5 Whitman Songs (W. Whitman), 1990

Other solo: Abelard's Monologue, Bar, orch, 1948; Missa patrinae rerum Domini, solo v, org, 1961

EDITIONS

E.-C. Jacquet de La Guerre: Sonata in D major (1707) (Pittsburgh, 1961)

J.F. Rebel: Sonata in G minor (1713) (Pittsburgh, 1961)

J.-J. Cassanéa de Mondonville: Jubilate (Pittsburgh, 1961)

A. Rener: Missa dominicalis in L. Duyler: *The Emperor Maximilian I and Music*, ii (London, 1973)

MSS in *CN*

WRITINGS

An Introduction to Elisabeth-Claude Jacquet de La Guerre (Brooklyn, NY, 1966)

Music of the Baroque (Dubuque, IA, 1970)

Music in Europe and the United States: a History (Englewood Cliffs, NJ, 1971/*R*)

ed.: *Notations and Editions: a Book in Honor of Louise Cuyler* (Dubuque, IA, 1974/*R*)

with M. Irvin: *Music in Perspective* (New York, 1976)

Three American Composers (Lanham, MI, 1986)

American Operas: a Checklist (Warren, MI, 1992)

Music Melting Round: a History of Music in the United States (New York, 1995/*R*)

BIBLIOGRAPHY

A. Franco: *A Study in Selected Piano Chamber Works by Twentieth Century American Women Composers* (diss., Columbia U., 1985)

J. Regier: *The Organ Works of Edith Borroff* (diss., U. of Oklahoma, 1993)

H.W. Heape: *Sacred Songs and Arias by Women Composers* (DMA diss., Southwestern Baptist Theological Seminary, 1995)

JANET REGIER

Borrowing. The use in a piece of music of one or more elements taken from another specific piece. Borrowing is a recurring theme in American music, encompassing a wide variety of practices.

From colonial times, Americans have created new songs by adapting existing music to new words. Hymnodists reshaped secular tunes as hymn tunes, including melodies by classical composers. Patriotic and protest songs often borrow tunes; even the national anthem, "The Star-Spangled Banner," joins words by Francis Scott Key to John Stafford Smith's tune for the English drinking song "To Anacreon in Heaven" (*c*1775). Satire, parody, and humor are often associated with setting new words to familiar melodies, from BALLAD OPERAS and MINSTRELSY to the music of Weird Al Yankovic. Adapting existing music in new media or new arrangements is equally common. Arrangements are generally received as versions of the original work, but variations, paraphrases, potpourris, medleys, and other works based on familiar tunes are clear instances of borrowing. Preludes and fantasies on hymn tunes, like Clarence Eddy's *Festival Prelude and Fugue on "Old Hundred"*, are staples of the church organist's repertoire.

Another form of borrowing is the use of an existing piece as a starting point or model. Examples abound in the classical tradition; for example, Edward MacDowell modeled his *Eroica Sonata* on Liszt's Piano Sonata in B Minor. Borrowing from a model is also evident in vernacular music. Melodies of some 19th-century American popular songs and hymns are related, as if a songwriter began with a fragment of a familiar tune and extended it.

Composers in the classical tradition have frequently adapted folksongs and other national melodies, using borrowing to give their music a national, regional, or ethnic flavor, as in Louis Moreau Gottschalk's piano pieces on melodies from Spain, the United States, and Latin America. In the early 1890s, Dvořák urged American composers to look toward African American spirituals, American Indian music, or Anglo-American folk music as sources for an Americanist style, and many composers adapted melodies from these traditions as themes. Charles Ives more often drew on popular and patriotic songs and hymns, believing that music in popular culture was most representative of America. His music illustrates the variety of borrowing procedures composers used, from traditional techniques such as modeling, variation, paraphrase, medley, and programmatic QUOTATION to innovations like cumulative form, in which the borrowed theme appears in full only near the end and is preceded by development of its motives. The effect or meaning conveyed varies as much as the methods, from depicting the performance of music and thus the situation in which it was heard (like the trumpet playing *Taps* at a memorial service in *Decoration Day*, *c*1913–19) to meditations on the musical material itself (as in his violin sonatas). Ives's most striking invention was COLLAGE, in which a swirl of quoted and paraphrased tunes is added to the musical fabric.

Postwar composers often reworked earlier music in order to address their relationship to the past musical tradition. In *Contra Mortem et Tempus* and *Music for the Magic Theater* (both 1965), George Rochberg juxtaposed passages quoted or derived from earlier composers with his own music, seeking to evoke "the many-layered density of human existence"; he called his *Nach Bach* (1966) for harpsichord a "commentary" on Bach's Partita no.6 in E minor, interspersing fragments and transformations of it with free atonal passagework. Lukas Foss's *Baroque Variations* (1967) distorts works by Handel, Domenico Scarlatti, and Bach by making parts inaudible, fading in and out, echoing passages in different rhythms, adding and subtracting notes, and using clusters, indeterminacy, and other avant-garde effects. In such works, the contrasts between the borrowed material and the often strange ways it is transformed or juxtaposed with quite different music can be fascinating and expressive, commenting on the fragmented, pluralistic culture and music of the modern era or on the gulf separating present from past. In *Cheap Imitation* (1969), John Cage used chance operations to reshape the melodic line of Erik Satie's *Socrate* by transposing segments of varying lengths into different keys, and his *Hymns and Variations* (1979) takes partsongs by William Billings and deletes portions of individual voices, again using chance; these works challenge received ideas of authorship, ownership, and the integrity of the musical work.

Since the 1980s, composers have often borrowed to represent a blending of idioms rather than disjunction. Philip Glass based his *Low Symphony* (1992) on themes drawn from the experimental pop recording *Low* by David Bowie and Brian Eno, drawing their work into the symphonic world. American composers of Chinese descent, such as Tan Dun and Bright Sheng, incorporated Chinese melodies and sounds into works in Western genres to create a hybrid that bridges both cultures.

Borrowing is also common in popular music. TIN PAN ALLEY songwriters of the 1890s through 1920s frequently quoted a familiar song just before the end of the chorus, as in Irving Berlin's "Alexander's Ragtime Band" (1911), which quotes Foster's "Old Folks at Home." The musical reference is normally alluded to in the text, which may borrow words from the quoted song or describe a performance of the quoted music. George M. Cohan's "The Yankee Doodle Boy" (1904) quotes "Yankee Doodle" like this in the chorus, but the verse is a PATCHWORK of patriotic tunes, a technique used by many songwriters. Quotation for humorous effect or in relation to a text continues to the present, as in Pam Tillis's 1992 country song that uses the much-quoted "hoochie-coochie" dance (first quoted in James Thornton's "Streets of Cairo" in 1895) to pun on the singer's comment that she is "the Queen of Denial" (i.e. "the Nile").

Musicians in popular traditions often rework or quote classical music. Numerous Tin Pan Alley and Broadway songs were about classical music or opera and quoted well-known works. Louis Armstrong quoted *Rigoletto*, *Pagliacci*, and other operas in his improvised solos. Robert Wright and George Forrest based their musical *Kismet* (1954) on melodies by Borodin. Duke Ellington adapted Tchaikovsky and Grieg for jazz band in his *Nutcracker Suite* and *Peer Gynt Suite* (1960). Emerson, Lake, and Palmer reworked Musorgsky's *Pictures at an Exhibition* and Copland's *Fanfare for the Common Man* as rock music, and Malcolm McLaren's songs "Madam Butterfly," "Death of Butterfly," and "Carmen" on his 1984 album *Fans* were intriguing retellings of the operas' stories in dance-pop style, woven around the heroines' most famous arias. The motivations for borrowing from classical sources have ranged from recycling good melodies to humor or commentary.

Reuse, reworking, and extension of existing music, all basic elements of West African musical practice, continued in African American music. BLUES and JAZZ involve improvisation and composition based on existing melodies and chord progressions, and similar practices continued into popular music derived from African American traditions, including RHYTHM AND BLUES and ROCK AND ROLL. Jazz improvisers quoted familiar tunes in their solos as a joke or meaningful ALLUSION, or borrowed passages from recorded solos by other artists. In the early 1940s, BOP artists created numerous "contrafacts," new jazz melodies to the chord "changes" (harmonic progressions) of popular tunes, such as Charlie Parker and Dizzy Gillespie's "Anthropology" and "Shaw 'Nuff"; both use the chord progression of George Gershwin's "I Got Rhythm," the most frequent source for contrafacts. This practice allowed artists to invent melodies in the new jazz style, yet continue to improvise on familiar harmonic patterns.

FILM MUSIC has relied on existing music from the beginning, as accompanists to silent films matched emotionally appropriate music to events on the screen. Orchestral scores for silent films, such as Joseph Carl Breil's score for *Birth of a Nation* (1915), and for early sound films such as *The Jazz Singer* (1927) often drew on existing music. When original scores were commissioned, composers used models or adapted music with strong associations. Max Steiner's music for *King Kong* (1933) adopted Wagner's leitmotif system and echoed the Fasolt and Fafner motive from *Das Rheingold* in Kong's leitmotif. Later film scores draw on all of these traditions. Some are pastiches, as in *American Graffiti* (1973), which uses American pop music of the 1950s to convey time, place, and situation; others are modeled on existing works, like John Williams's score for *Star Wars* (1977), which echoes passages from Gustav Holst's *The Planets*. Similar techniques are used in music for television and for advertising, where familiar music can lend certain associations to a product.

New forms of borrowing emerged with developments in recording technology in the late 20th century. Pop musicians overlaid new and borrowed elements in the recording studio; an early example was Simon and Garfunkel's "Save the Life of My Child" (1968), in which the opening of their first hit recording "The Sounds of Silence" (1965) was dubbed into an interlude. In the late 1970s, DISCO artists frequently used previously recorded bass and rhythm tracks as a backing for new songs. The new genre of RAP emerged from an African American practice of improvising rhymed poetry over instrumental passages from existing disco or funk recordings; the first rap recording to hit the top 40 in the pop charts, "Rapper's Delight" (1979) by the Sugar Hill Gang, used excerpts from Chic's slow disco hit "Good Times" (1979). The invention of digital sampling made manipulation of recorded material easier, and rap recordings began to include many more "samples," digitally recorded snippets of music, speech, or sounds. Public Enemy's "Night of the Living Baseheads" (1988) includes samples from 19 different songs, each of which adds meaning and resonance to the song's anti-drug and anti-racist message. Samples have been used by many others besides rap musicians, notably in the *Plunderphonics* (1989) of John Oswald, which directly engages issues of ownership through a kind of creative theft. Digital manipulation has grown in the 21st century with new software for music file sharing and editing. A characteristic new form is the MASH-UP, which combines layers or segments from multiple source recordings to create juxtapositions laden with meaning or humor.

BIBLIOGRAPHY

Grove7 ("Borrowing," J.P. Burkholder)

C. Kühn: *Das Zitat in der Musik der Gegenwart: Mit Ausblicken auf bildende Kunst und Literatur* (Hamburg, 1972)

Z. Lissa: "Historical Awareness of Music and Its Role in Present-Day Musical Culture," *International Review of the Aesthetics and Sociology of Music*, iv (1973), 17–32

J. Patrick: "Charlie Parker and the Harmonic Sources of Bebop Composition: Thoughts on the Repertory of New Jazz in the 1940s," *JJS*, ii (1975), 3–23

N.A. Huber: "John Cage: *Cheap Imitation*," *Neuland*, i (1981), 135–41

M. Hicks: *The New Quotation: its Origins and Functions* (diss., U. of Illinois, 1984)

D. Pesce: "MacDowell's *Eroica Sonata* and its Lisztian Legacy," *MR*, xlix (1988), 169–89

J.P. Murphy: "Jazz Improvisation: The Joy of Influence," *BPiM*, xviii (1990), 7–19

A.F. Block: "Dvořák's Long American Reach," *Dvořák in America, 1892–1895*, ed. J.C. Tibbetts (Portland, OR, 1993), 157–81

J.P. Burkholder: "The Uses of Existing Music: Musical Borrowing as a Field," *Notes*, l (1993–4), 851–70

A. Bartlett: "Airshafts, Loudspeakers, and the Hip Hop Sample: Contexts and African American Musical Aesthetics," *African American Review*, xxviii (1994), 639–52

D. Sanjek: "'Don't Have to DJ No More': Sampling and the 'Autonomous' Creator," *The Construction of Authorship: Textual Appropriation in Law and Literature*, ed. M. Woodmansee and P. Jaszi (Durham, NC, 1994), 343–60

J.P. Burkholder and others, eds.: *Musical Borrowing: an Annotated Bibliography* (1994–2013) <http://www.chmtl.indiana.edu/borrowing>

J.P. Burkholder: *All Made of Tunes: Charles Ives and the Uses of Musical Borrowing* (New Haven, CT, 1995)

A. Jones: *Plunderphonics, 'Pataphysics, and Pop Mechanics: an Introduction to musique actuelle* (Wembley, Middlesex, 1995)

T.G. Schumacher: "This is a Sampling Sport: Digital Sampling, Rap Music, and the Law in Cultural Production," *Media, Culture & Society*, xvii (1995), 253–73

R. Walser: "Rhythm, Rhyme, and Rhetoric in the Music of Public Enemy," *EthM*, xxxix (1995), 193–217

H. Davies: "A History of Sampling," *Organised Sound*, i (1996), 3–11

I. Monson: *Saying Something: Jazz Improvisation and Interaction* (Chicago and London, 1996)

S. DeVeaux: *The Birth of Bebop: a Social and Musical History* (Berkeley, CA, 1997)

K. Holm-Hudson: "Quotation and Context: Sampling and John Oswald's Plunderphonics," *Leonardo Music Journal*, vii (1997), 17–25

K. McLeod: "Bohemian Rhapsodies: Operatic Influences on Rock Music," *Popular Music*, xx (2001), 189–203

D. Metzer: *Quotation and Cultural Meaning in Twentieth-century Music* (Cambridge, 2003)

Y.U. Everett and F. Lau, eds.: *Locating East Asia in Western Art Music* (Middletown, CT, 2004)

J. Schloss: *Making Beats: the Art of Sample-Based Hip-Hop* (Middletown, CT, 2004)

E. Hung: "Hearing Emerson, Lake, and Palmer Anew: Progressive Rock as 'Music of Attraction,'" *CMc*, nos.79–80 (2005), 245–59

O.B. Arewa: "From J.C. Bach to Hip Hop: Musical Borrowing, Copyright, and Cultural Context," *North Carolina Law Review*, lxxxiv (2006), 547–645

P. Powrie and R. Stilwell, eds.: *Changing Tunes: the Use of Pre-existing Music in Film* (Aldershot, 2006)

P. Mercer-Taylor: "Mendelssohn in Nineteenth-century American Hymnody," *19CM*, xxxii (2009), 235–83

R.L. Schur: *Parodies of Ownership: Hip-Hop Aesthetics and Intellectual Property Law* (Ann Arbor, MI, 2009)

J. PETER BURKHOLDER

Bosch, Maura (Louise) [Hess, Marjorie Ann] (*b* Reading, PA, 8 Aug 1958). Composer. She studied at the Hartt College of Music (BM 1978) and Princeton University (MFA 1982, PhD 2008), where her teachers included Alexander Lepak, MILTON BABBITT, Edward T. Cone, and PETER WESTERGAARD. In 1998 she received a fellowship in composition from the McKnight Foundation, and in 2009 won a Bush Artist Fellowship. Bosch believes that all of her works "arise from a basic premise of performing music as theatre" and should be presented in "[their] own theatrical space," away from traditional venues of concert and opera. To this end, in 1990 she co-founded Corn Palace Productions, a music theater company in Minneapolis, to perform dramatic works by local composers. Her second opera, *Mirabell's Book of Numbers*, a surrealistic work based on poems by James Merrill, was completed in 1991, followed by *The Damnation of Felicity* in 1994. Her most recent dramatic work, *Art and Desire*, to her own libretto, was premiered at the University of Wisconsin, Madison, in 2009.

Bosch's eclectic style draws on both acoustic and electronic instruments. Although she has written for a variety of media, her compositions share a common focus on words. *Her Light Self* (1997), an "electro-acoustic collage," features phrases of text performed in canon with a recorded recitation of the same material. The *ZELDA* songs (1997), on feminist texts by the composer, are rooted in popular music idioms that provide a wide range of musical expression. The texts of *The Turning* (2007), written for the nine-voice male ensemble Cantus, takes its text from the words of male perpetrators of domestic abuse, collected and arranged by the composer. Her instrumental works also originate in texts that provide descriptive imagery or expressive intent. In addition to composing, Bosch is working on a book, *The Formation of My Musical World*, dealing with the ways people form their tastes in music and the arts.

WORKS

(selective list)

Ops: The Disappearance of Luisa Porto (M. Strand), 1989; Mirabell's Book of Numbers (J. Merrill), 1991; The Damnation of Felicity, 1994; Art and Desire (Bosch), 2009

Vocal: Theater Piece (Merrill), 1v, 1984; How She Was (Bosch), 1v, tape, 1988; The Oxen (T. Hardy), SATB, hp, 1993; 3 Hymns (Bosch), SATB, org, 1995; My Purity (Bosch), S, A, T, B, SATB, org, 1995; Bronte Songs (E. Bronte, Bosch), 1v, cl, vc, pf, 1996; Her Light Self (Bosch), 1v, accdn, tape, 1997; The Crossing (M.C. Wright), SATB, 1997; ZELDA (Bosch), 1v, ens, 1997; The Turning (Bosch), TBB, 2007; Interior Geometries (Juliet Patterson), S, pf, 2007; In the Meantime (Jim Moore), S, fl, 2007; Instructions for Life (Claudia Lindberg), SSA, 2010

Inst: Santuario, orch, 1992; About the Night, str qt, 1993; Sing to the Sun, nar, ob, str qt, mand, 1995; My Piano Journal, 8 pieces, pf (2005); 12 Preludes, pf, 2009

Principal publisher: Davidge

BIBLIOGRAPHY

J. Freese: "Tradition be Damned: Corn Palace Reinvents Opera," *Minnesota Women's Press* (7 Sept 1994)

K. Pendle: "For the Theatre: Opera, Dance and Theatre Piece," *CMR*, xvi (1997), 69–80

R. Rosario, Alliance Artist Management: "Making Music of Abusers' Words" <http://www.allianceartistmanagement.com/artist.php?id=cantus&aview=acclaim&nid=1093>

KARIN PENDLE

Bossa nova. In Brazilian popular music, a movement that originated about 1958–9 and effected radical stylistic changes in the classical urban SAMBA. The word "bossa," from Rio de Janeiro slang, means loosely "special ability," "shrewdness," "astuteness" and the like. The term "bossa-nova" first appeared in ANTONIO CARLOS JOBIM'S song "Desafinado" (1959) whose melody with complex intervals (diminished fourths, minor sixths) and a rather tortuous shape was intended to suggest the idea of a singer with a certain vocal insecurity. Its melodic and harmonic complexity was justified by the song text as "bossa nova." The originators of the new style included Jobim himself as a composer and JOÃO GILBERTO primarily as a singer and guitarist. Their first important recording was "Chega de Saudade" (March 1959). Although the samba figured prominently in their repertory it was not their exclusive genre.

One of the features of the new style, affecting popular music in general, and the samba in particular, was a deliberate avoidance of the predominance of any single musical parameter. Before bossa nova the melody was generally strongly emphasized, to satisfy the basic requirement of an easily singable tune; bossa nova, however, integrates melody, harmony, and rhythm. The performer has a vital role in this integration, but heavy emphasis on the singer's personality is altogether avoided. Strongly contrasting effects, loudness of voice, fermatas or scream-like high pitches are generally excluded from a proper bossa nova singing style; the singing should flow in a subdued tone almost like the normal spoken language. The characteristic nasal vocal production of bossa nova is a peculiar trait of the *caboclo* folk tradition of northeastern Brazil, but was rare in earlier urban music. As a soloist the interpreter no longer opposes the accompanying ensemble: they are reconciled. The guitar as an accompanying instrument is emphasized and, whether as a solo or accompanying instrument, may present a harmonic structure with two functions: one of traditional harmonic support, and the other a percussive function, stressing the rhythmic strokes chordally. Both functions are frequently integrated in the same chord entity, as shown in many performances of Baden Powell, Brazil's foremost guitarist in the 1960s. Certain harmonic formulae have almost become clichés since the advent of bossa nova, such as the shifting of major and minor modes in a tonic–dominant relationship (e.g., A minor to D major). The pattern of modulations is the opposite of those in jazz, which usually follow an ascending order in the circle of fifths and have greater harmonic tension. Except for certain processes of chord formation (particularly altered chords) there is less jazz influence than some early critics believed. A trait traceable to jazz and perhaps related to bebop is the highly improvised style on an implied theme of some bossa nova instrumental pieces. The most remarkable innovation of bossa nova music is in its rhythmic structure, which affects the very foundation on which the samba was built. The rhythmic structure of the bossa nova samba possibly had its origin in both the folk and the classical samba formulae (ex.1). João Gilberto was mainly responsible for extracting and isolating those elements that constitute his famous guitar stroke, called in Portuguese “violão gago” (“stammering guitar”; ex.2). Many variants of that basic rendering have developed, their common trait being the predominance of ternary divisions against the binary one, which occurs only once (exx.3a, b, and d) or not at all (ex.3c). These variants have been the point of departure for many ingenious drummers and guitarists toward a previously unknown rhythmic versatility. Bossa nova song texts are also innovatory, and are valued not only for their expressive content but also for the sonorous individuality of their words. Some affinity has been noticed between bossa nova texts and Brazilian concrete poetry. In several examples the lyrics seem to have been conceived together with the music, so close are the verbal rhythm and the melodic (compare with Jobim's *Samba de uma nota só*, *Desafinado*, and *A garota de Ipanema*).

During the early to mid-1960s bossa nova became linked with a social protest movement. Musically the introduction of international pop styles, especially rock music from England and the United States, gave rise to a dynamic hybrid style which reached its peak with the group Tropicália.

Ex.1 Classical samba rhythms

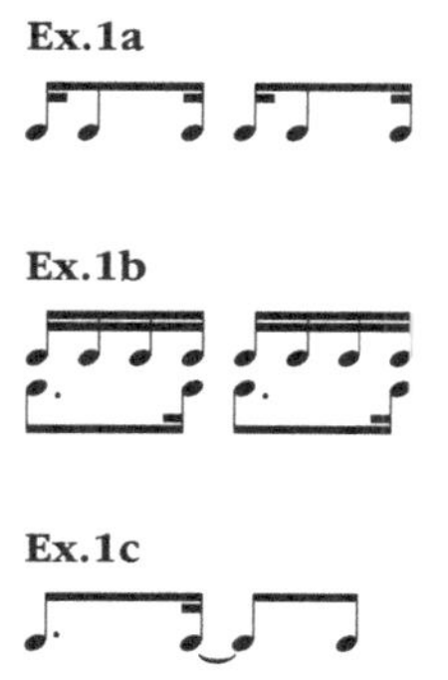

Ex.2 João Gilberto's characteristic bossa nova rendition of the samba rhythm Ex.3

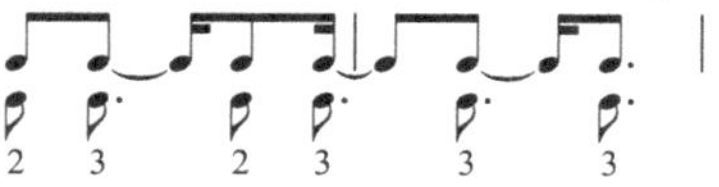

Ex.3 Bossa nova rhythmic formulae

Ex.3a

Ex.3b

Ex.3c

Ex.3d

BIBLIOGRAPHY

A. Ramalho Neto: *Historinha do desafinado* (Rio de Janeiro, 1965)
J.R. Tinhorão: *Música popular: um tema em debate* (Rio de Janeiro, 1966)
A. de Campos, ed.: *Balanço da bossa* (São Paulo, 1968)
B. Rocha Brito: “Bossa nova,” *Balanço da bossa*, ed. A. de Campos (São Paulo, 1968), 13
G. Béhague: “Bossa and Bossas: Recent Changes in Brazilian Urban Popular Music,” *EthM*, xvii (1973), 209–33
M. Budds: *Jazz in the Sixties* (Iowa City, IA, 1978)
J.S. Roberts: *Latin Jazz* (New York, 1999)
J.S. Roberts: *The Latin Tinge* (New York, 1979, 2/1999)
D. Treece: “Guns and Roses: Bossa Nova and Brazil's Music of Popular Protest, 1958–68,” *História: Questões & Debates*, 17/32 (Jan–June 2000), 121–65
S.C. Naves: *Da Bossa Nova à Tropicália* (Rio de Janeiro, 2001)
A. da Távola: *Bossa Nova* (Rio de Janeiro, 2002)

GERARD BÉHAGUE/R

Bostic, Earl (*b* Tulsa, OK, 25 April 1913; *d* Rochester, NY, 28 Oct 1965). Jazz alto saxophonist and arranger. During the early 1930s he worked in several bands in the Midwest before studying at Xavier University, New Orleans. He left Louisiana to tour with various groups, then moved to New York in 1938. He was featured in big bands led by Don Redman, Edgar Hayes, and Lionel Hampton, but was better known for work within his own small group. In the 1930s and 1940s Bostic was recognized as an accomplished saxophonist and a skillful arranger, but was not considered to be a major soloist. However, after recording “Flamingo” in 1951, he gained widespread fame and subsequently his records sold in vast quantities. On them, he often overemphasized glissandos and deliberately exaggerated his vibrato. Despite these inelegant effects, Bostic regularly showed that he retained considerable technical prowess, particularly in producing high harmonics—a skill he taught John Coltrane. Heart ailments curtailed his activities during the last decade of his life.

SELECTED RECORDINGS

Flamingo (1951, King); *Cherokee* (1952, King); *Indiana* (1956, King); *Exercise* (1957, King); *Answer Me* (1957, King); *Twilight Time* (1958, King)

BIBLIOGRAPHY

SouthernB
R. Cage: “Rhythm & Blues Notes,” *DB*, xxi/26 (1954), 8
H. Friedrich: “Earl Bostic Discography,” *Jazz Statistics*, no.4 (1956), 3; no.14 (1960), 2; no.17 (1960), 8
Obituary, *DB*, xxxiv/10 (1967), 13
V. Schonfield: “The Forgotten Ones: Earl Bostic,” *JJI*, xxxvii/11 (1984), 14

JOHN CHILTON/R

Boston (i). Capital city of Massachusetts (pop. 617,594; metropolitan area 4,552,402; 2010 US Census). Settled in 1630, it is the principal city of the region of the six northeastern states called New england. Distinguished by the breadth and intensity of its musical life, Boston has long been a leading center for composition, performance, music criticism, and music education, and an important seat of music publishing and instrument manufacture. Several politically independent municipalities, among them Cambridge and Wellesley, are here considered parts of "Greater Boston."

1. Early history. In 1620 separatists from the Church of England left the Netherlands and landed at what is now Plymouth, Massachusetts. They carried with them the psalter that Henry Ainsworth published in Amsterdam in 1612, which contained the psalms in English prose and verse, with the music of 39 tunes (borrowed from English, French, and Dutch psalters). In 1630 a Puritan group established the Massachusetts Bay Colony at Boston and quickly organized a complex society that, within ten years, founded Harvard College and a book press. They too restricted their music to songs based on the psalms, preferring Sternhold and Hopkins (London, 1562) and music from Ravenscroft's psalter (1621).

A group of 30 clergy from the colony devised new rhymed, metrical translations of the psalms, resulting in the *Bay Psalm Book* of 1640, the first North American book in English. The first edition known to include music was the ninth (1698), but meanwhile this American book had also been printed in England and was in relatively wide use there. The 13 tunes in the 1698 edition are from John Playford's *A Breefe Introduction to the Skill of Musick*.

By the mid-1660s the psalm tunes originally learned by rote were performed on both sides of the Atlantic by "lining out," a practice in which a precentor sang or declaimed a single line of text which the congregation then repeated in solo. After the turn of the century the feeling arose that lining out had outlived its usefulness and should be replaced by musically literate singing according to the rules of art music. New England clergy led the way toward reform through polemical tracts appearing in Boston from 1720. Singing schools were organized to teach it, and the appetite for music they created gave rise in turn to the "first New England School" of American composers; chief among the Yankee tunesmiths of the later 18th century was William Billings.

2. Concert life to 1881. The earliest documented public concert in America took place in Boston on 30 December 1731, in "Mr Pelham's Great Room." Among the city's leading musicians in subsequent decades was the organist William Selby, who came from England in 1771 and directed a performance of Handel's "Hallelujah" Chorus (accompanied by the 64th Regimental Band) two years later. A seminal figure was the German-born Gottlieb Graupner, who arrived in 1797 having served as oboist in Haydn's London orchestra. As conductor, publisher, and music and instrument dealer, Graupner was an entrepreneurial force. His Philo-Harmonic Society, begun in 1809 and lasting at least until 1824, resembled a club as much as a pioneering orchestra; its repertory included Haydn alongside many now forgotten composers. Graupner was also in 1815 a founding member of the Handel and haydn society, America's oldest enduring oratorio society. George K. Jackson, the first doctor of music to settle in America (in 1797), was another significant Boston proponent of Handel and the religious choral literature.

The centrality of sacred music, crowned by *Messiah*, was reinforced by Lowell Mason, Boston's leading music educator and a successful fashioner of hymns. Although Mason disdained the secular, the Boston Academy of Music (which he co-founded with George James Webb in 1833) formed an orchestra directed by Webb; it introduced Boston to seven Beethoven symphonies as well as to symphonies by Mozart and Mendelssohn. This group was succeeded, from 1839 to 1847, by a musicians' cooperative, the Boston Musical Fund Society.

The prevailing caliber of performance may be gleaned from an anecdote told by Thomas Ryan, an expert chamber musician who took part in a single unsuccessful rehearsal of Mendelssohn's *A Midsummer Night's Dream* overture as a member of the Musical Fund Society conducted by Webb; the work was abandoned as unplayable. An orchestra that specialized in Mendelssohn's overture was the Germania musical society, which first appeared in Boston in 1849 and later settled there before disbanding in 1854. This group not only set unprecedented performance standards throughout the United States, but dispersed influential musicians to individual American cities. In Boston the leading Germania alumnus was Carl Zerrahn, a conductor less progressive than New York's Carl Bergmann (also a former Germanian), but a constructive and inspirational force, as leader of the Handel and Haydn Society (1854–98).

A post-Germania landmark in orchestral performance was the 50th anniversary of the Handel and Haydn Society in 1865, for which an orchestra of 100, including former Germanians, was assembled under Zerrahn. In its wake, the Harvard Musical Association created for Zerrahn a semi-professional orchestra about half as large; begun in 1866 and discontinued in 1882, it was the primary local ensemble prior to the Boston SO. But Zerrahn's orchestra, however indispensable, was far from the polished group with which Theodore Thomas had begun to tour. An 1869 Boston visit by Thomas's orchestra was remembered by William Foster Apthorp for inflicting "humiliating lessons in the matter of orchestral technique." (But Thomas brought the Handel and Haydn Society to New York in 1873 when he needed an expert chorus for Handel, Beethoven, and Mendelssohn.) A jolt of another kind, also in 1869, was the five-day National Peace Jubilee and Musical Festival, for which Patrick S. Gilmore assembled an orchestra of 1000 and 10,000 choristers. The program for the opening concert listed (in the following order): a Lutheran chorale, the *Tannhäuser* overture (with a "select orchestra of 600"), a Mozart Gloria, the Bach–Gounod *Ave Maria* (with "the violin obbligato played by two hundred violinists"), "The Star-Spangled Banner" (with bells and cannon), an "American hymn," the *William Tell* overture, "Inflammatus" from Rossini's *Stabat mater*, the Coronation March from *Le prophète*, the Anvil Chorus from *Il trovatore* (with 100 anvils played by Boston firemen) and "My Country 'Tis of Thee" (with "the audience requested to join in singing the last stanza"). A popular and financial success, attended by President Grant and other dignitaries, the festival spawned a less successful sequel in 1872. (*See* Peace jubilees.)

A presiding influence on local musical growth, and a major factor in the evolution of musical high culture nationally, was the Transcendentalist and one-time Unitarian minister John Sullivan Dwight. Dwight considered great music "religious" and called Beethoven "sacred." He campaigned to purify "classical" music of such influences as Gilmore, Gottschalk, and Stephen Foster. His principal vehicles were *Dwight's Journal of Music* (1852–81), the leading American periodical of its kind, and the Harvard Musical Association, on whose committee he served. The Association's programming philosophy—to be "above all need of catering to low tastes," to promote "only composers of unquestioned excellence, and…nothing vulgar, coarse, 'sensational', but only such as outlives fashion"—embodied Dwight's severe conservatism; his enthusiasms stopped with Mendelssohn, Schumann, and Chopin.

If the Handel and Haydn Society, which resisted Berlioz and Brahms, reinforced local purism, other important Boston influences, notably the Wagnerite conductor B.J. Lang and Thomas Ryan's Mendelssohn Quintette Club, welcomed the music of the moment. Dwight had served to refine taste and promote appreciation, but by the 1880s was a retarding force; compared to New York, Boston was slow to accept Berlioz, Brahms, Liszt, and Wagner. In 1881 Dwight confessed: "What challenges the world as new in music fails to stir us to the same depths of soul and feeling that the old masters did and doubtless always will. Startling as the new composers are, [they] do not bring us nearer heaven." He added: "We revenge ourselves with pointing to the unmistakable fact, that in the concert-giving experience of to-day, at least in Boston, the prurient appetite for novelty…seems to have reached its first stage of satiety." Apthorp, in a shrewd eulogy for Dwight, summed up: "What he was, he was genuinely and thoroughly; fashion had no hold on him."

3. The Boston SO to World War I. Boston's need for a more professionalized, cosmopolitan, and focused musical community resulted in 1881 in the formation of the Boston SO. This was the brainchild of Henry Lee Higginson, a financier whose lifelong passion was music. Resolving to give Boston a "full-time and permanent" orchestra that would "offer the best music at low prices," Higginson created an ensemble soon regarded as peerless in the United States and comparable to the best abroad. He paid all salaries and deficits, but conferred artistic control on his conductors. Some recent accounts of his philanthropy stress the Gilded Age plutocrat rather than the cultural democrat. It is true that Higginson forbade his musicians to form a union or to play popular music on days they rehearsed or performed (a Wednesday-to-Saturday prohibition sometimes wrongly characterized as full-time); that his own musical tastes were relatively conservative; that his orchestra was a Brahmin cultural stronghold. At the same time, he reserved "rush seats" for non-subscribers and began "popular concerts"—the future Boston Pops.

The first Boston SO conductor, George Henschel (1881–4), was replaced by an Austrian disciplinarian, Wilhelm Gericke, whom Higginson heard in Vienna, and it was Gericke who polished and refined Boston's orchestra (1884–9). His successor, Arthur Nikisch (1889–93), was a Romantic in outlook and temperament, and less interested in precision; his interpretative liberties in Beethoven's Fifth caused a furor. The orchestra moved to Symphony Hall, its current home, in 1900. Nikisch was replaced by Emil Paur (1893–8), after which Gericke returned (1898–1906). Recent scholarship has established a greater frequency of performance in the early seasons of the Boston SO than had previously been acknowledged. In 1881–2, the orchestra offered 20 concerts and 20 "public rehearsals," plus six concerts in Cambridge. In 1882–3, the total number of concerts and public rehearsals grew to 77. By 1900, the orchestra was playing 100 times or more per season. By 1916, the "public rehearsals," long understood as de facto concerts, were no longer so termed.

Boston had by 1900 fostered a vigorous school of composers, to which the Boston SO was notably receptive. John Knowles Paine, whose professorship in music at Harvard University was unprecedented in the United States, was a father figure whose two symphonies (1875, 1879) pay homage to Beethoven and Schumann; but his late opera *Azara* (1883–98) is Wagnerian. Of Paine's progeny, G.W. Chadwick, whose music resonates with hymns, fiddle tunes, and popular song, may be considered Boston's first significant nationalist composer; his works were played 78 times by the Boston SO between 1881 and 1924. Other "Boston boys" (Chadwick's term) included Amy Beach, Arthur Foote, and Horatio Parker. The most progressive Boston composer was the German-born Charles Martin Loeffler, whose influences included the French symbolists. A true community, influential in its day, the pre-World War I Boston composers cannot be fairly described as "classicists" or Germanic clones; their worth is still not recognized. At the same time, Boston's discomfort with Dvořák's "New World" Symphony and "American" String Quartet, rebuked by local critics and composers (1893–4) for absorbing "barbaric" plantation songs and Native American chants, revealed a strain of elitist conservatism not evident in New York.

With the arrival of Carl Muck in 1906, the Boston SO obtained a world-class conductor who combined

Gericke's efficiency with energy and power; his Boston recordings, the orchestra's first, document an interpretative personality more restrained than Nikisch's (as documented by the latter's recordings in Berlin). Muck was followed by Max Fiedler (1908–12), but thereafter returned, only to fall foul of anti-German war sentiment; interned as an enemy alien, he left the United States in 1918 vowing never to come back. The same year, Higginson relegated control of the orchestra to a group of nine citizens, incorporated as the Trustees of the Boston SO. Postwar Germanophobia ensured that the orchestra would not have another German-born music director for decades to come; it also impugned the music of Chadwick and other German-trained local composers, whose works faded from the repertory.

4. Concert life after World War I. Muck's successors, Henri Rabaud (1918–19) and Pierre Monteux (1920–24), presided over a transitional period. In 1920 more than 30 players who wished to affiliate with the Boston Musicians' Protective Association, the local union of the American Federation of Musicians, went on strike and were replaced by musicians of Monteux's choice. (The Boston SO was the last important American orchestra to join the union, in 1942.) The glamorous Serge Koussevitzky (1924–49) influentially championed the music of Copland and such other postwar Americans as Barber, Bernstein, Hanson, Harris, Piston, and Schuman. It was under Koussevitzky that the orchestra took over the Berkshire Music Festival, acquired Tanglewood and in 1940 opened the Berkshire Music Center (renamed the Tanglewood Music Center in 1985; *see* Tanglewood) In the meantime, in 1929 Arthur Fiedler, a member of the orchestra since 1915, organized the Esplanade Concerts as free, outdoor programs of symphonic and light music in the band shell on the banks of the Charles River. In 1930 Fiedler succeeded Alfredo Casella as conductor of the Boston Pops, a position he held until his death in 1979. In 1980 he was succeeded by John Williams, who in turn was followed by Keith Lockhart in 1995. For the Boston SO's 50th anniversary season (1930–31) Koussevitzky commissioned Stravinsky's *Symphony of Psalms*, Hindemith's *Konzertmusik* and works by Copland, E.B. Hill, Honegger, Prokofiev, Respighi, and Roussel. Koussevitzky's successors were Charles Münch (1949–62), Erich Leinsdorf (1962–9), William Steinberg (1969–72), Seiji Ozawa (1973–2004), and James Levine (2004–11).

5. Opera and musical theater. Puritan traditions slowed the development of theater in Boston, but an anti-theater law of 1750 did not prevent "readings" of English ballad and comic operas. Over 150 ballad operas had been performed in Boston before 1800. In the late 1820s the resident opera company of New Orleans performed its French repertory in Boston, but Italian opera was not patronized by the upper classes in Boston to the extent that it was in New York. Therefore no serious attempts to promote Italian opera in Boston occurred before 1847, when an Italian company based in Havana played the first of two seasons in the Howard Anthenaeum. Traveling companies continued to visit during the next two decades, and opera in English opened at the new Boston Theatre in 1860. The Strakosch and Mapleson touring companies and others played in Boston, and a week-long Wagner festival in 1877 presented three early works and *Die Walküre*. The American premiere of *H.M.S. Pinafore* was given in Boston in 1878, and in 1883 the new Metropolitan Opera company of New York began its annual visits to Boston. The Boston ideal opera company (the Bostonians) was highly successful throughout America between 1879 and 1905.

In 1895–6 a season of opera, mostly light, French works sung in English by young Americans, was presented at the Castle Square Theatre by C.E. French. Charles A. Ellis, manager of the Boston SO, also presented an opera season early in 1899, with the New York SO in the pit and Walter Damrosch as both a business partner and conductor. Wagner enthusiasm peaked in Boston in the 1890s: Damrosch brought Wagner to the Boston Theatre, and B.J. Lang presented a concert version of *Parsifal* in 1891.

Increased public demand finally spurred the musical elite to push for Boston's first permanent opera company. Henry Russell and the department-store magnate Eben D. Jordan, Jr founded the city's first important resident company, the Boston Opera Company. Jordan invested more than $1 million in the new Boston Opera House and guaranteed the company's deficit for three years. The first season opened on 8 November 1909 with Ponchielli's *La Gioconda*, starring Lillian Nordica in the title role. In 1914 a costly spring season in Paris resulted in bankruptcy in 1915. During the next two seasons Max Rabinoff mounted the Boston Grand Opera Company, but thereafter there were only annual tours by the Chicago Opera between 1917 and 1932 and later the San Carlo Opera. The building was demolished in 1958.

There was no important local opera production again until Boris Goldovsky established the New England Opera Theatre in 1946. Goldovsky's former protégée Sarah Caldwell (with James Stagliano and Linda Cabot Black) formed a new company in 1958 first known as the Boston Opera Group and later as the Opera Company of Boston. It presented significant American and world premieres.

In 1976 a number of the city's smaller companies joined to form the Boston Lyric Opera, initially to provide performance opportunities for resident singers. Peter Sellars and the conductor Craig Smith, working with locally based singers, rehearsed their bold, updated productions of Handel and Mozart in Boston.

6. Choruses. The earliest choral singing in Boston was the first settlers' congregational psalm singing, which continued through later times of controversy over the relative virtues of the old style and the cultivated new style promoted in the singing schools. Church and community choirs were formed throughout New England from the 1750s. The work of George K. Jackson, who in 1812 organized a concert of Handel's music, was instrumental in broadening the musical repertory of Boston's churches.

The Handel and Haydn Society was formed for the purpose of "cultivating and improving a correct taste in the performance of sacred music, and also to introduce into more general practice the works of Handel, Haydn, and other eminent composers." It gave its first concert on 25 December 1815 and served as the prototype for similar organizations in other cities. At Christmas 1818 the society gave its first performance of the complete *Messiah*; on 16 February 1819 *The Creation* followed. The first edition of *The Boston Handel and Haydn Society Collection of Church Music*, anonymously edited by Lowell Mason (president of the society 1827–32), was published in 1822. Christopher Hogwood directed the society from 1986 to 2001, completing the transformation of the organization into a professional chorus accompanied by a period-instrument orchestra, expanding the group's reputation through recordings and tours, and fostering collaborative projects with other art forms (including jazz). Grant Llewellyn led the society from 2001 to 2006, and Harry Christophers became Artistic Director in 2009.

Several English-style glee clubs were the ancestors of three long-lived choral societies: the Apollo Club of about 50 male voices, founded in 1871 and led by B.J. Lang; the Boylston Club, founded in 1873 as a male-voice group devoted to relatively light music and converted in 1877 into a chorus of mixed voices with a serious repertory; and the Cecilia Society, established in 1874 under Lang to perform with the orchestra of the Harvard Musical Association. In 1877 it separated from the association, and under Lang presented the Boston or American premieres of 105 works. In 1889 it gave the first of more than 100 peformances with the Boston SO. Arthur Fiedler became its conductor in 1930, but the chorus declined after his departure until Donald Teeters assumed the conductorship in 1968.

The periods of greatest activity of these groups overlapped with current choral societies, many of which are affiliated with educational institutions. In 1912 A.T. Davison of the Harvard faculty took over direction of the glee club, and in 1913 he also took over the Radcliffe (College) Choral Society. In the late 1940s the Chorus Pro Musica was founded by Alfred Nash Patterson, and the New England Conservatory Chorus came under the direction of Lorna Cooke de Varon. The Tanglewood Festival Chorus was established in 1970 under John Oliver to perform with the Boston SO at Tanglewood and in Boston. Numerous other professional and amateur choral societies are currently active in Boston.

7. Other ensembles. In 1844 the Harvard Musical Association began a series of six annual chamber music concerts that continued for five years. The public performance of chamber music acquired an important place in musical life with the founding of the Mendelssohn Quintette Club in 1849 under the leadership of Thomas Ryan. The German pianist and composer Otto Dresel (1826–90), a pupil of Hiller and Mendelssohn, settled in Boston in 1852 and was much admired for his tireless efforts on behalf of J.S. Bach, Schumann, and Robert Franz. In 1858 B.J. Lang, who had been a member of the Liszt circle in Europe, returned to Boston to start an active career that included conducting the world premiere of Tchaikovsky's First Piano Concerto (1875) at Music Hall, with Hans von Bülow as soloist. The Euterpe Society was founded in 1879 as a membership subscription scheme for the presentation of chamber concerts and recitals.

The stability and skills of the Boston SO provided a new kind of community artistic resource. Franz Kneisel, who became leader in 1885, founded the Kneisel Quartet, which made its reputation during its 20 years in Boston. The success of the Longy Club, established in 1900, developed a new taste for French wind music, which was later featured by the Boston Flute Players Club, founded in 1920 under the direction of Georges Laurent. In the late 19th century Boston led America in the popular Victorian custom of "at homes," small-scale concerts in private residences.

The Boston Symphony Chamber Players were founded by the orchestra's management in 1964. A large variety of chamber organizations and series have prospered in the 20th century. The Pro Arte Chamber Orchestra, a professional cooperative founded in 1978, is one of the few musician-run groups in the United States. Concert series of broad general interest are presented under various auspices.

The "early music movement" has a long history in Boston. Interest in "original instruments" dates back to well before 1905, when Arnold Dolmetsch began to make them for the Chickering company. Ruth Charlotte Dana introduced Gregorian chant at Boston's Church of the Advent in the 1840s. On 22 January 1875 in Boston's Mechanics Hall, the first of "Four Historical Concerts" was presented by George Osgood and F. Boscowitz, featuring Josquin's *Tu pauperum refugium*, madrigals by Le Jeune and Morley, J.S. Bach's Italian Concerto, and other keyboard works by Bull, Byrd, Rameau, and Kuhnau performed on a harpsichord provided by Chickering.

In 1938 a group of string players from the orchestra formed the Boston Society of Ancient Instruments under Alfred Zighera. Bodky's Collegium Musicum, founded in 1942 and succeeded by the Cambridge Society for Early Music, established standards of performance nearer to those achieved today, and eventually the Boston Camerata, founded in 1954 by Narcissa Williamson and directed from 1969 to 2008 by Joel Cohen, became one of the country's best-known groups of this kind. Martin Pearlman's Boston Baroque, founded in 1973 as Banchetto Musicale, has acquired an international reputation. The Boston Museum Trio plays period instruments from the collections of the Museum of Fine Arts, and the Boston Early Music Festival and Exhibition, first held in 1981, has presented early music groups and instrument makers from Boston and around the world.

Influential contemporary music groups in Boston are Collage New Music, founded in 1972; Boston Musica Viva (founded 1969); Dinosaur Annex (founded 1975); and the Alea III (founded 1978).

8. Popular and traditional music. From the mid-19th century, popular musical entertainment has been an important feature of Boston's musical life. The English songwriter and entertainer Henry Russell lived in the city during the 1830s, and with the founding of Kendall's Boston Brass Band in 1835 a continuous tradition of significant band activities was initiated. Blackface minstrelsy emerged as a major pastime by the 1840s, including an early appearance by Dan Emmett and the Virginia Minstrels in 1843.

Beginning around 1850, the neighborhood surrounding Scollay Square (now Government Center) emerged as the city's main entertainment district. The area was home to major theaters and vaudeville houses including the Howard Athenaeum, B.F. Keith's New Theater, Scollay's Olympia, and the New Palace Theater. Programs generally included a mixture of music (including light opera, musical theater, minstrel songs, and ragtime), alongside dancers, comedians, skits, circus acts, and other fare. The dominance of Scollay Square would eventually give way to the city's South End, which became the center of jazz activity from the 1930s. Much of the area was later demolished during urban restructuring initiatives of the 1960s.

Boston's location as a port city has long made it a destination for immigrant communities, who brought their own musical practices. Irish residents fleeing the potato shortages in the mid-19th century arrived in large numbers, with many settling in the Roxbury neighborhood. Scores of Irish dance halls sprung up from the 1920s to the 1950s: listeners and dancers enjoyed a range of traditional and contemporary styles. While some groups focused exclusively on traditional reels and dances, others—such as the highly successful bandleader Johnny Powell—injected elements of American popular song. Both traditions remain active today, from traditional ensembles to more recent hybrid groups such as the Celtic-Punk band Dropkick Murphys.

Other traditional musics are performed regularly among the city's immigrant groups, which include large concentrations of Brazilian, Haitian, Dominican, Chinese, Vietnamese, and Cape Verdean residents. A large Jewish population—which grew in size throughout the 20th century in the neighborhoods of Roxbury, Dorchester, and Newton—also maintains an active musical life. In addition to practicing traditional dance and folk styles, these communities have also been involved in creating and supporting art music. For example, since 1952 the city's Armenian community (based mostly in nearby Watertown) has supported an annual "Armenian Night" presented by the Boston Pops Orchestra.

In the 1950s and 60s, Boston played a prominent role in the American folk music revival. Club 47 (now Club Passim), located in nearby Cambridge, was the centerpiece of the movement, and featured local artists such as the Charles River Valley Boys, Eric Von Schmidt, Mitch Greenhill, and others. The club's most highly-acclaimed performer was the young Joan Baez, who joined the folk scene after enrolling at Boston University in 1958. The city's preponderance of college campuses spurred connections between the folk revival and political movements.

Despite the city's high concentration of students, Boston was slow to have an impact on rock and roll, although a local scene did emerge in the 1960s in clubs including the Boston Tea Party, the Psychedelic Supermarket and the Crosstown Bus. In 1968, MGM records attempted to market a group of local psychedelic rock bands under the banner of "the Bosstown Sound," closely modeled after the "San Francisco Sound." The campaign ultimately proved a major financial and critical failure. Boston musicians found more success as part of the arena rock culture of the 1970s, as bands such as Aerosmith, the J. Geils Band, and the group Boston (iii) rose to prominence. The scene's alternative rock and hip hop scenes produced further successes during the 1980s and 1990s, including groups such as Mission of Burma, the Pixies, the Mighty Mighty Bosstones, and Gang Starr.

9. Jazz. The earliest announcements of jazz events in Boston appeared around 1917—roughly contemporaneous with its arrival in New York. In the 1920s, pianist Sid Reinherz contributed to the change in style from late rag to early stride, and Leo Reisman led a jazz-style big band in the Brunswick Hotel. Mal Hallett's popular band featured a distinguished membership that in 1933 included Gene Krupa and Jack Teagarden. The bandleader Vaughan Monroe began his career as a singer with the Jack Marshard "society orchestra" in 1936. Similar groups were led by Meyer Davis, Eddy Duchin, and Ruby Newman.

Beginning in the 1930s, the city's South End became a hub of jazz activity. Over the next several decades, the area served as home to major clubs including Wally's Paradise, the Savoy Café, and the Hi-Hat. The city's proximity to New York made it a frequent stop for nationally touring bands, and led to fruitful exchanges of talent. Several Boston musicians moved to New York to advance their careers, including pianist Charlie Johnson (who led the house band in Harlem's Small's Paradise from 1925) and Ellington saxophonists Johnny Hodges and Harry Carney. Other musicians from Boston to reach national prominence include Roy Haynes, Serge Chaloff, Paul Gonsalves, Tony Williams, and Chick Corea. Still others, like pianist Sabby Lewis, never developed national reputations but remained important staples of the local scene.

Although the South End clubs began to decline during the 1960s and 70s, jazz activity remained high through the support of local universities. The Berklee School of Music (originally founded as Schillinger House in 1945) was opened explicitly to teach jazz and popular music. The school gained full accreditation in 1966, making it the first college program to offer degrees in jazz performance. Three years later, the New England Conservatory (NEC) added its own jazz department, making it the first classical conservatory to incorporate a jazz curriculum. In 1973, NEC president Gunther Schuller (who had earlier performed with the Miles Davis Nonet) founded the school's Third Stream

Department (later renamed Contemporary Improvisation) to explore the overlap between jazz and classical music practices. Both schools remain crucial centers for jazz activity in the city. Their faculties have included many prominent musicians and theorists including Herb Pomeroy, Gary Burton, and Pat Metheny at Berklee and George Russell, Jaki Byard, and Thad Jones at NEC. Alumni from both schools have gone on to prominence in the jazz world over the past 50 years, ranging from avant-garde pianist Cecil Taylor (NEC, 1955) to bassist/vocalist Esperanza Spalding (Berklee, 2005).

10. Theaters and concert halls. Early public performances of music were organized in private homes, coffee houses, and religious meeting houses. A law of 1750, re-enacted in 1785, prohibited theatrical entertainments of all kinds, but it was commonly circumvented by billing such events as "lectures" or "readings." In 1792 the New Exhibition Room was opened for "lectures, moral and entertaining" with a "gallery of portraits, songs, feats of tumbling, and ballet pantomime" but it was promptly closed in 1793.

Public demand brought swift change, and in 1793, the Boston Theatre, designed by Charles Bulfinch to be one of the grandest in the United States, was opened. It was often called the Federal Street Theatre, especially after the Haymarket Theatre opened in 1796, and spoken drama and ballad opera were popular on both stages. Graupner later had a concert room in the same building as his home and shop. His Philharmonic concerts took place in Pythian Hall and later the Pantheon. The Handel and Haydn Society's early performances were given in churches such as Stone Chapel and then Boylston Hall. From 1835 to 1843 the Boston Theatre, remodeled and renamed the Odeon, was the home of the Academy of Music.

In 1827 the Tremont Theatre was built. After a fire, it was reopened as the Baptist Tremont Temple, which survives as rebuilt in the 1870s after another fire. The Lion Theatre of 1836, built for "dramatic and equestrian performances," taken over in 1839 by the Handel and Haydn Society and renamed the Melodeon, was the successor to the Odeon as Boston's leading concert hall.

In 1845 the Millerite Tabernacle was refitted as a theater, the Howard Athenaeum, which in 1847 saw Boston's first important season of Italian opera. It was closed in 1953, after long years of service as the Old Howard, a famous burlesque house, and was destroyed by fire in 1961. In the 1840s the Chickering firm's showrooms were the site of such serious musical events as the Harvard Musical Association's chamber concerts, and by the 1850s there was a Chickering Hall. Minstrel shows played at the Adelphi (opened 1847) and the Lyceum (1848). The Harvard Musical Association raised a construction fund of $100,000 for a new hall, and on 20 November 1852 they opened the 2700-seat Music Hall, which provided a new rallying point for the city's musical life.

In 1854 the New Boston Theatre opened, and from 1860 various operas were produced there. The Continental Theatre opened in 1866 and prospered with a long run of the musical *The Black Crook*. In 1876 Harvard's Memorial Hall had appended to it the 1400-seat Sanders Theatre, which became the university's principal auditorium and was the site of the Boston SO's Cambridge concert series for about 80 years. In 1896 the little Steinert Hall was opened by the Steinert Piano Co.

In the spring of 1893 Henry Lee Higginson said that he would discontinue maintenance of the Boston SO unless the Music Hall, endangered by planned street and subway construction, could be replaced within little more than a year. The estimated cost of $400,000 was quickly subscribed and McKim, Mead & White designed the New Boston Music Hall, later named Symphony Hall. The collaboration of Wallace C. Sabine, then a young member of the Harvard physics department, made this the first scientifically designed auditorium.

Jordan Hall (cap. 1019), built in 1908 at the New England Conservatory, is well suited to solo recitals and performances by smaller groups. In 1909 the 2700-seat Boston Opera House opened, its acoustic design also by Sabine. A theater-building boom occurred in Boston at the opening of the 20th century; in 25 years eight new playhouses and 16 movie theaters were constructed, with most theaters featuring live orchestras. The Metropolitan Theatre, opened in 1926 as a splendid vaudeville and movie palace and later used as an opera and ballet house (sometimes called the Music Hall or the Metropolitan Center), was closed in 1982. The Hatch Memorial Shell was built in 1940 for free outdoor concerts given on the Charles River Esplanade by Arthur Fiedler and members of the Boston SO. Massachusetts Institute of Technology opened its fine 1238-seat, general-purpose Kresge Auditorium in 1955.

11. Instruments. Before American independence almost all musical instruments used in Boston had been imported from England and later from the Continent; but by the mid-19th century Boston was exporting instruments to Europe and South America. Collections are owned by the Boston Public Library, the Boston SO, Boston University, Harvard University, the Museum of Fine Arts, and the New England Conservatory.

The first organ in New England, probably the second in the Colonies, was installed in the home of Thomas Brattle by 1711, and the first locally built organ was left unfinished by Edward Bromfield. A contemporary report of the period 1810–15 said that only six Boston churches then had organs. Among early organ builders were William Goodrich, the firms of Hayts, Babcock & Appleton and Hook & Hastings, and John Rowe. In 1854 a successful organ business was begun by Henry L. Mason and Emmons Hamlin, with financial backing from Lowell Mason and Oliver Ditson. Its products became well known in Europe, and its profits helped to finance the manufacture of the fine Mason & Hamlin pianos, begun in 1883, which eventually outweighed the reed-organ business in importance and resulted in its sale in 1911.

In 1855 a committee of citizens raised $10,000 to build an organ in the Music Hall. Ordered from the German firm of Walcker in Ludwigsburg, the organ was finally dedicated on 2 November 1863 by John Knowles Paine, B.J. Lang, and others. It was the largest organ in North America and one of the three or four largest in the world. It had fallen into disrepair by the early 1880s, however, and was eventually removed.

A spinet built by John Harris in 1769 was probably the first keyboard string instrument made in the Colonies. Benjamin Crehore, originally a cabinet maker, was building harpsichords and string instruments by 1792, and by 1797 he had begun to make pianos. Jonas Chickering made his first piano in 1823 and took out several important patents during the 1840s. The prospering Chickering company opened its new factory in 1855 as the second largest building in the country, exceeded in size only by the US Capitol. In 1927 the company moved to East Rochester, New York, as part the American Piano Company. In addition to Mason & Hamlin, several other Boston makers produced good pianos for home and school use, most of them ultimately absorbed by the Aeolian Corporation. Boston continues to support makers of fine harpsichords and other early keyboard instruments. William Dowd and Frank Hubbard, who established a joint workshop in 1949, worked independently from 1958. The Eric Herz workshop began operations in 1954. Jeremy Adams, who worked with Dowd, became an independent maker, restorer, and rebuilder in 1968.

A few early 17th-century settlers are believed to have brought viols to America. Within 50 years prosperous individuals were importing string instruments; Benjamin Crehore began to make them in Boston during the 18th century. George Gemunder, who trained in Paris under Vuillaume, and his brother August opened their shop in Boston in 1847, but moved to New York in 1851. The firm of J.B. Squier, established in 1886, was later remembered principally as a manufacturer of strings.

William Callender began to make wind instruments in 1796, and others continued the trade through the 19th century, though with little distinction until William S. Haynes started his flute company in 1900. Haynes and his foreman Verne Q. Powell were influential in establishing the silver flute in the United States. Powell started his own firm in 1926 and made Boston a leading center of flute making; in 1961 he sold it to a group of his employees. Brannen Brothers, founded in 1977, was joined in 1978 by the English flute maker Albert K. Cooper. In 1901 Cundy-Bettoney started to build woodwind instruments that were destined for the educational market, and in 1925 the firm began to produce what were said to be the first metal clarinets.

Boston became a center of brass-instrument manufacture after the establishment of Edward Kendall's Boston Brass Band in 1835. The firms of E.G. Wright and Graves & Co. combined about 1869 to form the Boston Musical Instrument Manufactory, known for its fine band instruments during the late 1880s. In 1884 Thompson and Odell founded the Standard Brass Instrument Co., which also made guitars and banjos; it was later taken over by the Vega company. George B. Stone started his business in percussion instruments in 1890. The Zildjian family's cymbal business, founded in Constantinople in 1623, moved to the Boston area in 1929.

12. Education and libraries.

(i) Education. Early settlers were concerned with musical education, and devotional singing is said to have had a place in the original curriculum at Harvard College, founded in 1636. The first published musical teaching material is the "admonition to the reader," in the Bay Psalm Book of 1640, and the instructive introductions to 18th-century tunebooks extended this practice. By 1720 the traditional "old way of singing" came under attack from those who favored musically literate "regular singing," and singing schools were established. A century of Yankee tunesmiths wrote and published the psalm settings and hymns that were their teaching pieces, but early 19th-century hymnodic reformers sought to replace earlier American psalmody with "scientific" European models.

Lowell Mason studied the methods of Swiss educational theorist Pestalozzi and applied them to the children's music classes that he taught in churches and private schools. In the Boston Academy of Music he held teacher-training classes in addition to its concerts. In 1837 he introduced music to the curriculum in the Boston public schools at his own expense, and in the following year the Boston school board created the first program of free, public-school instruction in music under his direction.

Harvard University, in Cambridge, was the first college in the United States, founded to train young men for the ministry. Its evolution into a secular university was slow, and music at first had a place there only in connection with religion. As early as 1808 there was interest enough in music among Harvard undergraduates for them to form the Pierian Sodality, whose members formed the basis of the Harvard Musical Association in 1837 (though the name was not assumed until 1840). It had no formal connection with the college but acted as a alumni advisory group, and in 1838 recommended that instruction in music be added to the curriculum. Its efforts had no effect, however, until 1862, when Harvard appointed John Knowles Paine to the post of college organist and instructor in music. In 1875 he became a full professor of music. During his long tenure (until his death in 1906), Paine taught many important composers and music historians during the height of the "Second New England School" of composers. Walter Piston taught several generations of composers at Harvard until his retirement in 1960.

The Perkins Institute and Massachusetts School for the Blind (founded in 1832) added music to its program in 1833, with Mason as teacher. Two new music schools opened in February 1867: the Boston Conservatory (founded under the direction of violinist and composer Julius Eichberg) and the New England Conservatory (founded by Eben Tourjée). The College of Music at Boston University was founded by Tourjée in 1872. In 1916 Georges Longy opened the school bearing his name, to offer instruction in solfège and theoretical subjects as taught in France. Schoenberg taught for one year at the Malkin Conservatory, which functioned from 1933 to 1954. The Berklee College of Music was founded by Lawrence Berk in 1945 to train professional musicians for work in jazz and other non-classical traditions. Among its graduates are Keith Jarrett, Ingrid Jensen, Quincy Jones, and Branford Marsalis.

There are many other institutions of higher education in which music has an important place, including Brandeis University (in nearby Waltham, founded in 1948 as the only non-religious Jewish-sponsored university in the United States), Massachusetts Institute of Technology, Northeastern University, Tufts University, and Wellesley College.

There is a long-standing tradition of community music schools in the Boston area. The Elma Lewis School of Fine Arts is a highly valued institution in the African American community, and earlier music schools were maintained by the city's Italian, Jewish, and Lithuanian communities.

(ii) Libraries. The principal music libraries in Boston proper are the collection (begun in 1859) at the Boston Public Library, whose enormous archival value can hardly be assessed from the admirable published catalogs (of 1910 and 1972), and those at Boston University, the Harvard Musical Association, the Massachusetts Historical Society, the New England Conservatory of Music, and the Boston Athenaeum. In Cambridge, Harvard's holdings are principally in the Houghton Library, the Isham Memorial Library, and the Eda Kuhn Loeb Music Library. Wellesley College also has a fine music library. At some distance from the city but of great importance for their collections of Americana are the Essex Institute in Salem and the American Antiquarian Society in Worcester. A librarians' informal discussion group that first met in 1974 became a productive consortium of 16 institutions called Boston Area Music Libraries, which in 1983 issued the monumental publication *The Boston Composers Project.*

13. Printing and publishing. The first music known to have been printed and published in North America appeared in the ninth edition of the *Bay Psalm Book* (Boston, 1698), in which 13 tunes are printed from woodblocks. The next appeared in two instruction books, one by John Tufts (1721 or earlier), the other by Thomas Walter (also 1721), which was probably the first North American music printed from engraved metal plates. Two collections by Josiah Flagg (1764 and 1766)

Charles Münch and the Boston Symphony Orchestra on the stage of Symphony Hall, c1955. (Photograph by Fay Foto, courtesy BSO Archive)

and at least part of William Billings's *The New-England Psalm-Singer* (1770) were engraved by Paul Revere. The first American set of type for printing music was cast in Boston by William (or possibly John) Norman, first used in the *Boston Magazine* in 1783.

Between 1798 and 1804 P.A. von Hagen (father and son) issued about 100 publications. Graupner was Boston's principal music publisher for about 25 years, beginning in 1802. The Handel and Haydn Society, which he helped form, paid him five cents per page, then a considerable sum, for the music of Haydn's *The Creation*. James Hewitt published in Boston from about 1812 to 1817. There were many other firms, and Ditson expanded and absorbed dozens before being absorbed itself by Theodore Presser in 1931.

In 1876 Arthur P. Schmidt founded a new firm that energetically published works by many American composers, including Beach, Bird, Chadwick, Foote, Hadley, MacDowell, Paine, and others. The Schmidt catalog is now owned by Summy-Birchard. Cundy-Bettoney, dating back to 1868 and specializing in wind music, is now part of Carl Fischer; the Wa-Wan Press, founded in 1901 by Arthur Farwell, was acquired by G. Schirmer in 1912. Specialist publishers include the firm of Robert King (established 1940), which was devoted to brass music until its expansion in 1982; it was acquired by the French publisher Alphonse Leduc in 1987. Other important firms included the Boston Music Company (founded 1885; closed 2003) and E.C. Schirmer (founded 1921), which is especially strong in choral music.

See also AMY MARCY BEACH; WILLIAM BILLINGS; SARAH CALDWELL; GEORGE WHITEFIELD CHADWICK; CHICKERING; JOEL COHEN; BENJAMIN CREHORE; OLIVER DITSON; JOHN SULLIVAN DWIGHT; ARTHUR FIEDLER; MAX FIEDLER; ARTHUR FOOTE; WILHELM GERICKE; PATRICK S. GILMORE; GOTTLIEB GRAUPNER; VON HAGEN; SIR GEORGE HENSCHEL; HENRY LEE HIGGINSON; GEORGE K. JACKSON; FRANZ KNEISEL; JOHN KNOWLES PAINE; SERGE KOUSSEVITZKY; ERICH LEINSDORF; JAMES LEVINE; KEITH LOCKHART; CHARLES MARTIN LOEFFLER; GEORGES LONGY; MASON; MASON & HAMLIN; PIERRE MONTEUX; CARL MUCK; CHARLES MÜNCH; NEW ENGLAND COMPOSERS, SCHOOLS OF; ARTHUR NIKISCH; SEIJI OZAWA; HORATIO PARKER; EMIL PAUR; WALTER PISTON; VERNE Q. POWELL; HENRY RUSSELL; ARTHUR P. SCHMIDT; WILLIAM STEINBERG; EBEN TOURJÉE; WA-WAN PRESS; JOHN WILLIAMS; CARL ZERRAHN.

BIBLIOGRAPHY

G. Hood: *A History of Music in New England* (Boston, 1846/*R*)
The Great Organ in the Boston Music Hall, being a Brief History of the Enterprise (Boston, 1865)
J.S. Dwight: "Music in Boston," *The Memorial History of Boston*, ed. J. Winsor, iv (Boston, 1881–3), 415–64
C.C. Perkins, and others: *History of the Handel and Haydn Society* (Boston, 1883/*R*)
M.A. de W. Howe: *The Boston Symphony Orchestra: an Historical Sketch* (Boston, 1914, enlarged 2/1931/*R* with J.N. Burk as *The Boston Symphony Orchestra 1881–1931*)
W.A. Fisher: *Notes on Music in Old Boston* (Boston, 1918/*R*)
J.H. Railey: *The New England Conservatory of Music, 1867–1927* (Boston, 1927)
W.R. Spaulding: *Music at Harvard: a Historial Review of Men and Events* (New York, 1935/*R*)
C.M. Ayars: *Contributions to the Art of Music in America by the Music Industries of Boston, 1640 to 1936* (New York, 1937/*R*)
A. Foote: "A Bostonian Remembers," *MQ*, xxiii (1937), 37–44
H.C. McCusker: *Fifty Years of Music in Boston, Based on Hitherto Unpublished Letters in the Boston Public Library* (Boston, 1938)
H.W. Foote: "Musical Life in Boston in the Eighteenth Century," *Proceedings of the American Antiquarian Society*, new ser., xlix (1939), 293–313
H.E. Johnson: "Early New England Periodicals Devoted to Music," *MQ*, xxvi (1940), 153–61
H.E. Johnson: *Musical Interludes in Boston 1795–1830* (New York, 1943/*R*)
H.E. Johnson: *Symphony Hall, Boston* (Boston, 1950/*R*)
J.W. Thompson: *Music and Musical Activities in New England, 1800–1838* (diss., Peabody College for Teachers, 1962)
Q. Eaton: *The Boston Opera Company* (New York, 1965/*R*)
H.E. Johnson: *Hallelujah, Amen: the Story of the Handel and Haydn Society of Boston* (Boston, MA, 1965/*R*)
B. Owen: *The Organs and Music of King's Chapel, 1713–1964* (Boston, 1966)
P.E. Paige: *Musical Organizations in Boston, 1830–1850* (diss., Boston U., 1967)
C.R. Nutter: *History of the Harvard Musical Association, 1837–1962* (Boston, 1968)
H.E. Dickson: *"Gentlemen, More Dolce Please!": an Irreverent Memoir of Thirty Years in the Boston Symphony Orchestra* (Boston, 1969)
Dictionary Catalog of the Music Collection (Boston, 1972–) [pubn of Boston Public Library]
L.J. Clarke: *Music in Trinity Church, Boston, 1890–1900: a Case Study in the Relationship between Worship and Culture* (diss., Union Theological Seminary, New York, 1973)
B.D. Wilson: *A Documentary History of Music in the Public Schools of the City of Boston, 1830–1850* (diss., U. of Michigan, 1973)
J. Baker-Carr: *Evening at Symphony: a Portrait of the Boston Symphony Orchestra* (Boston, 1977)
L. Snyder: *Community of Sound: Boston Symphony and its World of Players* (Boston, MA, 1979)
E. Von Schmidt and J. Rooney: *Baby Let Me Follow You Down: The Illustrated Story of the Cambridge Folk Years* (Garden City, NY, 1979)
B. Owen: *The Organ in New England* (Raleigh, NC, 1980)
D.A. Wood: *Music in Harvard Libraries: a Catalogue of Early Printed Music and Books on Music in the Houghton Library and the Eda Kuhn Loeb Music Library* (Cambridge, MA, 1980)
B. Lambert, ed.: *Music in Colonial Massachusetts, 1630–1820* (Boston, 1980–85)
P. DiMaggio: "Cultural Entrepreneurship in Nineteenth-Century Boston," *Media, Culture and Society*, iv (1982), 33–50, 303–22
The Boston Composers Project: a Bibliography of Contemporary Music (Cambridge, MA, 1983)
S. Ledbetter: *100 Years of the Boston Pops* (Boston, 1985)
D. McKay: "Opera in Colonial Boston," *AM*, iii/2 (1985), 133–42
A.W. Hepner: *Pro bonum artium musicarum: the Harvard Musical Association, 1837–1987* (Englewood Cliffs, NJ, 1987)
O.F. Saloman: "Margaret Fuller on Musical Life in Boston and New York, 1841–46," *AM*, vi (1988), 428–41
D. Whitwell: *The Longy Club: a Professional Wind Ensemble in Boston (1900–1917)* (Northridge, CA, 1988)
D. Kruh: *Always Something Doing: Boston's Infamous Scollay Square* (Boston, 1989, 2/1999)
M. Broyles: *"Music of the Highest Class": Elitism and Populism in Antebellum Boston* (New Haven, CT, 1992)
R.D. Cohen: *Rainbow Quest: the Folk Music Revival and American Society, 1940–1970* (Amherst, MA, 1992)
H. Pollack: *Harvard Composers: Walter Piston and His Students, from Elliott Carter to Frederic Rzewski* (Metuchen, NJ, 1992)
J. Wright: "Black Women in Classical Music in Boston during the Late Nineteenth Century: Profiles in Leadership," *New Perspectives in Music: Essays in Honor of Eileen Southern*, ed. J. Wright and S.A. Floyd (Warren, MI, 1992), 373–408
P. Fox: "Rebellious Tradition and Boston's Musical Spirit of Place: Elitism, Populism, and Lives Apart," *MQ*, lxxx (1994), 220–45
E. Hazell: *Berklee: The First Fifty Years* (Boston, 1995)
B. McPherson and J. Klein: *Measure by Measure: a History of New England Conservatory from 1867* (Boston, 1995)
P. Benes, ed.: *New England Music: The Public Sphere, 1600–1900* (Boston, 1998)

P. Benes and J.M. Benes, eds.: *Bibliography of Studies of New England Music Before 1900* (Boston, 1998)
R.P. Stebbins: *The Making of Symphony Hall* (Boston, 2000)
N. Hentoff: *Boston Boy: Growing Up with Jazz and Other Rebellious Passions* (Philadelphia, 2001)
K.K. Shelemay: "Case Study: Boston, U.S.A.," *Soundscapes: Exploring Music in a Changing World* (New York, 2001, 2/2006)
N.E. Tawa: *From Psalm to Symphony: a History of Music in New England* (Boston, 2001)
J. Horowitz: "Reclaiming the Past: Musical Boston Reconsidered," *AM*, xix/1 (2001), 18–38
A.A. Barnet: *Extravaganza King: Robert Barnet and Boston Musical Theatre* (Boston, 2004)
S. Gedutis: *See You at the Hall: Boston's Golden Era of Irish Music and Dance* (Boston, 2004)
J. Horowitz: *Classical Music in America: a History* (New York, 2005)
A.W. Adler: *"Classical Music for People who Hate Classical Music": Arthur Fiedler and the Boston Pops, 1930–1950* (diss., U. of Rochester, Eastman School of Music, 2007)
B. Milano: *The Sound of Our Town: a History of Boston Rock and Roll* (Beverly, MA, 2007)
J. Horowitz: *Moral Fire: Portraits from America's Fin-de-Siecle* (Berkeley, CA, 2012)

LEONARD BURKAT/PAMELA FOX (1, 10), JOSEPH HOROWITZ (2, 3, 4), MICHAEL C. HELLER (8, 9), LEONARD BURKAT/PAMELA FOX/R (5, 6, 7, 11, 12, I, II, 13)

Boston [Boston dip] **(ii)**. A waltz variation that first appeared in American ballrooms during the late 1860s. Each step to the dance was accompanied by a considerable bend of the knees, causing the entire body to sink down (the Boston "dip").

See WALTZ.

Boston (iii). Rock group. In 1970 Tom Scholz (*b* Toledo, OH, 10 March 1947; electric guitar, keyboards, and production) began collaborating with the musicians with whom he later formed Boston. An MIT graduate employed by Polaroid, he built a 12-track studio for developing his new band's sound. Harmonized vocal and guitar parts were painstakingly constructed through overdubbing. Scholz tried unsuccessfully to attract record company interest until Epic signed the group in 1975, at which time the band chose the name Boston. Their first album, *Boston* (Epic, 1976), was made up mostly of tracks that Scholz had assembled in his studio and became rock's fastest-selling debut, selling more than a million copies within three months and eventually selling more than 17 million. Hits from the album included "More than a Feeling," "Peace of Mind," and "Long Time." The band's touring personnel included Brad Delp (*b* Boston, MA, 12 June 1951; *d* Atkinson, NH, 9 March 2007; vocals), Barry Goudreau (electric guitar), Fran Sheehan (electric bass), and John "Sib" Hashian (drums).

Boston forged a style of rock built on the slow, precise construction of tracks in the studio, with guitar and vocal lines densely layered to create a thick, lush sound, owing much to Scholz's inventive experiments with electronics. The group's iconic sound influenced such melodic hard-rock groups as Journey, Foreigner, Styx, and Def Leppard. Although the group's second album was released only two years after their first, Scholz's perfectionism insured that each subsequent Boston album took seven years to produce. This led to diminishing commercial returns and caused friction with the band's record companies. Delp, whose bombastic tenor singing was a key part of Boston's style, took his own life in 2007.

SELECTED RECORDINGS

Boston (Epic, 1976); *Don't Look Back* (Epic, 1978); *Third Stage* (Epic, 1986); *Walk On* (MCA, 1994); *Corporate America* (Artemis, 2002)

CHRIS MCDONALD

Boston Academy of Music. American school founded in Boston in 1833 to train vocal music teachers. William Channing Woodbridge, Lowell Mason, George J. Webb, George H. Snelling, T. Kemper Davis, and Samuel A. Eliot influenced its establishment. A board of directors comprising approximately 50 businessmen and community leaders and a healthy student enrollment led the Boston School Committee to include the academy's leadership in discussions about adding music to the public school curriculum. An early academy leader, Lowell Mason, published the *Manual of Instruction of the Boston Academy of Music* (1834), which achieved nationwide popularity and added to the school's reputation. The academy offered public lectures, programs in private schools, music classes for children and adults, and served as a demonstration school. It advocated for improvement in church music and public school music. Hundreds of teachers received instruction during the school's 14 years of existence.

BIBLIOGRAPHY

E.B. Birge: *History of Public School Music in the United States* (Reston, VA, 1966), 25–8
M.L. Mark and C.L. Gary: *A History of American Music Education* (Lanham, MD, 3/2007), 141–6, 217

CAROLYN LIVINGSTON

Boston Ballet. Company founded by E. VIRGINIA WILLIAMS in Boston in 1963. An outgrowth of a civic ballet group, it was the first professional repertory ballet company in New England. It made its debut in 1964 at the Boston Arts Festival.

CLAUDE CONYERS

Boston Camerata. Ensemble of singers and instrumentalists founded in Boston in 1954 by Narcissa Williamson.

See EARLY-MUSIC REVIVAL.

Boston Festival Orchestra. Touring orchestra. It was founded in Boston in 1889 and was managed throughout its existence by George W. Stewart, a trombonist in the Boston SO; its purpose was to provide accompaniment for choirs at festivals and community events in places where orchestral resources were lacking. Generally numbering between 50 and 60 players, the ensemble specialized in oratorios and other standard festival fare. From 1889 to 1913 it made an annual spring tour along the Canadian border as far west as Minneapolis, then south by the Mississippi River to the Gulf of Mexico and up the Atlantic coast back to Boston. Carl Zerrahn led the first tour, and Victor Herbert those in 1890 and 1891; in the latter year he shared the conducting with Tchaikovsky, who traveled with the orchestra on his only visit to the United States. The conductor most closely associated with the orchestra, however, was EMIL MOLLENHAUER, who led the remaining 22 tours. He developed the orchestra's reputation as an accompanying ensemble, readily adaptable to working under many guest conductors, and reputedly able, if necessary, to transpose an aria from any oratorio at sight. After the orchestra ceased touring it was reconstituted annually in Boston for many years under Mollenhauer's direction to accompany the concerts of the Handel and Haydn Society chorus.

BIBLIOGRAPHY

H. Woelber: "Famous Bandmasters: Emil Mollenhauer," *International Musician*, xxx/6 (1932), 12

H. Woelber: "A Great Manager: George Washington Stewart," *International Musician,* xxxii/6 (1934), 19

E.N. Waters: *Victor Herbert: a Life in Music* (New York, 1955/*R*)

STEVEN LEDBETTER

Boston Ideal Opera Company [Bostonians; Ideals]. Opera company. In 1878 a Boston newspaper, critical of the performances of Gilbert and Sullivan's *H.M.S. Pinafore* that had been staged in the city, called for an "ideal" production. The singers' agent Effie H. Ober responded by forming the "Ideals," and staging a highly successful version of *Pinafore* on 14 April 1879. In the next years the troupe built a sizable repertory of contemporary comic operas and such works as Gaetano Donizetti's *L'elisir d'amore* and D.-F.-E. Auber's *Fra Diavolo*. It made annual countrywide tours and earned a reputation as the finest American ensemble of its kind. Aside from the troupe's chorus of 40 to 60 members, early featured singers included George Fessenden, Myron Whitney, Tom Karl, Adelaide Philips, and Mary Beebe. Trouble began for the Ideals in 1883, with the firing of a manager who was convicted as "insane from drink". In 1885 Ober stepped down as the troupe's manager. In 1887 an internal dispute prompted several of the leading players, including Barnabee, Cowles, Jessie Bartlett Davis, Karl, and W.H. MacDonald, to assume the group's management, at which time its name was changed to the Bostonians. The company presented several first performances of Victor Herbert's works, including *The Serenade* (1897), and became associated particularly with the operetta *Robin Hood* by De Koven and H.B. Smith, of which they gave the premiere in 1891. By 1898 the soprano Alice Nielsen had left the Bostonians to form her own company, taking with her several of its leading performers. This precipitated the group's financial demise, and it finally disbanded in 1905 after a theater fire in Red Bank, New Jersey claimed their entire stock of costumes and properties.

GERALD BORDMAN/STEPHANIE JENSEN-MOULTON

Boston Musical Instrument Manufactory. Firm of brass instrument makers. It was formed in 1869, when a group of brass instruments makers working at 71 Sudbury Street in Boston combined their skills and resources. The original group included George M. Graves, William E. Graves, E.G. Wright, Henry Esbach, and Louis F. Hartman, instrument craftsmen, and William G. Reed, bookkeeper. All except Reed were partners and workmen in the previous firms of E.G. Wright and Graves & Co. A case of brass instruments exhibited in September and October of 1869 at the Massachusetts Charitable Mechanic Association Fair won the new company a silver medal. It became a leading producer of brass instruments, notably "three star" cornets and trumpets, during the late 1880s. The company made instruments for several of the leading band soloists as well as for hundreds of community bands across the country. The building at 71 Sudbury burned in 1899, and the firm moved to 51 Chardon Street.

The firm was renamed in 1902 as the Boston Musical Instrument Company, incorporated in 1913 and sold to Cundy-Bettoney in 1919. The brand name was continued by Cundy-Bettoney until 1928. Boston Musical Instrument Manufactory instruments are found in most American collections, notably the John H. Elrod Memorial Collection, Germantown, Maryland; the Musical Instrument Museum, Phoenix, Arizona; the National Music Museum at the University of South Dakota; and the Essig Collection at the University of Missouri-Warrensburg.

BIBLIOGRAPHY

Waterhouse-LangwillI

C.M. Ayars: *Contributions to the Art of Music in America by the Music Industries of Boston, 1640–1936* (New York, 1937/R1969)

R.E. Eliason: "D.C. Hall and the Quinby Brothers," *JAMIS*, xxxiii (2007), 84–161

ROBERT E. ELIASON

Boston Music Company. Firm of music publishers. It was founded in 1885 by Gustave Schirmer Jr. (*b* New York, NY, 18 Feb 1864; *d* Boston, MA, 15 July 1907) and operated from premises at 2 Beacon Street, Boston; its first publication, Arthur Whiting's *Concert Etude* for piano, was issued the following year. The firm's large catalog, which includes many works by Ethelbert Nevin and Carrie Jacobs-Bond, is predominantly educational. Among its popular instructional series are the piano methods by John M. Williams (the "Blue Books"), C. Paul Herfurth's series *A Tune a Day* (for various instruments), and *Junior Hymnbooks* for piano by Rachael Beatty Kahl. Connections with the Schirmer family and firm remained close. Ernest Charles Schirmer, cousin of Gustave and founder of the E.C. Schirmer Music Company of Boston in 1921, was business manager and then partner, but left in 1917. On Gustave's death ownership passed to his son, also named Gustave (*b* Boston, 29 Dec 1890; *d* Palm Beach, FL, 28 May 1965), who engaged Carl Engel as editor and music adviser (1909–21), acquired catalogs of other publishers, and joined ASCAP (1924). In 1922 publication headquarters were moved to New York. The firm has long acted as agent for both domestic and foreign publishers. From 1968 to 1976 it was owned by the Frank Music Corp., then passed into the hands of CBS for a year, during which time it ceased to publish. Williamson Music took over from 1977 to 1979, when it was sold to William Hammerstein to become a division of the Hammerstein Music & Theater Company, Inc. The catalog of Boston Music Co. is now owned by Music Sales Corporation.

BIBLIOGRAPHY

W.A. Fischer: *One Hundred and Fifty Years of Music Publishing in the United States* (Boston, MA, 1933/*R*)

C.M. Ayars: *Contribution to the Art of Music in America by the Music Industries of Boston, 1640–1936* (New York, 1937/*R*)

GERALDINE OSTROVE/R

Boston Society of Ancient Instruments. Chamber ensemble founded in Boston in 1938.

See Early-music revival *and* boston (i).

Boston University. Private university founded in 1839, now the fourth largest private university in the United States. The School of Music was established in 1872 with Eben Tourjée as dean. Degrees are offered in composition, conducting, ethnomusicology, historical performance, music education, music theory, musicology, performance, and sacred music through three colleges: College of Fine Arts (BM, MM, DMA), College of Arts and Sciences (BA, MA, PhD), School of Theology (MSM), and a pre-professional certificate through the Opera Institute. The MM and DMA in music education have also been offered online since 2005. Research collections include the archives of the Hymn Society in the United States and Canada, Organ Library of the American Guild of Organists Boston Chapter, and collections of Arthur Fiedler, H.C. Robbins Landon, Charles Münch, and Kate Smith, among others, located in the Howard Gotlieb Archival Research Center. Resident ensembles include ALEA III, Boston Baroque, Boston Youth Symphony Orchestra, and the Muir String Quartet. The Boston University Tanglewood Institute, an intensive summer program for high school musicians, has been held as a counterpart to the Boston Symphony Orchestra's Tanglewood Music Festival since 1966.

BIBLIOGRAPHY

E. Nason: *The Lives of the Eminent American Evangelists Dwight Lyman Moody and Ira David Sankey, Together with an Account of Their Labor in Great Britain and America: and Also a Sketch of the Lives of Philip P. Bliss and Eben Tourjée* (Boston, 1877), 296

K. Kilgore: *Transformations: a History of Boston University* (Boston, 1991), 56

PATRICK M. JONES

Boswell, Connee [Connie; Constance Fooré] (*b* Kansas City, MO, 3 Dec 1907; *d* New York, NY, 11 Oct 1976). Singer. She changed the spelling of her name from Connie to Connee in the late 1940s. Raised in New Orleans, she spent most of her life in a wheelchair after a bout of polio as an infant. She and her sisters Martha and Helvetia each learned numerous musical instruments and formed the Boswell sisters, a vocal group that enjoyed much local popularity and made recordings in New Orleans as early as 1925. For their entire existence, the vocal and instrumental arrangements were written by the trio, with Boswell often taking the role of editor. Following the retirement of her sisters in 1936, Boswell toured by herself and recorded for Decca. She also appeared with the Casa Loma Orchestra, Bob Crosby, and Bing Crosby. Her vocal style was flexible and melodic following the example of jazz musicians of the period and she was credited by Ella Fitzgerald as a primary influence.

BIBLIOGRAPHY

L. Dahl: *Stormy Weather: the Music and Lives of a Century of Jazz Women* (New York, 1984)

E. Woodward and A. Hobson: *The Boswell Sisters and Connee Boswell: a Discography* (Oldbury, England, 1998)

JOHN L. CLARK JR.

Boswell Sisters. Vocal group. It comprised the sisters Martha (*b* Kansas City, MO, 9 June 1905; *d* Peekskill, NY, 2 July 1958), Connee (*b* Kansas City, 3 Dec 1907; *d* New York, NY, 11 Oct 1976), and Helvetia "Vet" (*b* Birmingham, AL, 20 May 1911; *d* Peekskill, 12 Nov 1988) Boswell. Raised in New Orleans, each of the sisters was introduced to a variety of instruments in their youth and received a thorough musical training. By the early 1920s they were performing as the Boswell Sisters, featuring intricate vocal and instrumental arrangements done by themselves. On the strength of a few early recordings, they moved to New York and began touring and appearing on radio; they also made several films and a series of recordings for Brunswick and Decca that are highly regarded. Martha and Helvetia retired from performing in 1936 to raise families, after which Connee embarked on a solo career despite being confined to a wheelchair since childhood (*see* Boswell, connee).

Initially, the Boswells provided their own accompaniment: Martha played piano, Helvetia violin, guitar, and banjo, and Connie cello, saxophone, trombone, and guitar. By the time they began recording in New York their recordings featured leading jazz musicians of the day, including the Dorsey Brothers, Joe Venuti, Eddie Lang, and Red Nichols, although the arrangements continued to be handled by the sisters, with Connie taking the lead role. Their vocals (for example, on "Heebie Jeebies," 1932, Brunswick) were loose and very modern for the early 1930s with much of their style sounding improvised and leaning toward the coming swing era. The Andrews Sisters were influenced by the Boswells and singers such as Ella Fitzgerald and Bing Crosby recalled them as inspirations.

BIBLIOGRAPHY

Linda Dahl: *Stormy Weather: the Music and Lives of a Century of Jazz Women* (New York, 1984)

E. Woodward and A. Hobson: *The Boswell Sisters and Connee Boswell: a Discography* (Oldbury, England, 1998)

L. Stras: "White Face, Black Voice: Race, Gender, and Region in the Music of the Boswell Sisters," *JSAM*, i (2007), 207–55

JOHN L. CLARK JR.

Bosworth & Hammer. Makers of historical oboes. Craftsman Jonathan Bosworth (*b* Ithaca, NY, 18 June 1938) and oboist, Stephen Hammer (*b* Rochester, NY, 14 April 1951), worked in partnership copying historical double-reed instruments from 1975. Their first project was a copy of an oboe by Thomas Stanesby Sr., then in the possession of Dr. Robert M. Rosenbaum. This was followed by copies of oboes by various 18th-century European makers, including Thomas Stanesby Jr., J. Denner, Charles Bizey, William Milhouse, C.A. and Heinrich Grenser, and J.F. Floth; oboes d'amore by Denner and J.H. Eichentopf; an oboe da caccia by Eichentopf; a tenor oboe by J.C. Denner; and shawms after anonymous specimens in Brussels and Prague museums. Working out of Acton, Massachusetts, they also began designing their own hybrid "Saxon" model patterned after several original oboes from Dresden and Leipzig makers. Production of this model was subsequently transferred to Joel Robinson of New York. At the time their partnership ceased in 2002, Bosworth and Hammer had made over three hundred instruments. Their oboes are represented in numerous recordings made by Hammer, notably the Mozart Oboe Quartet K370 (two-keyed classical oboe after Grenser; Academy of Ancient Music Chamber Ensemble, Decca, 1990), and Bach, *Six Favorite Cantatas* (oboe d'amore and oboe da caccia after Eichentopf; Bach Ensemble and Joshua Rifkin, Decca, 1997).

GEOFFREY BURGESS

Botsford, George (*b* Sioux Falls, SD, 24 Feb 1874; *d* New York, NY, 11 Feb 1949). Popular composer and arranger. Raised in Iowa, Botsford published his first copyrighted work, "The Katy Flyer," in 1899, marking the beginning of a prolific writing and publishing career, particularly in the two decades that followed. Shortly after "The Katy Flyer," he moved to New York, and composed a number of moderately successful songs in his first years there. His best known compositions appeared between 1908 and 1916, starting with the wildly popular "Black and White Rag" (1908), followed by the "Grizzly Bear Rag" (1910), which attained even greater popularity when Irving Berlin wrote lyrics for it, and "Sailing Down the Chesapeake Bay" (1913). Other titles from this period include the "Klondike Rag" (1908), "Pianophiends Rag" (1909), "Texas Steer" (1909), "Honeysuckle Rag" (1911), "Buck-Eye Rag" (1913), and "Boomerang Rag" (1916).

Botsford's rags exemplify a Midwestern school of rag composition that prominently featured folk or folk-like melodies, and included other ragtime composers such as Charles L. Johnson. In addition to folk-music influences, many of Botsford's rags are characterized by formal structures with a non-repeated "*A*" section, often using the structure *ABBACCB*. Many of his rags use a catchy "three over four" rhythm common at that time, so named because the pattern of accents on a set of twelve eighth notes—corresponding to a four-bar phrase in 2/4 time—would delineate four groups of three.

From 1911 through 1916, Botsford published a number of works in collaboration with songwriter Jean Havez, and in 1914, launched an unsuccessful venture to perform miniature operas staged with three or four performers. A charter member of ASCAP in 1914, he has remained best known for his ragtime works, but also managed harmony and quartet department for the music publisher Jerome H. Remick & Co., worked as music director for various stage productions, and directed the New York City Police Department Glee Club.

BIBLIOGRAPHY

"George Botsford: a Harmonious Blender of Quartet Music," *Metronome*, xxxix/9 (1923), 142

D.I. McNamara, ed.: *The ASCAP Biographical Dictionary of Composers, Authors, and Publishers* (New York, 1952)

R. Blesh and H. Janis: *They All Played Ragtime* (New York, 1966)

D.A. Jasen and T.J. Tichenor: *Rags and Ragtime: a Musical History* (New York, 1978)

RICHARD ZIMMERMAN/MARISTELLA FEUSTLE

Botstein, Leon (*b* Zürich, Switzerland, 14 Dec 1946). Conductor and music historian. He moved to New York with his family in 1949 and subsequently attended the University of Chicago and Harvard University, studying violin with Roman Totenberg and conducting with Richard Wernick and—much later—with Harold Farberman. In 1975 he was appointed president of Bard College, where he holds the Leon Levy Professorship of the Humanities. In 1990 he founded the Bard Music Festival, which each year focuses on a single composer through performances, symposia, and an acclaimed published volume of scholarly essays to each of which Botstein contributes a key entry. In 2004 the festival was extended to include fully staged opera and theatrical productions. Music director of the American SO since 1992, Botstein has restored the ensemble to prominence through thematic concerts, performances of rare repertory, and innovative educational programs. He was music director of the American Russian Youth Orchestra from 1995 to 2005, music director of the Jerusalem Symphony Orchestra, the radio orchestra of Israel, from 2003 to 2011, and has appeared extensively as a guest conductor in Europe, Asia, and South America.

Skeptical of inherited performing traditions, and impatient with sluggish pacing, Botstein is most at home in late 19th-century repertory, but is also firmly committed to the music of living composers. Among his many recordings are Dukas's *Ariane et barbe-bleue*, Popov's Symphony no.1, and Strauss's *Die ägyptische Helena*, as well as works by contemporary American composers. In 1992 he was appointed editor of *The Musical Quarterly*. Many of his writings place music in a larger cultural context, often revealing links with intellectual history as well as other arts such as painting and architecture.

WRITINGS

Judentum und Modernität: Essays zur Rolle der Juden in der deutschen und österreichischen Kultur, 1848–1938 (Vienna, 1991)

Jefferson's Children: Education and the Promise of American Culture (New York, 1997)

ed.: *The Compleat Brahms* (New York, 1998)

RICHARD WILSON

Bottesini, Giovanni (*b* Crema, Italy, 22 Dec 1821; *d* Parma, Italy, 7 July 1889). Italian double bassist, conductor, and composer. Following intensive early training by his father and then at the Milan Conservatory, Bottesini was engaged as principal bassist by the Teatro de Tacón in Havana, Cuba. Performance tours took the opera company to New Orleans, New York, and Boston in 1847. Serving as musical co-director with violinist Luigi Arditi, Bottesini also frequently performed solo intermissions to great public acclaim. In 1849 he traveled to London, but returned to the Americas in 1850 to continue his work with the Havana company, performing again in New York and in Philadelphia before returning to Cuba.

In 1853 Bottesini joined the immensely popular orchestra led by Louis-Antoine Jullien for its tour in the United States. He was a featured performer in the lavishly spectacular concerts throughout the season, which culminated with the Christmastime performances of William Henry Fry's "Santa Claus" Symphony. Early in 1854 Bottesini left Jullien's troupe to conduct opera in New Orleans and Mexico. He later returned to Europe, composing and conducting opera in Spain, Portugal, France, and England throughout the duration of his career.

BIBLIOGRAPHY

Grove7 (R. Slatford)

V.B. Lawrence: *Strong on Music: The New York Music Scene in the Days of George Templeton Strong*, i and ii (Chicago, 1988, 1995)

L. Inzaghi and others: *Giovanni Bottesini: virtuoso del contrabbasso e compositore* (Milan, 1989)

LAURA MOORE PRUETT

Botti, Susan (*b* Wichita Falls, TX, 13 April 1962). Composer and singer. She studied theater and French at Wellesley College (BM 1984), music at the Berklee College of Music (BM 1986), and composition at the Manhattan School of Music (MM 1990). Her teachers have included Hilda Harris, DREW MINTER, Myron McPherson, and Nancy Armstrong.

Botti has had a remarkable career as a performer and composer. Relationships with composers including Sofia Gubaidulina, Matthias Pintscher, and Toshio Hosokawa have played a crucial role in her development. Composer Tan Dun has created several significant works for her, including *Red Forecast* for soprano and orchestra and the role of Water in his opera *Marco Polo*. She has appeared as a soloist performing her own compositions with the New York PO, Cleveland Orchestra, BBC Scottish SO, and Los Angeles PO, among others.

Botti's sheerly beautiful scores often persuade the listener with soft elegies, ethereal interludes, and vigorous, lumbering dances; as is evident in her work *Translucence* (2005). Her diverse background and experiences are also reflected throughout her scores. *Impetuosity*, is a tribute to the freedom and exploration of momentum of many jazz artists, including John Coltrane, Thelonious Monk, and Gonzalo Rubalcaba. In *EchoTempo*, Botti sets translations of Native American texts for soprano, percussion, and orchestra. Rather than incorporate the original songs or dances with which the texts were conceived, Botti looked to the natural world, including animal movements and sounds as well as elemental and emotion-based sounds into her musical vocabulary. Her composition *Within Darkness* is an exploration of the textures and intensity found outside the light-filled intensity of her present life in New York City. Scored for solo violin and chamber orchestra the composition is inspired by the shadows of Vermeer paintings that reveal greater complexity as viewers move closer. In the composer's words, *Within Darkness* is an investigation of "what sounds within silence." *Gates of Silence*, a three-part commission from the Blakemore Trio of Vanderbilt University, was inspired by Virgil's *Aeneid*. The poetry written for this work by Linda Gregerson was awarded a 2011 Pushcart Prize.

Among her many awards are the Daniel R. Lewis Young Composer Fellowship with the Cleveland Orchestra (2003–5), a Guggenheim Fellowship (2005), and the Rome Prize (2005–6). Botti was a member of the composition faculty at the University of Michigan, Ann Arbor (2000–06); since 2006, she has been a member of the composition faculty at the Manhattan School of Music in New York City.

WORKS
(selective list)

Stage: Wonderglass (chbr op), 1993; Telaio: Desdemona (operatic soliloquy), S, str qt, hp, pf, perc, 1995

Orch: Within Darkness, fn, chbr orch, 2000; EchoTempo, S, perc, orch, 2001; Impetuosity, 2004; Translucence, 2005

Vocal: Jabberwock, 1v, perc, 1990; Cosmosis, S, wind ens, chbr chorus, 2005; Tagore Madrigals, SSATTB, 2006; Gates of Silence: 1 Lament: The Fallen City, vn, pf, 2 The Journey without her, pf trio, 3 Dido Refuses to Speak, S, pf trio, 2009–10; songs

ELIOT GATTEGNO

Bottje, Will Gay (*b* Grand Rapids, MI, 30 June 1925). Composer and flutist. He attended the Juilliard School, obtaining the BS in flute and the MS in composition (1947). Following several years as a freelance flutist, teacher, and conductor in western Michigan, he went to Europe on a Fulbright scholarship to study with Nadia Boulanger in Paris and Henk Badings in the Netherlands. In 1953 he enrolled at Eastman (DMA 1955), where he was a composition pupil of BERNARD ROGERS and HOWARD HANSON, studied conducting with Paul White, and flute with Joseph Mariano. He also studied at the electronic music studios of the University of Utrecht (1962–3) and the Stiftlesen in Stockholm (1973). Except for two years at the University of Mississippi (1955–7), his career as a teacher was spent at Southern Illinois University, Carbondale (1957–81), where in 1965 he founded and then directed the electronic music studio. After retirement, he was an adjunct instructor at Grand Valley State University (Michigan), where he also established an electronic music studio.

Bottje's works are performed most frequently on college campuses. He has won a number of prizes and received commissions from Washington University, Illinois State University, and Southern Illinois University, as well as other institutions and ensembles. Bottje's particularly adept writing for flute, piccolo, and other woodwinds is evident in many of his chamber works and in the *Concertino* (1956). His musical language has been described as experimental and dissonant, but is nevertheless accessible to both performers and listeners. He is drawn especially to writing for like groups of instruments (as in the *Quartet for Saxophones* and the

Chaconne for five guitars). One of his best-known works is the *Sinfonia concertante for brass quintet and band* (1961).

WORKS

Operas: Altgeld (Bottje), 1968; Root! (J. Maloon), 1971

Orch: Ballad Singer, 1951; Conc., fl, tpt, hp, str, 1955. Concertino, picc, orch, 1956; Sym. no.5, 1959; Pf Conc., 1960; Wayward Pilgrim (Dickinson), S, chorus, chbr orch, 1961; Rhapsodic Variations, va, pf, str, 1962; Tangents (Sym. no.7), 1970; Chiaroscuros, 1975; Tuba Conc., 1977; Mutations, small orch, 1977; Songs from the Land between the Rivers, chorus, orch, 1981; Conc., bn, ob, chbr orch/pf, 1981; Commentaries, gui/kbd, chbr ens/chbr orch, 1983; Sounds from the West Shore, 1983; Conc., vn, ob, small orch, 1984; Opener, 1987; Hn Conc., 1994; Flavors, 1995; Capriccio, 2 tpt, str, perc, 1998; other orch works

Band/brass ens: Contrasts, band, 1952; Sym. no.4, band, 1956; Conc., tpt, trbn, band, 1959; What is Man? (Whitman), chorus, band, 2 pf, nar, 1959; Sinfonia concertante, brass qnt, band, 1961; Sym. no.6, large brass ens, org, perc, 1963, also arr. kbd; Sym. Allegro, brass ens, perc, 1971; Facets, pf, band, 1975; Vc Conc., band, 1975; Conc., band, 1982; other band works

Chbr: 9 str qts, 1950, 1959, 1962, 1982, 1998, 2001, 2002, 2004; Diversions, ww qnt, pf, nar, 1962; Qt, s sax, a sax, t sax, b sax, 1963; Interplays, hn, hpd, pf, tape, 1970; Chaconne, 5 gui, 1975; Dances: Real and Imagined, gui, str qt, 1976; Pf Trio, 1978; Gui Sonata, 1980; Sym., vc, pf 4 hands, 1980; Fl Sonata, 1981; Qnt, cl, bn, hn, vn, db, 1983; Conc., 2 fl/pf, 1984; Mallers, xyl, mar, vib, 1984; *c*80 other chbr works

Vocal: Quests of Odysseus (N. Kazantzakis K. Friar), T, pf, 1960; In Caverns All Alone, 7 songs, T, fl, bn, pf, 1979; A Sentence once Begun (C. Fry), S, pf/str qt, 1982; Exhortation to the Dawn, SATB, org/pf/brass ens, 1984; Last Minute Message For a Time Capsule (P. Applebaum), SATB, perc, kbd, 1997; other songs and vocal works

Other: From the Winds and the Farthest Spaces (L. Eiseley), tape, ww qnt, nar, dancers, slides, 1977; To Charm the Cloudy Crvstal (Eiseley), chbr ens, 2 nar, dancer, 1983; other tape, mixed-media works; film music

Some early works withdrawn, incl. Syms. nos.1–3, 1946–53

Principal publishers: ACA, Robert King, Music for Percussion

BIBLIOGRAPHY

S. Cossaboom: *Compositional and Scoring Practices for Percussion in Symphonies Written for Concert Band: 1950–1970* (diss., U. of Connecticut, 1981)

BARBARA A. PETERSEN/KATIE BUEHNER

Boublil, Alain (*b* Tunis, Tunisia, 5 March 1941). French lyricist. Boublil and composer CLAUDE-MICHEL SCHÖNBERG are, along with composer Andrew Lloyd Webber's, largely the driving forces behind the dominance of the megamusical in the musical theater world since the 1980s. Educated in Paris at the Institute of Higher Commercial Studies, Boublil has no formal training in the arts but became interested in radio and writing lyrics. When Boublil saw Lloyd Webber's and Tim Rice's *Jesus Christ Superstar*, arguably the first of the megamusicals, he was inspired to create something equally epic, and teamed with Schönberg to write *La Revolution Française*, which ran in Paris in 1973. Their next project, *Les Misérables*, began as a concept album and caught the attention of powerful producer Cameron Mackintosh, who took the show to London in 1985 (with Boublil's libretto translated into English by Herbert Kretzmer) and then New York in 1987; it went on to become one of the largest American and international phenomena in musical theater history. On Broadway *Les Misérables* ran for 6,680 performances, until 2003. Boublil's next project with Schönberg, *Miss Saigon* (with some of Boublil's French lyrics translated and adapted by Richard Maltby), was nearly as successful, opening in London (1989), on Broadway (1991; it ran for ten years), and in resident and touring productions in numerous cities around the world. Boublil and Schönberg won Tonys for their book and score of *Les Misérables*, and were nominated for the same two awards for *Miss Saigon*. Later the pair created *Martin Guerre* (London, 1996) and *The Pirate Queen* (which had an 85-performance Broadway run in 2007), and Boublil wrote the lyrics with composer Michel Legrand for *Marguerite* (London, 2008).

BIBLIOGRAPHY

J. Sternfeld: *The Megamusical* (Bloomington, IN, 2006)

M. Vermette: *The Musical World of Boublil and Schönberg* (New York, 2007)

JESSICA STERNFELD

Bouchard, Linda (*b* Val-d'Or, QC, 21 May 1957). French-Canadian composer and conductor. She studied composition with HENRY BRANT at Bennington College, Vermont (BA 1979), and pursued graduate studies at the Manhattan School (MMus 1982). During the period 1985–90 she was the assistant conductor of the Children's Free Opera, New York, as well as the conductor of several new music ensembles, including Essential Music, the New Music Consort, New York New Music Ensemble, and her own group, Abandon. Upon her return to Canada she was appointed composer-in-residence for the National Arts Centre Orchestra, Ottawa (1992–5). She has taught at the Banff Centre for the Arts and the Université de Montréal. She has also guest conducted for the Vancouver Symphony, the National Arts Centre Orchestra (Ottawa), l'Orchestre Symphonique de Québec, and others. In 1997 she was awarded the *Prix Opus* as "Composer of the Year" by the Conseil Québécois de la Culture and won the Joseph S. Stauffer Prize from the Canada Council for the Arts for her outstanding contributions in music. She was composer-in-residence at the National Arts Centre Orchestra from 1992 to 1995 and has been artistic director and founding member of NEXMAP (New Experimental Music, Arts and Performance), San Francisco, since 2005.

Bouchard's primary compositional interests are timbre, structure, and spatialization. The specific placement of the performers is of the utmost importance in large-scale works such as *Triskelion* (1982), *Revelling of Men* (1983), and *Oracles* (1996). Experimentations with form and the use of a wide variety of contrasting materials led her to the development of "flexible structures," compositional plans that produce a kind of aleatory music. Works such as *Pourtinade* (1983), *Muskoday* (1988), and *Ressac* (1991) use "flexible structures" by leaving the specific order in which sections are played up to the performers or the conductor.

WORKS

STAGE

Triskelion (op), 1982; The House of Words (op), 2003; Sonic Forecast (multimedia), 2008; Murderous Little World (multimedia), 2009

INSTRUMENTAL

Orch: Essay 1, pf, perc, hp, str, 1979 [withdrawn]; Docile Demon, E tpt, perc, str, 1986 [withdrawn]; Fanorev, hpd, perc, str, 1986; Elan, pf, perc, hp, str, 1990; Marche, 2 a sax, 2 t sax, perc, timp, str, 1990 [withdrawn]; Ressac, pf, perc, str, 1991; Ire, 2 ens, 1992; Exquisite Fires, perc, str, 1993; Vertige, perc, str, 1994; Eternity, perc, str, 1995; Booming Sands, va, orch, 1999; The Open Life, 2000

Large chbr ens: Quican, fl ens, 1978 [withdrawn]; Of a Star Unfolding, 8 perc, prep pf, 1979 [withdrawn]; Rocking Glances, fl, ob, vn, va, vc, gui, mand, perc, 1979 [withdrawn]; Before the Cityset, ob, hn, 8 va, perc, 1981 [withdrawn]; Revelling of Men, 6 trbn, str qnt, 1983; Second Revelling, 6 trbn, 3 perc, 1984; Frisson "La vie," fl, va, str ens, 1992; Compressions, 2 hn, 3 tpt, 3 trbn, pf, perc, hp, str qt, 1996; Oracles, 3 str qt, 1996; L'échapée d'ailes, gamelan ens, 2 fl, ob, 2 cl, bc, bn, 2 hn, 2 tpt, 2004; Joint Venture, cl, b cl, hn, 2 perc, pf 4 hands, vn, 2 vc, 2008

Small chbr ens: Aspect d'un couloir, str trio/2 str, 1979 [withdrawn]; Chaudière à traction, fl, pf, 1979 [withdrawn]; Ma lune maligne, fl, va, hp, perc, 1981; Stormy Light, str qt, 1981; Viennese Divertimento, ob, va, vc, pf, perc, 1982; Circus Faces, fl, va, vc, 1983; Pourtinade, va, perc, 1983; Tossing Diamonds, brass qnt, tuba, 1983; Web-Trap, fl, bn, va, db, 1983; 5 Grins, fl, ob, vc, hpd, 1984; Icy Cruise, pic, tpt, va, vc, bn, hp, 1984; Propos III, 3 tpt, 1984; Propos IV, tpt qt, 1984; Forest, fl, cl, vc, pf, perc, 1985; Propos II, 2 tpt, 1985; Pulsing Flight, 2/4 pf, 2 taped pf, 1985; Rictus en miroir, fl, ob, vc, pf, perc, 1985; Possible Nudity, va, vc, bn, hp, perc, 1987, rev. va, vc, pf, 1988; Transi-blanc, fl, tpt, trbn, va, pf, perc, 1987, rev. fl, tpt, va, bn, hp, perc, 1987; Delicate Contract, fl, tpt, va, vc, bn, hp, perc, 1988; Muskoday, fl + a fl, va, vc, bn, hp, perc, 1988; Propos nouveaux, tpt, va, vc, bn, 1988; Amuser le temps, fl, ob, cl, vn, vc, db, pf, 1989; Le scandale, vn, va, vc, db, hp, perc, 1989; Swift Silver, hpd, cel, harm, 1989; Lung ta, str qt, 1992; Réciproque, vn, vc, pf, 1994; 7 couleurs, fl, cl, vn, vc, pf, perc, 1994; Traces, str qt, 1996; Liquid States, cl, b cl, vn, vc, perc, pf, 2004; 4LN, va, perc, elecs, 2008

Solo inst: Glances, vc, 1980 [withdrawn]; Propos, tpt, 1983; Tokpela, perc, 1988

VOCAL

Tout ça as thought (G. Beaudet), S, fl, vn, vc, pf, 1977 [withdrawn]; L'homme qui change (Beaudet), Bar, vc, bn, 1978 [withdrawn]; Anticipation of Priscilla (L. Bouchard), S, fl, vn, va, vc, pf, perc, 1980 [withdrawn]; Cherchell, nar, fl, vn, va, pf, 1982; Minotaurus, nar, fl + a fl, (s sax, va, vc, bn, hp)/(ob, bn, pf), perc, 1988; Black Burned Wood, S, vn + va, pf, perc, 1990; Mr Link, nar, pf, perc, timp, hp, str, 1993; Ocamow, Bar, gui, vc, perc, 1993; Risky, S, pf, db, 1993; Songs for an Acrobat, Bar, perc, str, 1995; Pilgrims' Cant, S, B, SATB, hpd, perc, 2 hp, str

Principal publishers: CMC, Doberman-Yppan

BIBLIOGRAPHY

EMC2 (D. Olds)

H. Plouffe: "Linda Bouchard," *Music Scene*, no.338 (1984), 13 only

SOPHIE GALAISE/ANYA LAURENCE

Boucher, William (*b* Germany, 1822; *d* Baltimore, MD, 11 March 1899). Instrument maker of German birth. He came to the United States around 1845 and worked as an instrument maker and dealer in Baltimore until 1891. In the 1840s he began making five-string banjos in Baltimore and was probably the earliest commercial manufacturer of banjos. He won medals for his violins, drums, and banjos in the 1850s. The Smithsonian Institution has three of his banjos (from the years 1845–7), donated by Boucher in 1890; the receipt for these identifies him as "the inventor of tightening banjo-heads by screw-fixtures. . . ." These banjos are characterized by heads of large diameter, thin but deep wooden rims, open backs, bracket systems for tightening the head, fretless fingerboards with one or more curves shaped into the side of the neck just below the fifth-string peg, and friction pegs. Boucher used several shapes for the peghead, but the most common was a scroll shape (like a violin peghead scroll turned sideways). As of this writing, approximately 45 Boucher banjos are known to be extant. The banjo in the well-known painting by William Sidney Mount, "The Banjo Player" (1856), has all the earmarks of a Boucher. Period photographs from the Civil War sometimes include Boucher banjos. Later Boucher banjos can be quite elaborate (with closed back and marquetry and carving) or quite plain. A number of banjo makers are currently making excellent reproductions of early Boucher banjos to serve a growing market of Civil War re-enactors and others seeking to accurately recreate the sound of mid-19th-century banjo music.

BIBLIOGRAPHY

L. Libin: *American Musical Instruments in the Metropolitan Museum of Art* (New York, 1985)

P. Gura and J. Bollman: *America's Instrument: the Banjo in the Nineteenth Century* (Chapel Hill, NC, 1999)

R. Carlin: *The Birth of the Banjo: Joel Walker Sweeney and Early Minstrelsy* (Jefferson, NC, 2007)

G. Adams: *Banjo Sightings Database* <http://www.banjodatabase.org/Browse3d.asp> [photos and detailed information on 16 Boucher banjos]

ROBERT B. WINANS

Boudousquié, Charles (*b* New Orleans, LA, 29 Feb 1814; *d* New Orleans, 23 Aug 1866). Impresario. He was the third and last director of the Théâtre d'Orléans, succeeding Pierre Davis, son of the theater's founder, in about 1853. The theater was important for its promotion of opera and Boudousquié did much to create its reputation. In 1858 he married the French soprano Julie Calvé, who had been prima donna at the theater from 1837 to 1846). In 1859 he left the Théâtre d'Orléans to build the French Opera House. This was formally opened on 1 December that year with Rossini's *Guillaume Tell*, in French. Under Boudousquié's brief but vigorous directorship, which saw the American premiere of Meyerbeer's *Dinorah* (1861, with Adelina Patti in the title role), the French Opera House quickly eclipsed the Théâtre d'Orléans as New Orleans's leading opera house.

JOHN JOYCE

Boudreau, Robert Austin (*b* Bellingham, MA, 25 April 1927). Conductor. After studies with Georges Mager in Boston, WILLIAM VACCHIANO at Juilliard, Raymond Sabarich at the Paris Conservatory, and performances with the Rhode Island Philharmonic, Boston Brass Quartet, Goldman Band and Metropolitan Orchestra, he taught at Ithaca College, Lehigh and Duquesne Universities. In 1957 he founded the American Wind Symphony Orchestra (AWSO) in Pittsburgh, an ensemble of young professionals that presented free concerts from a barge, towed by riverboat captains on inland waterways. In 1961 AWSO performed on the Rivers Thames, on a new float designed by architect Louis Kahn. Boudreau collaborated with Kahn in planning a self-propelled floating arts center, launched during 1976 Bicentennial celebrations. Of necessity, Boudreau learned to pilot and navigate this unique vessel on rivers, the Great Lakes, along the East Coast, and into the Caribbean. In 1989–91 AWSO presented acclaimed concerts in northern Europe, Scandinavia, and Russia. The AWSO has commissioned over 400 compositions from composers such as Penderecki, Villa-Lobos, Hovhaness, Amram, Françaix, Petrov, Mayuzumi, Loudová, Orrego-Salas, and Chou Wen-Chung that have been published by C.F. Peters. Boudreau's many honors include being knighted by the king of Sweden and acknowledged by *Time* magazine's statement (July 26, 1971) that "It may just be that there is no greater innovative force in American music than Robert Boudreau."

BIBLIOGRAPHY

J.H. Renshaw: *The American Wind Symphony Commissioning Project: a Descriptive Catalog of Published Editions, 1957–1991* (New York, 1991)

DAVID WHITWELL

Boulanger, Emile (*b* France, Sept 1844; *d* St. Louis, MO, 1908). Drum maker of French birth. Founder of the Duplex Drum Company in St. Louis, Missouri, he introduced a number of important innovations to the design of the snare drum. His family immigrated to the United States in 1854. In 1869, Emile and his father Louis were first listed in the St. Louis city directory as musical instrument makers and repairers. It is believed that Emile began building drums in 1882, and his first patent application dates from August of that year. Boulanger's patent was for a separate tension drum, which allowed the two drum heads to be tuned independently; it was awarded on 3 April 1883 (US Patent Number 274,900). This design would become the first commercially successful separate tension drum in the United States. Boulanger built drums with the name Duplex Drums as early as the 1880s, but did not incorporate the company until 1901. He also built metal shell drums, perhaps as early as the 1890s, patented a snare strainer, and introduced a muffler to the batter head of the snare drum. Duplex drums were sold primarily through the catalogs of musical instrument distributors, including Carl Fischer and Lyon & Healy. Boulanger continued to innovate and received several other patents for snare drum designs before his death in 1908. The Duplex company continued to operate until 1968.

BIBLIOGRAPHY

K.A. Mezines: *St Louis Duplex Drum Company, 1882 to 1968* (MS, Missouri Historical Society, St. Louis, n.d.)

J.K. Dobney: *Innovations in American Snare Drums, 1850–1920* (thesis, U. of South Dakota, 2003), 56–61

JAYSON KERR DOBNEY

Boulanger, (Juliette) Nadia (*b* Paris, France, 16 Sept 1887; *d* Paris, 22 Oct 1979). French teacher, conductor, organist, and composer. Her father, Ernest Boulanger (1815–1900), was a composer (winner of the Prix de Rome in 1836) and singing teacher at the Paris Conservatoire; her mother, the "Princess" Raïssa Mychetsky (1858–1935), had been one of her father's students. Boulanger entered the Conservatoire at the age of ten and studied harmony with Paul Antonin Vidal (1863–1931), organ with Louis Vierne (1870–1937) and Alexandre Guilmant (1837–1911), and composition with Charles-Marie Widor (1845–1937) and Gabriel Fauré (1845–1924), the latter remaining a favorite composer throughout her life. While at the Conservatoire she won a first prize in solfège in 1898, a first prize in harmony in 1903, and first prizes in fugue, organ, and piano accompaniment in 1904. In 1907 she reached the final round of the Prix de Rome, but her cantata, *Selma*, failed to win a prize. The following year she placed second in the Prix de Rome competition with her work *La sirène*. One of her first pupils, her younger sister Lili, became the first woman to win the Prix de Rome (1913). Lili's premature death in 1918 deeply affected Boulanger and influenced her to give up composing for a life of teaching.

Beginning in 1904 she began the teaching career that lasted until 1979. At first she taught solfège, harmony, counterpoint, fugue, piano, and organ privately, before accepting an appointment at the private Conservatoire Femina-Musica in 1907. She taught at the Ecole Normale de Musique in Paris from 1920 to 1939, where she was appointed teacher of composition in 1935 as successor to Paul Dukas (1865–1935), although her official role was as co-professor with Stravinsky. From 1921 she also taught at the Conservatoire Américain at Fontainebleau, an institution near Paris that operated for only three months each year. The conservatory was founded by Walter Damrosch and Francis Casadesus, Widor was the first director, and Boulanger became director in 1950. She was also professor of piano accompaniment at the Paris Conservatoire from 1946 to 1957. Boulanger first traveled to the United States in 1924 for her debut as organist in a performance of Copland's Symphony for Organ and Orchestra, a work she had convinced Walter Damrosch and Sergey Koussevitzky to commission from her student. In 1928 she became the first woman to conduct the Boston SO. During World War II she lived in the United States and taught in Massachusetts at Wellesley College and Radcliffe College, and in New York at the Juilliard School.

She became the leading music teacher of the 20th century, and was particularly influential with American composers. After Aaron Copland, Melville Smith, and Virgil Thomson "discovered" her in 1921, hundreds of Americans traveled to France to study with her. During the 1920s and 30s her influence on the musical development of the United States became such that Thomson once described every town as having "a five-and-ten-cent store and a Boulanger student." Known as the "Boulangerie," students journeyed year after year to her apartment on the Rue Ballu in Paris or to the American Conservatory where she taught harmony, counterpoint, analysis, composition, organ, and other musical subjects. She was possessed of phenomenal ability and thorough knowledge of all periods and styles of music. At her famous Wednesday afternoon classes young musicians could meet and hear works by the foremost figures in the arts of the day, including Boulanger's close friend Stravinsky. The performances of Monteverdi and Gesualdo madrigals at these gatherings played an important role in their rediscovery. In addition to Copland

and Thomson, among her most prominent American students were GEORGE ANTHEIL, MARC BLITZSTEIN, ELLIOTT CARTER, DAVID DIAMOND, PHILIP GLASS, ROY HARRIS, DOUGLAS S. MOORE, WALTER PISTON, ELIE SIEGMEISTER, and LOUISE TALMA.

Some students considered Boulanger a strict and demanding disciplinarian, but for those she deemed talented and sincere her devotion and efforts were tireless. Her many awards, honors, and decorations included a commandership in the Légion d'honneur, nomination as maître de chapelle to the Prince of Monaco, and membership in the American Academy of Arts and Sciences.

BIBLIOGRAPHY

(Letters to Nadia Boulanger in F-Pn)

A. Kendall: *The Tender Tyrant: Nadia Boulanger, a Life Devoted to Music* (London, 1976)

S.R. Hoover: "Nadia Boulanger," *The American Scholar*, xlvi/4 (1977), 496–502

R. Moevs and E. Rosand: "Nadia Boulanger (1887–1979)," *19CM*, iii/3 (1980), 276–8

B. Monsaingeon: *Mademoiselle: entretiens avec Nadia Boulanger* (Luynes, 1980; Eng. trans., 1985)

T. Walters: *Nadia Boulanger, Musician and Teacher: Her Life, Concepts, and Influences* (diss., Peabody Institute, Johns Hopkins U., 1981)

"Lili et Nadia Boulanger," *ReM*, nos.353–4 (1982) [Boulanger issue, incl. list of her students]

L. Rosenstiel: *Nadia Boulanger: a Life in Music* (New York, 1982)

D.G. Campbell: *Master Teacher: Nadia Boulanger* (Washington, DC, 1984)

J. Spycket: *Nadia Boulanger* (Lausanne, 1987)

C. Potter: "Nadia and Lili Boulanger: Sister Composers," *MQ*, lxxxiii (1999), 536–56

C.J. Harris: *The French Connection: the Neoclassical Influence of Stravinsky, through Boulanger, on the Music of Copland, Talma and Piston* (diss., State U. of New York, Buffalo, 2002)

C. Potter: *Nadia and Lili Boulanger* (Aldershot, 2006)

A. Laederich, ed.: *Nadia Boulanger et Lili Boulanger: témoignages et études* (Lyon, 2007)

A. Fauser: "Aaron Copland, Nadia Boulanger, and the Making of an 'American' Composer," *MQ*, lxxxix (2007), 524–54

VIVIAN PERLIS/CHRISTOPHER E. MEHRENS

Boulez, Pierre (*b* Montbrison, Loire, France, 26 March 1925). French composer, conductor, and theorist, active in the United States. He attended the Paris Conservatoire (1942–5) where he studied harmony with OLIVIER MESSIAEN and received private instruction in the 12-tone technique from René Leibowitz, a pupil of Arnold Schoenberg. By the age of 20, Boulez had developed a musical language based on the work and sensibility of Anton Webern, also a Schoenberg student. After that his compositions hardly veered from this grammar. Boulez first won acclaim in the United States as the composer of *Le marteau sans maître* (1954), a recording of which was released in the mid-1950s. Boulez came to the United States for the first time in 1953 as the conductor of the Compagnie Renaud-Barrault. Then on friendly terms with the American composer John Cage, whom he met in Paris in 1949, he stayed in Cage's loft in New York; Cage moved out so Boulez could move in. While there he attended a performance by David Tudor of his Second Piano Sonata. Also on the program was Cage's *Music of Changes*, a work so far removed from Boulez's in approach that the event precipitated a break that ended their friendship.

Boulez returned to New York with Barrault in 1958. He also went to Los Angeles on that trip where he conducted *Le marteau sans maître* at one of the Monday Evening Concerts, a series devoted to 20th-century music. In 1963, no longer working for Barrault, he appeared as Horatio Appleton Lamb Lecturer at Harvard University, where he spoke on the aesthetics of composition.

George Szell heard only positive comments about Boulez as a conductor from members of the Concertgebouw and invited him to conduct the Cleveland Orchestra in 1965 and 1967. Boulez became principal guest conductor of the Cleveland Orchestra in 1969. The same year Boulez appeared as guest conductor with four other major orchestras. After he conducted Stravinsky's *Le Sacre du Printemps* with the New York Philharmonic Orchestra, the board of directors appointed him the Music Director of the institution, succeeding Leonard Bernstein's long tenure there. He held the position from 1971 to 1977, concurrently serving as Music Director of the BBC Symphony Orchestra in London (1971–4).

Until 1969 Boulez conducted the 20th-century repertoire in which he believed, generating excitement in concerts that attracted those audiences interested in that music. But in New York, the same programs drove the traditional subscription audience from the concert hall. In order to guarantee the subscribers' continued support, Boulez compromised his idea that progress in art takes precedence over commercial success, and included more of the standard repertoire that the management then in power demanded.

On 5 January 1973, the Chamber Music Society of Lincoln Center gave the American premiere of *explosante-fixe* (for unspecified forces), the only major work Boulez composed during his time in New York. Boulez returned to Paris in 1978 as director of IRCAM, an institute for training and research in composition, electronic and computer techniques, acoustics, and instrument building. After leaving the New York Philharmonic, he made his first conducting appearance in the United States with the Los Angeles Philharmonic Orchestra on 13 May 1984, performing Elliott Carter's Symphony of Three Orchestras, a work he commissioned while music director in New York.

Americans continued to work for IRCAM and IRCAM continued to commission Americans. In the field of computer innovation, research, and interface controllers, Boulez's impact cannot be overstated. Changes of leadership occurred after Boulez retired from the presidency in 1995. Those who followed him have not been composers but, rather, festival producers. It is unclear whether a composer will ever again head the Institute.

Boulez apparently came to terms with the changing aesthetic that virtually annihilated his compositional agenda. He had begun to conduct in the 1950s in order to have his own and his composer-colleagues' works played, at the least, decently. No professional conductors of the time could succeed with this unfamiliar material. In the 1960s, when the grammar he had embraced was overshadowed by far less rigorous approaches, he decreased his composing and increased his conducting. Boulez never stopped thinking of himself as a composer; consider *Répons*, which emerged in three increasingly long versions in 1981, 1982, and 1984, lasting 17, 35, and 45 minutes respectively. Dedicated to Alfred Schlee, head of Universal Edition, the distinguished German music publishing house, and with a hidden musical reference to Paul Sacher, probably the 20th century's most progressive patron of music, *Répons* was distributed initially on CD by Deutsche Grammophon in the spring of 1999.

On the surface, conducting has been Boulez's primary occupation for half a century. He has never returned to guest conduct the New York Philharmonic, although the current management has invited him. He continues to instill admiration and affection with three American orchestras—Cleveland, Chicago, and Los Angeles. In June 1996 Boulez returned to the Ojai Festival Orchestra for a celebration of its 50th year.

Over and above everything else, Boulez's appointment as Carnegie Hall's Chair in Composition in 1999 may justifiably be viewed as an indication of the esteem in which he was still held as a composer. As for his role as conductor, it has been an extremely productive one. In the year 2000, Boulez was on the podium of Carnegie Hall's main venue for four concerts that included works by György Kurtág, Béla Bartók, Gustav Mahler, Salvatore Sciarrino, Luciano Berio, Schoenberg, Stravinsky, and Alban Berg, as well as his own *explosante-fixe*. He was also instrumental in the planning of Zankel Hall, a subterranean space that opened in 2003, one that most often presents innovative programming. On 16 May Boulez led his first performance with the Metropolitan Opera Orchestra. The *New York Times* reviewed it positively, singling out his "acute ear for color and texture" with an "urgent and memorable" performance. Trendy ensembles playing accessible, eclectic music may garner most of the public's attention, but Boulez has never complained that music has not gone his way. First, he is a stoic man. Second, no one can predict the future of art. Boulez's beloved musical language may well resurface.

BIBLIOGRAPHY

J. Peyser: *Boulez: Composer, Conductor, Enigma* (New York, 1976)
P. Griffiths: *Boulez* (London, 1978)
W. Glock, ed.: *Pierre Boulez: a Symposium* (London, 1986)
J.-J. Nattiez, ed.: *The Boulez–Cage Correspondence* (Cambridge, 1995)
R. Di Pietro: *Dialogues with Boulez* (Lanham, 2001)

JOAN PEYSER

Bounce. A style of hip-hop music associated with New Orleans, Louisiana. Bounce is oriented toward dancing, with performers calling out dance steps or prompting replies from the audience. Musical characteristics include call-and-response based upon repeated hooks, chants (influenced largely by Mardi Gras Indians), and brass-band music (regularly used for samples). Bounce features highly syncopated grooves often based on the "Triggerman beat," which is sampled from sources such as "Drag Rap" by the Showboys, "Brown Beat" by Cameron Paul, and "Rock the Beat" by Derek B. Much. Bounce is tied to specific New Orleans neighborhoods, its most common performance venues being clubs and large, outdoor, working-class parties. Lyrics often refer to these neighborhoods as well as cultural practices and explicitly sexual topics.

The term "bounce" appeared as early as 1968 on the Imperial album *Urban Blues: New Orleans Bounce*, referencing the city's long association with dance music. The term's usage in hip hop, however, can be traced to 1991, when MC T. T. Tucker and DJ Erv recorded "Where Dey At," a homemade cassette-only production that emphasized chanted lyrics and local place identification. DJ Jimi (and once again DJ Erv) covered "Where Dey At" in 1992 as "Where They At." This version, which exhibits more polished performance and production styles, is often considered the first bounce release.

By the mid-1990s bounce had become an essential New Orleans rap style with support from record labels, including Cash Money Records, Big Bang Records, and Take Fo'. In the late 1990s, artists such as B.G., The Hot Boys, Juvenile, and Lil Wayne charted nationally. Around 2000 the subgenre of "sissy bounce" emerged as an important trend in New Orleans' gay, lesbian, and transgender community. Although homophobia is widespread in rap, New Orleans's more traditionally tolerant attitude allowed this style to flourish. Important sissy bounce artists include Katey Red and Big Fredia.

Hurricane Katrina's 2005 devastation of New Orleans had a twofold effect on bounce music, not only emptying the city's neighborhoods of artists but also scattering many to other locations. While the latter may ultimately help spread bounce music, its source has suffered irreplaceable loss. Signs of bounce music's influence can be found in songs by non-New Orleans' artists that have incorporated bounce elements into their music. Beyonce's 2007 Columbia Records release "Get Me Bodied," for example, helped to bring the style to the international market.

BIBLIOGRAPHY

A. Edwards and A. Fensterstock: *Where They At: WTA Project* <http://www.wheretheyatnola.com/>
M. Miller: "Bounce: Rap Music and Cultural Survival in New Orleans," *Hyphenation: an Interdisciplinary Journal for the Study of Critical Moments Discussion*, i/1 (2006), 15–31

KENNETH KLESZYNSKI

Bourgeois, John Roy (*b* Gibson, LA, 31 Aug 1934). Conductor and arranger. He graduated from Loyola University in 1956, studying horn, and received some of his earliest conducting experience as back stage conductor at the New Orleans Opera. He joined the Marine Corps in 1956 and entered "The President's Own" band in 1958 as horn player and arranger. Named Director in 1979, he was promoted to colonel in 1983. During his tenure he participated in four Presidential inaugurations, performed at the White House more than any other musician during that period, and took the band on its first international tours, most notably to The Netherlands (1985) and the USSR (1990). He retired from active duty on 11 July 1996. Under his leadership the band retained and strengthened its reputation as one of the world's finest wind bands. Highlights of his many honors include the Mid-West International Band and Orchestra Clinic Medal of Honor (1993) and election into the National Band Association's Hall of Fame of Distinguished Band Conductors (2000). In his post-military career he has written on Sousa performance practice, is visiting professor at his alma mater and arranges for the wind series, "The Bourgeois Editions."

EVAN FELDMAN

Bowen, Gene [Eugene Everett] (*b* Biloxi, MS, 30 July 1950). Composer and performer. He studied at the California Institute of the Arts with HAROLD BUDD, MEL POWELL, Leonard Stein, and MORTON SUBOTNICK (1970–72). He was lecturer of modern American music at the University of Guadalajara in 1971 and taught electronic music at Moorpark (California) College from 1975 to 1980. His *Longbow Angels*, written for double bassist Buell Neidlinger, was awarded second place in a competition sponsored by the International Society of Bassists (1977). In the 1980s he collaborated with several contemporary composers, including Brian Eno (co-composing "Steal Away" for *Ambient 2: Plateaux of Mirror*, 1980), Daniel Lentz (*After Images*, 1981), and Budd (performing on *The Serpent [In Quicksilver]*, 1981, and *Abandoned Cities*, 1984). He co-founded Cantil Records in 1981 with Budd, and has produced music on the label Cold Blue Music.

Bowen composes in both classical and popular music idioms. His works present minimalist elements, a strong sense of lyricism, and sensitivity to folk and regional music, particularly that of Mexico, where he has traveled extensively. His 1994 album *The Vermilion Sea* resonates strongly with both Mexican harp and marimba traditions, and also features aspects of Native American and African traditions. Bowen recorded several original songs—himself on vocals and electric guitar—with Doors drummer John Densmore, saxophonist Art Ellis, and bassist Jimmy Hazz (*Hen House Studios Anthology Volume One*, 1999–2001).

WORKS

Casida del llanto (F. García Lorca), 2 solo vv, elecs, 1971; Longbow Angels, 5 db, 1974; Junkyard Pieces, perc ens, 1976; Jewelled Settings, S, pf, vib, vc, elecs, 1980; Desert's Edge, tape, vib, Chinese bells, synth, 1981; Steal Away, pf, 1981; The Vermilion Sea, Mexican hp, elecs, 1994; Pillar of Fire, vc, elecs, 1995

Principal publishers: Soundings, Sespe Music

RECORDINGS

Vermilion Sea (Gyroscope, 1994); Bourgeois Magnetic (Amorfon, 1997); Hen House Studios Anthology Volume One, 1999–2001 (Hen House Studios, 2001)

PETER GARLAND/TYLER KINNEAR

Bowen, George Oscar (*b* Castle Creek, NY, 9 Oct 1872; *d* Tulsa, OK, 3 Dec 1957). Music educator and choral conductor. He attended singing schools and later studied voice in Boston and in Providence, Rhode Island. He began his career teaching in the Courtland, New York, public schools (1897–1903). He attended the Sterrie Weaver Summer School in Massachusetts in 1900 and was influenced by Weaver's methods. After Weaver's death in 1904 he taught in the summer school through 1921. He was director of the Community Music Association in Flint, Michigan (1917–20), where he conducted mass sing-alongs for automobile factory workers. He taught at University School of Music in Ann Arbor, Michigan (1920–24) before becoming supervisor of music for the Tulsa, Oklahoma, Public Schools (1924–47). Bowen was president of the Music Supervisors (later Educators) National Conference (1928), and the national conference in Chicago during his presidency (1928) featured outstanding a cappella choirs. He was editor of *Music Supervisors* (later *Educators*) *Journal* (1921–6) and a prolific writer. His significant publications include *Graded Melodies for Individual Sight Singing* (1912), *Program Choruses: the Green Book* (1930), and *Song and Speech, a Coordinated Course in the Fundamental Production and Use of the Voice for Good Singing and Good Speech* (1954).

BIBLIOGRAPHY

A.L. Spurgeon: *George Oscar Bowen: his Career and Contributions to Music Education* (diss., U. of Oklahoma, 1990)

ALAN L. SPURGEON

Bowen, Jennifer Beth (*b* Mount Pleasant, MI, 11 May 1958). Librarian. She studied music history at Central Michigan University, Mount Pleasant (BM 1979) and received graduate degrees in library science (AMLS 1981) and historical musicology (MA 1982) from the University of Michigan. After serving as music cataloger at Detroit Public Library (1985–8), she was appointed music cataloger (1988–91), then Associate Head of Technical Services (1991–8), and Head of Technical Services (1998–2007) at Sibley Music Library of the Eastman School of Music. In addition, from 2000 to 2007 she held a concurrent position as head of cataloging at the University of Rochester Libraries, where she presently serves as director of metadata management.

Bowen has been active in committees related to cataloging in both the Music Library Association and the Association for Library Collections and Technical Services (ALCTS) and has given numerous presentations on the subject. She represented US libraries in the Joint Steering Committee for Revision of *Anglo-American Cataloguing Rules* (subsequently, Resource Description and Access or RDA), the main manual for descriptive cataloging. In recent years, Bowen has been developing descriptive metadata standards for music and other library materials. Her participation in the eXtensible Catalog Project resulted in open-source software that facilitates the implementation of the Functional Requirements of Bibliographic Records (FRBR), initiatives that enable users to view and understand the relationships between resources. Bowen received an ALCTS Presidential Citation in 2007 for her work on the development of RDA and a "Best of LRTS" award for the best article of 2006.

WRITINGS

"FRBR: Coming Soon to YOUR Library," *Library Resources and Technical Services*, xcix/3 (2005), 38–49

"Metadata to Support Next-Generation Library Resource Discovery: Lessons from the eXtensible Catalog, Phase 1," *Information Technology and Libraries*, xxvii/2 (2008), 6–19

MARK MCKNIGHT

Bowen, Jimmy (*b* Santa Rita, NM, 30 Nov 1937). Instrumentalist, record producer, and label executive. Bowen first made his mark as a recording artist with "I'm Stickin' With You" in 1957, which originally appeared as the B-side of Buddy Knox's "Party Doll." It peaked at number 14 on *Billboard*'s pop charts, sold a million copies, and was certified gold by the RIAA. In the early 1960s, Bowen moved to Los Angeles, where Frank Sinatra hired him as a producer at Reprise Records. He supervised his recordings as well as those by Dean Martin and Sammy Davis Jr., leading some to joke that Bowen had rejuvenated the Rat Pack for the youth market. Bowen also brought together producer-singer-songwriter Lee Hazlewood with Nancy Sinatra, and a sequence of hits ensued. Bowen ran an independent label, Amos Records, from 1969 to 1971, whose catalog includes some of the earliest work by future Eagles members Glenn Frey and Don Henley. He moved to Nashville thereafter and began his ascendance to the head of a sequence of labels, including MGM, Elektra, Warner Brothers, MCA, Universal, and Capitol, which he renamed Liberty. He oversaw the careers of such country stars as Hank Williams Jr., the Oak Ridge Boys, Reba McEntire, George Strait, Suzy Bogguss, and Garth Brooks. Bowen was known for his dedication to digital technology and desire to integrate out-of-town musicians with Nashville's session players. He retired in 1995 and published his autobiography in 1998.

BIBLIOGRAPHY

J. Bowen with J. Jerome: *Rough Mix* (New York, 1998)

DAVID SANJEK

Bowers, Thomas J. (*b* Philadelphia, PA, *c*1823; *d* Philadelphia, PA, 3 Oct 1885). Tenor. He studied organ with his older brother, John C. Bowers, whom he succeeded as organist at St. Thomas's African Episcopal Church, Philadelphia, about 1838. Yielding to his parents' desire that he devote his talents to sacred music, Thomas rejected a position in Frank Johnson's band. However, he studied singing with ELIZABETH TAYLOR GREENFIELD, with whom he appeared in a duo recital at the Sansom Street Hall, Philadelphia, in February 1854; reviewers dubbed him the "American Mario" and the "colored Mario," judging him to be the equal of the tenor Giovanni Matteo Mario. Later tours with Greenfield took Bowers from Canada to Baltimore (where he appeared only before unsegregated audiences). His repertory, which included arias by Friedrich Flotow, Verdi, and Donizetti, was intended to set him apart from the image of contemporary minstrelsy.

BIBLIOGRAPHY

SouthernB

J.M. Trotter: *Music and Some Highly Musical People* (Boston, 1881/*R*), 130

M.C. Hare: *Negro Musicians and their Music* (Washington, DC, 1936/*R*), 199

DOMINIQUE-RENÉ DE LERMA

Bowie [Jones], **David (Robert)** (*b* Brixton, London, England, 8 Jan 1947). English singer, songwriter, producer, and actor. Considered something of a musical chameleon, he has had a career marked by a series of often radical stylistic transformations. As David Jones, he released a succession of pop records in the mid-1960s that were indebted to traditional English music hall, before changing his name to avoid confusion with the Monkees' singer Davy Jones. After three modestly successful albums, he gained stardom in Britain with his pioneering glam-rock concept album *The Rise and Fall of Ziggy Stardust and the Spiders from Mars* (1972). Although none of his glam-rock tracks charted in the United States, his contributions to the genre exerted a major influence on such American glam-rock bands as the New York Dolls. His first hit in the United States came with the re-release in 1973 of his folk-rock single "Space Oddity," which had originally been released in 1969. During the mid-1970s his other US hits, "Young Americans," "Fame," and "Golden Years," saw him dabbling in blue-eyed soul and disco styles, and towards the end of the decade he released three albums (*Low*, *Heroes*, and *Lodger*) marked by their innovative incorporation of electronic synthesizers and minimalist song structures. Bowie achieved a string of US hits throughout the 1980s that were more conventionally dance-pop oriented, including three major hits from his album *Let's Dance* (EMI, 1983). From the 1990s his recordings began to rely more heavily on electronica and industrial-rock influences.

As a performer Bowie is known for presenting ambiguous or mysterious alter-egos like the androgynous alien Ziggy Stardust and the blue-eyed soul crooner the Thin White Duke. As a producer and arranger, he helped resuscitate the flagging careers of the British band Mott the Hoople (*All the Young Dudes*, 1973) as well as the American artists Lou Reed (*Transformer*, 1973) and Iggy Pop (*The Idiot*, 1977, and *Lust for Life*, 1977), producing artistic and commercial watersheds for all three. Bowie's modest chart successes in the United States have rarely reflected the influence he has exerted as an arbiter of musical style. Countless artists, from the first New York punk groups to Madonna, Nine Inch Nails, and the Smashing Pumpkins, have cited Bowie as having a musical and performative influence on their own work.

SELECTED RECORDINGS

The Rise and Fall of Ziggy Stardust and the Spiders from Mars (RCA, 1972); *Aladdin Sane* (RCA, 1973); *Young Americans* (RCA, 1975); *Station to Station* (RCA, 1976); *Low* (RCA, 1977); *Let's Dance* (EMI, 1983); *Earthling* (RCA, 1997)

BIBLIOGRAPHY

D. Thompson: *Moonage Daydream* (Medford, NJ, 1987)

E. Thomson and D. Gutman: *The Bowie Companion* (New York, 1996)

D. Buckley: *Strange Fascination* (London, 2000)

P. Auslander: *Performing Glam Rock: Gender and Theatricality in Popular Music* (Ann Arbor, 2006)

MARK MACAULAY

Bowie, (William) Lester (*b* Frederick, MD, 11 Oct 1941; *d* New York, NY, 8 Nov 1999). Jazz trumpeter and composer. He grew up in Little Rock and St. Louis, first studying the cornet with his father. He formed his first group, the Continentals, in 1954 and gained early musical experience with blues and rhythm-and-blues bands. After four years in the air force, Bowie studied briefly at North Texas State University and Lincoln University in St. Louis. He toured the South and Midwest with the bands of Little Milton, Albert King, Jackie Wilson, Rufus Thomas, and Solomon Burke and recorded in horn sections for the label Chess. In 1965 he moved to Chicago to become music director for his wife, the rhythm-and-blues singer Fontella Bass. There he became a founding organizer and the second president of the ASSOCIATION FOR THE ADVANCEMENT OF CREATIVE MUSICIANS (AACM), a collective of young African American improvisers who experimented with avant-garde forms. He performed and recorded with the saxophonist and fellow AACM member Roscoe Mitchell from 1966 to 1968 before moving to Paris. There in 1969 Bowie was a founding member with Mitchell, Joseph Jarman, and Malachi Favors of the ART ENSEMBLE OF CHICAGO, an eclectic and theatrical avant-garde group with which he recorded and performed into the 1990s. During the same period Bowie also explored many contexts, from solo concerts to appearances with fellow trumpeter Malachi Thompson, Sonny Murray, Archie Shepp, and Cecil Taylor. He was a member of Jack DeJohnette's New Directions Quartet and helped to organize the Black Artists Group and Great Black Music Orchestra in St. Louis.

Bowie led a number of bands including a gospel, jazz, and rock fusion group, From the Root to the Source, which was co-led by his wife. His New York Hot Trumpet Repertory Company (1982) featured Thompson, Olu Dara, Stanton Davis, and Wynton Marsalis. Within a year the group expanded to become Lester Bowie's Brass Fantasy, remaining active into the late 1990s. He helped organize an all-star avant-garde collective, The Leaders, in 1986 and established the New York Organ Ensemble in 1990. He was among the most original trumpeters in jazz with an impressive technique and an often irreverent style that drew on a large stock of effects.

RECORDINGS
(selective list)

Gittin' to Know y'all (1969, MPS); *Fast Last* (1974, Muse); *Rope-a-dope* (1975, Muse); *The 5th Power* (1978, Black Saint); *The Great Pretender* (1981, ECM); *All the Magic!* (1982, ECM)

BIBLIOGRAPHY

V. Wilmer: "Extending the Tradition," *DB*, xxxviii/9 (1971), 13
R. Townley: "Lester... Who?" *DB*, xli/2 (1974), 11
B. McRae: "Avant Courier: Lester Bowie," *JJI*, xxxiii/11 (1980), 12
J. Rockwell: "Jazz, Group Improvisation, Race & Racism: the Art Ensemble of Chicago," *All American Music: Composition in the Late Twentieth Century* (New York, 1983), 164
H. Mandel: "Lester Bowie M.D.: Magical Dimensions," *DB*, li/3 (1984), 14
B. Bennett: "The Brass Fantasies of Lester Bowie," *JT*, xxvii/8 (1997), 42
G.E. Lewis: *A Power Stronger than itself: the AACM and American Experimental Music* (Chicago, 2008)

LEE JESKE/BARRY LONG

Bowles, Paul (*b* Jamaica, NY, 30 Dec 1910; *d* Tangier, Morocco, 18 Nov 1999). Composer and writer. As a young man he studied with AARON COPLAND in New York, Berlin, and Paris. In 1931 they traveled to Morocco, where he completed his first chamber and solo piano works. He continued his studies with NADIA BOULANGER, ROGER SESSIONS, VIRGIL THOMSON, and ISRAEL CITKOWITZ. Further travel to Guatemala, Mexico, Ceylon, southern India, and the Sahara enabled him to explore indigenous musical styles which were to influence his own compositions. In 1937 he met the writer Jane Auer, whom he married the following year; together they traveled to Mexico, where he visited Silvestre Revueltas, whose compositional style had a considerable influence on his own.

Upon his return to New York, Bowles joined the musical milieu of Henry Brant, David Diamond, Citkowitz, and other members of the League of Composers. Between 1936 and 1963 he wrote several ballet scores for the American Ballet Caravan and incidental theater music for Orson Welles, John Houseman, William Saroyan, and primarily Tennessee Williams. He also composed under the aegis of the Work Projects Administration and the Federal Theatre Project. In 1943, Leonard Bernstein conducted the premiere of the zarzuela *The Wind Remains*, choreographed and danced by Merce Cunningham, at the New York Museum of Modern Art. Several Latin-inspired orchestral works followed. Under the guidance of Virgil Thomson, Bowles began writing music criticism for the *New York Herald Tribune* (from 1942), covering jazz and folk, as well as art music; he also contributed articles on these topics to *Modern Music*.

One of his most imaginative musical collaborations came with expatriate writer Gertrude Stein. He set four of her texts to music—one a verbatim postcard that she wrote him. Two of these songs appear in *Scenes from the Door* in his self-published music called *Éditions de la Vipère*. Under this title, Bowles published works by Diamond, Eric Satie, and himself.

Increasingly dissatisfied with his role as a composer of *Gebrauchsmusik*, Bowles left New York for Tangier in 1947. There he completed his first novel, *The Sheltering Sky* (London, 1949), the success of which encouraged him to become more active as a writer and translator. Despite his decision to leave the world of music and devote himself to prose, he composed one additional opera, *Yerma* (1948–55), for torch-singer Libby Holman, and continued to write songs throughout his life. His honors included a Guggenheim Fellowship (1941) and a Rockefeller grant (1959), which enabled him to pursue ethnomusicological research and record traditional music in Morocco. His collection now resides in the Archive for Folk Culture at the Library of Congress.

Bowles's compositional style is witty, aphoristic, and tuneful. He wrote almost exclusively in short forms that evoke, particularly in the solo piano works, American jazz and folk elements, Latin American dance rhythms, and Spanish harmonies. His operas are constructed as series of separate songs, each of which is unfailingly idiomatic. His orchestral music, which tends to be at once concise and kaleidoscopic, employing collage-like juxtapositions, displays little thematic development. Between 1997 and 2006, several thought-to-be-lost musical compositions have surfaced: *Tamanar* (1931) for solo piano, Bowles' one exploration into absolute dissonance; several piano works for dance (*Johnny Appleseed* and *Apotheosis*), which are lively and rhythmic; and Bowles's only chamber work adapted (from the piano) for small string orchestra and voice: *3 Pastoral Songs* (originally for voice and piano). A newly (2010) attributed work of *musique concrète* titled *The Pool K III* is Bowles's earliest known exploration in this genre—tones enhanced with echo-chamber effects in a rhythmic, repetitive atmosphere where seemingly random sounds gain significance in pitch and continuity over time. It was not his last foray into *musique concrète*. In his later years, he composed theater music for the American School in Tangier, which included *concrète* scores and percussion instruments such as cigar boxes and door bells.

Despite his fame as a writer, Bowles always thought of himself primarily as a composer. Even though many of his compositions remained unpublished at the time of his death, his music enjoyed a renaissance during the final decade of his life, inspiring numerous recordings and performances.

WORKS
(selective list)

DRAMATIC

Stage: Yankee Clipper (ballet), 1936; Denmark Vesey (op, C.H. Ford), 1939; Pastorela (ballet), 1941; The Wind Remains (zarzuela, after F. García Lorca), 1941–3, New York, 1943; Colloque Sentimental (ballet), 1944; Yerma (op, after García Lorca), 1948–55

Incid music: Doctor Faustus (C. Marlowe), 1936; Horse Eats Hat (M. Labiche), 1936; My Heart's in the Highlands (W. Saroyan), 1939; Love's Old Sweet Song (Saroyan), 1940; Twelfth Night (W. Shakespeare), 1940; Watch on the Rhine (L. Hellman), 1941; South Pacific (D. Heyward and H. Rigby), 1943; 'Tis Pity She's a Whore (J. Ford), 1943; Liberty Jones (P. Barry), 1944; Jacobowsky and the Colonel (F. Werfel), 1944; The Glass Menagerie (T. Williams), 1945; Summer and Smoke (Williams), 1948; In the Summer House (J. Bowles), 1953; Edwin Booth (M. Geiger), 1958; Sweet Bird of Youth (Williams), 1959; The Milk Train Doesn't Stop Here Anymore (Williams), 1963; *c*15 other incid scores; *c*11 film scores

INSTRUMENTAL

Ens and solo: Sonata, ob, cl, 1931; Suite, small orch, 1931–2; Scènes d'Anabase (St. J. Perse), T, ob, pf, 1932; Sonata, fl, 1932; Mediodia: Grupo de danzas Mexicanas, fl, cl, tpt, 7 strings, pf, 1937; Music for a Farce, cl, tpt, perc, perc, 1938; Romantic Suite, 6 wind, str, pf, 1938; Pastorela "First Suite," orch, 1947; Conc., 2 pf, wind, perc, 1947, orchd 1949

Pf: Tamanar, 1931; La femme de Dakar, 1933; Guayanilla, 1933; Impasse de Tombouctou, 1933; Nocturne, 2 pf, 1935; 2 Portraits, 1935; Prélude pour Bernard Suarès, 1936; Folk Preludes, 1939; Huapango I–II (El sol), 1939; Suite, 2 pf, 1939; El bejuco, 1943; El indio, 1943; La cuelga, 1946; Orosí, 1946; Sayula, 1946; Iquitos (Tierra mojada), 1947; Carretera de Estepona, 1947; 6 Preludes, 1947; Sonatina, 1947; Night Waltz, 2 pf, 1948; Dance, 1949; Sonata, 2 pf, 1949; Cross Country, 2 pf, 1976

VOCAL

Songs (for medium v, pf, unless otherwise stated): In the Platinum Forest (P. Bowles), 1931; Danger de mort (G. Linze), 1933; Scenes from the Door (G. Stein), 1933; Memnon (J. Cocteau), 5 songs, 1934–5; Green Songs (R. Thomas), 1935; Rain Rots the Wood (Ford), 1935; 6 American Folk Songs, 1939; 12 American Folk Songs, 1939; Love like Wildfire, 4 songs; [Untitled] (R. Hepburn), 1941; A Little Closer, Please (Saroyan), 1941; Two Skies (J. Bowles), 1942; Night Without Sleep (Ford), 1943; Sailor's Song (Ford), 1943; 5 Spanish Songs (García Lorca), 1943; An American Hero (A. Law, N. Niles), 1944; 3 Songs from the Sierras (old Sp.), 1944; A Quarreling Pair (J. Bowles), 2 songs, 1945; David (F. Frost), 1945; In the Woods (P. Bowes), 1945; Baby, Baby (Saroyan), 1946; Blue Mountain Ballads (Williams), 4 songs, 1946; Once a Lady was Here (P. Bowles), 1946; Song of an Old Woman (J. Bowles), 1946; Letter to Freddy (Stein), 1947; On a Quiet Conscience (Charles I), 1947; Three (Williams), 1947; *c*20 others

Other vocal: Par le détroit, S, 4 male vv, hmn, 1933; Tornado Blues, SATB, pf, 1939; 3 Pastoral Songs (anon., Canon Dixon, S. O'Sullivan), T, str qt, pf, 1944; A Picnic Cantata (J. Schuyler), 4 solo vv, 2 pf, perc, 1953, My Love Was Light (Williams) 1984

MSS at *AUS*

Principal publishers: G. Schirmer, Theodore Presser

BIBLIOGRAPHY

P. Glanville-Hicks: "Paul Bowles: American Composer," *ML*, xxvi (1945), 88–96

P. Garland: "Paul Bowles and the Baptism of Solitude," *Americas: Essays on American Music and Culture, 1973–1980* (Santa Fe, 1982), 186–218

J. Miller: *Paul Bowles: a Descriptive Bibliography* (Santa Barbara, CA, 1986)

G. Dagel Caponi: "A Nomad in New York: the Music of Paul Bowles, 1933–48," *AM*, vii/3 (1989), 278–314

C. Swan, ed.: *Paul Bowles: Music* (New York, 1995)

C.C. Blankenship: *The Unpublished Songs of Paul Bowles* (diss., U. of Memphis, 2003)

I. Herrmann: "Postcard from a Bohemian: Paul Bowles' Violin Sonata," *Strings Magazine*, xix (Dec 2004), 26–28

T. Mangan, and I. Herrmann, eds.: *Paul Bowles on Music* (Berkeley, CA, 2003)

Night Waltz: the Music of Paul Bowles, dir. O. Brown (Zeitgeist Films, 2000)

IRENE HERRMANN

Bowman, Brian L(eslie) (*b* Fort Dodge, IA, 22 July 1946). Euphonium performer and educator. Bowman began playing euphonium in his father's band. His early teachers included Robert L'Heureux, Sigurd Swanson, and Rex Conner. He completed the BM, MM, and DM degrees at the University of Michigan, where his principal teacher was Glenn P. Smith. In 1970 he joined the US Navy Band as euphonium soloist and section leader. In 1974 the US Armed Forces Bicentennial Band named him section leader, and in 1976 he joined the US Air Force Band, where he remained as soloist and section leader until 1991. During his time in the Air Force, he established himself as one of the leading American euphonium soloists, performing recitals and clinics in the United States and abroad. In 1976 Bowman gave the first euphonium recital at Carnegie Recital Hall.

While in Washington, DC, Bowman taught as adjunct faculty at numerous universities, and he helped create the DMA program in euphonium at the University of Maryland. Upon his retirement from the Air Force in 1991, Bowman joined the faculty of Duquesne University as professor and chair of brass performance. In 1999 he became the first Professor of Euphonium at the University of North Texas; he is the only full-time (non-adjunct) euphonium professor at an American university who does not teach another instrument.

Bowman has been active in the International Tuba-Euphonium Association, serving as president from 1981 to 1983. His articles have been published in the *TUBA*

Journal, *Accent*, and *The Instrumentalist*. Alfred Music published his *Practical Hints for Playing the Baritone (Euphonium)* in 1983.

BIBLIOGRAPHY

M. Meckna: *Twentieth-century Brass Soloists* (Westport, CT, 1994)

RICHARD PERRY

Bowman, Euday Louis (*b* Fort Worth, TX, 9 Nov 1887; *d* New York, NY, 26 May 1949). Composer and pianist. Bowman played the piano in Kansas City, Missouri, and named his "Twelfth Street Rag" (1914) after the city's main thoroughfare. He sold that composition, written with his sister Mary, to Jenkins of Kansas City and only in the latter period of his life did he receive royalties. It was written as a slow foxtrot and its recording by Louis Armstrong in 1927 (Col.) was at that tempo, and Armstrong continued to play it in that manner. Fletcher Henderson's 1927 recording was medium paced but Bowman's rag was more often played very fast—Fats Waller's 1935 version (Vic.) also almost ignores the melody and Sidney Bechet's 1941 New Orleans Feetwarmers session races at breakneck speed. Lionel Hampton and Basie both recorded it at that time, for "Twelfth Street Rag" was now a jazz classic. It was arranged for the accordion (1947) and in an up-tempo version sold three million copies in Walter "Pee Wee" Hunt's 1948 recording (Cap.). Hank Snow, Chet Atkins, and Liberace each recorded versions, Spike Jones's performance of it on television broadcast (1957) is readily available. The music was also arranged for guitar and piano and in 1990, for brass quintet. Bowman wrote other pieces that are known only because his "Twelfth Street Rag" had become an evergreen.

WORKS
(selective list)
(all for piano)

12th Street Rag, 1914; Sixth Street Rag, 1914; Tenth Street Rag, 1914; Petticoat Lane, 1915; Shamrock Rag, 1916; Eleventh Street Rag, 1917; Chromatic Chords, 1926

Principal publishers: J.W. Jenkins' Sons Music Company, Euday L. Bowman

BIBLIOGRAPHY

Obituary, *Kansas City Star* (5 June 1949)

E. Townley: *Tell Your Story: a Dictionary of Jazz and Blues Recordings, 1917–1950* (London, 1976), 367

A. Jasen and T.J. Tichenor: *Rags and Ragtime: a Musical History* (New York, 1978), 49

J. Chilton: *Sidney Bechet, the Wizard of Jazz* (London, 1987)

JEFFREY GREEN

Bowman, Wayne D(evere) (*b* Carrara, Italy, 16 Nov 1947). Music educator and scholar of Italian birth. He attended McPherson College and Wichita State University in Kansas, and received degrees from the University of Illinois at Champaign-Urbana (BME 1973, MM 1974, EdD 1980). He taught low brass, jazz, and courses in music education at Mars Hill College in North Carolina (1974–81). Since 1981 he has been on the music faculty at Brandon University, Manitoba, Canada, where he teaches primarily graduate courses in music education and music education philosophy. During some of this period he has been chair of graduate music studies, and he took a leave of absence to serve as a visiting professor at the University of Toronto (1995–7). Bowman's book *Philosophical Perspectives on Music* (Oxford, 1998) was named an Outstanding Academic Book by *Choice*. He served as associate editor of the journal published by the MayDay Group, *Action, Criticism, and Theory for Music Education*, from its establishment (2001) until he became editor (2007). He has written numerous articles and books on music and music education philosophy, including a chapter in the *New Handbook of Research in Music Education* (New York, 2002).

JERE T. HUMPHREYS

Boy bands. Term used to describe male popular music groups of the late 1990s and early 21st century. It refers to groups of three or more young male vocalists in the teen-pop genre who typically perform complex dance choreography. Popular American boy bands include the Backstreet Boys (whose albums include *Backstreet's Back*, Jive Records, 1997 and *Millenium*, Jive Records, 1999, among others), *NSYNC (*No Strings Attached*, Jive Records, 2000 and *Celebrity*, Jive Records, 2001), O-Town (*O-Town*, J Records BMG, 2001 and *O2*, J Records BMG, 2002), and LFO (*LFO*, Arista Records, 1999 and *Life is Good*, Arista Records, 2001). Boy bands from other Western countries that were popular in the United States include Westlife and Boyzone (both Ireland), Take That and 5ive (both Britain), and the trios soulDecision and b4–4 (both Canada). Bands often considered part of the genre include the Moffats, Hanson, and BBMak; however, these groups play instruments in concert and on their recordings.

In more generous usage, the term "boy band" might refer to all-male groups common in barbershop performance of the 1930s and R&B styles that developed throughout the late 20th century. Despite the boy band genre's stylistic roots in the music and dance aesthetics of African American culture, however, these musical styles pre-date the cultural understanding of the term "boy band" in the late 20th and early 21st centuries.

The boy band phenomenon was part of a wave of teen pop music which garnered a great deal of public attention in the late 1990s. Interested in the potential success of a staunchly pop-oriented version of New Kids on the Block, Lou Pearlman founded the Backstreet Boys in 1993 and *NSYNC in 1995. The boy-band genre, often dismissed as trite, attracted a high number of young fans—notably adolescent and pre-adolescent females. With florid vocal ornaments and modulation often used to authenticate the emotionality of their performances, boy bands sang about romantic love and desire with emotionally charged lyrics and musical aesthetics. Despite the frequent use of subtle sexual euphemisms, they typically emphasized emotional connection over physical, making the genre culturally appropriate for adolescent participation. They presented their lyrics through uncomplicated harmonies and accessible song structures. Group members were routinely positioned as objects of the gaze in accompanying music videos and visual depictions in popular culture. Each was presented to audiences as an individual with a distinct personality, style, and role in the group. Members' personae connect to common male archetypes in American teen-oriented popular culture—clown, jock, rebel, heartthrob, and so on—a boy band characteristic that has frequently been criticized. Disparate identities often translated into distinct vocal performance aesthetics within a group, although most boy-band singers employed a tenor range. In order to be recognizable to fans aurally, singers employ unique styles to differentiate themselves from their peers. Often a member utilized a strained, glottal style that added an erotic element to his singing, his performance often juxtaposed with that of a singer using a light and airy style or a forceful chest sound, among others.

BIBLIOGRAPHY

S. Hawkins: "[Un]Justified: Gestures of Straight-talk in Justin Timberlake's Songs," *Oh Boy! Masculinities in Popular Music*, ed. F. Jarmen-Ivens (New York, 2007), 197–212

F. Jarmen-Ivens: "Introduction," *Oh Boy! Masculinities and Popular Music*, ed. F. Jarmen-Ivens (New York, 2007), 1–20

G. Wald: "I Want it that Way: Teenybopper Music and the Girling of Boy Bands" (2002), <http://www.genders.org/g35/g35_wald.html>

CRAIG JENNEX

Boyd, John Pretz (*b* Kansas City, MO, 22 Sept 1944). Educator, conductor, composer, and arranger. Boyd received his BMusEd and MM from Northwestern University (1967, 1968), later earning a DMA from the University of Missouri–Kansas City (1981). He studied conducting privately with John P. Paynter, Bernard Rubenstein, Crawford Gates, and Glenn Block. In 1989, Boyd was appointed Director of Bands and coordinator of the Wind/Percussion Division at Indiana State University, retiring in 2010. Earlier, he served as Director of Bands at the University of Arizona (1986), Kent State University (1975), and Wichita State University (1971). He is frequently a clinician and adjudicator in the United States and Canada. In 1998, he co-founded with Frederick Fennell the professional wind orchestra Philharmonia à Vent, serving as conductor. Active internationally, he conducted at the Royal Northern College of Music (Manchester, UK, 1998, 2001), the Philharmonic Winds of Singapore (2009), the Central Conservatory Wind Orchestra (Beijing, 2008), the PLA Concert Band (Beijing, China, 2009), and served as the first conductor of the Conservatory Winds at the Yong Siew Toh Conservatory in Singapore (2006–7). Boyd has released more than 20 recordings featuring his conducting; over 60 compositions and arrangements are published with various firms. In 2002, Boyd was elected into the American Bandmasters Association.

VINCENT J. NOVARA

Boyd, Liona (Maria Carolynne) (*b* London, England, 11 July 1949). Canadian classical guitarist of English birth. After guitar studies with Eli Kassner as a teenager, she graduated from the University of Toronto in 1972, and then received further instruction from Alexandre Lagoya in Paris (1972–4). Boyd is well known as a classical-pop crossover artist. Her New York recital debut was at Carnegie Recital Hall in 1975, which inaugurated an international career as a concert artist, but she has also toured with folk-rock singers Gordon Lightfoot and Tracy Chapman. Her nearly 30 recordings show a similar diversity. Traditional classical repertoire is featured on *The Guitar* (1974; her first recording), *Miniatures for Guitar* (1977), and *Baroque Favorites* (1998, with Sir Andrew Davis and the English Chamber Orchestra), while *Persona* (1986) features appearances by rock guitarists Eric Clapton and David Gilmour, and *Camino Latino/Latin Journey* (2002) combines Boyd's guitar with Latin percussion and a variety of guest artists, including Al Di Meola and Steve Morse. On *The Romantic Guitar of Liona Boyd* (1985), she performs pieces by Andrew Lloyd Webber, Max Steiner, and Beethoven. Boyd has also written numerous original compositions for guitar, which are highlighted on the albums *Classically Yours* (1995) and *Passport to Serenity* (2000). In the early 2000s, Boyd became afflicted with focal dystonia, which caused her to abandon the recording studio and concert stage for several years. She re-established herself as a singer-songwriter, releasing two recordings in 2009: *Liona Boyd Sings Songs of Love* (with Srdjan Givoje) and *Seven Journeys: Music for the Soul and the Imagination* (with Peter Bond).

BIBLIOGRAPHY

L. Boyd: *In My Own Key: My Life in Love and Music* (Toronto, 1998)

M. Summerfield: *The Classical Guitar: its Evolution, Players and Personalities since 1800* (Blaydon on Tyne, UK, 1982, 5/2002)

M. Davis: "Latin Allure: Liona Boyd's Life-changing Musical Journey," *Guitar Player*, xl/12 (2006), 68–70, 72

D. Fox: "Liona Boyd," *Guitar Player*, xlv/1 (2011), 54, 57–9

LARS HELGERT

Boyer, Horace Clarence (*b* Winter Park, FL, 28 July 1935; *d* Amherst, MA, 21 July 2009). Singer, choral director, educator, and music historian. He studied at Bethune-Cookman College (BA 1957) and the Eastman School of Music (MA 1964, PhD 1973), and was Professor of Music Theory and African American Music at the University of Massachusetts, Amherst (1973–99). Boyer was a leading authority on African American gospel music, to which he made contributions as a scholar, editor, performer, and educator. With his brother James, he performed and recorded with major gospel stars and also as The Boyer Brothers duo. At the same time he toured widely as a soloist and directed many gospel choirs, including the Voices of New Africa House Workshop Choir (1973–7) and the Fisk Jubilee Singers during his tenure as United Negro College Fund Distinguished Scholar-at-Large (1985–7). He arranged spirituals and gospel songs and edited *Lift Every Voice and Sing: an African American Hymnal* (2/1993) of the Episcopal Church. His scholarship encompasses the musical and social history of gospel music as well as its analysis, and in addition to publications he compiled or contributed to several anthologies of recordings as well as video documentaries. In 1985–7 he was Curator of Musical Instruments at the National Museum of American History, Smithsonian Institution. Among many honors, he was named Chancellor's Distinguished University Lecturer at the

University of Massachusetts (1990), received an honorary doctorate from the University of Colorado (1996), and received the Lifetime Achievement Award from the Society for American Music (2009).

WRITINGS

"Contemporary Gospel Music. I: Sacred or Secular; II: Characteristics and Style," *BPiM*, vii (1979), 5–58

"Charles Albert Tindley: Progenitor of Black-American Gospel Music," *BPiM*, xi (1983), 103–32

"A Comparative Analysis of Traditional and Contemporary Gospel Music," *More than Dancing: Essays on Afro-American Music and Musicians*, ed. I.V. Jackson (Greenwood, CT, 1985), 127–46

"Tracking the Tradition: New Orleans Sacred Music," *Black Music Research Journal*, viii (1988), 135–47

"Gospel Blues: Origin and History," *New Perspectives on Music: Essays in Honor of Eileen Southern*, ed. J. Wright and S.A. Floyd (Harmonie Park, WI, 1992), 119–47

How Sweet the Sound: the Golden Age of Gospel (Washington, DC, 1995/*R*)

RICHARD WILL

Boykan, Martin (*b* New York, NY, 12 April 1931). Composer. He studied with WALTER PISTON at Harvard University (BA 1951), and with PAUL HINDEMITH, first at the University of Zürich (1951–2) and then at Yale University (MM 1953). Boykan also worked with AARON COPLAND at Tanglewood (1949, 1950), and studied piano with EDWARD STEUERMANN. An accomplished pianist, Boykan regularly accompanied soloists such as Joseph Silverstein and Jan de Gaetani; in 1964–5 Boykan appeared as pianist with the BSO. In 1953 Boykan went to Vienna on a Fulbright scholarship, and in 1957 he joined the faculty of Brandeis University, where he was appointed professor in 1976. Named the Irving G. Fine Professor of Music, Boykan is Professor Emeritus at Brandeis University having taught there for over 50 years. Boykan has lectured as Visiting Professor at Columbia and NYU, also serving as a Senior Fulbright Lecturer at Bar-Ilan University, Israel.

The recipient of several prominent awards and commissions, Boykan has been recognized by the Fromm Foundation (1976), the Martha Baird Rockefeller Fund (1977), the NEA (1983), the National Institute of Arts and Letters (1986), and the American Academy (1988). He also received a Guggenheim Fellowship (1984) and two Fulbrights (1953–5). Boykan has held residences at Yaddo (1981, 1991), the MacDowell Colony (1982, 1989, 1992) and the Virginia Center for the Creative Arts (1992, 2007, 2010), in addition to serving on the panels of prestigious competitions and awards, including the Rome Prize and the Fromm Commission.

Despite the tonal orientation of his principal teachers, Boykan's mature style is atonal and reflects the influences of Webern and the late music of Stravinsky, the respective subjects of his two most important articles ("'Neoclassicism' and late Stravinsky," *PNM*, i/2, 1963, pp.155–69, and "The Webern Concerto Revisited," *Proceedings of the American Society of University Composers*, iii, 1970, pp.74–85). His String Quartet no.1 (1967) is partly serial; his later works use 12-tone techniques. A characteristically American feature of his music is the long line, which for him is rhythmically flexible and extends across a wide registral range. He favors long works for small ensembles; a notable exception is his Symphony for orchestra and solo baritone (1989).

Boykan's body of work comprises compositions for a variety of instrumental combinations, including four string quartets, several duos, trios, and works for solo instruments, song cycles for voice and piano, a concerto for large ensemble, and choral music. His writings include the collections of essays *Silence and Slow Time: Studies in Musical Narrative* (Lanham, MD, 2004) and *The Power of the Moment: Essays on the Western Musical Canon* (Hillsdale, NY, 2011).

WORKS

(selective list)

Orch: Conc., 13 insts, 1971; Sym. Bar, orch, 1989; Conc., vn, pf, 2004

Choral: Psalm 128, chorus, 1965; Ma'ariv Settings, chorus, org, 1995

Chbr and solo inst: Str Qt no.1, 1967; Str Qt no.2, 1974; Pf Trio no.1, 1975; Str Qt no.3, 1984; Fantasy-Sonata, pf, 1986; Sonata no.2, pf, 1990; Nocturne, vc, pf, perc, 1991; Sonata, vc, pf, 1992; Impromptu, vn, 1993; Sonata no.1, vn, pf, 1994; Str Qt no.4, 1995–6; City of Gold, fl, 1996; Pf Trio no.2, 1997; Flume, cl, pf, 1998; Romanza, fl, pf, 1999; Songlines, fl, cl, vn, vc, 2001; Pf Trio no.3, 2006; Sonata no.3, pf, 2007; Sonata no.2, vn, pf, 2009

Vocal: Three Psalms, S, pf, 1993; A Packet for Susan, Mez, pf (J. Keats, J. Donne, W.S. Landor, E. Lear), 2000; Soliloquies for an Insomniac, S, pf (W. Merwin, W. Stevens, J.W. von Goethe, P. Sydney), 2008

Vocal with instruments: Elegy, S, fl, cl, vn, vc, db, pf (Goethe, G. Leopardi, G. Ungaretti, E. Dickinson, Li Ho), 1982; Epithalamium, Bar, vn, hp, 1987; Psalm 121, S, str qt, 1997; Motet, Mez, viol consort, 2001, second rev. Mez, cl, va, vc, 2005

BIBLIOGRAPHY

EwenD

J. Harbison and E. Cory: "Martin Boykan: String Quartet (1967), Two Views," *PNM*, xi/2 (1973), 204–48 [incl. score]

E. Cory: "Martin Boykan: String Quartet No.1 (1967)," *MQ*, lxii (1976), 616–20

H. Pollack: *Harvard Composers: Walter Piston and his Students from Elliott Carter to Frederic Rzewski* (Lanham, MD, 1992)

P.E. Anderson: "*Echoes of Petrarch*: Martin Boykan and Musical Narrative," *PNM*, xxxviii (2000), 168–81

D. Rakowski: "For Martin Boykan's Birthday Festschrift," *PNM*, xxxviii (2000), 199–207

STEVEN E. GILBERT/ELIZABETH PERTEN

Boyle, George Frederick (*b* Sydney, Australia, 29 June 1886; *d* Philadelphia, PA, 20 June 1948). Australian American pianist, composer, and teacher. He was first taught the piano by his mother and then, from 1901, by Sydney Moss. In the same year he made a concert tour of more than 280 towns and cities in Australia, Tasmania, and New Zealand; further tours followed. From 1905 to 1910 he studied in Berlin with Busoni. During these years of intensive study he performed extensively throughout Europe and conducted orchestras in the UK. After he settled in the United States in 1910, such notable pianists as Mark Hambourg, Ernest Hutcheson, and Backhaus continued to play his compositions in Europe. From 1910 until his death Boyle performed, taught, and composed in America. He held positions at three major American conservatories: the Peabody Conservatory of Music in Baltimore, as head of the piano department (1910–22), the Curtis Institute (1922–4), and the Institute of Musical Art, soon renamed the Juilliard School of Music (1922–40). In addition, he was on the faculty of Chestnut Hill College (1944–8) and was coordinator of the Boyle Piano Studios in Philadelphia from 1926 until his death in 1948.

Boyle composed in a late Romantic style. The works of his early period (1902–10) are short, small-scale pieces, characterized by simple harmonies, rhythms, and melodies. Many of them are dances in binary, ternary, or rondo forms. The 1909 Ballade for piano anticipated his middle period (1910–22), in which forms become larger, and rhythms and harmonies more daring in the manner of Debussy and Ravel or the later Rachmaninoff. Rich, often non-functional harmony and striking pianistic effects such as tremolos, long trills, alternating octaves, and fast repeated chords characterize such works as the Piano Concerto (1912), the Piano Sonata (1921), and the Habanera for piano. In Boyle's final period (1922–48), he returned to smaller forms, but now free-composed and with the advanced harmonies, chromatic melodies, and more complex rhythms of the middle period compositions. He wrote many pedagogical pieces during these later years.

WORKS

(selective list)

Stage: The Black Rose (operetta), unfinished

Orch: Pf Conc., d (New York, 1912); Slumber Song and Aubade, 1915; Sym. Fantasy (Philadelphia, 1916); Vc Conc., 1918; Pf Concertino, 1935; Holiday Ov.

Chbr: Canzone scherzoso, 1904; Quartette, str qt, 1916; Va Sonata, 1919; Vc Sonata, 1928; Ballade élégiaque, pf trio, 1931; Vn Sonata, 1933; other chbr music

Pf: Ballade, 1909; Nocturne (London, 1910); Morning: a Sketch for Pf (New York, 1911); 3 pièces, 1911: 1 La prima ballerina, 2 In tempo di mazurka, 3 La gondola; Pf Sonata, B, 1915; Habanera, 1919; Caprice, 1928; Obsession, 1928; Suite, 2 pf, 1931–2; numerous other pf pieces

Vocal: The Pied Piper of Hamelin (cant., R. Browning) (London, 1911); Don Ramiro (H. Heine), 1916; *c*50 songs (1909–43), incl. 6 Songs (Heine: *New Spring*), S, pf (London, 1909), La bonne chanson (P. Verlaine), 1v, pf (New York, 1911)

Principal publishers: Carl Fischer, Composers' Music Corp., Elkan-Vogel, Novello, G. Schirmer

BIBLIOGRAPHY

I.W. Peery: *George F. Boyle: Pianist, Teacher, Composer* (diss., Peabody Conservatory of Music, 1986)

IRENE WEISS PEERY

Boyle, J(ohn) David (*b* Gravette, AR, 1 Sept 1934). Music educator and scholar. He received degrees from the University of Arkansas (BSE 1956) and University of Kansas (MME 1960, PhD 1968). He taught music in the public schools of Cassville, Missouri (1956–9), and Lawrence, Kansas (1960–63), and was on the music faculties at Moorhead State College in Moorhead, Minnesota (1967–8), Pennsylvania State University (1968–81), and the University of Miami in Coral Gables, Florida (1981–2000). At the University of Miami he was chair of the Department of Music Education and Music Therapy (1981–92) and associate dean for graduate studies in music (1992–2000). Boyle's research interests include the writing of instructional objectives and evaluation of competencies; program evaluation, particularly of arts programs and comprehensive musicianship; and the psychology of music. He has published more than 50 articles and research papers, and co-authored (with Rudolf E. Radocy) four English editions, two Japanese editions, and a Korean edition of *Psychological Foundations of Musical Behavior* (English editions Springfield, 1979, 4/2003) and *Measurement and Evaluation of Musical Experiences* (New York, 1987). He also co-authored (with Richard K. Fiese and Nancy Zavac) *A Handbook for Preparing Graduate Papers in Music* (Houston, 2004).

JERE T. HUMPHREYS

Boys Choir of Harlem. Choir founded by WALTER TURNBULL in 1968.

Boyz II Men. R&B vocal group. After their initial success in the 1990s, the group has maintained a presence on the music scene for more than two decades. The four best-known members—Nathan Morris, Wanya Morris, Shawn Stockman, and Michael McCary—met at the Philadelphia High School for Creative and Performing Arts in 1988 and put together an ensemble called Unique Attraction. After changing their name to Boyz II Men, they were heard by the producer Michael Bivins, who arranged for the group to be signed to his parent label Motown Records. *Cooleyhighharmony* (Motown, 1991), their debut album, featured the sound of New Jack Swing complementing the soulful, tight-knit, complicated vocal harmonies for which they have become known. It spawned a series of top-selling singles, including "Motownphilly" and "It's hard to say goodbye to yesterday," and they won a Grammy for Best R&B Performance by a Duo or Group with Vocals. Their signature song, "End of the Road" (1992), set the record for longest stay at number one on the *Billboard* Hot 100 (13 weeks); the group broke this record with the song "I'll make love to you" (1994, 14 weeks) and their collaboration with Mariah Carey "One Sweet Day" (16 weeks). Following McCary's departure in 2003 for health reasons, the group has continued to tour around the world and record as a trio, discovering a particularly strong Asian fan base in the 2000s.

JONAS WESTOVER

Bozeman, George, Jr. (*b* Pampa, TX, 1936). Organ builder and organist. After graduating from North Texas State University, he served his apprenticeship with Otto Hofmann and Robert L. Sipe. In 1967 he received a Fulbright scholarship to study organ, harpsichord, and organ building in Austria, and upon his return went to work for Fritz Noack. In 1971 he established his own workshop in Lowell, Massachusetts, and the following year entered into partnership with David V. Gibson (*b* 1944) under the name of Bozeman & Gibson. The partnership dissolved in 1982, and in 1983 Bozeman moved his workshop to Deerfield, New Hampshire. Much of his work consisted of the rebuilding or restoration of older mechanical-action organs, but he also produced some significant new instruments, including those for St. Paul's Episcopal Church, Brookline, Massachusetts (1983), Eliot Congregational Church, Newton, Massachusetts (1988), and an organ based on the designs of 18th-century German builder Gottfried Silbermann for

SUNY, Stony Brook, New York (1985). Bozeman also built several small organs to a stock design called Cortez. His last organ was built for the First United Methodist Church of Denton, Texas in 1998, after which he devoted his time to giving organ recitals and consulting.

BIBLIOGRAPHY
U. Pape: *The Tracker Organ Revival in America* (Berlin, 1977)
G. Bozeman: "The Hook on the River," *The Tracker*, xxv/1 (1980)
L. Edwards, ed.: *The Historical Organ in America* (Hadley, MA, 1992)

BARBARA OWEN

Boziwick, George E(mil) (*b* Rockville Centre, NY, 23 Aug 1954). Music librarian and composer. He holds degrees in music composition from the State University of New York College at Oneonta (BA 1976) and Hunter College, CUNY (MA 1981), as well as in library science from Columbia University (MLS 1987). Boziwick joined the staff of the New York Public Library in 1986, served as Curator of its American Music Collection from 1991 to 2008, and was appointed Chief of the Music Division of the New York Public Library for the Performing Arts in 2006. In these roles he has worked closely with composers, performers, and musicologists to foster research on and documentation of American music.

An active composer, Boziwick's works have been performed by the Dorian Wind Quintet, the Modern Brass Quintet, and other ensembles. He has performed as an oboist and blues harmonica player. Boziwick has served on the boards of the Music Library Association and the Society for American Music.

JANE GOTTLIEB

Bozza, Anthony (*b* Brooklyn, NY, 19 March 1971). Critic and author. After graduating from Northwestern University with a concentration in African and Middle Eastern history, Bozza landed an internship at *Rolling Stone* magazine. He quickly climbed the ladder at the magazine; during his seven-year stint, he first volunteered to write unclaimed assignments, then edited the "Random Notes" section, and eventually wrote seven cover stories on such diverse subjects as Eminem, Cameron Crowe, Jennifer Lopez, Trent Reznor, Slipknot, and *NSYNC. Since his departure from *Rolling Stone* in 2002, Bozza has written books on Eminem and AC/DC and co-written six books, including the official biographies of Mötley Crüe drummer Tommy Lee, INXS, Slash, and Wyclef Jean. He has also published articles in such magazines as *Spin*, *Q*, *Mojo*, and *Radar*.

Bozza's key strength as a writer is his versatility. He is astute when he examines the social meanings of music; in *Whatever You Say I Am: the Life and Times of Eminem* (New York, 2003), he dissects what the rise of Eminem says about race relations in America at the turn of the 21st century. *Why AC/DC Matters* (New York, 2009) shows his skills at translating the experience of music into words and in writing musical analysis without technical terms. Bozza goes to great lengths to capture accurately the very different voices of the subjects of his official biographies; he even lived with Tommy Lee during the writing of *Tommyland* (New York, 2004).

With Neil Strauss, Bozza co-founded Igniter Literary Group, an imprint of Harper Collins's It Books. Dedicated to publishing "cutting-edge" nonfiction, it released its first two books in 2010.

ERIC HUNG

Brackeen [née Grogan], **JoAnne (Marie)** (*b* Ventura, CA, 26 July 1938). Jazz pianist, composer, arranger, and educator. Considered one of the most sophisticated jazz pianists of her generation, she is known for her forceful, harmonically rich, rhythmically complex approach. Largely self-taught, she began her professional career in the 1950s in Los Angeles, sitting in with Dexter Gordon, Charles Lloyd, and Bobby Hutcherson. One of the few women hired by top players in the 1960s and 70s, she worked with Art Blakey's Jazz Messengers (1969–72), Joe Henderson's group (1972–5), and the Stan Getz Quartet (1975–7). This led to offers to record as a leader. She is featured on more than 25 albums, including her original compositions as well as standards. Her signature tunes are "Haiti-B" (1971, in 7/4), "Habitat" (1978, in 10/4), and "Picasso" (1990, mixed meter). Notable albums include *Snooze* (1975, Choice), *Keyed In* (1980, Col. Tappan Zee), *Special Identity* (1981, Ant.), *Live at Maybeck Recital Hall Vol. I* (1989), and *Pink Elephant Magic* (2000, Arkadia), which was nominated for a Grammy Award. Since the mid-1970s Brackeen has primarily toured worldwide and recorded solo or with her own bands. A visionary teacher, she joined the faculty at the New School University in 1989 and the Berklee College of Music in 1994.

BIBLIOGRAPHY
U. Schlicht: *"It's gotta be music first": zur Bedeutung, Rezeption und Arbeitssituation von Jazzmusikerinnen* (diss., U. of Hamburg, 2000)
W. Enstice and J. Stockhouse: *Jazzwomen: Conversations with Twenty-one Musicians* (Bloomington, IN, 2004)

URSEL SCHLICHT

Brackett, David (Robert) (*b* Arlington, VA, 4 April 1958). Musicologist and composer. He studied at the University of California, Santa Cruz (BA 1981), the New England Conservatory (MM 1986), and Cornell University (DMA 1991), and taught at the State University of New York, Binghamton (1992–2003), before joining the faculty of McGill University in 2003. His *Interpreting Popular Music* is a landmark study in its marshaling of analytical and social-historical perspectives to address a wide array of music, including rock, soul, and country. He has also written extensively on issues of genre and categorization and edited a collection of source readings on popular music. From 1998 to 2000 he served as president of the International Association for the Study of Popular Music, US chapter. A composition pupil of KAREL HUSA, STEVEN STUCKY, and DAVID COPE, he has had works performed at many new music festivals and through the Society of Composers, and has won grants from the NEH and Meet the Composer among others.

WRITINGS
"The Politics and Practice of 'Crossover' in American Popular Music, 1963–1965," *MQ*, lxxviii (1994), 774–97

Interpreting Popular Music (Cambridge and New York, 1995, 2/2000)
"Banjos, Biopics, and Compilation Scores: the Movies Go Country," *AM*, xix (2001), 247–90
"Where's It At? Postmodern Theory and the Contemporary Musical Field," *Postmodern Music/Postmodern Thought*, ed. J. Lochhead and J. Auner (New York, 2002), 207–31
"What a Difference a Name Makes: Two Instances of African-American Popular Music," *The Cultural Study of Music: a Critical Introduction*, ed. M. Clayton, T. Herbert, and R. Middleton (New York, 2003), 238–50
"Elvis Costello, the Empire of the E Chord, and a Magic Moment or Two," *Popular Music* xxiv (2005), 357–67
"Questions of Genre in Black Popular Music," *Black Music Research Journal*, xxv (2005), 73–92
ed.: *The Pop, Rock, and Soul Reader: Histories and Debates* (Oxford and New York, 2005, 2/2009)

RICHARD WILL

Bradbury, William Batchelder (*b* York Co., ME, 6 Oct 1816; *d* Montclair, NJ, 7 Jan 1868). Composer, teacher, organist, publisher, and piano manufacturer. In 1830 his family moved to Boston, where he studied music with Sumner Hill and attended Lowell Mason's Academy of Music; he also sang in Mason's Bowdoin Street church choir and later became organist there. From 1836 he taught music classes and gave private piano lessons in Machias, Maine, then in 1838 became a singing-school teacher in St. John's, New Brunswick. Bradbury moved to New York in 1840 as choir leader of the First Baptist Church, Brooklyn, and the following year he accepted a position as organist at the Baptist Tabernacle in New York. He established singing classes for children similar to those of Mason in Boston; his annual music festivals with as many as 1000 children led to the introduction of music in New York's public schools. He also published his first collection, *The Young Choir* (1841), in association with Charles Walden Sanders. The music was later revised by Thomas Hastings, with whom Bradbury collaborated on four other collections, beginning in 1844 with *The Psalmist.*

Bradbury spent the years 1847 to 1849 in Europe, visiting London and Berne, and studying in Leipzig with E.F. Wenzel (piano), Moritz Hauptmann (harmony), and Ignaz Moscheles (composition). During this time he saw Mendelssohn conduct at the Gewandhaus Concerts and met Liszt and Robert and Clara Schumann. He wrote letters to the *New York Observer* and the *New York Evangelist*, describing his personal and musical experiences there.

Following his return to the United States, Bradbury lived in New Jersey and New York and continued teaching music to children, composing, and compiling numerous collections of music; he also conducted several musical conventions. Between 1850 and 1854 he was choir director at Broadway Tabernacle, New York, and in 1854 became associated with Mason, Hastings, and G.F. Root in their normal musical institutes, where he taught harmony. During the same year he began the manufacture of pianos with his brother Edward G. Bradbury and F.C. Lighte. The Bradbury piano received the endorsement of Theodore Thomas, William Mason, Gottschalk, and others, and in 1863 won first prizes at state fairs in New Jersey, New York, Illinois, Ohio, Pennsylvania, and Indiana. Following Bradbury's death the firm was controlled by F.G. Smith and was later absorbed into the Knabe Piano Company.

Bradbury composed, edited, and compiled numerous tunebooks, many of which were published by the firm he established in New York in 1861. Bradbury Publishers also issued a few compilations by other composers; after Bradbury's death it was taken over by Lucius Biglow and Sylvester Main to become Biglow & Main. Most of Bradbury's earlier works were designed for Sunday-school use and were exceedingly popular; an advertisement in the *New York Musical Gazette* in 1869 reported that three million copies of *The Golden Chain* (1861), *The Golden Shower* (1861), and *The Golden Censer* (1864) had been sold, and another collection, *Fresh Laurels* (1867), sold 1,200,000 copies. He compiled eight books of secular music, including *The New York Glee and Chorus Book* (1855). Bradbury wrote 921 hymn tunes, many of which, including those of the hymns "Jesus loves me," "Just as I am without one plea," "Sweet hour of prayer," "Savior, like a shepherd lead us," and "He leadeth me," remain in present-day hymnals. Correspondence, two unpublished works of biography and other papers are held in the Library of Congress.

WORKS
(selective list)
(all printed works published in New York)

Collections: The Young Choir (with C.W. Sanders, 1841); The Psalmodist (with T. Hastings, 1844); The Mendelssohn Collection (with Hastings, 1849); The Shawn (with G.F. Root, 1853); The Jubilee (1857); Cottage Melodies (1859); Oriola (1859), The Golden Chain (1861), The Golden Shower (1861); The Golden Censer (1864); Fresh Laurels (1867)

Cants.: Daniel, or the Captivity and Restoration (Root, C.M. Cady), collab., Root, solo vv. Chorus pf (1853); Esther, the Beautiful Queen (Cady), solo vv., chorus, pf (1856)

921 hymn tunes, mostly pubd in collections, incl. Angel Band; Rest; The God of love will sure indulge; Just as I am without one plea; Caddo; Olive's Brow; Holy Bible, book divine; Sweet hour of prayer; Savior, like a shepherd lead us; The sweetest name; Jesus loves me; Solid Rock; He leadeth me; Will the angels come to me?

30 anthems, incl. O magnify the Lord (collab. Hastings), 4vv, pubd in *The Psalmodist* (1844); Heavenly Love, 4vv pubd in *The Jubilee* (1857)

79 other sacred choral pieces

24 glees, incl. My home is on the mountain, pubd in *The New York Glee and Chorus Book* (1855)

77 other secular works, many pubd in *The Alpine Glee Singer* (1850)

Principal publishers: Bradbury, Ivison, Phinney & Col., Newman

BIBLIOGRAPHY

DAB (E. Salzer)
Obituary, *New York Musical Gazette,* ii (1867–8), 25
"William Bradbury," *New York Musical Gazette*, vii (1873), 65
F.J. Metcalf: *American Writers and Compilers of Sacred Music* (New York, 1925/*R*), 274ff
L. Ellinwood: "Bradbury, William Batchelder," *The Hymnal 1940 Companion* (New York, 1949), 385ff
A.B. Wingard: *The Life and Works of William Batchelder Bradbury, 1816–1868* (diss., Southern Baptist Theological Seminary, 1973)
V. Cross: *The Development of Sunday School Hymnody in the United States of America, 1816–1869* (diss., New Orleans Baptist Theological Seminary, 1985)

HARRY ESKEW

Bradford, Alex (*b* Bessemer, AL, 23 Jan 1927; *d* Newark, NJ, 15 Feb 1978). Gospel singer and composer. At the age of 13 he joined the Protective Harmoneers, a children's gospel group in Bessemer, and had his own radio show on a local station. He attended Snow Hill Institute in Snow Hill, Alabama, and as a student teacher acquired the title "professor," which he maintained throughout his career. While traveling with Mahalia Jackson in 1941–2, he copied down the names of promoters from her address book and left her employ to organize his own group, the Bradford Singers. When they made no great impression on the gospel field, Bradford joined Willie Webb and his singers, with whom he recorded "Every day and every hour" (1950). On the strength of its success he organized the Bradford Specials, an all-male group who sang in robes with pastel stoles and choreographed most of their songs. In 1953 Bradford wrote and recorded "Too close to heaven," which sold a million copies and received an award from the National Baptist Music Convention. A series of gospel recordings followed, and Bradford amassed a large following, not only for the beauty of his singing, marked by a throaty baritone and shrill falsetto, but his flamboyance as a stage personality and performer. In 1961 he turned to the theater and achieved a huge success in Langston Hughes's *Black Nativity* (1961), which then toured Europe and was broadcast nationwide on television in the United States. In 1972 he appeared on Broadway in *Don't Bother Me, I Can't Cope*, for which he won the Obie Award, and again in 1976 in *Your Arm's Too Short to Box with God*. He composed more than 300 gospel songs, including "He'll wash you whiter than snow" (1955) and "After it's over" (1963).

BIBLIOGRAPHY

SouthernB
Obituary, *BPiM*, vi (1978), 240 only

HORACE CLARENCE BOYER

Bradford, (John Henry) Perry [Mule] (*b* Montgomery, AL, 14 Feb 1893; *d* New York, NY, 20 April 1970). Jazz composer, pianist, and singer. He was raised in Atlanta, GA, where he had piano lessons as a child. After leaving home at an early age, he led a nomadic existence as a vaudeville performer and solo pianist before settling in Chicago in 1909 and moving to New York around 1912. He wrote, published, and energetically promoted his own music, but none of his efforts proved as rewarding as a 1920 Okeh Records release of Mamie Smith singing two of his songs, "That Thing Called Love" and "Crazy Blues." The release resulted from Bradford's persistent attempts to convince Okeh's Fred Hagar that there was a market for African American singers. It is generally recognized as the first commercial recording of a blues sung by a black performer. Sales reached a million copies, generated a blues craze that boosted the careers of such singers as Bessie Smith, Ma Rainey, and Ida Cox, and awakened the record industry to an untapped potential that ultimately changed the sound and direction of America's popular music.

Starting in 1923, Bradford himself recorded with various groups under his own name, often employing musicians of such caliber as James P. Johnson, Don Redman, and Louis Armstrong, but he remained best known for having stubbornly altered the course of American music. He died in relative obscurity, a bitter man who felt that his importance had been overlooked, and he wrote about it in a maundering autobiography (*Born with the Blues*, New York, 1965).

CHRIS ALBERTSON

Bradley, Carol June (*b* Huntingdon, PA, 12 Aug 1934; *d* Buffalo, NY, 27 July 2009). Music librarian, historian, and educator. She attended Lebanon Valley College (BS, Music, 1956), Western Reserve University (now Case-Western Reserve) (MS, Library Science, 1957), and the University of Florida (PhD 1978), and held positions at the Free Library of Philadelphia (1957–9), the United States Military Academy Library (1959–60), Vassar College (1960–67), and the State University of New York at Buffalo (1967–99) where, with James Coover, she established that institution's music library and its program in music librarianship.

Bradley's legacy falls into three areas: music cataloging and indexing; the history of music librarianship in America; and education for music librarianship. She was the leading authority on the Dickinson Classification for music, publishing a manual for its use in 1968. The *Index to Poetry in Music* is an example of her rigorous application of technical services skills to a public services problem. For her research into the history of American music librarianship, Bradley conducted hundreds of oral history interviews with pioneers in the field, producing two essential monographs and a series of vital articles that appeared in *Notes* between 1979 and 2007. Bradley edited two foundational volumes for the profession, including the *Reader in Music Librarianship* (Washington, DC, 1973), and compiled a comprehensive bibliography, *American Music Librarianship: a Research and Information Guide* (2005). In recognition of her contributions the Music Library Association awarded Bradley its highest honor, the MLA Citation and Honorary Membership, in 2001.

WRITINGS

The Dickinson Classification: a Cataloguing & Classification Manual for Music (Carlisle, PA, 1968)
Reader in Music Librarianship (Washington DC, 1973)
Music Collections in American Libraries: a Chronology (Detroit, 1981)
American Music Librarianship: a Biographical and Historical Survey (New York, 1990)
with J.B. Coover: "The Genesis of a Music Library: SUNY at Buffalo," *Notes*, lvii (2000–01), 21–45
Index to Poetry in Music: a Guide to the Poetry Set as Solo Songs by 125 Major Song Composers (New York, 2003)
American Music Librarianship: A Research and Information Guide (New York, 2005)

NANCY NUZZO

Bradley, [William] **Owen** (*b* Westmoreland, TN, 21 Oct 1915; *d* Nashville, TN, 7 Jan 1998). Record producer, arranger, and bandleader. Adept at piano and other instruments, he began playing professionally by age 15, following his family's move to Nashville. By 1940, he was leading his own dance band and broadcasting on local radio, and in 1942, with fellow WSM musicians

Marvin Hughes and Beasley Smith, he composed "Night Train to Memphis," a hit for rising *Grand Ole Opry* star Roy Acuff. After World War II, Bradley became WSM's music director.

In 1947, Decca Records country recording chief Paul Cohen tapped Bradley to head the company's Nashville office and assist in sessions. Bradley recorded for the Bullet, Coral, and Decca labels, and he made his reputation by working with Decca hit makers Ernest Tubb, Red Foley, Kitty Wells, Webb Pierce, Bobby Helms, and Brenda Lee, the last gaining pop stardom before releasing a series of country hits in the 1960s. After assuming Cohen's position in 1958, Bradley became a key architect of the pop-leaning Nashville Sound. For example, he enhanced Patsy Cline's country-rooted vocals with echo, dramatic chord changes, and background vocals to reach audiences in both markets.

Bradley and his brother Harold opened their first studio in 1952, and in 1955 their facility at 804 Sixteenth Avenue South launched Nashville's Music Row district. Along with Owen Bradley, producers from other labels used this studio and its adjacent Quonset-hut studio, recording hits such as Ferlin Husky's "Gone" (Cap., 1957) and Marty Robbins's "Don't Worry" (Col., 1961). After Columbia bought these facilities in 1962, the brothers built Bradley's Barn in nearby Mt. Juliet, Tennessee. The Barn (replaced when it burned in 1980) yielded hits by Conway Twitty, Loretta Lynn, Brenda Lee, k.d. lang, and others.

Bradley won election to the Country Music Hall of Fame in 1974 and left Decca two years later. Active until his death, he crafted soundtracks for the biographical films *Coal Miner's Daughter* (about Loretta Lynn, 1980) and *Sweet Dreams* (about Patsy Cline, 1985).

JOHN W. RUMBLE

Bradley, Scott (*b* Russellville, AK, 26 Nov 1891; *d* Chatsworth, CA, 27 April 1977). Composer and conductor. He studied organ and harmony with Horton Corbett. After working as a theater musician in Houston, Texas, he moved to Los Angeles in 1926 and played in theater and radio orchestras, including those affiliated with KHJ and KTM. He first became known in the early 1930s as a composer of tone poems and works for orchestra and chorus, including an oratorio, *Thanatopsis* (1934), which premiered the same year he married local professional singer Myrtle Aber.

Bradley was hired by animators Rudy Ising and Hugh Harman, formerly of the Warner Bros. animation studio, to provide music for a short sequence of animation in Paramount's 1933 feature adaptation of *Alice in Wonderland*. When the duo began producing animated shorts for MGM, Bradley was hired to score the cartoons, beginning with *The Discontented Canary* (1934). He stayed with the animation unit when they moved to the MGM lot in 1937. During the 1940s he studied with composer MARIO CASTELNUOVO-TEDESCO, who served as a teacher/mentor for many film composers in Hollywood at that time. Bradley maintained an active public profile as a composer, giving lectures and writing articles on film and cartoon music through the 1940s and 50s; he was also a member of numerous groups that supported new music, including the California Society of Composers. Bradley scored practically all MGM cartoons until the division was shuttered in 1957. He then retired from film composing, although his concert works—in particular *Cartoonia* (1938), inspired by cartoon scores—were performed in southern California and elsewhere in the United States through the 1960s.

Bradley's scores were unique among other cartoon composers of the time, and they stand out as some of the more experimental music created for mainstream Hollywood cinema, demonstrating his fondness for Hindemith and Schoenberg; his experiments with 12-tone rows can be heard in cartoon scores beginning in the early 1940s. His papers are held at the Cinema-Television Library at the University of Southern California.

WRITINGS

"Cartoon Music of the Future," *Pacific Coast Musician* (21 June 1941)

"'Music in Cartoons,' Excerpts from a talk given at The Music Forum, 28 Oct 1944," *Film Music Notes*, iv/3 (1944)

"Personality on the Sound Track," *MEJ*, xxxiii/3 (1947), 28–30

WORKS

(selective list)

Orch: The Valley of the White Poppies (1931); The Headless Horseman (1932); Thanatopsis (including soloists and choir) (1934); Cartoonia (1938)

FEATURE FILM SCORES (ALL PARTIAL CONTRIBUTIONS)

Courage of Lassie (1946), The Kissing Bandit (1948), The Yellow Cab Man (1950), Dangerous When Wet (1952), Blackboard Jungle (1955)

SHORT FILMS

The Discontented Canary (1934); A Tale of the Vienna Woods (1934); Honeyland (1935); Bottles (1936); Little Cheezer (1936); Swing Wedding (1937); Art Gallery (1939); The Bear That Couldn't Sleep (1939); The Blue Danube (1939); Peace on Earth (1939); The Mad Maestro (1939); The Fishing Bear (1940); Puss Gets the Boot (1940); Tom Turkey and His Harmonica Humdingers (1940); Romeo in Rhythm (1940); Abdul the Bulbul Ameer (1941); The Prospecting Bear (1941); Rookie Bear (1941); Dance of the Weed (1941); The Midnight Snack (1941); The Night Before Christmas (1941); Fraidy Cat (1942); Dog Trouble (1942); Puss N' Toots (1942); The Bowling Alley Cat (1942); The Blitz Wolf (1942); The Early Bird Dood It (1942); Fine Feathered Friend (1942); Barney Bear's Victory (1942); Sufferin' Cats (1943); Dumb Hounded (1943); Red Hot Riding Hood (1943); The Lonesome Mouse (1943); Who Killed Who? (1943); Yankee Doodle Mouse (1943); One Ham's Family (1943); War Dogs (1943); What's Buzzin' Buzzard (1943); Baby Puss (1943); Zoot Cat (1944); Screwball Squirrel (1944); Batty Baseball (1944); Million Dollar Cat (1944); Happy Go Nutty (1944)

The Bodyguard (1944); Bear Raid Warden (1944); Big Heel Watha (1944); Puttin' On the Dog (1944); Mouse Trouble (1944); Barney Bear's Polar Pest (1944); Screwy Truant (1945); Shooting of Dan McGoo (1945); Jerky Turkey (1945); The Mouse Comes to Dinner (1945); Mouse in Manhattan (1945); Tee for Two (1945); Swing Shift Cinderella (1945); Flirty Birdy (1945); Wild and Wolfy (1945); Quiet Please (1945); Lonesome Lenny (1946); Springtime for Thomas (1946); The Milky Waif (1946); The Hick Chick (1946); Trap Happy (1946); Northwest Hounded Police (1946); Solid Serenade (1946); Henpecked Hoboes (1946); Cat Fishin' (1947); Part Time Pal (1947); Hound Hunters (1947); The Cat Concerto (1947); Red Hot Rangers (1947); Dr. Jekyll and Mr. Mouse (1947); Salt Water Tabby (1947); Uncle Tom's Cabana (1947); A Mouse in the House (1947); Slap Happy Lion (1947); The Invisible Mouse (1947); King-Size Canary (1947); What Price Fleadom (1948); Little "Tinker (1948); Half-Pint Pigmy (1948); Old Rockin" Chair (1948); Lucky Ducky (1948); Professor Tom (1948); The Cat That Hated People (1948); Mouse Cleaning (1948); Goggle Fishing Bear (1949); Bad Luck Blackie (1949)

The Little Orphan (1949); Hatch Up Your Troubles (1949); House of Tomorrow (1949); Heavenly Puss (1949); Doggone Tired (1949); Cat and Mermouse (1949); Jerry's Diary (1949); Out-Foxed (1949); Tennis Chumps (1949); Little Quacker (1950); Saturday Evening Puss (1950); Texas Tom (1950); Jerry and the Lion (1950); Ventriloquist Cat (1950); Tom and Jerry in the Hollywood Bowl (1950); Casanova Cat (1951); Jerry and the Goldfish (1951); Daredevil Droopy (1951); Jerry's Cousin (1951); Symphony in Slang (1951); His Mouse Friday (1951); Car of Tomorrow (1951); Droopy's Double Trouble (1951); Flying Cat (1952); Magical Maestro (1952); Two Mouseketeers (1952); One Cab's Family (1952); Rock-a-Bye Bear (1952); Caballero Droopy (1952); Barney's Hungry Cousin (1953); Jerry and Jumbo (1953); Johann Mouse (1953); Little Johnny Jet (1953); That's My Pup (1953); T.V. of Tomorrow (1953); Three Little Pups (1953); Posse Cat (1954); Hic-Cup Pup (1954); Billy Boy (1954); Homesteader Droopy (1954); Mice Follies (1954); Farm of Tomorrow (1954); Neopolitan Mouse (1954); Dixieland Droopy (1954); Touché Pussy Cat (1954); Pup on a Picnic (1955); Field and Scream (1955); The First Bad Man (1955); Deputy Droopy (1955); Pecos Pest (1955); Cellbound (1955); Busy Buddies (1956); Muscle Beach Tom (1956); Millionaire Droopy (1956); Downbeat Bear (1956); Blue Cat Blues (1956); Barbecue Brawl (1956); Give and Tyke (1957) One Droopy Knight (1957); Happy Go Ducky (1958); Sheep Wrecked (1958); Robin Hoodwinked (1958); Droopy Leprechaun (1958); Tot Watchers (1958)

BIBLIOGRAPHY

I. Dahl: "Notes on Cartoon Music," *Film Music Notes*, viii/5 (1949), 3–13

D. Goldmark: *Tunes for 'Toons: Music and the Hollywood Cartoon* (Berkeley, CA, 2005)

DANIEL GOLDMARK

Braham, David (*b* London, England, Feb 1834; *d* New York, NY, 11 April 1905). Composer, theater orchestra director, and arranger. Born in London's East End, Braham's musical education was gained largely through his early education at the British Union School. He initially played the harp, but switched to the violin and became a skilled performer by the time he was 18. Rather than embarking on a career as a professional musician, Braham became a brass turner, making tubing for brass instruments, and supplemented his income by performing in theatrical orchestras in the evenings. In 1856, in the wake of a cholera epidemic that took his mother's life, he emigrated to New York, where he quickly found employment in theater orchestras. By 1857 he was a regular member of the orchestra attached to Matt Peel's Campbell Minstrels, and remained with this company, despite personnel conflicts and the reforming of the troupe under a modified name, until 1859.

That same year, Braham married Annie Hartley, a performer with the Ravel Pantomime company, and his need for a regular income that did not involve touring prompted him to become orchestra leader at Fox and Curran's Canterbury Music Hall. In the late 1850s variety entertainment was coming into its own, and Braham became one of the important orchestra leaders and composers associated with the form. As orchestra director for the Canterbury, and later for the Theatre Comique, Braham was responsible not only for directing the small theater ensemble but also for composing or arranging all of the music in each show. Singers sometimes traveled with their own arrangements, but when these were unsuitable Braham re-orchestrated them. He also provided arrangements for all of the "dumb acts" (i.e. non-singing acts such as dancers, jugglers, etc.) and for the burlesque after-piece that ended each performance. The orchestras in variety theaters also played overtures for each act for which the orchestra director was responsible.

By 1872 the Boston manager Josh Hart had taken over the lease of the Theatre Comique, where Braham was working. Braham's wife had recently given birth to the fourth of their eight children, and he was primarily concerned with providing for his growing family. In 1873, Hart brought a comic pair, Harrigan and Hart (no relation) to his stage. Braham's music for the songs and sketches Edward Harrigan wrote for his duo became the foundation on which they built the Mulligan Guard series of seven full-length topical urban musical comedies during the latter 1870s and 80s. The relationship between Braham and Harrigan was strengthened in 1876 when Harrigan married Braham's daughter Annie.

Braham's musical legacy includes more than 200 songs created with Harrigan and more than 50 songs written with other lyricists. He also composed or arranged many pieces of incidental instrumental music for the hundreds of shows on which he worked during his half-century career in American theater.

BIBLIOGRAPHY

E.J. Kahn, Jr.: *The Merry Partners: the Age and State of Harrigan & Hart* (New York, 1955)

J. Franceschina: *David Braham: the American Offenbach* (New York, 2003)

GILLIAN M. RODGER

Braham, John (*b* London, England, 20 March 1774; *d* London, England, 17 Feb 1856). English tenor and composer. He made his debut as a boy soprano at Covent Garden in 1787. He sang in Europe after his voice broke, returning to England at the turn of the century, where he established a reputation as one of the country's leading tenors. He traveled to the United States in the autumn of 1840 and, at the age of 68, "surpassed all expectations" with the "pathos, sublimity, power, and wonderful execution" of his voice. He appeared first in concert, with a selection of tenor and baritone airs from opera and oratorio mixed with popular ballads. His American operatic debut, at the Park Theatre in New York, was in Stephen Storace's *The Siege of Belgrade*, and he went on to re-create many of his famous roles, in Charles Horn's *The Devil's Bridge*, Thomas Dibdin's *The Cabinet*, and Weber's *Der Freischütz*. At one point he astonished audiences and critics by appearing in seven demanding roles in less than two weeks.

Braham was famed for the expressiveness and the floridity of his delivery; the richness of his embellishment helped establish a new school of vocal ornamentation in Britain. His vocal range exceeded two octaves, was perfectly modulated, and was renowned for its execution of the portamento. Sir Walter Scott described Braham as "a beast of an actor, though an angel of a singer." He composed songs and operas, including *The English Fleet in 1342* (1803), and also wrote arias for interpolation in the operas of other composers, particularly for his own roles. "All's Well" from *The English Fleet* was the most popular duet in the United States during the first half of the 19th century; other favorite songs were "Tho' love is warm awhile," "Is there a heart that never lov'd?," and "No more sorrow." These pieces are less formal and more directly expressive than the songs of many of Braham's British contemporaries.

He sang in various American cities before returning in 1842 to England and retiring from the stage in 1851. He is credited for decisively increasing American enthusiasm for opera.

BIBLIOGRAPHY

Grove7 (R. Crichton)
GroveO (R. Crichton)
W.T. Parke: *Musical Memoirs* (London, 1830)
A. Comtesse de Brèmont: *The World of Music: the Great Singers*, iii (New York, 1902), 1–13
G.C.D. Odell: *Annals of the New York Stage*, iv (New York, 1928/*R*)
W.B. Squire: "Braham, John," *DNB*
J.M. Levien: *The Singing of John Braham* (London, 1945)
R.J. Wolfe: *Secular Music in America, 1801–1825: a Bibliography* (New York, 1964)

CHARLES HAMM/KIMBERLY GREENE

Brailowsky, Alexander (*b* Kiev, Ukraine, 16 Feb 1896; *d* New York, NY, 25 April 1976). Pianist of Ukrainian birth. He studied with Pukhal'sky at the Kiev Conservatory and in 1911 went to Vienna, where he was a pupil of Theodor Leschetizky. During World War I he had lessons with FERRUCCIO BUSONI in Switzerland, and he made his debut in Paris in 1919. Thereafter he toured widely and in 1924 first appeared in New York. He made coast-to-coast tours in the United States, played in South America, and settled in New York. He continued to visit Europe and gave his first series of recitals of the complete piano works of Chopin in Paris in 1924; he later repeated these there as well as in New York in 1938. On the 150th anniversary of Chopin's birth in 1960 he again gave his complete piano works in New York and Brussels. Brailowsky's repertory consisted largely of the works of Romantic composers, particularly Chopin and Liszt, and he was usually regarded as an artist whose approach to pianism was that of a great virtuoso rather than an intellectual.

BIBLIOGRAPHY

K. Blaukopf: *Grosse Virtuosen* (Teufen, 1954); enlarged Fr. trans. as *Les grands virtuoses* (Paris, 1955), 217ff
"Brailowsky, Alexander," *CBY 1956*
A. Chasins: *Speaking of Pianists* (New York, 1957, 3/1981), 150ff

RONALD KINLOCH ANDERSON/R

Brainard, Silas (*b* Lempster, NH, 14 Feb 1814; *d* Cleveland, OH, 8 April 1871). Music publisher. He moved to Cleveland in 1834 and with Henry J. Mould opened a music shop, Brainard and Mould, two years later. By 1845 the company was known as S. Brainard and in that year began to publish music; this business (known as S. Brainard & Sons from 1866) became one of the most important in the country. Brainard published popular music, mostly pieces for piano and songs for solo voice with piano accompaniment, but also a few sacred hymns and quartets. Also in 1845 Brainard bought Watson Hall (built 1840, known as Melodeon Hall, 1845–60, and then Brainard's Hall until 1872), where many musical events took place. Brainard was a flutist who participated in and arranged works for musical organizations in Cleveland. The company opened branches in New York, Louisville, and Chicago (where it was eventually based), and in 1864 established an influential journal, *Western Musical World*, which became *Brainard's Musical World* in 1869. Brainard married Emily Mould in 1840. Two of their seven children, Charles Silas Brainard and Henry Mould Brainard, assumed responsibility for the firm on their father's death, changing its name to S. Brainard's Sons. The firm ceased operations in 1931.

BIBLIOGRAPHY

Dichter-ShapiroSM
K. Merz: "Silas Brainard," *Brainard's Musical World*, viii/May (1871)
L.A. Brainard: *The Genealogy of the Brainard-Brainard Family in America, 1649–1908*, i (Hartford, CT, 1908), 326
S.P. Orth: *A History of Cleveland, Ohio* (Chicago and Cleveland, 1910), 111, 200
M.H. Osburn: *Ohio Composers and Musical Authors* (Columbus, OH, 1942)
E.C. Krohn: *Music Publishing in the Middle Western States before the Civil War* (Detroit, 1972)
J.H. Alexander: *It must be Heard: a Survey of the Musical Life of Cleveland, 1836–1918* (Cleveland, 1981)
D.D. van Tassel and J.J. Grabowski, eds.: *The Encyclopedia of Cleveland History* (Bloomington, IN, 1987, 2/1996)
H.R. Witchey and J. Vacha: *Fine Arts in Cleveland: an Illustrated History* (Bloomington, IN, 1994)
Brainard's Biographies of American Musicians, ed. E.D. Bomberger (Westport, CT and London, 1999)

J.H. ALEXANDER/R

Branca, Glenn (*b* Harrisburg, PA, 6 Oct 1948). Composer and performer. Branca's musical interests began as a child, where he was a performer in musical theater at the Harrisburg Community Theater. Soon after, he became fascinated with rock music and began to play guitar at age 15, performing in the band, The Crystal Ship. Branca studied theater at Emerson College, Boston, and went to London after graduation. He returned to Boston in 1974, and started the Bastard Theater with John Rehberger in the following year. This gave him a chance to spotlight some of his early theatrical works, including *Anthropophagoi* (1975) and *What Actually Happened* (1976). Branca moved to New York City in 1976 and, with the composer and musician Jeffrey Lohn, he formed the experimental rock band Theoretical Girls (1977–9); even more extreme was Branca's other band, the Static (1978–9), with which he delved more deeply into the densities and loudness of electric guitars. He began creating longer, more austere and challenging works for ensembles of electric guitars and the drummer Stefan Wischerth. Such landmark compositions as *The Spectacular Commodity* (1979) and *The Ascension* (1980) introduced a visceral, high-volume, ecstatic music unknown to rock or the avant-garde. The harmonics of amplified electric guitars interacted and generated new kinds of sometimes unpredictable or uncontrollable acoustic phenomena. He developed larger ensemble works, such as 1981's 10-guitar *Indeterminate*

Activity of Resultant Masses, or Symphony no.1, which combined guitars and drums with keyboards, brass and percussion. The symphony received extensive attention, both affirmative and critical. For his Symphony no.2 (1982), he devised mallet guitars that gave the musicians more open strings. His research into the harmonic series led him to develop new tunings and new instruments, and he designed several keyboard instruments which were used to unique effect in his symphonies nos.3 (1983), 4 (1983), and 5 (1984). His notable later guitar works include symphonies nos.6 (1988), 8 and 10 (1994), and 12 (1998). A self-taught composer, Branca began receiving orchestral commissions in 1989, with his Symphony no.7. Although restrained in its loudness, his instrumental music can create sound fields of a hallucinatory density that rival his guitar music. Among his orchestral works are the dance scores *The World Upside Down* and *Les honneurs du pied*, and the symphonies nos.9 (1994) and 11 (1998), both for chorus and orchestra. The Glenn Branca Ensemble is the primary performing group for the composer's work, and although it features continually changing personnel, it has released several discs on the Atavistic label. Branca received a Foundation for Contemporary Arts grant in 2008.

WORKS
(selective list)

Orch: Sym. no.7, 1989; Shivering Air, 1989; Freeform, 1989; Harmonic Series Chords, 1989; The World Upside Down, dance score, 1990; Vacation Overture, 1991; Les honneurs du pied, dance score, 1991; Sym. no.9 (L'eve future), vv, orch, 1994; Sym. no.11 (The Nether Lands), Die Genenfeld, Part I, vv, orch, 1998

Gui/new-inst ens: (Instrumental) for Six Guitars, 1979; The Spectacular Commodity, 1979; Dissonance, 1979; Lesson no.1, 1979; The Ascension, 1980; Light Field, 1980; Lesson no.2, 1981; Mambo Diabolique, 1981; Sym. no.1 (Tonal Plexus), 1981; Indeterminate Activity of Resultant Masses, 1981; Music for Bad Smells, dance score, 1982; Sym. no.2 (The Peak of the Sacred), 1982; Sym. no.3 (Gloria), 1983; Acoustic Phenomena, 1983; Sym. no.4 (Physics), 1983; Sym. no.5 (Describing Planes of an Expanding Hypersphere), 1984; Chords, 1986; Music for the Murobushi Company, 1986; Hollywood Pentagon, 1986; Music for Edmond, theater score, 1986; Sym. no.6 (Angel Choirs at the Gates of Hell), 1987, rev. 1988 as (Devil Choirs at the Gates of Heaven); Syms. nos.8 and 10 (The Mysteries), 1994; Movement Within, 1997; Sym. no.12 (Tonal Sexus), 1998; Sym. no.13, 2001, rev. 2006

Other works: Anthropophagoi (music theater), 1975, collab. J. Rehberger; Percussion, Electronics, and Mouth [5], 1975; What Actually Happened (music theater), collab. Rehberger, 1976; Ballet Continuo, movement piece, 1976; Shivering Tongue Fingers Air (music theater), 1977; 14 Songs for Theoretical Girls, 1977; Cognitive Dissonance, theater, 1978; 20 Songs for the Static, 1978; Inspirez/Expirez, 1978; In Passions Tongue, op, 1986 [scene]; The Belly of an Architect (film score), str orch, 1986; Gates of Heaven, vv, 1989; Str Qt no.1, 1991; The Tower Opera, 1992, unperf.

BIBLIOGRAPHY

C. Gagne: "Glenn Branca," *Sonic Transports* (New York, 1990),15–78

C. Gagne: "*Glenn Branca*," *Soundpieces 2* (Metuchen, NJ, 1993), 1–21

B. Duckworth: "Glenn Branca," *Talking Music* (New York, 1995), 418–43

C.P. O'Meara: *New York Noise: Music in the post-industrial city, 1978–1985* (diss., U. of California,Los Angeles, 2006)

COLE GAGNE/JONAS WESTOVER

Brandeis, Frederic [Friedrich] (*b* Vienna, Austria, 5 July 1835; *d* New York, NY, 14 May 1899). Austrian pianist, composer, and organist. As a child in Vienna, Brandeis studied piano with J. Fischhoff and Carl Czerny, and composition with Johann Rufinatscha. He later studied under Wilhelm Meyerhofer of New York. Brandeis came to America in 1849, at the age of 14, and made his debut as a pianist in 1851, in New York. He published "Was It a Crime to Love Thee" a year later, aged 17. He toured the country with Vincent Wallace's concert company as a solo pianist and conductor, but finally became a teacher and composer in New York. He was also the organist from 1865 for the Roman Catholic Cathedral in Brooklyn and one of the large synagogues in New York. Brandeis's published works consist of numerous piano compositions and art songs. His unpublished, though performed, works include several large compositions for orchestra, string orchestra and military band; three ballades with orchestral accompaniment; a piano trio; and sextets for flute and strings. His vocal works comprise both sacred and secular themes.

BIBLIOGRAPHY

Baker4; *Grove3, Amer. suppl.*

W.L. Hubbard, ed.: *The American History and Encyclopedia of Music* (New York, 1908)

W.S. Pratt, ed.: *The New Encyclopedia of Music and Musicians* (New York, 1929)

W.T. Upton: *Art-Song in America* (Boston and New York, 1930)

JOSEPH A. BOMBERGER

Brandeis University. University founded in Waltham, Massachusetts, in 1948; *see* Boston (i).

Branscombe, Gena (*b* Picton, ON, 4 Nov 1881; *d* New York, NY, 26 July 1977). American composer and conductor of Canadian birth. Branscombe began playing piano at the age of five and was performing in public recitals soon afterwards. She studied at the Chicago Musical College with Rudolf Ganz (piano) and Felix Borowski (composition), twice winning the gold medal for composition (1901, 1902). She then taught at her alma mater while studying composition independently with Alexander von Fielitz. Branscombe also started the music department at Whitman College in 1907. After a year of further study in Germany, which included lessons with Engelbert Humperdinck, she moved in 1910 to New York and in the 1920s studied conducting with Chalmers Clifton and Albert Stoessel. She was active in women's arts organizations and as a choral conductor, notably of the Branscombe Choral (1933–54), a women's chorus for which she composed and arranged many works and commissioned works by other women composers.

A tireless advocate of contemporary music, she was awarded the annual prize of the League of American Pen Women for the best work produced by a woman composer (*Pilgrims of Destiny*, 1928, concerning the pilgrim fathers). Many of her songs and choral works were also inspired by historical events. Branscombe's most important orchestral work, *Quebec Suite*, was drawn from an unfinished opera on her own libretto, *The Bells of Circumstance,* which centers on 17th-century French-Canadian settlers. Although she was married, she decided to use her maiden name in publishing her works. Her earliest songs were published in the late 1890s in Chicago and Toronto, and she regularly published until her retirement from composition in the 1960s. Textual expression is of prime importance in her works and is achieved through an emphasis on late Romantic, richly textured harmony. This is especially apparent in Branscombe's songs, many of which can be heard on mezzo-soprano Kathleen Shimeta's compact disc, *Ah! Love, I Shall Find Thee: Songs of Gena Branscombe* (Albany Records, 2003).

WORKS

(texts of vocal works by Branscombe unless otherwise stated)

Vocal, orch: The Bells of Circumstance (op), 1920s, unfinished; Dancer of Fjaard, SSA, orch, 1926; Pilgrims of Destiny, S, B, chorus, 1928; Quebec Suite, T, orch, 1930; Youth of the World, SSA, chbr orch, 1932; *c*35 works, mostly choral arrs.

Songs (1v, pf, unless otherwise stated): Serenade (R. Browning), 1905; Autumn Wind, 1911; A Lute of Jade (Chin. poets), song cycle, 1911; The Sun Dial (K. Banning), song cycle, 1913; I bring you heartsease, 1915; 3 Unimproving Songs for Enthusiastic Children, 1922; Hail ye tyme of holiedayes (Banning), 1924; Wreathe the holly, SSAA, pf, 1938; Coventry's Choir, SSAA, pf, 1944; Bridesmaid's Song, SSAA, pf, 1956; A Joyful Litany, SSAA, pf, 1967; c100 others; *c*70 choral arrs.

Chbr and solo inst: Concertstück, pf, 1906; Sonata, vn, pf, 1920; Procession, tpt, pf, 1930; Pacific Sketches, hn, pf, 1956; American Suite, hn, pf, 1959; *c*20 ens works; *c*30 pf works; *c*15 vn pieces

Principal publisher: Arthur P. Schmidt

BIBLIOGRAPHY

L.A.E. Marlow: *Gena Branscombe (1881–1977)* (diss., U. of Texas, 1980)

"Gena Branscombe," *The Canadian Encyclopedia*, ed. J.H. Marsh <http://www.thecanadianencyclopedia.com/index.cfm?PgNm=TCE&Params=U1ARTU0000414>

LAURINE ELKINS-MARLOW/JONAS WESTOVER

Branson. City in Missouri (pop. 10,520; 2010 US Census). Located in the Ozarks of southwest Missouri, it was established in 1882 and incorporated in 1912. Despite its rural location and small population, Branson is known internationally as an entertainment tourism destination and attracts approximately eight million visitors annually.

The Branson area's natural and cultural features began attracting visitors as early as 1900. Tourism increased with the opening of folk-cultural theme park Silver Dollar City in 1960. Several regional ensembles, including the Baldknobbers and the Presleys, established theaters and began presenting string music and comedy performances reflecting the rural Vaudeville tradition prominent in the Ozarks and emphasizing "hillbilly" stereotypes and self-parody. In the late 1970s, several theaters began hosting appearances by famous country musicians, elevating Branson to prominence in the commercial country music world. In 1983, Roy Clark became the first country music celebrity to attach his name to a Branson venue and appear there regularly. Mel Tillis, Mickey Gilley, Loretta Lynn, Charley Pride, and many others subsequently did likewise. Mainstream popular musicians such as Andy Williams and Tony Orlando, musician-comedians Ray Stevens and Jim Stafford, and other performers opened theaters in the 1990s, diversifying Branson's entertainment offerings. Since then, musicians specializing in Southern gospel, bluegrass, Western swing, and many other genres have made Branson their base of operations. Shows commemorating icons ranging from Lawrence Welk to the Beatles, as well as Broadway-influenced musical theater performances, both secular and sacred, are staged frequently.

According to commentators, Branson combines Nashville's focus on country music and commodified manifestations of rural American culture with the theatricality, glitter, and glorification of celebrity characteristic of Las Vegas or Broadway while projecting an image of wholesomeness and moral inoffensiveness. Critics have suggested that Branson purveys kitsch and hokum, perpetuates detrimental caricatures of Upland Southern culture and superficial expressions of patriotic sentiment, and uncritically embraces Evangelical Protestant religiosity and white, middle-class hegemony. Such objections have not dimmed the enthusiasm of multitudes of visitors and supporters, many of whom identify strongly with Branson's cultural ethos.

BIBLIOGRAPHY

S. Faragher: *The Branson, Missouri Scrapbook: a Guide to the New Capital of Country Music* (New York, 1994)

R. Sylvester with J. Hampton: *Branson: Onstage in the Ozarks* (Fort Worth, TX, 1994)

J. Rodnitzky: "Back to Branson: Normalcy and Nostalgia in the Ozarks," *Southern Cultures*, viii/2 (2002), 97–105

A.K. Ketchell: *Holy Hills of the Ozarks: Religion and Tourism in Branson, Missouri* (Baltimore, MD, 2007)

MATT MEACHAM

Brant, Henry (Dreyfuss) (*b* Montreal, QC, 15 Sept 1913; *d* Santa Barbara, CA, 26 April 2008). Composer of Canadian birth. The son of a violinist, he developed his experimental attitude toward music in boyhood: at the age of nine he was composing for his own home-made instruments and organizing performances with them. He studied at the McGill Conservatorium, Montreal (1926–9), the Institute of Musical Art in New York (1929–34), and the Juilliard Graduate School (1932–4), also taking private lessons from WALLINGFORD RIEGGER, GEORGE ANTHEIL, and FRITZ MAHLER (conducting) during the 1930s. Having settled in New York, he earned his living by composing, conducting, and arranging for radio, film, ballet, and jazz groups, working for Benny Goodman, André Kostelanetz, and others. In the 1950s and 60s he extended his work in commercial music to Hollywood and Europe. He also taught composition and orchestration at Columbia University (1945–52), the Juilliard School (1947–54), and Bennington College (1957–80). His honors include two Guggenheim Fellowships (1947, 1956), and the distinction of being the first American composer to win the Italia Prize (1955). In 1979 he was elected to the American Academy and Institute of Arts and Letters.

From early on Brant was attached to unusual timbres and unconcerned with stylistic consistency. His *Music for a Five and Dime* (1932) is scored for E♭ clarinet, piano, and kitchen hardware, while *The Marx Brothers* (1938) features a tin whistle, accompanied by a chamber

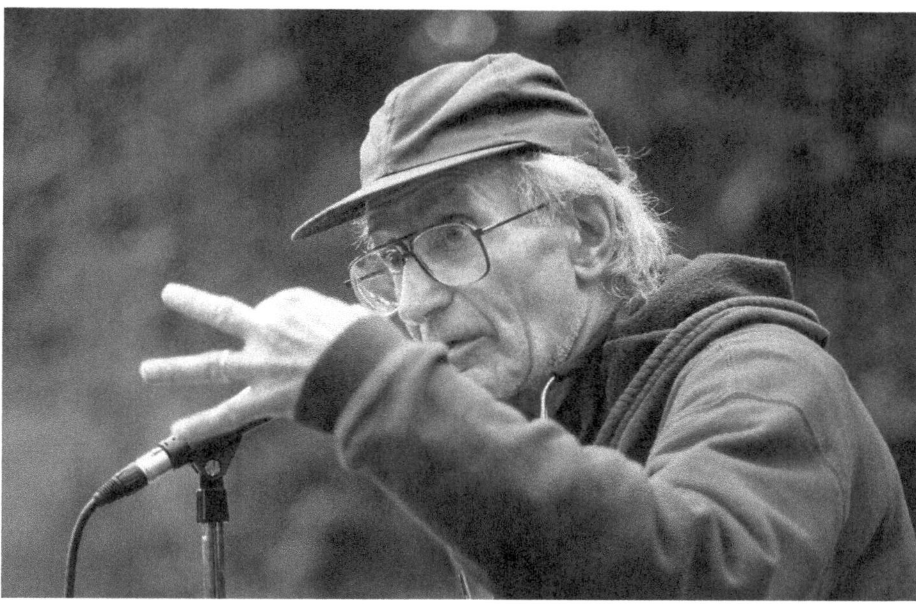

Henry Brant, 1999. (Kate Mount/Lebrecht Music & Arts)

ensemble. For a while he explored the idea of writing for multiples of the same instrument (a technique he returned to in later years), modifying instruments, when necessary, to obtain a smooth continuum of instrument sizes. His 1931 flute concerto, *Angels and Devils*, uses three piccolos, five normal flutes, and two alto flutes; his *Consort for True Violins* (1965) is written for the eight instruments of the New Violin Family, in whose conception and musical development he played a seminal role.

Brant is most closely associated, however, with spatial music, or music for spatially separated groups, a genre that he pioneered. Although inspired by the thick counterpoint of Charles Ives (and the angular melodic style of Carl Ruggles), he found that when he wrote 12 contrapuntual lines to be played simultaneously "you really couldn't identify the details in the compound result.... But there didn't seem to be a necessary reason why music should be limited to even twelve horizontal events at once. Why not more than twelve? The ear never said, 'I refuse to listen'." Taking a cue from Ives's *The Unanswered Question*, and also from Teo Macero's *Areas* for five separated jazz ensembles (1952), Brant found a solution to his perceptual problem in separating players from each other at distances of more than several yards. Space became, for Brant, music's "fourth dimension," after pitch, rhythm, and timbre.

A breakthrough came with *Antiphony I* (1953) for five widely separated orchestral groups, a work that predated the signal European spatial work, Stockhausen's *Gruppen*, by three years. Unlike Stockhausen, Brant developed Ives's ideas of stylistic contrast, and in most of his spatial works wrote music quite diverse in style, texture, and timbre for spatially separated groups. Achieving spatial separation often required the relinquishment of close rhythmic synchronization, so Brant began to explore controlled improvisation, often giving detailed instructions for register and timbre, but not pitch and rhythm. Because of the size of their forces and the logistical problems of placing ensembles around an auditorium, such mammoth Brant works as *Kingdom Come* for orchestra, circus band, and organ (1970), or *Orbits* (1979) for high soprano, organ, and 80 trombones (each of which plays an independent part, the coincidence of which often results in quarter-tone clusters), are staged only rarely, and recordings fail to capture the music's essentially spatial nature. Brant's frequent outdoor performances can also be difficult; a 1972 New York performance of *The Immortal Combat* was obliterated by traffic noise, a thunderstorm, and the fountain at Lincoln Center.

As early as 1950, Brant wrote that he had "come to feel that single-style music... could no longer evoke the new stresses, layered insanities, and multi-directional assaults of contemporary life on the spirit." In the 1980s he expanded his concept of stylistic diversity to include the musics of non-Western peoples; *Meteor Farm* (1982) is scored for Indonesian gamelan ensemble, jazz band, three South Indian soloists, and West African chorus with percussion, as well as conventional European performing forces. Steel drum bands and jazz bands began to appear regularly in his works. His *500: Hidden Hemisphere*, commissioned to celebrate the 500th anniversary of Columbus's discovery, positioned a steel drum band in one corner of Lincoln Center's outdoor courtyard and concert bands in the other three corners. In addition to using non-Western ensembles, Brant increasingly turned to improvisational scoring. When writing for jazz band, gamelan, or African ensemble, he explained that "I listen to their repertory and ask if I can have this piece or that, and they play at a certain point in their usual manner. I prefer to do that than modify the traditional music." Some of Brant's large works use a technique he called "instant music," which he described as "not notated. Based on precise prescriptions for range, dynamics articulation, timbre—not pitch arrangements, rhythm formulae or chance. Repeatable in recognizable form, not 'once only'."

As Brant gained recognition in his later years as a pioneer of both spatial music and multi-cultural style-mixing, he received more commissions for large works. He continued to eschew amplification of any kind (even refusing to use a microphone to lecture), and dreamed of developing larger, louder acoustic instruments similar to foghorns. In the 1980s he worked at designing a concert hall with movable plywood walls, which could be repositioned during a performance to make the acoustics of the room one of the changing components of the composition; though he toured with a cardboard model in search of support, the space was not made a reality.

Also recognized as a fine orchestrator, Brant labored for 30 years on the ultimate orchestral challenge, the scoring of Ives's dense *Concord Sonata* for orchestra, a project he completed in 1995. The following year he completed a "finished" version of Schubert's "Unfinished" Symphony in B minor. In 1997 Brant's entire archive, including all his manuscripts, was purchased by the Paul Sacher Stiftung in Basle. His 2001 work *Ice Field* won the Pulitzer Prize. Brant died in his home at the age of 94.

WORKS

(selective list; for fuller list of works composed before 1978 see GroveA)

WITH SPATIAL SEPARATION

Antiphony I, 5 orch groups, 1953, rev. 1968; Ceremony, triple conc., solo ob, solo vn, solo vc, S, A, T, B, wind, pf 4 hands, 4 perc, 1954; Millennium II, S, brass, perc, 1954; Conclave, Mez, Bar, tpt, trbn, pf, hp, timp, glock, 1955; December, spkrs, S, T, choruses, orch groups, 1955; Encephalograms II, S, 7 insts, 1955; Labyrinth I, 20 solo str, 4 female vv ad lib, str orch, 1955; Labyrinth II, 4 female vv ad lib, wind, 1955; The Grand Universal Circus (theater piece), 8 solo vv, 32vv, 16 insts, 1956; On the Nature of Things (after Lucretius), solo ww, str, glock, 1956; Hieroglyphics I, distant vv, va, timp, chimes, cel, org, hp, 1957; Millennium III, 6 brass, 6 perc, 1957; The Children's Hour, 6 solo vv, chorus, 2 tpt, 2 trbn, org, perc, 1958; In Praise of Learning, 16 S, 16 perc, 1958; Joquin, pic, 6 insts, 1958; Mythical Beasts, S/Mez, 16 insts, 1958; The Crossing, T, ob/s sax, glock, vn, vc, 1959

Atlantis, antiphonal sym., spkr, Mez, chorus, band, orch, perc, 1960; The Fire Garden, T/S, small chorus, pic, hp, pf, perc, 1960; Quombex, va d'amore, distant music boxes, org, 1960; Barricades, T, ob/s sax, cl, bn, trbn, pf, xyl, 4 str, 1961; Conc. with Lights, vn, 10 insts, lights, 1961; Feuerwerk (Brant), spkr, ww, chimes, timp, hpd, 2 vn, 2 va, 1961; Fire in Cities (Brant), choruses, orch groups, 2 pf, 8 timp, 1961; Headhunt, trbn, b cl, bn, vc, perc, 1962; The Fourth Millennium, 2 tpt, hn, euphonium, tuba, 1963; Underworld, sax, pipe org, 1963; Voyage Four, orch, 1963; Dialogue in the Jungle, S, T, 5 ww, 5 brass, 1964; Sing O Heavens, S, A, T, Bar, chorus, tpt, trbn, pf, perc, 1964; Odyssey—Why not? fl, fl obbl, 4 small orch groups, 1965; Hieroglyphics II, vn, cel, perc ad lib, pf ad lib, 1966; Verticals Ascending, 2 wind ens, 1967; Chanticleer, cl, str qt, pf, perc, 1968; Windjammer, pic, ob, hn, b cl, bn, 1969

Crossroads, tr vn, s vn, mez vn, a vn, 1970; Kingdom Come, circus band, orch, org, 1970; The Immortal Combat, 2 bands, 1972; An American Requiem, 5 wind groups, brass, perc, org, bell groups, church bells, opt. S, 1973; Divinity: Dialogues in the Form of Secret Portraits, 2 tpt, 2 trbn, hn, hpd, 1973; Sixty, 3 wind ens, 1973, rev. as 60/70, 1982; Nomads, solo v, solo brass, solo perc, orch/wind ens, 1974; Prevailing Winds, wind qnt, 1974; Six Grand Pianos Bash plus Friends, 2 brass, pics, pfs, perc, 1974; Solomon's Gardens, 7 solo vv, chorus, 3 insts, 24 handbells, 1974; A Plan of the Air, S, A, T, B, 10 wind and perc groups, Baroque org, 1975; Curriculum, Bar, b fl, b cl, va, vc, db, pf, timp, mar, 1975; Homage to Ives, Bar, 3 orch groups, pf obbl, 1975; American Commencement, 2 brass and perc groups, 1976; American Debate, wind and perc in 2 groups, 1976; American Weather, 8 solo vv, chorus, tpt, trbn, chimes, glock, 1976

Spatial Conc. (Questions from Genesis), 8 S, 8 A, orch groups, pf, 1976; Antiphonal Responses, 3 solo bn, 8 isolated insts, orch, 1978; Cerberus, S, pic, mouth org, db, 1978; Curriculum II, small orch groups, 1978; The $1,000,000 Confessions, 2 tpt, 3 trbn, 1978; Trinity of Spheres, 3 orch groups, 1978; Orbits, high S, 80 trbn, org, 1979; The Glass Pyramid, E♭-cl, eng hn, bn, dbn, 11 str, chimes, 1980; The Secret Calendar, 1v, solo insts, orch groups, org, 1980; Horizontals Extending, solo drum kit, 2 fl, 2 cl, 2 sax, brass qnt, timp, glock, 1982; Inside Track, solo pf, 1v, sax, 4 ww, hn, tpt, trbn, 7 str, perc, drum kit, 1982; Meteor Farm, 2 S, 3 South Indian pfmrs, 2 choruses, West African chorus, jazz band, gamelan, 2 perc ens, 1982; Revenge before Breakfast, fl, cl, vn, vc, pf/accdn, 2 perc, 1982; Desert Forest, 7 orch groups, pf ad lib, 1983; Litany of Tides, solo vn, 4 S, wind, 2 pf, mand, hp, perc, 1983

Lombard Street, org, chimes, vib, glock, 1983; Vuur onder Water [Fire under Water], planned improvisation, SATB, 4 fl, 2 vn, 4 vc, 4 hp, 4 mar, 1983; Bran(d)t aan de Amstel [Burning/Brant on the Amstel], environmental piece, 3 SATB, 100 fl, 3 bands, 4 hurdy-gurdys, 4 drum kits, 4 carillons, 1984; Mass in Gregorian Chant, 5 pic, 40 fl, 1984; Western Springs (Brant), 2 SATB, 2 jazz combo, 2 orch, 1984; Knot-Holes, Bent Nails, & a Rusty Saw, vn/mand, vib/mar, pf/hpd, 1985; Northern Lights Over the Twin Cities (Brant), 5 solo vv, choruses, bagpipe ens, jazz band, concert band, orch, perc ens, 1985; Autumn Hurricanes (Brant), 2 S, Bar, SA, TB, wind ens, str ens, jazz ens, 2 pf 4 hands, org 4 hands, perc ens, 1986; Four Mountains in the Amstel, 4 SATB, 4 tpt, 4 trbn, 4 perc, 1986; An Era Any Time of Year (L. Zukofsky), Bar, pf with perc mallets, timp, vib, chimes, 1987; Ghost Nets, solo db, fl, ob, cl, bn, hn obbl, 2 str qt, 1988

Flight Over a Global Map, 50 tpt, 3 perc, 1989; Rainforest (Moore), solo vv, SATB, wind qnt, tpt, trbn, hp, pf, perc, 11 str, 1989; Rosewood, 50 gui, 1989; Pathways to Security (G. Zrad), Bar, fl + pic, cl + b cl, timp + chimes + vib, pf, accdn, vn, va, vc, db, opt. hp, 1990; Skull & Bones (Brant), 5 solo vv, SATB, fl ens, jazz band, orch, org, perc ens, 1990; The Old Italians Dying (L. Ferlinghetti), spkr, 2 orch, 1991; 500: Hidden Hemisphere, 3 concert bands, steel drum band, 1992; Fourscore (Brant's 80th Birthday), 4 pieces, vn, va, t vn, vc, 1993; Homeless People, str qt, accdn, pf with perc mallets, 1993; If You Don't Like Comets, Get Out of the Solar System, 2 groups of fire truck sirens; Trajectory (silent film score, F. Diamand), S, A, T, B, 2 solo fl, cl, tpt, trbn, vn, va, vc, db, 2 accdn, 10 perc, 1994; Dormant Craters, perc orch, 1995; Plowshares and Swords, 9 orch groups, 1995; Jericho, 16 tpt, drums, 1996; Festive Eighty, concert band, 1997; Common Interests, brass ens, koto zither (Chinese), 3 viole da gamba, 2 pf, 2 perc, voice, vn, va, vc, db, 1998; Mergers, mezzo-sop, bar, 5 separated instrumental ensembles including ww, brass, 4 percussionists, pf, org, 2 harps, strings, 5 conductors, 1998; Crystal Antiphonies, orchestra, band, perc, pno, cel, hp (2 conductors), 2000; 4 Doctors, 4 trumpets (or sax or trom), chimes, 2001; Ice Field, separated orchestral groups, organ, 2 conductors, 2001; Wind, Water, Clouds & Fire (text by Leonardo da Vinci), trpt, org, mar, 4 choruses, wind groups, trp quartet, perc, pf, hpschd, hp, vns, 2004

OTHER WORKS

Orch: Angels and Devils, fl conc., 3 pic, 5 fl, 2 a fl, 1931, rev. 1956, 1979; Cl Conc., 1938; Fisherman's Ov., 1938; Whoopee in D, 1938; City Portrait (ballet), New York, 1940; Fantasy and Caprice, vn, orch, 1940; The Great American Goof (ballet excerpts), 1940; Rhapsody, va, orch, 1940; Vn Conc., 1940; Downtown Suite, 1942; Sym., 1942 [1st and 2nd movts withdrawn, last movt entitled An Adventure]; The 1930s, sym., 1945; Dedication in Memory of Franklin D. Roosevelt, 1945; Statements in Jazz, cl, dance orch, 1945; Jazz Cl Conc., cl, jazz band, 1946; The Promised Land, sym., 1947; Street Music, wind, perc, 1949; Origins, sym., 20 perc, org, 1950; Galaxy II, wind, timp, glock, 1954; Consort for True Violins, tr vn, s vn, mez vn, a vn, t vn, bar vn, b vn, cb vn, 1965; Glossary, mezzo-sop, fl, cl, sop/bar sax, 2 perc, pf, org, hp, mand; vn, va, vc, cb, 2000; Ghosts & Gargoyles, fl ens, jazz drummer, 2001; Climates violin family octet, 2007, unfinished

Choral: The 3-Way Canon Blues, unacc. vv, 1947; Credo for Peace, spkr, vv, tpt, 1948; County Fair, vv, 10 insts, 1949; Madrigal en casserole, vv, pf, 1949; A Plan of the Air II, SATB, 13 insts, 1979; Atlantis II, SATB, 10 insts, 1979; Prophets, 4 Jewish cantors, shofar, 2000; Tremors, vv, winds, sax, brass, perc, 2003

Arr.: Ives: Concord Sonata, orch, 1995; Schubert, Sym in B Minor, 1996

Chbr music, works for solo insts, film scores

MSS in *CH-Bps*; recorded interviews in *NHob*

WRITINGS

"Space as an Essential Aspect of Musical Composition," *Contemporary Composers on Contemporary Music*, ed. E. Schwartz and B. Childs (New York, 1967), 221–42

"Spatial Music Progress Report," *Quadrille*, xii/3 (1979), 20–22

BIBLIOGRAPHY

EwenD; *GroveA* (K. Stone); *VintonD* (J. Vinton)

S. Sankey: "Henry Brant's 'Grand Universal Circus'," *Juilliard Review*, iii/3 (1956), 21–37

K. Brion and J.E. Brown: "The Spatial Wind Music of Henry Brant," *The Instrumentalist*, xxx/6 (1976), 36–9

D. Drennan: "Henry Brant's Choral Music," *Choral Journal*, xvii/5 (1977), 27–9

C. Gagne and T. Caras: "Henry Brant," *Soundpieces: Interviews with American Composers* (Metuchen, NJ, 1982), 54–68

K. Gann: "Isn't that Spatial," *Village Voice* (15 Sept 1992)

K. Gann: "Space Master," *Village Voice* (15 Aug 1995)

K. Gann: "Now in Technicolor," *Village Voice* (12 March 1996)

D. Sykes: "Henry Brant: Spatialman," *Musicworks*, no.64 (1996), 42–8

M.A. Harley: "An American in Space: Henry Brant's Spatial Music," *AM*, xv/1 (1997), 70–92

KYLE GANN (WITH KURT STONE)

Brasfield, Rod(ney Leon) (*b* Smithville, MS, 22 Aug 1910; *d* Martin, TN, 12 Sept 1958). Comedian. For the decade prior to his death, Rod Brasfield was America's most popular country comedian, acting like a luckless bumpkin weekly for the *Grand Ole Opry*. His career began as the "straight man" in a comedic duo with his brother, traveling the South with Bisbee's Dramatic Shows in the late 1920s. In 1944, George D. Hay, announcer and innovator of the *Grand Ole Opry*, recruited Brasfield to join the program. With the *Opry*, Brasfield began a 12-year association with comedienne Minnie Pearl. Because of the *Opry's* large radio audience, their routines moved country humor away from a dependency on slapstick jokes and exaggerated visual gags, emphasizing instead quick-witted verbal repartee that allowed Pearl and Brasfield to alternately deliver punch lines. Although Brasfield's characters reveled in hillbilly stereotypes, they were portrayed with good-natured humor that Southern audiences did not find offensive; he was always laughing with them, not at them. Brasfield died of heart failure exacerbated by alcoholism. He was elected to the Country Music Hall of Fame in 1987.

BIBLIOGRAPHY

L. Jones: *Country Music Humorists and Comedians* (Urbana, IL, 2008)

CLAY MOTLEY

Brass band. A musical ensemble normally consisting of brass and percussion instruments.

See Band.

Braud [Breaux], **Wellman** (*b* St. James Parish, LA, 25 Jan 1891; *d* Los Angeles, CA, 29 Oct 1966). Double bass player, tuba player, violinist, guitarist, mandolinist, drummer, and trombonist. His principal instrument was violin from the age of seven until he moved in 1911 to New Orleans, where he learned mandolin, switched to double bass to join a string trio at Tom Anderson's Cabaret, and marched with brass bands playing trombone, his favorite instrument until developing lip problems in 1919. In 1917 he arrived in Chicago as the double bass player with Freddie Keppard, George Baquet, Roy Palmer, and Tubby Hall in the Original Creole Band (known as the Olympia Band in New Orleans). There, he studied double bass with Tony Jackson and worked at the Royal Gardens, Dreamland, the Pekin Inn, and the De Luxe Café. In 1923 he went to England with Will Vodery's Plantation Orchestra, in which he played both bass and trombone. He subsequently worked with Wilbur Sweatman in New York, played several revues before joining Duke Ellington (1927–35), initially sharing double bass and tuba responsibilities with Billy Taylor. Between 1929 and 1935 he appeared with the Ellington band in six films. He recorded with Sidney Bechet during the period 1940–41. In Harlem he opened his own Club Vodvil in 1935 and a pool room in 1945. In 1956 Braud toured the United States and Europe with Kid Ory and in the 1960s he played with Joe Darensbourg in Los Angeles. He was known for his tone, harmonic awareness, and off-beat slaps of his four-string bass. In 1970 Ellington chose the bass player Joe Benjamin to record *Portrait of Wellman Braud* (Atlantic).

BIBLIOGRAPHY

A. McCarthy: *Big Band Jazz* (London, 1974)

B. Russell: *Oh, Mister Jelly Roll* (Copenhagen, 1999)

S. Lasker: [disc notes] *The Complete 1932–1940 Brunswick, Columbia and Master Recordings of Duke Ellington and his Famous Orchestra*, Mosaic MD11-248 (2010)

PATRICIA WILLARD

Braxton, Anthony (Delano) (*b* Chicago, IL, 4 June 1945). Jazz alto saxophonist, contrabass clarinetist, sopraninoist, flutist, pianist, and composer. He studied clarinet with Jack Gell of the Chicago School of Music from 1959 to 1963 and music for one semester at Wilson Junior College in Chicago. In 1963 he entered the Music Corps of the US Army. After his discharge (1966), he returned to Chicago in order to study philosophy and composition at Roosevelt University (until 1968), with the objective of becoming a philosophy teacher. Following an invitation by Roscoe Mitchell he joined the newly formed musicians' cooperative the Association for the Advancement of Creative Musicians (AACM) during that time.

In 1967 Braxton founded with the violinist Leroy Jenkins and the trumpeter Leo Smith the trio Creative Construction Company which performed and recorded in New York. Along with other AACM members, the trio traveled to Paris in 1969, but Braxton himself was not well received and the group disbanded within a year. In 1970 he returned to New York and joined the Italian improvisation ensemble Musica elettronica viva, then played with Chick Corea, Dave Holland, and Barry

Altschul in the cooperative avant-garde quartet Circle (1970–71). After the breakup of that band in 1971 he lived in Paris again until 1974.

Braxton received widespread acclaim in 1972 following the release of the album *For Alto* (1968, Del.), the first for unaccompanied saxophone ever recorded. He was subsequently invited to present numerous solo concerts. In addition he performed frequently from 1971 to 1976 as the leader of his own quartets, which included Holland, Altschul, and a brass player: briefly the trumpeter Kenny Wheeler, then the trombonist George Lewis. His success in the 1970s was also thanks to a contract with Arista for which he recorded the albums *For Trio* (1977, Ari.), *For Four Orchestras* (1978, Ari.), and *For Two Pianos* (1982, Ari.). Displaying his growing interest in contemporary composers such as Schoenberg, Stockhausen, and Cage, Braxton became a controversial figure in jazz circles. He countered this disbelief with tribute sessions to Thelonious Monk and Lennie Tristano, a duo collaboration with Max Roach, and the album *In the Tradition* (1974, Ste.).

From 1983 to 1985 Braxton was based in New Haven before he accepted a termed professor of music position at Mills College in Oakland. In his last year in California he formed with the pianist Marilyn Crispell, the bass player Mark Dresser, and the drummer Gerry Hemingway an influential quartet, which remained active until 1994. In the 1980s Braxton composed a series of 12 operas called *Trillium*. This "ritual and ceremonial" work demonstrates Braxton's curiosity in mysticism, astrology, and numerology, as well as theater, dance and costume.

In 1990 Braxton began teaching composition, music history, and improvisation at Wesleyan University. The prestigious MacArthur Foundation award, which he received in 1994, enabled him to set up the Tri-Centric Foundation, a New York-based organization established for performing his multimedia works. In 1996 he began giving concerts of Ghost Trance Music, extensive performances navigating the boundaries between notated and improvised music. In the early 2000s he also recorded, primarily on piano, an impressive series of more traditional jazz material.

First influenced by John Coltrane, Paul Desmond, and Warne Marsh, Braxton has become a leading proponent of merging avant-garde jazz with contemporary art music. As a versatile innovator, he links such widespread areas as mathematics and African ritual practices with elements from free jazz to European art music.

BIBLIOGRAPHY

A. Braxton: *Tri-axium Writings* (n.p. [New Haven, CT], 1985)

G. Lock: *Forces in Motion: the Music and Thoughts of Anthony Braxton* (New York, 1988)

R.M. Radano: *New Musical Figurations: Anthony Braxton's Cultural Critique* (Chicago, 1993)

P.N. Wilson: *Anthony Braxton: sein Leben, seine Musik, seine Schallplatten* (Schaftlach, Germany, 1993)

G. Lock, ed.: *Mixtery: a Festschrift for Anthony Braxton* (Exeter, England, 1995)

M. Heffley: *The Music of Anthony Braxton* (Westport, CT, 1996)

A. Ford: *Anthony Braxton: Creative Music Continuums* (Exeter, England, 1997)

G. Lock: Blutopia: *Visions of the Future and Revisions of the Past in the Work of Sun Ra, Duke Ellington, and Anthony Braxton* (Durham, NC, 1999)

M. Heffley: "'O for a Thousand Tongues to Sing': Anthony Braxton's Speculative Musics," *JSAM*, ii/2 (2008) 203–33

S. Broomer: *Time and Anthony Braxton* (Toronto, 2009)

MICHAEL BAUMGARTNER

Bray, John (*b* England, 19 June 1782; *d* Leeds, England, 19 June 1822). Actor, composer, playwright, and arranger, active in Philadelphia, New York, and Boston from 1805 to 1822. He came to Philadelphia from England in 1805 as a member of Warren and Reinagle's theater company, and also acted in Charleston, New York, Richmond, and Baltimore. In 1815 he moved to Boston, where he remained active until the onset of his final illness, when he returned to England, settling in Leeds.

Most of Bray's compositions are songs for the stage, patriotic songs, and sacred works. His best-known work is the "Operatic Melo-Drame" *The Indian Princess*, to a libretto by J.N. Barker based on the story of Captain John Smith and Pocahontas. With Bray playing the role of Walter, it premiered at the new Chestnut Street Theater in Philadelphia on 19 April 1808; it was published the same year in a piano-vocal score that, besides songs and choruses, included the overture and instrumental background pieces for the scenes in melodrama—an unusually complete publication for the period. In 1814, he wrote both a musical farce, *Transformation, or Love and Law* (music lost) and a one-act play (without music) entitled *The Toothache, or Mistakes of a Morning*, and he contributed "additional sayings" for Samuel Beazley's musical farce, *The Boarding House, or Five Hours at Brighton*. In his Boston years from 1815 to 1820, he also composed several songs to texts by the author Susanna Rowson, including "Charity" and "Peace and Love" (music lost).

Bray's musical style as displayed in the piano-vocal score for *The Indian Princess* seems less polished than that of his American contemporaries Reinagle, Graupner, and Taylor, but this may be the result of arranging for amateur pianists and singers. His melodies are graceful and full of rhythmic variety; however, his piano textures, with their thin texture and reliance on broken-chord and murky basses, closely spaced triads, and infrequent modulations, are often awkward. His characterization of *The Indian Princess* as an "operatic melo-drame" followed the vogue set by Pelissier and others, but the 16 instrumental pieces, during which action was mimed, suggest musical tropes of earlier pantomime, especially the "hurry music" associated with fights between Smith and the Indians.

WORKS

(selective list)

(all published in Philadelphia; estimated dates of publication are given in brackets)

Stage: The Indian Princess, or La belle sauvage (op-melodrama, 3, J.N. Barker), Philadelphia, 6 April 1808, vs (1808), lib pubd separately (1808/*R*); Transformation, or Love and Law (musical farce, 2) Baltimore, 1814; 5 melodramas, 7 ops and pantomimes, lost, listed in Parker

Songs, all for 1v, pf, unless otherwise stated: Soft as Yon Silver Ray That Sleeps ([?1807]); The Rose ([?1807]); Il ammonitore dell'amore, or Love's Remembrancer, 6 songs ([1807]); Henry and Anna ([?1807]); Aurelia Betray'd! ([?1809]); Looney M'Gra ([?1809]); The Heath This Night ([c1812]); Hull's Victory ([?1812]/*R*); Our Rights on the Ocean, or Hull, Jones, Decatur & Bainbridge ([?1813]); The Cypress Wreath ([?1813]); Columbia, Land of Liberty! ([?1815]); The Columbian Sailor ([?1816]); Where Can Peace of Mind Be Found, 2v, pf (Boston, 1821)

Sacred: God Is There!, lv, pf (Boston, [?1818]); Peace and Holy Love, lv, pf (Boston, 1820); Child of Mortality, 2 solo vv, 4vv (Portsmouth, [c1824])

Inst: General Harrison's Grand March, pf ([?1812]); Madison's March, pf, fl/vn, in *Musical Olio*, iii (1814), 25

BIBLIOGRAPHY

J.R. Parker: "Mr. Bray," *The Euterpeiad*, i (1820), 11 [incl. list of stage works]

W. Dunlap: *A History of the American Theatre* (London, 2/1833)

C. Durang: "The Philadelphia Stage," *Philadelphia Sunday Dispatch* (1854, 1856, 1860)

H.E. Johnson: *Musical Interludes in Boston, 1795–1830* (New York, 1943)

G.C.D. Odell: *Annals of the New York Stage*, ii (New York, 1949/*R*), 289, 340, 373

H.W. Hitchcock: "An Early American Melodrama: *The Indian Princess* of J.N. Barker and John Bray," *Notes*, xii (1955), 375–88

R. Wolfe: *Secular Music in America, 1801–1825: a Bibliography* (New York, 1964)

A.D. Shapiro [McLucas]: "Action Music in American Pantomime and Melodrama," *AM*, ii/4 (1984), 49–72

V.F. Yellin: "Two Early American Musical Plays," *John Bray—The Indian Princess/Raynor Taylor—The Ethiop*, New World, CD 80232 (1996) [liner notes]

M. Pisani: *Imagining Native America in Music* (New Haven, CT, 2005), 73–74, 120

ANNE DHU McLUCAS

Brazilian American music. *See* Latino music.

Break (i). In jazz, a brief solo passage occurring during an interruption in the accompaniment, usually lasting one or two bars and maintaining the underlying rhythm and harmony of the piece. Breaks appear most frequently at the ends of phrases, particularly the last phrase in a structural unit (e.g. a 12-bar blues or a 32-bar song), or at the end of a 16-bar unit of a multi-thematic piece (e.g. a march or rag).

In rock vernacular any solo instrumental passage can be termed a break, such as a guitar break.

BARRY KERNFELD

Break (ii). Term with numerous meanings in hip-hop culture. As a verb, "to break" has often been used as a synonym for b-boying or breakdancing. In rap music, it has also been a popular slang term meaning "to flee." As a noun, break is used most consistently to refer to an instrumental "break down," also known as a breakbeat: the part of a record that DJs manipulated with turntables to create early hip-hop music.

Breakbeat. A sampled rhythmic fragment isolated from an extant sound recording and repurposed as a rhythmic hook in a new track.

The development of breakbeat techniques in early hip-hop culture during the late 1970s has been attributed to DJs such as Kool Herc and Grandmaster Flash, who used a setup of two turntables and an audio mixer to produce seamless rhythmic grooves for dancers at parties in New York's South Bronx (*see* Hip hop). These DJs learned that by manipulating two copies of the same record, playing one section on one turntable while recueing the same segment on the second one, they could weave the most rhythmically engaging elements of soul, funk, and disco tracks into extended loops.

The segments chosen from these recordings would often consist of the "breakdown," or simply the "break," a section of a funk or disco recording in which the vocalists, horn section, and other instrumentalists would cut out in order to foreground the rhythm section. Over time, DJs realized that "breakbeats" could be isolated from any compelling segment of any recording, and they began to amass a repertory of interesting segments from otherwise obscure or unremarkable records. Aspiring DJs became familiar with a canon of key "breaks," ranging from the Clyde Stubblefield drum break in James Brown's "Funky Drummer" to a bongo riff from the Incredible Bongo Band's "Apache." In early hip-hop culture, these breaks would often provide accompaniment for a distinctive virtuosic dance style known as "b-boying," later introduced and marketed to a national audience as "breakdancing."

With the advent of inexpensive digital samplers in the early 1980s, producers such as Marley Marl came to realize that they could use the devices to isolate and loop rhythmic breaks, enabling them to integrate the suppleness of conventional drumming into digitally sequenced tracks. As this practice became more widespread in rap production, it came to displace DJ Turntablism, or live instrumentation imitating DJ turntablism, as a key sonic component of rap. Throughout the late 1980s and 1990s, rap groups such as Public Enemy, N.W.A., Nas, and the Wu-Tang Clan based their sound around densely layered textures built from breakbeats. Since the late 1990s, breakbeat-based textures in rap and R&B have themselves been displaced by the reintroduction of sounds based upon drum machine programming, with producers such as Timbaland or Pharrell Williams emulating the textures of early electro or Miami bass.

Outside of American hip-hop culture, a single breakbeat known as the "Amen break" (after the Winstons' song "Amen, Brother") served as a crucial building block in countless tracks from the 1990s British dance music genre of Jungle/Drum 'n' bass. (*See also* Electronic dance music.) This two-bar drum pattern, derived from an obscure 1969 instrumental B-side by a soul band from Washington, DC, proved to be an exceptionally versatile rhythmic element in the hands of young, largely working-class London producers. In contrast to the conventional looping patterns used in hip-hop production, jungle producers spliced, segmented, and reordered the components of the "Amen break" to produce elaborate, seemingly improvised rhythmic patterns, generating maximal results with a remarkable efficiency of means.

BIBLIOGRAPHY

T. Rose: *Black Noise: Rap Music and Black Culture in Contemporary America* (Middleton, CT, 1994)

B. Noys: "Into the 'Jungle,'" *Popular Music*, xiv (1995), 321–32

S. Reynolds: *Generation Ecstasy: Into the World Of Techno and Rave Culture* (New York, 1998)
D. Toop: *Rap Attack 3: African Rap to Global Hip Hop* (London, 2000)
J. Schloss: *Making Beats: the Art of Sample-Based Hip Hop* (Middleton, CT, 2004)
J. Chang: *Can't Stop Won't Stop: a History of the Hip-Hop Generation* (New York, 2005)

DALE E. CHAPMAN

Breakdancing. A term often used synonymously with b-boying; a style of Hip-hop dance that became widely popular in the early 1980s. One of the key reasons for its rising appeal can be traced to the film *Flashdance* (1983), which introduced hip-hop dance to a worldwide audience.

Brecht, George (*b* Philadelphia, PA, 27 Aug 1926; *d* Cologne, Germany, 5 Dec 2008). Artist, composer, and conceptualist. Trained as a pharmacist, he had no formal schooling in the arts. In the early 1950s, he began to paint and, influenced by Dada and Eastern philosophy, developed (independently of John Cage) a number of indeterminate methods in reaction to the abstract expressionists; these years are chronicled in his book *Chance-imagery* of 1965. In 1958, he studied with John Cage at the New School for Social Research, New York. His fellow students included Dick Higgins, Allan Kaprow, and Jackson Mac Low, who, with Robert Watts, joined Fluxus, a group of avant-garde artists formalized by George Maciunas that gained prominence in the early 1960s. Brecht was a pioneer of intermedia and conceptual art, whose interests centered on minimalist performance events, experimenting with techniques involving theatrics and games. Many of his performance works from the 1960s and early 1970s draw attention to routine activities, aimed at the blending of art and life. These "event scores" are frequently humorous—for example, *Solo for Violin Viola Cello or Contrabass* (1962), in which the performer polishes the instrument rather than plays it, and *Drip Music* (1959), in which water drips from one container to another. An "event," as understood by Brecht, is a scene before an audience, containing an activity, whether brief or drawn out by means of repetition, ranging from an exercise in perception to the enactment of a basic metaphor. Brecht's art objects were sometimes recontextualized "found objects," a technique pioneered by Marcel Duchamp, such as his *Bottle Bottle-Opener* (1966), a wine bottle with a bottle opener mounted in place of a cork. Brecht's art objects also included games of his own design and handmade boxes that artfully enclosed a selection of his event scores. In 1989, he stated that he was "retired" from Fluxus. In 1970, Brecht moved to Cologne, Germany, where he lived until his death in 2008. A major retrospective of his work was staged in Cologne and Barcelona in 2005.

BIBLIOGRAPHY

J. van der Marck: "George Brecht: an Art of Multiple Implications," *Art in America*, lxii/4 (1974), 48
G. Brecht with P. Hughes: *Vicious Circles and Infinity: a Panoply of Paradoxes* (Garden City, NY, 1975)
M. Nyman: "George Brecht: Interview," *Studio International*, cxcii (1976), 256
G. Brecht, J. Robinson, and A. Fischer, eds.: *Events: a Heterospective* (Cologne, 2006)

DAVID COPE/ANDREW RAFFO DEWAR

Brecker, Michael [Mike] (*b* Philadelphia, PA, 29 March 1949; *d* New York, NY, 13 Jan 2007). Tenor saxophonist. Influenced by his father, an amateur jazz pianist who took his children to see Miles Davis, Thelonious Monk, and Duke Ellington, he started on the drums before moving to the clarinet at the age of seven. He switched to the alto saxophone in junior high after hearing a Cannonball Adderley record and then took up the tenor saxophone in high school; bop and the music of John Coltrane were formative influences. Brecker attended Indiana University for a year, working primarily in rock groups, before moving to New York in 1969 where he played rhythm and blues. That same year he formed the jazz-rock band Dreams with his brother, the trumpeter Randy Brecker, Billy Cobham, and John Abercrombie. After working with Horace Silver (1973–4) he led the Brecker Brothers with Randy. "Some Skunk Funk" (from the album *The Brecker Brothers*, 1975, Arista) epitomizes Brecker's preference for virtuosic, starkly angular, chromatically tinged melodies placed into an aggressive, syncopated, jazz-funk setting; a later album title described the style as *Heavy Metal Bebop* (1978, Arista). The group disbanded in 1982. The brothers also operated an influential New York club, Seventh Avenue South (1977–84). In 1979 Brecker established the group Steps (known from 1982 as Steps Ahead) with Mike Mainieri, Eddie Gomez, and Steve Gadd (later replaced by Peter Erskine). From 1970 he also worked frequently as a session musician with a number of jazz and rock artists, contributing to more than 400 projects. His collaborators included Eric Clapton, Chick Corea, Don Grolnick, John Lennon, Joni Mitchell, Pat Metheny, Charles Mingus, Jaco Pastorius, David Sanborn, Bruce Springsteen, James Taylor, and Frank Zappa. His characteristic style is perhaps best captured on Metheny's album *80/81* (1980, ECM), which also offers an exquisitely beautiful example of Brecker's ballad playing.

In 1987 Brecker toured the United States and Japan as a member of Herbie Hancock's quartet and recorded his first solo album as a leader (*Michael Brecker*, MCA), on which he may be heard playing a synthesizer controller known as the electronic wind instrument. The follow up, *Don't Try This at Home* (1988, MCA), earned Brecker his first of 13 Grammy Awards. Brecker subsequently reduced his studio work and toured widely as a leader and as a sideman with Paul Simon (1991–2), reformed the Brecker Brothers for two recordings (*Return of the Brecker Brothers*, 1992, GRP, and *Out of the Loop*, 1994, GRP), and performed and recorded with McCoy Tyner. Subsequent solo recordings include *Tales from the Hudson* (1997, Imp.), *Time Is of the Essence* (1999, Verve), and *The Nearness of You* (2001, Verve), the last with Hancock, Metheny, Charlie Haden, and Jack DeJohnette as sidemen. Brecker was diagnosed in 2004 with a bone marrow disorder, myelodysplastic syndrome. His subsequent worldwide blood drive inspired support and awareness of the disease. Despite his illness he completed a final album, *Pilgrimage* (2007, Heads Up), his first to feature entirely original compositions. He died of leukemia, leaving behind one of the strongest influences on young jazz tenor saxophonists after John Coltrane.

BIBLIOGRAPHY

R. Palmer: "Sneakin' up the Charts with the Brecker Brothers," *DB*, xlii/16 (1975), 12–13, 41

H. Mandel: "Steps Ahead," *DB*, l/8 (1983), 18–21

D. Demsey: "Michael Brecker," *Saxophone Journal*, xi/4 (1987), 22–8 [incl. discography]

B. Milkowski: "The Brecker Brothers: Boogie out of Africa," *DB*, lix/10 (1992), 16–8, 20

B. Milkowski: "Michael Brecker: a Musician's Quilt," *JT* (6/2006), also available at <http://jazztimes.com/articles/16921-michael-brecker-a-musician-s-quilt>

BRENDA PENNELL/BARRY LONG

Brecker, Randy [Randal Edward] (*b* Philadelphia, PA, 27 Nov 1945). Trumpeter, flugelhorn player, composer, arranger, and bandleader, brother of MICHAEL BRECKER. After graduating from Indiana University in 1966, he moved to New York, where he played with Clark Terry, Duke Pearson, and the Thad Jones–Mel Lewis Jazz Orchestra. A versatile musician, he worked with Blood, Sweat and Tears, performing on their debut album, played hard bop and soul jazz with the Horace Silver Quintet and Art Blakey's Jazz Messengers, and helped form the fusion group Dreams, which included his brother Michael, Billy Cobham, and John Abercrombie. During the 1970s he worked with Silver, Larry Coryell, Stevie Wonder, the Plastic Ono Super Band, and Cobham. He and Michael also performed and recorded (six albums) as the Brecker Brothers, garnering much critical acclaim. He continued to lead his own group into the 1980s and also recorded and toured with virtuoso performers Jaco Pastorious and Stanley Clarke. A reunion of the Brecker Brothers in 1992 led to new releases, including the Grammy-winning *Out of the Loop* (1994); numerous additional Grammys recognizing his solo releases have followed. In the 2000s, Brecker co-led the group Soulbop with the saxophonist Bill Evans. Equally at home in hard bop, fusion, jazz-funk, and Brazilian-influenced music, Brecker has been a highly sought-after collaborator, session player, and big band performer throughout his career. He has successively incorporated electronic effects for both trumpet and voice while maintaining a signature acoustic sound; as a composer, he has drawn on complex harmonic language to great effect.

JEFFREY HOLMES

Brehm, Alvin (*b* New York, NY, 8 Feb 1925). Composer, conductor, and double bass player. He studied double bass with Fred Zimmerman and orchestration with VITTORIO GIANNINI at the Juilliard School (1942–3) before becoming a composition student of WALLINGFORD RIEGGER at Columbia University (1946–52). He has been a member of the Contemporary Chamber Ensemble (1969–73), the Group for Contemporary Music (1971–3), and the Philomusica Chamber Music Society of Lincoln Center, and has also performed with the Guarneri, Budapest, Emerson, St. Petersburg, and Composers string quartets, the New York PO, the Pittsburgh SO, and as a recitalist. He has conducted the premieres of more than 50 works, both in guest appearances and with the Composers Theater Orchestra, which he co-founded with John Watts in 1967. His honors include commissions from the Chamber Music Society of Lincoln Center and the St. Paul Chamber Orchestra, grants from the Naumburg and Ford foundations, and a conducting residency at the American Academy in Rome. He has taught at SUNY, Stony Brook (1968–75), the Manhattan School of Music (1969–75), and SUNY, Purchase (from 1972), from where he retired as professor emeritus in 1996. The Purchase College Conservatory of Music now offers a prestigious award in composition in Brehm's name. He is currently on the Chamber Music faculty of The New School of Music (Mannes College). Brehm previously served as Dean of Purchase's Conservatory of Music and chairman of the national Chamber Music Panel of the Endowment for the Arts.

Once described as a "Heifetz of the big box," Brehm has drawn on his virtuosity as a double bass player to inform both his conducting and his composing. His haunting and dramatic song cycle on a text by García Lorca hints at the influence of Stravinsky and Schoenberg. His piano works, including the striking *Metamorphy*, are particularly powerful. Critics have remarked on the intensity, clarity of linear movement, and lyricism of his compositions. One of his primary interests is the energy that derives from conflicts between harmonic rhythm and melodic stress. Many of his works have been recorded.

WORKS
(selective list)

Orch: Hephaestus Ov., 1966; Concertino, vn, str, 1975; Pf Conc., 1977; Db Conc., 1982; Tuba Conc., 1982

Chbr and solo inst: Theme, Syllogism, Epilogue, pf, 1951; Divertimento, tpt, hn, trbn, 1962; Dialogues, bn, perc, 1964; Divertimento, wind qnt, 1965; Variations, vc, 1965; Brass Qnt, 1967; Variations, pf, 1968; Consort and Dialogues, fl, tpt, vc, pf, perc, 1973; Colloquy and Chorale, bn qt, 1974; Sonata, vc, pf, 1974; Quarks, fl, bn, str qt, pf, 1976; Sextet, str, pf, 1976; A Pointe at his Pleasure, Renaissance insts, 1979; Metamorphy, pf, 1979; AYU Variations, fl, gui, 1980; 3 canzoni, va, pf, 1980; La bocca della verità, fl, cl, vn, vc, pf, 1984; Children's Games, fl, cl, vn, va, vc, pf, 1984–5; By the Numbers, pf, 1994; Circles, pf, 1995; Lion's Den, vn, perc, 1995; Lament for the Victims of AIDS, str qt, 1996

Vocal: Cycle of 6 Songs (F. García Lorca), 1965

Principal publishers: General Music, Piedmont

MARGUERITA S. PUTNAM/ELIZABETH PERTEN

Breil, Joseph Carl (*b* Pittsburgh, PA, 29 June 1870; *d* Los Angeles, CA, 23 Jan 1926). Singer, composer, and conductor. He began to study piano and violin at the age of 11, and singing at 16. He attended St. Fidelis College, Butler, Pennsylvania, and Curry University, Pittsburgh, before going to Leipzig to study law. While in Leipzig he decided to pursue a career in music and took courses at the Conservatory and studied singing with Ewald. He also had singing lessons in Milan and Philadelphia (with Giuseppe del Puente) and sang as principal tenor of the Emma Juch Opera Company (1891–2). Then he settled in Pittsburgh, where he taught singing and was choir director of St. Paul's Cathedral (1892–7); for six years thereafter he worked for a variety of theater companies, and from 1903 to 1910 as an editor.

Breil first gained recognition as a composer with his incidental music to *The Climax* in 1909; three years later he wrote and conducted one of the first scores composed expressly for a film (*Queen Elizabeth*). Breil's association with D.W. Griffith resulted in several film scores, including *The Birth of a Nation* (1915) and *Intolerance* (1916). The former included selections from the symphonic repertory and popular songs from the Civil War as well as much original music by Breil. His one-act opera *The Legend* was produced at the Metropolitan Opera in 1919.

WORKS
(selective list)

Stage: The Climax (incidental music, E. Locke), 1909; Love Laughs at Locksmiths (comic opera, Breil), 1910; The Seventh Chord (incidental music, A. Miller), 1913; The Sky Pilot (incidental music, F. Mandel and G. H. Brennan), 1917; The Legend (opera, J. Byrne), 1919; Der Asra (opera, Breil, after H. Heine), 1925

Film scores: Queen Elizabeth, 1912; The Prisoner of Zenda, 1913; Cabiria, 1914; The Birth of a Nation, 1915; The Martyrs of the Alamo, 1915; The Lily and the Rose, 1915; Double Trouble, 1915; The Penetentes, 1915; The Wood Nymph, 1916; Intolerance, 1916; The Lost Battalion, 1919; The White Rose, 1923; The Green Goddess, 1923; The White Sister, 1923; America, collab. A. Finck, 1924

Vocal: sacred works, incl. 2 masses, solo vv, SATB; 3 partsongs

MSS in *DLC*

Principal publishers: Berge, Chappell

BIBLIOGRAPHY

D.J. Teall: "Mr. Breil's 'Legend' Embodies his Theories of Practical Democracy," *MusAm*, xxviii/22 (1918), 5

B.D. Ussher: "Joseph Carl Breil," *MusAm*, xliii/15 (1926), 39 [obituary]

E.E. Hipsher: "Joseph Carl Breil," *American Opera and its Composers* (Philadelphia, 1927), 87

M. Marks: *Music and the Silent Film: Contexts and Case Studies, 1895–1924* (New York, 1997)

A. Clyde: "Joseph Carl Breil and the Score for *The Birth of a Nation*," *Cue Sheet*, xvi/1 (2000), 5–31

J. Gaines and N. Lerner: "The Orchestration of Affect: the Motif of Barbarism in Breil's *The Birth of a Nation* Score," *The Sounds of Early Cinema*, ed. R. Altman and R. Abel (Bloomington, 2001), 252–70

R. Altman: *Silent Film Sound* (New York, 2004)

M. Cooke: *A History of Film Music* (Cambridge, 2008)

KATHERINE K. PRESTON/MARTIN MARKS/R

Bremner, James (*b* England; *d* Philadelphia, PA, or nr Philadelphia, Sept 1780). Composer, teacher, organist, and harpsichordist of English birth. He may have been related to the Edinburgh and London publisher Robert Bremner. He came to America in 1763 and settled in Philadelphia, where he taught harpsichord, guitar, violin, and flute, and served as organist at St. Peter's Church. By 1767 he was organist at Christ Church, where he remained until 1774 or later, but he may have spent some of this period in England, for a "J. Bremner" published music in London during the years 1770–75. Bremner and one of his pupils, Francis Hopkinson, often presented public concerts together. Hopkinson substituted as organist at Christ Church during Bremner's absence and wrote an ode on the occasion of Bremner's death. Four short harpsichord pieces and one arrangement by Bremner are in the Hopkinson manuscript collection at the University of Pennsylvania.

BIBLIOGRAPHY

O.G.T. Sonneck: *A Bibliography of Early Secular American Music* (Washington, DC, 1905; rev. and enlarged by W.T. Upton 2/1945/*R*)

O.G.T. Sonneck: *Francis Hopkinson, the First American Poet-Composer, 1737–1791 and James Lyon, Patriot, Preacher, Psalmodist, 1735–1794* (Washington, DC, 1905/*R*)

O.G.T. Sonneck: *Early Concert-life in America (1731–1800)* (Leipzig, 1907/*R*)

B.A. Wolverton: *Keyboard Music and Musicians in the Colonies and United States of America before 1830* (diss., Indiana U., 1966)

J.B. Clark: *The Dawning of American Keyboard Music* (New York, 1988)

R.B. Sher and J.R. Smitten: *Scotland and America in the Age of Enlightenment* (Edinburgh, 1990), 261–64

J. Ogasapian: *Music of the Colonial and Revolutionary Era, American History through Music* (Westport, CT, 2004), 82–3

J. BUNKER CLARK/R

Bresnick, Martin (*b* New York, NY, 13 Nov 1946). Composer. He studied at the University of Hartford, the Vienna Music Academy (1969–70), and Stanford University (DMA 1972). His principal teachers included Einem, Cerha, Ligeti, and JOHN M. CHOWNING. After serving on the faculties of the San Francisco Conservatory (1971–2) and Stanford (1972–5), he began a long and fruitful appointment as professor of composition at Yale University (1976). His many honors and awards include the Prix de Rome (1975), three NEA awards (1975, 1979, 1980), a MacDowell Colony Fellowship (1977), the Premio Ancona (1980), Lincoln Center's Stoeger Prize for Chamber Music (1996), the Charles Ives Living Award from the American Academy of Arts and Letters (1998), composer-in-residence, American Academy in Rome (1999), the ASCAP Foundation's Aaron Copland Prize for teaching (2000), and a Guggenheim Fellowship (2003). In 2006, he was elected to the membership of the American Academy of Arts and Letters. His commissions include works for the Koussevitzky and Fromm foundations.

Bresnick's early compositions are characterized by refined textures that develop through linear interplay. Dense webs of repeated and subtly varied interlocking melodic cells are manifest in such works as *Wir weben, wir weben* (1978) and the String Quartet no.2 "Bucephalus" (1984). With the Piano Trio (1988), he instilled in his increasingly lean contrapuntal writing a new harmonic discipline based on symmetrical sequences of melodic intervals. Throughout his oeuvre, unmistakable intellect undergirds dark expressivity; complex inspirations lie behind frequently abstract, programmatic titles. In the early 1990s, Bresnick composed *Opera della musica povera*, a series of pieces including *Follow Your Leader*, *Pigs and Fishes*, *The Bucket Rider*, and *BE JUST!*. These works impose severe limitations on musical material and embody longstanding trends in the composer's musical style, while hinting, from a detached perspective, at the progressive politics which have long played a role in his work. Recent works, such as *My Twentieth Century* (2002), *Ballade* (2004), and *Every*

Thing Must Go (2007) reflect the composer's eclectic stylistic influences, including minimalism, serialism, and neo-Romanticism.

WORKS
(selective list)

Dramatic: Stoneground, 1974; Ants (theater piece, M. Bresnick, R. Myslewski), S, Mez, T, B-Bar, ww qnt, str qt, db, perc, 1976; Arthur and Lillie (film score, dir. J. Else), 1976; The Day after Trinity (film score, dir. Else), 1980; Der Signal, 1982; Cadillac Desert (film score, dir. Else), S, Mez, ens, spkr, 1996; Muhammad (film score, dir. M. Schwarz) 2002; The Botany of Desire (film score, dir. Schwarz) 2009

Orch: Ocean of Storms, 1970; Wir weben, wir weben, 1978, arr. str sextet, 1980; ONE, 1986; Pontoosuc, 1989; Angelus novus, 1992; Falling, 1994; Pan Penseroso, 2009

Chbr and solo inst: Trio, 2 tpt, perc, 1965; B.'s Garlands, 8 vc, 1973; Conspiracies, 5 fl/(fl, tape), 1979; Bag O'Tells, mand, 1984; Bread and Salt, 2 ob, 2 cl, 2 bn, 2 sax, 2 hn, vc, db, 1984; Str Qt no.2 "Bucephalus," 1984; Just Time, ww qnt, 1985; Pf Trio, 1988; Str Qt no.3, 1992; The Bucket Rider, cl, vc, db, elec gui, perc, pf, 1995; BE JUST!, cl, vc, db, elec gui, perc, pf, 1995; ***, cl, va, pf, 1997; Fantasia on a theme by Willie Dixon, pno, amplified ensemble, 2001; My Twentieth Century, fl, cl, vln, va, vc, pno, 2002; Willie's Way, pno, 2006; Caprichos Enfáticos, 2007; Every Thing Must Go, 2007

Vocal: Alyosha (F. Dostoyevsky), Bar, pf, 1964; Where is the Way (Bible: *Job*), SATB, 1970; 3 Choral Songs, SATB, 1986 (Y. Amichai); Falling (D. Bottoms and K. Stripling Bayer), Mez, orch, 1994; The Human Abstract, Mez, pf, 2005

Elec-ac: PCOMP, tape, 1968; Lady Neil's Dumpe, synth, cptr, 1988

Principal publishers: Bote & Bock, CommonMuse

EDWARD HARSH/CHRISTINA TAYLOR GIBSON

Brewer, Christine (*b* Grand Tower, IL, 26 Oct 1955). Soprano. After graduation from McKendree College in Lebanon, Illinois, she worked for several years as a schoolteacher while taking private singing lessons. She subsequently studied for a short period in Germany with BIRGIT NILSSON, whom she cites as a major influence on her vocal development. Having joined the chorus of the Opera Theatre of St. Louis in 1980, she progressed, via small roles, to the part of Ellen Orford, her major operatic debut (1989). Other leading roles followed at St. Louis, including Donna Anna, Ariadne, Haydn's Armida, and Gloriana. Brewer made her New York City Opera debut, as the Countess in *Le nozze di Figaro*, in 1993, and her Covent Garden debut, in the same role, in 1994. Her sumptuous, soaring tone and gleaming top notes drew critical superlatives when she sang Ariadne at her ENO debut in 1997. She has since sung the role to equal acclaim in Lyon and Santa Fe, and for her Metropolitan Opera debut in 2003.

When Brewer sang her first Isolde, in concert performances at the Barbican in London in 2000, critics hailed her performance as the most affecting and beautifully sung in recent memory. She has since sung the role in the United States and at the 2005 Edinburgh Festival, and has recorded it. Another role with which she is closely associated is Leonore in *Fidelio*, which she sang at Covent Garden in 2006, having already recorded the part in English. In 2007 she scored a triumph at the Proms with her first Brünnhilde in *Götterdämmerung*. On the concert platform Brewer has been especially admired in works such as Beethoven's Ninth Symphony, Verdi's Requiem, and Richard Strauss's *Vier letzte Lieder*, which she has recorded with Donald Runnicles. Her other recordings include Donna Anna, Samuel Barber's *Vanessa*, Mozart's Requiem, and lieder by Schubert and Richard Strauss.

BIBLIOGRAPHY

H. Canning: "Christine Brewer," *Opera*, lxvii/9 (2006), 1048–53

RICHARD WIGMORE/R

Brewer, John Hyatt (*b* Brooklyn, NY, 18 Jan 1856; *d* Brooklyn, 30 Nov 1931). Organist and composer. He was a boy soprano in various Brooklyn and New York churches (1864–71) and studied organ and composition with DUDLEY BUCK. He served as organist of several Brooklyn churches and, for the last 50 years of his life, of the Lafayette Avenue Presbyterian Church. From 1899 to 1906 he taught at Adelphi College. An omnipresent leader of amateur choruses, Brewer conducted the Boylston, Brooklyn Hill, Damrosch, Flatbush, and Orpheus glee clubs, the Cecilia Ladies' Vocal Society, and the Hoadley Amateur Orchestra. In 1903 he succeeded Buck as conductor of the all-male Apollo Club, having since 1878 served as its accompanist. He was also active as a recitalist and was a Founder, Fellow, and Warden of the American Guild of Organists. In 1914 Brewer received an honorary doctorate of music from New York University. He composed more than 200 works, including church and organ music, a string quartet, and several pieces of programmatic chamber music, an orchestral Suite in G minor (1891) and several large-scale choral works, including *Lord of the Dunderberg* (1905), for male voices and orchestra, as well as other cantatas, both sacred and secular. The New York Public Library holds 24 folders of his manuscript scores.

BIBLIOGRAPHY

R. Hughes: *Contemporary American Composers* (Boston, 1900), 331–4

L. Ellinwood: *The History of American Church Music* (New York, 1953/*R*), 203f

WILLIAM OSBORNE

Brewster, W(illiam) Herbert (*b* Somerville, TN, 2 July 1897/1899; *d* Memphis, TN, 14 Oct 1987). Composer of gospel songs. He attended Roger Williams College in Nashville (BA 1922), then moved to Memphis to become dean of a proposed black seminary which, however, did not materialize, and in 1928 he accepted the pastorate of the East Trigg Baptist Church in Memphis. He also served on the Education Board of the National Baptist Convention and as dean of Shelby County General Baptist Association, and founded and directed the Brewster Theological Clinic at Memphis. Brewster is best known as a composer who made use of sophisticated biblical texts. His first song, "I'm leaning and depending on the Lord," was written in 1939; subsequently he contributed over 200 works to the repertory. Of these, "Move on up a little higher" (1946) and "Surely, God is able" (1949) were the first black gospel recordings to sell over a million copies. Mahalia Jackson, Clara Ward, Queen C. Anderson, and his own group, the

Brewster Ensemble, popularized most of his songs. Brewster also composed more than 15 biblical music dramas, one of which, *Sowing in Tears, Reaping in Joy*, was presented at the Smithsonian Institution (1982).

BIBLIOGRAPHY

A Retrospective of Gospel Music Composer Reverend William Herbert Brewster (Washington, DC, 1982)

H.C. Boyer: "William Herbert Brewster: the Eloquent Poet," *We'll Understand it Better By and By: Pioneering African American Gospel Composers*, ed. B.J. Reagon (Washington, DC, 1992), 211–31 [incl. list of works]

A. Heilbut: "'If I Fail, You Tell the World I Tried': William Herbert Brewster on Record," *We'll Understand it Better By and By: Pioneering African American Gospel Composers*, ed. B.J. Reagon (Washington, DC, 1992), 233–44

B.J. Reagon: "William Herbert Brewster: Pioneer of the Sacred Pageant," *We'll Understand it Better By and By: Pioneering African American Gospel Composers*, ed. B.J. Reagon (Washington, DC, 1992), 185–209

W.H. Wiggins: "William Herbert Brewster: Rememberings," *We'll Understand it Better By and By: Pioneering African American Gospel Composers*, ed. B.J. Reagon (Washington, DC, 1992), 245–51

H.C. Boyer: *How Sweet the Sound: the Golden Age of Gospel* (Washington, DC, 1995)

HORACE CLARENCE BOYER

Brice, Carol (Lovette Hawkins) (*b* Sedalia, NC, 16 April 1918; *d* Norman, OK, 15 Feb 1985). Contralto. She studied at Talladega College, Alabama, and the Juilliard School (1939–43), where she trained under Francis Rogers. While still a student, she appeared with Bill Robinson in *The Hot Mikado* at the New York World's Fair in 1939. In 1941 she sang at a concert to mark the third inauguration of President Franklin Roosevelt and made her recital debut in New York. In 1943 she became the first African American to win the Naumburg Award. Following her Town Hall debut (13 March 1945), she presented a recital on television (CBS, 1945) and appeared with the symphony orchestras of Pittsburgh (1945), Boston (1946), and San Francisco (1948). Her stage performances included the role of the Voodoo Princess in Clarence Cameron White's *Ouanga* (independently given at the Metropolitan in 1956 and at Carnegie Hall), Addie in Blitzstein's *Regina*, Kakou in Arlen's *Saratoga*, Queenie in Kern's *Showboat*, and Maria in *Porgy and Bess* (1961, 1976). Between 1967 and 1971 she appeared at the Vienna Volksoper in *Porgy and Bess*, *Showboat*, and *Carousel*. In 1974 she and her husband, the baritone Thomas Carey, established the Cimarron Circuit Opera Company. Brice's recordings include Falla's *El amor brujo* and arias by Bach; she also participated in the recordings of *Regina* and *Saratoga*, both in 1959, and the Houston Grand Opera's recording of *Porgy and Bess*, which won a Grammy Award in 1978.

BIBLIOGRAPHY

SouthernB

P. Turner: *Afro-American Singers* (Minneapolis, 1977)

DOMINIQUE-RENÉ DE LERMA

Brice, Fanny [Borach, Fania] (*b* New York, NY, 29 Oct 1891; *d* Beverly Hills, CA, 29 May 1951). Performer. Brice grew up in modest circumstances as the daughter of saloon keepers. In 1906, she won an amateur night contest at Frank Keeley's Fulton Street Theater, which aided her rise to stardom on the amateur circuit singing ballads and coon songs. Soon after she worked as a comic in burlesque. She sought out acquaintance Irving Berlin to suggest a number for a burlesque produced by Max Spiegel. Berlin recommended a comic spoof of Salome dancing, called "Sadie Salome." With Brice's Yiddish interpretation of the song, she received a seven-year contract to tour with Spiegel's *The College Girls*. While performing in this show she was officially discovered by Ziegfeld in April 1910. She appeared in the fourth edition of the Ziegfeld *Follies* in 1910, with eight more contracts to follow between 1911 and 1921. Brice debuted in vaudeville in 1911 and performed in other non-Ziegfeld revues, such as Irving Berlin's *Music Box Revue* (1924), and straight theater. She created the role of Baby Snooks in the *Good News of 1938* radio show, which became *The Baby Snooks Show* in 1941.

Brice excelled in improvisation and knew how to work the audience. However, she wanted to be recognized for being more than a comic actor. She possessed a strong alto voice with much flexibility. This allowed for clear text delivery, whether comic or sentimental. A unique song stylist, Brice sang a variety of repertoire from the tender ballad "My Man" to belting "When a Woman Loves a Man."

BIBLIOGRAPHY

B. Grossman: *Funny Woman: the Life and Times of Fanny Brice* (Indianapolis, 1991)

H. Goldman: *Fanny Brice: the Original Funny Girl* (New York, 1992)

SYLVIA STONER-HAWKINS

Brico, Antonia (*b* Rotterdam, Netherlands, 26 June 1902; *d* Denver, CO, 3 Aug 1989). Pianist and conductor of Dutch birth. She immigrated to the United States at the age of six and graduated in 1923 from the University of California at Berkeley. In 1920, she worked as assistant to the Director of the San Francisco Opera. Following further piano study with ZYGMUNT STOJOWSKI in New York, she pursued conducting in Germany at the Hochschule für Musik in Berlin and privately with KARL MUCK from 1927 to 1932. She made her debut as a conductor in Berlin in 1930 and subsequently was a guest conductor for many European orchestras and at the Hollywood (California) Bowl.

Brico returned to the United States in 1932, making appearances in New York with the Musicians Symphony Orchestra and orchestras sponsored by the Federal Music Project of the WPA. In 1934 she founded the Women's Symphony Orchestra of New York, which she conducted until 1938. In 1939 it became known as the Brico Symphony Orchestra. She conducted orchestras in Detroit, Buffalo, Los Angeles, and San Francisco, and in 1938 became the first woman to conduct the New York PO.

During the 1941–2 season, she settled in Denver, Colorado, where in 1948 she founded and conducted the semi-professional Antonia Brico Symphony Orchestra. Also in 1941 she founded a Bach Society and the Women's String Ensemble. After World War II, she was invited by Jean Sibelius to travel to Finland to conduct the Helsinki Symphony Orchestra in several concerts of his works. A documentary film, *Antonia*, made in 1974, about Brico's career and the discouragements she experienced on account of gender prejudice resulted in invitations to conduct leading symphony orchestras again. She also taught piano, conducting, and the history of opera.

CAROL NEULS-BATES/ANYA LAURENCE

Bridge. In popular music and jazz a term applied to a passage in which a formal transition is made. It is used to describe the penultimate section in the refrain of a Tin Pan Alley-style song, leading to the final repeat of the opening section (e.g., section *B* in the form *AABA*); the bridge provides a contrast, often tonal as well as harmonic and melodic, with the opening section. In ragtime and early jazz the bridge is a short section, normally of four or eight bars, that links the separate strains of multithematic compositions; it often incorporates a change of key. In the modal vamps of soul jazz and funk the bridge may simply be an alternative section, typically on the subdominant or dominant, without necessarily having such formal connotations. Rock musicians may call any different section that appears once within an otherwise repeating form the bridge or middle eight. Contemporary usage often tends toward a looser definition of bridge to indicate a contrasting passage.

Bridgewater, Dee Dee [Garrett, Denise Eileen] (*b* Memphis, TN, 27 May 1950). Singer and actress. Born in Memphis and raised in Flint, Michigan, she began singing at an early age and won local talent competitions with a vocal group while in high school. She enrolled in college at Michigan State University, but after playing a jazz festival at the University of Illinois, she accepted the host school's invitation to join their program. She toured with the University of Illinois jazz ensemble and married Illinois grad student and trumpeter Cecil Bridgewater; the two separated in 1972. In the early 1970s Bridgewater performed with the Thad Jones–Mel Lewis Orchestra and recorded with Max Roach, Dizzy Gillespie, and Sonny Rollins. In 1974 she was cast in the Broadway production of *The Wiz*, for which she won the Tony Award. She also made a recording as a leader in 1974, *Afro Blue*, followed by a series of pop-fusion and rhythm-and-blues albums. In the early 1980s Bridgewater moved to France, after traveling there with a touring production of *Sophisticated Ladies*. She found unprecedented success in France, drawing large audiences to stage productions such as *Lady Day* (in which she portrayed Billie Holiday) as well as to jazz concerts. Her recordings during this period were also well received, both in France and the United States. In the 1990s she released a number of albums focused on single artists, including Horace Silver. In 1997 she won the first of three career Grammy Awards for her tribute to Ella Fitzgerald, *Dear Ella*. Bridgewater returned to the United States in the late 1990s, where she began hosting the National Public Radio broadcast "JazzSet" in October 2001.

SELECTED RECORDINGS

Afro Blue (1974, Trio); *Dee Dee Bridgewater* (1976, Atlantic); *Live in Paris* (1986, Impulse!); *Keeping Tradition* (1992, Verve); *Love and Peace: a Tribute to Horace Silver* (1994, Polygram/Verve); *Dear Ella* (1997, Universal/Verve); *This is New* (2001, Universal/Verve); *J'ai deux amours* (2004, Sovereign Artists); *Red Earth* (2006, DDB/Emarcy); *Eleanora Fagan (1917–1959): To Billie with Love from Dee Dee* (2009, DDB/Emarcy)

BIBLIOGRAPHY

H. Reich: "Nobody knows the Trouble she's Seen: Dee Dee Bridgewater," *Let Freedom Swing: Collected Writings on Jazz, Blues, and Gospel* (Evanston, IL, 2010), 318–28

HILARY BAKER

Briegel, George F. (*b* Scranton, PA, 5 June 1890; *d* New York, NY, 12 May 1968). Bandmaster and publisher. He began studying the violin at the age of seven, and from 1905 to 1910 served in the United States Military Academy Band at West Point. He joined Shapiro, Bernstein & Company as a staff arranger and soon developed an excellent reputation that brought him work from many other publishers as well. He played with the 22nd (New York) Regiment Band under Victor Herbert, and then became leader (1914–17). He led a United States Navy band during the war, 1917–18. At one time he was leading six different bands in New York: the Fire Department Band (1920–58), Mecca Temple Shrine Band, Brooklyn Elks' Band, Brooklyn Edison Band, Metropolitan Life Insurance Band, and the 22nd Regiment Band, now renumbered the 102nd Engineer Regiment Band (1920–40). He operated his own music publishing and retail business from 1928 until his death in 1968.

BIBLIOGRAPHY

E. Wickes: "He Leads Five Crack Bands—and How: Meet George F. Briegel," *The Metronome*, xlv/4 (1929), 21, 35

W.H. Rehrig: *The Heritage Encyclopedia of Band Music* (Westerville, OH, 1991, suppl. 1996); CD-ROM (Oskaloosa, IA, 2005) [includes selective list of works]

RAOUL F. CAMUS

Brigham Young University. Private university founded as Brigham Young Academy in Provo, Utah, in 1875 by members of the Church of Jesus Christ of Latter-day Saints. In its second year the institution offered music in the form of extracurricular activities. The School of Music was formally established in 1902. The Music Department became part of the College of Fine Arts and Communications in 1964, and became the School of Music again in 1997. In 2010 the school enrolled 700 majors and employed 52 full-time and 58 part-time faculty members. It offers the following degrees: BA in Music History; BFA in Music Dance Theatre; BM in Jazz Studies, Media Music, Music Composition, Music Education, Performance, and Sound Recording Technology; MA in Musicology; MM in Composition, Conducting, Music Education, and Performance; and a Graduate Minor in Music. Music and Dance Library holdings are estimated at over 400,000 titles. Among its noteworthy special collections are the International Harp Archives and the Primrose International Viola Archive. Other important collections include the Gina Bachauer Archive, Percy Faith Archive, Capitol Records Archive, Joseph

Bonime Archive of Radio Music, RKO Vaudeville Orchestration Archive, John Seymour Collection of Opera and Ballet Scores, Film Music Archives, and items related to Max Steiner and Hugo Friedhofer.

CHRISTOPHER MEHRENS

Bright, Sol(omon) K(amaluhiakekipikealiikaapuniku kealaokamahanahana) (*b* Honolulu, HI, 9 Nov 1909; *d* Honolulu, 27 April 1992). Hawaiian singer, musician, bandleader, composer, and impresario. Sol Bright was a master entertainer of the old school: an energetic showman, accomplished musician, comic hula dancer, composer, raconteur, and entertainment director during Hawaiian music's era of greatest international appeal, the 1920s through the 1960s.

His professional experience began as a teenager playing drums with his sister Hannah's dance band. In 1928 an offer to play rhythm guitar and sing with Sol Hoʻopiʻi took him to *Kaleponi* (California), where a large community of Hawaiian musicians had formed. He started his own group, the Hollywood Hawaiians, in 1932. Playing steel guitar and singing, he recorded prolifically for major labels. He also appeared on radio and in four films: *South Sea Rose*, *Charlie Chan's Greatest Case*, *Flirtation Walk*, and *White Woman*. Bright composed a number of songs that have become standards, including the jazzy English language "Sophisticated Hula" and "Hawaiian Cowboy," a show-stopping novelty song in Hawaiian. With rapid-fire verses, reflective of fast *kepakepa* chanting, it remains an impressive display of virtuosity. In a follow-up, "Hawaiian Scotsman," Bright wore kilts and played bagpipes.

In the late 1940s, Bright kept five Hawaiian music shows going at the same time on the West Coast. Returning to Hawaii in the 1970s, he toured on behalf of Aloha Airlines, produced shows for the Japanese market and worked with many civic organizations. He helped found the Hawaiian Professional Songwriter's Society and was an active member of the Hawaii Steel Guitar Association. His last major appearance was in 1986 on the television movie *Blood and Orchids*.

JAY W. JUNKER

Brill Building. Located at 1619 Broadway in New York, the Brill Building housed the offices of some of the most commercially successful songwriters, producers, and music publishers working between the late 1950s and mid-1960s. The term "Brill Building" additionally has become a descriptor embracing a wide range of popular musical styles that were being created in New York in the early 1960s, including girl groups, bubblegum pop, vocal doo-wop, Latin pop, and soul. In addition to 1619 Broadway, other sites, notably the offices of Don Krishner and Al Nevins's Aldon Music at 1650 Broadway, were also locations that contributed to the Brill Building sound. The Brill Building is credited with fostering skillful songwriting and introducing innovations in popular music production models, following in the tradition of Tin Pan Alley.

Numbers 1619 and 1650 Broadway housed songwriters, producers, and publishers in dozens of small offices and cubicles, where collaboration took place daily. Songwriters, often working under salary, were able to pitch their work to publishers in the same building, while producers could solicit songs for their artists, hire musicians and arrangers, and make recordings in-house, resulting in what has been described as a vertically integrated production structure. This system has been likened to a conveyor belt and the Brill Building to a songwriting factory. While this characterization is accurate in some respects, scholars have argued that it undermines the creativity and innovation that emerged there as a result of close relationships between songwriters, publishers, producers, and artists.

The Brill Building was built in 1931 and originally housed the Brill Brothers clothing company, which began leasing offices to music publishers during the Great Depression. As New York became a major media center in the 1950s, the Brill Building increasingly became a nexus of activity for popular music. The songwriters and producers Jerry Leiber and Mike Stoller (*see* LEIBER AND STOLLER) moved their offices there in the 1950s and, along with DOC POMUS and Mort Shuman, wrote songs which became some of the most important early hits of the Brill Building era. Such songs as Pomus and Shuman's "Turn me loose," a hit for the teen idol Fabian in 1959, used the structures of rock and roll but smoothed out its harder sonic edges, a stylistic move that attracted a wide teenage audience.

In the years that followed, the Brill Building housed several renowned songwriting teams, including BURT BACHARACH and HAL DAVID, NEIL SEDAKA and Howie Greenfield, CAROLE KING and GERRY GOFFIN, Cynthia Weil and Barry Mann (*see* BARRY MANN AND CYNTHIA WEIL), and ELLIE GREENWICH and Jeff Barry. Most started working there while they were in their early 20s, only a few years older than the teenagers who were listening to their records. Their relative youth has been partially credited with their success, as it enabled them to write songs that spoke authentically to the concerns of the teen market. Likewise, women like King, Weil, and Greenwich made significant in-roads for women in the music industry, while writing songs that communicated with female listeners. Many Brill Building songwriters were Jewish, but brought together an array of compositional approaches, many of which had African American origins, including rhythm and blues, rock and roll, and vocal pop. Their songs were recorded by black and white performers alike. This diversity of approach is reflected in the range of artists who recorded Brill Building tunes; these included teen idols (notably Fabian and Bobby Vee), girl groups (the Shirelles, the Ronettes, and the Shangri-Las), singers (Dionne Warwick), and vocal groups (the Drifters and the Righteous Brothers). The producer PHIL SPECTOR also worked closely with Brill Building songwriters, notably Greenwich and Barry, and recorded songs including "Be my baby," with the Ronettes, and "River Deep, Mountain High," with Ike and Tina Turner.

While music publishers and record producers in the Brill Building had begun as distinct business entities, some publishers, taking advantage of the in-house production structure already in place, made the next logical step and began recording and releasing their own records. Such labels as Lieber and Stoller's Red Bird and Nevins and Krishner's Dimension increased the control that publishers had over songs, ensuring a larger share of the profits.

The Brill Building arguably set the stage for the rise of the singer-songwriter in the later 1960s, as its alumni King, Sedaka, and Jackie DeShannon went on to pursue fruitful solo careers. The in-house production model influenced the working practices of such record labels as Motown Records, and the high standard of songwriting that developed on Broadway has been cited as an influence by countless subsequent artists.

BIBLIOGRAPHY

M.E. Rohlfing: "Don't Say Nothin' Bad about my Baby: a Re-evaluation of Women's Roles in the Brill Building Era of Early Rock 'n' Roll," *Critical Studies in Mass Communication*, xiii/2 (1996), 95–114

T.E. Scheurer: "The Beatles, the Brill Building, and the Persistence of Tin Pan Alley in the Age of Rock," *Popular Music and Society*, xxiv/4 (1996), 89–102

I. Inglis: "Some Kind of Wonderful: the Creative Legacy of the Brill Building," *AM*, xxi (2003), 214–35

K. Emerson: *Always Magic in the Air: the Bomp and Brilliance of the Brill Building Era* (New York, 2005)

T. Fletcher: *All Hopped Up and Ready to Go: Music from the Streets of New York, 1927–1977* (New York, 2009)

J. Leiber, M. Stoller, and D. Ritz: *Hound Dog: the Leiber and Stoller Autobiography* (New York, 2009)

J. Stratton: "Jews Dreaming of Acceptance: from the Brill Building to Suburbia with Love," *Jews, Race, and Popular Music* (Farnham, 2009)

ALEXANDRA M. APOLLONI

Brindis de Salas, Claudio José Domingo (*b* Havana, Cuba, 4 Aug 1852; *d* Buenos Aires, Argentina, 1 June 1911). Cuban violinist. He was the son of the violinist, composer, and dance orchestra conductor Claudio Brindis de Salas (1800–72) and received his early musical training from him and from another black musician, José Redondo. His talent came to light at an early age, and he became a pupil of the Belgian José Van der Gucht, who played first violin in several groups in Havana. In 1869 Brindis de Salas traveled to Paris and entered the Conservatoire, where he studied with Charles Dancla, David, Sivari, and Léonard, and won a *premier prix*. He subsequently traveled to Milan, Berlin, St. Petersburg, and London. In 1875 he toured various cities of Central and South America, reappearing in Havana in 1877 to great critical acclaim. His success prompted the coining of such nicknames as "the Black Paganini" and "the King of the Octaves." He was much in demand in European and American concert halls, and occasionally returned to Cuba. From 1880 to 1900 he lived in Berlin, where he served Emperor Wilhelm II of Prussia, who made him a baron. He wrote a few pieces for violin, including a *barcarola*, but did not achieve recognition as a composer. His performances were noteworthy for their brilliance and subtlety, his agility in portamentos, his powerful and flexible bow, and perfect rendition of virtuoso passages. In later life his performing abilities declined, and he died in poverty.

BIBLIOGRAPHY

A. Carpentier: *La música en Cuba* (Mexico City, 1946, 2/1979)

E. Martín: *Panorama histórico de la música en Cuba* (Havana, 1971)

N. Guillén: *Brindis de Salas* (Havana, 1979)

A. Toledo: *Presencia y vigencia de Brindis de Salas* (Havana, 1981)

E. Casares Rodicio, J. López-Calo, and I. Fernandez de la Cuesta, eds.: *Diccionario de la música española e hispano-americana*, ii (Madrid, 1999), 701 only

R. Giró: *Diccionario enciclopédico de la música en Cuba* (Havana, 2007), i, 161–2

VICTORIA ELI RODRÍGUEZ

Brinkerhoff [née Rolph], **Clara M.** (*b* London, England, 8 Sept 1828; *d* after 1901). Soprano and music teacher of British birth. Born in London, she came to the United States as a young child. Her mother was a singer trained in the Italian school who provided her early musical education. At age 12, after her mother's death, she continued her studies with Henry Derwort, Mlle Arnault, George Loder, and Eliza Loder. Although she was encouraged to pursue an operatic career, she chose to concentrate on English song and oratorio singing. She made her debut in 1844 at age 16 at Apollo Hall in New York. She married C.E.L. Brinkerhoff in 1848 but continued to perform in New York and throughout the United States. In 1861 she traveled to Europe, singing in London and Paris, and attending voice classes at the Paris Conservatoire. Returning to New York, Brinkerhoff continued to sing and increasingly focused on teaching. In addition, she composed a number of songs, many of which became well known. She was well known in American musical circles, counting among her friends the pianist Louis Moreau Gottschalk.

BIBLIOGRAPHY

F.O. Jones, ed.: *A Handbook of American Music and Musicians* (Canaseraga, NY, 1886/*R*)

W.S.B. Mathews: *A Hundred Years Of Music in America* (Chicago, 1889/*R*)

F.E. Willard and M.A. Livermore, eds.: *Woman of the Century: Fourteen Hundred-Seventy Biographical Sketches Accompanied by Portraits of Leading Women in All Walks of Life* (Buffalo, NY, 1893)

"New York Letter," *Musical Record* (January 1897), 12

O. Thompson, ed.: *International Cyclopedia Of Music And Musicians* (New York, 1964)

LAURIE BLUNSOM

Brion, Jon (*b* Glen Ridge, NJ, 11 Dec 1963). Producer, composer, songwriter, drummer, guitarist, pianist, bass player, keyboard player, and vibraphonist. Born into a musical family he left high school early to play music. He performed in Boston in the late 1980s and then moved to Los Angeles, where he worked as a sideman, songwriter, and producer with various musicians he knew from Boston including the singer-songwriter Aimee Mann. He became known as an indispensible studio session musician and producer.

Although Brion is a prolific songwriter, he is perhaps best known for his varied projects as a producer and composer, which have spanned pop, rock, jazz, hip hop, and bluegrass. Among the artists that he has produced are Fiona Apple, Beck, Dido, Brad Mehldau, of Montreal, Elliott Smith, Rufus Wainwright, and Kanye West. Brion often plays and co-writes for his productions. He has also written scores for films, including

Magnolia (1999), *Punch-Drunk Love* (2002), *Eternal Sunshine of the Spotless Mind* (2004), *I Heart Huckabees* (2004), *The Breakup* (2006), *Synecdoche, New York* (2008), and *ParaNorman* (2012)

For almost ten years from 1997 Brion maintained a weekly residency at the club Largo in Los Angeles, where he garnered a dedicated underground following. At these solo concerts, which continues to hold monthly, he performed as a singer and instrumentalist, looped live mixes on stage, and eschewed a pre-determined setlist. He has released an album with the quartet the Grays (*Ro Sham Bo*, Epic, 1994) and another, *Meaningless* (Straight to Cutout, 2001), under his own name.

STEPHANIE CONN

Bristow, George Frederick (*b* Brooklyn, NY, 19 Dec 1825; *d* New York, NY, 13 Dec 1898). Composer, conductor, teacher, and performer. He was the son of English immigrants Anna (Tapp) and William Richard Bristow (1803–67), the latter a New York conductor, teacher, concert-organizer, and performer (organ and clarinet). Bristow's principal teachers were his father (piano), HENRY CHRISTIAN TIMM and George Macfarren (composition), and C.W. Meyrer, and OLE BULL (violin). An influential mentor was William Musgrif, an accomplished cellist and founding member of the Philharmonic Society.

Bristow made his first public appearance on piano at the age of nine and shortly thereafter joined his father in the orchestra of an unknown New York theater. Three years later both Bristows became members of the Olympic Theatre orchestra, a small ensemble of seven that accompanied burlesques, extravaganzas, and operas. Bristow later wrote that the technical demands he mastered because of this ensemble, combined with encouragement from Musgrif (another member), convinced him to pursue music as a career. In 1843 (not in 1842, as reported elsewhere), Bristow joined the first violin section of the Philharmonic Society of New York, which was in its second season; he remained a member (with one short hiatus) until 1879. As an active and accomplished freelance musician, Bristow performed regularly, accompanying singers and choral ensembles (organ and piano), playing chamber music and appearing as a soloist with the Philharmonic Society (piano and violin), and performing in orchestras such as the ensemble that accompanied Jenny Lind in her New York concerts (1850–51) and in Louis Jullien's Orchestra, which visited America in 1853–4. He began conducting in 1842 and was an active conductor for most of his life, later leading such choral groups as the New York Harmonic Society (1851–62), the Mendelssohn Union (1867–71), and the Harlem Mendelssohn Union (1871–3) in performances of large choral and orchestral works. He also served as choir director at a number of New York churches, including St. George's Chapel (1854–60) and (during the 1880s) Holy Trinity Church and the First Collegiate Reformed Church (both in Harlem), and the Church of the Divine Paternity and St. Ignatius Church (in Manhattan). Bristow also contributed significantly to music education throughout his life. He was a teacher in the New York public schools from 1854 to 1898, taught privately for most of his life, and wrote many pedagogical works.

Bristow began composing in his teens, and by the early 1850s had written over 30 works, most for piano, chamber ensemble, or orchestra. He earned some renown in New York with his early works for large ensemble, for his Overture in E♭ Major (op.3, 1845) was the first orchestral work by a native-born American that the Philharmonic Society performed. This ensemble also mounted performances of Bristow's first two symphonies, Sinfonia, op.10 (in an open rehearsal,1853) and Symphony No.2, "The Jullien," op.24 (in 1856). This attention to Bristow's orchestral music is particularly notable because during this period the Philharmonic Society programmed almost no other works by American composers. Bristow's compositions from this period are influenced by European style in harmonic, melodic, rhythmic, and formal characteristics, and reflect significant trends and tastes in New York at midcentury. His orchestral compositions are strongly influenced by the musical styles of Beethoven and Mendelssohn, whose works were performed frequently by the Philharmonic Society.

In early 1854 Bristow was drawn into a heated controversy between the Americanist William Henry Fry and the conservative music editor Richard Storrs Willis about American critics' responsibility to encourage native musicians. The focus of the argument quickly shifted to the Philharmonic Society's neglect of American composers, about which New York musicians had been complaining for years. The anti-Philharmonic Society perception was exacerbated by conductor Jullien's commissions of American works (including compositions by Fry and Bristow), and by his regular programming of pieces written in America. This "musical battle" had an important impact on Bristow. During the contretemps, he resigned from the Philharmonic Society orchestra and announced his intention to establish a rival American Philharmonic Society (which apparently never materialized). He rejoined the orchestra for the 1855–6 season, but later helped to establish other music groups in New York that had varying degrees of nationalistic purpose, including the American Music Association (1855–8) and the Metropolitan Music Association (1859). He also regularly programmed American as well as European works for his choral ensembles. Furthermore, although Bristow's subsequent compositions remained predominantly European in orientation, he increasingly turned his attention to Americanist subject matter; examples include the opera *Rip Van Winkle* (1855), *Columbus* Overture (1861), *Arcadian Symphony* (1872), *The Pioneer* (1872), *The Great Republic*: *Ode to the American Union* (1880), *Jibbenainosay* Overture (1889), and *Niagara Symphony* (1893). He remained a proselytizer for the development of American musical culture for the rest of his life.

Bristow functioned as a pillar of the New York musical community (as performer, composer, and teacher) for most of his life. He was a member (and sometimes officer) of the Philharmonic Society until 1879, wrote his final compositions in 1896, and was in a public school classroom when he collapsed and died in 1898. For decades a hard-working and conscientious musician, Bristow was well known and celebrated in New York even late in his career when he was no longer at the forefront of American music. Occasional biographical essays published in the 1880s and 90s (and obituaries) praised the composer, summarized his accomplishments, applauded his dedication to American music, and attributed his relative obscurity both to bias against American composers and to his modest and unassuming nature.

Bristow's best-known works include his opera *Rip Van Winkle* and oratorio *Daniel*; both are available in modern editions. His Symphony (Sinfonia) no.2 ("The Jullien," 1853), which Louis Jullien commissioned and performed in the United States and UK in the mid-1850s, has been edited and was published in the MUSA series. Three of his symphonies—no.2, no.3 (1858), and two movements of no.4 ("The Arcadian," 1872) were recorded in the 1960s in the Society for the Preservation of the American Musical Heritage series (Karl Krueger, conductor); Symphony no.3 was also released in 1993 on compact disc. A smattering of other works have been published or recorded. Many, however, remain undeservedly unknown. The chamber works, which were written during his early years, are especially laudable representatives of a genre rarely explored by American composers in the 19th century; notable examples include his two string quartets, two duos for violin and viola, and the violin sonata. These works—in addition to the "Arcadian" and "Niagara" symphonies, numerous songs, and piano pieces—reveal a talented 19th-century American composer. Holograph copies of his music are in the Bristow Collection at the New York Public Library. A valuable autobiographical sketch, "Life of a Musician" (also at *NYp*) shows a strong sense of humor and provides important information about his early life.

WORKS

(selective list)

printed works published in New York unless otherwise stated; MSS of unpublished works mainly in NYp; for more detailed list see Rogers

DRAMATIC

Rip Van Winkle (op.3, J.H. Wainwright, after W. Irving), op.22, 1852–5; New York, Niblo's Garden, 27 Sept 1855; rev. 1878–82 (J.W. Shannon), vs pubd (1882/*R*, ed. S. Ledbetter, New York, 1991)

Daniel (orat, W.A. Hardenbrook), solo vv, SATB, orch, op.42, 1866, lib. pubd (1867, facs. ed. D. Griggs-Janower, Madison, WI, 1999)

King of the Mountains (op, M.A. Cooney), op.80, 1894, inc.

SACRED VOCAL

(for SATB, org, unless otherwise stated)

To the Lord our God (sentence), SATB, op.15, 1850; I will arise (sentence) [op.23], ?1853; Morning Service (TeD, Jub, Ky), E♭, op.19 (1855), TeD pubd separately (1888); Gloria Patri, Praise to God, solo vv, SATB, orch, op.31, vs pubd as op.33 (Boston, MA, 1860); Evening Service (Bonum est, Benedic anima mea), op.36 (1865); Christ our Passover (Easter Anthem), op.39, ?1866; The Lord is in his holy temple (sentence), S, A, T, B, org, op.40, ?1866; rev. 1891 (inc.); 4 Offertories, op.48, ?1870; Morning Service (TeD, Bs), op.51, ?1873; TeD pubd (1873); Easy Morning Service, F [op.58], ?1881; There is joy today, SATB, pf, in *Tonic Sol-Fa Advocate* (Nov 1882); Holy Night, SATB, pf, in *Tonic Sol-Fa Advocate* (Nov 1884); Evening Service, G [op.56], 1885; Mass, C, solo vv, SATB, orch, op.57, 1885; Christmas Anthem (Light flashing into the darkness) (J. Elmendorf), op.73, 1887; O bells of Easter morning, SATB, pf, in *Tonic Sol-Fa Advocate* (March 1887); Where the holly boughs are waving, SATB, pf, in *Tonic Sol-Fa Advocate* (Nov 1887); Easter Anthem, solo vv, SATB, org [op.77], ?1894; Except the Lord build the house, SA, chorus, org [op.79], ?1894; Sweet is the prayer [after pf study by S. Heller], op.81, ?1894; Come ye that love the Saviour's name [after H. Praher]; I heard a voice from heaven, SATB, org; Oh that the salvation of Israel, SATB, pf/org; O Lord, thy mercy, my sure hope, SATB [op.76] (sketch); There's rest for all in heav'n, 1v, pf; *c*130 hymns, chants, ?1867

SECULAR VOCAL

Choral: Eleutheria. Festival of Freedom, cantata (G.H. Curtis) (1849); Ode, S, female vv, orch [op.29], ?1856; The Pioneer (H.C. Watson), cant., solo vv, SATB, orch, op.49, ?1872 [orig. intended as prel. to Arcadian Symphonie: *see* ENSEMBLE]; The Great Republic, Ode to the American Union (W.O. Bourne), solo vv, SATB, orch, op.47, vs pubd (1880); Niagara Symphony, solo vv, SATB, orch, op.62, 1893; The Bold Bad Baron, male vv, ?1896; Call John, SATB; Ode Written for G.S., 1v, SATB, kbd (kbd part inc.)

Songs, for 1 voice, piano, unless otherwise stated: Thine eye hath seen the spot, ?1846, inc., part quoted in W.T. Upton: *Art-Song in America* (Boston, MA, 1930/*R*; suppl. 1938); The Welcome Back (Boston, MA, 1848); I would I were a favorite flower, in *The Message Bird: a Literary and Musical Journal* (1 Dec 1849); The opening day (W.H. Carew), glee, SATB, pf, in *The Message Bird* (15 Feb 1850); The dawn is breaking o'er us, ?1852; Spring time is coming (Wainwright) (Springfield, MA, 1852); The Abode of Music (M. Marseilles), canzonet, op.31, 1855; The Cantilena: a Collection of Songs, Duets, Trios and Quartetts (1861) [130 works]; Keep step with the music of the Union, unison vv, orch, 1862, vs in *The Centennial School Singer*, ed. G.H. Curtis and W.O. Bourne (1876); Lily Song (1869); A Song of the Hearth and Home (W.P. Durfee) (1869); Only a little shoe (A.D.T. Cone) (1884); Woman's Love, ?1887; The ghost came bobbing up (Shannon); When morning's bright sun, 1v, orch

ENSEMBLE

Orch: Ov., E♭, op.3, 1845; Sinfonia, E♭, op.10, 1848; Captain Raynor's Quickstep, 1849; Serenade Waltz, 1849; Waltz, ?1849; La cracovian, vn, orch, op.13, 1850 [rev. of Duetto concertante, vn, pf, op.1, 1844]; Serenade Nocturne (1851), lost; Jullien Sinfonia, d, op.24, 1853, ed. K. Preston (2011); Winter's Tale, ov., op.30, 1856; Symphonie, f, op.26, 1858; Columbus, ov., op.32, 1861; Arcadian Symphonie, op.50, 1872; Fantasie cromatica con fuga, op.53, 1879 [arr. of J.S. Bach]; Jibbenainosay, ov., op.64, ?1889

Chbr: Duetto concertante, vn, pf, op.1, 1844, rev. as La cracovian, vn, orch, op.13, 1850; Fantasie Zampa, vn, pf, op.17, 1844; Duo no.2, g, vn, va, 1845; Duo no.3, G, vn, va, op.8, 1845; Quartetto, str, F, op.1, ?1849; Quartetto, str, g, op.2, 1849; Vn Sonata, G, op.12, ?1849; Friendship, vn, pf, op.25, ?1855; The Judge, march, pf, perc, op.60, ?1886

KEYBOARD

Pf: Celebrated Zip Coon, with Brilliant Variations (New York, 1840), ed. in J. Bunker: *American Keyboard Music through 1865* (Boston, MA, 1990); Rory O'Moore, variations (1842); Grand waltz de bravura, op.6 (1845); Grand duo…sur…La fille du régiment, pf 4 hands, op.7, 1845; Septour, pf duet, op.16, 1846; Dream of the Ocean (1849) [arr. of J. Gungl]; Duo La fille du régiment, 2 pf, op.5, 1849; Andante et polonaise, op.18, ?1850 (n.d.); A Life on the Ocean Wave, op.21, ?1852; Souvenir de Mount Vernon, op.29 (1861), ed. in J. Gillespie: *Nineteenth-Century American Piano Music* (New York, 1978); Eroica, op.38, ?1865; Raindrops, op.43, ?1867

Impromptu [op.76], ?1883, inc., ed. in S. Glickman: *American Keyboard Music 1866 through 1910* (Boston, MA, 1990); La vivandière, op.51, ?1884; Dreamland, op.59, ?1885; Saltarello [op.61], ?1886; March, op.69, ?1887; Marche-caprice, op.51 (1890); School March, op.63 (Boston, MA, 1893); Plantation Pleasures, op.82, ?1894; Plantation Memories no.2, op.83, ?1895; Plantation Memories no.3, ?1895; March Columbus, inc.; A Walk Around, inc.; arrs., transcrs.

Org: [53] Interludes, in Melodia sacra: a Complete Collection of Church Music, ed. B.F. Baker, A.N. Johnson, and J. Osgood (Boston, MA,

1852); Pot pourri, op.28, 1856; Impromptu Voluntaries, op.45, pubd as 6 Pieces (1883); 6 Easy Voluntaries, op.72, in *George F. Bristow's New and Improved Method for the Reed or Cabinet Organ* (1887)

PEDAGOGICAL WORKS

with F.H. Nash: *Cantata, or Teacher of Singing* (1866, enlarged 2/1868)

George F. Bristow's New and Improved Method for the Reed or Cabinet Organ (1887)

Bristow's Two-Part Vocal Exercises, op.75 (1890–95)

Principal publishers: Pond, G. Schirmer, Ditson, Dodworth

BIBLIOGRAPHY

ANB (J.W. Thomas); *DAB* (C.N. Boyd)

W.M. Thoms: "George F. Bristow, the American Composer," *American Art Journal*, xvi (1876), 133–3; also xxvii (1877), 17–9

K. Merz: "George F. Bristow," *Brainard's Musical World* (Nov 1877); repr. in *Brainard's Biographies of American Musicians*, ed. E. Douglas Bomberger (Westport, CT, 1999), 45–7

W.M. Thoms: "George F. Bristow," *American Art Journal*, xxxvii (1882), 241–2

G.H. Curtis: "G.F. Bristow," *Music* [Chicago], iii (1893), 547–64

"George Frederick Bristow," *The Choir Leader* (1898), 1–2

"George F. Bristow. Violinist and Composer; Sketch of his Life," *Music*, xv (1899), 471–3

D.D. Rogers: *Nineteenth-Century Music in New York City as Reflected in the Career of George Frederick Bristow* (diss, U. of Michigan, 1967)

B.F. Kauffman: *The Choral Works of George F. Bristow (1825–1898) and William H. Fry (1815–1864)* (diss, U of Illinois, 1975)

K.E. Gombert: *"Leonora" by William Henry Fry and "Rip Van Winkle" by George Frederick Bristow: Examples of Mid-Nineteenth-Century American Opera* (diss., Ball State U., 1977)

T.J. Dox: *American Oratorios and Cantatas*, i (Metuchen, NJ, 1986), 25–9, 326

G.M. Fried: *A Study of the Orchestral Music of George Frederick Bristow* (diss., U. of Texas, 1989)

T.J. Dox: "George Frederick Bristow and the New York Public Schools," *AM*, ix/4 (1991), 339–52

S. Ledbetter: *Introduction to George F. Bristow: Rip Van Winkle, Earlier American Music*, xxv (1991)

V.F. Yellin: "Bristow's Divorce," *AM*, xii/3 (1994), 229–54

D. Griggs-Janower: "Rescued from the Fiery Furnace: George Frederick Bristow's Oratorio of *Daniel*," *The Choral Journal*, xxxviii/9 (1998), 9–21

M. Pisani: "'I'm an Indian too': Creating Native American Identities in Nineteenth- and Early Twentieth-century Music," *The Exotic in Western Music*, ed. J. Bellman (Boston, 1998), 218–57

C.E. Gohari: "George Frederick Bristow: Incidental Gleanings," *Society for American Music Bulletin*, xxv (Summer 1999), 4–6

D. Von Glahn: *The Sounds of Place: Music and the American Cultural Landscape* (Boston, MA, 2004)

K.K. Preston: "Encouragement from an Unexpected Source: Louis Antoine Jullien, Mid-century American Composers, and George Frederick Bristow's *Jullien Symphony*," *Nineteenth-century Music Review*, vi/1 (2009), 65–87

K.K. Preston: "American Orchestra Music at the Middle of the Nineteenth Century," *George Frederick Bristow, Symphony no.2 in D Minor, Op. 24 "Jullien,"* Music of the United States of America, xxiii (Madison, WI, 2011)

KATHERINE K. PRESTON (Text, Bibliography);
DELMER D. ROGERS (List of works)

Britain, Radie (*b* nr Silverton, TX, 17 March 1899; *d* Palm Springs, CA, 23 May 1994). Composer. After studying the piano with European-trained teachers in Clarendon, Texas, and Eureka Springs, Arkansas, she enrolled at the American Conservatory, Chicago (BM 1921), where she studied with Heniot Levy, among others. She later studied the organ with Marcel Dupré in Paris (1923), the piano with Adele aus der Ohre in Berlin (1924) and composition with Albert Noelte in Munich (1924), where her first works were performed in 1926. Later that year, she accepted a post at the Girvin Institute of Music and Allied Arts, Chicago. Her orchestral work *Heroic Poem* won the Juilliard National Publication Prize in 1945; other orchestral works were performed by the Illinois SO and the Chicago SO. In 1935 and 1936 Britain was resident at the MacDowell Colony. She eventually settled in Hollywood, California, where she taught the piano and composition and continued to compose.

Britain's music is romantic, colorful, and often programmatic; melody plays a central role in her works and pitch material rarely strays from traditional tonal structures. One of her primary concerns was to forge an immediate connection with her audience. Nature, famous people, and current events inspired many of her compositions, a number of which evoke the American West. Her autobiography is titled *Ridin' Herd to Writing Symphonies* (Lanham, MD, 1996).

WORKS
(selective list)

Stage: Ubiquity (musical drama, L. Luther), 1937; Carillon (op, R. Hughs), 1952; Kuthara (chbr op, 3, Luther), 1960; The Dark Lady Within (musical drama, W. Shakespeare), 1962; Western Testament (musical drama, S.L. Stadelman), 1964; 4 ballets, 2 children's operettas

Orch: Prelude to a Drama (Ov. to Pygmalion), 1928; Sym. Intermezzo, 1928; Heroic Poem, 1929; Rhapsodic Phantasie, pf, 1933; Nocturn, 1934; Light, 1935; Southern Sym., 1935; Drouth, 1939; Ontonagon Sketches, 1939; Pastorale, 1939; Saturnale, 1939; Suite, str, 1940; St Francis of Assisi, 1941; San Luis Rey, 1941; Phantasy, ob, orch, 1942; Jewels of Lake Tahoe, 1945; Red Clay, 1946; Serenata sorrentina, 1946; Umpqua Forest, 1946; Paint Horse and Saddle, 1947; Cowboy Rhapsody, 1956; This is the Place, 1958; Cosmic Mist Sym., 1962; Kambu, 1963; Little Per Cent, 1963; Texas, 1987

Vocal (1v, pf, unless otherwise stated): Had I a Cave (R. Burns), 1925; Half Rising Moon (B. Tabb), 1925; Open the Door to Me (Burns), 1926; Hail Texas (Britain), 1927; Drums of Africa (R.L. Jenkins), chorus, 1934; Elegy (L. Luther), 1937; The Earth Does Not Wish for Beauty (Luther), 1940; Lasso of Time (A. Mckenzie), 1940; Love Still Has Something of the Sea (C. Sedley), 1952; The Star and the Child (J. Lancaster), chorus, 1956; Hush My Heart (A. Halff), 1961; Nisan (K. Hammond), chorus, 1961; Translunar Cycle (Hammond), 1970; many others

Chbr: Portrait of Thomas Jefferson (Epic Poem), str qt, 1927; Legend, vn, pf, 1928; Str Qt, 1934; Prison, vn, pf, 1935; Chipmunks, ww, hp, perc, 1940; Barcarola, vn, pf, 1948; Casa del sogno, vn, pf, 1955; In the Beginning, 4 hn, 1962; Processional and Recessional, 4 trbn, 1969; Hebraic Poem, str qt, 1976; Ode to Nasa, brass qnt, 1981; Soul of the Sea, vc, pf, 1984

Pf: Prelude, 1925; Western Suite, 1925; Dance Grotesque, 1929; Infant Suite, 1935; Wings of Silver, 1951; Cactus Rhapsody, 1953; Sonata, 1958; Les fameux douze, 1965; Epiphyllum, 1966; Ridin' Herd in Texas, 1966; Egyptian Suite, 1969; Invocation, 1977; Anwar Sadat, 1981; Upbeat, 1985; many others, incl. teaching pieces

MSS in Amarillo Public Library, Amarillo, TX; *AUS*; *BLu*; *CA*; Wyoming U. Library, Laramie, WY; *LAum*; *SPma*; *Wc*; *PHf*

Principal publishers: Clayton Summy, C. Fischer, Heroico, Kjos, Ricordi, Seesaw, Wilmark

BIBLIOGRAPHY

EwenD; *GroveW* (K.K. Preston) [incl. further bibliography]

C. Reis: *Composers in America: Biographical Sketches* (New York, 4/1947/R, rev. and enlarged edn of *American Composers*)

W.B. and N.G. Bailey: *Radie Britain: a Bio-bibliography* (Westport, CT, 1990)

WALTER B. BAILEY

British American music. *See* EUROPEAN AMERICAN MUSIC.

British invasion. A term which gained currency with critics and fans to describe the unprecedented popularity of British performers in the United States around the period 1963–6, beginning with the success of the Beatles' first North American tour; it makes ironic reference to the invasion of British armies during the American colonists' War for Independence. Many of the invasion's four-member male pop ensembles were such Beatles look-alike bands as Herman's Hermits and the Dave Clark Five, with lineups comprising two guitars, bass, and drums. Others, notably the Rolling Stones and the Animals, modeled themselves in opposition to the Beatles, with sounds closer to American rhythm-and-blues than to the Beatles' dulcet harmonies. Another important segment of the British invasion comprised solo singers: among these, Dusty Springfield, Petula Clark, Cilla Black, Lulu, and Tom Jones achieved the most enduring success. Taken together, British bands and solo singers left an indelible imprint on transatlantic popular music and culture in the 1960s, supplying some of the era's most memorable songs, many of which have become associated with mid-1960s swinging London. These include the Beatles' "I want to hold your hand" and "She loves you," Dusty Springfield's "I only want to be with you" (written by Ivor Raymonde), Petula Clark's "Downtown" (Tony Hatch), Lulu's "To Sir with Love" (Don Black and Mark London), Herman and the Hermits' "Mrs. Brown you've got a lovely daughter" (Trevor Peacock), and Gerry and the Pacemakers' "Ferry 'Cross the Mersey." In 1966 "Georgy Girl," composed by Tom Springfield and Jim Dale as the theme for a British film of the same name, was nominated for an Academy Award for Best Original Song.

The inspiration and stylistic foundation for the British invasion sound, including that of the Beatles, was American popular music—rock and roll, the girl groups, doo-wop, and even ersatz folk music—of the preceding era. Although British musicians were exporting their music to the United States, they were armed with American sounds. All of the British invasion bands and solo performers acknowledged a fundamental stylistic debt to Elvis Presley, Little Richard, Smokey Robinson and the Miracles, Chuck Berry, the Shirelles, the Chantels, Frankie Lymon and the Teenagers, the Ronettes, the Cookies, the Isley Brothers, and the Contours. They even presented cover versions of songs previously recorded by these artists to American audiences; for example, the Beatles' first two official US albums, *Meet the Beatles!* and *The Beatles' Second Album* (both Capitol Records), contained cover songs such as"Chains" (originally recorded by the Cookies), "Baby it's you" (the Shirelles), "Twist and Shout" (the Top Notes and the Isley Brothers), "Roll over Beethoven" (Chuck Berry), "You really got a hold on me" (Smokey Robinson and the Miracles), and "Please Mister Postman" (the Marvelettes).

While American markets welcomed the Beatles-led British invasion performers, American artists found it difficult to establish themselves in Britain because their US hits were covered in the UK by British performers just weeks after the original version had been released in the United States. For example, the Contours' "Do

The Who: Keith Moon (drummer), Roger Daltrey (singer), John Entwistle (bass guitar), and Pete Townshend (lead guitar), 1969. (RA/Lebrecht Music & Arts)

you love me" was covered there by Brian Poole and the Tremeloes, and Dionne Warwick's "Anyone who had a Heart" by both Cilla Black and Dusty Springfield. This practice effectively stopped once US labels, notably Motown, made transatlantic distribution deals allowing US artists to release their records abroad with little delay. US demand for British performers, while never rising to the level of the mid-1960s British invasion has remained consistently strong since that time.

BIBLIOGRAPHY

B. Miles: *The British Invasion: the Music, the Times, the Era* (New York, 2009)

P.J. Smith: "Brit Girls: Sandi Shaw and the Women of the British Invasion," *She's so Fine: Reflections on Whiteness, Femininty, Adolescence and Class in 1960s Music*, ed. L. Stras (Farnham, 2010), 137–62

ANNIE J. RANDALL

Britton, Allen P(erdue) (*b* Elgin, IL, 25 May 1914; *d* DeKalb, IL, 17 Feb 2003). Music educator, scholar, and administrator. He obtained degrees in instrumental music (BS 1937) and in education and English (MA 1939) from the University of Illinois at Champaign-Urbana, and in musicology from University of Michigan (PhD 1950). He taught music and English in the public schools of Griffith, Illinois (1938–41), and in the laboratory school at Eastern Illinois State Teachers College (1941–3). After serving in the US Army during World War II (1943–6), he completed his doctoral studies and joined the music faculty at the University of Michigan (1949), where he established a leading doctoral program in music education and directed 51 doctoral dissertations. He served as dean of the School of Music (1969–79) and retired from the faculty in 1984. Britton was president of the Music Educators National Conference (MENC) (1960–62) after serving on the MENC Music Education Research Council (1954–60) and editorial committee of the *Music Educators Journal* (1954–60). He participated in the Yale Seminar on Music Education (1963), Tanglewood Symposium on Music Education (1967), and numerous other important conferences, councils, and task forces. The author of 95 publications, Britton was an early leader in Americanist musicology and the history of music education, with special focus on colonial singing schools. He was editor of the *Foundations of Music Education* series (Englewood Cliffs, NJ, 1966–71), founded (with colleague Marguerite V. Hood) and edited the world's first scholarly journal in music education, the *Journal of Research in Music Education* (1953–72), and co-founded and edited (1982–85) the musicology journal *American Music*. Britton was inducted into the Music Educators Hall of Fame in 1986 and received the MENC Senior Researcher Award in 1990. The Britton Recital Hall at the University of Michigan was dedicated on 27 October 1996, and a symposium in his honor was held at the University of Maryland, College Park, in March 2000. His papers are held at the MENC Archives, University of Maryland.

BIBLIOGRAPHY

G.N. Heller: "Allen Perdue Britton and 'The Study of Music: An Academic Discipline," *Journal of Historical Research in Music Education*, xxii/2 (2001), 94–109

M. McCarthy and B.D. Wilson, eds., "Papers from the Allen P. Britton Symposium," *Journal of Historical Research in Music Education*, xxii/2 (2001) [includes lists of publications and dissertation advisees]

J.T. Humphreys: "A Tribute to *JRME* Founder Allen Perdue Britton," *JRME*, li/1 (2003), 4–5

PAULA MORGAN/JERE T. HUMPHREYS

Broadbent, Alan (*b* Auckland, New Zealand, 23 April 1947). Pianist, composer, and arranger of New Zealand birth. He was classically trained but developed a voracious appetite for jazz as a teenager and enrolled in the Berklee College of Music in 1966 to study composition and arranging. On weekends he traveled to New York for lessons with Lennie Tristano. He toured with Woody Herman from 1969 to 1972, which garned him a Best Arranger award from *Downbeat* and two Grammy writing nominations. After moving to Los Angeles, he spent ten years as Nelson Riddle's pianist and also worked with David Rose, Johnny Mandel, Henry Mancini, and Irene Kral. From 1987 he has played alongside Charlie Haden in the ensemble Quartet West. His albums as a leader include trio, duo, and solo settings. He has also collaborated with Michael Feinstein and the Israel Philharmonic Orchestra. Broadbent's arrangements, and his string writing in particular, are lush and inventive; this work, which has garnered two Grammy Awards, has graced projects with prominent artists such as Mel Tormé, Scott Hamilton, Natalie Cole, and Diana Krall.

JEFFREY HOLMES

Broadcasting. *See* Radio broadcasting; Radio, college; Radio, community; Television music.

Broadcast Music, Inc. [BMI]. Performing rights licensing organization founded in 1940. In addition to its primary activity of licensing the works of its writer and publisher affiliates to the users of music in copyright (*see* Performing rights societies), BMI sponsors the BMI-Lehman Engel Musical Theatre Workshop, the BMI Awards to Student Composers competition (founded 1951), and numerous symposia for songwriters around the country; additionally, it provides an advisory service to help writers and publishers with issues such as finance and investment. BMI also gives annual awards to songwriters, composers, and performers. The board of directors of BMI is drawn from the broadcasting industry. BMI is a member of CISAC.

For bibliography, *see* Copyright; Performing rights societies.

BARBARA A. PETERSEN/R

Broadhurst, Dorothea (*b* St. Mary Newington, Surrey, England, 1774; *d* Charleston, SC, 1 Oct 1802). British singer and actress. Broadhurst was performing on the New York stage as early as 1797, and in subsequent years participated in theatrical productions in several cities along the Atlantic coast, singing popular airs and in English operas. Contemporaries praised the quality of her voice and her vocal technique, but not the attractiveness of her person. Broadhurst spent the last year of her life in Charleston, South Carolina, where she had arrived with a theatrical group in the autumn of 1801. During her tenure there she performed at the Charleston Theatre, Vauxhall Garden, and at the exclusive subscription concerts of the St. Cecilia Society. She succumbed to "stranger's fever" (yellow fever) and was buried at St. Philip's Church. An obituary noted that Broadhurst was survived by her widowed mother, whom she had supported since her 14th year.

BIBLIOGRAPHY

C.W. Janson: *The Stranger in America: Containing the Observations Made During a Long Residence in that Country* (London, 1807)

G.C.D. Odell: *Annals of the New York Stage* (New York, 1927/*R*)

N.B. Butler: *Votaries of Apollo: the St. Cecilia Society and the Patronage of Concert Music in Charleston, South Carolina, 1766–1820* (Columbia, SC, 2007)

NICHOLAS MICHAEL BUTLER

Broadside. A single sheet, cheaply printed on one side, sold or handed out on the street or in public places, or posted on walls, containing anything from political messages to advertisements to announcements of the coming end of the world to song texts. In the context of American music it is the latter type that is relevant, and the term "broadside" is often used as shorthand for a song text printed on such a sheet. (*See also* SHEET MUSIC.)

They were also called song sheet, penny ballad, ballet, stall ballad, vulgar ballad, or "come-all-ye," the latter because of the common incipit. These song sheets consisted of one or several song texts arranged in one or two columns on the page, often with decorative woodcut illustrations and/or borders, publisher's name and address, and perhaps a price. Only occasionally was an author or copyright acknowledged. Rarely was music included, because of expense; more usual was a brief notation, "To the tune of…." The editing and assembly (and certainly the printing) of broadsides often took place at well-established print shops, but many sheets were printed at the request of a song's author or performer, and sold by him (very few, if any, were by identifiable women) on the street, in taverns, at markets, and similar locations; or, especially after the Civil War, by mail. Most broadside printers were not well-known sheet music publishers, but many identified themselves as booksellers.

A newspaper article of 1880 describing one publisher and his wares commented, "a majority of the songs that appear in the penny ballad series [owe their] present favor to being sung by a prominent minstrel troupe. A majority of the purchasers of the ballads are working girls, boys and young men who hear the verses sung at a theater or social gathering, where they catch the melody, and, at the expense of a cent for the words, are enabled to try their own vocal powers." (New York *Herald*, 2 Dec 1880)

Of particular interest to social historians and folklorists are songs or ballads addressing particular events: wars, disasters, crimes, political events, and so on, not because they present facts otherwise unknown but for the insights they provide into the attitudes of the public (or some segment of the public) at large. Etymologists sometimes find uses of slang and nonce terminology in cheap print well before occurrences in the mainstream press. Also useful to folklorists are broadsides that include texts of songs and ballads well known in oral tradition. In such cases, of interest is the antecedent, if any, of the text—sometimes a previous broadside (often, prior to the Civil War, a British imprint) or other cheap print document; sometimes from the printer/publisher's own memory; sometimes submitted to the printer by another person.

Important centers of broadside printing were the large northeastern cities, notably Boston, New York, Philadelphia, and Baltimore. Among the first broadside printers to achieve prominence were Nathaniel Coverly (?1744–1816) and his family. Coverly's earliest imprints appeared around 1767, successively in Amherst, Salem, and Boston. He was succeeded by his widow, Eunice Coverly, and then his son, Nathaniel Jr. (?1775–1824), who remained in business until his death. The Coverlys' broadsides included a great many traditional songs probably copied from British printings. They also

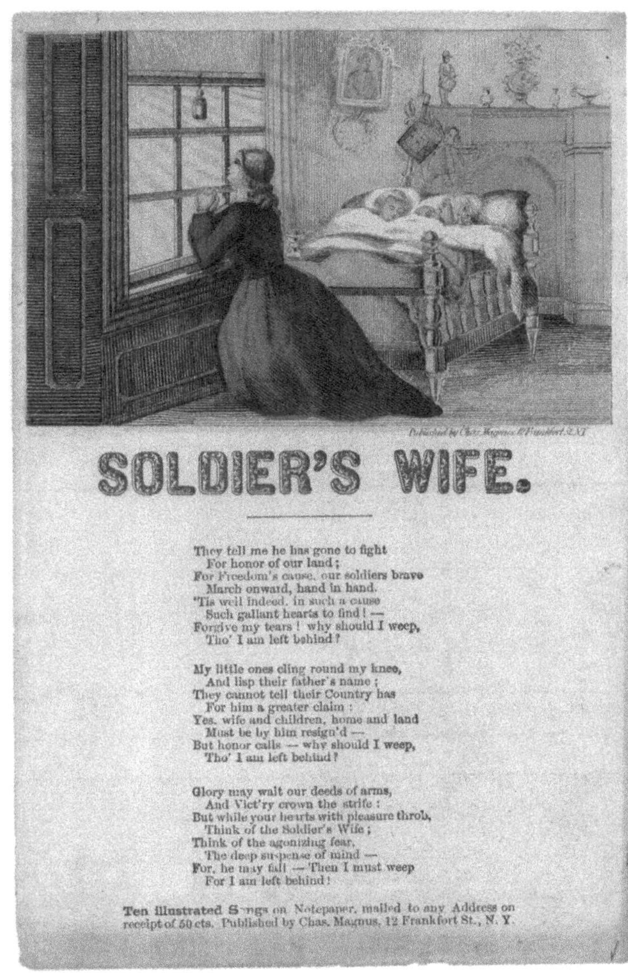

SOLDIER'S WIFE.

They tell me he has gone to fight
For honor of our land;
For Freedom's cause, our soldiers brave
March onward, hand in hand.
'Tis well indeed, in such a cause
Such gallant hearts to find! —
Forgive my tears! why should I weep,
Tho' I am left behind?

My little ones cling round my knee,
And lisp their father's name;
They cannot tell their Country has
For him a greater claim:
Yes, wife and children, home and land
Must be by him resign'd —
But honor calls — why should I weep,
Tho' I am left behind?

Glory may wait our deeds of arms,
And Vict'ry crown the strife:
But while your hearts with pleasure throb,
Think of the Soldier's Wife;
Think of the agonizing fear,
The deep suspense of mind —
For, he may fall — Then I must weep
For I am left behind!

Ten illustrated Songs on Notepaper, mailed to any Address on receipt of 50 cts. Published by Chas. Magnus, 12 Frankfort St., N. Y.

"Soldier's Wife," broadside published by Charles Magnus, Civil War era. (Library of Congress, Rare Book and Special Collections Division, America Singing: Nineteenth-Century Song Sheets)

printed a number of significant ballads from the Revolutionary War period and the War of 1812. An important early Coverly print was "The Yankees Return from Camp" (*c*1810–14), one of the earliest printings of "Yankee Doodle." Another major Boston broadside printer was Leonard Deming (*fl* 1829–40), whose catalog was similar to that of the Coverlys. Deming printed an early American text of a British imported ballad, "The Gosport Tragedy," that was still current in oral tradition in the American Northeast in the 20th century.

By the 1850s a major locus of broadside publishing was New York City, where a group of broadside printers were located at or near Chatham St. from the 1850s through the early 1900s. Prominent among them were John Andrews (*fl* 1853–69), his successor, Henry De-Marsan (1859–78), and Henry J. Wehman (*fl* 1875–1908).

While broadsides, like other forms of cheap print, were not intended for long-term use or survival, they were objects of great interest to some antiquarians, paper collectors, and historians. Large private collections eventually found their way into the hands of libraries, both public and private, whose staffs have had the foresight to treat them with greater reverence than did most of their original purchasers. It is due largely to the careful stewardship of these institutions that the survival of these fascinating pieces of popular literature has been assured. Among the most significant broadside collection owners are the libraries at Harvard, Yale, Princeton, and Brown Universities; the Universities of Pennsylvania, Michigan, and California; the Boston Atheneum, the American Antiquarian Society, the Library Company of Philadelphia, the New York Public Library, the New York State Library, the Massachusetts Historical Society, the Newberry Library, the Huntington Library, the Center for Popular Music at Middle Tennessee State University, and the Library of Congress. The latter two institutions are of particular interest because a large number of their broadside holdings are viewable on their websites. This list of institutions is by no means exhaustive.

BIBLIOGRAPHY

N. Paine: *A List of Early American Broadsides, 1680–1800 Belonging to the Library of the American Antiquarian Society* (Worcester, MA, 1897)

W.C. Ford: *Broadsides, Ballads &c. Printed in Massachusetts, 1639–1800* (Boston, MA, 1922/*R*)

O.A. Winslow: *American Broadside Verse from Imprints of the 17th & 18th Centuries* (1930/*R*)

E.L. Rudolph: *Confederate Broadside Verse: a Bibliography and Finding List of Confederate Broadside Ballads and Songs* (New Braunfels, TX, 1950)

E. Wolf, II: *American Song Sheets, Slip Ballads and Poetical Broadsides, 1850–70* (Philadelphia, 1963)

G.B. Bumgardner, ed. *American Broadsides: 60 Facsimiles Dated 1680 to 1800 Reproduced from Originals in the American Antiquarian Society* (Barre, ME, 1971)

J. Duffy, ed.: *Early Vermont Broadsides* (Hanover, NH, 1975)

M.I. Lowance and G.B. Bumgardner, eds.: *Massachusetts Broadsides of the American Revolution* (Amherst, MA, 1976)

W. Moss: *Confederate Broadside Poems: an Annotated Descriptive Bibliography based on the collection of the Z. Smith Reynolds Library of Wake Forest University* (Westport, CT, 1988)

A. Schrader: "Broadside Ballads of Boston, 1813: the Isaiah Thomas Collection," *Proceedings of the American Antiquarian Society*, xcviii (1988)

D. Yoder: *The Pennsylvania German Broadside: a History and Guide* (University Park, PA, 2005)

K.V.W. Keller: "Nathaniel Coverly and Son, Printers, 1767–1825," *Proceedings of the American Antiquarian Society*, lxvii (2007), 211–52

NORM COHEN

Broadway. Commercial name for the New York theater district. Few of the theaters are actually on Broadway, but many are in the Times Square area. The "Broadway" designation as a term, according to Actor's Equity, refers to a theater with at least 500 seats; off-Broadway houses are smaller.

See MUSICAL THEATER.

Brockenshire, James Opie (*b* Cornwall, England, Jan 1865; *d* Everett, WA, Dec 1938). Bandmaster and composer of British birth. He began studying music at an early age, playing organ in a local church at age six. He immigrated to the United States, and at age 19, enlisted in the band of the 7th Cavalry Regiment (Custer's Cavalry). He was promoted to bandmaster of that band several years later, a position he held until his retirement in 1915. Shortly after his retirement, the United States entered World War I and he was called back into service as a civilian inspector of music and instruments that were being purchased to equip army bands. He was stationed at the Philadelphia Arsenal and was in charge of all army music purchases until his retirement in 1938. Brockenshire wrote more than 20 pieces for band, including *General Chaffee's March*. Rudy Vallee used parts of the trio from the march to create "The Maine Stein Song," which he used as a theme song. Other well-known works include the marches *Glory of the Trumpets* and *The Cavalry Soldier*. Eight of his marches were included in Robert Hoe's *Heritage of the March* series (24).

BIBLIOGRAPHY

N.E. Smith: *Program Notes for Band* (Lake Charles, LA, 2000), 88–9

W.H. Rehrig: *The Heritage Encyclopedia of Band Music* (Westerville, OH, 1991, 2/1996); CD-ROM (Oskaloosa, IA, 2005) [includes selective works list]

WILLIAM H. REHRIG

Brockman, Jane (Ellen) (*b* Schenectady, NY, 17 March 1949). Composer, educator, and pianist. She studied briefly at the University of California at Santa Barbara and Michigan State University before settling at the University of Michigan to complete a BMus in music theory and embark on graduate studies in composition with George Balch Wilson, LESLIE BASSETT, and WALLACE BERRY. Immersed in electronic and experimental music, she also worked with the recently retired ROSS LEE FINNEY and distinguished herself as the first woman to earn a DMA in composition from the University of Michigan in 1977.

Fellowships from the Fulbright Foundation, the Alliance Française, and a Rackham Prize enabled her to study with Max Deutsch and Eugene Kurtz in Paris and Vienna. Other notable honors include a Sigvald Thompson Composition Competition Prize for her first orchestral piece and a Sundance Institute Film Composers' Lab Fellowship to work with Bruce Boughton, HENRY MANCINI, DAVID NEWMAN, and Alan Sylvestri. She has been awarded MacDowell Colony Fellowships on three occasions.

Brockman taught composition and theory at the University of Connecticut, where she established an electroacoustic music studio before moving to Los Angeles to pursue freelance composition in film and television. A persistent advocate of modern music, she served on review panels for the National Endowment for the Arts and on boards of directors for Women in Film and the Society of Composers and Lyricists. In 2005, Brockman established Music & Conversations, a salon-style chamber music concert series featuring world-class musicians and devoted to the performance of a wide array of music including world music and jazz improvisations.

Brockman's early works tend toward atonality. For example, *Tell-Tale Fantasy* (1978) for piano contains improvisational-sounding bursts of notes interrupted by brief contrasting segues that quote works including Arnold Schoenberg's *Six Little Piano Pieces*, op.19, and Charles Ives's *Concord Sonata*. Brockman's compositions frequently combine live performance with electronic media and MIDI technology, as in her work *Ningana* (1989) for clarinet with pitch-to-MIDI convertor and CD. Commissioned by F. Gerard Errante, *Ningana* (a Māori word meaning "resting place") employs tonally directed phrases enhanced with delays, reverb, and synthesized effects in a dreamy soundscape. Inspired by the success of the Music & Conversations series, Brockman's later works largely comprise compositions for small ensembles, such as *Dance of Spirals* (2008) for violin, cello, and piano that one reviewer declared a highly accessible work revealing a range of influence from Schubert to rock.

WORKS
(selective list)

Orch: Perihelion II, str, 1985; Prelude to Nibiru, orch, 1999

Chbr: Nibiru Trio, cl, vn, pf, 1999; Fantasy on a Vodoun Rhythm, vn, a sax, pf, 2003; From Secret Springs, fl, va, vc, pf, 2006; Scenes from Lemuria, cl, str qt, 2006; Law of the Jungle, mar, pf, 2007; Starsail Trio, vn, vc, pf, 2008; Departures, vn, vc, pf, 2009

Solo: Landscapes, pf, CD, 1990; Tenacious Turns, cl, elecs, CD, 1991; Circles in the Sun, cl, CD, 2002; Fireflies, fl, 2003; Mystique, pf 4 hands, 2009

BIBLIOGRAPHY

M.S. Jeffries: *Interviews with Six Women Composers in New England, with an Analysis of a Composition of Each One* (thesis, Connecticut College, 1984)

E. Hinkle-Turner: *Women Composers and Music Technology in the United States: Crossing the Line* (Burlington, VT, 2006)

GARY GALVÁN

Brockway, Howard (*b* Brooklyn, NY, 22 Nov 1870; *d* New York, NY, 20 Feb 1951). Composer, pianist, and teacher. He studied piano with H.O.C. Kortheuer and in 1890 went to Berlin, where he remained for five years, studying composition with OTIS BARDWELL BOISE and piano with Heinrich Barth. A successful concert of his chamber and orchestral pieces was given by the Berlin PO on 23 February 1895. Returning to the United States, he gave many concerts and taught at the Peabody Institute (1903–9), Mannes College, and, from 1910 to 1940, the Institute of Musical Art (which was taken over by the Juilliard Musical Foundation in 1926). He produced few original works after 1911, but his arrangements of Kentucky folksongs, collected with Loraine Wyman, enjoyed popularity in the United States and England. Brockway was a gifted composer, whose works display a rare sensibility and warmth of melody and harmony, best expressed in his numerous song settings. Notable among his larger-scale works are the Violin Sonata and the Cello Suite.

WORKS
(selective list)

Orch: Ballad, op.11, 1894; Sym., op.12, 1894; Cavatina, op.13, vn, orch (1895); Sylvan Suite, op.19 (1900); Scherzo (Scherzino), lost; Pf Conc., inc., lost

Chbr: Sonata, op.9, vn, pf (1894); Moment musical, op.16, vn, pf (1897); Romance, op.18, vn, pf (1897); 3 Compositions: Aria, The Coquette, Romance, op.31, vn, pf (1906); Suite, op.35, vc, pf (1908); Pf Qnt, ?op.38, lost; Fugue, 2 vn, pf

Choral: Cantate Domino, op.6, 1892; 2 Choruses: Wings of a Dove, Hey Nonino, op.24 (1899); Des Saengers Fluch, op.27 (1902); Herr Oluf (J. Herder), op.37 (1913); Matin Song (T. Heywood), op.40 (1911)

Pf: 2 Preludes, 1925, unpubd; other pieces incl. Dreaming, Unrest, At Twilight, An Idyl of Murmuring Water

Songs incl. Would thy faith were mine, Intimations, The Mocking Bird, An Answer

Folksong arrs. incl. Lonesome Tunes (New York, 1916), 20 Kentucky Mountain Songs (Boston, 1920)

MSS in *Wc* and *NYp*

Principal publishers: G. Schirmer, Schlesinger (Berlin), Church (Cincinnati), Margun Music

BIBLIOGRAPHY

R. Hughes: *Contemporary American Composers* (Boston, 1900, 3/1914), 298–304

H. Brockway: "The Quest of the Lonesome Tuner," *Art World*, ii/3 (1917–18), 227–30

Obituary: *New York Times* (21 Feb 1951), 27

BARTON CANTRELL/MICHAEL MECKNA

Broder, Nathan (*b* New York, NY, 1 Dec 1905; *d* New York, 16 Dec 1967). Editor and musicologist. He attended City College, New York, and studied music privately, but as a music scholar he was largely self-educated. His career in editing and music publishing began with his appointment as associate editor of *The Musical Quarterly* (1945–67) and manager of the publications department at G. Schirmer (1945–54); he subsequently became chairman of the publication committee of the American Musicological Society (1952–4), executive director of the American Section of *RISM* (1961–5) and music editor at W.W. Norton & Co., New York (1963–7). He also taught at Columbia University (lecturer 1946–52, associate professor 1959–62) and served as president of the American Musicological Society (1963–4). He received a Guggenheim Fellowship (1956) and a Ford Foundation Grant (1961).

Although Broder's career was devoted largely to guiding and publishing the work of others, he was himself a productive scholar. He published a book of essays, *The Great Operas of Mozart* (featuring the librettos translated by W.H. Auden and others), several articles on Mozart, and a standard edition of Mozart's piano sonatas and fantasias. His main interest was the 18th century, but he was not restricted to it: he also explored Schenkerian analysis, wrote on contemporary Americans including Samuel Barber and William Schuman, and assisted Reese in writing *Music in the Middle Ages* (New York, 1940). He was an energetic reviewer, and his contributions to dictionaries include 70 articles in *MGG1*. At his death he was working on a long-planned history of orchestral music.

WRITINGS

with A. Waldeck: "Musical Synthesis as Expounded by Heinrich Schenker," *The Musical Mercury*, ii (1935), 56–64

"American Music and American Orchestras," *MQ*, xxviii (1942), 488–93

"The Music of William Schuman," *MQ*, xxxi (1945), 17–28

Samuel Barber (New York, 1954/*R*)

"The American Representation in the *International Inventory of Musical Sources*," *FAM*, ix (1962), 15–16

BIBLIOGRAPHY

Grove7 (J. Newsom) [includes additional writings]

P.H. Lang: Obituary, *MQ*, liv (1968), 249–51

G. Reese: "Nathan Broder (1905–1967)," *JAMS*, xxii (1969), 526–27 [obituary]

JON NEWSOM/LAWRENCE SCHENBECK

Brodsky, Jascha (*b* Kharkov, Ukraine, 24 May 1907; *d* Ocala, FL, 2 March 1997). Violinist of Russian birth. The son of a violinist, Brodsky began playing violin at age 6. In his late teenage years, while a student of Eugène Ysaÿe, he won a concerto competition with Prokofiev's Violin Concerto no.1. After completing his studies at the Conservatory of Tiflis in 1924, Brodsky moved to the United States. He continued his training at the Curtis Institute of Music in 1930 and graduated with a Bachelor of Music in Violin and Chamber Music in 1934.

He began playing first violin in the Curtis string quartet in 1932 and continued performing in the quartet until 1981, the year of the death of the quartet's violist, Max Aronoff. This American-trained group was the first such ensemble to visit Europe, which it did in 1935 after being invited by the British Broadcasting Corporation. While at Curtis he was a student of Efrem Zimbalist and studied chamber music with Dr. Louis Bailly.

Brodsky was an instructor of violin at Curtis in 1932–3 and 1941–2, and from 1956 until he retired in 1996. He also taught at Philadelphia's New School of Music and Temple University. He received an honorary doctorate from the Curtis Institute in 1986 and in 1990 was awarded the American String Teachers Association's Artist Teacher Award. Many of his protégés are still active in both solo and orchestral careers, including Hilary Hahn, Joey Corpus, Elizabeth Pitcairn, and Daniel Yoo. He is remembered by his students as both an excellent performer and teacher, who took a very detail-oriented and meticulous approach, indicating how every phrase and note was to be practiced and performed. Such an approach seems natural in light of his belief that "music is the whole life." A small archive of Brodsky materials is held by the Curtis Institute Library.

BIBLIOGRAPHY

Obituary, *New York Times* (6 March 1997)

DANIEL JOHN CARROLL

Brody, Martin (*b* Chicago, IL, 8 July 1949). Composer and writer on music. The son of a jazz musician, he first studied the piano and cello, and later worked as a jazz and rock musician. He began composing music while a student of Lewis Spratlan and Donald Wheelock at Amherst College. After further study in composition at Brandeis University with Seymour Shifrin, and in computer music with Barry Vercoe at MIT, he was awarded a doctorate (1981) at Yale University, where his main teachers were Yehudi Wyner and Robert Morris. His honors include an Academy-Institute Award from the American Academy of Arts and Letters; commissions from the Fromm Foundation, the Massachusetts Cultural Council, and the National Endowment for the Arts; fellowships from the Bogliasco Foundation and the John Simon Guggenheim Foundation; and the Fromm Residency in Musical Composition at the American Academy in Rome. Brody has taught at MIT, Bowdoin College, Mount Holyoke College, and Brandeis, and in 1992 he was appointed Catherine Mills Davis Professor of Music at Wellesley College, where he had been a member of the faculty since 1979. He was also Executive Director of the Thomas J. Watson Foundation from 1987 to 1989, and for three years (2007–10) he served as Andrew Heiskill Arts Director at the American Academy in Rome.

Brody's compositional work encompasses music for the popular media in, for example, numerous productions for the Public Broadcasting System and the film *The Brother from Another Planet* (1980), as well as the concert hall. As his focus has shifted from densely woven atonal chamber music in such works as *What the Dead Know* (1987) to the more transparent textures of narrative theatrical works, his musical language has remained essentially harmonic: contrapuntal surfaces emerge from the prolongation of jazz-derived chords. *Heart of a Dog* (1990–92), which sets an early 20th-century Russian tale in an idiom that incorporates both operatic and rap styles, and *Earth Studies* (1993–5), which integrates dance and opera, both exemplify the power and flexibility of such a harmonic language. Following on these large-scale theatrical works, and in response to commissions often originating in the musical community of Boston, Brody has produced a steady succession of solo instrumental, vocal, chamber, choral, and orchestral compositions, characterized by a supple lyricism within an elastic rhythmic framework, both of which are enabled by an increasingly refined and fluid system of harmonic support. Together, these qualities have produced enthralling musical expressions of mystery and beauty.

Ranging from technical articles for a professional readership to general cultural criticism directed towards a broader audience, Brody's critical work has grown to constitute a contribution to the literature on American music unusually well focused on that music's relation to its broader cultural and political context. Among the

American composers on whom he has written are Harbison, Morris, Sessions, Copland, Wolpe, and Babbitt; for example, in "Music for the Masses: Milton Babbitt's Cold War Music Theory" (1993) he argues that the antecedents of late 20th-century American music theory can be found in the mid-century literary and political culture of the "New York intellectuals." Much of his work on American music has been concerned with tracing the transition in American musical culture from American regionalism to non-sovereign individualism.

WORKS

Stage: Heart of a Dog (chbr op, 1), 1990–2; Earth Studies (chamber ballet/orat.), 3 singers, 3 insts, tape, 6 dancers, 1994–6

Orch: Concertino, chbr orch, 1978; Ritornelli, pf, orch, 1985; Touching Bottom, 2011

Chbr: Duo, fl, pf, 1976; Music For Cellos, 2 vc, 1977; Commedia, vc, pf, perc, 1987; Anthem, 4 tpt, 1993; Reliquary: Nun Komm, ob, str trio, 1994; D.C., 4 perf, 1999; Book of Hours, pf trio, 2002; Chaconne, pf, vc, perc, 2006

Solo: Saxifrage, pf, 1975; Nocturnes, fl, 1979; Moments Musicaux, pf, 1980; Apparitions, pf, 1981; Voices, vn, 1983; G Corona, pf, 1998

Vocal: Casabianca, 3 songs (E. Bishop), S, ob, vn, 1988; La Tortuga (P. Neruda), S, vc, 1989; Millennium Sightings, Mez, 10 insts, 1999; Reasons for Moving, S, pf, 2000, vers. for S, 8 insts, 2002; Beasts (J. Merrill, W. Whitman, R. Wilbur), S, 10 insts, 2001; Tree of Life, S, ob, str qt, 2004; Muzot, Oct 1924, S, 6 insts, 2006; Until They Are Free, SATB, 2006

Elec: Turkish Rondo, tape, 1979; Doubles, ww quintet, tape, 1984; What the Dead Know, chbr ens, tape, 1986

WRITINGS

(selective list)

"Sensibility Defined: Set Projection in *Form*, for Piano, by Stefan Wolpe," *PNM*, xv/2 (1976–7), 3–22

"Roger Sessions on Music," *JMT*, xxvii/1 (1983), 111–9

"Criteria for Grouping in Milton Babbitt's *Minute Waltz (or 3/4 +/- 1/8)*," *PNM*, xxiv/2 (1986), 30–78

"MSHJ: Faith and Deeds in *The White Island*, by Donald Martino," *PNM*, xxix/2 (1991), 294–311

"Music for the Masses: Milton Babbitt's Cold War Music Theory," *MQ*, lxxvii/2 (1993), 161–93

"'Haunted by Envisioned Romance': John Harbison's Gatsby," *MQ*, lxxxv/3 (2001), 413–15

"Wolpe's Inner Beauty," *PNM*, xl/2 (2002), 174–82

"A Concrete Element You Work With: Wolpe and the Painters," in *The Fantasy Can Be Critically Examined: On the Music of Stefan Wolpe*, ed. A. Clarkson (Hillsdale, NY, 2003), 245–62

"The Scheme of the Whole: Black Mountain and the Course of American Music," *Black Mountain: an American Experiment*, ed. V. Katz (Cambridge, 2003), 237–67

"Founding Sons: Copland, Sessions, and Berger on Genealogy and Hybridity," *Aaron Copland and His World*, ed. C.J. Oja and J. Tick (Princeton, 2005), 15–46

"'Where to act, how to move': Unruly Action in Late Wolpe," *CMR*, xxvii/2 (2008), 205–25

BIBLIOGRAPHY

R. Taruskin: "Afterword: Nicht blutbefleckt?," *Journal of Musicology*, xxvi/2 (2009), 274–84

STEPHEN DEMBSKI

Broege, Timothy (*b* Belmar, NJ, 6 Nov 1947). Composer, harpsichordist, pianist, organist, and recorder player. Educated at New Jersey public schools and Northwestern University (BMus with highest honors 1969), Broege studied piano with Helen Antonides and Frances Larimer, composition with M. William Karlins and Alan B. Stout, harpsichord with Dorothy Lane, and recorder with Bernard Krainis. He has been organist and director of music at First Presbyterian Church, Belmar, New Jersey, since 1972; he also serves as organist at historic Elberon Memorial Church in Long Branch, New Jersey. His published compositions include the 21 *Sinfonias* for large ensembles, and eight sets of *Songs Without Words* for chamber ensembles. Best known for his band and wind ensemble works, he has also composed for keyboard, guitar, chorus, solo voice, and instrumental duos. Performed throughout the United States and Canada as well as Europe, China, Japan, and New Zealand, Broege's music has been praised for its stylistic diversity and structural integrity. He has appeared in concert in Boston, New York, Chicago, Dallas, Phoenix, and throughout New Jersey. He is published by Manhattan Beach Music, Boosey & Hawkes, Hal Leonard, and Daehn Publications.

BIBLIOGRAPHY

W.H. Rehrig: *The Heritage Encyclopedia of Band Music* (Westerville, OH, 1991, suppl. 1996); CD-ROM (Oskaloosa, IA, 2005) [includes selective list of works]

D.C. Fullmer: *A Comparison of the Wind Band Writing of Three Contemporary Composers: Karel Husa, Timothy Broege, Cindy McTee* (diss., U. of Washington, 2003)

DAVID WHITWELL

Broekman, Hendrik (*b* New York, NY, 11 April 1945). Harpsichord maker and harpsichordist. His father was a successful composer and conductor. He began his musical education at age 11, with lessons in piano and choral singing. He studied piano with John Goldmark at the Mannes College of Music (1963–9), and was later awarded a Harpsichord Music Society scholarship for study with Sylvia Marlowe. He developed an interest in the construction and maintenance of harpsichords, and during the 1960s worked for both Wallace Zuckermann and Eric Herz. Later, he served an apprenticeship with Frank Hubbard (1970–72). From 1972 to 1979 he maintained a shop in Hanover, New Hampshire, where he completed 18 instruments and undertook three restorations.

In 1979, three years after the death of Hubbard, he returned to the latter's shop as technical director. With the retirement of Diane Hubbard in 2000, Broekman became the principal owner of Hubbard Harpsichords, whose instruments have been signed "Hubbard & Broekman" since 1982. Broekman has been responsible for the production of more than 100 finished instruments as well as hundreds of kits. He redesigned the famous Hubbard French double-manual kit in 1979, and is highly regarded for his German instruments after Hieronymus Albrecht Hass. He has been successful in continuing the tradition of well-crafted, reliable instruments that have always been the hallmark of the Hubbard shop. Since the turn of the 21st century he has resumed a career as a harpsichordist, both as a soloist and a continuo player.

EDWARD L. KOTTICK

Brogue (Henning), Roslyn (*b* Chicago, IL, 16 Feb 1919; *d* Beverly, MA, Aug 1981). Composer and harpsichordist. She studied at Drake University, the University of

Chicago (BA 1937), and Radcliffe College (MA 1943, PhD 1947), where her teachers included WALTER PISTON. Among her teaching appointments were positions at the Harvard Summer School (1951–61), Boston University (1959–60), and Tufts University (1962–75); she also taught privately. EARLE BROWN was her best-known pupil. A versatile performer, she played the piano, organ, violin, and viola proficiently and also sang and conducted. Active in harpsichord building and restoration, she worked in the studio of Frank Hubbard and William Dowd for one year. Her other interests included classical paleography, poetry, sculpture, ceramics, and photography.

WORKS
(selective list)

Inst: Trio, ob, cl, bn, 1946; Suite, small orch, 1947; Allegretto, fl, pf, 1948; Qt (Fantasy on Mille regretz), str, pf, 1949; Sinfonia missae, org, 1949; Suite, rec ens, 1949; Str Qt, 1951; Duo lirico, vn, hpd, 1952; Quodlibet, fl, vc, hpd, 1953; Trio, vn, cl, pf, 1953; Parade, cl, pf, 1954; Andante and Variations, hpd, orch, 1954–6; Arabesque, vc, pf, 1955; Sonatina, fl, cl, hpd, 1957; Ww Qnt, 1970; Equipoise, a sax/cl, hpd, pf, 1971

Vocal: Mass, chorus, 1937–9; Childing (S. Slobodkin), concert aria, S, fl, vc, hp, 1957; 5 Songs of Courtly Love (Slobodkin), S, fl, hpd, 1958; Sonnets from the Portuguese (E.B. Browning), S, pf, 1959; Come, lovely and soothing death (W. Whitman), SA, 1960; Song of Exploration (cant., Whitman), S, fl, cl, vc, hpd, 1960; The Baite (J. Donne), B, vc, hpd, 1961; Speed we say (M. Rukeyser), S, fl, hpd, 1961; A Valediction: Of Weeping (Donne), S, hpd/pf, 1962; 4 Elegies (T. Hume, T.L. Beddoes, W.S. Merwin), S, hpd/pf, 1962; Juggler (R. Wilbur), S, vc, hpd, 1962

MARK DEVOTO

Brohn, William David (*b* Flint, MI, 30 March 1933). Orchestrator, conductor, and composer. His studies in music at Michigan State University and the New England Conservatory included composition, conducting, and double bass. Work as an instrumentalist was followed in the 1960s by conducting engagements for ballet and musicals. He has composed incidental music, songs, musicals, and dance works, and orchestrated for film (adaptations of Prokofiev film scores), recordings (for Jerry Hadley, Plácido Domingo, Marilyn Horne, and Joshua Bell, among others), and particularly for the stage. His Broadway work began with credits for additional orchestrations, followed by a series of new or revised orchestrations for compilations and revivals (*Jerome Robbins' Broadway*, *Carousel*, *Show Boat*, *Oklahoma!*), and by an impressive series of orchestrations of new works. These demonstrate Brohn's stylistic range, including the delicate chamber textures of *The Secret Garden*, featuring dulcimer, guitar, harp, and recorder; a classic Gershwin sound in *Crazy for You*; a tapestry of early 20th-century Americana for *Ragtime*, for which he won the Tony Award; the backstage atmosphere (including a parodied musical-within-the-musical) of *Curtains*. In addition to those already mentioned, such highly successful titles as *Miss Saigon*, *Wicked*, and *Mary Poppins* ensure that his work will remain familiar to audiences.

WORKS
(selective list)

Theater orchestrations (composers in parentheses): Timbuktu (R. Wright and G. Forrest; rev. of Kismet, after Borodin), 1978; King of Hearts (P. Link), 1978; Marilyn, 1983; The Wind in the Willows (W. Perry), 1985; Jerome Robbins' Broadway, collab. 1989; Miss Saigon (C.-M. Schönberg), 1989; The Secret Garden (L. Simon), 1991; Carousel (R. Rodgers), rev. 1992; Crazy for You (G. Gershwin), 1992; The Red Shoes (J. Styne), collab., 1993; Show Boat (J. Kern), rev. 1993; Oliver! (L. Bart), rev. 1994; Ragtime (S. Flaherty), 1996; High Society (C. Porter), 1998; Oklahoma! (Rodgers), rev. 1998; My Fair Lady (F. Loewe), rev. 2001; Sweet Smell of Success (M. Hamlisch), 2002; A Man of No Importance (Flaherty), 2002; Wicked (S. Schwartz), 2003; Mary Poppins (R.M. Sherman and R.B. Sherman), 2004; Dessa Rose (Flaherty), collab., 2005; Curtains (J. Kander), 2007; Porgy and Bess (Gershwin), rev. 2011

BIBLIOGRAPHY

W.D. Brohn: "An Arranger Evens the Score," *The Instrumentalist*, xlii/6 (1988), 20–26

"William David Brohn: the man behind a brand new set of Oliver! Orchestrations," *The Independent* [London] (24 Nov 1994)

JON ALAN CONRAD

Broiles, Mel(vyn) (*b* Coquille, OR, 4 Sept 1929; *d* New York, NY, 26 Aug 2003). Trumpeter. Broiles is recognized as an American trumpet virtuoso, orchestral musician, and teacher whose bizarre sense of humor equaled his reputation as a performer. He began playing trumpet in the second grade in Salina, Kansas, and for his high school years moved to Hollywood, California. There he performed with concert and dance bands. In 1950 he enrolled at the Juilliard School, where he studied with WILLIAM VACCHIANO. After one year he was drafted into military service and from 1951 to 1954 played in the West Point Academy Band. In 1954 the NBC Symphony's *Symphony of the Air* selected him to be a member, and he performed subsequently on numerous live radio broadcasts.

Broiles became principal trumpet of the Metropolitan Opera Orchestra in 1955, but after one year accepted a position as principal trumpet of the Philadelphia Orchestra. After being informed that his services were no longer needed, he returned to the Metropolitan Opera the following year and remained with that organization until his retirement in 2001. He is remembered as a flamboyant and strong player and an excellent teacher. His music library is housed at the University of Georgia.

BIBLIOGRAPHY

J. Falk: "Mel Broiles and His Magic Trumpet," *Journal of the International Trumpet Guild*, xi/4 (May 1987), 21–22

M. Laplace: *Trompette, Cuivres & XXe Siècle* (CD-ROM, Oct., 2008)

MICHAEL ELLZEY

Brombaugh, John (*b* Dayton, OH, 1 March 1937). Organ builder. After graduating from University of Cincinnati and Cornell University, he apprenticed with FRITZ NOACK and CHARLES BRENTON FISK (1964–7) before working as a journeyman for Rudolph von Beckerath in Hamburg, Germany, in 1967. The following year he established his workshop in Germantown, Ohio, in which he crafted virtually all components of his organs. From the beginning he followed historic principles of tonal and visual designs, an early organ in this style being that built in 1972 for Ashland Ave. Baptist Church, Toledo, Ohio, relocated to California State University in 2009. In 1976 he built an organ for the Lutheran Church of Eugene, Oregon, and relocated his workshop there the following year. During his career Brombaugh made several trips to Europe, particularly northern Germany, to study characteristics of historic 17th- and 18th-century organs, and was a leader in the movement to reproduce these characteristics in modern organs, with the result that several of his organs are employed as teaching instruments in educational settings such as Oberlin College (1981) and Duke University. Brombaugh builds exclusively mechanical-action organs, usually employing historic tuning temperaments such as Kellner, but in special instances also meantone temperament. Some significant organs include those in Southern College of Seventh-Day Adventists (1986), Lawrence University (1995), and First Presbyterian Church, Springfield, Illinois (2001); in 2002 he exported an organ to Toyota City Concert Hall in Japan. He also built several small practice and continuo organs. In all, he constructed 66 organs during his career, completing the last in 2005, after which he retired to continue his research into historic northern European organs.

BIBLIOGRAPHY

U. Pape: *The Tracker Organ Revival in America* (Berlin, 1977)

U. Pape: "John Brombaugh," *Organ Yearbook*, v/10 (1979)

K.M. DuPriest: "A Quest for Harmony," *Connoisseur* (July 1984)

J. Hamilton: "An Emerging US Organ-building Movement," *MT*, cxxv (1984), 347, 407

L. Edwards, ed.: *The Historical Organ in America* (Hadley, MA, 1992)

J. Ambrosino: "The Historical Organbuilders," *Choir & Organ* (Sept/Oct 2000)

BARBARA OWEN

Bronco [Grupo Bronco, El Gigante de América]. Mexican grupera ensemble. Formed by José Guadalupe Esparza, Ramiro Delgado, Javier Villarreal, and José Luis Villarreal in 1979, this band came together at a time when the genre later known as *onda grupera* was still in development. Influenced by the sounds of *cumbia* ranchera music, and romantic ballad, the band became a decisive factor in the commercialization of the *grupera* phenomenon. Not only did Bronco consolidate cowboy clothing as a *grupera* staple but they also pioneered the use of elaborate staging, fireworks, and gigantic screens in *grupera* concerts. After seven years of activity Bronco reached international popularity with the hit "Que no quede huella" (1989), and in 1993 starred in *Dos mujeres, un camino*, a soap opera that became a commercial hit in Latin America. Clothing, concert entertainment, television, and motion pictures brought international recognition for the band in the United States, Latin America, and Europe. Ultimately, these elements, accompanying Bronco's enormous record and ticket sales, marked the mainstream emergence of *onda grupera*. After announcing their retirement in 1997 the band reunited in 2003. However, due to copyright disputes with their former manager, the band re-emerged under the name El Gigante de América.

JESÚS A. RAMOS-KITTRELL

Bronson, Bertrand Harris (*b* Lawrenceville, NJ, 22 June 1902; *d* Berkeley, CA, 14 March 1986). Ballad scholar and musicologist. Like other ballad scholars such as Phillips Barry and S.P. Bayard, he studied English literature (Harvard University, MA 1922; Yale University, PhD 1927; Oxford University, MA 1929) and was able to use his expertise in literary studies in his scholarship on folksong. After teaching at the University of Michigan (1925–6), he joined the English department of the University of California, Berkeley, in 1927, and was appointed professor there in 1945; he retired in 1969.

While recognizing the achievement of F.J. Child in compiling ballad texts, Bronson insisted on the need to study the tunes and their variant forms. He conceived of the ballad as a structural unit within which text and tune were firmly wedded, and his major work, the four-volume *The Traditional Tunes of the Child Ballads* (1959–72), was important both for its research on tunes and the supplementary ballad texts. In his later writings, Bronson combed through different source material, including plainchant, collections of traditional ballads, and live recordings, to demonstrate that the ballad was a sung genre. He criticized literary scholars such as Kittredge for privileging text over tunes (*The Singing Tradition of Child Popular Ballads*, 1976), and in a series of essays spanning 30 years (published as a collection, 1969), he explored the identity of ballad tunes and how they are affected by features such as mode, contour, and final. Influenced by G.P. Jackson's theories on the "tune family," he classified tune variants for each ballad with a Child number not by mode but by melodic typology, showing how the "same basic tune may pass from mode to mode almost imperceptibly." Although he defended the use of church mode designations when this method was becoming unpopular, his perception of the structural dependence of the text and tune in the ballad remains an important contribution to the field.

WRITINGS

"The Riverside Recordings of the Child Ballads a Review Article," *Western Folklore*, xvi (1957), 189–94

The Traditional Tunes of the Child Ballads, i–iv (Princeton, NJ, 1959–72)

The Ballad as Song (Berkeley, 1969)

"Are the Modes Outmoded?" *YIFMC*, iv (1973), 23–31

The Singing Tradition of Child's Popular Ballads (Princeton, NJ, 1976)

"Let's Make It a Tradition," *YIFMC*, xi (1979), 27–39

BIBLIOGRAPHY

J. Porter, ed.: *The Ballad Image: Essays presented to Bertrand Harris Bronson* (Los Angeles, 1983)

A. Green: "Bertrand Harris Bronson (1902–1986)," *Journal of American Folklore*, c (1987), 297–9

JAMES PORTER

Bronson, Howard Curtis (*b* Algona, IA, 4 Nov 1889; *d* Richmond, VA, 23 Jan 1960). Military bandleader and clarinetist. After playing in local National Guard bands, Bronson joined the Navy in 1909 and became its youngest assistant bandmaster. He spent World War I as leader of the 51st Field Artillery Band, and later led a professional municipal band in Aberdeen, South Dakota.

Bronson served as a clarinetist in the Sousa Band between 1921 and 1929. He retired to direct the Kable Brothers 129th Infantry Band, an industrial-military ensemble in Mount Morris, Illinois. In 1941 Bronson became the War Department's first adviser on music and Chief of Bands. From this position he developed the modern training system for Army musicians and established instruction centers at Camp Lee and Fort Myer, Virginia, and Camp Crowder, Missouri. In order to bring music to deployed soldiers, Bronson helped to create monthly collections of popular songs. These Hit Kits were shipped overseas as piano arrangements and lyric sheets. He was also instrumental in the creation of the V-Disk series (recordings of bands and singers provided to deployed soldiers). Col. Bronson retired from the military in 1947 and was elected president of the American Bandmasters Association in 1948. He published one work for band: *General Marshall March* (New York, 1943). The ABA Research Center at the University of Maryland holds Bronson's own description of his activities for the War Department.

PATRICK WARFIELD

Brook, Barry S(helley) (*b* New York, NY, 1 Nov 1918; *d* New York, 7 Dec 1997). Musicologist. He took the BS at the City College of New York in 1939 and the MA at Columbia University in 1942. At Columbia his professors included Henry Lang and Erich Hertzmann, and he also studied with HUGH ROSS and ROGER SESSIONS. He received the doctorate from the Sorbonne in 1959. From 1945 he taught at Queens College, New York; he was a visiting professor at New York University (1964–5) and the University of Paris (1967–8). In 1967 he founded and became the executive director of the PhD program at the Graduate Center, CUNY, and taught doctoral seminars and advised doctoral students at the Juilliard School, 1977–88. He founded the DMA program at the Ecole Normale Supérieure, in 1986. He became professor emeritus at CUNY in 1989, after which he served as director of the Center for Music Research and Documentation, which he founded at the Graduate Center; the center has been since renamed in his honor. As visiting professor, Brook taught at nine other universities in the United States, Australia, and France. He received the Dent Medal of the Royal Musical Association (1965); the French government named him a Chevalier of the Ordre des Arts et Lettres (1972); and the Royal Swedish Academy of Music elected him to be among its fellows (1988). He served as the vice-president (1974–7) and president (1977–80) of the International Association of Music Libraries, Archives, and Documentation Centres (IAML), and the vice-president (1980–82) and president (1982–4) of the International Music Council (IMC).

Brook's interests were wide-ranging and pioneering in many areas, from music iconography, the history of thematic catalogs, the sociology and aesthetics of music, and the application of computers in musicology, to the 18th-century French symphony and the music of Haydn and Pergolesi. His dissertation is a groundbreaking study on the 18th-century French symphony, which provides extensive documentation, a thematic catalog of over 1200 works, and an edition of eight works. He initiated fundamental research on the history of thematic catalogs, publishing a facsimile of the Breitkopf thematic catalog and two editions of the annotated catalog of thematic catalogs. In source studies Brook developed a technique of analyzing composers' handwriting, demonstrating it by identifying Pergolesi's authentic opus and the body of Haydn's string trios. Initiating the publication of Pergolesi's collected works, of which he was the general editor, he founded the Pergolesi Research Center at the CUNY Graduate Center, which owns an extensive microfilm collection of Pergolesi sources. Under his editorship, a 60-volume series of symphonies from 1720 to 1840 and a dozen volumes in the series of French opera in the 17th and 18th centuries were published. In 1979 Brook initiated, under the auspices of the IMC, a global project, *The Universe of Music: a History*, intended to provide a comprehensive history of the musical cultures of the world.

Brook understood the enormous possibilities of computer applications in musicology, and already in the early 1960s he advocated their use for the control of music sources. In 1964 he made a proposal for the "Plaine and Easie Code," a system of notating music using ordinary typewriter or keypunch characters. The following year he founded *Répertoire International de Littérature Musicale* (*RILM*), the international annotated bibliography of music scholarship. At the 1971 St. Gall meeting of IAML, he initiated the *Répertoire International d'Iconographie Musicale* (*RIdIM*), an international project aiming to develop the methods, means, classification, cataloging, and research of iconographic sources relevant for music. Brook organized the Research Center for Music Iconography at the CUNY Graduate Center the following year, where he developed a vast archive of resources for study of music-related visual documentation. He was also a member of the RISM Commission Mixte (1986–97).

WRITINGS

ed.: *Musicology and the Computer: Musicology, 1966–2000* (New York, 1965 and 1966) [incl. "Music Documentation of the Future," 28–36; "The Plaine and Easie Code," 53–6]

"Music Bibliography and the Computer," *Computer Applications in Music* (Morgantown, WV, 1966), 11–27

"Music Literature and Modern Communication: some Revolutionary Potentials of the RILM Project," *AcM*, xlii (1970), 205–17

Thematic Catalogues in Music: an Annotated Bibliography (Hillsdale, NY, 1972, enlarged 2/1997)

"Music, Musicology and Related Disciplines," *A Musical Offering: Essays in Honor of Martin Bernstein*, ed. E.H. Clinkscale and C. Brook (New York, 1977), 69–77

"The Road to RILM," in *Modern Music Librarianship: Essays in Honor of Ruth Watanabe*, ed. A. Mann (Stuyvesant, 1989), 85–94

"Composer Sources and Resources," *Music Reference Services Quarterly*, iv/1 (1995), 1–42

BIBLIOGRAPHY

Grove7 (P. Morgan)

A. Atlas, ed.: *Music in the Classic Period: Essays in Honor of Barry S. Brook* (New York, 1985) [incl. list of publications, 359–74]

M Calderisi Bryce, ed.: The presidents [of IAML], *FAM*, xlviii/1 (2001), 49–70

PAULA MORGAN/ZDRAVKO BLAŽEKOVIĆ

Brooke, Thomas Preston (*b* Dubuque, IA, 1856; *d* Chicago, IL, 9 Sept 1921). Band composer and conductor. Early accounts indicate that Brooke left Dubuque as a young man to study theory and harmony in Boston (institution not known). While a student, Brooke was invited to conduct two of his marches with Patrick Gilmore's band. Soon after, Brooke won an audition as a trombonist and performed with Gilmore's band for two years. Brooke resigned in 1880, and, aside from returning to Dubuque to marry and compose, little is known of his activities before establishing the Chicago Marine Band in 1893. Brooke's band performed a series of winter concerts in Chicago, and spent summers touring the Midwestern and Eastern United States and Canada. His conducting career earned him the title of "Popular Music King," due to his innovative programming of ragtime and other music that appealed to the general public, in addition to serious classical repertoire. Brooke explored additional business ventures from 1903 through 1907 that resulted in bankruptcy and also brought about the end of his Chicago Marine Band. Following these failures, Brooke lived the remainder of his life in Chicago in poor health. His legacy includes over 80 known published marches, gallops, polkas, comic operas, and other works. Twenty-eight of his works were included in Robert Hoe's *Heritage of the March* series (27, SSS, DDDD).

BIBLIOGRAPHY

The Chicago Marine Band: Mr. T. P. Brooke, Conductor (Chicago, IL, 1899)

H.W. Schwartz: *Bands of America* (Garden City, NY, 1957)

W.H. Rehrig: *The Heritage Encyclopedia of Band Music* (Westerville, OH, 1991, suppl. 1996); CD-ROM (Oskaloosa, IA, 2005)

N.E. Smith: *Program Notes for Band* (Lake Charles, LA, 2000), 90–91

VINCENT J. NOVARA

Brookmeyer, Bob [Robert] (*b* Kansas City, MO, 19 Dec 1929). Jazz valve trombonist, arranger, and pianist. He studied at the Kansas City Conservatory and began his career as a pianist in various dance bands. In 1952 he settled on valve trombone and soon became an important figure in the West Coast style of jazz, particularly after replacing Chet Baker in Gerry Mulligan's "pianoless" quartet, in which he worked from 1953 to 1954. At the same time he continued to perform on piano, notably in a revealing duo album with Bill Evans (1959). In the early 1960s he played with Mulligan and also led a popular group with the trumpeter and flugelhorn player Clark Terry. He was also a founding member of the Thad Jones–Mel Lewis Orchestra (from 1965), for which he wrote several outstanding arrangements. From 1968 to 1978 Brookmeyer worked primarily as a studio musician on the West Coast and frequently played as a sideman with well-known mainstream jazz musicians. In 1981 he began to work mainly in Europe; there he established a music school in Rotterdam and formed his New Quartet and New Art Orchestra. The following decade he began teaching at the New England Conservatory, where he established the Jazz Composers' Workshop Orchestra. Brookmeyer is the first noteworthy jazz musician since Juan Tizol to specialize on valve trombone. He is an excellent soloist, playing in a good-humored linear style with, at times, pronounced overtones of blues and swing. As a pianist he has developed a distinctive percussive and dissonant manner entirely outside the main traditions of jazz pianism. A collection of his materials is held by the Miller Nichols Library at the University of Missouri, Kansas City.

BIBLIOGRAPHY

GroveJ2

L. Feather: "Brookmeyer's Tale of Three Cities," *DB*, xxii/18 (1955), 9

B. Coss: "Bob Brookmeyer: Strength and Simplicity," *DB*, xxviii/2 (1961), 19

D. Morgenstern: "Bob Brookmeyer: Master of the Brass Stepchild," *DB*, xxxiv/2 (1967), 14

M. Williams: "Giuffre, Brookmeyer Reunion," *DB*, xxxv/2 (1968), 15

"A Gallery of BMI Jazz Composers," *BMI: the Many Worlds of Music* (1981), no.3, p.25

W. Enstice and P. Rubin: *Jazz Spoken Here: Conversations with Twenty-two Musicians* (Baton Rouge, LA, 1992), 59

D. Ramsey: "Before & After: Bob Brookmeyer Searches for the Truth," *JT*, xxix/4 (1999), 91–3, 214

B. Donaldson: "Bob Brookmeyer," *Cadence*, xxvii/3 (2001), 5–14

D.N. Ware: "Bob Brookmeyer: Doin' it his Way," *Jazz Education Journal*, xxxvi/2 (2003), 42–8

E.A. Partyka: "Bob Brookmeyer," *ITA Journal*, xxxiii/1 (2005), 44–9

J. BRADFORD ROBINSON/R

Brooks, (Troyal) Garth (*b* Tulsa, OK, 7 Feb 1962). Country singer and songwriter. Born in Tulsa, Garth Brooks was four years old when his family moved to the small town of Yukon, Oklahoma. He was raised in a musical home, his mother having pursued a singing career in the 1950s. Brooks was particularly fond of singer-songwriter James Taylor and such 1970s rock groups as Boston, Journey, and KISS, but after hearing country star George Strait's "Unwound" in 1981, he became a country music convert. Brooks attended Oklahoma State University in Stillwater, where he participated in athletics and majored in advertising while performing in local clubs. He first visited Nashville in 1985, hoping to make his mark in country music, but was discouraged and quickly returned to Oklahoma to hone his skills. In 1987, he returned to Nashville and was introduced to ASCAP's Bob Doyle who, along with publicist Pam Lewis, formed Doyle/Lewis Management and signed Brooks in 1988. He first auditioned for Capitol in April of 1988, but it was his talent singing for a live audience in the intimate setting of the Bluebird Café just over a month later that convinced Capitol's Lynn Shults to offer him a recording contract. With Allen Reynolds as producer, Capitol released his debut album, *Garth Brooks* (1989), which yielded two number one singles, "If Tomorrow Never Comes" and "The Dance." Both this CD and its successor, *No Fences* (Cap./Liberty, 1990), were certified platinum in October 1990. Within the same week, Brooks became the 65th member of the Grand Ole Opry. In September 1991, he released *Ropin' the Wind* (Cap./Liberty) which entered *Billboard*'s country and "Top 200" charts at number one. *The Chase* (Cap./Liberty, 1992) was described by critics as more introspective, while *In Pieces* (Cap./Liberty, 1993) was viewed as freer and more representative of a live show. *The Hits*

(Cap./Liberty, 1994) sold over 10 million units. *Garth Brooks in... the Life of Chris Gaines* (Cap., 1999), the soundtrack for a film project which was to star Brooks as the fictional character Chris Gaines, met with mixed reviews. Throughout the 1990s, Brooks enjoyed sold-out concerts, numerous accolades, and continuous media attention. *Scarecrow* (Cap., 2001) was his 15th album. In 2006, he released *The Entertainer* (Wal-Mart), a five-DVD box set, and, in 2007, *Garth Brooks: Ultimate Hits* (Pearl Records). His charitable efforts include a series of concerts in Los Angeles, January 2008, to benefit victims of the California wildfires and in Nashville, December 2010, to raise funds for those affected by a local flood. To date, Garth Brooks has sold more than 128 million albums, debuting a remarkable seven times at number one on *Billboard*'s "Top 200" charts.

BIBLIOGRAPHY

M. McCall: *Garth Brooks, a Biography* (New York, 1991)
E. Morris: *Garth Brooks, Platinum Cowboy* (New York, 1993)
B. Feiler: *Dreaming Out Loud* (New York, 1998)
P.B. Cox: *The Garth Factor: the Career Behind Country's Big Boom* (New York, 2009)

LINDA J. DANIEL

Brooks, Hadda [Hapgood, Hattie L.] (*b* Los Angeles, CA, 29 Oct 1916; *d* Los Angeles, 21 Nov 2002). Jazz pianist, singer, and composer. She was raised in the Boyle Heights neighborhood of Los Angeles. After attending the University of Chicago, she worked as a dance studio accompanist in the early 1940s for the choreographer Willie Covan, who trained such figures as Fred Astaire and Shirley Temple. She began to mold her style in the manner of Albert Ammons and Meade Lux Lewis. The recording mogul Jules Bihari gave her the name Hadda Brooks, and it was for his label Modern Music Records that she recorded her first hit, "Swingin' the Boogie" (1945), after which she soon earned the billing Queen of the Boogie. Charlie Barnet suggested that Brooks learn to sing the song "You won't let me go," and it became her first vocal release in 1947. That same year Brooks was cast in the film *Out of the Blue* and her recording of the title song reached the rhythm-and-blues top ten list. This launched a successful film career for Brooks. She appeared in numerous films, often as a lounge pianist or singer, including *In a Lonely Place* (1950). Her alluring vocal quality and her sensitive piano technique made her ideal for such roles. In 1957 Brooks began hosting her own television show, a mixture of talk and musical performances; she was the first African American woman to do so. The show featured Brooks's signature tune "That's my desire" as its theme song. The show lasted only 26 episodes. Brooks performed less in the 1970s and 80s, but her career was rejuvenated in 1993 when she was awarded the Pioneer Award by the Rhythm and Blues Foundation. She once more began appearing in films, including *The Crossing Guard* (1995), and performing in nightclubs such as Johnny Depp's Viper Room.

BIBLIOGRAPHY

M.K. Aldin, with M. Humphrey: "Queen of the Boogie," *Living Blues*, no.118 (1994), 31
B. Vera: "Our Miss Hadda Brooks," *Grindstone Magazine*, no.9 (1999),

CHADWICK JENKINS

Brooks, Patricia (*b* New York, NY, 7 Nov 1937; *d* Mount Kisco, NY, 22 Jan 1993). Soprano. At the age of ten she won an award from the radio station WQXR for her solo playing in a Mendelssohn piano concerto. She studied music at the Manhattan School, but at 15 took up dancing, studying with Martha Graham. After injuring her knee, she turned to drama, appearing off Broadway in plays by Luigi Pirandello and Eugene O'Neill before deciding to become a singer. Having made her New York City Opera debut on 12 October 1960, as Marianne in *Der Rosenkavalier*, she soon graduated to Sophie, and then a leading role in Robert Ward's *The Crucible*, Violetta, Massenet's Manon, Leoncavallo's Nedda, Gilda, Lucia, and, perhaps most memorably, Mélisande. She made her Covent Garden debut as the Queen of Shemakhan in *The Golden Cockerel* in December 1969, and appeared at Chicago, San Francisco, Toronto, and Santiago, Chile. In 1974 she played Berg's Lulu at Santa Fe and later at Houston. Brooks was a highly individual actress, and her performances were often notable for their dramatic impact.

MARTIN BERNHEIMER/R

Brooks, Shelton (Leroy) (*b* Amesburg, ON, 4 May 1886; *d* Los Angeles, CA, 6 Sept 1975). Songwriter, pianist, and vaudeville entertainer of Canadian birth. He grew up in Detroit, where he taught himself music. For nearly half a century he toured the United States and Canada as an entertainer; he visited Europe with Lew Leslie's *Blackbirds of 1923* and appeared in a command performance for King George V and Queen Mary. Later he was a member of Ken Murray's successful revue *Blackouts* (1949). Although he never learned to read music, in the years around World War I he wrote a number of songs popularized by artists such as Sophie Tucker, Al Jolson, Mae West, Benny Goodman, and Ella Fitzgerald, including the highly successful "Some of these Days" (1910) and "Darktown Strutters' Ball" (1917). The brash, often sexually suggestive style of these songs appealed to an age looking for relief from the stuffiness of Victorian morality. Although many of his early works fit the mold of coon and minstrel songs, his later work breaks free from these genres. Brooks continued to compose songs until late in life, and long after the demand for his particular type of song had disappeared; by the time of his death he was almost completely forgotten as one of the most innovative and original songwriters of the early part of the century.

WORKS

(selective list)

(all published in Chicago unless otherwise stated; all lyrics by Brooks)

Songs: You ain't talkin' to me (M. Marshall) (1909); Honey Gal (1910); Some of these days (1910); Jean (New York, 1911); There'll come a time (1911); All Night Long (1912); You ain't no place but down South (C. Smith) (n.p., 1912); Rufe Johnson's Harmony Band (New York, 1914), collab. M. Abrahams; Walkin' the Dog (1916); Darktown Strutters' Ball (1917); I wonder where my easy rider's gone (n.p., 1929)

Principal publisher: Rossiter

BIBLIOGRAPHY

SouthernB
J. Burton: *The Blue Book of Tin Pan Alley*, ii (New York, 1965)
I. Whitcomb: "Shelton Brooks is Alive and Strutting," *Los Angeles Times Calendar* (18 May 1969)
W. Barlow and T. Morgan: *From Cakewalks to Concert Halls: an Illustrated History of African-American Popular Music from 1895 to 1930* (Washington, DC, 1992)
D. Jasen and G. Jones: *Spreadin' Rhythm Around: Black Popular Songwriters, 1880–1930* (New York, 1998)
M. Garber: "'Some of These Days' and the Study of the Great American Songbook," *JSAM*, iv/2 (2010), 175–214

SAM DENNISON/TIM SMOLKO

Brooks, William (Fordyce) (*b* New York, NY, 17 Dec 1943). Composer and musicologist. He studied music and mathematics at Wesleyan University (BA 1965) and then attended the University of Illinois, receiving degrees in musicology (MM 1971) and composition and theory (DMA 1976). His instructors included CHARLES HAMM in musicology and BEN JOHNSTON, KENNETH GABURO, and HERBERT BRÜN in composition. He taught at the University of Illinois (1969–73) and at the University of California, Santa Cruz (1973–4) and San Diego (1975–7). After ten years of freelance work as a composer, scholar, and performer, he returned to Illinois as associate professor in composition, theory, and musicology (1986–2003). Since 2000 he has been professor of music (composition and musicology) at the University of York, England. He was appointed Fulbright Professor at the University of Keele (1977–8) and has received Fellowships from the Smithsonian Institution (1979–80), NEA (1982), Institute for Studies in American Music, Brooklyn College (1983), Illinois Arts Council (1985), Newberry Library (2006), and the Orpheus Institute, Ghent, Belgium (2008–present). He has received commissions from the British Arts Council (1978), Gulbenkian Foundation (1981), Kronos Quartet (1986), Cleveland Chamber Orchestra (1990), University of Illinois (1994), University of Nevada (2001), and the Crash Ensemble (2008). Brooks has written on a wide variety of topics, primarily within the area of American music. He served as adviser on 19th-century music for *The New Grove Dictionary of American Music* and contributed two "overview" chapters to the *Cambridge History of American Music*, but his primary focus has been on Charles Ives and John Cage. A majority of his compositions are for voices, and he has sung with several vocal ensembles. His music frequently uses open-form structures, and it commonly mixes styles in a challenging or humorous way. A preoccupation with quotation, reference, and the intersection of high and low cultures characterizes Brooks's work in both musicological and compositional domains.

WORKS

Stage: Untitled (Borges), 8 solo vv, 2 speakers, 1972; The Legacy (chamber opera, Brooks), 4 solo vv, live elec, 4 opt actors, 1982–3, Metamorphoses (Ovid, trans Brooks), 2 solo vv, surround sound, projections, 2005

Inst: Poempiece I: whitegold blue, fl, 1967; Poempiece II: how I fooled the armies, b trbn, 1968; Bryant's Ridge Disco Phase no.1 (R. Madison), singers, disco band, 1978; Wallpaper Pieces, pf, 1979–; Footnotes, gui, 1981–4; March Peace, pc, 1988; Dancing on Your Grave, orch, 1990; For Violin, vn, 1990; The Kitchen Sink and the Water in It, 6 insts, 1991; Makers, quintet, 1992; Common Ground, wind ens, steel band, 1995; Small Talk, 4 insts, 2002; Canticanon, 12 insts, 2003

Vocal: Many Returns (Stein), 50 songs, Mez, pf, 1977; Medley (Stein), Mez, pf (1978); Madrigals (O. Gibbons, S. Foster, Brooks), amp SATB qt, 1977–8; Duets, 8 untexted pieces, 1v, live elec, 1978–9; De Harmonium (Stevens), amp SATB qt, amp st qt, prerecorded insts, 1986; A Peal for Calm (Joyce), SATB cho, pf, 1987; Vier Alte Lieder (Rilke), sop, vn, va, 1993; in memoriam reducere studemus (Joris), SATB cho, pf, 1996; Rubaiyat (Rumi), 2 sop, fl, vc, hp, 2001; Three Monodies (St. John of the Cross), ten, fl, prep pf, 2002; Three Songs (Rexroth), ten, pf, 2003; Six Mediaeval Lyrics (various), SSA trio, 2004; A Wake of Music (Dickinson), sop, cl, vc, pf, 2008

WRITINGS

"Unity and Diversity in Charles Ives's Fourth Symphony," *YIAMR*, x (1974), 5–49
"Ives Today," *An Ives Celebration* (Brooklyn, NY, and New Haven, CT, 1977), 209–23
"Competenza Maledetta," *PNM*, xviii (1979–80), 11–45
"Choice and Change in Cage's Recent Music," *TriQuarterly*, liv (1982), 148–66; repr. in *A John Cage Reader*, ed. P.G. Brent, J. Brent and D. Gillespie (New York, 1982), 82–100, repr (in Fr.) in *Revue d'Esthetique*, nos. xiii, xiv, xv (1988), 75–86
"On Being Tasteless," *Popular Music*, ii (1982), 9–18
"A Drummer-Boy Looks Back: Percussion in Ives's Fourth Symphony," *Percussive Notes*, xxii/6 (1984), 4–45
"Good Musical Paste: Getting the Acts Together in the Eighteenth Century," *Musical Theatre in America* (Westport, CT, 1984), 37–58
"Pocahontas: Her Life and Times," *AM*, ii/4 (1984), 19–48
"About Cage about Thoreau," *John Cage at Seventy-five*, ed. R. Fleming and W. Duckworth (Lewisburg, PA, 1989), 59–73
"The Americas, 1945–1970," *Man & Music*, viii: *Modern Times: from World War I to the Present*, ed. R.P. Morgan (London and Englewood Cliffs, NJ, 1993), 309–48
"John Cage and History: *Hymns and Variations*," *PNM*, xxxi/2 (1993), 74–103
"Music in America: an Overview," *The Cambridge History of American Music*, ed. D. Nicholls (Cambridge, UK, 1998, repr 2004), 30–48, 257–75
"Music II: from the Late 1960s," *The Cambridge Companion to John Cage*, ed. D. Nicholls (Cambridge, UK, 2002), 128–147
"Music and Society," *The Cambridge Companion to John Cage*, ed. D. Nicholls (Cambridge, UK, 2002), 214–226
"Simple Gifts and Complex Accretions," *Copland Connotations*, ed. P. Dickinson (Woodbridge, Suffolk, 2002), 103–117
"Music: Sound: Technology," *The Cambridge Companion to Modern American Culture* (Cambridge, UK, 2006), 332–353
"Pragmatics of Silence," *Silence, Music, Silent Music*, ed. N. Losseff and J. Doctor (Aldershot, UK, 2007), 97–126
"Sounds, Gamuts, Actions: Cage's Pluralist Universe," *MetaCage*, ed. W. Brooks (Leuven, Belgium, 2009)

KATHERINE K. PRESTON

Brooks & Dunn. Country music duo. Formed in 1990 by Leon Eric "Kix" Brooks (*b* Shreveport, LA, 12 May 1955) and Ronnie [Gene] Dunn (*b* Coleman, TX, 1 June 1953), Brooks & Dunn is the most celebrated country music duo in the history of the genre, having won a record 19 awards from the Country Music Association, including Vocal Duo of the Year 14 times (1992–9, 2001–6). Although neither Brooks nor Dunn was successful as a solo act in the 1980s, their debut album as a duo *Brand New Man* (Arista, 1991) was an instant success, producing four consecutive number-one hits, including "Brand New Man," "My Next Broken Heart," and "Neon Moon," landing Brooks & Dunn the Academy of Country Music's Top New Vocal Duet/Group award, and eventually selling over six million copies. The album's fourth number-one single, "Boot Scootin' Boogie," inspired a popular country line dance by the same name. Over the next few years, the duo released a series of hit albums, including *Hard Workin' Man* (Arista, 1993), *Waitin' on Sundown* (Arista, 1994), and *Borderline* (Arista, 1996), collectively selling 12 million copies and ultimately earning Brooks & Dunn awards for Entertainer of the Year in 1996 from both the Country Music Association and the Academy of Country Music. Dunn's soulful lead vocals combined with the strength of Brooks's vocal harmonies and ability to work the crowd and stage made the act a success on tour as well as on the country charts throughout the 1990s and into the new millennium. Later albums such as *Steers & Stripes* (Arista, 2001), *Red Dirt Road* (Arista, 2003), and *Hillbilly Deluxe* (Arista, 2005) produced additional number-one hits, including "Ain't Nothing 'Bout You" (2001), "Only in America" (2001), "Red Dirt Road" (2003), and "Play Something Country" (2005), resulting in over 27.5 million total albums sold and making Brooks & Dunn the best-selling country duo to date.

DAVID B. PRUETT

Broonzy, Big Bill [William Lee Conley] (*b* Scott, MS, 26 June 1893; *d* Chicago, IL, 14 Aug 1958). Blues singer and guitarist. He grew up in Arkansas, where he lived on a farm until his late 20s. After working as a fiddle player in the rural South, he settled in Chicago in 1920. There he learned to play guitar, on which he was already an outstanding performer when he began to record ten years later. In the late 1930s and the 1940s he was sympathetically supported at different times by the pianists Joshua Altheimer and Black Bob Hudson in a manner reminiscent of Leroy Carr and Scrapper Blackwell. One of the most prolifically recorded African American blues singers, Broonzy formed a link between the country and urban blues traditions, playing with a light, lilting style. Some of his recorded blues are poetic statements, complemented by moaning notes on the guitar, such as "Big Bill Blues" (1932, Champion) and "Friendless Blues" (1934, Bb), while others are of a ribald or "hokum" character, including "Keep your hands off her" (1935, Bb) and "Good Jelly" (1935, Bb). Broonzy was later one of the first blues singers to use trumpet and saxophone in small-band accompaniments, although recordings of these groups proved less successful than his earlier work. The decline of the blues' popularity in the United States coupled with the emerging interest in African American music abroad led Broonzy to make several visits to Europe in the 1950s, where he found audiences eager for the old country songs of his earlier years. He recorded more than 200 titles, including several versions of "John Henry" and the protest song "Black, Brown and White" (both 1951, Vogue). Broonzy's generosity, talents, and homely wit made him one of the most popular of all blues musicians, particularly in Europe, where he became close to such musicians as Alexis Korner and Chris Barber and was widely regarded as one of the last surviving exponents of authentic country blues. In this role he was often interviewed by emerging blues scholars and provided valuable information on the recording history and lives of older blues singers.

BIBLIOGRAPHY

W. Broonzy and Y. Bruynoghe: *Big Bill Blues* (London, 1955/*R*)

C. Smith: *Hit the Right Lick: the Recordings of Big Bill Broonzy* (Shetland, 1997)

R. House: *Blue Smoke: the Recorded Journey of Big Bill Broonzy* (Baton Rouge, 2010)

R. Riesman: *I Feel so Good: the Life and Times of Big Bill Bronzy* (Chicago, 2011)

PAUL OLIVER/CHRISTIAN O'CONNELL

Broude, Alexander. Firm of music publishers, distributors, importers, and exporters. Alexander Broude (*b* New York, NY, 1 Jan 1909; *d* Florida, 31 Dec 1997) was originally associated with his brother, Irving, in Broude brothers, and began publishing music in the 1930s in New York. In 1954 Alexander severed the association and founded his own company, Alexander Broude, Inc. (ABI Music), which from 1962 published music for all media, including educational materials and music textbooks. Twentieth-century American composers in the Alexander Broude catalog include Bales, Ruth Crawford, Dahl, Etler, Frost, Daniel Kessner, Alan Schulman, Elliott Schwartz, Riegger, and Westergaard. European composers of all periods, including Rachmaninoff, Casals, and Dallapiccola, are also published by the firm. Alexander Broude retired in 1970. In 1982 the company was bought by Michael Lefferts (president) and Dean Streit (vice-president).

W. THOMAS MARROCCO, MARK JACOBS/R

Broude Brothers. Firm of music publishers. Founded in New York in the 1930s by Irving and Alexander Broude, it publishes scholarly editions and reference books as well as performing editions of works by modern and older composers. Its projects have included new editions of the collected works of Buxtehude, Lully, Marais, Marenzio, and Rameau. It publishes the series Monuments of Music and Music Literature in Facsimile, as well as historical sets such as Tudor Church Music, Masters and Monuments of the Renaissance, and Music at the Court of Ferrara. Among 20th-century composers published by the firm are Babbitt, Bacon, Berger, Bloch, Duke, Herrmann, Hovhaness, Krenek, La Montaine, Lockwood, Messiaen, Nin-Culmell, and Rózsa. Alexander Broude left the organization in 1954 and established his own firm. Irving Broude's widow, Anne, took over the firm after her husband's death in 1973; when she retired in 1979, her son Ronald became president. The Broude Trust for the Publication of Musicological Editions was formed in 1981 to provide financial support for the preparation of the collected editions and historical sets.

W. THOMAS MARROCCO, MARK JACOBS

Broudy, Harry S(amuel) (*b* Fillipowa, Poland, 27 July 1905; *d* Urbana, IL, 24 June 1998). Philosopher of aesthetics and education of Polish birth. He earned degrees at Boston University (BA 1929) and Harvard University (MA 1933, PhD 1936), studying with Alfred North Whitehead at the latter institution. He was a supervisor with the Massachusetts Department of Education, and taught at Massachusetts State College

(1937–49) and Framingham State Teachers College (1949–57). He was a professor of the philosophy of education at the University of Illinois at Urbana-Champaign (1957–74), where he focused on society's demands on schooling and the aesthetic dimension of learning. He sought to establish that an educational commitment toward imaginative perception through the arts contributes to a society's wellbeing. A prolific author of numerous books and articles, Broudy was also editor of *Educational Forum* (1964–72), a member of the editorial committees of the *Music Educators Journal* and *Journal of Aesthetic Education*, and on the advisory board for the Getty Institute for Educators on the Visual Arts. He received honorary doctorates from Oakland University (1969), Eastern Kentucky State University (1979), and Massachusetts State College at North Adams (1981).

WRITINGS

Enlightened Cherishing: an Essay in Aesthetic Education (Urbana, IL, 1972/*R*)

The Role of Imagery Learning (New York, 1989)

MARK FONDER

Brougham, John (*b* Dublin, Ireland, 9 May 1810; *d* New York, NY, 7 June 1880). Playwright and comic actor of Irish birth. Most of his comedies used music extensively. Brougham was active in London during 1830–42 where he wrote his first play (a burlesque) in 1831. After managing the Lyceum theater (1840), he moved to the United States and made his New York debut on 4 October 1842. He toured widely in the United States, performing in Boston from 1846 to 1948, then settled in New York, where he starred at Burton's Theatre. On 23 December 1850 he opened Brougham's Lyceum, but the venture failed two years later. He edited a comic paper, *The Lantern* (1852). From 1852 to 1860 he acted at Wallack's and Burton's theaters and managed the Bowery. He founded and was president of the Lotus Club in New York. After spending five years in London, he returned in 1865 and acted in and wrote for several different theaters in Boston, Philadelphia, and New York. He opened Brougham's Theatre in New York on 25 January 1869, but soon after was forced by the owner, Jim Fisk, to step down. From 1870 to 1877, Brougham performed at Daly's and Wallack's theaters on Broadway and toured with stock companies. The following year his friends rescued him from destitution by organizing a benefit (17 January 1878), which provided him with an annuity for his last two years.

His *Little Nell and the Marchioness* (1867) became principal vehicle, but Brougham was best known for his burlesques: *Met-a-mora, or The Last of the Pollywogs* (1847), *Columbus el Filibustero!* (1857), *Much Ado about a Merchant of Venice* (1869), and especially *Po-ca-hon-tas, or The Gentle Savage* (1855; ed. R. Moody in *Dramas from the American Theater*, Boston, 1966). In these the musical references ranged from Meyerbeer to minstrelsy, with startling and hilarious juxtapositions; by elevating music to a central place, Brougham enriched the burlesque form and prepared the way for later genres.

BIBLIOGRAPHY

W. Winter, ed.: *Life, Stories, and Poems of John Brougham* (Boston, 1881)

W. Brooks: "*Pocahontas*: Her Life and Times," *AM*, ii/4 (1984), 19

D.R Sutton: *John Brougham: the American Performance Career of an Irish Comedian, 1842–1880* (diss., CUNY, 1999)

WILLIAM BROOKS/DENIZ ERTAN

Broughton, Bruce (*b* Los Angeles, CA, 8 March 1945). Composer, primarily for film and television. The son and grandson of Salvation Army musicians, he began studying piano and trumpet by the age of seven and traveled across the western United States throughout his youth, gaining practical experience as a performer in brass bands. He graduated *cum laude* from the University of Southern California with a composition degree in 1967 and worked at CBS Television through the mid-1970s, first as a music supervisor and then as a composer for series including *Gunsmoke* and *Hawaii Five-0*. He became one of television's leading composers, earning a record ten Emmy Awards from 1981 to 2005 (for such diverse fare as the drama series *Dallas* and the animated *Tiny Toon Adventures*; period miniseries like *The First Olympics, Athens 1896*; and television films including the Willa Cather adaptation *O Pioneers!* and the lighthearted *Eloise at the Plaza*).

Broughton's ease with Americana subjects—including the 1982 Civil War miniseries *The Blue and the Gray*—led to his first major feature, the Western *Silverado*, which earned a 1985 Oscar nomination. He quickly became a sought-after composer, especially for films that demanded symphonic treatment, among them *Young Sherlock Holmes*, *The Boy Who Could Fly*, *Harry and the Hendersons*, *The Rescuers Down Under*, *Honey I Blew Up the Kid*, *Tombstone*, and *Homeward Bound: the Incredible Journey*. He also composed the first orchestral score for a video game, *Heart of Darkness* (1999), a series of Roger Rabbit cartoon shorts, and a number of scores for Disney theme-park rides.

At the same time, Broughton became a leader in the Hollywood music community, serving as president of the Society of Composers and Lyricists, a governor of both the Academy of Television Arts & Sciences and the Academy of Motion Picture Arts & Sciences and eventually a member of the board of directors of ASCAP. In the late 1990s and early 2000s, Broughton turned more of his attention to concert work, composing dozens of new pieces for orchestra, band, and chamber ensemble.

WORKS

FILM AND TV SCORES

Feature films: The Prodigal, 1983; The Ice Pirates, 1984; Silverado, 1985; Young Sherlock Holmes, 1985; Sweet Liberty, 1986; The Boy Who Could Fly, 1986; Square Dance, 1987; Harry and the Hendersons, 1987; The Monster Squad, 1987; Big Shots, 1987; Cross My Heart, 1987; The Presidio, 1988; The Rescue, 1988; Moonwalker, 1988; Last Rites, 1988; Jacknife, 1989; Betsy's Wedding, 1990; Narrow Margin, 1990; The Rescuers Down Under, 1990; All I Want for Christmas, 1991; Honey I Blew Up the Kid, 1992; Stay Tuned, 1992; Homeward Bound: The Incredible Journey, 1993; So I Married an Axe Murderer, 1993; For Love or Money, 1993; Tombstone, 1993; Holy Matrimony, 1994; Baby's Day Out, 1994; Miracle on 34th Street,

1994; Carried Away, 1996; Homeward Bound 2: Lost in San Francisco, 1996; House Arrest, 1996; Infinity, 1996; Shadow Conspiracy, 1997; A Simple Wish, 1997; Krippendorf's Tribe, 1998; Lost in Space, 1998; One Tough Cop, 1998; Last Flight Out, 2004; Bambi II, 2006

TV series (*selective list*): Gunsmoke, 1973; Hawaii Five-0, 1973; Quincy, M.E., 1977; Dallas, 1979; How the West Was Won, 1979; Buck Rogers in the 25th Century, 1981; Two Marriages, 1983; Amazing Stories, 1985; Tiny Toon Adventures, 1990; Tales From the Crypt, 1991; Dinosaurs, 1991; Capitol Critters, 1992; JAG, 1995; First Monday, 2002

TV films and miniseries (*selective list*): Desperate Voyage, 1980; Killjoy, 1981; One Shoe Makes It Murder, 1982; The Blue and the Gray, 1982; Cowboy, 1983; This Girl for Hire, 1983; The Master of Ballantrae, 1984; The First Olympics: Athens 1896, 1984; Passions, 1984; Stormin' Home, 1985; George Washington II: The Forging of a Nation, 1986; The Thanksgiving Promise, 1986; Sorry, Wrong Number, 1989; The Old Man and the Sea, 1990; O Pioneers!, 1991; True Women, 1997; Glory & Honor, 1998; Jeremiah, 1998; Night Ride Home, 1999; The Ballad of Lucy Whipple, 2001; Roughing It, 2002; Damaged Care, 2002; Bobbie's Girl, 2002; The Locket, 2002; Eloise at the Plaza, 2003; Lucy, 2003; Eloise at Christmastime, 2003; Warm Springs, 2005; The Dive From Clausen's Pier, 2005; Safe Harbor, 2009

CONCERT MUSIC

Orch: Conc., tuba, orch, 1979; Conc., picc, chbr orch, 1992; English Music, hn, str, 1995; Modular Music I, II, 2003; And on the Sixth Day, ob, orch, 2004; Mixed Elements, orch, 2006; Saloon Music, tpt, pit orch, 2006; A Tiny Sym. for Str, 2007; Fanfares: Mosaic for Orch, 2008; Triptych: Three Incongruities, vn, chbr orch, 2008

Sym. band: Excursions, tpt, band, 1999; American Hero, 2001; New Era, 2008; Oliver's Birthday, tpt, band, 2008; In the World of Spirits, 2011

Brass band or brass ens: A Frontier Overture, brass band, 1982; Harlequin, brass band, 1984; California Legend, brass band, 1985; Concert Piece, 8 tpt, 1999; Euphonies, 8 hn, 1999; Masters of Space and Time, brass band, 2001; Fanfares, Marches, Hymns and Finale, brass, perc, 2004; Variations on a Sonata, double brass quartet, tuba, 2006; Hornworks, 5 hn, tuba, 2010

Chbr: General William Booth Enters into Heaven, Bar, pf, 1967; Sonata, tuba, 1979; Sparrows,4 fl, 1984; Toccata, 2 hp, mallet perc, 1986; Bipartition, vc, tuba, 1989; Ballad, trbn, pf, 1998; Tyvek Wood, hp, va, fl, 2001; Fingerprints of Childhood, fl, vn, va, 2002; Bounce, bn, 2 str qt, db, 2003; Sonata, hn, pf, 2004; Short Stories, mar, pf, 2005; A Primer for Malachi,fl, cl, pf, vc, 2005; Three American Portraits, brass qnt, 2006; Gold Rush Songs, vn, pf, 2006; Hudson River Valley, woodwind octet, 2006; Remembrance, a sax, pf, 2006; Sonata, vn, 2007; Conversations, cl, str qt, 2007; 5 Pieces, pf, 2009; when a body meets a body, brass qnt, 2009; Sonatina, vn, 2010

BIBLIOGRAPHY

T. Thomas: *Music for the Movies* (Beverly Hills, CA, 2/1997)

M. Schelle: *The Score: Interviews With Film Composers* (Los Angeles, 1999)

C. DesJardins: *Inside Film Music: Composers Speak* (Los Angeles, 2007)

J. Burlingame: "Bruce Broughton at 65," *Film Music Society* (2010) <http://www.filmmusicsociety.org/news_events/features/2010/030810.html>

JON BURLINGAME

Brouwer (Mezquida), Leo (*b* Havana, Cuba, 1 March 1939). Cuban composer, guitarist, and conductor. In 1953 he began his studies in the guitar with Isaac Nicola, and in 1955 he made his performance debut. In the same year, and self-taught, he started to compose (e.g. *Música para guitarra, cuerdas y percussion*, and Suite no.1 for guitar); his first works were published in 1956. He was awarded a grant (1959) for advanced guitar studies at the music department of the University of Hartford and for composition at the Juilliard School of Music in New York, where he was taught by Isadora Freed, J. Diemente, Joseph Iadone, Persichetti, and Wolpe. In 1960 he started working in cinema, as head of the department of music in the Instituto Cubano del Arte e Industria Cinematográficos (ICAIC); he has written scores for more than 60 films. He was involved in setting up (1969) and running the Grupo de Experimentación Sonora at ICAIC, becoming the teacher and mentor of its members, who included Silvio Rodríguez, Milanés, and other important figures of contemporary Cuban music. He worked as musical adviser for Radio Habana Cuba (1960–68) and for other Cuban institutions, and taught counterpoint, harmony, and composition at the Conservatorio Municipal in Havana (1960–67). His book *Síntesis de la armonía contemporánea* was a core text in his classes.

Together with the composers Juan Blanco and Carlos Fariñas and the conductor Manuel Duchesne Cuzán, Brouwer launched the avant-garde music movement in Cuba in the 1960s. He has been the most significant promoter of the bi-annual Havana Concurso y Festival de Guitarra, and in 1981 he was appointed principal conductor of the Cuban National SO. He has also conducted many other foreign orchestras including the Berlin PO and the Orquesta de Córdoba, Spain, which, under his direction, was formed in 1992. He is a member of the Berlin Akademie der Künste, of UNESCO, of the Real Academia de Bellas Artes Nuestra Señora de la Angustias in Granada (1996), and Honoris Causa Professor of Art at the Instituto Superior de Arte de Cuba (1996). For his contribution to the Cuban and international music scenes he was awarded the Orden Félix Varela, the highest honor granted by the Cuban state for culture. In 2010 the Sociedad General de Autores y Editores in Madrid awarded him the Premio Tomás Luis de Victoria.

Three phases can be identified in Brouwer's work: the first, nationalistic (1955–62); the second, avant-garde (1962–7); and a third in which avant-garde elements diminish and, particularly after 1980, a creative process described by the composer as "new simplicity" emerges. The first phase is characterized by the use of traditional musical forms, including sonata and variation form, and by tonal harmonic structures rooted in nationalism (e.g. in *Homenaje a Manuel de Falla*, 1957, *Tres danzas concertantes*, 1958, and *Elegía a Jesús Menéndes*, 1960, among others). During this phase, despite the prevailing use of tonality, a tendency to structural fragmentation may be discerned, as well as the employment of several simultaneous tonal centers, a device that has remained throughout his output.

Though never lacking formal rigor, Brouwer's works have in general sprung more from a sonic conception: "I use any form to help me find musical forms: that of a leaf, of a tree or geometric symbolisms. All these are also musical forms; despite the fact that my works appear very structured, what interests me is sound" (Hernández, 2000). This concentration on the sensory, and an accompanying use of extra-musical formal sources, is most to the fore in Brouwer's second phase, which was, with the Cuban avant-garde in general, heavily influenced by the Polish school; he first heard this music at the Warsaw Autumn in 1961. *Variantes* for solo percussion and in particular *Sonograma I* for prepared piano typify this phase, which also included a brief turn towards serialism, in works such as *Sonograma II* and *Arioso (Homenaje a Charles Mingus)*. Basic materials frequently comprise intervals of the second, fourth, and seventh and chords of superimposed sixths, ninths, 11ths, and 13ths. Complex polyphonic textures dominate, with thematic independence retained within the different planes of sound, and a resultant richness in rhythmic conjunction. Other common devices include pedals, ostinatos, sequences, and melodic and rhythmic echoing. One of Brouwer's most important avant-garde works, which has become a major piece of the guitar literature, is the solo *Elogio de la danza* (1964). In two movements—Lento and Ostenato—it was originally composed for dance with choreography by Luis Trápaga; it makes reference to primitive dances and to mysticism, and conveys an image of stamping feet and gyrations together with other dance elements.

Between 1967 and 1969 such works as *Rem tene verba sequentur*, *Cántigas del tiempo nuevo*, and *La tradición se rompe..., pero cuesta trabajo* approach what would now be the postmodern, characterized by sharply defined contrasts in structure and texture and employing references to various historical periods. In *La tradición se rompe..., pero cuesta trabajo*, for example, the interpolation and superimposition of elements of such composers as Bach and Beethoven in a suggestive heterophony borders on caricature; further, the participation of the audience is invited with a persistent "sh." All this is integrated into a process of thematic and instrumental development that evolves through a powerful, controlled aleatoricism.

In the 1970s Brouwer continued to work on post-serial and aleatory ideas, for instance in *La espiral eterna* for guitar. But by the 1980s a "new simplicity" had begun to take hold, involving neo-Romantic, minimalist, and newly tonal elements. There is a marked lyricism in this third period, the use of varying nuclear cells to generate development, and the return of traditional forms exemplified in works like *Canciones remotas*, *Manuscrito antiguo encontrado en una botella*, and *La región más trasparente*. His relationship with literature has remained a constant, as heard in pieces such as *Los Pasos perdidos* (1999) for contrabass and percussion, *Viaje a le semilla* (2000) for guitar, and *Vitrales de La Habana Vieja* (2007) for string orchestra, inspired by songs of A. Carpentier. His composed works, whether for guitar or for vocal and other instrumental forces, demonstrate wide-ranging breadth, diversity, and creativity. Organized annually since 2010, the Leo Brouwer Chamber Music Festival takes place in Havana.

WORKS

(selective list)

Orch: 3 danzas concertantes, gui, str orch, 1958; Balada, fl, str, 1963; Sonograma, 1964; Arioso (Homenaje a Charles Mingus), jazz combo, orch, 1965; Tropos, 1967; La tradición se rompe..., pero cuesta trabajo, 1967–9; Exaedros III, solo perc, 2 orch groups, 1970; Gui Conc., 1971; Conc., fl, str, pf obbl, 1972; Controversia (Sonograma IV), orch, 1972; El gran zoo (Guillén), nar, hn, orch, 1972; Vn Conc., 1978; Canción de gesta, 1979; Concierto de Liège (Quasi una fantasia), gui, orch, 1980; Concierto de Toronto, gui, orch, 1986; Concierto Elegíaco, gui, orch, 1988; Concierto (Helsinki), gui, orch, 1992; Wagneriana, str, 1992; Doble concierto "Omaggio a Paganini," vn, gui, orch, 1995; Lamento por Rafael Orozco, cl, str, 1996; Concierto "La Habana," gui, orch, 1998; Concierto de Benicassim, gui, orch, 2002; Concierto para dos guitarras. Libro de los signos, 2003–2004; Elegía por Víctor Jara, str orch, 2007; Las ciudades invisibles, 2008; Gismontiana, gui qt, orch

Vocal: Elegía a Jesús Menéndez (cant., N. Guillén), chorus, orch, 1960; Cantigas del tiempo nuevo, children's chorus, actors, 4 insts, 1969; Es el Amor quien ve...(J. Martí), high v, 6 insts, 1973; Cantata de Chile (Manns), male chorus, orch, 1975

Chbr and solo inst: Danza característica, gui, 1957; Homenaje a Manuel de Falla, fl, ob, cl, gui, 1957; Micropiezas (Homenaje a Milhaud), 2 gui, 1957; Piezas sin título nos.1 and 2, gui, 1957; 3 apuntes, gui, 1959; 2 bocetos, pf, 1959; Vc Sonata, 1960; Variantes, perc, 1962; Sonograma I, prep pf, 1963; Elogio de la danza, gui, 1964; Trio no.2, ob, cl, bn, 1964; 2 conceptos del tiempo, 10 insts, 1965; Conmutaciones, prep pf, 2 perc, 1966; Canticum, gui, 1968; El reino de este mundo, wind qnt, 1968; Epigramas, vn/vc, pf, 1968; Rem tene verba sequentur, str qt, 1968; Exaedros I–II, 6 insts/any multiple of 6 insts, 1969; La espiral eterna, gui, 1970; Per suonare a 3, fl, va, gui, 1971; Ludus metalicus, sax qt, 1972; Tarantos, gui, 1974; Acerca del sol, el aire y la sonrisa, gui orch, 1978; El decameron negro, 3 ballads, gui, 1981; La región más transparente, fl, pf, 1982; Manuscrito antiguo encontrado en una botella, vn, vc, pf, 1983; Sonata, sones y danzones, vn, vc, pf, 1992; In memoriam "Toru Takemitsu," gui, 1996; Cuarteto de cuerdas n°. 3, 1997; Como la vida misma, pf, vn, vc, perc, 1999; Los pasos perdidos, cb, perc, 1999; Viaje a la semilla, gui, 2000; Cuadros de otra exposición vn, vc, pf, 2005; El Triángulo de las Bermudas, vn, vc, pf, 2007; Rem tene verba sequentur II, str qt, 2007; Variaciones de un tema de Víctor Jara, gui, 2007

Tape: Sonata pian'e forte, pf, tape, 1970; Basso continuo I (cl, tape)/(2 cl), 1972; Per suonare a 2, gui, tape, 1972

Principal publishers: Empresa de Grabaciones y Ediciones Musicales, Eschig, Editora Musical de Cuba, Schott

WRITINGS

La música lo cubano y la innovación (Havana, 1982)

Gajes del oficio. Selección y prólogo I. Hernández (Havana, 2004)

BIBLIOGRAPHY

E. Martín: *Panorama de la música en Cuba* (Havana, 1971)

R. Giró: *Leo Brouwer y la guitarra en Cuba* (Havana, 1986)

D. Orozco: *Rasgos de identidad, entonación y universalidad en la creación musical cubana contemporánea: su singular proyección en 30 años de realidad social revolucionaria, Conferencia ofrecida en al Simposio de Música Contemporánea, UNEAC, 1989*

Z. Gómez and V. Eli Rodríguez: *Música latinoamericana y caribeña* (Havana, 1995)

Diccionario de la música española e hispano-americana, ed. E. Casares Rodicio, J. López-Calo, I. Fernandez de la Cuesta, vol. 2 (Madrid, 1999), 725–30

I. Hernández: *Leo Brouwer* (Havana, 2000)

J.M. Moreno Calderón: *Leo Brouwer y Córdoba* (Córdoba, 2005)

VVAA: *Leo Brouwer. Nombres propios de la guitarra* (Córdoba, 2006)

M. Rodríguez Cuervo, V. Eli Rodríguez: *Leo Brouwer. Caminos de la creación* (Madrid, 2009)

VICTORIA ELI RODRÍGUEZ

Brouwer, Margaret (Lee) (*b* Ann Arbor, MI, 8 Feb 1940). Composer and violinist. She studied violin at Oberlin Conservatory (BM 1962), and Michigan State University (MM 1963). She played with the Fort Worth Symphony and Opera Orchestras, and later the Dallas Symphony. During the same period she also played and recorded for commercial and pop artists, including Tony Bennett and Johnny Mathis. She composed during and after college but continued her professional violin career until 1984, when she began graduate studies in composition at Indiana University (DMA 1988), where she studied with DONALD ERB, HARVEY SOLLBERGER, and FRED FOX.

Before beginning her tenure as Head of Composition at the Cleveland Institute of Music (1996–2008) where she held the Vincent K. and Edith H. Smith Chair, she taught at Washington and Lee University (1988–96), and served as composer-in-residence for the Roanoke Symphony (1993–7). She has written for the Cleveland Chamber Symphony (*Mandala*, 2001), the Women's Philharmonic (*Sizzle*, 2000), percussionist Evelyn Glennie (*Aurolucent Circles*, perc, orch, 2002), the Detroit Symphony (*Rhapsody for Orchestra*, 2009), the American Composers Orchestra (*BREAKDOWN!* for video and orchestra, with video/sound artist Kasumi, 2009), and the Dallas Symphony Orchestra (Concerto for Viola and Orchestra, 2010). Brouwer has been recognized by the Guggenheim Foundation (2004), the Ohio Arts Council (2005), the American Academy of Arts and Letters (2006), and Meet the Composer/Commissioning USA (*Path at Sunrise, Masses of Flowers*, 2010). She has held residencies at Bellagio (Rockefeller Foundation) and the Charles Ives Center for American Music.

Brouwer's mostly tonal language, driven by lyricism and emotion, is colorful, lush, and imaginatively orchestrated, reflecting her experience as an orchestral violinist. Complementing this, she cites an eclectic array of influences from Renaissance and 20th-century classical music to minimalism, pop, rap, world music, and her years in the recording industry. Brouwer uses extended instrumental techniques, and often mixes styles and harmonic languages within a piece, such as in the Concerto for Violin and Orchestra (2007), which combines tonal chords with a 12-tone row. The result is always integrated, however, and never becomes pastiche. Her principal publisher is Carl Fisher, and her recordings are available on New World, CRI, Crystal, Centaur, Opus One.

AMELIA S. KAPLAN

Brower, Frank [Brower, Francis Marion] (*b* Baltimore, MD, 20/30 Nov 1820/1823; *d* Philadelphia, PA, 4 June 1874). Minstrel. His stage debut was in Philadelphia *c*1837. By spring 1840 he had teamed with DAN EMMETT, singing and dancing in blackface for the Cincinnati Circus Company. In July 1841 Brower began accompanying Emmett's banjo songs on bones, pioneering the use of this folk instrument in professional entertainment. After a stint with Raymond and Waring's Circus about 1841–2, the duo moved to New York. In early 1843 Brower, Emmett, BILLY WHITLOCK, and DICK PELHAM formed the VIRGINIA MINSTRELS, the first blackface minstrel troupe. Brower's boisterous performances in "Southern Negro character" encompassed playing bones on the right end (which led to the formal role of endman), songs, stump speeches, conundrums (a circus genre), and breakdowns. Patterned on black practice, Brower's dancing was distinctive for its jumps and leaps. He often danced while playing, his bones and feet creating a dense rhythmic texture, and he typically interrupted his dancing for brief comic dialogue. Brower and Pelham were considered premier dancers and were widely imitated by other minstrels, WILLIAM HENRY LANE among them. The last stage of Brower's career (from 1853) was associated with burlesques of *Uncle Tom's Cabin*, which he performed with various troupes. In an 1863 version of his "Happy Uncle Tom" Brower played a broken-down, near-deaf old man who sprang into a lively dance at the sound of a banjo. In 1867 Brower broke his leg while working as a circus clown and retired from the stage.

WRITINGS

Black Diamond Songster (New York, 1863)

BIBLIOGRAPHY

E. LeRice: *Monarchs of Minstrelsy, from "Daddy" Rice to Date* (New York, 1911)

H. Nathan: *Dan Emmett and the Rise of Early Negro Minstrelsy* (Norman, OK, 1962)

R.C. Toll: *Blacking Up: the Minstrel Show in Nineteenth-century America* (New York, 1974)

SANDRA JEAN GRAHAM

Brown, Angela (*b* Indianapolis, IN, 1 Dec 1964). Soprano. She studied with Ginger Beazley at Oakwood College and Virginia Zeani at Indiana University, and won the National Metropolitan Opera Council Auditions in 1997. Her 2004 Metropolitan Opera debut as Aida was a critical success. Other notable roles include the title role in *Ariadne auf Naxos*, Amelia in *Un ballo in maschera*, Serena in *Porgy and Bess*, Leonora in *Il trovatore*, Elisabetta in *Don Carlo*, Leonora in *La Forza del Destino*, Cassandra in Aleksandr Taneyev's *Agamemnon*, and Tosca. She has toured the United States, Canada, New Zealand, and Africa with a recital program, "Opera from a Sistah's Point of View," intended to bring opera to diverse audiences. In 1997 she performed and recorded selections from *Porgy and Bess* with Erich Kunzel and the Cincinnati Pops Orchestra for TelArc. In 2005 she sang Cilla in the Opera Company of Philadelphia's world premiere of *Margaret Garner* by Richard Danielpour and Toni Morrison, and in 2009 with the Pittsburgh Symphony she premiered the song cycle "A Woman's Life," which Danielpour wrote for her to texts by Maya Angelou. In addition to appearing regularly with orchestras throughout the United States, she has produced more intimate recordings such as *Mosaic* (Albany Records, 2004), which features African American spirituals with guitar and piano.

BETH McGINNIS

Brown, Anne (*b* Baltimore, MD, 9 Aug 1912; *d* Oslo, Norway, 13 March 2009). Soprano. Born to a music-loving mother and prominent physician father whose grandparents were slaves, Brown premiered the role of Bess in the original production of *Porgy and Bess* (1935). She studied music, first at Morgan State College and then the Juilliard School, where she was the first African American to win the Margaret McGill scholarship. Brown learned of Gershwin's new opera, then titled *Porgy*, while at Juilliard, and immediately requested an audition. She sang for Gershwin a few days later and left their meeting as Bess. Gershwin frequently invited Brown to his apartment to sing parts of the opera as he composed. As a result, Bess grew from a secondary character into one of the opera's leading roles.

After the original Broadway run and tour of *Porgy and Bess* ended in 1936, Brown continued with her career in the DuBose Heyward musicals *Mamba's Daughters* and *La Belle Hélène*. She also appeared as the soprano soloist in Beethoven's Ninth Symphony with the NBC Symphony Orchestra, and toured the United States as a recitalist.

Early the following decade Brown began to perform in Europe (including *Porgy and Bess* for Copenhagen's Royal Theatre, singing with the London Philharmonic Orchestra, and giving recitals) because of the racial prejudice she continually encountered in the United States. She permanently relocated to Norway in 1948 and performed professionally until 1953. She then became a private voice teacher, published her autobiography (1979), and won the 1998 George Peabody Medal for Outstanding Contributions to Music in America. Her archives are housed at Tulane University.

BIBLIOGRAPHY

R. Wyatt and J.A. Johnson: "Anne Brown: from an Interview by Robert Wyatt (1995)," *The George Gershwin Reader* (Oxford, 2004), 228–36

E. Berra: "Anne Wiggins Brown Papers, 1935–2002," Amistad Research Center <http://www.amistadresearchcenter.org/archon/?p=collections/findingaid&id=58&q=&rootcontentid=37212>

TRUDI ANN WRIGHT

Brown, Anthony (L.) [Tony] (*b* San Francisco, CA, 17 March 1953). Percussionist, composer, and scholar. He is a California-based artist and educator whose world travels and ethnic heritage have had a major influence on his musical career. His mother was a native of Tokyo, Japan, and his father was of African American and Choctaw descent. He grew up in a military family, moving between California, Germany, and Japan during his formative years. His career in music began in earnest after he returned to San Francisco in 1980. In 1985 he moved to New York and further developed his career while studying jazz performance at Rutgers University. He subsequently earned a PhD from the University of California, Berkeley, studying ethnomusicology, a field that allowed him to focus on the musical styles that reflected his cultural heritage. He then began an extensive relationship with the Smithsonian Institution working as the curator of American musical culture, director of the Jazz Oral History program, and a performer in the Smithsonian Jazz Trio. In 1997 he founded an ensemble, which later became known as Anthony Brown's Asian American Orchestra, as part of a touring project focused on Japanese American internment in World War II. Brown's music has blended elements from rumba, taiko, swing, and gagaku, among other styles, and has employed a variety of musical instruments including shakuhachi and erhu as well as Western instruments. His ensembles have interpreted the works of jazz greats such as Thelonious Monk, Duke Ellington, and George Gershwin as well as performing his own compositions. His creative activity also includes scholarly writing and a variety of musical endeavors such as the five movement *Incantation Suite* (1983) and his scores for the documentaries *Doubles: Japan and America's Intercultural Children* (1995) and *Witness to Hiroshima* (2008).

E. RON HORTON

Brown, Chris(topher Owen) (*b* Mendota, IL, 9 Sept 1953). Composer and pianist. He studied at the University of California, Santa Cruz (BA 1974) with WILLIAM BROOKS, GORDON MUMMA, and others, and at Mills College (MFA 1985) where his teachers included DAVID ROSENBOOM. He has taught at the San Francisco Art Institute (1985–92) and Mills College (from 1991), where he has served as co-director of the Center for Contemporary Music. During the 1980s he was active as an instrument builder, most notably of the "gazamba," a prepared electric piano. He later developed custom computer systems that interacted with and transformed live sounds. Often improvisatory, his music reflects his skills as a pianist. From the late 1990s he has designed computer network systems that allow musicians to interact with other musicians and computers over the Internet. In the 2000s he became interested in fostering audience participation in his music, creating works such as the *Transmissions* series, in which he used FM radio transmitters to broadcast sound to an audience carrying portable radios. He has collaborated with the Rova Saxophone Quartet, Glenn Spearman, Fred Frith, and others, and is a member of the computer network band The Hub. *Talking Drum* (1995) received honorable mention at the Prix Ars Electronica, Linz, in 1996.

RECORDINGS
(selective list)

Lava (1995 Tzadik 7002); Rogue Wave (2005, Tzadik 8014); Boundary Layer: The Hub (2008, Tzadik 8050–3)

WORKS
(selective list)

Sparks, pf, 1976; Quay, pf, 1977; Alternating Currents, orch, 1983; Conjunction, carillon, amp rods, 1983; Post Mortem, sax, pf, perc, elecs, 1984; Iceberg, perc, elecs, 1985; Obedience School, inst, elecs, 1985; Hall of Mirrors, sax, pf, perc, elecs, 1986; Snakecharmer, inst, cptr, 1987; Qt with Shadows, sax qt, elecs, 1989–90; Lava, brass, perc, elecs, 1992; Flies, vn, pf, perc, elecs, 1993; Tenebrae, vn, elecs, 1994; Talking Drum, insts, cptr, 1995; Inventions, kbd, cptr, 1997–2001; Transmissions, live cptr, radio broadcast (collab. Guillermo Galindo), 2002–06; TeleSon, for two "reacTables," 2005; Stupas, pf, vib, cptr, 2007

Principal recording companies: Artifact, Tzadik, Music & Arts, Centaur

WRITINGS

with J. Bischoff and T. Perkis: "Bringing Digital Music to Life," *Computer Music Journal*, xx/2 (1996), 28–32

"Some Thoughts about Improvising," *CMR*, XXV/5–6 (2006), 571–3

BIBLIOGRAPHY

J. Chadabe: *Electric Sound* (Upper Saddle River, NJ, 1997), 296–7

CARTER SCHOLZ/BENJAMIN PIEKUT

Brown, Chuck (*b* Gaston, NC, 28 Aug 1936; *d* Baltimore, MD, 16 May 2012). Bandleader, singer, guitarist, and composer. He was a musical icon of the Washington, DC, metropolitan area. He was widely known as "The Godfather of Go-go" and renowned for his live performances, which emphasize continuous, percussion-driven grooves and audience participation, all staples of the Go-go genre he developed in the 1970s. Brown's early years were marked by poverty and crime, first developing his guitar playing while incarcerated at the Lorton Penitentiary. With his band the Soul Searchers, Brown developed a distinctive sound that is grounded in funk and soul, but also heavily influenced by jazz and Latin genres. His hit songs include "Bustin' Loose," "We Need Some Money," and "Go-Go Swing." In 1992, Brown recorded *The Other Side* with vocalist Eva Cassidy, a critically-acclaimed album of jazz and blues material. He received a NARAS Governors Award and an NEA Lifetime Heritage Fellowship Award, and he continued to record and perform regularly until his death.

RECORDINGS
(selective list)

Your Game... Live at the 9:30 Club Washington, D.C. (Raw Venture, 2001); *The Best of Chuck Brown* (Liaison/Raw Venture, 2005)

BIBLIOGRAPHY

R.R. Parker: "Chuck Brown's Long Dance," *The Washington Post Magazine* (4 Oct 2009)

C. Lornell and C.C. Stephenson: *The Beat: Go-go music from Washington, D.C.* (Jackson, MS, 2009)

DAVID FONT-NAVARRETE

Brown, Clarence "Gatemouth" (*b* Vinton, LA, 18 April 1924; *d* Orange, TX, 10 Sept 2005). Blues singer and guitarist. A virtuoso guitarist and an icon on the Texas music scene, Brown mastered the guitar and the violin by age ten and later learned the fiddle, mandolin, harmonica, viola, and drums. He moved to Houston following the Second World War and became famous after filling in for an ailing T-Bone Walker at the city's Bronze Peacock nightclub in 1947. His performance of "Gatemouth Boogie" impressed the nightclub owner Don Robey, who founded Peacock Records to showcase his work. In 1949, Brown recorded two hits for the Peacock label, "Mary Is Fine"and "My Time Is Expensive," and recorded his signature tune "Okie Dokie Stomp" in 1954, an instrumental which captured his style of rapid, single notes on guitar over a forceful horn section. Throughout the 1950s, Brown recorded a number of sides for Peacock, including "Depression Blues," and "Hurry Back Good News." His later recordings synthesized the musical styles of jazz, zydeco, and Cajun music into his blues recordings. During his career, Brown played a variety of guitars, including the Gibson L-5 and Fender Telecaster, but his trademark guitar was a custom-made Gibson Firebird. Brown influenced other blues guitarists such as Johnny "Guitar" Watson, Albert Collins, and Guitar Slim. In 1982, Brown won a Grammy Award for Best Traditional Blues Album, *"Alright Again!"* His final album, *Timeless*, was released in 2004.

BIBLIOGRAPHY

L. Cohn: *Nothing but the Blues* (New York, 1993)

J. Rolf, ed.: *The Definitive Illustrated Encyclopedia of Jazz & Blues* (London, 2008)

DINA M. BENNETT

Brown, Clifford [Brownie] (*b* Wilmington, DE, 30 Oct 1930; *d* Pennsylvania, PA, 26 June 1956). Jazz trumpeter, composer, and bandleader. As a teenager at Howard High on Wilmington's east side, he studied music privately with Robert Lowry and won a math scholarship to Delaware State College. After transferring to Maryland State College to major in music, he arranged big band charts and played at jazz clubs in the Philadelphia area with Dizzy Gillespie, Charlie Parker, and Fats Navarro, in the process gaining widespread attention. After being seriously injured in a car accident in 1950, he was bedridden for a year but was constantly encouraged to continue his musical development by family, teachers, neighborhood musicians, and friends. With fierce determination, he rehabilitated, joined Chris Powell's Blue Flames (a rhythm and blues band), and made his first recordings in March 1952. The following year he took part in jam sessions in Atlantic City, New Jersey, with such bebop musicians as Gene Ammons, Red Garland, Benny Golson, Sonny Stitt, and the Heath brothers. His playing was so dominant that he was invited to record with Lou Donaldson, Tadd Dameron, and J.J. Johnson in June 1953. The latter session was interrupted by the producer Alfred Lion so that he could immediately sign Brown to work for Blue Note as a leader.

From August 1953 Brown worked with the Lionel Hampton band on a three-month tour of Europe, during which he was recorded by producers eager to satisfy European interest in hard bop. In these sessions he performed with Quincy Jones, Art Farmer, Gigi Gryce, and a host of European musicians including Henri Renaud. After returning to New York in December 1953, he was quickly contacted by several bandleaders who had heard about his European success. His next recording was a live album, *A Night at Birdland*, made in February 1954 with a band featuring Art Blakey, Horace Silver, and Lou Donaldson. Soon after this, he was invited by the drummer Max Roach to co-lead a new quintet and both performers left for California to audition musicians and develop ideas for the new group. Brown and Roach were immediately signed to a contract with EmArcy records and hired Harold Land, George Morrow, and Richie Powell for their quintet. Brown composed several selections for the group (including "Joy Spring" and "Daahoud"), which opted for tightly woven performances featuring economical improvisations along innovative harmonic lines. While touring and recording, the group broke attendance records (for example, at Basin Street in New York) and drew impressive critical reviews. It set a high-water mark for hard bop ensembles of the 1950s. In addition to his work with this quintet, Brown also recorded with the vocalists Sarah Vaughan, Helen Merrill, and Dinah Washington, organized and played at charitable musical events, mentored young musicians such as Lee Morgan, excelled at chess, and became a role model for musicians who struggled with substance abuse. He died in an automobile accident at the age of 25.

Brown's prescience and influence as a jazz trumpeter and virtuosic improviser has endured into the 21st century. His achievement with up-tempo, percussively articulated solos constructed along logical lines is unequaled. His preference for low-register, buttery-toned ballad playing on an instrument known for its high register is unique. His remarkable aesthetic achievement attained in just four years of studio recording remains unchallenged.

RECORDINGS
(selective list)

As leader: *Brownie: the Complete EmArcy Recordings of Clifford Brown* (Polygram, 1989); *The Clifford Brown Big Band in Paris* (Original Jazz Classics, 1987); *The Beginning and the End* (CBS, 1994); *The Complete Blue Note and Pacific Jazz Recordings* (BN, 1995)

As sideman: A. Blakey: *A Night at Birdland, Vol.I* (1954, BN); S. Rollins: *Sonny Rollins Plus Four* (1956, Prst.)

BIBLIOGRAPHY

Nat [N. Hentoff]: "Clifford Brown: the New Dizzy," *DB*, xxi/7 (1954), 15–16

Q. Jones: "A Tribute to Brownie," *DB*, xxiii (1956), 10

B. Gardner: "The Legacy of Clifford Brown," *DB*, xxviii/21 (1961), 17–21

M.L. Stewart: *Structural Development in the Jazz Improvisational Technique of Clifford Brown* (diss., U. of Michigan, 1973); pubd in *Jazzforschung/Jazz Research*, vi–vii (1974–5), 141–273

B. Weir: *Clifford Brown Discography* (Cardiff, Wales, 1982, rev. and enlarged 5/1990)

D. Morganstern: [disc notes] *Brownie: the Complete EmArcy Recordings of Clifford Brown,* EmArcy/Polygram Records 838 306–2 (1989)

N. Catalano: *Clifford Brown: the Life and Art of the Legendary Jazz Trumpeter* (New York, 2000)

H. Gillis and A. Hood: "Clifford Brown: a Short Life Well-Lived," *JT* (2010)

NICK CATALANO